THE BANTAM GREAT OUTDOORS GUIDE

is the most complete book on outdoor recreation and vacation travel in the United States and Canada. It is designed in an easy-to-use "A" to "Z" format, divided into Encyclopedia and Travel & Recreation Guide sections for each state and province.

THE ENCYCLOPEDIA

contains entries on accommodations, lodges and vacation resorts, airlines and charter fly-in services, backpacking and wilderness trails, canoeing and wilderness waters, recreation and scenic highways, fishing and hunting, maps and charts, guide services and outfitters, railway services, state and province record fish, ski touring centers and trails, and vacation travel services.

THE TRAVEL & RECREATION GUIDE

details source materials, maps, lodging and travel services for the national forests and parks, wild and scenic rivers, wilderness and primitive areas, national hiking trails, trophy fishing waters, alpine recreation areas, wilderness canoeing areas, and more.

More than five years in preparation, THE BANTAM GREAT OUTDOORS GUIDE was created and written by Val Landi, the president of Wilderness Sports Corporation. He is one of the nation's leading outdoor authorities and a contributing editor of *Outdoor Life*.

Literary Guild Book Club Alternate Selection
Outdoor Life Book Club Alternate Selection

THE BANTAM GREAT OUTDOORS GUIDE TO THE UNITED STATES AND CANADA

The Complete Travel Encyclopedia and Wilderness Guide

BY VAL LANDI

Illustrated by Gordon Allen
Region maps by Caroline Edwards

ACKNOWLEDGMENTS

I am deeply grateful to Angus Cameron of Alfred A. Knopf, whose kindness, generosity, and friendship made this book possible, and to Oscar Dystel, president of Bantam Books, for his unflagging support. I am indebted also to the staff of Wilderness Sports Corporation—A. Donald Grosset, Jr., Ann Paschke and Jacquelyn Brown—for their valuable contributions. To Lamar Underwood, editor in chief of *Outdoor Life* magazine, go my thanks for his inspiration, suggestions, and help.

Special thanks go the hundreds of United States and Canadian government fish and wildlife, forestry, park, and conservation authorities and their agencies (listed throughout the book) who contributed their time and expertise, and provided much of the source material that made the compilation of *The Bantam Great Outdoors Guide* possible.

My thanks go also to my editor, Beverly Teague, for her patience and kind assistance; to Sharon Earli and Natalie Parnass, for their participation in the typing of successive revisions of the manuscript; to Caroline Edwards for her unique region maps; and to Gordon Allen, for his superb and powerful sketches of the great outdoors.

—Val Landi

THE BANTAM GREAT OUTDOORS GUIDE
TO THE UNITED STATES AND CANADA
A Bantam Book / November 1978

All rights reserved.
Copyright © 1978 by Wilderness Sports Corporation

Cover photographs by Jay M. Steinberg

David Greenspan maps in the insert between pages 374 and 375.
Copyright © 1963 by American Heritage Publishing Co., Inc.
Reprinted by permission from the American Heritage Book
of Natural Wonders.

Map on page viii courtesy U.S. Geological Survey

ISBN 0-553-01112-X

Published simultaneously in the United States and Canada

Bantam Books are published by Bantam Books, Inc.
Its trademark consisting of the words "Bantam Books" and
the portrayal of a bantam, is registered in the United States
Patent Office and in other countries. Marca Registrada.
Bantam Books, Inc., 666 Fifth Avenue, New York, New York 10019.

PRINTED IN THE UNITED STATES OF AMERICA

0 9 8 7 6 5 4 3 2 1

CONTENTS

COLOR INSERT
THE GREAT
OUTDOOR ATLAS

Between pages 374 and 375

Yosemite National Park

Glacier National Park

Yellowstone National Park

Grand Teton National Park

Black Hills

Boundary Waters

Great Smoky Mountains

Mount Desert Island—Acadia National Park

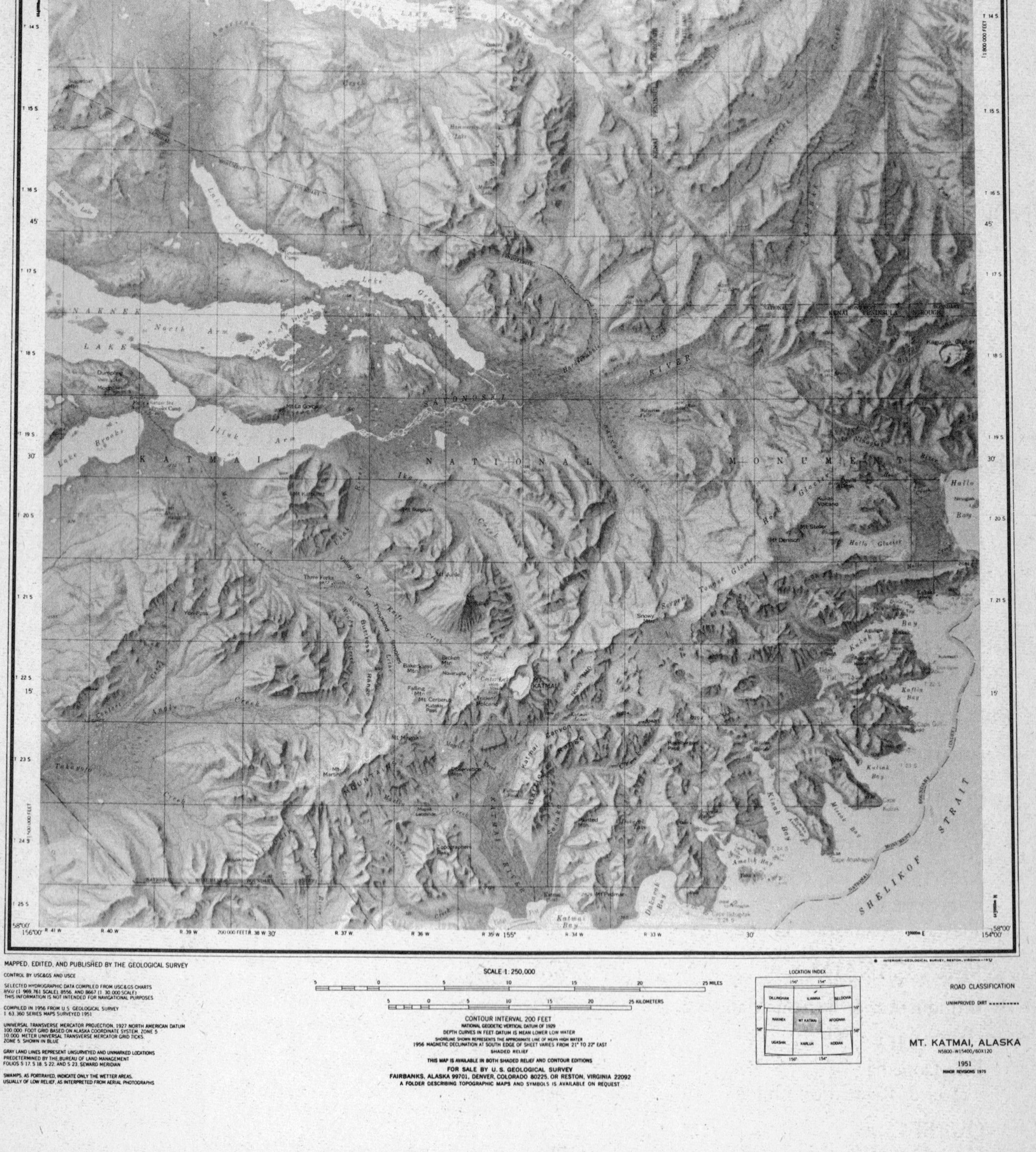

UNITED STATES
DEPARTMENT OF THE INTERIOR
GEOLOGICAL SURVEY

MT. KATMAI

ALASKA
TOPOGRAPHIC SERIES

MAPPED, EDITED, AND PUBLISHED BY THE GEOLOGICAL SURVEY

CONTROL BY USC&GS AND USCE

SELECTED HYDROGRAPHIC DATA COMPILED FROM USC&GS CHARTS
8552 (1:969,761 SCALE), 8556, AND 8667 (1:30,000 SCALE)
THIS INFORMATION IS NOT INTENDED FOR NAVIGATIONAL PURPOSES

COMPILED IN 1956 FROM U.S. GEOLOGICAL SURVEY
1:63,360 SERIES MAPS SURVEYED 1951

UNIVERSAL TRANSVERSE MERCATOR PROJECTION, 1927 NORTH AMERICAN DATUM
10,000 FOOT GRID BASED ON ALASKA COORDINATE SYSTEM ZONE 5
10,000 METER UNIVERSAL TRANSVERSE MERCATOR GRID TICKS.
ZONE 5 SHOWN IN BLUE

GRAY LAND LINES REPRESENT UNSURVEYED AND UNMARKED LOCATIONS
PREDETERMINED BY THE BUREAU OF LAND MANAGEMENT
FOLIOS 5-17, 5-18, 5-22, AND 5-23, SEWARD MERIDIAN

SWAMPS, AS PORTRAYED, INDICATE ONLY THE WETTER AREAS.
USUALLY OF LOW RELIEF, AS INTERPRETED FROM AERIAL PHOTOGRAPHS.

SCALE 1:250,000

CONTOUR INTERVAL 200 FEET
NATIONAL GEODETIC VERTICAL DATUM OF 1929
DEPTH CURVES IN FEET DATUM IS MEAN LOWER LOW WATER
SHORELINE SHOWN REPRESENTS THE APPROXIMATE LINE OF MEAN HIGH WATER
1956 MAGNETIC DECLINATION AT SOUTH EDGE OF SHEET VARIES FROM 21° TO 22° EAST
SHADED RELIEF

THIS MAP IS AVAILABLE IN BOTH SHADED RELIEF AND CONTOUR EDITIONS
FOR SALE BY U.S. GEOLOGICAL SURVEY
FAIRBANKS, ALASKA 99701, DENVER, COLORADO 80225, OR RESTON, VIRGINIA 22092
A FOLDER DESCRIBING TOPOGRAPHIC MAPS AND SYMBOLS IS AVAILABLE ON REQUEST

LOCATION INDEX

ROAD CLASSIFICATION
UNIMPROVED DIRT ==========

MT. KATMAI, ALASKA
N5800—W15400/60X120

1951
MINOR REVISIONS 1975

MOUNT KATMAI AND THE VALLEY OF 10,000 SMOKES (ALASKA)

READER'S GUIDE

The Bantam Great Outdoors Guide is the most comprehensive reference book ever published on outdoor recreation and vacation travel in the United States and Canada. Although its primary emphasis is on usefulness, the book is packed with the history, lore, and legends of the Indians, fur traders and trappers, explorers, mountain men, and early pioneers who blazed the trails followed by today's outdoor enthusiast. It contains thousands of little-known facts about the origin of place names, wildlife, flora, geology, climate and topography, and includes essays about such fascinating subjects as John Colter and the Discovery of Yellowstone, The Great Alaskan Moose, The Northern Lights, Wolverine-Indian Devil of the North, The Canadian Shield, Thoreau's Great Wilderness Canoe Journey, Wolves of the Great North Woods, and Admiralty Island and the Bald Eagle.

In addition to its authoritative, evocative descriptions of every important recreation area, the book contains the titles and sources of thousands of free, hard-to-find recreation maps, guides, booklets, and pamphlets, as well as the names, addresses, and descriptions of major fishing and hunting lodges, wilderness outpost camps, family vacation resorts, guest and dude ranches, wilderness fly-in services, fishing and hunting guides, wildlife photography guides, wilderness trip outfitters and packers, canoe services and wild river outfitters, wilderness instruction schools, fly-fishing and bass-fishing schools. It also provides the titles, sources, and prices of hundreds of regional guidebooks and specialty maps, and the names of the full-color U.S. Geological Survey and Canadian National Topographic Survey maps needed to cover every area described. (See the sample U.S. Geological Survey Map shown on the opposite page.)

The Great Outdoors Guide is designed in an easy-to-use "A" to "Z" format, divided into "Encyclopedia" and "Travel & Recreation Guide" sections. Each "Encyclopedia" section contains detailed entries about such varied subjects as accommodations, lodges & family vacation resorts, camping and state recreation areas, backpacking and wilderness trails, canoeing and wilderness waters, recreation and scenic highways, fishing and hunting, maps and charts, wilderness outfitting centers, state and province record fish, and ski touring. The "Travel & Recreation Guide" sections provide detailed descriptions and source materials and maps for the important outdoor recreation areas within each state and province: the wild and scenic rivers, national forests and parks, wilderness and primitive areas, national scenic hiking trails, trophy fishing waters, big game ranges, alpine recreation areas, wilderness and historic canoe routes, and more. (Readers should note that due to limited national recreation lands in several states, the Encyclopedia and the Travel & Recreation Guide have been combined.)

HOW TO ORDER MAPS & CHARTS

Detailed information on how to order the official United States and Canadian government topographic, shaded-relief, national park and specialty maps listed and described throughout the *Great Outdoors Guide* will be found by consulting the regional introductions to Alaska —The Last Frontier, Pacific Crest States, Rocky Mountain States, Northern Canada, and so forth.

When ordering maps and books direct from their publishers remember to include extra money (50¢ per book is the usual rule of thumb) for postage and handling. This will speed up delivery of your order by several weeks. Also, please note that listings of major outfitters, lodges, or guides are provided as a reader service and do not necessarily constitute endorsement due to possible changes from year to year. Always be sure to check references and plan your trips thoroughly.

REGION MAP LEGEND

▓▓▓▓▓▓▓▓▓▓▓▓▓▓	Railway
∿∿∿∿∿∿∿∿∿∿∿	Canadian Shield
⌒⌒⌒⌒⌒	National Park
—————○—————	Highway
ⱶ ⱶ ⱶ ⱶ ⱶ ⱶ ⱶ ⱶ	National Forest
♠ ♠ ♠ ♠ ♠ ♠ ♠ ♠	Tree Line
●●●●●●●●●●●	Ferry
>>>>>>>>>>>>	National Wild and Scenic River
= = = = = = = =	Foot Trail
✈ ✈ ✈ ✈	Outfitting Center
▬ ▬ ▬ ▬ ▬ ▬	State Forest
⬭⬭⬭	Primitive Area
⬯⬯	Wilderness Area

PART ONE
THE UNITED STATES

ALASKA— THE LAST FRONTIER

Introduction

Alaska, derived from the Eskimo word *Alayeska*, meaning "the great land," is one of the world's last great outdoor frontiers. Here, contained within an immense land area of 586,000 square miles, are several of the world's greatest remaining fishing, hunting, and wild river canoeing areas, set amongst a majestic wilderness of wave-swept coastal rain forests, towering glacier-studded snow-crowned mountain ranges and awesome volcanic highlands that reach up toward the clouds, eerie wind-swept sand dunes located north of the Arctic Circle, huge blue mountain-girded lakes, vast boreal forests and soft tundra barrens, wild torrential rivers, and seemingly endless mazes of mist-shrouded, evergreen-clad islands, inhabited by giant Alaskan brown bear, moose, Dall sheep, barren-ground grizzly, Roosevelt elk, wolves, caribou, and the nation's largest population of bald eagles. The remote, seldom-fished lakes and streams hold record-sized rainbow and lake trout, salmon, huge northern pike, arctic grayling, and giant mysterious sheefish—the "tarpon of the Arctic."

Southeastern Alaska, the ancient home and hunting grounds of the once-powerful Tlingit Indians, known as the "Panhandle," is encompassed within the vast boundaries of the Tongass National Forest. It includes a narrow strip of mainland and the adjacent labyrinth of picturesque, wave-lapped islands known as the Alexander Archipelago —including the prolific wilderness fish and game lands of Admiralty, Baranof, Chichagof, Kupreanof, Wrangell, Revillagigedo, and Prince of Wales islands, whose scenic shores are dotted with rustic fishing and logging villages—both of which stretch for 400 miles from the Alaskan mainland and the massive 16,000-foot peaks of the St. Elias Range southeastward along the beautiful Coast Range Mountains and the western boundary of British Columbia. The Panhandle is one of the scenic wonders of the modern world with its great glaciers, wild salmon and steelhead streams, awesome sheer-walled fjords, lush rain forests of western hemlock and towering Sitka spruce, and high mountains rising above a rocky, moss-covered, log-strewn coast, with dense alder thickets and alpine tundra meadows laced by an intricate network of deep mountain valleys and torrential whitewater streams. The coastal rain forests contain an almost impenetrable undergrowth of moss-carpeted down timber, giant ferns, spiny devil's club, salmonberry, salal, copperbush, Sitka willow, Alaska and dwarf blueberry, Nootka rose, Pacific red elder, alpine bearberry, dwarf arctic birch, mountain cranberry, sweetgale, silverberry, mountain ash, and buffaloberry.

South central Alaska lies to the northwest of the Panhandle. It includes Prince Edward Sound, the Kenai Peninsula and Cook Inlet regions of the southern coast, and adjacent wilderness areas and waterways that extend inland from the Gulf of Alaska through the Chugach National Forest to the soaring 14,000-foot peaks of the massive Alaska Range in central Alaska. North of the southern coastal regions, the Alaska Range sweeps across the state from the legendary big-game ranges of the Wrangell Mountains on the east, forming a gigantic arc, in places 150 miles wide, that reaches down into the unspoiled virgin wilderness of the Alaska Peninsula, where it merges with the remote Aleutian Range in the extreme southwest. Several large silt-laden rivers, such as the Copper and Susitna, break through the rugged Chugach Mountains fronting the Gulf Coast. The south central region embraces the renowned fishing, hunting, canoeing, and wilderness camping areas in the Kenai Mountains and Kenai National Moose Range, the remote headwater lakes of the Susitna and Copper rivers, the legendary big-game ranges of the Alaska Range, and Mount McKinley National Park.

The world-renowned trout and salmon fishing and trophy big-game

ALASKA

hunting areas of the Alaska Peninsula, Bristol Bay, and Aleutian Islands in southwestern Alaska are dominated by vast areas of rubble-strewn treeless tundra covered with low mats of dwarf willows, mountain cranberry, bog blueberry, Labrador tea, red and blue mountain heather, Lapland rosebay, and alpine azalea. Here, in this remote, seldom explored wild country are the trophy rainbow, lake trout, arctic grayling, salmon, and char waters of the Wood River–Tikchik Lakes chain, Nushagak River, Lake Iliamna, Brooks Lake and river, Naknek Lake, and the Ugashik Lakes; McNeil River Game Sanctuary; the awesome wilderness fishing and backpacking areas of Mount Katmai National Monument and the Valley of Ten Thousand Smokes; the legendary brown bear and moose ranges of Kodiak and Afognak islands, the Aleutian Range, and the remote Ahklun and Kilbuck mountains, located due west as the crow flies from the sparkling, jagged blue necklace formed by the great Tikchik Lakes chain.

The Great Interior, or central region, of Alaska stretches from the northern slope of the Alaska Range north beyond the Arctic Circle to the southern slopes of the massive Brooks Range, named in honor of Alfred Brooks, who served as chief Alaska geologist for the U.S. Geological Survey from 1903 to his death in 1924. This relatively low, rolling interior belt, dominated by taiga—the "land of little sticks"—of white and black spruce, quaking aspen, paper birch, and balsam poplar, extends from the Yukon Territory border west almost to the Bering Sea, slashed by the mighty Yukon and Kuskokwim rivers and the wild Yukon tributaries, including the Nation, Fortymile, Charley, Birch Creek, Koyukuk, and Beaver Creek rivers. The forests of the interior belt, which stretch in places for more than 300 miles from north to south and for 1,000 miles from east to west, have an understory of Labrador tea, crowberry, stunted willows, bearberry, bog and dwarf blueberry, mountain cranberry, and prickly rose, inhabited by moose, barren-ground grizzly, and caribou.

Arctic Alaska, the "land of the midnight sun," is located north of the Arctic Circle and embraces the lonely peaks of the fabled Brooks Range, a massive mountain chain first explored by the famous naturalist Robert Marshall, which stretches nearly 150 miles from north to south and more than 600 miles from east to west. It is formed, from west to east, by the big-game ranges of the Delong, Baird, Schwatka, Endicott, Philip Smith, Davidson, Franklin, Romanzof, and British mountains. Here, in the heart of the Arctic, are the Great Kobuk Sand Dunes and the remote, seldom-fished waters of the Noatak, Koyukuk, Alatna, Chandalar, Christian, and John rivers and their wild tributaries and the mountain-girded blue waters of wind-swept Walker, Wild, Chandalar, Elusive, Amiloyak, Feniak, Nutuvuki, Kurupa, and Old John lakes. The Brooks Range embraces the majestic 9,000-foot peaks and spires of the Gates of the Arctic National Park and the Arctic National Wildlife Range, inhabited by grizzly, moose, and barren-ground caribou. To the north stretches a forbidding land of treeless tundra plains to the frozen wastelands of the Arctic Ocean.

Weather, Bugs, & Beasts

Alaska has an enormous diversity and range of climate. The maritime climate of the Panhandle, warmed by the Japan Current, has mild winters, cool summers, and extremely heavy rainfall. In some areas of the Tongass Country, average annual precipitation exceeds 150 inches. In the high country of south central Alaska, snowstorms are likely to occur at all times of the year; bad weather conditions are the rule here. The inland valleys have moderate rainfall, short but rather warm summers, and winter temperatures not unlike those found in the northern prairie states of the U.S. The rugged, mountainous terrain of southwestern Alaska is generally wet, with mild foggy summers and harsh winters. South of the Aleutian Islands is an area of low pressure

with an east-west trend commonly known as the "Aleutian Low." Many of the cyclonic disturbances of the Northern Hemisphere swirl through this low-pressure trough. The Great Interior is a land of intensely hot summers and harsh, frigid winters. The subarctic far north regions have very short summers with little precipitation.

When fishing, hunting, or camping in the high country of southern Alaska, you should be alert for the violent and gusty wind known to the natives as the *williwaw*, which sweeps across the Bering Sea from Siberia, often reaching gale forces of up to 100 miles per hour on the high passes and leeward slopes of mountains. For protection against these fearsome winds, which have been known to flip over commercial salmon-fishing boats and bush planes and collapse tents, the smart woodsman will camp down low, pitching his tent in an isolated, protected stand of timber. Be sure in planning your trip to avoid the freeze-up, which lasts from the second week in October well into May, and even into mid-July in some high-country regions.

Alaska's grizzlies, both the barren-ground and giant Kodiak varieties, present potential hazards to the wilderness fisherman, hunter, backpacker, and paddler. Several unknowing backpackers have lost their lives or have been seriously maimed by foolishly camping along well-traveled bear trails. Andy Russell's classic book on grizzly behavior—which contains an excellent chapter on Alaska—is required reading for

anyone planning an Alaskan trip. *Grizzly Country* may be obtained for $7.95 (plus 50¢ postage) from Alfred A. Knopf, Inc., Mail Order Dept., 400 Hahn Rd., Westminster, MD 21157. To further enhance your knowledge and appreciation of the mysterious rhythms of life in the far north, read William Pruitt's classic account of the moose, wolf, and caribou in his famous book *Animals of the North*, available for $9.95 from Harper & Row, Mail Order Division, 10 E. 53rd St., New York, NY 10022.

The most ferocious beast of prey in this great land, however, is the voracious Alaskan mosquito. If you are planning a trip to Alaska, be sure to pack a good supply of Muskol, Mosquitone, Cutters, or Off! insect repellent. All of them contain concentrations of 50%-plus of DEET, the most effective known insect repellent. If you are planning an extended wilderness journey, a recommended dosage of 50 mg/day of Vitamin B-1 for a week prior to your departure and about 10 mg twice a day during the trip (check with your physican for his recommended dosage) is one of the most effective natural defenses against blackflies, mosquitoes, and no-see-ums to use in combination with an effective repellent. It's also advisable to take along a wide-brimmed hat, raingear, light-colored heavy cotton or wool shirt, and sunglasses.

Alaskan Maps & Charts—How to Order

Topographic map kits are a must for anyone planning a trip to the Alaskan wilderness. All maps listed in the Alaska chapter are full-color U.S. Geological Survey topographic maps (unless otherwise noted) at scales of 1:250,000, or 1 inch to 4 miles ($2 each), and 1:24,000, large-scale 7½-minute maps, 1 inch to 2,000 feet ($1.25 each). The maps show all natural and man-made features, including contours, falls, rapids, marshes, mountain ranges, glaciers, fjords, national forests and wilderness areas, wildlife refuges, roads, trails, lakes and streams, wilderness cabins, and highways. The maps (and a free *Alaska Topographic Map Index, Map Symbol Chart,* and *Topographic Maps* booklet) may be ordered from: Distribution Branch, U.S. Geological Survey, Federal Center, Denver, CO 80225. Be sure to order your maps by the individual map name and code; indicate scale when ordering 1:250,000-scale maps. To expedite delivery, include extra money for first-class postage. The U.S. Geological Survey publishes two useful, attractive overview maps of the state: the *Alaska Map B Topographic Edition* ($2), which consists of two sheets, each 36 × 51 inches, and shows all man-made and natural features, including contours; and the *Alaska Map E Shaded-Relief Edition* ($2), which has colored relief shading which gives the map the appearance of the sunlight striking the surface from the northwest. A free *Alaska Nautical Chart Catalog (3)—Including the Aleutian Islands,* is available from: Distribution Division (C44), National Ocean Survey, Riverdale, MD 20840.

A useful 214-page handbook for wilderness travel, *Be Expert with Map & Compass,* by Bjorn Kjellstrom, president and founder of Silva Compasses, may be obtained for $6.95 (plus 50¢ postage) from Charles Scribner's Sons, Bookstore Dept., 597 Fifth Ave., New York, NY 10017.

ALASKA ENCYCLOPEDIA

Accommodations— Vacation Lodges & Sporting Camps

A comprehensive listing of Alaska's hotels, motels, and inns—locally referred to as "roadhouses," and wilderness vacation, hunting, and fishing lodges in central, far north, southeast, and southwest Alaska is contained in the 54-page travel guide *The Worlds of Alaska*. The guide describes rates and lodge facilities and services, including trailer and camper parks, airstrips, cooking facilities, gear, guide and fly-in services, dining facilities, sleeping units, boats, motors, and fish and big-game species present. The guide is available free, along with the useful 20-page *Outdoor Guide of Alaska*, from: Division of Tourism, Department of Commerce and Economic Development, Pouch E, Juneau 99811. Vacation lodging and tour bookings may be made through *Alaska* Magazine Travel Service (which see) or Alaska Tour & Marketing Services, Inc., Suite 312 Park Place Bldg., Sixth and University St., Seattle WA 98101 (206–624–8551); (May–Sept.) Suite 106, 509 West Third Ave., Anchorage 99501 (907–274–7648). Ask for their free *Alaska Tour Destinations* booklet. (Listings of major lodges and camps are found throughout the "Encyclopedia" and "Travel & Recreation Guide" sections.)

Admiralty Island & the Bald Eagle

Admiralty, with its 678-mile coastline, is the second largest island in the massive Alexander Archipelago of southeast Alaska, and the most productive bald eagle habitat in the world. The eagle and the raven represented the two main clans of the Tlingit Indians, who lived in this region; the Tlingit totem poles usually had one or the other bird carved upon them. More eagles nest on this majestic island than the total number surviving in the lower 48 states. The mature bald eagle *(Haliaeetus leucocephalus)* is recognized by its distinctive white head and tail and a wingspread of 6–7½ feet. During the 17th and 18th centuries "bald" was commonly used to signify white; the adult bird's head feathers are white, thus the name "bald eagle." Admiralty's eagles nest in the tops of old-growth Sitka spruce or hemlock trees within a few hundred yards of the seacoast. The tall Sitka spruce, sometimes at least 2–3 centuries old, with their damaged, flattened tops, serve as natural platforms for the eagle's massive nests. The island has an estimated total of 1,000 of these great nests, averaging about two nests per mile, which attain tremendous size and weight and often survive the winter and are used again and again, for as long as 65 years. In order to reserve a sample of undisturbed eagle-nesting area where the bird can be studied and observed in its natural setting, several islands in the Seymour Canal on Admiralty Island have been designated as the Seymour Eagle Management Area. Spectacular concentrations can be seen feeding on the spring smelt runs in the Stikine River near Wrangell, the rivers of Berners Bay near Juneau, along the rivers entering Prince William Sound and Cook Inlet near Anchorage, and in the Chilkat Valley near Haines at the end of the Lynn Canal. For additional information and the free booklet *Bald Eagles in Alaska*, write: U.S. Fish & Wildlife Service, 313 D St., Anchorage 99501.

Admiralty's scenic wilderness, incredibly rich in fish and marine life, also has Alaska's highest-density population of brown bears. The Angoon Tlingit tribe's name for Admiralty was *Hutsnuwu*, meaning "Brown Bear Fort Island." The Tlingits had a great fear of the supernatural powers of the island's thick interior forests: the territory of the great bear. (Beautiful Thayer Lake on Admiralty is named for Jack Thayer, a U.S. Forest Service ranger who was mauled and killed by a brown bear.) The abundant wildlife of Admiralty that nourished the bear and the eagle also nourished the Tlingit tribes, who became a feared sea power, extending their trade routes from their coastal vil-

lages as far north as Prince William Sound and the upper Yukon and south to Puget Sound. Their great cedar war canoes lined the village beaches. Slaves captured from rival tribes labored to create totem poles proclaiming their ancient tribal symbols: the fierce superiority of the eagle and the precocious raven, and the beaver, killer whale, frog, and bear.

Airlines & Charter Fly-in Services

Several major airlines provide jet service and package wilderness hunting and fishing adventure trips to Alaska from the lower 48. Write or call the following airlines or your local travel agent for rates, flight information, and free wilderness adventure tour folders. *Alaska Airlines*, City Ticket Office, 418 University St., Seattle, WA 98101, connects Seattle with Sitka, Anchorage, and Fairbanks and also serves Cordova, Yakutat, and southeastern Alaska fish and game points. *Pan American World Airways*, 332 White-Henry-Stuart Bldg., Seattle, WA 98101, has daily nonstop service between Fairbanks and Seattle and New York with connections to all principal U.S. cities. *Northwest Orient Airlines*, White-Henry-Stuart Bldg., Seattle, WA 98101, has daily Boeing 747 nonstop service connecting major cities across the U.S. with Anchorage. *Western Airlines*, Sea-Tas International Airport, Seattle, WA 98158, has service from Seattle and Minneapolis and major cities of the West to Ketchikan, Juneau, and Kodiak. *Wien Air Alaska*, 4100 International Airport Rd., Anchorage 99502, and 6640 White-Henry-Stuart Bldg., Seattle, WA 98101, provides the only scheduled flights to Alaska's North Slope and serves over 150 outfitting centers and cities throughout the state, with B-737 jets to Anchorage, Bethel, Dillingham, Fairbanks, Homer, Juneau, Kenai, King Salmon, Kodiak, Kotzebue, Nome, and Point Barrow. Scheduled air and charter fly-in service and package tours within Alaska are provided by *Alaska Aeronautical Industries*, Box 6067, Anchorage 99502, to Kenai, Beluga River, Swanson River, Soldotna, Fire Island, and Homer. *Polar Airways*, 2600 E. 5th Ave., Anchorage 99501, has service to Gulkana, Tok, and Valdez. *Reeve Aleutian Airways*, Box 559, Anchorage 99510, has flights to points in the Aleutian Range and on the Aleutian and Pribilof islands. *Fairbanks Air Service*, Fairbanks 99701, has flights to Nenana, Clear, Usibelli, Healy, McKinley Park, Summit, Talkeetna, and Anchorage. *Air North*, Fairbanks 99701, flies to Fort Yukon, Chalkyitsik, Venetie, and Circle City. *Alaska Central Air*, Fairbanks 99701, has service to Galena via Tanana, Minto, Manley Hot Springs, and Ruby. *Coast Air*, Ketchikan 99901, has service to Craig, Hydaburg, Klawock, and nearby points. *Kodiak Western Alaska Airlines*, Kodiak 99615, serves Kodiak and Afognak islands and points in the Bristol Bay area with amphibious aircraft. *Shellbarger Flying Service*, Kotzebue 99752, has service to Shishmaref, Wales, and Tin City. *Munz Northern Airlines*, Nome 99762, flies to Stebbins, St. Michael, Cape Romanzof, Andreafsky, Bethel, Teller, Deering, King Island, St. Lawrence Island, Little Diomede Island, and points on the Seward Peninsula. *Eagle Air*, Sitka 99835, has service to Hoonah and Kake. In addition to scheduled airline service, there are close to 200 certified air charter bush pilots operating throughout Alaska to serve the fisherman, hunter, and wilderness paddler.

A listing of bush pilots who hold a valid air taxi certificate can be obtained by writing: Alaska Transportation Commission, 5410 International Airport, Anchorage 99510. A complete listing with descriptions of air taxis and air charter services, by city, is found in the 54-page travel guide *Worlds of Alaska*, available free from: Division of Tourism, Department of Commerce and Economic Development, Pouch E, Juneau 99811. Costs for fly-in services include the time required to fly to the designated hunting or fishing area and return flight to point of origin. Fly-in trips usually average $25–$40 a person.

Larger charters, such as an 18-passenger de Havilland Twin Otter can be chartered for about $150 per hour; the smaller 4-passenger Cessna 185 costs about $70 per hour. Often the size and bulk of your equipment, plus the number of passengers, determine the type of aircraft you will charter. Be sure to correspond with your pilot to determine how much weight the plane you will be flying will haul. It's best to pack your gear in several small bundles rather than a few large ones. A first-aid kit and survival gear are essential for wilderness fly-in trips in case of accident or sickness. Hunters should arrange with their pilot for cold-room storage or freezing of game. Transporting the antlers of trophy moose, elk, and caribou can present a problem in small aircraft due to new federal regulations prohibiting the carrying of antlers and other large objects on the struts of the plane. (Note: It is illegal to use helicopters in any manner to hunt in Alaska.)

Alaska Magazine Travel Service

The Alaska Northwest Publishing Company, one of the most renowned institutions of the "Last Frontier," publishes *Alaska* magazine, a beautifully illustrated full-color monthly which contains useful articles of interest to the outdoor traveler ranging from fishing to backpacking, where-to-go, history and lore, Alaska's great fish and game areas, and bush pilots and guides. The subscription cost, $12 per year for 12 issues, is worth every dime. Write: Alaska Northwest Publishing Co., Box 4-EEE, Anchorage 99509. The *Alaska Magazine*

Bald Eagles in Alaska

Travel Service will provide specific trip-planning assistance and provide tickets and reservations for Alaska tours, sportfishing packages, and carriers, including the Alaska state ferries. Address all inquires to: Alaska Magazine Travel Service, 139 Second Ave. S., Edmonds, WA 98020.

Alaska Railroad

The 470-mile-long Alaska Railroad is the nation's only government-owned railway. It winds north from Seward, on the scenic coast of the Kenai Peninsula, through Anchorage and Mount McKinley Park to Fairbanks. Passenger service is offered between Anchorage and Fairbanks, serving en route Mount McKinley National Park and the wilderness fishing and hunting areas along the Susitna, Nenana, and Yukon rivers and the Talkeetna Mountains. The railroad operates daily during the summer with drop-offs and pickups arranged at any point along the route; it also stops at any point along the track for the wilderness traveler who signals. For a free vacation travel brochure, rates and information write: Alaska Railroad, P.O. Box 7–2111, An-

chorage 99510. The Alaska Railroad and surrounding wilderness are shown on U.S. Geological Survey Maps, scale 1:250,000: Seward, Anchorage, Talkeetna, Tyonek, Healy, Fairbanks, Talkeetna Mountains.

Anchorage—Outfitting Center for the Alaskan Wilderness

(Pop. 180,000). This flat, sprawling city in south central Alaska was founded as a tent camp in 1914 during the construction of the Alaska Railroad. Anchorage is on an alluvial plain in upper Cook Inlet, surrounded by the peaks of the Chugach Mountains and dense forests of spruce, birch, and aspen. Anchorage is Alaska's largest city and the gateway to the wilderness recreation areas in the Alaska and Kenai peninsulas, Bristol Bay, the south-central coast, Mount McKinley National Park, and the Great Interior. Several of the state's foremost bush pilots, guides, and charter wilderness fishing and hunting fly-in services are headquartered here, including *Alaska Air Guides, Inc.*, 327 E. Fireweed La., 99503; *Alaska Bush Carrier*, 4801 Aircraft Rd., 99502; *Alaska Travel Air*, Box 4–2646, 99509; *Alyeska Air Service*, Box 5154 Annex, 99502; *Central Northern Ltd.*, Air Service 161, 7800 De Barr St., 99504; *Charlie Allen Flying Service*, Box 5105, 99502; *Denali Air Service*, Box 4–2769, 99501; *Great Northern Airlines*, 3400 W. Airport Rd., 99502; *Ketchum Air Service*, 2708 Aspen Dr., 99503; *Lee's Air Service, Inc.*, Box 4–2495, 99509; *Northwestern Air Service, Inc.*, 1704 E. 5th Ave., 99501; *Petco Aviation, Inc.*, Box 6358, 99502; *Rust's Flying Service*, Box 6301, 99502; *Spernak Airways, Inc.*, Box 2255, 99510; *Stoddard Aero Service, Inc.*, 2250 E. 5th Ave., 99501; and *Totem Airways, Inc.*, Box 4–2344, 99509. The city is reached by the major airlines, the George Parks and Glenn highways, and the Alaska Railroad.

Brown Bear, Alaska

The great, legendary Alaska brown grizzly *(Ursus horribilis)* is the largest of all bears, reaching heights as tall as 8 feet and weights up to 1,500 pounds. The Alaska brownie, of the same species as the

smaller barren-ground grizzly of the Great Interior, is a handsome, dish-faced fellow with a noticeable hump above his shoulders and a yellowish to chocolate brown coat. The Alaska brown, or Kodiak, bear inhabits the coastal forests and open country of the Alaska Peninsula, southern mainland, and the Panhandle and is found on St. Lawrence, Baranof, Chichagof, Admiralty, Kodiak, and Montague islands. The best hunting is found on the Alaska Peninsula and the Kodiak National Wildlife Refuge. Hundreds of centuries-old, deep, well-defined bear trails crisscross the coastal areas and islands. The bears have a sweet tooth for the elderberries that ripen in the warm sun of August and September, and in July and August are often found congregated along streams gorging themselves on spawning salmon. The big bears catch the spawned and dying salmon by pouncing with their forefeet to pin the fish to the streambed.

The ferocity of a wounded brown or grizzly bear is legendary, and a hunter or fisherman in bear country should carry at least a .30–06 power rifle. Many Alaskans will use nothing but their trusted .375 magnums. Always remember that these large, powerful animals are unpredictable and dangerous, and that each bear has a distinct personality and behavior. An old grizzly with an impacted tooth may charge in an instant should you cross his path. There are no formulas that apply to all bears, and unprovoked attacks on man in Alaska are not unusual. If you cross paths with one, yield the right of way. Never run. Any fast motion will excite the bear, and he may interpret your retreat as a follow-up of a hostile invasion of his territory. Always provide an escape route so this proud animal has a dignified exit. When traveling through Alaskan bear country, try to make a variety of noises by loud whistling, talking, or shaking pebbles in a can and always carry a rifle, if possible. Even though a bear's eyesight is poor, its senses of smell and hearing are excellent. The most dangerous situations are surprise meetings in brush thickets, dense forests, or tall grass; a feeding bear or "sorehead" with an impacted tooth or body wound; and a sow with cubs. Wind and rivers may muffle your noises. When fishing carry several large strong plastic bags to store your fish and hide odors.

Camping & Backpacking

Alaska has hundreds of well-maintained campgrounds and wilderness cabins scattered throughout the mountains and alpine tundra, lake country and coastal and interior forests, and along the highway systems of the Panhandle, Kenai and Alaska peninsulas, and the Great Interior. Nonresidents may purchase a $10 annual camping permit for Alaska's state campgrounds. For information about camping and state campgrounds write: Alaska Division of Lands, 344 E. 6th Ave., Anchorage 99501. The 20-page *Outdoor Guide of Alaska* lists all campsites and can be obtained free from: Division of Tourism, Department of Commerce and Economic Development, Pouch E, Juneau 99811. The free booklet *Alaska State Park System*, available free from the Department of Natural Resources, Division of Parks, 323 E. 4th Ave., Anchorage 99501, describes the recreational and wilderness campground facilities located in the Chugach and Denali state parks, Kachemak Bay State Wilderness Park, and the Captain Cook, Chena River, Harding Lake, and Nancy Lake state recreation areas. *Camps and Trails*, a guide to the campgrounds and public-use cabins located on the 283 million acres of national resource lands in Alaska, can be obtained free from: Bureau of Land Management, 555 Cordova St., Anchorage 99501, along with the *Alaska Recreation Guide Map*, which lists and describes all state, U.S. Fish & Wildlife Service, U.S. Forest Service, and National Park Service recreation areas and campgrounds. Write: National Park Service, 334 E. 5th Ave., Suite 250, Anchorage 99501, for information on camping and hiking in Mount

McKinley National Park and Katmai and Glacier Bay national monuments. For campground and trail maps of the Chugach and Tongass national forests write: U.S. Forest Service, P.O. Box 1628, Juneau 99801. Two useful guidebooks, *55 Ways to the Wilderness in South Central Alaska* and *Discovering Southeast Alaska with Pack & Paddle*, are available for $7.95 each, plus 50¢ handling and postage, from Alaska Northwest Publishing Co., Box 4-EEE, Anchorage 99509.

Canadian Customs & Citizen Band Radios

If you plan to travel to Alaska through Canada, you'll have to pass through Canadian customs. For information write: Customs & Excise Branch, Department of National Revenue, Connaught Bldg., Mackenzie Ave., Ottawa, Ont. If you plan on using a citizen band radio on your trip through Canada, a Canadian license is required. There is no charge for a license, however, and the application procedure is easy. Write: Regional Superintendent, Telecommunications Regulations Branch, Department of Communications, Room 320–25, 300 Financial Bldg., 10621 100th Ave., Edmonton, Alta. T5J 0B1, and request a license application form. Without a Canadian permit your CB set will be sealed at the border.

Canoeing & Wild Rivers

Alaska is blessed with many of the finest, and most dangerous, wilderness canoeing waters in North America. We recommend that the Alaska-bound wilderness paddler write for the *Alaska Canoe Trails* guide, available free from: Bureau of Land Management, 555 Cordova St., Anchorage 99501. This useful publication is a guide to highway-accessible canoe routes in Alaska. It includes maps and descriptions of the route, access, fish species present, and difficulty ratings for the Fortymile and Yukon rivers, Birch Creek, Chatanika and Chena rivers, Fish Creek, Delta River, Upper Tangle Lakes to Dickey Lake and Gulkana River, Kenai River, Swanson River and Swan Lake canoe routes, which are all clearwater except for the Yukon and Kenai rivers, which are swift, turbid glacial streams. Generally speaking, canoe travel on Alaska's clearwater rivers is 3–4 miles per hour; on glacial rivers, 5–7 miles per hour; and on lakes, 2 miles per hour. Be sure to write for the useful *Alaska Recreation Guide Map* and *National Wild & Scenic Rivers* booklet, available free from the Bureau of Land Management (address above). Proposed national wild and scenic rivers within Alaska include the Yukon-Charley National Rivers, 1.9 million acres near the eastern Yukon-Alaska border; Birch Creek National Wild River, a 135-mile stretch between Fairbanks and Circle; Fortymile National Wild & Scenic River, a 375-mile stretch along the Yukon-Alaska border; Beaver Creek National Wild River, a 135-mile stretch north of Fairbanks; and the Unalakleet National Wild River, a 60-mile stretch located 400 miles northwest of Anchorage on the Seward Peninsula. *Canoeing on the Kenai National Moose Range*, a detailed guide to the Swanson River route and Swan Lake route, is available free from: Superintendent, Kenai National Moose Range, Box 500, Kenai 99611. A fascinating guide to the remote wilderness canoe routes of scenic Admiralty Island in the Tongass National Forest, *Cross Admiralty Canoe Route*, is available free from: Supervisor, Tongass National Forest, Box 2278, Ketchikan 99901. Please note that Alaska's wilderness canoe routes travel through the heart of grizzly and brown bear country; they are extremely dangerous and should be attempted only by the experienced and well-prepared canoeist or with a registered Alaskan guide. Anyone planning an Alaska wilderness canoe trip is advised to read *Wild Rivers of Alaska*, a 176-page bible by Sepp Weber, published by Alaska Northwest Publishing Co., Box

4-EEE, Anchorage 99509 ($8.95, paperback). This handsome book contains more than 70 color photographs, maps, and charts and describes 53 wild rivers.

Guided wild river trips are provided by *Alaska Wilderness Expeditions, Inc.*, Box 882, Wrangell 99929; *Alaska Wilderness River Trips, Inc.*, Box 1143, Eagle River 99577; *Arctic Outfitters Ltd.*, Box 33, Kiana 99749 (Kobuk River); *Bear Bros. Whole Wilderness Experience*, Box 4–2969, Anchorage 99509 (kayak touring in Prince William Sound); *Wild Rivers North*, Box 151, McGrath 99627; and *Challenge Wilderness Adventure*, P.O. Box 4–2881, Anchorage 99509 (Yukon River).

Fairbanks—Outfitting Center for the Great Interior & Brooks Range

(Pop. 32,000). This former gold-mining community, known as the "golden heart of Alaska," is the state's second largest city and a renowned outfitting center and jumping-off point for the remote fishing and big-game hunting areas of the Great Interior and far north. Fairbanks, sited on a bend of the Chena River, is the northern terminus of the Alaska Highway and meeting point of the Elliott, Steese, George Parks, and Richardson highways. An extremely flat city, Fairbanks is surrounded by the White Mountains to the north, the foothills of the Alaska Range to the south, and low, rolling hills to the east and west. The University of Alaska Museum houses one of the finest collections of Eskimo, Aleut, and Indian artifacts, pioneer relics, and specimens of northern wildlife in Alaska. The city is home base for many of Alaska's great guides and bush pilots, and numerous air charter services serving the fisherman and hunter, including *Alaska Air Charter*, Box 80507, and *Al Wright Air Service, Inc.*, Box 60142, both College 99701; and *Elliot Air Service*, 5920 Airport Way, and *Great Northern Airlines, Inc.*, 3400 W. International Airport Rd., both Anchorage 99502. *Alaska Riverways*, Box G, 99701, offers sternwheeler cruises out of Fairbanks on the Tanana River. The *Itkillik Brooks Range Lodge*, 1206 Coppet St., 99701, has floatplane transportation from Fairbanks to lodges and cabins on the Itkillik River in the Brooks Range for arctic grayling, lake trout, and northern pike fishing. *Alaska Guide Service, Inc.*, Box 80929, College 99701, operates float trips, photography, and fishing at the Chatanika River Camp, north of Fairbanks.

Fenwick Alaska Fly Fishing School

The Fenwick Corporation's (world-renowned manufacturers of quality fishing rods and gear) 6-day Kulik River school, the oldest of all Fenwick fly fishing schools, operates during July, August, and September and is limited to fly fisherman (and their families) with some previous experience. The famous Kulik River, one of the nation's great wilderness rainbow trout streams, is located in the Bristol Bay Trophy Fish Area, 250 air miles southwest of Anchorage. The school's curriculum includes on-location fly casting and presentation; fly line, rod and reel construction, how to choose the proper tackle, and terminology; entomology, artificial fly construction, identification, choice of flies, and how to "match the hatch"; fly-fishing knots such as the "blood" and the ever-elusive "nail knot"; leader construction and uses; how to read the stream and wading. Tuition includes six nights lodging in rustic cabins at the Kulik River Lodge and meals. For free literature, rates, and info, write: School Coordinator, Fenwick Fly Fishing Schools, P.O. Box 729, Westminster, CA92683 (phone: 714–897–1066).

Fishing & Hunting in the Alaskan Wilderness

Alaska is separated from the lower states by British Columbia and the Yukon Territory and remains one of the least-developed areas in North America, with the exception of the vast barren lands of Canada's Northwest Territories. Its wild profusion of glacier-studded mountains, countless rivers and streams, immense lakes, thousands of square miles of boreal forests and barren tundra, dense coastal rain forests, and fish and wildlife have long been the dream of lower-48 sportsmen. The sheer immensity of Alaska is mind-boggling. If you were to place a map of Alaska over a map of the lower-48 states, it would cover Washington, Oregon, California, Idaho, Utah, and Nevada with a couple of Rhode Islands thrown in. Its 34,000-mile coastline is 50 percent longer than the rest of the U.S. coastline combined. At the northern end of the Panhandle, the massive 1,000-mile Alaska-Aleutian Range makes an arc from Yukon Territory, cutting across the southern half of the state down along the volcanic peaks of the Alaska Peninsula and through the stepping stones of the Aleutian Islands. Within the arc of the great range are the legendary big-game areas of the Chugach, Talkeetna, Mentasta, and Wrangell mountains. To the north lies the vast valley of the Yukon River, stretching from Yukon Territory on the east across to the Bering Sea on the west. North of the Yukon Valley is the remote Brooks Range, which sweeps for 600 miles across northern Alaska, separating the arctic coast from the Great Interior.

Trophy Fishing Waters

The Alaskan bush is a tough challenge for the outdoorsman—it's not a place for the weekend tenderfoot. The wilderness traveler should be prepared to encounter extremely rugged terrain, bears, moose in rut,

brawling rivers, voracious mosquitoes, and devil's club. The hazards come part and parcel with the rewards. The fishing in Alaska ranks with the finest in the world, but as in any true wilderness, the fishing varies greatly from one watershed to another. This is especially true of the sea-run, or migratory, species. Southwest and central Alaska generally have the best fishing for a mixed bag of salmon, rainbow and lake trout, northern pike, arctic char and grayling, and Dolly Varden. Fly-in guides operate charter aircraft throughout southwest and central Alaska from the Lake Hood seaplane base in Anchorage. Southeast Alaska is a top-ranked region for cutthroat trout, silver and king salmon, and steelhead trout. The remote lakes and rivers of the far north and the Brooks Range Wilderness hold lunker lake trout, grayling, sheefish, and great northern pike—often seen lined up along the shoals in the lakes like a fleet of submarines. A comprehensive guide to the fishing waters adjacent to Alaska's highway systems and fly-in waters, the *Alaska Sport Fishing Guide*, is available free from: Alaska Department of Fish & Game, Sportfish Division, Subport Bldg., Juneau 99801. The 96-page guide is packed with maps and lists the lakes and streams, location, and fish species present along the Alaska, Copper River, Taylor, Richardson, George Parks, Steese, Elliott, Denali, Glenn, Seward, Sterling, Slana-Tok Cutoff, and Palmer highways, along the Matanuska Valley, Skilak, and Nome-Solomon-Teller roads, and in the Brooks Range, Bristol Bay-Alaska Peninsula, Kotzebue-Kobuk, and Kodiak and Afognak Island fly-in waters. The Alaska-bound angler should also send for the *Alaska Sportfishing Seasons & Bag Limits*, a 69-page handbook published by the Department of Fish & Game. It describes and lists license fees and regulations, and contains a useful "Field Guide to Alaskan Game Species." The *Alaska Fishing Guide*, 171 pages, illustrated with maps, charts, and photos, is published by the Alaska Northwest Publishing Co., Box 4-EEE, Anchorage 99509, for $3.95, plus 50¢ handling and postage. This handy guide provides valuable info on planning an Alaskan fishing trip and describes the major fishing regions and 557 lakes and streams. The Department of Fish & Game provides daily prerecorded reports on sportfishing in central Alaska if you phone (907) 344–0566 in Anchorage or (907) 452–1525 in Fairbanks.

Trophy fish awards are issued by the Department of Fish & Game to anglers for fish that meet minimum weight qualifications for each species. Trophy fish rules and affidavits are available for each species at all license vendors and all Department of Fish & Game offices. Entries must meet these minimum weight requirements: rainbow-steelhead trout, 12 lb.; Dolly Varden-arctic char, 10 lb.; Lake trout, 20 lb.; eastern brook trout, 3 lb.; northern pike, 15 lb.; cutthroat trout (all species), 3 lb.; sheefish, 30 lb.; arctic grayling, 3 lb.; burbot, 8 lb.; red salmon (sockeye), 10 lb.; pink salmon (humpy), 7 lb.; silver salmon (coho), 18 lb.; king salmon, 60 lb.; halibut, 100 lb.; kokanee, 1 lb.; whitefish, 4 lb. Attractive 8 × 10-inch parchment certificates suitable for framing are issued to all contestants winning an award under the

ALASKA SPORT FISHING GUIDE

trophy fish program. The official records maintained by the Alaska Department of Fish & Game since the establishment of the trophy fish program in 1964 are as follows (larger fish may have been taken but were caught before the program was initiated or were not entered into competition):

ALASKA RECORD FISH

	Lb.–oz.	Length (inches)	Place	Year
Arctic char	17–8	36	Wulik River	1968
Arctic grayling	4–11	21½	Ugashik Lake Narrows	1975
Burbot	22–8	44	Lake Louise	1968
Chum salmon	27–3	39⅜	Raymond Cove	1977
Cutthroat trout	6–12	24½	Orchard Lake	1973
Halibut	340	90	Thomas Bay	1971
King salmon	91	50	Baranof Island	1977
Lake trout	47	44¼	Clarence Lake	1970
Northern pike	28–2	44¾	Wilson Lake	1971
Pink salmon	12–9	30	Moose River	1974
Rainbow/steelhead*	42–2	43	Bell Island	1970
Red salmon	16	31	Kenai River	1974
Sheefish	52–½	48	Kobuk River	1968
Silver salmon	23–10	35½	Behm Narrows	1973
Whitefish	5–8	22¾	Naknek River	1973

*World's record.

The *Bristol Bay Trophy Fish Area,* regulated by the Department of Fish & Game, offers some of the state's finest wilderness fishing for record arctic char, grayling, and rainbow trout up to 30 pounds. The area includes the Kvichak River watershed (except Lake Clark and its tributaries above Six-Mile Lake). The Kvichak includes the waters forming a ½-mile radius into Lake Iliamna.

Hunting in the Alaska Wilderness

The big-game species of Alaska offer some of the finest hunting remaining in North America. *The Alaska Hunter's Guidebook,* a useful and interesting 47-page guide, is a must for anyone planning an Alaskan trip. It describes the seasons, feeding habits, hunting methods, and trophy hunting areas for Alaska's big-game species with fascinating details on how to travel, selection of gear, and a section on trophy care and field handling of game. It is available free, along with the *Alaska Game Management Units Map, Alaska Hunting Regulations,* and *Upland Game Birds of Forest & Tundra,* from the Alaska Department of Fish & Game, Juneau 99801. The *Alaska Hunting Guide,* 170 pages, and *Fair Chase with Alaskan Guides,* 270 pages, are available for $3.95 each plus 50¢ postage and handling from the Alaska Northwest Publishing Co., Box 4-EEE, Anchorage 99509. All nonresident hunters are required to hire the services of a licensed guide. Alaska's largest moose trophies are taken in the Kenai and Alaska peninsulas. Moose with antler spreads exceeding 60 inches may be taken throughout southwest and interior Alaska if a hunter is lucky and persistent. Only a few of Alaska's caribou herds are accessible to the average hunter. The Nelchina herd, which numbers more than 60,000 animals, is one of the most accessible, generally found in an area bounded by the Alaska Range, the Talkeetna Mountains, and the Glenn and Richardson highways. Alaska's largest caribou are found on remote Adak Island, where bulls weighing up to 700 pounds have been

reported. Large Roosevelt elk in excess of 1,200 pounds are found in the alpine meadows and dense forests of Afognak and Raspberry islands in the southwest. Sitka black-tailed deer are found in the Panhandle, a few islands in Prince William Sound, and parts of the Kodiak island group. Deer country is often brown bear country, and experienced hunters will carry a rifle capable of stopping a "brownie." The Dall sheep, the white king of Alaska's high country, roams the towering peaks of the Wrangell, Chugach, and Talkeetna mountains, Alaska Range, Tanana Hills, Brooks Range, and Kenai Peninsula. Trophy Wrangell Mountain sheep are noted for their wide, flaring horns. Mountain goats dwell in the coastal mountains throughout the Panhandle to the Kenai Peninsula. The Alaska brown bear is found on Kodiak Island, Admiralty Island, and the Alaska Peninsula—where many blond-colored specimens are found. The grizzly is found throughout the Great Interior at or above timberline, particularly in the Alaska Range, Talkeetna Mountains, and on the south slope of the Brooks Range. Black bear range through the entire state, except the Alaska Peninsula and the arctic coast. Pack-hunting wolves are found wherever there are moose or caribou. (See "Guides & Wilderness Outfitters," "Airlines & Charter Fly-in Services," and "Travel & Recreation Guide.")

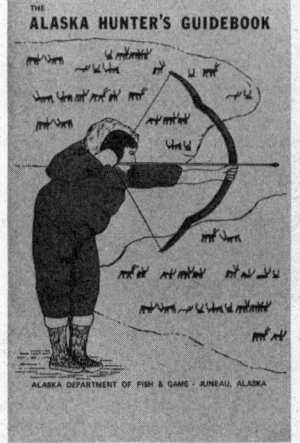

Guides & Wilderness Outfitters

Nonresident hunters and fishermen planning to travel into the Alaskan bush are well advised (and in certain instances are required) to hire the services of a licensed registered guide. *The Guide Register,* a

complete listing of the 400 master and registered Alaska guides, the species of game they hunt, and the type of transportation they offer, is available from the Department of Commerce, Division of Occupational Licensing, State of Alaska, Pouch D, Juneau 99811. A comprehensive listing of Alaskan wilderness hunting, fishing, photography, and canoe outfitters and gear rentals is found in the 54-page travel guide *Worlds of Alaska*, available free from: Division of Tourism, Department of Commerce and Economic Development, Pouch E, Juneau 99811. Alaska's hunting regulations specify that a nonresident hunter be accompanied by a guide when hunting grizzly or brown bear, Dall sheep, or polar bear. The majority of Alaska's guides charge a minimum of $150 per day for their services and require from one-third to one-half the price of the time scheduled for your hunting or fishing journey. Always keep in mind that a competent, ethical guide sells his time and expertise, not big-game heads or trophy fish. Fish and game conditions vary from year to year and place to place, even in the Alaskan wilderness. Most of Alaska's guides are certified bush pilots and hold air taxi certificates.

Alaska's renowned *master* guides, most of whom offer combined wilderness fly-in hunting and fishing trips, are: *Eldon Brandt*, Rte. C, Box 150, Palmer 99665 (907–822–3276); *Bud Branham*, Box 6128, Annex, Anchorage; *Dennis Branham*, Box 6184, Anchorage (907–277–9403); *Don De Hart*, Hart D Ranch, Gakona 99586; *Clark L. Engle*, 4129 Lana Court, Anchorage 99701 (907–479–6323); *Bud Helmericks*, 930 9th Ave., Fairbanks (907–452–5417); *Karl E. Lane*, Box 295, Juneau 99802 (907–586–3822); *John J. Lee*, Box 4, 2495, Anchorage 99509 (907–279–9549); *John H. McLay*, Box 754, Homer 99603 (907–235–8816); *Park Munsey*, Box 1186, Kodiak 99615 (907–486–3040);

George R. Pollard, Kasilof, 99610; *Frank See*, Hoonah 99829; and *Earl A. Stevens*, Box 1254, Homer 99603 (907–235–8630).

Before you hire a guide, ask him for half a dozen references and check them out thoroughly by correspondence or telephone (it's often easier to get an honest appraisal by phone than by letter; most people are busy and hesitate to put negative statements in cold print). Be sure to ask your guide for a list of recommended clothing and gear to bring, and what kind of living accommodations (a well-heated tent camp should be the minimum shelter in Alaska's bush) and food you can expect. These conditions will be stipulated in the guide-client contract

required by the Department of Fish & Game. Some guides will outfit you, if necessary, with sleeping bags, gear, and down clothing. The state encourages you to report both good and bad conduct of guides to: Investigator, Department of Public Safety, Fish & Game Protection Division, State of Alaska, P.O. Box 6188 Annex, Anchorage 99502.

Highways—Recreation & Scenic Routes

Alaska is served by an excellent system of paved and gravel-top highways that provide access to the major fishing, big-game hunting, and camping areas, and outfitting centers. The official *Highway Map of Alaska* is available free from: Alaska Travel Division, Pouch E, Juneau 99801. This useful full-color map describes access routes from the U.S. and shows the major highway routes in Alaska, Yukon Territory, and northern British Columbia as well as paved and gravel roads, marine ferry routes, railroads, glaciers, recreation areas, and other points of interest. It contains a recreation areas chart that lists camping units, boat-launching sites, shelter, drinking-water facilities, fishing, canoeing, and trails available for each area. The Alaska Department of Highways, P.O. Box 1467, Juneau 99811, publishes free, periodic *Highway Conditions Bulletins*. Driving on a gravel-surfaced highway can be a safe and pleasant experience if a few simple rules are followed: Do not accelerate excessively when passing another motorist as this can cause small stones to fly into the vehicle you are passing. Speeding up when passing also causes excessive dust. When meeting another vehicle, ease off the gas pedal. This is courteous as well as a good safety rule. Your slower speed reduces dust and the possibility of flying gravel. Cover your boat if you are trailing it on gravel roads. Rock guards are an important item for vacation trailers and exposed wiring on all trailers should be enclosed in plastic or a suitable tough material for protection from gravel. A rubber mat fastened to the underside of your car's gas tank will prevent damage from gravel. Headlights can be covered with clear plastic protectors specially made for this purpose. A wire mesh or fabric screen will prevent gravel and insect damage to radiators. Sliding or skidding on gravel can be prevented by avoiding sudden braking or abrupt steering movements under normal driving conditions. The full-color *Alaska Recreation Guide Map* shows all highways and Bureau of Land Management, Alaska Division of Lands, U.S. Fish & Wildlife Service, U.S. Forest Service, and National Park recreation areas and campgrounds in the Panhandle, Interior, Anchorage-Palmer, and Kenai Peninsula regions. It may be obtained free from: Bureau of Land Management, 555 Cordova St., Anchorage 99501. *The Milepost: All-the-North Travel Guide*, published by Alaska Northwest Publishing Co., Box 4-EEE, Anchorage 99509, for $5.95, is a must for anyone planning a car or recreational vehicle trip to Alaska. This extremely useful, large-format 498-page guide contains detailed maps, illustrations, and mile-by-mile descriptions of the Alaska Highway and major highway routes in Alaska and northwest Canada. A useful *Highway Guide to the Copper River* is available free from: Supervisor, Chugach National Forest, 121 E. Fireweed La., Suite 205, Anchorage 99503. A free travel information kit, *Touring the Prince of Wales Island Road System*, may be obtained by writing: Supervisor, U.S. Forest Service, Ketchikan Area, Box 2278, Ketchikan 99901. The kit contains detailed maps and nitty-gritty about key fishing sites, milepost attractions, forest development roads, campgrounds, trails and hiking, wildlife and hunting. Avis, Hertz, and National Car Rental services have offices in Anchorage, Cordova, Fairbanks, Haines, Homer, Juneau, Kenai, Ketchikan, Kodiak, Mount McKinley Park, Nome, Seward, Sitka, and Valdez. Campers may be rented at Winnebago Rentals, 2301 E. 5th Ave., Anchorage 99501; and Sport & Travel Equipment Co., 538 E. 5th Ave., Anchorage 99501. Listed below are brief descriptions of Alaska's great wilderness

and scenic highways along with their corresponding U.S. Geological Survey Topographic Overview Maps at a scale of 1:250,000, or 1 inch to 4 miles. (See "Fishing & Hunting in the Alaskan Wilderness" for descriptions of *Alaska Sport Fishing Guide.)*

Alaska Highway (2)

U.S. Geological Survey Maps: Big Delta, Fairbanks, Mount Hayes, Nabesna, Tanacross. The famous Alaska Highway is blacktopped from the Yukon border northwest to Fairbanks, with the usual number of bumps and dips caused by permafrost. This segment of the Alaska Highway passes through the great boreal forests and alpine tundra of the interior plateau past innumerable lakes and wild rivers. West of the Yukon border the highway passes through the Alaskan villages of Northway Junction, Tetlin Junction, Tok, Dot Lake, Delta Junction, Big Delta, Richardson, Salchaket, and North Pole to Fairbanks. The major features along the route include Tetlin Lake, Dot and Healy lakes, Alaska Range mountains, Gerstle and Little Delta rivers, Moose Slough, Craig Lakes, Tanana and Goodpaster rivers, and George and Blair lakes. There are campgrounds at Big Delta and Harding Lake Recreation Area.

Denali Highway (8)

U.S. Geological Survey Maps: Gulkana, Healy, Mount Hayes, Mount McKinley. This highway, once the only road link to Mount McKinley National Park, is a 2-lane gravel road which leads the traveler to the cloud-shrouded twin peaks of Mount McKinley. The highway winds through a land of arctic tundra, sparsely wooded hills, and shallow lakes from its junction with the Richardson Highway at Paxson, westward to its junction with the Anchorage-Fairbanks George Parks Highway 3. The region was once the home and hunting grounds of the semi-nomadic Athabascan Indians. Wildlife seen along the highway includes grizzly and black bear, caribou, bald eagle, moose, and Dall sheep. Major features shown on the maps include the Susitna River, Windy Creek, MacLaren River, Amphitheater Mountains, Reindeer Hills, and Mount McKinley National Park. There is good fishing for grayling, whitefish, and lake trout in the remote lakes and in the Delta, Gulkana, and Upper Tangle Lakes wilderness canoe trails. A handy guide, *Recreation Along Alaska's Denali Highway,* is available free from: Bureau of Land Management, 555 Cordova St., Anchorage 99501. The several roadhouses along the highway do not open until mid-June, and close early in September. Travelers should fill their gas tanks at Paxson or Cantwell. There are campgrounds at Brushkana Creek, Denali, and Tangle Lakes.

Elliott Highway (2)

U.S. Geological Survey Maps: Fairbanks, Livengood. The highway winds northwest from Fairbanks 156 miles to Manley Hot Springs, which is on a short tributary of the Tanana River. The Elliott is a well-maintained gravel road, but caution should be exercised when pulling trailers because of numerous steep hills and sharp turns. The highway provides access to the White Mountain Trail system. The summer trail is 23 miles long and traverses low marshy areas and high alpine tundra at Wickersham Dome. Access to the trail is at Mile 28. Three useful guides to the highway, *Alaska's White Mountain Trails, Recreation Along Alaska's Steese and Elliott Highways,* and *Alaska's Steese and Elliott Highways,* are available free from: Bureau of Land Management, 1028 Aurora Dr., Fairbanks 99701. The White Mountain Trail terminates at the Borealis LeFevre Cabin, which is open to public use for $2 per day by reservations through the Fairbanks district office of the Bureau of Land Management. The cabin is on the scenic grayling waters of Beaver Creek. The highway winds through the heart of grizzly and black bear, caribou, and moose hunting country and provides access to northern pike, sheefish, whitefish, and arctic gray-

ling fishing in the Tatalina and Tolovana rivers, Minto Flats, and Hot Springs Slough. There are campgrounds at Tolovana River and Manley Hot Springs.

George Parks Highway (3)

U.S. Geological Survey Maps: Anchorage, Tyonek, Talkeetna, Talkeetna Mountains, Healy, Fairbanks. The George Parks Highway, also known as the Anchorage-Fairbanks Highway, is the paved direct access route to Mount McKinley National Park. It winds for 359 miles through some of the most scenic, rugged wilderness in Alaska, from Anchorage northward through the fishing and hunting outfitting centers of Wasilla, Willow, Talkeetna, Colorado, Summit, Cantwell, McKinley Park, and Nenana to its terminus at Fairbanks. Major features along the route include the majestic peaks of the Talkeetna and Alaska Range mountains, Mount McKinley National Park, Broad Pass Lakes, and the Nenana, Chutitna, Talkeetna, and Sheep rivers. Campgrounds and recreation areas along the route include Rocky Lake, Big Lake, Willow Creek, Denali State Park, and Igloo Creek recreation areas and the Sanctuary River, Savage River, and Morina campgrounds. Advance campground reservations are required to drive past Savage River in Mount McKinley National Park.

Glenn Highway (1)

U.S. Geological Survey Maps: Anchorage, Gulkana, Nabesna, Talkeetna Mountains, Tanacross, Valdez. The highway is the major access route from the Alaska Highway southwest to Anchorage and the Kenai Peninsula in south central Alaska. The Glenn winds from the village of Tok on the Alaska Highway through a mountainous wilderness of alpine tundra and boreal forests surrounding the big-game hunting

and fishing areas at Tetlin Lake, Tok River, Cobb Lakes, Mentasta and Wrangell mountains, Gulkana and Copper rivers, Tazlina River, Talkeetna Mountains, and Matanuska River. The wilderness lakes and rivers accessible from the highway hold grayling, lake trout, and whitefish. The hunting and fishing outfitting centers along the route include the villages of Chistochina, Gakona, Gulkana, Glennallen, Eureka Lodge, and Sheep Mountain Inn. The Nabesna Gold-Mine Road winds from the Slana Roadhouse past Tanana Lakes to the old Nabesna gold mines on the Nabesna River. There are campgrounds at Lake Louise and Finger Lakes.

Richardson (4) & Edgerton Highways

U.S. Geological Survey Maps: Big Delta, Gulkana, Mount Hayes. The blacktopped Richardson Highway runs north from Valdez on Prince William Sound north through the 12,000-foot peaks and massive glaciers of the Chugach and Alaska Range mountains along the original route of the historic Abercrombie and Richardson trails to its junction with the Alaska Highway at Delta Junction. The highway passes through the villages of Tonsina, Copper Center, Glennallen, Gulkana, Sourdough, Paxson, Rapids, and Donnelly to Delta Junction. The major fish and game areas accessible from the highway include the Copper River, Chugach Mountains, Summit Lake, Alaska Range, and Gulkana and Delta River wilderness canoe trails. The Edgerton Highway, also known as the Edgerton Cutoff, runs for 33 miles from Milepost 82.6 of the Richardson Highway to the settlement of Chitina at the confluence of the Copper and Chitina rivers. The hundreds of lakes and rivers along the Richardson and Edgerton highways hold trophy grayling, northern pike, silver salmon, and lake and rainbow trout.

Steese Highway (6)

U.S. Geological Survey Maps: Circle, Fairbanks, Livengood. This map set shows the entire length of Alaska Route 6 and the topography of the surrounding wilderness from its origin at Fairbanks northeast to the picturesque village of Circle City, 50 miles south of the arctic circle on the Yukon River. The Steese, once used by prospectors freighting supplies by dogsled and wagon, is the gateway to the Circle Mining District of pre-Klondike fame. The area is famous for its grayling fishing, big-game hunting for grizzly and black bear, moose, and caribou, canoeing, hiking, wildlife, and alpine grandeur. Portions of the Steese-Fortymile caribou herd may be seen near Eagle Summit and Twelvemile Summit during their spring and fall migrations. The highway has two trailheads for the 24-mile-long Pinnell Mountain National Recreation Trail (shown on U.S. Geological Survey maps, Circle B-3, B-4, C-3, C-4). The trail winds through alpine terrain along high ridges and through mountain passes offering views of the "midnight sun" and scenic panoramas of the White Mountains, Yukon River Flats, Brooks Range, and Alaska Range mountains. The trail is above timberline, and water and a pocket stove should be carried. Three guides, *Alaska's Pinnell Mountain National Recreation Trail*, *Alaska's Steese and Elliott Highways*, and *Recreation along Alaska's Steese and Elliott Highways*, are available free from: Bureau of Land Management, 1028 Aurora Dr., Fairbanks 99701. The Steese provides access to the Chatanika and Birch Creek wilderness canoe trails. Facilities are limited along the highway; extra gasoline and tools should be carried. The Steese is paved for the first 40 miles, with the remainder gravel-surfaced all the way to Circle City. There are campgrounds at Cripple Creek, Chatanika River, Ketchem Creek, Circle City, and Bedrock Creek. The map set also shows the Chena Hot Springs Road and Circle Hot Springs Road.

Sterling & Seward-Anchorage Highways (1 & 9)

U.S. Geological Survey Maps: Seldovia, Kenai, Seward. This kit shows the entire length of the Sterling Highway on the Kenai Peninsula from Homer northeast through the famous fish and game wilderness areas of the Chugach National Forest and the majestic Chugach Mountains to its junction with the Seward-Anchorage Highway at Sterling. The highway provides access to the Kenai River, Quartz Creek Campground, Kenai Lake, Resurrection Pass Hiking Trail, Russian Lakes and River, Juneau and Swan lakes, Kenai National Moose Range, Forest Lakes, Hidden Lake and Petersen Lake campgrounds, Swanson and Moose rivers, Lake Tustumena, and Cook Inlet. Herds of white beluga whale can often be seen feeding on salmon and hooligan during incoming tides at the mouth of the Kenai River on Cook Inlet. The Seward-Anchorage Highway runs through the eastern section of the Kenai from Seward, northward past its junction with the Sterling Highway to Anchorage. The highway travels through the Chugach National Forest and provides access to the scenic Portage Glacier Wilderness. There are campgrounds along the route at Bertha Creek, Granite Creek, Beaver Pond, Williwaw, Tenderfoot Creek, Trail River, Ptarmigan Creek, Primrose Landing, First Lake, Caines Head Recreation Area, Tern Lake, Quartz Creek, and Crescent Creek.

Taylor Highway (5)

U.S. Geological Survey Maps: Eagle, Tanacross. This scenic highway extends for 162 miles northward along a narrow and winding route from Tetlin Junction on the Alaska Highway to the village of Eagle on the Yukon River near the Yukon-Alaska border. At Jack Wade Junction the Taylor connects with the Canadian Dawson Road. If you plan to drive into Canada, check on which hours the Alaskan-Canadian border is open before leaving Tok. There is no telephone service along the route or in Eagle. From Tetlin Junction the highway passes through low-wooded hills and then crosses the high divide that separates the Tanana River drainage to the south from the Fortymile River drainage to the north. The Taylor provides access to the famous Fortymile River country, so named because the mouth of the stream is about 40 miles below the site of Fort Reliance, a former trading post on the Yukon River. Gold was discovered along the Fortymile in 1886 and old cabins, gold dredges, and sluice boxes are still found along its banks. Place-names like Nugget Gulch, Discovery Creek, and Deadman Riffle are reminders of the romantic gold-rush days. The highway provides three major access points to the Fortymile River wilderness

canoe trail. Canoeists attempting this trip should use extreme caution due to the river's complete isolation and long stretches of severe rapids. The *Alaska's Historic Eagle & Taylor Highway* guide is available free from: Bureau of Land Management, 555 Cordova St., Anchorage 99501. There are campgrounds along the highway at Walker Fork, Liberty, and Eagle.

Juneau—Outfitting Center for Tongass National Forest

(Pop. 18,000). Alaska's capital is at the foot of 3,576-foot Mount Juneau on the scenic Gastineau Channel—the former water route to Skagway and the Klondike goldfields. The town was founded in the summer of 1880 when Joe Juneau and his sidekick Dick Harris discovered rich gold deposits in Silver Bow Basin, launching the first gold rush in Alaska. Thirteen miles north of Juneau, off the recently completed Glacier Highway, is the Mendenhall Glacier, where the U.S. Forest Service maintains an observatory and hiking trails. Juneau is the jump-off point for trout and salmon fishing and big-game hunting trips throughout the Tongass National Forest, which encompasses the whole of southeast Alaska. Air charter and fly-in services are provided by *Capitol Air*, RR5, Box 5112; *Channel Flying, Inc.*, RR3, Box 3577; *L.A.B. Flying Service*, Terminal Bldg., Municipal Airport; and *Southeast Skyways, Inc.*, RR5, Box 5112, all 99803. Juneau is served by major airlines and the Alaska Marine Highway System.

Kodiak & Aleutian National Wildlife Refuges

The first Alaskan wildlife refuges were established in 1908–12. They included some of the major seabird nesting islands of North America. Additional reserves for big-game species and sea mammals, and important nesting and resting grounds for migratory birds of the Pacific region, have been established since then. Several wilderness areas of the major refuges are open to the hunter and fisherman. A free informational leaflet, *Alaskan National Wildlife Refuges*, and booklets and brochures for the major refuges are available from: Supervisor, Alaskan Wildlife Refuges, Bureau of Sport Fisheries, Box 280, Anchorage 99510.

The *Kodiak National Wildlife Refuge* leaflet describes a 1.8-million-acre reserve in the Gulf of Alaska, due east of the Alaska Peninsula. The refuge provides a natural habitat for the great Kodiak brown bear. Hundreds of miles of brawling, wild rivers and streams are used by spawning salmon and support the important Kodiak commercial salmon industry. The refuge provides top-ranked hunting for trophy brown bear and often phenomenal fishing for salmon and rainbow trout. Chartered flights to the interior of the island for brown bear photography can be arranged through Wien Air Alaska with local bush pilots. Guiding service for hunting and photography, available in and around Kodiak, is required for nonresidents. *Munsey's Bear Camp*, Box 1186, Kodiak, offers photographic and hunting expeditions for Alaskan brown bear. For information write: Manager, Kodiak NWR, Box 825, Kodiak 99615. The refuge is shown on U.S. Geological Survey Topographic Maps, scale 1:250,000: Kodiak, Karluk, Trinity Islands, Kaguyak.

The *Aleutian Islands National Wildlife Refuge* and *Birds of the Aleutian National Wildlife Refuge* booklets describe a 2.7-million-acre refuge, the third-largest unit of the National Wildlife Refuge System. The Aleutian Islands, commonly called the "chain," are emergent peaks of a submarine mountain range. The often fog-shrouded archipelago includes 200 mountainous, volcanic islands dotted by thousands of lakes and crisscrossed by wild streams. The islands are a largely uninhabited wilderness, except for the Aleut villages of Atka and False Pass and a few active military installations. A high percentage of the world's emperor geese winter on the refuge. Bridging the north Pacific to Asia, the western Aleutians offer refuge to whooper swans, tufted ducks, and the Aleutian race of green teal. At the eastern end of the refuge, whistling swans, black brant, and the North American race of green-winged teal are found. Seabirds, including fulmars, storm petrels, cormorants, gulls, kittiwakes, murres, guillemots, murrelets, auklets, and puffins, nest in noisy colonies on the islands' cliffs and heather-covered hillsides. The once abundant Canada goose is dangerously near extinction as a result of blue fox introductions during the early fur-farming enterprises. The short-tailed albatross is almost extinct. Black-footed and Layson albatrosses, however, still soar offshore on motionless wings. The bald eagle and peregrine falcon are commonly sighted, and some gyrfalcons are also found. Sea otters have increased from near extinction to a population estimated at 20,000, and the northern sea lion is common. Unimak Island, an ecological extension of the Alaska Peninsula, is a stronghold of the Alaska brown bear. The island has over 1,000 caribou, and wolf and wolverine are common. Portions of the refuge are open to hunting of migratory and upland birds and big game. The wilderness lakes and streams hold trophy trout and salmon. Reeve Aleutian Airways provide access to the islands; for information, write: Manager, Aleutian Islands NWR, Cold Bay 99571. The refuge is shown on U.S. Geological Survey Topographic Maps, scale 1:250,000: Cold Bay, False Pass, Unimak, Unalaska, Umnak, Amukta, Samalga Islands.

For information on The Arctic National Wildlife Range, see the "Alaska Travel & Recreation Guide" section.

King Salmon—Gateway to Mt. Katmai & the Valley of 10,000 Smokes

(Pop. 202). This famous fishing and big-game hunting outfitting center, located on the west side of the Alaska Peninsula, is known as the gateway to the Katmai National Monument and the renowned Brooks River area and Valley of Ten Thousand Smokes, and to the trophy wilderness arctic grayling and salmon and rainbow trout waters of

Naknek, Iliamna, Kulik, Becharof, and Upper and Lower Ugashik lakes. There are guides, floatplanes, and lodging at Brooks Lodge in the Katmai National Monument; Enchanted Lake Lodge, 60 miles east of King Salmon; and North Country Lodge, Iliamna Outfitters, and Kvichak Lodge at Lake Iliamna. The No-See-Um Lodge is about 25 miles north of Naknek. The region is a fly-fisherman's paradise, and produces one of the finest natural food environments in the world for the tackle-busting rainbow trout and grayling which abound in these waters. Kulik Lodge on Nonvianuk Lake near the Katmai National Monument, operated by *Wien Air Alaska*, 4100 International Airport Rd., Anchorage 99502, is a short bush flight from King Salmon. The waters surrounding the lodge offer some of the best fly-fishing in North America for rainbow trout in the 10–12-pound class. *Griechen Air Taxi*, Box 271, 99613, offers chartered fishing and photography air service to Katmai National Monument and the McNeil River Bear Sanctuary. Wien Air Alaska and Kodiak Western Airlines have scheduled flights to King Salmon. *Glen Van Valin Air Charter* operates floatplanes and fishing camps at nearby Naknek; write: P.O. Box 155, Naknek 99633.

Malaspina—"Father of Glaciers"

The massive Malaspina Glacier at the head of Yakutat Bay near the southern border of the Yukon Territory is the largest piedmont glacier on the North American continent. This giant father of glaciers pours down from the towering 19,000-foot peaks of the St. Elias Range, forming an immense fan-shaped ice desert some 1,500 square miles in size. Near its center this great ice sheet is more than 2,000 feet thick. The giant glacier was named after the Italian-born explorer Alejandro Malaspina, who led the Spanish expedition of 1771 into the region in search of the legendary Northwest Passage. During the Klondike gold rush, a few ill-fated parties attempted to reach Dawson by crossing the

surface of this enormous ice mass, which is larger than the state of Rhode Island and notorious for its sheer canyons and crevasses. The glacier stretches along the coast of Yakutat Bay for nearly 50 miles. At the margin of the glacier a mile-wide strip of hemlock and Sitka spruce trees, some reaching heights of 75 feet and ages of 100 years, grows on top of a mantle of glacial ice 50–150 feet thick. The Bering Glacier, almost as large as the Malaspina, dominates the coastal region to the west.

Marine Highway System & the Inside Passage

The state of Alaska operates a fleet of modern ferryliners that transport both passengers and vehicles. The Southeast Marine Highway System operates from Seattle, Washington, and from Prince Rupert, British Columbia, and connects these ports with Ketchikan, Sitka, Petersburg, Wrangell, Juneau, Haines, and Skagway. The 1,130-sea-mile trip from Seattle to Skagway takes about 4 days. The ferryliners travel through the scenic Inside Passage, a series of protected waterways stretching from Seattle to Ketchikan, through a bewildering maze of islands bordered by massive glaciers and rain forests lush with ferns, mosses, spruce, and hemlock. Fogs and layers of mist are frequent along the Inside Passage, and the fragrant smell of spruce drifts from the labyrinth of evergreen-forested islands. Six ferries serve this route: the M.V. *Chilkat, Columbia, Le Conte, Malaspina, Matamuska,* and *Taku.* The smaller southeast Alaska communities of Hollis, Hoonah, Kake, and Metlakatla are serviced by the M.V. *Chilkat* and *Le Conte.* The Southwest Alaska Marine Highway System operates in Prince William Sound and in Cook Inlet waters. Two ferryliners, the M.V. *Bartlett* and *Tustumena,* serve this scenic region. The ferryliners are named after famous glaciers of Alaska, with the exception of the M.V. *Chilkat* (named for a Tlingit Indian tribe) and the *Bartlett* (named

for an Alaskan statesman). Advance reservations for stateroom and car deck space are required before departure. For rates, reservations, and the free 24-page *Alaska Marine Highway* schedule, write: Division of Marine Transportation, Pouch R, Juneau 99811, or phone (907) 465–3941. A free brochure, *Alaska by Sea*, is available from: Division of Tourism, Department of Commerce and Economic Development, Pouch E, Juneau 99811. Passengers are not permitted to sleep in their vehicles while traveling aboard the ferryliners.

Moose, Great Alaskan

The Alaskan moose *(Alces alces gigas)* is the largest and darkest of the species, a relic of the age of mammoths, found throughout Alaska (except in the woodless west) from the Stikine River in the southeast to the Colville River on the arctic slope. The moose is most abundant in the rich forage of birch, willow, and alder stands of second-growth forests, along timberline plateaus and major river valleys. An adult bull may stand 7½ feet tall, weigh close to 1,800 pounds, and carry more than 85 pounds of antlers with a spread of over 60 inches—the largest antlers in the world. The current Boone & Crockett world record, with a spread of 6½ feet, was taken in 1961 at Mount Susitna in the Alaska Range. The biggest specimens are generally found on the Kenai Peninsula. The Alaskan moose, also known as the Alaska-Yukon moose, ranges through the Yukon and the adjacent Mackenzie Mountains in the Northwest Territories and in northwest British Columbia. The most productive hunting season is usually mid- and late September, when most of the deciduous trees and shrubs have lost their leaves and the moose are easier to see and the bulls are entering the rut and beginning to roam in search of cows. By late September, moose in mountainous areas are often found above timberline, gathered in "rutting herds" along willow draws.

Sheefish of the Kobuk— The "Arctic Tarpon"

The sheefish, thought to originate from the Eskimo word *chi,* is the common name of the inconnu *(Stenodus leucichthys),* a unique predatory member of the whitefish family. The name inconnu, which means "the unknown," was given to the fish by Alexander Mackenzie's voyageurs during their exploration of the great northwest. It is also known as the cony and shovelnose whitefish in Alaska and as the white salmon in Russia. The deep-fighting sheefish is a prized trophy found in the great northern rivers of Alaska's interior. The Alaskan record is 52½ pounds and 48 inches long, caught in the Kobuk River north of the arctic circle at the foothills of the Brooks Range. Record sheefish, some up to 60 pounds, are also found in the Yukon, Selawik, and Kuskokwim rivers and tributaries. Like the tarpon, the sheefish has large silvery scales with a purple sheen when freshly caught. During their spawning migrations in late May or early June, the fish run up the great rivers, reaching their upper stretches in September, where they spawn when the water temperatures drop to 36° F. Sheefish, like salmon, don't feed during spawning, but will take a streamer fly and wobbling spoons and spinning lures.

Skagway—"Home of the North Wind" & Chilcoot Trail to the Klondike

(Pop. 850). This famous southeast Alaska town, originally known as Skaguay, "home of the north wind" in Tlingit dialect, is the state's oldest city and the site of the proposed Klondike National Park. It was the gateway to the White Pass Trail and the infamous Chilcoot Trail —the Trail of '98—which climbed over the Chilcoot pass to Lake Bennett and the Klondike goldfields. The journey from Skagway along the Chilcoot to Lake Bennett can also be made by the narrow-gauge White Pass & Yukon Railroad. The town still has a boomtown atmosphere with its boardwalks and weather-beaten false-front gold-rush

saloons and hotels. The town's major attractions include the Trail of '98 Museum and the Gold-Rush Graveyard, where Soapy Smith, the notorious Klondike con artist, is buried. *Skagway Air Service,* Box 357, 99840, provides fly-in services for the outdoorsman and sightseeing flights of the Chilcoot and White Pass trails. *Klondike Safaris,* Box 1898, 99840, has guided six-day hikes along the Chilcoot Trail and 700-mile Yukon River trips.

U.S. Forest Service Cabins

Forest Service wilderness cabins are located on remote lakes, streams, and coastal beaches throughout the Chugach, North Tongass, and South Tongass national forests. There are 150 cabins, accessible by floatplane, boat, or trail, that are available for public use for a fee of $5 per party per night. Reservations can be made a maximum of 6 months in advance by writing: Information Officer, U.S. Forest Service, 121 E. Fireweed La., Suite 205, Anchorage 99501. No reservations are accepted without payment of fee. Permits are issued on a first come, first served basis for periods not exceeding 7 nights. Boats are usually available with cabins located on lakeshores. A Coast Guard-approved flotation device is required to be on board for each passenger. Many of these cabins are located in brown bear country; you are encouraged to carry a .30–06 or larger caliber rifle. The cabins are equipped with oil- or wood-burning stoves, bunks, and outdoor sanitary facilities. Unauthorized use of these popular cabins is a violation of state and federal laws and regulations. (See "Travel & Recreation Guide" section: "Gulf Coast . . . Chugach National Forest"; "Tongass National Forest.")

Wild & Scenic River Maps

The following U.S. Geological Survey full-color large-scale (7.5 minute) maps show the entire lengths of Alaska's National Wild and

Scenic rivers, as well as the topography of the surrounding wilderness. *Charley National Wild River:* Charley River A-4, A-5, B-4, Eagle B-5, C-5, C-6, D-5, D-6; *Fortymile National Wild & Scenic River:* Eagle A-1, A-2, A-3, B-1, B-2, C-1, D-1, Tanacross D-2, D-3; *Beaver Creek National Wild River:* Circle B-1, Circle D-5, D-6, Fort Yukon A-5, A-6, B-5, B-6; *Birch Creek National Wild River:* Circle B-1, B-2, B-3, B-4, C-1; *Nation River:* Charley River A-1, A-2, B-1, B-2, C-1, C-2.

Wilderness Fishing & Adventure Trips

Alaskan expedition outfitters and tour operators offer a wide variety of wilderness adventure trips for the fisherman, photographer, and wilderness traveler. *North Country, Inc.,* Box 4–2331, Anchorage 99509, is a travel firm specializing in custom-tailored trips in the Alaskan wilderness ranging from sportfishing to shooting wildlife films. Research, editorial, and photographic support are also provided. *Southeast Waterway Adventures,* 328 Coleman Dr., Juneau 99801, offers the 38-foot twin-screw diesel yacht *Pacifica* for charter to Glacier Bay, Admiralty Island, and other wildlife areas of southeast Alaska. Trout fishing is their specialty. Available for daily or extended cruises. *Alaskan Wilderness River Trips, Inc.,* Box 1143, Eagle River 99577, has guided river float trips on a variety of central Alaskan rivers. Rates include bush flying, meals, equipment, and personnel. *Nova River Runners of Alaska, Inc.,* 7227 E. Duben St., Anchorage 99504, has charter trips and information on river floating on both slow and fast water. *Alaska Discovery Wilderness Adventures,* 6926 Town & Country Dr., Anchorage 99503, offers wilderness trips by canoe, kayak, and backpack to Glacier Bay National Monument, Admiralty Island, Tracy Arm, Klondike Trail, and the Yukon and Stikine rivers. *Alaska Wilderness Unlimited,* Box 4–2477, Anchorage 99509, offers guided wilderness backpacking and kayaking trips in the Brooks Range. *Alaska Sportfishing Packages,* Suite 312-A, Park Place Bldg., Seattle, WA 98101, offers complete guided fishing adventures to Alaska's trophy fishing waters. *Fish Alaska,* Box 316, Petersburg 99833, specializes in salmon fly-fishing charters for parties up to 4 persons for 7 to 10-day stays. Boat travel, accommodations, food, and guide service. *Genet Expeditions,* Talkeetna 99676, has year-round guide service for climbing, photography, cross-country skiing, fishing, and river trips. The firm specializes in Mount McKinley expeditions and May-June cross-country skiing expeditions, and operates a wilderness camp for teens and up to Pirate Lake to teach basic mountaineering and glacier technique, cross-country travel, rafting, log cabin building, fishing, and gold prospecting and panning. *Adventure Unlimited* offers sportfishing, photography, charters, and scientific expeditions. Write: Mike Branham, Box 6128, Annex, Anchorage 99502. *Alaska Marine Charters* is a central communications point for boat charters in the Ketchikan area of the Tongass National Forest. Write: 207 Main St., Ketchikan 99901. *Alaska Adventure* offers wilderness trail rides from Brushkana Creek headquarters at Mile 104 Denali Highway. Write: Keith Specking, Hope 99605. *Allen Marine Tours,* Box 1049, Sitka 99835, offers 2½-hour cruises aboard the 62-foot M.V. *St. Michael,* featuring wildlife, scenic beauty, and historical gold-mining areas of the Tongass National Forest. *Dick Cox,* Box 36, Yakutat 99689, offers river float trips, fly-in lake fishing, and stream fishing in the Tongass National Forest. *The Fisherman* offers fly-fishing only for remote trophy fishing and float trips. Write: Mike Herschberger, 2906 Will Rogers Place, Anchorage 99503. *Forbes Marine Service,* Box 557, Sitka 99835, offers custom sportfishing, sightseeing, and photography trips. *Glacier Bay Yacht Tours & Alaska Charters,* Box 424, Juneau 99802, specializes in close-up views of glaciers, icebergs, and wildlife in the Tongass Country. *Glacier Guides, Inc.,* RR5, Box 5610, Juneau 99803, offers cruises to Tracy Arm glaciers or Glacier Bay, with custom sportfishing, hunting, pho-

tography, and sightseeing cruises. *Dick Gunlogson,* Box 4–1062, Anchorage 99509, specializes in exploring and photography trips throughout Alaska, with float trips and trophy sportfishing in season.

The famous *Hart D Ranch,* MP1, Nabesna Highway, offers lodging, guides, sportfishing, packhorse, and boat trips. *Kodiak Charter Service,* Box 24, Kodiak 99615, provides a 35-foot cruiser for sportfishing, photography, and sightseeing. Master Alaska guide *Karl E. Lane,* Box 295, Juneau 99802, offers summer sportfishing and photography trips in southeast Alaska aboard the 58-foot charter M.V. *Heron. SEA Charters,* Rt. 1, Box 677, Ketchikan 99901, offers sportfishing charter cruises, with a 5-day, 170-mile cruise around Revillagigedo Island in the Tongass Country. *Bill Zaegel,* Box 3464, Anchorage 99501, specializes in guided canoe-fishing, river boating, and photography trips.

Air Alaska and Wien Air Alaska offer package trophy fishing trips to *Yes Bay Lodge* in the Behm Canal in the Panhandle; *Clover Pass Resort,* 15 miles by road from Ketchikan, aboard the sportfishing charterboat *Chaik; Glacier Bay Lodge; Kulik Lodge* on Nonvianuk Lake near the Katmai National Monument; and *Golden Horn Lodge* in the famous Wood River–Tikchik Lake region of Alaska. Write: Division of Tourism, Department of Commerce & Economic Development, Pouch E, Juneau 99811. (Additional information on specific area and regional outfitters is found throughout the "Encyclopedia" and "Travel & Recreation Guide" sections.)

Alaska Peninsula & Bristol Bay Trophy Fish Area

Alaska Peninsula Topo Maps

U.S. Geological Survey maps, scale 1:250,000: Naknek, Mount Katmai, Afognak, Ugashik, Karluk, Bristol Bay, Sutwik Island, Chignik, Stepovak Bay, Port Moller, Cold Bay, False Pass.

Bristol Bay Trophy Fish Area

U.S. Geological Survey maps, scale 1:250,000: Iliamna, Dillingham, Naknek, Nushagak Bay, Goodnews, Bethel, Taylor Mountains, Lake Clark.

Katmai National Monument

U.S. Geological Survey maps, scale 1:250,000: Afognak, Iliamna, Karluk, Mount Katmai, Naknek.

Lake Clark National Park

U.S. Geological Survey maps, scale 1:250,000: Lake Clark, Iliamna.

Lake Iliamna National Resource Range

U.S. Geological Survey maps, scale 1:250,000: Dillingham, Iliamna.

Wood River–Tikchik Lakes Trophy Trout & Salmon Waters

U.S. Geological Survey 1:250,000-scale overview maps: Dillingham, Goodnews, Bethel, Taylor Mountains.

The Bristol Bay area and the Alaska Peninsula offer some of the finest trophy fishing, big-game hunting, and wilderness adventure in North America. The narrow, mountainous peninsula stretches for 500 miles from the southwestern corner of Alaska into the northern Pacific along the volcanic snowcapped peaks of the Aleutian Range Mountains and the stepping stones of the remote Aleutian Islands. The world-famous grayling, rainbow trout, and salmon waters of the Bristol Bay uplands encompass the northwestern portions of the Alaska Peninsula, where it joins the mainland.

The Bristol Bay area is dominated by the craggy, glacier-studded peaks of the Aklun Mountains to the north and west and by the scenic Wood River–Tikchik Lakes country. This majestic chain consists of hundreds of cold, clear lakes connected by wild rivers and streams surrounded by boreal forests, muskeg, and alpine tundra. The area is dominated by the deep, cold glacier-formed waters of Nishlik, Upnuk, Nuyakuk, Tikchik, Kulik, Beverly, and Aleknagik lakes, and 29-mile-long Lake Nerka. The 2 million acres of mountains, forests, streams, lakes, and fjords of the Wood River–Tikchik Lakes region offer what is thought by many to be the world's finest fishing for record rainbow trout to 10 pounds, arctic char, grayling, steelhead, lake trout, northern pike, Dolly Varden, sheefish, and five species of salmon. King salmon up to 50 pounds run from late June through mid-July; red salmon to 10 pounds run July through August; and silver salmon to 13 pounds run late August through mid-September. Access to the Wood River–Tikchik Lakes region is via Wien Air Alaska from Anchorage to Dillingham and Kodiak Western Alaska Airlines. Several bush lodges in the region offer accommodations and outfitting services for fishing trips and big-game hunting in the high country wildlands for moose, grizzly bear, and caribou. The famous *Golden Horn Lodge*, operated by Wien Air Alaska, offers rustic lodging, with furnished rooms, private baths, family-style meals and lunches, and guides, powerboats, and floatplane fly-in fishing. Write: Box 546, Anchorage 99510. The *Bristol Bay Lodge* also has accommodations in the Wood River–Tikchik Lakes system, with floatplanes, jet riverboats, rubber

rafts, and guides. Write: John B. Garry, Box 148, Dillingham 99676. The *Tikchik Narrows Fishing Lodge*, Box 1631, Anchorage 99510, has full-service accommodations in the region, 63 miles north of Dillingham. The *Royal Coachman Lodge* is on the lakes chain and specializes in personalized trophy fishing with pilot guide. Booking is limited to 8 per fishing week. Season runs June 15 to October 15. Write: Alaska Sportfishing Guides, Inc., Box 1871, Anchorage 99510. The remote *Walton, Wood River Lodge,* located 50 miles north of Dillingham, offers sportfishing by boat and floatplane. Write: Box 246, Dillingham 99576.

The rainbow trout waters of the Lake Iliamna National Resource Range, a proposed 2¾-million-acre wilderness located in the northernmost part of the Alaska Peninsula due east of the Wood River–Tikchik Lakes region, are world-renowned. Lake Iliamna, Alaska's largest at 75 miles long and 20 miles wide and the seventh-largest lake in the United States, dominates the region. The lake and the surrounding network of lakes and wild rivers, including Kakhonak, Tazimina, Kukaklik, and Battle lakes and the Newhalen, Copper, Gilbratan, Kukaklik, and Kvichak rivers, hold trophy-size pink, king, and silver salmon, Dolly Varden, lake and rainbow trout, arctic char, grayling, steelhead, and northern pike. Lake Iliamna has been rumored to contain in its cold, clear depths a mysterious monster fish, believed to be perhaps a world's record lake trout, a prehistoric fish species that has somehow survived through the ages, or a beluga—a whale known to live in fresh water. The validity of these rumors, however, is doubtful. The Indians of Iliamna, who are usually the first to tell tall tales, have never reported seeing the giant mystery fish. To the north the waters of Lake Clark flow into Iliamna via the Newhalen River. The proposed Lake Clark National Park takes in 2.6 million acres of high country wilderness, varying from alpine tundra to Sitka spruce forests at the southernmost part of the Alaska Range and the northernmost portion of the Aleutian Range. This is a top wilderness fishing area for

rainbow, grayling, and lake trout to 30 pounds. Wildlife in the Iliamna–Lake Clark region includes wolf, black and brown bear, grizzly, moose, caribou, and the majestic golden-horned Dall sheep. The principal drainage of the area is through Lake Clark and the Iliamna lowlands into the Kvichak River trophy fish area, and then to Bristol Bay. The peaks of the Aleutian Range and the coastline of Cook Inlet form the eastern boundary of the Lake Clark–Iliamna region. The wilderness traveler may come upon several of the Eskimo–Athabascan Indian archaeological and prehistoric fossil sites that exist around Lakes Clark and Iliamna and along the Newhalen and Kvichak rivers.

The Lake Clark–Iliamna region has several wilderness fishing lodges and outpost camps with guides and fly-in service for trophy fishing and big-game hunting. The *Alaska Safari Fish Camp*, Box 6003, Anchorage 99502, has accommodations on lower Lake Clark and Lake Iliamna with floatplane service to outlying areas. The *Battle River, Wilderness Camp*, located south of Lake Iliamna in the Alaska trophy fish area, offers cabins, family-style meals, and guide service. Write: Ben. C. White, 1513 F St., Anchorage 99501. The *Copper River Fly-Fishing Lodge*, Box 250, Kenai 99611, has jet boats, canoes, meals, and tenthouses on the renowned Copper River in the Lake Iliamna area with fishing for rainbow trout, char, and salmon. The *Copper River Lodge* offers accommodations and guide service, 20 miles southeast of Lake Iliamna; write: Lloyd Samsal, 2733 W. 100th Ave., Anchorage 99502. *Iliamna River Outfitters*, Box 1711, Anchorage 99510, on the east end of Iliamna Lake, offers transportation from Iliamna Airport to lodge with double-occupancy room or cabin, floatplanes, boats, and tent camps. *Koksetna Camp*, Port Alsworth 99653, offers wilderness vacations on Lake Clark with lodging and meals for fly-in fishermen and hunters, bird-watching, and float trips on the Chulitna River. *Kvichak Lodge*, Box 37, Naknek 99633, is located on the Kvichak River at Lake Iliamna; it offers accommodations and guide service. *North Country Lodge*, Box 49, Iliamna 99606, has

modern accommodations near Lake Iliamna, with floatplane fly-outs, river float trips, and guiding service in designated trophy fish areas. *Van Valin's Island Lodge,* Box 155, Naknek 99633, has log cabin accommodations with private cabins on Lake Clark, accessible by floatplane, with trophy fishing, backpacking, and float trips. Access to lodges in the Lake Clark–Iliamna region is via fly-in service from major outfitting centers. The *Chulitna Lodge,* with a main lodge and cabins, provides daily fly-out fishing to Iliamna–Lake Clark–Tikchik Lake and guided trophy hunting. Write: Ken Owsichek, Box 6301, Anchorage 99502. *Kokhanok Lodge,* located on Lake Iliamna, has accommodations for 6 June through September. Write: Box 6128 Annex, Anchorage 99502. *Silvertip Lodge,* at the headwaters of the Talachulitna River, is accessible only by floatplane and offers wilderness fishing and vacationing. Meals are served family-style in the lodge. Write: Box 272, Anchorage 99510. Ray Loesche's famous *Rainbow King Lodge* (c/o Box 3446, Spokane, WA 99220), located at Lake Iliamna, offers elegant lodging and daily fly-out in Cessna 185 floatplanes to trophy rainbow trout, arctic char, grayling, and salmon waters.

Katmai National Monument, a tranquil 4-million-acre wilderness of unmatched natural beauty which was rocked in 1912 by one of the most violent volcanic eruptions in modern history, lies to the south of Lake Iliamna, encompassing the great peaks of the Aleutian Range; a segment of the Pacific ring of fire, one of the most active volcanic regions in the world, forming the mountainous backbone of the Alaska Peninsula; bowl-shaped calderas with crater lakes—depressions caused by the collapse of crater walls by erosion; novaruptas—newly erupted volcanic domes; massive glaciers; the steaming fumaroles of the awesome Valley of Ten Thousand Smokes; island-studded lakes fringed with coniferous forests, alpine streams, and braided rivers; a rugged coastline of fjords, bays, and surf-pounded beaches; and haunting "ghost forests" caused by the blasts of hot wind and gas of the cataclyism of 1912, which buried 40 square miles of lush green forests under volcanic ash as much as 700 feet deep and darkened the sky over most of the Northern Hemisphere with a haze of fine ash.

Today the snowcapped 7,000-foot peaks of the Katmai wildlands lie dormant. Mount Trident, however, has erupted four times during the past 20 years, the last time in 1969, and gray plumes of smoke rise from Mount Mageik and Mount Martin. A fascinating guide to the region, *Exploring Katmai National Monument,* is available for $7.50 from Alaska Travel Publications, P.O. Box 4–2031, Anchorage 99509. This useful 276-page paperback is packed with line drawings and vivid historical photographs of the great 1912 eruption, the early National Geographic Society expeditions, and the discovery of the Valley of Ten Thousand Smokes, and thorough descriptions of the climate and weather, wildlife, vegetation, fishing, travel, and back-country exploration of Katmai. The *Katmai* Map Brochure, *Brooks River Area,* and *Hiking the Katmai Back-Country* guides are available free from the Superintendent, Katmai National Monument, P.O. Box 7, King Salmon 99613. If you are planning a wilderness fishing trip into the Katmai region, write for the free brochure *Katmai—Angler's Paradise,* published by Wien Air Alaska, 4100 W. International Airport Rd., Anchorage 99502.

Due west of the great chain of volcanic peaks lie the famed fishing waters of Lake Naknek, the fourth-largest lake in Alaska (240 square miles); Lake Brooks and the renowned Brooks River; the turbulent Naknek River; King Salmon Creek; Colville and Grosvenor lakes; the Savonski, Ukak, and Rainbow rivers; and Becharof Lake and King Salmon River to the south and Nonvianuk and Kulik lakes to the north. The deep, clear waters of these glacially formed lakes and wild rivers offer trophy fly-fishing for rainbow, lake, and Dolly Varden trout, northern pike in the weedy shallow bays, arctic grayling and char

in the clearwater streams, and salmon. The village of King Salmon, located on the Naknek River, 17 miles downstream of Naknek Lake, is the headquarters for the monument and serves as the major outfitting center for trips to the Katmai wilderness and outlying fishing camps and lodges. *Brooks Lodge,* located below Brooks Falls near the mouth of the Brooks River on Naknek Lake in Katmai, offers some of the finest fishing in Alaska for record rainbow trout up to 12 pounds. The lodge operates daily bus tours to the Valley of Ten Thousand Smokes, passing en route the skeletal spruce trees of the ghost forest. A marked trail from the adjacent Brooks River Ranger Station leads to an Eskimo barabara, or pit house, dating from A.D. 1300. *Brooks Lodge* operates from June 10 to September 8. Write: Brooks Lodge, Wien Air Alaska, 4100 W. International Airport Rd., Anchorage

Exploring **Katmai** National Monument

and the Valley of Ten Thousand Smokes

99502. *Grosvenor Camp* is between Coville and Grosvenor lakes, 15 miles northeast of Brooks Camp, in spectacular mountain scenery and U-shaped lake valleys and offers two tent-frame cabins and fly-fishing for rainbow trout and arctic grayling. The camp opens June 10 and closes July 10. Write: c/o Wien Air Alaska (address above). *Enchanted Lake Lodge,* Box 97, King Salmon 99613, is 13 air miles north of the monument boundary; it offers fly-in fishing, guide service, boats, and meals. *Kulik Lodge,* outside the monument at the mouth of the Kulik River, provides wilderness lodging and fly-in and boat trips to the glacially carved Kulik and Nonvianuk lakes with guides. Accommodations up to 29. The lodge is operated by Wien Air Alaska. The *No-See-Um Lodge,* at Lovelock, 25 miles north of Naknek, provides freezing facilities, guides, boats, and floatplanes. *Becharof Lodge & Camps,* 40 miles south of King Salmon at the head of Egegik River, offers trophy fishing and wildlife and scenic photographic safaris. Write: Ben Guild, Box 632, Eagle River 99577. *Last Frontier Lodge,* within Katmai Monument near the western end of Naknek Lake, provides full sportfishing services with satellite camps located on the world-famous arctic grayling waters of the Ugashik River to the south and Alagnak River to the north. Services include riverboats and rubber rafts as well as floatplanes to outlying wilderness areas. Write: Box 42, King Salmon 99613. The *Alaska Peninsula Lodge* offers excellent accommodations, guided trophy fishing and hunting trips with floatplane fly-out service, river boats, and scenic float and photography trips. For rates and literature, write: Robert Cusack, 3300 Providence Dr., Suite 309, Anchorage 99504.

The boreal forests, valleys, mountain chains, alpine tundra, and rugged coastal regions of Katmai are inhabited by highsoaring bald eagles, which frequent the islands and coast of the Shilikof Strait, as well as petrels and eiders, auks, murres, moose, caribou, wolves, lynx, arctic hare, wolverine, beaver, and otter. The wilderness traveler should be alert at all times in Katmai country for brown bears. Their coloration serves as a natural camouflage, often difficult to spot. To avoid the potentially tragic mistake of jumping a bear, always make lots of noise and avoid dense alder patches and forests.

Going on down the peninsula, the Ugashik Lakes consistently produce char and record grayling up to 5 pounds, and the Meshik River is outstanding for bull Dolly Varden. The central region of the peninsula is renowned for its salmon streams and Alaskan moose, Dall sheep, and brown bear hunting. The Aniakchak is an especially good river for king and silver salmon up to 20 pounds. It flows through the 440,000-acre Aniakchak Caldera National Monument, noted for boiling sulfur pools, hot springs, and steam vents. At the tip of the peninsula is the 320,000-acre estuary of the Izembek National Wildlife Range. It is a good area for camping and has many rivers, lakes, lagoons, mountains, and heaths. It's also the only breeding ground in North America for the black brant. The wildlife range can be reached by sea from Cold Bay. The *Alaska Sportfishing and Waterfowl Hunting Camps*, located near Cold Bay, offer guided hunting trips and fishing for salmon, Dolly Varden, and rainbow trout. Throughout the peninsula, summers are often foggy with cold winds and frequent cold rains that sometimes last several days. If you plan on camping out, be prepared for rugged living and sudden high winds.

Access & Outfitting Centers

The Bristol Bay Area and Alaska Peninsula are reached by air from Anchorage via Wien Air Alaska to Dillingham and King Salmon. Charter fly-in air service is provided by Peninsula Airways, Kodiak Western Alaska Airlines, Katmai Air Taxi, and Wien Air Alaska to wilderness fishing and big-game hunting areas. Outfitting and supply services are located at Dillingham, Iliamna, and King Salmon.

Alaska Range & Mount McKinley National Park

Alaska Range Topo Maps

U.S. Geological Survey maps, scale 1:250,000: Gulkana, Healy, Iliamna, Kenai, Lake Clark, Lime Hills, Mount Hayes, Mount McKinley, Nabesna, Talkeetna, Talkeetna Mountains, Tancross, Tyonek.

Mount McKinley National Park

U.S. Geological Survey maps, scale 1:250,000: Healy, Mount McKinley, Talkeetna.

The snowcapped peaks of the Alaska Range, the highest in North America, form a sweeping 580-mile arc from the Yukon border across to the Alaska Peninsula, where they merge with the Aleutian Range. It is a high country wilderness of craggy summits, massive glaciers and icefields, dense aiga forests and alpine tundra carpeted by white-mountain avens, red and blue mountain heath, Labrador tea, crowberry, dwarf birch, and willows. This world-famous fishing and big-game hunting region is dominated by the spectacular peaks and wildlands of Mount McKinley National Park and by the Tanana, Ladau, Mac-Cleren, Nenana, Chistochina, Yentna, Kichatna, Skwentna, Chilligan, and Mulchatna rivers and the deep, clear waters of Lakes Chakachamna, Clark, Beluga, Minchumina, Kantishna, Chelatna, and the headwater lakes of the Amphitheater Mountains. The high country lakes, streams, and wild rivers hold arctic grayling, whitefish, lake

trout, northern pike, Dolly Varden, and rainbow trout. Don't forget that in some areas it is not safe to fish without carrying a rifle, and the Alaska Range is one of them. The range is one of Alaska's finest hunting regions for grizzly and black bear, caribou—found along the southeastern side of the range—moose, trophy Dall sheep, and wolf. Hunting the Dall sheep, the white king of Alaska's mountains, is usually hard work and requires a great deal of climbing. It pays to be in top physical condition before embarking on a sheep-hunting expedition. Most sheep hunters hike in or use riverboats, aircraft, or packhorses to reach the high country, then set up a base camp and hunt from there. Most sheep hunters use a good pair of binoculars (usually about 7 power), a spotting scope of 20 or 30 power, and a flat-shooting rifle equipped with a scope. With the exception of special hunts, only three-quarter-curl or larger rams may be legally taken.

To the ancient Athabascan Indians, Mount McKinley was known as *Denali*, "the great one." McKinley's summit soars to an altitude of 20,320 feet, rising 16,000 feet above the surrounding wilderness of Mount McKinley National Park, and forms a natural barrier between the coastal lowlands to the south and the great interior to the north. Mount McKinley was discovered in 1897 by William A. Dickey, a gold prospector who traveled inland to come upon the great mountain, and was established as a national park in 1917, due largely to the efforts of Charles Sheldon, a noted conservationist and member of the Boone and Crockett Club, who traveled McKinley's slopes to study Dall sheep and other wildlife. The great mountain dominates a wilderness of taiga, "the land of little sticks," a term of Russian origin that describes the scant forest growth near the arctic circle, found in narrow swaths that follow the winding course of rivers in the park, and, above timberline at 2,700 feet, on the wind-swept slopes are dwarf willows, birch, mountain cranberry and heaths, white mountain avens, and alpine bearberry. The taiga is mostly a land of white and black spruce, quaking aspen, paper birch, and balsam poplar, carpeted with a thick, springy mat of mosses and lichens. The Denali Fault, the largest crustal break in North America stretches for 1,300 miles across Alaska and passes through this wilderness of contrasting lowlands, braided rivers, and dark, somber mountains, brightly colored peaks, and sheer granite domes.

The U.S. Geological Survey publishes a beautiful 25 × 32-inch *Mount McKinley National Park Map* at a scale of 1:250,000. The map covers 8,634 square miles, is available in both a contour and a shaded relief edition, and costs $2.00. The major topographic features shown on the park map include Mount McKinley and the surrounding peaks and glaciers of the Alaska Range, Wyoming Hills, McKinley River, and the Foraker, Herron, Toklat, and Teklanika rivers. The U.S. National Park Service, Mount McKinley National Park, P.O. Box 9, McKinley Park 99755, offers several publications, including the free *Mount McKinley National Park* Map-Brochure which shows ranger stations, trails, campgrounds, gasoline stops-stores, paved and gravel roads; the free guide *How to Travel in Mount McKinley National Park*, which describes the public bus transportation system within the park; the free *Hiking in the Mount McKinley Back-Country Guide*, which provides tips on safe back-country use, including suggestions on equipment and ways to cope with glacial travel, stream crossings, and wildlife; *Today at Mount McKinley*, which describes places and times of dogsled demonstrations, wildlife tours, campfire programs, hikes, and a variety of other visitor services; the *Relief Model Map of Mount McKinley National Park* ($1), which is a molded plastic model 9½ × 6¾ inches at scale of 1:1,000,000, or 1 inch to 16 miles, printed in seven colors, with text and map showing glaciers, faults, tundra, and forests; *Wolves of Mount McKinley*, a classic book by the renowned Olas Murie, which describes wolf characteristics, habits, and behavior

and the relationship of the wolf to Dall sheep, caribou, moose, and bear, ($2.60, 238 pages, paperback); the 56-page *Mammals of Mount McKinley National Park*, by Olas Murie, available for $1.75; the *Tourist Guide to Mount McKinley National Park*, by Washburn ($4.35, paperback), which describes the park and Alaska Range mountaineering history and provides information on features along the park road and historical highlights; the *Horseshoe Lake Trail Guide*, available for 15¢, which covers the trail from McKinley Park Hotel to Horseshoe Lake with descriptions of plants, animals, and man's use of the area.

McKinley Park is a wilderness traveler's and naturalist's paradise. Caribou herds still follow their ancient migration patterns across the open tundra and through mountain passes. Dall sheep are found in the rugged high country, and moose in the pastures and willow thickets near the spruce forests, as well as wolves, grizzly, beaver, red squirrel, and bald eagle. The Sable Pass wildlife protection zone is prime grizzly bear habitat for the wildlife photographer.

There are few trails in the park. Wilderness travel is generally along river bars, gravel-covered ridges, or animal trails. Try to avoid, when possible, traveling through thick brush and marshy flats, low-lying tundra flats, tussocks and alder thickets on hillsides, and willows along river banks. The best time to hike depends on snow melt. General travel conditions tend to improve in July and are best in August. The mosquito is king between late June and mid-August. Even the caribou head for the snow patches of the high country during this time of the year to avoid the voracious warble and nostril flies. The last two weeks of August and the early weeks of September are prime time for cross-country hikes. Snowstorms may occur at any time of the year in the high country. Hunting is prohibited and there is little fishing, because most of the rivers contain a milky suspension of glacial silt,

or rock flour, which makes them uninhabitable. Wonder Lake, however, holds large lake trout.

Camp Denali, McKinley Park 99755, provides day or overnight hikes across the rolling tundra lands for up to 36 backpackers in camp from June through September, and provides sleeping bags, pack frames, and tents. *Genet Expeditions*, Talkeetna 99676, provides year-round guide service for climbing, wildlife photography, cross-country skiing, fishing, and river trips, specializing in Mount McKinley expeditions. Wilderness lodging and outpost camps in the Alaska Range and Mount McKinley region are provided by *Chulitna River Lodge*, Star Route, Box 381, Willow 99688, located 40 miles southeast of Mount McKinley in the foothills of the Alaska Range, with 4 log cabins on Ermine Lake. *Chulitna Lodge*, Box 6301, Anchorage 99502, has main lodge and daily fly-out trophy fishing and guided hunting expeditions. Lodging within the park is provided by the *McKinley Park Station Hotel;* for rates and literature, write: Outdoor World, Ltd., McKinley 99755 (phone: 907–683–2311). *North Face Lodge*, Box 66, McKinley Park 99755, is located in the Kantishna area on the north boundary of Mount McKinley National Park near an historic gold-mining area and offers one- and two-day wilderness experience trips. *Pirate Lake Training Camp*, Talkeetna 99676, has log cabins with Mount McKinley view and summer wilderness expeditions and rock, ice, survival, and leadership school. *Mountain Travel, Inc.*, 1398 Solano Ave., Albany, CA 94706, operates a summer *Mount McKinley Expedition*, with a base camp on the Kahitma Glacier at 6,000 feet. Climbers must be careful of carrying loads of more than 60 pounds.

Access & Outfitting Centers

The Alaska Range and Mount McKinley National Park are reached by charter fly-in service, the Alaska Railroad, and the Denali Alaska and Anchorage-Fairbanks highways. Outfitting and supplies are located at Talkeetna, Farewell, Skwentna, McKinley Park, Healy, Delta Junction, Dot Lake, Parson, Tanacross, and Fairbanks.

Far North & the Brooks Range Wilderness

Central Brooks Range & Gates of the Arctic National Park

U.S. Geological Survey maps, scale 1:250,000: Chandler Lake, Wiseman, Bettles, Ikpikpuk River, Killik River, Survey Pass, Hughes, Howard Pass, Ambler River, Shungnak.

Eastern Brooks Range & Arctic National Wildlife Refuge

U.S. Geological Survey maps, scale 1:250,000: Flaxman Island, Barter Island, Demarcation Point, Mount Michelson, Table Mountain, Arctic, Coleen, Christian, Chandalar, Philip Smith Mountains.

Western Brooks Range & The Great Kobuk Sand Dunes

U.S. Geological Survey maps, scale 1:250,000: DeLong Mountains, Misheguk Mountain, Noatak, Baird Mountains, Kotzebue, Selawik, Shungnak, Ambler River.

The great wilderness of Alaska's far north is bounded on the south by the Brooks Range Mountains, on the east by the Yukon border and the Porcupine Plain, and on the west by the Chukchi Sea. This rugged wilderness is dominated by the countless mountains, deep canyons, primeval valleys, and hundreds of height-of-land headwater lakes and wild rivers formed by the little-explored Brooks Range, which sweeps for 600 miles across Alaska's arctic from the Philip

Smith, Davidson, and Romanzof mountains on the east to the De-Long, Baird, and Waring mountains on the west. When the great explorer and conservationist Robert Marshall came upon the arctic divide and the massive gates of the arctic during his explorations of the Central Brooks Range in 1930, he observed the magnificence of a wild, timeless world filled with untold thousands of jagged spires, alpine valleys, lakes, and wild rivers teeming with arctic char and grayling, giant lake trout, and northern pike, previously unmapped, unnamed, and unknown. Today the great caribou, grizzly, and Dall sheep habitat of this magnificent central Brooks Range Wilderness has been irrevocably disrupted by the construction of the Alaska pipeline and the North Slope oil boom.

The Central Brooks Range wilderness, explored and mapped by Marshall during his journey to the headwaters of the upper Koyukuk River and across the arctic divide in the Endicott Mountains during the decade 1929–39, is encompassed within the proposed 8.36-million-acre Gates of the Arctic National Park. The massive spires and pinnacles of the gates of the arctic—Wien Mountain, Mount Doonerak, Hanging Glacier, the lofty snowcapped Boreal Mountain, the Six Darning Needles, Valley of the Precipices, and the snow-covered peaks of the arctic divide lie in the eastern region of the park and are described in Marshall's classic book *Alaska Wilderness—Exploring the Central Brooks Range,* available in paperback, 173 pages, for $2.95 from the University of California Press, Berkeley, CA 94720. Due east of the arctic divide and the gates of the arctic is the Trans-Alaska Pipeline corridor. The major features of the central and western park regions, an outstanding example of tundra country and taiga renowned for the stark, scenic grandeur of its vast open valleys and great sweeps of mountain slopes, include the Alatna, Killik, Noatuk, Tinayguk, Upper Kobuk, and John rivers; the jagged, dark spires of the Arrigetch Peaks, Mount Igikpak—the highest peak in the Central and Western Brooks Range—Alatna Hills, Anaktuvuk Pass; and the lunker lake trout and great northern pike waters of Walker, Chandler, Nutuvukti, Iniakuk, Minakokosa, Selby, and Narvak lakes; and the arctic foothills to the north. The Central Brooks Range and the gates of the arctic region still comprise one of the finest big-game hunting regions left in North America for barren-ground grizzly, Dall sheep, moose, and wolves. The biological resources of the region are of high scientific importance and value for wilderness recreation. It is located 200 air miles from Fairbanks, with fly-in charter service available at Bettles Field in Evansville. A descriptive *Map of the Proposed Gates of the Arctic National Park* is available free from the National Park Service, 334 W. 5th Ave., Suite 250, Anchorage 99501. The mountains of the Eastern Brooks Range, which joins the central and western portions of the range to form a continental divide between the arctic coastal plain and the Great Interior of the Yukon River system, form a great swath over 100 miles wide rising to a series of rugged, glacially eroded peaks 5,000–8,000 feet high from the Yukon border westward to the Sagavanirktok River. This land of permafrost, broad, colorful valleys, rock and alpine tundra, isolated stands of white spruce and poplar brush, muskeg bogs, lakes, and tundra meadows dominated by sedges, scattered willows, and dwarf birch, is encompassed within the 8.9-million-acre Arctic National Wildlife Range. The southern portion of the wildlife range contains fertile valleys, warmed by summer winds that flow from the Yukon River Basin, and carpeted by yellow snow buttercup, tundra rose, red shooting star, fireweed, blue Siberian aster, and fields of monkshood. Old Woman Creek and the Sheenjek River flow southward out of the mountains, winding through a valley floor of rich lakes, oxbow sloughs, and groves of spruce and cottonwood into the vast, densely forested plain of the Yukon River. In the north is the rolling tundra of the great treeless arctic plain. In the western part of the wildlife range lie Peters and Schroder lakes at the foot of Mount

Chamberain, each 5 miles long. The lakes contain grayling and large lake trout, and you can usually see white Dall sheep, caribou, and moose from the shores. In the eastern part of the range, the clear, cold Firth River flows past towering limestone ramparts and groves of cottonweed and white spruce.

If you're planning a fishing, hunting, or wilderness camping expedition into the region, be sure to write for the *Arctic National Wildlife Range* Map-Brochure, available free from the Bureau of Sport Fishery and Wildlife, 813 D St., Anchorage 99501. The range is one of the finest caribou-hunting zones in Alaska. The great porcupine caribou herd migrates through the region along deeply worn trails in the river valleys and mountain passes and on high slopes, similar to the buffalo trails on the Great Plains 100 years ago. The arctic range caribou winter on the Old Crow flats in the Yukon, then move to the calving grounds of the north slope in May. Moose are found scattered in the willow and poplar stands along valley bottoms and lakes of the southern portion of the range and to within 25 miles of the Arctic Ocean on the north side. A few barren-ground grizzly in color phases from dark brown to blond roam the high country along with Dall sheep, most easily observed in Hulahula, Jago, Opilak, and Chandalar valleys and above the shores of Peters and Schroder lakes. Other wildlife in the range includes large populations of hawks, eagles, and falcons, wolves, black bear, wolverine, lynx, fox, beaver, mink, marten, weasel, and snowshoe and arctic hares. Good hiking routes are found along the lichen-and-heath-carpeted uplands of the Brooks Range and along the headwaters of the Chandalar River and Hulahula River. Warm clothing, raingear, and plenty of insect repellent are a must. No campgrounds are available. Access is via charter fly-in from Arctic Village. *Wilderness Wildlife Camps,* located at Timber Lake on the south slope of the Brooks in the Junjik River Valley, about 40 miles west of the Arctic National Wildlife Range, offers canoe and river float trips,

wilderness hiking, and photographic safaris for youths, families, and small groups. Write: LTC E.M. Witt (Rct.), Mile 11, St. Steese Highway, SR 20579, Fox 99701. The *Itkillik Brooks Range Lodge* offers fishing for grayling, lake trout, and char, and lodge and cabins. Write: 1206 Coppet, Fairbanks 99701. *Gates of the Arctic Guide Service,* operated by Dan Wetzel, registered guide and biologist, provides trophy hunting and fishing trips in the Central Brooks Range. Write: Bettles 99726 (Winter, P.O. Box 80224, College 99708).

The Western Brooks Range takes in the DeLong, Baird, and Waring mountains and the vast wild country of scenic foothills, broad valleys, clear lakes and rivers, boreal forests and tundra, and prehistoric archa-

eological features surrounding the Noatak and Kobuk rivers. The lake region along the Selaivik River, the delta and inland valley of the Kobuk and Noatak rivers, and the lowlands near Cape Krusenstern contain large seasonal populations of loons, gulls, ducks, Canada geese, and whistling swans. The Grand Canyon section of the Noatak River is the nesting and hunting grounds for golden eagles, rough-legged hawks, gyrfalcons, and peregrine falcons. Black bear are found throughout the region, and grizzlies roam the highlands and valleys of salmon streams; a few polar bear are occasionally found along the ice floes of Kotzebue Sound. Portions of the arctic caribou herd winter in the lower stretch of the Noatak, the upper Kobuk, and along the Selawik Hills and Selawik River west of Inland Lake. Moose are found along the river valleys and lowlands, and Dall sheep are found among the peaks and alpine meadows of the Igichuk Hills and Baird and DeLong mountains. The Noatak, Kobuk, and Selawik rivers hold trophy chum salmon, arctic char, and sheefish.

The scenic wetlands, open tundra, barren jagged peaks, forested rolling hills, and the Great Kobuk Sand Dunes covering 25 square miles of the central Kobuk River Valley are encompassed with the proposed 1.85-million-acre Kobuk Valley National Monument. The proposed national monument is located north of the arctic circle between the Eskimo villages of Kiana and Ambler, about 100 miles east of Kotzebue. The famous Onion Portage Archaeological District—one of the most important sites in arctic North America to the understanding of the culture of early man in the New World and his relationship to Asia —lies just outside the eastern boundary of the proposed monument. Along the Chukchi Sea coast to the west lie the famous tundra lowlands, lava fields, and volcanic crater lakes of the proposed Chukchi-Imuruk National Reserve and the Cape Krusenstern National Monument, which embrace an ancient relic of the Bering land bridge. About 40,000 years ago, the sea level dropped during the last of the Pleistocene's great ice ages, and Alaska became linked to Asia by a 1,000-mile-wide land bridge across which prehistoric hunters are believed to have entered America. Maps of the proposed national reserve and monument are available free from Bureau of Sport Fishery and Wildlife, 813 D St., Anchorage 99501.

Access & Outfitting Centers

The far north and the Brooks Range are reached by scheduled and charter aircraft from Fairbanks and the arctic bush villages of Chandalar, Arctic Village, Fort Yukon, Bettles, Allakaket, Anaktuvik Pass, Deadhorse, Kiana, Ambler, and Kotzebue.

Great Interior: Yukon River Country

Upper Yukon River & Porcupine National Forest

U.S. Geological Survey maps, scale 1:250,000: Beaver, Fort Yukon, Black River, Christian, Coleen, Livengood, Circle, Charley River, Eagle.

Yukon-Kuskokwim National Forest

U.S. Geological Survey maps, scale 1:250,000: Nulato, Ruby, Unalakleet, Ophir, Medfra, McGrath, Iditarod, Holy Cross, Slutmute, Russian Mission.

Alaska's interior country is a vast 166,000-square-mile area which lies between the Brooks Range to the north and the Alaska Range to the south, dominated by the Yukon, known to the Athabascan Indians as "the great river," which flows for 1,200 miles through Alaska from the Yukon border to the Bering Sea, and its three major tributaries, the Porcupine, Tanana, and Koyukuk. The upper Yukon region includes the scenic section of the river and the surrounding wildlands between the Yukon-Alaska border at Eagle and Circle (the town, established as a trading post in 1887, owes its name to early traders and Klondike prospectors who mistakenly thought that the town was on the arctic circle). The upper Yukon is bordered by hills and the Crazy mountains, colorful bluffs, and bottomland forest, and is the principal segment of a network of wild and scenic rivers that include the Charley, Kandik, Tatonduk, and the renowned Nation rivers—the latter a wild, deep-flowing stream that offers some of the finest arctic grayling fishing in North America. Other wild and scenic streams and wilderness canoe routes in the region are the historic Fortymile River and

the Birch and Beaver Creek, which rise in the alpine uplands of the White Mountains. The entire Charley River Basin lies within the 1.97 million acres of the proposed Yukon-Charley National Wild and Scenic Rivers. The wild Charley River, one of Alaska's clearest and a top-ranked wilderness canoe route, has its headwaters in the primitive uplands area of the Tanana Hills. The dense bottomland spruce and poplar and the upland spruce-hardwood forests and low brush, alpine tundra, and hundreds of blue lakes form an important big-game and waterfowl hunting zone. Moose congregate along the river lowlands from late fall to spring. The Steese-Fortymile caribou herd roams the wildlands along the Taylor Highway. A small population of white Dall sheep inhabit the rugged glacier peaks between the Charley and Fortymile rivers. The peaks are designated a walk-in area where no vehicles or pack animals are allowed for hunting purposes. Wolves, wolverine, and black bear are common to the area, and grizzlies are found in the uplands. The remote headwater lakes and crystal clear tributaries of the "great river" are accessible by floatplane fly-in and canoe and hold record grayling, sheefish, northern pike, and king, silver, and sockeye salmon. The upper Yukon area is also considered to be the finest peregrine falcon habitat in Alaska, with one nest per 8 miles of river.

The great lake-dotted lowlands of the Yukon Flats and the Porcupine wetlands, encompassed within the remote 5.5 million acres of the proposed Porcupine National Forest, surround the confluence of the Porcupine and Yukon rivers at the historic Hudson's Bay Company trading post of Fort Yukon, northwest of Circle and the upper Yukon region. The Yukon-Porcupine Flats are Alaska's most productive waterfowl area. Ducks in untold thousands nest in the flats, including lesser scaup, widgeon, pintail, whitewinged scoter, green-winged teal, mallard, and one-fourth of the world's population of canvasbacks. The upper Porcupine River is an important area for the endangered peregrine falcon, gyrfalcon, and the golden eagle. Moose, wolves, grizzlies, and the Fortymile and Porcupine caribou herds are found through the lowlands and in the Hodzana Highlands.

Westward of Fort Yukon and the flatlands, the Yukon winds through its broad, densely forested valley, past the outposts of Beaver and Stevens Village, Mount Tozi, and the Rae Mountains to its confluence with the Tanana River, flowing on past the Kokrines Hills on the north and the Kaiyuk Mountains on the south to its confluence with the Koyukuk River and the Koyukuk Flats and the Nogahabare Sand Dunes, where it bends sharply and flows southwest through the wilderness of the proposed 7.3-million-acre Yukon-Kuskokwim National Forest and the lake-dotted "pothole country" of the Yukon Delta, to its mouth on the Bering Sea.

The Yukon and its tributaries, the Tanana, the Koyukuk, and the Porcupine, of the Great Interior are generally traveled with flat-bottomed riverboats, designed to carry large loads and to slide over riffles that are often a mere few inches deep. Moose hunting from an Alaskan riverboat, usually from 15 to 30 feet long and powered by outboards of up to 75 horsepower, is popular throughout the interior. Inflatable rubber boats are often used on fly-in fishing trips to the remote high-country headwaters and feeder streams of the Yukon. The renowned wilderness canoe routes along Birch and Beaver creeks, and the rugged Fortymile, Charley, and Nation rivers offer some of the finest canoeing and kayaking water in North America. The *Boater's Guide to the Upper Yukon River*, from Carcross, Yukon, to Fort Yukon, Alaska, is available in paperback, 66 pages, $3.95, from Alaska Northwest Publishing Co., Box 4-EEE, Anchorage 99509.

Access & Outfitting Centers

The Yukon country of the interior is reached by scheduled air service,

the Elliott and Steese highways, and charter fly-in service from Fairbanks. Outfitting and supplies are found at Eagle, Chatanika River, Circle Hot Springs, Circle, Fort Yukon, Livengood, Manley Hot Springs, Minto, Stevens Village, Beaver, Rampart, Tanana, Ruby, Galena, Koyukuk, Nulato, Kaltag, Grayling, Anvik, Holy Cross, Russian Mission, Marshall, St. Marys (Andreafsky), and Alakanuk.

Gulf Coast: Kenai Peninsula & Chugach National Forest

Chugach National Forest

U.S. Geological Survey maps, scale 1:250,000: Afognak, Bering Glacier, Blying Sound, Cordova, Kenai Middleton Island, Seldovia, Seward.

Kenai National Moose Range

U.S. Geological Survey maps, scale 1:250,000: Blying Sound, Kenai, Seldovia, Seward.

Wrangell Mountains

U.S. Geological Survey maps, scale 1:250,000: Nabesna, McCarthy, Gulkana.

The Chugach National Forest is one of Alaska's most scenic and popular areas for fishing, wilderness canoeing, cross-country hiking, and big-game hunting. The forest is named after the Chugach Eskimos of Prince William Sound and takes in 4¾ million acres of the mountainous, lake-studded Kenai Peninsula and a narrow strip of shoreline along the Prince William Sound and Boswell Bay of Alaska's Gulf Coast. It also includes the cluster of densely forested islands in Prince William Sound, including Afognak and Montague islands, which are covered with magnificent conifers, scenic fjords, log-strewn beaches, and quiet lagoons and spits, located between the peninsula and the mouth of the Cooper River. The major topographic features shown on the *Chugach National Forest Map*, available for 50¢ from the Supervisor, 121 W. Fireweed La., Suite 205, Anchorage 99503, include the renowned salmon, steelhead, arctic grayling, northern pike, lake trout, rainbow trout, and Dolly Varden waters of the Russian Lakes and River, Crescent Lake, Cooper River Delta, the massive Harding and Sargent icefields, Nellie Juan Wilderness, the rugged Kenai Mountains, and the Bear, Allen, Columbia, and Portage glaciers.

In the northernmost region of the forest, the Chugach Mountains range from Cook Inlet to Prince William Sound. The turbulent, silty Susitna and Copper rivers cut through this rugged chain of peaks, pouring their waters into the Gulf of Alaska. The upper Susitna and the headwater lakes of the Copper hold arctic grayling and lake trout to 40 pounds.

Several wilderness hiking trails provide access to the remote interior hunting, fishing, and scenic areas. Write the Forest Supervisor for the free *Forest Trails on Chugach.* The wilderness traveler should keep alert for brown bear and the williwaw, a sudden and violent gust of wind often reaching a gale force of up to 100 miles per hour. Hunting is good in the high country regions for white Dall sheep, mountain goat, and black bear, as well as for Sitka deer throughout Prince William Sound, and for Kenai moose, black-tailed deer, arctic hare, and brown bear along the coastal streams of lower Cook Inlet and the outer islands of Prince William Sound. Elk are found on Afognak Island and nearby Raspberry Island. An estimated 1,500 elk now range

these islands as a result of a transplant of 8 Roosevelt elk from the Olympic Peninsula in Washington to Afognak Island in 1929. One of the largest concentrations of trumpeter swans in North America and between 15,000 and 20,000 Canada geese nest in the 330,000-acre Copper Delta Game Management Area. Lynx, wolverine, and occasional wolves are reported in the central Kenai area. Wildlife seen along the rugged coastal areas include the majestic bald eagle and the legendary killer whale (actually a dolphin), the Minke, or little piked whale, humpback and gray whale, a few northern sea lion rookeries, sea otter, harbor seal and porpoise. The notorious killer whale, which has been observed at Chugach, is identified by the conspicuous white markings on a black background and the high, triangular-shaped dorsal fin up to 6 feet on the male. An informative guide, *The Ocean & the Forest,* is available free from the Chugach Forest Supervisor.

The free Forest Service publication *Recreation Cabins in the Chugach National Forest* describes the accommodations and area hunting and fishing for the 30 wilderness cabins open to the public at such re-

nowned areas as Afognak Lake, Crescent and Upper Russian lakes, Copper River Flats, Swan Lake, and Montague Island. The cabins range from simple A-frames to rustic log dwellings for 4–8 people and rent for $5 a night. Skiffs are available at most of the lakeside cabins. Reservations should be made at least 6 months in advance by writing to the Chugach National Forest Office at 121 W. Fireweed La., Suite 205, Anchorage 99503. Request application form R10–2300–21. The free publication also lists local charter aircraft fly-in services. The Chugach National Forest Office also publishes a free guide to the great tidal flats of the Copper River Delta, *Highway Guide to the Copper River Delta*, and the free guides *Nellie Juan Wilderness Study Area* and *Portage Glacier*. The Copper River region was the scene of the "copper rush" triggered by Captain Abercrombie's expedition in 1898 and his discovery of the famous Kennecott copper fields. It had been common knowledge for years that there was copper in the region. In precolonial days, the Indians from the Copper River area carried huge shields of copper when they traveled as far south as Sitka to trade. It took Abercrombie's discovery and building of the Copper River and Northwestern Railroad, between 1908 and 1911, to create one of the most intriguing sagas in American business history, immortalized in Rex Beach's gripping novel *The Iron Trail*.

The famous Kenai National Moose Range encompasses the major portion of the Kenai Peninsula wilderness to the south and west of the Chugach National Forest. The 1,730,000-acre refuge was established in 1941 by the U.S. Fish and Wildlife Service to protect the natural breeding and feeding range of the great Kenai moose, renowned for their palmated antlers in excess of 6 feet, and other native wildlife. The Moose Range is divided into two natural zones: a scenic mountain country with hundreds of lakes and glaciers, dominated by the huge Tustumena and Skilak lakes known as the Andy Simons Natural Area, and a lowland area dotted with over 1,200 lakes and dense forests of spruce, birch, and aspen.

The region was once the hunting grounds of the ancient Kenaitze Indians, who lived in pit houses known as barabaras along the shores of Cook Inlet and the Kenai River prior to the arrival of the early explorers led by Captain Cook, who claimed the territory for England in 1778. In 1786 the Russians established a fur-trading post and colony at the mouth of the Kasilof River. Until the 1890s the Kenai moose region was primarily a stone caribou habitat. At the turn of the century, however, a series of forest fires swept across the Kenai and created a lush second-growth habitat favorable to moose. Today wildlife populations include approximately 9,000 moose at lower elevations and about 1,000 Dall sheep, as well as black bear, wolves, wolverine, brown bear, mountain goat, coyotes, and caribou. Furbearers include beaver, muskrat, fox, otter, mink, and lynx.

Nearly 500,000 outdoorsmen visit the moose range each year to fish, hunt in the high country and lowlands, and canoe the wilderness water trails. The region provides excellent fishing in the Kenai and Russian rivers for record red salmon, silver salmon, and king salmon, running as large as 100 pounds. The wilderness lakes and rivers hold arctic char, Dolly Varden, lake trout, steelhead, and kokanee. The range offers scenic wilderness areas for alpine camping and wildlife photography, and canoeing along the Kenai, Swan Lake, Swanson River, and Moose River wilderness canoe routes. There are over 100 miles of well-marked hiking trails. Much of the lowland area is wet and swampy and requires waterproof footwear. Wilderness campsites are located in the interior regions. The moose range has 14 established campsites, varying from small, rustic overnight access camps to larger individual units with parking spurs, boat ramps, and water and sanitary facilities located at various scenic and popular fishing areas.

The refuge is the habitat of more than 146 species of birds, including grebes, loons, terns, and the graceful white trumpeter swan in the lake country, which reaches weights up to 33 pounds, with a wingspan of almost 8 feet, and has been known to live for over 32 years. Bald eagles, hawks, owls, and marsh and water birds are found throughout the moose range. Thousands of pintails, mallards, and lesser Canadian snow geese use the tidal waters of Chickaloon Flats during migrations.

The scenic, well-paved Sterling Highway runs across the northern half of the refuge, and the Swanson River Road and Skilak Loop Road wind through rolling hills of spruce and birch forests and a high country with views of deep valleys and hundreds of blue, gemlike lakes. The Kenai National Moose Range, P.O. Box 500, Kenai 99611, offers several useful free publications for the outdoorsman: the *Kenai National Moose Range* Map & Guide shows roads, range boundaries, canoe routes, trails, campgrounds, shelters, historical sites, and hiking trailheads and describes special regulations, accommodations, wildlife, and outdoor recreation; *Canoeing on the Kenai National Moose Range* describes the Swanson River and Swan Lake canoe routes and contains detailed maps showing routes, portages, and campsites; *Kenai National Moose Range Aircraft Regulations* describes landing regulations and contains an airstrip and closure area map. *Alaska Pioneer Canoers Association*, Box 931, Soldotna 99669, offers guided wilderness canoeing and fishing trips and rentals in the Kenai National Moose Range.

Due east of the Copper River lie the world-famous big-game hunting ranges of the Wrangell-Mentasta-Nutzotin mountains. This high country region is the premier Dall sheep hunting area in Alaska. Part of the wintering range for the Nelchina caribou herd, the most important in the state for the hunter, is located on the northwestern flank of the Wrangell Mountains. The smaller Mentasta and Chisana caribou herds roam the northern portion of the region year round. The boreal forests, lowlands, and alpine tundra of this high country are the habitat of moose, brown, grizzly and black bear, wolves, wolverine, and mountain goats. There are also two small herds of wild bison. The Wrangell Mountains take in the interior and coastal forests of the proposed Wrangell Mountains National Forest and the Wrangell–St. Elias National Park, which together form 14 million acreas of the greatest concentration of peaks over 14,500 feet in North America, including Mount St. Elias (18,008 ft.), Mount Blackburn (16,390 ft.), and Mount Sanford (16,237 ft.). The rugged coastline from Yakutat Bay to Prince William Sound, south of the Wrangell Mountains, is

prime habitat for bald eagles, harbor seals, sea otters, sea lions, and the endangered peregrine falcon.

Several wilderness lodges and outpost camps provide rustic accommodations and fly-in services on the Kenai Peninsula, Chugach Forest, and in the interior, northward to the Alaska Range. *Kenai Float Plane Service, Inc.*, Box 152, Kenai 99611, provides wilderness charter fly-in and fly-out service. *Alexander Lake Lodge*, Box 4–212, Anchorage 99509, offers fly-in fishing 50 miles northwest of Anchorage, and has cabin accommodations for 15. The remote *Bear Track Lodge*, Box 3–385, Anchorage 99501, has accommodations for 12, with 45-foot charter yacht for Prince William Sound glacier cruises, located 25 miles northwest of Cordova. *Bing Browns Sportsmen's Service*, Box 256, Star Rte. 2, Sterling 99672, provides camping accommodations and guided fishing trips. *Evergreen Lodge*, Box 264, Star Rte. C, Palmer 99645, provides accommodations, campgrounds, and fly-in services on Lake Louise off Mile 160 of the Glenn Highway. *Hayes River Lodge*, Box 6184 Annex, Anchorage 99502, is located in Susitna Valley 90 miles northwest of Anchorage with guide/pilot service for fishing trips. *Gwin's Lodge*, Mile 52, Sterling Highway, Copper Landing 99572, is located on the Kenai River, within 2 miles of the Russian River. *Mike's Kenai Fish Camp*, Box 75 SRA, Anchorage 99507, is located on Kenai River with guide service and fishing for steelhead, rainbow trout, Dolly Varden, and salmon. Vacation lodging on Afognak Island is provided by *Afognak Wilderness Lodge*, Seal Bay 99697.

Access & Outfitting Centers

The Kenai Peninsula–Gulf Coast Region is reached via scheduled airline service, charter aircraft, the Alaska Marine Highway System, and the Sterling, Seward-Anchorage, George Parks, Glenn, Edgerton, and Richardson highways. Outfitting and supply services are located at Kenai, Soldatna, Seward, Anchorage, Valdez, and Cordova.

Tongass National Forest & Alaska's Panhandle

Tongass National Forest Topo Maps

U.S. Geological Survey maps, scale 1:250,000: Bradfield Canal, Craig, Dixon Entrance, Juneau, Ketchikan, Mount Fairweather, Petersking, Port Alexander, Prince Rupert, Sitka, Skagway, Sundum, Taku River, Yakutat.

Admiralty Island

U.S. Geological Survey maps, scale 1:250,000: Sundum, Sitka, Juneau.

Glacier Bay National Monument

U.S. Geological Survey maps, scale 1:250,000: Juneau, Mount Fairweather, Skagway.

Prince of Wales Island

U.S. Geological Survey maps, scale 1:250,000: Petersburg, Craig.

The Tongass National Forest, a labyrinth of islands of the massive Alexander Archipelago, dense coastal forests of giant Sitka spruce and western hemlock, soaring snow-covered peaks and massive glaciers, rock-walled fjords, and clear mountain streams, is one of the most magnificent regions in North America and one of the least known. The forest covers the whole of the Panhandle, a narrow strip of land with heavy rains and mild winters along the British Columbia border. Tongass country is the ancestral home of the Haida and Tlingit Indians. Before the arrival of the white explorers and fur traders, the land was so plentiful with game and the wild, brawling rivers so rich with salmon that the Indians of Tongass, renowned for their haunting totems and huge cedar war canoes, were the wealthiest and most powerful of the Pacific Northwest tribes.

The *Tongass National Forest Map* (50¢) and *Recreation Facilities Guide* (free) are available from the Supervisor, North Unit, P.O. Box 1049, Juneau 99801, and Supervisor, South Unit, P.O. Box 2278, Ketchikan 99901. The Forest Service map shows all major features of Tongass's 16 million acres—the nation's largest national forest—including the Mendenhall Glacier Recreation area, the rugged cliffs and fjords of Rudyard Bay–Walker Cove Scenic Area, the iceberg-filled fjord of the Tracy Arm–Fjord's Terror Scenic Area, and remote wilderness of bald eagle, salmon, and brown bear country surrounding the Admiralty Lakes Recreation Area. The crazy-quilt maze of islands in the Tongass contain several proposed wilderness areas. The King Salmon Wilderness Area takes in 120,000 acres of ocean islands with scenic cliffs, capes, and log-strewn beaches and dense spruce and hemlock forests that are home of wolf, deer, black bear, and thousands of seals and sea lions. The beautiful Granite Fjords Wilderness, described in the free *Granite Fjords Wilderness Study Area* guide available from the Supervisor's Office, is characterized by rugged highlands cut by U-shaped glacial valleys, ancient stands of lichen-hung lodgepole pine, Sitka spruce, hemlock, and cedar, with icefields, glaciers, and muskeg bogs. Big Goat Lake is a top fly-in spot for goat hunting, and fishermen stalk the aristocratic steelhead in the deep pools and riffles of the wild Chickamin River. The free *Glacier Bay National Monument Map-Brochure* shows and describes the major features, the

active tidewater glaciers, deep fjords, and lush rain forests, of this 400-square-mile wilderness. Several glaciers, such as the Muir and John Hopkins, discharge massive icebergs as the ocean undermines the glacier lip, making it impossible to get within a 2-mile range of them. Mount Fairweather and surrounding peaks soar to over 12,000 feet and are surrounded by coastal highlands inhabited by the rare blue or glacier bear, wolf, moose, Sitka deer, and wolverine. Campers and hikers should be prepared for cool, damp weather, with temperatures seldom rising above 72° F. For free map-brochure and information write: Glacier Bay National Monument, Box 1089, Juneau 99801.

The dense coastal rain forests of Tongass with great profusions of mosses and the treacherous devil's club, blueberries, huckleberry, copperbush, and salal, and the great salmon-spawning streams provide prime cover and food for moose, along the river valleys, brown bear, and the world's greatest concentration of bald eagles (described, by the way, in the fascinating guide *Bald Eagles in Alaska*, available free from the Bureau of Sport Fishery & Wildlife, 813 D St., Anchorage 99501). The Forest Service maintains more than 20 recreational cabins, ranging from small A-frames to rustic log chalet-type cabins available to the public at $5 per night in the outlying hunting, fishing, and wilderness camping areas. The wilderness traveler using a cabin is advised to carry a .30–06 caliber or larger rifle for protection against a charging brown bear. Wilderness public-use cabins are located at Taku River, accessible by riverboat or floatplane, with salmon and steelhead fishing and moose hunting; Shelter Island Lake, accessible by floatplane, boat, and trail with fishing for cutthroat trout and deer hunting; the Admiralty Cove Cabin, accessible by floatplane or boat, offering stream and saltwater fishing, hiking, deer, and waterfowl hunting; and, at Distin Lake, Florence Lake, Laughton Glacier, Church Bight, Lake Alexander, Hasselborg River on Admiralty Island, and Lake Kathleen. Public campgrounds, maintained by the Forest Service with sanitary facilities, water systems, and sewage-dumping hookup, are available at Auka Village Recreation Area and Mendenhall Glacier. The Forest Service cabins and shelters (with assistance from organized sportsmen in Juneau) are maintained with fine woodpiles (always replace what you use), good skiffs, and stoves or fireplaces.

In addition to the Forest Service cabins, several wilderness lodges and

outpost camps provide accommodations and fly-in and guide service in the outstanding fishing, big-game hunting, and wilderness camping and wildlife photography areas of Tongass Country. The *Bell Island Hot Springs Lodge*, Bell Island 99950, located 42 miles north of Ketchikan, provides cabin accommodations and boats for steelhead and Chinook and coho salmon fishing. *Clover Pass Resort*, Box 2322, Ketchikan 99901, located 15 miles by road from Ketchikan, has a main lodge and 13 cabins, with fishing cruises, guide service, camper hookup, and fish-handling facilities. *Glacier Bay Lodge*, located 60 air miles northwest of Juneau in Glacier Bay National Monument, has charter fishing, marine fuel station, and sightseeing. Write: (Summer) Gustavus 99826; (Winter) Suite 312, Park Place Bldg., Seattle, WA 98101. *Glacier Bear Lodge*, Box 303, Yakutat 99689, has charter boat flightseeing and salmon and steelhead fishing with daily jet service from Anchorage and Seattle. *Hood Bay Wilderness Camp*, RR 5, Box 5610, Juneau 99803, is located on Admiralty Island near Angoon, reached by boat or air charter service from Juneau; it offers trophy fishing and wildlife photography. *Humpback Lake Chalet*, located 60 miles south of Ketchikan, offers trout fishing on a 5-mile-long glacier-carved lake. Write: Sportsman Paradise Tours, Box 812, Ward Cove 99828. *Prince of Wales Lodge*, Box 106, Klawock 99925, is located in a scenic Indian village with totem lights and fishing for salmon, trout, halibut, and steelhead. *Thayer Lake Lodge*, Box 416, Ketchikan 99901, is a wilderness retreat on Admiralty Island, accessible only by plane or trail; it offers trout fishing, boating, and hiking. *Yes Bay Lodge*, Yes Bay 99950, located 50 miles northwest of Ketchikan, has accommodations for 40, with fresh and saltwater fishing with fish smoking and packaging service, hiking, and wildlife photography. The beautiful *Waterfall Cannery Resort* offers outstanding family vacation facilities 62 miles west of Ketchikan. Write: Box 101, Ketchikan 99901.

Fish Alaska, Inc., Box 316, Petersburg 99833, specializes in salmon and steelhead fly-fishing charters throughout the Tongass National Forest. Wilderness charter fly-in service is provided by *Alaska Island Air, Inc.*, Box 508, Petersburg 99833; *B-Line Aviation*, Box 305, and *Gulf Air Taxi*, Box 37, both at Yakutat 99689; and, *Stikine Air Service, Inc.*, Box 631, Wrangell 99929. Air tours and charter service in the Glacier Bay National Monument region is provided by *Glacier Bay Airways*, Gustavus 99826.

Access & Outfitting Centers

Tongass National Forest and the Panhandle are reached by the Alaska Marine Highway System and scheduled airline and charter fly-in service from Prince Rupert, Ketchikan, Wrangell, Petersburg, Kake, Sitka, Hoonah, Juneau, Haines, Skagway, and Yakutat.

PACIFIC CREST STATES

Introduction

The sweeping forests, majestic snowcapped volcanic peaks, thousands upon thousands of remote blue lakes, quiet alpine meadows, and wild salmon, trout, and steelhead streams of the Pacific Crest Region stretch for 2,600 miles, from the British Columbia border south through Washington, Oregon, and California. The massive Cascade Range and the Sierra Nevada form the cloud-wreathed backbone of the region, bordered by the dense rain forests, snowfields, and glaciers of the Coast Range Mountains and the picturesque, wild, log-strewn beaches of the Pacific Ocean on the west; and by the ancient Columbia River Plateau and the arid sagebrush flats and canyons of the Great Basin on the east. This spectacular region, home of the legendary Bigfoot, embraces many of the nation's truly great hunting, backpacking, and wilderness camping areas and historic salmon, trout, and steelhead fishing streams. The Pacific Crest National Scenic Trail traverses the high country of the region, winding south from the North Cascades and following Washington's Cascade Crest Trail and Oregon's Skyline Trail until it enters California, where it follows the great lake-dotted arc of the High Sierra to the snowcapped summit of 14,494-foot Mount Whitney and beyond, along the edge of the Mojave Desert to the Mexican boundary.

Bordered on the north by British Columbia and the island-dotted Juan de Fuca Strait, on the east by Idaho, on the south by Oregon, and on the west by the Pacific and the beautiful San Juan Islands and the southernmost reaches of the fabled Inside Passage, the state of Washington covers 68,192 square miles and embraces the historic steelhead and trout waters of the wild Skagit River, the classic fly-fishing waters of the North Fork Stittaguamish River, the great salmon-fishing grounds of Puget Sound, the "lost" lakes and ancient dry falls of the Grand Coulee Country of the historic Columbia River, North Cascades National Park, Indian Heaven high country, the wild Olympic Peninsula—dominated by the massive glaciers and snowfields of the rugged Olympic Mountains, and the High Cascade alpine wilderness fish and game areas. The volcanic, snowcapped peaks of the Cascade Range, surrounded by fragrant coniferous forests, culminate at Mount Rainer (14,410 ft.), Mount Adams (12,307 ft.), Mount Baker (10,750 ft.), and Glacier Peak (10,436). The incredibly scenic coastal areas of the Evergreen State were explored in 1778 by the legendary British explorer Captain Cook, followed by Captain George Vancouver, who discovered, explored, and named the Gulf of Georgia, Hood Canal, Mount Baker, and Mount Rainier. The mouth of the historic Columbia River, the long-sought "River of the West," an ancient Indian water trail traveled by successive waves of explorers, voyageurs, and settlers, was discovered in 1792 by Robert Gray of Boston, followed in 1805 by Lewis and Clark on their epic overland westward journey along the Missouri, Snake, and Columbia rivers. In 1810, David Thompson, explorer and geographer of the North West Company, built Spokane House near the "Great Bend of the Columbia" to exploit the vast untapped fur forests of the Pacific Northwest. The Washington Territory was later ruled by fur traders of the Hudson's Bay Company, the lords of Rupert's Land.

The rich fish and game lands, forests, mountains, and wild rivers of Oregon are bordered on the north by the Columbia River and Washington, on the east by Idaho and the great canyons of the Snake River, on the south by California and the Siskiyou Mountains, and on the west by the rugged, wave-cut bluffs and wild sand dunes of the Pacific, rimmed by towering coastal forests of cedar, pine, spruce, and hemlock, with an understory of laurel, sweet gale and rhododendron, beautiful red-barked madronas, watery sphagnum bogs, and tangled thickets of the spiny devil's club. The Beaver State contains 96,981 square miles of varied topography, including several of the nation's

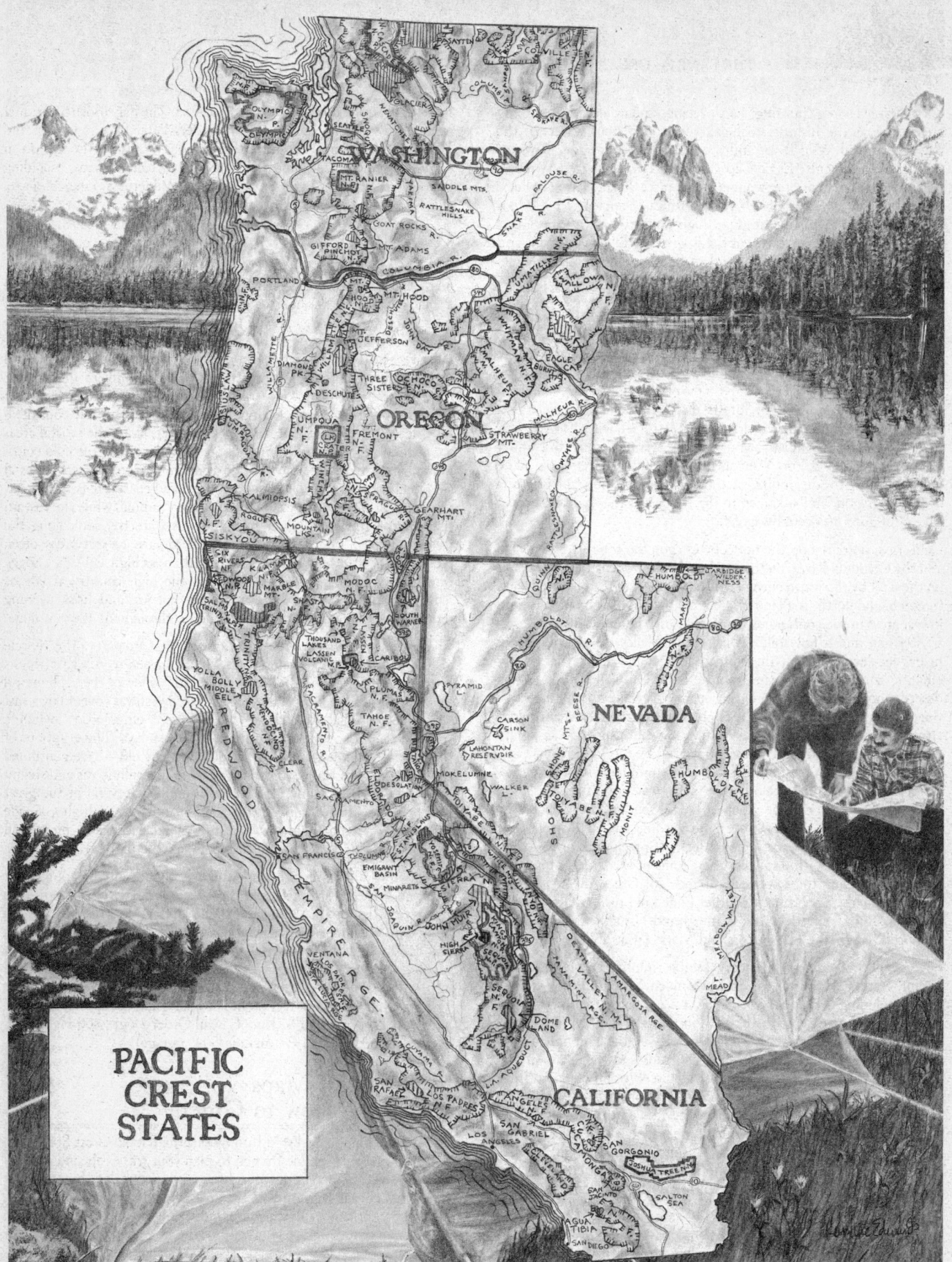

PACIFIC
CREST
STATES

outstanding fishing, hunting, backpacking, and wilderness camping areas, such as the historic steelhead and trophy trout waters of the Rogue National Wild River and the fabled Deschutes, or "River of Falls"; the spectacular Eagle Cap Wilderness in the rugged Wallowa Mountains; the haunting wonders of Crater Lake National Park, formed by the wrecking in prehistoric times of ancient 14,000-foot Mount Mazanna; the picturesque high country of the Sky Lakes wilderness and the headwaters of the Rogue; the Blue Mountains and Wenaha backcountry—the "Island of Shoshone"; the classic blue-ribbon fly-fishing waters of the North Branch of the Umpqua and Metolius rivers; the fabled waterfowl shooting areas and camas prairies of Malheur and Klamath lakes; the wild McKenzie River; and the spectacular "black forests" and wilderness areas of the High Cascades —culminating at 11,245-foot Mount Hood, the state's highest peak —carpeted along the alpine meadows and forest floors with sorrel, orchids, Indian pipe, the blood red snow plant, and the rare moccasin flower. The towering virgin forests of the Beaver State were first explored by the fur traders of John Jacob Astor's Pacific Fur Co. and the Hudson's Bay Company, who ruled the territory from 1821 under John McLoughlin at Fort Vancouver—"the Father of Oregon." The year 1842 saw the beginning of the "Great Migration" of pioneers over the Oregon Trail—known to the Indians as the "Great Road of the Whitetops" (covered wagons).

California, bordered on the north by Oregon, on the east by Nevada and the Colorado River, on the south by Mexico's Baja Peninsula, and on the west by the warm currents of the Pacific and the giant redwood forests of the north, is a land of great contrasts, with the highest and lowest areas in the contiguous United States: Mount Whitney rises to 14,494 feet and a few miles away, Death Valley drops to 282 feet below sea level. Within the state can be found all of the world's climatic zones but one—the tropical. Southern California is a vast desert panorama framed by rugged, sparsely vegetated mountains. To the northeast the great arc of the High Sierra Crest forms a continuous strip of sparkling blue alpine lakes, towering snowcapped peaks, granite pinnacles, and volcanic domes, traversed by the John Muir Trail, which stretches through some of the most stunning wilderness camping and alpine fishing country in North America, from Yosemite Valley south to the massive group of 14,000-foot peaks dominated by Mount Whitney at the headwaters of the Kings and Kern rivers. The eastern slopes of the Sierras, among the most precipitous in the country, plunge into beautiful valleys, where some of the nation's top trout streams, including the Owens River and Hot Creek, are fed by the high snowfields. The famous Mother Lode gold rush country of the Sierra foothills, dotted by ghost towns and abandoned mines, was immortalized by the forty-niners and Mark Twain's *Roughing It*.

Several of the nation's legendary fishing, hunting, and wilderness camping areas are found within the Golden State's 158,693 square miles, including beautiful Lake Tahoe at 6,225 feet elevation, Desolation Valley, the ancient Bristlecone Pine Forest, John Muir Wilderness, the steelhead waters of the Klamath River, the Yosemite Valley and backcountry, Lassen Volcanic Highlands and the Caribou and Thousand Lakes Wilderness areas, Hat Creek trophy trout waters, huge Lake Shasta, the classic fly-fishing waters of the McCloud River, the scenic Salmon-Trinity Alps, the wild Middle Fork of the Feather River, and Eagle Lake, the "lake that time forgot." The virgin California wilderness and the High Sierras—the "Range of Light"—were first explored in 1845 by Captain John C. Fremont, followed by the fur trader and explorer Jedediah Smith and the Walker Expedition.

To the east of the Sierra Nevada lies the state of Nevada, with 110,540 square miles in the Great Basin, a rugged arid plateau broken by north-south mountain chains enclosed on the north by Oregon and Idaho and on the east by Utah and Arizona. The Sagebrush State, first explored by Spaniards and the fur traders Peter Skeene Ogden and Jedediah Smith, and the site of the famous Comstock Lode rush in 1859, contains several renowned outdoor recreation areas, including Lake Tahoe, Pyramid Lake, the Jarbidge Wilderness, Lake Mohave, and the Lake Mead National Recreation Area.

Weather, Bugs, Beasts & the "Circle of Fire"

Pacific Northwest summers are usually cool and the winters mild, because of the warming effect of the Japan Current and the protection afforded by the Cascade Range. The southwestern Olympic Mountains receive the heaviest rainfall in the country, approaching 150 inches a year, while the northeastern Olympics, only 75 miles away, receive a scant 16 inches. The western slopes of the Cascades generally receive about 100 inches of rainfall a year in contrast to the considerably drier climate of the eastern slopes. Winters along the coastal areas are generally cloudy and damp, but are protected from the cold continental winds by the double barrier of mountains to the east. Coastal summers are mild, with light winds, mist, and coastal fogs. The western slopes of the Sierra Nevada receive heavy rainfall, while the eastern slopes are rather dry. Night fogs and mists are frequent along the western slopes. The Death Valley and Mojave Desert areas often record the hottest temperatures in the nation, as high as 129° F. Soggy trails of snow melt are often found in the high country as late as August. Violent electrical storms, snow flurries, and brisk evening temperatures may occur above timberline throughout the summer.

The ancient volcanoes of the Pacific Northwest are part of the "Circle of Fire" that rims the Pacific from Mount Lassen to Alaska's Mount Katmai with its eerie "ghost forests" and Valley of Ten Thousand Smokes. Seventy million years ago the Northwest was covered by a vast sea, which gradually receded. The continent emerged as awesome volcanic eruptions spread great flows of molten lava. The eruptions of the Cascade Range—less than 10 million years old—have continued almost to modern times. Emissions of hydrogen sulfide gas and steaming fumaroles are common near the summits of several of the great peaks. If you are planning a trip through one of the high Cascade wilderness areas, be sure to wear sturdy hiking boots as protection against the sharp, unstable cutting edges of the hardened lava flows.

Potential wildlife hazards include the occasional camp-invading black bear and western rattlesnakes at the lower elevations. Be sure to take along a good supply of insect repellent, preferably *Muskol, Mosquitone, Off!* or *Cutters*—all of which contain 50%-plus concentrations of DEET—a wide-brimmed hat, light-colored cotton shirts and a sweater, raingear, and sunglasses. A useful source of wilderness travel info is Colin Fletcher's classic 512-page book *The New Complete Walker*, on the joys and techniques of hiking and backpacking, available for $10 from Alfred A. Knopf, Mail Order Dept., 400 Hahn Rd., Westminster, MD 21157 (include 50¢ postage).

Pacific Crest Maps & Charts—How to Order

The topographic maps listed throughout the Pacific Crest States sections will make it possible for you to plan your trip easily and productively (as well as increasing your safety and knowledge) by providing you with a complete picture of the area where you plan to fish, hunt, camp, hike, or canoe. By traveling cross-country off the beaten path with a map and compass, you will be able to enjoy the experience of fishing unspoiled "lost" lakes and exploring seldom-traveled wild coun-

try. All maps listed (unless otherwise noted) are full-color U.S. Geological Survey overview maps with a scale of 1:250,000 ($2 each) or large-scale 7½-minute maps and 15-minute maps ($1.25 each). These useful maps show all man-made and natural features of the land, such as forests, mountain ranges, lakes and streams, roads and trails, glaciers, falls and rapids, dams, old logging roads, wilderness cabins, campgrounds, and contour lines. The maps and free *Topographic Map Indexes* of Washington, Oregon, California, and Nevada may be ordered (along with the free *Map Symbol Chart* and the booklet *Topographic Maps*) from: Distribution Branch, U.S. Geological Survey, Federal Center, Denver, CO 80225. Be sure to order the maps by their individual name (and scale, when ordering 1:250,000-type maps); to expedite delivery, include extra money for first-class delivery. A free *Pacific Coast Nautical Chart Catalog* may be obtained by writing: Distribution Division, National Ocean Survey, Riverdale, MD 20840.

The large, handsome U.S. Geological Survey *State Topographic Maps* and *State Shaded-Relief Maps* for Washington, Oregon, California, and Nevada are published with a scale of 1:500,000, or about 8 miles to 1 inch, and may be ordered for $2 each (the California map has 2 sheets and sells for $4 a set). The stunningly beautiful shaded-relief maps show all physical features with colored shadings which give the maps a 3-dimensional appearance of sunlight striking the surface from the northwest.

A useful 214-page handbook for wilderness travel, *Be Expert with Map & Compass,* by Bjorn Kjellstrom, the president and founder of Silva Compasses, may be obtained for $6.95 from Charles Scribner's Sons, Bookstore Dept., 597 Fifth Ave., New York, NY 10017. Full-color *Plastic Raised-Relief Maps* of all 1:250,000-scale overview maps listed in the Pacific Crest States may be ordered for $11.95 each from Hubbard Scientific Company, 1946 Raymond Dr., Northbrook, IL 60062 (a free catalog is available upon request). These useful maps provide a 3-dimensional model of the earth's surface and show all trails, falls, rapids, national forest and wilderness area boundaries, and so forth.

WASHINGTON ENCYCLOPEDIA

Accommodations— Vacation Lodges & Resorts

Washington's renowned wilderness fishing, hunting, and camping areas and family vacation areas in the North Cascades, Puget Sound, High Cascades, Mount Rainier National Park, Olympic Peninsula, and seven national forests are served by literally thousands of hunting and fishing camp, resort, and lodge operators. The Travel Development Division of Washington's Dept. of Commerce & Economic Development, General Administration Bldg., Olympia 98504, publishes a *Chamber of Commerce Directory*, available free upon request. The local chamber of commerce in the area you plan to visit will provide you with a listing of local resort, lodge, and camp operators. The useful publication *Resorts & Packers on the National Forests* contains a complete listing and description of lodges and facilities in the Gifford Pinchot, Mount Baker, Snoqualmie, Okanogan and Wenatchee national forests. This guide is available free by writing to: U.S. Forest Service, P.O. Box 3623, Portland, OR 97208. Washington's *Olympic Peninsula Directory*, available free from Olympic Peninsula Travel Association, P.O. Box 625, Port Angeles 98362, contains a useful listing and descriptions of fishing, hunting, and vacation resorts, lodges and camps, marinas, commercial campgrounds, and steelhead float trip operators. A complete listing of lodges and licensed outfitters in the North Cascade, Olympic, and Mount Rainier national parks and the national forest recreation areas is contained in the "Washington Travel & Recreation Guide."

Bald Eagle Natural Wildlife Area

The Skagit River Bald Eagle Natural Wildlife Area comprises more than 1,000 acres along a scenic stretch of the middle Skagit River between Rockport and the old logging town of Marblemount in northwestern Washington. This particular segment of key wooded bottomland and gravel bars is the winter gathering grounds for the largest known concentration of northern bald eagles anywhere on the West Coast of the continental United States. Each winter 100 to 300 eagles come to the Skagit to feed on spawned-out salmon, which line the river banks from December to March. While the eagles depend upon spent salmon for their staple winter diet, the primary purpose of the natural area is to provide a wilderness buffer strip or river corridor for feeding bars, perch trees, and roost trees. The huge raptors, with wingspreads up to 7½ feet, require tall trees for perching sites and gravel bars free from disturbance. Future plans of the State Game Department include camouflaged trails, a viewing tower, and blinds to allow public observance of the majestic birds.

Camping & Wilderness Trails

With a land area of 66,786 square miles, the Evergreen State is larger than all New England, and its seven natural physiographic regions— the Olympic Mountains, Willapa Hills, Puget Sound Basin, Cascade Mountains, Okanogan Highlands, Columbia Basin, and Blue Mountains—form many of the most famous camping and wilderness hiking areas in North America: the Lake Chelan country, Pasayten and Mount Baker wilderness areas, Goat Rocks wilderness area, Lake Crescent country in the Olympic Peninsula, Alpine Lakes and Enchantment wilderness areas. The rugged Pacific Crest National Scenic Trail winds north and south along the backbone of Washington's Cascade Mountains from Manning Park at the British Columbia border south to Oregon. The *Oregon, Washington National Forest Campground Directory* contains a comprehensive listing and description of services and facilities of all U.S. Forest Service Campgrounds in the Gifford

Pinchot, Mount Baker, Snoqualmie, Olympic, Okanogan, and Wenatchee national forests. This eminently useful 96-page camper's bible contains a full-color *National Forests Map of the Pacific Northwest Region* as well as individual national forest maps showing highways, forest roads, forest headquarters and district ranger stations, campgrounds, and winter sports areas. It may be obtained free along with wilderness travel and camping permits from: U.S. Forest Service, Pacific Northwest Region, P.O. Box 3623, Portland, OR 97208. A comprehensive listing and description of campgrounds in North Cascades National Park, Ross Lake and Lake Chelan national recreation areas, and in the Olympic and Mount Rainier national parks is contained in the free booklet *Camping in the National Park System,* available upon request by writing to: National Park System, Pacific Northwest Regional Office, 931 Fourth & Pike Bldg., Seattle 98101. A listing of *Primitive Camping Areas* in the state may be obtained by writing: Dept. of Natural Resources, Public Lands Bldg., Olympia 98504. A useful 18-page *Washington State Parks Outdoor Recreation Guide,* which describes all state park and recreation area facilities and activities, is available free from: State Parks & Recreation Commission, P.O. Box 1128, Olympia 98504.

Canoeing & Wilderness Waters

The Evergreen State's world-famous salmon and trout streams and the scenic wilderness waters of the North Cascades provide first-class canoe-camping opportunities surrounded by majestic alpine scenery. Two useful booklets of Signpost Publications, 16812 W. 36th Ave., W., Lynnwood 98036 will provide the Washington-bound wilderness paddler with an introduction to a few of the state's canoe and kayak routes. The 31-page *Water Trails of Washington* ($2.50) describes canoe routes along the Hoh, Humptulips, Satsop, Pilchuck, Upper Skagit, Sauk, Skykomish, Tolt, Nisqually, and Columbia rivers and the Grand Coulee Chain of Lakes, Deep Lake, the Deception Pass Area, and Banks Lake. *Kayak & Canoe Trips in Washington* ($2) describes water routes along the Quinault River, Sucia Island, Cedar River, Wenatchee and Cle Elum rivers, Crab Creek, and the Yakima River. *Northwest Alpine Guide Service,* 1628 Ninth at Olive, Seattle 98101, provides guided canoe trips in the Ross Lake and Lake Chelan national recreation areas in the North Cascades and on the Columbia River. *Rivers & Trails,* Box 86, Ashford 98304, provides guided canoe trips on Washington's Yakima, Skagit, and Cowlitz rivers, and on Montana's Missouri River and Idaho's wild St. Joe and Priest rivers. A unique canoe trip may be taken down the beautiful Quinault River, in the Olympic Peninsula, through the lush coastal rain forests and scenic interior wildlands of the Quinault Indian Reservation—the forest home of the Quinault Indians, a branch of the Salishan, as are all coastal tribes except the Makah. Indian guides are required for canoe travel through the reservation. Their service includes use of the traditional Quinault canoes—hand-carved, hollowed-out cedar logs about 30 feet long with a 30–36-inch beam. These beautiful canoes and the masterful boatsmanship of the Indian guides provide a rare, memorable wilderness experience. (See "Outfitters, Packers & Wilderness Guide Service.")

Fishing & Hunting in the Evergreen State

Washington's lofty mountains, wild rivers, scenic coastal rain forests, and sweeping high-country forests dotted by thousands of blue lakes, alpine meadows, and sagebrush flats have lured woodsmen and hunters since the golden era of the fur trade, when the territory was ruled by the Hudson's Bay Company.

The Evergreen State is the extreme northwesterly state of the contiguous United States, with a total land area of 66,786 square miles. The state is divided into eastern and western sections by the high, snow-capped peaks of the Cascade Range, which runs south from British Columbia to the Columbia River and Oregon. The turbulent, cascading streams that have carved deep forest valleys between the high summits give the range its name. The Cascades average about 8,000

feet in altitude, reaching their greatest height at the volcanic glacier-covered summits of Mount Rainier (14,410 ft.), Mount Adams (12,307 ft.), Mount Baker (10,750 ft.), Glacier Peak (10,436 ft.), Mount St. Helens (9,671 ft.), and Mount Stuart (9,470 ft.). These great peaks tower above scenic wilderness recreation areas and sprawling forests of cedar, fir, and spruce, which often reach 200 feet in height.

The Columbia River plains lie to the east of the Cascades, bounded on the north by the Okanogan Highlands. The Columbia plains, or basin, known as the Inland Empire, with Spokane as its capital, ranges in altitude from 500 to slightly over 2,000 feet, broken by depressions known as coulees and a few low hills alternating with vast level stretches. The center of the Columbia basin, known as the Great Bend Region, is the driest part of the state and contains a number of lost rivers and alkaline lakes. A number of these lakes occupy the ancient bed of the Columbia, known as the Grand Coulee, a major portion of which is dammed to form Roosevelt Lake. In the southeast the plains are broken by the rugged 7,000-foot summits of the Blue Mountains and the Umatilla National Forest lands, extending northward from Oregon.

West of the great mountain wall formed by the Cascades lie the scenic salmon waters of the Puget Sound basin. The Coast Range chain of mountains rises between the basin and the Pacific Ocean, increasing in height and ruggedness toward the northwest, where it forms the Olympic Mountains, which rise almost immediately from the sea, towering above lush rain forests and dominating the wildlands of the Olympic Peninsula. The snowcapped peaks of the range culminate in 7,954-foot Mount Olympus. The glaciers and snowfields of the range give birth to a number of the world's great salmon and steelhead fishing streams, which flow hell-bent through the wildlands of Olympic National Park and the national forest lands into the Pacific. These include the Queets, Quinault, Elwha, Soleduck, Hoh, Big, Humptulips, Hamma Hamma, Dosewallips, Clearwater, Duckabush, Big Quilcene, and Dungeness rivers.

Puget Sound lies at the north end of the basin—which slopes northward from the height-of-land at the Cowlitz River, a tributary of the Columbia—and is connected with the Pacific by the Strait of Juan de Fuca. The Hood Canal branches off Puget Sound and forms a narrow fjord thrusting inland for 60 miles to the southwest, close to the slopes of the Olympics, and then bends back upon the Kitsap Peninsula. The shores of the sound are dotted with salmon-fishing and lumbering centers, and a beautiful archipelago of islands, known as the San Juan Isles, forms the southernmost extension of the Inside Passage, which winds through the vast labyrinth of islands that stretch from Seattle northward for 1,000 miles along the British Columbia coast to Alaska.

From the remote high mountain lakes of the Olympic Peninsula and Cascade Range to the mighty Columbia, Washington has an outstanding variety of fishing conditions and fish species. The state's record game fish, compiled by the Department of Game, are as follows:

WASHINGTON RECORD FISH

	Lb.–oz.	Place	Year
Cutthroat trout (sea-run)	6	Carr Inlet	1943
Resident cutthroat (Crescenti)	12	Lake Crescent	1961
Eastern brook	6–1	Lake Cavanaugh	1969
Brown	22	Sullivan Lake	1965
Dolly Varden	22–8	Tieton River	
Mackinaw	30–4	Loon Lake	1966
Rainbow	22–8	Waitts Lake	1957
Rainbow (Beardslie)	15–4	Lake Crescent	
Steelhead*	32–10	Cowlitz River	1973
Blue catfish	17–12	Columbia River	1975
Channel catfish	25–8	Columbia River	1975
Bass, largemouth	11–8	Newman Lake	1966
Bass, smallmouth	8–12	Columbia River	1967
Bluegill sunfish	1–6	Potholes Reservoir	1973
Crappie	4–8	Lake Washington	1956
Yellow perch	2–4	Steilacoom Lake	1974
Walleye	12–9	Billy Clapp Lake	1973
Lake whitefish	3–5	Potholes Canal	1975
Mountain whitefish	3–13	North Fork Stillaguamish River	1975

*Washington-bound anglers should note that about 45 of the state's potential record-bearing steelhead streams, such as the wild Skagit, have restricted winter access due to Indian tribal fishing rights. Be sure to check with the Dept. of Game Information Office (phone: 206-753-5700) on the current status of the stream you plan to fish.

Steelhead, Trout, & Salmon

The state's major freshwater game fish is the rainbow trout, both in its nonmigratory status as a rainbow and as the larger steelhead in the sea-run variety. Rainbow are widely stocked; some 17 million are annually reared and released from Washington Game Department hatcheries. Although they thrive in a wide variety of habitats, large rainbow occur in greatest numbers in the insect-rich lakes of eastern Washington, where season-long hatches of chironomids, plus heavy damselfly and mayfly hatches in the spring and an abundant snail population help the trout grow to trophy weights.

The prized trophy fish of Washington is the steelhead, first described by Sir John Richardson from specimens caught near the mouth of the Columbia River in 1836 and named *Salmo gairdneri gairdneri* in honor of Dr. Meredith Gardner, a naturalist employed by the Hudson's Bay Company. The state has well over 100 major rivers that contain runs of steelhead at one time or another during the year. *Steelhead Fishing Maps* of the major rivers may be obtained by writing to the State Dept. of Game. Steelhead runs in the winter occur in most Washington streams and rivers west of the Cascades, which empty directly into either Puget Sound or the Pacific Ocean. The Columbia, Grande Ronde, and Snake rivers and their tributaries provide outstanding fishing for summer-run steelhead. Winter-run fish

move upstream from November to June and spawn in early spring. Summer-run fish generally travel upstream from June through September, but may be found as early as February in some streams. Summer-run fish lay over in deep pools until the following spring to spawn. Seaward migrants of both varieties move downstream with the spring runoff, peaking about the first of May in western Washington and about a month later in the Cascades.

The most productive of the state's more than 160 winter steelhead streams include the Skagit River, the state's top producer of trophy steelhead in the 20-pound-and-over class, and the Cowlitz, Humptulips, Snohomish, East Fork Lewis, Bogachiel, Chehalis, Elochoman, Naselle, Willapa, Lyre, Nooksack, North Fork Stillaguamish, Kolama, Snoqualmie, Washougal, Satsop, Main Stillaguamish, Dungeness, Whynoochee, Skykomish, Elwha, Grays, Queets, and the incredibly scenic and productive Quinault. The Snake and Columbia, above Bonneville Dam, are the largest producers of summer-run steelhead. The Snake usually supplies anglers with around 15,000 fish annually. Other famous summer-run rivers include the Grande Ronde, Kalama, Klickitat, Yakima, Big White, Salmon, Cowlitz, and Wind. The North Fork of the Stillaguamish is the state's most famous fly-fishing-only summer steelhead river.

Wild-reared steelhead spend two years in the stream after hatching, migrate to sea, and then return weighing around seven pounds. Steelhead of hatchery origin (the State Game Dept. annually plants over 3,000,000 winter-run and 2,000,000 summer-run steelhead) are now grown to migrant size one year after hatching and spend two years at sea prior to returning to spawn. A few steelhead stay in the Pacific 3–7 years, reaching weights up to 35 pounds. They achieve this tremendous growth feeding on greenling, squid, and amphipods. Steelhead tagged in Alaska have traveled over 2,500 miles to spawn in Washington streams.

Most Washington anglers use either stout fly rods with shooting-head lines or spinning gear. All anglers are required to have a steelhead permit card in their possession when steelhead fishing. The place and date of catch must be entered immediately upon landing a fish. Licenses and cards may be obtained at any of the 1,000 license dealers scattered throughout the state. Most steelhead fishing is done by wading from the bank. However, drifting in Rogue and McKenzie River-type guide boats is becoming increasingly popular.

Several other wild trout species are caught in Washington's lakes and streams. The cutthroat, *Salmo clarki clarki*, which was first described in 1836 by Sir John Richardson from fish caught in Oregon's Cathlapooth River and named for Capt. Clark of the Lewis and Clark expedition, occurs in the widest assortment of color patterns of any trout species. Washington varieties include the coastal cutthroat of western counties, found in streams as both resident and sea-run. The cutthroat of eastern Washington is often called the "native" and is similar to the Montana black-spotted cutthroat. Resident cutthroat prefer the colder sections of streams and thrive best in cold high-country lakes, up to 10,000 feet elevation. The Puget Sound region is centered within the sea-run's native range from northern California to southeastern Alaska. Sea-runs to 4 pounds are caught, although the average weight is 1–2 pounds. Cutthroat seem to favor lures with touches of yellow and red and nymphs, wet flies, bucktails, and live bait. Brown trout are found in a few scattered eastern Washington lakes and streams. Although trophy fish over 20 pounds have been taken from a few lakes, any brown exceeding 5 pounds is considered quite a trophy in Washington. The beautiful golden trout is found in a few remote High Cascade mountain lakes. The golden, originally introduced from wild stock of the northern California high country, is best adapted to high, rock-bound lakes of the Cascade wilderness

areas, where it thrives on a microcrustacea diet of straight plankton as well as caddis fly larvae and midges. The golden trout differs from the rainbow chiefly in its brilliant, distinctive coloration, which occurs during the spawning season, anytime from June to late August, depending upon time of ice-out on the lakes.

The brook trout, one of Washington's introduced species, is common in cool, clear headwater lakes, in spring-fed streams, and in large lakes with cool, well-oxygenated lower layers of water. Their dominant diet consists of caddis flies, insect larvae, and stone-fly nymphs. The brook trout was first described in 1815 by Samuel Mitchill from fish caught in New York State and was aptly named *fontinalis*, meaning "living in springs." The lake trout, also known as mackinaw, a member of the char family like the Dolly Varden and eastern brook trout, reaches weights of 30 pounds in Washington waters and has been successfully established in Cle Elum, Bonaparte, Deer, Eight-Mile, and Loon lakes. The lake trout was originally described in 1792 from fish taken in Hudson Bay and called *namaycush*, an Indian name. Lakers are usually found in cold, deep-water parts of the lake, but will move inshore to feed during the spring, before temperatures rise above 60° F. The Dolly Varden trout, a native Washington game fish, occurs most often in fast water at the headwaters or outlets of lakes on both sides of the Cascades. Many Dollys are taken as an incidental catch by anglers fishing for sea-run cutthroat and steelhead in downstream areas. In waters where saltwater migration is possible, Dollys take to the ocean and brackish areas for short feeding forays, migrating back to fresh water for parts of their life cycle. Dolly Varden have a preference for silver spoons. They average 1–3 pounds, but occasionally reach weights in excess of 20 pounds.

The Arctic grayling, renowned for its long, high, brilliantly colored dorsal fin, occurs in only a limited number of clear, cold High Cascade lakes. The "silver," a landlocked, freshwater silver salmon, is found in large, deep, cold lakes such as Goodwin, Blue, Park, and Washington. The silver is easily identified by its sweeping, sickle-shaped anal fin. It averages 7–14 inches by maturity. Silvers resemble the landlocked kokanee salmon; but, unlike the kokanee, silvers do not spawn naturally when landlocked and have been stocked in Washington lakes as fingerlings. The kokanee, a landlocked sockeye salmon, is found in large lakes with clearly defined thermoclines, such as Rimrock, American, Whatcom, and Chelan. It prefers temperatures close to 50° F. Large kokanee, also known as redfish, occasionally weighing up to 5 pounds, come from large lakes with a low relative density of population, where they feed on minute plankton. During spawning the kokanee turns a deep red, and the lower jaw of the male develops the characteristic hook common to most species of salmon. Kokanee are most often caught on flies, spoons, and salmon eggs. This soft-mouthed fish should be played carefully. Mountain whitefish, also known as mountain herring, are found in most of the major river systems on both sides of the Cascades. The lake whitefish, originally discovered in Roosevelt Lake, was introduced into Banks Lake and has since become distributed throughout the Columbia Basin irrigation system.

Back in the 1940s, the Washington Fly-Fishing Club initiated the state's fly-fishing-only waters program, which led to the protection of Pass Lake and the North Fork of the Stillaguamish. Today, Washington's list of fly-fishing-only waters has expanded considerably, and includes a "quality-waters" program, where fishing is restricted to artificial lures and flies with single barbless hooks. The lakes and streams protected under the fly-fishing-only and quality-waters programs provide some of the state's finest trophy fishing for cutthroat, rainbow, brown, and brook trout, steelhead, and transplanted Atlantic salmon (introduced from Quebec via Oregon's Wizard Falls hatchery

on the Metolius River). The state's quality fishing waters include Ell Lake in Okanogan County, Texas Ponds in Skagit County, and Dry Falls, Lenice, Merry, and Nunnally lakes in Grant County. Fly-fishing-only waters limited to dry flies, wet flies, bucktails, and nymphs include designated sections of the Green, Kalama, North Fork Stillaguamish, and Wind Rivers and Merrill, Long, Cady, Aeneas, Chopaka, Moccasin, Brown's Pass, Ebey, Squalicum, Granite, Leech, Bayley, and McDowell lakes. Fly-fishing with barbless hooks only is limited to the renowned Atlantic salmon waters of Quail Lake in Adams County, Rocky Ford Creek in Grant County, and Chopaka Lake in Okanogan County. Transplanted Atlantic salmon running up to 13 pounds have been successfully introduced to spectacular Dry Falls Lake, located in the catch basin of the ancient falls of the Columbia River—these great, towering coulees are several times higher than Niagara Falls—and Quail Lake, located in Adams County. The Washington Department of Game plans include stocking Atlantic salmon in larger Columbia Basin lakes and in the alpine lakes of the Olympic Peninsula.

Additional information on the steelhead, trout, and warm-water fisheries in the Evergreen State is contained in the following informative, illustrated guides, available free upon request from: Department of Game, 600 N. Capitol Way, Olympia 98504: *Trout of Washington,*

Fishing & Hunting in Washington, Washington Steelheading, and *Spiny-Rayed Fish of Washington.* The Department of Game also publishes a free *State Fishing Guide List* and fishing regulations booklets and information about public access, boat-launching sites, fly-fishing-only waters, and seasons. The color-coded *Columbia Basin Recreation Areas map,* available free from the Department of Game, shows the famous big-game and waterfowl hunting areas, fishing waters, and camping areas of the Columbia Basin.

The Evergreen State's incredibly scenic coastal waters provide top-ranked fishing for spring and fall chinook in the 20–65 pound range (the largest recorded chinook weighed 120 pounds, caught in a southeastern Alaska commercial net), coho, sockeye, and pink salmon—which appear only in odd-numbered years, when up to 9 million have been caught commercially during a single year in Puget Sound. Pacific salmon have many local names. Chinooks are known as tules and springs on the Columbia River, as king salmon on Puget Sound and in Alaska, and as tyees in British Columbia. Young, immature chinook are known as blackmouths. Coho are known as silver salmon, silversides, and hooknose; pinks as humpbacks; chum as dog or keta salmon. Male chinook, coho, and sockeye that return to spawn in their birth-streams at the age of 2 years instead of 3 are known as jack salmon. When a female coho matures ahead of schedule, it is known as a jell.

The state's major salmon charter fleets are located at Seattle serving Puget Sound; at Everett and Whidbey Island; at Bellingham and the San Juan Islands; at Port Angeles, Sekiu, and Neah Bay in the Juan de Fuca Strait; and at La Push, Ocean Shores, Aberdeen, Westport and Ilwaco along the Pacific Coast. With the increased development of dams and logging operations since the early 1900s, Washington's salmon populations have been increasingly augmented by hatchery-reared fish. Today, the progressive Department of Fisheries operates 26 salmon hatcheries, including the world's largest rearing station, located on the Cowlitz River, which annually rears and releases 100 million young salmon of migratory size. The *Washington Salmon Hatcheries Guide* contains a complete history of the state's salmon hatchery operations, including a description of natural and artificial salmon life cycles, distribution maps, and a listing and locations of state salmon hatcheries. The hatcheries guide and the useful publication *Tips for the Salmon Salt Water Angler,* which contains detailed descriptions of "mooching" methods and equipment and of types of herring bait used in Puget Sound, as well as a map of major salmon-fishing areas, may be obtained free from: Washington Dept. of Fisheries, Olympia 98504. The Dept. of Fisheries also publishes a free sportfishing regulation pamphlet giving fishing areas, an area map, the best fishing periods, tideland recreational areas for taking of shellfish, and freshwater areas for salmon, including the seasons. The department also publishes several books and guides that detail the methods of preparing and cooking Pacific salmon and the wide variety of marine life found in the coastal waters of the Pacific Northwest, including: *The Salmon Cookbook* (50¢), *Smokehouses & the Smoke Curing of Fish* (50¢), *The Marine Fish Cookbook* (50¢), *Shellfish Cookbook* (50¢), and the free publications *Washington State Shellfish Guide, Basic Marine Fish Recipes, Basic Shad Recipes, Basic Halibut Recipes,* and *Basic Salmon Recipes.*

Hunting

Washington's sweeping national forests, mountain wilderness areas, scenic coastal rain forests, logged-off areas, and sagebrush flats provide some of the nation's top-ranked big-game and upland game-bird hunting. Roosevelt elk, named in honor of Theodore Roosevelt, is found primarily in the Olympic Mountains and Tatoosh Range. Roosevelt elk *(Cervus canadensis roosevelti),* also called Olympic elk, are the largest of the elk species, noted for their massive antlers. Rocky Moun-

tain elk are found in greatest concentrations in the vast national forest and commercial forest lands and the high-country wilderness areas along the east slope of the Cascades in Yakima and Kittitas counties and in the rugged Wenaha backcountry area and Blue Mountains in the Umatilla National Forest in the southeast corner of Washington. Rocky Mountain elk neared extinction during the mining and logging boom days of the late 1800s and were reintroduced in 1912. Other big-game species include Rocky Mountain mule deer, whitetail deer in some eastern regions, blacktail deer in the western coastal mountains and Cascade Mountains, black bear, mountain goat, mountain lion, and a few bighorn sheep. An early September buck deer season is held in the Pasayten, Glacier Peak, and Daniel game management units. Several areas within the State Game Management units have been set aside for bow and arrow hunting only. Grizzly, moose, woodland caribou, timber wolf, and antelope are present, but are extremely rare. Upland game birds include pheasant (the most popular game bird in the state), quail, blue grouse, ruffed grouse, and Franklin grouse, as well as limited populations of sharptails and sage hens. Chukar partridge, introduced in 1938, provide excellent hunting in the steep, rocky slopes in the Columbia Basin. Puget Sound and the marshes, sloughs, and tidal flats of the western coastal regions and the grainfields of the Columbia Basin provide some of the finest waterfowl hunting in the Pacific Northwest. For detailed information on licenses, permits, and season limits, and for the free *Washington Deer Hunting Areas Map*, color-coded *Wildlife Recreation Areas Map*, and *Game Management Unit Map*, write: State Game Dept. 600 N. Capitol Way, Olympia 98504. (See "Outfitters, Packers & Wilderness Guide Service" in this section and the "Washington Travel & Recreation Guide.")

High Cascade Alpine Lakes & Wilderness Areas

Washington's majestic High Cascade lakes country offers some of the finest wilderness trout fishing and high-country hunting in the Pacific Northwest. The early High Cascade hunting season provides the alpine hunting enthusiast with an opportunity for deer, grouse, and black bear. He can hunt buck deer during the regular October season and elk during the November season. The heart of remote High Cascade wilderness lake country is embraced by the proposed Alpine Lakes Wilderness Area and the Cougar Lakes and Enchantment wilderness study areas. A *Wilderness Study Areas Map* may be obtained free from: Pacific Northwest Region, U.S. Forest Service, P.O. Box 3628, Portland, OR 97208. Access to the cutthroat, rainbow, Dolly Varden, and brook trout lakes of these remote areas is by hiking trails, packhorse safari, and forest road. The *Alpine Lakes Wilderness* straddles the crest of the Cascade Mountains in the Snoqualmie and Wenatchee national forests about 50 miles east of Seattle. The wilderness encompasses magnificent valleys, forests of Douglas fir and hemlock on the west slope and ponderosa pine on the east. Hundreds of remote blue lakes and tarns lie in basins gouged by Ice Age glaciers at elevations ranging from 2,500 feet in the heavily timbered Foss River Valley to over 8,000 feet in the barren Chiwaukum Range. The major features within this 162,400-acre wildland include the Snoqualmie River headwaters; Big Snow and Summit Chief mountains; Lake Dorothy; Waptus, Deep, and Marmot lakes; Cathederal Peaks; and the Cle Elum River. Hundreds of miles of wilderness trails provide access to the remote interior areas. The remote *Enchantment Wilderness* lies adjacent to the Alpine Lakes Area on the east. Known as the "Lost World Plateau," the Enchantment Wilderness encompasses some 30,700 acres of jagged granite spires, glacially carved slopes, and scenic lake basins interspersed with lush green mountain meadows at

elevations ranging from 3,000 feet to 9,470 feet at Mount Stuart. The area is reached by an extremely steep and rugged trail from the Icicle River. *Cougar Lakes Wilderness* encompasses 127,000 acres adjacent to the eastern boundary of Mount Rainier National Park in the Snoqualmie and Gifford Pinchot national forests. The wilderness is a summer range for elk and provides good rainbow and brook trout fishing in the American and Bumping rivers and Cougar and Bumping lakes. Access to the remote interior lakes and alpine meadow is by the Cascade Crest Trail over towering Chinook Pass and spur trails. One of the joys of high-country fishing in Washington and the Northwest lies in the fact that with a topographic map the angler can be his own explorer. He can discover lakes stocked years back by the Department of Game and the original trail blazers with native and black-spotted Montana cutthroat trout, golden trout, Montana grayling, and rainbow and eastern brook trout. Keep in mind, though, that it takes a bit of study to find these seldom-visited "lost" lakes. (For information on packhorses and guide service, see the "Washington Travel & Recreation Guide.")

The High Cascade lakes country is shown on the following large-scale U.S. Geological Survey maps. *Alpine Lakes:* Bandera, Baring, Benchmark Mountain, Big Snow Mountain, Labryinth Mountain, Monte

Crisco, Snoqualmie Pass, Kachess Lake, Mount Daniel, Poe Mountain, Snoqualmie Lake, Stevens Pass, the Cradle, Chiwaukum Mountain, Mount Stuart; *Enchantment Wilderness:* Mount Stuart, Liberty, Chiwaukum Mountains, Leavenworth; *Cougar Lakes Wilderness:* Bumping Lake, White Pass, Old Scab Mountain, Timberwolf Mountain, Rimrock Lake, Darland Mountain. Questions on fish and game in Washington's high-country wilderness should be directed to: State Game Dept., 600 N. Capitol Way, Olympia 98504. Travel restrictions and trail and campground information may be secured from: U.S. Forest Service, P.O. Box 3623, Portland, OR 97208.

Highways–Recreation & Scenic Routes

The Evergreen State's scenic and recreation routes, including Highways 123 and 410, which wind through Mount Rainier National Park and the Gifford Pinchot National Forest; Highway 2, which winds through Stevens Pass at 4,061 feet in the High Cascades region of Snoqualmie National Forest; Highway 542, which runs through Mount Baker National Forest to the Mount Baker Wilderness; Highway 20 in the North Cascades and Okanogan and Colville national forests; and Highway 101 through the scenic coastal rain forests and mountains of Olympic National Forest and Park, are shown on the

pounds and serves as a fall salmon migration route, lies in a primitive region of mountains and small alpine lakes, nearly 30 of which may be reached by trails that radiate from the Forest Service campgrounds. Spirit Lake's clear, cold waters reach depths of 1,300 feet, the bottom of which is white pumice. In some places the bottom has yet to be found! Spirit Lake was named by the Indians of the region, who interpreted many sounds of the lake and forest as the haunting voices of departed spirits. One legend tells of an Indian brave who, seeking food for his starving tribe, trailed a giant bull elk to the lake, only to be led by the phantom to his death in the water. The Indians were said to believe that each year both of them appeared over the lake on a certain night. Other legends attribute the name to the legendary *Siatcoes,* outcasts from other tribes, to whom were attributed supernatural powers. Mount St. Helens, one of the youngest volcanic peaks in the country, last erupted in 1842. To the Klickitat Indians, the mountain was known as *Tah-one-lat-clah,* meaning "Fire Mountain." Big game and wildlife that inhabit the high-country hunting areas include Roosevelt elk, black bear, deer, beaver, cougar, bobcat, eagle, and ruffed and blue grouse. The major features shown on the *Mount St. Helens–Spirit Lake map,* which comprises all 173,000 acres of the St. Helens Range District, include the Mount Margaret backcountry and Grizzly Lakes area, Goat Marsh Lake area, Cedar Flats natural

Washington State Highway Map, available free, from: Dept. of Commerce & Economic Development, Travel Development Div., General Administration Bldg., Olympia 98504. The map shows all major state and federal highways, roads, population centers, state parks and campsites, highway rest areas, points of interest, ski areas, trout and salmon hatcheries, toll ferries, airports, national parks, and forests. In addition, it shows the route of the historic Lewis and Clark Trail of 1805, Cariboo Trail of 1859–68 to the British Columbia gold fields, Old Stagecoach Road, Colville Road of 1826–81, and Mullan Road, and the sites of fur-trading forts and Indian rock paintings. (See "North Cascades Highway.")

Mount St. Helens & Spirit Lake High Country—Land of the "Fire Mountain"

This renowned fishing, hunting, and wilderness camping area is located on the St. Helens Ranger District in the Gifford Pinchot National Forest. Spirit Lake, which holds rainbow trout up to 7

area, and Elk, Tradedollar and Deadman lakes. This map, which is available for 50¢ from: District Ranger, St. Helens Ranger District, Cougar 98616, shows contours, primitive roads, campgrounds, wilderness campsites, and ranger stations. Spirit Lake Campground has 170 campsites, with facilities for auto and trailer camping. A public boat launching is located at Duck Bay. The Kalama Spring Campground provides camping facilities on Mount St. Helens south side. Mount St. Helens–Spirit Lake Area is shown on large-scale U.S. Geological Survey Topo maps Mount St. Helens and Spirit Lake. (See "Washington Travel & Recreation Guide" for Gifford Pinchot National Forest and Mount Margaret backcountry.)

North Cascades Highway

The North Cascades Highway (20), thought by many to be the most scenic wilderness recreation route in the United States, winds for 88 miles through the North Cascades high country from Marblemount, the oldest settlement in the Mount Baker region and once used as a supply base by prospectors; eastward through the foothills of the

Cascades through the Mount Baker National Forest and the North Cascades high country, paralleled on the north and south by the North Cascades National Park; past the town of Newhalem and the wild Skagit River, the town of Diablo and the beautiful blue-green waters of Diablo Lake (caused by the "rock flour," or fine sediment fed by glacial streams), Ross Lake National Recreation Area, which extends some 24 miles northward into Canada, the Pasayten Wilderness, and the incredibly scenic Washington Pass Overlook at 5,477 feet elevation; and again eastward through Okanogan National Forest, past the towns of Mazama, Winthrop, and Twisp to its junction with Highway 97 at Okanogan. Four miles east of Winthrop on Methow River Road is the North Cascades Smokejumper Base, home of the first airborne fire fighters in the Pacific Northwest. Harts Pass, the most northern access point to the Pacific Crest Trail in Washington, is reached via a 20-mile side trip from Mazama. The road, built during the 1890 gold rush, is very narrow; trailers are not allowed beyond the 10-mile point. A small campground can be used as a base for hikes to Slate Peak and old gold mines in the Harts Pass Area. Slate Peak provides a 360° panorama that encompasses several hundred square miles of wilderness mountain scenery, from Mount Baker on the west through the glaciated valleys and spruce and hemlock forests of the Pasayten Wilderness, to the sere eastern horizon, and south to the Glacier Peak Wilderness.

The *North Cascades Highway Map*, available free from: Mt. Baker National Forest, Bellingham 98225, shows the entire length of the highway, ranger stations, campgrounds, boating facilities, points of interest, mileage between points, wilderness areas, trails, national forests, parks, and recreation areas. In addition, the map provides a detailed history of the region and describes the climate, vegetation, geology, and glaciers of the North Cascades. The highway is served by the Marble Creek, Mineral Park, Early Winters, Klipchuck, and Lone Fir U.S. Forest Service campgrounds and by the Goodell Creek and Colonial Creek National Park Service campgrounds. The *North Cascades Highway Guide*, published by Fred T. Darvill, Jr., P.O. Box 636, Mt. Vernon 98273 ($1), is a handy companion to those interested in following this scenic drive (open mid-June to mid-November) or in exploring the numerous wilderness hiking trails leading from it. For additional info write or call: North Cascades National Park, Marblemount Ranger Station, Marblemount (206–873–4590); Mt. Baker National Forest, Baker River Ranger Station, Concrete (206–853–2851); or Okanogan National Forest, Winthrop Ranger Station, Winthrop (206–996–2266). (See "Highways—Recreation & Scenic Routes.")

Outfitters, Packers, & Wilderness Guide Service

The national forest wilderness and recreation areas of Washington are served by licensed outfitters and resorts that provide pack and saddle stock and guide service for the hunter, fisherman, or wilderness traveler. The free publication *Resorts & Packers on the National Forest,* available upon request from: Regional Forester, P. O. Box 3623, Portland, OR 97208, contains a complete listing of resorts and operators offering pack and saddle stock and guided camping, hunting, fishing, riding, and pack trips in the North Cascades, Glacier Peak Wilderness, Goat Rocks Wilderness, Umatilla, and Wenatachee, Mount Baker, and Okanogan national forests. A complete listing of *Big Game Hunting/Fishing Guides & Packers* may be obtained by writing to: Washington Dept. of Game, 600 N. Capitol Way, Olympia 98501. *Northwest Alpine Guide Service, Inc.,* 1628 Ninth at Olive, Seattle 98101, provides outfitting services, which include routing service, topo maps, stove, fuel, cooking utensils, and transportation to trailheads in

the Olympics and Cascades, as well as guided canoe trips on Ross Lake, Columbia River, and Lake Chelan; and guided ski touring, mountain climbing, and backpacking trips and wilderness Pacific hikes in the Olympic Peninsula and Cascade Mountains. Camps in the Olympic and Cascade mountains are situated to provide participants with maximum exposure to the greatest variety of flora and fauna, from the rain forests to the drier slopes of the eastern Cascades. In addition, Northwest Alpine Guide Service offers guided wilderness backpacking trips in northwest Vancouver Island, in Alaska's Brooks Range Mountains through the calving grounds of the porcupine caribou herd, along the Chilkoot Trail from Skagway to Bennett Lake, Queen Charlotte Islands, and the Carcajou Mountains in the Northwest Territories; and guided float trips along Alaska's Wild River, Alatna River, and North Fork Koyukuk River in the Gates of the Arctic Wilderness. (See "Washington Travel & Recreation Guide" for listings of regional outfitters and guide service.)

Pacific Crest National Scenic Trail

This famous trail, known in Washington as the Cascade Crest Trail, was designated in October 1968 as one of the two national scenic trails (the Appalachian Trail being the other). The trail follows the backbone of mountain ranges for 2,350 miles along ancient Indian footpaths from the Canadian border to the Mexican border. Clinton C. Clarke founded the trail when he organized the Pacific Crest Trail Conference, and today the Pacific Crest Club carries on his work and maintains the trail in much the same way as the Appalachian Trail Conference has been doing in the East. As in all designated wilderness and primitive areas, only horse and foot traffic are permitted on the route. Along the trail are numerous spur trails, diverging to areas of interest and beauty throughout the national parks and forests. Because of recent overuse, many campsites must be reserved through the local park rangers.

Supply points are infrequent, and the hiker can rely on several days' distance between most supply and communication points. The Washington Cascade Crest portion of the trail system follows the backbone of the Cascade Range, beginning at Monument 78 on the Canada-U.S. border; it winds for 457 miles through the Pasayten Wilderness, Okanogan National Forest, North Cascades National Park, Mount Baker Wilderness, Glacier Peak Wilderness, Wenatachee National Forest, Snoqualmie National Forest, Mount Rainier National Park, Goat Rocks Wilderness, Gifford Pinchot National Forest, and Mount Adams Wilderness.

The Cascade Crest Trail crosses historic routes traveled by trappers, miners, stockmen, and pioneers who blazed through the wilderness of the Cascades in the last century; at Harts Pass, where Colonel Hart built a narrow-gauge wagon road in the 1890s to reach the Slate Creek Mines, where the old town of Barron sprung up; at Stevens Pass,

selected by John F. Stevens, explorer for the Great Northern Railway, as a through-route for the railroad in 1890; at Naches Pass, site of the crossing of the Cascade Range by the Citizens Road into western Washington and Puget Sound; and, at Cispus Pass, where the old Klickitat Indian Trail is claimed to be the first trail between the east and west sides of the Cascades.

The *Pacific Crest National Scenic Trail Map & Trail Log,* available free from: Regional Forester, P. O. Box 3623, Portland, OR 97208, contains a detailed trail log and maps of the Cascade Crest Trail, showing primitive and dirt roads, spur trails, connecting trails, campsites, improved campgrounds, trail shelters, horse feed, district ranger and forest service stations, lookout towers, and airstrips. The forest supervisors in charge of the four national forests through which the trail passes will give travelers information regarding packers and outfitters, but arrangements should be made well in advance. Numerous spur trails along the route lead to hundreds of remote alpine lakes, many of which hold rainbow, brook, cutthroat, and Dolly Varden trout. A few elk and mountain goat may be seen in the rugged high country. Black-tailed deer are common along the ridges and creek bottoms of the western slope, and mule deer are found in the wild country of the east slope. Black bear are plentiful, particularly in the lush huckleberry patches during the late summer. Permits are required for entry into all wilderness and primitive areas, and may be obtained free on application from an area's headquarters or district ranger stations. If you plan to hike through several areas, you should request

a National Park Service–U.S. Forest Service Joint-Use Wilderness Permit. If you plan on hiking the entire Pacific Crest Trail, write to: Cleveland National Forest, 3211 5th Ave., San Diego, CA 92103. Self-addressed food and supply packages should be mailed to the following Cascade Crest Trail post offices: Stevenson 98648; Mount Rainier National Park 98397; Chelan 98816. For trail info in Manning Park, write to: Ranger, British Columbia Forest Service, Manning Park, B.C., Canada. For border-crossing info, write to: Canadian Government Office of Tourism, 150 Kent Street, Ottawa, Ontario, for the free booklet *Canada Border Crossing Information.* (See "Washington Travel & Recreation Guide" for outfitters, wilderness areas, specific trail descriptions, and U.S. Forest Service headquarters addresses).

REI Adventure Travel Service

The famous Recreational Equipment Inc. 700,000-member co-op op-

erates the REI Adventure Travel Service. This outstanding group of professionals runs guided backpacking and mountaineering trips in the North Cascades, Klondike, British Columbia, and Alaska, as well as foreign adventure trips to remote areas, including treks in the Himalayas to the Mount Everest Base Camp and cross-country skiing in Norway. For detailed information and rates, and a free *REI Adventure Travel* brochure and 83-page full-color *REI Catalog* of top-quality gear and accessories, write: REI, P.O. Box 22404, Seattle 98122 or phone (206) 323–8333.

San Juan Islands & the Inside Passage

The beautiful San Juan Archipelago includes some 172 islands and several hundred tide-washed rocks clustered in the northern waters of Puget Sound and the southernmost area of the Strait of Georgia. The archipelago is part of a submerged mountain chain that rises above sea level to a maximum of 2,454 feet at Mount Constitution and forms the southernmost extension of the famous Inside Passage, which winds through the scenic labyrinth of islands that stretches north from Seattle for 1,000 miles along the British Columbia coast to Alaska and Alexander Archipelago in the Tongass National Forest. The waters surrounding the maze formed by the San Juan Islands and Anacortes, Lummi, and Bellingham islands provide top-ranked fishing for coho, chinook, and humpback salmon. The rocky, jagged shores of the islands, many of which, such as Goose, Dot, Hat, Flattop, and Saddle Bag, are named for their unusual shapes, are covered by wind-stunted evergreens, with dense woodlands stretching inland. The picturesque isles are inhabited by eagles, deer, and wild goats. Deer are often seen swimming across the narrow channels between the islands in search of new browse. Several evergreen-fringed lakes nestled on the islands hold trophy trout and bass. Spring-fed Sportsman's Lake on San Juan Island offers top-ranked fishing for lunker smallmouth bass. Cascade Lake on Orcas Island holds big cutthroat, rainbow, and brook trout and kokanee salmon. Washington State Ferries provide access to the islands. Salmon-fishing camps and boat-rental docks are located on the major islands. For travel information write: San Juan Island Chamber of Commerce, P.O. Box 98, Friday Harbor 98250. For information concerning the proposed San Juan Wilderness, write: Manager, Willapa National Wildlife Refuge, Ilwaco 98624. The San Juan Islands are shown on U.S. Geological Survey map of Victoria, scale 1:250,000 ($2). (See "Washington State Ferries.")

Snake River Country

The middle, wild and free Snake River in southeast Washington flows through the beautiful, rugged country that was once the hunting grounds of the Nez Percé Indians, traveled by Lewis and Clark during their famous overland expedition of 1805. The last great chief of the Nez Percé, Hallshallakeen (Eagle Wing), or Chief Joseph as he was called by the white settlers, was born at the mouth of Joseph Creek, a tributary of the Grande Ronde, which flows into the Snake at Rogersburg near the Idaho boundary. The Middle Snake is a class-five white-water river, flowing through Hell's Canyon, the deepest natural gorge in North America. The canyon averages a mile deep, and the height from the river floor to the highest peak of the Seven Devils Mountains is nearly 8,000 feet. Hell's Canyon ends at Limekiln Rapids, a quarter mile upstream from the mouth of the Grande Ronde and the site of the largest natural deposit of lime in the Northwest. The Snake is known for its steelhead, salmon, native rainbow trout, trophy smallmouth bass, and channel catfish angling. Both the Idaho and Washington record steelhead were caught in the Middle Snake. Such famous rapids as Granite Creek, Wild Sheep, Bernard Creek, Rush Creek, Immaha, Wild Goose, and Dug Bar provide some of the most

exciting white water running in North America. The scenic, time-scarred peaks and richly colored yellow, brown, and vermilion canyon walls contain a number of ancient Indian pictographs. The surrounding wild country, with its rugged mountains and rocky draws, its broad, peaceful valleys and forests, provides top-ranked hunting for mule deer, Rocky Mountain elk, and the exotic chukar partridge. *Hell's Canyon Tours*, 118 Sycamore & 2nd, Clarkston 99403, provides charter jet boat trips up the Snake from April to October. Guided scenic float and fishing trips are provided by: *Snake River Packers*, Enterprise, OR 97828. Float trips on the Grande Ronde are provided by: *Blue Mountain Packers*, Troy Route, Wallowa, OR 97885. The Middle Snake River is shown on U.S. Geological Survey Topo Maps: Jim Creek Butte, Capt. John Rapids, Limekiln Rapids, Lewiston Orchards, South, Asotin, Clarkston, Silcott.

Ski Touring Outfitters for the High Cascades

Washington's national forests, wilderness areas, and parks have hundreds upon hundreds of miles of developed ski-touring trails and remote logging roads ideally suited to the cross-country skier and snowshoer. *The Cascades Corrals*, Stehekin 98852, is the ski-touring center for North Cascades National Park. The center offers equipment rentals, instructions, guides, and ski-touring trips along several of the North Cascades trails. Most of the park is subject to severe avalanche conditions and so is recommended for experts only. *Northwest Alpine Guide Service, Inc.*, 1628 9th Ave., Seattle 98101, provides guided ski tours in the Lake Wenatachee area, which has over two hundred miles of cross-country trails and logging roads. Accommodations are at *Cougar Inn* at the head of Lake Wenatachee. Mount Rainier National Park, Longmire 98397, offers practically unlimited opportunities for cross-country skiing, particularly in the Carbon River and White River areas. The *Paradise Lodge* provides access to Panorama Point, Camp Muir, and Nisqually Glacier. Ski tourers must report their route upon leaving and upon returning at either Paradise or Narado Falls. Be sure to write to the park supervisor for advance information, for some tours involve mountaineering skill and equipment. One of the state's most spectacular ski-touring areas is the Hurricane Ridge country, located at 5,000 feet elevation in open subalpine meadows in Olympic National Park, Port Angeles 98362. The high, open character of the area provides majestic views of the surrounding peaks and glaciers and the Strait of Juan de Fuca. Ski-touring instructions are available from the *Hurricane Ridge Ski School*, 3207 Maple Street, Port Angeles 98362.

Washington State Ferries

Washington State Ferries, the largest mass-transit passenger-vehicle ferry system in the United States, provides regularly scheduled service across Puget Sound to the San Juan Islands and Whidbey, Vashon, and Bainbridge islands, and the Kitsap Peninsula. The *Puget Sound & San Juan Islands Scenic Guide & Map*, available free along with rates, schedules, and travel information, from: Washington State Ferries, Seattle Ferry Terminal (Pier 52), Seattle 98104, contains a detailed map and descriptive information about the snow-fed rivers, mountain lakes, rain forests, and salmon-fishing meccas off Sekiu, Neah Bay, and La Push in the Olympic Peninsula and Hurricane Ridge area; the fjordlike Hood Canal, which stretches almost the entire length of the Olympic Mountain Range; the Kitsap Peninsula and Bainbridge Island; scenic Vashon Island and Tacoma; Saanich Peninsula and Victoria; the emerald-green maze of the scenic San Juan Islands; and picturesque Whidbey Island, the second-largest island in the contiguous United States.

Wildlife & Furbearers

The furbearers of Washington and the Pacific Northwest, which first attracted the explorers and trappers of the Hudson's Bay Company and the American Fur Company in the 1800s, include mink, long-tailed weasel, short-tailed weasel (or ermine), river otter, marten (also known as sable), fisher (found in the Olympic Peninsula, the Cascades, and parts of the Blue Mountains), sea otter, badger, bobcat, Canada lynx, western spotted skunk (or civet cat), striped skunk, coyote, lowland red fox, wolverine, beaver, muskrat, raccoon, nutria, fur seal, and opossum (originally brought into Washington during the 1920s). The gray wolf, the largest member of the wild dog family, is reportedly extinct in Washington, although there is the possibility of stray wolves entering the North Cascades region from British Columbia. Early settlers reported small wolf packs on the Olympic Peninsula, in the Okanogan Highlands, and in several other areas in western Washington. The last authenticated wolf was killed near Sherman Pass in Ferry County on August 9, 1950. The Cascade fox, a close cousin of the red fox, was introduced into the state in the 1920s and is indigenous to mountainous areas over 3,000 feet in elevation. The mountain beaver, thought to be the most primitive living rodent, is found west of the Cascades. Its total range is from San Francisco Bay north into southern British Columbia west of the major mountain ranges; it occurs nowhere else in the world. Generally considered a pest by timberland operators because of its fondness for Douglas fir, hemlock, cedar, Oregon grape, willow, and alder, it is virtually tailless, and not aquatic like the ordinary beaver. It is also much smaller, about muskrat size, and weighs only up to 3 pounds. It has a dark brown coat. The outer fur is pinkish cinnamon to light brown, with a few long black guard hairs on the backside. *Washington's Furbearers*, a useful guide that describes and illustrates the state's furbearing species, may be obtained free by writing to: Dept. of Game, 600 N. Capitol Way, Olympia 98504. *Washington Wildlife*, the official quarterly publication of the State Game Department, is distributed free of charge upon written request to: Washington Wildlife, c/o Dinner & Klein, P. O. Box 21188, Seattle 98111 and contains useful, informative articles about the state's wildlife, hunting, and fishing.

WASHINGTON TRAVEL & RECREATION GUIDE

Gifford Pinchot National Forest & Wilderness Areas

Gifford Pinchot National Topo Maps

U.S. Geological Survey overview maps, scale 1:250,000: Hoquiam, the Dalles, Vancouver, Yakima.

Goat Rocks Wilderness

U.S. Geological Survey large-scale maps: Wallput Lake, Jennies Butte, White Pass, Packwood.

Indian Heaven Wild Country

U.S. Geological Survey large-scale maps: Lake Butte, Sleeping Beauty, Steamboat Mountain, Wind River, Willard.

Mount Adams Wilderness

U.S. Geological Survey large-scale maps: Mount Adams East, Mount Adams West, Jungle Butte, Glaciate Butte, Green Mountain.

Mount Margaret Backcountry

U.S. Geological Survey large-scale map: Spirit Lake.

Pacific Crest Trail

The Gifford Pinchot National Forest segment of the trail through the Goat Rocks and Mount Adams wilderness areas to the Columbia River and the Oregon boundary is shown on the following large-scale U.S. Geological Survey maps: White Pass, Wallput Lake, Glaciate Butte, Green Mountain, Mount Adams West, Steamboat Mountain, Quartz Creek Butte, Lone Butte, Wind River, Willard, Hood River.

The 1,330,000-acre Gifford Pinchot National Forest (as big as Delaware) contains some of the most beautiful mountain wilderness in the United States. The forest is located in southwest Washington on the western slope of the Cascade Mountains and, to the south, borders the Columbia River Gorge in rough, heavily timbered terrain (route of the 1805–1806 Lewis and Clark expedition). Numerous trails, including segments of the Cascade Crest Trail, lead to the high peaks, glaciers, and meadows of the Mount St. Helens area, Mount Adams Wilderness, and the Goat Rocks Wilderness. Other backcountry trails lead to the Big Lava Beds, a 12,500-acre lava flow that issued from a cone with a 500-foot wide crater; to Cougar Lake; to the Mount Margaret area, a rugged alpine wilderness dotted with hundreds of small lakes; and to Indian Heaven Lakes, McClellan Meadows, Sawtooth Ridge, Shark Rock, and Silver Star Mountain.

The Indian Race Track at the south end of the lake-dotted Indian Heaven wild country was the site of pony races many years ago when the Indians hunted and camped in the area. A groove some 2,000 feet long and 10 feet wide, worn by the ponies' hooves, is still plainly visible. A portion of the large Twin Buttes huckleberry fields are reserved for the exclusive use of Indians in accordance with an old treaty agreement. Other historic huckleberry fields are located on the north side of Mount Adams, Nowich Butte–Bare Mountain Area, Mosquito Meadows, and Hamilton Mountain.

Hunting is very good throughout the forest for mule deer, elk, and black bear. Hikers who enjoy packing a fly rod should try the Packwood Lake area, located in a beautiful basin that can be reached only by the 4-mile trail from the Packwood Ranger Station. Fishing is good for rainbows from June through September. Good fishing for cutthroat, rainbow, Dolly Varden, and brook trout is found in the Cispus River, a large mountain stream with its source high in the Cascades between Mount Adams and Goat Rocks. The Upper Wind River and the Wind River Canyon along the lower river offer good fishing for sum-

mer and winter steelhead. The upper Wind area has numerous well-maintained camping grounds. The East Fork of the Lewis River, a noted steelhead stream with big fish up to 20 pounds not uncommon, flows in a westerly direction to join the main Lewis River near Woodland. The Lewis and Cowlitz rivers provide good early-season fishing before they turn milky with glacial till during the hot summer months. The Swift Reservoir, known for its scenic beauty and excellent fishing for rainbows up to 4 pounds and Dolly Varden to 10 pounds, is located 40 miles from Woodland on the Lewis River. Sudden violent storms can occur in any season at the higher elevations.

The famous Goat Rocks Wilderness encompasses 82,680 acres of rocky crags, meadows, glaciers, alpine lakes, and ridges, located high in the Cascades on the east flank of the great triangle formed by Mount Rainier, Mount Adams, and Mount St. Helens, with elevations ranging from 3,000 feet at Glacier Lake to 8,201 feet on Mount Curtis Gilbert. The wilderness derives its name from the bands of mountain goats that roam its high peaks. The Tieton and Klickitat rivers drain the eastern side of the area, and streams of the Cowlitz River system feed from the western side. The alpine central portion of the wilderness lies above timberline. The topographic U.S. Forest Service *Goat Rocks Wilderness Map*, available for 50¢ from Gifford Pinchot National Forest, P. O. Box 449, Vancouver 98660, shows the area's major features in full color at a scale of 1 inch to 1 mile, as well as boundaries, forest roads, Pacific Crest National Scenic Trail and other trails, forests in green, forest service stations and recreation sites, horse-loading ramps, boating sites, trail camps, winter sports sites, and alpine shelters. The map's contour interval is 80 feet.

The wilderness has approximately 95 miles of trails leading from dense forests and valleys up through broad meadows, ridges, and flower fields of lupine, heather, and phlox on up into the arctic-alpine mountain zone with its barren rocky soils, rock-conglomerate slopes, snowfields, and glaciers. The Cascade Crest Trail winds through the heart of the wilderness, with many side trails leading off to such places as Old Snowy Mountain, Goat Ridge, Cispus Pass, Devil's Horns, Beargrass Butte, Angry Mountain, Snowgrass Flats, and Packwood Glacier. Wallput, Packwood, Goat, and Lost lakes, plus many other lakes and streams in the area, provide good fishing for native cutthroat, brook, and rainbow trout. Access to the high lakes can be very difficult. For alpine enthusiasts, Goat Rocks is perfect for cross-country hiking and snowshoeing from White Pass to Hogback Mountain. Many of the trails are not free of snow until mid-August, and the weather is always unpredictable. The Klickitat River on the southern boundary of the wilderness lies within the Yakima Indian Reservation and is closed to the public. Big-game hunting is generally excellent throughout the area for elk, blacktail deer, black bear, and Rocky Mountain goat.

Indian Creek Corral, Star Route, Box 218-A, Naches 98937, provides pack trips into the Goat Rocks Wilderness area and fall elk hunts in the remote national forest high country. The *Packwood Lake Resort*, P. O. Box 302, Packwood 98361, serves as the northwestern portal to Goat Rocks Wilderness and provides accommodations, boats, fishing supplies, and horse rentals (in Packwood). Rocky Mountain elk may be observed during the summer in the meadows of Nannie Basin and upper Lake Creek Valley. Forest Service wilderness campsites are located at Alpine, Bypass, Chambers Lake, Dog Lake, La Wis Wis, Lost Lake, Midway, Packwood Lake, Wallput Lake, and White Pass. For wilderness travel, camping, fishing and hunting info write: District Ranger, *Packwood Ranger District*, Packwood 98361; or District Ranger, *Tieton Ranger District*, Naches 98937.

The bold, soaring summit of Mount Adams, towering above a sea of dense forest, dominates 32,400-acre Mount Adams Wilderness, located on the west slope of the High Cascades in the Gifford Pinchot

Forest adjacent to the Yakima Indian Reservation. Mount Adams, or "Pah-To" according to Indian legends, at 12,307 feet, is second only to Mount Rainier in height and bulk among Washington's peaks. The area is extremely rugged, having undergone successive volcanic convulsions. Mount Adams was formed by volcanic eruptions of ash and cinder accompanied by flows of basaltic and andesitic lava. Its largest glaciers and most severe examples of erosion are found on the northern and eastern flanks, where prevailing storm paths have caused large accumulations of snow and ice. The arctic-alpine zone near Mount Adams's summit includes many vents, blowholes, and caves. Hydrogen sulfide gas still issues from crevasses, and large deposits of sulfur cover the crater floor. The peak is adorned by the massive Mazama, Avalanche, White Salmon, and Klickitat glaciers, below which are lava crags and flows, alpine meadows, lakes, and forests of hemlock, pine, spruce, fir, and larch.

Numerous trails lead into the wilderness and join with the Round-the-Mountain Trail and the Cascade Crest Trail, which runs along the western side of the mountain and leads to Hellroaring Meadows, Lookinglass Lake, Bird Creek Meadows, Ridge of Wonders, and the Madcat Meadows. Hikers should detour to the north side of the mountain to gather some of the delicious wild blackberries and huckleberries found along the old burned-over areas. The fishing is generally poor, since the lakes are either too shallow or lack the necessary food to support a healthy fish population. The big-game hunting, however, is very good for mountain goat, elk, black bear, and blacktail deer. National Forest campgrounds are located on the western side and near the southern boundary of the wilderness.

The major features of the area are shown on the *Mt. Adams Wilderness Map*, available for 50¢ from: Regional Forester, P. O. Box 3623, Portland, OR 97208. The map shows wilderness boundaries, Yakima Indian lands, forest roads and trails, climbing routes, forest service and district ranger stations, recreation areas, and campsites located at Adams Fork, Council Lake, Horseshoe Lake, Midway Meadows, Morrison Creek, Olallie Lake, Spring Creek, Takhlakh Lake, and Timberline. The renowned *Mt. Adams Wilderness Institute*, Flying L Ranch, Glenwood 98619, offers a challenging program of instruction in mountaineering techniques and wilderness travel and alpine environment. For additional info on wilderness travel, camping, fishing, and hunting in the Mount Adams Wilderness, write: District Ranger, *Mt. Adams Ranger District*, Trout Lake 98650.

The Mount Margaret backcountry is a backpacker's paradise of flower-

studded alpine meadows and high mountain lakes separated by steep, rock-crested ridges, located due north of the Mount St. Helens–Spirit Lake area (see "Washington Encyclopedia" section) in the Gifford Pinchot National Forest. The trails and alpine trout lakes of this magnificent wilderness, including Grizzly, Obscurity, and Panhandle lakes, are shown on the *Mount St. Helens–Spirit Lake Map*, available for 50¢ from: Forest Supervisor, Gifford Pinchot National Forest, P. O. Box 449, Vancouver 98660. Elevations in the area range from 3,500 feet to 5,858 feet at Mount Margaret. The backcountry serves as the summer ranges for a herd of Roosevelt elk. Wildlife inhabiting the area include otter, beaver, marmot, cougar, osprey, eagle, hawks, loons, and ruffed and blue grouse. For wilderness travel, camping, hunting, and fishing info write: District Ranger, *St. Helens Ranger District*, Cougar 98616.

The useful *Gifford Pinchot National Forest map*, which shows wilderness areas, roads and trails, campgrounds, recreation and boat launching sites, and horse facilities may be obtained for 50¢ by writing: Forest Supervisor, Gifford Pinchot National Forest, P. O. Box 449, Vancouver 98660. *Ranger District Maps* of the St. Helens, Mount Adams, Packwood, Randle, and Wind River ranger districts may be

obtained free by writing to the Gifford Pinchot Forest Supervisor's office, along with the useful guides to *Mount St. Helens Snow Trails, Falls Creek Trail, Upper Wind River Winter Sports Area, Spirit Lake Campground,* and *Mount St. Helens Climbing Guide.* To obtain the latest info on local conditions of weather, roads, trails, campgrounds, fishing, hunting, berry status, and so forth, write to the forest supervisor's office or the district ranger at: St. Helens District, Cougar 98616; Mount Adams District, Trout Lake 98650; Packwood District, Packwood 98361; Randle District, Randle 98377; and Wind River District, Carson 98610.

Access and Outfitting Centers

Gifford Pinchot National Forest is reached via State Highways 141, 503, and 504 and U.S. Route 12. Lodging, supplies, outfitting, and guide service are available at Castle Rock, Morton, Stevenson, Vancouver, White Salmon, Randle, and Packwood.

Mount Baker–Snoqualmie National Forest & Glacier Peak Wilderness

Mount Baker National Forest Topo Maps

U.S. Geological Survey overview maps, scale 1:250,000: Concrete, Victoria.

Snoqualmie National Forest Topo Maps

U.S. Geological Survey overview maps, scale 1:250,000: Hoquiam, Wenatachee, Yakima.

Glacier Peak Wilderness

U.S. Geological Survey large-scale maps: Agnes Mountain, Cascade Pass, Dome Peak, Downey Mountain, Glacier Peak, Goode Mountain, Holden, Lucerne, McAlester Mountain, McGregor Mountain, Mount Lyall, Posiam Mountain, Smoking Mountain, Sonny Boy Lakes, Stehekin.

Pacific Crest Trail

The Glacier Peak Wilderness (including Wenatachee National Forest section) segment of the trail is shown on the following large-scale U.S. Geological Survey maps: Agnes Mountain, Holden, Glacier Peak; Glacier Peak to Alpine Lake Wilderness segment: Benchmark Mountain, Captain Point, Labyrinth Mountain, Stevens Pass; Alpine Lakes Wilderness segment: Stevens Pass, Scenic, the Cradle, Mount Daniel, Big Snow Mountain; Trail segment from Alpine Lakes to Crystal Mountain area and Mount Rainier National Park: Snoqualmie Lake, Snoqualmie Pass, Lester, Bumping Lake.

Mount Baker National Forest encompasses 1,283,000 acres of spectacular mountainous big-game and steelhead country in the upper northwest corner of the state and borders on British Columbia. Mount Baker was called *Kom Kulshan,* meaning "white and steep," by the aboriginal Lummi, Nooksack, and Skagit tribesmen. In 1792, thirteen years before the journey of Lewis and Clark, the English explorer Captain George Vancouver named the great peak soaring above the shoreline of upper Puget Sound Mount Baker in honor of his first lieutenant. The forest contains 40 percent of the glacier-covered area in the United States, excluding Alaska, and has more than 200 lakes at least an acre in size. Several outstanding trout and steelhead streams flow through the area, including the Suiattle, Sauk, Nooksack, and Skagit—one of the state's top streams for trophy steelhead. The large Nooksack River, flowing in a loop through northern Whatcom County, was at one time one of the Northwest's best steelhead streams, but present-day pressure from Indian tribal fishing rights has drastically reduced the catch. The Sauk River, a major tributary of the Skagit, holds some big Dolly Varden and cutthroat trout and has a good run of large winter steelhead. Baker Lake has good early-season fishing for kokanee and rainbow and Dolly Varden trout. The Cascade Crest Trail winds from Harts Pass through the Pasayten and Glacier Peak wilderness areas. Hunting is good for deer and black bear. The forest's major features, including the Mount Baker Recreation Area, Heather Meadows–Austin Pass Area, Boulder Creek–Summit Crater Area, Glacier Peak Wilderness, Crystal Mountain Area, Dalles Nature Trail, Pacific Crest Trail, and Alpine Lakes Area, are shown on the *Mount Baker–Snoqualmie National Forest Map,* available for 50¢ from: Supervisor's Office, Mt. Baker–Snoqualmie National Forest, 1601 Second Ave. Bldg., Seattle 98101. This useful, full-color map is published at a scale of ½ inch to 1 mile and shows forest roads, wilderness and ranger district boundaries, ranger cabins, campgrounds, trails and alpine shelters, and horse-loading and boat-launching ramps. Guided camping, hunting, fishing, riding, and pack trips in the Mount Baker National Forest Region, Glacier Peak Wilder-

ness, and the North Cascades are provided by: *Harold T. Olsen,* Route 3, Box 40, Arlington 98223; *Jim Clark,* Cascade Rt., Marblemount 98267; *Ralph Dexter,* Cascade Rt., Box 143, Marblemount 98267; *Donald L. Dayment,* Route 3, Box 257, Arlington 98223. The *Mt. Baker Lodge,* 1523½ Cornwall, Bellingham 98225, offers lodging and mountain-climbing and cross-country skiing instruction. *Tarrs Resort– Baker Lake,* Concrete 98237, provides lodging, boats and supplies.

The Snoqualmie National Forest preserves 1,211,901 acres of the majestic central Cascade Mountains, from Stevens Pass south to White Pass. Big-game hunting is good throughout the forest for elk, mule deer, black-tailed deer, black bear, and mountain goat. Renowned rivers such as the White, Skykomish, Snoqualmie, and Yakima flow through the forest and provide excellent fishing for steelhead, rainbow, brook, and cutthroat trout. Numerous trails pass through deep forests of giant fir and hemlock, fields of heather and snow lily, and high mountain meadows to such end points as the Alpine Lakes Wilderness, Bumping Lake, Cougar Lakes, Commonwealth Basin, McClellan Butte, Dutch Millers Gap, Mount Defiance, and the Tuscohatchie backcountry. The Cascade Crest Trail winds through the area from Cady Pass to Goat Rocks. The lovely roadless wilderness of the Alpine Lakes area contains over 700 lakes, most of which provide good fishing for the backpacker willing to tote along a fly rod. Bumping Lake offers good fishing for small kokanee and rainbow trout. Forest Service campgrounds near Bumping Lake are located at Cougar Flat, American River, and Cedar Springs. Access to the Cougar Lakes area is by trail from Swamp Lake. Flowing from its headwaters near Snoqualmie Pass (Snoqualmie means "moon people"), the lovely South Fork of the Snoqualmie River is famous for its excellent fishing, rapids, deep pools, and numerous waterfalls, including the 250-foot Twin Falls. Snow and Gem lakes, lying high in the mountains about 5 miles from Snoqualmie Pass, offer good fishing for cutthroats and rainbows.

Pack and saddle horses and guided hunting, fishing, and pack trips in the Snoqualmie National Forest are provided by: *Andy Brown,* P. O. Box 1465, Yakima 98901, with guided trips mostly from Fish Lake to Nelson Butte; *Bert Clark,* Star Route, Naches 98937, with guided trips into Goat Rocks Wilderness, Tumac Mountain Area, and Rattlesnake Drainage; *Bob Holeton,* Goose Prairie 98929, with guided riding and pack trips in the American Ridge and Swamp Lake areas; *Double K Mountain Ranch,* Goose Prairie 98929, mostly in the Bumping Lake Area; *L. E. Wyse,* 18680 Woodenville-Duvale Highway, Woodenville 98072, in the Rattlesnake Drainage; *Diamond Ring Guest Ranch,* Rt. 1, Box 148, Ellensburg 98926, pack trips into Menastash Canyon Area for hunting and fishing. Lodging, supplies, and outfitting in the Snoqualmie National Forest are provided by: *Alpental,* P. O. Box 578, Snoqualmie Pass Rural Branch Post Office, North Bend 98045, gateway to mountain lakes with registered touring

and mountain-climbing instruction; *Alta Silva,* Star Route, Enumclaw 98022, lodging at portal of entry to Mount Rainier National Park and Crystal Mountain Recreation Area; *Bumping Lake Resort,* RFD Box 185, Grandview 98930; *Crystal Mountain Resort,* Crystal Mountain 98022, portal of entry to Mount Rainier National Park, operates the Mt. Top Day Lodge, Alpine Inn, and Crystal House Lodge; *Dog Lake Boat Landing,* Star Route, Naches 98937; *Rimrock Landing,* North Side Rimrock Reservoir, Star Route, Naches 98937, cabins and boat rentals; *Silver Beach,* West End Rimrock Reservoir, 923 S. 23rd Ave., Yakima 98902; *Silver Springs Lodge,* Star Route, Enumclaw 98022, portal of entry of Mount Rainier National Park and Crystal Mountain Recreation Area; *Snoqualmie Summit Ski Area,* P. O. Box 476, Snoqualmie Pass Rural Branch P. O., North Bend 98045, gateway to Mountain Lakes and Pacific Crest Trail in Summit Area, with lodging, pack trips, and helicopter rides; *Stevens Pass Summit,* Star Route, Leavenworth 98826, day lodge with berry picking, hiking, skiing; *White Pass Resort,* P. O. Box 354, Yakima 98901, day lodge and supplies.

The majestic Glacier Peak Wilderness lies to the south of the North Cascades National Park, embracing the eastern and western slopes of the Cascades Range in Snoqualmie and Wenatchee national forests. This awesome 464,240-acre North Cascades wilderness area derives its name from Glacier Peak (10,436 ft.), the fourth highest mountain in the state, with its more than 30 sister peaks and massive icefields, Dome Peak, Spire Peak, and Sentinel Peak rising to 8,000 feet above the valleys. More than 90 glaciers lie within the area, giving rise to a number of rivers, including the Suiattle. To the northeast of the wilderness boundary are Stehekin River and Lake Chelan. The Stehekin, which flows into the head of Lake Chelan, is famous for its large rainbow and cutthroat trout. The Cascade Crest Trail is the major route through the wilderness, weaving its way north across mountain slopes, over passes, through alpine meadows, then west past Glacier Peak on along the Suiattle River, then eastward across Suiattle Pass and on down Agnes Creek to the Stehekin River. Connecting trails from both east and west provide opportunities for loop hikes and access to the Napeequa Valley, Entiat Glacier, Seven-Fingered Jack, Lyman Lake, Heather Ridge, Fourth of July Basin, the Seven Sisters, Mount Le Conte, White Rock Lakes, Mount Buckindy, and Hurricane Peak. The major trails leading through the rain forest to the glacial basins include the Suiattle Trail to Miners Ridge and Image Lake; White Chuck Trail, used by climbing parties to ascend Glacier Peak; Little Wenatachee Trail; Buck Creek Trail from the Chiwawa River area; and Railroad Creek Trail from Lucerne on beautiful Lake Chelan.

The fishing is good in most of the high mountain lakes for brook, rainbow, and cutthroat trout. It's a good idea to pack an inflatable boat to effectively fish the lakes. Many campsites lie within the area, and a number of simple shelters exist along the major trails. If you are planning to do some overnight camping, come well equipped for cold and violent weather. The wilderness is a first-rate hunting area for deer, black bear, mountain goat, and grouse. Much of the area lies within a special High Cascades early-season deer-hunting zone for those who enjoy high-mountain hunting.

Northwest Mountain Guides, 786 Commerce St., Tacoma 98402, offers alpine mountaineering instruction and guided expeditions in the Glacier Peak, Chimney Rock, and Dome Peak wilderness areas. The topographic *Glacier Peak Wilderness Map,* published at a scale of ¾ inch to 1 mile, may be obtained for 50¢ from: Forest Supervisor, Mt. Baker–Snoqualmie National Forest, Seattle 98101. This beautiful full-color map contains a detailed trail log of the Pacific Crest National Scenic Trail and other major trails in the wilderness and shows bound-

aries, forest roads and trails, forest service stations and recreation sites, campsites, forest cover, and lookout stations. The map has a contour interval of 100 feet. For additional info about trail conditions, camping, fishing, and hunting, write: Mt. Baker–Snoqualmie Forest Supervisor's Office or Forest Supervisor, Wenatachee National Forest, Wenatachee 98801. Detailed trail guides, ranger district maps, and additional info about the Mt. Baker-Snoqualmie National Forest recreation areas may also be obtained from the Forest Supervisor's Office.

Access & Outfitting Centers

The Mt. Baker–Snoqualmie National Forest recreation areas and Glacier Peak Wilderness area are reached via scenic Washington Highways 9, 530, and 542, North Cascades Highway 20, U.S. Route 2, and Interstate 90. Lodging, supplies, outfitting and guide service are available at Marblemount, Rockport, Concrete, Glacier, Mount Baker, Sedro Wolley, Darrington, Monte Cristo, Granite Falls, Silverton, Goldbar, Index, Skykomish, Snoqualmie, North Bend, Enumclaw, Roslyn, Cle Elum, Everett, Seattle, Tacoma, and Yakima.

North Cascades

North Cascades National Park Topo Maps

U.S. Geological Survey large-scale maps: Diablo Dam, Ross Dam, Crater Mountain, Marblemount, Eldorado Peak, Forbidden Peak, Mount Logan, Mount Arriva, Sonny Boy Lakes, Cascade Pass, Goode Mountain, McGregor Mountain, McAlester Mountain, Gilbert, Dome Peak, Agnes Mountain, Mount Lyall, Stehekin. U.S. Geological Survey 1:250,000 scale, overview map: Concrete.

Lake Chelan National Recreation Area

U.S. Geological Survey large-scale topo maps: Lucerne, Stehekin, Sun Mountain, McAlester Mountain, McGregor Mountain.

Pacific Crest Trail

The Pasayten Wilderness to North Cascades National Park segment of the trail is shown on the following large-scale U.S. Geological Survey maps: Castle Peak, Frosty Creek, Pasayten Peak, Slate Peak, Washington Pass, McAlester Mountain; North Cascades National Park segment: McAlester Mountain, McGregor Mountain, Mount Lyall, Agnes Mountain.

Pasayten Wilderness

U.S. Geological Survey large-scale topo maps: Ashnola Mountain, Ashnola Pass, Azurite Peak, Bauerman Ridge, Billy Goat Mountain, Castle Peak, Coleman Peak, Crater Mountain, Doe Mountain (15), Frosty Creek, Hozomeen Mountain, Jack Mountain, Lost Peak, Mazama (15), Mount Barney, Mount Lago, Pasayten Peak, Pumpkin Mountain, Remmel Mountain, Robinson Mountain, Ross Dam, Skagit Peak, Skull Mountain, Slate Peak, Tatoosh Buttes. U.S. Geological Survey 1:250,000 scale overview map: Concrete.

Ross Lake National Recreation Area

U.S. Geological Survey large-scale topo maps: Marblemount, Diablo Dam, Ross Dam, Pumpkin Mountain, Mount Prophet, Hozomeen Mountain, Mount Spickard, Skagit Peak.

Skagit Wild & Scenic River

U.S. Geological Survey large-scale topo maps: Diablo Dam, Finney Peak, Hozomeen Mountain, Illabot Peaks, Lake Shannon, Marble Mountain, Pumpkin Mountain, Rockport, Ross Dam.

Washington North Cascades is one of the great wilderness camping, hiking, fishing, and big-game hunting regions in North America. The major features of this majestic alpine country, including North Cas-

cades National Park, Lake Chelan and Ross Lake national recreation areas, and the Pasayten Wilderness, are shown on the U.S. Geological Survey *North Cascades Topographic Map* ($2). This full-color map has a scale of 1:250,000, is 30 × 40 inches in size, and shows trails, forest roads, campgrounds, ranger stations, lookout towers, elevations, and contours. The map's contour interval is 200 feet.

North Cascades National Park encompasses 1,053 square miles in the heart of the region. A majestic alpine wilderness area, the park embraces heavily forested valleys, deep glaciated canyons, snowfields, fjordlike lakes, jagged peaks, and more than 150 glaciers. The summits of Mount Challenger, Three Fingers, Del Campo, Mount Shuksan, the Picket Range Wilderness, and Eldorado Peaks Wilderness are composed of granitic gneiss, forming spires, horns, peaks, and ridges. More than 300 glaciers cling to these crags, and hundreds of lakes lie in the glacial cirques below. Numerous trails follow the long valley bottoms, leading through thick rain forests on the western slopes and through open sunlit woodlands to the east, winding out of the forests at 4,000 to 5,000 feet over high passes, through beautiful alpine meadows, and on up along the glaciers clinging to the high peaks. Many of the high trails have snow on them in July. High-water melt early in the season makes stream crossings particularly dangerous. Be sure to use extreme caution when crossing snow bridges.

Mountain goat, moose, elk, deer, black bear, a rare grizzly or two, wolverine, mountain beaver, and bald eagle range throughout the wilderness areas. Fishing is excellent in the hundreds of alpine lakes and streams for small cutthroat, rainbow, and brook trout, and in the large glacial rivers and lakes for steelhead and trout to lunker size. The remote wild Skagit River, originating in British Columbia's Cascade Range, once flowed through a mighty gorge emerging into the flatland of the Skagit Valley, which has since been dammed to form 24-mile-long Ross Lake. The Skagit, which flows on through the old logging-camp country of the Mount Baker National Forest region, yields some 35,000 steelheads up to 20 pounds each winter. The fishing in Ross is good for rainbows from 2 to 4 pounds and Dolly Varden up to 12 pounds. For much of its length this lake is walled by sheer granite peaks. Beautiful fjordlike Lake Chelan lies to the south. The largest lake in the state, it is over 52 miles long. Often referred to as the "Jewel of the American Alps," Lake Chelan provides very good early-season fishing for kokanee, rainbow, cutthroat, and large Dolly Varden. One of the most popular streams on the east slope of the Cascades is the Methow River, flowing southeasterly through the Cascades to join the Columbia River at Pateros. The Methow and its leading tributaries, Early Winters Creek, Lost River, and Wolf Creek, provide fine fishing for rainbow and cutthroat trout. The large, clear Skykomish River is an excellent steelhead stream. The Skykomish is formed by the meeting of its north and south forks near the village of Index; it then flows west for 23 miles before joining the Snoqualmie River, an excellent winter steelhead stream. Below the town of Snoqualmie, this latter river drops over a spectacular waterfall, then meanders northwesterly through a fertile valley where it joins the Skykomish to form the Snohomish River.

Other well-known lakes and rivers in the North Cascades include Lake Entiat, Lake Shannon, North Fork Thompson River, Tolt River, Rapid River, and the Chiwawa, White, and Wenatchee rivers. Camping in the wilderness is by permit only. Mountaineers must register with a park ranger in advance of all climbs. Campfires are prohibited in alpine and subalpine zones. Since very few trail shelters are available, it's wise to carry a lightweight plastic tarp or nylon tent for rain protection. Vehicle access campgrounds are located along North Cascades Highway 20 at Goodell Creek, with 26 camping sites suitable for both tents and small trailers, and at Colonial Creek on the shore of Diablo Lake, with 164 sites for walk-in use, trailers, or pickup campers.

The Superintendent's Office, North Cascades National Park, 311 State Street, Sedro Woolley 98284, publishes several useful maps and guides available free upon request. The *North Cascades National Park, Ross Lake & Lake Chelan National Recreation Area Map-Brochure*, contains useful descriptive info and shows roads, trails, glaciers, resorts, ranger stations, lookout towers, launching ramps, and campgrounds. The *North Cascades Main Trails & Backcountry Map* shows all trails, including the Big Beaver, Desolation, Lightning Creek, Rainbow Lake, and Warcreek trails, as well as primitive campsites and horse camps. The map also contains comprehensive backcountry rules for trailside and cross-country camping, climbing, and livestock use. The following information bulletins are also available free upon request: *North Cascades Campgrounds, Hiking in the North Cascades, Geologic History of the North Cascades, Weather and Climate of the North Cascades, Ross Lake National Recreation Area,* and *Campgrounds, Lakes & Glaciers in the Stehekin Ranger District.*

Wilderness outfitting and guided ski tours, pack trips, backpacking and hiking in the Sawtooth Ridge, Summit Trail, Lake Chelan, Washington Pass, and Cascade Pass areas of the North Cascades are provided by *Cascade Corrals,* Stehekin 98852 (509–663–1521). Horse and pack service is also provided by *Jim Clark,* Marblemount 98267, and *James Curran* (at Moore Point), Route 1, Box 8, Addy 99101. North Cascades wild-water trips are provided by *Bob Byrd River Raft Trips,* Stehekin 98852. Fly-in charter floatplane service is provided by *Chelan Airways,* Chelan 98816. Overnight accommodations are available at the rustic *Diablo Lake Resort,* Rockport 98283; *North Cascades Lodge,* Stehekin 98852; *Ross Lake Resort,* Rockport 98283; and *Stehekin River Resort,* Stehekin 98852. Boating services and rentals are provided by the Diablo Lake Resort, Ross Lake Resort, and North Cascades Lodge, and by the *Lake Chelan Boat Company,* Chelan 98816; *Cove Marina,* Route 1, Chelan 98816; *Granite Falls Marina,* Route 1, Chelan 98816; and *Joe Burnett,* Twenty Five Mile Creek, Chelan 98816.

The 505,514-acre Pasayten Wilderness forms a virtually unbroken fortress of wild backcountry in the Okanogan and Mount Baker national forests stretching along the boundary of the Ross Lake National Recreation Area. The wilderness was established in 1968 by the same congressional act that established the North Cascades National Park and Ross Lake and Lake Chelan national recreation areas. Most of what is now the Pasayten Wilderness was formerly included in the North Cascades Primitive Area. The wilderness is a primitive area of naked peaks composed of granite, marble, gneiss, schist, ice-scoured basins, U-shaped valleys, waterfalls, rock-strewn slopes, and sheer cliffs that provide a violent contrast to the open sunlit forests of spruce and fir, ponderosa pine, willows, birches, and groves of aspen and the vast meadows blanketed in the summer with Indian paintbrush, scarlet gilia, bluebells, violets, and yellow fireweed.

Hundreds of miles of trails wind through the Pasayten wilds, leading to such beckoning destinations as Setting Sun Mountain, Three Fools Pass, Chuchuwanteen Parks, Pistol Peaks, Cathedral Fork Valley, Lost River Gorge, and Jack Mountain (9,070 ft.), the highest point in the wilderness. Most of the area is accessible beginning in July and ending with the winter snows of October. Snow may be found on the high-country trails throughout the year. The Cascades Crest Trail passes through 27 miles of the wilderness from Monument 78 at the boundary with British Columbia south to Windy River Pass. Fishing is good in the high mountain lakes and in the Ashnola, Andrews River, and Middle Fork of the Pasayten for rainbow, cutthroat, brook, Montana black-spotted, Dolly Varden, and brown trout. The High Cas-

cades buck deer season and goat permit season in September result in a modest harvest.

The major features of the area as well as forest roads, recreation trails, horse facilities, boating ramps, wilderness trailheads, and primitive campsites are shown on the full-color U.S. Forest Service *Pasayten Wilderness Map,* available for 50¢ from: Forest Supervisor, Okanogan National Forest, Okanogan 98840. This useful map contains a "Wilderness Trip Planning Chart" for the area's major backcountry recreation sites. Travel prepared for inclement weather with possible snow and near-freezing weather. For free *Ranger District Maps,* trail info, and wilderness camping, fishing, and hunting information, write: District Ranger, Winthrop 98862, or District Ranger, Okanogan 98840. Guided high lakes fishing, camping, hunting, and scenic pack trips in the Pasayten Wilderness and adjacent North Cascades area are provided by *Hank Dammann,* Winthrop 98862; *Aspen Leaf Ranch,* Twisp 98856; *Clyde A. Scott,* Twisp 98856; and *Early Winters Resort,* Mazama 98833.

Access & Outfitting Centers

The North Cascades National Park, Lake Chelan and Ross Lake national recreation areas, and Pasayten Wilderness are reached via forest access roads off Washington's North Cascades Highway 20. Lodging, supplies, outfitting, and guide service are available at the old frontier logging and mining centers of Mazama, Stehekin, Newhalem, and Marblemount.

Okanogan-Colville National Forests & Grand Coulee of the Columbia

Okanogan National Forest Topo Maps

U.S. Geological Survey overview maps, scale 1:250,000: Concrete, Okanogan.

Colville National Forest Topo Maps

U.S. Geological Survey overview maps, scale 1:250,000: Okanogan, Sandpoint, Spokane.

Grand Coulee Dam National Recreation Area & Franklin D. Roosevelt Lake

U.S. Geological Survey large-scale maps: Electric City, Grand Coulee Dam, Wilbur, Keller, Lincoln, Turtle Lake, Wilmont Creek, Hunters, Inchelium, Bangs Mountain, Kettle Falls, Marcus.

The Okanogan National Forest is an outstanding fishing, hunting, and wilderness camping area, encompassing 1,521,000 acres of lovely valleys, alpine meadows and lakes, towering mountain ranges, and glaciers in north central Washington. *Okanogan* is the Indian word for "rendezvous," and applies to the area in the flatlands of the Okanogan Valley where the Indian tribes of British Columbia and Washington gathered for their annual potlatch. Over 1,200 miles of trail, including the Cascades Crest Trail from Manning Park on the Canadian border to Harts Pass, wind through the wild backcountry to such places as Great Goat Wall, a Yosemite-like glacier wall rising 2,000 feet above the valley floor; Slate Peak (7,500 ft.); Tatoosh Buttes; Lost River Canyon; Lake of the Woods; and the Pasayten Wilderness. Hunting is excellent throughout the forest for elk, deer, black bear, mountain goat, and moose. The waterfowl shooting is very good, since flocks of ducks and geese fly down the Columbia Basin through the Okanogan Valley during their annual migration. The high mountain lakes and major rivers, including the Methow, North Twisp, and Chewack, provide good fishing for rainbow, cutthroat, Dolly Varden, and brook trout. The once excellent fishing for steelhead and coho salmon in the

Okanogan River, a large tributary of the Columbia, has all but disappeared with the ever-increasing number of Columbia River reservoirs. Lake Bonaparte has good early-season fishing for large lake trout, kokanee, and brook trout, and is located near a well-maintained forest service campground.

The *Okanogan National Forest Map* (50¢) and free forest guides may be obtained by writing to: Forest Supervisor, Okanogan National Forest, P.O. Box 950, Okanogan 98840. This full-color map shows all major features, forest roads, Pacific Crest National Scenic trail, ranger stations, recreation sites, lookout stations, and boating and horse facili-

ties, and contains a listing of campgrounds and recreation facilities. Campgrounds providing pack and saddlestock facilities are located at Andrews and Cutthroat Creek, Fourteen Mile, Iron Gate, Lake Creek, Long Swamp, and Robinson Creek. The free 18-page *Okanogan National Forest Fishing Directory* contains useful information about the remote high-country lakes and streams, including location, elevation, size, fish species present, fishing conditions, and route of access. The free *Okanogan National Forest Roads & Trails Guide* is to be used as a companion to the forest recreation map and provides useful info about forest road and trail trips to the spectacular Salmon Falls, Salmon Meadows, Conconully Lake, Tiffany Meadows, Aeneas Valley, Strawberry Mountain, Bonaparte Lake, Big Trees Botanical Area, Camas Burn County, Black Pine Lake, Roads End, Sweetgrass Butte, and Harts Pass. For detailed wilderness travel, camping, hunting and fishing info, write: Forest Supervisor's Office or District Rangers at Tonasket 98855, Twisp 98856, or Winthrop 98862.

The Colville National Forest takes in 944,000 acres of the Selkirk Mountain Region in the northeastern corner of Washington, bordered on the north by British Columbia and on the east by Idaho. This forest region is known primarily for its excellent mule deer hunting, producing trophy bucks up to 440 pounds. Adjacent to the forest are the wildlands of the Colville Indian Reservation and Spokane Indian Reservation north of Roosevelt Lake and the Spokane River. The Roosevelt Lake area has some good hunting for whitetail deer, mule deer, and black bear, and wing shooting for quail, chukar partridge, mourning dove, pheasant, Canada goose, and brant.

The fishing in Roosevelt varies in quality with its water level for trout, bass, and walleye. Crescent Bay Lake near Grand Coulee is good for winter rainbow trout. The Grand Coulee Dam impounds the waters of the mighty Columbia for 151 miles to Arrow Lakes in British

Columbia. East of the Columbia River is the Pend Oreille River, flowing west out of Lake Oreille into Idaho at Newport and then north through the forest past Metaline Falls to Boundary Dam at the British Columbia border. The Pend Oreille has fine fishing for cutthroat, rainbow, and brown trout up to 5 pounds along its wild upper stretches. The Spokane River, flowing west from Coeur d'Alene Lake in Idaho through the Spokane Valley to its confluence with Roosevelt Lake, has good fishing for rainbow and brook trout in its upper portion. North of Colville, Big Sheep Creek flows into Roosevelt Lake from British Columbia. The creek's brushy banks, deep holes, and long stretches of white water provide an excellent habitat for good-sized rainbows and brookies. To the north of the Little Pend Oreille National Wildlife Refuge, the Little Pend Oreille chain of lakes offers excellent fishing for cutthroat trout. The Little Pend Oreille area lies in the heart of top hunting country for black bear, whitetail deer, grouse, and quail. The refuge draws heavy flights of mallards and Canada geese and provides some fine wing shooting in the adjacent areas.

A free *Colville National Forest Map* showing primitive forest roads, mines, ranger stations, cabins, lookout stations, forest service recreation sites, and points of interest, including Boundary Dam, Crystal Falls, Fort Colville Historical Monument, Maitlen Creek, and Salmo Basin research natural areas, may be obtained along with camping, fishing, and hunting info from: Forest Supervisor, Colville National Forest, Colville 99114.

The Coulee Dam National Recreation Area encompasses Roosevelt Lake and a narrow strip of land adjacent to the lakeshore. Franklin D. Roosevelt Lake stretches behind the dam for 130 miles almost to the Canadian border. A scenic highway follows the lake northeastward through the old fur-trading territory of the Northwest Company, rolling wheatlands, and evergreen forests past Fort Spokane and the Spokane Indian Reservation, Huckleberry and Kettle River mountains, to Gifford Ferry. Another scenic drive follows the Sanpoil River north through the Colville Indian Reservation to the old gold-mining town of Republic, through the national forest, then east over Sherman Pass. North of Kettle Falls, scenic roads follow the Columbia and Kettle rivers into Canada. Roosevelt Lake is the water gateway to the scenic Arrow Lakes region of British Columbia. Boaters planning to visit Canada are advised to inquire about inspection procedures from a park ranger or the U.S. customs service before crossing the international boundary.

The major features of the region are shown on the *Coulee Dam National Recreation Area Map-Brochure*, available free, from: Superintendent, Box 37, Coulee Dam 99116. This map/guide shows boat mileage, roads, ranger stations, developed resort areas, and Indian agency areas, and contains useful information about seasons and accommodations, boating signs, symbols, and rules. Campgrounds on the west arm of the lake are on open terraces, while those on the north arm are generally in forested areas. Hunting and fishing are permitted within sections of the national recreation area. Big game animals include black bear and whitetail and mule deer. Trout, walleye, and bass are most often found where lake waters meet cliffs and at the mouths of the Sanpoil River, Hawk Creek, Colville River, Kettle River, and Ninemile, Wilmont, Hunter's, Hall, Barnaby, and Sherman creeks. The Columbia River above Onion Creek has good fishing, as does Banks Lake southwest of Grand Coulee Dam. Other good areas are the base of the bluffs near Keller Ferry for trout and salmon, the Spokane River arm for walleye, the Kettle River arm for whitefish and bass, and the Little Dalles for trout. The free publication *Fishing Coulee Dam National Recreation Area* may be obtained by writing to the superintendent's office (address above). Dry Falls, located due

south of Banks Lake and west of Coulee City, is the skeleton of one of the most spectacular waterfalls in geological history, some 100 times more powerful than Niagara. It once roared over an 800-foot precipice near the Upper Coulee. Lenore Caves, located 10 miles south of Dry Falls near the north end of Lake Lenore, were shelters used by prehistoric man and are today accessible by trail.

Access & Outfitting Centers

Okanogan National Forest is reached via the North Cascades Highway 20, Washington State Highway 153, and U.S. Highway 97; lodging, supplies, wilderness outfitting, and guide service are available at Methow, Twisp, Winthrop, Mazama, Conconully, Okanogan, Tonasket, and Oroville. Colville National Forest is reached via Washington Highways 155, 20, 21, 25, and 31 and U.S. Highway 395; lodging, supplies, outfitting, and guide service are available at Republic, Kettle Falls, Northport, Metaline Falls, Marcus, Colville, Chewelah, Deer Park, Newport, and Spokane. Coulee Dam National Recreation Area is reached via State Highways 17, 155, and 21 and U.S. Highway 2.

Olympic Peninsula—
The Mountains, Forests & Waterways

Olympic National Forest Topo Maps

U.S. Geological Survey overview maps, scale 1:250,000: Cape Flattery, Copalis Beach, Seattle, Victoria.

Olympic National Park Topo Maps

U.S. Geological Survey overview maps, scale 1:250,000: Cape Flattery, Victoria, Copalis Beach, Seattle.

Hok River Rain Forest

U.S. Geological Survey large-scale maps: Destruction Island, Forks, Mount Tom, Spruce Mountain.

Olympic Range

U.S. Geological Survey large-scale maps: Mount Tom, Mount Olympus, Mount Angeles, Tyler Peak, Mount Christie, Mount Steel, The Brothers, Mount Tebo, Grisdale.

The famous rain forests, towering stands of ancient cedars and firs, rugged coastal shores, glacier-fed streams, and majestic mountains of the Olympic Peninsula offer some of the finest steelhead and trout fishing, wilderness camping and backpacking, and big-game hunting opportunities in the Northwest. The peninsula is bordered on the west by the Pacific Ocean, on the north by the Strait of Juan de Fuca, and on the east by the placid inland salmon waters of Puget Sound. The 622,000 acres of the Olympic National Forest encompass a major portion of the peninsula and contain some of the truly great steelhead streams of the Pacific Coast. The vast stretches of unsettled backcountry provide excellent hunting for deer, black bear, and Roosevelt elk. Numerous hiking trails and forest roads lead to Mount Jupiter, Marmot Pass, Mildred Lake, Silver Lake, and Mount Walker.

The great steelhead rivers of the Olympic Peninsula flow from their glacial headwaters in the pinnacles of the Olympic Range through dense rain forests and valleys and wilderness meadowlands bright with wild columbine, dogtooth violets and Indian pipes, forming numerous rapids, whirlpools, and deep holding pools along their course to the Pacific.

Some of the state's finest fishing for steelhead, native cutthroat, and rainbow trout is found in the famous Bogachiel River as it flows westerly from its source high in the Olympic Mountains to join the Calawah River below the town of Forks. The powerful glacial Hoh

River has its headwaters on the north slope of Mount Olympus and is one of the Northwest's great fishing streams for steelhead, chinook and coho salmon, and sea-run cutthroat. To round out the picture, the region's other outstanding steelhead and salmon streams include the Humptulips, Dungeness, Skokomish, Hamma Hamma, Quilcene, Wolfe, Soleduck, and Dosewallips rivers. In these big turbulent waters

roads and trails
OF OLYMPIC NATIONAL PARK

second revised edition
By FREDERICK LEISSLER

GUIDE TO
THE HOH RAIN FOREST

Guide to
HURRICANE RIDGE
Olympic National Park

Views   Plants
Roads   Animals
Trails   History

a good lead-core shooting head line should be used to get your fly down in front of the fish at depths not obtainable with ordinary lines. A powerful 8½ to 9½-foot rod and a reel with at least 100 yards of 15 to 18-pound test backing are strongly recommended. In certain rivers where steelhead in excess of 25 pounds are a possibility, it is advisable to use a reel that will hold at least 150 yards of backing. A sampling of a few of the popular steelhead fly patterns includes the Skykomish, Kalama Special, Sunrise, Thor, Van Luven, and Princess in sizes 6 to 1/0.

The major features of the forest, including the spectacular 300-foot-high old-growth Douglas fir, hemlock, cedar, and spruce of the Quinault Rain Forest, the Wynoochee River and gorge, Pioneer's Path Nature Trail, the renowned trout waters of Quinault and Cushman lakes, and the Humptulips Ridge, Quinault Ridge, Matheny Ridge, and Quilcene Range big-game hunting areas, are shown on the U.S. Forest Service *Olympic National Forest Map.* This full-color map is available for 50¢, along with the free *Quinault Rain Forest Guide,* from: Forest Supervisor, Olympic National Forest, Olympia 98501.

Pack and saddle horses and guided fishing, elk hunting, wilderness

camping, and pack trips throughout the forest and in the Olympic Mountains are provided by: *River Trails Ranch,* Quilcene 98376; *Drake's Lazy D Ranch,* Rt. 2, Box 238, Sequim 98382; *E. L. Crothers & R. B. Grinols,* Box 172, Port Angeles 98362; *4-Seasons Stables,* Rt. 2, Box 145, Port Angeles 98362; *Slash F Ranch,* Rt. 2, Box 101, Amanda Park. For hunting, fishing, wilderness camping, and trail maps and info write to: Olympic National Forest Supervisor's Office or to the following District Rangers: Hoodsport Ranger District, Hoodsport 98548; Quilcene Ranger District, Quilcene 98376; Quinault Ranger District, Quinault 98575; Shelton Ranger District, Shelton 98584; Soleduck Ranger District, Forks 98331.

The national forest forms a semicircle around Olympic National Park, a 1,400-square-mile wilderness in the heart of the peninsula. The park encompasses lush rain forests of giant Sitka spruce and hemlock towering above forest floors covered with thick mats of sphagnum moss, glacier-studded mountains, alpine lakes and meadows, rocky beaches and headlands, and powerful glacial streams renowned for their steelhead and salmon spawning runs. The park is dominated by the massive Olympic Mountains, which reach their greatest height at the summit of 7,954-foot Mount Olympus. Several other peaks tower above 7,000 feet, and the elevation of the ridges and crests lies between 5,000 and 7,000 feet. The Olympic Range contains over 60 glaciers; the three largest, White, Hob and Humes, are over 2 miles in length. The western side of the Olympic Peninsula has the wettest climate in the United States, with annual precipitation exceeding 140 inches. Mount Olympus and the high-elevation backcountry receive much more precipitation from snow. In contrast, the northeastern side of the peninsula has one of the driest climates on the Pacific Coast.

Park roads provide access to over 600 miles of trails that lead through rain forests dense with ferns to wide, gravelly valleys and such points as the Seven Lakes Basin, Bailey Range Mountains, Mount Tom, Marymere Falls, Hurricane Hill, Lake Crescent, Mount Storm King, Pyramid Peak, Flapjack Lakes, Mount Blue, Moose Lake, and Gravel Lake. The 50-mile-long Pacific Coast area has excellent wilderness beach trails along tough rocky headlands, around tidal pools, and by massive piles of driftwood. Be sure to obtain a tide table before you start your beach trek. This is tough hiking country, known for its slippery rocks and dense brush; getting lost is all too easy if you wander off the trail. A tide table, maps, and compass are essential.

Backcountry trails also lead to some of the finest steelhead and salmon streams on the continent. The East Fork of the Quinault River has excellent fishing for Dolly Varden, cutthroat, and brook trout and steelhead. The Quinault is paralleled by a trail through the Enchanted Valley, over Anderson Pass, and on to Dosewalips. Three miles beyond Enchanted Valley a spur trail leads to Marmot Lake, Hart Lake, and on to the Duckabush and Skokimish River trails. Shelters are located at O'Neill Creek and Enchanted Valley. The lovely Elwha River provides some of the best fishing in the state for rainbow, cutthroat, and brook trout, and is followed upstream by a trail for 25 miles with 9 shelters strung out along the way. The Hoh River trail parallels the upper portion of the stream to its headwaters near Elk Lake and Glacier Meadow, the starting points for ascents of Mount Olympus. About a half mile above the Olympus Patrol Cabin, a spur trail leads off to beautiful Hoh Lake, at 4,500 feet. The Hoh and its tributaries provide excellent fishing for winter steelhead up to 18 pounds, and cutthroat, rainbow, and Dolly Varden. Roosevelt elk, blacktail deer, and black bear are common throughout the forests.

Backcountry use permits are required for trail or beach camping. They may be obtained from the ranger station in the area where your hike originates. Mountaineering parties are asked to register at the ranger station nearest their route and to show that they have standard climb-

ing gear. Wilderness outfitting and guided expeditions in the Olympic Range are offered by *Lost Mountain Packing & Guide Service*, Rt. 1, Box 718, Sequim 98382.

The major features of the park and ranger stations, wilderness shelters and camps, campgrounds, trails, forest roads, and ferries are shown on the *Olympic National Park Map*, printed in shaded relief and available free upon request from: Park Superintendent, 600 East Park Ave., Port Angeles 98362. The map contains a detailed description of the park's geological history and a description of the major hiking trails. The full-color *U.S. Geological Survey Olympic National Park Map* ($2) shows the park and the adjacent wilderness, including the Quinault Indian Reservation, at a scale of 1:125,000, or about 1 inch to 2 miles. The map is 33 × 47 inches and is available in either a topographic or a relief edition, which gives the appearance of the sunlight striking the surface from the northwest.

The useful information bulletin *Climbing Mount Olympus* may be obtained free upon request by writing to the Park Superintendent's Office. Several useful and informative guides to the park and the surrounding wilderness areas are published by the *Pacific Northwest National Parks Association*, 2800 Hurricane Ridge Road, Port Angeles 98362: (1) *The Olympic Seashore*, Kirk, a comprehensive guide to the roads, trails, and natural and human history of the Pacific Coast Area of the Olympics, with detailed maps, Tidepool life sketches, 63 photos; paper, 88 pages, $2.25; (2) *The Olympic Rain Forest*, Kirk, a large-format book on this special environment covering forest relationships, geology, animals, and man; fully illustrated with 8 pages in color; cloth, 86 pages, $5.35; (3) *Roads and Trails of Olympic National Park*, Leissler, a trail guide with mileages, maps, descriptions, details; illustrated, paper; 101 pages, 1971 edition, $2.75; (4) *Geologic Guide to the Deer Park Area*, Tabor, 40¢; (5) *Geologic Guide to the Hurricane Ridge Area*, Tabor, 45¢; (6) *Wildflowers of the Olympics*, Stewart, $3.25, 100 flowers in color; best available for Olympics, paper, 64 pages; (7) *Backpacking in Mount Rainier, North Cascades and Olympic National Parks*, Maguire, pertinent for novices to Northwest hiking, illus., paper, 16 pages, 45¢; (8) *The Lowland Forest Community*, Wilkerson, 45¢; (9) *Indian Village Nature Trail*, Kaune, 45¢; (10) *Guide to Hurricane Ridge*, Stewart, brief history of ridge area, trail map information, 14 pages, 45¢; (11) *Guidebook to the Hoh Rain Forest*, Hanify and Blencowe, an interpretive handbook, pictures and text, 32 pages, $1.50; (12) *The Olympic National Park*, Bob and Ira Spring, an artistic pictorial with text, 10″ × 12″ photos, 28 pages, $3.20; (13) *Guide to the Geology of Olympic National Park*, Tabor, an introduction to the geology of the park, supplemented by description of pertinent geologic features along the main trails, 144 pages, illus., maps, bibliog., $4.20.

Two extremely useful guidebooks to the Olympic Peninsula are published by the University of Washington Press, Seattle 98105: Ruth Kirk's classic guide, *Exploring the Olympic Peninsula* ($4.95, 128 pages, paper), provides definitive coverage of the Olympic wildlands, including history, geology, plants, wildlife, and roads and trails, for the backpacker, fisherman, and family vacationer; Frederick Leissler's *Roads & Trails of Olympic National Park* ($3.95, 114 pages, paper) describes the 16 major roads and more than 600 miles of trails, with detailed maps and photographs.

Lodging facilities and services in Olympic National Park are provided by *Sol Duc Hot Springs Resort*, Star Route 1, Port Angeles 98362, in the scenic Soleduck River Valley; *Lake Crescent Lodge*, located 21 miles west of Port Angeles, on U.S. 101, *Lake Crescent Log Cabin Resort*, located on the northeast end of the lake 17 miles west of Port Angeles, and *Hurricane Ridge Resort*, all operated by National Park Concessions, Route 1, Box 416, Port Angeles 98362; *Kalaloch Beach Ocean Village*, Route 1, Clearwater 98399, located on U.S. 101, some 36 miles south of Forks; and *La Push Ocean Park*, La Push 98350, with housekeeping cabins, located 14 miles west of U.S. 101. Regularly scheduled airline service is available from Seattle to Port Angeles through *Pearson Aircraft, Inc.*, Fairchild International Airport, Port Angeles 98362. Regularly scheduled ferry service is available across Puget Sound via *Washington State Ferries*, Seattle Ferry Terminal, Seattle 98104, and between Victoria, British Columbia, and Port Angeles via *Black Ball Transport Inc.*, Foot of Laurel St., Port Angeles 98362.

Hunting and fishing lodging and steelhead guide service are available throughout the Olympic Peninsula. The deep waters of Lake Quinault and the famous steelhead waters of the Hoh and Quinault rivers in the Lake Quinault–Ocean Strip area are served by the *Lake Quinault Lodge* and *Rain Forest Resort*, Quinault 98575. The logging center of Forks and the Bogachiel, Forks, and La Push rivers and the Hoh River Rain Forest are served by the *Bogachiel Resort*, Star Route 1, Box 370, Forks 98331; *Forks Motel*, Box 510, Forks 98331; *Three Rivers Resort*, Star Route 2, Box 280, Forks 98331; and *Shoreline Resort*, La Push 98350. The famous salmon-fishing grounds of the Strait of Juan de Fuca, which extends from Crescent Beach to Neah Bay and Cape Flattery, are well served by fishing lodges and boat charter operators. Both big king and hard-fighting silver salmon are often caught near shore at protected Neah Bay, Sekiu-Clallam Bay, Agate-Crescent Bay, and Whiskey Creek. At Neah Bay, on the Makah Indian Reservation, sport and commercial fishermen cruise to salmon and halibut fishing grounds offshore. For lodging and outfitting services, write: *Agate and Crescent Beach Park*, Rt. 1, Box 294-D, Port Angeles 98362; *Whiskey Creek Beach Cabins*, c/o Schmitt-Pfaff, Joyce 98343; *Silver King Resort*, Star Route 2, Box 10A, Port Angeles 98362; *Coho Resort*, Middlepoint, Sekiu 98381; *Curley's Resort*, P.O. Box 265, Sekiu 98381; *Olson's Resort*, Box 216, Sekiu 98381; *Snow Creek Resort*, Sekiu 98381; *The Cove*, with fish storage and charter service, Box 216, Sekiu 98381; *Makah Resort*, P.O. Box 183, and *Thunderbird Resort*, Neah Bay 98357. Resorts located on the shores of glacier-fed Lake Aldwell on the Elwha River and Lake Sutherland include the *Maple Grove Resort*, Route 1, Box 426A, Port Angeles 98362; *Mallard Cove Resort*, Route 1, Box 433, Port Angeles 98362; and *Elwha Fishing Resort*, Route 3, Box 464, Port Angeles 98362. Resorts in the scenic Lower Hood Canal–Skokomish River Gorge Area and the beautiful Kitsap Peninsula include the *Siskam Resort*, Star Route 1, Box 525, Belfair 98528 on Hood Canal; *Miami Beach Resort*, Star Rt. 1, Box 150, Seabeck 98380; and *Puget Sound Salmon-land Cabins*, Hansville 98340.

Guided scenic float trips in Olympic National Park are provided by *Rivers Northwest*, Box 33, Amanda Park 98526; phone (206) 288–2383. Guided hiking and packhorse trips in the Olympic high country are provided by *Lost Mountain Ranch*, Rt. 6, Box 920, Sequim 98382; phone (206) 683–4331.

Access & Outfitting Centers

The Olympic National Forest Region and the National Park are accessible via scenic U.S. Highway 101, reached via Interstate 5 from Oregon. Lodging, supplies, outfitting, and guide service are available at the scenic logging and fishing centers of La Push, Ozette, Neah Bay, Sekiu, Clallam Bay, Joyce, Elwha, Dungeness, Discovery Bay, Quilcene, Staircase, Hoodsport, Grisdale, Quinault, Queets, Forks, Heart o' the Hills, and Humptulips.

Wenatachee National Forest & Mount Rainier National Park

Wenatachee National Forest Topo Maps

U.S. Geological Survey maps, scale 1:250,000: Wenatchee, Yakima.

Mount Rainier National Park Topo Maps

U.S. Geological Survey large-scale maps: Enumclaw (15), Greenwater, Lester, Golden Lakes, Mowich Lake, Sunrise, White River Park, Mount Wow, Mount Rainier West, Mount Rainier East, Chinook Pass, Bumping Lake, Randle, Packwood, White Pass.

Pacific Crest Trail

The Wenatachee National Forest segment of the trail from the Crystal Mountain Area in the Naches Ranger District through Mount Rainier National Park to the Goat Rocks Wilderness is shown on the following U.S. Geological Survey maps: Bumping Lake, White Pass, White River Park, Chinook Pass.

The Wenatachee National Forest, renowned for its outstanding wilderness camping, fishing, and big-game hunting areas, encompasses 1,602,000 acres along the eastern slope of the Cascades just south of North Cascades National Park. The Columbia River forms its boundary to the east. The major features of this high mountain country of sweeping forests, snowcapped peaks, and hundreds of alpine lakes, meadows, and streams are shown on the *Wenatachee National Forest Map*, available for 50¢ from: Forest Supervisor, P.O. Box 811, Wenatachee 98801. This useful, full-color map is printed at a scale of ⅜ inch to 1 mile and shows all campgrounds, forest roads, trails, and recreation sites.

Hundreds of miles of trails, shown on the map, provide access to the Chelan Mountains, Entiat Mountains, Stuart Range, Enchantment Lakes Basin, Glacier Peak Wilderness, Swauk Pass area, Wenatchee Mountains, Nason Ridge, Tumwater Meadows, and the Chiwaukum Mountains. The Cascades Crest Trail enters the region at Rainy Pass and winds past the North Cascades National Park boundary and the Glacier Peak Wilderness–Lake Chelan National Recreation Area. If you are traveling by pack horse, be sure to carry feed, since forage is scarce along the way. The trail follows Agnes Creek past Suiattle Pass and Glacier Peak Mines and heads for Fire Creek Pass, Sitkum Creek, and White and Cady passes, with high views of beautiful open meadows. Both water and campsites are scarce in this area. The trail continues on past Wenatachee Pass and Union Gap to Stevens Pass, where the Great Northern Railroad completed its Cascade crossing in 1893. The town of Skykomish, 16 miles to the west, is a good place to resupply. From here the trail passes through the heart of the High Cascade lake country leading to Trap Lake, Deception Pass, Dutch Miller Gap, Hardscrabble Creek Crossing, Goldmeyer Hot Springs, and on to Snoqualmie Pass. This last portion of the trail is inaccessible by saddle horse (and is also very risky on foot). Those using horses must use the Snow Creek Trail. The trail leaves the Wenatchee Forest on its way to Blowout Mountain to the south.

The clean-washed gravel beds of the Little Wenatachee and White rivers above Lake Wenatachee are among the few remaining natural chinook salmon spawning areas left in the Columbia River system. Both the glacial White and Little Wenatachee rivers provide good fishing for rainbows. Numerous trails provide access to their tributaries, such as Panther, Indian, and Boulder creeks, which offer excellent

fishing for limit catches of 8 to 11-inch cutthroat trout. The Wenatachee River (*Wenatachee* means "good place" or "river issuing from a canyon") has its source in the lake and is popular for cutthroat, rainbow, brook, and Dolly Varden.

The vast forest and mountain areas provide excellent hunting for deer, bear, elk, and bighorn sheep, particularly in the Colockum, Entiat, and Swakane Game Ranges. Blue grouse are numerous in the high timbered areas. Ruffed grouse are found scattered in the lower mountain altitudes in alder and other thickets along the mountain streams. Spruce, or Franklin's, grouse inhabit the subalpine coniferous forests, especially in the damp, dense areas. In the rugged wilderness parts of the forest you would do well to hire a guide and pack animal or use a 4-wheel-drive jeep to get in. Camping hunters will have no problem, since there are numerous well-maintained campgrounds located throughout the forest.

Several wilderness outfitters who provide pack and saddle horses and guided fishing and hunting trips into the remote Wenatchee backcountry area operate within the forest's boundaries: *Ray Courtney* and *Guy Imus,* Stehekin 98852, provide guided trips into the Lake Chelan area; *Gordon Stuart,* Domke Lake Resort, Chelan 98816, provides guided hunting trips into the Emerald Park area; *Jack White,* Manson 98831, operates in the Lake Chelan area; *Salmon la Sac Resort,* Box 68, Ronald 98940, has guided fishing, hunting, and riding trips in the Cle Elum River country; *Don Kilman,* Maverick Range, Star Rt. 157A, Leavenworth 98826, has guided pack trips in the Mad River and Mad Lake area; *Red Burkley,* Star Rt., Leavenworth 98826; *Wilfred Davey,* Box 324, Leavenworth 98826; *Bill Hansen,* Rt. 1, Box 122, Leavenworth 98826, has guided trips in the Icicle River country; *Rayrock Springs,* Star Rt., Leavenworth 98826; *Norm Trapp,* Star Rt., Leavenworth 98826; *William L. Sullivan,* Stehekin 98852, has trips to Upper Chelan district; *James W. Butterfield,* Star Rt., Leavenworth 98826, specializes in trips to Nason Creek Backcountry; *Robert H. Nicholson,* Rt. 1, Box 104, Spanaway, has trips in the Mount Baker and Wenatachee ranger districts. Lodging is provided by the *Domke Lake Resort,* Chelan 98816; *Ingalls Lodge,* Rt. 1, Leavenworth 98826; *Lucerne Park Resort,* c/o Ivan E. Jones, 417 Times Square Bldg., Seattle 98101, with pack trips in Glacier Peak Wilderness area arranged; *Mineral Springs Lodge,* Swauk Pass, Rt. 2, Cle Elum 98922; and *Salmon la Sac Resort & Co.,* P. O. Box 68, Ronald 98940.

In addition to the *Wenatachee National Forest Map,* other special guides, brochures, and maps, including the *Recreation Guide to the Naches and Tieton Ranger Districts,* are available from Ranger Stations or from the Wenatachee National Forest Supervisor's Office, P. O. Box 811, Wenatachee 98801. Free district trail guides, current area and trail restrictions, and snow trail info is available from the Forest Supervisor's Office.

The major features of Mount Rainier National Park, which encompasses some 235,400 acres of High Cascade natural areas south of the Ellensburg Ranger District, are shown on the *Mount Rainier National Park Topographic Map,* available for $2 from: Branch of Distribution, U.S. Geological Survey, Federal Center, Denver, CO 80225. This useful, full-color map is 22 × 26 inches, at a scale of 1 inch to 1 mile, and shows magnetic declination, contours, glaciers, trails, national forest boundaries, lakes, streams, marshes, and swamps. Mount Rainier (14,410 ft.), with its steep, unstable rock, heavily crevassed glaciers, and sudden devastating storms, is the highest peak in the Cascade Range and one of the supreme mountaineering challenges in North America.

There are over 350 miles of trails within the park. The Wonderland Trail is the longest, circling Mount Rainier for a distance of about 90 miles, crossing meadows, streams, mountain passes, and forested valleys, and reaching a maximum elevation of 6,500 feet at Pan Handle Gap. Other trails, including the Cascades Crest Trail, Nisqually Vista Loop, and Trail of the Shadows, lead to such backcountry places as Sunrise Point, Goat Island Mountain, Eagle Peak, Grove of the Patriarchs, Cowlitz Divide, Ohanapecosh Park, and the Elysian Fields.

For most of the year Mount Rainier lies under a blanket of snow, and even as late as July there may be 8-foot drifts in the sheltered coves. As the days grow warmer in the early summer months, the meadows become a brilliant sea of lupine, Indian paintbrush, marigold, and fawn lily. Then as summer turns to fall the forests and fields mellow with the deep reds of huckleberry, maple, and mountain ash. Climbing Mount Rainier is a dangerous feat and should be attempted only by the experienced mountaineer. For less experienced climbers, *Rainier Mountaineering, Inc.,* offers excellent 1-day snow and ice-climbing schools, guided summit climbs, and a 5-day climbing seminar. For information write: Rainier Mountaineering, 201 St. Helens Street, Tacoma 98402.

Fishing in the park can also be challenging. Generally, the clear lakes are small and not fertile enough to support a large fish population. Most of them lie at 4,000 to 6,000 feet and are not free of ice until July. Access to the lakes is by trail on foot or packhorse. A few of the more promising lakes to test your skill are Golden, Deadwood, Bear Park, Mowich, Mystic, and Palisades.

For detailed backpacking and trail information write: Backcountry Desk, Mount Rainier National Park, Longmire 98397. There are two excellent guidebooks available from the Mount Rainier Natural History Association, Longmire 98397: *50 Hikes in Mt. Rainier National Park* ($4.15) and *Guide to the Trails of Mt. Rainier* ($1.15). A 3-dimensional plastic *Relief Model of Mt. Rainier* may be obtained for $1 by writing to the park office.

Pack and saddle stock and guided wilderness camping, fishing, and pack trips in the park are provided by the *Alta Silva Resort,* Star Rt., Enumclaw 98022; *Indian Creek Corral,* Naches 98937; *Andy Brown,* P.O. Box 1465, Yakima 98901; and *Bob Holeton,* Goose Prairie 98929. Lodging in the park (with reservations) is available at *Paradise Inn* and *National Park Inn.* For rates and literature write: Mt. Rainier National Park Hospitality Service, P.O. Box 1136, Tacoma 98401 (phone: 206–475–6260).

Access & Outfitting Centers

Wenatachee National Forest is reached via Interstate 90, U.S. Routes 2 and 97, and Washington Highways 209, 207, 150, 151, and 28. Lodging, supplies, guides, and wilderness outfitting service are available at Cashmere, Chelan, Cle Elum, Ellensburg, Leavenworth, and Wenatachee. Mount Rainier National Park is reached via U.S. Highway 12 and Washington Highways 123, 410, 7, 706, and 165.

**OREGON
ENCYCLOPEDIA**

Accommodations—
Vacation Lodges & Ranches

Oregon offers a wide variety of hunting and fishing and family vacation accommodations, ranging from remote wilderness camps and cabins to deluxe ranch vacation resorts. For information write to: Oregon Travel Information, State Highway Bldg., Salem 97310. If you are planning to travel along the state's scenic 300-mile-long coastline, be sure to write to the Oregon Coast Association, Box 670, Newport 97365, for their two free accommodation guides: *Northwest Pacific Coast Travel-Mate* and *Northwest Pacific Coast Travel Guide*. Many of the state's hunting and fishing resorts, camps, motels, and lodges are described in a free guide distributed by the Oregon Motor Hotel Association, 11939 S.E. Stark St., Portland 97216.

A wide variety of ranch accommodations offering fishing, hunting, and wilderness camping services are found throughout the state, from the wilderness of the High Cascades and Wallowa Mountains in northeast Oregon to the famous steelhead and salmon waters of the Rogue River country in southern Oregon's Siskiyou Mountains. The *Take It Easy Ranch Resort & Hunting Lodge*, Box 408, Fort Klamath 97362, offers what is acclaimed by many as some of the finest fly-fishing for trophy trout in the country. The resort offers top-ranked fall shooting for ducks and Canada geese on 7,000 acres of grainfields and rough cover adjoining Agency Lake, one of the most productive hunting areas on the Pacific Flyway.

Sunnyside Cattle and Guest Ranch, located 12 miles from Interstate 5, just east of Grants Pass in the famous Rogue River country, offers trout fishing, hiking, gold panning, and Indian artifacts hunting. Near Crater Lake and Oregon Caves. For additional information contact: Mel and Medora Nankervis, Route 1, Box 100, Rogue River 97537. *Blue Mountain Hot Springs Guest Ranch,* 10 miles southeast of Prairie City in historic John Day country, offers homey country-style accommodations for the entire family. Exciting panoramas of the snowcapped Blue Mountains, mountain streams for rainbow trout fishing, and miles of trails for horseback riding. For rates and open dates, write Gene and Helen Ricco, Star Rt., Prairie City 97869.

Eagle Cap Wilderness Pack Station, 78 miles east of La Grande in the rugged Wallowa Mountains, features hunting and fishing trips, progressive pack trips, and horseback riding. Located in the heart of the resort area. Cabins and lodge accommodations nearby. Wallowa Lake State Park nearby for campers. Hunting seasons, rates, and additional information available from Dick and Barb Bloir, licensed guides and outfitters, Route 1, Box 416, Joseph 97846. *J Bar L Guest Ranch,* nestled in the Blue Mountains 10 miles south of John Day. For rates and information write: Denise and Jim Condren, Canyon City 97820.

Bar M Ranch, 31 miles from Pendleton on the Umatilla River, is ideal during June, July, and August for families with school-age children. September is excellent for couples or singles. Historic log ranch house, annex, and two big cabins provide accommodations. For rates and information write: Howard P. Baker, Route 1, Adams 97810. *Rock Springs Guest Ranch,* in central Oregon 9 miles north of Bend, offers all-new cottages for singles, couples, and families. Excellent fishing, horseback riding, chuck wagon cookouts. For information write: Donna Gill, Route 2, Box 1385, Bend 97701.

Tamarack Springs Ranch, 16 miles from La Grande in the beautiful Grande Ronde Valley of northeastern Oregon, is open year-round with accommodations in a large modern house. Wintertime activities include sledding, snowmobiles, and skiing. Summertime offers fishing, hiking, hunting (in season), rodeos, and Indian festivals. For rates and

information, write: Dorothy McCurdy, Route 1, Box 61, Summerville 97876. *Boulder Park Resort,* 54 miles east of La Grande and 18 miles east of Medical Springs, caters to families, children, and seasonal deer and elk hunters. Big-game archery. Special boys' camp season, June 15–August 15, offers fishing, horses, pack trips, and ranch activities. For detailed information contact: Larry Sweet, P.O. Box 417, La Grande 97859.

Minam Lodge, not a typical "guest ranch" but a vacation facility offering excellent wilderness hunting and fishing, is accessible only by airplane or horseback. Northeast of La Grande via a 20-minute flight or an 8-mile horseback ride into the heart of the Wallowa Mountains. Season: May 1 through elk-hunting season in November. For more information write: Duane Nelson or Ev Lawrence, 8810 S.W. O'Mara, Tigard 97223. *Red's Wallowa Horse Ranch,* accessible only by pack trip or airplane, is located deep in the Wallowa Mountains east of La Grande. It offers complete accommodations for every member of the family. Special vacation, fishing, or hunting packages available on request. For rates and information contact: Carol Higgins, Box 1, La Grande 97850.

Bar DL Guest Ranch, 35 miles north of Klamath Falls via U.S. Highway 97, features the very best of fishing on Spring Creek, unlimited horseback riding, boating, hunting, and exploring. Collier State Park Logging Museum is nearby. For more information contact: Don and Phyllis Lefler, P.O. Box 517, Chiloquin 97624. Other facilities offering accommodations are: *The Branding Iron-K Corrals,* Box 49, Joseph 97846, and *Trouthaven,* P.O. Box 288, Joseph 97846.

Additional listings and descriptions of vacation lodges and guest ranches are found throughout the "Oregon Travel & Recreation Guide."

Bigfoot Country

Could there possibly be a race of manlike creatures 7–12 feet tall weighing as much as 800 pounds roaming the 125,000-square-mile area from southern British Columbia to the Cascade regions of the northwestern United States? The native Salish and Hoopa Indians have thought so for years. They call him *Sasquatch* ("wild-man-of-the-woods") or *Omah* and have long regarded certain areas of the Klamath Mountains as sacred to these primitive beings. Footprints averaging 16 inches in length have been sighted since 1840, inspiring the appellation "Bigfoot" among early white settlers.

One contemporary authority who believes in the existence of the Bigfoot is Peter Byrne, a former professional hunter who runs the Bigfoot Information Center at The Dalles. The center has been in operation for five years, partially funded by the Academy of Applied Science, and receives accounts of glimpses of the Sasquatch or of his enormous footprints. So far Mr. Byrne has collected credible reports of almost 100 sightings and many more of prints. A network of volunteers, as zealous in their faith as the followers of the Loch Ness monster, is sent out to investigate the reports. Though some people cite a single blurred footprint, the more typical report describes a trail of huge tracks sometimes extending for miles.

Could the prints be an elaborate hoax? Some anthropologists are convinced they are real, and given the depth of the prints, have speculated that the prankster would have to carry at least 500 pounds of extra weight to create such a convincing indentation. The trails suggest a nomadic creature, and the prints themselves, showing an outsized big toe, differ from those of human feet or of any apelike animal. None of the wildlife of the region leaves a track remotely similar to that of Bigfoot.

Sightings of the creature usually describe a tall, heavy, broad-shouldered fellow covered with fur, with a lipless mouth and flattened nose. He is probably vegetarian and almost certainly harmless. Bigfoot is apparently somewhat shy; in virtually all reports, he simply walks away as soon as he knows he has been seen.

Among anthropologists there has been speculation that an extinct form of apeman, called *Gigantopithecus,* once roamed through Asia. Fossils have been found on that continent which corroborate the theory. If some of these animals found their way across the Bering land bridge into North America, then the Sasquatch may very well be their modern-day descendant. Anyone who has seen the frighteningly dense, virtually impenetrable forest covering the mountains of the Pacific Northwest will realize that there are vast unexplored areas where anything—and anyone—could survive for years, hidden from view and untouched by civilization.

Year-round search expeditions for Bigfoot in southwestern Oregon and northwestern California, led by scientists, naturalists, and professional trackers are provided by *Beamer Expeditions,* P.O. Box 285, Canoga Park, CA 91305.

Camping & State Recreation Areas

Oregon is one of the best places in the country for camping, thanks to the wealth of forestland, scenic shoreline, cold, clear rivers and lakes, and the towering mountain peaks. The state park system is outstanding, offering 238 parks and recreation areas, many of them dotting the coastline. Almost all of Oregon's state parks offer campsites with drinking water and firewood. The county and private park systems are also important additions to the network of campgrounds. Boating and fishing are available, and many extra facilities can often be found. *Oregon Parks,* a free map guide available from the Oregon State Highway Division, Travel Information Section, Salem 97310, gives a complete index of parks and facilities, as well as a basic set of rules and regulations. It also features a large map of the state, showing all state, national, county, and private parks and other points of interest. *The Pacific Northwest National Forest Campground Directory,*

available free from the U.S. Forest Service–Pacific Northwest Region, 319 S.W. Pine St., P.O. Box 3623, Portland 97208, lists each national forest in the state and gives complete information on facilities. Maps of each general area are provided. Situated in some of the most spectacular scenic areas, these campgrounds are well stocked and well maintained. This guide also includes designated wilderness areas, which forbid motor vehicles and provide limited, primitive camping.

The Bureau of Land Management manages one-quarter of Oregon, which includes 15.7 million acres of national resource land. Recreation sites maintained by the BLM are shown on the *BLM Recreation Guide for Oregon,* available free from the U.S. Dept. of the Interior, Bureau of Land Management, Oregon State Office, P.O. Box 2965 (729 NE Oregon St.), Portland 97208. The major feature is a large map that shows the national resource lands, national forests, national wildlife refuges, and popular rock-hounding areas. The department will also provide maps of individual recreation areas. The *Deschutes River Area Map* covers the Deschutes River area from the Columbia River to Madras. The scale is ½ inch to 1 mile. Each sheet is 20″ × 17″, and maps are 25¢ each or 75¢ for the set. The *John Day River Area Map* covers the John Day River from the Columbia River south and east to Kimberly. The scale is ½ inch to 1 mile. Each sheet is 20″ × 17″, and maps are 25¢ each or 75¢ for the set. The *Steens Mountain Area Map* covers the area from Princeton to Alvord Lake. The scale is ½ inch to 1 mile, the size is 22″ × 17″, and each sheet is 25¢, or 75¢ for the set. All maps show BLM lands, highways, roads, and recreation sites.

Drift-Boat Fishing & Wild River Guides

Oregon's scenic and wild rivers offer unsurpassed opportunities for the drift-boat fisherman, the wilderness canoeist, and the white-water enthusiast. Most of the state's wild rivers are what geologists term "young" rivers, rushing down from their volcanic High Cascade headwaters through densely forested steep slopes and into older valleys to the Pacific Ocean. The state's major drift-boat fishing and canoeing waters include the world-famous salmon, trout, and steelhead waters of the scenic Rogue and Illinois Wild and Scenic rivers, the Umpqua, McKenzie, Clackamas, Sandy, North and South Santiam, Deschutes, and John Day rivers, and the remote Grande Ronde, Owyhee, and Snake rivers, surrounded by haunting cliffs and dark, steep-walled canyons. These rivers are described in vivid detail in the useful *Oregon River Tours* guide ($4, 118 pages) by John Garrin, published by Binford & Mort, 2536 S.E. 11th, Portland 97207. This guidebook also contains useful info and charts on river roughness, discharge, mileage, drift time, velocity and types of river craft, and car shuttling.

Drift-boating is the preferred way to fish Oregon's powerful salmon and trout streams, because the water's depth and swiftness preclude wading in most places. The famous McKenzie and Rogue-type drift boat is accepted as the ideal craft for drifting down the scenic Oregon River in search of salmon, steelhead, and trout. The McKenzie drift boat has a "rocking chair" bottom and a high transom that allow the ends of the boat to be free of the water and make it extremely maneuverable. The boat was originally a "double-ender," with a V-shaped prow on its downstream end as well as on its bow to cut through the big white-water waves common to the Rogue and McKenzie. Eventually the original "double-ender" was modified; its pointed upstream end was replaced by a small transom for using a motor in quiet water stretches.

A comprehensive listing of the state's salmon, trout, and steelhead drift-boat fishing guides is contained in the *Official Oregon Guides & Packers Directory,* available free from Oregon Guides & Packers Inc., P.O. Box 722, Lake Oswego 97034. Several long-established members of the Oregon Guides & Packers Association offer guided scenic, white-water, and drift-boat fishing trips on the state's major salmon, trout, and steelhead streams. *Lute Jerstad Adventures,* P.O. Box 19527, Portland 97219, is one of Oregon's most renowned outfitters of drift-boat fishing and wilderness white-water trips. The trip down the Snake River, dammed into silence for most of its length, roars down through one of the country's deepest canyons, from Hells Canyon to Lewiston, some 100 miles below. This journey starts just below the dam and ends 80 miles downstream at the mouth of the Grande Ronde. The first 17 miles is through the rock walls of Hells Canyon and includes four major rapids. Below Hells Canyon, the river slows somewhat and its sides alternately widen out into huge grass-covered slopes and then close in again to narrow rock gorges. Wildlife in the canyon and a sense of isolation in the midst of scenic grandeur make this a journey into a different and rarely seen world.

The Rogue River trip covers about 45 miles from Alameda Bar, in the gold-rush country, to Illahee, about 30 miles from the Pacific. In this stretch, the Rogue cuts through the Siskiyou Mountains, gaining the character of a coastal river. The Rogue Canyon is steep-sided and narrow, graced by heavy timber, and the river cuts through solid rock,

alternating quiet stretches with sudden, chutelike rapids. Zane Grey, writing in *Rogue River Feud*, describes this section of the river as having "grown to superb maturity . . . here with brooding peace, and there with eddying poise." Twisting and chafing its way down through 40 named rapids in 30 miles, the Rogue flows in a sudden rage through Mule Creek Canyon before being combed by the huge boulders of Blossom Bar. Wildlife, including deer, black bear, otter, golden eagles and osprey, abounds, protected by the cover of heavy vegetation and the regulations attendant with the Rogue's classification as a National Wild and Scenic River.

The trip down the Lower Deschutes River, named by French trappers for a series of falls in its upper reaches, flows northward along the eastern edge of the Oregon Cascades and joins the Columbia River near The Dalles.

The Three Rivers Wilderness trip begins with a 9-mile horsepack trip into Red's Horse Ranch nestled high in the Wallowa Mountains, followed by a journey down the fast-flowing scenic Minam River. Flowing through the rugged Wallowa Mountains, this river is one of the very few left in North America that, from beginning to end, is in its completely wild state. The Minam produces some of the finest rainbow trout fishing in the Pacific Northwest. The run down the Minam is followed by a trip down the House Rock Drop and Blind Falls rapids of the glacier-fed Wallowa River. This river is little used, and you will see a variety of wildlife, such as deer, elk, mink, bald eagles, and hawks. The trip ends at the take-out point at Wildcat Creek.

The trip down the wide, fast-flowing *Grande Ronde* winds its way through a deep forested canyon in the Wallowa–Whitman National Forest. Next to the remote Owyhee, it is the least-used river in Oregon and provides the wilderness traveler with a sense of true isolation. With decent water conditions, fishing can be good to excellent. June and July are the prime water-level months and weather conditions are usually very pleasant, with warm days and cool nights.

The fishing and float trip down the Owyhee, known as the "Loneliest of Rivers," located in the far southeastern corner of Oregon, combines superb white water with incredible ever-changing desert canyon scenery. Its extremely remote location and lack of access makes it the least-used river in Oregon. The Owyhee's magnificent steep-walled canyon has numerous ancient Indian caves and petroglyphs, predating any known tribe. Wildlife along the river includes deer, hawks, eagles, chukars, mink, antelope, and bobcat. Depending upon water level, the lower river often provides excellent fishing for smallmouth bass and large rainbow trout.

Leisure Outfitters, P.O. Box 7144, Salem 97303, is a renowned outfitter of guided fishing excursions for winter steelhead on famous North Coast streams, including the Nestucca, Siletz, Alsea, Wilson, Trask, and Kilchis. Guided summer steelhead trips are offered on the North and South Santiam rivers and valley streams; on the famous Deschutes in scenic canyonlands for steelhead and large trout; and on North Coast streams. Leisure Outfitters sponsors a summer steelhead expedition on the Deschutes; river trips down the scenic Middle John Day, noted for its fossil beds, Indian sites, and wildlife; and expeditions down the Lower John Day Scenic and Wild River, and Owyhee and Grande Ronde rivers.

Several other outfitters offer statewide wilderness white-water and fishing trips. *Don L. Henry*, Box 7144, Salem 97303, provides statewide steelhead, salmon, and trout fishing, elk hunting, and scenic trips, as well as educational and recreation expeditions. *Dean Helfrich Guide Service Pacific Northwest Fishing & Camping Trips* provides packaged excursions down the Rogue and Owyhee rivers and Idaho's

Middle Fork Salmon River; write: 2722 Harvest Lane, Springfield 97477. *Whitewater Guide Trips, Inc.*, 12120 S.W. Douglas, Portland 97225, offers guided excursions and salmon, steelhead, and trout fishing trips on Hells Canyon of the Snake and the Deschutes, John Day, McKenzie, Grande Ronde, and coastal streams, and operates scenic fishing and youth camps. *Wilderness Water Ways*, 33 Canyon Lake Dr., Port Costa, CA 94569, offers guided white water raft trips on the Rogue, Illinois, and Klamath rivers.

River Trips Unlimited, c/o Irv Urie, 1810 Corona Ave., Medford 97501, offers a blend of rugged white-water travel and luxurious accommodations. All of the trips are completely planned and outfitted, with time out for fishing and swimming. Meals and lodgings are in comfortable rustic cabins. *Brigg's Guide Service*, 2750 Cloverlawn Drive, Grants Pass 97526, services the mighty Rogue River. They will provide rafts or kayaks and furnish cabins and meals. *B. A. & Elaine Hanten*, 8500 Galice Road, Merlin 97532, offer a 3-day trip down the Rogue, starting at Grants Pass. They provide rubber rafts, transportation, and deluxe lodging and meals. *Jerry's Rogue River Jet Boats and Wild River Trips* offers round-trip excursions from Gold Beach up to Agness or Paradise Bar. The boat pilots point out historic and natural sights along the way. Inflatable kayaks are the main feature of *Orange Torpedo Trips*, P.O. Box 1111, Grants Pass 97526. They equip river trips for the Rogue and the Deschutes. All services, including meals and transportation, are provided, and trips last 1–3 days. Experienced guides accompany all parties, and many of the first-timers are beginners. *Court's White Water Trips* provide excursion jet boats from Gold Beach to Clay Hill Rapids or Paradise Bar. Guides explain the sights along the river. Write to them at Box 1045, Gold Beach 97444. *The Hells Canyon Navigation Co.*, Box 145, Oxbow 97840, provides both jet boat and float trips down the Snake River. Hells Canyon provides a wide variety of wildlife and scenic beauty, and drop-off fishing trips are available in the summer.

If you are planning an Oregon river trip, be sure to write for the free *Oregon Boating Guide*, available from the Oregon State Highway Division, 101 State Highway Bldg., Salem 97310. This useful, efficient guide lists each water area and the facilities, location, and recreational

services available. The *Navigation Charts: Snake River, Oregon, Washington, and Idaho*, is available for $4 (postpaid, make checks payable to the Treasurer of the United States) from the U.S. Army Engineers District, Walla Walla, Washington. It provides aerial photos, river miles, and information on rapids. The *Willamette River Recreation Guide* is available free from the Oregon State Highway Division, Travel Information, Salem, 97310. The *River Forecast Center* in Portland gives information on water levels, stages, and discharges for most of the popular boating and fishing rivers. (See "Guides, Packers & Wilderness Outfitters.")

Fenwick Oregon Fly Fishing Schools

The Fenwick Corporation's Oregon fly fishing schools are located at the famous Tu Tu Tun Lodge 7 miles up the Rogue River and at the Kah-Nee-Ta Resort Hotel on Warm Springs River on the east slope of the Cascade Range. These 2 and 3-day July and September schools include intensive instruction in the art of fly casting, insects and their life cycle, gear, artificial flies, knots and leaders, fly presentation, how to read a stream, and wading. The Rogue River school, which is for steelhead, is limited to fly fishermen with some previous experience; the Warm Springs River school is open to all. For free literature, rates, and info, write: School Coordinator, Fenwick Fly Fishing Schools, Westminster, CA 92683 (phone: 714–897–1066).

Fishing & Hunting in Oregon

The Beaver State's 50,000 miles of fishing streams, 1,600 lakes, huge tracts of national forest lands, and High Cascade wilderness areas offer some of North America's best salmon, trout, and steelhead fishing and big-game hunting opportunities. The world-famous streams of the west slope of the Cascade Range, such as the Clackamas, the North and South Santiam, the McKenzie, Upper Willamette Forks, and Sandy, offer productive fishing for native rainbows and steelhead. The large lakes and impoundments located near the headwaters of Willamette Valley streams in the Mount Hood and Willamette national forests hold rainbow and brook trout and kokanee salmon. Among the most popular of these lakes are the North Fork Reservoir and Harriet and Timothy lakes on the Clackamas River and the Detroit, Foster, and Green Peter reservoirs on the Santiam River system.

Rogue & Umpqua Rivers

The renowned Rogue and Umpqua river systems in southwestern Oregon are seldom surpassed for trophy salmon and steelhead fishing and scenic beauty. The most productive rainbow trout fishing is found along the upper stretches and headwaters areas in the Umpqua River and Rogue River national forests. The lower stretch of the Rogue and its wild river tributary flow through the Siskiyou National Forest and hold good-sized cutthroat trout. The scenic Lemolo and Toketee reservoirs in the upper Umpqua hold large brown trout, and Diamond Lake, the headwaters of the north branch of the Umpqua, is an excellent producer of rainbow trout. Howard Prairie, Hyatt, Squaw Lake and Willow Creek reservoirs in the Upper Rogue River area are fine rainbow waters. Guides and wild river outfitters are available at Grants Pass for fishing trips in McKenzie drift boats through the awesome rapids of the Rogue River Canyon to Agness or Gold Beach (see "Drift-boat Fishing & Wild River Guides"). The canyon run is one of the finest wilderness boat trips in the Pacific Northwest. Reservations should be made well in advance.

Alpine Lakes

Hundreds of remote and seldom-fished lakes dot the High Cascade backcountry and provide the wilderness traveler with superb fishing and breathtaking alpine scenery. Several major highways cross the Cascade Range divides and serve as jump-off points for access into the wilderness lake country. Numerous spur roads will take the backpacker to trailheads that wind off to such lake groups as the Olallie Lake Basin, Mount Jefferson Wilderness, Marion Lake Area, High Rock, Bull of the Woods, Mount Washington Wilderness, Three Sisters Wilderness, Mink Lake Basin, Taylor Burn, Diamond Peak Wild Area, Sky Lakes Wilderness and Rogue Headwaters Area, and the Mountain Lakes Wilderness. These high-elevation lakes hold rainbow, eastern brook, brown, and golden trout. Midsummer through late fall is the most productive period.

Eagle Cap Lakes & Streams

Some of the finest, most remote trout fishing on the continent is to be had in the spectacular, jewellike high-country lakes and streams of the Eagle Cap Wilderness, situated in the Wallowa Mountains of northeastern Oregon. Here, the hardy wilderness fisherman can follow the famous Washboard Trail and Bowman Trail to the wild Minam and Lostine rivers and the awesome Grand Canyon of the Imnaha River and Bear, Aneroid, Minam, and Green lakes. The scenic Minam offers superb fly-fishing for native rainbows, steelhead, and salmon. The alpine lakes of the Eagle Cap group hold fat cutthroat and eastern brook trout. Packers are available at several trailheads in the wilderness (see "Guides, Packers & Wilderness Outfitters" and "Wallowa–Whitman National Forest & Eagle Cap Wilderness" in the "Oregon Travel & Recreation Guide" section). This is tough, rugged country, so come prepared for possibly severe conditions.

Northeast Waters

The major streams of northeastern Oregon are the John Day, Umatilla, Grande Ronde, Wallowa, Minam, Imnaha, Eagle, Burnt, and Powder. All produce good Dolly Varden and rainbow fishing; the most productive season begins in late May following the snowmelt. The wildly beautiful John Day River Gorge, a fascinating geological "museum," offers some of the finest steelhead fishing in Oregon. The river flows through many of the world's richest fossil beds and multicolored rock formations dating back 75 million years. The Wallowa River flows out of the Wallowa Mountains through Wallowa Lake and the "Land of Winding Waters" to its junction with the Minam and Lostine rivers and on into the Grande Ronde and the Snake. Numerous campsites provide access to this fine salmon and winter steelhead stream. The Grande Ronde flows through the canyon country of northeast Oregon and is an excellent producer of steelhead and native rainbows. A packhorse outfit will lead the angler along the Snake River trail over the high backbone of the Snake River Divide into the Hells Canyon area. You can also reach the area by charter boat service or float trip from the Hells Canyon Dam. The Snake offers choice smallmouth bass fishing. Jubilee Lake, located in the remote high ponderosa pine backcountry of the Umatilla National Forest in the renowned big-game hunting region bordering on the Wenaha Backcountry Area, offers often spectacular fishing for big rainbows.

Southeast Wild Waters

Southeastern Oregon includes great expanses of rangelands and semi-desert country, but nonetheless offers excellent fishing for trophy cutthroat and rainbow trout, which grow large and fast in the semi-alkaline waters. Some of the region's best rainbow fishing is found in the upper Malheur River and the lower Owyhee; in the Donner and Blitzen River draining the west side of the beautiful Steens Moun-

tains; and in Fish and Indian creeks. Access to the streams in the Steens is difficult, for they lie in deep canyons and are reached only by trail or jeep roads.

Fish Lake in the Steens is located in a high alpine setting and holds rainbows and brook trout. The only pack-in lake in the area is Wildhorse, one of the highest lakes in the state at 8,500 feet elevation. It holds cutthroats of good size and is reached by a steep, one-mile trail from the top of Wildhorse Rim. Brightly colored native cutthroats are found in the streams of Trout Creek Mountains south of the Steens. Other productive lakes in this high plateau country include Beulah, Malheur, Antelope, Crow, Campbells, Deadhorse, and Cow lakes. Strawberry Lake, a remote pack-in lake in the Strawberry Mountain Wilderness in the Malheur National Forest, offers good fall fly-fishing for eastern brook and rainbow trout.

East Slope Trophy Trout Waters

The scenic eastern slope of the Cascade Range and central Oregon is drained by the Deschutes River, flowing northward to the Columbia and the Klamath Basin, which drains to the south. The principal tributaries of the Deschutes, named *Rivière des Chutes* ("River of the Falls") by French Hudson's Bay Company trappers, are the Little Deschutes, Fall, Metolius, Crooked, and White rivers. In the Klamath Basin the major fishing streams are the Williamson, Sprague, Wood, and Klamath.

The Deschutes Basin encompasses about 15,000 square miles and represents one of the most important recreational and fishing areas of the state. All species of trout are found here, along with exotic Atlantic salmon in Hosmer Lake (transplanted from Quebec) and kokanee salmon. Until two concrete dams were built in the middle section of the Deschutes, forming Lake Simtustus and Lake Billy Chinook, the stream was one of the truly great trout and salmon streams in the world, flowing through one of the most awesome canyons in North America and fed by pure mountain springs. Prominent fly-fishermen came from all over the world to fish it, and in the late 1940s Governor Griswold of Neveda landed the world-record summer steelhead here on a Norwegian Moustache. It is still a formidable fishing stream—in spite of the dams. The river is famous for its fat rainbows, locally called redsides. Rainbow, eastern brook, and brown trout are taken in the upper river, and browns and summer steelhead are taken below Bend.

The Metolius is one of the nation's classic dry fly-fishing streams. It is located in a scenic, parklike pine forest, and the giant springs that issue from the base of Black Butte on the east slope of the Cascades make it a full-fledged river from the start of its 35-mile course along the southern boundary of Warm Springs Indian Reservation to its confluence with the Deschutes. The fishing here is for rainbows, large browns, and Dolly Varden. A 10-mile section of the stream is reserved for fly-fishing only. The Wizard Falls fish hatchery is located near Camp Sherman in the headwaters area. Lodging, guides, and supplies are available. Other famous and productive tributaries of the Deschutes include the scenic Fall, Crooked, and Little Deschutes. The Fall River is reserved for fly-fishing only, for rainbows, browns, and brook trout. Steelhead and trout fishing guide service on the Deschutes and its tributaries is provided by: *Sam Holmes, Jr.*, 13455 S.W. 2nd, Beaverton 97005; *Oscar Lange*, Madras 97741; and *Chet Oliver*, 115 E. 2nd St., The Dalles. (See "Oregon Travel & Recreation Guide.")

The Deschutes area of the Cascade slope is dotted by hundreds of remote alpine lakes, including the famous Atlantic salmon waters of Hosmer Lake. Flies with barbless hooks are the rule in Hosmer, and the fish must be returned to the lake unharmed. Mackinaw of 20

pounds and over are caught in Odell and Crescent lakes, along with kokanee salmon. Other lakes in the central Oregon area include Crane Prairie, Wickiup, Davis, Cultus, Elk, Blue, Sparks, East, and Paulina. Klamath Lake and nearby Agency Lake produce some of the largest rainbow trout in the state, some topping 20 pounds. These lunkers run up the Williamson and Wood rivers and provide exciting fishing during late May and June. The Wood River also holds large brown trout. Klamath Lake, over 40 miles long, is the largest natural body of fresh water west of the Rockies; the remnant of an ancient inland sea, it separates the pine-clad eastern slope of the Cascades from the gray, rim-rocked hills of the Central Oregon Plateau. Crater Mountain rises to the north, Mount McLoughlin looms to the west, and the white summits of Mount Shusta can be seen to the south. The Klamath-Agency lake region is one of the greatest waterfowl-hunting areas on the Pacific Flyway.

OREGON RECORD FISH*

	Lb.–oz.	Place	Year
Brook trout	5–0*	Muskrat Lake	1974
Brown trout	24–14	Wickiup Reservoir	1959
Brown trout	35–8	Paulina Lake	1965
Dolly Varden trout	12–12	S. Fork McKenzie River	1976
Mackinaw (lake) trout	36–8	Odell Lake	1976
Rainbow trout	24–4	Klamath Lake****	1956
Rainbow trout	24–2¼	Lake Simtustus	1974
Steelhead trout	31–4	Cascade Locks	1963
Chinook salmon	83	Umpqua River	1910
Chinook salmon	62 (dressed)	Nestucca River	1970
Coho salmon	25–5¼	Siltcoos Lake	1966
Coho salmon	23	Tillamook Bay	1963
Striped bass	64–8***	Umpqua River	1973
Striped bass	61	Umpqua River	1970
Whitefish	4–0**	McKenzie River	1974
Largemouth bass	10–8	Columbia Slough	1915
Smallmouth bass	5–2	Columbia R. Pothole	1970

*Unofficial records of the Dept. of Fish & Wildlife.

**Unofficial weight.

***New world's record for fly rod.

****Huge rainbow trout was taken from Klamath Lake in 1921; no weight record.

Maps & Guides

For detailed information about fishing and hunting regulations, seasons, wildlife code, and permits, write: Information Branch, Oregon Dept. of Fish & Wildlife, 1634 S.W. Alder St., P.O. Box 3503, Portland 97208. The Fish & Wildlife Department publishes several maps and guides of use to the fisherman and hunter, including the free guides *Fishing in Oregon*, *Hunting in Oregon*, *To Catch a Steelhead*, *A Guide to Salmon & Steelhead Hatcheries*, and *Lakes of Oregon's National Forest Series*; the free leaflets *Upland Game Birds*, *Salmon of Oregon*, *Mammals of Prey*, *Big Game*, *Trout of Oregon*, *Warm-Water Lakes with Public Access*, *Oregon's Furbearers*, *Pond & Diving Ducks*, *Geese of Oregon*, *Warm-Water Game Fish*, *Hawks*, *Rock, Surf & Bay Fishes*, *Owls*, *Long-Legged Wading Birds*, and *Shore Birds of*

Oregon; and the free *Oregon Wildlife* magazine, published monthly. The free *Oregon Game Management Unit Map* shows and describes all Big Game Management Units.

Hunting in the Beaver State

Oregon is one of the nation's great hunting states for deer, elk, upland game birds, and waterfowl. The black-tailed deer is found in the brushy, logged-over lands and Douglas fir forests westward from the crest of the Cascade Range and is unique in that it lives only in the Pacific Coast states. Mule deer inhabit the pine forests and sagebrush deserts of eastern Oregon. They occasionally mix with black-tailed deer on summer ranges in the Cascades, and crosses between the two subspecies are fairly common. White-tailed deer are relatively scarce but are found in scattered numbers on both sides of the Cascades.

Two kinds of elk are found in Oregon: Roosevelt elk, also known as Olympic elk, inhabit the rain forests of the Pacific Coast, and Rocky Mountain elk roam the northeastern corner of the state and west into the Ochoco Mountains of central Oregon. During the fall, Rocky Mountain elk are found in the high country of the Blue and Wallowa

mountains. Hunting pressure has caused elk to extend their range southward into Harney and Malheur counties and also to the west. Mountain mahogany, bitterbrush, chokeberry, and sumac are favorite browse plants of Rocky Mountain elk on winter range, and willow, cottonwood, and aspen are also sought. Roosevelt elk are most often sighted in openings in the forest where logging or fire has fostered growth of shrubs, grasses, weeds, and sedges. Fir thickets become hiding places when such shelter is needed, and despite their large size, elk can move through dense cover with awesome speed and silence.

The graceful pronghorn antelope inhabits the sagebrush country of southeastern Oregon. Once numerous, the pronghorn became alarmingly scarce during the 1930s, and all hunting was prohibited. Since then they have slowly increased, and limited hunting has been permitted in recent years. Although possessing keen eyesight with which to spot enemies and capable of great speed in flight, pronghorns are extremely curious critters. A piece of cloth waving on a bush or the reflection of a mirror will often lure them within range.

Cougar, once found throughout the forests of Oregon, are now restricted to the more remote wilderness areas of the Cascade and Siskiyou mountains and are found occasionally in the Fremont National Forest in southeastern Oregon. Black bear are most often sighted in cutover or down-timber lands overgrown with brush and huckleberry in forest areas throughout the state. Bighorn sheep, once native to the mountains and high plateaus of eastern Oregon, disappeared shortly after the turn of the century. California bighorn have been successfully reintroduced into the Hart Mountain area of southeastern Oregon and in the Steens Mountains, Strawberry Mountain Wilderness, and Owyhee Canyon. In 1970 and 1971 Rocky Mountain bighorns from Alberta were transplanted into the Wallowa Mountains. Shaggy-maned mountain goat have been introduced in the Wallowa Primitive Area in the northeastern corner of the state; their preferred range is the Hurwal Divide and Sacajawea and Matterhorn mountains.

Upland game-bird hunting is extremely popular in the state for ring-necked pheasant, chukar, partridge, Hungarian partridge, valley and bobwhite quail, blue and ruffed grouse, and sage grouse. Wild turkey transplanted from southwestern states are established in eastern Oregon, with the largest numbers present in the yellow pine and scrub oak stands along the east slopes of Mount Hood. The great marshlands in Klamath, Lake, and Harney counties provide excellent hunting for snow and cackling geese, along with white-fronted and Canada geese, mallards, and pintails. Some of the best mallard shooting in the state is available along the Snake River and in the Willamette Valley. (For additional fishing and hunting information, see the "Oregon Travel & Recreation Guide" section, and "Guides, Packers, & Wilderness Outfitters," "Drift-boat Fishing & Wild River Guides," and "Salmon-Fishing Waters & Charter Boat Services," in this section.)

Guides, Packers & Wilderness Outfitters

There are many guides, packers, and outfitters in this ruggedly beautiful state. Fishing and hunting servicers are available in every part of the state, and they provide instructions and equipment for all types of river, lake, and ocean fishing, as well as for camping and big-game hunting. The *Oregon Guides and Packers Directory,* free from P.O. Box 722, Lake Oswego 97034, lists guides and packers by regional area, stating which rivers, lakes, or land areas they service. The many wilderness sports opportunities available in Oregon's national forests are serviced by several outfitters, listed by forest in *Resorts & Packers on the National Forests,* free from the U.S. Forest Service, Pacific Northwest Region, 319 S.W. Pine St., P.O. Box 3623, Portland 97208. It tells the name and address of each operator, the services provided, season of use, and things to do, and includes a map of Oregon showing national forest land, resorts, pack and saddle stock, and highways and towns.

Leisure Outfitters, Inc., offers a wide range of guided wilderness trips, including an Olympic Range headwaters expedition and coast range excursions, and runs a Goat Rocks Wilderness trail camp, a high-country trail camp in the Oregon Cascades, a Rogue River trail camp, a father-son camp, Wilderness Academy for Scouts, and a backcountry pack camp in the Umatilla National Forest, with trail riding, nature photography, and deer and elk hunting camps in the ancient hunting grounds of the Umatilla, Cayuse, Walla Walla, and Nez Percé Indians. They also offer geological expeditions and explorations with a base at the Oregon Museum of Science & Industry Lon Hancock Science Camp. Leisure Outfitters offers spring bear-hunting expeditions, a High Cascades hunt, a primitive weapons hunt, and river boat elk-hunting & steelhead-fishing trips, and operates wilderness buck and elk hunting drop camps, spike camps, and trophy camps. Summer

fly-fishing instruction is offered on the McKenzie, the Santiam, High Cascades lakes, and coastal streams. Write for detailed information and catalog (which includes a wide mail-order selection of unusual, hard-to-find gear) to: Leisure Outfitters, P.O. Box 7144, Salem 97303 (Phone: 503–364–5532).

Lute Jerstad Adventures offers several unusual high-country horsepack, camping, and fishing trips. The *Imnaha River High Country Horsepack Trip* takes you through the heart of the Eagle Cap Wilderness. The major features of this excursion, which departs from historic Indian Crossing on the main Imnaha River, include camping along the South Fork, with side trips to Deadman Point and Boner Flats, up to the North Fork of the Imnaha to the Tenderfoot Basin, over Tenderfoot Pass, and down the east fork of the Wallowa River to the head of Wallowa Lake and Aneroid Lake. Wildlife includes deer, elk, bear, and mountain goat. Hikes can be taken to rims at 9,500 feet elevation with breathtaking views of this vast alpine country. The *Washboard Trail Wilderness Trip* combines high lakes fishing for cutthroat and eastern brook trout with a horsepack trip on one of the most spectacular horseback trails in North America. The Washboard Trail is cut into a rim at 7,600 feet, and 3,000 feet below runs the wild Minam River. The trip starts from the end of Bear Creek Road out of Wallowa and passes through the rugged Granite Prong country to Bear Lake and the remote Sturgill Basin in the Eagle Cap Wilderness. The great grass meadows of the Sturgill Basin were a summer hunting camp for the Nez Percé Indians and are now a high-country summer range for elk. The final camp is near the historic Stanley Guard Station, an old V-notched log cabin built and manned as a ranger station in 1908, and one of the few original stations still standing. The *Minam River and High Lakes* horsepack and fishing trip offers fly-fishing for native rainbow trout along the Lostine River to Minam Lake, nestled high in the Eagle Cap Wilderness at 7,400 feet elevation. The major features along this route include the Big Burn; West Minam Meadows, a wildflower sanctuary of great beauty and solitude; Green Lake, renowned for large, fat brook trout; and the famous Bowman Trail. Write to Lute Jerstad Adventures, P.O. Box 19527, Portland 97219 (Phone: 503–244–4364), for detailed info and their free *Adventures Catalog*.

Wilderness Pack Trips, P.O. Box 71, Rogue River 97537, offers guided base camp and drop pack trips into the Oregon Cascades and Klamath Mountain country of the Rogue River, Siskiyou, and Umpqua national forests. (For additional listings, see "Drift-Boat Fishing & Wild River Guides" in this section and "Oregon Travel & Recreation Guide" section).

Highways—Recreation & Scenic Routes

The Oregon highway system is among the best in the nation. What began as primitive Indian and pioneer trails developed into a streamlined, fast-moving network that takes care not to mar the beauty of the country. Some of Oregon's highways are panoramic as well as functional, fitting themselves easily into their magnificent surroundings. U.S. 101 travels down the 400 miles of coastline. From your car, you can see the broad, sandy beaches, rugged headlands, interesting rock formations, picturesque lighthouses, and varied wildflowers. Beachcombers can look for driftwood and sea shells or take time out to fish or dig for clams. Interstate 80N (or the alternate upper level Scenic Highway) follows the sweeping course of the Columbia River. Huge dams, rushing waterfalls, and lofty cliffs and mountains vie for your attention. The Hood River Valley is famous for apples and pears, and numerous state parks provide recreation areas. Spectacular views

of the Columbia Gorge are one of the highlights of this scenic highway.

The free *Official Highway Map of Oregon* is available from the Oregon Dept. of Transportation, State Highway Division, Salem 97308. It shows all major and minor roads, population markers, points of interest, state parks, rest areas, airports, lighthouses, fish hatcheries, winter sports areas, and national forest lands.

Pacific Crest National Scenic Trail

The Oregon stretch of the Pacific Crest National Scenic Trail begins at the Columbia Gorge above Bonneville Dam. From the time it climbs out of the Columbia River Gorge, it follows the Cascades at altitudes from 4,000 to 7,100 feet through Oregon for 420 miles. It winds southward high on the flanks of Mount Hood, past Mount Jefferson, Three-Fingered Jack, and Mount Washington. After passing the Belknap lava area and the Three Sisters, the trail goes through a beautiful lake region, including Waldo, Odell, Crescent, and Diamond lakes. Further south it traverses Crater Lake National Park, along the uppermost crest to Fourmile Lake on the side of Mount McLoughlin, and then across Lake of the Woods Highway 140 into California near the southern end of the Cascade Range.

The trail, also known as the Oregon Skyline Trail, uses some routes first followed by animals and later by Indians, whose folklore still clings to mountain peaks and fields where they gathered olallie (huckleberries) to dry for their winter supply of food. Early trappers and trailblazers also found their way over the Cascade summits, leaving several roads that are still in use today. Barlow Pass was the first wagon road across the Cascades into the Willamette Valley. Developed by Samuel K. Barlow in 1845, it enabled the immigrants to avoid the dangerous and expensive raft trip down the Columbia River from The Dalles. Santiam Pass was first crossed in 1859 by Andrew Wiley who explored an old Indian trail up the Santiam River and worked his way farther each year on his hunting expeditions from the Willamette Valley. McKenzie Pass was named for the river explored in 1811 by Donald McKenzie, a member of Astor's Pacific Fur Company. It was opened to travel in 1862, when Felix Scott and a party of 250 men chopped their way through the forest, building the road for their 106 ox-drawn wagons as they traveled. They crossed the divide by what is known as the Old Scott Trail, 2–3 miles to the south of the present route. The Dee Wright Observatory in the pass is a memorial to a trail builder and mountain guide who, with a few Indians, drove a pack train from the Molalla Valley along the crest of the Cascades over the route later

developed as the Skyline Trail. For 24 years he was a Forest Service packer. Eleven windows spaced at intervals in the lava walls each frame a mountain peak. Peak names and distances are carved into the window frames. The lava flow, one of Oregon's most recent, came from Belknap Crater.

Careful planning on the trail is a real necessity. If you want to hike for more than a few weeks, plan to mail yourself more supplies along the way. Food and extra footwear are the most pressing items. It's also important to be aware of land use regulations, all of which differ in national forest, BLM, Indian, and privately owned lands. Wilderness permits are required for entry to all wilderness areas. They can be obtained free from an area's headquarters or ranger district station. A National Park Service–U.S. Forest Service Joint-Use Wilderness Permit is useful (and all that is needed) if you plan to hike through several types of areas. For those who want to hike the entire trail, write for one to the Cleveland National Forest, 3211 5th Ave., San Diego, CA 92103. This permit is valid for the entire trail.

If you are in a nondesignated area, you may still need a campfire permit. Check with the Forest Supervisor or the local ranger districts for specific information.

A fishing license is always required if you intend to fish, but the type depends on your age, state of residency, and length of fishing time. For details write to: Oregon State Game Commission, 1634 S.W. Alder St., P.O. Box 3503, Portland 97208.

The useful *Pacific Crest National Scenic Trail Map & Trail Log* is available free from the Pacific Northwest Region Office, P.O. Box 3623, Portland 97208. It provides a complete trail log, history and description of the trail, and nine separate area maps that show national forest boundaries, roads, the trail route, mileage, trail shelters, campsites, improved campgrounds, horse feed, ranger stations, forest service stations, lookout stations, and airstrips. The eminently useful *Pacific Crest Trail Volume 2: Oregon & Washington* ($5.95, 287 pages) published by Wilderness Press, 2440 Bancroft Way, Berkeley, CA 94704, is a superbly accurate guide to the Oregon section of the trail; it contains 140 two-color topographic maps.

Rogue National Wild & Scenic River

In *Where Rolls the Rogue*, Zane Grey wrote of his love (of the sort that only a smitten fisherman could comprehend) of this majestic, historic river. "The happiest lot of any angler would be to live somewhere along the banks of the Rogue River, the most beautiful stream in Oregon . . . a moving medium of rose and lilac, incredible to the eye." Of the picturesque beauty of the wild Rogue below Grants Pass, he wrote: "The farther we went and the higher we climbed the more beautiful grew the vistas of river, seen through iron-walled gorges, or winding white-wreathed between dark and lofty timbered mountains, or meandering through a wide fertile valley of golden cornfields and fertile orchards . . . this was wild country. I saw cougar and bear tracks along the shore, and deer were numerous. The mountains high, cone-shaped, heavily timbered on some slopes. . . . Over the bare wind-swept hills lay the sea. We had indeed trailed the wild Rogue, shot and lined its rapids, rowed its canyon-walled lanes, and glided down its innumerable riffles to its home in the Pacific."

During his long restless days of exploring the far-flung oceans of the world for record marlin and swordfish, Zane Grey dreamed of the stillness, the verdant green, and the murmuring of the Rogue at his fishing camp on the boulder-strewn shores of Winkle Bar. No man was more responsible than this legendary fisherman and author for immortalizing the Rogue and securing the art of fly-fishing for steelhead as an American sport. The great runs of salmon and steelhead and the deep holding pools at Pierce Riffle, Chair Riffle, Leaning Tree Riffle, and Weatherby Riffle have endured the test of time and gained a firm place in the history of American fishing and outdoor lore.

The Rogue, equally famous today for its wild river boating as it is for its salmon and steelhead fishing, begins high in the Cascades near Crater Lake in Seven Lakes Basin, where it is a cold, clear stream, and carves its way west through the coastal mountains for 200 miles to the Pacific. The Rogue, named by early French fur trappers *la Rivière Aux Coquins*, "the River of the Rogues," after the warlike Indians in the area (another version has it that they named it *Rouge*, or "Red," for the color it takes on during flooding), is commonly divided into three sections by fishermen and boaters: Upper, Middle, and Lower. The upper river extends from below Grants Pass upstream through the Valley of the Rogue past Shady Grove, Needle Rock, and Cascade Gorge, through the Rogue River National Forest past Rogue River Camp, Union Creek Resort, and Minnehaha Camp to its High Cascade headwaters. The twisting Upper Rogue is a top-ranked trout stream with some healthy runs of summer and winter steelheads and chinook salmon, particularly in the famed Pierce Riffle below Savage Rapids Dam and in the Leaning Tree Riffle. Points of interest along the upper river include the scenic Mill Creek Falls, the Natural Bridge, and Rogue River Gorge. Several U.S. Forest Service campgrounds are located at strategic points along the upper river, surrounded by cool forests of Douglas fir, sugar pine, ponderosa pine, white fir, and white pine.

The wild river wilderness of the Middle Rogue flows from Grants Pass to Brushy Bar through the picturesque Hellgate and Mule creek canyons, past towering cliffs and timbered slopes, and through rocky chutes, rapids, riffles, and deep pools, including the historic Whitehorse Riffle, Brushy Chutes, Galice and Rocky riffles, Chair Riffle, Grave Creek Riffle, Wildcat and Tyee rapids, the Washboard, Windy Creek Chute, Black Bar Falls, Horseshoe Bend, Winkle Bar, Battle and Missouri bars, John's Riffle, Marial Lodge, Stair Creek Falls, Blossom Bar Rapids, Paradise Bar, Huggins Canyon, and Brushy Bar.

From Grants Pass to Hellgate Canyon, the Rogue is an easy 19-mile stretch of water with small, regular waves, clear passages, even riffles, and sandbars. The 13-mile stretch from Hellgate Canyon to Grave Creek has numerous rocks, eddies, and irregular waves, with clear but narrow passages. At Grave Creek the Rogue enters its 26-mile-long wilderness stretch, with a dizzying succession of long violent rapids, powerful and irregular waves, dangerous rocks, and swirling eddies. After the 6-foot drop at Grave Creek Falls is Rainie Falls, a vertical

10-foot drop requiring portaging or lining. The remaining stretch of the wild river, which brawls and spumes through Mule Creek Canyon, is a boiling white-water roller coaster with strange, violent cross currents and sudden eddies, surrounded by incredibly steep and extremely narrow canyon walls, in some places 50 feet high and only 15 feet across. Campgrounds along the Wild Rogue are located at Illake, Brushy Bar, Tucker Flat, Kelsey Creek, Meadow Creek, Horseshoe Bend, Russian Creek, Big Slide, Whisky Creek, and Rainie Falls.

The famed salmon and steelhead waters of the Middle Rogue are fished from shore or from guided drift boats. Flat-bottomed, high-bowed McKenzie-style drift boats and rubber rafts are generally used for floating the Rogue River. Boats should be broad-beamed to prevent capsizing and easily maneuverable with oars to avoid obstacles. Canoes and kayaks are unsafe in many of the rapids below Grave Creek, so their use should be limited to the river above that point. The wild river sections of the Rogue are for drift boats and rafts, but jet boats, outboards, and other major motorboats run the river above and below those sections. Commercially guided float trips begin at several boating sites between Grants Pass and Grave Creek. They offer trips of 3–8 days' duration. Some make overnight stops at commercial lodges along the river, while others camp out at public recreation sites. Be sure to write to: Supervisor's Office, Bureau of Land Management, Medford 97501, for regulations and boating permit information.

Grants Pass, the commercial outfitting center on the river, offers salmon and steelhead guide services and wild-water touring services. Several members of the Oregon Guides and Packers Association are headquartered at Grants Pass 97526. *Robert D. Bell*, 1176 Fruitdale Dr., offers guided salmon and steelhead-fishing trips on the Rogue and its wild-river tributary, the Illinois. *Briggs Guide Service*, 2750 Cloverlawn Dr., offers Rogue River Canyon fishing and scenic trips. *Tom Keith*, 788 Carol Dr., offers steelhead fishing in McKenzie drift boats on the Rogue and Illinois and scenic rubber raft trips. *Mel Norrick*, Box 841, offers fishing and scenic trips on the Rogue, Illinois, and Chetco rivers. *Bill Pruitt* offers guided fishing trips on the Rogue and Illinois and fall big-game hunting in the outlying wilderness. At nearby Medford, 97501, headquarters of the Rogue River National Forest, salmon, trout, and steelhead drift-boat fishing and scenic trips on the Rogue and Illinois rivers are offered by *Paul Brown*, P.O. Box 855; *Jerry Pringle*, 1570 Spring St.; and *Irv Urie*, 1810 Corona Ave., who also offers scenic 3 and 4-day trips for steelhead on the Rogue, Upper Rogue, Umpqua, Illinois, Chetco, Winchuck, Pistol, Smith, and Klamath rivers. For additional information write: *Rogue River Guides Association*, P.O. Box 792, Medford 97501, for free listing of over 70 members. For fishing and hunting lodge info write: *Grants Pass Chamber of Commerce*, 131 N.E. "E" St., Grants Pass 97526.

First-class accomodations, float-trip and guide service on the Rogue are provided by two rustic, long established fishing and vacation resorts: *Weasku Inn* (5560 Rogue River Hwy., Grants Pass 97526;

phone 503-479-2455) and *Morrison's Lodge* (8500 Galice Rd., Merlin 97532; phone 503-476-3825).

The Lower Rogue, from the town of Agness at the confluence of the Illinois Wild River tributary, is a mild, scenic stretch of water that flows through Copper Canyon and Crooked Riffle on to the mouth of the Rogue on the Pacific at Gold Beach, past the renowned steelhead and chinook and coho salmon fishing areas at Lobster Creek, Hawkins, Coal, and Gillespie riffles. The most popular fly patterns on the Rogue include the Rogue River Special, Silver Ant, Red Ant, Golden Demon, Juicy Bug, Weatherwax, and Royal Coachman Bucktail.

The wild Middle Rogue is paralleled by the Rogue River Trail from Grave Creek to Illahe. The trail is strictly for hikers and backpackers; it is closed to motorized vehicles, horses, and pack animals. The trail is well constructed and has moderate grades. If reasonable precautions are taken, the hike is comparatively safe, although hikers should always be wary of slides or washouts. Early summer and fall is the best time to hike the trail. Later in the season, temperatures are higher, but morning and evening hiking avoids midday heat.

Hikers normally take about 5 days for the entire distance. This allows time to stop and enjoy the scenery and to study the geology, plants, and wildlife along the way. A road reaches the river at Marial for those who want a shorter trip. Several primitive campsites are located along the trail, but facilities are limited.

The trail follows the most exciting part of the river. Grave Creek, the starting point, was named for the death of a young girl who was passing through with her family in 1846. The Indians dug up her body, stripped it of its clothing, and hung it over the branches of a tree as a mute, terrible warning to the white invaders. The beginning of the trail is very rocky. Old cabin sites and unusual rock formations occupy the banks, and hikers can stop to watch boats being lowered down treacherous Rainie Falls. After Tyee Rapids, a primitive campsite appears at Russian Creek. Tyee Bas was once a famous gold diggings. In the early days, some 300 Chinese took a million dollars in gold dust here. Deer and other wildlife stop to feed here, and interesting animal tracks can be detected in the soft sand. Bronco Creek, a few miles later, was originally named Jackass Creek in 1855 because of the loss of a pack mule as some men were trying to evade a band of Indians. Battle Bar is named after the skirmish that occurred during the Rogue River Indian War of 1855–56. Winkle Bar, a mile downstream from Battle Bar, is a stretch of rolling water named for pioneer prospector William Winkle and is the site of Zane Grey's famous summer steelhead fishing camp—now owned by the president of Levi Strauss Co. The Rogue River Ranch, at Mile 23, is managed by the Bureau of Land Management, and provides emergency aid. The first white man to settle in the area built a cabin just a short distance downriver from here, in 1880.

Mule Creek Canyon was named in the summer of 1852 when a company of soldiers from Fort Oxford tried to open a trail along the Rogue. A member of the party later related that a Lt. R. S. Williamson rode a mule named John. When the mule was turned loose to graze along the stream, it wandered off and was not found despite a thorough search. The men promptly named the stream John Mule Creek, but the name was later shortened. The story has a happy ending: years later Lieutenant Williamson found his mule in the possession of an Indian at Siletz.

Downriver from Mule Creek, you can overlook the famous Coffee Pot, a churning whirlpool of crosscurrents. Brushy Bar was the site of a large gold-mining operation around the turn of the century. In 1905

a fire burned all summer long, and the resultant vegetation was, for a time, low brush, hence the bar's name. Flora Dell Creek offers a trailside pool which is perfect for a restful swim.

The trail ends at the site of a historical Indian burial ground. Trenches, once built in the forest as fortification against the Indians, are still intact.

The observant wilderness traveler along the remote stretches of the Rogue may see great blue herons with their six-foot wingspread, common mergansers, belted kingfishers, water ouzels, cliff swallows and their mud-walled nests, ospreys, bald eagles, pileated woodpeckers, blue and ruffed grouse, California quail, and waterfowl. Rogue River country is also inhabited by black-tailed deer, Roosevelt elk, black bear, otter, raccoon, and rattlesnakes.

Vegetation along the river includes some botanical rarities. Trees include Oregon ash, bigleaf maple, Pacific madrone, Oregon white oak, western red cedar, Port Orford cedar, Pacific yew, canyon live oak, golden chinquapin, tan oak, Oregon myrtle, Douglas fir, western hemlock, grand fir, and sugar pine. Brewer spruce, knobcone pine, and pitcher plants are found in remote areas. Side streams are lined with rhododendrons, azaleas, Pacific dogwood, Oregon grape, salal, salmonberry, and a variety of ferns.

An excellent guide to the trail, *Rogue River Trail*, is available free from the Bureau of Land Management, 310 West Sixth St., Medford 97501. It provides a complete log of the trail, describing interesting points and campsites. It also provides information on and sketches of the foliage found along the river, and a foldout map that shows roads, campsites, and creeks that feed into the river. *The Rogue Wild &*

Scenic River Map is also available free from the Bureau of Land Management Office (address above). It gives a detailed description of the river and its history, including information on wildlife, major rapids, safety rules, and the Rogue River Trail. This large full-color map of the river shows forest and BLM lands, campsites, highways, roads and trails, recreation sites, boating sites, buildings, and mines. The river and its tributaries are also shown on the full-color *Rogue River National Forest Recreation Map*, available for 50¢ from: Super-

visor's Office, Rogue River National Forest, Medford 97501. A detailed guide, *West Coast River Touring—Rogue River Canyon and South,* provides descriptions of scenery and drainage, flow predictions, and ratings for canoes and rafts. Maps of the Rogue mark runs, creeks, roads, put-ins and take-outs. The book costs $6.95 and can be ordered from: Touchstone Press, P.O. Box 81, Beaverton 97005. The Rogue River is shown on the following U.S. Geographic Survey topographic maps: Agness, Butte Falls, Collier Butte, Diamond Lake, Galice, Garwood Butte, Glendale, Gold Beach, Gold Hill, Grants Pass, Lakecreek, Marial, Medford, Port Orford, Prospect, Rustler Peak, and Trail.

Salmon-Fishing Waters & Charter Boat Services

Captain Robert Gray sailed his ship *Columbia* into a great western river and found a tribe of Indians living on huge salmon, which abounded in this stream he named after his ship. The Indians were Chinooks, and the salmon became known by the same name. Both the chinook salmon and the smaller coho salmon are abundant in Oregon's waters. The most popular methods of salmon angling are trolling, anchoring, and mooching, depending on the current and type of water. Good strong gear is necessary, because chinooks often reach weights between 15 and 25 pounds. Some weighing nearly 100 pounds have been caught in the Columbia in nets, and the chance for a "sockdolager" of 50 or more pounds is always there.

Oregon Salmon Fishing, a free brochure available from the Oregon State Highway Division, Salem, describes all the major salmon streams, including the famed Rogue, Willamette, Nestucca, Siletz, Alsea, Siuslaw, Umpqua, Coquille, Chetco, Sides, Pistol, and Winchuck rivers and Tillamook Bay, and tells what kind of gear and bait to use. A map shows the location of the state's fisheries. A complete listing and description of salmon charter boat operators and fishing guides is contained in the *Oregon Guides & Packers Official Directory,* available free upon request by writing: Oregon Guides & Packers, Inc., P.O. Box 722, Lake Oswego 97034. (See "Fishing & Hunting in Oregon.")

Ski Touring & Snowshoeing

Oregon's vast national forest lands, high cascade wilderness areas, and thousands of miles of scenic logging roads and trails offer the cross-country skier and winter camping enthusiast unlimited opportunities. A free *Winter Travel in the National Forests* booklet and *Avalanche* brochure may be obtained by writing to: Pacific Northwest Region, U.S. Forest Service, 319 S.W. Pine St., P.O. Box 3623, Portland 97208. A useful paperback called *Oregon Ski Tours* is available from: Touchstone Press, P.O. Box 81, Beaverton 97005 for $5.95. It describes 65 cross-country ski tours in detail, with information on safety, equipment, and planning the trip. Simple maps for each area are included. A *General Guide to Central Oregon Cross-Country Skiing* may be obtained for $1 by writing to: Bend Chapter, Oregon Nordic Club, Bend 97701.

For information on ski-touring trails and tours in the *Anthony Lakes area* and the historic Elkhorn Mountains, accommodations, and transportation services write: Anthony Lakes Corporation, P.O. Box 1045, Baker 97814. Write to Cooper Spur Inc., Hood River 97031, for the nitty gritty about ski-touring and snowshoeing trails, rentals, and accommodations in the *Cooper Spur Area* located in the "weather lee" on the north side of Mount Hood. Beautiful *Crater Lake National Park,* located in the high Cascades of southern Oregon, offers scenic cross-country ski tours on trails around the rim of volcanic Crater Lake. Write: Superintendent, Crater Lake National Park, P.O. Box 7, Crater Lake 97604. The scenic Tipsoo, Thielsen, and Pacific Crest trails in the *Diamond Lake roadless area* of the Umpqua National Forest offer outstanding ski-touring and snowshoeing opportunities. For information and the free *Diamond Lake Snow Trails Map,* write: Diamond Lake District Ranger, Box 101, Idleyld Park 97447. The Hoodo Bowl on the crest of the Cascades at Santiam Pass offers cross-country trails and access to the Pacific Crest Trail and spur trails around scenic Three Fingered Jack. Write: Hoodo Ski Bowl, Box 20, Sisters 97759. The Mount Bachelor ski area and Three Sisters Wilderness to the west offer excellent cross-country skiing and snowshoeing trails. Write: Mount Bachelor Ski Area, Route 3, Box 450, Bend 97701. Spout Springs area in northeastern Oregon was the training site of the U.S. Olympic Nordic racing team and offers an excellent system of trails. Write: Spout Springs, Route 1, Weston 97886. (For more information on the national forests and wilderness areas, see the "Oregon Travel & Recreation Guide" section.)

Wild & Scenic River Maps

Useful, attractive wild-river scroll maps showing all rapids, falls, gradients, campsites, islands, and contours of canyons are available for the *Rogue River* ($5.60) and *McKenzie River* ($7.00) from: *Western Whitewater,* c/o Leslie Allen Jones, Star Rt. Box 13, Heber City, UT 84032. These handy waterproof maps also contain fascinating historical information and descriptions of river features.

The following U.S. Geological Survey topographic large-scale map kits show the entire lengths of several of the famous Oregon fishing streams (see "Oregon Travel & Recreation Guide" for additional listings) and the topography of the surrounding wilderness areas, including rapids, falls, trails, campgrounds, forest cover, contours, and wilderness cabins. *Chetco River:* Cape Ferrelo, Chetco Pk., Collier Butte, Mount Emily, and Pearsoll Pk.; *Clackamas River,* including North Fork, Oak Grove Fork, Roaring River, Timothy and Olallie buttes; *Upper John Day River:* Aldrich Mountain, Bates, Clarno, Dale, John Day, Kimberly, Kinzua, Monument, Mount Vernon, Picture Gorge, Prairie City, Ritter, Spray, and Susanville; *Little Deschutes River:* Anns Butte, Cryder Butte, Finley Butte, and La Pine; *Owyhee River & Lake:* Owyhee, Mitchell Butte, Grassy Mountain, Owyhee Dam, and Jordan Valley (1:250,000 scale map); *Walla Walla River:* Bone Spring, Bowlus Hill, Peterson Ridge, and Tollgate; *Grande Ronde River:* Andtone (WA), Limekiln Rapids (WA), Saddle Butte (WA).

OREGON TRAVEL & RECREATION GUIDE

Deschutes National Forest & High Cascades Wilderness Areas

Deschutes National Forest Topo Maps

U.S. Geological Survey overview maps, scale 1:250,000: Bend, Crescent.

Deschutes Wild & Scenic River—The "River of Falls"

U.S. Geological Survey large-scale topo maps: Ann Butte, Bend, Benham Falls, Dant, Eagle Butte, Erskine, Fly Creek, Forked Horn Butte, Gateway, Kaskela, La Pine, Madras W., Maupin, Pistol Butte, Redmond, Round Butte Dam, Seekseequa Jct., Sherers Bridge, Sinamox, Steelhead Falls, Summit Ridge, Tumalo, Wickiup Dam, and Wishram.

Diamond Peak Wilderness

U.S. Geological Survey large-scale maps: Chucksney Mountain, Waldo Lake.

Hosmer Lake Atlantic Salmon Waters

U.S. Geological Survey large-scale map: Elk Lake.

Metolius River Trophy Trout Waters

U.S. Geological Survey large-scale maps: Fly Creek, Sisters, Three-Fingered Jack, Whitewater River.

Pacific Crest Trail

U.S. Geological Survey large-scale maps: Three Sisters, Elk Lake, Packsaddle Mountain, Irish Mountain, The Twins, Waldo Lake, Odell Lake, Crescent Lake.

Three Sisters Wilderness

U.S. Geological Survey large-scale maps: Crane Prairie Reservoir, Elk Lake, Irish Mountain, Rocksaddle Mountain, Three Sisters.

The 1,588,000-acre Deschutes National Forest is located on the eastern slope of the southern Cascades in one of the great fishing regions of the Pacific Northwest and encompasses the headwaters of the Metolius and Deschutes rivers. Within this great forest rises Newberry Crater, an extinct volcano with cinder cores, boiling sulfur springs, fields of yellow and black and red obsidian glass, and blue mountain lakes. The name Deschutes derives from the fur-trading era, when the river was known as *Rivière des Chutes*, meaning "river of falls." The French trappers used the name because the stream poured into the Columbia River near the falls of that area in the days prior to The Dalles Dam. When Lewis and Clark passed its mouth in 1805, they referred to it in their journals by its Indian name, "Towahnah-looks," and renamed it for Captain Clark. But the name applied later by the fur traders of the Hudson's Bay Company prevailed.

The major features of the forest, including forest roads, trails, campgrounds, ranger stations, and portions of the Mount Jefferson, Three Sisters, Mount Washington, and Diamond Peak wilderness areas, are shown on the *Deschutes National Forest Recreation Map*, available for 50¢ from: Forest Supervisor, 211 Northeast Revere, Bend 97701. A network of over 400 miles of trails leads off to the remote interior areas, including the Pacific Crest Trail as it winds past Mount Jefferson, Three-Fingered Jack, and Mount Washington, through the Belknap lava fields, and on past the Three Sisters into the alpine lake country. The Deschutes River, a renowned canoe route and one of the most famous trout streams in the region, rises in the lava lakes and flows south for 85 miles through Crane Prairie and Wickiup reservoirs. The upper Deschutes has some excellent fly-fishing for good-sized

rainbows and browns. In some areas the river flows through private ranches, and permission should be obtained. Wickiup Reservoir has produced brown trout up to a hefty 24 pounds, and Crane Prairie Reservoir produces an occasional lunker rainbow up to 18 pounds. Crescent Lake, shadowed by Diamond Peak and surrounded by good forest roads, has superb early-season angling for kokanee, blueback salmon, rainbow, and some lake trout up to 25 pounds. The best time for the big lakers is just after ice-out, using lightweight tackle on the shoals near the east side of the lake. Odell Lake is one of the largest natural lakes in the state, located north of Crescent Lake on the east slope of the Cascades; it is well known for large rainbow, kokanee, Dolly Varden, and lake trout or mackinaws to over 25 pounds. Land-locked blueback salmon are abundant and grow to tremendous size in Odell. Well-maintained forest camps are located along the north, south, and east shores. To the south of Cultus Mountain, Big and Little Cultus lakes offer good fishing for rainbow, brook, kokanee, and lake trout. The hundreds of alpine lakes and streams hold rainbow, brook, cutthroat, and golden trout.

The high-country hunting in the forest is excellent for mule and blacktail deer, black bear, and Roosevelt elk. A few pronghorn antelope summer along the eastern edge of the forest. The majestic Roosevelt elk inhabit the Cascade and Olympic mountains from Vancouver through Washington and Oregon. Their antlers are noticeably thicker than those of the Rocky Mountain elk but are neither as long nor as wide, since the Roosevelt elk live in denser brush and forest. During the early fall days, the elk slowly begin to drift down from the high country as the rut and hunting season begins. With the onset of the mating season, their reddish brown summer coats turn slightly gray, and the bull elks' necks swell out as the big animals produce their whistling bugle call. A bull elk will usually take charge of a cow herd, driving the yearlings and older bulls out. The unattached bachelor bulls are those that will most often answer the elk whistle of a hunter or guide. In addition to the big game, there is good shooting along the large lakes for mallards and Canada geese. Upland game birds include the blue and ruffed grouse, valley and mountain quail, and chukar partridge.

The Three Sisters Wilderness is a vast, 196,708-acre preserve located astride the High Cascades in the Willamette and Deschutes national forests about 45 miles due east of Eugene. Of the Three Sisters, the North Sister, at 10,094 feet, is the most formidable climb. The main route is up the lower slopes of the North Sister to a col near the head of Collier Glacier. The climb then proceeds up a steep talus slope and includes a hazardous traverse of a large pinnacle at 9,825 feet. The Middle Sister requires the same approach up the north ridge to the peak. The popular South Sister nestles a crystal clear lake in a crater at 10,200 feet. The Three Sisters have fourteen glaciers on their slopes, including the massive 1½-mile-wide and ¾-mile-long Collier Glacier, the largest in Oregon. If you think you are seeing smoke clouds at the high elevations, they are most likely pulverized rock blown off the glaciers by the strong winds. Numerous trails lead into the interior hunting and camping areas near the Husband (7,520 ft.), Broken Top (9,165 ft.), Wife (7,045 ft.), and Little Brother (7,822 ft.), passing through lava fields, glaciers, meadows, high forests of fir and mountain hemlock, and along the shores of hundreds of mountain lakes and ponds. The trail network contains over fifty miles of the Pacific Crest Trail.

For the alpine fisherman, three chains of lakes lie off the western slope of the wilderness: Mink Lake Basin, the Horse Lake group, and the Sisters Mirror group. Mink Lake is the largest—350 acres of water lying at 6,000 feet elevation near the headwaters of the McKenzie River. Fishing here is good for brook trout from 6 to 20 inches. Access

is by the Skyline Trail or the Six Lakes Trail. Saddle horses can be rented at the Elk Lake resort. The Horse Lake chain, including Moonlight, Herb Park, and Mile lakes, offers good fly-fishing potential. The Sisters Mirror basin lies on Wickiup Plains, south of Three Sisters, with access by the Wickiup Trail, by the Skyline Trail from Horse Lake basin, or by a 4-mile hike from Devils Lake Camp. The fishing is only fair, but the alpine scenery is breathtaking. Nearby, the glacial Chambers Lake basin holds cutthroat trout. The wild interior areas of the Three Sisters have good hunting for trophy-size mule deer, elk, and some black bear. Blue and ruffed grouse are the main game birds. Campsites are numerous in the surrounding national forests. If you are planning midsummer hiking, be prepared for swarms of mosquitoes. The full-color *Three Sisters Wilderness Map*, showing all topographic features, forest service trails, shelters, campsites, ranger stations, woodlands, and the Pacific Crest National Scenic Trail, may be obtained for 50¢ by writing to the Deschutes National Forest Supervisor's Office (address above). For detailed hunting, fishing, and wilderness camping info write: Sisters Ranger Station, Sisters 97759.

The Diamond Peak Wilderness area embraces 35,400 acres astride the Cascade Crest in the southwestern portion of the forest, due west of scenic Odell and Crescent lakes. The major features of the wilderness, including Summit Lake, the Calapooya Mountains, and the Pacific Crest, Crater Butte, Diamond Peak, Bear Mountain, and Fawn Lake trails, are shown on the full-color *Diamond Peak Wilderness Map*. This map (50¢) and trail, mountain climbing, wilderness camping, fishing, and hunting information may be obtained by writing: District Ranger, Crescent Ranger Station, Crescent 97733. Diamond Peak, elevation 8,744 feet, is considered one of Oregon's ten major peaks by mountain climbers. Climbers should always travel in organized groups, fully equipped and under the leadership of competent and experienced guides.

For additional information about fishing and hunting, campgrounds, and wilderness permits and trails, and for the free publications *Deschutes National Forest Fishing Directory* and *Hunting in the Deschutes National Forest*, write to the Supervisor's Office (address above) or to the following District Ranger Offices: 211 Northeast Revere, Bend 97701; Crescent 97733; Sisters 97759. The fishing directory contains useful info about the forest's alpine fly-fishing lakes, big water lakes, rivers and streams, and reservoirs, including location, route of access, elevation, size, depth, and fish species present.

Wilderness outfitting, pack and saddle stock, and fishing and hunting guide service in the Deschutes National Forest and adjacent wilderness areas are provided by: *Buck Buckingham*, Sisters 97759, pack and hunting trips; *Crescent Lake Trail & Pack Service*, Crescent Lake 97425; *Hugh Harris*, Camp Sherman 97730, horse rentals and trail rides in the Camp Sherman–Black Butte area; *William J. Klein*, P.O. Box 349–C, Bend 97701, fall hunting and pack trips in Three Sisters Wilderness; *Ray Malott*, Rt. 1, Redmond 97756, fall hunting and pack trips in Three Sisters Wilderness; *Steve Van Sickle*, Box 42, Sisters 97759, guide services, pack and hunting trips in the Three Sisters Wilderness and Broken Top area. Lodging, supplies and boat rentals in the forest are provided by: *Bachelor Butte Lodge*, c/o Mt. Bachelor Inc., 930 Wall St., Bend 97701; *Camp Sherman Store*, Camp Sherman 97730; *Crescent Lake Resort*, c/o David F. Armond, Crescent Lake 97425; *Cultus Lake Lodge*, c/o William H. Wren, P.O. Box 262, Bend 97701; *East Lake Resort*, c/o Milton G. Apel, 525 State St., Bend 97701; Elk Lake Resort, P.O. Box 789, Bend 97701; *Gales Landing–Crane Prairie Reservoir and Lava Lake*, c/o K. Gales, 930 Newport Ave., Bend 97701, 36 boats, fuel, store; *Odell Lake Resort*, c/o D. L. Garcia, Crescent Lake 97425; *Odell Summit Lodge*, Odell Lake, c/o Flaten, Askew & Askew, Cascade Summit 97418; *Paulina Lake Lodge*, c/o Howard C. Reed, La Pine 97739; *Robideaux Landing*, Crane Prairie Boat Rentals, c/o R. F. Nelson, 1625 E. 12th St., The Dalles 97058; *Suttle Lake Resort*, Sisters 97759; *Shelter Cove Marina*, Odell Lake, Cascade Summit 97418; *Twin Lakes Resort*, c/o W. H. Wren, P. O. Box 262, Bend 97701. Lodging and guide service on the Metolius River is provided by *Ford's Metolius River Cottages* (Box 110) and *House on the Metolius*, both Camp Sherman 97730; and, *Deschutes Guide Service, Inc.*, 585 5th, Madras 97741.

Access & Outfitting Centers

The Deschutes National Forest is reached via U.S. Highways 20 and 97 and Oregon Highways 31, 51, 58, 126, 22, and 242. The Diamond Peak Wilderness can be reached from the Willamette Valley or central Oregon via the Willamette Highway (58) or forest roads. The Three Sisters Wilderness is accessible by the Willamette Highway, Oregon Highway 126, and forest roads. Lodging, supplies, guides, and wilderness outfitting service are available at Crescent, Crescent Lake, La Pine, Sunriver, Bend, Redmond, and Sisters.

Fremont National Forest & Gearhart Mountain Wilderness

Fremont National Forest Topo Maps

U.S. Geological Survey 1:250,000 scale overview maps: Crescent, Klamath Falls.

Gearhart Mountain Wilderness

U.S. Geological Survey large-scale maps: Fishole Mountain, Harvey Creek, Lee Thomas Crossing, Sandhill Crossing, Shake Butte.

The Fremont National Forest encompasses 1,194,000 acres in south central Oregon on the east slope of the Cascade Range. The forest, named after Capt. John C. Fremont, who along with Kit Carson, the guide and frontiersman, led one of the first exploration parties through southern Oregon, is divided into two distinct sections: one area encompasses the Warner Mountains from Abert Rim to the California border; the other encompasses the mountains between Lakeview and Klamath Falls, bordered by the Deschutes Forest on the north, the Winema Forest on the west, and California on the south. Numerous forest roads and trails provide access to interior areas such as the Black

Hills, Sycan Flat, Coleman Rim, Gearhart Mountain Wilderness, Lower Fishole, Barnes Rim, and Lake Abert. The Abert Rim, along the east side of Lake Abert, is the largest and most exposed geologic fault in North America, rising nearly 2,500 feet above the lakeshore, with a 640-foot vertical lava cliff at the topmost part. When Fremont saw Abert Lake in 1843, during his search for the mythical Buena Ventura River that was supposed to flow from Klamath Lake into San Francisco Bay, it was 50 square miles of water. In years when rainfall has been below normal, however, it has been completely dry.

Gearhart Mountain Wilderness contains some of the oldest volcanic domes in western Lake County. Gearhart Mountain, at 8,364 feet, is the highest and oldest. After the original volcanic material cooled and moistened, glaciers carved out a large amphitheater known as the Head of Dairy Creek. Today, its impressive headwalls tower over a primitive camping area of mountain meadows and springs. More than 20 miles of trails provide access to such areas as the Gearhart Marsh, Lee Thomas Meadow, Deadhorse Lake, Yoden Flat, Swing Field, Haystack Rock, and Campbells Lake. Three miles from the southeast entrance to Trail 100 lies the Dome, with its massively eroded cliffs 300 feet high stretching westward from the 7,380-foot dome for almost a mile. A half mile from the same trailhead are the stark sentinel-like hoodoos (columns of rock in fantastic shapes) of the Palisades. The wilderness is an important summer and fall range for Rocky Mountain mule deer. Other game includes black bear, wildcat, coyote, mountain lion, and blue grouse. For trail guides, a free *Gearhart Mountain Wilderness Map*, and regulations, write to: District Ranger, Bly 97622. Nearby, the Sprague River flows for about 90 miles, much of it through the Klamath Indian Reservation, and offers good fishing for rainbows to 3 pounds and browns. The Chewaucan River is the largest and finest trout stream in the forest. The river rises in the mountains northwest of Lakeview and flows in a northerly direction for about 50 miles into the Chewaucan Marsh. The Chewaucan offers superb dry fly-fishing for native rainbows. To the south, on the California-Oregon border, large, shallow Goose Lake is an excellent waterfowl shooting area.

The full-color *Fremont National Forest Recreation Map*, available for 50¢ from the Forest Supervisor, P.O. Box 551, Lakeview 97630, shows forest roads, trails, boating sites, ranger stations, campgrounds, and points of interest, including the Warner Canyon Ski Area, Slide Mountain Geologic Area, and Mitchell Recreation Area. For detailed fishing, hunting, and wilderness camping information, write to the Forest Supervisor or District Ranger at: Bly 97662; Lakeview 97630; Paisley 47636; or Silver Lake 97638.

Access & Outfitting Centers

Fremont National Forest is reached by U.S. Highway 395 and Oregon Highways 140 and 31. Lodging, supplies, fishing, and big-game hunting guides and outfitters are located at Bly, Lakeview, Valley Falls, Paisley, Summer Lake, and Silver Lake.

Malheur National Forest & Hart Mountain National Antelope Range

Malheur National Forest Topo Maps

U.S. Geological Survey overview maps, scale 1:250,000: Burns, Canyon City.

Malheur National Wildlife Refuge

U.S. Geological Survey large-scale maps: Dot Mountain, Lawen, Crane, Coyote Buttes, Jackass Butte NE, Diamond Swamp; and 1: 250,000 scale overview map: Burns.

Steens Mountain & Hart Mountain National Antelope Range

U.S. Geological Survey overview map, scale 1:250,000: Burns.

Strawberry Mountain Wilderness

U.S. Geological Survey large-scale maps: John Day, Logan Valley, Prairie City, Seneca.

The Malheur National Forest, an outstanding hunting, fishing, and wilderness camping region, encompasses 1,470,000 acres in the southwestern portion of the Blue Mountains and contains the headwaters of the Malheur, Silvies, and John Day rivers. The major features of the forest, including the Aldrick Mountains and Strawberry Mountains Wilderness, are shown along with campgrounds and recreation sites on the *Malheur National Forest Recreation Map,* available for 50¢ from: Forest Supervisor's Office, John Day 97845. Mule deer and Rocky Mountain elk range from the craggy peaks of the Strawberry Mountains to the sagebrush flats of the Oregon desert. The Canyon Creek archery range 16 miles southeast of John Day, and the Baker unit, east of Bates, are open to archers for deer and elk during the special seasons. Archery ranges have been established at the Ray Cole and High Desert areas. Upland bird hunters will find blue grouse along the high ridges, ruffed grouse in the timber, and chukar partridge along the grassy canyon bottoms. Wild turkey, black bear, bobcat, and mountain lion, though rarely seen, are fairly common.

The famous Malheur Lake National Wildlife Refuge and the adjacent marsh areas are prime country for mallards, pintails, and Canada, cackling, snow, and white-fronted geese. Malheur Lake and the nearby alkaline waters of Harney Lake, were discovered in 1826 by Peter Skene Ogden. Early settlers named them the Bitter Lakes. In 1908, the area was set aside by Pres. Theodore Roosevelt as a game and bird refuge. The Malheur River and its tributaries also have good shooting areas. Malheur Lake is an excellent trout fishery with limit catches, and fish to 4 and 5 pounds are not unusual. The upper stretches of the Middle Fork of the Malheur River, with headwaters in the Strawberry Mountain Wilderness, provide good fishing for rainbow trout. There are several forest camps near feeder streams along the upper river. Another good trout stream is the Silvies River, with its headwaters in the Blue Mountains near Seneca. The Silvies flows for 95 miles before merging with the Malheur Marsh. Hundreds of miles of forest roads and trails provide access to such interior backcountry areas as the Strawberry Mountain Wilderness and the high mountain areas near Baldy and Sheep mountains as well as those from Coal Pit Mountain to Fields Peak.

The Strawberry Mountain Wilderness lies along a high east-west divide south of the John Day River, with Slide Mountain on the east and craggy Canyon Mountain on the west. In the interior, numerous trails lead to Strawberry Mountain (9,044 ft.), Strawberry Lake, Pine Creek Mountain, Indian Creek Butte, and Rabbit Ears. There are five lakes in the area, and fishing is fair in some for brook and rainbow trout. Mud Lake, though it has no fish, is of interest as an "aquatic pasture" in its final stages, getting shallower and shallower each year as it fills with mineral deposits. Access is limited by snowpack during all seasons except summer, when wildflowers and bushes cover the meadows and hillsides, and the trails lead through open forests of pine and fir. Big-game hunting is good for deer and elk. The southwestern corner of the wilderness lies in the Canyon Creek Archery Area, where bow hunting is allowed. Other wildlife includes black bear, blue and ruffed grouse, and, for the birdwatcher, Traill's flycatcher. The wilderness derives its name, as do the mountain and lake, from a creek along which there is an abundance of wild strawberries, located at the northwest corner of the Canyon Creek area. For a *Strawberry Mountain Wilderness Map & Trail Log* (50¢) and camping information, write to: Bear Valley Ranger Station, 139 N.E. Dayton, John Day 97845. For additional information about the Malheur National Forest, write to: Supervisor, Malheur National Forest, John Day 97845.

The rugged, massive bulk of Steens Mountain lies to the east of the Malheur Refuge and dominates the landscape for 50 miles, rising nearly a mile above the surrounding plateau. Steens Mountain is actually a range with snow-covered crests, slopes clothed with sparse grounds of juniper and sagebrush, and cataracts pouring through small canyons to the lowlands. The Steens is a top-ranked hunting area for mule deer and antelope. The range was named for Maj. Enock Steen, head of a cavalry expedition that in 1860 drove a band of Snake Indians to the summit and then annihilated them. The famous Hart Mountain National Antelope Range lies westward of Steens Mountain. The refuge contains about 200,000 acres of rugged mountain and plateau country, dominated by the Warner Mountains. The refuge contains the largest herd of antelope in the United States. The Order of Antelope, organized around a campfire in the reserve in 1932 for the purpose of protecting this fleet-footed animal, holds an annual outing on the rugged slopes of Hart Mountain.

Access & Outfitting Centers

The Malheur National Forest and Strawberry Mountain Wilderness are reached via U.S. Highways 20, 26, and 395 and Oregon Highway 7. Lodging, supplies, guides and outfitters are located at John Day, Canyon City, Silvies, Prairie City, Long Creek, Mount Vernon, and Burns. Malheur National Wildlife Refuge is reached via state highways 78 and 205 and U.S. Highway 20. The Steens Mountain country is reached by all-weather roads off Oregon Highway 78. The Hart Mountain National Antelope Range is reached by unimproved roads off U.S. Highway 395 and Oregon Highway 140.

Mount Hood National Forest & Wilderness

Mount Hood National Forest Topo Maps

U.S. Geological Survey overview maps, scale 1:250,000: Bend, Salem, The Dalles, Vancouver.

Eagle Roadless Area

U.S. Geological Survey large-scale map: Bonneville Dam.

Mount Hood Wilderness

U.S. Geological Survey large-scale maps: Badger Lake, Bull Run Lake, Cathedral Ridge, Dog River, Government Camp, Hickman Butte, Mount Hood South, Rhododendron.

Pacific Crest Trail

U.S. Geological Survey large-scale maps: Bonneville Dam, Bull Run Lake, Government Camp, Mount Hood South, Mount Wilson, High Rock, Fort Butte, Breitenbush Hot Springs.

Olallie Butte Lakes

U.S. Geological Survey large-scale maps: Forte Butte, Breitenbush Hot Springs.

Rock Lakes Basin

U.S. Geological Survey large-scale maps: Fish Creek Mountain, High Rock.

Warm Springs Indian Reservation

U.S. Geological Survey overview maps, scale 1:250,000: Bend, The Dalles.

The Mount Hood National Forest, with a total of 1,118,000 acres, sweeps in a vast, panorama of snowcapped peaks and evergreen forests, rivers and lakes and cascades, from the banks of the Columbia River almost to the white bulk of Mount Jefferson, more than 100 miles south of the forest's northern boundary. Mount Hood, the monarch of Oregon's High Cascades peaks, towers over lesser mountains as it casts its long shadow across dense forests, deep ravines, alpine meadows, and lakes that reflect its splendor in their cold, tranquil depth. The headwaters of five rivers—the Bull Run, Sandy, Clackamas, Hood, and White—are in the forest, and countless swift small trout streams race down the high-country slopes.

The forest encompasses some of Oregon's finest camping, fishing, and hunting areas. Hundreds of miles of forest roads and trails lead to interior areas such as the Fish Creek Divide, Firecamp Area, Jefferson Park, Olallie Meadows, Bull Run Lake, Salmon River, Columbia Gorge, and the Mount Hood Wilderness. Trails in the Columbia Gorge area vary from relatively flat to steep and include the Oneonta-Horsetail Trail, Wahkeena Falls–Multnomah Falls Trail, Larch Mountain Trail, and the Eagle Creek Trail, which extends for 14 miles through wild backcountry flanked by solid rock walls before terminating at Wahtum Lake. The Bull of the Woods area has many miles of interconnecting trails passing along streams and lakes and through majestic stands of old-growth Douglas fir. The Pacific Crest Trail (also known as the Oregon Skyline Trail) winds south through the forest from the Columbia Gorge Work Center near Cascade Locks, past Wahtum Lake, and over Lolo Pass, and then skirts the west side of Mount Hood to Timberline Lodge. From here it passes Bird Butte, Little Crater, and Timothy Lakes as it meanders south and west between the forest and the Warm Springs Indian Reservation. The trail continues on through the high lake country and enters the Mount Jefferson Wilderness at Breitenbush Lake, from where it winds southward into the Willamette National Forest.

The forest is renowned for the excellent fishing in its many high-country lakes and streams. Breitenbush Lake basin, located on a plateau at the south end of the Olallie Lakes area just west of the Warm Springs Indian Reservation, has good fishing for brook and rainbow trout. A good fly-fishing stream is the White River, which rises in the glaciers on the south side of Mount Hood, flows south and east for 50 miles, and then joins the Deschutes River below the town of Maupin. The historic Clackamas River, brought to fame in stories by Rudyard Kipling for its fine salmon and steelhead fishing, heads high in the Mount Hood area near Olallie Lakes. With an 8-ounce rod, Kipling spent 37 minutes landing a 12-pound battling salmon. "That hour," he wrote, "I sat among crowned heads greater than all. . . . How shall I tell the glories of that day?" Fly-fishing is best in the fall months along the upper stretches of the Clackamas for rainbows, cutthroat, and Dolly Varden. Forest roads provide access to campgrounds along the upper river from Estacada on up to the headwaters. If you are in the area, you might want to try the Roaring River, a tributary of the Clackamas that heads in the scenic Rock Lakes Basin area. Access is by a trail knifing through a deep canyon, but anglers are often rewarded for their efforts by limit catches of rainbows and some brook and Dolly Varden trout. The Mount Hood region is also a first-rate High Cascades hunting range for Rocky Mountain elk, black-tailed deer, and black bear. Upland game birds include blue and ruffed grouse and quail. The best way to hunt this high country is by packhorse. Contact the Forest Service people for help in lining up a guide.

The scenic Mount Hood Wilderness, one of Oregon's most popular recreation areas, encompasses 14,160 acres of fragrant pine forests, alpine lakes, meadows, and wild streams, in the Zigzag Ranger District of the forest. The wilderness is dominated by the perpetually snowcapped peak of 11,245-foot Mount Hood, the state's highest mountain. North of Crater Rock, numerous mountain fissures still emit steam and hydrogen sulfide gas. On clear and windless days, these gas emissions, or fumaroles, are visible from as far away as Portland. Numerous glaciers, such as the Zigzag, White River, Newton Clark, Eliot, Coe, Ladd, and Reid glaciers, cling to its precipitous slopes. Below Mount Hood's towering bulk, numerous trails lead through the alpine and forested areas to such points as Crater Rock, Devils Kitchen, the Chimney, Cooper Spur, Langille Crags, Mississippi Head, Hot Rocks, Pinnacle Ridge, and Vista Ridge. The Timberline Trail is a relatively easy 37.6-mile route that weaves clear around Mount Hood. Several stone shelters with corrugated iron roofs unique to the wilderness were built during the construction of the Timberline Trail by the Civilian Conservation Corps over thirty years ago. Heavy snows, avalanches, and time have taken their usual toll, leaving the shelters at Gnarl Ridge, Cooper Spur, and Elk Cove in ruins. Mount Hood, although not an easy climb, is very popular. Caution and guides are highly recommended for the novice climber. Wood is scarce in the high country and a good fuel-burning stove is a must for long trips. The Timberline Lodge on the south side of the wilderness is the most

popular access point. The full-color Topographic U.S. Forest Service *Mt. Hood Wilderness Map* (50¢) shows all primitive roads, primary and spur trails, campgrounds, wilderness campsites, wooded areas, boundaries, and private lands, and contains a detailed "Trail Guide" to the wilderness. This map, and wilderness camping, mountain climbing, hunting, and fishing information may be obtained by writing: District Ranger, Zigzag District, Zigzag 97073 or Forest Supervisor, P.O. Box 16040, Portland 97216.

The forest lands that stretch south from the ancient Indian and fur-trade era water route of the Columbia River and the Great Gorge area form one of Oregon's most scenic wilderness camping, fishing, and big-game hunting areas. This region, described in ecstatic words by Lewis and Clark in their journal of 1805, is shown on the full-color U.S. Forest Service topographic *Forest Trails of the Columbia Gorge Map*, available for 50¢ from: District Ranger, Columbia Gorge District, Rt. 3, Box 44A, Troutdale 97060. This map of the Great Gorge forest area shows all major features, campsites, logging roads, fish hatcheries, and trails, including the scenic Multnomah Creek, Angels Rest, Horsetail Falls, Pacific Crest, Eagle Creek Larch Mountain, and Tanner Butte trails. The map also contains a detailed trail mileage and trip-planning guide. The slopes of the Great Gorge, which portray about 30 million years of geological history, and the sheer cliffs, picturesque waterfalls, and V-shaped upper valleys of Tanner Creek, Eagle Creek, and Herman Creek, are encompassed within the 52,000-acre Eagle Roadless area. The entire area is maintained by the Mount Hood National Forest for the use of wilderness campers and horsemen. Anyone interested in the fascinating history and lore of this region is advised to read Ward Jones's novel *Swift Flows the River*, based on the steamboat days of the Columbia, and Washington Irving's *Adventures of Captain Bonneville* and *Astoria*, the spellbinding story of John Jacob Astor and the Pacific Fur Company.

The major features of the entire forest, including the Mount Hood Wilderness area and the Pacific Crest Trail, Warm Springs Indian Land, primitive roads, campsites, ranger stations, and boat-launching and horse-loading ramps, are shown on the full-color *Mt. Hood National Forest Map*, available for 50¢ from: Supervisor's Office, 2440 S.E. 195 Avenue, Portland 97230. Special area maps for *Bull of the Woods, The Dalles Watershed, Bagley Hot Springs*, and *Rock Lakes Basin* are available free upon request. For detailed wilderness travel, camping, fishing, and hunting information, write to the Supervisor's Office.

For lodging information write: *Lost Lake Resort*, c/o Walter H. Loyd, Rt. 1, Box 93, Deer Island 97054 (winter) and Hood River 97031 (summer); *Olallie Lake Resort*, c/o Edward Upton, 1724 23rd Avenue, Forest Grove 97116 (winter) and Government Camp 97028 (summer); *Snowbunny Lodge*, Government Camp, 510 S.E. Morrison Street, Portland 97214 (dormitories for group use, with 300-bed capacity); *Timberline Lodge*, Government Camp, 97028; *Zigzag Auto Court*, Rhododendron 97049; *Multnomah Falls Lodge*, P.O. Box 64, Bridal Veil 97010.

The large, 300,000-acre Warm Springs Indian Reservation lies adjacent to the eastern boundary of the national forest. The remote backcountry of the reservation contains some interesting fishing waters. On the western boundary, the High Cascade lakes of the Mill Creek area, north of the Mount Jefferson Wilderness, lie clustered in a circle around Olallie Butte (7,215 ft.). These lakes provide good fishing for rainbow, native cutthroat, and brook trout. Access to the high lakes area is by trail and unpaved roads. Overnight camping is not permitted on most of the lakes. Fishing permits are required and are available from: Office of the Confederated Tribes of the Warm Springs Reservation, Warm Springs 97761. The famed Metolius River, one of

Oregon's classic dry fly streams, heads in the springs on the east slope of the High Cascades under the lee of Three-Fingered Jack and flows along the southern boundary of the reservation. Fishing is most productive along the upper fly-fishing-only stretches for rainbows and an occasional lunker Dolly Varden. Sections of the lower stream are inaccessible along the canyon in the Metolius Breaks area. Lake Simtustus, formed by the damming of the Deschutes River above Warm Springs, is located along the eastern edge of the reservation and has good fishing for rainbows, Dolly Varden, and an occasional Deschutes River steelhead passing through the lake. Lake Billy Chinook, just

north of Lake Simtustus, is in the form of three huge sprawling arms, formed by the damming of the Crooked, Metolius, and Deschutes rivers. Billy Chinook has good early-season trolling for large Dolly Varden, rainbow, and brown trout and lots of young silver and chinook salmon. Camping grounds and launching ramps are available at Cove Palisades State Park, adjacent to the lake, Day Creek, Blue Lake, Trout Lake, Indian Park, Kah-Nee-Ta Resort, Bear Springs, and Breitenbush. A *Warm Springs Indian Reservation Fishing Map* is available free from the headquarters office (address above).

Access & Outfitting Centers

Mount Hood National Forest and the Columbia Gorge area are reached via scenic Interstate 80N, U.S. Highway 26, and Oregon Highways 224 and 35. Lodging, supplies, guides, and outfitting services are available at Government Camp, Rhododendron, Zigzag, Mount Hood, Bull Run, Cascade Locks, Eagle Creek, Estacada, Hood River, Odell, Dee, Bonneville, Bridal Veil, Multnomah Falls, and The Dalles.

Ochoco National Forest

Ochoco National Forest Topo Maps

U.S. Geological Survey 1:250,000 scale overview maps: Bend, Burns, Canyon City.

Crooked River Backcountry

U.S. Geological Survey small-scale maps: Houston Lake, O'Neil, Opal City, Prineville, Redmond, Steelhead Falls.

Ochoco National Forest, a seasonal mule-deer hunting, fishing, and camping area, encompasses 845,855 acres of the Ochoco Mountains foothills and the Crooked River grasslands located at the western end of the Blue Mountains in the geographic center of Oregon. The first

explorers in this area were Peter Skene Ogden and his party of Hudson's Bay Company trappers in 1825. Nonresident hunters visiting the area are well advised to arrange for the services of a guide and horses or a four-wheel-drive jeep to get into the backcountry regions. Mule deer are plentiful throughout the forest, and a small band of pronghorn antelope inhabit the flatlands of the Big Summit Prairie during the spring, summer, and fall. Rocky Mountain elk are widely scattered in small groups throughout the area, particularly in the Battle Mountain–Black Canyon Creek area in the northeast. The hunting is also good for upland game birds, including pheasant, chukar partridge, the swift and erratic ruffed grouse, and valley quail in the canyons and brushy foothills. The best fishing in the forest is found in the Crooked River in the deep cold pools beneath the Prineville Reservoir Dam for rainbows around 3 pounds and an occasional fish up to 8 pounds. The Crooked River, a large tributary of the Deschutes River, heads in the Ochoco Mountains and flows west through the Prineville Reservoir

and on into Billy Chinook Lake adjacent to the Warm Springs Indian Reservation. There is also fair to good early-season trout fishing in the Monks, Wolf, Ochoco, Emigrant, Rock, and Silver creeks. The Prineville Reservoir, bordered by range land, canyon areas, bluffs, and picturesque rock formations, is a steady producer of 8 to 12-inch rainbows.

The major features of the region are shown on the *Ochoco National Forest Map*, available for 50¢ from: Forest Supervisor's Office, P.O.

Box 490, Prineville 97754. This full-color map shows campgrounds, boat ramps, horse facilities, trails and logging roads, ranger stations, and rock-hound areas. The forest is a top rock-hound area and is shown and described on the *Central Oregon Rockhound Guide Map*, available free from the Supervisor's Office. Additional wilderness travel, fishing, hunting, and camping information may be obtained by writing to the Forest Supervisor or to one of the District Rangers at: Big Summit Ranger District, Prineville 97754; Paulina Ranger District, Paulina 97751; Prineville Ranger District, Prineville 97754; Snow Mountain Ranger District, Hines 97738; Crooked River Ranger District, Prineville 97754.

Access & Outfitting Centers

Ochoco National Forest is reached via U.S. Highways 26, 395, and 20. Lodging, supplies, fishing and big-game hunting guides, and outfitters are available at Burns, Riley, Silvies, John Day, Mount Vernon, Paulina, Prineville, and Dayville.

Rogue River National Forest & Sky Lakes Wilderness

Rogue River National Forest Topo Maps
U.S. Geological Survey maps, scale 1:250,000: Medford, Weed.

Pacific Crest Trail
The Rogue River National Forest segment of the trail, from Crater Lake National Park through the Sky Lakes Wilderness to the California boundary, is shown on the following large-scale U.S. Geological Survey maps: Pelican Butte, Rustler Peak, Mount McLoughlin, Hyatt Reservoir.

Sky Lakes Wilderness
U.S. Geological Survey large-scale maps: Lake o' The Woods, Mt. McLoughlin, Pelican Butte, Rustler Peak.

The famous 621,005-acre national forest is dominated by the historic Rogue River and the Klamath and Siskiyou mountains in southwestern Oregon. The major features of the forest are shown on the full-color *Rogue River National Forest Map* (50¢), including forest service recreation sites, boating facilities, primitive logging roads and trails, campsites, Pacific Crest National Scenic Trail, ranger stations, horse facilities, points of interest such as the Blue Ledge Mine, Mammoth Sugar Pine, National Bridge, and Dutchman's Peak Lookout. Rogue River trails such as Beaver Meadows Trail, Frenchman Camp Trail, Hummingbird Meadow Trail, Red Blanket Trail, and numerous others, plus forest roads, provide access through the dense sugar pine and Douglas fir forests to the spectacular Rogue River Gorge, Fish Lake, Mount McLoughlin (9,497 ft.), and the Seven Lakes Basin in the Sky Lakes Wilderness.

The forest is a top-ranked hunting area for black bear, deer, Roosevelt elk, and mountain lion. Game birds include grouse, quail, ducks, geese, and doves. Wildlife present, but rarely seen, includes yellow-billed marmot, fisher, pine marten, timber wolf, and wolverine.

The Rogue River is perhaps the most famous fishing stream in the country, celebrated by Zane Grey for its great runs of steelhead and salmon. The river, once the battleground of the Rogue River Indian Wars and named the River of Rogues by the French fur trappers, flows through a dissected plateau for 200 miles from its headwaters near Beaver Meadows north of Crater Lake National Park to its mouth at Gold Beach. The lower Rogue is renowned for its large runs of coho salmon, chinook up to 30 and 40 pounds, and steelhead up to 8 and 10 pounds; the upper Rogue provides excellent fly-fishing for cut-

throat, rainbow, and brown trout. Float fishing is popular in flat-bottomed, high-bowed McKenzie drift boats and rubber rafts. Canoes and kayaks are unsafe in many of the rapids below Grave Creek. Rainie Falls, 1.7 miles downstream from Grave Creek, has a vertical drop of 10 feet. For information write: *Rogue River Boat Service*, Gold Beach 97444. From August through October, the half-pounders provide exciting steelhead fishing. Runs of heavier fish increase through the late winter season. The most popular lower Rogue riffles are the Gillespie, Lobster Creek, Coal, and Hawkins. The middle river canyon, with access by guided boat parties only, was famed in many a tale by Zane Grey, who maintained a fishing camp there and introduced the country to the sport of taking a steelhead on a fly. The upper river includes the famous Weatherby Riffle, the Pierce Riffle below Savage Rapids Dam, and the Leaning Tree Riffle. About 20 boat-launching ramps are maintained along the upper river. The river below Grants Pass is regularly serviced by licensed guides, and they will advise you through correspondence about the best time to fish for the various runs, and making reservations for trips of any duration. Popular Rogue River fly patterns include the Silver Ant, Royal Coachman, Juicy Bug, Rogue River Special, Golden Demon, and the Weatherwox.

To the east of the Rogue, the majestic Sky Lakes Wilderness and Rogue River Headwaters area lie along the Cascades for 27 miles, from Crater Lake south to the Lake of the Woods. This beautiful backcountry is a land of lofty peaks, blue lakes, and timbered slopes with elevations ranging from 3,800 feet in the canyon of the Middle Fork of the Rogue River to a lofty 9,497 feet at Mount McLoughlin. The Pacific Crest Trail follows the backbone for about 35 miles, with numerous spur trails leading off to the Devils Peak area, Wizzard Lake, Pelican Butte (8,036 ft.), and Squaw, Fourmile, Badger, and Wolf lakes, Blue Canyon Basin, Sky Lakes Basin, and Mudjekeewis Mountain. Be sure to carry food and water supplies, since there are no supply stores from Fourmile Lake to Crater Lake. Side treks to supply points at Butte Falls, Rocky Point, or Fort Klamath are not wise unless you have a vehicle at the trailhead. The major features of the wilderness are shown on the *Sky Lakes User's Map*. This extremely useful map shows topographic features, contours, trails and trailheads, springs, camps, logging roads, and horse-loading ramps. Both the Sky Lakes map and the Rogue River National Forest map may be obtained for 50¢ along with the free *Rogue Trails* booklet from: Forest Supervisor's Office, P.O. Box 520, Medford 97501.

For detailed info on trail conditions, wilderness camping permits, river running, fishing, and hunting, write to the Supervisor's Office or to the District Ranger Offices at: Butte Falls Ranger Station, P.O. Box 227, Butte Falls 97522, or Prospect Ranger Station, Prospect 97536. For info on the Winima National Forest portion of the Sky Lakes area, write: Klamath Falls Ranger Station, 1936 California St., Klamath Falls 97601. The *Rogue National Wild & Scenic River Map* and *Rogue River Trails* booklet may be obtained free by writing to: Bureau of Land Management, 310 W. Sixth St., Medford 97501. (See "Rogue National Wild & Scenic River" the "Oregon Encyclopedia" section.)

Guided high-country packhorse trips in the Rogue River National Forest and Sky Lakes Wilderness and in the Umpqua and Siskiyou national forests are provided by *Wilderness Pack Trips*, P.O. Box 71, Rogue River 97537; they offer moving, base camp, and drop trips.

Lodging, boat rentals, and supplies in Rogue River National Forest are provided by *Fish Lake Resort*, P.O. Box 40, Medford 97501, and by *Union Creek Resort*, P.O. Box 50, Prospect 97536. For a comprehensive listing of salmon and steelhead fishing guides and scenic trips by drift boat, raft, or kayak, write: *Rogue River Guides Association, Inc.*, P.O. Box 792, Medford 97501.

Access & Outfitting Centers

The forest and Sky Lakes Wilderness area are reached via Interstate Highway 5 and Oregon Highways 140, 62, 230, and 227. Lodging, supplies, guides, and outfitting service are available at Medford, Grants Pass, Eagle Point, Butte Falls, Trail, Shady Cove, Union Creek, Rogue River, Gold Hill, and Ashland.

Siskiyou National Forest & Kalmiopsis Wilderness

Siskiyou National Forest Topo Maps

U.S. Geological Survey overview maps, scale 1:250,000: Coos Bay, Midford.

Illinois Wild & Scenic River

U.S. Geological Survey large-scale maps: Agness, Cave Junction, Collier Butte, Pearsoll Peak, Selma.

Kalmiopsis Wilderness

U.S. Geological Survey large-scale maps: Cave Junction, Chetco Peak, Pearsoll Peak, Selma.

Klamath & Siskiyou Mountains

U.S. Geological Survey large-scale maps: Marial, Galice, Pearsoll Peak, Selma, Grants Pass, Cave Junction, Oregon Caves.

The Siskiyou National Forest, an outstanding fishing, hunting, and wilderness camping region, takes in 1,158,420 acres in the southwestern corner of Oregon, with a small extension into California. The forest encompasses a major portion of the rugged Siskiyou Mountains, joining the Cascade Range to the east and the Coast Range to the northeast. *Siskiyou* is the Indian word for a bobtailed horse. In 1828 Alexander McLeod, a Hudson's Bay trapper, was heading a party in the mountains and got lost in a snowstorm. The group suffered severe privations and lost several horses, among them the bobtailed racehorse belonging to McLeod. The mountain pass where they were became known thereafter as "the pass of the Siskiyou," a name that was later given to the entire range.

The forest has a large population of black-tailed deer and black bear. Roosevelt elk are found in the more restricted areas, especially in the Coquille River area. Mountain lion, bobcat, and coyote also inhabit the forest, but are rarely seen. Bird hunters will find plentiful grouse, doves, and quail. Numerous forest roads and trails wind through the backcountry to such areas as the Kalmiopsis Wilderness, Big Craggies, Coquille Falls, Vulcan Lake, Chetco Divide, Rogue River Canyon, and Elk River. The Illinois River Trail provides stunning views of the river canyon. The scenic Chetco River, flowing for 50 miles through a thick forest of myrtlewood trees, has good fishing for cutthroat, rainbow, and steelhead, and in its lower stretches are chinook and coho salmon. The 36-mile-long Sixes River is one of southern Oregon's best producers of steelhead. The Illinois River, a large tributary of the lower Rogue, is renowned for its tremendous autumn run of half-pound steelhead and chinook and coho salmon.

The unusual, 76,900-acre Kalmiopsis Wilderness is located in the Siskiyou Mountains in the central portion of the forest. A harsh, brushy area of low-elevation canyons, the wilderness contains the headwaters of the Chetco River, over 12 species of conifers, including the rare Brewer, or weeping, spruce, and the rare *Kalmiopsis leachiana*, a member of the heath family found only in the Chetco and Illinois river basins. This is a true primitive camping area, with a few shelters and old cabins left over from the early gold-mining days. The

trails are in fairly good condition, but tend to be steep and very rocky. The full-color U.S. Forest Service Topographical *Kalmiopsis Wilderness Map* shows primitive roads, trails, springs, woodlands, and the surrounding Siskiyou Highlands, including the Big Craggies Botanical Area. This map may be obtained for 50¢ by writing: District Ranger, U.S. Forest Service, Box 730, Brookings 97415. Access to the wilderness is via the Redwood Highway (Oregon 199) at Selma and Kerby, and via the Oregon Coast Highway to Brookings.

The full-color U.S. Forest Service *Siskiyou National Forest Map* (50¢) shows all major features, including the Kalmiopsis Wilderness, campgrounds, trails, ranger stations, forest roads, lookout stations, wilderness cabins, and boating sites. This map and detailed fishing, hunting, and wilderness camping information may be obtained by writing to: Forest Supervisor, P.O. Box 440, Grants Pass 97526, or to: Chetco Ranger District, Brookings 97415; Galice Ranger District, Grants Pass 97526; Gold Beach Ranger District, Gold Beach 97444; Illinois Valley Ranger District, Cave Junction 97523; or Powers Ranger District, Powers 97446. *Hiking the Bigfoot Country: The Wildlands of Northern California and Southern Oregon* ($7.95, 392 pages), published by Sierra Club Books, 1050 Mills Tower, San Francisco 94120, provides a detailed guide to the geology, flora and fauna, and trails in the Kalmiopsis Wilderness and High Siskiyou Wildlands.

Access and Outfitting Centers

The Siskiyou National Forest is reached via U.S. Highway 199 and the scenic Oregon Coast Highway 101. Lodging, supplies, guide service, and outfitters are available at Brookings, Pistol River, Gold Beach, Port Orford, Powers, Galice, Selma, Grants Pass, Cave Junction, and Elk Creek. *The Marial Lodge*, c/o Ted Camp, Star Rt., Box 84, Wolf Creek 97497, offers lodging and meals. This fishing lodge is reached by drift boat from Grants Pass down the Rogue River, or by car from Glendale.

Siuslaw National Forest & the Cascade Head

Siuslaw National Forest Topo Maps

U.S. Geological Survey overview maps, scale 1:250,000: Coos Bay, Roseburg, Salem, Vancouver.

Cascade Head Forest & Scenic Research Area

U.S. Geological Survey large-scale maps: Hebo, Euchre Mountain.

The Siuslaw National Forest, with a total area of 620,000 acres, stretches along the Pacific Coast from Coos Bay north almost to Tillamook, and inland to the slopes of the Cascade Range. Broken into many portions, the forest embraces many of Oregon's most famous beach resorts and is characterized by its dense stands of Sitka spruce, hemlock, cedar, and Douglas fir, its mountains, and its large coastal salmon and steelhead streams and wild, log-stream and rocky headland beaches. The name Siuslaw was taken from a small tribe of Yakona Indians who lived along the coast; it means "faraway waters." This is top elk, black bear, and steelhead country. Remote forest roads and trails lead to the best hunting and fishing areas, such as the Mill Creek Divide, Elos Prairie, Cascade Head, Mount Hebo, Marys Peak, and Tahenitch Lake. The upper stretches of the Siuslaw River, near the headwaters at Swisshome, have some good fly-fishing stretches for rainbows and native cutthroats; the lower river is good for steelhead, chinook, and sea-run cutthroat near its mouth at Florence. The famed Alsea and "Big Nestucca" offer outstanding angling for big steelhead trout and chinook salmon. The most popular spots along the "Big Nestucca" are Cottonwood Hole, Pipeline Hole, Three Rivers Drift, Orchard Hole, and the Lone Fir Hole. The big, fighting steelheads are most often caught on salmon eggs, crawfish tails, and wet flies such as the Bucktail Coachman and Caddis.

The 9,000-acre Cascade Head Scenic Research Area, established in 1974, and the surrounding experimental Cascade Forest are on the Hebo Range District and embrace the 1,600-foot Cascade Head and the beautiful Salmon River estuary. Sea Lion Point, south of Yachats, is the only known mainland sea lion rookery in the world. The Sea Lion Caves, located far below the Oregon Coast Highway 101 and accessible by an elevator, are inhabited during the winter by a herd of about 300 sea lions. The herd is ruled by an old bull whose throne is the center rock in the main cavern, a chamber 1,500 feet long and colored green, pink, and pale yellow. These huge Steller's sea lions found along the Oregon coast were named by Dr. Steller, a German scientist with the Russian expedition headed by the explorer Bering in 1741. During the summer months, they live on rocky islands off the coast of Alaska. They generally leave for the Oregon shore about the first of September.

The far-flung sand dunes, lakes, forests, and ocean beaches of the Oregon Dunes National Recreation Area extend for 40 miles along the Pacific Ocean from the Siuslaw River on the north to the Coos River on the south. At the widest point, the area extends inland approximately 2½ miles. The Oregon Dunes are the most extensive, spectacular dune landscape on the Pacific Coast. The dunes are accessible in a few places, such as Cleawox Lake, Sitcoos, Winchester Bay, and Horsefall Beach. These and other access points are shown on the *Oregon Dunes National Recreation Area Map-Brochure*, available free from: Superintendent's Office, Reedsport, 97467. This map also shows campgrounds, recreation sites, trails, and boat ranges. When traveling across the open sand, hikers should be aware that rain, dense fog, and wind may erase footprints and cause you to lose your way. The forest growth bordering the dunes is dense and lush, and spotting your trail back to your point of origin can be extremely difficult. Lodging is available at *Oregon Caves Chateau*, P.O. Box 128, Cave Junction 97523.

The full-color U.S. Forest Service *Siuslaw National Forest Recreation Map* shows all major features and adjacent fish and game lands, campgrounds, ranger stations, forest roads and trails, boat ramps, and recreation sites. The map costs 50¢ and may be obtained along with fishing, hunting, and wilderness camping info by writing to: Forest Supervisor, P.O. Box 1148, Corvallis 97330. A free *Northwest Pacific Travel Guide* listing lodges, resorts, and boat charters may be had by

writing: Oregon Coast Association, Box 670, Newport 97365. Guided coastal dune rides and sight-seeing trips are provided in the forest region by: *Dune Scooters,* c/o Norman Hanson, Rt. 1, Box 395, North Bend 97459; *Sand Dunes Frontier Inc.,* c/o R. E. Chapman, Rt. 1, Box 3625, Florence 97439; *Donald T. Wells,* Box 161, Florence 97439.

Access & Outfitting Centers

The major recreation areas of the Siuslaw National Forest are reached by auto along the incredibly scenic Oregon Coast Highway 101 and connecting state highways 38, 126, 34, 18, and 22 and U.S. Highway 20. Lodging, supplies, guides, and outfitting services are available at Florence, Reedsport, Yachats, Waldport, Newport, Corvallis, Lincoln City, Pacific City, Tillamook, Hebo, Cloverdale, Beaver, Toledo, Tidewater, Swisshome, Minerva, Cushman, Sitcoos, and Coos Bay.

Umatilla National Forest
& Wenaha Backcountry

Umatilla National Forest Topo Maps

U.S. Geological Survey maps, scale 1:250,000: Canyon City, Grangeville, Pendleton, Pullman, Walla Walla.

Wenaha Backcountry Area

U.S. Geological Survey, Oregon large-scale maps: Bone Spring, Eden, Elbow Creek, Flora, Troy, Wenaha Forks; Washington large-scale maps: Coppei, Deadman Peak, Diamond Peak, Eckler Mountain, Goodman Spring, Kooskooskie, Oregon Butte, Panjab Creek, Robinette Mountain, Stenty Spring.

The Umatilla National Forest encompasses the beautiful Blue Mountains Range, Oregon's oldest land, known to geologists as the "Island of Shoshone," and one of the top mule deer and elk-hunting regions in the United States. The forest takes in 1,400,000 acres in northeastern Oregon and extends in a northeasterly direction up into Washington. The forest and the Umatilla River take their name from an Indian word meaning "water rippling over sand." The forest region was first explored by members of the Lewis and Clark expedition during their trip down the Columbia River in 1805. The Old Oregon Trail, used by countless pioneers, crossed the Blue Mountains from the Grande Ronde Valley to the Umatilla Valley. The forest was once the scene of several Indian battles, beginning with the Whitman Massacre in 1847. Several gold-boom ghost towns and caved-in mines are found scattered through the backcountry.

Big-game hunters will find the highest concentration of Rocky Mountain elk in the northern part of the forest. There are also regulated seasons for Rocky Mountain sheep and wild turkey. Upland bird hunters will find blue grouse near the springs in the timbered areas adjacent to open ridges and chukar partridge in the arid, steep sagebrush country. A particularly good elk and mule deer area consists of the fir, spruce, and pine forests of the 111,200-acre Wenaha Backcountry Area located along the crest of the northern Blue Mountains. This roadless area is characterized by rugged basaltic ridges and outcroppings separated by deep canyons and white-water streams. There is a goodly population of whitetail deer along the banks of the Wenaha River during the fall months. Numerous forest roads and over 900 miles of trails provide access to many backcountry areas such as the Jump-Off Joe area and the Vinegar Hill–Indian Rock area—a tough, remote wilderness located on the boundary of the Malheur and Umatilla national forests. The Mill Creek Watershed is closed to all public entry except during special big-game hunting seasons. The headwaters of the Umatilla River are in the northern Blue Mountains and flows

for 70 miles through the Umatilla Indian Reservation past Pendleton and Hermiston into the Columbia River. The Bingham Springs area of the Umatilla has good fly-fishing for native rainbows. The forest's top-ranked trout streams include the Tucannon, Wenaha, Walla Walla, and North Fork John Day rivers. The scenic Grande Ronde runs through a deep gorge in the Blue Mountains and is a popular wildwater float trip between Rondowa and Troy in the Walla Walla Ranger District. The river is not difficult to navigate, but when the water is high and fast, experience is needed, and it is recommended that life preservers be worn at all times. Camping sites are located along the Grande Ronde at Meadow Creek, Alder Creek, Bear Creek, and Elbow Creek in the Walla Walla district. Rattlesnakes are found throughout the forest backcountry areas, so a snake bite kit should be part of your gear.

The major features of the forest, the Wenaha backcountry and the adjacent Umatilla Indian Reservation are shown on the *Umatilla National Forest Map.* This full-color map, which also shows forest roads and trails, horse-loading ramps, recreation sites, and campgrounds, may be obtained for 50¢ by writing to: Forest Supervisor's Office, Umatilla National Forest, 2517 S.W. Hailey, Pendleton 97801. For hunting, fishing, trail, and river information and the free publications *Umatilla Forest Facts* and *Trail Closure Map,* write to the Forest Supervisor's Office, or to District Ranger Offices at Dale 97880; Heppner 97836; Pendleton 97801; Pomeroy, WA 99347; Ukiah 97880; and Walla Walla, WA 99362.

Outfitting and guided elk-hunting trips in the Blue Mountains and Wenaha backcountry are offered by: *Heathman & Matheny,* Troy Rt., Wallowa 97885; *Aulden Kokel,* Box 290 E., Rt. 2., Canby 97013; and *LeRoy J. Wilson,* Troy Resort, Troy 97879. Pack and saddle stock service is provided by: *John E. Dausener,* 117 Poplar St., Milton-Freewater 97862, and *Keith M. Taylor,* 309 E. Logan, Enterprise 97828. *Blue Mountain Packers,* Troy Rt., Wallowa 97885, provides scenic river trips on the Grande Ronde, pack trips in the Wenaha backcountry, and guided fall hunts for elk, deer, black bear, and cougar.

Access & Outfitting Centers

The Umatilla National Forest and Wenaha backcountry are reached via Interstate 80N, U.S. Route 12, and Oregon Highways 204, 82, and

3 and Washington Highways 128 and 129. Lodging, supplies, guides, and outfitters are available at La Grande, Elgin, Wallowa, Minam, North Powder, Troy; and Walla Walla, Washington.

Umpqua National Forest & the North Umpqua River

Umpqua National Forest Topo Maps

U.S. Geological Survey overview maps, scale 1:250,000: Medford, Roseburg.

North Umpqua River

U.S. Geological Survey large-scale maps: Sutherlin, Glide, Mace Mountain, Illatree Rock, Toketee Falls, Summit Lake, Diamond Lake.

Pacific Crest Trail

U.S. Geological Survey large-scale maps: Crescent Lake, Burn Butte, Summit Lake, Miller Lake, Diamond Lake.

South Umpqua River

U.S. Geological Survey large-scale maps: Sutherlin, Roseburg, Canyonville, Days Creek, Tiller, Red Butte, Quartz Mountain, Garwood Butte.

The Umpqua National Forest, covering a total area of 984,000 acres, lies mainly within Douglas County in southeastern Oregon. The forest is named for the Umpqua Indians, who once fished its rivers and hunted in the great pine woods and high country. The renowned fly-fishing waters of the North and South Umpqua rivers, formed by tributaries in the Cascade and Calapooya mountains, flow through majestic evergreen forests and rugged wilderness valleys and unite to form the main Umpqua, which cuts through the Coast Mountains, the lower reaches forming a wide estuary. The world-famous steelhead trout waters of the North Umpqua, which have lured famous fly-fishermen such as Zane Grey and Herbert Hoover, rise in beautiful Diamond Lake, flow through the Umpqua National Forest, and join the main Umpqua below Roseburg. The scenic, swift-flowing North Umpqua is a difficult stream to wade, and the hardy steelheader must be able to handle a long line. The prime steelhead months are July through October; most fish go 6–8 pounds, with an occasional reel-stripper of over 10 pounds. The river is well served by excellent fishing camps, including the famous Gordon's North Umpqua Lodge. Lemolo Lake, located near the Diamond Lake headwaters, on the North Umpqua, holds large brown trout up to 15 pounds, plus rainbows and kokanee salmon. Good campgrounds are located at Lemolo Falls and at Kelsay Valley. Beautiful Diamond Lake, which reflects the snowcapped summit of Mount Bailey on its placid surface and looks across undulating forested hills at Mount Thielsen, is famous for its trophy rainbow trout. The scenic South Umpqua rises in Fish Lake high in the Cascades near Crater Lake and flows down through Umpqua National Forest to its confluence with the main Umpqua at Roseburg. This is a top-ranked salmon and steelhead stream. Numerous forest service campsites are located along its upper stretches.

Forest service roads and trails provide access to the remote wilderness camping and elk and deer-hunting areas found along the Calapooya Mountains, Dread and Terror Ridge, Thunder Mountain, Calapooya Divide, Beartrap Meadow, Skookum Prairie, Park Meadows, Devils Flat, and Rhododendron Ridge. The *Umpqua National Forest Map* shows the region's major features, recreation areas, Pacific Crest National Scenic Trail, logging roads and forest trails, ranger stations, horse and boat ramps, campgrounds, and trailheads. This U.S. Forest Service map may be obtained for 50¢, along with the free *Umpqua National Forest Pacific Crest National Scenic Trail Map, Douglas County Parks Map/Guide, Diamond Lake Snow Trails Guide,* and *South Cascades Snow Trails Map/Guide,* by writing: Forest Supervisor, Umpqua National Forest, P.O. Box 1008, Roseburg 97470. A guide to the old Bohemia Mining District, *Tour of the Golden Past,* is also available free from the Forest Supervisor's Office. This historic district covers about 225 square miles of mountainous country heavily timbered with old fir, spruce, and hemlock. Turbulent mountain streams, deep gorges, wooded scarps, and jagged peaks make this a region of great natural beauty. The district was named for "Bohemia" Johnson, who discovered gold-bearing quartz here in 1863. Detailed camping, fishing, and hunting information may be obtained by writing to the Forest Supervisor or to the District Ranger at: Cottage Grove 97424; Glide 97443; Steamboat District and Diamond Lake District, Idleyld Park 97447; Tiller 97484.

Guided fishing and scenic trips and pack and saddle stock are provided by *Diamond Lake Resort,* Diamond Lake Rural Sta., Chemult 97731 (winter: Wayne Watson, Broadbent 97414). Lodging and boat rentals in the forest are provided by: *Diamond Lake Resort,* Diamond Lake 97731; *Diamond Lake Trailer Court,* Diamond Lake 97731 (winter: c/o Mrs. I. F. Hall, 3017 W. Devonshire, Tucson, AZ 85007; *Lemolo Lake Resort,* P.O. Box 35, Roseburg 97470; and *Steamboat Inn,* Toketee Rt., Idleyld Park 97447, which also has private charter plane service.

Access & Outfitting Centers

The Umpqua National Forest is reached by Oregon Highways 227, 230, 138, and 62. Lodging, supplies, fishing and hunting guides, and outfitters are located at Tiller, Roseburg, Diamond Lake, Union Creek, Clearwater, Steamboat, Myrtle Creek, and Canyonville.

Wallowa-Whitman National Forest & Eagle Cap Wilderness

Wallowa-Whitman National Forest Topo Maps

U.S. Geological Survey maps, scale 1:250,000: Baker, Canyon City, Grangeville, Pendleton.

Eagle Cap Wilderness

U.S. Geological Survey large-scale maps: Cornucopia, Eagle Cap, Enterprise, Halfway, Joseph, Sparta.

Imnaha River High Country

U.S. Geological Survey large-scale maps: Cactus Mountain, Cornucopia, Dead Horse Ridge, Eagle Cap, Hare Butte, Homestead, Imnaha.

Lostine River Wild Country

U.S. Geological Survey large-scale maps: Eagle Cap, Enterprise, Sled Springs, Wallowa.

Minam River & Washboard Trail Wilderness

U.S. Geological Survey large-scale maps: Minam, Mount Moriah, Mount Fanny, Jim White Ridge, China Cap, Enterprise, Eagle Cap.

Snake National Wild & Scenic River

U.S. Geological Survey large-scale maps: Homestead, Cuprum, He Devil, Kernan Point, Kirkwood Creek, Grave Point, Wolf Creek, Cactus Mountain, Deadhorse Ridge, Wapshilla Creek, Jim Creek Butte.

The Wallowa-Whitman National Forest encompasses 2,238,000 acres of big-game hunting, fishing, and wilderness camping country in northeastern Oregon. *Wallowa* is a Nez Percé Indian word referring to the tripods placed in rivers to hold a pole lattice structure for catching salmon and trout. The Wallowa River Valley, known as the Valley of the Winding Waters, was the home of the elder Chief Joseph and his son Joseph of the Wallowa Nez Percé. The young Joseph is famous for his brilliant leadership in the Nez Percé War in 1877. The Whitman portion of the forest was named in honor of Dr. Marcus Whitman, who led a missionary party in 1836 from Missouri to Fort Walla Walla on the Columbia River. His group was among the first to traverse the Oregon Trail. The forest ranges from the gentle Blue Mountains and the rugged Wallowa Mountains down to the spectacular canyon country of the mighty Snake River on the border with Idaho. The short, snow-tipped Wallowa Mountain range thrusts up a mass of marble and granite reaching heights of 9,000 feet in an area covering less than 350 square miles. In their isolation, the Wallowas form an imposing sight. From their slopes flow a number of streams that have cut deep, rock-walled canyons. To the east is the broken Imnaha River Basin, the spectacular Hills Canyon of the Snake, and the lofty, snow-capped peaks of the Seven Devils Range.

Forest roads and trails lead to the interior big-game areas found along the Blue Mountains, to the rugged Wallowa Mountains, down to the Eagle Cap Wilderness, Grande Ronde River, and the historic Elkhorn Mountains, and to the Snake River Divide–Hells Canyon area. Hunting is good throughout the region for mule deer, black bear, mountain sheep (by permit only), pheasant, and blue and ruffed grouse. Hells Canyon of the Snake River is the deepest canyon in North America. Its steep walls rise on the Oregon side to 7,000 feet at Bear Mountain, with the Seven Devils Range of Idaho forming a majestic backdrop towering to 9,000 feet. The Snake National Wild & Scenic River has some of the finest smallmouth bass fishing to be found anywhere, with bronzesides to 5 pounds and over quite common. Good-sized rainbows are found at the mouths of feeder streams. The Snake also holds some giant sturgeon, and channel catfish up to 20 pounds. About the only way to fish the Snake effectively is by boat, floating down from below the rapids at Eagle Bar. Access is generally by horse trail or jet-powered boat from Homestead. The major features along the Oregon-Idaho wild and scenic stretch of the Snake include the Wild Sheep, Granite, China, High Range, Wolf Creek, Zigzag, and Frenchy rapids. For detailed information, maps, and permits, write: Hells Canyon National Recreation Area, P.O. Box 907, Baker 97814.

The remote Imnaha River, with its headwaters in the Wallowa Mountains, flows east and then north for 75 miles through the Imnaha

Canyon into the Snake. The Imnaha has good fishing for rainbows to 18 inches, Dolly Varden, steelhead, and salmon. Spinners, wobblers, hotshots, or wet flies should do the trick. Several forest camps are located along the upper river.

The majestic Eagle Cap Wilderness embraces 293,476 acres in the heart of the Wallowa Mountains. The massive Eagle Cap is the central peak, forming the hub of many streams and over 50 lakes that lie at the foot of its precipitous slopes or in the high mountain basins. The rugged granite and limestone peaks are nearly devoid of timber, and where there is soil present, whitebark pines cling to the ridges. The rough topography is broken by many deep canyons, towered over by some of the highest peaks in eastern Oregon, with Sacajawea, at 10,033 feet, the highest. Other peaks popular with mountaineers include the Matterhorn—whose white limestone peak is in vivid contrast to the reddish-brown color of the adjoining rock formations—Pete's Point, Brown Mountain, Aneroid Mountain, and Eagle Cap. When climbing these peaks, exercise caution at all times. At the lower elevations, primitive trails, including the spectacular Washboard Trail, lead through forests of pine, firs, and Englemann spruce and through meadows ablaze with colorful buttercups, lupine, fleabane, and fawnlily to such wild areas as Swamp Basin, Hurwal Divide, Big Sheep Basin, Lake Basin, Lostine River, Hurricane Divide, Minam River, and the Imnaha Divide.

The full-color *Eagle Cap Wilderness Topographic Map*, available for 50¢ from: Forest Supervisor's Office, P.O. Box 907, Baker 97814, is a basic necessity for the wilderness traveler. It shows the wilderness and national forest boundaries, primitive forest roads and trails, mines, ranger stations, lookout towers, recreation sites and campsites, horse facilities, and private lands. The map contains a useful Wilderness Trip Planning Chart and a Trail Mileage Chart and lists wilderness entry points. The map shows all topographic features, contours, and alpine lakes. The high-altitude lakes, such as Aneroid, Bear, Frazier, Crater, Lookingglass, Moccasin, and Pocket, offer good fishing for small brook and golden, cutthroat, and rainbow trout amid spectacular scenery. Lovely remote Mirror Lake, located in the Lake Basin in the western part of the wilderness, has good fishing for pan-sized and very hungry brookies. Access is by the East Fork Lostine River trail. There are a few good forest camps located nearby along the Lostine River Road, with guide service and saddle horses. Frances Lake, located high up on the Hurricane Divide east of the Lostine River, has excellent fishing in September for brook, rainbow, and cutthroat trout up to 15 inches. A few transplanted mountain goats were released in Eagle Cap in the 1950s, and their numbers have steadily increased. The Wallowa Mountains are top elk and mule deer range in the scrub, canyons, and foothills and up in the timber. Blue and ruffed grouse are plentiful in the lower thickets of willow or alder, openings, burns, and logged areas. Ptarmigan found in the Bonny Lakes area were introduced in 1967. The world's entire population of rare Wallowa gray-crowned rosy finch *(Leucosticte tephrocotis wallowa)* nests only in such selected areas of the wilderness as Pete's Point, Jewett Lake, and Glacier Lake near Eagle Cap Mountain. These birds, first discovered in 1923, prefer a habitat of snowfields, rocks, and meadow patches. For wilderness camping, fishing, hunting, and permit info, write to the Wallowa-Whitman Forest Supervisor's Office (listed above).

The *Wallowa-Whitman National Forest Map* (50¢) shows natural features, forest service roads and trails, ranger stations, recreation sites and campgrounds, horse-loading ramps, boating sites, and wilderness areas. This full-color map, wilderness camping, fishing, and hunting info, and free brochures on the Hells Canyon–Seven Devils Scenic Area, the Snake, Imnaha, Minam, and Grande Ronde rivers, and the historic Elkhorn Mountains may be obtained by writing to the Office

Snake River Packers & Outfitters, 207 N.W. 3rd, Enterprise 97828, offers wilderness float trips and guided steelhead-fishing and elk-hunting trips; Merton Loree, Box 36, Cove 97824, offers elk-hunting and pack trips in Hells Canyon area; *Greg Johnson,* P.O. Box 447, Enterprise 97828, has guided elk-hunting pack trips in Hells Canyon; *James B. Walker,* 207 N.W. 3rd, Enterprise 97828, offers hunting, fishing and float trips on the Snake River and Hells Canyon; *Wilson's Troy Resort,* Flora Rt., Enterprise 97828, provides complete outfitting, fishing, hunting, and scenic tours; *Divide Camp,* Box 49, Joseph 97846, deer and elk-hunting lodge offering Eagle Cap Wilderness area fishing pack trips; *Calvin Henry,* Box 26, Joseph 97846, has deluxe camps with hunting and fishing pack trips and fly-in and float trips in Hells Canyon; *Isley's Guide & Packing Service,* P.O. Box 519, Joseph 97846; *James D. Tippett,* Rt. 1, Box 141, Joseph 97846, offers Snake River boat trips, deer and bird hunting, fishing and photography trips; *Rivers Navigation Company,* 1115 11th Avenue, Lewiston, Idaho, are contract mail carriers on the Snake and offer float and sight-seeing trips; *Jim Zarelli,* P.O. Box 145, Oxbow 97840, offers boat trips from Hells Canyon Dam to Wild Sheep Rapids; *Charlie Short,* P.O. Box 7, Union 97883, offers guide service and wilderness fishing, deer and elk-hunting trips; *Lapover Pack Camp,* Bear Creek Road, Wallowa 97885, provides guided trout-fishing and elk-hunting trips throughout the national forest; *Minam River Lodge, Inc.,* c/o D. Ranney Munro, 507 Corbett Bldg., 430 SW Morrison, Portland 97204; *Ted Grote Air Service,* Joseph 97846.

Access & Outfitting Centers

The Wallawa-Whitman National Forest is reached via Oregon Highways 7, 237, 86, 203, 244, 204, 82, and 3 and Interstate Highway 80N. Lodging, supplies, guides, and outfitting services are available at Baker, Union, La Grande, Minam, Lostine, Imnaha, Lewis, Homestead, Halfway, Cornucopia, Medical Springs, North Powder, and Elgin.

Willamette National Forest & High Cascades Wilderness Areas

Willamette National Forest Topo Maps

U.S. Geological Survey overview maps, scale 1:250,000: Bend, Roseburg, Salem.

McKenzie River Trail

U.S. Geological Survey large-scale maps: McKenzie Bridge, Echo Mountain, Three-Fingered Jack.

McKenzie River—Wild Trout & Steelhead Waters

U.S. Geological Survey large-scale maps: Blue River, Echo Mountain, Eugene E., Leaburg, McKenzie Bridge, Springfield, Three Sisters, Walterville.

Mount Jefferson Wilderness

U.S. Geological Survey large-scale maps: Breitenbush Hot Springs, Mount Jefferson, Three-Fingered Jack.

Mount Washington Wilderness

U.S. Geological Survey large-scale maps: Broken Top, Sisters, Three-Fingered Jack, Three Sisters.

Pacific Crest Trail

U.S. Geological Survey large-scale maps: Mount Jefferson, Breitenbush Hot Springs, Three-Fingered Jack.

The wilderness camping, fishing, and hunting areas of the 1.6 million

of the Forest Supervisor, Box 907, Baker 97814 or to the District Ranger Offices at: Wallowa 97885; Enterprise 97828; Joseph 97846; La Grande 97850; Union 97883; Halfway 97834; Unity 97884. *Trailhead Horse Facilities* in the forest are located at Boulder Park, Cornucopia, Lillyville, North Catherine Creek, Sheep Creek, and West Eagle Meadow. *Hells Canyon Reservoir Boat Camps* are located at Kirby Creek, Leep Creek, Lynch Creek, and Vermilliao Bar. *Snake River Boat Camps* are located at Lookout Creek, Salmon Bar, and Salt Creek. Lodging, supplies, boat rentals, and saddle stock are provided by the *Anthony Lake Corp.,* P.O. Box 262, Baker 97814 and by *Wilderness Inc.–Boulder Park Resort,* c/o Donald A. Jordan, P.O. Box 417, La Grande 97850.

Several established wilderness outfitters offer pack and saddle stock and guided camping, fishing, and hunting trips in the Wallowa high country, Snake River and Grande Ronde country, and Eagle Cap Wilderness. The famous *Eagle Cap Pack Station* (P.O. Box 416, Joseph 97846, phone 432–4145), Oregon's largest riding and pack station, provides guided alpine fishing, camping, elk hunting, and riding trips in the Eagle Cap Wilderness and Hells Canyon country. It also provides "drop camp" service in the remote big-game hunting areas.

acre Willamette National Forest stretch for 110 miles along the western slope of the Cascade Range in northwest Oregon between the Mount Hood National Forest on the north and the Umpqua National Forest on the south. The Willamette, the largest of Oregon's national forests, embraces several of the highest peaks in the cascades; Mount Jefferson, Mount Washington, and Three-Fingered Jack tower above luxuriant growths of Douglas fir. The world-famous trout and steelhead waters of the McKenzie, Santiam, Calapooya, and Blue rivers rise among the forest's highlands, and, with their tributaries, spread a network of scenic waterways throughout the entire region.

Hundreds of miles of high-country trails and remote logging roads provide the wilderness traveler with access to such renowned hunting, fishing, and hiking areas as the Three Sisters Wilderness, Mount Jefferson and Mount Washington wilderness areas, and the Diamond Peak Wilderness; they pass through high mountain forests of alpine fir and hemlock and along steep ridges, glaciers, lava flows, rocky summits, and hundreds of mountain lakes and ponds. The Pacific Crest Trail enters the north part of the forest from the Wapinitia Pass area, winding south through the huckleberry fields of Olallie Meadows and on along the rough mountain terrain, to Breitenbush Lake Camp, Pamelia Lake, Minto and Santiam passes, McKenzie Pass, Sunshine Campsite, Horse Lake Forest Station, and beautiful lake country, with numerous spur trails leading off to Irish, Taylor, Waldo, Lily, Cultus, and Maiden lakes. The Diamond Peak (8,744 ft.) Wilderness occupies 35,440 acres in the Willamette and Deschutes national forests. The mountain was formed as a giant volcanic peak and was carved through the ages by large glaciers. The area is the home of black-tailed deer, mule deer, elk, black bear, snowshoe rabbit, pine marten, and fox. During the summer months the meadows provide a brilliant display of bright yellow mules-ears, white sego lilies, blue lupine, and dark red Indian paintbrush. The wilderness is a good fishing area for brook, golden, and rainbow trout.

From its headwaters in Clear Lake in the Three Sisters Wilderness, the famed McKenzie River, a former haunt of Zane Grey and one of the nation's historic trout streams, flows southeast through a beautiful forest for 60 miles to its mouth just north of Eugene. The upper stretches of the river have some spectacular white water and excellent fishing for cutthroats and the native McKenzie rainbows, known as redsides. As a conservation measure, all redsides caught over 14 inches must be released. No one should attempt to float the treacherous upper stretches without the services of a licensed guide. For information write to the *Mackenzie Guide Association*, Vida 97488. Several forest camps and state park campgrounds are located along the upper stretches of the river. For detailed river running, fishing, and camping info and for a free copy of the *McKenzie River Trail Guide*, write to: McKenzie Ranger District, McKenzie Bridge 97401. The McKenzie's Clear Lake headwaters lie in a depression 2,000 feet deep, and were formed by the damming of the old Santiam Valley by the great McKenzie lava flow. Fed by giant springs, the lake is the coldest in the Cascades and is of such crystal clearness that rocks can be easily seen on the bottom at depths of 40 feet. Another renowned river in the forest is the Santiam, which holds some lunker rainbows near Idanha and in the Big Meadows Camp area. The South Fork of the Santiam offers good trout fishing in the Cascadia Forest area.

Trails lead from all directions to Waldo Lake, nestled deep within the national forest due south of the Three Sisters Wilderness. The crystal clear and extraordinarily blue waters of the 6-mile-long lake lie high on the western slopes of the Cascades. The shores of this scenic lake (the second largest in Oregon) are covered by a green mantle of Douglas fir, hemlock, and pine. The lake is very deep and supports a population of kokanee salmon and rainbow and brook trout. Large

brookies have been seen and caught near Shadow Bay and Dam Camp. More than 226 camping units are located within three campgrounds along the eastern shore of the Lake. A free *Waldo Lake Recreation Area Map*, showing the Pacific Crest Trail (which passes just east of the lake), forest service trails, roads, and campgrounds, may be obtained along with detailed travel, fishing, and camping info by writing: Oakridge Ranger District, Star Rt. 130 B, Oakridge 97492.

The 46,655-acre Mount Washington Wilderness is located along the crest of the Oregon Cascades adjoining the Three Sisters Wilderness in the Willamette and Deschutes national forests. A desolate, remote country of great beauty, the area is dominated by 7,802-foot Mount Washington, which rises sharply above the lava-strewn plains. Mount Washington is a vivid example of a dissected volcano whose ancient ice flows denuded the summit, leaving only the most resistant lava fillings. The area adjacent to Mount Washington has experienced more recent volcanic activity than any other part of the Cascade Range. The lava sheet surrounding the Belknap Cones, commonly referred to as a "black wilderness," is one of the largest in the United States. Belknap Crater, located near the center of the McKenzie lava field, is a cinder and ash cone built up to an elevation of 6,872 feet. The volcanoes of the Northwest, including those in the Mount Washington area at McKenzie Pass, are part of the "circle of fire" that rims the Pacific Ocean. Seventy million years ago Oregon was covered by a shallow sea dotted with volcanic islands. As the sea gradually withdrew, the continent emerged in the form of volcanic eruptions, spreading vast flows of basaltic lava over eastern Oregon about 15 million years ago. The High Cascade peaks are less than 10 million years old, and the eruptions have continued almost to modern times. When hiking in the wilderness, don't attempt to walk on the lava flows, for the footholds are unstable and the rock is extremely sharp. Mount Washington is one of the most popular climbs in Oregon, but the final ascent to the summit through chimneys of sheer rock requires the most exacting safety precautions. There are about 28 lakes in the area, about half of which hold rainbow and brook trout. Trails lead through the barren and rugged backcountry to the Twin Craters, Patjens Lakes, Hidden Valley, Washington Ponds, the Knobs, Elf Lake, Scott Mountain, and Tenas Lakes. The Pacific Crest Trail winds south for 16 miles from the northern boundary near Big Lake, around the west side of Mount Washington, over the lava beds, and past the Dee Wright Observatory, where there are striking views of the mountains and lava fields. Hunting is good in this area for black-tailed deer and elk. Mule deer, which winter in the Metolius Valley, ascend the east slope in the summer to the Cascade Divide. Black bear, mountain lion, snowshoe rabbit, fox, and coyote also inhabit the area. Game birds are few, although blue and ruffed grouse may occasionally be seen. For camping and trail information, write to: District Ranger, McKenzie Ranger Station, McKenzie Bridge 97401. A full-color *Mt. Washington Wilderness Map*, showing all topographic features, Pacific Crest National Scenic Trail and forest trails, and campgrounds and containing a detailed log of the Pacific Crest Trail, may be obtained by sending 50¢ to the Mackenzie District Ranger's Office.

The Mount Jefferson Wilderness, a famous mountaineering and camping area, encompasses 99,600 acres of volcanic plateau country in the Deschutes, Mount Hood, and Willamette national forests. Mount Jefferson (10,495 ft.) was named by Lewis and Clark in 1806 in honor of Thomas Jefferson when they sighted the mountain from a spot near the mouth of the Willamette River. Both Mount Jefferson and the adjacent Three-Fingered Jack, an eroded volcanic cone at 7,841 feet, provide challenges to the experienced climber on their spirelike peaks. Mount Jefferson has five major glaciers and massive rock outcroppings and talus slopes. At the lower elevations, dense conifer forests of mountain hemlock and subalpine, silver, and noble

fir cover the deposits of pumice and glacial debris. Glacial erosion has formed many U-shaped valleys, alpine meadows, lakes, and streams. More than 160 miles of trails, including 36 miles of the Pacific Crest Trail, fan out into the interior areas, such as Sugar Pine Ridge, Bingham Basin, Eight Lakes Basin, and the Jefferson and Cabot creeks lava flows. For those willing to pack in a rod and reel, there is some excellent fishing to be had in the lovely high alpine lakes. Mowich Lake, located in the Eight Lakes Basin several miles northwest of Three-Fingered Jack, holds brook trout up to 16 inches. The fly-fishing is best during the early morning hours, when the water is tranquil and the mists are evaporating among the crags. An inflatable rubber boat will prove helpful in getting out to the cruising waters along the island shoals. Access to Mowich is by trail from Big Meadows Camp or by the Marion Lake Trail. Marion Lake is good for rainbows; a sizable number of 3–4 pound fish are taken each year. Nearby Pamelia Lake, just southwest of Mount Jefferson, has good early-season fishing for pan-sized cutthroat trout. The area is usually accessible by late May, but there is still lots of snow on the ground. For detailed wilderness camping, fishing, and travel info, and for the topographic U.S. Forest Service *Mt. Jefferson Wilderness Map* (50¢), write: Willamette National Forest, Eugene 97401.

The full-color U.S. Forest Service *Willamette National Forest Map* shows all forest service trails, Pacific Crest National Scenic Trail, logging roads, recreation and boat-launching sites, campgrounds, and major features, including the Quaking Aspen Swamp Botanical Area, Rebel Rock Geological Area, Lamb Butte Scenic Areas, the Willamette and McKenzie rivers, and the Three Sisters, Diamond Peak, Mount Jefferson, and Mount Washington wilderness areas. This map may be obtained for 50¢ along with the free 56-page booklet *The Forest by Road & Highway: A Motorist's Guide to the Willamette Trails—A Hiker's Guide*, by writing: Supervisor, Willamette National Forest, P.O. Box 1272, Eugene 97401. For detailed hiking, wilderness camping, fishing, hunting, and permit information, write to the Forest Supervisor's Office, or to the District Ranger Office at: Blue River 97413; Detroit 97342; Lowell 97452; McKenzie Bridge 97401; Westfir 97492; Oakridge 97463; Sweet Home 97386.

Wilderness outfitting, packing, and guide service in the forest is provided by *E. T. Ware*, Rt. 1, Box 181, Stayton 97382. Lodging facilities and services are offered by: *Breitenbush Hot Springs Cabins*, c/o Wayne Halseth, Star Rt., Detroit 97342; at Clear Lake by the *Santiam Fish & Game Association*, c/o E. J. Anderson, 570 Harden Drive, Lebanon 97355; *Detroit Lake Resort*, Detroit 97342; *Santiam Service Center* on Lost Lake, Sisters 97759; *Slayden's Resort* on Detroit Reservoir, Detroit 97342.

Access & Outfitting Centers

The Willamette National Forest and wilderness areas are reached via U.S. Highways 20 and 97, Oregon Highways 22, 126, and 242, and forest roads. Lodging, supplies, wilderness outfitters, and guide service are available at McKenzie Bridge, Blue River, Rainbow, Vida, Sisters, Oakridge, Sweet Home, and Eugene.

Winema National Forest & Crater Lake National Park

Winema National Forest Topo Maps

U.S. Geological Survey maps, scale 1:250,000: Crescent, Klamath Falls, Medford.

Crater Lake National Park

U.S. Geological Survey large-scale maps: Garwood Butte, Diamond Lake, Miller Lake, Welch Butte, Prospect, Leny, Rustler Peak, Pelican Butte, Chiloquin, and Crater Lake National Park Map ($2).

Klamath National Wildlife Refuge

U.S. Geological Survey large-scale maps: Klamath Marsh, Leny.

Mountain Lakes Wilderness

U.S. Geological Survey large-scale maps: Crater Mountain, Monroe.

Pacific Crest Trail

U.S. Geological Survey large-scale maps showing Crater Lake segment of the trail: Diamond Lake, Crater Lake National Park, Pelican Butte.

Winema National Forest encompasses 909,000 acres among the snow-capped peaks, valleys, and mountain lakes of the beautiful southern Oregon Cascades. This region, one of Oregon's finest wilderness camping, fishing, and hunting regions, is named after the Indian wife of the trapper Frank Riddle, and means "woman of the brave heart," in honor of Winema's valient efforts during the Modoc Indian War of 1873 to save the lives of many pioneers. Today, more than half of the forest consists of former tribal lands of the Klamath Indians, located in Klamath County. Recorded history in the Klamath Basin began with the explorations of Hudson's Bay Company fur trader, Peter Ogden in 1826. The name Klamath is believed to have been derived from the French *clair métis*, "land of the white fogs." The Klamath Indians, however, referred to themselves as *Ouxkanee*, meaning "people of the marsh." In the early 1870s, the Klamath country was the scene of a stubborn struggle between pioneers and Modoc Indians, whose descendants live on the Klamath Reservation adjacent to the forest. The conflict, which caused this region to be known as the "dark and bloody ground of the Pacific," lasted until the Modocs agreed to return to the reservation, after they had made their final stand at the Lava Beds near Oregon's southern boundary.

The forest is traversed by hundreds of miles of logging roads and wilderness trails, providing access to such outstanding hunting and fishing areas as the nearby Upper Klamath Lake National Wildlife Refuge; Lake of the Woods; at 4,950 feet, Fourmile Lake; Miller Lake, nestled in the Cascades at 5,600 feet with excellent fishing for brook, rainbow, and kokanee salmon; Yamsay Mountain, a broken volcanic cone rising to 8,196 feet; Ya Whee Plateau; Chiloquin Ridge; Sky Lakes Wilderness area; Mount McLoughlin; and the Mountain Lakes Wilderness. The Pacific Crest Trail enters the forest as it winds its way south from Crater Lake National Park, passing along Fourmile Lake and Devils Peak (where the hiker may encounter summer snow-drifts) and traversing the Oregon Desert for 10 miles. Numerous spur trails provide access to remote streams, alpine lakes, peaks, and primitive campgrounds. Trail elevations range from 4,000 to 7,000 feet. South of the forest boundary, the trail passes through private lands, and it is not as well maintained or marked. The last leg of the trail passes Lake of the Woods, with campgrounds and excellent fishing, and heads for Copco Lake, about 2 miles south of the Oregon-California border. Hunting is excellent throughout the forest for black-tailed and mule deer.

Some of the finest waterfowl shooting in the Northwest is found in the area around the Upper Klamath Lake Refuge, which includes the Klamath Marsh, Williamson River, Agency Lake, and Klamath River. Upper Klamath Lake is Oregon's largest natural freshwater lake, fed by the drainage from the High Cascades around Crater Lake. It forms the headwaters of the Klamath River. The Williamson River, with its headwaters in the Klamath Forest National Wildlife Refuge, was once one of the nation's great trout streams, holding rainbows up to 15 and 20 pounds. Unfortunately, the Williamson has declined in recent years because of heavy fishing pressure and easy access. Agency Lake, near the north end of Upper Klamath Lake, is a large shallow marsh area famous for its teeming waterfowl and spring fishing for giant rainbows up to 12, 14, and 20 pounds, that pass through the lake to spawn in the Wood and Seven Mile rivers. In the early 1880s, a huge grizzly bear, known as "Old Twisted Foot," roamed the Sprague River

country. Twisted Foot, whose paw left a track about the size of a Mexican sombrero, was one of the largest bruins ever known in southern Oregon. He was killed by Indian Dick in 1885, after slaughtering cattle herds and eluding hunters for several years.

Mountain Lakes Wilderness embraces 23,071 acres in the southern part of Winema National Forest and is renowned for its beautiful alpine lakes and timbered shorelines surrounded by high mountains. The area lies about 40 miles south of Crater Lake in a large glacial basin around which are 8 prominent peaks, including Crater Mountain (7,785 ft.), Greylock Mountain (7,747 ft.), Aspen Butte (8,208 ft.), and Whiteface Peak (7,706 ft.). A loop-trail system leads up through a forest of pine and fir to the lakes. Deep, lovely Como Lake is reached by trail from Harriette Lake above the Pelican Guard Station. Fly-fishing is good in Como for pan-sized brook trout. Harriette Lake, the largest in the wilderness, is surrounded by towering peaks with numerous meadows and lakes scattered nearby. Fishing is good here for brookies to 15 inches. Access is by the Moss Creek Trail and the Varney Creek Trail. Well-maintained campsites are found along the shoreline. During the summer months black-tailed deer are common among the groves of fir and hemlock. During the fall, ducks and geese are numerous. Mosquitoes are thick following the snow melt in late June. Thundershowers are frequent in July and August.

The major features of Winema National Forest and Mountain Lake Wilderness, including beautiful Lake of the Woods, Fourmile Lake,

Upper Klamath Lake, and the Klamath Forest National Wildlife Refuge, are shown on the *Winema National Forest Map*. This map, available for 50¢ from: Forest Supervisor's Office, P.O. Box 1390, Klamath Falls 97601, shows forest roads and the Pacific Crest National Scenic Trail, ranger stations, campgrounds, points of interest, and boating sites. For information about trail conditions, fishing, hunting, and wilderness camping, and for free *District Ranger Maps* and the *Winema Fact Sheet* write: Forest Supervisor's Office, or Klamath Ranger District, 1936 California Avenue, Klamath Falls 97601; Chiloquin Ranger District, P.O. Box 357, Chiloquin 97624; Chemult Ranger District, P.O. Box 150, Chemult 97731. Lodging, supplies, and boat rentals are available at *Fourmile Lake*, c/o Marvin Rush, P.O. Box 865, Klamath Falls 97601; *Lake of the Woods Resort*, Lake of the Woods 97603; and *Rocky Point Resort*, Klamath Falls 97601. Horse rental, packing, and guided trips in the Lake of the Woods area and Mountain Lakes and Sky Lakes wilderness areas are provided by *Robert Schott*, Lake of the Woods 97603.

The many geological wonders of Crater Lake National Park are located along the northwestern boundary of Winema National Forest. The park embraces 160,290 acres of the southern Cascade Range.

Crater Lake lies inside the great pit, or Caldera, created by the collapse of the Mount Mazama volcano in prehistoric times. This ancient volcano is one in a north-south chain of huge cones built during the last few million years along the crest of the Cascade Range, stretching about 600 miles from Lasser Peak in California northward to Mount Garibaldi, near Vancouver, British Columbia. Other prominent vol-

canoes in the chain include Mounts Shasta, Jefferson, Hood, Saint Helens, Adams, Rainier, and Baker. According to geologists, Mount Mazama once had an elevation of 14,000 feet. The upper portion of the mountain caved inward and left a craterlike rim rising to 2,000 feet. Today, the lake lies at 6,239 feet above sea level, is 4 miles wide and 6 miles long, and is the deepest body of freshwater in the United States, reaching depths in some places of nearly 2,000 feet. Crater Lake was discovered on June 12, 1853, by John Wesley Hillman, a young prospector and member of a party in search of a rumored "Lost Cabin Mine." Hillman named it Deep Blue Lake. Sixteen years later, it was changed to its present name. Multicolored rock walls 500 to 2,000 feet high surround the blue waters. The lake has never been known to freeze, and although it has no visible outlet, its waters are fresh. The Pacific Crest Trail passes around the western slope of the mountain, and short trails lead up and along the rim. Throughout most of the year, the area is covered by a deep blanket of snow. With the arrival of summer, the deep greens of the coniferous forests are patched with the brilliant meadow displays of phlox, monkeyflower, Indian paintbrush, lupine, and aster. Black bear, coyote, elk, bald and golden eagle, water ouzel, and mule and whitetail deer inhabit the wilderness.

The major features of the park, including Mount Mazama, Eagle Crags, Wizard Island, the haunting Phantom Ship, Palisades, and the Pumice Desert, are shown on the beautiful full-color *Crater Lake National Park Topographic Map* ($2) published by the U.S. Geological Survey. This map, which is also available in a shaded-relief edition, shows lake depth contours, the scenic Rim Drive, Crater Lake Lodge, and wilderness trails, including the Pacific Crest National Scenic Trail. The reverse side of the map contains a detailed geological history of the park and fascinating maps and charts showing the floor of Crater Lake, distribution of pumice deposits, and a geologic map of the lake and Mount Mazama.

Fishing, backcountry camping, trail information, and copies of the Crater Lake National Park U.S. Geological Survey map may be obtained by writing: Superintendent, Crater Lake National Park, P.O. Box 7, Crater Lake 97604. Fishing is fair at best for rainbows, Dolly Varden, and cutthroat trout in the lake. If you intend to fish in the lake, the best places are the shallows, such as those around Wizard Island. Boats are available for hire at the landing below the Rim Village at the southwest side of the lake. *Crater Lake Lodge*, Crater Lake 97604 (winter address: P.O. Box D, Beaverton 97005) provides lodging, meals, transportation, and boat services. Camping facilities in the park are located at Mazama Campground (198 sites), at Rim Village (54 sites), Lost Creek (12 sites), and the primitive Pinnacles campground. Several useful guidebooks to the park are available from the Crater Lake Natural History Association, Crater Lake 97604: *Along Crater Lake Roads*, Rukle, $1.00; *Ancient Tribes of the Klamath Country*, Howe, $5.95; *Birds of Crater Lake*, Farner, $2.50; *Crater Lake National Park*, Spring, $2.95; *Crater Lake: Story of its Origin*, Williams, $2.00; *Wildlife and Plants of the Cascades*, Yocum and Brown, $4.95. *Exploring Crater Lake Country* by Ruth Kirk, $4.95, is an excellent guide to the park's ancient geologic history, forests, wildflowers, wildlife, the Klamath Indians, settlement days and the Modoc War, the Rim Drive, boating, hikes, and trips beyond the park's boundaries.

Access & Outfitting Centers

Winema National Forest and Crater Lake are reached via Interstate Highway 97 and Oregon Highways 62, 232, 138, and 58. Lodging, supplies, guides, and outfitting service are available at Klamath Falls, Chiloquin, Beaver Marsh, Spraque River, Diamond Lake, and Chemult.

Accommodations— Vacation Lodges & Ranches

There is a wide variety of these accommodations throughout the state. The chamber of commerce in the area where you plan to travel will provide you with information on accommodations. To get the address of the local chamber, write to: California State Chamber of Commerce, P.O. Box 1736, Sacramento 95808. For information on family vacation guest ranches, resorts, and dude ranches, write: Guest Ranch Reservation Center, 6000 W. Sunset Blvd., Los Angeles 90028. Write Far West Ski Association, 812 Howard St., San Francisco 94103 and 1313 W. 8th St., Los Angeles 90017 for northern and southern California ski resort listings.

Listings and descriptions of many of the state's vacation lodges and resorts are found throughout the "California Travel & Recreation Guide."

American River Touring Association—North American Wilderness Expeditions & Instruction

The renowned American River Touring Association is a nonprofit organization that helps to support educational programs, including the River Classroom, the American White-water School, and river conservation and exploration. White-water workshops are designed for outdoor enthusiasts interested in mastering the techniques of white-water navigation and the essentials of river expeditioning, including the operation of both oar-powered and paddle rafts, kayaking, river-running logistics, minimal-impact camping, and outdoor cookery. Annual white-water workshops are held in California on the American, Stanislaus, and Tuolumne rivers; in Oregon on the Rogue, McKenzie, North Umpqua, and Klamath rivers; in Idaho on the main and middle forks of the Salmon River.

In addition to its wild-water education program, ARTA offers guided summer trips down the nation's great wild rivers and provides complete airline ticketing service for commercial flights to cities near the destination river. Guided River trips include the Rogue River camp and lodge adventures; the wild Illinois River, surrounded by Oregon's Siskiyou Mountains; the great canyon rivers of Utah, including the Green and Colorado rivers, Yampa River, and Green River Wilderness; Grand Canyon of the Colorado; Idaho's wild Selway River, between Whitecap and Selway Falls; the main and middle forks of the Salmon in the Idaho Primitive Area; California's gold-rush rivers, including the Stanislaus, Tuolumne and South Fork of the American, and the Klamath River; the Rio Grande River in Texas's Big Bend National Park; Colorado's wild Dolores River and the Slickrock Canyon; Wisconsin's St. Croix National Wild & Scenic River, the scenic Flambeau River, and the beautiful Apostle Islands canoe adventure (see Wisconsin in the "Great Lakes States").

The association also offers guided wilderness trips on British Columbia's Chilcotin and Fraser rivers as well as to the jungle wilderness headwaters of the Amazon and Urubamba rivers in the legendary Sacred Valley of the Incas surrounded by the primeval Amazon rain forest and the High Andes.

For detailed information and rates of the ARTA wild-water education programs and guided trips, and for a free copy of the *ARTA River Adventure Catalog*, write: American River Touring Association, 1016 Jackson St., Oakland, 94607 (phone: 415-465-9355).

CALIFORNIA ENCYCLOPEDIA

Baja California—Saltwater Fishing & Vacation Guide

Baja, California, one of the world's great saltwater fishing meccas, is a narrow, primitive, 800-mile-long mountainous peninsula on Mexico's west coast that reaches south like a long finger from just below San Diego to its southernmost tip at San José del Cabo. The peninsula is divided into the sparsely settled southern Territory of Baja California, or *Baja Sur*, central, and northern Baja; it is bounded on the west by the Pacific Ocean and on the east by the Gulf of California, also referred to as the "Sea of Cortez." The rugged, majestic southern cape of the Baja, reached by air or by car along the 1,000-mile-long narrow and treacherous Transpeninsular Highway, is a saltwater fisherman's paradise for striped marlin from February through June, broadbill swordfish year-round in the deep water off Cabo Pulmo south to San José del Cabo, big blue and black marlin during summer and early fall, roosterfish and dolphin (dorados) year-round with May through November the hot months, yellowtail during the massive January–May migration, Pacific sailfish during the summer and fall, and yellowfin tuna year-round. The surf-fishing and scuba diving in Baja Sur are superb. Awesomely scenic southern Baja has several of the world's most beautiful deluxe fishing resorts overlooking the ocean, flanked by mountains, which offer diesel fishing cruisers, tennis, hunting, riding, and skeet shooting. Three of the best known include Hotel Cabo San Lucas, Camino Real, and Hotel Finisterra. Central Baja offers excellent fishing on the Gulf of California for huge schools of marlin from late May through July, and for roosterfish, yellowfin tuna, dolphin, Sierra and giant grouper, as well as giant black snook up to 6 feet in the coastal rivers. The central Baja fishing vacation centers are at Mulegé, Santa Rosalía, and Loreto. Fishing in the northern Baja, a pale comparison to that found to the south, is headquartered at Ensenada.

Anyone planning a trip to the Baja is well advised to read Ray Cannon's classic, beautifully illustrated *Sea of Cortez*. Autographed copies are available for $12.10 (postpaid) from the author, Ray Cannon, 645 N. Serrano, Los Angeles 90004. The 168-page *Baja Book* by Tom Miller and Elmar Baxter contains 50 regional NASA satellite photo maps of the peninsula and the Baja Highway, which show secondary roads and 4-wheel drive trails, as well as towns and ranches, resorts, campgrounds, trailer parks, marinas, and airports, along with useful information about history, fishing, border regulations, and licenses. The book is available for $7.95 (postpaid) from Baja Trail Publications, Box 15444, Santa Ana 92705. Aeromexico has 10 nonstop flights weekly from Los Angeles. For detailed information about fishing, resorts, transportation, and other Baja info, write: Lewis Company Ltd., *Mexican National Tourist Council*, 8560 Sunset Blvd., Suite 500, Los Angeles 90069.

Camping & Wilderness Travel

California offers perhaps the widest spectrum of wilderness environments in which to camp and hike in the country. The state park system is outstanding. It includes 900,000 acres, nearly 9,000 campsites, and 700 miles of riding and hiking trails. The campsites dot an array of environments that range from deserts and rain forests to tundra. The state park system includes wildernesses, historical areas, and reserves (these usually have no facilities). A *Guide to the California State Park System* is available from: California Department of Parks and Recreation, P.O. Box 2390, Sacramento 95811. The guide groups the state parks into the Coast Redwoods, Coastal Mountains, Inland Mountains, Southern Inland, Central Valley, and North, Central, and South Coast regions. It maps and describes the state parks in each of these regions, noting which parks have primitive or family campsites and other facilities. The booklet also explains state park regulations and fees, and includes a list of publications that can be ordered from the Department of Parks and Recreation.

Camping is also available in the state's national forests and parks. U.S. Forest campsites are shown on all national forest recreation maps listed in the "California Map and Recreation Guide" section.

To the Wilderness Traveler is another useful free publication of the California Region Office (address above). This brochure describes the

4,500 miles of roadless areas in the state wilderness areas and the trails through them, gives information on backpacking and traveling with stock, and lists regulations for these areas. The map in the brochure marks the wilderness areas in national parks and forests and keys the location of ranger stations throughout the state, as well as national forest and national park headquarters. It also keys the U.S. Geological Survey topographic quadrangle maps in backcountry areas. A shorter pamphlet from the same office, entitled *The Wilderness Traveler*, gives travel advice, horse and pack stock information, and specific suggestions for waste disposal and firebuilding in the wilderness, along with information about getting a wilderness permit. A separate pamphlet (also free), *California Campfire Rules*, is also available from the California Region Office.

The Pacific Gas and Electric Company publishes a free map-guide to campgrounds on PG & E watershed lands and hydroelectric facilities from the Pit River in the Cascade Range to the Mokelumne of the Sierra Nevada. Elevation, facilities, and recreational opportunities are described. Write to: P.G. & E., Public Information Dept., Rm. 1730, 77 Beale St., San Francisco 94106.

Canoeing & Wild Rivers

There are no more inspiring paths through the unspoiled backcountry of California than its wild rivers. The wild sections of these rivers have been left in their natural state and are generally inaccessible except by trail. The scenic areas may be accessible at some points by vehicle, but remain largely undeveloped. The rivers also have recreational areas, which are developed for such use. California classified a number of its rivers into sections under the California Wild and Scenic Rivers Act

in 1972. The protected rivers include most of the Smith, Klamath, New, Salmon, Trinity, and South Fork Trinity; portions of the North Fork American and Scott; and large portions of the South, Middle, and North Forks of the Eel and the Van Duzen. The Eel and Van Duzen rivers are subject to changes in status after a review of the need for water in 1984. Other popular wild rivers in the state are the Stanislaus and Toulumne.

The Klamath rises in the eastern Oregon Cascades and enters the state below Copco Lake; it courses through the craggy canyons of the upper Central Valley, the deep, lonely chasms near Happy Camp, and through the majestic redwoods of the north to the sea. The North Fork of the Salmon begins among a group of jewellike lakes in the Marble Mountain Wilderness; the South Fork flows from a glacier bed high atop Thompson Peak in the Trinity Alps. The forks meet near Acorn Flat and plunge northward over a delightful white-water stretch to the confluence with the Klamath. The waters of the Trinity have lost some of their beauty as a result of projects to channel the river flow eastward into the Sacramento, but there are breathtaking wild stretches left along its 150-mile length. This river flows down from its source among the Scott and Salmon mountains to join the waters of the Salmon and form the Klamath. The Eel rises much farther south and flows north through rolling hills and coastal redwoods to plunge into the sea below Eureka. It is a changeable river, strewn with mud and debris during the furious flood waters of early spring and nearly dry in places by July.

The Wild and Scenic River classification has saved certain portions of the American River's North Fork from the hands of hydroelectric developers, but diversion dams have spoiled much of the distance for boating. But the river begins triumphantly, arising from the High Sierra and tumbling through the canyons and forests of the Mother Lode country.

The 108-mile Middle Fork of the Feather National Wild & Scenic River flows through the northeastern corner of the Sierra Valley in the Plumas National Forest, where Little Last Chance Creek joins it. It flows southwesterly through the forest and through a rugged canyon into Lake Oroville.

Down the Wild Rivers gives detailed descriptions of floatable sections of most of California's most beautiful streams and includes maps of the runs described which key the locations of diversions, canals, falls, tributaries, roads, put-ins, take-outs, and railroads. This 200-plus page book also gives important information on how and when to plan your trip. It costs $4.95 and is available from Chronicle Books, San Francisco.

An even more detailed guide, *West Coast River Touring—Rogue River Canyon and South,* describes 1,700 miles of river runs throughout the state. It includes both easy and difficult runs, location, scenery, U.S. Geological Survey topographical maps and National Forest maps available, flow predictions, scenery, drainage, and rating for canoes and rafts are given for each river run. Maps of the rivers mark runs, sections not run, towns and cities, creeks, good roads, poor roads, highways, and put-ins and take-outs. The book costs $6.95 and can be ordered from: Touchstone Press, P.O. Box 81, Beaverton, OR 97005. For a detailed description of the state's wild rivers, see the "California Travel & Recreation Guide" and "Guides, Packers & Wilderness Outfitters" in this section.

Death Valley

Death Valley presents a harsh and awesome environment to the wilderness traveler. The plants of this desert land are unique; they have evolved specialized means of obtaining and preserving precious water, because less than 2 inches of rain fall here yearly. The small animals of the area have adapted to a life with little water, while the larger ones seek it out or obtain it from the bodies of the animals on which they prey.

Strangely, many men inhabited this wilderness before our time and left their mark upon it. Prehistoric hunters and gatherers roamed the desert and left trails, rock drawings, and campsites. The Panamint Indians lived here when the Forty-niners arrived in search of precious metals. But the settlements were short-lived, and today the permanent population is negligible.

Death Valley National Monument covers about 3,000 square miles along the central portion of the state's eastern border. The monument encompasses dunes, salt flats, colorful canyons, and desert mountains that vary from 200 feet below sea level to 11,329 feet. The four campgrounds in the monument include Furnace Creek, Grapevine, Stovepipe Wells, and Wildrose Canyon. *The Furnace Creek Inn and Ranch* includes hotel rooms, cabins, food services, a store and garage, swimming, and horses. It offers limited services from November through April. For more information on the inn, write to Fred Harvey, Box 187, Death Valley 92328. *Stovepipe Wells Village* also offers overnight accommodations. Write to the village at Death Valley 92328.

If you decide to camp here, remember that the desert is an untamed wilderness. Never travel alone, and always tell someone where you are going and when you expect to return. Watch for flash floods when storms threaten. Carry water for you and your car. The extremely hot months—May through October—are only for the hardy. The monument is especially beautiful in early spring, when colorful desert flowers burst into bloom.

A *Death Valley National Monument* brochure describing its major features, accommodations and services, access, regulations, and trips through it is available free from: Supervisor, Death Valley Monument, Death Valley 92328. The brochure includes a map on a scale of 10 miles to 1 inch which keys the locations of campgrounds, secondary campgrounds, roads, jeep trails, and foot trails. Another brochure, *Camping in Death Valley,* describes bus service from Las Vegas to the monument, periods of heavy visitations, commercial services, and facilities, elevation, and location of campsites. It is available from: Death Valley Natural History Association, Inc., P.O. Box 188, Death Valley 92328. This organization also publishes a complete bibliography of books and maps about the area. Ask for its free list of publications. The U.S. Geological Survey publishes a full-color *Death Valley National Monument & Vicinity Topographic Map.* The map is 24 × 37 inches with a scale of 1:250,000 and costs $2.00.

Fenwick California Bass & Fly Fishing Schools

The world-famous Fenwick Corporation, makers of quality fishing rods and gear, operates bass and fly-fishing schools at several of California's renowned lakes and streams. The Fenwick fly-fishing schools, open to beginners through advanced fly-fishermen, offer instruction in fly casting and water safety, tackle, entomology and artificial flies, fly presentation, stream lore, and wading. The bass-fishing schools include intensive instruction in the anatomy of a bass and its life cycle, tackle, school fish behavior, deep-water versus shallow-water presentation, lures, casting and fishing, contour map reading, instruments and equipment (light meters, temperature gauges, oxygen meters, depth finders, trolling motors), and finding and patterning fish.

Fenwick's California fly fishing schools are headquartered at the famous Hartsook Inn on the *South Fork of the Eel River* in the heart of Redwood Country (2-day schools—May, June, September); at Putah Creek Park on 25-mile-long *Lake Berryessa*, which holds bass, kokanee salmon, landlocked steelhead, and trophy trout; at Coto de Caza in *Trabuco Canyon*, with 5,000 acres of open meadows and rolling hills in the Santa Ana Mountains, and with a large flat water area ideal for fly-casting instruction; at the Riverland Resort on the *Kings River*, near Kingsburg; and at the *Squaw Valley* base for both the Truckee River and beautiful Lake Tahoe. The *Fenwick Russian River Special Steelhead School* is on the river at Murphy's Ranch, a picturesque resort near Guerneville with rustic lodge accommodations and camping facilities nearby. The steelhead school curriculum includes special distance casting techniques, how to build your own shooting heads and leaders, fly construction and selection, and stream lore and wading.

The Fenwick bass fishing schools are headquartered at *Cachuma Lake* and *Lake Berryessa*. Cachuma Lake, located 24 miles northwest of Santa Barbara, is an outstanding fishery recognized by top bass fishermen as one of the most productive large and smallmouth bass lakes in California. There are 400 picturesque campsites for tents and trailers near the lake. Lake Berryessa, situated in northern California near Napa, is a top-ranked large and smallmouth bass fishery noted for its abundance of threadfin shad and varied types of bottom structures. Both of these 2-day schools operate during March and are open to beginners through advanced bass fishermen.

For free literature, rates and info, write: Director: Fenwick Fly Fishing School, Western Division, P.O. Box 1191, Novato, 94947 (415–883–3200).

Fishing & Hunting in California

The Golden State's huge tracts of national forests and high-country wilderness areas, great snowcapped mountain ranges, deep-flowing wild rivers and thousands of remote blue alpine lakes, and thousand-mile coastline offer an unsurpassed variety of freshwater and saltwater fishing and hunting opportunities. The state's scenic wild rivers and high-country lakes provide fishing for seven species of trout, including brown, cutthroat, rainbow, golden, eastern brook, Dolly Varden, and lake. Of these seven, the cutthroat, rainbow, golden, and Dolly Varden are natives, while the brown, eastern brook and lake trout have been introduced.

Rainbow Trout

The rainbow is by far the most widely distributed trout in California. Resident rainbow rarely attain a large size in the state, however, in lakes such as Eagle, Davis, Shasta, and Clair Engle, rainbows grow rapidly, and one weighing 18 pounds was recorded from Lake Almanor. Steelhead are found in many of the streams flowing into the Pacific. The most productive steelhead runs occur on the Smith, the northernmost coastal stream in California; on the big, turbulent Klamath and its scenic high-country tributaries, the Trinity and Salmon rivers; on the main Eel River and its Middle and South Fork; on Russian River; on the renowned Sacramento and its tributaries; and on the Mokelumne River. Fly-fishing for steelhead was firmly established as an American sport on the deep forest-bordered pools and riffles of the Klamath (and Rogue) River in the 1920s in the historic Happy Camp and Somes Bar areas by the legendary fisherman and author Zane Grey.

The famous Eagle Lake rainbow trout was originally native only to

Eagle Lake at 5,100 feet elevation in the Lassen National Forest and its tributary, Pine Creek, but it has been transplanted to several lakes in the Lassen and Modoc national forest regions. Beautiful Eagle Lake, known as the "lake that time forgot," lies within the Lahontan system, a drainage area of the Great Basin of North America with a number of fish species of unusual scientific interest. The Eagle Lake rainbows thrive in the lake's fertile alkaline water, where they feed on native tiu chubs and reach weights up to 11 pounds. (See "Lassen National Forest & Volcanic Park" in "California Travel & Recreation Guide.")

Golden Trout

The beautiful golden trout was originally limited to a few streams in the High Sierra headwaters of the Kern River, at elevations from 6,000 to 11,000 feet. California golden trout, which have been transplanted throughout the western and Rocky Mountain states, are now present in a number of remote scenic alpine lakes and streams, mostly at elevations over 8,000 feet, in the John Muir Wilderness Area in the High Sierras, and in the beautiful Salmon–Trinity Alps Primitive Area and Marble Mountain Wilderness of northern California. The extremely beautiful yellow and red coloration of the golden trout has resulted in its being named the state fish. Beautiful Virginia Lake, situated at 10,300 feet elevation, south of Yosemite in the Sierra National Forest, produced the state record 9 lb. 8 oz. golden in 1952.

The coastal cutthroat is a northern trout whose range extends only a short distance into California. Sea-run cutthroat are taken in Redwood Creek and in the Mad, Klamath, and Smith rivers in the Klamath and Six rivers national forests.

Cutthroat, Dolly Varden, Brown Trout & Chars

The Lahontan cutthroat trout (also known as the Tahoe and black-spotted trout) is a native of the Truckee, Walker, and Carson river systems. It was abundant in the crystal-clear waters of Lake Tahoe and in Nevada's Pyramid Lake until it became virtually extinct in the 1940s. Huge runs of Lahontan cutthroat up to 30 pounds once ascended the tributary streams of Tahoe to spawn in April. The most likely reason for its extinction was the introduction of lake and rainbow trout into the lake. (Tahoe, or "big waters," as it was originally known to the Washo Indians, was first called Mountain Lake by Capt. John Frémont, but appeared as Lake Bonplan—for the French botanist—on the map of his first passage of the Sierra Nevada.) The Piute cutthroat trout is restricted to upper Silver King Creek and its tributaries above Llewellyn Falls, an insurmountable barrier situated at the lower end of Fish Valley (and in Silver King Creek, a tributary of the East Carson River) in a remote region of Alpine County, east of the Sierra Divide. The Piute was separated a great many years ago from the Lahontan cutthroat living in the Carson River (named for Kit Carson, who with Capt. John Frémont explored the area in 1843–44 while searching for a direct overland route to California from the East) below the falls, and through the centuries developed a coloration pattern very similar to that of the golden trout.

The wild brown trout, introduced from Europe where it was originally described in 1758 by the great naturalist Linnaeus, is found widely scattered throughout the lakes and streams along both sides of the High Sierras. The Dolly Varden is found only in the McCloud River below the lower falls and the reservoirs connected with it. The name of the fish originated in California. In a publication in 1919, it was stated that: "When this fish was taken by scientists in the McCloud River, the resemblance to a dress goods with spots called Dolly Varden, and which was then the rage, led to its being given this name by lady members of the party, and 'Dolly Varden' it has been ever since." The eastern brook trout is found in high mountain lakes and

small streams at elevations between 5,000 and 11,000 feet from the San Bernardino Range northward through the High Sierras and wilderness areas of the Sierra, Stanislaus, Inyo, Plumas, Eldorado, Tahoe, and Lassen national forests to the Salmon-Trinity Alps and Marble Mountains near the Oregon border. The lake trout, or mackinaw, was brought to California in 1895 from Michigan and was planted in Lake Tahoe and Donner Lake, which make up its present-day range. Kokanee salmon, the red landlocked sockeye salmon, have been planted in about 35 lakes, including Donner Lake (named for the ill-fated Donner Party, whose members died near the lake in 1846).

Trophy Trout Waters

Several of California's streams are of national renown for their top-quality fishing for large wild trout. Scenic Fall River, a tributary of the Pit, located in Shasta National Forest, is one of the state's premier trout waters. During the summer of 1974, Department of Fish & Game biologists conducted a fish count on a small section of this stream using electrical-shocking gear. In one deep pool, they counted 27 trout over 12 pounds and one giant that tipped the scales at 18 pounds. Trout in the Fall include wild browns, rainbows, cutthroats, and brookies. The river must be fished from a boat or canoe due to restricted access. Located 35 miles north of Bishop in the Inyo National Forest, the Fall River is ranked as one of America's top 10 dry fly streams for rainbow and brown trout up to 9 pounds. The historic 170-mile-long Pit River, once one of the nation's great trout streams, still continues to yield big rainbows in spite of its 7 dams. The lightly fished waters of the Pit have good early and late season mayfly hatches. Wading can be hazardous because of the slick moss-covered boulders. The East Walker River, located due east of Yosemite and named for Capt. Joseph Walker, who led a trapping and exploring party into the area in 1833–34, is a trophy wild trout stream that holds some very large brown trout. The famous Kings River, which heads in the High Sierras in Kings Canyon National Park, is a rugged stream with large boulders and a slick, rocky bottom. It offers good fly-fishing for wild, spooky trout. (For additional information on California's wild trout, see "High Sierra Golden Trout Lakes & the John Muir Trail" in this section; for additional descriptions of alpine lakes and trout streams and topographic maps, see "California Travel & Recreation Guide.")

Several of California's nationally renowned trout streams are currently being managed as quality fly-fishing-only waters under the state's Wild Trout Program. The deep-flowing pools and rapids of these scenic Cascade–Sierra Nevada high-country streams offer excellent opportunities for trophy rainbow and brown trout. The state's managed quality fly-fishing-only waters include: the North Fork of the American River in Placer County, East Fork of the Carson River in Alpine County, Clavey River in Tuolumne County (for golden trout), Cottonwood Creek in Inyo County, Fall River in Shasta County, Middle Fork of the Feather River in Butte and Plumas counties, Hat Creek in Shasta County, Hot Creek in Mono County, Kings River and South Fork of the Kings in Fresno County, Klamath River from Copco Lake upstream to the Oregon border in Siskiyou County, McCloud River, South Fork of the Merced River in Mariposa County, Nelson Creek in Plumas County, Owens River in Inyo County, Rubicon River in Placer County, and Yellow Creek in Plumas County. For detailed information and special restrictions, write: California Dept. of Fish & Game, Resources Bldg., 1416 Ninth St., Sacramento 95814 and *Cal Trout/Wilderness Flyfishers*, P.O. Box 2046, San Francisco 94126.

Much of the wilderness fishing on California's remote High Sierra lakes and state-designated wild trout streams is done on a catch and release basis, often using barbless hooks, to protect the fragile stream ecology, spawning cycles, and slow growth rates of wild trout.

For more detailed information, consult the Department of Fish and Game's guide *Trout of California* (70¢), available from: Office of Procurement, Documents Section, P.O. Box 20191, Sacramento 95820. The book pictures and describes all of the trout species in the state, their distributions, and interesting facts about them. The book contains beautiful full-color plates of California trout and trout management, answers common questions, and provides suggested reading.

Largemouth & Smallmouth Bass

The large lakes and reservoirs of California produce some of the most spectacular largemouth and smallmouth bass fishing in America. The famous San Diego Bass Lakes, stocked with transplanted Florida bass in 1959, annually produce largemouths in the 17–20 pound class. The San Diego Lakes—Murray, Miramar, Lower Otay, Sutherland, San Vincent, Barrett, and El Capitan—are reported to hold bass exceeding the world record of 22 pounds 4 ounces, caught in Georgia's Montgomery Lake. Lake Berryessa in central California is one of the most productive lakes in the state for smallmouth and largemouth bass. Huge Lake Shasta in the northern portion of the state holds just about every species of freshwater game fish, including largemouth and smallmouth bass, Kamloops and native rainbow trout, and large brown

trout. Nearby Clair Engle and Lewiston lakes on the Trinity River provide often excellent fishing for kokanee salmon, rainbow trout, and bass. Famous Davis Lake in Plumas National Forest is a prolific producer of fat rainbow trout averaging 2½ pounds.

California's varied and productive fishing is highlighted by the state record freshwater fish compiled by the Department of Fish & Game.

CALIFORNIA RECORD FRESHWATER FISH

	Lb.–oz.	Place	Year
Brown trout	25–11	Crowley Lake, Mono County	1971
Cutthroat trout	31–8	Lake Tahoe, Placer & El Dorado counties	1911
Rainbow-Steelhead trout	27–4	Smith River, Del Norte County	1976
Eastern brook trout	9–12	Silver Lake, Mono County	1932
Golden trout	9–8	Virginia Lake, Fresno County	1952
Dolly Varden trout	9–11	McCloud Res., Siskiyou County	1968
Lake trout	37–6	Lake Tahoe, Placer & El Dorado counties	1974
Arctic grayling	1–12	Lobdell Lake, Mono County	1974
Kokanee salmon	4–13	Lake Tahoe, Placer & El Dorado counties	1973
Chinook salmon	85	Feather River	1935
Coho salmon	22	Paper Mill Creek Marin County	1959
Largemouth bass	20–15	Miramar Lake, San Diego County	1973
Smallmouth bass	7–11	Trapper Slough, San Joaquin County	1951
White crappie	4–8	Clear Lake, Lake County	1971
Black crappie	4	Mendota Pool, Fresno and Madera counties	1956
Bluegill	2–9	Middle Legg Lake, Los Angeles County	1971
Channel catfish	41	Lake Casitas, Ventura County	1972
Flathead catfish	51–8	Colorado River	1973
Striped bass	65	San Joaquin River	1951
White bass	5–5	Ferguson Lake (Colorado River)	1972
Sturgeon	420	Sacramento River	1973
American shad	6–15	Yuba River	1970

Saltwater Fishing

California's fabled Pacific coastline with its numerous bays and islands provides excellent surf and offshore saltwater fishing for striped bass, king and silver salmon, tuna, and bottom fish. The most productive salmon fishing is to be found in the Humboldt Bay, Shelter Cove, Fort Bragg, Trinidad, Tomales Bay, and San Francisco Bay areas. Salmon boat charters and accommodations are available along the coast. Some of the best saltwater fishing in the country is to be found off the southern California coast in the Channel Islands area for giant sea bass up to 400 pounds, yellowtail, barracuda, and for albacore during their northern migration. Swordfish, marlin, and bluefin tuna are found off the San Clemente, Santa Cruz, and Santa Catalina islands. The coast and bays offer excellent surf-casting and fly-fishing year-round for striped bass up to the state record 65-pound weight. Some of the best fishing for large stripers is to be had during their early spring and fall migrations up coastal rivers such as the Napa, Feather, and Sacramento.

Fishing and Hunting Maps & Guides

For fishing and hunting information, regulations, license and permit information, and hunting and wildlife management area maps, write: California Department of Fish & Game, Resources Bldg., 1416 Ninth Street, Sacramento 95814. The high-country wilderness fisherman will find the free publication *Where to Find California's Golden Trout* of interest. To obtain a copy, write to the Fish & Game Department (address listed above) and be sure to enclose a self-addressed, stamped, legal-size envelope. A wealth of useful Department of Fish & Game guides and maps may be obtained from: Office of Procurement, Documents Section, P.O. Box 20191, Sacramento 95820. The informative booklets *Offshore Fishes* and *Inshore Fishes* are available from the Documents Section for 70¢ each. Angler's Guides to *Striped Bass, Klamath River* and *Salmon and Steelhead* and Ocean Fishing Maps for *Del Norte, Humboldt and Mendocino Counties, Marin and Sonoma Counties, San Francisco, San Mateo and Santa Cruz Counties, Monterey and San Luis Obispo Counties* may be obtained from the Documents Section for 40¢ each. The following wildlife leaflets are available from the Documents Section free upon request: *Antelope, Bear, Bighorn Sheep, Canada Goose, Golden Trout, Striped Bass, Condor, Deer, Elk, Golden Eagle, Wolverine, Yellowtail, Wild Turkey, and Wood Duck.* Write to Chronicle Books, 54 Mint St., San Francisco 94119, for the following California Fishing Guides: *Trinity River, Klamath River, Shasta Lake, California Steelhead, California Trout, Lake Berryessa, San Diego Bass Lakes,* and *North Sierra Trout,* $1.95 each.

A complete guide to the *Anadromous Fishes of California* is available for 70¢ from: Office of Procurement, Documents Section, General Services Agency, P.O. Box 20191, Sacramento 95820. The 109-page book describes the steelhead trout and the various families and species of fish in California that migrate from salt or brackish water upstream to fresh water to spawn. It includes pictures of the individual species and descriptions of distinguishing characteristics, distribution, habits, and importance, as well as small distribution maps for each fish.

Another very helpful source of information is the *Salmon and Steelhead Fishing Map* (40¢) available from the same address. The large map is on a scale of 20 miles to 1 inch and shows streams that are open to steelhead fishing in the winter and a very few others where the runs start before the end of summer trout season (October 31). It also shows areas of ocean fishing for salmon. Information with the map describes the times of runs on the various rivers throughout the state and the areas where fishing is most successful. It describes the main species taken in the state and tells how to distinguish them.

Hunting

California's vast forest lands, mountainous high country, and wetlands offer an interesting variety of big game, upland game birds, and waterfowl hunting—the last of which is ranked among the finest in the nation. Big-game species include five subspecies of mule deer, including the Columbian black-tailed deer; black bear in the national forest regions of the north; wild European boars in Monterey County; and mountain lion in the Sierra and Siskiyou high-country wildlands. Small herds of Roosevelt elk are found in the coastal rain forests of the Six Rivers National Forest. The rare Tule, or dwarf, elk, once native to the interior foothills and valleys, are protected in small numbers in Owens Valley in Inyo National Forest. A few transplanted Rocky Mountain elk roam the remote areas of the High Sierras. The once vast herds of pronghorn antelope are today found in small bands in the Modoc and Shasta national forests. A few protected California bighorn sheep are found among the rugged snowcapped peaks of the High Sierra wild country. Upland game birds include pheasant in the San Joaquin and Sacramento valleys; quail throughout the state, along with chukar partridge, mourning dove, band-tailed pigeon, sage grouse, blue and ruffed grouse, and a few wild turkey. California's vast wetlands on the Pacific Flyway are the winter home of more migratory waterfowl than are found in any other state, and it is believed that the Tule-Klamath Basin in the northernmost region holds the greatest concentration of ducks and geese in the world. The major species and wetlands along the Pacific Flyway are described in detail in the useful guide *Waterfowl of California,* available for 70¢ from: Office of Procurement, Documents Division, Department of Fish & Game, P.O. Box 20191, Sacramento 95820. Also available are *Furbearers of California* (70¢) and *Upland Game of California* (70¢).

Fly Fisherman's Travel Service

Anglers Abroad Travel Service, operated by the editors of "Fly Fisherman" magazine, sponsors guided package trips to the legendary trophy trout and salmon waters throughout the world. These personalized trips are led by such world-renowned anglers as Ernie Schwiebert, author of "Matching the Hatch," and Phil Wright, known for his custom guiding service along Montana's blue-ribbon Big Hole River. Full-color brochures providing all details of itinerary, accommodations, guides, climate, services, equipment, and detailed maps and descriptions of the rivers and countryside, are available for trips to: Chile, Scotland, Ireland, England, Iceland, British Columbia, Alaska, Argentina, New Zealand, Spain, Eastern Canada, Baja, Bahamas, Yugoslavia, and France. Write: Fly Fisherman-Anglers Abroad Travel Service, 1766 Union St., San Francisco, 94123 (415–673–1999).

Guides, Packers, & Wilderness Outfitters

A useful *List of Licensed Fishing & Big-Game Hunting Guides* may be obtained by writing: Department of Fish & Game, 1416 Ninth St., Sacramento 95814. For listings of pack trip and saddle stock outfitters, write: *High Sierra Packers Association, Eastern Unit,* Box 147, Bishop 93514 or *High Sierra Packers Association, Western Unit,* P.O. Box 123, Madera 93637; *Shasta-Cascade Wonderland Association,* Box 1988, Redding 96002 (Northern California). Many of the major guides and outfitters in the state are listed in the "Travel & Recreation Guide" section.

American Safari, 386 60th St., Oakland 94618, offers many outdoor adventures, including camping trips between San Francisco and Las Vegas by way of Yosemite Valley, Lake Tahoe, Pyramid Lake in Nevada, Mount Whitney, and Death Valley, and an "Indian Country Trip" between San Francisco and Phoenix, Arizona. The trips are not strictly wilderness trips, as they include hotel accommodations as well as camping. Along the way are experiences in horseback riding, hang-gliding, sailing, river rafting, hiking, and gliding.

Adventours, Box B, Woodland 95695, specializes in float trips along California waterways, but it also offers bike tours, trail rides, snow mountaineering, rock climbing, and backpacking trips. *W. C. "Bob" Trowbridge* leads canoe and raft trips on the Russian, American, Sacramento, Feather, Colorado, Eel, and Klamath rivers. *The California Recreation Guides Association,* P.O. Box 1285, Monterey, 93940,

offers tours on rivers throughout the state. The Stanislaus and Tuolumne rivers are among the streams that Henry Falany runs in his *White Water Expeditions.* Write to him at P.O. Box 1249, Turlock 95380.

O.A.R.S., Inc., P.O. Box 67, Angels Camp 95222, is a top-notched outfitter offering a full line of wild-river trips in California and the western United States, including such widely diverse rivers as the San Juan, Dolores, Salmon, Rogue, and Tuolumne, in addition to the Colorado River trip it runs in cooperation with Mountain Travel Inc. Write for their free brochure and trip schedule. *Outdoors Unlimited,* 2500 5th Ave., Sacramento 95818, runs a number of rivers in the state. *River Adventures West,* P.O. Box 5219, Santa Monica 90405, leads float trips on the Stanislaus, Tuolumne, American, and East Carson rivers. *Martin's River Expeditions,* 1127 Rock Springs Hollow, Escondido 92026, include a run down Kings River in Kings Canyon and Sierra National forests. *River Rat Raft Rentals,* 5929 Fair Oaks Blvd., Carmichael 95608, runs the American River exclusively. *Outdoor Adventures* include paddle trips on the American, Stanislaus, East Carson, Klamath, and Eel rivers. Write to 21666 Arbor Ct., Hayward 94541. *Wilderness Water Ways, Inc.,* 33 Canyon Lake Dr., Port Costs 94569, offers float trips on a variety of California's rivers. *Wilderness World,* 1342 Jewell Ave., Pacific Grove 93950, offers float trips on California waterways, as well as a 5-day boatman's training course on the Stanislaus or the Rogue. *Wilderness Expeditions Inc.,* 1127 Rock Springs Hollow, Escondido 92026, offers guided trips on the Kings River and the Lower Colorado. (See "California Travel & Recreation Guide" for listings of fishing and big-game hunting guides and high-country packers.)

High Sierra Golden Trout Lakes & the John Muir Trail

The John Muir Trail winds for most of its 212-mile length along the western slope of the High Sierras through some of the most stunning wilderness camping and alpine fishing country on the continent. The great arc of the High Sierra crest forms a continuous strip of remote, sparkling, jewellike lakes and soaring snowcapped peaks, extending from Yosemite Valley to the massive 14,000-foot peaks dominated by Mount Whitney at the headwaters of the Kings and Kern rivers. From Yosemite, the trail passes through the Minarets Wilderness, winds on past the Devils Postpile National Monument and through the vast John Muir Wilderness in the Sierra National Forest, and enters the Sequoia National Park area, dominated by the Great Western Divide. The trail and numerous spur trails provide access to literally thousands of trout lakes, many of which hold thriving populations of prized golden trout, that lie in remote lake basins on both slopes of the High Sierra, including the Granite Area in the Minarets Wilderness of the Sierra National Forest, the Upper Bishop Creek Area in the John Muir Wilderness Area of the Inyo National Forest, and the Mono Creek Area, French Canyon and Humphreys Basin Area, and Bear Creek Area—all situated in the John Muir Wilderness in the Sierra National Forest. Wildlife often seen by the sharp-eyed wilderness traveler includes deer, the shrill-voiced coney, coyotes and weasels, and the tracks of the trout-loving pine marten. A few bands of bighorn sheep are occasionally sighted along the east slope of the Sierra crest from Convict Lake to Mount Whitney. Grouse and mountain quail are found throughout the timbered areas.

Many of the High Sierra lakes were originally barren of trout, but today hold healthy populations of eastern brook, rainbow, golden, and a few brown trout through intensive aerial stocking programs conducted by the California Department of Fish & Game. The brilliantly colored golden trout was originally found in a few small tributaries in the headwaters of the Kern River. The golden evolved through a process known to zoologists as "variation through isolation." It is believed that the ancestors of the golden were steelhead (sea-run) rainbows that became landlocked during the Ice Age, when the Kern River changed its course. The original descendants of the landlocked steelhead were the Gilbert rainbow trout (found today in Sequoia National Park), which evolved through isolation in "hanging valleys" blocked by impassable waterfalls. During the late 1800s, Basque shepherds of the High Sierra transported the goldens in coffee pots from the headwaters of the Kern to previously barren lakes. Through aerial stocking and transplanting, the original range of the California golden has been extended throughout the High Sierra and to high mountain lakes in Oregon, Washington, Wyoming, and Montana. The natural forage of goldens in the cold waters of the high-altitude lakes consists of caddis flies, midges, terrestrial insects, and small crustaceans. Although they are often caught with small spoons, spinners, and natural bait, fly-fishing them with dry flies, nymphs, midge patterns on hooks from No. 12 to 20, as well as bucktails and streamers, is by far more productive. California goldens range from pan-sized fish to occasional 2–3 pounders and up to the state record—9 lb. 14 oz.—caught in Virginia Lake at 10,300 feet elevation. Useful descriptions of the species are provided in the leaflet *Golden Trout,* available free from: Office of Procurement, Documents Section, P.O. Box 20191, Sacramento 95820. For detailed lake and fishing info, write: Department of Fish & Game, 9th & O Streets, Sacramento 95814, and ask for the free booklet *Golden Trout of the High Sierra.*

Several renowned golden trout lakes are located in a 60-square-mile wilderness in the *Mono Creek Area,* situated between the Fish Creek Drainage on the north and the Bear Creek Drainage on the south, in the John Muir Wilderness of the Sierra National Forest in northeastern Fresno County. Mono Creek, a tributary of the South Fork San Joaquin River, rises in the rugged, glaciated cirques and windswept peaks of the Sierra Nevada crest. The lake basin contains some 39 lakes that hold brown, rainbow, and eastern brook trout. Golden trout are found in 15 lakes and streams located at or above timberline, including rockbound Bighorn Lake, which occupies an open glacial pocket at the head of a canyon at 10,820 feet elevation; Golden Lake, located above timberline with an abrupt rocky shoreline at an altitude of 11,000 feet; Golden Creek, a steep, rocky, cascading stream located above Golden Lake; rockbound Upper Hopkins Lake, located at 11,050 feet in a glacial bowl above timberline; 3-mile-long Hopkins Creek, a small cascading stream heading in Upper Hopkins Lake; 50-foot-deep Upper Mills Creek Lake, which lies in a bare granite bowl at the head of a canyon above timberline, surrounded by a rocky shoreline with meadow fringe, and which flows into Lower Mills Creek Lake at 10,825 feet elevation and Mills Creek, with its numerous pools, falls, and slicks; Mono Creek and its North Fork, which cascade down a deep wooded canyon with high ridges rising on either side and many flat meanders, cascades, deep pools, riffles, and spawning areas; Pioneer Lake No. 6 in the Pioneer Basin Chain of Lakes, located in a glacial bowl above timberline; Silver Pass Lake, located in a granite basin with high cliffs on three sides, surrounded by meadows and a rocky shoreline; Upper and Lower Snow lakes, located in glacial pockets above timberline near the head of Fourth Recess Canyon; Third Recess Lake, which reaches depths of 50 feet in a glacial cirque near timberline; and Tough Lake (or Frog Lake), granitoid cirque on a bench high above Mono Creek at timberline.

The golden trout lakes and streams of the 180-square-mile *Granite Creek Area* lie to the north of Mono Creek in the Minarets Wilderness of the Sierra National Forest in a magnificent setting surrounded by the rugged sawtooth ridge dominated by Triple Divide Peak to the

northwest, beyond which lies Yosemite National Park; the yawning chasm of the San Joaquin River, which drops off in a blue haze to the south, with the jagged peaks of the Silver Divide off in the distance; and the spectacular summits of the Ritter Range and the Minarets across the canyon of the North Fork of the San Joaquin to the northeast. Golden trout are found in Alpine Lake; Isberg Lakes, located in shallow granite basins at timberline and above; Rutherford Lake, situated in a rocky basin at timberline; and Sadlor Lake, the largest lake in the East Fork of Granite Creek, surrounded by meadows and lodgepole pine forests.

The lakes and streams of the *Bear Creek Area* are located along the John Muir Trail in the John Muir Wilderness Area of the Sierra National Forest. All of the Bear Creek drainage, which rises in the spectacular glacial cirques and bare, ice-carved and wind-worn granite spires of the High Sierra Crest, was barren of trout until 1914, when some 200 golden trout were transplanted to the area by pack train. In 1928, wild golden trout were further transplanted to all tributaries and main lakes except for the lakes northeast of the Gables group, which were later stocked, beginning in 1943. The Bear Creek waters have been designated a golden trout area, and the South and East forks of Bear Creek are exclusively golden trout waters. Thirty-five lakes and lakelets in the area, including Three Island, Vee, Marie, Marshall, Rose, Brown Bear, Italy, Bear Twin, Apollo, Sandpiper, and Black Bear, contain trout populations, as follows:

Golden trout	26 lakes
Golden and rainbow trout	2 lakes
Eastern brook trout	6 lakes
Rainbow trout	1 lake

The wilderness fly-fisherman will also find good trout populations in Bear Creek above and below Kip Camp, East Fork of Bear Creek, the Seven Gables Branch, and in portions of the South and West forks, Rose Branch, and Hilgard Creek. A few of the lakes in the area have rustic camps built and maintained by the U.S. Forest Service. Camping, however, is not recommended at the rockbound lakes above timberline due to a lack of firewood. The heart of the Bear Creek lake basin, located astride the John Muir Trail, can be reached in about 5 hours by foot or pack train by trail from Bear Dam. As with all areas discussed in this essay, a campfire permit is a must and may be obtained from any U.S. Forest Service officer or from the High Sierra Ranger Station. The large meadows in the area provide ample stock feed, particularly near the mouths of Hilgard Creek and the East Fork of Bear Creek, at Sandpiper Lake and Rosemarie Meadow, and on the East Fork near Seven Gables Lake No. 1.

The French Canyon and Humphreys Basin Area, another state-designated golden trout area, is located due north of the Kings Canyon National Park in northeastern Fresno County within the John Muir Wilderness Area of the Sierra National Forest. The lakes and streams of this 42-square-mile area are drained by Piute Creek, a tributary of the San Joaquin River. The lake basins were originally stocked years ago with golden trout from the famous Cottonwood Lakes. The lakes of the French Canyon Basin lie above timberline (above 10,000 feet) in a rugged, glaciated, granite country surrounded by stunted conifers, tundralike meadows, and lakeside clumps of dwarf willow, Labrador tea, and mountain heath, broken by numerous benches and rocky ledges, open glacial flats, scours, talus slopes, and sheer-faced cliffs. The area is dominated by the cascading waters of French Canyon Creek and the remote, boulder-strewn shores of the Royce Lakes, French Lake, and La Salle, Steelhead, Alsace, L, Moon, and Merriam lakes. Royce Lake No. 4 contains a goodly population of 2–3 pound goldens.

Humphreys Basin, located due south of French Canyon, is a broad, barren, glacial basin of tundra meadows, rocky wind-swept ridges, jumbled boulder piles, glacial slicks, and some of California's premier golden trout lakes. Desolation Lake covers 22 acres at 11,000 feet elevation and produces goldens from 14 to 20 inches. Golden Trout Lake is a self-sustaining golden trout fishery with plenty of fish in the 6–9 inch range. Goithe Lake at 11,540 feet has a population of goldens up to 16 inches, sustained by occasional plantings. Other productive lakes in the basin include Humphreys (for goldens and large eastern brook trout), Lobe, Packsaddle, Muriel, Cony, Lost, Honeymoon, and Marmot. Twelve-mile-long Piute Creek contains wild goldens and brookies.

The French Canyon and Humphreys Basin Area is accessible from Bishop at Highway 395 by two main routes, a 4½-hour trip from the Pine Creek Pack Station over Pine Creek Pass into French Canyon and a 3½-hour trip from the North Lake Pack Station along the North Fork of Bishop Creek over Piute Pass to campsites on Golden Trout Lake in the middle of Humphreys Basin. The trail from North Lake joins the John Muir Trail at the junction of Piute Creek with the

South Fork of the San Joaquin River. Good camping areas are found along French and Piute creeks and at a number of locations where camps have been built up and maintained by local packers, fishermen, and deer hunters. Good supplies of stock feed are located at Hutchinson Meadow and lower French Canyon.

The *Upper Bishop Creek Basin* encompasses 50 square miles within the John Muir Wilderness area of the Inyo National Forest, southwest of Bishop. The 83 lakes of the area, including beautiful Lake Sabrina and Hungry Packer, Lamerch, Blue, Moonlight, Sky High, Sunset, South, and Echo lakes, offer the wilderness angler five species of trout, as follows:

Eastern brook trout	58 lakes
Rainbow trout	36 lakes
Golden trout	5 lakes
Brown trout	5 lakes
Kamloops rainbow	3 lakes

The Upper Bishop Creek lakes are located at 10,000 feet elevation or above, fed by the snowfields of the Sierra Crest. Bishop Creek and its tributaries offer excellent fishing for rainbow and brown trout. Golden trout are found in the Treasure Lakes chain, reached by trail from the roadhead at South Lake. U.S. Forest Service Campgrounds are located on Bishop Creek below South Lake and Lake Sabrina and above North Lake. Campsites are found at almost all lakes in the area below timberline. The area is reached by foot or on horseback from trailheads at South Lake, Lake Sabrina, and North Lake. Well-equipped pack sta-

tions serve the area as far as the upper reaches of the San Joaquin and Kings rivers beyond the Sierra Crest.

Detailed *Angler's Guides* with maps showing established horse trails, unmarked trails, major lakes and streams, and elevations are available for 40¢ each for Upper Bishop Creek, French Canyon, Humphreys Basin, Bear Creek Area, Granite Creek Area, and Mono Creek Area. Write: Office of Procurement, Documents Section, P.O. Box 20191, Sacramento 95820. *Sierra South* ($6.95, 287 pp.), by Winnett and Schwenke, is available from Wilderness Press, 2440 Bancroft Way, Berkeley 94704. It describes the wilderness trails of the High Sierra from Mono Divide south to Sequoia National Park, with maps and photos. *Fishing the California Wilderness* is an informative collection of essays of one couple's experiences of fishing the lakes, streams, and rivers of the High Sierras and other mountains of the California wild areas. The book offers good practical advice on how to prepare for a backpacking trip to the high country for trout. The book costs $2.95 and is available from Chronicle Books, 51 Mint Street, San Francisco. The indispensable *Starr's Guide to the John Muir Trail and the High Sierra Region* ($3.95, 156 pp.) published by Sierra Club Books, 530 Bush St., San Francisco 94108, contains detailed descriptions of the High Sierra trails and wild areas.

For information on packhorse outfitters, guides, and trips, write: *D. F. Pack Station*, P.O. Box 82, Raymond 93653 (western Sierra); *High Sierra Pack Station*, P.O. Box 396, North Fork 93643 (western Sierra); *Pine Creek Saddle and Pack Train*, Box 968, Bishop 93514 (eastern Sierra); and *Schober Pack Station*, Bishop 93514 (eastern Sierra). Additional information may also be obtained by writing: Bishop Chamber of Commerce, 690 N. Main, Bishop 93514. For detailed information on wilderness permits, trails, and fishing info write to the Forest Supervisor at Sierra National Forest, 1130 O Street, Fresno 93721 or at Inyo National Forest, 2957 Birch St., Bishop 93514. For detailed fishing and packer info write: Department of Fish & Game, 1234 E. Shaw Ave., Fresno 93721. For detailed topographic map info and expanded descriptions of the areas discussed above, see the "California Travel & Recreation Guide." The John Muir Trail is shown on these U.S. Geological Survey large-scale maps: Big Pine, Devils Postpile, Merced Peak, Mount Abbot, Mount Morrison, Mount Pinchot, Mount Tom, Mount Whitney, Yosemite.

Highways—Recreation & Scenic Routes

A free *California Highway Map* showing the Golden State's recreation and scenic highways, interstate and federal highways, points of interest, recreation area campgrounds, scheduled airline stops, ski areas, boat ramps, time zone boundaries, major mountain roads, national forests and parks, and cities and towns may be obtained by writing: California Chamber of Commerce, 455 Capitol Mall, Sacramento 94814.

Mountaineering Instruction & Mountain Travel Service

The majestic High Sierra Crest, one of the continent's truly great mountaineering areas, is served by several renowned wilderness schools and expedition outfitters. *The Palisade School of Mountaineering*, the oldest continuously operating school in the Sierra Nevada, operates under Forest Service permit in the Inyo National Forest at the Palisades, on the crown of the High Sierra Crest. The Palisades contain seven glaciers and five summits over 14,000 feet, as well as the best alpine climbing and scenery in the Sierra. The school is located near the base of these ragged cirques, where Big Pine Creek descends to

the east through granite domes, benches, and lakes. The school's top-ranked instructors and guides (with experience ranging from big wall climbing to expeditions in Yosemite, Canada, Alaska, the Andes, the Himalayas, the Karakoram, New Zealand, Britain, and the Alps) conduct intensive courses in ski mountaineering, mountain medicine and rescue, rock climbing, basic mountaineering, advanced mountaineering, and glacier travel. Complete meals are provided and all technical climbing equipment is supplied by PSOM. For brochures, applications, and reservations, write: Palisade School of Mountaineering, P.O. Box 694, Bishop 93514. Instruction and guided trips are also provided by *Frank Ashley,* Box 291, Culver City, 90320; *High Adventure,* 1067 N. Hanifax, Los Angeles 90046, in Wyoming's Wind River Range and the High Sierra; *Squaw Valley Mountaineering Center,* Box 2288, Olympic Valley 95730; and *Yosemite Mountaineering,* Yosemite National Park 95389.

One of the world's leading outfitters of mountaineering expeditions and outings is *Mountain Travel, Inc.,* 1398 Solano Ave., Albany 94706. This august firm offers guided trips under the leadership of experienced professional mountain guides to far-flung corners of the globe. The free 60-page *Mountain Travel Catalog of Expeditions & Outings to Remote Wilderness Areas of the World* describes and illustrates their worldwide program in depth, including the Himalayas, India, Africa, Pakistan, Galapagos, Patagonia, Peru, Alaska's Arctic National Wildlife Range and Mount McKinley. All guided trips in the *Mountain Travel Catalog* are described in greater detail in specific trip brochures, e.g., *Alpine Trekking in Nepal.*

The following maps may be purchased from Mountain Travel (address above): *Nepal Map,* Peace Corps Edition, 1:800,000, ($6); *Nepal,* East Sheet and West sheet ($3); *Research Scheme Nepal Himalaya Maps,* 1:50,000 (set $10); *Royal Geographic Society Mount Everest Region* ($10); *Kingdom of Sikkim,* 1:150,000 ($5); *Archipelago de Colen Galapagos,* 1:600,000 ($40); *Mount Kilimanjaro,* 1:100,000 ($2.50); and *Mount McKinley-Alaska,* 1:50,000 ($4.25).

Pacific Crest National Scenic Trail

The Pacific Crest Trail is a 2,600-mile pathway from Mexico to Canada, passing through 23 national forests, 14 wilderness areas, and 7 national parks along the way. Clinton C. Clarke proposed the trail for hikers and packers in the early 1930s. Soon the Oregon Skyline Trail and the Cascade Crest Trail in Oregon and the John Muir Trail and other segments in the California Sierra Nevada were under way. The trail is not yet complete, but when it is finished, it will wind through deserts to mountain forests, span a huge spectrum of elevations, and pass through wilderness and near city boundaries. In California, the proposed trail starts south of Observation Peak at the California-Oregon border, in the Siskiyou Mountains. When finished in this state, the trail will cover 1,660 miles, range in elevation from 500 to 13,200 feet, and end at International Border at Mexico, 2½ miles east of Tecate. Much of the trail, however, is uncompleted. At some points where the completed trail ends, the route transfers to other trails or rural roads, but elsewhere the uncompleted portions are unmarked. Be sure to check whether there are any unfinished stretches in the area you plan to hike before you begin. If you are unfamiliar with the rigors of hard mountain travel, do not attempt any part of the trail without the services of an experienced guide. Never travel alone. The rugged pathway weaves through areas where severe weather conditions are common and set in suddenly.

If you plan to hike the trail, you must obtain wilderness permits for all sections of the trail that pass through wilderness or primitive areas of the national forests. You may obtain the permits from the National

Forest headquarters or ranger station where your trip starts. In most areas along the trail, a campfire permit is also required. These permits are also available at the forest offices. If you plan to take horses, check here for special rules that apply to livestock.

The trail passes by many points of natural beauty and historic interest. South from the northern starting point of the trail is Grizzly Peak, where an early rancher shot and wounded a grizzly who nearly mauled him to death. Peter Lassen had a trading post just below the peak, which was the homeland of the last Yahi Indian. Aboriginal Indians inhabited Pit River, Mount Shasta, and Lassen Peak, east of the trail. Further south the trail passes through the magnificent land of the Feather River, which includes one of the highest falls in the country. Gold Lake in the Plumas National Forest was once rumored to be the source of all placer gold. On the ascent to Carson Pass is a spectacular view of Lake Tahoe. The Yokuts Indians inhabited the region of the Mono Craters and Mono Pass before the arrival of Spanish missionaries in 1770. Further on lie the wildflower meadows of the Tuolumne River and the High Sierra wilderness of Yosemite National Park. The Mojave Desert lies to the southwest, a barren wilderness that defeated many who challenged it to reach the land of plenty farther west. The trail moves on through Whitewater Canyon along the Whitewater River, at 1,185 feet, the lowest elevation of the entire trail within California. The San Jacinto Wilderness is another former Indian

domain, steeped in the legends of the Soboba tribe. The Indians sang in their dance houses near San Jacinto Peak, praying to the Great Spirit for successful hunting.

The Pacific Crest National Scenic Trail, California is a free brochure and map of the trail available from: U.S. Forest Service, Division of Information and Education, Room 531, 630 Sansome St., San Francisco 94111. The map describes the trail briefly, gives information on permits and preparation, and includes addresses for a number of sources of more detailed information. Those who plan to hike portions of the trail in California may be interested in *The Pacific Crest Trail Volume 1: California,* a detailed 287-page guide to the trail with a 16-page supplement, 26 photos, and 127 two-color topographic maps ($4.95) published by Wilderness Press, 2440 Bancroft Way, Berkeley 94704. A similar book describing the trail through Washington and Oregon, *The Pacific Crest Trail Volume 2: Oregon & Washington,* is available from the same address. To gain a historical perspective of the trail, write for a free book *Journey: Being an Historical Adventure through the Lands of the Pacific Crest Trail,* from: U.S. Forest Service Office, California Region, 630 Sansome St., San Francisco 94111. A

free 68-page booklet, *Pacific Crest National Scenic Trail*, which contains a set of maps showing the California portion of the trail and an index sheet to U.S. Geological Survey quadrangle maps of the route, is available at the same address.

Ski Touring Outfitters & Guided Trips

Royal Gorge Ski Touring, Inc., located north of the Yuba River in the mountain country of Tahoe National Forest, offers a tracks and trail system; a wilderness lodge program of High Sierra ski touring based at a large rambling hunting lodge, situated on a lake in the plateau area above the American River's Royal Gorge; Donner Pass overnight tours in the Paradise Valley or American River areas; and winter seminars in avalanches (includes weather, route finding, hazard evaluation, and rescue) and mountaineering medicine. Royal Gorge also offers guided ski-touring trips to Mounts Assiniboine and Skoki in the Slate Mountains of the Canadian Rockies and to Yellowstone National Park, with tours into the areas surrounding the Old Faithful Snow Lodge, Upper Geyser Basin, Cascades of the Fire Hole, and Fountain Paint Pot. Royal Gorge operates under outfitter-guide permits of the U.S. Forest Service. For rates, info, and a free brochure, write: Royal Gorge Ski Touring, Inc., P.O. Box 178, Soda Springs 95728. For additional information, write to the following organized ski-touring centers: *Alpine Meadows*, P.O. Box AM, Tahoe City 95730, for information about their High Sierra program called "The Wilderness Experience" for cross-country skiers, mountaineers, and winter campers; *Cal-Nordic Ski Touring Institute*, Tamarack Lodge, Mammoth Lakes 93546; *Kirkwood Ski Touring Center*, Kirkwood 95646, for Sierra ski touring in the Kirkwood Meadows; *Donner Ski Ranch*, P.O. Box 66, Norden 95724 in the Lake Tahoe area. See the "California Travel & Recreation Guide" for detailed information about the state's national forest and wilderness cross-country skiing, snowshoeing, and winter camping areas.

Ski Tours in California, published by Wilderness Press, is a comprehensive guide to mastering the sport and enjoying it in the major ski-touring areas of the state. The guide is an official publication of the Far West Ski Association. It includes chapters on equipment, techniques, food and cooking, waxing, route finding, shelter, first aid, and conservation, and descriptions of 38 tours. The tour descriptions list mileage, elevation gain, classification, climate, and topography, as well as route description. The 248-page book costs $4.95 and may be ordered from Wilderness Press, 2440 Bancroft Way, Berkeley 94704.

The Forest Service publishes three free brochures useful to the cross-country skier. *Winter Travel in the National Forests* is a general information pamphlet on winter sports, with sections on where to go, what to wear, hazards to avoid, how to handle emergencies, weather factors, frostbite, hypothermia, altitude sickness, hyperventilation, nutrition, and sanitation. *Avalanche* describes how to avoid and survive these winter hazards. *A General Bibliography of Ski Touring Literature* provides a comprehensive general list of reference material for the would-be or novice skier. These free materials may be ordered from: U.S. Forest Service, California Region, Room 531, 630 Sansome St., San Francisco 94111.

Sportfishing Adventures & Travel Service

Fishing International, one of the nation's foremost outdoor travel firms, offers complete worldwide fishing, vacation and travel service. They provide travel planning assistance suited to your specific fishing desires, be it fishing for trophy rainbow trout on the Alaska Peninsula or for giant marlin in the Sea of Cortez, and will help arrange your air transportation, lodging, and guide service. Free brochures are available upon request for the following trophy fishing destinations: Alaska's Bristol Bay trophy fish area; Alaska's Silvertip Wilderness Fly-in lodges on Judd Lake, Talachulitna River, and Unalakeet River for trophy Dolly Varden, grayling, rainbow, Arctic char, and salmon; British Columbia's Northern Lights Lodge on Lake Quensel and the famed Babine River Steelhead Resort; Klamath River Steelhead Fishing with the Somes Bar Guide Service; Baja California's Sea of Cortez for yellowfish, tuna, marlin, dolphin, roosterfish, yellowtail, and amberjack; Costa Rica's Isle de Pesca and famous Casa Mar in the remote rain forest of the East Coast, for trophy snook and Tarpon; Panama's Club Pacifico for sailfish, marlin, and other offshore big game; Pez Maya on the edge of Mexico's lush Yucatan jungle facing the blue Caribbean for offshore big game species; and the trophy trout fly-fishing waters of New Zealand's spectacular South Island and Lake Taupo. Write: Fishing International, P. O. Box 2132, 2310 4th St., Santa Rosa 95405 (phone: 707–543–4242).

Walker Expedition & the "Range of Light"

The second crossing of the "Range of Light"—the spectacular Sierra Nevada, was made from east to west in 1833, some six years after Jedediah Smith's epic journey. While the exact route followed and the details of the earlier venture remain somewhat obscure, the second expedition's travels are well documented thanks to the journals of one of the members, Zenas Leonard, who spared few words in describing the trails broken and hardships endured.

The party was headed by Joseph Reddeford Walker, an employee of Capt. B. L. E. Bonneville, whose fame would soon be guaranteed through Washington Irving's lengthy account, *The Adventures of Captain B. L. E. Bonneville, U. S. A., in the Rocky Mountains and the Far West*, published in 1837. In a few short years, the Rocky Mountain region had become overcrowded with itinerant trappers and company men in fierce competition for precious beaver pelts; the manic quest for fur had ensured the fortunes of some, destroyed others, and nearly doomed the beaver to extinction. Thus the primary goal of the Walker expedition was to discover new sources for fur and simultaneously to explore the unknown lands to the west.

Ski Tours
in California

by David Beck

An official publication of the Far West Ski Association

Thirty-five years old and already a veteran of the frontier, Walker was described by Irving as "about six feet high, strong built, brave in spirit, though mild in manners." His party included nearly 70 mounted men and extra horses carrying supplies. The group reached the eastern base of the Sierra late in October of 1833, and prepared to make the ascent about 60 miles southeast of Lake Tahoe, near the present-day town of Bridgeport. Walker's timing was bad from the start: the onslaught of winter was foreshadowed by piercing winds and gloomy skies. The group reached the summit with little trouble, but once at the crest the experienced band of trained mountain men shuddered at the country that unfolded before them: gaping canyons, black lakes, formidable peaks of granite—all seemed to stretch to infinity.

Poorly prepared for the rugged nature of the High Sierra and the length of time required to complete the crossing, the party's rations were quickly depleted. Soon horseflesh was the only alternative, and Walker gave permission to slaughter the animals when hunger became unendurable. As they pushed their way through snowfields and over rocky, barren terrain, alone in strange territory, and threatened with mutiny at several points, the mood of the party quickly turned sour. Leonard relates their growing despair:

> No one was acquainted with the country, nor no person knew how wide the summit of this mountain was. We had traveled for five days since we arrived at what we supposed to be the summit—were now still surrounded with snow and rugged peaks—the vigour of every man almost exhausted—nothing to give our poor horses, which were no longer any assistance to us in traveling, but a burden, for we had to help the most of them along as we would an old and feeble man.

The site chosen for the crossing was one of the wildest and most beautiful in the whole range. However, the half-frozen, half-starved wanderers were in no mood for sight-seeing. Making slow progress over high, broken ground through the region between the Merced and Tuolumne rivers, they soon came to an area where swift-flowing streams coursed into a huge canyon, falling over half a mile into the valley below. Leonard's journal gives short shrift to this phenomenon, but it now appears that the group was in the presence of the spectacular Yosemite Valley. The first white men to behold this wonder were probably grateful only for the fact that it signaled the beginning of the descent, for soon they found that snowfields were less frequent and the winds less fierce. They discovered an old Indian trail they could follow with relative ease, and when they halted at a precipice, they located a spot where the horses could be safely lowered by ropes. The horses must have heaved sighs of relief when the party stumbled upon deer and grizzlies to replace the stringy flesh of their tired mounts. During the course of the descent, the expedition sighted their second wonder —a grove of trees, each according to Leonard, "16 to 18 fathoms round the trunk at the height of a man's head from the ground." This entry in Leonard's diary marks the first mention of California's mighty redwoods. The grove he refers to was that of either the Tuolumne or the Merced.

From this point, the progress of the party was steady and uneventful, but the epic journey ends with a wry twist. Having forged their way through forests and foothills to the safety of the Central Valley, Walker's men were greatly vexed to find that among the herds of wild game roaming the area, their favorite delicacy—buffalo meat—was nowhere to be found.

Wild Areas of the Pacific Coast Forests

Several national forests and wilderness areas stretch inland from Cali-

fornia's scenic, frequently fogbound coastal areas, from the majestic redwood forests of the north to the fabled Big Sur country and beyond to the south. The Yolla Bolly–Middle Eel Wilderness contains 111,-000 acres in the Mendocino National Forest in the northwest region of the state. It contains the headwaters of the famed Eel River, South Fork Trinity River, and Stuart Gap (the main trailhead into the wilderness). For detailed info and a *Mendocino National Forest Map* (50¢), write: Forest Supervisor, 420 E. Laurel St., Willows 95988. The beautiful 98,112-acre Ventana Wilderness is situated in the Los Padres National Forest, stretching from the Big Sur River to the crest of the Coast Range. This backpacker's paradise, inhabited by bear, deer, and quail, embraces the Little and Big Sur river canyons and the Ventana Double Cone. The San Rafael Wilderness is also located in the forest and takes in the rugged *Sisquoc* River Valley and the *Sisquoc* Condor Sanctuary. For free wilderness maps, trail info, and the *Los Padres National Forest Map* (50¢), write: Forest Supervisor, 42 Aero Camino St., Goleta 93017. The 25,995-acre Aqua Tibia Primitive Area near the Mount Palomar Observatory is shown on the *Cleveland National Forest Map* (50¢) available from: Forest Supervisor, 3211 Fifth Ave., San Diego 92103. The 36,137-acre San Gabriel Wilderness is shown on the *Angeles National Forest Map* (50¢) available from: Forest Supervisor, 150 S. Los Robles, Pasadena 91101. The tiny, 9,022-acre Cucamonga Wilderness and the scenic San Gorgonio Wilderness, the 21,955-acre San Jacinto Wilderness, and the southernmost segment of the Pacific Crest Trail in the rugged San Bernardino Mountains are shown on the *San Bernardino National Forest Map* (50¢), available from: Forest Supervisor, 144 N. Mountain View Ave., San Bernardino 92408.

The following maps and guides are available from Wilderness Press, 2440 Bancroft Way, Berkeley 94704: *An Outdoor Guide to the San Francisco Bay Area* ($6.95); *Trails of the Angeles Trail Map* (75¢); and *San Bernardino Mountain Trails Map* (75¢).

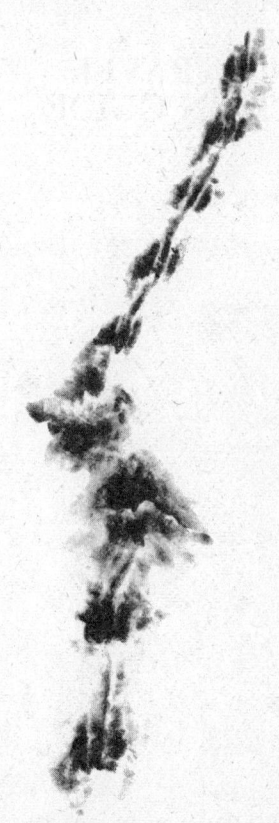

CALIFORNIA TRAVEL & RECREATION GUIDE

Eldorado National Forest— the Gold Rush Country

Eldorado National Forest Topo Maps

U.S. Geological Survey 1:250,000 scale overview maps: Chico, Reno, Sacramento, and Walker Lake.

Crystal Basin Recreation Area

U.S. Geological Survey large-scale topographic maps: Robbs Peak (7.5), Loon Lake, Riverton, Kyburz.

Desolation Wilderness

U.S. Geological Survey large-scale topographic maps: Echo Lake, Emerald Bay, Homewood, Loon Lake, Meeks Bay, Pyramid Peak, Rockbound Valley, Wentworth Springs.

Mokelumne Wilderness

U.S. Geological Survey large-scale topographic maps: Big Meadow and Silver Lake.

Pacific Crest Trail

U.S. Geological Survey large-scale topographic maps: Homewood, Rockbound Valley, Pyramid Peak, Silver Lake, Markleeville.

The Eldorado National Forest encompasses 700,000 acres, from the upper foothill country near Georgetown, extending through the dense sugar pine and white and red fir forests of the Crystal Basin, to the rugged granite slopes and snowcapped peaks of the Sierra Crest and Lake Tahoe. The Eldorado territory (Eldorado means "gilded one") was explored in 1827 by Jedediah Smith, who camped along the banks of the American River. The area now encompassed within the Lake Tahoe Basin Management Unit was explored in the winter of 1843–44, when John Frémont and Kit Carson crossed the Sierra and were the first white men to see Lake Tahoe, described, years later by Mark Twain in *Roughing It*, as ". . . a noble sheet of blue water . . . walled in by a rim of snow-clad peaks that towered aloft full 3,000 feet higher still. As it lay there with the shadows of the mountains brilliantly photographed upon its still surface . . . down through . . . these great depths, the water was not merely transparent, but dazzling, brilliantly so; we could see trout by the thousands winging about in the emptiness under us." The forest embraces a major portion of the legendary Mother Lode—a long narrow strip seamed and laced with gold stretching for 120 miles in the Sierra foothills. Ghost towns, abandoned mines, and romantic place names such as Placerville, Rough and Ready, Sutter Creek, Shirt Tail Canyon, Angels Camp, Sailors' Slide, Spanish Dry Diggins, and Dutch Flat are the legacy of the great gold rush and the hundreds of mining camps and thousands of adventurers and prospectors who invaded the territory in 1849, preserved in the stories of Bret Harte and Mark Twain.

The forest is a famed backpacking, fishing, hunting, and wilderness camping region. Hundreds of miles of forest roads and trails, including the Pacific Crest Trail, wind through the forest at elevations ranging from 3,000 to 10,000 feet and provide access to the North Fork of the Mokelumne River, Camp Creek, Crystal Range, Horneblende Mountains, the Cosumnes and Rubicon rivers, and the high peaks, meadows, jagged spires, and hundreds of remote alpine lakes in the Mokelumne and Desolation Valley wilderness areas.

The Desolation Wilderness is the northernmost of the High Sierra wilderness areas, embracing 63,469 acres due west of Lake Tahoe. Hundreds of forest lakes lie beneath the high glaciated peaks in the Tahoe Basin, at elevations ranging from 6,500 to 10,000 feet, at the

headwaters of picturesque Rubicon River, a top-ranked fly-fishing trout stream. Rockbound and Desolation valleys lie between the main crest of the Sierra Range to the east and the summits of the Crystal Range to the west. Pyramid Peak dominates a group of four high summits to the south. Over 75 miles of trails provide access through the forests, valleys, and alpine meadows and over high mountain passes to the lake country. The fishing is good for Kamloops, kokanee, brook, rainbow, and a few golden trout in Rubicon, Cascade, Fallen Leaf, Susie, Heather, Velma, and Gray lakes. The major trails are the Rockbound National Scenic Trail and the Tahoe-Yosemite segment of the Pacific Crest Trail, which passes Lake Aloha, Pyramid Peak, Echo Lake, and on to Carson Pass, through the lake country, and into the Mokelumne Wilderness. Many of the spur trails are poorly marked, so you will be wise to keep a topo map kit at hand. Be sure to travel prepared for cool nights and inclement weather. Carry a light waterproof ground tarp that can be rigged as a tent should it rain.

Fishing, packhorse, and trail information, wilderness permits, and a free *Desolation Wilderness Map* can be obtained by writing: Pacific Ranger Station, Pollock Pines 95726 (916–644–2348) or Lake Tahoe Basin Management Unit, Box 8465, 1052 Tata Lane, South Lake Tahoe 95731 (916–541–1130). The free map shows all natural features, trails, pack stations, recreation sites, boat-launching ramps, ski areas, and resorts. *Desolation Wilderness* ($3.95, 256 pp., with 26 photos, 19 drawings, and 23 maps) by Robert S. Wood describes over 200 miles of trail and 140 trout streams and lakes. This indispensable guide, published by Wilderness Press, 2440 Bancroft Way, Berkeley 94704, contains an up-to-date index of overused and underused places and an Angling Index that helps the backpacker to plan his trip. Wilderness Press also publishes a *Desolation Wilderness Trail Map* (75¢, 19¼ × 22¼ inches), which includes a trip-planning guide with specifics and remarks on the area's 27 major trails. Guided ski tours, orienteering, camping, and survival courses in the Desolation Wilderness are conducted by *Sugar House West*, Box 8135, South Lake Tahoe 95731 (916–541–6811).

The 50,400-acre Mokelumne Wilderness is located in the Eldorado and Stanislaus national forests near the crest of the Sierra Nevada Range, bisected by the North Fork of the Mokelumne River and surrounded by dense forests, the towering peaks of the Mokelumne Tetons dominated by Mokelumne Peak (9,332 ft.), deep mountain valleys, and alpine lakes. The word *mokelumne* is thought to be a derivation of *Muquelemnes*, the name of a tribe of Indians who occupied a Miwok Indian village formerly situated along the Mokelumne River near what is now Lockeford. Numerous foot and horse trails wind through the interior high country and provide access to the scenic Double Falls on the Mokelumne River, Camp Irene, Lake Valley, Munson Meadow, and primitive campsites developed over the years by fishermen, packers, and hunters at Moraine, Black Rock, Mosquito, Long, Cole Creek, Pardoe, Frog, Deadwood, Berbe, Grouse, and Fourth of July lakes. Rainbow and eastern brook trout are found in most of the alpine lakes and streams. The area is reached from the south by State Highway 4 to trailheads at Bear Valley and Lake Alpine; from the north by State Highway 88 to trailheads at Tragedy Spring, Silver Lake, Caples Lake, and Carson Pass; from the east via Blue Lakes; or from the west by way of Shriner Lake and Salt Springs Reservoir.

Information concerning wilderness permits, trails, and packers and a free *Mokelumne Wilderness Map* showing trails, camps, recreation sites, trailpoints, ranger stations, and pack stations may be obtained by writing: Amador Ranger Station, P.O. Box 1327, Jackson 95642 (209–223–1623); Lumberyard Ranger Station, Highway 88, Pioneer

95666; Arnold Ranger Station, Highway 4, Arnold 95223; Alpine Station, Bear Valley (209–753–2811). The *Silver Lake Guide* by J. R. Groden describes the Mokelumne Wilderness area, the least-used portion of the Tahoe-Yosemite Trail, where it runs along the giant 3,000-foot-deep canyon of the North Fork of the Mokelumne River. This guidebook costs $2.95 from Wilderness Press, 2440 Bancroft Way, Berkeley 94704.

Eldorado has 5 campgrounds exclusively for groups, over 1,260 improved single family camp units, and 6 boat-launching ramps. The Crystal Basin, located just west of Desolation Valley, and Lake Tahoe

areas receive heavy use. The forest is host to almost half a million skiers annually in the Freek Peak, Stevens Peak, Round Top, Thimble Peak, and Kirkwood Meadows areas. Additional information and a full-color *Eldorado National Forest Recreation Map* (50¢) may be obtained by writing: Forest Supervisor, Eldorado National Forest, 100 Forni Road, Placerville 95667 (916–622–5061). The Forest Service map contains a detailed recreation-site chart and shows all natural features and roads, trails, railroads, ranger stations, pack stations, resorts, ski areas, 4-wheel-drive trails, springs, lookout stations, trailer sanitary stations, and boat-launching ramps. Wilderness Press (address above) publishes two useful guides to the region: *Sierra North* ($4.95, 247 pp.) covers the Sierra from Desolation Wilderness south to the Mono Divide; and *The Tahoe-Yosemite Trail* ($4.95, 136 pp.) covers this 180-mile mountain route from Meeks Bay at Lake Tahoe to Tuolumne Meadows in Yosemite National Park.

Licensed guides serving the forest include: *Barry A. Gormen*, P.O. Box 424, Georgetown 95634 (packing); *Ralph R. Hernandez, Jr.*, 3356 Treehaven, South Lake Tahoe 95705 (fishing, hunting, cross-country skiing in the Caples Lake, Silver Lake, Markleeville, and Lake Tahoe areas); *John W. Gillespie*, P.O. Box 1584, South Lake Tahoe 95705 (fishing). Packhorse stations are located at Plasse-Stockton Muni Camp, at Silver Lake, at Meeks Bay at Lake Tahoe, and at Bear Valley south of the Mokelumne Wilderness in the Stanislaus National Forest.

Access & Outfitting Centers

Major routes to the Eldorado National Forest include Interstate 80 and U.S. Highways 50 and 395. Lodging, supplies, boat rentals, guides, and outfitters are available at Placerville, Pollock Pines, Markleeville, South Lake Tahoe, Camino, Eldorado, Coloma, Georgetown, Foresthill, Silver Lake, Caples Lake, Fallen Leaf, Meeks Bay, and Loon Lake.

Inyo National Forest & High Sierra Alpine Areas

Inyo National Forest Topo Maps

U.S. Geological Survey 1:250,000 scale overview maps: Death Valley, Fresno, Mariposa, Walker Lake.

Ancient Bristlecone Pine Forest

U.S. Geological Survey large-scale topographic maps: Blanco Mountain, Bishop, Mount Barcroft, White Mountain Peak.

Big Pine Alpine Lakes Basin

U.S. Geological Survey large-scale topographic maps: Big Pine and Mount Goddard.

California Bighorn Sheep Zoological Area

U.S. Geological Survey large-scale topographic maps: Mount Pinchot, Mount Whitney, Lone Pine, Kern Peak, Olancha.

Cottonwood Lakes Golden Trout Basin

U.S. Geological Survey large-scale topographic maps: Lone Pine and Olancha.

Hall Natural Area

U.S. Geological Survey large-scale topographic maps: Tuolumne Meadows and Mono Craters.

Hot Creek Wild Trout Waters

U.S. Geological Survey large-scale topographic map: Mount Morrison.

Kern Plateau Golden Trout Area

U.S. Geological Survey large-scale topographic maps: Olancha and Kern Peak.

Mammoth Lakes Alpine Area

U.S. Geological Survey large-scale topographic maps: Devils Postpile and Mount Morrison.

Owens River

U.S. Geological Survey large-scale maps, from Lone Pine upstream to headwaters: Lone Pine, Independence, Waucoba Mountain, Big Pine, Bishop, Mount Horn, Casa Diablo Mountain, Mount Morrison, Cowtrack Mountain, Devils Postpile.

Pacific Crest Trail

U.S. Geological Survey large-scale maps: Tuolumne Meadows, Mono Craters, Devils Postpile, Mount Morrison, Mount Abbot, Mount Goddard, Blackcap Mountain, Big Pine, Mount Pinchot, Mount Whitney.

The vast 1.8-million-acre Inyo National Forest lies east of Yosemite National Park and stretches south for about 160 miles along the eastern slope of the Sierra Nevada to the Nevada border in the eastern part of central California. The forest contains some of the most stunning wilderness camping and fishing areas in the West, including portions of the John Muir, Hoover, and Minarets High Sierra wilderness areas. Hundreds of miles of trails and Forest Service roads provide access to the famous wild trout waters of the Owens River, Hot Creek, and Cottonwood Creek, and to the remote alpine lakes and streams in the Hall Natural Area, Inconsolable Range, Little Valley, and Mammoth Lakes area. The native home of the golden trout is in the headwater lakes and streams of the Kern Plateau in the Forest, southwest of Lone Pine. The John Muir Trail segment of the Pacific Crest National Scenic Trail winds along the wind-swept peaks of the High

Sierra Crest in the John Muir Wilderness along the forest's western boundary. East of Owens Valley lie the White Mountains, the famous Ancient Bristlecone Pine Forest, and portions of the Inyo Mountains. Access to a large portion of the Sequoia–Kings Canyon and Yosemite national parks is through the west side of the Inyo National Forest.

The scenic northern district of the forest, located due east of Yosemite National Park, embraces several renowned fishing, backpacking, and wilderness camping and historic areas reached from trailheads and spur routes off U.S. Highway 359. Bodie Ghost Town is 20 miles north of Bridgeport via U.S. 395. From 1876 to 1880 this gold-rush town had a population of 12,000 and a reputation as one of the toughest and most lawless gold-mining camps in the West. It is surrounded by meager bunch grass, desert sage, and needle grass. Gold was first discovered in the Mono region in 1852, and the Mono Trail was blazed from Big Oak Flat through the present Yosemite National Park to Bodie and the Mono region. To the south at 6,409 feet elevation lies Mono Lake, covering 87 square miles. The lake is the third-largest natural body of water in California, formed more than 20,000 years ago by descending Sierra Nevada glaciers. Its blue waters are so impregnated with alkaline materials that nothing lives in its briny depths but one small species of saltwater shrimp and tiny black fly larvae. In *Roughing It*, Mark Twain tells a tale of a dog that hit a running speed of 250 miles an hour after taking a swim in the lake. Two large volcanic islands dot the lake's surface: Paoha, the larger, with its hot spring; and Negit, an old volcanic crater, with a rookery for sea gulls, or "mono pigeons," that have flown inland from the Pacific. South of the lake are the 20 Mono Craters, forming a crescent-shaped range and resembling gigantic ash heaps. Two campgrounds are located on the shores.

The beautiful alpine lakes and streams and forests of pine and fir in the southern portion of the Hoover Wilderness, the Hall Natural Area, and the Dana Plateau in the Minarets Wilderness lie due west as the crow flies from Mono Lake along the eastern slope of the High Sierra Crest, which forms the eastern boundary of Yosemite National Park. The Pacific Crest Trail winds through the area and provides access via spur trails to the Conness Glacier at 12,000 feet elevation and to the glacial brook and rainbow trout waters of Conness, Green, Treble, Big Horn Lakes, and Mine Creek Lakes in the Hall Natural Area. Saddlebag Lake, below the Tioga Crest, at 10,087 feet, holds large rainbows, cutthroats, and browns. The Saddlebag campground and Sawmill campground on Lee Vining Creek provide overnight camping facilities. Trails from the Tioga (Iroquois for "where it forks") Pass Ranger Station and the Tioga Road (Route 120) provide access to the beautiful Gaylor Lakes, the Tioga Tarns, Tioga and Ellery lakes, and the Lee Vining Canyon. The Tioga Road was originally a wagon road across Tioga Pass into Owens Valley, built by the Great Sierra Consolidated Silver Company in 1883. Camping facilities are available at Tioga and Ellery lakes and along Lee Vining Creek.

Rainbow, brook, brown, and cutthroat trout are found in June, Gull, Silver, and Grant lakes in the Reversed Creek Recreation Area, just west of the Minarets Wilderness and south of Mono Lake and the scarred, crumbled steps of the red Aeolian Buttes—the oldest volcanic formations on Mono Basin. The lakes and streams of the Reversed Creek Recreation Area lie in the ancient home and hunting grounds of the Yokuts Indians, who traded deer skins, willow bark baskets, and obsidian they obtained at the Mono Craters. The old Mono Trail was blazed by the Yokuts to trade their goods for the sinew-backed bows of the Paiutes in the eastern Sierras and for the berries of the Miwok in Yosemite Valley. Campgrounds and boat rentals are available along the shores of the lakes and along Reversed and Rush creeks.

Packhorse rentals, guides, and outfitters are available at the *Green Lakes, Virginia Lakes, Frontier, Bridgeport,* and *Silver Lake* pack stations, all Bridgeport 93517. Charter wilderness fly-in service to the remote High Sierra alpine lake areas is provided by *Bridgeport Aviation Service,* Bridgeport 93517.

The Pacific Crest Trail winds through the snowcapped peaks and alpine meadows of the Minarets Wilderness (see "Sierra National Forest & John Muir Wilderness") and past the sparkling, island-studded Thousand Island and Garnet lakes, which at 9,000 feet elevation, are surrounded by rocky islets, grassy shores carpeted with wild-flowers in season, and rugged, barren peaks, and which form the headwaters of the San Joaquin and Owens rivers. The trail winds out from the Minarets Wilderness and parallels the scenic rainbow and brook trout waters of the Middle Fork of the San Joaquin through the spectacular Devils Postpile National Monument. Several side trails follow old Indian paths to the Agnew Meadows Campground, Trinity Lakes, and the canyon of the Middle Fork of the San Joaquin. The sheer 40-foot cliff of the Devils Postpile, composed of columns that are nearly perfect vertical prisms, looms above the turbulent Middle Fork of the San Joaquin. Jumbled fragments of these blue-gray prisms lie at the base of the cliff, shaken down by some ancient earthquake. The postpile, a remnant of an ice flow, was worn smooth by glacial action during the last Ice Age. The monument is reached by the Pacific Crest Trail or by a narrow, winding gravel forest road that connects with a 10-mile-long paved road at Minaret Summit and passes eastward through Mammoth Lakes Post Office to U.S. 395. An overlook at Minaret Summit at 9,175 feet provides a sweeping view of the dark granite peaks of the Ritter Range. South of the Devils Postpile are the beautiful Rainbow Falls, where the San Joaquin plunges 140 feet into a box canyon with a deep green pool, creating a scene of mist-sprayed grandeur.

The famous brook and rainbow trout waters of the vast 200,000-acre Mammoth Lakes area form a chain of 19 lakes (including Mary, Crystal, George, Horseshoe, Mamie, and Twin) within a 5-mile radius, surrounded by beautiful woodlands and the peaks of the Mammoth Crest on the south. The Mammoth Lakes are one of the most popular recreation areas in the eastern Sierras. Numerous trails wind off through the surrounding wildlands, lakeshore campgrounds, and lodges. The Mammoth Lakes area was the scene of a mad gold rush in 1879, when a string of mining camps sprung up, only to be abandoned during the bitter winter of 1879–80. Forest Service trails provide access to the Mammoth Creek Indian Caves, Bald Mountain, and the Mammoth City Ghost Town. The Mammoth Lakes area is reached by Route 203 west from its junction with U.S. 395. Pack-horses, outfitting, and guide service in the Mammoth Lakes area are provided by *Red's Meadow Pack Train,* the *Mammoth Lakes Pack Outfit,* and *Agnew Meadows Pack Station,* all Mammoth Lakes 93546.

The beautiful blue rainbow, brook, and brown trout waters of Convict Lake, fed by Convict Creek with headwaters high in the John Muir Wilderness, are surrounded by colorful, rugged 12,000-foot mountains. The lake, reached along a short lateral road off Highway 395 about 5 miles south of Mammoth, is named for an episode that occurred here in 1871, when twenty convicts who had escaped from the Nevada State Penitentiary and killed a local mail carrier were tracked down and killed by a posse of outraged citizens. The summit of 12,245-foot Mount Morrison, which towers in the distance, was named for Robert Morrison, who was killed in the gun battle. Two campgrounds are located on the shores of the lake, and the *Convict Lake Pack Station* provides packhorses and guided trips into the John

Muir Wilderness. Accommodations are available at the *Convict Lake Resort,* Box 204, Bishop 93514.

The world-famous, spring-fed trout waters of Hot Creek lie due north of Convict Lake, just off U.S. 395, some 35 miles north of the eastern Sierra outfitting center of Bishop. This meandering stream, ranked as one of America's top 10 dry-fly streams, rises in the High Sierra and flows southeasterly to Hot Springs and the state fish hatchery. Here giant springs from the cold, crystal-clear waters of the main Hot Creek, which meanders for 15 miles through sagebrush flats to its junction with the upper Owens River. Below the state fish hatchery, the stream flows for 2½ miles through the meadows of the famous *Hot Creek Ranch,* a private fishing resort with dry-fly-only regulations and a two-fish limit. The waters above and below Hot Creek Ranch are open to public fishing. This classic dry-fly stream is loaded with trophy brown and rainbow trout and is included in the California Wild Trout Program. Most of the trout range between 1 and 2½ pounds. The stream record was a 9-pound brown, caught several years ago on a No. 16 Adams. The Hot Creek State Fishery, open to the public, produces 15 million trout eggs per year and stocks some 4 million fingerlings and 600,000 legal trout in eastern Sierra waters each year. The gin-clear waters of the Owens River, also included in the California Wild Trout Program (from Five Bridges crossing upstream to Pleasant Valley Dam in Inyo County), produces top-ranked fishing for rainbow trout and browns up to 9 pounds.

Bishop, the largest town in Owens Valley (named by Capt. Frémont for one of the men who accompanied him on his 1836 expedition), is a gateway and outfitting center for fishing, camping, and packing trips into the John Muir Wilderness area of the High Sierras, which rise more than 10,000 feet above the town on the west. The town is named after Bishop Creek (named for Samuel Bishop, a Fort Tejon stockman, who drove the first herd of cattle into the region in 1861), which flows 14 miles from the Lake Sabrina area in the High Sierras to its junction with the Owens River. Bishop Creek flows through a canyon with sheer cliffs rising to 1,000 feet and drops about 400 feet to the mile for the 14-mile stretch. The main stream is impounded with a series of seven power stations. Before the arrival of the white men, the primitive Paiute Indians lived along the banks of the creek, where they grew wild food plants. The Middle, North, and South forks of Bishop Creek rise in the John Muir Wilderness in scenic alpine country dotted by more than 200 inviting lakes along the eastern slope of the High Sierra. The lakes' basins are bounded on the east by the barren peaks of the Inconsolable Range. The high-country lakes in the area, including Hungry Packer, Schober Hole, Sunset, Sabrina, Piute, Sky High, Hell Diver, Fishgut, Blue Heaven, Tyee, Timberline, Inconsolable, and Chocolate, hold rainbow, eastern brook, golden, and a few brown and Kamloops trout. The wilderness fly-fisherman will find excellent fishing for brook and rainbow trout in the tributary streams that feed the lakes or flow from them. Bishop Creek proper holds a good population of brown trout. The area is reached by traveling west on State Route 168 from Bishop. Trails also enter the High Sierra lakes area from the western slope in the John Muir Wilderness via Piute Pass and Bishop Pass at 12,000 feet elevation. The most distant lake can be reached by foot or on horseback from trailheads at South Lake, Lake Sabrina, and North Lake. The *Schober Pack Station* at North Lake and *Rainbow Pack Station* at Parcher's Camp on the South Fork serve the entire Bishop Creek area and extend their services into the upper reaches of the San Joaquin and Kings rivers. Overnight accommodations are available at *Parcher's Camp Lodge, Habegger's Resort, Bishop Creek Lodge, Cardinal Valley Resort,* and *Camp Sabrina,* all Bishop 93514. Inyo National Forest campsites are located on Bishop Creek below South Lake and Lake Sabrina and above North Lake. Campsites are found on the shores of almost every

lake below timberline. A detailed map of the area is contained in the *Angler's Guide to the Lakes & Streams of the Upper Bishop Creek Area*, available for 40¢ from: Department of Fish & Game, Documents Section, P.O. Box 20191 Sacramento 95814.

The White Mountains rise to the east of Bishop and Owens Valley and contain the site of the world's oldest trees—the Ancient Bristlecone Pine Forest. It was thought for years that the world's oldest tree was the General Sherman sequoia in Sequoia National Forest. However, in 1956, Dr. Edmund Schulman established that the Pine Alpha bristlecone was indeed older than the ancient sequoias. A year later, an even older tree, named Methuselah, was dated at 4,600 years old. The wild, rugged 28,000-acre Ancient Bristlecone Pine Forest was established in 1958. The area has two hiking trails, the Pine Alpha Trail, which winds through living driftwoodlike stumps bleached and gnarled from centuries of wind, rain, and blowing sand to the famous Pine Alpha tree; and the 2-mile-long Methuselah Trail. The Patriarch Grove, named for the world's largest bristlecone tree, over 25 feet in height and 37 feet in diameter, is located at the north end of the forest. The forest lies at the crest of the White Mountains between 10,000 and 12,000 feet elevation, between Bishop and the California-Nevada border. A campground and the Sierra Viewpoint, which provides a spectacular view of the Eastern Sierra Nevada Range across Owens Valley, are located just south of the forest entrance. Piute, golden, and eastern brook trout are found in Cottonwood Creek, located at the northern edge of the forest, and Wyman Creek, which flows through the heart of the forest. Hunting for deer, quail, and chukar partridge is permitted in season. The forest is reached by the Westguard Pass Road, which branches northeast from U.S. 395 at Big Pine.

The High Sierra alpine lake basins surrounding the South and North forks headwaters of Big Pine Creek in the John Muir Wilderness form one of the most majestic areas along the eastern slope of the Sierra Crest. The two lake basins are walled in on the west by the towering, jagged Palisades Crest, dominated by three peaks over 14,000 feet, and are separated by a giant ridge dominated by Temple Crag at 12,999 feet. The massive Palisades Glacier at the upper end of the North Fork Basin is the southernmost glacier in the United States and the largest in the High Sierras. Several foot, horse, and jeep trails provide access to the remote blue high-country lakes located above 10,000 feet in the two basins, including Treasure Lakes (golden trout), Chocolate Lakes (brook trout), Long Lake (rainbow and brook trout), Ruware Lake (rainbows), Hidden Lake (golden trout), Black Lake (brooks, browns, rainbows), Big Pine Lakes (rainbow, brook, brown trout), Sam Mack Lake (brook trout), and Willow Lake (brook and rainbow trout). The tributaries and Big Pine Creek provide excellent fly-fishing for rainbow, brook, and brown trout. The *Glacier Pack Train* at Glacier Lodge, located at the junction of the North and South forks of Big Pine Creek, provides packhorse service and guided trips throughout the area. The Sage Flat, First Bridge, Big Pine Creek, Birch, and First Falls Forest Service campgrounds are located along Big Pine Creek. Overnight accommodations are available at *Glacier Lodge* and *Big Pine Creek Resort*, both Big Pine 93513. The area is reached by an 11-mile road from U.S. 395 at Big Pine.

The town of Independence on U.S. 395 is a renowned outfitting and jumping-off point for fishing, camping, and pack trips into the Onion Valley, Kearsarge Peak, Mount Gould, and Center Basin Crags areas of the John Muir Wilderness along the eastern slope of the High Sierra Crest. Independence is the site of the Eastern California Museum, which houses a collection of firearms used in the Indian wars, Indian relics, flora and minerals, historical documents, and photographs of Indian pictographs. The Mount Whitney State Fish Hatch-ery on Oak Creek is located 2 miles north of town. A road from Independence runs west along Independence Creek to Grays Meadow and the *Onion Valley Pack Station* (Independence 93526) and the Kearsarge Pass Trail, which climbs up to the Sierra Crest and to Golden Trout Lakes at 12,000 feet (golden and brook trout), Kearsarge Lakes at 10,000 feet (rainbow trout), and to Heart, Flower, and Gilbert lakes at 10,850 feet (rainbow and brook trout). Camping facilities are located at the Grays Meadow, Independence Creek, and Onion Valley campgrounds. Primitive campsites developed over the years by packers, fishermen, and hunters are located along the shores of most of the lakes below timberline.

The California Bighorn Sheep Zoological Area contains two management units surrounding Mount Baxter and Mount Williamson along the eastern slope of the High Sierra Crest in the John Muir Wilderness, due north and south of Onion Valley and the Kearsarge Pass. The California bighorn is occasionally sighted on the rugged peaks and ridges in the area above timberline. The bighorn is brown to grayish-brown with a creamy white rump. The male has massive, broomed horns that spiral back, then out and forward to complete an arc. The sheep are extremely alert and seldom wander far from steep escape routes. In keenness of vision, the bighorn is equaled or surpassed only by the pronghorn antelope. A sudden alarm will often send a spooked ram galloping across the terrain at over 35 miles an hour.

The famous outfitting center of Lone Pine, on U.S. 395, dates from the early 1850s and caters to fishermen, backpackers, and mountain climbers heading into the John Muir Wilderness area and alpine lakes country surrounding Mount Whitney and the legendary golden trout waters of the Cottonwood Lakes and Kern Plateau to the south. A forest road heads west from Lone Pine along Lone Pine Creek through Hunters Flat—a top-ranked hunting area in season for mule deer, black bear, sage hen, grouse, and quail—to the Whitney Portal Recreation Area and *Mt. Whitney Pack Station* (Lone Pine 93545). The Mount Whitney Trail climbs up over a well-graded trail to Outpost Camp, which lies below timberline in a setting of towering cliffs and green meadows surrounding Lone Pine Creek. The trail passes a series of falls and climbs past the beautiful trout waters of Mirror Lake into an area of spectacular granite walls and boulder-strewn basins, carpeted during the summer by lovely alpine wildflowers. The trail continues upward through perpetual snowfields to the lofty summit of Mount Whitney via Trail Crest. The Mount Whitney segment of the John Muir Trail continues on along John Muir Creek to the Crabtree Ranger Station in Sequoia National Park and its junction with the Pacific Crest Trail. The jewellike lakes of the Pine Creek Basin, including Mirror, Consultation, Meysan, Iceberg, and Boy Scout lakes, divided by the towering upthrusts of Wotan's Throne, Pinnacle Ridge, and Thois Peak at 12,300 feet, hold rainbow, brook, and golden trout. Mount Whitney was named by the noted geologist Clarence King in honor of Prof. J. D. Whitney, leader of the California Geological Survey party, which, in 1864, measured the peak at 14,494 feet—the highest peak in the continental United States, outside of Alaska. In 1871, King made the first attempt to scale Mount Whitney, but, confused by storm clouds, he unwittingly climbed Mount Langley (14,042 ft.) to the south by mistake. In 1873, W. A. Goodyear climbed Mount Langley, discovered King's marker, and published news accounts of King's mistake. King responded by rushing west from New York and climbing the true Mount Whitney on September 19, 1873, but lost the honor of making the first ascent by four weeks. On August 18, 1873, a party of three mountaineers had reached the level 3-acre summit and given the mountain the name of Fisherman's Peak. Nevertheless, King's original name for the great peak remained on the map. Forest Service campgrounds are located at Whitney Portal and Lone Pine. A free guide to *The Mount Whitney Trail* may be obtained

from the Supervisor's Office, Inyo National Forest, 2957 Birth St., Bishop 93514.

Several good forest roads lead from Lone Pine to the renowned golden trout waters of Cottonwood Creek and lakes, located south of Mount Langley near 10,875-foot Siberian Pass on the High Sierra Crest. Trails wind west from Last Chance Meadow at road's end and climb up along Cottonwood Creek to *Golden Trout Camp* (Lone Pine 93545) at its junction with Little Cottonwood Creek and continue on to the Cottonwood Lakes Basin to New Army Pass. The 13 Cottonwood lakes are the source of golden trout eggs for the entire state stocking program. Cottonwood Creek, a part of the California Wild Trout Program, offers unsurpassed fly-fishing for beautiful goldens in a magnificent wilderness setting, surrounded by fragrant pine and fir forests with the snowcapped peaks of the High Sierra Crest towering in the background. Packhorse and guide service in the area is provided by the *Cottonwood Pack Station* (Lone Pine 93545). Rocky Basin Lakes and Golden Trout Creek and the headwaters of the Kern River on the Kern Plateau are the original habitat of the golden, and provide excellent fishing for the species. Golden Trout Creek rises in the volcanic meadows near the Little Whitney Cow Camp on the plateau and flows westward through a stunning wilderness, passing beneath a natural bridge and plunging over Volcano Falls to its junction at the Kern River Canyon in Sequoia National Park. *Bob White's Flying Service & Tunnel Pack Station* (Lone Pine Airport, Lone Pine 93545), located at the Tunnel Air Camp on the Kern Plateau, provides packhorse and fly-in service and guided trips to the surrounding lakes and golden trout streams.

Several useful guides have been published for the wilderness traveler planning a fishing, camping, or backpacking trip into the High Sierra country of the Inyo National Forest. One of the most invaluable is *Starr's Guide to the John Muir Trail & the High Sierra Region*. This classic Sierra Club totebook provides detailed descriptions of the wilderness areas and Sierra trails along the eastern slope. Several informative guides are published by Wilderness Press, 2440 Bancroft Way, Berkeley 94704, including: *Sierra South* ($6.95, 287 pp.), which describes the Sierra trails from Mono Divide south to Sequoia National Park; *Mono Craters* ($3.95), which describes eastern Yosemite National Park and the June Lake Loop—the most diverse glacial-volcanic landscape in California; *Devils Postpile* ($1.95), which describes this favorite landscape of mountaineers, naturalists, and backpackers in northeastern John Muir Wilderness; *Mt. Whitney* ($2.95), with descriptions of parts of both the Sequoia and Kings Canyon national parks and cross-country hiking routes across the farthest reaches of the High Sierra; and *Kern Peak–Olancha* ($2.95), which describes the high-country wilderness bordering Sequoia National Park on the south.

The forest's natural features, trails, roads, recreation sites and campgrounds, pack stations, ranger stations, and lookout towers are shown on the full-color *Inyo National Forest Map* (50¢). The map and detailed fishing, camping, hiking, cross-country skiing, and hunting information may be obtained by writing: Forest Supervisor, Inyo National Forest, 2957 Birth Street, Bishop 93514 (phone: 714-873-5841).

Vacation lodging and wilderness guide service and pack trips in the region are provided by *Leavitt Meadows Lodge*, Sonora Pass, Bridgeport 93517 (winter: Box 25, Coleville 96107); *Minarets Pack Station*, 3218 N. Zediker, Sanger 93657; *Mono Hot Springs Resort*, Mono Hot Springs 93642; *Tioga Pass Resort*, Box 7, Lee Vining 93541 (winter: 15748 Condor Ridge Rd., Canyon Country 91351); *Twin Lakes Resort*, Box 248, Bridgeport 93517; *Woods Lodge*, Lake George, Mammoth Lakes 93546; *Saddlebag Lake Resort*, Box 36, Lee Vining 93541 (winter: 389 O'Connor St., Palo Alto 94303); *Red's Meadow-Agnes Meadow Pack Stations* and *Red's Meadow Resort*, both Box 395, Mammoth Lakes 93546; *Tamarack Lodge*, Mammoth Lakes 93546; *Mammoth Village*, Mammoth Lakes 93546. Guided nordic ski tours, instruction, and winter survival courses are provided by the famed *Mammoth Ski Touring Center*, Box 102 Mammoth Lakes 93546 (714-934-6955) and *Sports & Trails, Inc.*, 1491 Whittier Blvd., La Habra 90631 (phone: 213-694-2164).

Guided treks in the Mount Whitney area and climbing instruction are provided by the *Mt. Whitney Guide Service & Sierra Nevada School of Mountaineering*, Box 659, Lone Pine 93545 (phone: 714-876-4500). Fishing guide service and specific fishing, hunting, and High Sierra backpacking info are available at *Doug Kittredge Sport Shop*, Mammoth Lakes Village 93546 (phone: 714-934-2423).

Access & Outfitting Centers

The major automobile routes to the forest are U.S. Highways 395 and 6 and State Route 120 (east). Lodging, guides, supplies, boat rentals, and outfitters are available at Bridgeport, Lee Vining (Mono Lake), June Lake, Mammoth Lakes, Convict Lake, Rock Creek, Bishop, Bishop Creek Basin, Big Pine, Independence, and Lone Pine.

Klamath National Forest & the Salmon-Trinity Alps

Klamath National Forest Topo Maps

U.S. Geological Survey 1:250,000 scale overview maps: Alturas, Redding, Weed.

Klamath River Country

U.S. Geological Survey large-scale topographic maps: Condrey Mountain, Copco, Coyote Peak, Dillon Mountain, Forks of Salmon, Happy Camp, Hoopa, Hornbrook, MacDoll, Orleans, Requa, Seiad Valley, Ship Mountain, Te-tah Creek, Ukonom Lake.

High Siskiyou Wildlands

U.S. Geological Survey large-scale topographic maps: Gasquet, Preston Peak, Happy Camp, Seiad Valley.

Marble Mountains Wilderness

U.S. Geological Survey large-scale topographic maps: Forks of Salmon, Sawyers Bar, Ukonom Lake, Scott Bar, Dillon Mountain, Orleans, Etna, Fort Jones, Seiad Valley, Happy Camp.

Pacific Crest Trail

U.S. Geological Survey large-scale topographic maps: Seiad Valley, Ukonom Lake, Condrey Mountain, Scott Bar, Sawyers Bar, Etna, China Mountain, Coffee Creek, Bonanza King, Weed, Dunsmuir.

Red Buttes Wildland

U.S. Geological Survey large-scale topographic maps: Oregon Caves, Happy Camp, Seiad Valley.

Salmon River Country

U.S. Geological Survey large-scale maps: Forks of Salmon, Sawyers Bar, Cecilville, Coffee Creek.

Salmon-Trinity Alps Primitive Area

U.S. Geological Survey large-scale topographic maps: Helena, Trinity Dam, Schell Mountain, Cecilville, Coffee Creek, Bonanza King.

The 1.7 million acres of this large, rugged "big timber" forest contain some of the finest fishing, hunting, backpacking, and wilderness camping areas in the United States. The forest is located within the legendary Bigfoot country near Yreka in northwest California, due south of the Rogue River and Siskiyou National Forest in Oregon. Hundreds of miles of old logging and mining roads and scenic hiking trails wind from elevations ranging from 600 to 6,600 feet through forests of ponderosa pine, sugar pine, western white and Jeffrey pine, Douglas fir, white and red fir, incense cedar, mountain hemlock, the rare white-barked Brewer spruce, and lodgepole and knobcone pine, and provide access to the remote alpine camping areas in the Goosenest Range (a spur of the cascades in the eastern part of the forest) and Klamath, Salmon, Siskiyou, Marble, and Scott mountains—all parts of the Coast Range system—and to the Red Buttes Wild Area and Seiad Valley (which means, in the haunting call of the Yurok Indians, "faraway land"), Sleepy Ridge Hunting Area, Indian Tom Lake Hunting Area, and some of the world's most beautiful salmon, trout, and steelhead fishing, canoeing, and kayaking waters.

The forest's big-game animals include black bear, antelope, and mountain lion. Blacktail deer are found in the western part of the forest and mule deer in the eastern section. The Butte Valley area in the Goosenest Mountains and the Tule Lake and Lower Klamath Lake areas are located in the center of the Pacific flyway and offer some of the best waterfowl shooting in the Northwest. The beautiful forest mountain ranges are, for the most part, narrow ridges 5,000 to 8,000 feet high, separated by deep canyons. The hundreds of remote alpine lakes offer excellent fishing for golden, cutthroat, and brook trout, plus a few grayling. The famed Klamath River and its tributaries, the Shasta, Scott, Salmon, and Trinity, provide some of the state's finest salmon and steelhead fishing in a classic forest setting. The Klamath, a former fishing haunt of Zane Grey, and known during the fur trade and exploration era as the Clamitte, Klamet, or Indian Scalp, is a big turbulent stream with headwaters in Lake Ewauna near Klamath Falls; it flows through high mountains, valleys, and rugged canyons for 180 miles to its mouth at the Pacific Ocean. For much of its length, the Klamath flows through conifer forests and the rugged wildlands of the Klamath Mountains. It has three runs of steelhead—the popular fall run, the winter run, and the spring or summer run. Most of the early-run steelhead are half-pounders 10–14 inches in length. As the season progresses, the fish increase in size, up to 7 or 8 pounds and over. Dark flies such as the Silver Hilton and local patterns such as the "Brindle Bug," spinners, bait, and wobblers are the best producers. A strong wading staff is an important accessory on this deep, powerful stream. The upper Klamath, between the Copco Reservoir and the Oregon border, is managed as part of the state wild trout program and is the home of the famous fighting Klamath River rainbow. Most of the upper river is privately owned except for a small section of public land near the Oregon border. Brook trout are abundant in the high-country headwater lakes and streams. Several historic outfitting and fishing centers are located along the banks of the Klamath and its tributaries. Scott Bar is located in the deep gorge of the Scott River, which enters the Klamath about 2 miles upstream from the village of Hamburg and is an important spawning and nursery stream for salmon and steelhead. Once a center of feverish gold mining, Scott Bar is a popular jumping-off point for fishing trips up the steep 15-mile-long canyon for steelhead and an occasional large, buckskin-flanked brown trout. Famous Happy Camp, known to fly-fishermen and steelheaders the world round, is popular for year-round fishing and as an outfitting center and jumping-off point for trips into the Salmon-Trinity Alps Wilderness. Downstream from Happy Camp is Somes Bar, where the Salmon River joins the Klamath. Somes Bar, which began as a mining town, is a popular year-round salmon and steelhead fishing spot and departure point for trails heading into the western part of the Marble Mountains Wilderness. Another popular fishing center is Weitchpec, located at the confluence of the Klamath and Trinity rivers on the northern boundary of the Hoopa Indian Reservation, which occupies about 100 square miles of the Hoopa Valley. A useful *Angler's Guide to the Klamath River* contains a "Klamath River Fishing Chart" and a map of the river showing campgrounds, access sites, boat-launching areas, flight strips, ranger stations, roads, river mileage, and elevation. The guide may be obtained for 40¢ from: Office of Procurement, Documents Section, P.O. Box 20191, Sacramento 95820. *Klamath River Fishing* ($1.95) is a detailed guide to over 200 miles of Klamath River fishing, including maps, written by Jim Freeman and published by Chronicle Books, 54 Mint Street, San Francisco 94119.

The scenic Salmon-Trinity Alps Primitive Area contains 225,000 acres of some of the most rugged terrain in California north of the High Sierra. The alps include the high, rough mountain ridges and deep glacial canyons along the Salmon-Trinity Divide in sections of the Trinity, Shasta, and Klamath national forests. The region contains the headwaters of a number of large streams, such as the South Fork of the Salmon River, Coffee Creek, Swift Creek, Stuarts Fork, Canyon Creek, New River, and the North Fork tributaries of the Trinity River. Huge talus boulders and steep, jagged peaks characterize much of the area above the timberline. Fly-fishing enthusiasts will find numerous possibilities in the hundreds of alpine lakes, such as Grizzly Lake, which is seldom fished and full of fat 12-inch rainbows. Grizzly is reached by the Hunters Camp Trail from Hobo Gulch, where it begins its journey through tall stands of virgin Douglas fir and ponderosa pine, winding on along the granite slopes into the lush, green Grizzly Meadows. At the meadows, there is a breathtaking view of 9,000-foot-high Thompson Peak and the waterfall cascading 70 feet from the lip of Grizzly Lake at the base of the peak into Grizzly Creek. The hike from the meadow to the lake is about a 45-minute scramble up among large rocks and boulders. Stuarts Fork of the Trinity River has excellent angling for brook, brown, and rainbow trout in its headwaters in Emerald and Sapphire lakes and along its 14-mile course from there to Trinity Lake. In the fall, spawning kokanee run up the Stuarts Fork for about 3 miles from its mouth at Trinity Lake. The Morris Meadow area along the upper Stuarts Fork is an excellent fly-fishing stretch. The upper Trinity River is another superb trout stream, heading on the west slope of Mount Eddy (9,038 ft.) on the Trinity Divide and flowing southwesterly for 24 miles into Trinity Lake. Fly-fishing is superb for native rainbows and fall-run kokanee. Campgrounds and grazing areas are located at Eagle Creek and Horse Flat. Supplies and services are at Trinity Center and Coffee Creek. Near the Mumbo Creek Basin, the headwaters of the East Fork of the Trinity provide some great fishing for pan-sized rainbows, brookies, and browns. Access is by logging road from Whalen Station Road. The nearest campground is found at Jackass Springs on Trinity Lake. The scenic Salmon River has ideal fishing for large chinook, coho, and steelhead along its remote, heavily forested stretches of deep pools, cascades, runs, and broad riffles. The headwaters of this classic high mountain stream are in both the Marble Mountain and Salmon-Trinity Alps areas. The main Salmon is formed by the confluence of the North and South forks; it flows for 19 miles through the alpine forest, rushing along its final stretch through a deep canyon into the Klamath River. Wooley Creek, a major tributary of the Salmon, has some fine fishing for spring chinook and summer steelhead from its headwaters in Haypress Meadows downstream to its meeting with the Salmon. Golden trout averaging about 1 pound, with a rare fish up to 8 pounds, are found in many of the remote interior lakes. Popular fly patterns for this region include the Royal Coachman, Red Ant, Gray Hackle with yellow body, Mosquito, Grizzly King, Professor, and Black Gnat. The best lake fishing is during the spring and fall. During the hot mid-summer days it is best to fish over springs and in the deeper waters. Many of the trails in this rugged area are blind, forcing you to backtrack to reach other lakes and streams. Experienced backpackers have the advantage here, being able to travel cross-country. Good topographical maps and a working knowledge of the compass are essential.

The Salmon-Trinity Alps Primitive Area is located within two different ranger districts of the Shasta-Trinity National Forest and within two districts of the Klamath National Forest.

The District Rangers will be glad to help you plan a trip through the Primitive Area and to help answer questions you may have. The District Rangers are located at: Big Bar Ranger District, Big Bar; Weaverville Ranger District, Weaverville; Callahan Ranger District, Callahan; and Salmon River Ranger District, Sawyers Bar.

The invaluable *Angler's Guide to the Lakes & Streams of the Trinity Alps* (available for 40¢ from: Office of Procurement, Documents Section, P.O. Box 20191, Sacramento 95820) provides the wilderness fisherman with detailed descriptions of the wilderness area, access, and all lakes and streams, with elevation, characteristics, and fish species present. The guide contains a chart of campsites and boat-launching areas and a "Map of the Lakes of the Trinity Alps" that shows roads, trails, lookouts, ranger stations, Forest Service public camps, airports, marinas, and launching ramps.

The famous Marble Mountains Wilderness encompasses 213,363 acres of top-ranked fly-fishing, backpacking and hunting country north of the Salmon-Trinity Alps. Its dominant feature is the snow-white marble cap 700 to 1,000 feet thick at the top of Marble Mountain. The cap was formed from the bodies of sea organisms deposited when the peneplain formed the bottom of an ocean. This region is a mild and thickly forested country with gently rising trails. Numerous hiking and packhorse trails wind through this colorful wilderness, passing the majestic white of Marble Mountain, the lush green of Morehouse Mountain, and the deep blue of Cliff Lake, interspersed with various hues of sheer rock cliffs and dense stands of evergreens. Hundreds of lakes lie in the glaciated pockets forming the headwaters of many small trout streams. Most of the lakes in the wilderness hold either brook or rainbow trout. The lakes vary in size a half-acre to Ukonom Lake, the largest, 67 acres. Ukonom Lake is reached by a steep trail from Jacobs Ladder, at 6,000 feet. Pan-sized brook and rainbow trout abound in the upper reaches of Canyon, Elk, Shackleford, and Wooley creeks and the North Fork and Little North Fork of the Salmon River. Wooley Creek is also known for its excellent summer run of king salmon and steelhead. The hunting for deer and black bear is quite good. This region is known to produce the largest blacktail deer in California. The district ranger will give advice regarding trail conditions, licensed packers, campsites, and grazing pastures for saddle stock. Fire permits are required of all campers. Horse feed is plentiful along the main ridges and in the glaciated pockets. However, there is practically no feed below 4,500 feet elevation. Picketing animals in meadows is not permitted. Two kinds of outings are offered by the commercial packers. On a spot trip, your party is packed into an area and then packed out again on a given date. On the continuous plan, the packer and animals stay with your party, and you may move to new locations as you wish. You furnish all food and equipment and do all camp chores except wrangling and packing. The cost of saddle and pack stock is some $7 each per day; the packer and his horse cost about

$27 per day. Pack mules carry about 200 pounds if the load is not bulky. As a rule, allow one pack animal for carrying food and equipment for two people per week. A pack animal carries a top pack for bulky light pieces, and two side packs about $12'' \times 20'' \times 24''$; these are furnished by the packers. A list of packers is available from: Forest Supervisor, Klamath National Forest, Yreka 96097.

The *Marble Mountain Wilderness Area Map & Guide* (available free from the Forest Supervisor's Office, address above) contains a description of the area and a map showing all natural features and roads, trails, ranger stations, lookout towers, campsites, and improved campgrounds and base camps. The *Angler's Guide to the Lakes & Streams of the Marble Mountains* (available for 40¢ from: Office of Procurement, Documents Section, P.O. Box 20191, Sacramento 95820) contains detailed descriptions of the lakes and streams of the wilderness and a "Map of the Lakes & Streams of the Marble Mountains" showing trails, corrals, lookouts, roads, and campsites.

North of the Salmon-Trinity Alps and Marble Mountains wilderness areas are two of northern California's most remote, scenic wild areas —the High Siskiyou Mountains and the Red Buttes. The High Siskiyou Wildlands encompass some 200,000 roadless acres along the western reach of the Siskiyous. Numerous old Indian and hiking trails wind through a rugged glaciated landscape; through one of the richest coniferous forest areas in the United States, including dense montane forests and lovely stands of white and noble fir, several kinds of pines, the elegant white-barked Brewer spruce, and Alaska cedar at the higher elevations; and through lush forests of Douglas fir, western hemlock, cedars, and yew. They provide access to Youngs Valley, the East Fork of the Illinois River, Indian Creek, Clear Creek, Preston Peak, Devils Punchbowl, and Raspberry and Island lakes. This wilderness traveler's paradise was the ancient hunting grounds of the Totawa, Karok, and Yurok Indians and is the home of the mythical Bigfoot. The trails of this alpine area are bordered by great drifts of rhododendron, lush fields of colorful lilies, Pacific dogwood, pitcher plant beds, green-petaled coneflower, and pink deershead orchid, among others. The High Siskiyous are also inhabited by the wolverine —the "Indian devil" of the Far North—once believed to be extinct in California.

East of the High Siskiyous are the alplike highlands, broad highcountry, barren red desert, snowcapped crags, and densely forested valleys of the 90,000-acre roadless area known as the "Red Buttes"— named after a red rock, two-horned mountain. Numerous trails, including a segment of the Pacific Crest Trail, wind through this remote backpacking paradise and provide access to the Siskiyou Crest, Sucker Creek, Green Valley, Azela Lake, Portuguese Creek, the Middle Fork of the Applegate River, Cameron Meadows, Frog Pond, and the famous Oregon Caves. Both the High Siskiyou and Red Buttes wildlands are described in fascinating detail in *Hiking the Bigfoot Country*, a 398-page totebook by John Hart, available from Sierra Club Books, Box 7959, Rincon Annex, San Francisco 94104, for $7.95. The book contains topo maps of each area and useful info about weather, hazards and problems, following faint trails, walking light in Bigfoot country, geology, forests, flowers, wildlife, and much more.

The Klamath National Forest has 33 campgrounds, providing 451 family units. Most of these campgrounds are along the Klamath, Scott, and Salmon rivers. The forest's campgrounds, trails, roads, ranger stations, and natural features are shown on the full-color *Klamath National Forest Recreation Map* (50¢). This map and specific fishing, camping, hiking, hunting, canoeing, and kayaking info may be obtained from: Forest Supervisor's Office, Klamath National Forest, 1215 South Main, Yreka 96097 (phone: 916–842–2741).

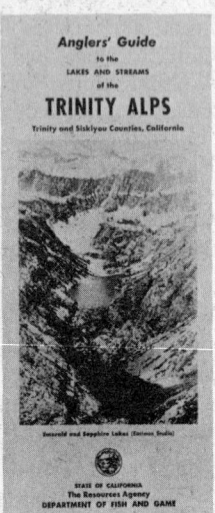

For detailed vacation accommodations information, write to the following Klamath National Forest lodges and fishing camps: *Rustic Inn* and *Anglers Motel*, both Happy Camp 96039; *Klamath River Lodge, Sportsman Lodge,* and *Beaver Creek Lodge*, all Klamath River 96050; *Kutzkey Resort* (steelhead fishing resort on the Klamath River), Hornbrook 96044; *Rainbow Resort*, Hamburg 96045; *Lor-O-Ranch,* Cecilville 96018; *Heart D Cattle & Guest Ranch* and *HR Place*, both Fort Jones 96032 in the Scott Valley-Salmon River area; *Trinity Alps Resort*, Lewiston 96052; *Eagle Creek Ranch, Coffee Creek Ranch, Seymours Ranch, Trinity Mountain Meadow Ranch,* and *Bonanza King* (Coffee Creek), all Trinity Center 96091. Guided fishing and hunting pack trips in the Trinity Alps wilderness are provided by *Trinity Pack Trains*, P.O. Box 277, Trinity Center 96091.

The famous *Somes Bar Guide Service & Lodge* (Somesbar 95568; phone: 916–469–3399) offers rustic accommodations, guided steelhead trips on the Klamath River using McKenzie River drift boats, pack-in fishing trips in the Marble Mountains Wilderness, rafting and kayaking trips, fly fishing instruction, and gold panning and gold mining expeditions. For Klamath and Salmon river wild water trips, write: *Wild Water Kayak Trips*, P.O. Box 158, Gasquet 95543.

Access & Outfitting Centers

The major routes to Klamath National Forest are Interstate 5, U.S. Highway 97 from Oregon, and California Highways 89, 299, 96, and 3. Lodging, supplies, canoe and boat rentals, guides, and outfitters are available at Seiad Valley, Horse Creek, Yreka, Scott Bar, Hamburg, Happy Camp, Clear Creek, Somes Bar, Forks of Salmon, Sawyers Bar, Etna, Cecilville.

Lassen National Forest & Volcanic Park

Lassen National Forest Topo Maps

U.S. Geological Survey 1:250,000 scale overview maps: Chico, Susanville.

Lassen Volcanic National Park Topo Maps

U.S. Geological Survey large-scale topographic maps: Manzanite Lake, Prospect Peak, Lassen Peak, Mount Harkness, Harvey Mountain, Chester.

Caribou Wilderness

U.S. Geological Survey large-scale topographic maps: Chester, Harvey Mountain.

Eagle Lake Area

U.S. Geological Survey large-scale topographic maps: Antelope Mountain, Fredonyer Peak.

Hat Creek Wild Trout Area

U.S. Geological Survey large-scale topographic maps: Burney, Jellico, Prospect Peak.

Pacific Crest Trail

U.S. Geological Survey large-scale topographic maps: Burney, Jellico, Prospect Peak, Mount Harkness, Jonesville, Almanor.

Thousand Lakes Wilderness

U.S. Geological Survey large-scale maps: Manzanita Lake, Burney.

The Lassen National Forest contains 1.2 million acres of renowned fishing, hunting, and wilderness camping country surrounding Lassen Volcanic National Park west of Susanville in northeastern California. The forest, which straddles the beautiful Cascade Range, is named after Peter Lassen, a frontiersman, trapper, miner, rancher, and trail guide who blazed a northwest route called the Lassen Road to lure settlers north to virgin goldfields and to the hoped-for settlement of Shasta County. The forest terrain consists of gently rolling mountains, dense forests of pine and fir, volcanically formed lakes, and meadows ranging in elevation from 1,200 to 10,000 feet. The sagebrush-covered Great Basin High Desert, east of the forest, is the winter range of antelope and Columbian blacktail and mule deer that live throughout the summer in the forest's deep valleys. The Lassen region is one of the state's top-ranked hunting areas for trophy mule deer. The Pacific Crest Trail and hundreds of miles of spur trails and winding forest roads provide access to the volcanic spring-fed waters of Hat Creek, Eagle and Almanor lakes, Painted Dunes, Rising River, the Susan River, and Willow Creek (a brush-lined gem that holds brown trout up to 5 pounds and more), and to the Caribou and Thousand Lakes wilderness areas.

Eagle Lake, 18 miles northwest of Susanville at 5,000 feet elevation, is the second-largest natural lake in California. It was formed by the receding alkaline waters of a primeval lake that was larger than Lake Erie. This nationally renowned trout lake, over 13 miles long, is often called "the lake that time forgot." The lake is the home of a unique species of rainbow trout that grows to lunker size in a period of about 3 years. The Eagle Lake rainbow was once near extinction, but has returned to its former abundance. Limit catches of rainbows averaging 2 to 3 pounds are common, and trout up to 11 pounds are caught each year from the lake's deep alkaline waters. The northern and middle sections of the lake are bordered by sagebrush-covered hills, and along the southern shoreline is a beautiful forest of pine and fir. Three campgrounds have been developed along the shoreline by the Forest Service and the Bureau of Land Management. The wildlands surrounding the lake are a top hunting area for large mule deer, and flocks of ducks and geese use the lake during their fall and spring migrations. Indian ruins, temporary shelters that were used while waiting for fish to dry that had been netted or speared as they migrated upstream to spawn, may be seen on Pine Creek near Spaulding tract.

The gentle, rolling, forested plateau of the Caribou Wilderness Area embraces some 19,080 acres of the forest along the eastern boundary of Lassen Volcanic National Park. The area's volcanic terrain is dominated by the Caribou Peaks and the Red Cinder Cone at 8,370 feet. A forest of Jeffrey and lodgepole pine mixed with white and red fir, western white pine, and hemlock at lower elevations provides cover for deer, black bear and the rare pine marten. Alpine fishing is good for rainbow and brook trout in Beauty, Long, Pasey, Triangle, Gem, Divide, Hidden, and Cypress lakes. Access to the remote interior lake basins is by hiking trail. Be sure to keep an eye out for rattlesnakes. The beautiful Thousand Lakes Wilderness is situated in the forest northwest of Lassen Volcanic National Park. It is dominated by the sparkling blue trout lakes of Thousand Lakes Valley, which is surrounded by towering peaks that reach their greatest heights at Magee Peak (8,550 ft.) and Crater Peak (8,677 ft.). This glacial valley is dotted by numerous small lakes and ponds surrounded by forests of ponderosa pine, white and red fir, and mountain hemlock and white bark pine above 8,000 feet. The Pacific Crest Trail and numerous spur trails wind through the wilderness and provide excellent opportunities for cross-country travel with the aid of a good map and compass. The Magee Trail winds up to Magee Peak and provides a spectacular view of the Sacramento Valley to the south, the Coast Range to the west, and the Warner Range to the northeast. Warner Valley, just inside the forest, commemorates William Warner, a captain in the U.S.

Army, who was killed in 1849 in a battle with the Modocs just south of the Oregon border while looking for a route across the mountains. A wilderness permit is required for both wilderness areas. The *Caribou Wilderness* and *Thousand Lakes Wilderness Map-Brochures* are available free from: Forest Supervisor's Office, Lassen National Forest, 707 Nevada St., Susanville 96130 (phone: 916–257–2151). The maps show roads, trails, and trailheads.

The famous rainbow and brown trout waters of Hat Creek, managed under the state's wild trout program, are thought to have been named for Hat-te-we-we of the Pit River Indians, or for an actual hat lost in the stream by a member of the Noble party, blazing trails in 1852. Hat Creek rises high in the volcanic crags of Lassen Park and flows northwest through the forest to its confluence with the Pit River. The Hat Creek Recreation Area offers camping facilities, fishing, and hiking. An archaeological site, the Subway Cave, lies in the Hat Creek area. This lava tube, 4 to 17 feet high, winds 1,300 feet through the lava flow that covered the Hat Creek Valley less than 2,000 years ago. A self-guided trail interprets the features of Subway Cave. A reliable lantern or flashlight must be carried.

The island-studded waters of Lake Almanor cover 75 square miles. This is one of the largest man-made lakes in California. Lying southeast of Lassen Volcanic Park, it offers fishing for trout and kokanee salmon. Campgrounds, boat rentals, and launching facilities are available. Evening campfire programs are held at the Almanor Campground Amphitheater.

The forest's wild high-country streams provide some of the finest wilderness fly-fishing in the state for rainbow, brown, and brook trout. The North Fork of the Feather River flows for 25 miles from its headwaters in Lassen Volcanic Park and empties into Lake Almanor. The North Fork has numerous campgrounds along its scenic route and holds brown trout up to 5 pounds and rainbows. Yellow Creek, a tributary of the North Fork, is a fly-fishing-only stream managed under the state's wild trout program; it provides excellent fishing for rainbows and browns. Pine Creek flows from its headwaters high in the Caribou Wilderness in an easterly direction for 35 miles and empties into Eagle Lake. Pine Creek has an abundant population of brook trout and has runs of large Eagle Lake rainbows. The largest stream

in the Lassen Forest region is the Susan River, which rises in the small lakes near the Caribou Peaks and flows southeasterly through aspen-bordered meadows. The upper stretches of the river produce large brown trout. Fly-fishermen will enjoy the cutbank holes and brushy pools along Willow Creek, a tributary of the Susan River that rises from springs near Eagle Lake.

The beautiful High Lakes Area lies in a subalpine setting in the forest, southeast of Butte Meadows. The area has glacial lakes, striations, and "erratics." Indian petroglyphs are inscribed on cliffs over Long Lake. The High Lakes are located at 6,800 feet elevation and are accessible only by jeep trail and spur trails of the Pacific Crest Trail. Forest Service campgrounds are located at Cherry Hill, West Branch, and Phibrook Lake. Unimproved roads in the area are very rough, rocky, and difficult to travel. Topo maps of the area are a must, and 4-wheel-drive vehicles are recommended.

Within the forest lies Lassen Volcanic National Park, known as the "sweathouse of the gods," encompassing 100,000 acres of rugged coniferous forest surrounding lava-devastated acres of sheer, jagged cliffs, fumaroles, boiling lakes, great weirdly shaped rocks, and bubbling mud pots. The park is dominated by 10,487-foot Mount Lassen, a plug-dome volcano situated at the southern tip of the Cascade Range. Mount Lassen is one of the most recently active volcanoes in the contiguous United States. Beginning in May 1914, eruptions occurred intermittently for more than 7 years. Evidence of the activity is visible in the beautifully symmetrical cinder cone, active hot springs, steaming fumaroles, and sulfurous vents. Other major features include the other-worldly scenery of Chaos Crags, a wild disarray of magnificent piles of pointed blocks surrounded by enormous banks of pointed talus reaching 1,000 feet high. Lake Helen, named for Helen Tanner Brodt, the first white woman to climb Lassen Peak, lies within the crater rim of ancestral Mount Tehama, once the dominant volcano of the region. The park has more than 150 miles of trails, including the Pacific Crest Trail, which wind through remote forests of pine, fir, cedar, and aspen and along waterfalls, alpine meadows, and lava flows leading to Kings Creek Meadows, Juniper Lake, Red Cinder Cone, Painted Dunes, Chaos Crags, Vulcan's Castle, Devil's Kitchen and Crystal Cliffs. Wilderness permits are required for all backcountry travel and camping. Beautiful Manzanita Lake has recently been closed to the public due to possible large-scale eruptions or a rockfall avalanche. Fishing in the park is good for rainbow, brook, and brown trout in Hat Creek, Lost Creek, Chester Lakes, Cliff Lake, and Big Bear and Widow lakes.

Campgrounds in the park are located at Summit Lake, Butte Lake, Warner Valley, Juniper Lake, and Chaos Crags. Lodging and cabins are available from *Lassen Guest Services*, Mill Creek 96061 (summer address: Drakesbad #2, via Chester) (phone: 916–595–3306); *Child's Meadows Resort*, Mill Creek 96061 (916–595–3391); *Deer Creek Lodge*, Mill Creek 96061 (916–258–2939); *Fire Mountain Lodge*, Mill Creek 96061 (916–258–2938); and *Mineral Lodge*, Mineral 96061 (916–595–4422).

A full-color U.S. Geological Survey *Lassen National Volcanic Park Topographic Map*, 24 ×30 inches, shows the park and adjacent area, trails, contours, campgrounds, and all natural and man-made features. This map, also available in a shaded-relief edition, costs $2. Detailed information, a free *Lassen Volcanic National Park Map-Brochure*, and information bulletins on fishing regulations, backcountry travel, campgrounds, and recreation fees may be obtained by writing: Superintendent, Lassen Volcanic National Park, Mineral 96063. The Loomis Museum Association, Mineral 96063, publishes several useful guidebooks to the park. These include the 56-page *Lassen Trails* booklet, with descriptions and maps of all park trails (50¢); *100 North-*

ern *California Hiking Trails*, with maps and photographs ($5.95); *Road Guide to Lassen Volcanic Park* (75¢); *Geology of Lassen's Landscape* (85¢); *Eruptions of Lassen Peak* ($1.25), an eyewitness account of 1914–15 eruptions with original Loomis photos; *Lassen— His Life & Legacy* ($1.25), story of Peter Lassen and the Lassen Trail; *Birds of Lassen Volcanic National Park* ($1); *Trees & Shrubs of Lassen Volcanic National Park* (85¢); and *Trail Leaflets* (10¢ each) for *Lassen Peak, Bumpass Hill, Cinder Cone, Lily Pond,* and *Boiling Springs Lake.*

Recreation site campgrounds in Lassen National Forest are located at Big Pine, Boundary, Bridge, Butte Creek, Cave, Hat Creek, Honn, Rocky, Wiley Ranch, and Willow Springs. A full-color *Lassen National Forest Map* (50¢), a free *Visitor Guide to Lassen National Forest,* and detailed hunting, fishing, and camping information may be obtained from: Forest Supervisor, Lassen National Forest, 707 Nevada St., Susanville 96130. The forest map shows all forest roads, trails, campgrounds, ranger stations, lookout towers, cabins, recreation sites, springs, and boat-launching ramps.

Lassen Ski Touring, c/o Child's Meadows Resort, Mill Creek 96061 (phone: 916–595–3306) offers guided tours, instruction, and winter survival courses in Lassen Park. Detailed fishing and stream information for Hat Creek, and the Fall and Pit rivers is available from the *Fall River Fly Shop,* Fall River Mills 96028 (phone: 916–336–6438).

Access & Outfitting Centers

The Lassen National Forest and Volcanic Park is reached via Interstate 5, U.S. Highway 395, and state routes 89, 139, 299, 44, 36, 99, and 32. Lodging, supplies, guides, and outfitters are available at Chester, Greenville, Quincy, Mineral, Red Bluff, Redding, Susanville, Westwood, Hat Creek, Burney, and Fall River Mills.

Modoc National Forest

Modoc National Forest Topo Maps

U.S. Geological Survey 1:250,000 scale overview maps: Alturas, Susanville.

Medicine Lake Volcanic Highlands

U.S. Geological Survey large-scale topographic maps: Medicine Lake, Hambone.

South Warner Wilderness

U.S. Geological Survey large-scale topographic maps: Eagle Peak, Emerson Peak, Jess Valley, Shield Creek, Soup Creek, Warren Peak.

The 1.7-million-acre Modoc National Forest, a renowned big-game and waterfowl hunting and backpacking area, is located in the northeast corner of California and includes the South Warner Wilderness, the Warner Mountains, Goose Lake, and Clear Lake National Wildlife Refuge. The setting of the forest is a complex geological region of recent volcanic activity. At the eastern border of the forest are the Warner Mountains, a spur of the Cascade Range to the north. The topography ranges from the alpine peaks, canyons, glades, and lush green meadows in the South Warner Wilderness to the rugged obsidian mountains, lava caves, and craters in the Medicine Lake Highlands, located along the west boundary of the forest, directly southwest of the Lava Beds National Monument. The sagebrush-covered grasslands and thick forests of ponderosa pine, red and white fir, and incense cedar were the ancient home and hunting grounds of the Modoc, Paiute, and Pit Indians. Fierce Indian wars took place between 1848 and 1911 against the invading white man, and the region

became known as the "bloody ground of the Pacific." The Modoc War of 1872–73 was the largest Indian war in California.

Many of the small streams draining eastward from the Warner Mountains into Surprise Valley hold wild trout populations. The South Warner Wilderness encompasses 68,507 acres along the southern Warner Mountains. Eagle Peak (9,906 ft.) and Warren Peak (8,875 ft.) dominate the area. The wilderness has a fairly extensive trail system for both the backpacker and horseman. Summit Trail follows

A Brief Guide to the Trails of Lassen Volcanic National Park

the backbone of the wilderness crest for 27 miles from Patterson Meadow, near the southern border, following the 9,000-foot contour for more than 15 miles north along a steep ridge. Numerous spur trails provide access to the forest's peaks, canyons, glacial lakes, and alpine meadows. Paterson Lake, nestled at the base of Warren Peak, offers a beautiful contrast to the massive backdrop of cliffs rising more than 800 feet to the top of the northern flank of the peak. Other trails lead to the interior hunting and fishing areas around Emerson Lakes, Duzenberry Peak, Mill Creek Mows, Poison Flat, Pine Creek, and Owl Creek. A portion of the wilderness lies within a game reserve. Most of the area, however, is open for hunting during deer season. This is considered a top-rate mule deer region. One of the forest's better lakes is Lake Annie, near the Fort Bidwell Indian Reservation at the north end of Surprise Valley. Lake Annie produces rainbow and brown trout to 2 pounds. Mule deer hunters should try the backcountry plateau, consisting of rocky lava flows, at the western border of the forest south of the Lost River. The divide along the western edge of the forest is formed by a chain of volcanic peaks and cones extending southward along the southern tip of the Cascade Range to Mount Shasta. To the northeast, the blue waters of Clear Lake National Wildlife Refuge hold huge but extremely wary brown trout. The Clear Lake and Goose Lake areas also offer some of the state's finest waterfowl shooting. Upland bird hunting is good throughout the forest for the handsome mountain quail, chukar partridge, sage grouse, and mourning dove. There is also limited hunting for antelope.

The Lava Beds National Monument and the Volcanic Medicine Lake Highlands are located in the northwestern portion of the forest. The lava beds were formed centuries ago by a group of volcanoes erupting masses of lava that cooled into a landscape of twisted lava flows, cinder buttes, ice caves, and spatter cones. A variety of wildlife can be seen

within the area, including bighorn sheep, which were reintroduced in 1971. The Medicine Lake Highlands, to the south of the lava beds, is an area of moderately sloping to steep mountains with numerous glass flows, lava caves, tubes, chimneys, cones, and craters and forests of sugar pine and red and white fir with an understory of bitterbrush, manzanita, and snowbrush. Medicine Lake has the forest's largest campground, which provides 88 family camping units. The cool, clear waters of the lake, situated at 6,676 feet elevation, hold rainbow and brook trout. The lake has 500 surface acres, a beach, and a new boat-launching ramp. Accommodations, supplies, and boat rentals are available at Medicine Lake Lodge. The Burnt Lava Flow Virgin Area is on the southern flanks of the highlands. This 9,000-acre area is a spectacular flow of jumbled black lava surrounding islands of 10 to 60 acres each on three old cinder cones cloaked by virgin stands of pine and fir.

The *Modoc National Forest Recreation Map* shows all campgrounds, trails, roads, ranger stations, natural features, springs, and recreation sites. This full-color map (50¢) and the free *Modoc National Forest Camping Guide* and *South Warner Wilderness Map* may be obtained by writing to: Forest Supervisor, Modoc National Forest, 441 N. Main St., Alturas 96101 (phone: 916–233–3521). There are 20 camp-grounds distributed throughout the forest, with a total of 283 camp-sites.

Licensed fishing and big-game hunting guides operating within the Modoc National Forest include: *David M. Capik,* 12th & Maine St., Alturas 96101 (waterfowl and deer); *Don Collis,* P.O. Box 476, Alturas 96101 (deer and goose hunting); *Dale H. Houston,* Box 68, Cedarville 96104 (waterfowl); *Gus W. Speridon,* P.O. Box 1248, Alturas 96101 (antelope, ducks, geese, and upland game birds).

Access & Outfitting Centers

The major routes to the forest include U.S. Highway 395 and state highways 139 and 299. Lodging, supplies, guides, and packhorses are available at Eagleville, Cedarville, Fort Bidwell, Davis Creek, Alturas, and Canby.

Plumas National Forest— Land of the Feather River

Plumas National Forest Topo Maps

U.S. Geological Survey 1:250,000 scale overview maps: Susanville, Redding, Chico, Ukiah.

Feather River—Middle Fork National Wild & Scenic River

U.S. Geological Survey large-scale topographic maps: Chilcoot, Reconnaissance Peak, Portola, Sierra City, Blairsden, Johnsville, Blue Nose Mountain, Onion Valley, Bucks Lake, Cascade, Brush Creek, Forbestown, Oroville Dam.

Lakes Basin Wild Area

U.S. Geological Survey large-scale topographic map: Sierra City.

Pacific Crest Trail

U.S. Geological Survey large-scale topographic maps: Almanor, Pulga, Quincy (7.5), Bucks Lake, Blue Nose Mountain, Mount Fillmore, Downieville.

Plumas National Forest encompasses 1,146,900 acres in the transition zone between the Sierra Nevada and the Cascade Mountains sur-rounding Quincy in northeastern California, and includes nearly the entire Feather River system. The terrain is mountainous, rugged, and exceedingly steep in some areas. The mountains, ranging in elevation from 1,000 to 8,372 feet, are cut by deep canyons, interspersed with large grassy valleys. Hundreds of miles of scenic trails, including the Pacific Crest Trail, and forest roads wind through colorful stands of sugar, ponderosa, and Jeffrey pine, white and red fir, Douglas fir, and incense cedar, and provide access to the remote Lakes Basin, Upper Canyon of the Middle Fork of the Feather River, Little Grass Valley, and Antelope, Bucks, Frenchman, and Davis lakes. The forest, estab-lished by Pres. Theodore Roosevelt in 1906, was once the home and hunting grounds of the Maidu Indians. The eastern portions of the forest were also used by the Washo, and possibly by the Paiutes. In the 1800s the area was explored by the Spanish, including Luis Ar-guello, captain of an expedition, who bestowed the name Feather River *(Rio de las Plumas)* because he is said to have seen a "great number of feathers of wild fowl floating on its bosom."

The Feather River country was virtually unexplored until the 1850s, when hordes of gold miners invaded the territory and boom towns sprang up almost overnight. The most productive gold-mining camps were strung along the Feather River. Bucks Creek, known as Buck's Ranch during the 1850s, was a landmark for stage drivers on the Oro-Quincy Road and a supply center for miners in the region. In 1851, Jim Beckworth found the lowest Sierra pass in the eastern part of what is now known as Sierra Valley. Indians had used this pass for thousands of years, and immigrants soon began moving through it and into the area. Spanish Creek, known to the pioneers as Spanish Ranch, is located in Meadow Valley in the forest and was the site of the famed Monte Cristo mine of the 1850s. It was during this era that competi-tive skiing originated in the United States and the world. Beginning around the towns of Johnsville, Onion Valley, and La Porte, the miners held competitive events on 12 to 14-foot skis known as "long boards."

Remnants of the gold rush days, including old machinery, abandoned water ditches, and trails, are found in the remote backcountry areas near the Middle Fork. The beautiful Middle Fork of the Feather, a national recreation area and wild and scenic river, flows southwesterly for 108 miles from the northeastern corner of Sierra Valley. It is joined by Last Chance Creek in a gentle valley, then switches into mountain-ous terrain, and finally plunges into the rugged canyons above Lake Oroville. Rainbow trout fishing is good along the entire length of the Middle Fork. Hunting is generally good throughout most of the re-mote backcountry areas for blacktail and mule deer, black bear, valley quail, Sierra grouse, sage grouse, and waterfowl. *The Middle Fork Feather River Map-Brochure,* available free from: Forest Supervisor, Plumas National Forest, 159 Lawrence St., Quincy 95971, shows the wild river zone, scenic river zone, recreational river zone, foot and 4-wheel-drive trails, primitive roads, and campgrounds. The recrea-tional zone of the Middle Fork flows for 65 miles from Last Chance Creek through small rocky canyons, timbered flats, and meadow lands to the quiet forest of the English Bar zone, where the river flows for 6 miles to the rugged, steep-banked Upper Canyon Wild River. Ac-cess to this section of the Middle Fork is by old mining and deer trails that skirt the break made by the river channel. The trail bridge and camp at Hartman Bar are on the crossing for the Pacific Crest Trail. The Middle Fork flows through the Upper Canyon zone for 27 miles into the forest of the Milsap Bar zone, where it flows over Seven Falls and continues on through the Bald Rock Canyon wild zone and pours into Lake Oroville. The Bald Rock Canyon area is dominated by huge boulders, rock cliffs, and sheer canyon walls; nearby is Feather Falls.

The Feather Falls Scenic Area includes portions of the Middle Fork and three of its tributaries—Fall River, the Little North Fork, and the South Branch Middle Fork Feather River. This 15,000-acre scenic

area embraces spectacular granite domes and Feather Falls on the Fall River, the sixth highest waterfall in the United States, which plummets 640 feet over a sheer granite cliff during its rush to meet the Middle Fork and Lake Oroville. Feather Falls was formed several million years ago when the Sierra Nevada tilted westward and erosion exposed a huge granite batholith that had fractured as it cooled. The Fall River eroded the soft fractured area back from the deep Bald Rock Canyon to hard solid rock at the brink of the falls. During March, April, and May, the water is at its highest flow and the falls are most spectacular. A foot trail provides easy access, and an overlook across from the falls provides an excellent view of one of the greatest scenic wonders in California. Another attraction in the scenic area is the South Branch Falls, a series of nine waterfalls varying in height from 30 to 150 feet, noted for their huge rock domes, boulders, and deep green pools. Hiking and riding trails wind throughout the scenic area and provide access to more than 22 miles of good rainbow trout streams, including the Little North Fork, a beautiful cascading stream that enters the Middle Fork near the Milsap Bar campground. Maidu Indian mortars and artifacts can be seen at Wagner Valley and Bald Rock Dome and along the Fall River. A free *Feather Falls Scenic Area Map-Brochure* may be obtained from the Forest Supervisor's Office (address above). For specific trail and road conditions, check with the Challenge or Oroville ranger stations.

Trails in the forest are, for the most part, in good condition. The Pacific Crest Trail and state roads provide access to the scenic Lakes Basin, a prime backpacking area, and Gold Lake. Here, overnight camping is permitted at Wade, Jamison, Rock, Grass, and Smith lakes. All other areas in Lakes Basin are restricted to day use. Gold Lake is believed to be the mythical "gold lake" of the miners and immigrants who believed it to be the source of all placer gold. The rumor of the lake started around 1849, when an immigrant by the name of Stoddard found incredible chunks of gold on the shores of a lake while lost in the highlands. Stoddard and anxious "gold-lakers," including Peter Lassen, were unable to relocate the area of his discovery during the ensuing years. Humbug Summit is thought to commemorate their frustrating experience. Other trails of interest to backpackers include Chambers Creek and Chip Creek trails, which wind through the ancient hunting grounds of the Maidu Indians in the vicinity of the North Fork of the Feather River near Belden. The trails pass through open high meadows, volcanic formations, and remote, seldom explored areas. The Pacific Crest Trail winds through the forest from Lassen National Forest on the north, crossing the North Fork near Belden and Lake Almanor to the east. The trail passes by Bucks Lake and across the Middle Fork of the Feather, veers southeast through the Lakes Basin area, and winds on into Tahoe National Forest on the south. Of the 67 miles of the Pacific Crest Trail in Plumas Forest, only 13 miles have been constructed and marked to date. The temporary route is marked by signs.

The forest has over 1,000 miles of trout streams and over 14,000 acres of natural and man-made lakes that hold large rainbow, brown, Kamloops, and brook trout, kokanee salmon, and largemouth bass. Five of the largest lakes have been set aside as U.S. Forest Service recreation areas. The Antelope Lake Recreation Area offers camping, hiking, hunting and fishing for rainbow and Eagle Lake rainbow trout. Large brown trout are caught in Indian Creek below the dam. The Forest Service maintains three family campgrounds, at Boulder Creek, Lone Rock, and Long Point, and a boat-launching ramp at Lost Cove Creek. The Antelope Lake area is within the summer range of the Rocky Mountain mule deer, which migrates east to the desert in winter. Beaver ponds and dams are found on Little Antelope Creek at the east end of the lake and along the main Lake Loop road. Write to the Forest Supervisor's Office for a free *Antelope Lake Recreation Area*

Map-Brochure. The Bucks Lake Recreation Area, located west of Quincy at 5,155 feet elevation, is a top-ranked camping, hiking, fishing, and hunting area for black-tailed deer, black bear, mountain lion, bobcat, snowshoe hare, ducks, and Canada geese. Bucks Lake has a 14-mile-long shoreline and good fishing for rainbow, brown, and brook trout and kokanee salmon. There are two Forest Service campgrounds here and three resorts, the Lakeshore Resort, Bucks Lake Lodge, and Valley Resort. The Pacific Crest Trail crosses Bucks Summit about 3 miles east of the lake. One of the unusual features of the area is the appearance of the brilliant red snow plant at 4,000 to 8,000 feet elevation during May, June, and July. Beaver ponds and dams are in Haskins Valley and in Bucks Creek near Whitehorse Campground. Unusual bird species found around Bucks Lake include the pileated woodpecker, osprey, and bald eagle. A free *Bucks Lake Recreation Area Map-Brochure* may be obtained from the Forest Supervisor's office.

Little Grass Valley Reservoir Recreation Area is located north of the old mining town of La Porte. With the discovery of gold and the rush of miners into this gold-rich country, Little Grass Valley became a supply post. It now provides fishing for rainbow and brown trout. Camping is provided at Running Deer, Red Feather, Little Beaver, and Wyandotte campgrounds—a total of 251 units. The Upper Canyon zone of the Middle Fork of the Feather River is located north of the lake, and Feather Falls Scenic Area is located to the southwest, near the town of Feather Falls. The major features of the area, includ-

ing trails, roads, boat ramps, and campgrounds are shown on the *Little Grass Valley Recreation Area Map-Brochure*, available free from the Forest Supervisor's Office. The Frenchman Lake Recreation Area in the easternmost section of the forest is a prime camping and mule deer hunting area. The lake holds rainbow, brown, and Kamloops trout. Camping is permitted in Chilcoot, Frenchman, Spring Creek, and Big Cove campgrounds—a total of 149 units. Cottonwood Springs Group Campground is by reservations only, from District Ranger, Milford 96121 (phone 916–253–2223). The meadows around the 21-mile-long shoreline of Frenchman Lake are the remnants of a prehistoric lake before it was drained by Little Last Chance Creek. Write to the Forest Supervisor's Office for the free *Frenchman Recreation Area Map-Brochure*, which shows the major features, trails, and campgrounds surrounding the 21-mile shoreline of this lake, located in Grizzly Valley. Camping is available at the Grizzly and Grasshopper campgrounds. An old sheep camp and adobe beehive often used by Basque sheepherders is located on the west side of the lake. The town of Beckwourth, southeast of Lake Davis along the north edge of Sierra

Valley, was established around 1850 by the black trapper and scout Jim Beckwourth. Lake Davis holds cutthroat, Kamloops, and brook trout.

Additional information and a *Plumas National Forest Map* (50¢) may be obtained by writing to: Forest Supervisor's Office, P.O. Box 1500, Quincy 95971 or by calling (916) 283–2050. The full-color forest map shows all trails, campgrounds, roads, recreation sites, cabins, ranger stations, boat-launching ramps, and lookout stations.

Full-service vacation accommodations in Feather River country are provided by *Elwell Lakes Lodge,* Beckwourth 96129; *Feather River Park Resort,* Box 37, Blairsden 96103; *Greenhorn Creek Guest Ranch,* Box 11, Spring Garden 95971; *Lakeshore Resort,* Box 266, Quincy 95971; *Layman Resort,* Box 8, Blairsden 96103; *Mohawk Valley Guest Ranch,* Box 124, Mohawk Valley, Clio 96106; *Mountain Base Camps, Ltd.,* Box 402, Graeagle 96103; *Plumas Pines Resort,* Almanor 95911; *River Pines Resort,* Box 117, Blairsden 96103; *Round Valley Lake Resort,* Box 65, Greenville 95947; *Ten-2 Resort,* Box 311, Meadow Valley 95956; *Tobin Resort,* Box 83, Storrie 95980; *Haskins Valley Resort* (rustic mountain lodge and cabins on Bucks Lake), Box 988, Quincy 95971.

Access & Outfitting Centers

Major routes to the Plumas National Forest include Interstate Highway 5, U.S. Highway 395, and state routes 49, 70, 99, 36, 139, 44, and 89. Accommodations, boat rentals, supplies, guides, and outfitters are available at the towns of Quincy, Challenge, Sierra City, Blairsden, Greenville, Crescent Mills, Oroville, Chico, Paradise, and Westwood.

Sequoia & Kings Canyon National Parks

Sequoia & Kings Canyon National Parks Topo Maps

U.S. Geological Survey 1:250,000 scale overview maps: Fresno, Mariposa; large-scale maps: Blackcap Mountain, Mount Goddard, Big Pine, Tehipite Dome, Marion Peak, Mount Pinchot, Giant Forest Triple Divide Peak, Mount Whitney, Kaweah, Mineral King, Kern.

Evolution Valley

U.S. Geological Survey large-scale topographic maps: Mount Goddard, Blackcap Mountain.

Giant Forest

U.S. Geological Survey large-scale maps: Giant Forest, Triple Divide Peak.

Great Western Divide & High Sierra Trail

U.S. Geological Survey large-scale topographic maps: Mineral King, Triple Divide Peak, Mount Whitney, Kern Peak.

Kern River Canyon

U.S. Geological Survey large-scale topographic maps: Kern Peak, Mount Whitney.

Kings Canyon Area

U.S. Geological Survey large-scale topographic map: Marion Peak.

Pacific Crest Trail

U.S. Geological Survey large-scale topographic maps: Mount Goddard, Blackcap Mountain, Big Pine, Mount Pinchot, Mount Whitney, Kern Peak, Olancha.

Roaring River Wildlands

U.S. Geological Survey large-scale topographic maps: Marion Peak, Triple Divide Peak.

Sequoia and Kings Canyon National Parks cover the most spectacular wilderness fishing, camping, and mountaineering country on the western slopes of the High Sierra. Sequoia covers 386,863 acres, stretching from the headwaters of the Kings River on the north to the headwaters of the Tule River on the south. A majestic arc of cloud-weathered High Sierra peaks—dominated by Mount Whitney (14,494 feet), the highest point in the contiguous United States—bounds the park on the east, sloping down to the foothills of the Sierras on the west. The Great Western Divide, a jagged granite ridge, bisects the park from north to south. Situated between the divide and the High Sierra crest are hundreds of remote blue alpine trout lakes and streams, the awesome Kaweah Peaks, the 3,000-foot walls of the Kern River Canyon (which parallel the divide for 25 miles), and the Chagoopa, Bighorn, and Boreal plateaus, formed in the Ice Age thousands of years ago. West of the Great Western Divide in the 4,000 to 8,000 feet elevations of the foothills are the park's major accommodations and the groves of giant Sierra redwoods, *Sequoia gigantea.*

Adjoining Sequoia on the north is Kings Canyon National Park, whose 460,331 acres embrace the renowned wilderness trout-fishing waters and camping areas of the rugged Kings-Kern Divide, Kearsarge Pinnacles, Painted Lady High Country, Sixty Lakes Basin, Kings Canyon, Cirque Crest, Upper and Lake basins, the Enchanted Gorge, the lake-dotted high country of the Goddard Divide and Evolution Basin, the Gorge of Despair, and hundreds of lush green alpine meadows, spurs, cascades, and valleys. The wild Middle Fork and South Fork of the Kings River and the South Fork of the San Joaquin River cut sheer-walled canyons on their journeys through the glacial high country of the park and provide top-ranked fishing for brook, brown, and rainbow trout.

The Sequoia–Kings Canyon country was once the hunting grounds of the Mono and Paiute Indians, who during their many crossings of the High Sierra mountain passes established many of the trails used today by backpackers and fishermen. Many of these trails, including the John Muir, Knapsack Pass, Cartridge Pass, Lost Canyon, Giant Forest, Indian Basin, and Sawtooth Pass trails, lead past old Indian camp-

sites and archaeological remains in Evolution Valley, Palisade Basin, Upper Basin, Quail Flat, and Five Lakes. The abundant game and beaver found in the area were first discovered in 1826 by Jedediah Smith. In 1858 Hale Tharp, a cattle rancher who lived on the Kaweah River near the present town of Three Rivers, traveled up the Middle Fork of the Kaweah guided by two Indians, and became the first white man to discover the magnificent sequoias of the Giant Forest. In 1869 Tharp mapped out a route along an old Indian trail in the Log Meadow area of the Giant Forest to serve as a summer trail and pasture for his herd of cattle, and built a summer home in a giant hollow log!

The first significant exploration of the Sierra high country and Kings Canyon was accomplished by the Whitney Survey of 1864 led by William H. Brewer. The Brewer party headed east from Big Meadows to the summit of a peak they named Mount Brewer at the northern end of the Great Western Divide. For the first time, the spectacular upper Kern River Canyon and numerous other canyons 2,000 to 5,000 feet deep; seemingly endless series of ridges with sharp needlelike pinnacles; hundreds upon hundreds of sparkling blue cloud-high lakes and glacial cirques; sweeping snowfields, glaciers, and barren, boulder-strewn meadows; giant, craterlike amphitheaters; and the soaring snow-capped 14,000-foot summits of the Southern Sierra Crest, were scientifically observed, and opened the way for further exploration and mapping of the Kings-Kern-Kaweah watersheds.

Clarence King broke off from the main party to explore the towering granite summit of the peak he named Mount Whitney. King followed the Hockett Trail on his journey to Whitney and fell short of reaching its level summit by some few hundred feet. King returned to the party's base camp, and the expedition set out with a small group of prospectors across the mountain precipices of Kings Canyon. Brewer compared the awesome grandeur of the canyon country with that of Yosemite. The members of the Whitney expedition also became the first white men to fish the "blue-ribbon" trout waters of the South Fork of the Kings, when, during a brief stop, they caught more than 70 cutthroats from its crystal clear waters.

As the news of the Whitney expedition spread, hunters, fishermen, mountaineers, and naturalists were lured into the majestic Kings Canyon country on the South Fork. In the summer of 1873, John Muir, accompanied by his mule, Brownie, explored the "Range of Light" and Kings Canyon country, and crossed the Middle and North forks of the Kaweah River into the giant sequoia country, which he aptly named the Giant Forest. Muir further explored the South and Middle forks of the Kings River in 1875 and 1877. The northernmost reaches of the region that was to become Kings Canyon National Park remained isolated and unexplored until Theodore Solomons discovered the alpine lakes and peaks surrounding the beautiful meadows of Evolution Valley in the mid-1890s.

The rugged grandeur of this country is shown on the full-color U.S. Geological Survey *Sequoia–Kings Canyon National Park Map* ($2, available in either a topographic or shaded-relief edition). This map, 30 × 41 inches with a scale of 1 inch to 2 miles, shows all trails (including the John Muir and High Sierra trails), campgrounds, ranger stations, shelters, contours, and natural features.

Several useful, engaging guidebooks covering the region are published by Wilderness Press, 2440 Bancroft Way, Berkeley 94704: *Sierra South* ($6.95, 287 pp.) covers the Sierra trails from Mono Divide to Sequoia National Park; *Mt. Goddard* ($1.95) covers the lakes, glaciers, and 13,000-foot peaks in eastern Kings Canyon National Park; *Mineral King* ($1.95) includes most of the spectacular Great Western Divide in southwestern Sequoia National Park and the endangered

Mineral King wilderness; *Mt. Whitney* ($2.95) describes cross-country routes into the farthest recesses of both Sequoia and Kings Canyon country; *Blackcap Mountain* ($2.95) describes Evolution Valley and the Le Conte Divide; *Marion Peak* ($2.95) covers western Kings Canyon–Sequoia national parks and the spectacular Kings Canyon, the most popular trailhead in the southern Sierra. The Sequoia–Kings Canyon country is also described in Starr's classic *Guide to the John Muir Trail and the High Sierra Region*, a Sierra Club totebook, available for $3.95 from: Sierra Club Books, Mills Tower, San Francisco 94120. A complete listing of Sequoia–Kings Canyon publications may be obtained free from: Sequoia National History Association, Ash Mountain, Three Rivers 93271.

Pack and saddle horses and guided wilderness pack trips in Sequoia National Park are provided by *De Carteret Pack Trains*, Lodgepole, Sequoia N.P. 93262 (winter address: 30547 Mehrten Dr., Exeter 93221); in Kings Canyon National Park, by *Kings Canyon Pack Station*, Cedar Grove, Kings Canyon N.P., 93633 (winter address: 31993 Ruth Hill Rd., Squaw Valley 93646) and by *Dick R. Wilson*, 1716 Meadow Lane, Visalia 93277. In addition, several licensed guides and outfitters operate in the Sequoia–Kings Canyon country. For rates and info, write: *Donald G. Abbott*, P.O. Box 504, Springville 93265 (pack trips, Sequoia); *Donald James Bedell*, P.O. Box 61, Three Rivers 93271 (Sequoia & Kings Canyon fishing and photographic trips); *High Sierra Pack Station*, P.O. Box 396, North Fork 93643 (fishing and pack trips in Sequoia–Kings Canyon); *Quaking Aspen Pack Station*, P.O. Box 756, Springville 93265 (Sequoia, fishing and pack trips).

The rustic *Montecito-Sequoia Lodge & Nordic Ski Lodge* offers year-round vacation accommodations and winter ski trails through a forest of giant sequoias and 35 miles of trails with views of the Great Western Divide. The lodge is in an alpine setting between Kings Canyon and Sequoia parks. Write: 1485 Redwood Dr., Los Altos 94022; phone (415) 968–8612. Guided tours, instruction, and lodging are provided by *Sequoia Touring*, Sequoia National Park 93262; phone (209) 565–3308. Marked trails wind through the Giant Forest, Tokapah Valley, and Big Meadow areas.

National park lodging and cabins are available at: *Giant Forest, Stony Creek*, and *Grant Grove* lodges (May–October); *Camp Kaweah*, cabins and motel-type rooms, year round; cabins at *Wilsonia* and motel-type rooms at *Stony Creek*, year-round. *Camp Kaweah* and *Meadow Camp* at Grant Grove offer housekeeping cabins. The *Bearpaw Meadow Camp* (wood-platform tents and meals) is located on the High Sierra Trail, 11 miles from Giant Forest. Reservations for lodges and cabins should be made by writing or phoning: *Sequoia and Kings Canyon Hospitality Service*, Sequoia National Park 93262 (phone: 209–565–3373); and *Wilsonia Lodge*, Kings Canyon National Park 93633 (phone: 209–335–2314).

For detailed wilderness camping, ski touring, fishing, and general information, and for the free *Sequoia and Kings Canyon Map-Brochure*, write: Superintendent, Lodgepole, Sequoia National Park 93262; or Grant Grove, Kings Canyon National Park 93633 (summer only).

Access & Outfitting Centers

Major routes to Sequoia and Kings Canyon national parks are Interstate 5 to State Routes 198 and 180, and U.S. 395. Lodging, supplies, and equipment outfitters are available at Three Rivers, Silver City, Mineral King, Sequoia, Visalia, Badger, Pinehurst, Pig Pine, and Independence. Generals Highway is the main road that connects the two. This all-weather road winds through the sequoia belt and covers 46 miles—a 2-hour drive from the Ash Mountain Entrance to Grant

Grove. Branch roads provide access to recreation areas and trailheads. From Grant Grove, you travel 30 miles on California 180 through Sequoia National Forest and along the South Fork of the Kings River to Cedar Grove. The road then continues for 6 miles through the solid granite walls of Kings Canyon that tower thousands of feet above the river floor. The road to Cedar Grove is closed from November 1 to May 1. Ski equipment and snowshoes may be rented in Sequoia at Wolverton.

Sequoia National Forest & High Sierra Wilderness Areas

Sequoia National Forest Topo Maps

U.S. Geological Survey 1:250,000 scale overview maps: Fresno, Bakersfield.

Dome Land Wilderness

U.S. Geological Survey large-scale topographic maps: Kernville, Lamont Peak.

High Sierra Primitive Area

U.S. Geological Survey large-scale map: Tehipite Dome.

Kings River Wild Trout Area

U.S. Geological Survey large-scale topographic maps: Pine Flat Dam, Trimmer, Patterson Mountain.

Mineral King Alpine Lakes Area

U.S. Geological Survey large-scale topographic map: Mineral King.

Pacific Crest Trail

U.S. Geological Survey large-scale topographic maps: Olancha, Monache Mountain, Lamont Peak, Onyx, Inyokern.

Quaking Aspen Area

U.S. Geological Survey large-scale topographic maps: Camp Nelson, Mineral King.

Upper Kern River Wildlands

U.S. Geological Survey large-scale topographic maps: Mount Whitney, Kern Peak.

The Sequoia National Forest encompasses 2 million acres of fishing, camping, backpacking, and hunting country along the southern Sierras in central California. It extends from the Kings River on the north to the Kern River Plateau on the south. The eastern boundary is on the Sierra Nevada Crest, where it joins the Inyo National Forest and portions of the Mojave Desert. The forest stretches westward to the brush-covered foothills along the San Joaquin Valley and is laced by a network of Forest Service roads and trails, including a segment of the Pacific Crest Trail, that provides access to the rugged 12,000-foot peaks of the High Sierra country on the north along the scenic South Fork of the Kings—which flows west out of Kings Canyon, over Grizzly Falls, past the Windy Cliffs, and around Horseshoe Bend to its union with the Middle Fork near Yucca Point—to the remote grandeur of the High Sierra Primitive Area along the Monarch Divide, to Hume Lake and Logger Flat, and to the renowned rainbow trout waters of the Kern River Plateau, Greenhorn Mountains, Dome Land Wilderness, and the headwaters of the Tule–Quaking Aspen area on the south. The forest contains several groves of the majestic giant sequoia redwoods, varying from a hundred trees or less to groves containing thousands of awesome specimens. Among the larger of the trees is the Boole sequoia, located northwest of Hume Lake on Con-

verse Mountain, with a base circumference of 90 feet and a height of 268 feet.

The Dome Land Wilderness takes in 62,206 acres at the southern end of the Kern Plateau between the South Fork and the main Kern River. Erosion and weathering have left the area strewn with oddly shaped rock outcroppings, giving the appearance of a "dome land." Backcountry trails lead to the "roughs" of the South Fork of the Kern River, Manter Meadows, Rockhouse Meadow, White Dome, Church Dome, Pilot Knob, and Trout Creek. The vegetation on the lower slopes is light, consisting mostly of piñon pine, mixed conifer, sagebrush, and rabbit brush. Access is by several spur trails off the Pacific Crest Trail, which winds south near the area's western boundary.

The famed Kern River, named by Frémont in honor of Edward Kern, the photographer and artist who nearly drowned while attempting to ford the river, flows south through the Hume Plateau wilderness in the southern portion of the forest from its headwaters high in the mountain wildlands of Sequoia National Park. The upper Kern enters the Tule River Ranger District of the forest east of the headwaters of the Kaweah River and the Great Western Divide at the Kern Canyon Ranger Station and the junction of Golden Trout Creek. The Kern River Trail follows the great canyon of the upper river, where sheer walls rise over 2,000 feet and reach their greatest height near the Red Spur of the Kaweah Peaks Ridge, where the west wall towers 5,000 feet above the river floor. The river flows south from the Kern Canyon Ranger Station through the heart of golden trout country. Several tributaries, including Big Kern Creek, Little Kern Creek and Coyote Lakes, and Grasshopper Creek, provide excellent wilderness fly-fishing for golden, rainbow, and brook trout. The river proper holds lunker rainbows and browns and flows out of its spectacular canyon, winding past Kern and Little Kern Lakes, the Grasshopper Flat Backcountry Campgrounds, Hole-in-the-Ground, Hells Hole, Kern Flat Backcountry Campgrounds, and Upper and Lower Pyles camps to the forks of the Kern and its junction with the Little Kern River, which rises high in the Mineral King alpine lakes basin beneath the western wall of the Great Western Divide. The northern tributaries of the Little Kern are paralleled by the Farwell Gap Trail and flow south through the beautiful high mountain country surrounding Mineral King, past the alpine trout waters of Bullfrog Lakes, the Broder Cabin site, the Rifle Creek Backcountry Campgrounds, Lion Meadows, Burnt Corral Meadows, Greg Meadows Backcountry Campgrounds, Deep Creek, Trout Meadows Creek, and Castle Rock, to its confluence with the Upper Kern at the "Forks." Numerous scenic foot and horse trails provide access to the remote wilderness fishing and camping areas in the plateau.

The beautiful high mountain country surrounding Mineral King at the headwaters of the Kaweah River lies within the Sequoia National Game Refuge, due south of Sequoia National Park and the Giant Forest. Several alpine lakes, including Franklin, Crystal, Monarch, Mosquito, Eagle, and White Chief, lie beneath the towering 12,000-foot peaks along the Great Western Divide. The lakes and streams hold sizable populations of rainbow and eastern brook trout. Some of the world's largest stands of foxtail pines are located near Timber Gap Pass. This famed wilderness fishing and camping area is reached via the Mineral King Road from Hammond to the west and by the Timber Gap–Black Rock Trail and the Soda Creek, Lost Canyon, Rattlesnake Creek, and Farwell Gap–Coyote Pass trails in the Tule River Ranger District. The Sunny Point and Cold Spring campgrounds provide overnight camping facilities. The tiny settlement of Mineral King, located at the base of 12,340-foot Sawtooth Peak, was founded in 1873 by three spiritualists who staked the White Chief Lode silver claim here. Their ill-fated venture was destroyed by an

avalanche in 1888. Wilderness pack trips in the Mineral King area are provided by the *Mineral King Pack Station*, Box 61, Three Rivers 93271 (winter: Creston Star Rt., Paso Robles 93446).

The outfitting centers of Camp Wishon, Camp Nelson, and the Quaking Aspen Ranger Station are popular jumping-off points for fishing, backpacking, hunting, and wilderness camping trips into the scenic backcountry surrounding the rainbow and brown trout waters of the Middle and North headwaters of the Tule River, Little Kern River, and Upper Kern River. This vast area lies south of Mineral King and west of the Upper Kern River. Scenic foot and packhorse trails wind through the remote interior areas of the Tule River Ranger District to Freeman Creek Grove, Peppermint Creek, Clicks Creek and Clicks Backcountry Campgrounds, Mountain Home State Forest, Dillonwood Grove, Mountaineer Creek, Loggy Meadows and Fish Creek, Flat Jacks and Alpine Meadow Backcountry Campgrounds, Pecks Canyon, Twin Lakes, Frog and Maggie Lakes, Soda Spring, Big Trees at Deadman Creek, Redwood Camp, Simmons Post Camp, and Black Mountain Grove. The Moorehouse Springs Fish Hatchery is located on State Highway 190, which provides access to the Tule River headwaters region. Packhorses and backcountry pack trips are provided by *Golden Trout Pack Trains, Inc.*, P.O. Box 407, Springville 93265 (at Quaking Aspen and Mountain Home State Forest); *Wishon Resort*, P.O. Box 664, Springville 93265 (Tule River); and *Quaking Aspen Pack Station*, P.O. Box 756, Springville 93265 (winter: 1030 Superba Ave., Venice 90291).

The eastern boundary of the Sequoia National Forest is formed by the wild South Fork of Kern River, which rises high on the Kern Plateau near Siberian Pass on the High Sierra Crest in the original range of the golden trout, flows south through beautiful coniferous forests and Big Whitney and Tunnel Meadows, past Monache and the Monache Cow Camps, and continues on through the Cannell Meadow Ranger District and Dome Land Wilderness into Isabella Lake and its confluence with the main Kern River. The Pacific Crest Trail follows the course of the Upper South Fork from Siberian Pass (named in the late 1800s for its bleak Russian steppes appearance) south to Fat Cow Meadow, where it swings southwesterly through the interior of the Cannell Meadow Ranger District to the Mojave Desert. The Monache Meadows on the Kern Plateau were once the home of the Monachi Indians, a subgroup of the Mono Tribe. The Monachi (meaning "fly people") based their livelihood on trading their chief source of food, the pupae of a fly, with neighboring tribes. Salmon Creek, below the beautiful cascades of the Salmon Creek Falls, provides fly-fishing for rainbow and brook trout; it is accessible by trail from the Horse Meadow Campground, due west of the Dome Land Wilderness. Several packhorse stations in the area provide guided pack trips to the noted golden trout waters high in the Kern Plateau and to the rainbow, brook, and brown trout waters of Fish Creek and the South Fork. For information and rates on overnight wilderness pack trips, write: *Kennedy Meadow Pack Station*, P.O. Box 966, Weldon 93283 (Troy Meadows); *Fairview Pack Station*, P.O. Box 81, Kernville 93238 (Weldon); *Jordon Hot Springs*, P.O. Box 31, Inyokern 93527 (Cannell Meadow); *Roads End Resort*, Star Rt., Kernville 93238 (lodging). For additional fishing, hunting, camping, and backpacking information, write: *Cannell Meadow Ranger District*, P.O. Box 6, Kernville 93238. Vacation accommodations in the Camp Nelson area are provided by *Camp Nelson Resort*, Camp Nelson 93208.

The northernmost portion of the Sequoia National Forest lies within the Hume Lake Ranger District. This outstanding backpacking, fishing, hunting, and wilderness camping area is in rugged high country with dense fir and pine forests, groves of giant sequoias, and scenic mountain trout streams, bordered on the south and east by Kings Canyon National Park and on the north by the Kings River and Pine Flat Lake and the Sierra National Forest wildlands. The rugged Kings River from Pine Flat Lake upstream 18 miles to the confluence with the South and Middle forks is managed as part of the state's wild trout program, and provides excellent, but often frustrating, fly-fishing for spooky, hook-jawed browns and pink-flanked rainbows. The scenic South Fork of the Kings from its confluence with the Middle Fork upstream to the western boundary of Kings Canyon National Park is also a top-ranked rainbow and brown trout fly-fishing stream, included in the California Wild Trout Program. The remote High Sierra Primitive Area, a part of the proposed Monarch Wilderness, is in the northeasternmost section of the district. The Primitive Area lies astride a portion of the Monarch Divide, a great mountain mass that separates the Sequoia and Sierra national forests and the South Fork and Middle Fork of the Kings River. This seldom-visited area is a land of high barren ridges and peaks, which fall in steep, unbroken slopes to the river canyons far below, with scattered stands of mixed conifers. The area is a summer range for mule deer, black bear, mountain lion, and a wide variety of birds and small mammals. Rainbow and brook trout are found in Grizzly Lake and Creek, while the Middle and South forks of the Kings River, to the north and south, offer trout fishing of a quality rarely found today. Scenic hiking and horse trails, jeep trails, and forest roads wind throughout the Hume Lake District and provide access to the Big Meadow, Stony Creek, Hume Lake, Landslide, Indian Basin, Redwood Mountain, Mill Flat, Aspen Hollow, and Logger Flat area campgrounds and to Weaver and Jennie lakes and the Kennedy Grove, Windy Gulch Grove, and Cabin Creek Grove of giant sequoias. For additional information, write: Hume Lake Ranger District, Miramonte 93641.

The U.S. Forest Service full-color *Sequoia National Forest Map* (50¢) shows all natural and man-made features, including campgrounds, roads, trails, ranger stations, cabins, lookout towers, and pack stations. The map and additional information about fishing, camping, hunting, backpacking, cross-country skiing, wilderness use permits, and backcountry campgrounds may be obtained by writing: Forest Supervisor, Sequoia National Forest, P.O. Box 391, 300 W. Grand Avenue, Porterville 93257 (phone: 209-784-1507). *Mineral King*, an informative, useful guide to the endangered Mineral King wilderness and the spectacular Great Western Divide, may be obtained for $2.95 from Wilderness Press, 2440 Bancroft Way, Berkeley 94704.

Access & Outfitting Centers

The major auto routes to the forest are U.S. 395 on the east and Interstate 5 on the west. State Route 178 bisects the southern portion of the forest, and hundreds of miles of secondary roads and Forest Service roads provide access to the interior recreation areas. Lodging, supplies, boat rentals, guides, and outfitters are available at Porterville, Camp Nelson, Kernvale, Woffard Heights, River Kern, Kernville, Greenhorn Summit, Pine Flat, Johnsondale, Camp Wishon, Springville, Mineral King, Silver City, and Hume Lake.

Shasta-Trinity National Forest

Shasta-Trinity National Forest Topo Maps

U.S. Geological Survey 1:250,000 scale overview maps: Alturas, Redding, Susanville, Weed.

McCloud River Country

U.S. Geological Survey large-scale topographic maps: Bartle, Big Bend, Bollibokka Mountain, Hambone, Shoeinhorse Mountain.

Mount Shasta Area

U.S. Geological Survey large-scale topographic maps: Shasta, Weed.

Trinity River Country

U.S. Geological Survey large-scale topographic maps: Black Rock Mountain, Bonanza King, China Mountain, Dubakella Mountain, Hayfork, Helena, Hayampom, Ironside Mountain, Pilot Creek, Schell Mountain, Trinity Dam, Weaverville, Willow Creek.

Pacific Crest Trail

U.S. Geological Survey large-scale topographic maps: Dunsmuir, Big Bend, Pondosa, Burney, Jellico.

Whiskeytown-Shasta-Trinity National Recreation Area

Includes Clair Engle, Whiskeytown, and Shasta Lakes, shown on large-scale U.S. Geological Survey topographic maps: French Gulch, Trinity Dam, Schell Mountain, Shasta Dam, Project City, Bella Vista, Lamoine, Bollibokka Mountain.

The Shasta-Trinity National Forest, once the home and hunting grounds of the Hoopa, Chilula, Whilkut, Nongathl, Wailaki, and Chimariko Indians, is located a few miles north of Redding in northern California. The forest overlaps into six counties. Its numerous old logging roads and trails, including over 150 miles of the Pacific Crest Trail, wind through grass and oak woodlands and heavily forested evergreen slopes, past soaring granite peaks, towering limestone bluffs, lakes, wild rivers, small mountain ranges near Shasta Lake, and deep, steep-sided canyons, and through gentle rolling plateaus to the interior fishing, hunting, hiking, and wilderness camping areas.

The Shasta Division encompasses one million acres east of the Trinity Forest in northern California and contains some of the state's most outstanding hunting, fishing, and wilderness camping areas. The Shasta area is comprised of geological formations related to the southern section of the Cascade Range, varying from the snowcap and perpetual glaciers of Mount Shasta to the colorful volcanic formations of the Medicine Lake Highlands to the east. Forest roads and trails provide access to the backcountry areas near Shasta Lake, Seven Lakes Basin at the Trinity Divide, Box Canyon Reservoir, Lake McCloud, Upper Sacramento River, and the Pit River. Hunting is good throughout the forest for blacktail deer, bear, pigeons, and quail. About 800 Rocky Mountain elk range near the Shasta Lake area, and to the north antelope and bighorn sheep roam the desertlike flats and craggy peaks. The Pacific Crest Trail winds through the region from the Salmon-Trinity Alps area, along the beautiful Scott Mountains, past the alpine trout lakes in the Eddy Mountains at the headwaters of the Sacramento River and the Seven Lakes Basin at the Trinity Divide. At Castle Crags near the town of Dunsmuir, the trail follows a route that passes along the lovely McCloud River, Grizzly Peak, and on to Lake Britton and into the Thousand Lakes Wilderness in the Lassen Forest. The Modocs, at the battle of Castle Crags in 1873, are believed to be the last Indian tribe to fight with bows and arrows. Joaquin Miller, known as the Poet of the Sierras, was wounded during the battle. Mount Shasta dominates the skyline in the north central part of the forest, due west of the Volcanic Highlands. This great mountain was discovered by the Spanish explorer Fray Norcisco Duran, who first sighted it in May 1817. Peter Skene Ogden, a trapper and fur trader, saw it in 1827 and gave it the name Sastie. About 14 years later, Lieutenant Emmons of the Wildes expedition showed it on his maps as Mount Shasta. The beautiful double cone of Mount Shasta is the largest of the Cascade volcanoes, composed of Shastina (12,330 ft.) on the west and Shasta (14,162 ft.), the main peak, on the east. This majestic mountain rests on a base 17 miles in diameter and is shrouded at its upper levels by unusual cloud formations, rapid and violent storms, dazzling light displays, and the rare and transient alpine glow of winter evenings. Mount Shasta has long been an object of awe and study by hikers, photographers, and mountaineers. Five perennial glaciers, Whitney, Bolam, Hotlum, Wintun, and Konwakiton, lie on the slopes above 8,500 feet. The glaciers form the headwaters of the McCloud, Shasta, and Sacramento rivers. To the north of Dunsmuir,

the exposed gravel beds gush large volumes of water, creating the beautiful Mossbrae Falls. On the lower slopes of Mount Shasta, plant life common to the High Sierra overlaps with plants common to the North Cascades, creating unique subspecies such as the beautiful and fragrant Shasta lily, Shasta daisy, and Shasta red fir. Manzanita and snowbrush have covered the old scars from the logging days. Wildlife in the Shasta area includes a few brown and black bear, bobcat, pine squirrel, chipmunk, porcupine, mountain quail, and speckled grouse. The Mount Shasta area was the hunting grounds of the Achomaivi ("dwellers by the river") clan of Pit River Indians. The Achomaivi trapped deer by digging pits around the base of Mount Shasta; netted salmon in the upper Fall River; and hunted geese and brant at the Tule Swamps. To the west of Mount Shasta lies the Trinity Divide, a maze of canyons, rivers, lakes, and peaks overlooked by Mount Eddy. The Sacramento River Canyon area to the south is dominated by the Castle Crags. To the north, the Black Butte cinder cone pierces the skyline, forming a miniature silhouette of Mount Shasta. If you are interested in climbing Mount Shasta, contact the District Ranger at Mount Shasta City.

The forest also contains some of California's finest trout streams. McCloud River, a classic trout stream, named for Alexander McLeod, a trapper who parted with Jedediah Smith in 1825 after becoming enchanted with the area, heads to the southwest of Mount Shasta, rising from the springs in the lava beds near Colby Meadows. The stream flows southwesterly for 45 miles through dense forests to its mouth at Shasta Lake. Fly-fishing is often superb for brown, brook, rainbow, and the state's only population of Dolly Varden, some reaching 9 pounds. The McCloud flows from its headwaters past the Algoma Campground, gathering strength from the creeks, springs, and seeps that join the flow of the stream, then passes through a small canyon into an open meadow. Between Lakin Dam and the first falls, the stream has a series of deep rapids and long, swift pools that provide excellent holding water for large trout. The stream flows on, rushing against the huge lava rocks below the Fowler Forest Camp and through the Bigelow Meadows. The beaver dam ponds above the meadows hold some of the largest rainbows and browns in the entire river. The McCloud flows on through the flooded area above Lakin Lake, past Cattle Camp, to the McCloud Canyon, where the ice-cold water gushes from the lava rock slides at Big Springs. The stream below Big Springs holds some giant brown and rainbow trout. Past the McCloud Reservoir, the stream flows along Ash Camp to the Ah Di Na Meadows, famous for their deep holes and big trout. For much of its length, the McCloud is heavily posted, and permission must be obtained to fish. A wading staff is an absolute necessity along most of the river. Favorite fly patterns on this wild-flowing stream are the high floating Bivisibles and deer hair flies such as the Horner Deer Hair or Brown Bivisible.

The four great fingers of Shasta Lake lie at the junction of the Klamath and Cascade ranges in the northern part of the Sacramento Valley. This largest of the man-made lakes in California has over 370 miles of shoreline sprawling across a land of ancient lava flows, dormant volcanoes, ice caves, and spectacular limestone caverns. The start of the famous Oregon Trail up the Sacramento River Canyon lies some 400 feet below the lake's surface. The trail was originally pioneered by the trapper La Framboise in 1834 for the Hudson's Bay Company. The Sacramento, Pit, and McCloud rivers and Squaw Creek feed the lake and form its four great fingers. Fishing has improved tremendously since the introduction of threadfin shad in 1960. The fishing varies from good to excellent, depending on the season, for Kamloops, native rainbow and brown trout, kokanee salmon, and largemouth and smallmouth bass. Kamloops are frequently caught in the 10-pound class, and brown are often reported in excess of 15 pounds. The experienced Shasta fisherman gets to know the habits of the massive schools of threadfin shad and watches for the large areas of flashing silver just below the surface of the water. The wise angler also keeps an eye out for diving gulls and terns.

The famous Upper Sacramento River, from Box Canyon Dam downstream for 36 miles to Shasta Lake, is considered one of the state's top trout streams. Both rainbows and browns 24 inches and longer are caught with regularity. This classic stream has some perfect stretches of fly-fishing water with numerous small cascades, long glides, deep pools, and rapids. Campgrounds along the river are: Pollard Flat, Sims Camp at Hazel Creek, Castle Creek, Castle Crags State Park, Mott Camp, and Lake Siskiyou Camp. Downstream from the icy waters of Keswick Dam, the lower Sacramento has wide, long, tree-lined pools and gravel riffles that provide excellent holding water for fall and spring-run chinook salmon up to 30 pounds and steelhead trout.

The renowned hunting and fishing areas of the Trinity Forest Division encompass about 1 million acres in north central California adjacent to the western boundary of Shasta Forest. In the forest are the Klamath Mountains, Coast Range Mountains, Trinity (Clair Engel) Lake, the Big Bar area, and the Yolla-Bolly Mountains in the southernmost section. This entire region was once the home and hunting grounds of the Whilkut, Nongatl, Wailaki, and Chimariko Indian tribes. Descendants of the region's once great Indian tribes live in the Hoopa Valley Indian Reservation northwest of the forest. This area was also the prospecting grounds for many of the old Forty-niners during the gold rush of the early 1850s. To the south of the Salmon Mountains lies the famed Big Bar area, which includes the western section of the scenic Trinity River and its tributaries, the New River, Canyon Creek, and the North Fork of the Trinity. The Trinity produces some of the country's finest steelhead trout fishing. It rises in the Salmon-Trinity Alps at more than 9,000 feet elevation and flows first southeast, then southwest, for 170 miles, forming Trinity and Lewiston lakes; it joins the Klamath River about 43 miles from the Pacific Ocean. The Trinity is known as a gentleman's stream, with easy wading and quick access by road and trail. Moving upstream from the mouth of the Trinity near Hoopa Valley, the angler will travel through scenic forested banks of pine and fir past many salmon and steelhead holding pools along the Trinity Gorge area, the Norton Creek Trail, the famous Cabin Riffle Trail, and the Red Rock Trail. Above the First Trinity Gorge are the Beaver Creek Riffle, Mill Creek area, Tish Tang Forest Camp area, Willow Creek Valley, Second Trinity Gorge, and Gray Falls. Above Gray Falls, the angler will travel through the extremely deep Third Trinity Gorge, with access by trail only, until he reaches the deep pools and riffles between China Slide and Cedar Flat. Some of the best big-fish water is found above Cedar Flat along the Hayden Flat, Big Bar, and Pigeon Point. The Trinity changes from its picturesque character above the mouths of the North Fork and Canyon Creek tributaries, becoming thick with brush, reeds, and willows because of the steady accumulation of silt from the Lewiston and Trinity dams. Popular fly patterns for the Trinity steelheads are the Comet, McGinty, Moth, Mickey Finn, Brindle Bug, Gray Hackle Yellow, and the Rust Nymph. Lewiston Lake, formed by the damming of the upper Trinity, is one of the finest trout lakes in the West. Located in the northeastern part of the forest, this large lake has cold clear waters regularly producing early and late-season limit catches of fat rainbows and browns of 5 pounds and more. Trinity Lake lies due north of Lewiston, and has some fine fishing for rainbows, kokanee salmon, and largemouth bass, particularly near the mouths of its feeder streams such as Stuarts Fork and Coffee and Papoose creeks, which rise high in the Salmon Trinity Alps. These gin-clear streams provide exciting fly-fishing for small rainbow and brook trout. Forest roads and trails provide access to the high-country

hunting areas for black-tailed and mule deer and a few black bear. Muskrat, beaver, mink, otter, and ermine, as well as bald and golden eagles and osprey, are found throughout the Trinity region. For camping, guide, and trail information, write: District Ranger, Big Bar 96010.

The Shasta-Trinity National Forest has 100 campgrounds containing over 2,000 family units and boat-access camping. Camping facilities are also available at the Whiskeytown-Shasta-Trinity National Recreation Area, which surrounds Whiskeytown Reservoir in Shasta County and is administered by the National Park Service. This island-dotted lake holds rainbow, brown, and Kamloops trout and kokanee salmon.

The U.S. Forest Service *Shasta National Forest Map* and *Trinity National Forest Map* cost 50¢ each and show all roads, trails, ranger stations, lookout towns, campgrounds, and recreation sites. The maps and additional hiking, hunting, fishing, and camping information may be obtained by writing: Forest Supervisor, Shasta-Trinity National Forest, 1615 Continental St., Redding 96001 (phone: 916–241–7100).

Vacation accommodations and services are provided by *Cooley's Circle Seven Guest Ranch*, McCloud 96057; *Shastina Properties Inc.*, Lake Shastina, Big Springs Rd., Weed 96094; *Shasta Lake's Holiday Harbor & Lakeshore Resort*, P.O. Box 112, O'Brien 96070; *Mountain Air Lodge*, 1121 S. Mt. Shasta Blvd., Mount Shasta 96067; *Swiss Holiday Lodge*, P.O. Box 335, Mount Shasta 96067; *Seldom Seen Ranch*, 2069 Lake Shastina, Weed 96094. Vacation lodging and guide service in the Trinity Forest Division is provided by *Corby's Steelhead Cottages*, and *Fish Tail Inn*, both Big Bar 96010, on the Trinity River; *Del Loma Lodge* on the Trinity at Del Loma, Big Bar 96010; *River Oaks Resort* on the Trinity at Junction City 96048; *Indian Creek Lodge* (Trinity River), Box 373, Douglas City 96024; *Timber Lodge* (Trinity River), Douglas City 96024; *Trinity River Lodge*, Lewiston 96052; *Wyntoon Park Resort*, Trinity Center 96091 and Cedar Stock Resort, Lewiston 96052, both on Trinity Lake.

Fishing information and guide service for the Upper Sacramento, McCloud, and Pit rivers are provided by *Ted Fay's Fly Casting Shop*, 4154 Dunsmuir Ave., Dunsmuir 96025; phone (916–235–2969).

Access & Outfitting Centers

The forest is reached via Interstate 5, U.S. Highway 97, and California routes 96, 3, 89, and 299. Lodging, supplies, boat and canoe rentals, guides, packers, and outfitters are available at Trinity Center, Big Bar, Junction City, Hayfork, Weaverville, Redding, Burney, Fall River Mills, Dunsmuir, McCloud, Weed, Mount Shasta.

Sierra National Forest & John Muir Wilderness

Sierra National Forest Topo Maps

U.S. Geological Survey 1:250,000 scale overview maps: Fresno, Mariposa.

Dinkey Lakes Alpine Area

U.S. Geological Survey large-scale topographic maps: Huntington Lake, Patterson Mountain.

John Muir Wilderness

U.S. Geological Survey large-scale topographic maps: Big Pine, Blackcap Mountain, Devils Postpile, Giant Forest, Independence, Kaweah, Kern Peak, Long Pine, Marion Peak, Mineral King, Mount Abbot, Mount Goddard, Mount Morrison, Mount Pine Hot, Mount Tom, Mount Whitney, Olancha, Tehipite Dome, Triple Divide Peak.

Minarets Wilderness

U.S. Geological Survey large-scale topographic maps: Devils Postpile, Merced Peak, Mono Craters, Tuolumne Meadows.

Monarch Wilderness

U.S. Geological Survey large-scale topographic maps: Tehipite Dome, Marion Peak.

Pacific Crest Trail

U.S. Geological Survey large-scale topographic maps: Devils Postpile, Mount Morrison, Mount Abbot, Blackcap Mountain.

Woodchuck Country

U.S. Geological Survey large-scale topographic maps: Blackcap Mountain, Tehipite Dome.

The vast Sierra National Forest encompasses some of the West's most spectacular wilderness camping and fishing areas. The forest lies east of Fresno in central California, west of the High Sierra Crest between Yosemite and Sequoia–Kings Canyon national parks. Hundreds of miles of trails, including the John Muir segment of the Pacific Crest Trail, and old mining and logging roads wind through the region from brushy front country to dense forests and barren alpine peaks and valleys, and provide access to the Minarets and John Muir wilderness areas, Silver Divide Lake Basin, Mono Divide Area, the Pinnacles, Humphreys Basin, Dinkey Lakes, Blackcap Basin, Woodchuck Country, North Fork of the Kings River, and the Monarch Divide wildlands. During the 1850s the Mariposa section of the forest was the center of gold-mining activity, and it later became important as a way station to Yosemite. Old logging-camp buildings can be seen at Sugar Pine and Central Camp.

In the northernmost section of the Sierra National Forest lies the famed Minarets Wilderness, a magnificent High Sierra hiking, camping, and fishing area that preserves 109,500 acres due northwest of the John Muir Wilderness. The northern portion of the Minarets extends into the Inyo National Forest. The wilderness has some excellent high-country fishing for rainbow, golden, and brook trout in the headwater lakes area of the Middle Fork and North Fork of the San Joaquin River. The largest lakes—Thousand Island, Garnet, and Shadow—and the Granite Creek Lakes lie on the eastern slope of the precipitous Ritter Range formed by the summits of Mount Davis (12,306 ft.), Banner Peak (12,957 ft.), and the Minarets (12,255 ft.). At its higher elevations, much of the area is barren, with rock outcroppings and red fir and some Jeffrey pine along the upper reaches of the San Joaquin River. Other sections of the wilderness are more alpine

in character, with scattered stands of lodgepole pine, mountain hemlock, and quaking aspen along the slopes and meadow edges. Both Inyo and California mule deer use the region as their summer range.

For most of its 212-mile length, the John Muir Trail leads through the strip of blue lakes along the western slope, or San Joaquin Valley side, of the High Sierra crest, stretching from Yosemite south to the massive group of 14,000-feet peaks at the headwaters of the Kings and Kern rivers to the south. As the Muir Trail enters the Minarets Wilderness, it swings eastward for a short distance to the San Joaquin Mountains along the east slope of the High Sierras. It climbs over Island Pass, then resumes its normal route along the western slope of the Sierra watershed. At Donohue Pass (11,050 ft.) the trail descends into beautiful lake country surrounded by high peaks; then it winds past the junction of Rush Creek Trail and climbs up over Island Pass to the dark ancient peaks and knife-edge ridges of the Ritter Range along the east slope. Climbing the Ritter Range peaks calls for extreme caution because of loose blocks of decomposing rock. The trail soon returns to the west slope and descends along the grassy shores of Thousand Island Lake, which forms the headwaters of the Middle Fork of the San Joaquin River. The trail follows the Middle Fork to Agnew Meadows, passes by the desolate shores of Garnet Lake, and winds on beneath the red, black, and silver flanks of Banner Peak. It continues on past Shadow Lake and Mount Ritter and its glacier, and zigzags on along the edge of the Minarets, with lovely Iceberg Lake nestled beneath its jagged spires and pinnacles. The trail winds past Lake Ediza and the bizarre black honeycomb cliff formation of the Devils Postpile National Monument; then travels the Middle Fork of the San Joaquin River to Red Meadows, about 2 miles upstream from the beautiful Rainbow Falls, which cascades 140 feet over dark cliffs into a deep green pool. At Mammoth Lakes, the trail enters the John Muir Wilderness area. You can pick up your wilderness camping permit at the Minarets Work Center, north of Mammoth Pool, or at the Minarets Entrance Station and Devils Postpile Road. Remember to carry a waterproof tarp to protect your provisions from the many sudden summer rainstorms.

The famous John Muir Wilderness covers 503,000 acres of the High Sierra, extending along the western slope of the Sierra Crest from Mammoth Lakes, south of the Devils Postpile National Monument, southeast for 30 miles, then around the boundary of Kings Canyon National Park to the Crown Valley and Mount Whitney region. This majestic land of snowcapped peaks contains literally thousands of trout lakes and streams, the headwaters of the San Joaquin River, Kern River, and the North Fork of the Kings River, and numerous creeks that drain from the eastern slope into Owens Valley. Fishing ranges from fair to excellent for rainbow, golden, and eastern brook trout in the Fish Creek area, Silver Divide area, Cascade Valley, Margaret Lakes, Mono Recesses area, Bear Creek, Seven Gables Peak area, French Canyon, Humphreys Basin, Mono Creek, Glacier Divide Area, The Palisades Group, Red Mountain Basin, and the Blackcap Basin. A few bands of mountain sheep are occasionally seen along the Sierra Crest on the east slope from Convict Lake to Mount Whitney. The wilderness is the summer range for over 50,000 mule deer, and grouse and mountain quail found throughout the timbered areas. Many of the least-known lakes of the wilderness have populations of trout and should not be overlooked. Most of the lakes below timberline have good camps built up over the years by packers, fishermen, and hunters.

The John Muir Trail enters the wilderness near Mammoth Lakes (8,900 ft.), a few miles south of Agnew Meadows and the Minaret Summit, and provides a sweeping view of the valley of the upper San Joaquin River, Banner Peak, Mount Ritter, and the Minarets. Here the trail enters the Middle Fork of the San Joaquin region, goes south past the Red Cones Trail and the Red Meadow Campground, crosses the Fish Creek–San Joaquin Middle Fork Divide, and climbs along the rim of the deep, densely forested Fish Valley with its high Yosemite-like cliffs. The trail winds on past the junction of the Duck Lake Trail and Purple Lake, crosses a divide along the east shore of Lake Virginia at 10,300 feet, and descends at Tully Hole to the headwaters of Fish Creek, down along a gorge to the beautiful green meadows at the head of Cascade Valley. Most of the lakes and streams of the Fish Creek area, both above and below timberline, hold rainbow, brook, and golden trout. Virginia Lake produced the state record 9 lb. golden.

The trail continues on past the Lake of the Lone Indian, climbs up between Chief Lake and Warrior Lake, and crosses the Silver Divide at Silver Pass (10,900 ft.), offering a windswept view of Mount Ritter and Banner Peak soaring in the distance. Spur trails branch off to the renowned trout waters in the beautiful Silver Creek lake basin, including Sedge, Rainbow, Fern, Big Margaret, Beetleberg, Ann, and Peter Pande lakes. From Silver Pass, the Muir Trail descends away from the crest through thick forests to the shores of Silver Pass Lake, and offers a spectacular view of Bear Ridge, Seven Gables, and Mount Hildegard. Winding on through Pocket Meadow, past Mott and Bighorn lakes to its junction with Mono Pass Trail, it crosses cascading streams and open meadows along the edge of the densely forested valley. The trail then enters the rugged high country of the beautiful Evolution Valley along the north side of Evolution Creek and climbs up along the gently sloping forest floor to McClure Meadow and then Colby Meadow (9,800 ft.), above which towers the Hermit and the cliffs of the Evolution Peaks. It goes along the lonely, grassy shores of Evolution Lake, where there's a good view of Mounts Fiske, Wallace, Haeckel, and Darwin and the glaciers and snowfields of the Goddard Divide. The trail passes Wand Lake and climbs up to the Muir Pass (11,955 ft.).

Along the Middle Fork of the San Joaquin region, several lateral trails provide access to the impressive mountains surrounding the Rock Creek Lakes chain in Owens Valley, to the Round Valley of the Owens River with the crest of the Sierras towering to the west and the Volcanic Tableland to the east, to Hell For Sure Pass, to Blayney Meadows, and to the beautiful rolling country of the North Fork of the Kings River with its headwaters high in the peaks along the crest of the Le Conte Divide at 12,000 feet elevation. The Owens River is an excellent fly-fishing stream and a good producer of brown trout up to 9 pounds, with lots of trout in the 2-pound class. Many of the remote alpine lakes along the Muir Trail hold golden trout averaging about 1 pound, with a rare fish up to 5 pounds. Most of these lakes must be reached by packhorse.

From the summit at Muir Pass, the trail descends into the lovely wild country of cascading streams, meadows, canyons, alpine basins, and towering peaks of the Middle Fork of the Kings Fork region. The trail follows the Middle Fork Kings down from its headwaters in Helen Lake to Little Pete Meadow, surrounded by huge cliffs, and winds along the floor beneath the granite walls of Le Conte Canyon to the boggy Grouse Meadows. The trail continues on past the black pinnacles of Devils Crags and through the long, thickly timbered Deer Meadow; then it ascends the stepping ledges of the Golden Stairway. Here there is a breathtaking panoroma of the massive summits of the Palisades Group, perhaps the mightiest of all the Sierra peaks, with their ancient snowfields and glacial amphitheaters. Lateral trails in the Middle Fork of the Kings River region lead to Crown Valley, Blue Canyon, and Tehipite Dome. The Crown Valley–Blackcap Basin area

is dotted by hundreds of glacial lakes, such as Horsehead, Bighorn, Twin Bucks, and Lone Doe, renowned for their fly-fishing for rainbow, golden, brook, and a few brown trout. From Mather Pass (12,080 ft.) the Muir Trail continues along the crest and descends into the basin of the South Fork of the Kings River, goes on past the Taboose Pass Trail and the Bench Lake Trail, and then winds through a long lake basin to the sheer dark wall of peaks above Woods Lake at Pinchot Pass. The trail descends down along the crags, beaches, and grassy shoreline of Rae Lakes, and passes the jagged Kearsarge Pinnacles and Vidette Spires on its way to the top of the Kings-Kern Divide at Forester's Pass (13,200 ft.).

Numerous lateral trails lead off to the forbidding mountain mass of the Monarch Divide and to the lakes and meadows of Kennedy Canyon, Volcanic Lakes, Kings River Canyon, and Scaffold Meadow. The Monarch Divide separates the deep canyons of the Middle and South forks of the Kings River and is located within the High Sierra Primitive Area on the western boundary of Kings Canyon National Park. The area is so rugged, and the canyons so deep, that the U.S. Geological Survey team that studied the area for reclassification as the Monarch Wilderness had to set up field camps by helicopter. California mule deer use the higher elevations of the Monarch Divide Wilderness as summer range, migrating down to winter in lower Kings Canyon. Black bear inhabit the area, and Sierra blue grouse and golden eagle are sighted occasionally. The area reportedly contains quite a few mountain lion. Rainbow trout are found in most streams, and golden trout have been planted in upper Grizzly Creek. The Middle Fork is

renowned as an exceptionally fine trout stream, often producing limits of large rainbows. Because of the ruggedness of the terrain, both fishermen and hunters face a real challenge in this area. From the high summit at Forester's Pass, the Muir Trail zigzags down along the slopes into the Sequoia National Park region, which is dominated by the Great Western Divide running parallel to the western slope of the Sierra Crest and dividing the headwaters of the Kern and Kaweah rivers. The Giant Forest lies to the west of the Great Divide, and consists of 22 groves of giant sequoias. At Junction Pass (13,888 ft.) just to the east of Forester's Pass, a sweeping view can be had across the headwaters of the Kern River to the Kaweah Peaks, and across the Great Western Divide to the Kings-Kern River Divide. The Muir Trail descends along the high sandy plateau of Sandy Meadow, past the Crabtree Ranger Station, and up along the banks of Whitney Creek to the Mount Whitney Trail. From here, the trail climbs up a steep talus slope to the 14,494-foot summit of Mount Whitney—the highest point in the United States besides Alaska's Mount McKinley. In the western section of the park, the famous High Sierra Trail winds for 49 miles from Crescent Meadows in the Giant Forest to the head of the Kern River, across the Great Western Divide, and up along the Kern River Canyon, to join the Muir Trail at Wallace Creek.

Several useful guidebooks and maps have been published to aid the wilderness fisherman, backpacker, and hunter planning to travel in the John Muir and Minarets wilderness areas. *Angler's Guides*, containing detailed maps, are published for *Granite Creek Area*, *Fish Creek Area*, *Bear Creek Area*, *Humphreys Basin–French Canyon Area*, and *Crown Valley–Blackcap Basin Area*. They are available for 40¢ each from: Dept. of Fish & Game, Documents Section, P.O. Box 20191, Sacramento 95820. Wilderness Press, 2440 Bancroft Way, Berkeley 94704, publishes guides to: *Mt. Abbot* ($1.95), which describes the deep side canyons and alpine lakes of the northern John Muir Wilderness and includes 14 pages of trail profiles; *Blackcap Mountain* ($2.-95), which describes the west central John Muir Wilderness, including Evolution Valley and Le Conte Divide; *Devils Postpile* ($1.95), which describes the monument and northeastern John Muir Wilderness; and *Sierra South* ($6.95), a comprehensive guide to John Muir Wilderness from Mono Divide south to Sequoia National Park. *Starr's Guide to the John Muir Trail and the High Sierra Region* ($3.95), published by Sierra Club Books, 530 Bush St., San Francisco 94108, has long been recognized as the bible to the trails and wilderness areas in this region.

The most popular recreation campgrounds in the Sierra National Forest are at Bass Lake, Mammoth Pool, Shaver Lake, Huntington Lake, Mono Hot Springs, Lake Edison, and Dinkey Creek. The Forest Service campgrounds are open year-round, though no piped water is available during the winter, along the Merced River, at Bass Lake, and at Pine Flat Reservoir. All other campgrounds in the forest are usually closed from November 1 to May 1. Off-road vehicles are restricted above 6,000 feet to specified trails and existing roads. All campgrounds, trails, ranger stations, lookout towers, boat-launching ramps, and pack stations are shown on the *Sierra National Forest Map* (50¢). The map also shows the John Muir Trail segment of the Pacific Crest Trail, the Minarets Wilderness, and John Muir Wilderness. The map and detailed fishing, camping, hunting, and wilderness travel info may be obtained by writing: Forest Supervisor, Sierra National Forest, 1130 O St., Fresno 93721 (phone: 209–487–5155).

Packhorse stations and outfitters in the forest are located at Wishon Village, Dinkey Creek, Badger Flat, Mono Hot Springs, Blayney Meadows–Muir Trail Ranch, Florence Lake, and Warm Creek Meadow–Vermillion Recreation Area. High Sierra wilderness pack trip service in the region is provided by the *High Sierra Pack Station*, Mono

Hot Springs 93642 (winter: Box 396, North Fork 93643); *D & F Pack Station*, P.O. Box 156, Lakeshore 93634 (winter: Box 82, Raymond 93653); *Dean & Dave's Pack Train*, Dinkey Creek 93617 (winter: Box 383, Raymond 93653); *Minarets Pack Station*, 3218 N. Zediker, Sanger 93657; *Yosemite Trails Pack Station*, Fish Camp 93623 (winter: 8314 Santa Fe Dr., Chowchilla 93610).

Vacation accommodations and High Sierra wilderness fishing and pack trips are provided by *Canadian Village* (Box 177) and *Muir Trail Ranch* (Box 176), both in Lakeshore 93634. For additional listings of guides and packers serving the region, see "Inyo National Forest & High Sierra Alpine Areas."

Access & Outfitting Centers

Major routes to the forest are U.S. Highway 395 and state highways 120, 108, 140, 41, 180, and 168. Lodging, supplies, boat rentals, guides, and outfitters are available at Dinkey Creek, Lakeshore, North Fork, Oakhurst, Mariposa, and Mammoth Lakes.

Six Rivers National Forest

Six Rivers National Forest Topo Maps

U.S. Geological Survey 1:250,000 scale overview maps: Eureka, Redding, Weed.

Mad River

U.S. Geological Survey large-scale topographic maps: Arcata N., Black Rock Mountain, Blocksburg, Blue Lake, Iaqua Buttes, Pickett Peak, Pilot Creek, Shannon Butte, Tyee City.

Smith River

U.S. Geological Survey large-scale topographic maps: Smith River, Crescent City (7.5), Hiouchi, Gasquet, Preston Peak, Ship Mountain, Dillon Mountain.

Van Duzen River

U.S. Geological Survey large-scale topographic maps: Blocksburg, Fortuna (15), Iaqua Buttes, Pickett Creek, Pilot Creek, Scotia, Weott.

The 960,000-acre Six Rivers National Forest is located along the western slope of the Coast Range Mountains down to the Pacific Coast from the Oregon border southward for 130 miles. The six major salmon and steelhead streams that flow from the mountain valleys through dense cool forests of fir and giant coastal redwoods into the Pacific are the Smith, Klamath, Trinity, Mad, Van Duzen, and North Fork of the Eel River. U.S. 101, the famed Redwood Highway, parallels the inland forest in a north-south direction on the coast side. The forest is just east of Redwood National Park. Hunting in Six Rivers country is good in the remote backcountry areas near the Hoopa Valley Indian Reservation, the Peaks, Mount Lassic, South Fork Mountain, Spike Buck Mountain, and Last Chance Ridge for black-tailed deer, black bear, blue grouse, and valley and mountain quail. Wild turkeys were introduced along the Mad River in 1971 and should soon offer some fine hunting. The forest terrain is generally mountainous in the north and moderately rolling in the south, with elevations ranging from 500 to 7,000 feet.

The salmon and steelhead fishing in the mighty Klamath River is a modern legend, famous throughout the world wherever steelheaders gather to spin the yarn. King salmon also enter the Klamath and provide excellent fishing at the mouth of the river during August and September. In the lower reaches, fishing is done by trolling spoons and spinners. About 3 miles upstream from the mouth, the fly-fishing begins. The North Fork of the Eel, the Mad River, and the Van Duzen are all good producers of large steelhead, with the runs usually beginning after the first fall rains. The king, or chinook, salmon, considered by many anglers the monarch of game fish, is also known as the tyee, spring, quinonat, and snow salmon. The big kings run up the Klamath about the first week of July, and reach their peak between the middle of August and the first week of September. The spawning activity starts about the end of September, peaking in October, and continues as late as December. The Klamath chinook average about 12 pounds in weight, ranging from 2 to 28 pounds. The annual run of chinooks in the Klamath averages about 168,000 fish. Also abundant in the Klamath is the fighting silver, or coho salmon, known for its long powerful runs and savage leaps. The coho first enter the Klamath about the middle of September and continue running through November and even later. They have no reservations about smacking a streamer fly. The average weight of the silver salmon is about 9 pounds.

Other attractions to the forest are floating the Klamath and Trinity rivers, the meadows of beautiful wildflowers in late April and May, water sports at Ruth Reservoir, and the perennial search for the elusive, legendary Bigfoot. There are 372 camping units in 15 Forest Service campgrounds. Many more primitive campsites are scattered throughout the remote backcountry areas. The local District Ranger should be contacted for information on the locations of such wilderness camps. The major features of the forest are shown on the full-color *Six Rivers National Forest Map*, available for 50¢, along with additional information from: Forest Supervisor, Six Rivers National Forest, 710 E. St., Eureka 95501 (phone: 707-442-1721). The free *Six Rivers National Forest Camping Guide* may also be obtained from the Forest Supervisor's Office. This guide contains listings and descriptions of all Forest Service campgrounds, and maps. For lodging and steelhead and salmon fishing info write: Del Norte County Chamber of Commerce, Crescent City 95531.

Vacation lodging and guide service in the Six Rivers Forest region is provided by *Flying Double AA Ranch*, Mad River 95552; *Six Rivers Lodge & Resort*, Mad River 95552; *Six Rivers Sportsman Inn*, Mad River 95552; *New Pioneer Ranch*, Hayfork 96041; *Ruth Lakeside Resort*, Mad River 95552.

Wild-water trips down the Klamath and Trinity rivers are provided by *Wilderness Water Kayak Trips*, P.O. Box 158, Gasquet 95543. The firm provides complete outfitting service from car shuttle to gear.

Access & Outfitting Centers

Major access routes to the forest include the spectacular "Redwood Highway" U.S. 101, U.S. 199 from Oregon, and state highways 299 and 96. Lodging, supplies, boat and canoe rentals, guides and outfitters are available at Smith River, Gasquet, Fort Dick, Klamath, Crescent City, Requa, Orick, Orleans, and Weitchpec.

Stanislaus National Forest & Emigrant Basin Primitive Area

Stanislaus National Forest Topo Maps

U.S. Geological Survey 1:250,000 scale overview maps: Mariposa, Sacramento, San Jose, Walker Lake.

Emigrant Basin Primitive Area

U.S. Geological Survey large-scale topographic maps: Dardenelles Cone, Pinecrest, Sonora Pass, Tower Peak.

Pacific Crest Trail

U.S. Geological Survey large-scale topographic maps: Markleeville, Dardanelles Cone, Sonora Pass, Tower Peak.

This 1.1 million-acre central High Sierra forest, once the hunting grounds of the Maidu Indians, is famous for its wilderness fishing, hunting, and camping areas. The region is primarily rugged mountainous forest along the west slope of the Sierras, traversed by the deep canyons of the Merced, Tuolumne, Stanislaus, and Mokelumne rivers. Elevations vary from 1,100 feet at the western edge to 11,570 feet at Leavitt Peak. The famous Mother Lode gold belt, formed by older metamorphic rocks, runs along the western edge of the forest. Scenic trails provide access to the remote Dardanelles Cone and the Columns of the Giants, Jawbone Ridge, Cherry Lake, Highland Lakes, and Iceberg Reservoir. Fishing is good in most of the high-country lakes for golden, rainbow, and brook trout. The Pacific Crest Trail enters the region at Carson Pass and descends through the beautiful lake country around Blue and Meadow lakes, passes Grover Hot Springs near the Mokelumne Wilderness, and climbs over Ebbetts Pass. The trail winds on past Highland Peak and Sonora Peak, over Sonora Pass, and skirts the Emigrant Basin Wilderness, entering Yosemite near Tower Peak. The Middle Fork of the Stanislaus River holds rainbow and brown trout. The Middle Fork of the Stanislaus, including Kennedy and Beardsley lakes and the Donnells and Lyons reservoirs, are noted brown trout waters. Kamloops rainbow have been stocked in Beardsley Lake, and kokanee salmon are found in Pinecrest Lake. Many of the forest's remote alpine lakes and streams hold rainbow, eastern brook, and a few golden trout. Wildlife species found in the region include raccoon, fox, black bear, mule and blacktail deer, fisher, martin, cougar, and the rare wolverine. The forest is the winter range for the large Yosemite and Jawbone mule deer herds.

Crossed by the Tahoe-Yosemite Trail, the 98,000-acre Emigrant Basin Primitive Area is located in the forest, bordered by the High Sierras to the east, Yosemite to the south, and high ridges to the west and north. The region is a favorite haunt of hunters seeking deer and bear and fishermen after trout in the headwaters area of the Tuolumne and Stanislaus rivers. Numerous trails cross the soft meadows, forests of pine and aspen, and patches of dark volcanic rock to Kennedy Mountain, Black Hawk Mountain, Bigelow Mountain, Huckleberry Lake, Gillet Mountain, Relief Lake, and Laurel Lake. The Emigrant Meadow area was used by travelers on the trans-Sierra Trail seeking gold in the mountains beyond. The high mountain lakes are well stocked with trout, but they are often very difficult to catch. Summit Creek forms a natural boundary between the coarse, dark brown lava to the north and the glacially polished light gray granite rocks to the south. Elevations vary from 5,200 feet near Cherry Bluffs to 11,570 feet at the top of Leavitt Peak.

The lakes and streams shown on the *Angler's Guide to the Waters of the Emigrant Basin Area map* (40¢, from Office of Procurement, Documents Section, P.O. Box 20191, Sacramento 95820) hold varying populations of trout, as follows:

Rainbow	42 lakes
Eastern brook	28 lakes
Golden	6 lakes
Rainbow and eastern brook	2 lakes
Brown and rainbow	1 lake

Most of the lakes in the basin are in the Cherry Creek drainage, and some drain into Lily Creek—both tributaries of the Tuolumne River. The area is accessible by foot and horse trails from Pinecrest, 30 miles from Sonora or Kennedy Meadow. The southern portion of the area can be reached from Cherry Valley Dam, about 40 miles from Groveland by surfaced road.

The majority of the lakes in the Primitive Area lie in glacial bowls at elevations ranging from 8,000 to 9,800 feet. Small, beautiful Blackhawk Lake lies on the northwest slope of Blackhawk Mountain and holds golden trout. Cow Meadow Lake covers 60 acres and holds a healthy population of rainbow trout. Fly-fishing is often excellent in the lagoons and its feeder, Cherry Creek, for rainbows up to 15 inches. Deer Lake, situated at 9,000 feet elevation, provides fly-fishing for a large, self-sustaining population of rainbow trout. Glacial Emigrant Lake, covering 230 acres, is one of the largest lakes in the area, with a population of rainbows up to 28 inches. The lake has good campsites, a fair amount of stock feed, and a limited supply of firewood. Emigrant Meadow Lake is an alpine meadow lake situated above timberline at 9,350 feet. The lake provides excellent fly-fishing for rainbows. Huckleberry Lake covers 200 acres at 7,700 feet and has eastern brook and rainbow trout. Constant flow releases from dams on Snow and Bigelow lakes provide good spawning and nursery areas and make the lake entirely self-sustaining. Nearby, the East Fork of Cherry Creek has long stretches of splendid trout fishing. Iceland Lake, reached cross-country from Relief Valley or from Lewis Lakes, is a high mountain stream. Nearby Rockbound Lake, at 9,100 feet, is stocked annually with golden trout. The lightly fished Lost Lake has lava and talus-covered shores and is located above timberline at 10,240 feet. The lake, reached cross-country from the Lunch Meadow–Emigrant Meadow Trail, provides excellent fly-fishing for hordes of eastern brook trout. Because of a scarcity of firewood at the higher rockbound lakes, camping is not recommended. Most of the lakes below timberline have campsites for overnight stays. The larger meadows provide stock feed for several days, and some of the smaller meadows will support a few head overnight. Packhorse stations and outfitters are located at Leavitt Meadows, northeast of the Primitive Area in the Toiyabe National Forest and the Stanislaus National Forest at Kennedy Meadow Resort to the north, Strawberry and Kerrick Corral in Aspen Valley, to the west, and Cherry Valley, to the south.

Much of the Stanislaus gold-rush country is rich in early California history, particularly in the Emigrant Basin, Sonora Pass, and Ebbetts Pass areas. The old gold-rush ghost town at Columbia was once the home of 15,000 prospectors, 143 faro games, 30 saloons, 4 banks, 27 produce stores, 3 express offices, and an arena for bull-and-bear fights, which were described by Horace Greeley in the old New York *Tribune* and were said to have given Wall Street one of its best-known phrases. The Sierra Nevada Mountains were first crossed in 1827 by Jedediah Smith, about 8 miles south of Sonora Pass. Other explorers, including Frinnt, Ebbetts and Goddard, followed, looking for easy routes for wagon trains and railroads, but moved north to the less arduous routes through the Lake Tahoe country. The pink volcanic ridges of the Sierra Crest at Sonora Pass marked the Emigrant Trail along the Walker River, across Emigrant Pass, and down rocky Dodge Ridge to the Mother Lode gold mines. It has been said that the Emigrant Trail was easy to follow, being well marked by broken wagons and the skeletons of dead animals. A full-color *Sonora Pass Area Map* may be obtained free from: Forest Supervisor's Office, 175 S. Fairview Lane, Sonora 95370.

The U.S. Forest Service *Stanislaus National Forest Map* shows all campgrounds, trails, roads, ranger stations, pack stations and resorts, lookout towers, and natural features. This full-color map may be obtained for 50¢ from the Forest Supervisor's Office (address above), along with specific wilderness camping, fishing, ski-touring, and hunting info. The Pioneer Group Campground at Pinecrest is available to groups of 15 to 200 people; write to the Summit Ranger Station or phone (209) 965-3434 for info and reservations. Fascinating small museums depicting the early pioneer and gold-rush days are located

in most of the old Mother Lode towns scattered around and within the forest boundaries.

The wilderness fisherman and backpacker planning a trip into the Stanislaus National Forest region is recommended to consult the following guidebooks published by Wilderness Press, 2440 Bancroft Way, Berkeley 94704: *Tower Peak* ($2.95) by Ken Fawatt, a guide to the long lakes and rugged granite landscapes of the Emigrant Primitive Area and northern Yosemite National Park; *Sierra North* ($4.95), a complete guide to the Sierras from Desolation Valley south to the Mono Divide; and *The Tahoe-Yosemite Trail* ($4.95).

Vacation lodging, guides, and wilderness pack trips are available at *Kennedy Meadows Resort*, Star Rt., Box 1490, Sonora 95370 (winter: Box 401, Sonora 95370); *Mather Pack Station*, Camp Mather via Groveland 95321 (winter: 12930 Lancaster Rd., Oakdale 95321); *Alpine Lake Lodge*, Lake Alpine 95235; *Tamarack Lodge*, Box 67, Bear Valley 95223. Guided cross country ski tours, instruction, winter camping and survival courses are provided by *Bear Valley Nordic Ski School & Touring Center*, Box 5, Bear Valley 95223 (phone: 209–753–2844); *Ebbetts Pass Ski Touring Center*, Tamarack Lodge, Box 67, Bear Valley 95223 (phone: 209–753–2121); and *Sonora Mountaineering*, 171 N. Washington, Sonora 95370 (phone: 209–532–5621). Scenic air tours of the High Sierra gold rush country are provided by *Yosemite Airlines*, Box 330, Columbia 94310 (for reservations, call: 209–532–6946).

Access & Outfitting Centers

Major routes to the forest include U.S. 395, 99, and 50 and state highways 49, 120, 4, 108, 89, 88, and 104. State Highway 4, once known as the Big Trees Road, passes east from Angels Camp through the historic gold-rush communities of Vallecito and Murphys before

entering the forest near Red Apple at an elevation of 3,200 feet. Designated by the state as a Scenic Highway from Arnold eastward, the road winds through dense forests and alpine meadows and peaks, offering sweeping vistas of the Stanislaus River Canyon and beyond to the Dardanelles and distant snowcapped peaks of the High Sierra Crest. As far as Lake Alpine, the road is a two-lane highway. Proceed-

ing eastward, it becomes increasingly narrow and winding, with steep grades, and is inadequate for autos towing large trailers. The highway also passes through Calaveras Big Trees State Park, famous since its discovery in 1852 for its magnificent stands of *Sequoia Gigantea*. Angels Camp was the scene of Mark Twain's story "The Celebrated Jumping Frog of Calaveras County," based on a tale heard one winter's night in the old Hotel Angels barroom. Today, the village holds an annual Jumping Frog Jubilee. Highway 120, a historic route better known as the Big Oak Flat Road, was a pack trail from Stockton in 1849, and by 1874 it was a wagon road which reached Yosemite Valley. Historic Highway 108 follows the old Sonora and Mono Toll Road. Lodging, supplies, boat rentals, guides, and outfitters in the forest region are available at Arnold, Sonora, Mi-Wuk Village, Groveland, Pinecrest, Dardanelles, Pioneer, Coulterville, and Lake Alpine.

Tahoe National Forest & Alpine Areas

Tahoe National Forest Topo Maps

U.S. Geological Survey 1:250,000 scale overview maps: Chico, Sacramento.

American River, Middle & North Forks

U.S. Geological Survey large-scale topographic maps: (Middle Fork), Auburn (7.5), Bunkerhill, Georgetown (7.5), Granite Chief (7.5), Greek Store, Greenwood, Michigan Bluff, Pilot Hill, Royal Gorge; (North Fork), Auburn (7.5), Colfax (7.5), Duncan Peak (7.5), Dutch Flat, Foresthill, Greenwood, Norden, Pilot Hill, Royal Gorge, Westville.

Grouse Lakes Alpine Area

U.S. Geological Survey large-scale topographic maps: Emigrant Gap, Blue Canyon, Cisco Grove.

Pacific Crest Trail

U.S. Geological Survey large-scale topographic maps: Sierra City, Emigrant Gap, Donner Pass, Granite Chief (7.5), Tahoe City, Homewood, Rockbound Valley.

Sierra Buttes Alpine Lakes Area

U.S. Geological Survey large-scale topographic map: Sierra City.

The Tahoe National Forest encompasses 698,000 acres northeast of Sacramento, in the central portion of the Sierra Nevada Mountains, and extends from Lake Tahoe to north of the massive and spectacular Sierra Buttes. The forest's name, taken from the famed Lake Tahoe, is thought to derive from a Washo Indian word meaning "big water." The Tahoe region was once the home and hunting grounds of the Maidu and Washo Indians and today offers renowned fishing, hunting, backpacking, canoeing, and wild-river canoeing. The Steven-Townsend-Murphy party, the first white men to explore the area, opened the Overland Emigrant Route through the forest in 1844. In 1846, the doomed Donner Party passed into the area. Their final campsite is located in the Donner Camp historical area near Truckee. Many abandoned mining camps, mines, and trails left from the goldrush era may be seen scattered throughout the remote backcountry area. Hundreds of miles of forest roads and trails, including the Pacific Crest–Rockbound national scenic trails, provide access to the remote backcountry areas near the Rubicon River, Grouse Lakes, Sagehen Valley, French Meadows, Bullards Bar, Fall Creek Mountain Lakes, Royal Gorge, Desolation Valley, Yuba River, Jackson Meadow Reservoir, Old Man Mountain, and the Sierra Buttes lake basin (8,587 ft.) north of the Wild Plum Guard Station. The Pacific Crest Trail enters

the Tahoe region as it winds south from the Feather River country and passes into the scenic lake region along the Milton and Jackson Meadow reservoirs, Bowman Lake, Weber Lake, and Summit Lake. It continues south through Emigrant Gap into the Lake Tahoe area along the French Meadows Reservoir, past Squaw Valley, through Alpine Meadows, along Wentworth Springs and Loon Lake, and into the Eldorado National Forest and the Desolation Wilderness.

North of Lake Tahoe is the picturesque Truckee River. The Truckee flows from the north end of Lake Tahoe and has some excellent fishing for good-sized rainbows and browns up to record size. Fishing pressure is heavy along this river, because it is close to a main east-west highway. Clear blue Lake Tahoe, the original home of the giant Lahontan

cutthroat, is an extinct volcano 1,600 feet deep lying at an altitude of 6,229 feet. Tahoe's water is so crystal clear that you can see small pebbles on the bottom at depths down to 50 feet. A stocking program was developed in 1949, and the quality of the fishing has improved almost to its peak in the "old days." Lake Tahoe has produced the California record cutthroat (31 lb. 8 oz.), kokanee slamon (4 lb. 13 oz.), and lake trout (37 lb. 6 oz.). Deep line trolling is most productive for kokanee salmon, Lahontan trout, Yellowstone cutthroat, Kamloops, brook trout, and rainbows up to 10 pounds. During the early spring months, top-lining close to shore and along the shoals provides some exciting fishing for cruising lake trout, rainbows, and browns. The *Angler's Guide to Lake Tahoe* provides a complete description of the lake and its fish species as well as a useful lake contour map. It may be purchased for 50¢ by writing: Office of Procurement, Documents Section, P.O. Box L0191, Sacramento 95820. Donner Lake to the northwest has some good early-season fishing for 10- to 20-pound lake trout and rainbows and browns up to 10 pounds.

The major trout-fishing waters in the interior areas of the forest for brook, rainbow, and browns are the wild North Fork of the American River, Middle Fork of the American River including the French Meadows Reservoir, and the Middle, North, and South forks of the Yuba River. The wilderness traveler will find excellent fly-fishing for large rainbows and browns in the spectacular Royal Gorge of the North Fork of the American River. Several designated fishing, hiking, and camping areas are located in the Tahoe region. The Grouse Lakes area encompasses 18,000 acres of meadowlands, granite-bound lakes, and aspen groves. Some 125 lakes including French, Faucherie, Culberston, Rock, Hidden Island, Beyers, and Bowman provide fishing for trout and bass. The Bowman Road provides access to the area. Camping facilities are available at the U.S. Forest Service campgrounds at Fuller Lake, Grouse Ridge, Jackson Creek, and Canyon Creek. To the

north lie the high mountain lakes and streams dominated by the spectacular Sierra Buttes. This area offers outstanding fishing, hiking, hunting, and wilderness camping opportunities. Family camping facilities are available at the Sardine Campground, Salmon Creek Campground, and Snag Lake Campground, all situated above 5,000 feet altitude. Access to the Sierra Buttes area is by the Gold Lake Highway. Supplies are available at Sierra City. Other Forest Service recreation and camping areas are located at Bullards Bar Reservoir, Donner Summit area, Stampede Reservoir, Jackson Meadow Reservoir, South Yuba River, Foresthill Divide–Big Reservoir Area, Truckee River, the French Meadows Reservoir, and Granite Chief area.

The Tahoe forests of mountain chaparral, mixed conifer, alpine, lodgepole pine, piñon-juniper, and sage-bitterbrush provide cover and excellent hunting in season for mule deer, black bear, and upland game birds.

The Granite Chief Area (Foresthill and Truckee Ranger Districts), which embraces the headwaters of the North Fork of the American River and the Grouse Lakes Area (Nevada Ranger District) have been closed to all types of motorized vehicles. Information and the free *Granite Chief Area Map* and *Grouse Lakes Area Map* may be obtained from the District Ranger Stations and from the Forest Supervisor's Office in Nevada City. The *Tahoe National Forest Map* (50¢) and hunting, fishing, hiking, camping, and wilderness travel information may be obtained by writing: Tahoe National Forest Headquarters, Highway 49, Nevada City 95959 (phone: 916–265–4531); or by writing to the District Ranger Offices at Foresthill 95631, Sierraville 96126, Downieville 95936, and Truckee 95734. The full-color Forest Service map shows all natural features, trails, roads, campgrounds, ranger stations, and recreation sites. The following Forest Service publications may be obtained free from the Forest Supervisor's Office: *French Meadows–Hill Hole Recreation Areas, Jackson Meadow Recreation Area, Woodcamp Creek Interpretive Trail, Washo Snowmobile Area, Washo—Indian Peoples of the Washo Territory, Bullards Bar Recreation Area, Glacier Meadow Loop Trail, Rock Creek Nature Study Area, Birds of the Tahoe National Forest & Vicinity,* and the *Tahoe National Forest Camping Guide.*

Wilderness pack trip service in Tahoe National Forest is provided by *Cascade Stables,* Box 7034, South Lake Tahoe 95731; *Cold Stream Corral* and *Camp Richardson Corral,* Box 8335, South Lake Tahoe 95731. Vacation lodging is available at *Big Chief Lodge* (Box 89), *Tahoe Donner Resort* (Box 538Y), *Red Bandana Cabins,* and *Northstar at Tahoe* (Box 129), all Truckee 95734; *Donner Ski Ranch* (Box 66), *Donner Summit Lodge* (Box 115), both Norden 95724; *Palisades, Donner Summit Lodge* (Box 115), *Serene Lodge* (Box 164), and *Soda Springs Lodge* (Box 36), all Soda Springs 95705. Wilderness ski tours, instruction, and lodging are provided by *Big Chief Guides,* Box 2427, Truckee 95734 (phone: 916–587–4723); *Kirkwood Ski Touring Center,* Box 77, Kirkwood, South Lake Tahoe 95731 in the Carson Pass backcountry (phone: 209–258–8864); *Royal Gorge Wilderness Lodge,* Box 178, Soda Springs 95728 (phone: 916–426–3793); *Tahoe Donner Nordic Center,* Truckee 95734 (phone: 916-587-2551); and *Northstar Nordic Center,* Box 120, Truckee 95734 (phone: 916-562-0396).

The *Squaw Valley Mountaineering Center,* Box 2288, Olympic Valley 95730, offers 5-day outings in the Granite Chief Wilderness Area, fly-fishing excursions, and nature hikes. The center also sells backpacking and climbing gear and topo maps and provides backcountry info. The Squaw Valley Center also runs *Alpine Meadows* and *Tahoe Nordic Ski Center.* For information, call (916-583-4316).

Access & Outfitting Centers

The major routes to the Tahoe National Forest are Interstate 80, U.S. Highway 50, and California Routes 28, 20, 49, and 89. Resorts, lodges, supplies, boat and canoe rentals, guides, and outfitters are available at Nevada City, Emigrant Gap, Cisco, Norden, Truckee, Boca, Graniteville, Sierra City, Meeks Bay, Tahoe City, Emerald Bay, South Lake Tahoe, Sierraville, and Downieville.

Toiyabe National Forest & The Hoover Wilderness

Toiyabe National Forest Topo Maps

U.S. Geological Survey 1:250,000 scale overview maps: Walker Lake, Sacramento, Reno.

East Fork of the Carson River

U.S. Geological Survey large-scale topographic maps: Sonora Pass, Topaz Lake, Markleeville, Mount Siegel.

Hoover Wilderness

U.S. Geological Survey large-scale topographic maps: Matterhorn Peak, Tower Peak, Pickel Meadow, Fales Hot Springs (7.5).

Walker River—East Fork

U.S. Geological Survey large-scale topographic maps: Bridgeport; (Headwaters area): Bodie, Matterhorn Peak, Fales Hot Springs (15).

The scenic Sierra Division of the Toiyabe National Forest, named after the Shoshone Indian word meaning "black mountains," embraces the massive wall of snowcapped peaks, blue alpine lakes, and tall trees along the eastern slope of the Sierras from Lake Tahoe south to Yosemite National Park. The wilderness of this historic fur-trapping and gold-mining region was first explored in 1827, when Jedediah Smith crossed the Sierra crest along the pink volcanic ridges of Sonora Pass (some historians now place the crossing at Ebbett's Pass), from west to east, in search of new trapping grounds, as well as the mythical Buenaventura River, which was believed to originate in the Rocky Mountains. Its course was shown on early maps as flowing through Great Salt Lake across the Great Basin southwesterly through a deep gorge in the High Sierras on its way to the Pacific. Smith was followed

in 1834 by Joseph Walker, a guide, mountaineer, and trapper, who discovered Walker Pass, a 5,000-foot divide on the Sierra crest. Walker first came to California in the company of Bonneville trappers in the 1830s. John Frémont explored the northern area of the forest in 1844 with his scout Kit Carson and crossed the high divide at Carson Pass, from which he looked down upon the awesome grandeur of Lake Tahoe.

One of the most daring characters who traveled the old Toiyabe trails was "Snowshoe" Thompson, who made the winter mail run between Placerville, on the overland trail, and Genoa, the first settlement in Nevada. Thompson made his daring treks through the frozen reaches of the Sierra Nevada on skis (or snowshoes, as they were then known), which he had learned to use in his native Norway. Thousands of frenzied prospectors invaded the Toiyabe trails with the discovery of placer gold at Godtown and Manoville on the eastern Sierra slope in 1859. Booming gold-rush camps such as Aurora, Lundy, Masonic, and Bodie, one of the wildest of the western mining camps, dotted the rugged eastern foothills.

Today fishermen, backpackers, hunters, and mountaineers follow the hundreds of miles of old Indian exploration and pioneer trails that wind through the forest and provide access to the Hoover Wilderness and Virginia Lakes, Eagle Creek, Hanging Valley, Piute Meadows, the headwaters of the West Walker River, Sweetwater Mountains, Corral Valley, Sunset Lakes, Wolf Creek Highcountry, Leavitt Creek Alpine Lakes, and Fishlake Valley. Silver King Creek in Fishlake Valley is the native home of the endangered Piute trout. The alpine meadows and rugged slopes of the Toiyabe are top-ranked mule deer country and are inhabited as well by black bear, bobcat, chukar partridge, and sage grouse.

The wilderness fly-fisherman will find brook, rainbow, cutthroat, and a few golden and brown trout here in many of the alpine lake basins and streams along the east slope of the Sierra crest. Two of California's top-rated trout streams, the East Fork of the Carson River and East Fork of the Walker River, rise in the forest's high country. The East Fork of the Carson is managed as part of the state's wild trout program and holds good-sized rainbows, browns, cutthroats, and eastern brook trout. The turbulent, boulder-studded waters of the East Walker River below Bridgeport Reservoir are a trophy wild trout stream for large, wily buckskin-flanked browns.

The Hoover Wilderness covers 42,800 acres of rugged high country, stretching north from the northeastern boundary of Yosemite National Park. Wilderness trails provide access by foot or packhorse to the fishing and primitive camping areas of Blacksmith Creek, Glacier Lake, Page Peaks, Mill Creek headwaters, Steelhead Lake, Green Creek high country, Little Walker River, Lee Vining Creek, and the Virginia Lakes—home of the state record golden trout (9 lb. 8 oz.). The white granitic cliffs and serrated peaks of the wilderness are a popular mountaineering area. A variety of routes on the Sawtooth Ridge provide access to Coodad, Three Teeth, Grey Tooth, Sawblade, Cleaver, Matterhorn, and Dunderberg (12,347 ft.) peaks. The area is a summer range for mule deer. Black bear, bobcat, coyote, and mountain lion roam the deep canyons. Mountain quail are found in the high country, and sage grouse inhabit the lower elevations.

The *Hoover Wilderness Map* and *Toiyabe National Forest Recreation Map* are available for 50¢ each, along with the free guide *Recreation on the Toiyabe National Forest*, from: Forest Supervisor, P.O. Box 1331, Reno, NV 89504. Specific fishing, camping, hunting, and wilderness travel information may be obtained by writing to the Forest Supervisor's office. Packhorse stations and outfitters are located in the forest at Trumbull Lake Resort, Green Creek, Mono Village, Fales Hot Springs, and Snodgrass Creek. Lodging and wilderness fishing and hunting pack trips are provided by *Little Antelope Pack Station & Lodge*, Box 105, Coleville 96107 (winter: 19553 E. Dawson, Glendora 91740).

Access & Outfitting Centers

Major auto routes to the forest are U.S. 395 and state routes 108, 4, 88, and 89. Lodging, supplies, guides, and outfitters are available at Bridgeport, Dardanelle, Lake Alpine, Walker, Coleville, Markleeville, Woodfords, and South Lake Tahoe.

Yosemite National Park & High Sierra Camps

Yosemite National Park Topo Maps

U.S. Geological Survey large-scale maps: Pinecrest, Tower Peak, Matterhorn Peak, Bodie, Lake Eleanor, Hetch Hetchy Reservoir, Tuolumne Meadows, Mono Craters, Kinsley, El Portal (7.5), Feliciana Mountain, Buckingham Mountain, Yosemite, Merced Peak, Devils Postpile, Mariposa (7.5), Stumpfield Mountain, Bass Lake, Shuteye Peak, Kaiser Peak.

Cathedral Range

U.S. Geological Survey large-scale topographic maps: Tuolumne Meadows, Merced Peak.

Grand Canyon of the Tuolumne

U.S. Geological Survey large-scale topographic maps: Hetch Hetchy Reservoir, Tuolumne Meadows.

Merced River & Headwaters

U.S. Geological Survey large-scale topographic maps: Feliciana Mountain, Kinsley, El Portal, Yosemite, Merced Peak.

Pacific Crest Trail

U.S. Geological Survey large-scale topographic maps: Tower Peak, Matterhorn Peak, Tuolumne Meadows, Mono Craters, Devils Postpile.

Ritter Range

U.S. Geological Survey large-scale topographic maps: Merced Peak, Devils Postpile.

Yosemite Valley

U.S. Geological Survey large-scale topographic maps: Hetch Hetchy Reservoir, Tuolumne Meadows, Yosemite, Merced Peak.

This 1,189-square-mile national park lies on the western slope of the Sierra Nevada in east and central California and contains the greatest concentration of natural grandeur along the entire 400-mile length of the Sierras. During the fall, Yosemite is a backpacker's paradise with its brilliant colors, granite domes and monoliths, trout streams, glaciers, great waterfalls that plunge over perpendicular cliffs as high as 1,612 feet, mountain chains soaring to over 10,000, and extensive forests of pine, fir, and oak. The park is bisected from east to west by Yosemite Valley to the south and the Grand Canyon of the Tuolumne to the north—both gouged down thousands of feet into solid rock when great rivers of ice advanced through Yosemite during the Ice Age.

In 1833, far beyond the High Sierras, in Wyoming's Snake River country, Capt. B. L. E. Bonneville rendezvoused his men on the upper Green and detached a division of more than 70 men under the command of one of his most trusted lieutenants, Joseph Reddeford Walker, to explore the unknown beaver country towards the Pacific. After a series of back-breaking misfortunes and near starvation, the Walker expedition, struggling through the rugged, barren peaks, rocks, and timberline snowfields near the northern headwaters of the Tuolumne River, crossed the High Sierra Crest and, following the old Mono Indian trail west of Tuolumne Meadows, became the first white men to see the natural wonders of Yosemite and the *Sequoiadendron giganteum*—the Big Trees of the Sierra.

The spectacular U-shaped trough of Yosemite Valley was first explored, accidentally, on March 25, 1851, by Maj. James D. Savage and Dr. L. H. Bunnell when, leading the Mariposa Battalion in an expedition to capture the warring Miwok Indians, they stumbled out of the forest at Inspiration Point, where the primeval valley lay spread out before them cut by the winding blue waters of the Merced River. Bunnell was so entranced by the beauty of the valley that he gave up his chase. While camping on the banks of the Merced that night, he named the valley Yosemite, from the Miwok Indian word for grizzly bear, *Uzumati,* one of the tribal divisions, or totems. Afterward, Bunnell's book, *Discovery of Yosemite,* spread the fame of the valley's natural wonders far and wide.

Yosemite Valley lies at 3,985 feet altitude and is 7 miles long, with an average width of 1 mile, carved out of the granite slopes of the High Sierra by stream erosion and massive glacial action. The level, parklike floor is sunk 3,000 feet below the rim of the park, and the once famed trout waters of the Merced River meander through the green meadows and forests, dominated by immense domes and rock masses which form a sheer wall surrounding the valley. The valley was once the home of the Miwok Indians, who called it *Ahwahnee,* meaning "deep grassy valley."

The wild Yosemite North Country is a hiker's paradise offering sculptured peaks and domes, waterfalls, valleys, meadows, groves of giant 3,000-year-old sequoias, alpine lakes and streams, and extensive forests of pine, fir, cedar, hemlock, oak, maple, western yellow pine, Jeffrey pine, and black oak. Glacial action has carved broad, U-shaped valleys and hundreds of lake basins along the crest of the High Sierras at elevations up to 13,000 feet. The Pacific Crest Trail enters the Yosemite region near Tower Peak (11,704 ft.), to the north of Stubblefield Canyon, and winds along the crest past Buckeye Pass, Kerrick Meadow, Burro Pass, and Fingers Peak, through the Matterhorn Canyon, to the grassy floor of Tuolumne Meadows at 8,600 feet—the largest subalpine meadow in the High Sierras and the jumping-off

point for trips by foot or horse down the Grand Canyon of the Tuolumne by way of the old Glen Aulin High Sierra Camp to Waterwheel Falls and the High Sierras. The Tuolumne Grove of Giant Sequoias, near the headwaters of Crane Creek, was discovered in 1833 by Joseph Walker's expedition. At Tuolumne Meadows the Pacific Crest Trail merges with the John Muir Trail and begins the 150-mile route along the grand crescendo of the High Sierras to the headwaters of the Kern River and the towering summit of Mount Whitney. To the west of the meadows, the Tuolumne River makes its wild and tumultuous descent through the Grand Canyon of the Tuolumne and through Muir Gorge. The Tuolumne flows from its headwaters near Lambert Dome and rugged flanks of the reddish Mounts Gibbs and Dana at the upper end of the Meadow past the massive Kuna Crest dominating the horizon along the central part of the meadow and, at the lower end, past the spires of Cathedral Peak and Unicorn Peak. The 24-mile-long section of the John Muir Trail from the Yosemite Valley north to its junction with the Pacific Crest Trail at Tuolumne Meadows begins where the rippling Merced River enters Yosemite Valley through the canyon at the rocky Happy Isles. The trail winds past the junction of Mist Trail and the 317-foot-high Vernal Falls, past the mist-filled chasm and rocket sprays of Nevada Falls, and on through Little Yosemite Valley, past the junction of Half Dome Trail, Clouds Rest Trail, Merced Lake Trail, and Forsyth Trail, and continues northeasterly along the eastern ridge of Sunrise Mountain.

The trail now passes through the scenic country at the Sunrise High Sierra Camp in Long Meadow, past the junction of Echo Creek Trail, and climbs up to Cathedral Pass, at 9,700 feet, where it provides a sweeping view of the upper Merced River and the towering peaks of the Cathedral Range, dominated by the spire of Cathedral Peak (10,-940 ft.) with its beautiful lake basin. The Muir Trail descends from Cathedral Pass and joins with Tenaya Lake in Tuolumne Meadows Trail, crossing the Tinza Road and Tuolumne River to the Tuolumne Ranger Station. Tenaya Lake is one of the most beautiful glaciated lakes in all the High Sierras. The Indians called it *Pyweack,* meaning "lake of the shining rocks," because of the glacier-polished granite in the depths of the lake and along its shores. Old Chief Tenaya and his renegade band of Yosemites were run down and captured here in 1851. Lateral trails in this region provide access to the backcountry near Babcock Lake, Emeric Lake, Ireland Lake, High Sierra Camp, Bernice Lake, and to the headwaters of the Merced River. The Isberg Pass Trail climbs to the summit of the divide separating the Merced and San Joaquin river watersheds, where it provides a spectacular view of the Clark Range to the west and the Cathedral Range and Merced Canyon to the north. At Tuolumne Meadows the Pacific Crest Trail joins the John Muir Trail; it winds southeasterly through the flat meadows and forest floor of the Lyell Fork Canyon and passes the ranger station and the excellent campsites and grazing area at the Lyell base camp; it then climbs rapidly up a steep granite slope to Donohue Pass, with its grand view of Mount Lyell and Maclure glacier, Mount Conness, and the dark ancient peaks of the Ritter Range. From Donohue Pass, the Muir Trail descends into the Minarets Wilderness Area.

There is fishing along the way for golden, cutthroat, and brook trout. Camping is permitted only in areas designated by the Park Service. Supplies, saddle horses, and guides are available at Wawona, White Wolf, Yosemite Valley, Tuolumne Meadows, and Mather Ranger Stations. The Curry Company provides corral and feed at its stables a mile downstream from Happy Isles at the upper end of Yosemite Valley on the Merced River. At all times, practice minimum-impact traveling and camping. Try to schedule your visit during the fall and spring to avoid the summer crowds.

High Sierra Camps

High Sierra backcountry tent camps in Yosemite include the *Glen Aulin Camp*, located at 7,800 feet on the White Cascade of the Tuolumne River near the scenic Tuolumne Canyon and the famed Waterwheel Falls, where the river, John Muir wrote, "is one wild, exulting, onrushing mass of snowy purple bloom . . . gliding in magnificent silver plumes, dashing and foaming against huge boulder dams, leaping high in the air in wheel-like whirls . . ."; *May Lake Camp*, located at 9,400 feet on the Sunrise Trail, with excellent fishing for rainbow and eastern brook trout and a 180-degree panoramic sweep of the High Sierra peaks; *Vogelsang Camp*, located at 10,000 feet— the highest camp, nestled at timberline among magnificent peaks; and *Merced Lake Camp*, located at the headwaters of the Merced River at 7,100 feet, accessible by 13 miles of trail from Yosemite Valley, with good fly-fishing for wild trout. For rates and information write: Reservation Department, Yosemite Park and Curry Co., Yosemite National Park 95389; or call toll-free in California (800) 692–5811; out-of-state, call (209) 372–4671.

Guided High Sierra pack trips are operated within Yosemite from July to early September. The 3-day saddle trip to Merced Lake leaves Yosemite Valley stable each Sunday morning. An experienced fishing guide escorts groups of ten to Merced Lake Camp. A 4-day saddle trip leaves Tuolumne Meadows each Saturday, with overnight stops at Glen Aulin Camp, May Lake Camp and Sunrise Camp. A 6-day saddle trip leaves Tuolumne Meadows each Sunday, with overnight stops in five High Sierra camps. A 7-day hiking trip leaves each Monday morning from Tuolumne Meadows with a ranger naturalist and explores the high country, circling all six High Sierra camps. For rates and information, write or call Yosemite Park and Curry Co. (address and phone number above).

Yosemite Maps & Guides

Backpackers and fishermen planning a cross-country or wilderness trip through the remote interior areas may obtain a free wilderness permit at one of the following locations: Valley Visitor Center, Happy Isles Trail Center, Tuolumne Meadows Ranger Station, Lee Vining Ranger Station, Glacier Point Ranger Station, White Wolf Ranger Station, Wawona Ranger Station, or Big Oak Flat Entrance Station. Reservations for backcountry trips may be made between February 1 and May 31 by writing: Superintendent, Yosemite National Park, Yosemite 95389. Some of the state's finest fly-fishing is along the 15-mile stretch of the South Fork of the Merced River from its confluence with the main stem of the Merced upstream to the western boundary of Yosemite. Fishing is for wild rainbow and brown trout. Please note that bears are numerous at the following areas: all High Sierra camps, Little Yosemite Valley, Cathedral Lakes, Lyell Canyon, Pate Valley, Rancheria Falls, Pleasant Valley, Ten Lakes, and Laurel Lake. Backcountry use regulations and the free publication *The Yosemite Backcountry* may be obtained by writing the Superintendent's Office, address above.

The invaluable U.S. Geological Survey *Yosemite National Park & Vicinity Topographic Map* ($2—also available in a beautiful shaded-relief edition) is 29 × 31 inches, with a scale of 1:125,000, or 2 miles to 1 inch, and shows all contours, natural features, campgrounds, ranger stations, wilderness shelters, trails, footbridges, and roads. The U.S. Geological Survey *Yosemite Valley Topographic Map* (also available in shaded-relief) is 19 × 42 inches, with a scale of 1:24,000, or 2,000 feet to 1 inch, and shows all natural and man-made features. A text on the reverse side of the map contains an illustrated description of the natural features of the valley. Several Yosemite trail map/guides

are available from the Yosemite Natural History Association, P.O. Box 545, Yosemite 95389: *Trails of Yosemite Valley* (35¢), which contains a map and description of trails in the Yosemite Lodge, Mirror Lake, Happy Isles, and Cathedral Rocks areas; *Giant Stairway* (50¢), a map/guide to the trails of the Happy Isles, Glacier Point, and Half Dome areas; *High Sierra Loop* (50¢), which describes trails around the rim of Yosemite Valley; *Snow Trails* (50¢), which describes the major park cross-country ski trails; *Tuolumne Country* (50¢), which describes trails in the Tuolumne Meadows area; *Yosemite Inyo-Tuolumne to the Devils Postpile* (50¢), which describes the John Muir trail and spur trails in this area; *Yosemite Trail Guide Packet* ($2.65), which includes all six of the above; the classic *Starr's Guide to the John Muir Trail & High Sierra Region; Climber's Guide to Yosemite Valley* ($6.95), the climber's bible, describing 482 climbing routes in the valley; *Yosemite* ($2.95), a Wilderness Press guide with a large-scale map of Yosemite Valley and its adjacent trails, plus a complete map of the Yosemite quadrangle; *Tuolumne Meadows* ($1.95), a Wilderness Press guide to day hikes and backpack trails, with diagramed trail "profiles" showing all the ups and downs; *Matterhorn Peak* ($2.95), a Wilderness Press guide to the northeastern section of Yosemite and the rugged Sawtooth Ridge, which cuts across the center of this spectacular area, complete with fishing facts on the area's lakes and streams; *Merced Peak* ($1.95), which describes the wilderness and trails centered about the Clark Range, including Mount Lyell, Yosemite's highest peak, in the southeastern section of the park; *Hetch Hetchy* ($1.95), a Wilderness Press guide to the area in western Yosemite Park dominated by the Grand Canyon of the Tuolumne River and its wild, remote north-bank tributaries, including all trails that lead north from Yosemite Valley; *Mono Craters* ($3.95), a Wilderness Press guide to this eastern Yosemite area and the June Lake Loop, the most diverse glacial-volcanic landscape in California.

Yosemite has more than 200 miles of historic, scenic roads that wind through the remote backcountry and the heart of the High Sierra. The Big Oak Flat Road (Route 120 West), named for an old gold-mining settlement, begins its winding mountain journey at the lower end of Yosemite Valley, 6 miles west of Yosemite Village, and provides spectacular views of the 620-feet-high Bridal Veil Falls, Big Meadow (remnant of an ancient glacial lake), Clark Range, San Joaquin Valley, and the wildlands and conifer forests of the Yosemite North Country. This mountain route provides access to Crane Flat, a High Sierra meadow, with a ranger station and public campground; Merced Grove of Giant Sequoias; Hodgdon Meadow Campground; and the "49er Route," Highway 49, which leads to many of the historic mining camps and towns of Mother Lode country. The Glacier Point Road winds for 16 miles from Chinquapin to Glacier and provides access to the 4,500-foot-deep gorge of the Merced River, Badger Pass Ski area, Bridal Veil Creek Campground, Pothole Meadows, and the spectacular vistas of the High Sierra from Glacier Point at 7,214 feet. The Hetch Hetchy Road, or Mather Road, winds for 16 miles to Hetch Hetchy Reservoir and provides access to the South Fork of the Tuolumne River, Middle Fork of the Tuolumne Campground, and Mather Ranger Station. The Merced Road (Route 140) winds down from Yosemite Valley along the beautiful Merced River past Cascade Falls to the park boundary at El Portal. The scenic Tioga Road (Route 120 East) climbs through the wildlands of Yosemite's High Sierra to Tioga Pass at 9,941 feet—the highest auto pass in the Sierra Nevada. The Tioga Road provides access to the Old Big Oak Flat Road and the Tuolumnel Grove of Big Trees, Smoky Jack Campsite (named for a man for whom John Muir herded sheep), Red Fir Forest, White Wolf Campground (named by a sheepherder who claimed to have seen a white wolf there), Yosemite Creek, Porcupine Flat Primitive

Campground, May Lake Junction and High Sierra Camp, Tenaya Lake and the Tenaya Branch of the Tuolumne River, the Ghost Forest, Tuolumne Meadows and High Sierra Camp, old Mono Indian Trail, Dana Meadows, and Lee Vining Canyon. The Wawona (thought to be the Indian word for "big tree"), or Fresno (Spanish for "ash tree"), Road (Route 41) follows the route of the Mariposa Battalion when, in pursuit of the Miwok Indians in 1851, it entered Yosemite Valley. This route provides access to Bridal Veil Falls, the South Fork Canyon of the Merced River, Wawona Campground, and Wawona. Detailed descriptions of the routes discussed above are contained in the 77-page *Yosemite Road Guide,* available for $1.25 from the Yosemite Natural History Association, Yosemite 95389.

The Yosemite Natural History Association also makes available several guides to the natural history, wildlife, and exploration of Yosemite of interest to the wilderness traveler. Titles of historical interest include *Guide to the Pioneer Cemetery* (50¢), the story of those who made Yosemite's history and were buried there; *The Tioga Road* ($1), history of the Great Sierra wagon road; *Yosemite—Story of an Idea* (75¢), by the noted historian Huth, who traces the significance of the world's first national park; *Ghost Mines of Yosemite* ($1.50), history and anecdotes of the old mining days; *Guardians of Yosemite* ($2.50), the story of the first rangers; *Short Line to Paradise* ($2), a classic account of the old Yosemite Valley Railroad; *Thunder over the Mountains* ($7.95), the story of High Sierra logging; *Yosemite Yarns* ($1.50), lively tales of the old days in Yosemite; *The Ahwahneechees* ($2.50), the story of Yosemite Indians; *John Muir in Yosemite* ($1.50), the story of Muir's residency, work, and studies in Yosemite; and *The Yosemite* ($1.25), John Muir's sensitive study of Yosemite Valley. Titles on natural history and geology include: *Sierra Nevada* ($7.95, 281 pp.), a living picture of the range, including natural and human history and ecology; *Yosemite Butterflies* ($2); *Yosemite Wildflowers & Their Stories* ($1.50); *The Incomparable Valley* ($2.95), a fine geologic interpretation of Yosemite; and *Yosemite—The Story behind the Scenery* ($1.50), authoritative text with excellent illustrations of Yosemite's geology. King's classic *Mountaineering in the Sierra Nevada* ($2.25) describes the experiences of a geographer in the 1860s.

For additional information and bulletins about skiing (downhill and cross-country), fishing regulations, campgrounds, wilderness use permits, backpacking, geology, weather, an equipment check-list for summer backpacking, fees, and the free *Cycle Guide to Yosemite Valley* and *Yosemite National Park Map-Brochure,* write: Superintendent, Yosemite National Park 95389 (phone 209–372–4532).

Access & Lodging

Major routes to the park are State Highways 140 and 120 and U.S. Highway 395. Lodging and accommodations are available in Yosemite at *The Ahwahnee* (121 rooms); *Curry Village* (116 bungalows, 80 wooden cabins, 418 tent cabins, 300 housekeeping cabins); *Tuolumne Meadows Lodge* (66 canvas cabins); *Wawona Hotel* (63 rooms, 14 housekeeping cabins); *White Wolf Lodge* (13 cabins); *Yosemite Lodge* (281 hotel rooms, 65 redwood cabins, 90 cabins without bath, and 19 housekeeping cabins). For rates and reservations, write: Yosemite Park & Curry Co., Yosemite 95389 (phone toll-free in California, 800–692–5811; or out-of-state 209–372–4671). Camping and cross-country ski equipment can be rented at Curry Village in Yosemite Valley. Mountaineering and cross-country skiing instruction, seminars, and guided trips in the park backcountry are provided by *Yosemite Mountaineering Inc.* at Curry Village. For rates, information, and the free publication *Yosemite Ski Touring,* write: Yosemite Mountaineering, Yosemite 95389. For weather, road conditions, etc., phone: 209–372–4222.

NEVADA ENCYCLOPEDIA

Accommodations— Vacation Lodges & Resorts

For detailed information about fishing, hunting, and vacation lodges and resorts, write: Travel and Tourism Division, Nevada Dept. of Economic Development, Carson City 89701, or the local Chamber of Commerce of the area you plan to visit.

Campgrounds & State Recreation Areas

There is lots of room to roam on Nevada's expanse of land, and camping facilities are numerous. The *Guide to Bureau of Land Management Campgrounds* is available free from: Bureau of Land Management, Room 3008 Federal Bldg., 300 Booth St., Reno 89502.

Free brochures are also available on the following outstanding camping areas. *Ruby Marsh Campground* is an excellent access spot to fishing, hunting, bird hunting, and mountain scenery in the colorful Ruby Valley. *Indian Creek Reservoir,* on the eastern slope of the Sierra Nevada, provides water sports and fishing among the lush pine forests. *Walker Lake Recreation Site* offers camping and fishing around the rocky, rugged terraces of Lake Walker. The *Curtz Lake Environmental Study Area* provides educational trails through forest and lake country, and the area is filled with small mammals and woodland birds. These areas are managed by the Bureau of Land Management, and free information can be obtained from the Carson City District, 801 North Plaza St., Carson City 89701.

Guide to BLM's Nevada Campgrounds, free from the State Office of the BLM in Reno, is an index to all BLM-managed camping areas in the state. Additional camping information is available free from: Travel and Tourism Division, Nevada Dept. of Economic Development, Carson City 89701.

Fishing & Hunting in Nevada

Nevada offers some of the best trout and bass fishing and hunting opportunities in the Far West. Lake Tahoe, nestled among the towering Sierras on the state's western boundary, is one of the West's premier trout waters. The lake is 21 ½ miles long and 12 miles wide and has a delightfully irregular rocky shoreline thickly forested with evergreens. With the peaks of the High Sierras in view above the trees, the lake is a brilliant blue-green, owing to its great depth—1,776 feet at one point. It is the tenth-deepest lake in the world and the second-clearest in the United States. The fishing in Tahoe was nearly destroyed near the turn of the century when hundreds of tons of the native Lahontan cutthroat trout, also known as black spotted trout, were taken for commercial purposes and shipped to markets as far away as San Francisco. During the 1870s, the lake was stocked with Atlantic king and silver salmon; rainbow, brown, golden, and Mackinaw trout; and Great Lakes whitefish. Subsequent stockings of trout, including the native Lahontan cutthroat, and kokanee salmon, beginning in 1949 have brought the fishing close to its former level of excellence.

First recorded knowledge of the lake is in the report of Frémont's expeditions. When he was encamped at Pyramid Lake near the mouth of the Truckee River in 1844, Indians "made a drawing of the Truckee River, which they represented as issuing from another lake in the mountains three or four days distant, in a direction a little west of south; beyond which they drew a mountain, and farther still two rivers, on one side of which, the Indians said, people like ourselves traveled." Frémont then crossed the Sierras over Carson Pass and saw Lake Tahoe, which he later called Mountain Lake. The name of the lake

was changed many times, and finally the name Tahoe was put together from several Indian words.

There are numerous camping spots and trails in this area. Among wildflowers are the snow plant, red and white heather, gentian, water lily, wild marigold, Indian paintbrush, pennyroyal, and primrose. Small trees include the ash laurel and holly; the larger trees include several varieties of pine, firs, alpine spruce, cedar, and tamarack. There is also a great variety of songbirds.

The beautiful Truckee River, flowing out of Lake Tahoe, flows through a scenic wooded valley and holds rainbows and browns up to 15 pounds. Topaz Lake, on the California border, holds cutthroat, brown, and rainbow trout, as does 20-mile-long Walker Lake, which is fed by the East Walker River. Pyramid Lake is one of the West's outstanding rainbow and cutthroat trout fisheries. (See "Pyramid Lake.")

Some of the state's finest trout fishing is in the wilderness areas of the Humboldt River tributaries, rising high in the scenic Ruby, Jarbidge and Independence mountains in the northeast. These less-known lakes and streams offer wonderful opportunities for fishing and camping free from crowded conditions and misuses. Many of the high-country lakes are situated amidst rugged and beautiful scenery and are accessible only by foot and horseback. The wilderness fisherman can enjoy roughing it for days in complete solitude. Along the crest of the Ruby Range, Snake Range, and Schell Creek Range lie hundreds of scenic alpine lakes and streams which hold cutthroat, eastern brook, brown, rainbow, and, in the Jarbidge area, an occasional Dolly Varden. The Utah cutthroats found in a few of these high mountain streams are believed to be the only remaining populations of this pure trout strain in existence.

The Independence–Mountain City area in the Humboldt National Forest contains a number of small mountain streams which provide often excellent fishing for wild cutthroat, rainbow, and brook trout. These include Jack Creek, the North Fork of the Humboldt River above the forest boundary, the East Fork of the Owyhee River, Bull Run Creek, and the Bruneau River and its tributaries. Populations of native cutthroat are found in a number of streams in the Tuscarora Mountains and Independence Range. Some of the finest trout fishing

in the region can be found on the following streams and creeks: Beaver, Bluejacket, Columbia, Gance, McDonald, Merritt, Snow, Trail and Van Duzer. Several improved public campgrounds are found in the forest region.

In the beautiful rugged Jarbidge Wilderness, the East Fork of the Jarbidge River and the headwaters of the Marys River provide fly-fishing for rainbows and Dolly Varden. Pan-sized trout are found in the O'Neil Basin in the headwaters of Canyon Creek, and in Wilson, Camp, and Sun creeks. The Salmon Falls River, which drains the basin, holds some lunker rainbow and cutthroat trout. In the extreme northeastern corner of the state, wild cutthroat are found in the seldom-fished Big Goose Creek and its Piney and Coon creek tributaries. A U.S. Forest Service campground is located on the West Fork of the Jarbidge.

Wilderness fly-fishing for wild rainbow, cutthroat, and brook trout may be found in the scenic high-country lakes and streams of the Ruby Mountains in the Humboldt National Forest in northeastern Nevada. The South Fork of the Humboldt River and the Lamoille Creek are accessible by road. Hiking and pack trails provide access to the following streams and their alpine headwaters: Boulder, Pole Canyon, Secret, Long Canyon, Soldier, and North Feerlong creeks. The spring holes of the famed Ruby Marsh National Wildlife Refuge, located along the eastern slope of the range, hold some monster browns and rainbows in excess of 10 pounds. The largest fish caught to date was a 17-pound brown trout. Some 30,000 to 50,000 deer range through the Ruby and Butte mountains area, and deer weighing over 250 pounds have been reported. The Ruby Valley, crossed by the Frémont expedition in 1845, was once the home and hunting grounds of the Shoshone Indians. The Ruby Mountains were named for "rubies" (actually worthless garnets) found in an early gold pan.

Favre Lake in the Ruby Range is one of the most scenic of the alpine lakes, and in the early morning it reflects surrounding peaks as though it were beveled grass. In the summer a meadow sloping down to the shore is frequented by grazing sheep. Lamoille Creek in the Ruby Mountains is a cold, clear, tumultuous stream that feeds from snow-covered peaks rising as high as 11,000 feet. Mountain mahogany and aspen blend into patches of pine and stunted willow, and a wide variety of wildflowers blooms on the stream's canyon floor.

In southern Nevada, the Colorado River and its impoundments, Lakes Mead and Mohave, a deep blue in their desert brown setting, attract thousands of anglers each year. Lake Mead began to fill in 1935 upon completion of Hoover Dam, and by 1941 had reached its maximum elevation along the 550-mile shoreline. By 1941 (when a 13 lb. 14 ounce largemouth was caught) the lake's bass-fishing reputation had spread across the nation. Lake Mohave, 67 miles long, is impounded by Hoover Dam and provides excellent fishing for rainbow trout, coho and kokanee salmon, and largemouth bass from Eldorado Landing, to the south. The swift, frigid, crystal-clear tailrace waters below Hoover Dam yield lunker rainbows up to 21½ pounds.

The Nevada Trophy Fish Program, initiated in 1968 and designed to recognize exceptional angling feats, also provides the State Department of Fish & Game with valuable records of the state's fisheries.

NEVADA RECORD FISH*

	Lb.–oz.	Place	Year
Bass, largemouth	11	Lake Mohave	1972
Bass, smallmouth	2–14	Carson River	1977
Bass, striped	48–12	Colorado River	1977
Bluegill	1–2	Lake Mead	1972
Bullhead	2	Ft. Churchill Pond	1973
Carp	29–7	Lake Mohave	1973
Catfish, channel	29–8	Lahontan Reservoir	1974
Catfish, white	11	Lahontan Reservoir	1969
Crappie, black	3	Lake Mead	1972
Crappie, white	2–8	Lahontan Reservoir	1968
Northern pike	23	Cummins Lake	1978
Salmon, kokanee	16–4	Lake Tahoe	1973
Salmon, silver	4–13	Lake Mead	1974
Trout, brook	8–12½	Round Mtn. Reservoir	1972
Trout, brown	5–4	Comins Lake	1973
Trout, cutthroat**	23–8	Pyramid Lake	1977
Trout, cutthroat & rainbow hybrid	19–9	Pyramid Lake	1974
Trout, rainbow	16–4	Lake Mohave	1971
Trout, mackinaw	37–6	Lake Tahoe	1974
Walleye	6–5	Ryepatch Reservoir	1974
Whitefish, Mtn.	2	E.F. Carson River	1974

*Note: These records are officially recorded in the Nevada Fish and Game records as established from the year 1968, the first year of the Nevada Trophy Fish Program. It is recognized that earlier fish of larger size have been taken from Nevada waters. These records include fish taken in interstate waters including Lake Tahoe, Lake Mead, Lake Mohave and the Colorado River.

**The all-time world's record cutthroat of 41 pounds also came from Pyramid Lake, in 1925.

The Department of Fish & Game publishes several useful, information-packed fishing guides, which cost 25¢ each, and the free *Angler's Map of the Fishing Waters of Nevada. The Angler's Guide to Northeast Nevada* contains detailed area maps and descriptions of fishing in the Independence–Mountain City area, the Jarbidge–O'Neil area,

and the Ruby Range. *The Angler's Guide to Eastern Nevada* contains maps and useful info about fishing in the Wayne E. Kirch Wildlife Management Area, Snake Range, Schell Creek Range, Illipah Creek–White River Area, Eureka County and Newark Valley, and Nye County. *The Angler's Guide to Lake Tahoe* and *The Angler's Guide to Lakes Mead, Mohave & the Colorado River* each contain a useful lake contour map and info about the fish species present and their feeding habits.

Nevada *Fishing Seasons & Regulations, Deer Seasons and Regulations* (which contains a Mule Deer Hunting Map), and *Trophy Hunt Seasons & Regulations* (for elk, antelope, bighorn sheep, and mountain lion, which contains a Management Area Map) may be obtained by writing to the Department of Fish & Game. The department will provide big-game hunting guide and outfitter information upon request.

Nevada is an excellent mule deer hunting state and has limited hunting by permit only for antelope, elk, and bighorn sheep. The upland game bird hunting is for chukar partridge, quail, sage grouse, and mourning dove. The state has surprisingly good hunting for ducks and geese in its numerous marshlands and wildlife management area wetlands, particularly in the renowned Ruby Marshes in Elko County.

Highways—Recreation and Scenic Routes

The Nevada State Highway Map, available free from the Travel and Tourism Division, Nevada Dept. of Economic Development, Carson City 89701, shows all roads and highways, recreation areas, national forest land, towns, lakes and streams, airfields and railroads, and public lands.

Lake Mead National Recreation Area

This outstanding recreation area lies along the spectacular Grand Wash Cliffs, surrounded by stark, colorful desert landscapes. Lake Mead stretches 115 miles up the old course of the Colorado River from Hoover Dam to the Grand Canyon. Its 550-mile shoreline has

wide, sandy beaches, shadowed coves, and steep canyon walls, providing opportunities for fishing and beach camping. The famous rainbow trout waters of Lake Mohave reach northward 67 miles to the base of Hoover Dam. The whole area is surrounded by rugged desert country that provides scenic views and excellent hiking. Desert animals and plants include creosote bush, yucca, Joshua tree, and of course cactus, and kit fox, kangaroo rats, bighorn sheep, and a variety of reptiles and birds. Mule deer are common on the plateaus. Juniper, piñon pine, and Gambel oak populate the woodland regions. Ducks, gulls, and grebes feed on the surface of the water, and largemouth black bass, rainbow trout, and black crappie are caught around the submerged cliffs. Rainbow trout make up the majority of the catch in Lake Mohave, along with coho salmon, catfish, bluegill sunfish, and threadfin shad. There are several recreation areas and campsites in this area, accommodating fishermen and families.

The Lake Mead–Mohave region was first explored in 1826 by Jedediah Smith on his first southwest expedition in search of beaver. Smith was followed by a long list of explorers, including John C. Frémont and Maj. John Wesley Powell. The ancient Lost City Pueblo and the Virgin River salt quarries of the once-great Pueblo Indian culture lie submerged at the bottom of the reservoirs.

Several publications are available which provide information on history, Indians, fishing, and recreation areas. *Lake Mead National Recreation Area*, available free from: Supervisor, 601 Nevada Highway, Boulder City 89005, provides a good overall map of the region. *Angler's Guide*, with information about fishing and the kinds of fish available, as well as maps and descriptions of facilities, can be obtained for 25¢ from the Nevada Dept. of Fish and Game, P.O. Box 10678, Reno 89510. Complete fishing information, including Davis Dam, Willow Beach, Eldorado Canyon, and Cottonwood Cove, is provided in *Boating Guide to Lake Mohave*, available for 50¢ from the Southwest Parks and Monuments Association, Box 1562, Globe, AZ 85501. *Indians of the Lake Mead Country* can be obtained for 50¢ from the same organization. It provides an unusual insight into the earliest history of the area by telling plausible stories about ancient and recent Indians at various points throughout their history. It begins with cavemen and ends with the arrival of the white explorers. *Nautical Charts* are also available for $3.25, and *Recreational Boating Guide* is available for $1.20.

A float trip by canoe, kayak, or raft below Hoover Dam in the Black Canyon area and Upper Lake Mohave area can be an exciting and rewarding experience. The water is cold and the current is often slow, but the rapids and strong winds provide challenges. Park rangers will take visitors on hikes through the desert, forest, and mountain country where no trails are present. Information on float trips and hikes can be obtained by writing: Lake Mead Recreation Area, Boulder City 89005.

The many recreation services around the Lake Mead area include *Lakeshore Trailer Village*, Boulder Beach, Boulder City 89005, which provides accommodations and facilities for fishing and camping. *Lake Mead Yacht Tours*, 5030 Paradise Road, Las Vegas 89119, offers deluxe cruises of Hoover Dam. *Lake Mead Marina*, P.O. Box 96, Boulder City 89005, provides luxurious rooms and many water sport and fishing facilities.

There are several resorts and suppliers in the Lake Mead area. These include: *Cottonwood Cove Development Corp.*, P.O. Box 1000, Cottonwood 89046; *Echo Bay Resort, Inc.*, P.O. Box 384, Overton 89040; *Forrest Enterprises, Inc.*, Boulder City 89005; *Callville Bay Trailer Village*, 2103 Western Ave., Las Vegas 89102; *Lake Mohave Resort,*

Inc., Bullhead City, AZ 86430; *Overton Beach Resort, Inc.*, P.O. Box 714, Overton 89040; *Temple Bar Marina, Inc.*, Temple Bar, AZ 86443; *Willow Beach Resort, Inc.*, P.O. Box 187, Boulder City 89005; *Lake Mead Ferry Service, Inc.*, 5441 Paradise Road, Suite A-101, Las Vegas 89109; and *Las Vegas Boat Harbor, Inc.*, P.O. Box 771, Henderson 89015.

Information on boating regulations is supplied in *Boating Regulations for Nevada-Arizona Interstate Waters*, available free from the State of Nevada Dept. of Fish and Game.

The Lake Mead National Recreation Area is shown on the following U.S. Geological Survey Topographic 15-minute quadrangle maps: Black Canyon, Hoover Dam, Davis Dam, Iceberg Canyon, Mount Perkins, Overton Beach, Spirit Mountain, Virgin Basin.

Pyramid Lake & the Lahontan Cutthroat Trout

Located in the desert in western Nevada, northwest of Lake Tahoe, 30-mile-long Pyramid Lake is the remnant of a vast, ancient sea once 500 miles long and 300 miles wide. When Pyramid was first seen by Frémont in 1844, its waters teemed with giant Lahontan cutthroat trout, and it was the prize fishing grounds of the Paiute Indians. The world-record cutthroat (41 lb.) was caught here in 1925, and a 65-

pound cutthroat was reportedly taken here at the turn of the century. Today, the lake once again is providing fishing for rainbows to 12 pounds and cutthroats.

Pyramid Lake, the largest remnant of the ancient Lahontan Sea, is a sparkling blue body of water surrounded by colorful, deeply eroded hills. The lake, which has no outlet and is slowly receding from its former shoreline (marked by a white ribbon composed of the dead bodies of minute algae), is thought to have been named by Captain Frémont for the spectacular pyramid rising 475 feet above the surface just north of Anaho Island. Paiute Indian lore says the pyramid is the home of the lake spirit, which devours humans swimming in its waters.

The surface of the lake is studded with tufa islands, including 248-acre Anaho Island near the southeastern shore, which contains the West's largest rookery of pelicans. North of Pyramid Island on the eastern shore is an unusual tufa formation known as the Squaw with a Basket. At the northern end of the lake is a cluster of sharp stone spires rising from the water known as the Needles.

The Paiute tribal lands of the Pyramid Lake Indian Reservation surround the lake, and a tribal fishing permit is a necessity here.

136 · THE BANTAM GREAT OUTDOORS GUIDE

Pyramid Lake is shown on the following U.S. Geological Survey topographic maps: Dove Creek, Fox Range, Kumiva Park, Needle Rocks, Nixon, Pyramid N.E., Pyramid S.W., Sutcliffe, Tohakum Park N.E., Tohakum Park N.W., and Tohakum Park S.E.

Wildlife Refuge & Recreation Areas

Desert National Wildlife Range is an extensive area northwest of Las Vegas. Desert bighorns and mule deer are the major species, but other desert mammals and birds occupy the area. Mule deer can be hunted by special permit, but there are no camping facilities. The mailing address is 1500 North Decatur Blvd., Las Vegas 89108.

Ruby Lake National Wildlife Refuge contains 37,631 acres of marsh, lake, and sagebrush habitat for trumpeter swans, Canada geese, ducks, sandhill cranes, shorebirds, and sage grouse. Waterfowl hunting and fishing are permitted. The mailing address is Ruby Valley 89833.

Sheldon National Antelope Refuge and *Charles Sheldon Antelope Range* comprise 580,000 acres of high desert land. Besides antelope, there are mule deer, bighorn sheep, sage grouse, waterfowl, coyotes, bobcats, wild horses, and other desert species. Camping and hunting are permitted in certain areas. Write to Box 111, Lakeview, OR 97630.

Humboldt National Forest

Humboldt National Forest Topo Maps

U.S. Geological Survey 1:250,000 scale overview maps: Caliente, Elko, Ely, Lund, McDermitt, Wells.

Jarbidge Wilderness Area

U.S. Geological Survey large-scale topographic maps: Black Butte, Buena Vista Ranch, Charleston Reservoir, Elk Mountain (15), Gilmer Ranch, Hanks Creek, Hot Creek, Jarbidge (15), Marys River Basin N.E., Marys River Basin N.W., Stag Mountain, Stormy Peak, Sun Creek N.W.

Ruby Range Alpine Lakes Country

U.S. Geological Survey large-scale topographic maps: Cold Creek Ranch, Sherman Mountain, Station Butte, Ruby Lake N.W., Franklin Lake S.W., Jiggs, Franklin Lake N.W., Lee, Lamoille.

Wheeler Peak Scenic Area

U.S. Geological Survey large-scale topographic maps: Wheeler Peak, Garrison, Sacramento Pass.

This vast 2.5-million-acre reserve contains several divisions in northeastern and north central Nevada, embracing some of the finest big-game hunting and fishing water in the West along the spring-fed Ruby Lake marshes set high in the beautiful Ruby Mountains, close to the trail that early pioneers followed on their way to the California country. In the potholes and canals of the marshes, trout grow exceptionally large; rainbows reach weights up to 13 pounds, brook trout to 6½ pounds, and brown trout up to 6 pounds. Largemouth bass up to 8 pounds are common. West of the Ruby Range, near the Duck Valley Indian Reservation, lies Wilson Reservoir, noted for its rainbows up to 5 pounds. To the west of the Jarbidge Wilderness, at an elevation of 5,400 feet, lies the famed Wild Horse Reservoir, formed by the damming of the Owyhee River. Fishing is for rainbows averaging 3 pounds. The alpine fly-fishing buff will find brook trout fishing in Lamoille, Favre, Echo, Soldier, and Robinson lakes at 10,000 feet elevation in the Ruby Dome wilderness area. Access is by trail. The vast expanses of roadless backcountry offer some of the finest trophy mule deer hunting in the state.

Rich in mining and ranching history, this land was visited by many explorers in the nineteenth century. It was named after Baron Alexander von Humboldt, a German explorer and naturalist.

The White Pine Ranger District is rough and steep, ranging from the juniper belt to bristlecone pine forest at over 10,000 feet. Three limestone terraces in the War Mountains offer excellent hiking and camping areas and provide a stunning view of the valley below. Once a busy mining center, there are several ghost towns in the area. The most famous is Hamilton, which once produced millions of dollars' worth of silver. The old Hamilton Pioche Stage Route is one of many dirt roads that traverse the region.

The Ely Ranger District includes the Wheeler Peak Scenic Area, bristlecone pine forests, the Lehman Caves National Monument, the spectacular Asilo Verde Drive, and solitary, massive Mount Moriah. Mount Moriah rises above the desert in a giant wilderness of unnamed peaks and rugged canyons. A few trails are the only access to this lonely wilderness.

Wildflowers in the area include larkspur, monkshood, lupine, heart-leafed arnica, aster, elephanthead, Indian paintbrush, hawksbeard, sego lily, and marsh marigold.

The Humboldt National Forest White Pine and Ely Ranger District

NEVADA TRAVEL & RECREATION GUIDE

Recreation Map, available for 50¢ from Ely District Ranger, P.O. Box 539, Ely 89301, shows all roads and trails, recreation areas, ranger stations, and lakes and streams.

The Wheeler Peak Scenic Area is named for Wheeler Peak, which rises to over 13,000 feet. The area earned recognition for its outstanding geologic, scenic, and botanical attractions. The top of Wheeler Peak was used as a heliograph point for flashing messages with mirrors between Troy Peak in Nevada and Mount Nebo in Utah.

Hiking is popular in the scenic area. The Baker Creek Trail, Solace Trail, and Wheeler Peak Trail provide interesting, challenging, and scenic hikes uphill to beautiful lake areas. New Bristlecone and Icefield Trail passes both young and old bristlecones, and on to the icefield which falls from the glacial head wall. An interesting alternate route to the Scenic Highway is the Lehman Creek Trail, which connects the Lehman and Wheeler Peak campgrounds. Horse owners may ride up the Stella Lake Horse Trail.

The *Wheeler Peak Scenic Area Recreation Map* is available for 50¢ from: Ely Ranger District, P.O. Box 539, Ely 89301. It shows all roads and trails, ranger stations, lakes, and recreation sites.

The Ruby Division of the Humboldt National Forest contains the Ruby Mountain Range and the East Humboldt Range. The two ranges appear to be continuous, but they are in fact divided by Secret Pass. The mountains were explored by Peter Ogden, a trapper, and later by John C. Frémont, who studied the area in depth. The Ruby Mountains were named by soldiers looking for gold in the mountains, who found garnets they hoped were rubies. The Ruby Mountains Scenic Area extends from Overland Lake on the south to Verdi Peak on the north, and includes the 11,000-foot Ruby Dome. The canyons have sheer walls rising 2,000 feet above the valley floor, and narrow waterfalls flow from scenic hanging valleys. Camping and hiking are very popular. Major hiking trails include the Ruby Crest, Kleckner, Smith Creek, and Overland.

The *Humboldt National Forest—Ruby Division Map* is available for 50¢ from: Ruby Mountains Ranger District, Wells 89835. It shows all roads and trails, historic routes, ranger stations, recreation sites, and lakes and streams.

The Santa Rosa District and the Humboldt District on the northern border of Nevada are lands of contrasts. Traces of ancient lakes can be found in the rugged mountains formed by volcanoes, glaciers, and huge land faults. Here Indians encountered early explorers, followed by miners, followed by ranchers who settled the land. Jarbidge is one of the mining towns that stayed alive. The name is a Shoshone word meaning "weird beastly creature." Legend says that the Indians chased such a creature into a cave, where they trapped it with boulders and rocks.

Streams and rivers on the Humboldt Division are headwaters of the north fork of the Humboldt River, east and south forks of the Owyhee River, and the Bruneau River. The Wild Horse Reservoir provides excellent fishing opportunities. The Santa Rosa Division boasts three major streams—east and south forks of the Quinn River, the north fork of the Little Humboldt, and Martin Creek.

Wildlife includes mule deer, antelope, bighorn sheep, mountain lion, and bobcat. Upland game birds include sage grouse, blue grouse, chukar partridge, and various species of duck. Mink, otter, and beaver are also common.

The Jarbidge Wilderness is a rugged mountainous region bounded by the Columbia River Plateau on the north and the Great Basin Desert

on the south. Rising abruptly between Marys River and the headwaters of the Jarbidge River is a 64,830-acre area that is often considered to be the most wildly beautiful mountain range in Nevada. Marys River and the east fork of the Jarbidge are the major streams, and there are eight peaks that exceed 10,000 feet in elevation. The range is characterized by U-shaped canyons, brilliant wildflowers, yellow and orange quaking aspen in the autumn, and some of the largest trophy-size mule deer in the state.

The *Humboldt National Forest Map for the Humboldt and Santa Rosa Districts* is available for 50¢ from: Forest Supervisor, Humboldt National Forest, Elko 89801. It shows all roads and trails, recreation sites, lakes and streams, and ranger stations.

Access and Outfitting Centers

The Humboldt National Forest is reached via U.S. Highways 93, 40, 50, and 6 and Nevada State Highway 51. Lodging, supplies, and outfitting centers are available at Ely, Mountain Creek, Jarbidge, Lamoille, Elko, and Winnemucca.

Toiyabe National Forest

Toiyabe National Forest Topo Maps

U.S. Geological Survey 1:250,000 scale overview maps: Goldfield, Mariposa, Walker Lake, Tonopah, Millett, Las Vegas.

West Walker River & Lake

U.S. Geological Survey large-scale topographic maps: Topaz Lake, Desert Creek Peak, Wellington, Yerington, Wabuska.

The name Toiyabe is derived from the Shoshone word for "black mountains" and refers to the dark color of the beautiful piñon-covered slopes in the area. The forest is divided into three sections, which include the Carson Ranger District, the Las Vegas Ranger District, and the Central Nevada Division.

The Central Nevada Division is the largest region, encompassing rugged terrain, green meadows, rolling hills, sagebrush, piñon, and juniper. The Shoshone Indians were the first inhabitants of this rugged land, and they left ancient petroglyphs painted on the walls of caves.

The Simpson Road, built by Capt. James Simpson in 1849, was used by the Pony Express and the Concord Stagecoach line. It became a route for settlers undergoing the perilous trek from Salt Lake City into the rich valleys in California. As with many areas of the Old West, a mining boom began here suddenly in 1862, when a Pony Express rider accidentally discovered a silver mine on the Reese River. Prospectors came flooding into the region, and boom towns sprang up.

The many mountain ranges in this part of the forest include the Paradise, Shoshone, Toiyabe, Toquima, and Monitor ranges. They were created by long blocks of the earth's crust being pushed and dropped together over thousands of years. The mountains provide rugged, rocky settings in the desert, with green oasis patches on the cooler, higher elevations.

Write to the Forest Supervisor, Toiyabe National Forest, 111 N. Virginia St., Reno 89504, for detailed information on the forest. Ranger Districts in the Central Nevada Division include the Tonopah Ranger District, P.O. Box 989, Tonopah 89040; Austin Ranger District, Austin 89310; and Fallon Ranger District, Fallon 89406. The *Toiyabe National Forest—Central Nevada Division Map* is available for 50¢ from the Forest Supervisor. It shows all roads and trails, recreation sites, ranger stations, and historic sites.

The Las Vegas Ranger District bears none of the familiar glitter and tinsel usually associated with the name. Instead, it offers abundant wildlife and vegetation and stunning desert scenery. It includes the Spring Mountain Range, standing out like a green oasis in the hot Nevada sun. The Anasazi Indians, who were the earliest inhabitants of this land, raised squash and corn in the Moapa Valley. They disappeared and were replaced by the Paiutes, whom the Spanish found when they came and explored the area. The Old Spanish Trail was one of the first routes to California. It was used by Capt. John C. Frémont and Kit Carson in 1844, when they were returning through the region from California on one of their many expeditions. The Mormons also came into the region to harvest timber in Kyle Canyon.

This is a fascinating area geologically. The highest mountain in the Spring Mountain Range, Charleston Peak, was once the floor of an ancient sea. Fossils of oyster and clam shells are found near the top of the 11,918-foot peak. The layers of rock folded, shifted, and faulted into the rugged cliffs and towers that exist today.

Deer, elk, an occasional antelope, and wild turkey are the major game species in this area. The high elevations provide many different life zones. Cactus, yucca, and creosote bush cover the desert floor. The gradual elevation begins to reveal juniper and piñon pines, and mountain mahogany and oakbrush appear further up the slope. The highest peaks abound with bromegrasses and wild strawberry, evergreens and aspen, chokeberry, and heart-leafed arnica.

The bristlecone pine, considered to be the oldest living thing in the world today, lives up on these rocky peaks. These twisted and gnarled veterans have adapted amazingly well to their somewhat harsh environment, growing rapidly in favorable years and remaining dormant in adverse years. Several specimens have been found which approach 5,000 years in age. Elk and deer also roam these high, rocky ranges.

The *Toiyabe National Forest—Las Vegas Ranger District Map* is available for 50¢ from: District Ranger, Las Vegas District, 1217 Bridger St., Las Vegas 89101. It shows all roads and trails, ranger stations, and recreation sites.

The Carson Ranger District bordering the eastern shoreline of Lake Tahoe received its towering, rugged appearance from millions of years of carving by drastic movements of the earth's crust, lava flows, and glaciers. Lake Tahoe is an example of a recent fault which created a huge basin. There are many scenic areas in the Carson District, laden with history and teeming with wildlife. Scenic Dog Valley was named after the packs of wild dogs that once roamed the area. The Grigsby-Ide Party, the first emigrant train to California, was followed by many other emigrants through the Carson District—including the Donner Party, which met with disaster. Mount Rose is the dominant peak over Lake Tahoe; it offers a spectacular view to those who climb to the top. It was named for Jacob Rose, who first brought Chinese laborers in from California to work in the mines. Lake Tahoe is one of the most scenic sites in the country, and the Tahoe Basin contains the Desolation Wilderness, accessible only by foot or horseback.

The *Toiyabe National Forest—Carson Ranger District Map* is available for 50¢ from: District Ranger, 1536 South Carson St., Carson City 89701. It shows all roads and trails, recreation sites, ranger stations, landmarks, and boat ramps.

Access and Outfitting Centers

The Central Nevada District is reached via U.S. 50 and Nevada State Highways 82, 91, and 89. The Las Vegas Ranger District is reached via Nevada State Highways 39 and 52. The Carson Ranger District is reached via U.S. Highways 50 and 395 and Nevada State Highways 57 and 28. Lodging, supplies, and outfitting services are available for the Toiyabe National Forest at Reno, Washoe City, Lake Tahoe, Genoa, Glenbrook, and Carson City.

ROCKY MOUNTAIN STATES

Introduction

The towering, snow-crowned peaks, glaciers, timberline tundra meadows and lakes, turbulent free-flowing streams, deep valleys, and cathederal-like forests of the Rocky Mountains—once the floor of a shallow sea that stretched from the Gulf of Mexico to the Arctic Ocean—sweep across the continent for 2,200 miles, through the United States and Canada from northern New Mexico to the Yukon Territory. The great Continental Divide winds along the backbone of the Rockies—actually a complex system of separate ranges broken by the Yellowstone Plateau and the Great Divide Basin in southern Wyoming—from Colorado northwest to the Peace River in British Columbia. Set among the craggy heights of the Rockies are several of the nation's truly great fishing, hunting, and wilderness camping areas.

In the Southern Rockies of Colorado and Utah, the mountains reach their greatest elevations and width—300 miles across. Colorado contains 46 snowcapped peaks exceeding 14,000 feet, culminating at Mount Elbert (14,431 ft.), the second-highest peak in the United States. The state's 104,247 square miles are bordered on the north by Wyoming and the Central Rockies, on the east by the Great Plains of Nebraska and Kansas, on the south by New Mexico, and on the west by Arizona and Utah. The Centennial State contains the Rocky Mountain headwaters of the historic Colorado, the "River of the Shining Mountains"; the beautiful Sangre de Cristo Range; the nationally renowned trophy trout waters of the upper North Platte, Yampa, Blue, Gunnison, Elk, South Platte, Animas, Michigan, Canadian, and Cache la Poudre rivers and creeks and the headwaters of the Rio Grande; the beautiful Indian Peaks wild country and Never Summer Range in Rocky Mountain National Park; the famous fishing, backpacking, and elk-hunting areas of the Grand Mesa high country and Flattops Primitive Area; and the remote fish and game lands of the Rocky Mountain high wilderness areas. The Colorado territory was first penetrated by Coronado in 1540, during his search for the fabled Seven Cities of Cibola. Fur traders and a host of explorers and surveyors followed, including Zebulon Pike, who in 1806 discovered the famous peak bearing his name while mapping the headwaters of the Arkansas River.

Utah, once the home and hunting grounds of the Ute Indians, and long called Deseret, which in the *Book of Mormon* means "land of the working bee," encompasses Great Salt Lake, a remnant of the ancient Lake Bonneville, arid deserts, vast colorful canyonlands, and the Wasatch and Uinta ranges of the Rocky Mountains. The Beehive State is bordered on the north by Idaho, on the west by Nevada and the Great Basin, on the south by Arizona, and on the east by Wyoming and Idaho. It contains within its boundaries the world-record trout waters of Flaming Gorge Reservoir, the alpine lakes and elk meadows of the High Uinta Primitive Area, the Green River Wilderness and Dinosaur National Park, the beautiful Fishlake Hightops, the trophy bass and trout waters of Lake Powell National Recreation Area, and the awesome pink, yellow, red, white, and black cliffs of Canyonlands National Park and the Colorado River. The first Americans to explore the Utah territory were the mountain men and fur traders of the Rocky Mountain Fur Company, including the legendary Jim Bridger, who is credited with the discovery of Great Salt Lake. The most famous settlers were the Mormons led by Brigham Young.

Wyoming's Central Rocky Mountains are one of North America's great trout-fishing, hunting, and wilderness vacation areas. Its high-country names are those of a legendary outdoor paradise: the Trois Tetons, Jackson Lake, Wind River Range, Beartooth High Lakes country, Teton Wilderness, Bighorn Mountains, Jackson Hole,

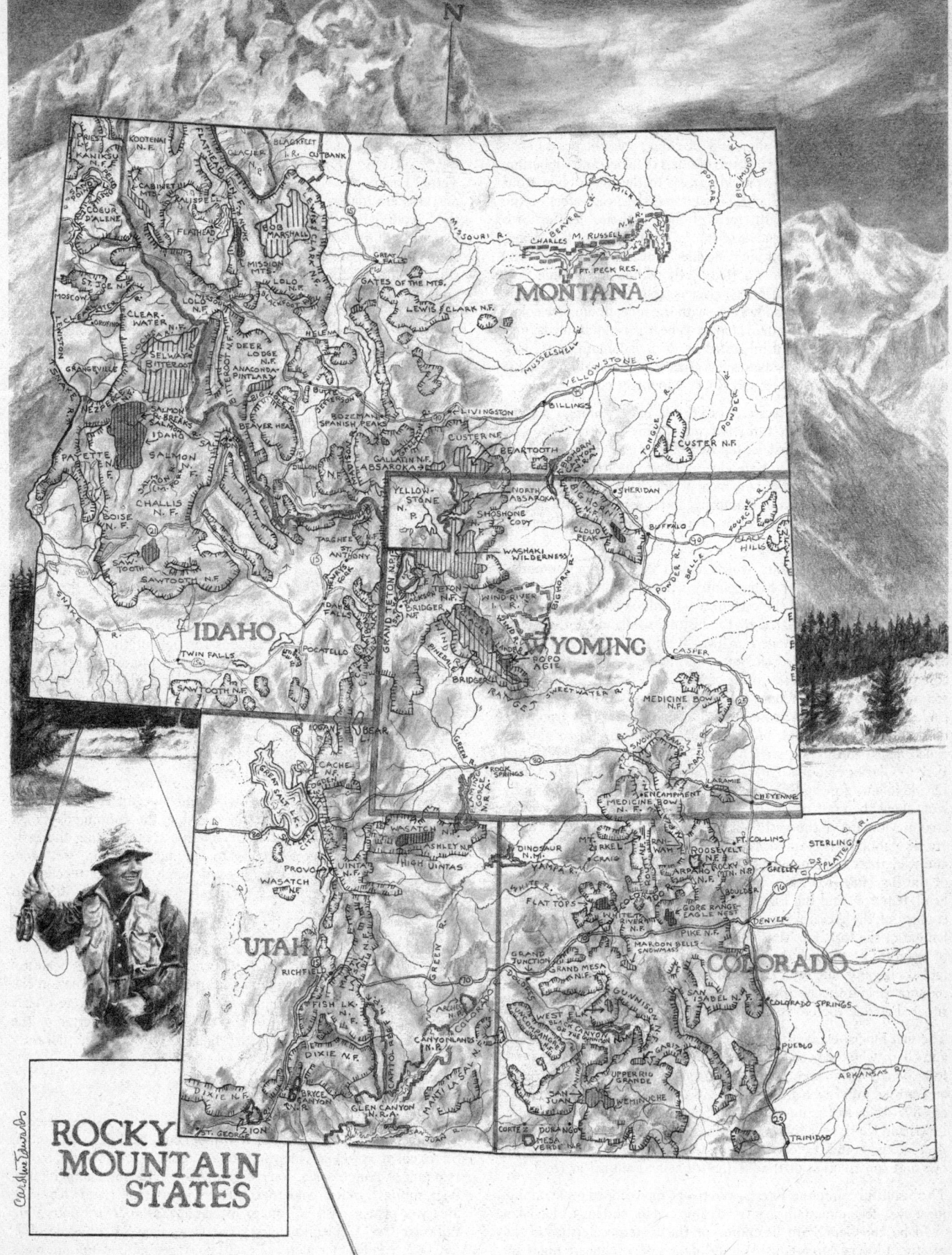

ROCKY
MOUNTAIN
STATES

Bridger Wilderness and Popo Agie Primitive Area, Medicine Bow Mountains and the Snow Range, Yellowstone National Park, Cloud Peak Wilderness, Wapiti Valley, and the craggy volcanic peaks of the massive Absaroka Range. Thousands of miles of hiking and timberline pack trails and forest roads provide access to the blue-ribbon trout waters of the upper Snake and Yellowstone, the headwaters of the Green, the North and South forks of the Shoshone; to the Gros Ventre wildlands; to the renowned trophy trout waters of the Wind, North Platte, Madison, Gardiner, Bechler, Gallatin and Bighorn rivers; and to remote wildlands dotted by thousands of sparkling blue lakes surrounded by jagged peaks, glaciers, fragrant spruce and pine forests, and lush alpine meadows alive with the brilliant rainbow colors of Indian paintbrush, mountain cranberry, bearberry, andromeda, rosy sedum and cassiopeia, and inhabited by deer, mountain lion, black bear, upland game birds, wolves, a few grizzly, and the nation's largest population of bighorn sheep and Rocky Mountain elk.

The Rockies cover the western two-thirds of Wyoming's 97,914 square miles; the eastern third is Great Plains country. The wild Wyoming frontier was first visited by the French explorers and fur traders François and Louis Verendrye; followed by the trapper John Colter, the legendary mountain men of the Rocky Mountain Fur Company and American Fur Company, and successive waves of government hunters and surveyors, adventurers, pioneers, cattlemen, and sheepherders.

Montana, the Treasure State, which adjoins Wyoming on the north, contains the magnificent high-country wilderness of the Northern Rockies in the west, and the eastern two-thirds of the state is part of the Great Plains, dominated by the historic wildlands of the upper Missouri River and the huge Fort Peck Reservoir surrounded by the elongated Charles M. Russell National Wildlife Refuge, a 1 million-acre preserve bordering 180 miles of the river's course, inhabited by sharp-tailed grouse, pronghorn antelope, peregrine falcon, osprey, bald eagle, bison, elk, Canada goose, and black-footed ferret. The backbone of the Northern Rockies, broken by deep luxuriant valleys (locally called holes) and basins, stretches north from Yellowstone National Park to Glacier National Park and the Alberta boundary. The Great Divide follows a meandering route north and south, turning abruptly west along the crest of the Bitterroot Mountains into Idaho, which adjoins Montana on the west. Within Montana's 147,138 square miles are several of North America's legendary fishing, big-game hunting, and wilderness camping areas, including the blue-ribbon trout waters of the Big Hole, Madison, Yellowstone, Beaverhead, Gallatin, Flathead, Jefferson, and Big Blackfoot rivers; the scenic, lake-dotted high country of the Absaroka and Beartooth primitive areas; the grizzly habitat of the vast Bob Marshall Wilderness; the trophy trout waters of beautiful Flathead Lake, known as the "gem of the Rockies"; the fabled big-game ranges of the Bearpaw, Mission, Cabinet, and Swan mountains; and the awesome scenic beauty of Glacier National Park, situated astride the crown of the Great Divide.

The first official exploration of the Montana Territory was by Lewis and Clark, who followed the Missouri up to the confluence of its three forks, where they ascended the Jefferson River to the Great Divide and crossed into Idaho at Lolo Pass during their epic overland journey of 1805–1806 to the mouth of the Columbia River and the Pacific. Lewis and Clark were followed by fur traders, missionaries, gold prospectors, and homesteaders, who were lured by the luxuriant hay meadows and construction of the Northern Pacific Railroad in 1883.

The beautiful coniferous forests, wild rivers, snowcapped peaks, alpine meadows, deep mountain valleys, volcanic craters, and huge blue lakes of Idaho, the Gem State, lie entirely on the western watershed of the Northern Rocky Mountains. Within Idaho's 83,557 square miles are several of the nation's great fishing, hunting, and unspoiled wilderness camping areas: the eerie volcanic lava flows and cinder cones of the "Craters of the Moon" in the southern plain; the blue-ribbon trout waters of Henrys Fork of the Snake and Henrys Lake country in the Teton Basin; the rugged Selway-Bitterroot Wilderness along the northeastern Idaho-Montana boundary; the interior wildlands around the Salmon River (the historic "River of No Return") in the Chamberlain Basin of the vast Idaho Primitive Area, an area several times larger than Switzerland, bounded on the south by the snowcapped crags of the Sawtooth Mountains and Sun Valley; the famous elk-hunting ranges and wild rivers of the Clearwater country north of the Salmon River, traversed east and west by the ancient Nez Percé hunting trail, known as the Lolo Trail, which was traveled by the Lewis and Clark expedition; and the great lakes region of the sparsely settled Northern Panhandle, dominated by the deep, clear trophy lake and rainbow trout waters of Pend Oreille, Priest, Coeur d'Alene, and Spirit lakes, dense boreal forests, and the rugged peaks of the Selkirk Mountains. Lewis and Clark were followed by fur traders of the Hudson's Bay Company (based at Lake Pend Oreille) and the Missouri Fur Company (based on Henrys Fork of the Snake), as well as by successive waves of mountain men, gold prospectors, and homesteaders via the Oregon Trail.

Weather, Bugs & Beasts

The mild, sunny summer months in the Rockies are punctuated by near-daily thunderstorms, which strike with intensity in the tundra country among the high peaks above timberline. Strong winds whistle through the mountain passes throughout the year, and sudden snow flurries can occur at high elevations throughout the summer. The moist westerly winds have dropped much of their moisture before they reach the Rockies, although the western slopes of the Great Divide receive considerable rain as the winds drop what moisture they hold during their ascent over the slopes. Many of the valleys, parks, and canyons, however, have near-desert conditions: Colorado's San Luis Valley receives about 6 inches of rain and snowfall a year; Idaho's Salmon River country, about 7 inches.

Most outdoor recreation in the high country begins about mid-July, depending on the level of the spring runoff, as the warming days melt the snow patches and begin to dry off the trails. During the early summer, clouds of mosquitoes swarm around the damp, wet high-country areas. Be sure to carry a good supply of insect repellent—Muskol, Mosquitone, Off!, or Cutters, all of which contain 50%-plus concentrations of DEET. The ideal months for travel in the Rocky Mountains are August and September, when the days are warm, the trails dry, the nights cool, and the mosquitoes diminishing in numbers and strength. The crisp golden days of early fall are the most beautiful and rewarding. Potential wildlife hazards include rattlesnakes in the arid, rocky low country, camp-invading black bears, the rare grizzly with cubs or a body wound in the remote wilderness areas of the Northern Rockies, and hot-blooded bull moose during the fall rut.

Rocky Mountain Maps & Charts—How to Order

The topographic map kits listed throughout the Rocky Mountain States chapters will provide you with a complete picture of the mountain ranges, remote lakes, trails, logging roads, streams, campgrounds, bogs, springs, glaciers, wilderness shelters, dams, rapids, and falls of the area you plan to visit. All maps listed (unless otherwise noted) are full-color U.S. Geological Survey overview maps with a scale of 1: 250,000, 4 miles to 1 inch ($2 each) or large-scale 7½-minute maps

and 15-minute maps ($1.25 each). These maps and free *Topographic Map Indexes* of Colorado, Utah, Wyoming, Montana, and Idaho may be ordered (along with a free *Map Symbol Chart* and *Topographic Maps* booklet) from: Distribution Branch, U.S. Geological Survey, Federal Center, Denver, CO 80225. Be sure to order the maps by their individual name (and indicate scale when ordering 1:250,000 scale maps); to expedite delivery, include extra money for first-class delivery.

Large, attractive U.S. Geological Survey *State Topographic Maps* and *State Shaded-Relief Maps* of Idaho, Montana, Wyoming, Utah, and Colorado are published with a scale of 1:500,000, or about 8 miles to 1 inch, and may be ordered for $2 each. Please note that the Montana topographic map consists of 2 sheets, and sells for $4 a set. The strikingly beautiful shaded-relief maps have colored shading that gives the maps a 3-dimensional appearance of the sunlight striking the surface from the northwest.

A useful 214-page handbook for wilderness travel, *Be Expert with Map & Compass,* by Bjorn Kjellstrom, the president and founder of Silva Compasses, may be obtained for $6.95 from: Charles Scribner's Sons, Bookstore Dept., 597 Fifth Ave., New York, NY 10017. Full-color *Plastic Raised-Relief Maps* of all 1:250,000 scale overview maps listed in the Rocky Mountain States section may be ordered for $11.95 each from: Hubbard Scientific Company, 1946 Raymond Dr., Northbrook, IL 60062 (a free catalog is available upon request). These useful maps provide an actual 3-dimensional model of the earth's surface and show all man-made and natural features.

IDAHO
ENCYCLOPEDIA

Accommodations—Rocky Mountain Vacation Lodges & Ranches

A free pamphlet, *Idaho Outfitters and Guides Association*, lists the names and addresses of members of the association and briefly describes their facilities and services. Many of these outfitters lead big-game hunting, fishing, pack, or float trips. Some own guest ranches and lodges which provide supplies, accommodations, and other tourist services. Others lead wilderness training courses. Most of the guides and outfitters provide all basic equipment from the association at P.O. Box 95, Boise 83701.

The Idaho Innkeepers Association has published a free directory of travel accommodations and recommended restaurants called *Idaho, The Place to Go.* It lists hotels, motels, and housekeeping units by city, and gives their locations, facilities, prices, and nearby recreation opportunities. Request a copy of it from: Division of Tourism and Industrial Development, Room 108, Capitol Bldg., Boise 83720. The pamphlet also describes each of the major regions of Idaho, provides an overview of recreation opportunities, and lists addresses where you may obtain additional travel information.

For listings and descriptions of the state's major lodges and guest ranches, see "Wilderness Outfitters, Guides, & Guest Ranches" in this section and the "Idaho Travel & Recreation Guide."

Aircraft—Wilderness Fly-in Services

A number of Idaho guides and outfitters operate fly-in services for hunting, fishing, or float expeditions. Some air services provide transportation to the starting point of your wilderness trip, with pick-up service at your base camp. Among them are: *Flying W Ranch,* Rex E. Lanham, Rt. 2, Box 242, Emmett 83617 (hunting and fishing); *Mackay Bar Lodge,* Drawer F, Suite 1010, One Capital Center, Boise 83702 (hunting, fishing, and float trips); *Sulfur Creek Ranch,* Box 131, Boise 83707 (hunting, riding, and fishing); *Pinnacle Ranch,* c/o Marty and Dorothy Rust, P.O. Box 8003, Boise 83707 (hunting, fishing, riding, and rock-hounding); *Valley Flying Service,* Challis Municipal Airport, Box 156, Challis 83226 (hunting, fishing, ski touring); *Boise Air Service,* Boise Municipal Airport, Boise 83701 (backcountry flying into all primitive areas); *Salmon Air Taxi,* P.O. Box 698, Salmon 83467 (hunting, boating, fishing); *Air Unlimited,* Box 656, Challis 83226 (hunting, fishing, float trips); *ACME Air Taxi,* Box 521, Salmon 83467 (hunting, fishing); *Gaige Aviation,* Boise Municipal Airport, Boise 83701 (flying to all backcountry fields); and *Teton Aviation,* Driggs 83422. Write to the individual outfitters and air services to find where they fly and what guide services and equipment they supply.

An *Idaho Airport Directory, Idaho Aeronautical Chart,* and other flight information are available from: State Department of Aeronautics, 2103 Airport Way, Boise 83705.

Camping & Backpacking

Whether you choose the stream-laced fields of the central valleys, the forests and lakes of the snowcapped northern mountains, or the white-water rivers and sage-covered plateaus of the south, scenic camping areas are plentiful in Idaho. There are clean, well-equipped recreation sites in every section of the state as well as undeveloped sites open to campers looking for a more secluded wilderness experience. In all, more than 2,800,000 acres have been set aside as wilderness and primitive areas.

The *Idaho Recreation Guide*, available from the Division of Tourism and Development for 50¢, lists and describes the public recreation sites, historic trails, national forests and parks, wilderness areas, and related recreational areas of the state. The guide has 22 full-color maps showing campgrounds and other recreational facilities accessible by road, trail, or boat. Send your order to: Tourism Division, State Capitol Building, Boise 83720.

If you plan to camp or hike in northern or southern Idaho, the free *National Forest Camp and Picnic Area Guides* for the northern and intermountain regions will be helpful. These directories list developed camp and picnic grounds, boat-launching sites, and beaches in the forests of northern and southern Idaho. The guides identify the facilities available at all the camp and recreation sites and give the access roads to them. For your copies, write: U.S. Forest Service, Northern Region Federal Building, Missoula, MT 59801, or Intermountain Region, 324 25th Street, Ogden, Utah 84401.

There are seven national forests in southern Idaho, including the Caribou, Boise, Challis, Targhee, Sawtooth, Salmon, and Payette. The Forest Service provides a free directory to the recreation sites in these forests entitled *A Guide to National Forest Recreation in Southern Idaho.* The directory lists all recreation sites in the forests, including campgrounds and picnic areas, and describes the available facilities, recreational opportunities (hunting, fishing, etc.), and special features nearby for each site. Small maps throughout the guide key the locations of these sites. For a copy, write: Forest Service, Intermountain Region (address above).

The Division of Tourism and Industrial Development publishes a comprehensive overview of the state's outdoor recreation opportunities in its *Idaho Parks and Outdoor Recreation Guide*, a map and guide brochure which lists and keys the state's campgrounds, parks, rivers, rock-hound areas, lakes, and other features. The guide lists campgrounds and recreation sites by region in state parks, national forests, and other public lands. Write: Division of Tourism and Industrial Development, State Capitol Building, Boise 83720. A listing of Bureau of Land Management recreation area campgrounds may be obtained by writing: B.L.M., Federal Bldg., 550 W. Fort Street, Boise 83720.

If you plan to journey into the backcountry, write to the superintendent of the national forest or primitive area where you plan to go for a listing of trails and primitive camping areas. A good pamphlet on this subject entitled *Leading a Back Country Outing* is available free from: Forest Service, Intermountain Region, 324 25th St., Ogden, Utah 84401. The pamphlet gives important tips on leadership of backcountry parties, equipment, food emergencies, immunization, clothing and footwear, backcountry manners, and first aid.

Canoeing & Wild Rivers

The rivers of Idaho offer a wide variety of canoeing opportunities. Because two-thirds of the state is public land, access to the rivers is no problem. Campgrounds and facilities lie along the rivers in national forests. One river, the Middle Fork of the Salmon, has limitations on float trip usage. Before you set out for a canoeing expedition, however, check at one of the six Fish and Game Regional Offices, located at Coeur d'Alene, Lewiston, Boise, Jerome, Pocatello, and Idaho Falls, for current water conditions.

All of the major river systems in Idaho offer areas of good canoeing waters. These river systems, from north to south and east, include: the Kootenai, Pend Oreille, Spokane, Clearwater, Salmon, Weiser, Payette, Boise, Lost, Henrys Fork, Snake, Bruneau, Owyhee, Wood, Raft, and Bear. *Canoe Waters of Idaho*, a guide describing the areas of these rivers most suitable for canoeing, is available free from: Idaho Department of Fish and Game, P.O. Box 25, 600 South Walnut, Boise 83707.

Experienced guides lead expeditions down the wild rivers of the state, making trips safer and more enjoyable. For a complete free listing of outfitters and guides in the state, write: Idaho Outfitters and Guides Association, P.O. Box 95, Boise 83701. For more information, see also "Wilderness Outfitters, Guides & Guest Ranches," "Wild & Scenic River Maps," and the "Travel & Recreation Guide" section.

Craters of the Moon National Monument

The eerie, blackened landscape of the Craters of the Moon National Monument bears testimony to a violent geologic past. Cinder cone–studded lava fields stretch across the face of south central Idaho; the monument itself is part of a 200,000-square-mile lava field stretching westward to the Columbia Plateau. The 83 square miles of the monument were formed less than 2,000 years ago, when lava boiling at 2,000°F poured forth from thousands of fissures in the earth. The lava floods destroyed all vegetation and left the land so barren that only a few of the hardiest plants could survive. Today, however, more than 200 plants are native to the area, including sagebrush, antelope bitterbrush, and mock orange. Wildflowers burst into bloom in the spring, lacing the blackened earth with magenta, yellow, and pink. Caves, natural bridges, terraces, and piles of stone add to the grotesquerie and unearthly splendor of the monument.

Sixty-eight square miles of the weird and fantastic formations of the Craters of the Moon are inaccessible by road—one of the four designated wildernesses in the National Park System. This is true wilderness, cut only by three short trails (aside from deer trails). Maps and compasses are a necessity, as is a topographical map of the area (available at the visitor center). Permits are required. Bring your own water into this extremely dry area, and remember to wear sturdy shoes. In the summer, temperatures reach the 90s; in the winter they fall below zero.

The wilderness is never more beautiful than in the winter, when snow transforms the eerie shapes and carpets the rocky lava surface. Snowshoeing and cross-country skiing are among the best ways to experience this strange land.

There are no motel, hotel, or eating accommodations at the monument. The nearest towns are Arco (pop. 1,500), 18 miles to the east, and Carey (pop. 750), 24 miles to the west. For more information about the Craters of the Moon National Monument, write: National Park Service Office, Craters of the Moon National Monument, Arco 83213.

A 24 × 33 inch U.S. Geological Survey topographical map of the monument on a scale of 2 inches to 1 mile is available for $2 from: Branch of Distribution, U.S. Geological Survey, Federal Center, Denver, CO 80225.

Fishing & Hunting in Idaho

Few states in the Union have more to offer in quality hunting and fishing and remote, scenic high-country wilderness areas than Idaho. This beautiful state, whose name is said to be a contraction of the Shoshone Indian words *Ee-dah-how*, meaning the "sun is coming down the mountains" and often incorrectly translated as "gem of the mountains," is a patchwork of topographic regions, containing parts of the Middle and Northern Rocky Mountains, the Great Basin, and the Columbia Plateau. A slice of the Continental Divide separates Idaho from southwestern Montana, while a segment of the Snake River forms part of the state's boundaries with Oregon and Washington.

All of central Idaho and most of the northern Panhandle are covered by the Northern Rockies; a slender wedge of the Middle Rockies is found along the Idaho-Wyoming border. The mountainous Panhandle is densely forested and strewn with lakes left when glaciers melted thousands of years ago. The central wilderness of Idaho, bounded on the east by the Bitterroot Range and on the west by the Seven Devils Mountains, contains some 20 of Idaho's 81 distinct mountain ranges and is covered by rugged, primitive terrain similar to that found in Alaska. South of this area is the huge, crescent-shaped Snake River Plain, built up by basaltic lava flows, which are visible on the surface in such areas as the Craters of the Moon National Monument. Along most of the Utah-Idaho border is a small triangular section of the Great Basin. The southern mountains area, bordering Wyoming and covering the southern extremity of the state, includes such mountains as the Bannock and Wasatch ranges, interrupted by deep valleys, grasslands, plateaus, and small lakes.

The Snake River flows east to west through the southern part of the state, coursing through North America's deepest gorge (1 mile), Hells Canyon, and magnificent Shoshone Falls. The major tributary of the Snake, the Salmon River, drains the Chamberlain Basin in the central wilderness. A fisherman's paradise, Idaho contains over 2,000 natural lakes.

Prevailing winds from the Pacific bring moist, warm air over most of the northern third of Idaho, and the mountains to the east tend to hold back the cold winter air from Montana and Wyoming. The high mountain areas are extremely cold in winter, but very few of the larger towns have more than 10 days of zero weather. Summer temperatures in the major urban centers average 75°F at Lewiston and Boise and 70° in Coeur d'Alene. The January mean in these areas varies from 27° to 30°. Rainfall averages 30 inches annually in the northern Panhandle and a scant 10 inches on the arid Snake River Plain. The high mountain regions receive abundant snowfall, sometimes exceeding 200 inches annually.

Big-Game & Upland Game Bird Hunting

Big-game hunting in the vast national forest lands is renowned for elk, mule, and whitetail deer, and to a lesser degree for mountain goat, antelope, black bear, and a few moose. Mule deer are especially numerous in the rugged Chamberlain Basin and Selway-Bitterroot Primitive Area, as well as along the Middle Fork of the Salmon River and the headwaters of the Payette and Boise rivers, and in the Kaniksu and Priest river areas in the northern Panhandle. Moose (an Indian word for "twig eater") are found primarily in the Lochsa and Selway rivers area in the north and in the Island Park area west of Yellowstone National Park. Idaho is one of the top elk-hunting states in the country. Elk herds are most numerous in the Clearwater, Selway, Lochsa, and St. Joe river regions in the north, and in the Chamberlain Basin. Elk are found along the Boise and Payette rivers and in the Seven Devils Mountains area. Antelope are found in the Pahsimeroi Valley and in the southwest corner of Owyhee County. Mountain goats are plentiful throughout the Selkirk Mountains, in the Selway and Lochsa river high country, in the Bitterroot Mountains, and up in the highlands of the Middle Fork of the Salmon. Rocky Mountain bighorn sheep are found in greatest numbers along the Middle Fork of the Salmon, particularly in the Camas Creek, Loon Creek, and Big Creek areas. Mountain lion are most numerous in the Priest Lake region and in the country around the Selway, Middle Fork of the Salmon, and Payette rivers. Black bear are fairly common throughout all national forests except those in the extreme south. A few protected grizzlies roam in the remote high country of the Selway-Bitterroot Wilderness and in the Selkirk Mountains north of Priest Lake.

Chief among the upland game birds is the ring-necked pheasant, which is common to the farmlands. This handsome bird, eagerly sought by the Idaho sportsman, is invaluable as a destroyer of insects. Big blue, or Franklin, grouse and ruffed and spruce grouse are found in the foothills and mountains of the state's evergreen forestlands. Other upland game birds popularly hunted in the state include the Hungarian and chukar partridge; Gambels, California, and mountain quail; mourning dove; Merriam's turkey; and sage and sharptail grouse. The large rivers and lakes in Idaho offer excellent fall shooting for Canada geese, mallards, and several other species, including the handsome canvasback and green-winged teal. The greatest migration concentration areas in the state include the American Falls Reservoir near Pocatello, Deer Flat Wildlife Management Area, C. J. Strike Reservoir, Hagerman, Camas, North Lake and Minidoka areas in the southern portion of the state and along the lower Coeur d'Alene River, Pend Oreille River, Round Lake, and the Benewah-Chatcolet and Hoodoo areas.

Wild Rivers, Lakes & Streams

Idaho's thousands of remote blue high-mountain lakes, wild rivers, and great northern lakes, such as Pend Oreille, Priest, and Coeur d'Alene, are world-famous for thriving populations of rainbow, cutthroat, brook, brown, Dolly Varden, lake, and golden trout. Idaho's northern lakes, renowned for the spectacular scenic beauty of their sparkling blue waters and evergreen-clad shores backed by snowcapped peaks, have produced several record trout. Pend Oreille Lake was the home of the world-record 32-pound Dolly Varden and 37-pound Kamloops rainbow trout. Beautiful Priest Lake in the majestic Selkirk Mountains, north of Pend Oreille Lake, has produced lake trout up to 57 pounds and is justly famous for the large number of Mackinaw in the 20–45 pound range taken there each year. The diversity and quality of the fishing is underscored by the Idaho all-time record fish.

IDAHO RECORD FISH

	Lb.–oz.	Place	Year
Mackinaw (lake trout)	57–6	Priest Lake	1971
Kamloops trout	37	Pend Oreille Lake	1947
Rainbow trout	19	Hayden Lake	1947
Steelhead trout	30–2	Clearwater River	1973
Cutthroat trout	18–15	Bear Lake	1970
Cutthroat-rainbow	23–4	Blackfoot Res.	1957
Brook trout	6–12¾	Henrys Lake	1972
Brown trout	25–12	Palisades Res.	1969
Dolly Varden	32	Pend Oreille Lake	1949
Golden trout	5–2	White Sands Lake	1958
Chinook salmon	45	Salmon River	1964
Coho salmon	4–10	Brown Lee Res.	1977
Sockeye salmon	5	Redfish Lake	1970
Kokanee salmon*	6–9¾	Priest Lake	1975
Sturgeon	394	Snake River	1956
Smallmouth bass	6–13	Brown Lee Res.	1978
Largemouth bass	10–15	Anderson Lake	—

*World's record.

The state's finest steelhead and salmon fishing is found along the Clearwater and Salmon river systems in central Idaho. The Island Park area in the Targhee National Forest is a renowned trout-fishing region, particularly in the insect-rich waters of Henrys Lake, Island Park Reservoir, and the Henrys Fork of the Snake River. For more detailed information about the state's fish and game areas and map coverage, see the "Idaho Travel and Recreation Guide." Write to the Idaho Dept. of Fish & Game, P.O. Box 25, Boise 83707, for fishing and hunting seasons, regulations, special permits, *Wildlife Management Area Maps, Public Access Areas, Hunting Zone Maps,* and the useful, free guides *Hunting & Fishing in Idaho* and *Idaho Lakes & Reservoirs,* which provide detailed info, such as access, fish species present, campsites, and facilities for over 200 lakes, including Coeur d'Alene, Priest, Bear, Blackfoot, Hayden, Pend Oreille, and Spirit. The Dept. of Fish & Game also publishes an invaluable free guide, *Mountain Lakes of Idaho,* which contains detailed descriptions and access and fishing info for the Selkirk Mountains, Sleeping Deer area, Cabinet Mountains, Surveyors Ridge area, Five Lake Butte area, Selway Crags, Buffalo Hump area, Seven Devils area, Bighorn Crags, White Cloud Peaks, Cooper Basin, and Big Wood River headwaters.

Good highways and forest service roads provide automobile access to all parts of Idaho. Air service is available on a scheduled or a charter basis. Charter pilots are experienced and familiar with remote, backcountry airfields used as jumping-off points to the wilderness fishing and hunting areas. The state has about 180 licensed outfitters and 220

guides for fishing trips and big-game hunting in season. Hunters are not required by Idaho law to hire outfitters or guides, but they generally prove invaluable to nonresidents. Some game management units lie partly or completely within federal wilderness or primitive areas. Motorized travel is prohibited within those areas, except for aircraft using established landing fields. Otherwise, travel is restricted to foot, horseback, boat, and float raft. (For detailed fishing and hunting info, see the "Idaho Travel & Recreation Guide" and "Wilderness Outfitters, Guides & Guest Ranches" in this section.)

Hells Canyon–Seven Devils Scenic Area

The 130,000-acre Hells Canyon–Seven Devils Scenic Area straddles the Snake River Canyon on the Idaho-Oregon border. Ninety-seven thousand of these acres lie within Idaho. This land is within the borders of the Nez Percé, Payette, and Wallowa-Whitman national forests. The Seven Devils Mountains of this area take their name from the legend of an Indian brave who became lost among the jagged peaks and encountered seven demons before he found his way back to his tribe. The volcanic mountain range reaches heights of over 8,000 feet. Hells Canyon cuts through the range to a depth of 7,900 feet from He Devil Peak; it is the deepest and narrowest gorge on the North American continent. In some areas the canyon walls are richly hued in red, orange, and yellow.

Much of the area is accessible only by river or trail. Many of the trails lead up into the high country of the Devils, where you can see miles of Oregon, Washington, Idaho, and Montana stretching before you. The white waters of the Snake in this area are wild, comparable in volume and gradient with the Cataract, Marble, and Grand canyons of the Colorado or the Hells Half Mile–Disaster Falls rapids of the Green. Unless you are a highly skilled white-water runner, hire a licensed guide or outfitter to take you down the rapids, and let the area Forest Ranger know of your plans. Wild Sheep rapids and Granite Creek rapids are extremely dangerous for boating, and amateurs should remember that chances of resuming in case of upset are poor.

The Sheepeaters, Paiutes, and Nez Percé Indians were among those who inhabited these lands before the arrival of white men. During the Nez Percé War of 1877, Chief Tu-hul-hut-sut led these Indians in the

struggle to retain their lands. He later joined Chief Joseph and died in Montana in the last battle in the Little Bear Mountains. Today little is left of these civilizations and those before them, but the artifacts and petroglyphs along the Snake River Canyon still remain.

The mountains where the Indians fished and hunted still yield a variety of wildlife. The high mountain lakes (about 7,000 ft.) east of the river in Idaho offer cutthroat, Dolly Varden, rainbow, and brook trout. Horse feed is scarce at these elevations, and the area is open to

recreational use only during the months of July, August, and September. The Snake River is another good angling spot for some of the above-mentioned trout, in addition to sturgeon, chinook salmon, channel catfish, and smallmouth bass. Elk, mule deer, mountain goat, white-tailed deer, bear, cougar, and bobcat inhabit the area. Bald and golden eagles, vultures, and owls are often sighted among the peaks. Game birds include blue, Franklin, and ruffed grouse; chukar and Hungarian partridge; turkey; and California and mountain quail.

A free *Hells Canyon–Seven Devils Map-Brochure* is available from: Northern Region Headquarters, Forest Service, Federal Building, Missoula, MT 59801. The map, on a scale of about 2 miles to 1 inch, shows highways, roads, trails, recreation sites, natural features, and forest service stations. The brochure describes the location of and facilities at each of the recreation sites in the area. The Hells Canyon–Seven Devils Scenic Area is shown on the large-scale U.S. Geological Survey maps of Cuprum and He Devil.

Highways—Recreation and Scenic Routes

A free full-color *Highway Map of Idaho* is published by the Idaho Department of Transportation, P.O. Box 7129, Boise 83707. The map shows highways and roads (including paved, improved, and unimproved roads), major geographical features, cities and towns, rest areas and interchanges, points of interest, winter sports areas, campsites, time zone lines, state parks and recreation areas, state monuments and historic sites, and historic trails, including the Lewis & Clark trail, Mullan Road, Lolo Trail, Nez Percé and Oregon trails, and Lander and Kettan roads. The map also lists the state parks and recreation areas and the facilities available at each, and gives camping fees and hunting and fishing license fees. A smaller, simplified map shows historic, geological, and recreational sites throughout the state.

Lolo—Great Nez Percé Hunting Trail

The Idaho section of the historic Lolo Trail extends westward through the beautiful high-country wildlands of the Clearwater National Forest for about 90 miles, from 5,187-foot Lolo Pass over the Bitterroot Mountains to the village of Weippe, adjacent to the Nez Percé Indian Reservation located due east of Lewiston and the Snake River. A dim trail through a primeval land, this east-west route follows the ancient Nez Percé hunting trail, traveled over the ages by the Nez Percé Indians from their homeland on the Columbia River through the Northern Rockies for 250 miles to the buffalo-hunting grounds of the Missouri River in the Deer Lodge Valley of Montana. In 1805, Lewis and Clark used the trail and pass to cross the rugged Bitterroot Range on their epic westward journey to the mouth of the Columbia River on the Pacific Ocean. The legendary Sacajawea (Indian for "boatpusher") led them through this wilderness on her own journey home from the Crows, who had stolen her many years earlier. On their return from the Pacific, Lewis and Clark retraced the path, living off the wild berries and game, including deer, crawfish, salmon, trout, and an occasional stray Indian horse.

The hostile Nez Percé, under Chief Joseph, traveled the Lolo Trail on their famous trek of 1877. Some 700 Indians with several thousand horses left their homeland by way of this trail, followed by Gen. O. O. Howard's army with artillery and supply trains. Today the Lewis and Clark Highway (U.S. 12) parallels the historic trail for about 4 miles west of the Montana line. The major features of the Lolo Trail and the surrounding wilderness camping areas are shown on the *Lewis & Clark Trail Map-Brochure*, available free, along with detailed trail info for backpackers, from: Supervisor's Office, Clearwater National Forest, Orofino 83544. Additional information about the trail and historic sites on it may be obtained by writing: Superintendent, Nez Percé National Historical Park, P.O. Box 93, Spalding 83551. The Lolo Trail is shown on the U.S. Geological Survey 1:250,000 scale map of Hamilton.

The Nez Percé National Historical Park contains 23 historic sites, including the Lolo Trail, scattered over 12,000 square miles of northern Idaho. The major historical sites, shown on the free *Nez Percé National Historical Park* brochure (write to Superintendent's Office, above), include the Musselshell Meadow, one of the last active gathering spots of wild camas for the Indians; Weippe Prairie; Canoe Camp, where Lewis and Clark camped in the autumn of 1805 and built canoes and cached their supplies, and from where they headed down the Clearwater River to the Snake; the Pacific Fur Company Post, established in 1812; Lewis & Clark Long Camp, site of the expedition's month-long encampment on the banks of the South Fork of the Clearwater River during the spring of 1806 on the homeward journey;

and the Whitebird Battlefield, where the Nez Percé defeated one-third of General Howard's troops in the opening engagement of the Nez Percé War. There is a free guide to these areas, describing the locations, access, operating schedules, uphill facilities, maximum vertical drops, teaching facilities, lodging, and other services. It is available by writing to: Division of Tourism, Statehouse, Boise 83720.

Selway-Bitterroot Wilderness

This rugged mountain territory straddling the Montana-Idaho border is the largest federally classified wilderness in the continental United States. It covers more than 1.25 million acres. The Selway (from the Nez Percé Indian word *Selwah*, meaning "smooth water"), Bitterroot, and Lochsa rivers wind through the Bitterroot Range here, at the lower elevations. In the higher reaches of the mountains, sparkling snow-fed lakes dot the wilderness in cirques carved by ancient glaciers.

Most of the trails follow stream bottoms at the lower elevations. Some of them were made by Indians who fished here for the abundant ocean-run salmon and steelhead trout before the first white men arrived. The spectacular scenery of the high country rewards those who make the effort of cross-country travel. The best season for visiting the high country is from mid-July through September, although cross-country ski touring is becoming popular in snow months. The lower elevations are snow-free from mid-March through November. The wilderness lies on both sides of the rugged Bitterroot Range, which forms the border between Idaho and northwest Montana and includes some of the toughest mountain terrain in the world, with thousands of high peaks, steep valleys, deep forests, and wild rivers. This is prime chinook country; salmon to 45 pounds are caught in the Selway, Clark Fork, Lochsa, and Middle and North forks of the Clearwater. Numerous trails lead to remote areas with such colorful names as Grizzly Saddle, Otter Butte, Sneakfoot Meadows, and Wahoo Pass. The hardy outdoorsman who is looking for a remote alpine fishing and big-game area should explore the scenic Selway Crags, located in the heart of the Clearwater River drainage between the Lochsa and Selway rivers. Access is by way of the Fenn Ranger Station above the mouth of the Selway, where a steep road winds its way up to the Big Fog Saddle. Old Indian trails at Big Fog lead into the lake basin area. Brook and cutthroat trout fishing is good in Old Man, Legend, Big Fog, Lone Creek, Florence, and Lizard Creek lakes. During the summer months the scenery is stunning; wildflowers and rose heather carpet the meadows and slopes. Be sure to check trail conditions with the District Forest Service Ranger on arrival. The wilderness has one of the country's largest elk herds, as well as moose, sheep, deer, and black bear.

The Selway River is recognized as one of the most challenging small rivers for white-water runners. Many of its rapids are rated as Class IV (very difficult) and above. Schedule float trips for May through July, because low water prevents continuous floating at other times. If you wish to hire a guide, contact the *Idaho Outfitters and Guides Association*, Box 95, Boise 83701, or *Bitterroot Outfitters and Guides*, Sula, MT 59871.

For a *Selway Bitterroot Wilderness Map-Brochure* (50¢), write: Forest Supervisor, Bitterroot National Forest, 316 N. Third Street, Hamilton, MT 59840. The map, on a scale of 4 miles to 1 inch, shows highways and roads, trails, roads to entrance points, ranger stations, recreation sites, and heliports. The brochure gives information on using the wilderness area and preparing for your trip, and lists additional sources of information.

The U.S. Geological Survey topographical map of the region is Hamilton, on a scale of 1:250,000.

Ski Touring in the Idaho Rockies

Idaho's mountain valleys and vast national forests and wilderness areas offer some of the finest opportunities for ski touring and winter camping in the nation. Scores of ski touring areas dot the northern and southeastern regions of the state. One of the oldest and most famous of these is the Sun Valley area (see the "Idaho Travel & Recreation Guide" section). The Division of Tourism (Statehouse, Boise 83720) publishes a free guide to these areas. It describes locations, access, lodging, and instruction services. First-class accommodations in the Sun Valley area are provided by *Sun Valley Lodge*, *Sun Resorts*, and *Tamarack Lodge*, all Sun Valley 83353. For detailed information and literature on lodging, instruction, and trails in the Sun Valley area, write: *Nordic Ski Center*, Box 272, Sun Valley 83353 (phone: 208–622–4111). For detailed information on winter lodging in the national forests, write to the vacation ranches and lodges listed under "Wilderness Outfitters, Guides & Guest Ranches" in this section and throughout the "Idaho Travel & Recreation Guide."

A free *National Forest Ski Guide* describing Idaho's forest service ski touring areas—including the Lost Trail Ski Area in the Bitterroot National Forest and the Schweitzer and Chewelah basins in the Kaniksu National Forest—may be obtained by writing: U.S. Forest Service, Northern Region, Federal Bldg., Missoula, MT 59801. The Northern Region Office also publishes several useful, free booklets: *General Bibliography of Ski Touring Literature*, *Avalanche*, *Four Lines of Defense Against Hypothermia*, and *Winter Travel in the National Forests*.

Snake River Birds of Prey Natural Area

The Snake River Birds of Prey Natural Area covers 31,000 acres of the Snake River Canyon surrounded by deserts and fields in southwestern Idaho. The canyon's pinnacles and rocky ledges attract more raptorial (meat-eating) birds than any other area of similar size in the country. Eagles, ospreys, falcons, owls, and hawks glide the canyons and hunt the fields. Of these magnificent birds, the golden eagle and the prairie falcon are the most abundant.

Near the river grow willow rushes and other water plants. Further away from the banks through the desert and fields, shrubs and grasses predominate. The birds of prey compete with coyotes and bobcats for the rodents and rabbits on which they feed. The golden eagles and great horned owls occupy the area year-round. Prairie falcons arrive late in February, after the owls and eagles have begun to nest. Most wintering raptors arrive earlier, in November or December. The American rough-legged hawk, which nests far to the north in Canada and Alaska, occupies this area in January, as do sparrow hawks, North American falcons, goshawks, bald eagles, and ospreys.

The birds of prey share their nesting grounds here with a variety of other wildlife, including mule deer, beaver, mink, waterfowl, and a variety of smaller birds. All of the raptors are completely protected under the Migratory Bird Treaty Act, the Bald Eagle Protection Act, and the Endangered Species Act. No discharging of firearms is allowed here between March 1 and August 31.

The communities of Boise, Nampa, Grand View, and Bruneau offer accommodations near the area. There are campsites at Bruneau Sand Dunes State Park and at the C. J. Strike Cove Site Recreation Area between Grand View and Bruneau. Summers here are hot, often reaching to 100° or more. During the winter the temperatures rarely drop below zero.

Although most visitors come to the area to see the birds, it is also used by hunters and fishermen. A free *Snake River Birds of Prey Natural Area Map* shows each of the species of the area in full color and describes them in detail. The map shows roads, power lines, historic trails, canyon rims, and springs. For the map brochure or other information about the area, write: Manager, Birds of Prey Natural Area, Boise District Office, Bureau of Land Management, U.S. Department of the Interior, 230 Collins Road, Boise 83702. The natural area is shown on the following large-scale U.S. Geological Survey maps: Walters Butte, Initial Point, Coyote Butte, Sinker Butte, Wild Horse Butte, Castle Butte, Jackass Butte, Dorsey Butte, Vinson Wash, Grand View.

Wild & Scenic River Maps

Beautiful western white-water maps published by the renowned map maker Leslie Allen Jones, Star Rt. Box 13, Heber City, Utah 84032, may be purchased for the *Hells Canyon of the Snake* ($11.50 waterproof, $2.50 paper), *Middle Fork of the Salmon* ($11 waterproof, $3.50 paper), *Main Salmon River* ($17 waterproof, $5 paper), and the *Selway, Lochsa* and *Clearwater* (each $12 waterproof and $4 paper). These useful scroll maps show river gradient, falls, rapids, and canyons and contain interesting notes about the rivers' geology and history. The *Bruneau Wild & Scenic River*, located in the southwest corner of the state is shown on the following large-scale U.S. Geological Survey maps: Mouth of Bruneau, Bruneau (7.5), Sugar Valley, Hot Spring, Winter Camp. For additional listings, see the "Travel & Recreation Guide" section.

Wilderness Outfitters, Guides & Guest Ranches

Whether you plan to make a white-water or steelhead fishing trip down the Salmon or a hunting and packhorse expedition into the mountains of the northern region, there are scores of experienced guides and outfitters in Idaho to provide you with lodging and the needed wilderness supplies and lead you through the backcountry. A comprehensive guide to all licensed outfitters and guides is the 64-page

MIDDLE FORK of the SALMON

U.S. DEPARTMENT OF AGRICULTURE · FOREST SERVICE · INTERMOUNTAIN REGION · OGDEN, UTAH

Idaho Outfitters and Guides Association Catalog, available from that group at Box 95, Boise 83701. Additional information on professional river guides may be obtained by writing to: *Western River Guides Association,* 904 Denver St., Salt Lake City, UT 84111. The high country ranches listed below offer vacation lodging in addition to their outfitting and guide services, and will provide literature and rates on request.

Among the major outfitters in the northern portion of the state is the *Lochsa River Outfitters,* a guide and outfitting service for fishing and big-game hunting expeditions in the Selway and Lochsa river country, based at *Cool Water Ranch,* Kooskia 83539. The *Flying W Ranch,* run by Rex E. Lanham, Rt. 2, Box 242, Emmett 83617, is a guide and outfitter for big-game hunting and fishing with fly-in or pack-in services and lodging in the heart of the Idaho Primitive Area. *Mackay Bar Lodge,* also in the Primitive Area, offers float trips as well as fish and game expeditions. Write to Drawer F, Suite 1010, 1 Capital Center, Boise 83702. *Triangle C Ranch,* Cliff and Nancy Cummings, Box 1187, North Fork 83466, offers float trips on the Middle Fork of the Salmon, big-game hunting, and winter sports. In the Selway-Bitterroot area, the *Nitz Brothers Outfitters* lead big-game hunting and fishing trips. They are based at Elk City 83525. *Gillihan's Guide Service,* Rt. 2, Box 242, Emmett 83617, leads fishing trips to the high mountain lakes of the state, scenic trail rides, and big-game hunts. Stanton C. Miller leads backpacking, steelhead and salmon fishing, and float trips down the wild Selway, Snake, Owyhee, and Middle Fork and Main Salmon rivers. Write for more information to: *Primitive Area Float Trips, Inc.,* Box 585, Salmon 83467. Another Salmon River country outfitter-guide is *Nez Percé Outfitters and Guides,* P.O. Box 1454-A, Salmon 83467. They lead pack as well as float trips. Eldon Handy's *Salmon River Expeditions* also include trips down the Hells Canyon of the Snake. They may be contacted at Box 015, Jerome 83338.

Western River Expeditions offers float trips down the Selway, Middle Fork of the Salmon, and the Main Salmon. Write to: P.O. Box 5339, Salt Lake City, UT 84106. *Ken Wolfinbarger* of North Star Ranch offers hunting trips in the Selway-Bitterroot Wilderness. Write to him at Box 65, Darby, MT 59829. The *Quarter Circle A Outfitters* lead hunting trips both on the Selway and along the Middle and Main forks of the Salmon. Write to them c/o Rick Hussey, Star Rt., Salmon 83467.

In Caribou National Forest, the *Revell Ranch* offers fishing and hunting. Write to P.O. Box 674, Soda Springs 83276. A smaller ranch, the *Indian Guest Ranch,* located 10 miles down the Salmon from North Fork, offers lodging and fishing, hiking, and riding. Write to Jack or Lois Briggs, Box 1089, Salmon 83467. *Bob and Ken Smith,* Box 1185, North Fork 83466, are also located near the Salmon. They lead float trips on the Salmon and the Snake, as does *Everett Spaulding,* Box 302, Lewiston 83501.

The *Allison Ranch,* 5727 Hill Rd., Boise 83707, offers fishing, swimming, accommodations, and on-site recreation facilities in the Idaho Primitive Area along the Middle Fork of the Salmon. The *Devil's Bedstead Guest Ranch* in the White Cloud Mountains area offers pack trips, 30 trout lakes, 200 miles of trout streams, and luxury accommodations. Write: Box 328, Mackay 83251. *River Adventures West,* P.O. Box 5219, Santa Monica, CA 90405, leads trips down the Middle Fork and Main Salmon. *Wilderness World,* 1342 Jewell Avenue, Pacific Grove, CA 93950, also offers Salmon River trips, and leads float trips down Hells Canyon.

Boulder Creek Pack Camp offers big-game expeditions and fishing and photography trips in the Selway-Bitterroot Wilderness. For information, write: Herman Kuykendall, Rt. 1, Box 12, Peck 83545. *Fog Selway Mountain Outfitters* also offers services in the Selway-Bitterroot Wilderness, including float trips. Write: S. C. Miller, Box 851-B, Salmon 83467. Another guide in this area is *Carl Hagaman*, P.O. Box 294, Quincy, WA 98848. *Teton Expeditions* leads fly-fishing expeditions into the Teton River country, pack trips, and float-fishing trips on the Snake, Teton, Blackfoot, and Salmon rivers. Contact: J. D. Foster, 427 East 13th St., Idaho Falls 83401. Guided horsepack trips into the Bighorn Crags area of the Salmon National Forest are provided by *Yellowjacket Ranch*, P.O. Box 44, Cobalt 83229.

The majority of large guide and outfitter groups are based in Salmon River country, though not all of them serve only that area. *Happy Hollow Camps* are based in the Idaho Primitive Area along the Middle Fork, and offer trail rides and pack trips, boat trips, fishing, winter sports, and a youth camp. Write to *The Martin Capps*, Box 694, Salmon 83467. *Whitewater Adventures*, P.O. Box 184, Twin Falls 83301, offers float and fishing trips on the Middle and Main forks of the Salmon, Hells Canyon of the Snake, and the Selway River. *Bill Guth and Sons*, Box 705, Salmon 83467, leads float trips on the Middle Fork, elk hunts, and bear hunts in the Idaho and Salmon River Breaks Primitive Areas. *Snake River Outfitters*, 811 Snake River Avenue, Lewiston 83501, lead float trips through Hells Canyon and on the Salmon.

Idaho Wilderness Camps, c/o Gary D. Merritt, Salmon 83467, offer fishing and elk, deer, sheep, goat, cougar, and bear hunting. *Wilderness River Outfitters & Trail Expeditions* lead float trips in the Salmon, Owyhee, Bruneau, Snake and Green river wilderness, cross-country ski tours, and backpacking expeditions. Write: The Tonsmeires, P.O. Box 871, Salmon 83467. *Whitewater Outfitters* offers accommodations, boating, trail rides, high lake pack trips, and big-game hunting. Write: Zeke and Marlene West, Whitewater Ranch, Salmon River Air Route, McCall 83638. *Nicholson and Sons* lead float trips on the Middle Fork. Contact: R. L. Nicholson, Route 3, Twin Falls 83301. The *Salmon River Lodge* offers accommodations, big-game hunting, Middle Fork and Main Salmon float trips, steelhead fishing, and primitive area pack trips.

Sulphur Creek Ranch, Box 131, Boise 83707, is a fly-in-only ranch, offering fishing, hunting, and accommodations. In the Sawtooth Wilderness is the *Mystick Saddle Ranch*, which leads pack trips into the alpine lakes of the area for fishing and hunting expeditions and offers horseback riding. Write: Max J. Bitton, Box 461, Mountain Home 83647, in the winter, or Stanley 83340 in the summer. Another fly-in ranch, *Pinnacle Ranch*, is located in the Owyhee River Breaks, Malheur County, Oregon. Accommodations, game-bird hunting, deer hunting, rock-hounding, fishing, and trail rides are available here. Write: Marty and Dorothy Rust, P.O. Box 8003, Boise 83707. *Rawhide Camps* also offers backcountry hunting and fishing and pack trips. Contact: Mike Loening, Box 5461, Boise 83795.

Idaho Adventures, P.O. Box 834, Salmon 83467, are licensed guides and outfitters for float trips, fall fishing and hunting, and scenic photography trips in the Hells Canyon, Salmon River, and Middle Fork of the Salmon areas. *Elk Creek Ranch* offers guided fall hunts for elk, mule deer, and bear in the Elk Creek and South Fork of the Salmon River area, and summer high-country fishing, pack trips, and camping in the Payette National Forest. Write: Box 987, McCall 83538. *Packer John Outfitters*, Box 952, Salmon 83467, has big-game hunting, fishing, and float and pack trips in the Idaho Primitive Area. *Clearwater Outfitters*, P.O. Box H, Elk River, offers summer fishing, pack trips, and fall hunting in the Clearwater National Forest. For outstanding trout fishing and wilderness accommodations write: *Middle Fork Lodge* (on the Middle Fork of the Salmon River), Thomas Creek

Landing, Air Star Rt., Boise 83707. *Rock'n-H Packers*, P.O. Box 294, Quincy, WA 98848, operate fall elk-hunting trips in Selway River country. *Peck's Ponderosa*, Box 57B, Challis 83226, offers guided big-game hunting and combination float and pack fishing trips for steelhead, salmon, and trout in the Idaho Primitive Area.

Most of Idaho's guides and outfitters will supply you with detailed literature about their services and trips, as well as maps, free upon request. Just drop them a line and state the type of trip you are interested in. In the Nez Percé National Forest, *Red River Corrals*, Elk City 83525, offers fishing, hunting, packhorse, and backpacking trips, as do the *Elk Head Ranch* and *Wally York & Son, Inc.*, also of Elk City. The *Middle Fork Ranch*, Box 7594, Boise 83707, provides fishing, big-game hunting, and packhorse trips in the Idaho Primitive Area. The Payette National Forest is served by *Johnson's Fly Service*, Payette Lakes Airport, P.O. Box 925, McCall 83638, which offers scenic pack and photographic trips, big-game hunting, and fishing. The *Moose Creek Ranch*, Lucile 83542, offers fishing, hunting, backpacking, packhorse, and wild-river float trips, as does *Wilderness Encounters and Ranches, Inc.*, P.O. Box 232, Cambridge 83610. The *Crowfoot Ranch*, Box 500, McCall 83638, offers guided big-game hunting and fishing trips. Guided fishing, hunting, packhorse, and backpacking trips in the Challis National Forest region are provided by *Camas Creek Outfitters*, P.O. Box 566, Challis 83226; *Flying Resort Ranches*, Box 59, Idaho City 83631; *Hidden Valley Ranches*, Challis 83226 (wilderness fly-in service, steelhead fishing, and big-game hunting trips); and *Stanley Basin Ranch*, Stanley 83278.

The *Muleshoe Wilderness Camp*, at the gateway to the Selway-Bitterroot Wilderness, is located at the scenic Elk Summit Road, which winds through the Clearwater National Forest to the Muleshoe base camp. Muleshoe is the sole officially designated licensed outfitter for 250 square miles of the Selway-Bitterroot Wilderness. The base camp has cabin accommodations and platform tents and offers fall hunting trips and wilderness pack and fishing trips for rainbow, brook, steelhead, cutthroat, and Dolly Varden trout in Hoodoo Creek, which runs through the center of the camp, and in the high-country lakes and rivers of the Selway-Bitterroot country. Camp services include pickup at the Missoula Airport. For information, literature, the *Muleshoe Hunting Bulletin*, and rates, write: Box 83, Harrison 83833.

See the "Idaho Travel & Recreation Guide" for additional listings of guest ranches, licensed guides, packers, and outfitters operating within the national forests and wilderness areas.

IDAHO TRAVEL & RECREATION GUIDE

Caribou National Forest

Caribou National Forest Topo Maps

U.S. Geological Survey 1:250,000 scale overview maps: Brigham City, Driggs, Pocatello, Preston.

Blackfoot River & Reservoir

U.S. Geological Survey large-scale topographic maps: Upper Valley, Lower Valley, Henry, Portneuf, Paradise Valley, Higham Peak, Goshen, Lincoln Creek, Blackfoot.

Caribou Mountain Range

U.S. Geological Survey large-scale topographic maps: Commissary Ridge, Red Ridge, Herman, Big Elk Mountain, Poker Peak, Alpine, Caribou Mountain, Tincup Mountain, Etna, Freedom.

The Caribou National Forest lies on a high plateau along the Continental Divide in southeastern Idaho. Much of the old-growth timber has disappeared here to reveal rough mountainlands, once the hunting grounds of the Shoshone, Bannock, and Lemhi Indians. White settlers began to arrive in significant numbers in the 1850s. After decades of bloodshed, they pushed the Indians onto several reservations. But even after defeating the Indians, they found the business of eking out an existence difficult; the land itself was inhospitable. Over the generations these people and their descendants upset the fragile ecology, overcutting the timber and depleting once-abundant game through uncontrolled hunting. Game management and conservation after the establishment of the national forest have helped the wildlife make an encouraging comeback.

The forest's 980,000 acres of mountains and valleys still encompass much backcountry wilderness. The forest has 20 developed camp and picnic areas, 4 summer home areas, 4 youth camps, and a winter sports area. One of the most popular recreation sites is Palisades Reservoir between Swan Valley, Idaho, and Alpine, Wyoming, where visitors boat, fish, camp, and hike.

Some of the region's best fishing is found in Bear Lake, with cutthroat and lake trout up to 25 pounds. North of Bear Lake the vast salt-grass marshes of the Dingle Swamp provide excellent shooting for mallards and Canada geese. Other productive waterfowl areas include Soda Springs, Grays Lake, America Falls Reservoir, and the Snake River. The Blackfoot Reservoir is a productive fishery; fishermen occasionally take trout in the 20-pound class.

Backpackers and cross-country hikers will enjoy the beautiful alpine backcountry of the Elk Peak (9,000 ft.) and Bonneville Peak (9,260 ft.) areas.

The region is well known for its sizable mule deer and elk populations, as well as black bear and moose. The best hunting is found in the high wilderness areas of the Wasatch Range, Caribou Mountains, Bannock Mountains, Portneuf Range, Malad Range, Sublett Range, Webster Range, and Wooley Range, whose names reflect the French Canadian trappers and American mountain men who first entered this Indian hunting grounds. Upland game birds found in the foothills and forested areas include ruffed, blue, and sage grouse, chukar partridge, and mourning dove. Other wildlife includes lynx, bobcat, badger, skunk, beaver, and snowshoe rabbit.

For the full-color *Caribou National Forest Recreation Map* and more information on camping and trails, write: Supervisor, Caribou National Forest, 427 North 6th Ave., Pocatello 83201. District Ranger Stations for the forest are located in Idaho Falls, Malad, Montpelier, Pocatello, and Soda Springs, Idaho, and in Freedom, Wyoming.

Several licensed fishing and big-game hunting guides and wilderness outfitters operate within the forest region, including *Lynn M. Davis*, Clifton 83677 (big game, fishing, backpacking, cross-country skiing, float trips); *Marriner R. Jensen*, Montpelier 83254 (big-game hunting and fishing); *Wayne Robinson*, Pocatello Creek Rd., Pocatello 83201 (hunting, fishing, and pack trips); *Nicholson & Faber Float Trips, Inc.*, Rt. 3, Twin Falls 83301 (wild rivers); *Kenneth E. Masoner*, P.O. Box 184, Twin Falls 83301 (fishing, backpacking, and wild-river float trips).

Access & Outfitting Centers

The forest is accessible by way of U.S. 91, 191, and 30N. In addition to the forest's 21 camping areas, resort and motel accommodations are available in the nearby towns of Idaho Falls, Malad City, Montpelier, Pocatello, Soda Springs, and Swan Valley, Idaho, and Afton, Wyoming. The forest also has a winter sports area.

Clearwater National Forest & Wild River

Clearwater National Forest Topo Maps

U.S. Geological Survey 1:250,000 scale overview maps: Elk City, Hamilton.

Middle Fork of the Clearwater National Wild & Scenic River

including the Lochsa and wild Selway rivers and headwaters shown on the following large-scale U.S. Geological Survey maps: *(Middle Fork of the Clearwater)* Kooskia, Glenwood, Big Cedar, Syringa, Lowell; *(Selway River)* Lowell, Goddard Point, Stillman Point, Selway Falls, Fog Mountain, Mink Peak, Moose Ridge, Dog Creek, Gardiner Peak, Spot Mountain, Burnt Strip Mountain, Beaver Jack Mountain, and Wood Hump; *(Lochsa River):* Lowell, Coolwater Mountain, McLendon Butte, Huckleberry Butte, Greenside Butte, Holly Creek, Greystone Butte, Bear Mountain, Tom Beal Peak, Cayuse Junction, Rocky Point, Roundtop.

Powell Alpine Lakes Area

U.S. Geological Survey large-scale topographic maps: Tenmile Lake, Saddle Mountain, Wahoo Peak, Cedar Ridge, Jeanette Mountain, Blodgett Mountain, Grave Peak, Savage Ridge, White Sand Lake, Rocky Point, Roundtop, Ranger Peak, St. Joseph Peak, West Fork Butte, Dick Creek.

Selway Crags Alpine Lakes Wild Area

U.S. Geological Survey large-scale topographic maps: Selway Falls, Fog Mountain, Mink Peak, Chimney Peak, Fenn Mountain, Big Rock Mountain.

The evergreen mantle of the Clearwater National Forest stretches westward from the high, snowcapped peaks of the Bitterroot Range along the Montana-Idaho border, covering 1,677,000 acres of canyon-furrowed mountain country. The forest shares the 1.2-million-acre Selway-Bitterroot Wilderness, the largest classified wilderness in the country, with three other national forests. The boulder-strewn wildwaters of the Clearwater Middle Fork, Lochsa, and Selway rivers plunge through the canyons of the forests; hot springs warm their snow-fed tributaries.

Hundreds of named peaks, buttes, streams, lakes, and campsites reveal the rich human history beneath the forest's cloak of wilderness. The Flathead Indians named the Lochsa River ("rough water"); the Nez Percé named the Selway ("smooth water") and Kooskia ("little river"). When Lewis and Clark arrived in the area, guided over the Lolo Trail by the Shoshone woman Sacajawea, about 6,000 Nez Percé Indians inhabited the region, drawing their physical and spiritual sustenance from the mountains. The tribe greeted the explorers as friends; they exchanged gifts with Lewis and Clark, gave feasts in their honor, and sent six of their chiefs to accompany the white men to the mouth of the Columbia River.

Fur traders followed these first explorers. The Nez Percé at first received them in friendship, but became increasingly concerned at the traders' slaughter of their game. The traders, however, managed to hold the Indians' trust with continued protestations of friendship, and even interested them in Christianity. Soon settlers began pouring into the region, overrunning the homelands of the Nez Percé and their neighbors. In 1855, several of the enraged Northwest tribes joined in an uprising that might have succeeded if the Nez Percé had participated. The resulting treaty gave the Nez Percé and the other tribes land in Idaho, Oregon, Washington, and Montana. But by 1863 the whites had decided they wanted these lands, too, because gold had been discovered on them. They attempted to negotiate back this land, but Nez Percé Chief Joseph refused to cede any of his lands, and Indian attacks on settlers throughout the state sprang up frequently in the 1860s and 1870s. The U.S. Army stepped in and battled where necessary to force the Indians out of their lands and into reservations, and by 1872 nearly all of the northwest Indians but the Nez Percé had agreed to give up their lands. In the meantime, Chief Joseph had died, but his son Joseph pledged never to cede the Wallowa. In 1877 the U.S. Government called a council at the proposed Lapwai Reservation, demanded that the Indians give up their lands, and arrested their holy man. It appeared that the Indians would finally surrender, but on the final day allotted to them on their lands, a band of the Nez Percé under the young Chief Joseph attacked the settlers of the Salmon River country. The government sent out Captain Perry of the U.S. Cavalry and two companies, but they were defeated with heavy losses. The government then sent out 600 more men under General Howard, who managed to force the Indians' retreat after a two-day battle. Chief Joseph decided to retreat to safety across the border in Canada over the Lolo Trail with his people, and would have eluded his pursuers had not the U.S. forces telegraphed troops in Montana to head off the Indians. Chief Joseph won two battles with them and escaped. But as autumn fell the Nez Percé were forced to surrender at the Battle of Bear Paw Mountain to a force of soldiers twice their number. The remnant of the Indian group agreed to return to the Lapwai Reservation, but the government failed to live up to even this agreement. They sent the Indians to Fort Leavenworth and then transferred them to the Indian Territory in the South. Finally, after many petitions to the government, the Indians were allowed to return to a reservation in their native Northwest.

The Forest Service has preserved a portion of the trail between Kamiah, Idaho, and Lolo Pass in the Bitterroots along the Idaho-Montana border. The *Lewis & Clark Trail Map-Brochure* describing historic sites and showing camps, streams and springs, lakes, and prominent topographic features is available free from: Forest Supervisor, Clearwater National Forest, Orofino 83544. The Lewis and Clark Highway (U.S. 12) parallels this trail across the southern boundary of the forest to Lolo Pass.

A portion of the trail runs through the Selway-Bitterroot Wilderness. Salmon and steelhead trout run up the area's streams each year; rainbow, brook, cutthroat, German brown, and Dolly Varden trout, as well as whitefish, are also taken. Elk, deer, bighorn sheep, mountain goat, and black bear are among the big-game animals of the area. Osprey, bald eagles, and golden eagles hunt the wilderness mountains. It is no wonder the Indians fought so obstinately for these lands and

held them sacred; the Selway Waterfall on the river is among the most beautiful in the state, and hot springs dot the area.

The renowned float-fishing and kayak waters of the Middle Fork of the Clearwater National Wild & Recreation River include the Middle Fork from Kooskia to Lowell, the wild Selway River from Lowell to Race Creek and from Paradise to the Magruder Ranger Station, and the Lochsa River from Lowell to the Powell Ranger Station—a total of 131 river miles. The Selway wild river segment flows for 54 miles from its headwaters to the Magruder Ranger Station and from the Paradise Guard Station to Race Creek. This wilderness river area is reached by trail and charter fly-in service in the Lowell and Smith Creek–Syringa areas. The 56,000-acre area provides top-ranked float-fishing for brown, cutthroat, rainbow, brook, and Dolly Varden trout and seasonal fishing for migratory salmon and steelhead. Access to the Middle Fork, Lochsa, and Selway is via U.S. Highway 12 from Kooskia. For detailed info on these scenic, wild, and often hazardous rivers, write: Lochsa Ranger District, Kooskia 83539.

The remote, high-country headwaters areas of the North Fork of the Clearwater, Selway, and Lochsa rivers provide often excellent wilderness fishing for brook, rainbow, and cutthroat trout. The beautiful Selway Crags area is located between the Lochsa and Selway rivers in the heart of the Clearwater River drainage. Access is by a steep forest road from Selway Falls that winds its way uphill to Big Fog Saddle, where primitive hiking and packhorse trails lead to the alpine basin dotted by the blue waters of Lizard Creek, Lone Creek, and Old Man, Three Links, Cove, and Big Fog lakes, surrounded by spruce-fir forests and towering granite crags. The scenic, high-country Powell Area at the headwaters of the Lochsa River is reached via the Lewis and Clark Highway eastward from Kooskia. Rugged forest trails climb up to the remote blue, gemlike waters of Beaver Ridge, Big Sand, Colt, Duck, Hoodoo, Skookum, Spruce Creek, Walton, Goat, and Wind lakes. Packers operate from the Powell and Elk Summit areas. Write to the Powell Ranger Station, Powell, for outfitter and trail information.

The forest's big-game population includes whitetail and mule deer, black bear, moose, a few wary mountain lion, and the largest elk herd in the continental United States. The best time to hunt is from dawn to midmorning, along the slopes and meadows near the edge of the

forest. Elk prefer to bed down on the high slopes, where a wide view and rising air currents allow them to sense danger from below. During a strong wind, look to the lee slopes, timber ravines, and thickets. Elk are most active on rainy or cool days, when they are likely to move into open areas.

For the wing shooter, the forest contains a large population of Franklin, blue, and ruffed grouse. One of the major attractions of this region is the unique steelhead and chinook salmon spawning run on the Clearwater River and its tributaries. These large fish, averaging about 15 pounds, travel from the Pacific Ocean the entire length of Oregon into Idaho, fighting their way up to the remote headwaters of the Clearwater to spawn. In banner years, the steelhead catch has run as high as 15,000 to 20,000 fish. The largest recorded chinook caught in the Clearwater weighed 45 pounds. Fishing is at its best from about July 1 to mid-August.

A U.S. Forest Service *Clearwater National Forest Map* is available from the Forest Supervisor's Office (address above) for 50¢. The map, on a scale of 4 miles to 1 inch, shows the locations of highways, roads (state and secondary), trails, mileage points, wilderness areas, water features, recreation sites, supervisors' headquarters, ranger stations, and points of interest. A recreation site directory gives the map locations, camp units, picnic units, and trailer units for picnic and camp sites in the forest. A text on the reverse side of the map describes the history, natural setting, and recreational possibilities of the forest.

Ranger stations are located at Bungalow, Canyon, Kelly Forks, Kooskia, Kamiah, and Powell. For detailed information on camping in the forest, write or visit one of the ranger stations or write for the free *National Forest Camp and Picnic Areas—Forest Service/Northern Region.* The guide gives access, elevations, locations, facilities, and attractions for campsites within the forest as does the booklet *Camp and Picnic Areas in the Clearwater Forest.* Both are available from the Forest Supervisor's Office (address above).

Also available free from the Clearwater National Forest Supervisor's Office are detailed maps of the individual ranger districts of the forest. These large maps are on a scale of 2 miles to 1 inch.

Several licensed big-game hunting and fishing guides and packers and outfitters operate within the forest and Selway-Bitterroot Wilderness. For literature and detailed information, write: *Frank L. Askin,* P.O. Box 86, Alberton, MT 59820 (fishing, hunting, packhorse, and backpacking); *Earl S. Brown,* Box 763, Orofino 83544 (fishing, hunting, packhorse, and backpacking); *Don K. Cooper,* Rt. 2, Box 1094, Kendrick 83537 (hunting and fishing); *Leo Crane,* P.O. Box H, Elk River 83827 (fishing, hunting, packhorse trips); *Bobby Ray Crick,* Rt. 1, Box 99A, Victor, MT 59875 (fishing, hunting, packhorse, and backpacking); *John A. Dark,* Box 222, Kooskia 83539 (fishing, hunting, packhorse trips); *John C. Dorsey,* Star Rt., Box 33, Kooskia 83539 (hunting); *Clifford E. Gallaugher,* Box 358, Elk City 83525 (hunting and packhorse trips); *Lester R. Grasser,* Rt. 4, Box 10, Orofino 83544 (fishing, hunting, packhorse); *Charles Grotzinger,* White Bird 83554 (big-game hunting); *William E. Heinrich,* Box 117, Weippe 83553 (hunting and fishing); *Indian Lake Outfitters,* Box 423, Darby, MT 59829 (fishing and big-game hunting); *Don Jackman,* Box 427, Lolo, MT 59847 (fishing, hunting, packhorse, backpacking); *Larry Jarrett,* Rt. 1, Kuna 83634 (hunting, fishing, packhorse trips); *Gene E. Kuykendall,* 529 Warner, Lewiston 83501 (fishing, hunting, packhorse); *Jack Lykins,* Box 202, Hamilton, MT 59840 (big-game hunting); *Ronald L. Malone,* Box 239, Challis 83226 (fishing, hunting, packhorse, backpacking); *G. M. Matteson,* Box 1, Grangeville 83530 (hunting, fishing, trail rides, backpacking); *Robert T. Muks,* 1819 Powers, Lewiston 83501 (hunting); *Don Nitz,* Elk City 83525

(fishing, hunting, packhorse); *Richard L. Norris*, P.O. Box 1181, Orofino 83544 (fishing, hunting, packhorse); *Jack Nygaard*, Star Rt., Kooskia 83539 (fishing, hunting, packhorse); *Lochsa Lodge*, Box 68, Lolo, MT 59847 (big-game hunting, fishing, packhorse); *Ralph & Arnolt Oswold*, Kamiah 83536 (fishing, hunting, packhorse); *Everett L. Peirce*, Box 1100, Hamilton 59840 (fishing, hunting, packhorse, backpacking); *Jim Renshaw*, Star Rt., Box 115, Kooskia 83539 (fishing, hunting, packhorse); *Homer K. Rhett*, Box 19, Lenore 83541 (fishing, hunting, packhorse, backpacking, wild-river float trips); *Jerry D. Spear*, Box 1040, Hamilton, MT 59840 (fishing, hunting, packhorse, backpacking); *Raymond L. Tarbox*, RR2, Box 92, Potlatch 83855; *Timber Ridge Ranch*, P.O. Box 83, Harrison 83833 (fishing, hunting, backpacking, packhorse); *Harry W. Vaughn*, 418 S. Van Buren, Moscow 83843 (fishing, hunting, packhorse, backpacking); *Wally York & Son, Inc.*, Box 319, Elk City 83525 (fishing, big-game hunting, packhorse, backpacking); *Travis W. York*, Box 319, Elk City 83525 (fishing, hunting, packhorse, backpacking); *Allison Ranch*, 5727 Hill Road, Boise 83703 (fishing, hunting, packhorse, backpacking, wild-river float trips).

Access & Outfitting Centers

The forest is reached via the paved two-lane Lewis and Clark Highway (U.S. 12). This all-weather highway cuts across the southern edge of the forest, crossing the Bitterroot Mountains at Lolo Pass (5,233 ft.), and parallels the route of the 1805–1806 Lewis and Clark expedition. Points of historical interest are marked along the highway by Forest Service signs. Numerous campsites are located along the highway. Lodging, supplies, guides, boat rentals, packers, and outfitters are located at Orofino, Kooskia, Bungalow, Canyon, Kelly Forks, Kamiah, and Powell, Idaho; and Missoula, Montana.

Coeur d'Alene National Forest

Coeur d'Alene National Forest Topo Maps

U.S. Geological Survey 1:250,000 scale overview maps: Elk City, Hamilton.

Coeur d'Alene Lake Area

U.S. Geological Survey large-scale topographic maps: Coeur d'Alene, Lane, Plummer, St. Maries.

Coeur d'Alene Mountains & River

U.S. Geological Survey large-scale topographic maps: Plummer, St. Maries, Lane, Kingston, Kellogg, Burke, Pond Peak, Taylor Peak, Spyglass Peak, Jordan Creek, Cathedral Peak, Packsaddle Mountain, Clark Fork.

Hayden Lake Area

U.S. Geological Survey large-scale topographic maps: Lane, Hayden, Hayden Lake, Coeur d'Alene.

Spirit Lake Area

U.S. Geological Survey large-scale topographic maps: Spirit Lake West, Spirit Lake East.

The fish and game areas of the 725,000-acre Coeur d'Alene National Forest are bounded by the Bitterroot Range on the Montana-Idaho border on the east, the St. Joe Mountains on the south, and the Purcell Trench on the west. The smaller Shoshone Range flanks the Bitterroots to the west, and beyond it lie the Coeur d'Alene Mountains, whose wooded foothills border the quicksilver waters of Coeur d'Alene Lake beyond the forest's western border.

Coeur d'Alène means "heart of an awl." Authorities believe the name is derived from a derogatory appellation used by the Indians who lived here to describe the Canadian trappers who entered the area in the early 1800s. The trappers responded by applying the term to the Indians themselves. The tribe, otherwise known as the Skitswish, were actually a docile people who were friendly to the early whites in the region. But repeated invasions of their lands throughout the first half of the nineteenth century led them to warfare with the whites. They attacked the forces of Col. E. J. Steptoe at Walla Walla, after he entered their lands to investigate the murders of two miners by Palouse Indians, and nearly exterminated his force of 155 men. Another group led by Col. George Wright set out to punish the tribes. Wright routed the band at Four Lakes (16 miles southwest of the present Spokane), slaughtered their horses, and defeated them, thereby setting the stage for the eventual internment of the Northwest tribes.

Beautiful Lake Coeur d'Alene is 30 miles long and has 104 miles of shoreline. The best fishing for kokanee salmon, Dolly Varden, cutthroat, and rainbow trout is at the south end of the lake along the west shore from Conkling Park to Windy Bay, and at the north end from Wolfe Lodge Bay to Arrow Point. Fishing is best in June and July.

The Coeur d'Alene River provides some of the best fly-fishing in the northern Panhandle for rainbows and cutthroats up to 5 pounds. Hayden Lake, on the western edge of the forest above Coeur d'Alene Lake, also has excellent spring and fall fishing for large rainbow and cutthroat. The lake yielded the Idaho state-record rainbow (19 lb.). Most trout caught in Hayden average between 1 and 3 pounds. Hayden, like Coeur d'Alene, is shored by evergreens and sheltered by mountains. It has two public access areas, one at Honeysuckle Beach on the west end and another at Sportsmans Park at the north end. Resort accommodations and boat rentals are available at the lake. Coeur d'Alene has about 30 points of access, and there are resort accommodations around the lake and at St. Maries and Coeur d'Alene. It is accessible by several roads from U.S. 95 on the west.

Blue fields of huckleberries cover the slopes of the Coeur d'Alene Mountains. Forests here are of Douglas fir, white and yellow pine, larch, cedar, western hemlock, Engelmann spruce, and lodgepole pine. Just west of Cataldo near the forest border is the Cataldo Mission, built in 1848 by Indians under leadership of Father Ravalli. The mission was abandoned in 1887 and fell into ruin, but citizens of area communities restored it in 1930. It holds two of the original Indian dye paintings that decorated the mission walls, one of heaven and the other of hell. The forest stretches to the north and east. Trails lead from McGee Ranger Station to Grizzly Ridge, McDonald Peak, Grassy Mountain, Lookout Peak, Cathedral Buttes, Elkhorn Peak, and McGee Peaks. Hundreds of mountain streams drain the forested hills, which harbor lynx, beaver, marten, bear, deer, and elk.

Interstate 90 provides access to the forest from the south, but only a few roads reach up into the remote north. In winter a thick blanket of snow covers the slopes and valleys; if you decide to ski the forest trails during these months, be alert for avalanche-prone areas. The Northern Region Office of the Forest Service (Federal Bldg., Missoula, MT 59801) publishes a free guide to *Snowmobiling Trails in the Coeur d'Alene National Forest*, which includes safety tips and a wind chill chart.

A U.S. Forest Service *Coeur d'Alene National Forest Map* is also available from the Northern Region Office (address above). The full-color map is on a scale of 2 miles to 1 inch and shows all major man-made and natural features, including trails, roads, and campgrounds. A recreation site directory with the map gives the map locations, facilities, and nearby ski and fishing areas of the recreation

sites. It costs 50¢. The Northern Region Office also publishes a free guide to *Camp and Picnic Areas in Coeur d'Alene National Forest.* It describes access, facilities, and attractions for campgrounds throughout the forest.

Further trail and camping information can be obtained at the forest headquarters at 218 North 23rd St., Coeur d'Alene 83814, or at the ranger stations at Coeur d'Alene (Fernan and Magee districts), Kingston (Kingston District), and Wallace (Wallace District). The *Timber Ridge Ranch* (Harrison 83833) is a lodge near the forest border which offers trail riding, ski touring, riding instruction, fishing, and hiking. The *Bar BQ Ranch* (Box 173, Harrison 83833) provides pack trips into the backcountry of the forest. *Brooks Seaplane Base*, Coeur d'Alene, provides Cessna charter fly-in service.

Access & Outfitting Centers

Major routes to the forest include Interstate 90 from Spokane, Washington, on the west and Missoula, Montana, on the east; and U.S. Highway 95 from Moscow on the south and Sandpoint on the north. Lodging, supplies, boat and equipment rentals, guides, and outfitters are available at Coeur d'Alene, Kellogg, Spirit Lake, Hayden, Twin Lakes, Rathdrum, Hauser, Chilco, Garwood, Hayden, Harrison, and Pinehurst.

Kaniksu National Forest & Lake Pend Oreille

Kaniksu National Forest Topo Maps

U.S. Geological Survey 1:250,000 scale overview maps: Clifty Mountain, Leonia.

Lake Pend Oreille

U.S. Geological Survey large-scale topographic maps: Elmira, Sandpoint, Eagle, Packsaddle Mountain, Coccolahia, Bayview, Lakeview, Clark Fork.

Priest Lake Fish & Game Area

U.S. Geological Survey large-scale topographic maps: Priest Lake N.W., Priest Lake N.E., Priest Lake S.W., Priest Lake S.E., Outlet Bay, Coolin.

Selkirk Crest Special Management Area

U.S. Geological Survey large-scale topographic maps: Priest Lake S.E., Mount Roothan, Dodge Peak, Priest Lake N.E., the Wigwams, Roman Nose, Caribou Creek, Smith Peak, Pyramid Peak.

Some of the most outstanding fishing waters in North America lie in this 1,600,000-acre preserve extending from western Montana across the northern Panhandle of Idaho into eastern Washington. Its northern boundary is formed by the province of British Columbia. The entire region is well served by highways, Forest Service roads, and trails leading to such famous destinations as Pend Oreille Lake, the glaciers of 8,712-foot Snowshoe Peak, the Selkirk and Cabinet mountains wilderness areas, Clark Fork of the Snake River, Kootenai River, Myrtle Creek Game Preserve, Purcell Mountains, Priest Lake Area, and the Purcell Trench.

The beautiful evergreen-covered shores of 43-mile-long Pend Oreille Lake lie among the Selkirk Mountains. The Pend Oreille Indians once inhabited the surrounding country and the lands along the Clark Fork River. Young braves approaching maturity were sent into the mountains, where they were to stay till they dreamed of some animal, fish, or bird, which then became their "medicine." Each of the braves wore

a tooth, claw, or feather from this creature to protect him from evil. The Indians held the islands of Warren, Cottage, Pearl, and Memaloose on Pend Oreille sacred, and used them as burial grounds. Instead of burying the dead, however, they suspended them from trees.

Huckleberry, elderberry, and syringa cover the shores of the lake, which reaches depths of 1,800 feet. U.S. 10A runs along the north shore and western edge of the lake. The main public access areas on the lake are Garfield Bay, Sandpoint City Beach, Springy Point Camp Grounds, Bayview Public Dock, Blackwell Point Public Access, Pack River Bay Access Area, Samowens Recreation Area, Johnson Creek Recreation Area, and Morton Slough Access Area.

The lake is world-famous for its rainbow and Kamloops trout of up to 37 pounds and Dolly Varden trout up to the 32-pound world record. The months to fish the lakes are May and early June and October and November, when cooler temperatures bring the big fish to the surface. Pend Oreille also has good fishing for cutthroat, kokanee, perch, crappie, and largemouth bass.

The Pend Oreille River flows for 28 miles downstream to the Washington border. The backwater and slough areas created the Albeni Falls Dam provide some fine fishing for largemouth bass in the 1–6 pound class. Rainbows are taken upstream from the Priest River. Priest Lakes have good fishing for kokanee and Dolly Varden trout and are renowned for their large lake trout, or Mackinaw, up to 51 pounds. The kokanee salmon are vigorous fighters but have soft mouths, and a limber rod is recommended. Once caught, the salmon are delicious lightly smoked or kippered.

The main Priest Lake is about 19 miles long; Upper Lake, connected to the main lake by a 2-mile river, is 3 miles long. The main lake is accessible by way of State Highway 57 from Priest River and U.S. 2, but the upper lake is accessible only by trail or water travel. Resorts, cabins, and supplies are available at the main lake. Public access areas include: Coolin Public Access, Indian Creek State Park, and Kalispell Bay Recreation Area.

Dense pine and fir forests stretch out from the shores of the Priest Lakes, their verdant undergrowth challenging cross-country hikers. Smaller lakes and rarely fished streams lie throughout the surrounding country, which supports large populations of deer, bear, elk, and mountain goat. The free guide to *Nature Trails of the Priest Lake Ranger District* will help to identify some of the trees, plants, and shrubs along the Luby Bay, Hanna Flat, and other trails throughout the district. It may be obtained from: Northern Region Office, Forest Supervisor, Kaniksu National Forest, Sandpoint 83864.

North of the Pend Oreille area, the alpine lakes of the Selkirk Mountains provide excellent fly-fishing for cutthroat, brook, and rainbow trout and an occasional kokanee and landlocked sockeye salmon. The northwest division of this area extends from Canada to the south, encompassing Hidden Lake (50 acres), Myrtle Lake (20 acres), Two Mouth Lake (20 acres), and a number of smaller lakes with excellent fishing. Access to the area is by roads up Myrtle, Trout, and Smith creeks and trails from the west side of the road along the Kootenai Valley and Upper Priest and Priest Lakes.

Forest Service trails lead to Brush, Big Fisher, Pyramid, and Trout lakes in the northeast division of the Selkirk Mountains area. This high country of alpine meadows, virgin forests, and steep-walled canyons may also be reached cross-country from the Trout Creek Road. The lakes in this area yield rainbow, brook, golden, and cutthroat trout. Brush Lake also offers bass fishing.

The Moyie and Kootenai rivers have good populations of rainbow trout. The Moyie River plunges over the Moyie Falls, the glinting water cascading through a narrow gorge. Both rivers flow through some of the most scenic areas in the forest.

On the east of Priest Lake lies the southwest division of the Selkirk Mountains lakes area, drained by the Priest, Pack, and Kootenai rivers. Harrison, Brook, Bottleneck, Standard, Two Mouth, and several beautiful high-country lakes offer good to excellent fishing for cutthroat and brook trout. They are accessible by way of the Myrtle, Snow, and Ruby Creek roads from the east, the Pack River road from the south, and roads from Priest Lake from the west. Climbers will be interested in the glacially formed Chimney Rock formation in this area, which rises vertically 200 feet above the surrounding terrain to an elevation of 7,136 feet. Climbing equipment is needed to scale the rock. A goat trail leads along the northern side of the formation to a narrow ledge extending a half mile eastward.

The southeast division of the Selkirk lakes area includes drainages east of the Selkirk Range and south to Pack River. Most of them may be reached by short hikes from the roads serving the area. Rainbow, cutthroat, and brook trout offer good to excellent fishing at Bloom, Bottleneck, Brook, Roman Nose, Snow, and a number of smaller lakes. For more detailed information on these and other alpine lakes, write to the Idaho Fish and Game Department (600 S. Walnut, Boise 83707) for the free 55-page *Mountain Lakes of Idaho* guide. The Selkirk Crest Special Management Area takes in 35,780 acres of this scenic, rugged, glaciated country. The area contains more than 20 lakes, including Myrtle, Pyramid, Ball, Two Mouth, and Beehive, nestled in the cirque basins. Trails in the area are where you find them, with a few trails maintained to a low standard. The free *Selkirk Crest Map-Brochure* may be obtained by writing to the Forest Supervisor's Office (address above).

Throughout the forest there is good hunting for whitetail deer, mule deer, black bear, elk, moose, and a few mountain goats. Scant populations of grizzly and caribou range in the Selkirk Mountains.

The Cabinet Mountains Wilderness lies across the border in Montana. It includes 94,272 acres of high peaks and ridges, mountain lakes, forests, and streams. This area offers good hunting for mountain goats and other big game. Trails lead into the area from all sides. A Forest Service map of the *Cabinet Mountains Wilderness* is available free from: Northern Region Office, Forest Service, Federal Bldg., Missoula, MT 59801. The color map, on a scale of 2 miles to 1 inch, shows the locations of highways, roads (paved, dirt, primitive), trails (including marked trails and suggested routes), recreation sites, and forest and ranger stations. A directory to points of interest with the map gives the map location, facilities, elevation, season of use, and recreational opportunities for each marked site.

The Northern Region Office of the Forest Service (address above) publishes a free guide to *Camp and Picnic Areas in Kaniksu National Forest,* which gives access routes, elevations, locations, facilities, and attractions for all campsites listed. Information sheets on *Developed Recreation Sites on the Kaniksu National Forest* are available free from: Supervisor, Kaniksu National Forest, Box 490, Sandpoint 83864. The Scweitzer Basin Winter Ski Area lies near the southern shores of Pend Oreille Lake, and resorts, hotels, lodges, and cabins provide overnight accommodations in the forest vicinity.

A U.S. Forest Service *Kaniksu National Forest Map* is available from the Northern Region Office of the Forest Service (address above). The full-color map, on a scale of 2 miles to 1 inch, shows all man-made and natural features. The map includes an index to U.S. Geological Survey topographic maps.

Big-game hunting guide service in the forest region is provided by *Gerald W. Sturgis*, Star Rt., Coeur d'Alene 83814 and *Stanley A. Sweet*, Star Rt. 2, Bonners Ferry 83805. Lodging and charter services on Pend Oreille Lake are provided by *Boileau's Resort*, Bayview 83803; *Kamloops Resort*, Hope 83836; and *Sunset Beach Resort*, Sandpoint 83864; and on Priest Lake by *Outlet Resort*, Priest River 83856; *Grandview Lodge & Resort*, Nordman 83848; *Tillakum Resort*, Nordman 83848; *Kaniksu Resort*, Nordman 83848; and *Elkins Resort*, Nordman 83848.

Access & Outfitting Centers

Major routes to the forest include U.S. 95, 2, 195, and 10A and Washington Rt. 6. Lodging, supplies, boat rentals, guides, and outfitters are available at Priest River, Sandpoint, Bonners Ferry, Old Town, Clark Fork, Eagle, Hope, Cabinet, Nordman, Meadow Creek, and Coolin.

St. Joe National Forest & Wild River

St. Joe National Forest Topo Maps

U.S. Geological Survey 1:250,000 scale overview maps: Hamilton, Pullman, Wallace.

Mallard-Larkins Pioneer Area

U.S. Geological Survey large-scale topographic maps: Buzzard Roost, Mallard Peak, Pole Mountain, the Nub, Sheep Mountain, Thompson Point.

St. Joe Wild & Scenic River

U.S. Geological Survey large-scale topographic maps: Bacon Peak, Calder, Illinois Peak, St. Joe, St. Maries, Simmons Peak, Wallace, Chamberlain Mountain, Hoodoo Pass.

This beautiful 865,000-acre tract in north central Idaho embraces the St. Joe River (the highest navigable river in the world), St. Maries River, Potlatch River, Little North Fork of the Clearwater River, and the Mallard-Larkins Pioneer Area. These outstanding hunting, fishing, and backpacking areas are well served by a network of highways, forest service roads, and trails. Forests of lodgepole, fir, and spruce intermixed with hemlock and larch cover the rugged slopes, with an undergrowth of elder, syringa, dogwood, grape, heath, laurel, and huckleberry.

The river from which the forest takes its name flows down from the Bitterroot Mountains on the Montana border to the west. The St. Maries River flows northward through the forest to meet the St. Joe at the town of St. Maries. The Jesuit Father Pierre-Jean De Smet explored the lands of the lower St. Joe River in 1842 and named it the St. Maries. He founded the Sacred Heart Mission, which still stands in Desmet, and ministered to the Indians of the area.

The St. Joe River has more than 120 miles of free-flowing water whose foaming white waters and quiet fishing stretches attract canoers, kayakers, and rafters. At an elevation of 2,128 feet, tugboats can be seen towing large brails of logs to the mills at Coeur d'Alene. The scenery is outstanding, mostly in a primitive state, even though the river flows through somewhat populated areas. These tranquil waters lined with cottonwood trees give rise to the river's nickname, "the shadowy St. Joe." The lower 6 miles are on the "River through the Lakes," a unique phenomenon where the St. Joe River with its natural tree-lined levees meanders through Benewah, Round, Chatcolet, and Coeur d'Alene lakes. These levees are the summer home of the largest colony of osprey in North America. A trip from Heller Creek to Spruce Tree Campground runs through the furious white-waters of a 17-mile wilderness canyon; it makes a good 2-day trip for experienced white-water kayakers. The quiet waters from St. Joe City to Coeur d'Alene Lake offer outstanding scenery and easy camping. The Gold Creek to Bluff Creek Bridge stretch challenges the most experienced white-water kayakers and canoers. A guide to *St. Joe River Float Trips* is available free from: Northern Region, Federal Bldg., Missoula, MT 59801. It describes 6 trips between Heller Creek and Coeur d'Alene Lake, citing major rapids, hazardous areas, and difficulty ratings for each trip. A map of the river course shows the locations of creeks, campgrounds, and settlements along the way. District rangers at Red Ives, Avery, or St. Maries can provide more detailed information on float trips and current river conditions. The headwaters lakes of the St. Joe in the Five Lakes Butte Area at 6,700 feet elevation offer good fishing for brook, rainbow, and cutthroat trout. These blue, high-country lakes and vast expanses of rose heather and wildflowers make the area ideal for wilderness camping. Campsites are located near Gospel Hill and along Meadow Creek. Forage for packstock is available throughout the area.

The forest shares the 30,500-acre Mallard-Larkins Pioneer Area with the Clearwater National Forest. This area is a roadless subalpine wilderness on the high divide between the North and the Little North Fork of the Clearwater River. Lakes that fill the glacial cirques of the high country offer rainbow and cutthroat trout. Cutthroat average 10 inches in most lakes, but fish weighing several pounds have been taken from Heart Lake. During the early weeks of July, the ridge trail near Mallard, Heart, and Mud lakes passes through the best camping areas; mosquitoes are a problem at lower elevations. The area contains one of the state's largest bands of mountain goat and offers good hunting for mule deer, elk, bear, and moose. Many of the better lakes, including Crags, Larkins, Mud, Hero, and Heart, are lightly fished. Foot trails, generally in poor condition, lead to such interesting destinations as Black Buttes, the Nub, Devils Pulpit, Mulligan Hump, and Nub Lakes. Upland game birds include blue, ruffed, and Franklin grouse. The nearest access road is on Smith Ridge. Elevations range from 2,600 feet to over 7,000 feet at Black Mountain. The wilderness includes the beautiful Heritage Cedar Grove, one of the few groves

of ancient cedars that escaped catastrophic forest fires in the early part of the century. A map-guide to the *Mallard-Larkins Pioneer Area* is available from the Northern Region Office of the Forest Service (address above). The map, on a scale of 2 miles to 1 inch, shows streams, lakes, and peaks in the area. A short text describes the area and its recreational opportunities. More information can be obtained from: District Ranger, Red Ives Ranger District, St. Joe National Forest, Avery 83802.

The forest is also the site of the Emerald Creek Garnet Area, where gem garnet deposits are found in alluvial deposits and the mica schist parent material. The garnets in the alluvial deposits are usually found in a sand and gravel stratum just above bedrock. They range in size from the tiniest particle to 2 inches in diameter, and include star garnets with four- or six-ray stars. Garnet sand, made up of small dodecahedron garnet crystals, is abundant throughout the area. A permit at a small cost allows visitors to hunt the crystals. Rubber boots, round-point shovels, buckets, and screens are needed for the rockhounding. For a free *Emerald Creek Garnet Area Map-Brochure* and more information on this region, write: District Ranger, St. Maries District, St. Maries 83861.

The wild upper reaches of the St. Joe River offer some good stretches of dry fly water for rainbow and cutthroat trout. The lower stretches of the river east of the town of St. Maries are popular areas for cutthroat and Dolly Varden trout and largemouth bass.

The forest contains the North-South Ski Area (Washington State University, Wilson Compton Union B-27, Pullman, WA 99163), on Highway 95 Alternate 4 miles south of Emida. Cross-country trails wind through the forest; ski touring equipment is available in nearby towns. A guide to *Winter Recreation in St. Maries District of St. Joe National Forest* is available free from the Northern Region Office of the Forest Service (address above). A *Snowmobiling Guide Map* in the guide shows highways, roads, trails, land administration boundaries, roads normally plowed, roads used for snowmobiling when not plowed, snow play areas, known avalanche areas, information points, winter ranges of big game, and roads used for cross-country skiers. The guide also includes a wind chill chart and a trail access chart.

The Palouse Ranger District of the forest lies southwest of the major portion of the forest in the Elk River region along Elk Creek and other tributaries of the North Fork Clearwater River. An 81-mile system of trails leads to Sand Mountain (Trail 330), East Dennis (Trail 223), and other areas, and offers pleasant one-day hikes (2–12 miles). The Elk Creek Falls, a series of waterfalls along Elk Creek south of the town of Elk River, are lovely but accessible only by trail or poor roads. Those who make the trip up the stream will find good fishing for native eastern brook and planted rainbow. Rainbow are stocked in the Elk Creek Reservoir and stream near the community of Elk River, and in the vicinity of Laird Park upstream to the mouth of the North Fork of the Palouse. The best waters for eastern brook are the North Fork of the Palouse and the Palouse River headwaters. There are a number of small elk herds throughout the district. Mule deer range the higher elevations of Bald Mountain, Baby Grand, Shattuck Butte, and Elk Butte.

Winter sports are popular in this district. A brochure entitled *A Guide to Year Round Recreation: Use of Roads and Trails of the Palouse District* is available from the Potlatch or Moscow office of the Palouse District. This guide shows restricted areas where snow machines and mechanized vehicles are prohibited.

There are camping facilities throughout the forest at more than 15 developed camping areas. The Northern Region of the Forest Service

(address above) publishes a free guide to *Camp and Picnic Areas in St. Joe National Forest*, which describes and maps 13 campgrounds throughout the forest, along with their elevations, facilities, size, and special attractions. For more information on camping and trails, write: Forest Supervisor's Office, P.O. Box 310, Coeur d'Alene 83814.

Maps of the individual ranger districts showing trails, roads (paved, all-weather, dirt, primitive), ranger and forest stations, recreation sites, buildings, and water and topographic features are available free from the Forest Supervisor's Office (address above). The maps are on a scale of 2 miles to 1 inch and are black and white. The U.S. Forest Service *St. Joe National Forest Map* is on the same scale and shows all the above-mentioned features as well as ski areas, points of interest, and special use areas. This full-color map costs 50¢.

Several state-licensed guides, packers, and wilderness outfitters operate within the St. Joe National Forest. For literature, rates, and information, write: *Lawrence R. Bentcik*, Rt. 1, St. Maries 83861 (hunting, backpacking, wild-river float trips); *Les Crane*, P.O. Box H, Elk River 83827 (fishing, hunting, packhorse, backpacking); *Carl Nagel*, Rt. 3, Box 19, Hayden Lake 83835 (fishing, hunting); *Roy E. Powis*, Rt. 1, Box 10BB, Deer Park, WA 99006 (big-game hunting); *St. Joe Hunting & Fishing Lodge*, Avery 83802 (big-game hunting, fishing, packhorse trips); *Gordon Stimmel*, Box 367, Kooskia 83539 (fishing, hunting); *Floyd H. Weddle*, Rt. 3, Box 35, Orofino 83544 (fishing, hunting).

Access & Outfitting Centers

The St. Joe National Forest is accessible by way of U.S. 95A and Idaho 7, 8, and 43. There are dude ranches nearby and cabins available along the St. Joe River. Overnight accommodations, guide and outfitting services, supplies, and other services are available in the nearby towns of Avery, Clarkia, Moscow, Potlatch, and St. Maries.

Salmon River Wilderness & Idaho Primitive Area

Salmon River Wilderness & Idaho Primitive Area Topo Maps

U.S. Geological Survey 1:250,000 scale overview maps: Hailey, Challis, Dillon, Elk City, Grangeville.

Big Horn Crags

U.S. Geological Survey large-scale topographic maps: Aggipah Mountain, Hoodoo Meadows, Mount McGuire, Puddin Mountain.

Boise National Forest

U.S. Geological Survey 1:250,000 overview maps: Baker, Boise, Challis, Hailey.

Challis National Forest

U.S. Geological Survey 1:250,000 scale overview maps: Challis, Dubois, Hailey, Idaho Falls.

Middle Fork of the Salmon National Wild & Scenic River

U.S. Geological Survey large-scale maps: Aggipah Mountain, Aparejo Point, Buttes Creek Point, Greyhound Ridge, Long Tom Mountain, Norton Ridge, Puddin Mountain, Ramey Hill, Sliderock Ridge.

Nez Percé National Forest

U.S. Geological Survey 1:250,000 scale overview maps: Elk City, Grangeville, Hamilton.

Payette National Forest

U.S. Geological Survey 1:250,000 scale overview maps: Baker, Challis, Elk City, Grangeville.

Rapid National Wild River

U.S. Geological Survey large-scale topographic maps: Cuprum, Pollock Mountain, Heavens Gate, Pollock, Riggins.

Salmon National Forest

U.S. Geological Survey 1:250,000 scale overview maps: Dillon, Dubois, Elk City, Challis.

Salmon Wild & Scenic River

Salmon National Forest segment shown on large-scale U.S. Geological Survey topographic maps: North Fork, Ulysses Mountain, Shoup, Long Tom Mountain, Buttes Creek Point, Square Top.

The Salmon, known to the Shoshone as *Tom-Agit-Pah*, or "big fish river," rises in the Sawtooth and Lemhi valleys of east central Idaho, fed by the snows of the majestic Sawtooth and Salmon River mountains in the south and the Clearwater and Bitterroot mountains in the north. It flows north through the great Chamberlain Basin to Salmon and west to Riggins, then north again to meet the Snake. The Salmon runs through a wilderness course of still, deep waters followed by frothing rapids and many 4–8 foot waterfalls, and a rock-ribbed canyon that is one-fifth of a mile deeper than the Grand Canyon, surpassed only by the awesome, sheer walls of the Snake River Canyon. The Salmon River Gorge is more than one mile deep for a distance of 180 miles. Rising at elevations of 8,000 feet, the Salmon cascades along its 425-mile-long course to an elevation of 905-feet at its mouth on the Snake, draining a high-country wilderness of 14,000 square miles in the Sawtooth, Challis, Salmon, Bitterroot, Nez Percé, and Payette national forests.

The tortuous waters of the river for an 80-mile stretch between the road's end west of North Fork and Riggins has been known as the "River of No Return" since it defeated Lewis and Clark in their search for a northwest passage to the Pacific. In the 79 miles from the end of the North Fork road to the end of the Riggins road, one-half mile upstream from the Wind River bridge, the Salmon drops a total of 969 feet, approximately 12 feet per mile. Peak flows occur from the middle of May to July 1. It is at its lowest in January and February, but these highs and lows are subject to seasonal changes. River crossings 100 years ago in the "No Return" stretch were made by swimming or by raft, cable crossing bridge, or ferry. Today you will find pack bridges at Horse Creek, Campbell Ferry (Trout Creek), Fivemile Trail (Mackay Bar) and Wind River (at the end of the road from Riggins). The ancient Nez Percé trail, used by the Indians during their travels east to hunt buffalo on the plains, crosses the Salmon near Campbell Ferry Bridge.

The first known attempt by white men to navigate the Salmon ended in tragedy when four Hudson's Bay Company trappers left Salmon in March 1832 to float down the river in a small boat made of hides. Two of the men were lost in the boiling white fury of the rapids; the other two managed to reach Fort Nez Percé 30 days later. About 1890 Henry Guleke and a man named Sanderland successfully ran the Salmon River Canyon and rapids in wooden flatboats steered by large sweeps. A new boat was built for each trip to float miners, prospectors, and trappers into this vast wilderness, and was dismantled at downstream destinations. The lumber from these flatboats was used to build many a Salmon River gold-mining camp. Unless you are skilled in white-water river running, hire a good guide if you plan to float the river. You should inform a Forest Ranger in the area of your plan to travel down the river, and follow the Idaho boating regulations. Information on the regulations is available from the Idaho Fish and Game Department, Boise 83707. Vacation lodging and guided float trips, steelhead fishing, big game hunting, jet boat trips, and pack trips on the Big Salmon are provided by *Salmon River Lodge* (Box 58, Salmon 83467; phone: 208-756-2646) and *Mackay Bar Lodge* (Drawer F, Suite 1010, One Capitol Center, Boise 83702; 208-344-1881).

There are over 40 stretches of powerful brawling rapids on the main Salmon, including Ruby Rapids (3 miles of white water), Gun Barrel, Ranier, Salmon Falls, Bailey, Big and Little Mallard, Little Elk Horn, Johnson, Chittam, Five-Mile, Long Tom Creeks, and Pine Creek (considered the most hazardous by many), studded by huge boulders, jagged sawtooth rocks, sweepers, and numerous small chutes and cascades broken by quiet stretches of calm water and deep-flowing pools.

The first 30-40 miles of the Salmon, from its beginnings in the upper Sawtooth Valley, provide easy fishing from the shore or in float boats. Fishing this part of the river in the early morning mist, one is greeted by stunning vistas of the Sawtooth Mountains to the west and the famous White Cloud Peaks towering on the east. Fishermen start working the lower stretches for chinook in June, and as the runs grow larger, the anglers move upstream with the fish. The best fishing is usually in late June and July. Salmon eggs are the most effective bait, although large grass wobblers and spoons are also very productive.

The upper Salmon has good fly-fishing from July on for Dolly Varden and brook trout. The middle stretch of the Salmon is popular for fall and spring steelhead fishing and for the chinook run in late April and May. For 180 miles of its course, the Salmon surges through treacherous V-shaped canyons and gorges. In the most rugged part of this wilderness, the 216,870-acre Salmon River Breaks Primitive Area borders the river on the north for 40 miles between Riggins and North Fork. On the south side of the river are the wilds of the Idaho Primitive Area. This area encompasses some very hazardous terrain that can be reached only by boats or rafts, and furnishes services for float trips popular during the steelhead runs.

Lewis and Clark were the first white men to explore this wilderness.

After 15 exhausting miles down the Salmon River Canyon, they were forced to retrace their path and cross the Continental Divide at Lost Trail Pass. In 1879 the massive invasion of white settlers into the lands of the Salmon Mountains tribes resulted in scattered Indian reprisals. The U.S. Government wrongly blamed the massacre of settlers on the Sheepeaters and sent troops after them through the rugged mountain backcountry. The Indians held out for weeks, but were finally forced to surrender with the coming of autumn.

A few of the outstanding big-game areas within the region include the Yellowjacket Mountains, Salmon River Mountains, Lemhi Mountains, Beaverhead Mountains, and the Bitterroot Range. Bighorn sheep are found in great numbers in the Camas Creek–Loon Creek area of the Middle Fork. Sheep hunting is generally open to anyone, resident or nonresident, who possesses a valid hunting license and a sheep tag. Mountain goats are hunted under a permit system and are fairly plentiful throughout the higher elevations. Mule and whitetail deer are numerous; moose, bobcat, and black bear are spotted occasionally. The Lost River–Salmon River plains area provides the state's finest antelope hunting. Either sex of the animal may be hunted. Upland game hunters will find chukar partridge and sage, ruffed, and Franklin grouse. Backpackers will enjoy hiking the famous Lewis and Clark and Nez Percé trails.

Middle Fork of the Salmon

The Middle Fork of the Salmon joins the main Salmon about 20 miles west of Shaup. The Middle Fork pounds northward through steep-walled canyons from its source at the confluence of the Marsh and Bear Valley creeks through the 1¼-million-acre Idaho Primitive Area. It is this fork of the river that has been designated part of the National Wild and Scenic River System, preserved in its free-flowing state. The river flows through the Boise, Challis, Payette, and Salmon national forest sections of the Idaho Primitive Area before it meets the main Salmon. The rugged Bighorn Crags mountain range juts up near the confluence of the two rivers.

The mighty Middle Fork flows for 106 miles, plunging along its route through one of the deepest gorges in North America before joining the Salmon River. Near the junction of the Middle Fork and Salmon rivers loom the jagged peaks of the Bighorn Crags, one of the wildest and most rugged ranges in the Northwest. As in the main Salmon, deep-flowing pools dot the river between long stretches of dangerous rapids and falls. These scenic holding pools often provide excellent fishing for steelhead, cutthroat, rainbow, and Dolly Varden from spring through fall. Nearly one-third of the chinook salmon spawning nests (locally called redds) in the Salmon River drainage are found in the Middle Fork and its tributaries. The chinook is the largest of the Pacific salmon, averaging about 18 pounds, with recorded weights up to 126 pounds. The chinook leave the Pacific and migrate up the Columbia River from March through July, spawning in the Middle Fork during August and September. During the fall and winter months, the fighting steelhead migrate up the Salmon River to spawn in the Middle Fork in early spring. This is also top big-game hunting country for mule deer, whitetail deer, elk, moose, bighorn sheep, and mountain goat. Because of the hazardous terrain, many hunters prefer to float the Middle Fork and scan the banks and slopes for their quarry. Float trips down the river often start at Dagger Falls, where a fish ladder assists salmon in the final stages of their spawning journey. July, August, and September are the best months for these trips; the high-water period from late May through June makes trips during these months hazardous. In the late summer when the water is low, landing fields downstream from Dagger Falls are the best starting points. If you lack knowledge of the river or experience at river running, hire the services of a licensed guide. Along the way are the rugged spires of the

Bighorn Crags, Indian paintings and petroglyphs recalling a culture that existed 8,000 years ago, and the Sheepeater Hot Springs. Keep in mind that the Middle Fork Canyon is rattlesnake country. Numerous campsites are available along the Middle Fork, and many of them have spur trails leading out into the interior wilderness. Open flats along the river's edges and meadows in the high country provide natural campsites. For much of its distance, the Middle Fork is paralleled by a primitive trail. There are a number of small landing fields

along the river for charter flights into the Idaho Primitive Area. For boating, camping, and trail information write: Supervisor, Challis National Forest, Challis 83226. For listings of guides, packers, and outfitters that operate in the Primitive Area, see "Wilderness Outfitters, Guides & Guest Ranches" in the "Encyclopedia" section.

A guide to the wildwaters of the Middle Fork, *Middle Fork of the Salmon*, is available free from: Intermountain Region, Forest Service, 324 25th Street, Ogden, UT 84401. The guide includes a map of the length of the Middle Fork on a scale of 2 miles to 1 inch that shows river campsites, campgrounds accessible by road, rapids and falls, ranger stations, and cable crossings and pack bridges. This office publishes a similar free guide to the main Salmon, *The Salmon, River of No Return*. A map on the same scale showing the same features is included, as well as a useful "Salmon River Mileage Log." A *Lower Salmon River Guide* with a series of maps charting this portion of the river is available free from the Bureau of Land Management. This

18-page booklet describes rapids difficulty ratings, bridges, boat landings, and campgrounds along the way. Write to: Bureau of Land Management, Resource Area Headquarters, Rt. 3, Cottonwood 83522. Rustic vacation lodging and guided float trips, steelheading fishing, big game hunting, and pack trips on the Middle Fork of the Salmon are provided by the *Middle Fork Lodge*, Thomas Creek Landing Field, Air Star Route, Boise 83707.

The Middle Fork of the Salmon River, called the "Impassable Canyon" on Colonel Bernard's map of 1879, includes most of the spawning grounds for the chinook salmon in the Salmon River system. It has special regulations for trout fishing, so if you plan to fish here, write for a copy of the regulations to: Idaho Department of Fish and Game, 600 S. Walnut St., Boise 83707.

Idaho Primitive Area

The Idaho Primitive Area, lying partially within the Challis, Salmon, Payette, and Boise national forests, encompasses some 1,232,744 acres of the Chamberlain Basin in the geographic center of the state, bordered by the Middle Fork of the Salmon River to Rapid Creek on the south; the Bighorn Crags, Yellowjacket Range, and Sleeping Deer Mountain on the east; the main Salmon River on the north; and the western limit of the Marble, Monumental, Beaver, and Chamberlain creeks watersheds on the west. It is a majestic, wild area of rolling plateaus, high cliffs, alpine meadows, deep dark gorges, the beautiful high-country lakes of the Bighorn Crags, soaring 10,000-foot peaks, and, almost everywhere, forests. At the lower elevations grows western yellow pine; higher up are Engelmann spruce, limber pine, Douglas fir, and lodgepole pine. Hundreds of alpine lakes and streams offer excellent wilderness fishing, and hot springs bubble up here and there. Caves along the Big and Camas creeks and the Middle Fork of the Salmon bear the artwork of ancient inhabitants; brightly painted hieroglyphics, pictographs, and carved petroglyphs have withstood time and nature. Over 1,600 miles of wilderness trails wind through the Primitive Area, long famous for its outstanding big-game hunting for deer and elk, trout fishing, and wilderness camping to such destinations as the Bighorn Crags, Big Creek, Pistol Hot Springs, Phantom Meadow, Papoose Lakes, Rainbow Mountain, old mines and placer camps, cliff dwellings, and the Middle Fork of the Salmon River.

The Intermountain Region Office of the Forest Service publishes a free *Idaho Primitive Area Map & Guide* which describes the area, its wildlife, and its history. It also lists points of access to the area and directions on how to travel through it. The map, on a scale of about 4 miles to 1 inch, keys entrances, main roads, secondary roads, trails, landing strips, ranger and guard stations, campsites, and topographic features, and may be obtained by writing: Intermountain Region, U.S. Forest Service, 324 25th St., Ogden, UT 84401.

Salmon National Forest & Bighorn Crags

The major features of the Salmon National Forest are shown on the *Salmon National Forest Map*, available for 50¢ from: Forest Supervisor's Office, Salmon 83467. An outdoorsman's dream, this 1,768,000-acre tract located in east central Idaho was once the scene of the bloody Sheepeaters Indian War. Numerous trails, including the historic Nez Percé and Lewis and Clark trails, wind through the rugged wilderness along the Yellowjacket Mountains, Idaho Primitive Area, Lost River–Salmon River plains, Bitterroot Mountains, Salmon River Mountains, Beaverhead Mountains, and the Middle and North forks of the Salmon River. Elevations vary from 2,480 feet in the Salmon River Canyon to 11,350 feet at Big Peak near Leadore. The fishing is excellent in the Salmon and its tributaries for steelhead, cutthroat, Dolly Varden, and rainbow trout and chinook salmon. This wilderness

along the Continental Divide is one of the country's top big-game hunting areas for mountain goat and sheep, moose, bear, and deer. Another publication available free from the Forest Supervisor's Office is *Birds of the Salmon & Challis Forests*, a guide to 209 species and their habitats within the forest.

The forest encompasses portions of the Bighorn Crags area, a high mountain wilderness noted for its camping and big-game hunting for bighorn sheep, mountain goat, mule deer, and occasional elk and black bear. A special permit is needed when hunting sheep or goat. Elk and deer are included in the general license. Fishing is good for rainbow, cutthroat, and golden trout in the lake basins nestled beneath the high jagged peaks. The most productive lakes include Skyhigh, Ship Island, Big Clear, Glacier, Gooseneck, and Crater. A successful hunting or fishing trip to this remote portion of the Idaho Primitive Area requires detailed plans for either hiking or packing in, and most often requires the services of a guide. Crags Camp, the main trailhead, is reached by unpaved forest roads from either Challis or Salmon. Trails fan out from Crags Camp to the interior lakes, meadows, and peaks. Primitive campsites with scarce wood supplies and pit toilets are located at Birdbill, Heart, Big Clear, Terrace, and Welcome lakes. Travel prepared for rain and short but intense thunderstorms. Morning frost is common, and summer snowstorms can occur on occasion.

A Forest Service *Bighorn Crags Map* is available from the Salmon National Forest Supervisor's Office (address above). The map is on a scale of about ¾ of a mile to 1 inch and shows lakes, rivers, streams, peaks, campgrounds with road access, primitive area boundaries, and trails. A short text with the map describes trails and trail use, campsites, wildlife, and climate of the Bighorn Crags areas. For trail and camping information, write: District Ranger, Salmon Ranger District, Salmon 83467.

The Salmon National Forest is served by several guides and wilderness outfitters licensed by the Idaho Department of Fish & Game. For the nitty gritty on lodging, services, rates, and literature, write: *Camas Creek Outfitters*, P.O. Box 566, Challis 83226 (fishing, hunting, packhorse trips); *Diamond D. Ranch*, P.O. Box 1, Clayton 83227 (fishing, hunting, trail rides); *Flying Resort Ranches*, Box 59, Idaho City 83631 (fishing, hunting, backpacking, packhorse); *Hidden Valley Ranches*, Challis 83226 (big-game hunting, fishing, packhorse trips); *Rick Hussey*, Star Rt., Salmon 83467 (big-game hunting); *Idaho Adventures*, P.O. Box 834, Salmon 83467 (fishing, packhorse, backpacking, and wild-river float trips); *Stanton C. Miller*, Box 585, Salmon 83467 (big-game hunting, fishing, backpacking, packhorse, and wild-river float trips); *Nez Percé Outfitters & Guides*, P.O. Box 1454, Salmon 83467 (wild-river float trips); *Wild Rivers West*, Box 503, Salmon 83467 (wild-river floating & fishing); *Wilderness River Outfitters & Trail Expeditions*, P.O. Box 871, Salmon 83467 (fishing, backpacking, cross-country skiing, wild-river float trips); *Guth Enterprises*, Box 705, Salmon 83467 (hunting, fishing, packhorse, backpacking, wild-river floating); *Frontier Expeditions*, Box 1186, North Fork 83466 (wild-river float trips); *Triangle C Ranch*, North Fork 83466 (big-game hunting, float trips); *Williams Lake Resort*, Salmon 83467 (packhorse trips).

Nez Percé National Forest

The major features of the Nez Percé National Forest are shown on the *Nez Percé National Forest Map*, available for 50¢, along with fishing, hunting, and camping info from: Forest Supervisor's Office, Grangeville 83530. The forest covers 2 million acres from north central Idaho to the state's western border with northern Oregon; it is bordered by the Salmon River in the south, the South and Middle forks of the Clearwater further north, and portions of the Lochsa and Selway in Selway-Bitterroot Wilderness. The Snake River Canyon forms a portion of its westernmost border. It encompasses the mountainlands beyond the Bitterroots to the west, including the Gospel and Clearwater mountains. The forest is dominated by the world-famous rainbow and steelhead waters of the Clearwater River, which flows into the Snake River at Lewiston and forms one of the largest and most complex river systems in the northern Idaho fish and game country. In years past, the annual steelhead catch on the Clearwater often numbered as high as 20,000.

The Middle Fork of the Clearwater cuts a deep canyon through the forest mountain slopes, covered by dense stands of white and lodgepole pine, Douglas and alpine fir, Engelmann spruce, and western red cedar, with a lush undergrowth of dogwood, snowberry, mountain laurel, syringa, berry and currant bushes, and wild rose. The bracken, sword, and maidenhair ferns and a myriad wildflowers of the woods add to its luxuriance.

The Middle Fork is formed by the confluence of the wild Selway and Lochsa rivers in the northeastern portion of the forest. Further up the course of the Selway is the beautiful Selway Waterfall, and beyond it, high-country wilderness. Between the two rivers is the Selway Crags Area, an alpine lakes wilderness (see "Clearwater National Forest & Wild Rivers").

The South Fork of the Clearwater flows into the heart of the forest, an area of canyons and densely wooded mountain slopes. In the spring the river is thick and furious; in the autumn its clear waters reflect the brilliance of the hills. South of Crooked River is another alpine lakes wilderness; the lovely Crystal, Fish, Wildhorse, Rainbow, Deer, and Ruby lakes are accessible by road or trail.

The Nez Percé region is well known for its outstanding wingshooting for pheasant, Hungarian partridge, chukar partridge, sage grouse, and wild turkey. The backcountry near the Nez Percé Indian Reservation is particularly good for game birds. Unusually large populations of chukar partridge are found in the Hells Canyon of the Snake River between Lewiston and Weiser. This chasm, known also as the Seven Devils Gorge and the Grand Canyon, is the deepest in North America, reaching a depth from He Devil Peak (7 miles east of the river) of 7,900 feet. Sheer walls of red, orange, and yellow flank the narrow gorge. To the east, the wild fury of the Rapid National Wild River—a tributary of the Salmon—roars down from its headwaters in the Seven Devils Mountains through the wildlands of the Payette and Nez Percé national forests (for information on this violent stretch of water, write to the Supervisor's Office, Nez Percé National Forest).

Spring is the season for black bear hunting in the forest. Nonresidents should hire the services of an experienced guide who has thorough knowledge of the region. Black bear are most often found near blueberry bushes and streams where spawned-out salmon provide forage.

A few of the region's most productive hunting and fishing areas include the Snake River Canyon, Clearwater River, Lochsa River, Salmon River, and the Clearwater Mountains. The Lochsa River is one of Idaho's top-rated elk ranges. Before and during rut, bull elk can often be spotted in the open pastures where the herd browses on bluegrass, sedge, needlegrass, and wheatgrass. During early October, as the rutting season draws to a close, snowdrifts begin to force the bulls down to the dense wooded areas, where they feed on bog birch, mountain mahogany, willow, pine, aspen, berry bushes, and wild rose. By late October, the bulls have generally moved into the lower valleys and wooded slopes. The best hunting for trophy elk is usually during the late season in the forested areas with a good cover of tracking snow. A light wool shirt and hunting vest are suitable for the early season

at low elevations. For high elevations and late-season hunting, down clothing is highly recommended.

Payette National Forest

The 2.3 million-acre Payette National Forest extends from the southern shores of the Salmon River through the vast wilderness of the Idaho Primitive Area and the Salmon Mountains. Major streams originating in the forest include the Weiser River, North Fork of the Payette, Big Creek, and most of the South Fork of the Salmon. The Hells Canyon of the Snake River forms a portion of the forest's western border. The forest's 154 fishing lakes and 1,530 miles of streams include outstanding trout and salmon waters. Glaciers formed many of its cirques and canyons.

Hundreds of remote alpine lakes dot the evergreen-clad slopes and meadows north of Payette Lake and McCall. These jewel-like lakes offer good wilderness fishing for brook, rainbow, and cutthroat trout. The area surrounds the uppermost reaches of the North Fork of the Payette River and includes Hazard, Elk, Rainbow, Goose, Upper Payette, Twentymile, Loon, and Enos lakes. Much of the country lies at 6,000–8,000 feet elevation and is extremely rugged, laced by primitive trails that provide access to the lake basins. The trailheads in the area are reached by Idaho Route 15 and the Warren Wagon Road. State Highway 15 is one of the most scenic routes in the state.

Mule deer, black bear, and elk range throughout the forests, and whitetail deer inhabit the Salmon River country. Bighorn sheep roam the high country of the Idaho Primitive Area, and mountain goats range in the rugged country from McCall to the Middle Fork of the Salmon to the east. Cougar, beaver, fox, lynx, bobcat, marten, and muskrat are other forest furbearers. Game birds include Franklin, ruffed, and blue grouse and chukar partridge.

A full-color *Payette National Forest Recreation Map* may be obtained for 50¢ along with detailed fishing, hunting, and wilderness camping information from: Forest Supervisor's Office, McCall 83638.

Challis National Forest

The Challis National Forest, one of the finest backpacking, fishing, and big-game hunting areas in North America, takes in 2.4 million acres in the geographic center of Idaho. The forest, which includes parts of the Sawtooth and Idaho primitive areas, accessible only by foot, horse, or boat, is a top-ranked hunting area for deer, elk, mountain goat, bighorn sheep, antelope, and black bear. The Pahsimeroi Valley is the home of the state's largest herd of antelope. Waterfowl, upland game birds, hawks, and golden eagles are often sighted. Both these backcountry tracts and the forest's more accessible regions hold an abundance of wildlife. The Lost River Range sweeps down through the forest area, crowned by Mount Borah (12,655 ft.), the highest peak in Idaho. Parallel to this range on the east lies the Lemhi Range; on the west, the Salmon River Mountains; and below them, the alpine lakes of the White Cloud Peaks. The magnificent blue-spired ridges of the Sawtooth Mountains rise up further to the west. The headwaters of the Salmon River gather in the Stanley Basin among the shadows of these crags. The wildwaters of the Middle Fork of the Salmon flow northeast in the western portion of the forest along the southeast border of the Idaho Primitive Area. Primitive hiking and packhorse trails provide access to the remote alpine fishing, hunting, and wilderness camping areas in the Lost River Range, Sleeping Deer Area, and White Knob Mountains.

A U.S. Forest Service full-color *Challis National Forest Recreation Map* (50¢) and a free *Hiking Guide for Borah Peak* may be obtained along with detailed fishing, hunting, and wilderness camping info

from: Forest Supervisor's Office, Challis National Forest, Challis 83226.

Boise National Forest

The major features of the Boise National Forest are shown on the full-color *Boise National Forest Recreation Map* available for 50¢ along with fishing, hunting, and wilderness camping info from: Forest Supervisor's Office, 210 Main St., Boisie 83702. This outstanding fishing, hunting, and wilderness camping area encompasses 2,639,000 acres bordered on the west by the Snake River along the Oregon border and includes the headwaters of the Boise, Payette, and Salmon rivers, the Sawtooth Wilderness, Cascade, Bull Creek Trail, Anderson

Ranch, and Deadwood reservoirs, the beautiful snow-covered peaks of the Trinity Mountains Lakes Basin, and Seafoam Lakes Area. The hundreds of beautiful alpine lakes, such as Three Sisters, Big Roaring River, Big Buck, North Star, Cape Horn, Vanity, and Ruffneck Peak, offer good fishing for rainbow and cutthroat trout. Most of the lakes are at 9,000 feet elevation. This region is extremely rugged and the trails are steep.

Access & Outfitting Centers

The Salmon National Forest is accessible by way of U.S. 93 and Idaho 28. More than 20 developed camping areas dot the forestlands; primitive camping is also available. Dude ranches serve the area, and overnight accommodations, guide and outfitting services, and supplies are available at the nearby towns of Leadore, Salmon, and North Fork. The Nez Percé National Forest can be reached by way of U.S. 95 and Idaho 9, 13, and 14. There are only two access roads to the Salmon River between Riggins and the end of the North Fork Road (a distance of about 80 miles). Both approach the river from the north. The Dixie Ranger Station road runs from Mackay Bar north to the junction with the Elk City–Dixie Road at Jack Mountain. Lodging, gear, boat rentals, guides, and outfitters are available at Kamiah, Kooskia, Grangeville, Lewiston, Lowell, Nezperce, Golden, Elk City, Orogrande, Dixie, and Red River Hot Springs.

The Payette National Forest is reached via U.S. Highway 95 and Idaho Highways 71 and 55. Lodging, supplies, boat rentals, guides, and outfitters are available at McCall, New Meadows, Tamarack, Council, Cambridge, Weiser, Yellowpine, Burgdorf, French Creek, Bear, Cuprum, Riggins, and Big Creek. The Challis National Forest has 52 camping areas and 7 picnic sites. Resorts, hotels, cabins, dude ranches, and commercial guides and packers are available in and near the towns of Challis, Mackay, Salmon, and Stanley. The forest is

accessible by way of U.S. 20, 93, and 92A. Boise National Forest can be reached by way of U.S. 20, 30, and 95 and Idaho 15, 17, 21, 52, and 68. The forest has 116 campsites, 5 picnic sites, and 1 swimming site and includes the Bogus Basin Winter Sports Area. Resorts, motels, and dude ranches offer overnight accommodations in the surrounding towns of Boise, Cascade, Emmett, Horseshoe Bend, Idaho City, and Mountain Home. Guide and outfitting services and boat rentals are also available in these towns.

Sawtooth National Forest & Wilderness

Sawtooth National Forest Topo Maps

U.S. Geological Survey 1:250,000 scale topographic maps: Brigham City, Challis, Idaho Falls, Pocatello, Twin Falls, Wells.

Headwaters of the Salmon River

U.S. Geological Survey large-scale topographic maps: Galena, Frenchman Creek, Marshall Peak, Snowyside Peak, Alturas Lake.

Red Fish Lake Recreation Area

U.S. Geological Survey large-scale topographic maps: Mount Cramer, Stanley.

Sawtooth Wilderness & National Recreation Area

U.S. Geological Survey 1:250,000 scale map: Challis.

Sun Valley Area

U.S. Geological Survey large-scale topographic maps: Amber Lakes, Rock Roll Canyon, Griffin Butte, Sun Valley.

White Cloud Peaks Wilderness

U.S. Geological Survey large-scale topographic maps: (Boulder Mountains) Galena Peak, Ryan Peak, Meridan Peak, Herd Peak, Easley Hot Springs, Amber Lakes, Rock Roll Canyon, Phi Kappa Mountain; (White Cloud Peaks) Robinson Bar, Livingston Creek, Washington Peak, Boulder Chain Lakes.

The sharp-edged 10,000-foot peaks of this range dominate the 1,800,000 acres of the Sawtooth National Forest and Sawtooth Wilderness Area. The northern division of the forest in south central Idaho encompasses the Sawtooth National Recreation Area and the Sawtooth Wilderness, as well as the mountainlands of the famous Ketchum and Sun Valley area. The headwaters of the Middle and North Forks of the Boise, South Fork of the Payette, and the Salmon River gather among the jagged peaks of the Sawtooth Mountain Wilderness here, flanked by the White Cloud Peaks and the Boulder, Pioneer, and Smoky mountains. Most of the forest's southern division lies in southern Idaho, in the Cassia, Albion, Sublett, Black Pine, and Raft River mountains, cut by the tributaries of the Snake River. The major recreational facilities of the southern division are located at Rock Creek Canyon and Howell Canyon.

In the northern division, numerous trails and roads fan out into the wilderness from the Sawtooth Valley, leading to such famous hunting and fishing areas as Boulder Mountain, Big Wood River, the Smoky Mountains, the Soldier Mountains, and the White Cloud Peaks. This outstanding big-game region was the former hunting grounds of the Shoshone and Sheepeater Indians. The hunting today, though not nearly as good as it was in the old days, is for elk, mule deer, mountain goat, bighorn sheep, antelope, and black bear. There is excellent rainbow trout fishing if you hike up to the lovely wilderness lakes basin located on the eastern slope of the Smoky Mountain Range, which forms a long, jagged upthrust to divide the Big Wood River from the South Fork of the Boise. Camping facilities are located along the Big Wood River, and steep trails lead up from the valley floor to the high lakes. In the Sun Valley area to the southeast are the famous fly-fishing-only waters of spring-fed Silver Creek, a nationally renowned trophy rainbow fishery noted for its insect rich alkaline waters and abundant growths of watercress, tules, bullrushes, and water lilies. The headwaters of Silver Creek are reached via the old Sun Valley Ranch lands. Bird life often seen throughout the forest includes marsh hawks, redtailed hawks, osprey, goshawks, sandhill cranes, and golden eagles.

The jagged Sawtooth Mountain peaks are the setting for the 216,383-acre wilderness of the same name, whose wildlands were sculpted by the great glaciers of long ago. Hundreds of alpine lakes were carved by them; as they melted, the torrential streams formed deep gorges in the mountain slopes. Deer, elk, mountain sheep, and mountain goats roam the high country and provide outstanding hunting. The glacial lakes clustered at the headwaters of the Middle Fork of the Boise, South Fork of the Payette, and Salmon River are a trout fisherman's paradise. The major lakes of the Sawtooth Range and White-cloud Peaks region include Redfish, Pettit, Alturas, Stanley, Hell Roaring, Yellow Belly, and the spectacular Big Boulder and Boulder Chain lakes. Redfish is considered one of the world's most beautiful alpine moraine lakes. Most of the remote off-trail lakes provide fishing for Dolly Varden, rainbow, and brook trout, and Kokanee salmon—known locally as "redfish." The craggy Sawtooth peaks challenge the mountaineer. Atop the mountain, great snowbeds border wildflower meadows. This is the region of the Stanley Basin, where the mighty Salmon River is born. The brilliant yellows and blues of mountain buttercup and camas and dense evergreen stands cover the shores of Stanley Lake in summer; beyond them rise the great flanks of the Sawtooth Range.

The most popular entry points to the wilderness are the Pettit Lake Trail from Pettit Lake; Yellow Belly Trail; Hell Roaring Creek Trail; Redfish Creek Trail from Redfish Lake; and the Iron Creek Trail from Iron Creek Transfer Camp, all approaching the area from the east side of the Sawtooth Range. Most visitors enter the area in late July and August, although most trails are easily accessible in June, early July, and September. For more information on outdoor recreational opportunities in the Sawtooth Wilderness, write: Forest Supervisor, Sawtooth National Forest, 1525 Addison Ave. E., Twin Falls 83301; Sawtooth National Recreation Area Headquarters, Ketchum 83340; or Stanley Ranger Station, Stanley 83278.

Use permits (free) are required for all groups of 10 to 20 persons, stock use trips, and winter travel between November 15 and May 15. These are available at the Sawtooth National Recreation Area Headquarters (address above).

A *Sawtooth National Recreation Area & Wilderness Map-Brochure* is available free from the Forest Supervisor's Office (address above). It describes the area, gives tips on wilderness travel, and includes a detailed trail mileage chart. The map is on a scale of 2 miles to 1 inch and shows national forest boundaries, county boundaries, wilderness boundaries, roads (paved, secondary, dirt, and primitive), trails, ranger and forest stations, recreation sites, heliports, buildings, water features, and prominent topographic features.

The White Cloud Peaks and Boulder Mountains lie between the Salmon River on the north and west and the East Fork of the Salmon on the east. The Big Wood River borders the mountains on the south. The white limestone striations on the White Cloud Peaks give them their name, for they appear as summer clouds enshrouding the moun-

tains. The Boulder Range is a rugged, bare mass of peaks and spires varying in elevation from 6,500 feet to almost 12,000 feet.

More than a hundred alpine lakes dot the area, many of them formed in the cirques left by ancient glaciers. Clear mountain streams feed into the surrounding river systems. Elk and deer are plentiful throughout the area. At the higher altitudes among the rocky ledges and near the more remote lakes are mountain goats and bighorn sheep. Black bear and a few cougar also roam the area.

The most heavily used entrance point to the White Cloud Peaks area is by way of the East Fork of the Salmon. From this point lead the Big Boulder Creek Trail and the Little Boulder Creek Trail. The area may also be entered via road and trail at Slate Creek, Fourth of July Creek, Pole Creek, and Fisher Creek.

The Boulder Mountains are much less used. You can reach this area by the East Fork of the Salmon River, then by way of trails up West Pass Creek, South Fork of East Fork, and West Fork of East Fork. Access from the south is by way of U.S. Highway 93, up Boulder Creek, Gladiator Creek, and North Fork of the Wood River.

The free *White Cloud–Boulder Mountains Map-Brochure* is available from the Sawtooth National Recreation Area Headquarters, Ketchum 83340. The map, on a scale of 2 miles to 1 inch, keys the location of roads, highways, trails, ranger stations, recreation sites, landmark objects, and houses or cabins, as well as lakes and streams.

In addition to the developed campsites marked, camping is permitted in most areas at least 100 feet from lakes, streams, and trails. Pack and saddle stock use is permitted on all trails in the wilderness. The area is open to winter travel, but winter packers should be aware that avalanches are common in this area. Another sport gaining popularity in the area is mountain climbing.

Fishing is good in many of the region's cirque lakes such as Baron, Bear, Big Boulder Chain, Chamberlain, Frog, and Rainbow for brook, California golden, and Dolly Varden trout and grayling.

The Boulder Mountains on the north, the Smokies on the west, and

the Pioneers on the east are among the lands of the Ketchum Ranger District. The Pioneer Range is the second-highest of Idaho's mountain ranges, its peaks rising 11,000 to 12,000 feet. Trail Creek, Warm Springs Creek, North Fork, East Fork, and Deer Creek flow down from the mountains to feed the quicksilver waters of the Big Wood River. This beautiful mountain and valley area was once among the homelands of the Northwest Indian tribes. White settlers entered the Wood River Valley after the last of the Indian wars in 1879. Boom towns arose in the 1880s after rich ores were discovered in the area. Towns like Ketchum and Hailey fell on hard times after the closing of the mines. Then in 1936 the Union Pacific Railroad chose the site of Sun Valley, just outside Ketchum, to create the famous ski resort that attracts some 200,000 people a year today. North of Ketchum are the wildlands of the Sawtooth National Forest, where Ernest Hemingway found inspiration for his work. A half mile past Sun Valley, a Hemingway memorial is inscribed: "Best of all he loved the fall/ The leaves yellow on the cottonwoods/ Leaves floating on the trout streams/ And above the hills, the high blue windless skies/ Now he will be a part of them forever."

Snow-fed streams, hot springs, lakes, and canyons lace the forest country. All of the area's streams and most of its lakes offer trout fishing. Brook trout are found in beaver ponds, and cutthroats in the high lakes. Rainbow are also common. Elk and deer range the southern slopes in Trail Creek, Warm Springs Creek, Deer Creek, and North Fork during the winter months. Ski touring, as well as downhill skiing, has been popular here since the 1930s, when the Pioneer Cabin was built as a ski-touring hut by Sun Valley. The landmark lies along the western edge of the Pioneer Mountains and offers brilliant mountain vistas.

A guide to the *Ketchum District* is available free from the Forest Supervisor's Office (address above). The guide describes the area and its history, major features, access roads and trails, and camping facilities. A large map of the ranger district is included. It shows forest boundaries, roads (paved, secondary, dirt, primitive), trails, forest and ranger stations, recreation sites, points of interest, buildings, water features, and prominent topographic features.

A U.S. Forest Service *Sawtooth National Forest Map* is available from the Forest Supervisor's Office (address above) for 50¢. It shows all the features included in the Ketchum District map, as well as adjacent national forests of ski areas. A directory to recreation sites throughout the forests is included; it gives the map locations, elevations, facilities, and recreational opportunities of each site. The Forest Supervisor's Office (1525 Addison Ave. E., Twin Falls 83301) also publishes large maps of the northern and southern divisions of the forest, with scales of 2 miles to 1 inch. These maps cost $2 each. They provide a detailed inventory of individual areas within the forest boundaries. District Rangers of the forest are located at Hailey, Ketchum, Fairfield, Twin Falls, Burley, and Malta.

A *Motorized Vehicle Information Map of Sawtooth National Recreation Area* is available free from all Sawtooth NRA offices. This map shows most of the features shown in the Forest Service maps in black and white. It also shows roads open to vehicle use, trails open to motorbike travel, areas open to over-snow vehicles, big game habitats, and cross-country ski areas closed to over-snow vehicles.

Guided cross country ski tours along the 45-mile long Sawtooth Hut System (the huts are five to seven miles apart) are provided by *Leonard Expeditions*, Box 98, Stanley 83278 (208–774–3325).

Several guides and wilderness lodges provide services in the Sawtooth region. For detailed info, rates, and literature, write: *E. D. Bennett,* Box 286, Ketchum 83340 (hunting, fishing, trail rides); *Maxwell J.*

Bitton, Box 461, Mountain Home 83647 (big-game hunting, fishing, trail rides, backpacking); *Phillip A. Johnson*, Clayton 83227 (fishing, hunting, trail rides, backpacking, float trips); *Frank A. McMaster*, Star Rt., Ketchum 83340 (fishing, hunting, packstock); *Paul Ramlow*, Sun Valley 83353 (fishing, hunting); *Stanley Basin Ranch*, Stanley 83278 (fishing, trail rides, and backpacking in the Sawtooth Wilderness); *Fishin' Fool Fly Shoppe*, 760 Main Ave. N., Twin Falls 83301 (professional guide service for Silver Creek and Big Wood River system); *Sun Valley Co.*, Sun Valley 83353 (fishing, packhorse, backpacking, cross-country skiing, mountain climbing); *Sevy Brothers Guide Service*, Box 164, Sun Valley 83353 (fishing, backpacking, wild-river float trips); *Sawtooth Mountaineering, Inc.*, 5200 Fairview Ave., Boise 83704 (fishing, backpacking, cross-country skiing, mountaineering); *Redfish Lake Lodge*, Stanley 83278 (packhorse trips); *Galena Lodge*, Star Rt., Ketchum 83340 (backpacking, cross-country skiing). Professional guide service for fly-fishing in the Sun Valley area as well as access and information on most western trout waters, fly-fishing instruction, and guided backpacking and cross-country skiing trips are provided by *The Snug Company*, P.O. Box 598, Sun Valley 83353 or phone (208) 622-9305.

Other full-service vacation lodges in the Sawtooths are *Torrey's Burnt Creek Inn, Mountain Village Lodge, Idaho Rocky Mountain Ranch* (since 1932), all in Stanley 83278. The rustic *Robinson Bar Guest Ranch*, Clayton 83227 offers full fishing guide service and pack trips in the White Cloud Wilderness. For detailed fishing and hunting info in the Sun Valley area, write or call: *Sun Valley Sports Center*, Sun Valley Mall (phone: 208–622–4111) and *Dick Alf's Fly Shop*, Main St. (208–726–5282), both Sun Valley 83353.

Access & Outfitting Centers

The forest is accessible by way of U.S. 30N, 30S, and 93. It has 64 camping areas, 8 winter sports areas, and nearby resort, dude ranch, hotel, motel, and cabin accommodations. Accommodations, supplies, and outfitting services are available at the nearby communities of Burley, Gooding, Sun Valley, Twin Falls, Ketchum, and Hailey.

Targhee National Forest & Henrys Fork Trophy Trout Waters

Targhee National Forest Topo Maps
U.S. Geological Survey 1:250,000 scale overview maps: Ashton, Driggs, Dubois, Idaho Falls.

Alaska Basin Wildlands
U.S. Geological Survey large-scale topographic maps: Mount Bannon, Grand Teton (Wyoming).

Henrys Fork of the Snake River
U.S. Geological Survey large-scale topographic maps: Big Springs, Island Park, Last Chance, Lookout Butte, Snake River Butte.

Henrys Lake Fish & Game Area
U.S. Geological Survey large-scale topographic maps: Targhee Peak, Targhee Pass, Sawtell Peak, Big Springs.

Island Park Fish & Game Area
U.S. Geological Survey large-scale topographic maps: Icehouse Creek, Bishop Mountain, Island Park Dam.

Snake River Range
U.S. Geological Survey large-scale topographic maps: Garns Moun-

tain, Driggs, Swan Valley, Thompson Peak, Palisades Peak, Palisades Dam, Mount Baird.

This 1,700,000-acre forest, famous for its fishing, backpacking, canoeing, hunting, and wilderness camping, forms a great semicircle around the headwaters of the Snake River near the western borders of Yellowstone and Grand Teton national parks. It encompasses the mountains and valleys north from the Grand Canyon of the Snake and the crest of the Teton peaks and west to the Little Lost River, and includes the nationally renowned trophy trout waters of Henrys Lake and Henrys Fork of the Snake—one of the great historic trout streams, considered by many to be the best dry-fly stream in the West. Henrys Fork is the largest spring-fed creek in the world. The forest extends north and south from the Continental Divide to the Upper Snake River Valley. Lodgepole pine dominates the densely wooded river region, intermixed with stands of alpine and Douglas fir and Engelmann spruce. The high-country slopes and meadows are resplendent with colorful wildflowers in late spring and summer.

The famous trout waters of Henrys Lake lie nestled at 6,500 feet elevation beneath the Red Rock, Reynolds, Targhee, and Boot Jack mountain passes, surrounded by evergreen forests. This mountain-fed lake is a vestige of the lakes of the Pliocene period, which then filled valleys throughout the region. When the ancient Indian tribes inhabited the lands of the forest, mysterious islands composed of a spongy grass-covered substance periodically rose and sank in the lake. According to legend, the Indians refused to explore these islands for many years before they decided to use them as burial grounds. The Indians believed that by the time the scaffolds erected for the dead sank, the souls of the dead Indians would be free from worldly cares. Over the years the burial grounds would sink and reappear from the clear, warm spring-fed waters of the lake, bearing their haunting burden of the dead.

Chief Joseph and his people, the Nez Percé, came this way on their retreat from U.S. troops over the Lolo Trail. They fought a skirmish with a group of soldiers at the lake in an attempt to throw off their followers and escape through Yellowstone to safety in Canada. According to an early account, the forest is named after an Indian who died in this battle.

Camping areas dot the forest's mountain slopes, canyons, lakeshores, and riverbanks. The camping areas on the main highway to Yellowstone Park have better facilities and attractive settings, but they are usually filled to capacity by early evening in summer. More primitive and secluded camping areas lie within the forest interior. July, August, and September are the best camping months; June may bring a light snow.

Although there are no formally classified wilderness areas within the forest, the quiet magnificence of the forest offers backpacking and hiking trips varying from short, easy treks to extended backpacking over steep, rugged trails challenging to the most experienced backpacker. The west slope of the Tetons provides spectacular backcountry scenery.

Three ski areas with excellent skiing terrain and snow conditions serve the forest area—Kelly Canyon, Bear Gulch, and Grand Targhee. Cross-country skiing is gaining popularity, although there are no marked cross-country trails in the forest. Other winter activities include snowshoeing, sledding, and snowmobiling (trails available).

The Snake River is the most popular waterway in the forest for rafting, canoeing, kayaking, and boating. The North Fork (Henrys Fork) of the Snake crosses the northeastern portion of the forest in a generally placid course with some white-water stretches. The South Fork of the Snake forms the border between Targhee and adjacent forests along the south and southeast. The canyon of the South Fork offers exciting white waters. Both forks of the river are floated by commercial outfitters and private parties. There are no fees, permits, or formal restrictions on use of the river by private parties. Before you set out on a float trip, however, contact experienced river runners in the area or a Forest Service Office to obtain current conditions and detailed information.

Among the suggested rivers and stretches for canoeing are the upper portion of the Snake River South Fork, the South Fork of the Snake through the Grand Canyon of the Snake (hazardous—experienced float-boaters with larger boats only), and from Palisades Reservoir to the Forest Service Guard Station near Poplar and Kelly Canyon (some fast stretches); the head of Henrys Fork from Big Springs to Upper Coffee Pot campground, Box Canyon to Osborne Bridge, and Warm River to Ashton Reservoir; the Buffalo River from the Split Creek Road to Island Park Village; and the upper stretches of the Teton River. For more information about the Teton River, inquire at the Teton Basin Ranger District office at Driggs. For more information on the upper portion of the South Fork of the Snake River, write: Grand Teton National Park, Moose, WY 83012; or Teton National Forest, Jackson, WY 83001.

Forest Service information bulletins on camping, backpacking, ski areas, snowmobiling, canoeing, river running on the Snake River Grand Canyon, boating, and points of interest are available from: Forest Supervisor, Targhee National Forest, St. Anthony 83445.

The Targhee National Forest is an outstanding big-game region with excellent hunting in the Snake River Range, Big Hole Mountains, Moose Creek Plateau, Teton Range, Lemhi Range, and the Snake River plain for Shiras moose, Rocky Mountain elk, antelope, mule deer, and black bear. Game birds include geese, ducks, and grouse. The Targhee is the home of Idaho's largest moose herd, and the state's largest antelope herd is found in and adjacent to the forest in the Birch Creek Area. A few silver-tip grizzlies and bighorn sheep inhabit the remote high-country areas. The Island Park area, including Henrys Fork of the Snake River, is one of the two most important wintering areas in the United States for the trumpeter swan.

The Snake River System, perhaps the finest trout fishery in the Rocky Mountain region, is the area's foremost attraction. Henrys Fork, particularly the famous Railroad Ranch stretch, is famous for its big rainbows, cutthroats, and browns, with fish in the 10–12 pound class always a possibility. Below the Ashton Reservoir Dam, Henrys Fork annually yields 10-pounders to experienced fly-fishermen. Nymphs, fished in September or early October, are the bill of fare for the lunker trout. The main Snake River is well known for its excellent smallmouth bass fishing, as well as for channel catfish and sturgeon up to 400 pounds.

Henrys Lake, which lies northwest of the headwaters of Henrys Fork at Big Springs, has excellent fishing for brook, cutthroat, and rainbow trout in the 5 to 10-pound class. The lake's warm spring-fed waters are rich in insect life and provide blue-ribbon fly-fishing for large cutthroats and brook trout. (Use dragonfly and shrimp nymph imitations.) Due south as the crow flies, Island Park Reservoir, at 6,300 feet, is an outstanding producer of big brook and hybrid trout and coho and kokanee salmon. After maturing to a weight of 2–3 pounds, the landlocked kokanee migrate back up the streams to the place of their birth to spawn. En route, the male develops a humpback, a pronounced hooked jaw, and a coloration change to bright red. Several Forest Service campgrounds dot the scenic shoreline of Island Park.

The deep-flowing, boulder-strewn pools of the upper Teton River located to the north of the Snake River on the Idaho-Wyoming border offer excellent dry fly-fishing for 2–3 pound rainbows and cutthroats. If you're in the area, you might want to try the lovely, much underrated Falls River for good-sized browns up to 5 pounds. Popular local fly patterns include the Quill Gordon, Adams, Mosquito, Ginger Quill, Iron Blue Dun, Red Variant, and the Irresistible. Come prepared for deer flies and mosquitoes.

Numerous wilderness trails lead to such interesting areas as Sawtell Peak (9,902 ft.) and the renowned Alaska Basin, characterized by its raw peaks, alpine lakes, and wildflower meadows. Access to the Alaska Basin is by trail from the Grand Teton National Park or from the end of the canyon road east of Driggs.

For additional hunting and fishing information write: Supervisor, Targhee National Forest, St. Anthony 83445. The U.S. Forest Service *Targhee National Forest Map* is available from the Forest Supervisor's Office (address above) for 50¢. It is on a scale of 6 miles to 1 inch and

shows all man-made and natural features including, highways, trails, forest and ranger stations, recreation sites, ski areas, water features, and prominent topographic features.

Several guides and wilderness outfitters licensed by the Idaho Department of Fish & Game operate within the forest. For detailed info, rates, and literature, write: *A. W. Angell*, Rt. 1, Box 202E, St. Anthony 83445 (hunting, fishing, packstock and float trips); *Rhett M. Bradford*, Box 105, Irwin 83428 (big-game hunting); *Vaughn Haderlie*, Box 126, Freedom, WY 83120 (fishing, hunting, packhorse, backpacking, float trips); *Lyle Kunz*, Box 253, Driggs 83422 (fishing, hunting, packhorse and float trips); *Fremont Outdoor Education & Recreation*, 249 W. 4th North St., St. Anthony 83445 (fishing, float trips); *Glen J. Park*, Irwin 83428 (fishing, big-game hunting, packstock); *Dale Robson*, Felt 83424 (fishing, hunting, packstock); *Thomas K. Woolstenhulme*, Victor 83455 (big-game hunting, fishing); *Teton Expeditions*, 427 E. 13th St., Idaho Falls 83401 (fishing, packhorse, backpacking, wild-river float trips); *Ee-Da-How Mountain & Guide Service*, Box 207, Ucon 83454 (backpacking, mountaineering); *A. E. Pat Barnes*, Box 296, West Yellowstone, MT 59820 (float fishing); *James R. Danskin*, Box 276, West Yellowstone, MT 59758 (fishing); *Will's Fly Fishing Center*, Box 68, Island Park 83429 (fishing, backpacking, float trips); *Seldon M. Jones*, Box 111, West Yellowstone, MT 59758 (fishing); *Greg A. Lilly*, Box 387, West Yellowstone, MT 59758 (fishing, floating); *Henrys Fork Anglers, Inc.*, Island Park (complete guide service and fishing information on area conditions and hatches; address: Box 487, St. Anthony 83445). Guided fly-fishing trips on the Snake River and lodging are provided by *South Fork Expeditions*, 1880 Malibu, Idaho Falls 83201. Scenic glider flights of the Grand Tetons and Yellowstone and Cessna charter flights are available at the *Red Baron*, Teton Peaks Airport, Driggs 83422 (208–354–8131).

Rustic vacation accommodations on Henrys Fork are provided by *Last Chance Resort* at Last Chance in Island Park, Star Rt., Ashton 83420 (208–558–9966) and by the *Island Park Company*, SR Box 12, Macks Inn 83433. Vacation accommodations in the Teton Valley are available at *Grand Targhee Resort*, Driggs 83422 and *Melehe's Teton Tepee*, Alta 83422. Guided pack trips and hunts are provided by *Teton Creek Ranch*, Driggs 83422.

Access & Outfitting Centers

The major routes to Targhee National Forest are U.S. Highways 191/20 and 26, Interstate 15, and Idaho Routes 47, 84, 31, 32, 33, and A2. Lodging, resorts, cabins, supplies, boat and canoe rentals, guides, packers, and outfitters are available at Island Park, Lake, Ashton, Drummond, Lamont, Felt, Tetonia, Driggs, St. Anthony, Rexburg, Swan Valley, Alpine, and Idaho Falls, and Jackson, Wyoming.

MONTANA
ENCYCLOPEDIA

Accommodations—Rocky Mountain Vacation Lodges & Ranches

Several free guides are available to help you find vacation accommodations throughout Montana. Listed in these directories are lodges, guest ranches, resorts, and outfitters and guides. The *Montana Farm & Ranch Vacation Guide,* published by the Cooperative Extension Service, Montana State University, Bozeman 59715, lists farm and ranch hosts throughout the state and describes services, type of accommodations, activities, and types of visitors desired (sportsmen, families, young people, etc.). An *Accommodations Guide to Montana* is provided free by the Montana Travel Hosts Council, Montana Chamber of Commerce, P.O. Box 1730, Helena 59601. This guide lists ranches, resorts, hotels, and motels throughout the state, describing their size, facilities, services, and special activities (pack trips, hunting, fishing, etc.). The same organization publishes a short list of *Montana Outfitters and Hunting and Fishing Guides* and their addresses.

Among the many vacation lodges and resorts throughout the state are the following ranches: *Hole-in-the-Wall Lodge,* Box 86, Alberton 59820, offers pack trips, hunting, and fishing for 30 guests. *JJJ Ranch,* P.O. Box 383, Augusta 59410, provides accommodations (housekeeping cabins) for 8, pack trips, fishing and hunting, trail rides, and hiking. *Chief Mountain Guest Ranch,* Box 45, Babb 59411, with 7 rooms, has fishing and horseback riding. There are 20 rooms at *Flathead Lake Lodge,* Box 248, Bigfork 59911, which offers pack trips, fishing, and lake cruises. The well-known *Big Sky of Montana* resort, Box 1, Big Sky 59716, has 204 rooms, resort facilities, dude ranch facilities, restaurant services, and condominiums. Two dorms and 4 private family accommodations are available at *Rush's Lakeview Ranch,* 2905 Harrison, Butte 59701. The ranch offers pack trips, fishing, hunting, and cross-country skiing.

At *C-Bar-M Ranch,* Box A.E., Clyde Park 59018, 8 rooms are available to guests. The operating cattle ranch leads pack and fishing trips and offers room and board. *Chief Joseph Guest Ranch,* P.O. Box 48, Darby 59829, has 10 rooms and group facilities and offers family-style meals or individual cooking facilities. Activities include pack trips, hunting, fishing, backpacking trips into Selway, and horseback riding. *Covered Wagon Ranch* and *Nine Quarter Circle Ranch* offer lodging, pack trips, fishing, and hunting in Yellowstone country. Covered Wagon has 7 rooms, Nine Quarter Circle 41. Write to either ranch at Gallatin Gateway 59730. The Nine Quarter Circle Ranch also runs a September fly-fishing school with famous instructors on the blue-ribbon stretch of the Yellowstone and Gallatin rivers. The rustic *Boulder River Ranch,* McLeod 59052, offers lodging and fly-fishing for wild rainbows and brookies on 2 miles of private stream.

Fairmont Hot Springs Resort, Gregson 59711, has 190 rooms, with extensive facilities. *Wilderness Lodge & Ranch,* Box 391, Hungry Horse 59919, offers a much more rustic range of activities, including pack trips, hunting, fishing, float trips, and camping. The *Sixty Three Ranch,* Box 676, Livingston 59047, has 29 rooms, fishing and hunting, pack trips, and all cattle ranch activities. *Chico Hot Springs Lodge,* Pray 59065, offers both resort and rustic facilities and activities, including 63 rooms and a free 30-space campground.

Table Bay Resort, Rollins 59931, has 8 rooms, a campground, and a trailer court. It offers fishing, boating, and swimming. *Montana Sports Ranch,* Seeley Lake 59868, offers fishing and hunting, pack trips, and rooms for 12. *Roger Guest Ranch,* Swan Lake 59911, also leads fishing and hunting trips. *Elk Horn Ranch,* Victor 59875, has accommodations for 8 and leads pack, hunting, and fishing trips.

Desert Mountain Lodge, Box 155, West Glacier 59936, has 20 rooms

and leads pack trips and hunting and fishing trips, as well as trail rides. *Lake Five Resort*, Box 338, West Glacier 59936, has a 36-space campground and lakeshore cottages. *Blacktail Ranch J*, Wolf Creek 59648, is an operating horse ranch which offers fishing and hunting, trail rides, and family-style meals in the ranch house. *Boulder River Ranch*, McLeod 59052, provides lodging and fly-fishing on 2 miles of private stream for wild rainbow and brookies. The renowned *Nez Percé Ranch* is located in the Bitterroot National Forest and is the last stop before entering the majestic Selway-Bitterroot Wilderness. Numerous logging roads provide quick access to remote elk, deer, moose, mountain sheep, and goat-hunting country and high mountain lakes. The ranch is located at the banks of the West Fork of the Bitterroot on the historic Nez Percé Trail. The ranch offers rustic cabin accommodation, western cooking, and wilderness fly-ins, hiking, float trips, horseback riding, wildlife photography, and cross-country skiing. For literature and rates write: Nez Percé Ranch, West Fork Route, Darby 59829. (For additional listings of Montana guest ranches and lodges offering fishing, hunting, and wilderness pack trips, see "Rocky Mountain Outfitters, Guides & Guest Ranches" and the "Montana Travel & Recreation Guide" section.)

Aircraft—Charter Fly-in Services

For a listing of charter fly-in services, aeronautical charts, and information, write: Division of Aeronautics, Department of Intergovernmental Relations, Capitol Station, Helena 59601.

Bear Trap Canyon Primitive Area

The Bear Trap Canyon Primitive Area covers 3,639 acres in southwestern Montana beyond the northern tip of the Beaverhead National Forest. The Bear Trap is a 9-mile gorge carved through the Madison Mountains by the river of the same name. The craggy canyon walls rise nearly 1,500 feet above the water. Birds of prey soar among the timbered slopes and rocky cliffs. Mule deer are abundant here, and bobcats and coyotes are sometimes sighted. A variety of waterfowl nest along the river.

The Montana Stream Classification Committee has designated this stretch of the Madison as a "Blue Ribbon Trout Stream," the highest classification given to a fishing stream in the state. Many fishermen float the river from the powerhouse 9 miles downstream to the Red Mountain Campground. Shore fishing is also popular. The stream yields sizable rainbow and brown trout.

A number of camping sites are located in the gorge, and firewood is plentiful. Water from the streams may be used, but boiling or purification tablets are advised.

Motorized vehicles are prohibited in the Primitive Area. The most heavily used access to the area is a foot trail beginning at the Montana Power Company plant at the upper, or south, end of the gorge. Wear sturdy boots, for the terrain is rough and rock-strewn in places. The trail follows the east side of the river, offering spectacular views. The Primitive Area is about 30 miles west of Bozeman by way of State Highway 289. The route takes you to the Red Mountain Campground at the north end of the canyon. The area is also accessible by taking U.S. 287 from Ennis to McAllister, then east along the north shore of Ennis Lake. This route leads to the Montana Power Company plant at the southern end of the canyon.

A map and brochure, *Bear Trap Canyon Primitive Area*, is available free from: Bureau of Land Management, Montana State Office, 316 North 26th St., Billings 59101. The small map gives an overview of the Primitive Area, keying quadrangles within the area to *National*

Resource Lands in Montana maps provided free by the BLM office at the above address. The Primitive Area is shown on U.S. Geological Survey topographic maps of Norris and Ennis.

Camping & Backpacking in the Northern Rockies

Campgrounds throughout the state of Montana are listed and described in *Montana, Last of the Big Time Splendors*, a free booklet published by the Montana Department of Highways. The booklet describes the facilities and recreational opportunities at each campground, along with points of interest in each area. It also identifies good fishing areas, state and national parks and monuments, trails, and areas known for fly-in vacations, dude ranch vacations, backpacking, float trips, and skiing. Write: Montana Department of Highways, Advertising Unit, Helena 59601.

National Forest Camp and Picnic Areas in the Northern Region, a booklet published by the Forest Service, describes all campsites in Montana's national forests, giving access routes and naming attractions and facilities for each. For this free guide, write: Northern Region Office, U.S. Forest Service, Federal Building, Missoula 59801. Commercial campgrounds are listed by city and described (size, facilities, locations) in *An Accommodation Guide to Montana*, available free from the Montana Travel Hosts Council, Montana Chamber of Commerce, P.O. Box 1730, Helena 59601.

Camping the Big Sky, a free brochure of the Bureau of Land Manage-

ment (316 N. 26th St., Billings 59101), describes the state's BLM campgrounds in detail.

Several Montana outfitters specialize in guided backpacking and mountaineering trips. *Wildlife Outfitters*, Rt. 1, Victor 59875, offers backpacking trips in the Selway–Bitterroot Wilderness Area. *Backpacking with Barrow*, 282 W. 6th, Whitefish 59937, offers scheduled and custom trips in the Bob Marshall Wilderness Area of the Flathead National Forest. *Mountaincraft Inc.*, Box 821, Big Sky 59716, offers guided trips and mountaineering seminars in the Big Sky area and Beartooth Mountains Primitive Area. *High Country Adventures*, P.O. Box 176, Helena 59601, is a licensed outfitter of wilderness backpacking trips into the most spectacular backcountry of the Northern Rockies. Backpackers are offered expertly guided and fully equipped outings into such areas as the Madison Range, Yellowstone National Park, and the Bob Marshall, Selway-Bitterroot, and Beartooth wilderness areas. *Highcountry Outfitters*, Rt. 1, Box 99, Victor 59875, offers summer wilderness living classes in the majestic Bitterroot Mountains. *The Mountain Man Experience*, Box 222, Darby 59829, operates a unique school in the Bitterroot Mountains wilderness with professional instruction in the arts and crafts of the mountain men.

Fenwick West Yellowstone Fly Fishing School

The Fenwick Corporation's nationally famous West Yellowstone school of fly fishing is surrounded by the legendary trout waters of the Firehole, Snake, Madison, Gallatin, and Yellowstone rivers. You can choose a 3-day school that includes technique, development, and on-stream practice, or a 5-day school that adds a special guided wader trip and a float trip. Special advanced schools, limited to fly fishermen with previous experience, provide intensive instruction while you are actually fishing the fabled streams of West Yellowstone. The curriculum for all schools includes the art of fly casting; types of fly line and rod and reel construction; insects and their life cycles; artificial fly construction, identification, choice of flies, and how to match the hatch; knots; leader construction and uses; how to read a stream, where the fish lie, and why they do so; and wading. Family accommodations are available at nearby motels, hotels, guest ranches, and U.S. Forest Service campgrounds. For free literature, rates, and info, write: School Coordinator, Fenwick Fly Fishing Schools, P.O. Box 729, Westminster, CA 92683 (phone: 714-897–1066).

Fishing & Hunting in Montana

Montana is a stunningly beautiful and rugged state, which ranks as one of the West's truly great fishing and big-game hunting areas. The early Montana territory, rich in furbearers and big game, was explored successively by French fur traders, by Lewis and Clark, and by the mountain men and fur traders of the old North West Company, the Rocky Mountain Fur Company, and the "Upper Missouri Outfit" of the American Fur Company.

Hunting

The sheer abundance and exploitation of game during Montana's hunting and trapping era is illustrated by a colorful episode that occurred in 1854, when Sir St. George Gore, a wealthy Irish sportsman, entered the Powder River country (named for the fine black sand along its banks that resembles gunpowder) with the legendary Jim Bridger as his guide and a retinue consisting of 40 servants, 112 horses, 14 hunting dogs, 12 yokes of oxen, enough guns and ammo for a small army, and 6 wagons and 21 carts carrying every conceivable luxury from bound volumes of Shakespeare to telescopes. Although they barely made a dent in the wildlife population, Gore's party slaughtered so much game that they aroused the wrath of the Blackfeet, and were forced to flee south along the old Bozeman Trail into Wyoming territory.

Today the state has one of the country's largest herds of elk in the national forests of western Montana, as well as a large population of mule deer extending from the Rockies to the plains of the southeast. Whitetail deer are found throughout the national forestlands; the best hunting is in the Snowy and Big Snowy Mountains in Lewis and Clark National Forest and in the Longpine Hills of Custer National Forest in the southeast. Antelope range along the eastern prairies and in the foothills east of the Continental Divide. Yellowstone moose are found in the lake country of the southwest and northwest. Limited numbers of mountain goat and sheep and a steadily diminishing number of silver-tip grizzlies (known to Lewis and Clark as the "great white bear") roam the remote high country and wilderness areas of the foothills in the northwest. The prairies and scenic evergreen forestlands offer upland game bird shooting for grouse, chukar, pheasant, and wild turkey and waterfowl hunting for ducks and Canada geese along the Central and Pacific flyways. Montana's world-renowned big-game hunting regions include the Sun River Game Range, Painted

Robe Region, and the Crow Line, Castle Butte, Bull Mountains, Stillwater, Missouri River Breaks, Bitterroot, Blackfoot-Clearwater Game Range, Tobacco Root Mountains, Absaroka and Pioneer mountains, Sweetgrass Hills, Cut Bank, Blacktail, Kootenai, Swan, and Mission Mountains regions.

Trophy Fishing Waters

Montana is world-famous for the excellence of its scenic trout-fishing waters. The Big Hole, Flathead, Madison, Missouri, Rock Creek, West Gallatin, and Yellowstone rivers are classified as blue-ribbon trout streams and annually produce trophy browns and rainbows in the 10, 12, and 20-pound class. Equally renowned trout waters are the beautiful Big Blackfoot, Gallatin, Jefferson, Bitterroot, Boulder, Swan, and Sun rivers and scenic Flathead Lake, Georgetown Lake, and Duck Lake in the Blackfeet Indian Reservation. Georgetown and Duck lakes consistently produce enormous rainbows in the 14–15 pound class. Most of the state's trout are wild and temperamental, and will provide the most skilled angler with an exciting and often frustrating challenge. In the remote high country in the Selway–Bitterroot, Mission Mountains, Beartooth Plateau, and Bob Marshall Wilderness areas, the angler will find hundreds of isolated, primitive lakes accessible only by foot or packhorse, which hold cutthroat and rainbows, and some have grayling and golden and brook trout. Good bass fishing is found, surprisingly, in the numerous lakes and ponds in the scenic Flathead Valley, including the Ninepipe and Kickinghorse reservoirs and Thompson, Echo, Blaine, and Flathead lakes, to name a few. Northern pike up to 30 pounds are found in the Flathead River below Kerr Dam, in Fort Peck Reservoir, and in the Missouri and lower Yellowstone rivers. Montana's big fish waters, the Madison 20-mile Beartrap Canyon, the Yellowstone, Jefferson, Middle and North forks of the Flathead, lower Kootenai, Missouri, Big Hole, and Blackfoot, are ideal for float-fishing trips. The following table lists state's all-time record fish caught by rod and reel.

MONTANA RECORD FISH

	Lb.–oz.	Place	Year
Brook trout	9–1	Lower Two Medicine Lk.	1940
Brown trout*	29	Wade Lk.	1966
Black crappie	3–2	Tongue Rv. Res.	1973
Bluegill	2–8	Dengel Res.	1967
Burbot (ling)	12–9¾	Missouri Rv.	1977
Coho	4–14	Fort Peck Res.	1973
Cutthroat trout	16	Red Eagle Lk.	1955
Dolly Varden	21–7	Flathead Lk.	1957
Golden trout	1–6¼	Island Lk.	1973
Grayling	2–10	Handkerchief Lk.	1974
King salmon (Chinook)	4–7	Missouri Rv.	1972
Kokanee salmon	5–4	Helena Valley Res.	1969
Lake trout	28–5	Flathead Lk.	1974
Lake whitefish	No record		
Largemouth bass	7–6	Ninepipe Res.	1973
Mountain whitefish	4–9¾	Blackfoot Rv.	1977
Northern pike	37–8	Tongue Rv. Res.	1972
Paddlefish	142–8	Missouri Rv.	1973
Pallid sturgeon	38	Tongue Rv.	1950
Perch (yellow)	2	Nelson Res.	1974
Rainbow trout	20	Cliff Lk.	1952
Rainbow-cutthroat hybrid	17–10	Ashley Lk.	1973
Sauger	5	Tongue Rv.	1974
Smallmouth bass	4–4	Loon Lk.	1971
Sturgeon (shovelnose)	10–8	Yellowstone Rv.	1977
Sturgeon (white)	96	Kootenai Rv.	1968
Walleye	14	Nelson Res.	1974

*It's highly probable that the next Montana and world record brown trout will be caught in the big, turbulent waters of the Upper Missouri River below Canyon Ferry Dam. Documented sightings of giant browns in the 50 pound and over class have been reported there.

Maps, Guides & Booklets

Nonresident big-game hunters and fishermen are well advised to hire the services of an experienced guide or wilderness outfitter. Their knowledge of the region will increase your enjoyment and chances of success tenfold. Be sure to plan your trip well in advance and write to the Montana Dept. of Fish & Game, Helena 59601, for detailed information about seasons, permits, and regulations, and for a free *Fisherman's Log, Fishing District Maps, Hunting Zone Maps, Popular Float Streams Guide,* and *Montana Hunting & Fishing Booklet.* The Mountain Press Publishing Company, 287 West Front St., Missoula 59801, publishes two useful, info-packed guidebooks: *Montana's Fishing Guide Volume 1: Waters West of Continental Divide* ($6.95, 325 pp.) and *Montana's Fishing Guide Volume 2: Waters East of Continental Divide* ($6.95, 359 pp.). Volume 1 covers the Bitterroot, Clark Fork of the Columbia, Flathead River and Lake, the Middle, North, and South forks of the Flathead, the Kootenai, and the Swan, and Glacier National Park. Volume 2 gives the lowdown on the Beaverhead, Big Hole, Boulder, Gallatin, Jefferson, Missouri (Upper & Lower), Yellowstone, Teton, and Sun rivers. Both volumes describe river and lake characteristics, insect life, and recommended techniques and hot spots, and contain useful lake survey contour maps and photos.

Blue-Ribbon Trout Streams & Angling Guides

Montana's scenic "big water" streams and lakes offer a wide choice of trophy trout fishing. The world-renowned blue-ribbon trout waters of the upper Yellowstone flow for 104 miles from Yellowstone Na-

tional Park north through a succession of 10 to 20-foot-deep pools, riffles, and a scenic, rugged country of gorges, Yankee Jim Canyon, and beautiful Paradise Valley below the famous outfitting center of Livingston. Yankee Jim Canyon was named for James George, who, almost single-handedly, built the road into Yellowstone National Park on what became the Northern Pacific Railroad, paralleling the present-day U.S. Highway 89. Rudyard Kipling visited this colorful trapper and guide in 1890 and described the experience in a volume on his American travels. The Yellowstone from Livingston to its mouth on the great Missouri was followed by Lewis and Clark on their return trip through Montana from the Pacific.

The Yellowstone holds some monster browns and rainbow and cutthroat trout. Many of the trophy trout are taken on this classic fly fishing stream with streamers imitating the abundant muddler minnows and dry fly imitations of small midge flies and "salmon" flies. An indication of the quality of fishing on this historic river is found on the "Wall of Fame" in Dan Bailey's Fly Shop in Livingston, a collection of several hundred wooden plaques containing the silhouettes of Yellowstone trout 4 pounds and over taken on a fly. The largest "Wall of Famer" is a giant brown (14 lb. 4 oz.). The names of many famous American outdoorsmen and personalities are honored on Bailey's wall, including Joe Brooks (5 lb. 5½ oz. brown, muddler minnow) Art Flick (5 lb. 4 oz. brown, multicolored marabou), novelist and screenwriter Tom McGuane (5 lb. brown, spuddler), and cartoonist V. T. Hamlin (of *Alley Oop* fame, 4 lb. 5 oz. brown, Dadger Yellow). Dan Bailey's Fly Shop, an American institution among fly-fishing enthusiasts, produces over 750,000 trout flies annually (many on custom order) and provides guide and float-fishing service on the Madison and Yellowstone. A catalog of the shop's unique selection of trout flies and fishing gear is free upon request from *Dan Bailey's Fly Shop*, 209 W. Park St., Livingston 59047 (406–222–1673).

Several historic "Old West" towns are located along the Yellowstone and provide lodging, guides, and outfitting service for the river and the surrounding fishing and big-game hunting grounds in the Gallatin National Forest and Absaroka Range. They are Emigrant, Chico Hot Springs, and Gardiner—the home of Park's Fly Shop, which provides guide service into Yellowstone National Park and Absaroka Primitive Area and float-fishing trips. Gardiner is situated on the old hunting grounds of the Crow Indians and was named for Johnston Gardiner, a trapper who ran his lines along the upper Yellowstone and its tributaries in the 1830s.

The Yellowstone has several nationally renowned tributaries that provide top-ranked trout fishing. The Boulder River of the Yellowstone is a beautiful fast-flowing stream with deep pools and scenic cascades. It flows north from its headwaters high in the Absaroka Mountains for 50 miles through the Gallatin National Forest into the Yellowstone at Big Timber. The river is one of the state's finest trout streams for rainbows and browns up to 10 pounds. The outfitting center of Big Timber, named for the creek that rises in the Crazy Mountains and flows into the Yellowstone opposite the town, was originally called Rivers Across by Lieutenant Clark of the Lewis and Clark expedition because both the Boulder River and Big Timber Creek flow into the Yellowstone here. The headwaters area of the Clarks Fork of the Yellowstone on the Beartooth Plateau offers scenic wilderness fly fishing for golden, brook, and rainbow trout in high-country alpine waters such as Arctic, Hellroaring, Big Moose, September Morn, and Timber lakes and Lake of the Winds. The Shields River flows into the Yellowstone 4 miles east of Livingston after a 44-mile journey from its headwaters in the Crazy Mountains. The Shields holds some good-sized browns and rainbows.

The Big Hole River, a state-designated blue-ribbon trout stream, rises in the Bitterroot Mountains and flows through a deep canyon and the Valley of 10,000 Stacks, with many deep pools and riffles, to its confluence with the Jefferson River at Twin Bridges. The Big Hole is surrounded by the Beaverhead and Deerlodge national forests and offers unsurpassed fishing for large hook-jawed brown trout up to 17 pounds, rainbows up to 7 pounds, brook trout, and arctic grayling. The tributaries of the Jefferson, which flow into the river near the outfitting center of Twin Bridges, were originally named Philosophy, Wisdom, and Philanthropy by Lewis and Clark for Pres. Thomas Jefferson's cardinal virtues. With the passing of time, Philosophy became known as Wisdom Creek, Wisdom became the Big Hole, and Philanthropy became first the Passamari (Shoshone for "evil smelling") or Stinking Water, and finally the Ruby River. The earlier Indian name referred to the sulfur springs near the river. As with all great trout streams, the Big Hole can be very temperamental, and the refrain "you should have been here last week" often holds true.

The Jefferson River flows for 60 miles from its source at the confluence of the Big Hole and Beaverhead past the majestic Tobacco Root Mountains and old Indian caves that are visible from the river, through large deep pools and a towering limestone canyon, and past the famed Lewis and Clark Caverns to its confluence with the Madison and Gallatin at the outfitting center of Three Forks, where they form the mighty Missouri River. The long, flat, deep-flowing pools of the Jefferson, a state-designated red-ribbon trout stream, yield rainbows and browns up to 4 and 5 pounds. The largest brown taken on the Jefferson was a hefty 12-pounder.

The Gallatin River rises in Yellowstone Park and flows to its junction with the Madison River to form the Missouri. This scenic river yields brook, rainbow, cutthroat, and brown trout. The Bozeman vicinity is one of the best fishing areas on the river. Madison River is among the renowned trout streams of the world. The river rises in Yellowstone Park and courses through meadows and pine-covered mountains through Hebgen Lake, Ennis Lake, and Bear Trap Canyon to join the Missouri at Three Forks. Fishing is outstanding along this river; the Ennis vicinity is known for whitefish as well as for rainbow and trophy brown trout. The Madison flows through the Beaverhead National Forest surrounded by the majestic Tobacco Root Mountains on the west, the amethyst peaks of the Madison Range on the east, and the slate-colored Gravelly Range near the upper river. The Upper Missouri offers some of Montana's top fishing for trophy rainbows and browns up to 12 pounds, and for coho salmon/rainbow hybrids. Fly fishermen do well using big yellow perch streamers along the sandbars. The outfitting center of West Yellowstone, the gateway to the upper Madison and Yellowstone National Park, lies in the lands of the Sheepeater Indians, known as the "Country of the Painted Rocks."

The beautiful pools of the Gallatin River are served by float-trip and guide services available at the outfitting centers of Gallatin Gateway and Bozeman and reached by U.S. 191, known as the Gallatin Way, which winds up the rugged Canyon of the Gallatin between the Gallatin and Madison mountains in the Gallatin National Forest and skirts the western edge of Yellowstone National Park for nearly 30 miles.

For detailed information on stream conditions, hatches, lodging and where-to-go advice in Montana's "trophy trout" country, write or call the angling specialists listed below, all of whom offer top-ranked professional guide service and float fishing trips. The following firms are located in West Yellowstone (zip code 59758; area code 406): *Pat Barnes Tackle Shop* (Snake, Big Hole, Madison, Yellowstone), Box 296 (646–7564); *Bud Lilly's Trout Shop* (wading or McKenzie River driftboat trips on the Henrys Fork in Idaho and Madison with custom trips in Yellowstone Park), Box 387 (646–7801); *Jim Danskin Tackle*

Shop (Firehole, Madison, Yellowstone, Henrys Fork, Henrys Lake, Hebgen Lake), Box 276 (646–7663); *Bob Jacklin's Fly Shop* (Madison and Yellowstone Park waters), Box 604 (646–7336). Other area "blue-ribbon" guides include: *Beaver Pond Sport Specialists* (Big Hole, Beaverhead Madison, Gallatin, Yellowstone, Upper Missouri), 1716 W. Main, Bozeman 59715 (406–587–4261); Phil Wright's *Complete Fly Fisher* (Big Hole, Madison, Beaverhead Falls, Bitterroot, Gallatin), Box 105, Wise River 59762 (406–839–2243); *Will Godfrey's Fly Fishing Center* (Henrys Fork, Henrys Lake, Yellowstone Park), Box 68, Island Park, ID 83429 (208–558–9960); *Henrys Fork Anglers, Inc.* (Henrys Fork, Henrys Lake, Firehole, Madison, Yellowstone, Spring Creek), Box 487, St. Anthony, ID 83445 (summer: 208–558–7525; winter: 208–624–3595).

Far to the north, the beautiful Blackfoot rises high on the west slope of the Rocky Mountains and flows through the Helena and Lolo national forests and some of the best big-game country in the West to meet the Clark Fork of the Columbia near Missoula. The Blackfoot holds some lunker rainbow and cutthroat trout. The Swan River flows from high on the crest of the Mission Range through Gray Wolf, Whelp, Lindberg, and Swan lakes to the northern end of Flathead Lake at Bigfork. The upper stretches between the Bob Marshall and Mission Range wilderness areas have some of the country's finest cutthroat fishing, as well as rainbow, brook, and Dolly Varden to 10 pounds.

Flathead Lake, known as the "Gem of the Rockies," lies in the Flathead National Forest along the western foothills of the Mission Mountains. The lake is 28 miles long and 15 miles wide and holds cutthroat, kokanee, and Dolly Varden. It also yields large lake trout, as well as some bass and perch, and provides excellent angling for whitefish.

Above Flathead Lake on the blue-ribbon stretch of the Flathead River, cutthroat and large Dolly Varden predominate, and kokanee can be caught in the fall; below Flathead Lake are cutthroat and rainbow. The wild Middle Fork of the Flathead rises high on the west slope of the Continental Divide in the Bob Marshall Wilderness and flows through narrow, rugged canyons, glacial valleys, and evergreen forests. This beautiful crystal-clear wild river holds cutthroat averaging about a pound and huge Dolly Varden often in the 15–20 pound range. The mercurial North Fork of the Flathead is a large, crystal-clear float-fisherman's dream. It flows south from British Columbia along the western boundary of Glacier National Park through Flathead National Forest to its confluence with the main river. The North Fork offers variable fishing for migratory Dolly Varden. The headwaters area of the South Fork of the Flathead in the scenic Rocky Mountain high country of the remote Bob Marshall Wilderness offers superb wilderness fly fishing for cutthroat trout up to 3 pounds and bull Dolly Vardens up to 20 pounds. The South Fork has been cut off and isolated from the main Flathead and Flathead Lake by the construction of the Hungry Horse Reservoir.

Fishing guides and outfitters serving the Flathead River country and the Bob Marshall Wilderness are located at Kalispell, the seat of Flathead County, and surrounding towns. Kalispell lies in the beautiful Flathead Valley, known to the Salish Indians as the "park between the mountains," surrounded by Whitefish Range on the north and the sheer Swan Range on the east. Accessible only by the Old Tobacco Plains Trail, the Flathead Valley remained unexplored until the arrival of David Thompson of the North West Company in 1809, and no permanent settlement was made there until 1881.

The wilderness traveler in Montana should keep an eye out for the Rocky Mountain rattlesnake, the least venomous of the species, which is found in the high, dry rocky areas of the state.

For rates and info write: *Gary Abbey*, Box 219, Ronan 59864 (Middle Fork Flathead and Bob Marshall Wilderness); *Shirley M. Barrow*, Box 183, Whitefish 59937 (Bob Marshall–Gorge Creek drainage); *Roland O. Cheek*, Rt. 1-A, Box 202, Columbia Falls 59912 (Bob Marshall); *Vern "Bud" Cheff*, Charlo 59824 (Bob Marshall Wilderness, Mission Mountains); *Russell Deist*, Rt. 3, Kalispell 59901 (Bob Marshall–Schaffer Meadows area); *Milton Hopkins*, Rt. 1, Bigfork 59911 (Bob Marshall Wilderness); *R. H. "Buff" Hultman*, Seeley Lake 59868 (Bob Marshall, Swan Valley); *Ronald M. Hummel*, Seeley Lake 59868 (Mission Mountains); *Frank Jette*, Seeley Lake 59868 (Mission Mountains, Lindberg Lake); *Ambrose L. Kolby*, Lakeside 59922 (Flathead); *Eugene P. Lee*, Box 391, Hungry Horse 59919 (Bob Marshall Wilderness); *W. E. McClellan*, Box C, Lakeside 59922 (Flathead Lake); *James Madden*, Box 125, Martin City 59926 (North & Middle forks of the Flathead); *Dave W. Morris*, Box 554, Whitefish 59937 (Bob Marshall Wilderness); *Jim Noffsinger*, 239 Columbia Ave., Whitefish 59937 (Middle Fork of the Flathead); *Fred Norris*, Seeley Lake 59868 (Swan Valley, Bob Marshall Wilderness); *Harlan Pollman*, Box 1513, Rolson 59860 (Flathead Lake); *Lee Rost*, Bigfork 59911 (South Fork of the Flathead); *William Smith*, Rt. 1, Ronan 59864 (Bob Marshall Wilderness); *Art Strackbein*, Box 841, Whitefish 59937 (Bob Marshall Wilderness); *Pat Timmons*, S. Karrow Rd., Whitefish 59937 (South Fork of the Flathead); *Thomas C. Triplett*, Box 653, Kalispell 59901 (Flathead National Forest); *M. L. West*, Box 65A, Eureka 59917 (Bob Marshall Wilderness–Eureka area); *Harry Workman*, Box 84, Eureka 59917 (Flathead country); *Don Worley*, Box 124, East Glacier 59434 (Middle Fork of the Flathead).

Montana Outdoors, a beautiful full-color magazine published by the progressive Montana Dept. of Fish & Game, contains useful articles about fishing, hunting, backpacking, wilderness camping, wildlife, and conservation. It costs $3 per year for 6 issues and may be obtained by sending a check or money order to: Montana Outdoors, Dept. of Fish & Game, 1420 E. Sixth, Helena 59601.

For additional listings of guide services and descriptions of Montana's major fishing and big-game hunting areas, see "Montana Travel & Recreation Guide," and in this section see "Rocky Mountain Outfitters, Guides & Guest Ranches," and "Fenwick West Yellowstone Fly Fishing School."

Highways–Recreation & Scenic Routes

A free, comprehensive *Montana Official Highway Map* is distributed by the Montana Dept. of Highways, Helena 59601. The map includes descriptions of the history, geology, physical features, major regions, and recreational opportunities of the state. Montana state parks and monuments, historic sites, and points of interest are also indicated. All highways and roads, historic trails, airports, ski areas, campsites, rest areas, cities, and towns are keyed.

Two major trails cross through Montana on modern highways. The Old West Trail is a self-guiding automobile tour through five western states. Scenic and historic sites are marked with a Buffalo head symbol. In Montana the Old West Trail includes city circle tours of Billings, Butte, Fort Benton, Great Falls, and the Fort Peck area, and such sites as the Boothill Cemetery, historic riverboat landings, and museums of the Old West. The route through the state includes a tour of the mansion of a copper millionaire, the famous Big Sky of Montana resort, and a 14-mile round-trip river canyon excursion. A brochure on the *Old West Trail* is available free from: Old West Trail Foundation, P.O. Box 2554, 405 East Omaha St., Rapid City, SD 57701.

The Lewis and Clark Highway closely follows the route of Lewis and Clark between Lolo and Kooskia in 1805–1806. The highway winds through the beautiful Bitterroot Mountains. Campsites, hot springs, forests, and clear mountain springs dot the mountains along the historic route. For more information, see "Lewis & Clark Highway."

A leaflet distributed free by the Montana Dept. of Highways, Advertising Unit, Helena 59601, marks 4 scenic routes across the state between West Yellowstone and West Glacier. It describes the cities, lakes, rivers, forests, and mountains along these beautiful routes and places them in the context of the history of the state. Write to the Dept. of Highways and request *Montana between Glacier & Yellowstone National Parks*.

Humbug Spires Primitive Area

This Primitive Area covers 7,041 acres in hilly terrain about 25 miles south of Butte near the southern slopes of Mount Humbug. The slopes are covered with forests of ponderosa pine and studded with hundreds of white granite spires. Nine of the spires tower between 300 and 600 feet above the surrounding terrain, offering spectacular climbing for experienced mountaineers. One monolith overhangs on all sides and is yet unclimbed. Other spires offer climbs ranging from relatively easy to very difficult. If you climb here, recognize the limits of your experience and ability. Rescue operations for the area have not yet been established.

Among the animals of the area are black bear, whitetail and mule deer, and a few elk, moose, and bighorn sheep. Birds of prey soar among the rocky spires and peaks, and blue and ruffed grouse are found on the lower slopes.

Good primitive campsites are located here, and firewood is plentiful. Moose Creek, Lime Gulch, and Tucker Creek provide water, but boiling or purification tablets are advised. The area has no established trails, but the terrain is not terribly difficult.

For a brochure (including a small map) on the *Humbug Spires Primitive Area*, write: Montana State Office, Bureau of Land Management, 316 North 26th Street, Billings 59101. The BLM also publishes a series of maps of individual regions of the state, including this one, entitled *National Resource Lands in Montana*, which keys recreation areas and campsites and boundaries of national forests and monuments, state parks and monuments, and other lands. To find the map you need, obtain the free *BLM Recreation Guide*, a map of these lands throughout the state. These maps are available at the BLM Montana State Office at the above address. The primitive area is shown on the large-scale U.S. Geological Survey topographic maps of Butte South, Melrose, and Wickiup Creek.

Lewis & Clark Highway

This historic highway closely follows the route of Lewis and Clark through Montana for 133 miles between Lolo and Kooskia, Idaho. The highway winds through mountains covered by forests of pine, fir, cedar, larch, and spruce and dotted with hot springs. Lewis and Clark passed through this area of the Bitterroot Mountains in 1805–1806. Today the area includes parts of the Lolo and Clearwater national forests. The streams that lace these lands still yield trout and salmon, and elk, moose, mountain goat, and bear roam the mountain woods. Along the highway are spots for camping, picnicking, mountain climbing, fishing, hunting, and looking into the historic past. About 15,000 elk winter in the Selway-Bitterroot Wilderness across the Lochsa River to the south of the highway.

Fatigue and hunger nearly ended the Lewis and Clark expedition going west from Lolo to the Weippe meadow. The Nez Percé Indians had used this path before Lewis and Clark. It was their "buffalo road" across the Bitterroots to hunt the buffalo on the plains to the east. They guided the Lewis and Clark party when they crossed back over

the trail to the east, waiting at the Weippe meadow in June until they judged the snow had melted enough to permit passage.

A brochure describing the historic sites and recreational opportunities along the *Lewis and Clark Highway* is available free from: Northern Region Office, U.S. Forest Service, Missoula 59801. The brochure includes a map which marks camp and picnic areas, ranger stations, lookouts, and points of interest along the highway. (See also "Highways—Recreation & Scenic Routes.")

Outdoor Recreation Maps & Guides

All the public lands of Montana, state fishing or boating access sites, recreation and camp sites, highway rest areas, and ski areas are shown on a free map of the state published by the Bureau of Land Management. The map, on a scale of 20 miles to 1 inch, keys national forests and recreation areas, national parks, BLM lands, and lands administered by the Bureau of Sport Fisheries & Wildlife. The map also provides the names and addresses of other sources of information on outdoor recreation in the state.

Individual *B.L.M. Quadrangle Maps* for 42 areas within the state are also available free from the bureau. These maps include Glacier, Blackfoot, Tiber, Fresno, Havre, Belknap, Bowdoin, Glasgow, Poplar, Muddy, Seeley, Sun River, Cascade, Highwood, Judith, Breaks, U.L. Bend, Haxby, Circle, Savage, Granite, Avon, Townsend Castles, Snowy, Roundup, Sinatra, Custer, Fallon, Big Hole, Madison, Park, Beartooth, Pryor, Crow, Tongue, Powder, Box Elder, Red Rock, and Centennial. These maps show man-made and natural features including streams, ditches, reservoirs, dry lakes, springs, wells, windmills, oil or gas wells, mines, buildings, schools, recreation sites, highways, roads, jeep roads and trails, and boundaries. Both this series of maps, *National Resource Lands in Montana*, and the state map, *Montana BLM Recreation Map*, are available from: Bureau of Land Management, Montana State Office, 316 North 26th St., Billings 59101.

Rocky Mountain Outfitters, Guides & Guest Ranches

Montana Licensed Outfitters, a 31-page booklet provided free by the Montana Dept. of Fish & Game, Helena 59601, lists and describes all licensed outfitters in the state. The booklet gives the name, address, phone, hunt area, accommodations, and species hunted for each outfitter. A regional listing of the major outfitters and vacation guest ranches follows.

Spotted Bear Ranch, Hungry Horse 59919, leads hunting (big-game and birds) and fishing trips into the Bob Marshall area and has lodge, cabin, and tent accommodations. *Warren Johnson* of the Bear Creek Guest Ranch, Box 28, East Glacier 59434, leads cross-country skiing and pack trips and hunting and fishing expeditions into the Flathead National Forest and Bob Marshall Wilderness Area (big-game hunting and fishing are excellent in these areas). *Andrew Koch* of the Desert Mountain Lodge leads statewide big-game hunts and fishing expeditions. The ranch, at West Glacier 59936, has lodge and tent accommodations. *Rogers Guest Ranch*, Box 107, Swan Lake 59911, offers big-game hunting and fishing in the Swan Lake and Bob Marshall areas. The *Cheff Ranch*, Charlo 59824, provides guided fall hunting trips in the Bob Marshall Wilderness and Gorge Creek area. Guided fishing and hunting trips in the Bob Marshall Wilderness are also provided by the *Walking/Bar Nine*, Seeley Lake 59868, and *M Lazy Ranch*, Marion 59925. The *Bear Creek Guest Ranch*, Box 38, East Glacier 59434, offers guided hunting and fishing trips throughout

the Flathead National Forest and Bob Marshall Wilderness. *Holland Lake Lodge*, Seeley Lake 59868, offers fishing and hunting trips in the Bob Marshall area. All these outfitters are based in northwestern Montana.

In the west central portion of the state, the *White Tail Ranch* owned by Jack Hooker offers hunting and fishing trips to the Bob Marshall area and has lodge, cabin, and tent accommodations. The ranch is located at Ovando 59854. Paul Murphy of the *Murphy Ranch*, also in Ovando, leads hunting and fishing expeditions on the upper South Fork of the Flathead River. Tent accommodations are provided. Frederick Tedesco of *Streamside Anglers* leads hunting and fishing trips (tent accommodations) on the North Fork of Deep Creek, Sun River, and Rock Creek and in the Clark Fork Drainage. His address is: 1109 W. Broadway, Missoula 59801.

There are a number of well-known guides for southwestern Montana's numerous wilderness areas and national forests. Among them are: *Jim Anderson*, Lone Mt. Ranch, Big Sky 59716, who leads fishing trips in the Spanish Peaks, Yellow Mules, South Fork Drainage, West Fork of the Gallatin River, Thompson Lake, and Beaverhead National Forest areas; *Dan Bailey*, an eminent fly-fisherman and guide, leads fishing expeditions into Park, Gallatin, Sweet Grass, and Madison counties and their adjacent drainages (his address is 209 W. Park St., Livingston 59047); and Thomas Brogan of *Big Sky Guide and Outfitters*, Wilsall 59086, who offers hunting and fishing trips throughout southwestern Montana. Robert Furu of the *Big Sky Lodge*, West Yellowstone 59758, leads fish and game trips through Madison and Gallatin counties. *Devers Brothers*, Rt. 1, Box 27C, Dillon 59725, lead hunting and fishing expeditions throughout the state. Clinton C. Huth, *Wisdom Pack Station*, Wisdom 59761, leads hunting expeditions into Ravalli, Madison, Beaverhead, Silver Bow, Jefferson, Flathead, Gallatin, Deer Lodge, and Park counties, and fishing trips statewide. Accommodations include lodge, tent, and motel. Howard Keyes specializes in day trips statewide for hunting and fishing parties. Contact him through *Cottonwood Guide Service*, Rt. 2, Wilsall 59086. *Blue Sky Outfitters*, Rt. 1, Box 23, Dillon 59725, guides hunters and anglers in the renowned Big Hole and Beaverhead rivers country. *Bridger Mountain Guide Service*, Wilsall 59086, operates in the scenic Bridger and Crazy mountains. *Jim Danskin* of Jim Danskin Tackle Shop, Box 276, West Yellowstone 59758, guides fly-fishermen on all rivers and lakes in Gallatin, Madison, and Yellowstone counties. *Will's Fly Fishing Center*, located across the border at P.O. Box 68, Island Park, ID 83429, guides fishermen along the Madison, Gallatin, Big Hole and Yellowstone rivers. The rustic *Sundance Lodge*, Wise River 59762, provides guided fishing and hunting in the Beaverhead National Forest and Anaconda-Pintlar Wilderness. *Medicine Lake Guide Service*, Hebgen Lake, West Yellowstone 59758, serves fishermen and hunters in the Gallatin National Forest. The *Tobacco Root Guest Ranch*, Sheridan 59749, provides statewide guided fishing and big-game hunting trips. The rustic *Big Hole Lodge*, Wise River 59762, guides hunters and fishermen in the Beaverhead National Forest, Big Hole River area, and Anaconda-Pintlar Wilderness. *Park's Fly Shop*, Box 196, Gardiner 59030, guides fishermen along the famous upper Yellowstone and Missouri river areas. *Angler's Paradise Lodge*, Melrose 59743, has guide service for hunters and fishermen along the Big Hole and Beaverhead rivers. *Reed Outfitting & Guide Service*, P.O. Box 645, Ennis 59729, operates in the Gallatin and Madison mountains. *Lakeview Ranch*, 2905 Harrison, Butte 59701, provides statewide fishing and hunting guide service. *Wise River Club*, Wise River 59762, offers fishing and hunting guide service throughout the Beaverhead National Forest. The renowned *Parade Rest Ranch*, Star Route, W. Yellowstone, serves the Madison and

Gallatin, and Yellowstone Park's Firehole and Gibbon rivers. *Valley View Ranch*, Ennis 59729, guides big-game hunters and fishermen in the Beaverhead, Gallatin, and Yellowstone national park areas. Philip Wright of the *Complete Fly Fisher*, Box 105, Wise River 59762, guides anglers along the Big Hole, Madison, Beaverhead, Falls, Bitterroot, and Gallatin rivers. *Beaver Pond Sport Specialists*, 1700 West Main, Bozeman 59715, provides professional guide service and trips on the Big Hole, Beaverhead, Madison, Gallatin, and Yellowstone rivers.

North central Montana is a land of wide prairie ranges and the sun-whitened Missouri River Breaks. Among the guides of this area are Roy Coghill of the *Ford Creek Ranch*, Box 67, Augusta 59410, who leads hunting and fishing parties through the Flathead and Lewis and Clark national forests; Bud Heckman of the *Benchmark Wilderness Ranch*, Box 190, Augusta 59410, who works in the same areas; Arthur Goss of *Goss Hunting Camp*, Box 187, Augusta 59410 who specializes in big-game hunting along Smith, Petty, Jakie, and Goss creeks; N.K. Sayres of the *Mountain Palace Bar*, Cascade 59421 who takes fishing and game expeditions through the Upper Dearborn and Upper Blackfoot areas; and Art Weikum of the *Hidden Valley Ranch*, Augusta 59410, a hunting and fishing guide and outfitter for the Flathead and Lewis and Clark national forests and the White and Sun rivers. *D C Outfitting*, Hilger 59451, operates in the renowned fish and game areas of the Lewis and Clark National Forest. The *Klick K-Bar L Ranch*, Augusta 59410, guides big-game hunters in the Bob Marshall Wilderness and Sun River area. The *Circle Bar Ranch*, Utica 59452, provides guide service along the Judith River. *Hidden Valley Ranch*, Augusta 59410, guides fishermen and hunters by horse and jeep in the Flathead and Lewis and Clark national forests and along the Sun and White rivers.

The Yellowstone River winds north through the mountains of south central Montana, where big-game hunting and fishing are outstanding. In this area *Boulder River Ranch*, McLeod 59052, leads big-game parties along the Boulder River drainage. *Big Horn Outfitters*, Route 1, Box 171, Joliet 59041, is a guide and outfitter for hunting and fishing expeditions in Park and Stillwater counties and the Gardiner and Jardine areas. The Beartooth Ranch, Nye 59061, leads hunting

and fishing trips in the Stillwater River, Slough Creek, and Lake Abundance Creek areas. Accommodations include cabins and tents. Florence Paulson of *Paintbrush Trails*, Box 902, Red Lodge 59068, specializes in day trips for hunting and fishing parties in the Custer National Forest. *Scott Brothers Outfitters*, 1925 Grand Ave., Billings 59102, lead day trips in the Yellowstone River area and in the Broadus and Powder River country. Edward Whaley of *Wilderness Outfitters and Guides*, Box 452, Hardin 59034, is a guide for hunting and fishing expeditions statewide. *Beartooth Plateau Outfitters*, Red Lodge 59068, guides fishermen by pack train in the high lakes country of Carbon and Stillwater counties. *Beartooth Ranch*, Nye 59061, guides guests along the Stillwater River. The *33 Ranch*, McLeod 59052, guides hunters and fishermen in the Crazy Mountains and Custer National Forest. The *Hawley Mountain Guest Ranch*, Box 4, McLeod 59052, provides fishing and big-game hunting guides. *Rocky Mountain Outfitters*, Box 108, Roberts 59070, provide guided big-game hunting trips in Carbon, Stillwater, and Park counties.

In the plains of northern and northeastern Montana are the *K. C. Outfitters*, 1274 Boulevard Ave., Havre 59501. They lead fishing and hunting trips into the Strawberry Creek and South Fork Flathead River areas; the Flathead National Forest; Flathead, Blaine, and Phillips counties; and the Bob Marshall Primitive Area.

Outfitters and guides serving southeastern Montana include *Paul Ellis* of the Tongue River Stage, Miles City 59301, who leads hunting and fishing parties into Custer and Powder River counties; *Dan Keltner Outfitters*, Terry 59349, who lead fishing and hunting expeditions throughout the area; and *John Trumbo*, of Hell Creek Ranch, who leads day trips into the Garfield, Prairie, and Rosebud areas for fish and game. His address is: Jordan 59337.

Trail Riders of the Wilderness, operated by the American Forestry Association, sponsers summer high-country pack trips in the Bob Marshall Wilderness in the South Fork of the Flathead and Chinese Wall areas. The association also sponsors a scenic fall-color pack trip and photographic safari in the wilderness. For information and rates write: American Forestry Association, 1319 18th St., N.W., Washington, D.C. 20036.

The following members of the Montana Wilderness Guides Association—master blue-ribbon guides—offer professional guided wild-country fishing, hunting, and packhorse trips: *Monture Lodge*, Box 46, Ovando 59854; *Cheff Guest Ranch*, Box 124, Charlo 59824 (Bob Marshall Wilderness and Mission Mountains Primitive Area); *Wild Country Outfitters*, 713 W. Poplar, Helena 59601 (Scapegoat and Bob Marshall Wilderness); *Double Arrow Outfitters*, Box 104, Seeley Lake 59868; *V-A Ranch*, Box 162-B, Lincoln 59639 (Bob Marshall and Scapegoat Wilderness); *Wilderness Outfitters*, Rt. 6, E. Rattlesnake, Missoula 59801; *K Lazy Three Ranch*, Lincoln 59639.

Almost all of these guides provide complete outfitting for hunting and fishing parties, saddle and pack animals, and related services for backcountry and wilderness trips. Many of them provide vehicles for transportation into the backcountry.

If you plan to make a pack trip into the wilderness of the high country, the free booklet *Suggestions for Using Horses in the Mountain Country* will help you to plan your trip. Available from the Montana Fish & Game Dept., Helena 59601, it describes preparations for the trips, care of horses in the wilderness, and protection of the delicate environment of the wilderness. See the "Montana Travel & Recreation Guide" section for additional listings, and see "Camping & Backpacking," "Fishing & Hunting in Montana," and "Wildwater Outfitters & Missouri River Expeditions" in this section.

Ski Touring in the Montana Rockies

Thousands of square miles of public lands across Montana offer gently sloping meadows, forests, frozen snow-covered lakes, and slick mountain runs to the cross-country skier. Ski areas in the state include miles of developed and undeveloped ski terrain and lodges for overnight accommodation.

Cross country ski touring centers, lodging, instructions, and guided tours are provided by: *Bridger Bowl Ski School*, Box 846, Bozeman 59715 (phone: 406–862–3511), with accommodations at the Bridger Mountain Lodge; *Woody Creek Cross Country*, Box 1044, Cooke City 59020 (phone: 406–838–2305), site of the U.S. Nordic Team summer training camp, with guided tours into the Beartooth Primitive Area and Yellowstone National Park and accommodations at the Watuck Lodge; *Lone Mountain Guest Ranch–Big Sky of Montana*, P.O. Box 1, Big Sky 59716 (phone 800–548–4486 toll free or 406–995–4644) provides rustic lodging, trails, and guided tours in the Spanish Peaks Wilderness, Gallatin and Yellowstone backcountry; *Northern Nordic*, P.O. Box 895, Whitefish 59937 (phone: 406–862–3200), offers a summer training camp, instruction, and guided tours in the beautiful Flathead Valley west of Glacier National Park; *Whitefish Nordic Ski Center*, 15 Central Ave., Whitefish 59937 (phone: 406–862–5294), offers instruction, guided tours, and survival seminars; *Yellowstone Nordic*, Box 488, West Yellowstone 59758 (phone: 406–646–7319), offers first-class tours and lodging in the Yellowstone and Gallatin wildlands.

Wildwater Outfitters & Missouri River Expeditions

There is no special directory of river outfitters and expeditions in Montana, but the general guide *Montana Licensed Outfitters* includes some guides who lead river trips in addition to on-land fishing, hunting, and hiking excursions. Write for the free booklet to: Montana Dept. of Fish & Game, Helena 59601. This office will also provide you with a complete list of popular float streams and recreation areas, suggested gear, and water safety laws.

One well-known guide to the Missouri River is Bob Singer of *Missouri River Cruises*. He offers canoe trips and cruise services down the historic river, recalling the Lewis and Clark expedition on the wild section of the river stretching 160 miles below Fort Benton. A variety of trips are offered, most of them from 2 to 5 days in duration. Write to: Bob Singer, Missouri River Cruises, P.O. Box 1212, Fort Benton 59442.

The 2,466-mile-long Missouri, believed to have been named for a tribe of Sioux living near the river and called the Emessourita, meaning "dwellers on the Big Muddy," forms a wild, untamed stretch, designated as a national wild and scenic river, between historic Fort Benton and the huge Fort Peck Reservoir. It flows through the rugged White Cliffs area of the Missouri River Breaks—between the Little Rockies and Bearpaw and Highwood mountains—with their spectacular, colorful eroded sandstone formations. A boat trip down to the "wild" Missouri passes through ancient Indian hunting grounds marked by tepee rings and "Pishkun," or buffalo jumps, along the high cliffs and bluffs and historic landmarks that note the passing of the Hudson's Bay Company and Northwest Company, trappers, the Lewis and Clark expedition, Manuel Lisa and John Colter, and countless other explorers, fur traders, mountain men, and adventurers. A series of five boater campsites are situated at intervals on the Missouri between Virgelle and James Kipp State Recreation Area in Charlie Russell country at Coal Banks Landing, Cow Island Landing, Judith Landing, Hole-in-the-Wall, and Slaughter River on the route of Lewis and Clark. Downstream from Fort Benton—once the major supply depot of the American Fur Company for camp traders in Montana, Idaho, and Canada and outfitting center for thousands of tenderfeet heading into the gold-rush country—are the faint remains of historic Fort McKenzie near the mouth of the Marias River, and Fort Cook, Fort Clagett, and Fort Chardon near the mouth of the Judith River. The Fort Benton Museum contains a reproduction of an early keel boat of the type used by Lewis & Clark during their arduous upstream exploration of the Missouri. Boaters on the "wild" river stretch may see golden eagles, pelicans, cliff swallows, elk, and bighorn sheep, described in *The Journals of Lewis & Clark 1804–06 Expedition*. This stretch of the Missouri above Fort Peck Reservoir holds northern pike up to 20 pounds and prehistoric paddlefish. Fascinating *1893 Maps of the Missouri River* (6 sheets), with historical notes on the Missouri from the mouth of the Marias to Fort Peck Reservoir, may be obtained free upon request from: National Park Service, Rocky Mountain Region, P.O. Box 25287, Denver, CO 80225. These historical maps, with a scale of 1 inch to 1 mile, show the shoreline and topography of the Missouri, mileages, and historical sites and river features, including Fort Benton, Lewis and Clark's campsites, Fort McKenzie, Brule Bar, Black Bluffs Rapids, Spanish Islands, Three Islands, Crow Coulee Bar, Butcher Knife Canyon, Hole in the Wall, the Pinnacles, Sheath Bottom, Steamboat Rock, Gallatin and Bear Rapids, Chimney Bend, and Little Dog Rapids. For additional information on the Missouri National Wild & Scenic River, write: Bureau of Land Management, P.O. Box 30157, Billings 59107. The "wild" upper Missouri from Fort Benton to the head of Fort Peck Reservoir is shown on the following large-scale U.S. Geological Survey topographic maps: Fort Benton, O'Hamlon Coulee, Loma W., Loma E., Stranahan, Boggs Island, Verona, Lonetree Coulee, Big Bend School, Pilot Rock, Eagle Buttes, Dark Butte, Last Chance Butte, Starve Out Flat, PN Ranch, Council Island, Gallatin Rapids, Leroy, Taffy Ridge, Bird Rapids, Sturgeon Island, Cow Island, Baker Monument, Bell Ridge W., Bell Ridge E., Hessler Ridge, Carter Coulee. The "wild" river section is shown on U.S. Geological Survey 1:250,000 overview maps of Great Falls and Lewistown.

MONTANA TRAVEL & RECREATION GUIDE

Beaverhead National Forest & Big Hole Trophy Trout Country

Beaverhead National Forest Topo Maps

U.S. Geological Survey 1:250,000 scale overview maps: Bozeman, Butte, Dillon, Dubois.

Beaverhead River

U.S. Geological Survey large-scale topographic maps: Garfield Canyon, Red Rock, Dalys, Gallagher Mountain, Dillion W, Dillion E, Glen SE, Beaverhead Rock SW, Beaverhead Rock, Beaverhead Rock NE, Twin Bridges.

Big Hole River Blue-Ribbon Trout Waters

U.S. Geological Survey large-scale topographic maps: Beaverhead Rock, Block Mount, Dewey, Dickey Hills, Earls Gulch, Glen, Lincoln Gulch, Lower Seymour Lake, Melrose, Mud Lake, Pine Hill, Twin Bridges, Virond Park, Wisdom, Big Hole Pass, Issac Meadows, Big Hole Battlefield.

Jefferson River

U.S. Geological Survey large-scale topographic maps: Jefferson Island, Three Forks, Twin Bridges, Vendome, Waterloo, Whitehall.

Red Rock River & Lakes

U.S. Geological Survey large-scale topographic maps: Upper Red Rock Lake, Lower Red Rock Lake, Antelope Peak, Wolverine Creek, Monida, Lima Dam, Henry Gulch, Lima, Dell, Briggs Ranch, Kidd, Red Rock.

Ruby River

U.S. Geological Survey large-scale topographic maps: Monument Ridge, Stonehouse Mountain, Spur Mountain, Varney, Home Park Ranch, Ruby Dam, Belmont Park Ranch, Metzel Ranch, Alder, Laurin Canyon, Sheridan, Beaverhead Rock NE, Twin Bridges.

Situated in southwestern Montana, this 2,195,166-acre reserve encompasses the rugged Beaverhead Mountains and some of the finest stretches of trout water in the country, including the Madison, famous for its lunker browns and rainbows; Big Hole, called simply "the Hole" by early trappers and the Wisdom River by Lewis and Clark, which flows through a broad valley bottom and holds some giant rainbows and browns; and the mighty Jefferson River. Elevations in the forest range from 5,200 feet in the vicinity of Melrose east of Sheridan and Ennis Lake to 11,316 feet at Hilgard Peak in the Madison Range. From the lower elevations, where semidesert conditions prevail, lofty snow-covered mountains can be seen thrusting above the timberline, and although nearly 40 peaks exceed 10,000 feet, all of them can be climbed without special technical equipment. The Continental Divide Trail and many forest roads lead to the deep pools and riffles of the Beaverhead River; the challenging summits of the Snowcrest, Greenhorn, and Tobacco Root mountains; Schultz Lakes; Wade Lake; Echo Lake, nestled on the crest of the Madison-Gallatin Divide; the Pioneer Mountains; and Taylor Peaks.

The Beaverhead River, a slow, meandering stream that flows between the major units of the forest through the broad Beaverhead Valley, begins at Clark Canyon Reservoir, at the junction of the Red Rock River and Horse Prairie Creek, and heads north for 33 miles to its confluence with the Jefferson. The river's deep holes, gravel bars, and riffles offer good fishing for whitefish and for brown trout up to 8 pounds. Most fishermen descend the river by canoe or inflatable boats, because the brushy shore makes casting difficult. There is also hunting in the river valley for sage and mountain grouse, chukar partridge,

pheasant, duck, and goose in season. From the Beaverhead's headwaters, Captain Meriwether Lewis crossed the Great Divide through Lemhi Pass (7,373 ft.) in August of 1805. Sacajawea, his famous guide, recognized the unusual formation of Beaverhead Rock rising near the shores of the river and realized that she was not far from her native tribal lands. Short of rations and supplies, the Lewis party stumbled upon a Shoshone camp and offered gifts in the hopes of receiving help and food in return. As luck would have it, the Shoshone Chief Cameahwait was none other than Sacajawea's brother; the storybook reunion between long-lost brother and sister guaranteed the friendly reception of the Lewis party and the continued survival of the struggling expedition on its westward trek.

Flowing through the "Valley of 10,000 Stacks" into the Beaverhead from the north is the Big Hole River, named after the trapper's term for a large mountain valley. The Big Hole Battlefield, at the junction of Trail Creek and the North Fork of the Big Hole, marks the site of Chief Joseph's defeat of General Howard in 1877 during the flight of the Nez Percé along the arduous Lolo Trail towards Canada. In the Big Hole Basin, the river flows through lush meadows dotted by thousands of haystacks. Men once traveled here from far and wide during the late hay harvest to earn a summer's pay in this fastness of the Old West. This historic blue-ribbon trout stream is one of the nation's truly great fly-fishing waters for trophy grayling and brook, rainbow, and brown trout, the latter up to 20 pounds. In late summer, wading the Big Hole is hazardous because moss covering the underwater rocks is thick and slippery; chain creepers or waders with felt soles are a must. The remote alpine lake headwaters of the Big Hole feeder streams on the Beaverhead Mountains, including Swamp, Big Lake, Miner, Hamby, Pioneer, and Darkhorse creeks, offer unsurpassed high-country fishing for grayling and cutthroat, brook, and rainbow trout, and hunting for moose, elk, deer, and black bear. Traveling upriver, the Jefferson, formed by the confluence of the Beaverhead and Big Hole, flows northeast for 70 miles, where it joins with the Madison and Gallatin at Three Forks, an ancient battleground of Crow and Blackfeet Indians, and marks the beginning of the mighty Missouri. Lewis and Clark named the Jefferson in honor of the great statesman responsible for the exploration and acquisition of the western United States. The river is best known for its rainbow and brown trout, with browns averaging about 2 pounds and some lunkers up to 7½. The upper Madison River is famous for its salmonfly hatch, which reaches a peak during the last week of June, the same time as the giant stone fly hatch. The proliferation of insects works the giant rainbows and browns into a feeding frenzy. Echo Lake yields 2 to 3-pound rainbows when the fishing is good. This beautiful spot is a mile west of Echo Peak, below the amethyst-colored crests of the Madison Range. The best way to get there is via the Moose Creek Trail along the top of the Madison-Gallatin Divide. There is also some hunting for mountain goat here. Ennis Lake, a flooded hay meadow, has some real lunker rainbows and browns, and Wade Lake, deep in a steep-walled canyon, produced the state-record brown trout (29 lb.). A high alpine lake west of Mount Takepia, Schultz Lake, holds cutthroat and rainbow trout that average 1–2 pounds, plus a few big ones to 5 pounds. The evergreen forests and breathtaking high country also offer top-ranked hunting for elk, mule deer, Yellowstone moose, antelope, bear, mountain goat, and bighorn sheep. Upland game bird hunting is good for Franklin, blue, ruffed, and sage grouse.

Other big-game mountain ranges within this immense reserve include the Snowcrest, Greenhorn, Gravelly, Ruby, Bitterroot, and Tobacco Root ranges. Along the slopes of the Tobacco Root Mountains grows a variety of bitterroot called *quee* by the Shoshone and *racine de tabac* (tobacco root) by French voyageurs who discovered that the roots of the plant gave off a pungent nicotine odor when cooked. While the hardy Indians had no trouble digesting the root, white visitors found that the strange plant produced effects equivalent to eating straight tobacco. To the south of the Tobacco Root Mountains is the Ruby Range, once thought to be a source for more precious stones than the common garnets actually found by disappointed prospectors. In the southeastern reaches of the forest are the slate-colored slopes of the Gravelly Range, resembling vast banks of flowing sand. The mountains of the Beaverhead National Forest are rich in the history of Montana's great gold rush, and old ghost towns, such as Elkhorn near the Pioneer Range, offer mute testimony to the days of the mining boom, when Virginia City's population swelled to 10,000 and the Alder Gulch produced over $9 million in gold in a single year. Abandoned mines, battered railroad grades, ancient charcoal kilns, and primitive roads are all that remain of this frenetic and short-lived era.

Several tributaries of the Beaverhead and Big Hole rivers rise in the forest's famous big-game-hunting high-country areas and offer some of the finest wilderness trout fishing in the West. The Ruby River, a designated red-ribbon trout stream, heads high among the peaks of the Gravelly and Snowcrest mountains and flows down, northward, through a broad open valley to its junction with the Beaverhead near Twin Bridges. The Ruby and its reservoir hold wild rainbow, cutthroat, and brown trout up to 10 pounds. The remote high-country alpine lakes surrounding the Wise River, Willow Creek, Cherry Creek, Trapper Creek, and Canyon Creek tributaries of the Big Hole River, which rise in the Pioneer Mountains, provide often unsurpassed wilderness fly-fishing for cutthroat, brook, rainbow, and lake trout, grayling, and whitefish. Many of these lightly fished gems hold trophy fish in the 5-pound-plus class. Several Forest Service campgrounds are scattered throughout the area; access is by logging roads and trails. The Red Rock River rises high on the Continental Divide near the Henrys Lake area of the Targhee National Forest and flows through alpine meadows and precipitous gorges, plunging through Hell Roaring Creek Canyon and the beautiful Alaska Basin, into Centennial Valley and the Red Rock Lakes National Wildlife Refuge, and winds westward through the Lima Reservoir, past the towns of Lima and Dell into the Clark Canyon Reservoir. The nesting areas in the 40,000-acre Red Rock Lakes National Wildlife Refuge, the single most important breeding grounds in the United States for the endangered trumpeter swan, are closed to fishing. The Red Rock from Dell to the Clark Canyon Reservoir is designated a red-ribbon trout stream and holds rainbow, cutthroat, and brown trout up to 7 pounds. Below Clark Canyon Dam, the Red Rock becomes the Beaverhead River.

In the northwest reaches of the forest are 72,000 acres of the magnificent Anaconda-Pintlar Wilderness, which straddles the Continental Divide and extends into parts of the Beaverhead, Bitterroot, and Deerlodge national forests. The Anaconda Range is a true sierra, encompassing spectacular cirques, glacial moraines, sparkling streams fed by perpetual snowbanks above the timberline, numerous lakes, and high, secluded mountain meadows. On Rainbow Mountain, Pintlar Peaks, and at other points along the Continental Divide, hikers and horseback riders can view the Mission Mountains to the northwest and the mountains marking the Idaho-Montana boundary to the southwest. The wilderness can be reached by horse or foot over trails from the Big Hole, Bitterroot, Rock Creek, and Warm Springs Creek valleys. Motorized travel in the area is not permitted.

For information about camping, hunting, and fishing regulations in the forest, write: Forest Supervisor, Beaverhead National Forest, Dillon 59725. The *Beaverhead National Forest Map* is available for 50¢ from the supervisor. It shows all roads and trails, recreation sites, ranger stations, and points of interest, including the major routes of the Lewis and Clark expedition through the forest. Individual black-

and-white maps of each ranger district, showing roads, trails, mountains, caves, recreation sites, lakes, streams, and other features, are available from the Ranger Stations at Ennis, Dillon, Sheridan, Wisdom, and Wise River.

Rustic family vacation accommodations and guided fishing, hunting, and packhorse trips are provided by the *Big Hole Lodge*, Wise River 59762 and *Canyon Creek Guest Ranch*, Melrose 59743.

Access & Outfitting Centers

The Beaverhead National Forest is reached via U.S. Highways 287, 91, and 15 and Montana State Highways 287, 41, 257, 278, and 43. Supplies, guides, and outfitting services are available at Cameron, Alder, Virginia City, Norris, Nevada City, Pony, Dell, Lima, Jackson, Wisdom, Divide, Wise River, and Melrose.

Bitterroot National Forest & Alpine Wilderness Areas

Bitterroot National Forest Topo Maps

U.S. Geological Survey 1:250,000 scale overview maps: Butte, Dillon, Elk City, Hamilton.

Anaconda-Pintlar Wilderness

U.S. Geological Survey large-scale topographic maps: Long Peak, Pine Hill, Pintlar Lake, Warren Peak, Foolhen Mountain, Lower Seymour Lake, Mount Evans, Storm Lake, Carpp Ridge; and Dillon and Butte (1:250,000 scale maps).

Bitterroot River Fish & Game Country

U.S. Geological Survey large-scale topographic maps: Boulder Peak, Burnt Ridge, Corvallis, Darby, Florence, Hamilton N., Hamilton S., Medicine Hot Springs, Painted Rock Lake, Piquet Creek, Robbins Gulch S.W., Missoula, Stevensville.

Selway-Bitterroot Wilderness Alpine Lakes Country

U.S. Geological Survey large-scale topographic maps: Shoup, Painted Rock Lake, Blue Joint, Nez Percé Peak, Watchtower Peak, Mount Jerusalem, Boulder Peak, Tin Cup Lake, Trapper Peak, Hunter Peak, El Capitan, Como Peaks, Saddle Mountain, Tenmile Lake, Ward Mountain, Blodgett Mountain, Printz Ridge, White Sand Lake, Gash Point, Ranger Peak, St. Joseph Peak, Dick Creek.

The Bitterroot National Forest encompasses 1.5 million acres of snow-capped peaks, alpine lakes and meadows, rushing mountain streams, and some of the most remote high-country wilderness in the West. The forest is located in west central Montana and takes in the rugged Anaconda-Pintlar Wilderness and a large portion of the vast Selway-Bitterroot Wilderness, which straddles the Montana-Idaho boundary along the crest of the Bitterroot Mountains. The Bitterroot River rises high in the alpine lakes of the wilderness along the western slope of the Continental Divide and meanders in a broad valley through the heart of the forest for 70 miles. The west and east branches of the Bitterroot meet at Conner, once known as the "Place of Many Roads," where the long-gone trails of the Nez Percé and Salish crossed on their way east to the northern plains buffalo hunting grounds. A renowned float-fishing stream, the Bitterroot was named by the Salish Indians after the flower classified *Lewisin rediviva* by Meriwether Lewis in 1805 and found among the cottonwood stands that line the riverbanks. The Bitterroot holds large rainbow, brown, cutthroat, and brook trout. The rugged upper stretches of the river, including the West and East forks, provide top-ranked float-fishing for large rain-

bows. Its many oxbows and sloughs are fine shooting areas for duck and Canada goose. The Bitterroot high country and foothills provide hunting in season for mountain goat, deer, elk, and moose.

The Montana portion of the vast 1-million-acre Selway-Bitterroot Wilderness contains scores of sparkling blue alpine trout lakes at elevations ranging from 8,000 to 10,000 feet, which form the headwaters of the turbulent mountain tributaries that feed into the Bitterroot River. These high-country gems, such as Lake of the Rocks, Tin Cup, Canyon, Boulder, Big Creek, Totem Peak, Fred Burr, and Grizzly lakes, and the snow-fed mountain streams lie in the heart of elk and grizzly country and provide good fishing for rainbow, brook, and cutthroat trout. Access to the eastern slope of the range is by foot and packhorse trails, which are readily accessible from Highway 93 and the Nez Percé Trail road along the Selway River in Idaho.

The Indians made little use of this wilderness area. Their trails linking Idaho's Clearwater Valley with the Bitterroot Valley ran to the north and south, avoiding the rugged high country of the Bitterroot Divide. Their summer encampments were along the upper Selway (from the Nez Percé word *Selwah* meaning *"smooth water"*), lower Bear Creek, and Moose Creek areas, where they fished for salmon and steelhead and hunted the natural mineral licks for mule deer and elk. Wilderness campers in the area may see the remains of marten sets notched in trees and old line cabins built by trappers who once worked the area. The design of the marten set notches varied by trapper from a cathedral or rounded shape to a rectangular notch. Backpacking trips and trail rides in the Selway-Bitterroot Wilderness are sponsored by *Rocky Mountaineers*, P.O. Box 1575, Missoula 59801; *Montana Wilderness Association*, Box 548, Bozeman 59715; *Sierra Club*, Box 315, Missoula 59801; *Wilderness Society*, 729 15th Street, N.W., Washington, DC 20005; and *American Forestry Association*, 919 17th Street, N.W., Washington, DC 20006. A listing of professional outfitters and guides serving the wilderness may be obtained by writing: *Bitterroot Outfitters & Guides*, Sula 59871; *Montana Outfitters & Dude Ranchers Association*, Bozeman 59715; and *Idaho Outfitters & Guides Association*, Boise, ID 83701. A full-color *Selway-Bitterroot Wilderness Map* may be obtained for 50¢ by writing: Forest Supervisor, Bitterroot National Forest, Hamilton 59840.

The 157,803-acre Anaconda-Pintlar Wilderness lies due east from the Selway-Bitterroot Wilderness astride the Continental Divide for 30 miles in the Anaconda Range of the Rocky Mountains. The rugged Anaconda Range is a true sierra, with spectacular cirques, U-shaped valleys, glacial moraines in the foothills, and turbulent streams that plunge down through alpine forests and steep canyons from the high-country meadows and lakes. The wilderness is laced by a network of hiking trails, including a 45-mile trail along the crest of the Great Divide, which provide access to the high peaks and to the East Fork of the Bitterroot and its headwaters at Ripple, Kelly, and Hidden lakes, situated beneath Bitterroot Pass. The East Fork and its alpine headwaters hold cutthroat and rainbow of 4 pounds and over. From the Pintlar Peaks, named for Charles Pintlar, a pioneer trapper in the Big Hole country, the wilderness traveler can view the Mission Mountains to the northwest and the Bitterroot Range to the west. Pintlar Creek, a feeder of the Big Hole River, holds cutthroat, brook trout, and a few grayling. Sawed Cabin on Pintlar Creek was built by the fabled woodsman "Seven Dog" Johnson, who is said to have trapped mountain goats and packed them out of this high country to sell to zoos. The wilderness traveler in this remote area will pass through stands of alpine larch and pine and fields of mountain heather and wildflowers. One may see the tracks and signs of marten, mink, badger, cougar, and lynx. The Anaconda Range and the gentle slopes of the Sapphire Range, which adjoins the wilderness on the northwest, are

a top-ranked hunting zone for Rocky Mountain elk, moose, deer, and black bear.

Detailed information concerning camping, trails, wilderness permits, fishing, and hunting and an *Anaconda-Pintlar Wilderness Map* (50¢) showing trails, campgrounds, ranger stations, and roads may be obtained by writing: Sula Ranger Station, Bitterroot National Forest, Sula 59871.

Full-service vacation accommodations and guided fishing, hunting, and packhorse trips are provided by the famous *Trapper Peak Ranch* (they also operate the *Indian Lake Outfitting Service*, and *Rainbow Wilderness Camp* for young adults), P.O. Box 246, Darby 59829 (406–821–3407); *Cash Creek Guest Ranch*, Box 99A, Victor 59875.

Additional information concerning fishing, hunting, camping, and outfitters and packers may be obtained along with the *Bitterroot National Forest Map* (50¢) from: Forest Supervisor, Bitterroot National Forest, Hamilton 59840. Wilderness charter fly-in service is provided by *Hamilton Aircraft*, Hamilton 59840. For information on canoeing the Bitterroot, write: *Richard Schloemen*, Box 58G, Victor 59875. For information on Selway River float trips, contact the West Fork Ranger District, Darby 59829.

Access & Outfitting Centers

The Bitterroot National Forest is reached via U.S. Highways 93 and 10 and Montana State Highway 38. Supplies, guides, and outfitting services are available at Sula, Missoula, Hamilton, Darby, Conner, Woodside, Victor, Stevensville, Bonner, and Clinton.

Custer National Forest & Beartooth Primitive Area

Custer National Forest Topo Maps

U.S. Geological Survey 1:250,000 scale overview maps: Bozeman, Billings, Hardin, Ekalaka.

Beartooth Primitive Area

U.S. Geological Survey large-scale maps: Alpine, Castagne, Cooke City, Crow Butte, Cutoff Mountain, Emerald Lake, Garnet Mountain, Mackay Ranch, Mount Douglas, Mount Hood, Mount Maurice, Roscoe.

Lake Plateau High Country

U.S. Geological Survey large-scale topographic maps: Mount Douglas, Cutoff Mountain.

Stillwater River

U.S. Geological Survey large-scale topographic maps: Cooke City, Cutoff Mountain, Mount Douglas, Mount Wood, Beehive, Cow Face Hill, Sandborn Creek, Absarokee, Whitebird School, Columbus West.

Divided into four major units scattered across the southern part of the state, Montana's share of the Custer National Forest covers nearly 1,100,000 acres of staggering mountain peaks, scenic lakes, glaciers, rushing waterfalls, and high plateaus. The stark granite outcroppings of the Beartooth Range dissolve into forested slopes in the east and then into rolling prairie in the Long Pines of eastern Montana. Many plateaus in the forest, each extending over several square miles, exceed levels of 11,000 feet. The granddaddy of the Beartooth Mountains and Montana's highest mountain, Granite Peak (12,799 ft.), dominates the perpetual snowfields. Of the many lesser peaks, twenty-five tower above 12,000 feet. Exposed rock in the Beartooths, the oldest known in North America, is some 2.7 billion years old. Climbing the peaks

is difficult going, and just to get within striking distance of Granite Peak takes at least 10 hours of strenuous travel. There are 45 miles of trails within the Beartooths, and the main ones, such as Wounded Man, Horseshoe Brand, and East Rosebud to Russell Creek, are along the Stillwater River. Near Granite Peak is the trail forged by Chief Joseph and his Nez Percé followers on their futile flight to Canada. After refusing to be herded into a northern Idaho reservation, the Nez Percé led the United States Army a long and difficult chase over 1,600 miles and several states. In the Bearpaw Mountains of north central Montana, the exhausted remnants of this proud tribe finally surrendered on October 8, 1877, after a four-day battle.

Straddling the peaks of the Beartooth Range near the Wyoming border, the 230,000-acre Beartooth Primitive Area covers about half of the westernmost unit of Custer National Forest and spills over to the south into the Gallatin National Forest. Much of the wilderness area and surrounding forestland is above the timberline at 9,000 feet, and the country is rugged in the extreme, encompassing rock-strewn plateaus, high mountain peaks, steep canyons, glaciers, and some 300 mountain lakes which hold grayling and golden, brook, rainbow, and cutthroat trout. Near the western periphery of the primitive area flows the Stillwater River, a designated red-ribbon trout stream for browns, rainbows, and some brookies. Cutthroat are taken in Goose Lake, a deep, 120-acre lake surrounded by a grassy mountain meadow 7½ miles north of Cooke City. Spectacular fishing for golden trout is available in the upper reaches of Woodbine Creek, one of the many mountain streams that feed the Stillwater. The six small, unnamed lakes below Pinchot Lake, on the magnificent Lake Plateau, where goldens are often crossed with rainbow, can be reached by a fisherman's trail from Wounded Lake, an equally fine spot for rainbows and cutthroat, located a half-mile to the northwest. In addition to excellent lake fishing, the Beartooth region offers rugged hiking over primitive roads and trails, which skirt snow-covered mountains and rocky plateaus and provide access to the many alpine lakes. In the eastern reaches of the primitive area is Beartooth Mountain, one of many ochre-tinted peaks in the region, distinguished from its sister mountains by the Bear's Tooth, a rocky projection which gives the range its name. Nearby Beartooth Falls forms a silvery cascade against the dark green of a tree-rimmed gorge and is especially spectacular in June, when snow on the mountains begins to melt. Another fascinating sight in Beartooth country is the Grasshopper Glacier, just north of Cooke City, named for the millions of ice-trapped insects lining the almost perpendicular face of this 80-foot cliff. Succeeding swarms of grasshoppers, chilled in passing over the glacier, fall each year and become embedded in the layers of black-flecked ice reaching depths of over 60 feet. A free map of the *Beartooth High Lake Country*, available from the Forest Supervisor, Custer National Forest, 2602 First Avenue North, Billings 59103, shows roads, trails, campsites, lakes, creeks, rivers, ranger stations, and towns. The reverse of the map offers advice on fishing and camping in the area. *Beartooth High Lakes Country Index of Lakes*, a companion folder, lists all the major fishing lakes in the area with information on access and species of fish present.

Several licensed packers and fishing, hunting, and wilderness backpacking guides serve the Beartooth divisions of the forest. For rates and literature, write: *Wm. E. Butler*, Silesia 59080 (Beartooth and Pryor mountains, fishing, hunting); *Big Horn Outfitters*, Route 1, Box 171, Joliet 59041 (fishing, hunting); *Otter Creek Ranch*, Big Timber 59011 (hunting); *Beartooth Plateau Outfitters*, Red Lodge 59068 (fishing, hunting); *Ted Dinsdale*, General Route 1, Bridger 59014 (fishing, hunting); *Maurice N. Flanagan*, Big Timber 59011 (fishing, hunting, backpacking); *Arnold H. George*, Roscoe 59071 (Beartooth Mountains, fishing, hunting); *The 33 Ranch*, McLeod 59052 (fishing,

hunting, backpacking); *Carl O. Huff*, P.O. Box 112, Absarokee 59001 (fishing, hunting); *Shane Ridge Guide Service*, Box 561, Columbus 59019 (hunting, Stillwater River area); *Hailstone Ranch Co.*, Big Timber 59011 (hunting); *Beartooth Ranch*, Nye 59061 (Stillwater River, fishing, hunting); *Paintbrush Trails*, Box 902, Red Lodge 59068 (fishing, hunting); *O'Hang'n Tree Guide Service*, Nye 59061 (hunting); *Nelson Sanford*, Box 126, Bridger 59014 (fishing, hunting); *William Schlachter*, Box 31, Absarokee 59001 (fishing, hunting); *Bill Tratton*, Box 245, Boyd 59013 (Beartooths, fishing, hunting); *Wilderness Outfitters & Guides*, Box 452, Hardin 59034 (fishing, hunting); *Rocky Mountain Outfitters*, Box 108, Roberts 59070 (hunting).

The *Montana School of Fly-Fishing*, located on the Stillwater River 36 miles northeast of Yellowstone National Park adjacent to the Beartooth Primitive Area, offers expert fly-fishing instruction, wilderness fishing expeditions, pack trips, and lodging at the Stillwater River Ranch. For info on rates, clothing, and pick-up services at Billings, write: Montana School of Fly-Fishing, Nye 59061 (phone: 406-327-4365).

The drive from the ranch to the northeast Cooke City entrance to Yellowstone Park is one of the most spectacular paved highways in the world. Rising to an elevation of almost 11,000 feet at Beartooth Pass, the Beartooth Highway winds past dozens of glacier-fed emerald lakes and alpine meadows of wildflowers.

Between the Beartooth and Ashland divisions of the Custer National Forest lie the Crow and Northern Cheyenne Indian reservations, encompassing the Bighorn Lake and River, Rosebud and Bighorn mountains, and the Custer Battlefield National Monument. Just off U.S. 90, the Custer Monument and battlefield cemetery are reminders of that hot Sunday in June 1876 when the controversial Lt. Col. George A. Custer and 261 of his men met their death in an ill-fated encounter with Sioux and Cheyenne warriors. Most of the Bighorn country is the original home of Crow Indians, who called it the "good country" in recognition of the peaceful existence they led there. Winding through the Bighorn Mountains, the 3,000-foot-high rust-colored cliffs of the Bighorn Canyon tower above the river of the same name. River, mountains, and canyon all take their name from the bighorn, or Rocky Mountain, sheep native to the area. To the east, the Cheyenne Indian Reservation, wedged between the Tongue River

and the Crow Reservation, covers rolling grasslands and occasional forested areas. Although the Cheyenne called themselves *tsis-tsis-tas*, their present-day name is thought to derive from either the Sioux word *shahiena* or the French *chien*, meaning "dog." The Dog Soldiers, a fierce, powerful group of Indian braves, were a select society within the Cheyenne nation. The removal of these nomadic people to the reservation occurred only a year after Custer's defeat at Little Bighorn. Between the Ashland unit and the reservation, the twisting Tongue River offers good spring fishing in its lower reaches for walleye pike, and catfish. Below the Tongue River Reservoir, fair fishing is available for the rainbows that are stocked here annually.

Within the forest itself, grayling are stocked in Froze-to-Death Lake on Phantom Creek, and golden trout in Cairn, Medicine, Fossil, Echo, Big Park, Dewey, and Martin lakes. Hunting in the area is good for moose, mountain goat, and mountain sheep. Big-game hunters are required to wear fluorescent orange, and cleated shoes are recommended, because the mountainsides are often muddy and slippery.

The *Custer National Forest Map* is available for 50¢ from: Supervisor, Custer National Forest, 2602 First Avenue North, Billings 59101. It shows all roads and trails, mountains, lakes and streams, ranger stations, points of interest, and boat access centers.

Access & Outfitting Centers

The Custer National Forest is reached via U.S. Highways 212 and 310 and Montana State Highways 307, 397, 323, and 308. Supplies, guides, and outfitters are available at Ekalaka, Mill Iron, Fishtail, Roscoe, Red Lodge, Cooke City, Warren, Belfry, Ashland, and Birney. Ranger stations are at Ashland, Fort Howes, Red Lodge, Camp Crook (S. Dakota), and Meyers Creek.

Deerlodge National Forest

Deerlodge National Forest Topo Maps

U.S. Geological Survey 1:250,000 scale overview maps: Bozeman, Butte, Dillon, White Sulphur Springs.

Boulder River of the Jefferson

U.S. Geological Survey large-scale topographic maps: Elk Park, Basin, Jefferson City, Boulder, Devils Fence, Jefferson Island.

Clark Fork—Upper River & Headwaters

U.S. Geological Survey large-scale topographic maps: Fred Burr Lake, Silver Lake, West Valley, Anaconda, Racetrack, Deer Lodge, Conleys Lake, Garrison, Drummond, Bearmouth, Ravenna, Clinton, Bonner.

This 1,357,500-acre reserve, astride the Continental Divide in southwestern Montana, takes its name from a curious natural landmark, an ash-colored mound shaped like a gigantic haystack which once sat in the middle of the valley at the head of Clarks Fork. On cold mornings, a column of steam would rise from its summit, like plumes of smoke from a distant chimney. Closer inspection revealed that the mound was actually a boiling spring surrounded by a self-formed block of cement. Snake Indians called the object the "White-Tailed Deer Lodge" because deer, abundant in the nearby swamps, would come to lick the salt deposited on the mound's sides. On winter mornings, the steam that rose from the top of the mound resembled smoke coming out of the peaks of Indian lodges.

The forest is situated within the headwaters of the historic Jefferson and Clark Fork rivers, both renowned to fly-fishermen for brown and rainbow trout, and embraces a number of spectacular natural attractions, including the Tobacco Root and Highland mountains, Georgetown Lake, the Boulder River of the Jefferson, and Flint Creek Range.

The upper and middle reaches of Fish Creek, one of many streams of the Jefferson River drainage, provide spectacular scenery and fishing for brook, and occasionally cutthroat, trout. The lower stretches of the Boulder River, which flows into the Jefferson near Cardwell, form a rocky, sandy-bottomed stream bordered by cottonwood and aspen and inhabited by muskrat, mink, and river otter. Fishing here and in the tributary creeks is good for pan-sized cutthroat and brook trout to 10 inches. Just south of the forest are the waters of the famous Big Hole River, one of the best trout streams in the nation, where trophy-sized rainbows and browns are the rule occasionally rather than the exception. Fly-fishermen will find that big Muddlers, Maribou Muddlers, Haystacks, Sofa Pillows, Matukas, Black Creepers, and Wooley Worms are most effective here. Early morning and late evening are favored times for fishing the river and its many tributary streams, such as Sevenmile, Deep French, Jerry, and Moose creeks. Rock Creek, a blue-ribbon trout stream that originates in the Anaconda-Pintlar Wilderness and flows into the Clark Fork River east of Missoula, and Homestake Lake, a small man-made lake off Interstate 90 south of Butte, are also popular with fishermen. Georgetown Lake, a big body of water at 6,300 feet elevation, offers brown, rainbow, and cutthroat trout, sockeye and coho salmon, and grayling.

The high alpine peaks and meadows, mountain valleys, and dense forests are top hunting grounds for elk, moose, black bear, antelope, and deer. Most of the forest is above 5,000 feet, providing the preferred habitat for blue grouse. In the spring the birds move into the foothills to mate, nest, and raise their young. In autumn they move up to the higher alpine meadows, offering good Indian summer sport. Deep gorges and narrow canyons within the area's several mountain chains offer a challenge to the hunter, who should be prepared for some tricky climbing. There is also hunting here for elk, Shiras moose, antelope, black bear, and deer, although the game is diminishing.

Elevations in the forest vary from 4,360 feet at Whitehall to 10,604 feet at Mount Jefferson in the Tobacco Root Mountains. Vegetation varies with the elevations in the valleys and on southern exposures. Douglas fir is the predominant tree species, with lodgepole and limber pine at higher elevations. A colorful array of wildflowers enhances the beauty of the forest understory and alpine meadows. Glacier lilies, alpine poppies, columbines, white dryads, Indian paintbrush, violets, asters, and white and purple heather are among the delicate sights within the forest. Straddling the Continental Divide for 30 airline miles in the Anaconda Range of the Rocky Mountains is the spectacular Anaconda-Pintlar Wilderness, which can be reached by horse or foot along several routes in the Deerlodge, Bitterroot, and Beaverhead national forests. The 45-mile Highline Trail and other trails offer fine opportunities for hikers to explore this vast mountain wilderness. Visitors not familiar with the region are advised to check with a forest ranger or experienced guide before setting foot in these rugged reaches.

The Deerlodge area covers some of the richest mineral deposits in the state. Rock-hounds and fortune hunters will find that the forest offers plenty of opportunities for pursuing their favorite pastimes. Panning for gold has frustrated many a modern-day prospector, but those who are willing to settle for brilliance instead of value will discover abundant deposits of fool's gold. Rubies have been found in Cottonwood and Upper Rock creeks in Granite County and in the Ruby River within Madison County. Placer gravels in the Tobacco Root and Ruby mountains hold garnets, and industrial-quality sapphires are found in the westernmost section of the Deerlodge.

Like many other regions of Montana, Deerlodge was once the scene of furious activity, when gold was suddenly discovered in the second half of the nineteenth century. The hopes and heartbreaks of that incredible era are spelled out by such names as Lost Dutchman, Miner's Gulch, Homestake Creek, Silver Hill, and Gold Creek. Abandoned mining towns, like Granite and Pioneer, are forlorn reminders of the boom towns that mushroomed overnight and then disappeared when the rush was over. Elkhorn, near the present-day town of Boulder, is another ghost settlement that prospered after 1872, when gold and silver were discovered in the area. Fourteen old saloons in this one tiny town, their walls riddled with bullet holes, testify to a hell-roaring past, when disputes were settled with fists or shotguns.

Less ominous and certainly more breathtaking is the Lewis and Clark Cavern, off U.S. 10 just southeast of the forest. The third largest series of caves in the United States, Lewis and Clark Cavern is a succession of passageways and vaulted chambers studded with stalagmites and hung with a broken curtain of stalactites. Tortuous paths lead to the various recesses—the Cathedral Room, the Coffin, the Deepest Room, and the Lion's Den—where underground formations provide natural pillars, domes, spires, and colorful mosaics streaked with shades of golden brown and amber. The full tour requires steady footing and an expert guide equipped with a miner's lamp.

Other attractions of the Deerlodge area include the neighboring Bitterroot and Beaverhead national forests, Helena National Forest and the Big Belt Mountains, and the Skalkaho Game Preserve. The *Deerlodge National Forest Map*, showing trails, mountains, roads, recreation sites, rivers, streams, and lakes, is available for 50¢ from: Forest Supervisor, Deerlodge National Forest, P.O. Box 400, Federal Building, Butte 59701. Free black-and-white maps of individual ranger districts can be obtained from the relevant district office: Deer Lodge 59722; Whitehall 59757; Philipsburg 59858; and Butte 59701. *Welcome to the Deerlodge*, a free 14-page booklet describing fishing, camping, skiing, canoeing, and points of interest in the forest, is available from the Supervisor at the above address.

Access & Outfitting Centers

The Deerlodge National Forest is reached via U.S. Highways 10 and 91, Interstates 91 and 15, and Montana Highways 41, 287, 48, 274, 348, and 43. Supplies, information, outfitting services, and guides are available at Butte, Boulder, Twin Bridges, Whitehall, Jefferson City, Basin, Wickes, Deer Lodge, Elk Park, Divide, Warmsprings, Opportunity, Anaconda, Hall, and Philipsburg.

Flathead National Forest & Bob Marshall Wilderness

Flathead National Forest & Bob Marshall Wilderness Topo Maps

U.S. Geological Survey 1:250,000 scale overview maps: Choteau, Cut Bank, Kalispell, Wallace.

Flathead Lake

U.S. Geological Survey large-scale topographic maps: Bigfork, Bull Island, East Bay, Polson, Rollins, Somers, Wild Horse Island, Woods Bay.

Flathead National Wild & Scenic River

U.S. Geological Survey large-scale topographic maps: *(Main Stem)*, Big Fork, Buffalo Bridge, Bull Island, Columbia Falls N., Columbia Falls S., Caston, Dixon, East Bay, Elmo, Hungry Horse, Kalispell, McDonald, Perma, Plains, Polson, Rollins, Round Butte, St. Regis, Sloan, Somers, Wild Horse Island, Woods Bay; *(North Fork)*, Cyclone Lake, Demer Ridge, Huckleberry Mountain, Hungry Horse, Kintla Lake, McGee Meadow, Polebridge, Trail Creek; *(South Fork)*, Circus Peak, Felix Peak, Hungry Horse, Mount Grant, Nyack S.W., Pioneer Ridge, Quintonkon, Tin Creek; *(Middle Fork)*, Blacktail, Essex, Hungry Horse, Hyde Creek, Lake McDonald E., Lake McDonald W., McGee Meadows, Mount Bradley, Mount Jackson, Nimbo, Nyack, Pinnacle, St. Anton Lake, Summit, West Glacier.

Jewel Basin Wild Country

U.S. Geological Survey large-scale maps: Crater Lake, Jewel Basin, Pioneer Ridge, Big Hawk Mountain.

Mission Mountains Wilderness

U.S. Geological Survey large-scale topographic maps: Cedar Lake, Gray Wolf Lake, Hemlock Lake, Mount Harding, Peck Lake, Piper Crow Pass, St. Mary Lake, Salmon Prairie.

Sun River Wildlands

The following U.S. Geological Survey large-scale topographic maps show the North & South forks of the Sun River in the Sun River Game Preserve Area of the Bob Marshall Wilderness: *(North Fork)*, Patricks Basin, Arsenic Peak, Glenn Creek, Gates Park, Porphyry Reef, Mount Waight; *(South Fork)*, Patricks Basin, Benchmark, Flint Mountain.

Swan River Wildlands

U.S. Geological Survey large-scale topographic maps: Bigfork, Big Hawk Mountain, Condon, Crater Lake, Doris Mountain, Gilly Creek, Hash Mountain, Jewel Basin, Nyack Mountain, Peak Lake, Pioneer Ridge, Salmon Prairie, Swan Lake, Yew Creek.

Named for the tepee-dwelling tribe that settled along the shores of Flathead Lake and in the Bitterroot Valley, this majestic forest reserve encompasses 2.5 million acres along the northern Rockies of northwestern Montana. Timbered mountains towering high above clear lakes, fast-flowing streams and falls are the dominant features of this outstanding big-game hunting, wilderness fishing, and camping area. An excellent network of forest trails and roads winds through seemingly endless acres of larch, western white and yellow pine, Engelmann spruce, Douglas fir, and other virgin species that have escaped the chainsaw and axe, and provides access to the forest's superb fishing, hunting, and wilderness camping areas: Flathead Lake, Mission Mountains Primitive Area, Spotted Bear River, Jewel Basin, Swan River, Stillwater River, Bob Marshall Wilderness, Great Northern Mountains, and the north, south and middle forks of the Flathead

River, one of the country's great wild rivers, with superb fly-fishing for rainbow, cutthroat, and lunker Dolly Varden trout up to 20 pounds.

The first white men to explore this rugged high country were members of the adventurous Vérendrye family, the French trader Pierre Gaultier, Sieur de la Vérendrye and his sons, François and Pierre. Inspired by Indian stories of a river that led to the Western Sea, the elder Vérendrye sent his willing offspring west from Montreal to find the mythic stream. In January 1743, after the long, dreary trek across the Dakota Plains, they first sighted the "Shining Mountains"—the lofty, snow-covered peaks of the Northern Rockies standing brilliant in the midwinter sun. Then for over sixty years, until David Thompson entered the Flathead Valley and established a post there in 1811, the area remained the province of the Flathead (Salish), Kootenai, and Kalispel tribes. Unlike their counterparts in the coastal regions, the Flatheads never flattened the heads of infants, but probably received their distinctive name from western neighbors whose heads were comparatively more pointed. Called *Ootlashoots* by Lewis and Clark, the Flatheads were never numerous, although their ferocity and skill in battle were highly respected by other local tribes. Even more warlike were the Kootenai, friends and allies of the Flatheads, who lived in southeastern British Columbia, northwestern Montana, and northern Idaho. Famous for their hunting prowess, the Kootenai were also noted for unusual birchbark canoes with undershot ends—a vessel more common along the Amur River in Siberia than on the streams of North America. The third tribe native to the region, the Kalispel, dwelt mainly in the Flathead Valley and were closely related to the Pend d'Oreilles.

Framed by the sheer-walled mountains of the Swan Range on the east and the Whitefish Range to the north, the Flathead Valley offers a haven in the midst of rocky peaks, and was called by the Indians "the park between the mountains." Entrance to the valley was a difficult and hazardous feat, and no permanent settlement in the area was accomplished until 1881. With the arrival of the Great Northern Railroad 10 years later, both lumbering and agriculture stimulated further growth and development. The valley is covered in part by the waters of Flathead Lake, just west of the national forest. One of the largest natural freshwater bodies within the continental United States, the lake is 28 miles long and 10 miles wide and is studded with tree-covered islands near its western shore. Just beyond the town of Dayton is a series of painted rocks, colored pictographs left by an early Indian artist. The lake offers fine fishing for trout, salmon, bass, and whitefish, as well as opportunities for swimming, boating, and water-skiing. Two campgrounds are located south of Woods Bay on the eastern shore.

Two large sections of the Flathead have been set aside as roadless wilderness areas: the Mission Mountains Primitive Area in the Swan Lake Ranger District and the Bob Marshall Wilderness encompassing the Big Prairie Ranger Station and parts of other ranger districts. Trail systems in both areas permit backcountry travel on horseback, but no motorized vehicles or equipment are allowed.

The 75,000 acres comprising the Mission Mountains Primitive Area offer a high-country retreat of seldom paralleled scenic beauty: rugged shining peaks, several small glaciers, alpine lakes, meadows, and clear cold streams. The topography is generally rough and broken, especially in the southern portion. Forming the western margin of the wilderness are the Mission Mountains themselves, the age-old summer hunting grounds of the Salish, named for the St. Ignatius Mission established by Jesuits in 1854. In the northern reaches of the wilderness, the terrain is more heavily timbered and less strenuous in terms of backpacking or hiking. Throughout the area are many near-vertical cliffs,

flat slablike boulders, and talus slopes. Elevations range from 4,500 to 9,000 feet, averaging about 7,000 feet. There are over 65 miles of forest system trails in the Mission Mountains, most of them better suited to hiking than to horseback riding. Few of the trails can be classified as easy, and some are especially difficult because of the precipitous landscape. Old Indian and packer trails winding through various sections of the mountains are usually steep and difficult to follow. The hiker looking for a challenge will find it here. Access points into the area from the Swan Valley include Glacier Creek, Cold Lakes, Jim Lake, Fatty Creek, and Beaver Creek. There are also several access points from the Flathead Indian Reservation. A free black-and-white topographic map of the *Mission Mountains Wilderness* (scale 1 inch to 1 mile) showing trails, streams, creeks, contours, and lakes is available from: U.S. Forest Service, Swan Lake Ranger Station, Bigfork 59111. The Forest Service also publishes a free 7-page *Guide to the Mission Mountains Wilderness* describing the history and physical features of the area, with advice on backpacking, equipment, and camping.

There is hunting in the Mission Mountains Wilderness for mountain goat, elk, black bear, whitetail deer, and an occasional moose. The clear and beautiful Swan River, which rises below Gray Wolf Glacier and flows down a steep subalpine valley through Gray Wolf, Whelp, and Lindbergh lakes, has fishing for brown trout, rainbow up to 4 pounds, cutthroat, and Dolly Varden in the 4–10 pound range. Skyline

Lakes, high in the mountains, are good from late July to September, after the fish have spawned and are eager for flies and grasshoppers. Lost Lake, secluded between Goat and Daughter of the Sun Mountains, has cutthroat from 3 to 5 pounds. Recommended fly patterns, in either number 8 or 10, are the Wulffs, Muddlers, Gray Drakes, Light Cahills, and Brown Bombers.

To the east of the Mission Mountains, the Bob Marshall Wilderness lies along the Continental Divide for 60 miles within the Flathead and Lewis and Clark national forests. This vast million-acre wildland is the summer range for three major elk herds and one of the last strongholds of native black-spotted cutthroat. The beauty of the rugged peaks and cold alpine lakes is heightened by the 12-mile-long escarpment known as the Chinese Wall, with its 1,000-foot vertical face through which there are only three passes. The terrain varies abruptly between 4,000-foot valleys and 9,000-foot cliffs. There is good fly-fishing for 3-pound rainbows and black-spotted cutthroat in the South Fork River, which rises on the western side of the Continental Divide and flows north into the Flathead, and in the tributaries that flow into it. There are also Dolly Varden—an occasional 20-pounder—and the ever present whitefish in the Big Salmon, Sunburst, Spotted Bear and Lena rivers. The wilderness is famous for its elk, mule deer, whitetail deer, black bear, and mountain goat; this is also the spring, summer, and fall range of the state's largest herd of bighorn sheep. Mountain goats are especially numerous along the cliffs of the Chinese Wall, and Shiras moose

roam the Youngs, Basin, upper Middle Fork, and Danaher Creek valleys. Canada lynx, cougar, marten, coyote, and wolverine are present in the wilderness, although they are rarely seen. Even if you've set your sights for big game, you may also want to hunt the area's numerous Franklin, blue, and ruffed grouse. Don't forget that this is grizzly country. One of the best ways to hunt or fish this region, and many others for that matter, is through the offices of an outfitter. He will supply you with horses, camping equipment, food, and a guide. If you are going after big game, you must be accompanied by a guide or licensed outfitter; this rule does not apply to small or upland game. Some of the outfitters in the region, many of which offer lodge or tent accommodations, include *Cheff Ranch,* Charlo 59824; *Spotted Bear Ranch,* Hungry Horse 59919; *Walking Y Bar Nine,* Seeley Lake 59868; *M Lazy Ranch,* Marion 59925; *Bear Creek Guest Ranch,* Box 38, East Glacier 59434; *Desert Mountain Lodge,* West Glacier 59936; *Holland Lake Lodge,* Seeley Lake 59868; *Rogers Guest Ranch,* Box 107, Swan Lake 59911; *5 Bars Ranch,* Trout Creek 59874. For a complete listing of outfitters and advice on hunting, float trips, and pack trips, write: Montana Outfitter and Guides Association, Billings 59101.

In addition to hunting and fishing, the Bob Marshall Wilderness offers a superb network of trails for short or long high-country camping trips on foot or horseback. Established paths lead through forest growth typical of the region: Engelmann spruce, ponderosa pine, western larch growing to heights of 150 feet, Douglas fir, string-straight lodgepole, and a full complement of wildflowers such as flamboyant lupine, pink and yellow monkeyflowers, and multicolored Indian paintbrush. Some of the outstanding features of the wilderness accessible by trail include Prairie Reef, a rugged, 8,868-foot peak offering an excellent view of the Chinese Wall and Lower Sun River Canyon; the tumbling waters of Needle Falls underlain by a clear pool where cutthroat trout are often caught; the ice-filled caves of Bullet Nose Mountain; and Dean Falls, a small waterfall situated in a narrow gorge of the Spotted Bear River. Trails, lakes, streams, camping spots, peaks, and other wilderness features are shown on the *Bob Marshall Wilderness Map,* available for 50¢ from: Forest Supervisor, Flathead National Forest, Kalispell 59901. The reverse of the map contains abundant information on wildlife, trees and plants, hunting and fishing opportunities, and suggested wilderness trips.

Aside from the Bob Marshall and Mission mountain areas, which together account for more than half of the forest landscape, the Flathead National Forest offers fine opportunities for boating and fishing on Tally, Swan, Whitefish, Lindbergh, Ashley, and Holland lakes. Eight miles north of Whitefish in the northern part of the forest is the Big Mountain Recreation Area, with ski trails for beginners and experts alike. Chalet and lodge accommodations, double chair lifts, T-bars, and rope tows are available. In the heart of the forest is the Hungry Horse Reservoir, surrounded by a key big-game range, beaches, campgrounds, and boat-launching ramps. Trolling for cutthroat trout is popular at the north end of the reservoir, and Dolly Varden are often caught along the southern end. Many side creeks also provide excellent trout fishing. A *Hungry Horse Reservoir Recreation Area Map* showing campsites, side creeks, boat ramps, water levels, roads, and hazard areas is available free from: Hungry Horse Ranger Station, Hungry Horse 59919.

The scenic Jewel Basin near the Bob Marshall Wilderness and due west of Hungry Horse Reservoir embraces exquisite gemlike lakes at the head of Graves and Aeneas creeks. The Jewel Basin wild country offers spectacular backpacking and wilderness camping opportunities among high-country crags and meadows.

The forest's high country is one of the state's great big-game hunting areas for elk, deer, mountain goat, Shiras moose, and black and grizzly bear. Bear hunting is a special challenge here because the use of dogs is forbidden. The black bear can be hunted from spring through fall, and because it has been designated a trophy animal, its flesh does not have to be used. Grizzlies range almost exclusively between the South and Middle forks of the Flathead, which starts in the Bob Marshall Wilderness and flows through handsome timbered mountains and glaciated valleys. One of the better ways to get to the Middle Fork is to fly into Schafer Meadows Airport, which is about 26 miles from Highway 2. Your outfitter can meet you there. If you are going by horse or foot, there are trails from Spotted Bear Ranger Station. The most popular float stretch on the Middle Fork is the 28-mile run between Schafer airstrip and Bear Creek. The Flathead area has not only good hunting but good fishing as well. Flathead Lake, called the "Gem of the Rockies," holds cutthroat, Dolly Varden, and kokanee; Lone Pine Reservoir contains the only northern pike in western Montana, some reaching 27 pounds; Little Dry Lake has whopper perch up to 21 inches; Tranquil Basin Lake has 2–3 pound cutthroat, plus rainbow and golden trout, the latter averaging about 18 inches. Dark fly patterns, from number 8 to 14, are best. For spinning, medium or large spoons bounced off the bottom are most productive, and a 1-ounce-or-heavier red-and-white hammered brass or copper spinner makes a good lure. The wild North Fork of the Flathead, rising high in the Canadian Rockies and flowing fast and furiously into the Middle Fork, also offers excellent fishing. Some sportsmen descend the river in rubber rafts, and if you decide to make such a float trip, you should wear a life jacket. Dolly Varden is the fish of the upper Flathead, and specimens 10–20 pounds have been caught. The fish winter in Flathead Lake, feeding on kokanee, and head up the North Fork with the spring runoff; in September they spawn in the upper tributaries. Black-spotted cutthroats, the delight of both fly fisherman and gourmet, make their annual run at the same time as the Dolly Varden. Recommended dry fly patterns for both fish are Black Gnat, Polar Bear, Bunyan Bug, and Sofa Pillow; good wet flies are the Mickey Finn, Bloody Pitcher, Lady Mite, and Sandy Mite; and the best live bait is the reliable grasshopper. The South Fork is also known for lunker Dolly Varden, as well as whitefish and cutthroat. The main stem of the Flathead from the lake upstream to the confluence of the North and Middle forks is designated a blue-ribbon trout stream and offers outstanding fishing for cutthroat trout and tackle-busting bull Dolly Vardens up to 30 pounds. Two other good fishing streams are the Little Salmon River and the Spotted Bear. Both have bull Dolly Vardens, and the Spotted Bear has cutthroat and whitefish.

Some of the most spectacular wilderness trout fishing in the Flathead National Forest region is found along the rugged high-country wildlands of the Swan River, which serves as a gateway for the backpacker and packhorse fisherman to the Mission Mountain Wilderness and Bob Marshall Wilderness, and along the remote North Fork and South Fork headwaters of the Sun River. The Swan rises high in the Mission Mountains, where it flows from its headwaters in Gray Wolf and Crystal lakes, and plunges some 450 feet per mile through the mountain highlands into Lindbergh Lake on the valley floor. It winds from the lake through a beautiful timbered valley, forming a series of deep-flowing pools and rapids, into Swan Lake, from which it meanders on to its mouth at Big Fork on the northeast end of Flathead Lake. The Swan and its tributaries, which include Glacier, Elk, Beaver, Gold, Jim, Dog, Lion, Goat, Lost, and Porcupine creeks, provide good fishing for large Dolly Varden during their upstream spawning runs from Swan Lake, for brook and cutthroat trout, and for pink-slashed rainbows up to 5 pounds. The remote high-country lakes in the Mission Mountains headwaters, such as Jim Creek, Glacier, Holland, Crystal, Lindbergh, and Gray Wolf, hold rainbow, cutthroat, Dolly Varden, brook, and golden trout, occasionally up to 4 and 5 pounds, and kokanee salmon. These remote high-country gems are reached by old logging roads and trails off of Route 209, which runs parallel to the Swan for its entire length. U.S. Forest Service campgrounds are located at Holland Lake (be sure to check out the beautiful Holland Creek Falls at the head of the lake) and Lindbergh and Swan lakes. The North Fork and South Fork of the Sun River flow through the high mountain wildlands of the Sun River Game Preserve, along the eastern boundary of the forest in the Bob Marshall Wilderness, and hold good-sized rainbow and cutthroat trout. The North Fork, which rises below the Sun River Pass at 7,800 feet, is a top-ranked fly-fishing stream in the deep pools and riffles formed along its 25-mile-long journey through a deep timbered valley in the Sun River Preserve to the Gibson Reservoir. The remote stretches of the North Fork produce an occasional hook-jawed rainbow in the 10–12 pound class. Both the North and South forks are paralleled by Forest Service trails.

Ranger Districts in the Flathead National Forest include Big Prairie, Condon, Coram (at Hungry Horse), Glacier View (at Big Creek), Hungry Horse, Spotted Bear, Swan Lake (at Bigfork), and Tally Lake (at Whitefish). Forest rangers are always glad to answer questions, and it is often advisable to consult one before heading into a wilderness area. The *Flathead National Forest Map* is available for 50¢ from: Forest Supervisor, 290 North Main, Kalispell 59901. It shows all roads and trails, recreation sites, ranger stations, lakes, streams, and towns in and around the forest. *The Forest Visitors Map to the Flathead National Forest,* also available for 50¢ from the Forest Supervisor, shows the area in greater detail at a scale of ½ inch to 1 mile. Individual ranger district maps indicating roads, trails, recreation sites, lakes, streams, mountains, and points of interest in black and white are available from the respective ranger stations.

Full-service family vacation lodging and services in the region are provided by *Flathead Lake Lodge,* Bigfork 59911; *Elks Resort* (Flathead Lake), Somers 59932; *Wilderness Ranch & Lodge* (one mile south of Spotted Bear Airport), Hungry Horse 59919; *Rogers Guest Ranch,* Box 107, Swan Lake 59911.

The major features of the Flathead Indian Reservation, which covers a vast area from the shores of Flathead Lake (the southern half of the lake lies within the reservation) some 60 miles to the south, and from the Rocky Mountains on the east to the Salish Mountains on the west, are shown on the *Flathead Indian Reservation Map.* The map, on a scale of about 2 miles to 1 inch, marks recreation areas, boat launches and marinas, fisheries, lakes, streams, rivers, roads, and closed areas.

This map, along with a free copy of hunting, fishing, and recreation regulations, may be obtained by writing to: Flathead Agency, Bureau of Indian Affairs, Drawer A, Ronan 59864.

Access & Outfitting Centers

The Flathead National Forest is reached via U.S. Highways 2 and 93 and Montana State Highways 200, 40, 35, and 28. Outfitters, guides, supplies, and lodging are available at Kalispell, Polson, Whitefish, Columbia Falls, Hungry Horse, Coram, Martin City, Swan Lake, Creston, Bigfork, Somers, Kila, Marion, Elmo, Proctor, Arlee, St. Ignatius, Dixon, Perma, Ovando, Pablo, and Ronan.

Gallatin National Forest & the Absaroka Range

Gallatin National Forest Topo Maps

U.S. Geological Survey 1:250,000 scale overview maps: Billings, Bozeman, White Sulphur Springs.

Absaroka Primitive Area

U.S. Geological Survey large-scale topographic maps: Abiathar Peak, Cutoff Mountain, Emigrant, Gardiner, Mount Bower, Mount Douglas, Mount Wallace, Tower Junction.

Gallatin River

U.S. Geological Survey large-scale topographic maps: Belgrade, Bozeman, Crown Butte, Fridley Peak, Garnet Mountain, Manhattan, Miner, Spanish Peaks, Tepee Creek, Three Forks.

Madison River Blue Ribbon Trout Waters

U.S. Geological Survey large-scale topographic maps: Cameron, Cliff Lake, Ennis, Hebgen Dam, Madison Junction (Wyo.), Manhattan, Norris, Spanish Peaks, Sphinx Mountain, Tepee Lake, Three Forks, West Yellowstone.

Spanish Peaks Primitive Area

U.S. Geological Survey large-scale topographic maps: Garnet Mountain, Spanish Peaks.

Yellowstone River Blue Ribbon Trout Waters

U.S. Geological Survey large-scale topographic maps: Brisbin, Emigrant, Fridley Peak, Gardiner, Mammoth, Livingston, Miner.

The world-famous fishing and big-game hunting area of the 1¾-million-acre Gallatin National Forest in the Rockies lies directly north of Yellowstone National Park, Wyoming, and encompasses a land of high peaks, wild rivers and crystal-clear lakes, brilliant green alpine meadows, and timbered hills. Elevations range from 4,000-foot valleys to 12,000-foot summits. Within Gallatin National Forest are the Gallatin, Jefferson, Madison, and Yellowstone rivers, the Spanish Peaks and Absaroka primitive areas, and the Beartooth Mountains. Above all, this is a prime backpacking and alpine trout-fishing region. Some of the more interesting areas are Hyalite Range, with good hiking trails and climbing through scenic canyons, around lakes and waterfalls, and up 10,000-foot peaks; Boulder River high country, with its steep canyons, high peaks, and plateaus; West Boulder River Valley, a narrow canyon valley running parallel to the Absaroka Range; Mount Cowen, a challenge to even the most experienced climbers; Crazy Mountains, isolated to the east in the prairie, with peaks higher than 11,000 feet and deep canyons radiating out into the plains; Taylor and Hilgard peaks, part of the Madison Range, with its high peaks and alpine trout lakes; Bridger Mountains, made up of 9,000-

foot limestone peaks extending for 20 miles from Bozeman to Sixteen Mile Creek; Coffin Mountain in the Continental Divide, a good cross-country hiking area with old and not carefully maintained Indian trails; and Gallatin Petrified Forest, in the Tom Miner area, a popular spot for climbers and rock-hounds.

The Gallatin also has both bird and big-game hunting. There are sharptail sage, blue, and Franklin grouse, chukar pheasant, wild turkey, duck, and Canada goose. In the fall months hunters find moose, elk, deer, mountain sheep, black bear, mountain goat, and an occasional protected grizzly. Deer is one animal in Montana you can be sure you'll get. In some districts, because the population is so great, you can often take more than one deer per season, and the Gallatin is one of these. The Yellowstone River, which flows through the forest, is a world-renowned trout river. The Yellowstone flows 104 miles through a blue-ribbon trout fishing area and has pools 10–20 feet deep and riffles. The best time to fish the Yellowstone is September and October, for lunker rainbow, brown, and cutthroat trout, averaging 2–3 pounds. The scenic West Gallatin, with its clear water and gravel bottom, is beautiful to fish, and it has whopper rainbow, brook, and brown trout, with the average take anywhere from 1 to 3 pounds. The east bank of the Gallatin flows through open meadows and has brushy undercut banks. Brush-pile and log jams harbor rainbows and browns sometimes up to 17 pounds. The Gallatin River area also has some mallard shooting.

The most famous river that flows through the forest, however, is the legendary Madison, one of the world's truly great trout streams. From its headwaters in Yellowstone Park, this officially designated blue-ribbon trout stream flows through Hebgen and Earthquake lakes in the Madison River Canyon Earthquake Geological Area formed by the 1959 earthquake, and on through Ennis Lake and the rugged Beartrap Canyon Primitive Area to its confluence with the Gallatin and Jefferson rivers at the head of the mighty Missouri. The 20-mile-long headwaters area of the Madison in Yellowstone is classic dry fly-fishing water; flowing lazily through lush alpine meadows and evergreen forests, its deep pools and warm thermal waters rich in insect life hold fat trophy brown trout, many 10–15 pounds. The wilderness fly-fisherman wading this stretch of the Madison will often see elk, mule deer, buffalo, geese, and an occasional trumpeter swan. The crystal-clear, placid water and sandy bottom with patches of moss and weeds here and there allow for leisurely wading and fishing. The Upper Madison between Earthquake and Ennis lakes, long famous among fly-fishermen for its prolific June salmonfly hatch, is a 50-mile-long riffle with a slick, moss-covered, smooth-stone bottom. During the lower 40-mile stretch of the Madison between Ennis Lake and the Missouri, it roars hell-bent for 7 miles through the sheer rock walls of Bear Trap Canyon. The huge, boulder-studded pools of the canyon harbor lunker brown and rainbow trout. Public access sites and camping facilities located along the Madison include Bakers Hole, Cabin Creek, Madison River, West Fork, West Fork Bridge, Palisades, Ruby Creek, Varney Bridge, Eight Mile Ford, Burnt Tree Hole, Ennis, Valley Garden, and Greycliff. Fishing grades, gear, and supplies are available at Ennis or West Yellowstone.

The Boulder River of the Yellowstone is a beautiful trout stream with deep-flowing pools. It has its source in its East and West forks, high in the Absaroka Range north of Yellowstone National Park, and flows north through the Gallatin National Forest for 50 miles before it empties into the Yellowstone at Big Timber. The Boulder is considered one of Montana's finest trout streams, holding fat rainbows and browns up to 10 pounds. One of the most famous features of the Boulder is the beautiful Natural Bridge Falls. The jewel-like headwater lakes of the East Fork on the Lake Plateau of the Beartooth Moun-

tains offer excellent wilderness fly-fishing for rainbow, brook, cutthroat, and golden trout and grayling.

The abundance of wildlife in the Gallatin area was noticed as early as 1806 when Lieutenant Clark recorded in his journal: "I saw elk, deer and antelopes, and a great deal of old signs of buffalo. The roads are in every direction—immense quantities of beaver on this Fork—and their dams very much impeed the navigation of it." Today hunters come from all over the state during the fall season to stalk the elk that drift over from Yellowstone Park when the snow is deep. Mule deer, whitetail deer, mountain sheep, black bear, and a few grizzly also inhabit the forest. Marten, mink, beaver, badger, weasel, and skunk are the principal furbearing animals. Ruffed and blue grouse are plentiful as well.

The Gallatin National Forest takes its name from the 90-mile-long Gallatin River, a broad, clear ribbon of water fed by numerous trout streams as it makes its way through the forest. In 1805, while camped near the Three Forks of the Missouri, Lewis and Clark named the three streams that join there after prominent contemporary statesmen: Jefferson, Madison, and Gallatin. In summer, the lower Gallatin Valley is covered with brilliant wildflowers. Old Indian legends tell of a bloody battle that took place here between Sioux and Nez Percé tribes. On the third day of fighting, the sun was obscured by clouds and darkness fell over the valley. Suddenly the voice of the Great Spirit cut through the gloom, commanding the rival warriors to lay down their weapons and put an end to the bloodshed, for they were defiling the beauty of the "Valley of Peace and Flowers." When the sun emerged once again, the Sioux and Nez Percé promised to live forever in friendship.

More credible, perhaps, are the stories of early prospectors in the region and of the days when "great spirits" meant something quite different from peace-making Indian deities. To the north of the forest is the village of McLeod, once a collection of saloons, gambling dives, and "dance halls." The owner of one such establishment, a certain Kitty O'Leary, a.k.a. Madame Bulldog, used her 190-pound bulk to discourage any rough or drunken behavior, thereby saving herself the wages of a bouncer. Among her memorable customers were Kid Brown, Soapy Smith, and Calamity Jane. West of McLeod is Bozeman, named for the first man to lead wagon trains of settlers into the Gallatin Valley, in 1864. Jim Bridger, the legendary mountain man and expert guide, followed shortly afterwards with another train of settlers. Mountain passes used by these formidable pioneers still bear their names, and once formed the first leg of a race between Bridger and Bozeman to see who could reach Virginia City first.

Just west of the Gallatin River within the forest is the 50,000-acre Spanish Peaks Primitive Area, named for Spanish beaver trappers killed by Crow Indians in 1836. Beaver still inhabit the area along with mule deer, moose, elk, bear, coyote, and bobcat. The foremost big-game attraction, however, is mountain sheep—the largest band in the whole area roams this roadless backcountry. A challenge to the most hardy hunter or angler, the Primitive Area is extremely rugged, with elevations varying abruptly from 6,000 to 11,000 feet. Some of the noted peaks are Wilson and Blaze, the Table Mountains, and Indian Ridge. There are many icy streams and more than twenty cold, crystal-clear lakes, including Cascade, Chilled, and Spanish lakes, and Hellroaring, Burnt, Asbestos, Deer, and Dudley creeks. In addition there are over 50 miles of trails within the Spanish Peaks, and the area is only 25 miles from Bozeman. A free list of *Spanish Peaks Primitive Area Trails*, describing length, difficulty, and location, and a simple black-and-white map of the area are available from: Forest Supervisor, Gallatin National Forest, Box 130, Bozeman 59715.

Parts of the Gallatin were once the domain of the powerful Crow Indian tribe, who called themselves the Absarokee and settled along the Yellowstone, Powder, and Bighorn rivers. Some interpretations maintain that their original Indian name was understood by French traders as *gens de corbeaux*, or "people of the raven." Older members of the Crow nation state that it was their hated enemy, the Sioux, who pinned the unflattering name on them and perpetuated the error. Crow custom and legend have been responsible for the names of several natural landmarks in the area. In Bridger Canyon, for example, stands the rocky pinnacle known as the Stone Maiden, a comely Indian girl literally petrified by grief when her lover failed to return with other members of a victorious Crow war party.

In the south of the forest along the Wyoming border is the 64,000-acre Absaroka Primitive Area, a majestic alpine trout-fishing and camping area. The terrain here varies from mountains near the head of Bull Creek to broad valleys created by Hellroaring and Slough creeks. Elevations range from 6,000 feet near Hellroaring Cabin to 10,218 feet at Roundhead Butte. Most of the Absaroka, however, is high plateau country with scattered meadows and deep valleys. Lodgepole pine, Engelmann spruce, and alpine fir grow in the moist basins, while whitebark pine covers the high ridges. Crisp fall days offer

hunting here for mule deer, elk, moose, black bear, and grizzlies, along with an occasional coyote or bobcat. There is also trout fishing in Hellroaring, Buffalo, and Slough creeks, and in some of the lakes. Whether you go to fish or hunt, you have to take in all your camping equipment and food. The best way to reach the Primitive Area is via packhorse on the trails from Jardine, Cooke City, Mill Creek, Passage Creek, or Lambert Creek, by the Stillwater Trail from Nye, or via trails originating in the south out of Yellowstone Park.

To the north of the Absaroka area are the many spectacular peaks of the Absaroka Range, including the Pyramid, Boulder Mountain, and Old Baldy, called Crow Test Peak by early settlers. Young Crow Indians, naked and weaponless, proved their courage and strength by keeping long winter vigils on the summit, spending their days in sacrifice and prayer to the Great Spirit. Those who survived this strenuous test of manhood were considered full-fledged braves and admitted to the tribal council. The northernmost range within the forest, the Crazy Mountains, were a source of awe and terror to both the Indians, who called them the "Mad Hills," and later white settlers, who avoided their frightening heights. A geologically young range, the mountains form an isolated, jagged upthrust of rock over 11,000 feet in height, punctuated by oddly shaped canyons through which violent

winds continually blow. Around the north end of the Crazy Mountains flows the Shields River, a fair-sized fishing stream with numerous deep holes. Fall fishing for 2–5 pound brown trout and rainbows up to 12 inches is especially good. This seldom-fished stream also offers whitefish in winter and occasional brook and cutthroat trout during the summer months.

South of the forest lies the Yellowstone area, known to the Indians as the "Land of the Evil Spirits" and avoided by most of the local tribes, who feared the miraculous spouting geysers, hot springs, and bubbling "paint pots." The only Indians to live in what is today National Park Land were the Sheepeaters, a peaceful, cliff-dwelling people who hunted the wild mountain sheep of the area and fashioned obsidian arrowheads of such an exquisitely intricate design that they were also known as the Arrow Makers. Near West Yellowstone, in an area called by the Indians the "Country of the Painted Rocks," the Sheepeaters carved tribal emblems and rough outlines of tiny men and women. Thought to be either the remnant of a non-Indian race or descendants of the Bannock and Shoshone, the Sheepeaters themselves maintained that their ancestors had lived in the geyser country "from the beginning" and that a large number of their followers had been destroyed by a cataclysmic upheaval near the Upper Geyser Basin.

The Gallatin National Forest Map, available from the Forest Supervisor, Box 130, Bozeman 59715, for 50¢, shows all roads and trails, lakes, mountains, streams and creeks, ski areas, boat access points, recreation sites, ranger stations, and lookouts. The individual Ranger Districts will also provide you with free black-and-white maps of their areas: Big Timber, Livingston, Bozeman, Gardiner, Squaw, Creek, and Hebgen Lake. A free leaflet, *Camp and Picnic Areas*, listing attractions and facilities at each major campsite, is available from the Forest Supervisor.

Guided wilderness packhorse and high-country fishing trips are provided by: *Black Otter Guide Service*, Box 93, Pray 59065 (Absaroka and Beartooth primitive areas); *Inverness Rawhide Outfitters*, Rt. 38, Livingston 59047 (Absaroka Primitive Area and Yellowstone National Park); *Nine Quarter Circle Ranch*, Gallatin Gateway 59730 (Taylor Peaks and Yellowstone National Park); *Sixty-Three Ranch*, Livingston 59047 (Absaroka Range); *Wood Guide Service*, Box 1153, Livingston 59047 (Absaroka Primitive Area and Yellowstone National Park). Detailed fishing information, guide service, and float trips on the region's trophy trout streams are provided by *Bud Lilly's Trout Shop* (Box 387, West Yellowstone 59047); *Jim Danskin Tackle Shop* (Box 276, West Yellowstone 59758) and *Dan Bailey's Fly Shop* (Livingston 59047)—see the "Montana Encyclopedia" for additional listings. Vacation accommodations in the Gallatin region are provided by: (West Yellowstone 59758) *Bar N Ranch, Diamond P Ranch, Madison Fork Ranch, Parade Rest Ranch, Watkins Creek Ranch;* (Gallatin Gateway 59730) *Castle Rock Inn, Almart Lodge, Covered Wagon Ranch, Elkhorn Ranch, 320 Ranch, Nine Quarter Circle Ranch;* (Livingston 59047) *Boulder River Ranch, Yellowstone Valley Guest Ranch;* (Pray 59065) *Snowy Range Ranch;* (Big Timber 59011) *Lazy K Bar Ranch, Spring Creek Trout Camp;* (Cooke City 59020) *Sky Top Ranch, Rawhide Motel;* (Emigrant 59027) *BW Guest Ranch, Point of the Rocks Lodge;* (Nye 59061) *Beartooth Ranch, Double Y Bar Ranch*. Marina and lodging services are provided by *Hebgen Lake Lodge*, West Yellowstone 59758, overlooking beautiful Lake Hebgen. Charter air service and scenic flights throughout the region are provided by *Yellowstone Aviation*, Box 178, West Yellowstone 59758.

Access & Outfitting Centers

The Gallatin National Forest is reached via U.S. Highways 191, 287, 10, and 89 and Montana State Highways 87, 293, 243, 298, and 339.

Lodging, guides, supplies, and pack and outfitting services are available at Bozeman, West Yellowstone, Jardine, Gallatin Gateway, Livingston, Big Timber, and Clyde Park. Cooke City, once a prosperous mining settlement, lies nestled in an alpine setting along the scenic Beartooth Highway and serves as the center of outdoor recreation and jumping-off point for hikers, fishermen, hunters, skiers, and campers heading into Yellowstone National Park and the Absaroka and Beartooth mountains.

Glacier National Park

Glacier National Park Topo Maps

U.S. Geological Survey 1:250,000 scale overview maps: Cut Bank, Kalispell.

This world-renowned wilderness camping, hiking, and fishing area, often called "the crown of the continent," lies astride the Great Divide of the Rocky Mountains in the northwest corner of Montana. The Park encompasses more than 1,500 square miles of snowcapped peaks, sharp spires, deep green alpine valleys and meadows, and hundreds of azure lakes and glacial streams. It stretches south from the Canadian boundary for 50 miles to the Flathead National Forest, and from the wild North Fork of the Flathead River east to the borders of the Blackfeet Indian Reservation. An intricate network of hiking and packhorse trails winds along ancient Indian and fur trade routes through the wildlands of this mountain vastness, known to the Blackfeet as the "backbone of the world," and provides access to the Continental Divide, which meanders from the Lewis Range to the Livingston Range, with numerous spurs broken at intervals by the evergreen forests of lake-studded valleys; to Stoney Indian Peaks, named for the tribe of Stoney Indians who once inhabited the area near the headwaters of the Mokowania River; and to the ancient Grinnell and Sperry glaciers, beautiful Lake McDonald, known to the Indians as "Sacred Dancing Lake," Swiftcurrent Valley, Logging and Kintla lakes, and hundreds of other remote backcountry fishing and camping areas.

The Indian hunting grounds, which extended from the dense forests and elk, deer, and grizzly country surrounding the Lewis Range across to the great buffalo herds on the rolling plains to the east and southeast, were once roamed by the Flatheads, Nez Percés, Snakes, Stoneys, and Kootenais. In the late 1700s, the Blackfeet, having acquired horses and white man's weapons, moved south from Alberta and drove the rival tribes into the Yellowstone country. The first white man to travel in the area that is now Glacier Park was probably Peter Fidler, a young surveyor for the North West Company, in 1792, followed in 1806 by Captain Meriwether Lewis, who attempted on his return trip from the Pacific to locate the headwaters of the Marias River, named in honor of Lewis's cousin, Maria Wood. Lewis camped on the banks of the river with his men in hopes of making astronomical observations. After four days of overcast weather, they aptly named the place Camp Disappointment and set out to rejoin the main part of the expedition. The first white resident of the area bordering the present-day park was the Hudson's Bay Company fur trader Hugh Monroe, who was assigned in 1815 to live for a year with the Piegan Blackfeet under the leadership of Chief Lone Walker. On his return to the Hudson's Bay post a year later, Monroe severed his association with the company and returned to live out his life with the tribe, as Rising Wolf, "the white Blackfoot." The towering summit of Rising Wolf Mountain near Two Medicine Lake bears his Indian name.

The glacier region was successively traveled, exploited, and explored by trappers, fur traders, the surveyors for the Great Northern Railroad,

military reconnaissance men, prospectors, scientists, and pioneers, including the legendary John George "Kootenai" Brown, hunter, trapper, guide, and first pioneer in the northern reaches of Glacier country. In 1877 he became the first resident of the Kootenai Lakes country, and in 1910 became a ranger and acting superintendent of the Canadian Waterton National Park. Efforts to preserve Glacier country as a national park began in 1885, when George Bird Grinnell, the naturalist, conservationist, and editor of *Forest and Stream,* explored the region. Captivated by the area, Grinnell returned annually, and labored courageously for 25 years to have it set aside as a national park. Grinnell's friend and advisor was James Willard Schultz, author of such classics as *Signposts of Adventure* and *Blackfeet Tales of Glacier National Park.* Schultz, like his predecessor, Hugh Monroe, lived in the Glacier country as a member of the Blackfeet tribe, using his Indian name Apikuni, meaning "Spotted Robe." Finally, in 1910, President Taft signed a bill establishing Glacier National Park.

Glacier's magnificent trails, which wind through the Rocky Mountain wildlands to more than 700 remote campsites and alpine lakes and streams that hold native cutthroat, lake trout, Dolly Varden, and arctic grayling, are shown on the full-color U.S. Geological Survey *Glacier National Park Topographic Map.* This map ($2) is 38″ × 42½″ with a scale of 1:100,000 and shows contours and all man-made and natural features. Careful study of the map will provide the backpacker and fisherman with an invaluable guide to the hundreds of intriguing mountain trails.

Many of Glacier's trails follow old game, Indian, and exploration routes. The old saying among mountain men holds true for the Glacier region: "The deer made the first trails; the elk followed the deer, the buffalo the elk, and the Indians the buffalo; after the Indians came the trapper; then an army officer came along and discovered a pass." The most ancient of the aboriginal trails in the region was the Great North Trail, also known as the Travois Trail, which ran from Athabasca to present-day Mexico. An old Indian trail that led from Waterton Lakes south to Lake McDonald was used by trappers on their way to Flathead country. Numerous other Indian trails led into the valleys of the Cut Bank, Two Medicine, and Swiftcurrent and across the Red Eagle, Marias, and Stoney Indian passes on the Great Divide. Today, hundreds of miles of park trails wind through the majestic highlands and valleys and across the high mountain passes to remote wilderness fishing and camping areas, including the St. Mary Lakes on the eastern slope of the Lewis Range, Swiftcurrent Valley, and Grinnell, Sherburne, St. Mary, Waterton, Red Eagle, Two Medicine, Avalanche, Logging, Bowman, and Kintla lakes on the western slopes of the Great Divide. Lake trout up to 30 pounds are taken from Lakes St. Mary, McDonald, Waterton, Kintla, and Cosley. Great northern pike up to 20 pounds are found in Sherburne Lake. Arctic grayling, cutthroat, rainbow, and Dolly Varden are found in most of the lakes and streams in the Hudson Bay and Flathead River drainages. Glacier's wildlife includes the Rocky Mountain bighorn, mountain goat, moose, elk, silvertip grizzly, black bear, mule and whitetail deer, cougar, beaver, hoary marmot, lynx, river otter, wolverine, marten, pika, and other, smaller mammals. Birds of Glacier include great concentrations of bald eagles during the kokanee salmon spawning run in the Apgar region along McDonald Creek between the Middle Fork of the Flathead River and the foot of Lake McDonald, and osprey, water ouzel, ptarmigan, Clark's nutcracker, thrushes, and sparrows.

Nearly 1,000 species of plant life are found in Glacier country. On the arctic tundra of the windblown summits, there are only lichens, moss, and the hardiest of alpine plants. In the valleys of the west slope of the Continental Divide are dense Pacific-type forests. The plains on the Atlantic watershed side of the Divide provide an expansive view

of grassy, flower-covered meadows in startling contrast to the dark rugged wall of peaks in the distance. The western slopes, benefiting from warm, moist Pacific winds, have dense forests of spruce, fir, larch, and lodgepole pine. The eastern slopes, exposed to cold winds and less rainfall, have open forests of spruce, lodgepole pine, Douglas fir, and limber pine. The park's brilliant wildflower displays begin in early spring and continues up the mountainsides as the snow recedes. In the alpine meadows among stunted, gnarled fir and whitebark pine are delicate glacier lilies, fringed parnassia, red and yellow mimulus, wild fragrant heliotrope, heather, gentian, and the showy, beautiful beargrass. On the meadows and slopes at lower elevations are a vast array of Great Plains flora, including shooting star, pasqueflower, Indian paintbrush, red and white geraniums, gaillardia, and asters.

All wilderness travelers who intend to have a fire or camp overnight must obtain a Backcountry Camping Permit, which can be obtained from any ranger or information center during the summer. Permits are issued on a first-come-first-served basis, and no earlier than 24 hours before departure time. In winter, and generally in late fall and early spring, permits may be obtained at Park Headquarters or at the St. Mary Ranger Station. Paved park roads provide access to eight of Glacier's campgrounds—Apgar, Avalanche Creek, Fish Creek, Many Glacier, Rising Sun, St. Mary, Two Medicine, and Sprague Creek. Primitive roadside campsites are located at Bowman Creek, Kintla Lake, Cut Bank, Logging Creek, and Quartz Creek. Saddle stock and packhorses are provided by *Rocky Mountain Outfitters Inc.,* Box 776, Columbia Falls 59912.

There are many excellent books, pamphlets, and guides available that will help you plan your trip to Glacier National Park. *Glacier,* available

free from the Glacier Natural History Association, Inc., Glacier National Park, West Glacier 59936, includes an excellent map of the area, showing all major lakes, peaks, contours, trails, and recreation sites. This office will also provide you with the following material. *Backcountry*, a free folder, describes different trails and hiking situations, as well as information on fishing, bears, and camping. It includes a recreation site index and map. *Fish and Fishing in Glacier National Park* shows the best fishing areas on a small map and describes the

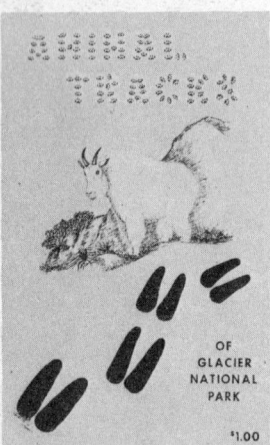

most common park species. *In Grizzly Country* talks about bears and how to respond if you run into one. Pamphlets on the many scenic trails are available for 10¢ each. These describe the various kinds of trees, flowers, and wildlife seen along the most popular and beautiful trails. *Ski Touring and Snowshoeing* describes the many ski areas and the terrains, hazards, and highlights of each.

The following publications are available from the same office: *Family Fun in Waterton-Glacier International Peace Park* ($1); *Roads and Trails, Waterton-Glacier National Park* ($1.95); *Rocks, Ice, and Water—The Geological Story of Glacier National Park* ($2.95); *Glaciers* ($1.25); *Wild Flowers of Glacier National Park* ($1.50); *Birds of Glacier National Park* ($1.50); *Through the Years in Glacier National Park* ($1.50); *Plastic Relief Map of Glacier National Park* ($1). The *Motorist's Guide* ($1.50) is a 47-page booklet that includes many color-photographs, mileage estimates, and descriptions of the park's spectacular areas. *Roads and Trails* describes each highway and road in detail, highlighting major features. It includes photographs, maps, and drawings.

National Parkways in Glacier and Waterton Lakes National Parks is a magnificently illustrated 72-page book that features beautiful full-color photos of the park's numerous scenic sights, descriptions of each area, and information on recreation sites and facilities. It can be obtained from the World-Wide Research and Publishing Co., National Parks Division, Box 3073, Casper, WY 82601, for $2.50. *Animal Tracks*, available for $1 from the Glacier Natural History Association (address above), features descriptions and black silhouettes of the tracks of every major animal species found in the park.

The vast wildlands of the Blackfeet Indian Reservation, which stretch eastward from Glacier National Park, encompass several recreational sites and camps, including Chewing Blackbones, Lower Two Medicine, and Duck Lake campgrounds, historical sites, and the fascinating Museum of the Plains Indians. All are shown on free maps available from the Blackfeet Agency, Browning 59417, along with the free publications *Blackfeet Indian Reservation, Fishing Regulation, Blackfeet Country,* and *Browning, Montana—Home of the Blackfeet Indians.* The Cree Indians named this once feared tribe *Siksika,* or "Blackfeet," because their moccasins were blackened by soot from prairie fires or paint. Beautiful Duck Lake is a renowned trophy rainbow trout fishery and has produced some giant rainbows of 14–15 pounds.

Access & Lodging

Glacier is on U.S. Highway 2 and 87, and near U.S. 91 and 93. Access to recreation areas within the park is provided by Going-to-the-Sun Road for 50 miles from West Glacier to St. Mary; by the Camas Creek Road, an 11-mile short route from Going-to-the-Sun Road near Apgar to Camas Entrance and the Forest Service North Fork Road and Polebridge; by North Fork Road, a narrow, primitive 43-mile road that parallels the North Fork of the Flathead from Going-to-the-Sun Road near Apgar to Kintla Lake; by U.S. Highway 2 for 55 miles from West Glacier to East Glacier Park; by the Blackfeet Highway, which parallels the Front Range of the Rockies from East Glacier Park north to Carway, Alberta; by Two Medicine Road for 12 miles from East Glacier Park to historic Two Medicine; by Many Glacier Road for 12 miles from Babb to Many Glacier; by Chief Mountain International Highway from Babb for 39 miles to Waterton, Lakes National Park, Alberta. Lodging and meals in the park are provided by Benton Chalets Inc., Box 188, West Glacier 59936 (phone: 406 888–5511) at the *Granite Park Chalet* (12 rooms) and *Sperry Chalet* (17 rooms). Lodging, meals, and camping supplies are provided by Glacier Park, Inc., East Glacier Park 59434 (phone: 406 226–4845) at the *Glacier Park Lodge* (155 rooms), *Lake McDonald Lodge* (101 rooms), *Many Glacier Hotel* (191 rooms). (Winter address: 1735 E. Fort Lowell, P.O. Box 4340, Tucson, AZ 85717.) *Glacier Park Boat Company, Inc.,* East Glacier 59434, provides boat rentals and launches at Swiftcurrent, Josephine, Two Medicine, McDonald, and St. Mary Lakes.

Helena National Forest & Gates of the Mountains

Helena National Forest Topo Maps

U.S. Geological Survey 1:250,000 scale overview maps: Butte, Choteau, White Sulphur Springs.

Gates of the Mountains Wilderness

U.S. Geological Survey large-scale topographic maps: Beartooth Mountain, Candle Mountain, Nelson, Upper Halter Lake.

Scapegoat Wilderness

U.S. Geological Survey large-scale topographic maps: Benchmark,

Danaher Mountain, Lake Mountain, Flint Mountain, Olson Peak, Scapegoat Mountain, Trap Mountain, Spread Mountain, Wood Lake.

Upper Missouri River Trophy Trout Waters

U.S. Geological Survey large-scale topographic maps (show river from Three Forks to Great Falls): Three Forks, Manhattan, Toston, Duck Creek Pass, Townsend, Canyon Ferry, East Helena, Upper Halter Lake, Beartooth Mountain, Sheep Creek, Wolf Creek, Craig, Mid Canon, Hardy Rocky Reef, Cascade, Antelope Butte, Southwest Great Falls.

This 900,000-acre reserve, first explored by Lewis and Clark, embraces the beautiful Blackfoot River, the Elkhorn and Big Belt mountains, Baldy Lakes, the Lincoln backcountry, and the Gates of the Mountains and Scapegoat Wilderness areas. Within the forest, the waters of the historic Upper Missouri River and its many tributary creeks offer some of the finest big trout fishing in Montana. Seldom fished stretches like Duck, Cottonwood, and Beaver creeks and Confederate Gulch offer fair to good catches of cutthroat, rainbow, brown and brook trout, and most of them are easily reached by Forest Service roads. Canyon Ferry Reservoir, 7½ miles long and more than a mile wide, is popular with fishermen for 12–14 inch rainbows, occasional browns, and a few walleye and yellow perch. Numerous recreation areas and campgrounds, boat ramps, and an inviting forest setting have made the lake a favorite focus for outdoor recreation. Park Lake, a jewel of a mountain lake just 8 miles southwest of Helena, offers a well-maintained campground and fishing for rainbows to 2 pounds as well as an occasional grayling to 12 inches. Perhaps the most spectacular fishing along the entire length of the Missouri is at the base of Canyon Ferry Dam, where trophy-size rainbow and brown trout congregate when they find their journey upstream from the Hauser Reservoir blocked. Biggest catches are made from boats 14 feet long or larger in the middle of the Missouri's fast waters, but many fish are also taken at the shoreline.

Once the hunting grounds of the Blackfeet Indians, the forest is still an excellent big-game area for antelope, mule deer, mountain goat, and black bear. There are also waterfowl, geese, and sage, blue, and Franklin grouse. Within the woods, the combination of a long growing season, ditch banks, and cattail marshes provide essential cover and food supply for ringnecks. Because the wily pheasant is unsurpassed in the art of hiding when crippled, only a well-placed shot can bring one down for good. Other game birds found within the Helena area include Hungarian partridge, wild turkey, and a variety of ducks.

One of the most spectacular sights within the forest is the Gates of the Mountains, discovered and named by Lewis and Clark in July of 1805, when they first entered the Missouri River Canyon. "The most remarkable cliffs that we have yet seen," Captain Lewis wrote in his journal, "the cliffs rise from the water's edge on either side to the height of 1,200 feet." Southeast of the Gates of the Mountains lie the many ochre-tinted peaks of the Big Belt Range, including Willow, Sacajawea, Moors, Sawtooth, Middleman, and Needham, with elevations varying between 6,500 and 9,000 feet. The mountains take their name from a prominent encircling "belt" of limestone outcroppings. Another breathtaking canyon within the region, the Big Belt Canyon, is composed of lofty walls streaked with shades of green, red, and yellow, which vary from iridescent brilliance to subtle, shadowy tones, depending on the amount of sunlight. A popular drive within the forest along the scenic, 42-mile figure-eight route passes through the mountains and Helena's "canyon country," offering panoramic vistas of Trout Creek and Beaver Creek canyons. The side trip to Hogback Mountain (7,813 ft.) leads to a magnificent view of the Helena Valley and part of the Gates of the Mountains Wilderness.

Much of the present-day forestland was once the highly prized hunting grounds of the Blackfeet, famous warriors and horsemen who staged surprise campaigns as far west of the Rockies as the Great Salt Lake. After the passage of Lewis and Clark through the area in the summer of 1805, no white men visited the region until the great Montana gold rush of 1858, when, almost overnight, swarms of fortune hunters began prospecting in the streams and valleys. In 1864, gold was discovered in Last Chance Gulch, now the main street of Helena, one of the few towns to survive after the mining boom had played itself out a few years later. Numerous towns in the area that were once prosperous mining settlements hastily thrown together out of tents, rickety buildings, and dirt roads are today little more than ghost communities, either sparsely populated or totally deserted. Marysville, a ghost town just east of the Continental Divide, boasted a population of 5,000 when the famed Drumlummon gold mine opened in 1876, and eventually produced over $50 million in gold.

In the northern reaches of the forest is the magnificent Scapegoat Wilderness, a 450,000-acre tract shared with Lewis and Clark and Lolo national forests. This huge tract straddles the Continental Divide and offers a landscape of incredible beauty, with limestone cliffs rising sharply against broad expanses of alpine meadows and numerous creeks and trails winding through dense forest growth. Stonewall Creek, skirting the base of Stonewall Mountain, has good fishing for 8–12 inch cutthroat, brook, and brown trout, plus some Dolly Vardens to 12 pounds. In the upper reaches of Copper Creek, followed for much of its length by a good jeep road, there is fair to good fishing in the numerous beaver dams for cutthroat to 15 inches. Bighorn Lake, a remote backcountry cirque lake just below the Continental Divide, can be reached by an unmarked trail from the Bighorn Creek Trail and is reputedly excellent for whopper cutthroats and rainbows. Other fine trout streams in the wilderness include Landers Fork, Arrastra Creek, and Falls Creek. The *Scapegoat Wilderness Map*, available for 50¢ from the Helena National Forest Supervisor, 616 Helena Avenue, Helena 59601, shows all roads, trails, mountains, lakes, and streams.

Other attractions within the Helena National Forest include the McDonald Pass Vista Point, Crow Creek Falls, Ophir Cave, and the rugged but scenic Hanging Valley Trail. In the winter, the forest offers recreational opportunities for skiers, snowmobilers, and snowshoers. There are two fine ski areas nearby: Grass Mountain, located on national forest land 23 miles east of Townsend, and the Belmont Ski Area, near Marysville, 25 miles northwest of Helena. The forest also has more than 100 miles of marked snowmobile trails. The *Helena National Forest Map* shows all recreation areas, points of interest, roads, trails, streams, lakes, campgrounds, and boat access points and is available for 50¢ from the Forest Supervisor at the above address.

Access & Outfitting Centers

The Helena National Forest is reached via U.S. Highways 12, 91, and 287, Interstate 15, and Montana State Highway 200. Supplies, guides, and outfitting services can be found at Helena, East Helena, Lincoln, Blackfoot City, Avon, Wickes, Jefferson City, Clancy, York, Jimtown, Canyon Ferry, Whites City, Diamond City, Townsend, Hassell, and Radersburg.

Kootenai National Forest & Cabinet Mountains Wilderness

Kootenai National Forest Topo Maps

U.S. Geological Survey 1:250,000 scale overview maps: Kalispell, Sandpoint, Wallace.

Cabinet Mountains Wilderness

U.S. Geological Survey large-scale topographic maps: Crowell Mountain, Ibex Peak, Snowshoe Peak, Smeads Bench, Elephant Peak, Edward Lake, Goat Peak, Silver Butte Pass, Howard Lake, Treasure Mountain, Kootenai Falls, Scenery Mountain.

Kootenai River

U.S. Geological Survey large-scale maps showing float-fishing stretch from Libby Dam to Idaho border: Alexander Mountain, Tony Peak, Swede Mountain, Vermiculite Mountain, Libby, Scenery Mountain, Kootenai Falls, Troy, Kibrennan Lake, Leonia.

This 1.8 million-acre tract is located in central northwest Montana and embraces the wilderness stretches of the Upper Kootenai River, Salish Mountains, Purcell Mountains, Cabinet Mountains Wilderness, Tobacco River, Ten Lakes Area, and Yaak and Fisher rivers. The forest is named for the warlike Kootenai Indians, who were driven west of the Rockies by their archenemies, the Blackfeet, and settled in northwestern Montana and southeastern British Columbia. Renowned as great deer hunters and skillful tanners, the tribe very appropriately derives its name from the Indian word for "deer robes." Reminders of Kootenai domination in the area are found throughout the forest. Just south of Libby along the Kootenai River are the remains of ceremonial sweat baths used in Indian purification rites. After steaming himself in shallow pits heated by red-hot rocks, the Kootenai bather plunged into the icy waters of the river in a ritual not so far removed from the practices associated with Finnish saunas. The deep, swift Kootenai River, once a waterway favored by both Indians and fur traders, sweeps down from British Columbia and makes a 174-mile bend through Montana and Idaho around the Purcell Mountains before turning back toward Canada. A major tributary of the Columbia, the Kootenai, below Libby Dam, offers fishing for trophy-sized rainbow and cutthroat trout and white sturgeon up to 67 pounds. Most standard flies do the trick if the fish are taking, but spinners, spoons, and grasshoppers do well too. Unfortunately, all but the lower 38 miles of this once majestic emerald green wild river have been impounded behind the U.S. Army Corps of Engineers Libby Dam to form Lake Koocanusa. The only free-flowing stretch left is from the dam to the Idaho border. The cold spring-fed section of the Kootenai near the mouth of the Yaak River holds trophy rainbows from 5 to 12 pounds.

West of the Kootenai River are the rocky peaks of the Purcell Mountains, a region of steep canyons and numerous waterfalls. The Yaak River flows near the Canadian line through the wilderness for 28 miles before joining the emerald green waters of the Kootenai. A good-sized stream bordered by a gravel road for its entire length, the Yaak is popular for 10–12 inch rainbows, cutthroat, and brook trout to 27 inches. Kilbrennan Lake, a 59-acre lake about 10 miles north of Troy, offers equally fine fishing for brook and rainbow trout and is bordered by a public campground with boat ramps. Winter visitors to the Purcell Mountains region can enjoy the unsurpassed ski slopes of Turner Mountain, a few miles east of Kilbrennan Lake.

The Cabinet Mountains, just below the Purcell Range, were named by French Canadian trappers who discovered boxlike openings resembling cabinets in the gorge of Clark Fork near the Montana-Idaho border. Between the Clark Fork and Kootenai River lies the Cabinet Mountain Wilderness, a beautiful, lake-studded high-country reserve encompassing 94,272 acres within the Kaniksu and Kootenai national forests. The landscape here varies from high, snow-clad peaks to mountain lakes to timbered valleys, with elevations rising from 3,000 feet to 8,712 feet at the top of Snowshoe Peak. Alpine fir and spruce,

with snowbrush and huckleberry undergrowth, cover the mountains, whose granite crags rise steeply, overlooking boulder-strewn slopes. This is primarily a hiking and fishing area, and most people enter on horseback, a service easily arranged through local outfitters. Licensed outfitters in the region include: *Robert W. Boothman*, Rt. 1, Box 1258, Libby 59923; *Edna Hill*, Trout Creek 59874; *Wayne E. Leighty*, Rt. 1, Eureka 59917; *Lewis N. Sprout*, Rt. 1, Whitefish 59937; *Edward Vance*, Rt. 2, Troy 59935; and *Harry Workman*, Box 84, Eureka 59917. Fishermen will find brook trout and rainbows up to 7 pounds in Leigh Lake; Leigh Creek, which flows out of the lake for 5 miles down a steep canyon, contains brook trout in the big flat just below the lake. Most lakes in the Cabinet Mountains can be reached by backcountry roads in Idaho from Trestle Creek, Clark Fork, or Antelope Lake. The logging road on the South Fork of Callahan Creek in Montana is the best route to Callahan Lake. Other fishing lakes include Wishbone, Hanging Valley, Sky, Cedar, Snowshoe, Tahoka, Wanless, and Bear. The *Cabinet Mountains Wilderness Map*, available free from the Forest Supervisor, Kootenai National Forest, Box AS, Libby 59923, shows roads and trails, recreation sites, ranger stations, streams, and lakes. A free list of *Cabinet Mountains Trails* is also available.

Other features of the Kootenai National Forest include Kootenai Falls, a dramatic series of tumbling cascades that descend over 200 feet along the river east of Libby. David Thompson, the first white man to explore and map the Kootenai River, made the difficult portage around the falls in 1808 and called them the Lower Dalles. A trading post established by Thompson near the falls soon became a key stopover for trappers traveling the waterways of Montana. Many years later, between 1890 and 1902, steamboats plied the Kootenai between Jennings and Fort Steele in British Columbia. A short distance from the falls is the Kootenai Gorge, a narrow canyon, through which the raging white water rushes with a deafening, ominous roar.

With its Douglas fir and lodgepole pine, its many streams, mountains and willow-lined swamps, the forest provides good hunting for Shiras, or Yellowstone, moose; mountain goat and bighorn sheep high in the Purcell and Cabinet mountains; mule and whitetail deer; and Franklin, blue, and ruffed grouse. Over 1,000 miles of Forest Service trails lead deep into the forest, along shaded streams, through flower-decked woods, past swampy "moose pastures," and to wind-swept lookout towers. Trails, roads, points of interest, campgrounds, boat access points, and lookout towers are all indicated on the *Kootenai National Forest Map*, available for 50¢ from the Forest Supervisor at the above address. An index to *Camp and Picnic Areas* in the forest is free on request.

Access & Outfitting Centers

The Kootenai National Forest is reached via U.S. Highways 2 and 93 and Montana State Highways 37 and 200. Lodging, supplies, guides, and outfitting services are available at Libby, Troy, Rexford, Eureka, Leonia, and Gateway. Ranger stations in the forest are at Troy, Libby, Raven, Eureka, Warland, Sylvanite, and Murphy Lake.

Lewis & Clark National Forest

Lewis & Clark National Forest Topo Maps

U.S. Geological Survey 1:250,000 scale overview maps: Choteau, Cut Bank, Great Falls, Roundup, White Sulphur Springs.

Big Spring Creek Trophy Trout Waters

U.S. Geological Survey large-scale topographic maps: Lewistown, Glengarry, Spring Creek Junction, Danvers.

Sun River Game Preserve

U.S. Geological Survey large-scale topographic maps: Bungalow Mountain, Three Sisters, Gates Park, Amphitheatre Mountain, Slategoat Mountain, Glenn Creek, Haystack Mountain, Prairie Reef, Pretty Prairie, Pilot Peak, Trap Mountain, Benchmark.

The Lewis & Clark National Forest lies in the heart of Missouri River country and is composed of two divisions: the 1 million-acre Rocky Mountain Division, encompassing the headwaters of the Sun, Teton, and Dearborn rivers high in the Sun River Game Preserve portion of the Bob Marshall Wilderness; and the 786,072-acre Jefferson Division, which encompasses the famed lands of the Big Snowy, Crazy Highwood, and Little Belt mountains and the renowned trout waters of Judith River, Big Spring Creek, and Smith River Canyon. The forest is a top-ranked big-game hunting area for antelope along the Musselshell River Flatlands, for Rocky Mountain elk in the Little Belt and Castle mountains, and for deer, black bear, and grouse forestwide. The Missouri River, which forms a natural demarcation between the two forest divisions, was first explored by Lewis and Clark during their westward expedition of 1805. The party spent a month making a portage around the white fury of Great Falls (located north of the Jefferson Division), using a primitive cart along a well-traveled buffalo migration route. Lewis wrote on his return to the area the following year that "there were not less than 10,000 buffalo within a circle of two miles." Jim Bridger, of the Rocky Mountain Fur Company, was the next white man to explore the region, followed by Andrew Henry and his fur-trading party in 1823, who pushed up as far as Great Falls, where he was turned back by the warring Blackfeet. He was followed in 1828 by Kenneth McKenzie of the American Fur Company, who successfully obtained the trade of the Blackfeet and built Forts Piegan, McKenzie, Chardon, and Benton on the banks of the great river.

The Judith River, named by Captain Clark for his fiancé, rises in the Little Belt Mountains in the Jefferson Division of the forest and flows through the undulating flatlands of the Judith Basin into a scenic canyon, where it winds through the "breaks" to its mouth at the Missouri. The upper stretches of the river provide good fishing for rainbows. The most famous feature of the Judith River is its tributary, Big Spring Creek, which holds giant brown trout to 20 pounds and over in its deep-flowing pools. This trophy stream rises in the Big Spring at the Lewistown Fish Hatchery and winds for 20 miles through low rolling hills to its mouth on the Judith. The beautiful Smith River, a state-designated red-ribbon trout stream, rises in the Castle Mountains and flows northward for 90 miles between the Big and Little Belt Mountains through a picturesque limestone canyon to its mouth on the Missouri near Great Falls. The Smith's deep crystal-clear pools, rapids, and limestone ledges hold trophy rainbow and brown trout in the 5-pound-and-over class. Float fishing by canoe or rubber raft is the best way to tackle this wildwater gem. The upper stretches of the Musselshell River (which rises along the southern slopes of the Little Belt and Big Snowy Mountains and flows through the heart of antelope, mule and whitetail deer country in central Montana to its mouth on the Fort Peck Reservoir) hold brown trout.

In the Rocky Mountain Division of the forest are the renowned fish and game lands of the Dearborn, Teton, and Sun river drainages. The Dearborn River, whose lower stretches offer some of the nation's finest fly-fishing for rainbow and brown trout up to 12 pounds, rises high in the Scapegoat Wilderness Area and flows eastwardly for 62 miles through rugged high country, broad valleys, and canyons to its mouth on the Missouri, 30 miles south of Great Falls. Much of the Dearborn flows through private lands and must be floated. The picturesque Sun River and its remote North and South forks, which rise high in the

Bob Marshall Wilderness and Sun River Game Preserve, flow through scenic high country and deep, wide canyons to their mouth on the Missouri near Great Falls. The North Fork of the Sun, beginning high in the Sun River Game Preserve below Sun River Pass on the Continental Divide at 7,800 feet, offers often superb wilderness fly-fishing for wild cutthroats and pink-slashed rainbows, with an occasional lunker tipping the scales at 10–12 pounds. The wilderness upper stretches of the Sun are reached by backpacking or packhorse. The small Teton River, which rises north of the Sun near the Continental Divide, offers fair fishing for brook, rainbow, and cutthroat trout.

Gibson Reservoir

The *Lewis & Clark National Forest Map* shows all forest roads, highways, and trails, which provide access to the most remote fish and game areas, as well as campsites, ranger stations, lookout towers, recreation sites, and boat access sites. This full-color map may be obtained for 50¢ along with free fishing, hunting, camping, and wilderness permit information, by writing: Forest Supervisor, Lewis & Clark National Forest, Box 871, Great Falls 59401.

Licensed fishing and hunting guides serving the Jefferson and Rocky Mountain divisions of the forest include: *Edward F. Arnott*, Utica 59452 (Judith Basin, fishing, hunting); *Charles Blixrud*, Choteau 59422 (Sun River); *Alston S. Chase*, Millegan Rt., Great Falls 59401 (Smith River); *Ford Creek Ranch*, Box 67, Augusta 59410 (fishing, hunting); *DC Outfitting*, Hilger 59451 (fishing, hunting); *Benchmark Wilderness Ranch*, Box 190, Augusta 59410 (fishing, hunting); *Klick K Bar 1 Ranch*, Augusta 59410 (Bob Marshall Wilderness & Sun River, hunting); *John W. McMahon*, 2225 11th Avenue, Helena 59601 (Bob Marshall Wilderness & Smith River, fishing, hunting); *Black Tail Ranch*, Wolf Creek 59648 (South Fork Dearborn, Scapegoat & Bob Marshall Wilderness, fishing, hunting); *Eldon Snyder*, Box 1099, Lewistown 59457 (fishing, hunting); *Circle Bar Ranch*, Utica 59452 (Judith River, fishing, hunting); *Arthur Stevens*, Box 237, Augusta 59410 (Sun River Area, fishing, hunting); *Hidden Valley Ranch*, Augusta 59410 (Sun River Country, fishing, hunting); *Canyon Ranch*, White Sulphur Springs 59645 (fishing, hunting).

Access & Outfitting Centers

The major automobile routes to the Jefferson (eastern) Division of the forest are U.S. Highways 89, 12, and 87 and Interstate 90. Lodging, guides, supplies, boat rentals, and outfitters in the Jefferson Division are available at White Sulphur Springs, Harlowton, Thale, Neihart, Stanford, Monarch, Lewistown, and Great Falls. The Rocky Mountain (western) Division of the forest is reached via Interstate 15 and U.S. 287 and 89. Accommodations, supplies, guides, boat rentals, and outfitters are available at Cut Bank, Shelby, Conrad, Great Falls, Choteau, Augusta, Bowman's Corner, and Wolf Creek.

Lolo National Forest & Blackfoot River Country

Lolo National Forest Topo Maps

U.S. Geological Survey 1:250,000 scale topographic maps: Butte, Choteau, Hamilton, Wallace.

Blackfoot River Fish & Game Country

U.S. Geological Survey large-scale topographic maps: Bonner, Blue Point, Sunflower Mountain, Potomac, Greenaugh, Bata Mountain, Woodworth, Ovando, Chamberlain Mountain, Browns Lake, Marcum Mountain, Moose Creek, Lincoln, Swede Gulch, Stemple Pass, Cadotte Creek, Rogers Pass.

Rock Creek Blue Ribbon Trout Waters

U.S. Geological Survey large-scale topographic maps: Ravenna, Cleveland Mountain; and Butte (1:250,000 scale map).

This historic fishing, hunting, and camping region embraces 2 million acres of rugged high country surrounding Missoula and the Clark Fork of the Columbia and Blackfoot rivers in northwest Montana. The Clark Fork, once a major water trail for the Northwest explorers and fur traders, bisects the forest, flowing from its headwaters in Deerlodge National Forest in a northwesterly direction past Bearmouth, Medicine Tree Hill, the mouths of Rock Creek and the Bigfoot River, through Hell Gate Canyon, Missoula, past the mouths of the St. Regis, Flathead, and Thompson rivers, and forms the Noxon Reservoir in Kaniksu National Forest before flowing into Idaho. The forest is laced by a network of logging roads and old Indian trails that wind through forests of pine, fir, hemlock, spruce, and quaking aspen, along rolling hills, and through the renowned big-game hunting and fishing country surrounding the Sapphire and John Long mountains, Garnet Range, the Bitterroot, Coeur D'Alene, and Cabinet mountains, and along the Clark Fork, Blackfoot, Clearwater, Thompson and St. Regis rivers and the trophy trout waters of Rock Creek. The forest was once traversed by the old Kootenai Trail of the Salish Indians and traveled by David Thompson, Finan McDonald, Jacque Finley, and other fur traders of the Northwest Company in the early 1800s and by prospectors and pack trains during the boom days of the Coeur d'Alene and Kootenai mines in the 1860s. Within the forest is the site where, in 1805, Lewis and Clark set up the camp called Traveler's Rest on the Bitterroot River near the mouth of Lolo Creek. On their return trip from the Pacific they separated there, and Clark traveled south up the Bitterroot while Lewis crossed the Missoula flats through Hell Gate Canyon and followed the beautiful Blackfoot along the Salish (or Kootenai) Trail. Hell Gate Canyon of the Clark Fork, known to the French Canadian trappers as *Porte de l'Enfer*, or "Gate of Hell," is the site of present-day Missoula, which lies on the level bed of a prehistoric lake at the mouth of the canyon and is named after the Salish Indian word *Im-i-sul-ol*, meaning "by the chilling waters." Missoula was visited in 1812 by the explorer-surveyor David Thomp-

son, who went through the forest along the Clark Fork and Kootenai Trail and became the first white man to follow the Columbia River from its source to its mouth on the Pacific Ocean, traveling more than 50,000 miles on foot, on horseback, and by canoe. Near Thompson Falls on the Clark Fork, Thompson built Salish House (believed to have been the first roofed habitation built by a white man in the territory of present-day Montana) on a site from which he could see Indian war parties crossing Bad Rock on the Kootenai Trail. Thompson, with his compass and sextant, was regarded with superstitious awe by the Indians, who called him *Koo-koo-sint*, meaning "man who looks at stars."

Today the former Indian hunting and trapping grounds of the forest provide top-ranked high-country hunting for Rocky Mountain elk, whitetail deer, mule deer, black bear, moose, mountain goat and sheep, and Franklin and ruffed grouse. Several tributaries of the big Clark Fork of the Columbia provide superb fishing for trophy trout in a wilderness setting. The once-famed trout waters of Clark Fork proper, however, have suffered from pollution. The most renowned tributary is Rock Creek, a state-designated blue-ribbon trout stream, which flows for 50 miles from the junction of its north and middle forks through densely timbered hills between the Sapphire Mountains on the west and the Long John Mountains on the east to its junction with the Clark Fork. The famous Blackfoot River flows for most of its length through some of the finest big-game country in the West. From its source high on the Continental Divide, the Blackfoot flows through the Helena and Lolo national forests to its confluence with the Clark Fork just east of Missoula. This incredibly scenic wild river holds large, spooky brown, rainbow, cutthroat, and Dolly Varden trout. The Clearwater River, a tributary of the Blackfoot, and the Clearwater Chain-of-Lakes (Salmon, Placid, Seeley, Inez, Alva, and Rainy) hold rainbow, cutthroat, Dolly Varden, and whitefish. Other important trout fisheries of the Clark Fork include the St. Regis, Thompson, and Vermilion rivers. A group of remote, seldom fished alpine trout lakes, including Deer, Duckhead, Arrowhead, Frog, Porcupine, Terrace, Stony, and Fishtrap, lie high in the Cabinet Mountains in the heart of grizzly country, due west of the Thompson River. The lakes are reached by pack trail and forest roads.

Additional information and the *Lolo National Forest Map* (50¢), showing all roads and trails, recreation sites, ranger stations, boat access points, ski areas, points of interest, caves, houses, mines, schools, and churches, are available from the Forest Supervisor, Bldg. 24, Fort Missoula, Missoula 59801. Individual ranger districts will also provide you with maps and information about their areas: Missoula Ranger District, 2801 Russell St., Missoula 59801; Ninemile Ranger District, Huson 59846; Plains Ranger District, P.O. Box 429, Plains 59858; Seeley Lake Ranger District, Seeley Lake 59868; Superior Ranger District, Superior 59872; and Thompson Falls Ranger District, Thompson Falls 59873. The *Lolo National Forest Campground Directory* is available free from the Forest Supervisor.

Access & Outfitting Centers

The Lolo National Forest is reached via U.S. Highways 2, 12, and 10, Interstate 90, and Montana State Highway 200. Information, lodging, supplies, guides, and outfitters are available at Missoula, Ovando, Seeley Lake, Evaro, Huson, Stark, Frenchtown, Alberton, Plains, Superior, Thompson Springs, Paradise, St. Regis, Greenough, Potomac, and Bonner. For a listing of outfitters for fishing, hunting, and wilderness pack trips in the Lolo National Forest, write: Dept. of Fish & Game, 490 Meridian Road, Kalispell 59901.

Accommodations—Rocky Mountain Vacation Lodges & Ranches

The Wyoming Travel Commission publishes a free directory, *Big Wyoming Dude Ranches, Lodges, & Resorts*, which provides a comprehensive listing of such accommodations by county throughout the state. The guide lists locations, type of accommodations, services and activities, rates, and addresses and phones of each lodge or resort. It includes a map of the state with locations of the resorts and ranches; national parks, monuments, forests, and recreation areas; and state and U.S. highways. It also includes a listing of special camps, schools, and wilderness schools throughout the state. Write: Wyoming Travel Commission, 2320 Capitol Avenue, Cheyenne 82002. Also available free from this address is a thorough directory to *Big Wyoming Hotels and Motels*, which lists accommodations by city. It gives number of units, cooking facilities, rates, dining facilities, pet regulations, bar facilities, special services, credit cards accepted, and address and phone of each hotel and motel.

If you plan to visit a national forest area, the free booklet *National Forest Vacations* may be helpful to you in finding accommodations. This book describes the national forest areas briefly, tells if there are motels and dude ranches nearby, and gives the names of towns and communities in the area which offer accommodations. This booklet covers the entire United States and is available for 90¢ from: Superintendent of Documents, U.S. Government Printing Office, Washington, DC 20402.

Listings of the major guest ranches and vacation lodges are found throughout the "Wyoming Travel & Recreation Guide."

Bighorn Canyon National Recreation Area—"The Land that Time Forgot"

The Bighorn Basin is a natural valley covering more than 13,000 square miles (over 8 million acres) in Big Horn, Park, Washakie, and Hot Springs counties of northwestern Wyoming. The bighorn sheep of the Absaroka Mountains to the west and the Bighorns to the east gave the basin its name.

The Bighorn River bisects the valley. Along with its tributaries, the Shoshone and the Greybull rivers, it provides top-ranked fishing for rainbow, brown, and cutthroat trout. The legendary John Colter was the first white man to pass through this country, by way of the Pryor Gap of the Bighorn Mountains in 1807, on the trek that led him to the discovery of the natural wonders now called Yellowstone National Park. Later in the year a trapping party led by Ezekiel Williams traveled up the Bighorn River through what was then Crow Indian country. Edward Rose, a member of the party, remained here to become the first known permanent white resident of the valley.

Today, the Yellowtail Dam across the Bighorn River in Montana has created the 47-mile-long Bighorn Lake, the setting of the Bighorn Canyon National Recreation Area. This area of spectacular scenery is known as "the land that time forgot." Tremendous geologic forces have metamorphosed once level layers of rock surrounding the basin into immense walls, or anticlines. The largest of these great arches is the Bighorn, which extends south from Yellowtail Dam to form the Bighorn Mountains. The river has cut deeply into the arch upstream of the dam, creating colorful cliffs rising almost one-half mile over the river, and exposing fossil-rich rocks up to 500 million years old.

The mountains are carpeted with forests of lodgepole and timber pine, fir, and spruce. Dwarf juniper, mountain mahogany, sumac, choke-

WYOMING ENCYCLOPEDIA

cherry, buffalo berry, and sage cover the foothills. Black bear, mule deer, elk, grouse, chukar and Hungarian partridge, waterfowl, pheasant, rabbit, muskrat, beaver, and mink inhabit the area, and wild horses roam the slopes. The Bureau of Land Management has established the 31,000-acre Pryor Mountain Wild Horse Range to preserve the habitat of the more than 200 wild horses that live beyond the western boundaries of the recreation area. Access to the range is by four-wheel drive.

Activities in the recreation area include hunting, boating, fishing, camping, and hiking. Bighorn Lake has an excellent walleye population, with a bonus of trophy-sized rainbow and brown trout. Another fascinating attraction in the area is the mysterious Medicine Wheel, left here by a prehistoric Indian culture. It is a circle of flat white stones 245 feet in circumference with 28 spokes, the monument of a vanished culture and religion. Other nearby features include the geologic marvels of Sheep Mountain and the Devil's Kitchen area north of Greybull. Wilderness campers will enjoy the remote beauty of the Cloud Peak Wilderness in the Bighorn National Forest about 40 miles east of Greybull. A free *Bighorn Canyon Pryor Mountain Area Map & Guide* may be obtained by writing: Bighorn Canyon National Recreation Area, National Park Service, P.O. Box 458, Fort Smith, MT 59035.

The Bighorn Canyon is accessible from Lovell via State Secondary 37 to Horseshoe Bend, or to Kane Bridge by way of U.S. 14A. Dude ranches and resorts in the area include: *B Bar Ranch*, Shell 82441; *Paintrock Outfitters*, Box 509, Greybull 82427; *Earl Brost & Sons*, Owl Creek Route, Thermopolis 82443; *Broken H Ranch*, North Fork Star Rt., Cody 82414; *Circle H Ranch*, M.E. Hall, Wapiti 82450; *Crossed Sabres Ranch*, Box WTC, Wapiti 82450; *Elk Creek Ranch*, c/o The Ridgeways, 802 Lane Drive, Cody 82414; *Grizzly Ranch*, North Fork Rt., Cody 82414; *Meadowlark Lodge*, Ten Sleep 82442; and *Deer Haven Lodge*, Box 121, Ten Sleep 82442. There are hotel and motel accommodations in Greybull and Lovell.

U.S. Geological Survey topographical maps of the area include Dead Indian Hill, East Pryor Mountain, Hillboro, Kane, Little Finger Ridge, Mystery Cave, Natural Trap Cave, and Sykes Spring.

Black Hills Fish & Game Region

The rich game lands and blue-ribbon trout streams of the Black Hills National Forest were once the sacred land of the Sioux Indians, for whom the hills were the home of many spirits. The Indians often camped on the edge of the Black Hills, or *Paha Sapa*, which they named for the darkness of the timbered slopes. But they ventured into the sacred hills only when it was necessary to hunt and fish, gather medicinal herbs, or obtain lodgepoles. Vast herds of antelope and buffalo grazed the nearby plains, providing the tribe with plentiful meat and skins. When white men moved into the territory in the mid-1800s, the Sioux under Sitting Bull fought to hold them back. At first the government attempted to keep out the gold seekers who streamed into the region after the discovery of the precious metal on French Creek near what is now Custer, South Dakota. But by 1876 the Indians had relinquished the territory between the Platte and Powder rivers to the white men. Thousands of gold-hungry settlers streamed north from Cheyenne and Rawlins. Such historical characters as Wild Bill Hickok, Calamity Jane, and Buffalo Bill were among the many travelers between Cheyenne and Deadwood.

Today, a few deep ruts remain in the soil of the region to remind us of the rush, and arrowhead-strewn fields recall the battles that preceded it. The initial rush gave way to a steady stream of newcomers, who rode the newly built Union Pacific Railroad to their destination.

The buffalo are gone now, and many of the antelope, but the Black Hills remain a region of great natural beauty rich in wildlife. The area supports mule deer and elk and the state's largest concentration of whitetail deer and wild turkey. Such streams as Sand Creek, Cold Springs Creek, Redwater Creek, Beaver Creek, and the Belle Fourche River, as well as Lake Cook, offer excellent trout fishing for trophy rainbow, brook, and brown trout. Hiking and camping are popular among the birch and oak-covered slopes, as is ski touring during the winter months. Famous Sand Creek in the Sundance area, a designated blue-ribbon stream, is fed by a giant spring and offers excellent fishing for trophy hook-jawed browns up to 12 pounds. There are 6 miles of public access as well as "pay as you go" fishing on Belle Fourche Club lands.

The *Flying V Guest Ranch* has resort accommodations in nearby Weston County, with horseback riding, hunting, and rodeos. The address is: Flying V Cambria Inn, P.O. Box 158, Newcastle 82701. The towns of Moorcroft and Sundance outside the national forest area have hotel and motel accommodations, as well as camping facilities.

Sundance is a town rich in history. It is located at the foot of Sundance Mountain, known to the Sioux as *Wi Wacippi Paha*, "Temple of the Sioux." Legend says that the "Sundance Kid" (Harry Longabaugh) earned his title here. Sundance, a member of Butch Cassidy's Hole in the Wall Gang, left for remote portions of the state after killing a deputy sheriff near the town. The imposing Devil's Tower, 28 miles northwest of Sundance, is composed of a mass of rock columns 1,000 feet across at the bottom and 275 feet wide at the top. It looms 1,280 feet over the Belle Fourche River, rising to a height of 5,117 feet above sea level. The Indians called the tower *Mateo Tepee*, or "Bear Lodge," and gave it an important role in their mythology. It later became a landmark for explorers, trappers, and pioneers. The fluted, polygonal columns were formed by the cooling and crystallization of molten rock. The tallest formation of its kind in the country, it was named a national monument by Pres. Theodore Roosevelt in 1906. For a full-color *Black Hills National Forest Map* (50¢) and detailed fishing, hunting, camping, and wilderness travel information, write: Bearlodge Ranger District, Sundance 82729. The Black Hills region and the small Wyoming portion of the Black Hills National Forest are shown on the following 1:250,000 scale U.S. Geological Survey overview maps: Gillette, Newcastle, Torrington.

Camping & Backpacking

The Wyoming Travel Commission publishes a free guide to camping throughout the state, *Camping Big Wyoming*. This comprehensive guide lists campgrounds throughout the state in national parks, forests, and recreation areas. It also lists commercial campgrounds throughout the state by county. The directory gives the name, location, and type of each campground, as well as the number of tent and trailer sites, open season, limit of stay, free facilities, activities, special attractions, and nearest town and supplies. It designates campgrounds administered by the Forest Service, National Park Service, Bureau of Land Management, Wyoming State Parks, Wyoming Game and Fish Commission, and Natrona County Parks Board. A map in the guide keys the location of each campground described and the counties, parks, and forests in which they are located. Only federal and state highways and certain forest roads are shown on the map, but information in the guide shows you how to get from the main highways to campgrounds well off the main roads. To reach the more remote campsites, consult a Wyoming highway map, and inquire locally at chambers of commerce and park or forest offices for more specific travel instructions. The guide includes the addresses of information sources for Wyoming State Parks, the Wyoming Game and Fish Commission, and national

forests and national parks in the state. To order the map, write: Wyoming Travel Commission, 2320 Capitol Ave., Cheyenne 82002.

If you plan to camp in a wilderness area, remember to obtain a wilderness permit from a ranger station or forest supervisor's office in the forest in which you plan to travel. The addresses of individual offices are given in the Encyclopedia sections on the individual forests. In most cases you may obtain your permit by mail, but you must register at a forest office before entering a wilderness area.

Backpacking—Climbing Big Wyoming, a free brochure published by the Wyoming Travel Commission, outlines the major sources of information for backcountry travel throughout the state. The brochure lists several good reference books on backpacking and mountain climbing in Wyoming and tells where to order them. It also gives the addresses of information sources for fishing and hunting, state parks and historic sites, geology, rock-hounding, and topographical maps. It tells where to write for information on hiking and backpacking in national parks, national forests, national recreation areas, national monuments, and other public lands. Special camps, wilderness schools, and mountain-climbing schools are also described in the guide, and their addresses are listed. To order the brochure, write: Wyoming Travel Commission, 2320 Capitol Ave., Cheyenne 82002.

Canoeing & Wild-River Floating

Wyoming's waterways are born in the grandeur and solitude of her wildlands and reflect their character. Many of these scenic lakes, streams, and rivers are readily accessible by good all-weather roads and highways.

The free brochure *Family Water Sports—Big Wyoming* lists all the major fishing streams accessible by road or highway, the species of fish they hold, their length or surface area, and the nearest town. A map included in the brochure keys all waters open to public access for fishing. The map can be used to reach the approximate location of a fishing area; highway signs throughout the state mark the exact location of access points. The brochure is available from: Wyoming Travel Commission, 2320 Capitol Ave., Cheyenne 82002.

Wyoming's national forests, parks, and recreation areas, and state parks include some of the outstanding canoe and float streams and lakes in the state. Among these areas are Grand Teton National Park and Jackson Hole, Yellowstone National Park, Bighorn National Forest, Black Hills National Forest, Bridger National Forest, Medicine Bow National Forest, Shoshone National Forest, Teton National Forest, Bighorn Canyon National Recreation Area, Flaming Gorge Na-

tional Recreation Area, and Alcova, Big Sandy, Boysen, Glendo, Guernsey, Keyhole, Seminoe, Curt Gowdy, and Sinks Canyon state parks. The Wyoming Travel Commission booklet mentioned above lists the waterways in each of these areas, their boating, camping, and picnicking facilities, other activities, and nearest towns or concessions.

Canoe, kayak, and rubber raft floaters will find a myriad of waterways to run, whether they are beginners at the sport or experienced white-water boatmen. Wyoming's historic water highways include the Green River (southwest), the Salt River (west), the Snake River (northwest), the Shoshone River (northwest), the Bighorn River (west central), and the North Platte River (southeast). Before you set out, however, familiarize yourself with river characteristics and local conditions in the area where you plan to travel. Find out about hazards and obstructions, upstream water releases from reservoir dams, weather and water temperature conditions, and streambank ownership. If you plan to float the Snake in Grand Teton National Park, check and register with the Chief Ranger's Office at Park Headquarters in Moose before starting your trip. Special regulations apply to the use of canoes, kayaks, and rubber rafts in this park.

If you are not an experienced white-water runner but want to experience the wildwaters of the state's famous rivers, you might hire the services of an experienced white-water guide, who can introduce you to remote waterways. For a listing of white-water guides, see "Jackson Hole" in "Rocky Mountain Outfitting Centers & Services" and the "Wyoming Travel & Recreation Guide." The *Family Water Sports* guide described above lists a number of these guides and their addresses.

The upper Snake River winds through the majestic Teton country, passing through one of the most spectacular wildlands of our nation. Many guides are available to lead you down the course of the river; but experienced river runners may want to challenge it on their own. Be sure to inquire locally, study your proposed course, and obtain permits where necessary before setting out. The *Grand Teton National Park Snake River Guide*, available for $4.95, is an excellent guide to this portion of the river. The book describes the course of the river from the Yellowstone South Entrance Station south to Alpine, discussing the history, geology, wildlife, and natural features of the lands along the way. Detailed maps of the course show mileage from the Yellowstone South Boundary, dikes and levees, rapids and falls, highways, secondary highways, light-duty roads, unimproved roads, elevation of shore areas, campgrounds, towns and settlements, ranger stations, trails, special features such as hot springs, and access points. To order the book write: Westwater Books, P.O. Box 365, Boulder City, NV 89005.

Colter, John—The Discovery of Jackson Hole & Yellowstone

John Colter, the first white man believed to have entered Jackson Hole and explored the Yellowstone region, was born toward the end of the eighteenth century, probably around 1775. The first written mention of him is made in connection with his enlistment with the Lewis and Clark expedition of 1803. After serving with Lewis and Clark on their westward journey, Colter was on his way back to St. Louis in the late summer of 1806 when he encountered two trappers en route to the rich beaver lands of the upper Missouri and promptly joined his fortune with theirs. The trapping venture proved short-lived, and the following spring Colter again headed for St. Louis. This was not, however, the end of Colter's involvement with the fur trade, for he met yet another party heading up the Missouri in search of pelts. The leader of this brigade was a young Spaniard named Manuel Lisa, an enterprising and adventurous businessman determined to develop his

own interests in the unexploited regions north of St. Louis. Though a seasoned trader, Lisa was totally unfamiliar with the wilderness. In Colter he recognized a man of experience and ability whose knowledge of the area would be worth any price. Accordingly Colter was pressed into service and once again turned his back on civilization for a sojourn in the unknown.

In late November of 1807, Lisa chose a site for his trading post at the junction of the Yellowstone and Bighorn rivers. He named the log structure Fort Raymond, after his son, but the building was popularly known as Manuel's Fort or Fort Lisa. Soon after settling in, Colter was sent out with the most rudimentary equipment to fulfill Lisa's objectives of exploring the trapping country to the west and persuading the Indians to trade at the post. The exact details of Colter's route are unknown, but it now appears that he journeyed across Pryor's Fork, down Gap Creek to its junction with the Bighorn, and from there up to the Shoshone (called the Stinking Water River because of its sulfurous fumes). He was the first white man to enter the Bighorn Basin, where he was cordially received by Crow Indians. On the Shoshone, Colter discovered an area of considerable thermal activity, which was later dubbed "Colter's Hell" because of his descriptions of subterranean fires, underground rumblings, and gases escaping in great gusts. Later historians mistakenly attributed Colter's account to one or more of the geyser or hot spring regions of Yellowstone, but present-day evidence points to the existence of a Colter's Hell near de Maris Springs, just outside Cody.

On the Idaho side of the Teton Range, the first evidence of Colter's winter whereabouts in 1807–1808 was discovered some 40 years ago. In the spring of 1930, young William Beard unearthed a curiously shaped stone while plowing his father's farm near Tetonia, Idaho. The stone had been crudely worked to resemble a human head in profile; on one side appeared the words *John Colter;* the other side bore the barely legible date 1808. The stone's authenticity has been widely doubted, yet the Beards had never heard of John Colter before, and it seems improbable that anyone anxious to perpetrate a hoax would have gone to such lengths to hide a fake relic, burying it almost two feet underground in a remote corner of Idaho. Since the material from which the head is fashioned is a kind of soft, easily shaped lava, one can imagine Colter passing a winter's night or keeping himself amused while snowbound by chipping away at the stone and incising his name and the date.

From Idaho, Colter made his way back to Manuel's Fort in south central Wyoming, probably by following the Yellowstone River and crossing Clark's Fork and Pryor's Fork. He returned in February or March of 1808, stayed at the fort just long enough to rest from his arduous 500-mile trek, then was dispatched by Lisa once again to drum up trade among the Indians.

Late in 1808 Colter and another veteran of the Lewis and Clark expedition, John Potts, were captured on the Jefferson River by Blackfoot Indians. Potts made the fatal mistake of trying to escape and was killed and dismembered while his companion was forced to watch. Colter himself was no stranger to the Blackfeet; on his second expedition from Manuel's Fort, he had encountered the hostile tribe while traveling with a party of their archenemies, the Flatheads and Crows. Severely crippled in the ensuing skirmish, Colter had painfully limped back to the fort. Now the Blackfeet were given a second chance to destroy the white man who roamed their territory and consorted with the enemy. Deeming an easy death too good for Colter, they decided to have some sport before closing in for the kill. Colter was stripped naked and told to run for his life. In spite of a wounded leg, he managed to elude all the braves except one. Certain that he could not outdistance the one remaining warrior, Colter turned in despair and

prepared to meet his end. As the Indian lunged, Colter seized his lance. Caught off guard, his opponent stumbled and fell, and the intended victim, favored with yet another reprieve, plunged the weapon into the red man's chest.

Emaciated and barely able to crawl, Colter somehow covered the 300 miles back to Manuel's Fort. He made two more expeditions into the wilderness and suffered similar narrow escapes from the Blackfeet. In 1810 he guided Colonel Menard to Three Forks, where a new fort was constructed. This outpost, too, was subject to constant Blackfoot harassment. Shortly afterward Colter decided enough was enough. Vowing never to return to the wilderness, he made his way back to St. Louis, bought a small farm in Missouri, and spent the three years left to him peacefully tilling the land, far from the nightmare of murderous Indians.

Fishing & Hunting in Wyoming

Jagged snowcapped peaks, vast evergreen forests, remote alpine wilderness, hundreds of miles of blue-ribbon trout streams, thousands of sparkling, sapphire-hued lakes, world-famous high-country big-game ranges, and millions of acres of game-rich sagebrush and prairie country combine to make Wyoming one of the great wilderness recreation regions in North America. The richly varied topography of this beautiful Rocky Mountain state offers spectacular fishing for big cutthroat trout, pink-slashed rainbows, hook-jawed trophy brown trout, and hordes of ravenous brook trout, particularly in the high-country lakes and streams. Rare golden trout and grayling inhabit the watersheds of the remote high-country, and big lake trout cruise the depths of many of the pure, cold lakes, particularly in the mountain areas. The prolific kokanee and Rocky Mountain whitefish are present in large numbers, and walleyes, northern pike, largemouth and smallmouth bass, catfish, and panfish occupy the warmer waters of lakes and rivers in the plateau areas. The hunter can find elk, bear, moose, and sheep in the magnificent high-country big-game ranges, and deer almost everywhere in the state. Antelope are abundant in the plateau country, and game birds, waterfowl, and small game animals are found throughout the state.

Wyoming occupies 97,914 square miles of sparsely settled land. The land tilts upwards in a westerly path from the prairie, butte, and sagebrush country of the Great Plateau to the snow-crowned crags of the Rocky Mountain heartland. Elevations vary from about 3,100 feet, where the Belle Fourche River leaves the state at the South Dakota border in the Black Hills of the northeast, to the majestic summit of Gannett Peak (13,785 ft.) in the Bridger National Forest–Wind River range country. The geological magnificence of Yellowstone National Park with its thermal springs, geysers, rainbow-hued mineral deposits, and fascinating rock formations is home to an abundance of elk, moose, bear, and deer, which roam the thick forests and meadowlands. The trout fishing in the numerous streams and lakes for cutthroats, browns, and rainbows is legendary.

Thumbs of high country protrude towards the center of the state from the Montana and Colorado borders. The Continental Divide, separating the Atlantic and Pacific watersheds, follows an erratic, southerly course through the western mountains. The region contains headwaters of the Colorado and Columbia rivers flowing toward the Pacific, and those of the Missouri which flow to the Atlantic.

This vast land of contrasts has a mean altitude of 7,000 feet and is home to only a few more than 300,000 residents. This means that there is plenty of space for you to pursue your favorite outdoor sport. Summer weather conditions range from the unpredictable, sometimes severe conditions in the highest elevations to the dry heat of the plateau. Evening temperatures are generally on the cool side throughout the state. Early spring and fall conditions are very changeable, and freezing storms sweep down from the north, particularly in the mountains, bringing snow and ice—so be prepared! If possible, drive across the state and watch the country change abruptly from grassland to sagebrush to alpine forest. There are few gradations, and the terrain lines are very distinct. As you cruise along, the great peaks of the Rockies will loom in the distance for hundreds of miles with their promise of wilderness adventure.

Almost 50 percent of Wyoming's 30 million acres are composed of public lands managed by the federal government. Of these, 9 million acres are managed by the U.S. Forest Service, including the national forests and the national grasslands, the largest of the latter being the 600,000-acre tract of Thunder Basin near the South Dakota border.

The Bureau of Land Management areas are located mainly in the plateau lands outside of the mountain areas and contain limitless opportunities for fishing and hunting. Write for the free BLM publication *Wildlife and Recreation on Public Lands in Wyoming* to: Bureau of Land Management, Department of the Interior, 2002 Capitol Ave., Cheyenne 82001. The BLM also produces a series of maps of the various tracts under its jurisdiction.

Wyoming owns or cooperatively administers numerous lands, including Wildlife Units and Public Hunting and Fishing Areas. Write for the free booklet *Public Hunting and Fishing on Wyoming Game and Fish Commission Areas* to: Wyoming Game & Fish Commission, Box 1589, Cheyenne 82001.

The superlative quality of Wyoming trout fishing is well known throughout the angling world. The plateau lakes and impoundments yield some eye-popping brown trout and rainbows, and the Wyoming Rockies conjure visions of trophy trout fishing in the cold, pristine streams and jewel-like lakes and ponds of the rugged, ice-capped mountain wilderness areas and alpine meadowlands. Walleye, northern pike, largemouth and smallmouth bass, assorted panfish, and catfish of several varieties are abundant in the warmer waters, as well as the tasty, grotesque freshwater cod, the burbot, which inhabits the cold depths of many lakes.

The impressive Wyoming fishing records are indicative of what may be expected. These statistics show that, with few exceptions, the trophy trout were yielded by the waters of the Rocky Mountain highlands on the western border, and that the warm water fish came from the plateau.

Because of the diversity and extremes of topography, generalities are dangerous and local exceptions the rule. However, the best stream fishing usually begins in late July and August, after the waters have cleared and dropped, following the prodigious spring runoff from the snowfields, and continues into October. Bait fishermen employ the standard night crawlers, live bait, salmon roe, etc., and spin fishermen prefer an assortment of wobblers, spoons, spinners, and plugs, particularly the Finnish minnow types and the banana or flatfish models. The fly-fisherman is faced with an enormous amount of variance in physical characteristics and underwater life in the thousand streams, lakes, and ponds, and the size of the fish and their preferences fluctuate accordingly. For example, alpine brook and golden trout live in a vastly different environment from that of the sleek brown trout, which inhabit the alkaline thermal waters of the Firehole River in Yellowstone Park. In general, trophy trout in the lower elevations prefer big flies, such as the Muddler Minnow, Spruce Fly, Sofa Pillow, Matukas, Gray and Black Ghosts, and Squirrel Tails; standard wet flies such as the Grizzly King, Western Bee, and, above all, the various Wooly Worms; dry flies such as the Wulff series, the Humpy, grasshopper patterns, and popular classic dries and assorted nymphs, again, with many on the large size. The importance of checking conditions and local patterns for each area to be fished cannot be overemphasized.

Trophy Fishing Waters

Wyoming is divided into five fishing areas and seasons; creel limits and regulations vary from area to area, and there are internal exceptions as well. For the free *Wyoming Fishing Regulations* booklet, which includes the above information, a fishing district map, and rules for the national parks and Indian reservations, write: Wyoming Game & Fish Dept., Communications Branch, Cheyenne 82002. The free *Wyoming Stream Fishery Classification Map*, published by the Fish Division of the Game & Fish Commission, Cheyenne, shows and classifies all fishing streams in terms of scenic beauty, accessibility, and size of trout population. Wyoming's Class 1, blue-ribbon streams include the Snake, Green, and North Platte rivers and Sand Creek.

The Game & Fish Dept. also offers a free booklet called *Wyoming Fishing Guide*, which describes the waters within each numbered zone, gives the fish species present, size, access, and facilities available, and pinpoints the various lakes and streams on a series of zone maps.

Cutthroat trout, the native species of the Rockies, are dispersed across the watersheds of the western mountain areas. Famed cutthroat waters include Yellowstone Lake and River, the nearby Lamar and Shoshone river regions, the Green River and its tributaries in the Bridger National Forest area, the Snake and Gros Ventre rivers, and numerous streams and ponds in the remote areas of the mountains. The record

15-pound cutthroat came from Native Lake in the Bridger National Forest area, and Bridger Lake in the general vicinity is noted for excellent fishing. Cloud Peak Reservoir in the Bighorn National Forest produces some lunker cutthroats as well.

WYOMING RECORD FISH

	Lb.–oz.	Place	Year
Cutthroat trout	15	Native Lake, Sublette Co.	1959
Rainbow trout	23	Burnt Lake, Sublette Co.	1969
Brown trout	23–3	Flaming Gorge Res., Sweetwater Co.	1977
Golden trout*	11–4	Cook's Lake, Sublette Co.	1948
Brook trout	10	Torrey Lake, Fremont Co.	1933
Lake trout	44	Jackson Lake, Teton Co.	1967
Grayling**	—	—	—
Whitefish (Rocky Mountain)	4	Wind River, Fremont Co.	unknown
Walleye	14–4	Keyhole Res., Crook Co.	1973
Sauger	6–8	Wind River, Fremont Co.	1942
Largemouth bass	7–2	Stove Lake, Goshen Co.	1942
Smallmouth bass	4–6	Acme	1974
Black crappie	1–7	Boysen Res., Fremont Co.	1968
Burbot	19–4	Pilot Butte Res., Fremont Co.	1965
Northern pike	16–12	Keyhole Res., Crook Co.	1975

*World's record.

**No official record. Wyoming Fish & Game personnel reported a 4-lb. specimen in 1933.

Brown trout are found almost everywhere in the state, and they are big, as attested to by the frequent catches of arm-length fish reported from the Green River impoundment of Flaming Gorge Reservoir, in the southwest part of the state, which yielded the state record (22 lb. 1 oz.). The Green River produces stream fishing for brownies to better than 10 pounds from the Bridger National Forest highlands on down into the meadowlands. Perhaps the premier brown trout stream, all factors considered, is the North Platte River in the Medicine Bow– Snowy Range region. Here you may set your hook to a gentle rise and find a 15-pound brown trout careening downstream and stripping your reel in the process. A tributary stream, the Encampment, also offers fishing that borders on the legendary. The Yellowstone Park region includes such famous waters as the Yellowstone, Firehole, Gibbon, and Madison rivers, where brown trout grow to impressive proportions but become progressively wary as their poundage increases. Lake Hat-

tie near Medicine Bow National Forest, Jackson Lake in Teton National Forest, Seminoe Reservoir near Rawlins in central Wyoming, and Lake de Smet near Bighorn are among the noted flat water trout holes.

Rainbow trout are abundant in streams, lakes, and impoundments all over Wyoming. The North Platte, Green, Snake, Yellowstone, Madison, Firehole, and Lamar rivers consistently produce great fishing, and the bows run big, particularly in the Green, North Platte, Madison, and Snake. Burnt Lake, near the Green River in Sublette County, yielded the 23-pound record. Ross Lake in the Wind River country holds trophy fish, as do Lake de Smet, near Bighorn National Forest, and Pathfinder and Seminoe reservoirs in south central Wyoming.

Brook trout inhabit high-country streams, lakes, and ponds, particularly in the Wind River Range and the Shoshone, Bridger, Teton, Medicine Bow, and Bighorn national forests. Alpine waters usually teem with small brookies, but some of these hold fish to 5 pounds. The record speckled trout come from Torrey Lake in the Wind River Range, which also has some big browns.

The rare golden trout, a transplant from California, prefers the frigid, pure watersheds of the distant alpine peaks, where only the hardiest, most persistent angler ever sets foot. A backpacking trip into the haunting grandeur and solitude of Wyoming's roof to fish for the exquisite crimson-slashed golden trout with its white-edged fins makes memories that will last a lifetime. The Shoshone National Forest, which sprawls southward through the Absaroka and Wind River ranges, offers some fine golden trout fishing in the Copper Lakes, in the Middle Fork of the Popo Agie River, in Lower Deep Creek Jug, and in Boat Lakes. The majestic Wind River Range produces more goldens than any other region. Dinwoody Lake, Golden Lake in the Dry Creek area, Lost Lake, Marion Lake, and lakes Klondike, Titcomb, and Sledgehammer are among noted producers, as is Pyramid Lake in the Bridger National Forest, which yields goldens to 20 inches. Teton National Forest contains goldens, and one of the better areas is the Buffalo River area. Bighorn National Forest has golden trout in the Ten Sleep areas, and fine fishing is found in Lost Twin Lake #2. The Medicine Bow National Forest provides some good fishing in the snowy range, particularly in Bear, Arrow, and North Gap lakes.

The swift, graceful grayling also shows a decided preference for the lonely alpine terrain and cannot survive heavy fishing pressure. The Tetons, Wind River Range, Medicine Bow–Snowy Range area, Bighorn National Forest (especially the Cloud Peak Primitive Area), the Bridger National Forest, Shoshone National Forest, and Medicine Bow National Forest contain the best waters. Lake of the Woods, near Dubois in the Wind River Range, has some large fish. Meadow Lake in the Green River headwaters of Bridger National Forest and Beartooth Lake in Shoshone National Forest offer excellent fishing. Grayling prefer small flies, particularly wets such as the Black Gnat and dries such as the Gray Hackle, yellow body. Be sure to have some patterns on #20 hooks. This lavender-hued, black-dotted creature with its sweeping dorsal fin complements the beauty of this primeval environment.

Lake trout, known locally as Mackinaw, occur in many of the deep cold lakes of the mountain areas. Jackson Lake in Teton National Park and Fremont to the southeast in the Bridger National Forest both produce trophy fish, Jackson being the source of the current 44-pound record. Kearney Lake in the Bighorn National Forest region, Buffalo Bill Reservoir near Cody on the edge of Shoshone National Forest, and Louis Lake in the Shoshone Forest, near Lander, all produce lakers in excess of 20 pounds. Beartooth Lake and Flaming Gorge Reservoir are other good bets.

Rocky Mountain whitefish are abundant in many of the drainage systems of the western highlands. Not held in the same esteem as trout, they are willing strikers and are excellent table fare. The Wind River, source of the 4-pound record, is noted for their abundance. Whitefish provide some of the finest angling in the winter and readily take web flies, nymphs, and small natural bait.

Kokanee, a landlocked sockeye salmon strain, are found in a number of Wyoming lakes, where they furnish some fast fishing and provide rich feed for some of the larger predatory trout. De Smet near Bighorn National Forest and Fremont Lake in Bridger National Forest are hot spots too.

Walleyes occur in many of the low country lakes and streams. Keyhole Reservoir in Crook County gave up the 14¼-pound record, and other good bets include Boysen Reservoir at the east tip of the Wind River Reservation, Wardell Reservoir near Basin to the west of Bighorn National Forest and Bighorn Lake, and Wheatland Reservoir, north of Laramie. Northern pike are common in the same range as walleyes. Keyhole produced the state record (16 lb. 2 oz.), and numerous other impoundments and large river stretches offer pike fishing. Black bass are found in lakes such as Wild Horse Reservoir near Casper, Boysen Reservoir and Ocean Lake in the Wind River Reservation Area, and Lake Cameahwait near Boysen Reservoir, as well as in the Wind River Indian Reservation region. Bass are also taken in Keyhole Reservoir in the northeast's Crook County.

Panfish including crappie, perch, sunfish, bullhead, and rock bass are found together or singly in Lake de Smet, Boysen Reservoir, Packer's Lake, Ocean Lake, Keyhole, Wheatland, and Glendo reservoirs, and in other lakes, impoundments, ponds, and sluggish rivers and streams. Write to the Wyoming Travel Commission for the free map/brochure *Family Water Sports—Big Wyoming.* This publication lists 62 lakes and rivers and gives the fish species found in each, availability of boats, guides, and bait and tackle in each area, and acreage of lake or length of stream. Each "water hole" is numbered, and the number appears in its appropriate location on the map. Public fishing areas are marked on the map with an *F* and marinas with an *M.* Included in this publication are license details; water skiing, canoeing, kayaking, and rafting information; a list of outfitters who conduct float-fishing trips on principal waters; a list of marinas; general national and state park details; and a list of national parks, national forests, and other recreation areas, outlining the various water sports and facilities offered.

Big-Game Hunting

Wyoming ranks as one of the very best hunting regions in the United States. Big-game opportunities include elk, moose, and bear in the mountain country, mountain sheep and goats (extremely limited) in the most remote wilderness areas, and antelope in the plateau areas all over the state. Mule deer are well dispersed across Wyoming, while whitetails are found primarily in the Black Hills area. In addition, there is a small population of mountain lions, still classified as predators, which inhabit the high-country reaches, but there is not much hunting interest.

Big-game hunting is rather complicated in Wyoming. Each species has special regulations, or "hunting orders," and numbered areas placed on a map, and these areas differ from species to species. Seasons are established for each numbered area, and special regulations as well. In addition, several game varieties are under a quota kill plan, and in some cases the number of licenses issued is limited during any given season. License applications must be submitted during a set period, usually in May, and be accompanied by a bank draft, money order, or certified check. The hunter must be familiar with the multiplicity of

rules and regulations that apply to various species and areas. The free *Wyoming Hunting Guide* leaflet, produced by the Wyoming Game & Fish Dept., Cheyenne 82002, describes general laws, firearm codes, fee schedules, application schedules and details, general species information including small game, and other basic input. A companion free leaflet, *Issuance of Licenses and Special Permits,* gives the necessary instructions for submitting and ordering big-game licenses by species. The Big Game Orders for each species can be obtained free from the Game & Fish Dept. They contain the previously mentioned numbered area map, a description of each area, the season for each area, special limitations in regards to number of permits or restrictions on game, a list of check stations, and the general hunting laws for the species. Companion area maps with the numbered area regulations described above and pocket regulation cards with application dates and seasons are available for ready reference. In Wyoming it is important to remember that nonresidents must be accompanied by a guide in designated wilderness areas.

Considering all the available national forest lands, state forests, Bureau of Land Management tracts, and Public Hunting Areas, the problem is not *where* to hunt; it's *what* to hunt. Deer are found everywhere except the high peaks areas. Mule deer compose the bulk of the 80,000 or so deer shot in an average year. The Black Hills region in the northeast is excellent and also contains many of the state's whitetails. Medicine Bow National Forest, Bighorn National Forest, and Bridger National Forest are all good bets. In Bridger, Soda Lake PHA, Half Moon PHA, and Green River PHA offer excellent deer hunting, as does Pemrock Mountain PHA in the Medicine Bow National Forest.

The swift, graceful antelope, Wyoming's state animal, is found in the rolling plateau country, which covers much of Wyoming. The biggest herds are in the eastern half of the state, but excellent hunting occurs right up to the border in the southwest corner. Crook, Weston, Niobrara, and Campbell counties are prime areas, as are the open lands south of Casper, and the Lander region. Wyoming boasts a high kill-to-hunter ratio, but this is due largely to the abundance of the pronghorn. Possessed of great speed and exceptionally keen eyesight, this strikingly colored animal of tan, brown, black and white hues makes an exciting quarry. When startled, it streaks away in a wink, its rump flashing white as it disappears from view down an intervening gully. Once on the verge of extinction, the antelope is now abundant, and upwards of 35,000 animals are killed in a good season.

Wyoming supports one of the largest elk herds on the North American continent. This great majestic deer, which can weigh over 1,000 pounds, prefers the mountain uplands. Once pursued to the point of extinction, the elk has staged an amazing comeback, aided in large part by the protection afforded by preserves such as Yellowstone Park and intelligent game management. The Wyoming kill varies between 10,000 and more than 20,000 animals. The Bighorn National Forest, the Teton National Forest and its Gros Ventre watershed—probably the best single area in the state—Bridger National Forest, Shoshone National Forest, and Medicine Bow National Forest constitute the cream of the elk-hunting areas.

The Shiras moose, an incredible combination of grandeur and homeliness, inhabits the thickets and swamps of the Rocky Mountain highlands. Managed on a strict quota system, the abundant moose is another species with a high kill ration. The Bridger National Forest area provides exceptionally good hunting, particularly in the Gros Ventre basin east of Jackson, the Pinedale area, and the reaches of the Upper Green River. Yellowstone National Park is closed to hunting, but it serves as a source of animals for the Shoshone, Teton, and Bridger national forests to the east and south.

Hunting for the nimble, sure-footed bighorn sheep, with its massive curl of horn, is confined to the high peak areas of Wyoming. In the topmost slopes near and above the timberline, the bighorn thrives, descending into the forests in the winter. Shoshone, Bridger, and Teton national forests offer the bulk of the hunting, and severely limited permits are assigned to Medicine Bow National Forest. Guides are a requirement for nonresidents throughout many of the hunting zones and should be used by all but the most experienced hunters. Patience, stealth, and good binoculars are the essentials of success, not to speak of a good dollop of luck. Sheep have uncanny vision and an acute sense of smell.

The cloud-wreathed crags and ice-rimmed ledges of the Rocky Mountain primitive areas are home to the unbelievably agile, glue-hooved mountain goat. This animal's ability to pick its way along inches-wide ledges with thousands of feet of open space yawning up is legendary. Hunting for this rare trophy is limited to a handful of permits for a single zone in the Beartooth region of the Montana border tip of Shoshone National Forest.

Bear hunting is not popular in Wyoming, which is surprising, because the black bear is a common animal in the mountain forests, as any national park or forest visitor can attest. All of the national forests harbor substantial populations of black bear. The grizzly is protected, and only a few animals remain from the great numbers which once ruled the western mountains. The Yellowstone region contains most of the remnant population of this dangerous, awesome carnivore.

Mountain lions, too, are scarce and are classified as predators. These animals prefer upland areas, but not the thick forest ever prevalent in Wyoming. The Utah-Colorado border areas harbor most of the population, but through a quirk in the hunting laws, nonresidents cannot hunt cougars.

Upland Game Birds & Waterfowl

For small-game hunters, the Game & Fish Dept. puts out two free booklets. The first is *Wyoming Hunting Guide, Upland, Small Game, Waterfowl.* It contains general hunting rules and regulations, license fee schedules, and species maps. The state is divided into seven game division districts, and each species is described in detail, including its habits, terrain preferences, and other interesting facts. Each article is accompanied by the seven-district map, which is shaded to show distribution patterns. Game species include sage grouse, pheasant, mourning dove, chukar partridge, Hungarian partridge, blue grouse, ruffled grouse, sharp-tailed grouse, turkey, ducks and geese, snowshoe and cottontail rabbits, gray and red squirrels, snipe and rail, and sandhill cranes. The last section of the guide rates the hunting conditions for the various varieties in each of the seven districts. The free *Wyoming Bird Regulations,* available from the Game & Fish Dept., gives the specific season rules and hunting zone instructions for each game variety. Some small-game species have a statewide season, while others are confined to numbered hunting zones. As in the big-game setup, the zones differ from one species to another, and differ from the game division districts. There are many variances within each varietal numbered zone, as well.

Pheasants are found predominantly in the irrigated agricultural lands of the plateau. PHAs such as Springer, Bump Sullivan, and Reservoir in Goshen County offer a chance for good hunting. The Bighorn–Sheridan area has good ringneck hunting, and the big Yellowtail PHA on the shore of Yellowtail Reservoir is both productive and popular. Since the best pheasants are in farmlands, hunters must ask permission to get at the cream of the hunting. Check the PHA booklet, because

there are public lands in almost all of the pheasant counties. Fifty thousand to one hundred thousand birds are shot each year, but this reflects hunting pressure rather than abundance.

Sage grouse, the big Wyoming native bird, inhabits the sagebrush plains across the state. This bird ranks second to the pheasant in numbers killed, but it is present in greater numbers. Carbon and Sweetwater counties on the Colorado border are the best districts in the state. Bureau of Land Management tracts offer limitless opportunities to hunt sage grouse. One of the best PHAs is the Upper North Platte–Ryan Park unit in Carbon County, and there are several others in the general area. Chukar partridge are found in semiarid hilly areas, especially in the north and north central counties, such as Park, Washakie, Hot Springs, and Bighorn. Yellowtail PHA on the west border of Bighorn National Forest is a good chukar habitat and a very popular location. Blue and ruffled grouse are found in the mountain forests of Bridger, Teton, Medicine Bow, Shoshone, and Bighorn national forests. Few hunters pursue these birds, and the very modest kill does not reflect the ample supply of both species. Sharp-tailed grouse are scarce and are found principally in Sheridan, Campbell and Crook counties, which sprawl along the Montana border between Bighorn National Forest and the Black Hills and in Goshen County in the southeast. It is a marginal game bird and there is little hunting interest. Merriam's turkey has been successfully stocked in the Laramie Mountains, the Black Hills, and the Bighorn Mountains, and spring and fall seasons have been established. Mourning doves are hunted all over the state with the exception of the high mountain country. Ducks and geese provide good hunting everywhere except the most arid areas. The wetlands of Albany County are wintering grounds for redheads, canvasback, and scaup. Other common species are the mallard, widgeon, teal (all varieties), gadwall, and pintail. Reservoirs and river areas

offer good shooting for those who take advantage of the potential. Bighorn, Goshen, and Fremont counties all have major wintering grounds. Write to the Game & Fish Dept. for the free *Waterfowl Regulations* leaflet, which gives the seasons, bag limits, general regulations, closed areas, shooting hours, and a time zone and Goose Management area map.

Snowshoe rabbits are common in the upland forests, and cottontails abound in the foothills and plateau areas. Red and fox squirrels, too, are abundant in the state for those who enjoy the sport.

The Wyoming Game & Fish Dept. publishes a monthly magazine, *Wyoming Wildlife*, which includes features on the state's most scenic and interesting wildlife areas, how-to articles on such wilderness pastimes as fishing, and informative essays on the biology and ecology of the state's wild animals. The magazine features beautiful color photographs of the state's backcountry and its inhabitants. The subscription rate is $3 a year or $7.50 for 3 years in the United States, Canada, and Mexico. Write to: Wyoming Wildlife, State of Wyoming, Game and Fish Department, Cheyenne 82002.

High-Country Outfitters & Guides

A guide to *Wyoming Outfitters*, prepared by the Wyoming Game & Fish Dept., lists licensed big-game hunting and fishing outfitters and guides in the state, their counties, their addresses, and the species they hunt. The guide is available free from: Wyoming Game & Fish Department, Cheyenne 82002. Another source of information on guides is the *Wyoming Outfitters Association*, c/o Leo Tass, Kaycee Route, Box 14, Buffalo 82834.

See "Jackson Hole" in "Rocky Mountain Outfitting Centers & Services" and check the section of the "Wyoming Travel & Recreation Guide" which describes the area in which you plan to hunt, camp, or fish for outfitters and guides in the area.

Highways— Recreation & Scenic Routes

Wyoming's highways wind through some of the most awesome country in the United States and make some of the remote regions accessible. The *Wyoming Official Highway Map* shows these roads on a shaded relief background. The map also clearly marks streams and lakes, cities and towns, highways and roads (multilane, paved, gravel, graded, and earth), roadside parks, county seats, railroads, commercial and municipal airports, ski areas, and historical trails. Short descriptions of points of interest and historical sites are given on the map. Vicinity maps of the larger cities are included, as is a mileage chart for distances between cities. The map is available free from: Wyoming Travel Commission, 2320 Capitol Ave., Cheyenne 82002.

For more detailed information on the areas through which you plan to travel, use the free Big Wyoming region maps available from the Travel Commission, including *Central Big Wyoming*, *Western Big Wyoming*, *Northern Big Wyoming*, and *Southern Big Wyoming*. Each area map shows highways, cities and towns, historical sites, major natural features and points of interest, lakes and rivers, and wildlife of the area. Included with each map are extensive descriptions of the areas within the region, as well as information on outstanding natural features (fishing waters, rock formations, scenic backcountry, hunting areas), national forests, history, and wildlife. The maps covering areas of many waterways include charts describing "Fishing Holes," which list camping, lodging, and boating facilities, nearest towns, lengths of the streams, and species of fish indigenous to the streams. These guides also list the addresses of additional sources of information on recreation in the regions they cover. The maps are free from: Wyoming Travel Commission, Cheyenne 82002. A fascinating map/guide to the Old Oregon Trail and Auto Route, *The Guide to the Lander Cut-off Oregon Trail*, is available free from: Bureau of Land Management, Box 1828, 2120 Capitol Ave., Cheyenne 82001.

Mountain Men, Beaver, and the Great Rendezvous

In March 1822 the following notice appeared in the St. Louis newspaper *Missouri Republican*:

> To Enterprising Young Men. The subscriber wishes to engage one hundred young men to ascend the Missouri River to its source, there to be employed for one, two or three years. For particulars inquire of Major Andrew Henry, near the lead mines in the county of Washington, who will ascend with, and command, the party; or of the subscriber near St. Louis.
>
> William H. Ashley

With these few brief sentences the Rocky Mountain fur trade was officially opened, thus signaling the genesis of a venture that would result in the trailblazing of vast, unexplored reaches of the West and the birth of a new breed of pioneer-trapper known to history as the mountain man. Among those who responded to Ashley's call were Jim Bridger, David Jackson, William Sublette, Thomas Fitzpatrick, Jedediah Smith, and others who became famous as fur traders, guides, and scouts.

After several serious skirmishes with the Blackfoot and Arikara tribes, the company succeeded in establishing a trading post on the Yellowstone River. Ashley's original intention was to confine trapping and trading activities to the Missouri Valley, but competition forced his men further and further into the unknown corners of the Rockies. Working the area alone or in small groups, the trappers forged the earliest trails to Oregon and California, trails which eventually became the routes of the first westward settlers and the major highways of today.

Necessity dictated entirely different methods of trapping and bartering from those of Ashley's counterparts in Canada, the employees of the Hudson's Bay and Northwest companies. Mounted on horseback, the Rocky Mountain trappers had to be skilled riders able to handle a rifle with deadly aim. In this vast and rugged wilderness—uncharted, unsettled, and ruled by hostile Indians—fixed forts or trading posts were impossible to maintain. Instead, itinerant trappers roamed the lonely territory and met at an annual rendezvous where furs were traded for supplies, ammunition, and sometimes money. The rewards

of such an existence were few; only a handful realized any sort of substantial profit and many lost their lives. It has been calculated that well over half the men who worked for Ashley and his successors were killed by Indians. Yet the lure of adventure kept the ranks filled with restless young men until the early 1840s, when felt hats were no longer fashionable and the beaver from which they were made had virtually disappeared.

The annual rendezvous held among Indians and trappers became legendary as an occasion for business, brawling, gambling, and disruptive behavior in general. From nameless woods and valleys, scores of trappers converged on a preselected spot, such as Henrys Fork of the Green River or the Great Salt Lake. Indians in all their finery appeared, eager to trade pelts for whisky, beads, or trinkets. Long trains of wagons or packmules made their way over poorly marked trails carrying commodities such as salt, traps, guns, flour, and a few luxuries —mirrors, clothing, sugar. Rival companies pitched camp and competed for coveted pelts and the services of the best trappers for the year to come. The gathering, which began in 1824 and included only Ashley's immediate band, grew into an annual celebration, impatiently awaited and sometimes attended by more than 1,500 trappers.

The Rocky Mountain fur trade was a short-lived era in the history of the West, dependent on the fluctuations of demand and the supply of furbearing animals. By 1840, the price of pelts had dropped radically, the fur trade declined, and trappers became scouts and guides. Leading missionaries and homesteaders over trails they had forged, the mountain men were instrumental in the settlement of the gradually shrinking frontier.

Rocky Mountain Outfitting Centers & Services

The historic frontier towns of Jackson, Cody, Dubois, and Pinedale, situated in the vastnesses of the majestic Rocky Mountain high country in western Wyoming, are the headquarters for one of North America's greatest concentrations of wilderness outfitters and packers, schools of wilderness instruction, and fishing, hunting, and float-trip guides. During the summer and early fall, they serve as popular jumping-off places to some of the most famous blue-ribbon trout streams and remote unspoiled wilderness camping, fishing, and hunting areas remaining in the contiguous United States—the Jackson Hole country and Teton Wilderness, the massive Absaroka Range, and the spectacular Wind River Range and Upper Yellowstone River wildlands— where faint trails reach back into rugged country beyond which few men have traveled since the golden era of the fur trade during the 1830s.

These nationally renowned Rocky Mountain outfitting centers lie sheltered in the valleys of the Upper Snake, Big Wind, Shoshone, and Upper Green rivers and provide convenient access to thousands of miles of hiking and packhorse trails that climb up through boreal forests and meadows to a God's country of glimmering blue rock-bound lakes and connecting streams surrounded by alpine tundra and boulder-strewn parks, barren volcanic crags, and wind-swept, snow-capped peaks. Many of these high-country trails follow an intricate network of ancient game and Indian routes, some of which have been deeply furrowed from successive use over the years by the moccasins, boot leather, and saddle stock of the early explorers, Rocky Mountain Fur Company trappers, government hunters and surveyors, sheep herders, and a host of legendary characters such as John Colter, discoverer of Jackson Hole and Yellowstone; Capt. L. E. Bonneville; mountain men and guides Kit Carson and Jim Bridger, whose tales of the Yellowstone headwaters were once regarded as the colorful vapors of

a mind to which truth had long been a stranger; Buffalo Bill Cody, who guided the likes of Grand Duke Alexis of Russia on big-game hunts from his lodge on the North Fork of the Shoshone; and the flamboyant Irish baronet and big-game hunter Sir St. George Gore, who traveled through the region in 1856 with a retinue of 40 servants, 6 wagons, 21 carts, 12 yoke of cattle, 14 dogs, and 112 horses!

Wyoming's blue-ribbon rivers and untold thousands upon thousands of alpine lakes and streams in the heart of the Rocky Mountains offer what is considered to be some of the nation's top-ranked fishing in a wilderness setting for big buckskin-flanked browns, rainbows, native cutthroats, temperamental goldens, splake, goldbows (rainbow-golden hybrids), lake trout, hordes of hungry brook trout, and a few Montana grayling. Although not as numerous as they were 20 years ago, the big fish are still there. Many of the distant, seldom fished lakes and connecting streams clustered in obscure valleys at the headwaters of the wilderness tributaries of the Upper Green, Wind, Popo Agie, Snake, and Yellowstone rivers—originally stocked from milk cans packed in on horseback and foot by outfitters, trappers, hunters, forest rangers, and Fish and Game personnel—hold trophy-sized trout as long as your arm that complete their life cycle never having eyed a fisherman's fly.

Trophy fish in the rugged high-country wilderness areas are hard earned, and fishing success varies directly with your experience and knowledge of the area you plan to fish, water conditions, and timing. As a general rule, the farther back you travel off the main trails, the better your chances for success. The most productive and rewarding fishing is found by backpacking cross-country with topo maps and compass to the remote lakes hidden in obscure, trailless valleys nestled beneath the towering peaks along the crest of the Great Divide.

Fishing and backpacking in the high country begins about mid-July, depending on the level of the spring runoff, when the water goes down and the sunny but brisk days begin to dry off the spongy trails. In the Wind River Range and the Tetons, there are brief electrical storms and stiff winds almost every afternoon, with occasional snow flurries. As the weather warms, the elk and moose begin to move up the slopes from the river valleys and bogs to the mountain meadows. The nights are cold, and above timberline the temperature dips close to freezing. During July the mosquito is King, aided in its brief career of torture by a tiny gnat which flourishes early in the season. Clouds of mosquitoes swarm around melting snow patches, marshes, lakes, and damp meadows. If you plan on early-season fishing, be sure to carry a healthy supply of repellent and netting for your tent. By August, the trails and streams are generally in great shape, and the days are hot, the nights cool. The brisk golden days of late September and early fall are the most beautiful and rewarding on both stream and trail.

Jackson Hole and Yellowstone Outfitters & Guides

For detailed information, rates, and literature on licensed hunting and fishing guides and outfitters headquartered in Jackson (zip code: 83001), write: Richard Allen, *Boots Allen & Sons*, Box 1176. For info on wilderness pack and backpacking trips: Alden L. Burdick, Jr., *Mad Dog Outfitters*, Box 1449; Jack H. Dennis, Box 286; Frank S. Ewing II, Box 1243; George T. Kelly, Box 668; James W. Kinker, Box 1346; Virgil F. Lowder, Box 42A, Star Rt.; John E. Rummer, *Jackson Lake Lodge;* Keith Stilson, Box 1885; Wm. F. Thomas, *Bar T-5 Outfitters*, Box 2140. Jay Buchner of *High Country Flies* (Box 1022, Jackson), a fly-tying and fishing business, has been guiding and outfitting fishermen in the Jackson Hole and the Green River system for the last eight years. The free *High Country Flies Catalog* contains a large selection of quality hand-tied flies, including such Jackson Hole country favor-

ites as Humpys (Goofus Bugs), the Wulff series, muddler minnows, hoppers, and Matukas. For the nitty gritty on Jackson Hole country guides headquartered in Moran (zip: 83013), write: Russ Doty, *Diamond D Ranch & Outfitters*, Box 11 (trips into the Teton Wilderness and Two Ocean Pass); Lewis Price, Jr., *Mountain View Ranch* (Teton Wilderness backpacking and fishing trips); Dr. Wm. R. Hurst, *Heart 6 Guest Ranch*, Box 70 (wilderness pack/fishing trips in Teton Wilderness); Walter M. Korn, *Box K Ranch;* Robert W. Sandison, *Leek's Lodge*. The Turner brothers of *Triangle X Ranch*, Moose 83012, offer guided fishing and pack trips into the Teton Wilderness and Yellowstone National Park. *Sleeping Indian Fishing Excursions, Inc.*, Box 18, Wilson 83014, offers guided trips on the Snake, Madison, Yellowstone, Lamar, and Gallatin rivers and Yellowstone and Lewis lakes. Arnold and Al Gaub of *Jackson Hole Country Outfitters*, Box 28, Alpine 83127, provide guided hunting and fishing trips on the Gros Ventre and Snake rivers and backpack pack-in trips to high mountain lakes. *Three Eagles Expeditions*, Box 2606, Jackson Hole 83001, specializes in guided backpack fly fishing trips to high country lakes and the headwaters of the Snake, Yellowstone, Madison, and Green rivers.

Licensed guides and outfitters serving the Thorofare Plateau country in the Teton Wilderness, North Absaroka Wilderness, and Yellowstone Lake & Lamar River Wildlands headquartered in the Cody area (zip code: 82414) include: Dr. DeWitt Dominick, *Seven D Ranch*, Box 109 (pack/fishing trips into Sunlight Basin and Mirror Plateau); Joseph A. DeSarro, *A-2-Z Ranch*, South Fork Rt.; Jerome C. Asay, Box 1318; Robert Model, *Majo Ranch;* Joseph E. Tilden, *Castle Rock Ranch;* C. O. Wheeler, Jr., Box 941; Keith Dahlem, Box 960, *Shoshone Lodge;* Donald Schmatz, Box 604; Dean Johnson, Box 1535; Mike Miller, Box 451. In Wapiti, (zip: 82450) write: David F. Houtz, *Crossed Sabres Ranch*, and Jan F. Schoonover, *Rivers Rest Ranch*. *Yellowstone Wilderness Guides*, Crossed Sabres Ranch, Wapiti, is based 9 miles from East Gate of Yellowstone National Park and provides custom guide service into the Yellowstone backcountry and adjacent wilderness areas, and backpacking and cross-country travel instruction.

EXUM MOUNTAIN GUIDES

Wilderness Instruction & Schools

The famous *Fenwick School of Fly-Fishing*, located on the Madison River near West Yellowstone (Montana), offers intensive instruction in the art of fly-fishing from June to September. Course includes casting, fly lines and leaders, mending the line, setting the hook, entomology and artificial flies, presenting the fly, and on-stream fishing on the Madison, Gallatin, Firehole, Gibbon, or Bechler in Yellowstone Park. For rates, info, and free literature, write: Ms. Jody

Nelson, Fenwick, P.O. Box 729, Westminster, CA 92683. *Exum Mountain Guide Service*, Moose 83012, offers mountaineering courses in the Teton Range. *Jackson Hole Mountain Guides* offers climbing instruction seminars and guide service in the Tetons. Write: Teton Village 83025. *Wilderness Expeditions*, Box 471, Jackson 83001, offers summer backpacking expeditions and instruction in the Teton, Gros Ventre, and Wind River ranges. The *Grand Teton Climbers Ranch* (c/o 113 E. 90th St., New York, NY 10028), located in Grand Teton National Park between Moose and Jenny lakes, offers a mountain retreat for all persons engaged in registered climbing in the Tetons. For additional literature and information about wilderness instruction and field trips, write: *Audubon Workshop of Wyoming*, c/o National Audubon Society, P.O. Box 3232, Boulder, CO 80303; *Jackson Hole Summer Ski Camp*, Jackson Hole Ski Corporation, Teton Village 83025; *National Outdoor Leadership School* (a 35-day course which includes instruction in backpacking, mountaineering, conservation, fly-fishing, horsemanship, survival, and expedition planning), Box AA, Lander 82520; *Rawhide Ranch Camps* (for young adults), Teton Valley Ranch, Kelly 83011 (winter: 916 S. 11th St., Laramie 82070); *Skinner Brothers Wilderness Schools*, Box B, Pinedale 82941, one of the nation's top schools for outdoor living and adventure, adult and family group pack trips and fishing trips, and big game guides for trophy hunts; *Valley Center for Ecology*, Thorne Ecological Institute, 1405 Broadway, Boulder CO 80302, and South Fork Star Rt., Cody 82414; *Wind River Wilderness Camps* (for young adults), c/o Rod Mines, Box 38, Farson 82932, or Roland Ryand, 6678 Arapahoe Dr., Littleton, CO 80120.

Guided high-country and float-fishing trips, pack trips, photography and scenic sight-seeing trips, and guided fall hunts for elk, moose, deer, bear and sheep are provided by the following Jackson Hole ranches and outfitters: *Boreal Outfitters*, Box 1645, Jackson 83001 (phone: 307–733–3729), in the Glacier Wilderness area of the Wind River Range; *Box Y Ranch*, Box 1172, Jackson 83001 (307–733–4329), located in a secluded mountain valley along the Greys River in the Bridger and Teton national forests; the *Broken Arrow Ranch*, Box 45, Jackson 83001 (307–733–2173), located 17 miles south of Jackson on the Hoback River; *Goose Wing Ranch*, Box 496, Jackson 83001 (307–733–2768), offering lodging and guided hunts and pack trips in the spectacular Gros Ventre Range; the *Flying V Ranch*, Kelly P.O., Jackson Hole 83011 (307–733–2799), located on the Gros Ventre River directly across Jackson Hole Valley from 13,766-foot Grand Teton; *Riddle Hunting Camp*, Box 691, Jackson 83001 (307–733–2918), offering guided fall hunts from base camp to North Fork of Fall Creek, Elk Creek, Taylor Creek, and Cottonwood Creek; *Lost Creek Ranch*, Box K95, Moose 83012, located 70 miles north of Moose with 120 acres, bordered by Grand Teton National Park and Teton National Forest; *Moose Head Ranch*, Moose 83012 (307–733–3141), located within the boundaries of Grand Teton Park, 15 miles north of Moose; *Heart Six Guest Ranch*, Moran P.O., Jackson Hole 83001, 4 miles east of Moran Junction, bordering the Grand Teton National Park and the Teton Wilderness; *Spotted Horse Guest Ranch;* Jackson 83001 (307–733–2097), on the scenic Hoback River with scenic summer float-fishing trips on the Hoback, Snake, and Salt rivers; *R Lazy S Ranch*, Box 97, Moose 83012 (307–733–2655), located at the base of the Tetons with pack trips into the Gros Ventre and Yellowstone; *Trail Creek Ranch*, Wilson 83014, at the foot of Teton Pass in the cattle-raising section of Jackson Hole, specializing in pack trips along the Skyline Trail; *White Grass Ranch*, Moose 83012 (307–733–3329), the oldest dude ranch in continuous operation in Jackson Hole, offering its famous fall 100-mile horse drive through the mountains, valleys, and meadows of the Gros Ventre and Wind River ranges; *Triangle X Dude Ranch*, Moose 83012 (307–733–2183), located in

the heart of Grand Teton National Park with full services including cross-country skiing; and *Turpin Meadow Ranch*, Moran 83013 (307–733–2496).

Transportation Services

The Jackson Hole Airport is served daily by *Frontier Airlines* (Box 1618, Jackson 83001, phone 307–733–3100) prop-jet flights from Denver, Salt Lake City, and Billings. Charter fly-in service is provided by *Alpine Air Service*, Box 28, Alpine 83127; *Imeson Aviation*, Box 573, Jackson 83001; and *Elgin Flying Service*, Box 551, Cody 82414. For lodging information write: Jackson Hole Chamber of Commerce, Box E, Jackson 83001 (phone: 307–733–3316).

Wind River Range Outfitters & Guides

For detailed information, rates, and literature on licensed fishing guides and outfitters headquartered in Dubois (zip: 82513), write: Larry Stetter, *Dunoir Outfitters, Inc.*, pack fishing, and hunting trips into Glacier Peak, Washakie Wilderness, and Wind River system headwaters; Donald L. Hessling, *Wind River Ranch*. For guides in Cora (zip: 82925), write: Larry F. Vance, Box 24; Ronald Krause, Box 27; A. J. McGuire, *Circle S Ranch;* Dick Thompson, Box 17; Irv Lozier, *Box R Ranch* (fishing and pack trips). For guides headquartered in Pinedale (zip: 82941), write: Dick Stott, Box 654; James Thomas, Box 667; Monte B. Skinner, *Skinner Bros. Outfitters*, Box B; Richard Miller, Box 35; Harold Lee, Box 82; James L. Evans, *Green River Outfitters*, Box 727; D. S. "Ben" Bennett, Box 784; Grant Beck, *Two Spear Ranch*, Box 251 (Bridger Wilderness pack trips); Hank Snow, *Fall Creek Ranch*, Box 181; Keith Anderson, *Bridger Wilderness Outfitters; White Pine Lodge*, Box 833 (float trips); *Seteton Pack Ranch* (fishing, float trips).

For information on lodging, supplies, and equipment rentals, write: Dubois Chamber of Commerce, Dubois 82513; Pinedale Chamber of Commerce, Pinedale 82941; Lander Chamber of Commerce, Lander 82520. The Lander–Popo Agie area is served by Frontier Airlines to Riverton.

Ski Touring in the Wyoming Rockies

Ski touring opens up the snow-whitened wilderness of Wyoming, where mountain meadows are dotted by hot mineral springs and bursting geysers, and thousands of miles of winter fishing streams wind through deep green forests of pine, fir, and spruce. The state offers a full spectrum of cross-country skiing experiences, from conducted ski treks through the slopes and valleys of the Tetons to rugged high-country touring through the Wind River Range. The Shoshone National Forest has established a special ski-touring course in the Wind River District of the forest, about 20 miles west of Dubois. Other excellent ski-touring areas include Libby Flats, Medicine Bow Peak, Browns Peak, and Sugarloaf in the Medicine Bow and Sierra Madre mountains; the forest slopes and meadows of the Bighorns; the beautiful Jackson Hole Valley in the Teton, Targhee, and Bridger national forests and the Grand Teton National Park and the surrounding slopes; and miles of trails in Yellowstone National Park. Between December and March, try the Casper Mountains in central Wyoming.

The state offers a number of cross-country ski-touring guide services. Those serving the national forests include: *Bear Lodge Resort*, Bear Lodge 82836 (guide service, lodging, meals in the Bighorn National Forest); Fred Klein, *Hogadon Basin Ski Area*, Box 621, Casper 82601 (ski rentals in Casper, food service at area); *Box Y Ranch*, Box 1172, Jackson 83001 (lodging, meals, equipment rental, guided tours into Bridger National Forest); *Diamond D Ranch*, Box 1048, Jackson

83001 (lodging, meals, guided tours); *Game Hill Ranch*, Bondurant 82922 (lodging, meals, equipment, tours in Gros Ventre and Teton areas); *Grand Targhee Resort*, Rt. 1, Alva 82711 (lodging, meals, guides, equipment rental); *Heart Six Ranch*, Box 39, Moran 83013 (meals, lodging, equipment, tours in Teton Wilderness); *Jackson Hole Mountain Guides*, Box 124, Teton Village 83025 (tours in Tetons, Wind Rivers, and Absarokas); *Parklands Expeditions*, Box 371, Jackson 83001 (ski tours in Yellowstone and Jackson Hole); *Powderhound Ski Tours*, Box 286, Wilson 83014 (equipment rentals, tours in Grand Teton National Park and Teton National Forest); *Rimrock Guest Ranch*, Box 485, Jackson 83001 (meals, lodging, guided tours); *Sundance Ski Tours;* Box 1226, Jackson 83001 (accommodations, guided tours into Teton, Yellowstone, and Wind River areas); *Teton Village Resort Association*, Teton Village 83025 (books a number of ski tour operators in Jackson Hole and Grand Teton National Park); *Triangle X Ranch*, Moose 83012 (lodging, meals, guided tours into Grand Teton National Park and Teton National Forest); *Turpin Meadow Ranch*, Box 48, Moran 83013 (lodging, meals, ski tours in Teton Wilderness); *Len's Sport Shop*, Box 875, Saratoga 82331 (meals, tours into Medicine Bow National Forest); *Absaroka Mountain Lodge*, Box 7, Cody 82414 (meals, lodging, group tours into Yellowstone National Park and Shoshone National Forest); and *Yellowstone Park Company*, Yellowstone National Park 82190 (guides, instruction, equipment rentals, meals and lodging at Old Faithful Snow Lodge).

The Guide to Ski Touring in Jackson Hole (available for $3.50 from Allumette Studio, Ltd., Box 1550, Jackson 83001) provides complete descriptions of 18 tours in Grand Teton and Yellowstone national parks.

Wilderness Waters & Trophy Fishing Area Maps

The following large-scale (7.5 and 15 minute) U.S. Geological Survey full-color topographic maps show Wyoming's major wilderness camping areas and trophy fishing waters. For additional listings of map kits, see the "Travel & Recreation Guide" section. *Lewis River & Lake:* Huckleberry Mountain, West Thumb; *Shoshone Lake:* Old Faithful, West Thumb; *Falls River:* Warm River Butte, Grassy Lake Reservoir; *Heart Lake & River:* Frank Island, Mount Hancock; *Gibbon River & Grebe Lake Headwaters:* Mammoth, Norris Junction, Madison Junction; *New Fork River & Headwaters:* New Fork Lakes, Warren Bridge, Cora, Mount Airy, Pinedale, Boulder Lake, Boulder, Two Buttes Reservoir, Olsen Ranch, Rosa Butte; *South Fork of the Shoshone & Bliss Creek Meadows:* Shoshone Pass, Younts Peak, Hard Luck Mountain, Fall Creek, Clouds Home Peak, Valley, Ptarmigan Mountain, Wapiti; *Green River Lakes:* Green River Lakes; *Thorofare Plateau & Creek:* Thorofare Plateau, Yellow Mountain; *Two Ocean Plateau:* Eagle Peak, Two Ocean Pass; *Gros Ventre River:* Grizzly Lake, Upper Slide Lake, Burnt Mountain, Ouzel Falls, Darwin Peak; *Jackson Lake:* Jenny Lake, Mount Moran, Moran, Colter Bay, Huckleberry Mountain.

WYOMING TRAVEL
& RECREATION GUIDE

Bighorn National Forest & Cloud Peak Wilderness

Bighorn National Forest Topo Maps

U.S. Geological Survey 1:250,000 scale overview maps: Arminto, Hardin, Sheridan.

Cloud Peak Wilderness

U.S. Geological Survey large-scale topographic maps: Allen Draw, Brokenback Narrows, Cloud Peak, Dome Lake, Lake Angeline, Lake Helen, Lake Solitude, Little Goose Peak, Meadowlark Lake, Park Reservoir, Powder River Pass, Shell Lake, Spanish Point, Willow Park Reservoir.

The Bighorn National Forest covers 1,115,125 acres in the heart of the Bighorn Mountains in north central Wyoming. The range rises like a giant wall out of the Great Plains to snowy peaks ranging in height from 9,000 to almost 14,000 feet. The lower levels of this north-south range are carpeted with pine, fir, and spruce. Lakes dot the eastern slopes of the mountains, and many streams are born here. The glacier-covered Cloud Peak (13,165 ft.) is the highest mountain on the range.

Sioux, Crow, and Cheyenne Indians lived and hunted here before whites settled in the area. The region was the scene of many conflicts between the tribes and the ways of life they represented. But none of these conflicts approached the fury of those fought against white intruders. In December 1866, along the eastern slopes of the Bighorns, Red Cloud and Sioux Indians ambushed Capt. William Fetterman and 81 soldiers and civilians in the state's worst military disaster. On the Red Fork of the Powder River south of this area, the Cheyenne warriors led by Dull Knife made their last stand against General Mackenzie's bluecoats.

The entire Bighorn region is drained by major tributaries of the Yellowstone River, including the Tongue, Bighorn, and North Fork Powder rivers. The beautiful Cloud Peak lake area has some outstanding fishing for brown, rainbow, Rocky Mountain cutthroat, brook, and golden trout from 8 to 10 inches, with an occasional fish tipping the scales at 3 pounds. A few of the Cloud Peak lakes hold Mackinaw up to a whopping 35 pounds—not bad for wilderness mountain fishing. The remote Wyoming lakes and streams hold some real lunkers. Fly-fishermen will do well in the North Fork of the Powder River, since 8–12 inch rainbows, cutthroats, and browns are common. Along the lower stretches, the North Fork holds some trophy-sized rainbows and browns. The angler with an urge for some rugged exploration should try the remote water of the Powder River Canyon. Lake de Smet, north of the town of Buffalo, has good fishing for rainbows and browns up to 4 pounds. Kearney Lake, in the Blacktooth Mountain lake basin, contains a good-sized population of rainbows and lake trout up to 20 pounds. Almost all of the hundreds of small streams that shed off the crest of the Bighorns have good fly-fishing for pan-sized rainbows, browns, and brookies. The Bighorn region is the range for one of the state's largest elk herds, and there are also a large number of bighorn sheep. Upland game birds include sharptail grouse, a few bobwhites, and excellent pheasant shooting in the Bighorn Basin. All nonresidents must be accompanied by a guide when hunting deer, moose, sheep, goat, elk, or bear in the national forest. Be sure to check the elk-hunting orders map issued by the Fish and Game Commission for the regulation season dates in the Bighorns. For information write: Supervisor, Bighorn National Forest, Sheridan 82801.

The forest is near to the famous "Hole-in-the-Wall" country that harbored Butch Cassidy and the Wild Bunch. This historic area west

of Kaycee is a huge, verdant valley hemmed in by a steep wall of red rocks. To reach the area you must have four-wheel drive and be willing to hike. It is on private land, so obtain the permission of the owners before you explore.

There are 58 campgrounds and picnic areas in the forest; most are easily accessible, but a few, for the sake of the wilderness traveler, are more remote. Winter sports are popular here, as well as wilderness camping, hiking, and trout fishing. The forest's wooded slopes and rolling meadows offer excellent ski touring.

The Cloud Peak Wilderness encompasses 93,880 acres of rugged wildlands, stretching for 27 miles along the backbone of the Bighorn Range. Elevations in the wilderness vary from 8,500 feet to 13,165 feet at the summit of Cloud Peak. At elevations reaching above 10,000 feet are 256 alpine lakes and 49 miles of streams, including the headwaters of Big and Little Goose Creek, a tributary of the Tongue River; Piney and Rock creeks and Clear Creek, tributaries of the Powder River; and Ten Sleep, Paintrock and Shell creeks, tributaries of the Bighorn River, which hold rainbow, Mackinaw, cutthroat, brook, and the prized grayling and California golden trout. Among the trails that

wind up to these lofty lands are the Misty Moon Trail, Angeline Trail, and Seven Brothers Trail. Among the better-known lakes are Sherd, Seven Brothers, Elk, Geneva, Solitude, Helen, and Lakes of the Rough. In all, 81 miles of trails lead to 10 wilderness campgrounds. Popular entrances to the Cloud Peak area are via Battle Park, Circle Park, Coffeen Park, and Hunter Creek, Paintrock Lakes, and West Tensleep Lake.

Nonresident big-game hunters seeking elk, moose, deer, mountain sheep, or black bear are well advised to engage the services of an outfitter and guide. The present-day moose population in the Cloud Peak area and the Bighorns is the result of a 1942 transplanting from the mountains of western Wyoming. Moose were extremely scarce in the early days of the Wyoming territory, and they were rarely reported in the journals of the trappers and scouts. It was not until the early 1900s that they began to migrate into the territory in steadily increasing numbers.

Among the features of the area are the formidable gray granite west face of Cloud Peak, the ultimate challenge to the experienced mountaineer; Blacktooth and Mather peaks; and the glacial Solitude, Cra-

ter, Cliff, and Geneva lakes. Travel here is by foot or horseback only; trails are the only means of access. No mechanized equipment of any kind is permitted. The primitive campsites are located at Sherd Lake, Medicine Cabin Park, Seven Brothers Lakes, Elk Lake, Lake Geneva, Cliff Lake, Upper and Lower Lake Solitude, and Upper and Lower Lake Helen. If you are new to wilderness travel, go with an experienced friend or contact a professional guide or packer.

A free map & guide, *Cloud Peak Primitive Area*, is available from: Forest Supervisor, Bighorn National Forest, Sheridan 82801. The brochure describes the area and includes a small map which marks trails (and names them), secondary roads, lakes, streams, prominent mountains, and camps. A full-color Forest Service *Bighorn National Forest Map* is available for 50¢ from the same address. The map, on a scale of 2 miles to 1 inch, marks natural features such as lakes, streams, and peaks, as well as highways and roads (paved, dirt, all-weather, and four-wheel drive), trails, railroads, ranger and forest stations, recreation sites, ski areas, overlooks, forest supervisors' headquarters, points of interest, buildings, and wells. It identifies Bighorn National Forest, Bureau of Land Management, state, and national park lands.

The same office publishes a free black-and-white *Bighorn National Forest Travel Map*. This map is also on a scale of 2 miles to 1 inch and identifies the same features, with the exception of identification of the various public lands. In addition, information with the map

explains the travel restrictions and regulations for all trails and areas within the forest, including times of year each trail and area is open.

For information on dude ranch accommodations with wilderness outfitting and guiding services in the national forest area, write to: *HF Bar Ranch*, Saddlestring 82480; *Paradise Guest Ranch*, Box 790, Buffalo 82434; *French Creek Ranch*, Box 143, Buffalo 82443; and *UM Ranch*, Kim Love, Buffalo 82434. Lodges and resorts in the area offering wilderness pack trips and fishing and fall big-game hunting trips include: *Caribou Resort*, Rt. 16 West, Buffalo 82434; *Pines Lodge*, A. L. Harvey, Box 100, Buffalo 82434; and *South Fork Inn*, P.O. Box 218, Buffalo 82434. High in the Bighorn Mountains are the *Meadowlark Lodge* and *Deer Haven Lodge*, both Ten Sleep 82442; and *Bear Lodge Resort*, Bear Lodge 82836.

Wyoming licensed professional fishing guides and outfitters serving the Bighorn National Forest and Cloud Peak Wilderness include *Delbert Jenkins*, Rt. 1, Box 236 and *Erling Granstrom*, 338 Western Ave., both of Buffalo 82434; and *Allen C. Anderson*, Box 37, Ten Sleep 82442. Guide packhorse trips into the Cloud Peak Wilderness and Bighorn Mountains are provided by: *Souder's Wilderness Camp*, 850 N. 5th St., Greybull 82426, based in Paintrock Basin at the edge of the Cloud Peak Wilderness; *North Piney Corral*, Box 395, Story 82842, offering moving, base, and drop packhorse trips; and *Spear-O-Wigwam Ranch*, Box 1081, Sheridan 82801. *Paintrock Outfitters, Inc.* (Box 509, Greybull 82426) is located high in the Bighorns on the border of the Cloud Peak Wilderness, offering rustic lodging, guide service, and pack trips.

Access & Outfitting Centers

The Bighorn National Forest is readily accessible from the east by taking Interstate 90 to U.S. 87 (with which it merges just north of Buffalo), then turning west onto U.S. 14 near Sheridan. U.S. 14 and 14A lead into the forest from Cody to the west. Lodging, meals, guides, outfitters, and supplies are available at Lovell, Greybull, Buffalo, Ten Sleep, Dayton, and Sheridan.

Grand Teton National Park & Teton Wilderness

Grand Teton National Park Topo Maps

U.S. Geological Survey 1:250,000 scale overview maps: Ashton, Driggs.

Teton National Forest Topo Maps

U.S. Geological Survey 1:250,000 scale overview maps: Ashton, Cody, Driggs, Thermopolis.

Gros Ventre Range

U.S. Geological Survey large-scale topographic maps: Blue Miner Lake, Bull Creek, Burnt Mountain, Cache Creek, Camp Davis, Darwin Peak, Doubletop Peak, Granite Falls, Grizzly Lake, Gros Ventre Junction, Ouzel Falls, Shadow Mountain, Tosi Peak, Turquoise Lake, Upper Slide Lake.

Jackson Hole of the Snake River

U.S. Geological Survey large-scale maps: Jackson, Cache Creek, Teton Village, Gros Ventre Junction, Grand Teton, Moose, Jenny Lake, Shadow Mountain, Moran.

Teton Range

U.S. Geological Survey large-scale maps: Jackson, Teton Pass, Teton Village, Rendezvous Peak, Grand Teton, Mount Bannon, Mount

Moran, Granite Basin, Ranger Peak, Rammel Mountain, Grassy Lake Reservoir.

Teton Wilderness

U.S. Geological Survey large-scale topographic maps: Angle Mountain, Crater Lake, Dundee Meadows, Gravel Mountain, Green Mountain, Joy Peak, Kisinger Lakes, Lava Mountain, Mount Hancock, Rosies Ridge, Togwotee Pass, Tripod Peak, Two Ocean Pass, Ferry Lake, Thorofare Plateau, Open Creek, Thorofare Butte, Yellow Mountain, Younts Peak, Shoshone Pass, Esmond Park.

Headwaters of the Snake

The wide, crystal-clear, blue-ribbon trout waters of Wyoming's picturesque 100-mile portion of the Snake River—once known to the Shoshonean Snake Indians as *Yam-pah-pa*, for a plant with long pencillike roots that grew along its banks, and to the French-Canadian voyageurs who attempted its treacherous canyon as *la Maudite Rivière Enragée*, the "Accursed Mad River"—rise in the rugged volcanic high country along the west slope of the Great Divide on the Two Ocean Plateau in the Teton Wilderness just south of Yellowstone National Park. The headwaters of the Snake flow northerly into Yellowstone, receiving the waters of Heart and Lewis rivers, and flow southward out of the park due north of Jackson Lake, beginning their long, turbulent westward journey to the Columbia River and the Pacific Ocean.

The first official exploration of the headwaters of the Snake was accomplished by the heroic Doane Expedition of 1876–77, one of the most unusual and bizarre sagas in the history of the West. Lt. Gustavus C. Doane, 2nd Cavalry (the commander of the military escort that accompanied the famous Yellowstone Expedition of 1870, who wrote the first official report on Yellowstone and served with the Hayden Survey of 1871), was ordered to lead a party of 6 during the late fall and winter of 1876 through the wilderness from Yellowstone Lake, southward through the Valley of the Snake (Jackson Hole) and the "Mad River" Canyon, to the Columbia River and the Pacific, outfitted with pack animals, camp gear, a 22-foot-long double-ended boat, and a portable shelter known as an "Indian lodge," constructed from army wagon covers. The voyage down the Snake from Yellowstone Basin, along the rugged forests on the western shore of Jackson Lake beneath the awesome, jagged peaks of the Teton Range, and through Jackson Hole and the icy torrents of the Grand Canyon of the Snake was a harrowing, subzero winter ordeal during which the party was forced to kill off their horses for meat, suffered violent sickness from spoiled venison, lost their boat and gear, including blankets, in the violent rapids of the "Mad Canyon," and barely survived the last three days without food of any kind. The party was rescued in January by a detachment from Fort Hall (in Idaho Territory), and Doane was ordered to return to his post at Fort Ellis near Three Forks (Montana Territory)—saving the expedition from almost certain death in the icy, brawling rapids of Hells Canyon of the Snake.

In Yellowstone, the Snake River Pack Trail parallels the river from the Fox Creek Patrol Cabin northwestward past several narrow rock gorges, hot springs, flowering meadows, and moose pastures near its confluence with the Heart River, where it swings southwesterly around the famed elk range at Big Game Ridge to its junction with the South Boundary Trail. Beautiful Heart Lake, named for an old hunter who was killed here by a war party of Crows in 1852, is rimmed on the west by the Red Mountains. It holds large cutthroats and produced the Yellowstone record 43-pound lake trout. The brilliant blue pools and bright orange algae terraces of the Rustic Geyser, in the geyser basin on Witch Creek near the Heart Lake Patrol Cabin, are surrounded by a mysterious cordon of logs placed there by Indians or trappers years ago. The Shoshone Lake Trail, reached from the Heart Lake and South Entrance trails, winds through lodgepole forests and beautiful meadows to the picturesque wilderness shoreline of 12-square-mile Shoshone Lake—the headwaters of the Lewis River, a top-ranked brown trout stream.

The Lewis River flows from the southeast outlet of Shoshone Lake into Lewis Lake, before flowing south over Lewis Falls through its canyon into the Snake. Shoshone Lake to the Lewis River and Lake provides an excellent wilderness canoe route with good fishing along the way for large lake, brown, and brook trout up to 3 pounds. The brown trout fishing in the Lewis River is often spectacular during the fall, when the spawning browns begin to congregate and move upstream from the lake. With the first chills of late September and October, lake trout can be caught along the shoals of Lewis, Heart, and Shoshone lakes on a fly rod with white millers and wooly worms. In 1890 the U.S. Fish Commission stocked lake and brown trout in Lewis and Shoshone lakes and introduced 10,000 yearling lake trout into the Yellowstone River. Today, lake trout distribution in Yellowstone is limited to Heart, Lewis, and Shoshone lakes and to the Lewis, Heart, and Snake rivers.

The Snake flows out of Yellowstone at the Snake River Ranger Station, and flows south through a scenic meadow inhabited by Yellowstone moose and bald eagles and a white-water stretch formed by the narrow gorge of Flagg Canyon through the Teton National Forest into Jackson Lake in Grand Teton National Park—named for David Jackson, one of the original partners of the Rocky Mountain Fur Company. The frigid, clear waters of this magnificent lake, which lies at an altitude of 6,770 feet, reach depths of 445 feet. The lake has more than 80 miles of shoreline and is one of the state's top-ranked fisheries for trophy brown, cutthroat, and Mackinaw trout up to 30 and 40 pounds. The awesome scenic beauty of the lake, framed on the west by the jagged peaks of the Tetons and dense evergreen forests, was first discovered in 1807 by the fur trader John Colter, who left the Lewis and Clark expedition to explore the beaver country to the west of the Bighorn River. It was first named Lake Biddle by Lieutenant Clark in honor of Nicholas Biddle, who provided the world with the first authentic edition of the *Journals of Lewis and Clark*. Several primitive trailheads, reached by boat from Colter Bay and other launching points along the eastern shoreline, are located along the rugged western shores and provide access to several trails that climb up through a wild country of great canyons, soaring snowcapped peaks, and alpine meadows in the Teton Range. This wild, primitive country is inhabited by summering bands of bighorn sheep, elk, Shiras moose, and an occasional grizzly. Guides, boats, and canoe rentals are available at Leeks Lodge Marina, Colter Bay Marina, and Signal Mountain Marina.

Jackson Hole

The Snake flows southward from Jackson Lake for 60 miles through Grand Teton National Park and its incredibly scenic valley known as Jackson Hole to its confluence with the Hoback River, beyond which it enters the treacherous Grand Canyon, with its roaring whitewater, whirlpools, and turbulent crosscurrents. Jackson Hole lies about 30 miles west of the Great Divide and the towering peaks of the Wind River Range and is one of the largest enclosed valleys in the Rocky Mountains. It varies in width from 6 to 12 miles for some 60 miles north to south, and covers an area of 400 square miles. This awesome, mountain-bound valley is girded on the west by the stunning gray crags, sheer canyons, and perennial snowfields of the Tetons, which rise abruptly from the broad, peaceful cobble-strewn plain and sagebrush flats to form one of the most precipitous mountain fronts in North America, reaching to heights of 13,770 feet at the raw, jagged peaks of the historic Trois Tetons (or "Three Breasts," as they were

known to the woman-starved French Canadian fur traders), which were important landmarks to the trappers and explorers of the early nineteenth century; on the north by the Yellowstone Plateau; and on the east and south by the peaks of the Absaroka Mountains and Mount Leidy Highlands, Gros Ventre Range, Wind River Range, and Hoback Range.

From the time of John Colter's explorations in 1807, on the journey that also led to his discovery of the Yellowstone country, until about 1840, Jackson Hole was the crossroads of the western fur trade, intricately laced with a network of trapper's trails which led into and out of the valley. Besides providing the most practical passage across the Rockies, the area abounded with beaver and wild game. Traditionally, a "hole" referred to any sizable valley containing prime trapping spots. The areas were named for their discoverers or dubbed in honor of some famous trapper, for instance, Gardiner's Hole in Yellowstone country to the north; Pierre's Hole (Pierre was massacred by hostile Blackfeet in 1827) in the Teton Basin to the west; and Brown's Hole, at the base of the Uinta Mountains on the Green River to the south. Jackson Hole (originally known as Jackson's Big Hole, but later abbreviated) was named in 1829 for David Jackson of the Rocky Mountain Fur Company.

Today, Jackson Hole is noted for its luxuriant hay meadows and sagebrush flats, ranches, a great variety and abundance of wildlife, and some of the best trout waters in the nation. Shiras moose are often seen feeding along the marshy shores of the lakes and streams and in the meadow wetlands. Mule deer and a few whitetails roam the backcountry, and thousands of Rocky Mountain elk leave the winter browsing grounds of the National Elk Refuge near the outfitting center of Jackson and move up into the high country of the Teton National Forest and Yellowstone National Park to the north and east. A few small herds summer on the slopes of the Tetons to the west. Antelope roam the aptly named Antelope Flats, and bighorn sheep frequent the crags and ridges of the Tetons and the Gros Ventre Range to the east. Beaver lodges and dams are commonly seen along the Snake, and extensive beaver flows border the remote shores of Jackson Lake. Several pairs of bald eagles nest along the Snake along with a great variety of birdlife common to the area, including sandhill cranes, trumpeter swans, red-tailed hawks, osprey, great blue herons, and white pelicans.

Floating the Snake

The big, clear world-famous fly-fishing waters of the Snake along its serpentine course through Jackson Hole are characterized by several braiding channels, islands, bars, and glacial gravels, which are often blocked by shallow riffles and down trees. Flanked along its banks by groves of aspen, blue spruce, tall cottonwoods, and willows, this beautiful blue-ribbon section of the Snake headwaters offers some of the nation's finest fishing for native Snake River cutthroat, averaging about 11 inches and attaining trophy weights of 6–7 pounds, and a few rainbows and browns. The most effective fly patterns on the Snake include large Muddlers, Jois Hopper, Yellow Maribou Muddlers, Humpys, Royal Wulf's, red flying ant imitations, and Golden Stone nymphs, depending on water conditions and hatch cycles. One of the most productive ways to fish the Snake is by floating it. A scenic, productive 27-mile swift-flowing stretch of the river winds through Grand Teton National Park from below Jackson Lake, swings around Oxbow Bend and flows through Jackson Hole southwest past the mouth of Buffalo Fork and the small outfitting centers of Moran and around the infamous Deadmans Bar bordered on the west by the Potholes and Burned Ridge, and meanders on between Baseline and Antelope Flats past the outfitting center of Moose and Blacktail Butte to the South Park Boundary and its confluence with the Gros Ventre River north of Jackson.

The Snake should be attempted only by experienced boatmen or in the company of one of the licensed Jackson Hole float-fishing guides headquartered at Jackson, Moose, Moran, Alpine, and Wilson (see "Jackson Hole" in "Rocky Mountain Outfitting Centers & Services" in the Encyclopedia section for listings). The river current is deceptively swift and variable. The air temperature is about 5 degrees cooler than on nearby land, and the water temperature is 40 degrees during spring runoff and rises to only about 55 degrees at the warmest period of the year. Floating permits for the Snake may be obtained at any ranger station in the park. Several campgrounds are located along the Park-to-Park Highway, which parallels the river for its entire length through Jackson Hole to Yellowstone.

The free booklet *Floating the Snake River in Grand Teton National Park* describes the flora and fauna along the river, gives safety and trip-preparation tips, lists regulations governing float trips, and includes a map of the river's course and a mileage chart with travel times. It may be obtained by writing: Superintendent, Grand Teton N.P., Moose 83012. The useful *Snake River Guide* ($4.95) provides detailed descriptions of the river, along with historical annotations and maps of its course from the South Entrance of Yellowstone to Alpine Junction at the terminus of the Grand Canyon of the Snake. To order a copy, write: Westwater Books, P.O. Box 365, Boulder City, NV 89005.

Guided float-fishing trips on the Snake are provided by the following Jackson Hole outfitters: Jay Buchner, owner of *High Country Flies*, Box 1022, Jackson 83001, who is one of the best guides in the area and operates float trips on the Snake, Green, and New Fork; *Jackson Hole Country Outfitters*, Box 28, Alpine 83127, which provides guided float-fishing trips on the Snake, Gros Ventre, Greys, and Salt river drainages; Mike Taylor, *Fish Creek Ranch*, Wilson 83014; *Mad Dog Enterprises*, Box 1449, Jackson 83001; *Parkland Expeditions*, Box 371, Jackson 83001, which offers spring and fall "Parkland Fishing Camps" for Snake River cutthroat, a Grand Teton canoe voyage and wilderness by horseback and canoe trip; *Signal Mountain Lodge*, Moran 83013; *Triangle X Ranch*, Moose 83012; Richard Winger, *Jackson Hole Fish & Game*, Jackson 83001; *Boyer's Rod & Reel Shop*, Box 647, Jackson 83601, which is located in the center of Jackson Hole and offers fishing trips on the Green, New Fork, and Snake; *Fort Jackson Inc.—Boots Allen & Sons*, Box 1176, Jackson 83001; *Robert Garrett, Custom Rods*, Box 1433, Jackson 83001; *Heart Six Ranch*, Moran 83013.

The Teton Range

The wilderness backpacker will find some good fishing for small brook and cutthroat trout and spectacular alpine camping areas in Grand Teton National Park along the rugged trails that climb up through the Teton Range from trailheads at the Granite Canyon Ranger Station, White Grass Ranger Station, and Jenny Lake Ranger Station, and at remote points along the western shoreline of Jackson Lake. These rugged Teton trails, including the primitive Teton Crest Trail, reach up above timberline through beautiful alpine meadows and forests of limber and whitebark pine to wind-swept, boulder-strewn parks, canyons, snowfields, and barren jagged peaks, pinnacles, and crags and provide access to the remote wilderness camping areas at Marion Lake, Death Canyon, Mount Jedediah Smith, Alaska Basin Lakes, the Paintbrush Divide, Sunset Lake, Hurricane Pass, Cascade Canyon, and the Wigwams. The Teton trails serve as convenient jumping-off points for the experienced cross-country traveler striking out with topo maps and compass to explore the remote trailless country surrounding Snowshoe Canyon and Dudley Lake, Wilderness Falls and Waterfalls Canyon, Colter Canyon, Moose Basin and Webb Canyon, and the old Jackass Pass Indian trail along the western shore of Jackson Lake. The wilderness traveler in Teton country should attempt to plan an early fall trip to avoid the usual summer crush in the popular areas.

The clear blue waters of Jenny and Leigh lakes, the source of Cottonwood Creek, a tributary of the Snake, lie south of Jackson Lake at 6,000 feet altitude, mirroring the towering stark peaks of the Tetons, and hold cutthroat and some large lake trout. Jenny Lake also provides good early-season fishing for brookies, rainbows, and whitefish. Leigh Lake, reached by a one-mile hike or packhorse along Valley Trail, was named for Richard Leigh, known as "Beaver Dick," a noted hunter, trapper, and guide in Jackson Hole country. The Indians called him "the Beaver," not for his exploits as a trapper, but because of the striking resemblance of his two upper front teeth to those of a beaver. Nearby Jenny Lake to the south was named for his Indian wife.

Grand Teton Maps & Guides

A written, nonfee permit is required for overnight backcountry use in the park, and may be obtained at any ranger station. A 3-night maximum stay is in effect in any one area, and reservations may be made for camping within 30 percent of the available areas. The rest are issued on a first-come-first-served basis. One of the most comprehensive guides to the Teton Range is *Hiking the Teton Backcountry*, a Sierra Club Totebook. This useful guide provides detailed information on all park trails and connecting trails in the Targhee National Forest on the west and in Teton National Forest on the north and south. It may be obtained for $4.95 from: Sierra Club Books, 1050 Mills Tower, San Francisco, CA 94104. *Teton Trails*, a 56-page booklet available for $1 from the Grand Teton Natural History Association, Moose 83012, describes the major trails in the range, their trailheads, distances, hiking time, and prominent features and wildlife found along the way.

Many hikers return to the Tetons to snowshoe and ski-tour. Taggart and Bradley lakes offer some of the best traveling conditions during the months of February, March, and April. Moose Visitor Center is open all year and is the headquarters for all permits and registrations during the winter months. *Winter in the Tetons*, a free pamphlet available from the Grand Teton Natural History Association, Moose 83012, or at the visitor center, summarizes the services and recreational opportunities available in the park during winter months. The pamphlet includes a short guide to nordic skiing trails throughout the park. These are short cross-country trips which require no special experience. If you prefer a guided ski tour, write to one of the following:

The Jack Pine Ski D.B.A. *Quiet Country Tours*, Jackson 83001; *Jackson Hole Ski Corporation*, Teton Village 83025; *Powderhound Ski Tours*, Box 286, Wilson 83014; and *Sundance Ski Tours*, Box 1226, Jackson 83001. The pamphlet includes the names and addresses of lodges open during the winter, as well as supply centers.

The park is one of the finest areas in the country for mountaineering; Teton Rock is rated excellent, and snow slopes are usually moderate. The higher peaks are usually climbed from a high camp or bivouac in two or more days. All climbers must register, sign out prior to, and sign in immediately after each climb. Jenny Lake Ranger Station is the center for mountaineering registration and information from early June to mid-September. Obtain information during the remainder of the year from Park Headquarters at Moose. For mountaineering guide service information, write: Glenn Exum, Box 103, Moose 83012; or *Jackson Hole Mountain Guides*, Teton Village 83025. General mountaineering information is available free from: Superintendent, Grand Teton National Park, Moose 83012. Request the free handout *Mountaineering in Grand Teton National Park. A Climber's Guide to the Teton Range* ($2.95) is a 144-page guide including off-trail routes to some canyons and major peaks. Write: Grand Teton Natural History Association, Grand Teton National Park, Moose 83012. It may also be purchased over-the-counter at the park's visitor centers.

The full-color U.S. Geological Survey *Grand Teton National Park Map* (available for $2.50 in either a topographic or a beautiful shaded-relief edition, which gives the appearance of sunlight striking the map's surface from the northwest) shows all natural and man-made features including depth contours of Jackson Lake, and all roads, trails, campsites, ranger stations, glaciers, marshes, rapids, and falls in the Snake River and Jackson Hole, Teton Range, and portions of the adjacent Targhee and Teton national forests. A text on the reverse side of the map describes the history and geology of the area. The map is 34 × 50 inches with a scale of 1 mile to 1 inch. Write: Superintendent's Office, Grand Teton National Park, Moose 83012, for the following free publications: *Weather Information, Fee Information, Fishing Information & Regulations, Hiking & Backcountry Camping, Campground Information, Accommodations Information*, and the *Grand Teton Shaded-Relief Map* at a scale of 2 miles to 1 inch. The spellbinding *Campfire Tales of Jackson Hole* describes the early history of the region, including the trappers, fur traders, mountain men,

and explorers, and may be obtained for $1 from: Grand Teton Natural History Association, Moose 83012. For nitty-gritty on current park road and weather conditions, facilities, and recreation info, call *Dial-A-Park* (307–733–2220); for campground and specific fishing and wilderness travel info, call 307–733–2880.

The major features of the Teton National Forest to the east and northeast of the Jackson Hole outfitting centers, including packhorse and hiking trails, forest service roads, campsites, and ranger stations, are shown on the huge, full-color, 3 × 6 foot *Teton National Forest Map*, available for $2 along with detailed camping and trail information from: Forest Supervisor, Teton-Bridger National Forest, Jackson 83001 (phone: 307–733–2752). A smaller *Teton National Forest Map* may be obtained from the same address for 50¢. The major features shown on the maps of this 1.7 million-acre forest include the Two

Ocean and Thorofare plateaus and the headwaters of the Yellowstone River in the Teton Wilderness, and the majestic wildlands surrounding the top-ranked cutthroat pools and riffles of the Upper Gros Ventre River (pronounced "Grow Vaunt," a typically vivid French Canadian voyageur's name, meaning "big belly," to describe the Indian sign language of passing both hands over the stomach to convey hunger, given to a local tribe of Arapahos) from its headwaters at Grizzly Basin above Upper and Ouzel falls downstream to its confluence with Fish Creek. The 500,000 acres of wild country surrounding the Upper Gros Ventre are criss-crossed by a network of rugged packhorse and hiking trails that wind up through the highlands to the scenic primitive camping areas at the Meadows and the Six Lakes, Darwin Peak, Buffalo Meadow, Washakie Park, and Fish Lake Mountain on the west slope of the Wind River Range.

Teton Wilderness & the Yellowstone Headwaters

About 20 years before the journey of Lewis and Clark, the French Canadian voyageurs of the North West Company learned from the Mandan Indians in the Upper Missouri country of a distant river known as the *Mi-tsi-a-da-zi*, which they translated to *Rivière au Roche Jaune*, or "Yellow Rock," which described the coloring of the Grand Canyon of the river we know today as the Yellowstone. The waters of this world-famous blue-ribbon trout stream rise high in the heart of the Rockies on the east slope of the massive Absaroka Range at 12,165-foot Younts Peak in the remote, seldom traveled Thorofare Plateau country of the vast 563,000-acre Teton Wilderness. The wilderness is bordered on the north by the wildlands of the Yellowstone Plateau, on the west and south by the Snake River and Jackson Hole country, and on the east by the Shoshone National Forest and the great wall of the Absaroka Mountains, so-called after the Crow Indians, who called themselves *Absarokee*, meaning "People of the Raven."

To the west of the Yellowstone headwaters are the Great Divide, which bisects the Teton Wilderness in a northwesterly direction, and the Two Ocean Plateau and sheer Big Game Ridge, one of the favorite summer ranges of the Jackson Hole elk herd. At the 8,150-foot Two Ocean Pass, situated on the Continental Divide in a nearly level park, is a shallow marshy area known as "the parting of the waters," where a single stream divides, with part flowing to the Pacific Ocean via Pacific Creek and the Snake River, and part flowing to the Atlantic Ocean via Atlantic Creek and the Yellowstone and Missouri Rivers— a continuous water connection of some 6,000 miles. Two Ocean Pass, discovered by the legendary Jim Bridger in 1830, bears a direct link to the renowned cutthroat trout fishery found above the 109-foot-high Upper Yellowstone Falls in Yellowstone Lake and the headwaters above the lake. During the early explorations of Yellowstone country, it was observed that all streams were barren of trout above their falls, except for one—the Yellowstone. One theory has it that the cutthroat entered Yellowstone Lake and the upper river by migrating from the Snake River up Pacific Creek and over the Divide at Two Ocean Pass. Cutthroat trout on the east slope of the Great Divide have evolved into the Yellowstone Lake form, while the Snake River cutthroat, which differs from the Yellowstone fish by its more numerous and smaller black spots, has developed on the west slope of the Divide.

Outfitter trails wind throughout the wilderness, along timbered slopes and ridges and through deep canyons and mountain meadows with forest borders of pine, fir, spruce and aspen, inhabited by elk, Shiras moose, bighorn sheep, black bear, marten and beaver, and a few grizzlies and wolves. Trailheads are located just outside the wilderness boundaries in the Teton National Forest at the Snake River, Lava Creek, Hatchet, and Turpin Meadow campgrounds and provide access to remote interior wilderness camping and fishing areas along Pacific Creek (a good early-season fly-fishing stream for cutthroats), North Buffalo and South Buffalo forks of the Snake, and the South Fork Falls, Pendergraft Meadows, and the high-country lakes of the Buffalo Plateau, and to the wildlands of the Thorofare Plateau, along the southeastern boundary of Yellowstone Park. The rugged canyons and large stream-side meadows of the Thorofare may also be reached from Yellowstone Park along the South Boundary Trail and Thorofare Pack Trail, which parallels the Yellowstone upstream from its famous lake through some of the wildest and most beautiful country in the park. Thorofare Creek, a deep tributary of the Yellowstone, provides often spectacular fly-fishing for cutthroat 17–22 inches and over during their awesome early summer spawning run upstream from Yellowstone Lake. Keep an eye out for grizzlies, which feed along the stream during the spawning run from about mid-July to mid-August.

The major features and trails of this renowned fishing and backpacking region are shown on the full-color *Teton Wilderness Map*, which may be obtained for 50¢ along with info on wilderness permits, camping, and backpacking by writing: District Ranger, Buffalo Ranger District, Box 78, Moran 83013.

Teton Country Lodges & Guest Ranches

There is a wide selection of dude ranches, resorts, and lodges which offer wilderness pack trips, fishing, and big-game hunting trips into the Teton Forest and Wilderness. Dude ranches include: *Anchor Ranch*, Mrs. Frederick Hiller, Wilson 83014; *Box Ranch*, c/o Walter M. Korn, Moran 83013; *Bonanza Butte Ranch*, Arthur F. Lange, Box 982, Jackson 83001; *Broken Arrow Ranch*, Box 45, Jackson 83001; *Darwin Ranch*, Box 511, Jackson 83001; *Diamond D Ranch & Outfitters*, Jackson Hole, P.O. Box 11, Moran 83013; *Fish Creek Ranch*, Box 48, Wilson 83014; *Flying V Ranch*, Roy and Becky Chambers, P.O. Box 105, Kelly 83011; *Heart Six Guest Ranch*, Moran 83013;

Lost Creek Ranch, Moose 83012; *Mad Dog Ranch*, Box 1645, Jackson 83001; *Moose Head Ranch*, Box 214, Moose 83012; *Mountain View Ranch*, P.O. Box 248, Moran 83013; *Rimrock Ranch*, Box 485, Jackson 83001; *Spotted Horse Ranch*, Jackson 83001; *Trail Creek Ranch*, Wilson 83014; *Triangle X Ranch*, Moose 83012; *Turpin Meadow Ranch*, Box 48, Moran 83013; *White Grass Ranch*, Frank and Nona Galey, Moose 83012; *Fir Creek Ranch*, Moran 83013; *Goosewing Ranch*, Harold Shervin, Box 496, Jackson 83001; *Twin Creek Ranch*, Hugh Soest, Box 958, Jackson 83001; *Wilderness Ranch*, Bud Nelson, Box 409, Jackson 83001.

Lodges and resorts include: *Jackson Hole Ski Area*, Teton Village Resort Association, Teton Village 83025; *Alpenhof*, Teton Village 83025; *Hilton Inn*, Box 21, Teton Village 83025; *The Hostel*, Teton Village 83025; *Crystal Springs Inn*, Teton Village 83025; *Hotel Rendezvous*, Box 26, Teton Village 83025; *Sojourner Inn*, Teton Village 83025; *Beard Mountain Ranch*, Lyle Beard, Box 295, Driggs, ID 83422; *Colter Bay Cabins*, Teton Lodge, Moran 83013; *Grand Targhee Resort*, Driggs, ID 83422; *Flagg Ranch*, Leo Dentino, 640 E.

High Point Terrace, Peoria, IL 61614 (winter) or Moran 83013 (summer); *Jackson Lake Lodge*, Grand Teton Lodge Company, Moran 83013; *J Circle S Ranch*, Jackson 82001; *Jenny Lake Lodge*, Grand Teton Lodge Company, Moran 83013; *Signal Mountain Lodge*, Moran 83013; *Teton Village Resort Association*, Teton Village 83025; *Timbercrest Lodging*, Box 1185, Jackson 83001 (summer) or Bradley Hollis, 2710 Broadway, Ft. Wayne, IN 46807; *Togwotee Mountain Lodge*, Box 8, Moran 83013; *Ramada Snow King Inn*, Jackson 83001; and *Jackson Hole Racquet Club*, Box 362A, Star Route, Jackson 83001 (call toll free 800–525–4200).

Resort accommodations and dude ranches in Grand Teton National Park include: *Grand Teton Climber's Ranch* (for registered climbers), P.O. Box 157, Moose 83012; *Grand Teton Lodge Company*, Moran 83013, which operates Jackson Lake Lodge, Jenny Lake Lodge, Colter Bay Cabins, Colter Bay Tent Village, and Colter Bay Village Trailer Park; *Leek's Lodge*, Moran 83013; *Signal Mountain Lodge*, Moran 83013; *Triangle X Ranch*, Moose 83012; *Flagg Ranch*, Moran 83013; *Huckleberry Hot Springs*, Box 1934, Jackson 83001; *Bar B-C Ranch*,

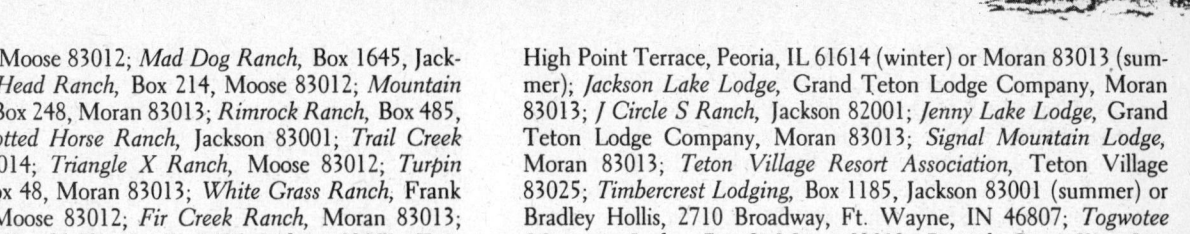

Moose 83012; *Circle D*, Kelly 83011; *Kent's Korner*, Kelly 83011; *Moose Head Ranch*, Moose 83012; *Spur Ranch*, Moose 83012; *Wolff Ranch*, Moran 83013; *X Quarter Circle X Ranch*, Moose 83012; and *Whitegrass Ranch*, Moose 83012. Information on accommodations in Jackson Hole may be obtained by writing: Jackson Hole Chamber of Commerce, Jackson 83001. Short descriptions of the above accommodations are obtainable from: Supervisor, Grand Teton National Park, Moose 83012.

Access

Grand Teton National Park is reached via U.S. Highways 16, 14–20, 89, 191, 187, and 287. Teton National Forest and Wilderness is accessible from the south by way of U.S. 189–187 leading north from Interstate 80.

Medicine Bow National Forest & the Snowy Range

Medicine Bow National Forest Topo Maps

U.S. Geological Survey 1:250,000 scale overview maps: Casper, Cheyenne, Greeley, Rawlins, Torrington.

Encampment River Trophy Trout Waters

U.S. Geological Survey large-scale maps: Dudley Creek, Encampment, Cow Creek Ranch, Cow Creek.

North Fork Platte River Trophy Trout Waters

U.S. Geological Survey large-scale maps: Cow Creek, Dudley Creek, Encampment, Finley Reservoir, Gunst Reservoir, Lone Haystack Mountain, Overland, Overland Crossing, Saratoga, Savage Ranch, Sinclair, Walcott.

Snowy Range Mountains

U.S. Geological Survey large-scale topographic maps: Centennial, Medicine Bow Peak, Morgan, Sand Lake, Rex Lake, White Rock Canyon, Albany, Lake Owen.

The magnificent high country and lakes and streams of the Medicine Bow National Forest offer some of the West's top-ranked trophy trout fishing, big-game hunting, and wilderness camping opportunities. The mists of time and white men's confusion about the Indian's ways have clouded over the origin of this forest's name. The generally accepted version is that white settlers took the name from two sources. The Indian tribes gathered in the forest valleys each year to make bows from the rich mahogany wood found here, and held ceremonial pow-wows during these gatherings to cure disease; the settlers merged ideas of making medicine and making bows and called the forest Medicine Bow. Later, Owen Wister's novel of the Old West, *The Virginian*, made the name immortal.

Among the first mountain men to visit this region were Ezekial Williams and his party, who passed southward through the area in 1810 from Montana on their way to the Arkansas River in Colorado. Ten years later Jacques La Ramie visited the area and met his death at the hands of Indians. Capt. John C. Frémont made the first extensive exploration of the area in 1843–44 and noted the beauty of the mountains' flowers and wildlife in his report on the region.

The Medicine Bow Forest covers 1,398,288 acres. Three of its four divisions lie within the arc made by the North Platte River here, and the fourth (the Hayden Division) lies west of the river. The Medicine Bow Range, known locally as the Snowy Range, borders the Medicine Bow Division of the forest; its slopes are carpeted by forests of lodgepole pine, fir, and aspen. Many streams course through this division

of the forest. Hundreds of lakes lie among the mountains at higher elevations. These glacial lakes vary in size from potholes to basins of a hundred acres and yield a variety of trout.

This region is one of the state's top fishing and big-game hunting areas for mule deer, elk, and antelope. Foot trails lead to the high-altitude Snowy Range trout lakes, such as Telephone Lake and Klondike, Lewis, Gap, Shelf, Meadow, and Arrowhead lakes. Brook trout are found in most of the lakes at 9,500 to 11,000 feet elevation, along with grayling, cutthroat, and California golden trout. A major portion of the Snowy Range lakes area is closed to all motor vehicles except snowmobiles. Nearby, the Big and Little Laramie rivers hold plenty of 10- to 12-inch brown and rainbow trout. The blue-ribbon waters of the North Platte and Encampment rivers flow through the Hayden region and provide some of the finest fishing in southern Wyoming. The lightly fished upper reaches of the North Platte hold some real lunkers; 3- to 4-pound rainbows and browns are common, and an occasional tackle-buster will run up to 18 pounds. The most productive way to fish this big river is by rubber raft or boat. The best fly-fishing is from the beginning of August to the end of October. The most productive dry flies on the North Platte include the Gray Hackle, Sofa Pillow, Red Variant, Humpy, Silver Blue Dun, Joe's Hopper, Gray Wulf, and Black Gnat; the best wet flies include the Muddler, Red Squirreltail, Gray and White Ghost. The lovely, winding Encampment River, with its deep holes and overhanging brush, is one of the finest trout streams in the West; the rainbows and browns usually average between 1 to 4 pounds. The largest brown trout caught in the Encampment tipped the scales at 15 pounds. Hunting for sage grouse, deer, and antelope is excellent in the Upper North Platte River–Ryan Park, Pennock Mountain, and Medicine Bow public hunting areas. Some of Wyoming's finest hunting for mule deer, antelope, and bighorn sheep is found in the Laramie Peak area of the Laramie Mountains—a part of the Front Range of the Rocky Mountains. The rugged, rocky slopes are bordered by open grass and sagebrush lands on all sides. Beautiful mountain parks and deep valleys lie between the rugged breaks.

The Hayden Division of the forest runs along the Sierra Madre Range (Continental Divide) north from the Colorado-Wyoming boundary. The eastern slope of the mountains, drained by the North Platte River, is covered by stands of lodgepole pine and Engelmann spruce. Quaking aspen and brush carpet the western side.

The Pole Mountain Division covers more than 52,000 acres between Cheyenne and Laramie. Open forests of pine, fir, and aspen cover the rolling hills that surround Pole Mountain, offering fishing, camping, hiking, riding, and skiing (Happy Jack Ski Area). Elk, deer, black bear, antelope, coyote, beaver, badger, and marmot are among the species that inhabit Pole Mountain. Rainbow, brook, and native trout are found in the many streams and beaver ponds of the area.

Weird rock formations create an unearthly landscape along Middle Crow Creek. The outstanding features of this area include Turtle Rock, the Devils Playground, and Vedauwoo Glen, which forms a natural two-stage theater in granite. The word *Vedauwoo* means "earthborn" in the Cheyenne Indian language. The Indians believed that playful spirits of men and animals had formed the unusual rock features. This area is heavily used; it is easily accessible by way of Vedauwoo, Happy Jack, and Telephone roads from Interstate 80.

The largest of the four divisions is the Snowy Range area, where the peaks of the Medicine Bow Range are veiled in white year-round. The Snowy Range Division and the Sierra Madre area across the North Platte River to the west offer both highly developed recreation areas and more remote areas where horsepacking, backpacking, cross-coun-

try skiing, and hiking are popular. In the more remote areas the pathways are closed to use by motorized vehicles. Elk and mule deer are often seen in the mountain country. Other wildlife species include black bear, bobcat, mountain lion, and coyote. A myriad of mountain streams and lakes offer some of the best trout fishing in the West.

This area is full of the history of the Old West. The town of Centennial lies near the entrance to the forest on Wyoming 130 (open during summer only). The town grew up after the discovery of a quartz gold mine was discovered here in 1876, and was named in honor of the U.S. Centennial. A rich lode was found here, but unfortunately lost, giving rise to the legend of the "Lost Centennial Lode."

The summer route to the forest, Wyoming 130, is approachable by way of Interstate 80 on the north or Wyoming 230 on the south. In wintertime, the forest is accessible from Arlington, Centennial, Foxpark, and Ryan Park. The Medicine Bow Ski Area on Wyoming 130 provides a good base-camp for cross-country skiing.

The Laramie Peak lies among the Laramie Mountains, part of the Front Range of the Rockies, rising from the Great Plains. High rocky pinnacles, impressive granite walls, and deep, boulder-strewn canyons characterize this region. Above the prairie grass and sagebrush rise slopes of pine and fir. Among the rugged peaks are verdant forests and valleys. Elk, mule deer, black bear, bobcat, and coyote range the slopes.

The central feature of the district is the imposing Laramie Peak, towering 10,274 feet above the prairie floor. In the days of the westward movement, fur traders, trappers, settlers, and gold seekers looked

for this great landmark along the Oregon Trail. The mountain and region were named for Jacques La Ramie, a French mountain man who died at the hands of hostile Indians.

Guided wilderness and trophy trout-fishing trips in the Medicine Bow region are provided by the following licensed fishing guide outfitters headquartered in Saratoga 82331: *Leonard B. Johnson*, Box 211; *Charlie Gould*, Box 626; Herb Shaeffer, *Elk Mountain Safari; Brady Len Bensen*, Box 875; and, by *Larry Richard*, 715 Hancock, Laramie 82070.

Dude ranches in the vicinity of the forest include: *T Bar Guest & Cattle Ranch*, Rex Rt., Laramie 82070 (trout fishing, hunting, rockhounding, riding); *Two Bars Seven Ranch*, Box 67-W, Tie Siding 82084 (fishing, hunting, pack trips); *Mountain Meadows Cabins*, Box 157, Meriden Rt., Cheyenne 82001 (fishing, riding, hiking); *Old Corral*, Centennial 82055 (fishing, hunting, skiing); *A Bar A Ranch*, Box 36, Encampment 82325 (resort facilities, fishing, riding); *Boyer YL Ranch*, Savery Post Office 82332 (riding, fishing, hunting); *Medicine Bow Lodge*, P.O. Box 16, Ryan Park 82330 (riding, pack trips, float trips, fishing, hunting); *Moore Guest Ranch*, Box 293, Encampment 82325 (riding, fishing, pack trips); *Snowy Range Cabins*, Saratoga 82331 (fishing, hunting); *Sand Lake Lodge*, Centennial 82055 (summer) or Gene Alloway, 1634 Jim Bridger, Casper 82601 (pack trips, fishing, hunting, boating); *Saratoga Inn*, Box 867, Saratoga 82331 (resort facilities, float trips, fishing); *Treasure Island Cabins*, Jack & Clara Maenoell, Box 444, Saratoga 82331 (fishing); *Silver Spruce Ranch*, Glenrock 82637 (riding, fishing, mountain climbing, pack trips, hunting).

A full-color Forest Service map, *The Medicine Bow National Forest in Wyoming*, is available from the U.S. Forest Service, Rocky Mountain Region, Federal Center Bldg. 85, Denver, CO 80225, for 50¢. A recreation directory with the map charts the locations, elevations, units for camping, and facilities at campgrounds and recreation areas throughout the forest. A *Travel Map of the Medicine Bow National Forest*, showing most of the same features in black and white, is available free from the same address. This map includes a section on regulations and restrictions of travel in the forest.

For general information on the Medicine Bow National Forest, write: Supervisor, Medicine Bow National Forest, 605 Skyline Drive, Laramie 82070. The address of the Laramie Peak District of the forest is: Medicine Bow National Forest, Laramie Peak District, Douglas 82633.

Access & Outfitting Centers

Major auto routes to the Medicine Bow National Forest are Interstate Highways 80 and 25. Numerous secondary and forest service roads provide access through the forest districts. Lodging, supplies, guides, and outfitters are available at Laramie, Albany, Woods Landing, Centennial, Elk Mountain, Encampment, Medicine Bow, Casper, Douglas, and Cheyenne.

Shoshone National Forest & the Absaroka Range

Shoshone National Forest Topo Maps

U.S. Geological Survey 1:250,000 overview maps: Ashton, Cody, Driggs, Lander, Thermopolis.

Beartooth High Lakes Country

U.S. Geological Survey large-scale maps: Pilot Peak, Beartooth Butte, Deep Lake, Clark, Cooke City, Alpine, Mount Maurice, Red Lodge.

North Absaroka Wilderness

U.S. Geological Survey large-scale topographic maps: Dead Indian Peak, Pat O'Hara Mountain, Pilot Peak, Sunlight Peak, Pelican Butte, Eagle Creek, Chimney Rock, Clayton Mountain, Flag Peak.

Sunlight Basin & Copper Lakes

U.S. Geological Survey large-scale maps: Sunlight Peak, Dead Indian Peak, Deep Lake.

Wapiti Valley

U.S. Geological Survey large-scale topographic maps: Eagle Creek, Chimney Rock, Flag Peak, Wapiti.

Washakie Wilderness

U.S. Geological Survey large-scale maps: Eagle Creek, Chimney Rock, Clayton Mountain, Flag Peak, Wapiti, Pinnacle Mountain, Sheep Mesa, Lake Creek, Ptarmigan Mountain, Open Creek, Thorofare Buttes, Clouds Home Peak, Valley, Irish Rock, Thorofare Plateau, Yellow Mountain, Fall Creek, Emerald Lake, Mount Burwell, Needle Mountain, Ferry Lake, Younts Peak, Hard Luck Mountain, Francs Peak, Shoshone Pass, Five Pockets, Snow Lake, Wiggins Peak, Dunrud Peak, Dick Creek Lakes, Twin Peaks, Ramshorn Peak, Indian Point, Castle Rock, East Fork Basin, Monument Peak.

This magnificent forest reserve encompasses 2,431,000 acres in north central Wyoming and includes some of the finest fishing, hiking, and big-game hunting areas in the West. Shoshone was the first national forest in the United States, created by Pres. Benjamin Harrison in 1891. Elevations range from 4,600 feet near Cody to 13,785 feet at Gannett Peak, the highest mountain in Wyoming. It is the only national forest in the state in which elk, mule deer, whitetail deer, mountain sheep, mountain goats, antelope, moose, black bears, and grizzly bears share a common range. Bald eagles, golden eagles, wolves, coyotes, waterfowl, and songbirds also inhabit the forest. Its streams feed the Clarks Fork, Shoshone, Greybull, and Wind rivers of the Missouri River Basin. The forest lies among the Wind River and Absaroka Mountain ranges, where vast areas of sheer rock, alpine meadows, and evergreen forests make up the varied and spectacular scenery. (The majestic Absaroka Mountains were named after the Crow Indians, who called themselves *Apsaruke* or *Absarokee*, *"People of the Raven."*)

The Wapiti District, the largest of the five Shoshone National Forest districts, encompasses the beautiful Wapiti ("elk") Valley, so named for the elk which abound here, as well as 550,000 acres within the North and South Absaroka Mountains Wilderness. The Shoshone Indians, for whom the forest was named, once used this valley as part of their hunting grounds. The North Fork of the Shoshone River runs through the valley, separating the North Absaroka region from the 679,520 acres of the Washakie Wilderness.

The North Absaroka contains 353,103 acres along the northeastern border of Yellowstone Park. Alpine lakes dot the peaks of this region, which rise to heights of 12,000 feet; fishing varies from good to excellent. Glaciers cap many of the peaks; meadows and forests cover the lower slopes. The Copper Lakes of the Sunlight Basin area offer good fishing for cutthroat and the prized golden trout (up to 20 inches) early and late in the season. A gravel road leads from the Sunlight Creek camping grounds through the Sunlight Basin Public Hunting Grounds to the long-abandoned Lee City. From the roadside a steep foot trail leads up to Copper Lakes.

The Washakie Wilderness, which borders Yellowstone National Park to the southeast, encompasses 679,520 acres of the southern Absaroka

Mountains. Its barren, volcanic terrain, sparse forests, and rocky crags offer top-ranked hunting for elk, moose, deer, and black bear. These mountains, like the Yellowstone Plateau, were formed through the alternating flows of lava and buildups of ash beds. Erosion has stripped these mountains of some of their former grandeur; eventually, it will wear them to rubble. If you plan to hike in this high country, wear sturdy shoes, as the rocks are sharp and jagged. It is an eerie country, strewn with the remnants of former forests and plants, fossilized by the repeated lava flows. A few of the tree trunk remains still stand upright near the head of Frontier Creek, where they lived millions of years ago.

Fishing in this barren high country (average elevation 10,000 feet) is unpredictable, although 16 lakes and more than 100 miles of streams are scattered through the wildlands. In spite of the uncertain angling, backpacking and horsepacking are challenging and well worth the effort here. Such trails as the Wind River Trail, Wiggins Fork Trail, South Fork Trail, and the natural Creek Trail provide access to the remote Five Pockets Area, the Ramshorn, Ishawood Mesa, Eagle Creek Meadows, and Frontier Creek.

The spectacular Beartooth High Lakes Plateau, once the summer hunting grounds of the Mountain Crow and Arapaho Indians, takes in the northernmost portion of the Shoshone National Forest, where it adjoins the 230,000-acre Beartooth Primitive Area in Montana's Custer National Forest on the north. This renowned wilderness fishing and backpacking area embraces a scenic high country of stark, barren crags, ochre-tinted peaks, and ancient rock outcroppings surrounding rolling, boulder-strewn, arcticlike tundra plateaus at 9,000 to 10,000 feet elevation, broken by deep canyons, finger ridges, meadows, and hundreds of remote, blue, rock-bound lakes inhabited by grayling, rainbow, brook, cutthroat, golden, and lake trout and fringed by gnarled, stunted conifers which provide striking examples of krummholz (a German word meaning "crooked wood"). The packhorse and hiking trails, campsites, ranger stations, access roads, and lakes of the area, including Beautiful Island, Little Bear, Sheepherder, Night, Emerald, Grayling, Hauser, Reno, Beartooth, and Big Moose, are shown on the *Beartooth High Lake Country Map*, available free from the Shoshone National Forest Supervisor's Office, W. Yellowstone Hwy., P.O. Box 961, Cody 82414. The *Beartooth High Lakes Country—Index of Lakes*, a free 32-page companion booklet, lists 134 major lakes in the area clustered at the remote headwaters of the Boulder River, Clarks Fork of the Yellowstone, Stillwater River, and Rock, Slough, Rosebud, and Hellroaring creeks, along with useful information on access and fish species present. The Beartooths, which offer generally unpredictable fishing, are inhabited during the summer by elk, mule deer, moose, and mountain goat, and by bighorn sheep in the Monument Peak–Haystack Peak area and in the high country east of Wounded Man Lake.

The Beartooth Highway, between Red Lodge (Montana) and Yellowstone National Park, is considered one of the nation's most spectacular scenic routes and provides access to the High Lakes Plateau in the Shoshone National Forest. Trailheads located off the highway provide access to the remote lakes and high-country wilderness camping areas. U.S. Forest Service campgrounds are located at Beartooth Lake, Lake Creek, and Fox Creek.

Guided packhorse trips into the North Absaroka Wilderness and Beartooth High Lakes Plateau and Yellowstone National Park are provided by *Morning Creek Outfitter*, Box 101, Cody 82414. Guided wilderness and trophy fishing trips in the Shoshone National Forest region are provided by the following licensed fishing guide outfitters: *Larry Miller*, Burris 82511; in Cody 82414, by *Joseph A. DeSarro*, A-2-Z Ranch, South Fork Rt.; *Jerome C. Asay*, Box 1318; *Robert*

Model, Majo Ranch; *Joseph E. Tilden*, Castle Rock Ranch; *Pete Wheeler, Jr.*, Box 941; *Donald C. Schmaltz*, Box 604; *Keith Dahlem*, Box 960; *Dean Johnson*, Box 1535; *De Witt Dominick*, Box 109; and *Mike Miller*, Box 451; by *Donald Hessling*, Wind River Ranch, Box 278, Dubois 82513; and by *David F. Houtz*, Crossed Sabres Ranch, and *Jan F. Schoonover*, both of Wapiti 82450.

Dude ranches, lodges, and outfitters are plentiful in this area and provide guided wilderness camping and pack trips, fishing and fall big-game hunting. For information on dude ranch accommodations and outfitting services in the east slope of the Wind River region of the forest serving the Washakie Wilderness and Glacier and Popo Agie primitive areas, write to the following addresses: *Amoretti Ranch*, Janice & George Peck, Box 307, Dubois 82513; *Brooks Lake Lodge*, Box 333, Dubois 82513; *CM Ranch*, Les E. Shoemaker, Dubois 82513; *Cross Mill Iron Ranch*, Larry Miller, Burris 82511; *Highland Meadow Guest Ranch*, Dubois 82513; *Lazy L and B Ranch*, Barnard F. Didier, Dubois 82513; *Pilot Lake Ranch, Inc.*, West Rt., Pavillion 82523; *T Cross Ranch*, Dubois 82513; *Timber Line Ranch*, Dubois 82513; *Triangle C Ranch*, Dave Addy, Dubois 82513; *Wiggins Fork Ranch*, Wyoming Safari, Inc., Box 607, Saratoga 82331 (winter) or Box 747, Dubois 82513 (summer); *Lava Creek Ranch*, Box 557, Dubois 82513; *Louis Lake Ranch*, Box 482, Lander 82520; *Ocean Lake Resort*, Riverview Route, Riverton 82501; *Pinnacle Motor Lodge & Ranch*, Dubois 82513; *Red Rock Lodge*, Burris 82551; *Wind River Ranch*, Dubois 82513; *Earl Brost & Sons*, Owl Creek Rt., Thermopolis 82443.

For literature, rates, and information on lodging, pack trips, wilderness camping, fishing, and big-game hunting trips in the eastern Park County region of the forest serving the North Absaroka and Washakie Wilderness areas, Teton Wilderness, and Yellowstone National Park, write: *Broken H Ranch*, North Fork Star Rt., Cody 82414 (with excursions to Yellowstone); *Circle H Ranch*, Wapiti 82450 (located 25 miles east of Yellowstone); *Crossed Sabres Ranch*, Wapiti 82450 (9 miles east of Yellowstone); *Elk Creek Ranch*, c/o the Ridgeways, 802 Land Drive, Cody 82414 (with trips to Yellowstone, the majestic Copper Lakes and Beartooth Mountains); *Grizzly Ranch*, North Fork Rt., Cody 82414 (located halfway between Cody and Yellowstone National Park); *Hidden Valley Ranch*, Rt. 2, Box 3650, Cody 82414 (with pack trips into Yellowstone Park, Teton and Absaroka Wilderness areas); *Hunter Peak Ranch*, Box 255, Cody 82414 (with hunting camps in Clarks Fork area); *Rimrock Dude Ranch*, Cody 82414; *Sweetwater Lodge & Guest Ranch*, Wapiti 82450 (located on Sweetwater Creek deep in Shoshone National Forest); *Seven D Ranch*, Box 109, Cody 82414; *Siggins Triangle X Ranch*, Cody 82414 (located on the South Fork of the Shoshone River, surrounded by the Shoshone National Forest and Washakie Wilderness); *Valley Ranch*, South Fork Star Rt., Cody 82414 (located on the South Fork of the Shoshone at the East Entrance to Yellowstone); *Few Acres Ranch*, Box 1567, Cody 82414 (located in Sunlight Basin on Clarks Fork of the Yellowstone).

Lodges and resorts with wilderness outfitting services located in the eastern region of the forest include: *Absaroka Mountain Lodge*, Box 7, Cody 82414 (12 miles east of Yellowstone); *Eagle Valley Guest Ranch*, Northfork Rd., Cody 82414; *Elephant Head Lodge*, Wapiti 82450 (located 11 miles from East Entrance to Yellowstone); *Pahaska Tepee*, Box 491, Cody 82414 (Buffalo Bill's old hunting lodge, located 2 miles east of Yellowstone); *Flying L Skytel*, Box 1136, Cody 82414 (a working cattle and sheep ranch adjacent to Shoshone Forest with private airstrip and scenic flights over Yellowstone and Tetons); *Goff Creek Lodge*, Box 167, Cody 82414; *Lakeview Resort*, Rt. 2, Box

4760, Cody 82414 (located near Buffalo Bill Reservoir); *Rivers Rest Ranch*, Wapiti 82450; *Bill Cody's Ranch Inn*, P.O. Box 1390, Cody 82414 (operated by the grandson of Buffalo Bill, located in Shoshone National Forest on the road to Yellowstone); *Shoshone Lodge*, Box 960, Cody 82414 (outside the East Entrance to Yellowstone); *South Shoshone Guest Ranch*, Southfork Rt., Cody 82414; *UXU Lodge*, Wapiti 82450 (located in the heart of beautiful Wapiti Valley on Yellowstone Highway); *Wapiti Valley Inn*, Wapiti 82450.

Guided trout fishing and float trips on the Shoshone River and its headwaters area are provided by *Crossed Sabres Resort*, Wapiti 82450, and *Shoshone River Float, Inc.*, Box 1635, Cody 82414.

Two full-color U.S. Forest *Shoshone National Forest Maps* (North & South) are available for 50¢ each from: Forest Supervisor, Shoshone National Forest, P.O. Box 961, Cody 82414. A chart with each map gives the locations, elevations, camp units, and facilities of recreation sites in the forest. *South Half Shoshone National Forest* and *North Half Shoshone National Forest*, showing most of the same features in black and white, are available free from the same address and describe restrictions and regulations on travel throughout the forest. A map/-guide on the *Wapiti Valley* is also available free from this address. It describes the wildlife, natural features, and recreation opportunities in this portion of the forest, and has maps of the area showing the locations of roads, trails, buildings, and recreation sites.

For further information on the forest, write: Forest Supervisor, Shoshone National Forest, P.O. Box 961, Cody 82414. District Rangers are located in Cody, Powell, Meeteetse, Dubois, and Lander.

Access & Outfitting Centers

The Shoshone National Forest and Wapiti Valley are reached via U.S. Highways 16, 28T, Alternate 14, 212, and 310. Wyoming routes 296, 120, and 290 also provide access to the forest. Lodging, meals, supplies, guides and outfitters are available at Wapiti, Pahaska, Meeteetse, Sunshine, Dubois, and Cody. The Beartooth Lakes country services and facilities are available at Red Lodge and Cooke City, Montana.

Wind River Range— The "Crest of the World"

Wind River Range Topo Maps

U.S. Geological Survey large-scale maps: Alpine Lake, Bridger Lake, Christina Lake, Cony Mountain, Downs Mountain, Esmond Mountain, Fayette Lake, Fish Creek Park, Fish Lake, Fremont Peak N., Fremont Peak S., Gannett Peak, Green River Lakes, Horseshoe Lake, Ink Wells, Kisinger Lakes, Moccasin Lake, Mount Bonneville, Simpson Lake, Sweetwater Gap, Sweetwater Needles, Union Peak, Warm Spring Mountain.

Bridger National Forest Topo Maps

U.S. Geological Survey 1:250,000 scale overview maps: Driggs, Lander, Preston, Thermopolis.

Bridger Wilderness

U.S. Geological Survey large-scale topographic maps: Big Sheep Mountain, Boulder Lake, Bridger Lake, Fayette Lake, Fremont Lake N., Fremont Lake S., Gannett Peak, Horseshoe Lake, Alpine Lake, Mount Bonneville, Scab Creek, Square Top Mountain.

Glacier Primitive Area

U.S. Geological Survey large-scale topographic maps: Alpine Lake, Blue Holes, Bob Lakes, Bridger Lake, Burris, Downs Mountain, Fremont Peak N., Fremont Peak S., Gannett Peak, Hays Park, Ink Wells, Kirkland Peak, Paradise Basin, Simpson Lake, Torrey Lake, Wilderness.

Headwaters of the Green River

U.S. Geological Survey large-scale maps (shows upper river to Pinedale): Gannett Peak, Square Top Mountain, Green River Lakes, Big Sheep Mountain, Klondike Hill, Dodge Butte, Warren Bridge, Daniel Junction, Mount Airy.

Popo Agie Primitive Area

U.S. Geological Survey large-scale topographic maps: Christina Lake, Cony Mountain, Moccasin Lake, Sweetwater Gap, Sweetwater Needles.

Wind River Headwaters

U.S. Geological Survey large-scale maps: Kisinger Lakes, Esmond Park, Warm Spring Mountain, Dubois, Masson Draw, Torrey Lake, Blue Holes, Wildernesss.

The ancient, jagged, snowcapped peaks of the Wind River Range, revered by the Shoshone Indians as the "crest of the world," rise abruptly from the Great Divide Basin and Central Plains and wind along the backbone of the Continental Divide from historic South Pass—a broad grassy gateway on the old Oregon Trail, known to the Indians as the "Great Road of the White Tops" (covered wagons), originally used by the trappers of the Rocky Mountain Fur Company en route to the Green River Valley and "rendezvous" points to the north and south—northwest for more than 100 miles to Togwotee Pass, where they merge with the massive volcanic crags of the Absaroka Range. To the northwest lie the cobble-strewn flood plains of Jackson Hole and the headwaters of the Snake, the Trois Tetons, and the wild headwaters of the Yellowstone.

This majestic 2 ¼-million-acre range is one of North America's most spectacular wilderness fishing and backpacking regions. It encompasses portions of the Bridger and Shoshone national forests, the Glacier and Popo Agie primitive areas, part of the Wind River Indian Reservation, the 383,400-acre Bridger Wilderness with its 800 miles of trout streams and 140 square miles of glaciers, the headwaters of the Wind and Green rivers, and some 4,000 granite-bound lakes surrounded by towering spires, barren crags, steep-walled valleys, and alpine meadows inhabited by Rocky Mountain elk, Shiras moose, bear, mule deer, and the nation's largest population of bighorn sheep.

Headwaters of the Wind

One of the most rewarding and least publicized fishing and backpacking areas in the Wind River region is found in the Shoshone National Forest along the upper stretches of the Big Wind River and its remote wilderness tributaries and headwater lake basins on the east slope of "the Winds" in the Glacier Primitive Area and in the vast Washakie Wilderness—a consolidation of the old South Absaroka Wilderness and Stratified Primitive area, located north of the rustic outfitting center of Dubois, the hub for entry into this vast unpopularized wilderness region. The fishing potential of the upper Wind River and its remote tributary lakes is highlighted by the never-before-published record fish caught in the region.

WIND RIVER SYSTEM RECORD FISH*

Trout	Lb.–oz.	Place	Year
Rainbow	14	Upper Wind River	1947
Brown	11–4	Upper Wind River	1952
Brook**	12–4	Lake Louise–Torrey Creek	1933
Mackinaw	22	Brooks Lake	1954
Cutthroat	7	Murray Lake–Dunoir Creek	1976
Golden	8	Golden Lake–Dinwoody Creek	1971

*Source: Jack Conley, Supervisor, Wyoming Game & Fish Dept., State Fish Hatchery, Dubois. These are local records, not confirmed state records.

**This fish was caught (but not photographed) when brook trout were first discovered in Lakes Louise and Torrey on the Torrey Creek lakes chain in the Glacier Primitive Area. It's remarkable that this small lake produced a fish in the same league as the world-record squaretail.

The Wind River, named for the constant gusts that rush down the area the Indians knew as the "Valley of the Warm Winds," flows from its headwaters in Wind River Lake, high against the east slope of the range, in a southeasterly direction past the mouths of its Dunoir, Warm Spring, Horse, Jakeys Fork, Torrey, and Dinwoody creek tributaries, and swirls beneath the towering Red Walls through the 200,000-acre Wind River Indian Reservation (presently closed to public entry), beyond which it swings northward into the Boysen Reservoir and its great canyon carved through the Owl Creek Mountains. Beyond this point, at a place called the "wedding of the waters," the name changes to the Bighorn.

The Upper Wind above the outfitting center of Dubois is open 12 months a year and has a 25-mile stretch downstream from the thermal springs of its Warm Spring Creek tributary that never freezes over. This upper stretch of river, surrounded by the towering peaks of the Wind River Range on the south and by the Absaroka Range on the north, provides some exciting fishing from August 15 to October 15 for large, hook-jawed browns, rainbows, cutthroat, and brook trout. The Upper Wind is designated as a red-ribbon Class 11 stream because of limited public access, and is most effectively fished by floating it with one of the licensed fishing guides headquartered in Dubois on

U.S. 287. For info on fishing outfitters headquartered in Dubois, see "Jackson Hole" in "Rocky Mountain Outfitting Centers & Services" in the Encyclopedia section.

At the head of the Wind River Mountains, to the north of Dubois, is the vast Washakie Wilderness, which encompasses the southern Absarokas and scenic Brooks Lake, the renowned rainbow and cutthroat trout waters of the Dunoir Glacier lakes chain, the Ramshorn Basin, Five Pockets, Wiggins Fork, and East Fork drainages—which serve as trailheads for wilderness outfitters, backpackers, and fishermen heading into the remote interior of the "Yellowstone Thorofare" during the spawning run of cutthroat trout up from Yellowstone Lake. Nestled under the Dunoir Butte on the east are Upper and Lower Watkins lakes and on the west are Clendenning, Froms, and Murray lakes, holding cutthroat trout up to 7 pounds. On the extreme west side of the Dunoir drainage, under the rugged Pinnacle Mountains, are the picturesque Kisinger Lakes, which produce trophy brook trout in the 4–6 pound class. The isolated, rarely fished "big" brook trout waters of the South Fork of the Shoshone River along the Bliss Creek Meadows are reached by backpacking over the rim of Shoshone Pass from the head of the East Fork of Dunoir Creek.

Some of the region's finest wilderness fly-fishing and alpine backpacking country is found within the majestic 182,510-acre Glacier Primitive Area, just south of Dubois along the east slope of the Wind River Range. This little-known, largely trailless area, first explored in 1833 by Captain Bonneville, the legendary fur trader and explorer, is dominated by the towering 13,000-foot peaks along the crest of the Great Divide, culminating at 13,785-foot Gannett Peak (the highest point in the state), flanked on its east face by the massive Bull Lake, Fremont, Dinwoody, Gannett, and Grasshopper glaciers. Beneath the crest of the Divide is an unfolding panorama of glistening blue lakes and torrential streams that twist through deep gorges and sheer cliff-walled valleys towards their confluence with the Wind River. Mount Sacajawea, towering above the Fremont Glaciers and the headwaters of the North Fork of Bull Lake Creek, is named for the Shoshone squaw known to the Indians as the "Boat Pusher," who guided Lewis and Clark during their epic westward journey to the Pacific. Sacajawea is buried on the Wind River Indian Reservation, which borders the Primitive Area on the east.

Several rugged packhorse and hiking trails shown on the topo maps of the Glacier Primitive Area climb up above timberline through the deep canyons and mountain valleys past ancient Indian petroglyphs, artifacts, and the remains of corrals and runways built long ago by the Sheepeater Indians to stampede and trap bighorn sheep, to the remote lakes clustered beneath the crest of the Great Divide at the head of the East and West forks of Torrey Creek, Dinwoody Creek and Downs Fork, Dry Creek, and Bull Lake Creek. Many of these seldom-fished lakes, including Snowbridge and Milky lakes on Bull Lake Creek, Native and Phillips lakes on Dry Creek, Dinwoody and Golden lakes on Dinwoody Creek, and Mile Long, Bomber, Ross, Hidden, and Louise lakes on Torrey Creek, surrounded by barren crags, cliffs, and stunted growths of spruce and pine, hold trophy golden trout up to 8 pounds, cutthroats up to 7 pounds, and brown, Mackinaw, brook, and rainbow trout, and a few Montana grayling and splake. Fish species generally vary from lake to lake.

The major campsites, packhorse and hiking trails, forest roads and jeep trails, and lakes and streams in the Washakie Wilderness, Glacier Primitive Area, and the Popo Agie Primitive Area to the southeast are shown on the full-color *Shoshone National Forest Map*, "North Half" and "South Half," available for 50¢ each along with fishing, camping, backpacking, and wilderness permit information from: District

Ranger's Office, Wind River Ranger District, Shoshone National Forest, Dubois 82513.

Popo Agie Primitive Area— "Beginning of the Waters"

The barren, wind-swept crags and spires, sawlike ridges, moonlike alpine meadows, and granite-bound lakes and turbulent streams of the rugged 70,000-acre Popo Agie Primitive Area, pronounced "Po-poz'-ee-uh" from the Crow Indian word meaning "beginning of the waters," are located southwest of the old outfitting and supply center of Lander along the eastern slope of the southern peaks of the Wind River Range, and offer some of the region's finest high-country wilderness fishing and backpacking opportunities. Legend has it that Butch Cassidy, who frequented Lander in the 1890s during his travels with his "Wild Bunch" from their Hole-in-the-Wall hideout in the Bighorns along the old Outlaw Trail, with its elaborate hollow-tree and hole-in-the-rock post offices, once cached $70,000 in this area of "the Winds," when hard-pressed by a posse—and returned to look for the hidden gold in 1936, some 27 years after his reported death in South America.

The breathtakingly beautiful lake basins nestled beneath the awesome Cirque of the Towers, flanked by Mount Washakie (12,524 ft.) to the west, Lizard Head (12,842 ft.) on the east, Wind River Peak (13,400 ft.), and Roaring Fork Mountain (12,490 ft.), at the head of the South Fork Little Wind, North Fork Popo Agie, Deep Creek, and Middle Fork Popo Agie rivers, hold golden, rainbow, goldbow, brook, brown, lake, and cutthroat trout up to trophy weights. Many of these lakes, reached by packhorse and foot along the old Washakie, Lizard Head, Bears Ears, Pinto Park, High Meadow, North Fork, and Stough Basin trails shown on the U.S. Geological Survey topo maps and the *Shoshone National Forest Map*, are located in wind-swept basins above timberline, and many are barren of fish. Some of the most productive fishing is found along the headwaters of the South Fork Little Wind River, located just south of the Wind River Indian Reservation Roadless Area, in South Fork, Loch Leven, Valentine, Macon, and Grave lakes, and in Washakie Lake, located beneath the towering summit of Mount Washakie on the crest of the Divide, which holds some eye-popping golden-rainbow hybrids in the 10-pound-and-over class. Back in the old days, Valentine Lake is reported to have held world-record-sized goldens in the 13-pound range. Loch Leven Lake, reached by a spur route off the Washakie Trail, holds some wary trophy browns in the 8–9 pound class. Lonesome Lake, nestled beneath the wind-swept Cirque of the Towers, the headwaters of the North Fork of the Popo Agie and Washakie Creek, is a top-ranked cutthroat fishery.

Elsewhere in the Popo Agie wildlands, the wilderness fisherman will find grayling up to 16 inches in Squirrel Lake in the Tayo Creek high country and in the beautiful Middle Fork Popo Agie River. At the headwaters of Tayo Creek, beneath the crest of the Great Divide, pure rainbows are found in Hanks Lake; crosses of cutthroat, golden, and rainbows are caught in Poison Lake; and Coon and Mountain Sheep lakes hold cutthroat-golden hybrids. The lakes of the Stough Creek drainage hold big brookies and cutthroat trout in the Stough Creek Basin on Roaring Fork Mountain. Gustave and Christina lakes in the Little Popo Agie Basin hold rainbows and lake trout up to 20 pounds. Atlantic Lake, located in the Atlantic Can beneath the crest of the Divide, holds some big brookies and splake. The remote Deep Creek and Ice lakes in the Wind River Peak area hold brook, golden, and cutthroat trout. Bears Ears Lake on Sand Creek south of the Wind River Indian Reservation holds some big cutthroats. Some excellent wilderness fishing may be found along the Little Popo Agie River, which rises here and flows through the Moxon Basin and the Popo Agie Canyon, the Middle and North forks of the Popo Agie, and especially along the spectacular South Fork of the Little Wind River in the far northwest corner of the Primitive Area. The main stem of the Popo Agie, a major tributary of the Wind River, has produced rainbows up to 3 pounds and browns up to 10 pounds.

For detailed fishing, camping, backpacking, and trail information, write: District Ranger's Office, Shoshone National Forest, Lander 82520.

Bridger Wilderness & Headwaters of the Green

The Bridger Wilderness, named for the yarn-spinning Rocky Mountain trapper and guide Jim Bridger and often referred to as the "land of 1,000 lakes," stretches for more than 90 miles south of Gannett Peak along the west slope of the Wind River Range. Gannett Peak crowns the rugged beauty of this formidable wilderness, towering over the valleys of the Green and New Fork rivers, where freezing temperatures, severe electrical storms, and clouds of mosquitoes test the prowess of the fisherman and backpacker. A great deal of the wilderness is trailless and should be explored only by experienced cross-country travelers with topo maps and compass. The lakes and streams, campsites, and trails, including the Highline Trail (the old Fremont sheep trail) from Big Sandy Opening to Green River Lakes, Island Lakes, and New and Middle Fork lakes, are shown on the *Bridger Wilderness Map Set*, available for $1.50 along with wilderness travel and permit

info from: District Ranger's Office, Bridger National Forest, Pinedale Ranger District, Pinedale 82941.

The extensive glacial gouging of the last ice age has left nearly 1,300 rock-bound lake basins and potholes that dot a benchlike high-country wilderness between 9,000 and 11,000 feet in elevation surrounded by barren tundralike meadows covered by jumbled rocks and glacial debris, jagged glacier-studded peaks, and deep picturesque mountain valleys with numerous cascades and waterfalls. The wilderness has hundreds upon hundreds of lakes clustered beneath the awesome crest of the Great Divide at the headwaters of the Green River, Clear Creek, East Fork River, Big Sandy River, and Trapper, Pole, Boulder, Pine, Halls, and Washakie creeks, which hold brook, rainbow, brown, and cutthroat trout up to trophy weights. The prized golden trout is found in Pyramid, East Fork, Cook, Wall, Elbow, Stonehammer, Titcomb, Faller, Peak, Tommy, and Nelson lakes, and in Surprise Lake, which is utilized as a spawning station for state fish hatcheries and has a restricted season. Native Lake at the remote headwaters of the boulder-studded Roaring Fork, a tributary of the Green, produced the state-record 15-pound cutthroat. The choice of lakes and streams facing the fisherman not intimately familiar with the area can be absolutely bewildering. About 25 percent of the lakes in the Bridger Wilderness are barren of fish, including most of the lakes north of the Green River Lakes, and many of the underfished lakes, such as the once famous golden trout waters of Cook's Lakes, are presently overpopulated with legions of hungry, big-headed, snake-bodied brookies. Several of the remote (and productive) lakes do not even appear on the topo maps of the area. The big "finger lakes" located just south of the wilderness boundary, including tub-shaped 12-mile-long Fremont Lake, which reaches depths of 126 feet, and New Fork, Boulder, Halfmoon, and Burnt lakes, hold big rainbows and lake trout up to 40 pounds. The state-record 23-pound rainbow trout was taken from Burnt Lake, located between Boulder and Halfmoon lakes.

The legendary blue-ribbon trout waters of the Green River, once known as the "Spanish River" and later named by Gen. William H. Ashley, founder of the Rocky Mountain Fur Company, for one of his associates, rises high against the crest of "the Winds" near Green River Pass beneath Gannett Peak and flows through a majestic mountain valley, beginning its long wild journey southwestward through Flaming Gorge, Red Canyon, Dinosaur National Park, and the brawling rapids of the Desolation Wilderness to its confluence with the Colorado in Utah's Canyonlands National Park. In the Bridger Wil-

derness, the Green forms a great bend, flowing through the early-season lake trout, cutthroat, and rainbow trout waters of the Green River Lakes, dominated by the stark granite walls of 11,679-foot Square Top, a great landmark of the Green River Canyon which looms above Lower Green Lake, and begins its serpentine journey south. The upper river flows through deep, boulder-studded pools past the Kendall Warm Springs and the mouths of its high-country tributaries through the Green River Valley to the Daniel Fish Hatchery and its junction with the New Fork River near the outfitting center of Pinedale. The upper Green, from its headwaters downstream to Pinedale, is a classic freestone mountain stream; below its junction with the New Fork, it changes to a big, wide, meandering course.

The magnificent evergreen, aspen, and cottonwood-fringed headwaters of the Green and its upper valley beneath the towering green-gray, snowcapped peaks of the Wind River Range were the historic center of operations for the Rocky Mountain Fur Company. The first "Green River Rendezvous" was held here in 1824, organized by Thomas Fitzpatrick, known to the Indians as "Broken Hand, Chief of the Mountain Men," and attended by the legendary fur traders and explorers Jedediah Smith, David Jackson, William Sublette, whose massive frame gave rise to his Indian name of "Mountain Thunder," and the wily Jim Bridger. The colorful annual "rendezvous," which replaced the fixed trading post and was a forerunner of the cattle roundup, continued as an annual event, attended by as many as a thousand "free trappers," mountain men, and Indians from across the West, until the end of the free trapping era in the 1840s.

The blue-ribbon waters of the Green, particularly the popular float-fishing stretch from Warren Bridge downstream to the Daniel Fish Hatchery and its confluence with the New Fork, hold an abundance of rainbows and browns in the 1–2 pound class. The largest reported fish caught here was a "lunker" hook-jawed 12-pound brown. Much of the upper river and its tributaries flow through private property and are best fished with one of the licensed guides headquartered at the old frontier town of Pinedale. Some of the finest, least-known fishing on the Upper Green is found along the deep pools and beaver flows of its remote tributary creeks, including Piney, Rock, Big Twin, Horse (named in 1823 by trappers who discovered a large herd of wild horses grazing along its banks), Wagon, and Tosi (a rarely fished top-ranked trophy fishery), which rise high in the surrounding wildlands of the Bridger National Forest. The brook trout fishery of the torrential Roaring Fork has suffered from high spring runoff, which has gutted its beaver pond nursery areas. The New Fork tributary, a slow, meandering meadow stream which rises in the Bridger Wilderness near New Fork Park and flows south through the New Fork Lakes, has been pounded mercilessly although it is still producing fish, mostly browns from 1 to 2 pounds.

Hatch cycles vary as always with weather and water-level conditions. On streams fed by warm springs, you may find trout rising to emerging and spinner hatches of caddis, stone, and may flies from the opening to the closing of the fishing season. Standard wet and dry fly patterns are effective, as well as western favorites such as Humpys (Goofus Bugs), Hoppers, the Wulff series, Matukas, and Wooly Worms. The most effective spinning lures in Wyoming's wilderness lakes and streams include the Rapala Count-Down Minnow, Wonderlure, Krocodile, Dardevle, Panther Martin, Thomas Cyclone, Flatfish, Thomas Buoyant Minnow, Rooster Tail (darker colors), Jake's Stream-A-Lure (brass), and the Nebco Flashbait.

Guided float-fishing trips on the upper Green and New Fork rivers are provided by the *Green River Outfitters*, Box 727, Pinedale 82941. Guided fishing trips in the upper Green River wilderness are also provided by: *Len Benson*, Saratoga 82331 (from Big Piney area); *Joe*

Hicks, Pinedale 82941; *Robert F. Garrett*, Box 1433, Jackson 83001; *Harold Lu*, Pinedale 82941; *Richard Miller*, Pinedale 82941; *Lane Pen Eyck*, Pinedale 82941; and *Triangle R Lodge*, Pinedale 82941.

A detailed *Upper Green River Map* from Green River Lakes to Daniel, showing every bend, rapids, and falls in the river, including descriptions, campsites, historical annotations, and a useful cross-section of the river's gradient, may be obtained from Leslie A. Jones, Star Rt. 13-A, Heber City, UT 84032, for $2.50. *Wind River Trails*, a classic guide by the Wind River Range naturalist and outdoorsman Finis Mitchell, is packed with useful info about the Bridger Wilderness and the Glacier and Popo Agie primitive areas, and with fascinating lore of the region. This bible of "the Winds" is required reading for both the fisherman and backpacker and may be obtained for $2.95 (postpaid) from: Wasatch Publishing Co., Idlewild Rd., Salt Lake City, UT 84117. An autographed, postpaid copy at the same price may be had by writing to the author, Finis Mitchell, 336 P St., Rock Springs 82901.

There are developed camping and recreation areas near many of the most scenic areas of the Bridger National Forest in addition to the plenitude of natural campsites in the more remote wilderness areas. *A Guide to National Forest Recreation in Western Wyoming* lists each of the recreation sites in the forest, its elevation, season of use, access, camping and picnicking facilities, numbers of units, activities and attractions, and special features nearby. It also describes resorts and cabins in the forest. The free guide is available from: Forest Supervisor, Bridger-Teton National Forest, Pinedale 82941. Also available from this office is a *Bridger National Forest* map (50¢), which describes the area. The map, on a scale of 10 miles to 1 inch, shows the location of lakes and streams, paved roads, gravel or dirt roads, ranger stations, recreation sites, points of interest, guard stations, airports, ski areas, wilderness and primitive area boundaries, and adjacent national forest lands. Comprehensive recreation site information is included in a chart identifying available facilities and activities at each site.

In Lincoln County there are several dude ranches and resorts that offer wilderness outfitting and guide service and provide easy access to the forest and wilderness. Dude ranches include the *Box Y Guest Ranch*, Box 1172, Jackson 83001; and the *Forest Dell Guest Ranch*, Box 33, Smoot 83126. Lodges and resorts include: *Flying Saddle Ranch*, Al-

pine 83127; *Jay Box Dot Guest Ranch,* Everett and Beth Peterson, Box 224, Cokeville 83114; and *Silver Stream Lodge,* Afton 83110.

The many dude ranches in Sublette County include: *Boulder Lake Ranch,* P.O. Box 725, Pinedale 82941; *Box R Ranch,* Cora 82925; *Fall Creek Ranch,* Hank and Melita Snow, Box 181, Pinedale 82941; *Hoback Basin Guest Ranch,* Star Rt., Box 61, Jackson 83001; *Middle Butte Ranch,* and *Teton Pack Ranch,* P.O. Box 265, both Pinedale 82941; *Sweetwater Gap Ranch,* P.O. Box 26, Rock Springs 82901; *Triangle F Ranch,* Bondurant 82922; *Two Bar Spear Ranch,* Grant Beck, Box 251, Pinedale 82941; and *Game Hill Ranch,* Bondurant 82922.

Lodges and resorts offering wilderness guide service in this county include: *Big Sandy Lodge,* Joe and Lynn Thomas, Boulder 82923; *Lakeside Lodge,* Box 194, Pinedale 82941; *Ponderosa Lodge,* P.O. Box 827, Pinedale 82941; and *White Pine Resort,* Box 128, Pinedale 82941.

Bridger Wilderness Outfitters, located 4 miles north of U.S. 187 on State Secondary 352, the Green River Entrance to the Bridger Wilderness, offer some of the area's best guiding services. They offer spring bear hunting during April, May, and June; summer pack trips in July, August, and until September 15; and fall hunting trips during September, October, and November. Accommodations are in modern housekeeping cabins, and supplies are sold at an old general store. The outfitters also offer horseback riding and youth trail rides. Special rates are available for pack trips and trail rides in groups of 6 to 10 persons. For rates and additional information write: Keith Anderson, Bridger Wilderness Outfitters, Pinedale 82941.

Access

The west slope of the Wind River Range and the Bridger Wilderness is reached via Wyoming 28 and U.S. 189 and 187 off Interstate 80. The east slope of the range is reached via Wyoming 28 off U.S. 187 and by U.S. 287 off Interstate 80.

Yellowstone National Park

Yellowstone National Park Topo Maps

U.S. Geological Survey 1:250,000 scale overview maps: Ashton, Cody.

Cascade Corner & Bechler River

U.S. Geological Survey large-scale maps: Warm River Butte, Grassy Lake Reservoir, Old Faithful.

Firehole River Area

U.S. Geological Survey large-scale maps: Old Faithful, Madison Junction.

Gallatin River Area

U.S. Geological Survey large-scale maps: Mount Holmes, Tepee Creek, Crown Butte.

Gardiner River Area

U.S. Geological Survey large-scale maps: Mount Holmes, Mammoth, Gardiner.

Madison River Area

U.S. Geological Survey large-scale maps: West Yellowstone, Madison Junction, Norris Junction.

Mirror Plateau & Lamar River

U.S. Geological Survey large-scale maps: Sunlight Peak, Pelican Cone, Abiathar Peak, Cutoff Mountain, Tower Junction.

Thorofare Plateau & Upper Yellowstone

U.S. Geological Survey large-scale maps: Younts Peak, Ferry Lake, Thorofare Plateau, Two Ocean Pass, Eagle Peak.

Yellowstone Lake Country

U.S. Geological Survey large-scale maps: Frank Island, Eagle Peak, West Thumb, Canyon Village.

Yellowstone River— The Grand & Black Canyons

U.S. Geological Survey large-scale maps: Canyon Village, Norris Junction, Tower Junction, Mammoth, Gardiner.

Yellowstone, our oldest and largest national park, contains within its 2 million acres some of the most spectacular and beautiful wilderness fishing, backpacking and canoeing country in North America, including the headwaters and Black Canyon of the Yellowstone, the Lamar River and Mirror Plateau Region, the remote upper stretches of the Firehole River, and the rugged highlands, falls, cascades, canyons, and hot springs of the Gardiner, Madison, and Gibbon rivers, and the Bechler River in the serene Cascade Corner. Few outdoorsmen realize that in spite of all its visitors, more than 97 per cent of the park remains in a wilderness state, much of it rarely seen by human eyes.

The Yellowstone region was known to the Indians as the "Land of Evil Spirits" and the "Burning Mountains" and was avoided by most of the local tribes, who feared the awesome spouting geysers, thermal springs, and boiling "paint pots." The early trappers reported that Indian guides consistently lost their bearings when they entered the region. The only tribe to live permanently in what is today national park land was the Sheepeaters, a peaceful, cliff-dwelling tribe who hunted the wild sheep of the area and fashioned obsidian arrowheads of such an intricate design that they were also known as the Arrow Makers. The Sheepeaters maintained that their ancestors had lived in the geyser country "from the beginning" and that a large number of their following had been destroyed by a cataclysmic upheaval near the Upper Geyser Basin. An ancient Indian trail, known as the Great Bannock Trail, often used by the early trappers and explorers of Yellowstone (and still visible in places) extended from Henry's Lake in Idaho across the Gallatin Range, eastward through the northern regions of the park, to the Shoshone River and Bighorn Basin.

Many of the geographical place-names on the topo maps of Yellowstone are derived from the early fur traders, trappers, and explorers who traveled through the region prior to the famous Yellowstone Expedition of 1870. Colter Peak, located southwest of Yellowstone Lake in the Thorofare country, is named for John Colter, the fur trader and discoverer of Yellowstone. Jim Bridger, mountain man, guide and one of the original partners of the Rocky Mountain Fur Company, camped at the beautiful lake that now bears his name east of the Upper Yellowstone River in the Teton Wilderness, just south of the park's boundary. Bridger's unsurpassed knowledge of the Yellowstone country dated back to 1830. With the decline of the fur trade after 1840, he discovered that his invaluable experience of the region could be put to good use as a scout for army expeditions. Officers vied for his services and gladly suffered their guide's erratic schedule (he ate and slept when he chose, sometimes stopping at high noon for a 4-hour siesta; often after eating, he would beat a tom-tom and howl Indian chants well into the night). It was said that he could draw an accurate map of the Yellowstone region from memory with only a piece of charcoal and buffalo hide. Annoyed with the disbelief he encountered at his descriptions of the boiling springs, petrified forests, 100-foot geysers, and the huge "lake in the mountains" in Yellowstone country, the wily guide took perverse satisfaction in em-

bellishing the truth with details fueled by his powerful imagination. He told yarns that led to the use of the expression "old Jim Bridger lies"—of a glass mountain that magnified an elk grazing 30 miles away, of a petrified forest where "a peetrified bird setting in a peetrified tree sang peetrified songs," and of Echo Peak, which he claimed to use as an alarm clock from his distant campsite because if he bellowed out "Time to get up," sure enough, six hours later his alarm would roll back through the camp!

Of all the stories told by and about Bridger, the one related by Father de Smet, the famous missionary known to the Indians as Kaniksu, or "Black Robe," best demonstrates the rugged endurance and gruff humor of the Rocky Mountain trappers—which gave rise to the slogan "a trapper is either tough, or dead." In an encounter with hostile Blackfeet, Bridger was wounded, and spent three painful years with the arrowhead lodged in his back. The missionary had it removed and asked Bridger why the wound never became infected. Never at a loss for an explanation, the resourceful guide winked and replied, "In the mountains, meat never spoils."

Upper Yellowstone River & the "Lake in the Mountains"

The Yellowstone Thorofare, one of the nation's most beautiful and least traveled wilderness areas, embraces the vast southeast corner of the park, dominated by Yellowstone Lake and the Upper Yellowstone River, which flows through the Thorofare Plateau and Two Ocean Plateau areas of the Teton Wilderness, bound on the east by the craggy 10,000-foot peaks of the Absaroka Range. Yellowstone Lake and the upper river contain the largest population of native cutthroat trout in North America. The great fleets of white pelicans on Yellowstone Lake reportedly devour nearly half a million of the golden green fish a year. Unequaled fishing can be found along the Upper Yellowstone and its Thorofare Creek tributary during the annual summer spawning run upstream from the lake (the season runs from mid-August to mid-October; be sure to check with park headquarters for individual stream regulations). Dry fly-fishing picks up during early July, when the streams have cleared and the salmon fly (stone fly) hatch is on. By late July and through August and September, grasshopper imitations size 6 to 14, such as Joe's Hopper, the Quill Gordon, and bright patterns such as the Royal Coachman are good all-around dry flies. The best fishing is to be had by matching the hatch. Wooly worms and the muddler minnow are effective wet fly patterns throughout the season.

The Upper Yellowstone River, from its source at Younts Peak (named for an old hunter and guide) in the Teton Wilderness to its mouth

on the Southeast Arm of Yellowstone Lake, is one of the nation's great wild trout streams. The upper river meanders through Yellowstone Meadows, where it picks up the waters of Atlantic Creek, and winds on past the Hawks Rest Patrol Cabin and Bridger Lake into the park, flowing on past its junction with Thorofare Creek through extensive moose meadows, willow brush, and lodgepole forests, forming numerous oxbows along its serpentine course. The wild country surrounding the Upper Yellowstone is prime grizzly and moose habitat and serves as the summer range for the northern Yellowstone elk herd. During early summer, grizzlies are often seen along the river feeding on migrating cutthroat. Beaver dams and lodges are found along nearly all the streams in this region. Birdlife most commonly seen by fishermen along the Upper Yellowstone includes white pelicans, grebe, great blue heron, sandhill crane, water ouzel, and golden and bald eagles. Nests of the numerous fish hawk, or osprey, are often sighted atop slender lodgepole pines and on rock pinnacles.

Famous Yellowstone Lake, the sprawling "lake in the mountains," whose shape was compared by the early explorers to the gnarled hand of an old trapper, is surrounded by dense boreal forests and the high-country wildlands of the snowcapped Absaroka Mountains on the east, and the Great Divide and Two Ocean Plateau to the west and south. Yellowstone is the largest lake in North America above 7,500 feet elevation, with a maximum depth of 300 feet and an average depth of 30 feet. Its icy cold waters, crystal clear and transparent to great depths, are fed almost entirely from the springs and snowfields of the Absaroka Range. The surface of the lake once stood 160 feet higher than at present, covering an area to the southern base of Mount Washburn, some 20 miles to the north, and its waters flowed into Heart Lake and the Snake River. The lake's southern outlet was dammed up by glacial ice, and its waters rushed over the eastern base of Mount Washburn, carving a deep gorge into the lava beds and forming the Yellowstone River.

The remote wildlands along the lake's southern arms are a premier wilderness canoeing and backpacking region. The wilderness paddler can make arrangements with the Yellowstone Boat Co. for transportation to the southern canoe country, where he can explore the shoreline from Eagle Bay to Flat Mountain Arm, the South Arm, the Southeast Arm, and the mouth of the Upper Yellowstone. This wild big lake canoe country is noted for its extensive birdlife, big game meadows, willow brush and moose pastures, marshlands, and beaver flows. The Molly Islands in the Southeast Arm are the nesting area for Wyoming's only breeding colony of white pelicans, which often appear in the distance like a large fleet of small white boats on the lake's blue surface. At the southernmost tip of the Southeast Arm is the Trail Creek Patrol Cabin, where you can cache your canoe and backpack along Trail Creek Trail, which heads west through wild lodgepole forests and grizzly country, past flowering meadows and sloughs inhabited by moose and elk to Heart Lake. Trail Creek often provides excellent fishing for spawning cutthroats. East of the Patrol Cabin, the trail winds along the shoreline of the Southeast Arm past extensive marshes and meadows to the Thorofare Pack Trail and the Upper Yellowstone River. The Thorofare Trail skirts the entire length of the eastern shoreline and parallels the Upper Yellowstone to the Teton Wilderness and Thorofare Plateau. Only experienced wilderness paddlers and cross-country travelers should attempt this rugged country. Strong winds stir up a heavy sea nearly every afternoon during the summer, and severe storms frequently churn the lake into a dangerous frothing sea of whitecaps.

The clear waters of the lower Yellowstone flow in a northerly direction from Yellowstone Lake through the heavily used Canyon Village vacation area, where it is paralleled by the Grand Loop Road, past

numerous mud pots and hot springs to Upper and Lower falls, where it enters the dazzling shades of yellow, red, orange, brown, and purple of the Grand Canyon, bordered on the east by the wildlands and petrified forests of the Mirror Plateau and on the west by the Washburn Range. The Yellowstone flows down through its rugged 20-mile-long trailless chasm, which reaches a maximum width of 1,500 feet and a depth of 750 feet, past small geysers and hot pools set deep in the canyon floor and the deep, boulder-filled, seldom fished cutthroat pools at Threemile Hole and Sevenmile Hole (reached by a spur route off the Howard Eaton Trail) to the Narrows and its confluence with the Lamar River near Tower Falls. Below Tower Falls the Yellowstone flows through the dark-shaded walls of the Black Canyon into Montana near the park's North Entrance at Gardiner. The beautiful Black Canyon section of the river, with its deep-flowing pools, riffles, and 15-foot falls, is paralleled by the Yellowstone River Trail and is a top-ranked trophy fishery for cutthroat, brook, rainbow, and, below Knowles Falls, brown trout up to 6 pounds.

Yellowstone Wild Trout Country—West

To the west of the Yellowstone River are the headwaters of several of the nation's great blue-ribbon trout streams and some of the most isolated wilderness fishing and backpacking country in the region. The renowned Bechler and Falls rivers rise in the remote "Cascade Corner" region in the southwest portion of the park adjacent to the Idaho boundary and Targhee National Forest. The insect-rich trophy brown trout waters of the Firehold River—named for its valley, called Burnt Hole by the early trappers, from a great forest fire that had swept over it—with its falls, cascades, canyon, quiet pools, and grassy banks interspersed with rocky channels and rapids, fringed by dense stands of evergreens, thermal springs, and awesome geysers, rise to the north of the Cascade Corner along the east slope of the Divide in small Madison Lake on the Madison Plateau. The remote roadless section of the Firehole above the Kepler Cascades is paralleled by the Howard Eaton Trail (named for the famous horseman and early Yellowstone guide) and holds rainbow and brook trout up to 18 inches. The famous

rainbow, brown, and brook trout waters of the scenic Gibbon River, which joins the Firehole to form the headwaters of the Madison and was named for Gen. John Gibbon, who explored this region in 1872, rise high in the grayling waters of Grebe, Wolf, and Ice lakes in the 8,000-foot Washburn Range off the Howard Eaton Trail, and flow southwest through Virginia Meadows, over Virginia Cascade, and through a series of rapids, falls, and geyser basins to Madison Junction.

The classic blue-ribbon rainbow, brown, and grayling waters of the Madison River flow lazily in a westward direction through evergreen forests and lush green brightly flowered meadows inhabited by buffalo, moose, and elk; through Madison Canyon into Montana, past the Barns near West Yellowstone, and on into Hebgen Lake. The Madison, paralleled by the West Entrance Road, offers some excellent fall fishing for large browns during their upstream migration from Hebgen Lake. The beautiful Gallatin River, which holds rainbow and cutthroat trout, rises to the north of the Madison in the roadless wild country of the Gallatin Range in the northwest corner of the park, in Gallatin Lake at 9,956-foot Three Rivers Peak, and flows northwesterly through scenic forests and meadows into Middle Basin and the Gallatin National Forest in Montana. The renowned Gardiner River, named for one Johnson Gardiner, a so-called "free trapper" who lived in the area during the 1830s, rises high on the east slope of the Gallatin Range and flows east through the large trailless meadows of Gardiners Hole and the Sheepeater Cliffs, where it flows over Osprey Falls and swings north to its junction with the Yellowstone at Gardiner, Montana. The lower stretches of the Gardiner below Osprey Falls hold buckskin-flanked browns up to trophy weights; the wild upper stretches of the river, paralleled by the Sportsman Lake Trail near its headwaters, hold rainbow and cutthroat trout.

The remote moose and elk country of the Bechler River region in the Cascade Corner, located west of the bizarre, primeval landscapes and lava flows of the Pitchstone Plateau and south of the Madison Plateau, is one of Yellowstone's truly magnificent wilderness fishing and backpacking areas. The gentle wild country of the Cascade Corner, also

known as "waterfalls country," is dominated by the Bechler River and the headwaters of the Falls River, which contain 21 of the park's 41 waterfalls and are framed on the south by the smoky blue peaks of the Tetons. The Bechler, named for a topographer in the Snake River Division of the 1872 Hayden Expedition and once known as the world's premier dry-fly cutthroat stream, holds rainbows and cutthroats up to 4 pounds. It rises high on the Madison Plateau, surrounded by forests of large spruce, fir, and aspen, with an undergrowth of ferns, mosses, and innumerable raspberry and huckleberry bushes, and flows from the confluence of its remote tributaries at Three Rivers Junction southward past hot springs, through the Bechler Canyon and several cascades and terraced falls, to the huge Bechler Meadows and its union with the Falls River. The top-ranked rainbow and cutthroat waters of the Falls River rise in Beula Lake south of the Pitchstone Plateau and flow in a southwest direction over numerous cascades and rapids to the Falls River Basin, where they merge with the Bechler. The seldom visited wild country in the interior of this region is reached from trailheads at the Bechler River Station along the South Boundary, Old Marysville Road, Boundary Creek, and Bechler River trails. Two primitive campsites are located along the Bechler, at Colonnade Falls and Three Rivers Junction.

Yellowstone Wild Trout Country—East

The rugged fishing and backpacking areas of the Mirror Plateau and Lamar River wildlands lie to the east of the Yellowstone River in the northeast corner of the park, dominated by extensive thermal basins, a 40-square-mile fossil forest at Specimen Ridge—where ancient walnut, dogwood, oak, maple and hickory trees "frozen" nearly 55 million years ago by lava flows stand upright—beautiful meadows and valleys, and the 10,000-foot snowcapped peaks of the Absaroka Range, bordered on the east by the golden trout waters of the Sunlight Basin Area of the North Absaroka Wilderness in the Shoshone National Forest. The Lamar River rises high against the west slope of the Absarokas in the spectacular, unearthly wildlands of the Hoodoo Basin area, named for the eroded, gnomelike rock formations from 50 to 300 feet high separated by tortuous passages, known as hoodoos. The Lamar, although not a major trout stream, offers some good fishing for small cutthroats along its upper stretches and tributaries, and for rainbows in the lower Lamar Valley region below Cache Creek (designated as "catch and release" waters). Contrary to old legends, the small hydrogen sulfide emissions in Death Gulch off of Cache Creek are of little consequence to the wilderness traveler. They have, however, caused the deaths of old, senile animals.

The Lamar flows from its timberline headwaters down past the mouths of its Cold, Miller, Calfee, Cache, and Soda Butte tributaries, paralleled by the Lamar River Trail, through scenic Lamar Valley elk range and the Lamar Canyon past the mouth of Slough Creek to its confluence with the Yellowstone. Spur trails off the Lamar River Trail wind up along tributary streams of great length and beauty to the seldom explored crest of the Northern Absarokas and offer some remarkable fishing for small brook and cutthroat trout when the water is clear. Surrounded by beautiful meadows, Trout Lake, the site of an old fish hatchery off of Soda Butte Creek, has a terrific food supply and holds some huge wary rainbows in its deep clear waters. During the summer, moose, elk, buffalo, and the signs of grizzly and black bear are often seen along the trails. Lamar Valley, the largest treeless tract in the park, is a summer antelope range.

Yellowstone Maps, Guides & Lodges

For detailed fishing regulations and backcountry camping and canoeing permits and info, write: Superintendent, Yellowstone National Park 82190. Cross-country travel in Yellowstone with topo maps and compass should be attempted only by experienced wilderness backpackers and fishermen. Special permission from park rangers is required for all off-trail travel.

A variety of ski-touring treks is available in Yellowstone. If you are interested in ski-touring the park, see "Ski Touring in the Wyoming Rockies." Snowshoeing is another favorite winter sport here.

There are several lodges and resorts within the park. *Lake Village*, located at the northern end of Yellowstone Lake, includes cabins and a hotel. Meals are available in the main dining room, and fishing boats may be rented here. The following resort services are available throughout the summer season, June 11 to September 6. For more information, write to: Yellowstone Park Company, Travel Dept., Yellowstone National Park 82190. *Mammoth Hot Springs Inn & Cabins* offers a variety of resort services during the summer and winter, as well as outfitting services for horsepacking and ski touring. The lodge includes the Mammoth Museum, which offers displays of the geology, natural history, and human history of Yellowstone. *Old Faithful Inn* lies in the area surrounding Old Faithful Geyser. The inn has 360 rooms; nearby *Old Faithful Lodge* has 300 cabins. A wide variety of tourist services is available. *Roosevelt Lodge Rough Rider Cabins* offers tourist services and outfits and conducts cross-country pack trips through the wilderness areas. The season is from June 8 to August 31. *Canyon Village*, the most centrally located lodging in the park, has 100 luxury cabins and 498 standard cabins in the Hayden Valley and Central Plateau area. *Lake Yellowstone Hotel*, overlooking Yellowstone Lake, has 281 guest units.

Numerous private dude ranches and resorts offer accommodations in national forests bordering Yellowstone, and many of them lead pack trips, hunting trips, fishing expeditions, and ski-touring treks into the park area. For the addresses of these resorts and ranches, see also "Shoshone National Forest" and "Grand Teton National Park & Teton Wilderness" in this section, and "Jackson Hole" in "Rocky Mountain Outfitting Centers & Services" in the "Encyclopedia" section.

If you plan to visit Yellowstone to observe its wildlife, *Yellowstone Wildlife*, a guide on sale by the U.S. Government Printing Office, will be helpful to you. The book lists the major species found in the park, describes them in the context of their environment, and tells where to look for them. The book includes a number of color photographs.

YELLOWSTONE AND GRAND TETON
wild life

It costs 45¢ and may be ordered from: Superintendent of Documents, U.S. Government Printing Office, Washington, DC 20402.

Fishermen will appreciate *Yellowstone Fish and Fishing* ($1.15), a guide which describes both native and introduced fish in the park in detail and gives a clear guide to their distribution. The book includes color illustrations of the more common trout, whitefish, and grayling in the park. Order it from: Yellowstone Library and Museum Association, P.O. Box 117, Yellowstone National Park 82190.

Fly fishing instruction and guide service is provided on the Firehole, Madison, and Yellowstone rivers (with advance reservations) by *Fly Fishing Service*, Yellowstone Park Company, Yellowstone National Park 82190; phone (307) 344–7311.

Ruth Kirk's *Exploring Yellowstone* ($2.95), also available from the Yellowstone Library and Museum Association, is a comprehensive guide to the park divided into sections on the early explorers and Indians of the region, natural phenomena, and automobile trips and trails within the park.

Yellowstone National Park by Hiram Martin Chittenden is a classic historical account of the park from the times before its discovery by white man to the late nineteenth century, when it was written. Its author was the builder of more than 400 miles of road construction in the park and the famous Roosevelt Memorial Arch at its northern entrance. The book costs $2.50 and may be ordered from the Yellowstone Library and Museum Association (address above). *Journal of a Trapper* is taken from the original manuscript by Osborne Russell, a member of Jim Bridger's brigade of Rocky Mountain Fur Company men. The unembellished narrative of mountain experiences from 1834 to 1843 imparts the rough-and-ready flavor of the fur era in Yellowstone country. The book costs $2.75 and is available from the Yellowstone Library and Museum Association. *Colter's Hell and Jackson's Hole* by Merrill J. Mattes ($1) is a history of the discovery and exploitation of the Yellowstone-Teton region by fur traders. The book, available from the Yellowstone Library and Museum Association, describes the deeds of such legendary adventurers as John Colter, Jedediah Smith, Jim Bridger, and William Sublette. Another historical book available from the Library and Museum Association is *Chief Joseph's People and Their War* (25¢). This short book describes the futile flight and tragic encounter of the Nez Percé in 1877. An 8-page booklet called *The Bannock Indian Trail* describes the famous Indian trail through the park and includes a map of the trail. It costs 10¢ and is available from the same address as the books mentioned above.

The special U.S. Geological Survey *Yellowstone National Park Topographic Map* is on a scale of 1:250,000, or about 2 miles to 1 inch. The map measures 38 × 41 inches and shows roads and buildings, trails, campgrounds, streams, depth contours of Yellowstone Lake, intermittent streams, cascades and falls, geysers, hot springs, mudpots, springs, lakes and ponds, marshes, contours, and elevations. Also available in a shaded-relief edition, either edition costs $2.

Access & Outfitting Centers

Yellowstone Park is reached from Idaho via U.S. Highway 191–20; from Montana via U.S. Highways 191, 89, and 212; in Wyoming along U.S. Highways 212, 287–89, and 14–20. Lodging, meals, guides, supplies, and wilderness outfitters are available at West Yellowstone, Gardiner, Cooke City, and Mammoth Hot Springs in Montana; at Ashton, Idaho; and at Cody, Wapiti, Pahaska, Moran, Moose, and Jackson in Wyoming.

Accommodations— Vacation Lodges & Resorts

The *Utah Travel Guide,* published by the Utah Innkeepers' Association, lists hotels, motels, housekeeping units, and resort lodges (including those with dormitory accommodations) throughout the state. It gives the location, facilities (including on-site recreation activities for resorts), and phone number of each. It lists accommodations by city and region, gives a short description of historic or scenic areas, and mentions local points of interest and nearby recreation areas. For a free copy of the booklet, write: Utah Travel Council, Council Hall, Capitol Hill, Salt Lake City 84114.

For listings of major vacation lodges and guest ranches, see the "Utah Travel & Recreation Guide."

Camping & Wilderness Trails

Hundreds of camping sites dot Utah's vast outdoors. Several free guides are available to help you find them. The Utah Travel Council publishes two good booklet guides to campgrounds throughout the state, *A Guide to Utah's Camp and Picnic Areas* and *Utah's Part of the Earth Campground Directory.* Both guides list campgrounds in national parks, monuments, recreation areas, and forests; Bureau of Land Management campgrounds; and private campgrounds. They give the number of camping units at each site, the available facilities, and nearby recreational opportunities. The Bureau of Land Management publishes a leaflet listing and describing its recreation sites in the state, most of which are free. The publication, *BLM-Developed Recreation Sites in Utah,* gives location, size, and access for each of the campgrounds, and describes the facilities at each one. A small map designates each site. For the Travel Council Guides, write: Utah Travel Council, Council Hall, Capitol Hill, Salt Lake City 84114. For the BLM publication, write: Bureau of Land Management, Utah State Office, P.O. Box 11505, Salt Lake City 84111.

A set of eight *Utah Multipurpose Maps* is available free from the Utah Travel Council. The maps include guides to national forest parks and recreation areas. Each guide gives available facilities, number of camping units, and limit of stay for each campground. The maps, on a scale of 4 miles to 1 inch, show campsites, recreation areas, highways and roads, and special lands such as national parks and public lands. The maps include Southeastern Utah, Southeastern Central Utah, Northeastern Central Utah, Northeastern Utah, Southwestern Utah, Southwestern Central Utah, Northwestern Central Utah, and Northwestern Utah. To order, write: Utah Travel Council, Council Hall, Capitol Hill, Salt Lake City 84114.

Canoeing & Wildwater Touring

The great Colorado and its tributaries helped to carve the wonders of this monolithic land. Spectacular arches and spires of rock alternate with verdant shores, and quiet waters burst into furious white water along the state's many waterways. Utah's rivers include 400 miles of floatable sections, ranging in degrees of difficulty from waters safe for the novice to those which challenge the experts.

For novice river runners, whether their trips will be by canoe or rubber raft, the rivers offer many miles of placid water and small riffles. Jordan River in Salt Lake County offers a variety of opportunities for short stretches or for the entire length between Utah Lake and the Great Salt Lake, a distance of 30 miles. Provo River in Utah County, from the base of Deer Creek Reservoir Dam to the area of the Bridal Veil Falls Resort, makes another good day trip. In Summit County, Weber

UTAH ENCYCLOPEDIA

River offers a beautiful stretch from the base of Rockport Reservoir Dam to the Echo Reservoir (about 8 miles). Another fine canoeing area lies on the Bear River from the Cutler Dam near Collingston to Corrine, approximately 17 miles. Sevier River in Piute and Sevier counties is very floatable from the base of the Piute Reservoir to the town of Sevier, a 15-mile trip. There are also some floatable stretches downstream in Juab and Millard counties from below the dam on the Sevier Bridge Reservoir down to the D.M.A.D. reservoir near Oak City.

For those who prefer the more spectacular, the Green and Colorado rivers offer some of the most breathtaking white waters in the country. One of the most beautiful sections of the Colorado suitable for white-water canoeing lies between the Cisco Bridge in Grand County and the potash plant area below Moab. The Green River includes nearly 100 miles of canoeable water between the Price River confluence above the town of Green River down to the Spring Canyon access road or the Mineral Canyon road near the confluence of the Green and Colorado rivers.

Before you embark on a trip, remember to assess current water conditions and your own experience, equipment, and expertise. River levels and currents vary from year to year and month to month. On the Green and Colorado rivers, be sure you know the departure and access roads and their conditions.

A free booklet, *Running the Green River from Sand Wash to Green River, Utah,* is available from: Bureau of Land Management, Utah State Office, Salt Lake City 84111. It includes an informative map of that section of the river, the Desolation Canyon. The map marks all major rapids and rates them in degree of difficulty. It also shows unimproved roads, jeep trails, hard-surface roads, and streams running into the river, as well as campsites and points of interest along the way. The booklet includes bits of history, archaeology, geology, and wildlife lore that will add to your river experience, and describes the most difficult rapids.

Remember—don't try a trip on the Green through the canyons of Dinosaur Monument unless you are skilled in boat handling and know the river well. You must have a permit from the monument superintendent or be accompanied by a competent guide who has a permit to run this section. To obtain a permit, write or visit the Superintendent, Dinosaur National Monument, P.O. Box 101, Dinosaur, CO 81610.

A good pamphlet to help get you acquainted with the Green River below Flaming Gorge Dam, *Three Faces of the Green River,* is available free from: District Ranger, Flaming Gorge National Recreation Area, U.S. Forest Service, Dutch John 84023. (See also "Green River Wildlands.")

More complete guides to the wildwaters of the Green and Colorado rivers are available from Westwater Books, P.O. Box 365, Boulder City, NV 89005. The three books that describe these wildwaters include *Desolation River Guide, Dinosaur River Guide,* and *Canyonlands River Guide,* all available in a standard edition for $4.95 or a waterproofed edition for $6.95. Detailed maps in each of the guides show rapids, campgrounds, unimproved dirt roads, light duty roads, heavy duty roads, boat ramps, elevations, and topographical features of the shoreline. The guides also give in-depth descriptions of the regions through which the rivers run, including their geology, history, fishing, and wildlife. The text is illustrated by photographs of the lands bordering the rivers and their peoples and wildlife.

For river buffs, Westwater Books has a full inventory of books, both paperback and hardbound, which illuminate the history, geology, and

life of the rivers. Their offerings include river guides, rim and trail guides, and books on geology of rivers and the surrounding areas, natural history, historic expeditions, history, biography, and environment and conservation. For a copy of their catalog, *Books for River Runners*, write to Westwater Books at the address above. (For more information on Utah's rivers, including fishing opportunities and white-water expeditions, see also "Wild & Scenic River Maps" and "Wildwater Expeditions.")

Canyonlands National Park & Wildwater Wilderness

The great twisting blue forks formed by the confluence of the Green and Colorado rivers in the heart of the "Land of the Stand Rocks" are surrounded by a labyrinth of upheaved domes, red and orange cliffs, Indian ruins, deep red sandstone chasms, pinnacles, and needle-like spires of the awesome 337,258-acre Canyonlands National Park. The first trip through the Canyonlands on the Green and Colorado rivers was made by Denis Julien, a French trapper. He was followed by Major Powell's expedition in 1869 and the ill-fated Brown-Stanton expedition. The Green River flows through the deep, colorful Labyrinth and Stillwater canyons; surrounded by red buttes, spires, and mesas, this is the longest smooth-water stretch of the river. The major features of the Canyonlands—the roaring, foaming waters of Westwater Canyon, the Spur, Housethief Point, the ancient cliff dwellings at the Island in The Sky, the Grabens, Orange Cliffs, the Needles, Dead Horse State Park, and the twisting waters and islands of the Colorado River—are shown on the beautiful U.S. Geological Survey *Canyonlands National Park & Vicinity Shaded-Relief Map* ($2). The map shows all towns, canyons, campgrounds, and hiking and jeep trails. Two useful guidebooks, *Canyon Country Scenic Tours* ($1.95) and *Canyon Country Hiking & Natural History* ($3.95) may be obtained from: Wasatch Publishers Inc., 4647 Idlewild Rd., Salt Lake City 84117.

The sinuous canyons and white water of the Green and Colorado are among the nation's most popular river-touring areas. For a listing of river-touring guides and outfitters, see "Wildwater Outfitters & Expeditions" and "Canoeing & Wildwater Touring." Motor vehicle tours and hiking trips in the Canyonlands are provided by *Canyonland Tours*, 295 Blue Mountain, Monticello 84535. Vehicle tours are provided by *Lin Ottinger Tours*, 137 North Main Street, Moab 84532. Hiking trips are provided by *Peace and Quiet, Inc.*, P.O. Box 15742, Salt Lake City 84115. Horse and four-wheel-drive tours are provided by *Outlaw Trains, Inc.*, P.O. Box 336, Green River 84525. *Tex Tours, Inc.*, P.O. Box 67, Moab 84532, offers boat trips and provides shuttle transportation for boaters. A comprehensive listing of Canyonlands guidebooks is contained in the free catalog *Books for River Runners* available from: Westwater Books, Box 365, Boulder City, NV 89005. Lodging, food, and supplies are available at Green River, Moab, and Monticello. For a free *Canyonlands Map-Brochure* and information, write: Superintendent, Canyonlands National Park, 446 South Main St., Moab 84532.

Fishing & Hunting in Utah

Utah's stunningly scenic canyonlands, plateaus, and awesome lake-dotted high country offer some of the West's best trout fishing as well as hunting for mule deer and upland game bird. Beautiful Flaming Gorge Reservoir, which straddles the Utah and Wyoming boundary, produced the world-record brown trout (31 lb. 12 oz.) and is believed by many pros to be the world's outstanding trophy brown trout fishery. Flaming Gorge also yields trophy rainbow, cutthroat, and lake trout.

The state's other popular and productive trout-fishing waters include the remote, scenic High Uinta Lakes, Boulder Mountain Lakes, Panguitch and Fish lakes, Weber River, the scenic blue-ribbon trout waters of the Green River below Flaming Gorge, and the famous Logan and Blacksmith Fork rivers. The crystal-clear waters of lovely Fish Lake, nestled among the Hightops in the Fishlake National Forest (200 miles south of Salt Lake City), hold record-sized Mackinaw (lake trout), brook, cutthroat, and brown trout, and kokanee salmon. Rainbow trout were introduced in 1915 and have since become the most commonly caught species in the lake. Mackinaw from 1 to 35 pounds are taken each year. Cutthroat trout, native to the lake, have become almost extinct. The lake occupies a depression caused by a geological fault at 8,000 feet elevation and is fed by six small streams that enter on the northwest shore. Boats can be launched at several areas adjacent to the highway that runs along the northwest shore, including Lakeside Resort, Fish Lake Lodge, and Bowery Haven Resort. Utah's premier trout fishery is beautiful Panguitch Lake, annually yielding more than 100,000 rainbow and cutthroat trout and kokanee salmon. The lake lies high in the Markagunt Plateau of Dixie National Forest at 8,250 feet elevation, due west of Bryce Canyon National Park in the southwest portion of the state. Access to the lake is by a paved highway from the town of Panguitch. Lodging, supplies, and boats are available along the lake's shore at the Lake View Resort, Panguitch Lake Resort, Rustic Lodge, and Beaver Dam Lodge.

The crystal-clear Logan and Blacksmith Fork rivers, located just south of the Idaho border at the top of the state, are two of the West's best trout streams. The Logan River, which has produced brown trout up

to 26 pounds, rises in the Bear River Range at an elevation of 8,500 feet, while the Blacksmith heads at a somewhat lower elevation about 8 miles southeast of the Hardware Ranch elk management area. The Logan and its tributaries (the Beaver, Franklin Basin, Temple Fork, and Right Fork creeks) provide about 70 miles of fishable water above its confluence with the Blacksmith Fork. The Blacksmith Fork and its tributaries (the Curtis, Left Fork, and Rock creeks) provide some 60 miles of fishing water. Large, temperamental brown trout feed on the abundant insect life in the main stems of both streams. Cutthroat and brook trout are found primarily in the headwaters and tributaries. The Logan River is reached by U.S. Highway 89 and the Blacksmith Fork by Utah Highway 242. Well-maintained campgrounds are located along both streams.

Highcountry Fishing Guides

The following series of guides to the remote wilderness high-country lakes of Utah are available for 50¢ each from the Utah Division of Wildlife Resources, 1596 W. North Temple, Salt Lake City 84116: *The Aquarius Plateau and Thousand Lake Mountain Guide* and the *Lakes of the High Uintas Series*, which includes the following individual booklets: *Ashley Creek, Burnt Fork Creek, Sheep Creek–Carter Creek, and Whiterocks River Drainages; Weber, Provo, and Duchesne River Drainages; Rock Creek and Lake Fork River Drainages;* and *Yellowstone, Swift Creek, Dry Gulch, Uinta River Drainages.*

UTAH RECORD FISH

	Lb.–oz.	Place	Year
Brown trout*	33–10	Flaming Gorge Res.	1977
Cutthroat trout	26–12	Strawberry Res.	1930
Rainbow trout	21–8	Mill Creek Res.	1947
Lake trout	36	Fish Lake	1960
Kokanee salmon	4	Utah Lake	1967
Walleye	10	Provo River	1967
White bass	4–1	Utah Lake	1970
Brook trout	7–8	Boulder Mountain Lake	1971
Black crappie	2–5	Lake Powell	1974
Largemouth bass	10–2	Lake Powell	1974
Northern pike	15–14	Lake Powell	1977
Golden trout	1–13½	Atwood Creek	1977
Striped bass	6–6½	Lake Powell	1977

*World's record.

The 44-page booklet *Popular Utah Fishing Waters* is a must for anyone planning a fishing trip to the state. This useful guide contains detailed descriptions of the most productive fishing spots, with info about access, lodging, and services. You can get a copy by sending 50¢ to: Division of Wildlife Resources, 1596 W. North Temple, Salt Lake City 84116.

The *Fenwick Fly Fishing School* runs its Utah school in June at Wasatch State Park, a 30-mile drive from Salt Lake City and near Heber City. For literature and information, write: Director, Fenwick Fly Fishing School, Western Division, P.O. Box 1191, Novato, CA 94947 (415–883–3200).

Hunting

Utah's scenic high country and vast national forest lands provide excellent hunting for mule deer. Areas renowned for outstanding mule deer hunting include the Dixie National Forest, Book Cliffs, Daggett

Range, Moab and Blue Mountain areas, the Price region, and the remote scenic country of the southwest. Moose (hunting is limited to residents) are found in the dense forests of evergreen and quaking aspen and willow bottom swamplands of the Uinta Mountains in Summit and Weber counties. The state also has limited populations of elk, antelope, desert bighorn sheep, cougar, and black bear, and a wild herd of buffalo in rugged Henry Mountain country. The grizzly bear, the "Ole Ephraim" of the mountain men, is extinct in the state. Utah once had a species of grizzly bear *(Ursus Utahonsis)* that has not been found elsewhere. It was identified from a skull in 1914; no specimens have ever been seen alive. Utah's wild marshlands and waterfowl management areas provide some of the best duck and goose hunting in the nation. The vast saltgrass marshes of the Bear River National Wildlife Refuge (located at the mouth of the Bear River) form one of the country's top-ranked waterfowl shooting (and photography) areas. Autumn upland game-bird hunting is popular for ring-necked pheasant in the farmlands; exotic chukar and Hungarian partridge in the steep, rocky slopes and canyons where they feed predominantly on "cheatgrass"; sage grouse in the sagebrush plains, foothills, and mountain valleys; ruffed grouse (locally referred to as willow grouse) in the brushy woodlands of the Wasatch and Uinta mountains and Wasatch Plateau; blue grouse in open stands of conifers or aspen in the state's mountainous areas; California quail along farmland streams and in foothill areas along the Wasatch Range; Gambel's quail in brushy areas of southern Utah; wild turkey in the ponderosa pine areas of mountain ranges in the southern part of the state; and mourning dove throughout the state.

Write to the Utah Division of Wildlife Resources (address listed above) for fish and game seasons and regulations, license and permit information, *Waterfowl Management Area* and *Deer Management Unit Maps,* and the useful 40-page *Utah Fishing and Hunting Guide* (50¢), *Waterfowl Hunting in Utah* (50¢), and *Utah Upland Game Birds* (50¢). (For additional fishing and hunting info, see the "Utah Travel & Recreation Guide" section.)

Flaming Gorge National Recreation Area & Trophy Trout Waters

Flaming Gorge country has two distinct districts: a desert area across the border in Wyoming composed of small hills and shale badlands, and a mountainous area in Utah embracing canyons and forests. The Green River enters the Uinta Mountains of Utah through a brilliant red canyon, named Flaming Gorge by Maj. John Wesley Powell. In 1962 the Flaming Gorge Dam was built to impound the waters of the river. Today Flaming Gorge Lake extends 91 miles to the north and has fast become one of the world's most prolific producers of trophy, hook-jawed browns in the 10, 15, 20, and 30-plus pound class, metallic-flanked rainbows up to 18 pounds, cutthroat trout up to 10 pounds, and fast-growing trophy Mackinaw up to 20 pounds. The monster trout gorge themselves on the chubs and small rainbows that feed just below the surface of the lake. The most effective fishing method for the great browns is to slow-troll a Rapala Sinking Countdown plug (which resembles a wounded chub) at the base of the canyon walls on the cold deep Utah side of the lake; in the Goosenecks, Bear Canyon, Jarvie Canyon, Hideout Canyon, and Gold Point areas; and at the mouths of feeder streams and the ledges along the old Green River channel. Flaming Gorge recently produced the new world-record brown (the old record brown—39 lb. 8 oz.—taken in Scotland in 1866 was snag-hooked and recently declared ineligible for world-record status) and is reported to hold monster browns of 35–40 pounds.

The Green River continues through the Red Canyon below the dam.

Here a family can enjoy a river trip in comparative safety. The first 12 miles below the dam, known as Utah's "Blue Ribbon Trout Stream," offers one of the best chances to catch trophy rainbow trout in the state. The lake and the stream below are very cold much of the year and are often whipped by strong winds, so upsets can be uncomfortable and sometimes dangerous. Be cautious. Because of these conditions, life preservers are required, as are extra paddles and a bail bucket.

Browns Park, a long valley where the Green River wanders through low hills, is an important wintering place for deer and elk. Here many species of waterfowl and animals benefit from enlarged nesting and forage areas. Hunting and fishing are allowed during specified seasons. Duck and goose hunting are particularly good, and ice fishing is popular on the lake during the winter.

As the Green River flows south from the Flaming Gorge area, it slices through the canyons of the Dinosaur National Monument. In this area the rapids become fast and furious, and only the highly skilled can challenge them. The Dinosaur National Monument superintendent requires you to obtain a permit or to travel this section of the river with a guide who holds such a permit. A free pamphlet on the Green River below the dam, *Three Faces of the Green River*, is available from: District Ranger, Flaming Gorge National Recreation Area, U.S. Forest Service, Dutch John 84023. A more complete guide to the Dinosaur area of the river is available from: Westwater Books, P.O. Box 365, Boulder City, NV 89005. The guide, entitled *Dinosaur River Guide*, costs $4.95, or $6.95 for a waterproofed edition.

Utah Highway 44 north from Vernal and Wyoming Highway 530 south from Green River provide access to the lake. Overnight accommodations are available at two lodges in the southern part of the recreation area. For information write to either the *Red Canyon Lodge* or the *Flaming Gorge Lodge*, both Dutch John 84023. *Cedar Springs Marina, Inc.*, Dutch John 84023, provides boat rentals, tackle, and lake tours. *Dutch John Service*, Dutch John 84023, is located three miles below Flaming Gorge Dam and offers raft rentals for Red Canyon trips, pick-up service, and fishing supplies.

Campgrounds with modern facilities are located at Bootleg, Lucerne Valley, Antelope Flat, and Buckboard Crossing. A free brochure, *Flaming Gorge National Recreation Area*, available from the District Ranger, U.S. Forest Service, Box 157, Dutch John 84023, describes all camping sites within the recreation area and their facilities. It also includes a color map of the area and a description of the recreation opportunities in the area.

Flaming Gorge National Recreation Area is shown on the following U.S. Geological Survey topographical maps: Buckboard, Dutch John, Firehole, Flaming Gorge, Manila, and McKinnon Junction. (See also "Green River Wildlands.")

Glen Canyon National Recreation Area & Lake Powell

The principal feature of the Glen Canyon National Recreation area is Lake Powell, a body of water 186 miles long with 1,960 miles of canyon-indented shoreline. The lake was formed by the Glen Canyon Dam, built by the Bureau of Reclamation between 1956 and 1964 on the Colorado River in southern Utah. The rough canyon country of the Colorado Plateau has been known to various Indian tribes for 2,000 years. The name Glen Canyon was given to this area of the Colorado River by John Wesley Powell, who led explorations of the region in 1869 and 1871.

Today the lake is a recreation center for fishermen, boaters, and campers. Lake Powell provides easy access to the Rainbow Bridge National Monument, which contains the largest natural stone bridge in the world. At Bridge Canyon, a foot trail about ½ mile long leads to the natural bridge. Towering sandstone walls edge the river upstream from Lees Ferry, and the cold, clear channels of this area hold trophy trout. Canyons easily accessible by boat from Wahweap include Antelope, Navajo, Dungeon, Cathedral, Driftwood, and Cascade.

Throughout Lake Powell the fishing is good for rainbow trout, largemouth bass, and kokanee salmon. Catches of trout and bass up to 10 pounds are common, particularly in the spectacular, steep-walled Lost Canyon area.

Wahweap, just upstream from the dam, offers camping and boating facilities and supplies, including boat rentals and a campground with 178 sites for tents and trailers (no utility hookups). Other outfitting and supply centers include Page, Bullfrog, Lees Ferry, Halls Crossing, Hite, and Rainbow Bridge Floating Marina. For more information about the supplies and services at each of these communities and addresses of concessioners, write to the Superintendent, Glen Canyon National Recreation Area, Box 1507, Page, AZ 86040, and ask for the free brochure *Glen Canyon Dam and National Recreation Area*. The brochure includes a map of the area on a scale of 4 miles to 1 inch which marks roads, trails, floating signs, and combination facilities, as well as major geological features.

Vacation lodging and services are provided by *Bullfrog Resort & Marina*, Hanksville 84734; and the *Lake Powell Motel*, *Wahweap Lodge*, and *Wahweap Trailer Village & Cabins*, all c/o Canyon Tours, Inc., P.O. Box 1597, Page 86040.

Glen Canyon is accessible by U.S. 89, which intersects east-west routes north and south of Glen Canyon. Page has bus service from Flagstaff, Ariz., and Salt Lake City, and scheduled flights from Phoenix and Grand Canyon, Ariz., and Salt Lake City. Roads of the area are always open, and the main waterways of the lake are open all winter.

A U.S. Geological Survey *Glen Canyon Recreation Area Topographic Map* on a scale of 1:250,000 is available for $2. This full-color map is 32 × 36 inches and shows all natural and man-made features, including primitive roads, dams, and campgrounds.

Green River Wildlands & Dinosaur National Monument

When Maj. John Wesley Powell passed through this area in 1869 on the first scientific explorations of the Green and Colorado rivers, he called it an area of "wildest desolation." Powell was not the first to run the Green since the upper river had been traveled by mountain men in search of beaver. Gen. William Ashley, father of the Rocky Mountain Fur Company, made the first recorded boat trip on the Green in 1825 in search of fur-trading sites. The Ashley expedition traveled in rawhide-covered canoes to the mouth of the Duchesne River. Today the tortuous canyons, frothing rapids, and deep flowing pools lure wild-river floaters and fishermen from across the nation. Among the canyons of the Green are traces of the Fremont culture, Indians who inhabited this area 800 years ago. Among their legacy are petroglyphs, pottery, stone ruins, and arrowheads. The Utah Indians came here after the Fremont people left, and met the first white explorations of the area during the early 1800s. The Green was known to the early Utah Indians as the Bitterroot. The Crows, who hunted in its Rocky Mountain headwaters, called it the Seedskeedee Agie, or "Prairie Hen," river. To the trappers of the American Fur Company, it was known as the Colorado or Spanish River. General Ashley correctly believed it to be the "Rio Colorado of the West" and is credited with renaming it the Green after one of his partners in the Rocky Mountain

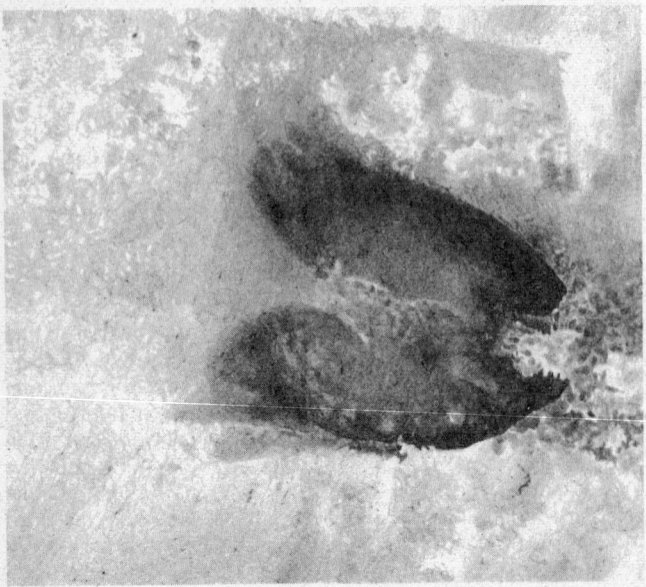

Fur Company. Most rivers of the West served as natural water highways for exploration, but the imposing canyons, treacherous rapids, and wildlands of the Green and the other wild rivers of the Colorado Basin presented effective obstacles to travel and were among the last frontiers in the region to be explored.

The Green rises high in Wyoming's Bridger Wilderness and flows down the slopes of the Rockies, where it meanders across a long highland valley and enters Utah's Uinta Mountains through the brilliant Red Canyon, named Flaming Gorge by Major Powell. Before the Flaming Gorge Dam was built in 1962, the riverbed through the Uintas was little more than a sluiceway for glacial debris washing off the Wind River Range. The Green now flows for its first 18 miles in Red Canyon through Flaming Gorge Lake (one of the nation's top brown trout fishing areas) and for its second 12 miles through a stretch of frigid, deep, state-designated blue-ribbon rainbow and brown trout waters. Motors are not permitted on the 12-mile stretch between the dam and Red Creek. A riverside foot trail follows this part of the river. Most boating parties leave the river at Little Hole. At the lower end of Red Rock Canyon, below Little Hole, is Red Creek Rapids, a frothing mass of churning water and rocks. For detailed fishing and boating info on this stretch of the river, write: District Ranger, Flaming Gorge National Recreation Area, U.S. Forest Service, Dutch John 84023.

The Green flows from Red Canyon through the low hills and wide river bottoms of Browns Park, a long, mountain-rimmed valley that straddles the Utah-Colorado boundary. Isolated by its mountain fastness, the area was a favorite winter retreat of the mountain men during the early 1800s and was named after the fur trader Baptiste Brown. Old cabins located not far from the river once provided refuge for the Wild Bunch led by Butch Cassidy. The roughness and ruggedness of the area, its proximity to three state lines, and its strategic position between Hole-in-the-Wall, Wyo., and Robber's Roost, Utah, made this area a gathering place unsurpassed for its number of unsavory characters. The valley is a major wintering range for deer and Rocky Mountain elk. The Browns Park National Wildlife Refuge embraces a part of the Colorado portion of the river. This meandering section of the Green holds trophy rainbows and browns in the 10-pound-and-over class and provides excellent duck and goose hunting. For the nitty-gritty on the Browns Park area of the Green, write: Bureau of Land Management, Vernal 84078; or Browns Park National Wildlife Refuge, Bureau of Sport Fisheries & Wildlife, P.O. Box 398, Vernal 84078.

The Green flows from the Browns Park area through the imposing Gates of Lodore into the spectacular Dinosaur National Monument, an area of about 330 square miles of rugged and scenic wilderness in the eastern Uinta Mountains. Paved roads lead into the area from Monument Headquarters at Dinosaur, Colo., and from Jensen, Utah, near the famous quarry. John Wesley Powell saw "reptilian remains" in the monument area in 1871, but it was Earl Douglass, of Pittsburgh's Carnegie Museum, who found the "Dinosaur Ledge" quarry in 1909, when he discovered the tail bones of a *Brontosaurus*. The scenery of the monument is dominated by the towering limestone and shale canyons of the Green and Yampa rivers. Both rivers flow placidly through broad green valleys before plunging headlong through, not around, the mountains into their respective canyons. The major features of the Green River Wildlands in the monument—the awesome Canyon of Lodore (where Powell lost one of his boats, the *No-Name*, at Disaster Falls), Hills Half Mile, Steamboat Rock, the fierce Whirlpool Canyon, the verdant meadows of Island and Rainbow parks, Moonshine Rapids, and the wild roller-coaster rapids and eddies of Split Mountain Canyon—are shown in stunning full-color on the U.S.

Geological Survey *Dinosaur National Monument Shaded-Relief Map* ($2). This beautiful map, which measures 30 × 51 inches, shows all ranger stations, trails, and campgrounds located along the Green and Yampa rivers. Major Powell's excellent exploratory maps, and others prepared by the surveys of Clarence King and F. V. Hayden, were for half a century the only maps available of the vast Uinta Mountain wilderness of which Dinosaur National Monument is a part. For detailed info on this section of the Green, and a free *Dinosaur National Monument* map and brochure, river-running and backcountry travel permits write: Dinosaur National Monument, Box 101, Dinosaur, CO 81610. A *River Runners' Guide to Dinosaur National Monument and Vicinity* ($3.50, postpaid) may be obtained by writing: Dinosaur Nature Association, Box 127, Densen 84035.

The Green River leaves the Split Mountain Canyon, meanders through the Uinta basin, flows through the large wooded islands and bottomlands of the Ouray National Wildlife Refuge, and enters the famous wildlands of Desolation Canyon, surrounded by the colorful Book Cliffs on the west and by the Uintah and Ouray Indian Reservation lands on the east. The refuge provides excellent opportunities to observe blue heron, ducks, geese, and beaver. The Green flows through the precipitous walls of Desolation and Gray canyons, forming numerous frothing white-water rapids, eddies, and crosscurrents, and winds on through the great Canyonlands to its junction with the Colorado River.

For free information on outfitters offering guided trips on this section of the Green River, write: Bureau of Land Management, Box 11505, Salt Lake City 84111. The bureau also distributes private permit information. For info about *Ute Trails and Rivers,* a guide service for hunting, fishing, and rafting trips run by the Ute Indian Tribe, write: Ute Trails and Rivers, Fort Duchesne 84026.

Two detailed guides to the river in this area, entitled *Dinosaur River Guide* and *Desolation River Guide,* are available from Westwater Books, P.O. Box 365, Boulder City, NV 89005, at $4.95 each ($6.95 for a waterproofed edition). The guides include an in-depth map of the route of the river in the wilderness, including unimproved dirt roads, light duty roads, medium duty roads, heavy duty roads, rapids, campgrounds, boat landings, and rapids. Facts about the history, geology, and wildlife of the area are also included. The following may also be obtained from Westwater at the address above: *The Wild Bunch at Robber's Roost* ($6.95), about Butch Cassidy and his compadres, by Pearl Baker; *Dinosaur National Monument & Vicinity* ($3); *Desolation and Gray Canyons* ($3).

The Green River Wilderness, including Dinosaur National Monument and Desolation Canyon, is shown on the following large-scale U.S. Geological Survey maps: Jones Hole, Stunty Reservoir, Island Park, Split Mountain, Dinosaur Quarry, Jensen, Rasmussen Hollow, Vernal SE, Brennan Basin, Ouray SE, Ouray, Uteland Butte, Nutters Hole, Firewater Canyon, Flat Canyon, Range Creek, Gunnison Butte, Green River, Bowknot Bend, the Knoll, the Spur, Upheaval Dome, the Needles.

Highways—Recreation & Scenic Routes

The Utah Travel Council publishes a free full-color *Utah Highway Map* which shows geographical features, highways, roads, trails, cities and towns, national and state parks, forests, and recreation areas, campsites, and other points of interest. The map, on a scale of about 17.4 miles to 1 inch, is available from the council, Capitol Hill, Salt Lake City 84114.

For those particularly interested in the spectacular land formations of Utah, the American Association of Petroleum Geologists has published a free *Geological Highway Map of the Southern Rocky Mountain Region* (including Utah, Colorado, Arizona, and New Mexico). This brightly colored map, on a scale of about 30 miles to 1 inch, shows the major land features of these areas and the age and type of the rocks of each area. The map also includes a mileage chart for distances between the various cities in these states.

The Utah Travel Council publishes a free guide for motoring tourists called *Utah! 24 Discovery Tours.* The guide, available from the council address above, outlines points of interest, routes, and seasonal events for tours through northern Utah, the eastern shore of Great Salt Lake, Wasatch Front Pioneer Trail, Salt Desert, Salt Lake City, Salt Lake Canyons, and many other tours throughout the state.

Another free series of maps available from the Utah Travel Council (address above) is the *Utah Multipurpose Map* series of eight maps of the different sections of the state. The multipurpose map for Northwestern Central Utah shows, among many other features of interest, jeep trails which wind through scenic sections of the state.

National Parks & Monuments

Utah is known as the national park state, and the five national parks here encompass some of the most beautiful wilderness in the country. Arches National Park is sandwiched into a triangle of the Colorado River, Interstate 70, and U.S. 163 in the southeast corner of the state. The park was named for its many arches, the largest concentration of these natural wonders in the world, ranging from holes hardly large enough to crawl through to massive sandstone bridges. The arches were formed by wind, water, and frost erosion over thousands of years. Foot trails lead to some of the park's most interesting features.

A number of Bureau of Land Management–administered campgrounds are in nearby areas. Write to the Bureau of Land Management, Utah State Office, P.O. Box 11505, Salt Lake City 84111, for their free pamphlet, *BLM-Developed Recreation Sites in Utah.*

Of all the national parks here, Bryce Canyon National Park is probably

the best suited to day hikers. The park is a series of deep crevices in 12 huge natural amphitheaters slicing down a thousand feet through many layers of pink and white limestone. Situated on an 8,000–9,000 foot plateau in southwestern Utah, the park encompasses hundreds of geological formations which range in appearance from the ruins of ancient temples to the forms of men marching across the great plateau. Many trails wind throughout, and horses are available for riding trips. This small park (56.3 square miles in central Utah, 11 miles east of Torrey via State Route 24) includes huge natural arches, petrified forests, and beautiful pinnacles and gorges of colorful rock. The park is named for huge rock formations with white-capped domes resembling the nation's capitol. The domes are part of a hundred-mile bulge in the earth's crust containing eroded pockets that catch thousands of gallons of water each rainfall.

Zion National Park lies deep in southwestern Utah, covering over 229 square miles of canyon country. The park includes a huge main canyon and several side gorges sliced out of a high plateau by an ancient river. Colorful sheer rock walls create some of the most spectacular natural beauty of the southern-Utah-northern-Arizona landscape. Some of the major formations include the Great White Throne, Angels Landing, Cathedral Mountain, and the Pulpit, all easily visible from the roadside. Horseback and foot trails also wind through this rocky wonderland.

Star Route 15, branching off Interstate 15 north of the Arizona border, winds through Zion. For more information on the park, write: Superintendent, Zion National Park, Springdale 84767.

Family vacation accommodations are provided by *Bryce Canyon Lodge* and *Zion Lodge*, both Box 400, Cedar City 84720 (phone toll-free for reservations: 800–662–4246). Rustic accommodations are also offered by *Chateau Meadeau View Lodge*, Box 356, Cedar City 84720. Vacation accommodations in Capitol Reef National Monument are provided by *Sleeping Rainbow Guest Ranch* and *Capitol Reef Lodge*, both Torrey 84775.

Full-color U.S. Geological Survey maps are available for the following national parks: *Bryce Canyon National Park Map* (either contour or

shaded-relief edition, scale of ½ mile to 1 inch, $2); *Cedar Breaks National Monument*, scale 4 inches to 1 mile, $1.25); *Zion National Park Map*, Kolob Section, scale of 2 miles to 1 inch, also published in a shaded-relief edition, $2).

Recreation & Wildlife Maps

The Bureau of Land Management has published a series of free maps detailing recreation lands and wildlife in the state. The maps, entitled *Recreation and Wildlife on BLM Lands*, show in full color BLM-administered land, state land, national forests and parks, Indian reservations, wildlife refuges, and private lands in the respective regions of the state. The maps also show elevation and mark all-weather roads, seasonal roads, four-wheel-drive roads, trails, and recreation sites and campgrounds, on a scale of 4 miles to 1 inch. On the reverse side of the large map are a number of smaller maps, which delineate the foraging and nesting areas of the region's wildlife. Major features of each section of the state, along with short descriptions of points of interest, are included. The maps may be ordered from: Bureau of Land Management, 125 South State St. Salt Lake City 84114.

The regional *Utah Multipurpose Maps*, available from the Utah Travel Council, are another valuable resource for visitors to the state. This series of eight regional map/guides includes descriptions of many outdoor recreational centers and points of interest in each of the regions, which are keyed on the map. The maps, on a scale of 4 inches to 1 mile, mark private land, Indian reservations, public lands, state lands, national parks and monuments, national forests, primitive areas, national recreation areas, and military reservations. Among the points of interest keyed on the map are picnic areas, campsites, historical sites, view points, ruins, geological formations, rock-hounding areas, golf courses, boat launch sites, marinas, ski areas, snowmobile trails, game reserves, and bird refuges. The map/guides also contain campground guides, which describe the size, location, and recreational opportunities at public campsites in each region. Order the maps from: Utah Travel Council, Council Hall, Salt Lake City 84114.

Ski Touring & Snowshoeing

The mountains and canyons of Utah sparkle with soft powdery snow during the winter months, and there are many ways to explore them. For cross-country skiers, there are miles of trails. *Utah Multipurpose Map No. 5, Southwestern Utah*, describes and marks a number of trails and is available free from: Utah Travel Council, Council Hall, Salt Lake City 84114. In addition, many of the ski resorts named above have trails for cross-country skiers. To arrange a ski vacation to suit your own needs, whether they be cross-country or downhill, write: Utah Ski Reservation Center, Council Hall, Capitol Hill, Salt Lake City 84114. *Utah Multipurpose Maps* of the various regions of the state (available free at the address above) describe and mark ski trails and resorts. The maps also give detailed information on snowshoeing in the state and mark snowshoe trails and areas. The most complete guide to skiing in the state, titled *Ski Utah* and including detailed descriptions of resorts, accommodations, and access to ski areas, is available free from the Ski Reservation Center at the address above.

First-class accommodations, nordic instruction, and trails are available at *Mount Majestic Lodge*, Brighton Ski Bowl, Brighton 84121 (phone: 801–359–3283); *Snowbird*, c/o Information Director, Snowbird Corp., Snowbird 84070 (Phone: 801–742–2222); *White Pine Lodge & Touring Center*, 463 W. 200 South, Heber City 84032 (phone: 801–654–3300). Backcountry skiing in the Wasatch National Forest is provided by *Wasatch Touring Company*, 779 E. 3rd St. S., Salt Lake City 84111 (801–359–9361).

Wild & Scenic River Maps

Beautiful, professional scroll maps showing every bend, island, rapid, fall, campsite, and contour of the *Green River* ($4, showing Red Canyon, Canyon of Lodore, Whirlpool Canyon, Split Mountain Canyon, Desolation Canyon, and Gray Canyon); *Colorado River* ($3, Gore Canyon to Grand Junction); *Westwater Canyon* ($3); *Cataract Canyon* ($3); *Yampa River* ($2.50); *Dolores River* ($3.50); *San Juan River* ($2.25); *Lake Powell* ($5); and *Flaming Gorge* ($3) are available from Western Whitewater Co., Star Rt. 13, Heber City 84032. These maps, painstakingly produced by riverman Leslie Jones, include fascinating historical annotations, difficulty ratings, and river-running and scouting advice. Each scroll map comes with a transparent, watertight case.

Wilderness Outfitters & Guides

Guides for the entire state include *Dave Peterson*, RFD 1, Morgan 84050, and *Martin W. Kordas, Jr.*, Diamond Hitch Outfitters, 550 North St. Ogden 84404; both are guides for hunting trips in the Promontory Mountains, Bear River Refuge, and adjacent marshes for big game and waterfowl. For more information write to *Promontory Club & Guide Service*, 616 West 5th North, Brigham City 84302. *Piute Creek Outfitters*, 2490 South 2300 East, Salt Lake City 84109, conducts camping and pack trips and hunting expeditions, plans ski tours, and rents campsites, shelters, and burros in High Uintas in northeastern Utah. Another guide operation in the area is the *Defa Dude Ranch*, Hanna 84031, which offers fishing, hiking, camping, and pack trips in the Grandaddy Lakes Basin and North Fork Duchesne River country.

Pack trips into the Uinta Primitive Area are conducted by *Western Outfitters & Guides*, 325 South Third East, Salt Lake City 84111. *Lloyd & Bill Branch* of the U-Bar Ranch offer fishing, hunting, and pack trips in the Uinta Mountains. Write to Neola 84053 during the winter. *Piute Creek Outfitters*, at the address listed above, also guides trips in this area. In the High Uintas, *Bull Canyon Guides* offers fishing float trips on the Green River and big-game hunting expeditions. Write to them at 116 Fourth Avenue, Dutch John 84023.

In central Utah, *Del Strickland* rents boats and cabins and sells supplies to visitors to the Heber Valley. His address is 3701 South 7200 West, Magna 84044. *John H. Gledhill*, Marysvale 84750, guides fishing, hunting, and pack trips in this part of the state. In the Beaver Mountains, *Robert Schramm* offers fishing and hunting, cabins, and supplies. His address is Beaver 84713. *Mat & Hazel Houston*, Box 445, Panguitch 84759, guide hunting, fishing, and pack trips and offer lodging.

In the south, *Milt Holt* guides mountain lion hunting expeditions and offers accommodations. Contact him at Gunlock 84733. In the Lake Powell area, *Earl Johnson* offers jeep and boat tours, fishing tours, and accommodations and supplies. His address is *Canyon Tours*, Box 1597, Page, AZ 86040.

The Eastern Utah Landowners Association offers guide service in the southeastern part of the state and rents camps and lodging during the summer. Contact *Funnon Shimmin*, 711 North Fifth East, Price 84501. *Waldo Wilcox* is another hunting guide in this area who has lodgings. Write to: Box 337, Green River 84525. *Joe L. Lemon*, Box 910, Moab 84532, is a deer hunting and fishing guide in the area. *Tag-A-Long Tours*, directed by Mitchell M. Williams, 452 North Main Street, P.O. Box 1206, Moab 84532, guides hunting and fishing tours and special interest backcountry outfitting. Pete Steele of *Horse-*

head Pack Trips guides pack trips into Canyonlands National Park, Grand Gulch, and Dark Canyon. His address is P.O. Box 974–U, Monticello 84535. *Kent Frost* is another guide for the Canyonlands country. Write to: 295 Blue Mountain Drive, Monticello 84535. *Eugene D. Foushee* gives geologist-naturalist guided trips into southeastern Utah's red-rock canyon country. Write to him at: Bluff 84512. At Lake Powell, Jerry Sampson, *Lake Powell Ferry Service*, Blanding 84511, offers fishing and boating trips, trailer accommodations, and supplies. For information on river expeditions and outfitters, see "Wildwater Expeditions."

Several Utah guides and outfitters operate within the national park, monument, and recreation areas. In Bryce Canyon National Park, *Bryce-Zion Trail Rides*, P.O. Box 368, Fredonia, AZ 86022, offers saddle and pack animal services. Canyonlands National Park is served by *Canyonlands Tours*, 295 Blue Mountain, Monticello 84535, offering motor vehicle tours and hiking trips; *Horsehead Pack Trips*, P.O. Box 974, Monticello 84535; and *Peace & Quiet Inc.*, P.O. Box 15742, Salt Lake City 84115; for hiking trips; and four-wheel jeep tours in Capitol Reef National Monument are provided by *Rim Rock Motel & Tours*, Torrey 84775, and *Sleeping Rainbow Tours*, Torrey 84775. In Zion National Park, *Thomas Brereton*, P.O. Box 277, Springdale 84767, provides guided hiking trips and *Jack H. Church*, Tropic 84767 offers saddle and pack animal services.

Wildwater Expeditions

The Colorado and Green rivers join forces in the heart of Utah to create some of the most breathtaking and challenging white-water runs in the country. Elsewhere, the Green and the Colorado flow more peacefully through the state's backcountry. In all, Utah's rivers include more than 400 miles of floatable waterways. Unless you are a highly skilled white-water runner, the best and safest way to explore Utah's wildwaters is to hire an experienced guide or to join an expedition organized by knowledgeable outfitters. Detailed information on professional wild-river guides may be obtained by writing: *Western River Guides Association*, 904 Denver St., Salt Lake City 84111.

Western River Expeditions offer river raft trips in wilderness areas including Canyonlands National Park and Dinosaur National Monument. For information write: Jack L. Currey, *Western River Expeditions, Inc.*, P.O. Box 6339, Salt Lake City 84106. *Hatch River Expeditions* leads trips in the same areas. Write to them at 411 East Second North, Vernal 84078. *Tag-Along Tours*, led by Mitch Williams, 452 North Main, Moab 84532, offers land and river combination tours in the wilderness areas of the Green and the Colorado. *Holiday River Expeditions* also offers a variety of river expeditions through such Green and Colorado wildwater areas as Desolation Canyon of the Green River Wilderness and the Granite Canyon of the Westwater Wilderness. For information write: Holiday River Expeditions Inc., 519 Malibu Drive, Salt Lake City 84107.

Outlaw Trails, based in the slick-rock country of southeastern Utah, also guides land and water expeditions through the wilderness river areas of the state. Their address is: P.O. Box 336, Green River 84525. *Moki Mac River Expeditions* leads several wild-river tours on the Green and Colorado. Write to 6829 Bella Vista Drive, Salt Lake City 84121, for more information.

Fastwater Expeditions guide tours through the Green River Wilderness, and may be contacted at P.O. Box 365, Boulder City, NV 89005. *Canyonlands Expeditions, Inc.*, specialize in guiding visitors through the waters of the Green and Colorado in Canyonlands National Park. Write to them at P.O. Box O, Kanab 84741. The *American River Touring Association* also offers raft expeditions on

the Green and Colorado. Their address is 1016 Jackson Street, Oakland, CA 94607.

White-water trips in the Canyonlands, Desolation, and Dinosaur areas are provided by several other well-established professional guide and outfitting services. For free literature, rates, and detailed information, write: *Colorado River & Trail Expeditions*, 1449 E. 30th S., Salt Lake City 84106; *Harris Boat Trips*, P.O. Box 521, Kanab 84741; *North American River Expeditions*, P.O. Box 1107, Moab 84532; *San Juan Expeditions*, P.O. Box 1206, Moab 84532; *Tour West*, P.O. Box 333, Orem 84057; *World Wide Expeditions*, 445 Scott Avenue, Salt Lake City 84115; *Cross Tours & Exploration*, 274 W. 1400 S., Orem 84057; *Mountain River Guides*, 3325 Fowler Ave., Ogden 84403; *Travel Institute*, 714 Ninth Avenue, Salt Lake City 84103.

Some of these outfitters provide all necessary equipment and supplies for your expedition. Others may require that you bring some of your own gear. Different outfitters emphasize different aspects of the trip, such as camping, geological and natural history study, or white-water thrills. The information you order from the individual guides will help you make your choice.

Ashley National Forest & Red Canyon of the Green

Ashley National Forest Topo Maps

U.S. Geological Survey 1:250,000 scale overview maps: Price, Salt Lake City, Vernal.

Red Canyon of the Green Blue-Ribbon Trout Waters

U.S. Geological Survey large-scale maps: Flaming Gorge, Dutch John, Clay Basin, Warren Draw, Swallow Canyon.

Sheep Creek Geological Area

U.S. Geological Survey large-scale topographic maps: Phil Pico Mountain, Jensen Butte, Manila.

Ashley National Forest covers 1,398,986 acres in northeastern Utah and southwestern Wyoming, ranging from the heights of the majestic Uintas to the brilliance of the Green River's Flaming Gorge. The forest is named after Gen. William H. Ashley, who led parties of fur traders into Utah territory in 1825. He traveled down the Green River, then circled the Uintas on his way to a rendezvous up Henrys Fork. The alpine lakes of the high country reflect the beauty of Utah's highest mountain, Kings Peak (13,498 ft.). Below the timberline lie 650,000 acres of virgin timber, including lodgepole and ponderosa pine, Engelmann spruce, and Douglas fir. The forest abounds in big game, especially mule deer and elk. Black bear, moose, and antelope also roam the slopes, and a few Rocky Mountain bighorn sheep can be found. Game birds of the high country include the sage, ruffed, and blue grouse. At lower elevations are the California quail and chukar partridge.

Some of the best fishing in the state is found in the lakes of the High Uintas Primitive Area, straddling both the Ashley and Wasatch (q.v.) national forests. The snowfields and spectacular alpine lake basins of these high peaks give birth to four of Utah's major rivers: the Duchesne, Provo, Weber, and Bear. Most of the wilderness lakes, such as those clustered at the headwaters of Ashley Creek, Burnt Fork Creek, Sheep Creek, Yellowstone River, Carter Creek, and Whiterocks River, have been stocked by plane with rainbow, native or cutthroat, brown, and brook trout and Montana grayling. (For fishing and camping information on the alpine lakes, see "Fishing & Hunting in Utah" in the "Encyclopedia" section.) An invaluable guide for both fishermen and backpackers, *High Uinta Trails* ($3, 132 pages) may be obtained by mail from Wasatch Publishers, Inc., 4647 Idlewild Rd., Salt Lake City 84117.

Utes and Shoshones once roamed this land. In July 1825, the first American fur trappers' rendezvous of the Old West took place here on the Henrys Fork near Flaming Gorge. About a thousand trappers, most of them Indians organized by General Ashley, traded and celebrated. The northeastern section of the forest, including the Sheep Creek Geological Area and Flaming Gorge, bears testimony to many geological ages and events. The Sheep Creek Area has massive, colorful walls and spires of rock. The Green River enters the forest in its brilliant Red Canyon. The Bureau of Reclamation's Flaming Gorge Dam has created a 66-mile reservoir among these canyons. Float trips are popular in the Green River Corridor below the dam.

In 1869, Maj. John Wesley Powell led an expedition down the Green through the Red Canyon and the present-day Dinosaur National Monument, which lies due east of the Ashley Forest. The major, who had lost his right arm in the Battle of Shiloh, narrowly escaped death while climbing the cliffs of Green River Canyon. He left a vivid

UTAH TRAVEL & RECREATION GUIDE

description of the river from the summit on the east side of Split Mountain Canyon: "We are standing three thousand feet above its waters, which are troubled with billows, and white with foam. Its walls are set with crags and peaks, and buttressed towers, and overhanging domes. Turning to the right, the park is below us, with its island groves reflected by the deep, quiet water. Rich meadows stretch out on either hand to the verge of a sloping plain that comes down from the distant mountains. These plains are of almost naked rocks, in strange contrast to the meadows; blue and lilac colored rocks, buff and pink, vermillion and brown, and all these colors clear and bright. A dozen little creeks, dry the greater part of the year, run down through the half circle of exposed formations, radiating from the islands-center to the rim of the basin. Each creek has its system of side streams, and each side stream has its system of laterals, and again, these are divided, so that this outstretched slope of rock is elaborately embossed. Beds of different colored formations run in parallel bands on either side. The perspective, modified by the undulations, gives the bands a waved appearance, and the high colors gleam in the midday sun with the luster of satin. We are tempted to call this Rainbow Park. Away beyond these beds are the Uinta and Wasatch Mountains, with their pine forests and snow fields and naked peaks. Now we turn to the right, and look up Whirlpool Canyon, a deep gorge with a river in the bottom—a gloomy chasm, where mad waves roar; but, at this distance and altitude, the river is but a rippling brook, and the chasm a narrow cleft. The top of the mountain on which we stand is a broad grassy table, and a herd of deer is feeding in the distance. Walking over to the southeast, we look down into the valley of White River, and beyond that see the far distant Rocky Mountains, in mellow, perspective haze, through which snow fields shine."

Campsites are scattered over the entire forest area. The *Ashley National Forest Map* (50¢) includes a chart which keys the location of each and its facilities. The map, on a scale of 6 miles to 1 inch, shows all roads and highways, trails, ranger stations, recreation sites, and primitive areas. Write to: Forest Service, Ashley National Forest, Vernal 84078.

Lodging, guide service, and pack trips to the head of Henrys Fork and Painter's Basin in the High Uintas are provided by *U Bar Ranch*, Box 254, Neola 84503 (winter: Box 314, Myton 84052). Elsewhere in the High Uintas Primitive Area lodging and guide service is provided by

Spirit Lake Lodge, Manila 84046 (Sheep Creek Area). See "Wasatch National Forest & High Uintas Primitive Area" for additional listings.

Access & Outfitting Centers

The Ashley National Forest and Green River country is reached by auto on U.S. Highway 40 and Utah Highways 44 and 330. Lodging, guides, supplies, and outfitters are available at the towns of Vernal, Whiterocks, Bridgeport, Dutch John, Duchesne and Manila.

Cache National Forest

Cache National Forest Topo Maps

U.S. Geological Survey 1:250,000 scale overview maps: Brigham City, Ogden, Preston.

Bear River Range Mountains

U.S. Geological Survey large-scale topographic maps: Porcupine Reservoir, Hardware Ranch, Logan Peak, Mount Elmer, Boulder Mountain, Temple Peak, Tony Grove Creek, Naomi Peak.

Blacksmith Fork River

U.S. Geological Survey large-scale maps: Red Spur Mountain, Boulder Mountain, Hardware Ranch, Porcupine Reservoir, Logan Peak, Paradise, Logan.

Logan River

U.S. Geological Survey large-scale maps: Logan, Logan Peak, Mount Elmer, Temple Peak, Tony Grove Creek.

This 679,000-acre tract straddles the boundary between Utah and Idaho and extends from the Weber River on the south to Soda Springs on the north. The first white men to visit the region, in 1824, were American beaver trappers who *cached*, or hid, their furs in present Cache Valley. The trappers used the area as their winter quarters to take advantage of the bison and other game in "Willow Valley," as they called it. Major features of the forest include the Bear River Range, Wellsville Range, Logan River, Dingle Swamp, and Bear Lake. The Bear River Range is a northern extension of the Wasatch Mountains. The Bear River rises southeast of the forest in the Uinta Mountains, circles around into Idaho, flows down along the western side of the Bear River Mountains, and empties into Great Salt Lake. Among the fine trout streams and lakes in the forest are Pineview Reservoir, White Pine and Deep lakes, and the Blacksmith Fork, well known for its brown trout. The Logan River, southwest of Bear Lake, has produced a record 27-pound brown trout. A good number of 10–20 pound browns are caught here each year. Big game in the forest includes elk, mule deer, and black bear. Many nongame species, including bobcat, cougar, mink, and fox, add to the beauty of the wildlife of the area.

Logan Canyon between Logan and Bear Lake on Highway 89 is a mile-deep chasm carved by the ceaseless force of the Logan River, named for Ephraim Logan, an early trapper. It is most spectacular in the fall, when the brilliant colors of changing leaves add to the hues of the canyon itself. Minnetonka Cave in St. Charles Canyon 8 miles west of St. Charles, Idaho, extends about 2,200 feet into the limestone mountain. Guided tours into its beautiful stalactite and stalagmite formations are conducted from June to September. At Hardware Ranch in Blacksmith Fork Canyon, a herd of elk is fed each winter. Boating and fishing are popular at Pineview Reservoir.

Cache Trails ($1.50; 96 pages), a useful guide by Mel Davis to the trails in Cache Valley—including the Wellsville Mountains, Logan Peak area, Mount Naomi area, and Highline Trail area—is available

by mail from: Wasatch Publishers, Inc., 4647 Idlewild Rd., Salt Lake City 84117.

Campgrounds and overnight accommodations are available at the larger towns surrounding the forest, including Garden City (6 motels and hotels); Logan (8 motels and hotels, 3 trailer parks, 1 resort); Brigham City (9 motels, 2 trailer parks, nearby camping facilities); and Ogden (12 motels, numerous hotels and motor hotels, 6 trailer parks). For specific information describing the available accommodations, write to the Utah Innkeepers' Association, Newhouse Hotel, 4th South at Main St., Salt Lake City 84101.

There are numerous campsites throughout the forest. *Cache National Forest Map* (50¢), published by the forest administrators, describes each of the camping sites. The map, on a scale of 4 miles to 1 inch, marks roads, trails, ranger stations, lakes, and streams. The map and brochure are available from: Forest Supervisor's Office, 427 North Sixth Avenue, P.O. Box 4189, Pocatello, ID 83201.

Access & Outfitting Centers

The forest is reached by Interstate 80N off Interstate 80, north of Coalville, or by driving north on Interstate 15 from Salt Lake City. Interstate 80N can also be taken south into the forest area from Idaho. Lodging, guides, supplies, and outfitters are available at Lewiston, Smithfield, Logan, Garden City, Laketown, Randolph, Woodruff, Huntsville, Devils Slide, Ogden, Wasatch, Paradise, and Brigham City.

Dixie National Forest & High-country Lakes

Dixie National Forest Topo Maps

U.S. Geological Survey 1:250,000 scale overview maps: Cedar City, Escalante, Richfield, Salina.

Aquarius Plateau High Lakes Country

U.S. Geological Survey large-scale maps: Rogers Pea, Posy Lake, Big Lake, Jacobs Reservoir, Loa N.E., Grover.

Escalante Mountains High Lakes Country

U.S. Geological Survey large-scale maps: Sweetwater Creek, Grass Lakes, Griffin Point, Barker Reservoir, Antimony, Pollywog Lake.

Thousand Lake Mountain High Country

U.S. Geological Survey large-scale maps: Loa N.E., Torrey.

This 2 million-acre reserve, known as the "Land of the Rainbow Canyons," straddles the Divide between the Great Basin and the Colorado River in southern Utah. The land varies from mountains of over 11,000 feet to broad mesa and rolling hills to steep-walled gorges. Many trails and forest roads wind through green high-country forests and amber hills along the Markagunt, Paunsaugunt, and Aquarius plateaus. The Aquarius Plateau, also known as Boulder Mountain, is one of the largest and highest timbered plateaus in America. It is dotted with hundreds of trout-bearing alpine lakes at altitudes of 10,000–11,000 feet. A 400–800 foot rim of lava rock around the edge of the plateau separates the lakes on the top from those just under the rim. Many of the remote wilderness lakes, surrounded by high alpine tundra meadows and beaver flows, have been aerial stocked with rainbow, brook, and cutthroat trout and a few grayling. The lakes are reached by foot or packhorse and provide excellent wilderness base camps. *The Lakes of the Aquarius Plateau Guide*, available for 50¢ from the Utah Division of Wildlife Resources, 1596 W. North Temple, Salt Lake City 84116, describes access, lakes, and fish species present for the West Escalante Slope, North Creek Lakes, Griffin

Top, South and East Boulder Slopes, Boulder Top, North Boulder Slope, Solomon Basin, and Thousand Lake Mountain.

Major features of the area include the Escalante River (which later empties into Lake Powell), the Antelope Range, Harmony Mountains, Pine Valley Mountains, Beaver Dam Mountains, Santa Clara River, Hurricane Cliffs, Sevier River, Navajo Lake, Cedar Breaks, Henry Mountains, and the Virgin River.

Panguitch Lake, which fills a volcanic basin a mile long and three-quarters of a mile wide, has excellent fishing for rainbows and kokanee salmon. The wilderness hiker will find good fly-fishing along the park-like Duck Creek and Navajo and Aspen-Mirror lakes. The Escalante has good cutthroat, and the Santa Clara has some big rainbows and brown trout.

The forest is known for its excellent mule deer hunting. Hunters usually find muleys high in the mountains during Indian summer, especially on cool northern slopes, but as cold weather sets in the deer move further down to the warmer slopes. In late fall it is usually best to hunt lowland flats, canyons, and draws, and to scan oak, cedar, and piñon stands. Where cover is sparse, look for deer on the shady north slopes of depressions or shady ridges.

Other animals of the forest include black bear, cougar, bobcat, and coyote. Ruffed and blue grouse, chukar partridge, and wild turkey are among the game birds of the area.

The forest meadows are carpeted with brilliant wildflowers, grass, shrubs, and trees during the warmer months. Before white men walked here, these lands were the home of the Piute Indians and of a mysterious group archaeologists refer to as the Mesa Verde branch of the Anasazi culture. For protection from marauding tribes and the elements, the Mesa Verde people built cliff dwellings high on the canyon walls of the Colorado tributaries. The people vanished long before the white man arrived, but their dwellings are still visible from the road near Escalante.

The *Dixie National Forest Map* is available for 50¢ from: Forest Supervisor, Dixie National Forest, Cedar City 84720. The map, on a scale of 4 miles to 1 inch, marks roads and highways, trails, ranger stations, streams, and improved recreation areas. A chart gives the size and available facilities of the campgrounds within the forest. Two detailed trail guides describing flora and fauna, geological features, and other points of interest along the trails are also available from the Forest Supervisor's address. The guides, *Bristlecone Pine Trail* and *Lost Hunter Trail* are free. The Forest Service also publishes a free guide to the flowers of the forest, *How to Know Wildflowers Near Your Camp*, which is available at the same address.

Vacation lodging, guide service, and pack trips are provided by *Panguitch Lake Resort, Rustic Lodge, Lake View Resort, Houston Ranch,* and *Beaver Dam Lodge,* all Panguitch 84759.

Access & Outfitting Centers

To reach the forest, drive east on State Rt. 14 from Cedar City, north on U.S. Highway 89 from Kanab, or dip south on U.S. 89 from Interstate 70 at Salina. Lodging, supplies, and guides are available at St. George, Enterprise, Cedar City, Panguitch, Escalante, Beaver, Boulder, Antimony, and Teasdale.

Fishlake National Forest

Fishlake National Forest Topo Maps

U.S. Geological Survey 1:250,000 scale overview maps: Delta, Richfield, Price, Salina.

Fish Lake Hightops

U.S. Geological Survey large-scale maps: Burrville, Fish Lake, Mount Terrill, Hilgard Mountain.

This 1.5 million-acre reserve is located in central Utah at the southern end of the Great Salt Lake Basin. It embraces three longitudinal strips of the High Utah Plateau, including part of the Wasatch, Aquarius, Sevier, and Tushar plateaus and all of the Fish Lake and Pavant plateaus. The forest is named after the beautiful Fish Lake, the state's largest natural freshwater lake, nestled beneath the Fish Lake Hightops. Glacial deposits formed the lake's basin and dammed its waters. Fish are unusually active in the icy waters of the 8,800-foot-high lake. Among them are lunker rainbow and Mackinaw trout ranging in size from 1 to 35 pounds.

The tops of the plateaus are generally small, either flat or rolling, and the sides slope gently to deep valleys carved by radiating canyons. The plateaus rise from 5,500-foot valleys to their 10,000-foot summits. Backpackers will find the mountain trails up to the Fish Lake Hightops challenging. They will also find good fishing in the lakes of the heavily wooded Aquarius Plateau. The top of this scenic tableland, with an area of 49 square miles, is crowned with dense stands of aspens and evergreens. The Aquarius is a remnant of a vast plateau that once extended east and south of the present-day Green and Colorado rivers, attaining, in prehistoric times, heights of nearly a mile above those of today. Here the wilderness traveler enters a land of wide, sage-silvered deserts, colossal mesas, pinnacles and spires that spring from the sand, and floorlike areas jumbled with vividly colored rocks. Other good fishing streams are the Beaver and Fremont rivers, and the Clear, Fish, Monroe, Salina, Gooseberry, and Seven Mile creeks, all of which hold rainbows and browns.

The forest is also known for its large herds of mule deer. Black bear and mountain lion roam the area, and a small herd of elk flourishes on the Fish Lake Plateau. Upland game includes sage, ruffed, and blue grouse. Limited numbers of waterfowl nest among the lakes and streams.

The Forest Service publishes a *Fishlake National Forest Map* (50¢), which describes its major features, recreational opportunities, and wildlife in some detail. The map, on a scale of 4 miles to 1 inch, marks trails, roads and highways, ranger stations, lakes and streams, and improved recreation sites. A chart in the guide gives the sites, camping units available, facilities, and recreational opportunities at each. Write: Supervisor, Fishlake National Forest, Richfield 84701.

Rustic vacation accommodations and guided pack trips are provided by *Fish Lake Lodge, Lakeside Resort,* and *Bowery Haven Resort,* all Richfield 84701.

Access & Outfitting Centers

The forest is easily accessible from the east by way of Interstate 70; from the south, take U.S. 91 and Interstate 15 north. Lodging, meals, supplies, guides, and outfitters are available at Beaver, Monroe, Richfield, Torrey, Salina, Redmond, Ephraim, and Gunnison.

Manti–La Sal National Forest & the Colorado River

Manti–La Sal National Forest Topo Maps

U.S. Geological Survey 1:250,000 scale overview maps: Cortez, Moab, Price.

Colorado River

U.S. Geological Survey large-scale maps: Brown's Rim, Castle Valley, Cisco, Coates Creek, Hatch Point, Lake Canyon, Mancos Mesa, Moab, Mount Ellsworth, Mouth of Dark Canyon, Navajo Mountain, Orange Cliffs, the Needles, the Rincon, Upheaval Dome, Westwater S.E., Westwater S.W.

This forest is a 1¼ million-acre tract in the heart of Utah, surrounding the La Sal and Abajo mountains. The La Sal Mountains are the second-highest range in the state, roughly 15 miles long and 6 miles wide, with high mesas radiating from the main mass covering a much larger area. Mount Peale, the highest peak, has an elevation of 13,089 feet. Green forests of pine, fir, and aspen cover the higher slopes while cedar, scrub oak, and sagebrush grow at lower elevations. Above all, this is big-game country, although there is also some good fishing. Game animals of the area include elk (especially around the Price area), black bear, blacktail deer, bobcat, cougar, and blue, ruffed, and sage grouse. Wild turkey have been introduced to the Moab and Monticello ranger districts, and the mourning dove is the most common game bird, consequently receiving the most pressure. Backpackers and hikers will enjoy the Narrows Trail, which winds for 8 miles from Pinchot Campground to Skyline Drive in the Gunnison Valley, past many beaver dams. Other backcountry trails include Dry Creek, Oak Creek, Canal Canyon, Black-Reeder Canyon, Bear Creek, Ferron Canyon, and Tie Fork to Pole Canyon trails.

To the west of the forest, the silt-laden Colorado River, which rises near the Continental Divide in Rocky Mountain National Park, Colo., flows through the awesome Upper Grand Canyon, where the face of the earth breaks away into a 3,000-foot chasm, offering perhaps the most sensational canyon panorama in Utah. At Dead Horse Point, south of Moab, the hiker is able to overlook 5,000 square miles of the red and rugged Colorado Plateau. This majestic view sweeps east to the La Sal Mountains, south to the Abajo Mountains, southwest to the Henry Mountains, west to the Aquarius Plateau, and down into a tremendous gorge, at the bottom of which, in a canyon within a canyon, the Colorado flows through a maze of buttes and mesas. Aeons ago, the Colorado was a wide, shallow stream flowing aimlessly across the flat and unscarred Colorado Plateau. As the surrounding land uplifted, the river cut deeper and deeper into the red sandstone.

Today, the river roars between steplike walls some 3,000 feet below the surface of the plateau.

Near Moab is the famous *Petroglyph of the Mastodon*, known as the "riddle of the Colorado." The "mastodon" is an ancient drawing chipped in red sandstone, measuring 42 inches from trunk to rump. The petroglyph was discovered in 1924, but little information regarding the strange carving was available until 1933, when Dr. Laurence M. Gould, a noted geologist-geographer on Byrd's first Antarctic Expedition, visited and photographed it. The weathering of the sandstone in which the drawing is carved proves that it is very old, as does the fact that it is located 300 feet above the present riverbed—far above other petroglyphs of lesser age along the Colorado. If it is true that early man carved only images of what he actually saw, the petroglyph was carved some 30,000 years ago after the mastodon became extinct. Or perhaps the drawing proves that a group of mastodons survived in isolation to a much later age.

The Manti-La Sal National Forest is divided into two portions. The La Sal Division lies half a day's drive to the north of the main portion, the Manti. In both sections, the forest is a place of contrast. The orange, buff, and red sandstones of the cliffs and canyons stand out against the green patches of ponderosa pine, spruce, and fir. Abajo Peak, in the Manti Forest Division, provides a sweeping panorama of the Colorado Plateau broken eastward only by the San Miguel and La Plata mountains, southward by Black Mesa, westward by the Kaiparowits and Aquarius plateaus, and northward by the Book Cliffs.

The major features shown on the *Manti–La Sal National Forest Map* (50¢) include Scofield Reservoir, Robertson Pasture, Chipean Rocks, Mount Linnaeus, Babylon Pasture, Bear Ears, Monticello Lake, Mount Mellentthin, and Mount Tukuhnikivatz. This map and brochure is available from: Manti–La Sal National Forest Supervisor, 350 East Main Street, Price 84501. The map, on a scale of 4 miles to 1 inch, shows roads, highways, trails, ranger stations, and improved recreational campsites. A chart on the map describes the location, size, and facilities at the campgrounds within the forest.

Vacation accommodations and services are provided by the rustic *Blue Mountain Ranch*, Box 758, Monticello 84535 and *Tavaputs Plateau Ranch*, Box 786, Price 84501.

Access & Outfitting Centers

The Manti section of the forest is accessible by taking U.S. 163 south from Interstate 70. Follow U.S. 163 south past the turnoff to the Manti section to reach the La Sal section of the forest. Lodging, supplies, big-game hunting guides, packers, and outfitters are available at Blanding, Monticello, La Sal, Paradox, and Moab.

Uinta National Forest

Uinta National Forest Topo Maps

U.S. Geological Survey 1:250,000 scale overview maps: Price, Salt Lake City.

Reaching from the Provo River of north central Utah south to Nephi, this forest has 780,000 acres of good climbing, hunting, and fishing. Mule deer and elk are the biggest of the game, and trout is king among fish. The Provo River has good trout fishing, and below the dam at Heber is some of the best brown trout fishing in the state. Strawberry Reservoir, up Daniels Canyon, is well known for rainbow and record cutthroat up to 28 pounds. Backcountry lovers will find good climbing among the snowcapped mountains and excellent fishing in the high lakes and icy streams. The forest is known for its alpine wilderness and

the Sheeprock Mountains, Utah Lake, Payson Lakes, San Pitch Mountains, Strawberry River, and Deer Creek Reservoir.

More than 50 campsites and picnic areas, including over 1,100 family units, are available. Camping is permitted only in designated areas. For a good map of the region and a guide to the available campsites and recreational facilities in the forest, write to the Utah Travel Council, Council Hall, Salt Lake City 84114, for the free *Utah Multipurpose Map No. 3.*

To obtain a copy of the *Uinta National Forest Map* (50¢) and detailed fishing, hunting, and camping info, write: Forest Supervisor, Uinta National Forest, 290 North University Ave., Box 1428, Provo 84601.

Access & Outfitting Centers

The forest is easily accessible by way of U.S. 15 south from Salt Lake City. Lodging, supplies, guides, and outfitters are available at Orem, Provo, Springville, Pleasant Grove, and Spanish Fork.

Wasatch National Forest & High Uintas Primitive Area

Wasatch National Forest Topo Maps

U.S. Geological Survey 1:250,000 scale overview maps: Delta, Ogden, Salt Lake City, Tooele.

Henrys Fork of the Green High Country

U.S. Geological Survey large-scale maps: Mount Powell, Bridger Lake, Gilbert Peak.

High Uintas Primitive Area

U.S. Geological Survey large-scale topographic maps: Mirror Lake, Whitney Reservoir, Iron Mine Mountain, Hayden Peak, Christmas Meadows, Red Knob, Explorer Peak, Two Rose Pass, Kidney Lake, Oweep Creek, Mount Lovenia, Lake Fork Mountain, Garfield Basin, Mount Powell, Kings Peak, Mount Emmons, Burnt Mill Spring, Hellers Lake, Bollie Lake, Fox Lake, Chepeta Lake, Rasmussen Lakes, Whiterocks Lake, Paradise Park, Ice Cave Peak. The Primitive Area is also shown on U.S. Geological Survey 1:250,000 scale Salt Lake City and Vernal maps.

The Piute and Ute Indians once lived in the mountains and semidesert valleys of this million-acre forest, and they gave it its name, which means "high mountain pass." The rugged, scenic country of the Uinta Mountains ranges from 4,000 feet to 13,528 feet at Kings Peak, the highest point in Utah. The canyons of the Wasatch-Uinta region have echoed over the years to the passage of Indians, trappers, explorers, Pacific emigrants, Mormon pioneers, wagon freighters, California gold seekers, Pony Express riders, Overland Stage drivers, and travelers of every description. Hunting and fishing are excellent in this vast region dotted and laced by hundreds of lakes and streams, and grassy alpine meadows and tundra.

The rugged Uinta Mountains run east-west (the largest such range in the United States) at elevations from 12,500 to 13,500 feet along the crest. They lie within both the Ashley and Wasatch national forests and contain some of the finest wilderness fishing and camping areas within the state. The Ute and Piute Indians hunted and fished for centuries in the part of the High Uinta Mountains that was incorporated into the Wasatch National Forest in 1906. The word *Wasatch,* meaning "high mountain pass," is taken from their language. Early in the 1800s, explorers and trappers followed the ancient Indian and game trails across the mountain passes to the Kamas Valley and into Salt Lake Basin. Following the exploration trails blazed by the legend-

ary Kit Carson, Jedediah Smith, and Jim Bridger, wagon trains of pioneers and forty-niners took the trail from Wyoming over the Uinta and Wasatch ranges through the Salt Lake Valley to California. Hundreds of miles of trails and forest roads wind through the Uintas, following the old paths along the Whiterocks River, Big Bush Creek, Duchesne River, Blacks Fork and Lake Fork rivers, Sheep Creek Canyon, Spirit Lake, Chepeta Lake, and the Green River. Deep green meadows and pine forests cover the high country, where the hunting along the northern slopes is excellent for deer, bear, elk, and moose. Most mountain streams are muddy in the early season and are best suited to bait fishing. Fly-fishermen come into their own later, when the water clears and drops. Many of the remote, "lost" alpine lakes and their feeder streams, reached only by backpacking cross country, hold grayling and rainbow, brown, brook, and cutthroat trout up to trophy weights.

An invaluable guide for wilderness fishermen, backpackers, and hunters called *High Uinta Trails* (132 pp.) provides detailed descriptions of the trails (including the spectacular Highline Trail) and natural features in the Mirror Lake, Grandaddy Basin, Rock Creek, Brown Duck Basin, Lake Fork River, Suasey Hole, Yellowstone Creek, Chain Lakes, Swift Creek, Uinta River, Whiterocks River, West Fork of the Blacks Fork, East Fork of the Bear, Stillwater Fork, Henrys Fork, East Fork of Smiths Fork, East and Middle Fork of Blacks Fork, Spirit Lake, Kabell Creek, Middle and West Fork of Beaver Creek, and Burnt Ridge high-country alpine lakes areas. The guide may be obtained for $3 from: Wasatch Publishers, Inc., 4647 Idlewild Rd., Salt Lake City 84117. See "Highcountry Fishing Guides" in the "Encyclopedia" section for details on how to order *Lakes of the High Uintas* fishing guides.

Although most of the trails are in good condition, backpackers and wilderness fishermen should be alert for bogs, wet fields, and mud holes. All of the larger rivers but the Yellowstone have bridges across them. Even in summer, temperatures can dip below freezing at night. In addition to good boots and long johns, rain gear is advisable, for thunderstorms are frequent and sudden during the summer.

The Wasatch National Forest Map (50¢), available from the Supervisor, Wasatch National Forest, 125 South State St., Salt Lake City 84111, describes the forest and the campsites available there. The map shows roads, trails, lakes, campsites, streams, ranger stations, and ski areas in the forest.

The Uinta Primitive Area was named after the Uintah Indians, a branch of the Ute tribe that once inhabited the area. The Uintahs hunted here before the coming of the white man, following the game up the mountains in summer, drying the meat, tanning the hides, and gathering and drying berries. Elevations range from about 8,000 feet in the lower canyons to 13,528 on Kings Peak. This relatively large wilderness tract (237,177 acres) is a scenic coniferous forest interspersed with cool mountain lakes. Rocks of the area include multicolored quartzites and shale, and their rich red contrasts with the green trees.

The scenic High Uintas Highland Trail runs in a general east-west direction along the crest of the mountains. A network of trails across the area, with the Highline Trail the trunk or main artery, provides access to Mirror Lake, Four Lake Basin, Rocky Sea Pass, Rainbow Lake and Rock Creek, Deadhorse Pass (perpetual cool winds blow over this high pass and the view from the summit is breathtaking), Red Knob Pass, North Star Lake, Chain Lakes, North Fork of the Uinta River, Gunsight Pass (from which the vast meadows of Henrys Fork drop off to the north), Henrys Fork Lake, Glass and Bear lakes, and Fish Lake and through dense timber and lush meadows to Henrys

Fork Park, the eastern terminus of the Highline Trail. Somewhere in Upper Rock Creek Valley is reportedly one of the "lost" Caleb Rhodes gold mines. No one has ever been able to find a trace of the lode mine, but it is well established that Rhodes left a fortune when he died.

There is big-game hunting for moose, elk, mule deer, and black bear, but no open season for mountain sheep of the area. If you plan a trip to the area, do it between June 10 and September 15, as the mountains are usually snowbound for the rest of the year. Even in the summer the weather is unpredictable and thunderstorms are frequent, often moving faster than 25 miles per hour. Don't try to outrun one, but look for a place to hide, preferably between two flat rocks or under a flat-rock ledge. If you are out in the open, jettison all your steel equipment and crouch low on something made of rubber. Stay at least 50 feet from the face of a cliff. Remember, thunder is nature's warning, so heed it.

Write to the Supervisor, Wasatch National Forest, 125 State St., Salt Lake City 84111, for camping and trail information. A free informational guide and brochure, *High Uintas Primitive and Related Areas,* gives important backpacking information, including a map on a scale of about 3 miles to 1 inch which marks trails, forest routes, roads, streams, and lakes. Request it from the Forest Supervisor at the address above.

A useful 77-page guide to the trails and old logging and mining roads of the Wasatch Mountains, which range north-south to the west of the Uintas, called *Wasatch Trails,* may be obtained for $1.50 from the Wasatch Mountain Club, 3155 Highland Drive, Salt Lake City 84106. The guide describes trails and natural features in the Parley's Canyon, Wasatch Front, Miles Creek, Big Cottonwood Canyon, and Little Cottonwood Canyon backcountry.

Lodging and pack trip service in the primitive area is provided by *Defa Dude Ranch* (Grandaddy Lakes Basin), Hanna 84031; *Moon Lake Resort* (Lake Fork Creek Area), Mountain Home 84051; *Rock Creek Ranch* (Rock Creek High Country), Duchesne 84021; and *Trial Lake Lodge* (Provo River Headquarters), Kamas 84036.

Access & Outfitting Centers

The Wasatch National Forest is reached by U.S. Highway 40, Utah Highway 44, and Wyoming Highway 414 from Lonetree. Lodging, supplies, guides, and outfitters are available at Vernal, Whiterocks, Holiday Park, Mountain Home, Defas Park, Ogden, Heber City, Brigham City, and Logan.

COLORADO ENCYCLOPEDIA

Accommodations—Rocky Mountain Vacation Lodges & Ranches

The *Colorado Year 'Round Vacation Guide* provides a comprehensive listing of accommodations, restaurants, tourist services, and recreational activities throughout the state. The free booklet is published by the Convention & Visitors Bureau/Denver & Colorado (those listed are bureau members), located at 225 West Colfax Ave., Denver 80202. Descriptions of lodgings include rates, facilities, number of units, nearby recreational activities, and credit cards accepted. Services are listed by cities, which are described and designated on a map in the guide. Recreational highlights of many cities are included in the descriptions. Accommodations listed include motels, hotels, lodges, resorts, and some campgrounds.

For specific lodging and guest ranch information, see the "Colorado Travel & Recreation Guide" section and "Rocky Mountain Wilderness Outfitters & Guest Ranches" in this section.

Air Charters & Rocky Mountain Vacation Services

Rocky Mountain Airways, Hangar 6, Stapleton International Airport, Denver 80207, provides charter fly-in and scheduled service to the most remote wilderness fishing, camping, ski-touring, and big-game hunting areas throughout the state's vast national forest lands. For detailed trip information and rates, write or call (303–355–6241).

Aspen Airways, Hangar 5, Stapleton International Airport, Denver 80207, has four pressurized convairs flying to Aspen daily and provides charter fly-in service throughout the state. For information rates and charter info write or call (303–398–3747).

Frontier Airlines, Inc., 8250 Smith Road, Denver 80207 (303–399–0808), serves 32 major ski and national forest areas and 14 national parks, including Grand Teton and Yellowstone, via Boeing 737 jets and Convair 580 jet props.

Black Canyon of the Gunnison

The eroding forces of wind, water, and glaciers have sculpted the Black Canyon of the Gunnison River out of the mountains of central Colorado. The Black Canyon of the Gunnison National Monument includes 10 miles of the most scenic portion of the 50-mile canyon. Sheer walls rise 3,000 feet at their highest point, forming the deepest gorge in Colorado, which narrows in places to a mere 10 feet. Near the center of the monument, erosion has created a fantastic display of spires, pinnacles, and knobs of rock along the 2,400-foot walls. Here the gorge opens to a width of 150–300 feet, revealing its colorful crystalline walls. Granite, gneiss, and schists glint in the sun in an array of color ranging from white to red, black, and blue. The canyon is at its most beautiful when the autumn reds and yellows of scrub oak, mountain mahogany, aspens, and willows flash amidst the green of pine and spruce. Elk, bear, and an occasional mountain lion range the canyon rims; beaver, muskrat, and mink live along the river. The deep-flowing, boulder-studded pools of the Black Canyon stretch of the Gunnison hold trophy rainbows.

The river that courses through the canyon was named for Capt. John W. Gunnison, who explored the river in 1853 but was forced to turn back when he reached the dark depths of the canyon.

For detailed information and a free *Black Canyon of the Gunnison* map and brochure, write: Superintendent, Box 1648, Montrose 81401.

A special U.S. Geological Survey map, *Black Canyon of the Gunnison National Monument, Colorado,* is available for $2 from: Distribution Section, U.S. Geological Survey, Federal Center, Denver 80225. The map, on a scale of 2,000 feet to 1 inch, is available in either a contour or a shaded-relief edition. It is 23 × 30 inches.

Camping & Backpacking

Hundreds of scenic campsites dot the state's wildlands on both public and private lands. *Camping in the National Park System* is a free booklet which lists and describes all campgrounds in national parks and monuments throughout the country. Charts list the camping seasons, number of sites, facilities, fees, and recreational activities available for each campground. Order the booklet from the Superintendent's Office of the park you plan to visit.

The Bureau of Land Management administers a number of camping areas throughout the state. These are listed in *Camping on the Public Lands,* a publication listing BLM campgrounds across the country. This booklet gives elevation, location, number of sites, facilities, and recreational opportunities for each campsite. Order it from: Bureau of Land Management, Federal Building, Room 14023, 1961 Stout St., Denver 80202.

If you plan to camp in a national forest, check the "Travel & Recreation Guide" entry describing the forest for the address of the Forest Superintendent, and order the Forest Service Map of the area. These maps key the locations of campsites and describe the facilities and recreational opportunities at each recreation site. Should you intend to camp or backpack in a Wilderness or Primitive Area, write to the superintendent of the forest administering the area and learn the special travel regulations that apply to the area. *Off on the Right Foot,* published by the Wilderness Society, is a free guide to wilderness use available from the society at 729 Fifteenth St., N.W., Washington, D.C. 20006. The booklet covers preparations, what to take on backpacking and horse pack trips, safety, conservation, and sources of more detailed information on wilderness travel.

The Colorado Dept. of Natural Resources (Division of Parks and Outdoor Recreation, 1845 Sherman, Denver 80203) publishes a free *Guide to Colorado's State Park & Recreation Areas.* The guide lists numbers of campsites, facilities and services, recreational opportunities, size, elevation, and location of each of the state parks and recreation areas, and shows the locations on a map. The guide also includes information on fees and lists regulations for the areas.

Colorado Private Campgrounds is a free publication available from: Colorado Campground Association, Inc., P.O. Box 965, Colorado Springs 80901. Campgrounds throughout the state are listed by city. Locations, fees, facilities, rates, size and number of units, season, and nearby recreational activities are given for each campground listed. The locations of these campgrounds are keyed on a large, detailed map of the state.

Canoeing & Wild Rivers

Colorado's great wild rivers, which rise high in the lofty, snowcapped peaks of the Rocky Mountains, offered a course of travel over the centuries to the Indians, traders, and trappers who explored the scenic wildlands of western America.

The state's major wildwater float and trout-fishing streams include the Black Canyon of the Gunnison and the rocky, narrow Arkansas Valley of the Arkansas River, famous for the canyon of the Royal Gorge; the boiling rapids and rock formations of the scenic Glenwood Canyon

and Gore Range Red Gorge and Little Gore canyons of the Colorado River; the Green River and the awesome Canyon of Lodore; the scenic Lower Dolores Canyon of the Dolores River; the massive, narrow, red sandstone gorges of the Dolores and Slickrock canyons of the Dolores River in the San Juan National Forest; the world-renowned trout waters of the North Platte River and the boiling rapids of the beautiful North Gate Canyon in the Medicine Bow National Forest bordering Colorado into Wyoming; and the scenic canyon country of the Yampa and White rivers. (See "Wild River Outfitters & Float Trips.")

The U.S. Geological Survey topographical maps for the outstanding high-country and wildwater streams located on the eastern and western slopes of the Rocky Mountains are listed in the "Travel & Recreation Guide" section. The wilderness traveler should note the numerous beaver ponds shown along the feeder streams on his map set. Many hold tackle-busting cutthroat and rainbow trout.

Fishing & Hunting in Colorado

Colorado has long been famous for the trout fishing in its numerous rushing streams and icy mountain lakes, and the legendary big-game hunting offered by the evergreen-forested Rocky Mountain high country, foothills, and rolling sagebrush plains and tablelands. Small-game hunting and warm-water fishing also provide excellent sport. The Continental Divide separates the eastern two-thirds from the rest of the state, and 75% of all of the land over 10,000 feet in the United States lies within Colorado's borders. The Rocky Mountains, with their snowcapped peaks, and the vast plateau lands, which occupy much of the state, offer suitable habitat to a great variety of popular fish and game species. Over one-third of the state consists of public lands contained in national forests and parks, Bureau of Land Management properties, and state-owned or managed tracts. The most important lands from the sportsman's view are the eleven national forests, which have a combined area in excess of 13 million acres.

The Bureau of Land Management, State Office, 910 15th St., Denver 80202 (phone: 303–534–4151 ext. 8402), produces a free *Hunting and Fishing Colorado Map & Guide,* which describes the public lands and outdoor recreation programs and has a map section to show the BLM

acreage. The *Colorado Land and Water Use Information* booklet, produced free by the Division of Wildlife, 6060 Broadway, Denver 80216, presents the general regulations that apply to usage of lands and waters, except for those that apply specifically to hunting hours, seasons, limits, etc. Information about campground permits and park passes is also included.

Trophy & Wilderness Fishing Waters

Colorado offers some exceptional fishing opportunities for rainbow, brown, brook, and cutthroat trout; however, the best cutthroat fishing is found in the least accessible high-country waters. Lake trout and kokanee are found in a number of lakes, golden trout and grayling are found in a very few isolated wilderness streams and lakes, and whitefish contribute variety to the trout fishing in many areas. Warm-water fish include black bass, crappie, white bass, walleye, northern pike, yellow perch, sunfish, bullheads, catfish, and Sacramento perch, which primarily frequent the lakes, impoundments, and slower rivers of the plateau lands and foothills. The esteemed striped bass of saltwater fame has been introduced into selected waters, such as Sterling Reservoir, in the northeast sections of the state. Colorado has over 10,000 miles of streams and thousands of acres of lakes and ponds, but it also boasts a population in excess of 2,200,000, in contrast to its sparsely settled neighbors to the north, and so is subjected to heavy pressure. This means that, with a few exceptions, it is necessary to get away from the well-traveled roads and fish the more remote waters to reach the cream of the angling. Roadside angling yields mainly freshly stocked fish, which the state furnishes with a generous hand. Premium trout habitat, consisting of gentle, meandering high-country meadowlands, is rather limited in the state, because the Colorado Rockies have tight, precipitous stream valleys and the rivers rush out of the peaks and spill into the lowlands, which are traversed by the state's well-developed highway system. Cold high meadow streams, lakes, and the remote alpine waters, reached by foot or horse, offer some of the best opportunities for trophy fish, particularly the native cutthroat. Among the notable exceptions are the White, Yampa, Gunnison, North Platte, Laramie, Animas, and Rio Grande watersheds, which are accessible by road, but, as in much of Colorado, a significant amount of the best fishing is on private lands and permission must be secured. Write to the Division of Wildlife for the free *Colorado Fishing Statutes and Regulations* pamphlet.

In spite of heavy pressure from a large, enthusiastic, outdoors-oriented population, superb fishing exists, as indicated by the state fishing records. It is interesting to note that many of the trophies were taken during the last seven years. The best stream fishing begins after the snow-melt runoff subsides in late June or July and continues into October. Generally, dry fly fishing improves as fall approaches, and golden autumn days spent searching the pools and runs of mountain-bordered streams with high-riding dries can be memorable. The big fly–big fish equation, true in much of the West, also applies to Colorado. Muddlers, minnows, willow flies, spruce flies, wooly worms, streamers, and big nymphs produce well, as do bushy floaters, such as the Irresistible, Humpy, assorted Wulffs, and Grass Hoppers. Standard Western wet flies and dry flies take their share of fish, and in the high elevations it is particularly important to carry some very small flies, since a great deal of alpine insect life is minute. Standard spoons,

spinners, and wobblers are effective, and nightcrawlers, minnows, live insects, roe, and other popular natural baits yield a lot of fish, particularly in the early season. Lake fishing starts as soon as the ice leaves in the spring and continues into the fall, with the quality of the fishing governed by water temperature. While certain flies and lures are popular throughout Colorado, it is absolutely imperative to check local sources for the best lures and patterns at a given time, because tremendous variations exist, and adjacent rivers or lakes may require entirely different lures and methods at any given point in time.

Denver has some surprisingly good angling within a short distance. The South Platte River, which runs from Pike National Forest through Denver on a northeasterly course, produced the state-record rainbow trout, and in the Fort Collins area, a little over 50 miles due north, are the Thompson, its North Fork, the Cache La Poudre system, the St. Vrain Creeks, and the Fall River, which furnish some impressive fishing for rainbow, brown, and some brook trout. Horsetooth Reservoir yielded the record smallmouth bass, and Estes Lake and Rattlesnake and Carter reservoirs also contain trout.

COLORADO RECORD FISH

	Lb.–oz.	Place	Year
Rainbow trout	18–5¼	So. Platte River	1972
Brook trout	7–10	Unknown	1940
Brown trout	24–10	Vallecito Res.	1972
Cutthroat trout	16	Twin Lakes	1964
Lake (mackinaw) trout	36	Deep Lake	1949
Splake	19	Island Lake	1976
Golden trout	1–15	Kelly Lake	1977
Kokanee	3–15	Eleven Mile Res.	1972
Grayling	1–7	Zimmerman Lake	1964
Whitefish	4–3	White River	
Northern pike	30–1	Vallecito Res.	1971
Walleye	16–8	Cherry Creek Res.	1973
Smallmouth bass	4–3¼	Kendricks Lake	1977
Largemouth bass	9–6	Cherry Creek Res.	1970
Striped bass	10–4	North Sterling Res.	1977

The Laramie River, flowing north from its alpine headwaters in Roosevelt National Forest into Wyoming, has some big trout, plus the added bonus of spectacular scenery, especially in the headwaters skirting the beautiful remote Rawah Wilderness Area. The North Platte River, in the Roosevelt and Routt national forest regions of northern Colorado, and its tributaries, such as the Canadian River, yield some trophy browns and rainbows before entering Wyoming, where some spectacular catches are made. The Yampa River, flowing west out of Routt National Forest in the northwestern part of the state, is highly regarded by many fishermen, but the best fishing is away from the road that parallels much of the stream. The White River and its tributaries, flowing west out of the ice-crusted crags of the White River National Forest in north central Colorado, are considered by many trout anglers to be the finest streams in the state. Rainbow, brown, and brook trout grow to trophy size in the cold, deep, forest-shrouded pools. Since much of the water is on ranches, club stretches, and other private land, fishermen should request permission before fishing. The waters of Trapper Lake on the North Fork are noted for some of the finest lake fishing in the state for trophy trout.

The Colorado River, flowing west from its headwaters in Rocky

Mountain National Park through Arapaho, Routt, and White River national forests, provides some fast fishing for rainbows and browns in the vicinity of Glenwood Springs and upstream. The best fishing, however, is in tributaries such as the Frying Pan and Roaring Fork rivers near Aspen and the gin-clear waters of the exquisite Crystal River, which enters the Colorado near Carbondale.

The Gunnison River in the Gunnison National Forest area of west central Colorado has perhaps the greatest reputation of the state's streams. Brown and rainbow trout commonly run to 2 pounds, but fish in excess of 10 pounds are taken every year, and the river holds some cutthroat and brook trout as well. The famed Black Canyon area holds some real trophies in its rugged, hard-to-reach stretches. Tributaries such as the Taylor and East rivers and Tomichi and Powderhorn creeks offer excellent opportunities. Taylor Lake above the dam on the Taylor is famed for big rainbows.

The Animas River in the southwest corner offers good rainbow trout fishing in the San Juan National Forest area north of Durango, and the Rio Grande National Forest area of the Rio Grande River northwest of Del Norte is another favorite southern trout stream. The Arkansas River, in the Leadville region of central Colorado, has a reputation for excellent angling down through the San Isabel National Forest to the region just north of Pueblo. Some lunker trout are taken every year from the deep pools that are common throughout this stretch.

Many lakes and ponds offer superlative trout fishing. Twin Lakes Reservoir in the Flattops Primitive Area of White River National Forest produced the 16 lb. record cutthroat trout. Vallecito Reservoir to the northeast of Durango in the San Juan National Forest yielded both the 24 lb. 10 oz. record brownie and the record 30 lb. 1 oz. northern pike. Other noted trout producers include Deep Lake, in the scenic Flattops Primitive Area, home of the 36 lb. record lake trout; Lake John in the North Platte headwaters; Grand, Shadow Mountain, and Granlby lakes in the southwest corner of Rocky Mountain National Park northwest of Boulder; Williams Fork Reservoir to the southwest, near Parshall; Sweetwater Lake above Glenwood Springs in the White River National Forest; Monument Lake near Trinidad and the border with New Mexico in south central Colorado; the Williams Creek Reservoir in the vicinity of Pagosa Springs in San Juan National Forest; Vega Reservoir in the Grand Mesa National Forest area; and Eleven Mile Canyon and Antero reservoirs in the South Platte River headwaters. High-country lakes such as Emerald, Flint, Hassick, Rock, and Four Mile to the northeast of Vellecito Reservoir in San Juan National Forest offer quality trout angling amid spectacular alpine scenery. In the remote Rocky Mountain areas, hundreds of small lakes, ponds, and beaver dams provide some of the best fishing in the state.

Warm-Water Fishing

Colorado offers a variety of warm-water fishing for walleye, northern pike, large- and smallmouth bass, and panfish such as crappies, perch, sunfish, white bass, and bullheads. Channel catfish, drum, and a variety of coarse species are also available. Foothill and plateau lakes, impoundments, ponds, and sluggish river stretches are the principal habitat for these fish. The area between La Junta and Lamar in southeast Colorado on the lower reaches of the Arkansas River has fishing for walleye, channel catfish, white bass, and a variety of panfish. So do Adobe Creek and Horse Creek reservoirs and the group of "Nee" reservoirs and adjacent waters to the south of Eads, and portions of the Arkansas and Purgatoire are also worth trying. Further north near the Kansas border is Bonny Reservoir, on the Republican River, noted for walleyes, largemouth bass, white bass, crappie, drum,

and catfish. In the northeast corner of the state in the vicinity of Sterling, the North Sterling and Julesburg reservoirs produce large crappies, walleyes, white bass, largemouth bass, catfish, and other panfish. Many anglers consider these waters the best warm-water fishing in Colorado. In the Loveland area due north of Denver are Boyd, Lone Tree, and Horseshoe lakes and some good local reservoirs and ponds that contain crappie, bass, yellow perch, and bullheads. The lower reaches of the Green, White, Yampa, Gunnison, and Colorado rivers offer the best warm-water fishing in western Colorado. There are not many impoundments and lakes in the western plateau country, so flat-water fishing opportunities are limited.

Hunting

Colorado has long enjoyed a reputation for excellent hunting. Big-game species include elk, deer, antelope, bear, mountain lion, and a few mountain sheep and mountain goat. Small-game varieties are pheasant; blue and sage grouse; chukar partridge; mourning doves; band-tailed pigeons; blue, or scaled, Gambel's, and bobwhite quail; and turkey, ptarmigan, snipe, rails, sandhill cranes, ducks, geese, cottontail and snowshoe rabbits, and squirrels.

Write to the Colorado Division of Wildlife for the free *Colorado Regular Big Game Seasons* folder, which gives the statutes and regulations pertaining to big-game hunting, license information, season dates, restricted areas, specific rules by species, area and unit provisions, permit qualifications, and other pertinent data. The state is divided into more than one hundred big-game management units, and there are many seasonal and regulatory differences among the various divisions. A map of these units is in this pamphlet.

The mule deer is the most popular large game species, and the premium hunting areas are in the western half of the state, with the best hunting regions in national forests. A few whitetail deer have migrated into the northeast from Kansas. Over 100,000 are killed in a normal season, and the real trophies are concentrated in the remote portions of the national forests. Good deer hunting can be found in almost every part of the state, and many of the public hunting areas offer excellent opportunities. As is the case with most western states, the deer regulations require careful study, because management units are individually controlled on the basis of herd requirements, and hunting provisions vary from one unit to another. Antelope are scattered all over the state but are numerically concentrated in the eastern portion. Hunters have to enter a draw by application to secure a permit to hunt in specific units. The annual kill normally exceeds 5,000 animals, and the hunter-kill ratio is excellent for the lucky permit winners. Ranch areas provide the best opportunities for success but require permission to hunt. Elk, too, are managed by individual units under an application-draw system for a limited number of permits. Black bear are found in the forested areas, and again the national forests offer the best opportunities for success. The Uncompahgre National Forest has one of the best seasonal averages in Colorado. The grizzly bear is rare in the state, and the small population is protected. Black bear can be hunted in certain units during a special early season and have a statewide season in the fall. Mountain lions are pursued across Colorado in the fall, with a special winter season in designated units. Mountain sheep and goats are confined to the most remote areas of the high peaks country. Sheep are by far the more plentiful, but both are scarce compared to deer, elk, and antelope. Permits are extremely limited, on an application-and-draw basis, and goat hunting is further restricted to residents only; only a handful of goat permits are issued.

Colorado's upland game hunting offers unusual variety, ranging from the chukar partridge, which is native to the semiarid draws and gullies of India, to the white-tailed ptarmigan, which prefers the tundra and willow thickets of the Far North. Pheasants constitute the biggest kill of any single species of upland bird. The best areas are concentrated in the northeastern counties, particularly in the agricultural land serviced by the vast irrigation system, and hunting the irrigation ditches usually brings success, because ringnecks like to stay relatively close to water. Other good areas include the Gunnison, Arkansas, and Rio Grande river valleys. Seasons are set by management unit. For small-game hunting, all of Colorado is divided into management units, which differ completely from the big-game units. Write to the Colorado Division of Wildlife for the free *Colorado Season Information for Small Game* pamphlet, which includes the basic rules and regulations, general seasons for each species, and a game unit map which defines the limits of each unit. Remember, there are many individual unit variances.

Blue grouse and ptarmigan are creatures of the vast national forests. The blue grouse prefer the thick evergreen cover of the lower portions of the mountains, while ptarmigan like the brush and rubble found near and above the timberline. The grouse harvest approaches 30,000 in a good year, while the ptarmigan kill numbers a few thousand. Ptarmigan inhabit very rugged, remote terrain and are difficult to hunt. Sage grouse are found in the sagebrush plains of northern and western Colorado, and many prime areas are contained in the Bureau of Land Management lands. Chukars are spread through the western foothills of the state and favor semiarid canyons and rubble-strewn hill country. The kill is small, a few thousand birds. The mourning dove is found in the grainfields of the agricultural districts along the major river systems. The beautiful band-tailed pigeon prefers the forest and is a prized game species, as well as a treat on the table. Merriam's turkey is found in the mountainous country, and the national forests offer much of the best hunting. There is a general season in the fall of a week's duration, and a restricted spring season. Some of the turkey hunting is by permit and draw, so it is wise to check the regulations. Sharp-tailed grouse inhabit the foothills of the western slope, but are not found in great numbers throughout the state. The kill numbers a few thousand birds, and the population is drastically reduced from its once great abundance.

Ducks and geese provide some of the best shooting in the state. Mallards predominate in the east, and various flight varieties are found throughout Colorado. Certain duck species, such as canvasbacks and redheads, are under a point system, which restricts hunters' kills of these birds. Write for the free *Waterfowl Season Information* folder produced by the Colorado Division of Wildlife, which defines the general regulations and statutes that apply to waterfowl, the special rules and regulations that pertain to the Pacific and central flyways dividing Colorado, and the special restrictions and closures that apply to specific locations, and which provides a "goose area map" showing the limited hunting zones. Look for the best wild-fowling in lakes, impounds, and sluggish lower reaches of the big rivers. The area around and in the Monte Vista National Wildlife Refuge in south central Colorado near Alamosa and the Alamosa National Wildlife Refuge provides some of the best gunning in the entire state.

Rails, snipe, and sandhill crane round out the migratory game list. They are found in wetlands and adjoining agricultural areas. Cottontail and snowshoe rabbits are plentiful, the former preferring open country and farmlands, the latter inhabiting the vast evergreen forests. Squirrels, too, may be hunted, but are not a popular game species.

The Colorado Division of Wildlife publishes an excellent bimonthly magazine, *Colorado Outdoors*, which costs $2 per year or $5 for three years and may be ordered from the magazine's office at 6060 Broadway, Denver 80216. It contains how-to and where-to information, history, humor, wildlife vignettes, and a good deal of full-color artwork and photography. The magazine cuts across just about every area of outdoor interest and is a valuable tool in learning about the prime recreational opportunities.

Colorado has very strict gun and safety clothing rules for outdoorsmen and requires a hunter safety certificate before a hunting license can be issued. Nonresident hunters must take the course or present a certificate from their home state. For definitive information, write the Division of Wildlife c/o the Hunter Safety Section for the free *Hunter Safety Bulletin* leaflet.

For additional fishing and hunting info, see the national forest and wilderness areas described in the "Colorado Travel & Recreation Guide" section, and "Rocky Mountain Wilderness Outfitters & Guest Ranches" in this section.

Garcia Bass & Fly Fishing Schools

The Garcia Corporation, famous manufacturers of quality fishing gear and accessories, operates a Steamboat Springs fly fishing school and the Lake Powell Bass School in cooperation with the American Sports-

man's Club. The 3-day Lake Powell (Utah) bass fishing seminars beginning April 27 cover bass biology, the latest electronic gear, reading structure, techniques with crank baits, and more. Tuition fee includes meals, equipment, and lodging at the Bullfrog Marina on Lake Powell. Fully equipped bass boats and professional guides are included in the tuition fee. The Garcia Steamboat Springs Fly Fishing School, headquartered at the American Sportsman's Club Lodge, offers 3-day sessions from July 11 to August 4 for advanced and beginning fly fishermen. The subjects covered include the art of casting, stream entomology, biology, reading the stream, small and big water fishing and wading on the Elk and Yampa rivers. Reservations are accepted on a first-come-first-served basis. For information, rates, and free literature, write: Garcia Fishing Schools, American Sportsman's Club, 650 S. Lipan St., Denver 80223 (phone: 303–744–1881).

Highways—Recreation & Alpine Scenic Routes

The free Colorado highway map *Colorful Colorado*, a shaded relief map in full color, shows interstate, U.S., state, and county highways and roads, mileage between points, interchanges, points of interest, mountain passes, Continental Divide areas, ranger headquarters, roadside parks, campgrounds, national and state forests, national parks and monuments, government reservations, airports, streams, lakes, and reservoirs. The reverse side of the map tells motorists where to find such features as the Continental Divide, highest altitude, colleges and universities, museums, mineral hot springs, and national parks and monuments. A key to the points of interest marked on the map identifies them and groups them into such categories as state and national parks or recreational areas, national historic landmarks, state fishing and hatchery areas, and ski and winter sports areas. Colorado peaks and mountain passes are also listed in the map guide, and vicinity maps of Boulder, Denver, Colorado Springs, and Pueblo are included. The map may be ordered from: Colorado Marketing Section, 602 State Capitol Annex, Denver 80203.

Also free from the Marketing Section at the above address is the booklet *Colorado Top of the Nation Mini-Tours*. The booklet is a guide to 15 automobile circle tours through some of the most scenic and historic areas of the state. The tours included are Standing Up Country (316 miles), in the Grand Junction area; Mountains to Prairies (190 miles), a circle from Fort Collins to Denver; Land of Lakes (265 miles), the Gunnison National Forest area; Gateway to Gold (184 miles), the mountain mining country of Idaho Springs, Central City, and other boom towns; Land of Long Ago (273 miles), a tour of the Steamboat Springs area and the mountains, canyons, and forests to the east and south; Spanish Conquistador Land (292 miles), through the old Indian hunting grounds of the Rio Grande National Forest; Productive Plains (245 miles), through the high plains of Colorado; the Shining Mountains (216 miles), a tour of the Continental Divide area; the Navajo Trail Country (318 miles), through Pueblo and the Great Sand Dunes National Monument; the Smoky Hill Trail (310 miles), which leads through a high plains area rich in history; Santa Fe Trail (305 miles), the route of the Pike expedition; Crown Jewel of the Rockies (206 miles), a tour of central Colorado; San Juan Country (251 miles), through the rugged wilderness of the San Juan Mountains; and Dinosaurland (236 miles), from the hills surrounding Craig to the valleys of the Yampa and Green rivers.

The Marketing Section also publishes a free 50-page book, *Colorful Colorado Invites You*, which describes each of the tour areas in detail and provides a map of the region showing the location of points of interest, campgrounds, ghost towns, boat launches, roadside rests,

historical markers, ski areas, and other recreational sites. The book describes the wildlife, geology, history, and recreational opportunities of different areas of the state. It also lists additional sources of information on travel throughout the state and includes a short article on how to take good color pictures. This publication may be ordered from the Marketing Section at the address given above.

If you plan to drive through Colorado, remember that road conditions change as quickly as the weather, especially at high altitudes. To find out the latest road conditions, call 303–630–1234 or 303–630–1515 for recorded reports. For specific information on highway and driving regulations, contact the Department of Highways, 4201 E. Arkansas Ave., Denver 80222.

Jeep Tours & Rentals

Four-wheel-drive roads and jeep trails lead through some of the most rugged mountain backcountry and desert wilderness areas of the state. The wild-river areas of the Green and Yampa white waters are accessible by jeep, as are the vast white sands of the Great Sand Dunes National Monument and the high-country wilderness areas of the Elk Mountains. For information about jeep tours and rentals in the state, write to: *San Juan Jeep Trails*, Ouray 81427; *Lake City Jeep Rentals & Tours*, Lake City 81235; *Vail Jeep Guides*, Vail 81657; *Cloud 9 Guided Jeep Trs.*, P.O. Box 344, Aspen 81611; and *Ghost Town Scenic Jeep Tours*, R.R. #1, Box 290, Salida 81201.

Powderhorn Primitive Area

This 40,400-acre wilderness managed by the Bureau of Land Management embraces a vast expanse of tundra at 12,000 feet elevation and forests of spruce, fir, and pine on the Cannibal and Calf Creek plateaus southwest of Gunnison. The rugged mountains of the region yielded fortunes in gold and silver during the 1890s, making the area Colorado's richest of the day. Among the famous mines of the area were the Headlight, the Old Lott, and the Anaconda.

The wide, chill stretches of Cannibal Plateau recall a grisly episode from the days of the Old West. A party of prospectors from Utah reached the nearby home of Ouray, chief of the Ute, who warned the men to wait for the spring before challenging the tundra. Six men, including Alferd Packer, pushed on in spite of the chief's advice. Packer turned up at a white settlement six weeks later, claiming that his companions had deserted him in the wilds, leaving him to forage for roots and hunt small game to survive. The story seemed suspicious, as Packer's first request was for whiskey, not food. He appeared in another settlement several days later with a good deal of money, which he spent drinking and gambling.

An Indian arrived at one of the towns with strips of flesh from human bodies he had found along the prospectors' trail, and Packer was arrested. In the spring a photographer from *Harpers Weekly* discovered the bodies of Packer's companions, their skulls crushed. Local authorities arrested Packer and chained him to a rock to await trial, because there was no jail. He escaped. He was recaptured in Wyoming ten years later, tried and convicted of murder and cannibalism, and sentenced to hang. But he won the right to a new trial on a technicality and was sentenced instead to 40 years in prison for manslaughter. He was granted parole a few years later and died a free man in Denver in 1906.

In spite of its gruesome history and formidable backcountry wilderness, this area is a top-ranked hunting area. Alpine lakes dot the high reaches, providing good wilderness fishing. The Utes once hunted these high plateaus where mule deer, black bear, and coyote roam. A part of the area serves as wintering grounds for Rocky Mountain elk. Beaver dams dot the streams of the region, which offer excellent trout fishing. Bald eagles soar above the chilly plateaus.

This remote area is accessible by way of State Highway 149, which runs southeast from Gunnison. U.S. Highway 50 runs east to Gunnison from Pueblo. Guides and outfitters for the Primitive Area may be found in Gunnison. *Powderhorn Hunting Camp*, Box 595, Gunnison 81243, is the base for deer and elk hunts in the Primitive Area. For additional information write: State Director, Bureau of Land Management, 1961 Stout St., Denver 80202.

U.S. Geological Survey topographic maps of the Powderhorn Primitive Area include: Alpine Plateau, Cannibal Plateau, Lake City, Powderhorn Lakes.

Rocky Mountain Trails—Maps & Guides

Colorado's majestic Rocky Mountains offer the wilderness traveler a wealth of incomparable backcountry—sheer granite walls that challenge the most experienced mountaineers, gently sloping wildflower meadows and deep green forests that welcome world-weary campers, and high-country glacial lakes and sparkling streams abundant in trout —and much of it is accessible by foot or horse trail.

Many areas are easily reached in a day trip; others are best appreciated in trips of several days. *Rocky Mountain Trails* by Louis Kenofer is a detailed 23-page guide to the major trails through the park. The book includes reproductions of U.S. Geological Survey 7.5-minute maps of each trail area discussed, along with a full-sized topographical map of the entire Rocky Mountain National Park. The book describes trails in the Wild Basin area, a large valley in the southeastern part of the park that contains clear glacial lakes, waterfalls, and excellent trout-fishing streams; the Tahosa Valley, an attractive area within a short drive of Estes Park; Bear Lake country, containing the highest peak of the park; Glacier Gorge and the lakes and glaciers of Loch Vale on the slopes of Longs Peak; the cirques, waterfalls, and aspen groves of the Moraine Park–Odessa Gorge region; the remote backcountry of the Mummy Range; Lumpy Ridge's unusual rock features; the renowned trout waters of the North Fork Big Thompson River; the starkly beautiful tundra country of the Great Divide; the Milner Pass, with splendid views of the Never Summer Range; Kawuneeche Valley, land of the North Fork of the Colorado; and the major lakes of the western slopes of the park. The book costs $4.45 and may be ordered from the Rocky Mountain Nature Association, Estes Park 80517.

Trails of the Front Range is the second volume of Kenofer's Rocky Mountain trails guide. It costs $4.95 and is available from the same

source. The trails included here are among those penetrating the Front Range area south from the Rocky Mountain National Park. The Indian Peaks area of this region, rivaling the grandeur of its northern neighbor, encompasses the Continental Divide area that borders the Rocky Mountain National Park. The book also covers the trails of the Boulder Creek area, ranging from Nivot Ridge south to Rogers Pass.

One of the most comprehensive trail guides to this part of the Rockies is the *Guide to the Colorado Mountains* by Robert Ormes with the Colorado Mountain Club. The guide (in hardback) costs $7.95 and may be ordered from: Colorado Mountain Club, 2530 W. Alameda Ave., Denver 80219. (Add 35¢ for mailing.) This is the sixth revised edition of the well-known book, first published in 1952. It describes the whole of the Colorado Rockies, which cover all of the state to the west of Denver. The guide is written for cross-country skiers and mountaineers as well as for trail hikers and includes descriptions of technical climbs throughout the state. The areas described are depicted in maps throughout the book, which should be used in conjunction with U.S. Geological Survey topographical maps of the areas in which you plan to travel. The book includes short chapters on ski touring, rock climbing, caves and spelunking, white-water boating, and general information on mountain climbing, but the largest portion of the book is a concise and factual description of the trails and climbing routes.

The Colorado Mountain Club provides a variety of other publications dealing with the Rocky Mountains. Among these are the following guidebooks: *Boulder Trail Map* ($1), *Colorado Fourteens* ($1.25), *Front Range—Indian Peaks* (75¢), *Guide to the New Mexico Mountains* ($3.45), *Hikes and Climbs from Crystal* (50¢), *Mt. Evans above Timberline* ($2), *Roads and Trails, Front Range* ($2.50), *Route of the Rocky Mountain Trail* (50¢), *Colorado Front Range Ski Tours* ($5.95), *80 Northern Colorado Hiking Trails* ($4.95), *50 West Central Colorado Hiking Trails* ($4.95), *Mountain Search and Rescue Techniques* ($4), *Backpacking* ($3.75), *Basic Mountaineering* ($2.50), *Freedom of the Hills* ($11.95), *Mountaineering First Aid* ($2.50), *Practice Climbing* ($1), *Nordic Skiing* ($2), *Winter Mountaineering Notes* ($2), *Lightning* (10¢), and *ABC of Avalanche Safety* ($1.50).

Colorado Mountain Club books on the flora of the Rockies include: *Alpine Wild Flowers* ($1.25), *Colorado Wildflowers* ($1.50), *Mountain Wild Flowers of Colorado* ($1.50), *Mushrooms of Colorado* ($2.25), and *Wild Flower Name Tales* ($6.95). Other books available from the club include: *Fourteen Thousand Feet—A History of the Naming and Early Ascents of the High Colorado Peaks* ($1.50), *Roof of the Rockies* ($9.95), *Front Range Panorama* ($3.75), *High Country Names* ($2.25), *Colorado Skylines 1—Front Range* ($3.50), *II—The Parks* ($5.50), *III—Colorado River Basin* ($5.50), *IV—Southern Section* ($5), and *Birds of North America* ($3.95). The club also offers the

following periodicals (nonmember rates): *Trail and Timberling* monthly magazine ($4/yr. or 50¢/copy), *Summer Schedule for the Club* ($2.50), and *Winter Schedule for the Club* ($2). Add 35¢ mailing cost for books; 20¢ for periodicals, pamphlets, or maps; and 50¢ for summer and winter schedules.

The Colorado Mountain Club has conducted hikes, climbs, snowshoe treks, ski tours, local walks, mountaineering training schools, and other activities in the mountains since 1912. Write to the address given above for membership information. Dues vary from club to club, and special rates are available for students and persons under 21. If you are interested in trips conducted by the club, write to their address for a free listing of current trips.

Rocky Mountain Wilderness Outfitters & Guest Ranches

Colorado's many high-country and wilderness areas offer excellent alpine fishing and big-game hunting opportunities and challenge the most experienced backpackers and climbers. A wide variety of guides and outfitters are available to equip and/or lead your backcountry hiking, fishing, canoeing, or ski-touring expedition. The most comprehensive listing of these professionals is the free *Licensed Outfitters and Guides*, available from: Colorado Division of Wildlife, 6060 Broadway, Denver 80216. This 33-page booklet lists all licensed professional outfitters in the state, the game management units they serve, their licensed guides, and their addresses.

The state's Outfitters Professional Society publishes a free brochure, *Colorado—Wilderness in the Rockies*, which describes the organization and its guide and outfitting services. The brochure includes a form for you to use to describe the services you need and the area and length of trip in which you are interested. The organization then provides you with at least one prospective outfitter for your trip. Write to: The Outfitters Professional Society, Inc., Trappers Lake Rt., Box 45, Meeker 81641.

Much of the remote mountain high country is best seen with an experienced guide and outfitter. Scores of professional guides are available throughout the state; for detailed information on individual guides, see the "Travel & Recreation Guide" section, and "Wilderness Society—North American High-Country & Wildwater Trips" and "Wild River Outfitters & Float Trips" in this section. In addition to the guides and outfitters mentioned there, special wilderness outings and trips are conducted by the following individuals and organizations: *Rocky Mountain Expeditions, Inc.*, P.O. Box CC, Buena Vista 81211 (backpacking, fishing, ski touring, and river float trips in the Rocky Mountains); *Telluride Mountaineering School*, Box 4, Aspen 81611 (skills are taught on backpacking trips into Colorado's high mountain country and on float trips through the wild-river canyons of the state); *Wilderness Adventures Inc.*, Box 265, South Fork 81154 (horsepacking, backpacking, hunting, fishing, and snow camping trips in the Rio Grande National Forest; Rio Grande River float trips; and wilderness workshops); *The Mountain Men*, 11100 East Dartmouth 219, Denver 80232 (4-wheel-drive mountain wilderness tours, camping trips, fishing and hunting expeditions in the Colorado high country); *American Wilderness Experience*, Rt. 2, Nebraska Way, Longmont 80501 (horsepack and river expeditions through the mountains and rivers of the San Juan Wilderness, Colorado, as well as in two other states); *The Bob Culp Climbing School*, 1329 Broadway, Boulder 80302 (climbing in the Flatiron Range near Boulder); *Colorado Wilderness Experience Trips*, 2912 Aspen Drive, Durango 81301 (camping and climbing trips in the San Juan Wilderness); *Adventure Bound, Inc.*, 6179 So. Adams Dr., Littleton 80121 (float trips through-

out the wilderness waters of the Green, Yampa, and Colorado rivers); and *Rocky Mountain Ski Tours & Backpack Adventures,* P.O. Box 413, 172 E. Elkhorn Ave., Estes Park 80517 (backpacking and ski touring in the Rocky Mountain National Park and Routt and Roosevelt national forests).

Dude ranches dot the state and offer every possible kind of wilderness and backcountry travel and recreation. The *Arapaho Valley Ranch* (Box 1420, Granby 80445), a family ranch resort on the south fork of the Colorado, offers horseback riding, pack trips, fishing, boating, canoeing, and cabin accommodations. *Bar Lazy J Guest Ranch* (Chuck & Phyl Broady, Box ND, Parshall 80468) is another family ranch with riding, fishing, hiking, and nearby resort facilities. *The Bar X Bar Ranch* (P.O. Box 27X, Crawford 81415), surrounded by the Gunnison National Forest, offers fishing, pack trips, auto trips, and riding. *Beavers Guest Ranch* (Box 43, Winter Park 80482) lies in the Arapaho National Forest and has riding, fishing, resort facilities, pack trips, raft trips on the Colorado, and scenic auto trips. *Black Mountain Ranch* (Box 607 D, McCoy 80463) adjoins the Routt National Forest and offers pack trips, fishing, child care, and riding. The *C Lazy U Ranch* (Box 518A, Granby 80446) has resort facilities, riding, and a well-stocked stream and lake. *Colorado Trails Ranch* (Box 848, Durango 81301) has riding, archery, riflery, fishing, pack trips, ranch activities, and child care. *Columbine's Double JK Ranch* (Longs Peak Route, Box D, Estes Park 80517) lies between Rocky Mountain National Park and Roosevelt National Forest. It is a family ranch, with resort facilities, on-site activities, child care, and fishing. *Coulter Lake Guest Ranch* (Box 906A, Rifle 81650), located in White River National Forest, offers riding, fishing, on-site activities, and big-game hunting. The *Don K Ranch* (2677 S. Siloam Road, Pueblo 81004), in the San Isabel National Forest area, has riding, child care, and resort facilities. *Drowsy Water Ranch* (Box 147A, Granby 80446) adjoins a national forest area and provides riding, pack trips, ranch activities, fishing in the Colorado and nearby streams and ponds, and child care. *Deer Valley Ranch* (Box P, Nathrop 81236) has two natural hot springs on its acreage and offers jeep trips through the mountains, fishing, riding, and pack trips. *Futurity Lodge Guest Ranch* (Box 9, Nathrop 81235), surrounded by San Isabel National Forest, offers cross-country hiking and riding. *Focus Ranch* (P.O. Box 22, Slater

81653) lies near the Medicine Bow National Forest and offers mountain climbing, riding, hiking, jeep rides, big and small-game hunting, and on-site activities. *Harmel's Ranch Resort* (P.O. Box 9440, Gunnison 81230) has fishing, wilderness pack trips, riding, river rafting, ranch activities, and resort facilities. *The Horseshoe Bend Guest Ranch* (Meredith 81542), located high in the White River National Forest, is a 100-year-old resort offering fishing, jeep trips, pack trips, and hunting. *Idlewild Guest Ranch* (Box 1, Hideway Park 80450), in the Fraser Valley, has fishing, hiking, riding, resort facilities, and on-site activities. The *Indian Head Ranch* (P.O. Box 2200, Estes Park 80517), surrounded by Roosevelt National Forest and Rocky Mountain Park, has riding and trout fishing in a beaver-dammed creek. *Lake Mancos Ranch* (Box 218A, Mancos 81328), in the San Juan Mountains, has riding, lake and stream fishing, jeep trips, child care, ranch activities, and a swimming pool. The *Lazy H Guest Ranch* (Allenspark 80510) has resort facilities, trap shooting, pack trips, stream fishing, hiking, and riding. *Lost Valley Ranch* (Deckers 80135), in Pike National Forest, offers resort facilities, trout fishing, child care, a special teen program, riding, and on-site activities. *Peaceful Valley Lodge & Guest Ranch* (Dept. C6, Star Rt., Lyons 80540) offers jeep trips, trail rides, pack trips, riding instruction, cross-country skiing and instruction, and an indoor riding hall and pool. *Rainbow Trout Lodges & Dude Ranch* (Antonito 81120), located on the Conejos River of the San Juan Mountains, offers fishing on 50 miles of stocked trout streams, river rafting, riding, pack trips, supervised children's activities and on-site recreation, and resort facilities. *Rawah Ranch* (Glendevey, Colo., Rt., Jelm, WY 82053), near Big Laramie River, offers excellent trout fishing, hiking, riding and instruction, and side trips. *Saddle Pocket Guest Ranch* (P.O. Box 53, Slater 81653) in the Little Snake River Valley offers trout fishing, riding, jeep trips, hiking, hunting, cross-country skiing, on-site recreation, and ranch activities. *Seven W Guest Ranch* (Sweetwater Creek, Gypsum 81537) near the White River National Forest has fishing, pack trips, hiking, hunting, and on-site recreation. *Sitzmark Guest Ranch* (Box 65DR76, Winter Park 80482) has float trips, pack trips, riding, resort facilities, and on-ranch recreation. *Sky Corral Ranch* (Mark & Amey Crubbs, Bellvue 80412) offers fishing, hiking, riding, pack trips, and on-site activities. Surrounded by the Arapaho National Forest, the *Snowshoe Ranch* (Box 23/0, Kremmling 80459) has fishing, hunting, big-game hunting, cross-country skiing, and on-site recreation. *Sun Valley Guest Ranch* (Box 470–A, Grand Lake 80447) adjoins the Rocky Mountain National Park and offers riding and instruction, pack trips, hiking, hunting, and resort facilities. At the *Swiss Village Guest Ranch* (Longs Peak Route, Box A, Estes Park 80517), near Rocky Mountain National Park and Roosevelt National Forest, there are riding, hiking, resort facilities, and on-site recreation. *Sylvan Dale Ranch* (2939 N. Country Rd. 31D, Loveland 80537) offers riding, pack trips, ranch activities, trout fishing, and on-site recreation. *Tarryall River Ranch* (Box A5, Lake George 80827) in Pike National Forest has pack trips and trail riding. *Tally Ho Ranch* (Box 51, Winter Park 80482), surrounded by the Arapaho National Forest, offers riding, fishing, and a special children's program. At the *Triple B Guest Ranch* (Woodland Park 80863) in the Pikes Peak area are horseback riding and a wide variety of on-site activities. *Tumbling River Ranch* (Grant 80448) in the Pike National Forest area offers riding, instruction, pack trips, jeep rides, stream and lake fishing, and children's counselors. *Two Bars Seven Ranch* (Box 39, Virginia Dale 80548) has riding, ranch activities, pack trips, fishing, hunting, and on-site activities. *U–T Bar Ranch* (Glendevey) offers trout fishing, riding, on-ranch activities, and outfitting for special groups into the Rawah Wilderness. *Waunita Hot Springs Ranch* (Rt. 2, Box 56, Gunnison 81230) has riding, fishing, hot springs swimming, and ski touring. *Wilderness Trails Ranch* (Bayfield 81122) offers riding, fishing, pack trips, sailing, and children's

counselors. *Wind River Ranch* (Estes Park 80517) offers riding, instruction, pack trips, fishing, children's counselors, and other on-site activities. *Winding River Ranch* (Box 16, Grand Lake 80447) provides riding, nearby fishing, skiing, and resort facilities. *Tall Timber,* a rustic luxury resort in the San Juan National Forest region, offers trophy trout fishing on the Animas River and is accessible only by a historic narrow-gauge railroad; for info and literature write: Box 90, Durango 81301.

Additional ranches, lodges, and individuals providing guide and outfitting services are listed throughout the "Colorado Travel & Recreation Guide" section.

Ski Touring in the Colorado Rockies

The thick snowbeds carpeting the Colorado Rockies during the winter offer outstanding ski mountaineering and touring and some of its most scenic winter camping. The Front Range is a mountain land of many faces and ages. But the constantly changing environments of the range offer challenge as well as pleasure; be prepared for sudden drops in temperature, wind chill, and avalanche-prone cornices along ridges. *Colorado Front Range Ski Tours* is a comprehensive guide to tours throughout the Front Range for skiers at all levels of experience. The book covers 54 tours of half-day, one-day, and overnight duration. The book costs $5.95 and is available from: Touchstone Press, P.O. Box 81, Beaverton, OR 97005.

National forests and parks may require mountaineering permits for those ski touring within their boundaries. Check with the forest or park supervisor in the area you plan to tour. If you plan to camp, make sure you are properly equipped. Go with an experienced winter camper your first time, if possible; winter weather brings unexpected difficulties to the novice. Be aware of the possibility of sudden snowstorms, avoid avalanche-prone areas, and keep warm. Hypothermia can be a killer. Learn to avoid it.

The Roosevelt National Forest offers excellent ski mountaineering and tours. The Poudre and Redfeather Ranger Districts, 148 Remington St., Fort Collins 80521, offer a guide to winter wilderness travel in this area. This free guide, *Winter Backcountry Use Information—Ski Touring & Ski Mountaineering,* describes about 20 tours for cross-country skiers throughout the forest and in Rocky Mountain National Park.

For general information on ski touring in Colorado, write to: *Colorado Ski Country,* 1461 Larimer Sq., Denver 80202; or *Colorado Ranch & Ski Tours,* 3113 E. Third Ave., Denver 80206. For information on snow conditions throughout the state, call 303-893-2201.

For literature and rates on Rocky Mountain cross country skiing centers, guided tours, instruction, lodging, and ski mountaineering, write: *Bear Pole Ranch,* SR 1, Steamboat Springs 80477; *Rocky Mountain Outfitters,* Box 85, Granby 80446; *Ashcroft Ski Touring Center,* Box 1572, Aspen 81611; *Breckenridge Ski Touring School & Mountain Guide Service,* Box 1058, Breckenridge 80424; *C Lazy U Ranch,* Box 378, Granby 80446; *Copper/Ski Escape Ski Touring School,* Box 1, Copper Mountain 80443; *Crested Butte Ski Area,* Box 528, Crested Butte 81224; *Devils Thumb Cross Country Center* (Arapaho National Forest), Box 25, Winter Park 80482; *Glen Eden Ranch,* Box 867, Clark 80428; *Keystone Resort* (in Montezuma Quadrangle area), Box 38, Dillon 80435; *Box Canyon Ski Tours,* Box 435, Ouray 81427; *Rocky Mountain Expeditions,* Buena Vista 81211; *Rocky Mountain Ski Tours,* P.O. Box 413, Estes Park 80517; *San Juan Alpine Tours, Inc.* (Weminuche Wilderness), Box 457, Silverton 81433; *Scandinavian Lodge* (run by Sven Wiik, former U.S. Olympic coach), Box 5040, Steamboat Springs 80499; *Snowmass Ski Touring Center,* Aspen 81611; *Steamboat Springs Ski Area,* Box 1178, Steamboat Springs 80477; *Telluride Ski Touring,* Box 672, Ophir 81426; *Vail Ski Touring School,* P.O. Box 1000, Vail 81657; *Vista Verde Guest Ranch* (Routt National Forest), Box 465, Steamboat Springs 80477; *Wildernest* (Arapahoe National Forest), Silverthorne 80498.

Wilderness Society—North American High-Country & Wildwater Trips

The renowned Wilderness Society, a nonprofit organization founded in 1935 to preserve the nation's wild lands, sponsors a wide variety of guided summer wilderness trips to the remote unspoiled areas of the United States and Canada. Membership in the society is not a requirement for participation in their trip offerings (most of which are of 7–10 days' duration and are planned for family participation). *Packhorse Trips* are offered in Superstition Wilderness (Arizona), Pisgah Wilderness (North Carolina), Pecos Wilderness (New Mexico), La Garita Wilderness (Colorado), Lincoln-Scapegoat Wilderness (Mon-

tana), Weminuche Wilderness (Colorado), Bob Marshall Wilderness (Montana), Wind River and Absaroka Wilderness (Wyoming), Sun River Wilderness (Montana), and Yellowstone Wilderness. *Backpacking Trips* (lightweight equipment provided) are offered in the wild Escalante Canyon and High Uintas Wilderness (Utah), Mummy Range and Eagles Nest Wilderness (Colorado), Jewel Basin and Ruby Mountains (Montana), Great Smoky Mountains, Canyonlands Wilderness (Utah), Mount Zirkel and Flattops Wilderness Areas (Colorado), Sawtooth Wilderness (Idaho), Gates of the Arctic Wilderness and Kenai National Moose Range (Alaska), Adirondacks (New York), Beartooth Primitive Area (Montana), and the West Elk Wilderness and Holy Cross and Collegiate Ranges (Colorado). *Base Camp Hiking Trips* are provided in Alaska's Mount McKinley National Park. Wilderness *Hiking Trips with Packstock* are offered in the Grand Gulch Wilderness (Utah), Gros Ventre Range and Teton Wilderness (Wyoming), Mission Mountains and Selway-Bitterroot Wilderness (Montana), Wind River Range and Washakie Wilderness (Wyoming), Yellowstone Wilderness, and in Colorado's La Garita, Weminuche, and Uncompahgre wilderness areas.

Wilderness Canoe Trips are offered each year through Florida's Everglades National Park, Big Bend Country of the Rio Grande (Texas), Okefenokee-Suwannee River Wilderness (Georgia), Algonquin Provincial Park (Ontario), Boundary Waters Canoe Area and Voyageurs National Park (Minnesota), Missouri River Wildlands (Montana), and the Green River–Canyonlands Wilderness (Utah). *Wild Water Rafting Trips* are run down the Grand Canyon of the Colorado, Hells Canyon of the Snake, Yukon River Wilderness (Yukon, Canada), North Platte Wildlands (Wyoming), Green River–Cataract Canyon (Utah), and the Salmon River and Middle Fork Wilderness (Idaho).

For detailed trip literature, schedules, rates, and reservations, write: Trip Department, The Wilderness Society, 4260 East Evans Ave., Denver 80222 (phone: 303-758-2266).

Wild River Outfitters & Float Trips

For the adventurous, the Yampa and Green rivers in the rugged canyon country of the Dinosaur National Monument provide some of the most exciting white-water running in the country. The Colorado courses through magnificent mountain country. Among the many outfitters and guides who offer trips down these and other wildwaters throughout the state are: *Adventure Bound, Inc.* (6179 So. Adams Dr., Littleton 80121), which offers guided trips through the Yampa and Lodore canyons of Dinosaur National Monument, along the Colorado River, and through the wild rivers of Utah; *Rocky Mountain Expeditions* (P.O. Box CC, Buena Vista 81211), which offers river float trips in the Rockies; *Telluride Mountaineering School* (Box 4, Aspen 81611), which combines mountaineering instruction with float trips through the wild-river canyons of the state; *Wilderness Adventures* (Box 265, South Fork 81154), offering Rio Grande float trips as part of its program; *American Wilderness Experience* (Rt. 2, Nebraska Way, Longmont 80501), which leads float trips through the rivers of the San Juan Wilderness; *Baars Canyon Tours* (2909 Balsam Dr., Durango 81301, Attn. Don Baars), which offers river float trips on the San Juan River and the Desolation and Gray canyons of the Green River; *International Aquatic Adventures* (1127 W. Elizabeth, P.O. Box 1396, Fort Collins 80522), with trips on the Cache La Poudre, North Platte, Arkansas, Dolores, and Colorado rivers; *Rocky Mountain River Expeditions* (P.O. Box 1394, Denver 80201), which offers float trips on rivers throughout Colorado and three other states (*Rocky Mountain River Expeditions* also offers horse-pack trips into the scenic alpine high country of the Mount Zirkel Wilderness and combination river-backpacking trips into the Lost Park Area/Arkansas

River, Never Summer Range/North Platte River, and Gore Range/Upper Colorado River, and winter cross-country ski-touring trips in the Rockies.); *Slickrock River Co.* (SRCDA, P.O. Box 10543, Denver 80210), whose Colorado river trips are on the San Juan River, in the Desolation and Gray canyons of the Green River, and in the Westwater Canyons of the Colorado.

Arapaho National Forest & the Gore Range–Eagles Nest Primitive Area

Arapaho National Forest Topo Maps

U.S. Geological Survey 1:250,000 scale overview maps: Craig, Denver, Greeley, Leadville.

Gore Range–Eagles Nest Primitive Area

U.S. Geological Survey large-scale topographic maps: Dillon, Minturn, Mount Powell, Ute Peak.

Headwaters of the Colorado

U.S. Geological Survey large-scale maps: Bowen Mountain, Fall River Pass, Granby, Grand Lake, Hot Sulphur Springs, Kremmling, Mount Richthofen, Shadow Mountain, Strawberry Lake, Trail Mountain.

Indian Peaks Roadless Area

U.S. Geological Survey large-scale topographic maps: Monarch Lake, Ward, East Portal.

Rabbit Ears Range

U.S. Geological Survey large-scale topographic maps: Buffalo Peak, Hyannis Peak, Lake Agnes, Mount Warner, Parkview, Parkview Mountain, Rabbit Ears Peak, Rand, Spicer Peak, Walton Peak, Whitchy Peak.

The Arapaho National Forest covers a million acres of public wilderness camping, fishing, and big-game hunting country along the Continental Divide in the area of the headwaters of the Colorado River. On the opposite side of the Great Divide, the historic Platte River flows along its long, shallow course towards the Atlantic. The forest is divided into three divisions, two small ones west of Loveland and a larger one south of these and west of Denver. The Rabbit Ears Range, part of the Continental Divide, forms the natural northern border of the forest. The mountains form the southernmost peaks of the North Park Range and run east from the end of this range to the boundaries of the Rocky Mountain National Park. The last portion of the range east of the Rocky Mountain National Park area is called the Never Summer Range, so named because of its perennially snowy peaks, which rise to heights of more than 12,000 feet. Among the better-known peaks of this range are Baker Mountain (12,406 ft.), Mount Nimbus (12,730 ft.), Red Mountain (11,505 ft.), Mount Cumulus (12,724 ft.), and Mount Richthofen (12,953 ft.). The Arapahos gave the Never Summer Range its name, and white settlers translated it into English.

The scenic Gore Range forms a southern extension of the North Park Range, connecting Rabbit Ears Pass and Fremont Pass. The mountains are the namesake of Sir St. George Gore, who traveled through the North, Middle, and South Park Mountains in 1855 with the legendary Rocky Mountain trapper and scout Jim Bridger as his guide. With his retinue of 40 retainers, 112 horses, 6 wagons, 14 dogs, 21 carts, and 12 yoke of oxen, he managed to kill some 3,000 buffalo, 40 grizzly bear, and huge numbers of antelope and deer. The Indians of the area, horrified by this senseless slaughter and fearful for their food supply, considered wiping out the party, but did not. The flamboyant nobleman entertained Bridger along the way by reading him the plays of William Shakespeare.

The Gore Range–Eagles Nest Primitive Area takes in more than 61,000 acres of alpine fishing, camping, and hunting country in the Arapaho and White River national forests. Trails lead up into the craggy heights of Meridian Mountain and Climbers Lake (11,000 ft.); Eagles Nest Mountain (13,397 ft.); Mount Powell (13,534 ft.); the

alpine Boulder Lake; and the lake basins of Red Peak and Buffalo Mountain. The Gore Range Trail runs for 50 miles along the east slope of the range, winding past crystal lakes and turbulent streams. This rugged, roadless area west of Dillon Reservoir is accessible only by foot and horse. Remember that arctic weather conditions exist above timberline; summer temperatures can drop to below freezing within an hour, and sudden severe thunder and wind storms are common. Bring warm clothes, and adapt yourself to the thin air before you attempt a strenuous trip.

The southern portion of the forest encompasses the mountains of the Front Range, which run from Longs Peak on the north to Mount Evans on the south. The 14,264 foot Mount Evans has North America's highest paved highway, which runs through 14 miles of alpine tundra. This verdantly forested area is crossed by trout streams and dotted with campgrounds. Another area of the Continental Divide runs through the high-country meadows and forests of this region. Atop Arapaho Peak lies the Arapaho Glacier, a remnant of the great ice masses of the Pleistocene era which carved cirques and canyons into the craggy mountains. Nearby, the jagged peaks of Kiowa, Navaho, and Apache mountains surround a huge natural basin that holds the spectacular Isabelle Glacier. The glacier is accessible by trail from the campground at Brainard Lake at the foot of the Continental Divide; the climb provides a pleasant day trip.

These mountains were the setting for the first important gold strikes in the state. By 1859, hundreds of miners and prospectors had swarmed into the area to make their fortunes. The boom town of Idaho Springs, known before the rush as Sacramento City, Jackson Diggings, and Idahoe, became a well-known health spa in the 1860s. The name is thought to be derived from *Ee-da-how*, an Indian word signifying that the sun is coming down the mountains. It boasted elaborately furnished parlors, dressing rooms, and shower baths. New York *Herald Tribune* editor Horace Greeley visited nearby Central City shortly after the rush began to investigate the claims of gold. Miners complied with his request by "salting" a placer mine (shooting gold into it with a shotgun). He was properly impressed, and his fervent account of the riches of these hills intensified the rush. By 1872, however, the veins had been depleted, and Central City languished amid abandoned mines and mills.

Among the craggy peaks of the Front Range south of Rocky Mountain National Park lies the Indian Peaks Special Management Area, another roadless wilderness along the Continental Divide. The spirelike ridge of Lone Eagle Peak (11,920 ft.) can be reached by the Cascade Creek Trail, running east from the north side of Monarch Lake to Crater Lake, which lies under the peak at 10,500 feet. Those who attempt the climb to the summit should be experienced mountaineers; the peak has claimed the lives of several challengers. Other peaks of the area, including Ogalalla Peak (13,138 ft.), Paiute Peak (13,088 ft.), and Shoshoni (12,967 ft.), also provide challenging climbs.

A full-color U.S. Forest Service *Arapaho National Forest Map* is available for 50¢, along with camping, fishing, hunting, and wilderness travel info from: Forest Supervisor, Arapaho National Forest, 1010 Tenth St., P.O. Box 692, Golden 80402. A black-and-white *Arapaho National Forest Travel Map* showing most of the same features (no recreation directories included) is available free from the same address. This map explains special restrictions on travel throughout the forest. Also available from the Forest Supervisor's Office is a free booklet describing a self-guided auto tour through the Arapaho and Roosevelt national forests, *The Moffat Road*. The tour shows you the former "hill" route of the Moffat Railroad, which led a tortuous course up the mountains of the area and crossed the Continental Divide through Rollins Pass. The line was started in 1903 and finished in 1927.

Another free brochure from the Rocky Mountain Region Office is the guide to *Dillon Reservoir Recreation Area*. Built in 1964, the reservoir provides boating and camping opportunities. The brochure includes a map and description of the area.

Vacation lodging and fishing, backpacking, and pack trips in the Arapaho National Forest are provided by *High Country Inn*, Box 96, Winter Park 80482 (big-game hunting); *Ptarmigan Lodge*, Box 218, Dillon 80435, with view of scenic Lake Dillon; *Drowsy Water Ranch*, Box 147, Granby 80446; *Arapaho Valley Ranch*, Box 142C, Granby 80446; *Bar Lazy J Guest Ranch*, Parshall 80468, a family vacation resort with trout fishing on the Colorado River or in Williams Fork Lake; *Tiger Run, Inc.*, Box 1418, Breckenridge 80424, offering scenic jeep tours.

Access & Outfitting Centers

The forest is accessible by way of State Rt. 72 running north from Interstate 70 or State Rt. 119 running west from Interstate 25. Accommodations, guides, and equipment rentals are available at Dillon, Golden, Granby, Grand Lake, Hot Sulphur Springs, Idaho Springs, and Kremmling.

Grand Mesa National Forest & Alpine Lakes Country

Grand Mesa National Forest Topo Maps

U.S. Geological Survey 1:250,000 scale overview maps: Grand Junction, Leadville, Moab, Montrose.

Grand Mesa Land o' Lakes Country

U.S. Geological Survey large-scale topographic maps: Indian Point, Hells Kitchen, Skyway, Grand Mesa, Leon Peak, Chalk Mountain.

The Grand Mesa National Forest encompasses 368,418 acres of glacier-carved canyon country, carpeted with evergreen forests and wildflower meadows. The forest is named for Grand Mesa, the nation's largest table-topped mountain, rising some 10,000 feet above the confluence of the Colorado and Gunnison rivers at Grand Junction. This vast mesa, the largest in the country, offers wild-country fishing for rainbow, brown, cutthroat, and brook trout in its more than 300 gin-clear alpine lakes, including Cottonwood, Mesa, Island, Eggleston, Big Battlement, Ward, and Griffeth, and camping along the Land o' Lakes Trail. For those who prefer a more accessible retreat, many of the turquoise cirques near the mesa rims are easily reached by car. Gravel-surfaced roads provide access to much of the lake area, and two paved roads cross the mesa. Those who prefer the solitude of wilderness travel should try the many remote lakes accessible only by four-wheel drive, horseback, or foot. More than 4,000 mule deer and 200 elk are taken each year by big-game hunters in the forest. Black bear also inhabit the mesa country.

The great mesa is covered each winter by a snowpack 5–10 feet deep. The forest offers many open slopes and exciting cross-country runs. Major ski areas in the forest include Powderhorn Ski Area on the north side of the Mesa and Rim Rock Ski Area near Alexandra Lake. The mesa was formed by a lava flow 100–400 feet thick which covered the softer sedimentary rock of the area. Eventually the forces of erosion wore away the sedimentary rock around the area of the lava flow, leaving this immense tabletop high above the surrounding country.

The Ute found a mystical beauty in this high and isolated wilderness and called it *Thigunawat,* "Home of Departed Spirits." According to their myths, the north rim of this mesa hunting ground once held the ghosts of three pairs of great eagles, or thunderbirds *(Bahaa-Nieche).* These birds were believed to prey on Indian children as well as deer and antelope, and one day one of the thunderbirds carried away the son of Sehiwaq, a chieftain. The chieftain wrapped himself in the bark of the sacred red cedar and scaled the mesa slopes in his disguise. Finally he reached the nest of the thunderbirds and threw the young eaglets down the side of the mesa, where they were gobbled up by the giant serpent Batiqtuba. When the thunderbirds returned and realized the young birds were gone, they seized the serpent, carried him high into the air, and tore him to pieces. The pieces fell to the earth and formed great pits in the mesa. The rage of the great birds caused torrential thunderstorms, and the rains filled the pits of the mesa, forming its many lakes.

Several trails wind through the mesa country. One of the most scenic is the Crag Crest Trail, which starts at Crag Crest Campground, runs along a ridge rising 1,000 feet over the mesa, and ends at Highway 75 near Island Lake. Another favorite trail is the Land o' Lakes Nature Trail. Coal Creek, Kannah Creek, and Spring Camp trails also lead the hiker through the mesa backcountry. More than 40 developed campsites dot the mesa, and camping in the backcountry is also permitted. Come prepared for chilly nights; snow may remain in some campgrounds early in the season. Expect afternoon showers in July and August. September is pleasant and colorful, but cool. Bring plenty of insect repellent.

Accommodations are available in and around the forest, among them four lodges on Grand Mesa itself. Private resorts, hotels, motels, dude ranches, restaurants, guides, and outfitters are also available in and around the forest. For more specific information, write to the chamber of commerce of such nearby communities as Grand Junction or Ouray.

A U.S. Forest Service *Grand Mesa National Forest Map* is available for 50¢ from the Rocky Mountain Region, Federal Center, Bldg. 85, Denver 80225. A smaller map on the reverse side shows the major fish-supporting lakes, ski areas, lodges and resorts, campgrounds, picnic grounds, fishermen's parking areas, youth organization camps, trails, highways, and roads.

Additional free information on camping, fishing, trails, and recreation is available from the Grand Mesa–Uncompahgre & Gunnison National Forest Supervisor, P.O. Box 138, Delta 81416. A *Travel Map of the Grand Mesa National Forest* is free from the Forest Service, Rocky Mountain Region Office, Federal Center, Bldg. 85, Denver 80225. It shows most of the same features as the official Forest Service map but is not in color. The map explains travel restrictions in force throughout the park. These restrictions are shown on the map where possible.

Rustic vacation accommodations, guide service, and pack trips in the Grand Mesa National Forest are provided by the following resorts, guest ranches, and outfitters: *Alexander Lake Lodge* (Grand Mesa), *Grande Mesa Lodge* (Grand Mesa), and *Spruce Lodge* (Grand Mesa),

all Cedaredge 81413; *El Rancho Cimarron Resorts* and *Pleasant Valley Ranch,* both Cimarron 81220; *Mesa Lakes Resort* (Grand Mesa) and *Powderhorn Lodge Corporation,* both Mesa 81643; *Trail's End Ranch* (Box 202) and *Vega Lodge,* both Collbran 81624; *San Miguel Ranch,* Norwood 81423; *V-M Guide Service & Guest Ranch,* Unaweep Canyon, Gateway 81522; *Esperanza Ranch,* Rt. 1B, Collbran 81624; *Roberts Outfitting & Guide Service,* Mesa 81643; *Baier Guiding & Outfitting Service,* Little Creek Ranch, Collbran 81624; *Colorado West Guide Service,* P.O. Box 382, Mesa 81463 (guided hunting, fishing, and family vacations); *K & H Outfitters,* Collbran 81624 (pack trips and big-game hunting); *Lyons Guide Service,* P.O. Box 3373, Collbran 81624.

Access & Outfitting Centers

The Grand Mesa National Forest and lake country is reached from Grand Junction via Interstate Highway 70 and U.S. Highway 50 and Colorado Highways 65, 92, and 133. Lodging, meals, guides, supplies, and outfitters are available at Grand Junction, Rifle, Grand Mesa, Molina, Collbran, Plateau City, and Bowie.

Gunnison National Forest & West Elk Wilderness

Gunnison National Forest Topo Maps

U.S. Geological Survey 1:250,000 scale overview maps: Durango, Leadville, Montrose.

Gunnison River Headwaters

U.S. Geological Survey large-scale topographic maps: Crystal Creek, Matchless Mountain, Cement Mountain, Almont, Signal Peak, Gunnison.

West Elk Wilderness

U.S. Geological Survey large-scale topographic maps: Anthracite Range, Squirrel Creek, West Beckwith Peak, West Elk Peak, West Elk Peak S.W.

This famous fishing, big-game hunting, and wilderness camping area embraces 1,773,589 acres on the western slopes of the Rockies. The forest is bounded on the north by the peaks of the Elk Range, on the east and south by the Continental Divide, and on the west by Uncompahgre Valley. The forest was named for Capt. John W. Gunnison, who explored this area in 1853 in search of a route for the proposed transcontinental railroad; he met his death at the hands of hostile Indians in Utah that same year.

Rainbow, native cutthroat, eastern, brook, and trophy brown trout are found in the many streams of the forest, which drain into the famed trout waters of the Gunnison River. The swift, deep-flowing Gunnison is one of the nation's top trout streams for trophy rainbows and browns up to 10 pounds. The once free-flowing middle portion of the Gunnison (before it flows through the Black Canyon) has been dammed to form the Blue Mesa and Morrow Point reservoirs. The wildlife, too, is plentiful; mule deer, black and brown bear, mountain sheep, and elk range the remote forest areas.

The forest offers 45 well-developed camp areas. In Taylor Park around Taylor Park Reservoir, camping is permitted only in developed campgrounds, but camping in the backcountry is not restricted. Many of the campgrounds and lakes are located at elevations ranging from 9,000 to 11,000 feet, and nights here are chilly. Afternoon showers are common in July and August, and September is cool. The La Garita and West Elk wilderness areas are closed to motorized vehicles and offer scenic backcountry retreats for wilderness campers.

Backcountry trails wind through the evergreen forests and wildflower meadows of the lower elevations and up into the high country. The Summerville Trail is a challenging 11-mile path running from the Taylor River Canyon about a mile below Lodgepole Campground through Crystal Creek Drainage to Fossil Ridge, an area of remote and rugged backcountry. The Washington Gulch Trail leads from the Gothic Campground to the old townsite of Elkton (about 3 miles), offering some scenic vistas of the mountains and streams around Crested Butte. The Lion Gulch Trail heads about ⅛ mile inside the forest boundary on Red Creek Road and leads to West Elk Creek (about 5 miles). The trail winds over some rough terrain, but offers splendid mountain views and leads through some unusual geological formations. The short (½ mile) Beaver Ponds Trail begins off the Ohio Creek Road and leads to a picnic ground beside a beaver pond that is good for fishing. The Texas Creek Trail heads at the end of Texas Creek 4WD Road and leads through an area of alpine scenery and old mine workings to Waterloo (5 miles), Magdalene Gulch (8 miles), South Texas Creek (7 miles), and Browns Pass (7 miles). The Timberline Trail, which starts just below Mirror Lake Campground and meanders through 8.5 miles of scenic views to Cottonwood Pass Road, is an easy trip for the beginning hiker. Trails to Henry Lake and Mysterious Lake provide access for backcountry fishing enthusiasts. The Mineral Creek and Skyline trails lead through the backcountry of the La Garita Wilderness. The Skyline Trail covers more than 25 miles between Stewart Creek and Cebolla Creek, and ties into the Mineral Creek Trail on the west side of the Wilderness.

The West Elk Wild Area of the forest covers 62,000 acres of rugged canyons, high mountain meadows, dense forests, and fantastic rock formations. Elevations here range from 8,000 to 12,920 feet. Mountains of the West Elk Wild Area include the Beckwith Mountains, the West Elk Range, and the Anthracite Range. Wilderness fly-fishermen will find cutthroat trout in the remote alpine lakes and feeder streams.

Costo Lake in the eastern West Elk area offers a good day hike, with trout fishing and scenic views. The alpine meadows of the Baldy Mountains are another easily accessible retreat, offering views of distant peaks and Beaver Basin. An overnight trip from Mill Creek to Castle Creek includes spectacular views of "The Castles," a huge formation of rock spires. Another two-day trip, from the trailhead at Horse Ranch Park over trail 438 through Beckwith Pass, offers superb views of Beckwith Mesa, Beckwith Mountains, and the Anthracite Range. The three-day trip from Rainbow Lake southwest of the Wild Area Soap Park takes the hiker through the alpine regions of the Baldy Mountains. Large numbers of deer and elk range the high country of the Wild Area during the summer; bear, mountain sheep, and a wide variety of furbearers also inhabit this area.

A full-color U.S. Forest Service *Gunnison National Forest Map* is available for 50¢, along with fishing, camping, hunting, and wilderness travel info from: Forest Supervisor, Gunnison National Forest, 216 N. Colorado, Gunnison 81230. A recreation site directory on the reverse side names all campgrounds within the forest and gives their locations, elevations, and facilities. A *Travel Map of the Gunnison National Forest,* available free from the same office, keys the locations of many of the same features in black and white and describes travel restrictions in effect throughout the forest. The office also publishes a free guide to the *West Elk Wild Area.* This guide describes the area, its wildlife, and its major features. A map in the brochure shows the locations of trails, secondary roads, and unimproved campsites and indicates the mileage between points on the trails. The guide also describes some interesting day hikes and extended trips through the Wild Area.

Guided packhorse, fishing, and elk and deer hunting trips in the Gunnison National Forest are provided by *Gunnison Guides & Tours,* Box 913, Gunnison 81230 (also ski touring, backpacking, and float trips); *Heart of the Rockies Outfit,* 10210 Co. Rd. 160, Salida 81201; *Joe Pecharich, Jr.,* Paonia 81428 (big-game hunting in the West Elk Wilderness); *Sid Simpson Guide Service,* RR 1, Paonia 81428 (hunting expeditions and pack trips in West Elk Wilderness); *Steve's Trophy Hunts,* P.O. Box 184, Montrose 81401 (western Colorado); *Waunita Hot Springs Ranch,* Rt. 3, Box 26, Gunnison 81230 (pack trips and big-game hunting); *Char-B Resort,* Box 277, Almont 81210 (in Spring Creek Canyon, 2 miles from Taylor River); *Harmel Ranch Resort,* Box 944, Gunnison 81230 (family vacations); *Wagon Wheel Guest Ranch,* 16760 County Rd. 220, Salida 81201 (family vacations); *Cement Creek Ranch,* Star Rt., Crested Butte 81224 (a rustic family wilderness resort in a remote valley at 9,000 ft.); *Crested Butte Resort,* Box 565, Crested Butte 81224 (instruction and guide service for horseback riding, kayaking, river rafting, rock climbing; ski school and trails); *Bar X Bar Ranch,* Box 27, Crawford 81415 (packhorse and big-game hunting trips); *Ragged Mountain Guest Ranch,* Somerset 81434 (a remote guest ranch nestled at the foot of the Ragged Range, with private stream and lake fly-fishing, elk and deer hunting, and horseback riding). For additional full-service vacation accommodations, write: *Spring Creek Resort,* Almont 81210; *Ute Trail Ranch,* Rt. 4, Box 11, Powderhorn 81243; *White Water Resort,* Almont 81210; *Three Rivers Mountain Resort* (guided float trips on the Gunnison), RR 3, Gunnison 81230; *Char-B Resort,* an alpine resort in Spring Creek Canyon, Box 279, Almont 81210.

Access & Outfitting Centers

State Rt. 133 runs south from Interstate 70 to the forest area. The forest is also accessible by taking State Highway 789 south from Interstate 70 near Grand Junction to Delta, then picking up State Highway 92. Ranger station offices are located at Gunnison and Paonia. Lodging, guides, supplies, and outfitters are available at the towns of Cimarron, Gunnison, Almont, Crested Butte, Marble, Tincup, Paonia, Crawford, Maher, and Aspen.

Pike National Forest

Pike National Forest Topo Maps

U.S. Geological Survey 1:250,000 scale overview maps: Denver, Leadville, Montrose.

Abyss Lake Scenic Area

U.S. Geological Survey large-scale topographic maps: Windy Peak, McCurdy Mountain, Cheesman Lake, Green Mountain.

Big Chief Mountain Area

U.S. Geological Survey large-scale topographic maps: Mount Big Chief, Cheyenne Mountain, Mount Pittsburg, Timber Mountain.

Lost Creek Scenic Area

U.S. Geological Survey large-scale topographic maps: Windy Peak, McCurdy Mountain, Cheesman Lake, Green Mountain.

Pikes Peak High Country

U.S. Geological Survey large-scale topographic maps: Signal Butte, Mount Deception, Palmer Lake, Black Forest, Falcon N.W., Elsmere, Fountain, Big Bull Mountain, Cascade, Cheyenne Mountain, Cripple Creek N., Cripple Creek S., Divide, Manitou Springs, Mount Big Chief (7.5), Pikes Peak, Pikeview, Woodland Park.

This 1,105,000-acre forest is dominated by the towering grandeur of famous Pikes Peak (14,110 ft.). In 1803, Lt. Zebulon M. Pike first saw the majestic mountain of central Colorado that now bears his name. He estimated its height at 18,000 feet and described it as "so remarkable as to be known to all savage nations for hundreds of miles around, to be spoken of with admiration by the Spaniards of New Mexico, and to be the bounds of their travels northwest." In 1820, Dr. Edwin James, botanist and historian, made the first recorded ascent of the mountain. During the gold rush of 1859, thousands of Conestoga wagons crossed the plains bearing the motto "Pikes Peak or Bust!" on their sides. The grand mountain was the gateway to gold country.

Some of the state's finest elk, deer, mountain sheep, antelope, and bear hunting is found in the Pikes Peak region and the surrounding mountains. Wildflower meadows share the lower elevations of these mountains with forest floors of blueberry shrubs, bluebells, purple monkshood, and yellow butterweed. Nearer the timberline grow forget-me-nots, mountain pinks, and alpine gentian. Hundreds of miles of forest roads and trails weave through the forest and provide access to the headwaters of the Platte and Arkansas rivers, South Platte River, Rampart Range, Tarryall Mountains, Mosquito Range, Kenosha Mountains, Pigmatite Points, Devil's Head, and the scenic Windy Ridge–Bristlecone Pine Botanical Area, the Lost Creek Scenic Area, and the Abyss Lake Scenic Area.

The Lost Creek area is the most spectacular and rugged of the backcountry areas, encompassing 15,120 acres on the northeastern slopes of the Tarryall Mountain Range. There are no roads in this area, and motorized vehicles are prohibited. A number of foot and horse trails lead through the area. The Goose Creek Trail is accessible by Forest Road 211; take it from its intersection with the Tarryall Road (State Highway 77) near Lake George, or its intersection with the Buffalo Creek–Deckers Road (State Highway 126) near Deckers. The trail ascends to the crest of the Tarryalls by way of Hankins Pass, or follows Goose Creek into the interior of the Scenic Area. The Twin Eagles Trail heads on the Tarryall Road and ascends the southwest face of the Tarryalls. The Lost Park Trail begins at the Lost Park Road off U.S. 285 near Jefferson and leads to East Lost Park and Wigwam Creek, or to Bison Pass, Bison Peak, and McCurdy Park. Hikers may camp anywhere within the Scenic Area; camping and fire permits are not required. Be properly equipped if you decide to backpack here. Summer thunderstorms are frequent. If you are caught in a storm, avoid mountain peaks, rock outcrops, and other prominent points during lightning activity. Bring warm clothing and rain gear.

The area is named for the elusive Lost Creek that emerges and sinks at nine different points in this backcountry. The peaks of this area offer good rock climbing, and its streams provide good trout fishing. Deer, elk, bear, and the Rocky Mountain bighorn sheep frequent the area. A free map and guide to the *Lost Creek Scenic Area* is available free from: Supervisor, Pike National Forest, 403 South Cascade, Colorado Springs 80907. The guide describes the history, wildlife, recreational opportunities, and major features of the area. The map shows trails through the area, forest road points of access to these trails, and campgrounds near trailheads leading into the area.

The forest's Rampart Recreation Area offers fishing and boating at the Rampart Reservoir, hiking along the 13-mile Lakeshore Trail, and winter ski-touring.

A U.S. Forest Service *Pike National Forest Map* is available for 50¢ from: Pike National Forest Carpenters Hall, 403 Cascade Ave., P.O. Box 2380, Colorado Springs 80901. Free from the same source is a *Pike National Forest Travel Map*, which shows most of the same features as the official service map in black and white and describes travel regulations and restrictions in effect throughout the forest. The office also distributes a free brochure, *Pikes Peak*, describing the history, surrounding topography, and flora and fauna of this outstanding feature. The forest, which includes all of the life zones found in Colorado, supports a rich variety of bird life. A *Checklist of Birds* includes 261 species that inhabit the forest or migrate through it. This list is available free from the Rocky Mountain Region Office (address above). A beautiful shaded-relief map, *Pikes Peak & Vicinity* (also available in a topographic edition), 32 × 32 inches, is available from the Distribution Branch, U.S. Geological Survey, Federal Survey, Denver 80225 for $2. On the reverse side of the map, is the geologic story of Pikes Peak and the adjacent area.

If you plan to drive through this area, write to the Rocky Mountain

Region Office for a free copy of *The Short Line Gold Camp Auto Tour*, a guide to a car tour that includes such sites as the Silver Cascades, the precarious railroad switchbacks that early locomotives followed over the mountains of the gold country, and such famous boom towns as Cripple Creek, where the discovery of the precious metal marked the beginning of the 1859 gold rush.

Guided fishing, packhorse, and hunting trips in Pikes Peak country are provided by the following outfitters, guest ranches, and resorts: *Cotton Gordon Guiding & Outfitting Service*, Box 122, Lake George 80827 (pack trips and big-game hunting in the Tarryall Mountains); *Tarryall River Ranch*, Box B–5, Lake George (located 17 miles northwest of Lake George in the scenic Tarryall Mountains); *Tumbling River Ranch*, Grant 80448 (a family resort surrounded by national forest lands, Mount Evans, and the snowcapped Continental Divide); *Triple B Guest Ranch*, Woodland Park 80863 (a family resort located 20 miles south of Colorado Springs at 8,700 feet in the heart of Pikes Peak country).

Access & Outfitting Centers

The forest is accessible by U.S. Highway 185 south from Denver, U.S. Highway 24 from Colorado Springs, or State Highway 9 north from Route 50, which runs west from Pueblo. Lodging, guides, supplies, and outfitters are available at the towns of Woodland Park, Manitou Springs, Monument, Shamballa, Colorado Springs, Westcreek, Deckers, Lake George, Estabrook, Buffalo Creek, South Platte, and Tarryall.

Rio Grande National Forest & Wilderness

Rio Grande National Forest Topo Maps

U.S. Geological Survey 1:250,000 scale overview maps: Durango, Montrose, Pueblo, Trinidad.

La Garita Wilderness

U.S. Geological Survey large-scale topographic maps: Bowers Peak, Grouse Creek, Lake Mountain, Lookout Mountain, Mesa Mountain, Saquache Park.

Rio Grande Headwaters

U.S. Geological Survey large-scale topographic maps: Alamosa E., Bristol Head, Creede, Del Norte, Finger Mesa, Homelake, Indian Head, Kiowa Hill, Lasauces, Little Squaw Creek, Mesita Reservoir, Monte Vista, Mount Pleasant School, Pikes Stockade, Sevenmile Plaza, Sky Valley Ranch, South Fork E., South Fork W., Weminuche Pass, Workman Creek.

Upper Rio Grande Wild Area

U.S. Geological Survey large-scale topographic maps: Little Squaw Creek, Rio Grande Pyramid, Weminuche Pass.

This 1.8 million-acre reserve of scenic high-country forest lies along the eastern slope of the Continental Divide, embracing portions of the spectacular San Juan and Sangre de Cristo mountains. This is the region of the headwaters of the historic Rio Grande del Norte, the "Great River of the North," whose famous trophy rainbow and brown trout waters plunge through the rugged Upper Rio Grande Wild Area. Between the 14,000-foot heights of the ranges, the fertile San Luis Valley of southern Colorado stretches for a hundred miles. The Alamosa ("Cottonwooded"), Conejos ("Rabbits"), and Rio Grande rivers flow easterly to the valley where they form the Rio Grande del Norte. The "Great River of the North" makes an oxbow bend in the valley and heads south to New Mexico, where it begins a long journey to the Gulf of Mexico far beyond. The San Juan Mountains in the western portion of the forest had their beginnings some 60 million years ago with a great outpouring of molten lava from beneath the earth. Later, faulting raised the mountains higher. Streams falling from great heights carved deep canyons. Today the mountain slopes are covered with fir, blue and Engelmann spruce, and aspen. In autumn the aspen flashes gold amid the green. Cottonwood groves border the river, and ponderosa pine grows in the drier areas. The scenic 58,014-acre Upper Rio Grande Wild Area includes the Rio Grande Reservoir, Vallecito Trail, Ute Creek, Simpson Mountain, Rio Grande Pyramid, and Weminuche Pass. Big game includes elk, mule deer, black bear, bobcat, mountain lion, and a few bighorn sheep.

The Upper Conejos River flows through these mountains in the southeastern portion of the forest. The headwaters of the river offer miles of unposted wild-country trout fishing and high-country trout lakes. Game includes deer, elk, bear, and grouse.

The forest has hundreds of miles of remote wilderness trails for hiking, backpacking, horseback riding, and pack trips. One of the most exciting backcountry areas of the forest is the famous La Garita Wilderness lying astride the Continental Divide, the natural barrier between the Rio Grande National Forest and Gunnison National Forest to the northwest. The wilderness encompasses some 49,000 acres of alpine meadows, rushing streams, and towering peaks. The mountains rise to the heights of San Luis and Stewart peaks, over 14,000 feet in elevation. Glaciers have carved steep talus slopes and formed rocky deposits in the craggy heights where bear, coyote, and mountain lion roam. In the summer elk, deer, and mountain sheep range the heights; ptarmigan, blue grouse, and coney also inhabit the slopes. Beaver dams are found along the snow-fed streams, whose waters hold native cutthroat and eastern brook trout.

Closed to motorized vehicles, the area offers a real wilderness experience to the hiker, horsepacker, or backpacker. There are no developed campsites; wilderness travelers may camp wherever they choose. Summer storms and cold nights are the rule in this rugged high country, so come prepared. The La Garita Area is usually accessible between June 15 and October 15. For information on which trails are open, write the Supervisor (Rio Grande National Forest) at either Monte Vista or (Gunnison National Forest) Gunnison.

La Garita Wilderness Map-Brochure is available free from: Forest Supervisor's Office, Rio Grande National Forest, 1803 W. Hwy. 160, Monte Vista 81144. The brochure describes the terrain, wildlife, waters, and recreational opportunities in the wilderness and includes a map on a scale of 2 miles to 1 inch showing the trails and waterways of the wilderness and the mileage between major points.

A full-color U.S. Forest Service *Rio Grande National Forest Map* (scale 2 miles to 1 inch) is also available from the Forest Supervisor's Office (address above). It costs 50¢. A *Travel Map of the Rio Grande National Forest* is available free from the same source. It shows many of the same features, but in black and white, so they are not as easy to distinguish. The map shows travel restrictions and regulations in effect on areas, roads, and trails within the forest.

Also available free from the Rocky Mountain Region Office of the Forest Service (address above) is a *Guide to High-Country Auto Tours, Rio Grande National Forest*. The guide covers three car tours which begin in the San Luis Valley between the two major sections of the Rio Grande National Forest, swing up into the mountains surrounding the valley in different directions, and swing back down again into another part of the 100-mile valley. Areas visited include the San Juan and Sangre de Cristo mountains and the headwaters of the Conejos, Alamosa, and Rio Grande rivers.

Guided fishing, packhorse, and big-game hunting trips in the Rio Grande wild country are provided by the following outfitters and guest ranches: *Dickey Brothers' Outfitters & Guides*, Rt. 1, 80186 West, Del Norte 81132 (elk hunts); *Phipps Ltd.*, Del Norte 81132 (guided big-game hunts in Upper Rio Grande area); *Rainbow Trout Lodge*, Box 36, Antonito 81120 (winter: Rt. 5, Box 80, Evergreen 80439), a full-service family vacation resort, located at 9,000 feet, with excellent trout fishing and pack trips; *Broadacres Guest Ranch*, Box 37, Creede 81130 (private trout-fishing river, lake, and stream, with good elk and deer hunting); *Sky Hi Ranch*, Monte Vista 81149 (on the Rio Grande River on the boundary of the Weminuche Wilderness); *Wilderness Adventures, Inc.*, Box 265, South Fork 81154 (located at the *Moon Valley Resort* on the South Fork of the Rio Grande, on Wolf Creek Pass, near the Continental Divide; guided packhorse, backpacking, Navajo trail rides, Rio Grande River trips, snowcamping, fishing and hunting trips, and summer wilderness skills workshops); *Colorado Back Country Pack Trips*, P.O. Box 110, La Jara 81140 (located at Aembres Pass and Wolf Creek Pass on the Great Divide).

Access & Outfitting Centers

The forest is reached via U.S. Highways 50, 160, 84, and 285 and via Colorado Highways 149 and 114. Lodging, guides, supplies, and outfitters are available at the towns of Del Norte, Monte Vista, Alamosa, La Garita, Saguache, Baxterville, Creede, and Wagon Wheel Gap.

Rocky Mountain National Park & Shadow Mountain Area

Rocky Mountain National Park Topo Maps

U.S. Geological Survey 1:250,000 scale overview map: Greeley.

Headwaters of the Colorado River

U.S. Geological Survey large-scale topographic maps: Shadow Mountain, Grand Lake, Fall River Pass.

Mummy Range

U.S. Geological Survey large-scale topographic maps: Trail Ridge, Comanche Peak, Pingree Park, Estes Park.

Never Summer Mountains

U.S. Geological Survey large-scale topographic maps: Bowen Mountain, Mount Richthofen, Fall River Pass, Chambers Lake.

Shadow Mountain National Recreation Area

U.S. Geological Survey large-scale topographic maps: Granby, Strawberry Lake, Monarch Lake, Trail Mountain, Shadow Mountain, Isolation Peak.

Wild Basin Backcountry

U.S. Geological Survey large-scale topographic maps: Allenspark, Isolation Peak.

This famous wilderness fishing, backpacking, and camping preserve lies in a spectacular setting of high peaks and mountain valleys, forests, and alpine tundra along the central Front Range stretch of the Continental Divide. Here, nestled among the high peaks, lies Grand Lake, the state's largest natural body of water and the headwaters of the mighty Colorado River. Huge glaciers have carved gulches, canyons, and hundreds of cirques into the mountains. At the time our country declared its independence, this area formed part of New Spain's northern frontier and was inhabited by Hopi Indians. It was not until 1860 that Joel Estes, the first known American settler of the area, arrived here. (He later moved his family out of the area, after two or three

other families followed him, complaining of too many people.) The beauty of the region soon became famous. The Rocky Mountain National Park was created in 1915.

The Rockies had their beginnings when the area rose up from shallow inland seas in a great faulting action 300 million years ago. Alternating periods of uplift, volcanic activity, and erosion followed. After the last uplift five to seven million years ago, the mountains achieved their present altitudes of nearly 12,000 feet. Eventually the glaciers carved their marks into the mountains and left sheer rock faces and masses of debris known as moraines. Streams connecting the many glacial cirques hold brown, brook, rainbow, and cutthroat trout. More than 300 miles of trails lead through such remote sections of the park as the Wild Basin Area, a mountain valley with a spectacular variety of lakes, waterfalls, and icy mountain streams; Tahosa Valley; Bear Lake country in the heart of the park; Glacier Gorge and Loch Vale in the famous Longs Peak area; the glacial lakes of Moraine Park and Odessa Gorge; the distant Mummy Range; the rock formations of Lumpy Ridge; and the trout waters of the North Fork Big Thompson River.

A detailed guidebook to these trails of the Rocky Mountain National Park is *Rocky Mountain Trails* by Louis Kenofer ($4.45). The book describes trails in the various areas of the park and shows them on reproductions of U.S. Geological Survey 7.5-minute maps. Write to: Rocky Mountain Nature Assoc., Inc., Rocky Mountain National Park, Estes Park 80517.

Douglas fir, Colorado blue spruce, lodgepole pine, ponderosa pine, and aspen carpet the lower elevations of the mountain forests; Engelmann spruce, limber pine, alpine fir, arctic willow, and black birch grow at higher levels. Columbine, mariposa, lilies, phlox, Indian paintbrush, asters, and marigolds brighten the meadows and woods. Elk, deer, and bighorn sheep range the high country during the summer and descend to the warmer valleys for the winter. A few bear and mountain lion roam the remote high country, and a wide variety of birds and small game are found here.

The park requires backcountry use permits for overnight trips into the backcountry and all technical climbs, and permits must be obtained before you start your trip. They are issued on a first-come-first-served basis unless a reservation is made two weeks ahead of time. For a reservation, write: Superintendent, Rocky Mountain National Park, Estes Park 80517. The permits may be picked up at Park Headquarters or the West Unit Office throughout the year, and in the summer, also at the Wild Basin and Longs Peak Ranger Stations.

Other trail guides available from the Rocky Mountain Nature Association, Inc. (address above) include the short nature trail guides to *Bear Lake* (35¢), *Moraine Park* (25¢), and *Tundra World* (15¢); and the comprehensive backcountry guide *Outdoorsman's Guide to Rocky Mountain National Park* ($2.15). The guides to *Alpine Wildflowers of Rocky Mountain National Park* ($1.20) and *Rocky Mountain Mammals* ($1.70) will help you to identify the flora and fauna of the backcountry. *Raising the Roof of the Rockies* ($1.70) describes the geology of the mountains. These are available from the same source.

The backcountry terrain of Rocky Mountain National Park offers excellent and varied ski mountaineering for experienced skiers familiar with Colorado snow and weather conditions. Snow cover (moderate to heavy) fills the valley from late December into May. Tundra areas have good touring conditions in late April and May. Many winter days are clear in the park. A free pamphlet, *Ski Mountaineering in Rocky Mountain National Park,* available from the Rocky Mountain Nature Association (address above) provides brief information about terrain, equipment, weather, safety, avalanches, and suggested tours, and includes regulations on winter use of the park. For further information, stop at the Park Headquarters near the Beaver Meadows Entrance or the West District Office near Grand Lake. Another invaluable free publication for winter travelers from the same source is *Hypothermia,* a booklet on how to avoid exposure sickness.

Several mountain roads cut through some of the most scenic areas of the park. The Trail Ridge Road winds up into the mountains from Estes Park to an elevation of 12,183 feet and then descends to the Grand Lake area, offering superlative views of glacier-carved peaks. The *Trail Ridge Road Guide* describes the most interesting features along this highest continuous road in the country. It is free from the Rocky Mountain Nature Association, Inc. (address above). The Fall River Road, a segment of the original road crossing the mountains, is open one-way from Horseshoe Park Junction to Fall River Pass, over gravel switchbacks up a narrow mountain valley. The road is closed to trailers and motorized vans. The *Old Fall River Road Guide* explains the history of this road. It is also available from the Rocky Mountain Nature Association, Inc., and costs 35¢.

The park has five roadside campgrounds: Moraine Park, Glacier Basin, Aspenglen, Longs Peak, and Timber Creek. Camping stays are limited to 3 days at Longs Peak and 7 days at other campgrounds. These camps are usually filled to capacity every day throughout the summer. The organization campsites at Aspenglen and Glacier Basin campgrounds, however, can be reserved. None of the camps have electrical, water, or sewer connections.

Additional camping facilities are available at the Shadow Mountain National Recreation Area bordering the southwestern corner of the Rocky Mountain National Park. Lake Granby and Shadow Mountain Lake are man-made reservoirs in this area which fill portions of the Colorado River valley. The area is open to boating, fishing, and hunting. Deer, coyote, bobcat, red fox, yellowbelly marmot, chipmunk, badger, pine squirrel, ground squirrel, and beaver inhabit the region. Rainbow, lake, and brown trout and kokanee salmon are taken in the two major lakes.

Campgrounds at Shadow Mountain, Green Ridge, Stillwater, Willow Creek, and Arapaho Bay provide more than 350 campsites. The camping limit is 7 days, and individual campsites may not be reserved. Groups may write for reservations to: West Unit Manager, Shadow Mountain National Recreation Area, P.O. Box 100, Grand Lake 80447. There are no hookups for recreational vehicles or shower facilities at these campgrounds, and the camps are fully open only during the summer months. Shower facilities and other services are available in Grand Lake.

A *Shadow Mountain National Recreation Area Map-Brochure* is available free from: Superintendent, Rocky Mountain National Park, Estes Park 80517. The map describes the features, flora and fauna, and recreational opportunities of the area. The map is on a scale of 1 mile to 1 inch and keys the locations of environmental study areas, picnic areas, information stations, ranger stations, campgrounds, lookout towers, boat ramps, roads (paved and unpaved), and trails. A publication describing *Camping in Shadow Mountain National Recreation Area* is also available free from the same office.

The *Hidden Valley Ski Resort* is located in the park. For more information on it write to the *Rocky Mountain Park Company*, 2817 East Third Ave., Denver 80226 (winter); or P.O. Box 1020, Estes Park 80517 (summer). The *Fantasy Ridge School of Alpinism* (Michael Covington, P.O. Box 2106, Estes Park 80517) offers mountaineering instruction and mountain guide service within the park. For information on horse rental and pack service, write to: *Hi Country Stables*, Rex & Queeda Walker, P.O. Box 1735, Estes Park 80517 (summer); or Boulder Airport, Boulder 80301 (winter).

A *Rocky Mountain National Park Map-Brochure* is available free from: Superintendent, Rocky Mountain National Park, Estes Park 80517. The guide describes the history, recreational facilities and opportunities, geology, wildlife and vegetation, and accommodations and access roads of the park. A large shaded-relief map in the brochure (scale 2 miles to 1 inch) shows historic sites, scenic overlooks, roads (paved, light-duty, and dirt), trails, environmental study areas, campgrounds, ranger stations, launching ramps, visitor centers, liveries, picnic areas, and water features. A chart lists trail distances throughout the park.

A special U.S. Geological Survey *Rocky Mountain National Park Map* shows the park and adjacent areas on a scale of 1 mile to 1 inch. It is published in a 29 × 39 inch shaded-relief or contour edition for $2. The full-color U.S. Geological Survey *Denver Mountain Area Map* (available for $2 in either a shaded-relief or a topographic edition) shows the eastern slope of the Front Range of the Rockies, including Rocky Mountain National Park and portions of the Arapaho, Roosevelt, and Routt national forests.

Guest ranches and resorts located in or adjacent to the park include: *Brookside Resort*, Box 1982, Estes Park 80517; *Columbine's Double JK Ranch*, Longs Peak Rt., Box V, Estes Park 80517 (located at 9,000 feet in secluded area 9 miles south of Estes Park); *Circle A Lodge*, P.O. Box 1354, Estes Park, 80517 (located near Fall River Entrance of the park and Hidden Valley Ski Area); *Lane Guest Ranch*, Box

1766, Estes Park 80517 (located high in Rockies adjacent to the park); *Lazy H Guest Ranch*, Box 217, Allenspark 80510 (a rustic mountain ranch); *Swiss Village Guest Ranch*, Longs Peak Rt., Estes Park 80517 (located at base of Longs Peak); *Wind River Ranch*, Longs Peak Rt., Estes Park 80517 (at base of Longs Peak); *YMCA of the Rockies— Estes Park Center*, Association Camp 80511 (winter: 25 E. 16th Ave., Denver 80202); *Arapaho Valley Ranch*, Box 142, Granby 80446 (offers family vacations and packhorse trips into the park high country and Indian Peaks to the south); *C Lazy U Ranch*, Granby 80446; *Double A Bar Ranch*, Star Rt., Granby 80446 (located on the Colorado River just below Shadow Mountain Dam); *YMCA of the Rockies—Snow Mountain Guest Ranch*, Box 558, Granby 80446; *Sun Valley Guest Ranch*, Box 470, Grand Lake 80447 (provides lodging and packhorse trips in the park and Arapaho National Forest).

Access

The park is accessible by State Highway 72 running northwest from Denver, or U.S. Highway 34 running west from Interstate 25 through Loveland.

Roosevelt National Forest & Rawah Wilderness

Roosevelt National Forest Topo Maps

U.S. Geological Survey 1:250,000 scale overview maps: Denver, Greeley, Craig.

Cache La Poudre River

U.S. Geological Survey large-scale topographic maps: Fall River Pass, Trail Ridge, Comanche Peak, Chambers Lake, Boston Peak, Kinikinik, Rustic, Big Narrows, Poudre Park, La Porte.

Laramie Range

U.S. Geological Survey large-scale topographic maps: Sand Creek Pass, Deadman, Boston Peak, Chambers Lake.

Laramie River

U.S. Geological Survey large-scale maps: Old Ranch, Crazy Mountain, Glendevey, Rawah Lakes, Boston Peak, Chambers Lake, Clark Peak.

Medicine Bow Mountains

U.S. Geological Survey large-scale topographic maps: Kings Canyon, Old Roach, Shipman Mountain, Johnny Moor Mountain, Rawah Lakes, Clark Peak.

Rawah Wilderness

U.S. Geological Survey large-scale topographic maps: Clark Peak, Eagle Hill, Glendevey, Johnny Moor Mountain, Kings Canyon, Old Roach, Rawah Lakes, Shipman Mountain.

The Roosevelt National Forest encompasses 776,000 acres of top-ranked fishing, wilderness camping, and big-game hunting country along the Continental Divide north and east of Rocky Mountain National Park. This is the region of the Laramie and Medicine Bow mountains arching down from Wyoming and the remote Mummy Range. The Laramie, St. Vrain, Boulder, and Cache La Poudre rivers flow through the evergreen and broadleaf forests of the mountain high country. The famous rainbow and brown trout waters of the Cache la Poudre rise in the Divide area at Poudre Lakes and roar through steep-walled canyons to the valleys of the High Plains. The name of the river derives from a tale of the Old West. In 1836 a group of French trappers were traveling by wagon through the rugged high

country of the region, and a snowstorm overtook them. They were forced to lighten their wagon loads and cache their supplies, including a large amount of gunpowder, in the Rist Canyon area at the site of the present-day Early Trappers Monument. The name Cache la Poudre means "cache of powder." They recovered their hidden supplies the following spring. The canyon of the Cache la Poudre River is a popular vacationing area with good trout fishing.

The Brainard Lake Recreation Area in the forest is a popular gateway to the Indian Peaks backcountry. Glaciers carved these mountains about 100,000 years ago, creating their striking features. The Isabelle and Arapaho glaciers are remnants of these huge ice masses. Snowbeds lace the mountain crags, and glacial lakes fill the cirques left by the glaciation. The Indian Peaks area straddles the border between the Roosevelt and Arapaho national forests. About 55,000 acres of this area have been closed to motor vehicle travel and man-made developments and are being considered for inclusion in the National Wilderness System. Such trails as the Arapaho Pass, Arapaho Glacier, Devil's Thumb Pass, Kings Lake, High Lonesome, and Corona wind through the high country of these 12,000-foot peaks. Some of the trails are accessible from the Brainard Lake recreation area.

Another remote area, the Rawah Wilderness, encompasses some of the most beautiful backcountry in the forest. The wilderness area includes 27,000 acres of isolated alpine lakes, rocky peaks, evergreen forests, and abundant wildlife. Elevations in this majestic "island of wilderness" range from 9,500 to nearly 13,000 feet. Thick blankets of snow cover the area from November to June, providing water for the plains below. The area contains some beautiful wilderness stretches of the famed Laramie River, one of Colorado's top fly-fishing streams for rainbows and browns in the 5–7 pound class. The 26 high-country lakes of the wilderness area, including Camp, Rawah, Chambers, Twin Crater and Island, and its many streams provide excellent fishing for rainbow, brook, native, Mackinaw, kokanee, and grayling. Mountain sheep, black bear, mule deer, and occasional elk roam the mountain heights. Other wildlife includes beaver, coyote, fox, mink, marten, rabbits, and squirrels. Mountain ptarmigan and grouse are the game birds of the area.

This rugged high country can be reached by an hour or two of hiking or horseback riding from roads' ends at trailheads and guest ranches. As in all wilderness areas, motorized travel is forbidden. About 75 miles of trails lead through the Rawahs, most of them well marked and numbered. Access trails include: Medicine Bow Trail, leading south along the crest of the ridge from a trailhead off Wyoming Highway 230; Mount Home Link Trail, leading from Browns Park Campground into the area; Ute Pass Trail, leading at Holligan's Roost Campground near Glendevey and following McIntyre Creek; Rawah

and West Branch trails leading from the Laramie River Road at Rawah Guest Ranch (see "Rocky Mountain Wilderness Outfitters & Guest Ranches" and "Wilderness Society—North American High-Country & Wildwater Trips" in the "Encyclopedia" section) and Tunnel Campground, respectively; and Blue Lake Trail, leading into the area from the parking lot at Chambers Lake Campground on Colorado Highway 14.

The Forest Service has built primitive campground facilities at the four major lakes of the area. Campers, however, are permitted to camp wherever they wish, as long as they take the proper wilderness camping measures to protect the fragile alpine environment. Wilderness travelers should first register at trail registration boxes (at trailheads). Rangers at the Stub Creek Ranger Station will provide you with current trail, fishing, and general information. Mountain climbing is popular here; if you go climbing, stay within your range of ability and experience, be alert for rotten rock, and go properly equipped. For additional detailed information on this area, write to: *Redfeather Ranger District*, 148 Remington Street, Fort Collins 80521.

A brochure and *Rawah Wilderness Map* is available free from the Forest Supervisor, Roosevelt National Forest, Fort Collins 80521. The brochure describes the natural features, wildlife, flora, trails, camping facilities, and other recreational possibilities in the wilderness. It also describes two 1-day trip possibilities and four possible overnight trips through the wilderness. The map shows and numbers the trails running through the wilderness, the developed campsites, nearby roads, mileage between points on the trails, resorts, trailheads, water features, and some topographical features.

The full-color U.S. Forest Service *Roosevelt National Forest Map* is available from the same office for 50¢. A *Travel Map* of the forest showing most of the same features in black and white, and describing travel restrictions, is available free from the same address.

Fishing, hunting, and vacation resorts in the forest region include: *Glen Echo Resort*, Poudre Canyon Drive, Fort Collins 80521, located on the banks of the Cache la Poudre River; *Sylvan Dale Guest Ranch*, Loveland 80537, on the banks of the Big Thompson River; *Trout Lodge*, at Red Feather Lakes; *Arapaho Ranch*, Eldora 80437 (winter: 1730 Cook St., Denver 80201), a 680-acre mountain ranch with exclusive trout fishing on 3-mile stream, with 2 scenic lakes; *Sky Corral Dude Ranch*, Bellvue 80512, which offers packhorse and hunting trips and runs a school of dude wrangling, packing, and outfitting.

Access & Outfitting Centers

The forest is accessible by way of State Highway 119 west from Boulder or State Highway 7 leading west from Interstate 25. Lodging, guides, supplies, outfitters, and high-country packers are available at Fort Collins, Poudre Park, Owl Canyon, Rustic, Livermore, Virginia Dale, Red Feather Lakes, Logcabin, Loveland, Longmont, and Boulder.

Routt National Forest & Mount Zirkel Wilderness

Routt National Forest Topo Maps

U.S. Geological Survey 1:250,000 scale overview maps: Craig, Rawlins, Vernal.

North Platte River & Headwaters

U.S. Geological Survey large-scale topographic maps: Spicer Peak, Buffalo Peak, MacFarlane Reservoir, Coalmont, Delaney Butte, Lake John, Cowdrey, Northgate.

Park Range Alpine Lakes Area

U.S. Geological Survey large-scale topographic maps: Buffalo Pass, Teal Lake, Mount Werner, Rabbit Ears Peak, Walton Peak, Lake Agnes.

Mount Zirkel Wilderness

U.S. Geological Survey large-scale topographic maps: Buffalo Pass, Teal Lake, Mount Ethel, Pitchpine Mountain, Mount Zirkel, Boettcher Lake, Davis Peak, Pearl.

This 1,125,000-acre forest reserve is located in high country along the Continental Divide near Steamboat Springs. The forest was named for Col. John N. Routt, the last territorial and first state governor of Colorado. The famous deep-flowing trophy brown and rainbow trout waters of the North Platte River, a tributary of the Missouri and Mississippi, drain the North Park Region in the eastern portion of the forest. The wild Yampa, flowing toward the Green and Colorado rivers, drains the waters on the west. Atop the Great Divide lies the 72,472-acre Mount Zirkel Wilderness. Elevations in the forest range from 7,000 to 13,000 feet. Remote high-country trails and forest roads provide access to the wilderness trout fishing and camping areas along the headwaters of the famed Encampment and Little Snake rivers, Williams Fork, Elkhead Mountains, and the remote tributaries and headwaters of the North Platte. The North Platte flows in sheer walled canyons through the wild Windy Hole, Narrow Falls, Cowpie, and Stovepipe rapids, surrounded by evergreen forests and meadows. The major tributaries of the North Platte—the Canadian, Michigan, and Illinois rivers—rise to the east of the forest high on the east slopes of the Medicine Bow and Never Summer ranges and offer some of the state's top-ranked rainbow and brown trout fishing.

U.S. Highway 40 now cuts through the forest mountains at the site of the historic Rabbit Ears Pass. The two rocky towers that mark the pass here became a landmark first for the Indians, then for the explorers and Rocky Mountain trappers, and eventually for emigrants.

The Park Range Trail leads from the end of a road running 2 miles north from Rabbit Ears Pass on U.S. 40 to the famed peaks of the Mount Zirkel Wilderness. This rugged high-country area, famous for its excellent alpine fishing and camping, is about 20 miles long and 5 miles wide and comprises the main ridge of the North Park Range. Glaciers have carved lakes and river canyons out of the underlying volcanic and metamorphic rock. Backcountry trails wind through the beautiful Sawtooth Range, which forms the nucleus of the wilderness area and provides access to Big Creek and Rainbow lakes, the Dome, Red Elephant, and 12,220-foot Mount Zirkel. The area is a summer range for Rocky Mountain elk and mule deer.

To the northwest of the North Park Range lies the smaller Elkhead Range; to the southwest lie the Flattops. The Flattops Wilderness embraces this high plateau of forests and lakes. The wilderness lies between the famous ski resort area of Steamboat Springs and Glenwood Springs. The plateau itself is covered with smaller mesas and cliffs. Trails lead throughout the wilderness area to the lakes and to the peak tops. They include Derby Creek Trail, Park Creek Trail, South Fork Trail, and Lost Solar Creek Trail.

The beautiful trout waters of the Elk River and the famed Encampment River rise in the forest and flow to their respective confluences with the Yampa and North Fork Platte. In the northeast corner is the region of the Big Creek Lakes. A 6-mile side road southwest from Pearl in the northwestern North Park area leads to the Big Creek Lakes Campground. The Seven Lakes trail heads here and runs west to fishing areas in the remote lakes along the Great Divide.

Elk and deer range throughout the forest in the summer; mountain lion, coyote, bear, bighorn sheep, and antelope also inhabit the area, along with beaver, marmot, ptarmigan, osprey, eagle, and other small game animals.

Here and there throughout the park are the ruins of old mine shafts and cabins, the remnants of the boom towns of the gold rush and the hard days of the Old West.

A full-color U.S. Forest Service *Routt National Forest Map* is available for 50¢ from the Forest Supervisor, 137 10th St., Steamboat Springs 80477, along with detailed fishing, hunting, camping, and wilderness travel information. A *Travel Map of the Routt National Forest* with many of the same features in black and white is available free from the same office. The map includes information on the travel restrictions and regulations in effect throughout the forest.

Guided fishing, hunting, wilderness pack trips, and vacation lodging are provided by the following outfitters and guest ranches: *Big Creek Reserve,* Big Creek R.F.D., Steamboat Springs 80477 (pack trips to Mount Zirkel Wilderness, ski tours, and hunting); *Cherokee String*

Guide & Outfitters, Clark Rt., Steamboat Springs 80477; *Del's Triangle Three Ranch,* P.O. Box 14, Steamboat Springs 80477 (Mount Zirkel Wilderness); *S Bar S Ranch,* Steamboat Springs 80477 (family vacations, wilderness pack trips, fall hunting, fishing).

Access & Outfitting Centers

U.S. 40, which runs from the Denver area northwest to the forest, U.S. 34 from Loveland, and State Highway 14 from Fort Collins provide access to the forest areas. Lodging, guides, supplies, outfitters, and packers are available at Craig and Steamboat Springs.

San Isabel National Forest & the Spanish Peaks

San Isabel National Forest Topo Maps

U.S. Geological Survey 1:250,000 scale overview maps: Leadville, Montrose, Pueblo, Trinidad.

Sangre de Cristo Alpine Lakes Country

U.S. Geological Survey large-scale topographic maps showing alpine lakes region including Comanche Lake, Lake of the Clouds, and the Rainbow, Crossover, and Comanche Venable Pack Trails: Electric Peak, Horn Peak, Crestone Peak, Crestone, Beck Mountain, Midano Pass.

Spanish Peaks

U.S. Geological Survey 1:250,000 scale overview map: Trinidad.

This 1,106,000-acre reserve in southern Colorado encompasses some of the most spectacular mountain wilderness areas in the state, including the hundreds of alpine lakes and meadows, canyons, waterfalls, and dense forests within the beautiful peaks of the Sangre de Cristo Range, Spanish Peaks, Collegiate Peaks, and the Sawatch Range. The Spanish Peaks, among the most important landmarks of the West for the Indians and early Spanish and French explorers, lie in the southernmost sector of the forest. The peaks rise abruptly out of the Great Plains, their great dikes and ridges radiating out like the spokes of a wheel. These dikes were once intrusions of volcanic material into the overlying sediment. Erosion eventually wore away the softer sedimentary rocks, leaving the impressive morphology of the Spanish Peaks.

Long before the first Spanish explorer saw these mountains, Indians had revered them. The sudden summer thunderstorms that erupt over the peaks were thought by the Ute, Apache, and Comanche to mark the home of the Rain God. The Indians named the mountains *Wahatova,* or "Breasts of the World." The first known Spanish explorer to pass by the peaks was Juan de Ulibarri, who reached the area from Santa Fe in 1706. After him came many others, including Gov. Juan Bautista de Anza, founder of San Francisco and conqueror of the Comanches. Lt. Zebulon Pike explored the newly acquired area for the United States after the Louisiana Purchase in 1803.

The peaks harbor a wide spectrum of plant and animal life. Bristlecone, limber, and ponderosa pines, alpine, white, and Douglas firs, and Engelmann spruce grace the mountainsides. Aspen and oak brush add fall color. The Purgatoire and Cucharas rivers and Bear, Blue, North, Monument, Martin, Horseshoe, and La Veta lakes offer good trout fishing. Campgrounds are located at Blue Lake, Bear Lake, and along Cucharas Creek. There are also resorts, cabins, and private and state campgrounds in the area. A free *Spanish Peaks Area Map-Brochure* is available from: Forest Supervisor's Office, San Isabel National Forest, P.O. Box 753, Pueblo 81002. The guide describes the history, geology, natural history, recreation facilities, and the Apishapa scenic drive in the Spanish Peaks. A map of the area on a scale of 3 miles to 1 inch shows national forest land, roads (paved, gravel, dirt, and primitive), trails, prominent dikes, recreation sites, BLM land, and state lands.

The Lake Isabel area lies in the northeastern sector of the forest, among the Wet Mountains. The 35-acre lake is the result of damming of the St. Charles River. Trout fishing is good here and in nearby streams. Hiking trails wind through the mountains, and there are developed camping facilities in the Lake Isabel area. Motorboats are not allowed on the lake. A guide to the *Lake Isabel Recreation Area,* including a map and brief description of the area, is free from the Forest Supervisor's Office (address above).

The northernmost sector of the San Isabel Forest encompasses the spectacular peaks of the Sawatch Range, crowned by Mount Elbert (14,433 ft.), the second-highest mountain in the 48 contiguous states. Nearby Mount Massive (14,421 ft.) rivals Elbert in height, as do 19 other peaks in the forest over 14,000 feet. Mount Massive is named for its size; it actually encompasses seven peaks over 14,000 feet and 70,000 acres of alpine tundra above timberline. A trail to the summit of Mount Massive wanders through alpine flower fields and near the remnants of an old glacier. Both Mount Elbert and Mount Massive can be climbed by persons with no technical experience, but good physical condition is a prerequisite for the trips.

Should you decide to climb the high peaks, remember the suddenness of weather changes and storms at high elevations, and do not underestimate the cold. Hypothermia is a real, if avoidable, threat at elevations where summer temperatures rarely rise above 50° and often drop below freezing. A brochure on *Climbing Mt. Elbert/Mt. Massive* is available free from the Forest Supervisor's Office (address above). It includes a description of the area and tips on climbing the peaks. A map in the brochure keys the locations of trailheads, highways, roads (forest routes, paved, all-weather, dirt, primitive, trail, and 4-wheel drive), trails, district ranger stations, Forest Service stations, recreation sites, overlooks, points of interest, and buildings.

South of Mount Elbert and Mount Massive, at the foot of the snow-covered Sawatch Range peaks, lie Twin Lakes, a scenic area accessible by paved road, with camping areas nearby. Mackinaw trout fishing is popular here.

A full-color *San Isabel National Forest Map* is available for 50¢ from the Forest Supervisor, P.O. Box 753, Pueblo 81002. A guide to forest

recreation sites is included with the map. It lists the map locations, elevations, camp units, and facilities of all Forest Service recreation sites in the forest. A *Travel Map of the San Isabel National Forest* showing most of the same features in black and white is available free from the same source. It also describes travel regulations and restrictions in effect throughout the forest.

The *Ponderosa Guest Ranch*, 9010 County Rd. 240, Salida 81201, offers lodging, pack trips, big-game hunting, and trout fishing. The *Wagon Wheel Guest Ranch*, 16760 County Rd. 220, Salida 81201, offers lodging and fishing and big-game hunting. ·

Access & Outfitting Centers

The northern sector of the forest is accessible by way of U.S. 50 west from Pueblo. The southern portion may be reached by taking Interstate 25 south from Pueblo, then traveling west from it on State Highway 12. The Lake Isabel area and the Wet Mountains are accessible by taking Interstate 25 south from Pueblo, then traveling west on State Highway 165. The town of Leadville serves the northernmost portion of the forest as an outfitting and supply center. Numerous guides and dude ranches are located nearby. Salida and Westcliffe serve the Sangre de Cristo Mountains section of the forest in this capacity; to the east, Pueblo is the main outfitting center.

San Juan National Forest & Weminuche Wilderness

San Juan National Forest Topo Maps

U.S. Geological Survey 1:250,000 scale overview maps: Cortez, Durango, Trinidad.

Animas River Trophy Trout Waters

U.S. Geological Survey large-scale maps: Basin Mountain, Bondad Hill, Durango East, Electra Lake, Engineer Mountain, Hermosa, Loma Linda, Long Mountain, and Needle Mountains

Mesa Verde National Park

U.S. Geological Survey large-scale maps: Cortez, Mancos, Moccasin Mesa, Point Lookout, Trail Canyon, Wetherill Mesa.

Needle Mountains Alpine Lakes Country

U.S. Geological Survey large-scale topographic maps: Electra Lake, Engineer Mountain, Snowden Peak, Storm King Peak, Needle Mountains, Rio Grande Pyramid.

Weminuche Wilderness

U.S. Geological Survey 1:250,000 scale overview map of Durango and

small-scale topographic maps: Little Squaw Creek, Rio Grande Pyramid, Weminuche Pass, Workman Creek, Bristol Head, Finger Mesa, Needle Mountains.

Wilson Mountains Primitive Area

U.S. Geological Survey large-scale topographic maps: Dolores Peak, Gray Head, Little Cone, Mount Wilson.

This 1,866,000-acre tract embraces some of the finest wilderness camping, fishing, and hunting areas in the Rocky Mountain region, including the alpine lakes and meadows, canyons, cascades, and spruce, pine, and fir forests of the Weminuche Wilderness, Needle Mountains, and San Juan Mountains. The Forest's rugged interior wildlands are the last refuge of the few remaining Colorado grizzles. Golden, rainbow, brook, brown, and cutthroat trout grow to record size in the wild Animas River and in such lakes as crystal-clear Vallecito, Lemon, and Williams Creek. Vallecito Reservoir, with 22 miles of shoreline, is located in the heart of the forest and is nationally famous for its trophy rainbow and brown trout, northern pike, and kokanee salmon fishing. The Colorado record 30 lb., 1 oz. northern pike and 24 lb., 10 oz., brown trout were taken here.

The forest bears the marks of both man and nature. Unusual geologic formations dot the high country, while abandoned mines recall the gold rush days. The ruins of cliff dwellings inhabited thousands of years ago can also be seen here; after the cliff dwellers came the Utes, Navajos, and Apaches. The first white men to enter the area came with Juan Vásquez de Coronado in 1541. The next recorded expedition occurred over two centuries later, the journey of Escalante and Dominique to California. Prospectors entered the area in the 1860s. The last narrow-gauge passenger train in the country still makes the Durango-Silverton trip, a remnant of the Old West. *Along the Narrow Gauge* is a free brochure describing the historic sites and outstanding natural features along this route. Order it from: Rocky Mountain Region Office, U.S. Forest Service, Federal Center, Bldg. 85, Denver 80225.

The Needle Mountains tower to heights of over 14,000 feet, embracing some of the roughest high country in the United States. The mountains have few roads and trails; mountaineering is popular here. Most of them lie between the Animas and Vallecito rivers, both roadless in this area. The main peaks are most easily accessible by railroad.

The Weminuche Wilderness, the largest wilderness area in Colorado, encompasses 316,833 acres of the old San Juan and Upper Rio Grande primitive areas, much of it within the Needles. Some 250 miles of trails wind up through the high country, often gaining 5,000 feet in 4–5 miles. The Pine River Trail over Weminuche Pass was a route over the Great Divide used by the Weminuche Indians. Mount Aeolus, Sunlight, and Wisdom peaks in this area reach heights of over 14,000 feet. At the lower elevations grow Douglas fir, ponderosa pine, blue spruce, and aspen. Wildflowers carpet these slopes from spring till late autumn. Among them are orchids, buttercups, violets, lupines, geraniums, paintbrush, phlox, beardtongues, daisies, marsh marigolds, the rare wood lily, and the mariposa lily. At higher altitudes Engelmann spruce dominates the forests; alpine fir is also common. Wildflowers here include the columbine, larkspur, gentians, monkshood, and glacier lilies. On the high alpine peaks grow hardy wildflowers and lichens. These high-country wildflowers are at their peak in mid-July.

Wildlife is abundant here; big game includes elk, mule deer, black bear, coyote, and bighorn sheep in the Ammarona Peak and Sheep Mountain areas. A few mountain lions range the rugged slopes. Birds

of the area include the mountain ptarmigan and blue grouse. Hawks and eagles are often seen soaring among the craggy heights.

The lakes and streams of this mountain wilderness hold native cutthroat, along with the stocked rainbow, brook, and brown trout. Fishing is excellent in Emerald, Flint, Rock, Hossick, and Fourmile lakes, Pine River, and Weminuche Creek.

Outstanding features of the Weminuche Wilderness include Chicago Basin, the site of early mining interests; the 13,830-foot Rio Grande Pyramid, a mountain whose shape recalls the pyramids of Egypt; the Window, a natural gateway through a solid rock wall on a trail to Weminuche Pass; the Knife Edge, a huge wedge of volcanic rock that has been exposed by the forces of erosion; Emerald Lake, the site of several backcountry campgrounds; the Trinity Peaks, three mountains over 13,000 feet in the Grenadier Range; and hot springs on the West Fork of the San Juan River. There is no frost-free period here; temperatures fall as low as −30°F in the winter. Summer highs may reach 80°.

It is not necessary to check with a district ranger prior to your visit. Annual trips into the area are conducted by the American Forestry Association, 919–17th St. N.W., Washington, DC 20006. Trip information is also available from: Wilderness Society, 2144 P Street N.W., Washington, DC 20037.

A free *San Juan Primitive Area Map-Brochure*—a portion of the Weminuche Wilderness—is available from the same office. The brochure describes the flora and fauna, history, geology, outstanding features, and camping and hiking opportunities of the area in detail. A map in the brochure shows fishing lakes, campgrounds, trails, fishing streams, the Continental Divide, mountain peaks, mountain passes, and mileage between major points in the San Juan Primitive Area portion of the newly formed wilderness. The brochure includes a chart of 15 suggested trips through the wilderness of 1–10 days.

A *Weminuche Wilderness Map-Brochure* is available from: Forest Supervisor, San Juan National Forest, P.O. Box 341, Durango 81301. The pamphlet describes the newly formed wilderness area and gives information on backpacking, camping, fire regulations, weather, horse travel, and general wilderness travel. The brochure includes a large map of the wilderness on a scale of 2 miles to 1 inch. This map shows lakes, streams, trails, and camping areas. Check with district rangers at Durango, Bayfield, Pagosa Springs, or Creede for more detailed maps.

The smaller Wilson Mountains Primitive Area (27,000 acres) encompasses two groups of peaks in the San Miguel Mountains. The Wilson Group in the east is the larger cluster, and includes Mount Wilson

(14,246 ft.), El Diente Peak (14,159 ft.), Wilson Peak (14,017 ft.), and a summit locally known as South Wilson (14,110 ft.). Two miles to the east is the spectacular Lizard Head formation, a rocky pinnacle soaring 300 feet above a conical base to 13,113 feet. The western cluster is the Dolores Peak Group, reaching a maximum elevation of 13,290 feet. In this area temperatures dip below freezing throughout the year, and several permanent snow masses carpet the craggy slopes.

For a comprehensive information source, request the 9-page booklet *San Juan National Forest* from the Forest Supervisor's Office (address above). This booklet describes the general topography, wildlife, geology, history, and recreational possibilities of the forest. It gives specific information on the forest's wilderness and primitive areas, as well as general information on camping and hiking in national forests. A full-color U.S. Forest Service *San Juan National Forest Map* is available from the same source for 50¢.

The prehistoric cliff dwellings and ruins of Mesa Verde National Park lie to the south of the forest boundary on a majestic plateau rising abruptly out of semi-arid land bordering the high country of the Continental Divide. Six mountain ranges in four states can be viewed from Park Point. Detailed information and a free *Mesa Verde National Park Map-Brochure* may be obtained by writing: Mesa Verde National Park 81330. A full-color U.S. Geological Survey *Mesa Verde National Park Shaded-Relief Map* is available for $2. Campsites are available at the *Morfield Campground Village*. Deluxe family vacation accommodations·in the park are available at the *Far View Motor Lodge* (for reservations, call toll-free 800–525–5421), c/o Mesa Verde Company, Box 277, Mancos 81328.

Vacation lodging and guided fishing, packhorse, and big-game hunting trips in the San Juan National Forest are provided by: *Colorado Trails Ranch*, Box 848, Durango 81301 (family vacations, pack trips, and big-game hunting trips); *Cottonwood Cove Lodge*, Box 2, Wagon Wheel Gap 81154 (packhorse trips in the Weminuche and La Garita wilderness areas); *Packsaddle Ranch, Inc.*, P.O. Box 81, Chimney Rock 81127 (big-game hunting and summer pack trips into high-country wilderness for lake and stream fishing); *Ah Wilderness Guest Ranch*, Box 997, Durango 81301 (trap shooting, fishing, pack trips for family vacations; located on the famed Animas River); *Silver Streams Hunting & Fishing Lodge*, Rt. 1, Bayfield 81122 (located at north end of Vallecito Reservoir, surrounded by beautiful mountain scenery, with fishing for trophy rainbows, browns, and northern pike; family vacations); *Tall Timber Resort*, Box 90, Durango 81301 (family vacations); *Pine River Lodge*, Rt. 1, Bayfield 81122 (family vacations, overlooking Vallecito Reservoir); *Red Mountain Lodges*, P.O. Box 355, Silverton 81433 (located 50 miles north of Durango on Million Dollar Highway U.S. 50 at Durango-Silverton Railroad Loop; family vacations, with rainbow trout fishing on lodge lands, pack horses, and wilderness lakes and streams nearby); *Thunderbird Lodge Guest Ranch*, P.O. Box 4015, Pagosa Springs 81147 (located high in San Juan Mountains; family vacations); *Lake Mancos Ranch*, Box 218, Mancos 81328 (family vacations, fishing, pack, and jeep trips; close to Mesa Verde National Park and Durango-Silverton Narrow-Gauge Railroad). *Colorado Wilderness Experience Trips*, 2912 Aspen Dr., Durango 81301, offers backpacking trips in the Weminuche Wilderness. The *San Juan Scenic Jeep Tours Company*, Ouray 81427, provides 4-wheel-drive trips through the forest scenic wild areas. Write to the *San Juan Basin Packers & Outfitters Association*, c/o Chamber of Commerce, Durango 81301, for additional information. Other first-class vacation ranches and resorts in the forest region include the *Tamarron*, P.O. Box 3131, Durango 81301 and *Wilderness Trails Ranch*, Vallecito Reservoir, Bayfield 81122. Guided float trips on the Animas, Dolores, and San Juan rivers are provided by *Colorado Rivers*,

Box 1386, Durango 81301. For reservations on the *Durango-Silverton Narrow Gauge Railroad,* write: 479 Main Ave., Durango 81301.

Access & Outfitting Centers

The forest is reached from Cortez and Durango along U.S. Highway 160 and State Highway 145. U.S. Highway 550 runs north through the forest from New Mexico to Ouray, Montrose, Delta, and Grand Junction. Lodging, guides, supplies, outfitters, and packers are available at Cortez, Dolores, Durango, Pagosa Springs, Hermosa, Trimble, La Plata, Vallecito, Silverton, and Telluride.

Uncompahgre National Forest & Wilderness

Uncompahgre National Forest Topo Maps

U.S. Geological Survey 1:250,000 scale overview maps: Cortez, Moab, Montrose, Durango.

Lake Fork of the Gunnison

U.S. Geological Survey large-scale maps: Redcloud Peak, Lake San Cristolme, Lake City, Alpine Plateau, Powderhorn Lakes, Gateview.

Uncompahgre Wilderness & Alpine Lakes Country

U.S. Geological Survey large-scale topographic maps: Handies Peak, Ironton, Mount Sneffels, Ouray, Redcloud Peak, Telluride, Uncompahgre Peak, Wetterhorn Peak, Lake San Cristobal, Lake City, Sams.

The remote alpine wilderness areas of the Uncompahgre National Forest located in southwest Colorado are renowned for their trout fishing, camping, and big-game hunting. The northern section of this million-acre forest reserve lies along the crests and slopes of the rolling, mesalike Uncompahgre Plateau; the southern portion embraces the rugged northern slopes of the San Juan Mountains. Sharp, rugged canyons cut through the Uncompahgre Plateau tableland and into the pinyon-juniper hills below. In the fall, quaking aspen groves flash gold against the evergreens. The Ute who once roamed the area believed the aspen once refused homage to the Great Spirit, who decreed thereafter that its leaves should tremble whenever looked upon.

The San Juan Mountains portion of the forest encompasses high rocky peaks, their slopes slit by deep, narrow canyons in some places and covered by alpine grasslands elsewhere. Snowcaps on the high summits feed plunging streams culminating in breathtaking waterfalls. Among

the major mountains of this area are Uncompahgre Peak (14,309 ft.), Mount Sneffels (14,150 ft.), and Wetterhorn Peak (14,017 ft.). A variety of trails wind through this remote high-country area, the land of the Uncompahgre Wilderness. Jeeps may be helpful in getting to some trailheads, but motorized vehicles are not permitted in the wilderness area. Camping is somewhat unrestricted in this backcountry; check with a ranger on wilderness travel regulations and restrictions.

Ute Indians called the areas north of Ouray *Uncompahgre,* meaning "Red Water Springs." Spanish explorers entered the area in 1777, and Rocky Mountain fur trappers worked their lines here during the 1830s and 1840s. The discovery of gold gave birth to the area's first settlement, Mineral Point, in 1873. By the 1880s many settlers had arrived. The towns of Lake City, Ouray, and Telluride had populations of several thousand people, and smaller settlements, such as Sherman, Capitol City, Red Mountain, Ironton, Alta, and Mineral Point, dotted the mountain valleys. All of the smaller settlements are now ghost towns. Most of these abandoned mining camps are on private property within the forest, and their buildings are often hazardous—so look, but don't trespass.

The Lake Fork of the Gunnison River, Big Blue Creek, Big and Little Cimarron Rivers, San Miguel River, and Henson Creek flow through the forest. The best fishing for rainbow, brown, and cutthroat trout is found in the San Miguel River and Cimarron and Hensen creeks. The remote alpine areas throughout the forest provide excellent fall hunting for black bear, mule deer, elk, and upland game birds.

Among the scenic trails through the backcountry are the Blue Lakes Trail, starting east on Dallas Creek about 7 miles off Highway 62 and leading to the Blue Lakes of the Uncompahgre Primitive Area, where fishing is fairly good; the Woods Lake Trail into the Wilson Mountain Primitive Area of the San Juan National Forest; the Bilk Creek Trail into the Wilson area; the Lizard Head Trail to the rocky pinnacles of the Lizard Head formation; the Wetterhorn Basin Trail, leading through the alpine country of the Uncompahgre Primitive Area; the Big Blue Trail, starting at the Alpine Guard Station and following Big Blue Creek, then ascending Uncompahgre Peak at a distance of about 11 miles; the Dallas Trail, 22 miles to the North Pole Peak area; Horsethief Trail, from the end of Dexter Creek road 3 miles northeast of Ouray through 15 miles of spectacular mountain country and precipitous ledges (not for the timid) to American Falls; and the Portland Cascade System, leading over Hayden Mountain with steep climbs and beautiful vistas.

A full-color U.S. Forest Service *Uncompahgre National Forest Map* showing all man-made and natural features is available for 50¢, along with fishing, hunting, camping, and wilderness travel information from: Forest Supervisor, Post Office Bldg., Box 138, Delta 81416. A recreation site directory with the map lists the map locations, elevations, and facilities of all Forest Service recreation sites. A *Travel Map of the Uncompahgre National Forest* is available free from the same source. It shows most of the same features, but in black and white. It also describes and illustrates travel restrictions and regulations in effect throughout the forest.

Colorado Adventures, Box 128, Lake City 81235, offers guided high-country camping, backpacking, horsepacking, and hiking trips in the high San Juan Mountains. Lodging and jeep trips are provided by *Red Mountain Lodge*, Ouray. *Stewart Bros. Guides & Outfitters*, Rt. 2, Montrose 81401, offers packhorse and big-game hunting trips in the Uncompahgre Wilderness.

Access & Outfitting Centers

To reach the forest, take State Route 146 south from Interstate 70 to State Route 141 and continue southwest to the forest border, or take State Route 789 south from Montrose on U.S. 50. Ouray, Telluride, Montrose, and Lake City are among the outfitting and supply centers in the area.

White River National Forest & Alpine Wilderness Areas

White River National Forest Topo Maps

U.S. Geological Survey 1:250,000 scale overview maps: Craig, Leadville, Montrose, Vernal.

Flattops Primitive Area

U.S. Geological Survey large-scale topographic maps: Meadow Creek Lake, Blair Mountain, Deep Lake, Sweetwater Lake, Sugarloaf Mountain, Buford, Oyster Lake, Big Marvine Peak, Trappers Lake, Dome Peak, Lost Park, Ripple Creek, Devils Causeway, Orno Peak, Dunkley Pass, and Sand Point.

Maroon Bells–Snowmass Wilderness

U.S. Geological Survey large-scale topographic maps: Aspen, Capitol Peak, Hayden Peak, Highland Peak, Marble (7.5), Maroon Bells, Redstone, Snowmass.

White River

U.S. Geological Survey large-scale maps: Banty Point, Barous Creek, Big Beaver Reservoir, Buckskin Point, Buford, Cactus Reservoir, Divide Creek, Fawn Creek, Gillam Draw, Lost Park, Meeker, Rangely, Rattlesnake Mesa, Rough Gulch, Smizer Gulch, Veatch Gulch, Walsh Knolls, and White River City.

This 1,960,000-acre forest located northwest of Glenwood Springs embraces some of the finest wilderness stretches of the renowned White River, a fine summer stream for rainbow, brown, and brook trout. Hundreds of miles of hiking trails and forest roads wind through this spectacular high-country region to such wilderness areas as Eagle River, Hanging Lake, Bridal Veil Falls, Elk Range, Flattops Primitive Area, Sawatch Range, Gore Range–Eagles Nest Primitive Area, Roaring Fork, Ten-mile Range, and the Maroon Bells–Snowmass Wilderness. The forest is an excellent elk and mule deer range. The Flattops Primitive Area lies within the 400 square miles of the White River Plateau, about 20 miles north of Glenwood Springs and 30 miles southwest of Steamboat Springs. The plateau, a lava-capped dome bordered by rimrock, is most prominent at the "Devil's Causeway," a ridge between the drainages of the East Fork of the Williams Fork River and the North Fork of the White River. The forces of time and nature have carved deep canyons far into the plateau. This superb green wilderness is a land of violent contrasts, with steep cliffs, sparkling blue lakes, jagged rocks, snowcapped peaks, meadows,. and densely timbered valleys. A bark beetle infestation in the 1940s left 68,000 acres of spruce devastated, but spruce and alpine fir are beginning to regenerate the forest. If you travel through this area, be aware of the dangers of falling trees and the path obstructions they create.

About 160 miles of trails wind through the wilderness; from them experienced cross-country hikers can explore untracked valleys and plateaus and more than 30 fishing lakes, including, Wall, Marvine, Big Fish, Island, Muskrat, Twin, Sable, and the renowned trophy trout waters of Trappers Lake. Half of the area's 100 miles of streams also offer good to excellent fishing for native cutthroat, rainbow, and Eastern brook trout. One of the most beautiful wilderness camping areas is the Lost Lakes Peaks, located due north of Trappers Lake.

The Flattops are a top-ranked hunting area for elk, mule deer, and black bear. Blue grouse, white-tailed ptarmigan, and snowshoe rabbits are the area's small game animals. Bobcats, coyotes, badgers, foxes, beavers, martens, minks, mountain lions, and a variety of smaller animals inhabit the wilderness. A free *Flattops Wilderness Map-Brochure* is available from: Forest Supervisor's Office, White River National Forest, Old Federal Bldg., P.O. Box 948, Glenwood Springs 81601. It describes the flora and fauna, topography, and recreational opportunities of the wilderness and gives tips on wilderness use. The brochure includes a black-and-white map of the wilderness area on a scale of 2 miles to 1 inch, showing major features and boundaries. The map should be used in conjunction with U.S. Geological Survey topographical maps of the wilderness, which include the Craig and Leadville overview maps, both on a scale of 1:250,000.

The Maroon Bells–Snowmass Wilderness area of the White River National Forest encompasses 66,380 acres of the central Elk Range, including some of the most breathtaking landscapes in all of Colorado. Peaks such as Capitol, Snowmass, Maroon Bells, Castle, and Pyramid range from 12,000 to 14,259 feet. Plunging streams and fine, large alpine lakes grace the heights of formidable, often richly colored peaks, unmarred by old mining claims. Much of the wilderness is above timberline where small clumps of trees cling to the precipitous valley walls. Through these canyon valleys flow Snowmass, Maroon, Geneva, and Conundrum creeks. Below timberline, groves of aspen are inter-

spersed with Engelmann spruce and subalpine fir. Wildflowers carpet these lower stretches and bloom prolifically on the tundra as well. Forget-me-nots, alpine lilies, alpine phlox, moss campion, and Indian paintbrush are just a few of them.

Almost 130 miles of trails wind through the wilderness, providing access to the spectacular lake and mountain scenery and alpine camping and fishing at Capitol, Avalanche, Willow, Geneva, and Snowmass lakes. The relatively inaccessible Pierre Lakes provide good trout fishing for those who wish to make the long hike.

The White River National Forest Supervisor's office (address above) offers a free brochure on the *Maroon Bells–Snowmass Wilderness*. The brochure describes the topography, wildlife, plants, trails, the camping, hiking, and mountaineering opportunities, and the fishing areas of the wilderness. The brochure includes a map of the region on a scale of 2 miles to 1 inch which shows trails and trail numbers, mileage between points, water features, prominent topographical features, and wilderness boundaries.

Commercial packers and big-game hunting and fishing guides make horsepack trips into the area, and adjoining ranches rent horses for daily trips. *K.E. Shultz* (Ponderosa Road, Glenwood Springs 81601) offers big-game hunting trips into the area for deer, elk, and bear and summer pack trips for high-country camping and cutthroat trout fishing. Most hunting is done on foot, with horses for transportation and to pack out game.

The White River National Forest shares the Eagles Nest Wilderness amidst the Gore Range with neighboring Arapaho National Forest. Trails in this remote area lead into the areas of Meridian Mountain and Climbers Lake (11,000 ft.), Eagles Nest Mountain (13,397 ft.), Mount Powell (13,534 ft.), and the alpine Boulder Lake. A free black-and-white map of the area showing the preliminary boundaries for this

wilderness is available free from the Rocky Mountain Region Office of the Forest Service at the above address. The map also shows national forest boundaries, trails, and good and poor motor roads. For more information on this area, write: Forest Supervisor, White River National Forest, Old Federal Building, P.O. Box 948, Glenwood Springs 81601.

A U.S. Forest Service *White River National Forest Map* is available for 50¢, along with detailed campground, fishing, hunting, and wilderness travel info from the Forest Supervisor's office (listed above). A recreation site directory describes the map locations, elevation, and facilities of all Forest Service recreation sites within the forest boundaries. A *Travel Map of the White River National Forest* is available free from the same source. It shows most of the same features as the color map, but in black and white. It also outlines travel regulations and restrictions in effect throughout the forest.

A wide assortment of ranches, lodges, and camps located in the White River region provide the services of guides and outfitters for their guests, including packhorse trips, wilderness stream and lake fishing, and fall elk and deer hunts. The major outfitters, ranches, and lodges include: *Adams Lodge*, Box 50A, Trappers Lake Star Rt., Meeker 81641; *Dean Chambers Elk Creek Lodge*, Trappers Lake Rt., Meeker 81641 (Flattops Wilderness); *Coulter Lake Guest Ranch*, Box 906, Rifle 81650; *7L Guest Ranch*, 52 Trappers Lake, Meeker 81641; *B & J Guide & Outfitter Service*, 9 Mile Gap, Meeker 81641 (elk and deer hunting); *Buckskin Ranch Outfitters & Guides*, New Castle 81647 (fishing, hunting, packtrips in the Flattops); *Green Acres Ranch*, Rt. 1, Box 3X, Oak Creek 80467 (located in the beautiful Yampa River Valley to the northwest of the White River); *E-Quarter Circle Ranch*, Gypsum 81637 (elk and deer hunts); *Cherokee Guide Service*, Sugarloaf Star Rt., Boulder 80302 (trophy hunts for elk, deer, and bear in the Flattops; pack trips in Rocky Mountain National Park); *Sleepy Cat Guest Ranch*, Trappers Lake Rt., Meeker 81641 (big-game hunting and two miles of fishing on White River running through ranch). *Rocky Mountain River Expedition Inc.*, P.O. Box 1394, Glenwood Springs 81601, offers 2–5 day float trips on the North Platte, Green, Dolores, Arkansas, and Colorado. *Eagle Rock Lakes Lodge*, Box 164V, Yampa 80483, offers fly-fishing on private mountain lakes. The famed *Horseshoe Bend Guest Ranch*, Meredith 81642, is located at 9,000 feet overlooking beautiful Lake Nast 17 miles north of Aspen. *Ripple Creek Lodge*, Craig 81625, is located 8 miles from Trappers Lake. *Seven W Guest Ranch*, Gypsum 81637, is located on Sweetwater Creek. *Anderson River Expeditions*, Gypsum 81637, offers trips of from ½ to 3 days' duration on the Colorado River in northwestern Colorado.

Budge's South Fork Resort, in the heart of the Flat Tops, is a wilderness vacation resort specializing in elk hunting, pack trips, and family vacations. Write: Box 71, Glenwood Springs 81601; phone (303) 442-7195 winter; (303) 328-6544 summer. Other vacation facilities in the Glenwood Springs (zip code: 81601) area of the forest include: *Okanela Lodge*, with three trout streams crossing the ranch; *Ponderosa Lodge* overlooking the Colorado River; *Rock-N-Pines Guest Ranch*, with 15 miles of trout stream and ponds, lodges with fireplaces, hiking trails, guide service, and big-game hunting on private land with cabins; and *Apple Inn* (Box 360), a ski lodge-summer resort.

Access & Outfitting Centers

The forest is easily accessible from Interstate 70, which runs between two of its major districts. Colorado Route 82 dips south of Interstate 70 and enters the forest near Aspen. Aspen, Yampa, Glenwood Springs, Trapper, and Leadville provide overnight accommodations and outfitting, guide, packhorse, and supply services.

SOUTH- WEST STATES

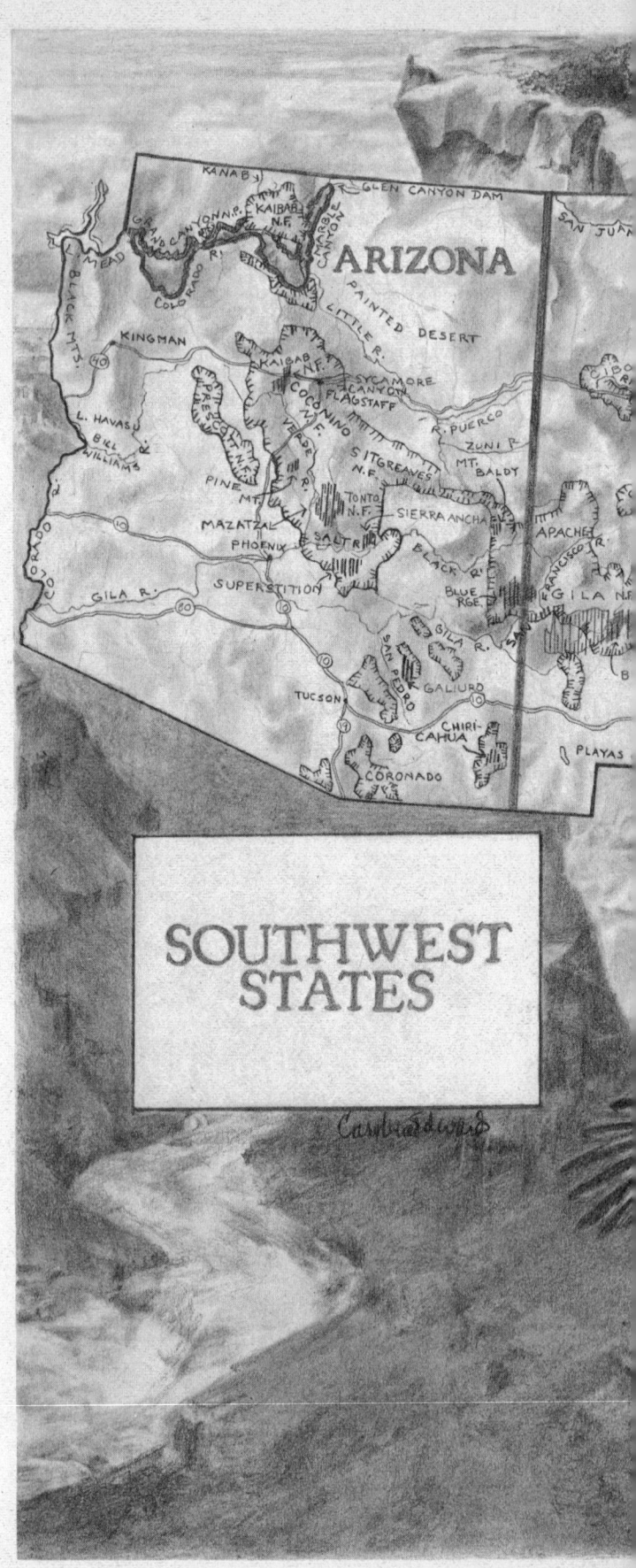

ARIZONA

SOUTHWEST
STATES

Introduction

The great open spaces, rugged mountains, eerie wind-tortured deserts and rolling sagebrush flats, evergreen-clad highlands, awesome canyons, and huge reservoirs of the American Southwest offer a wide variety of outdoor recreation opportunities, including fishing, hunting, wilderness camping, and wild-river touring. Arizona, known as the "Apache" or "Grand Canyon" state, is divided into three distinct regions: the first is the Colorado Plateau region, which occupies some 45,000 square miles in the northern area of the state, including the high prairie and conifer forests north of the Mogollon Rim and the densely forested, mountainous country of the Kaibab Plateau, which stretches north from the rim of the Grand Canyon of the Colorado; the second region is a broad zone of greatly eroded ranges and gently sloping valleys with crests rising to 5,000 feet above the plains; the third, or desert, region occupies the southwestern quarter of the state. Arizona's wild country, portrayed in the rough-'n'-ready tales of Zane Grey, and famed recreation areas include spruce-and-alpine-meadow God's Country of the Apache National Forest and the trout lakes of the White Mountains; the Grand Canyon Game Preserve established by Theodore Roosevelt and the backpacking and big-game-hunting lands of the Kaibab National Forest; the Tonto National Forest fish and game lands; and the trophy bass waters of the Lake Mead National Recreation Area and the fire-red Grand Wash Cliffs, Buckskin Mountains, Topock Swamp area, and lakes Mohave and Havasu in the vast 1.5-million-acre Kingman Resource Area.

New Mexico, the "Land of Enchantment," is bordered on the north by Colorado, on the east by Oklahoma and the panhandle plains of Texas, on the south by Mexico and Texas, and on the west by Arizona. Located on the eastern slope of the Great Divide, New Mexico contains several renowned fishing, hunting, and camping areas, including the trophy trout waters of the wild Rio Grande and Upper Pecos rivers, the beautiful snowcapped peaks and alpine meadows of the Sangre de Cristo Mountains—the southernmost extension of the Rocky Mountains—the canyonlands and ancient cliff dwellings of the remote Gila Wilderness, the trophy brown trout waters of the Chama and San Juan rivers, and the arctic tundra meadows of the scenic Wheeler Peak Wilderness and high-country elk meadows of the beautiful San Pedro Parks Wilderness. New Mexico is the home of the historic Santa Fe Trail to Missouri and the notorious Lincoln County cattle war, starring Billy the Kid Bonney.

Oklahoma, the "Sooner State," which joins New Mexico on its western boundary, has a surprisingly varied terrain, dotted by numerous sparkling blue lakes formed by impounding its major rivers: in the northeast, the Ozarks sprawl into the state from neighboring Arkansas; in the southeast are the famed game lands and wild areas of the Kiamichi and Ouachita mountains slashed by high-country streams; to the west are the Prairie Plains and bottomlands along the Red River and the Arbuckle Mountains and Wichita Range to the southwest; in the central and northwest regions are the Redbed Plains and High Plains. Oklahoma's major fishing, hunting, and camping areas include the renowned trout waters of the Illinois River with its numerous falls and deep pools; the trophy bass waters of huge Lake Texoma and Lake Tenkiller, nestled among the Cookson Hills; the fabled goose-hunting lands surrounding Great Salt Plains Lake; the oak and pine forest game lands of the Tiak National Forest; and the rugged trails of the Wichita Mountains Wildlife Refuge. To the south are the vast fish and game lands of Texas, including the nationally famous bass-fishing waters of Toledo Bend Reservoir and Caddo Lake, surrounded by pine forests; the huge international fisheries formed along the Mexico boundary by Amistad and Falcon lakes; and the saltwater fishing meccas along the Gulf of Mexico.

Weather, Bugs & Beasts

The climate throughout the Southwest is uniformly warm, often extremely hot, and dry. Sudden violent electrical storms occur frequently during summer afternoons throughout the high-country areas. Canoeists and wild-river travelers should keep alert for flash floods following intense storms. Snow flurries may occur throughout the year at the highest elevations of the New Mexico Rockies. Strong winds whip through the deserts year round, causing sandstorms which can obscure the sun, creating a strange, eerie midday dusk. Sometimes the hot winds form whirlwinds, known locally as "dust devils." Most times, in arid regions, the thunderstorms produce little actual rain, the precipitation evaporating as it falls. Summer and early spring weather in Texas' Gulf Coast and southernmost tropical areas is often hot, humid, and stormy. Potential hazards throughout the Southwest include the common western rattlesnake, sunstroke, scorpions, mosquitoes in the wetland areas, and a few camp-invading black bears in northern New Mexico. Be sure to wear long pants, sturdy boots, and carry a walking staff when traveling in rattler country. Also carry a good snakebite kit, such as a Cutter Compak Suction Kit, and by all means turn out your boots (for scorpions) in the morning and check out your sleeping bag before slipping in.

Southwest Maps & Charts—How to Order

The topographic maps listed throughout the Southwest States chapters will provide you with an invaluable guide to the area you plan to visit—showing all mountains, lakes, streams, springs, canyons, roads, trails, rapids and falls, wilderness shelters, campgrounds, national forests and parks, wildlife management areas, wilderness areas, wildlife refuges and game preserves, and state forests and parks, as well as land contours. All maps listed (unless otherwise noted) are full-color U.S. Geological Survey overview maps, 1 inch to 4 miles ($2 each) or large-scale 7½-minute and 15-minute maps ($1.25 each for either). These maps and free *Topographic Map Indexes* of Arizona, New Mexico, Oklahoma, and Texas may be ordered (along with a free *Map Symbol Chart* and *Topographic Maps* booklet) from the Distribution Branch, U.S. Geological Survey, Federal Center, Denver, CO 80225. Be sure to order the maps by their individual names (and indicate scale when ordering 1:250,000 type maps); to expedite delivery, include extra money for first-class postage.

Large, useful U.S. Geological Survey *State Topographic Maps* of Arizona, New Mexico, Oklahoma, and Texas (4 sheets, $8 a set) may be ordered from the above address for $2 each. Beautiful full-color *Shaded-Relief Maps* of Arizona and New Mexico are also available for $2 each; they show relief by shading, which gives the appearance of sunlight striking the maps' surface from the northwest. *Plastic Raised-Relief Maps* of all 1:250,000-scale maps listed in the Southwest States may be ordered for $11.95 each from Hubbard Scientific Company, 1946 Raymond Dr., Northbrook, IL 60062 (a free catalog is available upon request). These useful full-color maps provide an actual three-dimensional model of the earth's surface and show all manmade and natural features.

Accommodations— Vacation Lodges & Ranches

Arizona provides a complete range of hotels, motels, guest ranches, and hunting and fishing vacation resorts that offer a variety of services. A free booklet called *The Arizona Accommodations Directory* and a free *Arizona Directory of Guest Ranches & Ranch Resorts* may be obtained upon request from the Arizona Office of Tourism, 1700 W. Washington, Phoenix 85007 (602-271-3618).

Listings of the state's major vacation ranches and lodges are found throughout the "Arizona Travel & Recreation Guide."

Camping & Campgrounds

Arizona's mountain forests, sweeping canyons, and expansive desert country offer many different kinds of camping opportunities. Visitors can find themselves thousands of feet above sea level, deep in the plunging gorges, or flat on the hot desert sand.

National Forest Camp and Picnic Grounds, a free booklet available from the U.S. Forest Service, Southwestern Region, Albuquerque, NM 87101, lists and describes every recreation site in each of the great national forests of the area. It includes an index of facilities for each

forest, and a map of each forest showing major roads, campsites, streams, and ranger stations. *Amazing Arizona: Camping & Campgrounds* is another very useful and compact guide. It is also available free, from the Arizona Office of Tourism, 1700 W. Washington, Phoenix 85007. It divides Arizona into five major recreation areas, listing sites and their facilities under each area. All the sites are shown on a large map of the state that also indicates roads and cities.

Fenwick Lake Powell Bass Fishing School

The famous Fenwick Corporation's Arizona bass fishing school is headquartered at the Wahweap Lodge in the wild Glen Canyon National Recreation Area near Page on Lake Powell, with its 1,900 miles of shoreline and a fish population of trophy largemouth and striped bass, walleye, rainbow, and brown trout. This two-day May school, open to beginners through advanced bass fishermen, includes intensive instruction in the anatomy of bass and life cycle, tackle, school fish behavior, deep-water vs. shallow-water presentation, lures,

ARIZONA
ENCYCLOPEDIA

casting and fishing, contour-map reading, finding and patterning fish, instruments and equipment (light meters, temperature gauges, oxygen meters, depth finders, trolling motors). There is a complete marina service, with fine motels and camping facilities, and some of the nation's best campout-cruise tours to famous Rainbow Bridge, rubber-raft tours on the Colorado River, and ghost towns. For free literature and rates, write: School Coordinator, Fenwick Bass Fishing Schools, P.O. Box 729, Westminster, CA 92683.

Fishing & Hunting in Arizona

Arizona's 113,956 square miles of diverse and contrasting topography, vast national forest lands and waters, offer some surprisingly productive trout and bass fishing and hunting for Rocky Mountain mule deer, javelina, wild turkey, upland game birds, and waterfowl. The state contains three distinctive physical areas, each with its own more or less individual climate, flora, and wildlife. The northern part of the state, an area of approximately 45,000 square miles, lies within the Colorado Plateau region and is distinguished by its great canyons, including the Grand Canyon of the Colorado River. The San Francisco Plateau, the portion of the Grand Canyon region lying south of the Colorado River, is covered with lava flows and dotted with several hundred volcanic cones. The San Francisco Mountains rise above the surrounding tablelands culminating in Humphreys Peak, an extinct volcano, which has a height of 12,611 feet and is the highest point in the state. The area is drained by the Colorado, Little Colorado, and Verde rivers. The northeastern region is a canyon-cut, broken tableland studded with hills, buttes, and mesas. The mountain region lies between the plateau country and the plains to the south. The broad ridge that forms the edge of the Colorado Plateau narrows in this mountain region to the Mogollon River. A great unbroken stretch of fragrant pine forest lies along this great ridge. The great plains district lies partly in central and mostly in southern Arizona and consists largely of vast stretches of desert plains, broken by short mountain chains from 1,000-feet height.

Colorado River Lakes

The state's most important river is the Colorado, which flows through the northwestern part of the state and forms the state's western boundary with Nevada for nearly all its remaining course. The great Colorado River impoundments, including lakes Mead, Mohave, Havasu, Cibola, Mittry, and Martinez, offer often excellent fishing for largemouth bass, crappie, and catfish. The famed sloughs of the Toppock Swamp, between lakes Mohave and Havasu, produce outstanding fishing for bass and crappie. The frigid, turbulent tailrace waters below the giant dams offer some of the country's finest early season drift-boat fishing for large, hard-hitting rainbow trout up to 20 pounds. Campgrounds, boat-launching sites, and rentals are available along the Colorado River lakes. The remote tributary streams in the Grand Canyon area of the Colorado, located in the Kaibab National Forest, offer exciting fishing for pan-sized rainbows. The wilderness fly-fisherman may reach these streams only by a long hike or pack-horse trip. The most productive of these scenic, wild streams are North Canyon Creek, Clear and Bright Angle creeks, Thunder River, and Tapeats Creek. The quality of the Colorado River system fishing is best illustrated by its record fish.

ARIZONA'S COLORADO RIVER RECORD FISH

	Lb.–oz.	inches	Place	Year
Bass, largemouth	11–2	24.0	Lake Mead	1950
Bass, smallmouth	4–6.6	19.5	Deer Lake, Colorado River	1973
Bass, striped*	59–12	—	Colorado River	1977
Bass, warmouth	0–12	10.0	Senator Lake, Colorado River	1974
Bass, white*	5–5	19.6	Imperial Reservoir	1972
Bluegill	1–9	9.0	Lake Havasu	1960
Carp	28–0.5	37.5	Imperial Dam	1972
Crappie, black	2–11⅜	16.2	Lake Mohave	1977
Catfish, channel	35–4	38.0	Topock Marsh	1952
Catfish, flathead	52–8	46.0	Colorado River	1974
Pike, walleye	8.1	—	Lake Powell	1977
Sunfish, redear	1–0	10.7	Imperial Dam	1972
Tilapia	3–7.3	16.3	Salinity Canal, Yuma	1973
Trout, brown	17–0	32.0	Last Chance Bay, Lake Powell	1971
Trout, rainbow	21–5.5	—	Colorado River	1966
Trout, cutthroat	8.6	—	Lake Mohave	1978

*World's record.

Trout & Bass Waters

Some of the finest trout fishing in the Southwest is found in the high-country lakes of the White Mountains in the Apache National Forest at the extreme eastern edge of the state. The lakes of the White Mountains, including Big, Becker, Lee Valley, Luna, Rainbow, Show Low, and Fool's Hollow, lie at elevations ranging from 7,000 to 9,000 feet. Big Lake is one of the state's premier trout fisheries, having produced an 8 lb. 3 oz. brook trout; 6 lb. 9 oz. cutthroat trout; and a 1 lb. 7 oz. grayling. The White River flows from its headwaters in the mountains and through the Apache National Forest and Fort Apache Indian Reservation and provides excellent fishing for rainbow trout. The rare Gila trout *(Salmo gilae)* is found in Ord Creek in the White Mountains and in Grant Creek in the Mount Graham area of southeastern Arizona.

Some fine fishing for rainbow and brown trout can be had in the lakes and streams of the Cococino National Forest in the north-central part of the state, particularly in Oak Creek and the Kinnikinick Lake area. Ashurst Lake, southeast of Flagstaff, has been stocked with kokanee salmon (as has Luna Lake in the White Mountains). Other productive trout-fishing streams include Tonto Creek and the East Verde River and Pine Creek in the Mazatzal Mountains country of the Tonto National Forest.

Fishing for warm-water species is productive on the Gila, the second-largest river, which crosses the state from east to west and flows into the Colorado near Yuma. Its major impoundment, San Carlos Lake, holds largemouth bass, crappie, and bluegills. The lakes of the Salt River, a tributary of the Gila formed by a union of the Black and White rivers in the Mogollon Mountains, include Theodore Roosevelt, Apache, Suguaro and Canyon lakes, all of which are popular fishing holes for bass and crappies. Other major warm-water fishing areas are found along the Verde River, a tributary of the Salt, which has its source in a series of springs in Chino Valley in the great Colorado Plateau; the Little Colorado, which rises in the Sierra Blanca range near the eastern boundary of the state in the Apache National Forest, only a short distance from the sources of the San Francisco, Black, and Salt rivers, and flows northwesterly to enter the Colorado at the Grand Canyon. Its first important tributary is the Zuni River; farther on, it is joined by the Rio Puerco; and about 10 miles from this junction it receives Lithodendron Creek, on the banks of which is the famous Petrified Forest. The state's inland record fish are as follows:

ARIZONA'S INLAND RECORD FISH

	Lb.–oz.	inches	Place	Year
Arctic grayling	1–5¼	—	Lee Valley Lake	1977
Bass, largemouth	14–2	26.0	Roosevelt Lake	1956
Bass, smallmouth	6–12	22.0	Black River	1974
Bass, white	4–11.7	19.5	Upper Lake Pleasant	1972
Bass, yellow	1–9	—	Saguaro Lake	1977
Bluegill	3–5	13.0	San Carlos Reservation	1965
Carp	23	—	Lake Pleasant	1978
Catfish, blue	31–0	40.0	Randolph Park, Tucson	1970
Catfish, channel	24–3	37.0	Saguaro Lake	1963
Catfish, flathead	65–0	52.0	San Carlos Lake	1951
Crappie, black	4–10	—	San Carlos Lake	1959
Crappie, white	2–0.4	16.0	Bartlett Lake	1973
Pike, northern	21–9	42.5	Lake Mary	1974
Pike, walleye	7.7¾	—	Canyon Lake	1977
Sunfish, green	0–12	—	Saguaro Lake	1973
Trout, brook	4.5½	—	Hawley Lake	1977
Trout, brown	14.4	—	River Res.	1978
Trout, cutthroat	3–10	22.0	Bear Canyon Lake	1975
Trout, rainbow	10–0	31.2	Becker Lake	1958

Several fish records, believed to be authentic, were compiled before the Arizona Game and Fish Department established formal procedures for recognizing record catches based upon weight on state-certified scales and two witnesses. These are all from unknown anglers and include a 14 lb. 10 oz. largemouth bass from Roosevelt Lake; a

1 lb. 7 oz. grayling from Big Lake in the White Mountains in 1942; a 12 lb. 2 oz. brown trout from the Little Colorado River in 1948; an 8 lb. 3 oz. brook trout from Big Lake in 1943; and a 6 lb. 9 oz. cutthroat trout from Big Lake in 1943.

Fishing & Hunting Guides

Arizona fishing and hunting regulations, permits, hunting-zone species maps, and information may be obtained by writing: Game & Fish Dept., 2222 West Greenway Rd., P.O. Box 9099, Phoenix 85068. The department also publishes the following free guides: *Arizona Fishing Holes* gives the locations and facilities of important fishing areas managed by the department; *Arizona Game Bulletins*, information sheets describing the state's important wildlife species and groups; *Emergency Code Card*, giving ground to air emergency code symbols; *Hunting and Fishing in Arizona*, designed to inform about the state's wildlife resources; *Now That You Got It* provides info about field care of your game and gives suggestions and procedures for handling and preparation of game and fish; and *Survival*, detailing the effects of being lost and a plan for a simple survival kit.

Hunting

The state's national forest lands and wilderness lands offer excellent fall hunting for Rocky Mountain mule deer, which range over the northern part of the state in the forested highland areas. Desert mule deer and the Arizona whitetail or Coues deer, seldom exceeding 100 pounds dressed, are found in the southern hunting zones. Rocky Mountain elk are found in the high-country areas of the Apache, Tonto, Sitgreaves, and Cococino national forests. The rare desert bighorn sheep is found in the Kingman Resource area, Kofa Game Refuge, and Galiuro Mountains Wilderness area. The javelina is one of the state's most popular big-game animals and is found throughout the brushy desert floors and foothills of the national forest lands, along with a few small remaining herds of pronghorn antelope. Large Merriam turkey are found in the forest regions from the Kaibab National Forest, north of the Grand Canyon, south to the Mexican border. The most important upland game bird in Arizona is the mourning dove, which ranges throughout the state. Waterfowl hunting for ducks and geese is generally best along the marshlands of the Colorado and Salt river systems, with limited shooting along the Gila and Verde rivers.

Grand Canyon National Park & the "River of the Shining Mountains"

The Grand Canyon is one of the world's most awesome and spectacular natural structures. It provides unforgettable river trips, hiking trips, mule rides, and dazzling views. The dark pines of the Kaibab National Forest conceal the Grand Canyon until the rim is reached. There, spread out for miles and miles, is an ocean of color. From misty blue depths rise gigantic islands of crimson sandstone, with undulating bands of reds and purples growing softer in color and outline toward the horizon. The immensity is staggering, the boldness of its contours overwhelming. Colors change continually as the sun moves across the sky, creating new shadows and illuminating new contours.

The Grand Canyon is more than 1½ billion years old. The many ancient layers of rock were pushed into high mountains by movements of the earth's crust and contain fossils and remnants of early plant and animal life. Compared to the age of its rocks, man's advent in the canyon is very recent. The earliest ruins are those of the Pueblo Indians, from about A.D. 1200. The first explorers to see the canyon were the Spaniards. Coronado and his men tried to climb down, but they wisely abandoned the effort. The Colorado River was finally navigated in 1869 by John Wesley Powell, a one-armed veteran of the

Civil War. Powell and his expedition of 10 men set off from Green River City, Wyoming on May 24, 1869, in three small rowboats 21 feet long and one 16-foot boat. One of the boats was smashed to splinters at Disaster Falls. The expedition passed through Marble Canyon (whose walls were described by Powell as towering more than half a mile above the river floor, with hundreds of buttresslike projections and domed recesses) to the mouth of the Little Canyon and on through the raging waters of the Granite Gorge of the Grand Canyon. The trip through the gorge was marked by unending toil and a series of narrow escapes, inspiring Powell to write that at times their danger was so great that they "forgot the danger till they heard the roar of a great fall below." Three of the men who refused to tackle the succession of falls and rapids below Diamond Creek left the expedition and were killed by Paiutes, the rest survived and made it to the mouth of the Virgin River on August 13, ninety-eight days after they had started. Undaunted, Powell returned to explore the Colorado a second time. News of the canyon brought many more explorers and eventually tourists. In 1909, Julius Stone's expedition made a complete photographic record of the canyon.

A wide range of plant and animal life complements the beauty of the canyon. Desert cacti flourish along the river, and blue spruce and Douglas fir grow along the rim. Many flowers are present, including delphinium, white sego lily, white thistle poppy, scarlet bugle, blue locoweed, prickly pear, and the yucca plant. Wildlife includes the Kaibab squirrel, a dark animal with a plumy white tail and tufted ears, whose habitat is limited to the North Rim. There are also beaver, deer, mountain sheep, porcupine, a few mountain lions, some beautifully colored lizards and snakes, meadowlarks, mockingbirds, long-tailed chats, spurred towhees, water ouzels, and roadrunners.

The two most popular hiking trails on the canyon are the Bright Angel Trail and the Kaibab Trail. The Bright Angel Trail, originally used by Havasupai Indians of the South Rim, has two campgrounds and several rest houses with water. The Kaibab Trail links the north and south ends of the canyon. The South Kaibab Trail has no campgrounds, no water, and little shade. It descends down into Bright Angel Campground and Phantom Ranch, where it meets the North Kaibab Trail. This trail is a little more receptive, with campgrounds and water at two locations.

The Grand Canyon is generally referred to in terms of the North Rim and the South Rim. The road to the North Rim winds through forests of ponderosa pine, spruce, aspen, and occasional mountain meadows. A hike to the canyon bottom will take you through as many life zones as there are between Canada and Mexico. The North Rim is generally cooler than the South Rim, because the elevations are higher. However, it is closed during the winter. The South Rim includes many overlooks and rim trails. The Grand Canyon is one mile deep, and while its size can readily be measured, its impact on the human spirit cannot. People standing on the rim can look down to the tops of mountains that are thousands of feet high. The Colorado River was the chief architect of the canyon, and remains a staggering living example of the power of moving water. Each layer of the canyon was revealed by the insistent flow of the river, recording the evolution of life forms. Nowhere else on earth is such a complete geological record exposed. Each layer and climate supports its own distinct groups of plant and animal life. The gorges are desert regions, but the rims are covered with forests. It's the elevation that makes the difference. Many day hikes can be taken from the rims, but hikers should remember that the canyon is an upside-down mountain—the second half of the trip will be more strenuous than the first.

One of the most rewarding ways to see the Grand Canyon is to take a trip down the Colorado River. The same falls and rapids that greeted John Wesley Powell are still there, but modern equipment has greatly reduced the risks. The exhilaration, the terror, the excitement, and the gloom experienced by Powell and his men are described in the *Powell Centennial Grand Canyon River Guide*, available for $4.95 from Westwater Books, Box 365, Boulder City, NV 89005. A continuing strip map of the river extends throughout its pages, accompanied by many photographs of historic figures and points on the river as well as excerpts from Powell's journal. This is an excellent and informative guide to the Colorado River.

The *Inner Canyon Hiking Booklet* (90¢), a guide to the abandoned trails of Grand Canyon National Park and monument, and *Grand Canyon Wildflowers* ($2.50, an annotated checklist with key; illustrated in color and black and white) may be obtained from: Grand Canyon Natural History Assn., Box 219, Grand Canyon 86023 (include 20¢ for postage). *Guidebook to the Colorado River*, Part I, Lee's Ferry to Phantom Ranch ($1.75); and Part II, Phantom R Ranch to Temple Bar ($2.25), may also be obtained from the same address. The beautiful *Grand Canyon Scroll Map*, Lee's Ferry to Temple Bar ($3.50), is available from Leslie A. Jones, Star Route, Box 13A, Heber, UT 84032. *Maps & Profiles of the Colorado River*, Lee's Ferry to Temple Bar ($5.00), is available from the American River Touring Assn., 1016 Jackson St., Oakland, CA 94607. *The Exploration of the Colorado River and Its Canyons*, the classic by John Wesley Powell ($3.00), may be obtained from Dover Publications, Inc., 180 Varick St., New York, NY 10014. *River Runners' Guide to the Canyons of the Green and Colorado Rivers*, Vol. III, Marble Gorge and Gravel Canyon ($4.00), may be obtained from the Powell Society, 750 Vine St., Denver CO 80206. A complete listing of Colorado River guidebooks is contained in the free catalog *Books for River Runners*, available upon request from Westwater Books, Box 365, Boulder City, NV 89005.

Grand Canyon White Water & Backpacking Trips

Many outfitters and wild-water and backpacking guides service the Grand Canyon and the Colorado River. *Colorado River & Trail Expeditions, Inc.*, 1449 East 3000 South, Salt Lake City, UT 84106, will send a free brochure on request. They provide many river and hiking trips for singles or groups. Other outfitters include the *American River Touring Association*, 1016 Jackson St., Oakland, CA 94607; *Arizona River Runners, Inc.*, Box 2021, Marble Canyon 86036; *Cross Tours and Explorations, Inc.*, 274 West 1400 South, Orem, UT 84057; *Georgie's Royal River Rats*, P.O. Box 12489, Las Vegas, NV 89112; *Grand Canyon Dories, Inc.*, P.O. Box 5585, Stanford, CA 94305; *Grand Canyon Expeditions, Inc.*, Kanab, UT 84741; *Grand Canyon Scenic Rides*, North Rim, 86022; *Grand Canyon Trail Guides, Inc.*, P.O. Box 957, Flagstaff 86001; *Grand Canyon Youth Expeditions*, Route #2, Box 755, Flagstaff 86001; *Harris Boat Trips*, Box 521, Kanab, UT 84741; *Hatch River Expeditions, Inc.*, 411 East 2nd North, Vernal, UT 84078; *Hualapai Grand Canyon River Runners*, Hualapai Tribal Enterprises, P.O. Box 274, Peach Springs 86434; *Moki Mac River Expeditions*, 6829 Bella Vista Drive, Salt Lake City, UT 84121; *Mule Train Tours*, P.O. Box 231, Fredonia 86022; *O.A.R.S., Inc.*, Box 67, Angels Camp, CA 95222; *Outdoors Unlimited*, 2500 Fifth Ave., Sacramento, CA 95818; *Sanderson River Expeditions*, P.O. Box 1535, Page 86040; *Tour West, Inc.*, P.O. Box 333, Orem, UT 84057; *Western River Expeditions, Inc.*, P.O. Box 6339, Salt Lake City, UT 84106; *White Water River Expeditions*, P.O. Box 476, Kanab, UT 84741; *Wilderness World*, Box 1882, Flagstaff 86001; *Wonderland Expeditions*, P.O. Box 338, Green River, UT 84525. One of the best of the many Grand Canyon guide and outfitting services is *Canyoneers, Inc.* (P.O. Box 2997, Flagstaff 86001), located in the historic old Santa Fe railroad depot near El Tovar Hotel at Grand Canyon. They offer first rate guided river and trail trips, trailhead service, and equipment rentals.

Scenic air tours of the Grand Canyon country are provided by: *Grand Canyon Airlines*, P.O. Box 186, Grand Canyon 86023; *Grand Canyon Helicopters*, P.O. Box 455, Grand Canyon 86023; *Northland Aviation, Inc.*, Pulliam Airport, Flagstaff 86001.

Grand Canyon Lodges & Maps

Hotels and rustic lodges near the rims include the *Grand Canyon Lodge* (North Rim), operated by TWA Services, Inc., Box 400, Cedar City, UT 84720, phone (801) 586–9476; and *Bright Angel Lodge, El Tovar, Grand Trailer Village, Kachina Lodge, Motor Lodge, Phantom Ranch* (reached by hiking or mules only), *Thunderbird Lodge, Old Yavapai Lodge,* and *New Yavapai Lodge* (South Rim), all operated by Fred Harvey Inc., Grand Canyon 86023, phone (602) 638–2631.

Trail maps, tour information, and transportation schedules are available free from the Park Supervisor, Grand Canyon National Park, Grand Canyon 86023.

An excellent selection of topographic and shaded relief maps is available from the U.S. Geological Survey, Federal Center, Denver, CO 80225. *The Grand Canyon National Monument Map* shows the monument and adjacent area. The scale is 1:48,000, or one inch to 4,000 feet. Size is 33 by 42 inches. It is available for $2.00. The *Grand Canyon National Park and Vicinity Map* shows the entire park and the adjacent area. The scale is 1:62,500, or about one inch to one mile. Size is 38 by 60 inches. The topographic and shaded-relief edition is $2.00. A *Map of the Bright Angel Area* is also available, which includes a brief geologic history on the back of the map. The scale is 1:62,500, or about one inch to one mile. Size is 17 by 21 inches. Both a topographic and shaded-relief edition are available for $1.25 each. (See

also "Kaibab National Forest & The Grand Canyon" in the "Travel & Recreation Guide" section.)

Guides & Wilderness Outfitters

A free listing of Arizona licensed guides is available from the Arizona Game and Fish Dept., 2222 W. Greenway Rd., Phoenix 85068, covering big-game hunting and fishing in the following areas: White Mountains, Springerville, Alpine, Show Low, Prescott, Arizona Strip, Kaibab, Upper and Lower Colorado, Kingman Resource Area, Seligman, North Central, Yuma, Parker, Central Arizona, Globe, Payson, Tucson, Flagstaff, Nogales, Ft. Huachuca, Southeastern Clifton, Safford, Willcox, and Douglas.

Highways—Recreation & Scenic Routes

Arizona's magnificent landscape makes driving a pleasant experience throughout this land of contrasts. Indian ruins, historic sites, recreational areas, and astounding terrain are never very far away. *Explore Arizona*, a map guide of the state, is available free from the Office of Economic Planning and Development, 1645 W. Jefferson, Phoenix 85007. It divides the state into five regions, providing a highway map and description of each one. *County Road Maps*, showing highways, campgrounds, and recreation areas, are also available free from the Arizona State Highway Dept., Administrative Services, 206 S. 17th Ave., Phoenix 85007.

The *Arizona State Highway Map*, showing all highways and roads, national forests, recreation areas, towns and settlements, lakes and streams, and airfields and railroads, is available free from the Arizona State Highway Depart. (address above).

Kingman Resource Area

This 1.5-million-acre reserve is located in northwestern Arizona and contains the spectacular peaks of the Hualapai Mountains, Lake Mead National Recreation Area, the fire-red Grand Wash Cliffs, the scenic Buckskin Mountains and the Needles, Cerbat Mountains, Lake Mohave, Bill Williams River, Topock Swamp Area, Lake Havasu, the Black, Big Sandy, and Aquarius mountains, Mojave Canyon, Kofa Game Range (a 660,000-acre preserve for the desert bighorn sheep), and the Imperial National Wildlife Refuge, which stretches along both sides of the Colorado River for some 30 miles above Imperial Dam.

The Kingman Resource Area Recreation Map is available free from the Kingman Resource Area Office, Box 386, Kingman 86401. It shows all public and Indian lands, roads, towns, springs and wells, mines, points of interest, recreation sites, airfields, and railroads. It also includes a close-up map of the Hualapai Mountains.

The Kingman Resource Area is shown on the following U.S. Geological Survey topographic maps: Kingman, Las Vegas, Needles, Prescott, and Williams.

Paria Canyon Primitive Area

This wilderness gorge is flanked by red cliffs, and embraces 18,726 acres in Arizona and 8,726 acres in Utah. The Paria River flows through the canyon for 45 miles from the Bryce Canyon National Park area to its confluence with the Colorado River at Lee's Ferry.

The Paria Canyon deepens rapidly, with sheer walls towering 1,500 feet above the riverbed. About eight miles before the river joins the Colorado at Lee's Ferry, the Canyon changes into terrain of rolling hills and sand dunes. At one spot along the canyon the river roars through at the Narrows, a 12-foot-wide space flanked by vertical walls. Some fine fishing for rainbow trout can be found along the Colorado River below the Glen Canyon Dam near Lee's Ferry. The Paria River,

however, holds no game fish. But there are several species of wildlife, including raccoon, fox, bobcat, and swarms of white-throated swifts and cliff swallows. Eagles, crows, and hawks circle in the sky, looking for prey, and an occasional duck, dove, or killdeer can also be found.

The largest and most spectacular tributary to the Paria Canyon is Buckskin Gulch. This is a twisting labyrinth carved millions of years ago by the steep stream gradient. The canyon has numerous natural arches, stairwells, and caves, and in some places the gorge is less than two feet in width and the undulating, near vertical walls block skyward vision.

Because this area can often be hazardous, a permit is required from the Kanab District Office. A simple map and log of the Paria Canyon is available free from the Bureau of Land Management, Kanab District Office, 320 North 1st East, Kanab, UT 84741.

The Paria Canyon Primitive Area is shown on the following U.S. Geological Survey topographic maps: Lee's Ferry, Paria, and Paria Plateau; 15-minute quadrangle maps of the Paria Canyon—Paria (Utah), Paria Plateau (Arizona), and Lee's Ferry (Arizona)—are available from the Distribution Branch, Federal Center, Denver, CO 80225.

Apache National Forest & the White Mountains

Apache National Forest Topo Maps

U.S. Geological Survey Overview Maps, scale 1:250,000: Clifton, Mesa, and St. Johns.

Blue Range Primitive Area

Large-scale U.S. Geological Survey Topographic Maps: Alpine, Big Lake, Blue, and Hannagan Meadow.

Mount Baldy Wilderness

Large-scale U.S. Geological Survey Topographic Maps: Hawley Lake and Mount Ord.

White Mountains Lake Country

Large-scale U.S. Geological Survey Topographic Maps: Hawley Lake West, Hawley Lake East, Corn Creek Plateau, Marshall Butte, Mount Ord, Bonito Rock, Big Lake, Alpine, McNary, Horseshoe Cienaga, Greens Peak, Greer, Eagan, Nelson Reservoir, Loco Knoll.

This region, known as "God's Country," encompasses 1,808,000 acres of cool fir and spruce forests, mountains, and meadows in eastern Arizona and extends partway into New Mexico. The headwaters of the Black, Little Colorado, Blue, and San Francisco rivers rise in the Apache. Forest roads and trails lead to the renowned fishing waters of the White Mountains, Big Lake, Crescent Lake, Luna Lake, Mangas Mountains, Gallo Mountains, Mexican Hay Lake, Blue Range Mountains, Greer Lakes, San Francisco Mountains, and the Mount Baldy Wilderness. This region was once the hunting grounds of Ben Lilly, the legendary lone hunter who killed bears with his knife and, according to local lore, treed over 50 mountain lions in one season.

Big-game hunting is still excellent in the wild backcountry areas for mule and whitetail deer, elk, javelina, antelope, black bear, cougar, and wild turkey. Hunting camps that operate out of Blue, Arizona, and Luna, New Mexico, are famous for their high rate of big-game trophies. Arizona considers the wild turkey big game, and the Apache is prime gobbler territory. The Merriam's turkey is a bird of big timber and high slopes and ridges. A mature Merriam gobbler usually weighs between 15 and 20 pounds; hens between 9 and 12 pounds. When the pioneer settlement cut away the original open mature forests, the turkey became rare or nonexistent in many parts of the country. Today, with the growth of the forests, the turkey has experienced a dramatic comeback. "Roosting," or stand-hunting, is the most common and productive way to hunt this wary bird. Drab or camouflage clothing is a must. Turkeys have superb hearing, and like most diurnal birds, possess a keen ability to distinguish colors.

Fishing and hunting are good in the headwaters area on the West Fork of the Little Colorado in the Mount Baldy Wilderness. Elevations in the wilderness vary from 8,700 feet to 11,000 feet, from gently sloping timbered benches to extremely steep, rock-strewn mountainsides cut by deep canyons. Volcanic Mount Baldy (11,590 ft.) dominates this 7,000-acre blend of remote mountains, forests, valleys, and streams located on the border between the Apache Forest and the Fort Apache Indian Reservation. Two main trails lead to the summit of Mount Baldy, passing through forests of Douglas, white, and corkbark fir, blue and Engelmann spruce, and white and ponderosa pine, and along meadows ringed with quaking aspen. Another outstanding hiking and hunting region is the Blue Range Primitive Area, encompassing 173,713 acres along the southern edge of the Colorado Plateau. Old Apache Indian trails lead past the barren lava pinnacles, timbered ridges, gray cliffs, and deep canyons found along the Mogol-

ARIZONA TRAVEL & RECREATION GUIDE

lon Rim, to the spectacular Blue River Canyon, Saddle Mountain, Whiterocks Mountain, and the Bear and Alder mountains. Big-game hunting is good throughout the area for deer, elk, bear, and the elusive mountain lion.

The White Mountain region, located in the cool spruce and fir forests at the eastern edge of the state boundary, is perhaps the most important trout-fishing area in Arizona. The White Mountains embrace more than 24 major trout lakes and over 600 miles of streams. The lakes in the eastern portion of the White Mountains, including Rainbow Lake, Show Low Lake, and Fool's Hollow Lake, have first-rate fishing for large rainbow trout. Good populations of cutthroat and rainbow trout are found in Becker, Lyman, Mexican Hay, Luna, Lee Valley, Greer, Big, and Crescent lakes. Along the western section of the White Mountains are the trout streams and lakes of the Fort Apache Indian Reservation. The Apache tribe, with the assistance of the U.S. Fish and Wildlife Service, keeps the streams and lakes well-stocked with fat rainbow and brown trout. The White River flows through a major portion of the reservation, and provides good fly fishing for cutthroats and rainbows. Reservation permits and the regular Arizona fishing licenses are required to fish the Apache waters. The White Mountains are also first-rate big-game country for deer, elk, and bear. Upland game birds include blue grouse, pheasant, mourning dove, and quail. For a free *Fort Apache Indian Reservation* map-brochure and fishing, hunting, camping, and boating regulations, write: White Mountain Recreation Enterprise, P.O. Box 218, Whiteriver 85941.

There is a steady 10-mile climb between Springerville and the summit of the White Mountains. Sheep and cattle graze on the abundant grass, and the wooded peaks rise more than 10,000 feet above sea level.

An *Apache National Forest Map* and recreation site index is available for 50¢ from the Forest Supervisor, Apache-Sitgreaves National Forest, P.O. Box 640, Springerville 85938. It shows all roads, recreation sites, streams, ranger stations, and points of interest. A small map of the *Mount Baldy Wilderness* is also available free from the Forest Supervisor.

Rustic vacation accommodations in the White Mountains Country are provided by the following lodges and guest ranches: *Canyon Cove* (with miles of trout streams), Box 363, Springerville 85938; *South Fork Guest Ranch* (a family resort in the heart of the White Mountains), P.O. Box 627, Springerville 85938; *Mountain High Lodge*, Box 151, Alpine 85920; *Sprucedale Ranch* (a working ranch with modern guest cabins), Alpine 85925.

Access & Outfitting Centers

The Apache National Forest is reached via U.S. highways 60, 180, and 666, and Arizona State Highway 73. Lodging, supplies, guides, and outfitting services are available at Alpine, Springerville, Greer, Clifton, Morenci, and Nutrioso.

Cococino National Forest

Cococino National Forest Topo Maps

U.S. Geological Survey Overview Maps, scale 1:250,000: Flagstaff, Holbrook, Prescott.

Sycamore Canyon Wilderness

Large-scale U.S. Geological Survey Topographic Maps: Bill Williams Mountain, Clarkdale, Grand Prairie, Loy Butte, Sycamore Point.

This 1.8-million-acre reserve stretches from the desert country near Camp Verde up over the Mogollon Rim to the San Francisco Peaks

and from the wild Sycamore Canyon on the west to the cool, tall-timbered lake country above Mormon Lake. Major features include Lake Mary, Kinnikinick Lake, Beaver Creek, Blue Ridge Reservoir, Stoneman Lake, and the Elden Mountains. Wildlife includes Rocky Mountain mule deer, antelope, turkey, a few black bears, and, in the lower elevations, javelina.

Cococino is a Hopi word for "piñon-nut people." The Hopis used it to describe their neighbors, the Havasupai. Much of the Cococino lies on the Colorado Plateau, part of the massive geologic uplift through which the mighty Colorado has cut its course. The region occupies a section of the plateau that is an irregular tableland of pine forest. The Mogollon Rim to the south is part of a great fault that runs for 200 miles across Arizona from the southeast to the northwest. The San Francisco Peaks, the tallest of Arizona's mountains, rise from the vast Colorado Plateau and are remnants of an ancient volcano that may well have reached 15,000 feet at the peak of its activity. The beautiful lake country, a remnant of ancient lake beds, is located southeast of Flagstaff and has good bass fishing in Mary and Mormon lakes. Kinnikinick Lake, to the south, has fishing for cutthroat trout. Oak Creek, about 15 miles farther south, holds rainbows and browns. Forest roads and trails provide access to the backcountry areas along Beaver Creek, Blue Ridge Reservoir, Stoneman Lake, Sycamore Canyon, and the Elden Mountains. The Sycamore Canyon Wilderness is reached by a gravel road 12 miles north of Clarkdale. This 49,575-acre region winds for 20 miles along the red-rock canyon of Sycamore Creek, which cuts through the southern edge of the Colorado Plateau. Numerous trails lead through forests of ponderosa pine and alligator juniper and along red, white, and yellow rock formations to White Horse Lake, Ruin Mountain, Casner Mountain, and the Verde River.

A *Cococino National Forest Map* is available for 50¢ from the Forest Supervisor, Cococino National Forest, Flagstaff 86001. It shows all roads and trails, ranger stations, streams and lakes, points of interest, and towns. It also includes an index to recreation sites in the area.

Access & Outfitting Centers

The Cococino National Forest is reached via U.S. highways 89, 66, and 180, and Arizona highways 87, 209, and 79. Lodging, supplies, guides, and outfitting services are available at Flagstaff, Cosnino, Winona, Angell, Mountainaire, Bellemont, Sedona, Cornville, Bridgeport, Happy Jack, and Camp Verde.

Coronado National Forest

Coronado National Forest Topo Maps

U.S. Geological Survey Overview Maps, scale 1:250,000: Douglas, Mesa, Nogoles, Silver City, and Tucson.

Chiricahua Mountains Wilderness

Large-scale U.S. Geological Survey Topographic Maps: Cochise Head, Chiricahua Peak, Portal.

Galiuro Mountains Wilderness

Large-scale U.S. Geological Survey Topographic Maps: Galiuro Mountains, Klondyke, Redington, Sierra Bonita, and Winchester Mountains.

This 1,791,000-acre tract is located in south-central Arizona and embraces the Santa Catalina Mountains, Sonora Desert, Sabino Canyon, and a portion of the Chiricahua Mountains. The old Swift Trail winds along the crest of the Grahams Range, the highest of the Coronado Mountains, reaching 11,000 feet at Mount Graham. Heliograph Peak is one of a chain of mountaintop sun-signal stations used by the army

during the years of the Apache wars. Other features include the Whetstone Mountains, Tumacaroi Mountains, Chiricahua Wilderness, Galiuro Wilderness, and the Rincon Mountains.

The deep-blue waters of Parker Canyon Lake, at 5,400 feet, and Pena Blanca Lake are located in the semidesert foothills of the Atacosa and Pajarito mountains and provide good sport for bass, catfish, and crappies. The rugged pine-clad peaks of the 18,000-acre Chiricahua Mountain Wilderness rise from the desert floor and dominate an area of precipitous canyons and towering cliffs. This is some of the roughest country in southeastern Arizona, with elevations ranging from 9,797 feet at Chiricahua Peak to 6,100 feet at the floor of South Fork River. Dense timber stands, along with a heavy accumulation of dead and down trees, cover the wilderness floor. Old burns, rock outcroppings, and a few natural parks provide the only openings. Big-game hunting is good in the area for whitetail deer, black bear, and mountain lion. The rare Chiricahua fox squirrel is found in the mountains. Black-spotted and rainbow trout are found in the upper reaches of Cave Creek and in Rucker Canyon. The four main wilderness entrances are at Turkey Creek, Rucker Canyon, Rustler Peak, and Cave Creek.

The 52,717 acres of the Galiuro Mountains Wilderness enclose a double range bisected by two main canyons—Rattlesnake and Redfield. Cleared and graded trails pass through dense stands of manzanita, oak, juniper, Arizona cypress, pine, and fir; along brightly colored cliffs and steep brushy slopes to Bassett Peak (7,671 ft.), Kennedy Peak (7,540 ft.), and Sunset Peak (7,094 ft.) along the east divide; and to Rhodes Peak (7,116 ft.), Maverick Mountain (6,990 ft.), and Kielberg Peak (6,880 ft.) along the west divide. Three trail heads are located on the east slope of the mountain. The major wilderness trails include the 25-mile Aravaipa Canyon trail to Powers Cabin, the seven-mile-long Deer Creek Road to Powers Garden, the four-mile-long Pipestem Canyon Trail, the 22-mile-long Jackson Cabin Trail to Maverick Mountain, Redfield Canyon, and the West Divide, and the Powers Garden Trail to Old Tent Lookout. Big-game hunting is good throughout the Coronado Forest for desert mule deer, whitetail deer, black bear, javelina, and cougar. The javelina, or peccary, is descended from giant pigs that lived about 25 million years ago, and is related to swine and wild boar. A mature animal will weigh between 30 and 65 pounds, stand about 18 to 22 inches high, and measure about 30 to 38 inches in length. The javelina will fight ferociously when cornered by men or dogs. The hunter may occasionally find javelina foraging at altitudes as high as 6,000 feet on the gentler mountain slopes. Favorite haunts are found near caves, old mine tunnels, cool hollows, protracted draws, washes, gullies, and patches of prickly pear, mesquite, oak, and brush. Upland game birds include quail, dove, and band-tailed pigeon. There are also wild turkeys, and a few scattered bands of desert bighorn sheep.

Madera Canyon provides conditions that are unique in the United States. The combination of climate, moisture, and elevation creates an atmosphere that harbors such creatures as the trogon, a colorful, red-breasted, parrotlike bird that is more commonly seen in Mexico. There are more than 200 species of birds in the canyon. The Spaniards named the canyon Madera for its heavy timber supply. Cactus and other low desert vegetation give way to ponderosa pine on the upper elevations. A few abandoned frontier army posts remain nearby. They were built to ward off attacks from the Apaches, but were destroyed by Confederate troops during the Civil War.

The Santa Catalinas are an excellent recreation area, with 12 camp and picnic grounds. They are close to Tucson, and are very popular with families in the summer months.

Tantalizing bits of history are present at Cochise Stronghold Canyon,

located in the heart of the Dragoon Mountains. It is a rugged natural fortress, bordered by granite domes and sheer cliffs, and covered with beautiful natural forest land. Cochise, the Apache chief, lived here with his clan and was never conquered or captured by white men. He is buried somewhere in or near his impregnable fortress, but no one knows the exact spot. The area contains several ghost towns that were once livestock and mining centers. The only one left is Tombstone, with its famous Boot Hill Cemetery. Campgrounds and trails provide recreational opportunities, and the ruins of the Dragoon Springs station, a favorite target of the Apaches, can still be seen.

For detailed information, write to the Forest Supervisor, Coronado National Forest, Federal Bldg., 301 Congress (West), Tucson 85701. They will also provide you with a *Coronado National Forest Map* for 50¢, which shows all roads and trails, recreation sites, streams and lakes, ranger stations, and points of interest. Free maps of the *Pena Blanca Lake* and the *Madera Canyon Recreation Area* are also available.

Vacation accommodations in the region are provided by *Circle Z Ranch* (a working ranch famed for its riding), Patagonia 85624; *Elkhorn Ranch*, Sasabe Star Rt., Tucson 85736; *Double U Ranch* (in the foothills of the Santa Catalina Mountains), P.O. Box 6148, Tucson 85733; *Hacienda Del Sol*, Tucson 85718; *Lazy K Bar Ranch* (over-

looking the Santa Cruz Valley), Rt. 9, Box 560, Tucson 85704; *Price Canyon Ranch* (a full-service family ranch in the Chiricahua Mountains), P.O. Box 1065, Douglas 85607; *Rancho Santa Cruz* (in the beautiful Santa Cruz River Valley), P.O. Box 8, Tumacacori 85640; *Rex Ranch*, P.O. Box 87, Amado 85640; *Saddle & Surrey Ranch* (a picturesque ranch resort nestled in the desert foothills on a game reserve surrounded by six mountain ranges), 4110 Sweetwater Dr., Tucson 85705; *White Stallion Ranch* (at the base of the rugged Tucson Mountains on a 100,000-acre game preserve), Rt. 9, Box 567, Tucson 85704; *Wild Horse Ranch Club*, Box 5505, Tucson 85703.

Access & Outfitting Centers

The Coronado National Forest is reached via U.S. highways 80, 666, 89, 70, and 10. Lodging, supplies, guides, and outfitting services are available at Safford, Tucson, Douglas, Nogales, Dragoon, Sonoita, Patagonia, Lochiel, Arivaca, Tubac, Amadc, Greaterville, Rosemont, Bonita, Oracle, Klondyke, and Aravaipa.

Kaibab National Forest & the Grand Canyon

Kaibab National Forest Topo Maps

U.S. Geological Survey 1:250,000 scale overview maps: Flagstaff, Grand Canyon, Marble Canyon, Prescott, Williams.

Grand Canyon National Monument

Large-scale U.S. Geological Survey Topographic Maps: National Canyon, Kanab Point, Tuckup Canyon, Vulcans Throne, Whitmore Rapids, Mount Trumbull NW, Mount Trumbull NE, Mount Trumbull SE, Mount Logan.

Grand Canyon National Park

Large-scale U.S. Geological Survey Topographic Maps: Nankoweap, Vishnu Temple, Bright Angel, Havasupai Point, Grandview Point, De Motte Park, Powell Plateau, Supai, and Kanab Point.

Marble Canyon of the Colorado River

Large-scale U.S. Geological Survey Topographic Maps: Vishnu Temple, Nankoweap, Emmett Wash, Tanner Wash, Lee's Ferry.

This 1.7-million-acre reserve is located in northwestern Arizona and is divided into northern and southern sections by the Grand Canyon. The Kaibab Plateau, north of the Grand Canyon, was established as the Grand Canyon Game Preserve by Theodore Roosevelt. Hunting is regulated by special permit for elk, bear, and deer. Hundreds of miles of hiking trails wind through the forests and canyons to such areas as the Cockscombs, Marble Gorge, Havasu Creek, Squaw Cockscombs, Kaibab Lake, White Horse Lake, Eagle Nest Mountain, Deer Creek Falls, Thunder River, Kanab Creek, Colorado River, and the Havasupai Indian Reservation.

Since primitive times, the Kaibab Plateau has been a choice hunting ground. Indian legends tell of hunting seasons in which more than a thousand deer were shot. Wilderness trails provide access to the deep canyons along the low desert country near the Colorado River. The hiker should be well versed in the techniques of desert travel before attempting to explore this wild and often hazardous region. On the north side of the Grand Canyon, the Deer Creek and Thunder River trails descend from the north rim just beyond Indian Hollow Campground. Thunder River, an enormous spring, roars out of Thunder Cave, following a steep course to Tapeats Creek past lush green carpets of fern, mimulus, columbine, box elder, willow, and cottonwood. In Surprise Valley, the Deer Creek Trail winds down the convoluted narrows (this trail is frequently exposed at great heights, frightening for those hikers who are subject to vertigo) to the otherworldly specter of Deer Creek Falls. Kanab Creek, gathering its waters from the Kaibab Plateau and the mountains of southern Utah, has cut a huge, little-visited canyon between the Kanab and Kaibab plateaus. The character of Kanab Canyon varies as it cuts through successive layers of paleozoic rock formations on its course to the Grand Canyon. At one point, it meanders across undulating "sliderock" platforms, eroded into complex knobs and fins; at another location Kanab Creek has formed a deep and sinuous gorge. The spring-fed North Canyon Creek originates about 500 feet below the east rim of Kaibab Plateau, flowing along its 1½-mile course through a thick border of aspen, fir, berry bushes, and wildflowers, creating a rainbow-green beauty found nowhere else on the Kaibab. Although small in size, and seldom fished, North Canyon Creek holds pan-sized gila trout. The streambed may be followed by trail to the "Cockscombs," large sandstone fins that line the base of the East Kaibab Escarpment. The Hualapai Trail is the major route to Havasu Canyon and the emerald waters of Havasu Creek, which plunges over four waterfalls along its 15-mile course before it flows into the Colorado River in the bottom of the Grand Canyon. Supai Village, the only post office in the United States to be serviced by pack mule, is located about eight miles from Hualapai Hilltop. Because of heavy precipitation, the Kaibab Plateau region is a verdant island within the desert, a stark contrast to the more arid region along the South Rim of the Grand Canyon. The Paiutes called it a "mountain lying down," and it is indeed an oasis that harbors its own flourishing greenery.

Kaibab National Forest Maps (north and south sections) are available for 50¢ each from the Forest Supervisor, Kaibab National Forest, P.O. Box 817, Williams 86046. They show roads and trails, forest lands, Indian lands, ranger stations, mines, schools and churches, recreation sites, points of interest, ski areas, and lakes and streams.

Vacation accommodations in Grand Canyon Country are provided by *Grand Canyon Lodge*, North Rim 86052; *Jacob Lake Inn* and *Kaibab Lodge*, both North Rim 86052; and *Red Feather Lodge* (Box 520) and *Moqui Lodge* (Box 369), both South Rim 86023. For additional listings see "Grand Canyon National Park" in the "Encyclopedia" section. Lodging in the Marble Canyon area is provided by *Cliff Dwellers Lodge*, Box H, Page 86040.

Access & Outfitting Centers

The Kaibab National Forest can be reached via U.S. highways 89 and 66, and Arizona state highways 67 and 64. Lodging, supplies, guides, and outfitting services are available at Fredonia, Jacob Lake, and the town of Grand Canyon.

Prescott National Forest

Prescott National Forest Topo Maps

U.S. Geological Survey Overview Maps, scale 1:250,000: Phoenix, Paria, and Paria Canyon.

Pine Mountain Wilderness

Large-scale U.S. Geological Survey Topographic Maps: Tule Mesa, Verde Hot Springs, Bloody Basin.

This forest, high but somewhat drier than the other areas along the Mogollon Rim, encompasses 1,250,000 acres of top-rate mule-deer country in central Arizona. The forest includes the western edge of a stand of ponderosa pine that stretches 350 miles across central Arizona and into New Mexico. Other trees include Douglas fir, white fir, and limber pine, found at elevations from 3,000 to 8,000 feet. Rocky Mountain mule deer are plentiful and widely distributed. The trophy bucks tend to retreat to the steep, brushy slopes, where plenty of skill, patience, and stamina are needed to stalk them. The big-game hunter may also have a shot at antelope, javelina, whitetail deer, and possibly black bear. Forest roads and trails lead to the more remote hunting and camping areas around Pine Mountain, Sycamore Canyon, Agua Fria River, Lyn Lake, Longfellow Ridge, Connell Mountains, Limestone Canyon, and Hassayampa Lake. Upland game-bird shooting is good for wild turkey, band-tailed pigeon, dove, and quail.

Pine Mountain wilderness area lies along the high Verde River Rim. It stands as an island of tall, green timber, surrounded by desert mountains with hot, dry mesas and deep canyons. Major features include Mocking Bird Pass, Pine Mountain, and Turret Peak.

The Prescott National Forest Map is available for 50¢ from the Forest Supervisor, Prescott National Forest, Box 2549, Prescott 86301. It shows all roads and trails, towns, points of interest, streams, ranger stations, and recreation sites.

Family vacation accommodations in the Forest are provided by the beautiful *Quail Springs Ranch*, P.O. Box 21, Cottonwood 86326. This working cattle ranch, located on the eastern slope of Mingus Mountain, offers guided pack trips and overnight trail rides.

Access & Outfitting Centers

The Prescott National Forest is reached via U.S. Highway 89, and Arizona state highways 279, 69, 79, and 255. Lodging, supplies, guides, and outfitting services are available at Whipple, Humbolt, Dewey, Cordes, Bumble Bee, Paulden, Iron Springs, Walker, Groom Creek, Crown King, Walnut Grove, Cherry, Jerome, Drake, and Simmons.

Sitgreaves National Forest

Sitgreaves National Forest Topo Maps

U.S. Geological Topographic Maps, scale 1:250,000: Holbrook and St. Johns.

This region contains 800,000 acres of green meadows and pine forests at elevations ranging from 5,500 feet to 9,000 feet on the Mogollon Plateau in north-central Arizona. The spectacular 1,000-foot vertical cliffs on the Mogollon Rim (or Tonto Rim) have figured in many a tale by Zane Grey. The lakes along the Mogollon Rim provide some of the finest fishing in the state. There is a good amount of trout fishing in this region, much of it requiring a pack trip or a day-long hike into the remote areas. Clear Creek is an ideal fly stream and is well known for its big rainbows. Fool's Hollow, Show, Whipple, Sponseller, Rainbow, and Woodland lakes and Lake-of-the-Woods all have fishing for rainbows. Grayling can be found in Bear Canyon Lake. Fishing is best in the early spring and autumn, when the forest surrounding the lake country is ablaze with the brilliant shades of red, yellow, and brown.

The Merriam elk, once native to the forest, was killed off by the early pioneers, and was replaced in the 1920's by the introduction of Rocky Mountain elk from Yellowstone. Today the forest is a major elk range. Big-game hunting is also good for mule deer, whitetail deer, antelope, and wild turkey. In season, wing-shooting is excellent for mourning dove, band-tailed pigeon, and duck. For camping information, write to the Supervisor, Sitgreaves National Forest, Holbrook, 86025.

The *Sitgreaves National Forest Map*, available for 50¢ from the Forest Supervisor, P.O. Box 640, Springerville 85938, shows all roads and highways, lakes and streams, recreation areas, towns, and ranger stations.

Access & Outfitting Centers

The Sitgreaves National Forest is reached via Arizona state highways 377, 277, 77, 173, and 87, and U.S. Highway 60. Lodging, supplies, guides, and outfitting services are available at Vernon, Pinetop, Lake-

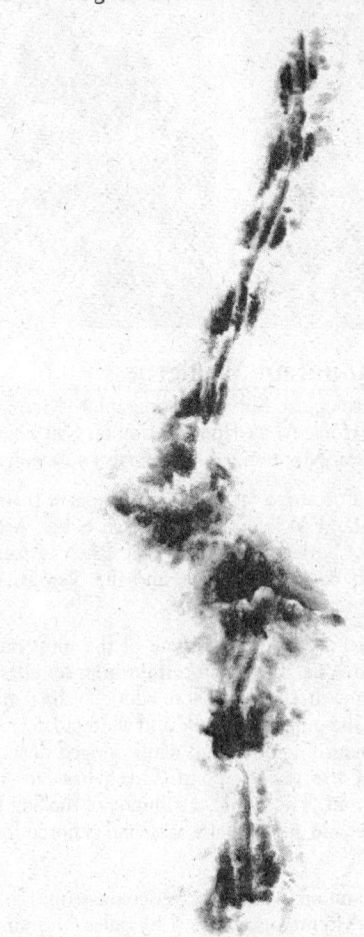

side, Silver Creek, Shumway, Show Low, Linden, Pinedale, Clay Springs, Heber, Aripine, and Overgaard.

Tonto National Forest & Superstition Mountains

Tonto National Forest Topo Maps

U.S. Geological Survey Overview Maps, scale 1:250,000: Holbrook, Mesa, Prescott.

Sierra Ancha Wilderness

Large-scale U.S. Geological Survey Topographic Maps: Armer Mountain, Copper Mountain, McFadden Park.

Mazatzal Mountains

Large-scale U.S. Geological Survey Topographic Maps: Verde Hot Springs, Cane Springs Mountain, Cypress Butte, Table Mountain, Mazatzal Peak, Lion Mountain, Reno Pass, Kayber Butte, Boulder Mountain, Tonto Basin, Mini Mountain, Four Peaks, Horse Mesa Dam, Theodore Roosevelt Dam, Pinya Mountain, Two Bar Mountain, Iron Mountain, Haunted Canyon.

Superstition Mountain Wilderness

Large-scale U.S. Geological Survey Topographic Maps: Florence Junction, Goldfield, Horse Mesa Dome, Mormon Flat Dam, Pinyon Mountain, Superstition Mountains SW, Weaver's Needle.

The Tonto National Forest is a 1.5-million-acre reserve that embraces the Mazatzal Mountains Wilderness and Cave Creek Area, Verde River, Camp Creek, Barlett Reservoir, Salt River, Apache Lake, Sahuaro Lake, Tonto Basin, the Gorge, and the New River Mountains.

The Tonto National Forest contains some of the most outstanding wilderness areas in Arizona, ranging in terrain from semidesert to the cool pine forests beneath the Mogollon Rim. Javelina inhabit the semidesert areas and the pine zone. Mule and whitetail deer, elk, black bear, turkey, quail, mourning dove, and white-winged dove are found scattered throughout the region. Tonto Creek has fair fishing for rainbow and brown trout. The Verde, a tributary of the Salt River, has good fishing for large- and smallmouth bass, and is noted for its trout fishing.

The Superstition Mountains Wilderness, encompassing 124,117 acres of the Superstition Mountains, offers 140 miles of trails winding through rugged land. According to an Indian legend, a group of Indians once sought shelter on the mountaintop during a great flood and were warned not to make a sound until the waters receded. They disobeyed and were turned to stone.

The Lost Dutchman Gold Mine, reputedly located near Weaver's Needle, is the subject of a brutal and frightening legend. The story opens with a young Mexican, fleeing the wrath of his sweetheart's father. He discovered a gold mine in the Superstition Mountains, and his entire community made the trek into the wilderness to mine as much gold as they could. On their way home, they were attacked by Apaches, and the whole party—400 men—was killed, except for two boys who hid safely under a bush. These two children found their way back to Mexico, but returned to claim their heritage many years later. While they were digging, the Dutchman came along. He was Jacob Wolz, or Walz; after befriending the Mexicans, he murdered them and jealously guarded the stolen property from 1870 until his death. On his death bed, he gave directions for finding the mine to a neighbor. Unfortunately, one of the landmarks could not be found, and thousands of would-be prospectors have been looking for it ever since. Some have never returned, some come back with pieces of human skeletons, and some are mysteriously shot in the wild canyons.

The most frequently used trail heads are at Peralta and First Water. Across the Tonto Basin, about 35 miles southeast of the Mazatzal Mountains, is the exceptionally rough, scenic, and often inaccessible country of the Sierra Ancha Wilderness. This 20,850-acre reserve is a land of precipitous box canyons, high vertical cliffs, prehistoric cliff dwellings, and rugged trails leading to Devil's Chasm, Deep Creek, Center Mountain, Aztec Peak, and Cherry Creek.

The Mazatzal Mountains, on the western horizon, were the scene of several skirmishes between General Crook and the Apaches. Four Peaks, a group of rocky heights in the southern part of the Mazatzals, are said to have ended the migration from Mexico of an Indian tribe that considered the number four to be sacred, signifying finality, or the end of life. When they reached the Salt River Valley, they gazed in awe at these four equally high peaks, which, they decided, must mark the edge of the world.

Big-game animals in the area include the mule and whitetail deer, antelope, elk, black bear, and javelina. Game birds include turkey, quail, mourning dove, and white-winged dove. There are a number of recreation areas at Horseshoe Lake, Bartlett Lake, Saguaro Lake, and Canyon Lake.

The *Tonto National Forest Map*, available for 50¢ from the Forest Supervisor, 102 S. 28th St., Phoenix 85034, shows all highways and roads, recreation sites, ranger stations, streams and lakes, mines, and points of interest. Maps of the *Superstition Wilderness* and the *Cave Creek–Mazatzal Mountains Area* are also available, for 50¢ each, showing all roads and trails, streams, ranger stations, and points of interest.

Rustic family vacation accommodations are provided by *Sahuaro Lake Ranch Resort*, 13020 Bush Highway, Mesa 85205 and *Kohl's Ranch*, Payson 85541, with 60 rustic units on the banks of Tonto Creek surrounded by 4 million acres of pine country with excellent trout fishing and hunting. Guided trail rides in the Superstition Wilderness are provided by *Superstition Inn Stables*, Apache Junction 85220.

Access & Outfitting Centers

The Tonto National Forest is reached via Arizona state highways 288, 260, 188, 87, and 205. Lodging, supplies, and outfitting services are available at Pleasant Valley, Payson, Pine, Strawberry, and Punkin Center.

NEW MEXICO ENCYCLOPEDIA

Accommodations—Vacation Lodges & Ranches

New Mexico's resort guest ranches offer a full spectrum of outdoor sports and activities, in addition to basic tourist accommodations and services. A free brochure listing resort ranches is available from the New Mexico Dept. of Development, Tourist Division, 113 Washington Ave., Santa Fe 87501. For information about other accommodations (hotels, motels, housekeeping units, cabins), contact local Chambers of Commerce. For listings of the state's major high-country and wilderness fishing, hunting, and family vacation resorts and lodges, see "High-country Guest Ranches & Lodges" in this section.

Camping and Wilderness Trails

Hundreds of campsites dot New Mexico's wide expanse, which ranges from the mystical desert mesas of the Navajo, Zuni, and Pueblo Indians to the mountains that sweep the state from north to south. In the southern part of the state, and at lower altitudes, the weather is mild year round. Be prepared for cool nights in the mountains. Campers will find accommodations in all areas of the state on state or federal lands. In some areas a fee is charged; in others, camping is free.

A booklet listing the state's campgrounds, *Camping—Hunting—Fishing in New Mexico*, is available free from the Department of Development (address above). The booklet describes the size, available facilities, and cost of the campgrounds. It lists state parks and national forests and their fees and rules, describes the fish and game of the state, and offers fishing- and hunting-license information. It includes a state road map that shows major geographical features, national forests, Indian reservations, and points of interest.

Another map and camping guide, *New Mexico Outdoors*, may be helpful to use along with the booklet, and is available (also free) from the same place. While the booklet groups its campground listings by geographical area, this guide tells who administers them. In addition to the information given in the booklet, the guide lists special features of the campgrounds, such as wilderness access. The 25-page booklet *National Forest Camp & Picnic Grounds in Arizona & New Mexico* may be obtained free by writing: U.S. Forest Service, Southwest Region, Federal Bldg., Albuquerque 87101.

Those who seek the more remote reaches of the wild country will find them in the upper Pecos Wilderness of the southern Sangre de Cristo Mountains. Spectacular peaks ranging to over 13,000 feet rise from the area's main divides on the west and north. Gently sloping ridges and mesas separate the deep canyons that characterize the area. In the areas below the timberline, spruce, aspen, and meadows full of wildflowers carpet the earth. A *Trail Guide to the Geology of the Upper Pecos* describing fifteen trail logs for hiking and horseback riding in this area, may be ordered from the New Mexico Bureau of Mines and Mineral Resources, Publications Room, Socorro 87801, for $3.50. It includes a geology and trail map.

The Bureau of Mines also publishes the guide *Zuni-Cibola Trail* (see Cibola National Forest) for $2.00. This guide summarizes the geologic features of the landscape on the trail, and describes archaeologic and recent events that have influenced the culture along it. The guide includes several trips out of Grant: lava flow to Zuni Mountains, across Continental Divide to El Morro National Monument, Ramah, and Zuni Pueblo. Also from the Bureau of Mines, *Mosaic of New Mexico's Scenery, Rocks and History* ($2.50), gives an overview of landscapes, flora and fauna, geology, recreation spots, and history.

Fenwick New Mexico Fly Fishing School

The Fenwick Corporation's New Mexico fly fishing school is head-quartered at Vermejo Park, a 750-square-mile privately owned guest ranch and working cattle ranch with miles of streams and dozens of lakes that provide fly fishing for cutthroat, rainbow, brook, and a few golden trout. The school curriculum, open to beginners through advanced fly fishermen, includes intensive instruction in the art of fly casting, tackle, entomology, artificial flies, knots, fly presentation, stream lore, and wading. The school runs for three days during July, with special three-day advanced schools limited to fly fishermen with some previous experience. Family activities at this scenic wilderness-type resort include backpacking in the surrounding Rocky Mountain high country. For free literature, rates, and info: School Director, Fenwick Fly Fishing School, Vermejo Park, Drawer E, Raton 87740 (505-445-3097).

Fishing & Hunting in New Mexico

Within the borders of New Mexico, the fifth largest state in the United States, lies some of the most varied topography in the country. Sagebrush, rimrock lands, sand deserts, prairie, and oak-scrub tracts contrast sharply with the soaring majesty of the Rocky Mountains, whose green, forested flanks rise to heights of over 13,000 feet. Much of this high country is contained in the six national forests: Carson and Santa Fe in north-central New Mexico; Cibola, sprawling across the central and west-central part of the state; Lincoln, in the south; and Apache and its southern neighbor, Gila, in the southwest corner. Much of the best trout fishing, big-game hunting, camping, canoeing, and hiking are located in these great land areas. Over one-half of New Mexico is publicly owned, including the national forests, state parks, one national park, Bureau of Land Management acreage, Game and Fish Department property, and National Grasslands. In addition, there is a vast amount of Indian reservation territory where fishing and hunting can be enjoyed on a fee basis. An excellent road network traverses the state, bringing the outdoors enthusiast to the edge of the wildest areas. Write to the State of New Mexico Department of Development, 113 Washington Ave., Santa Fe 87501, for the free booklets Camping—Hunting—Fishing in New Mexico and New Mexico Fishing Waters, which give an overview of the state's hunting and fishing opportunities, license information, and photographs of wildlife. Included also is a list by area of the campgrounds maintained by the state and federal governments and private owners, which provides

information about capacity, facilities, location, altitude, and fees. A full-color map of the state and a map showing state-park locations complete this useful publication. Another helpful campground information source is the free map/brochure New Mexico Outdoors, published by the Department of Development, which breaks down camping areas by national forest, Indian reservation, wildlife refuge, etc., and expands on the facilities contained in the booklet mentioned above. A full-color map shows the national forests, Indian reservations, major river systems, important lakes, wildlife refuges, and campsites, and lists state, federal, and Indian agencies that provide information for the sportsman, plus other useful material.

Trophy Fishing Waters

New Mexico's varied terrain makes possible an impressive list of fish species, especially for a state that is noted for its dry climate. The state fishing records indicate that many opportunities for good fishing exist:

NEW MEXICO RECORD FISH

	Lb.–oz.	Place
Rainbow trout	11–10	San Juan River
Brown trout	20–4	Chama River
Cutthroat trout	6–12	Brazos River
Brook trout	3–0	Seven Lakes
Bluegill	3–1½	Lovington Lake
Channel catfish	22–9	Ute Lake
Crappie	3–9	Ute Lake
Flathead catfish	73–6	Elephant Butte Lake
Largemouth bass	11–0	Ute Lake
Smallmouth bass	6–8¾	Ute Lake
Northern pike	36–0	Miami Lake
Walleye	10–8	Ute Lake
White bass	4–0	Elephant Butte and Red Bluff Lake
Yellow (ring) perch	1–13½	Miami Lake
Striped bass	13–0	Elephant Butte Lake

As can be seen from the records, New Mexico produces some excellent angling for rainbow, brown, brook, and cutthroat trout, and warm-water species such as large- and smallmouth bass, white bass, walleye, northern pike, crappie, bluegill, yellow perch, channel and flathead catfish, and coarse fish. One of the latter, the Colorado squawfish, which inhabits large swift river stretches and attains weights to fifty pounds, is a voracious, jumbo-sized member of the minnow family. Striped bass, an import from saltwater, is becoming established in a few lakes, such as Elephant Butte, and shows signs of adding a significant new factor to New Mexico's angling situation.

Write to the New Mexico Department of Game and Fish, State Capitol, Santa Fe 87503, for the free New Mexico Fishing Information folder, which gives the seasons' bag limits, general rules and regulations, Indian reservation laws, and new fishing developments. For boating ordinances, write for a free booklet, New Mexico Boating Law, produced by the New Mexico State Park and Recreation Commission, Box 1147, Santa Fe 87501. This publication also provides the various usage rules and conduct codes for the state's recreation areas and parks.

Trout fishing is confined predominantly to the mountainous areas of New Mexico, particularly near the six national forests. Generally, the northern section of the state offers the best opportunities, because the

elevation is higher and the temperatures are cooler. Trout are also found in scattered lakes in the plateau areas around the state, where they share the habitat with warm-water species. A very useful free publication of the Department of Game and Fish is the map/brochure *Fishing Waters—Trout Waters, Warm Waters*. The full-color map shows the trout waters in blue and the warm-water-fish areas in red, and assigns a number to each of the important streams and lakes. The map alphabetically lists each major fishing place, gives its number and location on the map, describes the fish species present, and suggests where to fish. These areas are also cross-indexed by their watershed. This color-coded fishing guide should be obtained by anyone planning to fish in New Mexico. A free companion booklet, produced by the Department of Game and Fish, splits the state into six zones, and describes the fishing waters in each zone, again identifying them by number and map location on accompanying zone maps.

The Rio Grande River enters the state from the center of the border with Colorado in the Carson National Forest and has the reputation for producing the best trout fishing in New Mexico. The wild, formidable Rio Grande Gorge encloses the river for the first 70 miles, of which the first 50 miles are almost roadless. Rainbow and brown trout abound in this gorge, with walls scaling 800 feet in places. There are a lot of fish to 5 pounds, and a number of big browns exceed 15 pounds. Many of the Rio Grande's tributaries and headwaters have excellent trout angling. Chief among these is the Chama, which flows southeasterly through the mountains to meet the Rio Grande at the town of Espanola, just south of Carson National Forest. The Chama, which yielded the 20 lb. 4 oz. state-record brown trout, contains some big cutthroats and rainbows, as well. El Vado Lake, formed by a dam on the Chama, is one of the better rainbow- and brown-trout lakes in the state, and the cold tailrace waters below the dam, where the record brown was caught, are well known for lunker trout. Another great section of the Chama is the portion from El Vado Lake north to Colorado. The Brazos River enters the Chama above El Vado and has a rugged box-shaped canyon and beautiful meadow areas that are among the most productive waters in the state, especially for cutthroat trout, and the record 6¾ lb. fish was taken in the box canyon. Valleceto Creek spills into the Chama south of El Vado and offers rainbow- and cutthroat-trout fishing, and Hopewell Lake in its headwaters area has good populations of cutthroat, rainbow, and brook trout. Rio Los Pinos, a Rio Grande tributary, flows along the Colorado border for a short distance and is considered a prime, if short, stretch of trout water. The twenty miles of river in New Mexico have often great fishing for cutthroat and brown trout.

Other good Rio Grande tributaries and headwaters in the Carson National Forest area include the Hondo and Red rivers—the latter with a wild 800-foot-deep gorge—Costilla River and Reservoir, and the Seven Latin Lakes. There are many excellent headwater lakes, ponds, and beaver dams in this section of northern New Mexico. Cutthroats are found in the higher elevations, along with a scattered population of brook trout, while browns and rainbows prefer the lower stream portions and lower lakes. The Pueblo and Santa Barbara rivers to the south are beautiful streams, but are fished hard.

From the Espanola area south, the Rio Grande is mostly a warm-water fishing environment, with the exception of the cold waters that issue from the dam at Elephant Butte Lake and provide some exceptional rainbow-trout angling. To the east of Espanola lies Santa Cruz Reservoir, impounding waters of Rios del Medio and Frijoles, which is well-stocked with large rainbow trout.

In the section to the west of Carson National Forest, near Farmington, is sprawling Navajo Lake and its outlet, the San Juan River, a

tributary of the Colorado. The river has excellent fishing for rainbows —it produced the 11 lb. 10 oz. record—and brown trout for about twenty miles below the dam. Navajo Lake, the largest in the state, also is a fine producer, and contains kokanee salmon as an added attraction. One hundred miles south of Farmington, in the Gallup area, is McGaffey Lake, which has been the object of extensive fisheries management and yields some very fast trout fishing, with rainbows to about five pounds.

The eastern slope of the snow-capped Sangre de Cristo Range in the Carson and Santa Fe national forests region yields some fine trout angling in the tributaries, headwaters, and lakes of the Canadian and Pecos river systems. Eagle Nest Lake, in the headwaters of the Cimarron, a Canadian River tributary, is one of the most famous rainbow-trout lakes in the state, and the Cimarron for twenty miles below the lake is a good rainbow and brown trout fishery. South of the Cimarron, near the town of Wagon Mound, are the two Charette Lakes, which produce some of the best rainbow fishing in the state. Stone Reservoir, to the north of Las Vegas, and McAllister Lake, to the south, provide

rainbow-trout angling, and the quality of McAllister's fishery is famous throughout the state thanks to the efforts of the Game and Fish Department. Fast growth rates produce excellent fishing for rainbows to about six pounds.

The Pecos River and its feeder streams flow out of the Sangre de Cristo Range and offer some of the most scenic trout angling in New Mexico. The river above the town of Pecos contains browns, rainbows, and cutthroat—the last-named increase with the altitude, and some lunkers are taken in the deep pools and runs. The Mora, a Pecos River tributary, has exceptional fishing for rainbows and cutthroat, as does Cow Creek. In the Pecos Wilderness Area are numerous jewel-like alpine lakes, such as Truchas, Lost Bear, Spirit, and North Fork, that contain cutthroat, brook, and rainbow trout.

The Jemez Mountains are located in Santa Fe National Forest, between Santa Fe and Los Alamos, and contain good trout waters, such as Jemez River, Rio de Los Vacas, Clear Creek, Rio Caballa, Fenton Lake, and San Gregorio Lake, which produce rainbows, browns, and cutthroat. Heavy fishing pressure reduces the average size, because the area is both lower in elevation than the national-forests sections to the north and closer to populated areas.

The southern mountain areas of Mexico have much more limited trout fishing. In the Gila National Forest, the Gila River and its tributary, the Mogollon, have the best angling, and in the Apache National Forest, the San Francisco River System and upper Gila River

The area around Raton, in the northeast section of the state, has some reservoir trout fishing, especially in Lake Maloya, which provides superb rainbow-trout angling; and Clayton Lake, near the town of Clayton, in the northeast corner, is a fine rainbow-trout spot.

New Mexico provides some quality warm-water fishing in impoundments, lakes and ponds scattered around the plateau areas. Channel catfish are found in the lower portions of some of the river systems that support trout, such as the Rio Grande, San Juan, Canadian, Mora, Pecos, Gila, and San Francisco rivers, as well as in numerous lakes and impoundments; and scattered populations of smallmouth bass are established in some of the same rivers.

Elephant Butte Lake, below Socorro, on the Rio Grande, in west-central New Mexico, contains black bass, striped bass, channel catfish, crappies, yellow perch, walleyes, and bluegills. Its downstream neighbor, Caballo, has white bass, crappie, largemouths, and channel catfish.

The Pecos River has a number of impoundments that provide good fishing for warm-water species; Alamogordo Reservoir, near Fort Summer, in the east-central area, holds largemouth bass, crappies, bluegills, and catfish; Better Lakes and Lake Van, downstream, near Roswell, contain bass and bluegills; McMillan, Avalon, Municipal, Six Mile, Harroun Dam, and Harroun Lake produce crappie, bluegill, largemouth bass, and catfish; and Red Bluff Lake, on the Texas border, provides fast fishing for largemouth bass, bluegills, catfish, and white bass—it shares the record for whites with Elephant Butte Lake.

The Canadian River system, in eastern New Mexico, is another prime warm-water fishing area. Beautiful Conchas Lake, to the northwest of Tucumcari, produces excellent fishing amid spectacular scenery caused by damming a deep rock gorge. Bass, walleyes, crappies, bluegills, and channel catfish reward the skilled fisherman. Downstream, near Logan, is perhaps the best warm-water fishing in the state—Ute Lake, near the Texas border, in eastern New Mexico. This impoundment claims the records for channel catfish, 22 lb. 9 oz.; crappie, 3 lb. 9 oz.; largemouth bass, 11 lb.; smallmouth bass, 6 lb. 8¾ oz.; and walleye, 10 lb. 8 oz. Crappies, bluegills, and other panfish add to the variety. Miami and Springer lakes, to the west of Springer, on the upper Canadian, offer northern pike fishing, and the former yielded the impressive 36 lb. state record, as well as the record yellow perch.

Hunting

New Mexico has an innovative, progressive Department of Game and Fish, which continually works on management of the state's diverse wildlife and imports new species that might fit into the richly varied topography and climatic conditions of the state. Big-game varieties include mountain lion, elk, mule and whitetail deer, antelope, mountain sheep, black bear, and javelina, plus exotics such as Barbary sheep (aoudad), oxyx, kudu, and ibex. Game-bird species consist of Merriam's and Rio Grande turkeys; scaled (blue), Gambel, and bobwhite quail; dusky (blue) grouse; lesser prairie chickens; ringneck pheasants; mourning and white-winged doves; band-tailed pigeons; ducks; geese; snipe; rails; sandhill cranes; rabbits; and squirrels. Afghan pheasants have been successfully introduced, and attempts have been made to establish other exotics such as francolin, chukar, and Hungarian partridge.

Write to the Department of Game and Fish for the free *Hunting-Zone Maps* and for information on hunting rules and regulations pertaining to big-game species, upland game, and migratory birds.

Mule deer are the principal big-game species located in almost every part of the state except the eastern counties bordering Texas and scattered vacuums in other areas. The best hunting opportunities are

headwaters contain the best angling opportunities. In this region, rainbow and cutthroat trout predominate, and it is wise to packback in to the most remote areas to reach the best fishing. There is limited fishing in the White Mountain area of Lincoln National Forest in Rio Ruidoso, Eagle Creek, Carrizo Creek, Bonito Creek and Lake, and in a few other areas.

found in the national forests, with trophy specimens concentrated in the more inaccessible ranges, such as the Wheeler Peak Wilderness in Carson National Forest, Black Range in Gila National Forest, and the Pecos Wilderness in Santa Fe National Forest. Whitetail deer are found in the Sangre de Cristo region, Lincoln National Forest, the Texas border area, and a few other locations, but the populations, composed of two subspecies, is small. Antelope are not abundant, but are well established in the plateau lands, such as Socorro, southeast to the Black Range, the area to the southeast of Rosewell, and in the northeast part of the state. Scattered populations occur in other locations, and hunting is by draw and permit.

New Mexico is divided into four management zones, which are further divided into management units. Seasons, draws and permits, special regulations, and application procedures are set by individual units for many species. Write to the Game and Fish Department for information.

Elk prefer the green fastnesses of the national forests, and the best hunting is in the northern ranges and in the southwest high country. The kill is small when compared to the more northern Rocky Mountain states, and hunting is by draw and permit. The best elk territory is in the Carson and Santa Fe national forests, particularly in the high mountain country of the Sangre de Cristos. Black bear also prefer the forested slopes, but the kill is small. Cougar are found in several parts of New Mexico, and the rugged southwest wild areas contain the most animals. Javelina inhabit the extreme southwest corner of the state near the Mexican border in rugged country such as the Animas Mountains. The hunting is by permit and draw, and both the kill and the population are small. Bighorn sheep and aoudad are scarce, and hunting is prohibited. Bighorn prefer the upper peaks of the Rockies, while aoudad inhabit rugged semiarid lowlands and foothills.

Mourning doves are shot over grain fields throughout New Mexico, and the best gunning occurs in the eastern half of the state. Whitewinged doves live in the agricultural lands of the southwest, while band-tailed pigeons select the pine forests of the mountain ranges as their prime habitat. Quail are popular game birds, with the scaled quail being the most abundant. These birds like the plateau lands, particularly the grasslands of the eastern half of the state, but they are well dispersed into the south and southwest. Gambel quail primarily inhabit river bottoms in the southwest and central parts of the state, but isolated populations occur in other locations. Bobwhite are thinly established in the sandy plains terrain adjacent to the Texas border. Turkeys roam the mountain areas of national forests, such as Gila, Lincoln, Cibala, and Santa Fe and the adjacent foothills. Dusky grouse, too, prefer the evergreen forest areas of the high country, especially in the Sangre de Cristo Range. Prairie chickens are confined to the extreme eastern counties and are not abundant anywhere. Ringneck pheasants are found in only a few areas in the eastern and central parts of New Mexico. Of far greater promise is the Afghan pheasant, an importation, which has established itself in the Gila River basin and in the southwest corner of the state. Unlike the ringneck, which needs the proximity of water in the Rio Grande and Pecos watersheds, the Afghan can survive in semiarid badlands and may become a significant resource in the future. Waterfowl opportunities are somewhat limited, because of the relative scarcity of water in New Mexico. Lakes, impoundments, rivers, and streams give wildfowlers some good shooting, particularly in areas adjacent to the several wildlife refuges and in areas where grain fields lie close to water. Sandhill cranes, snipe, and rails round out the gunner's menu, but the latter two species are scarce, and it is difficult to find a place where enough birds exist to make a hunt worthwhile. The sandhill crane is a large, meaty bird, which is decoyed in grain fields and is delicious

on the table. New Mexico also offers rabbits and squirrels, but they are not popular.

Remember that New Mexico is infested with rattlesnakes, from the plateau on up into the mountains, and the outdoorsman must be careful at all times to watch where he places his feet.

New Mexico Wildlife, a bimonthly magazine produced by the Department of Game and Fish, costs two dollars a year, or five dollars for three years. It contains fascinating articles about fish and game species, where-to-go and how-to information, as well as material on wildlife management. The magazine provides a wealth of information for anyone planning a trip to the state's outdoor recreation areas.

For additional fishing and hunting information, see "High-country Guest Ranches & Lodges" and "Rio Grande National Wild River," in this section, and the New Mexico "Travel & Recreation Guide" section.

High-Country Guest Ranches & Lodges

Several long-established wilderness trout-fishing, hunting, and family-vacation guest ranches and resorts are located near or within the boundaries of New Mexico's national forests and wilderness areas, and provide guided fishing, hunting, and pack trips.

The *Bar X Bar Ranch,* one of the West's most beautiful ranches, is located at 8,400 feet in the Manzanares Valley near the Pecos Wilderness in the Santa Fe National Forest. The fishing at Bar X Bar Ranch is unexcelled in the Southwest for rainbows, browns, brooks, and cutthroats, ranging in size from 8 inches to 8 pounds. There are 33 lakes and four streams on the ranch, including the crystal-clear waters of Cow Creek, which flow over the falls at the head of Box Canyon. The ranch also owns the state's oldest private hatchery. The scenic, rugged mountains and forests of blue and silver spruce, pine, fir, and quaking aspens offer good hunting for turkey, mule deer, black bear, grouse, and Rocky Mountain elk. For information and rates, write: P.O. Drawer 2, Pecos 87552; phone (505) 757–8500.

Chama Land & Cattle Company, located 3 miles south of Chama, high in the San Juan Mountains, is a working ranch that offers accommodations and guided fishing, hunting, hiking, and pack trips. Transportation facilities include a 6,000-foot landing strip. For info and rates, write: P.O. Box 85, Chama 87520; phone (505) 756–2133.

Conchas Lake Lodge is located 30 miles northwest of Tucumcari on the banks of Conchas Lake. Facilities include main lodge with dining room, marina, and 5,000-foot landing strip. Write: Box 1045, Conchas Dam 84416; phone (505) 868–2211.

The *Spanish Stirrup Guest Ranch,* located 10 miles southeast of Deming at the base of the Florida Mountains in desert terrain, is one of two working guest ranches in the state, offering hiking, horseback riding, hunting, and sightseeing. Write: Route 1, Box 206, Deming 88030; phone (505) 546–3165.

Stone Lake Lodge is located 20 miles southwest of Dulce, on the Jicarilla Apache Indian Reservation at the Colorado border. The lodge offers boating, fishing, hiking, and big-game hunting with guides. Write: P.O. Box 147, Dulce 87528; phone (505) 759–3242.

The *Boca Grande Angel Fire Resort* is located 30 miles northeast of Taos in the scenic Sangre de Cristo Mountains in the Carson National Forest, and offers boating, fishing, hiking, trapshooting, horseback riding, and cross-country skiing. Facilities include a 7,968-foot landing strip. Write: Eagle Nest 87718; phone (505) 377–2301.

Elephant Butte Inn is situated 3 miles north of Truth or Consequences, on the banks of Elephant Butte Lake, with fishing, hiking,
boating, and big-game hunting with guides. Write: P.O. Box 5, Elephant Butte 87935; phone (505) 894–6631.

Los Alamos Guest Ranch offers accommodations, fishing, biking,
horseback riding, hunting, and sightseeing in the Mogollon Mountains near the Gila Wilderness, 65 miles northwest of Silver City.
Facilities include a 3,000-foot landing strip. Write: Box 127, Glenwood 88039; phone (505) 539–2311.

Taos-Red River-Eagle Nest,
New Mexico
Circle Drive

Frijoles Canyon Lodge is located 13 miles south of Los Alamos at the
Bandelier Indian cliff ruins. Activities include hiking and sightseeing.
Write: Bandelier National Monument, Los Alamos 87544.

Tres Lagunas Ranch is located in the Pecos River Canyon, near the
scenic Pecos Wilderness in the Santa Fe National Forest, with fishing
(ponds and trout streams on premises), hiking, horseback riding, and
big-game hunting with guides. Write: Route 2, Box 100, Pecos 87552;
phone (505) 757–6194.

The *Singing River Guest Ranch,* P.O. Box 245, Questa 87556, is
located 25 miles north of Taos in the Carson National Forest, near
the Rio Grande Wild River area. The ranch provides accommodations, fishing, hiking, and pack trips.

Vermejo Park Ranch is located 40 miles south of Raton in the Sangre
de Cristo Mountains and provides backpacking, fishing, hiking, and
big-game hunting with guides. Special activities, such as bird-watching
and archaeology field trips, are available to groups by prearrangement.
Facilities include a landing strip and pickup service from Raton.
Ranch vehicles are available for use on premises. Write: Drawer E,
Raton 87740; phone (505) 445–3097.

The *Lazy H Guest Ranch* is located 3 miles northeast of Red River
in the high Sangre de Cristo Mountains in the Carson National Forest
region, and offers cabin accommodations and wilderness fishing, hiking, trail rides, and pack trips, and guided big-game hunting. For info
and rates, write: P.O. Box 908, Red River 87538; phone (505) 754–
2221.

Gascon Ranch, a working guest ranch, is located 29 miles northwest
of Las Vegas in the Sangre de Cristo Mountains, and offers trout
fishing, hiking, and horseback riding. Write: Rociada 87742; phone
(505) 425–7038.

The *Pendaries Village Inn* is located 26 miles from Las Vegas at the
edge of the Santa Fe National Forest and offers fishing, hiking, pack
trips, and hunting (no guides). Facilities include a 5,000-foot landing
strip, with pickup services from Albuquerque and Santa Fe. Write:
Rociada 87742; phone (505) 425–6076.

Bishop's Lodge offers fishing, hiking, horseback riding, skeet- and
trapshooting in the Tesuque Valley of the Sangre de Cristo Mountains, 5 miles north of Santa Fe. Write: P.O. Box 2367, Santa Fe
87501; phone (505) 983–6378.

Rancho Encantado is located 7 miles north of Santa Fe on the edge
of the Santa Fe National Forest; activities include fishing and hunting
by arrangement, skeet- and trapshooting, horseback riding, sightseeing, and skiing at the Santa Fe Ski Basin nearby. Write: Route 4, Box
57-C, Santa Fe 87501; phone (505) 982–3537.

The *Bear Mountain Guest Ranch* is situated 5 miles northwest of
Silver City at the edge of the Gila Wilderness, and provides guided
field trips in bird-watching, botany, rocks and geology, and astronomy,
with wilderness hiking and horseback riding nearby. Write: P.O. Box
1163, Silver City, 88061.

The *Taos Ski Valley* is located about 20 miles northeast of Taos in
the Sangre de Cristo Mountains near the Colorado border, and offers
fishing, hiking, horseback riding, and skiing. Accommodations ranges
from dormitories to hotel rooms to apartments and luxury chalets. For
info and rates, write: Taos Ski Valley 87571; phone (505) 776–2266.

The *Los Pinos Ranch* is located 21 miles north of Pecos in the Pecos
River Canyon, near the Pecos Wilderness. The ranch offers wild trout
fishing on the Pecos River and nearby lakes, hiking, and pack trips.
Write: Route 3, Box 8, Terrero 87573.

The *Inn of the Mountain Gods* is situated on the Mescalero Indian
Reservation near Ruidoso, 220 miles southeast of Albuquerque and 40
miles northeast of Alamogordo. Activities include boating, fishing,
riding, hiking, and hunting. Write: Mescalero 88340; phone (505)
257–5141.

Highways—Recreation & Scenic Routes

An official road map of New Mexico is included in the free booklet
Camping—Hunting—Fishing in New Mexico, available from the
New Mexico Dept. of Development, 113 Washington Ave., Santa Fe
87501. The map shows the state's major geographical features, national forests, parks and monuments, Indian reservations, state parks,

and points of interest. Complete campground listings for the state, and hunting and fishing information are also included in the booklet.

The New Mexico Bureau of Mines and Mineral Resources has published a series of good guides for the highway traveler entitled Scenic Trips to the Geologic Past. The individual guides include *Santa Fe* ($1.50), *Taos-Red River-Eagle Nest, New Mexico* ($1.50), *Roswell-Capitan-Ruidoso and Bottomless Lakes State Park* ($1.50), *Southern Zuni Mountains, Zuni-Cibola* ($2.00), *Silver City-Santa Rita-Hurley*, ($1.50), *High Plains Northeastern New Mexico-Capulin Mountain-Clayton-Rayton* ($2.00), *Mosaic of New Mexico's Scenery, Rocks and History* ($2.50), *Albuquerque—Its Mountains, Valley, Water and Volcanoes* ($2.50), and *Southwestern New Mexico* ($1.50). Write to: New Mexico Bureau of Mines and Mineral Resources, Socorro 87801.

Public Lands Recreation Map

The U.S. Bureau of Land Management has published a free map and guide to *Public Lands in New Mexico*. The guide summarizes the major features of the 13,600,000 acres of public land in the state, and describes its most plentiful fish and game. It also lists regional offices where visitors can inquire about the boundaries of the public lands. The multicolor map, with a scale of 20 miles to the inch, marks public domain, national forests, Indian reservations, military reservations, land grants, wildlife refuges, and private lands. It also shows major highways, gravel roads, unimproved roads, parks and monuments, Indian pueblos, and points of interest. Write to: U.S. Bureau of Land Management, New Mexico State Office, P.O. Box 1449, Santa Fe 87501.

Rio Grande National Wild River

The majestic Rio Grande, known to the Spanish conquistadors as the "Great River of the North" and from the legends of the Rocky Mountain trappers and early explorers as the "River of Ghosts," is one of the great wild rivers and one of the most productive natural trout fisheries in all the West. The river rises high in the mountain wilderness of Colorado's Rio Grande National Forest and flows through the weather-worn walls of the remote and rugged 70-mile Rio Grande Gorge, where the river cuts southward into New Mexico and continues on its spectacular 2,200-mile journey to the sea. The champagne-like flows of frigid, crystal-clear water from gigantic clusters of huge springs produce the world-famous trout fishing found in the canyon country along this wild river. Trophy rainbows and hook-jawed browns up to 20 pounds lurk in the deep-flowing holes and feed on crayfish and other "hardshells" in the fast water and eddies that swirl around huge boulders. It also, surprisingly, holds northern pike that have drifted down into the Rio Grande Gorge from stockings made in Colorado.

The river flows from its Rocky Mountain headwaters through the San Luis Valley of southern Colorado, enters the great gorge some seven miles upstream from the New Mexico–Colorado border, and begins its tortuous 70-mile journey through the ancient layers of gray, black, salmon-pink, brown, and orange lichen-covered volcanic flows—reaching depths of 800 feet where an early lava flow crystallized into the black basalt now lining the bottom of the gorge—surrounded by colorful yellow bluffs, plains, and sagebrush-carpeted benchlands broken by fields and pastures. At the bottom of the gorge, the banks of the Rio Grande are covered by woodbine, stinging nettleweed, cockleburs, willows and waist-high grass, apache plume, the beautiful yucca, columbine, and benches of piñon, juniper, sagebrush, narrowleaf cottonwood, chamisa, and a few small oaks.

The major features of interest to the trout fisherman and river runner, shown on the topographic maps of the wild river, beginning at the

Colorado border and following the river south through the gorges, include: Costilla Creek, which enters the river from the east; volcanic Ute Mountain, which leans against the gorge, soaring to 10,000 feet above the canyon floor; the primitive Lee Trail, on the east rim of the gorge at 220 feet elevation between Ute Mountain and the mouth of Latin Arroyo west of Cerro, often used by fishermen and float trippers packing out their craft; fierce rapids, falling 650 feet during the 12-mile stretch between Latin Arroyo and the junction of the Red River, roaring and boiling around giant boulders, polishing the basalt bed to glasslike smoothness; the Chiflo Mountain Trail; the six-mile

stretch of trophy trout water formed by the giant cold-water flows of the misnamed Big and Little Arsenic springs, accessible by trail from Cerro; the confluence of the Red River, which flows into the Rio Grande from the east through its own 1,300-foot-wide and 800-foot deep gorge, and Carson National Forest campsites; the Arroyo Hondo Creek and San Cristobal Creek tributaries and the cool bubbling flows of Cedar Springs; Manby Spring, where the remnants of an old wagon road wind down to the river from the east and west rims of the gorge and where the ruins of an old stone hut enclose the warm-water spring; the 600-foot overlooks and picnic sites at the Rio Grande Gorge High Bridge; the narrow, wild rapids from the gorge bridge to Taos Junction, known to the old-timers as Rio Bravo, or "wild river," forming an unbroken stretch of foaming white water, 20-foot-deep holes, gi-

gantic boulders, and violent whirlpools. The national wild river ends at the Taos River Bridge.

Wildlife inhabiting the wild-river gorge include muskrat, mule deer, coyote, and bobcat. Bird life includes the snowy egret, quail, merganser, raven, golden eagle, blue heron, innumerable songbirds, and swallows.

A more detailed geological history and description of the river and gorge is contained in *The Rio Grande—First to Go Wild*, a New Mexico travel guide, by Doyle Kline, available for 50¢ from New Mexico Magazine, P.O. Box 2988, Boulder, CO 80302. The Bureau of Land Management maintains 48 family picnic and camp shelters plus roads and trails on the east bank, where the Rio Grande and Red River meet below Questa. Several are situated at the bottom of the gorge near good springs and the rivers. The wild river and campsites, springs, trails, roads, cliffs, tributaries, and national forest boundaries

are shown on the *Map-Guide to the Rio Grande Gorge*, available free, along with detailed fishing, camping, and river information from the Bureau of Land Management, New Mexico State Office, P.O. Box 1449, Santa Fe 87501.

If you are planning to fish, camp, or float on the Rio Grande Gorge, the following large-scale U.S. Geological Survey Topographic Maps are absolutely essential: Ute Mountain, Sunshine, Guadalupe Mountain, Arroyo Hands, Los Cordovas, and Taos SW.

Wilderness & Wild River Outfitters

Southwest Safaris, based in Santa Fe, is the best-known wilderness outfitter in the state. The group specializes in taking people to the more remote areas of scenic beauty and historical interest in the southwestern United States. Southwest Safaris uses airplane travel to transport trip members from one area to another in order to allow the study of huge geological formations and widely separated Indian ruins, and to cut down traveling time. At the various points of interest, trip members are met by jeeps, horses, rafts, or cars. Tour members camp out during the spring, summer, and fall, but take lodging in the winter. All camping equipment is provided.

Southwest Safaris' tours vary from one to twelve days, and include jaunts to Colorado, Utah, and Arizona, as well as New Mexico. The group also offers short air tours (one to four hours) covering Santa Fe, Taos, the Jemez Mountains, Sangre de Cristo Mountains, Rio Grande River, northeast Arizona, and southeast Utah.

The seven-day "Southwest Safari" including lodging in Santa Fe before and after the trip is the most popular. The first flight includes the mesa, mountains, ruins, and great rivers of northwest New Mexico. A guided hiking tour of the famous cliff dwellings of the Anasazi Indians is a highlight of the day, along with a swim in Navajo Lake. The tour continues to Arizona, Colorado, and Utah by air, land, and water. Although the trips are scheduled for certain dates each year, private safaris are arranged all year by special request. On all tours, the pilot doubles as guide, conducting informal orientation sessions before flights and leading the explorations en route.

For information on individual tours, write to P.O. Box 945, Santa Fe 87501; phone (505) 988–4246.

A number of other groups lead wilderness tours throughout the state. For information about *Sierra Club* field trips and workshops, write to Bob Howard, 1522 Stanford NE, Albuquerque 87106. The *Wilderness Society* offers a "Way to the Wilderness Program," with guided backpack trips to the Pecos Wilderness. For details, write to the regional office, 4260 E. Evans Avenue, Denver, CO 80222. *New Mexico Mountain Club* climbing-hiking school and trips are open to nonmembers by arrangement. To find out more about the trips, write to the club at Box 4151, Albuquerque 87106.

Commercial backpacking guides offering trips in New Mexico include *Base Camp Outdoor Supply Store*, 121 W. San Francisco, Santa Fe 87501; *Live! Wilderness Expeditions*, Box 157, Glenwood 88039; *Deep Creek Ranch*, Glenwood 88039; *Southwestern Expeditions for Youth*, Box 40451, Indianapolis, IN 46240; Wes Adams, *Wilderness Society Outfitter*, Star Route, Melrose 88124; *Wilderness Adventure*, Box 1259, Taos 87571; *Wilderness Experiences for Youth*, Box 12586, Albuquerque 87105; and *Wilderness and Wheels*, 1612 Brae Street, Santa Fe 87501. For mountain climbers, several mountain-climbing schools offer adventure, including *Realidad Ultima*, 1410 Cerro Gordo, Santa Fe 87501; and the *Natural High*, c/o 121 W. San Francisco, Santa Fe 87501. The *Bear Mountain Guest Ranch*, managed by Fred and Myra McCormick, Box 1163, Silver City 88061, offers commercial botany/birding workshops and hikes.

Commercial river guides operating float trips down New Mexico's wild rivers include *Get Down Rivers*, Doug Murphy, 9212 Bellehaven NE, Albuquerque 87112; *Live! Wilderness Expeditions*, Box 157, Glenwood 88039; *Southwest Safaris* (river trips as part of flying tours), Box 945, Santa Fe 87501.

New Mexico offers excellent cross-country ski-touring opportunities on the hundreds upon hundreds of miles of old logging roads and hiking trails in the national forest lands and wilderness areas. Commercial ski-touring guides operating in the state include *Trail Adventures de Chama*, Box 86, Chama 87520 (summer address: 4839 Idlewilde Lane SE, Albuquerque 87108); *Base Camp Outdoor Supply Store*, 121 W. San Francisco, Santa Fe 87501; and *Wilderness Adventure*, Box 1259, Taos 87571.

Carson National Forest & Alpine Wilderness Areas

Carson National Forest Topo Maps
U.S. Geological Survey Overview Maps, scale 1:250,000: Atec and Raton.

Eagle Nest Lake High Country
Large-scale U.S. Geological Survey Topographic Maps: Eagle Nest, Ute Park, Palo Flechado Pass, and Tooth of Time.

Latir Lakes High Country
Large-scale U.S. Geological Survey Topographic Maps: Cerro, Latir Peak, Red River, Amalia, and Sunshine.

Wheeler Peak Wilderness
Large-scale U.S. Geological Survey Topographic Maps: Eagle Nest, Palo Flechado Pass, Pueblo Peak, and Wheeler Peak.

This great fishing and hunting region embraces 1,440,000 acres of the Carson National Forest in northern New Mexico. Named after Kit Carson, the forest encompasses some of the most spectacular mountain areas in the Southwest, including the Sangre de Cristo Range and the 13,160-foot Wheeler Peak—the highest point in the Southwest. Big-game hunting is good throughout the region for elk, mule deer, antelope, black bear, Rocky Mountain bighorn sheep. The Jicarilla Apache Indian Reservation, a 758,000-acre wild area within the environs of the forest, is one of the state's top mule-deer hunting areas. Excellent mule-deer hunting is also found in the mountains and foothills near the Chama River, the Red River Canyon, and Eagle Nest Lake.

Some of the finest trout fishing in the country is found along the turbulent stretches of the Upper Rio Grande River as it winds its way south from the Colorado border for some 80 miles through an awesome 200- to 800-foot deep gorge of sheer cliffs and boulders. Its very inaccessibility and deep rushing waters produce large wild rainbows and browns that are frequently 8 pounds or more. The upper regions of the Rio Grande also produce fighting smallmouth bass up to 6 pounds. The headwaters area of the Chama River above the El Vado Dam holds lunker brown trout up to 20 pounds, and fish up to 6 pounds are caught consistently each season. To the east, the snow-capped peaks of the Sangre de Cristo Range hold numerous alpine lake basins and small, rushing trout streams. One of the more famous lake basins is the Latir Lakes nestled below the towering Latir Peaks. Access to the Latir Lakes area is by trail. Twenty miles to the south, a cluster of alpine lakes forms the headwaters of the Red River and offers excellent trout fishing in a pure wilderness setting. Eagle Nest

NEW MEXICO TRAVEL & RECREATION GUIDE

Lake, situated in the Merino Valley at an elevation of 8,400 feet, is another top trout-fishing lake. The famous wilderness hiking region, dominated by majestic Wheeler Peak, is located about 20 miles northeast of Taos. The tundra that covers Wheeler Peak and the other adjacent summits is rarely found in the Southwest. This region is infamous for sudden afternoon electrical storms. Make an early start and keep a watchful eye out for weather conditions. For the *Carson National Forest Map* (50¢) and for camping and trail information, write to the Carson National Forest, Box 558, Taos 87571.

The most famous of the Indian villages along the Rio Grande is the Taos pueblo, located just outside the boundaries of the forest. The Taos Indians have inhabited its two large five-storied structures for at least 800 years. The Indians farm their lands, raise cattle and horses, and work at jobs outside the pueblo, participating in the other cultures of the area while maintaining their own. The pueblo is entirely self-governing. An elected governor serves as civic head, while the *cacique* (priest) and the clan groups are still instrumental in the life of the pueblo. The ancestral religious ceremonies are still observed with traditional songs and dances.

The forest area offers excellent skiing from December through April, for both cross-country and downhill enthusiasts. Ski resorts within 25

miles of Taos include Taos Ski Valley, Sipapu Lodge and Ski Area, and Angel Fire Ski Basin and Country Club. Write to the Taos Chamber of Commerce, Drawer 1, Taos 87571, for more information about them. Red River Ski Valley is another nearby resort; for a description of the facilities, write to the Red River Chamber of Commerce, Red River 87558.

Another showplace of the north, Wheeler Peak Wilderness, preserves the rugged beauty of the highest mountain (Wheeler Peak, 13,161 feet) in the state. High peaks characterize this 6,027-acre preserve in the Carson National Forest.

The plant life here varies from a tundralike subalpine turf to Engelmann spruce, cork-bark fir, and bristlecone pine. Four alpine lakes and several streams with access by trail lie within the boundaries of the wilderness and offer good trout fishing. Game species include mule deer, elk, bear, grouse, marmot, pike, and marten.

The best time to visit the wilderness is early June or September, when fewer people are here and the weather is crisp and clear. If you visit in July, be prepared for afternoon thundershowers daily. It is warm during the day, but temperatures often dip below freezing at night.

Snowfall usually begins in November, slowing ground travel. The wilderness is open to cross-country skiing and snowshoeing during these months, but there are no ranger patrols in the area during the winter.

If you wish to travel in the wilderness, you must obtain a wilderness entry permit (groups traveling together need only one permit). The permit is free and is available, along with camping and trail information, from the District Ranger's office at Taos or Questa.

Access & Outfitting Centers

Major routes to the Carson National Forest include U.S. Highway 64 off Interstate 25; U.S. 285 and state routes 38 and 3. Lodging, guides, supplies, and outfitters are located at Chama, Cimarron, Espanola, Farmington, Taos, and Tierra Amarilla.

Cibola National Forest & the Sandia Crest Trail

Cibola National Forest Topo Maps

U.S. Geological Survey Overview Maps, scale 1:250,000: Fort Sumner, Gallup, St. Johns, Santa Fe, Socorro, Tularosa.

Sandia Crest Trail

Large-scale U.S. Geological Survey Topographic Maps: Bernalillo, Placitas, Sandia Crest, Tijeras.

This 1,660,630-acre forest lies south of Albuquerque in a region of great natural beauty where the Apache once roamed and hunted. Here the widely scattered ranges of the Datil, Gallina, Magdalena, Manzano, Sandia, San Mateo, Cebolleta, and Zuni mountains rise from the desert of central and western New Mexico. Big-game hunting is good throughout the mountainous backcountry for mule deer, bear, turkey, mountain lion, and Rocky Mountain bighorn sheep. Elk and antelope inhabit some areas of the forest.

Wilderness camping areas are plentiful in the rugged Sandia Mountains, particularly where they rise abruptly to 10,600 feet at the eastern edge of Albuquerque to form the 55,000-acre Sandia Recreation Area. The Sandia Crest Trail passes through the area, beginning at the terminus of Canyon Estates Road and extending north for 18 miles along the crest to North Sandia Creek. Many natural campsites can

be found among the juniper, pine, and spruce-fir forests that cover the mountains to the timberline.

Elephant Butte Reservoir and Caballo Lake have good fishing for black and white bass, walleye, and channel catfish, along with some fine fishing for large rainbow trout in the cold tailrace waters beneath the Elephant Butte and Caballo Dams. Bluewater and McGaffey lakes are also good trout waters.

The 57,200-acre Bosque del Apache National Wildlife Refuge lies above Elephant Butte Reservoir and preserves the river bottomlands along the Rio Grande. This "Apache Forest" of Rio Grande cottonwoods provides a sanctuary for ducks, geese, sandhill cranes, and quail. Most of the refuge beyond the river bottomlands is sparsely covered dry desert lands.

Nearby the forest are Indian pueblos, prehistoric ruins, ice caves, and lava flows. Windmills mark infrequent habitations. This is old prospecting country, a land of long-lost mines. The area is open to recreational use all year, although the high-country winter is severe. Sandia Peak Ski Area attracts downhillers. For more information and the *Cibola National Forest Map* (50¢), write to the Supervisor, Cibola National Forest, Box 1826, Albuquerque 87103.

Access & Outfitting Centers

The forest is reached by spur routes 142, 52, 78, and 107 off Interstate 70 and U.S. Highway 60. Lodging, guides, supplies, and outfitters are available at Albuquerque, Datil, Grants, Gallup, Magdalena, Mountainair, and Socorro.

Gila National Forest & Wilderness Areas

Gila National Forest Topo Maps

U.S. Geological Survey Overview Maps, scale 1:250,000: Clifton, Las Cruces, and Tularosa.

Black Range Primitive Area

Large-scale U.S. Geological Survey Topographic Maps: Bonner Canyon, Hay Mesa, Lookout Mountain, Reeds Peak, Victoria Peak.

Gila Wilderness

Large-scale U.S. Geological Survey Topographic Maps: Bearwallow Mountain, Black Mountain, Buckhorn, Burnt Corral Canyon, Canteen Canyon, Canyon Creek Mountains, Canyon Hill, Coppinas Peak, Diablo Range, Gila Hot Springs, Grandy Mountain, Grouse Mountain, Lilley Mountain, Little Turkey Peak, Loco Mountain, Middle Meso, Mogollon Baldy, Negrito Mountain, North Star Mesa, Rice Ranch, Shelley Peak, Spring Canyon, Wall Lake, Woodland Park.

This vast 2,694,471-acre forest encompasses some of the most primitive wilderness areas in the Southwest. The forest, located in southwestern New Mexico, is a land of steep mountains, rough canyons, mesas, river channels, and flood plains. The Continental Divide snakes through this awesome canyon country for about 150 miles, with elevations ranging from 4,500 feet to 11,000 feet. Forest roads and trails provide access to the remote hunting, fishing, and camping areas in the Big Burro Mountains, Mogollon Mountains, Diablo Mountains, Black Range Primitive Area, Gila Wilderness, and the Tularosa Mountains.

The deep and sinuous gorges of the Gila River country were set aside as the Gila Wilderness in 1924 as a tribute to the forester Aldo Leopold; it was the country's first roadless wilderness. The 429,506-acre wilderness and the surrounding 135,978-acre Gila Primitive Area

embrace the Mogollon and Diablo mountains. The deep canyons of the Gila River dissect the region, which is surrounded by a jumbled terrain of rocky spires and broad pine-covered flats, rolling hills, and grassy beaches. The outermost boundaries lie in the desert foothills, but the area itself reaches upward through juniper woodland to ponderosa pine and on to spruce-fir forests interspersed with meadows and stands of aspen.

The finest trout fishing in the forest is found in the interior of the Gila Wilderness. The middle and west forks of the Gila River and Mogollon Creek offer fair to good fishing for rainbows and browns. Trout are also found in Roberts, Snow, and Wall lakes, about 10 miles south of the Beaverhead Ranger Station. Big-game hunting is good throughout the forest for mule deer, Sonoran whitetail deer (or "fantailed" deer), bighorn sheep, antelope, and javelina.

Most of the main trails are well maintained and easy to follow. Trails following the river bottoms are occasionally flooded by flash storms or spring runoff. Flooding frequently affects the trails along the west fork, middle fork, and main Gila River. There are numerous crossings, but you should be prepared to get wet. Light canvas shoes are recommended. The trails starting on the south and west side of the Gila Wilderness and in the Gila Cliff Dwellings Area begin at low elevation

and climb steadily uphill. In the Willow Creek–Snow Lake area the trail heads are at high elevation, eliminating the necessity of long climbs out of deep valleys. Be alert for rattlesnakes. Use a walking stick to poke ahead of you where overhanging vegetation covers your view of the trail.

Man has lived in the Gila country for 10,000 years. The ancient Gila Cliff Dwellings are situated deep in the canyons, accessible only by foot or horseback, and are preserved as a national monument. Members of the Mogollon culture built the cliff dwellings and occupied them until about A.D. 1300, when they abandoned their home for unknown reasons. Spanish explorers entered the area in the early 1500s and gave the country its name, after a Yuma Indian word meaning "running saltwater." Still later, such historical characters as Geronimo, Billy the Kid, and Butch Cassidy were associated with the Gila.

The Black Range Primitive Area encompasses 169,356 acres of rugged, rocky canyons, forested peaks, old burns, and remote streams due

east of the Gila Wilderness. Several primitive trails wind through the remote interior wilderness camping areas and provide access to the Continental Divide, Diamond Creek, Granite Peak, Reeds Peak, and the headwaters of the Members River. The Black Range was used by the infamous Apache Chief Geronimo as a hideout. The rare Gila trout is found in a few of the remote streams.

A *Gila National Forest Map* that shows recreation sites, trails, roads, and points of interest is available free from the Forest Supervisor, Gila

whitetail, which usually weighs about 140 pounds. Black bear are less common, with perhaps no more than 24 taken each year. Wild turkey are found throughout the timbered areas of the forest. Upland game birds include Gambel and scaled quail on the forest fringes, and mourning dove, chukar partridge, and band-tailed pigeon.

For the *Lincoln National Forest Map* (50¢) and information on camping and trails in the forest, write to the Superintendent, Lincoln National Forest, Lincoln, 88338.

National Forest, 301 W. College Avenue, Silver City 88061. Write to the Supervisor's Office for additional camping, fishing, hunting, and wilderness travel info.

Access & Outfitting Centers

The Gila National Forest is reached by spur routes 90, 180, and 61 off Interstate Highway 10 and by state routes 90 and 52 off Interstate 25. Lodging, supplies, guides, packers, and outfitters are available at Glenwood, Reserve, Silver City, Truth or Consequences, Luna, Quemado, and Lordsburg.

Lincoln National Forest & White Mountains Wilderness

Lincoln National Forest Topo Maps

U.S. Geological Survey Overview Maps, scale 1:250,000: Carlsbad and Roswell.

White Mountains Wilderness

Large-scale U.S. Geological Survey Topographic Maps: Sierra Blanca Peak, Carrizozo, and Little Black Peak.

This million-acre forest embraces the lofty Capitan, Guadalupe, Sacramento, and White mountains in southern New Mexico. The forest contains the finest mule-deer range in the state. Three types of deer roam the juniper- and brush-covered foothills: the Rocky Mountain mule deer, the desert mule deer, and the whitetail. The Rocky Mountain mule deer is the largest, with mature bucks weighing up to 250 pounds. The desert mule deer, a somewhat smaller member of the family, is most common in the Guadalupe Mountains. The Sacramento Mountains above Alamogordo are inhabited by the Texas

The White Mountains Wilderness rises abruptly from the Tularosa Basin, starting from 6,000 feet and reaching an altitude of 11,400 feet, crossing 5 different life zones, and encompassing 31,171 acres of high-country meadows and mixed conifer forests. Primitive trails provide access to Big Bear Canyon, Nogal Peak, Church Mountain, Thra River, and Bonito Creek. Big-game species in the wilderness include mule deer, black bear, a few elk, and wild boar. There is fair trout fishing in several high-country lakes and streams. Winter activities include cross-country skiing and snowshoeing.

The Capitan Mountains, located due east of the White Mountains Wilderness, were the birthplace of Smokey Bear, discovered by firefighters after a 17,000-acre forest fire in 1950.

Access & Outfitting Centers

The Lincoln National Forest is reached by U.S. highways 82, 70, 54, and 380. Accommodations, guides, supplies, and outfitters are located at Alamogordo, Artesia, Capitan, Carlsbad, Cloudcroft, Roswell, and Ruidoso.

Santa Fe National Forest & Alpine Wilderness Areas

Santa Fe National Forest Topo Maps

U.S. Geological Survey Overview Maps, scale 1:250,000: Albuquerque, Aztec, Raton and Santa Fe.

Pecos Wilderness & Alpine Lakes Country

Large-scale U.S. Geological Survey Topographic Maps: Aspen Basin, Cowles, Elk Mountain, El Valle, Jicarita Peak, Pecos Falls, Rociada, Sierra Mosca, and Truchas Peak.

San Pedro Parks Wilderness

Large-scale U.S. Geological Survey Topographic Maps: Arroyo Del Aqua, Cuba, Gallina, Jarosa, Nacimiento Peak, and Regina.

The Santa Fe National Forest is a majestic mountainland richly covered with pine, aspen, fir, and wildflower meadows. The forest, located in northern New Mexico, offers some of the finest fishing, hunting, and wilderness camping in the Southwest. Within the forest's bounds lies the Pecos Wilderness, where the 13,101-foot Truchas Peak shares winter snows with other lofty mountaintops and the San Pedro Parks Wilderness. The wilderness headwaters of Pecos River contain forests of aspen, pine, fir, and spruce. Sloping gradually southward, the forest's Pecos Division is some 50 miles long and 25 miles wide. It includes the popular Santa Fe Ski Basin on the west, and farther south, historic Glorieta Pass and the old Santa Fe Trail.

Hundreds of alpine lakes, beaver ponds, and wild streams, such as Spirit, Baldy, Truchas, Encantada, Ruth, North Fork, the Upper Pecos, and Mora rivers, have fishing for native cutthroat, rainbow, and brown trout.

The forest has the finest Rocky Mountain elk and mule deer hunting range in the state. Other game species here include black bear, mountain lion, bobcat, coyote, weasel, badger, raccoon, marten, mink, and muskrat. Game birds are geese, ducks, dusky grouse, wild turkey, quail, and band-tailed pigeon. The major big-game areas lie in the interior of the forest among the Jemez, San Pedro, and Sangre de Cristo mountains, and along the Rio Grande and Guadalupe rivers.

More than 1,000 mapped trails wind through the forest. Forest roads also run through the area, and developed campsites are scattered throughout.

The U.S. Forest Service publishes a full-color *Santa Fe National Forest Map* to the forest. The map, with a scale of 4 miles to the inch, shows improved recreation sites, highways, forest roads, other roads, important recreation trails, streams, and ranger and forest stations. The map lists and describes all campsites within the forest. It is available for 50¢, along with camping and trail information, from the Supervisor, Santa Fe National Forest, Box 1689, Santa Fe 87501.

The rugged 167,416-acre Pecos Wilderness encompasses the headwaters of the Pecos River at the southern end of the Sangre de Cristo Mountains in the Carson and Santa Fe national forests. The Upper Pecos, a scenic white-water river, drains a huge horseshoe-shaped basin with streams radiating out on either side, and has good fishing for wild rainbow, cutthroat, and brown trout.

The wilderness encompasses magnificent forests of aspen, pine, fir, and spruce to the timberline of the high mountains. They are crowned by the 13,101-foot Truchas Peak. Elsewhere in the wilderness, deep canyons slice gently sloping ridges and mesas.

Eagles are often sighted among the treeless peaks, while elk, black bear, mule deer, grouse, and turkey populate the meadows of the lower elevations. The wilderness is a top-ranked fall hunting area. Beaver dams are a common sight in the high country, and a few mountain lions, bobcats, bighorn sheep, marten, minks, and muskrat inhabit the area.

Horses are available from several dude ranches along the borders of the wilderness. Hikers can approach the high country from Cowles, Panchuela, Jack's Creek, or Iron Gate campgrounds at the head of the Pecos Canyon Road. Wilderness trails, including the beautiful Skyline Trail, provide access to Truchas Peak, Santa Fe Mountains, Rio Mora River, Truchas Lakes, Joe Vigil Lake, Serpent Lake, Rio Medio River, Lost Bear Lake, Horsethief Meadows, and Pecos Baldy Lake.

A 116-page *Trail Guide to the Upper Pecos*, describing 15 trail logs for hiking and horseback riding, is available from the New Mexico Bureau of Mines and Mineral Resources, Publications Room, Socorro 87801. The trail guide includes a geology and trail map. It costs $3.50. A free *Visitor's Guide to the Pecos Wilderness* may be obtained by writing the Pecos District Ranger, Santa Fe National Forest, Pecos 87552. The guide contains a map showing the major features and entrance points to the wilderness and Upper Pecos.

The San Pedro Parks, a beautiful backpacking paradise, covers 41,132 acres along the San Pedro Mountains in the western part of the Santa Fe National Forest. The wilderness is a land of gently rolling grass parks and boggy meadows interspersed among dense stands of spruce and mixed conifers at an elevation of 10,000 feet.

Clear streams meander through the meadows of brilliant wildflowers and beaver ponds. For the hunter who enjoys a pack trip, the beautiful meadows and parks offer some of the finest elk and trophy mule deer opportunities in the state, as well as blue grouse, turkey, squirrel, wild turkey, and black bear.

Backpackers should be prepared for showers in July and August. Daytime temperatures in the summer are often in the seventies, but nights vary from to cool to cold. Snowfall usually begins in November. The wilderness is open to skiing and snowshoeing.

A wilderness entry permit is required for single travelers or groups. The permit, which is free, is available at the District Forest Ranger offices in Cuba and Coyote. You may also order the permit by mail from the same offices, or from the Forest Supervisor, Santa Fe National Forest, Santa Fe 87501. Permits obtained by mail must be validated at one of the two district offices before the visitor enters the backcountry.

Many wilderness visitors travel through the backcountry by horse. Group size is limited to 25 animals to minimize the environmental impact.

Commercial guide-outfitters are not permitted on the San Pedro Parks Wilderness because of its small size.

A free *Visitor's Guide to the San Pedro Parks Wilderness* is available from the Forest Supervisor (address above). The guide describes the area, and gives rules and regulations for visitors. Its map designates roads, trails, national forest lands, and wilderness boundaries. It divides the wilderness into 12 travel zones.

Access & Outfitting Centers

The Santa Fe National Forest is reached by Interstate 25, U.S. Highway 84, and state routes 63, 475, 76, 283, 266, 94, 3, 38, and 121. Lodging, guides, supplies, packers, and outfitters are available at Cuba, Espanola, Las Vegas, Los Alamos, Pecos, and Santa Fe.

Accommodations— Vacation Lodges & Resorts

For information about Oklahoma's varied vacation resorts, lodges, and motels, write: Oklahoma Dept. of Tourism & Recreation, 504 Will Rogers Bldg., Oklahoma City 73105.

There are a number of good lodges situated in Oklahoma's state parks. The *Roman Nose Lodge*, Box 61, Watonga 73772, is named for a legendary Cheyenne chieftain. It is a rugged retreat, and the lodge and park are the gateway to Oklahoma's great Northwest. *Quartz Mountain Lodge*, Lone Wolf 73655, is surrounded by the grandeur of ancient hills and peaceful Lake Altus-Lugert. Southern hospitality is the keynote at *Lake Murray Lodge*, Ardmore 73401. The old West comes to life with daily stagecoach runs through Indian country, on the peninsula of 2,800-acre Sequoyah Park, where clear waters lap the shore at the *Western Hills Lodge*, Box 509, Wagoner 74467. *Texoma Lodge*, Box 248, Kingston 73439, built on the shores of Lake Texoma, provides almost 2,000 acres of unspoiled parkland. Recreation and relaxation are the keys to *Fountainhead Lodge*, Checotah 74426, whether you fly into the lighted, paved airstrip or motor the scenic routes via I-40 or U.S. 69. *Arrowhead Lodge*, Box 57, Canadian, 74425, lies on Lake Eufaula's southern shore. A free brochure describing these lodges in detail may be obtained by writing to the Oklahoma Dept. of Tourism & Recreation, address above.

Camping and Backpacking

There are many facilities available in Oklahoma's comprehensive system of campgrounds. *Oklahoma Campers Guide* lists all major areas and towns in the state, and the camping facilities convenient to each. It may be obtained free by writing to the Oklahoma Dept. of Tourism & Recreation, 504 Will Rogers Bldg., Oklahoma City 73105.

Public Recreation Areas of Oklahoma, available free from Dept. of Wildlife Conservation, 1801 North Lincoln, Oklahoma City 73105, lists major public recreation areas in the state, and which services are provided. A complete description of state-park facilities is provided in *Oklahoma State Parks*, which profiles 30 parks and lists state lodges and recreation areas. Information is available free from the Oklahoma Dept. of Tourism & Recreation, 504 Will Rogers Bldg., Oklahoma City 73105.

The same office will also provide free information on hiking opportunities in state parks. The most popular areas are the Ouachita National Forest and the Charon Gardens Wilderness in the Wichita Mountains Wildlife Refuge. Abandoned logging trails and tall, cool forests are the attractions in the Ouachita National Forest, which is dotted with clear lakes and streams. More rugged challenges are offered by the Charon Gardens Wilderness area, which was once used as a religious site by the Comanche Indians. Hikers must cope with near-vertical rock walls; and deer, elk, and buffalo are common.

Oklahoma is a melting pot of Indian cultures, with 35 tribes inhabiting the state. Complete information about events and important sites is given in *Oklahoma and the Indian*, a free map/guide available from Oklahoma Indian Affairs Commission, 4010 Lincoln Blvd., Oklahoma City 73105.

Canoeing & Float Fishing

There are many excellent canoeing opportunities in Oklahoma, and there are float streams to suit all levels of experience. The most popular river is the Illinois, which combines good fishing with a scenic, mild-

OKLAHOMA ENCYCLOPEDIA

mannered river. Smallmouth, largemouth, and spotted bass, channel catfish, white bass, rock bass, and colorful sunfish provide good fishing, and there are many outfitters and services along the river to help you plan your trip. From such streams as the Kiamichi, Mountain Fork, Glover, Big Eagle, Eagle Fork, and smaller creeks, canoe fishermen take smallmouth and rock bass, channel catfish, sunfish, goggle-eyed perch, drum, and buffalo; and in doing so, they pass down shadowed canyons, scramble through cliffside underbrush and over high-piled rocks that give character to this southeastern corner of the state. The Kiamichi is the most important river of the region, but the Mountain Fork is the most beautiful, plunging down to the Little River over riffles and falls and between rock cliffs overhung by willows and tall gum trees.

A free map/guide, *Floating the Illinois*, may be obtained by writing to the Dept. of Wildlife Conservation, 1801 N. Lincoln Blvd., P.O. Box 53465, Oklahoma City 73160.

Oklahoma canoeing and float streams are shown on the following large-scale U.S. Geological Survey Topographic Maps. *Mountain Fork:* Goodwater, Broken Bow, Cove, Smithville; *Glover River:* Golden, Bethel (shaded relief); *Little River & Black Fork:* Albion SE, Albion SW, Wildhorse Mountain, Nashoba, Caney Mountain, Sobol, Alikchi, Wright City, Golden, Garvin, Idabel, Shutts, Goodwater, Cerrogordo; *Eagle Fork River:* Smithville, Page, Ludlow; *Illinois River & Tenkiller Ferry Reservoir:* Siloam Springs NW, Kansas, Chervey, and Moody's large-scale maps and the Tulsa and Fort Smith 1: 250,000-scale maps; *Flint Creek:* Siloam Springs NW; *Cimarron River:* 1:250,000-scale Woodward, Oklahoma City, Enid, Tulsa, and Fort Smith maps; *Canadian River* is shown on 1:250,000-scale maps: Woodward, Clinton, Oklahoma City, Ardmore, and Fort Smith; *Blue River:* Caddo NW, Durant N., Caddo S., Wade.

Fishing & Hunting in Oklahoma

Oklahoma's great lake impoundments, with over two million surface acres of water, and mountainous plateau country provide some good fishing and hunting opportunities. The Grand Lake of the Cherokees, located on the Grand River in the northeastern corner of the state, is the state's largest body of water, with close to 1,000 miles of shoreline, and offers excellent fishing for largemouth bass and crappies. Rainbow trout, an exotic fish in Oklahoma, are caught in the cold, turbulent tailrace waters below Tenkiller Reservoir and in the 12-mile stretch of the Illinois below Tenkiller Dam. The waters of the lower Illinois are drawn from the bottom of Lake Tenkiller, which maintains a constant temperature of 60 degrees throughout the year. When the river's water level begins to rise during generation of the hydroelectric dam, the big rainbows often go on a feeding binge, and fly fishermen often land hookjawed lunkers. Once the river has risen, float fishermen in canoes or johnboats have the advantage. Another rainbow-trout fishery has been established on the beautiful spring-fed clear-running Blue River in southeast Oklahoma on the Blue River Public Hunting and Fishing Area. The Blue's numerous falls, deep pools, boulders, and small islands provide excellent trout habitat. The current state record 10 lb. 4 oz. rainbow was caught in the Illinois River in June 1966.

Largemouth bass is the number-one sport fish in Oklahoma and is present in nearly every lake and stream, along with schools of white bass, channel catfish, and bluegills. The record largemouth in the state is 11 lbs. 5 oz. The average size is one and a half to four pounds in weight. The smallmouth bass is restricted to the cool, swift-flowing mountain streams of eastern Oklahoma, namely, the Mountain Fork River and the tributaries of the Grand and Illinois rivers. Oklahoma smallmouths seldom exceed two pounds. Walleye have been well

established in the state as a result of an intensive stocking program that began during the spring of 1961 in the state's outstanding system of reservoirs. Large flathead catfish up to 66 pounds and channel cats are found in the large lakes and rivers. Big blue catfish up to 50 pounds are found in the lakes and rivers of southern Oklahoma, especially in the Red River system. The state's great lakes and reservoirs, which together include more shoreline than the Atlantic and Pacific coasts, are described in detail in the free guide *Oklahoma Lakes*, available from the Dept. of Tourism & Recreation, 504 Will Rogers Bldg., Oklahoma City 73105.

The major lakes and reservoirs include Lake Texoma, a superb fishery for striped bass up to 40 pounds; 42,000-acre Robert S. Kerr Lake, a top-ranked fishing and waterfowl hunting area, with peak populations of ducks and geese numbering well over 50,000; long, winding 26,300-acre Keystone Reservoir, another fine striped-bass fishery nestled among scenic rolling hills; the renowned largemouth and smallmouth bass, and walleye waters of beautiful 12,500-acre Lake Tenkiller, nestled among the historic Cookson Hills, once a retreat for outlaw gangs and the former hunting grounds of the Cherokee Indians; the bass and walleye waters of beautiful Lake Wister, the gateway to the "Kiamichi Country" and Ouachita National Forest in southeastern Oklahoma; the prolific trophy largemouth-bass waters of Spavinaw and Eucha

lakes in the east; the northern pike waters of Lake Corl Etling, nestled in the primitive reaches of "Black Mesa" country; scenic Broken Bow Reservoir, in the foothills of the Ouachita Mountains, with its 180-mile pine-fringed shoreline and island-dotted smallmouth- and largemouth-bass waters; the fabled goose-hunting lands surrounding Great Salt Plains Lake in northwestern Oklahoma; Oologah Lake, named for a famous Cherokee chief, meaning "Dark Cloud," adjacent to the birthplace of humorist Will Rogers; the trophy "big bass" waters of beautiful 12,000-acre Lake Hudson—site of the state's first trading post, established in 1796; beautiful Greenleaf Lake in the verdant Cookson Hills; and the clear, deep waters of 2,349-acre Arbuckle Lake, nestled amid the rugged outcroppings of the Arbuckle Mountains, with good fishing for bass and northern pike. The state's warm-water and trout-fishing opportunities are illustrated by the state's record fish.

OKLAHOMA RECORD FISH

	Lb.–oz.	inches	Place	Year
Bass, largemouth	11–15	28	Kiamichi River	1941
Bass, smallmouth	4–12	21	Mountain Fork River	1968
Bass, spotted	8–2	23½	Pittsburg Co. Pond	1958
Bass, striped	32–0	37½	Lake Eufaula	1972
Bass, white	4–14	20	Lake Eucha	1969
Buffalo, bigmouth	43–8	32	Washita River	1973
Carp	32–12	38	Lake Rush	1968
Catfish, blue	69	—	Lake Texoma	1977
Catfish, channel	30–0	39½	Washita River	1974
Catfish, flathead	66–0	48½	Lake Spavinaw	1970
Crappie, black	4–10	20¼	Lawyer Pond	1974
Crappie, white	4–13	19	Tillman Co. Pond	1967
Drum, freshwater	35–4	38	Lake Texoma	1967
Pickerel, chain	2–8	21	Guthrie Farm Pond	1973
Pike, northern	20–0	40½	Lake Vincent	1974
Sunfish, bluegill	1–15	10	Caddo Co. Pond	1968
Sunfish, green	2–7	13	Pontotoc Co. Pond	1972
Sunfish, redear	2–1¼	12¾	Logan Co. Pond	1973
Trout, rainbow	10–4	27	Illinois River	1966
Walleye	11–4	30	Lake Hefner	1967

Detailed information on float fishing on Oklahoma's scenic mountain streams and rivers is contained in the section "Canoeing & Float Fishing."

Oklahoma fishing and hunting regulations may be obtained from the Dept. of Wildlife Conservation, 1801 North Lincoln Blvd., P.O. Box 53465, Oklahoma City 73160. The department also publishes the following free guides, available from the address listed above: *Crow Shooting on Fort Cobb Public Hunting Area; Sport Fish of Oklahoma; Fish Facts; Floating the Illinois; McCurtin County Wilderness Area; Oklahoma Game Birds; Oklahoma Mammals; Rio Grande Turkey Management; Trout Fishing in Oklahoma;* and free maps of the Canton, Choctaw, Fort Gibson, and Lexington public hunting areas. The handy full-color booklet *Fishes of Oklahoma* may be obtained from the department for 50¢. The Dept. of Wildlife Conservation also publishes *Public Lands of Oklahoma* (25¢), an extremely useful large-format booklet that contains maps and descriptions of all public hunting lands in the state.

Hunting

Although much of the state's land is privately owned, there are some 500,000 acres of public hunting areas managed for wildlife and hunting by the Department of Wildlife Conservation, as well as national grasslands and 250,000 acres of the Ouachita National Forest, which sprawls across the border from Arkansas. These public hunting lands provide excellent cover for whitetail deer and upland game birds. Whitetails are found throughout the state, with the best hunting in the cypress swamps and conifer forests of the southeast. Other big-game species include a small number of antelope in the Panhandle and a small herd of Rocky Mountain elk in the Wichita Mountains Na-

tional Wildlife Refuge. Hunting for both species is by special permit only. Small game animals include cottontails, jackrabbits, and gray squirrels in the oak and hickory forests of the east, and fox squirrels along the rivers and forest ravines of the west. The Fort Cobb Public Hunting Area has the largest winter crow roost in North America, numbering some ten million birds. The state also offers some of the best hunting in the country for coyotes, bobcats, and raccoons.

Highways—Recreation & Scenic Routes

Oklahoma's transportation system provides easy access to all recreation areas. The free *Oklahoma State Highway Map,* available from the Oklahoma State Highway Commission, shows all major roads and highways, towns and settlements, lakes and streams, national forest land, airfields and railroads, and recreation sites.

Oklahoma Tours is a free brochure that lists several different possible road tours of the state, with descriptions of various scenic attractions and points of interest. It is available from the Tourism Promotion Divison, Oklahoma Tourism & Recreation Dept., 504 Will Rogers Bldg., Oklahoma City 73105.

Red Wolf & Southern Bald Eagle

There are eleven wildlife species known to exist in Oklahoma that are considered endangered. Loss of habitat, pesticide poisoning, certain forestry practices, and illegal shooting are the major causes of a threat that could mean the end of several species.

Among them is the red wolf, which has been forced out of its range in southeastern Oklahoma. The red wolf is usually larger than the coyote, sometimes weighing up to 80 pounds. Despite its name, the red wolf is a combination of black, buff, and gray, and is often mistaken for a coyote.

The southern bald eagle is another endangered species. This magnificent bird of prey is a junior cousin of the bird that is our national emblem. It is dark brown or gray in its early life, but its head and tail turn distinctly white later on. Despite its tremendous soaring ability, superb vision, and impressive size, it has been the victim of just about all of man's destructive intrusions.

For complete information about all of Oklahoma's endangered wildlife, write for a free copy of *Oklahoma's Endangered Species:* Dept.

of Wildlife Conservation, 1801 North Lincoln Blvd., Oklahoma City 73160.

Wichita Mountains Wildlife Refuge

The Wichita Mountain Range comprises 61,480 acres, extending northwest and lying largely within Comanche country. The rounded summits of its granite peaks average 650 to 700 feet in height. Classed among the older mountains in the United States, they are interesting both geologically and scenically, and have attracted many thousands of Oklahomans, as well as tourists from other states.

Until the middle of the nineteenth century, the only inhabitants of this area were Indians. The onetime presence here of a tribe of Wichita Indians has been substantiated, and remains of other tribal lodges have been found.

President Theodore Roosevelt first proclaimed this area a wildlife preserve. Thanks to his initial efforts, the region is now a haven for buffalo. Other wildlife preserved in the refuge include elk, white-tailed deer, Texas longhorns, wild turkeys, and various birds.

The buffalo herd in the Wichita Mountains Wildlife Refuge now numbers about a thousand head. Old records reveal that "Black Dog," a bull of the original herd, lived to achieve the reputation as the largest buffalo, with an estimated weight of 2,800 pounds. The heaviest weights of bulls now on the range are in the 1,600- to 2,000-pound class. These big animals are not often seen by the public, as they tend to range apart from the rest of the herd. Every effort has been made to keep the herd in as natural condition as possible. The dozen refuge lakes that are open for fishing are stocked with bass, sunfish, crappie, and channel catfish.

Included in the Wichita Refuge are nearly 8,900 acres of wilderness —land as wild as ever, little touched by the hand of man. The Charon Gardens Wilderness Area of 5,000 acres and the North Mountains Wilderness Area of 3,900 acres encompass some of the most rugged landscape in the Wichitas.

A two-hour hike will take you into the center of the Charon Gardens Wilderness, but the going is rugged and you should be in good physical condition before trying the more broken sections. There are no marked trails or drinking water.

The North Mountain area is designated as a research area. It is reserved for research studies and is not open to the public.

A free map/guide, *Wichita Mountains Wildlife Refuge*, is available from the Refuge Manager, Wichita Mountains Wildlife Refuge, P.O. Box 448, Cache 73527. It shows all recreational facilities, lakes, contours, trails, campgrounds, and study areas. The same office will also provide you with information on the buffalo herd and a free pamphlet on the *Wichita Mountains Wildlife Refuge Regulations*.

The Wichita Mountains Wildlife Refuge is shown on the following large-scale U.S. Geographic Survey Topographic Maps: Meers, Mount Scott, Saddle Mountain, Quanak Mountain, Odetta, Indiahoma, Post Oak Creek, Cooperton, Glen Mountains, and Snyder.

TEXAS
ENCYCLOPEDIA

Accommodations—
Vacation Resorts & Lodges

Write to the Division of Travel and Information, State Dept. of Highways & Public Transportation, Austin 78701 for complete listings of ranches, lodges, resorts, and hotels. For listings and descriptions of fishing and hunting vacation resorts, write: Guides, Outfitters & Resorts, 3444 Northaven Rd., Dallas 75229.

Big Bend National Park
& the "River of Ghosts"

This 708,221-acre preserve encompasses the wild country of spectacular canyons, bluffs, stark desert, and mountains bordered on three sides by the "Big Bend" of the Rio Grande—the international boundary between Mexico and the United States—known to the Spanish conquistadors as the "Great River of the North" and to the early pioneers as the haunting "River of Ghosts." This rugged wilderness, once the home and hunting grounds of the Comanche Indians, is inhabited by mule deer, javelina, mountain lion, pronghorn antelope, gray fox, and bobcat. The rugged Chisos Mountains—the Apache word for "ghostly"—with their red, yellow, blue, and purple slopes, dominate the landscape north of the "Big Bend." The major features along the Rio Grande as it flows through the park include the awesome Mariscal Canyon; the Break—where the canyon walls recede from the river for a distance of one-fourth mile; the short but scenic San Vicente and Hot Springs canyons; and Boquillas Canyon. Old Comanche trails, petroglyphs, dugouts, and numerous caves are located along the dark, shadowed floors of the canyons.

Write to Big Bend National Park 79834 for complete information on canyons, the Rio Grande, hiking, float trips, camping, fishing, rules and regulations, safety, and use of horses and vehicles. The *Big Bend Map/Guide*, available free, provides a contour map and description of the park, and indicates services, facilities, roads, trails, and campgrounds. Overnight lodging is available at *Chisos Mountains Lodge* in the basin. Reservations are advisable. Write to National Park Concessions, Inc., Big Bend National Park 79834; phone (915) 477–2291. There are also food services, trailer parks, stores, and gas stations. *Villa de la Mina, Inc.*, provides river float trips and cabins. Write to Glen Pepper, Box 47, Terlingua 79852, for further information.

The Big Bend Natural History Assn., Big Bend National Park 79834, publishes three illustrated guides: *Hiker's Guide* (50¢), *Road Guide* (50¢), and *Guide to the Backcountry Roads and the River* (50¢). Each of these 32-page booklets gives detailed descriptions of the natural and scenic wonders in the park. Other publications available from the Natural History Assn. include *The Big Bend of the Rio Grande Guidebook* (138 pp., $2.50), *Birds of Big Bend & Vicinity* ($4.95), *Wildflowers of the Big Bend Country* ($5.00), *Guide to Texas Snakes* (75¢), and the U.S. Geological Survey *Terlingua-Chisos Mountains Map* (scale, 1:130,000; $1.00).

Campgrounds are located at Chisos Basin and Rio Grande Village. Guided packhorse trips are provided by *Chisos Remuda*, Big Bend National Park 79834; phone (915) 477–2374. Guided Rio Grande float trips are provided by *Villa de la Mina*, P.O. Box 47, Terlingua 79852; phone (915) 364–2446.

Big Bend National Park is reached via U.S. 90, 385, 80, and 67, Interstate Highway 10, and Texas State Highway 118 and Texas Ranch Road 170—the Camino Real. Supplies and services are available at Boquillas, Rio Grande Village, Castolon, Santa Elena, Study

Butte, Terlingua, and Lajitas. Big Bend is shown on the U.S. Geological Survey Emory 1:250,000-scale map.

Braniff Outdoor Adventures Travel Service

Braniff Airlines publishes a free, full-color catalog, *Outdoor Adventures*, which describes 60 worldwide fishing and hunting tours. The fin and feather adventures described range from trophy fishing for rainbows and salmon in the Alaska wilderness, to outings on the wild highcountry lakes and rivers of the Andes Mountains in Chile and Argentina for giant brown, rainbow and brook trout; as well as such exotic trips as an Ecuador jungle safari, goose hunting in Patagonia, and trekking in the remote Galapagos Islands. For a copy of the catalog and detailed trip planning information, write: Braniff Outdoor Council, Room 1003, Exchange Park, Dallas 75235.

Campgrounds & State Recreation Areas

The hundreds of campgrounds in this wide and varied state provide excellent facilities and access to natural areas. *Texas Public Campgrounds,* available free from the Travel & Information Division, State Dept. of Highways & Public Transportation, P.O. Box 5064, Austin 78763, lists and describes all the public camping areas in the state. *Texas—A Land of Contrasts,* a free and enormously useful 205-page book with many color illustrations, lists local, state, and federal campgrounds as well as complete information on virtually every recreational facility and service in the state. It is available free from the same office, and it includes maps of every region in the state, information on trails, state parks, forest lands, hunting and fishing, rocks, minerals, flowers, birds, special events, tourist bureaus, and weather.

Canoeing & Float Trips

Texas has a great diversity of scenic and wild waterways. The East Texas rivers, characterized by a lush, junglelike climate, fragrant pine- and cypress-covered banks, and meandering currents, are noted for their log jams, overhanging branches, and trophy-sized largemouth bass. The major East Texas rivers include the Angelina, Neches, Red, Sabine, West Fork San Jacinto, Sulphur, and Trinity, and the Big Cypress Bayou, Attoyac Bayou, Pine Island Bayou, and Village Creek. The Big Cypress Bayou, noted for its log jams and its two major impounds, beautiful Caddo Lake and Lake o' the Pines, flows through dense forests and offers top-ranked float fishing for bass. The Central Texas rivers, including the Basque, Brazos, Colorado, Concho, Frio, Guadalupe, Medina, Pedernales, and Wichita, flow through the hill country and often have stretches of white water. The 840-mile-long Brazos River—the largest river between the Rio Grande and the Red River—provides excellent canoeing and float fishing along the scenic and wild 41-mile stretch below Possum Kingdom Lake, where the river flows through a rugged region of beautiful cedar-covered hills, surrounded by high bluffs, forests, spectacular rock outcroppings, and views of the Palo Pinto Mountains. The river's numerous gravel bars and islands provide excellent campsites. A 22-mile section of the Guadalupe River flows through an incredibly scenic area of high limestone bluffs, with pecan, cottonwood, giant bald cypress, oak, palmettos, and a variety of vines, shrubs, and forbs lining the river. This stretch of the Guadalupe, with its islands, falls, and rapids, is considered the most scenic in Texas.

The waterways of West Texas—the historic Rio Grande, Pecos, and Devils rivers—flow through an extremely arid country with spectacular bluffs and great canyons. Flash floods and rattlesnakes are potential hazards. The wild and scenic Rio Grande flows for 1,248 miles along the southern border of Texas through a series of some of the most rugged canyons in the United States. The Lower Canyons of the Rio Grande rank only behind the Grand Canyon of the Colorado and Hells Canyon of the Snake, and should be attempted only by experienced river runners. Lower Canyons, located just outside the eastern boundary of Big Bend National Park, forms a series of rapids and flows through the Black Gap Wildlife Management Area, past Outlaw Flats, Big Canyon, Reagan Canyon, Hot Springs Rapid, Daggar Mountain, Panther Canyon Rapids, San Francisco Canyon Rapids, and El Indio Canyons. Numerous old Indian trails, rock paintings, dugouts, and caves are located along the riverbanks. The names on the land suggest the wild and harsh nature of this old West wilderness. Beyond the Lower Canyons, the Rio Grande flows through the great Amistad and Falcon reservoirs into the Gulf of Mexico. A National Park Service camping and boating permit is required for travel through Big Bend National Park.

Fishing & Hunting in Texas

Texas, the largest of the contiguous states, containing 265,986 square miles, offers some excellent fishing and hunting opportunities in the forestlands and sagebrush flats, mountain and canyon country, and 6,000 square miles of freshwater lakes and streams, plus scores of tidal bays and 624 miles of shoreline along the Gulf of Mexico.

Piney Woods Region

The state is rimmed on the north by the Red River, on the east by the Sabine, and on the west and south by the historic Rio Grande, all of which contain a series of large impoundments. The scenic green-canopied Piney Woods and Big Thicket region of East Texas offers some of the state's finest whitetail deer, wild turkey, and upland game-bird hunting and trophy largemouth-bass fishing in the Southwest. Here are the vast, fragrant pine forests of the Angelina, Davy Crockett, Sabine, and Sam Houston national forest lands, and the lunker-bass waters of famous Lake Caddo and Lake o' the Pines, Livingston, Palestine, Sam Rayburn, Wright Patman, and Toledo Bend reservoirs, set among scenic, rolling forestlands. Huge 32,700-acre Caddo Lake, which straddles the Texas-Louisiana border, is renowned for its trophy bass and primeval beauty—fringed by dense moss-covered forests. Caddo, believed to have been created by the great New Madrid earthquake of 1811, has a confusing maze of

channels, 42 miles of which have been marked as "boat roads" by the state.

"Gateway" Region

To the west, in the "Gateway" region between the rolling prairies and the Brazos Valley, are the bass waters: 33,750-acre Cedar Creek Lake, one of the most popular in north-central Texas; Eagle Mountain Lake, noted for its huge schools of white bass; and Granbury Lake on the Brazos River, Grapevine Lake, and Lewisville, Lavcon, and Palestine lakes. Some of the state's best bass fishing is found here in huge 89,000-acre Lake Texoma; in 36,700-acre Lake Tawakoni, with its more than 5 miles of submerged timber and countless coves and inlets; and in the clear blue waters of 15,760-acre Lake Whitney, with its towering cliffs and sheltered coves and inlets.

Brazos River Country

The woodlands and glades of the Brazos River Valley to the south, named Brazos de Dios, the "Arms of God," by the Spaniards, provide good hunting for deer and wild turkey, and bass fishing in Mexia, Somerville, Waco, and Stillhouse Hollow lakes. The "Ranch and Hill" country to the west provides fishing for rainbow and brown trout on the Guadalupe River below the Canyon Lake Dam, and for trophy bass in the submerged brush areas of the upper reaches of 22,050-acre Corpus Christi Lake. Scenic 19,800-acre Possum Kingdom Lake, in the rolling prairie country to the north, is a popular bass-fishing and hunting area. Greenbelt Lake, on the Salt Fork of the Red River, is known as the "northern pike capital of Texas," and produced the state-record 18 lb. 2 oz. northern. To the west of the rolling prairie country are the arid flatlands of the Texas High Plains, the wetlands of the Buffalo Lake National Wildlife Refuge, and the beautiful blue waters of Lake Meredith and the Sanford Recreation Area, set among the colorful buttes and cliffs of the Canadian River Valley.

Pecos River Country

To the south is the rugged Pecos River Country, home of Pecos Bill, legendary king of the cowboys, and Judge Roy Bean—the "Law West of the Pecos." The clear blue waters of the huge 67,000-acre Amistad Reservoir—a joint project of the United States and Mexico and a national recreation area—impounds the waters of the Rio Grande just below its confluence with the Devils River. The numerous coves and inlets of the great lake—which extends for 74 miles up the Rio Grande, 13 miles up the Pecos River, and 25 miles up the Devils River, surrounded by rugged wild lands—provides top-ranked fishing for trophy largemouth bass. For detailed information about fishing, regulations, accommodations, fishing guide service, and marinas, write: Amistad National Recreation Area, Del Rio 78840.

"Big Bend" Country

To the west lie the lofty mountains and spectacular canyons of the "Big Bend" Country of the Rio Grande and the rugged Guadalupe Mountains. The near-tropic region to the east, along the Gulf of Mexico, encompasses the famed trophy bass and catfish waters of the huge 78,340-acre Falcon Reservoir, straddling the U.S.-Mexico boundary, and the renowned saltwater fishing centers at Port South Padre Island, Aransas Pass, Corpus Christi, and the Padre Island National Seashore. During the early 1900s, the Mustang Island area was one of the world's great tarpon centers, but it has rapidly declined over the years.

The renowned saltwater fishing meccas along the Gulf of Mexico on Texas' 624-mile east coast provide fishing for tuna, marlin, sailfish, pompano, snook, king and Spanish mackerel, wahoo, speckled trout, flounder, grouper, jewfish, red snapper, sheepshead, drum, bluefish, southern kingfish, and several varieties of sharks. The coastline teems with gulls, egrets, pelicans, and roseate spoonbills, plus a few rare whooping cranes that winter at the Aransas National Wildlife Refuge.

TEXAS RECORD FRESHWATER FISH

	Lb.–oz.	Place	Year
Largemouth bass	13–8	Medina Lake	1943
Spotted bass	5–9	Lake o' the Pines	1966
Striped bass	27–5	Red River/Denison Dam	1974
White bass	5–4¼	Colorado River	1968
Northern pike	18–2	Greenbelt Lake	1975
Walleye	8–14	Lake Meredith	1972
Rainbow trout	4–12	Guadalupe River	1968
Chain pickerel	4–7	Caddo Lake	1976
White crappie	4–9	Navarro Mills Lake	1968
Channel catfish	36–8	Pedernales River	1965
Flathead catfish	67–0	Lake Tyler	1972
Freshwater drum	22–6	Eagle Mountain Lake	1974
Paddlefish	7–1	Pat Mayse Lake	1973
Bluegill	3–4	Form Pond	1966
Alligator gar	279–0	Rio Grande River	1951
Bowfin	17–3	Toledo Bend Reservoir	1972

TEXAS RECORD SALTWATER GAMEFISH

	Lb.–oz.	Place	Year
Amberjack	71–8	S. of Freeport	1974
Barracuda	45–0	SE of Freeport	1974
Bluefish	8–3	Buccaneer Rig	1975
Bonefish	2–9	Aransas Rock	1974
Bonito	27–0	Freeport	1969
Dolphin	57–0	Gulf of Mexico	1976
King mackerel	68–0	Port O'Connor	1971
Spanish mackerel	7–6	Port Aransas	1971
Blue marlin	547–0	Port Aransas	1963
White marlin	106–0	Port Aransas	1963
Pompano	6–1	Port Aransas	1970
African pompano	19–0	Port Aransas	1972
Sailfish	95–0	East Breaks	1972
Sawfish	736–0	Galveston	1939
Mako shark	325–0	Port Aransas	1973
Tiger shark	815–0	Galveston Jetties	1975
Snook	57–6	Padre Island	1937
Tarpan	210–0	South Padre Island	1973
Speckled trout	13–9	Laguna Madre	1975
Yellowfin tuna	155–8	Port O'Connor	1976
Wahoo	112–8	Port Aransas	1975

Hunting

Texas is thought by many to be the nation's number one deer state. Whitetails are found throughout the state, but are hunted most successfully in the hill country, where they are found in greater numbers than anywhere else in the United States. Mule deer and pronghorn

antelope are found in the rugged western portions of the state, along with javelina and wild boar. Game birds include huge numbers of ducks and geese, which winter in the state, as well as wild turkey, mourning and white-winged doves, pheasant, prairie chickens, chachalacas, sandhill cranes, and several types of quail. Unfortunately, most of the hunting lands in Texas are privately owned, requiring permission from the landowner before entering or hunting, or the payment of a "lease" or fee. Hunting arrangements can be made through *Guides, Outfitters & Resorts,* 3444 Northhaven Rd., Dallas 75229. An excellent source book containing hunting locations, types of big and small game, and hunting fees is *The Hunter's Guide to Texas* (Pembeaton Press), available by mail order for $3.95 (plus 40¢ postage and handling) from P.O. Box 12013, Austin 78711. Fishing and hunting seasons, size limits, bag and possession limits and special regulations are contained in the free publications *Texas Hunting Guide* and *Texas Fishing Guide,* available from the Texas Parks & Wildlife Dept., John H. Reagan Bldg., Austin 78701.

Guadalupe Mountains National Park

Once the home and hunting grounds of the Apache, this new park, established in 1972, preserves 77,518 acres of desert wilderness dominated by El Capitan, surrounded by deep canyons, towering cliffs, high parklike valleys, ghostly white salt flats, countless caverns, and spectacular mountain vistas in northwest Texas, just south of the New Mexico line. The mountain slopes are covered with Texas madrona, Douglas fir, limber pine, aspen, and ponderosa pine, and are inhabited by mule deer, elk, bobcats, coyote, and a few mountain lions. Access to the interior is limited to hiking and wilderness camping. Only experienced, well-equipped backpackers should enter the rugged backcountry. A small, primitive campground is at the Pinery, near Pine Springs on U.S. 62/180. For information, write: Superintendent, Guadalupe Mountains National Park, 3225 National Parks Hwy., Carlsbad, NM 88220.

Highways—Recreation & Scenic Routes

The free *Texas Official Highway Travel Map* is available from the State Dept. of Highways & Public Transportation, Travel & Information Division, P.O. Box 5064, Austin 78763. It shows all highways and roads, towns, lakes and rivers, and tourist bureaus. Detailed folders are available from the State Dept. of Highways & Public Transportation for the following vacation travel trails—great circle loops of from 500 to 700 miles along hard-surfaced byways off the beaten path of fast-moving freeways and Interstate routes: *Pecos Trail, Plains Trail, Mountain Trail, Lakes Trail, Independence Trail, Tropical Trail, Brazos Trail, Hill Country Trail, Forts Trail,* and the *Texas Forest Trail.* A detailed guide to the highways and byways, scenic and recreation attractions, and just about everything you need to know about travel in the Lonestar State, including weather information, is contained in the giant 205-page *Texas—A Land of Contrasts* travel guide, available free upon request from the Travel & Information Division (address above).

"Piney Woods" National Forests & Big Thicket Reserve

National forestlands in Texas include the Angelina, Davy Crockett, Sam Houston, and Sabine national forests, located in the "Piney Woods" region in eleven East Texas counties, with a combined total of 658,023 acres. The Angelina National Forest, the smallest, with 154,389 acres, is a great pine forest and game preserve bordered in part by the Angelina River, Shawnee Creek, and Ayish Bayou, all of which offer good float fishing. Camping facilities, boat-launching sites, and hiking trails are located at Boykin Springs, Letney, Townsend, Harvey, Caney Creek, Sandy Creek, and Bouton Lake recreation areas. Huge, 113,410-acre Sam Rayburn Lake, with a 560-mile shoreline, is the largest lake in the state, with vast areas of flooded timber providing prime trophy bass habitat. The Sabine National Forest lies adjacent to the Louisiana border, and covers 183,843 acres on the Toledo Bend Reservoir—one of the nation's finest trophy bass fisheries. Forest Service campgrounds along Toledo Bend include Indian Mounds, Willow Oak, Ragtown, and the Lakeview primitive camping area. The scenic Davy Crockett National Forest encompasses 161,556 acres in Houston and Trinity counties and contains the Neches Bluff, Ratcliff Lake, and Kickapoo recreation areas. Sam Houston National Forest encompasses 158,235 acres and contains a portion of the vast two-million-acre Big Thicket National Biological Reserve—a wild, jungle-like region of tangled, often impenetrable pine and hardwood forests, vines, shrubs, creepers, rare ferns (some over 6 feet tall), orchids, and remote ponds surrounded by wild flags, white and red lilies, and cattails.

The *National Forests in Texas Recreation Map,* available for 50¢ from the Forest Supervisor, Box 969, Lufkin 75401, shows all roads and trails, streams, lakes, campgrounds, ranger stations, trail shelters, boat ramps, and points of interest. These East Texas National Forests are reached via Interstate 90, 10, and 45; state highways 21, 7, 150, 87, 147, 13, and 94; and U.S. highways 96, 287, and 59. Accommodations, supplies, and services are available at Houston, Conroe, Lufkin, Center, Huntsville, and San Augustine. The forests are shown on the following U.S. Geological Survey 1:250,000-scale Overview Maps: Angelina N.F., Davy Crockett N.F., Sabine N.F., Palestine, Sam Houston N.F., Beaumont.

Texas Forest Trails

The pine forests of Texas are covered with a network of trails. They offer scenic beauty as well as glimpses of wildlife, forest plants and vegetation, wildflowers, and birds. Along the state's trails, you may discover a bird sanctuary or such small animals as raccoons, minks, squirrels, muskrats, foxes, and rabbits. Relics of Indian life and lore are present, as well as mute remains of pioneer history. There are several recreation areas, and good fishing in the lakes and streams. *Ride the Texas Forest Trail,* a list and description of Texas trails, is available free from the Texas Highway Dept., Austin 78701. It includes an overall map indicating highways, towns, and farms.

GREAT PLAINS STATES

Introduction

The Great Plains States cut a wide swath from Canada's Prairie Provinces south through the Dakotas, Nebraska, and Kansas, as well as the eastern regions of the Rocky Mountain States, to the High Plains, the Rio Grande, and the Mexican border. The foothills of the Rockies form the western limit of the plains; to the south of the Rockies, the rolling plains reach westward to the Pecos River Valley.

Several famous fishing, hunting, camping, and family vacation areas are set amid the grasslands and short grass steppes of these big, wide-open spaces. North Dakota, the Flickertail State, first explored by Pierre La Vérendrye, who in 1738 crossed the Assiniboine River in Canada to the Missouri River, searching for a "river to the west," contains the noted fish and big-game country of the Upper Missouri and its great impoundments—the Garrison and Oahe reservoirs, which provide some of the nation's finest fishing for big northern pike and walleye—and the scenic lakes and woodlands of the Turtle Mountain country in the northernmost reaches of the state.

South Dakota contains the remote trophy trout waters and rugged big-game ranges of the Black Hills National Forest and the Badlands, with their fantastic pinnacles of rainbow-hued sandstone in the westernmost portion of the state, extending to the Bear Lodge Mountains in Wyoming; the nationally famous great northern pike and walleye waters of the great lakes of the Missouri, Lake Kampeska, and the hauntingly named Enemy Swim Lake Country. The Sunshine State, explored by Lewis and Clark during their 1805 expedition up the Missouri, and the home of Sacagawea, Sitting Bull, and Crazy Horse, was the site of the great Dakota Gold Boom and the 1890 massacre of Indian families at Wounded Knee.

The Great Plains of Nebraska, which slope gently toward the Missouri River (the eastern boundary of the state), provide some of the nation's finest pheasant hunting and encompass the famous fishing and waterfowl hunting areas of the Sand Hills, the rugged Pine Ridge country, and the noted striped bass, walleye, and northern pike waters of McConaughy Reservoir. The broken tablelands in the westernmost portions of the Cornhusker State mark the eastern limit of the Rocky Mountain foothills. Kansas, known as the Sunflower State, with its rolling fields of wheat, provides excellent upland game-bird shooting, as well as fishing for smallmouth and largemouth bass, walleye, and northern pike in its numerous clearwater reservoirs.

Weather, Bugs & Beasts

Nearly everywhere in the Great Plains there is a lack of forest cover, because of an arid climate, extremes in temperature, and the high winds that blow across the land. During the summer the Plains States have long days of sunshine with hot winds; temperatures can rise above 100°. July mean temperatures in the north are around 70°, and above 80° in the southern regions. Rainfall ranges from about 20 inches a year in the eastern portions to 15 inches a year in the west, with higher rainfall along the extreme southern and eastern borders. Blizzards often sweep the plains during the bitter winters, with temperatures well below freezing.

The Great Plains are prime rattlesnake country. Avoid dark hollows, hidden ledges, woodpiles, rocky slopes—any likely place that might harbor a coiled, red-eyed rattler. Keep in mind that snakes do not always give a warning before striking. A snake-wise person traveling through this country will pack an Antivenin kit such as that produced by Wyeth Laboratories—a standard item at many pharmaceutical stores. Mosquitoes and horseflies are a nuisance in the wetland areas.

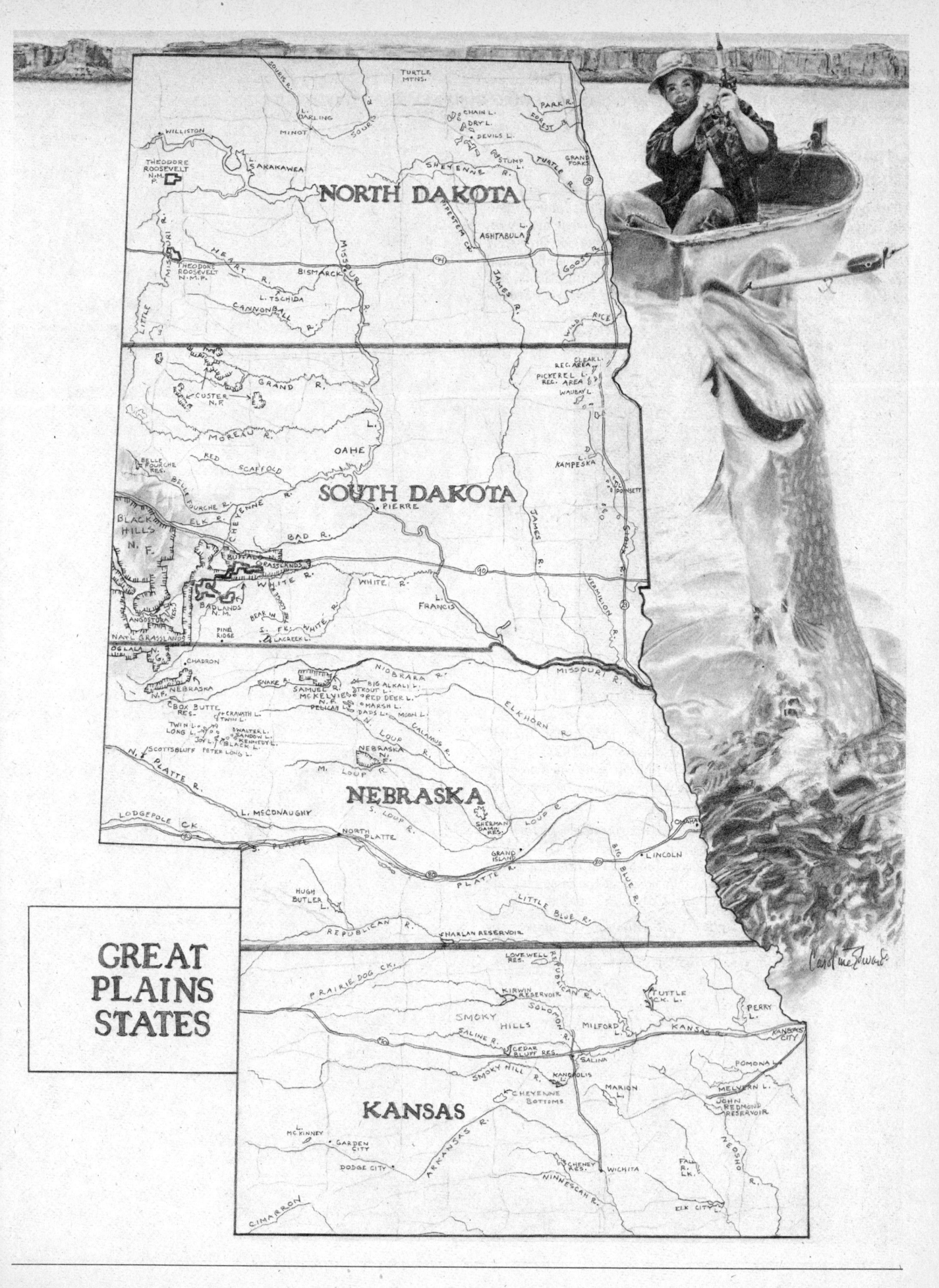

GREAT
PLAINS
STATES

Great Plains Maps & Charts—How to Order

All topographic maps listed in the Great Plains chapters (unless otherwise noted) are full-color U.S. Geological Survey overview maps with a scale of 1:250,000, or 1 inch to 4 miles ($2 each) or large-scale 7½-minute and 15-minute maps (both $1.25 each). These maps and free *Topographic Map Indexes* of North Dakota, South Dakota, Nebraska, and Kansas may be ordered (along with a free *Map Symbol*

Chart and *Topographic Maps* booklet) from: Distribution Branch, U.S. Geological Survey, Federal Center, Denver, CO 80225. Be sure to order your maps by individual names (indicate scale when ordering 1:250,000-scale maps); to expedite delivery, include extra money for first-class postage.

Large-size U.S. Geological Survey *State Topographic Maps* for each of the Great Plains States are published with a scale of 1:500,000, or 1 inch to 8 miles, and may be ordered for $2 each from the above address. Beautiful full-color shaded relief maps at the same scale are available for North Dakota and South Dakota ($2 apiece).

A useful 214-page handbook, *Be Expert with Map & Compass*, by Bjorn Kjellstrom, president and founder of Silva Compasses, may be obtained for $6.95 from Charles Scribner's Sons, Bookstore Dept., 597 5th Ave., New York, NY 10017.

Accommodations— Vacation Lodges & Resorts

For information on North Dakota's lodging facilities—hotels, motels, fishing and hunting lodges, or whatever you desire—contact the following agencies: Travel Director, Highway Dept., State Capitol Grounds, Bismarck 58505, phone (1–800) 472–2100 between 8:00 A.M. and 5:00 P.M., toll free, May through October 1; Lake Sakakawea Assn., Box 515, Riverdale 58565; Turtle Mountain Assn. (Peace Garden), O. A. Parks, Bottineau 58318: and local Chambers of Commerce.

Campgrounds & State Recreation Areas

A helpful source of information on campgrounds and recreation areas is the free 32-page booklet *Rough Rider Guide to North Dakota.* Charts are provided, listing campgrounds and state parks and showing exactly what facilities are available in each area. There is also information on trailer regulations and traveling with pets. The booklet can be obtained by writing: Game & Fish Dept., 2121 Lovett Ave., Bismarck 58505.

Another helpful publication is a free brochure available from the State Park Service, Fort Lincoln State Park, Rte. 2, Box 139, Mandan 58554, entitled *North Dakota State Parks.* It describes briefly each state park, giving the reader an idea of the type of country, and extent of facilities available. A chart of parks and their facilities is also provided; the brochure is attractively illustrated with full-color photographs.

Canoeing & Trophy Fishing Waters

North Dakota has several lakes and streams offering outstanding wild and scenic canoeing as well as excellent fishing for walleye and northern pike up to record weights. The state's major canoeing and fishing waters include the famous Devils Lake country, whose name is derived from the Sioux *Minewaukan,* "mystery" or "spirit water"; Lake Ashtabula country, which offers good fishing for walleye and big northerns up to 30 pounds; Arrowhead Lake country; the rugged Lake Sakakawea country; Garrison Dam, which impounds the legendary Missouri River and is known as the northern pike capital of the United States; the Little Missouri River, flowing through the rugged Badlands, named by the French fur traders who first traveled through the region; the Knife River, on whose banks Sacagawea lived with her French trapper husband when Lewis and Clark employed her for their epic journey to the Pacific in 1805; Goose River, first explored by the voyageurs who called it Rivière aux Outardes ("River of Geese") because of the great number of wild geese that nested along its banks; Lac aux Mortes country (French for "Lake of the Dead"), named by the French trappers who visited the area in the early 1860s during a severe Indian smallpox epidemic; the Park River, named for the Indian corrals or "parks" once used to corral and kill great herds of buffalo; Pembina and historic Red River of the north; Souris (French for "mouse"), named by the early explorers for the numerous field mice found along its lands; and Wild Rice River and Turtle Mountains Lake country—the latter, named by the Indians for its shape, includes Metigishe, Boundary, Upsilon, and Lords lakes.

The Wakopa Game Management Area in the beautiful Turtle Mountains of north central North Dakota is a top fishing and canoeing area. Its 5,178 acres consist mainly of tree-covered rolling hills with a heavy sprinkling of natural lakes and potholes. Aspen, birch, oak, and wild fruits are among the common trees and shrubs of the area. It is

currently being developed by the Game & Fish Department as a semiwilderness area. The natural habitat—woody hills, grassy meadows, lakes, and marshes—makes the area ideal for fishing and canoeing. Lake Upsilon is good for pike, and trout fishing is excellent in Gravel Lake. Rainbows up to 5½ pounds have been taken here. The WGMA has two marked canoe trails. You can put in along the highway into Laird Lake and follow the trail 1½ miles into Hooker Lake with a ¼-mile portage. Those desiring a longer trip can put in at the public boat ramp on Lake Upsilon and canoe through Upper Walker Lake and make a short portage into the channel leading to Laird Lake, then continue through Rames and Island lakes and a short portage into Hooker Lake. This trail is 4 miles long and is clearly marked with signs. A free informative brochure on the area can be obtained by writing: Game & Fish Dept., 2121 Lovett Ave., Bismarck 58505.

Custer National Forest & Theodore Roosevelt National Memorial Park

This million-acre reserve embraces the rugged hill country and Little Missouri grasslands of western North Dakota. The major features of this area include the Badlands of the Little Missouri, Knife, Heart, Green, Missouri, and Cannonball rivers, Garrison Reservoir, and Theodore Roosevelt National Memorial Park. The Badlands are a fantastic array of buttes and mesas in which layers of brick-red scoria and gray, blue, and yellow clays are exposed. Among them is 3,468-foot Black Butte, the state's highest point. The Garrison Reservoir

offers some of the state's finest fishing for giant walleye and northern pike. This is a top-ranking hunting region for whitetail deer, antelope, big whitetail jacks, snowshoe hare, upland game birds, wild turkey, and waterfowl. The area can be located on the following U.S. Geological Survey Maps: Dickinson, Watford City, Williston. Visitors to the area may obtain a *Custer National Forest Map* (50¢) as well as fishing, hunting, and camping information, by writing: Custer National Forest, Billings, MT 59102.

Theodore Roosevelt National Memorial Park honors the former president and his interest in national conservation of our natural resources. Its 70,436 acres take in the Badlands, which include the site of Roosevelt's Elkhorn Ranch in western North Dakota. Major features include petrified forests, deep canyons, rolling prairies, and the Little Missouri River. Wildlife includes bighorn sheep, bison, and antelope. The Badlands straddle the final 320 kilometers (200 miles) of the Little Missouri River and span its valley for 8 to 48 kilometers (5 to 30 miles). Moving waters carved out this valley, one of many that have cut into ancient preglacial plains. The park is open year round, but the best time to visit is from May through October (during the winter, portions of the park road may be closed because of snow). The park offers interpretive programs and an extensive system of backcountry trails for those who wish to leave their vehicles at one of the roadside pullouts to explore the Badlands on foot. The marking and mapping of trails in the north and south units is not completed; visitors are advised to obtain directions from a park ranger before setting out. The Caprock, Coulee, and Squaw Creek trails are open, marked, self-guiding trails. Hikers are not restricted to the existing trails and are invited to explore at their leisure. The weather here is prone to extremes: proper clothing, head protection against the sun, and good boots are essential.

Snowmobiling can be enjoyed during the winter months within the banks of the natural channel of the Little Missouri. A map of authorized trails and a set of regulations is available free from: Superintendent, Theodore Roosevelt NMP, Medora 58645.

Visitors should obtain the U.S. Geological Survey's *Theodore Roosevelt National Memorial Park Map*, North Unit and South Unit ($1.25 each). These topographic maps have a scale of 1:24,000 and show roads, trails, and other features including campgrounds, corrals, longhorn herds, ranger and information areas, and wildlife water areas. The park may be located on the following large-scale U.S. Geological Survey Maps: Fryburg NE, Fryburg NW, Gorham SW, Lone Butte, Long X Divide, Sperati Point, Tepee Butte.

Fishing & Hunting in North Dakota

The Sioux State offers some of the nation's top northern pike and walleye fishing waters, as well as hunting in season for deer, upland game birds, and rafts of waterfowl. North Dakota is a transitional state separating the Great Lakes country of Minnesota on the east from Montana's Upper Missouri River plains and towering Rocky Mountain high country on the west. Its flat to gently rolling prairie lands, characterized by sloughs and thousands of small ponds or potholes, which form one of the most important waterfowl areas in the United States, are joined on the north by Canada's Prairie Provinces—Manitoba and Saskatchewan—and on the south by South Dakota. Major hunting and fishing areas include the huge Oahe and Sakakawea Reservoirs on the Missouri River and the Badlands surrounding the Little Missouri in the western half of the state; the Central Lakes country; the scenic Turtle Mountains in the north; and the Red River of the North and Bois de Sioux rivers, which form the eastern boundary.

Great Northern Pike Country

The state's premier fishing is found along the vast 200-mile-long course of Lake Sakakawea (also known as Garrison Reservoir), with its numerous bays and coves. Lake Sakakawea offers some of the nation's top-ranked fishing for northern pike up to 30 pounds and over, as well as walleye, sauger, crappie, white bass, rainbow trout, coho salmon, goldeye, and channel catfish. Boat ramps, tackle, cabins, and campgrounds are available at most of the major fishing areas along the lake's twisting, snakelike shoreline, such as Whitetail, Bear Den, White

Earth, McKenzie, Charging Eagle, Nishu, and Little Missouri bays. The frigid tailrace waters below Garrison Dam yield large rainbow trout, sauger, walleye, pike, and channel cats. A few rainbows and browns are taken upstream from the mouth of the Yellowstone at the top of Lake Sakakawea just east of the Montana boundary. To the south lies the state's second great Missouri River impoundment, Lake Oahe, which straddles the boundary of the two Dakotas. The Oahe Reservoir is another top-ranked trophy northern pike and walleye fishery. The reservoir's major fishing areas are at the Oahe Game Management Area backwaters, Huffard-Fort Rice areas, and Badger, Cannonball, Porcupine, Battle, Beaver, Red Horse, and Cattail bays.

Other North Dakota walleye and northern pike waters include Lake Tschida, Long Lake National Wildlife Refuge, Lake Ashtabula—famed for its giant northern pike—Jim Lake, Spiritwood Lake, Arrowwood Lake National Wildlife Refuge, Sully's Hill National Game Preserve & Devils Lake Country, Lake Darling-Upper Souris National Wildlife Refuge, Buffalo Lodge Lake, J. Clark Salyer Refuge on the Souris River, the Turtle Mountain Indian Reservation lakes, the Red River, and the Sheyenne, Heart, Cedar, Cannonball, and James rivers. Spiritwood Lake is another top-ranked smallmouth bass and muskellunge fishery. Gravel Lake in the Wapoka Game Refuge area of the Turtle Mountains produced the state record 40-pound tiger muskellunge. The scenic lakes of the Turtle Mountains in the northern prairie region yield walleye, pike, smallmouth bass, and trout.

The fishing potential of North Dakota's lakes and streams is illustrated by a list of state record fish caught on rod and reel, compiled by the Game & Fish Department.

NORTH DAKOTA RECORD FISH

	Lb.–oz.	Place	Year
Northern pike	37–8	Sakakawea Reservoir	1968
Muskellunge	40	Gravel Lake	1975
Walleye	15–12	Wood Lake	1959
Sauger	8–12	Sakakawea Reservoir	1971
Rainbow trout	13.2	Garrison Tailrace	1977
Brown trout	14.2	Garrison Tailrace	1977
Lake trout	5	Garrison Tailrace	1978
Coho Salmon	6–12	Garrison Tailrace	1977
Largemouth bass	7–12	Welk Dam	1953
Smallmouth bass	4	Sakakawea Reservoir	1977
White bass	4–4	Sakakawea Reservoir	1969
Bluegill	2–12	Strawberry Lake	1963
Crappie	3	James River	1958
Yellow perch	2–4¾	Devils Lake	1978
Sturgeon	41	Missouri River	1975
Paddlefish	93	Missouri River	1977
Channel catfish	26–8	Sakakawea Reservoir	1968

A free complete *North Dakota Fishing Waters* guide may be obtained from: Game & Fish Dept., 2121 Lovett Ave. Bismarck 58505. The department also publishes a free *Game & Fish Management Areas* guide, *Game Management Area Maps, Fishing and Hunting Regulations,* and a *Map of North Dakota's Fishing Waters.*

Hunting

North Dakota offers sharptail grouse and duck hunting in the grasslands and pothole country. In addition, the state provides hunting for ringneck pheasant, Hungarian partridge, sage grouse in the extreme southwest, wild turkeys along the Upper Missouri River, whitetail deer, and mule deer in the Badlands of the southwest, as well as snowshoe hares, red fox, and bobcats. The state's major game lands include the Little Missouri National Grasslands, Custer National Forest, federal waterfowl production areas, and state-managed fish and game areas. (See "Lake Contour Fishing & Hunting Maps.")

Those interested in wildlife and game in North Dakota will want to subscribe to *North Dakota Outdoors,* a magazine published monthly by the Game & Fish Department. Subscription rates are $2 for one year, $5 for three years. Club rates of $1.50 are available to organizations ordering 25 or more subscriptions in a single year. Single-copy price is 25¢. Remittance should be made by check or money order (no stamps) payable to: Game & Fish Dept., 2121 Lovett Ave., Bismarck 58505. The magazine publishes interesting and informative articles on various aspects of game and wildlife management in the state, written by experts in the field and illustrated by photographs.

Highways—Recreation & Scenic Routes

To help you get where you are going the *North Dakota Official Highway Map* is an essential tool. You can get your copy free from: Highway Dept., State Capitol Grounds, Bismarck 58505. The map shows all roads and highways, boundaries, railroads, and route markers. It also shows the locations of national parks, state parks, rest areas, airports, the Lewis and Clark Trail, Explorers Highroads, game preserves, fish

hatcheries, ski areas, the Old West Trail, and other points of interest. There is a location index for the state's principal cities, towns, and villages as well as a chart for computing mileage distances between points shown on the map. A handy summary of traffic regulations and a list of radio stations are also provided.

Lake Contour Fishing & Hunting Maps

Individual county maps are available from: Highway Dept., Map Sales, Bismarck 58501, for 75¢ per section; most counties are divided into two sections, a few into three. Topographic maps for the counties of Benson, Richland, Barnes, Cass, Traill, Steele, Griggs, Foster, Eddy, Grand Forks, Walsh, Pierce, Rolette, Towner, Nelson, Ramsey, Ransom, Cavalier, Pembina, and most of McHenry and Sargent are available from: Water Commission, Bismarck 58501, for 75¢ per section. Each map covers a 7½-minute quadrangle. *Maps of North Dakota Fishing Waters* are available at no cost from: Game & Fish Dept., 2121 Lovett Ave., Bismarck 58501. Check with the department to ascertain whether the map you are seeking is currently available; however, there are maps currently available for most of the major fishing waters. *Maps of Waterfowl Production Areas* are available free from: U.S. Bureau of Sport, Fisheries, & Wildlife, Bismarck 58501. The *Oahe Boating & Recreation Map* can be obtained by writing: U.S. Corps of Engineers, Omaha, NE. Cost is 65¢. A *Lake Sakakawea Sportsman's Map* is available for $2.50 from: Northwest Mapping Co., Box 1234, Bismarck 58501. The same company will provide a *Lake Oahe Sportsman's Map* ($2.65), a *Badlands Sportsman's Map* ($3), and *Sportsman's County Hunting Maps* ($3 each) available for the following counties: Benson, Bowman, Burleigh, Dickey, Emmons, Kidder, La Moure, Logan, Mercer, McIntosh, Morton, Nelson, Ramsey, Ransom, Richland, Sargent, Stutsman.

Packhorse Outfitters

Several packhorse outfitters provide guided trail rides through the Badlands and Turtle Mountain country. *Little Missouri Trail Rides*, Rhame, offers 2-4-day summer trail rides in the scenic western North Dakota Badlands. Guides, meals, and sleeping facilities are provided. *Medora Trail Rides*, Medora, offers guided rides through the Badlands from June through August. *Tescher Trail Rides*, Theodore Roosevelt National Memorial Park, offers guided summer trail rides through the park portion of the Badlands. *Roy Bird Ranch*, New Town, has guided trail rides through the scenic Fort Berthold Indian Reservation part of the Badlands.

Upper Missouri Outfit & Fort Union Trading Post

On their epic 1805 journey to the Pacific, the Lewis and Clark expedition spent the winter at the small Mandan Indian village of cottonwood log huts known as Fort Mandan at the mouth of the Knife River on the Upper Missouri River. It was during this fierce North Dakota winter, with its mixture of arctic gales and long windless cold spells that produce sun dogs (the "false suns"—haloes around the moon), that Lewis and Clark hired Sacagawea of the Snake Nation, their famous squaw guide known to the Indians as "Boat Pusher," and learned of the Great Falls of the Missouri and the Rocky Mountain headwaters beyond. With the arrival of spring, the expedition traveled up the Missouri in wooden keelboats on their historic journey west that was to open the Rocky Mountain fur country and the lands beyond to the traders of John Jacob Astor's American Fur Company.

In the summer of 1828 Kenneth McKenzie—head of the American Fur Company's Upper Missouri Outfit, known as the "King of the Missouri"—dispatched the keelboat *Otter* from the Mandans to the mouth of the Yellowstone to establish Fort Union for the Assiniboine fur trade. Soon a string of trading posts along the Upper Missouri, served by the steamboats of the American Fur Company—such as the *Yellowstone*, known to the Indians as "the big medicine canoe with eyes"—brought immense wealth to the New York financiers and helped secure the westward course of the American empire. In 1865, with the decline of the American buffalo robe market, Fort Union was sold to the Northwestern Fur Company and in a few years was abandoned and dismantled by the army.

Today Fort Union is being reconstructed as a national historic site. Travelers can reach the site via U.S. 2 and County Road 4 from Williston, which is 25 miles to the southwest. A free *Fort Union Trading Post* map-guide, which contains a complete history of the post and a *Map of Upper Missouri Area Fur Trading Posts & Prominent Indian Tribes*, may be obtained by writing: Superintendent, Theodore Roosevelt NMP, Medora 58645.

Accommodations— Vacation Lodges & Resorts

For detailed information on fishing, hunting, vacation lodges, hotels, motels, or whatever type of accommodations you are seeking, write to: Dept. of Economics & Tourism Development, Pierre 57501, or to the local Chamber of Commerce of the area you plan to visit. For additional lodging and travel information, write: Northeast Lakes Assn., Watertown 57201; for central South Dakota, write: Great Lakes Assn., Pierre 57501; for western South Dakota, write: Black Hills Badlands & Lakes Assn., Sturgis 57785.

Badlands

South Dakota's haunting Badlands—known to the Indians as *Mako Sica* and to the early French explorers as *Mauvaises Terres*, both meaning literally, "Bad Land"—were described by General George A. Custer as "a part of hell with the fire burned out." The Badlands lie just east and north of the Black Hills, dominated by the Badlands Wall: a range of grassless, eroded multicolored peaks of gray, tan, buff, olive, deep rose, and cream. It is a barren country of ghostly peaks, lofty pinnacles, terraces, and cathedrallike spires which rise above eroded, rounded domes, with washed-out gaps forming natural windows. The Fossil Trail winds through an ancient region once roamed by giant saber-toothed tigers, dog-sized camels, titanotheres, and hyracodons.

Historic Big Foot Pass lies in the heart of the Badlands. It was through this opening that Indian Chief Big Foot, with his band of 400 warriors, eluded the U.S. Cavalry. After his escape from the Badlands, Big Foot and his braves met their gruesome fate at the Battle of Wounded Knee—the last conflict between the whites and the Indians and the culmination of the Messiah War.

Visitors to this area should obtain a copy of the U.S. Geological Survey *Map of Badlands National Monument and Vicinity* ($2), showing the Badlands National Monument and adjacent areas in Pennington, Jackson, Shannon, and Washabaugh counties and contours, roads, cities, towns, borders, campgrounds, streams, lakes, and ponds. The size is 48 × 24 inches, scale, 1:62,500. For information, write: Badlands National Monument, Interior 57750.

Black Hills National Forest

This 1,223,000-acre preserve, whose name is a direct translation of the Sioux term *Paha Sapa*, is in the wildlands of western South Dakota and extends into the Bear Lodge Mountains region of Wyoming. This jumbled region of ponderosa pine forests, rushing streams, deep canyons, and cascades is a top-ranking deer and elk hunting area. Fly fishing is good for brook, brown, and rainbow trout up to 4 and 5 pounds in Spring, Spearfish, Beaver, Elk, Redwater, and Box Elder creeks, and in Cox's Creek and Mirror lakes. Forest roads provide access to the Taylor Divide, Belle Fourche River and National Wildlife Refuge, Elk Mountains, Mount Rushmore, Pactola Lake, Cheyenne River, and the Angostura Reservoir—one of the state's finest lakes for walleye, northern pike, and black bass to 6 pounds.

When white men first discovered gold in the hills, they proceeded to invade this sacred land of the Sioux, first by force, then by treaty. Remains of old mining towns can still be seen.

Anyone planning a trip to the Black Hills area should send for the *Black Hills National Forest Map* (50¢) from: Forest Supervisor, P.O. Box 792, Custer 57730. This full-color map shows all roads, trails,

SOUTH DAKOTA ENCYCLOPEDIA

railroads, forest supervisors' quarters, ranger and forest service stations, recreation areas, lodging sites, and other points of interest. There is also a directory of recreation sites showing elevation and facilities available in each area.

The Black Hills National Forest is shown on the following U.S. Geological Survey 1:250,000-scale Maps: Hot Springs, Gillette, Newcastle, Rapid City.

Campgrounds & State Recreation Areas

Anyone planning to camp in South Dakota should send for an informative *Directory of Campgrounds in South Dakota,* available free from: South Dakota Campground Owners Assn., 1035 Lawrence St., Belle Fourche 57717. The brochure contains descriptions of the association's member campgrounds, listing facilities and phone numbers, and including a map so that you can see where each campground is. It is best to check with the campground in question before setting out, to determine what the current rates are and to get information on rules and regulations.

Canoeing & Trophy Fishing Waters

South Dakota's major canoe routes and fishing waters are shown on the following large-scale U.S. Geological Survey Maps. *Beaver Creek:* Boland Ridge, Buffalo Gap, Wind Cave; *Belle Fourche River* (once a crossing for prospectors in search of gold in the Black Hills): Belle Fourche, Dalzell NE, Dalzell NW, Elm Springs, Elm Springs SW, Fruitdale, Hereford, Hereford SW, Newell, Nisland, Rapid City NE, The Forks, Vale NE, Vale SE, Volunteer; *Big Sioux River* (including Pelican, Poinsett, Clear, and Oakwood lakes): Brookings, Bruce, Castlewood, Dempster, Estelline, Flandreau NW, Lake Poinsett, Midway, Pelican Lake, Volga, Watertown E, Watertown W, Watertown SE; *Bois de Sioux River* (including Big Stone, Traverse, and Bleska lakes): Beardsley, Big Stone Lake, Ortonville, Peever, White Rock; *Elk Creek* (named for the large number of elk that once inhabited the area): Dalzell NE, Dalzell NW, Elm Springs, Elm Springs SW, New Underwood, Quanka NW, Viewfield; *Enemy Swim Lake Country* (perhaps the state's best area for lunker walleye and northern pike): Milbank; *Fort Randall Reservoir* (including Lewis and Clark Lake): Mitchell, O'Neill; *Deerfield Lake:* Deerfield; *Pactola Reservoir:* Silver City, Pactola Dam; *Sheridan Lake:* Mount Rushmore; *Spring Creek:* Caputa SW, Creston, Folson, Hermosa NE, Hermosa SW,

Hermosa SE, Hill City, Mount Rushmore, Rockerville, Scenic SW; *Lake Preston:* Erwin, Lake Preston, Lake Preston NE, Lake Preston W; *Oahe Reservoir Country* (including Long, Tschida, Stony, and Rice lakes): Bismarck (ND), McIntosh, Pierre (1:250,000 scale).

Fishing & Hunting in South Dakota

Few people are aware that South Dakota's great lakes and the wide-open spaces of its vast rolling grasslands and rugged hill country offer some of the finest fishing and hunting in the United States. The Sunshine State, also long known as the pheasant capital of the world, is divided into two parts by the Missouri River, which flows through the middle of the state from north to south. The eastern half of the state holds rich glacial farmlands and, in the northeast, hundreds of natural blue lakes carved out by the receding glacial ice cap. Rising from the great plains to the west of the Missouri are the rugged Badlands and Black Hills, crowned by 7,242-foot Harney Peak, the highest point in the state and the highest point in the nation east of the Rocky Mountains.

Great Lakes of the Missouri

When Lewis and Clark traveled up the Missouri in the early 19th century it was a wild river, a challenge to conquer. Today it has been tamed by four large dams—Oahe, Big Bend, Fort Randall, and Gavins Point—built by the U.S. Army Corps of Engineers, creating deep blue-water lakes. There is a 2,300-mile shoreline extending along the prairie grassland in the shadow of rising bluffs.

Anglers can find isolation and year-round trophy fishing in this wilderness paradise. The Missouri River and its great lakes claim 20 South Dakota fishing records, including a 35-pound 8-ounce northern pike, a 113-pound paddlefish, and a 7-pound 7-ounce sauger. There are outstanding facilities for boating, hunting, camping, exploring, and hiking.

Lake Oahe, impounded by the Oahe Dam above Pierre, is one of the nation's top-ranked northern pike and walleye fisheries. The reservoir impounds 370,000 surface acres and winds for 230 miles from Pierre to Bismarck, North Dakota. Lake Sharpe to the south is impounded by Big Bend Dam at Fort Thompson. The lake stretches for 80 miles along prairie bluffs and grassy lowlands. Further south lie Fort Randall Dam, which impounds Lake Francis Case, and Lewis and Clark Lake. All of the great lakes hold trophy-sized walleye, northern pike, white bass, channel catfish, and white and black crappie. The cold, tailrace waters below the dams offer outstanding fishing for sauger (known locally as "sandpike"), walleye, catfish, paddlefish, and sturgeon. There are boat-launching sites at major fishing access areas along the great lakes. Fishing supplies, equipment, and boat rentals are available at the major outfitting centers located along the lakes.

A useful full-color *Map of the Great Lakes of South Dakota* contains a Lake Oahe Area Map and Lake Sharpe Area Map, a facilities chart, and shows all principal highways, secondary roads, elevations, boat ramps, parks and recreation area campgrounds, historical sites, airports, Indian Reservation lands, and rangelands. It describes historical sites and points of interest, including the ancient Arikara Indian fortress and village predating Columbus; Fort George, established as a trading post of the Missouri Fur Company in 1819; Little Eagle, where Sitting Bull was killed at his cabin on Grand River in 1890; and Fort Manuel, established as a trading post in 1812 by Manuel Lisa and the purported gravesite of Sacagawea. (More than 80 historic sites lie beneath the waters of Lake Oahe, including Lewis and Clark campsites, Indian missions, trading posts, and Indian villages. For information, write: South Dakota Historical Society, Pierre 57501.) The map of the great lakes may be obtained free by writing: Information & Education Branch, Dept. of Game, Fish, & Parks, State Office Bldg. 1, Pierre 57501. This department also publishes a free pamphlet on the *Missouri River Waterfowl Refuges,* renowned for their mallard and Canada geese hunting. The finger-like draws along the lakes harbor grouse, Hungarian partridge, pheasant, deer, and antelope.

Northeastern Lake Region

The beautiful gravel-bottomed, forest-fringed lakes of the northeast lake region provide some of the state's finest fishing for walleye and trophy northern pike. Here, amid the state's greatest concentration of natural lakes, are the legendary waters of Enemy Swim, Blue Dog, Kampeska, and Buffalo lakes. The region's major lakes include 4,820-acre Lake Kampeska; 2,800-acre Lake Pelican; 513-acre Punished Woman Lake; 320-acre Willow Lake; 1,502-acre Blue Dog Lake; 2,150-acre Enemy Swim Lake; the famed 5,000 acres of North and South Waubay lakes; 2,300-acre Rush Lake; 1,161-acre Round Lake; 1,146-acre Lake Alice; 365-acre Lake Cochrane; 7,866-acre Lake Poinsett, the state's largest natural lake; the 2,200 acres of North and

South Buffalo lakes; 1,700-acre Roy Lake; 21,280-acre Big Stone Lake, straddling the South Dakota-Minnesota boundary; and the 2,480 acres of North and South Drywood lakes. Rainbow trout are caught in the Kampeska Trout Ponds and Amsden Lake. The scenic mixed hardwood and evergreen forests of the northeast lake country are slashed by several swift-flowing streams and rivers: the Big Sioux River holds northern pike, walleye, and panfish; Gary Creek yields brook trout; the South Fork of the Yellowbank River holds brook trout; and Sieche Hollow holds some big brown and rainbow trout. A free *Map of the Northeastern Lake Region* may be obtained by writing: Northeastern Lake Region, P.O. Box 783, Watertown 57201.

The wide-open spaces of the north-central region are dotted with natural and artificial lakes which yield walleye, crappie, largemouth bass, northern pike, yellow perch, and panfish. Major lakes include Byron, Elm, Richmond, Pocasse, South Scatterwood, Twin, and Cottonwood. The James and Elm rivers yield channel catfish, walleye, northern pike, and panfish. The hundreds of lakes, streams, and ponds in the southeastern region offer record-sized walleyes, northern pike, and largemouth bass. The region's major lakes include Campbell, Hendricks, Oakwood, Andes, Mitchell, Brant, Herman, Madison, and McCook. The major rivers—Big Sioux, Vermilion, James, and Missouri—yield walleye, pike, sauger, channel catfish, and panfish.

Black Hills Country

The state's premier trout waters are set amid the rugged elk country of the Black Hills in far western South Dakota. Here are the nationally

renowned trophy brown and rainbow trout waters of Pactola Reservoir —home of the state record 22-pound 8-ounce brown trout—and Canyon, Sheridan, Horsethief, Deerfield, and Canyon lakes, surrounded by the Black Hills National Forest. Angostura Reservoir to the south yields walleye and largemouth bass; Belle Fourche Reservoir to the north yields walleye and white bass. Top rainbow trout streams of the Black Hills include Englewood, Kirk, Redwater, Spearfish, Hanna, Crow, Sand, Cold Spring, Bear Butte, Elk, Boxelder, Rapid, Castle, Spring, Battle, French, Beaver, Fall, Cascade, and Blockade Beaver creeks.

The fishing potential and diversity of the Sunshine State's lakes and streams is highlighted by the record South Dakota fish caught on rod and reel, as compiled by the Department of Game, Fish, & Parks.

SOUTH DAKOTA RECORD FISH

	Lb.–oz.	Place	Year
Northern pike	35–8	Lake Sharpe	1972
Walleye	15	Lake Kampeska	1960
Smallmouth bass	3–7	Fort Randall Tailwaters	1977
Largemouth bass	8–12	Fraiser Lake	1974
Brown trout	22–8	Pactola Reservoir	1973
Brook trout	5–6	Deerfield Reservoir	1966
Rainbow trout	12–8	Oahe Dam Tailwaters	1974
Kokanee salmon	2–11	Pactola Reservoir	1974
Coho salmon	3–5	Oahe Dam Tailwaters	1974
Sauger	7–7	Oahe Dam Tailwaters	1960
Black crappie	3–2	Fort Randall Reservoir	1964
White crappie	3–9	Hughes Co. Pond	1974
Paddlefish	113	Big Bend Dam	1974
Flathead catfish	49–6	Fort Randall Reservoir	1964
Channel catfish	55	James River	1949
Blue catfish	97	Missouri River	1959
Lake sturgeon	25	Missouri River	1968
Buffalo	38	Lake Mitchell	1977
Bluegill	2–4½	Leola Lake	1971
Yellow perch	2.5½	Haakon County	1977
White bass	4–2	Enemy Swim Lake	1972
Bullhead	3–5	Waubay Lake	1972
Rock bass	1–8	Enemy Swim Lake	1974
Burbot	12–3	Lake Sharpe	1974

*World's record.

Several publications of use to South Dakota-bound anglers and hunters may be obtained free from: Information & Education Branch, Dept. of Game, Fish, & Parks, State Office Bldg. 1, Pierre 57501, including the 35-page *South Dakota Anglers Almanac*, a guide to the state's public fishing waters; *South Dakota Fishing Guide*, which contains regulations, seasons, and limits; *South Dakota Guide to State Public Shooting Areas & Federal Waterfowl Production Areas; Know Your South Dakota Fishes; Nonresident Fall Hunting;* and the *South Dakota Hunting Guide*, which includes regulations, seasons, and special permit information.

Hunting

South Dakota offers excellent and varied hunting for pheasant, sharptail grouse, prairie chicken, and bobwhite quail in the southeast, Hun-

garian partridge and ruffed grouse in the Black Hills, mourning doves and wild turkey in the Black Hills and West River plains, whitetail deer and mule deer in the West River and Black Hills country, and antelope, a few Rocky Mountain elk, protected mountain goat and bighorn sheep in the Black Hills. South Dakota offers some of the nation's top hunting for Canadian geese, snows and blues, and mallards in the wetlands and sloughs of the northeast lake region and along the great lakes of the Missouri. Other top-ranked waterfowl hunting areas include the game lands surrounding the Lake Andes, Sand Lake, Waubay, Madison, and La Creek national wildlife refuges. The Sand Lake refuge in Brown County shelters a flock of giant Canada geese, once believed to be extinct.

Highways—Recreation & Scenic Routes

In order to be sure of taking the most direct highway route to your destination in South Dakota, write for the free *South Dakota Official Highway Map* to: Dept. of Economics & Tourism Development, Pierre 57501. The map shows all roads and highways, national forests, parks and monuments, Indian reservations, national grasslands areas, roadside rest areas, airports, railroads, and other points of interest. A location index of cities and towns is provided. The reverse side of the map indicates a number of scenic and recreational attractions that would make enjoyable family excursions. Inserts detail Rapid City, Sioux Falls, and Aberdeen.

Along the highways of South Dakota there are various Tipi Rest Areas. These areas, characterized by a distinctive, 56-foot-high steel and concrete tipi framework, provide rest rooms and tourist information centers. The buildings themselves are fashioned after the sod houses and dugouts that dotted the prairies during pioneering days.

Lake Contour Fishing Maps

These useful maps, which show water depth, bottom composition, dams, and contours, are available free upon request for most major South Dakota lakes including famous Enemy Swim, Punished Woman, Pelican, Poinsett, Kampeska, Kampeska Gravel Pits, Waubay, Nine Mile, Bear Butte, East Vermilion, Blue Dog, Red Iron, and Cottonwood, to name a few. Write to: Information & Education Branch, Dept. of Game, Fish, & Parks, State Office Bldg. 1, Pierre 57501, for a free map listing.

Accommodations— Vacation Lodges & Resorts

A complete guide to lodges, resorts, and motels in the Cornhusker State is contained in the free booklet *Nebraska Lodging*, available from: Tourist Information Branch, Dept. of Economic Development, State Capitol, Box 94666, Lincoln 65809, phone (402) 471–3111, which will also provide a free Nebraska Travel Pack and specific information about the area you plan to visit.

Camping & State Recreation Areas

Nebraska's major state recreation and camping areas—including the 3,000 acres of wooded bluff lands of Indian Cove, Ponca and Niobrara state parks, and the Wildcat Hills Recreation Area with its herds of buffalo and elk—are described in the useful booklet *Nebraska Parklands*, available free from: Game & Parks Commission, P.O. Box 30370, Lincoln 68503. It describes and lists, in chart form, all the recreational facilities run by the commission, showing exactly what facilities are available in each area. It is lavishly illustrated with color photographs. Anyone planning on camping in Nebraska should send for the free brochure *Nebraska Camping Guide*, available free from the commission. This handy publication contains a chart listing all the state recreation areas, state parks, state wayside areas, state special use areas, and federal areas, showing facilities available in each area. Rules and regulations governing the use of these areas are also noted in capsule form (area regulations; camping; fires, smoking; pets; fishing, hunting, and trapping; etc.).

Canoe Routes & Fishing Waters

Nebraska's major canoe routes are described in the informative booklet *Canoeing in Nebraska*, available free from: Game & Parks Commission, P.O. Box 30370, Lincoln 68503. The canoe routes described include the winding Niobrara River, with its panoramic scenery and spring-fed tributaries, which hold rainbow and brown trout; the small (80-mile-long) Dismal River, which flows through the Sand Hills; Elkhorn River, one of the most overlooked canoe routes in the state; serene Calamus River in the Sand Hills country; the historic North Platte River, with its island-dotted channels; the Republican River and the 60-mile stretch of the great Missouri between Gavins Point Dam and Ponca; the Big Blue River, with its frequent logjams and thick vegetation; and the historic Platte River, known to the early pioneers as "too wet to plow, and too thick to drink."

The booklet also has some tips on how to make your trip safer and more enjoyable; it contains a brief section on Nebraska lakes, pointing out that although lake travel can be less demanding than river travel and access is usually easier, lakes can be rough during high winds, so they should be approached with caution.

Fishing & Hunting in Nebraska

The Cornhusker State's big open spaces, forests, and rugged hill country, dotted by more than 3,300 lakes and slashed by 11,000 miles of streams, offer some surprisingly excellent fishing and hunting opportunities. Nebraska's Panhandle, the northwest corner of the state, offers fly fishing and spin casting for rainbow and brown trout and trolling for walleyes and rainbows in the reservoirs, and is top-ranked for mule deer, antelope, wild turkey, and upland game birds in the Pine Ridge division of the Nebraska National Forest, Oglala National Grasslands, Crescent Lake National Wildlife Refuge, and state game lands and recreation areas. The shallow, natural lakes of the famous

NEBRASKA ENCYCLOPEDIA

Sand Hills region hold some big northern pike, largemouth bass, and panfish. Fine hunting in the Sand Hills country for deer, antelope, grouse, pheasant, quail, dove, and waterfowl is found in the Valentine National Wildlife Refuge, Samuel R. McKelvie National Forest, Bessey division of the Nebraska National Forest, and state-managed game lands and recreation areas. The lakes and streams of the northeast, southwest, and southeast regions offer fishing for walleye, northern pike, bass, catfish, and panfish; their forests, grasslands, and wetlands provide excellent hunting for deer, upland game birds, waterfowl, and small game on state recreation areas such as the Dead Timber, Lewis and Clark Lake, and Branched Oak Lake recreation areas; state special use areas such as the Limestone Bluffs, Medicine Creek, Red Willow Reservoir, Cornhusker, and Iron Horse Trail areas; and on federal reservoir waterfowl areas such as Harvard Marsh, Macon Lakes, Killdeer Basin, Harlan County Reservoir, Clark Lagoon, and Atlanta Marsh.

The fishing potential of Nebraska's lakes and streams is mirrored in the listing of state record fish caught on rod and reel, as compiled by the Game & Parks Commission.

NEBRASKA RECORD FISH

	Lb.–oz.	Place	Year
Northern pike	27–8	Lake McConaughy	1962
Muskellunge	18–4	Merritt Reservoir	1969
Smallmouth bass	5–14	Red Willow Reservoir	1974
Largemouth bass	10–11	Columbus Sandpit	1965
Striped bass	26.5	Lake McConaughy	1977
Coho salmon	5–12	Lake McConaughy	1971
Kokanee salmon	4–2	Lake McConaughy	1971
Brown trout	20–1	Snake River	1973
Rainbow trout	14–2	Keith Co. Canal	1975
Brook trout	5–1	Pawnee Springs	1965
Walleye	16–2	Lake McConaughy	1971
Sturgeon	45–4	Niobrara River	1973
Yellow perch	2–3	Merritt Reservoir	1978
Bluegill	2–13	Grove Lake	1977
White bass	4–15	Grand Island Sandpit	1962
Blue catfish	100–8	Missouri River	1970
Channel catfish	37	Fremont Recreation Area	1972
Flathead catfish	76	Missouri River	1971
Black crappie	3–15	Lake McConaughy	1962
Sauger	8–5	Missouri River	1961
Paddlefish	91	Gavins Point Dam	1975
Freshwater drum	28–4	Gavins Point Dam	1971

The Panhandle

The streams of the Panhandle offer some of the state's top trout fishing. Brown and rainbow trout up to 5 pounds are taken from the North Platte during their early spring and late fall migrations up from Lake McConaughy. Some excellent backcountry fly fishing is found along tributaries of the North Platte such as Dry Sheep, Sheep, Spotted Tail, Pumpkin, Lodgepole, Wildhorse, Nine Mile, and Lawrence Fork creeks. Lake Minatare, northeast of Scottsbluff, holds walleye, largemouth and smallmouth bass, rainbow trout, and channel catfish. The remote streams of the Pine Ridge and Niobrara valleys hold browns and rainbows. Most of the streams, including Monroe, Sow-

belly, Hat, Soldier, Larabie, Chadron, Bordeaux, Beaver, and Pine creeks and the White and Niobrara rivers, flow through private ranchlands, and permission of the landowner is required. The major impoundments of the Panhandle—Whitney, Kimball, and Box Butte—hold northern pike, walleye, largemouth and smallmouth bass, white bass, and channel catfish. Island and Crane lakes in the Crescent Lake National Wildlife Refuge hold northern pike and largemouth bass.

Sand Hills Country

The feed-rich, shallow, weed-filled lakes of the famous Sand Hills region provide excellent fishing for big northern pike and largemouth bass, plus yellow perch, crappie, and bluegills. The renowned lake-dotted 71,516-acre Valentine National Wildlife Refuge offers fishing for the major species in Watts, Dewey, Ballards Marsh, Duck, Rice, Clear, Pelican, and West Long lakes. Each year thousands upon thousands of mallards, pintails, redheads, and teals nest in the refuge. The major Sand Hills lakes surrounding the refuge include Shell, Cottonwood, Round, Big Alkali, Long, Fish, Atkinson, Overton, Victoria Springs, Arnold, and Frye. The Merritt Reservoir on the Snake River offers excellent fishing for big rainbow trout, walleye, largemouth and smallmouth bass, crappie, bluegill, yellow perch, and white bass. Merritt produced the state record 18-pound 4-ounce muskellunge. The Snake River produced the state record 20-pound 1-ounce brown trout. The major Sand Hills brown trout tributaries of the Niobrara include Fairfield, Coon, Long Pine, Plum, and Schlagee creeks. The Dismal River west of Dunning also holds some big browns. The deep-flowing pools and sloughs of the Calamus River hold northern pike and channel catfish.

Southwest

To the south are the trophy fishing waters of 35,000-acre Lake McConaughy—the state's largest body of water and top "big fish" lake. The bays, coves, and shoals along the 105-mile shoreline of "Big Mac," as the lake is known locally, yield northern pike to 25 pounds, walleye to 16 pounds, and hordes of white bass, rainbow trout, crappie, yellow perch, and striped bass, which grow to record weights on the large schools of threadfin shad. During May and August large schools of white bass drive the shad to the surface during feeding sprees, where they attract noisy flocks of diving, swooping gulls. Lake McConaughy has been stocked periodically with kokanee and coho salmon. Other major lakes of southwestern Nebraska, which hold big northerns, walleye, largemouth bass, channel catfish, and panfish, include Harlan County and Harry D. Strunk reservoirs, Hugh Butter Lake, Red Willow Reservoir, Lake Ogallala, Medicine Creek Reservoir, Gallagher Canyon Reservoir, Midway Canyon and Jeffery Canyon reservoirs, Maloney Reservoir, Platte Valley Canal, Sutherland Reservoir, Wellfleet Lake, and the Sandy Channel Wildlife Area. Otter Creek, a feeder stream of Lake McConaughy, yields some big browns and lake-run rainbows. The North Platte River offers excellent fishing above Lake McConaughy for northern pike and channel catfish in spring and early summer. Red Willow Creek holds northern pike, largemouth and smallmouth bass, channel cats, crappie, and bluegill.

The northeast region of the state is dominated by the Missouri River and its Lewis and Clark Lake impoundment, which yields big walleye, sauger, channel catfish, crappie, white bass, and freshwater drum. The free-flowing, unchannelized stretch of the Missouri is the last of the "Big Muddy" that resembles its condition when traveled by Lewis and Clark in 1805. Here its shallow bars, undercut banks, and meandering channels yield walleye, catfish, sauger, white bass, and primitive paddlefish. The hundreds of farm ponds and sandpits scattered throughout the region hold largemouth bass, bluegill, and crappie. Major rivers include the Cedar, Elkhorn, and North Loup. Brown trout are found in the North, Middle, and East branches of Verdigre Creek, and Steel Creek. In the southeast are the long-famous channel, flathead, and blue catfish waters of the Missouri, Platte, Blue, Nemaha, and Republican rivers. The region's hundreds of farm ponds, sandpits, and lakes, and the flood control reservoirs of the Salt Valley near Lincoln, yield some big largemouth bass, walleye, catfish, crappie, northern pike, and bluegill.

A number of free information publications of interest to Nebraska-bound anglers and hunters are available from: Game & Parks Commission, P.O. Box 30370, Lincoln 68503, including the 24-page *Boating Guide;* the 16-page booklet *Safe Boating;* the 16-page *Fishing Guide,* which contains fishing regulations; a full-color, 16-page *Fishing Nebraska Guide* to public fishing areas and species available; *Ice Fishing Guide, the Fishes of Nebraska* (98 pages, 50¢), which contains full-color plates, species information, and range maps; *Billfold Cards of Nebraska Hunting Seasons; Field Care of Big Game;* the 16-page *Hunting Guide; Where to Hunt in Nebraska,* a list of state and federal public hunting areas; the full-color, 16-page booklet *Crane River,* story of sandhill cranes and their annual spring sojourn on the Platte River; *Fremont Lakes Map-Guide;* the 16-page, full-color booklet *Outdoor Recreation in Nebraska;* Two Rivers Recreation Area Map-Guide; wildlife publications including *The Bobwhite Quail, Duck Identification Guide for Hunters, Facts About the Pheasant, Deer of Nebraska* (32 pages, full color), *Mourning Dove, The Ring-Necked Pheasant in Nebraska* (32 pages, full color); and the "Your Wildlife Lands" series —*The Panhandle, The Platte Valley,* and *The Sand Hills.* A valuable pocket-size guide, *Waterfowl Identification in the Central Flyway* (52 pages, 35¢), contains beautiful full-color plates of waterfowl species, showing winter and fall plumage, with brief descriptions.

Grande Domaine U.S. and Canadian Fishing & Hunting Lodges

The famous Grande Domaine Retreats—founded by Nebraska's Jack Cole—offers some of North America's finest fishing, hunting, and family vacations at their network of United States and Canadian fishing and hunting lodges. Packaged vacations include Canadian fly-in fishing, big-game hunting, Atlantic salmon fishing, pack trips by horseback, float trips, father-and-son fishing trips, wild turkey hunting, family vacations, Florida Keys fishing, trout fishing, upland and migratory bird hunting, fly fishing schools for private groups, and corporate programs.

Grande Domaine's North American network of fishing and hunting lodges includes Saskatchewan's *Highrock Lodge* at Highrock Lake, one of Canada's top lakes for northern pike up to 29 pounds, lake trout, grayling, and whitefish; *Grayling Lodge,* at Careen Lake on the Black Birch River, one of the world's best arctic grayling streams. Facilities in British Columbia include the *Wapiti River Outfitters* Belcourt Lake base camp, near Dawson Creek, with spring and fall hunting for grizzly, mountain goat and sheep, moose, black bear, elk and caribou, and wilderness fishing; and *Omenica Wilderness Lodge* at Tutizzi Lake, with fishing for trophy rainbow, Dolly Varden, lake trout, and grayling. Grande Domaine Montana retreats include *Spotted Bear Ranch* near Hungry Horse, with cutthroat and Dolly Varden fishing and mule deer and mountain goat hunting; and *Canyon Creek Ranch,* for trophy Big Hole River browns and elk and mule deer hunting. Northwest Territories facilities include *Henik Lake Lodge; Dubawnt Trophy Trout Camp,* with arctic grayling and lake trout to 62 pounds; and the *Wilson River Char Camp* at Hudson Bay. New Brunswick Atlantic salmon fishing lodges include the *Fourmen Lodge* on the Northwest Miramichi, *Square Forks Salmon Club* on the

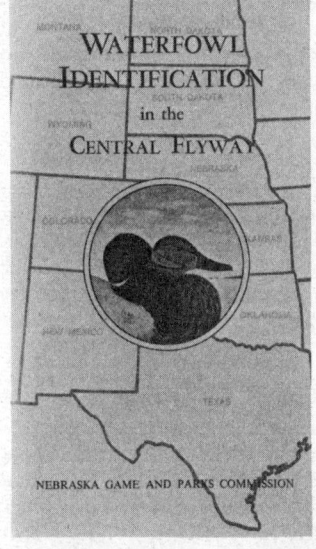

Sevogle River, and *Gauges Salmon Club* on the Little Southwest Miramichi. *Reids' Stork Lake Lodge* at Long Legged Lake, Ontario, offers quality fishing for muskellunge, walleye, and northern pike. The *Florida Keys Fishing Retreat* at Islamorada offers fishing for bonefish, tarpan, snook, and sailfish. In eastern Wyoming is the Grande Domaine *Wyoming Antelope Camp*. In Nebraska, the *Pine Ridge Sportsman's Lodge*, overlooking Deadman Valley at Crawford, offers family vacations and hunting for wild turkey and mule deer; the *Willow Lake Sportsman's Lodge* offers some of the Midwest's top duck hunting, plus upland game birds.

For detailed information, rates, and a full-color brochure, write: Dana Cole, Grande Domain Retreats, Fishing & Hunting Lodges, 801 P St., Lincoln 68508, phone (402) 477–9249.

Highways & The Great Platte River Road

A free *Official Nebraska Highway Map & Travel Guide* may be obtained by writing: Tourist Information Office, Dept. of Economic Development, State Capitol, Box 9466, Lincoln 65809. This useful full-color map shows all major highways and secondary roads, campgrounds and state recreation areas, airports, national forests and wildlife refuges, lakes and streams, waysides, historic sites, and points of interest. It also contains an inset map of the Great Platte River Road (Interstate 80), known to the Indians as the "Big Medicine Trail" and to the pioneers as the Oregon Trail.

Lake & Reservoir Maps

Free maps of Nebraska's major lakes and reservoirs, including Lewis and Clark Reservoir, Lake McConaughy, Harlan County Reservoir, and Crescent, Island, and Twin lakes, are available from: Game & Parks Commission, P.O. Box 30370, Lincoln 68503. These maps show boat ramps, campgrounds, trailer spaces, river channels, deep water, and surface areas.

Nebraska National Forest

This 225,000-acre reserve is scattered in several divisions throughout the famous Sand Hills region in northwestern Nebraska. The major features of this area include the North, Middle, and South Loup rivers, Valentine National Wildlife Refuge, the Niobrara, White, Upper Snake, North Platte, and South Platte rivers, and McConaughy Reservoir, which offers the state's finest fishing for walleye and northern pike up to 27 pounds. The entire region provides the state's best hunting for pheasant, quail, sharptail and prairie grouse, wild turkey, waterfowl, mule and whitetail deer, antelope, and bobcat.

The Game & Parks Commission, P.O. Box 30370, Lincoln 68503, offers an informative free brochure on *Nebraska and Samuel R. McKelvie National Forest*. The Nebraska National Forest's Bessey district contains a completely man-made forest planted in 1902. A beautiful panoramic view rewards visitors at the Scott Lookout Tower. The Bessey recreation complex is located along the Middle Loup River 2 miles west of Halsey, and has excellent camping facilities. A large part of this area (about 16,000 acres) was destroyed by a major forest fire that swept through the area in 1965—there are still traces of the devastation. So far about 1,000 acres have been reforested. In the brochure, a map of the area shows roads, boundaries, and forest plantations.

Pine Ridge Fish & Game Lands

The famous Pine Ridge fish and game lands, located in the distant northwestern corner of Nebraska's Panhandle, include the rugged

Badlands, Pine Ridge, and High Plains. The Badlands and 4,000-foot-high Pine Ridge country were cut by ancient rivers and have been eroded by millennia of violent, sand-carrying winds. The area was the site of numerous Indian skirmishes: Buffalo Bill is said to have taken his first scalp here to avenge Custer's defeat at Little Bighorn. This unspoiled, pine-clad bluff country offers top-ranked hunting for wild Merriam's turkey, mule deer, pronghorn antelope, sharp-tailed grouse, and a few pheasant. Brown and rainbow trout are found in Monroe, Sowbelly, Hat, and Soldier creeks and in the White River. Box Butte Reservoir holds northern pike, walleye, largemouth and smallmouth bass, white bass, and channel catfish.

If you plan to visit this interesting, varied area, send for an informative map-guide *Recreation Guide Map—Nebraska Pine Ridge Area*. It contains a map of the entire area showing wooded areas, national parks, forest service lands, Game & Parks Commission lands, federal and state camping areas, roads and trails, lakes and reservoirs, rivers and streams, towns and villages, and boundaries. Historic trails are outlined (Laramie, Wyoming, to Fort Robinson, the Fort Robinson-Hat Creek Stage Road military telegraph line, Laramie Spottedtail, and Fort Robinson Road). Areas where hunting is prohibited are indicated. A sunrise/sunset schedule is provided, as well as a chart showing recreation and wayside areas and the facilities available at each. The reverse side contains information on the history, recreation, wildlife, management, and plant life of the area. It is illustrated with attractive color photographs. A copy of this map-guide can be obtained free from: Game & Parks Commission, P.O. Box 30370, Lincoln 68503.

KAN

S

ENCYCLOPEDIA · 329

Accommodations—
Family Vacation Facilities

For complete information on hotels, motels, campsites, or whatever type of accommodation you are seeking, write to: Dept. of Economic Development, State Office Bldg., Topeka 66612, or to the local Chamber of Commerce where you plan to visit.

Campgrounds & State Recreation Areas

Campers in Kansas should obtain a copy of the helpful free brochure *Camping & Campsites,* which lists and describes campsites, noting facilities available at each area, outstanding recreational activities, and the best approach by car. The exact location of each campsite is shown on a map that marks the highway routes leading to the areas. A handy chart showing federal lakes, recreation areas, and facilities is provided, and explicit auto route approaches are also given. A chart of state fishing lakes, state parks, and recreation areas is shown and details the facilities available at each area. A list of safety rest areas is provided, as well as rules and regulations governing forestry, fish and game, state parks, and motor vehicle information. You can write to: Dept. Of Economic Development, State Office Bldg., Topeka 66612, for your copy.

Fishing & Hunting in Kansas

The Sunflower State's rolling hills and grasslands, broad valleys, woodlands, and large impoundments boast some excellent hunting for deer, waterfowl, and upland game birds and fishing for largemouth bass, walleye, northern pike, transplanted striped bass up to 20 pounds and over, and giant catfish. Topographically the state is divided into three natural regions: the High Plains of the west; the Great Bend Prairie or Low Plains in the center of the state; and the beautiful Flint Hills region, or Bluestem Belt in the east, with its picturesque, rolling uplands interspersed with limestone bluffs. In the central region lie the Smoky Hills and Blue Hills uplands. South of the prairie region are the heavily eroded cliffs and terraces of the Cimarron Breaks, bordering the Cimarron River. The treeless High Plains were formed by the

**KANSAS
ENCYCLOPEDIA**

course of ancient streams that flowed eastward from the Rocky Mountains and deposited huge loads of gravel and debris. Major rivers include the great Missouri along the northeastern boundary, the Kansas and its tributaries, the Big Blue, Solomon, Republican, and Smoky Hill; the Neosho and its tributaries, the Cottonwood and Fall; and the Arkansas and its feeders, the Pawnee, Little Arkansas, Minnescah, Walnut, Rattlesnake, and Whitewater.

Several lakes in the northeastern corner of the state provide excellent fishing for walleye, largemouth bass, crappie, and white bass including 6,930-acre Melvern Reservoir, on the Marais des Cygnes River south of Topeka; beautiful 12,600-acre Perry Reservoir on the Delaware River—one of the top channel catfish streams in the state; 4,000-acre Pomona Reservoir, with its submerged timber, coves, flats, and rocky bluffs; 15,800-acre Tuttle Creek Reservoir in the Big Blue River Valley—one of the nation's top crappie fisheries, with its jagged 112-mile shoreline outlined by dead timber and hidden coves; and the Deep Creek and Rocky Ford state fishing areas. In the southeast region of the state, fishermen will find crappie, white bass, largemouth bass, channel catfish, and a few striped bass in 4,400-acre Elk City Reservoir, with its 50 miles of shoreline ranging from steep, wooded slopes to rolling grasslands and big channel and flathead catfish, white bass, and crappie in 9,400-acre John Redmond Reservoir on the Neosho River, nestled in the scenic Flint Hills. The Flint Hills National Wildlife Refuge is located on the upper end of the lake. Other fishing lakes in the southeast include the Lake Crawford State Park, Marais des Cygnes Waterfowl Management Area, Neosho Waterfowl Management Area, strip-mine lakes scattered throughout Linn, Crawford, Bourbon, and Cherokee counties, and the Big Hill Lakes.

In the north central portion of the state are the V-shaped 3,280 acres of Council Grove Reservoir, offering 27 miles of shoreline and fishing for white bass, catfish, crappie, and walleye—particularly below the dam in the outlet waters. The 3,550-acre Kanopolis Reservoir in the Smoky Hill River Valley, with its Indian rock carvings and fossils, holds huge schools of white bass and crappie, as well as walleye, flathead, and channel catfish. Other major fisheries in the north central area include Lovewell Reservoir; huge 16,187-acre Milford Reservoir on the Republican River—one of the state's top-ranked striped bass lakes, with a large population of white bass and crappie; beautiful 12,586-acre Waconda (Glen Elder) Reservoir on the Solomon River, featuring 100 miles of scenic shoreline and striped bass fishing; and 9,000-acre Wilson Reservoir, with its jagged 100-mile boulder-strewn shoreline and top-ranked crappie, white bass, walleye, largemouth bass, and striper fishing.

In south central Kansas, the sprawling 9,500-acre Cheney Reservoir, 20 miles west of Wichita, home of the state record 33-pound 12-ounce striped bass, provides good fishing for largemouth bass, crappie, and channel catfish, in addition to trophy-sized stripers. The 2,600-acre Fall River Reservoir is noted for the large early spring migration of white bass up its Otter Creek and Fall River feeders. The 6,160-acre Marion Reservoir, with its 60 miles of shoreline nestled in the Cottonwood River Valley, holds a large variety of fish including walleye, white bass, crappie, largemouth bass, channel catfish, and a few blue catfish. Toronto Reservoir, which covers 2,800 acres in the Verdigris River Valley, produced the world record 5-pound 4-ounce white bass.

In the High Plains of northwest Kansas lie the crystal-clear, trophy smallmouth bass waters of 6,869-acre Cedar Bluff Reservoir surrounded by jagged 50-mile shoreline. Kirwin Reservoir, which covers 5,080 acres in the Solomon River Valley, is noted for its early spring walleye migration and fishing for white bass, channel catfish, and crappie. The 2,187-acre Norton Reservoir with its 67-mile shoreline provides good fishing for trophy-sized smallmouth bass, crappie, northern pike, walleye, bluegill, and catfish. The 3,445-acre Webster Reservoir is noted for large numbers of big walleye. The major fishing areas in southwest Kansas include numerous state fishing lakes and the Cheyenne Bottoms, Lake Meade State Park, Morton County Wildlife Area on the Cimarron Grasslands, and Lake Scott State Park.

The fishing potential of the Sunflower State's lakes and streams is reflected in the list of state record fish compiled by the Forestry, Fish, & Game Commission.

KANSAS RECORD FISH

	Lb.–oz.	Place	Year
Largemouth bass	11–3	Bourbon Co. Lake	1965
Smallmouth bass	2–9½	Norton Reservoir	1972
Striped bass	33–12	Cheney Reservoir	1975
Northern pike	24–12	Council Grove Reservoir	1971
Walleye	12–1	Rocky Ford Area	1972
White bass	5–4	Toronto Reservoir Spillway	1966
Bluegill	2–5	Scott Co. Farm Pond	1962
Black crappie	4–10	Woodson Co. Lake	1957
White crappie	4–¼	Greenwood Co. Lake	1964
Yellow perch	0–12	Lake Elbo	1970
Sturgeon	4	Kaw River	1962
Paddlefish	74–8	Dam below Chetopa	1973
Blue catfish	33–12	Kansas River	1974
Channel catfish	32	Gardner City Lake	1962
Flathead catfish	86–3	Neosho River	1966
Bullhead catfish	5	Fish & Game Strip Pit	1974
Gar	31–8	Perry Reservoir Outlet	1974

A free 40-page guide, *Fishing in Kansas Lakes & Reservoirs*, may be obtained free upon request from: Forestry, Fish, & Game Commission, Box 1028, Pratt 67124. In addition, the commission publishes free *Kansas Fishing Regulations*, *Hunting Seasons & Regulations*, *Boat & Water Safety Laws*, and *Public Hunting in Kansas* brochures.

The more than 304,000 acres of public hunting and game management lands in Kansas provide excellent uncrowded hunting in season for ducks, geese, doves, bobwhite quail, and pheasant. The Flint Hills country of eastern Kansas contains the largest single concentration of greater prairie chickens in the United States. Squirrel hunting is popular in the eastern regions and along the timbered streams in western Kansas. Other popular small-game species include cottontails, jackrabbits, and crows. Coyote range throughout the state. A growing whitetail deer herd is found along the state's woodland river valleys. The major state game management areas (GMA) include 7,958-acre Cheney GMA, 12,254-acre Cheyenne Bottoms Waterfowl Management Area, 11,834-acre Cedar Bluff GMA, 10,092-acre Fall River GMA, 25,100-acre Glen Elder GMA, 3,353-acre Lovewell GMA, 4,043-acre Kingman GMA, 3,000-acre Kingman Management Area, 15,660-acre Milford GMA, 2,016-acre Neosho Waterfowl Management Area, 4,757-acre Pratt Sandhills GMA, 5,979-acre Strip Pits Wildlife Management Area, and 13,000-acre Tuttle Creek GMA.

Highways & Frontier Trails

A free official *Kansas Highway Map* showing all major roads, highways, campgrounds, points of interest, and natural features may be obtained by writing: Dept. of Economic Development, State Office Bldg., Topeka 66612. The free map-guide *Frontier Trails of Kansas* may be obtained from the same address. This interesting publication shows and describes the state's historic exploration and pioneer routes, and the location of historic markers along major auto routes. The frontier trails described include the famous Chisholm Trail, named after Jesse Chisholm, an Indian trader who first marked it for his

wagons—beginning in 1867 it became the major cattle trail to the Abilene stockyards; Lewis and Clark Trail, which traces the expedition's trail through Kansas to the mouth of the Kansas River and up the Missouri—the gateway to the northern Rockies and the Lolo Trail to the Columbia River and the Pacific Ocean; the Oregon Trail, which beginning in the early 1840s was known to westward-bound trappers as the Rocky Mountain Trail, to Mormons as the Great Salt Lake Trail, and to gold seekers as the California Trail; Pony Express Route, which carried mail overland from St. Joseph, Missouri, to Sacramento, California, in 10 days, using a system of 9-to-15-mile relays; and the Santa Fe Trail, which opened the great Southwest. The map-guide also shows and describes the state's major historic sites, including the beautiful Flint Hills and the last remaining expanses of native tall-grass prairies, which at one time covered 400,000 square miles of the United States; Dodge City, "Queen of the Cow Towns" and Boot Hill Cemetery; and the Pawnee Indian Village Museum at Republic.

GREAT
LAKES
STATES

Caroline Edwards

GREAT
LAKES
STATES

Introduction

The lake-dotted evergreen forests of the glacially scoured Canadian Shield, historic north-country canoe routes, and ancient highlands surrounding the rugged boulder-strewn beaches and cliff-lined shores of the Upper Great Lakes—Superior, Michigan, Huron—form one of the nation's most popular outdoor recreation and vacation areas. Here, in the rugged Laurentian uplands of northern Minnesota, Wisconsin, and Michigan, are thousands upon thousands of sky-blue lakes, brawling wild rivers, great lowland areas of bogs, tea-colored muskeg streams, and the incredibly wild and scenic granite cliffs, bays, coves, and countless rocky islands scattered along the rugged, wave-pounded shores of the Upper Great Lakes. In the southern regions of the states, glacial deposits have formed gently rolling plains, crossed here and there by wide valleys.

The often storm-tossed and fog-bound waters of lakes Superior, Huron, and Michigan have inspired a body of folklore and numerous tales of the supernatural, ranging from Paul Bunyan's gouging out the lakes to provide ponds for his sawmills to rumors of ghost ships, vessels lost to the deeps, which still haunt the coastline. Frequent disasters on these great inland seas have also given rise to tales of sunken treasure: rich cargoes of gold coin and valuable metals that have been claimed forever by the frigid depths. At the bottom of Lake Michigan's Saginaw Bay lies the schooner *Fay*, holding $200,000 worth of steel billets; and the richest prize of all, some 5 million dollars' worth of gold bullion, is reputedly locked in the safe box of a vessel that sank near Poverty Island off Lake Huron's Big Bay de Noc.

Minnesota, known as the "Land of 10,000 Lakes," the westernmost of the Great Lakes States, bounded on the east by Lake Superior and Wisconsin, contains the headwaters of the mighty Mississippi—which begins its long, meandering 3,710-mile journey south into the Gulf of Mexico from its source in beautiful Lake Itasca in the north-central part of the state—and several of the nation's outstanding fishing, canoeing, and wild and scenic north-woods vacation areas, including the famous trophy muskellunge of lakes Leech, Cass, and Winnibigoskish in the Mississippi headwaters country of the Chippewa National Forest; the Red Lake canoe country; the great glacially gouged Boundary Lakes, such as Rainy, Namakayan, Lac La Croix, Basswood, Gunflint, Saganaga, Kabetogama, and Mountain—which stretch like a ragged necklace of blue jewels along the Minnesota-Ontario border; the wild rivers and remote blue lakes of the Boundary Waters Canoe Area in the Superior National Forest; the historic Grand Portage Trail and brawling, deep-flowing trophy steelhead streams along Lake Superior's rugged North Shore.

The "North Star State," located in the geographic center of North America, contains several distinct outdoor recreation regions within its 84,068 square miles: the "arrowhead" region in the northeast—a southern extension of the great Canadian Shield, with rocky highlands, swampy marshes, and ancient volcanic rock, and both the highest and lowest elevations in the state (2,230 feet in the Masquah Hills and 660 feet at Lake Superior); the central hill and lake country, with its mixed hardwood and coniferous forests and wetlands; the ancient bed of glacial Lake Agassiz in the northwest—which at one time covered an area 700 miles long and 200 miles wide, leaving traces of its lowering beach lines in the many sandy ridges still visible here—dominated by the southern reaches of beautiful island-dotted Lake of the Woods (1,485 square miles), Rainy Lake (345 square miles) and Red Lake, the state's largest body of water, covering an area of 494 square miles, all draining northward into Canada's Hudson Bay. The virgin forests and waterways of Minnesota, the original home and

hunting grounds of the Chippewa and Sioux Indians, were first explored by the hardy fur traders and voyageurs of the old Northwest Company, followed by Lieutenant Zebulon Pike, who took possession of the region for the United States under President Thomas Jefferson.

Like neighboring Minnesota, northern Wisconsin boasts several of the nation's most renowned fishing, hunting, canoeing, wilderness-camping, and family-vacation areas and one of the greatest concentrations of lakes in the world. Over 8,500 have been charted throughout the state, the largest of which is Lake Winnebago, with an area of 215 square miles, but a comparatively shallow average depth of 15 feet. Situated within the Badger State's 56,134 square miles are the scenic evergreen forests and trophy fishing waters of the Northern Highlands; the nationally renowned muskellunge waters of the Chippewa Flowage–Hayward Lakes Region; the historic fur-trade canoe routes of the Bois Brule and Flambeau rivers; the famous trophy trout and smallmouth-bass waters off the evergreen-clad shores of Lake Superior's Apostle Islands; the St. Croix and Namagakon rivers; the scenic Wisconsin River Dells (gorges); and the famed brown-trout waters of the Wolf National Wild River. The virgin forests and waterways of the Badger State were first explored by the French voyageurs in their search to find the legendary "Northwest Passage." Jean Nicolet was the first European to penetrate the Wisconsin Territory in 1634, having been sent by Samuel Champlain to investigate rumors of a distant race called the "People of the Sea," who, it was believed, might be Asiatics, but were actually the populous tribe of Winnebago Indians.

Michigan's 58,216 square miles border on four of the five Great Lakes, divided into an Upper and Lower Peninsula by the picturesque Straits of Mackinac, which links Lake Michigan with Lake Huron. The two peninsulas are connected by the Mackinac Bridge, with its 3,800-foot suspension span—the third longest in the U.S. The Wolverine State is one of North America's most popular fishing, hunting, camping, canoeing, and family-vacation areas. The awesomely productive trophy fishing waters of lakes Michigan, Huron, and Superior, managed by Michigan's progressive Department of Natural Resources, hold, without a doubt, yet-to-be-caught world-record muskellunge, brown trout, northern pike, rainbow trout, walleye, and coho salmon. The mitt-shaped Lower Peninsula, a low-lying region of rolling hills and mixed hardwood and coniferous forests, contains several nationally famous recreation areas, including the historic trout waters of the Au Sable and Père Marquette rivers, the famed ruffed-grouse lands of the Pigeon River State Forest, and the nationally renowned salmon and steelhead waters of the wild Big Manistee, Boardman, Platte, Au Gres, and St. Joseph rivers.

The remote wildlands of the beautiful Upper Peninsula, with its ancient mountains, sandy plains, rocky ridges, vast swamplands, and boreal forests, boasts the renowned trout waters of the scenic Big Two Hearted and Tahquemenon rivers and the rugged, picturesque South Shore of Lake Superior, Lake Huron's beautiful Les Chenaux Islands, the Porcupine Mountains Wilderness, the famed fishing and game lands of the Ottawa and Hiawatha national forests, and the remote Isle Royale of Lake Superior. The sandy plains areas, in part burned over by the Indians, are covered with jack pine, scrub oak, aspen, and huckleberry bushes. The tea-colored cedar swamps of the Upper Peninsula, with their numerous beaver flows, offer one of the nation's last remaining wild brook trout frontiers. Michigan, the ancient home and hunting grounds of the Chippewa, Ottawa, and Huron Indians, was an important center of the fur-trade era, with a major fort at Michilimackinac (Mackinac Island), and later became a part of the United States' old North-West Territory.

Weather, Bugs & Beasts

The Upper Great Lakes have a significant influence on the climate of Minnesota, Michigan, and Wisconsin, absorbing heat from warmer air and warming the colder winds. In the summer, prevailing westerly winds are cooled by the waters. Summers are often hot, with sudden storms and foggy conditions along the coastal areas. Travelers by small craft or canoe on the Great Lakes should hug the shoreline and be alert at all times for the sudden squalls that can turn the coastal waters into a frothing sea of whitecaps, occasionally smashing small boats and canoes against the towering cliff-lined shores. The north woods of the Upper Great Lakes are infamous for their swarms of mosquitoes, black flies, deer flies, horse flies, moose flies, and no-see-ums during the early summer. If you are planning a north-country trip, be sure to take along a good supply of Off!, Muskol, Mosquitone, or Cutters insect repellent —all of which contain a 50%-plus concentration of DEET, the most effective known insect repellent. It is advisable to bring a wide-brimmed hat, light-colored shirt, raingear, head net, and sunglasses. If you plan an extended wilderness trip, a recommended dosage of 50 mg/day of vitamin B1 for a week prior to your departure and about 10 mg twice each day during the trip is one of the best natural defenses against insects (check with your physician for his recommended dosage).

Great Lakes Maps & Charts—How to Order

The topographic map kits listed throughout the Great Lakes States chapters will provide you with a valuable picture of the area you plan to visit—showing all mountains, bogs, rivers, lakes, campgrounds, springs, wilderness cabins, national forests and parks, wildlife-management areas, wildlife refuges, wilderness areas, state parks and forests, roads, trails, clearings, rapids and falls, as well as the contours of the land. All maps listed (unless otherwise noted) are full-color U.S. Geological Survey overview maps, scale 1:250,000, 1 inch to 4 miles ($2 each) or large-scale 7½-minute and 15-minute maps ($1.25 each for either). These maps and free *Topographic Map Indexes* of Minnesota, Wisconsin, and Michigan may be ordered (along with a free *Map Symbol Chart* and *Topographic Maps* booklet) from: Distribution Branch, U.S. Geological Survey, 1200 S. Eads St., Arlington, VA 22202. Be sure to order maps by their individual names (and indicate scale when ordering 1:250,000-scale maps); to expedite delivery, include extra money for first-class postage.

Large, attractive U.S. Geological Survey *State Topographic Maps* of Michigan, Wisconsin, and Minnesota are published, scale 1:500,000, or 1 inch to 8 miles, and may be ordered for $2 each from the address above. The Michigan Topographic map consists of 2 sheets (each $2). A stunningly beautiful *Wisconsin Shaded-Relief Map* at the same scale is available for $2; its colored shading gives the map a three-dimensional appearance of the sunlight striking the surface from the northwest. A free catalog, *Great Lakes Nautical Charts*, may be obtained by writing: National Ocean Survey, Distribution Division (C44), Riverdale, MD 20840. The catalog contains a complete listing of small-craft and recreational craft charts and Great Lakes nautical publications.

A useful 214-page handbook, *Be Expert with Map & Compass*, by Bjorn Kjellstrom, the president and founder of Silva Compasses, may be obtained for $6.95 from Charles Scribner's Sons, Bookstore Dept., 597 5th Ave., New York, NY 10017

Accommodations—
Vacation Lodges & Resorts

The following guides to lodging, facilities, motels and hotels, and services in Minnesota's great outdoor vacation regions may be obtained free upon request: *Arrowhead Country,* a guide to the state's scenic and wild northeastern corner, may be obtained from the Minnesota Arrowhead Association, Hotel Duluth, Duluth 55802, phone (218) 722–0874; *Tip o' the Arrow* is a 23-page booklet to rugged Cook County—the easternmost point of Arrowhead country between Saganaga Lake, Jacoinette Harbor, and Grand Portage—available from the Tip of the Arrowhead Association, Grand Marais 55604; *Heartland,* a 55-page guide to north-central Minnesota, known as the "Muskie Capital of the World," is available from Heartland Inc., P.O. Box 443, 411 Laurel St., Brainerd 56401, phone (218) 829–1615; *Viking Land U.S.A.,* a 23-page booklet about the northwest region, believed to have been visited by the Norsemen in 1362, may be obtained from Viking-Land USA, Box 545, Battle Lake 56515; *Hiawathaland,* a 55-page guide to the southeastern region, is available from Hiawathaland, 212 1st Ave., SW, Rochester 55901; *Pioneerland,* a guide to the state's southeastern corner, is available from Pioneerland Inc., Chamber of Commerce Bldg., Box 999, Mankato 56001.

Further information on resorts throughout the state can be obtained from the Minnesota Resort Association, 2001 University Ave., St. Paul 55104. The Minnesota Hotel and Motor Hotel Association, at the same address, will also be glad to provide details on statewide accommodations. Information on motels alone is also available from the Minnesota Motel Association, 2901 Pleasant Avenue, Minneapolis, MN 55408.

A toll-free phone number is also available to Minnesota's visitors for information on Minnesota vacations. Dial 1 (800) 652–9008 for information on resorts, hotels, motels, attractions, calendar events, camping, and driving tours of the state. Twin Cities residents should use the regular tourist center number, (612) 296–5029. Residents of Illinois, Iowa, Kansas, Michigan, Missouri, Nebraska, North and South Dakota, and Wisconsin should call toll-free 1 (800) 382–9161 for Minnesota vacation information.

Listings of major lodges and resorts are found throughout the "Minnesota Travel & Recreation Guide" section.

MINNESOTA
ENCYCLOPEDIA

Aircraft—Wilderness Fly-in Service

The Grand Marais Municipal Airport at Devils Track Lake offers facilities for both land-based aircraft and seaplanes. Customs officers are on duty here for flights returning from Canada. *Wilderness Wings Airways* (Box 188, Ely 55731, phone (218) 365–4449) offers fly-in service, hunting trips, seaplane training, and tours in the heart of the Superior National Forest and surrounding Arrowhead terrain. *Lac La Croix Quetico Air Service,* Crane Lake 55725, phone (218) 993–2361, provides charter fly-in and pickup service throughout the famed Quetico-Superior canoeing and fishing country.

Based at Duluth International Airport (Duluth, 55811), *Halvair Airways* features a charter service, scenic rides, and air-taxi facilities. *Messabi Airlines* in Grand Rapids, 55744 phone (218) 326–6657, has scheduled daily flights from Minneapolis-St. Paul and will provide charter flights anywhere. Rentals, Cessna sales and service, and float certification are also provided. (See "North Country Wilderness Canoeing & Fishing Outfitters" for additional listings.)

Boundary Waters Lake Charts

Charts of the Minnesota-Ontario border lakes showing navigation routes, portage trails, and topography of the surrounding North Country wilderness are available from the Distribution Division (C44), National Ocean Survey, Riverdale, MD 20840. The following charts sell for $1.25 each (be sure to order by chart number and make checks payable to NOS-Dept. of Commerce) and are at a scale of 1:42,240 unless otherwise specified: 14982 *North Lake;* 14983 *Northern Light Lake;* 14984 *Sea Gull Lake;* 14985 *Saganaga Lake;* 14986 *Knife Lake;* 14987 *Basswood Lake,* Eastern Part; 14988 *Basswood Lake,* Western Part; 14989 *Crooked Lake;* 14990 *Basswood River* (1:10,-000); 14991 *Lac La Croix;* 14992 Sand Point Lake to Lac La Croix, including Crane Lake and Little Vermilion Lake; 14993 *Namakan Lake,* Eastern Part; 14994 *Namakan Lake,* Western Part, and *Kabetogama Lake,* Eastern Part; 14995 *Kabetogama Lake,* Western Part; 14996 *Rainy Lake-Big Island,* Minn., to Oakpoint Island, Ont. (1:25,000), and Kettle Falls (1:12,500); 14997 *Rainy Lake-Dryweed Island, to Big Island* (1:25,000); 14998 *Rainy Lake-International Falls to Dryweed Island* (1:25,000); 14999 *Lake of the Woods* (1:120,000), *Warroad Harbor* (1:20,000), and *Rainy River* (1:20,000).

Camping & Wilderness Trails

Minnesota's innumerable lakes, rugged wilderness areas, and scenic mixed hardwood and evergreen forests offer excellent opportunities for camping. The *Minnesota Camping Guide,* a 57-page sourcebook for campers, lists almost all campgrounds and recreation areas in the state. The booklet is divided into sections on state, national forest, and private camping sites and Mississippi River recreation areas. Listings are alphabetical by townsite and include location, rates, telephone numbers, activities and facilities available, including boat rentals, sewage hookup, laundry facilities, fireplaces, picnic tables, swimming beaches, fishing outfitters, and the like. The *Minnesota Camping Guide* is available free from the Publicity and Promotion Division, Dept. of Economic Development, 480 Cedar St., St. Paul 55101.

Another *Minnesota Camping Guide,* prepared by the Minnesota Association of Campground Operators, lists state-licensed association members throughout the state. Again, listings are alphabetical by town and indicate addresses, number of sites, facilities, telephone numbers, and directions to the campsite from many of the major cities. A road map showing the various campgrounds and major highways is in-

cluded. The 23-page booklet is available free from the Minnesota Assn. of Campground Operators, P.O. Box 3440, Elk River 55330. MACO recommends making all reservations for campsites in advance, and will be happy to answer any questions you have about camping in Minnesota.

Minnesota's state and national forests offer abundant outdoor camping sites beside still lakes or in thickly wooded settings, in well-developed campgrounds with many modern conveniences or in primitive areas where you're totally on your own. Many of these sites are listed in the camping guides described above; forest maps will also help in locating the best spots, and the appropriate forest supervisors will be glad to provide additional information (see "Chippewa National Forest" and "Superior National Forest" in the "Travel & Recreation Guide" section).

Forest maps and literature also offer descriptions of a wide variety of hiking trails for both novices and experienced hikers. In addition, there are innumerable old logging roads and undeveloped trails winding through public forests and wilderness areas where you can blaze your own route and explore primitive terrain. Hikers will also enjoy the challenge of the Grand Portage Trail, perhaps the oldest path in the state; this same rugged forest roadway in Minnesota's Arrowhead was used extensively by voyageurs carrying heavy packs between the trading post of Grand Portage and the way station of Fort Charlotte (see "Grand Portage—the 'Great Carrying Place' ").

Canoeing & North Country Waters

Minnesota, "the Land of Sky-blue Waters," offers a canoeist's jackpot in swift-flowing rivers and intricate networks of waterways. Inland waters alone cover an area equal in size to that of the combined areas of Rhode Island and Connecticut. Together with hundreds of tributary systems, the Mississippi, Minnesota, St. Croix, Red, and St. Louis rivers make up more than 25,000 miles of flowing water. But of all the state's renowned canoe routes, perhaps those of the far north and northwestern regions, including the unparalleled complex of the Boundary Waters Canoe Area, offer the finest opportunities for challenging white-water runs and extended trips through vast labyrinths of inter-connected rivers and lakes. Here rock-bottomed, swift streams with many waterfalls flow along the forested North Shore, while others find their origin in the "Big Bog" of northwestern Minnesota, a muskeg wilderness of tamarack, low shrubs, black spruce, and spongy sphagnum moss lying in the ancient basin of glacial Lake Agassiz. Streams originating in this swampy wilderness feed the Red River, eventually reaching the waters of Hudson Bay.

The region laced by these waterways resounds with the history of the fur trade and of voyages which led to the discovery and exploration of the far Northwest. In the fall of 1731, the Sieur de La Vérendrye struggled up an old Indian portage trail and ascended the upper Pigeon River, aided by a rough map sketched on birchbark and by valuable Indian guides, experts who had paddled these waters for hundreds of years. Beyond the height of land dividing the Hudson Bay and Atlantic drainages lay a wilderness thickly studded with beaver lodges on the many ponds and along marshy creeks. Vérendrye never realized his original goal of finding a passage to the Pacific, the great "Western Sea" sought by every self-respecting eighteenth-century explorer, but he did succeed in opening one of the most important trade routes in history. The Pigeon River bypass, soon known as Grand Portage, provided the gateway to a vast and complex network of river systems: the Winnipeg, Assiniboine, Red River of the North, Saskatchewan, Athabasca, Vermilion, Peace, and others. These waters formed the highway of the fur trade; voyageurs paddled their craft from the central post at Grand Portage over half a continent and back

before the end of the short northern summer, sometimes covering over 3,000 miles in less than nine months. No mean feat by any standards.

The same rivers traveled by trappers and traders over 200 years ago still provide some of the finest canoeing in the country, and the variety of trips that can be planned from a central locus such as Ely, Minnesota, is mind-boggling. A typical week's trip, for instance, might take the paddler from the Moose River down to Lac La Croix, returning via Iron and Crooked lakes, then Basswood River and Lake, over portages beaten solid by centuries of use. Another satisfying run takes the canoeist on a 30-mile trip from Fowl Lake to the lower end of Gunflint Lake through a succession of waterways with connecting portages. Trout fishing is excellent along this route, especially near the south shore of Rose Lake. Between North and South lakes lies a 500-year-old portage where novice voyageurs, or "porkeaters," were officially initiated into the ranks of the full-fledged "Nor'westers." After a mock-baptismal rite in which the greenhorns were sprinkled with a few drops of water from a cedar bough and asked to repeat a litany of "sacred" vows, the ceremony would reach a festive conclusion with dancing and rum all around. The initiates were now permitted to sport colored plumes in their headgear, proud badges signifying the successful completion of an arduous route and membership in a daring

and difficult society. Still other routes follow the paddles of voyageurs through Gunflint to Knife Lake along shores lined with virgin timber; down the Basswood River to Crooked Lake, where a series of thousand-year-old Indian rock paintings showing crude but graceful representations of men and animals can be examined; and through the island-studded waters of Lac La Croix, enhanced by superb fishing and a nearby village of Chippewa Indians.

Many different publications offer excellent guides to these waters; some are pocket-sized, providing only maps and basic route information, and others are more extensive, covering many runs and offering explicit and detailed information on technique, equipment, and even the history of the area traversed. Of the latter category, *Whitewater, Quietwater—The Wild Rivers of Wisconsin, Upper Michigan, & NE Minnesota,* by Bob and Jody Palzer, is a 157-page guide to canoe streams and rivers personally traveled and recorded by the authors. *Whitewater, Quietwater* is concerned with those waters that are still mainly for canoes; hence, wide rivers, lakes, and flowages are not described. Over 80 trips are mapped and detailed; in addition, fifteen trips are outlined without maps. Each river run is a one-day trip between landings accessible by car. Length of the run, time required, gradient, hazard rating, and water conditions are described for each

route. Also included are comments on the scenery, geology, fishing, campgrounds, and local history. The 32-page introductory section describes equipment, including the various types of canoes—open, decked, and kayaks—paddles, protective aids, rafts, and other important gear. Descriptions of canoeing techniques, paddling methods, portaging, and tips on maneuvering in rapids and water safety are also offered. Profusely illustrated, this section contains detailed but highly readable explanations of all data relevant to the canoeist. A substantial bibliography is also provided. Appendixes at the end of the guide offer additional river information, an explanation of the International Scale of River Difficulty, plus lists of periodicals, clubs, maps, technique manuals, and equipment sources. Priced at $7.95, *Whitewater, Quietwater* is available from Evergreen Paddleways, 1416 21st St., Two Rivers, WI 54241.

Another comprehensive guide to canoe runs along the state's waterways, *Minnesota Voyageur Trails*, outlines many routes originally traveled by French fur traders and early explorers. Seventeen routes on such rivers as the Big Fork, Kettle, Des Moines, Mississippi, Snake, and Rum are described in abundant detail. Additional facts on the history of the region are woven into the text. Also provided is a mile-by-mile guide to the terrain and local points of interest, along with names and addresses of contacts who will be glad to supply additional information. *Minnesota Voyageur Trails* is available for $2.00, tax included, from the Minnesota Dept. of Natural Resources, Division of Parks and Recreation, 320 Centennial Bldg., St. Paul 55155.

Also available from the department are six pocket-size, spiral-bound boating guides providing aerial photographic descriptions of canoe routes along Minnesota's rivers. Written descriptions of the trips are brief, detailing mileage, scenic areas, locations of rapids, bridges, etc., but the numerous maps following, showing each stretch of the route, contain abundant directions superimposed in code. Small (about 4 by 6 inches), lightweight, and easily portable, the guides are available for each of the following runs: *Crow River*, from Forest City to Albright Mills County Park (9–46; $1.49); *Kettle River*, between Willow Road and the confluence with the St. Croix River through Hells Gate Rapids, white water navigable only by seasoned experts (9–41; $1.20); *Rum River*, from Princeton to the Mississippi River in Aroka (9–42; $1.49); *St. Croix River, Book 1*, from Danbury to Taylors Falls (9–43; $1.49); *St. Croix River, Book II*, from Taylors Falls to the Mississippi River (9–44; $1.20); and the *Snake River* from McGrath to Gaston (9–45; $1.20). Booklets may be ordered by the code numbers and at the prices cited above, tax included, from the Minnesota Dept. of Natural Resources, 140 Centennial Bldg., St. Paul 55155.

A second series of free, compact, brochure-type guides describes 10 different canoe trips in Minnesota. A detailed map for each run, indicating campsites, rest areas, rapids, portages, and mileage is accompanied by a mile-by-mile route description, general trip information, tips on packing and safety, and, in some guides, a checklist of equipment. In addition, the surrounding terrain is briefly described—the landscape, wildlife, and possibilities for fishing. The following routes are each described in individual brochures: *Pine River*, from Cross Lake Dam through Pine Lake to the Mississippi River; *Mississippi River*, from Lake Winnibigoshish through Schoolcraft State Park and Grand Rapids to Jackson; the *Mississippi Headwaters*, from Lake Itasca past Rice and Boat lakes and through Lake Irving to Lake Bemidji; *Vermilion River*, from Vermilion Lake past Shively and Liftover falls, across De Caigny Rapids to Crane Lake; *St. Louis River*, from the access point near U.S. 53 across the White Face River through Boulderfield Rapids to Spafford Park at Cloquet; *Kettle River*, from the access point near Kennedy bridge through heavily forested

Banning State Park and Hell's Gate Rapids to State Highway 27; *Rum River*, from Anoca through Cambridge, Princeton, and the Milaca Dam to Mille Lacks Lake; *Cloquet River*, from Island Lake through Alden Lake over Dr. Barny's Portage to Indian Lake; *North Fork Crow River*, from Lake Koronis Dam through Forest City and the Crow Hassan Park Reserve to the Mississippi; and *Root River*, from Houston over a lengthy stretch of white water between Rushford and Chatfield. The canoe routes are free from the Minnesota Department of Natural Resources at the above address.

The guides described above will help you plan your route, and the various outfitters described in the "Travel & Recreation Guide" will be glad to help you with equipment, river advice, and miscellaneous trip information. (See "Boundary Waters Lake Charts," "Superior-Quetico Maps & Charts," and "North Country Wilderness Canoeing & Fishing Outfitters.")

Ely Outfitting Center—Gateway to the Boundary Waters Canoe Area

Situated on the shores of Lake Shagawa in the heart of Superior National Forest, Ely is the major outfitting center and gateway to the renowned wilderness of the Boundary Waters Canoe Area. Nearby attractions include Bear Island State Forest, Tower-Soudan State Park, and dozens of lakes containing smallmouth bass, northern pike, walleyes, and trout. The area offers an invigorating spring season, pleasantly warm summers, and spectacular autumn and Indian summer seasons, when the forest cover of birch and aspen dons its colorful fall foliage.

Ely is the home of Sigurd Olson, considered by many to be the country's most famous living woodsman and author. This modern-day voyageur, who over the years has explored the ancient Indian water trails and canoe routes throughout the Superior-Quetico Wilderness

and the remote, seldom-explored hinterlands of Canada's Great North Woods, has described his adventures in the vast grandeur of the north country and the lonely lands of the Canadian Northwest in a series of classic books that are required reading for the wilderness paddler. The following books (hardbound) by Sigurd Olson may be obtained from Alfred A. Knopf Inc., Mail Order Dept., 400 Hahn Rd., Westminster, MD 21157: *The Lonely Land* ($7.95), *Reflections from the North Country* ($7.95), *Runes of the North* ($7.95), *Listening Point* ($7.95), *The Singing Wilderness* ($6.95), *The Wilderness Days*

($13.95). Be sure to enclose 50¢ per book to cover postage and handling.

Ely, Minnesota, a 15-page brochure available free from the Chamber of Commerce, Tour/Travel Center, Ely 55731, lists and describes resorts, lodges, canoe outfitters, flight and portage services, campgrounds, motels, dining rooms, and other services in the area. The Ely area is shown on U.S. Geological Survey large-scale 7.5-minute maps: Ely and Shagawa Lake. (See also "North Country Wilderness Canoeing & Fishing Outfitters" and the "Minnesota Travel & Recreation Guide" section.)

Fishing & Hunting in the North Star State

The North Star State's huge expanses of scenic northern hardwood and evergreen forests, wetlands, and 4,900 square miles of water (excluding the state's portion of Lake Superior), including more than 10,000 "sky-blue" lakes and wild, twisting rivers, provide unrivaled fishing and hunting opportunities.

Trophy Walleye & Muskellunge Waters

The walleye, the "King of Minnesota Fishes," is caught to trophy size along the wave-swept shores and on gravel and rock reefs in the expansive north-central lakes such as Red, Leech, Cass, Mille Lacs, and Winnibigoshish and in Kabetogama, Rainy and the scenic, island-studded Lake of the Woods to the north. The elusive, temperamental muskellunge (Algonquian for "ugly fish") are caught up to trophy weights of 40 pounds and over in the lakes and streams in central and northern Minnesota. The most productive natural muskie waters are the huge lakes in the Mississippi Headwaters and Park Rapids areas and Lake of the Woods. Among the most famous muskellunge waters are Leech, Cass, and Winnibigoshish lakes in the Mississippi Headwaters, and Mantrap, Bad Axe, and Bottle lakes in the Park Rapids area in its original range. In recent years, its range has been extended to other lakes in the central and northern regions of the North Star State, including Moose and Spider lakes in the northeast, near Grand Rapids, and the Woman Lake chain. In 1955, a phenomenon known as the "mad muskie days" occurred on Leech Lake in the Chippewa National Forest, when amazed muskie fishermen took 163 trophies in the 19- to 44-pound class in only 5½ days. This elusive, moody lone-wolf hunter, a savage, tackle-busting fury "leaping for heaven and diving for hell" when hooked, is most often caught over dense weed beds in 6 to 15 feet of water, and near rocky points, mouths of feeder streams, fallen timber, open-water sandbars and cliffs, using live suckers and lures such as big Suick and Rapala plugs, which imitate wounded suckers darting just under the lake's surface.

Northern Pike & Smallmouth Bass

Northern pike are common throughout the state and reach weights of 25 pounds and over in Mississippi Headwaters lakes such as Leech, Red, Cass, Ball Club, and Winnibigoshish. Scrappy smallmouth bass in the 2- to 5-pound range are caught in the scenic canoe country lakes and streams of the Superior National Forest and the Quetico-Superior Boundary Waters. Rainy Lake, and Saganaga, Basswood, Brule, Greenwood, Gunflint and Lac La Croix are among the nation's most productive smallmouth waters. The cold, clear, rockbound lakes of Minnesota's northeast corner hold splake (a hybrid lake and brook trout) and lake trout in the 5- to 20-pound class. The most productive deep, cold-water lakes of the Arrowhead Region include Snowbank, Gunflint, Seagull, and Mountain lakes, and of course, the wind-swept 1,290-foot depths of Lake Superior.

Lake Superior Salmon, Trout, & Steelhead

Minnesota has 1,500 miles of cold-water trout streams. Brook and rainbow trout are most numerous in the Lake Superior tributaries of the northeast and in the rugged valleys and the Root and Whitewater rivers of the southeast. The black-water streams of the rugged Arrowhead Region along the famed North Shore of Lake Superior have spawning runs of rainbows, or steelheads, from 2 to 12 pounds, as well as brook trout, coho and chinook salmon. The picturesque gorges of the North Shore provide excellent trophy fishing for spectacular hard-fighting, metallic-flanked steelhead up to 12 pounds. The brawling, tempestuous gravel-bottomed Lake Superior steelhead streams, which rise in the alder swamps and brush-choked mixed hardwood and conifer forests on the southern slope of the Laurentian Divide in the Superior National Forest, include the Baptism River; Brule (also known as the Arrowhead) River; Sucker River; the deep pools of the wild Devils Track River—a top-ranked wilderness river; and Knife River—the state's longest steelhead stream, with over 70 miles of accessible water. Other trophy salmon and steelhead waters along Lake Superior's North Shore include the French River, Beaver Bay, Lester River, Silver Bay Harbor, and Cascade River. All told, there are 59 scenic North Shore streams that support steelhead spawning streams and provide some 132 miles of accessible fishing water. Some excellent trout fishing is to be had in the famous Straight River near Park Rapids and in the dense forest streams of the Mississippi River Headwaters and in the Rainy River country and St. Croix River system. Excellent catches of smallmouth bass, crappies, and walleye are made in warm-water rivers such as the Crow, Rum, Kettle, Snake, Cloquet, St. Louis, Crow Wing, Root, Big and Little Fork, and St. Croix.

The quality and diversity of Minnesota's legendary fishing waters is reflected in the state record fish, compiled by the Division of Fish & Wildlife (p. 341).

Maps & Guides

Two publications, *The Story of the Walleye* and *The Story of Minnesota's Pike,* available free from the Dept. of Natural Resources, Information & Education, 350 Centennial Office Bldg., St. Paul 55155, include a wealth of facts about walleye, northern pike, and muskie fishing in Minnesota, including spawning and growing patterns and fishing methods.

MINNESOTA RECORD FISH

	Lb.–oz.	Place	Year
Brook trout	9–0	Ash River	1958
Rainbow trout	17–6	Knife River	1974
Brown trout	16–8	Grindstone Lake	1961
Walleye	16–11	Basswood Lake	1955
Lake trout	43–8	Lake Superior	1955
Northern pike	45–12	Basswood Lake	1929
Muskellunge	56–8	Lake of the Woods	1931
Splake	9–6	Pierz Lake	1971
Chinook salmon	18–8	Sucker River	1973
Sturgeon	236–0	Lake of the Woods	1911
Largemouth bass	10–2	Prairie Lake	1961
Smallmouth bass	8–0	West Battle Lake	1948
Crappie	5–0	Vermilion River	1940
Bluegill	2–13	Lake Alice	1948
Perch	3–4	Lake Plantaganette	1945
Sauger	6–2½	Mississippi River below Alma Dam	1964

Fishing and hunting regulations, seasons, permits, and specific area information are available from the Division of Fish & Wildlife, Dept. of Natural Resources, 390 Centennial Bldg., St. Paul 55155. For waterfowl hunters, the Division of Fish & Wildlife publishes a useful, free *Minnesota Wildlife Lands Map*, showing the locations of 848 wildlife-management-area wetlands. Department of Natural Resources Five Plan Maps are available to sportsmen who hunt in Minnesota. Each map covers 36 square miles (except in border areas). The scale is 2 inches to 1 mile, and details shown include rivers, lakes, railroad tracks, fire towers, and the logging roads. The maps are reproduced on plastic-coated paper and sell for 75¢. A free *Index to Fire Plan Maps*, giving range, township, and ordering instructions, may be obtained by writing: Documents Section, Room 140 Centennial Bldg., 658 Cedar St., St. Paul 55155. Several useful field guides are available from the Documents Section of the Division of Fish & Wildlife (address above): *Beaver in Minnesota* (9–14, $1.50, 87 pp.) describes the history of the beaver and contains a guide to beaver trapping and grading; *Big Game in Minnesota* (9–15, $2.50) provides a useful, fascinating guide to the state's big-game past and present, including whitetail deer, bear, moose, elk, and caribou; *Steelhead of the Minnesota North Shore* (9–8, $1.00) provides a technical study of the steelhead trout of the Great Lakes; *Timber Wolf in Minnesota* (9–18, $1.15) is a field study of the timber wolf on the Superior National Forest. Make checks or money orders payable to: State of Minnesota, Documents Section.

Hunting & Wildlife

Minnesota was once inhabited by grizzly, which were hunted along the western boundary, and by buffalo, elk, antelope, and woodland caribou. The last known band of caribou reportedly roamed in the border area of Upper Red Lake over thirty years ago. The cougar, never common to the state, has been exterminated, but its two smaller relatives, the Canada lynx and bay lynx, or bobcat, although rarely seen, inhabit the northern woods. Black bear are found throughout the vast forest regions of the northeast. Whitetail deer are found throughout the state. Superior National Forest has one of the highest population densities of timber wolves in the U.S. The state's large forest tracts and wildlife-management areas offer excellent whitetail-deer

hunting. Minnesota is a top-ranked Mississippi Flatway state for ducks and geese. The extensive wetlands, grain fields, beaver ponds, and wild-rice beds lure large flocks of mallards, bluewing teal, ringnecked ducks, wood ducks, pintails, scaups, canvasbacks, snow and blue geese, and white-fronted geese. Upland game birds include pheasant, ruffed and sharptail grouse, and Hungarian partridge. (For additional information, see "Lake Contour Fishing Maps," "North Country Wilderness Canoeing & Fishing Outfitters," "State Forest Reserve Maps," and the "Travel & Recreation Guide" section.)

Grand Portage— "The Great Carrying Place"

If the enterprising but loosely federated traders who traveled the waterways of the great Northwest in pursuit of pelts and profits could have chosen a capital city for their wilderness kingdom, it most certainly would have been Grand Portage, the "great carrying place" on the extreme northeastern tip of Minnesota's Arrowhead. Even before the signing of the Declaration of Independence in "old" Philadelphia, a busy settlement replete with shops, French fashions, saloons, and even a police force had been established more than 1,000 miles away. By 1792 the flourishing fur trade demanded a center equal to its prosperity; a Great Hall, 16 log buildings, a stockade, fur press, and kitchen building gave Grand Portage an air of civilization at odds with its wild and rugged surrounding terrain. Beyond the immediate town complex were the camps of "porkeaters," as tenderfoot canoeists were called, and clusters of Indian wigwams. A canoe yard was built for the shelter and maintenance of more than 150 canoes, to which some 70 new craft were added each year.

On any given summer day, French voyageurs, the true fathers of the fur trade, could be seen swaggering about the streets of Grand Portage, on "vacation" after the long, cold months in the far north. It was French fishermen who originally started the practice of trading with Indians along the banks of Newfoundland and the mainland coast. Furs gathered by the French for sale in Europe soon became the cash crop of New France. When fur-bearing animals, particularly beaver, became scarce, the French traders searched westward. Blocked to the north by the British fur domain of the Hudson's Bay Company, the French traders were forced over a long water and land route from Montreal through the Ottawa River to Grand Portage—gateway to the untapped fur riches of the Northwest.

Under British auspices after 1763, the route over the Grand Portage was inherited by independent traders who founded the North West Company. Theirs was a fur-trade empire based primarily on the exportation of beaver fur to supply the particular whims of fashionable Europeans. Beaver pelts, from which the finest quality felt hats were made, were in tremendous demand.

In July the post at Grand Portage was the scene of the North West Company's annual rendezvous. Trading negotiations were usually completed by this time, after which there always followed a celebration attended by a motley crowd of factors, voyageurs, and Indians, some from many miles away. The generous opening banquet was followed by dancing in the mess hall, where, to the tune of flutes, violins, and bagpipes, and under the influence of many gallons of rum, the voyageurs and their Indian partners danced the night away. The festivities over, the trappers returned to the wilderness in their canoes, now freshly loaded with camp goods and trinkets for barter.

Today Grand Portage National Monument offers a re-creation of the 200-year-old buildings that comprised this key trading post. The Great Hall, scene of many business negotiations and equally heated social

occasions, has been reconstructed around the remains of the foundation and fireplace ruins discovered by archaeologists in 1937. Nearby is the company stockade, consisting of palisade, blockhouse, and gates, originally intended not so much for defense as for quieter quarters during the furious activity of the rendezvous. Reconstruction of the canoe warehouse followed excavation on the site in 1963–64. Its location outside the stockade probably indicates that it was built by an independent trader. Possibly it was owned by a competitor who later joined with the more powerful North West Company. Originally, trade goods or furs were stored here. Other buildings—a fur press, a nineteenth-century cabin, and the town kitchen—have also been re-created in the most authentic detail possible. *Grand Portage,* a brochure available free from the Grand Portage National Monument, Grand Portage 55605, describes the various buildings and local trails and offers a concise but fascinating history of the fur trade.

A short distance from the national monument, Grand Portage Trail winds through the woods to the site of Fort Charlotte, 8½ miles away on the Pigeon River. Fort Charlotte once served as a way station for furs arriving from the Northwest in transit to the stockade at Grand Portage. Voyageurs shouldered heavy packs of furs over this trail, completing the trip in about 2½ hours, a hiking time which today's visitor may find hard to match. The trail offers the same difficulties and challenges faced two centuries ago—mud, rocks, mosquitoes, and flies. A few earthen mounds and depressions mark the place of Fort Charlotte. A primitive campsite near the river offers overnight camping before the strenuous return trip to Grand Portage. Another nearby trail climbs Mount Rose knoll behind the stockade and affords splendid views of Lake Superior. Complete trail information on both routes is available free from the Grand Portage National Monument at the above address.

Deluxe vacation lodging and services are provided by the *Radisson Inn Grand Portage,* Grand Portage 55605 (phone toll-free for reservations: 800-228-9822).

Daily boat service from Grand Portage to Isle Royale National Park (see the "Michigan Map & Recreation Guide" section) is provided by *Grand Portage-Isle Royale Transportation Lines, Inc.,* 363–6 Lake Ave., South, Duluth 55802 (218–722–2609).

Grand Portage (including Grand Portage State Forest) is shown on the following large-scale U.S. Geological Survey maps: Farquhar Park, Grand Portage, Hovland, Marr Island, Mineral Center, Pigeon Point, Pine Lake E., South Fowl Lake, The Cascades, Tom Lake.

Gunflint—Arrowhead Trails & Lake Superior North Shore Scenic Drive

Beginning at Grand Marais on Lake Superior, the Gunflint Trail winds inland for 58 miles through the heavily forested terrain of the huge Superior National Forest. Originally used by Chippewa Indians as a winter trail, the route later became the main transportation link for travel into the vast forest and lakes area by explorers and trappers. Today, most of the road is well-paved and open to automobiles.

The trail passes through the magnificent stands of pine, spruce, balsam, birch, and aspen that cover the ancient Laurentian Highlands, the geologic reminder of the prehistoric chain of hills that once

covered a large area of Minnesota. Along much of the route, the famous chain of glacial lakes bordering the Boundary Waters Canoe Area offers excellent opportunities for camping, canoeing, and fishing for lake trout, brookies, walleyes, northerns, and bass. Near Poplar Lake, the trail crosses the Laurentian Divide, where the watershed divides, with water falling on the south side flowing into Lake Superior, and water falling on the north side traveling toward Hudson Bay. The route ends near the cold, clear waters of Saganaga Lake, named for a Chippewa term meaning "lake with many islands."

East of the Gunflint Trail, the 18-mile-long Arrowhead Trail pursues a parallel route through the wilderness of Grand Portage State Forest. Beginning at Hovland on Highway 61, the trail winds through dense spruce, balsam, birch, and pines and terminates at McFarland Lake, a short distance south of the Canadian border. Like the Gunflint trail, this paved road offers an introduction to the remote wilderness of Minnesota's Arrowhead Country: pine forests as far as the eye can see, and clear lakes and swift-flowing streams that hold smallmouth bass, walleye, steelhead, and salmon.

Two other scenic trails explore the wilds of Arrowhead country and lead to the famous Boundary Waters Canoe Area. The region's first major entrance to the BWCA, the 24-mile Sawbill Trail, begins near Tofte and runs parallel with the Temperance River for several miles. The route then crosses Parent Lake Road and ends at Sawbill Lake, a long L-shaped body of water studded with numerous small islands. Caribou Trail, beginning just north of Lutsen, winds its way into the interior of Arrow Tip region along many smaller lakes and rivers, ending at Brule Lake, the second major boundary lake for the BWCA.

The Lake Superior North Shore Scenic Drive passes through Grand Marais as it makes its way between Duluth and Thunder Bay in Ontario. The drive follows a hard-paved road near the edge of Lake Superior and passes through almost all towns along the lakeshore: Two Harbors, Castle Danger, Beaver Bay, Little Marais, Grand Marais, Hovland, and Grand Portage. Sprawling vistas of the lake are available from craggy cliffs all along the drive. North of Two Harbors, picnic and camping sites offer fine views of the cascading waters of Gooseberry Falls.

Highways—Recreation & Scenic Routes

The first roads in what is now Minnesota were trails of the American Indians, followed by wilderness routes forged by the voyageurs and fur traders—down from Hudson Bay and Fort Garry in the Red River Valley, from Pembina as far as Red Lake and Lake Traverse. Grand Portage, the most notable of these trails, still exists and retains the primitive and rough character of 200 years ago.

Today, the state boasts a vast network of roads and highways, including some spectacular scenic drives such as the North Shore Drive along the craggy cliffs bordering Lake Superior and the wilderness Gunflint and Arrowhead trails (see "Gunflint & Arrowhead Trails), paved roads open to automobiles leading through the rugged terrain of northeast Minnesota. These and other roads and highways are shown on the *Minnesota State Highway Map*, available free from the Minnesota Highway Dept., Administrative Services Section, State Highway Bldg., St. Paul 55165. The map shows all varieties of goods, including interstate highways, divided and undivided highways, gravel-surfaced roads, railroads, airports, towns and cities, parks, forests, rest areas, and historical sites.

Minnetours, an attractive booklet with many handsome photographs, describes 11 tours by automobile through every part of Minnesota, including the "voyageurs' empire," the Lake Superior region, and the

heartlands of the old Sioux Indian nation. Explicit directions and alternate routes are provided for each trip, along with information on accommodations, campgrounds, rest areas, picnic sites, restaurants, and other facilities along the route. Points of historical and natural interest are also described, with directions for finding the best "lookouts" and panoramic views. The booklet is available free from the State of Minnesota, Dept. of Economic Development, 480 Cedar St., St. Paul 55101.

International Falls Outfitting Center—Gateway to Rainy Lake & Voyageurs National Park

Called "lac de la pluie" by the French explorer La Vérendrye, who crossed its waters in 1732, Rainy Lake separates Voyageurs National Park in northern Minnesota from the province of Ontario. Colorful rock escarpments rich in mineral deposits and shorelines blanketed with dense evergreen forests have earned this body of water the more flattering title of "Queen of the Lakes." Measuring about 50 miles in length and from 3 to 15 miles in width, Rainy Lake features innumerable long arms and bays, giving it a total area of about 325 square miles. Over 1,600 evergreen-clad islands are scattered off shore, varying in size from small upthrusts of rock to areas of several square miles.

Rainy Lake offers some of North America's top smallmouth-bass, walleye, and northern-pike fishing. Excellent northern-pike fishing is also found in Black Bay, at the foot of Rainy Lake south of Island View. The whole Black Bay district east of International Falls offers a superlative landscape of great natural beauty; within a two-mile radius are dozens of densely wooded islands affording spectacular panoramas of the lake.

International Falls is located on Rainy River, two and a half miles west of Rainy Lake on the old Voyageur's Highway. A base for logging operations in the early 1900's, the town today is the major outfitting center and jumping off point for Rainy Lake and Voyageurs National Park. Fly-in charter fishing and hunting trips and canoe trip outfitting are provided by *Bohman Airways, Inc.*, the international seaplane base on Jackfish Bay of Rainy Lake (Island View Rt. B, Ranier 56668) and by *Einarson Bros. Flying Service*, Falls International Airport, Rogers Rt. 1, International Falls 56649. Cruises of Rainy Lake and Voyageurs National Park are provided by *Rainy Lake Cruises* (Box 303, Island View Rt., Ranier 56668) and *Viking Cruises* to Kettle Falls and Voyageurs National Park (Box 432, Island View Rt., International Falls 56649).

Vacation lodging and services on Rainy Lake are provided by *Camp Idlewood* (County Rd. 20, Island View Rt.), *Island View Lodge* (Island View Rt., Highway 11 E.), *Northernaire Floating Lodges* (County Rd. 94), *Rainy Lake Houseboats* (Thunderbird Rd., Highway 11 E., P.O. Box 408), and *SHA SHA Resort* (Highway 11 E., Black Bay, Island View Rt.)—all International Falls 56649. *Musket Inn* (P.O. Box 121, Ranier 56668) is located at Jackfish Island of Rainy Lake.

International Falls is reached via U.S. Highway 53 from Virginia and Duluth and via State Highway 11 from Warroad and the Lake of the Woods area.

Rainy Lake is shown on the full-color U.S. Geological Survey 1: 250,000-scale International Falls topographic overview map.

Lake Contour Fishing Maps

Contour maps of more than 3,500 lakes in Minnesota showing the

configuration of the shoreline, inlets and outlets, islands, depth contours, underwater bars, and drop-offs have been developed and drawn up by the state Fisheries Research Unit for careful studies of the life patterns of native fish. The finished map provides biologists with a picture of the lake basin as it would appear without water in it. Specialists use the maps as tools for determining the migration routes of fish, locating possible natural spawning sites, and calculating chemical treatments for control of water plants and fish removal. Because the physical features are so well delineated, the maps are of great value to fishermen, who can obtain them at a price of $1.50 for each lake, tax included, from the Documents Section, State of Minnesota, 140 Centennial Bldg., 658 Cedar St., St. Paul 55155. These maps are *not* intended for navigation, since hazards are not marked.

All lake maps are printed on sturdy, plastic-coated paper, and most are 17 by 22 inches in size; however, some maps vary from 8½ by 11 inches to 24 by 36 inches. Just about every minor and major lake imaginable has been mapped by the Fisheries Unit, including Inguadona, Tamarack, Swan, Leech, Winnibigoshish, Mud, Big Sandy, Gunflint, Seven Beaver, and many others. Special prices on lake-map sets are available for *Lake Pepin* (B–303), 4 sheets, $4.00; *Big Stone* (B–37), 4 sheets, $4.00; *Vermilion* (St. Louis County—B–272), 6 sheets, $6.00; the *Whitefish Chain* (Crow Wing County), 8 sheets, $8.00; the *St. Croix River* (B–289), 9 sheets, $9.00; *Kawishiwi River* (uncoated paper only), 18 sheets, $10.00. *Namakan Lake* in St. Louis County on the Canadian border has recently been sounded, and a plastic-coated, 3-by-7-foot map is now available for $10.00. This is the first time one of the larger border lakes has been completed in its entirety. It covers 24,000 acres and has 140 miles of shoreline in St. Louis County; maximum depth is 150 feet.

Maps should be ordered by name, county, and code number from the address above. The free *Index of Minnesota Lake Maps* is also available from the Documents Section and lists all maps and their code numbers alphabetically by county. Prepayment is required, and checks should be made payable to the State of Minnesota.

Lake of the Woods Fish & Game Region

With a lakeshore shared by both Canada and Minnesota, Lake of the Woods, in the remote northern wilderness, covers more than 200 square miles of surface and offers some of the finest fishing in the nation for smallmouth bass, northern pike, walleye, muskellunge, perch, and whitefish. Warroad, the only American port on Lake of the Woods, is the starting point for vacationers and anglers bound for this famous body of water studded with 14,000 islands and offering more miles of shoreline than any other lake on the North American continent.

Several lodges and resorts provide accommodations near the lakeshore, and charter boats are available for both fishing and excursions on the lake. *Nipped Bay Resort* (Williams 56686), open year round, offers cabins, boat ramps and rentals, guides, and winter fishing. The *Trail's Edge Lodge* (Baudette 56623), located on Lake of the Woods, has facilities for cross-country skiing, snowmobiling, and ice fishing as well as attractive rooms, a heated pool, boat rentals, and fishing excursions. Guided launch services are available at *Border View Lodge* (Box H, Baudette 56623), along with lodge rooms, cabins, and a dining room. Other accommodations and charter services are listed and described in the *Heartland* booklet mentioned under "Accommodations."

When the treaty that gave the United States her independence was signed in Paris in 1783, the Mississippi River was commonly believed to be west of Lake of the Woods. This geographical mistake gave the United States not only the southern shore of the lake, but also many islands and the Northwest Angle, the most northerly point of the forty-eight contiguous states. Entirely isolated from the mainland, the Angle offers true wilderness country with few roads and magnificent forests of spruce and pine. The area is rich in the history of explorers and fur traders. The famous French explorer and first man from the east to see the Rocky Mountains and the Sioux, La Vérendrye, founded Fort St. Charles on the Angle in 1732. Four years later, 21 Frenchmen—including La Vérendrye's son—perished in a surprise attack of Sioux Indians on what today is known as Massacre Island. Their bodies were brought back to the fort and buried under the chapel. A reconstruction of Fort St. Charles can be visited today by air charter.

Accessible only by air or water, a number of fine resorts are located on the Angle and on nearby Flag, Oak, and Penasse islands. The Chamber of Commerce, Box 34, Warroad 56763, will supply information on vacation, fishing, and moose and waterfowl hunting accommodations and outfitters in these and other Lake of the Woods areas.

All of the U.S. islands in the lake are magnificently forested with spruce and pine, in spite of their predominantly rocky composition. Cracked and broken rock surfaces here alternate with ankle-deep carpet moss and scrubby underbrush. Intricate designs are traced on craggy outcroppings by a gray-green lichen indigenous to the area; and rare flowering plants, saxifrage and fleabane, grow on rough ledges.

Seventeen miles southeast of Lake of the Woods is Baudette, billed as the "walleye capital of the world" and situated on the cold, deep waters of the Rainy River. The last seven miles of this river and its tributary streams form a weather-safe harbor for the 26 resorts along its banks, including *KOA Kampground* (Box 132H, Baudette 56623), offering a complete marina, heated pool, and nearby golf course; *Wigwam Resort* (Baudette 56623), with its cabins, hotel rooms, heated pool, and launching ramp; the *Sportsman's Lodge* (Baudette 56623), offering both cabins and motel rooms, boats, launches, and guides, an indoor pool, and saunas; and the *Red Carpet Lodge* (Baudette 56623), providing boats, motors, cabins, launch services, and guides. Boats by the hundreds use the Rainy River as a highway to such famous fishing areas as Morris Point, Four Mile Bay, Light House Gap, Wheeler Point, and Pine, Sable, and Curry islands. Almost 3,000 acres of wild land just west of Baudette on the south shore of Lake of the Woods are now being developed as Nipped Bay State Park, with primitive campsites now available. A 50-mile wilderness trail just south of Baudette offers visitors a chance to see deer, bear, grouse, moose, and other wildlife. Write the Chamber of Commerce in Baudette or Warroad for more information on accommodations and outfitters. While in the Lake of the Woods area, be prepared for lengthy bouts of daylight. Baudette boasts the longest vacation day in the U.S., with as many as 18 hours from sunrise to sundown.

The Baudette International Airport is an international (U.S.-Canada) point of entry with both land and seaplane facilities. An airport at Warroad offers three charter, seaplane, and fly-in services: *Carlson Flying Service, Hanson's,* and *Warroad;* write c/o Warroad Airport, Warroad 56763, for details.

Lake of the Woods is accessible via State Highway 11 from Rosseau, Roosevelt, and Williams; and via Minnesota 172 from Baudette. Lake of the Woods is shown on U.S. Geological Survey 1:250,000-scale map: Kenora.

North Country Wilderness Canoeing & Fishing Outfitters

The virtually limitless opportunities for outdoor adventure and wilderness travel within Minnesota have given rise to an equally staggering number of outfitters and expedition services, offering jaunts ranging from short canoe trips along a placid stretch of water to longer excursions where "roughing it" is the order of the day. Backpacking tours, camping trips, fishing expeditions, fly-in hunting and fishing trips, and other wilderness experiences are sponsored in Minnesota's far north, along with many excellent outfitting and equipment sources. Listed below are many of the more outstanding services offered in this incomparable wilderness of lakes, rivers, and virgin forests.

Bill Zup's Lac La Croix Outfitters, Crane Lake 55725 (winter: 611 E. Harvey St., Ely 55731), offers complete fly-in fishing and canoe outfitting services for the Lac La Croix area of the Quetico Wilderness. Write for free literature and Lac La Croix-Quetico maps.

Sawbill Canoe Outfitters, on Sawbill Lake near the end of Sawbill Trail, provides access to the entire Boundary Waters Canoe Area and complete or partial outfitting for canoe trips. Located next to a 50-unit U.S. Forest Service Campground, Sawbill Outfitters offers groceries, gasoline, a sauna and showers, and a laundry. For a free brochure and price list, write to Sawbill Canoe Outfitters, Tofte 55615.

Wild Places, Inc., Box 758, Ely 55731, has a lodge and base on secluded Jasper Lake and specializes in personalized service for families and individuals. Whether you envision a leisurely fishing and camping trip, or one designed to meet the challenge of remote areas, Wild Places will help you plan and pursue a trip tailor-made to meet your expectations. A recently developed program, called "Venture Out and In," offers 16-day wilderness sessions that introduce participants to outdoor skills such as wilderness and water safety, rock climbing, canoeing and navigation, portaging and camping, and just getting in touch with the surrounding terrain.

A unique outfitter offering personalized services for the beginning to advanced canoeist, backpacker, and bicyclist, *Bear Track Outfitting, Inc.*, near Grand Marais on Highway 61, also boasts the latest equipment and fine food. A wilderness canoe and backpacking camp for children is also sponsored. Write to Box 505, Mazomanie, WI 53560, for details.

Irv Funk Canoe Outfitters, located in the heart of the Crow Wing River Canoe Trail, maintains a fleet of 70 to 80 canoes and a complete line of camping equipment for expeditions along the Crow Wing River, varying in length from 1 to 8 days. Available May through October, canoe trips take advantage of numerous camping grounds in the area and the superb fishing on the river. Swimming, many hiking trails, and 90 miles of developed horseback trails are additional attractions. Brochures and information are available from Route 2, Box 51, Sebeka 56477.

Wilderness Outfitters, in Ely, based on Basswood Lake, offers canoe expeditions and fly-in fishing trips to remote cabins on Lac des Mille Lacs in Canada. Basswood Lake itself also provides excellent fishing for lake trout, northern pike, walleyes, and small- and largemouth bass; Wilderness Outfitters provides guides, equipment, and tent-cabins. An efficient launch service to all points on the lake via Fall Lake and the Four Mile Portage is also available. Write to 1 East Camp Street, Ely 55731, for additional details.

Also located in Ely, *Carlson's Quetico-Superior Outfitters*, P.O. Box 89, Ely 55731, has been outfitting canoeists from their strategic base on Moose Lake for 26 years. Carlson's services are devoted entirely to outfitting canoe parties, providing fine guides, equipment, and personal gear. Trips are customized to fit your itinerary and the number of people in your party. Write to the above address for free brochures and maps.

Another outfitter based on Moose Lake, *Canadian Border Outfitters*, offers trips that follow the time-honored routes of the Indians and voyageurs. Outfitting facilities, motel and bunkhouse accommodations, saunas, a boat-launching ramp, towboat and float-plane services are all located at the lakeshore base. Other activities include wilderness fly-in trips, combination hunting-fishing trips, and boat camping. Brochures describing rates and services are available from Box 117, Ely 55731.

Jocko's Canoe Outfitters on the Gunflint Trail in Grand Marais, sponsors canoe-camping and fishing trips to remote lakes in or near the BWCA. Complete outfitting, expert advice, and seasoned guides will all help you plan personalized trips. Lodge accommodations and a bunkhouse are also available. Write to Jocko's Clearwater Canoe Outfitters, Box 31, Grand Marais 55604, for information.

Located in downtown Grand Marais, *Grand Marais Northwoods Outfitters* is excursion-trip headquarters for escorted nature hikes and canoe trips of up to a week's length. Canoe rentals and north-woods supplies are also offered. For information, contact B. Kerfoot, Box 100, Grand Marais 55604.

The only outfitter on beautiful East Bearskin Lake, *Bearskin Canoe Outfitters*, offers direct access to the BWCA through the long, narrow, all-weather lakes in the vicinity. A small family outfitter in a relatively uncrowded area, Bearskin discourages large parties but especially welcomes beginners and families. Brochures and further details can be obtained by writing to Bearskin Canoe Outfitters, Box A, Grand Marais 55604.

Duane's Canoe Outfitters in Babbitt is a complete service for canoe excursions on the Boundary Waters, boat fishing trips, fly-in canoe trips, and partial equipment rentals. Experts will help you plan and map individualized routes. A bunkhouse, showers, and sauna will welcome you back to civilization after your journey through the wilderness. Write to Highway 21, Babbitt, 55706, for brochures and rates.

Tuscarora Canoe Outfitters, located 50 miles up the Gunflint Trail on the edge of the BWCA, is strategically situated near the "paddle zone" and provides access to the Boundary Waters Canoe area and Canada's Quetico Park. Private bases are located on Round and Saganaga lakes. Modern overnight lodge accommodations and a free bunkhouse and shower facilities are additional attractions. For further information, write to Box C, Grand Marais 55604.

Tailored trips are also a specialty of *Bill Rom's Canoe Country Outfitters*, in Ely. Fly-in fishing trips, motel accommodations, and fine campsites are additional attractions. The Moose Lake landing is only a brief paddle from the Canadian ranger and customs stations and is one of the best starting points for American or Canadian trips. Brochures and rates are available from 629 E. Sheridan St., Ely 55731.

Headquarters for *Moose Lake Wilderness Canoe Trips* are located on the shores of Moose Lake, 20 miles northeast of Ely and 5 miles by water from the Canadian border. From this strategic point, completely outfitted canoe and wilderness fishing trips are planned and launched. They specialize in ultralightweight canoe outfitting and offer fly-in canoe trips, fishing expeditions, guide services, and overnight accommodations. Write to Box 358, Ely 55731, for brochures and rate schedules.

Situated on Saganaga Lake at the end of Sea Gull River, and easily accessible from the Gunflint Trail, *Blankenburg's Canoe Outfitters* offer lightweight canoes, up-to-date equipment, expert instruction for beginners, and personalized service to all. For details, write to R. Blankenburg, Grand Marais 55604.

The original canoe outfitter in the Quetico Area, *Canadian-Quetico Outfitters*, in Ontario, sponsors expeditions through Quetico Park and the surrounding network of waterways, including Pickerel, Crooked Pine, Mercutio, and Marmion lakes. The new Quetico airport is only 2½ miles from the base camp, which offers lodge accommodations and complete outfitting services for wilderness fishing excursions. A cabin outpost on Elbow Lake, fly-in hunting and fishing trips, and numerous hiking trails through the nearby park are additional attractions. Brochures and further details are available from P.O. Box 910, Atikokan, Ontario, Canada.

Chik-Wauk Canoe Outfitters, on Big Saganaga Lake, provides easy access to the BWCA and Quetico Provincial Park and complete or partial outfitting for any expedition. Overnight accommodations are offered in the bunkhouse or adjoining lodge. A tow service is also available across the lake. Write to R. Griffis, Box 170, Grand Marais 55604, for information.

Situated on a point of land jutting into the BWCA boundary, *Northpoint Outfitters* is surrounded by water to either side, with the Seagull River on the west and an arm of Lake Saganaga on the east. The Gunflint Trail leads practically to their doorstep. Complete outfitting and customized expeditions on the Boundary Waters and through Quetico Park are offered. Expert guides and advice, fly-in trips, and the requisite licenses and permits are all offered at their headquarters. Detailed booklets and maps can be obtained free by writing to Box 427, Grand Marais 55604.

Friendly, courteous service with expert advice on camping, canoeing, fishing locations, scenery, and wildlife are the specialties of *Tip of the Trail Outfitters*. Overnight accommodations, fly-in and tow services, and boat-camping are offered. For a free brochure and further information, write: Box 7, Gunflint Trail, Grand Marais 55604.

Backed by 13 years of service, *Canadian Waters, Inc.*, based in Ely, offers free transport to 5 put-in points, guides, and package canoe and boat fishing trips. Special air charter package trips from Chicago are also offered. Organized groups will be especially interested in this outfitter. For rate schedules, a trip-planning kit, and descriptive material, write to 111 E. Sheridan St., Ely 55731.

Nor' Wester Lodge & Canoe Outfitters are located at Poplar Lake on the Gunflint Trail in the Superior National Forest near the Canadian border. For details, write to lodge at Grand Marais 55604.

Border Lakes Outfitters, in Winton, offers complete and partial outfitting for canoe trips into the heart of the Quetico-Superior wilderness. Fishing and canoeing excursions are planned from their jump-off point on lovely Fall Lake. For additional information, write to P.O. Box 158, Winton 55796.

The Superior-Boundary Waters wilderness is also served by the long-established *Gunflint Northwoods Outfitters*, Box 100, Grand Marais 55604, located on the Gunflint Trail and offering complete canoe-fishing outfitting services, including guided backpacking trips along the primitive Kekakabic Trail in Superior National Forest and on Isle Royale National Park.

Crane Lake Outfitters, Box 74, Crane Lake 55725, provides complete outfitting services at Crane Lake, with guides and wilderness fly-in service and pickup at Hibbing, Orr, and Duluth.

Vermilion Canoe Outfitters, Star Route, Box 144, Tower 55790, serves the Boundary Waters Canoe Country with complete outfitting service, guides, and canoe rentals.

For free literature and information about Bill Pucel's *Boundary Waters Canoe Outfitters*, write: Box 447, Ely 55731.

Portage Canoe Outfitters, Box 126, Grand Marais 55604, is located 55 miles northwest of Grand Marais on Seagull Lake, offering quality lightweight canoes and gear at reasonable rates.

Saganaga Outfitters, Box 148, Grand Marais 55604, is located one mile beyond the tip of the Gunflint Trail and offers wilderness canoe trips in the Boundary Waters Canoe Area and Canada.

Northern Wilderness Outfitters Ltd., Box 98, Ranier 56668, offers deluxe fly-in fishing trips to northern Ontario for trophy walleye, brook and lake trout, and northern pike.

The *Pipestone Outfitting Co.*, P.O. Box 780, Ely 55731, located on Fall Lake, a major gateway to the Boundary Waters Canoe Area, provides complete outfitting and custom trip service.

Wilderness Waters Outfitters, Box 398, Grand Marais 55604, provides guided trips and outfitting for the Arrowhead Country of Superior National Forest. Write for their free 32-page wilderness canoe trip informative booklet.

In Crow Wing River country, *Huntersville Outfitters* sponsors canoe and camping trips, horseback riding, and snowmobiling. Nearby are Menahga, Wadena, Sunnybrook, and Sebaka parks. A recently added attraction is the five-day horseback-riding and camping package. Write to R.R. 4, Menahga 56464, for further details.

Ski Touring Trails & Centers

Once the winter season begins, around Thanksgiving, Minnesota offers four solid months of prime snow-sport weather: downhill and cross-country skiing, snowshoeing, and snowmobiling can all be enjoyed on the many slopes and in the vast open areas throughout the state. Overnight ski trips can be planned around campgrounds at Eagle Mountain, Golden Gate to Fun, Quadna Mountain, and Spirit Mountain. Cross-country skiers looking for winter campsites will find both primitive and modern camping areas right near the trail in many parts of the state, and those who are always scouting for new cross-country trails will appreciate the recent expansion of ski touring areas. The introduction and popularity of Nordic skiing has resulted in a corresponding expansion of facilities to meet the increased demand. In addition, many resorts prohibit snowmobiling to ensure quiet, uninterrupted exploration of Minnesota's outdoors.

A source book to cross-country and major downhill skiing areas in the state, *Guide to Skiing in Minnesota,* provides lists of lodges, campgrounds, forests, and resorts. Some of the cross-country and downhill areas covered include Wolf Lake Resort, George Washington State Forest, McCarthy Beach State Park, Cannon River Wilderness Area, Cedar Hills, Eagle Mountain, Sugar Hills, and Mount Itasca. Maps showing locations for the various facilities are provided in the 18-page booklet, and each listing offers all information relevant to ski touring or downhill areas. *Guide to Skiing in Minnesota* is available free from the Publicity and Promotion Division, Dept. of Economic Development, 480 Cedar St., St. Paul 55101.

State park maps showing old logging roads, trails, campsites, and major ski trails for the outstanding cross-country ski areas, including *Remote Lake Solitude Area, St. Croix State Park, Savanna Portage State Park,* and the *Lake Itasca Wilderness Area,* are available free from the Division of Parks & Recreation, 320 Centennial Bldg., St. Paul 55155.

Two nationally renowned ski touring centers in Northern Minnesota offer vacation package plans, lodging, maintained trails, instruction and guide service: *Lutsen Resort* (Lutsen 55612; phone: 218-663-7212) is located in the Poplar River Valley with access to Superior National Forest trails; the beautiful *Radisson Inn Grand Portage* (Box 307, Grand Portage 55605; phone: 218-475-2401) offers a 50-mile trail system and tours of the historic Grand Portage Trail—the old voyageur route from the shores of Lake Superior to the Pigeon River Cascades.

Lynx Track Winter Travel, a nonprofit educational organization, offers seminars in all forms of winter travel in the northern forest wilderness —including dog-sledding, cross-country skiing, snowshoeing, winter camping, maps and compass use, igloo building, ice safety, first aid, fire, survival techniques, stargazing, and winter nature lore. The seminars include all meals and sleeping-bag accommodations at their base camp north of Ely near the Boundary Waters Canoe Area in heated arctic tents and Indian tepees. Advanced courses include a 9-day crossing of the Boundary Waters Canoe Area via cross-country skiis,

snowshoes, and dog sled, and a ski-touring expedition in Wyoming's Cloud Peak Wilderness in the Bighorn Mountains. For rates and free literature, write: 5375 Eureka Rd., Excelsior 55331, phone (612) 474-5190.

State Forest Reserve Maps

Minnesota's forest cover varies from region to region. In the upper north and east are the great coniferous forests of white, jack, and red or Norway pine, mixed with stands of white spruce and balsam fir at the higher altitudes. The only deciduous tree to grow abundantly side by side with the evergreens is the white birch; however, aspen and poplar, black and mountain ash, red maple, pine cherry, and yellow birch are also scattered throughout the area. The northern reaches of the state also contain many swamp areas, fertile terrain for black spruce, Tamarack and white cedar. Smaller shrubs in the northern forests include wintergreen, dwarf kalmia, sweetfern, elder, dwarf birch, and many varieties of honeysuckle, and blueberries and cranberries.

Minnesota's scenic state forest lands and wildlife-management areas, provide excellent canoe-camping, hiking, fishing, and hunting in season for whitetail deer, black bear, upland game birds, and waterfowl. The following U.S. Geological Survey large-scale topographic maps show Minnesota's major wildlife-management areas and state forests. The maps show each area's major natural and manmade features, including logging roads, lakes and streams, swamplands, falls and rapids, campgrounds, and trails. *Rosseau River Wildlife Area:* Caribou, Caribou NE, Badger NW, Badger NE, Pinecreek; *Thief Lake Wildlife Area:* Thief Lake SE, Thief Lake NE, Wannaska SW, Wannaska, Skime; *Beltrami Island State Forest & Red Lake Wildlife Management Area:* Roseau and Bemidji 1:250,000-scale maps; *Pine Island & Koockicking State Forests:* Roseau, International Falls, and Hibbing 1:250,000-scale maps; *Kabetogama State Forest,* including Pelican and Vermilion lakes and the Ash, Black Duck, Vermilion, and Pelican rivers: International Falls and Hibbing; *Smoky Bear State Forest:* Devlin, Pelland, Little Fork NW, Little Fork; *George Washington State Forest:* Hibbing 1:250,000-scale map; *Grand Portage State Forest:* Grand Portage, Mineral Center, The Cascades, Hovland, Farquhar Peak, South Fowl Lake; *Finland State Forest:* Finland, Little Marais, Cramer; *Cloquet Valley State Forest:* Two Harbors 1:250,000-scale map; *Fond du Lac State Forest:* Cromwell, Sawyer, Iverson; *Savanna State Forest,* including the Savanna Portage & Big

Sandy Lake: Minnewawa, Tamarack, Wright, Libby, Balsam, Little Prairie Lake, Vanduse Lake, Island; *Hill River State Forest & Moose-Willow Wildlife Area:* White Elk Lake, Swatara, Hill City, Bain, Rabey, Sanders Lake, Ball Bluff, Libby; *Land o' Lakes State Forest:* Thunder Lake, Remer, Shingle Mill Lake, Shovel Lake, Edna Lake, Roosevelt Lake; *Crow Wing State Forest:* Lower Whitefish Lake, Cross Lake, Pelican Lake, Trommald; *Mississippi Headwaters State Forest:* Wilton, Alida, Grant Lake, La Salle Lake, Lake Itasca, Anchor Hill; *Mud-Goose Wildlife Area:* Goose Lake, Bay River, Nushka Lake, Ball Club; *Foothills State Forest:* Hackensack, Backus, Bungo Creek, Spider Lake; *Northwest Angle State Forest:* Angle Inlet, Angle Inlet SW, Buffalo Bay NW, Buffalo Bay, Flag Island, Garden Island West; *White Earth State Forest:* Ebro, Ebro NW, North Twin Lake, Beaulieu, Tulaby Lake, Long Lost Lake, Big Rush Lake, Many Point Lake; *Mille Lacs Wildlife Area & Rum River State Forest:* Wahkon South, Isle SW, Ann Lake, Milaca Lake, Page; *St. Croix & Nemadji State Forests:* Danbury, Webster, Holyoke; *Salana State Forest:* Solana, Split Rock Lake, Thor NE, Thor SW; *Chengwatana State Forest:* Grantsburg, Pine City; *Whitewater Wildlife Area:* Cochrane, Plainview; *Memorial Hardwood State Forest:* St. Paul, Eau Claire, Mason City, and La Crosse 1:250,000-scale maps.

Superior-Quetico Maps & Charts

Maps compiled, lithographed, and published by the W. A. Fisher Company are designed as aids for those who travel the waters in northern Minnesota and southern Ontario. All maps of the border waters show shorelines, lakes, streams, rivers, BWCA motor and snowmobile routes, roads, highways, and other features, and may be ordered at the prices quoted below from the W. A. Fisher Co., Box 1107, Virginia 55792. Be sure to indicate code numbers and titles when ordering, and request a free chart index.

The basic Superior-Quetico map series (size 17 by 22 inches, scale ⅝ inch to 1 mile, waterproof) includes fifteen maps, numbered 101 to 115. The Minnesota-Canadian border country between Grand Portage on Lake Superior and International Falls on Rainy Lake is mapped in detail. All of the Canadian Quetico Park, Boundary Waters Canoe Area, and most of Minnesota's Superior National Forest are covered. Campsites and portages are updated annually. These maps are specifically designed for the fisherman and canoeist. An index chart illustrating the 15 maps and the area they cover is available on request. Maps are priced at 50¢ each.

All 15 maps in the Superior-Quetico series have been combined in book form (17 by 22 inches, printed on regular paper). Also included is a historical map of the entire area. The *Superior-Quetico Map Book* costs $4.00 plus postage.

Enlarged Superior-Quetico maps (22 by 34 inches, scale 1¼ inches to 1 mile, waterproof), which are similar in nature to the regular maps, place greater emphasis on detail, such as incorporation of some reef markers, water levels, campsites, BWCA boundaries, motor routes, etc. The following maps are available in these editions: E–1 *Crane, Sandpoint, Namakan;* E–2 *Lac La Croix;* E–3 *Crooked, Basswood, Agnes;* E–4 *Saganaga, Saganagons, Seagull;* E–5 *Brule, Alice, Sawbill;* E–19 *Winchell, Arrow, Fowl lakes* (slightly smaller scale); E–20 *Namakan.* The above maps are priced at $1.00 each.

Enlarged maps of both *Saganaga Lake* (E–6) and *Northern Lights Lake* (E–7) are 17 by 22 inches, at a scale of 1½ inches to 1 mile, and show most of the islands and landmarks. They are waterproof and cost 50¢ each. The *Seagull Lake Hydrographic Map* (E–8, 17 by 22 inches, scale 3½ inches to 1 mile, waterproof) is similarly enlarged and designed for maximum detail, showing the lake-bottom contour at

depth intervals of 10 feet. Price is also 50¢ each. Enlarged maps are also available for *Kabetogama Lake* (E–9) and *Namakan Lake* (E–10), 17 by 22 inches, at a scale of 1 inch to 1 mile, priced at 50¢ each.

The *Rainy Lake Boaters Map* (E–11, 22 ½ by 35 inches, scale ⅝ inch to 1 mile, waterproof) is priced at $1.00 and shows all of the lake, with special attention to accuracy of shoreline detail. The *Pelican Lake Hydrographic Map* (E–12, 17 by 22 inches, scale 2½ inches to 1 mile, waterproof) shows bottom contours, landmarks, islands, and reefs, and is priced at 50¢. Divided into its east and west sections, the *Lake Vermilion Hydrographic Map* (East E–13, West E–14, 22 by 33⅝ inches, scale 2⅛ inches to 1 mile, waterproof) shows the lake bottom contour, reefs and buoy information. The two maps overlap and cost $1.00 each.

A comprehensive map of the area within, and of the surrounding Boundary Waters Canoe Area, the *Minnesota-Canadian Wilderness Area Map* (E–15, 22 by 34 inches, scale 1 inch to 3 miles, waterproof) shows the region from Crane Lake on the west to Gunflint Lake on the east. Also designated are the Superior National Forest, Quetico Provincial Park, BWCA, and international boundaries. Outboard-motor and snowmobile routes within the BWCA are also shown. Maps cost $1.00 each.

The *Trout Lake Hydrographic Map* (E–16, 17 by 22 inches, scale 2 ⅛ inches to 1 mile, waterproof) is priced at 50¢ each and shows Trout and surrounding lakes. Lake-bottom contours are shown at depth intervals of 20 feet. The adjacent portion of Lake Vermilion and connecting motorized portage are also indicated. *Kabetogama Lake Hydrographic Maps* (E–17, 22 by 34 inches, scale 2⅛ inches to 1 mile, waterproof) shows coast-guard buoys, reefs, shallows, and lake-bottom contours at intervals of 10 feet. Maps cost $1.00 each. Enlarged hydrographic maps are also available for *Leech Lake* (E–18, 22½ by 29¼ inches, scale 1 1/6 inches to 1 mile, waterproof) and for *Lake Winnibigoshish* (E–21, 22½ by 35 inches, scale 1¼ inches to 1 mile, waterproof) showing contour intervals at five feet, reefs, buoys, and shallows. Each hydrographic map is priced at $1.00 each.

The Fisher Map of *Southwestern Ontario* (R–2, 22 by 27¼ inches, scale ¼ inch to 1 mile, waterproof) also costs $1.00 and shows Rainy Lake, the western portion of Lake of the Woods, and the area east of Lake of the Woods, spanning a distance of about 125 miles. The map is of interest primarily to those traveling north and east of International Falls, Minnesota, and south and east of Kenora, Ontario, Canada.

A small map is also available of the *Orr Region* (R–3, 11 by 17 inches, scale ⅜ inch to 1 mile, waterproof), including Pelican Lake and the area to the immediate north and west, at a price of 35¢ each. The *Ely Area Map* (R–4, 17 by 22 inches, scale ¼ inch to 1 mile, regular paper) shows lakes in the Superior-Quetico region from Atikokan on the north to Babbitt on the south and is also priced at 35¢. A similar edition of the *Gunflint Trail Area* (R–5) at the same scale, size, and price shows lakes in the Superior-Quetico region from Basswood Lake on the west to Whitefish Lake on the east. Maps are also available for the *Western Entry to the Canoe Country* (R–6, 17 by 22 inches, scale 1 inch to 3 miles, regular paper) at a price of $.50 each, indicating the Minnesota-Canadian border lakes accessible from Crane Lake, including Lac La Croix, Beaverhouse, Basswood, and Crooked lakes.

W. A. Fisher also publishes a special map of the *Old Voyageurs Highway* (C–1, 19 by 24 inches, embossed-finish paper), colorfully decorated with sketches and historical information, showing the country from Grand Portage on Lake Superior to Rainy Lake. The Voyageurs maps cost 50¢ each.

Chippewa National Forest & The Mississippi Headwaters

Chippewa National Forest Topo Maps
U.S. Geological Survey Overview Maps, scale 1:250,000: Bemidji, Brainerd, Duluth, Hibbing.

Cass Lake Trophy Fishing Waters
U.S. Geological Survey large-scale maps: Pike Bay, Cass Lake, Pennington.

Lake Winnibigoshish Trophy Fishing Waters
Large-scale U.S. Geological Survey maps: Raven Lake, Portage Lake, Bena, Dixson Lake, Pigeon Dam Lake, Max, Little Winnibigoshish Lake.

Red Lake Indian Reservation & Canoe Country
U.S. Geological Survey Overview Maps, scale 1:250,000: Roseau and Bemidji.

Leech Lake & the Inguadona Canoe Route
Large-scale U.S. Geological Survey maps: Sucker Lakes, Portage Lake, Bena, Sugar Point, Federal Dam, Bay River, Tobique, Laura Lake, Thunder Lake, Whipholt, Jack Lake, Walker, Steamboat Bay.

Mississippi Headwaters & Lake Itasca
Large-scale U.S. Geological Survey maps: Lake Itasca, La Salle Lake, Alida, Grant Lake, Bemidji West, Bemidji East, Cass Lake, Pennington, Raven Lake.

Located in north-central Wisconsin, the Chippewa National Forest covers 640,000 acres of mixed hardwood and conifer forests, swamps, sparkling lakes, and meandering wilderness streams. The Mississippi River, the "father of waters," little more than a country stream at its Lake Itasca headwaters, enters the forest on the western boundary at Andrusia Lake. It sweeps past the end of Star Island in Cass Lake, through Knulson Dam, where seasonal boat passage is provided, winds into Lake Winnibigoshish—the fifth-largest body of water in Minnesota—then travels southeast across the forest on its long journey to the Gulf of Mexico. The river's waters are swollen by Leech Lake River and by other major rivers in the watershed: Steamboat, Turtle, Pigeon, Boy, Bear, Shingobee, and others.

The many tongue-twisting and exotic names given to the major forest landmarks—Winnibigoshish (locally shortened to "Winnie"), Inguadona, Shingobee, Ah-gwah-ching, Wabana—are reminders of this area's early inhabitants, the Chippewa Indians, properly called the Ojibway. The tribe was named for its moccasins, since Ojibway literally means "gathering" and describes the leather footgear gathered over toe and instep worn by these people. One of the largest Algonquian tribes north of Mexico, the Chippewa lived in loosely federated villages across the north-central Midwest. They lived off the land, harvesting planted crops, hunting, gathering wild rice, and intermittently making war on their neighbors, the Sioux and Fox Indians. From the outset, they depended on the intricate travel routes provided by inland waterways, and they learned to navigate the huge network of lakes and rivers—eventually guiding the trappers and explorers who first discovered the area's rich beaver lands and mighty forests in the mid-seventeenth century. The introduction of firearms a short time later gave the Chippewa temporary sway over rival tribes, but by 1832 the discovery of the Mississippi's source attracted increasing numbers of white men. The influx of fur traders, trappers, lumbermen, and settlers brought many changes to the wilderness, most of them detrimental to the forest's primeval glory. The loggers who came to Min-

MINNESOTA TRAVEL & RECREATION GUIDE

nesota, romanticized in the folklore of Paul Bunyan, came from the East, where a growing nation's demand for timber had all but exhausted the land. Pressure from conservationists gradually persuaded a sympathetic government of the need for protection of forest lands, and in 1908 President Theodore Roosevelt proclaimed this area the Minnesota National Forest. Lands were purchased from the Chippewa Indians; the region's name was changed in 1928 to honor the original rulers of the forest.

Today many areas of the forest offer a wilderness experience as rugged and unspoiled as that encountered by the Indians and first white men. Canoe tours explore the same waters braved by trappers in search of a fortune in furs. While the Mississippi remains a favorite route for canoeists, other rivers with rich historical pasts are becoming equally popular. The Turtle River, for instance, was first navigated by followers of La Salle in vain pursuit of the elusive Northwest Passage. The

The Turtle River Canoe Tour
CHIPPEWA NATIONAL FOREST

The Inguadona Canoe Tour
CHIPPEWA NATIONAL FOREST

Turtle River Canoe Tour, a free brochure/map published by the Forest Service, describes the river's course from Lake Julia through Turtle and Three Island lakes into Turtle River Lake, where it enters Chippewa National Forest and finally Cass Lake. Sights along the way include blue herons, wild-rice beds, remains of an old splash dam and sawmill, and the site of an American Fur Company post operative around 1820. The map shows access points, stopover areas, resorts, and points of interest; its reverse side explains the tour and offers a brief history of the area. Write the Forest Supervisor, Chippewa National Forest, Cass Lake 56633, for a free copy.

A similar brochure/map for the *Rice River Canoe Tour*, also available free from the above office, describes the river route from Clubhouse Lake in the forest's northeastern corner through East, Slauson, and Cameron lakes to the terminus at Big Fork, a total length of 18 miles. The tour covers clear, usually tranquil waters as they wind through the forest and past the remains of old logging camps, the homestead of an early settler and a farm reputedly taken over by a small population of skunks.

The *Inguadona Canoe Tour* offers a map and directions for the canoe trail from Lower Trelipe Lake southeast of Leech Lake through Inguadona Lake along the Boy River to a terminus some 20 miles north. A generally easy route, with one stretch of fast-moving water, the tour explores an early "highway" of the fur trade called "Equademog," meaning edge of a slope, by the Chippewa who paddled these waters

in canoes laden with pelts. The name eventually metamorphosed into Inguadona, perhaps because it was found more manageable by French and English tongues. Points of interest along the way include the site of an early Chippewa village, nests of native bald eagles, and the extensive beds of wild rice in the area. Also available free from the Forest Supervisor, the brochure/map shows and describes the route, including access points, resorts, stopover areas, rapids, and other information helpful to the canoeist.

In addition to the innumerable streams and rivers in Chippewa National Forest, there are 499 major lakes, of which the most popular, at least with fishermen, are probably Winnie, Leech, and Cass. The two latter have gained national reputations as muskie lakes and offer excellent northern pike and walleye fishing as well. Most of the lakes in the forest are ideal for boating and are generally fine for canoeing, although squalls can develop quickly on the large lakes, and it is always best to skirt the shoreline. The remote unspoiled wilderness areas of Upper and Lower Red Lake—the state's largest body of water—located to the north in the Red Lake Indian Reservation, and the meandering Red Lake River, provide outstanding canoeing and fishing opportunities.

Many species of wildlife inhabit the forest, including the rare and majestic bald eagle. Of the estimated 600 breeding pairs in the United States today, Chippewa National Forest supports about one-sixth of the population of our endangered national emblem. Most readily sighted between March 15 and November 30, the bald eagle is distinguished from vultures and osprey of the area by its magnificent flat wings spreading over seven feet. Huge nest structures, sometimes measuring ten feet in diameter, are easily spotted in tall pine trees along the lakeshores. The *Bald Eagle in the Chippewa National Forest*, a 6-page brochure summarizing the life patterns and habits of this regal bird, is available free from the Forest Supervisor, Chippewa National Forest, Cass Lake 56633.

Other winged residents of the forest include the Canada goose, mallard, loon, goldeneye, teal, and many other waterfowl and songbirds. White-tailed deer, bear, moose, gophers, otter, mink, bobcats, and others roam the open lands, swamps and forests of birch and pine. While the most common species of trees include Norway and jack pines, aspen and spruce, the various swamplands offer certain seldom-seen varieties: black spruce, northern white cedar, and tamarack. The Avenue of Pines, a scenic drive along State Highway 46, offers a fine introduction to the different pine trees of the forest, including 100-year-old red pines.

Over forty recreation sites on the Chippewa offer camping facilities, trails, boat ramps, picnic grounds, and other opportunities for outdoor activities. The *Chippewa National Forest Map* (50¢) lists and locates these facilities and shows lakes, rivers, highways, trails, roads, canoe routes, and boat-launching sites as well. Also included are descriptions of the forest's history and many points of interest. Maps and other free information are available from the Forest Supervisor, Chippewa National Forest, Cass Lake 56633 or from any of the District Rangers at Bena, Blackduck, Cut Foot Sioux, Marcell, Remer, and Walker. For additional accommodations and descriptions, consult the *Heartland Country* booklet described under "Accomodations."

Canoeing and backpacking trip service and outfitting in the Mississippi Headwaters Canoe Country is provided by *Papoose Outfitters Canoeing & Backpacking*, Niava Star Rt., Park Rapids 56470; phone 218-732-3065.

Vacation lodges, resorts, and trophy fishing camps in the Leech Lake area include *Chase on the Lake Lodge*, Walker 56484; *Big Rock*

Resort, Walker 56484; *Sugar Point Resort,* Federal Dam 56641; *Leech Lake Lodge,* Walker 56484; *Walker Bay Resort,* Walker 56484; *Shelter Cove Resort,* Walker 56484. Lodges and resorts in the Cass Lake area include *Wolfview Resort* (Big Wolf Lake), Cass Lake 56633; *Cass Lake Lodge,* Cass Lake 56633; *The Birchmont Resort* (Lake Bemidji), Bemidji 56601; *McArdle's on Lake Winnibigoshish,* Bena 56626; *Northland Lodge* (Lake Winnibigoshish), Deer River 56636; *Nodak Lodge* (Lake Winnibigoshish), Bena 56626; *Little Itasca Resort* (Deer Lake), Deer River 56636; *Finn'n Feather Resort* (Lake Andrusia), Bemidji 56601; *Isle O'Pines Resort* (Big Wolf Lake), Bemidji 56601.

Access & Outfitting Centers

Chippewa National Forest is easily reached via State Highway 46 from Deer River and Grand Rapids east of the forest. Cass Lake, another major outfitting and supply center, provides access to the forest at its western boundary. Other towns within and near the area include Walker, Blackduck, Bigfork, and Northome.

Superior National Forest & Boundary Waters Canoe Area

Superior National Forest & Boundary Waters Canoe Area Topo Maps

U.S. Geological Survey Overview Maps, 1:250,000 scale: Hibbing, International Falls, Quetico, and Two Harbors.

Basswood Lake Area

Including Sarah, Knife, Ensign, Newfound, Kekekabic, Wind, and Snowbank lakes, shown on large-scale U.S. Geological Survey Maps: Basswood Lake, Ensign Lake, Kekekabic Lake, and Dutton Lake.

Crane Lake Area

U.S. Geological Survey large-scale maps: Crane Lake, Johnson Lake, Echo Lake, Kabustasa Lake.

Ely Area

U.S. Geological Survey large-scale maps: Crab Lake, Ely, Eagles Nest, Bear Island, Angleworm Lake, Fourtown Lake, Kangas Bay, Gabbro Lake.

Gunflint Trail Area

U.S. Geological Survey large-scale maps showing the entire length of the trail and surrounding wilderness, including the Brule River and Saganaga, Poplar, Trout, and Bearskin lakes: Conners Island, Long Island Lake, Gunflint Lake, South Lake, Hungry Jack Lake, Crocodile Lake, Northern Light Lake, Pine Mountain, Grand Marais.

Lac La Croix Trophy Fishing Waters

Includes U.S. portion and Agnes, Iron, and Crooked lakes, U.S. Geological Survey large-scale maps: Snow Bay, Takucmich Lake, Coleman Island, Lake Agnes, Iron Lake, Friday Bay.

Pigeon River & The Cascades

Includes North and South Fowl lakes headwaters, U.S. Geological Survey large-scale maps: South Fowl Lake, The Cascades, Grand Portage, Pigeon Point.

Encompassing the famous Boundary Waters Canoe Area and most of Minnesota's Arrowhead Country, the 3-million acre Superior National Forest contains 2,000 portage-linked lakes and streams, dense evergreen forests, muskeg, islands, stark outcroppings of weathered granite, and the ancient Nesabi and Vermilion mountain ranges. The

forest straddles the southern extension of the vast Canadian Shield, a 2½-billion-year-old granite intrusion that covers a total area in excess of two million square miles. Great glaciers stretched across the area three times during the Ice Age, carving countless valleys and ridges, and leaving over 5,000 lakes, ranging in size from a few acres to 70 square miles, in their wake. For hundreds of years Indians paddled the quiet waters and braved the treacherous river rapids between the shores of Lake Superior and the international boundary. Later, Jesuit fathers, traders, and voyageurs became the first white men to explore this wilderness. While the white traders of the rival Hudson's Bay and North West companies fought for supremacy of the fur empire, Chippewa and Sioux tribes fought vicious battles over the land itself. Eventually, both the Chippewa and Hudson's Bay were victorious, each according to its own methods.

The forest, of course, remained neutral to human differences, and today offers little testimony to its rich history, beyond the portages blazed by voyageurs or wild-rice beds harvested by Indians. Even the effects of the logging industry have been largely effaced. From a nucleus of 36,000 acres established in 1909, the forest has grown to its present mammoth size, blanketed by healthy stands of balsam, spruce, tamarack, aspen, and paper birch. The forest cover is complemented by lichen-quilted rock outcroppings and numerous plants and flowers, among them the delicate pink lady slipper, Minnesota's state flower. Other varieties of flowers include wild iris, marsh marigold, wild rose, daisies, and dogwood. Mushrooms and several kinds of berries—raspberry, strawberry, chokeberry, and juneberry—are also abundant throughout the forest.

The forest is a top-ranked hunting area for whitetail deer and upland game birds. Moose, protected in Minnesota since 1922, range across the Forest's 185-mile long northern tip. Woodland caribou, once common to the region, were last seen in the Red Lake area more than 30 years ago, and are presumed to be extinct. Other common game species include black bear, red and gray fox, raccoon, upland game birds, and waterfowl. Diligent wildlife watchers may be lucky enough to sight the tracks of the elusive eastern timber wolf. Classified as an endangered species, the timber-wolf population today is limited largely

to Minnesota and Superior National Forest, the latter offering refuge to about half the nation's wolf population.

At least thirty different species of fish are found in the lakes and streams of the Superior National Forest and its famous Boundary Waters Canoe Area. Among others, these include muskellunge, northern pike, walleye, and large and smallmouth bass up to record weights in such famed Boundary Waters lakes as huge Saganaga—considered one of the nation's top trophy walleye lakes—Gunflint, Vermilion, Sea Gull, Namakan, Basswood, and sprawling Lac La Croix. Sprawling, island-dotted Lac La Croix and the Bottle River and the hidden bays and coves of Iron, Crooked, and Knife lakes along the boundary waters chain provide some of the premier smallmouth bass fishing in North America. Inland, the forest's deep, cold-water lakes offer almost every kind of fishing challenge, from deep-water trolling for lake trout and splake to fly fishing for lake-run steelhead, browns, and trophy brook trout in the deep pools of the turbulent North Shore streams.

In the north, abutting the Quetico Provincial Park in Ontario, is the largest water-based wild region in the country, the Boundary Waters Canoe Area. Set aside in 1926 as a roadless area to preserve its primitive character, the BWCA consists of more than one million acres of land and water covering the northern third of the forest. Stretching approximately 200 miles along the Canadian boundary, the BWCA offers more than 1,200 miles of canoe routes. Portages here, worn deep from use over several centuries, were used by such notables as Jacques de Noyons, believed to be the first white man to travel the border waters; Sieur de La Vérendrye, who left a record of his travels through the area; and Alexander Mackenzie, a traveler along this route on his epic journey to the Pacific. The real fame of the area came in 1731 with the arrival of Vérendrye and the opening of the fur trade. In the spring of 1732, the Vérendrye party and others paddled their narrow birchbark canoes over what are now the waters of the BWCA, establishing posts on the border lakes. Later, settlers, loggers, missionaries, miners, and farmers plied these waters on their way across Minnesota to the north and inland. *The Boundary Waters Canoe Area*, a brochure available free from the Forest Supervisor, Superior National Forest, Duluth 55801, describes the BWCA, its history, regulations governing the area, tips for travelers, and offers several campfire recipes. U.S. Geological Survey maps, listed at the end of this chapter, are essential guides to the remote wild areas, as are the maps cited under "Boundary Water Canoe Charts." A number of outfitters headquartered at Ely and Grand Marais supply everything needed except personal articles at very reasonable rates, which include food, canoe, tent, ax, cook kits, and detailed items such as insect repellent. They will also rent any item of equipment needed.

The most popular entry routes into the Boundary Waters Canoe Area include the Ely area entry points at Moose Lake, Fall Lake, and Lake One; at Saganaga, Seagull, and Sawbill lakes on the east; and the more remote wilderness entry points such as those at Crab Lake, Fourtown Lake, and Horse Lake (20 miles to the northwest of Ely), at Moose River (at the Echo Trail crossing, 40 miles northwest of Ely), at Little Indian Sioux River (50 miles northwest of Ely on the Echo Trail), and at Magnetic and Round Lakes (45 miles from Grand Marais on the Gunflint Trail). Be sure to check with the Forest Supervisor's Office for the "BWCA User Distribution Program" regulations. Entry points into Canada's Quetico Wilderness from the BWCA are located at Basswood Lake, the Cache Bay Ranger Station, and Saganaga Lake Customs.

The Superior Forest–Boundary Waters Canoe Area contain literally hundreds of renowned, historic canoe-camping and wilderness fishing lakes and streams, including the famous tributaries of Minnesota's

North Shore region of Lake Superior. Many plants not found elsewhere in Minnesota grow along the North Shore and in the surrounding forests: stands of leatherleaf cover; acres of muskeg; abundant Labrador tea; billberry, which grows only in this upper tip of the state. Swamp laurel, bog and autumn willow, and black currant are plants characteristic of the region. Trailing arbutus is found in the sandy forests, and aromatic wintergreen covers the forest bed in much of the drier area. The major features of the North Shore region include the Grand Portage Trail (this 9-mile portage was used by voyageurs and fur traders to avoid falls and rapids in the Pigeon River) and the famous black-water trout and steelhead waters of the Reservation River, Arrowhead and Cascade rivers, and the Temperance, Knife, Poplar, Devil Track, Manitou, and Brule rivers—the last named after Etienne Brule, who explored the foot of Lake Superior in 1622—which rise out of Tamarack and Alder swamps along the southern slope of the Laurentian Divide and flow along wild boulder-studded courses into frigid Lake Superior. Crane Lake, to the northwest, is renowned for its walleye and northern-pike fishing and serves as a gateway to the chain of wilderness boundary lakes. From Crane Lake are accessible some of the greatest inland canoeing-fishing waters on the continent, and the scenic wilderness camping areas of Voyageurs National Park. This great chain of border lakes—including Rainy, Namakan, Lac La Croix, Iron, Crooked, Basswood, Knife, Saganaga, Gunflint, Mountain, and South Fowl—now so sparsely settled, was once the scene of great historic conflicts. It was on these lakes that the Sioux fought losing battles in their retreat before the ruthless, savage Chippewa, who had determined to secure for themselves the rewards of the fur trade. The region's remote lakeshores and rivers contain numerous Indian petroglyphs and ancient dams constructed of huge rounded boulders, often several tons in weight, and situated where such boulders are naturally scarce. To the south and east of Crane Lake lie beautiful Vermilion Lake, known to the Chippewa as the "Lake of the Sunset Glow," and the famous Boundary Waters outfitting center of Ely. The region was developed through the Vermilion Iron Range mining industry. Campgrounds and excellent smallmouth-bass, walleye, and northern-pike fishing in the Ely area are found at the South Kawishiwi River, Birch Lake, Burntside Lake, Moose River, South Hegman, Fenske, Big, and Second lakes, and along the Moose, Sioux, and Hunting Shack rivers. Fascinating, informative histories of the Boundary Waters Canoe Area, Rainy Lake Wilderness, and the North Shore of Lake Superior are published by the University of Minnesota Press, Minneapolis 55455: *Portage into the Past: By Canoe Along the Minnesota-Ontario Boundary Waters* ($6.50), BY J. Arnold Bolz; *Canoe Country* ($4.50), by Florence Page Jacques and Francis Lee Jacques, is a beautiful book about the Big North canoe country; *Snowshoe Country* ($5), by Florence Page Jacques and Francis Lee Jacques, captures the wild charm of dog-sled and snowshoe travels through the great Rainy Lake Country and includes a wealth of information on wildlife, geography, and geology.

Several useful guides to the Boundary Waters-Quetico Canoe Country may be obtained from Waters, Inc., 111 East Sheridan St., Ely 55731 (phone: 218-365-3206): *The Quetico-Superior Canoeist's Handbook* ($2.50), by Mark Fisher; *The Voyageur's Highway* ($3.50), by Grace Lee Nute, the definitive history of the fur traders' canoe route between Lake Superior and Rainy Lake; *The Voyageur* ($5), by Grace Lee Nute, a colorful and authoritative history of men who opened the great fur empires of the North; *Superior-Quetico Canoe Country* ($1) by W.A. Fisher Co., a photo guide to the Boundary Waters Canoe Area.

For those who prefer touring the forest on dry land, there are a number of hiking trails, ranging from easy to challenging, winding through the remote wilderness regions and beside clear streams. The three-mile-long Eagle Mountain Trail leads to the highest point in Minnesota and provides access to a six-mile branch tour leading to Brule Lake tower. Recommended only to experienced hikers, the Kekekabic Trail winds for 38 miles over low flatland and rolling terrain, heavily wooded with balsam, aspen, and stands of red and white pine. Parts of the route are wet, rough, and brushy. Obstructed by windfalls at many points, the Sioux-Hustler Trail also offers a challenge to even the hardiest. The trail forms a loop over streams that must be waded, and through heavily wooded lands. Improved campsites offer overnight facilities at Devil Cascade, Emerald Lake, and Pageant Lake. Norway Trail, 8 miles long and considerably less difficult, leads to Trout Lake over gently rolling lands covered with aspen and paper birch. These and other trails are indicated on the full-color *Superior National Forest Map* (50¢), which also shows the Boundary Waters Canoe Area, campgrounds, ski areas, highways and roads,

THE VOYAGEUR
Grace Lee Nute

canoe routes, recreation sites, landing fields, snowmobile trails, and numerous other forest features. The map and lists of hiking trails describing trail conditions, access points, and mileage are available free from the Forest Supervisor, Superior National Forest, Box 338, Duluth 55801. If you are interested in the Kekekabic Trail, the Forest Service also issues a separate flyer on this trail alone, covering historic and scenic points, trail conditions and modes of travel, camping, and

safety tips. Write to the above address requesting *Kekekabic Trail # 147.* Novice campers and canoers will appreciate another free publication of the Forest Service, *Canoeing-Camping in the Superior National Forest,* an 18-page brochure offering advice on portaging, paddling, and pitching camp. The booklet also gives details on how and what to pack for a canoe trip.

Canoe portage service in the forest and Boundary Waters Canoe Area is provided by *Wilderness Portage Service* (Moose Lake), Ely 55731. Fly-in service is provided by *Wilderness Wings Airways,* Box 188, Ely 55731, which also serves the Quetico country to the north. Wilderness and family vacation lodges and resorts in the remote, lake-studded Crane Lake Area of the forest (which includes Sandpoint, Little Vermilion, Loon, and Namakan lakes, and Lac La Croix) include *Pine Point Lodge, Nelson's Resort, Olson's Borderland Lodge,* and *Ostlund's Resort*—all Crane Lake 55725. *Bob Anderson's Canoe Outfitters,* Box 66, Crane Lake provides package fly-in trips into Beaverhouse or Lac La Croix. Lodges and resorts on beautiful Lake Vermilion—which sprawls along the edge of the Superior National Forest and Boundary Waters Canoe Area and offers trophy fishing for walleye, great northerns, and smallmouth bass—include *Bay View Lodge, Pike Bay Resort, Everett Bay Lodge, Pine Trees Resort,* and *Vermilion Beach Resort,* all Tower 55790. *Bill Zup's Lac La Croix Fishing Camp,* Crane Lake 55725 (winter: 611 E. Harvey St., Ely 55731), offers deluxe vacation lodging, guide service, and remote outpost camps in the Quetico Wilderness with fly-in fishing to some of the best smallmouth bass waters in North America.

Wilderness and family vacation lodges and resorts in the Ely area of the forest (write to resort name, plus Ely 55731) include *Aki-Nibi Resort* (Farm Lake), *Anderson's Lodge* (Moose Lake), *Bear Island Resort, Beaver Lodge* (Burntside Lake), *Burntside Lodge, Canadian Border Lodge* (Moose Lake), *Coral Ridge Resort* (Bear Island Lake), *Deer Trail Lodge* (Twin Lakes), *The Escape* (Bear Island Lake), *Holt's Superior Forest Lodge* (Farm Lake), *Jackpine Lodge* (Snowbank Lake), *Jasper Lake Resort, Johnson's Fall Lake Resort, Kawishiwi Lodge* (Lake One), *Kirk's Lodge* (Moose Lake), *Marleau's Garden Lake Resort, Moose Lake Lodges, National Forest Lodge* (Lake Gegoka, Isabella 55607), *Northernair Lodge* (Mitchell Lake), *Pine*

Point Lodge (White Iron Lake), *River Point Resort* (Birch Lake), *Shagawa Inn Resort* (Shagawa Lake), *Snowbank Beach Resort, Snowbank Lodge, Squaw Bay Resort* (Fall Lake), *Sunny Dene Resort* (Fall Lake), *Sun-Set Lodge* (White Iron Lake), *Tanglewood Trail Resort* (Moose Lake), *Timber Bay Lodge* (Birch Lake, Babbit), *Timber Trail Resort* (Farm Lake), *Whispering Pines Lodge* (Big Lake), *White Iron Beach Resort, White's Shig-Wak Lodge* (Little Long Lake).

Full-service vacation lodges and resorts in the Gunflint Trail area of the forest include *End of the Trail Lodge* (Lake Saganaga), *Gunflint Lodge, Trail Center* (Poplar Lake), *Gateway-Hungry Jack Lake Lodge, Trout Lake Lodge, Sea Gull Resort and Motel* (Sea Gull Lake), *Loon Lake Lodge, Rockwood Lodge* (Poplar Lake), *Land of the Voyageur Lodge & Canoe Outfitters, Fowl Lake Lodge, Bearskin Lodge* (East Bearskin Lake), and *Borderland Lodge* (Granite River)—all Grand Marais 55604. *Wilderness Retreat Resort,* Hovland, 55606, offers lodging and fly-in service into Fowls and adjoining lakes.

Access & Outfitting Centers

The Superior National Forest is reached by numerous scenic forest roads off the Lake Superior North Shore Drive (U.S. 61), U.S. Highway 53, Minnesota highways 1, 169, 135, and secondary roads 23, 24, 18, 15, 16, 7, 6, and the Sawbill Trail (116). Lodging, supplies, hunting and fishing guides, wilderness outfitters, and fly-in services are available at Grand Portage, Grand Marais, Two Harbors, Sawbill Landing, Forest Center, Ely, Soudan, Tower, Buyck, and International Falls.

Voyageurs National Park

Voyageurs National Park Topo Maps

U.S. Geological Survey large-scale maps: Ash River NE, Cranberry Bay, Crane Lake, Daley Bay, Hale Bay, Johnson Lake, Kabetogama, Kempton Bay, Kettle Falls, Namakan Island, Red Horse Bay, Soldier Point.

This 219,400-acre wilderness encompasses the Kebetogama Peninsula, a heavily forested region of fir, spruce, pine, aspen, and birch, broken by bogs, ancient rock outcroppings, sandy beaches, and towering cliffs. Bounded in part by three major glacial lakes—Rainy, Kabetogama, and Namakan—Voyageurs National Park offers top-ranked trophy fishing, canoeing, and wilderness lakeshore camping. The main body of land, the 75,000-acre Kabetogama Peninsula, is accessible principally by water, and its interior holds a number of lakes that can be reached only on foot. The north shore of the peninsula features a sharply broken front with many small bays and hidden coves. Off the south shore lie innumerable tiny islands; smooth, glaciated rocks along both shores offer ideal sites for camping.

The earliest chapters in the human history of the North American continent opened in the forested lake country of Minnesota's northern border when descendants of the Asiatic people wandered south thousands of years ago and settled along the shoreline. These people are known to have been in Minnesota as early as 11,000 years ago, the first known existence of man in America. The remains of one of their descendants, "Minnesota Man," was found in 1931 near Pelican Rapids. "Minnesota Man" was actually a teenage girl who drowned in glacial Lake Pelican, part of the vast waters of ancient Lake Agassiz. From these early peoples the Sioux Indians evolved into the first tribal inhabitants of the area. Thanks to the rich sources of game—deer, moose, and caribou—and the abundant fish in the lakes and streams, the Sioux developed a highly prosperous hunting and gathering society which thrived until 300 years ago, when Algonquian Indians, also known as Ojibways, and their relatives the Ottawas moved westward from the Ohio and Michigan area. The Ojibways, commonly called

Chippewas, intruded upon the highly desirable lands of the Sioux. After many battles lasting several generations, the Sioux were forced from northern Minnesota by Chippewa tribes, who then held sway over the lakes and forests until the coming of the white man.

Beginning in the mid-seventeenth century and for a century and a half thereafter, French Canadian voyageurs, led or assisted by Indians, plied this maze of lakes and streams in slender canoes, transporting huge quantities of furs and goods between Montreal and the far Northwest. Thus opened one of the most colorful and adventurous eras in the history of the great Northwest; names like Sieur de La Vérendrye, Pierre Esprit Radisson, and Sieur des Groseillers still evoke an aura of romance and daring, of incredible prosperity coupled with hard work, tremendous hardship, danger, and sheer cunning. The portage paths blazed by the Indians and French Canadian explorers were traveled during the nineteenth century by the fur traders of the American Fur Company, who established trading posts in the North Country at Fond-du-Lac, Grand Portage, Grand Marais, Vermilion Lake, Moose Lake, Basswood Lake, Rainy River, Rainy Lake, Rosseau Lake and Lake of the Woods. The latter part of the nineteenth and early twentieth centuries saw the influx of loggers and gold prospectors, who followed the old Indian trail from Duluth to beautiful Lake Vermilion, called *Sak-Ga-Ee-Gum-Wah-Ma-Mah-Nec,* or "Lake of the Sunset Glow," by the Chippewa.

Though the hardy voyageur—with his lusty songs, colorful sash, red stocking cap, pipe, and vermilion-tipped paddle—is gone, the land is not. From the water this stretch of lake country looks today much as it did during the heyday of trapping and trading. It has all the wildness and immense scale associated with the northern lakes region—a land surface shaped by continental glaciation into an endless and intricate system of waterways complemented by the vast green mantle of lush forests.

Water sports have naturally become the major attraction of the area. Game-fish populations, especially walleyes, provide excellent fishing opportunities in Kabetogama, Namakan, and Rainy lakes. Northern pike, trout, and smallmouth bass are other frequently caught species. Boating is also popular on the many lakes. Boaters not familiar with the waters are advised to obtain the services of a guide or detailed charts, which are available locally. The large lakes can quickly become very rough, and it is imperative to keep an eye on weather conditions at all times. Users of small boats and canoes should be particularly cautious and prepared to wait out rough water.

Private campgrounds are located near International Falls at the western end of the park, and around Lake Kabetogama. The Boise Cascade Corporation operates a number of camping sites open to the public. In addition, the state of Minnesota and the U.S. Forest Service also provide camping facilities in or near the park. The *Voyageurs National Park Map-Guide* will help to locate campgrounds, lakes, streams, forest roads, and other park features. A brochure, *Voyageurs National Park Backcountry Travel,* provides valuable information for campers and visitors, including park regulations, hints on backcountry travel, and a list of lake charts indispensable for navigation. The park service also issues lists of local resorts, canoe outfitters, campgrounds, houseboat rentals, and fly-in services. All of the above materials are free on request from Voyageurs National Park, P.O. Box 50, International Falls 56649.

The park's wildlife is also a source of continuing fascination and delight. Black bear and deer are common sights, as are ruffed grouse and snowshoe hare. Shorebirds are fairly scarce, although the solitary sandpiper sometimes nests in the area. Northern owls, the great gray, boreal, and hawk owls can often be seen silhouetted against the winter sky, along with merlins and ravens. The principal species sought by the voyageur—beaver, otter, mink, Canada lynx, muskrat, and fox—are still found in good numbers throughout the park, with over 200 beaver colonies scattered along inland streams. A 26-page brochure on *The Fish and Wildlife of Voyageurs National Park* indicates the relative scarcity or abundance of fish and game and describes the best places for finding them. The brochure includes an excellent park map showing the concentration of various trees, rock outcroppings, marshes, and swamps, and is available free from the National Park Service, Voyageurs National Park, 405 2nd St., International Falls 56649.

Vacation lodging and resort facilities in the National Park area include *Berggren's Whispering Pines Resort* (Lake Kabetogama), Orr 55771; *Ash Trail Lodge* (on Ash River), Orr 55771; *Meadwood Resort* (Lake Kabetogama), Ash River Trail, Orr 55771; *Minnesota Vogageur Houseboats,* Orr 55771; *Ash-Ka-Nam Resort* (on Ash River), Ash River Trail, Orr 55771. The following lodges and resorts are located on Lake Kabetogama in the township of Ray 56669: *Rocky Point Resort, Moose Horn Resort, Pinecrest Lodge, Kec's Kove,* and *Voyageur Park Lodge.* For additional information and a free illustrated brochure, write: Kabetogama Lake Assoc., Ray 56669.

Access & Outfitting Centers

Voyageurs National Park is easily approached by surfaced roads from four points along U.S. 53 traveling from Duluth. County Route 23 from Orr leads to Crane Lake at the eastern end of the planned park; County Route 122, just south of International Falls, provides access to the south shore of Lake Kabetogama; Minnesota 11 from International Falls approaches the park area at Black Bay and Neil Point; County Route 765, or Ash River Trail, provides access to Namakan Lake. There are no roads into the interior, so access is primarily by boat. Major outfitting centers are Crane Lake and International Falls (which see).

Accommodations— Vacation Lodges & Resorts

Listings of resorts, lodges, and other accommodations are contained in the 40-page *Wonderful Wisconsin Accommodations Directory,* available free from the Wisconsin State Vacation & Travel Service, Dept. of Natural Resources, Box 7921, Madison 53707. In addition, a useful 500-page *Wonderful Wisconsin Vacation Guide* ($2.50) contains comprehensive listings and descriptions of resorts, motels, and skiing facilities, as well as a complete campground guide. To obtain a copy, write: Wisconsin Vacationland, Inc., Box 407, Fontana 53125.

Indian Head Country, so called because its 18 counties form the profile of an Indian chief when viewed on a map, boasts more state parks and forests, famous fishing streams, and spectacular waterways than any other Wisconsin vacation area. The 1976 *Travel Directory to Indian Head Country of Wisconsin* provides comprehensive, town-by-town listings of campgrounds, resorts, motels, sporting-goods stores, special services, and other sources of accommodations and outfitting in this scenic western region. The 47-page guide, which includes an index to points of interest within each county, is available free from Wisconsin Indian Head Country, Inc., 101 Heritage Plaza, 1316 Fairfax St., Eau Claire, 54701.

Listings of major resorts, lodges, and sporting camps are found in the "Wisconsin Travel & Recreation Guide."

Apostle Islands of Lake Superior

The Bayfield Peninsula, a large promontory off the coast of northern Wisconsin, juts into the waters of Lake Superior like a giant thumb pointing toward Canada. Off the shores of this hilly protrusion lie 22 islands, called the Twelve Apostles by Frenchmen arriving from Sault, who counted only a dozen on first sighting the group. Originally there were probably eight or nine additional islands, now reduced to rocky shoals scattered throughout the archipelago. All of the islands bear evidence of the effects of repeated glaciation and wave erosion; each is composed of red sandstone bedrock blanketed by a layer of glacial till—rocks, clay, and boulders. Along the shores of many of the Apostles, wave action has produced intricate, sometimes grotesque carvings in the 10- to 60-foot cliffs fringing the coastlines. The interior landscapes are characterized by unspoiled white sand beaches, thick evergreen forests, and marshes—habitats of deer, mink, beaver, muskrat, and many species of migratory waterfowl.

The earliest inhabitants of the region were called the Mound Builders, a group of prehistoric Indians who lived near the shores of Lake Superior some 12,000 years ago. More recently, shortly before the discovery of America, Ojibway or Chippewa tribes built a settlement on Madeline Island, the largest of the Apostles, and dubbed the area *Monigwunakauning,* meaning "home of the golden-breasted woodpecker," because of the thousands of birds that stopped on the island during their annual migrations. According to the Chippewa legend, the islands were made by Manitou, or Spirit, who pursued a stag as far as the shores of Lake Superior, unsuccessfully firing arrows at the animal. When the deer jumped in the water, Manitou became so angry that he picked up handfuls of rocks and threw them at the escaping animals. These rocks became the Apostle Islands.

The first white man to visit the Apostles was probably Etienne Brule, who arrived in 1622 in search of the Northwest Passage. Later, other French explorers—Nicolet, Groseillers, and Radisson—also stumbled on the islands. The two latter built a cabin on Chequamegon Bay, near the present city of Ashland, in 1659. Missionaries and fur traders

WISCONSIN ENCYCLOPEDIA

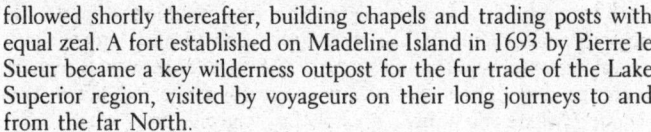

followed shortly thereafter, building chapels and trading posts with equal zeal. A fort established on Madeline Island in 1693 by Pierre le Sueur became a key wilderness outpost for the fur trade of the Lake Superior region, visited by voyageurs on their long journeys to and from the far North.

Many of the legends connected with the islands and a full history of Madeline are recounted in *Madeline Island & the Chequamegon Region*, a 59-page paperbound narrative. The story of the fur trade in the Apostles is told in full detail as is the subsequent history of the lumbering industry and the archipelago's development as a summer resort. The book is priced at $1.00 and is available from the National Park Services, Apostle Islands National Lakeshore, 1972 Centennial Dr., Bayfield 54814.

The Apostles provide a spectacular unspoiled setting for wilderness camping, canoeing, fishing, and hunting. Fishing on the Sioux and Onion bays for lake, brown, and rainbow trout and coho salmon is a popular activity, as is seining for smelts along shallow beach areas during late April. Chequamegon Bay enjoys a reputation for excellent catches of trophy northern pike, smallmouth bass, walleye, and yellow perch, and chinook and coho salmon. Bayfield County Forest, Chequamegon National Forest, and Apostle Islands National Lakeshore lands are all open in season for public hunting for black bear, ruffed grouse, snowshoe hare, woodcock, and whitetail deer.

The *Guide to the Apostle Islands and the Bayfield Peninsula*, a comprehensive booklet describing the individual islands and the mainland in terms of their history and recreational opportunities, is available for $2.80 from the Cartographic Institute, 330 Garfield Ave., Eau Claire 54701. Many photographs of the area and maps detailing the shorelines and depth contours are included, along with full descriptions of the area's outstanding natural features. Another publication, *Chequamegon Bay and Apostle Islands*, is devoted primarily to historical sketches of the region, and contains several interesting articles on early settlements and missions, old buildings and local notables, and the growth of various industries in the area. The 18-page booklet also features chronologies and a wealth of illustrations—old drawings, photographs, and engravings. Priced at $1.00, *Chequamegon Bay and Apostle Islands* is available from the National Park Service, Apostle Islands National Lakeshore, 1972 Centennial Dr., Bayfield 54814. The Park Service also publishes a free brochure, *Apostle Islands*, describing the history of the archipelago, natural attractions, and flora and fauna.

The easiest way to see all 22 of the Apostles is to sign up on one of the excursion-boat cruises that leave the Bayfield City Dock daily from June 10 through the month of September. A 50-mile cruise on the *Chippewa*, offered daily, tours the islands and makes a stop at Devils Island to inspect the sandstone caves and Coast Guard Lighthouse. Two shorter trips of 25 miles each are also made daily aboard the *Islander. Apostle Island Outfitters*, Mellen 54814, offers charter services to anyone wishing a private tour or to campers in need of transportation to island campgrounds. Charter motor- and sailboats are available at Bayfield Marina, Port Superior Marina, and Madeline Island Marina.

Walking tours are another enjoyable way to become acquainted with the islands and their history. *Historic Chequamegon*, a 15-page booklet offering a historical introduction to the region, includes self-guiding tours. It's available for $1.00 from the National Park Service at the above address.

The town of Bayfield can be reached via State Highway 13 from Park Falls, Mellen, and Ashland. From Duluth, Minnesota, or Superior, take U.S. 535 southeast, then travel northeast on 13.

The Apostle Islands are shown on the following U.S. Geological Survey maps: Sand Island, Mount Ashabay, Bayfield 7.5, Madeline Island 7.5, American Point, Oak Island, Stockton Island, Michigan Island, York Island, Bear Island, Rocky Island, Cat Island, Outer Island. The Bayfield Peninsula is shown on the Ashland 1:250,000 U.S. Geological Survey Overview Map.

Bois Brule State Forest— Trophy Fishing & Canoe Country

Long famous for its superb brook-trout fishing, the historic Bois Brule River, once an important exploration and fur-trade route to the headwaters of the St. Croix and thence to the Mississippi, is also one of the North Country's great canoe routes. This scenic north-woods gem provides outstanding fishing for Lake Superior-run rainbows, salmon,

and lunker brown trout. Fed by numerous springs and bordered by a dense northern coniferous forest, the river flows in the former channel of a larger waterway which drained the waters of the melting ice of glacial Lake Duluth thousands of years ago. The upper and lower stretches of the Bois Brule River differ greatly in character. The lower Brule, from the start of the Copper Range to its mouth on Lake Superior, is a swift-moving run marked by almost continuous rapids as it flows through a deep and narrow valley. Flanked by forests of aspen, birch, and balsam fir, this section of the river drops 328 feet in 19 miles. The 30-mile section of the upper Brule is by contrast placid and slow-moving, coursing through a broad, flat, bog-filled valley, its banks lined with towering cedar, tamarack, and spruce.

A 33,000-acre forest provides the setting for this majestic river and is a prime hunting ground for whitetail deer, black bear, ruffed grouse, and waterfowl in the Merriam Swamp area. The forest also offers excellent opportunities for backpacking and hiking. Winding through the southeastern part of the forest, the Brule-St. Croix Portage Trail crosses a historic carrying place used by Indians, explorers, and fur traders traveling along the Mississippi-Lake Superior waterway. Other trails follow the course of clear fishing streams or explore the shores of Lake Nebagamon and Lake Minnesuing. The 26-mile Brule-St. Croix Lake Trail is groomed for snowmobiling in winter and also offers excellent hiking during the summer months. The trail is marked with standard snowmobile marking signs and parking areas are provided at both ends.

Camping is available at the Bois Brule Campgrounds along the banks of the river one mile south of Highway 2, and at the Copper Range Campground along the Brule, 4 miles north of the village of Brule on Highway H. Overnight camping for canoeists at designated canoe

campsites while traveling by watercraft on the Brule River is free and no permit is required.

Perhaps the most popular attraction of the Brule River State Forest is the famous Bois Brule River canoe trip, from Stones Bridge over the privately owned Cedar Island estate through Big Lake to Lake Superior. From the Copper Range Campground to Superior, the river contains some of the most dangerous rapids of its entire length and only the most skillful canoeist—one who is willing to risk frequent spills and portages—should attempt this part of the Brule. About two miles from Lucius Lake, the route passes through a two-mile stretch known as "Winneboujou," undoubtedly the most scenic on the entire river with its many beautiful summer homes hidden among large pines. Winneboujou is named for a Chippewa deity, a roving god who guarded the tribes and occasionally administered a rough and capricious justice. His forge was supposedly located some 20 miles south in the Smoky Mountains, where he fashioned the native copper into fearsome weapons. Since much of his blacksmithing was done by moonlight, the ringing blows from his hammer were heard at night by Indians along the entire shore of Lake Superior. Winneboujou's grandmother, Amik, rebelled against the stronger god's authority and was transformed into a beaver. Three-quarters of a mile from the railroad station named for this mighty blacksmith is Hall's Rapids, followed by the treacherous Little Joe Rapids, a narrow stretch of white water lined by sharp rocks.

A map and description of the *Brule River Canoe Trip*, including most of the forest features such as campgrounds, parking lots, picnic areas, falls and rapids, foot trails, and roads, is available free from the Information Branch, Dept. of Natural Resources, Box 7921, Madison 53707. The *Brule River State Forest Map-Guide* also offers information on trails, the Brule fish hatchery, campgrounds, and other points of interest. The forest is shown on U.S. Geological Survey Topographical Maps: Solon Springs, Ellison Lake, Brule, Lake Nebagamon, Cloverland, Poplar NE, Poplar.

Campgrounds & State Recreation Areas

Wisconsin offers a full sixteen weeks of fine camping weather along many of the state's clear rivers, beside stunning blue lakes, or in heavily wooded forests far from the bustle of civilization. Once you've consulted the maps, circled your camping targets, and made a final inventory of equipment, you may want to consult *Woodall's Trailering Parks & Campgrounds*, a 32-page comprehensive guide to the state's many camping areas. Woodall makes annual inspections of all campgrounds and recreational vehicle areas and lists only those facilities which meet or surpass their minimum standards of cleanliness and maintenance. *Woodall's Trailering Parks and Campgrounds* is available free from the Dept. of Natural Resources, Box 7921, Madison 53707.

Another handy guide for campers is the *1976 Visitor's Guide to Wisconsin's State Parks, Forests, and Other Recreation Lands*, a brochure listing campsites throughout the state parks and forests, available free from the Department of Natural Resources at the above address.

Canoeing & Wilderness Waters

Drained by a network of incomparable wild rivers and streams, Wisconsin has been a favorite area with canoeists since Indians and voyageurs first plied these waters hundreds of years ago. Long before the covered wagon, Wisconsin's rivers provided the swiftest and most efficient links in a vast highway of waters extending thousands of miles

northward into Canada, knitting together innumerable scattered trading posts and settlements. Canoeists today can still enjoy long or short runs along waterways through some of the finest north-woods regions in the country. The secret of any successful canoe trip lies in the planning: where you want to go, how fast you will travel, what activities—fishing, hiking, exploring—you want to enjoy along the way. Wisconsin offers a staggering variety of trails—some navigable only by white-water experts, others ideal for beginners, families, and fishermen. The publications described below will help in selecting a route tailored to individual abilities and tastes.

A source book to canoe streams and rivers personally traveled by the authors, *Whitewater; Quietwater—the Wild Rivers of Wisconsin, Upper Michigan & NE Minnesota* describes the state's major canoe routes. Length of the run, time required, gradient, hazard rating, and water conditions are detailed for all runs. Also included are comments on the scenery, geology, fishing opportunities, campgrounds, outfitters, and history of the area. Among the rivers described are the St. Croix, Namekagon, Wisconsin, Wolf, Brule, Flambeau, Menominee, and Peshtigo. Appendixes give additional river information, an explanation of the International Scale of River Difficulty, plus lists of periodicals, clubs, maps, technique manuals, and equipment sources. Priced at $7.95, the 175-page guide is available from Evergreen Paddleways, 1415 21st Street, Two Rivers 54241.

Canoe Trails of North-Central Wisconsin ($4.00) describes a variety of trips along ten different streams: the Chippewa, Flambeau, Couderay, Jump, Turtle, Yellow, Manitowish, and Thornapple rivers, and Deertail and Main creeks. Written descriptions include information on rapids, campgrounds, scenery, fishing, and historical points of interest. Maps accompanying each description show rapids, best channels, campsites, boat landings and access, points of interest, hazard ratings, nearby creeks, and other reference points for the canoeist. Similar in format, *Canoe Trails of Northeastern Wisconsin* ($4.75) offers the same kind of information and maps for the Brule, Deerskin, Embarrass, Manitowish, Menominee, Oconto, Pelican, Peshtigo, Pike, Pine, Popple, Red, Spirit, Tomahawk, Wisconsin, and Wolf rivers. *Canoe Trails of Southern Wisconsin* ($4.95) offers maps and descriptions for canoe trips on the Baraboo, Crawfish, Crystal, Fox, Kickapoo, La Crosse, Lemonweir, Manitowoc, Mecan, Milwaukee, Pecatonica, Pine, Rock, Sugar, Waupaca, Wisconsin, and Yellow rivers. The guides are available at the prices quoted above from Wisconsin Trails, P.O. Box 5650, Madison 53705.

Canoeing the Wild Rivers of Northwestern Wisconsin ($3.50), published by Wisconsin Indian Head Country, Inc., 1316 Fairfax St., Eau Claire 54701, contains maps for trips on the Brule, St. Croix, Namekagon, Totogatic, Eau Claire, Yellow, and Clam river systems. A free

brochure from the Vacation and Travel Service, Box 450, Madison 53701, *Canoeing in Wisconsin*, offers tips on river safety and planning for canoe trips. The Service also has publications available for all of the above rivers and surrounding areas, along with information on lodging, campsites, and area attractions. (See "St. Croix & Namekagon National Scenic Rivers" and "Wolf National Wild & Scenic River.")

Fenwick Wisconsin Fly Fishing & Musky Schools

The renowned Fenwick Corporation's Wisconsin schools of fly fishing are located at Silver Springs Trout Farm in the center of a 350-acre ice-age park in the heart of Kettle Moraine country and at Seven Pines Lodge in beautiful, natural woodlands near Lewis, an hour and a half from the Twin Cities. These two-day May and June schools are open to beginners through advanced fly fishermen and include intensive instruction in fly casting, insects and artificial flies, knots, fly presentation, stream lore, and wading. For free literature, rates, and info, write: Director, Fenwick Fly Fishing School, Midwest Division, 309 S. 11th Ave., Wausau 54401 (715-842-9879).

Fenwick's Musky Schools are run in June and October at the Trees for Tomorrow Center on the beautiful Chain of Lakes in Northern Wisconsin. The school curriculum includes intensive study of habitat, electronic equipment, structures, contour map reading, casting techniques, equipment and lures, motor trolling, finding and patterning fish, and fish behaviour. For literature and rates, write: Director, Fenwick Musky Schools, Rt. 1, Box 94, Manitowish Waters 54545 (715-543-2271).

Fishing & Hunting in the Badger State

Within the borders of Wisconsin are some of the United States' finest blue-ribbon fishing and canoeing waters, small-game cover, wildfowl wetlands, and deer and bear haunts. Wisconsin's 56,154 square miles include an unusual diversity of topography, fish and wildlife, and forest types. There are more than 6½ million acres of public fishing and hunting lands contained in the fragrant north woods of three-sectioned Chequamegon National Forest and Nicolet National Forest, several state forests that total over 400,000 acres, county forests that exceed 2,000,000 acres, more than 500,000 acres of Department of Natural Resources owned and leased lands, and the recreational acreage made available by power and forest products companies. Much of this acreage can be utilized for hunting, as well as for fishing, canoeing, and hiking. Large, malevolent muskellunge, lunker trout, acrobatic bass, trophy walleyed pike, sleek coho and chinook salmon, voracious northern pike, log-sized sturgeon, and hordes of panfish share these expanses with white-tailed deer, the black bear, ruffed grouse, pheasant, woodcock, sharp-tailed grouse, Hungarian partridge, ducks and geese, cottontails and snowshoe hares, squirrels, and other small-game animals. Information pamphlets describing the county and state forests are available free from the progressive State of Wisconsin Dept. of Natural Resources, Box 450, Madison 53701.

The excellence and diversity of Wisconsin fishing opportunities is well documented by the list (to the right) of Badger State record fish compiled by the Department of Natural Resources.

Incidentally, the 14 lb. 11¾ oz. tiger trout is the world's record, and the state record 69 lb. 11 oz. muskellunge held the world's record for a number of years, being surpassed by only a few ounces by the current titleholder, taken from the St. Lawrence River, New York.

Hayward, Wisconsin, often called "The Muskie Capital of the World," is the home of the National Fresh Water Fishing Hall of Fame, which is building a museum to contain current and historic items of fishing tackle and related gear, memorabilia, record fish mountings, fishing feats of interest, and a "Hall of Famers" section. Fishermen who have historical or unusual tackle, fish mountings, pictures, tales of unusual adventures, and related material are encouraged to contact Executive Director Steve Henry, National Fresh Water Fishing Hall of Fame, Box 33, Hayward 54843. Acceptable pieces donated or lent will be displayed on a permanent or rotating basis, and the donor will be given credit for each item used.

WISCONSIN RECORD FISH

	Lb.–oz.	Place	Year
Largemouth bass	11–3	Lake Ripley	1940
Smallmouth bass	9–1	Indian Lake	1950
Rock bass	1–12	Big Green Lake	1971
White bass	3–12	Pelican Lake	1963
Yellow bass	2–2	Lake Monona	1972
Bluegill	2–4	Squash Lake	1971
Bullhead			
(black)	2–9	Trappe Lake	1967
(brown)	3–12	Nelson Lake	1972
(yellow)	3–3	Nelson Lake	1972
Channel catfish	44–0	Wisconsin River	1962
Flathead catfish	61–0	Fox River	1966
White crappie	4–8	Gile Flowage	1967
Muskellunge	69–11	Lake Chippewa Flowage	1949
Muskellunge (hybrid)	50–4	Lac Vieux Desert	1951
Northern pike	38–0	Lake Puckaway	1952
Perch (yellow)	3–4	Lake Winnebago	1954
Sauger	4–5	Mississippi River	1970
	4–5	Mississippi River	1971
Atlantic salmon	12–0	Lake Michigan	1975
Coho salmon	24–6	Lake Michigan	1975
Chinook salmon	40–4	Menominee River	1973
Sturgeon	94–3	Menominee River	1968
	(hook & line)		
Sturgeon (lake)	180–0	Lake Winnebago	1953
	(spearing)		
Brown trout			
(Great Lakes–run)	29–9	Lake Superior	1971
(inland)	14–8	Rush River	1974
Lake trout			
(Great Lakes-run)	47–0	Lake Superior	1946
(inland)	35–4	Green Lake	1957
Rainbow trout	24–4	Lake Michigan	1973
Splake (hybrid)	14–4	Ada Lake	1967
Tiger trout (hybrid)	17*	Lake Michigan	1977
Walleye	18–0	High Lake	1933

*World's record.

For detailed information on fishing waters, local stream and lake conditions, write or call the following DNR district offices: *Southern*, Rt. 1, Wakanda Dr., Waunakee 53597 (608-266-0585); *Southeast*, 9722 W. Watertown Plank Rd., Milwaukee 53226 (414-257-6543); *North Central*, Box 818, Rhinelander 54501 (715-362-7616); *Northwest*, Box 309, Spooner 54801 (715-635-2101); *West Central*, 1300 W. Clairmont Ave., Eau Claire 54701 (715-836-2956); *Lake Michigan*, Box 3600, Green Bay 54303 (414-497-4064).

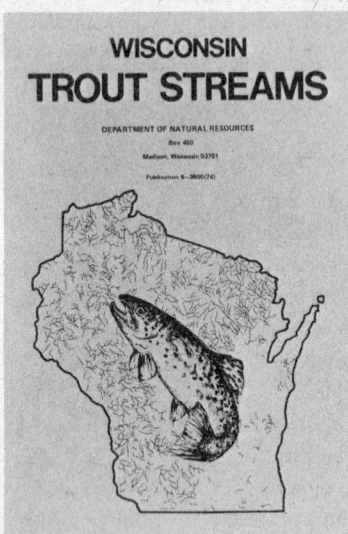

Trout Streams & Lakes

Trout of one kind or another is found in almost every part of the state. Orange-bellied brook trout need very cold, clean water and are found predominately in the heavily forested northern tier in spring-fed streams and ponds and in the headwaters of many of the large river systems. Feeder streams of the Menominee River in the northeast corner such as the Brule, Popple, and Pine rivers are noted for brookies, as are the headwaters of the Wolf, Pike, and Montreal rivers, all in the northern section of the state. Spring and fall are the best times to go after brook trout, because warm weather and summer water temperatures force these fish into spring holes. An autumn trip into a spring, pond, or stream in the Chequamegon or Nicolet national forest after brookies is a memorable experience; the reds and golds of the leaves rival the brilliant red-orange flanks of the male brook trout.

Brown trout are found throughout the state and range in size from the pan-size feeder brook fish to the tackle-busting Great Lakes prowlers, the "beer barrel" browns, which reach 30 pounds. The Wolf River via the northeast is considered by many anglers to be one of the top brown-trout streams in the nation. The river near Keshena is particularly prized for its deep, wild water, and for the hook-jawed trophy browns that lurk in the deep holes and underneath snags and ledges. Tributaries of the Wolf, such as the Little Wolf, Red, and Embarrass rivers, offer superb fishing for trophy brownies. Among other highly rated streams are the Lower Pike, Pine, Popple, and Upper Peshtigo in the north and northeast. The Montreal and Bois Brule rivers in the northwest region afford fine brown-trout fishing and also pay host to the Great Lakes spawning run of yardstick-size trout. The east-central Sand County area offers classic meadow angling in pastoral surroundings, where "matching the hatch" is a favored technique during the profuse mayfly-emergence period. The nationally renowned Mecan and Lower Pine rivers are popular and productive fly-fishing streams of natural beauty, as is the Crystal River. The hill country of

the southwest corner has many streams noted for good brown-trout fishing.

Rainbow trout are found in North Country streams, such as the Pine, Popple, and Brule, and in some of the state's central and southern waters, but reach their zenith in the Great Lakes and their tributaries, where they reach sizes in excess of 20 pounds, and in spawning season, invade rivers as silvery, pink-sided steelhead to test the angler's nerves and tackle. The Bois Brule, Iron, and Flag rivers, which flow into Lake Superior, and the Door County Green Bay Tributaries of Lake Michigan are favored locations.

Lake trout were decimated by the lamprey invasion that reached its peak of devastation in the 1950s and 1960s. Control efforts and stocking, along with the increase in forage fish, have combined to produce an impressive comeback. The scenic, evergreen-clad Apostle Islands in Lake Superior off Chequamegon Bay, and the string of islands at the tip of the Door Peninsula in the mouth of Green Bay on Lake Michigan, are hot spots. Inland lakes scattered around the state offer lake-trout angling, especially Green Lake, in the east-central region.

For detailed info on Northern Wisconsin trophy trout stream conditions and hatches, write or call: *Chuck Billie's Northern Wildlife*, P.O. Box 116, Lake Nebagamon 54849 (715-374-2408). Be sure to request a copy of their catalog/newsletter, *The Northern Angler*. This nationally famous firm also offers guided trips on the Bois Brule, White, Namekagon, Iron, and Black rivers for rainbows, browns, and brookies, and on Lake Superior for trophy trout and salmon.

Coho & Chinook Salmon

Coho and chinook salmon were introduced into Lake Michigan in the 1960s to combat the hordes of alewives, a slim, oily bait fish that invaded the Great Lakes along with the sea lamprey and created an odoriferous nuisance by washing ashore in the tens of millions. A spectacular new fishery was born, as the exotic Pacific salmon found the new environment much to their liking. Numerous tributary rivers pay host to vast runs of spawning salmon. Lake fishermen troll and cast in Michigan for the salmon and enjoy superb results. The abundant coho reach 30 pounds but average much smaller, usually 6 to 15 pounds, while the scarcer chinook reach weights in excess of 50 pounds. These fish are widely dispersed in Lake Michigan, and success depends on water temperature and bait-fish location. The Root River in Racine is a Chinook hot spot in the fall. (See "Great Lakes Trout & Salmon.")

Warmwater Fish

If the muskie (see "Muskellunge—Trophy Fishing Waters") is the premier game fish of Wisconsin waters, the bread-and-butter fish is surely the walleye. This largest member of the perch family provides more fun and good eating than any other game species. Lakes like sprawling Winnebago support substantial populations of these fish, and the spring runs up the Wolf River from Winnebago, Lake Buttes des Morts, Lake Winneconne, and Lake Poygan are legendary. Other prime areas include the Namekagon River near Hayward, Monitowish River and Lake, Wisconsin River and Lake, Rock and Upper Fox rivers, and the Great Lakes. Most larger lakes and streams support populations of walleye.

Smallmouth bass are found throughout much of the state, but the best sections are generally in the countless lakes, ponds, and streams of the north country, the watersheds of south-flowing rivers such as the Wolf, Wisconsin, and St. Croix, and along the shores of both Great Lakes. Wisconsin has superb smallmouth fishing, and these bronzed

acrobats reach large sizes, particularly in places such as Green Bay on Lake Michigan, Manitowish Lake and River in the Flambeau area of the north, the Bad, Potato, White, and Marengo rivers near Ashland, the Menominee and Peshtego rivers on the border with Michigan, numerous lakes in the Northern Highlands, the Hayward-Chippewa area, the Namekagon, Big Eau Pleine, and Big Rib rivers.

Largemouth bass are found in warm waters throughout the state in innumerable farm ponds, lakes, Mississippi flow lakes, and sluggish streams.

Northern pike inhabit many of the lakes and rivers all over the state, such as Winnebago, the Flambeau and Chippewa flowages and watersheds, lower Wisconsin and Wolf rivers, the St. Croix, the Mississippi and her flow lakes, and countless lakes such as Buckaway, which produced the state record. Pike are found just about everywhere throughout the state and afford a great deal of excitement with their slashing strikes at plugs, spoons, and spinners.

Panfish are the most prolific and most sought-after fish in the state. Yellow perch, white and yellow bass, bluegill, crappie, bullheads, rock bass, warmouth, and other species populate nearly every piece of water in Wisconsin. Noted panfish producers are lakes Winnebago, Mendota, Chequamegon, Michigan, Superior, and Pepin.

Sturgeon, the world's most ancient freshwater fish, give anglers the chance to indulge in some big-game fishing. This species attains weights in excess of 300 pounds, although the Wisconsin record is only half that figure. This armor-plated, vacuum-mouthed monster requires heavy tackle, and can be taken in the fall on worms and minnows in rivers such as the Wisconsin, Menominee, St. Croix, and Monitowish. A special spearing season during the month of February on Lake Winnebago gives ice fishermen the opportunity to participate in an ancient sport that dates back to the days of the Indian. Wooden fish decoys are lowered through the ice in hopes of luring curious sturgeon within range of the spear. A harpooned log-sized fish makes a formidable opponent, and the fisherman should take care to avoid injury during the ensuing fireworks.

Maps & Guides

The following useful DNR publications are available free upon request (single copies only): *Fishing, Spearing & Netting Regulations, Wisconsin Game Fish, Wisconsin Trout Streams, Wisconsin Walleye, Wisconsin Lakes, Largemouth Bass, Brook Trout, Brown Trout, The Lake Sturgeon, Muskellunge,* the 68-page guide *Forest Trees of Wisconsin, Wild Flowers of Wisconsin, Wetlands, Upland Trees, Forests,* and *Endangered Animals in Wisconsin.* Write to: Department of Natural Resources, Box 450, Madison 53701 (608-266-2621).

Hunting & Wildlife

At one time animal life in Wisconsin was as diversified as the state's climate and topography. It was the fur-bearing mammals that first attracted white men to the area, and early traders and explorers in the far north would have encountered elk, moose, wolverines, and Canada lynx in addition to the more commonly sought species such as beaver, otter, and mink. The state still boasts a varied animal population, but many of the original mammals, including elk, moose, cougar, and the bison, have disappeared entirely. Black bear, whitetail deer, common coyotes, red fox, snowshoe hare, woodchucks, and raccoons are plentiful today and provide sport for hunters and wildlife enthusiasts alike. Recent reports would seem to indicate that mountain lions still have a foothold in Forest County, one of the most heavily wooded regions in the state. For the last twenty years occasional sightings of the lean, rangy beasts have led residents to believe that the big cat still hides out somewhere in the north woods. The most recent sighting was reported in the fall of 1973, when a local couple spied a full-grown but pitifully thin mountain lion near Hiles.

Hunting opportunities are best in Wisconsin because of the abundance of game and the immense tracts of hunting lands contained in the national forests, state forests, county forests, DNR lands, and corporate lands mentioned earlier, which exceed five million acres; there are numerous campsites throughout these areas.

Whitetail deer are the number one big-game quarry. The best hunting is found in national forests, such as the Chequamegon, state forests such as Northern Highlands, and the county forests. Best geographic areas are the Northern Tier and the west-central region. The south and east-central areas yield the fewest deer, but the animal is found throughout the state. A taste of Wisconsin deer-hunting nostalgia in the "good old days" is contained in *The Bucks Camp Log*, published by the Wisconsin Sportsman, P.O. Box 1307, Oshkosh 54901, $5.95 postpaid. The book records the absorbing adventures and misadventures of the members of Bucks Camp, written in the camp log of that north-woods camaraderie of hunters from 1916 to 1928.

Black bear are found predominantly in the Northern Tier, in the more remote areas of tracts such as Chequamegon National Forest, and legal hunting is restricted to the top part of the state. In the topmost hunting zone, hunting with dogs is allowed.

Write to the DNR for the free map and chart, *Public Lands Open to Hunting*, and *Wisconsin Hunting and Trapping Regulations* booklet, which describes license-fee information, hunting restrictions,

snowmobile and off-the-road vehicle regulations, protected species, firearm restrictions, big- and small-game seasons and bag limits, special rules, and trapping laws. The DNR also publishes a fascinating 64-page guide, *Birds of Prey of Wisconsin* (50¢). Numerous illustrations will help you identify the different species by their markings and tracks, as will the section on "How to Read Sign."

Ring-necked pheasants are found in all areas with the exception of the heavily forested tracts. Ringnecks are most abundant in the agricultural areas of southern Wisconsin.

Ruffed grouse are found in many sections of Wisconsin, but the best hunting is in the heavily forested Northern Tier in locations such as Northern Highlands State Forest and Chequamegon and Nicolet national forests. The west-central region also produces good gunning, particularly where woodlands meet farms and orchards. About 500,-000 grouse fall to hunters' guns in a good year. Hungarian partridge are found in the agricultural lands of the east-central region and the south and taper off to the west. The western and northern areas are closed to hunting for this exotic. Sharp-tailed grouse are hunted only in the Northern Tier, and the annual bag is very small. In some years, there is no season. Woodcock are found in swales and in alder thickets throughout the state, and the best hunting occurs in the Northern Tier and east-central area.

Ducks and geese are found in marshes, lakes, backwaters, and farmlands all over Wisconsin. The biggest flights come into the southeastern part of the state. Horicon Marsh, south of Fond du Lac on Winnebago, is the premium goose-hunting area and offers excellent duck hunting as well. The Mississippi River, with its flow lakes and backwaters, is another prime wildfowling location, as are the wild-rice-bordered lakes in the north.

Quail are scarce, and the hunting is confined to the southwest corner. Cottontail rabbits are abundant, as are squirrels, and the northern forests have large populations of snowshoe hares.

Wisconsin Sportsman magazine is a bimonthly devoted to fishing and hunting in Wisconsin. Anyone who lives in the state or plans to fish or hunt in the state would do well to take out a subscription, which costs $4.00 per year to $17.50 for five years. Write to the magazine at P.O. Box 1307, Oshkosh 54901. Much invaluable specific fishing, hunting, and camping where-to-go and how-to information is contained between the covers of this fine publication, which deals exclusively with the Wisconsin outdoors.

Great Lakes Trout & Salmon

Trout and salmon fishing in the Great Lakes of Wisconsin, Superior and Michigan, vastly differs from the angling found inland, as do fresh- and saltwater fishing on the two seaboards. Lake Michigan covers 22,400 square miles, and Superior sprawls over 31,800 square miles. Wisconsin has 495 miles of shorelines on Lake Michigan and 325 miles on Lake Superior. The scale of lake life is more akin to oceanic conditions than to fresh water as most people know it. The lakes kick up thundering whitecaps, which explode on the shore as crashing breakers. Waves reach heights in excess of 20 feet, backed by strong, gusting winds that are a chronic feature of these landlocked seas. Boats suited to fishing some favorite interior lake are an invitation to disaster on the "Lakes."

The fish, too, exist in a completely different environment than do their inland counterparts: cool water—the temperature seldom rises above the low 60s—unlimited living space with depths to many hundreds of feet, a great choice of forage and vast schools of bait fish, and less competition for their life needs (with the exception of the presence

of the lethal, parasitic lamprey, which decimated the various trout species in the Great Lakes system in the 1940s, 1950s, and 1960s, after this parasite gained access following completion of the Welland Canal around Niagara Falls). Lampreys were accompanied by the oily, prolific alewife, a member of the herring family. As the predatory trout declined, the alewife population ballooned, to the disgust of shorefront residents, who had to contend with the stench of windrows of bleached alewives. Lamprey poison in the upstream spawning areas has helped to control this menace, and the native trout species and the Pacific salmon feast on the alewives and other bait fish, becoming big and combative.

Brook, brown, and rainbow trout all lose their normal coloration in Great Lakes water, becoming silvery on the sides, with dark backs and a marked disappearance of characteristic colors and spots. Splake (brook and lake trout hybrids) and tiger trout (brook and brown trout hybrids) also undergo a change of coloration. These fish have been introduced into a number of inland waters, as well as the Lakes. Trout prefer the shallower areas of the Great Lakes, while lake or gray trout inhabit deep, cold water and are found in the shallows only for a short time after ice-out and again in the fall. All trout species average much larger in size than their inland counterparts. Brook, brown, and lake trout are fall spawners, while rainbows ascend the rivers in the spring.

Wisconsin's major Lake Michigan steelhead streams include the Manitowoc, Kewaunee, and Ahnapee rivers and Hiblard's, Whitefish Bay, Riebotts, and Heins creeks. Several scenic north-country Lake Superior streams offer top-ranked fishing for these metallic-flanked aristocrats, up to weights of 12 pounds, including the famed Bois Brule River, with its deep pools and shallow gravel bars; the Cranberry River near Ashland, noted for heavily brush-lined banks; and Fish Creek, which offers an interesting combination of pastoral and wild country fishing.

The rise of salmon fishing has created a need for information about the new sport form. Erwin Bauer's *New Guide to Salmon & Trout Fishing*, $2.00 postpaid, available from Lawrence Electronics, 12000 East Skelly Drive, Tulsa, OK 74128, provides a great deal of information on techniques and fishing areas.

The DNR publishes *Fishing Wisconsin's Great Lakes for Trout and Salmon*, available free in single copies (25¢ per copy in multiples). This guide describes the general characteristics and vital statistics of the two Great Lakes and provides a history of the fishery, record fish, thumbnail sketches of the various species, and fishing techniques for each of the lakes and their tributaries. For example, trolling lures that resemble alewives in 5 to 25 feet of water are recommended for brook,

brown, and rainbow trout, as are casting lures from docks and piers in Lake Michigan. Lakers and salmon have to be fished for with deep-water gear by trolling alewive-type lures in deep water. Occasionally, lucky fishermen find coho schooling on the surface and can cast flies and lures to them, which is a thrilling method of fishing. The DNR booklet includes a listing by county of the tributaries with good spawning runs, as well as info about access sites and boat ramps. Write: DNR, Box 450, Madison 53701.

Another useful book is *Coho Fishing Guide*, a 12-by-16-inch map/guide published by the Wisconsin Wildlife Federation, P.O. Box 208, Kaukauna 54130. The cost is $3.75 postpaid; the guide covers the 495 miles of Lake Michigan shoreline in a series of maps showing harbor depths, bottom contours, and tributary streams. The *Compleat Guide to Fishing the Great Lakes*, a comprehensive 218-page paperback, provides the where-to-go and how-to info for fishing the Great Lakes and includes maps, drawings, and photographs. It can be obtained for $5.95 from Greatlakes Living Press, 3634 W. 216th St., Matteson, IL 60443.

Whether you pursue lakers, salmon, or trout, the Great Lakes coasts of Wisconsin will present you with a fascinating challenge for which the rewards are big, pugnacious lake-run fish.

Highways—Recreation & Scenic Routes

Travelers to Wisconsin's state and national forests, scenic lakes, wild rivers, and other wilderness areas will appreciate the comprehensive *Wisconsin State Highway Map*, available free from the Dept. of Transportation, Division of Highways, 4802 Sheboygan Ave., Room 2B, P.O. Box 40, Madison 53701. The map indicates every type of road within the state, from unsurfaced county trunks to interstate highways, as well as cities, towns, rivers, lakes, state and national forestlands, airports, information centers, historical sites, wayside facilities, Indian reservations, public hunting and fishing grounds, and other information of interest to visitors and residents alike.

Another valuable handbook for visitors to Wisconsin is the *Guide to Fun in Wisconsin*, a 112-page, atlas-sized source book containing a wealth of information on all areas of the state. The book is primarily a collection of full-sized maps for every county, state, and national forest and other recreation areas. Each map is accompanied by a description and inserts giving facts about wildlife in the area, campgrounds, and lakes and rivers. The book is especially valuable for the lists of camping areas and public hunting and fishing grounds, the latter giving acreage, lists of wildlife, access points, and information

on regulations. Priced at $4.95, the book is available from the Clarkson Map Co., Box 208, Kaukauna 54130.

The full-color 111-page *Atlas of Wisconsin* offers a thorough geographic inventory of the state for both sportsmen and visitors. The atlas features all major roads and highways and many minor roads; contours, elevations, forested lands, streams, and lakes; parks and preserves; and township lines. Locations of any of the 14,000 names in the gazetteer (including streams, rivers, lakes, etc.) can be easily found by using the various keys. The clothbound *Atlas of Wisconsin* can be ordered for $5.95 from the Wisconsin Sportsman, P.O. Box 1307, Oshkosh 54901. Please include 50¢ for postage and handling. For the serious connoisseurs of ghost towns, the Wisconsin Sportsman publishes a *Map of Ghost Towns, Old Mining and Logging Towns of Northern Wisconsin and Michigan* ($3).

Ice Age Trail

Still under construction in many areas of the state, the marathon Ice Age Trail will eventually cover a route of more than 600 miles through the hilly, lake-strewn wilderness left in the wake of Wisconsin's last great glacier. The trail will link nine units of the Ice Age National Scientific Reserve and will also connect many already established campgrounds with primitive camping areas and shelters planned for other spots along the route. Intended for use by backpackers and hikers during the summer months, the trail should also provide excellent opportunities for snowshoeing and cross-country skiing.

The Two Creeks Buried Forest Unit, located in northeastern Manitowoc County, will mark the Ice Age Trail's eastern terminus. From there, the route travels southwest through Northern Kettle Moraine State Forest, then reaches its southernmost point in South Kettle Moraine State Forest. Looping northward to Cross Plains, then over the Wisconsin River, the trail will eventually wind through Devils Lake State Park and continue in a northerly direction to Standing Rock County Park in Portage County. After entering the Kettlebowl Ski Area, the major path winds west through county forestlands, then follows a 30-mile stretch of heavily wooded terrain through the Chequamegon National Forest. Continuing in a largely westerly direction, the trail will cross the Chippewa Moraine Unit, Barron County, and Polk County before reaching its terminus at Interstate Park.

In its own way, the Ice Age Trail is as ambitious a project as its more lengthy eastern and western counterparts, the great Appalachian and Pacific Crest trails. Certainly it is the longest trail project of its kind ever attempted through Wisconsin. Some sections, such as the Northern Kettle Moraine stretch, are complete and open to hikers. Others have been laid out and marked, and lack only the finishing touches. Still other segments are in the preliminary planning stages.

For detailed information, write: Ice Age Park and Trail Foundation, 780 N. Water St., Milwaukee 53202.

Lake Contour & Trout Stream Maps

Lake contour maps for over 30,000 Wisconsin Lakes showing lake-bottom composition, depth, access, campgrounds, resorts, shore features, vegetation, and fish species present are listed in the 48-page *Wisconsin Mapped Lakes Catalog* ($1), available from Clarkson Map Company, 724 Desnoyer St., Kaukauna 54130. These maps may be ordered direct for 75¢ each (plus 40¢ postage and handling) and are available for every major lake in the state, including such nationally renowned fishing waters as *North Twin Lake, Eagle Lake, Chippewa Flowage, Lac Court Oreilles, Totogatic Flowage, Lac Vieux Desert,*

Big Sand Lake, and the *Turtle-Flambeau Flowage.* The Clarkson Map Company also publishes special purpose maps ($1 each) of the famous outdoor recreation areas: *Boulder Junction* (Vilas County) Land of the Muskie, *Minocqua, Shawano Lake, Wolf River* (includes lakes Poygan, Winnecone, and Butte Des Morts), *Lake Winnebago, Menominee County, Three Lakes* (includes the beautiful 27 lakes chain in Oneida County), *Waukesha Area* (includes Pewaukee, Nagawicka, Oconomowoc, Okauchee lakes), and the *Waupaca Chain.*

Trout stream maps ($2 each) showing fishing, wading, boat conditions, width and depth of channel, trout population, public access, and campgrounds are available for the *Bois Brule* and *Mecan* rivers from Hendrickson's, P.O. Box 207, New Glarus 53574.

Muskellunge—Trophy Fishing Waters

If there is one fish that represents Wisconsin to a majority of fishermen, it is that great toothy, gape-jawed member of the pike family, the muskellunge. The fish's name is a French-American adaption of the Indian name *maskinononge,* meaning "ugly fish." However, no angler fortunate to put a hard-won 30- or 40-pound muskie on the floorboard of his boat would consider his prize to be anything but beautiful. The state's 312,000 acres of muskellunge water include 649 lakes and flowages and 43 streams. The original range in the state was concentrated in the watershed lakes and rivers of the Black, Wisconsin, Tomahawk, and Chippewa rivers in northern Wisconsin and the Ammicon in the northwest corner. Today, the greatest concentration of muskie water is found in the northern area of the state in the heart of its original range, the headwaters of the Chippewa, Wisconsin, and Flambeau rivers, in the Hayward-Chippewa Flowage area, and Lac du Flambeau Indian Reservation.

Muskies are solitary fish that prefer clear shallow water, weed beds, snags, and submerged trees where they can lurk, waiting for unwary prey, from pelicans to small fish. The muskie likes to stake out an area as his domain and stay put. Fishing methods include trolling large plugs, bucktail baits, spoons, and bait, particularly 9- to 12-inch suckers, and casting the same lures to choice locations. The most popular lures for "old long face" include the Muskie Monk Plug, Pflueger Globe Plug, Rapala Magnum Plug, Suick Plug, and Mepps Giant Killer. The explosive strike of a large fish at a surface plug is an unforgettable experience. Make sure that your hooks are strong and needle-sharp, because this fish has a hard, long jaw, and throws lures under the best of circumstances. Muskies are caught all season long, but the fish do not take lures as well in the summer. Many fishermen prefer the fall for the fastest fishing and the beauty of the autumn leaves, and some of the best fishing is in raw November, when the fish feed voraciously to store up nourishment for the winter.

Some of the better waters besides the locations mentioned are the Turtle-Flambeau Flowage, Escanaba, High, Big Twin, the Eagle Chain, Lac Vieux Desert, Big Sand, Buckatabon, the St. Germaine, Tomahawk, and Pelican lakes in the northern section; Green and Little Green Lakes near Ripon; the Waupaca Lakes near Waupaca in the east-central area; and the Black River and Potter Flowage in the west-central area. Muskies are found in the Great Lakes, but they are spread *very* thinly.

The DNR produces a very useful booklet, *Wisconsin Muskellunge Waters*, free for single copies (25¢ each for multiple copies), which describes the muskie's history and original range, producing acreage, habits and habitat, management, and fishing tips, as well as an illustration showing the differences between muskies, pike, and pickerel. A map shows the number of muskellunge lakes in each county. The northern region of the Chippewa-Flambeau area has more than the rest of the state combined. In addition, there is a listing of lakes and rivers alphabetically within each county, and the counties are listed alphabetically. The list gives the section, township, and range of each lake, or other location information, its acreage, maximum depth, classification of fishing quality, and public access. Write: DNR, Box 450, Madison 53701.

North Country Canoe Trip Outfitters

The renowned American River Touring Association (ARTA) offers summer North Country canoe trips along several of Wisconsin's historic wilderness waterways, including the 60-mile *St. Croix River Trip,* the beautiful *Flambeau River Trip* through Flambeau River State Forest and the famed Cedar and Beaver Dam rapids, and the *Apostle Islands Canoe Adventure,* using 34-foot Montreal canoes to island-hop along Superior's scenic south shore and explore caves, arches, cliffs, and rocky wave-swept beaches, starting in Bayfield and ending in the fishing village of Cornucopia. This week-long trip includes overnight camping in the Apostle Islands National Lakeshore Area. For more information about these programs, as well as short two-day outings along the beautiful cliff-lined shores of Lake Michigan in Door County and the Mississippi River in Minnesota, write: ARTA North Country, 5375 Eureka Rd., Excelsior, MN 55331; (612) 474–5190.

North Country Trail

This 60-mile wilderness trail crosses the northern half of the Chequamegon National Forest from Ruth Lake, 3 miles south of Iron River on County Trunk A, to Forest Road 390, about 2½ miles west of Mellen. The trail's eastern half winds through the Penokee Hills, a region of granite outcroppings, boulder-strewn ridges, and scenic overlooks. The western half follows a gently rolling combination of upland and swamps. About 7 miles from the Ruth Lake entry point,

WISCONSIN MUSKELLUNGE WATERS

DEPARTMENT OF NATURAL RESOURCES
MADISON
PUB. 1–3600 (73)

the North Country Trail enters the Rainbow Lake Wilderness, a lake-strewn, forested area encompassing 6,583 acres, carefully maintained in its primitive, unspoiled state, free from motorized vehicles or developed recreational facilities. Hikers should note that a free permit is required to enter the wilderness. Since the trail crosses some 20 roads, the route can be explored in short, easy segments, ideal for weekend or day trips.

Three Adirondack shelters are located along the trail, and are designated specifically for trail use. Fire rings and refuse containers are the only amenities available at the shelters located at Seitz Lake, Marengo River, and Porcupine Lake. There are also four campgrounds adjacent to or within one mile of the trail, offering sites for a small, daily-use fee.

The many wilderness attractions of the route—dense forests, craggy ridges, and a variety of wildlife—are enhanced by the 23 lakes near the trail, all of them fine sources for walleye, northerns, small- and largemouth bass, panfish, and trout. In addition to the larger rivers, such as Brunsweiller and Marengo, there are a number of seldom-fished trout streams off the main trail.

Early May, when the spring flowers begin to bloom, is a favorite time for hiking the trail, as is October, when the spectacular fall foliage provides miles of brilliant forest scenery. In winter, the trail may be used for cross-country skiing, although the route does contain many steep hills and sharp turns that may prove difficult for less experienced skiers. The Forest Service sternly warns that all ski travel on the trail should be done with caution and adequate preparation, both for survival and physical ability.

Detailed information, including trail descriptions, points of interest, and mile-by-mile trail data, and a map of the North Country Trail are available from the District Forest Rangers at Glidden 54527, telephone 1 (715) 264–2511; at Hayward 54843, telephone 1 (715) 634–4821; and at Washburn 54891, telephone 1 (715) 373–2667. North Country Trail is shown on the following U.S. Geological Survey maps: Delta, Drummond, Diamond Lake, Marengo, Grandview.

St. Croix & Namekagon National Scenic Rivers

The historic St. Croix, an ancient Indian and fur trade canoe route, flows from its source, the St. Croix Flowage, through scenic north country forests past numerous evergreen-clad islands, swamps, and towering sandstone bluffs, winding southward for 174 miles before emptying into the "Father of Waters," the Mississippi. Near Big Island, the river is joined by its beautiful tributary, the Namekagon (the Chippewa word for sturgeon), whose waters swell the St. Croix to more than twice its original size; then for 80 miles the river traces the boundary between Minnesota and Wisconsin. Flowing silently between the sandy banks of an ever-widening glacial valley, the St. Croix is fed by numerous other tributaries, and changes in character from a narrow trout stream to a broad, lake-like flowage of almost imperceptible movement. In the first 12½ miles of its journey, it forms 35 rapids of low to medium risk. The rest of its length is marked by waters with some moderately challanging rapids, currents varying from slow to fast, and one high-risk rapid at Big Fish Trap in the St. Croix River Forest. Historic points of interest along the route include the remains of a primitive Indian village near the confluence with the Lower Tamarack River and Sioux Portage Creek, the main artery of travel for trappers and Indians on their way to Yellow Lake.

Both the St. Croix and Namekagon (see "Wisconsin Travel & Recrea-

tion Guide") are shown and described in the free *St. Croix* map/brochure, available from the Superintendent, P.O. Box 579, St. Croix Falls 54024, which also provides background on the river's history and character along with a list of mileages between the most widely used put-in and takeout points. The same office offers free one-page fliers on camping sites along the St. Croix and Namekagon, guidelines to follow when traveling the riverway, and lists of outfitters in the immediate area. Both rivers are fully described in *Whitewater; Quietwater,* the wild-river touring guide listed under "Canoeing & Wilderness Waters."

The St. Croix and Namekagon hold muskellunge, northern pike, walleye, smallmouth bass, trout, and panfish. The Namekagon is especially noted for its trophy brown trout. On that portion of the St. Croix forming the boundary between Wisconsin and Minnesota, a license from either state is valid for those fishing from a boat.

The scenic mixed hardwood and evergreen forests adjacent to the riverway support an abundance of bird and wildlife, including whitetail deer, black bear, snowshoe hare, ruffed grouse, coyote, beaver, mink, otter, golden and bald eagles, woodcock, great blue heron, kingfisher, waterfowl, and a wide variety of hawks.

Both rivers have their source in lakes, and the entire region is studded with scenic ponds and lakes, each more secluded and beautiful than the last, making this region a camper's and hiker's paradise. Numerous campgrounds are scattered along the banks of both national scenic riverways, and are indicated on the map included in the free *St. Croix* brochure, and on lists available from the riverway superintendent at the address given above. Visitor information offices in Trego and Grantsburg, Wisconsin, will also be happy to supply information for canoeists, campers, and hikers. Since both rivers are easily navigable by beginners and experts, guide services are not needed for canoe trips. However, there are many outfitters and canoe-rental services in the area, some of which include: *Buck's Sportsman Headquarters,* Minong 54859; *Camp One,* Route 1, Box 606, Danbury 54830; *Canfield's Campground,* Trego 54888; *Ed's Service Center, Inc.,* Cable 54821; *Four Rivers,* Highway 77, Co. Road H, Webb Lake 54892; *Jack's Boat & Canoe Rental,* WI Hwy. 35, Markville, MN 55048; *Marine Canoe Rental,* Sid Cornell, Marine on St. Croix, MN 55047; *St. Croix Scenic River Outfitters,* Route 1, Pine City, MN 55063; *Taylors Falls Canoe Company,* Taylors Falls, MN 55084; *The Wild River Canoe Rental & Sales,* John Kass, Trego 54888; *Voyageurs Canoe & Bicycle Rental,* 2150 Greenview Dr., St. Paul, MN 55112; *Voyageurs Canoe Outfitters,* Hayward 54843; *Voyageurs Canoe Rental,* St. Croix State Park, Hinckley, MN 55037; *Water Trails, Inc.,* Grantsburg 54840; *Wild River Inn,* Hayward 54843; *Wild River Outfitters,* Grantsburg 54840.

St. Croix National Wild & Scenic River is shown on the following large-scale U.S. Geological Survey maps: Danbury, Grantsburg, Milltown, Minong, Pine City, Rush City, Solon Springs, Webb, Webster. Namekagon National Wild & Scenic River is shown on U.S. Geological Survey large-scale maps: Danbury, Hayward, Minong, Spooner, Stone Lake, Webb Lake, Cable, Lake Takodah, Namekagon Lake, Seely.

Ski Touring Trails & Centers

With more than 175 ski-trail areas, almost 80 marked cross-country routes, and a climate and terrain that have been compared to Sweden and parts of Norway, Wisconsin offers some of the finest ski touring available in the country today. The state's first settlers early discovered the advantages of winter travel on skis, although some nonskiing residents thought the skinny tracks discovered across their homestead belonged to a rare, narrow-footed beast. Among the first cross-country

buffs to achieve renown on a pair of skis, "Snowshoe" Thompson earned his niche in the annals of the sport by carrying the mail across western Wisconsin and later over the Sierras. Inhabitants of the remote reaches of Wisconsin still understand the value of snowshoes and skis when weather conditions make other forms of travel impossible.

Both the Chequamegon and Nicolet national forests provide opportunities for ski touring in areas closed to snowmobiles and other motorized vehicles. Both forests also feature hundreds of miles of unplowed logging roads and trails for cross-country use. While the North Country Trail winding through the northern part of the Chequamegon is not recommended for beginners, its many steep hills and sharp turns should provide challenging travel to the more experienced skier. The *Wisconsin Ski Touring Directory,* available free from the Dept. of Natural Resources, Box 7921, Madison 53707, lists both public and private marked trails in each county throughout the state and offers information on locations, trail descriptions, comments on trail difficulty, and miscellaneous information concerning the kind of terrain traversed and facilities available—shelters, campgrounds, resorts, etc.

The nationally renowned *Telemark Lodge,* Cable 54821 (phone: 715–798–3811) offers lodging, touring trails, and nordic instruction. Other top-ranked Badger State cross country centers include: *Wolf River Lodge,* Langlade 54491; *Thunder Lake Ski Touring Center,* Box 215,

Rt. 2, Eagle River 54521; *Port Mountain,* Box 840, Bayfield 54814; *Olympia Sport Village* (with 100 miles of old logging roads), Box 3, Lake O'Brien, Upson, 54565; *Omnibus Ski Area* (Door County), Fish Creek 54212; *Green Lakes Winter Sports Center,* Green Lake 54941; *Game Unlimited Cross Country Ski Area,* Rt. 2, Hudson 54016; *Chanticleer Inn* (on Eagle Lakes Chain), Rt. 3, Box 577, Eagle River 54521.

Skiers looking for luxurious accommodations, ski clinics, and a choice of downhill or cross-country trails will enjoy the atmosphere at *White-cap Mountains,* a resort and ski lodge tucked among three mountains near Montreal, Wisconsin. More than 20 miles of skiing for beginners and experts, seven ski lifts, a ski school, and lodging are available. In addition, Whitecap Mountains offers a Nordic ski clinic designed to prepare novices for cross-country ski trips, and special weekend packages including lodging, meals, and instruction. Write to Whitecap Mountains, Montreal 54550, for further information.

Additional information on activities in Wisconsin, arctic and Nordic skiing, and ski reports is available from the Dept. of Natural Resources, Box 7921, Madison 53707, and the Dept. of Business Development, Division of Tourism, Box 177, Madison 53707. (See also "Ice Age Trail" and individual sections on Wisconsin state forests.)

Wild & Trophy Fishing Waters

Listed below are large-scale U.S. Geological Survey topographic map kits showing the entire lengths, including headwaters, and the topography of the surrounding wildlands of several of Wisconsin's nationally renowned fishing streams and canoe routes (see "Wisconsin Map & Recreation Guide" for additional listings). *Amnicon River:* Lyman Lake, Parkland, Poplar NE, South Range; *Little Wolf River:* Rosholt, Tigerton NW, Iola, Big Falls, Tigerton, Symco, Manawa, Northport; *Popple River:* Alvin SE, Florence SE, Florence SW, Iron Mountain SW; *Evergreen River:* White Lake, Langlade; *Brule River:* Beechwood, Iron River (7.5), Gaastra, Fortune Lakes, Nautts, Florence W., Florence E., Randville, Iron Mountain SW, Iron Mountain (7.5); *Lac du Flambeau:* Flambeau Flowage, Butternut, Mercer; *Peshtigo River:* Athelstane, Coleman, Goodman, Laona, Little Sturgeon, Marinette W., Porterfield, Thunder Mountain; *Oconto River:* Gillett, Langlade, Mountain, Oconto, Oconto Falls; *Montreal River:* Ironwood, Little Girls Point, N. Ironwood; *Marengo River:* Marengo, Mellen; *Moose River:* Clam Lake, Clam Lake NE, Clam Lake SE, Glidden, Moose Lake; *Manitowish River & Chain of Lakes:* Boulder Junction, Mercer; *Upper Wisconsin River* (from Lac Vieux Desert to Wausau): Eagle River E., Eagle River W., Heafford Junction, Merrill, Phelps, Rhinelander, Spirit Falls, Starks, Star Lake, Three Lakes, Tomahawk, Wausau; *Totagatic River* (including Pokegama, Minong and Totagatic flowages): Chittamo, Hayward, Minong, Totagatic Lake; *White River:* Ashland E., Ashland W., Delta, Grandview NW, Marengo, Odanah; *Red River* (including Moose and Shawano lakes): Antigo, Gillett, Gresham, Shawano, White Lake; *Deerskin River:* Eagle River E., Anvil Lake, Phelps; *Spirit River & Flowage:* Rib Lake, Spirit Falls, Tomahawk.

Wolf National Wild & Scenic River

This nationally famous big-water fly fishing stream and national scenic waterway, considered the Badger State's most dangerous canoe trail, forms its headwaters near the small village of Hiles in northeastern Wisconsin and flows south some 400 miles into Lake Poygan. The remote wild stretches of the upper Wolf flow through the Menominee Indian Reservation and Big Smoky Falls area, Wolf Rapids, Otter Slide, Big Eddy Falls, Tea Kettle Rapids, Keshena Falls area, and the beautiful Dalles of the Wolf. Fly fishing in this stunning north-woods wilderness is good for brown trout up to 5 pounds. Although only one 24-mile stretch of the Wolf has been classified as a wild and scenic river, the shortest such segment included among the first nine rivers protected by the 1968 legislation passed by Congress, many other runs along the river offer equally spendid scenery and adventurous white water. The scenic-river portion of the Wolf runs for 23½ miles between the Menominee-Langlade county line and Keshena Falls. Because of the heavy concentration of visitor accommodations and other commercial enterprises, the last half-mile before the town of Keshena has been designated "recreational." Most runs along the river include rapids of considerable difficulty, and this particular stretch, encompassing such evocative white-water milestones as Shotgun Eddy, Gilmore's Mistake, White Rapids, and Big Eddy Falls, is no exception. The run is thus not recommended for beginners, and even experts are strongly advised to scout the water situation in advance at Boy Scout, Gilmore's, and Shotgun rapids.

Another run along the Wolf north of the scenic portion of the river follows a 15-mile stretch between the confluence with the Lily River and Langlade in the county of Langlade, Wisconsin. This section of the Wolf—indeed, all of the river above Keshena—is nationally renowned for its brown trout fishing. Rapids vary from easy white water at Big Slough Gundy and Hollister to the more challenging waters of Cedar Rapids, laced with granite boulders and large waves. This stretch can easily be cut into two runs of 7 and 8 miles each at the takeout/put-in site of Hollister. Other segments of the river are fully described in *Canoe Trails of Northeastern Wisconsin* and *Whitewater, Quietwater* (see "Canoeing & Wilderness Waters").

The countryside surrounding the Wolf River is hilly, and, for the most part, sparsely populated—a wild region blanketed with white pine and hardwood forests of ash, yellow birch, aspen, and maple, offering spectacular fall scenery. Big-game animals indigenous to the terrain around the river's northern stretches include deer and black bear; of the smaller mammals, porcupine, otter, muskrat, beaver, and snowshoe hare are most common. Fishermen should note that the areas around the Trip Rapids, Duckness Falls, and Sullivan Falls have been set aside for fly fishing only. Brown trout, along with some walleyes and white bass, are the most popular species taken. The slower-moving, marshy stretches near Lake Poygan are famous for tremendous runs of spring walleye and northerns to 30 pounds.

Campgrounds along the Wolf include the developed sites at Boulder Lake in Nicolet National Forest (write the U.S. Forest Service, Lakewood 54138 for information) and 10 primitive campsites located near Pissmire Rapids at the County Highway WW Bridge in Menominee County. The *Wolf River Lodge* (c/o R. C. Steed, White Lake 54491) offers a comfortable inn with food, lodging, and drink; tree-shaded campsites; ski touring along the Lake Superior and Oxbow trails; trout fishing and outfitting; and raft rentals. Rafts may also be rented from *Shotgun Raft Rental* (c/o J. A. Peters, Langlade 54491), *River Forest Lodge* (c/o J. Stecher, Langlade 54491), *Herb Buettner* (White Lake 54991), and *Robert Walters,* Northern Light Bridge (White Lake 54491). Trout-fishing guide services are available through *William E. Kern* (P.O. Box 170, Rt. 1, Cascade 53011).

For detailed river and permit information, write: Menominee Restoration Committee, P. O. Box 397, Keshena 54135.

Wolf National Wild & Scenic River is shown on the following large-scale U.S. Geological Survey maps: Argonne, Bear Creek, Crandon, Elcho, Hortonville, Lake Poygan, Langlade, Leeman, Lily, Lunds, Nashville, Readfield, Shawano, Shiocton, White Lake, Weyauwega.

Chequamegon National Forest & Flambeau River Country

Chequamegon National Forest Topo Maps

Includes the Red Cliff Lac Court Oreilles, and Lac du Flambeau Indian reservation lands and trophy muskellunge waters. U.S. Geological Survey Overview Maps, scale 1:250,000: Ashland & Rice Lake.

Chippewa Flowage—Hayward Lakes Trophy Muskellunge Country

Large-scale U.S. Geological Survey Topographic Maps includes Round, Grindstone, Tiger Cat, Ghost, Lost Land, Teal Lakes, and Totagatic Flowage: Radisson (15-minute map), Chief Lake, Reserve, Hayward, Seeley, Moose Lake.

Flambeau River State Forest

Large-scale U.S. Geological Survey Topographic Maps including the Flambeau, Holcombe, and South Fork flowages: Butternut, Butternut Lake, Exeland, Ingram, Kennan, Kennedy, Lac Sault Dore, Ladysmith, Lugerville, Mercer, Oxbow, Park Falls.

Situated south of the Apostle Islands and Lake Superior's Chequamegon Bay in northwestern Wisconsin, this reserve encompasses 838,000 acres of gently rolling terrain, conifer and hardwood forests, and over 400 evergreen-rimmed lakes, including some of the nation's great muskie waters in the famed Hayward Lakes–Chippewa Flowage area and the adjacent Lac du Flambeau Indian Reservation waters. Its name derives from *sho-wah-ma-gon*, a Chippewa Indian term for the "place of shallow waters," referring to the Chequamegon Bay. The forest's major waterways—the Flambeau, Chippewa, Yellow, and Namekagon—and their tributaries form a network of more than 632 miles of streams, once the travel routes of Indians, missionaries, voyageurs, and loggers. Today these same streams provide superlative canoe routes and excellent fishing for muskie, northerns, walleye, bass, panfish, and trout.

Three proposed wilderness areas within the Chequamegon have been carefully maintained as unspoiled forest tracts. Approximately one mile north and west of Drummond, the Flynn Lake Wilderness Study Area offers 15 undeveloped lakes and 31 ponds, all of them essentially landlocked, since there are no existing streams within the 6,321-acre area. The Flynn Lake Wilderness offers fine examples of northern hardwood, balsam fir, natural and planted pine, and aspen/paper birch stands on rolling glaciated-lake-country terrain. The only signs of development within this primitive expanse are a one-mile section of the North Country Trail in the northeast corner of the area, numerous old railroad grades and logging roadbeds, and two private cabins located on private lands. Wildlife common to the northern Wisconsin forests include deer, black bear, ruffed grouse, red fox, coyote, skunk, otter, beaver, muskrat, and weasel. Most of the species of fish common to the area are found in the numerous lakes—such as Cisco, Arrowhead, and Star—and provide excellent fishing. At present, the Flynn Lake Wilderness is intended for day use only, but Perch Lakes Campground, some 2 miles north of the northeast corner of the area, offers 16 sites and is within easy reach of the wilderness. Horses, outboard motors or mechanical devices, motorized vehicles, and nonmotorized wheeled vehicles are forbidden. No special permits are needed to visit the area.

Northwest of Flynn Lake is the Rainbow Lake Wilderness, a similarly primitive forest tract covering 6,583 acres and containing 15 lakes and 9 ponds. Much the same fauna and flora are found in the area, and, as in the Flynn Lake region, fishing is tops for bass, perch, trout,

WISCONSIN TRAVEL & RECREATION GUIDE

crappie, bluegill, and northern pike. The only developed recreation facility within the area is the section of cross-country trail; old logging roads provide access to other parts of the area. Permits, available from the District Ranger Offices, are required for entrance to the Rainbow Lake Wilderness.

Located 18 miles due east of Park Falls, the Round Lake Wilderness Area encompasses the 2,900-acre Doering Tract, mature stands of aspen, paper birch, and yellow birch, and 25,000 feet of frontage on both sides of the South Fork of the Flambeau River. Aside from Round Lake, other bodies of water within the area include Tucker, Jupa, and Ole's lakes. The South Fork of the Flambeau River rises in the Round-Pike lake chain and flows for some 2 ½ miles through the wilderness study area. In spring and early summer, the river is navigable by canoe from the Round Lake outlet. Later in the summer, numerous shallows and rapids offer difficulties for less experienced canoeists and may require portaging. The first rapids, Fishtrap, is located on the western boundary of the Round Lake Wilderness. In addition to offering a real challenge in season to white-water enthusiasts, the Flambeau provides fine fishing for walleye, muskellunge, northern pike, bass, and panfish. The only developed recreation facility in the study area is a portage trail between Tucker and Round lakes; primitive type roads and old logging trails provide access to other parts of the area and make excellent hiking trails through this dense northern hardwood forest. There are three nearby national-forest campgrounds and one canoe camp providing overnight facilities to visitors to the wilderness. Round Lake is open for day use only, but no permits are required for entry. As in the other wilderness study areas, horses, motorized vehicles, mechanical devices, outboard motors, and aircraft are forbidden.

Free maps and descriptions of each of the above areas—*Flynn Lake*, *Rainbow Lake*, and *Round Lake*—are available from the Forest Supervisor, Chequamegon National Forest, Federal Bldg., Park Falls 54552. The maps show lakes, streams, trails, and the surrounding forestlands, while the descriptions cover regulations, history, access points, wildlife, and forest growth.

Among the more unusual scenic attractions in the forest are the Morgan Falls, fifteen miles west of Mellen, Wisconsin, where a small stream falls over 70 feet down a rock cliff to a small pool, then tumbles downward once again to a second pool fringed by tall conifers. From there the stream flows through a small valley, paralleled for a short distance by high rock bluffs. The highest point within the forest is known as St. Peter's Dome, near Morgan Falls, a lofty, pink granite outcropping affording fine views of Lake Superior 25 miles to the north.

Many superb large and small remote lakes, framed by secluded shores and conifer forests, fall within and adjacent to forestlands. They range in size from one acre to 17,000-acre Chippewa Lake just outside the southwest corner of the Chequamegon. A number of the large lakes within the forest, and many smaller bodies of water, hold trophy-size northern pike, muskellunge, walleye, small- and largemouth bass, several species of panfish and trout. Several streams and spring ponds hold rainbow, brook, and brown trout. Several of the deep, cold-water lakes have been treated by the Fisheries Division of the Wisconsin Department of Natural Resources to remove undesirable species; these have been restocked with rainbows, which have reproduced in sufficient quantities to provide good catches.

The forest's populations of black bear, whitetail deer, raccoon, snowshoe rabbit, squirrel, and ruffed grouse offer superb hunting in season, while the many predators, such as coyote, fox, and bobcat may also be taken. During September bear-hunting season, several large, trophy-size black bear have been bagged by successful hunters. In recent years the DNR has permitted the use of bear hounds to hunt bear. In October and November, the ruffed grouse, or "partridge," is the most popular game bird hunted in this area. The forest's most popular big-game animal, whitetail deer, is scattered uniformly throughout the forest. During the late-November season, their natural wariness offers a challenge to even the most experienced hunter. Waterfowl hunting in the Chequamegon is limited and considered average at best, although a number of shallow impoundments have been developed in an effort to improve local waterfowl habitat conditions.

A network of old logging roads, seeded to clover and mowed to retard brush growth, and forest service roads provide access to the Riley Lakes Wildlife Area, Blockhouse Lake, the Moquah Barrens Wildlife Area, and to Moose, Teal, Lost Land, Owen, Pigeon, Namekagon, and scores of remote seldom-fished wild-country lakes. Several logging roads are gated during the hunting season and provide the sportsman with many hours of good hunting without being disturbed by motorized hunters. Adjacent to the forest are the superb fishing waters of the Red Cliff Lac Court Oreilles, Lac du Flambeau, and Bad River Indian reservations.

Of the innumerable rivers and streams that flow through the Chequamegon, the Flambeau, Chippewa, and Namekagon rivers are considered top-ranked canoeing waters. Designated a Wild and Scenic River by Congress in 1968, the Namekagon, flowing from Namekagon Lake, is generally runnable for its entire length all summer long and, within forest lands, flows through a relatively unspoiled stretch of terrain and numerous low marshy areas. The river's name derives from an Ojibway expression meaning "where the sturgeons are plentiful" —a deceptive appellation, since one of the outstanding features of the Namekagon stretch is the number of fine trout streams adjoining the river, including Cap Creek and Big Brook. The Jump and Yellow rivers, northwest of Medford, are also good canoeing streams with several white water stretches. The upper reaches of all of these rivers are often shallow in the late summer and early fall, so be prepared to portage around shallow stretches. Specific information on a canoeing stream or lake within the Chequamegon National Forest can be obtained by contacting the District Ranger's Office, cited at the end of this section, nearest your point of interest. (See also "Canoeing & Wilderness Waters" in the "Encyclopedia" section.)

Three major trail systems, complemented by seven short paths, offer fine routes on foot or on horseback. The Flambeau Trail System, a network of almost 100 miles in length, passes through varying types of forest cover and crosses several streams and creeks, including the South Fork of the Flambeau River. Because there are 12 different trails with lengths from one to 24 miles, the system appeals to both the casual hiker and serious backpacker. The seventeen-mile Mount Valhalla Loop Trail passes through forests of jack pine, aspen, and white birch and winds around the Valhalla Overlook, a high hill offering beautiful views of Lake Superior. The 16-unit Birch Grove Campground and Long Lake Picnic Grounds are situated within easy reach of this route. Other attractions along the Mount Valhalla Trail include a ridge-top section and the Sunbowl, a large valley with exceptional one-mile views from its surrounding rim. Information on the Flambeau and Mount Valhalla trails and other hiking routes within the forest is available from the Forest Supervisor, Chequamegon National Forest, Federal Bldg., Park Falls 54552. A separate flier giving detailed information on snowmobiling and skiing is also available from the above address. (See also "North Country Trail" in the "Encyclopedia" section.)

The *Chequamegon National Forest Map* (50¢) will also help to locate

camping facilities as well as streams, lakes, rivers, trails, campgrounds, roads, surrounding towns, winter sports areas, historical sites, and other forest features. Recreation folder maps and all general information concerning the forest can be obtained directly from the Forest Supervisor, Federal Bldg., Park Falls 54552. In addition, the Forest Service also publishes three maps sheets covering separate ranger districts within the forest. Even though the basic information is essentially the same as in the recreation map, scale for these maps is ½ inch to the mile, so they are four times larger. The *Medford* and *Park Falls Ranger District* maps are approximately 17 by 20 inches in size and cost 50¢ each. The *Glidden-Hayward-Washburn Ranger Districts Map* is printed on a 32-by-47-inch sheet and is priced at $1.00. All three maps are available from the Forest Supervisor at the above address or from the Regional Forester, U.S. Forest Service, 633 W. Wisconsin Ave., Milwaukee 53203.

Covering over 86,000 acres just south of Chequamegon National Forest, the Flambeau River State Forest was originally created to preserve the great natural wilderness area along the North Fork of the Flambeau. The name "Flambeau" was given to the river by early French voyageurs, who discovered Indians spearing fish by torchlight in the big lake to the east. Ever since that time, the Lac du Flambeau —"Lake of the Torch"—and its river have been famous for both trophy muskellunge fishing and canoeing; today the river and its surrounding wooded terrain are renowned as one of the few unspoiled and noncommercialized areas left in Wisconsin.

The forest itself offers two family campgrounds of 30 sites each on Connors Lake and Lake of the Pines, 50 miles of snowmobile trails, 13 canoe campsites, a large beach and picnic area, and both hiking and nature trails. Northern hardwoods, aspen, hemlock, and other conifers form lofty canopies for a rich understory of mosses and wildflowers, while waterfowl and occasionally bald eagles soar overhead; beaver, black bear, and deer inhabit the forestlands. Beautiful lakes offer-

ing panfish, muskie, bass, and walleye, along with several nearby trout streams, have made the area popular with fishermen. The autumn season is often best for fishing, and the entire forest is open to public hunting for deer, woodcock, grouse, and other species.

By far the greatest attraction of the area is the Flambeau River, praised by beginners and experts alike as one of the finest and most scenic canoe runs in the state. A 12-mile run from Nine Mile Creek on Highway 70 to Oxbow passes through acres of virgin hardwood and hemlock and has only one stretch of fast water worth mentioning, the Barnaby Rapids below Nine Mile Creek. Several trout streams, including Butternut and Log creeks, enter this section of the river, which also passes through Dead Man's Slough, named for an unfortunate logger who met his end during one of the treacherous highwater periods. Still other portions of the river pass through miles of heavy timber, including the "Big Block," a solitary stand of old-growth hemlock running for about three miles, or over perilous white water such as Cedar Falls, Beaver Dam, and Flambeau Falls. See "Canoeing & Wilderness Waters" in the "Encyclopedia" section for information on guides to the area.

Summer is the canoeist's season in Flambeau State Forest; winter is reserved for snowshoers, skiers, and snowmobile enthusiasts. The area is traversed by 53 miles of marked and maintained snowmobile trails, plus connecting links from Rusk County to the Tuscobia-Park Falls State Park Trail. Snowmobilers must stick to the designated trails, but snowshoers and cross-country skiers are free to travel anywhere.

Trails, campsites, canoe campsites, rapids, access points, highways, portage trails, and roads are all indicated on the *Flambeau River State Forest Map,* available free from the Wisconsin Dept. of Natural Resources, Box 7921, Madison 53707.

For detailed vacation-resort information in the Hayward Lakes Region, write: Recreation Assn., Hayward 54843. Canoe rental and shuttle-service info may be obtained by writing: *Chippewa Trails Canoe Rentals,* U.S. Hwy. 8, Bruce 54819; *Flambeau Lodge,* Rt. 1, Ladysmith 54848; *Taylor Falls Canoe Co.,* Taylor Falls 55084 (St. Croix-Namekagon); *Water Trails Inc.,* Box 336, Grantsburg 54840 (Lake Namekagon and St. Croix).

Vacation accommodations are offered by the following lodges and resorts (write to resort name, plus town and zip code for literature and rates): (Cable 54821) *Hemlock Circle Resort, Lake Owen Lodge, The Lakewoods, Mogasheen Resort, Rohr's Otter Bay Resort;* (Hayward 54843) *Arrowhead Resort, Big Musky Resort, Broken Arrow Lodge, Ciceronia Resort* (on Lac Court Oreilles), *Clements Lake Chippewa Resort, Dun Rovin Lodge, Lake Land Resort, Lost Land Lake Lodge, Northland Lodge, Pine Manor Resort, Rolly's Resort, Timberland Resort, Virgin Timber-All Season Resort* (Moose Lake), *Wild River Inn Motel* (Namekagon River), *Williams Grindstone Lake Resort;* (Iron River 54847) *Pine Point Lodge* (Eagle-Pine Lakes Chain), *Tower Trail Resort;* (Winter 54896) *Adams Flambeau Forest Resort, Big Bear Lodge.* For additional listings and information, write to the local chambers of commerce.

Access & Outfitting Centers

Chequamegon National Forest is easily reached via State Highway 64 from Medford; via County Route H from Phillips; via state highways 182 and 13 from Park Falls; and via County Road GG from Mellen. From the Bayfield Peninsula and Chequamegon Bay region, the forest is accessible via State Highway 112 from Ashland; from Bayfield and Red Cliff take State Highway 13 south to Washburn, then proceed west on County Road C.

Nicolet National Forest & the Northern Highlands

Nicolet National Forest Topo Maps

U.S. Geological Survey topographic overview maps, scale 1:250,000: Iron Mountain, Iron River.

Northern Highlands State Forest

Large-scale U.S. Geological Survey topographic maps: Boulder Junction, Dam Lake, Eagle River N., Fence Lake, Lac du Flambeau, Mercer Lake, Minocqua, St. Germain, Star Lake, Sugar Camp, Winchester.

American Legion State Forest

Large-scale U.S. Geological Survey topographic maps: Eagle River W., Dam Lake, Minocqua, Heafford Junction, Sugar Camp.

Lac Vieux Desert Country

Including North Twin, Big Sand, and Long lakes, large-scale U.S. Geological Survey topographic map: Phelps.

Pine River Wild Trout & Canoe Country

Large-scale U.S. Geological Survey topographic maps: Alvin SW, Alvin SE, Alvin, Long Lake, Tipler, Long Lake SE, Long Lake NE, Naults.

Bounded on the north by the twisting Brule River, Nicolet National Forest stretches over parts of six northeastern counties, embracing nearly 650,000 acres of mixed hardwoods and evergreens just south of the Northern Michigan-Wisconsin border, and hundreds of sparkling blue lakes, including the famed trophy muskie waters of Big Sand, Lac Vieux Desert, and North Twin lakes, and the headwaters of five of the top-ranked trout streams in the Upper Great Lakes Region—the Pine, Popple, Peshtigo, Oconto, and Wolf. Many of the forest's remote "lost" lakes provide excellent fishing for trout, bass, northern pike, and walleye for the adventuresome wilderness angler. The Pike River, which rises just east of the forest boundary and flows for 90 miles into Lake Michigan's Green Bay, floated the world's record amount of lumber during the logging era, and today its deep marshy waters offer quality fly fishing for large browns and brookies. The famed Deerskin River, home of the old 10 pound world-record tiger trout, flows through the northeast corner of the forest.

The forest is named for Jean Nicolet, an early French explorer and emissary of Governor Champlain of New France, who landed near Green Bay in 1634. Certain that he had at last discovered the route to China and would be greeted by mandarins as soon as he stepped off his ship, Nicolet arrived dressed in elaborate robes, firing pistols with both hands. Instead, groups of naked Indians emerged from the forest, bowing and singing praises before this splendid deity. Though he never did reach the Orient, Nicolet was the first white man to touch soil now governed by Wisconsin, and as such he claimed the land surrounding Green Bay—Indians and all—for New France.

The wild Wolf River, the Pine, the Popple and Wisconsin, the Peshtigo, and the Oconto were well-traveled highways of the fur trade during the eighteenth and early nineteenth centuries. Beaver were so abundant in the forest that Nicolet reported being served 120 of the animals as the main course at a feast given by Indians in his honor. For almost two centuries, pelts, and especially beaver skins, were the standard currency. Today beaver are still present in the national forest sharing the terrain with popular game species, including whitetail deer and ruffed grouse. Many of the more remote beaver ponds shown on

the topo maps provide excellent fishing in a wilderness setting for fat orange-bellied brook trout.

Numerous trails, many of them groomed for multiple use—hiking, hunting, skiing, and snowmobiling—wind through the forests and around scenic lakes. The Butternut Lake interpretive trail forms a mile-long loop for shorter jaunts, with informative stations spaced along the route. More strenuous trails pass from Boulder Lake in the south of the Nicolet (pronounced nick-oh-lay) northward to Boot, Ada, Richardson, Bear, Morgan, and Chipmunk lakes and Chipmunk Rapids. Campgrounds are strategically situated at each of these lakes, most of them offering fine opportunities for boating and fishing. The Anvil Trail, designed for both skiers and hikers, crosses gently to hilly terrain near Upper Nine Mile Lake. McCaslin Mountain, a 25-square-mile region featuring the highest point in the area, is a roadless, undeveloped area containing eleven small lakes, several streams, and unlimited exploring and hiking. Other wilderness areas, especially Florence County in the northeastern corner of the forest, provide ample opportunities for backpacking and primitive camping. The Forest Service publishes many maps of trails in individual areas, showing marked routes, lakes, streams, swamps and bogs, parking areas, roads, private and forest lands, shelters, mileage, and the like. Free maps are available from the Forest Supervisor, Nicolet National Forest, Federal Bldg., Rhinelander 54501, for the following areas: *Riley Lake Unit, Laona Ranger District, Anvil Trail, Catwillow Creek Area, Jones Springs Unit, Kimball Creek Unit, Alvin Creek.* The above maps form useful supplements to the *Nicolet National Forest Map*, available at 50¢ from the Forest Supervisor at the above address. In addition to showing all major forest features—trails, roads, towns, lakes, streams, boat-launching sites, recreation sites, winter sports areas, ranger stations, and historical points of interest—the map provides information on camping and recreation areas, wildlife-management areas, snowmobile trails, and auto tours.

White-water canoeing is another popular activity in the forest, especially on the rough-and-tumble Wolf River, where summer races held annually offer exciting and competitive sport. Gentler but nonetheless invigorating canoeing rivers include the Pine, Popple, Oconto, Wisconsin, and Peshtigo. One stretch of the Peshtigo River canoe trail, traced on the *Laona Ranger District Map* mentioned above, takes the canoeist over gently flowing quiet water for an 8-mile run from "Big Joe" landing to the CCC Bridge. Requiring three hours to complete, this section is ideal for beginners. From the CCC Bridge to Burnt Bridge, a distance of about 9 miles, the river character changes, and experienced canoeists will delight in the challenges offered by many rapids and swift water. The final leg of the trip, an 8-mile stretch between Burnt Bridge and Burton Wells Bridge, requires two portages at Michigan Rapids and the Dells and crosses numerous smaller rapids. For an adventurous, long-distance canoe trip, try the Wisconsin River, which flows south from its headwaters at Lac Vieux Desert and leads ultimately to the heart of Mardi Gras country in New Orleans. Further information on wilderness canoeing in the forest is offered in the *Whitewater; Quietwater Guide* described under "Canoeing & Wilderness Waters." (See also "Wolf National Wild & Scenic River" in the "Encyclopedia" section.)

Wildlife-management areas and innumerable lakes and streams make the Nicolet National Forest a favorite haunt for all sportsmen, especially fishermen and hunters. The six management areas—Alvin Creek, Catwillow Creek, Colburn Creek, Jones Spring, Kimball Creek, and Riley Lake—are fine examples of the maintenance of wildlife habitats and are favorite hunting grounds for grouse and whitetail deer as well as black bear, fox, and snowshoe hare. Maps of trails and other facilities within the individual areas are available from

the Forest Supervisor, Nicolet National Forest, Federal Bldg., Rhinelander 54501, or from the relevant District Ranger's Offices listed on page 374. In addition, many of the campgrounds throughout the park are situated on fine fishing lakes, including Kentucky, Lost, Laura, Stevens, Bear, and Franklin, and most camping sites are only a short walk from equally bountiful streams and rivers. *The Nicolet Is Camping,* a brochure available free from the Forest Supervisor, describes the various campgrounds and their recreational opportunities. Used in conjunction with the *Nicolet National Forest Map*, the guide should help in selecting a site to meet every camper's needs and outdoor interests.

Detailed information on specific areas of the forest, including maps, lists of campsites and trails, and wildlife-management areas, can be obtained from the following District Rangers: Three Lakes 54562; Eagle River 54521; Florence 54121; Lakewood 54138; and Laona 54541. Other free publications of interest to visitors available free from the Forest Supervisor's Office in Rhinelander are *Outdoor Safety Tips*, a brochure offering basic first-aid information and hints on safe camping; *Play Safe with Snowmobiles*, 14 pages of illustrations and advice on snowmobile use and etiquette; and the basic forest *Regulations*, a list of requirements every camper and visitor should be thoroughly familiar with.

The Northern Highlands State Forest, established in the early part of this century to protect the headwaters of the two great rivers that lie within its boundaries—the Flambeau and the Wisconsin—covers 140,000 acres of glaciated terrain in north-central Wisconsin. The forest also encompasses many miles of water frontage and provides access to most of the 150 lakes within its borders. The relentless, sweeping action of glaciers, which several times covered the area, created the present rolling topography and numerous crystal-clear lakes, and formed the sandy, gravelly soils that supported the towering pine forests of ages past. Today the predominant tree species in the forest are aspen and white birch, with a secondary cover of pine, oak, maple, tamarack, and black spruce.

Only three other regions in the world can match northern Wisconsin in density of lake surface per square mile—Minnesota, Ontario, and Finland. The high concentration of lakes within the forest is indicated by the fact that although the largest of these bodies of water, Trout Lake, covers only 6½ square miles, the lakes and ponds of Vilas

County alone occupy 140 square miles, or over 15 percent of the area. Together with the Flambeau and Wisconsin rivers, these waterways offer unparalleled opportunities for fishing and canoeing, and the Northern Highlands forest area has been especially tailored to meet the growing demands of canoeists, with portages, access points, and canoe-campgrounds located throughout the region.

The lakes, rivers, and streams within the forest generally feature clear water with sand and gravel bottoms. Currents are slow to medium, affording plenty of time to enjoy the spectacular northern forest scenery—with some fast water below dams. Since there are few dangerous rapids, these waters are ideal for families and beginners. However, there are some stretches of white water that may have to be portaged. Caution is urged when crossing the larger lakes on windy days or when sudden squalls might occur. During periods of low water there are portions of the rivers and streams that may require wading or short portages. *Northern Highlands Canoe Trails,* an informative map/guide available free from the Dept. of Natural Resources, Rt. 1, Box

45, Boulder Junction 54512, shows canoe routes, campsites, portage trails, rapids, and other forest features, and includes descriptions of the surrounding terrain, waterways, and regulations. Other guides and publications mentioned under "Canoeing & Wilderness Waters" provide information on neighboring canoe runs and offer general advice on navigating and enjoying Wisconsin's waterways.

Besides canoeing, Northern Highlands State Forest offers a wealth of other opportunities for outdoor adventure. Rustic family campgrounds are located throughout the forest, most of them on wooded lakeshores where fishing and boating can be enjoyed. Campgrounds vary in size from the 27 sites on Upper Gresham Lake to the 102 units on Crystal Lake, and all camping areas feature widely spaced individual sites with wells and pit-type toilet facilities nearby. In keeping with the rustic forest atmosphere, running water and electrical outlets are not provided. For those who want true woodland solitude, ten wilderness campsites with limited access are available, in addition to the more than one hundred canoe campsites. Beach and picnic areas within the forest have also been developed for day use.

Three self-guiding trails ranging from ½ to 2½ miles in length explore wooded lakeshores, swamplands, and upland timber groves. Interpretive stations are scattered along the routes. For snowmobilers, the forest offers over 40 miles of interesting trail riding in the Boulder

Junction, Sayner, and St. Germain-Arbor Vitae area. A shorter scenic Camp Lake Trail is located west of Highway 15.

The forest's many lakes, including Trout, White Sand, Partridge, and Clear, offer excellent fishing for muskie, walleye, rainbow and brown trout, largemouth and smallmouth bass, and northern pike. Developed boat landings on the major lakes provide easy access. Active timber-management programs within the forest allow access, cover, and food for deer and grouse, and prime habitats for bear, squirrels, and other game animals. In addition, the Powell Marsh Waterfowl Area has increased the number of ducks and geese available to the hunter.

A free *Northern Highlands State Forest Map* shows all information of interest to campers, fishermen, hunters, and canoeists, including campsites, canoe routes, hiking and portage trails, boat-launching sites, forest roads, and natural features. Maps and information are available from the Dept. of Natural Resources, Box 450, Madison 53701.

The major features of neighboring American Legion State Forest—including Buck-Track Trail and the muskellunge waters of Clear, Big Buckskin, Tomahawk, Cupard, and Little Bass Lakes—are shown on the *American Legion State Forest Map,* available free upon request from the Dept. of Natural Resources (address above).

Vacation accommodations and services in the Nicolet National Forest and Northern Highlands region are provided by the following lodges and resorts (write to resort name, plus town and zip code for literature and rates): (Boulder Junction 54512) *Dona & Walts Musky Lodge, Wildcat Lodge, Zastrows Lynx Lake Lodge;* (Eagle River 54521) *Chanticleer Inn Resort, Eagle Waters Resort, Pike Bay Lodge, Timberlands Resort, Yutch's Duck Lake Resort;* (Lac du Flambeau 54538) *Baldwins Golden Arrow Resort, D.J.'s Pine Forest Lodge, Fence Lake Lodge, Sandy Point Resort;* (Lake Tomahawk 54539) *Coy's Bayview Resort;* (Land O' Lakes 54540) *Maple Grove Resort* (Lac Vieux Desert), *Wind Drift Resort;* (Manitowish Waters 54545) *Coun-Tree Acres Resort, Deer Park Lodge, Voss' Birchwood Lodge, Voss' Breezy Point Resort;* (Mercer 54547) *Anglers Acres Resort* (Fisher Lake), *Beaver Lodge;* (Minocqua 54548) *Bobkat Resort* (Lac du Flambeau), *Schmalzer's Back Bay Inn, Siech's Chain O' Lakes Resort;* (Phelps 54554) *Holiday Lodge Resort;* (Rhinelander 54501) *Dorich's Pine Isle, Fease's Shady Rest Lodge, Holiday Acres;* (St. Germain 54558) *Cox's Estrold Resort, Esch's Serenity Bay Resort* (Little St. Germain Lake), *The Musky Inn, Osier's St. Germain Lodge, Pride O' Th' North* (Little St. Germain Lake), *Twin Waters Resort* (Big St. Germain Resort), *Whispering Wind Resort;* (Sayner 54560) *Ed Gabe's Lost Lake Resort, Froelich's Sayner Lodge, Lehor's Twin Cabin Resort, Wah-Wah Taysee Resort;* (Three Lakes 54562) *Northernaire;* (Woodruff 54568) *Buck Horn Lodge* (Arbor Vitae Lake); (White Lake 54491) *Wild Wolf Inn.* For additional listing and information, write to the local chambers of commerce.

Access & Outfitting Centers

Northern Highlands State Forest is accessible from Rhinelander via State Highway 47; via State Highway 70 from Eagle River; via State Highway 182 from Park Falls; and via U.S. Highway 51 from Ironwood, Michigan. Other outfitting centers surrounding or within the forest include Arbor Vitae, Boulder Junction, Star Lake, Manitowish, and Presque Isle. Nicolet National Forest can be reached via State Highway 70 from Eagle River; via U.S. Highway 32 from Crandon; via State Highway 73 or 189 from both Stambaugh and Caspian in Michigan; and via State Highway 17 north from Rhinelander to Eagle River, then east on 70.

THE
GREAT OUTDOORS
ATLAS

This special insert contains a selection of unique, full-color, shaded-relief maps of major outdoor recreation areas in the United States and Canada, drawn with great skill and craftsmanship by David Greenspan. These beautiful, panoramic maps will provide both the armchair traveler and trip planner with vivid and useful reference tools by giving an overview of the great outdoor recreation areas. If you're planning a trip to one of the areas illustrated on the maps, be sure to send for the appropriate official national forest, park, and/or wilderness area maps (listed and described throughout the book) showing the latest, up-to-date changes in campground locations, ranger stations, and trails.

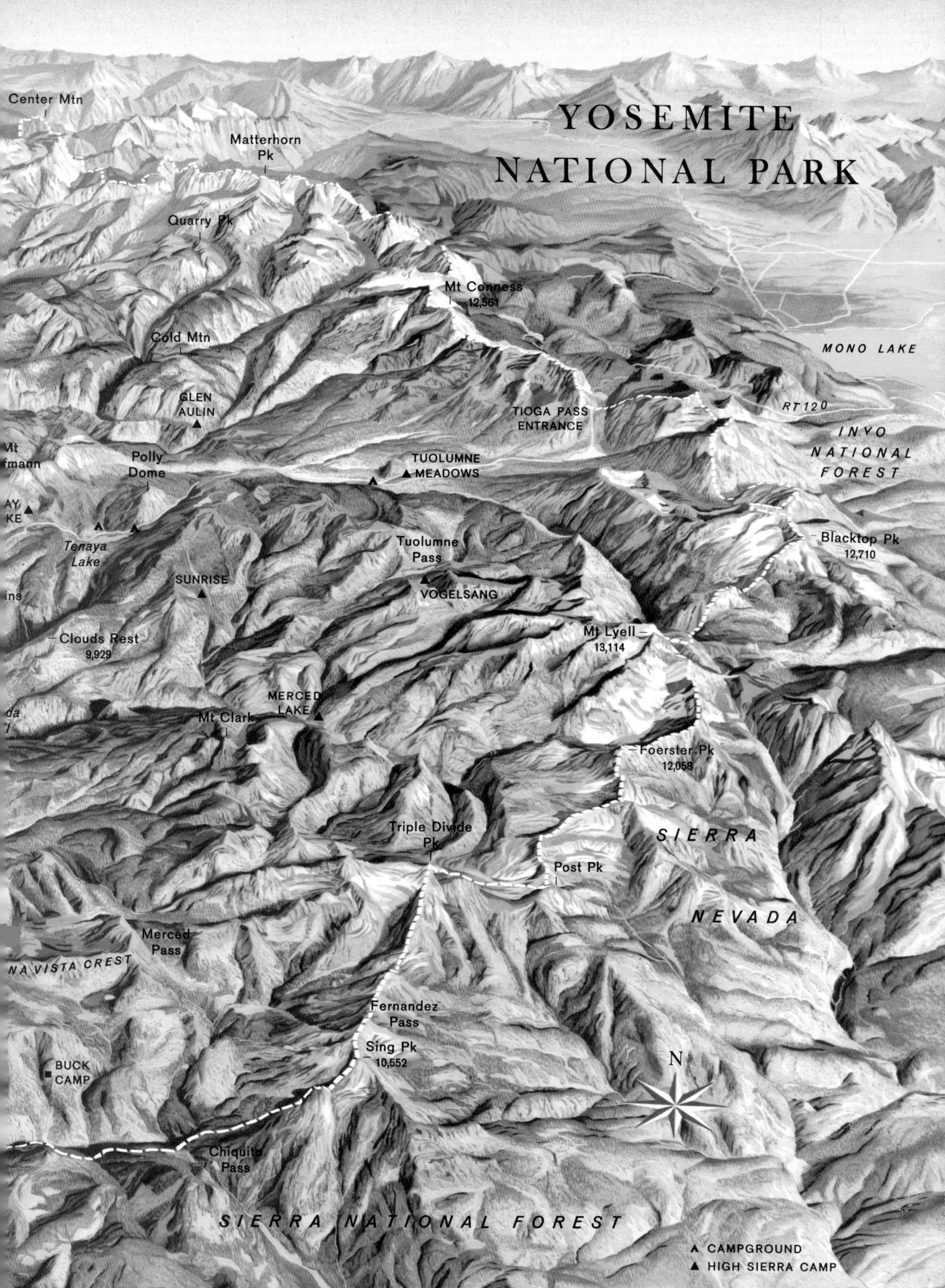

YOSEMITE NATIONAL PARK

Center Mtn

Matterhorn Pk

Quarry Pk

Mt Conness
12,561

Cold Mtn

MONO LAKE

GLEN AULIN ▲

RT 120

TIOGA PASS ENTRANCE

INYO NATIONAL FOREST

Mt fmann

Polly Dome

TUOLUMNE ▲ MEADOWS ▲

AY KE ▲

Tenaya Lake

▲ ▲

Tuolumne Pass

Blacktop Pk
12,710

SUNRISE ▲

▲ VOGELSANG

— Clouds Rest
9,929

Mt Lyell —
13,114

ins

da 'l

Mt Clark ▲

MERCED LAKE ▲

— Foerster Pk
12,058

SIERRA

Triple Divide Pk

Post Pk

NEVADA

Merced Pass

NA VISTA CREST

Fernandez Pass

Sing Pk
10,552

N

BUCK CAMP ■

Chiquito Pass

SIERRA NATIONAL FOREST

▲ CAMPGROUND
▲ HIGH SIERRA CAMP

WATERTON
LAKES
NATIONAL PARK

Mt Dungarvan

Mt Crandell

Waterton
Lake

Mt Cleveland
— 10,448

CANADA
UNITED STATES

Kintla
Pk
10,110

Upper
Kintla
Lake

Kintla
Glacier

Carter Glaciers

Flattop
Mtn

Rainbow
Glacier

Longfellow
Pk

Kintla
Lake

Vulture
Glacier

Wolf Gun
Mtn

Heavens

Bowman
Lake

Quartz
Lake

Logging
Lake

NORTH FORK FLATHEAD RIVER

FLATHEAD

NATIONAL FOREST

APGAR MTNS

Lake McDO

APGAR
VILLAGE

WE
GLA

N

PA

TO KALISPELL RT U.S. 2
GREAT NORTHERN RY

▲ CAMPGROUND
■ ENTRANCE STATION

DaviGreenson

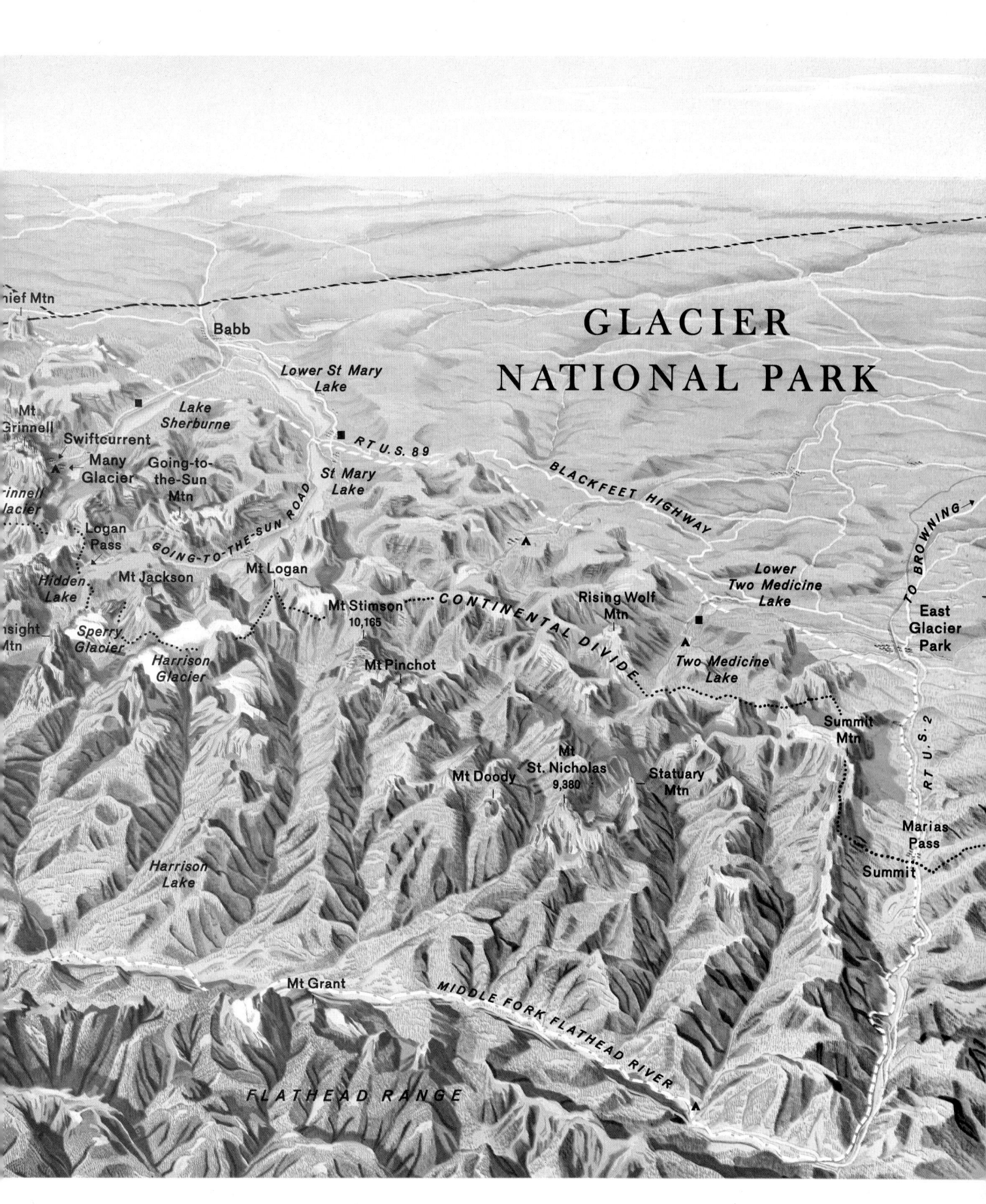

GLACIER
NATIONAL PARK

hief Mtn

Babb

Lower St Mary
Lake

RT U.S. 89

Mt
Grinnell

Swiftcurrent

Lake
Sherburne

Many
Glacier

St Mary
Lake

Going-to-
the-Sun
Mtn

BLACKFEET HIGHWAY

TO BROWNING

rinnell
lacier

Logan
Pass

GOING-TO-THE-SUN ROAD

Lower
Two Medicine
Lake

East
Glacier
Park

*Hidden
Lake*

Mt Jackson

Mt Logan

Rising Wolf
Mtn

nsight
Mtn

*Sperry
Glacier*

Mt Stimson
10,165

CONTINENTAL DIVIDE

Two Medicine
Lake

RT U.S. 2

*Harrison
Glacier*

Mt Pinchot

Summit
Mtn

Mt
St. Nicholas
9,380

Mt Doody

Statuary
Mtn

Marias
Pass

*Harrison
Lake*

Summit

Mt Grant

MIDDLE FORK FLATHEAD RIVER

FLATHEAD RANGE

YELLOWSTONE
NATIONAL PARK

Hellroaring
Pk

Petrified
Tree

Tower Jct

Mt Washburn
10,243

nraven Pass

Inspiration
NYON Pt

Artist Pt
Yellowstone Falls

AYDEN
ALLEY

Mud
Volcano

Natural
Bridge

Fishing
Bridge

Lake

Steamboat
Pt

GRAND CANYON

YELLOWSTONE
LAKE

heridan
0,308

HEART LAKE
GEYSER BASIN

Heart
Lake

KE RIVER

TETON
NATIONAL
FOREST

Slough
Creek

Soda
Butte

Lamar

Fossil Forest

MIRROR
PLATEAU

Pelican
Cone

Lake Butte

Sylvan Lake

The
Promontory

TWO OCEAN
PLATEAU

Abiathar Pk
10,928

NORTHEAST ENTRANCE

Cache
Creek

ABSAROKA

LAMAR RIVER

RANGE

Avalanche Pk
10,566

Sylvan Pass

YELLOWSTONE

RIVER

THOROFARE

Bridger
Lake

MONTANA

WYOMING

RT U.S. 212

Pollux Pk Hoodoo
11,067   Basin

EAST
ENTRANCE

Eagle Pk
11,358

The
Trident

CAMPGROUND

Driggs

UNION PACIFIC

IDAHO

WYOMING

Rendezvous
Pk

Mt
Hunt

Buck Mtn
11,923

South
Teton

Nez
Perce —
Pk

Grand Teton
13,766

Mt
Owen
— 12,922

Teewinot Mtn
12,317

Mt St J
11,419

Jenny
Lake

JENN
LAKE LO

← TO TETON PASS

Phelps Lake

Moose ■

PARK
HEADQUARTERS ←

RTS U.S. 187 89 26

Blacktail
Butte —

SNAKE RIVER

← TO JACKSON

GROS VENTRE RIVER

JACKSON HOLE HIGHWAY

NATIONAL
ELK
REFUGE

Kelly

Lower
Slide Lake

N

TETON
NATIONAL FOREST

▲ CAMPGROUND
△ PICNIC GROUND
■ ENTRANCE STATION

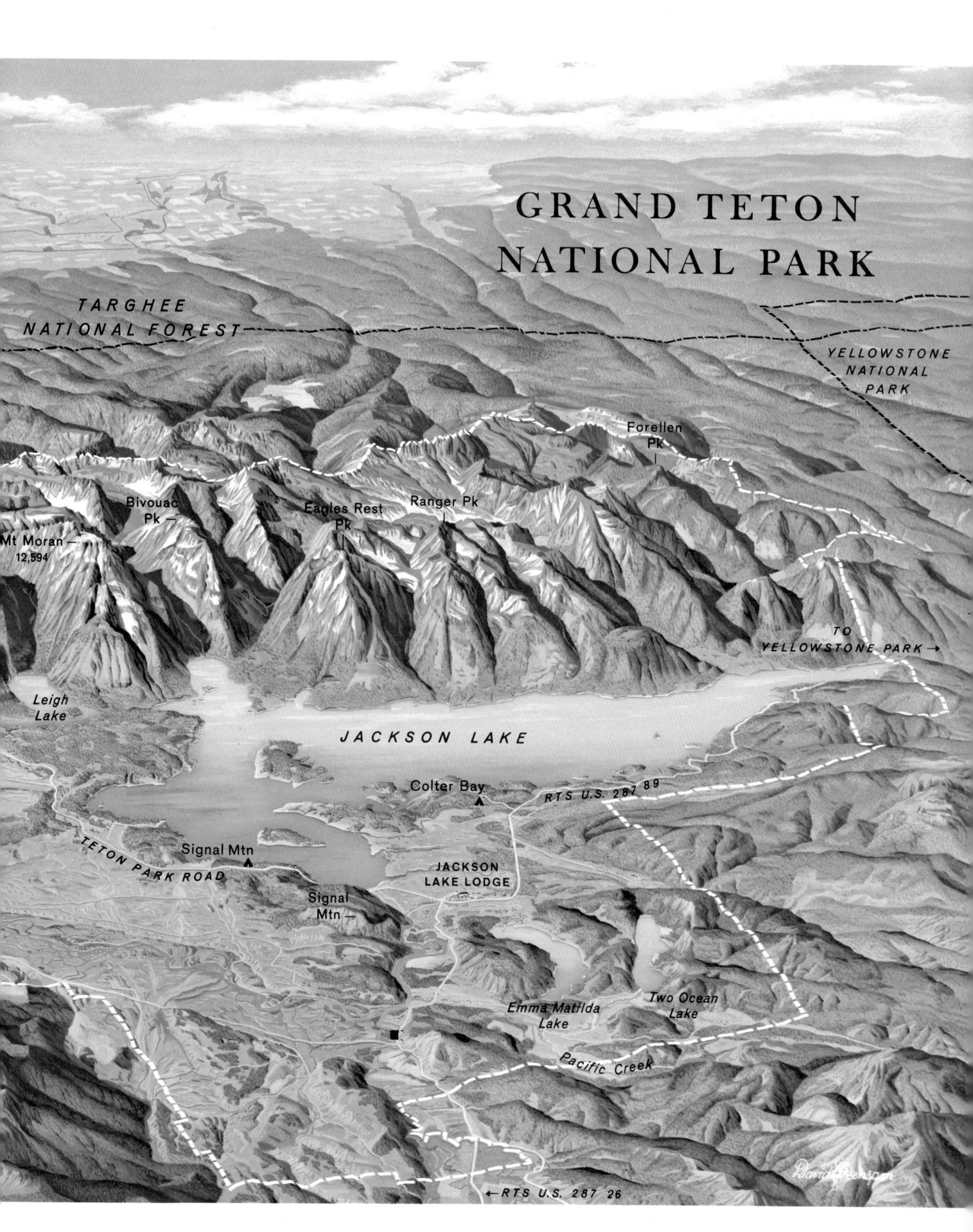

GRAND TETON
NATIONAL PARK

TARGHEE
NATIONAL FOREST

YELLOWSTONE
NATIONAL
PARK

Forellen
Pk

Bivouac
Pk

Eagles Rest
Pk

Ranger Pk

Mt Moran
12,594

TO
YELLOWSTONE PARK →

Leigh
Lake

JACKSON LAKE

Colter Bay

RTS U.S. 287 89

TETON PARK ROAD

Signal Mtn

JACKSON
LAKE LODGE

Signal
Mtn

Emma Matilda
Lake

Two Ocean
Lake

Pacific Creek

← RTS U.S. 287 26

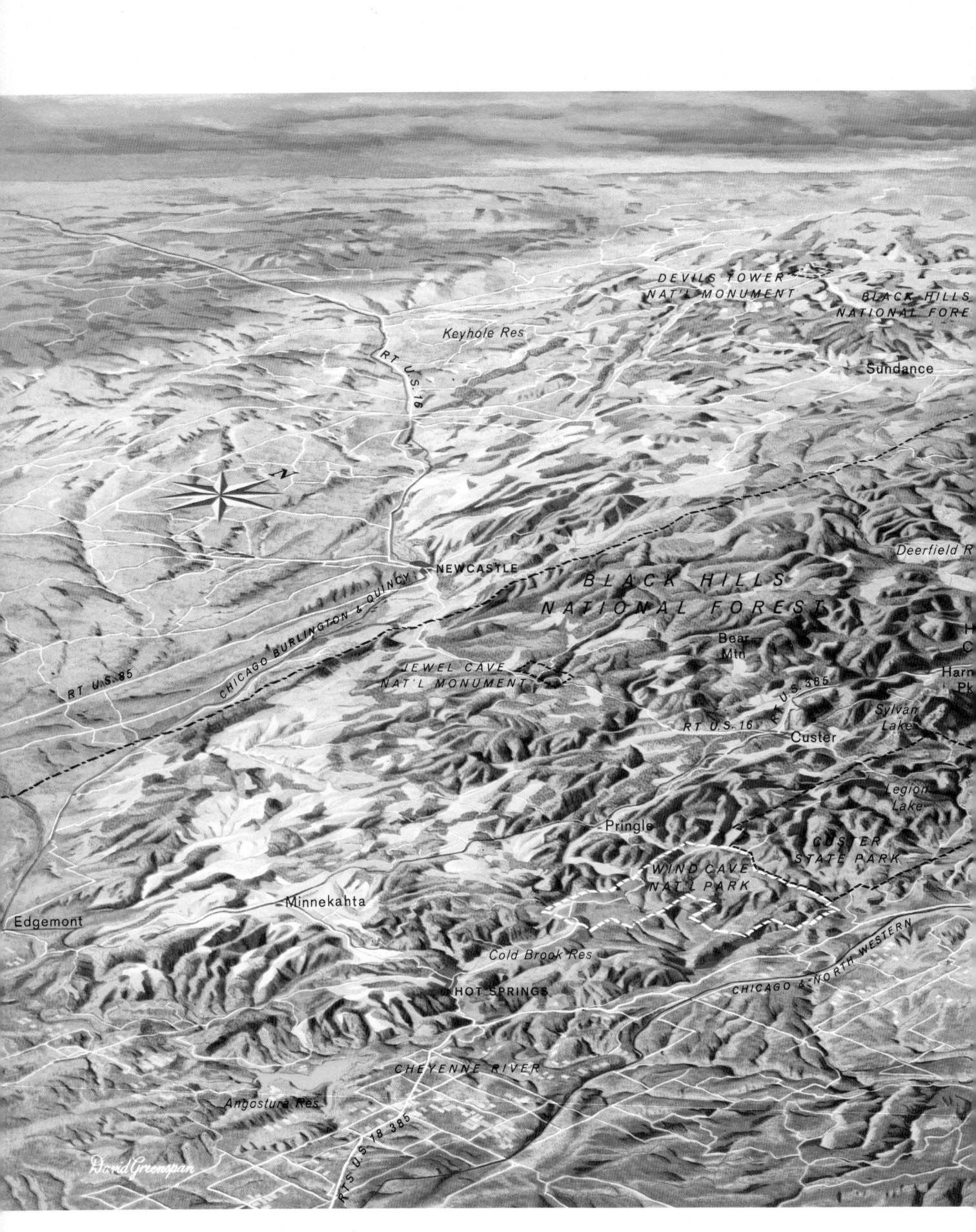

DEVILS TOWER
NAT'L MONUMENT

BLACK HILLS
NATIONAL FORE

Sundance

Keyhole Res

RT U.S. 16

Deerfield R

BLACK HILLS
NATIONAL FOREST

NEWCASTLE

Bear
Mtn

H
C

CHICAGO BURLINGTON & QUINCY

JEWEL CAVE
NAT'L MONUMENT

RT U.S. 85

RT U.S. 385

RT U.S. 16

Harn
Pk

Sylvan
Lake

Custer

Legion
Lake

Pringle

CUSTER
STATE PARK

WIND CAVE
NAT'L PARK

Minnekahta

Edgemont

Cold Brook Res

CHICAGO & NORTH WESTERN

HOT SPRINGS

CHEYENNE RIVER

Angostura Res

RT. U.S 18 385

David Greenspan

BLACK HILLS

WYOMING   SOUTH DAKOTA

RT U.S. 14

Belle Fourche

Spearfish   Belle Fourche
                                  Res

Terry   Central
Pk   City
     Lead   Deadwood

                        Sturgis

Silver
City

Pactola Res

Sheridan Lake

Mt
more

Keystone

RUSHMORE
'L MEMORIAL

RT U.S. 16

RT 79

Hermosa

RAPID CITY

INTERSTATE 90

CHICAGO & NORTH WESTERN

INTERSTATE 90

CHICAGO MILWAUKEE ST PAUL & PACIFIC

RT 40

CHEYENNE RIVER

BADLANDS
NATIONAL MONUMENT

Sheep
Mtn

Cirrus Lake

Pickerel Lake

Kasakokwog Lake

QUETICO
PROVINCIAL PARK

Sturgeon Lake

MALIGNE RIVER

Poohbah Lake

Lac La Croix

Crooked Lake

Basswood Lake

ELY - BUYCK ROAD

Snow La

Moose Lake

Cummings Lake

Trout Lake

Burntside Lake

ELY

White Iron Lake

RT 1

Bald Eagle Lake

RT 1

Vermilion Lake

David Greenspan

▲ CAMPGROUND ACCESSIBLE BY AUTO
▲ PICNIC GROUND

BOUNDARY WATERS
CANOE AREA
SUPERIOR NATIONAL FOREST
MINNESOTA

N

Saganaga Lake

Northern Light Lake

Whitefish Lake

Arrow Lake

North Lake

Gunflint Lake

CANADA

ED STATES

Greenwood Lake

Elton Lake

Brule Lake

SUPERIOR

Lake Alice

Lake Insula

Devils Track Lake

Isabella Lake

NATIONAL FOREST

Parent Lake

GRAND MARAIS

RT. U.S. 61

LAKE SUPERIOR

GREAT SMOKY MOUNTAINS
NATIONAL PARK

KNOXVILLE

RT U.S. 441

Sevierville

LITTLE
PIGEON RIVER

RT U.S. 41

RT U.S. 441

RT U.S. 411

Wildwood

GATLINBURG

PARK
HEADQUARTERS

Cove
Mtn

SUGARLAN
VISITOR CEN

RT 73

Maryville

CHILHOWEE MTN

Elkmont

Townsend

Tremont

LITTLE   RIVER

Cerulean
Knob

FOOTHILLS
← PARKWAY

CADES COVE

Look
Rock

Hatcher –
Mtn

CADES
COVE

Gregory
Bald

Parson
Bald –

Happy
Valley

Parson
High Top

Mt
Lanier –

Dalton
Gap

Bunker –
Hill

Abrams
Creek

Deals Gap

Panther
Creek

RT U.S. 129

TENNESSEE

NORTH
CAROLIN

LITTLE
TENNESSEE
RIVER

David Greenspan

Newport

Cosby

TENNESSEE

NORTH CAROLINA

PIGEON RIVER

Mt Sterling
5,835

Mt Cammerer

RT 32

COSBY

Mt Guyot
6,621

Mt Chapman
6,430

Cataloochee
Mtn

Chiltoe
Mtn

BALSAM MTN

RT 73

Mt
Le Conte
6,593

LE CONTE
LODGE

Newfound
Gap

RT U.S. 441

SMOKEMONT

BLUE RIDGE
PARKWAY →

PIONEER
MUSEUM

Cherokee

Chimney
Tops

Clingmans Dome
6 643

THOMAS DIVIDE

CHIMNEYS

Silers
Bald

NOLAND
DIVIDE

DEEP CREEK

Bryson
City

erhead
Mtn

FORNEY
RIDGE

WELCH
RIDGE

LOCUST
RIDGE

Blockhouse
Mtn

Hazel
Creek

RT 28

kstack

NTY MILE
GE

APPALACHIAN TRAIL

Stecoah

FONTANA LAKE

Fontana
Village

Cheoah

NANTAHALA NATIONAL FOREST

▲ DEVELOPED CAMPGROUND
△ PRIMITIVE CAMPGROUND
▲ SHELTER CABIN

MOUNT DESERT

ACADIA
NATIONAL PARK

TO BANGOR

RT 102

RT 3

Lamoine

EASTERN BAY

Salsbury Cove

FRENCHMAN BAY

RT 186

Town Hill

MOUNT DESERT
ISLAND

BAR
HARBOR

PARK
HEADQUARTERS

Eagle Lake

Cadillac
Mtn
1,532

Anemo
Cave

WESTERN BAY

RT 198

Sargent
Mtn

Somesville

The
Bubbles

Jordan Pond

Sand
Beach

BARTLETT
ISLAND

SOMES SOUND

Echo Lake

Seal
Harbor

OCEAN DR

Long Pond

Beech
Mtn

Bernard
Mtn

Northeast
Harbor

Center

ISLESFO
HISTOR
MUSE

Seal Cove Pond

Southwest
Harbor

Manset

Seal
Cove

RT 102

GRE
CRANB
ISLA

BLUE HILL BAY

Bernard

McKinley

ATLANTIC OCEAN

▲ CAMPGROUND
△ PICNIC GROUND
■ PARK ENTRANCE

Greenspan

Accommodations— Vacation Lodges & Resorts

For detailed travel and vacation accommodations information about the Wolverine State, write to the Michigan Travel Bureau, P.O. Box 30226, Law Building, Lansing 48909 (phone: 517–373–0670). For regional vacation travel and lodging info, write: West Michigan Tourist Assn. (136 Fulton E., Grand Rapids 49503), request their free accommodations guide, *West Michigan Host Directory;* East Michigan Tourist Assn. (Log Office, Bay City 48706) and request their free *East Michigan Auto Guide to Lodging;* Upper Peninsula Travel & Recreation Assn. (P.O. Box 400, Iron Mountain 49801) and request their free *Travel Service Directory to Michigan's Upper Peninsula;* and the Southeast Michigan Travel & Tourist Assn., Executive Plaza, 1200 6th St., Detroit 48226. The free guides contain the nitty gritty about lodging, campgrounds, dining, charter boat and canoe rental services.

Listings of major lodges and resorts are found throughout the "Michigan Travel & Recreation Guide" section.

Au Sable State Forest & the Historic "River of Sands"

This scenic 152,000-acre north-country reserve is located in the north-central part of the Lower Peninsula and is bordered on the south by the clear, pale sand-and-gravel-bottomed waters of the historic Au Sable River—one of the nation's classic fly-fishing streams for trophy browns. The Au Sable, named the Rivière aux Sables—the "River of Sands"—by the French voyageurs, was traveled for centuries by the Chippewa and Ottawa Indians, trappers, and explorers and provided a valuable waterway between 1870 and 1890 for logs destined for the sawmills of East Tawas, Tawas City, and Oscoda. This classic limestone trout stream, noted for its mazes of deadfalls, log jams, and sweepers, rises in the marl swamps of Otsego County and flows southeast for 200 miles through sandy country of jack-pine forests, bogs, cedar swamps, and limestone outcroppings to its mouth on Lake Huron at Oscoda. Its famous tributaries—including the tea-colored Middle Branch; the East Branch, which rises in the marl bogs and spring-fed Loon Lake above Grayling; the legendary North Branch, which rises in the frigid springheads above Lovells; and the famed fly-fishing waters of the South Branch's Mason Tract—offer another 300 miles of highly alkaline, insect-rich trout water. The once awesome runs of big Lake Huron steelhead up the Au Sable were brought to an abrupt end with the construction of 6 dams along the lower river. Today, fishing for the big lake-run rainbows up to 20 pounds is confined to a stretch of river below Foote Dam. This great historic river, which has contributed immeasurably to American angling lore, has been floated by fishermen since the turn of the century in the fabled flat-bottomed Au Sable longboats. (For additional information, see "Huron National Forest & the Au Sable River" in the "Travel & Recreation Guide" section.) The forest itself includes other fine fishing streams and lakes, such as the East and Middle branches of Big Creek, the North Branch of the Au Sable, Little Shupac, and Lost and Big Blue lakes. Many of the lakes are also stocked with rainbow trout. Foremost among these are Log, Bear, Starvation, Big Blue, Twin, Big Guernsey, Oxbow, and Selkirk.

The Au Sable Forest is located in Crawford and Kalkaska counties, two of Michigan's top-ranked hunting areas. Deer are found throughout the region, with the best opportunities in cutover areas, swamp edges, and old orchards. Ruffed grouse and woodcock are often found in young aspen stands and along the brushy stream areas. In the

MICHIGAN ENCYCLOPEDIA

southern part of the forest's eastern division, the Conners Marsh Flooding has long been a favorite with duck hunters. Snowshoe hare are most plentiful in pine plantations, conifer swamps, and stands of young aspen; while squirrel abound along the Au Sable River and in mature oak areas.

Campgrounds are situated at Big Creek Forest near Lewiston, and beside Guernsey, Houghton, and Shupac lakes. Nearby attractions include the Huron National Forest to the south and west, Lake Margarethe, Hartwick Pines State Park, and the Houghton Lake State Forest. Portions of the Shore-to-Shore Trail (see "Campgrounds & State Recreation Areas") also fall within the Au Sable State Forest.

The Au Sable State Forest is reached via State Highway 144 from Roscommon and via State 72 from Luzerne and Grayling. *Carlisle Canoes*, 110 State St., Grayling 49738, provides complete canoe rental, outfitting, and pickup service for the Au Sable.

The Au Sable State Forest is shown on the following large-scale U.S. Geological Survey Maps: Alba, Big Bradford Creek, Comstock Hills, Cote Dam Marie, Eldorado, Fletcher, Grayling 7.5, K-P Lake, Lake Margarethe, Lovells, Luzerne, Luzerne NW, Pere Cheney, Red Oak, Roscommon N., Wakeley Lake.

Beaver Island

Known as "America's Emerald Isle," Beaver Island lies in upper Lake Michigan, 32 miles west of the harbor of Charlevoix. The island is 14 miles long and up to 6 miles wide, the largest of a group of 13 that includes Hog, Gull, Squaw, Trout, Garden, and Whiskey islands. To the southwest of Beaver Island are the Fox Islands and the Manitou, two small groups that complete the archipelago.

Archaeological evidence indicates that the first people to inhabit the island were mound builders, primitive tribes whose mounds for burial and for worship mark the terrain in many places. In the seventeenth century, Chippewa and Ottawa Indians owned the archipelago and became notorious for their canoe-raiding parties. When a passing vessel was sighted, groups of Indians would swiftly paddle out in their birchbark craft, board the ship, torture the crew, and make off with all valuables. The first white men in the area were French *coureurs de bois*, itinerant adventurers who roamed the woods and trespassed on Indian hunting grounds for possibly a century before permanent settlements were made in Michigan. Calling Beaver Island *Isle du Castor*, they set up headquarters and makeshift farms near St. James as early as 1603. After the disappearance of the French, no attempt was made to settle the islands until the territory came into American possession, even though the archipelago remained a popular stopover for missionaries and voyageurs on their way west and north.

In 1847 a scouting party for the eastern branch of the Mormons, led by James Jesse Strang, found Beaver Island admirably suited for a religious colony where members could live and worship undisturbed by outsiders. By 1850 Strang had laid out the town of St. James, built a tabernacle, and persuaded most of the Mormons from the mainland to join him on the island.

Today only a few buildings in the town of St. James bear witness to this short and fascinating chapter in Beaver Island's history. The island is now one of the world's unique vacation retreats. Seven inland lakes, including Geneserath, Fox, Greens, and Font lakes, offer fine fishing for game and panfish. The run of perch in St. James Bay each spring and fall is rated among the finest in the Great Lakes. The island also has improved dock and marina facilities in a fine natural harbor. Charter boats are available to Garden Island, renowned for smallmouth bass and pike fishing, and the site of numerous burial mounds,

some of them thousands of years old. The island's 54 square miles are covered with dense forest growth, providing cover and fall hunting for grouse, deer, geese, ducks, squirrels, and rabbits. Fox and coyote hunting has also become popular. "America's Emerald Isle" is shown on the U.S. Geological Survey Beaver Island map.

Vacation accommodations are provided by the *King Strang Hotel* (c/o 46950 Six Mile Rd., Northville 48167) and *Isle Haven Tourist Court* and *Wojan Harbor View Motel*, both Beaver Island 49782. Regular ferry service between Beaver Island and Charlevoix is provided by *Beaver Island Boat Co.*, Beaver Island 49782 (phone: 616–547–2311). Air service between Charlevoix and the island is provided by *McPhillips Flying Service*, Charlevoix 49720 (phone: 616–547–2141).

Campgrounds & State Recreation Areas

Michigan's many lakes and scenic wooded areas offer fine opportunities for all kinds of camping—in rustic out-of-the-way spots or in developed campgrounds with all the latest conveniences. A special reservation system has been established in state parks permitting campers to make arrangements for sites in advance. Fifty percent of the campsites in each park are available on a reservation basis, leaving the remaining sites open to campers on a first-come system. Application forms for reservation requests are available for any state park from the Parks Division, Dept. of Natural Resources, Lansing 48926. Lists of camping sites in state parks and a description of the reservation system are available from the Parks Division at the above address. For those who are not familiar with Michigan's camping facilities, the Department of Natural Resources publishes a free map/guide, *Michigan State Parks*, including a checklist of campgrounds with addresses, number of sites, general camping information (toilets, showers, fees, boat-launching sites, etc.), day-use facilities, activities, and special features.

Michigan State Forests Campground Directory lists camping facilities in all 33 state forests and correlates individual campgrounds with highway maps of the Upper and Lower peninsulas. Various charts for each forest give all information relevant to campers: number of sites, special attractions, addresses, phone numbers, and opportunities for boating, canoeing, fishing, and hiking. Write to the Dept. of Natural Resources, Forestry Division, Lansing 48926, for a free copy of the brochure and further information on campgrounds in the state forests.

For detailed, state-wide camping information (after Memorial Day), call the *Michigan Camping Hotline*, operated by the DNR, (517 373–1279).

Michigan's Shore-to-Shore Riding-Hiking Trail is a fine way to see the state on horseback or on foot. The trail stretches from the Lake Michigan shore on the west to the shores of Lake Huron on the east, crossing scenic countryside, beautiful rivers, and dense hardwood and pine forests. Public trail camps along the route, as well as private facilities and services, are available for trail users. Two brochures offer information on the trail—*Michigan's Shore-to-Shore Riding-Hiking Trail* and *Michigan Riding & Hiking Trails*—and include a map of the route, approximate distances between major points, and general information on trail camps. Both brochures are available free from the Michigan Dept. of Natural Resources, Lansing 48926.

A useful 104-page *Great Lakes Nature Guide* by Dr. Paul A. Herbert, describes in words and drawings more than 400 species of mammals, birds, fish, reptiles, amphibians, insects, trees, shrubs, mushrooms, and grasses common to Michigan and neighboring states. Copies may be obtained for $1 each, including postage and tax, from Michigan United Conservation Clubs, Box 30235, Lansing 48909.

Canoeing & Wild Rivers

Canoeists planning to ply the waters of the Wolverine State will find that an astounding repertory of trips is possible. With its 34 major river systems, the state offers streams differing markedly in character and difficulty, from the gentle, pastoral rivers of the Lower Peninsula to the brawling and wild waters of the Upper Peninsula.

The names of Michigan's rivers testify to the prominent role they have played in the history of the state, beginning with the days when Indians paddled the waterways in search of game, through the times of early settlement. Names like Au Sable, Père Marquette, and Brule are reminders of the loosely-knit empire of the fur trade in the seventeenth and eighteenth centuries, when rugged French voyageurs, 10 hardy men in 36-foot canoes, paddled the thousand-mile journey from Michigan posts to the great Northwest, then returned over the same route in a single summer.

Taking its name from the Indian term for "river with marshes," the deep Muskegon River flows through the longest and narrowest valley in the state, and was noted for the high timber lining its shores by Jean Nicolet as early as 1634. Fur trading was active in the region on and off for almost a hundred years, with a permanent trading post established on Bear Lake around 1812. Later, during the heyday of the lumber industry, the valley resounded with the blows of the trailblazer's ax, and the town of Muskegon soon earned the reputation as the "Gambling Queen" or "Saloon Queen" when river drivers or mill men, locally known as "Timber Beasts," came to town to spend their money on less-than-respectable amusements. For canoeists, the stream offers even-tempered waters with no dangerous rapids in its upper half. However, from the Reedsburg Dam campground to the Missaukee-Clare County line, fallen trees can be a hazard. The 227-mile trip can be accomplished in one to two weeks, or broken into shorter stretches at various put-in and takeout points. The West Branch of the Muskegon offers 8 miles of paddling through some very scenic swampland and hardwoods, but numerous beaver dams and log jams may require careful navigation.

Another waterway down which logs were floated during the lumber boom, the Au Sable River is renowned as a trout stream and canoe route navigable as far as Oscoda. Since canoe traffic is often heavy immediately below Grayling, many canoeists prefer to begin the trip at Wakeley Bridge a few miles to the east. Canoe rentals and pickup service are available at Grayling, Wakeley Bridge, Mio, McKinley, Glennie, and Oscoda. The Au Sable's South Branch is a crooked stream running through wild country, with many shallow pullovers and jams, and is recommended for more experienced paddlers. The lower stretch passes through the scenic Mason Tract, a wild-land preserve.

Many other rivers in the Lower Peninsula offer fine opportunities for canoeing, with numerous possibilities for extended trips along adjoining streams. The Little Manistee's fast waters pass an old ghost town by the same name; the historic Père Marquette features many quick turns, and crosses several tricky rapids; the scenic Ocqueoc, for experts only, flows north through several small lakes, swamps, forests, and plains; and the placid waters of the Clinton offer easygoing waters with minimum portaging. The above rivers, as well as the St. Joseph, Black, Thornapple, Paw Paw, Flat, Red Cedar, Rifle, Chippewa, and many others are described in *Canoeing in Michigan*, a booklet available free from the Michigan Dept. of Natural Resources, 905-A Southland Dr., Lansing 48910. Directions, put-in and takeout points, length, points of interest, location of campsites, and the possibilities for extended trips are all described. Maps and details on Upper Peninsula rivers such as the Carp, Sturgeon, Escanaba, Brule, Menominee and others are included as well. Sections on "paddling pointers" and "reading white water," with several illustrations, are also provided, and the short introduction will help you decide which streams are best suited to your interests and abilities. The Department of Natural Resources also publishes a free pamphlet, *Michigan's Natural Rivers Program*, that describes the state's proposed wild and scenic rivers. For more detailed information on the Huron and Clinton rivers, write for the free *Huron River Canoeing Guide* from the Huron-Clinton Metropolitan Authority, 3050 Penobscot Bldg., Detroit 48826.

Canoeists will find that Upper Peninsula rivers generally offer more challenging runs than the streams in the state's southern reaches, with rapids and turbulent water the rule rather than the exception. Forming part of the boundary between Michigan and Wisconsin, the Brule River flows through stunning scenery, with wooded shorelines dominated by pines, aspen, birch, and various hardwoods. The marshlands that alternate with forested stretches are favored by deer, beaver, blue herons, and various types of waterfowl. After about 54 miles, the Brule joins the Paint and Michigamme rivers and becomes known as the Menominee; here the water flow is more than triple that of the section above the Brule River Flowage. The major attraction of this last stretch of the river is the Big Bull Rapids, consisting of large waves that develop upstream. Scouting from a large island near the right bank is imperative, since open canoes are often swamped in these waters.

In the extreme northwestern part of the peninsula are the wild waters of the Ontonagon River, named for an Indian word meaning "place of the bowl." Ever since the arrival of white men in the region, rumors circulated concerning the existence of a great mass of copper some nine miles upstream from the town of Ontonagon. In 1766 Alexander Henry reported the existence of a five-ton boulder veined with ore so pure and malleable that he easily extracted a mass of copper weighing 100 pounds. The curiosity aroused by this huge and valuable rock naturally directed attention to the Porcupine Mountain region and opened up mining operations, which continued until the 1840s, when numerous prospectors, disillusioned by the absence of other sources of "loose" copper, drifted westward in search of higher stakes. The river today flows through rugged wilderness country long abandoned by commercial enterprises, with abundant wildlife and wildflowers lining the steep clay banks. Some good canoe stretches are available along the Ontonagon's four branches, including a 30-mile segment along the main stream from Military Bridge on U.S. 45 to Lake Superior.

Less strenuous canoeing is possible on the Escanaba River, named for the Indian word *eshkonabang,* meaning "land of the red buck." The upper stretches of the river are marked by several interesting rock cliffs, while the lower sections pass through scenic farmlands and swampy areas. Low water from mid-July through August makes the trip inadvisable at this time. Several state-forest campgrounds and primitive camping sites line the river, and fishing for bass and trout above the Boney Falls Flowage is excellent.

Winding through the varied wilderness of the eastern Upper Peninsula, the Tahquamenon River passes extensive willow marshes and riverbanks supporting dense, tall stands of timber. In some places, steep stone cliffs up to 100 feet in height line the stream's course. The Upper and Lower Tahquamenon falls offer some breathtaking cascades but must be portaged. Before the takeout on Whitefish Bay, there are three campgrounds—Natalie, Camp 16, and Tahquamenon River Campground.

Other Upper Peninsula rivers—the Indian, Sturgeon, Fox, Waiska, and Carp, to name but a few—offer exciting canoe runs. While most of these are described in the *Canoeing in Michigan* guide mentioned above, more detailed information is available in *Whitewater; Quietwater—The Wild Rivers of Wisconsin, Upper Michigan & NE Minnesota,* a 157-page source book to canoe streams and rivers personally

traveled and recorded by the authors. Each of the 80 river runs described is a one-day trip between landings accessible by car. Explicit maps, length of the stretch concerned, gradient, hazard rating, and water conditions are included for each trip. Also provided are comments on the scenery, geology, history, fishing, and campgrounds in the area. Some of the Upper Peninsula rivers mapped and described include the Black, Brule, Escanaba, Ford, Menominee, and Ontonagon. One of the most comprehensive guides available on Upper Peninsula rivers, *Whitewater; Quietwater* is priced at $7.95 and can be obtained from Evergreen Paddleways, 1416 21st St., Two Rivers WI 54241.

Fenwick Michigan Fly Fishing Schools

The Fenwick Corporation, manufacturers of quality fishing rods and gear, operates its Michigan fly fishing school on the banks of the famed Au Sable River, near Grayling. This two-day school in June is open to beginners through advanced fly fishermen and includes intensive

instruction in the art of fly fishing, rod-and-reel construction, how to choose proper tackle, terminology, insects and their life cycles, artificial-fly construction, identification, fly-fishing knots, leader construction and uses, how to read a stream, and wading. The school headquarters is at the Gates Au Sable Lodge. Family activities include canoeing and camping locations at the nearby Kneff Lake and National Forest campgrounds. The Fenwick Boardman River School is based at Ranch Rudolph, a unique wilderness ranch on the Boardman River, surrounded by Fife State Forest. The ranch offers superb cuisine, lodgings, canoeing, hiking, horseback riding, and more. For free literature and rates on Fenwick's Michigan schools, write: Director, Fenwick Fly Fishing School, Midwestern Division, 309 S. 11th Ave., Wausau, WI 54401 (715–842–9879).

Fishing & Hunting in the Wolverine State

"Michigan," derived from the Chippewa Indian word *Mischaganong,* meaning "big water," has been endowed with an abundance of natural riches: millions of acres of mixed hardwood and evergreen forests; thousands of clear, cold streams, rivers, ponds, and lakes, including the frigid blue depths of lakes Michigan, Superior, Huron, and St. Clair, and the many miles of the Great Lakes interconnecting waterways; a fish population of tremendous diversity, running in size from the small silvery smelt to the ponderous, armorplated sturgeon, which attains weights in excess of 300 pounds; a richly varied game population; and some of the most spectacular north-woods scenery in America. The Wolverine State can be called a land of surprises. A population of about nine million people lives in a territory that offers some of the best fishing and hunting on the continent. The more densely populated mitt-shaped Lower Peninsula (LP) is separated from the long, icicle-shaped Upper Peninsula (UP) by the Straits of Mackinac and by the urban and industrial orientation of the southern population centers, such as Detroit, versus the rural, north-woods emphasis of the UP. The dichotomy almost makes one think of the two areas as different states, and, indeed, the beautiful north woods of the Upper Peninsula are reminiscent of Canadian wilderness along Lake Superior's North Shore. Muskellunge, walleye, and northern pike are caught in the productive waters of Lake St. Clair within sight of the skyline of Detroit, and 30-pound Chinook salmon are taken within the limits of some of the state's manufacturing cities. Of the state's 37,000,000 acres, some 7,000,000 are public lands, contained in four national forests—Ottawa and Hiawatha in the Upper Peninsula, and Huron and Manistee in the Lower Peninsula—almost 4,000,000 acres in state forests (many of which exceed 100,000 acres, and one of which, Houghton Lake, is almost 300,000 acres), and thousands of acres in state parks, state game areas, wildlife areas, and refuges. Michigan boasts over 11,000 sparkling blue lakes and ponds, 36,000 miles of fishing and canoeing streams, and 3,000 miles of Great Lakes coastline. In many areas of Michigan, the outdoors enthusiast can fish for lunker trout or perch from a city pier, backpack in to some remote wilderness trout pond, shoot ducks within sight of skyscrapers, and run a white-water river in a canoe, all within the radius of 100 miles. A great deal of credit for maintaining the quality of fishing and hunting in Michigan goes to the Department of Natural Resources, which has been able to balance the recreation needs of a large army of outdoorsmen with the productive capacities of the environment through a skilled, innovative program of fish-and-game management. The excellence and variety of Michigan's fishing can be determined by examining the list of state record trophies, compiled by the Department of Natural Resources.

MICHIGAN RECORD FISH

	Lb.–oz.	Place	Year
Rainbow (steelhead) trout	26–8	Lake Michigan	1975
Brown trout	31–8	Lake Michigan	1976
Brook trout	6–2	Big Bay de Noc	1974
Lake trout	53–0	Lake Superior	1944
Splake	16–4	Lake Huron	1977
Tiger trout	9–4	N. Branch, Manistee River	1975
Coho salmon	30–8	East Arm, Grand Traverse Bay	1971
Chinook salmon	44–2	St. Joseph River	1975
Atlantic salmon	22–1	Lake Charlevoix	1976
Pink salmon	2–7	Silver River	1975
Kokanee salmon	1–14	Clinton River	1975
Lake whitefish	12–3	Lake Michigan	1975
Menominee whitefish	1–9	East Arm, Grand Traverse Bay	1975
Cisco (lake herring)	3–13	Big Pleasant Lake	1974
Muskellunge (Great Lakes)	62–8	Lake St. Clair	1940
Muskellunge (northern)	40–15	Lake Michigamme	1976
Muskellunge (tiger or hybrid)	32–0	Hamlin Lake	1976
Northern pike	39–0	Dodge Lake	1961
Smallmouth bass	9–4	Long Lake	1906
Largemouth bass	11–15	Big Pine Island Lake	1934
	11–15	Bamfield Dam	1959
Walleye	17–3	Pine River	1951
Sauger	6–6	Torch Lake	1973
Yellow perch	3–12	Lake Independence	1947
Black crappie	4–2	Lincoln Lake	1947
White crappie	2–10	Kent Lake	1977
Rock bass	3–10	Unknown, Lenawee Co.	1965
Bluegill	2–10	Silver Lake	1945
White bass	2–11	Thunder Bay	1975
Lake sturgeon	193–0	Mullett Lake	1974
Channel catfish	47–8	Maple River	1937
Flathead catfish	38–2	Grand River	1974
Sheepshead	26–0	Muskegon Lake	1973
Carp	61–8	Big Wolf Lake	1974
White sucker	2–10	East Arm, Grand Traverse Bay	1975

It is interesting to note that of the 35 species listed, 22 record fish were taken within the last five years, that the champion northern muskie, tiger muskie, brown trout, splake, and Atlantic salmon were landed in 1976, and surprisingly, that only 6 winners came from the wild Upper Peninsula. Write to the Michigan Dept. of Natural Resources (DNR), 905-A Southland Dr., Lansing 48926, for the free *Michigan Fishing Guide* booklet, which defines the seasons, bag limits, and approved fishing methods for the various game fish, and lists the general laws, waters with special rules, and the location and telephone number of DNR field offices. For detailed, state-wide fishing information, call the *Michigan Fishing Hotline*, operated by the DNR, (517–373–0908).

Trout & Salmon Waters

Trout species include brook, brown, rainbow (steelhead), lake, splake, and tiger. Brook trout are found in the cold, clean headwaters of a few northern Lower Peninsula streams, such as the Black in Cheboygan County, the Manistee, and the Au Sable, but the prime squaretail fishing is found in the UP in the deep coniferous forests and vast northern boglands. Ernest Hemingway vividly described the joys of Michigan trouting in his superb short story *The Big Two Hearted River*. You may still take large brookies in this great river on a grasshopper and greased line, as did his protagonist, Nick Adams. Among other great brook-trout streams are the Fox, Whitefish, Upper Pine, Iron, Teaspoon, Escanaba, Tahquamenon, Paint, Brule, Montreal, Black, and Sturgeon rivers. Big squaretails are taken along the Great Lakes shorelines, where they are called "coasters," one of which, a 6 lb. 2 oz. fish from Big Bay de Noc in Lake Michigan, holds the state record.

Brown and rainbow trout are found throughout both peninsulas and attain hefty sizes, particularly the migratory steelhead and "beer-barrel" browns, which seasonally leave the depths of the Great Lakes and invade the coastal rivers, giving shore-bound anglers a chance at great hook-jawed trophy fish. Spawn sacs, night crawlers, yarn lures, spinners, spoons, plugs, and big flies are the preferred lures for these jumbo-size battlers.

The streams of the Lower Peninsula include the hallowed waters of the Au Sable, Manistee, Père Marquette, Jordan, and Boardman rivers, which have spawned a rich tradition in American fly-fishing lore. Many great anglers fish these streams, particularly during the emergence of an extraordinarily large mayfly, the "Michigan Caddisfly" (giant mayfly), which hatches in mid- to late June and causes lunker trout to lose all caution and feed with reckless enthusiasm. The Père Marquette, Grand Rapids, and Indiana, and the Ann Arbor railroads did much to popularize the trout fishing of the northern part of the LP in the years following the turn of the century by producing colorful and provocative folders depicting the angling delights to be enjoyed by merely boarding any one of the many excellent trains and traveling into the magnificent forests north of Grand Rapids and Saginaw. In addition to the Au Sable, other streams flowing to Lake Huron produce excellent brown and rainbow-trout fishing, such as the Au Gres, Thunder Bay, Pigeon, Sturgeon, Pine, Tobacco, and Rifle rivers. Famous trout rivers spilling into Lake Michigan on the western shore of the LP include the Betsie, Platte, Muskegon, Little Manistee, Big Sable, Pentwater, Boyne, and Bear rivers. The larger of these rivers provide spectacular fishing for steelhead, coho, and Chinook salmon. The salmon are primarily late-summer and autumn spawners, while the steelhead migrations are concentrated in the late winter and early spring, with a smaller run in autumn. The beautiful spring-fed Jordan River in the northwest corner of the LP flows for 22 miles from its headwaters through cedar and spruce swamps, past abandoned farmlands, into the south arm of Lake Charlevoix and provides top-ranked fishing for trophy brookies, brown trout and steelhead. The Jordan has a spectacular run of giant lake-run browns during the June mayfly hatch.

The more remote Upper Peninsula has many beautiful trout streams, which flow through the magnificent forests of conifers and hardwoods

and from the vast boglands that run the length of the peninsula's spine. The quality of UP trout fishing can be experienced through the books of former Michigan Supreme Court jurist John Voelker, who wrote under the name of Robert Traver *(Anatomy of a Murder)*. His *Anatomy of a Fisherman*, McGraw-Hill, 1964, was written in collaboration with photographer Robert W. Kelley, and is a poetic and visual hymn to the splendor of the interior of the UP. Great UP rivers include the Big Two Hearted, Otter, Black, Chocolay, Salmon Trout, Ontonagon, Manistique, Sturgeon, Whitefish, Fox, Tahquamenon, Escanaba, Michigamme, Paint, Brule, Yellow Dog, and Carp. Many of these rivers have steelhead, Chinook, and coho runs in season. The Manistique and Menominee rivers support big salmon runs, and the former has earned a reputation for large steelhead, as have the Montreal, Huron, Big Two Hearted, Black, Pine, Millecoquin, Carp, and Ontonagon rivers, and the area below Soo Rapids.

Lake fishing for trout can be found throughout the state. The three Great Lakes offer excellent fishing for all species, with the exception of Huron, which has a limited lake-trout population. Coho and Chinook salmon abound in these great bodies of water and provide fast fishing for the big Pacific-coast imports from ice-out until late fall. In the LP, Grand Traverse Bay, Little Traverse Bay, Leelanau, and Charlevoix lakes in the northwest offer excellent angling for big sleek rainbow, brown, and lake trout. Charlevoix contains some Atlantic salmon, and the two Traverse bays are renowned for superb coho and Chinook fishing. On the eastern side of the northern LP, Thunder Bay Lake is a hot spot for browns and rainbows, Burt Lake for rainbows, and Mullett Lake for splake. In the southern LP, Gull Lake holds browns, rainbows, and Atlantic salmon. Cass Lake has rainbows and lakers, and Proud and Cedar lakes yield fine rainbows.

The UP has hundreds of lakes and ponds that provide first-rate fishing for brook, brown, and rainbow trout, as well as splake, which have been widely stocked in this region. The best opportunities are found in the more inaccessible interior of the peninsula in waters such as Fence Lake (Baraga Co.), Bass Lake (Marquette Co.), and Mishkike Lake (Gogebic Co.). Isle Royale National Park, 60 miles to the north of Keweenaw Peninsula in Lake Superior, has scores of good trout lakes in its rugged interior. Lake trout are found along the Great Lakes coasts and in some inland lakes such as Chicagon, Clear, Dodge, and Island, in the UP.

Michigan's Better Summertime Fishing Waters, compiled by Stanley L. Lievense, a free booklet published by the Travel Bureau, Michigan Dept. of Commerce, Lansing 48913, splits Michigan into geographic regions and lists the principal lakes, ponds, brooks, and rivers for each species—trout, muskellunge, walleye, bass, etc., and by county within each region. Fishing techniques and tips round out this extremely useful publication, and anyone planning to fish in the state should secure a copy. *Fishing in Michigan*, published by the Michigan Tourist Council, Michigan Dept. of Commerce, Suite 102, 300 S. Capital Ave., Lansing 48296, is a free illustrated booklet describing in general the fishing, major species, techniques, and some cooking tips. A list of regional member tourist associations is provided where you can write for additional information about the area you have chosen. The DNR can also supply this booklet, and offers its own free folder, *Michigan Fish and How to Catch Them*, which covers the same general material. The DNR also publishes a free *Michigan Boat Launching Directory* for users of trailer-borne boats, car-top boats, and canoes, and lists and describes all state boat-launching facilities.

The standard reference book for non-resident and resident anglers alike, *Trout Streams of Michigan*, published by the Michigan United Conservation Clubs, contains detailed descriptions and maps of more than 300 trout streams, including such nationally renowned north country trout, steelhead, and salmon streams as the Escanaba, Fox, Ontonagan, Paint, Whitefish, Blind Sucker, and Big Two Hearted rivers in the Upper Peninsula and the Jordan, Père Marquette, Rifle, and Little Manistee rivers in the Lower Peninsula. Individual stream descriptions cover species present, habitat, insect life, access, stream bottom composition, tributaries, holding pools, historical info, and topography. This eminently useful large-format book is edited by Thomas E. Huggler and contains an introduction by Robert Traver. It may be ordered for $2.95 (plus 50¢ postage) from: MUCC, Box 30235, Lansing 48909.

Muskellunge Lakes

Michigan has three varieties of muskellunge: the large Great Lakes species; the northern muskie; and the smaller northern-pike hybrid, the tiger muskie. These large fish prefer slow rivers, backwaters, lakes, and flowages, and hit large plugs, spoons, bucktail spinners, and live bait, particularly suckers if about one foot in length. Spring and fall produce the fastest fishing, especially with artificials, such as noisy surface plugs. However, some very large fish are taken in midsummer at the height of the tourist season. At this time, live bait seems to be the most effective, and suckers are fished around dropoffs, weed beds, and areas where there is good cover in water 10 to 15 feet deep. These great members of the pike family are well dispersed throughout the state, and while the more remote waters generally have better fishing, Lake St. Clair, which yielded the state record and still has fine muskie fishing, lies in the shadow of Detroit's skyline. The wild forested tracts of the UP contain numerous remote primeval flowages, rivers, and lakes where trophy muskies lurk among the weeds and stumps, waiting for unwary prey. Boglands, log-strewn shorelines, and floodlands, crested by dams, make this primitively beautiful area an exceptional habitat for this toothy, gape-jawed predator. Among the well-known UP waters are Lac Vieux Desert, Lower Tahquamenon River, Craig Lake, the two Bays de Noc, Lake Michigamme, Net River Dam Flowage, Munuscong Bay, Iron Lake, and Caribou Lake. The LP offers many opportunities for quality muskellunge fishing, and these fish are caught in the beautiful north-woods lakes, rivers, and wetlands of the northern section, as well as in the more urban areas of the southern half. Some waters with long-established reputations for muskies include Dumont, Silver, Big Platte, Boardman, Hamlin, Manistee, Portage, Père Marquette, Muskegon, Lansing, Houghton,

Thornapple, and White Lakes, Grass Lake Flooding, Mud Lake Flooding, Saginaw Bay, and Thunder Bay, the Red Cedar, Tihabawassee, Shiawassee, Muskegon, and Père Marquette rivers.

Northern Pike

Northern-pike fishing is found in every part of Michigan, but waters near population centers contain mostly small "snakes," because these ready strikers seldom last long enough under conditions of intense fishing pressure to reach the impressive proportions that come only with age. Spoons, spinner baits, plugs, and live bait all produce well, but the greatest thrill is seeing a surface plug or fly rod popper disappear in an explosion of spray, as a big pike inhales the lure on some quiet snag and lily-pad-filled wilderness lake. Almost all of the places mentioned under muskellunge are also excellent pike-fishing waters. Some UP waters worthy of special mention include Dodge Lake, Les Cheneaux Islands, near the Straits of Mackinac, Michigamme Reservoir and River, and Big Manistique River and Lake. In the LP, Saginaw Bay, Douglas Lake, Tawas Bay, Tomahawk Flooding, and the Au Gres river-mouth area are good pike producers.

Walleye

Walleyes are considered the bread-and-butter gamefish of Michigan and are present in great schools in sections of the Great Lakes and in many inland lakes and streams. Walleyes prefer deep water during the day and move into shoal areas around drop-offs in the evening and at night. These giant members of the perch family take deep-running plugs, jigs, spinner-and-bait combinations, and still-fished minnows and night crawlers. Spring spawning runs up rivers like the Muskegon give stream fishermen a chance to harvest these savory prizes. Lake Gogebic in the UP offers superb fishing for walleyes, and some other favorite places are Munuscong Bay, Potagonnissing Bay, Lake Nicolet, Au Train Lake, Tahquamenon River, Michigamme Reservoir and Lake, Lac Vieux Desert, Ontonagon River, Big Manistique River, Les Cheneaux Islands, and the mouth of Montreal River. In the LP, Lake St. Clair and the St. Clair River, lakes Cadillac, Mitchell, Manistee, Portage, Houghton, Burt, Mullett, Douglas, and Kent, Cook Dam tailwaters, Pine Creek, and the Grand River are among the more popular walleye spots, but good fishing is found all over.

Trophy Bass Waters

Smallmouth and largemouth bass thrive in the waters of both peninsulas, but the bigmouth has a somewhat limited range in the UP. Plugs, spinners, spoons, bucktail baits, bass bugs, streamers, plastic worms, and live bait are popular lures. Smallmouth are more partial to live bait and prefer smaller artificials than do largemouths. Fly rodders particularly enjoy fishing the rock-strewn shoals, shallow weed beds, lily pads, and snags of wilderness lakes with popping bugs and seeing the explosive strikes of trophy smallmouths shatter the still surfaces. In the UP, the Paint River, St. Marys River, Michigamme Reservoir, Menominee and Escanaba rivers, Big and Little Bay de Noc, Les Cheneaux Islands, and Munuscong and Potagonnissing bays are among the better smallmouth hot spots. Iron Lake has some trophy largemouths, and Chicagon, Brevoort, Whitefish, and Bass lakes contain plenty of fish.

In the LP, Grand Traverse Bay and adjacent regions of Lake Michigan offer some superb fishing for smallmouths to six pounds. Lake Huron, Lake St. Clair, numerous points along Lake Michigan, Au Sable River, Tihabawassee River, Tawas Bay, and Douglas, Houghton, Higgins, Long, Missaukee, Lime, Bear, Harvation, and Leelanau lakes all attract dedicated smallmouth fishermen. Bigmouth are found throughout the peninsula, particularly in the southern tier. Some of the best waters are Martin, Pigeon, Cass, Pontiac, Big Crooked, and Win-

newana lakes, Saginaw Bay, Lake St. Clair, and the Grand River, but good fishing is found everywhere.

Lake St. Clair

Lake St. Clair deserves special mention, because it produces excellent fishing for muskellunge, northern pike, walleyes, largemouth and smallmouth bass, crappies, bluegills, white bass, channel catfish, rock bass, bullheads, sturgeon, sheepshead, and, above all, huge quantities of yellow perch. All of this fish production comes from a lake that is bounded by Detroit on its west shore and by Ontario towns and villages on its east shore and that receives heavy pressure during the winter from thousands of ice fisherman who set up villages of ice shacks during the long winter months. Write to the DNR for the free folder/map *Fishing Lake St. Clair*, published in conjunction with the Michigan Marine Dealers Association. The various species are discussed, including best areas, optimum fishing information, and cooking hints. The map splits St. Clair into zones and pinpoints the prime areas for the principal fish species.

Panfish

Panfish are found throughout the state from the white-bass and yellow-perch waters of Lake Erie to the mouth of the Montreal River, at the northwestern tip of the UP, which pays host to vast hordes of perch in late summer. Perch also swarm in season in lakes Huron and Michigan, and the fishing can be fantastic for big fish up to two pounds in weight. Les Cheneaux Islands, at the north end of Huron, draw thousands of fishermen each year to fish for the big perch schools that appear in the fall. Every lake, pond, and stream, with the exception of a small number of pure trout waters, offers assorted panfish. Channel catfish are found in lakes and rivers, along with flathead catfish. Enormous sturgeon inhabit the Great Lakes and some large inland lakes and large river systems. Coarse species, such as sheepshead, carp, eels, and suckers, are found in hundreds of lakes, ponds, and streams.

Hunting & Wildlife

Michigan has always been rated a superior hunting state and annually pays host to almost one million hunters, who pursue deer, black bear, grouse, woodcock, pheasant, quail, ducks, geese, shorebirds, rabbits,

squirrels, and other small game in the millions of acres of national and state forests, and state-owned game and wildlife areas, marshes, and on private lands where permission must be secured. Write to the DNR for the free *Michigan Hunting* folder, which describes the zone system, principal game species, and general hunting information, and contains a series of maps that indicate the public lands in the southern part of the LP. The DNR produces the free *Michigan Big Game-Small Game Hunting Guide,* which defines the game species, bag limits, seasons, general regulations, license fees, special restrictions, permit-application data, and contains a list, along with telephone numbers, of DNR field offices. A free companion pamphlet, *Michigan Waterfowl Hunting Guide,* provides equivalent information about migratory birds.

The Wolverine State offers some of the nation's best hunting for whitetail deer, wild turkey, ruffed grouse (partridge), woodcock, snowshoe hare, and gray, black, and fox squirrels. In the northern Lower Peninsula, deer, bear, ruffed grouse, and woodcock are found in Pigeon River State Forest, which has the best grouse and woodcock cover in Michigan, Au Sable State Forest, Hardwood State Forest, Houghton Lake State Forest, Thunder Bay State Forest, Manistee National Forest, and Huron National Forest. Famous UP big-game ranges and upland covers include the wild Huron Range, Porcupine Mountains Wilderness Reserve, Baraga State Forest, Iron Range State Forest, Lake Superior State Forest, Hiawatha National Forest, Ottawa National Forest, Menominee State Forest, and the Sturgeon River State Forest. The western end of the Upper Peninsula is considered the most productive black-bear region in the state. A small protected moose herd exists in the Isle Royale National Park and in the boglands and lake shores of the Upper Peninsula wildlands. Sharptail-grouse hunting is restricted to six Upper Peninsula counties. Pheasants are still abundant in the southern half of the Lower Peninsula, but the population has been in a decline for many years because of overhunting and a steady attrition of habitat. Bobwhite quail are confined to the farmlands of the southern tier, particularly the counties along the Ohio and Indiana borders.

Michigan offers some outstanding waterfowl hunting for Canada and blue geese, scaup, teal, baldpate, pintail, gadwall, black duck, mallard, shoveler, and the scarce wood duck, redhead, and canvasback. Prime areas include the famous Lake Erie marshes, where luxurious duck clubs once controlled the hunting, the Lake St. Clair marshes, the Manistee, Muskegon, Shiawassee, Tihabawassee, Kalamazoo, and Detroit river marshes, Saginaw Bay, and lakes Houghton, Hemlin, and Leelanau. In the UP, better areas include Les Cheneaux Islands, areas around the vast Seney Wildlife Refuge, the St. Marys River area,

particularly Potagonnissing and Munuscong bays, Whitefish Bay, Big and Little Bay de Noc, Manistique Lake, and the Portage Lake marshlands on Wild Keweenaw Peninsula. Check the *Michigan Big Game-Small Game Hunting Guide* for public hunting lands located near lakes and river bottoms. Michigan's thousands of marshes, potholes, logans, streams, lakes, and grain fields bordering water offer good hunting opportunities when the flights funnel in from Ontario. Snipe and rails round out the migratory birds list, but the hunting interest is limited.

Write to DNR for the free booklet *Game Recipes,* which will help you to cook your game after a successful hunt, and recipes run the gamut from fried pheasant to muskrat meatloaf.

Two publications are of special interest to Michigan outdoorsmen. *Michigan Natural Resources* is produced by the DNR and costs $3.00 for six bimonthly issues. Each copy contains articles on fishing, hunting, camping, natural history, conservation, and practical field biology. Where-to-go and how-to articles round out a very useful publication for anyone planning to enjoy Michigan's outdoors. A similar excellent magazine is the monthly *Michigan Out-of-Doors,* published by the Michigan United Conservation Clubs, a group of nearly 400 affiliated conservation-oriented sportsmen's clubs and environmental groups who act as a unit to promote legislation beneficial to the state's wildlife and environment. The magazine contains a wealth of useful and interesting information for Michigan sportsmen and is free with a membership in MUCC. For information, write to the MUCC, P.O. Box 30235, Lansing 48909. (For additional fishing and hunting info, see "Michigan Travel & Recreation Guide" section and "Great Lakes Trout & Salmon," "Lake Contour & Trout Stream Maps," and "Wild & Trophy Fishing Water Maps.")

Great Lakes Trout & Salmon

Two major factors are responsible for an amazing resurgence in the quality of fishing for members of the trout and salmon families in Michigan's Great Lakes waters, primarily lakes Michigan, Superior, and Huron, and to a lesser extent in the small margin along Lake Erie: a method to control the deadly sea lamprey that devastated the lake trout and steelhead populations from the 1940s until the 1960s, and the importation of coho, Chinook, and Atlantic salmon, which quickly grow to trophy size by feasting on the vast schools of alewives that accompanied the lampreys through Ontario's Welland Canal into the four upper Great Lakes. A new deep-sea fishery, complete with charter boats, has sprung up since 1968, when the salmon explosion burst upon the astonished biologists and incredulous sports fishermen, following initial plantings in 1966. Nourished by the hordes of oily alewives, salmon have flourished to a degree undreamed of by even the most optimistic members of the DNR. Lake, steelhead, and brown trout, too, have profited from the lamprey control and the abundance of forage, and have staged a vigorous comeback from a point where disappearance from the lakes was a real possibility. Write to the DNR, 905-A Southland Dr., Lansing 48926, for the free booklet *Catching Great Lakes Salmon and Trout,* by Stan Lievence, which describes the principal species, their histories in the lakes, their habits, and fishing methods. A second free DNR pamphlet, *Know Your Great Lakes Salmon and Trout,* by biologist Ned E. Fogle, describes in text and drawings the identification characteristics of the various species. *The Compleat Guide to Fishing the Great Lakes* ($5.95, by Patrick K. Snook), is a comprehensive where-to-go and how-to guide to fishing the Great Lakes. This 218-page paperback contains useful maps, drawings, and photographs; it may be obtained from Greatlakes Living Press, 3634 W. 216th St., Matteson, IL 60443.

Coho are taken off the Michigan coasts of lakes Huron, Michigan, and

Superior and are by far the most abundant of the various salmon species. These powerful, silvery scrappers provide action in the lakes from ice-out until the fall spawning season in August and September, when they congregate in their home rivers and ascend them to spawn. Hooking a fresh coho in running water is an unforgettable experience, particularly on a fly rod. Coho are caught on spoons, spinners, plugs, flies, live bait, worms, cut baits, and flies. Hot spots include the mouths of large rivers such as the Au Sable, Au Gres, Thunder Bay, Muskegon, Manistee, Pere Marquette, and St. Joseph, all on the LP, and the Manistique, Menominee, Huron, and Escanaba, on the UP, as well as bays such as Saginaw, Grand Traverse, Little Traverse, and Platte, on the LP, and Big Bay de Noc, Little Bay de Noc, Whitefish, and Keweenaw, on the UP. Coastal lake fishing depends on the migratory movements of the salmon and their prey, the alewife, and varies with the time of the year from location to location.

Chinook salmon, although larger, are not as abundant as coho. Their habits and life histories are rather similar, but Chinook seem to prefer cooler water than silver salmon and are fished for in generally deeper water. The same lures and baits are used for both species, and Chinook fishing can be found in the same areas as coho, particularly the Menominee, Manistique, Thunder Bay, Au Sable, Muskegon, and St. Joseph rivers and the Saginaw, the Big and Little Bay de Noc, and the

Traverse bays. Write to the Michigan Tourist Council or the DNR for Stan Lievence's free pamphlet, *Catching Fall-Run Chinook Salmon*, which describes the Chinook's habits and fishing methods. Two strains of Atlantic salmon, one from Canada and a landlocked species from Sweden, have been stocked, but it is too soon to determine the results of this unusual and innovative attempt to establish the aristocrat of game fish in Michigan waters and help to perpetuate an endangered species. Lake Charlevoix produced a 22 lb. 1 oz. fish in 1976, so there is some success. Pink salmon and kokanee are also taken in the lakes, and these small Pacific salmon add variety to the cold-water fishing. Pink salmon were accidentally stocked in Lake Superior more than 20 years ago and are taken along with trout in stream fishing. The best kokanee runs occur in Lake Huron, where a lot of stocking has been done, and these fish turn streams to flame in the fall, when they assume their bloodred spawning colors on their final journey to the place of their birth.

Steelhead are caught along the shores of all the Great Lakes and in the larger tributary streams. Spinners, spoons, plugs, roe, live and cut bait, and flies all produce well. The steelhead's willingness to hit flies has endeared this fish to generations of fly fishermen. A major spawning run in the spring and a smaller one in the fall give stream fishermen two chances at this great silver and pink-tinted prince of freshwater

game fish. The Wolverine State's premier "trophy" Lake Michigan steelhead streams include: the Betsie River, a consistent producer of big steelhead from 10 to 18 pounds, located near Beulah; the gin-clear water of the Platte River; the "big fish" waters of the Muskegon River from its mouth upstream to the tailwaters of the huge Croton Dam; the famous waters of the turbulent Big Manistee and the Little Manistee—one of the nation's top streams, with huge runs of steelhead in the 10- to 20-pound class; the Boardman River in Traverse County, primarily a small-fish river; the Black River near South Haven in southern Michigan, with runs of rainbows up to 15 pounds; St. Joseph River—a top-ranked stream for steelhead up to 20 pounds, located in the southern part of the state; and the Elk and deep-flowing Grand rivers. Large spawning runs of Lake Huron steelhead occur on the famous Au Sable and Au Gres rivers for fish up to 15 pounds; on the Rifle River; Sturgeon River and the Ocqueoc River, noted for its deep

holding pools and trophy fish up to 15 pounds. The magnificent wild rivers that flow into Lake Superior on the Upper Peninsula provide often unsurpassed fly fishing for trophy lake-run rainbows in a scenic evergreen north-country setting. The major UP steelhead streams include the placid tea-colored waters of the renowned Two Hearted River, flowing through remote, sandy pine forests; the log-jammed waters of the Mosquito River, located northeast of Munising; the beautiful Middle Branch of the Ontonagon in the Ottawa National Forest Region, upstream to the towering cascade at Agate Falls; the dark, acid-stained waters of the Chocolay River near Marquette; in the Montreal River along the Michigan-Wisconsin boundary and in the Black and Presque Isle rivers. A successful fall steelhead trip along one of Michigan's white-water rivers with the maples and birches flaming against the somber green background of conifers makes memories that last a lifetime. The useful guide *Coho, Chinook, and Steelhead in Michigan* may be obtained free from the Department of Natural Resources (address above).

Lake trout are found all over lakes Michigan and Superior and prefer shoals and reefs in the spring, descending into very cold water as the surface areas warm with the approach of summer. In the summer, sunken reefs and drop-offs along shoal areas, where the water temperature is in the 45–55-degree range, are good bets. Lake Michigan waters of the northern LP, both shores of the UP, and the Isle Royale coast have the biggest lake populations. Deep trolling with lures or "Coro-

bells" and sewn bait, and still fishing with large live bait, are traditional methods, and some of the new salmon lures, such as minnow-type plugs and spoon-fly combinations, have proved effective. Some of the best areas are the two Traverse bays, the two de Noc bays, the Straits of Mackinac, Huron Bay, Keweenaw Bay, Whitefish Bay, Eagle Harbor, and the Grand Marais areas of Lake Superior.

Brook and brown trout are also found in the lakes. Brookies are called "coasters," and the best fishing is in the northern LP and the UP. Brown trout grow to huge size in the alewife-rich waters of the lakes, and are called "beer-barrel" browns because of their rotund, deep shapes. Lake browns provide excellent trolling, as well as casting opportunities from boat and shore. The fall spawning runs of both lake-run browns and brookies give stream fisherman a crack at great hook-jawed trophies under optimum conditions.

Boat owners planning to fish for these "deep-sea" prizes should write to the DNR for the free booklet *Michigan Harbors Guide*, which describes and lists the various harbors and facilities on lakes Michigan, Superior, Huron, and Erie and provides aerial photographs of principal marinas, as well as the services available at each one; a list of sewage pump-out stations by marinas is also included.

Fishermen planning to charter a boat and guide to pursue salmon, lakers, and steelhead should write to the Michigan Travel Commission, Lansing 48913, for the free booklet *Michigan Charter Boat Directory by Port*, which lists boats and captains by lake and alphabetically within each lake region by port. Boat lengths, rates, and address and telephone numbers of the skippers are provided in each listing.

Highways—Recreation & Scenic Routes

Visitors to Michigan's numerous lakes and wilderness areas will find the *Michigan Official Transportation Map* an invaluable guide to routes within the Upper and Lower peninsulas. All interstate, U.S., and state routes are indicated, as well as country roads, state parks, rest areas, roadside parks, airports, seaports, county lines, ferries and boatlines, cities, towns, villages, and many other features. The map is available free from the Michigan Dept. of State Highways and Transportation, Lansing 48904. The same office also offers free maps to individual counties, showing roads and recreation facilities (total map limit: 1).

A useful *Map Guide to Michigan* is a large bound book that contains individual color maps for each of Michigan's 83 counties, packed with info about hunting, state forests, public access sites, game and fish reports, and campgrounds. It may be ordered for $5.80 from Michigan United Conservation Clubs, P.O. Box 2235, Lansing 48911.

The atlas-sized, fact-filled *Guide to Fun in Michigan* contains a wealth of information of interest to sportsmen, campers, and travelers. The book is basically a compendium of county maps with insets offering information on visitor attractions, natural resources, hunting, fishing, and other recreational activities. There are also map/guides to ski areas, snowmobile trails, and recreational harbor facilities. The index to state and county parks and recreation areas offers camping information and details on day-use facilities. This useful guide to the Great Lake State is available paperbound for $5.95 from the Michigan United Conservation Clubs (address above).

A fascinating *Map of Ghost Towns, Old Mining and Logging Towns of Northern Wisconsin and Michigan* may be obtained for $3 from Wisconsin Sportsman Inc., P.O. Box 1307, Oshkosh, WI 54901. It contains historical descriptions of all ghost towns shown on the maps.

Lake Contour & Trout Stream Maps

Contour lake maps are available for all major Michigan lakes, including Cisco, Lac Vieux Desert, Indian, Michigamme, Caribou, and Gogebic, for 75¢ each (plus 40¢ postage and handling) from the Michigan United Conservation Clubs, P.O. Box 2235, Lansing 48911. A handy catalog, *Michigan Mapped Lakes and Campgrounds*, offers both a county-by-county index of contour maps and a useful explanation of how such maps allow you to determine the best fishing spots. The catalog also contains a guide to forest and private campgrounds throughout the state, with charts indicating location and recreational opportunities, including fish species available in nearby lakes. At the end of the catalog is a "Michigan Guide to Easy Canoeing" describing rivers in the state that can be navigated by canoe easily, leisurely, and with a minimum of danger. The *Michigan Mapped Lakes and Campgrounds* guide is available for $1.00 from the Michigan United Conservation Clubs at the above address.

A paperbound volume, *25 Upper Peninsula Hydrographic Lake Maps*, offers 12-by-16-inch contour maps for 25 lakes, including Thousand Island, Brevoort, Gogebic, Manistique, Au Train, Caribou, Deer, Lac Vieux Desert, Michigamme, and other favorite fishing lakes in the Upper Peninsula. Similar volumes of *25 Southern Michigan Hydrographic Lake Maps* and *25 Central Michigan Hydrographic Lake Maps* are available at a price of $2.00 each from the Clarkson Map Co., Kaukauna, WI 54130. Clarkson will also mail you a complete list of approximately 2,200 hydrographic maps available from the Michigan Conservation Department if you send a stamped, self-addressed envelope to the above address.

Trout and salmon stream maps ($2 each) showing fishing, wading, boating conditions, width and depth of channel, trout population, public access areas, and campgrounds are available for the *Pere Marquette, Manistee, Boardman, Sturgeon, Pigeon, Black, Au Sable,* and *Rifle* rivers. They may be ordered by mail from Hendrickson's, P.O. Box 207, New Glarus, WI 53574.

Lake Superior State Forest

Stretched across Luce and Chippewa counties in the unsettled wilderness of the Upper Peninsula, this 175,749-acre area offers unparalleled canoeing, hunting, and fishing just north of the Hiawatha National Forest. The forest encompasses both the rugged Lake Superior shoreline and several major inland bodies of water, including Muskallonge, Betsy, Little Two Hearted, Bear and Sheephead lakes, which hold wild brook trout, bass, northern pike, and walleye. Two historic north country gems, the Tahquamenon and Big Two Hearted rivers, are top-rank canoe routes and fishing streams for wild red-bellied brook trout and rainbows, surrounded by scenic conifers and mixed hardwoods, beaver meadows, tag alder, cedar and spruce swamps. The Tahquamenon, sometimes called the "dark" or "golden" river, flows through marshy lowlands, past densely wooded ridges, and between towering rock cliffs as it makes its way through the forest and neighboring Mackinac State Forest to the waters of Whitefish Bay. The river figures prominently in Longfellow's epic poem *Hiawatha*, where it marks the watery grave of Kwasind, the friend of Hiawatha who is killed in a mighty battle with the scheming otters. Between the towns of Newberry and Paradise are the legendary Tahquamenon Falls, known as the "Little Niagara," tumbling down the face of a 40-foot cliff. Six miles downstream from the Big Falls are the Cataracts, or Lower Falls, from which point the river broadens over wide ledges, then swirls through impressive stretches of thundering rapids until it finally comes to rest in Lake Superior. The Tahquamenon offers good canoeing between McMillan and Whitefish Bay during all months except June and July, when black flies make the trip unbearable. Canoeists should plan on paddling 15 miles the first day, since campsites are not available in the extensive willow marshes that line this first stretch of the route. The upper and lower falls must be portaged. A 25-mile trip for experts is also possible on the Two Hearted River between the High Bridge on County Road 407 and the stream's mouth at Lake Superior. Fast water, occasional portages, and wild and rolling country are the characteristics of this particular run. About seven miles downstream is the Two Hearted River Canoe Campground, and another state campground is five miles farther, at Reed and Green Bridge, a good spot for pickup or overnight camping. Beyond the Two Hearted River Forest campground, another state facility at the river's mouth, the land adjoining the river is suitable for camping almost anywhere.

Besides canoeing and trout fishing, the interior wild lands of this old logging country provide top-ranked hunting for whitetail deer, black bear, and ruffed grouse. Nearby attractions and major features of the forest include the Tahquamenon Falls State Park, Grand Sable Sand Dunes, Seney National Wildlife Refuge, and the Hiawatha National Forest. Campgrounds are located on Pratt, Holland, Perch, Culhane, and Bodi lakes, and at the High and the Reed and Green bridges.

Access from Newberry, Eckerman, and Trout Lake is via State Highway 123 North. County Road H58 leads east from Grand Marais.

Lake Superior State Forest is shown on the following large-scale U.S. Geological Survey Maps: Betsy Lake N., Betsy Lake NW., Betsy Lake S., Betsy Lake SW., Emerson, Grand Marais NE, Grand Marais SE, Muskallonge Lake E., Muskallonge Lake SE, Muskallonge Lake SW, Muskallonge Lake W., Sheephead Lake, Shelldrake, Timberlost, Vermilion, Vermilion SE, Whitefish Point.

Pictured Rocks National Lakeshore & the Grand Sable Banks

Along a 15-mile stretch of the Lake Superior shoreline are the multicolored sandstone cliffs of the Pictured Rocks escarpment, rising abruptly to heights of 200 feet and overshadowing the coastal waters northeast of Munising. Wind, driving rain, and the erosive action of ice during glacial periods have carved many weird and beautiful formations: columns, arches, towers, domes, promontories, and thunder caves. Over the years, soluble oxide deposits have stained the intricate patterns incised by nature on the exposed sandstone, creating tableaux colorful enough to rival any artist's canvas.

The Pictured Rocks National Lakeshore offers outstanding opportunities for wilderness camping, backpacking, and encompasses the scenic trophy trout and steelhead waters of the Miners, Mosquito, and Hurricane rivers, surrounded by tag alder, wooded dunes, conifer and mixed hardwood forests. These wild north country streams are noted for their deep pools, log jams, falls, and overhanging brush.

The beauty of these rock sculptures and the pounding of breakers in the caverns filled the Indian natives with awe. Chippewa tribes who camped here each summer believed the underground hollows to be the home of the gods of thunder and lightning. Evil spirits also lurked in hidden caves and had to be appeased at frequent intervals with offerings of tobacco and food. Hiawatha, the Chippewa man-god, hunted in the woods surrounding the rocks and gouged out holes in the cliffs with his mighty fist. The first white settlers were equally impressed by the strange rock formations. Pierre Radisson reported that "waves go into these cavities with great force and make the most horrible noises, like the shooting of great guns."

Many of the individual rock formations have acquired names descriptive of their shape or history. A white sandstone escarpment resembling the prow of a man-of-war has been dubbed Battleship Rock. Noted for their bright vermilion streaks, the Colored Caves were feared by the Indians because the red tints suggested fresh blood. The Chippewa thought the caves were used for torture or execution, and called them the "caverns of the bloody chiefs." Near the center of the Pictured Rocks escarpment is the Rainbow Cave, so called because the waters around the entrance reflect the colored walls, creating brilliant kaleidoscopic effects. Chapel Rock, also called Pulpit Rock, rises majestically above the water line and is approached by a steep stairway of natural stone steps. Within is a natural auditorium with a lofty vaulted ceiling, perpendicular walls, and a small stone bench resembling an altar. Other interesting formations include the Grand Portal, Indian Drum Cave, and Flower Vase Rock.

In the eastern section of the national lakeshore are the spectacular Grand Sable Banks and Dunes. Extending for 5 miles along the Lake Superior shorelines and rising to a height of 275 feet above the lake level, the Grand Sable Banks are the remnant of a vast glacial deposit left by melting sheets of ice thousands of years ago. Perched on top of the banks are the Grand Sable Dunes, rising an additional 85 feet and covering an area of 5 square miles. The sand was blown into great dunes at the edge of the ancient lake that preceded Superior. Wind off the lake is slowly blowing the dunes inland, where they are partially stabilized by plant growth.

Much of the inland portion of the national lakeshore is thickly wooded with northern hardwoods, pine, spruce, hemlock, and fir. Spring flowers and autumn foliage make the area particularly spectacular in season. In some burned-over areas, there are large, almost pure stands of lovely white birches. Arborvitae and tamarack, along with leatherleaf and other northern bog plants, are common in marshy areas and around ponds and lakes.

At Hurricane River, Little Beaver Lake, and Twelve-Mile Beach there are primitive camping areas accessible by car. Backcountry camping is permitted in many remote areas of the park, but a special camping permit, available from park headquarters or any park ranger, should be obtained first. Winter activities in the national lakeshore include snowmobiling, cross-country skiing, and snowshoeing.

A free map/brochure, *Pictured Rocks National Lakeshore*, showing major park features, roads, lakes, and other points of interest, is available from the Superintendent, Pictured Rocks National Lakeshore, Munising 49862. The Park Service also publishes free fliers on hiking, skiing, snowshoeing, boating, fishing, hunting, and camping. Guided cruises of the area are provided by *Pictured Rocks Cruises, Inc.*, Box 355, Munising 49862 (906–387–2379).

Pictured Rocks National Lakeshore is accessible via County Road H58 from Grand Marais to the northeast of the park and via State Highway 28 from Munising and Marquette. From Manistique, take State High-way 94 north. Other nearby outfitting centers include Wetmore, Shingleton, and Meistrand.

Pictured Rocks National Lakeshore is shown on the following large-scale U.S. Geological Survey Maps: Munising, Wood Island, Grand Portal Point, Au Sable Point, Au Sable Point SW, Grand Sable Lake, Grand Marais.

Porcupine Mountains Wilderness

One of the wildest areas left in the Midwest, the Porcupine Mountains Wilderness State Park covers 58,000 acres along the shores of Lake Superior about 17 miles west of Ontonagon in Michigan's Upper Peninsula. Towering stands of virgin pine and hemlock, four secluded lakes, and miles of wild rivers and streams combine to make this one of the most beautiful and challenging areas in the state for backpacking, fishing, and camping. The "Porkies," densely wooded mountains reaching heights of 1,900 feet, were named by Chippewa Indians who thought their rolling, forested outlines resembled crouching porcupines. The only road in this primitive wilderness skirts the south and east borders of the park and leads motorists to within a quarter-mile of spectacular views of the Lake of the Clouds.

The Department of Natural Resources maintains over 80 miles of foot trails and rustic trailside cabins for use by the public. Strategically designed to reward hikers with breathtaking views of tree-rimmed lakes and forested ridges, the trails are rugged with steep grades and many stream crossings. The 16-mile Lake Superior Trail, longest in the park, follows the rugged lake shoreline and offers both outstanding views and excellent fishing for lake trout, rainbows, and salmon at the mouths of the many streams that empty into Lake Superior. Two short trails, the East and West River trails, follow the Presque Isle River, largest and most beautiful of the streams in the Porcupines. Before it reaches the waters of Lake Superior, the Presque Isle rushes from the tableland through narrow, precipitous gorges over a series of spectacular waterfalls and rapids. The Big Carp River Trail, nine miles in length, offers perhaps the widest variety of wilderness scenery in the park. For the first two miles the trail parallels the escarpment; then it descends into the valley of the Big Carp River, where excellent brook-trout fishing and turbulent rapids are found all the way to the river's mouth. Shining Cloud Falls, the second longest in the park, are located approximately one mile upstream from the mouth. The four-mile Escarpment Trail begins where the Carp River route leaves off and leads over Cloud and Coyahoga peaks, then down to the north end of the Government Peak Trail. Striking rock formations and panoramic views of Lake of the Clouds are the major attractions of this footpath. These and other trails are described and mapped in the *Porcupine Mountains Wilderness State Park Map-Brochure*, available free from the Porcupine Mountains State Park, Star Route, Ontonagon 49953. The map/guide also contains information on modern and rustic campgrounds and trailside cabins. The cabins are available for rent between April 1 and November 30, and reservations should be made in advance with the Park Supervisor. Adirondack shelters have also been developed for trail hikers and are available on a first-come basis. Backpackers must register at the park office before entering the wilderness.

Hunting for deer in season and cross-country skiing are other favorite activities in the Porcupine Mountains. Write to the Park Supervisor at the above address for ski- and snowshoe-trail maps and information on hunting. For canoeists there is the Carp River Canoe Trail, with its many beautiful cascades, including the Explorers, Trappers, Trader, Greenstone, and Shining Cloud falls. Complete outfitting and resort-type accommodations are available in nearby Ontonagon.

Porcupine Mountains Wilderness is shown on the following large-scale U.S. Geological Survey Maps: Bergland 15, Carp River, Thomaston, White Pine 15.

Ski Touring Trails & Centers

Cross-country skiing and snowshoeing are among the most peaceful and enjoyable winter activities in Michigan. The following pathways and areas have been set aside for hiking, skiing, and snowshoeing in state forestlands. All motorized vehicles, including snowmobiles, are prohibited from operating on marked pathways or within the areas listed.

Maps of most state-forest pathways and areas are available through the Dept. of Natural Resources, Forestry Division, Lansing 48926. *Winter Quiet Areas,* a brochure available free from the same office, offers lists of skiing and snowshoe trails within state forests, game areas, and parks and recreation areas.

The state's major cross-country ski areas include: *Timberlane Ski Touring Lodge* and *Camp Martin Johnson,* both Irons 49644, in the Manistee National Forest, with equipment rentals and instruction; *Boyne USA Resorts* (Boyne Falls 49713; phone: 616–549–2441), with 30 miles of trails, lodging, and instruction; *Hinchman Acres Resort* (Box 146, Mio 48647; phone: 517–826–3991) with lodging, trails, and instruction along the Au Sable River bordering the Huron National Forest; *Lost Lake Resort* (Paradise 49768; phone: 906–492–3464), with lodging and trails near the Lake Superior State Forest; *Schuss Mountain,* Mancelona 49659 (phone 616–587–9162); *Shanty Creek Lodge,* Bellaire 49615 (phone: 616–533–8261); *Sugar Loaf Mountain Resort,* RR 1, Cedar 49621 (phone: 616–228–5461). Hundreds of miles of old logging roads and trails are open to nordic skiers in the state and national forest backcountry areas. Guided ski tours in the Ottawa National Forest are provided by *Sylvania Outfitters,* Watersmeet 49969 (906–358–4766).

One of the most popular cross-country skiing areas in the Lower Peninsula is *Ranch Rudolf,* a unique wilderness resort in the scenic Boardman River Valley surrounded by the 100,000-acre Fife Lake State Forest. The ranch offers lodging, free use of trails, and rentals and professional instruction through the Boardman Valley Outfitting Company owned and operated by the ranch. Group lodging is available at the rustic Homestead bunkhouse; campgrounds are open and maintained during the winter. Write or call Ranch Rudolf, P.O. Box 587, Traverse City 49684 (phone: 616–946–5410).

Sleeping Bear Dunes & the Manitou Islands

An old Chippewa Indian legend tells of a mother bear who once attempted to swim across Lake Michigan with her two cubs. As the trio approached the shoreline, the exhausted cubs began to lag behind. On reaching dry land, the mother bear climbed to the top of a high bluff to watch and wait for her offspring, but they never rejoined their anxious parent, who can still be seen today as the "Sleeping Bear," a solitary dune covered with dark trees and shrubs in the wilderness of northwestern Michigan. Her unfortunate cubs, now the Manitou Islands, lie a few miles offshore.

The Sleeping Bear Sand Dunes, today part of a varied and fascinating national lakeshore, rise as much as 460 feet above Lake Michigan. These and other dunes along the shoreline are in a state of constant flux; wind continually blows sand off the beaches and up the side of

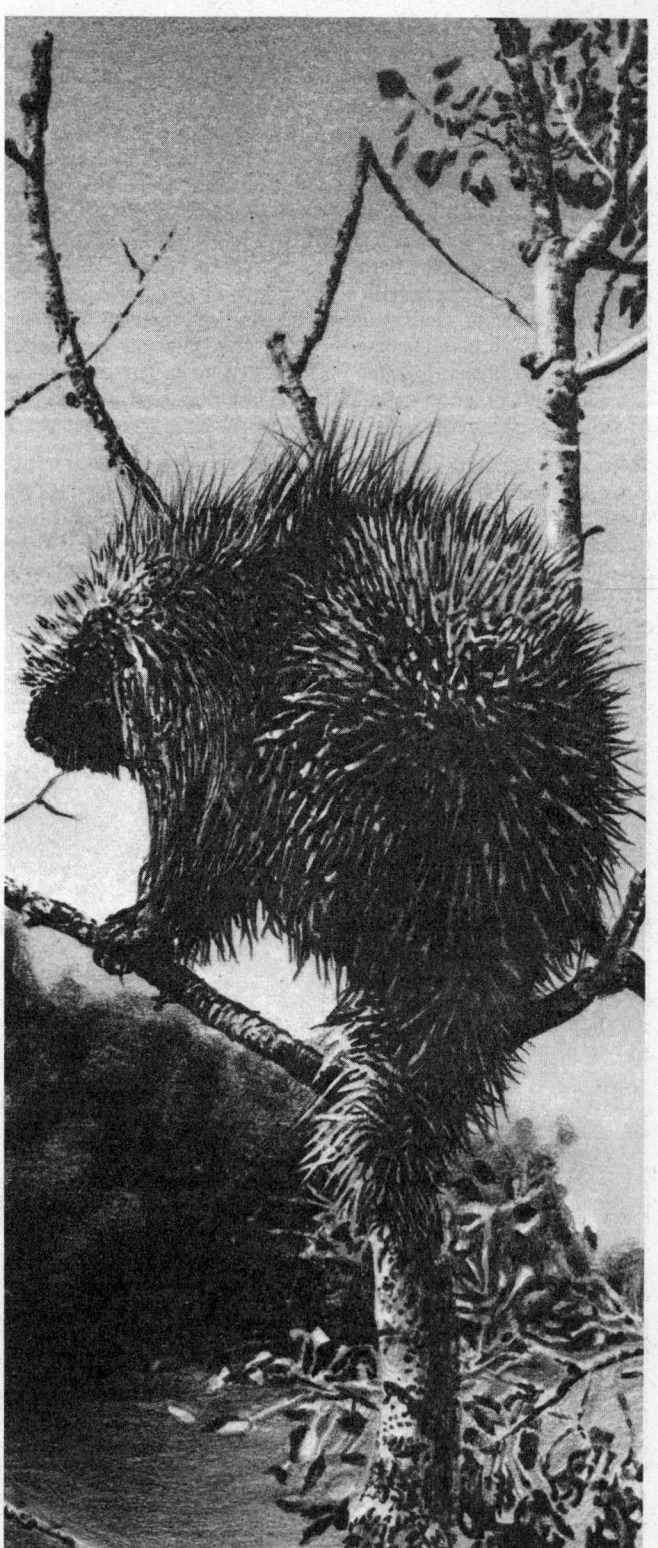

bluffs, forming dunes perched high above the lake. A protected dune climb takes visitors to the top of Sleeping Bear, where sand dunes of all shapes and sizes, sparse clumps of cottonwoods, and forests of bleached wood can be explored.

A living essay in the geologic history of the area, the national lakeshore's sinuous outline, consisting of rounded headlands and sweeping embankments, traces the rough outline of the last great glacier as it paused in its retreat northward. As the ice disappeared during the great thaw, a tremendous quantity of rock, sand, and silt was deposited by the glacier or sluiced by its meltwater to create the ridges, hills, lowlands, and lakes of the present park landscape. Today this variety of landforms supports a rich diversity of plant and animal life. Sand-dune deserts form a striking contrast with hardwood forests that explode in a glow of color during the fall season. Beech, basswood, maple, and oak alternate with dense stands of green and aromatic pines, cedar swamps, chalk-white birches, and an occasional unsteady bog of sphagnum moss. Where there are trees, there are also porcupines, sometimes seen gnawing on the green inner bark of a young tree. Deer hide in the aspen thickets; and in winter, bobcat tracks can be sighted in the fresh snow.

Seven miles by water from Glen Have, South Manitou Island also forms part of the Sleeping Bear Dunes National Lakeshore. The island's 12 miles of shoreline, deep natural harbor, and thick virgin forests attracted European settlers as early as 1830. Since that time South Manitou's natural resources have been used by various interests—lumbermen, farmers, the coast guard, and more recently vacationers and fishermen. The Valley of the Giants in the southwestern part of the island offers a remnant of the magnificent forest that once covered the whole region: tall white cedars, some more than 500 years old, common and redberry elder, white ash, basswood, mountain and sugar maple. The native understory of shrubs and flowers makes hiking in the region a particularly inviting adventure. Gull Point, the island's northwestern "hook," is a major nesting area for herring and ring-billed gulls. Although the point is closed to visitors, a trail around the colony permits observation of these noisy but graceful winged residents. Perched more than 350 feet above Lake Michigan, the high dunes on the west side of the island rest on bluffs of glacial moraine and are intersected by marked paths leading to spectacular views of the lake. Three camping areas with primitive facilities are located on the east side of the island. On the mainland, the Platte River and D. H. Day campgrounds, operated by the National Park Service, are also available to visitors. Camping is limited to 14 days, and campgrounds are usually filled to capacity during the summer.

The park's numerous lakes, including Platte, Crystal, Loon, Glen, and giant Lake Michigan, offer trophy fishing for salmon, walleye, trout, northern pike, and bass. During the autumn season, when coho salmon run, fishing fervor reaches its greatest peak. Canoeists will enjoy the quiet waters of the Platte River, running through some of the loveliest scenery in northern Michigan.

For more information on the Sleeping Bear Dunes National Lakeshore, write to the Superintendent, 400½ Main Street, Frankfort 49635. A free *Sleeping Bear Dunes Map-Brochure* describing the area, as well as a flyer on South Manitou Island, is available. For information on accommodations and services in the area, write to the Sleeping Bear Dunes Area Chamber of Commerce, P.O. Box 505, Beulah

49617. Ferry service to the Manitou Islands is provided by *Manitou Islands Boat Cruise,* Leland 49654 (616–256–9116).

Sleeping Bear Sand Dunes is shown on the following large-scale U.S. Geological Survey Maps: Frankfort, Empire, Maple City, North Manitou.

State Forest Reserves & Maps

The following full-color, large-scale U.S. Geological Survey topographic maps show the topography of the Wolverine State's vast forest reserve and game lands. These scenic north country reserves offer nationally renowned fishing, canoe-camping, backpacking, cross-country skiing, and hunting in season for whitetail deer, black bear, small game, waterfowl, and upland game birds. See the "Travel & Recreation Guide" section for additional listings.

The *Baraga State Forest & Huron Mountains* (U.S.G.S. Topo Maps: Greenland, Herman, Keweenaw Bay, Pelkie, Point Mills, Sidnaw, Skanee, Winona) takes in 67,000-acres in the western UP and embraces the famed Copper Range and Huron Mountains; Otter, Mountain, and Prickett Lakes; the scenic canoe routes and steelhead waters of the Firesteel, Portage, Ontonagon, Otter, Sturgeon, Huron, and Salmon Trout rivers; and the adjacent L'Anse Indian Reservation lands.

The *Black Lake State Forest* (U.S.G.S. Topo Maps: Cheboygan, Grace, McRae Bay, Onaway, Round Island, Tower) takes in 146,000 acres south of Lake Huron in the northernmost part of the Lower Peninsula and includes the trophy fishing and canoeing waters of the Ocqueoc River and Lake (the Chippewa word for "sacred place," where the aged and crippled members of the tribe plunged to their death where the Ocqueoc enters the bay), Black and Rainy rivers, Black Mallard Lake, and scenic Bois Blanc Island situated along the old voyageur route due east of the Straits of Mackinac in Lake Huron's South Channel.

The *Escanaba River State Forest* (U.S.G.S. Topo Maps: Gladstone, Northland, Schaffer, Watson) embraces 142,000 acres of roadless wildlands of dense conifer forests, rolling hills, swamps, bogs, and beaver ponds surrounding the famous boulder-studded trout and steelhead waters of the Escanaba River.

Fife Lake State Forest (U.S.G.S. Topo Maps: Cadillac N., Central Lakes, Copemish, Elk Rapids, Empire, Fife Lake, Frankfort, Kingsley, Maple City, Mesick, Onekama, Thompsonville, Traverse City) encompasses 103,000 lake-dotted acres north from the Manistee National Forest to the wild shores of Lake Michigan and Grand Traverse Bay in the northwestern section of the Lower Peninsula and includes the renowned canoe routes and trophy salmon and steelhead waters of the Boardman, Platte, and Betsie rivers, Betsie River State Game Area, the Shore-to-Shore Trail, and Long, Glen, Green, Duck, Arbutus, Elk, and Woodcock lakes. Lake Leelanau, a long, slender body of water in the Chippewa "Land of Delight," is famed for its lunker brown trout up to 15 pounds.

The *Hardwood State Forest* (U.S.G.S. Topo Maps: Bayshore, Big Stone Bay, Cross Village, Gaylord, Hetherston, McGulpin Point, Mullett Lake, Pellston, Petoskey, Wolverine) takes in 188,000 acres of coniferous and mixed hardwood forests, rolling hills, swamps, large blue lakes, and wild rivers south of the majestic Straits of Mackinac in the northernmost part of the Lower Peninsula and includes a southern arm of Mullett Lake—second largest of Michigan's inland waters; the renowned trout, salmon, and smallmouth bass waters of the Pigeon, Sturgeon, Carp, Bear, and Black rivers; the northern-pike, muskellunge, walleye, and lake-trout waters of Burt and Douglas lakes;

and Little Traverse Bay, one of the state's salmon and trout hot spots.

Houghton Lake State Forest (U.S.G.S. Topo Maps: Harrison, Houghton Lake, Lake City, Lyon Manor, Marion, Meredith NW, Meredith SW, Prudenville) encompasses 282,000 acres stretching south from Grayling and the Huron National Forest in the north-central region of the Lower Peninsula and includes Houghton Lake, the largest inland lake in the state, Higgins Lake, Muskegon River, Lake Missaukee, and the Deadstream Swamp Area.

The *Iron Range State Forest* (U.S.G.S. Topo Maps: Amasa, Crystal Falls, Florence E., Florence W., Fortune Lake, Gibbs City, Kelso, Kiernan, Lake Mary, Ned Lake, Perch Lake, Sunset Lake, Witch Lake) takes in 78,000 acres covering most of the eastern part of Iron County in the western UP and includes the scenic lakes and woodlands surrounding the Michigamme Reservoir and the famous trout waters and canoe routes of the Paint, Net, Hemlock, Fence, and Michigamme rivers. The Paint is renowned as one of the state's top smallmouth bass streams.

The *Menominee State Forest* (U.S.G.S. Topo Maps: Bark River, Cedar River, Escanaba, Foster City, Gladstone, Mariette, Norway, Pembine, Powers, Schaffer, Stephenson, Wausaukee), named for the Chippewa word meaning "wild-rice country," encompasses 90,000 acres of wilderness in the UP, stretching between the Menominee River east to the shores of Lake Michigan's Green Bay and Little Bay de Noc. The forest area was the site of the Indian Sturgeon War, fought when the Menominee Indians dammed the river to prevent sturgeon from reaching the Chippewa settlements upstream. The major features of the forest include the canoeing and fishing waters of the Menominee, Ford, Escanaba, Bark, Big Cedar, Shakey, and Little rivers. The Menominee has produced record-sized chinook salmon up to 40 pounds.

The scenic *Michigamme State Forest* (U.S.G.S. Topo Maps: Big Bay, Champion, Huron Mountain, Ishpeming, Michigamme, Negaunee, Republic, Skanee, Witch Lake) is spread over 116,000 acres in the UP encompassing the famous fishing and canoe-camping waters of beautiful Lake Michigamme and the Fence, Sturgeon, Michigamme, Black, and Yellow Dog Rivers. To the north of the Sturgeon River area are the Burnt Plains, once the prized hunting grounds of the Wisconsin Indians. In late summer, the natives set fire to the forests and easily slaughtered the hordes of fleeing deer, moose, and caribou, drying and curing the meat for food during the long winter. The fresh grass and undergrowth that covered the region in the spring once again attracted more game, and the same process would be repeated, until the larger trees were destroyed and the charred grounds became a grassy plain.

The majestic *Pigeon River State Forest* (U.S.G.S. Topo Maps: Alba, Beaver Island, Big Bradford Lake, Boyne City, Boyne Falls, Central Lake, Comstock Hills, Elk Rapids, Gaylord, Heatherton, Johannesburg, KP Lake, Lewiston, Lovells, Otsego Lake, Turtle Lake), which contains some of the finest grouse cover in the state, encompasses 90,000 acres of north country wildlands surrounding the Pigeon River watershed in the northern Lower Peninsula and includes the beautiful evergreen-rimmed Torch Lake Chain—so-called because the Indians once speared fish there at night, using torches as a source of light, as well as Otsego, Opal, Big Bear, Tuttle, Big Wolf, Six Mile, Tea, Bradford, and Emerald lakes and the famous trout and salmon waters of the Jordan, Big Manistee, Upper Au Sable, Sturgeon, Black, and Pigeon rivers. Elk, originally native to Michigan, were brought into the region about 40 years ago, and today the forest supports a modest herd.

The 176,000-acre *Thunder Bay River State Forest* (U.S.G.S. Topo

Maps: Atlanta, Comins, Hillman) embraces the wildlands surrounding the Thunder Bay River in the northeastern region of the Lower Peninsula and includes Canaca Creek, Rush, Grass, and Muskallonge lakes. Thunder Bay River has good fishing in its headwaters area for rainbow and brook trout, and in the lower stretches the fishing is superb for northern pike, smallmouth bass, and hard-hitting muskies up to 36 pounds.

Upper Peninsula—the Mountains, Forests, Lakes, & Wild Rivers

A rugged, unspoiled region of wild rivers, clear, deep lakes, and heavy forest growth, Michigan's Upper Peninsula has long been favored by outdoor travelers looking for a north-woods atmosphere within the boundaries of the United States. The Upper Peninsula is connected to the Lower Peninsula by the Mackinac Bridge, which spans the awesomely beautiful Straits of Mackinac between lakes Huron and Michigan—dominated on the east by the historic wilderness fur trade capital of Mackinac Island, known to the Indians and voyageurs as *Michilimackinac,* or "the great turtle" because of its appearance as it rises from the Straits.

Dramatic rocky shorelines of lakes Superior, Huron, and Michigan, where dunes and beaches alternate with craggy outcroppings, outline this geologically ancient country. The western half of the peninsula offers a sharp contrast with the rest of Michigan, providing both

Map and Guide to Travel and Recreation

michigan's Upper Peninsula

The clean air, clear water country

spectacular topographic beauties and unparalleled mineral wealth. From the evergreen and northern hardwood forests of Huron Mountains westward, the land is wild in the extreme, culminating in the northwestern Porcupine Mountains, where towering stands of virgin timber cover the state's highest peaks. The peninsula's eastern portion is composed of low-lying lands and swamps. Marshy, often barren areas along the Tahquamenon River are bordered to the north by the sandstone tablelands of Alger and Marquette counties and to the south by rolling limestone hills. Throughout the peninsula there are numerous state forests, each offering its own particular wilderness character as well as opportunities for outdoor experiences in unspoiled settings.

In contrast to the southern regions of the Lower Peninsula, where

mixed hardwood forests are the rule, the Upper Peninsula is blanketed with coniferous species, especially jack pine and spruce. Across the eastern half of the peninsula, the Hiawatha National Forest forms two vast green belts, while the Ottawa National Forest in the western part offers a lake-strewn woodland bordered by Lake Superior. Both national forests and smaller state lands feature numerous evergreen varieties and diverse hardwood species such as sugar maple, aspen, red oak, basswood, and hemlock. The forest understory is adorned with a rich growth of shrubs, berry bushes, and briers. Wildflowers, including orchids, lady's slippers, anemones, phlox, violets, wild roses, and tiger lilies, complete the beauty of the woodland setting.

Upper Peninsula streams hold trophy-sized brook, brown, and rainbow trout, migratory salmon, steelhead, and great-northern pike, walleye, and smallmouth bass. The thousands of remote seldom-explored coves, bays, and rocky islands along the incredibly picturesque shores of the Upper Great Lakes offer some of the nation's truly great fishing for smallmouth bass, salmon, northern pike, yellow perch, lake, rainbow and brown trout up to record weights. Inland are the scenic trophy northern-pike, walleye, and smallmouth-bass waters of island-dotted Lake Michigamme and Thousand Island, Brevoort, Beatons, Gogebic, Indian, Betsy, Crooked, Manistique, Millecoquin, Au Train, Caribou, Cisco, Deer, Medora, and Golden lakes, and the trophy muskellunge waters of beautiful Lac Vieux Desert. Here are thousands of remote beaver ponds, many of which harbor fat orange-bellied brook trout and the renowned trout and steelhead waters of the Big Two Hearted, Fox, Whitefish, Escanaba, Paint, Blind Sucker, Ontonagon, and Otter rivers, surrounded by north country wildlands of conifers and tag alders, spruce and cedar swamps, jack and red pine plains, meadows, and tangles of willow, huckleberry, and dogwood. Caribou, once native to the peninsula, have vanished, but other game animals and birds common throughout the region, including deer, black bear, grouse, cottontail rabbit, red fox, and bobcat, still provide the hunter with challenging quarry. Wolves have been sighted in sparsely settled regions of the Upper Peninsula, especially on Isle Royale, where a sizable population of moose makes its home. Two national wildlife refuges, the Huron Refuge on Keweenaw Bay and Seney Refuge in the center of the peninsula, attract a broad variety of migratory and native birds, including the bald eagle, sandhill crane, and a variety of hawks.

Visitors to the Upper Peninsula can obtain a number of free publications especially written to increase enjoyment of this wilderness playground. *The Upper Peninsula Campground Directory* lists almost all camping areas in the region, both public and private, with sections on sites with state parks, state forests, and national forests. Location, activities available, special regulations, and number of acres are all included. *Finest Attractions in Michigan's Upper Peninsula,* a glove-compartment-size brochure, describes various highlights, including the Pictured Rocks boat cruises, Copper Peak, Mackinac Island boat cruises, the Soo Locks tour train, and other activities. Over 150 waterfalls are found along the Upper Peninsula's swift, roaring streams, many of which can be easily reached by car. Grand Sable Falls at Grand Marais, Presque Isle River Falls north of Wakefield, and the famous Tahquamenon Falls between Newberry and Paradise are included in the *Upper Peninsula Waterfalls Guide,* a brochure listing 117 superb cascades with a keyed map and brief directions for finding the falls. For those interested in touring the peninsula by car, the folder entitled *Fall Color Tours* describes eight trips, from 70 to 223 miles in length, that thoroughly explore some of the region's most spectacular natural attractions. Included are tours through the remote Keweenaw Peninsula, along the shores of lakes Superior and Michigan, beside sand dunes and tumbling rivers, and through several ghost towns, abandoned since nineteenth-century mining days. Explicit di-

rections and maps are provided. Fine introductory descriptions of attractions in the region are offered on the reverse of the *Map and Guide to Travel and Recreation in Michigan's Upper Peninsula,* a special edition of the Michigan State Highway Map. Historic forts, Mackinac Island, shoreline drives, mountains, fishing, hunting, boating and water sports, winter activities, and many other features are described, while the detailed road and highway map will help you find your way. All of the above publications are available free from the Upper Peninsula Travel & Recreation Assn., P.O. Box 400, Iron Mountain 49801.

For winter-sports enthusiasts, the Travel & Recreation Association also publishes a free *Winter Activities and Recreation Guide* listing ski areas and snowmobile trails. Slopes, lifts, trails, rentals, accommodations, and other facilities are all indicated for such prominent skiing attractions as Porcupine Mountain, Big Powderhorn, Pine and Brule mountains, Ottawa National Forest, and other areas. The *Calendar of Winter Events* lists special races and winter festivals.

Wild & Trophy Fishing Waters Maps

Listed below are large-scale U.S. Geological Survey Maps showing the entire lengths, including the headwaters and topography of the surrounding wildlands, of Michigan's famous canoe routes and salmon, trout, and steelhead streams. The paddler should note that many stretches of these rivers are extremely dangerous and may require numerous portages around falls, rapids, and log jams.

Au Gres River: Au Gres, Hale SE, National City, Sage Lake, South Branch, Whittemore; *Au Sable River:* East Tawas, Hale, South Branch, Tawas City; *Au Sable Middle Branch:* Alba, Grayling, Lake Margarethe, Luzerne NW, Red Oak, Wakeley Lake; *Au Sable North Branch* (including Otsego and Turtle Lakes): K-P Lake, Lovells, Luzerne NW, Otsego Lake, Red Oak, Turtle Lake; *Au Sable South Branch:* Eldorado, Luzerne NW, Pere Cheney, Roscommon N.; *Au Train River:* Au Train, Rapid River, Trenary; *Bark River:* Bark River, Escanaba, Schaffer; *Betsie River:* Frankfort, Kingsley, Onekama, Thompsonville; *Big Sable River* (including Little Manistee River and Hamlin Lake): Freesoil, Manistee, Willston; *Big Two Hearted River:* Betsy Lake N., Betsy Lake NW, Betsy Lake S., Betsy Lake SW, Grand Marais, Grand Marais SE, Muskallonge Lake E., Muskallonge Lake SE, Muskallonge Lake SW; *Boardman River:* Fife Lake, Kalkaska, Kingsley; *Carp River:* Carp River, White Pine; *Cedar River:* Bark River, Cedar River, Foster City, Powers; *Chippewa River:* Lake, Mecosta, Mount Pleasant, Sanford, Shepherd, Sherman; *Escanaba River:* Gladstone, Northland, Schaffer, Watson; *Fence River* (including the Hemlock River and Ned Lake): Kiernan, Ned Lake, Witch Lake; *Firesteel River:* Greenland, Rousseau, Winona; *Ford River:* Escanaba, Foster City, Gladstone, Northland, Ralph, Schaffer, Watson; *Huron River* (including the Huron Mountains): Michigamme, Skanee; *Laughing Whitefish River:* Au Train, Gladstone, Rapid River, Rock, Skandia, Trenary; *Menominee River:* Chappee Rapids, Iron Mountain, Iron Mountain SW, Mariette E., Mariette W., Norway, Pembine, Randville, Stephenson, Vulcan, Wausaukee; *Michigamme River* (including Lake Michigamme): Channing, Florence E., Kiernan, Lake Mary, Michigamme, Republic, Republic SW, Witch Lake; *Muskegon River* (including Houghton Lake): Big Rapids, Evart, Fremont, Harrison, Houghton Lake, Lake Harbor, Marion, Sand Lake, Twin Lake, Woodville; *Ned River:* Ned Lake, Perch Lake, Sidnaw, Sunset Lake; *Ontonagon River* (including the West, East, and South branches, and Potato, Flintsteel, Middle, and Tenderfoot rivers): Bergland, Greenland, Matchwood, Ontonagon, Rockland, Rousseau, Thayer, Watersmeet; *Otter River and Lake:* Pelkie, Winona; *Paint River:* Amasa, Crystal Falls, Florence W., Gibbs City,

Kenton, Perch Lake, Sunset Lake; *Pigeon River* (including Mullett and Burt lakes): Gaylord, Heatherton, Tower, Wolverine; *Presque Isle River:* Boulder Junction, Marenisco, Thomaston, Wakefield; *Rifle River:* Omer, Omer SW, Selkirk, Skidway Lake, Standish NE, Sterling, West Branch; *Salmon Trout River:* Champion, Huron Mountain; *Shiawassee River:* Chesaning, Corunna, St. Charles; *Sturgeon River* (including Lake Michigamme): Chassell, Herman, Michigamme, Pelkie, Point Mills, Sidnaw, Three Lakes; *Thunder Bay River:* Alpena, Comins, Hillman, Lachine, Lake Winyah; *Tittabawassee River:* Auburn, Edenville, Edwards, Hope, Midland S., St. Charles, Sanford, Secord Lake, Wooden Shoe Village; *White River:* Hesperia, Montague, Twin Lake, White Cloud; *Yellow Dog River:* Big Bay, Champion, Negaunee.

For additional listings, see the "Travel & Recreation Guide" section.

MICHIGAN TRAVEL & RECREATION GUIDE

Hiawatha National Forest & Les Cheneaux Islands

Hiawatha National Forest Topo Maps

U.S. Geological Survey Overview Maps, scale 1:250,000, also showing the adjacent Grand Sable, Lake Superior, Mackinac, Manistique, Escanaba River, and Munuscong state forests and the Fox, Whitefish, and Blind Sucker rivers: Escanaba, Marquette, Sault Ste. Marie.

Bay de Noc—Grand Island Trail

Large-scale U.S. Geological Survey Topographic Maps: Rapid River, Trenary, Au Train.

Betchler Lake Wilderness

Large-scale U.S. Geological Survey Topographic Map: Strongs.

Indian River Country & Big Island Lakes Wilderness

Includes Indian, Thunder, Minerva, Bass, Triangle, Byers, Twilight, Big Island, Round, Klondike, Deep, Grassy, Fish, Halfrom, and many other headwater area lakes, and the entire length of the Indian River, shown on large-scale U.S. Geological Survey Topographic Maps: Cooks, Steuben, Corner Lake, and Munising.

Les Cheneaux Islands

Large-scale U.S. Geological Survey Topographic Maps: St. Martin Island, Goose Island, Cedarville, Prentiss Bay, and Allany Island.

This famous 860,000-acre forest embraces a wild, lake-dotted country of dense evergreens and mixed hardwoods, wetlands, and scattered rolling hills interlaced by hundreds of miles of rushing, free-stone streams and wild rivers. The forest takes its name from Henry Wadsworth Longfellow's famous *Song of Hiawatha*, the epic poem celebrating the deeds of an extraordinary Indian brave. Stretched across the eastern segment of Michigan's Upper Peninsula, the two units of the Hiawatha National Forest open onto the wave-pounded shorelines of lakes Huron, Michigan, and Superior, the last of which was described by Longfellow as the "Shining Big-Sea Waters." Here are ancient Indian cliff paintings and the famed smallmouth bass, steelhead, brown trout, and northern pike waters of Big and Little Bay de Noc of Lake Huron, and the beautiful Laughing Whitefish Falls. Remote trails and old logging and Forest Service roads provide access to the brook-trout and steelhead waters of the Indian, Manistique, Au Train, Rapid, and Tahquamenon rivers and to the wild, scenic Rock River Canyon, Betchler Lake Wilderness, and to the swamps, glacial moraines, and giant buck trees of the Big Island Lake Wilderness. The proposed 23,000-acre Betchler Lake Wilderness contains the Laurentian Divide and the headwaters of streams that flow into both Lake Superior and Lake Michigan, surrounded by swamps, eskers, and chaotic glacial moraines. The wild fish and game lands of the Munuscong, Mackinac, Manistique, Lake Superior, Escanaba River, and Grand Sable state forests lie adjacent to the national forest boundaries. To the north are the Grand Sable Sand Dunes and ancient Indian burial grounds at Grand Island and Lake Superior.

The forest's domain includes Round and Government islands surrounded by the clear waters of Lake Huron off the southern shores of the eastern unit. Government Island is the only one of the beautiful Les Cheneaux Islands in public ownership. Like the other 34 members of this archipelago located just south of Cedarville and Hessel, the island is heavily wooded and offers superb fishing offshore for northern pike, yellow perch, and smallmouth bass, as well as hunting in season

for deer and small game. Government Island was a popular stopover for explorers and voyageurs en route from Montreal and Mackinac, and from 1874 to 1939 it served as a U.S. Coast Guard station. On the northwest end of this uninhabited island are the remains of a dock and manmade clearings. Water channels leading to Government Island are popular for small boating and fishing, and small craft can be beached at two widely separated primitive picnic sites on the sheltered side of the island. The name "Les Cheneaux" derives from the French word for "the channels." Known locally as "The Snows," the islands vary in size from Marquette Island, over 6 miles long, to Dollar Island, barely large enough to accommodate a single summer cottage. Les Cheneaux have been popular with summer vacationers since the turn of the century. All the islands are heavily wooded, with numerous trails leading through forests of cedar, pine, and balsam. From a distance, the group gives the appearance of floating rafts of greenery, while tall conifers lend an illusion of great height.

Sandwiched between Mackinac and Bois Blanc islands, Round Island has changed very little since the Indians called it *Minnisais* ("little island"). An old lighthouse on the northwest end of the island, built in 1873 and abandoned in 1935, is the only permanent testimony to the white man's presence here. Round Island can be reached by boat in summer or over ice in wintertime. Both Government and Round islands have been classified as scenic areas and are carefully managed to preserve the natural wilderness conditions favorable to forest plant and animal life. A varied and fascinating community of plant life flourishes on the islands throughout the spring and summer. Bunchberry and bearberry carpet wide areas; twin flowers, trillium, ground hemlock, and pyrola thrive deep in the woods; and rare and delicate orchids are found growing wild and undisturbed. Present everywhere is a variety of trees, shrubs, ferns, lichens, and mosses. Wildlife of the mainland, varying in size from the deer mouse to the whitetail deer, are able to cross the water to visit or live on the islands. Bird life of the area includes ducks, woodpeckers, sparrows, warblers, sandpipers, hawks, and owls. No campgrounds have been developed on either Round or Government Island, but picnic sites and primitive trails make both areas ideal for day trips. A free brochure, *The Islands*, describes both Round and Government islands and is available from the Forest Supervisor, Hiawatha National Forest, Escanaba 49829.

Other attractions of the Hiawatha National Forest's eastern unit include the Point Iroquois Lighthouse, a picturesque abandoned structure at the mouth of the St. Marys River affording splendid views of Canada, Lake Superior, and of oceangoing freighters, or "salties," plying the river and lake. The Big Sea Water Area offers miles of sandy Lake Superior shoreline with handsome scenery and panoramic overlooks. The Bay View and Monocle Lake campgrounds near Lake Superior offer 24 and 59 campsites each and opportunities for fishing and boating. Other campgrounds in the eastern unit are located on the shores of Brevoort Lake, along Carp River, at Soldier Lake, and near Foley Creek. Just outside the forest's southern boundary is St. Ignace, second oldest settlement in Michigan, officially founded by Father Jacques Marquette and visited during its early history by such notables as Jean Nicolet and the Sieur de La Salle.

In the western part of the forest is the famous Grand Island-Bay de Noc Trail, following an old Indian route along the Whitefish River bluff. Au Train, just north of the lake of the same name, was a favorite camping ground for Chippewa Indians and an important stop for voyageurs on their trips along the south shore of Lake Superior. A modern campground with opportunities for fishing and boating is nestled among Norway pines on the south shore of Au Train Lake. Many other campgrounds in the western unit are situated near lakes,

including Camp, Little Bass, Petes, Pole Creek, and Corner. Canoeing is popular on the Whitefish, Sturgeon, and Au Train rivers.

Campgrounds, picnic sites, winter-sports areas, Forest Service stations, trails, roads, lakes, streams, and many other forest features are all shown on the *Hiawatha National Forest Map*, available for 50¢ from the Forest Supervisor, U.S. Forest Service, Escanaba 49829. The Forest Service will also be glad to answer any questions you may have on campgrounds and outdoor activities in the area.

Innumerable species of wildlife contribute to the beauty and fascination of the national forest. Whitetail deer and black bear are among the largest species, but there is also an abundance of snowshoe hare, beaver, squirrel, porcupine, coyote, weasel, red fox, and raccoon. In addition, the rare pine marten, previously extinct in this part of the country because of trapping and changes in habitat, has been reintroduced. Although the chances of sighting them are extremely remote, there have been reports of both timber wolves and moose in the Hiawatha. In addition to the wide variety of mammals, game birds—including ruffed and sharp-tailed grouse, woodcock, and a diversity of waterfowl—provide top hunting opportunities. In the waters of the Hiawatha, Thunder, Hulbert, Pendrills, Manistique, and Brevoort lakes, and the forest's many rivers hold trophy-sized trout, bass, perch, walleye, northerns, coho salmon, smelt, and steelhead.

The wildlands of red pine and marshes of the Seney National Wildlife Refuge located to the west of the forest in the Great Manistique Swamp, are shown on the free *Seney Wildlife Refuge & Wilderness Tract Map* available from the Refuge Manager, Seney National Wildlife Refuge, Seney 49883. The wild Fox River, which flows from its headwaters through the Seney Swamp, is one of the state's top trophy brook trout streams.

Towns within and surrounding the Hiawatha National Forest offer campgrounds, accommodations, and outfitting services within easy reach of forest lands and other Upper Peninsula attractions. In St. Ignace, the *Fort Aux Chenes Resort* (c/o C. Stoyka, Rt. 2, St. Ignace 49781), 10 miles west of the Mackinac Bridge, offers a sand beach on Lake Michigan, swimming, boating, fishing, and attractive cabins and housekeeping cottages. On Brevoort Lake, within the forest, *Kemeny's Sunset Bay Resort* (c/o Bill Kemeny, Moran 49760) features lakeside cottages, 915 feet of safe, sandy beach, boating, and fishing for muskie, pike, bass, walleye, and panfish. Housekeeping cabins are also available

at *Miles Cabins* (877 N. State St., St. Ignace 49781) on Lake Huron overlooking Mackinac Island. The *Lake Shore Park Campground* (c/o W. J. Heck, St. Ignace 49781), on beautiful Lake Michigan, offers fine family camping just 1½ miles west of the Mackinac Bridge near U.S. 2. Picnic tables, hook-ups, fireplaces, showers, and a nearby laundry are all available.

City Limits Cabins (Rt. 3, Box 53, Sault Ste. Marie 49783), 3 miles south of the Soo Locks, features kitchenettes and sleeping cabins, heated showers, and groceries, and is open from early May through late October. An all-new campground 2 miles south of the locks, *Chippewa Travel Park* (Box 606, Sault Ste. Marie 49783), has space for 100 campers, shower rooms, electricity to all sites, picnic tables, and a laundry. The campground is open May through mid-October and is situated near prime hunting areas. Located on the St. Marys River, *Riverview Cabins & Campgrounds* (Rt. 1, Box 54, Sault Ste. Marie 49783) is open year round, offering cabins and campsites, boats, motors, docking and launching facilities. Hunting, fishing, and snow-mobile guide services are available upon request. During the fall and early winter, a deer-hunting guide service (firearm or bow-and-arrow) is offered.

In Manistique, the *Anchorage Resort* (c/o F. R. Lowman, Manistique 49854), on Indian Lake, offers clean, comfortable cottages on a safe, sandy beach and is centrally located for the best fishing spots on the lake. Housekeeping cottages are also available at *Brady's Resort* (Star Route, M-94, Box 33, Manistique 49854), on Island and Dodge lakes. Open May through October, *Nor-Land Cabins* (Box 264, RFD 1, Manistique 49854), on the east side of Indian Lake, offers boating, swimming, and fishing. Also situated on Indian Lake is the *Mountain Ash Resort* (R.R. 1, Indian Lake, Manistique 49854), with its water-front housekeeping cottages, private dock, boats, and several acres of private, wooded lands. *Sequoya Resort* (Rt. 1, Box 309, Manistique 49854) offers cabins on Indian Lakes, excellent fishing for walleye, perch, and pike, and an attractive sand beach.

Simpson's Lakeside Cottages (Rt. 2, Box 106, Ford River Road, Escanaba 49829) is located just 2½ miles south of the Escanaba city limits on M-35. Housekeeping cottages, free boats, and a beautiful sand beach on Green Bay are some of the attractions.

In Munising, the *Sunset Resort Motel* (c/o W. Truckey, Bay St., Munising 49862), on Munising Bay facing Grand Island, offers knotty-pine-paneled cottages, a private swimming beach, and boats and motors for the best in trout, whitefish, and coho fishing. Also located on the bay, *King Kole Kabins* (c/o D. Toebe, Munising 49862) offers modern housekeeping cabins and a pleasant swimming beach. The *Wandering Wheels Campground* (c/o T. Hardley, Munising 49862), 3½ miles east on Munising in the Pictured Rocks National Lakeshore Parks, has 100 sites, a heated swimming pool, playground, a laundry, and a grocery store. Within the Hiawatha National Forest just southwest of Munising, the *Otter Lake Hiawatha Campgrounds* (c/o B. Graham, P.O. Box 237, Munising 49862) offers 72 scenic sites on 100 acres of private lands. Open year round, the campground also features swimming, boating, ice fishing, snowshoeing, and cross-country skiing, with rental equipment for most activities.

A number of resorts are available in Au Train north of the forest on Lake Superior: *Bark's Resort* (c/o E. Bark, Au Train 49806), on Au Train Lake, offers modern, rustic cedar-log housekeeping cottages on the lake, a private beach, good fishing and hunting, and special off-season rates. On the west side of Au Train Lake, *Dana's Lakeside Resort* (c/o D. Frick, Box 61, Au Train 49806) features two- and three-bedroom housekeeping cottages, sand beach, fiberglass boats, and other facilities for both fishermen and vacationers. Also on Au

Train Lake is *Dick Perry's Resort* (Au Train 49806) with 17 deluxe log cabins surrounded by lofty pines along the lakeshore, good fishing, boats, motors, and waterbikes. On Lake Superior's Shelter Bay, *Kimar's Resort & Charter Boats* (c/o D. Kimar, Shelter Bay, Au Train 49806) has rental seaworthy craft for deep-sea fishing as well as housekeeping cottages, good swimming beaches, fishing, boating, and water-skiing. An experienced, licensed pilot who knows the best fishing grounds is available for guided charter trips. *Ben Har's Au Train Lake Resort* (c/o B. McCollum, Au Train 49806) offers completely modern cabins, boats, trout fishing, and deer hunting and is open from April 10 to December 1. Open May 1 through December 1, the *Riverside Resort* (c/o D. Peck, Au Train 49806) on the Au Train River features one-, two-, and three-bedroom cottages, boats, and tackle. On Lake Superior are the *Rock River Cottages* (c/o B. Braamse, Au Train 49806), with a sand beach, lakefront cottages, and excellent fishing right at your doorstep.

Situated on 11 acres surrounded by the Hiawatha National Forest, *Twin Point Cabins* (S.R., Box 114, M-94, Boot Lake, Manistique 49854) offers completely modern cabins, boats, excellent fishing, hunting, and an area for snowmobiling. The *Midway Resort and Campground* (Wetmore 49895) has both housekeeping cabins and a campground and trailer park. Hunting, fishing, and snowmobiling are available nearby. Open year round, the *Camel Rider's Restaurant and Resort* (c/o J. Herro, Star Rt., Wetmore 49895) offers access to the four lakes and Indian River by boat, housekeeping cabins, excellent fishing and hunting, and a fine restaurant.

In Les Cheneaux, *Loreli Lodges* (c/o L. Smith, Les Cheneaux 49754), on Hessel Bay, features four modern housekeeping lodges with fireplaces, boats, motors, bait, and tackle. *Barefoot's Resort* (c/o W. Barefoot, Cedarville 49719) has modern lakefront cottages, a sandy beach, boats, motors, and a small camping area and trailer park. Just east of Cedarville is the *Island View Resort* (c/o B. DeLong, Cedarville 49719) with its housekeeping cottages, boats and motors, and fine fishing. Housekeeping cottages are also available at the *Rustic Resort* (Cedarville 49719), along with excellent fishing, hunting, boat and motor rentals, and a guide and charter-boat service.

Located on the famous Lake Superior sand dunes, *J&J's Bay View Cabins* (Grand Marais 49839) offers housekeeping cabins in the heart of fine hunting and cross-country ski terrain. Also on the shores of Lake Superior is *Welker's Lodge & Motel* (c/o Mrs. C. Welker, Grand Marais 49839), with both a motel and housekeeping cottages near a fine sand beach.

Vacation lodging facilities, charter boats, and guides on beautiful Drummond Island—known as the "Gem of Lake Huron" and renowned for its superb duck shooting in Potagonnissing Bay and offshore fishing for trophy salmon and trout—are provided by *Drummond Island Yacht Haven, Lakeview Resort, H & H Resort,* and *Cedar View Resort*—all Drummond Island 49726. The island is reached by ferry from the village of De Tour.

Complete outfitting is available at *Northland Outfitters* (P.O. Box 65, Germfask 49836), which also sponsors wilderness canoe-camping trips on the beautiful Manistique River and in the Seney Wilderness Tract mid-May through October. Sales, service, and equipment rentals are also offered. Write for a free brochure.

Access & Outfitting Centers

From Sault Ste. Marie take U.S. 75 south, then State Highway 28 west. U.S. 75 also leads north from Mackinaw City and St. Ignace. From Escanaba and Gladstone, take U.S. 41 north.

Huron National Forest & the Au Sable River

Huron National Forest Topo Maps

U.S. Geological Survey Overview Maps, scale 1:250,000: Traverse City, Tawas City; *Middle Branch of the Au Sable:* Alba, Big Bradford Lake, Lake Margarethe, Grayling, Otsego Lake, Wakeley Lake, Luzerne NW; *North Branch of the Au Sable:* K-P Lake, Lovells, Luzerne NW, Otsego Lake, Turtle Lake.

Au Sable River

Large-scale U.S. Geological Survey Topographic Maps: East Tawas, Hale, South Branch, Tawas City.

Au Sable–South Branch State Fishing Area

Large-scale U.S. Geological Survey Topographic Maps, including Canoe Harbor Campground: Luzerne NW, Eldorado, Roscommon N.

Rifle River State Recreation Area

Large-scale U.S. Geological Survey Topographic Maps, showing Au Sable, Rifle, Grousehaven, Lot, Grebe, Devoe, and Jewitt lakes headwaters: South Branch, Hale, Sage Lake, Selkirk.

Stretching west from the shores of Lake Huron, this renowned forest covers some 415,000 acres in east-central Michigan. The Au Sable River, lifeline of the Huron National Forest, is the largest of over 650 miles of streams that crisscross the wooded landscape and form a network of prime canoeing and fishing waters. During the days of

Michigan's lumber boom, the Au Sable was one of the principal channels down which logs were floated to Lake Huron. Today the fertile, insect-rich alkaline waters of the Au Sable are renowned for excellent brown-trout fishing and challenging canoe trips, especially below Mio, where the waters are faster and dams must be portaged. Grayling, a sizable town along the Au Sable a few miles west of the forest, is named for the now-extinct game fish that once flourished in these waters. Grayling were caught by the thousands until the early 1880s, when the species began to dwindle, then virtually disappeared

because of extensive logging activities. Brook trout, introduced in 1884, and subsequent stockings of brown trout, and the famous June mayfly hatch have earned the Au Sable the reputation of one of the finest trout streams in the nation.

Another animal species in danger of extinction, the Kirtland's warbler, has found a sanctuary on the Huron. Because there are presently only 400 of these tiny songbirds left in the world, a management area of 4,010 acres has been provided to improve the habitat of this rare warbler, which nests only in eastern Michigan. To the southeast of the forest is the Tuttle Marsh Wildlife Area, another region on the Huron set aside for the protection of birds and mammals. The marsh inlets near Lake Huron and other waters of the forest have long been favored by a wide variety of waterfowl: green and blue-winged teals, wood duck, bufflehead, merganser, black duck, widgeon, pintail, canvasback, and shoveler.

Other attractions of the Huron National Forest include the winter-sports areas at Mio, Oxbow, and Pioneer Hills, the last of which is just outside the forest's southwest corner. Twelve campgrounds are scattered throughout the area, many offering opportunities for fishing, swimming, and boating. In addition to the Au Sable River, there are numerous fine fishing streams and lakes, including Horseshoe, Island, Jewell, Kneff, Round, Loon, and Mack lakes. The Huron is also one of the best hunting areas in the state for black bear, deer, and upland game birds. Campgrounds, trails, roads, lakes, streams, and other features are described in and shown on the *Huron National Forest Map*, available for 50¢ from the Forest Supervisor, Cadillac 49601. District Ranger Stations are located at Mio, East Tawas, and Harrisville. The forest map also shows the Au Sable River–South Branch State Fishing Area, and the Rifle River State Recreation Area, adjacent to the forest's south-central boundary.

Vacation accommodation in the Au Sable River region of the forest are provided by *Edgewater on the Au Sable*, (Rt. 2, Box 2822) and *Penrod's Au Sable River Resort* (P.O. Box 432), both Grayling 49738; *Hinchman Acres Resort & Au Sable River Canoe Rental*, Box 146, Mio 48647. Canoe rentals, guide and pick-up service on the Au Sable are provided by *Borcher's Au Sable Canoe Livery* (also serves the upper Manistee River), *Carr's Pioneer Canoe Livery* (also Manistee), *Penrod's Au Sable Canoe Trips*, *Long's Canoe Rental*, and *Ray's Canoe Livery*—all Grayling 49738. Other lodges and resorts in Huron country include: *Boyd's Resort* and *Weed's Maple Sands*, both Glennie 48737 on the lower Au Sable; *Pines Hotel* on Bois Blanc Island 49775; *Big Lake Resort* (Box 345) and *Northwoods Resort* (Rt. 2, Box 600, on Otsego Lake), both Gaylord 49735; *Huronic Beach Resort* and *New Au Sable Beach Resort*, both Oscoda 48750. The *Sawyer Canoe Co.*, 234 State St., Oscoda 48750, provides rentals and float trips on the lower Au Sable. For additional info on vacation lodging and services, write: East Michigan Tourist Association, 1 Wenonah Park, Bay City 48706 (517–895–8823).

Access & Outfitting Centers

The Huron National Forest is accessible via Highway 55 from Tawas City and East Tawas. From West Branch, take State Highway 55 east, then 33 north. From Loena, take U.S. 23 south. Lodging, guides, supplies, and canoe rentals are available at numerous towns within the forest, including East Tawas, Glennie, Mio, South Branch, Luzerne, Eldorado, and Grayling.

Isle Royale National Park

Isle Royale National Park Shaded-Relief Map

This beautiful, full-color U.S. Geological Survey Map ($2, also availa-

ble in a standard topographic edition) is 39 by 54 inches with a scale of 1 inch to one mile and shows all major features of the island, including harbors, neighboring islands, lakes, ridges, campgrounds, streams, rapids and falls, and trails.

The largest of Michigan's islands, Isle Royale, forms a majestic forested wilderness camping, backpacking, and fishing paradise 15 miles from the mainland shores of the Keweenaw Peninsula in the extreme northern part of the Upper Peninsula. Isle Royale is renowned for the scenic beauty of its wild, log-strewn beaches, dense forests, 1,000-foot-high hills, fjordlike natural harbors, deep blue lakes, and fast-flowing streams. The island is approximately 45 miles long and 3 to 9 miles wide, with a rugged, irregular coastline notched with excellent harbors, including Rock Harbor in the northeast, considered by many to be the finest port of anchorage in the Great Lakes. The surrounding waters of Lake Superior are studded with more than 200 small (often fog-

shrouded) islands and atoll-like reefs, visited regularly by excursion and fishing boats. The interior of Isle Royale offers a truly unspoiled landscape, free from roads or towns. Spruce and balsam forest alternate with fine stands of white and black birch; pure hardwoods grace the upland regions; and the cool, moist shores and lake borders support mixed evergreens. A few crystal-clear streams and emerald-blue lakes, such as Lake Desor, Siskiwit Lake, Sargent Lake, the Little and Big Siskiwit rivers, and Tobin Creek, dot the rugged forest mantle.

Isle Royale's history begins millions of years ago with the glaciers that covered the island time and again. Massive sheets of ice ground smooth the surfaces of its rocks, gouged out basins that are now lakes,

and exposed layers of sandstone, subsequently eroded by water into valleys extending the length of the island. Between the valleys are rock beds of hard basalt forming long ridges, including the massive Greenstone Ridge, Isle Royale's bulky and impressive spine. At frequent intervals, the linear ridges are broken by cross-cutting ravines or depressions, much to the dismay of the less hardy hiker, who finds himself going endlessly up and down on the more than 160 miles of foot trails. The topography, geologic history, and rich mineral treasures of the island are described in *The Geologic Story of Isle Royale National Park*, a generously illustrated 66-page paperbound guide available for $1.00 from the Isle Royale National History Assn., P.O. Box 27, Houghton 49931. (Please add 15 percent handling charge for all books ordered.) The text and photographs trace Isle Royale's natural history and offer explanations for the formation of such geologic spectacles as Monument Rock, one of the numerous "sea stacks" lining the coast, and the huge wave-cut arches on Amygdaloid Island to the northwest of Isle Royale.

Long after the retreat of the glaciers, prehistoric races settled here and mined the extensive copper deposits, using alternate applications of hot and cold water to cause the rock to crack then pounding out the small particles of copper with stone hammers. Archaeologists have excavated their primitive shallow mining pits and the remains of crude tools, some of which date as far back as 4,500 years. Theories concerning the identity of these tribes range from Phoenicians from the Near East to Norsemen to early American Indians. When the French took possession of the island in 1671, they found Indians living here who could not remember the copper miners of old. A scholarly study of Great Lakes prehistory, *Lake Superior Copper and the Indians,* is sold for $2.50 by the Isle Royale Natural History Association (address above). More than 200 pages of essays and plates tell the story behind the artifacts discovered, the early history of the Lake Superior copper district, and the folklore surrounding early mining operations. A map of Isle Royale allows you to trace the steps of archaeologists in their attempts to reconstruct the culture of these ancient peoples.

The first white man known to have visited Isle Royale was Etienne Anton Brule, followed by Jean Nicolet in 1643. Nicolet's report on the island, stating that "gold, rubies, and precious stones are found in abundance," caused considerable excitement in Paris and Montreal and probably did a great deal to incite further exploration in the New World. French traders, lured to the island in pursuit of fur-bearing animals, gave the area its name. Isle Royale passed into American hands in 1783, largely through the insistence of Ben Franklin, who had heard tales of the rich copper deposits and was determined to obtain the island in the terms of the Treaty of Paris.

Until 1842 Isle Royale was recognized as Chippewa territory. After the Indians ceded the island to the Federal government, commercial mining became the chief activity in the region, continuing intermittently until 1899. Prospectors swarmed over the island, burning acres of forested land to expose copper outcroppings and clear space for mining settlements. It was not until the early 1900s that Isle Royale was discovered as a summer retreat; its establishment as a national park in 1940 guaranteed the protection of this unique and stunning archipelago. Descriptions of the rough-and-tumble—and often hazardous—existence led by early miners on the island are included in the 20-page booklet *Historic Mining on Isle Royale*. The story of the mining boom is supplemented by photographs and firsthand accounts from contemporary newspapers and nineteenth-century miners. Priced at 60¢, *Historic Mining* is available from the Isle Royale Natural History Association at the above address.

One of the island's most valuable and fascinating natural resources is

its varied wildlife. The only animals that live here today are those that could fly, swim, drift across the water barrier, or cross the ice that occasionally forms a bridge to Canada. Of the many common mammals that make their home here—including beaver, red fox, coyote, muskrat, and weasel—undoubtedly the most spectacular is the moose. Standing almost seven feet high and weighing as much as 1,000 pounds, these impressive beasts have been on Isle Royale since 1912, when a few of them straggled fifteen miles over ice from Canada and became stranded during the spring thaw. Although they are most often seen wading in the shallow inland lakes, moose are common throughout the park and form one of the largest herds in the United States. Wolves, rarely seen by visitors, prey upon the moose population, culling the herds and keeping the numbers down to levels the island can support. Those interested in an in-depth study of these "gray ghosts" will find fascinating reading in *The Wolves of Isle Royale*, a 200-page study available for $1.75 (including postage) from the Isle Royale Natural History Association (address above). The book explores the ecological relationships between moose and wolf packs as well as the habits and behavior patterns of Isle Royale wolves.

Bird life on the island is largely dominated by waterfowl, including the wild ducks and geese that feed on the lakes throughout the warm weather. By day, the raucous cries of gulls fill the air, while summer nights are often interrupted by the shrill laugh of native loons. Eagles, red-shouldered hawks, and great horned owls prey on the island's smaller birds and rodents. Other species common to the area are robins, warblers, wrens, and redheaded and downy woodpeckers. The informative, useful booklet *Birds of Isle Royale National Park* is available from the Natural History Association for 60¢.

Hunting is not allowed on the island, but Isle Royale has long been a favorite rendezvous for fishermen eager to try their luck on the more than 70 inland lakes and connecting streams, and in the frigid waters of Lake Superior. Brook, brown, rainbow, and lake trout, steelhead, northern pike, and muskellunge up to 25 pounds are the most common species taken. A few fortunate anglers have landed lake trout weighing over 30 pounds. *Fishes and Sport Fishing in Isle Royale National Park*, a handy, pocket-sized guide available for 60¢ from the Isle Royale Natural History Assn., P.O. Box 27, Houghton 49931, offers descriptions and illustrations of native fish, maps of the island, and tips on finding and landing each species. The *Rock Harbor Lodge* and *Windigo Inn*, both located on the island, offer guided fishing excursions, as well as lodgings, dining rooms, boat rentals, and sightseeing trips. For information from June to September on either lodge, write to the National Park Concessions, Inc., P.O. Box 405, Houghton 49931. During the winter, write to National Park Concessions, Inc., Mammoth Cave, KY 42259, for free brochures and lists of rates. Michigan fishing regulations apply on Isle Royale, and a state license is required in all Lake Superior waters, but no license is necessary for the island's inland lakes or streams. Both the store at Rock Harbor and the Windigo Inn offer complete outfitting.

Despite a relatively short summer growing season, the island offers several hundred species of wildflowers, which greatly enhance the pleasure of hiking trips and form a delicate counterpoint to the lofty green of Isle Royale's forests. Early spring brings bluebells and common violets, while white daisies, over 30 varieties of wild orchids, and jack-in-the-pulpits appear in full force during the summer months. *The Wildflowers of Isle Royale National Park* describes 101 different flowers on the island, with black-and-white illustrations to help you identify the various species. The 84-page booklet, fully indexed and including a flowering timetable, is available for $1.00 from the Isle Royale Natural History Association at the above address. A similar guide, entitled *Forests and Trees of Isle Royale National Park*, pro-

vides a history of the island woodlands and detailed descriptions of native trees, as well as illustrations of leaves and evergreen needles. Priced at 60¢, the 34-page guide is also available from the Isle Royale Natural History Association.

In addition to fishing, camping and hiking are perhaps the most popular activities on the island. Because motor vehicles are prohibited in the park, travel must be accomplished solely by boat or on foot, with the latter form of transport fast becoming the most enjoyable way to explore the rocky, wooded wilderness. An extensive trail system offers hikes to suit just about every taste—long, short, easy, or rugged, each revealing a different corner of the island's unspoiled beauty. One of the longer routes in the park, the Rock Harbor Trail, follows the rocky shore of the harbor to its head some 10½ miles away, passing an inland sea arch and the Daisy Farm Lakeside Camp, one of the largest

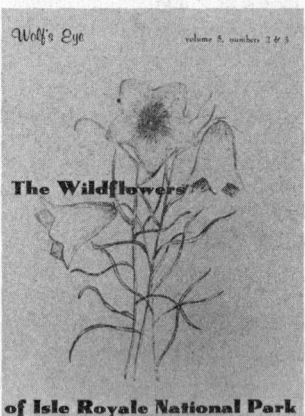

campgrounds in the park. The 2.2-mile Mount Franklin Trail leads from Rock Harbor to Mount Franklin and continuously alternates between ridge and valley until it reaches the summit with its spectacular view of the north side of the island. By far the longest and most rugged path in the park is the wild and primitive Greenstone Ridge Trail, recommended for the seasoned hiker only. Winding across the forested interior of the island atop the Greenstone Ridge some 40 miles between Rock Harbor Lodge and Windigo Inn, the footpath passes through diverse scenery within easy reach of three lakeside campgrounds. Descriptions of these and other Isle Royale trails are found in *Wilderness Trails—A Guide to the Trails in Isle Royale National Park*, available for 75¢ from the Isle Royale Natural History

Assn., P.O. Box 27, Houghton 49931. Maps, points of interest, location of campgrounds, mileage, and other trail data are all included.

The island offers 24 lakeside and trailside campsites with a maximum of 23 tent spaces. All camping parties, including those traveling in their own boats, are required to obtain a camping permit and/or boat registration upon arrival. No fee is charged for admission to the park or for camping. Campsites cannot be reserved and are operated on a first-come basis. Basic food staples, specialized camping foods, and white gasoline may be purchased at the Rock Harbor store or at Windigo. Disposable items such as bottles, cans, and other nonburnables are prohibited in Isle Royale's backcountry. A description of the Isle Royale camping system is found in *Camping and Hiking in Isle Royale National Park*, a brochure available free from the Superintendent, 87 North Ripley St., Houghton 49931. Another folder available at no cost from the Superintendent, *Isle Royale*, offers an introduction to the natural and human history of the park, along with a map and brief descriptions of opportunities for boating, hiking, camping, and other activities.

Access & Outfitting Centers

Isle Royale National Park is open to visitors from about May 15 to October 20. Transportation from the mainland to the island is by boat or floatplane only. For schedules, rates, and reservations on the National Park Service boat *Ranger III* from Houghton to Rock Harbor (May to October), write to the Superintendent, Isle Royale National Park, Houghton 49931. The *Isle Royale Queen II* (Copper Harbor 49918) runs between Copper Harbor and Rock Harbor between late June and Labor Day and also offers pre- and post-season charter trips. For information on boat service between Grand Portage and Windigo (late June to Labor Day) and between Grand Portage and Rock Harbor via Windigo, write to *Sivertson Brothers*, 366 Lake Ave. S., Duluth, MN 55802. One boat circumnavigates Isle Royale and will discharge and pick up passengers at various points. The *Isle Royale Seaplane Service* (Box 371, Houghton 49931) offers flights between Houghton and Windigo via Rock Harbor from late June to Labor Day. Because the waters of Lake Superior are often rough, it is not safe to use boats of 20 feet or less to go to the island. However, such boats can be transported to Isle Royale on the *Ranger III*. The private boat operators mentioned above will transport small runabouts and canoes. Gasoline for your boat cannot be carried on commercial boats or planes, but may be purchased at Rock Harbor and Windigo.

Manistee National Forest & Père Marquette River

Manistee National Forest Topo Maps

U.S. Geological Survey Overview Maps, scale 1:250,000: Manitowoc (WI), Midland, Milwaukee (WI), Traverse City.

Big Manistee River

Large-scale U.S. Geological Survey Topographic Maps: Alba, Bar Lake, Black Lake, Cadillac N., Copemish, Fife Lake, Fletcher, Kalkaska, Lake Margarethe, Mancelona, Mesick, Onekama.

Little Manistee River

Large-scale U.S. Geological Survey Topographic Maps: Manistee, Freesoil, Willston, Luther.

Pentwater River State Game Area

Large-scale U.S. Geological Survey Topographic Maps: Ludington, Hart, Hesperia.

Père Marquette River

Large-scale U.S. Geological Survey Topographic Maps, including the Big South Branch: Baldwin, Custer, Ludington, White Cloud, Woodville.

This 500,000-acre mixed hardwood and conifer forest is located in the northwestern part of the Lower Peninsula east of Lake Michigan and is renowned for its salmon, trout, and steelhead streams and canoe-camping routes. The major features include the historic Père Marquette and wild Big Manistee rivers—both are truly great fishing streams for large, hook-jawed brown trout to 8 pounds, steelhead to 20 pounds, and coho and Chinook salmon up to 36 pounds. Manistee Lake, bordering the Manistee River State Game Area, is well-stocked with largemouth bass, perch, and pike and offers excellent duck hunting as well. Flowing out of the lake, the Big Manistee River twists through cedar swamps and forests with campgrounds situated all along the route north of the lake as far as Crawford County. The legendary Little Manistee, located between the Big Manistee and Père Marquette rivers, is one of the Wolverine State's finest trophy fishing streams for giant metallic-flanked steelheads and brown trout. This wild, turbulent river, noted for its deep pools and log jams and scenic red and white pine borders, was once the scene of numerous logging drives. Its famous Indian Club, Old Grade, Bear Track, and Sawdust Pile pools have been immortalized in angling history. Named for the seventeenth-century Jesuit missionary who founded St. Ignace, the Père Marquette River flows through lake-studded regions of the forest on its swift course, marked by numerous tricky rapids, deep pools, overhangs, log jams, and eddies. The legendary Père Marquette (once renowned for its grayling fishing) and its historic trout pools—the Birch Hole, Whirlpool, Claybanks, Grayling Hole, and First Rollway —offers some of the nation's finest fishing for trophy brown and lake-run rainbows. The main Père Marquette and its tributaries provide 138 miles of trout water noted for its deep pools and log jams, surrounded by scenic forests, jack pine plains, and marshes. Its backwaters hold big northern pike. A good put-in site for canoeists is the public access site south of Baldwin. Numerous campgrounds line the river's course with canoes and supplies available at Baldwin, Branch, Custer, and Scottsville. The 7-mile stretch of the river from M-37 down to Gleason's Landing is fly fishing only, year-round.

Hunting is also excellent in the Manistee National Forest. Deer are found throughout Manistee County, but the best hunting is on the public lands near swamps, river bottoms, and in jack-pine and oak forests. Grouse and snowshoe hare inhabit the swamp edges, some pine plantations, and brushy areas adjacent to swamps. Rivers, lakes, and Lake Michigan shoreline provide hunting for dabbling ducks, divers, and geese. Wild turkey are found in some parts of the forest, but special regulations govern hunting.

Nearby attractions in the vicinity of the forest include the Mena Creek Waterfowl Area; the White, Muskegon, and Little Manistee river canoe routes; Pentwater River State Game Area; Lake Michigan Recreation Area; Big Star, Tippy Dam, Hamlin, and Mitchell lakes; and the adjacent Fife Lake and Père Marquette state forests. Campgrounds are located beside Lake Mitchell, near the Hodenpyle Dam, at the Peterson Bridge, on Dorner Lake, and near the Deer Lake Bayou. The *Manistee National Forest Recreation Map* (50¢) shows all major forest features, including campsites, rivers, creeks, game areas, forest roads, trails, and the like. Additional information is available from the Forest Supervisor, 421 S. Mitchell Street, Cadillac 49601.

Four-season vacation accommodations in the Manistee National Forest region are provided by: *Sportsmen's Lodge* (Brethren 49619; 616-477-5588), on Big Manistee River; *Coho Center Resort* (Manistee

49660; 616–889–4253), on Portage Lake; *Leelanau's Rustic Resort* (on Lake Leelanau; 616–288–5900), *Ranch Rudolf* (P.O. Box 587; 616–946–5410; on Boardman River), *Sugar Loaf Mountain Resort* (616–228–5461), and *Windjammer Resort* (on Spider Lake; 616–946–6229)—all Traverse City 49684; *Homestead Resort* (on Betsie River; 616–882–4163), Benzonia 49616; *Swiss Hideaway* (on Jordan River), Mancelona 49659; *The Logs Resort*, Fife Lake 49633; *Barothy Lodge* (on Père Marquette River, Box 165; 616–898–2340) and *Fox Lake Resort, Long Lake Resort;* and *Timberlane Resort* (Long Lake), all Walhalla 49458; *Portage Point Inn* (Lake Michigan and Portage Lake; 616–889–4222), Onekama 49675; *Brierwood Resort* (RR 2, Box 278) and *Fisherman's Retreat*, both on Big Muskegon River, Newaygo 49337; *American Resort* (Little Platte Lake, RR 1, Box 64) and *Platte Lake Resort* (8483 Deadstream Rd.), *Rustic Resort* (RR 1, Box 30), and *Thompson's Resort* (RR 1, Box 32), all on Big Platte Lake, Honor 49640; *Beaver Resort* (Burt Lake), Brutus 49716; *Wolf Lake Ranch*, Box 243, Baldwin 49304; *Cedar Rest* (Lake Charlevoix, South Arm), East Jordan 49727; *Big Log Cabin Resort* (Round Lake) and *Hobby Crest Resort* and *Sauble Resort*, both on Hamlin Lake, all Ludington 49431; *Boyne Valley Lodge* (Bear and Jordan rivers; Box 25; 616–535–2475), *North Arm Resort*, and *Village Resort* (Box 220), all Walloon Lake 49796.

For detailed info on steelhead and salmon fishing, stream and lake conditions, canoe rentals and guide service, write or call: *Trout & Salmon Pro Shop*, Bear Lake 49614 (616–864–3000); *Baldwin Boat & Canoe Livery* (Père Marquette, Pine, and Little Manistee rivers), Box 518, Baldwin 49304 (616–832–5027); *Betsie River Campsite* (fishermen's headquarters for Lake Michigan and Betsie River), Frankfort 49635 (616–352–9535); Casey's Corner (info and rentals for Platte River), Honor 49640 (616–325–3636); *Big Manistee River-view Campgrounds* (boat rentals and guide service), Manistee 49660 (616–723–3821); *Rip's Betsie River Canoe Trips*, Thompsonville 49683 (616–378–2386). For additional listings and info, contact: West Michigan Tourist Assn., 136 Fulton E., Grand Rapids 49503 (616–456–8557).

Access & Outfitting Centers

Manistee National Forest is accessible via State Highway 55 from the town of Manistee. From Cadillac, take the Cadillac Highway (M115) northwest. State 42, leading west from Manton, also offers access to forestlands. Lodging, supplies, guides, canoe rentals, and outfitters are available at numerous towns within and surrounding the forest, including Muskegon, Big Rapids, Ludington, Pentwater, Scottville, Walhalla, Manistee, Little Manistee, and Boon.

Ottawa National Forest & Sylvania Recreation Area

Ottawa National Forest Topo Maps

U.S. Geological Survey Overview Maps, scale 1:250,000: Ashland, Iron River.

Black Wild & Scenic River

Large-scale U.S. Geological Survey Topographic Maps, including Chippewa, Algonquin, Great Conglomerate, Sandstone, and Rainbow falls, and the Potawatomi & Gorge Falls Scenic Area: Ironwood 15, Bessemer (7.5), Wakefield (7.5), Thomaston, North Ironwood.

Lake Gogebic Country

Large-scale U.S. Geological Survey Topographic Maps: Bergland, Marenisco 15.

Sylvania Recreation Area

Large-scale U.S. Geological Survey Maps, including the Cisco Chain of Lakes and Whitefish, Clark, Loon, Lac Vieux Desert, Deer Island, Crooked, Bear, Big Bateau, Thousand Island, Devils Head, and Duck lakes: Phelps, Starlake, Thayer, Watersmeet.

The famous fishing, hunting, and canoe-camping areas of this 910,000-acre reserve embrace wild, second-growth hardwoods and conifers, rolling hills, remote blue lakes, and fast deep-flowing streams, located in the western section of the Upper Peninsula, south of Lake Superior and the Keweenaw Peninsula. The forest terrain varies from the level, sandy plains covered with second-growth pine to the rugged hills of the Gogebic Range. Black River Harbor, in the westernmost sections of the forest, has been called the most picturesque harbor in Michigan and offers charter boats for salmon, steelhead, and lake trout in Lake Superior. The wild and scenic Black River is one of the north country's most picturesque streams, with 11 scenic cascades and rapids. The Black is also renowned for its superb trout fishing and canoe-camping. The Ottawa Country contains several of the Wolverine

State's outstanding trophy fisheries for northern pike, walleye, small-mouth bass, and muskellunge, including Lake Gogebic, Lac Vieux Desert on the Wisconsin boundary, Thousand Island Lake, Cisco Chain Lakes, Presque Isle Flowage, Chaney and Langford Lakes, and the adjacent rainbow, salmon, and brook-trout waters of the Montreal and Brule rivers. The Ontonagon River system, including its nationally renowned Middle Branch and its famous Agate Falls pool, provides fishing for brook and brown trout up to trophy weights, and Lake Superior steelhead. The Middle Branch from Bond Falls to Agate Falls—surrounded by an evergreen wilderness—is considered the top brook and brown trout water in the Upper Peninsula.

Perhaps the most spectacular region on the Ottawa is the Sylvania Recreation Area, encompassing Whitefish, Clark, Loon, Deer Island, Devils Head, and Duck lakes in the southern reaches of the forest. Spread out over 21,000 acres, the old-growth forests of birch, maple, hemlock, pine, spruce, and fir are still largely virgin timber, huge trees that burst into full color during the fall season. The water quality of the lakes here is as high as or higher than most other inland lakes in the United States, with a transparency seldom exceeded in lakes of other regions. Because these lakes were at one time inaccessible to fishermen, a virgin-type fish population developed. Most fish, though relatively large, are quite old, making the fish population similar to what might have been found by the first white men to visit the Upper Peninsula. The lakes contain bass, lake trout, walleye, northern pike, perch, and sunfish. Mammals of the Sylvania area include whitetail deer, black bear, skunk, otter, raccoon, beaver, muskrat, coyote, mink, and fox. A variety of water and forest birds, including the loon and bald eagle, may be seen in their natural habitats. Hunting and fishing are permitted in season with a valid state license. Numerous campsites, many of them situated on lakeshores, are scattered throughout the area and are available on a first-come basis. Fine hiking trails wind around the southern shores of Clark Lake, around Deer Island Lake, and through dense, unspoiled forests. Lake canoeing is also popular, with the major lakes linked by established portage routes. A *Sylvania Recreation Area Map-Brochure* showing hiking trails, canoe routes, campsites, boat-launching sites, lakes, forest roads, picnic grounds, and other features of the region is available free from the Forest Supervisor, Ottawa National Forest, Ironwood 49938.

Other attractions of the forest include the series of waterfalls south of Black River Harbor, including Rainbow, Standstone, Potawatomi, Great Conglomerate, and Algonquin falls. Southwest of Paynesville,

the Agate Falls, reached by a 200-yard footpath along the riverbank, drop over an 80-foot ledge that crosses the Ontonagon River. The four branches of the Ontonagon offer some very good canoe stretches, including the main stream from Military Bridge on U.S. 45 to Lake Superior, a pleasant 30-mile paddle with a few rapids that are easily portaged. The scenery along the river is wild and rugged, with little or no development near the shoreline. Nestled in a deep valley with steep clay bluffs to either side, the Ontonagon is particularly lovely in late spring, when banks of delicate lady's slippers bloom near the shoreline. *Whitewater; Quietwater,* the canoeing guide described under "Canoeing & Wild Rivers" in the "Encyclopedia" section, gives further details on running the river. The Paint River and its North and South branches also offer excellent canoeing in the south-western reaches of the forest.

Once the hunting and trapping grounds of the Ottawa Indians, the forest still provides excellent hunting for whitetail deer, black bear, and upland game birds. The forest is a top-ranked fishing area for large steelhead and brown trout from Lake Superior found in the many miles of deep-flowing streams, including the Ontonagon, Deer Creek, Presque Isle River, and Cherry and Warbler creeks. In fall, these two species, plus salmon, enter forest streams on their annual spawning runs. Walleye and northern pike; brook, rainbow, and brown trout; splake; muskies; and small and largemouth bass are other game fish found in the 700-odd lakes and 2,000 miles of streams.

In wintertime, downhill skiers can enjoy the major ski hills near Iron-wood, Iron River, and in the Porcupine Mountains just north of the forest. In the western part of the Ottawa is the Copper Peak Ski Flying Hill, the largest ski jump in the Western Hemisphere, offering breath-taking views of Lake Superior from its lofty summit. Many trails wind through all sections of the wilderness, exploring remote woodlands, clear blue lakes, and cascading streams. The Beaver Lodge Trail, beginning at the Bob Lake Campground, passes an active beaver colony near Leveque Creek.

Twenty-four campgrounds on the Ottawa offer additional outdoor activities such as swimming, boating, and interpretive trails. Many campgrounds are located beside unspoiled lakes, and some feature fine sand beaches. The recreation sites index on the *Ottawa National Forest Map* indicates the number of sites and kind of activities available. The map also shows forest roads, recreation areas, ski areas, hiking trails, lakes, streams, rivers, boat-access sites, and other attractions of the Ottawa, including nearby towns, the Porcupine Mountains State Park, and adjoining lands of the Nicolet National Forest, Copper Range State Forest, and Baraga State Forest. The map is available for 50¢ from the Forest Supervisor, Ottawa National Forest, Ironwood 49938.

The nearby towns of Watersmeet and Bessemer offer accommodations and complete outfitting for visitors to the Ottawa National Forest. *Gray's Crooked Lake Cabins* (Star Route, Watersmeet 49969) features modern housekeeping cabins, boats, motors, and good trout, bass, and pan fishing in Crooked Lake near Sylvania, 4 miles west of the U.S. 2 and State Highway 45 junction. Located 12 miles west of Watersmeet, *Cisco Lake Resort* (c/o B. Krummel, Watersmeet 49969) also offers housekeeping cabins by the lakeshore. Other attractions are a sandy beach and 200 acres of resort land for hiking and nature study. Boating on Cisco Lake, headwaters of the famous Cisco chain of 15 lakes, is another favorite pastime. Also situated on Cisco Lake, the *North Shore Resort* (c/o D. Murphy, Cisco Lake Road, Watersmeet 49969), near the Sylvania Recreation Area, offers good swimming, deluxe housekeeping cottages, boats, a modern lodge and dining room. Boat rentals, motors, and tackle are also available. The *Arrow Lodge Resort and Restaurant* (c/o D. Yakel, Thousand Island

Lake Road, Watersmeet 49969), on a bay of clear, beautiful Thousand Island Lake, is surrounded by fabulous wilderness scenery and open year round, with housekeeping cottages, a shallow sand beach area, and boat and motor rentals. *Jay's Resort* (c/o J. Shifra, Thousand Island Lake Road, Watersmeet 49969) features housekeeping cabins, boats, motors, bait, canoes, and a playground for children. Housekeeping cabins, a sandy beach, and a boat with every cottage are the attractions of the *Indian Head Resort* (c/o B. Moore, Watersmeet 49969), just outside the Ottawa National Forest. *Lac LaBelle Resort* (c/o D. Vernier, Watersmeet 49969), near the Sylvania Recreation Area on Thousand Island Lake, offers housekeeping cottages, hookups for trailers, boats, motors, canoes, bait, and a nearby swimming area. Also adjacent to the Sylvania Recreation Area is *Vacationland Resort* (c/o A. Fiorucci, P.O. Box 5, Iron Mountain 49801), with its one- to three-bedroom cottages, beach, boat and motor rentals, and other recreational attractions.

Sylvania Outfitters, headquarters for canoe-camping and ski touring, sponsors wilderness flat-water and white-water canoe trips as well as complete outfitting for both canoeing and cross-country skiing. Cabin rentals, cross-country ski trails, ski instruction, and a lounge are additional drawing cards. Contact Bob Zelinski, West US-2, Watersmeet 49969, for further information.

A number of fine accommodations are available in Bessemer, due south of the Ottawa's western reaches. These include the *Chippewa Lodge* (c/o R. Bianchi, Hedberg Road, Bessemer 49911), offering individual and family accommodations in a rustic chalet a short distance from Black River Harbor, Copper Peak, Ski Flying Hill, and the Big Powderhorn and Indianhead Mountain ski areas. Other features are a sauna, canoe rentals on the Black River, a toboggan hill, and 40 miles of snowmobile trails. At Big Powderhorn Mountain, the *Viking Inn* (Rt. 1, Box 85, Bessemer 49911) provides lodging for skiers, a capacious lounge, sauna, and breakfasts and lunches. Located between Bessemer and Wakefield, the *Alpine Trailer Park and Campground* (c/o N. Sanders, Rt. 1, Box 296, Bessemer 49911) offers excellent campsites with trailer hook-ups, stocked trout ponds, hot showers, a sauna, laundry, picnic tables, and stoves. Open year round, Alpine will accept reservations with a deposit.

Gallery Canoe Trips (US-2, Bessemer 49911) offers three-day package trips in the Ottawa National Forest, including guides, meals, and lodging. Float-fishing trips for trout, pickup and delivery services for canoe trips, and canoe rentals are additional features. Gallery also sells canoes and related equipment.

Vacation lodges and resorts on beautiful Lake Gogebic—the largest lake in the U.P.—include *Bailey's Rustic Resort,* Box 207; *Cordy's Gogebic Lodge;* and *The Fisherman Resort,* Box 175—all Marenisco 49947.

Strategically located in the most rugged country of Michigan's Upper Peninsula, the Ottawa National Forest forms a jump-off point for extended wilderness travel. To the north are the Porcupine Mountains, the Copper Range State Forest, and the wild Keweenaw Peninsula. The Baraga and Iron Range state forests lie just west of the Ottawa, and to the south is the renowned Nicolet National Forest of Wisconsin. The possibilities for canoeing, camping, hunting, and fishing trips, and adventurous backpacking are virtually unlimited.

Access & Outfitting Centers

Ottawa National Forest is easily reached on State Highway 2 from Ironwood, Bessemer, and Ramsay. From Ontonagon, take State Highway 45 south. State Highway 2 also leads to the forest on the east from Iron River, Stambaugh, and Caspian.

CENTRAL STATES

Introduction

The Central States contain several outstanding fishing, hunting, canoeing, camping, and backpacking areas. Arkansas, the "Land of Opportunity," takes in the scenic pine, oak, and beech forests, deep, clear river, and spectacular bluffs and highlands of the Ouachita and Ozark national forests. Here, flowing through the beautiful highlands, are the renowned float fishing waters of the Buffalo, the Ouachita, and the crystal-clear White River, which offers nationally renowned fishing for giant rainbow trout in the frigid water below Bull Shoals Dam. Arkansas's great sprawling lakes and reservoirs, among them Bull Shoals, Beaver, and Ouachita, offer top-ranked fishing for trophy largemouth bass and trout. Rugged hiking trails and old forest roads provide access to wild forests inhabited by whitetail deer, bobwhite quail, wild turkey, raccoon, and red fox. Arkansas's northern Ozark neighbor, Missouri, contains the famous canoe-camping, fishing, and hunting areas of the Clark National Forest; the Eleven Point and Current national scenic rivers, surrounded by a wild backcountry of rolling hills, barren rock outcroppings, sinkholes, limestone caves, and thick forests of oak and native shortleaf pine in the Mark Twain National Forest; and the beautiful Lake of the Ozarks, with its jagged twisting shoreline and trophy bass fishing.

The gently rolling farmlands, lakes, streams, and woodlands of Iowa, Indiana, Illinois, and Ohio lie to the north of the Ozarks, south of the Great Lakes region, east of the Great Plains, and west of the Appalachians. The major outdoor recreation features of these great Central States include the famous goose and duck hunting areas along the Mississippi Flyway, Iowa's "Great Lakes" region, Indiana's Hoosier National Forest and Wild Country, Lake Michigan's trophy salmon and trout waters, Illinois's Shawnee National Forest, and Ohio's Lake Erie-Bass Islands salmon, smallmouth bass, and muskellunge fishing areas and the rolling hills, spectacular rock outcroppings, lakes, streams, and woodlands of the Wayne National Forest. Kentucky, situated along the southern rim of the Central States, contains the historic Cumberland Gap backcountry—blazed by Daniel Boone and his axmen to create the famous Wilderness Road, the trophy smallmouth bass and walleye waters of beautiful Dale Hollow and Cumberland lakes and the scenic rivers, towering sandstone bluffs, woodlands, natural arches, and rolling hills of the Daniel Boone National Forest.

Weather, Bugs, & Beasts

The Central States have warm, humid summers, with July mean temperatures of about 75° to 80°, with summer temperatures over 100° not unusual. Summer nights are also warm, rarely dropping below 65° in July. Summer thunderstorms and hailstorms are common. Mosquitoes are a problem throughout the damp wet areas of the Central States and travelers to these areas should carry an adequate supply of insect repellent. Timber rattlesnakes and copperheads are found throughout the rocky forest areas; cottonmouth moccasins are common in the lake country and swamp areas of the southern Central States.

Central States Maps & Charts—How to Order

The topographic maps listed in the Central States chapters (unless otherwise noted) are full-color U. S. Geological Survey overview maps, scale 1:250,000, or 1 inch to 4 miles ($2 each) or large-scale 7½-minute and 15-minute maps ($1.25 for either). These maps and free *Topographic Map Indexes* for the Central States may be ordered (along with a free *Map Symbol Chart* and *Topographic Maps* booklet)

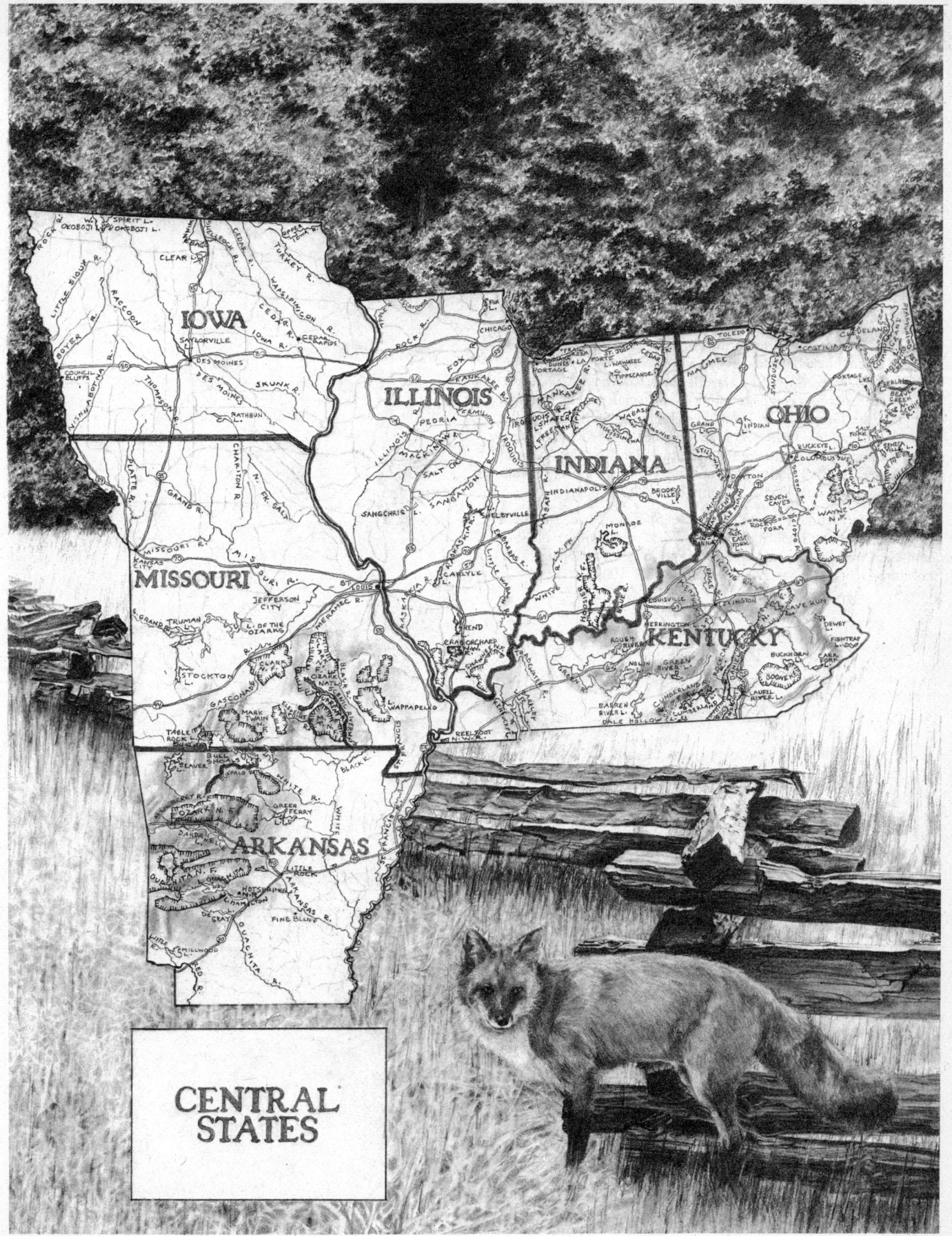

CENTRAL
STATES

from: Distribution Branch, U. S. Geological Survey, 1200 S. Eads St., Arlington, VA 22202. Be sure to order maps by their individual names (and indicate scale when ordering 1:250,000-scale maps); to expedite delivery, include extra money for first-class postage. Maps of Arkansas, Missouri and Iowa should be ordered from the Distribution Branch, U. S. Geological Survey, Federal Center, Denver, CO 80225.

Large, attractive U. S. Geological Survey *State Topographic Maps* of Arkansas, Missouri, Iowa, Indiana, Illinois, Ohio, and Kentucky are available, scale 1:500,000, or 1 inch to 8 miles, and may be ordered for $2 each from the above address. Strikingly beautiful U. S. Geological Survey *Shaded-Relief Maps* of Arkansas, Missouri, Ohio, and Kentucky may be purchased at the same scale for $2 each; colored shading gives the maps a three-dimensional appearance of the sunlight striking the surface from the northwest. A free catalog, *Great Lakes Nautical Charts,* may be obtained by writing: National Ocean Survey, Distribution Div. (C44), 6501 Lafayette Ave., Riverdale, MD 20840. The catalog contains a complete listing of small-craft and recreational craft charts for Lake Michigan and Lake Erie, along with Great Lakes nautical publications. Waterproof, 23×35-inch *Lake Contour Maps* showing all underwater structures and features for 200 major Central and Southern United States lakes and reservoirs are available from Lakes Illustrated, Box 4854 GS, Springfield, MO 65804.

An eminently useful 214-page handbook, *Be Expert with Map and Compass,* by Bjorn Kjellstrom, the president and founder of Silva Compasses, may be obtained for $6.95 from: Charles Scribner's Sons, Bookstore Dept., 597 5th Ave., New York, NY 10017.

Accommodations— Vacation Lodges & Resorts

Iowa has accommodations to suit every vacationer's needs—for complete information, write: Development Commission, 250 Jewett Bldg., Des Moines 50309; or the local Chamber of Commerce of the area you plan to visit. Some state park and recreation areas offer modern family cabins, each of which can house 4 persons with ease. Electricity, water, dishes, cooking utensils, refrigerator, and kitchen stove are included with each cabin; the renter must provide bedding, pillows, towels, and personal items. Reservations must be made through the park ranger; reservations for a minimum of a week are accepted. Cabins are rented for stays of less than 1 week on a first-come, first-served basis. The number of cabins available in each area is as follows: Backbone, 18; Lacey-Keosauqua, 6; Lake of Three Fires, 6; Lake Walleop, 12; Pine Lake, 4; Palisades-Kepler, 4; and Springbrook, 6. Palisades-Kepler has two cabins that can each accommodate 8.

Camping & State Recreation Areas

State park and recreation area camping sites are located in scenic areas throughout the state. For complete information on facilities of each state park or recreation area, consult the useful brochure *Iowa State Parks and Recreation Areas*, available free from: Conservation Commission, 300 4th St., Des Moines 50309. There is a convenient chart listing each recreation area, its mailing address, telephone number, highway location, and available facilities. The same information is also provided for the state forests. The areas are location-keyed to a map, and the brochure includes a chart describing the areas of the state preserves system. There is a section of rules and regulations, and information on reservations for the camping and recreational facilities.

Canoeing & Quality Fishing Waters

Iowa's historic canoe routes—the Des Moines, Iowa, Cedar, Raccoon, Wapsipinicon, Maquoketa, Skunk, Turkey, Nishnabotna, Upper Iowa, Mississippi, Missouri, Yellow, Boone, Red Cedar, Shell Rock, Volga, and Big Sioux rivers—are described (with maps) in the large-format, 14-page *Iowa Canoe Trips* guide, available free upon request from: Conservation Commission, 300 4th St., Des Moines 50309. Several of the outstanding canoe routes flow through narrow valleys, bounded by rugged scenic bluffs and woodlands along ancient Indian,

IOWA ENCYCLOPEDIA

fur trade, and pioneer routes. The historic and recreation points of interest along Iowa's major waterways are thoroughly described in the guide.

The following full-color large-scale U.S. Geological Survey Maps show the state's major canoe routes and fishing waters and the topography of the surrounding countryside, including rapids, falls, bridges, trails, roads, woodlands, lakes, campgrounds, orchards, and shelters. *Iowa Great Lakes Region:* Harris, Ocheyedan, Lake Park, Okoboji, Spirit Lake, Superior, Estherville, Lake Park SE, Milford, Spirit Lake SE; *Little Sioux River:* Little Sioux, Pisgah, Moorhead NW, Castana, Onawa, Smithland, Oto, Correctionville SE, Correctionville, Washta, Quimby, Cherokee S, Cherokee N, Peterson SW, Sutherland E, Peterson, Sioux Rapids, Webb, Gillett Grove, Dickens, Spencer, Milford, Okoboji; *Rock River:* Rock Rapids, Doon, Hull, Rock Valley, Fairview, Hawarden N; *Big Sioux River,* scale 1:250,000: Sioux Falls, Sioux City, Fremont, Omaha, Nebraska City; *Raccoon River* (including North Fork), scale 1:250,000: Fort Dodge, Omaha, Des Moines; *Nishnabotna River,* scale 1:250,000: Nebraska City, Omaha; *Des Moines River,* scale 1:250,000: Fairmont, Fort Dodge, Omaha, Des Moines, Centerville, Burlington; *Boone River,* scale 1:250,000: Mason City, Waterloo; *Cedar & Wapsipinicon Rivers,* scale 1:250,000: Mason City, Waterloo; *Turkey River,* scale 1:250,000: Mason City, La Crosse; *Yellow River:* Frankville, Rossville, Monona, Girard, Waterville, Prairie du Chien; *Upper Iowa River,* scale 1:250,000: Mason City, La Crosse.

Fishing & Hunting in the Hawkeye State

Iowa's lakes, streams, woodlands, rolling uplands, loess hills (bluffs), big river oxbows and floodplain sloughs, marshes, and crop fields offer a surprising diversity of fishing and hunting opportunities. The Hawkeye State lies wholly within the prairie region and contains 56,290 square miles bordered on the north by Minnesota; on the west by Nebraska and the Big Sioux and Missouri Rivers; on the east by Wisconsin, Illinois, and the Mississippi River; and on the south by Missouri. The 50 natural glacial lakes in northwest Iowa, known as the Iowa Great Lakes region, offer some of the best fishing in the central United States for smallmouth and largemouth bass, northern pike, channel catfish, white bass, yellow perch, walleye, crappie, and a few elusive muskellunge up to trophy weights in West Okoboji and Clear lakes. The best fishing is found over the weed beds and brush piles and

along the rocky shorelines, reefs, and sandbars in Spirit, East and West Okoboji, Clear, Storm, Silver, Trumbull, North Twin, Pine, Briggs Woods, Swan, Badger, Beeds, Arrowhead, Black Hawk, Crystal, Five Island, Upper and Lower Gar, and Little Spirit lakes. Beautiful Spirit Lake is a top-ranked walleye fishery with fish taken up to 14 pounds. For specific information on Iowa's Great Lake region, write: Spirit Lake Fish Hatchery, Spirit Lake 51360.

The upland lakes and streams of northeast Iowa, known as "Little Switzerland," offer the state's top-ranked smallmouth bass and trout fishing. The Upper Iowa River, proposed for inclusion in the National Wild & Scenic River System, holds smallmouth bass up to 6 pounds, brown and rainbow trout, white bass, walleye, and channel catfish. The Upper Iowa flows past limestone bluffs, including the massive 200-foot Chimney Rocks, and several beautiful tributary trout streams such as Coldwater and Canoe Creeks. The Turkey and Big Wapsipinicon and Maquoketa rivers contain a wide variety of fish including smallmouth bass, northern pike, walleye, channel catfish, and crappie. The Elk Creek tributary of the Turkey River produced the state record 12-pound 14½-ounce brown trout. The farm ponds and lakes of the region—including Backbone, Fontana, Cedar Falls, Hendricks, Meyers, Hickory Hills, Sabula, and Sweet Marsh—hold largemouth bass, crappie, northern pike, and channel cats. The tailrace waters beneath the hydroelectric dams yield walleye, smallmouths, channel cats, and a few large northern pikes.

The big impoundments and rivers of central and southern Iowa yield largemouth bass, northern pike, crappie, and large catfish. The 11,000-acre Rathbun Reservoir on the Chariton River, known as "Iowa's ocean," has been stocked with striped bass and muskellunge from South Carolina's Santee-Cooper Reservoir. Lake Geode consistently yields bunker largemouth bass in the 5–8-pound class. The big inland rivers yield northern pike, channel catfish, carp, walleye, and bullhead. The North Raccoon and scenic Middle Raccoon and Upper Des Moines and Iowa rivers yield smallmouth bass. Northern pike up to trophy weights are taken from the upper reaches of the Des Moines, Little Sioux, Winnebago, Iowa, Shell Rock, and Cedar rivers. The state's mighty boundary rivers, the Big Sioux and Missouri rivers on the west and the Mississippi on the east, with their numerous lakes, oxbows, sloughs, chutes, and backwaters, yield giant catfish, walleye, sauger, largemouth bass, and hordes of crappies and bluegills.

The potential of Iowa's lakes and streams is illustrated by the state's all-time record fish caught by rod and reel (p. 407).

The Iowa Conservation Commission publishes several free fishing and hunting guides, maps, and booklets, including *Iowa Fishing Regulations, Iowa Trout Maps, Iowa Mammals, Common Wildlife Tracks, Iowa Hunting & Trapping Laws, Public Hunting Areas, Upland Game Bird Hunting, Iowa Deer Hunting, Pheasant & Quail Distribution Maps, Deer Distribution Map, Red Rock Game Management Map, Bays Branch Public Hunting Area, Duck Point System Sheet, Lake Odessa Public Hunting Area, Iowa Woodland Flowers, Iowa Prairies, Simple Key to Iowa Trees, Yellow River Forest, Missouri River Spring Goose Migration, Stephens State Forest, Shimek State Forest, Boating Regulations,* and *Mississippi River Boating Facilities Guide.* The 31-page *Iowa Fishing Guide* (50¢) contains detailed descriptions of the state's major lakes, streams, and reservoirs as well as maps and charts. The Conservation Commission also publishes a free *Iowa Trout Fishing Guide,* which shows and lists all trout streams by county. The 35-page *Iowa Hunting Guide* (25¢) contains maps and indepth descriptions of the waterfowl flyways and the Big Sioux, Ingham High, Rice Lake, Upper Iowa, Ruthven, Big Marsh, Sweet Marsh, Missouri River, Blackhawk, Saylorville, Otter Creek, Maquoketa, Bays Branch, Red Rock, Coralville, Riverton, Mount Ayr, Rathbun, Wapello, and

Odessa wildlife management units. The publications listed above and free maps of the *Big Sioux, Mount Ayr,* and *Otter Creek* wildlife management units may be ordered from: Conservation Commission, 300 4th St., Des Moines 50309.

IOWA RECORD FISH

	Lb.-oz.	Place	Year
Largemouth bass	10–5	Farm Pond	1970
Smallmouth bass	6–7	Upper Iowa River	1976
Muskellunge	38	West Okoboji Lake	1975
Northern pike	25–5	West Okoboji Lake	1977
Walleye	14–2	Spirit Lake	1968
Rainbow trout	13–8	Richmond Springs	1968
Brown trout	12–14½	Elk Creek	1966
Brook trout	1–14	Snowy Magill Creek	1975
Sturgeon	12	Des Moines River	1974
Yellow perch	1–15	Spirit Lake	1974
Sauger	6–8	Missouri River	1976
Crappie	4–1	Farm Pond	1969
Yellow bass	1–½	Clear Lake	1976
White bass	3–14	West Okoboji Lake	1972
Rock bass	1–8	Mississippi River	1973
Channel catfish	30–4	Viking Lake	1974
Flathead catfish	62	Iowa River	1965
Paddlefish	83	De Soto Bend	1973
Sheepshead	46	Spirit Lake	1962
Bluegill	2–5	Farm Pond	1966

The Hawkeye State ranks among the nation's leading pheasant, quail, and goose hunting states. It also offers excellent hunting for deer, squirrels, cottontails, and mallards. Some of the best pheasant shooting is found in the "Cash Grain" region of central Iowa. There are red fox, Hungarian partridge, raccoons, crows, jackrabbits, and a few coyotes and wild turkey in the eastern woodlands. Cornfield mallard shooting is popular late in the waterfowl season. Small crop fields, timbered creek bottoms, and brushy draws generally produce excellent hunting for upland game birds. The state's numerous rivers and streams provide excellent wood duck hunting early in the season. The Missouri River country is one of the nation's prime hunting areas for snow geese and rafts of mallards, teal, wood duck, widgeon, and gadwall. One of the most scenic hunting areas in the state is the White Pine Hollow Preserve in the extreme northwest corner of Dubuque County. It has been designated as a National Natural Landmark because of its virgin stands of white pine, large cold-air slopes of Canada yew, and the rare monkshood. The White Pine Hollow has a stable population of whitetail deer and ruffed grouse as well as pheasants along the forest borders.

Highways & Recreation Routes

The motorist traveling through Iowa should obtain a copy of the *Official Iowa Highway Map* which is distributed free by the Iowa State Highway Commission, 826 Lincoln Way, Ames 50010. The map shows all major roads and highways, both existing and proposed. It also indicates route markers that indicate different types of roads. Recreational facilities are also shown, such as state parks with and without camping, state and U.S. fish hatcheries, information centers, travel trailer disposal stations, scenic areas, and points of interest where local

inquiry is advisable. A distance table showing mileage between major cities and towns is provided, and there is a chart showing state parks and recreation areas and the facilities provided in each.

Iowa Mountaineers—Rocky Mountain Schools & Expeditions

The Iowa Mountaineers, a prestigious nonprofit organization founded in 1940, organizes summer mountain camps and foreign expeditions in such outstanding scenic climbing and backpacking areas as the Lake of the Hanging Glaciers in the Canadian Rockies, Colorado's San Juan Mountains, Montana's spectacular Beartooth High Lakes Plateau, and the majestic Peruvian highlands and east Africa; an intensive 7-day rock-climbing course; basic mountaineering courses held in the Rocky Mountains; backpacking outings in Arizona's Grand Canyon Country; and cross-country skiing and winter survival courses. The club's safety record is flawless. For information on membership and current outings, write: Iowa Mountaineers, P.O. Box 163, Iowa City 52240, phone (319) 337-7163. The club boasts members from all parts of the country, and anyone interested in serious wilderness travel would do well to consult this organization.

Lake Contour Fishing Maps

The following lake contour fishing maps showing depth and major hydrographic features may be purchased for $1 each by writing: Conservation Commission, Information and Education Section, 300 4th St., Des Moines 50309: *Clear Lake Depth Map, Storm Lake Depth Map, East Okoboji Depth Map, West Okoboji Depth Map, Spirit Lake Depth Map,* and *Rathbun Depth Map.* You can also obtain the following free: *Chartered Maps of Iowa Lakes, List of Artificial and Natural Lakes, Meandering Rivers, Rathbun Reservoir Recreation Map, Red Rock Recreation Map,* and *Guide to Iowa Great Lakes.* Small topo maps of the following lakes are available free upon request from the Iowa Conservation Commission (address above): Silver, East Okoboji, West Okoboji, Lost Island, Clear, Spirit, Five Island, Storm, North Twin, Upper and Lower Gar, Black Hawk, Meadow, Anita, Red Hawk, Ahquabi, Wapello, Geode, Little Spirit, Nine Eagles, Keomah, Iowa, Big Creek.

MISSOURI ENCYCLOPEDIA

Accommodations— Vacation Resorts & Lodges

For detailed information about accommodations, resorts, and lodges in Missouri, write: Division of Tourism, P.O. Box 1055, Jefferson City 65101, phone (314) 751-4133); Missouri Innkeeping, Resort, & Travel Assn., 122½ E. High St., Jefferson City 65101, phone (314) 635-3536); and Missouri Hotel & Motel Assn., 1800 Southwest Blvd., Jefferson City 65101, phone (314) 636-2107).

Camping & Hiking Trails

Missouri offers many different kinds of camping facilities. Lakesides, forests, Ozark hills, and farmlands are all scenic settings for excellent campground services. *Camping in Missouri*, available from: Division of Tourism, 308 E. High St., Jefferson City 65101, lists every campground owned or operated by the state or federal government as well as privately owned campgrounds. It tells you the name and address of each campground, access and routes, number of acres, number of trailer sites, tent sites, the basic fee, length of the season, and the time limit for guests. It also lists the available facilities and activities. An extra feature is a list of hiking and riding trails which indicates the name and location of the trail, and its length in miles.

Hiking in Missouri can uncover many surprises. Twenty-six outstanding trails are listed in the 58-page booklet *Missouri Hiking Trails*, which can be ordered from: Dept. of Conservation, P.O. Box 180, Jefferson City 65101, for $1. It provides a clear black-and-white map for each trail, with a brief description of the area and a log. Among the trails described are the Whites Creek Trail, which runs through the heart of the Irish Wilderness Area in the Mark Twain National Forest; Monteau Wilderness Trail in the Rudolf Bennett Wildlife Area, which winds past the boyhood home of General Omar Bradley and an old Indian village and burial ground; Woodchuck Forest Trail, which winds along the Current National Scenic River past cranebreak (bamboo) and giant bubbling springs; and the scenic Big Piney and Rock Pile Mountain wilderness trails.

A useful 270-page guide, *Missouri Wildflowers*, may be obtained for $4 from the Dept. of Conservation (address above). This durable, pocket-size field guide to the wildflowers of Missouri includes description of almost 400 species, with 249 of them pictured in full color. A color key, habitat information, distribution, and flowering dates make this book easily utilized by the beginner. The book is divided into two parts. The first includes color photos and a brief description of where the flowers are found and when they bloom. The second part gives detailed descriptions of the plants and flowers and interesting information about them.

Fishing & Hunting in Missouri

The Show Me state's national and state forests, wildlife management areas, great lakes, and meandering, spring-fed Ozark float streams offer some of the top hunting and fishing opportunities in the Central United States. This great state, once a frontier mecca and jumping-off place to the wilderness fur kingdom of the Upper Missouri River country and the Rocky Mountains, is divided into four natural regions: the glaciated plains located north of the Missouri River; the old plains located south of the Missouri River and west of the Ozark Highlands; the Missouri River Plains; and the south and central Ozark Highlands. Missouri has an area of 69,686 square miles, 19,000 miles of rivers, 718,000 acres of lakes, and 200 species of fish, including bass, walleye,

muskellunge, northern pike, rainbow and brown trout, pan fish, and giant catfish.

Several of the state's best smallmouth, largemouth bass, walleye, and trout waters are found in the Big Springs region of the southeast, including Clearwater and Wappapello lakes and the nationally renowned Ozark float streams—the Eleven Point, St. Francis, Black, Current, Jacks Fork, North Fork, and Big Piney rivers surrounded by the beautiful green Ozark Hills in the Clark and Mark Twain national forests. Several of the nation's top-ranked trophy bass impoundments are found in the scenic Ozark Highlands of the southwest—Table Rock, Bull Shoals, Norfork, Stockton, Taneycomo, and Pomme de Terre reservoirs. The giant spring-fed waters of the Roaring River and Bennett Spring on the Niangua River in the Ozark Highlands hold lunker rainbow trout up to 14 pounds. The famous Lake of the Ozarks in the central portion of the state, surrounded by colorful hills and bluffs of the forested northern Ozarks, has approximately 1,375 miles of shoreline, making it one of the largest man-made lakes in the world. Known as the "dragon lake" for its serpentine shape, this giant lake offers top-ranked fishing along its numerous cliffs, bays, hidden coves, and dead timber areas for lunker largemouth bass, striped bass, crappie, catfish, and the primitive paddlefish (known locally as spoonbill).

The quality and diversity of fishing in Missouri is highlighted by the record fish caught by rod and reel, compiled by the Conservation Department.

MISSOURI RECORD FISH

	Lb.-oz.	Place	Year
Rainbow trout	15	Current River Headwaters	1977
Brown trout	15–11	Current River	1977
Walleye	20	St. Francis River	1961
Largemouth bass	13–14	Bull Shoals Lake	1961
Smallmouth bass	6–7	Valley Dolomite Pond	1952
Muskellunge	27–4	Pomme de Terre River	1975
Northern pike	18–9	Stockton Lake	1974
Striped bass	22–9	Lake of the Ozarks	1974
Chain pickerel	6–3	Duck Creek Lake	1977
Yellow perch	0–15	Butter City Lake	1977
Rock bass	2–12	Big Piney River	1968
Sturgeon	5–3	Missouri River	1950
Freshwater drum	34	Warsaw	1959
Green sunfish	2–2	Stockton Lake	1971
Bluegill	3	Pond at Bevier	—
Kentucky bass	7–8	Table Rock Lake	1966
White bass	5–2	Table Rock Lake	1973
Bowfin	19	Duck Creek	1963
Buffalo	40	Current River	1971
Carp	47–7	Busch Wildlife Area	1974
Blue catfish	56	Osage River	1961
Channel catfish	30–14	Valley Lake	1975
Flathead catfish	61	New Madrid Co.	1963
Black crappie	4–8	Farm Pond—Clay Co.	1967
White crappie	3–12	Sugar Creek Lake	1964

The Missouri Department of Conservation publishes several free booklets and guides to the state's fish, game, flora, and wildlife: *Where to Fish, Where to Hunt, Wildlife Code of Missouri, Fishing Seasons & Limits, Show-Me Squirrel Hunting, How to Catch Fish, Deer Hunting in Missouri, Ducks at a Distance, Missouri Game Animals & Furbearers, Life History of Important Hook & Line Fishes in Missouri, Life History Chart of Missouri Mammals, Missouri Trees, Snakes & Facts About Them, Rare & Endangered Animals in Missouri, Rare & Endangered Fauna of Missouri*, and the following free mammal leaflets—*Beaver, Bobcat, Cottontail Rabbit, Coyote, Fox, Mink, Muskrat, Opossum, Prairie Chicken, Raccoon, Skunks, Squirrels, Whitetail Deer*, and *Woodchuck*. Single copies may be ordered by writing: Dept. of Conservation, Information Section, P.O. Box 180, Jefferson City 65101. The department also publishes free map-guides to Missouri's state forests and wildlife management areas, which offer excellent opportunities for fishing, primitive camping, and hunting in season.

Missouri Hiking Trails

WHERE TO FISH IN MISSOURI

A *Lake of the Ozarks Contour Map* ($6) is available from: Structure Graphics, 917 Pyramid Dr., Valley Park 63088. Contour maps of *Bull Shoals Lake* and *Table Rock Lake* may be obtained for $2.95 each from: Lakes Illustrated, Box 4854 G.S., Springfield 65804.

The state's vast wetlands, rolling hills, prairies, and scenic forests of oak, hickory, and shortleaf pine offer top-ranked hunting for deer, quail, mourning doves, wild turkey, ducks and geese, squirrels, rabbit, coyote, red and gray fox, woodchucks, and a few pheasant. Some of the finest hunting in the nation for Canada geese, mallards, pintails, teal, and wood ducks is found during the fall along the Mississippi and Missouri lowlands.

(For additional fishing and hunting information see "Ozark Float Fishing & Scenic Waterways" in this section and the "Travel & Recreation Guide" section.)

Highways—Recreation & Scenic Routes

The *Official Missouri Highway Map*, published by the State Highway Commission, shows every major road in the state, indicating the width and number of lanes. It also features toll bridges and ferries, state patrol offices, caves, forest towers, hospitals, highway interchanges, frontier trails, points of interest and historical markers, airports, and roadside parks and rest areas. A population chart and a mileage chart are included, as well as an index of towns and villages. The reverse side of the map provides the traveler with detail maps of major cities. The city maps show parks, hospitals, universities, and airports along with main thoroughfares. There is also a state park index, which lists the recreational facilities offered in each of Missouri's 37 state parks. The map is free upon request by writing to: Division of Tourism, 308 E.

High St., Jefferson City 65101. The division also publishes a free full-color 43-page travelers' guide to the state, *Seven Ways to Get Away in Missouri*, which describes the seven major vacationlands: Pony Express, Mark Twain, Kansas City, Lake of the Ozarks, St. Louis, Big Springs, and Ozark Highlands regions.

Ozark Float Fishing & Scenic Waterways

Missouri's famous johnboat float streams include the Sac, Pomme de Terre, Niangua, Moreau, and Osage rivers in the Lake of the Ozarks region; the historic, 300-mile-long Gasconade, Little Piney, Osage Fork of the Gasconade, and the wild, spring-fed Big Piney River in the Central Ozark region; the wild, spring-fed tributaries of the Mara-mec River Valley; the Spring River, Big Sugar Creek, and Shoal Creek in the southwestern region; the renowned smallmouth bass waters of the James River, Roaring River, Bull and Beaver creeks, and the clear, spring-fed North Fork White River in the White River region; and the big, spring-fed waters of the nationally renowned Current, Jacks Fork, Eleven Point, Black, and St. Francis rivers in the Big Springs region of the Ozarks. Fallen trees, sweepers, log jams, "willow jungles," swinging bridges, and low-water bridges present occasional hazards along the Ozark waterways.

A useful 117-page booklet, *Missouri Ozark Waterways*, is available for $1 from the Dept. of Conservation, Information Section, P.O. Box 180, Jefferson City 65101. It divides the waterways into six regions, and describes the navigation of each river in depth. A map is featured for each river, showing access points, scenic sites, caves, springs, campsites, lookout towers, and dams. The rivers are graded according to difficulty and scope, and a detailed log of the river is provided. Information on equipment safety, river pointers, conservation, private lands along the rivers, and difficulty ratings is also given.

A free booklet, *Missouri Float Fishing Outfitters*, may be obtained by writing: Division of Tourism, P.O. Box 1055—Dept. FFO, Jefferson City 65101.

The major waterways in the Ozark region are shown on the following large-scale U.S. Geological Survey Topographic Maps. *Beaver Creek:* Bradleyville, Fordland, Forsyth, Hilda, Mincy; *Black River:* Clearwater Dam, Ellington, Hanleyville, Hendrickson, Lesterville, Lesterville SE, Mill Spring, Oglesville, Poplar Bluff, Vastus, Williamsville; *James River:* Aurora, Galena, Galloway, Highlandville, Hurley, Nixa, Oak Grove Heights, Reed Springs, Republic, Shell Knob; *North Fork White River:* Cabool SW, Topaz 15, Cureall NW, Bakersfield, Udall; *Niangua River:* Macks Creek, Long Lane, Buffalo, Charity, Niangua;

Roaring River: Cassville, Shell Knob; *Bull Creek:* Branson, Day, Selmore, Chadwick; *Lake of the Ozarks:* Barnumton, Bollinger Creek, Boylers Mill, Camdenton, Edwards, Gravois Mills, Green Bay Terrace, Knobby, Lake Ozark, Lakeview Heights, Lincoln SE, Proctor Creek, Rocky Mount, Shawnee Bend, Sunrise Beach, Toronto, Warsaw E, Warsaw W; *Little Niangua River:* Barnumton, Branch, Climax Springs, Green Bay, Terrace; *Little Sac River:* Aldrich, Bassville, Bearcreek, Bona, Caplinger Mills, Ebenezer, Morrisville, Roscoe, Stockton, Willard, Vista; *Osage River Lower:* Bagnell, Eugene, Iberia, Meta, Mokane, Osage City; *Osage River Upper:* Iconium, Lowry City, Monegan Springs, Osceola, Papinsville, Rich Hill, Rockville, Roscoe, Shawnee Bend, Taberville, Valhalla, Warsaw W; *Osage Fork River:* Drew, Dry Knob, Lebanon, Niangua, Rader, Rickland; *St. Francis River:* Coldwater, Fisk, Fredericktown, Greenville, Greenville SW, Hendrickson, Kennett, Marmaduke, Patterson, Piggott, Shook, Valley Ridge, Wappapello; *White River:* Branson, Forsyth, Garber, Lampe, Mincy, Protem SW, Reed Springs, Shell Knob, Table Rock Dam.

(For information on the Big Piney River, the Eleven Point National Scenic River, the Current River, and the Jacks Fork River, see the entries on those areas in the "Travel & Recreation Guide" section.)

Clark National Forest & Big Piney River

Clark National Forest Topo Maps

U.S. Geological Survey Overview Maps, scale 1:250,000: Poplar Bluff, Rolla, St. Louis, Springfield.

Bell Mountain Wilderness

Large-scale U.S. Geological Survey Maps: Banner, Edge Hill, Johnson Mountain, Johnson Shut-ins.

Big Piney River

Large-scale U.S. Geological Survey Maps: Bordo, Beulah, Big Piney 7.5, Cabool NE, Devils Elbow, Dixon, Houston, Prescott, Slabtown Springs.

Deer Run State Forest

Large-scale U.S. Geological Survey Maps: Ellington 7.5, Exchange, Garwood, Van Buren N.

Gasconade River

Large-scale U.S. Geological Survey Maps: Bland, Brownfield, Dixon, Drew, Dry Knob, Hancock, Linn, Manes, Morrison, Newburg, Ozark Springs, Richland, Vienna, Waynesville, Winnipeg.

Indian Trails State Forest

U.S. Geological Survey large-scale maps: Steelville, Stone Hill.

This renowned canoe-camping, fishing, and hunting area embraces 800,000 acres along the Ozark Plateau in southern Missouri. The forest is a wild country of connecting ridges, rolling hills, deep hollows, clear, deep limestone streams, dense forests of oak, hickory, red cedar, and shortleaf pine, and caves and sinkholes. The major features of the forest include the famous smallmouth bass waters and canoe trails of the Current, Black, Gasconade, St. Francis, and Big Piney rivers, Lake Wappapello State Park, Clearwater Lake, Johnson Shut-ins State Park, and the Huzzah Wildlife Management Area. This is one of the finest wild turkey, deer, and upland game-bird hunting areas in the state.

The primitive 13,000-acre Bell Mountain Wilderness lies in the St. Francis Mountains within the Iron County Ranger District of the forest. The wilderness lies on the highest part of the Ozark Plateau and embraces the pools and falls of Shut-in Creek, numerous glades, deep gorges, and thick forests of oak, hickory, and red cedar. The wilderness is an outstanding scenic hiking, primitive camping, and hunting area.

Two of the state's finest hiking, camping, and hunting areas for deer, crow, squirrel, wild turkey, and upland game birds—the Deer Run and Indian Trails state forests—lie adjacent to the national forest boundaries. The scenic 13,255-acre Indian Trails State Forest lies adjacent to the western boundaries of the Clark National Forest, due east of the village of Salem. The major features of the area include Kiln Pond, Fishwater Creek, and the Meramec River. The 120,000-acre Deer Run State Forest—the largest state-owned forest reserve—lies between the Clark and Mark Twain national forests adjacent to Current River and Logan Creek.

Several of the state's outstanding float fishing streams for smallmouth bass and walleye flow through the rolling hills and woodlands of the forest, including the Gasconade, Osage Fork, Little Piney, Black, St. Francis, and the renowned spring-fed Big Piney—considered by many to be the state's number one float fishing stream. This wild and unspoiled free-flowing stream, the largest tributary of the Gasconade River, flows through scenic pine forests and past spectacular limestone

---

**MISSOURI TRAVEL
& RECREATION GUIDE**

bluffs and hollows. Use of johnboats is restricted to the long, deep pools and eddies. Two portages are located within the Fort Leonard Wood Area. Access points along the 83-mile floatable stretch of the Big Piney are at Baptist Church Camp, Dog's Bluff, Mineral and Boiling Springs, Mason Bridge, Cave Eddy, Six Crossings, Ross Bridge, East Gate-Fort Wood, Spring Creek, Booker Tract, and Confluence of Gasconade and Big Piney.

The major man-made and natural features of the region including highways, roads, mines, ranger stations, recreation sites, trails, hunting camps, boat-launching and fishing access sites, and the Karkaghone Scenic Drive are shown on the full-color *Clark National Forest Map,* available for 50¢ from: Forest Supervisor, P.O. Box 937, Rolla 65401, phone (314) 364-4621. The Forest Supervisor's office also publishes a free guide, *The Big Piney River.*

A complete listing of float fishing outfitters and canoe rental services on the Gasconade, Big Piney, and Osage Fork is contained in the *Missouri Float Fishing Outfitters Guide,* available free upon request from: Division of Tourism, P.O. Box 1055, Jefferson City 65101.

Access & Outfitting Centers

The forest is reached via U.S. Highways 60, 61, 66, and 67; Missouri Routes 8, 17, 21, 32, 49, and 72. Overnight accommodations, supplies, guides, and boat rentals are available at Rolla, Fredericktown, Piedmont, Potosi, Ironton, Poplar Bluffs, Salem, and St. Louis.

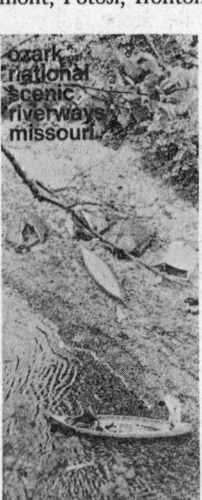

Mark Twain National Forest & Ozark National Scenic Rivers

Mark Twain National Forest Topo Maps

U.S. Geological Survey Overview Maps, scale 1:250,000: Harrison, Poplar Bluff, Rolla, Springfield.

Current & Jacks Fork National Scenic Waterways

Large-scale U.S. Geological Survey Maps. *Current River:* Big Spring, Cedargrove, Doniphan, Eminence, Grandin SW, Lewis Hollow, Powder Mill Ferry, Round Spring, Stegall Mountain, The Sinks, Van Buren N, Van Buren S; *Jacks Fork:* Alley Spring, Clear Springs, Eminence, Jam Up Cave, Pine Creek.

Eleven Point National Scenic River

Large-scale U.S. Geological Survey Maps: Bill More, Birch Tree, Montier, Riverton, Wilderness, Willow Springs.

Irish Wilderness

Large-scale U.S. Geological Survey Maps: Bardley, Hanley, Riverton, Wilderness.

The four divisions of the famous 620,000-acre Mark Twain National Forest embrace the Ozark canoe trails along the Eleven Point and Current national scenic rivers surrounded by a wild backcountry of rolling hills, barren rock outcroppings, numerous sinkholes, limestone caves, and thick stands of oak and native shortleaf pine. The major features include Table Rock Reservoir—one of the state's best for lunker bass, trout, and walleye up to 17 pounds—Beaver Creek, Bull Shoals Lake, James and North Fork rivers, Roaring River State Park, Carman Springs Wildlife Refuge, Peck Ranch Wildlife Management Area, and the Irish Wilderness. The forest is one of the state's finest hunting regions for deer, waterfowl, wild turkey, and upland game birds.

The famed smallmouth bass and walleye waters of the spring-fed, clear Ozark National Scenic Waterways—the deep-flowing Current and Jacks Fork rivers—are shown on the free map-brochure *Ozark National Scenic Riverways,* available from: Superintendent, Ozark National Scenic Riverways, Van Buren 63965. The map shows all campgrounds, access points, springs, trails, and unimproved roads along the rivers. The Current River, named *La Rivière Courante*—"The Running River"—by the French trappers who first explored the region from their base on the upper Great Lakes, flows through the ancient Ozark Hill country surrounded by giant springs, caves, and lush forests of oak, hickory, shortleaf pine, sycamore, sassafras, blackgum, maple, and birch with a colorful understory of hawthorn, dogwood, bittersweet, redbud, and beautiful rose azalea, inhabited by deer, wild turkey, mink, bobcat, raccoon, opossum, gray and fox squirrels, osprey, owls, kingfish, green heron, and great blue heron. The Current is one of the state's top-ranked streams for walleye (known locally as "jack salmon) up to 20 pounds. The Current also produced the state record 14-pound 10-ounce brown trout. The major features along the Current include the trout springs in Montauk State Park, Medlock Spring and Cave, Welch Cave and Spring, the large sinkholes known as "Burr Oak Basin" and "The Sunkland" in the Akers Hieronymus Hollow, Rock House Cave, Bee Bluff, Paint Rock Bluff and Gravel Spring, Big Spring State Park, Bog Hollow, and Goose Lake—a pond in the river. The major features along the wild and scenic Jacks Fork River, a tributary of the Current, include the Prongs, Chimney Rock Cave, Jam Up Bluff and Cave, Ebb and Flow Springs, Bucks Hollow, Blue Spring, Sinking Branch, and Horse Hollow. The upper reaches of the Jacks Fork offer superb fly fishing for smallmouth bass. If you plan on floating the Current or Jacks Fork keep an eye out for root wads, obstructions caused by exposed roots and trunks of fallen trees. The major center of activity on the Jacks Fork is at Alley Spring; and at Akens, Pulite Spring, and Round and Big springs on the Current.

A beautifully crafted, large-format *River Maps of the Current & Jacks Fork* is available for $2.75 from: Ozark National Riverways Historical Assn., Van Buren 63965. Individual maps include an 1826 edition of the State of Missouri, as well as maps of Montauk–Akers, Akers–Round Spring, Junction–Jacks Fork, Owls Bend–Blue Spring, Van Buren–Big Spring, Buck Hollow and Alley Spring, Alley–Spring Junction, and The Sinks. Mileage logs are provided, as well as indications of rivers, wet weather creeks, springs, roads, trails, sinks, caves, access points, interest points, and campsites. This guide offers a rare close-up view of the wild springs and individual sections of these two rivers. They are navigable throughout the year, as crystallized mist freezes the water on the trees, but not in the rivers.

Several other publications of interest are available from the Ozark

National Riverways Historical Assn. (address above): *Ozark Stories of the Upper Current* ($4.50, 95 pp., large-format); *Pioneers of the Ozarks* ($16, 193 pp., large format), profiles and sketches of the early Ozark people; *History of Carter County* ($2.50, 142 pp.); *Foxfire Book I* ($3.95, 384 pp.), hog dressing, log cabins, mountain crafts and food, planting by the signs, snake lore, hunting tales, faith healing; *Foxfire II* ($4.50, 410 pp.), ghost stories, wild plant foods, spinning, weaving, corn shuckins, and more affairs of plain living; *Foxfire III* ($4.95, 485 pp.), animal care, hide tanning, and much more.

The enchanting Eleven Point National Scenic River lies within the boundaries of the Winona and Doniphan Ranger districts of the forest. Starting at Thomasville, the river channel is narrow and easy to locate. Long stretches are separated by shallow riffles. Below Green Springs the volume of water increases as well as the speed and size of the rapids. The Eleven Point, which is fed by several of the most beautiful wild springs in the Ozarks, flows through the 17,880-acre Irish Wilderness—an unspoiled primitive camping and backpacking area marked by numerous caves and sinkholes, traversed by the Whites Creek Hiking Trail. The major features of the river—shown on the *Eleven Point National Scenic River Map-Brochure*, available free from: Forest Supervisor, Fairgrounds Rd., Box 937, Rolla 65401 —include Posy, Roaring, Blowing and Graham springs, Cane Bluff, Greer Spring, Graveyard Springs, Horseshoe Bend, Whites Creek, Boze Mill Springs, and The Narrows, McCormack Lake, Camp Five Pond, Greer Crossing and Buffalo Creek are national forest campgrounds located near the Eleven Point. Greer Crossing—a ford once used by the Osage Indians and horse-drawn wagons—is the focal point of activity on the river and the starting point for many float trips. Old Greer Mill, still standing on the hilltop south of the crossing, was powered by a unique cable system from a waterwheel in the spring.

The major features of the forest, including scenic roads, trails, campgrounds, float camps, ranger stations, and recreation sites, are shown on the *Mark Twain National Forest Map*, available from: Forest Supervisor (address above), whose office also publishes a free guide to *National Forest Hiking & Riding Trails*. Auto access to some of the forest's most scenic areas is provided by the Skyline Drive and Gladetop Trail.

Guided Ozark canoe trips and expeditions are provided by *Pack N' Paddle Wilderness Expeditions Ltd.*, P.O. Box 5002, Springfield 65801, and *Wilderness Ridge Resort*, Big Piney Rte., Newburg 65550. For a complete listing of float fishing guides and canoe rental services along the Current, Jacks Fork, and Eleven Point write for the *Missouri Float Fishing Outfitters Guide*, available free from: Division of Tourism, P.O. Box 1055, Jefferson City 65101.

Access & Outfitting Centers

The forest is reached via U.S. Highways 60, 63, 66, and 160; Missouri Routes 5, 14, 39, 76, 87, 95, 125, 148, and 173. Overnight accommodations, supplies, guides, and canoe and johnboat rentals are available at West Plains, Willow Springs, Van Buren, Doniphan, Cassville, Ava, Willow Springs, Winona, Salem, Eminence, Alley Spring, Round Spring, Jadwin, Gladden, and Alton.

ARKANSAS ENCYCLOPEDIA

Accommodations—Vacation Resorts & Sporting Camps

The *Arkansas 1976 Tour Guide*, a 112-page booklet, is available free from: Dept. of Parks & Tourism, State Capitol, Little Rock 72201. It gives information on specific attractions and areas of interest in the state, listing local Chambers of Commerce, and state park facilities. It features maps for each recreational region, and describes local points of interest, as well as hotels and inns.

The department also offers free booklets on specific vacation areas. *Greater Beaver Lake Area: Queen of the White River Lakes* includes a map and brief description of the area, and several suggestions for accommodations. *Hot Springs National Park: Diamond Lakes Country* describes the local parks, lists major annual events, features a clear highway map of the immediate area, and includes a complete listing of downtown hotels, lakeside resorts and campsites, and Hot Springs bathhouses, as well as churches and convention facilities. *The Lake Dardanelle Recreation Area* features a map, camping facilities, hotel listings, and brief descriptions of Mount Nebo, Mount Magazine, and Petit Jean Mountain. A colorful map and camping and hotel listings are contained in *Greers Ferry Lake & Little Red River.* The booklet *North Central Arkansas* (Independence, Izard, Sharp, Jackson, Stone, and Fulton counties) describes the Ozark Gateway region, and provides hotel and campground listings. *Delta Highlands* (Cross, Crittenden, St. Francis, Phillips, and Lee counties) describes local state parks, provides a simple, clear map, gives a brief history and scenic description of each county, and provides suggestions for accommodations.

The 44-page *Ozark Mountain Region* booklet, available free from Ozark Mountain Region, Inc., P.O. Box 122, Mountain Home 72653, describes vacation accommodations in the Bull Shoals Lake, White River, Lake Norfolk, and Buffalo National River areas.

Major vacation resorts, lodges, and fishing guide services in the Ozark Mountain country include: (Bull Shoals Lake) *Lakeview Boat Dock & Marina* (Lakeview 72642), *Sunset Point Resort* (Rt. 1, Box 166, Midway 72651), *Wilson's Bait-n-Hook It Resort* (Rt. 1, Midway 72651), *Tucker Hollow Lodge & Boat Dock* (Rt. 4, Harrison 72601), *Bass Bay Resort* (Rt. 1, Box 107M, Mountain Home 72653), *Edgewater Resort & Lodge* (Rt. 1, Box 150–08, Mountain Home 72653), *Waterfront Resort* (Box 374–0, Lakeview 72642), *Chit-Chat-Chaw Resort* (Rt. 1, Promise Land Rd., Mountain Home 72653), *Crow Barnes Resort on Bull Shoals Lake* (Bull Shoals 72619), *Bull Shoals Lake Boat Dock* (Bull Shoals Landing, Box 348, Bull Shoals 72619), *Carter's Lighthouse Resort* (Rt, 1, Box 183, Bull Shoals 72619). The White River area is served by *Sportsman's Resort & Trout Dock* (Rt. A, Box 115, Flippin 72634; 501–453–2424), *Gaston's White River Resort* (Lakeview 72642; 501–431–5202), *Stetson's Fishing Resort* (Rt. A, Box B, Flippin 72634; 501–453–2523), *White Hole Acres Trout Lodge* (Rt. A, Flippin 72634; 501–453–2913), *Hurst Fishing Service* (P.O. Box 129B, Cotter 72626; 501–435–6414), *Cotter Trout Dock* (Box 96W, Cotter 72626, float trips on the White and Buffalo rivers), *Miller's White River Float Service* (Box 277, Cotter 72626). For info on Lake Norfork resorts, write: Lake Norfork Recreation Assn., P.O. Box 3044, Mountain Home 72653. For additional listings, see "Fishing & Hunting in Arkansas" in this section and the "Travel & Recreation Guide" section.

American Institute of Bass Fishing Schools

The American Institute of Bass Fishing offers annual 5-day courses at

several of the nation's top bass fishing lakes such as Clark Hill Reservoir and California's Lake Shastina. Courses are conducted by well-known anglers and cover spin casting, baits, lures, equipment, school fish behavior, bass biology, deep-water and shallow water fishing. Rates include lodging, meals, and marina facilities. Write: Box 2342, Hot Springs 71901 (phone: 501-624-0997).

Camping & State Recreation Areas

Arkansas's 18 million acres of forest lands, two mountain ranges, and the remote country surrounding its wild and scenic rivers provide unlimited opportunities for camping and backpacking. The vast high country forest regions are crisscrossed by old logging roads, firebreaks, and abandoned railroad beds that make excellent paths into seldom explored areas. The state's public camping areas are in the state parks, Buffalo River and Hot Springs national parks, Ozark and Ouachita national forests, and Corps of Engineer recreation areas, including the Arkansas River Development Project, Beaver Lake, Blue Mountain Lake, Bull Shoals Lake, Greers Ferry Lake, Nimrod Lake, Lake Ouachita, Norfork Lake, and De Gray, Millwood, and Table Rock lakes. The camping areas are listed and described in the 32-page *Arkansas Camper's Guide*, available free upon request along with detailed camping information from: Travel Division, Dept. of Parks & Tourism, State Capitol, Little Rock 72201.

Canoeing & Float Fishing— the Ozark Wild & Scenic Rivers

Arkansas's magnificent wild and scenic rivers offer some of the nation's finest canoeing and float fishing for smallmouth bass and trophy rainbow and brown trout. The famed Buffalo, a national wild and scenic river, is one of North America's great canoe routes; it flows east from its headwaters in the Ozark Mountains for 150 miles through lush forests, past towering spectacular 700-foot multicolored limestone bluffs, in a serpentine course characterized by numerous rapids, gravel bass, and gin-clear pools, to its confluence with the White River in the Sylamore district of the Ozark National Forest. The Buffalo offers top-ranked float fishing in a setting of great wilderness beauty for hard-hitting smallmouth bass up to trophy weights. Several primitive campsites are located along gravel bars on the river's twisting course, and maintained campgrounds, hiking trails, and rustic cabins, situated on high bluffs overlooking the river, are available at the Buffalo Point recreation area. Wilderness paddlers who plan to camp along the banks of the Buffalo should keep in mind that a heavy overnight rainfall can transform the river into a raging torrent.

Float fishing, which first originated here on the often otherwise inaccessible wilderness streams of the Ozarks, is popular using canoes or flat-bottomed johnboats. Fly fishing or spin casting from a canoe or johnboat allows the fisherman to cover deep pools, submerged ledges, and riffles along great distances that would be impossible to fish from the banks of the spring-fed Ozark streams, which are often densely forested with thick tangles of underbrush. Experienced float fishermen will periodically beach their craft on gravel bars to thoroughly fish promising-looking stretches. The primary advantage to floating Arkansas's Ozark streams is the thrill of exploring great tranquil stretches of magnificent green wild country.

The headwaters of several other wildwater float streams are found in the Boston Mountains at 2,400 feet elevation in the Ozark National Forest in northwestern Arkansas, including the Big Piney (a 25-mile float), Illinois Bayou, and the Mulberry (a 55-mile float), which flow southward to their confluences with the mighty Arkansas River. These

rugged, remote wilderness streams have an average gradient of 20 feet per mile and should be attempted only by experienced canoeists familiar with the challenges and joys of wilderness camping. Several renowned canoeing and float fishing streams flow northward from the Boston Divide, including the upper White River (a 30-mile float) and the King (a 28-mile float); they all provide often spectacular fishing for explosive smallmouth bass. Crooked Creek, one of the South's top-ranked smallmouth streams, is a tributary of the White River which flows for 30 miles before coursing into underground caves along its lower reaches.

The White River below Bull Shoals Lake Dam is world famous for its float fishing for trophy rainbow trout ranging from 4 to 19 pounds and for monster hook-jawed brown trout up to weights of 30 pounds. The North Fork of the White below Norfork Lake Dam is equally famed for its quality float fishing for trophy-sized trout. To the east of the White River are the renowned Eleven Point and Spring rivers, which flow south into the Arkansas and offer excellent scenic canoeing and float fishing for bronzebacks. Other Ozark wild and scenic float streams include the Little Red River and Caldron Creek, the Strawberry River, and the Illinois and Lee Creek, which flow westward from their Ozark headwaters into Oklahoma.

For additional information about Arkansas's Ozark wild and scenic float streams, write for the following publications. *The Float Streams of Arkansas* is available free from: Dept. of Parks & Tourism, State Capitol, Little Rock 72201. *Buffalo River Canoeing Guide* ($1), *Buffalo River Country* ($4.95), *Mulberry River Canoeing Guide* ($1), and reprints of guides to other Arkansas streams ($2.50) are available from: Ozark Society Book Service, Box 725, Hot Springs 71901. *Buffalo National River* (50¢), an illustrated booklet with a useful river map, is available from: Superintendent, Buffalo National River, P.O. Box 1008, Harrison 72601. Maps of the *Spring River & South Fork, Little Red River, White River Trout Fishing*, and *Buffalo River*, showing public access, boat dock and fishing services, portage points,

graveled roads, and trout areas, are available free upon request from: Game & Fish Commission, State Capitol Mall, Little Rock 72201. The commission also publishes a free *Guide to the Smallmouth Bass Streams of Arkansas.*

(For additional info, see "Ozark National Forest & Buffalo National Wild River" in the "Travel & Recreation Guide" section.)

Fishing & Hunting in Arkansas

Arkansas's great wild, gin-clear rivers, huge sprawling stump-filled lakes and moss-fringed bayous, and dense mixed hardwood and pine forests located in the ancient summits, sheer limestone bluffs, and jagged promontories of the Ozark Mountains, the wildlands of the Ouachita Mountains, once the hunting grounds of the Caddo Indians, and the great Mississippi Delta and Grand Prairie form one of the nation's truly great fishing and hunting regions. The 9,000 miles of streams and rivers and 2.5 million acres of lakes provide good fishing for big largemouth bass, battling bronze-backed smallmouths, monster hooked-jawed browns, and acrobatic trophy rainbows. The two magnificent mountain ranges, and vast tracts of wilderness in the Ozark and Ouachita national forests and wildlife management areas, laced by old logging roads and trails, provide top-ranked hunting for wild turkey, waterfowl, red fox, squirrel, quail, and whitetail deer.

The awesome potential and variety of Arkansas's trophy fishing lakes and streams is illustrated by its record fish, as compiled by the Game & Fish Commission.

ARKANSAS RECORD FISH

	Lb.-oz.	Place	Year
Largemouth bass	16–4	Lake Mallard	1976
Smallmouth bass	7–5	Bull Shoals Lake	1969
Northern pike	16–1	De Gray Reservoir	1973
Walleye	19–12	White River	1963
Rainbow trout	19	White River	1976
Brown trout	33–8	White River	1977
Chain pickerel	7–3	Little Red	1976
Striped bass	40–9	Lake Ouachita	1976
Bluegill	2–1	Farm Pond	1970
Black crappie	4–9	Oladale Lake	1976
White crappie	4–3	Ulm	1975
Spotted bass	6–9	Bull Shoals Lake	1971
White bass	4–15	White River	1969
Sauger	6–12	Arkansas River	1976
Flathead catfish	48	Arkansas River	1974
Blue catfish	47–8	Arkansas River	1976
Channel catfish	18	Fayetteville Lake	1963
Alligator gar	215	Arkansas River	1964

White River Trophy Trout Waters

Several crystal-clear wild and scenic rivers, shadowed by staggering limestone bluffs, and inhabited by trophy smallmouth bass and trout, rise among the ancient summits of the Ozark Highlands in the northwest portion of the state. The White River, once famous for the quality of smallmouth bass fishing, has gained worldwide fame for its float fishing for giant rainbows and browns in the 70-mile stretch of cold, clear water below Bull Shoals Dam. The trophy waters of the White annually yield thousands of rainbows from 4 to 19 pounds and buckskin-flanked browns in the 4-to-25-pound range. The White, framed on the east from Buffalo Shoals to Sylamore by the beautiful Ozark National Forest lands, is best fished by floating using a johnboat equipped with a 9- or 10-horsepower motor. Float fishing service along the river is provided by *Gaston's White River Resort,* Bull Shoals 72619; *Hurst Fishing Service,* P.O. Box 129, Cotter 72626; *Miller's Float Service,* P.O. Box 297, Cotter 72626; *Jenkins Fishing Service,* P.O. Box 303, Calico Rock 72519; and *Jack's Fishing Service,* Sylamore Rte., Mountain View 72560. For comprehensive fishing camp, lodge, and guide service info, write: *Ozark Mountain Region,* P.O. Box 668, Harrison 72601. A listing of the many first-class fishing resorts and camps where you can be outfitted with a johnboat and an expert guide is contained on the *White River Trout Fishing Map,* available free from the Game & Fish Commission, State Capitol Mall, Little Rock 72201. The map also shows boat docks, public access areas, hard-surfaced roads, graveled roads, and shoals, including the famed Wildcat, Rim, Buffalo, Shipp, Bone Island, and Lion Creek shoals.

Camping in White River country is permitted in the largely undeveloped public access areas and along the scenic gravel bars. Be sure to guard against quick river rises and to check locally for the power-generating schedule of the Bull Shoals Dam. When the dam is not generating, the water level drops rapidly, making it difficult to get boats upstream over shoals, where the current is deceptively swift. Wading on the White is limited and can be extremely dangerous on this deep "big-water" river.

Beaver Lake

The headwaters of the Upper White River rise in the Ozark National Forest and flow northward where the river's impounded waters form the massive, sprawling Beaver Lake. The White flows out of Beaver Lake into Missouri, where it swings east through Table Rock Lake and then south back into Arkansas and Bull Shoals Lake. The clear, deep waters of 28,000-acre Beaver Lake, also fed by the top-ranked smallmouth bass waters of War Eagle Creek, hold trophy-sized largemouth bass, walleye, crappie, and landlocked striped bass in the 20-pound-and-over class. This beautiful lake, lined with sheer towering limestone bluffs, has been the site of several major bass tournaments and has been a regular stop on the B.A.S.S. pro tour for several years. Beaver Lake also holds northern pike and giant rainbows in the frigid tail waters beneath the dam. Boat rentals, guides, and gear are available along the shoreline at Lost Bridge, Starkey, Rocky Branch, Prairie Creek, Horseshoe Bend, Hickory Creek, and War Eagle.

Bull Shoals Lake

The crystal-clear waters of massive Bull Shoals Lake, with its sprawling cove-indented 1,000 miles of shoreline surrounded by the hardwood and pine-clad hills of the Arkansas-Missouri Ozarks, is one of the nation's top-ranked trophy largemouth bass waters. Bull Shoals annually produces thousands of lunker "bucketmouth" bass in the 4-to-11-pound class, and holds rainbows up to 8 pounds, and smallmouth bass, walleye, crappie, and spotted bass up to record weights. The lake reaches depths of 200 feet near the Bull Shoals Dam—the fifth-largest concrete dam in the United States. Specific information about lodging, boat rentals, and fishing guides may be obtained by writing: Bull Shoals Lake, White River Assn., P.O. Box 311, Bull Shoals 72619.

Norfork Lake & Little Red River

Famous Norfork Lake—located to the southeast of Bull Shoals on the North Fork River, a major tributary of the White, in the Ozark highlands—is considered by many fishermen as the nation's top large-

mouth bass lake. Norfork, with its 500 miles of shoreline surrounded by scenic wooded hills inhabited by deer and wild turkey, produces largemouth bass up to 12 pounds, smallmouths up to 6 pounds, and trophy-sized walleye, white bass, and crappie. The frigid, turbulent North Fork River below the dam holds rainbows in the 8-to-15-pound class. The U.S. Bureau of Sport, Fisheries, & Wildlife Federal Trout Hatchery—the largest in the U.S.—is located below the dam, and is responsible, along with the Arkansas Game & Fish Commission, for the excellence of White River country trout fishing. The bureau also operates a trout hatchery on the Little Red River, another tributary of the White, located just below the Greers Ferry Lake Dam. The turbulent, 30-mile, island-dotted, shoal-lined stretch of the Little Red below the dam is nationally renowned for its float fishing for trophy rainbow trout up to 15½ pounds. The major features of the river, including boat docks and fishing services, public access areas, roads, and the Cow, Ritchey, Winkley, Moss Dam, Scroncher, Mossy, and Dunham shoals are shown on the *Little Red River Map*, available free from the Game & Fish Commission (address above). The crystal-clear waters of the 40,000-acre Grass Ferry Lake provide excellent fishing for largemouth and smallmouth bass, walleye, and crappie. Lodging is available at luxurious lakeside resorts, or you can pitch your tent at one of the many campgrounds provided by the Corps of Engineers.

Arkansas Game & Fish Commission

Ouachita Lakes & Streams

The free-flowing smallmouth bass streams of the Ozark National Forest, which protects more than a million acres in one of the nation's most scenic natural areas, are described above in "Canoeing & Float Fishing—the Ozark Wild & Scenic Rivers" and in the "Travel & Recreation Guide" section, and also in the free publication *Smallmouth Bass Streams of Arkansas*, available upon request from: Game & Fish Commission (address above). The major warmwater fisheries located south of the Ozark highlands include beautiful blue mountain lakes on the Petit Jean River, huge Lake Ouachita encircled by the craggy bluffs and dense green forests of the million-acre Ouachita National Forest, De Gray Reservoir on the Caddo River, Lake Greeson on the Little Missouri, Lake Dardanelle and the historic Arkansas River—surrounded by the plain of the Arkansas River Valley, and the oxbows of the meandering Mississippi on the eastern boundary, and the Spanish-moss-lined sloughs and bayous of the southern forests, bisected by the Ouachita River. Trophy rainbows and browns are found in the cold tailrace waters below the Gruson Reservoir and Lake Ouachita dams. Huge alligator gars up to 200 pounds are caught and sometimes landed on the lower White River, Red River, and the lower sluggish stretches of the Ouachita.

Arkansas fishing and hunting regulations, license and seasons information, and the free booklet *Public Owned Fishing Lakes* may be obtained from: Game & Fish Commission, State Capitol Mall, Little Rock 72201. Many of the state's old logging roads and deserted railroad beds which provide access to the remote fishing and hunting areas are shown on *Arkansas County Maps*, available for 50¢ each from: Highway Dept., Little Rock 72201.

The state's scenic farmlands, mountains, swamps, mixed hardwood and pine forests, and gum- and cypress-fringed bayous of the southern bottomlands provide excellent big and small game, upland game-bird, and waterfowl hunting.

Highways—Recreation & Scenic Routes

The free *Arkansas State Highway Map* includes all major and minor roads, cities and towns, railroads, colleges and universities, roadside tables, campsites, national forests, wildlife management areas, and estimated mileage between major points. It also features detail maps of Little Rock and North Little Rock, Jonesboro, West Memphis, Pine Bluff, El Dorado, Fort Smith, Blytheville, Texarkana, Springdale, Hot Springs National Park, Fayetteville, Camden, and Conway. Write: Dept. of Parks and Tourism, State Capital, Little Rock 72201.

Wild & Trophy Fishing Waters Maps

Arkansas's famed wild and scenic canoeing and float fishing streams and lakes are shown on the following full-color, large-scale U.S. Geological Survey Maps. These invaluable maps will provide you with a complete physical inventory of the stream or lake you plan to fish or float, including the topography of the surrounding countryside, rapids, falls, springs, campsites, islands, woodlands, footbridges, and roads and trails. *White River Trophy Trout Waters* (Bull Shoals Dam to Melrose): Bull Shoals, Cotter, Mountain Home W, Buffalo City, Norfork, Norfork Dam S, Calico Rock, Boswell, Sylamore, Guion, Mount Pleasant, Bethesda, Almond; *Norfork River Trophy Trout Waters:* Norfork Dam N, Norfork Dam S, Norfork; *Crooked Creek Smallmouth Bass Waters:* Harrison, Bergman, Everton, Zinc, Pyatt, Bruno, Yellville, Rea Valley, Buffalo City; *Spring River* (from Missouri line to Powhatan): Mammoth Springs, Stuart, Hardy, Sitka, Williford, Ravenden, Imboden, Powhatan; *South Fork of the Spring River:* Salem, Agnos, Stuart, Hardy; *Eleven Point River:* Dalton, Warm Springs, Ravenden Springs, Ravenden Springs SE, Powhatan; *Current River:* Supply, Reyno, Pocahontas, Manson, Powhatan; *War Eagle Creek:* Spring Valley, War Eagle, Hindsville; *Little Red River* (from Greers Ferry Dam): West Pangburn, Pangburn, Steprock, Judsonia, Bald Knob, West Point, Georgetown; *Beaver Reservoir:* Pea Ridge, Beaver, Nundell, War Eagle, Rogers, Sonora, Spring Valley; *Bull Shoals Lake:* Omaha NE, Diamond City, Peel, Cotter NW, Bull Shoals, Cotter, Cotter SW, Cotter; *Norfork Lake:* Clarkridge, Gamaliel, Mountain Home E, Norfork Dam N. (For additional map kit listings, see the "Travel & Recreation Guide" section.)

Ouachita National Forest & Caney Creek Backcountry

Ouachita National Forest Topo Maps

U.S. Geological Survey Overview Maps, scale 1:250,000: Fort Smith, Russellville, McAlester, Little Rock.

Caney Creek Backcountry & Wildlife Management Area

Large-scale U.S. Geological Survey Maps: Umpire, Athens.

Lake Ouachita Fish & Game Area

Large-scale U.S. Geological Survey Maps (includes upper Ouachita River): Mount Ida, Fannie, McGraw Mountain, Crystal Springs, Mountain Pine, Avant, Hamilton, Acorn, Mena (7.5), Board Camp, Oden.

This 1.5-million-acre oak, beech, and pine forest reserve is located due west of Little Rock, encompassing the rugged mountainous backcountry surrounding the headwaters of the Little Missouri, Cossatot, Fourche la Fave, and Caddo rivers. The Choctaw district of the forest sprawls across the Arkansas boundary into Oklahoma. The major features of this outstanding camping, fishing, and hunting region include the Ouachita, Kiamichi, and Winding Stair mountains, the renowned smallmouth bass and crappie waters of beautiful Ouachita, Nimrod, Winona, and Hamilton lakes, Blue Mountain Lake, and the Caney Creek and Muddy Creek wildlife management areas. The 14,433-acre Caney Creek Wilderness is the largest roadless mountain area in the central United States. There are several rugged hiking trails and old forest roads which provide access to the remote interior wildlife management areas where the hunting is excellent for bobwhite, wild turkey, deer, raccoon, red fox, and opossum. Lake Ouachita is nationally renowned for its striped bass to 17 pounds and rainbows to 10 pounds.

The Forest Supervisor, Ouachita National Forest, Hot Springs 71901, will be glad to provide you with free maps of the forest, hiking trails, and the *Ouachita River Float Trip* and *Charlton Recreation Area*

ARKANSAS TRAVEL & RECREATION GUIDE

guides. *The Ouachita National Forest Map* (50¢) shows all boundaries, highways, roads and trails, points of interest, district ranger stations, landing fields, lookout stations, and recreation and camping sites, and includes an index of recreational facilities. *Trails on the Ouachita National Forest* shows existing trails, proposed trails, hiking trails, interpretive trails, and information points. It describes each trail briefly, and provides information on preparation, camping, campfires, and the Talimena Scenic Drive—a 55-mile road which affords spectacular views of the Ouachita Mountains, especially in the spring, when the fruit trees, dogwood, and redbud are in bloom, and in the fall, when a panorama of color sweeps over the forest.

The Upper Ouachita River above the lake to its headwaters offers a camping and float fishing stream for smallmouth bass and lunker rainbows. The tailrace waters below the Lake Ouachita Dam hold trophy rainbows to 10 pounds and over. Float fishing base camps located on the Ouachita River include the *Rocky Shoals Float Camp*, 2 miles southeast of Pencil Bluff; *River Bluff Float Camp* and *Fulton Branch Float Camp*, both 1 mile northeast of Mount Ida; *Dragover Float Camp*, 4 miles east of Sims; and *Sims Float Camp*, 1 mile south of Sims.

Access & Outfitting Centers

The forest is reached via U.S. 71, 270, 64, and 70, and Interstate Routes 40 and 30. Overnight accommodations, supplies, guides, and boat rentals are available at Mountain Pine, Mena, Hartford, Hot Springs, Mansfield, and Hartfield (Arkansas), and Heavener (Oklahoma).

Ozark National Forest & Buffalo National Wild River

Ozark National Forest Topo Maps

U.S. Geological Survey Overview Maps, scale 1:250,000: Tulsa, Fort Smith, Harrison, Russellville.

Buffalo National River

Large-scale U.S. Geological Survey Maps: Fallsville, Boxley, Osage SW, Ponca, Jasper, Hasty, Mount Judea, Western Grove, Snowball, Maumee, Marshall, Cozahome, Rea Valley, Big Flat, Buffalo City.

The Ozark National Forest embraces 1,103,000 acres of scenic mixed hardwood and pine forests, deep clear rivers, and spectacular limestone bluffs in the Ozark Highlands in northwestern Arkansas. Rugged backcountry trails and forest roads provide access to the major recreation areas and fish and game lands, including the Ozark and Boston mountains; Hurricane Creek Scenic Area; Illinois Bayou Bluffs; the streams, caves, lakes, and picturesque bluffs of the Blanchard Springs Recreation Area; the rugged Magazine Mountain Recreation Area; Upper Buffalo Wilderness at the headwaters of the river, surrounded by high rocky bluffs and canyons; and the renowned smallmouth bass waters of the Upper Buffalo, White, Mulberry, War Eagle, Big Piney, and Illinois rivers. The forest is a top-ranked hunting area for deer, wild turkey, red fox, raccoon, and squirrel.

The wild and scenic Buffalo River rises in the Boston Mountains and flows northeast through a lush green region hemmed by towering multicolored bluffs, caves, and spectacular waterfalls, past old backcountry hamlets with odd names like Lick Skillet, Blue Eye, and Bug Scuffle. The deep-flowing pools of the Buffalo are nationally renowned for trophy smallmouth bass. Camping facilities and canoe rentals are available at Buffalo Point Campgrounds, 17 miles south of Yellville. Guided float trips are provided by *Buffalo River Fishing Resort*, Yellville 72687, and *Hedge Canoes*, Ponca 72670. Write to the Ozark

Mountain Region, P.O. Box 668, Harrison 72601, for a complete listing of outfitters and fishing guides serving the Buffalo. A detailed *Buffalo River Canoeing Guide* may be obtained for $1 from the Ozark Society, Box 2914, Little Rock 72203. For detailed camping and river travel info, write: Superintendent, Buffalo National River, P.O. Box 1173, Harrison 72601.

Rustic vacation lodging on the river is provided by *Buffalo Point Concession*, Rt. A, Box 214, Yellville 72687. Guided backpacking and canoe trips are provided by the *Buffalo Outdoor Center*, from two locations on the Buffalo: Ponca 72670 (501–861–5590) and Hasty 72640 (501–429–6433).

The scenic Mulberry River, one of the few remaining free-flowing rivers in the state, rises high in the Ozarks and flows southwest to its confluence with the Arkansas River. The Mulberry is one of the best smallmouth bass rivers in the state and is characterized by quiet gin-clear pools interspersed by numerous shoals and rapids. Canoeists who plan an overnight float trip down the river should avoid camping on islands and should have easy access to high ground, because of the "quick-rise" nature of the river. Camping facilities are available at the Shores Lake, Redding, and Wolf Pen recreation areas. A free *Mulberry River Map* may be obtained by writing: Forest Supervisor, Ozark National Forest, Box 340, Russellville 72801.

A full-color *Ozark National Forest Map* (50¢) showing forest roads, trails, campgrounds, points of interest, ranger stations, trail shelters, and recreation sites may be obtained from the forest supervisor's office (address above).

Access & Outfitting Centers

The forest is reached via U.S. 65, 64, 62, and 71, and Interstate 40. Accommodations, supplies, guides, and outfitters are available at Ozark, Clarksville, Russellville, Harrison, Van Buren, Norfork, and Fayetteville.

ILLINOIS
ENCYCLOPEDIA

Accommodations—Family Vacation Lodges & Resorts

For information about Illinois's wide variety of motels, hotels, and fishing, hunting, and family vacation lodges, write: Division of Tourism, 222 S. College St., Springfield 62704. For information and reservations for state park cabins and lodges, write: Giant City State Park, Makanda 62958, phone (618) 457-4921); Illinois Beach State Park, Zion 60099, phone (312) 244-2400; Pere Marquette State Park, Box 325, Grafton 62037, phone (618) 786-3351; Starved Rock State Park, Box 116, Utica 61373, phone (815) 667-4211; and White Pines Forest State Park, RR1, Mount Morris 61054, phone (815) 946-3817.

Campgrounds & State Recreation Areas

Illinois provides many opportunities for campers to enjoy the beauties of the state's natural areas. Campers should obtain the free booklet *Illinois Camping Guide,* available from: Division of Tourism, 222 S. College St., Springfield 62704. This publication lists and describes Illinois's major camping areas, organizing them by region. The camping areas are presented in chart form, noting the season open, number of campsites, facilities, and other information available for each area.

A useful free brochure, *Illinois Department of Conservation Recreation Areas,* provides a handy chart listing state parks, historical memorials, conservation areas, and state forests, and the facilities available at each area. Each area is location-keyed to a map. Camping permits must be obtained upon arrival at each campsite from the manager or nightwatchperson. Camping is limited to 14 nights. Boat rentals in some areas are in operation only during the summer or on weekends; and in some areas, such as refuge areas, motors are not allowed at certain times of the year. It is advisable to check with the management of the area you're planning to visit in advance. For additional information on state recreation areas and campgrounds, write to: Information/Education Section, Dept. of Conservation, 605 State Office Bldg., Springfield 62706.

Canoeing & Quality Fishing Waters—Maps, Guides, & Outfitters

Illinois's major canoeable waterways, several of which were originally traveled by the French-Canadian voyageurs, are described in the 64-page *Illinois Canoeing Guide* available free from the Dept. of Conservation, 605 State Office Bldg., Springfield 62706. The major routes—including the Cache, Des Plaines, Embarras, Fox, Illinois, Kankakee, Iroquois, Mackinaw, Pecatonica, Rock, Sangamon, Vermilion, and Spoon rivers—are presented in detail, with maps accompanying each route, indicating access, bridges, dams, campsite locations, points of interest, and locations of state parks. There is also a useful equipment checklist.

The historic Fox Valley Canoe Trail between Yorkville and Wedron in northeast Illinois is the state's most popular canoe route, flowing past caves, springs, numerous islands, exotic plants, and a relic glacial forest. The major features along this scenic wild river include Old Mill, Glass House, the Slooper Settlement of Norway, Dells of the Fox, Sank Ford where Lincoln is believed to have camped, and the Indian Creek Massacre site. The Kankakee River, traveled by La Salle into the Illinois country in 1683, is one of the state's top-ranked fishing streams and canoe routes. The Kankakee flows over a limestone bed past bayous, islands, canyons, caves, rapids, and large beds of mallow and lotus. The "Big" Vermilion River, famous for its spring run of striped bass, is one of the best whitewater streams in the state. The beautiful, unspoiled Mackinaw River flows past high bluffs and the Bloomington Moraine—a remnant of the Wisconsin Ice Age. The scenic, gravel-bottomed Kishwaukee River flows through wooded hills and meadows with good fishing for walleye, smallmouth bass, and northern pike. The Sangamon—the first Illinois stream to be dedicated as a canoe trail—is a beautiful, winding woodland stream that flows through the heart of Lincolnland. The 70-mile stretch known as the "Lincoln Heritage Canoe Trail" flows past the sternwheeler *Talisman*—a replica of the one young Lincoln once piloted down the river. The majestic Rock River—known as the "Hudson of the West"—flows for 150 miles through Black Hawk country past many islands, rolling hills, and pine-clad bluffs. The Cache River, named by the French-Canadian voyageurs, flows through towering forests past numerous islands, ancient Indian campsites, beaver dams, cypress swamps, cliff and fossil beds. Overnight campers on the Illinois canoe trails should be alert for rattlesnakes, copperheads, and cottonmouths.

The Chicagoland Canoe Base, 4017 N. Narragansett Ave., Chicago 60634, phone (312) 777-1489, offers complete canoe rental and trip outfitting services. It also offers free *Chicagoland Canoe Trails* and *Historic Fox Valley Canoe Trail* guides, a *Des Plaines River Marathon Canoe Map* (50¢), *Midwest Canoe Livery Guide* ($1.50), *Illinois Country Canoe Trails, Vol. I:* Fox, Mazon, Vermilion, and Little Vermilion ($1.25), and *Illinois Country Canoe Trails, Vol. II:* Du Page, Kankakee, Des Plaines, and Aux Sable ($1.25). Add 25¢ per copy to cover postage and handling.

The major waterways of the Inland Empire are shown on the following full-color large-scale U.S. Geological Survey Maps. *Big Muddy River:* Ashley, Carbondale, Christopher, Crab Orchard Lake, De Soto, Du Quoin, Gorham, Herrin, Ina, Neelys Landing, Murphysboro, Oraville, West Frankfort 7.5, Wolf Lake; *Cache River:* Anna, Cache, Cairo, Cypress, Dongola, Karnak, Makanda, Mount Pleasant, Pulaski, Tamms, Vienna; *Des Plaines River:* Berwyn, Channahon, Elwood, Englewood, Juliet, Palos Park, Romeoville, Sag Bridge; *Embarras River:* Birds, Chauncey, Greenup, Landes, Lawrenceville, Newton, Oakland, Oblong S, Stoy, Thomasboro, Toledo, Urbana 7.5, Villa Grove; *Fox River:* Aurora N, Aurora S, Barrington, Crystal Lake, Elgin 7.5, Fox Lake, Geneva 7.5, Newark, Ottawa 7.5, Plano, Serena, Sheridan, Wauconda, Wedron; *Kankakee River:* Bourbonnais, Gilman, Herscher, Kankakee, Wilmington 7.5; *Kickapoo River:* Hanna

City, Oak Hill, Peoria W; *Little Wabash River:* Albion NW, Carmi, Clay City, Edgewood, Emma, Enterprise, Flora 7.5, Golden Gate, Mount Erie, New Haven, Sailor Springs; *Mackinaw River:* Delavan N, Hopedale, Mackinaw, Morton, Pekin, South Pekin; *Rock River:* Coal Valley, Dixon, Erie, Green Rock, Kishwaukee, Milan, Morrison, Oregon, Port Byron, Prophetstown, Rockford N, Rockford S, South Beloit, Sterling; *Sangamon River:* Argenta, Athens, Beardstown, Bement, Biggs, Chandlerville, Decatur 7.5, Easton, Gibson City, Mahomet, Mechanicsburg, Monticello, Niantic, Petersburg, Rising, Salisbury, Springfield E, Springfield W, Taylorsville; *Skillet River:* Boylestown, Carmi, Enfield, Wayne City; *Spoon River:* Avon, Duncan Mills, Havana, Lewistown, Smithfield; *Vermilion River:* Cullom, Flanagan, La Salle, Pontiac, Sibley, Streator; *Fox Chain O' Lakes:* Fox Lake, Antioch, Wauconda, Grayslake; *Crab Orchard Lake:* De Soto, Herrin, Carbondale, Crab Orchard Lake, Marion; *Devil's Kitchen Lake:* Lick Creek, Crab Orchard Lake; *Strip Mines Country:* Collison, Royal.

Fishing & Hunting in Illinois

The heavily populated Inland Empire, as the state is popularly known, offers some surprisingly good, if limited, fishing and hunting opportunities. This river-slashed, intensely farmed and settled plains state contains 56,400 miles bordered on the north and northeast by the glacial uplands of Wisconsin and Lake Michigan; on the east and southeast by Indiana and the Wabash and Ohio rivers; on the west by Iowa, Missouri, and the Mississippi River; and on the south by Kentucky and the Ohio River. The great Mississippi Flyway has long made the state famous for its Canada goose and duck hunting. Inland some excellent goose and duck shooting is found on crop fields, marshes, lakes, and river bottomlands. The scenic Shawnee National Forest and state forests and wildlife areas offer good, but crowded, hunting in season for whitetail deer and upland game birds, as well as cottontails, squirrels, crows, red and gray fox, raccoon, and woodchuck.

Lake Michigan Trophy Fish

The state's premier trophy fishery is Lake Michigan—the sixth largest lake in the world, 22,400 square miles in surface area. The Illinois portion of the lake takes in 7% of its total surface area and offers top-ranked fishing for brown trout up to 28 pounds, brook trout up to 4 pounds, rainbow trout in the 20-pound-plus class, tiger trout and rod-busting Atlantic, coho, and Chinook salmon, as well as lake trout, yellow perch. Lake Michigan has a relatively smooth, gently sloping bottom in its southern region and an irregular bottom, with numerous scenic islands in the northern regions. Salmon were first introduced, unsuccessfully, into the lake between 1873 and 1880. The recent, spectacularly successful introduction into Lake Michigan began when the Michigan Department of Natural Resources obtained 1 million coho salmon eggs from Oregon in 1964. The fish were hatched and reared in a Michigan hatchery for 18 months until they reached smolt size and were released into the Big Huron River in the Upper Peninsula, and the Platte River and Bear Creek in the Lower Peninsula. In the fall of 1966 several thousand coho jacks ranging from 2 to 7 pounds returned to their parent streams. The following fall, 35% of the original stock returned to spawn and complete their life cycle. The results of this first spawning run have become a modern legend, with coho and Chinook salmon growing to record weights on the enormous alewife population found throughout the lake and its tributaries. Illinois's Lake Michigan hot spots include the Great Lakes Naval Station, Belmont, Waukegan, Diversey Harbor, Jackson Harbor, Winnetka, Chicago, Illinois Beach, Poevell Park, Kellog Ditch, Roosevelt Park, Burnham Harbor, and Highland Park areas. Anyone planning a Lake

Michigan fishing trip should read *The Complete Guide to Fishing the Great Lakes* ($5.95, 218 pp.), published by Great Lakes Living Press, 3634 W. 216th St., Matteson 60443.

For info on daily condition and salmon fishing on Lake Michigan, call the *Salmon Unlimited Hotline* (312) 267–6800. The useful 47-page guide, *Illinois Fishery of Lake Michigan,* shows boat and bank fishing areas, rigs, launch sites, and contains charter boat info. It may be obtained free upon request from: Dept. of Conservation, Division of Fisheries, 605 State Office Bldg., Springfield 62706. For info on Lake Michigan trout and salmon charters, write or call: Chicago Sportfishing Assn., 25 E. Washington, Suite 823, Chicago 60602 (312–922–1100) or Waukegan Charter Assn., 207 Water St., Waukegan 60085 (312–244–3474).

Inland Lakes & Streams

While not as dramatic as the spectacular Great Lakes trophy salmon and trout fishery, the lakes and streams of the Inland Empire provide often excellent fishing for largemouth and smallmouth bass, walleye, northern pike, crappie, sunfish, and a few trout. The glacially formed waters of Fox Chain O' Lakes in the northeast region of the state—comprised of Fox, Long, Nippersink, Pistakee, Grass, Petite, Bluff, Marie, Katherine, and Channel lakes—hold walleye, northern pike, channel catfish, panfish, bass, and northern pike. Marie Lake produced the state record 22-pound 12-ounce northern pike. Beautiful Grass Lake, with its large beds of snow-white lotus lilies, is one of the chain's best producers of largemouth bass. Several northern Illinois rivers—among them the Rock, Kishwaukee, Sugar, Coon, Du Page, Fox, Kankakee, Iroquois, and Vermilion rivers and Big Indian Creek—provide fishing for smallmouth bass, walleye, yellow perch, and channel and flathead catfish. Cliff-lined Apple River in the rugged uplands of northwest Illinois is one of the state's top rainbow and brown trout streams. The major fishing waters in central Illinois include the primitive Spoon River—immortalized in Edgar Lee Masters's *Spoon River Anthology*—the club-owned Strip Mines lakes, Sangamon River, La Moine Creek, Kickapoo River, Salt Creek, Middle Fork of the Vermilion River, and the wild and scenic Mackinaw River. The fishing is primarily for smallmouth bass, walleye, and catfish. The Little Vermilion River, a fine limestone smallmouth bass stream, flows past numerous cliffs and Troy Grove—the birthplace of Wild Bill Hickok. The rugged backcountry lakes and streams of southern Illinois, known as "Little Egypt," provide the state's top trophy largemouth bass fishing. Little Grassy, Devil's Kitchen, and Crab

Orchard lakes in the Crab Orchard National Wildlife Refuge, situated in the heart of the Shawnee National Forest region, provide consistently good fishing for largemouth bass up to 6, 7, and 8 pounds in the numerous shallow submerged timber areas. Other productive lakes in the Shawnee Hills region include Kincaid, Horseshoe, Dutchman, Lake of Egypt, Glendale, and Glen O. Jones Lake in the Wildcat Hills country. The rugged Cache and Big Muddy (Aux Vases) rivers are the region's top streams. The giant navigation pools, sloughs, backwater lakes, and weed-filled bays of the island-dotted, meandering Mississippi River provide often excellent fishing for lunker bass, crappie, walleye to 10 pounds, and giant catfish.

The fishing potential of Illinois lakes and streams is highlighted by the state record fish, as compiled by the Department of Conservation.

ILLINOIS RECORD FISH

	Lb.-oz.	Place	Year
Largemouth bass	13–1	Stone Quarry Lake	1976
Smallmouth bass	5–15½	Kankakee River	1974
Striped bass	19–6	Saline River	1975
Muskellunge	24–12	Spring Lake	1977
Northern pike	22–12	Marie Lake	1976
Brook trout	4–1	Lake Michigan	1970
Brown trout	28–8	Lake Michigan	1975
Rainbow trout	22–1	Lake Michigan	1976
Tiger trout	8–12½	Lake Michigan	1977
Atlantic salmon	6–6	Lake Michigan	1977
Coho salmon	20–9	Lake Michigan	1972
Chinook salmon	37	Lake Michigan	1976
Walleye	14	Kankakee River	1961
Yellow perch	2–8¾	Arrowhead Club Lake	1974
Black crappie	4–8	Rend Lake	1976
White crappie	4–7	Farm Pond	1973
White bass	3–13½	Baldwin Lake	1974
Spotted bass	6–10	Charleston Stone Co. Lake	1972
Rock bass	1–9	Strip Mine Lake	1968
Bluegill	2–10	Strip Mine Lake	1963
Blue catfish	65	Alton Lake	1956
Channel catfish	28–6	Farm Pond	1976
Flathead catfish	51	Hennepin Canal	1950
Sturgeon	57	Mississippi River	1971
Alligator gar	157	Mississippi River	1944
Buffalo	48	Mississippi River	1936

Single copies of the following booklets may be obtained free upon request from the Dept. of Conservation, Division of Fisheries, 605 State Office Bldg., Springfield 62706: *Carlyle Lake Fishing Guide, Lake Shelbyville Fishing Guide, Rend Lake Fishing Guide, Fishing the Mississippi, Fishing the Rock, Pond Fish & Fishing, Fishing the Kankakee, Fishing the Big Muddy.* The following brochures may be obtained free from the Southern Illinois Tourism Council, 2209 W. Main, Marion 62959: *Southern Illinois Lake Guide* and *Recreation Map of Southern Illinois.*

An *Illinois Fishing Information* brochure (which contains regulations, seasons, and a listing of state-managed public fishing areas and facilities) and *Illinois Hunting Information* brochure (with regulations,

seasons, and public hunting areas) may be obtained free from: Dept. of Conservation, 605 State Office Bldg., Springfield 62706.

Highways—Recreation & Scenic Routes Map

Anyone planning on driving in Illinois should have a copy of the free *Illinois Highway Map*. It can be obtained by writing: Division of Tourism, 222 S. College St., Springfield 62704. It indicates all roads and highways, route markers, access points, and junctions. Also shown on the map are the Great River Road, Lincoln Heritage Trail, state parks or conservation areas, rest areas, airports, and other points of interest. A location index of cities and villages and points of interest is provided, as well as a chart of recreation areas showing facilities available in each, and its location on the map. A mileage distance chart showing distances between principal towns and cities is also included.

Lewis and Clark Trail & National Scenic Trails System

The National Trails System Act passed by Congress in 1968 provided funds for the establishment of the Pacific Crest National Scenic Trail and Appalachian National Scenic Trail. In addition, it called for the study and construction of the following scenic and historic trails along ancient Indian, exploration, fur trade, and pioneer routes: *Lewis & Clark Trail*, from Wood River, Illinois, to the Pacific, following the epic 1805–1806 routes of the Lewis & Clark Expedition; *Continental Divide Trail*, a 3,100-mile trail extending from Glacier National Park in Montana south along the Great Divide to the Mexican border; *Old Cattle Trails of the Southwest*, extending from San Antonio, Texas, for 800 miles through Oklahoma to Fort Scott, Kansas, including the Chisholm Trail; *North Country Trail*, stretching from the Appalachian Trail in Vermont for 3,200 miles across the continent to the Lewis & Clark Trail in North Dakota; *Oregon Trail*, extending from Independence, Missouri, for 2,000 miles to Fort Vancouver, Washington; *Santa Fe Trail*, stretching for 800 miles from Independence, Missouri, to Santa Fe, New Mexico; *Long Trail*, an existing trail (see Vermont) which follows the Crest of the Green Mountains for 255 miles from the Massachusetts border northward through Vermont to the Quebec border; *Pacific Northwest Trail*, extending for 1,000 miles from the Continental Divide in Glacier National Park westward through several of the nation's most spectacular wilderness areas to Washington's Olympic Mountains and the Pacific Ocean; *Nez Perce Trail*, extending from the vicinity of Wallowa Lake, Oregon, to the Bear Paw Mountains in Montana; *Indian Nations Trail*, extending from the Red River in Oklahoma approximately 200 miles northward through the former Indian nations to the Kansas border; *Daniel Boone Trail*, stretching from Statesville, North Carolina, to Fort Boonesborough, Kentucky; *Florida Trail*, extending north from Everglades National Park through Big Cypress Swamp and the Kissime Prairie to the Blackwater River State Forest (400 miles of this trail have been built; see Florida); *Bartram Trail*, extending from North Carolina to Mississippi; *Desert Trail*, extending from Idaho to the Mexican border; *Dominguez-Escalante Trail*, extending 2,000 miles northward from Santa Fe, New Mexico, along the San Juan, Dolores, Gunnison, and White rivers in Colorado, to Utah Lake, and southward to Arizona and returning to Santa Fe following the route of the 1776 Spanish expedition; *Natchez Trace Trail*, from Nashville, Tennessee for 600 miles to Natchez, Mississippi; *Gold Rush Trails* in Alaska; *Mormon Battalion Trail*, extending 2,000 miles from Mount Pisgah, Iowa, through Kansas, Colorado, New Mexico, and Arizona to California; *El Camino Real Trail*, from St. Augustine for 20 miles along the

St. Johns River to San Mateo, Florida; *Kittanning Trail* in Pennsylvania (q.v.).

For additional information about these proposed national scenic trails and the free booklet *National Scenic & Recreation Trails*, write: Information Office, Bureau of Outdoor Recreation, Dept. of the Interior, Washington, D.C. 20240.

Shawnee National Forest

This 240,000-acre reserve is made up of rolling hills, lakes, and towering limestone bluffs, stretching across southern Illinois from the Mississippi River to the Ohio. The major features include the La Rue-Pine Hills Ecological Area, Oakwood Bottoms Greentree Reservoir, Garden of the Gods, Rimrock Forest Trail, Bell Smith Springs, Lusk Creek Wild Area, Lake of Egypt, Crab Orchard National Wildlife Refuge, Kincaid, Devil's Kitchen, and Little Grassy lakes, and prehistoric stone forts and Indian burial mounds. The forest is an outstanding fishing, hunting, and camping area. Game animals include whitetail deer, drumming grouse, red fox, and raccoon.

The La Rue-Pine Hills Wilderness is one of the outstanding hiking and natural areas in the Midwest, embracing 19,000 acres of deep, forested ravines, hill prairie, wet pin-oak flatlands, springfield swamps, and sheer limestone river bluffs in the northwestern section of the Shawnee National Forest. Wildlife includes whitetail deer, bobcat, red fox, raccoon, and beaver. The 15,000-acre Lusk Creek Wild Area is located in the Greater Shawnee Hills in the eastern section of the Shawnee National Forest, embracing the spectacular Indian Kitchen of Lusk Creek Canyon. The area, renowned for its natural beauty, is an outstanding hiking and hunting region.

An informative free booklet, *The Shawnee Is Camping*, is available from: Division of Tourism, 222 S. College St., Springfield 62704. It provides information on facilities in each of the forest's many recreation areas—picnicking, camping, boating, hiking, etc. Small maps for the main areas are shown, indicating the locations of campgrounds, bodies of water, hiking trails, etc. Bell Smith Springs, Garden of the

Gods, Illinois Iron Furnace, Pale of Egypt, Lake Glendale, Ohio River, Pine Hills, Pounds Hollow, and Tower Rock are presented in this manner; the rest of the areas are noted in chart form.

Visitors to the Shawnee National Forest should obtain a copy of the *Shawnee National Forest Map*, available for 50¢ from: Supervisor's Office, Shawnee National Forest, Harrisburg 62946. This excellent map of the entire Shawnee area shows all roads and highways, boundaries, trails, mines, recreation sites with and without camping facilities, horse trails, boat-launching sites, ranger stations, and other points of interest. A chart of the various recreation areas and facilities provided in each is also included. The map is attractively illustrated with full-color photographs and some information on the various recreational opportunities offered in the forest.

The forest is reached via U.S. Highways 45 and 51 and Illinois routes 1, 3, 34, 127, 144, 145, 146, and 151. Overnight accommodations, supplies, and equipment rentals are available at Anna, Cairo, Carbondale, Harrisburg, Metropolis, and Murphysboro; also, Paducah, Kentucky, and St. Louis, Missouri.

The Shawnee National Forest is shown on the Paducah, Kentucky, U.S. Geological Survey Map, scale 1:250,000; *La Rue-Pine Hills Wilderness:* Cobden, Jonesboro, Ware, Wolf Lake; *Lusk Creek Wild Area:* Brownfield 7.5, Eddyville, Harrisburg 7.5, Herod, Rudement, Shelterville, Waltersburg.

Sport Fishing Adventures & North American Travel Service

PanAngling Travel Service, one of the nation's finest outdoor recreation travel firms, matches the fisherman with the type of fishing he desires. The firm arranges all air travel, lodging and guide service, and provides its clients with recommended lists of clothing, tackle, and detailed information about the specific area he plans to visit.

PanAngling Travel Service offers a wide spectrum of different fishing trips available throughout the world. While the firm is heavily involved with Canada and Central America, its scope is almost worldwide. To give you an idea of their range here are some species and fishing trips available through the services of PanAngling: *Black Marlin:* Cairns, Australia, Club Pacifico of Panama, and Tropic Star (also Panama); *Striped Marlin:* Salinas, Ecuador, Mazatlan, Mexico, Baja California; *Pacific Sailfish:* Club Pacifico of Panama, Trop Star, and Costa Rica's Bahia Pez Vila; *Atlantic Sailfish:* Cozumel, Mexico; *Pacific Blue Marlin:* Kona, Hawaii; *Wahoo:* Club Pacifico of Panama, Bahia Pez Vela; *Tarpon & Snook:* several camps on East Coast of Costa Rica; *Bonefish:* Boca Paila, Mexico, Turnefee Islands in Belize, Deep Water Cay Club in Bahamas, Mexico; *Trophy Rainbow Trout:* Alaskan camps, North Island of New Zealand, Argentina; *Brown Trout:* South Island of New Zealand and Argentina; *Trophy Brook Trout:* Minipi Waters of Labrador, several Quebec Rivers, and Argentina; *Arctic Char:* Umiakovik Camp in Labrador, Tree River and Victoria Island in Canada's Northwest Territories, and Ilkalu Lodge in northern Quebec; *Northern Pike:* throughout Canada, but Brabant Lodge in N.W.T. among the best; *Arctic Grayling:* numerous Canadian waters, particularly Kasba Lake Lodge in N.W.T.; *Lake Trout:* throughout northern Canada, particularly Great Bear Lake in N.W.T.; *Atlantic Salmon:* Alta River in Norway, Laxa i Kjos in Iceland, and the Restigouche in Quebec; *Smallmouth Bass:* Rainy Lake (with Fontana's Houseboats) and other lakes in Ontario.

PanAngling caters to fishermen who are interested in fly fishing for relatively small species, such as trout or grayling, and to those anglers who like to tussle with big marlin for several hours. Some clients like to fish for exotic species in remote areas regardless of whether sport is good or not, while others are interested in a great deal of action. For detailed trip brochures, rates, and travel planning information, write: *PanAngling Travel Service*, 180 N. Michigan Ave., Chicago 60601 (phone: 312–263–0328).

Accommodations— Family Vacation Resorts

For complete information on where to stay in Indiana, send for the free 124-page booklet *Indiana Camping & Outdoor Recreation Guide*. This publication lists and describes camping areas and resorts, giving locations, facilities available, length of the season, rates, and of course, addresses and phone numbers. Each area is location-keyed to a map on the inside front cover of the book. The booklet and additional information may be obtained from: Dept. of Commerce, Rm. 336, State House, Indianapolis 46204. Several major resorts in Hoosier country include *Broomsage Ranch*, North Vernon 47265, phone (812) 346-2246; *Lake Manitou Resort & Marine*, Rochester 46975, phone (219) 223–6217; *Lukens State Resort*, Box 141, Roann 46974, phone (317) 833–2778; *Twin Mills Resort*, RR3, Howe 46746, phone (219) 562–8969; *Abe Martin Lodge* (Brown County State Park), P.O. Box 116, Nashville 47448; *Clifty Inn & Motor Lodge* (Clifty Falls State Park), P.O. Box 443, Madison 47250; *Canyon Inn* (McCormick's Creek State Park), P.O. Box 71, Spencer 47460; *Spring Mill Inn* (Spring Mill State Park), RR2, P.O. Box 127, Mitchell 47446; *Turkey Run Inn*, Marshall 47859, phone (812) 597–2211; *Sycamore Spring Farms*, Box 224, Churubusco 46723, phone (219) 693–3603.

Camping & Backpacking

Indiana's national and state forests, parks, and wildlife management areas provide excellent scenic and primitive camping, hiking, and backpacking areas. Several of the major state-managed areas include the Pike State Forest, Patoka Fish and Wildlife Area, Green-Sullivan State Forest, Starve Hollow State Forest, Pigeon River Fish and Wildlife Area, and Salamonie River and Yellowwood state forests. Other scenic camping and backpacking areas include the large tracts of virgin forest and deep, rock-walled canyons and gorges of the Turkey Run area; the dense stands of pines, juniper, blueberry thickets, shifting dunes of the famous Indiana Dunes on Lake Michigan; the Chain O' Lakes area with its nine natural connecting lakes; the ravines, sinkholes, abandoned quarries, and deep stone gullies of the McCormick's Creek area; and scenic woodlands, lakes, streams, and rolling hills of the Brown County backcountry.

A comprehensive listing of state camping areas and facilities is contained in the 124-page *Indiana Camping & Outdoor Recreation Guide*, available free upon request from: Dept. of Commerce, Rm. 336, State House, Indianapolis 46204. Free maps of Indiana state forest reserves and wildlife management areas may be obtained from: Dept. of Natural Resources, Indianapolis 46204.

Canoe Trails—Maps & Outfitters

Several of the Hoosier State's streams and rivers—including the historic Tippecanoe, Iroquois, Kankakee, Fawn, St. Joseph, Elkhart, Salamonie, Wild Cat, Deer, Wabash, Eel, and White rivers—provide excellent scenic canoeing and float fishing opportunities. Many of the waterways are rich in historic Indian and exploration lore. The Eel River, near the town of Hoosier Highlands, served as a common hunting ground for the Indian tribes in the area. Old legends have it that they panned gold here from the highland streams. The river was called *Shakamak* by the Delaware Indians and *Kena Pocomoco* by the Miami—both meaning "eel" or "snakefish." The Kankakee, used by the French explorer La Salle and the voyageurs as a connecting waterway between the Mississippi and Great Lakes, is derived from the Indian word *A-ki-ki*, meaning "wolf." Near Argos, on the south bank

INDIANA
ENCYCLOPEDIA

of the famed Tippecanoe, is the site of the Chippewanuing Indian village, one of the last of the Potawatomi Indian villages. Paddlers with an interest in Indian history and lore should send for the 24 × 36-inch *Historic Indian Map* (Publication 122), available for 50¢ from: Dept. of Natural Resources, Map Sales, Rm. 604, State Office Bldg., Indianapolis 46204.

If you are interested in renting canoes and related equipment, contact *Whitewater Valley Canoe Rental*, P.O. Box 2, Brookville 47012, or RR1, Metamora 47030, 24-hour telephone (317) 647–5434, which runs many canoe trips of varying lengths through the Whitewater River and historic Whitewater Canal. The firm also rents and sells equipment, and arranges field trips and outdoor recreation programs for schools and groups. *Clements Canoes,* 911 Wayne Ave., Crawfordsville 47933, phone (317) 362–6272, on weekends (317) 362–9864, runs canoe trips on scenic Sugar Creek, in the Turkey Run backcountry, which flows through deep rock-walled canyons and gorges. Call or write for free brochure describing the route along the creek, as well as information on rates and put-in and pickup service. Canoe rental and passenger pickup service, and free camping for canoeing patrons, are provided by *Turkey Run District Canoe Rental,* 311 W. Ohio St., Rockville 47872, phone (812) 569–6705. For additional info on Indiana canoe rental services write for the *Midwest Canoe Livery Guide* ($1.50), available from: Chicagoland Canoe Base, 4019 N. Narragansett Ave., Chicago, IL 60634. Include 25¢ for postage and handling.

A 100-page *Indiana Canoe Guide* ($2) providing complete details on the state's 21 top-ranked canoe trails, may be obtained from the Division of State Parks, Dept. of Natural Resources, 608 State Office Bldg., Indianapolis 46204.

Indiana's major canoe routes and float streams are shown on the following large-scale U.S. Geological Survey Maps. *Eel River:* Churubusco, Columbia City, Huntertown, Laud, Logansport, North Manchester N, North Manchester S, Peru, Roann, South Whitley E, South Whitley W, Twelve Mile; *Elkhart River,* including Lake Wawasee: Elkhart, Goshen, Lake Wawasee, Ligonier, Millersburg, North Webster; *Fawn River,* including Snow, Pleasant, and James lakes: Angola, Bronson, Burr Oak, Kinder Hook, Orland; *Iroquois River:* Goodland, Kentland, McCoysburg, Mount Ayr, Parr, Rensselaer, Sheldon; *Kankakee River:* Demotte, English Lake, Hamlet, Hebron, Illiana Heights, Kingsford Heights, Knox, Kouts, San Pierre, Schneider, Shelby, Wheatfield; *Pigeon River,* including George and James lakes: Angola, Angola W, Ashley, Lagrange, Mongo, Orland, Shipshewana; *St. Joseph River:* Bristol, Elkhart, Middlebury, Osceola, South Bend E, South Bend W, Topeka; *Tippecanoe River,* including Tippecanoe and Webster lake headwaters: Argos, Bass Lake, Brookston, Buffalo, Burket, Culver, Kewanna, Leesburg, Mentone, Monticello N, Monticello S, North Webster, Pershing, Rochester.

Fishing & Hunting in the Hoosier State

From the scenic woodlands of the northern lake country through the central agricultural plain to the rugged hills, shard ridges, rounded knolls, and waterfalls of the southern lowlands, the Hoosier State offers some surprisingly varied fishing and hunting opportunities. The state-managed forests and fish and game areas, and the Hoosier National Forest lands provide hunting in season for bobwhite quail, pheasant, ruffed grouse, whitetail deer, cottontails, fox and gray squirrels, red fox, raccoons, and fair hunting in wetland areas for a few Canada geese and ducks. The major public hunting areas include the Pigeon River, Jasper-Pulaski, Kingsbury, Winamac, Atterbury, Patoka, Momoe, Hovey Lake, Springs Valley, Brush Creek, Willow Slough, Kankakee, and La Salle state fish and game areas and the Yellowwood, Salamonie River, Clark, Pike, Harrison-Crawford, Ferdinand, Jackson-Washington, Frances Slocum, Martin, Monroe-Morgan, Owen-Putnam, and Greene-Sullivan state forest reserves.

Lake Michigan Trophy Fish

The vast, wave-capped waters of Lake Michigan in the extreme western corner of the northern lake region are the state's premier trophy fishery. More than 50,000 coho and Chinook salmon, steelhead trout, brown trout, and lake trout are caught along Indiana's Lake Michigan shoreline each year. Brown trout and lake trout are stocked directly in the lake, while coho and Chinook salmon and steelhead trout from

the Mixsawbah State Hatchery are introduced into Trail Creek and the east branch of the Little Calumet River. The giant, state record 18-pound 13-ounce brown trout was caught in Trail Creek in 1975. Fishing for coho from 4 to 10 pounds and Chinook from 12 to 30 pounds and over is excellent in the tributary streams during the fall spawning run. Most of the steelhead are in the streams by October, where they remain until February or March of the following year. Although fewer fish are caught during the fall than in the spring, their average size is much larger. For additional information, write for the free publication *Fishing Indiana's Lake Michigan Shoreline,* available from: Dept. of Natural Resources, Indianapolis 46204. A wealth of useful information is contained in the 218-page *The Compleat Guide to Fishing the Great Lakes,* available for $5.95 (include 50¢ postage and handling) from: Great Lakes Living Press, 3634 W. 216th St., Matteson, IL 60443.

Northern Lake Country

The state's premier lake and stream fishing for holdover rainbow and brown trout, northern pike, walleye, largemouth bass, crappie, and huge catfish is found in the northern lake country with its hundreds of small lakes, ponds, and streams surrounded by low rolling hills left by retreating glaciers. The swift flowing waters of the historic Tippecanoe River, once considered one of the top smallmouth bass streams in the nation, yields smallmouth bass, northern pike, rock and white bass, and channel and flathead catfish up to trophy weights. In the scenic lake-dotted northeast region are several of the state's top trout and bass streams and lakes, including famous Gage Lake, Lake James, Oliver Lake, Pigeon River, Lake Hamilton, and Fawn, Emma, Little Elkhart, Elkhart, and St. Joseph rivers. Deep, clear Lake Gage yielded the state record 13-pound 5-ounce rainbow and 3-pound 15-ounce brook trout. Other premier lakes and streams in the northern lake country include the Indian Lakes, Pine Creek, and Hudson, Koontz, Freeman, Wolf, Flint, Pine, Stone, Clear, Ball, Snow, Troxall, Fox, Fish, Story, Flatbelly, Waldron, Chain O' Lakes, Wawasee, Syracuse, Bixler, and Tippecanoe lakes. The Kankakee River yields northern pike and walleye up to record weights.

Central and Southern Lakes & Streams

The major streams in the central region of Indiana—a great level till plain of deep glacial deposits of soil and gravel—and the east-to-west succession of lowlands and uplands in the southern region are the White River and its tributaries: the Wabash, Eel, West Fork White River, East Fork White River, Blue River, Patoka River, and Mascatatuck River tributaries. The fishing is primarily for largemouth bass, white crappie, rock bass, yellow perch, channel and flathead catfish, a few walleye and smallmouth bass, as well as for freshwater drum, buffalo, and the primitive paddlefish (also known as the spoonbill). A few small muskellunge up to 12 pounds are taken from the Blue River and its tributaries. The major lakes in the central and southern region include Hominy Ridge, Prairie Creek, Mississinewa, Loon, Salamonie, Palestine, Mansfield Reservoir, Rockville, Brookville Reservoir, Waveland, Whitewater, Manlove, Monroe, Dogwood, West Boggs Creek Reservoir, Wampler Pit, West Twin Pit, Island Pit, Indian, Celina, Ferdinand, Tipsaw, Saddle, Versailles, Cypress, Grouse Ridge, Greensburg Reservoir, Hardy, Crosley Fish & Wildlife Area, Clark State Forest, and Starve Hollow. Yellowwood Lake in the scenic Yellowwood State Forest east of Bloomington in Brown County and the Willow Slough State Fish & Wildlife Area north of Morocco in Newton County are two of the state's top lunker largemouth areas.

The potential and diversity of the Hoosier lakes and streams are illustrated by the state record fish caught on rod and reel, compiled by the Department of Natural Resources.

INDIANA RECORD FISH

	Lb.-oz.	Place	Year
Largemouth bass	11–11	Ferdinand Reservoir	1968
Smallmouth bass	6–8	Rush County Stream	1970
Northern pike	26–8	Lagrange Co. Lake	1972
Walleye	14–4	Kankakee River	1974
Muskellunge	12	Little Blue River	1965
Steelhead	20–11	Lake Michigan	1972
Rainbow trout	13–5	Lake Gage	1973
Brown trout	18–13	Trail Creek	1975
Brook trout	3–15	Lake Gage	1973
Lake trout	21	Lake Michigan	1975
Coho salmon	20–12	Lake Michigan	1972
Chinook salmon	37–4	Lake Michigan	1974
White bass	4–3	Lake Freeman	1965
Spotted bass	5–1	Howard Co. Lake	1975
Rock bass	3	Sugar Creek	1969
Bluegill	3–4	Greene Co. Pond	1972
Crappie	4–7	Posey Co. Pond	1965
Sauger	5	Wabash River	1964
Yellow perch	2–1	Crooked Lake	1974
Channel catfish	27	Tippecanoe River	1970
Flathead catfish	79–8	White River	1966
Blue catfish	57	Clark Co. Lake	1975
Freshwater drum	30	White River	1963
Paddlefish	62	Farm Pond	1975
Buffalo	47–2*	Lake Tippecanoe	1975
Bullhead	3–13	Delaware Co. Pond	1970

*World's Record.

A comprehensive listing and description of the state's fish and wildlife areas, state forests, hunting preserves, state recreation areas, and hunting and fishing resorts is contained in the 61-page booklet *Indiana Hunting, Fishing, Boating,* available free upon request from: Dept. of Commerce, Rm. 336, State House, Indianapolis 46204. The following publications may be obtained free upon request from the Dept. of Natural Resources, Division of Fish & Wildlife, Indianapolis 46204: *Where to Fish in Indiana, Indiana Fishing Regulations, Indiana Hunting & Trapping Regulations, Deer Distribution Map, Pheasant & Quail Distribution Map,* and *DNR Property Guide,* as well as free maps of Indiana state forests and fish and wildlife areas. The DNR also publishes a 53-page *Guide to Indiana Lakes* (52¢). *Lake Survey Reports,* free from the Division of Fish & Wildlife, are available for about 100 lakes. Be sure to specify both lake name and the county it's in when ordering.

Highways—Recreation and Scenic Routes

A free *Official Indiana Highway Map* showing all interstate, U.S., and state routes, points of interest, airports, recreation sites, fish hatcheries, national and state forests, cities, and towns, is available upon request from: Dept. of Commerce, Rm. 336, State House, Indianapolis 46204.

Indiana Sceni-Circle Drives is an excellent, informative 126-page booklet designed to get the traveler off the speedy interstate road system and onto leisurely secondary roads where a wealth of scenic wonders and points of interest await discovery. Visitors may trace Abraham Lincoln's footsteps along the Lincoln Heritage Trail, or recapture the life-style of simpler days in Amishville, near Berne. This free booklet describes 13 scenic drives ranging from 82 to 268 miles. It is attractively illustrated with line drawings. You can obtain a copy free of charge by writing to: Dept. of Commerce (address above).

★ A pleasant State to be in.   ★ A Great State to be in.

Hoosier National Forest

This 117,906-acre reserve is located in the Crawford and Norman uplands in southern Indiana. It is a scenic area of rolling hills, sharp ridges, numerous lakes and streams, and colorful stands of hardwoods and evergreens with an understory of dogwood and redbud; it embraces the old buffalo migration trail between the western plains and French Lick. The major features of this outstanding hiking, camping, fishing, and hunting region include German Ridge, French Lick, and Monroe reservoirs; the Patoka, White, Salt, Lost, Little Blue, and Anderson rivers; the Yellowwood, Washington, Wyandotte Caves, and Harrison-Crawford state forests; Brown County State Park; and lakes Celina, Indian, Tipsaw, Saddle, and Starve Hollow. Wildlife includes deer, red fox, raccoon, upland game birds, and wild turkey.

The proposed Hoosier Wilderness takes in 80 square miles of rolling hills, marshlands, and woodlands in the northern division of the Hoosier National Forest, Brown County State Park, and Yellowwood State Forest. This is the largest roadless wild area in the state and is an outstanding hiking and hunting zone. The major features in the area include Lemon, Yellowwood, Ogte, and Strahl lakes, Hardin Ridge Recreation Area, and the North, Middle, and South Forks of the Salt River.

If you are planning to visit this area, write to: U.S. Forest Service, Bedford 47421, for the useful full-color *Hoosier National Forest Map* (50¢), which shows all roads and highways, state parks, state forest lands, state fish and game areas, forest service and other recreation sites with or without camping facilities, and boat-launching sites, district ranger stations, and other points. There is also an index of recreation sites showing their locations on the map and facilities available in each area. Rules, regulations, and addresses of forest rangers are provided on the reverse side. The map is attractively illustrated with color photographs. The Forest Service also has available a free map of

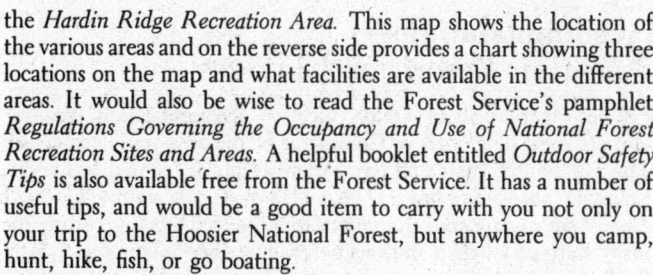

the *Hardin Ridge Recreation Area*. This map shows the location of the various areas and on the reverse side provides a chart showing three locations on the map and what facilities are available in the different areas. It would also be wise to read the Forest Service's pamphlet *Regulations Governing the Occupancy and Use of National Forest Recreation Sites and Areas*. A helpful booklet entitled *Outdoor Safety Tips* is also available free from the Forest Service. It has a number of useful tips, and would be a good item to carry with you not only on your trip to the Hoosier National Forest, but anywhere you camp, hunt, hike, fish, or go boating.

The Hoosier National Forest is reached via U.S. Highways 50 and 150 and Indiana routes 37, 46, 62 and 64. Overnight accommodations, supplies, and equipment rentals are available at Bedford, Evansville, Jasper, Paoli, Tell City, and Bloomington.

The forest is shown on U.S. Geological Survey Maps, scale 1:250,000: Evansville, Indianapolis, Vincennes. The *Hoosier Wilderness Area* is shown on large-scale U.S. Geological Survey Maps: Allens Creek, Bartlettsville, Belmont, Elkinsville, Kurtz, Nashville, Norman, Story, Unionville.

Lake Contour & Stream Fishing Maps

Fishermen and boaters will be interested in the lake maps available from: Dept. of Natural Resources, Map Sales, Rm. 604, State Office Bldg., Indianapolis 46204. Maps of Indiana's major lakes; *Reservoir Depth Maps* (Morse, Geist, Hardy, Cataract); *Reservoir Area Maps* (Monroe, Mansfield, Salamonie, Mississinewa, Huntington, Eagle Creek), size 22 × 28 inches, are available at 60¢ each. The following state maps are also available: *Streams and Lakes of Indiana*, scale 1: 250,000, size 47 × 72 inches, $2; and *Streams and Lakes of Indiana*, scale 1:500,000, size 24 × 36 inches, 50¢. A 10% postage and handling charge must be enclosed with all mail orders. Prepayment must accompany the orders (no stamps). Make your check or money order payable to Dept. of Natural Resources. The lake and reservoir maps show fishing ponds, stumps, brush piles, standing timber, picnic areas, boat ramps, and areas where shoreline fishing is permitted. Mooring areas, camping sites, and other important features are also shown.

OHIO
ENCYCLOPEDIA

Accommodations—
Vacation Resorts and Lodges

For information about Ohio's vacation accommodation facilities, write to local Chambers of Commerce of the area you plan to visit. The Division of Parks and Recreation, Dept. of Natural Resources, Fountain Sq., Columbus 43224, will provide you with *Ohio State Parks Lodge and Cabin Accommodations,* a free brochure listing the many state park lodges and vacation cabins. (See "Camping & State Recreation Areas.")

For additional vacation lodging and services info, write: Office of Travel & Tourism, 30 E. Broad St., Columbus 43215; Lake Erie Tourist Information Center, 1018 Ramada St., Sandusky 44870, covers North-Central Ohio and Lake Erie Islands; Buckeye Tourist Council, Box 307, Cambridge 43725, covers East-Central Ohio; Tecumseh Tourist Council, RR 2, West Liberty 43357, covers West-Central Ohio; and Toledo Convention & Visitors Bureau, 218 Huron St., Toledo 43604.

Camping & State Recreation Areas

Ohio's scenic mixed hardwood and conifer forests, valleys, lakeshores, and meadowlands in the state forest reserve and park lands feature literally hundreds of family campgrounds and primitive backcountry campsites. Rustic lodges and cabins are available by reservation at Burr Oak, Hueston Woods, Mohican, Punderson, Salt Fork, and Shawnee, Deer Creek, Dillon, Geneva, Hocking Hills, Hueston Woods, Lake Hope, Pymatuning, and South Bass state parks. Descriptions of campgrounds, lodges and cabin accommodations, and reservation information for all of Ohio's state forests and parks are contained in the following publications, available free upon request from: Division of Parks & Recreation, Dept. of Natural Resources, Fountain Sq., Columbus 43224: *Ohio State Forests, Ohio State Parks Lodge & Cabin Accommodations, Ohio State Parks Camping Information, Ohio State Parks Area Facilities.* You can get free *Ohio State Park Maps* for all state park areas from the address above.

A 16-page *Hocking Hills State Park Hiking Trails Guide,* describing the scenic backpacking trails that wind through these rugged, forested hills, steeped in Indian and colonial lore, may be obtained free from the Division of Parks & Recreation (address above). Numerous trails reach back through this 10,000-acre backcountry of hills; deep, damp gorges; dry, sandy ridgetops; forests of eastern hemlock, black birch, Canada yew, mountain laurel; and a profusion of ferns and wildflowers to Old Man's Cave, Ash Cave, Cedar Falls, beautiful Conkle's Hollow, the massive cliff of Black Hand sandstone known as "Rock House," and the steep Cantwell Cliffs on Buck Run.

Canoe Trails & Scenic Waters

Ohio offers a small but varied selection of scenic canoe streams. These include the Cuyahoga River, the Great Miami River, the Little Miami River, the Maumee River, the Sandusky River, and the Mohican, Walhonding, and Muskingum rivers.

The Little Miami River and Little Beaver Creek are part of the national wild and scenic river system. Little Beaver Creek, noted for its boulder outcroppings and beautiful wooded slopes, is a tributary of the Ohio River in the extreme southeast corner of the state. The scenic Little Miami River is located just northeast of Cincinnati and offers an unusual unspoiled canoeing experience for Ohio. For detailed information about the state's scenic river system, write: Department

of Natural Resources, Div. of Natural Areas & Preserves, Fountain Sq., Columbus 43224.

The Cuyahoga originates in sugarbush country, traveling through glacial plains, and drops over a series of falls and rapids in the Akron-Cuyahoga Falls area, following a wide gorge to Lake Erie. The river flows through scenic pasture and forest land, and the bass fishing is excellent. The current varies from mild to dangerous. The Great Miami offers almost 140 miles of navigable water, ending in the rugged hill country of the southwestern corner of the state. The entire route is mild and easy to canoe, and fishing is good for smallmouth bass. The Little Miami cuts through a deep gorge filled with scenic beauty. Challenging canoeing is the main attraction on the Maumee, with several portages, rapids, and dams. The Sandusky offers picturesque farmland and excellent fishing for smallmouth bass, rock bass, channel catfish, bullhead, crappie, and white bass. The name Sandusky is derived from an Indian word meaning "water within water pools." The continuous stretch formed by confluences of the Mohican, Walhonding, and Muskingum rivers is often considered the most scenic in Ohio. Many colorful river towns are passed, and good fishing conditions are prevalent up and down the route. The mixed hardwood forests along the shores are inhabited by gray squirrels, raccoons, red fox, mink, ducks, deer, blue herons, and osprey.

For more information and the free booklet *Ohio Canoe Adventures*, with descriptions and maps of numerous river trips, write to: Publications Center, Dept. of Natural Resources, Fountain Sq., Columbus 43224.

The following Ohio streams and quality fishing waters are shown on these U.S. Geological Survey Topographic Maps. *Ashtabula River:* Ashtabula N, Ashtabula S, Gageville, Leon, Pierpont; *Black River:* Avon, Grafton, Lagrange, Loran; *Cuyahoga River:* Akron E, Akron W, Aurora, Burton, Chardon, Cleveland N, Cleveland S, Hudson, Kent, Northfield, Peninsula; *Grand River:* Ashtabula S, Geneva, Jefferson, Mentor, Painesville, Thompson; *Hocking River:* Athens, Coolville, Cutler, Gore, Jacksonville, Logan, Nelsonville, Rockbridge, Stewart, Union Furnace; *Huron River:* Bellevue, Flat Rock, Huron, Kimball, Milan; *Killbuck River:* Coshocton, Killbuck, Holmesville, Millersburg, New Pitsburg, Randle, West Salem, Wooster; *Little Miami River:* Bellbrook, Xenia, Mason, Oregonia, Pleasant Plain, Yellow Springs, South Lebanon, Waynesville; *Little Scioto River:* Beaver, Minford, New Boston, Stockdale; *Maumee River:* Antwerp, Bowling Green N, Colton, Defiance E, Defiance W, Florida, Grand Rapids, Maumee, Napoleon E, Napoleon W, Oregon, Paulding, Rossford, Sherwood, Toledo, Woodburn N; *Muskingum River:* Adamsville, Baltic, Conesville, Coshocton, Dresden, Fleming, Fresno, Low-

ell, Lower Salem, Marietta, McConnelsville, Philo, Rokeby Lock, Stockport, Wills Creek, Zanesville E, Zanesville W; *Ohio Brush Creek:* Belfast, Concord, Hillsboro, Lynx, New Market, Peebles, Sinking Spring, Sugar Tree Ridge; *Portage River:* Bradner, Elmore, Jerry City, Lacarne, Lindsey, North Baltimore, Oak Harbor, Pemberville; *Raccoon Creek:* Apple Grove, Mercerville, Mineral, Mulga, Rodney, Vales Mills, Vinton, Wilkesville; *Toussaint River:* Dunbridge, Elmore, Genoa, Lacarne, Oak Harbor 7.5, Pemberville; *Tuscarawas River:* Bolivar, Canal Fulton, Dover, Doylestown, Gnadenhutten, Massillon, Navarre, Newcomerstown, New Philadelphia; *Vermilion River:* Berlin Heights, Clarksfield, New London, Vermilion W; *Cold Creek:* Castalia, Vickery; *Mohican River:* Greer, Brinkhaven, Walhonding; *Bass Islands—Lake Erie:* Put-in-Bay, Gypsum, Kelleys Island; *Buckeye Lake:* Millersport, Thornville; *Little Beaver Creek:* Lisbon, Elkton, West Point, East Liverpool North.

Fishing & Hunting in the Buckeye State

The Buckeye State's terrain unfolds from the highlands of West Virginia and Pennsylvania into soft undulating hills and fertile valleys and flattens out into broad woodlands which reach to Indiana on the west. The mighty Ohio River flows in a sweeping arc forming the state's southern and eastern boundaries, and the southern shoreline of Lake Erie forms a wave-swept boundary along nearly three-quarters of the northernmost reaches of the state. Ohio's 41,222 square miles contain over 500,000 acres of mixed hardwood and conifer forests, meadows, bogs, and beaver flows on state forest and public game lands which provide good hunting in season for whitetail deer, waterfowl, small game, and upland game birds. Its 200 square miles of lakes and streams hold trophy-sized largemouth and smallmouth bass, walleye, muskellunge, northern pike, striped bass, hordes of panfish, a limited number of trout, and Great Lakes Chinook and coho salmon.

The fishing potential and variety of the Buckeye State's lakes, streams, and ponds are illustrated by the record fish caught by rod and reel, as compiled by the record fish committee of the Outdoor Writers of Ohio.

OHIO RECORD FISH

	Lb.-oz.	Place	Year
Largemouth bass	10–11	Wellston Strip Pond	1974
Smallmouth bass	7–6	Mad River	1941
Muskellunge	55–2	Piedmont Lake	1972
Chain pickerel	6–4	Long Lake	1954
Northern pike	18–10	East Harbor—Lake Erie	1975
Chinook salmon	26–6	Daniels Park—Lake Erie	1972
Coho salmon	10–15	Chagrin River	1974
Striped bass	25–4	Lake St. Mary	1975
Brown trout	13–8	Cold Creek	1942
Rainbow trout	15–6	Cold Creek	1975
Brook trout	2–11	East Branch—Chagrin River	1955
Walleye	15	Pymatuning Reservoir	1951
Bluegill	2–5	Magadore Reservoir	1974
Yellow perch	2–8	Lake Erie	1954
Black crappie	3–6	Scioto Lakes	1968
White crappie	3–3	Muzzy Lake	1968
Spotted bass	5–4	Lake White	1967
White bass	4–2	Lake Erie	1972
Sauger	3–4	Sandusky River	1977

Lake Erie & the Bass Islands

Ohio's premier fishing area is the vast southern waters of Lake Erie surrounding the famous archipelago north of Sandusky and Port Clinton formed by Kelleys Island, South Bass Island and Put-in-Bay, Middle Bass Island, and North Bass Island and Isle St. George. The reefs, shoals, sandbars, and rock and gravel bottoms surrounding this renowned summer vacation region provide often spectacular fishing for fat yellow perch and scrappy smallmouth bass, and an occasional walleye, muskellunge, northern pike, coho salmon, or sturgeon. The Bass Islands area is one of the hottest smallmouth bass fishing spots in the Midwest. The best time to fish the islands is in May when the water temperature varies from 54° to 60°. Fly fishing, bait fishing, and spin casting using emerald shiners, crayfish, and a variety of lures are effective when fished over reefs, gravel, and sandbars. Acrobatic bronzebacks, one of the truly great sport fishes, caught here average from ¾ to 1½ pounds and range up to 7 pounds. Chinook salmon and the beautiful silver-blue coho can be caught in Lake Erie throughout the year and many are taken by shoreline fishermen using large plugs, flashy spinners and spoons, and by offshore trolling. During the fall when the water temperature is 45°–50°, Chinook and coho migrate up such Lake Erie tributaries as the Chagrin River, Conneaut Creek, and Huron River. Northern pike, which once were abundant and grew to monster lengths in Lake Erie before 1900, are today confined to Sandusky Bay, Maumee Bay, and the marshlands and tributary streams adjoining these areas. As the ice breaks up during late February or early March, the great northerns move from Lake Erie into the adjoining bays and marshes to spawn.

Elsewhere in Lake Erie, smallmouth bass are found along the gravel bottoms, shoals, and reefs along Kelleys Island, Huron-Vermilion Reef, and the Port Clinton Reef. Big largemouth bass are found in all boat harbors and weed-filled inlets and bays, along with buckets of scrappy crappies. Legions of white bass are found off the Bass Islands, Kelleys Island, Mouse Island, and the Port Clinton Reef areas.

Inland Lakes & Streams

Inland from the once pristine waters of Lake Erie, smallmouth bass are found in clear, cold impoundments and lakes, and streams with good gravel or rock bottoms and a visible current in every county of the Buckeye State, as are largemouth bass, walleye, and crappie. The top-ranked smallmouth, largemouth, and walleye waters in the lake country of northeastern Ohio include Pymatuning Lake (which holds muskies up to 30 pounds and walleye up to 18 pounds), Clendening Lake, Berlin Lake, M. J. Kirwan Reservoir, Mosquito Creek Lake, Tappan Lake, and Lake Milton. Premier lakes and streams in the northwest include the Huron River, Killdeer Reservoir, Clear Fork Reservoir, Pleasant Hill Lake, Beaver Creek Reservoir, and Lost Creek, Amick, Bresler, and Metzger reservoirs. The top-ranked waters of central Ohio, surrounded by scenic mixed hardwood forests and marshlands, include the famous Buckeye Lake, the Delaware Wildlife Area ponds, island-studded Indian Lake, Hoover Reservoir, Knox

Lake, Hargus Lake, Kokosing Lake, Mohican and Kokosing rivers, Deer, Paint, Big Darby, and Big Walnut creeks, and the Olentangy River. The major fishing waters in southwestern Ohio include Acton, Rocky Fork, Grand (St. Marys) Lake, C. J. Brown, Clark, Cowan, and Rush Run lakes, and the Great Miami and Little Miami rivers. In the rugged backcountry woodlands of southeastern Ohio are Burr Oak Lake, Muskingum River, Scioto Brush Creek, Lake Logan, Wellston Reservoir, and Snowden Lake.

Largemouth bass are caught in the bays, coves, and submerged log piles and dead timber areas, using plugs, spinners, and live bait. Walleyes are taken by trolling spinners with night crawlers and drifting minnows over old roadbeds, rip-rap areas, and gravel bars adjacent to deep drop-offs. The elusive muskellunge is caught most often during the "mad" muskie days during the fall turnover around filled trees, brush piles, and stumps, and clear cold waters with sandy bottoms and aquatic vegetation.

The cannibalistic muskie, whose name is derived from an Ojibwa Indian word meaning "long snout," are most often caught on live suckers and floating, diving plugs, spoons, jointed lures, and feathered spinners. Muskies were rarely found in Ohio's lakes and reservoirs before the Division of Wildlife started stocking them in 1953. Today, muskies of 5 to 25 pounds and up to 50 pounds are found in Piedmont, Leesville, Rocky Fork, Clear Fork, Dillon, Cowan, Hargus, Delaware, Knox, and Deer Creek reservoirs, Grand and Little Muskingum rivers, and Paint, Olive, Meigs, Wolf, Rocky Fork, Scioto Brush, Wills, and Ohio Brush creeks. The Ohio Huskie Muskie Club awards certificates to anglers who catch trophy-sized muskellunge (regular membership is awarded for fish over 20 pounds and 40 inches or more in length). Membership applications are available at Muskie Lake marinas and the Division of Wildlife, Fountain Sq., Columbus 43224.

Trout are limited to several localities in Ohio. Rainbow trout are found in Clear Creek on the Erie and Sandusky county border and in the Mad River. The Mad River rainbows and browns are thought to be fish that have escaped from the privately operated Zanesfield Rod & Gun Club lands during periods of high water. Carry-over rainbows are also found in the Chagrin River, Conneaut Creek, and Beaver Creek in Seneca County and in Punderson, Oberlin, and Forked Run lakes. The state record 13-pound 8-ounce brown and 15-pound 6-ounce rainbow were caught in the privately operated Castalia Trout Club stretch on Cold Creek. Brook trout are found in Cold Creek and in the Mad River and its Macocheek Creek and Cedar Run tributaries.

Maps & Guides

The Ohio Dept. of Natural Resources (DNR), Information Office, Fountain Sq., Columbus 43224, publishes reams of useful free publications, including *Ohio Fishing & Hunting Areas*, which contains listings and a "Map of Public Fishing & Hunting Locations"; a 58-page *Guide to Boating in Ohio; Lake Erie Fishing Services; Ohio Fishing Regulations Booklet; Fish Identification Chart;* the 18-page booklet *When & Where to Fish; Ohio Hunting Regulations;* an *Ohio Licensed Shooting Preserves* booklet; and the following Ohio information leaflets: *Bait Fish, Rainbow Trout, Brown Trout, Brook Trout, The Pickerels in Ohio, Muskellunge in Ohio, Muskellunge Fishing in Ohio, Northern Pike in Ohio, Northern Smallmouth Blackbass, Coho Salmon in Ohio, Fish Dehydration Guide, Fish Smoking, Endangered Wild Animals in Ohio, Red Fox in Ohio, Ringnecked Pheasant, Wild Turkey, Whitetail Deer, Woodcocks,* and *Hawks in Ohio.* The DNR also honors big Ohio bass by awarding anglers with Master Certificates for 4-pound smallmouth or 7-pound largemouth bass, and Expert Certificates for 3½-pound smallmouth or 6-pound largemouth.

The Division of Wildlife (Fountain Sq., Columbus 43224) publishes free *Wildlife Area Maps*—including the Brush Creek, Copper Hollow, Deer Creek, Delaware Reservoir, Grand River, Indian Creek, Killdeer Plains, Mosquito Creek, Sunday Creek, Willard Marsh, Wolf Creek, and Dillion Reservoir areas—showing trails, campgrounds, natural features, target ranges, and facilities for hunters and fishermen.

Hunting

Hunting in the Buckeye State is popular on the Wayne National Forest, state forest and wildlife area lands, and private clubs and preserves for ringnecked pheasant, ruffed grouse, bobwhite quail, ducks and Canadian geese, woodcock, fox and gray squirrels, cottontail rabbits, whitetail deer, raccoon, woodchuck, red fox, and a few wild turkey. The following licensed shooting preserves are open to the public: *Elkhorn Lake Shooting Park*, Rte. 2, Bucyrus (pheasant); *Dray's Shooting Preserve*, Rte. 1, Box 31, Bluffton (pheasant); *Tallmadge Pheasant Farm & Shooting Preserve*, Co. Rd. 1975 RD2, Jeromeville; *Adar Valley Hunting & Fishing*, RD6, Wooster (pheasant, quail, chukar partridge); *Wooster Duck & Pheasant Shooting Preserve*, 470 Carter Dr., Wooster (pheasant, quail, chukar partridge). (For additional information see "State Forest Reserves," and "Canoe Trails & Scenic Waters.")

Highways—Recreation & Scenic Routes

The *Ohio Transportation Map*, available free from Dept. of Transportation, 25 S. Front St., Columbus 43215, shows all highways and roads, lakes, rivers, and streams, towns and settlements, county lines, railroads, ferries, tolls, dams, points of interest, state forests, airports, rest areas, parks, fairgrounds, highway patrol posts, and first-aid stations. It includes close-up maps of Cleveland, Cincinnati, Columbus, Youngstown, Dayton, Toledo, and Canton, and an index of state park camping facilities.

Lake Contour Fishing Maps

Lake contour maps showing boat-launching points and harbors, gas stations, wooded areas, highways, towns, bridges, county lines, railroads, and lake features including bottom type, dead timber areas, streams, and depth contours, are available for all major lakes including Seneca, Pymatuning, Killdeer, Logan, Indian, Deer Creek, Burr Oak, Clendening, Buckeye lakes, Lake Erie Islands, and Berlin, Milton, Mosquito, Portage, Mogadore, Atwood, Leesville, Tappan, Piedmont, Pleasant Hill, Delaware, Hoover, Rocky Fork, Grant, Cowan, Acton, Clark, Indian, Kiser, and Dillon. Maps are free up to 5 copies; over 5 they are 10¢ each. Each map includes a "peak action calendar." A complete set of bound maps is available for $7.65 from: DNR, Fountain Sq., Columbus 43224.

State Forest Reserves

Ohio's state forests offer excellent backpacking and primitive camping opportunities and good hunting in season for whitetail deer, ruffed grouse, raccoon, wild turkey, and red fox. Free *State Forest Maps* showing roads, streams, campsites, points of interest, trails, and towns are available from: Division of Forestry and Reclamation, Dept. of Natural Resources, 815 Ohio Depts. Bldg., Columbus 43215. These include Shade River State Forest, Shawnee State Forest, Brush Creek State Forest, Blue Rock State Forest, Scioto Trail State Forest, Dean State Forest, Fernwood State Forest, Hocking State Forest, Maumee State Forest, Mohican and Memorial state forests, Pike State Forest, Tar Hollow State Forest, and Zaleski State Forest.

The major Buckeye state forests are shown on the following large-scale 7.5-minute U.S. Geological Survey Topographic Maps. *Brush Creek:* Byington, Otway, Rarden, Wakefield, West Portsmouth; *Pike:* Bainbridge, Byington, Latham, Morgantown; *Scioto Trails:* Chillicothe, Richmond Dale, Waverly N; *Shawnee-Roosevelt:* Blue Creek, Buena Vista, Friendship, Jaybird, Otway, Pond Run, Rarden, Vanceburg 7.5, West Portsmouth; *Tar Hollow:* Hallsville, Laurelville, Londonderry, Ratcliffburg; *Zaleski:* McArthur, Mineral, Vales Mills, Zaleski.

Wayne National Forest

This scenic 106,000-acre reserve is composed of three forest divisions in southeastern Ohio. The major features of this outstanding backpacking and hunting country of rolling hills, spectacular outcroppings of sandstone and shale, and numerous streams include the Hanging Rock Region, Lake Vesuvius Recreation Area, Dean State Forest, Trimble and Wolf Creek state wildlife areas, Strouds Run State Park, Waterloo State Forest, Burr Oak Reservoir, and Symmes, Hocking, Raccoon, and Little Muskingum rivers. The beautiful Little Muskingum River, with its several covered bridges and scenic woodlands, holds a good population of smallmouth bass. Burr Oak Reservoir holds big largemouth bass and walleyes. This is the state's top hunting area for whitetail deer, red fox, raccoon, wild turkey, and upland game birds.

The Hocking Caves region presents many interesting geological formations. Trails and camping facilities are numerous. Ash Cave was once the site of countless Indian fires, and Old Man's Cave was the longtime residence of an anonymous hermit more than 100 years ago.

There are district ranger stations at Athens and Ironton. Complete information and a 50¢ full-color *Wayne National Forest Map* showing all roads and trails, railroads, ranger stations, recreation sites, points of interest, boat-launching sites, and lakes, ponds, and streams are available from: Forest Supervisor, 1615 J St., Bedford, IN 47421.

The Wayne National Forest is reached via U.S. Highways 33 and 52, Interstate 70, and Ohio State Highways 7 and 93. Supplies, guides, and outfitters are available at Athens, Ironton, Marietta, Grandview, Wade, Newport, Fly, Ellisonville, Lisman, Hanging Rock, Nelsonville, Corning, New Straitsville, Greendale, and Shawnee.

The Wayne National Forest is shown in the following full-color U.S.

Geological Survey Topographic Overview Maps, scale 1:250,000:
Charleston, Clarksburg, Columbus, Huntington.

Wildcat Hollow Primitive Weapons Hunting Area

This primitive weapons deer hunting area is located in the northeast
section of Burr Oak State Park, near Glouster. The rugged, scenic
49,000-acre area includes pasture, brushfields, woodlands and streams,
and is composed of 6,938 acres of the Wayne National Forest and the
3,500-acre Wolf Creek Wildlife Area. A free *Wildcat Hollow Primitive Weapons Area Map* may be obtained from: Division of Wildlife,
Dept. of Natural Resources, Fountain Sq., Columbus 43224. It shows
highways, roads, camping areas, public hunting land, and primitive
weapons area boundaries. The area is shown on the following large-
scale U.S. Geological Survey Maps: Deavertown, Corning, Rokeby
Lock, Ringold.

Wilderness & Backcountry Outfitters

Alder's *Wilderness Trails Outfitters,* 728 E. Prospect Ave., Cleveland
44115, provides all kinds of equipment, guides, and several trips and
wilderness expeditions. Their five-day survival school teaches anyone
who wants to improve his wilderness skills, emphasizing direction,
shelter, fires, and first aid. Two-day Pennsylvania trips are introductory
backpacking trips into the Allegheny Mountains. A 30-day expedition
takes participants into Wyoming's spectacular Wind River Range.
Mountaineering and expedition skills involved include glacier work,
fishing, rock climbing, mountain rescue, first aid, cooking, survival,
and navigation. Ohio natural areas trips provide short-range trips into
natural areas at Eagle Creek and Black Hand Gorge.

Accommodations— Vacation Resorts & Lodges

The *Kentucky Travel Guide*, an 84-page booklet available free from: Division of Travel & Promotion, Dept. of Public Information, Frankfort 40601, contains a complete listing of fishing, hunting, and family vacation resorts, hotels, and restaurants, alphabetically by town within regional districts. It includes regional and city maps, lists special events and interesting sights, museums, industrial tours, schools and churches, and state parks and national forests. Information on fishing, boating, skiing, swimming, hiking, and camping is provided, and tidbits of Kentucky statistics and trivia are sandwiched in with concise, practical suggestions and listings.

The Division of Travel & Promotion will also provide free booklets on *Kentucky Lake Vacationland* and *Kentucky's Lake Cumberland-Dale Hollow and Green River Lake.* Kentucky Lake is extremely popular all year round for fishing and water sports. The booklet provides information on the different kinds of fish in the lake, seasonal weather and recreation, annual events in the area, and complete listings of motels, resorts, campgrounds, houseboats, attractions, restaurants, realtors and subdivisions, grocery supplies, and other general services. A pullout map of the whole area is included.

For detailed information about Kentucky's State Park Lodge System —with family lodges and cabins available at Kenlake, Audubon, Kentucky Dam Village, Lake Barkley, Rough River Dam, Barren River Lake, Cumberland Falls, General Butter, Lake Cumberland, Buckhorn Lake, Carter Caves, Wiley, Natural Bridge and Pine Mountain state parks—write: Dept. of Parks, Capitol Tower Plaza, Frankfort 40601, phone (502) 223–2326.

Campgrounds & State Recreation Areas

The 46-page *Kentucky Campgrounds Guide* contains a comprehensive listing of all public and commercial campgrounds with descriptions of facilities and recreation activities available. The guide covers all state park, forest, wildlife management and recreation areas, including the Turkey Foot, Hurricane Creek, Grand Rivers, Rockcastle, Mammoth Cave, Rodburn Hollow, and Windy Hollow lakes. The campgrounds guide may be obtained free upon request from: Division of Travel & Promotion, Dept. of Public Information, Frankfort 40601.

Canoe Trails & Float Streams

Kentucky's scenic streams provide excellent early season canoeing and float fishing for muskellunge, walleye, largemouth and smallmouth bass, and rainbow trout. The state's major canoe routes and float streams include the Red River, with its spectacular gorge—known as "the Grand Canyon of the East"—high bluffs, rapids, and the surrounding Daniel Boone National Forest lands; the scenic and wild Elkhorn River; the beautiful Green River, which winds through the cave-studded rolling hills of the Mammoth Cave National Park; the Big South Fork of the Cumberland River, one of the most beautiful rivers in the Southeast, proposed for inclusion in the National Wild and Scenic Rivers System; and the boulder-studded Rockcastle River, a Kentucky-designated scenic and wild river, which winds along its rapids-filled course through the Daniel Boone National Forest. A free *Kentucky Canoeing Waters* guide may be obtained by writing to: Division of Travel & Promotion, Dept. of Public Information, Frankfort 40601.

The following canoe routes and float streams are shown on large-scale

KENTUCKY ENCYCLOPEDIA

U.S. Geological Survey Topographic Maps. *Bark Camp Creek:* Sawyer, Wofford; *Beaver Creek Wilderness:* Hail, Wiborg; *Big South Fork of the Cumberland River:* Barthell, Burnside, Frazer, Nevelsville, Oneida N; *Jellico Creek:* Hollyhill, Jellico W, Ketchen, Williamsburg; *Laurel Creek:* Corbin, Sawyer, Vox; *Marsh Creek:* Cumberland Falls, Hollyhill, Whitley City, Winfield; *Red River:* Cannel City, Clay City, Hazel Green, Landsaw, Lee City, Palmer, Pomeroyton, Slade, Stanton; *Rockcastle River:* Ano, Bernstadt, Billows, Livingston, Parrot, Sawyer; *Station Camp Creek:* Irvine, Leighton, McKee, Panola; *Kinniconick Creek:* Burtonville, Strickett, Head of Grassy, Vanceburg, Garrison; *Elkhorn Creek:* Switzer, Frankfort E, Stamping Ground, Midway, Georgetown, Centerville, Lexington E, Versailles, Lexington W.

Cumberland Gap Roadless Area & the Boone Trace

The Cumberland Gap Roadless Area embraces 20,169 acres of mixed hardwood forests, knifelike ridges, valleys, streams, caves, and limestone sinks along the Allegheny Plateau in the Cumberland Gap National Historic Park. A backpacking trail winds across the length of the park, passing through scenic forests of pine, oak, and hickory, with a lush understory of rhododendron, mountain laurel, dogwood, and redbud inhabited by deer, ruffed grouse, raccoon, and red fox.

The historic Boone Trace, and its successor, the Wilderness Road, one of the most famous trails in American history, originated at Cumberland Gap and crossed the Cumberland River where it followed the ancient Warriors Path—known to the Indians as *Athiamionee*, meaning "path of the armed one"—across the state to the Daniel Boone National Forest and beyond through the Great Valley to Pennsylvania. The legendary Boone Trace, originally a game trail followed by the buffalo and Indians, and later by the French fur trappers, was blazed by Daniel Boone and 30 companions. From about 50 miles north of Cumberland Gap, Boone followed the Warriors Path. The Boone Trace later became the Wilderness Road, followed by intrepid pioneers heading west. The old route of the Boone Trace and Wilderness Road will be followed by the proposed Daniel Boone National Scenic Trail, which will extend from North Carolina to Fort Boonesborough State Park, Kentucky.

For backpacking and camping info in the Cumberland Gap backcountry, write: Superintendent, Cumberland Gap National Historic Park, Box 340, Middlesboro 40965. The park and roadless area are shown on the following large-scale U.S. Geological Survey Maps: Middlesboro S, Ewing, Middlesboro N, Varilla, Wheeler, TN.

Daniel Boone National Forest

This forest reserve takes in 460,000 acres of towering sandstone bluffs, woodlands, waterfalls, natural arches, and rolling hills on the western rim of the Cumberland Plateau between the mountains of eastern Kentucky and the bluegrass country. The major features of this hunting, camping, and canoeing region include the 7,000-acre Pioneer Weapons Hunting Area—set up for the use of only old-time weapons including flintlock and percussion cap rifles, muzzle-loading shotguns, longbows, and crossbows—the Red River Gorge Scenic Area, Licking River, Beaver Creek Wilderness, Rockcastle River, and Lake Cumberland. The Big South Fork of the Cumberland, a proposed national wild and scenic river, is one of the most spectacular rivers in the eastern U.S.; it flows through the forest surrounded by a wild country of giant sandstone bluffs, scenic waterfalls, and deep woodland valleys. There is good hunting in season for gray squirrel, ruffed grouse, white-

tail deer, and wild turkey. Cave Run, Wood Creek, Buckhorn, and Laurel River lakes provide good fishing for trophy bass and pan fish. Lake Cumberland, created by Wolf Creek Dam, provides 250 miles of national forest shoreline and provides top-ranked fishing for trophy walleye, largemouth bass, white bass, and crappie. The scenic Red River yields muskellunge up to 20 pounds. Fly fishermen will find large holdover rainbow trout along the remote backcountry reaches of Craney Creek, Beaver Creek, Brushy Creek, Bark Camp Creek, Big Buck Lick, Dogslaughter Creek, Hawk Creek, Buckhorn Lake, Indian and War Fork Creeks, Laurel Fork, and Swift Camp Creek. A segment of the Boone Trace or Wilderness Road has been marked at several places in the forest, including the site of Wood's Block House at "Hazelpatch," which furnished the only refuge from the Indians to pioneers on their way to Boonesborough.

The *Daniel Boone National Forest Map* shows recreation sites and facilities, boundaries, highways and roads, trails, railroads, lookout stations, boat launches, natural arches, points of interest, historical points, and lakes and streams. Information is also given on hunting and fishing, camping, wildlife, climate, and boating. The map is available for 50¢ from: Forest Supervisor, Winchester 40391. Free map-brochures are available from the same address for the *Pioneer Weapons Hunting Area*, *Red River Gorge*, *Natural Bridge*, and *Yahoo Falls Scenic Area*. The primitive weapons area map shows gravel roads, trails, primitive camping areas, water holes, bottomlands, and wildlife openings.

The forest is reached via U.S. Highways 25, 27, 60, 421, and 460. Motels and cottages are available at the boat docks on Lake Cumberland at the confluence of the Laurel and Rockcastle rivers. Accommodations, supplies, and equipment rentals are available at Boonesboro, Corbin, and Lexington.

The Daniel Boone National Forest is shown on the following U.S. Geological Survey Topographic Maps, scale 1:250,000: Cumberland, Corbin, Huntington, Jenkins, Winchester. The Primitive Weapons Area is shown on large-scale U.S. Geological Survey Topographic Maps: Bangor, Salt Lick.

Fishing & Hunting in Kentucky

The Bluegrass State's great reservoirs, streams, thousands of productive farm ponds, national and state forest lands, and wildlife management areas offer superb fishing and hunting opportunities. Kentucky's topography consists of a scenic blend of mountains and gently rolling uplands. The eastern mountain region contains the state's highest elevations, slashed by hundreds of numerous rushing creeks and streams. Moving westward from the Daniel Boone National Forest, the mountains gradually give way to an irregular plain known as the Knobs and the famous bluegrass country; at the southern end of the central plain are broad valleys, gently rolling farmlands, and rocky forested hillsides. The terrain gradually levels off into plains and the swampy bottomlands along the Mississippi and Ohio rivers which form the state's western boundary.

Trophy Lakes

Several of the nation's top-ranked bass and walleye lakes are found in Kentucky. The famous Dale Hollow Lake, covering 4,300 acres, straddles the central Kentucky-Tennessee border. The world's record 11-pound 15-ounce smallmouth bass was taken from the deep, clear waters along the Kentucky side of the lake in 1955. In addition to trophy bronzebacks, Dale Hollow yields hordes of white bass and crappie, as well as large rainbow trout and an occasional muskie. The gently rolling creek bottoms and steep ridges of the 3,000-acre Dale Hollow Wildlife Management Area wind along the shoreline of the lake. Just north of Dale Hollow are the sprawling waters of huge 50,250-acre Lake Cumberland—one of the most scenic and productive fishing areas in the state for trophy largemouth, smallmouth, and Kentucky bass, white bass, crappie, big rainbow trout, walleye, and landlocked striped bass. Cumberland yielded the state record 21-pound 8-ounce walleye. The big frigid tailrace waters below the Wolf Creek Dam hold trophy metallic-flanked rainbow trout up to 14 pounds. During the hot summer months night is the most productive time to fish for the big Lake Cumberland rainbows. The gently sloping creek bottoms, ridges, hardwood forests, old farmlands, and wildlife food plots of the 23,000-acre Lake Cumberland Wildlife Management Area border portions of the lake's irregularly shaped shoreline. Beautiful 6,000-acre Laurel River Lake lies due east of Lake Cumberland, surrounded by the forested hills and rocky bluffs of the Daniel Boone National Forest. This incredibly scenic lake yields smallmouth bass, panfish, and rainbows.

Mountain Country Lakes & Streams

The rugged uplands of eastern Kentucky shelter several outstanding lakes and streams. Buckhorn Lake has 1,250 acres surrounded by mountains and yields good strings of largemouth bass around submerged brush areas as well as white bass, crappie, and bluegill. Rainbows are caught beneath the dam from spring through fall. Portions of the shoreline are hemmed by the primitive gamelands of the 2,580-acre Buckhorn Lake Wildlife Management Area. Scenic Fishtrap Lake, the easternmost of Kentucky's major lakes, covers 1,130 acres in Pike County with fishing for bluegill, channel catfish, smallmouth, and white bass. The dense hardwood forests and steep mountainous terrain of the 10,000-acre Fishtrap Lake Wildlife Management Area borders portions of the lake's shoreline. Cave Run Lake on the Licking River covers 8,300 acres in the northern part of the Daniel Boone National Forest and yields smallmouth bass, crappie, bluegill, and a large population of elusive muskellunge. The deep-flowing pools of the Licking River and its tributaries provide some of the state's best smallmouth bass and muskie float fishing. Other top-ranked eastern Kentucky fisheries include Kinniconick Creek for muskie, bass, and trout; Tygart Creek, a renowned muskie stream; Grayson and Greenbo lakes on the Little Sandy River for trophy bass, crappie, bluegill, and trout; Red River for smallmouth bass and muskie; and the scenic South Fork of the Cumberland and Dewey Lake on Levisa Fork.

Central Lakes & Streams

Several major lakes and float streams are located in the beautiful, gently rolling central bluegrass country. Herrington Lake stretches for 35 miles and has a huge spring spawning run of white bass up the Dix River. Herrington's 1,860 acres also produce good catches of largemouth bass, crappie, and bluegill. Green River Lake in south central Kentucky yields trophy largemouth bass, crappie, and bluegill. The wooded hills of the 14,625-acre Green River Wildlife Management Area border portions of the lake's shoreline. The North, South, and Middle forks of the Kentucky River provide excellent float fishing for muskellunge and smallmouth bass. The Little Kentucky River is an excellent early season smallmouth bass stream. The scenic and wild, gravel-bottomed Elkhorn Creek is considered one of the nation's top smallmouth bass streams. Other productive central Kentucky game-fish streams include the Rolling Fork and its Beech Fork, Chaplin River, and Little Beach Fork tributaries; Salt River and Floyd's Fork; Guist Creek Lake; and Eagle Creek, a good panfish stream.

Western Lakes & Streams

In western and west central Kentucky huge Barkley Lake and Kentucky Lake offer some of the state's premier largemouth bass and crappie fishing along the numerous coves, submerged brush areas, and riprap banks where large schools of fish gorge on threadfin shad. The tailwaters below both lakes hold giant channel and blue catfish. The two giant TVA impoundments surround the 100,000-acre Land Between the Lakes Wildlife Management Area, with its forests, clearings, old farm sites, and gently rolling terrain (for info, write:

Information Office, Land Between the Lakes, Golden Pond 42231). Other major western Kentucky lake and stream fisheries include the oxbows and sloughs of the Mississippi River; Green River, an excellent float stream for bass, crappie, and muskie; Rough River Lake, which holds both largemouth and smallmouth bass, crappie, and walleye; Nolin River Lake and Lake Beshear; Green River Lake, which holds bass, muskie, striped bass, and crappie; and the noted bass and muskie waters of the Barren River and 10,000-acre Barren River Lake, famous for black bass and crappie fishing in brushy coves and along rocky points and deep banks, and for a spring run of white bass.

The outstanding fishing potential and diversity of Kentucky's lakes and streams is illustrated by the list of state record fish compiled by the Department of Fish & Wildlife Resources.

KENTUCKY RECORD FISH

	Lb.-oz.	Place	Year
Largemouth bass	13–8	Greenbo Lake	1966
Smallmouth bass	11–15	Dale Hollow Lake	1955
Muskellunge	43	Dale Hollow Lake	1978
Walleye	21–8	Lake Cumberland	1958
Chain pickerel	3–2½	Clear Lake	1974
Rainbow trout	14–6	Cumberland River	1972
Crappie	4–3	Lake Pewee	1969
White bass	5	Kentucky Lake	1943
Kentucky bass	7–10	Nelson Co. Lake	1970
Blue catfish	100	Tennessee River	1970
Channel catfish	15–6	Beaver Lake	1973
Flathead catfish	97	Green River	1956
Sturgeon	36–8	Lake Cumberland	1954
Paddlefish	72	Lake Cumberland	1957
Sauger	6–1	Kentucky Lake	1972
Bluegill	3–6	Buckanon Pond	1955
Striped bass	45–8	Lake Cumberland	1978

Maps & Guides

Several useful free fishing and hunting guides, maps, and booklets may be obtained by writing to: Division of Public Relations, Dept. of Fish & Wildlife Resources, Capitol Plaza Tower, Frankfort 40601. The 29-page guide *Fishing in Kentucky* contains descriptions of all major lakes and streams, as well as a "Kentucky Fishing Map," regulations, and a handy fishing resort and marina guide. The 29-page guide *Hunting in Kentucky* contains regulations and license information, seasons and limits, and descriptions of game species. Additional free Fish & Wildlife Resources publications include a *Kentucky Trout Waters Map, Guide to 28 Public Fishing Lakes, Kentucky Lake Fish & Fishing, Hunting Digest, Deer Hunting Guide, Waterfowl Hunting Guide, Waterfowl Identification,* and *Places to Hunt—a Guide to 45 Public Hunting Areas in Kentucky,* which describes all state forest reserves and fish and wildlife management areas. Boating information and regulations may be obtained from: Division of Boating, Dept. of Transportation, State Office Bldg., Frankfort 40601.

Hunting

The Bluegrass State's scenic forest reserves and wildlife management areas provide excellent hunting opportunities for deer, upland game birds, and small game. The mountainous eastern portion of the state provides choice habitat for ruffed grouse, gray squirrel, bobwhite quail, red fox, cottontail rabbit, whitetail deer, and wild turkey in the wooded hills, narrow valleys, and cleared farmlands. The major public hunting areas in eastern Kentucky include the Daniel Boone National Forest, Kentenia State Forest, Mead Forest, Kentucky Ridge State Forest, Olympia State Forest, Tygarts State Forest, and the primitive gamelands of the Beaver Creek, Beech Creek, Buckhorn Lake, Cranks Creek, Dale Hollow, Dewey Lake, Fishtrap Lake, Grayson Lake, Pine Mountain, and Stearns wildlife management areas and the Pioneer Weapons Hunting Area.

The rich farmlands, woodlands, and gently rolling hills of central Kentucky, including the famous bluegrass region, offer prime hunting for rabbits, doves, quail, deer, red fox, squirrels, and raccoon. The major public hunting areas in central Kentucky include the Knob State Forest and the Barren Lake, Central Kentucky, Curtis Gates Lloyd,

Fort Knox, Green River, Lake Cumberland, Mullins, Nolin Lake, Rough River, and Twin Eagle wildlife management areas.

The farmlands, forests, and sloughs and river bottomlands along the Mississippi Flyway in western Kentucky provide the state's premier duck and goose hunting as well as rabbits, quail, raccoon, and deer. The major public hunting areas in western Kentucky include Ballard County, Barkley Lake, Fort Campbell, Kentucky Lake, Land Between the Lakes, Pennyrile Forest, Reelfoot Lake, Sloughs, Tradewater, and West Kentucky wildlife management areas.

Highways—Recreation & Scenic Routes

The Dept. of Public Information, Frankfort 40601, will provide a free *Kentucky Official Highway & Parkway Map.* It shows all cities and towns, roads and highways, airports, forests and parks, lakes and rivers, plus populations and mileage markers. Close-up maps of Ashland, Owensboro, Lexington, Louisville, and Covington-Newport are provided, as well as detail maps of major parkways and highways. These include Pennyrile Parkway, Cumberland Parkway, Audubon Parkway, Daniel Boone Parkway, Mountain Parkway, Blue Grass Parkway, Purchase Parkway, Western Kentucky Parkway, Green River Parkway, and Interstates 64, 71, 65, and 75. Toll charts are included, plus an index of state park facilities. A mileage chart showing distances between major points is featured.

A bound book of *Kentucky County Highway Maps* is available for $8 from: Map Sales Office, Dept. of Commerce, Main & Ann Sts., Frankfort 40601.

Outdoor Recreation Instruction & Wilderness Expeditions

SAGE, School of the Outdoors, Outfitters, and Expeditioners, specializes in wilderness instruction and adventure travel throughout the United States. SAGE courses include instruction in canoeing, kayaking, climbing, sailing, and wilderness survival. The SAGE wilderness adventure travel services include guided Red River Gorge canoe trips,

Elkhorn River canoe trips, Green River canoe and kayak journey, Big South Fork of the Cumberland canoe trips, Rockcastle River canoe trip, Buffalo River (Tennessee) canoe trip, Cumberlands backpacking trip, Louisiana bayou float trip, Smoky Mountains Wild River trip, Colorado Rocky Mountain climbing seminars, Cape Hatteras National Seashore and Dismal Swamp exploration, northern Ontario wilderness canoe trip, and Hiwassee River, Okefenokee Swamp, Suwannee River, and Chattoga Wild River trips. The SAGE Supply Division sells and rents quality backpacking, mountaineering, canoeing, and kayaking equipment. For free literature, rates, and current trip schedules, write: SAGE, 209 E. High St., Lexington 40507, phone (606) 255–1547.

Trophy Fishing Lake Maps

A free index of TVA Navigation Charts may be obtained from the Map Sales Office, Dept. of Commerce, Main & Ann Sts., Frankfort 40601, or from TVA Maps, 400 Commerce Ave., SW, Knoxville, TN 37902. A *Kentucky Lake Recreation Map*, available free from the Tennessee Valley Authority, shows recreation areas and facilities, public lands, boat docks, wildlife management areas, boat-launching sites, and roads. The following full-color, large-scale U.S. Geological Survey Maps show the Bluegrass State's major lakes and surrounding game lands. *Barkley Lake:* Cadiz, Canton, Cobb, Eddyville, Grand Rivers, Mont, Fenton; *Barren Lake:* Austin, Glasgow S, Holland, Lucas, Fountain Run; *Beaver Lake:* Ashbrook; *Beshear Lake:* Dawson Springs, Dawson Springs SW; *Boltz Lake:* Williamstown; *Buckhorn Lake:* Buckhorn, Hyden E, Hyden W, Krypton; *Bullock Pen Lake:* Verona; *Cave Run Lake:* Bangor, Ezel, Salt Lick, Scranton, West Liberty, Wrigley; *Cumberland Lake:* Burnside, Cumberland City, Delmer, Eli, Faubush, Frazer, Jabez, Jamestown, Mill Springs, Parnell, Somerset, Wolf Creek Dam; *Dale Hollow Lake:* Albany, Byrdstown, Dale Hollow Dam, Dale Hollow Reservoir, Frogue, Moodyville, Savage; *Dewey Lake:* Lancer; *Fishtrap Lake:* Lick Creek, Millard; *Grayson Lake:* Ervin, Grayson, Willard; *Green River Lake:* Campbellsville, Cane Valley, Dunnville, Knifley, Mannsville; *Greenbo Lake:* Argillite, Oldtown; *Guist Creek Lake:* Shelbyville, Waddy; *Herrington Lake:* Bryantsville, Wilmore; *Kentucky Lake:* Birmingham Point, Briensburg, Buchanan, Calvert City, Fairdealing, Fenton, Grand Rivers, Hamlin, Hico, Mont, New Concord, Rushing Creek, Paris Landing; *Laurel Lake:* Ano, Corbin, London SW, Sawyer, Vox; *Nolin Lake:* Clarkson, Cub Run, Millerstown, Nolin Reservoir; *Rough River Lake:* Custer, Kingswood, Madrid, McDaniels.

GULF
COAST
STATES

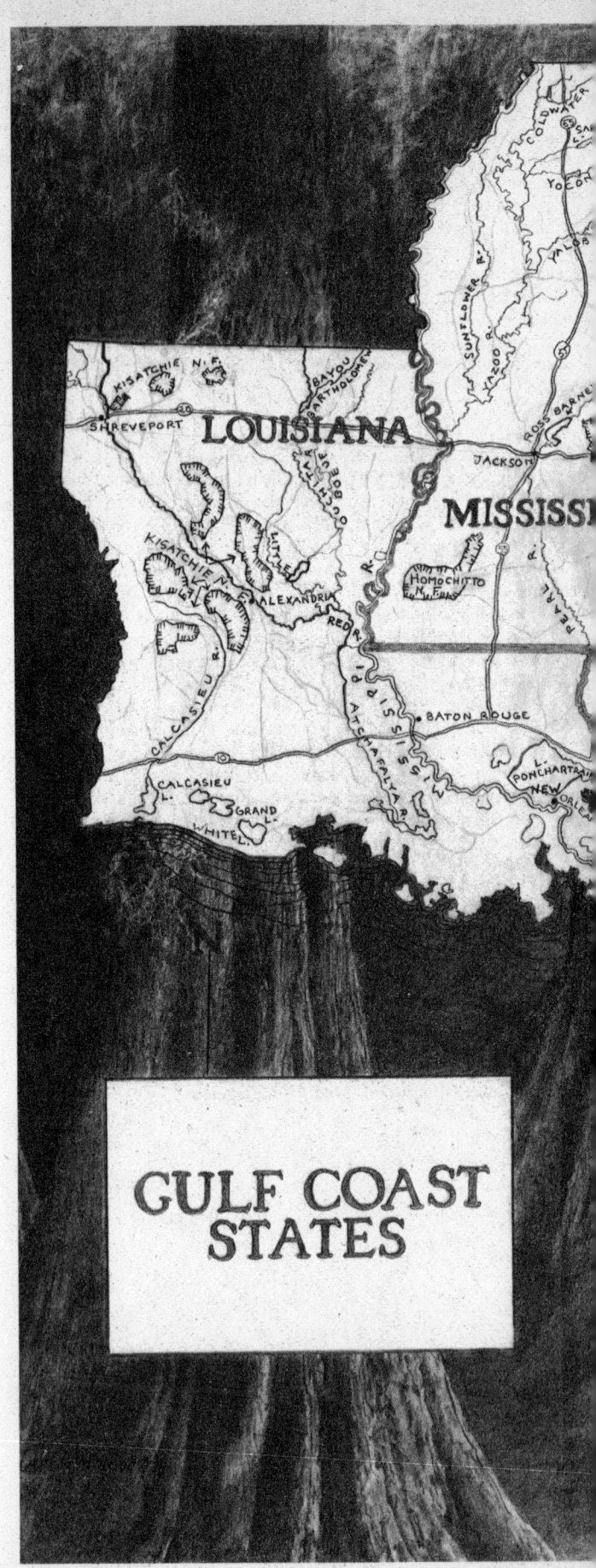

GULF COAST
STATES

Introduction

The generous pine and hardwood forests, rolling fields, lakes and reservoirs, beautiful moss-draped cypress bayous and meandering rivers, and the sun-drenched isles, lagoons, reefs, and flats of the Gulf Coast offshore waters offer some of the nation's finest trophy bass fishing, hunting, camping, and saltwater-fishing opportunities. The famous bayou country of the lower Mississippi and the Florida Everglades support swampland forests of cypress and tupelo gum, with stands of ash, poplar, and fragrant magnolia. These areas are clotted with swamp lilies and other water plants, and are inhabited by an incredible variety of wildlife, including deer, black bear, panther, bald eagle, osprey, sandhill cranes, great blue herons, alligators, and several varieties of poisonous snakes. In the warm tidal inlets of southern Florida and the Ten Thousand Islands in the backwaters of the Florida Keys, dense mangrove thickets provide havens for trophy snook and silver tarpon.

Weather, Bugs & Beasts

Winters in Louisiana, Mississippi, Alabama, and Florida are mild, with January mean temperatures of about 40 degrees, although on occasion temperatures drop well below freezing. Summers are hot and humid, with means between 75 and 85 degrees. The coasts of Louisiana and Mississippi have the hottest weather. Average yearly precipitation ranges from 40 to 60 inches, with more rain falling in the summer. Violent hurricanes whip the coast in the late summer and early fall.

Potential wildlife hazards include black bear in the remote wild country of Florida's interior, alligators, and poisonous timber rattlesnakes, coral snakes, cottonmouth moccasins, and copperheads. Fishermen, canoeists, and hunters planning trips in the bayou country and interior forests are advised to carry antivenom kits and a good supply of insect repellent; use Muskol, Mosquitone, Cutters or Off!—all of which contain a 50%-plus concentration of DEET, the most effective known repellent. It is advisable to bring a wide-brimmed hat, light-colored shirts, rain gear, and Polaroid sunglasses to cut the water glare.

Gulf Coast Maps & Charts—How to Order

The topographic maps listed throughout the Gulf Coast States chapters will provide you with a valuable guide to the area you plan to visit, and show all manmade and natural features, including contours, swamps, rivers, lakes, clearings, springs, roads, trails, rapids, islands, hills, national forests and parks, wildlife management areas, wildlife refuges, and state forests and parks. All maps listed (unless otherwise noted) are full-color U.S. Geological Survey overview maps, scale 1: 250,000, 1 inch to 4 miles ($2 each), or large-scale 7½-minute and 15-minute maps ($1.25 each for either). These maps and free *Topographic Map Indexes* of each of the Gulf Coast States may be ordered (along with a free *Map Symbol Chart* and *Topographic Maps* booklet) from the Distribution Branch, 1200 S. Eads St., Arlington, VA 22202. Maps of Louisiana should be ordered from the Distribution Branch, U. S. Geological Survey, Federal Center, Denver, CO 80225. Be sure to order maps by their individual names (and indicate scale when ordering 1:250,000-scale maps); to expedite your order, include extra money for first-class postage.

Large, useful U.S. Geological Survey *State Topographic Maps* of Louisiana, Mississippi, Alabama, and Florida are published with a scale of 1:500,000, or about 1 inch to 8 miles, and may be ordered for $2 each from the addresses listed above. A free catalog, *Atlantic and Gulf*

Coasts Nautical Charts, may be obtained by writing: National Ocean Survey, Distribution Division (C44), Riverdale, MD 20840. The catalog contains a complete listing of small-craft and recreational craft charts and Gulf Coast nautical publications. Waterproof, 23 × 35-inch *Lake Contour Maps* showing all underwater structures and features are available for 200 Southern United States lakes and reservoirs. For a free listing of mapped lakes and prices, write: Lakes Illustrated, Box 4854 GS, Springfield, MO 65804.

A handy 214-page guidebook, *Be Expert with Map and Compass,* by Bjorn Kjellstrom, the president and founder of Silva Compasses, may be obtained for $6.95 from Charles Scribner's Sons, Bookstore Dept., 597 Fifth Ave., New York, NY 10017.

Accommodations

For information about Louisiana's fishing and hunting lodges, family-vacation resorts, and hotels and motels, write to the Tourist Development Commission, P.O. Box 44291, Baton Rouge 70804, or to the local Chamber of Commerce of the area you plan to visit. Vacation cottages are available at the Chicot, Chemin-A-Haut, Lake Bistineau, and Sam Houston state parks.

Camping & State Recreation Areas

This land of forests, rolling fields, scenic moss-hung cypress swamps, bayous, rivers, and lakes provides excellent opportunities for family vacations as well as primitive camping. A guide to all state-park camping areas is contained in the *Louisiana State Parks* brochure, available free upon request from the State Parks & Recreation Commission, P.O. Drawer 1111, Baton Rouge 70821. It also describes recreation facilities in all state-park areas. Free information about fees, facilities, and regulations may be obtained at the same address.

Fishing & Hunting in the Bayou State

Louisiana's winding bayous, lakes, swamp streams, coastal marshes, forests, and rolling fields offer some superb fishing and hunting opportunities. The northern and central regions of the Bayou State are composed of gentle hills, pine forests, and thick pockets of cypress swamps, laced by bayous and dotted with lakes and sprawling reservoirs. Huge 250,000-acre Toledo Bend Reservoir—formed by damming the Sabine River along the Louisiana-Texas border—is the region's major body of water and offers some of the South's top fishing for big largemouth bass and crappie. Toledo Bend is also the state's top striped-bass fishery. The state record 25 lb. 4 oz. striper was taken here in 1976. Turkey Creek Lake and D'Arbonne Lake are among the most productive trophy bass and crappie lakes in the state. The latter lake also holds striped bass, stocked by the Wildlife and Fisheries Commission. Other top-ranked fishing waters in northern and central Louisiana include 13,500-acre Black Lake, and Chicot, Claiborne, Nantachie, and Vernon lakes. The shallow, cypress-studded backwater lakes and beautiful long, narrow oxbow lakes along the mighty Mississippi, known to the Indians as the "father of waters," provide good fishing for crappie, bream, bass, and catfish. The major fishing waters include the "flats" of False River Lake, noted for their spectacular bluegill fishing, and Bruin, St. John, Providence, and Concordia lakes. Some 850,000 acres of game-management areas in the northern and central regions provide good hunting in season for whitetail deer and small game.

Southern Louisiana has a varied terrain, which includes a region of bayous and swamps in the southeast, the 4-million-acre Atchafalaya Swamp, prairie country in the southwest, and pine forests laced by swift streams north of Lake Pontchartrain. The famous Atchafalaya Swamp (derived from the Choctaw Indian word meaning "long river") has good deer and duck hunting, canoe-camping, and fishing for trophy largemouth bass, crappie, and bream in Henderson, Catahoula, Grand, Dauterive, and Six-mile lakes and in Bayou Sorrel, Little Bayou Pigeon, Big Bayou Pigeon, the Upper Grand River, and in countless named and unnamed bayous to the west of the Atchafalaya River. Detailed topo maps are a must in this labyrinth of islands, bayous, and unmarked trails. The clear, fast-flowing streams of the bayous in the Florida parishes, located north of lakes Maurepas and Pontchartrain, provide good fishing for spotted bass, warmouth, rock bass, crappie, and catfish. Some excellent float fishing, using live bait such as shiners, night crawlers, crawfish, and crickets, or joined

surface lures and Rapala-type lures, may be found in the Amite River, Bayou Sara, Bayou Lacombe, and the Blind, Natallany, Pearl, Pushepatapa, Tanipahoa, Tchefuncte, and Tickfaw rivers.

The coastal marshes of Louisiana provide superb duck and goose shooting, plus fishing in the brackish tidal inlets and bays for speckled trout, redfish, and flounder. The major inland coastal fishing areas include the Sabine, Lacassine, and Rockefeller wildlife refuges; Calcasieu Lake, noted for its superb speckled-trout fishing; and the Point-au-Chien, Salvador, Wiener, Biloxi, and Bohemia wildlife-management areas in the southeast. The offshore waters of the Gulf of Mexico offer red snapper, cobia, bluefish, African pompano, dolphin, tarpon, amberjack, Spanish and king mackerel, particularly around the oil-

drilling platforms, which serve as a natural sanctuary for bait fish. Trophy billfish ride the "Loop" current each summer across the gulf. The major charter-boat centers for offshore fishing along the gulf shore are headquartered at Grand Isle, Empire, and Cameron.

The fishing potential of the Bayou State's lakes and streams and tidal waters is reflected in the listing (p. 445) of record fish, compiled by the Wildlife and Fisheries Commission.

The coastal lakes, grain fields, wooded swamps, marshes, and rivers of Louisiana form the major wintering area for ducks and geese east of the Rocky Mountains. Whitetail deer are found throughout the state, with the prime hunting grounds found in the hardwood deltas along

the Mississippi and Atchafalaya rivers and in the central and northwest pine-woods areas. The greatest concentrations of wild turkey are found in the forested Florida parishes (counties) and northeast parishes along the Mississippi River. Bobwhite quail range throughout the state, with the best wing shooting found in the cutover pine woods in the south-central region. Louisiana is the major wintering area of the North American woodcock—also known as the "timberdoodle" or, locally, as the "bec." Woodcock range throughout the state, particularly in the forested areas with wet soils, where they probe with their long bills for earthworms. Other popular bird and game species include gray and fox squirrels, swamp and cottontail rabbits, and waterfowl.

LOUISIANA RECORD FISH

	Lb.-oz.	Year
Freshwater Fish		
Largemouth bass	12–0	1975
Spotted bass	4–14	1976
Striped bass	25–4	1976
Bream	2–8	1959
White bass	3–14	1969
Largemouth bass on flyrod	8–8	1971
Crappie	6–0	1969
Warmouth	1–8	1973
Catfish	62–0	1970
Saltwater Fish		
Tarpon	206–0	1973
Cobia	96–0	1973
Dolphin	71–4	1976
Speckled trout	12–6	1950
Amberjack	101–12	1975
Spanish mackerel	10–9	1972
African pompano	23–2	1975
Redfish	56–8	1968
Pompano	8–8	1969
King mackerel	72–0	1976

For additional fishing and hunting information and regulations, write to the Wildlife and Fisheries Commission, 400 Royal St., New Orleans 70130. The commission publishes the following free fishing and hunting guides: a 39-page *Guide to Fishing in Louisiana*, a comprehensive illustrated guide to the major fishing areas and species; and a 67-page illustrated *Guide to Hunting in Louisiana*, which provides descriptions of game species and all state wildlife-management areas.

Highways—Recreation & Scenic Routes

The state of Louisiana Dept. of Highways, Baton Rouge 70804, will send you a free *Louisiana State Highway Map*. It shows cities and towns, major and minor roads, route markers and population symbols, access points, mileage between major points, state parks, forests, wildlife preserves, rest areas, boat launching ramps, points of interest, ferries, airports, and campsites. It also includes an index of recreation sites and a mileage table. Close-up maps of New Orleans, Lafayette, Lake Charles, Monroe, Alexandria, Baton Rouge, and Shreveport are provided, as well as detailed close-ups of the Interstate highways entering these cities. A special feature is a chart of highway signs.

Kisatchie National Forest

This 595,000-acre forest reserve varies in terrain from dark, cathedral-like cypress swamps with hanging moss to the famous sandstone Kisatchie Hills. The forest—which encompasses the Cloud Crossing Recreation Area, Saline Lake, Kincaid Reservoir, Saline Bayou, and the Catahoula, Fort Polk, and Red Dirt game-management areas in central Louisiana—provides excellent opportunities for fishing, hunting, canoeing, camping, and backpacking.

The *Kisatchie National Forest Recreation Map*, available for 50¢ from the Forest Supervisor, Kisatchie National Forest, 2500 Shreveport Highway, Pineville 71360, shows major and minor roads, parish and state lines, landing fields, boat ramps, rest areas, points of interest, hunting camps, district ranger stations, lookout stations, campgrounds, and work centers. It also includes a recreation-site facilities index and a general description of the area.

A GUIDE TO FISHING IN LOUISIANA
THE SPORTSMAN'S PARADISE
Paul M. Jackson and Dan Timmer, Jr.
Wildlife Education Specialists
Louisiana Wildlife and Fisheries Commission

The forest is reached via U.S. highways 71, 165, 167, and 84, and Louisiana state highways 19, 21, and 28. Overnight accommodations, supplies, and equipment rentals are available at Alexandria, Leesville, Minden, and Winnfield. The forest is shown on the following U.S. Geological Survey 1:250,000-scale Topographic Maps: Alexandria, Lake Charles, and Shreveport.

MISSISSIPPI ENCYCLOPEDIA

Accommodations

For detailed information on fishing and hunting lodges, vacation resorts, motels, and hotels throughout the state, write to the Travel/-Tourism Department, Mississippi Agricultural & Industrial Board, P.O. Box 849, Jackson 39205, or to the local Chamber of Commerce of the area you plan to visit. A complete listing of state-park lodges and cabin facilities is contained in the 95-page *Mississippi Travel Guide,* available free upon request from the Travel/Tourism Department (address above).

Camping & State Recreation Areas

Comprehensive listings and descriptions of all commercial, state-park, and national-forest campgrounds are contained in the free 95-page *Mississippi Travel Guide,* available upon request from the Travel/-Tourism Department, Mississippi Agricultural & Industrial Board, P.O. Box 849, Jackson 39205. This indispensable guide also contains a listing of all Mississippi lake and reservoir campgrounds, and descriptions of types of facilities available, including trailer camping, tent camping, group camping, and primitive camping as well as boat-launching sites, trailer-hook-up sites, tent showers, and recreation attractions.

Fishing & Hunting in Mississippi

Mississippi's scenic pine and hardwood forests, rolling fields, coastal waters, lakes, streams, reservoirs, cypress-shaded bayous, and marshlands provide excellent fishing and hunting opportunities. The state's major freshwater fish species include largemouth, spotted, striped, and white bass; blue and channel catfish; and hordes of white perch, bream, and crappie. The state's 19 upland wildlife areas, national-forest game lands, 9 waterfowl areas, and 2 national wildlife refuges provide outstanding hunting in season for whitetail deer, gray (or cat) fox and squirrel, rabbits, wild turkey, and rafts of dove, quail, mallards, black ducks, and pheasant. In addition to the public game lands, the state licenses 75 shooting preserves, where hunting is permitted on payment of a fee.

The northern Lakes and Hills Region of the Magnolia State contains the foothills of the Great Smokies and the "great lakes"—huge reservoirs that have hundreds of miles of shoreline, marvelous fishing for trophy bass and bream, and some of the nation's top duck-hunting lands. Pickwick Lake, on Tennessee's TVA Pickwick Dam on the Tennessee River in the northeast corner of the state, offers fishing for largemouth bass, striped or white bass, walleye, crappie, and bream. Pickwick is Mississippi's largest body of freshwater. Other major bass lakes and streams include Arkabutla Reservoir, which covers 52 square miles, surrounded by 28,200 acres of public hunting lands; Y-shaped Grenada Reservoir, with 75,000 acres of public game lands; and Log Loader Lake, Sunflower River, Black Bayou, Six-Mile Lake, and Horn, Beaver, Lamar Bruce, Lee, and Dumas lakes and the Sardis River, which extends up the Little Tallahatchie River for 30 miles. The prime public game lands in the northern lake and hill country include Holly Springs National Forest and the reservoir waterfowl areas, and Malmaison and John Bell Williams wildlife-management areas, and Yellow Creek Waterfowl Area on Pickwick Reservoir.

The fertile Mississippi Delta Region, which stretches along the western boundary of the state, has good fishing for bass, crappie, bream, and catfish in the innumerable lakes formed by the ever-changing Mississippi, Sunflower, and Yazoo rivers. The major lakes of the region include Beulah, Bolivar, Old River, De Soto, Horseshoe, Tchula, Little Eagle, Chotard, Yazoo, McIntyre Scatters, Lower Ossy, Mink, Buzzard Bayou, and 17-mile-long Tunica Cutt-off lake (an old bed of the Mississippi), Moon Lake (a cut-off bend in the "Ole Miss"), and Ferguson, Washington, and Deer lakes. The 30,000-acre Ross Barnett Reservoir, in the southwest corner of the state, is the site of the annual National Bass Anglers Sportsman Society Tournament (BASS). The lake's 150 miles of shoreline, with its numerous bays and dead timber areas, provide top-ranked fishing for trophy black bass, sea-run striped bass, crappie, bluegill, and catfish. The acorn-bearing hardwood forests, marshlands, and beautiful moss-hung, cypress-studded bayous provide good hunting for deer, dove, duck, quail, rabbit, squirrel, and turkey. The major public hunting areas include the Assaquena and Sunflower wildlife-management areas, Delta and Homochitto national forests, and the Indian Bayou Waterfowl Area, and Pearl River Waterfowl and Upland Birch Area.

The lakes, streams, gently rolling hills, extensive cornfields, and woodland borders on the Plains Region, in the east-central part of the state, the legendary hunting grounds of the Choctaw Indians, provide numerous hunting and fishing opportunities. Within the region is Nanih Waiya, an Indian mound considered to be the fabled birthplace of the Choctaw nation. The Chickasawhay River, which flows for 96 miles through the plains past high bluffs and limestone banks lined with southern pines and cypress, provides good float fishing for bass and bream. The major lakes include Long Creek Reservoir, American Legion Lake, Bluff and Loakfona lakes in the Noxubee National Wildlife Refuge, Lake Tiak-O'Khata, and the Big Noxubee River and Lobutchia, Noxapater, and Tallalaga creeks. The Plains Region provides good hunting in season for deer, wild turkey, mallard and black duck, and pheasant on its numerous private shooting preserves and on the Tombigbee and Bienville National Forest game lands, and the Tallalaga Creek Wildlife Management Area and Noxubee National Wildlife Refuge.

The southern Gulf Coast Region, with its hundreds of fishing camps, provides excellent bass, crappie, and bream fishing in the scenic Black and Beaver Dam creeks, Lake Bogue Homa, and countless remote lakes, ponds, and bayous. Hunting in season is for deer, turkey, rabbit, quail, and waterfowl on the De Soto National Forest game lands and on the Red Creek, Chickasawhay, Hugh L. White, Wolf River, Leaf River, and Little Biloxi state wildlife-management areas, as well as on several licensed shooting preserves. The tidal waters of the Gulf Coast and Mississippi Sound are havens for big redfish, speckled trout, white trout, flounders, bluefish, croaker, sheepshead, and tripletail. Famous Chanderbur Island and the isles of the Gulf Islands National Seashore—Ship, Horn, and Petit Bois—provide scenic unspoiled surf fishing. This beautiful string of islands protects the sound from the offshore winds. Charter boats from Biloxi and Gulfport provide offshore fishing for saltwater big-game fish, including tarpon.

For additional Magnolia State fishing and hunting regulations and information, write to the Game & Fish Commission, Box 451, Jackson 39205. The commission has available upon request the free publications *Hunt in Mississippi, Mississippi Commission Lakes,* and wildlife-management-area regulations sheets. The bimonthly magazine *Mississippi Game & Fish* is available free upon request to residents of the state from the commission (address above). A complete listing and description of state wildlife-management and waterfowl areas, lakes, reservoirs, streams, and fishing camps and licensed shooting preserves is contained in the 95-page full-color *Mississippi Travel Guide,* available free from the Travel/Tourism Department, P.O. Box 849, Jackson 39205.

Highways & Mississippi Recreation Travel Guide

Detailed highway maps of the state, including the Lakes and Hills, the Delta, the Plains, the Old and New South, and the Gulf Coast vacation regions, are contained in the 95-page *Mississippi Travel Guide,* available free upon request from the Travel/Tourism Department, Mississippi Agricultural & Industrial Board, P.O. Box 849, Jackson 39205. This eminently useful travel guide is packed full with information about Mississippi's weather and climate, little-known facts, natural resources, national forests, geography, hunting and fishing, pilgrimages, and region-by-region/county-by-county descriptions of historic sites and buildings, county fairs and festivals, scenic attractions and museums, recreational activities, reservoirs, campgrounds, rock- and fossil-collecting areas, and shooting preserves.

The "travel guide" also contains a detailed *Natchez Trace Parkway Map* as well as descriptions of all major recreation and historic attractions along this famed scenic route, which winds from Natchez, Mississippi, to Nashville, Tennessee. This national parkway, maintained and administered by the National Park Service, crosses the state from its northeast corner to its southwest boundary, passing through beautiful forests of majestic pines and moss-hung oaks, along the ancient Natchez Trace Indian Trail and pioneer route. The major features shown along the trace include Emerald Mound—a temple mound built by an unknown tribe of Indians—Owl Creek Indian Mounds, Pigeon Roost, Bynum Mounds, the legendary Witch Dance, De Soto's Crossing, and the old Chickasaw Village. This ancient wilderness route once connected the Natchez, Choctaw, and Chickasaw Indian villages. For detailed recreation travel information along the route, write: Natchez Trace Parkway, P.O. Box 948, Tupelo 38801.

An excellent guide, *Fossil & Mineral Collecting Localities in Mississippi,* available for $1.50 from the Geological Economic & Topographical Survey, 2525 Northwest St., P.O. Box 4915, Jackson 39216, gives explicit directions and maps to collections throughout the state.

National Forests in Mississippi

Mississippi's 1.5 million acres of national forestlands range from flat, black marshlands and spectacular bluffs to cypress-shaded bayous and dense cathedral-like pine and hardwood forests. The 177,000-acre *Bienville National Forest,* located in central Mississippi, includes

Coastal Plain second-growth pine and hardwood forests and the 189-acre virgin loblolly pine forest surrounding the Bienville Ranger Station. The 23-mile Shockaloe Riding Trail provides access to the scenic interior areas. The forest game lands provide hunting in season for quail, deer, and wild turkey. The forest is reached via U.S. 80 and State Highway 85. The 59,000-acre *Delta National Forest* in the west-central part of the state contains the Greentree Reservoir waterfowl-hunting area and the Red Gum Natural Area, a natural bottomland hardwood stand. The forest is reached along U.S. 61 and state routes 16, 14, and 3. The 500,000-acre *De Soto National Forest,* situated in the southeast corner of the state, is the site of the South Mississippi Gun and Dog Club field trials and includes the Tuxachanie Trail, which winds through pine forests and scenic bottomland hardwoods, and two of the nation's most scenic float-fishing streams, Black Creek and Beaver Dam Creek. The forest's acorn-bearing hardwoods make the area a hunters' mecca for deer, wild turkey, and waterfowl. Other features in the forest include Airey Lake, Big Biloxi River, and Thompson Creek. The forest is reached via U.S. 11, 49, and 90 and State Highway 26. *Holly Springs National Forest,* which encompasses 145,000 acres in northern Mississippi, is the site of annual bird-dog field trials at Holly Springs, and the Chewalla Lake and Puskus Lake fish and game areas. The forest provides top-ranked hunting in season for whitetail deer, quail, squirrel, and wild turkey. The forest is reached via U.S. 72 and 78 and Mississippi 7 and 15. The 192,000-acre *Homochitto National Forest* in southwest Mississippi offers fishing, hiking, and primitive camping opportunities in the Clear Lake, Woodman Springs, and Pie's Lake areas, and top hunting in the Amite and Franklin wildlife-management areas for deer, wild turkey, and squirrel. The forest is reached via U.S. highways 61 and 84 and State Route 33. *Tombigbee National Forest,* encompassing 65,000 acres in the northern portion of the state, contains Upper Coastal Plain pine and hardwood forests, ancient Indian mounds, Davis and Choctaw lakes recreation areas, and a portion of the Natchez Trace Parkway. Beautiful 200-acre Davis Lake, near the Owl Creek Indian Mounds, is close to the site of explorer Hernando de Soto's winter camp. The forest provides good hunting in season for deer and quail. Access is via U.S. 82, the Natchez Trace Parkway, and Mississippi routes 8 and 15.

Specific fishing, hunting, camping, hiking, and canoeing information may be obtained from the Forest Supervisor, National Forests in Mississippi, Box 1291, Jackson 39205. A full-color *De Soto National Forest Recreation Map* (50¢) may be obtained from the Supervisor's office, along with the following free publications: *Outdoors in Your Southern National Forests, National Forests in Mississippi, Black Creek Float Trip* (De Soto National Forest), *Tuxachanie Trail* (De Soto National Forest), *Chewalla Recreation Area* (Holly Springs National Forest), *Clear Springs Recreation Area* (Homochitto National Forest), *Big Foot Horse Trails* (De Soto National Forest), and *Shockaloe Trail* (Bienville National Forest).

Accommodations

For information on Alabama's vacation lodges and resorts, motels, and hotels, write the Alabama Travel Department, State Capitol, Montgomery 36104 (call toll free (800) 633–5761). Additional information may be obtained by writing to the local Chamber of Commerce of the area you plan to visit.

Camping & State Recreation Areas

Alabama's state-park recreation areas provide a complete range of camping facilities, from primitive backcountry campsites to modern family campgrounds with complete connections for large motor homes or trailers. A comprehensive listing of state-park and Corps of Engineers campgrounds, including descriptions of facilities and recreation activities, is contained in the 58-page *Alabama Travel Guide*, available free upon request from the Alabama Travel Department, State Capitol, Montgomery 36104. Alabama's state parks range from De Soto State Park on Lookout Mountain in the foothills of the Smokies, surrounded by pine forests, with fishing and canoeing in Little River Canyon, to Gulf State Park, overlooking the Gulf of Mexico. A free guide, *Alabama State Parks*, may be obtained by writing: Division of State Parks, 64 North Union St., Montgomery 36104.

Fishing & Hunting in Alabama

Alabama's Gulf of Mexico coastal waters, inland lakes, reservoirs, scenic rivers, and national forest and state wildlife-management-area game lands offer some outstanding fishing and hunting opportunities.

The Cotton State's sprawling reservoirs, ranging in size from 560 acres to 67,086 acres, dot the Mountain Lake Country of the northern region and the Black Belt Country of the Central Region, and provide good seasonal angling for a wide variety of fish, including chain pickerel; largemouth, smallmouth, and spotted bass; crappie, walleye, bluegill, white bass, warmouth, and a few stocked striped bass up to trophy weights. The major impoundments in central Alabama include 9,200-acre Bankhead Lake on the Black Warrior River, with a sinuous shoreline of over 400 miles; Warrior Lock and Dam Lake on the Black Warrior River, which covers 7,800 acres with a 300-mile shoreline; 5,850-acre Lake Tuscaloosa on the North River, with a 177-mile shoreline; 10,000-acre Demopolis Reservoir on the Tombigbee River; deep, rocky 6,800-acre Lake Jordan, which offers striped-bass fishing below Mitchell Dam; 22,000-acre Miller's Ferry Reservoir on the Alabama River, which provides good spring fishing for chain pickerel, channel catfish, and a few striped bass; and sprawling Lake Eufaula, once considered by many to be one of the nation's top trophy largemouth-bass lakes, which covers 45,000 acres on the Chattahoochee River. Other productive central Alabama lakes include Holt, Oliver Pool, Claiborne, Big Creek, Shelby, Jones Bluff, Yates, Thurlow, Bartlett's Ferry, Goat Rock, Oliver, Columbia, and Gantt.

The great reservoirs of northern Alabama, surrounded by the rolling foothills of the ancient Appalachian Mountains, offer some of the nation's top-ranked trophy largemouth and smallmouth bass fishing. Pickwick Lake, which straddles the Alabama-Tennessee border on the Tennessee River, is one of the nation's top smallmouth-bass lakes, as is Wilson Lake, the oldest of the four TVA reservoirs in Alabama. Impounded in 1924, Wilson has yielded trophy smallmouths that grow to trophy weights of 10½ pounds, feeding on the large schools

of gizzard shad found in all the TVA impoundments. Wheeler Lake, a 67,100-acre TVA impoundment, is noted for its crappie, bass, bream, and striped-bass fishing. Huge 69,100-acre Guntersville Lake, the largest lake in the state, provides often spectacular fishing for crappie and bream during the June willow-fly hatchings, and trophy largemouth bass during the spring and early summer. The hundreds of acres of flooded woodlands in 12,000-acre Lay Lake yield huge stringers of big largemouth and spotted bass and crappies. Other major lakes of the northern mountain country include Smith, Weiss, Neely, Henry, Logan Martin, Mitchell, and Martin lakes and the beautiful unspoiled Inland Lake, which provides good fishing for rainbow trout.

Float Fishing the Wild & Scenic Rivers

The beautiful, wild West Fork of the Sipsey River, a feeder stream of the Lewis-Smith Reservoir, rises in the rugged backcountry of northwest Alabama and flows through the Bee Branch Scenic Area and a wilderness of narrow ridges, canyons, deep valleys, waterfalls, sheer rock bluffs, and lush vegetation in the Bankhead National Forest to its mouth on the reservoir. This beautiful stream offers unspoiled float fishing for spotted bass, white bass, and fat bluegills. May, June,

September, and October are the most productive months to float the Sipsey. The beautiful Cahaba River rises in Lake of the Woods in the Central Region and flows for 162 miles past scenic woodlands—with thick undergrowths of colorful dogwood, wild azalea, and mountain laurel—and sheer rock bluffs to its mouth on the Alabama River at Old Cahaba. The Cahaba provides good float fishing along its entire length for walleye and river redhorse and for bream and spotted bass in the upper stretches, and largemouth bass, crappie, and bluegill along the lower coastal-plain stretches. Numerous sand and gravel bars provide natural campsites. The sunken logs and weed beds of the Tallapoosa River, upstream from Lake Martin, provide excellent fishing for scrappy spotted bass and largemouths. The scenic, wild, boulder-strewn waters of the upper river provide superb float-fishing opportunities. Other top-ranked float-fishing streams that offer long stretches of wild country include the upper Black Warrior River, Coosa River, and Little River.

The angling potential of Alabama's lakes and streams is illustrated by the state record fish, caught on rod and reel, compiled by the Department of Conservation & Natural Resources.

ALABAMA RECORD FISH

	Lb.-oz.	Place	Year
Largemouth bass	14–4	Private Pond	1976
Smallmouth bass	10–8	Wheeler Dam	1950
Walleye	8–4	Tallapoosa River	1970
Muskellunge	79–8	Wilson Dam	1972
Striped bass	55–0	Tallassee	—
Rainbow trout	5–13½	Lewis Smith Reservoir	1973
Chain pickerel	6–5½	Dyas Creek	1976
Crappie, black	4–5	Lay Lake	1978
Sauger	5–2	Wilson Dam	1972
Spotted bass*	8–10½	Lewis Smith Lake	1972
Redeye bass*	6–½	Hallawakee Creek	1967
White bass	4–4	Lake Jordan	1972
Bluegill	4–12	Ketona Lake	1950
Blue catfish	46–4	Guntersville Dam Tailrace	1976
Channel catfish	40–0	Inland Lake	1967
Flathead catfish	40–0	Tallapoosa River	1973
Yellow bass	1–9½	Inland Lake	1974
Redear sunfish	4–4	Chattahoochee Park	1962
Alligator gar	120–0	Mobile Bay	1974
Spoonbill catfish	38–8	Tennessee River	1976

*World's record.

Saltwater Fishing

Alabama offers an interesting variety of saltwater fishing in its bays, tidal streams, and offshore waters. The rivers and bayous of the great 40-mile-long Mobile Delta—including the bays of the lower delta, Tensaw River, Johns Bend, and the bayous and lakes of the middle and upper delta—provide fishing for crappie, yellow bass, white bass, striped bass, catfish, huge alligator gars often in excess of 100 pounds, as well as for speckled trout (weakfish) and white trout, redfish, croaker, and flounder in the bays and tidal streams. Charter boats and skiffs provide seasonal offshore fishing for tarpon—the state fish—and for king mackerel, kingfish, bluefish, barracuda, blackfin tuna, dolphin, snapper, cobia, ladyfish, pompano, big sharks, amberjack, channel bass, sea trout, and sailfish.

Hunting

The state's rolling hill country, fields, woodlands, and wild marshes offer hunting in season for quail, dove, whitetail deer, wild turkey, and ducks and geese in the Mobile Delta and Tennessee Valley of northern Alabama.

For detailed hunting and fishing information, regulations, and free *Wildlife Management Area Maps*, write: Department of Conservation & Natural Resources, Montgomery 36130.

Highways—Recreation & Scenic Routes

The free *Alabama State Highway Map* is available from the Alabama Travel Dept., State Capitol, Montgomery 36104. It shows all major and minor routes, mileage between major points, points of interest, state parks, airports, rest areas, and national and state forests. It includes a state-park index and many color pictures of the state's attractions. A free travel guide to vacation highlights off the Interstate highway system, *Interstate Interludes*, may be obtained by writing the Alabama Travel Dept. (address above).

National Forest Reserves

A full-color map, *Alabama National Forests*, showing major roads, trails, trail shelters, boat ramps, forest-service recreation sites, lookout stations, and hunting camps, may be obtained for 50¢ from the Forest Supervisor, P.O. Box 40, Montgomery 36101. This useful map shows the fishing, hunting, and camping areas of the 360,000-acre Talladega National Forest in the northeast corner of the state at the southernmost thrust of the Appalachian Mountains, including the South Sandy Wildlife Management Area, 2,407-foot Mount Cheaha (the highest point in the state), Lake Chinnabee, Choccolocco Wildlife Management Area and Sweetwater Lake, Hollins Wildlife Management Area, and the scenic Skyway Motorway and Talladega Scenic Drive; the 181,000-acre Bankhead National Forest, in the northwest region of the state, which includes the bass waters of sprawling Lake Lewis Smith with its sheer rock-wall-lined shoreline, the famed Black Warrior Wildlife Management Area, Bee Branch Scenic Area, and the deep canyons of the wild Sipsey River; the 85,000-acre Conecuh National Forest; and the 11,000-acre Tuskegee National Forest.

Tennessee Valley Lakes— Maps & Navigation Charts

Recreation on TVA Lakes, available free from the TVA Map Sales Office, Union Bldg., Knoxville, TN 37902, describes the entire region, provides information on public access, public parks, boat docks and resorts, fishing, boating, camping, water safety, and the Land Between the Lakes Recreational Area. The map shows lakes, rivers, forests, state parks, and roads and includes a close-up of the Land Between the Lakes. Complete listings are given for boat docks, resorts, state parks, U.S. Forest Service camp areas, and county and municipal parks with docks or camping areas.

Recreation maps of *Pickwick Lake, Guntersville Lake*, and *Wheeler Reservoir* are available free from TVA Map Sales (address above). They show public-use areas, public lands, commercial recreation areas, commercial boat docks, public parks, wildlife-management areas, boat-launching sites, and private lands. They also show roads, lakes, rivers, and parks. A free *Index to Navigation Charts & Maps of TVA Reservoirs* may be obtained upon request from the TVA Map Sales Office.

FLORIDA
ENCYCLOPEDIA

Accommodations— Vacation Resorts & Lodges

Travelers in Florida should consult the *Florida Hotel & Motel Guide* for information on where to stay. This free publication is available from the Florida Hotel & Motel Association, Inc., P.O. Box 8788, Jacksonville 32211. The booklet contains information about rates and facilities of all Florida Hotel & Motel Association members at the time of compilation of the publication. The accommodations are listed alphabetically by town, and there is a handy form included so that you can make reservations by mail if you wish. Several toll-free reservation numbers (for phoning in Florida only) are provided, should you wish to reserve or obtain additional information.

For further information on any of the Dept. of Natural Resources vacation facilities, write to the Department, Bureau of Education and Information, Room 321, Crown Building, Tallahassee 32304; phone (904) 488–7326. The Dept. of Natural Resources will send you a free *Vacation Cottages and Group Camping* describing the cabins and camping areas and providing information on current rates and reservation policies of each park.. Another helpful agency is the Dept. of Commerce, Tallahassee 32304. They will be glad to provide you with information on accommodations and vacation resorts in Florida.

Apalachicola National Forest

This scenic 556,480-acre reserve, from the Indian word meaning "people on the other side," lies in the eastern portion of the Florida panhandle and includes the renowned bass waters of the Ochlockonee River (Indian for "red oak") canoe trail, Lake Talquin, and the New, Sopchoppy, and Apalachicola rivers. Wildlife includes whitetail deer, black bear, the beautiful wood duck, southern bald eagle, sandhill crane, alligator, and panther. Campgrounds are located at Wright, Silver, Lost, and Moore lakes and at Trout Pond. The entire forest is a designated wildlife-management area, with hunting by special permit only.

Visitors to the Apalachicola National Forest will want to send for the *Apalachicola National Forest Map.* A copy can be obtained for 50¢ from the Forest Supervisor, P.O. Box 1050, Tallahassee 32302. This map shows roads and highways, wildlife-management areas, recreation areas, undeveloped sites, ranger headquarters, and work centers. The Forest Service also has available a free pamphlet describing the *Silver Lake Recreation Area,* noting the facilities available in the area, along with a map. For further information on Silver Lake, contact the District Ranger, P.O. Box 68, Crawfordville 32327.

The forest is reached by U.S. highways 98 and 319 and Florida 20, 65, and 369. Accommodations, supplies, and equipment rentals are available at Apalachicola, Blountstown, Bristol, and Tallahassee. The forest is shown on U.S. Geological Survey Overview Maps, scale 1: 250,000: Apalachicola and Tallahassee.

Boating & Intercoastal Waterways

Florida offers unlimited opportunities for pleasure cruising, exploration, and fishing along its 8,426 miles of coastal shoreline and hundreds of navigable lakes and scenic rivers. The Sunshine State's major waterways, including the Hawk Channel from Miami to Key West, West Coast Intercoastal Waterway, Okeechobee Waterway, St. Johns River, Oklawaha River, Kissimmee Waterway, Apalachicola River, and Suwannee River, are described in the free 100-page booklet *Florida Boating Safety,* available from the Division of Marine Resources, Crown Bldg., Tallahassee 32304.

This excellent booklet is chock-full of information on all aspects of boating—including tips on selecting and using a trailer to transport your boat, safety equipment (both that required by law and equipment not required but good to have on board), facts about fueling, boarding a boat, launching, "rules of the road," and a comprehensive directory of marine facilities in Florida listed by county. The booklet also has information on navigation, buoys, and weather, and includes a number of small maps. There are also brief sections on skin diving, sailing, and canoeing. Emergency measures and a glossary of nautical terms are also provided. This is a publication that every boater, from novice to expert, should have before setting out on a Florida boat trip.

Another useful publication is *Facts for Florida Boat Owners*, available free from the Dept. of Natural Resources, Crown Bldg., Tallahassee 32304. This brochure contains helpful facts on registration, fees, classification, and other rules and regulations regarding boat ownership and operation in Florida. For additional information, contact the Division of Marine Resources (at address above).

Camping & State Recreation Areas

Florida is a year-round camping paradise, and the Sunshine State offers extensive public and privately owned facilities ranging from fully developed parks to remote, primitive retreats. There are a number of booklets and brochures that provide listings and descriptions of Florida's many camping areas, so that you can select one that fits your desires and requirements.

The Florida Dept. of Commerce, Crown Bldg., Tallahassee 32304, has prepared an extensive, informative free booklet, *Florida Camping*, which lists, by region, camping areas in chart form, indicating available facilities in each area. A map inside the back cover will show you the location of each region. The ownership or administration of each area is also given (private, state park, national forest, etc.). It is wise to contact the campsite you are considering for current information on fees and availability of space (most private and public campgrounds accept reservations by phone *only*). If you write to the Florida Campground Assn., Inc., P.O. Box 10084, Tallahassee 32302, they will send you their free brochure *Private Campgrounds in Florida*, which contains a listing and brief description of Florida's private campgrounds. Their locations are shown on a road map, and the campgrounds are also listed in chart form, showing facilities available and proximity of facilities if they are not on the campground itself.

Two comprehensive guides to state parks and camping facilities— *Florida Camping & State Parks Guide* and *Camping in Florida's State Parks*—may be obtained from the Dept. of Commerce, Tallahassee 32304.

Canoe Trails & Float-Fishing Streams

The Florida Dept. of Natural Resources has established the Canoe Trail System, currently composed of sixteen wild and scenic rivers and creeks, including the Suwannee Wild and Scenic River, and the Kissimmee, St. Johns, Loxahatchee, Manatee, Escambia, Oklawaha, Withlacoochee, Peace, Chipola, Wacissa, Econfina, and Yellow rivers. These waters include renowned bass meccas that produce fish in the 10-pound class up to weights of 20 pounds. If you are planning a canoe trip in Florida, send for the free *Florida Canoe Trail Guide*. This useful, interesting 40-page booklet describes all the Florida canoe trails, and has illustrative maps showing the exact courses the trails take. The maps also show campsites, boat ramps, and wayside parks. You can get your copy by writing to the Dept. of Natural Resources, Division of Recreation and Parks, Larson Bldg., Tallahassee 32301.

The state's major float-fishing streams and trophy bass waters are shown on the following large-scale U.S. Geological Survey Topographic Maps. *Escambia River*, noted for its lagoons, reedy islands, and fishing camps: Century, Milton, Muscogee, Pensacola; *Kissimmee River and Lake*, one of Florida's largest trophy bass lakes: Basinger, Basinger NW, Basinger SW, Ft. Basinger, Ft. Kissimmee NW, Lake Marion NW, Lake Marion SW, Lake Weohyakapka, Lake Weohyakapka SW, Okeechobee NW, Taylor Creek; *Loxahatchee Recreational Area*, including Loxahatchee River (one of the South's last great wild rivers) and Slough trophy bass waters: Delat, Jupiter, Road, W. Palm Beach Farms; *Manatee River*, named for the odd herbivorous

mammal once plentiful in the tidal waterways: Duette, Kenntown, Myakka City NW, Parrish, Rye, Verna; *Withlacoochee River* (Indian for "little great river"), a top-ranked wild river that flows through some of the South's most picturesque swamp country, noted for its rapids, springs, and high waves: Borough, Branch, Dade City, Dunnellon, Dunnellon SW, Inverness, Lacoochee, Lake Panasoffkee NW, Nobleton, Rutland, St. Catherine, Stokes Ferry, Weldwood, Yankeetown, Yankeetown SW; *St. Johns River—Headwaters at Lake Helen Blazes to Lake George*, including Woodruff, Monroe, Harney, and Poinsett lakes trophy bass waters: Astor, Deer Park, Geneva, Lake Poinsett, Lake Poinsett NW, Lake Poinsett SW, Lake Woodruff, Orange, Osceola, Osteen, Sanford, and Titusville; *St. Johns River—Lake George to Jacksonville*: Astor, Fleming Island, Green Cove Springs, Hastings, Jacksonville, Orangedale, Orange Park, Palatka, Picolata, Riverdale, Salt Songs, Satsuma, Wilaka, Wilaka SE; *St. Marys River*: Boulogne, Folkston, Kings Ferry, Kingsland, Macclenny E., Macclenny NE, Macclenny NW, Macclenny W, Moniac, St. George, St. Marys, and Toledo; *Suwannee Wild & Scenic River*: Benton, Branford, Dowling Park, East Pass, Ellaville, Falmouth, Fargo SW, Fort Union, Hatchblend, Hillcrest, Live Oak, Manatee Springs, Mayo, Mayo SE, Suwannee, Suwannee River, Vista, Wanee, White Springs E, and White Springs.

Everglades National Park & Ten Thousand Islands

The famous fishing and canoeing area and wilderness reserve takes in the largest subtropical forest in the United States. The reserve covers

a vast wildland of beautiful, mangrove-bordered waterways along the famous trophy tarpon- and snook-fishing areas of the Ten Thousand Islands, inland to limestone flats, cypress swamps, sloughs, hammocks, dense tropical hardwood forests, and open woods of slash pine and saw palmetto inhabited by crocodiles, bald eagles, man-o'-war birds, wood ibis, rare manatees, alligators, flocks of white ibis, deer, and bear. The thousands of miles of interconnecting waterways and lakes, including vast Lake Okeechobee and the Loxahatchee Slough, offer some of the finest fishing in the country for tarpon, snook, and largemouth bass up to 18 pounds. Other features of the region include Okaloochee Swamp, Corkscrew Swamp, Big Cypress Indian Reserve, and Tamiami Canal. Some of the biggest tarpon caught in the state are found along the passes, creek mouths, and outside channels of the Ten Thousand Islands.

For information about guided park tours, hikes, and canoe adventures, write: Superintendent, Everglades National Park, Box 279, Homestead 33030.

For free maps that show the canal system of Florida from Orlando to the Everglades National Park, detailing locks, spillways, pump stations, and major roads, as well as a booklet, *Recreation in the Everglades,* containing maps described above and also launching ramps, write to: Central and Southern Florida Flood Control District, P.O. Box V, West Palm Beach 33402.

The park is reached via the Tamiami Trail, U.S. Route 41, and Florida 27 from Miami. Lodging, meals, marina services, charter fishing boats, and sightseeing boat trips are provided by *Everglades Park Catering, Inc.,* 301 Miamarina Parkway Dr., Miami 33132; phone (305) 358–5480. Boats, motors, fishing, and tour guides are provided by *Sawgrass Recreational Area,* P.O. Box 22755, Ft. Lauderdale 33315, and *Everglades Holiday Park,* P.O. Box 22750, Ft. Lauderdale 33315.

The Everglades and Ten Thousand Islands are shown on the following U.S. Geological Survey Overview Maps, scale 1:250,000: Key West, Miami, W. Palm Beach.

Fishing & Hunting in the Sunshine State

Florida is nationally famous for its trophy largemouth bass and saltwater fishing. This 447-mile-long peninsula is divided into four geographic regions: the eastern Atlantic coastal strip, bordering the Atlantic to Key West; the rolling central lake district; the western coastal region; and the western panhandle, which includes the hill country along the north shore of the Gulf of Mexico. The Everglades, until 1842 a mysterious, unexplored region known only to the Seminole Indians, form one of the nation's largest wilderness areas. The famous snook and tarpon waters of the Ten Thousand Islands, fringing the lower gulf and the Whitewater Bay and Florida Bay, are a labyrinth of mangrove-tangled islets broken by swift-running tide channels. An estimated 30,000 lakes dot the low-lying terrain of the Sunshine State, ranging in depth from 2 to 27 feet and in size from small ponds to giant Lake Okeechobee, which has a surface area of 717 square miles.

Saltwater Fishing

Florida's east and west coasts and the Florida Keys have long been famous for the quality of their saltwater fishing. The cooler waters of the eastern Atlantic coast provide seasonal fishing for bluefish, Spanish mackerel, giant spotted sea trout up to 13 pounds, tarpon, red and black drum, sheepshead, whiting, crevalle, ladyfish, snook, and tarpon, and Gulf Stream gamefish including sailfish, blue marlin, blackfin tuna, dolphin, kingfish, yellowtail, amberjack, and wahoo. Popular east-coast fishing areas include the inshore tidal waters and offshore waters in the St. Augustine, Daytona, Jacksonville, New Smyrna,

Halifax, and Tomoka rivers, Indian River, Banana River, Mosquito Lagoon, Cocoa Beach, St. Lucie River, Stuart, Palm Beach, Boynton, and the tidal canals and offshore waters of the Miami area. Excellent seasonal fishing is found in Biscayne Bay (Miami) for bonefish along the grassy flats, mackerel, bluefish, ladyfish, big schools of marauding jack crevalle, barracuda, snook, tarpon, and permit along the edges of the deep flats.

The western coast, along the Gulf of Mexico, offers nationally famous spin and fly fishing for giant tarpon to well over 100 pounds, and snook along the beautiful mangrove-tangled Ten Thousand Islands and the Shark River wilderness in Everglades National Park; Boca Grande, at the mouth of the Myakka and Peace rivers; and at nearly every point along the coast north to Pensacola for most marine gamefish, including red drum, mangrove snappers, spotted sea trout, grouper, bluefish, sheepshead, red snapper, and king and Spanish mackerel. Along the northwest coastal areas, sailfish move in close to the shoreline and remain until the cold water forces them to follow the "Loop" current south. A dramatic run of cobia, or "ling," occurs off northwest Florida's "Miracle Strip" on the Gulf Coast beaches after the first of April.

Hundreds of party boats, locally called "head boats," for drifting and bottom fishing, and charter boats for deep-water trolling and drifting the reefs for sailfish, marlin, dolphin, bonito, kingfish, mackerel, and an occasional tuna, are anchored at the major fishing centers up and down both coasts and provide convenient access to the offshore hot spots. "Tarpon boats," used for shoal-water fishing, are common in the Keys and along the lower west coast. Skiffs and other small craft (available at hundreds of fishing camps that dot the Florida coastal areas) are used along the Inland Waterway, Key flats, and the thousands of bays, passes, and tidal rivers.

Mangrove snappers, channel bass, snook, and jack crevalle are easily reached by inshore small-craft boaters. Tarpon, which are caught on trolled spoons, plugs, and flies with feathers, are caught during the spring and year-round in the Keys and on the southern coast. Trophy snook are taken along the east-coast Inland Waterway in the Lake Worth vicinity during the summer on plugs and live mullet. Big snook, which reach record weights of up to 50½ pounds, are best caught during the ebb tide, when the receding waters pull schools of baitfish out of the mangrove mazes into the open holes.

Florida Keys & the "Gray Ghost"

The beautiful Florida Keys, curving into the Gulf of Mexico from Florida's southern tip for over 100 miles from Key Largo to Key West, are world-famous for their year-round fishing for bonefish, permit, tarpon, barracuda, snook, jacks, ladyfish, blackfin tuna, sharks, kingfish, mackerel, and redfish. The elusive, spooky bonefish, commonly known as the "gray ghost," are caught on weighted jigs, shrimp, and flies along the shallow, sun-drenched flats of the Keys. Stalking this aristocratic powerhouse—infamous for its searing, tackle-busting runs—is as much a matter of trophy hunting as it is fishing. Fly fishing along the grassy flats for "tailing" bonefish ranks among the world's most challenging (and often frustrating) sports. The inexperienced angler is strongly advised to hire the services of a knowledgeable local guide, with a skiff and pole. The major fishing areas include the Islamorada Area, Marathon Area, and Smith Shoals, Demolition Key, Fleming Key, Northwest Channel, Boca Grande Key, Snipe and Barracuda keys, and Calda Banks in the Key West area. The chain of islands is connected by the Florida Overseas Highway.

Resort lodging and guide services for sport fishing on the Keys is provided by the famous *Cheeca Lodge,* Islamorada 33036, phone (305) 664–4651; *Indies Inn,* Duck Key, Marathon 33050, phone (305)

289–1783; and *Rainbow Bend Fishing Club*, patterned after the old Florida Keys fishing clubs, located on Grassy Key, P.O. Box 2447, Marathon Shores 33052, phone (305) 289–1505. Sport fishing guide service is provided by *Gris Bettle*, 618 Fleming St., Key West 33040, phone (305) 294–5398; *Jack Kertz*, Box 628, Islamorada 33036, phone (305) 664–2461; and *Bob Carter*, 777 Copland Ave., Everglades City 33929. In Everglades National Park and Ten Thousand Islands, for snook, *Nat Ragland*, P.O. Box 1151, Marathon 33050, phone (305) 743–6376; *Steve Huff*, 7991 Shark Dr., Marathon 33050, phone (305) 743–4361; *Lefty Reagan*, 2923 Harris Ave., Key West 33040, phone (305) 296–9958; and *John Eckard*, 2207 Juanita Lane, Key West 33040, phone (305) 296–8179.

Fishing the Florida Keys, the definitive guide by Stu Apte, a Pan Am pilot who has guided in the Keys for many years, provides the nitty-gritty about the types of fishing available, where to fish, effective lures and baits for each species. It also contains 15 location fishing charts and lists of recommended fishing camps, marinas, and fishing-tackle shops, as well as a useful section on fishing knots. This invaluable paperback may be ordered for $3.20 (postpaid) from: Windward Publishing, Inc., P.O. Box 370233, Miami 33137.

Detailed saltwater-fishing information and the free information guide *Facts for Florida Fishermen*, which contains saltwater-fishing laws and seasons, may be obtained by writing the Division of Marine Resources, Crown Bldg., 202 Blount St., Tallahassee 32304. A *National Wildlife Refuges of the Florida Keys* map/guide, which contains detailed info about the Key West, National Key Deer, and Great White Heron refuges, may be obtained free from the Refuge Manager, P.O. Box 510, Big Pine Key 33043.

Trophy Florida Bass Waters

Florida's shallow, weedy, stump-filled lakes and meandering cypress-lined rivers are inhabited by a subspecies of the northern bass known as the Florida largemouth—a strain that grows to trophy weights of more than 20 pounds and provides the legendary fishing that gave birth to the state's nickname as "The Bass Capital of the World." Other freshwater species caught in Florida's lakes and streams include chain pickerel, several sunfishes, catfishes, crappie, and gar. Florida record freshwater fish, as reported by the Department of Natural Resources, are as follows:

FLORIDA RECORD FRESHWATER FISH

	Lb.-oz.	Place	Year
Largemouth bass	19–0	Lake Tarpon	1961
Chain pickerel	8–0	Lake Talquin	1971
Bluegill	3–5½	Crystal Lake	1950
Redbreast	1–8	Lake Iamania	1972
Warmouth	1–6½	Tiger Lake	1970

Each year, hundreds of trophy bass in the 10- to 14-pound class are caught in the lakes and streams throughout the state. The trophy waters of the western panhandle region include the Chipola River and Dead Lake—tributaries of the Apalachicola River; sprawling Lake Seminole, which straddles the Florida-Georgia border; Lake Talquin, on the Ochlockonee River, which flows through the Apalachicola National Forest; and Lake Iamonia and Lake Jackson. The moody Ochlockonee River flows through banks of high, pine-clad bluffs and dense cypress and hardwood forests. It can be treacherous during the flood season. Dead Lake, named for the countless dead cypress, oak, and pine trees submerged in the overflow from the Chipola River, offers some excellent fly fishing for big bass in the shallow, stump-filled

areas and along the maze of forest-covered islands. Lodging and fishing guide service in the Apalachicola Swamp and Dead Lakes area is provided by *Breakaway Lodge*, Box 606, and *Bay City Lodge*, Box 172, both Apalachicola 32320.

The trophy bass waters in the famous northeast region of the Sunshine State include the Suwannee River, St. Johns River, Lake George, Lake Crescent, Oklawaha Lake and River, Waccasassa Bay, and Lochloosa, Orange, Newmans, and Magnolia lakes. The St. Johns River, whose nationally famous bass waters are suffering from the environment effects of an increasing population, still provides stretches of pastoral beauty along its shores, and excellent fishing in the cathedral-like cypress backwaters and sloughs. The St. Johns—the only major river in the United States that does not freeze over—rises in the flat, marshy treeless plains near Lake Helen Blazes and meanders north through a famed chain of bass lakes that include Sawgrass, Winder, Washington, Poinsett, Puzzle, Harney, Monroe, Mullet, Jessup, Beresford, Woodruff, Dexter, and Spring Garden, and huge

Lake George. The central section of the St. Johns provides excellent fishing during the winter for American shad. Salt Cove, on the northwest side of Lake George, and the eastern shore of the lake yield good-size bass. The mouth of the Oklawaha River is a popular area, as are the waters around Turkey Island and Seven Sisters Islands. The prime fishing months are December through April for bass and January through April for crappie. The *Bass Capital Sportsman's Assn.* will provide free maps and information on big-bass spots and resorts in the St. Johns area; write: Box 550 C, Palatka 32077. A 60-page paperback guide to fishing, camping, and canoeing on the legendary Suwannee River, *Suwannee Country*, may be ordered for $4.50 from the Council Company, P.O. Box 5822, Sarasota 35579.

The fabled central lake region of Florida contains the largest number of trophy largemouth bass waters, including the cypress-lined shores of the wild Withlacoochee River, Rainbow and Hillsborough rivers, and Apopka, Tsala, Rousseau, Hamilton, Larkin, Louisa, Hart, Tohopekaliga, Myrtle, Preston, Cypress, Hatchineha, Kissimmee, Weohyakapka, Caloosa, Tiger, Marion, Pierce, June in Winter, and

Istokpoga lakes. These scenic lakes and rivers, fringed with hammock growth of oak, hickory, cypress, and magnolia, provide fishing for pickerel, perch, bream, and catfish, in addition to lunker bass in the tangled, shallow, weedy, and dead-timber areas. Write to the *Hunting and Fishing Association*, Dunnellon 32630, for free information on fishing, guides, and lodges in the Withlacoochee and Rainbow river areas. Free recreation map/guides to the *Kissimmee Waterway* may be obtained by writing: Central and Southern Florida Flood Control District, P.O. Box V, West Palm Beach 33402.

The southern wild Everglades country offers the nation's top big-bass fishing in a wilderness setting along the innumerable backwaters, sloughs, and cypress-fringed shores of huge Lake Okeechobee, Loxahatchee Slough and National Wildlife Refuge, and Big Cypress Swamp areas of the Everglades. Some of the best trophy bass fishing (as well as giant snook up to 25 and 30 pounds, and tarpon) is found in the weed-free Hillsborough, Miami, St. Lucie, and Tamiami canals. Write to the Southern Florida Flood Control District (address above) for detailed fishing information on the Everglades canal system. For detailed maps and information on the nationally renowned trophy bass waters of the Loxahatchee National Recreation Area and Wildlife

Refuge, with its 220 square miles of sloughs, sawgrass marshes, tree islands, and wet prairies, inhabited by bobcats, ducks, rare Everglade kites, alligators, Florida panther, bald eagle, ibis, egrets, great blue herons, and Florida sandhill cranes, write: Refuge Manager, Rte. 1, Box 278, Delray Beach 33444, and Dept. of Natural Resources, Room 320, Crown Bldg., Tallahassee 32304. For information about lodging facilities, fishing conditions, boat rentals, guides, and airboat tours, write: Loxahatchee Recreation Inc., Rte. 1, Box 6428, Pompano Beach 33060. Another top-ranked trophy bass area of the southern region is the remote, seldom-fished Okaloacoochee Slough in the wild, aptly named Devils Gardens Country, southwest of Lake Okeechobee. The southern region and the Everglades are reached via Interstate 95 and 75. The Big Cypress Swamp Country of the Everglades is traversed by the Everglades Parkway (Route 84, known as "Alligator Alley").

For detailed fishing and hunting information, regulations, and the following free publications, write to the Information Office, Dept. of Natural Resources, Crown Bldg., 302 Blount St., Tallahassee 32304: *Florida's Fish Management Areas; Florida Sport Fishing Guide*, which includes full-color illustrations of freshwater and saltwater game fish, fishing tips, laws, first aid, fishing rigs and natural baits, and a

chart for regional fishing areas and species present; *Facts for Florida Fishermen; Archery and Special Managed Hunt Information; Migratory Game Bird Regulations; State Forest Maps;* and *Hunting & Freshwater Fishing Regulations*.

Southern Guide Fishing Maps showing all man-made and natural features including camps, boat-ramps, roads, water depths, stump and lily pad areas, and trophy bass spots are available for Juniper, Dead, Talquin, Jackson-Orange-Lochloosa, Rodman, George, Tohopekaliga, Kissimmee, and Okeechobee lakes. Each map sells for $1.90 (postpaid) and may be ordered from: Southern Guide Fishing Maps, 1325 E. Tennessee St., P.O. Box 1106, Tallahassee 32302.

Florida's game-management areas and national forestlands offer excellent hunting in season for whitetail deer, black bear, wild hogs, fox and gray squirrels, rabbits, wild turkey, quail, doves, red fox, bobcat, ducks, and a few geese.

Florida Trail

The 475-mile Florida Trail, which will eventually stretch for 1,300 miles as a national scenic hiking trail, begins in the Big Cypress Swamp just north of the Everglades National Park and ends in the Blackwater River State Forest near Pensacola. The trail passes through some of the wildest and most scenic portions of Florida's interior, and provides access to many seldom-explored bass lakes and wilderness camping areas. The best time to hike the trail is winter, when temperatures are moderate and insects less troublesome than during the spring and summer. For information, a free *Florida Trail* pamphlet, and a *Florida Trail Map Kit* ($2.50, postpaid), write: Florida Trail Assn. Office, P.O. Box 13708, Gainesville 32604.

Highways—Recreation & Scenic Routes

If you are driving in Florida, you should obtain a copy of the *Florida Official Road Map*. This excellent road map shows all roads and highways, including Florida toll roads (which are conveniently broken down in a separate legend, state parks and recreation areas with and without campsites), airports, welcome stations, rest areas, and points of interest. There is a list of the Florida Trail sites (see section on this trail), with each point location keyed on a small map. A chart of public recreation areas (state parks and historic memorials), U.S. Park and Forest Service, and Division of Forestry (state forest) areas is provided, showing the facilities available in each area. There is a handy mileage index, showing distances in miles between major points on the map. The map is attractively illustrated with color photographs. For your copy, or further information, write to: Florida Dept. of Commerce, Collins Bldg., Tallahassee 32304.

Individual *County Maps*, showing highways, secondary roads (including dirt roads), lakes, streams, and structures, printed in black and white, are available from the Library, Room 57, Dept. of Transportation, Hayden Burns Bldg., Tallahassee 32304, at a cost of 30¢ per chart (½ inch:one mile) or $1.50 per chart (1 inch:one mile). Most counties are shown on one sheet.

Ocala National Forest

This outstanding bass-fishing, camping, canoeing, and hunting reserve takes in 336,000 acres of vast sand-pine forests, meandering crystal-clear streams, huge bubbling springs, and hundreds of natural lakes between the Oklawaha and St. Johns rivers in central Florida. The major features of the region include Junipers and Alexander Creek canoe trails, Ocala Trail, Buckskin Prairie, and the renowned large-

mouth-bass waters of Lake George and of Dorr, Ker, Bryant, Dexter, and Halfmoon lakes, and the Lake Woodruff National Wildlife Refuge. The forest also includes the whitetail-deer, black-bear, and wild-turkey hunting areas of the F. McCoy and Lochloosa wildlife-management areas.

The Ocala Trail, a 64-mile portion of the Florida Trail, which eventually will run the 700-mile length of Florida in much the same way as the Appalachian Trail crosses the eastern mountains, passes about 60 natural ponds and plunges through cypress and gum swamps on winding boardwalks. The trail also traverses the rolling, open, longleaf-pine forests and scattered clumps of dwarf live oaks. The rolling sand dunes of the ancient Florida coastline are now covered with sand pine. This unusual tree, with its dense scrub understory, is the only major species of tree capable of growing on these very dry dunes. A descriptive folder on the Ocala National Forest is available free from the Forest Service, P.O. Box 1050, Tallahassee 32302. This attractive full-color brochure provides the forest visitor with a map showing all primary and secondary recreation areas and roads. A brief description of the extent of the forest's variety and beauty is also included. For further information on the forest, you may contact: Lake George Ranger District, Ocala 32670, phone (904) 622–6577; Seminole Ranger District, Eustis 32726, phone (904) 357–3721; or Forest Supervisor, P.O. Box 1050, Tallahassee 32302. The Forest Service will also provide a free folder on the *Ocala National Trail*. It contains a map of the trail, showing campgrounds, water sources, lookout towers, roads, and other useful points of interest to the hiker. Mileage between points on the trail is also provided, and different vegetation areas are also delineated. This brochure is useful not only to the beginner but to anyone who is planning to hike this most interesting trail for the first time.

Professional guide service for the trophy bass waters of the Ocala National Forest and Central Florida is provided by *Bass Champions*, Route 2, Box 2047, Ft. McCoy 32637. Bass Champions also arranges guided bass fishing trips throughout the Southern United States, plus big-game saltwater fishing trips.

All visitors to the Ocala National Forest should obtain a copy of *The Ocala National Forest Map*, available for 50¢ from the Forest Supervisor, P.O. Box 1050, Tallahassee 32302. This excellent map shows all boundaries, roads, canoe runs, developed and primitive recreation sites, boat ramps, swamps and marshes, lakes and ponds, wayside areas, and other points of interest. A legend of federal recreation symbols is also provided to aid motorists. The map includes a chart showing principal, secondary, and primitive recreation areas, their locations on the map, and the facilities available at each individual area.

Free maps/guides to the *Alexander Springs Recreation Area* and *Juniper Creek Canoe Run* may be obtained by writing to the Forest Supervisor's Office.

The forest is reached via U.S. highways 98 and 319 and Florida 20, 65, and 369. Accommodations, supplies, and equipment rentals are available at Apalachicola, Blountstown, Bristol, and Tallahassee.

Ocala National Forest is shown on the following U.S. Geological Survey 1:250,000-scale maps: Daytona Beach and Orlando.

Sport Fishing Adventures & Caribbean Travel Service

Worldwide Sportsman, Inc.—Safaris and Outfitters, of Islamorada, offers complete travel-planning and trip-outfitting services (including air transportation, lodging, and guides) for vacations at several world-

renowned trophy fishing meccas, including the tarpon and bonefish waters of the Florida Keys; Mexico's Pez Maya on the Yucatán Peninsula; Casa Mar Camp on the northeast Caribbean coast of Costa Rica for giant snook and tarpon; and the famed bonefish flats of the Turneffe Islands in Central America. For free literature, rates, and information, write Worldwide Sportsman, Inc., P.O. Drawer 787, Islamorada 33036; or call, toll free, (800) 327–2880.

Florida Trail
ASSOCIATION

The world-renowned bonefish flats of the Turneffe Islands, located 30 miles off the coast of Belize (formerly known as British Honduras) in Central America, lie nestled inside the second-largest barrier reef in the world. The area encompasses 125 low-lying sun-drenched islands, and mangrove-tangled cays, flats, natural creeks, and cuts inhabited by bonefish, tarpon from 20 to 70 pounds, jacks, permit, big barracuda, and snappers. Beyond the reef are offshore big-game fish. The beautiful grass-covered flats of the islands are a fly fisherman's paradise, famous for one of the world's largest concentrations of bonefish. Luxury accommodations, meals, and English-speaking guides and fiberglass skiffs are provided on this virgin fishing area by the American-owned and -managed *Turneffe Island Lodge*, P.O. Box 430732, Miami 33143, phone (305) 666–0984.

For additional vacation, resort, and fishing information in the Caribbean, write: (Bermuda) Director, Fishing Information Bureau, Dept. of Tourism, P.O. Box 465, Hamilton 5, Bermuda, phone 2–0023; (Bahamas) Director, Fishing Information Bureau, Ministry of Tourism, Nassau, Bahamas, and to the Deep Water Cay Club, P.O. Box 1145, Palm Beach 33480, phone (305) 655–2988; (Mexico) Dirección General de Turismo, Avenida Juarez 89, Mexico D.F., Mexico.

SOUTHERN APPALA-CHIAN STATES

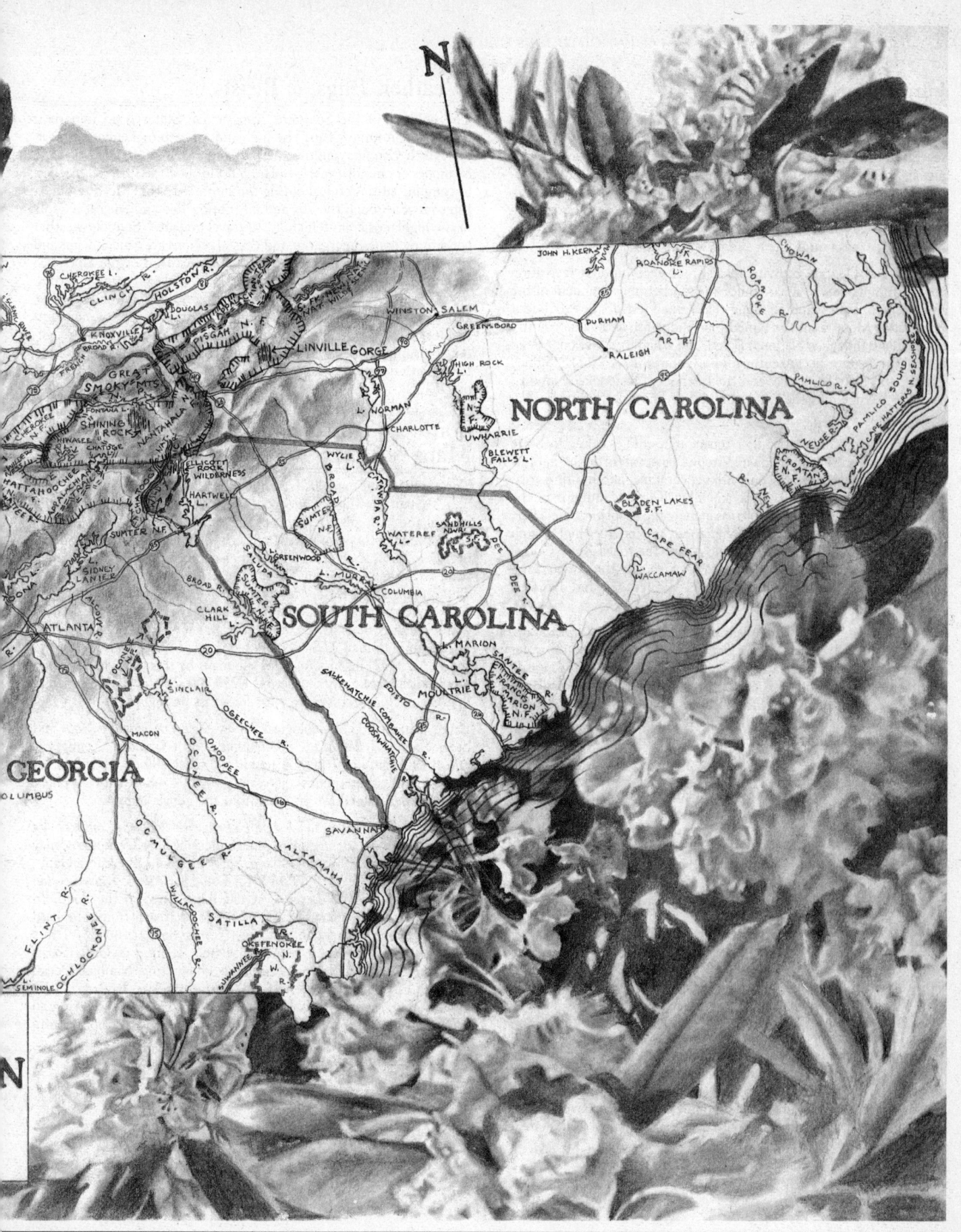

Introduction

The ancient Southern Appalachian Mountains, which form wave upon wave of massive summits and spectacular "balds," embrace several of the nation's most scenic and wild fishing, camping, canoeing, and hunting areas. The famed Appalachian Trail begins its 2,000-mile-long journey to Maine's Mount Katahdin here, winding northeastward through Georgia, North Carolina, and Tennessee along the ridge crests and valleys of the often mist-shrouded Blue Ridge, Nantahala, Unaka, and Great Smoky mountains.

The State of Georgia contains several renowned outdoor recreation areas within its 58,876 square miles: the southernmost segment of the Appalachian Trail, winding along the scenic crest of the 4,000-foot Blue Ridge Mountains; the famed Blue Ridge fish and game country of the Chattahoochee National Forest; the Chattooga National Wild River; the waters of Lake Burton, Chestatee River, Lake Sidney Lanier, and Lake Seminole; and the legendary Okefenokee National Wildlife Refuge and the headwaters of the historic Suwannee National Scenic River.

South Carolina contains 31,055 square miles. The Palmetto State embraces the nationally renowned trophy bass waters of the Santee-Cooper Reservoir and the scenic fishing, camping, and hunting areas of the Sumpter National Forest and Blue Ridge Mountains in the northwest. The wild and scenic areas include the beautiful Blue Ridge highlands of the Ellicott's Rock Wilderness, the shoulder-high switch cane of the Long Cane Creek Scenic Area, Chattooga River Gorge, Clarks Hill Reservoir, Indian Camp Wild Area, and the remote tumbling trout waters of the Chauga, Little, Whitewater, and Toxaway rivers.

North Carolina, known variously as the Tar Heel or Old North State, rises from the low coastal plain, dominated by the fabled saltwater fishing grounds of Cape Hatteras and the Outer Banks, to the central Piedmont plateau, and in the west, to the scenic highlands of the Nantahala, Blue Ridge, and Great Smoky mountains, culminating at 6,684-foot Mount Mitchell—the highest point in the East. Within the state's 52,586 square miles are 300 miles of the Appalachian Trail; the famed wildlands and backpacking trails of Great Smoky National Park; the Pisgah National Forest and the Linville Gorge and Shining Rock Wilderness Areas; the Nantahala National Forest; the Snowbird Creek Wilderness and wilderness camping areas of the Joyce Kilmer Forest and Standing Indian Country; and the nationally renowned fishing waters of beautiful Fontana Lake, Big Pigeon River, Nantahala Lake and River, Hiwassee River and Lake, New River, and Lakes Santeetlah and Chatuge.

Tennessee contains 42,244 square miles of varied terrain with the scenic Great Valley separating the Cumberland Plateau from the Great Smokies on the eastern border; the rolling hills and bluegrass country of the central basin, sloping to the Mississippi River bottomlands along the western boundary. The Volunteer State contains several famous fishing, hunting, and wild country camping areas, including Reelfoot Lake; the western highlands and remote mountain coves of the Great Smoky Mountains National Park; Cherokee National Forest, which embraces a narrow strip of rugged highlands along the Unaka and Great Smoky mountains; and the trophy bass, walleye, and trout waters of the Tellico River, Doe Creek and Watauga Lake, Dale Hollow Lake, Caney Fork of the Cumberland, Obed River, South Fork of the Cumberland, and South Holston, Wilbur, Norris, Great Falls, and Center Hill lakes.

Weather, Bugs, & Beasts

The weather in the Southern Appalachian States is an important consideration for any trip. The highlands of eastern Tennessee, western North Carolina, and northern Georgia receive as much as 60 to 80 inches of rainfall a year—the heaviest in the East. Careful selection of camping sites is crucial during the summer season. Mean temperatures range through the 70s and 80s during July and August. Nights in the highlands are often chilly, so travel prepared. Summer weather conditions along the interior and coastal regions are generally hot and very humid. Potential wildlife hazards in this land of the Cherokee include camp-invading black bears, cornered wild boars, timber rattlesnakes in the rocky high country areas, copperheads at lower elevations, and water moccasins and cottonmouths in the swampy coastal plains regions. Mosquitoes carry on their relentless career of torture throughout the summer. Be sure to carry a good supply of Muskol, Mosquitone, Cutters, or Off!—all of which contain a 50%-plus concentration of DEET.

Southern Appalachian Maps & Charts—How to Order

The topographic maps listed throughout the Southern Appalachian States chapters will provide you with a physical inventory of the natural and man-made features of the area you plan to visit. All maps listed (unless otherwise noted) are full-color U.S. Geological Survey overview maps, scale 1:250,000, 1 inch to 4 miles ($2 each) or large-scale 7½-minute maps and 15-minute maps ($1.25 each for either). These maps and free *Topographic Map Indexes* of Georgia, North Carolina, South Carolina, and Tennessee may be ordered (along with a free *Map Symbol Chart* and *Topographic Maps* booklet) from: Distribution Branch, U.S. Geological Survey, 1200 S. Eads St., Arlington, VA 22202. Be sure to order the maps by their individual names (and indicate scale when ordering 1:250,000 scale maps); to expedite delivery, include extra money for first-class postage.

Large, attractive U.S. Geological Survey *State Topographic Maps* and *State Shaded-Relief Maps* of Georgia, North Carolina, Tennessee, and South Carolina (there is no shaded-relief edition published for South Carolina) are published, scale 1:500,000, or 1 inch to 8 miles, and may be ordered for $2 each from the above address.

A useful 214-page handbook, *Be Expert with Map & Compass*, by Bjorn Kjellstrom, the president and founder of Silva Compasses, may be obtained for $6.95 from: Charles Scribner's Sons, Bookstore Dept., 597 5th Ave., New York, NY 10017. Full-color *Plastic Raised-Relief Maps* of all 1:250,000 scale overview maps listed in the Southern Appalachian States may be ordered for $11.95 each from: Hubbard Scientific Co., 1946 Raymond Dr., Northbrook, IL 60062 (a free catalog is available upon request). A free *Atlantic & Gulf Coasts Nautical Chart Catalog* may be obtained by writing: National Ocean Survey, Distribution Div. (C44), 6501 Lafayette Ave., Riverdale, MD 20840. Waterproof 23 × 35-inch *Lake Contour Maps* showing all underwater features and structures are available for 200 trophy southern lakes and reservoirs. For a free listing of mapped lakes and prices, write: Lakes Illustrated, Box 4854 GS, Springfield, MO 65804.

GEORGIA ENCYCLOPEDIA

Accommodations— Vacation Lodges & Resorts

For information on hotel and motel accommodations in Georgia write: Georgia Hotel and Motel Assn., 1410 Rhodes Haverty Bldg., Atlanta 30303. Specific details on state parks and historical points of interest can be obtained from: Public Relations and Information Section, Dept. of Natural Resources, 270 Washington St., SW, Atlanta 30334. The Bureau of Industry and Trade, Tourist Division, P.O. Box 38097, Atlanta 30334, will be glad to provide information and suggestions on vacation and travel within the state.

Georgia Days, a handsome, illustrated 47-page booklet available free from the Bureau of Industry and Trade at the above address, contains a wealth of interesting information on the state's many outdoor attractions. Divided into three major sections on the mountains, piedmont, and coastal plain, the guide offers town-by-town listings of camping areas, historical sites, lakes, hunting areas, state parks, and annual events. Charts for the various state parks indicate number and kinds of facilities available: picnic areas, campsites, hiking trails, boat rentals, etc. Detailed and comprehensive road maps for each region are also included. For more specific information on any area, activity, or attraction, the authors of *Georgia Days* advise writing the Chamber of Commerce for the community listed.

Appalachian National Scenic Trail

After crossing the Nantahala National Forest in North Carolina, the Georgia section of this famous footpath enters the state at Hightower Bald and winds for its final 79 miles along the rugged crest of the 4,000-foot Blue Ridge Mountains in the Chattahoochee National Forest. The trail terminates at Springer Mountain, the southernmost limit of the Blue Ridge chain. Some of the forest features explored along the way are the headwaters of the Chattahoochee River, Slaughter Gap, and Blood Mountain, the latter named for a fierce battle between warring Creek and Cherokee Indians. So savage was the fighting that mountain streams ran red with blood, staining the lichenous plants that cover the slopes. During late spring and early summer, sections of the trail are transformed into flower-lined paths as laurel, rhododendron, and flame azalea bloom in vivid profusion.

The *Guide to the Appalachian Trail in the Great Smokies, the Nantahalas, and Georgia* (see "North Carolina: Appalachian National Scenic Trail") provides full trail data and describes the area traversed, including its natural and human history. The guide contains three explicit maps and is available for $6.70 from: Appalachian Trail Conference, Box 236, Harpers Ferry, WV 25425. A useful, free *Chattahoochee National Forest Appalachian Trail Map & Guide* may be obtained by writing: Forest Supervisor's Office, P.O. Box 1437, Gainesville 30501. This full-color, waterproof map shows the Adirondack shelters along the trail, as well as approach trails, campsites, drinking water, supply areas, and recreation sites.

The Appalachian National Scenic Trail is shown on the following large-scale 7.5-minute U.S. Geological Survey Maps: Courock, Dahlonega, Ellijay, Hightower Bald, Jacks Gap, Neels Gap, Noontootla, Osborne, Suches, Tickanetley, Tray Mountain.

Camping and Blue Ridge Trails

Campgrounds in the Blue Ridge include the Lake Blue Ridge Camping Area, off U.S. 76 near the town of Blue Ridge. Open between May 1 and October 31, the area is operated by the U.S. Forest Service and offers tent and trailer camping, water skiing, swimming, nature trails,

fishing, and a boat ramp, all on 15 forested acres adjoining the lake. Slightly northwest of the Lake Blue Ridge Camping Area, Morgantown Point, also off U.S. 76, offers similar opportunities for outdoor recreation on 12 acres of national forest land. The privately owned Skeenah Creek Campgrounds, 16 miles east of Blue Ridge via State Highway 60, is open year round for trailer and primitive camping, hiking and bicycle trails, and trout fishing. Also privately owned, Whispering Pines Camping Area, 8 miles east of Blue Ridge, features year-round tent and trailer camping, nature trails, fishing, a swimming pool, and a playground. A third Forest Service campground 18 miles east of Blue Ridge via State Highway 60, Deep Hole Recreation Area, offers camping, hiking, and fishing between May 1 and October 31.

Many other campsites are scattered throughout the state, providing facilities and activities for every taste and budget. Consult the *Georgia Days* booklet (see "Accommodations—Vacation Lodges & Resorts") or write to: Georgia Campground Owners Assn., P.O. Box 5487, Columbus 31902. Supervisors for the state parks and national forest will also be glad to supply details on camping areas within their jurisdiction.

Besides the Appalachian Trail, a number of interesting hiking paths wind through the high country wilderness of Chattahoochee National Forest. A 2½-mile side trail near Chattahoochee Gap explores the remote reaches of Brasstown Bald, highest point in Georgia and the site of unusual forest plants, some of them of a distinctly northern origin. Fort Mountain in the Cohutta Range is accessible via a good trail beginning at Hassler's Mill, northeast of Chatsworth. The challenging climb up the mountain's steep, almost perpendicular sides leads to the ruins of an old fort, rumored to be the work of an unknown race of white men who settled in the area before the arrival of Cherokee Indians. Other trails within the forest meander along the clear waters of Panther Creek, past De Soto Falls, and through the unspoiled watersheds of the Cohutta Wilderness. The *Chattachoochee National Forest Recreation Map* (see "Chattahoochee National Forest") shows many of the trails. Further information can be obtained from the forest supervisor or by consulting the *Guide to the Appalachian Trail in the Great Smokies, the Nantahalas, and Georgia.*

Canoe Trails & Trophy Fishing Waters

The following U.S. Geological Survey Map Kits show the entire lengths, including headwaters and surrounding topography, of the major canoe routes and trophy fishing lakes and streams in the Blue Ridge country of the Chattahoochee National Forest, central and southern Georgia. There is excellent fishing in the deep, cool waters of Blue Ridge Lake for smallmouth bass and walleye and on the Toccoa River for hard-hitting muskellunge up to 36 pounds as well as large smallmouth and largemouth bass, and walleye. Both the Tallulah River and Lake Burton hold big rainbows and browns in the 8–10-pound class. See "Chattahoochee National Forest" for additional information.

The state's major canoe routes and fishing waters are shown on the following large-scale U.S. Geological Survey Maps. *Chattahoochee River* (including Mossy Creek): Clarkesville, Gainesville, Lead, Lula, Tallulah Falls; *Chattooga National Wild River:* Cashiers, Rainy Mountain, Satolah, Tamassee, Tugaloo Lake, Whetstone; *Chestatee River and Lake Sidney Lanier:* Buford Dam, Chestatee, Clermont, Cleveland, Coal Mountain, Dahlonega, Flowery Branch, Gainesville, Lula, Murrayville, Neels Gap; *Coosawattee River:* Calhoun, Ellijay, Sugar Valley, Talking Rock; *Upper Etowah River and Allatoona Lake:* Acworth, Allatoona Dam, Campbell Mountain, Canton, Coal Mountain, Dawsonville, Matt, South Canton, Suches, Tate; *Hiawassee*

River (including Trodder, Soapstone, Carbin, and Hightower creeks): Hiawassee, Macedonia, Tray Mountain; *Jacks River:* Dyer Gap, Hemp Top; *Nottely River & Lake:* Blairsville, Coosa Bald, Jacks Gap, Nottely Bald; *Soque River:* Clarkesville, Lake Burton; *Suwannee River:* Billys Island, Cravens Island, Dinner Pond, Fargo, Fargo SW, Strange Island, The Pocket, Waycross; *Tallulah River* (including Burton, Seed, Rabun, and Tallulah lakes): Hightower Bald, Lake Burton, Tallulah Falls, Tiger, Tugaloo Lake; *Toccoa River & Blue Ridge Lake:* Blue Ridge, Mineral Bluff, Noontootla, Suches, Wilscot; *Lake Lanier:* Murrayville, Clermont, Lula, Gainesville, Chestatee, Flowery Branch, Coal Mountain, Buford Dam; *Chattahoochee River Trophy Float Fishing Waters* (Buford Dam to Norcross): Buford Dam, Suwannee, Duluth, Norcross, Chamblee; *Clark Hill Reservoir:* Calhoun Falls, Chennault, Wilmington, Lincolnton, Plum Branch, Parksville Leak, Clarks Hill; *Hartwell Reservoir:* Avalon, Oakway, Lavonia, Reed Creek, Hartwell NE, Hartwell, Hartwell Dam; *Rock Creek Trophy Trout Waters:* Crandall, Ramhurst, Calhoun NE, Dalton S; *Coosawattee River & Carters Lake:* Webb, Ramhurst, Talking Rock, Oakman, Rosebud, Calhoun N; *Lake Seminole:* Steam Hill, Fairchild, Reynoldsville, Smeads, Chattahoochee, Bainbridge.

Chattahoochee National Forest & Blue Ridge Wilderness

This renowned hunting, fishing, hiking, and canoe-camping area, once the hunting grounds of the Cherokee Indian Nation, covers 700,000 acres of Blue Ridge wilderness country in northern Georgia. The forest is joined on the north by the Cherokee and Nantahala national forests of Tennessee and North Carolina. Two of the Chattahoochee's major features are the Appalachian Trail (see "Appalachian National Scenic Trail") and a 50-mile stretch of the Chattooga National Wild River, rated by experts as one of the most perilous whitewater canoe runs in the United States. The wild Chattooga roars through a deep gorge with sheer walls up to 400 feet high. The major features along this violent wild river, which rises in the scenic highlands of the Nantahala National Forest, include: Silver Slipper Falls, Big Bend Falls, Big Shoals, Rock Garden, the Narrows, Eye-of-the-Needle, Painted Rock Rapids, Deliverance Rock, Raven Chute, Crack-in-the-Rock, and Sock-em-dog. Below U.S. 76 the river is for advanced paddlers only. Write to the Forest Supervisor's Office (address below) for detailed information.

The forest offers excellent hunting for whitetail deer, ruffed grouse, and wild turkey in the interior wildlands of the Warwoman, Russell Lake, Swallow Creek, Lake Burton, Chattahoochee, Chestatee, Cooper's Creek, Blue Ridge, Rich Mountain, Cohutta, and Johns Mountain wildlife management areas. There is good fishing for brook, brown, and rainbow trout in the highland streams and fine canoe camping along the Toccoa, Nottely, Hiawassee, Jacks, Conasauga, and Tallulah rivers.

Primitive hiking trails and old abandoned logging roads provide access to the distant pools and riffles of the forest's premier fly fishing waters, where rainbow, brook, and brown trout grow to record weights. These picturesque streams, which are managed for artificial lures and flies only, are located in scenic mountain valleys surrounded by mixed hardwoods and dense thickets of laurel and rhododendron. The major streams include the Chattahoochee River, Coleman River, Jones and Noontootla creeks on the Blue Ridge WMA (Wildlife Management Area), Moccasin Creek on the Lake Burton WMA, Mountaintown Creek on the Cohutta WMA, Stanley Creek on the Rich Mountain WMA, Tate Branch on the Coleman River WMA, scenic Tuckaluge Creek, and Walnut Fork and Hood creeks on the Warwoman WMA.

Water Creek on the Chestatee WMA produced the state record 5-pound 5-ounce brook trout, is managed as a "trophy" stream for barbless hooks only, and annually yields rainbows up to 10 pounds and brown trout to 8 pounds. Rock Creek on the Blue Ridge WMA produced the state record 18-pound 3-ounce brown trout, and consistently yields trophy browns up to weights of 8 pounds.

In the northwestern portion of the forest is the Cohutta Wilderness, 61,500 acres of primitive mountains and forest, the largest protected Forest Service Wilderness in the East. The land here is steep and deeply scored by the Conasauga and Jacks rivers and their many tributary streams. The rough topography, rocky bluffs, and absence of major roads make the area almost completely inaccessible except to hikers and backpackers, who will find innumerable deep, quiet pools interrupting the boulder-strewn stretches of river. The Jacks River flows through a wild gorge, dropping over 400 feet in 2 miles, and is additionally enhanced by a spectacular waterfall, Ball-Peen Falls. The waters of the two adjacent watersheds of the Conasauga and Jacks rivers harbor naturally reproducing stocks of trout, testimony to the quality and purity of these streams as they flow through virtually undisturbed areas. In the southern reaches of the wilderness, tall stands of virgin hemlock and oak blanket the slopes of Cohutta Mountain. Camping facilities are available on Conasauga Lake at the foot of the mountain.

The *Chattahoochee National Forest Map* (50¢) shows the Cohutta Wilderness Area, the numerous wildlife management areas, streams, lakes, rivers, all recreation and camping sites, roads, trails, and other forest attractions. The surrounding terrains, including highways and nearby towns, are also indicated. Forest maps and the free *Canoeing Routes Guide, Trail Guide,* and *Guide to Outdoor Recreation on the Cohutta District* are available from: Forest Supervisor, Chattahoochee National Forest, U.S. Forest Service, P.O. Box 1437, Gainesville 30501. Another useful guide to the wilderness, *Wildlife on the Chattahoochee National Forest,* describes and illustrates the black bear, deer, bobcat, raccoon, and other animals found in the forest. The booklet contains much useful information concerning animal habits and habitats, tracks, breeding patterns, and the like and is available free from the Forest Supervisor at the above address.

The Chattahoochee National Forest is easily reached via State Highway 11 north of Gainesville. Other nearby towns include Toccoa, Clarkesville, and Chatsworth. The Chattahoochee National Forest is shown on the following U.S. Geological Survey Maps, scale 1:250,000: Greenville, Rome.

Fishing & Hunting in Georgia

Georgia, the largest state east of the Mississippi, has an old and rich hunting tradition (it was known for years as the quail capital of the world) in its scenic forests and wildlife management areas for whitetail deer, ruffed grouse, squirrel, raccoon, red fox, quail, waterfowl, wild turkey, and a few black bear and has some of the finest fishing in the eastern U.S. for bass and chain pickerel up to world's record size, brown trout up to 8 pounds, rainbows to 12 pounds, walleye to 11 pounds, acrobatic bronzebacks up to 7 pounds, giant stripers up to 60 pounds, and schools of perch, crappie, and bluegills in its 17 major reservoirs, 3,500 miles of warmwater streams, 40,000 small lakes and ponds, and some 700 miles of scenic mountain trout streams in the northern Blue Ridge wildlands in the vast Chattahoochee National Forest (q.v.). The state is divided into five major physiographic provinces: the Appalachian plateau, the valley and ridge region, the Blue Ridge country, the Piedmont plateau, and the coastal plain.

The extreme northwestern corner of the state, separated by mountain ridges from the rest of Georgia, ranges in altitude from 800 to 2,000 feet. Most of north Georgia is covered by ranges of the southern Appalachians, the Blue Ridge mountains on the east and the Cohuttas —a continuation of the Smoky Mountains—on the west. Numerous cross ranges are separated by valleys such as the Hiawassee and Nottely river valleys. The ridge separating these two valleys features Georgia's highest peak, Brasstown Bald or Mount Etowah, 4,784 feet in altitude. Many of the state's major rivers—the Savannah, Toccoa, Chattahoochee, and Tennessee—have their sources in the Blue Ridge, where the clear, swift-flowing headwaters descend in many waterfalls.

Almost a third of Georgia's territory and most of its major cities fall within the rolling uplands of the middle or Piedmont region. The landscape here is broken occasionally by deep rivers and a few bold ridges and hills rising as high as 1,000 feet above the surrounding terrain. Formed of a highly resistant rock, the most conspicuous of these hills are Kennesaw Mountain near Marietta and Stone Mountain outside Atlanta. The red or reddish-yellow waters of the Savannah, Ocmulgee, Oconee, and Chattahoochee rivers drain the Piedmont.

CHATTAHOOCHEE National Forest GEORGIA

Below the fall line, which extends from Augusta to Columbus, the southern half of Georgia is part of the coastal plain. Rivers descend in many small rapids from hills along the highlands, some of which exceed elevations of 600 feet. Five coastal "terraces" cover the southeastern corner of the plain; the best known of these, the Okefenokee Terrace, ranges in elevation from 100 to 160 feet and contains the magnificent Okefenokee Swamp, second-largest freshwater swamp in the country. Often submerged at flood tide, the shorelands of the coastal plain are cut by tidal rivers and studded with grassy marshes. Many sandy islands—including St. Catherines, St. Simon, Jekyll, Cumberland, and Sapelo—fringe the Georgia coastline.

Long summers and short winters are characteristic of the state's climate. The average annual temperature ranges from 57° in the mountain towns to 68° in southern Georgia, where subtropical conditions occur along the coast and near the Florida line. Minor windstorms are not unusual, and the prevailing westerlies sometimes bring sudden cold waves.

The superb fishing potential and variety of the state's lakes and streams is highlighted by the state record fish caught in the annual Big Fish Contest sponsored and run by the Georgia Wildlife Federation and *Outdoors in Georgia* magazine, published by the Department of Natural Resources.

GEORGIA RECORD FRESHWATER FISH

	Lb.-oz.	Place	Year
Largemouth bass	22–4	Montgomery Lake	1922
Smallmouth bass	7–12	Lake Nottely	1972
Muskellunge	38	Blue Ridge Lake	1957
Brook trout	5–5	Water Creek	1973
Brown trout	18–3	Rock Creek	1967
Rainbow trout	12–4	Coosawattee River	1966
Walleye	11	Lake Burton	1963
Chain pickerel	9–6*	Homerville	1961
Striped bass	63	Oconee River	1967
Spotted bass	7–12	Lake Chatuge	1973
Shoal bass	7–8	Flint River	1975
White bass	5–5	Lake Lanier	1971
Redeye bass	2–10	Jacks River	1967
Bluegill	3–5	Shamrock Lake	1972
Black crappie	4–4	Lake Spivey	1975
Flathead catfish	51–15	Lake Nottely	1972

*World's record.

Chattahoochee National Forest Wild & Trophy Waters

The scenic mountain streams and sprawling TVA lakes in the Chattahoochee National Forest, surrounded by the Appalachian and Blue Ridge highlands, provide the state's premier trout, smallmouth bass, and walleye fishing. The deep, clear waters of Blue Ridge Lake on the Toccoa River are the state's top-rank walleye and smallmouth bass habitats, and hold Georgia's only population of elusive, tackle-busting muskellunge, reaching weights up to 30 pounds and over. Two Forest Service campgrounds are located on the shores of this lake. The shallow green waters of Nottely Lake, located 30 miles to the east just south of the North Carolina boundary, hold largemouth bass up to 12 pounds, striped bass up to 25 pounds, and some huge channel and flathead catfish. The deep, cool waters of Lake Chatuge, which sprawls across the Georgia-North Carolina line, provide superb fishing for scrappy smallmouths up to 7 pounds, walleye, rainbow and brown trout, largemouth and spotted bass, and hordes of bream and crappie. The huge, sprawling blue waters of Lake Burton on the Tallulah River, located to the south of the TVA lakes, surrounded by great "Balds" of the southern Appalachians and beautiful mixed hardwood forests and dense masses and thickets of azalea, rhododendron, and laurel, hold trophy rainbows, walleye, largemouth bass, and striped bass up to 30 pounds. The beautiful tumbling mountain streams of northern Georgia in the wild country of the Chattahoochee National Forest provide excellent fly fishing for brook, rainbow, and brown trout. The best fishing is found by backpacking off the main trails and forest roads to the deep-flowing, boulder-studded pools with their cut banks and mossy ledges, along remote upper stretches of these streams surrounded by the majestic Appalachian and Blue Ridge highlands. The major Chattahoochee trout streams include the trophy waters of Rock Creek (browns and rainbows up to 10 pounds) and Noontootla Creek

in the 36,000-acre Blue Ridge WMA, located on the Blue Ridge Mountain Divide north of Dahlonega; Moccasin, Wildcat, and Dicks creeks on the 13,000-acre Lake Burton WMA; the headwaters of the Chattahoochee River, Duke Creek, and Spoilcane Creek on the primitive 23,000-acre Chattahoochee WMA north of Robertstown; the headwaters of the Chestatee River and Boggs, Dicks, and Waters creeks on the 19,000-acre Chestatee WMA north of Dahlonega (Waters Creek is a state-designated "trophy" stream which yields some huge pink-slashed rainbows up to 10 pounds, browns, and brook trout up to 4 and 5 pounds); the Conasauga River, Jacks River, and Mountaintown Creek on the huge 95,000-acre Cohutta WMA wilderness; the Coleman River, Tate Branch, and Mill Creek surrounded by the rugged, steep highlands of the 11,000-acre Coleman River WMA on the North Carolina border; Cooper, Sea, Mulky, Petty-Bryant, and Burnett creeks on the mountainous 34,000-acre Cooper Creek WMA in Fannin and Union counties; Fir, Flat, Worley, Trails, and Mountaintown creeks on the rugged 24,000-acre Coosawattee WMA in Gilmer and Murray counties; Johns Creek in the mountainous 23,000-acre Johns Mountain WMA in far northwest Georgia; Cartecay River, Turpintown, Big, Stanley, and Rock (big hook-jawed browns here up to 8, 12, and 18 pounds!) creeks on the 45,000-acre Rich Mountain WMA in Gilmer and Fannin counties; the Middle Broad River, which flows through the 17,000-acre Lake Russell WMA northeast of scenic Lake Russell; Corbin, Mill, and Swallow creeks on the steep, rugged 19,000-acre Swallow Creek WMA surrounded by dense mixed hardwood and evergreen forests; and Finney, Sarah's, Walnut Fork, and Tuckaluge creeks on the isolated highlands of the 14,000-acre Warwoman WMA in Rabun County.

An overview of northern Georgia's trout streams and rugged wildlife management is provided by a full-color *Chattahoochee National Forest Recreation Map* (50¢), available from: Forest Supervisor, Chattahoochee National Forest, U.S. Forest Service, P.O. Box 1437, Gainesville 30501. A set of full-color U.S. Geological Survey large-scale topo maps will prove an invaluable aid to the wilderness fly fisherman (see "Canoe Trails & Trophy Fishing Waters"). Nonrelief *Wildlife Management Area Maps* are available free from: Information Section, DNR, 270 Washington St., SW, Atlanta 30334, phone (404) 656–3530. Nonrelief *County Maps* showing roads, many smaller trout streams, and boundaries of wildlife management areas may be obtained for 25¢ each from: Department of Transportation, Rm. 354, 2 Capitol Sq., Atlanta 30334. The *Guide to Georgia Trout Regulations* contains a detailed map of the Chattahoochee River from Buford Dam to Morgan Falls Dam, a map of Georgia's streams, rivers, and reservoirs, a map of trout streams of Georgia, and regulations of managed stream directions and fishing schedule. An *Oconee National Forest Map* (50¢) showing all fish and game lands, campgrounds, trails, and forest roads may be obtained from the Supervisor, Oconee National Forest, Monticello 31064.

Trophy Bass Lakes

Huge island-dotted Lake Lanier, located south of the Chattahoochee National Forest, where it is fed by the clear, frigid waters of the Chestatee and Chattahoochee rivers, provides some of the state's best fishing for trophy largemouth bass and brown trout. The clear, 30-mile long tailrace waters below Lake Lanier provide some of the best float fishing in the South for large rainbows and buckskin-flanked browns up to 9 pounds. Lake Allatoona to the west on the Etowah River holds some lunker bass, and Lakes Rabun, Seed, Tugaloo, and Hartwell on the Tallulah River to the east hold large bass and a few trophy-sized rainbows and browns. The lakes of northern Georgia are generally clear year round with excellent launching and rental facilities scattered along the access area.

The huge Clark Hill Reservoir, Lake Blackshear, Walter F. George Reservoir, and Lake Seminole—often referred to as the bass capital of the world—with their sprawling, stump-filled irregularly shaped shorelines in central and southern Georgia, offer some of the South's finest fishing for trophy largemouth bass. The meandering, deep, dark waters of the scenic Flint, Chattahoochee, Ocmulgee, Oconee, Ogeechee, Ohoopee, Altamaha, Savannah, and Satilla rivers, which flow through the central plateau and coastal lowlands surrounded by moss-draped cypress trees, thick green floodplain forests, and swamplands, provide excellent canoe camping and float fishing for big largemouth bass, bluegills, redear sunfish, and voracious chain pickerel as long as your arm. Fishing camps and float fishing outfitters are located along most of the rivers. The lower reaches and tidewater areas of the coastal streams provide good seasonal fishing for migrating shad and striped bass up to 50 pounds. The limpid green headwaters of the beautiful Suwannee River in the vast primitive wildlands of Okefenokee National Wildlife Refuge (q.v.) hold some monster largemouth bass and lean green chain pickerel.

Saltwater Fishing

Georgia's warm Gulf Stream waters and irregularly shaped coastline, with the Inland Waterway, bays, and scenic islands, provide good surf (particularly on the beautiful unspoiled Golden Isles) and offshore fishing in season for tarpon up to 100 pounds, red drum, sailfish, barracuda, the "mad chopper" (bluefish), weakfish (called summer trout locally), albacore, cobia, kingfish, striped bass, and during the winter months for spotted sea trout and American shad.

The Georgia Big Fish Contest, sponsored annually by the Georgia Wildlife Federation and *Outdoors in Georgia* magazine, awards certificates and prizes, provided courtesy of the Garcia and Pflueger corporations, to resident and visiting anglers who enter their trophy fish. For application forms and regulations, write: Outdoors in Georgia, Rm. 714, 270 Washington St., SW, Atlanta 30334 (this beautiful full-color magazine, published by the Department of Natural Resources, costs $3 per year for 12 issues).

A free *Guide to Georgia Freshwater Sportfishing Regulations* and a free 30-page *Georgia Hunting Regulations and Game Management Area Guide* may be obtained from: Information Office, DNR, 270 Washington St., SW, Atlanta 30334. The management area guide contains detailed descriptions of Georgia's game management areas and a Map of Georgia's Hunting Areas. The useful, beautifully written

Prince of Game Birds—the Bobwhite Quail, by Charles Elliot ($5.50) may be obtained from: DNR (address above).

Georgia's vast national forests and game management lands provide excellent hunting in season for quail, whitetail deer, ruffed grouse in the northern highlands, mourning doves, rails and snipe along the coastal marshlands, wild turkey in the Clark Hill WMA and Chattahoochee National Forest, black bear in the dark interior of the Okefenokee Swamp, and squirrels, cottontails, raccoons, red fox, and waterfowl on the coastal plain wetlands. (See "Canoe Trails & Trophy Fishing Waters.")

Okefenokee National Wildlife Refuge

A few miles south of Waycross, the Okefenokee Swamp spreads across the southeastern corner of the state to an indefinite termination south of the Florida line. Covering an area of close to half a million acres, the Okefenokee is some 40 miles long and up to 25 miles wide. Geologists believe the swamp was once a shallow ocean sound, cut off by a 100-mile-long sandbar now called the Trail Ridge. Sometime during the Pleistocene era, a half million to a million years ago, the large body of water was trapped and its salt content gradually flushed away by heavy rains. Sandbars scattered beyond the Trail Ridge became islands. Aquatic plants first found a favorable environment in the tepid shallows, than decayed and formed layers of peat, rich deposits capable of supporting other forms of plant life. Eventually a forest took root throughout the swamp. Fires leveled the forest growth, resulting in the swamp prairies of today.

In this vast swamp, sizable bodies of water stretch through dense mazes of moss-covered cypress trees. Against the prevailing silvery-green of cypress and tupelos, white and golden water lilies along with other flowering plants add bright splashes of color. Lakes, islands, and prairies interrupt the moist expanse. "Houses," clumps of bushes and trees underlain by smaller plants, are formed when gases produced by decaying vegetable matter force masses of plant growth from the bottom of the water. The surface of this mucky stuff rises several inches above the surrounding water and becomes covered in time by bushes, water weeds, and grass. This living island floats until it becomes entangled in a thicket of trees, gathering seeds from cypress and other trees until it forms a "house." Many houses never stabilize but sway and tremble under the slightest disturbance, hence the origin of area's name: Okefenokee is derived from a Choctaw Indian term meaning "quivering earth."

Depending upon the place and time of day, the waters of the swamp vary in color from dark brown to pitch, stained from the tannic acid released by decaying plants. On clear days the water acts as a dark mirror, reflecting a steady image of cypress trees, clouds, and sky. Legend has it that persons lost in the swamp have jumped into the waters as into a mirage, mistaking the liquid illusion for solid land. Indeed, the sense of mystery and otherworldliness pervading the swamp has given rise to numerous irresistible tall tales and myths. The region was once part of the lower hunting ground of Creek Indians, who told an 18th-century traveler that the swamp harbored the most blissful island on earth. A group of hunters had glimpsed the island, but were unable to pass through the labyrinth of trees and water surrounding the spot. Lost and close to starvation, they were met by several ethereally beautiful women who offered them fruit, marsh eggs, and corn pone. Warning them that their husbands would slaughter all intruders, they pointed out a passage by which the warriors could return safely home. Stories about these ravishing visions inspired other hunters to enter the swamp country in pursuit of them. Many

tried and many became hopelessly lost, but none were ever able to rediscover the enchanted island or the "daughters of the sun."

Visitors to the Okefenokee Swamp may never run across lovely Indian women, but its great profusion of wildlife offers equally fascinating sights and sounds. Some nine-tenths of the area has been designated a wildlife refuge. Ring-necked, pintailed, and black ducks make their winter home here, sharing the terrain with robins, cardinals, buzzards, red-winged blackbirds, owls, catbirds, osprey, and many other species. Except during the stillness of midday, the squealing cries of wood ducks and the discordant squawks of herons and egrets are heard repeatedly. Add to this the constant plops and splashes of over twenty species of frogs, the hammering of woodpeckers, and the occasional deep-throated bellowing of alligators in the canals, lakes, and deeper pools, and you have a veritable symphony of the swamp. In the tangled forests of cypress, bay, and gum adorned with streamers of Spanish moss are raccoons, bobcats, opossums, and otter. There are also abundant signs of bear and white-tailed deer.

The principal outlet of the swamp, the Suwannee River, drifts southwestward to empty into the Gulf of Mexico. Though much of the Suwannee runs through wild, rough country, its shores were at one time punctuated with prosperous plantations as well as remote camps of runaway slaves who found allies among the nearby Seminole tribes.

For its entire 250-mile length, from the edge of the Okefenokee through Florida to the Gulf, the river is navigable by small boats. Canoe runs, described later in this section, are possible along all of its course. Another river freighted with rich historical associations, the St. Marys, once called the "Seine" by homesick French settlers, winds toward the Atlantic and drains the southeastern part of the swamp. In these and other waters there is prime fishing throughout the year under Georgia State regulations. Trophy largemouth bass, bluegill, warmouth, catfish, and chain pickerel up to 3 feet long are among the most commonly caught of the more than 50 species found here. Tiny tropical fish, including the rare rainwater fish *(Lucania parva)*, flash brightly in the dark waters of quiet lakes and pools.

Three public entrances provide access to the Okefenokee Wildlife Refuge: the west entrance at Stephen C. Foster State Park near Fargo, the Suwannee Canal Recreation Area near Folkston on the east, and the northern entrance in Okefenokee Swamp Park. At each entry point guided tours, walking trails, swamp exhibits, and picnic facilities are available. Typical activities include guided boat tours leaving several times daily for trips over watery swamp trails into the heart of the refuge; a mile-long boardwalk trek over the wetlands to an observation tower; and self-guiding canoe and motorboat rentals over marked water trails. Camping is not permitted in the swamp itself, but camping facilities, hotels, motels, and restaurants are available at Folkston. For an *Okefenokee National Wildlife Map-Guide* and other free information, write: Okefenokee Swamp Park, Waycross 31501.

A map and folder on *Wilderness Canoeing in Okefenokee*, describing trips over Floyd's Island, through Minnie's and Big Water lakes, and across Chase and Mizell prairies, is available free from: Refuge Manager, Okefenokee Wildlife Refuge, P.O. Box 117, Waycross 31501. Canoe trails allow you to explore the boundaries of Billy's Island (named for the Seminole chief Billy Bowlegs), for many years the home of Daniel Less and his family, the only white people living in the swamp's interior. When timber crews first arrived in the late 19th century, the Lees evacuated the island but were so homesick they returned a few months later. A lumber camp, stores, a school, and a movie house thrived on the island for a short time but have long been abandoned. Floyd's Island, a favorite overnight stop for canoers, features bogs of muck and moss so dense it is impossible to walk on them. Hundreds of spotted pitcher plants, able to ensnare flies in their tubelike leaves, are found here growing to the unusual height of 3 feet. Canoers will have to use their paddle every inch of the way, as there is no fast-moving water within the swamp. Because there is little dry land and much shallow water, you may have to get out of your craft and push across peat blowups and low-water pools. Reservations for canoe trips are advisable but not necessary. Permits are required. For both reservations and permits, write: Refuge Manager (address above).

The Okefenokee National Wildlife Refuge is shown on the following large-scale U.S. Geological Survey Maps: Billy's Island, Blackjack Island, Chase Island, Chesser Island, Colon, Council, Cravers Island, Dinner Pond, Double Lake, Eddy, Fargo, Fort Mudge, Moniac, Sargent, Spooners, Strange Island, The Pocket, Waycross SE.

Wilderness Outfitters & Expeditions

Based in Savannah, Wilderness Southeast offers a wide-ranging spectrum of outdoor activities from hiking in the Great Smokies to canoeing in the Okefenokee Swamp and the Big Cypress Wilderness in Florida, and the Suwannee and Chattooga Rivers in Georgia. Groups of 20 or less are guided by experienced members on backpacking trips through the Appalachians of North Carolina (April to October); around Cumberland Island's freshwater lakes and intricate shifting

dunes (September through May); through the marshes of Wassaw Island; and across the subtropics of south Florida. Other canoe and backpacking trips explore the watery wilderness of Okefenokee Swamp with its lush cypress trees and network of twisting waterways and the side lakes and channels of the Ogeechee River. Weekend and longer trips are sponsored year round with special rates for organizations, families, and organized groups. For complete information, write to: *Wilderness Southeast*, Rte. 3, Box 619, Savannah 31406, or telephone (912) 355-8008. Summer wilderness camps and special trips for children and teenagers are also offered.

A nonprofit educational organization, Wolfcreek Wilderness, located near Blairsville, provides both a series of seminars in outdoor skills and a program of wilderness adventures for young people 14 years and older. Seminars vary from 2 to 12 days and are generally held at Wolfcreek Lodge. Subjects include leadership courses in rock-climbing, outdoor emergency medical aid, and winter leadership. Skills development seminars explore mountaineering rock craft, introductory backpacking and winter camping, caving, and wilderness cookery. The 3-week wilderness experiences for young people in groups of 8 are guided backpacking trips through the mountains of northern Georgia and western North Carolina. Write to: *Wolfcreek Wilderness*, P.O. Box 596, Blairsville 30512, for further details.

SOUTH CAROLINA ENCYCLOPEDIA

Accommodations— Vacation Lodges & Resorts

For complete information on and listings of lodges, resorts, and hotels and a free, full-color 48-page *South Carolina State Parks Guide*, write to: local Chambers of Commerce or the Dept. of State Parks, Recreation and Tourism, Edgar A. Brown Bldg., 1205 Pendleton St., Columbia 29201. Many state parks provide cabins with excellent facilities and services. Parks with cabin accommodations include Cheraw, Edisto Beach, Givhans Ferry, Hickory Knob, Hunting Island, Myrtle Beach, Oconee, Pleasant Ridge, Poinsett, Santee State Resort, and Table Rock.

Campgrounds & State Recreation Areas

The Palmetto State has over 16,000 campsites from the banks of the wild Chattooga in the beautiful Blue Ridge Mountains south through the state to the sand dunes of the Atlantic coastline. Camping areas with complete facilities and services are available in Sumpter and Marion national forests and in all of the state parks. There is a wide variety, from primitive camping areas to full-service family campgrounds. A free *South Carolina Camping Guide* is available from: Division of Tourism, P.O. Box 71-C, Columbia 29202. The *South Carolina State Parks Guide* is a free, illustrated brochure which lists and describes the many parks and their excellent services in detail. (See "Accommodations—Vacation Lodges & Resorts.")

For a free listing of commercial campgrounds in the state, write to: Myrtle Beach Chamber of Commerce, P.O. Box 1326, Myrtle Beach 29577; Pendleton District Historical and Recreational Commission, P.O. Box 234, Pendleton 29670; or Santee-Cooper Counties Promotion Offices, P.O. Box 12, Santee 29142.

Canoe Trails & the Chattooga Wild River

The major whitewater stream in South Carolina is the Chattooga. This river provides some of the finest trout fishing in the region, and various stretches of the river offer different degrees of canoeing difficulty. There are many rapids and falls here, but beginners can pick out easily navigable areas. The Chattooga River was the scene of the disastrous expedition in the film *Deliverance*, and while you will doubtless not meet up with a similar fate, you are well advised to take stock of the river's rugged, temperamental character. The river starts in the Carolina highlands at the peak of the Appalachians. It winds down 50 miles of rugged, wild, and spectacular country, falling through deep, rocky canyons and towering cliffs. Waterfalls, pools, strange rock formations, and vegetation provide constant interest on this challenging, exotic river.

A free *Canoeing the Chattooga Map-Guide* is available from: Sumpter National Forest, 1801 Assembly St., Columbia 29201. *Wildwater*, Longcreek 29658, is an outfitting service that provides equipment, guides, and instruction on the Chattooga and the Nolichuckey.

Other major canoe routes and float streams in the state include the Cooper, Chauga, Congaree, Keowee, Santee, and Wateree rivers.

Fishing & Hunting in South Carolina

The state of South Carolina, specifically the famous Santee-Cooper watershed, offers some of the best largemouth and landlocked striped bass fishing in the nation. Roughly a triangle in shape, the state covers

31,055 square miles (775 of which consist of lakes and streams), bordered on the east and north by North Carolina and the beautiful Blue Ridge Mountains (which occupy an area about 500 square miles in the northwest portion of the state), on the west by the wild Chattooga and the Tugaloo, and the historic Savannah River and its Hartwell and Clark Hill reservoirs, and on the south by the warming currents of the Atlantic Ocean. From the scenic highlands of the soft Blue Ridge Mountains the terrain drops gradually to the rolling hills, mixed hardwood and pine forests, and red clay country of the Piedmont plateau and the Sand Hills, to the vast swamplands and tidewaters of the coastal plains, a distance of about 235 miles. The climate ranges from temperate in the Blue Ridge highlands to semitropical in the southeast, with long, hot summers, tempered by sea breezes near the coast. Possible hazards common to all southern states confronting the outdoorsmen include mosquitoes and poisonous snakes—water moccasins, coral snakes, and copperheads.

The quality and diversity of the state's freshwater fishing is reflected by the record fish caught on rod and reel, as compiled by the Wildlife & Marine Resources Department.

SOUTH CAROLINA RECORD FRESHWATER FISH

	Lb.-oz.	Place	Year
Largemouth bass	16–2	Lake Marion	1949
Smallmouth bass	5–4	Toxaway River	1971
Striped bass	55	Lake Moultrie	1971
Walleye	9	Lake Hartwell	1974
Chain pickerel	6	Lake Marion	1962
Brown trout	13–4	Chauga River	1961
Rainbow trout	5–8	Hartwell Dana Tailrace	1971
Brook trout	2–5	Oconee Co.	1975
Bluegill	3–4	Lancaster Co. Pond	1973
Yellow perch	1–10	Richland Co. Lake	1972
Black crappie	5*	Lake Moultrie	1957
White crappie	5–1	Lake Murray	1949
Channel catfish	58*	Lake Moultree	1964
Flathead catfish	42	Congaree River	1975
Blue catfish	21	Diversion Canal	1975
White catfish	31–8	Cooper River	1975
Bullhead catfish	6–3	Edisto River	1973
Bowfin	19–12*	Lake Marion	1971

*World's record.

Sumpter National Forest Wild & Trophy Waters

Trout fishing in South Carolina is limited to the cold clear streams of the Blue Ridge Mountains in the Sumpter National Forest. Wilderness fly fishermen will find good fishing along the upper reaches of the wild Chattooga River and its East Fork and Whetstone Creek tributaries for native and stocked rainbows and browns. The Chauga River and its Cedar Bore, Hell Hole, and West Village Creek headwaters are top-ranked brown trout waters surrounded by the scenic Blue Ridge high country and mixed hardwood forests with thick undergrowths of mountain laurel and rhododendrons. The remote wild stretches of the Whitewater River above Lake Jocassee hold large resident populations of rainbow and brown trout. The cold, gin-clear headwaters of Big Eastatoe Creek, a feeder stream of the Keowee-

Toxaway Reservoir, hold rainbows and browns. Other top-ranked rainbow and brown trout streams in the forest include North and Middle Saluda rivers, South Pacolet River, and the remote wild country stretches of Matthews, Cane, and Laurel Fork creeks, which hold native populations of small, orange-bellied brookies.

The major impoundments in Sumpter National Forest, including Yonah, Tugaloo, Keowee, and Jocassee reservoirs, provide good year-round fishing for bream, largemouth bass, crappie, and yellow perch. The Tugaloo River branch of Hartwell Reservoir is noted for its late winter spawning run of walleyes upstream to Yonah Lake Dam. The sprawling, island-studded waters of 61,350-acre Hartwell Reservoir on the Savannah River, and its many branches and feeder streams, provide top-ranked fishing along the shoals, rocky shorelines, and dead-timbered areas for largemouths, and schools of white bass, crappie, bream, and catfish. Huge 78,500-acre Clark Hill Reservoir, a famous impoundment on the Savannah River to the south of Lake Hartwell, bordered on the east by the Long Cane Division of Sumpter National Forest and on the west by Georgia's Piedmont plateau, has huge schools of threadfin shad and provides excellent fall fishing for surface-churning schools of largemouth bass up to trophy weights in the 10-pound-plus class. During the spring spawning run, big bass are caught along the lake's Long Cane, Little River, and Buffalo Creek feeders, and at Hollings Landing and Hester's Bottoms at the mouth of Newford Creek. Clark Hill also offers good year-round fishing for crappies around shallow stump-filled areas, brush piles, and submerged islands, using popping bugs and live worms. Large rainbows are occasionally caught in the cold, dangerous tailrace waters below Clark Hill Dam. The Savannah, which forms the boundary between Georgia and South Carolina, flows south from the dam in a meandering course with numerous oxbows to its mouth at the Atlantic Ocean, and provides often excellent fishing for largemouth bass and spring-run striped bass. The most popular local artificial lures include rebels, hellbenders, plastic worms, bombers, devil dogs, brown-pike lures, thin fins, mirror lures, shysters with doll flies, nepps spinners, jumbo minnows, and a variety of surface lures and live bait.

Santee-Cooper & Trophy Bass Waters

The world-famous Santee-Cooper lakes with their 450 miles of shoreline formed by 110,000-acre Lake Marion and 60,400-acre Lake Moultrie, joined by a 7½-mile diversion canal, offer some of the South's finest fishing for trophy largemouth bass and landlocked striped bass up to monster weights during the spring spawning period at the famed Low Falls, Jacks, and Wybow creeks, Santee, Congaree, and Wateree rivers, and the Diversion Canal area. In addition to spectacular bass fishing the Santee-Cooper lakes provide excellent fishing with live minnows around submerged debris during the spring and fall for crappie up to world's record weights, and good but unpredictable fishing for large chain pickerel and catfish. Other top-ranked bass waters in the Santee-Cooper watershed include the 11,400-acre Lake Greenwood and 50,800-acre Lake Murray on the Congaree River and

13,710-acre Lake Wateree on the Wateree River. Marina fish camps, boat landings, and campgrounds are available at all major lakes in the Santee-Cooper country. The most popular striped bass lures include White Dudes, bucktails, striper swipers, and live gizzard shad and cut herring bait. Effective largemouth bass lures include Johnson spoons with pork rind, little Cleos, rebels, plastic worms, hellbenders, Bayou boogies, thin fins, white bucktails, and pot guts. During the hot summer months, largemouth bass, stripers, and crappies are most successfully caught by trolling over cold deep water holes. For the nitty-gritty on accommodations, fishing guides, boat rentals, and gear, write: Santee-Cooper Country, P.O. Box 12, Santee 29142, phone (803) 854-2131. A *Santee-Cooper Lake Contour Map* ($3) may be obtained from Lakes Illustrated, Box 4854 GS, Springfield, MO 65804.

Maps & Guides

Detailed descriptions of the major lakes and streams, including the Savannah River Watershed, Coosawhatchie, Combahee, and Ashepoo watersheds, Santee-Cooper Watershed, Peedee Watershed, and Edisto and Ashley watersheds, are contained in the *Guide to Fishing in South Carolina*, available free upon request from: Wildlife & Marine Resources Dept., P.O. Box 167, Columbia 29202. This invaluable guide also contains a detailed Watershed Map of the state, a Map of Trout Waters in South Carolina, and a listing of managed public fishing lakes. A free *Guide to South Carolina Hunting & Fishing Regulations* may be obtained from the same address. The 22-page *South Carolina Game Management Areas Guide*, available free from the Dept. of Wildlife & Marine Resources, contains detailed maps and descriptions of the renowned game lands in the scenic Mountain, Western Piedmont, and Central Piedmont hunt units in the Sumpter National Forest. A *South Carolina Boat Landings Map & Guide* and *Boating Regulations Guide* may be obtained free from: Division of Boating, P.O. Box 167, Columbia 29202.

South Carolina's beautiful Atlantic coastline, with its numerous islands, provides excellent saltwater fishing during the spring and fall for inshore species including sea bass, porgy, flounder, snapper, and grunt; and offshore trolling in the Gulf Stream waters for sailfish, kings, bonito, marlin, wahoo, barracuda, amberjack, dolphin, kings, mackerel, cobia, and jacks. A free *Map of South Carolina's Offshore Bottom Fishing & Trolling Areas*, which shows depths, general compass headings frequently used, artificial reefs, buoys, and wrecks, may be obtained from: Wildlife & Marine Resources Dept. (address above).

Long famed for its rich hunting tradition, South Carolina's most productive game lands are, for the most part, on privately held property. The bulk of the state's 1.4 million acres of public game management area lands are located on the Sumpter and Francis Marion national forests. The primary game species include quail, wild turkey, waterfowl, ruffed grouse, whitetail deer and a few black bear, and squirrels, rabbits, red fox, and raccoons.

Highways—Recreation & Scenic Routes

A *South Carolina State Highway Map* is available free from: Map Sales Section, Highway Commission, Drawer 191, Columbia 29202. It shows all roads and highways, towns, lakes, rivers and streams, parks, points of interest, railroads, airfields, national and state forests, fish hatcheries, campgrounds, and rest areas.

Sumpter National Forest & Blue Ridge Mountains

This scenic 346,000-acre reserve, once the home and hunting grounds of the Cherokee Indians, encompasses the pine, oak, yellow poplar, and hardwood forests of the northwestern section. The forest has three major divisions: the Andrew Pickens district, known as the Gateway to the Mountains, in the Blue Ridge Mountains; and the Enoree and the Long Cane districts, in the rolling Piedmont. Many old logging roads and trails, including the Foothills Trail, provide access to such remote interior wild areas as the beautiful highlands of the Ellicott's Rock Wilderness, the shoulder-high switch cane of the Long Cane Creek Scenic Area, Broad River Scenic Area, Chattooga River Gorge, Clarks Hills Reservoir, Indian Camp Wild Area, and the trout waters of the Chauga, Little, Whitewater, and Toxaway rivers. This is the state's top hunting area for whitetail deer, quail, and wild turkey.

The high mountains and plateaus of this area were the last stronghold of the Cherokees before they moved out in 1792. The Ellicott's Rock Scenic Area looks much as it did when the Indians lived in it. There is excellent hunting in the Enoree and Tyger districts, and there are several campsites set up for hunters. The Fairfield Primitive Weapons Area caters to those who want to try their skill with an old-fashioned muzzle-loader or a bow and arrow. The Edgefield-Long Cane District also has excellent wildlife populations.

Recreation maps of the *Sumpter National Forest* and the *Andrew Pickens ranger district, Enoree and Tyger districts,* and the *Long Cane division* are available for 50¢ each from: Supervisor, Francis Marion & Sumpter National Forests, 1801 Assembly St., Columbia 29201. They show roads and trails, ranger stations, mountains, lakes, streams, recreation sites, and points of interest. Rangers are at Walhalla, Greenwood, Edgefield, and Newberry.

Sumpter National Forest is reached via Interstates 20 and 26, U.S. Highways 25 and 176, and South Carolina State Highways 28, 9, and 72. Guides, supplies, and outfitters can be found at Union, Whitmire, Newberry, Greenwood, Walhalla, Augusta, Edgefield, McCormick, and Calhoun Falls.

Sumpter National Forest is shown on the following large-scale U.S. Geological Survey Topographic Maps. *Long Cane Ranger District:* Calhoun Creek, Calhoun Falls, Chennault, Clarks Hill, Lincolnton, McCormick, Parksville, Plum Branch, Willington, Winterset, Verdery; *Andrew Pickens Ranger District:* Cashiers, Holly Springs, Rainy Mountain, Reid, Salem, Satolah, Tamassee, Tugaloo Lake, Walhalla, Whetstone. The forest is also shown on the following 1:250,000-scale overview maps: Athens, Augusta, Greenville, Knoxville, Spartanburg.

Accommodations— Vacation Lodges & Resorts

For hunting, fishing, and family vacation resort information, write to: Travel Development Section, Dept. of Natural & Economic Resources, Raleigh 27611; North Carolina Citizens Assn., P.O. Box 2508, Raleigh 27602; or the local chamber of commerce of the area you plan to visit.

For listings of vacation lodges and resorts see the "North Carolina Travel & Recreation Guide" section.

Appalachian National Scenic Trail

For almost 193 miles, the Appalachian Trail follows the North Carolina-Tennessee state line between the wildlands of the Pisgah and Cherokee national forests. Much of the route is mountain crest travel, with considerable distances over 5,000-foot elevations forming a breathtaking introduction to the majestic southern Appalachians. Wave upon wave of massive summits and spectacular "balds" swell toward the horizon, making this one of the loftier and more rugged segments of the entire Appalachian chain. During June and early July a wealth of flowering shrubs blankets the mountain meadows.

Even higher and more primitive is the 70-mile segment of trail within the Great Smoky Mountains National Park. Again, one of the prime seasons for following the trail is early summer when flame azalea and rhododendron put on their annual extravaganza. The advantage of travel at this season is unfortunately offset by the increased probability of heavy rains characteristic of the region. Less ostentatious but perhaps more interesting to the naturalist or observant hiker are the many varieties of trees in the area. Great Smoky National Park alone contains more species of trees than all of Europe. While the magnificent spruce and balsam forests have largely fallen victim to the lumber industry, and the once abundant chestnut has been destroyed by blight, the vast slopes of the Smokies still offer forests like those seen by the first settlers: red and white oak, yellow poplar, hickory, maple, dogwood, and many kinds of evergreens are all found in great profusion. Within the park, the trail winds along roaring mountain streams through numerous forests and over many high peaks, including Gregory Bald, called *tsistuyi* ("the rabbit place") by Cherokee Indians, who believed the mountains to be the site of many rabbit "town houses" and the home of Great Rabbit, the huge chief of the bunnies with feet the size of skis.

Beyond the Great Smokies is a difficult 27-mile section of trail through the Yellow Creek-Wauchecha-Cheoah Range. The route turns south at the Nantahala River to enter the Nantahala National Forest, where 5,000-foot peaks and gaps almost as steep form a worthy counterpart to the Smokies. After passing over Wesser and Wayah balds, through Wayah Gap and over Panther Knob, the trail culminates in Standing Indian (5,498 feet), called the "Grandstand of the Southern Appalachians" because of the extraordinary views offered in all directions from its long ridge. The deeply cut gorge of the Tallulah River directly below to the west is especially impressive. North of Standing Indian, the trail passes through Deep Gap, then winds south around Courthouse Bald and enters Chattahoochee National Forest in Georgia.

Two publications of the Potomac Appalachian Trail Club are a great help in following the trail through North Carolina: the *Guide to the Appalachian Trail in Tennessee and North Carolina* (see Tennessee: "Appalachian National Scenic Trail") and the *Guide to the Appalachian Trail in the Great Smokies, the Nantahalas, and Georgia.* In format, the Great Smokies guide is nearly identical to the first publica-

NORTH CAROLINA ENCYCLOPEDIA

tion, describing the trail southwest of Pisgah National Forest through Great Smoky Mountains National Park, the Yellow Creek-Wauche-cha-Cheoah Range, Nantahala National Forest, and Georgia's Chattahoochee National Forest. The guide contains a history of the region, descriptions of fauna and flora, suggestions for extended trips, information on trail shelters and other accommodations, and three explicit maps of the trail. Trail data is given in full detail, including mileage, points of interest, difficulty, access points, and side trails. Priced at $6.70, the guides are available from: Appalachian Trail Conference, P.O. Box 236, Harpers Ferry, WV 25425. Allow 3 weeks for delivery or add $1 for special mailing.

The U.S. Forest Service also publishes maps of the *Appalachian Trail in Pisgah and Cherokee National Forests* and in *Nantahala National Forest*. Each map shows the route of the trail, nearby roads and highways, major forest features, towns, streams, rivers, lakes, trail shelters, recreation areas, water sources, and the like. Maps are available free from: Forest Supervisor, Plateau Building, 50 S. French Broad Ave., Asheville 28801.

The North Carolina Appalachian Trail is shown on the following large-scale U.S. Geological Survey Maps. *Pisgah National Forest Trail Segment:* Davy Crockett, Flag Pond, Greystone, Hot Springs, Lemon Gap, Sams Gap, Spring Creek, Waterville; *Nantahala National Forest Trail Segment:* Dillard, Hightown Bald, Prentiss, Rainbow Springs, Santeetlah Creek, Tapoco, Wayah Bald, Wesser; *Yellow Creek Trail Segment:* Fontana Dam, Hewitt, Wesser.

Camping & Wilderness Trails

North Carolina's scenic high country wilderness areas provide excellent opportunities for camping and hiking. *Camping in North Carolina*, a 28-page guide available free from: Travel Development Section, Dept. of Natural & Economic Resources, Raleigh 27611, lists public and private campgrounds within the state. Number and kinds of campsites, location, seasons, nearby attractions and activities available at each campground in the major forests and parks are all described. In addition to the 60 public campgrounds, there are over 300 private camping facilities in North Carolina, many of which are listed. The directory also includes a short description of parks and forests giving the location of ranger headquarters and nearby towns. At the back is a handy equipment checklist for the camper.

Another valuable guide for campers and hikers is *North Carolina Outdoors*, available free from the same address. The booklet is basically an expanded version of *Camping in North Carolina* with the listings of outdoor recreation areas keyed to coordinates of the official North Carolina Highway Map (see "Highways & the Blue Ridge Parkway"). In addition to the detailed descriptions of camping facilities, both public and private, the brochure includes brief paragraphs on fishing and hiking opportunities, wildlife, and scenic attractions in the various parks and forests. Concise directions to the different campsites and a list of campgrounds near the Blue Ridge Parkway are also included.

North Carolina offers hundreds of miles of hiking trails winding through nearby impenetrable forests, over lofty summits in the western part of the state and through lowlands, pocosins, and along fine sandy beaches in the east. *Trails and Streams of North Carolina*, a 20-page booklet free from the Travel Development Section (same address), offers a brief guide to the 200 miles of Appalachian Trail and its system of trail blazes and to other mountain trails within the state: Clingmans Dome, Cheoah Bald, Black Mountain, Mount Mitchell, Table Rock, and many others. Trail data is concise, giving mileage, access and exit points, difficulty, and sights to watch out for along the way. Trails within the state parks, such as Mount Jefferson, Morrow

Mountain, and William B. Umstead, are also briefly outlined. Canoers and rock climbers will appreciate the brochure's list of favorite river runs and rugged rock faces within the state. The Travel Development Section also publishes the free booklet *The Mountains of North Carolina.* This attractive guide provides interesting information about the state's high country and contains beautiful full-color photographs.

The 18-page *Directory of National Forest Recreation Areas* in North Carolina, is a must for the camper, fisherman, canoeist, hunter, or wilderness traveler planning a visit to the Croatan, Pisgah, or Nantahala national forests. This free booklet will help you locate both developed and primitive recreation areas and campsites in the national forests, and provides information on the facilities you will find at each site and tells you how to get there. Primitive camping is allowed anywhere in the national forests unless posted otherwise. Permits are not needed for primitive camping. However, permits are required for entrance to Linville Gorge and Shining Rock Wilderness; they can be obtained at the district ranger stations that administer these areas.

Canoe Trails & Wild Rivers

Canoeing is a favorite activity in all parts of North Carolina. The western region of the state, with its many hair-raising white-water runs along the French Broad, Nantahala, South Fork New, Little Tennessee, and Oconaluftee rivers, offers maximum excitement and the greatest challenge to experienced canoers. Although streams and rivers in eastern North Carolina are not as rapid as those in the highlands, some of the coastal streams offer many rich and rewarding experiences to the canoer in search of uncommon species of wildlife such as the osprey, alligator, and bald eagle. Amateurs and experts will enjoy runs along the fast-moving swamp water of the Lumber River, through the cypress forests lining Merchants Millpond, and down the fine fishing waters of the Black River. Another favorite coastal run follows the White Oak River through Croatan National Forest, where alligators, unusual vegetation, and rare bird species are commonly sighted. The 27-mile wilderness stretch of the South Fork of the New National Wild and Scenic River offers some of the finest white-water canoeing in the East. For detailed information, write: Stone Mountain State Park, Star Route 1, Box 17, Roaring Gap 28668.

Trails and Streams of North Carolina, a booklet available free from: Travel Development Section, Dept. of Natural & Economic Resources, Raleigh 27611, lists the various rivers frequented by canoers in the mountains, Piedmont, and coastal areas of the state. Location, difficulty, principal access points, and a short description of the run are included.

The following U.S. Geological Survey Map Kits show the entire lengths and headwaters as well as the surrounding topography of the state's major wilderness trout streams and white-water canoe routes in the Great Smokies and the Pisgah and Nantahala national forests. These remote highland streams offer some of the finest fishing in the eastern United States of large, wild brook, brown, and rainbow trout up to 14 pounds. The fly fisherman should be prepared to fish along stream banks overgrown with laurel and rhododendron. *Big Pigeon River & Waterville Lake:* Clyde, Cove Creek Gap, Fines Creek, Waterville; *Cheoah River:* Fontana Dam, Tapoco, Robbinsville; *French Broad River:* Asheville, Brevard, Horse Shoe, Hot Springs, Leicester, Marshall, Pisgah Forest, Rosman, Skyland, Spring Creek, Weaverville; *Hiwassee River & Lake:* Hayesville, McDaniel Bald, Murphy, Persimmon Creek, Unaka; *Linville River:* Ashford, Grandfather Mountain, Linville Falls, Newland, Oak Hill; *Little Tennessee River & Lake Fontana:* Alarka, Corbin Knob, Fontana Dam, Franklin, Noland Creek, Prentiss, Scaly Mountain, Tapoco, Tuckasegee,

Wesser; *North Fork New River:* Baldwin Gap, Grassy Creek, Jefferson, Mouth of the Wilson, Warrensville; *South Fork New River:* Boone, Deep Gap, Glendale Springs, Laurel Springs, Jefferson, Mouth of the Wilson, Todd; *Nolichuckey River:* Bakersville, Burnsville, Celo, Chestoa, Huntdale, Micaville; *Nottely River:* Culberson, Murphy, Persimmon Creek; *Oconaluftee River:* Clingmans Dome, Mount Guyot, Smokemont; *Roaring River:* Glade Valley, McGrady, Roaring River, Traphill, Whitehead.

Cape Hatteras National Seashore & the Outer Banks

This world-famous island reserve, established more than 40 years ago as the nation's first national seashore, embraces 71 miles of wild, undisturbed sand dunes and crashing surf, forming one of the last great natural formations in the country. The shoals that extend seaward from the cape are littered with broken, rusted skeletons of long forgotten ships wrecked by furious storms or destroyed by enemy torpedoes during two world wars. These great offshore waters are renowned for their "big-game" fishing for dolphin, sailfish, amberjack, barracuda, bluefin and yellowfin tuna, wahoo, cobia, and white marlin, and are fished by fleets of charter boats based at Oregon Inlet and at Hatteras. Hatteras is known as "Gamefish Junction," the meeting place of northern and southern species, where the cold green waters of the northern Labrador current flow against the Gulf Stream and force the northbound flow of warm tropical water away from the coast. The Gulf Stream waters off Cape Hatteras produce some of the country's top-ranked fishing for trophy blue marlin. Fish up to 1,140 pounds have been taken off Hatteras, with the average running close to 300 pounds. The marlin begin to appear in the offshore waters late in May and continue to strip line from whirring reels through late October. Hatteras boats fish the 12 miles of turbulent Diamond Shoals and the Gulf Stream waters which start at the Diamond Light Tower stationed on the eastern tip of the shoals. Oregon Inlet charter boats fish the Platt and Wimble shoals and the Gulf Stream waters beyond. "Headboats" fishing out of the harbors drift and bottom-fish the coral reefs for a grab bag of porgies, groupers, grunts, triggerfish, red snappers, sea bass, and an occasional amberjack or dolphin.

Surf fishing along Cape Hatteras is unsurpassed for channel bass in the 20 to 50 pound class, bluefish, striped bass during the crisp fall months, spotted sea trout during the rising tide of cool fall mornings, and pompano, flounder, and kingfish. The all-tackle world's record bluefish weighing 31 pounds 12 ounces was caught near Hatteras Inlet in 1972.

The great Hatteras dunes, marshes, and woodlands of holly, oak, and pine are inhabited by thousands of migrating Canada and snow geese during October, and by herons, egrets, seabirds, and soaring gulls.

Surf fishermen and family vacationers will find dune buggy rentals, bait and tackle shops, accommodations, and supplies at the towns of Rodanthe, Waves, Saho, Avon, Burton, Hatteras, Ocracoke, and at Oregon Inlet. A free ferry connects Hatteras Island with Ocracoke Island. The lowdown on local fishing conditions can easily be obtained from the local marinas and bait and tackle shops. For info write: *Avon River & Recreation Enterprises,* P.O. Box 35, Avon 27915; *Cape Hatteras Fishing Pier,* Hatteras 27943; *Chicamacomico Enterprises,* Rodanthe 27968; and *Oregon Inlet Fishing Center,* P.O. Box 342, Manteo 27954.

For detailed maps and information write: Superintendent, Cape Hatteras National Seashore, P.O. Box 457, Manteo 27954. The national seashore recreation area is traversed by State Route 12 and is reached by U.S. Highways 64, 264, and 158.

Fishing & Hunting in North Carolina

The variety and quality of North Carolina's fishing—ranging from wild brook trout to trophy blue marlin—and hunting is unmatched in the eastern United States. The turbulent white-water mountain streams and rivers in the western part of the state, which rush down from their forest headwaters in the Blue Ridge Mountains on the east, the Great Smokies and Unakas on the west, and transverse ranges like the Nantahala, Black, and Pisgah mountains, creating a stepladder effect in between, offer a wide range of water conditions and fishing. In the lower mountain valleys there are big lakes, such as the Hiwassee, Santeetlah, Cheoah, and Nantahala, that hold lunker largemouth and smallmouth bass, walleye, rainbow trout, crappie, and white bass. The higher-elevation streams in the remote highlands of the Nantahala National Forest hold brown and rainbow trout, and in the deep pools high up in the mountain ridges are the cold-water brook trout, or "speckles" as they are known to the natives.

Highcountry Trout Waters

North Carolina's 25 mountain counties encompass dense highland thickets of rhododendron, laurel, and azalea and colorful forests of yellow poplar, red oak, sugar maple, spruce, and black cherry and thousands of miles of crystal-clear, cold streams and lakes in the Nantahala and Pisgah national forests which produce trout ranging in size from pan-sized brookies to hook-jawed browns up to 10 pounds, and in the lakes, rainbows to 14 pounds.

Many of the more inaccessible streams in the remote highland wilderness areas hold wild brook and brown trout; natural reproduction keeps these waters near their carrying capacity. Many of these streams are located at elevations exceeding 6,000 feet and are noted for their deep staircased pools. Streams like Forney, Eagle, Hazel, and Noland creeks in the Great Smokies stretch back through the roadless cathedrallike forests toward the crest of the great range and can be reached only by crossing Fontana Lake by boat. Streams such as Horsepasture, Whitewater, and Toxaway in Transylvania County are seldom fished because their rugged, steep-walled gorges discourage all but the most determined wilderness fly fishermen. The same is true of the scenic high country wilderness threaded by the famous trophy brook trout waters of Big Snowbird Creek in the Nantahala National Forest and the whitewater and deep pools of the Linville River in the Linville Gorge Wilderness area of the Pisgah National Forest. The great brown trout waters of Slickrock Creek in the Great Smokies are likewise visited only by fishermen willing to hike several miles of mountain ridge trail.

There are literally hundreds of miles of great trout streams designated public mountain trout waters, managed by the North Carolina Wildlife Resources Commission and the U.S. Forest Service, located on the state game lands, including Green River Game Lands in Henderson and Polk counties, Nantahala National Forest Game Lands, Caney Fork Game Restoration Area in Jackson County, Pisgah National Forest Game Lands, South Mountains Game Land in Burke County, Thurmond Chatham Game Land in Wilkes County, and Toxaway Game Land in Transylvania County. Several of these public mountain streams have been further designated as native trout waters and hold wild trophy brook and brown trout. The most renowned of these waters include Big Snowbird Creek above Mouse Knob Falls in Graham County, Caney Fork Creek in Jackson County, Fires Creek in

Clay County, North Fork of the French Broad River in Transylvania County, and Slick Rock Creek on the Tennessee line and in Graham County.

Trophy Trout Waters

A few of the premier state game land streams are managed as trophy trout waters where the minimum legal size for rainbow and brown trout is 16 inches and the minimum size for brook trout is 12 inches. These renowned trout waters include Lost Cove Creek in the Avery County section of Pisgah National Forest, the rainbow trout waters of Nantahala River from the high concrete bridge at Standing Indian Campground downstream to the Bear Sanctuary line in the Macon County region of the Nantahala National Forest, South Mills River in Henderson and Transylvania counties, and a section of Wilson Creek in the Avery County region of the Pisgah National Forest.

Anyone planning to fish the public mountain waters, native trout waters, or trophy trout waters must have a game lands use permit in addition to the regular North Carolina fishing license and special trout license. The game lands use permit is not required to fish in the section of Slick Rock Creek which coincides with the Tennessee state line, or when fishing from a boat on Calderwood Reservoir. On these streams only artificial lures having a single hook are allowed; only artificial flies may be used on the trophy trout waters.

A free 70-page booklet, *Hunting and Fishing Maps for North Carolina Game Lands,* may be obtained by writing: Game Land Maps, Wildlife Resources Commission, Albemarle Bldg., 325 N. Salisbury St., Raleigh 27611. Information and regulations pertaining to the Great Smoky Mountains National Park waters may be obtained from: Superintendent, National Park Service, Gatlinburg, TN 37738, phone (615) 436-5615.

Trophy Bass Lakes

Some of North Carolina's best smallmouth bass fishing is found in the scenic valleys along the New River, including the North and South Forks, in Ashe and Alleghany counties, and along the Watauga, Upper Yadkin, Johns River, Elk Creek, and Lower Wilson's Creek. Many of the TVA lakes, such as Chatuge, Hiwassee, Lure, Calderwood, Cheoah, Santeetlah, and Fontana, provide outstanding fishing for largemouth bass up to 10 and 12 pounds during the spring and fall months when the fish are in the shallows and for walleye, smallmouth bass, and crappie. Fontana Lake, Hiwassee Reservoir, and Lake Santeetlah have been ranked among the top 100 bass lakes in the United States. Some exciting fishing can be had for large rainbow trout in Lake Fontana at the mouths of Forney, Hazel, Eagle, and Noland creeks when the fish begin their annual spawning run. Some good fishing can be found in the small sparkling blue lakes that dot the highlands of western North Carolina. Rainbow and brook trout are found in the headwater lakes of the East Fork of the Tuckasegee River; Bear Creek, Wolf Creek and Tennessee lakes; Price's Lake off the Blue Ridge Parkway near Blowing Rock; the Daniel Boone Wildlife Management Area; and in Bec Tree Lake near Asheville, to name a few.

Accommodations ranging from luxury resorts to cabin camps are found within easy access of the major roadways throughout the mountain country. Primitive camping facilities are provided in the Pisgah and Nantahala national forests (q.v.) and in most of the state game lands for the wilderness fisherman.

The diversity and quality of fishing in the mountain, Piedmont, and upper coastal regions of North Carolina is illustrated by the state's all-time big-fish records.

NORTH CAROLINA RECORD FRESHWATER FISH

	Lb.-oz.	Place	Year
Largemouth bass	14–15	Santeetlah Reservoir	1963
Smallmouth bass	10–2	Hiwassee Reservoir	1953
Bluegill	4–5	Edneyville Pond (Henderson Co.)	1967
Shellcracker	4–4	Lee Co. Pond	1968
Chain pickerel	8	Gaston Reservoir	1968
Channel catfish	40–8	Fontana Reservoir	1971
Brook trout	3–9	Oconaluftee River	1971
Rainbow trout	14–1	Glenville Reservoir	1949
Brown trout	10–9	Jonathan Creek	1973
Crappie	4–13	Jordan's Lake	1961
Walleye	13–4	Santeetlah Reservoir	1966
White bass	4–15	Fontana Reservoir	1966
Sauger	5–15	Lake Norman	1971
Striped bass (landlocked)	39–4	Lake Hickory	1969
American shad	7–9½	Tar River	1972
Hickory shad	2–9	Contentnea Creek	1971
Warmouth	1–8	Ellis Creek (Bladen Co.)	1971
Bowfin	13–8	Tar River (Pitt Co.)	1973

Tidal Fishing Waters

Some exceptional fishing for striped bass, largemouth and smallmouth is found in the lakes and rivers of the hilly Piedmont region, which unfolds eastward from the foothills of the Blue Ridge. Each April huge schools of striped bass move up the Roanoke River from Albemarle Sound to the edge of the Piedmont plateau to spawn, and good catches are made at the mouths of the rivers on cut bait, bucktails, and spoons. The headwaters area of the Yadkin River produces first-class largemouth and smallmouth bass fishing. The best fishing in this vast midstate area, however, is found in enormous impoundments such as the Roanoke River's Kerr Reservoir, which has 800 miles of shoreline straddling the Virginia-North Carolina boundary and is recognized as one of the nation's top 100 bass lakes and also provides some of the state's finest fishing for landlocked striped bass. Several other Piedmont reservoirs provide outstanding fishing, including James, Rhodhiss, Hickory, Norman, Mountain Island, and Wylie lakes on the Catawba River and High Rock, Badin, Tillery, and Blewett Falls lakes on the Great Pee Dee River. Lake James is one of the state's best walleye waters, producing fish up to 10 pounds, and Lake Hickory is a top-ranked largemouth and striped bass lake, producing stripers ranging in size up to the 39-pound 4-ounce state record.

The brackish tidewaters of the renowned Currituck, Albemarle and Pamlico sounds, which flow into the Atlantic through the four inlets of the Outer Banks, provide some of the finest largemouth bass fishing in the United States—producing fish in the 1–5-pound class in astonishing numbers. The freshwater natural lakes and creeks of the tidewater region, a low-relief belt of swamp forest, dotted with pocosins and savannahs and laced by a complex network of blackwater streams typical of southern swamp country extending from the Dismal Swamp near the Virginia line south to the broad bottomlands of the Cape Fear River, hold lunker bass and hordes of scrappy, colorful panfish. The best fishing in the tidewater region is found in Lake Mattamus-

keet, the area's largest with 30,000 acres, Lake Phelps in Hyde County, Alligator River and Merchants Mill Pond in Gates County, Lake Waccamaw in the southeast and in the tributaries of the Tar, Black, Roanoke, North, Yeopin, and Chowan rivers. Freshwater fishing licenses are required when fishing in brackish waters, except for Albemarle Sound. Nonresident anglers are recommended to hire the services of a local guide, available at most villages along the sounds, to help navigate the intricate waterways and to help keep the boat within casting range when the wind is up. The usual guide fee is $35.40 a day for a party of two. The Wildlife Resources Commission maintains boat-launching sites at most of the major waters mentioned above.

Cape Hatteras & the Outer Banks

The wild sand dunes and vast stretches of isolated thundering surf along Cape Hatteras, Cape Lookout, and Cape Fear and the world-famous shoals that extend seaward from these capes, littered with the skeletons of long forgotten ships wrecked by the fury of these seas, produce some of the world's greatest surf and offshore fishing for

bluefish, stripers, giant blue marlin, and a veritable host of other saltwater game fish species. This renowned region known as the Outer Banks runs in a sandy strip 175 miles long from Virginia south to Cape Lookout, where it curves back to the mainland.

The offshore hot spots are fished for amberjack in the 10-20-pound class up to 123 pounds, dolphin in the 5-20-pound range, blue marlin up to 1,140 pounds, sailfish to 76 pounds, white marlin averaging close to 60 pounds, barracuda averaging 10 pounds with fish up to 44 pounds, cobia up to 90 pounds over the offshore wrecks, and large numbers of bluefin tuna, yellowfin tuna, Atlantic big-eyed tuna, little tunny, skipjack tuna, wahoo, and Atlantic bonito. The offshore waters of the northeastern coast are fished by fleets of charter boats, based at Oregon Inlet, which fish the Platt and Wimble shoals and the Gulf Stream waters beyond; and by the famous fleet of Hatteras boats that fish the 12 miles of treacherous Diamond Shoals and the warm sapphire Gulf Stream waters which begin at the Diamond Light Tower on the east tip of the shoals. The reefs and wreckages of Lookout Shoals and beyond are fished by the charter boat fleet based at Morehead City. Off Cape Fear, the blue waters of Frying Pan Shoals are fished by charter boats from Carolina Beach, Southport, Wrightsville Beach, and Shallotte. The seashore along the Outer Banks, pierced by Oregon Inlet and Hatteras, Ocracoke, Beaufort, Swash, and Drum inlets, provides world-renowned surf fishing for powerful channel bass and tremendous periodic runs of giant bluefish and striped bass.

Maps, Guides & Information

North Carolina fishing and hunting regulations, seasons, and information about special permits and free publications may be obtained by writing to: Wildlife Resources Commission, Albemarle Bldg., 325 N. Salisbury St., Raleigh 27611. The following fishing publications are available free from the commission: *Belew Lake, Fish Facts, Fishing at Lake Toisnot, Lake Waccamaw, Largemouth Bass in North Carolina, Rainbow Trout in North Carolina, The Bluegill in North Carolina,* and *The Chowan River.* Free publications about game birds and wildlife published by the commission include *Adventures with the Wood Duck, The Squirrel* (fox and gray), and *The European Boar in North Carolina.* Other free publications and regulations booklets published by the commission include *Boating in North Carolina Waters, Ecology Reprints, Designated Public Mountain Trout Waters, North Carolina Fishing Rules, North Carolina Game Lands, Hunting & Trapping Regulations,* and *Motorboat Owner's Guide.*

The useful, free publication *Fishing in North Carolina,* a full-color 32-page booklet, contains descriptions and illustrations of popular lures and fish species, a map of the piers on the North Carolina coast, and detailed descriptions of offshore, surf and pier, inshore, inlet and sound, brackish water, midstate, and mountain waters fishing. The free 24-page booklet *Fishing North Carolina Waters* provides a handy guide to fishing for striped bass, spring shad, fall speckled trout, winter chain pickerel, summer white perch, largemouth bass, trout, and panfish in eastern, western, and Piedmont regions of the state. The 38-page guide *Hunting in North Carolina* contains game species distribution maps and useful information about the black bear, wild boar, whitetail deer, raccoon, opossum, squirrel, rabbit, quail, wild turkey, fox, wildcat, upland game birds, and waterfowl hunting in the state. The free 70-page booklet *Hunting & Fishing Maps for North Carolina Game Lands* contains detailed maps of all state game lands, including the Nantahala, Pisgah, Green River, New Hope, Uwharrie, Holly Shelter, Croatan, Big Pocosin, Goose Creek, and Toxaway state game lands. All four publications are available free from the Wildlife Resources Commission.

Four useful, informative publications, *Fishing Currituck Sound, Offshore Fishing in North Carolina, Outer Banks Surf Fishing,* and *Bass Fishing in North Carolina,* are available free from: Travel Development Section, P.O. Box 27687, Raleigh 27611. Lake Survey Maps, some showing depth and bottom contours, are available for *Kerr Reservoir,* free from: W. Kerr Scott Reservoir, Box 182, Wilkesboro 28697; a *Lake Gaston Atlas* ($3.88) and *Kerr Reservoir Atlas* ($5.41) are available by mail from: Alexandria Drafting Co., 417 Clifford Ave., Alexandria, VA 22305. Maps of the *Upper Lakes* (James, Rhodhiss, Hickory, and Lookout Shoals), the *Lower Lakes* (Mountain Island and Wylie), *Lake Norman,* and *Belew Creek* Lake are available free from: Duke Power Co., P.O. Box 2178, Charlotte 28232. Navigation maps of Lakes Chatuge, Fontana, Hiwassee, and Apalachia are available at 45¢ each from: Tennessee Valley Authority (see "Tennessee Valley Lakes Recreation Maps"). There are 2 navigation maps for Hiwassee, 3 for Fontana, and 1 each for Apalachia and Chatuge.

Hunting

The hunting picture in North Carolina matches the stunning scenery of its varied terrain. Nearly 2 million acres of land is open to public hunting under the Wildlife Resources Commission's game lands program. Game lands are located in all sections of the state from the Great Smoky Mountains to the coast and provide a cross section of all types of hunting available in North Carolina. In addition, there are 1,125,196 acres of national forest lands in the state, including the pine and swamp-hardwood forests of the Croatan National Forest, with

hunting for waterfowl, black bear, whitetail deer, quail, and wild turkey; the dense rugged highland forests and thick undercover of rhododendron and azalea of the Nantahala National Forest, with top-ranked hunting in season for wild boar, black bear, deer, and ruffed grouse; the scenic mountains and forests of the Pisgah National Forest, with wild boar, whitetail deer, upland game birds, and small game; and the small Unwharrie National Forest, with 43,571 acres, located in the center of the state. *U.S. Forest Service Maps* of the Croatan and Unwharrie national forests may be obtained for 50¢ each from the Supervisor's Office, U.S. Forest Service, P.O. Box 2750, Asheville 28802

Black bear, the state's largest game animal, frequently attaining weights in excess of 500 pounds, are confined to the vast forests of the western highlands and eastern swamps. In an effort to preserve the species and improve hunting, several bear sanctuaries have been established, including the Daniel Boone Bear Sanctuary in Avery, Burke, and Caldwell counties; Pisgah Bear Sanctuary in Buncombe, Haywood, Henderson, and Transylvania counties; the Mount Mitchell Bear Sanctuary in McDowell and Yancey counties; and the Standing Indian, Wayah Bald, and Rich Mountain bear sanctuaries in Macon County. While not designated as such, the Great Smokies National Park serves as the largest and most productive sanctuary in western North Carolina.

North Carolina is one of the few states in the country with hunting for wild boar (originally introduced through a private stocking on Hoopers Bald in Graham County) on public game lands. The Santeetlah Wildlife Management Area in Graham County is the focal point of boar hunting in the state, but boar are also found in several surrounding communities. Whitetail deer, scarce in the state at the turn of the century, is the major big-game species today. A population of 400,000 deer range throughout the state.

Wild turkey is the state's largest game bird, with trophy toms often exceeding 20 pounds. Turkey were once in a serious decline because of overhunting, but North Carolina today has some excellent spring turkey hunting ranges, especially in the hardwood bottoms of the Nantahala National Forest and on the Daniel Boone, Santeetlah, Standing Indian, and Wayah Bald wildlife management areas. Bobwhite quail are the king of game birds in the state, with an average of 2 million taken each year by some 250,000 Tarheel hunters. Quail are found throughout the state, with highest-density populations in the coastal plains. With the decrease of patch farms in the state, quail have been moving from the diminishing fields of broomstraw into woodlands, which provide an abundance of fall and winter foods such as acorns, sweet gum buds, dogwood berries, and pine mast. The most productive hunting areas are the edges of large fields, cutover woods with scattered large sweet gum trees, and open stands of pine, particularly after a good seed fall. Other popular upland game birds include ruffed grouse in the forest mountain country of western North Carolina, grape tangles, abandoned cabin sites, rhododendron slicks, logged and uncut areas, hemlock and pine patches, and hardwood; woodcock in the coastal plains region; and mourning dove, best hunted in freshly cut silage fields.

Coastal North Carolina is considered one of North America's truly great waterfowl hunting grounds for 37 species of ducks and Canada geese. Currituck Sound is one of the nation's top-ranked duck and Canada goose shooting grounds and Mattamuskeet Lake was once the winter headquarters for geese on the east coast of the United States. The drop in the number of geese wintering in North Carolina in recent years is due for the most part to shortstopping in the northern states. The U.S. Fish & Wildlife Service has suspended waterfowl hunting in Mattamuskeet Lake to help restore the overwintering goose population there.

North Carolina also offers hunting for raccoon—nature's smartest bandit; squirrel in mature hardwood forests, timberland borders of cornfields, and along Piedmont and eastern streams; fox squirrels, usually found in longleaf pine areas; red or "loomer" squirrels in the spruce and fir forests on the higher mountains; cottontail and bluetail or marsh rabbits; red and gray foxes; the groundhog, woodchuck, or "white pig" in the open pasturelands in the northwestern part of the state; and wildcats, found throughout the state in areas of extensive woodlands.

The attractive full-color magazine *Wildlife in North Carolina* is available for $2 per year (12 issues) from: Wildlife, Albemarle Bldg., 325 N. Salisbury St., Raleigh 27611. It is published by the progressive Wildlife Resources Commission and contains interesting and informative articles about hunting, fishing, game and fish species, wildlife photography, conservation, canoeing and wild rivers, and hiking and backpacking in the Tarheel State.

Great Smoky Wilderness Camping & Fishing Areas

A short distance southwest of the Great Smoky Mountains National Park lie several remote high country wild areas in the Nantahala National Forest that offer some of the finest backpacking and wilderness fly fishing and camping opportunities in eastern America. The Joyce Kilmer Wilderness Area, a 32,500-acre tract of rugged terrain in the Nantahala National Forest, straddles the Tennessee-North Carolina line. In the heart of the wilderness is the Joyce Kilmer Memorial Forest, dedicated to the author of "Trees." The forest covers 3,840 acres, the entire watershed of Little Santeetlah Creek, and is surrounded by mile-high ridges curving around the stands of virgin timber like a giant horseshoe. In 1935, when the forest tract was chosen, it was recognized as the finest remainder of our eastern primeval forest then in Forest Service ownership. Today, as then, it is a prime example of the wilderness found by white men when they first ventured into the southern Appalachians. Huge poplars and hemlocks in the lower cove create green, canopied chambers with mossy floors. In the higher elevations, towering oaks and maples predominate.

Adjoining the Kilmer Forest is another roadless valley, the watershed of Slickrock Creek. Tributary streams flowing down the steep surrounding ridges have sculpted the valley's sides while the creek itself runs clear and pure, cascading over two beautiful waterfalls. Slickrock

is especially famous as one of the finest brown trout streams in the East. First stocked in the 1930s, the creek's fish now reproduce naturally, and grow to trophy weights in the remote, deep-flowing pools.

To the east of Slickrock is the valley of Yellowhammer Creek and on the west, the undeveloped half of the drainage of Citico Creek. All four creeks have carved extraordinary valleys where their tributaries have incised deep V-shaped troughs transforming the mountainsides into a series of serrated furrows. The topography of the wilderness, which includes a total of 10,000 acres of virgin timber, is rugged and steep, ranging in elevation from 1,086 feet at Calderwood Lake to 5,341 feet at Stratton Bald. The high dividing ridges, nearly level for long distances, usually exceed altitudes of 5,000 feet.

The entire area is generously crisscrossed with foot trails offering excellent opportunities for hiking, camping, hunting, and fishing. The size of the area offers the backpacker routes on which he can travel for days without doubling back or retracing steps. A large number of trail entry points also make for a variety of day hikes.

Slightly east of the Joyce Kilmer Forest is the Cheoah Bald Wilderness, halfway between Bryson City and Andrews. The central feature of the area, the hub of the whole 19,000-acre tract, is Cheoah Bald itself with an elevation of 5,062 feet. Some 12 miles of the Appalachian Trail, regarded by many as the most spectacular segment of the trail in the Southeast, pass over the top of the Bald, offering a splendid panorama of the Smokies and surrounding terrain.

The south slope of Cheoah Bald forms one side of the Nantahala Gorge, a canyon so deep and narrow that sunlight rarely hits the valley floor.

The area's steep terrain is covered by substantial stands of virgin timber. The same precipitous slopes create numerous waterfalls and cascades, the best known of which are found along Ledbetter Creek. A few old logging trails, well mossed over, make excellent hiking trails through the remote reaches of the wilderness. Wildlife, including the elusive black bear, is abundant.

The 15,000-acre wilderness area surrounding Snowbird Creek is practically guaranteed to keep wilderness fly fishermen in a state of permanent bliss. This stream and its major tributary, Sassafras Creek, are entirely contained within the Nantahala National Forest and have been rated among the eight best trout fishing streams in western North Carolina. All sections of Snowbird Creek offer excellent fishing, but the stretch above Big Falls offers a population restricted solely to "wild" brook trout, making the creek the largest in the state with a population limited to brook trout. The wilderness is also renowned for its many waterfalls and stands of hardwood and pine, generously nourished by the annual 80-inch rainfall. Trails follow old logging roads up Snowbird Creek and wind through the many spectacular balds of surrounding ridges, including the Snowbird and Cheoah mountains.

Highways & the Blue Ridge Parkway

Stretching for 460 miles through the southern Appalachians, the Blue Ridge Parkway follows the mountain crests to link Shenandoah National Park in northern Virginia with the Great Smoky Mountains National Park in North Carolina and Tennessee. Designed especially for motor recreation, the parkway provides quiet, leisurely travel, free from commercial development and the congestion of high-speed highways. From Shenandoah National Park for 355 miles, the parkway follows the Blue Ridge Mountains, eastern rampart of the Appalachians, entering North Carolina near Cumberland Knob. Then, skirting the southern end of the Black Mountains, it weaves through the Craggies, the Pisgahs, and the Balsams to the Great Smokies.

In North Carolina, the land crossed by the parkway becomes higher and more sparsely settled. Rolling bluegrass pastures terminate in precipitous bluffs. Lush gardens of rhododendron bloom throughout Doughton Park, about 20 miles south of the Virginia-North Carolina line, in early June. Some of the more spectacular sights easily accessible from the parkway include Linville Falls, a rugged gorge and waterfalls reached by a short trail; Craggy Gardens with its lovely purple rhododendron blooming in mid-June; and the Devil's Courthouse, a rock affording 360-degree views across the mountains of the Carolinas, Georgia, and Tennessee. Many campgrounds, picnic areas, restaurants and self-guiding trails are located along the parkway. The *Blue Ridge Parkway Map* for North Carolina and Virginia describes the area traversed and shows the route in its entirety from Shenandoah National Park to the Cherokee Reservation in North Carolina. Points of interest, mileage, campsites, trails, picnic areas, points of access, nearby towns, and major highways are all indicated on the map, which is available free from: Superintendent, Blue Ridge Parkway, P.O. Box 7606, Asheville 28807. Another brochure available free from the Parkway Superintendent, *Blue Ridge Parkway Visitor Activities*, lists various attractions and visitor centers in Virginia and North Carolina—Peaks of Otter, Rocky Knob Campground, Doughton Park, Linville Falls, Crabtree Meadows, and others—and gives hours and special features. Self-guiding trails along the parkway are also listed.

Those seriously considering camping or exploring trails near the parkway may want to consult the *Camper's and Hiker's Guide to the Blue Ridge Parkway*, an 80-page paperbound booklet describing the various campgrounds, trails, and scenic attractions. Maps, trail data, tips on camping and hiking, a chart of visitor services and facilities, and fairly detailed descriptions of accommodations are included. Published in cooperation with the National Park Service, the guide is priced at $1.95 and is available from: Chatham Press, 15 Wilmot La., Riverside, CT 06878.

In North Carolina, three vacation lodges near the parkway offer rooms, cabins, and meals. *Pisgah Inn* (Rte. 2, Box 441, Canton 28716, phone (704) 648-5661), near Mount Pisgah, has 52 rooms available in the lodge, cabins, and motel. In Doughton Park, *Bluffs Lodge* and *Rocky Knob Cabins* offer eight rustic cabins; both c/o National Park Concessions, Mammoth Cave, KY 42259 (phone: 502–758–2217). In Virginia, *Peaks of Otter Lodge* offers 58 rooms; write: P.O. Box 489, Bedford, VA 24523 (703–586–1081).

The Blue Ridge Parkway is also shown on the *North Carolina Highway Map*, an invaluable aid to anyone traveling around the state. State and U.S. highways, cities, towns, roads, state and national forests, railroads, ferries, airports, rest areas, park campsites, lakes, rivers, and streams are all shown on the map, which also provides insets showing routes in and through major cities. The reverse side of the special 1976 Bicentennial Edition describes North Carolina's participation in the American Revolution and shows Cornwallis's march through the state. The map is available free from: Dept. of Natural & Economic Resources, Travel Development Section, Raleigh, NC 27611.

Ski Touring & Snowshoeing

Sections of the Blue Ridge Parkway are closed to motor vehicles in the winter and provide good ski touring, depending on snow conditions. The trip committee of the Le Conte chapter of the Sierra Club occasionally sponsors ski tours in the Boone-Blowing Rock area. Other sections where satisfactory snow conditions may occur include the Craggy Gardens-Mount Mitchell area and the Mount Pisgah-Balsam

Mountain Range southwest of Asheville. For information contact Blue Ridge Parkway Headquarters, Asheville, phone (704) 258-2850, or the Balsam Gap and Gillispie Gap Ranger Stations, Waynesville and Spruce Pine.

Much of the North Carolina high country falls within Pisgah National Forest. Weather permitting, the Shining Rock Wilderness north of Brevard offers some excellent terrain for ski touring. Ski access is via the Blue Ridge Parkway from Wagon Road Gap (U.S. 276) or Balsam Gap. For information, contact Forest Service district rangers at Pisgah Ranger Station, Pisgah Forest (Shining Rock); Toecane Ranger Station, Burnsville (Roan Mountain): or the Forest Supervisor, National Forests in North Carolina, Asheville 28801, phone (704) 258-2850.

The highest point east of the Mississippi, Mount Mitchell (6684 feet), offers some fine ski touring country if you can get to it. Although the state park is open year round, the only auto access route via the Blue Ridge Parkway is often closed when snow conditions are best for skiing but worst for driving. The combination of skiing the parkway from the nearest access point and from there the side road up to Mount Mitchell is often too much for a day trip. Old logging roads in the Camp Alice area make good cross-country routes. For information on snow conditions and winter camping contact State Park Headquarters by phoning (704) 675-4611.

Tennessee Valley Lakes Recreation Maps

Excellent maps published by the large power companies as a public service are available for many of the large lakes in North Carolina. The Tennessee Valley Authority offers maps of Fontana and Hiwassee lakes (the latter also shows Apalachia, Chatuge, Nottely, and Blue Ridge lakes), and several other lakes in Georgia and Tennessee. Each map shows the lakes and surrounding terrain, cities and towns, roads and highways, public lands, wildlife management areas, national forest lands, boat docks and launching ramps, recreation areas, and canoe access points. Also available through TVA is a recreation folder showing boat docks and facilities at the lakes and a companion map showing principal highways in the TVA region. Single copies of lake maps, *Index to TVA Navigation Charts & Maps*, and a guide, *Recreation on TVA Lakes*, are available free from: TVA Maps & Engineering Records Section, 400 Commerce Ave., SW, Knoxville, TN 37902.

The TVA also has available a beautiful full-color *Plastic Relief Map of the Tennessee Valley*. This 30 × 50-inch three-dimensional map includes the interstate highway system and a diagrammatic profile of the nine main stream lakes. The map costs $12.50 (plus $10 if you want the maps shipped in a protective carton). *Tennessee River Tributary Watershed Maps*, lithoprinted in color showing drainage, drainage basin, topography, woodlands, roads and railroads, highways, and towns, with a contour interval of 100 feet, are available for the *Upper French Broad River* (17 × 22 inches, 45¢), *Yellow Creek* (22 × 34 inches, 75¢), *Little Tennessee River* (22 × 34 inches, 75¢) and *Hiawassee River* (22 × 34 inches, 75¢).

Duke Power also issues excellent, full color maps of its lakes and all are free. There are maps available for Lakes Norman, James, Rhodhiss, Hickory, Lookout Shoals, Mountain Island, Wylie, Fishing Creek, and Wateree. Copies may be obtained from: Public Relations, Duke Power Co., P.O. Box 2178, Charlotte 28232.

John H. Kerr Reservoir maps can be obtained free from the Kerr Reservoir Commission, Stovall 27582. Another map of the reservoir is available from: Kerr Reservoir Manager, Box 76, Route 1, Boydton, VA 23917.

Wilderness Outfitters & Expeditions

North Carolina's mountain country and many wilderness areas offer countless opportunities for outdoor adventures. Two experienced outfitters within the state sponsor varied expeditions tailored to appeal to different age groups and different tastes. *Mondamin Wilderness Adventures* offers trips into the wilderness by foot, horse or float year round to inexperienced and seasoned wilderness travelers. Eight hundred acres of woodlands just south of Asheville, adjoining hundreds of acres of privately owned terrain and several large watersheds, provide the setting for trips ranging from a few days to a week. Mondamin also offers 10-20-day expeditions through other parts of North America: Canada, Mexico, and the western United States. Some of the adventures available include "introductory" backpacking trips along trails of easy or moderate difficulty; longer backpacking hikes through nearby national forests; canoe and raft runs along the white-water stretches of the Green and Nantahala rivers; and horseback trips in Smoky Mountain National Park and Pisgah National Forest. Seminars are also given in basic wilderness skills: backpacking, canoeing, rafting, camping, sailing, and horseback riding. For more information, write to: Frank T. Schell, Mondamin Wilderness Adventures, Box 8, Tuxedo 28784, phone (704) 693-7446 or 684-9002.

Nantahala Outdoor Center, on the banks of the Nantahala River, also offers a broad spectrum of wilderness activities. White-water rafting on the Chattooga River guarantees unparalleled excitement for those seeking the challenge of really big rapids. Less perilous runs in 12-foot, heavy-duty rubber rafts are offered on the Nantahala's clear, cold waters through a steep gorge lined with rhododendron, laurel, and "Princess" trees. Trips generally range from 3 hours to a full day. Other adventures—backpacking, horseback riding, rock climbing, hiking, nature walks, and winter camping—are sponsored too. The center maintains an outpost camp on the Chattooga and provides equipment, instruction, and guides. Lodging and meals are available at the motel, campgrounds, and restaurant operated by the center. There is an outfitter shop with all kinds of equipment—including the materials and assistance necessary to build or repair kayaks and canoes. The center's chief guide, Payson Kennedy, served as river guide and "canoeing double" in the filming of James Dickey's *Deliverance*. Information can be obtained by writing or calling: Nantahala Outdoor Center, Star Rte., Box 68, Bryson City 28713, phone (704) 488-6407.

The French Broad River and its majestic mountain setting in western North Carolina provide the backdrop for trips sponsored by *Smoky Mountain River Expeditions*. White-water runs in sturdy rubber rafts are offered daily May through October (weekends only, May and October; 7 days a week, June through September) for individuals or groups. Reservations are necessary. Write: Smoky Mountain River Expeditions, P.O. Box 252, Hot Springs 28743, phone (704) 622-7260, for details.

Scenic New River Canoe Trips (Box 57, Boone 28607, phone (704) 295-3751, sponsors day and overnight runs combining easy floats and some white-water. Trips are offered April through October and are directed by a naturalist/guide to introduce canoeists to the plants and wildlife along the New River.

Horseback enthusiasts will find the *Cataloochee Ranch* (Rte. 1, Box 500, Maggie Valley 28751, phone (704) 926-1401), near Great Smoky Mountains National Park, a fine source for moving and base camp trips through the splendid high country and neighboring forests. Open May through October, the ranch sponsors trips of 2–10 days in groups of 8–16 riders. Swimming, fishing, and camping along the trails and streams are some of the sideline attractions offered.

Designed to provide a meaningful wilderness experience for young people, the *Mountaineer Travel Camp* offers trips through the Appalachians in coed groups of 24. Minimum age is 12 years for backpacking, rock climbing, kayaking, and canoeing in the North Carolina Wilderness; and 15 years for the camp's more rugged western trips through the Rockies and Tetons. For information, write to: Mountaineer Travel Camp, c/o Asheville School, School Rd., Asheville 28806, phone (704) 254-6345.

Nantahala National Forest & Highlands

Nantahala National Forest Topo Maps

U.S. Geological Survey Overview Topographic Maps, scale 1:250,000: Chattanooga, Greenville, Knoxville, Rome.

Fires Creek Wildlife Management Area

Large-scale U.S. Geological Survey Topographic Maps: Andrews, Hayesville, Peach Tree, Shooting Creek, Topton.

Fontana Lake Wild & Trophy Fishing Waters

Includes Cheoah Lake and wilderness feeder streams, shown on large-scale U.S. Geological Survey Topographic Maps: Fontana Dam, Tuskegee, Noland Creek.

Joyce Kilmer Forest & Santeetlah Wildlife Management Area

Includes Santeetlah Lake and Cheoah Bald Wilderness, shown on large-scale U.S. Geological Survey Topographic Survey Maps: Big Junction, Fontana Dam, Robbinsville, Santeetlah Creek, Tapoco.

Nantahala Lake & River

Includes the Wayah and Standing Indian WMA's and entire length of the Nantahala River, shown on large-scale U.S. Geological Survey Topographic Maps: Hewitt, Noland Creek, Prentiss, Rainbow Springs, Shooting Creek, Topton, Wayah Bald, Wesser.

Snowbird Creek Wilderness

Large-scale U.S. Geological Survey Topographic Maps: Andrews, Big Junction, Marble, Robbinsville, Santeetlah Creek.

Unicoi Mountains Wildlands & Lake Hiwassee

Includes Apalachia and Cherokee lakes, shown on large-scale U.S. Geological Survey Topographic Maps: Unaka, Bald River Falls, McDaniel Bald, Big Junction, Persimmon Creek, Murphy.

This sprawling 420,000-acre forest reserve, once the heart of the Cherokee Indian Nation and named after the Cherokee word for "Land-of-the-Noon-Day Sun," takes in some of the finest fishing, camping, hunting, and wilderness backpacking areas in the East, including the towering 5,000-foot peaks of the Nantahala Range in the northwestern part of the state. Old logging roads and hundreds of miles of rugged wilderness trails, including the Appalachian Trail, provide access to the Joyce Kilmer Forest, Nantahala, Tallulah, and Little Tennessee rivers; the Snowbird, Valley, Tusquitte, Cheoah, and Cowee Mountains; and to Fontana, Santeetlah, Hiwassee, Chatuge, and Cheoah lakes. The remote Snowbird Creek Wilderness offers some of the finest fishing in the eastern United States for large, wild brook trout. The forest and state wildlife management areas provide top-ranked hunting in season for whitetail deer, wild turkey, grouse, quail, and wild boar.

Several large lakes and powerful white-water mountain streams in the Nantahala Forest highlands offer nationally renowned fishing for large rainbow, brown and brook trout, largemouth and smallmouth bass, and kokanee salmon.

Beautiful Nantahala Lake, formed by the damming of the swift, deep-flowing Nantahala River (a renowned rainbow trout stream that provides natural spawning beds for the large lake-run fish), provides excellent fishing for hook-jawed kokanee and rainbow trout. Large Lake Hiwassee, located to the west of Nantahala Lake and formed by the damming of the Hiwassee River, holds lunker largemouth and smallmouth bass and walleye, as does Lake Santeetlah, formed by the impoundment of the Little Tennessee River. Huge Fontana Lake is

NORTH CAROLINA TRAVEL & RECREATION GUIDE

bordered on the north by the Great Smoky Mountain National Park, on the west by Cheoah Lake, on the east by the Tuckasegee River Valley, and on the south by the Cheoah Mountains and Nantahala National Forest and is fed by the Nantahala, Little Tennessee, and Tuckasegee rivers and by the cold, clear mountain waters of Hazel, Eagle, Forney, Sawyer, Noland, Panther, and Alaska creeks. Situated at 1,710 feet elevation, the lake has a surface area of 10,670 acres, a 248-mile-long irregularly shaped shoreline, and a maximum depth of 440 feet. Fontana offers renowned fishing for walleye, largemouth and smallmouth bass, crappie, and white bass. The cold, deep blue-green waters of beautiful Cheoah Lake, located just below the great Fontana Dam, hold some huge tackle-busting rainbows. Many small lakes and remote ponds located at elevations ranging from 2,000 to 6,000 feet dot the highlands of the forest and provide good fishing for those willing to hike in for pan-sized trout and bass. These small gemlike lakes and beaver ponds are easily identified on U.S. Geological Survey Maps of the region.

The mountain streams of the Cherokee Indian Reservation, north of the forest, are heavily stocked with rainbow and brook trout, and many of the trout are quite large. The Indians and federal authorities manage the Cherokee waters under a special permit system. To get a copy of the regulations and information on the permits, write: Cherokee Fish & Game Management Enterprise, Box 302, Cherokee 28719.

Nine developed campgrounds with more than 400 family units are scattered throughout the forest. Some of the more popular include the 66 sites on Hiwassee Lake, the beautiful new camping area at Cable Cove on Fontana Lake, and the Tsali Campground with 42 sites, also near Fontana Lake. The *Nantahala National Forest Map* indicates the location of each campground and the facilities available. The map also shows major forest features, lakes, streams, trails, roads and highways, ranger stations, landing fields, and other points of interest and may be obtained for 50¢ from: Supervisor's Office, U.S. Forest Service, P.O. Box 2750, Asheville 28802.

Vacation lodging and services in the Nantahala National Forest region are provided by *Fontana Village Resort,* Fontana Dam 28733 (704–498–2211); *Nantahala Village Resort,* Bryson City 28713 (704–488–2826), in the Great Smoky Mountains near Fontana Lake; *Hemlock Inn,* Bryson City 28713 (704–488–9820), alpine setting in heart of the Great Smokies; *Tapoco Lodge Resort,* Box 57, Tapoco 28780 (704–498–2290), a scenic alpine location at Cheoah Lake in the Great Smokies; *Snowbird Mountain Lodge,* Robbinsville 28771 (704–479–3433), a secluded mountain resort bordering the Joyce Kilmer Memo-

rial Forest; *Skyline Lodge* (Box 630; 704–526–2121) and *Lee's Inn* (Box 520; 704–526–2171), both Highlands 28741, surrounded by the Nantahala Forest Highlands and the Primeval Forest Reserve.

Access & Outfitting Centers

Nantahala National Forest is accessible via U.S. Highway 19 from Asheville; U.S. Highway 23 from Waynesville; and U.S. 129 from Knoxville, Tennessee. Other nearby towns include Franklin, Andrews, Sylva, and Bryson City.

Pisgah National Forest & Wilderness Areas

Pisgah National Forest Topo Maps

U.S. Geological Survey Overview Maps, scale 1:250,000: Charlotte, Johnson City, Knoxville, Winston-Salem.

Linville Gorge Wilderness

Large-scale U.S. Geological Survey Topographic Maps: Ashford, Grandfather Mountain, Linville Falls, Newland, Oak Hill.

Pisgah Forest Highlands & Wildlife Management Area

Large-scale U.S. Geological Survey Topographic Maps: Sam Knob, Shining Rock, Pisgah Forest, Dunsmore Mountain, Cruso, Horse Shoe, Enka.

Shining Rock Wilderness

Large-scale U.S. Geological Survey Topographic Maps: Cruso, Shining Rock.

This renowned hiking, fishing, canoe-camping, and hunting area in northwestern North Carolina covers 478,000 acres of wild rivers, deep gorges, cascading waterfalls, thickets of rhododendron and azalea, and colorful forests of yellow poplar, red oak, sugar maple, spruce, and black cherry. The forest cover provides superb hunting for whitetail deer, black bear, ruffed grouse, wild turkey, and boar.

The biblical name Pisgah was given to a prominent peak near Asheville by a pioneer mountain preacher. Nearby is Rat Mountain, resembling a rodent with tail extended and head lowered between its front paws. When snow covers the northern slope of Pisgah, the twin peaks of Rat and Mount Pisgah are said to resemble a bride and groom standing out in heroic stature against the landscape.

In the Toecane district of the forest is Roan Mountain (6286 feet), famed for its spectacular display of native purple rhododendron in bloom the last two weeks of June. Awesome views of the surrounding countryside are available from the trails winding toward the lofty summit. The top of the mountain is relatively broad, level, and almost treeless. Each June the flowering of the rhododendron is celebrated by a festival atop the mountain.

In the forest's Grandfather district, the Linville Gorge area, a 7,600-acre tract, is maintained as a primitive, natural environment, an unspoiled setting for native fauna and flora, including many rare plant species. Cliffs of the Linville Mountains rim the gaping crevice on the west, with the rugged broken range of Jonas Ridge forming the eastern wall of the canyon. The steep sides of the gorge enclose the wild Linville River, which makes a dizzying descent of 2,000 feet in only 12 miles. Hunting and fishing are permitted here under state regulations. Primitive camping is also available. Access is via foot trails leading from State Highway 105. Free permits, available at the district ranger's office, are needed to enter the area. Since the Linville Gorge

Wilderness is a challenge to even the most experienced hiker, anyone using the trails is advised to inform the National Forest District Ranger's Office at Marion of all hiking plans within the gorge.

Like the Linville Gorge, the Shining Rock Wilderness Area has been set aside as a carefully protected reserve beyond the reach of man's influence. The outstanding feature of this 13,600-acre tract is Shining Rock Mountain, an outcropping of white quartz with elevations ranging from 3,500 to over 6,000 feet. The area is accessible by trails from U.S. 276 North off the Blue Ridge Parkway at Wagon Road Gap. Again, primitive camping is available, and a permit is required to enter the area.

Over 600 miles of trails, including 80 miles of the Appalachian Trail (see "Appalachian National Scenic Trail" in the "Encyclopedia" section), provide access to the remote wilderness highlands, Black Mountain peaks, the scenic waterfalls and virgin hemlock stands of the Craggy Mountain area, to Lakes James and Cane, and the many rivers and streams, including the Cane, Watauga, Big Pigeon, and Broad rivers. Special challenges for the hiker are the Black Mountains and Mount Mitchell, highest peak in the eastern United States. Campsites are available at Bald Mountain, Black Mountain, Carolina Hemlocks, Coontree, Mortener, North Wells River, Powhatan, Rocky Bluff, and White Pines.

Major forest features, recreation areas, campsites, streams, rivers, trails, roads and highways, points of interest, and surrounding towns are all shown on the *Pisgah National Forest Map*, available for 50¢ from: Forest Supervisor, Plateau Bldg., 50 S. French Broad Ave., Asheville 28801. The Forest Service also publishes the free *Shining Rock Wilderness Map* and *Linville Gorge Wilderness Map* (same address).

Vacation accommodations in the Pisgah National Forest region are provided by the following lodges and resorts: *Roaring River Chalets* (704–295–3695), *New River Inn* (Box 670; 704–295–3101), and *Hound Ears Lodge & Club* (Box 188; 704–963–4321)—all at Blowing Rock 28605; *Pisgah Inn*, Canton 28716 (704–648–5661); *Bluffs Lodge*, Blue Ridge Parkway, Laurel Springs 28644 (704–372–4499); *Eseeola Lodge*, Linville 28646 (704–733–4311), a rustic lodge on Lake Kawana; *Big Lynn Lodge*, Box 459, Little Switzerland 28749 (704–765–4257); *Falling Waters* (Box 476; 704–926–1107), *Meadowbrook* (Box 596; 704–926–1821), and *Rocky Waters* (Box 515; 704–926–1585) lodges and *Cataloochee Ranch* (Box 500; 704–926–1401) —all at Maggie Valley 28751 adjacent to Great Smoky National Park and the Blue Ridge Parkway.

Access & Outfitting Centers

The Pisgah National Forest is reached via U.S. 40 from Asheville. The Blue Ridge Parkway traverses portions of the forest north and west of Asheville.

TENNESSEE
ENCYCLOPEDIA

Accommodations—
Vacation Lodges & Resorts

A comprehensive directory compiled for the visitor to Tennessee, the 69-page *East Tennessee Tourist Directory* lists just about every local attraction, outdoor and indoor activity, and accommodation imaginable. The directory is devoted primarily to the 16-county East Tennessee Development District. However, the entire Cherokee National Forest and Great Smoky Mountains National Park are covered as well as all state parks in East Tennessee. Listings for hotels and motels with addresses and phone numbers, aircraft charters and rentals, canoe rentals and trails, hunting lodges, game and fish preserves, camping equipment, and campsites, ski resorts, and points of historical interest are included. There are entries for caves, annual features, babysitters, and liquor stores. A Map of East Tennessee is provided in the directory, which is available free from: Knoxville Tourist Bureau, P.O. Box 237, Knoxville 37901, phone (615) 523–2316.

Hunting and fishing lodges include the *Caryonah Hunting Lodge*, Rte. 1, Grossville, phone (615) 277–3113; *Clark Range Hunting Preserve*, Rte. 1, Clarkrange 38553; *Crooked Creek Hunting Lodge*, Rte. 1, Jamestown 38556, phone (615) 879–8440 or 879–8089; *Hunter's Haven*, P.O. Box 36, Walland 37886, phone (615) 982–5505; *Loudon Hunting Preserve*, Box 351, Loudon 37774; *Parch Corn Creek Lodge*, Box 667, Jamestown 38556, phone (615) 879–8149; *Renegade Range*, Box 304, Grossville, phone (615) 354–2368; *Telleco Junction Hunting Preserve*, Englewood 37329 (615) 887–7819.

Appalachian National Scenic Trail

From Damascus, Virginia, the Appalachian Trail ascends Holston Mountain, then after 4 miles enters the State of Tennessee. Between the state line and McQueens Knob to the southwest, the trail falls entirely within the Watauga district of the Cherokee National Forest. From McQueens Knob, national forest land is to the right of the trail with mostly private land to the left. Holston Mountain is paralleled by Iron Mountain; both ridges are of almost equal height and extend side by side in a southwesterly direction for almost 35 miles. They are connected by Cross Mountain near their center, forming a great letter *H*. The trail follows the level crest of Holston Mountain for some 18 miles, then crosses to Iron Mountain and proceeds southwestward along the narrow summit for 15 miles. This segment of the trail passes through lush forest growth with no abrupt changes in elevation. Some of the sights to watch out for are a high rock outcropping near Flint Mill Gap overlooking the Holston River Valley and South Holston Lake, and the Holston High Knob, where a Forest Service fire tower offers splendid views of the area. At the southwest end of Iron Mountain, the trail begins a descent of 1,500 feet to cross the Watauga River. A mile below the Watauga Dam is a narrow, sheer-faced gorge and nearby horseshoe-shaped Wilbur Lake. Beyond the dam, the trail makes a substantial climb which, while strenuous and fairly steep, offers its own rewards in the form of beautiful scenery and numerous views of the lake and gorge.

For a short distance, the ridge crest of Iron Mountain again provides the backbone of the trail, which bears left and winds down the mountain's south slope, from which point it leads southeast for 18 miles, passing first through the magnificent gorge of the Laurel Fork and then along White Rocks Mountain to the North Carolina line. Both the gorge and mountain along this segment are well worth any backaches or sore feet acquired along the way. Sheer cliffs, wooded slopes, waterfalls, rapids, and dense rhododendron and laurel transform the Laurel Fork Gorge into a proscenium of breathtaking natural beauty.

Moving from the intimate to the panoramic, the summit of White Rocks Mountain affords superb views of a king's ransom in mountains: Holston and Iron mountains on the north, Grandfather and Beech mountains to the east, and Roan and Unaka mountains to the south and southwest.

Next the trail follows the main crest of the Unakas southwest along the Tennessee-North Carolina border, passing over a section of lofty balds that culminate in Roan Mountain (6,285 feet). The crest of the Roan features large mountain meadows and open grasslands punctuated by dense stands of fir trees. Some 1,200 acres of catawba rhododendron bloom annually in natural, untended splendor. Catawba Indian tribes believed the garden to be the site of a great war between their people and all other nations of the earth. The victory of the Catawba was assured after many battles and considerable bloodshed. Forever after the garden bloomed bright red in honor of the tribe's fallen warriors.

From Roan Mountain the trail generally follows the Tennessee-North Carolina line all the way to Doe Knob in the Great Smokies. It reenters the state briefly at Curley Maple Gap, then continues along the state line and beyond through Pisgah National Forest in North Carolina.

A continuous chain of lean-tos is offered along the Appalachian Trail in Tennessee and North Carolina. Lean-tos are three-sided watertight structures with open fronts, usually fitted with bunks or a wooden floor for sleeping bags. A spring, toilets, and tables are usually situated nearby. In the Great Smoky Mountains National Park, camping permits are required for either camping or use of lean-tos. Stays in the structures, which are available on a first-come, first-served basis, are limited to 1 night. In Cherokee National Forest, 12 lean-tos are scattered at fairly even intervals from Abingdon Gap to Sams Gap.

Anyone seriously planning a trip along the Appalachian Trail in Tennessee should consult the *Guide to the Appalachian Trail in Tennessee and North Carolina*. Published by the Appalachian Trail Conference, the book includes three detailed maps and extensive trail data: mileage, difficulty, directions, points of interest, historical information on the area traversed, national park and forest regulations, etc. The trail is covered from both north to south and south to north, so there is no backtracking of information to find your way. A general history of the Appalachian Trail is also included. Priced at $6.70, the guide may be ordered from: Appalachian Trail Conference, P.O. Box 236, Harpers Ferry, WV 25425. Checks should be in U.S. dollars only, payable to Appalachian Trail Conference. Allow 3 weeks for delivery or include $1 for special mailing and note the addition with your order. The following U.S. Geological Survey maps cover the Appalachian Trail: Bakersville, Bald Creek, Carter, Carvers Gap, Chestoa, Damascus, Doe, Elizabethton, Elk Park, Huntdale, Iron Mountain Gap, Laurel Bloomery, Sams Gap, Shady Valley, Unicoi, Watauga Dam, White Rocks Mountain.

Camping & Wilderness Trails

Over 250 campsites are scattered throughout Tennessee, some near urban centers offering all the comforts of home, others hidden deep in the wilderness far from the sights and sounds of civilization. Tennessee's wild climate makes year-round camping possible in many of the campgrounds that remain open and operative year round. *Camping in Tennessee* lists 252 campsites that have been approved by the Tennessee Department of Public Health, alphabetically by the nearest town or city. Each listing includes the name of the campsite, address and directions where available, seasons, type of camp, and

facilities including showers, toilets, boat rentals, hunting and fishing opportunities, swimming, and laundries. Two types of camps are listed in the guidebook: travel camps house provisions for travel trailers, truck coaches or campers, tent campers, tents and vehicles, whole primitive camps are sites established primarily for tent camping, which permit tents, travel trailers, truck coaches, and tent campers. Camping in Great Smoky Mountains Park in areas other than specified campgrounds requires a special permit, which may be obtained at the Sugarlands Visitor Center. *Camping in Tennessee* is available free from: Tennessee Tourist Development, 505 Fessler La., Nashville 37210.

For listings of hiking, horse, and nature trails in Tennessee, see pages 34–38 of the *East Tennessee Tourist Directory* (see "Accommodations"). The directory lists almost all trails in Anderson County, the Cherokee Lake Area, Cherokee National Forest, and Great Smoky Mountains National Park. For more detailed information on the 650 miles of horse and foot trails in Great Smoky Mountains National Park, write to: Park Headquarters, GSMNP, Gatlinburg 37738.

Some camping and backpacking equipment supply stores in Knoxville include *Camel Tent Awning Co.*, 111 Jackson Ave., E, Knoxville 37915, phone (615) 525–3114; *Gateway Sporting Goods Center*, 3413 Chapman Highway, S, Knoxville 37920, phone (615) 577–5811; *Outdoor America Outfitters*, 6610 Kingston Park Dr., SW, Knoxville 37919, phone (615) 584–8961; *Smoky Mountain Outfitters*, 6600 Kingston Park Dr., SW, Knoxville 37919, phone (615) 584–9432; and *Surplus City*, 3211 Chapman Highway, S, Knoxville 37920, phone (615) 577–5571. Camping equipment may be rented from Watts Bar Lake Koa in Kingston off State Highway 58, phone (615) 376–5880, or from Camel Tent Awning Co. in Knoxville (listed above). Equipment may also be rented in Knoxville from the *Taylor Rental Center*, 116 Sandwood Rd., N, phone (615) 693–9524.

Canoeing & Trophy Fishing Waters

Tennessee boasts a number of fine rivers and streams inviting to white-water enthusiasts and fishermen alike. On the Tennessee-Kentucky border, the South Fork of the Cumberland River has hollowed out a wild, magnificent canyon perfect for float trips, which can be divided into two runs: one from New River to Leatherwood Bridge, and the other from the bridge to State Highway 92. The entire trip takes 3 days or longer, depending on whether one stops to fish or explore the area. Put-in for the upper run is off Highway 27 at the

town of New River. The first 9 miles travel the placid waters of the New River through a steep-faced canyon. Near the confluence with the South Fork of the Cumberland are some easy rapids followed by a scenic run through a handsome gorge with 400-foot-high sandstone cliffs. Dogwood, hardwoods, and lofty pine trees grow near the river's edge. Next comes Jake's Hole and a series of breathtaking drops as the river rushes through boulder masses, creating a confusion of turbulent, class IV white water, navigable only by experts.

Angel Falls, a boulder garden just below Leatherwood Bridge in Scott State Forest, is no place for the novice either. Experts have run the left side under certain water conditions, but saner and less experienced people portage. Excellent smallmouth bass fishing is available at the gorge as well as several nearby spots for camping. There are Indian cliff

dwellings located beneath the canyon rim, but they are accessible only to those with rock-climbing skills and equipment. Just across the Kentucky line is perilous Devil's Jump Falls, which can be run at certain water levels but must be portaged if the river is up.

Like the South Fork of the Cumberland, the Obed National Wild and Scenic River in the Catoosa Wildlife Management Area north of Rockwood, has carved a precipitous and rocky gorge with a floor of unpredictable white water. The 12½-mile trip through the gorge can be made in one day, but the clear pools filled with huge muskie, lovely sand beaches, and natural swimming holes will prove too tempting to pass up. Two or 3 days with frequent stops will make for a most enjoyable journey.

Put-in for the Obed run is at the bridge on Big Daddy Creek, 16 miles from Crossville. The most perilous rapids (rated class IV) in the gorge is about 3 miles below the confluence of Big Daddy and the Obed. Following this stretch are a number of class III rapids. The river becomes more peaceful below Clear Creek with less powerful rapids and long pools. Takeout is at Nemo Bridge, a short distance below where the Obed meets the Emory River. Take your fishing gear— muskie, bluegill, catfish, and bass are plentiful in these rivers.

Other trips along the Obed and Emory are described in *Obed-Emory Canoe Trails,* a brochure and map available free from: Recreation Resources Branch, TVA, Knoxville 37902. Canoe routes described include runs along Daddy's Creek, Clear Creek, and White Creek as well as the Obed and Emory rivers. All information, including location of rapids and pools, river difficulty, portages, trip length, and the like, is provided. The three-color map is fairly explicit, showing roads, highways, the major runs described, towns, paved and gravel roads, and access points. For detailed information on the beautiful Obed National Wild and Scenic River and its Clear Creek Tributary, write: Obed Wild & Scenic River, P.O. Box 477, Oneida 37841.

Tennessee Valley Canoe Trails is another useful aid for river runs in the Tennessee Valley. Varied types of river canoeing from serene trips on certain portions of the French Broad and Nolichuckey rivers to exciting white water on other sections of the same streams are described and identified on a map of the valley. Other bodies of water covered include White's, Clear, and Daddy's creeks; the Obed, Oconaluftee, Hiwassee, Tuckasegee, and Tellico rivers; the Watauga and Raven Fork. Mileage, river difficulty, and stream gauge readings are provided. Point-by-point descriptions of each route are not included. Copies of this brochure and pamphlets on the Obed and Elk rivers and streams in the Little Tennessee Valley Watershed are available free from: Recreation Resources Branch, TVA, Knoxville 37902.

Little Tennessee Valley Canoe Trails is a guide to the middle portion of the Little Tennessee River and four of its tributary streams—the Nantahala, Raven Fork, Oconaluftee, and Tuckasegee rivers—all of which are used extensively by canoers. These streams, which have their beginning on the western side of the Appalachian Mountains in North Carolina, flow generally east to west and provide a variety of river runs, from the easygoing to the treacherous. The guide includes a very basic map showing access points, major routes, bridges, towns, and roads. Detailed descriptions of each stream provide mileage, access points, stream difficulty and stream gauge, and a list of canoe safety tips. The brochure may be obtained free from: *TVA Canoe Trails,* 301 Cumberland Ave., SW, Knoxville 37902.

Still another guide to Tennessee's waters, the *Elk River Guide,* describes the river (called Chuwalee by the Indians), which rises on the edge of the Cumberland Plateau in middle Tennessee and flows southwest to the Tennessee River near Wheeler Dam. The Elk is an easy stream to float and is ideal for beginners or family expeditions. The

brochure includes a simple map of the river's course between Jim's Ford Dam to the Old Stone Bridge near Fayetteville, a distance of a little over 40 miles. Tips on floating the Elk and a brief description of the river are also included in the folder, which is available free from: Elk River Development Assn., Municipal Bldg., P.O. Box 507, Fayetteville 37334.

Buffalo River Canoe Rental will rent 17-foot Grumman 3-man aluminum canoes, paddles, and life jackets for expeditions on the Buffalo River in middle Tennessee. The river is a basically pastoral stretch of water, with some turbulent water in the upper sections. Year-round floating is available, with tributary streams providing interesting diversions. Located on Highway 13, 10 miles south of Linden and 16 miles north of Waynesboro, the company also offers a primitive-type campground at Slink Shoals provided for customers at no cost. A brochure describing the rental service and access sites along the Buffalo and Duck rivers is available free from: *Buffalo River Canoe Rental Co.*, Flat Woods 38458, phone (615) 589–2755.

Other canoe and float rentals in Tennessee and nearby North Carolina include *Fontana Village Resort*, Fontana Dam, phone (704) 498–2211, near Fontana Lake; *Stone Mountain Recreation Park*, U.S. 25–70, Del Rio, for float trips on the French Broad; *Hiwassee Float Service*, U.S. 411, phone (615) 263–5581, offering both canoes and floats; the Crosseyed Cricket, located 20 miles west of Knoxville off Interstate 40, phone (615) 986–5435; *Chilhowee Shoals Landing*, Tallassee, phone (615) 856–3721, for floating on the Little Tennessee; *Big Ridge State Park*, State 61, Maynardville, phone (615) 992–5523, for the Norris Lake area; and *Camp 'n Aire*, Townsend, State 73, Townsend, in the Smokies area.

The following U.S. Geological Survey Map Kits show the entire lengths, including the headwaters and surrounding topography, of the state's major canoe trails and lakes, and the famous wild highland brook trout streams in the Cherokee National Forest. Most of the larger lakes and rivers offer excellent fishing for smallmouth bass, walleye to 20 pounds, and record-size rainbow and brown trout in cold tailwaters below the large reservoirs. *Big Pigeon River:* Hartford, Newport, Waterville; *Doe River:* Elizabethton, Iron Mountain Gap, White Rocks Mountain; *French Broad River* (including Lake Douglas): Boyds Creek, Chestnut Hill, Douglas Dam, Hot Springs, Jefferson City, Neddy Mountain, Newport, Paint Rock, Rankin, Shady Grove, Shooks Gap, White Pine; *Hiwassee River:* Benton, Calhoun, Charleston, Farmer, McFarland, Oswald Dome; *South Fork Holston* (including Boone and South Holston lakes): Bluff City, Boone Dam, Carter, Holston Valley, Indian Springs, Keenburg, Kingsport; *Little River* (including West and Middle forks): Clingmans Dome, Gatlinburg, Kinzel Springs, Maryville, Silers Bald, Thunderhead Mountain, Wear Cove, Wildwood; *Little Pigeon River:* Douglas Dam, Mount Guyot, Mount Le Conte, Pigeon Falls, Richardson Falls; *Little Tennessee River:* Calderwood, Concord, Lenoir City, Loudon, Meadow, Tallassee, Tapoco, Vonore; *New River* (including South Fork of the Cumberland): Barthell SW, Block, Duncan Flats, Honey Creek, Huntsville, Norma, Oneida S, Petros, Windrock; *Nolichuckey River* (including Davy Crockett Lake): Cedar Creek, Chestoa, Chuckey, Davy Crockett Lake, Erwin, Greeneville, Parrotsville, Rankin, Springvale, Telford; *Obed River:* Alpine, Byrdstown, Clark Range, Crawford, Obed City, Riverton, Wilder; *Ocoee River:* Benton, Caney Creek, Oswald Dome, Parksville; *Sequatchie River:* Billingsley, Brockdell, Daus, Denson Gap, Ketner Gap, Melvine, Mount Airy, Pikeville, Sequatchie, Whitewell; *Tellico River* (including Sycamore Creek and North River): Bald River Falls, Big Junction, Rafter, Tallassee, Tapoco; *Watauga River:* Bluff City, Boone Dam, Elizabethton, Elk Mills, Elk Park, Johnson City, Watauga Dam.

Fishing & Hunting in Tennessee

Tennessee's spectacular mountains and verdant green valleys, plateau country, turbulent mountain streams, scenic lakes, and timbered bottomlands, extending from the over-6,500-feet elevation of the Great Smoky Mountains in the east to the flatlands bordering the Mississippi River on the west, and encompassing 41,951 square miles, provide some of the best and most varied fishing and hunting in the eastern United States.

TVA Lakes

The famous Great Lakes of Tennessee impoundments built by the Tennessee Valley Authority and the U.S. Corps of Engineers, range in size from 900-acre Davy Crockett Lake in the Cherokee National Forest in the eastern section of the state to the huge 158,300-acre Tennessee-Kentucky Lake, with its 2,380 miles of shoreline, in the west. The TVA lakes (see "Tennessee Valley Lakes Recreation Maps") are located on the Tennessee River system stretching from the northeast corner of the state southward into Alabama and then north through western Tennessee. Corps of Engineers impoundments include Dale Hollow on the Obed River, Woods Reservoir on the Elk River, Center Hill on Caney Fork and Barkley, Cheatham, and Old Hickory on the Cumberland. All of the state's major impoundments, including Berkley, Kentucky, Cheatham, Old Hickory, Percy Priest,

Woods, Tims Ford, Center Hill, Cordel Hill, Nickajack, Great Falls, Dale Hollow, Chickamauga, Watts Bar, Melton Hill, Norris, Fort Loudon, Chilhowee, Cherokee, Douglas, Fort Patrick Henry, South Holston, Boone, Wilbur, and Watauga reservoirs are renowned to fishermen far and wide for often spectacular fishing for largemouth and smallmouth bass, spotted or Kentucky bass, white and black crappie, walleye, sauger, white bass, rock, bass, bluegill, muskellunge, rockfish, rainbow, brown and brook trout, and several species of catfish.

All of the major impoundments have good to excellent fishing for largemouth or smallmouth or both. Dale Hollow Reservoir on the Obed River provides nationally ranked fishing for largemouth bass, walleye, and muskellunge and produced the world's record 11-pound 15-ounce smallmouth bass. The cold tailwaters below Dale Hollow Dam are renowned for their outstanding rainbow trout, and produced the state record 26-pound 2-ounce brown trout. Good tailwater fishing for lunker rainbows and brown trout is found below the dams of Lakes Watauga, Norris, Chilhowee, Dale Hollow, South Holston, and Center Hill. The tailwaters flowing through the dams from the bottom of the reservoirs are extremely cold and rich in insect life and schools of minnows and threadfin shad. The best time to fish the tailwaters is when the generators are shut off, and the pots and rapids are easily reached. High water scatters the fish and makes access more difficult. Several of the great lakes are world renowned for walleye fishing, including Woods, Dale Hollow, Norris, Watauga, and Old Hickory—which holds the world's record of 25 pounds for this species. A few

488 · THE BANTAM GREAT OUTDOORS GUIDE

of the lakes and float streams of the Cumberland Plateau have native populations of muskellunge. Dale Hollow Lake and Woods Reservoir in Franklin County and Norris Reservoir, which backs up the Clinch and Powell rivers, are among the state's best muskie waters, producing trophies up to 20 pounds. The Tennessee muskie, often referred to as a subspecies, *Esox masquinongy ohionensis*, is a silvery fish with vertical bar markings and seldom weighs more than 5 pounds. Watauga Lake, which impounds the waters of the Watauga River in the beautiful mountain country of Cherokee National Forest (see "Cherokee National Forest" in the "Travel & Recreation Guide" section) offers some of the state's finest trout fishing when lunker rainbows up to 10 pounds move into Doe Creek tributary during their winter spawning run.

Cherokee Wild Trout

The scenic mountain streams, with their deep staircased pools and rapids, in the Cherokee National Forest and Great Smoky National Park of eastern Tennessee provide excellent fishing for wild trout in the remote headwaters of the Unaka and Great Smoky mountains. These wild, turbulent streams surrounded by lush grass meadows and dense hardwood forests of yellow buckeye, white ash, black cherry, mountain silverbill and beech, colorful hemlock forests of red and sugar maples, yellow and sweet birches, holly, black and pin cherries with undergrowths of rosebay and catawba rhododendrons, and fragrant spruce and fir forests at the higher elevations hold wild brook, rainbow, and brown trout. Many of the most productive trout streams, managed by the state, are in rugged, wild country and are often accessible only by hiking up packhorse trails that follow old Indian paths and logging railroad beds. The most productive streams are located on the several units of the vast Cherokee Wildlife Management Area and include Paint Creek, Laurel Fork Creek, Tellico River, Citico Creek, and Green Cove Pond. Trout fishing in these streams and in the state-designated wild trout streams—North Fork of Citico Creek, North River, Bald River, Sycamore Creek, and their tributaries —is by special permit only, available from: Wildlife Resources Agency, P.O. Box 40747, Nashville 37204.

Several of the state's large rivers and streams offer good float fishing with a johnboat or canoe. Canoe rentals and float-trip guides are located along most of the major rivers. The major float-fishing waters include the Buffalo River for smallmouth bass, bream, and pickerel; Duck River for smallmouth bass and rock bass in the upper section; Obed River for smallmouth and rock bass; Hiwassee River for brown and rainbow trout; Little Tennessee River for brown and rainbow trout; French Broad River for largemouth bass, catfish, and sauger; the lower portions of the Nolichuckey River for smallmouth bass and channel catfish; and the South Fork Holston River for excellent brown and rainbow trout fishing below South Holston Dam.

The great diversity and quality of the state's fishing waters is underscored by a study of the all-time record fish caught by rod and reel, listed below.

TENNESSEE RECORD FISH

	Lb.-oz.	Place	Year
Bass:			
Coosa	0–12	Brymer Creek	1977
Rock	2–8	Stones River	1958
Smallmouth	11–15*	Dale Hollow Reservoir	1955
Largemouth	14–8	Sugar Creek	1954
Spotted	5–4	Chickamauga Lake	1976
Striped	48–0	Norris Reservoir	1977
White	4–10	Pickwick Lake tailwaters	1949
Rockfish (hybrid)	18	Norris Lake	1974
Sunfish:			
Bluegill	3–0	Falls Creek	1977
Pumpkinseed	0–3	Private pond	1975
Green	0–11¾	Farm pond, Jackson	1971
Longear	0–7	Surgoinsville Creek	1968
Redbreast	1–5	Holston River	1974
Redear	2–10	Private pond, Cumberland Co.	1976
Warmouth	1–4½	Pipkins Pond, Knox Co.	1961
Crappie:			
Black	2–14	Meadow Park Lake	1975
White	5–1	Garner Brown's Pond, Dickson Co.	1969
Perch:			
Yellow	1–4½	Fort Loudon Dam tailwaters	1974
Sauger	7–6	Chambers Creek, below Pickwick Dam	1973
Walleye	25*	Old Hickory Lake	1960
Pike:			
Northern	6–15½	South Holston Reservoir	1973
Muskellunge	42	Dale Hollow Reservoir	1975
Chain pickerel	6–9	Kentucky Lake	1951
Trout:			
Brook	3–14	Hiwassee River	1973
Brown	26–2	Dale Hollow Lake tailwaters	1958
Cutthroat	0–6	Obed River, below Dale Hollow Dam	1969

	Lb.-oz.	Place	Year
Trout (cont.):			
Rainbow	14–8	Obed River, below Dale Hollow Dam	1971
Catfish:			
Blue	115	Kentucky Lake, near Clifton	1971
Brown bullhead	1–15½	Forded Deer River	1968
Channel	24–3⅕	Laurel Hill Lake	1967
Flathead	74	Powell River	1969
Bowfin	14–11	Reelfoot Lake	1974
Black buffalo	52	Kentucky Lake	1973
Carp	42–8	Boone Lake	1956
Paddlefish	88	Center Hill	1976
Drum	54–8	Nickajack Dam	1972
Gar	23	Pickwick Lake tailwaters	1963
River herring	2–15	Watts Bar Reservoir	1976

*World's record.

Maps & Guides

Tennessee fishing and hunting regulations and information about special permits and season are available along with the publications listed below, from: Wildlife Resources Agency, P.O. Box 40747, Nashville 37204. The free *Tennessee Fishing Guide* contains a fishing map of the state, laws and regulations, license information, and a listing of wildlife officers and agency-managed lakes. The free, full-color *Fishing Tennessee* booklet contains illustrations and descriptions of the state's principal game fish, a *Tennessee Fishing Map* showing reservoirs, streams, and major roads, and a *Map of Floatable Streams in Tennessee*. Fishing pamphlets are available from the agency for *Watts Bar, Norris Lake, Fort Loudon, South Holston, Cherokee, Douglas, Boone,* and *Watauga* reservoirs. The free *Guide to Hunting in Tennessee* contains regulations, laws, license information, and a comprehensive listing and descriptions of the state's Wildlife Management Areas (see "State Forest Reserves & Game Lands"), including the vast Cherokee Wildlife Management Area and its Tellico Pond Mountain and Ocoee bear reserves and Tellico, Ocoee, Andrew Johnson, Kettlefoot, Laurel Fork, and Unicoi game units. The *Tennessee Turkey Hunting Guide* contains a listing of laws, regulations, and county checking stations. The agency also publishes a free *Wildlife Management Areas Map* showing state and Cherokee National Forest game units. A *Reelfoot Wildlife Refuge Map* and a *Directory of Reelfoot Lake Camps* (includes guides, lodging, and boat rentals) may be obtained free from the Refuge Manager, Box 295, Samburg 38254.

Hunting

Tennessee's rugged and scenic Cherokee National Forest highlands and widely scattered wildlife management area lands and public hunting areas provide excellent fall hunting opportunities for whitetail deer, upland game birds, waterfowl, and limited numbers of black bear and wild European boar—both by special permit only. The Pond Mountain, Tellico and Ocoee bear reserves in Cherokee National Forest are closed to bear hunting. The vast hardwood and conifer forests of the Cherokee Wildlife Management Area units in the Cherokee National Forest are among the state's finest public hunting grounds: the Tellico WMA unit (80,000 acres of spectacular mixed hardwood and pine forests), Ocoee WMA unit (40,000 acres of moun-

tainous conifer and hardwood forests), Laurel Fork WMA unit (10,000 acres of mixed hardwoods), Kettlefoot WMA unit (39,000 acres of mixed hardwoods and rugged highlands), and the huge Unicoi WMA provide good hunting for deer, wild boar, grouse, woodcock, raccoon, opossum, bobcat, fox, black bear, rabbit, gray and fox squirrel, and wild turkey.

The state's great reservoirs and lakes are prime resting and nesting areas for large flocks of ducks and Canadian geese. Reelfoot Lake, created by an earthquake, is a bass fisherman's and waterfowl hunter's paradise located up in the extreme northwest corner of the state near the Mississippi River. The Mississippi itself has long been famous as a migration route for large flocks of ducks and honkers.

As a note of caution, both fishermen and hunters should have an eye out for rattlesnakes, copperheads, and a few cottonmouth moccasins found scattered throughout the fish and game regions of the state.

Highways—Recreation & Scenic Routes

The state's scenic and recreation highways and roads that wind through the beautiful forest highlands of the Great Smokies along the eastern border, along the large man-made impoundments of the Great Valley of the Tennessee River, and through the Cumberland Mountains, plateau, and the central basin and the famed bluegrass country are shown on the *Official Tennessee Highway Map*, available free from: Division for Tourist Development, 1028 Andrew Jackson Bldg., Nashville 37219. In addition, this useful map shows state parks and recreation areas, campgrounds, lakes and streams, towns, and the Cherokee National Forest lands.

Land Between the Lakes

In western Kentucky and Tennessee is a long, narrow strip of land, surrounded nearby by two large man-made lakes and covered by a green, forested canopy. This 170,000-acre peninsula, known as Land Between the Lakes, is being developed by the Tennessee Valley Authority as a national demonstration in outdoor recreation and environmental education. Situated between TVA's Kentucky Lake and the U.S. Corps of Engineers' Lake Barkley, Land Between the Lakes is about 8 miles wide and stretches over 40 miles north to south.

Camping is especially popular in the area, with facilities ranging from large campgrounds with all modern conveniences to secluded lakeside sites. Three large family campgrounds on Kentucky Lake offer more than 800 well-equipped campsites. Hillman Ferry, about 3 miles south of Barkley Canal in the northern section, and Piney, near the southern entrance about 3 miles off U.S. Highway 79, are open year-round. Rushing Creek, near the midway point of Land Between the Lakes, is open spring through fall. All three offer a variety of shaded tent and trailer sites overlooking the lake. Each of the family campgrounds has a marked swimming area, playgrounds, electrical outlets, boat-launching ramps, and picnic tables and grills. Sections of the family campgrounds can be reserved by camping clubs, associations, and other organized groups. In addition to the family campgrounds, there are lake access centers scattered along the shorelines of the two lakes that are designed specifically for campers, fishermen, picknickers, and day use. Most of the access sites are located on good fishing embayments and provide tables, grills, boat-launching ramps, and sanitary facilities.

Other activities in the Land Between the Lakes include archery, field trials, bow hunting in season for deer and wild turkey, and hiking. A short, navigable canal between Kentucky Lake and Lake Barkley joins two of the top bass and crappie fishing lakes in the nation. These two great lakes have more than 3,500 miles of shoreline and hundreds of

deep, quiet coves. Kentucky Lake has long been noted for its populations of crappie, and Lake Barkley is considered one of the best bass lakes in the Southeast. Catfish, bluegill, stripes (white bass), and sauger are also taken year round. Boats, motors, and guides are available at many docks just outside Land Between the Lakes.

Hunting is also popular during the fall and winter. Over ten kinds of wildlife, including deer, wild turkey, quail, and Canada geese, inhabit the scenic woodlands and marshes in the peninsula. For the hiker, there are more than 400 miles of backcountry roads and trails winding throughout the area. A 26-mile historical trail system has been developed in the southern portion of the area, tracing General Grant's troop movements from Fort Henry to Fort Donelson just south of Land Between the Lakes.

Among the most unusual attractions of the area is the herd of buffalo that grazes in a 200-acre pasture alongside The Trace near the former site of Model, Tennessee. Bald and golden eagles can also be seen in the area, soaring above the quiet coves of the two lakes or perched high above the lakeshore.

Land Between the Lakes, a brochure published by the Tennessee Valley Authority, includes a map and describes the area in full detail. This booklet and further information can be obtained free along with a free *Hunting Guide* from: Land Between the Lakes, TVA, Golden Pond, KY 42231, phone (502) 924-5602.

A full-color *Land Between the Lakes Topographic Map*, size 22 by 34 inches, scale 1 inch to 4,000 feet, may be purchased for $1.25 from: TVA Map Office, 400 Commerce Ave., SW, Knoxville 37902.

Ski Touring & Snowshoeing

Good opportunities for cross-country skiing are available in Great Smoky Mountains National Park and Cherokee National Forest. Access to Great Smoky is via U.S. 441 to Newfound Gap (elevation 5,048 feet) between Cherokee, North Carolina, and Gatlinburg, Tennessee. A round trip of 14 miles is possible on the Clingmans Dome Road (elevation 6,643 feet) during winter months when the road is closed. Tours may also be made either north or south on the Appalachian Trail. Overnight tours require a camping permit which will not be issued unless clothing, camping gear, equipment, and food are considered safe and adequate upon inspection by a ranger. Trailside shelters are available, but overnight use is by reservation only and plans must be cleared from park headquarters before a permit can be obtained. Day touring parties are urged to inform park headquarters near Gatlinburg or the Oconaluftee Ranger Station near Cherokee of the trip schedule and route.

The Cherokee National Forest encompasses the southern Appalachian Mountains both to the north and south of the Great Smoky

Mountains National Park. Although snow conditions are not as reliable as in the park because of lower elevations, there are nonetheless a number of reliable areas exceeding 5,000-foot elevations. These include Camp Creek Bald, site of the former Viking Mountain Ski Area, and Roan Mountain, shared with the Pisgah National Forest in North Carolina. Wind conditions may cause spotty snow in some areas. Several trail shelters are located along the Appalachian Trail, which crosses both forests. For more information contact the U.S. Forest Service district rangers at Greeneville (Camp Creek Bald) or Erwin (Big Bald, Roan Mountain, Yellow Mountains).

State Forest Reserves & Game Lands

The following U.S. Geological Survey maps show the topography of the state's major wildlife management areas, wilderness areas, forest reserves, and parks. These reserves offer outstanding wilderness, fishing, and backpacking opportunities, and excellent hunting in season for whitetail deer, ruffed grouse, wild turkey, raccoon, red and fox squirrel, and wild boar. *Andrew Johnson WMA* (Cherokee National Forest; includes Paint Creek, Rich Laurel WMA, and Bald Mountains): Davy Crockett Lake, Hot Springs; *Catoosa WMA:* Camp Austin, Cardiff, Fox Creek, Herbertsburg, Jones Knot, Lansing; *Chickasaw State Forest,* Bolivar E, Medon, Silerton, Teague; *Chuck Swan WMA:* Demory, Well Spring, White Hollow; *Falls Creek State Park:* Brockdell, Sampson, Smart Mountain, Spencer; *Kettlefoot WMA:* Carter, Doe, Holston Valley, Keenburg, Laurel Bloomery, Mountain City, Shady Valley; *Laurel Fork WMA* (Cherokee National Forest): Watauga Dam, Whiterocks Mountain; *Marion Franklin State Park:* Orme, Sinking Cove; *Morgan State Forest:* Camp Austin, Fork Mountain, Gobey, Petros; *Natchez Trace State Forest:* Buena Vista, Chesterfield, Holladay, Parsons, Seventeen Creek, Yuma; *Ocoee WMA* (Cherokee National Forest; includes Carey Creek and Parksville Lake): Benton, Carey Creek, Oswald Dome, Parksville; *Pickett State Forest:* Barthell SW, Sharp Place; *Prentice Cooper State Forest:* Gap, Wauhatchie; *Roan Mountain State Park* (Cherokee National Forest): Iron Mountain Gap, White Rocks Mountain; *Standing Stone State Park:* Hilham, Livingston; *Tellico WMA* (Cherokee National Forest; includes Citico, Sycamore, Doublecamp, Bald and Turkey creeks, North River, and Unicoi Mountains): Bald River Falls, Big Junction, Rafter, Tallassee, Tapoco; *Unaka Mountains* (Cherokee National Forest): Huntdale, Iron Mountain Gap, Unicoi; *Unicoi WMA* (Cherokee National Forest; includes Clark and Bonipace creeks and Rich Mountain): Erwin, Flag Pond, Telford.

Tennessee Valley Lakes Recreation Maps

The Tennessee Valley Authority has developed some 36 lakes in the seven Tennessee Valley states, offering more than 600,000 acres of water surface and 11,000 miles of shoreline. Detailed recreation maps for nine lakes in Tennessee are available from: TVA Map Office, 400 Commerce Ave., SW, Knoxville 37902, or Chattanooga 37401. Single copies of the maps are free on request. Each lake recreation map describes points of interest in the area, opportunities for fishing, hunting, and outdoor activities, boating requirements and water safety, and the topographic features of the lake. The map shows the lake and surrounding terrain, public and TVA dam reservation lands, commercial boat docks, boat-launching sites, public parks, wildlife management areas, roads, highways, and nearby towns. Maps are available for the following lake areas: *Nickajack Lake* is near Raccoon and Sand mountains on the Tennessee River. The *Upper Holston Lakes* include Fort Patrick Henry Dam, Boone Lake, South Holston Lake, Watauga Dam and Lake, and Roan Creek—all in and around the Cherokee

National Forest and the nearby towns of Johnson City, Elizabethton, Bristol, and Kingsport. *Chickamauga Lake* lies between the Watts Bar and Chickamauga dams just outside Chattanooga. Bordering the lake are Harrison Bay and Booker T. Washington state parks, both of which are indicated on the map. The *Cherokee-Douglas Lakes* include Davy Crockett Lake and a segment of the French Broad River. Neighboring towns include Morristown and Rogersville. *Watts Bar Lake* adjoins Chickamauga Lake near Kingston, Harriman, and Rockwood. The map of *Melton Hill Lake* shows the Clinch River Floatway, situated near the towns of Oak Ridge and Clinton. *Fort Loudoun Lake* is just outside of Knoxville on the Tennessee River; *Norris Lake* adjoins the Central Peninsula and Cove Creek Peninsula wildlife management areas near the town of La Follette. The *Hiwassee Lakes* include Appalachia Lake in the Nantahala National Forest of Tennessee and Blue Ridge and Nottely lakes in Georgia's Chattahoochee National Forest.

Navigation charts and maps have also been published by TVA for its major lakes. They show water depths, the location of public recreation areas, boat docks, resorts, and roads. Charts for the mainstream lakes of the Tennessee River show navigation channels, buoys, lights, and other navigation aids. Maps for tributary lakes show the location of numbered boards the TVA has installed at strategic locations on shore to aid fishermen and recreation boaters in locating their positions. A free Index of TVA navigation charts, maps, and other charts may be purchased from: TVA Maps (Knoxville and Chattanooga addresses above).

A brochure published by the TVA, *Recreation on TVA Lakes*, offers a general description of recreational opportunities on the lakes, including fishing, boating, and camping, and a list of addresses for further information. A map of TVA lakes with a detailed listing of recreation areas on each lake giving addresses and facilities is also provided. The brochure, a useful supplement to the recreation maps, is available free from the addresses above.

Tennessee River Tributary Watershed Maps, lithoprinted in color, showing drainage, topography, woodlands, highways and roads, cities and towns, with a contour interval of 100 feet, are available from: TVA Map Office (addresses above) for *Bear Creek* (45¢), *Upper French Broad River* (45¢), *Sequatchie River* (45¢), *Duck River* (75¢), *Elk River* (75¢), *Little Tennessee River* (75¢), *Emory River* (75¢), and *Hiwassee River* (75¢).

Wilderness Outfitters & Expeditions

The fairly recent completion of a dam on Hiwassee Lake in the Nantahala National Forest just inside North Carolina has made rocky and challenging float trips possible on the Hiwassee River. *Hiwassee Float Service*, Delano 37325, phone (615) 263–5581, offers 3- to 8-hour trips on both the Hiwassee and Ocoee in rafts for 2 to 4 passengers navigated by expert guides. The Lower Hiwassee is also offered for smoother expeditions. Stops are made along the way to hike, fish, or explore. Nearby are stores for food and fishing supplies, campgrounds, and in the river itself beautiful blue ribbon rainbow trout. Hiwassee Float Service will also outfit smooth and white-water canoeing. *The Trail Riders of the Wilderness Program* (sponsored by: American Forestry Assn., 1319 18th St., NW, Washington, DC 20036) offers spring and fall packhorse trips along the crest of the Great Smoky Mountains. (See also Buffalo River Canoe Rental Co., under "Canoeing and Trophy Fishing Waters.")

TENNESSEE TRAVEL & RECREATION GUIDE

Cherokee National Forest

Cherokee National Forest Topo Maps.

U.S. Geological Survey Overview Maps, scale 1:250,000: Chattanooga, Johnson City, Knoxville, Rome (GA), Winston-Salem (NC).

Bald River Wilderness

Large-scale U.S. Geological Survey Topographic Maps: Bald River Falls, Unaka, Big Junction.

Cohutta Wild Area

Large-scale U.S. Geological Survey Topographic Maps: Cohutta, Felker, McDonald.

Frog Mountain Wilderness

Large-scale U.S. Geological Survey Topographic Maps: Carey Creek, Hemptop.

Gee Creek Wilderness

Large-scale U.S. Geological Survey Topographic Maps: Etowah, McFarland, Mecca, Oswald Dome.

Unaka Mountains

Large-scale U.S. Geological Survey Topographic Maps: Huntdale, Iron Mountain Gap, Unicoi.

Unicoi Mountains

Large-scale U.S. Geological Survey Topographic Maps: Unaka, Bald River Falls, Big Junction, Whiteoak Flats.

This 614,000-acre highland reserve, renowned for its outstanding fishing, hunting, hiking, and canoe-camping areas, takes in a long, narrow strip of mountainous terrain along the Great Smoky and Unaka mountains of the Tennessee-North Carolina border. The forest is divided into two major segments—the Unaka and Cherokee divisions—which are connected by the Great Smoky Mountains National Park, shared by Tennessee with North Carolina. Numerous forest roads and hiking trails, including the entire Tennessee section of the Appalachian Trail (see "Appalachian National Scenic Trail" in the "Encyclopedia" section), provide access to the remote wilderness backpacking and hunting areas within the forest. The *Cherokee National Forest Map* shows all major natural features, roads, trails, recreation and campsites, trail shelters, landing fields, district ranger stations, and points of access and is available for 50¢ from: Forest Supervisor, Cherokee National Forest, P.O. Box 400, Cleveland 37311. Backpackers, hikers, hunters, horseback riders—in short, anyone using roads or trails within the forest—will find the *Road and Trail Maps* for individual ranger districts especially useful. Maps are available for the Tellico, Hiwassee, Ocoee, Nolichuckey, and Unaka ranger districts. Each map shows highways; horse trails; foot trails; paved, gated, all-weather, and gravel roads; National Forest System roads; and routes on which automobiles and motorcycles are permitted. National forest lands are carefully distinguished from private property, and natural features—mountains, lakes, streams, rivers, and the like—are indicated too. Maps are available free from: Forest Supervisor (address above). Be sure to specify which ranger district you are requesting. For those who prefer to enjoy the park in the relative safety and comfort of an automobile, the Forest Service also publishes a map for a self-guiding 15-mile auto tour through part of the Nolichuckey ranger district of the Cherokee National Forest. The 2-hour trip over well-graded gravel roads winds along the banks of the French Broad River to the crest of Meadow Creek Mountain. The Brush Creek Auto Map shows the complete route, describes points of inter-

est along the way, and is available free from: District Ranger, U.S. Forest Service, Greeneville 37743.

A number of wilderness areas, small and large pockets of unspoiled natural beauty, lie within Cherokee National Forest. In the southwest section of the forest, bounded by Starr and Chestnut mountains on the west and east and Gee Knob to the south, is the Gee Creek Wilderness Area, encompassing the entire Gee Creek Watershed. The creek itself contains large numbers of brown trout and flows through a magnificent gorge with 5–25-foot waterfalls. Prime timber and rhododendron thickets cover its steep sides. The heart of the gorge is true wilderness—not even a trail interrupts its primitive setting.

The mountains which surround Gee Creek provide a fitting complement to the stream flowing from their slopes. Starr Mountain on the west and Chestnut Mountain on the east reach elevations of 2,480 and 2,500 feet, respectively; Gee Knob on the south is a little over 2,000 feet in height. All three mountains are heavily forested with a variety of evergreen and deciduous trees and provide splendid views of the gorge area, the peaceful Hiwassee River, and the mountains to the east. In spite of an abundance of wildlife, the area is not part of any designated wildlife management area. Access to the wilderness is provided by Forest Service Road 115 following the ridge line on the northern end of the watershed.

Northeast of the Gee Creek Wilderness in Monroe County are 13,900 acres of mountain terrain comprising the Bald River Wilderness. For virtually its entire length, the Bald River in the southern half of the roughly oval-shaped area is filled with rippling, shooting cascades and many falls beneath which lie deep crystal pools and swift-flowing clear mountain water. As it enters the Tellico, the river makes a dramatic plunge over the 100-foot Bald River Falls. Dense mountain laurel and rhododendron outline all streams in the watershed in a profusion of broad-leafed evergreen and brightly colored blossoms. Populations of rainbow and brown trout reproduce naturally in the Bald and its tributary streams—Henderson Branch, Brookshire Creek, Kirkland Creek, Big Cove Branch, and Waucheesi Creek. The upper reaches also support native populations of brook trout. It is estimated that this watershed alone contains half of the brook trout in the southern section of the forest. Since it is considered part of the Tellico Wildlife Management Area, the Tennessee Game and Fish Commission has imposed certain restrictions on fishing in the wilderness: Henderson Branch is closed to fishermen in order to encourage nature production, and the Bald has been defined as a wild trout stream to be fished with wet or dry flies only with reduced bag and increased size limits.

An 8-mile gravel road with a 20-foot stone bridge crosses the watershed. At Holly Flats is a Forest Service campground with picnic tables and fireplaces. These and a few trails are the only visible evidence of man in this wild and unspoiled setting.

Access to the area is from Forest Road 210, which connects with State Highway 68 southeast of Madisonville.

In the extreme southwestern reaches of the forest is the Frog Mountain Wilderness, a 15,000-acre area adjoining the Coheetia Wilderness in Georgia's Chattahoochee National Forest. Swift streams in the north side of Frog Mountain flow into the broad Ocoee River. A part of the Ocoee Wildlife Management Area, the area supports good populations of game and nature trout. (See "State Forest Reserves & Game Lands" in the "Encyclopedia" section.) Also included are some lands which now border on the portion of the Conasauga River, designated a Wild and Scenic River by the State of Tennessee. Nearby are campgrounds at Sylco, Tumbling Creek, and Thunder Rock. Ac-

cess is from Forest Road 45 off U.S. Highway 64 northwest of Copperhill.

There are a variety of other scenic attractions in Cherokee National Forest, including a number of lakes—Watauga, Holston, Chilhowee, and Parksville—with nearby campsites. (See "Tennessee Valley Lakes Recreation Maps" in the "Encyclopedia" section.) Parksville, a 1,900-acre Tennessee Valley Authority Lake, provides beautiful waters for fishing and boating. Seven-acre Chilhowee Lake, nestled on the top of Chilhowee Mountain, provides numerous camping facilities and astounding views of the surrounding countryside. Hiking trails traverse the area and lead to the nearby waterfalls. *The Chilhowee, Quinn Springs, Parksville Lake Recreation Areas Map* is available free from: Forest Supervisor, Cherokee National Forest, P.O. Box 400, Cleveland 37311, and shows the major features of the area as well as points of access and major roads. A list of campsites and recreation areas is also included.

Another free brochure from the forest supervisor, *Outdoors in the Unaka Mountains*, shows streams, hiking trails, roads, highways, and recreation areas in the Unicoi-Erwin area in the central region of the northern (Unaka) division of the forest. The Rock Creek Recreation Area in this section lies along a cascading mountain stream and provides several trails leading to waterfalls, mountain peaks, and coves in the neighboring mountains. The Raven's Lore Walk, a self-guiding trail, winds through majestic Unaka Mountain and offers an introduction to the history and natural wonders of the area.

Another publication issued free by the Forest Service, *Endangered, Rare and Uncommon Wildflowers*, is a 20-page booklet with beautiful color photographs, describing 62 varieties of rare wildflowers. The booklet tells how to recognize each flower, where to find it, and includes an index and the scientific name for each species.

If you are planning an extended stay in the forest, be sure to write the forest supervisor for *Regulations Governing the Occupancy and Use of National Forest Recreation Sites and Areas*.

Access & Outfitting Centers

State Highway 32 and U.S. Highway 25 both provide access to the southern end of the forest's Unaka division from the nearby town of Newport. State Highways 70 and 107 lead from Greeneville to the Unaka division, as does U.S. Highway 23 from Johnson City. The

forest's southern or Cherokee division is reached via U.S. Highway 64 from Cleveland and State Highway 30 from Athens and Etowah.

Great Smoky Mountains National Park

Great Smoky Mountains National Park Topo Maps

Large-scale U.S. Geological Survey 7.5-minute North Carolina Maps: Tapoco, Fontana Dam, Tuckasegee, Noland Creek, Bryson City, Whittier, Calderwood, Cades Cove, Thunderhead Mountain, Silers Bald, Clingmans Dome, Smokemont, Bunches Bald, Delwood, Luftee Knob, Cove Creek Gap. Large-scale 7.5-minute Tennessee Maps: Mount Le Conte, Blockhouse, Kinzei Springs, Wear Cove, Gatlinburg, Mount Guyot, Richardson Cove, Jones Cove, Hartford, Waterville.

Appalachian National Scenic Trail

Park segment is shown on large-scale 7.5-minute U.S. Geological Survey Series Maps: Cades Cove, Clingmans Dome, Fontana Dam, Hartford, Luftee Knob, Mount Guyot, Mount Le Conte, Silers Bald, Thunderhead, Waterville.

Boundary Trails Region

The following large-scale 7.5-minute U.S. Geological Survey Maps show the entire trail system along the northwestern boundary of the park: Blockhouse, Cades Cove, Calderwood, Kinzei Springs, Wear Cove.

The most massive and lofty mountain range in the eastern United States, the Great Smoky Mountains fall within the larger system of the southern Appalachians, a roughly oval-shaped chain of ranges running northeast to southwest. The Great Smokies themselves march for about 70 miles on an almost east-to-west line between North Carolina and Tennessee, bordered on the east by the Big Pigeon River and on the west by the Little Tennessee. In the eastern part of the Smokies, 16 peaks exceed 16,000-foot elevations. To the west, crests are generally lower, forming the bald (or forest) country, where grassy meadows blanket the mountaintops, affording spectacular views in all directions. With outlines softened by dense forest growth, the mountains seem to billow and stretch in sweeping troughs as far as the eye can see. The name Great Smokies is derived from the smokelike haze that envelops the mountains.

Situated between three national forests—the two segments of the Cherokee in Tennessee, and Pisgah and Nantahala forests in North Carolina—the Great Smoky Mountains National Park contains vast areas of virtually unspoiled forests, similar to those found by the early pioneers who settled in isolated mountain valleys. The first settlers arrived in the area late in the 18th century and established simple farms in the coves and valleys. As the years passed, the outside world changed under the impetus of progress while the mountain culture remained untouched by events beyond the Smokies—an early 19th-century farming community totally oblivious to the trappings of the modern world. Many of the old log cabins and barns still stand as monuments to the pioneer existence that has all but vanished from the mountains.

Fertile soils and heavy rains over a long period have caused a world-renowned variety of flora to develop within the park. Some 1,400 kinds of flowering plants bloom in the hills and valleys. Within the coves, broadleaf trees predominate; along the 6,000-foot-high crests, conifer forests similar to those of Canada find a climate suitable for dense growth.

The main roads offer only a cursory introduction to the beauties of the Smokies. At Cades Cove an 11-mile loop road leads past open fields, pioneer homesteads, and little frame churches where the mountain people lived and worshiped almost unnoticed for a century. Another scenic high mountain road winds its way through Newfound Gap to Clingmans Dome; there, a ½-mile walk to an observation tower provides an excellent panorama of the countryside. Summer brings extremely heavy traffic to this route. Both roads can be traced on the *Great Smoky Mountains National Park Map*, which also describes points of interest, camping facilities, accommodations, and general park features. The map shows access points, major highways surrounding the park, park roads, campsites, ranger stations, trail shelters, horse and foot trails, creeks, and other features. The map is available free from: Superintendent, Great Smoky Mountains National Park, Gatlinburg 37738.

For those who prefer to avoid the beaten track, there are 600 miles of horse and foot trails winding along streams and through forests into the high country. The spectacular views and waterfalls on many streams are popular objectives. The Park Headquarters publishes a free list of trails, including Abrams Bald, Laurel Falls, Mingus Creek, Newton Bald, and Spruce Mountain trails. Elevations, hiking difficulty, mileage, and starting points are indicated. Write to the superintendent in Gatlinburg for a copy of *Favorite Hiking Trails* in the Great Smokies National Park. For other trails and more detailed information, try the *Hiker's Guide to the Smokies*, a Sierra Club Totebook including a map of the park and environs and 370 pages of explicit information. The guide, coauthored by Dick Murlless and Constance Stallings, offers a brief history of the park, notes on the weather, a geologic history of the Smokies, descriptions of flora and fauna, tips on off-trail hiking, and a list of park regulations. Various trails are described in the Tennessee and North Carolina divisions of the park. The 14 sections on both states are each prefaced by a general history of the area, describing its early settlement and natural attractions. The trails following the introduction are outlined in abundant detail including point-by-point trail data, mileage, difficulty, elevations, U.S. Geological Survey maps covered, trail connections, and more. An invaluable source for the serious hiker in the Smokies, the guide is priced at $7.95 and can be ordered from: Sierra Club, Box 7959, Rincon Annex, San Francisco, CA 94104.

A backcountry camping permit is required for all overnight hiking

parties in the Great Smokies National Park; it can be obtained free of charge at any ranger station, visitor center, or park headquarters. Because of overcrowding, it has become necessary to ration overnight use of the 68 miles of Appalachian Trail within the park. Four other popular areas, Mount Le Conte, Laurel Gap, Kephart Prong, and Moore Spring, are rationed also. Arrangements for a permit must be made after you arrive in the park. There are many uncrowded trails in the park offering trailside campsites, a list of which *(Backcountry Map & Camping Guide)* is available from the Park Superintendent at the Gatlinburg address. Permits for winter camping between November and March will be issued only after winter gear and clothing are approved by a ranger as adequate for survival in deep snow and 20° weather.

In addition to the backcountry camping sites, the park offers seven developed campgrounds (at Smokemont, Balsam Mountain, Cosby, Elkmont, Deep Creek, Cades Cove, and Look Rock) and three primitive camping areas (at Cataloochee, Davenport Gap, and along Abrams Creek). Fees are charged at the developed campgrounds, which feature water, fireplaces, tables, comfort stations, and tent and limited trailer space. Visitors should bring their own tents and other camping equipment, since no shelters are provided. There are no showers or hookups for trailers. From June 1 through Labor Day, the camping limit is 7 days. Primitive campgrounds have no developed water supply. All water must be boiled or chemically treated before drinking. Camping at primitive areas is also limited to 7 days. Camping permits are not necessary for campgrounds reached by car, but registration is required upon arrival. Write to park headquarters for more details on individual campsites or consult *Camping in Tennessee* (see "Camping & Wilderness Trails" in the "Encyclopedia" section).

Several of the park's remote backcountry areas offer unsurpassed wilderness fishing and primitive camping opportunities. The remote Big Creek area in North Carolina, in the heart of old logging country, provides excellent fishing for wild brook and rainbow trout, and camping at the Big Creek Primitive Campground and the Walnut Bottoms backcountry camp. The area is laced by primitive footpaths, including the Big Creek Trail, which provides access through the scenic hardwood and moss-covered balsam and red spruce forests. The pastoral backcountry surrounding Cataloochee Creek (Cherokee for "wave upon wave of mountains") and Cataloochee Primitive Campground in North Carolina is a renowned backpacking area laced by numerous trails. Numerous hiking trails wind through second-growth forests of river birch, basswood, yellow poplar, majestic eastern hemlocks, oaks, maples, magnolia, and tulip poplar in the backcountry surrounding the trout waters of Deep and Indian creeks and the Patch Pole backcountry camp and Deep Creek campground in North Carolina. Miles of scenic trails wind through hardwood forests, large grassy balds, spruce and fir stands, and tangles of flame azalea and purple rhododendron surrounding the renowned wild trout waters of Noland, Forney, Hazel, Eagle and Twentymile creeks, which feed into the northern shoreline of huge Lake Fontana; backcountry campsites are located along the creeks. Hazel Creek and its Cold Spring branch, Sugar Fork, and Bone Valley Creek tributaries is nationally famous for its trophy rainbow and brook trout fishing. Remnants of old logging railroads that traversed the majestic virgin forests during the early part of this century and spectacular displays of rare yellow-berried dogwoods, yellow iris, kerria bush, monkshood, bluebead lily, wild ginger, pawpaw bushes, and flame azalea border the old Cherokee trails and trout pools that make this area a backpacker's and wilderness fly fisherman's paradise. Hundreds of miles of primitive trails wind through the scenic meadows, flats, valleys, and high country red spruce and Fraser fir forests and balds throughout the Great Smoky Park to Mount Le Conte, Greenbrier Cove, Little Pigeon River, Little River, Slickrock Creek,

Joyce Kilmer Forest, Oconaluftee (Cherokee for "near the river") Valley, and the beautiful, verdant green of Cades Cove. Campers and fisherman should keep in mind that black bear and wild boar are common in many of the remote interior areas.

Two park streams are set aside as "fishing for fun" streams, where trout or bass under 16 inches must be returned immediately. The regular season is from April 15 through September 15. A Tennessee or North Carolina fishing license is required, but not trout stamps. Local regulations are posted on streams and can be obtained at any park ranger station or visitor center. *Camping-Fishing Great Smoky Mountains National Park*, a brochure available free from the Gatlinburg office, lists the various fishing streams, regulations, open waters, campgrounds, and horseback concessionaires.

Most of the neighboring towns have gas, food, lodging, and camping supplies. Many private campgrounds operate outside the park. For information, write the chambers of commerce of nearby towns in North Carolina and Tennessee. For those in search of more luxurious accommodations, *Le Conte Lodge*, within the park, offers cabins and lodge rooms from mid-April to late October. Allow a half day's hike up a mountain trail to reach this secluded retreat. Reservations are necessary; write or call: Le Conte Lodge, P.O. Box 350, Gatlinburg 37738, phone (615) 436–4473.

Saddle horses for the Great Smoky pack trails are provided by *Cades Cove Riding Stables*, Cades Cove Star Route, Townsend 37882; *McCarters Riding Stables*, Gatlinburg 37738, at Tuomide Branch; *Smokemont Riding Stables*, Route No. 1, Cherokee, NC 28719, at Smokemont Creek; and *Smoky Mountain Riding Stables*, P.O. Box 445, Gatlinburg 37738, at Dudley Creek.

A U.S. Geological Survey Map, *Great Smoky Mountain National Topographic Map* (2 sheets), is available showing the eastern and western halves of the park. Each is 28 × 32 inches with a scale of 1:62,500 or about 1 inch to 1 mile, and each sheet is priced at $2. A complete U.S. Geological Survey Park Map, scale: 1:125,000, is also available showing the park and adjacent areas. It covers approximately 2,730 square miles and is issued in both contour and shaded-relief editions. This map shows roads, trails, including the Appalachian Trail, shelters, ranger stations, fire towers, and campgrounds. A text printed on the reverse side of the map discusses the geology and history of the region, and offers other information of interest to visitors. Either the contour or relief edition is priced at $2. A *1934 Edition of Great Smoky Mountains National Park U.S. Geological Survey Map* may be obtained from: TVA Map Office, 400 Commerce Ave., SW, Knoxville 37902. This full-color topographic map shows old roads, trails, and railroads not shown on the new park map. Set of 2 sheets, each 28 × 34 inches, scale 1:62,500 (1 inch to 1 mile). Price $4 per set.

Access & Outfitting Centers

Great Smokies National Park is reached from Nashville via Interstate Highways 24, 40, and 75; from North Carolina via Interstate Highways 26, 40, 59, and 75; from Knoxville via U.S. Highway 129; and from the east via Interstate 381. Lodging, supplies, and canoe rentals are available at Gatlinburg, Townsend, Maryville, Sevierville, Cherokee, North Carolina, and several other towns and villages surrounding the park in Tennessee and North Carolina.

MID-APPALA-CHIAN STATES

Introduction

The Mid-Appalachian States, which encompass several nationally renowned fishing, camping, hunting, backpacking, and canoeing areas, stretch from Virginia north to the St. Lawrence Lowlands in New York, and from the Atlantic Coastal Plain west to the Central Lowlands. Beyond the famous waterfowl hunting grounds of the Atlantic Coastal Plain lies the rolling Piedmont country and, to its west, the beautiful Blue Ridge Mountains. The great Appalachian National Scenic Trail winds along the crest of the ancient mountain chain and provides access to hundreds of remote blue lakes, ponds, and streams surrounded by mixed hardwood and conifer forests and thick undergrowths of holly, winterberry, hazelnut bushes, witch hazel, sassafras, alder, sweetfern, willow, bayberry, and rainbow-hued waves of shrubs and wildflowers, including bog rosemary, bluebell, rhododendron, mountain laurel, trillium, and wild lily of the valley.

Virginia, known as the Old Dominion, encompasses the famed saltwater fishing and waterfowl hunting grounds of the Tidewater region; the rugged slopes, valleys, lakes and streams, and peaks of the beautiful Blue Ridge and Allegheny mountains in the Jefferson and George Washington national forests; the magnificent high camping and hiking areas of the Mount Rogers National Recreation Area; Shenandoah National Park, which extends for 80 miles along the Blue Ridge Mountains, traversed by the scenic Skyline Drive; remote forest reserve and fish and game lands, inhabited by whitetail deer, ruffed grouse, black bear, fox squirrel, red fox, raccoon, and wild turkey; and the nationally renowned smallmouth bass waters of the North and South forks of the Shenandoah River.

West Virginia is a land of surprises. The Mountain State embraces some of the eastern United States' most spectacular wild country, much of which is reminiscent of the north country of eastern Canada. The Monongahela National Forest in the Allegheny Mountain Range encompasses the arcticlike wild sphagnum and cranberry bogs, mats of heath shrubs, huckleberry plains, beaver ponds, and swift-flowing runs of the Cranberry backcountry—once known as the "Wilds of Pocahontas"—and the often fog-shrouded Dolly Sods backcountry. The forest also takes in the wild trout waters of Seneca Creek, Shavers Fork, and the Cranberry River, which holds transplanted golden-rainbow hybrids; the trophy muskellunge waters of the Elk River; and the wild and scenic South Branch of the Potomac, the best smallmouth bass stream in the East, with a wild 7-mile gorge.

Maryland, the Old Line State, stretches from the Atlantic Ocean to the Allegheny Mountains and takes in the nationally famous striped bass waters and duck and goose hunting grounds of Chesapeake Bay. Inland are the trophy smallmouth bass waters of the North Branch of the Potomac and the backpacking and camping areas of the state forest reserves and game lands, which offer good hunting in season for whitetail deer, wild turkey, upland game birds, and waterfowl. Delaware, to the east, is known primarily for its superb waterfowl hunting and saltwater fishing.

Pennsylvania, with its vast tracts of "big-woods" state forest reserves and game lands, wild high country areas, thousands of lakes and ponds, trophy muskellunge and smallmouth bass rivers, scenic canoe routes, and nationally famous limestone trout streams—including the Yellow Breeches, Letort, Brodhead, Big Spring, Loyalstock, and Penns Creek—offers some of the East's finest canoe-camping, fishing, hunting, and backpacking opportunities. In the northwest region of the Keystone State are mixed hardwood forests, rolling hills, marshlands, and hundreds of miles of remote wild trout streams in the beautiful Allegheny National Forest. The scenic Upper Delaware River, which forms the natural boundary between Pennsylvania and New Jersey, is one of the

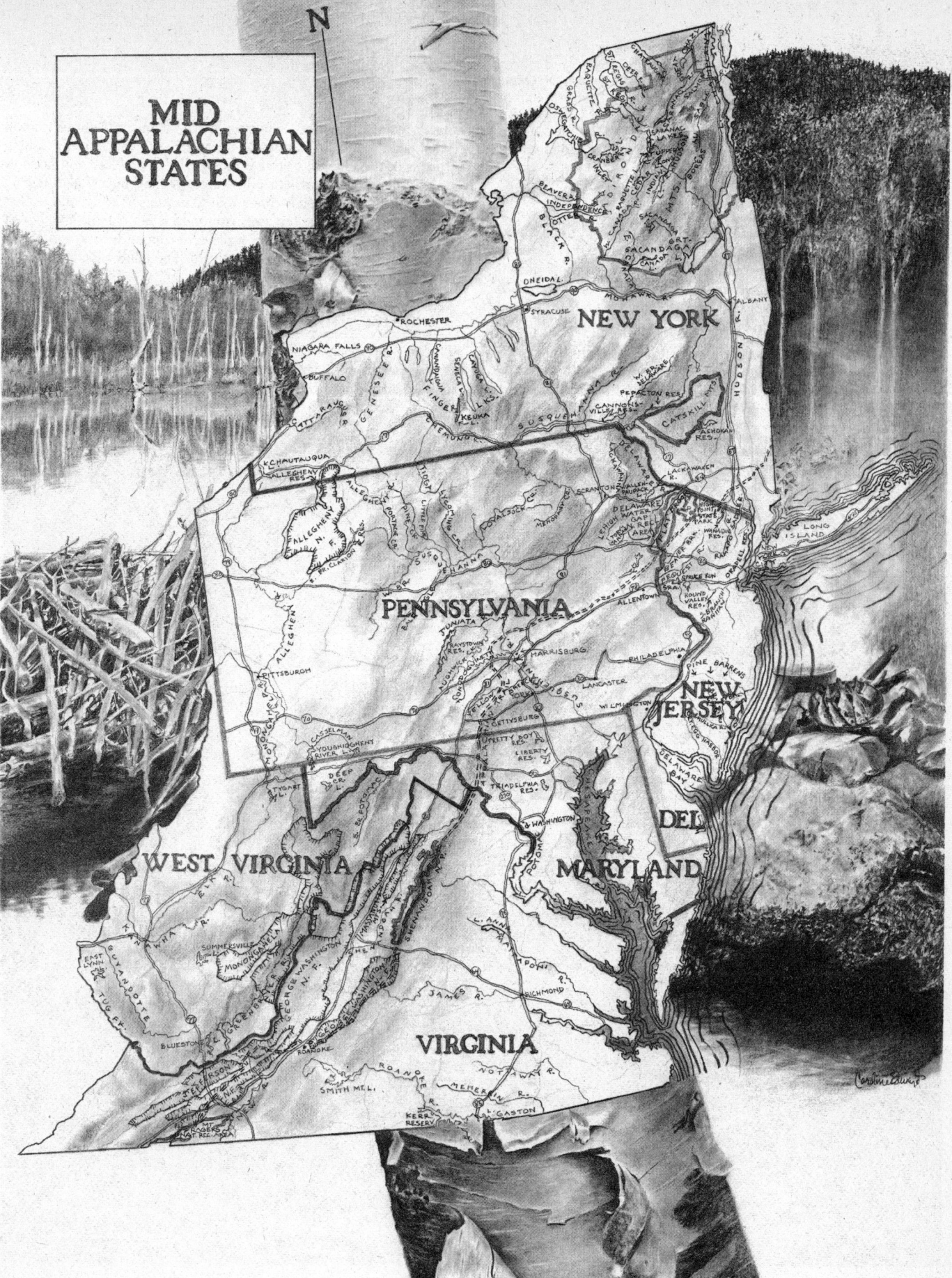

MID APPALACHIAN STATES

East's top walleye and rainbow trout streams and canoe routes, noted for its deep-flowing pools, islands, rapids, and swirling eddies.

New Jersey, known as the Garden State, embraces one of the nation's largest wild areas, the haunting Pine Barrens, with its primeval swamps, bogs, cranberry glades, and tea-colored "cedar" rivers, which hold voracious, arm-length chain pickerel; the renowned trout waters of Big Flat Brook; the beautiful island-dotted waters of Lake Hopatcong, one of the East's top-ranked lakes for tackle-busting brown trout and largemouth bass; the trophy rainbow and brown trout waters of Spruce Run and Round Valley reservoirs; and the long famous saltwater fishing meccas of the Jersey coast.

The vast reaches of New York State, with its coastal saltwater fishing areas, historic trout streams, extensive game lands, and sprawling island-dotted north country lakes, wild rivers, and high peaks, form one of the nation's most popular outdoor recreation areas. The Empire State's major attractions include the world-famous striped bass runs off Montauk Point; the nationally renowned brown trout fly fishing streams of the Catskill Forest Preserve; the trophy lake and rainbow trout, walleye, and northern pike waters of the Finger Lakes region; the beautiful north woods canoe routes, fishing, hunting, and wilderness camping areas of the vast Adirondack State Park and Forest Preserve; and the muskellunge, walleye, smallmouth bass, and northern pike waters surrounding the beautiful Thousand Islands of the St. Lawrence River.

Weather, Bugs & Beasts

The Mid-Appalachian States offer a wide range of climates ranging from generally mild days in the coastal areas to often cool days in the high country areas. Summers in the central lowlands are hot and humid, often reaching 90°, with frequent thunderstorms. Heavy pre-

cipitation falls throughout the year; deep snows blanket the states in winter.

The coastal and inland areas are infamous for swarms of voracious mosquitoes; in the north country the mosquitoes are joined in their brief career of torture by blackflies, deerflies, "bulldogs," and no-see-ums. A good supply of insect repellent is a must for summer survival. The forest regions and woodlands are inhabited by timber rattlesnakes and copperheads; the swamps and marshes by cottonmouth moccasins. The snakewise woodsman will pack an antivenin kit such as that produced by Wyeth Laboratories and stocked in many drugstores. The remote forest areas of Virginia, West Virginia, Pennsylvania, and New York are inhabited by black bears, which present an occasional nuisance rather than a common hazard. Of each 1,000 black bears encountered, something like 999 will avoid all contact with man, but like all wildlife, they are unpredictable and one may attack without provocation.

Mid-Appalachian Maps & Charts—How to Order

The topographic maps listed throughout the Mid-Appalachian States sections will provide you with a valuable picture of the area you plan to visit, showing all mountains, bogs, rivers, lakes, campgrounds, springs, roads, trails, shelters, orchards, footbridges, national forests and parks, wildlife management areas, refuges, rapids and falls, as well as the contours of the land. All maps listed (unless otherwise noted) are scale 1:250,000 U.S. Geological Survey Maps, 1 inch to 4 miles ($2 each) or large-scale 7½- and 15-minute maps ($1.25 each for either). These maps and free *Topographic Map Indexes* of the Mid-Appalachian States may be ordered (along with a free *Map Symbol Chart* and *Topographic Maps* booklet) from: U.S. Geological Survey, Eastern Distribution, 1200 S. Eads St., Arlington, VA 22202. Be sure to include extra postage to expedite delivery of your order. Maps must be ordered by their individual names (indicate scale when ordering scale 1:250,000 maps).

Large-size, full-color U.S. Geological Survey *State Topographic* Maps of Virginia, West Virginia, Maryland, Delaware, Pennsylvania, and New Jersey are available with a scale of 1:500,000, or about 1 inch to 8 miles, $2 each. Strikingly beautiful U.S. Geological Survey *Shaded Relief Maps* of West Virginia, Virginia, Pennsylvania, New Jersey, and New York are available for $2 each. These magnificent maps are works of art, presenting a three-dimensional picture of the land's surface by the use of color shadings which give the map the appearance of sunlight striking its surface from the northwest. A free catalog, *Atlantic & Gulf Coasts Nautical Charts,* may be obtained by writing: National Ocean Survey, Distribution Branch (C 44), Riverdale, MD 20840. The catalog contains a complete listing of small-craft and recreational craft charts and nautical publications.

A useful 214-page handbook, *Be Expert with Map & Compass,* by Bjorn Kjellstrom, president and founder of Silva Compasses, may be obtained for $6.95 from: Charles Scribner's Sons, Bookstore Dept., 597 5th Ave., New York, NY 10017. Full-color *Plastic Raised Relief Maps* of all scale 1:250,000 overview maps listed in the Mid-Appalachian States sections may be obtained for $11.95 each from: Hubbard Scientific Co., 1946 Raymond Dr., Northbrook, IL 60062 (a free catalog is available upon request). These useful maps provide an actual three-dimensional model of the earth's surface and show all man-made and natural features.

Waterproof *Lake Contour Maps* of several of the Mid-Appalachian lakes and reservoirs, including Pennsylvania's famous Allegheny Reservoir, may be obtained from Lakes Illustrated, Box 4854 GS, Springfield, MO 65804. Write for free brochure and price list.

WEST VIRGINIA
ENCYCLOPEDIA

Accommodations— Vacation Resorts & Lodges

West Virginia's state parks offer excellent, inexpensive lodgings. Special low-priced park and forest family licenses are available to visitors. Detailed hunting and fishing regulations are available free on request at any field office or by writing: Travel Development Division, Dept. of Commerce, State Capitol, Charleston 25305.

All state park lodges operate year round, except for Mountain Creek (at Pipestream) and Tygart Lake, which are both closed during the winter season. Requests for reservations will be confirmed upon payment of the first night's lodging which should be included with the reservation request. If cancellations are received at least 48 hours prior to the reservation date, the deposit will be refunded. Current rate sheets for all lodges may be obtained from: Dept. of Commerce (address above).

Park/forest cabins are available in sizes accommodating from 2 to 8 persons. Additional cots may be reserved for most cabins to increase capacity. Not every facility has cabins of each size available. Rate sheets and applications for cabin reservations are available from any park or from the Charleston office, and these sheets list exact availabilities of cabins in individual parks and forests.

Reservations for cabins are made with: Cabins Reservation Office, Division of Parks and Recreation, State Capitol, Charleston 25305, phone (304) 348–2766. Reservations for the summer months are for 1 or 2 weeks only. After Labor Day through the second Monday in June, cabins in Canaan Valley can be reserved (only by the week) for ski season, which extends through December, January, February, and March. Any cabin not reserved by November 1 for 1-week periods will be available by the day or weekend.

West Virginia Hotels & Motels, an alphabetical listing by town, gives rates, number of units, facilities available, addresses, and phone numbers and can be obtained free from: Dept. of Commerce (address above). Descriptions of the state parks and forests, including detailed information on accommodations and public hunting and fishing areas, are contained in the booklet *West Virginia State Parks and Forests,* also available at no cost from the department.

Camping & State Recreation Areas

West Virginia's campgrounds are rapidly expanding to meet the boom in outdoor recreation, with new camping facilities opening each season. All campsites in the public hunting and fishing area campgrounds are rented on a first-come first-served basis with no advance reservations accepted. At many parks there are overflow areas which can handle limited extra campers on a 1-night basis in case late arrivals find all the permanent sites filled.

Four types of campsites are available. *Deluxe* campsites provide a grill or stove, tent pad, pull-off for trailers, hot showers, flush toilets, electric-sewer-water hookups on some sites, dumping station, and picnic table. The *standard* campsites are similar to the deluxe but with no hookups available. *Rustic* campsites provide pit toilets, well water, and improved sites with limited facilities. The *primitive* sites are just that —undeveloped areas designated for use by campers, primarily hunters and fishermen. Some have basic water and sanitation facilities.

Checkout time is 3:00 p.m. at campgrounds. Most campgrounds open in mid- to late April and close about November 1. Campers must pay a small fee for use of swimming areas and game courts. All park guests

are welcome to participate in nature programs, tours, and other organized activities.

Camping West Virginia, a brochure available free from: Travel Development Division, Dept. of Commerce, State Capitol, Charleston 25305, lists all campgrounds alphabetically by city, giving addresses, phone numbers, number and type of campsites, and a brief description of facilities. A list and map of public hunting and fishing area campgrounds is also found in *West Virginia State Parks & Forests*.

Canoeing & Wild-Water Expeditions

In spite of its name, the New River of West Virginia is geologically one of the oldest rivers in the country; rocks of extremely ancient origin have been found where the river cuts across the Narrows of Virginia, and before the Ice Age, it flowed as far north as the Great Lakes. Originating high in the Blue Ridge of North Carolina, the New River crosses Virginia and rushes noisily from the Appalachian foothills, entering "the Grand Canyon of the East" just southeast of Charleston. A raucous and wild 30-mile stretch of water between Prince and Fayette Station features powerful rapids and enormous waves and is generally run only by more intrepid experts. The second half of this run, between Thurmond and Fayette Station, is particularly treacherous. An ordinary riffle may suddenly turn into major rapids when the canoer realizes he is in a funnel with water precipitously converging toward a huge double wave.

Wildwater Expeditions Unlimited, P.O. Box 55, Thurmond 25936, a group of competent and experienced outdoorsmen, sponsors daily float trips on this exciting stretch of the New River. All trips begin and end in Thurmond, and *Wildwater Expeditions* provides transportation to the put-in at McCreery Beach near Prince, and return transportation from Fayette Station to the base camp near Thurmond. Trips are made on sturdy rubber rafts, 8 by 18 feet, and are divided into two parts, each about 15 miles—or both may be combined into a 2-day package. The first day's journey, beginning at 9:00 a.m., follows the river downstream through modest white-water rapids and ends at Thurmond, where guests are served dinner and sleep overnight in tents. The second phase of the trip, from Thurmond to Fayette Station down the New River Canyon, crosses some of the most impressive water in the East—waves from 8 to 16 feet rise between the sheer canyon walls, producing foaming wild water and an exciting, pitching, but ultimately safe adventure. Explicit instructions on water safety and life jackets are provided prior to the trip. The operators run a tight ship and warn that no matter what the circumstances, no infringements of the carefully articulated rules will be allowed. Stops are made for fishing, swimming, and a shore lunch each day. Trips on the Gauley River three times a year and fishing excursions on the Greenbrier River are also featured.

The New River offers other, gentler pleasures: relaxing trips where minimal effort allows the canoer to enjoy the lovely scenery along its shores. An 11-mile stretch of water between the Bluestone Dam and Sandstone has something for everyone: a scenic valley to pass through, flat water and easy rapids, and spectacular Brooks Falls, an impressive drop over the complete width of the river. Excellent fishing and numerous campgrounds have made the 15-mile run between Sandstone and McCreery equally popular, especially for overnight trips.

The New flows in an almost straight line through West Virginia, draining most of the state. Innumerable small tributaries flow in all directions from the river, but the most important are the Bluestone and the Greenbrier. A small river through out-of-the-way backcountry, the Bluestone was dubbed *Momongosenaka* ("big stone") by local Indians. A 25-mile run along the river from Spanishburg to Bluestone

State Park flows through an impressive narrow gorge lined with 200-foot waterfalls. Mountain Creek Lodge, a luxurious restaurant and inn, miraculously appears after 16 miles of wilderness and rapids, offering overnight accommodations for the weary paddler.

By far the most historic of West Virginia rivers, the great Potomac and its tributaries offer unlimited scenic wonders and white-water challenges. Huge cliffs and bizarre rock formations line the Cacapon and South Branch tributaries; Gaudy's Castle, Royal Glen, and Chanipe Rocks are only a few of the better-known "big rocks." Hundreds of other formations, seldom seen and unnamed, are known only to the white-water paddlers who brave the rapids in kayak or canoe. The canoeist will also find an underground paradise of caves in the South Branch highlands, where subterranean rivers have carved a labyrinth of damp chambers into the soft sedimentary rocks.

Following the many stretches of the Potomac and its branches—Abram Creek, Stony River, Seneca Creek, and Moorefield River—is much like tracing paths in America's past. Early explorers and settlers looked for a new land along these waters, and political boundaries were decided by the rivers themselves or their watersheds. The most celebrated of the Potomac's early navigators was George Washington. His hope of finding waterways connecting the Potomac and Ohio River basins was never realized, but the journals and records kept by Washington influenced subsequent exploration.

Major and minor runs on the New, Potomac, and other rivers and streams of West Virginia—the North Branch, Dry Fork, Juggart,

Blackwater, and more—are fully described in *Wild Water West Virginia,* by Bob Burrell and Paul Davidson. Each of the 9 chapters in this 162-page guide is prefaced by a regional introduction which points out history, scenic attractions, economics, natural history, and environmental threats for each area. Detailed information is provided for white-water paddlers for each river, carefully explaining access points, general hydrologic characteristics, key rapids, danger points and difficulties, and other characteristics helpful in planning a trip on each river. The book costs $6 and is available from: Paul Davidson, Dept. of Medicine, West Virginia University, Morgantown 26505. Include 3% West Virginia resident sales tax plus 25¢ for postage.

U.S. Geological Survey Maps for West Virginia's canoe trails show the entire length and the surrounding backcountry for the state's canoe routes and fishing streams (see "Wild River & Trout Stream Maps").

Cranberry Backcountry

This 53,000-acre area of dense forests, rushing streams, hills, and cranberry bogs, once known as the "Wilds of Pocahontas," is located in the Monongahela National Forest on the Allegheny Plateau. The area was logged extensively until 1934 when the backcountry was acquired by the U.S. Forest Service, but since opening to the public in 1945, the second-growth timber has developed into some of the

finest northern hardwood and red spruce stands in the East. The 750 acres that comprise the Cranberry Glades, presently designated a pioneer area, contain the southernmost extension of several northern forms of flora and fauna—plants and animals pushed south by glaciers thousands of years ago and now unique to this part of the country. In terms of terrain, the glades are actually a large sphagnum bog, similar to arctic tundra.

In spite of the relatively small deer population, the area is popular with hunters, who manage to bag substantial numbers of grouse and turkeys, as well as a few deer, each year. Designated a black bear sanctuary by the state, the backcountry's bear population, ranging from 75 to 200, roams the area unmolested by visitors or hunters.

By far the greatest attraction of the Cranberry Backcountry is the superb fishing in Cranberry River and the 2 miles of its South Fork, both of which are stocked with trout each week during April and May and again in the fall during small-game season. State hunting and fishing licenses and National Forest stamps are required in this area and may be obtained from county clerks or authorized license agents. Further information is available in the form of a brochure-map, free from: District Ranger, U.S. Forest Service, Richwood 26261, phone (304) 846–6558. A more extensive 41-page text describing the history of the area, its wildlife and terrain, mineral resources, and recreational opportunities, entitled *Cranberry Backcountry,* can be obtained for 90¢ from: Highlands Conservancy, Box 711, Webster Springs, 26288.

There are no roads in the Cranberry Backcountry—old jeep trails and logging roads have reverted to trails overgrown with vegetation. The landscape is particularly attractive to the hiker, especially the naturalist-hiker interested in unusual plant forms. Broad, forested ranges and narrow valleys, low cliffs, house-size boulders, and other rock outcrops are scattered throughout the area. Elevations range from 2,350 feet at Three Forks of the Williams River to 4,625 feet at the summit of Black Mountain. Backcountry trails provide access to the interior areas along the Middle Fork of the Williams and Cranberry rivers and to the Cranberry Glades. Cranberry Backcountry is shown on large-scale U.S. Geological Survey Maps: Lobelia, Merlinton, Mungo, Webster Springs SE, Webster Springs SW.

Dolly Sods Backcountry

This rugged backcountry wilderness of sphagnum bogs, extensive mats of heath shrubs, and scattered spruce forests is on the Allegheny Plateau adjacent to the Monongahela National Forest. The canyon of Red Creek cuts about 2,000 feet deep into the high plateau that forms most of the Dolly Sods. Its banks lined with dense rhododendron thickets, Red Creek is a swift stream flowing over large smooth rocks forming pools and waterfalls. Bare rocky outcrops at the canyon rim provide panoramic views. The plateau country in the Dolly Sods has an average elevation of almost 4,000 feet, with weather and vegetation characteristic of areas much farther north. Large areas of bog and meadow, where mosses and grasses are the predominant vegetation, give the Dolly Sods a degree of openness unusual in the central Appalachians. In appearance the area is similar to the tundra in northern Canada, with windblown spruces growing individually or in sparse clusters. Breeding birds include such northern species as the hermit thrush and winter wren. Beavers are common—the many dams they have constructed are among the main attractions of the area.

The Dolly Sods area remained a wilderness long after settlers had built their homes in the nearby valleys. During the Civil War a group of Confederate scouts reputedly built a fire that went out of control and

burned the Roaring Plains. Family expeditions to the high, open ridges where blueberries and cranberries grow in wild profusion were as popular in the 19th century as they are today. The meadows of the area, regions similar to the "balds" of the southern Appalachians, were used as grazing lands for sheep and cattle and were called sods by the local inhabitants. Because the Dolly (or Dahle) family used the meadows in the southern end of the Rohrbaugh Plains, the whole region eventually became known as the Dolly Sods. At one time the magnificent spruce forests sheltered mountain lions, elk, and wolves—big-game animals long extinct in this part of the country.

A 69-page paperbound *Guide to the Dolly Sods Backcountry,* describing the history of the area, major trails (such as Bald Knob, Bear Rocks, and Big Stonecoal), natural resources, hunting and fishing regulations, and containing several maps, is available for 90¢ from: Highlands Conservancy, Box 711, Webster Springs, 26288.

The U.S. Forest Service offers two maps that are useful for getting around: *Monongahela National Forest* (50¢) shows the entire forest and environs in a color topographic map (¼ inch to 1 mile); *Spruce Knob-Seneca Rocks National Recreation Area* (free) includes the Dolly Sods area (½ inch to 1 mile), and is not a topographic map. Both maps can be ordered from: U.S. Forest Service, Box 1231, Elkins 26241. (See "Monongahela National Forest" and "Spruce Knob-Seneca Rocks Backcountry" for further map information.)

Additional information, including the maps just described, can be obtained from: Potomac District Ranger's Office, Petersburg 26847, phone (304) 257-7111. The office, just west of Petersburg on Route 4–28, is open 8:00 to 5:00 on weekdays only. It is advisable to call here for snow information before planning trips in late fall, winter, or early spring.

Dolly Sods Backcountry is shown on the following large-scale U.S. Geological Survey Maps: Blackbird Falls, Blackbird Knob, Hopeville, Laneville. Maps for Mount Storm Lake and Davis, also available from the U.S. Geological Survey, are needed too for the northern Canaan Valley and the upper Stony River Watershed.

Fishing & Hunting in West Virginia

West Virginia's rugged Appalachian Highlands, national and state forest lands, remote wild areas, and wild, turbulent rivers and mountain streams offer some of the finest hunting and fishing opportunities in the eastern United States. The Wildlife Resources Division of the Department of Natural Resources maintains 35 areas for hunting, fishing, camping, or access to the prime fishing and hunting lands, including the Monongahela and portions of the Jefferson and George Washington national forests, and nine state forests. West Virginia offers over a million acres of public lands to the outdoorsman. Basically the state is divided into two physiographic regions by the Allegheny Front. The Allegheny Plateau covers the western two-thirds of the state, where hundreds of streams cut the region into a maze of wooded valleys and rolling hills. The scenic highlands in the northeast portion of the plateau, where more than 40 peaks exceed 4,000-foot elevations in the Monongahela National Forest, give rise to fast-flowing trout streams that form the headwaters of the state's major rivers, including the famous smallmouth bass waters of the South Branch of the Potomac, and the wild Cheat, Elk, Gauley, Tygart, and Greenbrier rivers. The Monongahela, Kanawha, and the wild New River tributaries of the Ohio River drain an area of approximately 21,000 square miles.

The state's principal game fish are the scrappy, acrobatic smallmouth bass, found in most warmwater streams of the state; the elusive mus-

kellunge, found in the big-river tributaries of the Ohio; and brook, brown, and rainbow trout in the lakes and streams of the eastern highlands. The diversity and potential of the state's fishing opportunities are illustrated by a list of West Virginia record fish, compiled and maintained by the Department of Natural Resources.

WEST VIRGINIA RECORD FISH

	Lb.	Place	Year
Largemouth bass	10.0	Coal River	1968
Smallmouth bass	9.75	South Branch, Potomac	1971
Muskellunge	43.5	Elk River	1955
Northern pike	11.25	Elk River	1973
Brook trout	3.76	Rich Creek	1969
Brown trout	16.0	South Branch, Potomac	1968
Golden-rainbow trout hybrid	4.5	Fly Fishing Section, Shavers Fork	1975
Rainbow trout	10.0	Spruce Knob Lake	1956
Walleye	16.19	New River	1967
Yellow perch	1.75	Pond (Monongalia Co.)	1971
Rock bass	1.7	Big Sandy Creek	1964
Spotted bass	3.2	South Fork, Hughes River	1966
Striped bass	11.75	Ohio River	1977
White bass	4.0	Kanawha River	1964
Bluegill	2.31	Farm Pond (Pendleton Co.)	1973
Bowfin	4.5	Little Coal River	1975
Carp	40.1	New River	1970
Bullhead catfish	3.9	Ohio River	1975
Channel catfish	22.75	Farm Pond (Jefferson Co.)	1975
Shovelhead catfish	70.0	Little Kanawha River	1956
Chain pickerel	4.1	Back Creek	1968
Crappie	4.05	Meathouse Fork	1971
Paddlefish	70.0	Little Kanawha River	1965
Sauger	2.01	Ohio River	1974
Skipjack	1.9	Ohio River	1960
Sturgeon	12.5	Ohio River	1949
Fallfish	3.5	North Fork of South Branch	1970
Freshwater drum	25.0	Little Kanawha River	1954
Gar (longnose)	17.5	Elk River	1975
Goldeye	2.75	Middle Island Creek	1963

Mountain Lakes & Streams

As the state records show, the rushing mountain streams and lakes hold smallmouth, largemouth, and spotted bass; brook, rainbow, golden-rainbow, and brown trout; walleye, muskellunge, white bass, crappie, bluegill, channel catfish, and the recently introduced striped bass and voracious northern pike. The most productive smallmouth bass waters include the famous South Branch of the Potomac, home of the state record, and the Greenbrier, Little Kanawha, and Ohio rivers. The smallmouth is often caught by spin casting with medium, light, and ultralight tackle using Mepps spinners and artificial lures resembling minnows, crayfish, frogs, and night crawlers.

The most productive trout fishing is found in the remote backcountry glades of the picturesque Cranberry River in the Monongahela Na-

tional Forest, and in the Williams, South Branch of the Potomac near Petersburg, North Fork of the Cheat River, Shavers Fork of the Cheat, and the Elk River above Webster Springs. Some of the state's finest trout fishing is found among the tundralike bogs, beaver meadows, and wilderness highlands of the Monongahela National Forest. Access is by hiking trails and packhorse. The state has established quality trout fishing "catch and release" regulations on the Back Fork of the Elk River in Webster County, beginning 2 miles upstream from Webster Springs, extending upstream 4 miles; and on the Shavers Fork, a 5½-mile section in the Monongahela National Forest in Randolph County, north of U.S. 250, extending downstream to the mouth of McGee Run. The Back Fork can be reached from state secondary routes 29 and 24/3; Shavers Fork can be reached from National Forest Route 92, which intersects U.S. 250, 4 miles west of Cheat Bridge.

"Fly fishing only" sections for wild trout enthusiasts have been established on Edwards Run in a marked area within the boundaries of the Edwards Run Public Hunting & Fishing Area in Hampshire County; on Otter Creek and tributaries in the Monongahela National Forest in Randolph and Tucker counties, with year round fishing permitted; and on scenic Rich Creek in a marked area offering year-round fishing in Monroe County. All fish caught in these waters must be released.

The useful *West Virginia Stream Map,* showing the Mountain State's major trout and fishing streams and illustrations of the major game fish, may be obtained free by writing: Division of Wildlife Resources, Dept. of Natural Resources, State Capitol, Charleston 25305. This large, handy map shows the locations of all lakes and streams stocked with trout. The state's progressive stocking program releases over 1 million trout each year.

Trophy Muskellunge Waters

Temperamental, tackle-busting muskellunge up to 43 pounds are caught in the Elk River, called *Tis-chil-waugh* by the Shawnee Indians, meaning "river of plenty fat elk," downstream from Sutton. The Elk is West Virginia's largest river, flowing for 172 miles from its headwaters in western Pocahontas County to its confluence with the Kanawha River at Charleston. The state record musky was caught on a spinner in the Elk in 1955 at the mouth of the Birch River. Other important muskellunge waters include the Little Kanawha and Hughes rivers and Middle Island Creek. The most productive fishing is during the fall months, using live creek chubs, suckers, or large minnows. The West Virginia Husky Musky Club is an organization established for the recognition of state-caught muskies. To be eligible for membership an angler must catch a legal-size musky (28 inches) from West Virginia waters. The angler submitting an application with a witness and (if possible) a color photo, automatically becomes a club member and will be presented with a membership certificate at an annual awards banquet. Special certificates will be awarded to fishermen who catch a musky at least 40 inches in length. Applications should be mailed to: Division of Wildlife Resources, Dept. of Natural Resources, Rte. 2, Belleville 26133.

Fat walleyes up to 15 pounds are caught on minnow imitations, spinners, and live minnows in the Greenbrier, Ganby, New, and Elk rivers. The state's most productive white bass waters are the New River drainage, especially Bluestone Lake, where bass up to 3 pounds are caught on doll flies, lures, streamers, and live minnows. The best crappie waters are the Bluestone, Sutton Reservoir on the Elk River, and Summerville Lake. Channel catfish, bluegills, and largemouth bass are found in practically all warmwater streams, lakes, and state impoundments.

Float-Fishing Waters

The state's wide, swift trophy smallmouth bass, muskellunge, and walleye rivers are best fished from a boat. These streams offer excellent float-trip fishing, where water conditions are suitable, and allow access to the large- and smallmouths and walleye that feed among the huge boulders and limestone ledges of these deep-flowing streams. Float-trip outfitters serve the state's major rivers. (See "Wilderness & Wild River Outfitters.") Some of the more popular trips recommended by the Department of Natural Resources are listed below.

SOUTH BRANCH FLOAT TRIPS

From	To	Miles
Smoke Hole P.O.	Pendleton-Grant Co. line	3.0
Pendleton-Grant Co. line	Redman Run	8.0
Redman Run	Mouth of North Fork	3.25
Mouth of North Fork	Petersburg Bridge	4.0
Petersburg Bridge	Petersburg Gap (220)	2.5
Petersburg Gap (220)	Fisher Bridge	8.0
Fisher Bridge	Mouth of South Fork	1.75
Mouth of South Fork	Oldfield Bridge	3.0
Oldfield Bridge	McNeil (R.R. trestle)	5.0
McNeil (R.R. trestle)	Glebe	6.0
Glebe	Romney	10.0
Romney	Hanging Rock	4.5
Hanging Rock	Blue Beach (above ski area)	3.25
Blue Beach (Bridge)	Milleson Mill	7.0
Milleson Mill	Iron Bridge	2.5
Iron Bridge	Blue Ford	4.75
Blue Ford	Indian Rock	4.0
Indian Rock (Horse Shoe Bend)	Mouth of South Branch	4.0
Virginia line	Smoke Hole P.O.	33.25

CACAPON RIVER FLOAT TRIPS

From	To	Miles
Yellow Spring	Where road leaves river above Hooks Mill	4.5
Where road leaves river above Hooks Mill	Capon Bridge	7.0
Cold Stream	Rte. 45 Bridge	7.0
Rte. 45 Bridge	Largent	16.5
Largent	Rte. 9 Bridge	8.0
Rte. 9 Bridge	Dam—power plant	7.0

GREENBRIER RIVER FLOAT TRIPS

From	To	Miles
East end of Alderson	Pence Springs Bridge	8.5
Pence Springs Bridge	Talcott Bridge	4.5
Talcott Bridge	Willow Wood Bridge	10.0
Anthony Bridge	Caldwell Bridge	12.7
Harpers Sliding	Ronceverte	9.0

The float from Talcott to Willow Wood has two falls to be portaged.

NEW RIVER FLOAT TRIPS

From	To	Miles
Below Sandstone Falls	Prince	12.0
Prince	Thurmond	12.0

Only experienced canoeists and boaters should attempt to float fish the New River. Portaging some areas will be necessary.

West Virginia fishing and hunting regulations, bag and possession limits, opening and closing dates; a trout stocking schedule listing each stream, county location, and frequency stocked; a listing of public fishing lakes and pounds, indicating trout waters, stocking schedules, tailwaters, boating, and camping; and bear and turkey hunting maps may all be obtained free by writing: Dept. of Natural Resources (Charleston address above).

Hunting

The state's scenic Appalachian highlands, mixed conifer and hardwood forests, valleys, and gently rolling hills offer excellent hunting for ruffed grouse, quail, pheasant, woodcock, wild turkey, gray squirrel, cottontails, raccoon, bobcat, deer, and black bear. The whitetail deer population, near extinction at the turn of the century from logging and mining activities, today is over 100,000 and growing. The best hunting areas are found in the uplands of the Monongahela National Forest region. The dwindling population of black bear, which once roamed in good numbers throughout the state, are now protected in the Otter Creek and Cranberry Glades backcountry areas of the Monongahela National Forest. Wild turkey, brought close to extinction because of slaughter for food during the early pioneer days, have been brought back to former population levels and today offer excellent fall hunting on the state and national forest public hunting lands. The handsome ruffed grouse is the state's most important upland game bird, found along the primitive roads, streams, and burns in the mountainous state and national forest hunting areas. The bobwhite quail is concentrated along the scenic wooded river valleys and farmlands in the eastern counties. A substantial number of woodcock are shot each year, especially in the Canaan Valley. The state also offers limited shooting for pheasant, wood ducks, and a very few mallards, blacks, teal, and Canada goose.

Highways—Recreation & Scenic

The state's highway and road system is shown on a full-color *West Virginia Highway & Tourist Map* available free from: Travel Development Division, Dept. of Commerce, State Capitol, Charleston 25305. The map shows all major and secondary roads, airports, points of interest, and state and national forests. It also contains a state park and forests facilities chart and camping information. One of the major features of the state's scenic highway system is the New River Bridge, which carries the Appalachian Corridor "L" highway across a scenic gorge deep in the hills of Fayette County. The bridge is the world's longest steel arch, with a main span of 1,700 feet across the canyon.

Monongahela National Forest

The Monongahela, which includes such wilderness areas as Dolly Sods, Otter Creek, and Cranberry Backcountry, stretches over 830,000 acres of the Allegheny Mountain range. The highest peak in this mountainous wilderness and also the highest point in West Virginia is Spruce Knob (4,862 feet), in the Spruce Knob-Seneca Rocks National Recreation Area. To the northeast of Spruce Knob, still within the recreation area, are the Seneca Rocks—sheer-faced, towering rocks which erupt dramatically nearly 1,000 feet out of the edgeline forest of rolling pasture land. Within the forest boundaries are the headwaters of three major river systems; the Monongahela, Potomac, and Greenbrier.

Auto touring is a popular way of getting around the park, but there are also many trails for hikers along clear mountain streams, through forested valleys, and across highland bogs. In many reaches of the park, the harsh climate and rocky soil will support little vegetation except mosses, ferns, and sparse shrubbery. Interesting features of the park include Smoke Hole, where cool air from the many caves meets the moist warm air from the gorge, forming a smoky mist, and the Falls of Hills Creek—three stunning waterfalls along a short stretch of the creek. Remnants of a vast virgin spruce forest still stand near Gaudineer Scenic Area. The *Monongahela National Forest Map*, showing these and other recreation sites, highways, campgrounds, historical sites, railroads, ranger stations, and major topographic features, is available for 50¢ from: U.S. Forest Service, Box 1231, Elkins 26241. Access and supply centers include Marlinton, Webster Springs, Monterey, Cherry Grove, Petersburg, and Beverly.

Even though Monongahela's trees were extensively felled during the early part of this century, the second-growth timber that now blankets the area provides a wide diversity of species. The forest is essentially an eastern hardwoods area, but many highland regions are reminiscent of the dense forests of eastern Canada. Forest and valley alike abound with many forms of plant and animal life, including the timid black bear and wild turkey. Trout, muskie, catfish, and smallmouth bass are found in the park's numerous streams, including the Cranberry, Upper Potomac, and Elk rivers. Members of the plant kingdom are also a source of fascination: the forest floor supports mosses and ferns in lush profusion, and the waxy-leaved laurel and rhododendron have found a comfortable habitat in the cathedral-like spaces between tall trees.

West Virginia Stream Map

Tips on hiking year round and descriptions of trails are provided in a *Hiking Guide to Monongahela and Vicinity*, a 147-page guide to all parts of the area (except Dolly Sods and Otter Creek, which are covered under separate titles). Maps, descriptions of interesting features, and an extensive bibliography to the hiker's West Virginia are included. Priced at $1.50 the book is available from: Highlands Conservancy, Canaan Valley, Davis 26260. (For additional information on parts of Monongahela, see "Dolly Sods Backcountry," "Otter Creek Backcountry," and "Spruce Knob-Seneca Rocks Backcountry.")

Monongahela National Forest is shown on U.S. Geological Survey Maps (scale 1:250,000): Charleston, Charlottesville (VA), Clarksburg, Cumberland (VA).

Otter Creek Backcountry

Nestled among the mountains in northeastern West Virginia, Otter Creek backcountry in the Monongahela National Forest is a remote 20,000-acre wilderness of unspoiled streams and valleys, forests, and mountains. The Otter Creek Valley is a complete drainage basin with no roads, dwellings, or other visible signs of civilization to mar its natural beauty. Running for 11 miles through the valley and followed by an excellent trail along its 1,200-foot drop to the Dry Fork River, Otter Creek itself has become the area's primary attraction. The course of the creek is often turbulent, as swiftly flowing waters pass through mazes of boulders and ledges. Parallel mountain ridges, reaching heights of 3,800 feet, encircle a 4-mile-wide oval basin, with a system of small streams draining down to the main creek. The area includes three bogs containing unusual plant species and a stand of virgin hemlock. Extensive parts of the area are blanketed with nearly impenetrable masses of waxy-leaved rhododendrons—harmless but dense obstacles to traveling off the trails.

A network of more than 40 miles of well-maintained foot trails plus many unmarked paths through solitary valleys have made Otter Creek a mecca for hikers and backpackers. A 31-page description of the area, *Otter Creek* (90¢) containing information on trails and maps, is available from: Highlands Conservancy, Box 711, Webster Springs, 26288. The booklet outlines the backbone of the entire system, the Otter Creek Trail, plus several other, shorter trails and points of interest along the way. A simple map of the area can also be obtained free from: Cheat District Ranger, U.S. Forest Service, Parsons 26287. Trails shown on this map are generally well cleared and signed, with most marked by blue paint on trees; however, the trails may often be wet and muddy. Otter Creek is usually less than knee deep where the trails cross the stream, but it may be above the waist and fast-moving during high water following periods of prolonged rain. The trails are not suitable for horses. There are two Adirondack-type shelters in the wilderness, each of which will accommodate 6 people, available on a first-come first-served basis.

One of West Virginia's finest hunting areas, Otter Creek backcountry supports a varied wildlife population, including white-tailed deer, wild turkey, grouse, snowshoe hare, and cottontail rabbits. The area is one of about four in the state large and wild enough to harbor a breeding population of black bear. A small number of brook trout may soon be increased by regular stocking of streams; fishing is permitted downstream of Turkey Run and in all tributaries. Hunting and fishing are subject to state regulations. Special fishing regulations are in effect for Otter Creek. Check the state regulations before pursuing either sport.

Otter Creek Backcountry, is shown on the following large-scale U.S. Geological Survey Maps: Bowden, Harman, Mozark Mountain, Parsons. The Forest Service advises that these maps are excellent for topographic information, but trail locations shown are not all correct.

Ski Touring & Snowshoeing

Of West Virginia's several excellent ski facilities, *Snowshoe Resort*, a private 6,000-acre development, offers one of the most comprehensive cross-country ski programs in the South. Located in the Monongahela National Forest near the site of the pioneering village of Old Spruce, Snowshoe features 10 miles of well-maintained ski touring trails with a system of warming huts. Among the more popular tours are Bear Pen

Ramble, 3½ miles from the resort center on a gradual descent down the northwest bowl returning via Cup Run lift, and Shavers Run, 4 miles from the resort center, southeast around part of Snowshoe basin rim with a gradual descent into the valley terminating at Shavers Pond. For novice skiers there is the Leather Bark Loop, a gentle 1.5-mile loop trail along the top of Snowshoe basin. Snowshoe also offers 4½ miles of slopes, a luxurious lodge and resort center, and special vacation packages. For information, write: Snowshoe, Slatyfork 26291; phone (304) 799–6600.

There are several other areas in Monongahela National Forest with good ski touring potential. Since forest roads are closed in winter, the Bear Rocks, Dolly Sods, and other areas in West Virginia are often inaccessible in winter except to the skier or snowshoer. For information on the high, treeless plains with altitudes of 4,000 to 6,000 feet in the Dolly Sods, Bear Rocks, and Otter Creek contact: District Ranger, U.S. Forest Service, Parsons 26287. The Seneca Rocks-Spruce Knobs National Recreation Area, featuring West Virginia's highest peak at 4,863 feet, has many miles of trails suitable for ski touring. Additional attractions are the waterfalls along Spruce Forest and shelters near Judy Springs. Contact: District Ranger, U.S. Forest Service, Petersburg 26847, for details.

A 1,700-acre state park near Davis with 70–100 inches of snow annually and miles of trails, Blackwater Falls is open year round and is a good base for day ski tours. Nearby Canaan Valley State Park receives up to 140 inches of snow and offers many side trails leading from the downhill ski slopes. For additional information, write: Blackwater Falls Lodge, Davis 26260, phone (304) 259–5216; or Canaan Valley Resorts, P.O. Box 368, Davis 26260, phone (304) 866–4121.

Coopers Rock State Forest, a 13,000-acre area near Morgantown and the Pennsylvania line, includes a small ski area—a good starting point for ski tours on backwoods roads throughout the forest. Contact Coopers Rock State Forest Headquarters, Bruceton Mills 26525.

Free maps are available for Spruce Knobs-Seneca Rocks National Recreation Area and Monongahela National Forest from: Forest Service, U.S. Dept. of Agriculture, Elkins 26241.

Spruce Knob-Seneca Rocks Backcountry

Some of the most rugged country in West Virginia is found in the Seneca Rocks-Spruce National Recreation Area, a 100,000-acre wilderness situated just below Otter Creek and the Dolly Sods on the Monongahela National Forest. The terrain offers sharp contrasts as bold mountain peaks rise from thick stands of pine trees, then fall away along sheer-faced cliffs to rolling valleys and open pasturelands. Spruce Knob itself is the high point of Spruce Mountain and, at 4,862 feet, the highest point in the state. An area of windblown red spruce and rock outcrops, it is easily accessible by road and affords excellent views of the mountains to the east and west. Seneca Rocks, a 1,000-foot-high quartzite formation, rises above the North Fork Valley at the mouth of Seneca Creek. Renowned as the best rock climb in the East, the rocks have been nicknamed the "Face of 1,000 Pitons" because of the many spikes driven by climbers into the stubborn surface. Nearby and rivaling the famous Seneca Rocks are the similar formations of Champe Rock, Blue Rock, and Chimney Rock. Another spectacular rock formation is Eagle Rock, named for Colonel William Eagle, who enlisted in the army at the age of 15 and fought at Valley Forge. He died in 1848 and is buried near the base of the rock.

Other places of interest especially favored by hikers include North Fork Mountain, or North Mountain, in the eastern part of the Spruce Knob-Seneca Rocks backcountry. Extending the length of the area,

the mountain is threaded with several trails which offer panoramic views of the park. Seneca Creek, originating on Spruce Mountain, is an exceptionally beautiful stream with spectacular waterfalls and some of the best trout fishing around. Again, well-maintained trails follow the creek's course, some of which are actually old railroad grades, reminders of the area's exploitation by timber barons in the earlier part of the century. Descriptions of these and other trails—among others, Big Rock, Allegheny, and Horton-Horserock—are found in the *Hiking Guide to Monongahela and Vicinity* (see "Monongahela National Forest"). The *Spruce Knob-Seneca Rocks Area Map*, defining trails, roads, recreation sites, campgrounds, and points of interest, is available free from: U.S. Forest Service, Box 1231, Elkins 26241.

Three tracts of land within the area—around Seneca Creek, Smoke Hole, and Hopeville Gorge—have been declared pioneer zones and are managed as unspoiled wilderness areas by the U.S. Forest Service. Of particular interest is the Smoke Hole, a canyon through which the South Branch of the Potomac flows for 20 miles; for over half the distance it is flanked by a quiet, scenic road. Smoke Hole Cave, a circular chamber about 40 feet high and 15 feet in diameter, was allegedly used by Indians as a smoke curing chamber for preserving meat. Another explanation for its name derives from the shroud of smokelike mist which forms when moist air rising from the caves meets the cooler air outside. Spruce Knob-Seneca Rocks Area large-scale U.S. Geological Survey Maps: Bowden, Circleville, Glady, Omega, Sinks of Ganby, Spruce Knob, Whitmer.

Wilderness & Wild River Outfitters

The Appalachian Trail Conference, responsible for the building and maintenance of the 2,000 miles of trail winding from Maine to Georgia, lists over 100 affiliate clubs with programs for year-round camping, hiking, ski touring, and mountaineering. For information, write: ATC, Box 236, Harpers Ferry 25425, phone (304) 535-6331.

The only guide service for hikers in the wilds of the New River Canyon, *Pack Trips Unlimited*, P.O. Box 55, Thurmond 25936, phone (304) 469-2551, sponsors hikes through 15 miles of gentle to rugged terrain in the company of an experienced guide and trusty pack mules. Trips through the canyon, surrounding plateau area, and several ghost towns are offered December through March, 2–7 days, for small groups of hikers. Custom-tailored hikes are also available.

Honey C Stables, in the Rock Gap-Berkeley Springs region of northeast West Virginia, offers "walking trips" on horseback through the area. Groups of 12 to 15 riders are guided by expert horsemen on trips ranging from 1 to 7 days. Deer, wild turkey, and bobcats are often encountered; rivers are crossed on horseback; a float trip is even offered. For details, write: Honey C Stables, Rte. 1, Berkeley Springs 25411. Regularly scheduled and custom expeditions are offered.

Float trips covering 12 miles of wild water on the great Cheat River are offered by *Cheat Canyon Expeditions*, Box 194, Albright 26519. Billed as the "great-grandaddy of all eastern white-water runs," the Cheat belies the fraudulent overtones of its name, guaranteeing more bumps, waves, and rapids than any other run of its length in the East. Six-hour trips are offered April to June on 12- and 20-foot rafts. A shuttle service, lunch, and experienced guides are included. *Cheat River Outfitters*, Box 117, Albright 26519, phone (304) 465–1608, also offers white-water adventures along 13 miles of the river. In top-quality 8-man rafts navigated by seasoned experts, anyone from 14 years up can enjoy the challenge of over 38 rapids of class 3, 4, and 5 difficulty. Two trips per day are sponsored.

Transmontane Outfitters, an extension of *Wildwater Expeditions Unlimited* (see "Canoeing & Wild-Water Expeditions"), sponsors activities for youth groups and families in the heart of the Monongahela National Forest that cover a broad range of outdoor experiences: canoeing through the bogs of the Blackwater, Cheat River, Shavers Fork, Smoke Hole, Hopeville Canyon, Laurel Fork, Glady Fork, and Dry Fork Canyon; backpacking in the arctic tundra of Dolly Sods, Otter Creek Wilderness, Canaan Mountain Area, and Laurel Fork Wilderness; caving in the Sinks of Ganby; and ski touring and snowshoeing. A skills workshop for each adventure and seminars in wildlife photography and mountain crafts are also offered. The Appalachian Mountains are the base for all operations, June through August 1. For information, write: Transmontane Outfitters, Main St., Davis 26260. (September to May, write: G. M. Bowers III, 215 W. Brook Run Dr., Richmond, VA 23233). The *Trail Riders of the Wilderness* program sponsored by: American Forestry Assn., 1319 18th Street, NW, Washington, DC 20036, offers July pack trips into the rugged Cacapon Mountains, along its rim to Bear Wallows and Seldom Seen Valley, with a 1-day float on the Cacapon River.

Wild River & Trout Stream Maps

The following large-scale U.S. Geological Survey Topographic Map Kits show the entire lengths and surrounding backwoods of West Virginia's renowned wild rivers and blue-ribbon trout streams. The maps will provide the wilderness paddler and angler with a complete three-dimensional picture of the area he plans to visit, including trails, logging roads, swamps, falls, rapids, footbridges, gradient, and contours. The canoe-fishing along many of these streams, such as the Cheat and New rivers, is excellent for walleye, smallmouth bass, and trophy muskellunge up to 40 pounds. *Blackwater River:* Parsons, Mozark Mountain, Blackwater Falls, Davis; *Cacapon River:* Wardensville, Yellow Spring, Capon Springs, Capon Bridge, Largent, Ridge, Great Cacapon; *Cheat River:* George, Kingwood, Lake Lynn (PA), Masontown, Parsons, Rowlesburg, Valley Point; *Cranberry River:* Lobelia, Marlinton, Mingo, Webster Springs SE, Webster Springs SW; *Dry Fork:* Mozark Mountain, Harman, Whitmer; *Otter Creek:* Bowden, Parsons, Mozark Mountain; *Horse Shoe Run:* St. George, Lead Mine, Aurora; *Mill Creek:* Upper Tract, Mozer, Petersburg W, Petersburg E; *Back Fork of Elk & Sugar Creek:* Webster Springs, Bergoo, Skett, Pickens; *Glady Creek Fork:* Glady, Bowden, Harman, Mozark Mountain; *Stony River & Lake:* Blackbird, Knob, Mount Storm Lake, Greenland Gap, Gorman, Mount Storm; *South Fork:*

Palo Alto, Sugar Grove, Brandywine, Fort Seybert 7.5, Mozer, Milam, Petersburg E, Lost River State Park, Moorefield; *Rich Creek:* Matoaka, Athens; *Lost River & Trout Run:* Bergton (VA), Orkney Springs (VA), Lost City, Needmore, Baker, Wardensville, Wolf Gap; *Seneca Creek:* Spruce Knob, Whitmer, Onego; *Ganby Creek:* Spruce Knob, Sinks of Ganby, Whitmer, Harman; *North Fork:* Snowy Mountain, Spruce Knob, Circleville, Onego, Upper Tract, Hopeville, Petersburg W; *Laurel Fork:* Sinks of Ganby, Glady, Whitmer, Harman; *Elk River Float Trip:* Bergoo, Big Chimney, Blue Creek, Charleston E, Clay, Clendenin, Diana, Elkhurst, Gassaway, Herold, Ivydale, Mingo, Newton, Newville, Pickens, Skett, Strange Creek, Sutton, Webster Springs; *Greenbrier River:* Cass, Durbin, Lobelia, Marlinton, Mingo, White Sulphur Springs; *New Wild & Scenic River* (including Bluestone Reservoir): Beckley, Beckwith, Cedar Grove, Charleston E, Eechwah, Fayetteville, Forest Hill, Meadow Creek, Montgomery, Peterstown, Pipestem; *South Branch Potomac River:* Circleville, Hanging Rock, Keyser 15, Moorefield, Oldtown, Petersburg E, Petersburg W, Rig, Upper Tract; *Shavers Fork River:* Beverly E, Bowden, Cass, Durbin, Elkins, Glady, Parsons; *Tygart Valley River:* Beverly E, Beverly W, Durbin, Elkins.

Accommodations—
Vacation Resorts & Lodges

For listings of local hunting, fishing, and vacation resorts write to: Chamber of Commerce, 611 E. Franklin St., Richmond 23219; Travel Service, 911 E. Broad St., Richmond 23219, or to the local chamber of commerce of the area you plan to visit.

Appalachian National Scenic Trail

Of the 14 states through which the Appalachian Trail passes on its 2,000-mile long journey, Virginia boasts the largest share of this historic footpath. About 500 miles of trail, or one-fourth the total mileage, winds through the state, beginning at Snickers Gap near the West Virginia border and ending in the Jefferson National Forest from which it enters Cherokee National Forest in Tennessee.

The first segment of the Appalachian Trail to be established between New York State and the Great Smokies was opened in 1927 south of Harpers Ferry, West Virginia, by the nascent Potomac Appalachian Trail Club. Within 2 years the trail became a reality, passing through Shenandoah National Park as far as Rockfish Gap. South of Rockfish Gap the trail follows the same narrow ridge as the Blue Ridge Parkway, crossing the confused jumble of ridges that stretch north to south with cross ranges separated by high gaps and deep valleys. Farther south the trail enters the Pedlar district of George Washington National Forest, following peaks which parallel the Blue Ridge Parkway. Side trails lead away from the main path, exploring the summits of the Religious Range, 50 miles of mountain region whose high points were piously christened the Friar, Little Friar, Priest, Little Priest, and Cardinal. Beyond the James River the trail crosses the Glenwood district of the Jefferson National Forest and is again on the borderlands of the parkway. The trail crosses the Valley of Virginia about 10 miles north of Roanoke and enters the Allegheny Mountains, following that range throughout the rest of Virginia. After reentering the Jefferson National Forest it reaches the end of the Virginia stretch at Damascus, just north of the Virginia-Tennessee line. (See "Jefferson National Forest" in the "Travel & Recreation Guide" section.)

Since most of the Appalachian Trail in Virginia winds through publicly owned lands—Shenandoah National Park, Jefferson and George Washington national forests, and lands bordering on the Blue Ridge Parkway—the scenery and wildlife tend to be unspoiled and well protected. For the most part the country is rugged, and the main footpaths and side trails penetrate heavily forested areas or skirt the summits of high cliffs, affording wide and spectacular vistas. Each season imposes its own particular beauty. In spring, carpets of flowers in riotous colors grace the area. Lush azaleas and rhododendrons are so profuse in summer that travel on side trails often becomes difficult. In autumn, the colorful foliage of southern hardwoods is justifiably famous. Even winter has its attractions: broad, snow-covered stretches, glimpsed between naked branches, and streams choked with ice floats. Various species of wildlife are often sighted along the trail; white-tailed deer are most common, but an occasional black bear, gray fox, or bobcat may put in a sudden appearance.

Trail guides published by the Appalachian Trail Conference are invaluable in following the footpath. For Virginia, three guides to the Appalachian Trail are needed to complete the entire route. The *Susquehanna River to the Shenandoah National Park and Side Trails* ($4.79; no maps) covers the trail from Clarks Ferry Bridge in Pennsylvania through Maryland, West Virginia, and northern Virginia as far as Shenandoah Park. The *Guide to the Appalachian Trail & Side Trails in Shenandoah National Park* ($4.79; no maps) covers the major

and minor trails through the whole of the park, between Chester and Rockfish gaps. *Central and Southwestern Virginia* ($6.10; including maps) follows the trail from Rockfish Gap through Jefferson and George Washington national forests to the Tennessee border. Each guide contains profuse trail data (from north to south *and* from south to north), including mileage, difficulty, points of interest, campgrounds, recreation areas, and points of access and exit. The natural and human history of the area and the story of the Appalachian Trail are provided in some detail. Guides may be ordered from: Appalachian Trail Conference, P.O. Box 236, Harpers Ferry, WV 25425. Please allow 3 weeks delivery, or to expedite shipment include $1 for special mailing and note the addition with your order.

Maps for the trail may also be ordered separately: PATC Map #7 covers the North Virginia trail section from Harpers Ferry to Snickers Gap ($1); PATC Map #8 follows the trail between Snickers and Chester gaps ($1); PATC Maps #9, 10, and 11 show the trail in the Shenandoah National Park ($3.25). Each map shows the Appalachian and side trails, shelters, lookout towers, names of mountain ridges, rivers and creeks, roads, towns, and highways. Maps may be ordered from: ATC (above address). National forest and park maps also show the trail, though not in such concentrated detail, and may be obtained from the appropriate forest or park supervisor's office. (See all three parts of the "Travel & Recreation Guide" section.)

The following U.S. Geological Survey Map Kits cover the Appalachian Trail. *Harpers Ferry:* Ashby Gap, Bluemont, Charles Town (WV), Harpers Ferry (WV), Linden, Round Hill, Upperville; *Jefferson National Forest:* Arnold Valley, Buchanan, Daleville, Montvale, Snowden, Villamont; *Shenandoah National Park:* Bentonville, Chester Gap, Elkton, Madison, Stony Man, Thornton Gap, University, Waynesboro; *Brushy Mountain:* Atkins, Damascus, Konnarock, Trout Dale, Whitetop Mountain; *Southwest Virginia to Catawba Mountain:* Catawba, Craig Springs, Daleville, Glenvar, Looney, McDonalds Mill, Newport, Salem; *Southwest Virginia to Mouth of Daniel Creek:* Atkins, Big Bend, Bland, Cedar Springs, Garden Mountain, Long Spur, Mechanicsburg, Rural Retreat; *Southwest Virginia to Sinking Creek:* Interior, Lindside (WV), Narrows, Newport, Pearisburg, Waiteville (WV), White Gate.

Campgrounds & Recreation Areas

Virginia's vast national and state forest and park lands offer hundreds of well-maintained campgrounds and recreation cabin facilities. State park recreational campground areas include Bear Creek Lake, adjoining Cumberland State Forest near the Willis River and the town of Dillwyn; Chippokes Plantation State Park, on the James River across from Jamestown; Clayton Lake State Park, near Pulaski and Radford in western Virginia (cabins); Douthat State Park, near the Allegheny Mountains and the city of Clifton Forge (cabins); Fairy Stone State Park, next to the Philpott Reservoir (cabins); Goodwin Lake State Park, off Route 460 in southern Virginia; Holiday Lake, on the Appomattox River in south central Virginia; Hungry Mother, just north of Marion and the Mount Rogers National Recreation Area (cabins); Natural Tunnel, in southwest Virginia off Route 23 (cabins, camping); Occoneechee, near Clarksville on Buggs Island Lake; Pocahontas State Forest and Park, about 10 miles southwest of Richmond; Prince Edward, off Route 360 in south central Virginia (cabins); Seashore State Park, near Norfolk and Virginia Beach (cabins); Staunton River State Park, on Buggs Island Lake (cabins); and Westmoreland, on the Potomac (cabins). For information and reservations in state forests and parks containing cabins or campsites write: Division of Parks, 1201 State Office Bldg., Richmond 23219.

National park campground facilities along the Blue Ridge Parkway include Otter Creek Campground, about 15 miles northwest of Lynchburg; Peaks of Otter, about 10 miles north of Bedford; Roanoke Mountain, just outside Roanoke; and Rocky Knob, 20 miles west of Philpott Reservoir (cabins). In the Shenandoah National Park, major recreation areas are Big Meadows (cabins); Lewis Mountain (cabins); Loft Mountain, Matthews Arm Campground; and Skyland (cabins).

Major national facilities in George Washington National Forest are Sherando Lake, and Todd Lake. In Jefferson National Forest, the major recreation areas include Cave Mountain Lake; Cave Springs; and the Mount Rogers National Recreation Area. (See also "Travel & Recreation Guide" section.)

Canoeing & Scenic Rivers

A short 50 miles from Washington, D.C., lies one of the finest wilderness runs in the East: a 29-mile stretch of the Rappahannock River between Remington and Fredericksburg. Over a century ago General Grant marched his Army of the Potomac through the woods shared by this river. Nearby are battlefields—Brandy Station, Chancellorsville, Manassas—where Civil War campaigns were planned and fought. Since this stretch is seldom fished, the river is not only rich in a sense of history and lovely, wooded scenery, but is loaded with smallmouth bass as well. Put-in for the run is close to Remington with the first real white water, Kelly's Ford Rapids, about 5 miles downstream. About 1¼ miles of rapids follow along this wide section of the river; the safest course after the first ¼ mile is well to the left bank. For some 26 miles below Kelly's Ford there are no convenient takeout points until close to Fredericksburg. Nor are there any roads, farms, or other signposts of civilization near the river's edge. A ½-mile sweep of white water near the Rappahannock's confluence with the Rapidan River can prove perilous for even expert canoers; again, the left bank is the safest bet. Many other shoals along this stretch make the trip an exciting and potentially dangerous one. The takeout is 3 miles from Fredericksburg above a sharp left bend where a road reaches the river's right bank.

Less than 30 miles south of Lynchburg, a 60-mile stretch of the Roanoke River between Leesville Dam and the head of the Kerr Reservoir offers equally fine white water and freedom from reminders of human activity. Both scenery and rapids are especially spectacular between Long Island and Brookneal. Close to the North Carolina border, the river passes through rich tobacco country. Few roads come close to the shoreline; and otter sliding down the slippery banks can still be sighted here.

Including the Roanoke and Rappahannock, some 29 rivers have been proposed for the state's Scenic River System. Recommended stretches of water for canoe runs include 39 miles of the Blackwater River (Route 603 to Franklin); the entire length of Cedar Creek; 73 miles of the Cowpasture River from its headwaters to the Jackson River; 21 miles of the Jackson (U.S. 220 to Gathright Reservoir); the entire Northwest River near the North Carolina line; and two trips along the Rapidan from its headwaters to the town of Rapidan (42 miles) and from there to the Rappahannock River (35 miles). Further descriptions of these and other runs are found in *Virginia's Scenic Rivers*, a booklet available free from: Commission of Outdoor Recreation, 803 E. Broad St., Richmond 23219. Also free, from: Commission of Game & Inland Fisheries, P.O. Box 11104, Richmond 23230, is *An Outline for Safe Canoeing in Virginia*, a 7-page guide containing tips on water safety, signs of a river in flood stage, notes on equipment and preparation, and a description of the International River Classification System.

Shenandoah River Outfitters, RFD 3, Luray 22835, phone (703) 743–4519, offers complete outfitting year round for up to 1 week on the Shenandoah River as it follows its course along the George Washington National Forest. Backed by six years of service, the outfitters also offer shuttle service, guides, and group rates. The firm is the largest and most experienced canoe outfitter in the Mid-Atlantic region.

Fishing & Hunting in Virginia

The four natural regions of the Old Dominion—the Tidewater region bordering the Atlantic Ocean, Piedmont Plateau, with its scenic rolling hills and large coldwater limestone streams, the Shenandoah Valley and Blue Ridge Mountains, and the Appalachian Plateau in the extreme southwest corner of the state—provide some excellent fishing and hunting opportunities.

Virginia's lakes and rivers offer a startling variety of game fish species. Two of the finest streams are the scenic Clinch and Halston rivers, tributaries of the Mississippi, and the major streams in the Appalachian Plateau. These wide, deep-flowing rivers offer excellent fishing for smallmouth bass, and some largemouth, crappie, and walleye. The Clinch is best fished by drifting in a flat-bottomed floatboat. The upper portion of the South Fork of the Holston is stocked with trout. South Holston Reservoir, a 7,586-acre TVA impoundment on the Virginia-Tennessee border, holds large walleyes, white bass, and largemouth bass. Some excellent trout fishing is found in the headwaters of the Pound and Levisa rivers in the Clinch ranger district of the Jefferson National Forest (q.v., in the "Travel & Recreation Guide" section), in Big Stony, Big Wilson, Bark Camp, Wolf, and Whitetop Laurel creeks, and in Big and Little Tumbling creeks in the Clinch Mountain Wildlife Management Area, including Laurel Bed Lake and Creek.

The New River flows north through the state from the North Carolina highlands forming a series of deep pools and rapids on its way through the Appalachian Plateau to the Ohio River. The New is one of Virginia's top streams for large, hard-hitting smallmouth bass in the 6-to-7-pound class, and is the state's top walleye water, with the best fishing found below Claytor Lake during the winter months. Claytor Lake is the home of the state record smallmouth bass and produces lunker walleye up to 15 pounds. The Roanoke and Dan rivers are famous for their annual runs of spawning striped bass, and for smallmouth bass, and trout in the upper reaches. Drift-boat fishing during April and early May is often spectacular for 10-pound-and-over stripers as the big fish move upstream to Brookneal on the Roanoke and to Danville on the Dan to spawn.

The beautiful Blue Ridge Mountains and valley country of central Virginia offer hundreds of miles of wild trout streams, remote blue lakes, and scenic, nationally renowned smallmouth bass waters in the Jefferson and George Washington national forests and Shenandoah National Park. The headwaters of the James River, formed by the Jackson and Cowpasture rivers in the George Washington National Forest, hold good-sized smallmouth bass and trout in the upper sections. The stretch of the Jackson flowing through the Gathright Wildlife Management Area offers top-ranked fishing for rainbow and brown trout. Beautiful Back Creek, which rises in the Gathright WMA, produced the state record brook trout. The remote mountain streams and ponds of the James River and Warm Springs ranger districts of the George Washington National Forest, particularly the renowned Bullpasture River and Big Lick, Dry Run, and Wolf Run creeks, provide good to excellent fishing for rainbow, brook, and brown trout. The famous smallmouth bass and canoeing waters of the winding North and South forks of the Shenandoah surround the Lee ranger

district of the George Washington National Forest before their union at Front Royal to form the main branch of the Shenandoah. The headwaters and forest tributaries of the North Fork of the Shenandoah, including the Big and Little Stony creeks, offer trout fishing. Shenandoah National Park offers fishing for wild trout in the Blue Ridge headwaters of the Rapidan, Rivanna, and Moormans rivers. The Rappahannock offers some top-ranked smallmouth bass fishing and canoeing from its headwaters, including the Rapidan and Hazel Creek, downstream to the dam at Fredericksburg. The upper stretches of the Potomac, which forms Virginia's northern border for 156 miles, hold a large population of smallmouth bass.

State-managed "fish-for-fun" areas, where anglers are limited to artificial lures and single barbless hooks and all trout caught must be returned to the stream, are established on the Rapidan River in Madison County, Big Cedar Creek in Russell County, Dan River in Patrick County, Little River in Floyd County, Snake Creek in Carroll County, Little Stony Creek in Carroll County, and on Passage Creek. Large rainbows up to 24 inches and brook trout about a foot long are commonly caught on the fish-for-fun section of the Rapidan. Pay-as-you-go trout fishing is offered on the upper reaches of Big Tumbling Creek, including Laurel Bed Lake and Creek, in the Clinch Mountain Wildlife Management Area and in Douthat State Park Lake, including a portion of Wilson Creek upstream to the Park boundary; these are stocked regularly throughout the season. Fishermen are required to buy a $1 daily permit in addition to having an applicable fishing license.

Virginia's finest fishing for trophy rainbow and brown trout, walleye, muskellunge, lake trout, and northern pike is found in the renowned lakes and reservoirs of the Piedmont Plateau, the state's largest geographic area. Philpott Reservoir, on the Smith River, and Carvins Cove, a 640-acre reservoir on Carvins Cove near Roanoke, are the state's hot spots for trophy-sized rainbow and brown trout in the 5-to-10-pound (and up) class. Philpott also produces lake trout (recently introduced by the Commission of Game & Inland Fisheries) up to 5 pounds. The 7-mile stretch of cold Tailrace waters below Philpott Dam provide outstanding float fishing for the lunker trout. Both lakes offer consistently good fishing for largemouth and smallmouth bass. Huge Smith Mountain Lake on the upper Roanoke River is one of Virginia's premier bass waters and is the home of some giant muskellunge (including the state record muskie). Famous Kerr Reservoir, a 50,000-acre impoundment which backs up the silty Dan and Staunton rivers at their junction at Buggs' Island and straddles the Virginia-North Carolina border, is the home of king-sized striped bass up to 39 pounds. These handsome lunkers, which grow rapidly on the lake's huge schools of threadfin shad, were trapped in the lake during their spawning run when the river was sealed off by the dam. The shallow, stump-lined shores of Gaston Reservoir, located just downstream from Kerr, surround water containing a few large stripers, crappie, largemouth bass, and pickerel. The great James River, which flows across the center of the Piedmont Plateau from its headwaters in the George Washington National Forest, is renowned for its often superb float fishing for smallmouth bass.

Tidewaters

Virginia's tidewater region offers both fresh- and saltwater fishing opportunities. The lower reaches of the Appomattox, a major tributary of the James River, hold largemouth bass and pickerel as well as good seasonal runs of white shad and herring. Another tributary of the James, the Chickahominy River, provides excellent fishing along its weedy shores below Walkers Dam for largemouth bass, panfish, and channel cats. The locks at Walkers Dam are one of the state's hot spots for hordes of silvery herring about the first of May. The Pamunkey River and its sister stream, the Mattaponi, and the beaver ponds along the small tributaries hold largemouth and smallmouth bass, pickerel, and pike. The wildlands of the Dragon Run, a short, twisting stream with scenic, tree-studded channels in the Northern Neck area, hold largemouth bass and large pickerel. The Blackwater River, noted for its cypress-covered banks and dark, moss-stained waters, has good fishing for chain pickerel, largemouth bass, and crappie. The nearby Nottoway River holds large walleye and largemouth bass. Virginia's top-ranked pickerel waters lie clustered around the town of Suffolk south of Portsmouth and include Kilby, Kahoon, Meade, Prince Western Branch, and Burnt Mills lakes. Western Branch Lake has produced as many as 135 pickerel weighing 4 pounds or more, including two 7-pounders during a recent season. Chickahominy Lake and its sister, Diascind, are noted for their productive weedy shorelines, which hold lunker largemouth bass, crappie, pickerel, and panfish. Occoquan Reservoir in northern Virginia provides excellent fishing for largemouth and smallmouth bass and for voracious northern pike, recently introduced by the Commission of Game & Inland Fisheries.

Virginia's state forest reserves offer excellent fishing opportunities for largemouth bass, pickerel, bream, and crappie. The Cumberland State Forest contains Bear Creek Lake (55 acres), Winston Lake (10 acres), Arrowhead Lake (6 acres), Oak Hill Lake (6 acres), and 20 miles of fishing on the Willis River. The Appomattox-Buckingham State Forest contains Holiday Lake (145 acres) and the Prince Edward State Forest has Prince Edward Lake (37 acres) and Goodwin Lake (12 acres). Swift Creek Lake (100 acres) is in the Pocahontas State Forest.

Access roads, boat-launching ramps, and parking areas have been constructed at convenient locations.

VIRGINIA RECORD FISH

	Lb.-oz.	Place	Year
Brook trout	4–2	Back Creek	1973
Brown trout	14–6	Smith River	1974
Rainbow trout	10–12	Philpott Dam	1974
Coho salmon	8–12	Philpott Dam	1971
Carp	60	Private Lake	1970
Lake trout	5–6	Philpott Dam	1966
Channel catfish	30–3	Smith Mountain Reservoir	1975
Crappie	4–14	Lake Conner	1967
Flathead catfish	57	South Holston	1972
Gar	20–8	Northwest River	1973
Grindle (bowfin)	17–8	Chickahominy Lake	1964
Kentucky bass	5–12	Claytor Lake	1973
Lake trout	5–6	Philpott Dam	1966
Largemouth bass	14–2	Gaston Lake	1975
Smallmouth bass	8	Claytor Lake	1964
Muskellunge	31–8	Smith Mountain Lake	1975
Chain pickerel	8–4	Gaston Lake	1973
Rock bass	2–2	Pigg River	1964
Striped bass	39–8	Dan River	1975
Sunfish (redear)	4–8	Private Pond	1970
Sunfish (bluegill)	4–8	Private Pond	1970
Walleye	22–8	New River	1973
White bass	4	Claytor Lake	1974
Yellow perch	2–4	New River	1972
White perch	2–4	Lake Smith	1973
Sauger	5–8	South Holston Lake	1972

Maps & Guides

Virginia fishing and hunting regulations, and the following free publications may be obtained by writing to: Commission of Game & Inland Fisheries, P.O. Box 11104, Richmond 23230. The free Boating Access Map to Virginia Waters shows all boat-launching ramps in the state managed by the commission. The useful free guide *Freshwater Fishing in Virginia* describes license requirements, reservoirs, streams, and public fishing waters; it contains a map of Virginia waters and a Virginia fishing calendar. The free 24-page *Virginia Hunters' Guide* describes license requirements, hunting seasons, distribution of game, hunting methods, and hunting on private lands; it contains a useful map of public hunting lands, and lists and describes bow-hunting areas, shooting preserves, sportsman's organizations, and annual harvest records by county. In addition, the commission publishes two free guides to the state's game lands: *Wildlife Management Areas* and *The Sportsman's Guide to the Goshen-Little North Mountain Wildlife Management Area* in the remote western Blue Ridge Mountains. The *Sportsman's Guide to Virginia's Piedmont State Forests* may be obtained free from: Division of Forestry, Box 3758, Charlottesville 22903. The commission also publishes an attractive full-color monthly, *Virginia Wildlife* magazine. This informative magazine contains articles on hunting, fishing, scenic rivers and canoe routes, hiking, wildlife, and conservation of Virginia's lakes, streams, and wild areas.

Hunting

The commission's 155,000 acres of wildlife management area lands, George Washington and Jefferson national forest lands, some 250,000 acres of state forest and park lands, and 700,000 acres of private hunting lands permit areas offer top-ranked hunting in season for whitetail deer, black bear, upland game birds, waterfowl, and small game. Deer are found throughout the state, with the heaviest concentrations in the Dismal Swamp, Northern Neck, Central Piedmont, and Blue Ridge Mountains and valley country. A few oriental sika deer are found on Assateague Island on the eastern shore where they are hunted under special permit. Virginia has one small herd of elk, in Botetourt and Bedford counties primarily on Blue Ridge Parkway land. The herd was reestablished from Rocky Mountain stock following the extermination of the once native herds in the 19th century. Wild turkeys are abundant in the large, remote, mature hardwood forests in Virginia's mountains and ranges over most of the Piedmont Plateau. Gray squirrel are found throughout the state in mature forests with nut-producing hardwoods. A few colonies of the larger fox squirrel inhabit the river valleys in western Virginia. Cottontail rabbits are most abundant around farmlands in the Tidewater and Piedmont regions and in the western mountains. Quail are found throughout the state along farmlands and adjacent woodlands. Young second-growth pine forests are in the valleys of the mountain country. They are most abundant in the Piedmont region. Ruffed grouse are found in young second-growth hardwood forests and around abandoned farmlands from the Blue Ridge Mountains west and along the James River in the western Piedmont. The woodcock, known as the "timber doodle," is common throughout the state in wet, boggy woodlands. Mourning doves are also found throughout the state, with the largest concentrations on the Piedmont during early fall.

Virginia's coastal marshes and tidal rivers are renowned for their great variety of migrating waterfowl. Chesapeake Bay is the best bet for diving ducks such as canvasbacks, redheads, scaup, and ringnecks. The coastal marshes are best for black duck. Mallards, blacks, and wood ducks can be found on rivers across the state to the Blue Ridge Mountains; a few diving ducks are found along the large reservoirs. Canada geese are abundant throughout the tidewater region. Virginia's Atlantic Coast is on the major migration route for American brant: good shooting is available along the eastern shore. Other game birds and animals in the state include snipe, rails, raccoon, red and gray fox, opossum, and bobcat in the mountains and swamplands, including the great Dismal Swamp, in eastern Virginia.

The George Washington and Jefferson national forests encompass 1,500,000 acres of some of the best deer, bear, grouse, squirrel, and turkey hunting areas in the mountains of western Virginia. A $1 national forest stamp is required of all hunters using these lands.

(For additional fishing and hunting information, see the "Travel & Recreation Guide" section.)

Highways—Recreation & Blue Ridge Scenic Routes

Beginning at the southern end of the Skyline Drive in Rockfish Gap, the Blue Ridge Parkway extends for 469 miles through George Washington and Jefferson national forests to Cherokee, North Carolina, just south of the Great Smoky Mountains National Park. Constructed for recreational purposes only, the route is limited to passenger vehicles and consists of a two-lane roadway running through a strip of parkway varying in width from 500 to 1,200 feet on either side. The landscape bordering the drive has been left as unspoiled as possible, affording a panorama of striking scenery ranging from superb mountain vistas to quiet rural farmlands.

Originally much of the Blue Ridge Parkway's route through Virginia was part of the Appalachian Trail. The trail has been relocated to lands on either side of the parkway, usually in the national forest preserves. Because it crosses the parkway in many places along its route through the national forests, easy access to the trail is provided by the parkway, making short trips of 1–3 days possible (see "Appalachian National Scenic Trail").

There are many picnic areas with water supply, toilet facilities, and concession stands in summer along the parkway. Overnight and restaurant accommodations are available at Doughton Park, North Carolina, and Rocky Knob. A free *Blue Ridge Parkway Map-Brochure* describing points of interest and listing mile posts along the parkway may be obtained from: Superintendent, Blue Ridge Parkway, P.O. Box 1710, Roanoke 24008. Descriptions of concessions and lodgings with a reservation request form are found in a leaflet issued free by: National Park Concessions, Blue Ridge Parkway Operations, Laurel Springs, NC 28644. For the Blue Ridge Parkway, see these U.S. Geological Society maps (scale 1:250,000): Bluefield, Charlotte (NC), Charlottesville, Knoxville, Roanoke, Winston-Salem (NC).

An *Official Virginia Highway Map* may be obtained free by writing to: Dept. of Highways & Transportation, 1221 E. Broad St., Richmond 23219. This useful full-color map shows state parks and forests, national forests, highways and roads, ferries, travel information stations and rest areas, national and state fish hatcheries, national wildlife refuges, and other points of interest.

Mount Rogers National Recreation Area

The highest mountain in Virginia at 5,729 feet, Mount Rogers is joined by a saddle to nearby Pine Mountain (5,526 feet). The area formed by these two mountains, managed as part of the Jefferson National Forest, is unusual for a number of reasons. Fraser fir and red spruce caps, even at the highest elevations, are unique in Virginia. Below these fir caps are northern hardwood forests (beech, oak, and hickory), which are generally indigenous only to the northern United States and Canada. In addition, the high plateau and open meadows characteristic of most of the region give the area a strikingly anomalous alpine flavor, as though a high Swiss mountain plateau had been miraculously transplanted to the rugged lands of southwest Virginia. These features give the Mount Rogers area a feeling of height and vastness, and a mood found nowhere else in the state.

The area abounds in opportunities for outdoor adventures: fishing in Straight Branch, Jones Creek, and the Holston River; horseback riding in the mountains; and hiking on many trails including the Iron Mountain and a section of the Appalachian. Winter sports (see "Ski Touring & Snowshoeing") are popular, as well as swimming, hunting, and canoe trips. There are campgrounds, including some with showers and flush toilets, at Bear Tree, Comers Rock, Grindstone, Hurricane, Shepherds Corner, and Raccoon Branch. Nearby are the New River, Buck Lake, Rural Retreat Fishing Lake, and the Grayson Highlands State Park. A map of the Jefferson National Forest, including the Mount Rogers National Recreation Area, is available from: Forest Supervisor, Jefferson National Forest, 3517 Brandon Ave., SW, Roanoke 24018. (See "Jefferson National Forest" in the "Travel & Recreation Guide.") Further information on accommodations and facilities may be obtained from the same address or from the state departments of commerce and travel (see "Accommodations—Vacation Resorts & Lodges").

Mount Rogers National Recreation Area, is shown on the following large-scale U.S. Geological Survey Maps: Atkins, Cedar Springs, Chilhowie, Grayson (NC), Konnarock, Marion, Middle Fox Creek, Nebo (NC), Park, Rural Retreat, Speedwell, Trout Dale, Whitetop Mountain.

Ski Touring & Snowshoeing

Virginia's national forest and park lands, and hundreds upon hundreds of miles of old logging roads and scenic hiking trails, provide unsurpassed cross-country skiing and snowshoeing.

Within the Mount Rogers National Recreation Area, a 154,000-acre alpine lake setting administered as part of the Jefferson National Forest, is a mile-high range including Virginia's highest point, Mount Rogers (5,729 feet). This land is designated the Crest Zone and is closed to snowmobiles.

For information on snow conditions and overnight camping at Mount Rogers check with: National Recreation Area Headquarters, U.S. Forest Service, Marion 24354, phone (703) 783–5196.

Mountain Lake, a 1,500-acre scenic area within the Jefferson National Forest, offers 4½ miles of trails 12 miles north of Blacksburg. Elevations range from 3,900 to 4,300 feet. There is a large tract of private land on Salt Pond Mountain near the Mountain Lake resort which is posted and patrolled. Be sure to stay on the state highway right-of-way or Forest Service land. The road along the crest of Potts Mountain on the northern edge of the area offers good ski touring east to Stony Creek (1 mile) and west to Butt Mountain Fire Tower (5 miles).

Elevations here range from 3,500 to 4,200 feet. Part of the route follows the Appalachian Trail.

A 5,000-acre basin in the Jefferson National Forest facing northeast with elevations averaging 3,750 feet, the Angels Rest-Mill Creek Watershed area is laced with Appalachian Power Company service roads (gated to vehicles), wildlife trails, and part of the Appalachian Trail. Access is from Pearisburg, Virginia, south on Virginia 100 to Virginia 663, west 5 miles to U.S.F.S. 199, and north 3 miles to the Narrows Watershed sign at the Appalachian crossing, where trail access begins.

For information on snow conditions at Mountain Lake and Angels Rest, contact: Blacksburg Ranger Station, U.S. Forest Service, Blacksburg 24060, phone (703) 552–4641.

State Forest Reserves & Game Lands

The following large-scale U.S. Geological Survey maps show the topography of the state's major forest reserves and wildlife management areas (WMA). These rugged, wild tracts offer outstanding camping, backpacking, fishing, and hunting in season for whitetail deer, grouse, black bear, fox squirrel, raccoon, and wild turkey.

Buckingham-Appomattox State Forest: Andersonville, Appomattox, Holiday Lake, Pamplin; *Prince Edward & Gallion State Forest:* Green Bay, Meherrin; *Pocahontas State Forest:* Hallsboro, Chesterfield, Beach, Winterpock; *Little North Mountain & Goshen WMAs:* Augusta Springs, Brownsburg, Churchville, Craigsville, Elliot Knob, Goshen, Greenville; *Goshen WMA:* Augusta Springs; *Big Laurel WMA:* Big Levels, Sherando, Vesuvius; *Clinch Mountain WMA:* Elk Garden, Honaker, Richlands, Saltville; *Fairy Stone WMA:* Charity, Philpott Reservoir; *Gathright WMA:* Falling Spring, Healing Spring, Minnehala Springs, Mountain Grove, Sun Rise, Warm Springs; *Highland WMA:* Deerfield, McDowell, Monterey SE, Williamsville; *Wunder WMA:* Orkney Springs, Timberville. *Peaks of Otter Backcountry:* Peaks of Otter, Sedalia, Arnold Valley, Snowden.

George Washington National Forest

George Washington National Forest Topo Maps

U.S. Geological Survey Overview Maps (scale 1:250,000): Bluefield, Charlottesville, Cumberland, Roanoke.

Crawford Mountain Wilderness

Large-scale U.S. Geological Survey Maps: Churchville, Elliot Knob, Stokesville, West Augusta.

Laurel Fork Wilderness

Large-scale U.S. Geological Survey Maps: Snowy Mountain, Thornwood.

Little River Wilderness

Large-scale U.S. Geological Survey Maps: Palo Alto, Reddish Knob, Stokesville, West Augusta.

Ramseys Draft Wilderness

Large-scale U.S. Geological Survey Maps: McDowell, Palo Alto, West Augusta.

Rich Hole Wilderness

Large-scale U.S. Geological Survey Maps: Collierstown, Longdale Furnace, Millboro, Nimrod Hall.

Shenandoah River, North & South Forks

Large-scale U.S. Geological Survey Maps: (North Fork) Bergton, Broadway, Edinburg, Front Royal, Fulks Run, New Market, Rileyville, Strasburg, Timberville, Toms Brook; (South Fork) Bentonville, Elkton E, Elkton W, Front Royal, Hamburg, Luray, Rileyville, Stanley, Strasburg, Tenth Legion.

The George Washington National Forest in northwest Virginia includes over 1 million acres of rugged mountains and hiking, fishing, hunting, and wilderness camping country in a dozen counties. About 100,000 acres of the forest spill over into West Virginia. Hundreds of miles of forest roads, canoe trails, and hiking trails, including the Appalachian Trail, provide access to the Ramseys Draft, Crawford Mountain, Little River, Rich Hole, and Laurel Fork wilderness areas, the Highlands, Little North Mountain, Goshen and Wunder wildlife management areas, the Maury, James, Bullpasture, Dry, Cowpasture, Jackson, and North Fork Shenandoah rivers, and Elkhorn, Hearthstone, and Sherando lakes. The forest and the 70,000 acres of state wildlife management areas have some of the finest hunting in the East for whitetail deer, black bear, wild turkey, grouse, quail, and raccoon. The highland headwaters offer good fishing for pan-size rainbow and brook trout.

Among the many untamed areas of the forest, Crawford Mountain, just south of U.S. 250 and 10 miles west of Staunton, is a surprisingly intact, roadless, and self-contained wilderness covering about 17,000 acres. The most prominent feature of the area is the mountain itself, part of the long range of Great North Mountain. The ridge runs generally northeast to southwest, everywhere exceeding elevations of 3,000 feet to a maximum of 3,770. A curving trail following the ridge, unbroken by any road and closed to motor vehicles, offers some 10 miles of scenic hiking. Other attractions within the forest include a 70-mile portion of the Appalachian Trail; Woodstock Tower, offering one of the finest views of the Seven Bends of the Shenandoah River; Crabtree Falls, leading to the base of the waterfalls; and Kennedy Peak, with its outstanding panoramas of the Shenandoah and Blue Ridge mountains. Trails within the forest, campgrounds, recreation sites, roads, shelters, streams, rivers, and other major features are all

VIRGINIA TRAVEL & RECREATION GUIDE

shown on the *George Washington National Forest Recreation Map*, available for 50¢ from: Forest Supervisor, George Washington National Forest, Federal Bldg., Harrisonburg 22801, phone (703) 433–2491, which also will supply a free list of hiking trails with descriptions and directions.

The national forest and the 70,000 acres of wildlife management areas offer hunting opportunities unsurpassed in the East. Hunters annually take about 9,000 deer from the 12-county area. This is also the state's best bear hunting area and the home of the largest populations of wild turkey. The wooded terrain offers top quality squirrel and grouse hunting. Quail and rabbit are found around the open lands and abandoned farms in the hollows. Raccoon hunters will find abundant game on forest- and commission-owned lands, where dove and waterfowl are also legal game.

Over 150,000 pan-sized rainbow and brook trout are stocked annually in streams on the national forest and nearby wildlife management areas, such as the Cowpasture River, Buffalo and East Dry Branch, Jackson River, Pads Creek, and Midday Run. Some streams offer good fishing for scrappy native brook trout. *Sportsman's Guides to the George Washington National Forest* specifically tailored for hunters and fishermen, showing stocked streams, forest and wildlife management areas, campsites, highways, roads, fish hatcheries, and parking and recreation areas, are available for the Deerfield, Lee, Pedlar, Dry River, James River, and Warm Springs ranger districts. These free maps as well as information on hunting and fishing regulations are available from: Commission of Game & Inland Fisheries, P.O. Box 11104, Richmond 23230.

Of particular interest to hunting and fishing enthusiasts is the Ramseys Draft area in the Deerfield and Dry River ranger districts. The draft is a clear trout stream arising about 25 miles northwest of Staunton; it drains the narrow valley between the parallel ridges of the Shenandoah Mountains on the west and Bald Ridge on the east. The area was the first portion of the George Washington National Forest to be purchased when the forest was being established, and it has never been logged. As a consequence, Ramseys Draft is unique in Virginia because of its large area of virgin timber: extremely tall hemlocks, giant white pines, and tulip trees grow in the valley and along the draft and its tributary creeks. This substantial roadless area provides a habitat for many wildlife species including a sizable population of black bear. Still essentially an isolated wilderness with little evidence of human activity, the terrain is characterized by steep slopes almost everywhere except near the eastern periphery. A few trails, such as Jerrys Run and

Ramseys Draft Trail, wind through the region. See the *Deerfield Ranger District Map* (described above) for further features of the area.

South of U.S. Highway 250 about 10 miles west of Staunton, the Crawford Mountain Wilderness is a rugged, isolated area of some 17,000 acres. The most prominent feature of the wilderness is the mountain itself, part of the long range of Great North Mountain. The ridge runs generally northeast to southwest, with elevations between 3,000 and 3,770 feet. Crawford Knob, a separate peak, rises to 3,728 feet. The minimum elevation is about 1,700 feet on the eastern boundary. On the west the area is drained by the Calfpasture River; on the north and south, by the Jennings and East Dry branches, respectively, of the Middle River.

There are no roads within the wilderness, and most trails have been officially closed to motor vehicles because of their steepness and erosion potential. An unbroken trail winds along the ridge for about 10 miles, with several splinter trails providing access to the area. Hunters who venture in on foot find the game, including grouse, turkeys, and deer, exceptionally plentiful. Occasional bobcat and black bear roam the area. Ravens and pileated woodpeckers are the most common of the many bird species. Impressive stands of white pine and hemlock are scattered throughout the forest and share the terrain with the numerous hardwoods along streams at lower elevations. Virtually untouched by human activity, the Crawford Mountain area is one of the few roadless scenic areas within the national forest.

Shared by both the Warm Springs ranger district and the Potomac ranger district of West Virginia's Monongahela National Forest, Laurel Fork Wilderness contains 17,262 acres and is laced with a network of beautiful clear streams and beaver ponds. Some of the streams providing excellent wild trout fishing are Laurel Fork and its several branches, and Buck, Christian, Bearwallow, and Lost runs. The area is excellent for hunting: many deer, black bear, squirrel, snowshoe hare, woodcock, turkey, and grouse are bagged every year. The *Warm Springs Ranger District Sportsman's Guide* (described above) is especially helpful for getting around the area.

Before its acquisition by the U.S. Forest Service in 1922, the area was widely logged and burned. Most timber in the area is 40 to 60 years old, with handsome stands of spruce, white pine, beech, maple, and hemlock providing a luxuriant forest cover. At lower elevations, the laurel thickets which give the area its name transform streamside trails into laurel-lined avenues. The Laurel Fork Wilderness is also known for its abundance and variety of mushrooms.

A number of old logging roads and jeep trails within the area have reverted to foot trails—which, with only two exceptions, are closed to public vehicles. A picnic and camping area at Locust Spring in the wilderness features primitive campsites, a three-sided shelter, fire rings, a protected spring, and picnic tables.

Little River Wilderness of the Dry River ranger district is immediately north and east of the Ramseys Draft, to which it is linked by a foot trail, offering circuit hikes of several days' duration. Other trails and roads crisscross the area, including Wolf Ridge, California Ridge, and Sand Spring Mountain trails. The Little River and its North and South forks, and the North River provide trout fishing. Hunting for white-tailed deer, black bear, quail, and grouse is equally popular. The *Dry River District Map* of the forest (described above) is an invaluable aid for hunters, hikers, and fishermen, showing trails, streams, campsites, roads, and parking areas. Campgrounds and a picnic area border Todd Lake within the wilderness. Nearby are Hearthstone Lake and the surrounding ridges of Chestnut, Grooms, Hearthstone, Wolf, and Timber.

The 6,000 acres of the Rich Hole Wilderness Area in the James River district are covered by a virgin stand of Appalachian hardwood forest. Along the streams—short offshoots of the Cowpasture River's South Fork—grow large hemlocks of apparent great age. The solitude and unspoiled beauty of the area are such that entering the wilderness from nearby U.S. 60 is like leaving the sights and sounds of our high-speed technology for a walk through the remote past. Northern red oak, basswood, and tulip poplar share the wilderness with a variety of game animals: black bear, white-tailed deer, raccoon, gray squirrel, ruffed grouse, and wild turkey. Two small headwater creeks provide a habitat for the native brook trout which spawn in them, and a pair of trails—Rich Hole and North Branch—meet near Brushy Mountain, in the heart of the wilderness. Nearby are the Rockbridge Alum Springs, the North Mountains, and Simpson Creek. *The Sportsman's Guide to the James River District* (described above) is a useful guide to Rich Hole and the surrounding region.

Campsites and recreation areas are scattered throughout the forest. Among the more popular are Brandywine and Sherando lakes, which feature water sports; Elizabeth Furnace with its campfire theater and historic iron furnace; and Camp Run, in a primitive forest setting. Lists of campsites and facilities, with descriptions and information on fees, regulations, and seasons, are available at no cost from: Forest Supervisor (address above).

Access & Outfitting Centers

The major routes leading to the forest are Interstate 64 from the east and west, and Interstate 81 from the north and south. The forest is traversed east and west by U.S. 33 and 250, and by U.S. 220 from the north and south. Lodging, supplies, gear, and canoe rentals are available at many towns and villages in the forest vicinity, including Clifton Forge, Milboro Spring, Staunton, Waynesboro, Head Waters, Sun Rise, Mountain Grove, Brandywine, Sugar Grove, and Natural Bridge.

Jefferson National Forest

Jefferson National Forest Topo Maps

U.S. Geological Survey Overview Maps (scale 1:250,000): Bluefield, Jenkins, Johnson City, Roanoke, Winston-Salem.

Hunting Camp Creek Backcountry

Large-scale U.S. Geological Survey Topographic Maps: Garden Mountain, Big Bend, Bastian.

James River Face Backcountry

Large-scale U.S. Geological Survey Maps: Arnold Valley, Snowden.

Mountain Lake-Peters Mountain Wilderness

Large-scale U.S. Geological Survey Maps: Eggleston, Interior, Waiteville (WV).

White Rocks Recreation Area

Large-scale U.S. Geological Survey Maps: Craig Springs, Eggleston, Interior, Lindside (WV), McDonalds Mill, Newport, Pearisburg, Waiteville (WV).

Sprawled across 575,000 acres of the Blue Ridge and Allegheny mountains of Virginia, Jefferson National Forest offers many opportunities for just about every form of outdoor recreation. The forest's liberal seasons and bag limits permit excellent hunting opportunities for deer, black bear, wild turkey, ruffed grouse, and fox squirrels. Fishermen will find native brook trout in the high headwater streams of the James river and stream-raised brown and rainbow at lower elevations. The larger streams—Hunting Camp Creek, Laurel Creek, Dry Branch,

Johns Creek, and others—are heavily stocked throughout the season. Nearby reservoirs such as the Gatewood and Big Cherry offer fine fishing for small- and largemouth bass, pickerel, panfish, walleye, and muskellunge.

The Appalachian Trail winds for 95 miles through the Jefferson National Forest. Through Iron, Walker, Brushy, and Creek mountains the trail is well marked with white paint blazes, standard Appalachian Trail markers, and with Forest Service and state highway signs at intersections, shelters, and points of interest. A map, *Appalachian Trail on the Jefferson National Forest,* showing the major approach and side trails, shelters, campsites, ranger stations, roads, streams, and major towns, is available free from: Forest Supervisor, Jefferson National Forest, 3517 Brandon Ave., SW, Roanoke 24018. Other trails, such as the Iron and Catawba mountain trails, as well as major park features, roads, highways, recreation sites, campgrounds, shelters, rivers, and streams, are shown on the *Jefferson National Forest Map* (50¢; same address), available from the forest supervisor's office. (See also "Appalachian National Scenic Trail" in the "Encyclopedia" section for hiking guides to the area.)

Immediately adjacent to the Blue Ridge Parkway, the James River Face forms the easternmost portion of the forest and is just 35 miles northeast of busy Roanoke. The wilderness has rugged terrain, with a network of steep ridges and hollows and a precipitous drop to the James River. Views of the James River Gap are particularly spectacular. The area is traversed by a section of the Appalachian Trail, and a number of old logging roads provide additional trails through the area. A trail shelter not far from the James River and campsites near Cave Mountain Lake offer opportunities for a breather or for overnight camping.

Also located in the Jefferson National Forest is the Mountain Lake-Peters Mountain Wilderness, 10,000 acres intersected by the Appalachian Trail and several streams: Johns Creek, and Little Stony Creek and its North and South forks. The 1,500 acres of land around Mountain Lake have been designated a scenic area and contain protected stands of native spruce and hemlock.

The Mount Rogers National Recreation Area (q.v.) and the White Rocks area, the southernmost extension of the forest, duplicate the look and atmosphere of a Swiss Alpine setting with stands of deep green spruce and high mountain vegetation. At 5,729 feet, Mount Rogers is the highest point in Virginia. Recreational activities include a variety of winter sports, hunting, fishing, hiking, camping, and horseback riding through bucolic valleys and fir forests bordering vast open lands.

Detailed *Sportsman's Guides to the Jefferson National Forest* with maps for three ranger districts within the forest—Glenwood, New

Castle, and Clinch—are available from the Forest Supervisor (address above). Each map shows the major features of the district: trails, roads, wildlife management areas, campsites, ranger stations, streams, rivers, and major mountain ridges, and describes the major scenic attractions, hunting and fishing opportunities, and wildlife in the region.

Access & Outfitting Centers

The major routes to Jefferson National Forest are Interstate Highways 81, 77, 581, and 64. Lodging, supplies, fishing, hunting and camp gear, and canoe rentals are available at Wytheville, Bluefield, Rural Retreat, Marion, Tazewell, Narrows, Pearisburg, Blacksburg, Dublin, Pulaski, Buena Vista, New Castle, Salem, Roanoke, and Chilhowie.

Shenandoah National Park

Shenandoah National Park Topo Maps

U.S. Geological Survey Maps (each section $2): Northern Section, Central Section, Southern Section.

Headwaters of the Rapidan

Large-scale U.S. Geological Survey Topographic Maps: Rochelle, Stanardsville, Madison, Fletcher, Big Meadows.

Extending for 80 miles along the Blue Ridge Mountains between Front Royal on the north and Waynesboro on the south, the Shenandoah National Park covers about 193,500 acres, over 300 square miles, of northwestern Virginia. Sixty peaks, ranging in elevation from 3,000 to 4,000 feet, rise within the park, providing the backbone for the famous Skyline Drive. Following the older Appalachian Trail most of the way along the crest of the ridge, the drive offers a continuous, almost numbing series of spectacular views over wooded ravines and occasional rocky crags to the undulating Piedmont Plateau on the east and across the rolling farmlands of the Shenandoah Valley to the Alleghenies on the west.

The area presently covered by the park was once farmed and extensively lumbered. Its most prosperous period occurred between the mid-18th and late-19th century when farming and, later, mining were the chief activities of the region. Late in the 19th century the demand for mountain handicrafts waned and a blight destroyed most of the chestnut trees. With the decline of interest in mining and agriculture, families began to move away from the area and the population dwindled. Soon the forest began to take over, and today nearly all the land within the park is heavily wooded with oak, pine, and other species. There are over 900 different kinds of flowering plants in the area. Just as the forest returned after human activity declined, so the wildlife began to make a comeback. Among the larger mammals, white-tailed deer are most common; other animals, including bobcat, gray fox, black bear, and woodchuck, may also be glimpsed in dense forest areas.

In addition, many small feeder streams such as Big Ugly Run, Big Creek, Brokenback Run, Rose River, and Overall Run provide some of the few remaining strongholds of native eastern brook trout in the southeastern United States. Because of the park's long, ridgelike topography, streams tend to be short with steep gradients. Trout found within the streams are small, rarely exceeding 12 inches and usually measuring from 5 to 8 inches. There are several other species of fish within the park streams, but trout are the only fish that may be legally caught. Because of the size of the streams and density of the forest cover, fishermen will find most of the waters very brushy with little casting room. The best way to fish the streams is from the lower boundaries of the park. Fishing is not permitted near any of the park campgrounds or Skyline Drive. Any serious fisherman in the park should secure a good set of maps, such as those issued by the U.S.

Geological Survey. Regulations (a license valid for 3 days is required) and descriptions of fishing possibilities (*Fishing in Shenandoah Park*—a 1-page flyer) are available from: National Park Service, U.S. Department of the Interior, Shenandoah National Park, Luray 22835. A list of trout streams in the three districts (*Trout Streams; Shenandoah National Park*), giving access points, is available free from the same address.

There are nearly 370 miles of foot trails in Shenandoah National Park, including a 95-mile section of the famous Appalachian Trail. *Circuit Hikes in the Shenandoah National Park* ($1.25) is available from: Potomac Appalachian Trail Club, P.O. Box 236, Harpers Ferry, WV 25425). It describes a collection of 1-day hikes in the area, including Bluff Trail, Trayfoot Mountain, Lewis Falls, and Stony Man Mountain. Discussions of each hike give mileage, directions, and points of interest and are accompanied by a simple map. The *Guide to the Appalachian Trail and Side Trails in Shenandoah National Park* (see "Appalachian National Scenic Trail") goes into greater detail about the main footpath, side trails, and history of the area.

Most of the park is open to "backcountry camping," defined by park officials as any use of portable shelters or sleeping equipment in areas of the park that are more than 250 yards from a paved road, and more than ½ mile from any park facilities other than trails, unpaved roads, and trail shelters. Permits are required and are available from park headquarters, visitor centers, and all entrance stations. There are also 6 fully equipped, locked cabins in backcountry areas, able to accommodate a total of up to 12 people. Reservations are necessary and can be made with: Potomac Appalachian Trail Club, 1718 N St., NW, Washington, DC 20036.

There are 4 family campgrounds within the park. Big Meadows in the central section near Fishers Gap is the largest of these and is open year round. 253 campsites are available, as well as showers, a laundry, and nearby food services. Horseback riding, an amphitheater, and fishing streams are additional attractions. Also in the central park section is Lewis Mountain Campground, open mid-May to October and offering 32 sites. Matthews Area in the northern section near Hogback Overlook off Knob Mountain Road offers 186 campsites and is open Mid-April to October. Loft Mountain near Big Run Overlook on the Skyline Drive in the southern section offers 31 campsites, showers, a laundry, and a nearby store, and is open mid-April to October. Available only to organized youth groups, Dundo Campgrounds is open April to October and must be reserved in advance from park headquarters. Tables and fireplaces are provided at all campsites, with piped water, comfort stations, and sewage disposal stations nearby. There are no trailer hookups. Camping limit is 14 days. For further information, write: National Park Service (address above).

Access & Lodging

For those who desire more luxurious accommodations, overnight and dining facilities and housekeeping cabins are available at *Big Meadows Lodge & Cabins* (open mid-May to late October, 93 rooms); *Lewis Mountain Lodge & Cabins* (mid-April to late October, 8 rooms); *Skyland Lodge & Cabins* (late March to early November, 158 rooms); and *Big Meadows Wayside* (year round, 30 rooms). For information and reservations write to: ARA Virginia Sky-Line Co., P.O. Box 727, Luray 22835, phone (703) 743–5108.

Major routes leading to Shenandoah National Park include Interstate 81 and 66, and Interstate 64 from Richmond. The park is traversed north and south by the scenic Blue Ridge Parkway. Lodging, supplies, and canoe rentals are available at towns and villages surrounding the park, including Front Royal, Luray, Elkfort, Waynesboro, and Charlottesville.

Accommodations

Maryland has accommodations to suit the needs of every vacationer, including hotels, motels, fishing and hunting lodges, resorts, and campsites. For information on where to stay, write to: Division of Tourist Development, Dept. of Economics & Community Development, 1748 Forest Dr., Annapolis 21401. A detailed traveler's guide to the state is contained in the *Maryland Guidebook,* available free upon request from the same address.

Appalachian National Scenic Trail

The 38-mile Maryland section of the Appalachian Trail parallels the ancient route of the Great Indian Warpath (a system of old Indian trails) along the northernmost Blue Ridge Mountains through Civil War battlefields to the Virginia line at Weverton. The 35-mile stretch from Pen Mar to Weverton passes along a narrow ridge crest through a scenic forest area and an area of historic interest. From Weverton the trail follows the abandoned Chesapeake & Ohio Canal towpath west and crosses the Potomac River via the bridge at Sandy Hook, Virginia.

If you are planning to hike the Appalachian Trail in Maryland, you will want to consult *The Appalachian Trail,* (publication #17, 25¢), Appalachian Trail Conference, P.O. Box 236, Harpers Ferry, WV 25425, a booklet which contains a brief history of the trail and a description of the route, including maps and a complete list of publications sold by the conference. You should also look into *Suggestions for Appalachian Trail Users* (70¢), same publisher, which includes information on trip planning, accommodations, safety precautions, maps, equipment, and other important aspects of using the trail. This publication is essential for all trail users. The *ATC Guidebook—Susquehanna River to Shenandoah National Park* ($4.75) describes the Maryland segment of the Appalachian Trail in detail. The Appalachian Trail in Maryland can be located on the following U.S. Geological Survey Maps: Blue Ridge, Harpers Ferry (WV), Keedysville, Middletown, Myersville, Smithsburg.

Campgrounds & State Recreation Areas

With over 10 state forests, 20 state parks, and dozens of private campgrounds, Maryland provides the camper with a variety of choices in every region ranging from full-service family campgrounds to remote primitive sites and Adirondack shelters. The 25-page *Directory of Maryland Campgrounds* lists and describes all privately operated campsites and trailer parks, state forest and park campsites, and national and regional campsites. The directory may be obtained free from: Division of Tourist Development, Dept. of Economics & Community Development, 1748 Forest Dr., Annapolis 21401, phone (301) 267–5517. Most campsites are available on a first-come first-served basis. At Assateague, Deep Creek Lake, and Shad Landing state parks, campsites have been set aside as reserved areas for family groups and may be reserved in advance for 1-week periods. For campsite permit regulations, and reservation information, write: Park Service, Dept. of Natural Resources, State Office Bldg., Annapolis 21401. For 24-hour recorded, up-to-date state park camping information, call (301) 768–0895.

Detailed *State Park Map-Brochures* are available free upon request for all state park recreation areas from: Park Service (address above). For information on state forest campsites write to: Maryland Forest Service (same address). A free guide, *Maryland—the Mountains, the Bay,*

MARYLAND ENCYCLOPEDIA

520 · THE BANTAM GREAT OUTDOORS GUIDE

the Ocean, Recreation in Maryland's Parks & Forests, may be obtained from: Park Service (same address).

Canoe Trails & Quality Fishing Waters

Maryland's major canoe trails and trout streams are shown on the following large-scale 7.5-minute U.S. Geological Survey Maps. These invaluable full-color maps show the topography of the surrounding countryside, including contours, lakes and parks, rapids, falls, footbridges, orchards, woodlands, trails, and campsites. *Antietam Creek:* Funkstown, Hagertown, Keedysville; *Casselman River:* Avilton, Bittinger, Grantsville, McHenry; *Catoctin Creek:* Middletown, Myersville, Point of Rocks; *Gunpowder Falls River* (including Prettyboy and Loch Raven reservoirs): Edgewood, Hereford, Lineboro, New Freedom (PA), Phoenix, Towson, White Marsh; *Deer Creek:* Aberdeen, Bel Air, Delta (PA), Fawn Grove (PA), Jarrettsville; *Monocacy River:* Buckeystown, Frederick, Poolesville, Walkersville, Woodsboro; *Patapsco North Branch:* Finksburg, Sykesville, Reisterstown, Westminster; *Patapsco South Branch:* Damascus, Sykesville, Woodbine; *Patuxent River:* Benedict, Bowie, Bristol, Clarksville, Ellicott City, Laurel, Lower Marlboro, Odenton, Savage, Sykesville, Woodbine; *North Branch Potomac:* Artemas (PA), Bellegrove, Cresaptown, Cumberland, Davis (WV), Gorman, Great Cacapon (WV), Hancock, Keyser (WV), Kitzmiller, Mount Storm (WV), Oldtown, Patterson Creek, Paw Paw (WV), Westernport; *Savage River:* Avilton, Barton, Bittinger, Frostburg, Westernport; *Town Creek:* Flintstone, Oldtown; *Winters Run:* Bel Air, Edgewood, Jarrettsville, Phoenix; *Youghiogheny River:* Deer Park, Friendsville, McHenry, Oakland, Sang Run. The state's *Highway and Resources Map* (q.v.) contains a listing of trout streams, location-keyed to the road map.

Chesapeake Bay Fish & Game Region

Chesapeake Bay, which covers 3,237 square miles, is one of the nation's great fishing, boating, and waterfowl hunting regions. This vast semi-enclosed body of water, a mixture of sea and river some 185 miles long, varies from 3 to 22 miles wide, with an average depth of 21 feet. The deepest area, off Bloody Point at the southern tip of Kent Island, reaches down 174 feet. The food-rich waters of this great bay are fed by 46 rivers and streams, including the "father of rivers"—the Susquehanna—and the Northeast, Bohemia, Elk, Bush, Sassafras, Gunpowder, Patapsco, Choptank, Potomac, Pocomoke, and Patuxent riv-

ers. Its 4,100 miles of tidal shoreline in Maryland provide the finest Canada goose shooting on the Atlantic seaboard. More than 430,000 geese and 402,000 ducks winter in the tidewater region during a typical season, along with innumerable quail, dove, rails, woodcock, and jacksnipe. The tidal flats and marshlands are also inhabited by whitetail deer and annually produce the nation's second-largest number of muskrat pelts.

The bay is the nation's prime producer of striped bass (known south of the Mason-Dixon line as "rockfish"). The best striper fishing is from mid-June to mid-September when the schools begin the annual fall migration toward their winter homes in the Potomac and Susquehanna rivers. The most popular fishing methods include bait fishing with peeler crabs, drifting soft-shell crabs and live eels, and casting with surface plugs, bucktails, spoons, and surgical hose eels. The bay provides often spectacular fishing for black drum around the marshy islands of Tangier Sound, cobia around wrecks in the lower Chesapeake, and spotted sea trout, bluefish, big largemouth and smallmouth bass, northern pike, chain pickerel, and crappie in the tidewater areas, such as the Susquehanna, Northeast, and Pocomoke rivers, and elsewhere. Fly fishing with streamers, poppers, and shad flies is becoming increasingly popular in the bay region.

The tremendous fishing potential of Chesapeake Bay (it is estimated that on an average summer weekend 100,000 people fish with rod and reel in the bay; they annually land nearly 70 million pounds of fish) is illustrated by the record fish summaries compiled by the Maryland Sportfishing Tournament office.

A detailed guide to Chesapeake Bay is contained in the 32-page *Tidewater Fishing Guide*, available free from: Dept. of Natural Resources, Tarves State Office Bldg., Annapolis 21401. The guide also contains a synopsis of laws, seasons, dividing lines, public launching ramps, state fishing reefs, full-color hydrographic sectional charts, a Maryland fish table, and a fish identification chart. Chesapeake Bay is shown on National Ocean Survey Nautical Charts 12260 and 12220, available for $3.25 each from: Distribution Division (C44), National Ocean Survey, Riverdale 20840.

Fenwick Maryland Fly Fishing School

The Fenwick Corporation operates two classes for beginning through advanced fly fishermen (April and May) and two classes limited to fly fishermen with some previous experience (June and July) at Cunningham Falls Lake, which covers 43 acres and is filled with trout. The school is only minutes away from Catoctin Mountain National Park (site of the Camp David presidential retreat). Family recreational activities include hiking, camping, and sightseeing. The curriculum includes the art of fly casting and tackle, entomology, artificial flies, knots, fly presentation, stream lore, and wading. It includes slides, films, demonstrations of all phases of fly presentation, and extensive individual casting practice. Fenwick supplies complete balanced tackle for your use. Comfortable lodging is available at the Cozy Motel Inn and Cottages. School headquarters are only 20 minutes from historic Gettysburg, Pennsylvania and 1 hour from Washington, D.C. For free literature, rates, and information, write: Director, Fenwick Fly Fishing School, Eastern Division, 2202 Glen Court, Rt. 7, Frederick 21701 (301–663–3966).

Fishing & Hunting in Maryland

Although Maryland is small, encompassing only 10,577 square miles, its varied topography provides some of the finest fishing and waterfowl hunting opportunities in the eastern United States, ranging from the

CHESAPEAKE BAY RECORD FISH

	Lb.-oz.	Place	Method*	Bait	Year
Hickory shad	4	Susquehanna River	CG	Shad dart	1972
White shad	8–2	Wicomico River	CG	Shad dart	1975
Flounder	8–1	Chesapeake Bay	BF	Peeler crab	1964
Smallmouth bass	6	Susquehanna River	CG	Rebel	1971
Largemouth bass	9–1	Pocomoke River	CG	Plastic worm	1975
Black drum	103–8	Buoy No. 16	BF	Peeler crab	1973
Norfolk spot	1–4	Snake Reef	BF	Bloodworm	1967
	1–4	Magothy River	BF	Peeler crab	1969
Channel bass	70	Tangier Sound	BF	Peeler crab	1974
Spotted seatrout	11–12	Adams Island	CG	Peeler crab	1974
Gray trout	13–6	Tangier Sound	BF	Peeler crab	1975
Bluefish	21	N. of Bloody Point Light	D	Cut spot	1975
Striped bass	54	C & R Buoy	T	White #19 Tony	1975
Yellow perch	2	City Yacht Basin	BF	Shiner	1965
White perch	2–8	Devil's Hole	T	Spoon	1967
Chain pickerel	6–8	Susquehanna River	BF	Minnow	1965
Catfish	16–4	Spesutie Narrows	BF	Clam	1974
Cobia	97–12	Middle Grounds	BF	Eel	1969
Carp	35	Susquehanna River	CG	Shad dart	1970
		Salt Peter Creek	BF	Doughball	1974
Crappie	**	Pig Point	BF	Minnow	1972
		Sassafras River	CG	Bucktail	1971
Croaker	4	Buoy 16-AA	BF	Peeler crab	1964
		Buoy 16-AA	BF	Peeler crab	1964

*BF-bottom fishing; CG-casting; D-drifting; T-trolling.

**18 inches.

CHESAPEAKE BAY FLY FISHING RECORDS

	Lb.-oz.	Place	Method*	Bait	Year
Striped bass	11	Susquehanna River	CG	White streamer	1969
White shad	3–8	Port Deposit	CG	Shad fly	1975
Hickory shad	2–2	Susquehanna River	CG	White streamer	1969
Largemouth bass	5–4	Susquehanna River	CG	Popper	1969
Smallmouth bass	4–5	Susquehanna River	CG	Popper	1969
Spotted seatrout	6–1	Tangier Sound	CG	White streamer	1972
Gray trout	2–3	Tangier Sound	CG	White streamer	1975
Bluefish	8–6	Mouth of Chester River	CG	Popping bug	1974
White perch	1–4	Susquehanna River	CG	Shad fly	1973

*CG-casting.

flat lowlands of tidewaters of the Coastal Plain, through the low-lying Eastern Shore and the higher Western Shore of the 20,000-square-mile inland area of Chesapeake Bay, and the rolling, orchard-studded hillsides of the Piedmont Plateau region, to the rugged beauty and scenic mountain streams, valleys, and mixed hardwood and conifer forests of the Appalachian Mountains in the western counties—which reach their greatest height at the peak of Backbone Mountain (3,360 feet) in Garrett County. The state's 9 forests and 33 parks and wildlife management areas cover 170,000 acres in the mountains and on the ocean, bays, and rivers. There are 35 public hunting grounds covering 70,788 acres. Seventy-two ponds, lakes, and reservoirs make up the state's freshwater fishing area, along with the historic waters of the Susquehanna River in the northeast corner, the winding riverbanks of the Patapsco, and the famed smallmouth bass waters of the North Branch of the Potomac. The major lakes include scenic Deep Creek Lake, Youghiogheny Lake, and Savage River Reservoir in the western highlands, and Liberty, Prettyboy, and Loch Raven reservoirs in the north central region. The state's generally moderate climate varies from mild to hot in summer and mild in winter to moderate in the east and south to bitter cold in the western mountains.

Freshwater Fishing

The major fishing waters in the Appalachian Highlands and forests of northwest Maryland include Deep Creek Lake, the state's largest body of fresh water, and the brook, rainbow, and brown trout waters of the beautiful Savage River, which flows through Savage River State Forest, torrential Youghiogheny River, Bear Creek, Salt Block Run, Mill Run, Muddy Creek, and Buffalo, Puzzley, and Glade runs in Garrett County and Evitts Creek, Flintstone Creek, and Laurel Run in Allegany County. Scenic Youghiogheny Reservoir, which sprawls across the Maryland-Pennsylvania boundary surrounded by dense conifer forests and highlands, holds muskellunge, northern pike, rainbow and brown trout, walleye, and smallmouth bass up to trophy weights. The waters of the renowned North Branch of the Potomac, with its deep pools and rocky ledges forming the southern boundary of the northwest region at the West Virginia line, are a fly fisherman's paradise for explosive smallmouth bass up to 4 and 5 pounds. Bass fishermen get the best results using poppers, large streamer flies and bucktails, muddler minnows, and dry flies such as the Wulff series and Brown Hackle.

Sprawling Deep Creek Lake, surrounded by the Appalachian Highlands and evergreen forests, covers 3,900 acres and has a 62-mile-long shoreline. The predominant fish species include smallmouth bass, largemouth bass, black crappie, bluegill, yellow perch, chain pickerel, and trout. Northern pike and walleye have been stocked to control rough species, resulting in the state record 15-pound 15-ounce great northern, caught here in 1974. The Department of Natural Resources annually stocks 10,000 brook, brown, and rainbow trout. Drift fishing over the weed beds surrounding McHenry Point and Cove is productive for bass and northern pike. Other top areas on the lake include the state park docks for yellow perch; stump-filled State Park Cove; Harveys Cove for perch and pickerel; Sky Valley Cove for bass, bluegill, and pike; Beckmans Island; Stump Point; Cat Rocks for smallmouth bass and walleye; Holy Cross Area for northern pike; Turkey Neck Point; and Poland Run. Shoreline fly fishing is effective using streamers, wet and dry flies, "go-go" poppers, and the fly-rod mouse. The most effective spinning lures include the Rapala, Yellow Shyster, Mepps Spinner, frog-colored Beno, black rubber worms with spinner, Jitterbug, Crazy Crawler, and L & S Mirrolures.

The major features of the lake and depth contours are shown on the *Fisherman's Map of Deep Creek Lake*, available free from: Information Division, Dept. of Natural Resources, Tarves State Office Bldg., Annapolis 21401. Campgrounds are available at Deep Creek Lake State Park; for additional information and reservations, write: Park Superintendent, Rte. 2, Swanton 21561.

Rainbow, brook, and brown trout are found to the east, in north central Maryland's Beaver Creek (the state record brown trout was taken here), Little Antietam Creek, and Sideling Hill Creek in Washington County and in the Big Hunting, Little Hunting, Fishing, Owens, Friends, and Middle Creek watersheds in Frederick County. Other stocked trout streams in central Maryland include the Patuxent River from Triadelphia Lake Dam to Rocky Gorge, the Little Seneca Watershed, and Beaver Run, Deer Creek, and the Jones Falls, Little Falls, Bee Tree Run, and Big Gunpowder Falls watersheds. Triadelphia Lake, shown on the *Fisherman's Map of Triadelphia Lake* (which includes a detailed *Map of the Patuxent River Watershed*), available free from the DNR (address above), holds some lunker largemouth and smallmouth bass, northern pike, and chain pickerel. Liberty Reservoir to the north on the Patapsco River, shown on the free DNR *Fisherman's Map of Liberty Reservoir*, holds largemouth and smallmouth bass, crappie, and bluegills. Scenic Prettyboy Reservoir, on the Gunpowder Falls River, has a 46-mile-long, irregularly shaped shoreline with numerous bays, coves, and islands inhabited by some trophy-sized smallmouth and largemouth bass and black crappies. Major features of this important lake, which is surrounded by beautiful northern hardwood forest and swamps dotted by numerous beaver dams, are shown on the free *DNR Fisherman's Map of Prettyboy Reservoir*. The sprawling clear blue waters of Loch Raven Reservoir, located to the south of Prettyboy Reservoir on the Gunpowder Falls

Reservoir, provides often excellent fishing along its stump and boulder-filled shoreline and rocky ledges and shoals for great northern pike, walleye, smallmouth and largemouth bass, and crappie up to trophy weights. The prime fishing areas shown on the free DNR *Fisherman's Map of Loch Raven Reservoir* include the Oak Tree Foundation, Old Faithful Log Jam, Warren Point, Dead Man's Cove, East and West Bosley Island, Peach Orchard Area, large Feather Island, the Cliffs Sand Bar, Seven Stumps Area, and the Old Limestone Quarry.

The most popular lures used in the central Maryland reservoirs include black plastic minnows, a purple worm rig for lunker bass, black rascal (pork rind), Fenton Fly (a small Shad Dart), Mepps Spinners fished deep, Tiny Torpedo, Sputterbug, and the deep-running Water Dog. The baits include minnows, crayfish, night crawlers, and hell-grammites. Boating permit applications for Prettyboy and Loch Raven reservoirs may be obtained from: Watershed Operations, Bureau of Operations, 3001 Druid Park Dr., Baltimore 21215.

The famous tidewater areas of the tributary rivers that flow into Chesapeake Bay, such as the great Susquehanna, Northeast, Pocomoke, Magothy, Bush, Gunpowder, Severn, Patuxent, Allens Fresh, and Port Tobacco rivers and the Choptank, Nanticoke, Wicomico, and Manokin rivers on the rural Eastern Shore provide often spectacular fly and spin fishing along the marshy coves and flats for large white and hickory shad, northern pike, chain pickerel, and largemouth and smallmouth bass.

The fishing potential of Maryland's lakes and streams is illustrated by a list of state record freshwater fish, compiled by the Maryland Sportfishing Tournament headquarters.

MARYLAND RECORD FRESHWATER FISH

	Lb.-oz.	Place	Method*	Bait	Year
Largemouth bass	10–4	Prettyboy Reservoir	CG	Prowler	1974
Smallmouth bass	8–4	Liberty Reservoir	BF	Crawfish	1974
Yellow perch	1–15	Liberty Reservoir	BF	Crawfish	1974
Chain pickerel	5–8	Leonard Pond	BF	Minnow	1975
Catfish	24–14	Potomac River	BF	Cut bait	1975
Carp	36	Patuxent River	—	—	1977
Crappie	3–14	Depot Lake	—	—	1977
Bluegill	2–2	Farm Pond	—	—	1978
Muskellunge	18–5	Susquehanna River	—	—	1977
Northern pike	19–8	Deep Creek Lake	—	—	1977
Brown trout	9–4	Beaver Creek	BF	—	1974
Rainbow trout	5–4	Gunpowder River	CG	Worm	1974
Brook trout	2–5	Steiner's Farm Pond	BF	Worm	1974
Walleye	9–8	Patapsco River	BF	Bull minnow	1975

*BF-baitfishing; CG-casting.

**18 inches.

Sport Fishing Tournament

The Maryland Sportfishing Tournament, sponsored by the Department of Natural Resources, honors resident and visiting anglers with awards and trophies for eligible species meeting the following minimum weight requirements, in pounds:

Largemouth bass	5	Muskellunge	10
Smallmouth bass	3	Northern pike	8
Yellow perch	⅞	Brook trout	2
Chain pickerel	4	Rainbow trout	2
Catfish	5	Walleye	5
Carp	15	Redear sunfish	1½
Crappie	¾	Bluegill	1

Fishing & Hunting Guides

For complete descriptions of the freshwater, Chesapeake Bay, and Atlantic coast divisions, write for the free *Maryland Sportfishing Tournament* brochure to: Bill Perry, DNR, Tarves State Office Bldg., Annapolis 21401. The DNR also publishes the following free fishing and hunting guides: *Maryland Sportfishing Guide*, which contains detailed information about licenses, season and special fishing areas, regulations, trout streams, lakes and ponds open to the public, a fish identification chart, all-purpose fisherman's knots, and live baits; a 32-page detailed *Tidewater Sportfishing Guide;* a 36-page *Maryland Hunting Guide;* a *Marylander's Guide to Venomous Snakes & Snakebite Treatment* (rattlesnakes and copperheads); and *Fish & Wildlife News,* a bimonthly publication available free on request.

Saltwater Fishing

Maryland's famous saltwater fishing potential in the Ocean City area —long known as the White Marlin Capital of the World—and the Atlantic shore and ocean and its renowned bays, including the Isle of Wight, Sinepuxent, Assawoman, Assateague, and Chincoteague, some 80 miles from the great inland sea of Chesapeake Bay (see "Chesapeake Bay Fish & Game Region"), is illustrated by the saltwater fishing records, as compiled by the Maryland Sportfishing Tournament headquarters.

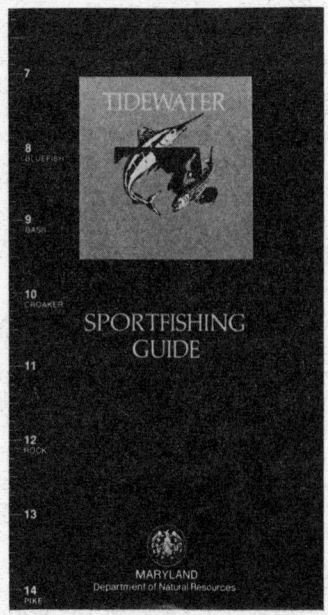

MARYLAND RECORD SALTWATER FISH

	Lb.-oz.	Place	Method*	Bait	Year
White marlin	119–8	S.E. Ocean City	T	Mackerel	1972
Blue marlin	569	Wilmington Canyon	T	Mullet	1975
Black drum	60–8	Ocean City	BF	Squid	1972
Tuna	625	45 mi. E. Ocean City	T	Mullet	1975
Shark	279	Sinepuxent Bay	BF	Bonito	1965
Striped bass	45	Assateague Island	S	Eel	1975
Dolphin	65	Off Ocean City	T	Eel	1973
Mako shark	224	Sugar Lump	T	Knucklehead	1969
Bluefish	23–8	Assateague Island	S	Cut spot	1974
Flounder	17	Assateague Island	S	Cut spot	1974
Tautog	18	African Queen	BF	Clam	1972
Seabass	7–8	Fenwick Shoal	BF	Clam	1973
Spotted seatrout	13	Sinepuxent Bay	BF	Cut spot	1973
Gray trout	12–4	Ocean City Inlet	BF	Squid	1975
Porgy	6–3	Fenwick Shoal	BF	Clam	1966
Kingfish	2–8	Assateague Island	S	Squid	1975
Wahoo	98–4	50 mi. 120° off Ocean City	T	Cut mullet	1972
Channel bass	67–8	Assateague Island	S	Croaker head	1974
False albacore	18–8	13 mi. E.S.E. Ocean City	T	Spoon	1971
		Bass Grounds	T	Spoon	1974

*BF-bottom fishing; S-surf casting; T-trolling.

ATLANTIC COAST FLY FISHING RECORDS

	Lb.-oz.	Place	Method*	Bait	Year
False albacore	8–1	Bass Grounds	CG	Streamer	1975
Bluefish	10–12	Winter Quarter Shoal	CG	Streamer fly	1975
Gray trout	5–9½	Bass Grounds	CG	Yellow streamer	1975
Shark	32	Atlantic Ocean	CG	Fly	1974

*CG-casting.

Hunting

Maryland's scenic rural farmlands, Appalachian Highlands, state forest lands and wildlife management areas, and vast coastal wetlands provide excellent hunting in season for whitetail deer, bobwhite quail, mourning doves, woodcock, snipe and rails, ducks and geese, and a few wild turkey in Savage River State Forest, Potomac State Forest, Green Ridge State Forest, and in the Dana Mountain, Mount Nebo, Warrior Mountain, Sideling Hill, and Bill Meyer wildlife management areas in the northwestern highlands.

Highway & Natural Resources Map

For anyone planning a trip through the state, the *Maryland Highway & Natural Resources Map* is essential. It shows all highways and other roads, route markers, population size of towns and cities, and special features such as forests and parks, information centers, picnic areas, airports, state and federal wildlife areas, camping areas, and rest areas. There is a mileage diagram showing distances between points. A chart of forests and parks is provided, showing facilities available in each. A list of lakes and ponds open to public fishing is provided, and the coordinates for location on the map are shown, as well as winter warmwater fishing areas, fish hatcheries and rearing stations, trout streams, wildlife management areas and sanctuaries, public hunting grounds, and public boat-launching ramps (listed by county). For a free copy, write to: Division of Tourist Development, Dept. of Economics & Community Development, 1748 Forest Dr., Annapolis 21401.

State Forest Fish & Game Lands

The Maryland state forests and game lands provide many opportunities for backpacking and camping, as well as good hunting in season for ruffed grouse, wild turkey, quail, mourning doves, waterfowl, whitetail deer, gray squirrel, and rabbit.

Savage River State Forest, in central and eastern Garrett County, is the largest Maryland state forest, encompassing about 53,000 acres of near wilderness. The forest, which completely surrounds the Savage River Dam, a strategic watershed area, is classified as a northern hardwood forest, and includes wild cherry, sugar and red maple, yellow and black birch, beech, basswood, white pine and hemlock, tulip poplar, and hickory. It can be located on the following U.S. Geological Survey Maps: Accident, Avilton, Barton, Bittinger, Frostburg, Grantsville, Lonaconing, McHenry.

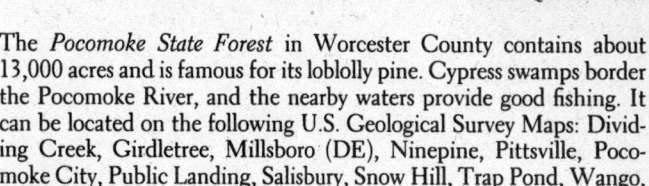

Swallow Falls State Forest, 5 miles northwest of Oakland, off U.S. 219, is the site of the initiation of Maryland's scientific forest program. Here one can find some of the best red pine plantations in the mid-Atlantic area, with abundant wildlife as well as some of the state's most beautiful scenery. It can be found on U.S. Geological Survey Maps: Oakland, Sang Run.

Potomac State Forest, in southeastern Garrett County off Maryland 135, contains approximately 12,500 acres of rugged mountain where the Potomac River's headwaters are situated. Timber is harvested regularly here, and the area is vital in the management of wildlife and watershed programs. It can be located on the following U.S. Geological Survey Maps: Artemas (PA), Bellegrove, Cresaptown, Cumberland, Davis (WV), Gorman, Great Cacapon, Hancock, Keyser (WV), Kitzmiller, Mount Storm (WV), Oldtown, Patterson Creek, Paw Paw (WV), Westernport.

Green Ridge State Forest, about 20 miles east of Cumberland in eastern Allegany County, off U.S. 40, is a large forestland containing about 28,000 acres. It has an abundance of wildlife, including wild turkey, grouse, deer, and squirrel. It can be located on these U.S. Geological Survey Maps: Artemas (PA), Bellegrove, Flintstone, Oldtown, Paw Paw (WV).

Doncaster State Forest, in western Charles County, contains yellow poplar, red gum, curly poplar, chestnut, and pine throughout its 1,500 acres. Locate it on U.S. Geological Survey Maps: Indian Head, Nanjemoy.

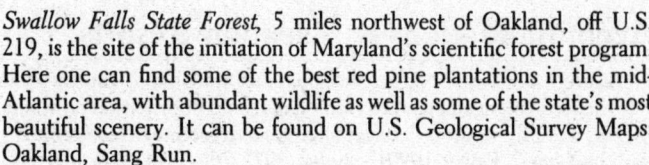

Elk Neck State Forest, in Cecil County off U.S. 7, comprises about 3,000 acres, and is a prime deer habitat. Wildlife food plots are maintained throughout the forest, and a fishing pond has been developed in cooperation with the Fish and Wildlife Administration. It can be found on one U.S. Geological Survey Map: Elkton.

Cedarville State Forest, northeast of Waldorf, is used for forestry research and demonstration, and is popular with hikers and backpackers. It can be located on U.S. Geological Survey Maps: Brandywine, Hughesville.

Wicomico State Forest, just south of Pittsville, contains about 1,100 acres of woodland, primarily used for research in loblolly pine. It is on one U.S. Geological Survey Map: Wango.

The *Pocomoke State Forest* in Worcester County contains about 13,000 acres and is famous for its loblolly pine. Cypress swamps border the Pocomoke River, and the nearby waters provide good fishing. It can be located on the following U.S. Geological Survey Maps: Dividing Creek, Girdletree, Millsboro (DE), Ninepine, Pittsville, Pocomoke City, Public Landing, Salisbury, Snow Hill, Trap Pond, Wango, Whaleysville.

Consult the excellent free brochure entitled *Maryland: The Mountains, The Bay, The Ocean, Recreation in Maryland's Parks & Forests*. One can be obtained from: Park Service, Tarves State Office Bldg., Annapolis 21401.

DELAWARE ENCYCLOPEDIA

Accommodations & Vacation Resorts

Delaware has a variety of accommodations available to the traveler. For the free 16-page *Delaware Hotel Guide* and information on where to stay, write to: Visitors Service, Division of Economic Development, 45 The Green, Dover 19901, phone (302) 678–4254. You may also contact local chambers of commerce.

Camping & State Recreation Areas

State campgrounds are maintained at Lum's Pond State Park in the Chesapeake & Delaware Canal Wildlife Area, northern Delaware, and at Trap Pond State Park, in southern Delaware. Trap Pond is surrounded by picturesque pine and hardwood forests, and contains the northernmost natural stands of cypress trees in the United States. Primitive camping and backpacking opportunities are available in several of the state forest and wildlife area game lands. For information on camping regulations, seasons, and reservations, write: Division of Parks, Recreation, & Forestry, Dept. of Natural Resources, William Penn St., Dover 19901.

Canoe Trails & Quality Fishing Waters

Canoeing in Delaware is limited by the terrain. Most of the state is situated in the Atlantic Coastal Plain. The relatively flat courses of the rivers and creeks do not lend themselves to extensive canoeing.

The northern portion of the state is in the hilly Piedmont Plateau. The chief waterway in this area is historic Brandywine Creek. This is a lovely 1-day trip by canoe. The creek flows through a very picturesque area. Symmetrical slopes, rising 200 feet above the water, line the shores of the upper course. Although the upper river is aesthetically more pleasing, the white-water enthusiast will enjoy views of the terracing slopes of the Brandywine battlefield above the northeastern shore. In the lower reaches of the Brandywine much of the industrial history of the United States and Delaware was written. Gristmills, textile mills, and other water-powered factories once stood on these shores. Most impressive are the mills of the Hagley Yards where the Du Pont company was founded in 1802 and where black powder was manufactured until the mid-1920s. It is now an industrial museum.

The Brandywine course begins at Lenape (PA), State Route 52, and ends directly above the Market Street Bridge in Wilmington at the tidewater mark. For further information, write: Division of Economic Development, 45 The Green, Dover 19901.

Fishing & Hunting in Delaware

Tiny Delaware, the nation's second-smallest state, offers some surprisingly good freshwater and saltwater fishing and hunting. Its 2,057-square-mile area, which is divided into two natural regions—the Piedmont Plateau in the extreme north and the low-lying Coastal Plain—is drained by the Delaware River, and the Murderkill, Mispillion, Indian, and Nanticoke rivers. During the spring, summer, and fall, its 50 ponds and streams yield largemouth and smallmouth bass, chain pickerel, black crappie, bluegills, trout, and white and yellow perch, shad, and striped bass in the tidewater areas. The Diamond State, which is in the eastern part of the Delmarva Peninsula, formed by Chesapeake Bay and the estuary of the Delaware River, has long been known for the quality of its coastal waterfowl shooting and surf and offshore saltwater fishing in the Bower Beach, Slaughter Beach, Mispillion Light, Breakwater Harbor, Lewes Beach, and Indian River areas. A daily *Fishing Forecast for Delaware Tidal Waters* may be

obtained by dialing (1–800) 282–8511. The climate is generally humid and mild, with cool winds warmed by the ocean currents. A healthy supply of insect repellent is advised during the mosquito-plagued summer months.

The quality and variety of the state's freshwater and saltwater fishing is illustrated by the Delaware record fish caught on rod and reel, as compiled by: Sportfishing Tournament, Division of Fish & Wildlife, D St., Dover 19901.

DELAWARE RECORD FRESHWATER FISH

	Lb.-oz.	Place	Year
Largemouth bass	9–8	Noxontown Pond	1969
Smallmouth bass	5–5	Red Mill Pond	1968
Chain pickerel	7–3	Horsey's Pond	1972
Rainbow trout	6–10	Brandywine Creek	1975
White shad	6–12	Brandywine Creek	1972
White perch	2–4	Red Mill Pond	1975
Yellow perch	2–5	Red Mill Pond	1975
Crappie	3–3	Noxontown Pond	1967
Bluegill	2	Red Mill Pond	—

DELAWARE RECORD SALTWATER FISH

	Lb.-oz.	Place	Year
White marlin	120	Baltimore Canyon	1972
Blue marlin	305	Baltimore Canyon	1975
Shark	390	Bowers Beach	1967
Tuna	153	Baltimore Canyon	1972
Black drum	113–1*	Cape Henlopen	1975
Channel bass	63–¾	Slaughter Beach	1971
Cod	44	Five Fathom Bank	1975
Dolphin	38	"B" Buoy	1974
False albacore	17	Atlantic Ocean	1971
Striped bass	48	Indian River Inlet	1974
Bluefish	21	Dewey Beach	1974
Flounder	17–5	Indian River Inlet	1974
Sea trout	13–15	Lewis Beach	1974
Atlantic mackerel	3	Atlantic Ocean	1973
King mackerel	22–8	Dewey Beach	1973
Wahoo	84–¾	Baltimore Canyon	1974
Kingfish	4	Bathing Beach	1973
Porgy	4–1	Fenwick Shoal	1975

*World's record.

For further information, including a listing of the official tournament weighing stations, contact: Division of Fish & Wildlife (address above).

Warmwater species are found in all Delaware's heavily fished ponds and larger streams, including Trap Pond in Trap Pond State Forest, Killen Pond in Killen Pond State Park, and Tub Mill, Coursey, Ingrams, Blair's, Griffith, McGinnis, Garrison's, Becks, and Lum's ponds, as well as the state record-producing waters listed above. Rainbow, brook, and brown trout are stocked seasonally in White Clay Creek, Brandywine Creek, Christina Creek, Beaver Run, Red Clay Creek, and Wilsons Run. Red Clay Creek from the Pennsylvania line to Yorklyn is restricted to fly fishing only. Fishing and hunting regulations may be obtained by writing: Division of Fish & Wildlife (address above).

Delaware's coastal wetland areas and central farmlands provide some of the East's finest shooting for Canada geese and ducks. The scenic interior woodlands and swamp areas provide good hunting in season for whitetail deer, rabbit and squirrel, bobwhite quail, mourning doves, woodcock, red fox, raccoon, and woodchuck. The Division of Fish & Wildlife publishes *Wildlife Area Maps*, available free on request.

Highway & Outdoor Recreation Map

The motorist will need the essential *Delaware Highways Map*, which shows principal highways and other roads, route markers, access points, airports, fish hatcheries, charter boat fishing, state park or recreation area, state police offices, campsites, lighthouses, and other features. Population of cities and towns are also indicated. There are insets showing Dover, Wilmington, northern New Castle County, and the Atlantic Ocean area. There is an index of cities and towns whose locations are shown on the map.

The reverse side contains an outdoor recreation guide to Delaware. Some scenic and historic routes are described, and outlined on an illustrative map. There is a chart of state parks and state forests showing the facilities available at each area. A chart of areas managed by the Division of Fish & Wildlife is also shown. Each area is location-keyed to the road map, and the chart shows which activities are available to sportsmen and vacationers (hunting, fishing, boat launching, etc.) at each area. There are capsule descriptions of state parks and state forests. The map is attractively illustrated with photos of Delaware attractions. To get your free map, write to: Visitors Service, 45 The Green, Dover 19901, phone (302) 678-4254.

PENNSYLVANIA
ENCYCLOPEDIA

Accommodations— Vacation Lodges & Resorts

Pennsylvania has vacation accommodations to suit every taste and pocketbook, encompassing the entire spectrum of standards of luxury. For information on where to stay, write to the local Chamber of Commerce of the town you plan to visit, or: Bureau of Travel Development, Dept. of Commerce, South Office Bldg., Harrisburg 17120, or the local chamber(s) of commerce of the town(s) you plan to visit. Many of the state's premier fishing and hunting lodges are open to private club members only. Several, however, such as the *Allenberry Inn* (Bolling Springs 17007) on the Yellow Breeches and the *Nemacolin Trail Hunting Resort* (P.O. Box 67, Farmington 15437) on Beaver Creek, are open to the public.

Allegheny National Forest

This renowned camping, fishing, and hunting region embraces 495,-000 acres of mixed hardwood forests, rolling hills, marshlands, and hundreds of miles of remote, wild trout streams along the Allegheny Plateau in northwest Pennsylvania. The major features include the Hearts Content and Tionesta virgin timber stands, Allegheny Reservoir, Minister Valley Backcountry, State Game Lands #28–29, Beaver Meadows Lake, Tracy Ridge and Hickory Creek wild areas, and the North Country, Tanbark, Twin Lakes, and Tracy Run trails. The forest is a top hunting area for whitetail deer, red fox, wild turkey, ruffed grouse, raccoon, and snowshoe hare.

Canoeing in Kinzua Country (available for $1 from: Kinzua Dam Vacation Bureau, 305 Market St., Warren 16365) contains detailed paddling info for Tionesta Creek, Conewango Creek, Brokenstraw Creek, and the famed bass, walleye, and muskellunge waters of the Allegheny and Clarion rivers. Canoe outfitting and guide services are provided by *Allegheny Outfitters*, P.O. Box 211, Clarendon 16313, phone (814) 726–1232; and *Indian Valley Campground & Canoe Livery*, Box 36, West Hickory 16370, phone (814) 755–3578.

Write to: Forest Supervisor, Allegheny National Forest, Warren 16365, for detailed fishing, camping, hiking, and hunting information and for the full-color *Allegheny National Forest Recreation Map* (50¢) and the free *Kinzua Dam-Allegheny Reservoir Map.* A complete listing of area accommodations, resorts, services, and recreational activities and facilities is contained in the 60-page booklet *Kinzua Country,* available free upon request from the forest supervisor. The forest is reached via U.S. 6, 62, and 219. Overnight accommodations, supplies, and equipment rental are available at Bradford, Kane, Ridgway, Sheffield, Tionesta, and Warren.

The Allegheny National Forest is shown on one U.S. Geological Survey Map (scale 1:250,000): Warren.

Appalachian National Scenic Trail

This renowned highland trail winds through the state for 225 miles and parallels, in some portions, the course of the Great Indian Warpath. The trail enters the state at the Delaware Water Gap, and follows the Blue Mountain Range, crosses the Cumberland Valley, and winds through the northernmost Blue Ridge Mountains.

Anyone planning to hike this great trail in Pennsylvania should obtain a copy of the comprehensive *Guide to the Appalachian Trail in Pennsylvania* ($9.25, 150 pp.), published by the Keystone Trails Association. It can be ordered from: Appalachian Trail Conference, P.O. Box 236, Harpers Ferry, WV 25425. The book contains information essen-

tial to the trail hiker, including the nature of the trail in Pennsylvania, trail markings, maintenance, fires, shelters and cabins, uniform distress signal, snakes, historical information, and organizations involved in trail maintenance such as the Keystone Trails Association. The trail is described in detail in 14 sections, reading north to south and south to north. A summary of distances is provided. There is an appendix, and some brief notes on other Pennsylvania trails.

The Appalachian Trail in the Delaware Gap area can be found on the following large-scale U.S. Geological Survey Maps: Kunkletown, Palmerton, Saylorsburg, Stroudsburg, Windgap. The Lehigh Gap Area Maps are: Auburn, Cementon, Hamburg, New Ringgold, New Tripoli, Palmerton, Slatedale. The Clinton Area of the trail is on the following maps: Auburn, Fredericksburg, Friedensburg, Indiantown Gap, Pine Grove, Swatara Gap. The Susquehanna River Area can be found on the maps for: Blue Ridge Summit, Caledonia Park, Dickinson, Duncannon, Iron Springs, Mechanicsburg, Mount Holly Springs, Scotland, Smithsburg (MD), Walnut Bottom, Waynesboro, Wertzville. The Swatara Gap Area is on these maps: Duncannon, Enders, Grantville, Halifax, Indiantown Gap.

Backpacking & Primitive Camping

Pennsylvania is one of the best backpacking and primitive camping states in the eastern United States. Thousands of miles of remote, scenic trails and old logging roads wind through the state's vast mixed hardwood and conifer forestlands and high country past meadows and valleys, wild mountain trout streams and bogs, lakes and ponds, beaver dams, canyons, and marshlands. The major trail systems in eastern Pennsylvania include the famed Appalachian National Scenic Trail (q.v.), the granddaddy of hiking trails, with 8 Adirondack shelters along the route between Lehigh Gap and the Susquehanna, and the Horse Shoe and Loyalstock trails to the north. The state forests of central Pennsylvania are traversed by the Appalachian Trail and numerous spur routes: the 400-mile-long Tuscarora Big Blue Trail, which leaves the Appalachian Trail west of the Susquehanna River and winds along the Blue Mountains until it joins the Appalachian again in Virginia's Shenandoah National Park; the primitive 55-mile-long ridgetop Mid-State Hiking Trail; the Penns Creek Trail, which follows an abandoned railroad bed for 8 miles through a beautiful mountain gorge; the Quehanna Trail, which winds through the remote 46,163-acre Quehanna Wild area in the Elk and Moshannon state forests; the 85-mile-long Susquehannock Trail, which loops through the state forest wildlands in Potter County; the 40-mile-long Black Forest Trail in Lycoming County; and the scenic Grand Canyon trails—the Turkey Path and Barbour Rock Trail—in the Tioga State Forest and the Donut Hole Trail system in the Sproull State Forest.

The highlands and forests of western Pennsylvania are traversed by the North Country Trail and Tanbark Trail in the Allegheny National Forest; the 32-mile-long Laurel Highland Trail in Somerset and Cambria counties—designed primarily for backpacking; the Forbes Road Historic Trail in Fulton County, which follows a portion of the old Forbes Road—an overland trail first blazed during the French and Indian War to enable a military expedition to move west to drive the French and Indians from the forks of the Ohio River; the 33-mile-long Traders Path in Westmoreland, Indiana and Armstrong counties—an important Indian trail during the 18th century; the High Point Trail, which winds through Armstrong, Indiana, Jefferson, and Forest counties, past several primitive campsites and 11 Adirondack shelters before it joins the North Country Trail in the Allegheny National Forest; and the Warriors Trail, an ancient Indian footpath, which winds for 67 miles in southwestern Pennsylvania and West Virginia.

For comprehensive, detailed information on backpacking and hiking in Pennsylvania, a number of free publications are available. The definitive guide to Pennsylvania trails is the Keystone Trail Association's excellent *Pennsylvania Hiking Trails in State Parks, Game Lands, and Elsewhere*. This 91-page book ($2.50) is available from: Appalachian Trail Conference, P.O. Box 236, Harpers Ferry, WV 25425. It contains useful general information on maps, state game lands, and forests and parks. It also contains a list of motels, restaurants, inns, private campgrounds, etc., located near hiking areas, moderately priced, and where hikers are welcome. Thirty-four major and minor hiking trails are described, with a sketch map of each trail on a facing page. Descriptions of each trail include map information, camping data, and addresses where you can write for further information. The Department of Environmental Resources has two free brochures: *Hiking Trails of Pennsylvania* and *Natural Areas in Pennsylvania*. These publications list and describe popular hiking trails and natural areas. For additional information on trails, you can write to: Keystone Trails Assn., RD2, Coopersburg 18036; or to: Bureau of Forestry, Dept. of Environmental Resources, P.O. Box 1467, Harrisburg 17120.

For the nitty-gritty on backpacking and primitive camping, information as well as guides and maps for specific trail systems, write to the following organizations. Baker Trail and Traders Path: American Youth Hostels, 6300 5th Ave., Pittsburgh 15232. A *Baker Trail Guide Book* is available for $1 (the *Old Traders Path*, a 23-page booklet is available free from: Moraine Trails Council, 830 Morton Ave., Butler 16001). Black Forest Trail: Tiadaghton State Forest, 423 E. Central Ave., South Williamsport 17701 (a *Black Forest Map-Guide* is available for $1—make check payable to Tiadaghton Forest Fire Fighters Assn.). Donut Hole Trail: Sproull State Forest, Box 247, 150 6th St., Renovo 17764 (ask for free *Donut Hole Trail System Map*). Horse Shoe Trail: Trails Chairman, 623 Righters Mill Rd., Narberth 19072. Laurel Highland Trail: Laurel Ridge State Park, RD3, Rockwood 15557. Loyalstock Trail: Alpine Club, P.O. Box 501, Williamsport 17701. Mid-State Trail: Penn State Outing Club, 60 Recreation Bldg., Penn State University, University Park 16802. Susquehannock Trail: Potter County Recreation, P.O. Box 245, Warren 16365. Warrior Trail: W. Bertram Waychoff, 405 Huffman St., Waynesburg 15370. A *Hiker's Guide to the Forbes Road Historic Trail* is available for 80¢ postpaid from: Mason-Dixon Council, P.O. Box 2133, Hagerstown, MD 21740.

HIKING TRAILS OF PENNSYLVANIA

COMMONWEALTH OF PENNSYLVANIA
DEPARTMENT OF ENVIRONMENTAL RESOURCES
HARRISBURG, PENNSYLVANIA

Bald Eagle State Forest

The fish and game lands of the 180,000-acre Bald Eagle State Forest in Snyder, Union, Centre, and Mifflin counties encompass the nationally famous trophy limestone trout fishing waters of Bald Eagle, Penns, Laurel Run, Little Fishing, Buffalo, and Jacks creeks. The forest contains several hundred miles of scenic hiking trails and old logging roads that provide access to the interior backpacking, fishing, hunting, and primitive camping areas in the virgin white pine and hemlock forests of the 77-acre Joyce Kilmer Natural Area; the 5,119-acre Hook Natural Area of mixed oak forest along the North Branch of Buffalo Creek; the old-growth hemlocks and sandstone outcrops of 600-acre Mount Logan Natural Area; the mountain bogs and cranberry, mountain holly and high bush blueberry thickets of the 140-acre Rosecrans Bog; the virgin pine-hemlock and pitch pine wilds of the 500-acre Snyder-Middlesworth Natural Area; the beautiful, remote 1,000-acre Tall Timbers Natural Area on Swift Run, with its second-growth oak, white pine, hemlock, and hard pine-oak forests; and the 3,581-acre White Mountain Wild Area along the deep trout pools and riffles of famous Penn Creek. For detailed information, write: Supervisor, Bald Eagle State Forest, Mifflinburg 17844.

The forest is shown on the following U.S. Geological Survey Maps: Beaver Springs, Beavertown, Carroll, Centre Hall, Coburn, Hartleton, Jersey Shore, Loganton, Madisonburg, McClure, Middleburg, Mill Hall, Millheim, Mingoville, Richfield, Spring Mills, Weikert, Williamsport, Woodward.

Boone & Crockett Club

The Boone & Crockett Club, established in 1887 by Theodore Roosevelt at the age of 29 along with a small group of progressive sportsmen, is best known today for its activities in recording and publicly recognizing outstanding trophies of the 32 species of North American mammals which the club considers as qualified by game using its official scoring system. The coveted Sagamore Hill Medal, first awarded in 1948 for the outstanding trophy in the big-game competitions, has been presented nine times over the years for trophy Alaskan brown bear, mountain goat, wapiti, woodland caribou, white sheep, stone sheep, mule deer, and whitetail deer.

The club's progressive conservation activities over the years have saved the small herd of bison that were being poached and slaughtered in Yellowstone Park at the turn of the century; led to the exploration and creation of Glacier National Park through the efforts of one of its founders, George Bird Grinnell, editor of *Forest and Stream;* explored and established Mount McKinley National Park in Alaska, spearheaded by the efforts of Charles Sheldon, hunter, conservationist, and scientist; was instrumental in the organization of the Save-the-Redwoods League in California; led to the establishment of the Charles Sheldon Antelope Range and the preservation of the key deer in Florida; and has undertaken preservation studies of the cougar, grizzly, polar bear, and most recently, the wolf.

The *Records Book of North American Big Game* (403 pp., $15), available from: Boone & Crockett Club, 424 N. Washington St., Alexandria, VA 22314, lists nearly 5,000 individual trophy specimens of North American big game in 32 categories, giving the rank of each trophy, its detailed measurements, and name of hunter and place taken. It reproduces each of the official scoring charts, instructions for measurements, and rules of fair chase. The book contains 47 photographs of the ranking trophies, in addition to other photographs, maps, and drawings, and articles by the world's leading hunting authorities.

Campgrounds & State Recreation Areas

The Bureau of Travel Development has published a free 37-page booklet entitled *Four-Season Camping in Pennsylvania.* This publication lists, in handy chart form, private campgrounds as well as state parks, providing travel directions, mailing addresses and phones, and facilities available at each area. For the traveler's convenience the state is broken down by region (there is a map in front showing where each of these regions is), each consisting of a number of counties. For information on individual campgrounds you should write or call the campground operators. A copy of this informative booklet can be obtained by writing to: Bureau of Travel Development, Dept. of Commerce, South Office Bldg., Harrisburg 17120.

For information on Pennsylvania's state parks, you can consult the free brochure *State Parks,* which provides names, counties, addresses, and phone numbers of all state parks, presenting in chart form the recreational facilities currently available in each. For a copy of this brochure, or further information on specific parks, cabin rentals, park activities, and other questions, write to: Office of Public Information, Dept. of Environmental Resources, Box 1467, Harrisburg 17120.

If snowmobiling is your forte, you should send for the free *Pennsylvania Snowmobile Trail Directory,* available from: Bureau of Travel Development (address above). This publication lists, by county, all the state's snowmobile trails on public lands, indicating mileage and agency to contact for each trail. The locations are shown on a map, differentiating among state forest and park trails, state game-land trails, and so on.

Canoeing & Wild-Water Outfitters

Pennsylvania has a great variety of scenic and wild-water rivers that provide excellent canoe-camping, white-water, and fishing opportunities along the way for rainbow, brook, and brown trout, largemouth and smallmouth bass, pickerel, walleye, and a few voracious muskellunge. The canoe routes found within the state's three major river basins—the Delaware, Susquehanna, and Ohio—are shown and described in detail in the *Pennsylvania Canoe Country Map-Guide,* available free upon request from: Bureau of Travel Development, Dept. of Commerce, South Office Bldg., Harrisburg 17120. This useful guide contains a map showing the major canoe trails during normal water conditions, with color codes to indicate expected degree of difficulty. The guide also contains detailed descriptions of each canoe route and charts showing public lakes available for canoeing as well as facilities available (launch ramps, boat moorings, campgrounds). A 3 × 5-foot *Stream Map of Pennsylvania* is available from Pennsylvania State University for $1 plus 6¢ resident tax. Write: Stream Map of Pennsylvania, Box 6000, University Park 16802. White-water canoeists and kayakers are urged to wear a life vest, a good crash helmet—and, when the water temperature is below 50°, a wet suit to survive the paralyzing effect of ice-water immersion. Canoeists are urged to contact the State Fish Commission in Harrisburg before their trip, to determine water conditions.

The state's major canoe routes include the scenic upper Allegheny River from Kinzua Dam downstream past numerous islands, valleys, and scenic mixed hardwood and evergreen forests; the Clarion River, a tributary of the Allegheny—a good early season route with excellent scenery; the wild and powerful Youghiogheny River in the southwest, a tributary of the Monongahela and one of the premier white-water streams in the eastern United States; the main branch of the Susquehanna River, once the main north-south travel route for the six Iroquois nations, which winds for nearly 500 miles through central

Pennsylvania's scenic woodlands and valleys, past Standing Stone—a huge remnant of the glacial age—the cliffs of the Wyalusing Rocks, which tower 500 feet above the river, Wyoming Valley, McKee Half Falls, eroded ledges, channels, and several dams; the beautiful West Branch of the Susquehanna, a magnificent canyon river which flows from its wild headwaters deep in the forests of north central Pennsylvania to its confluence with the main branch at Williamsport; the remote, unspoiled stretches of Pine Creek in the heart of the wild forestlands of the north central region, which flows through its awesome gorge known as the "Grand Canyon of Pennsylvania"; Moshannon Creek, or the "Red Mo" as it is commonly called, a white-water wilderness stream flowing through the forests of the central region, with a yellowish red streambed from abandoned coal mines; the beautiful wild water, rapids, and famous trout waters of Loyalstock Creek, a tributary of the West Branch Susquehanna, in Lycoming and Sullivan counties; the slow-flowing, meandering Juniata River, with its many boulders, shoals, and eel traps; and the magnificent big waters of the historic upper Delaware River, and its renowned white-water tributaries—the Lackawaxen and Lehigh rivers.

Guided wild-water and scenic canoe trips, rentals, and gear are provided by the following canoe trip outfitters. For the Youghiogheny River, contact *Mountain Streams & Trails*, Box 106, Ohiopyle 15470; *Whitewater Adventures*, Box 31, Ohiopyle 15470; and *Wilderness Voyageurs*, P.O. Box 97, Ohiopyle 15470. Elsewhere in the state, contact *Kittatinny Canoes*, Silver Lake Rd., Dingmans Ferry 18328 (for Delaware and Lackawaxen rivers); *Norse Paddle Co.*, P.O. Box 77, Pine Grove Mills 16868; *Dauber Canoe & Kayak Headquarters*, P.O. Box 59, Washington Crossing 18977 (Delaware River); *Laurel Highland River Tours*, 1286 Washington St., Indiana 15701 (summer: Box 86, Rte. 381, Mill Run 15464); the *Pocono Boathouse*, Old Rte. 940, Pocono Pines 18350; and *Allegheny Outfitters*, P.O. Box 211, Clarendon 16313 (Allegheny River and National Forest). For additional wildwater outfitting information, write: *Eastern River Guide Assn.*, P.O. Box 33, Ohiopyle 15470.

Fenwick Pennsylvania Fly Fishing Schools

The world-famous Fenwick Corporation operates 2-day fly fishing schools during August on Spruce Creek—one of the fabled Appalachian limestone streams. The school is held on private waters, which include 6 meandering miles of Spruce Creek and a small lake used as a casting pond. Spruce Creek is the stream President Eisenhower used to fish, and one of the Fenwick instructors used to coach Ike. On-stream and classroom instruction includes use and types of fly line, rod and reel construction, how to choose tackle and terminology, entomology, choice of flies and how to match the hatch, fly fishing knots, casting technique, reading the stream, and playing the fish. Accommodations are available at Spruce Creek Lodge—15 miles west of State College in the center of Pennsylvania. Fenwick also runs 2-day schools at the huge Seven Springs Mountain Lodge in Champion, during April, May, and June. Both schools are open to beginning through advanced fly fishermen.

For free literature, rates, and registration information, write: Director, Fenwick Fly Fishing School, Eastern Division, 2202 Glen Court, Rt. 7, Frederick, MD 21701 (301-663-3966).

Fish & Game Frontiers Travel Service

Fish and Game Frontiers, one of the nation's most renowned firms specializing in outdoor recreation travel, offers guided trips and travel service for freshwater and saltwater fishing, Atlantic salmon fishing, big game hunting, wingshooting, Africa photo tours, and special tours, as well as foreign independent travel. Free brochures are available upon request for the following package trips (include air transportation, lodging, meals, and professional guide services): Columbia Special Summer Quail/Dove Hunt; Birdshooting at Snook Inn on Mexico's Yucatan Peninsula; Trophy Tarpon and Snook Fishing at Casa

Mar Lodge, Costa Rica; Bonefishing Adventure at Boca Paila on the Mexican Caribbean; Quebec's Mistassini Reserve Trophy Fishing; Atlantic Salmon Fishing on Iceland's famed Laxa; New Mexico Antelope Hunt; Alaskan Wood River—Tik Chik Lake Chain Wilderness Fishing; Labrador Trophy Squaretail and Salmon Fishing; Rainbow King Lodge—Iliamna Lake, Alaska; African Hunt Safaris; Pheasant Shooting in Denmark; Club Pacifico-Panama Sportfishing Camp; and, New Zealand Trophy Trout Fishing. For the trip brochures listed above, rates, and custom travel planning service, write: *Fish & Game Frontiers*, P.O. Box 161, Pearce Mill Rd., Wexford, PA 15090 (phone: 402–931–6640).

Fishing & Hunting in Pennsylvania

Pennsylvania's forest-mantled mountain ranges and extensive river systems offer some of the East's finest hunting for whitetail deer, wild turkey, and ruffed grouse and fishing for large, wary trout, trophy muskellunge, and hard-hitting smallmouth bass. Much of the state is covered by mountains: the Alleghenies to the west; the curious "breadstick"-shaped ridges of the Appalachian system, linking the southern mountains with the Poconos and Catskills to the northeast, which begin the northern Appalachian Range; and the central and north-central ranges, which contain some of the wildest territory in the state. An extensive system of springs produces the clear, sparkling mountain streams and rich, limestone creeks which crisscross the state, most of them converging in three great watersheds: the Allegheny, Susquehanna, and Delaware rivers. There are millions of acres of public forests, fields, and marshes contained in one national forest—the Allegheny—a large number of state forests and parks, state game lands, and cooperating farm tracts open to sportsmen. Though Pennsylvania boasts an outdoors-oriented population of over 11 million, abundant recreational resources and progressive, dedicated fish and game commissions furnish quality fishing and hunting. The state is dominated by the Allegheny River on the west, the sprawling Susquehanna system, draining the central, north-central, and south-central portions of the state, and the Delaware, which forms the eastern border with New York and New Jersey.

The Keystone State provides fishing for a great variety of species, including brook, brown, rainbow, lake, and steelhead trout; coho, Chinook, and kokanee salmon; muskellunge, northern pike, both kinds of bass, walleye, shad, catfish, and assorted panfish. The state trophy fish records indicate the angling potential of Pennsylvania's waters.

PENNSYLVANIA RECORD FISH

	Lb.-oz.	Place	Year
Brook trout	5–11½	Bald Eagle Creek	1977
Brown trout	24	Lake Wallenpaupack	1967
Lake trout	24	Crystal Lake	1952
Rainbow trout	10–4	Yellow Breeches Creek	1974
Steelhead trout	11	Twenty Mile Creek	1977
Coho salmon	*	Lake Erie	1972
Chinook salmon	23	Trout Run	1975
Largemouth bass	8–8	Stillwater Lake	1936
Smallmouth bass	6–2	Conodoguinet Creek	1937
Muskellunge	54–3	Conneaut Lake	1924
Northern pike	21–4	Lake Erie	1971
Chain pickerel	8	Shohola Falls	1937
Walleye	12	Allegheny River	1951
American white shad	7–4	Delaware River	1965
Yellow perch	*	Oneida Dam	1936
Crappie	31–4	Pinchot State Park Lake	1971
Bluegill	1–8	Pymatuning Lake	1974
Rock bass	3–2	Elk Creek Lake	1971
Brown bullhead	*	Forest Lake	1975
Channel catfish	35	Allegheny River	1970
Flathead catfish	35	Allegheny River	1975
Carp	52	Juniata River	1962

*Weights unknown. Lengths: coho salmon, 31 inches; yellow perch, 18 inches; brown bullhead, 18 inches.

Allegheny River Country

The famed Allegheny River rises in the timbered ridges and mountain slopes of north central Pennsylvania near Coudersport. The laurel-shaded headwaters furnish good fishing for brook trout, and as the stream approaches Coudersport, brown and rainbow trout grow in both numbers and size. From the town downstream to the New York border (it flows in a northerly direction in this segment), the Allegheny becomes a full-fledged river and produces some trophy trout: big, hook-jawed browns and rainbows reaching record weights, as well as chunky brook or speckled trout. As the river widens, smallmouth bass, muskies, and panfish add to the angling thrills along this excellent stretch of water.

The Allegheny flows north out of Pennsylvania into New York State for about 30 miles and spills into the top of the long, cove-indented expanse of Allegheny Reservoir, one of the best lakes in the state, which brings its flow back into Pennsylvania. The clean waters of this big impoundment skirt the western edge of the Allegheny National Forest and produce exciting fishing for big muskies, trout, smallmouth bass, walleye, and panfish. After passing out of the lake through the Kinzua Dam, the river starts on its final journey to Pittsburgh, where it joins the Monongahela to form the Ohio River. As the river broad-

ens, trout gradually disappear, but the muskies, smallmouth, and walleyes are joined by voracious great northern pike. The Allegheny National Forest portion of the river from the Kinzua Dam to Tionesta Station at the forest's southwest edge is one of the premium fishing stretches in the state, particularly for big muskellunge. The French Creek system enters the Allegheny at Oil City, and this stream and its tributaries provide fine angling for muskies and smallmouths. Good fishing continues down to the Kittanning area about 40 miles northeast of Pittsburgh, where water quality declines.

Susquehanna River System

The broad Susquehanna, one of the East's major rivers, meanders in a northwesterly direction from its confluence with Chesapeake Bay in Maryland upstream to Sunbury, where it forks into North and West branches. At the downstream end in the Maryland border area there are three big impoundments: Conowingo, Haltwood, and Safe Harbor dams. The lakes and dam tailrace waters furnish good angling for smallmouth and largemouth bass, muskies, northern pike, walleyes, catfish, and panfish, particularly crappies and bluegills. The Susquehanna, including both branches and most tributaries, provides some of the finest smallmouth fishing in the East, and as one progresses upstream the quality of the fishing improves with the scenery. Muskies, pike, walleyes, pickerel, catfish, and panfish are found in both forks. From Sunbury, the North Branch winds upstream in a northerly path to the New York line at South Waverly. The fishing in this swift fork is superb, especially for smallmouths, and many of the tributaries, such as the Lackawanna and Tunkhannock, offer fine trout angling. The West Branch drains the center of the state as it flows east to Sunbury from its headwaters to the south of Allegheny National Forest in Clearfield, Jefferson, and Indiana counties. This part of the river contains the same general species as the north segment, and the beauty of the mixed hardwood forests in this mountainous area complements the excellent fishing, with muskies, smallmouths, and walleyes being the most prized quarries. Some of Pennsylvania's prime trophy trout streams, both freestone and limestone, are tributaries of this beautiful, swift-flowing river.

Delaware River

The rapid-filled upper reaches of the Delaware enter Pennsylvania at the northeast corner of the state near Hancock, and the river forms the eastern border as it flows south through the forested margins of the Catskill and Pocono mountains, the pastoral Pennsylvania German country, and the industrial regions of Philadelphia and Wilmington to spill into the tidewaters at Delaware Bay. Hordes of deep, silvery shad endure the industrial wastes of the lower reaches, as the spawning urge propels them upstream to the tributaries. Shad attain weights in excess of 10 pounds, and are powerful, determined battlers, giving them the name "poor man's salmon." They will strike small spoons, shad darts—a small jig, dressed with bucktail or marabou—and shad flies, which have a tinsel body, and sparse hair or feather wings. Bright red, orange, or pink beads are often placed ahead of the eye of the hook for added attraction. In shad fishing the important thing is to keep the lure, whether cast or trolled, just off the bottom. A big shad, hooked in fast water, makes strong runs, occasional jumps, and uses its deep body to advantage in the current. The savory, although bony flesh and delicious roe of the hen fish make this big herring an angler's delight. The best fishing is above Easton, particularly upstream through the magnificent, steep-sided Delaware Water Gap to the Port Jervis, New York, area.

From Easton north, the Delaware becomes increasingly clean and more beautiful and is a treat for fishermen and canoeists. Bass, particularly smallmouth, muskies, pickerel, walleye, and panfish, are found throughout the length of the river, and to the north, the classic streams of the Poconos and Catskills add trout to the deep boulder-strewn pools and frothing runs of upper stretches. Anglers who know the water take some enormous rainbows and browns on spinning lures and bait, and fly fishermen score well with nymphs, streamers, Muddler Minnows, and dry flies. Of the latter, an Adams-type pattern with a silver body is a particular killer when the big trout are feeding on the surface. Walleye and bass are taken on bait—minnows, night crawlers, hellgrammites, and, above all, small lampreys, as well as standard spinners, spoons, jigs, and plugs. Fly fishermen do well on smallmouth using streamers, bushy dry flies, and surface bugs.

Fishing Guides, Maps & Charts

Anglers should write to: Fish Commission, P.O. Box 1673, Harrisburg 17120, for the free *Summary of Fishing Regulations and Laws*, which furnishes the usual rules, restrictions, seasons, and limits, and lists the fly fishing-only waters, the fish-for-fun areas, special season streams and lakes, and approved trout waters. Regional commission offices and fish wardens are listed, with addresses and telephone numbers. The commission produces an extremely useful, free booklet, *List of Pennsylvania Fishing Waters*, which specifies the state's principal lakes and streams by region and alphabetically within each region by county and indicates the fish species present in every listing. In addition, the commission publishes the following angler's aids, available free upon request: *Fishing in Pennsylvania, Favorite Trout Waters, Favorite Lakes of Eastern Pennsylvania, Favorite Lakes of Western Pennsylvania, Fly Fishing-Only Waters, 100 Best Fishing Spots, Salmon Fishing Guide, Ice Fishing,* and *Pennsylvania Boating Guide*. A beautiful full-color 32-page booklet, *Pennsylvania Fishes*, is available from the commission for $1 along with the full-color *Fish Chart* ($1) and the handy *Fly Tying Guide* ($1.50), by George Harvey.

Waterproof *Lake Contour Maps* showing underwater natural and man-made structures and hydrographics are available for $2.95 each (include 50¢ postage) for the following Pennsylvania lakes and reservoirs: Allegheny, Crooked Creek, East Branch (Clarion), Loyalhanna, Mahoning Creek, Shenango, Tionesta Creek, and Youghiogheny. Order direct from: Lakes Illustrated, Box 4854 GS, Springfield, MO 65804.

Trophy Trout Streams

Pennsylvania has been famous for trout fishing since classic fly fishing began after the Civil War. The Pocono Mountains area, with its thick

hemlock and hardwood forests and beautiful rhododendron- and laurel-shaded streams and rivers, has added a great deal to the literature of fly fishing. Streams such as the twisting Lehigh River System, spilling into the Delaware at Easton; Brodhead Creek and its exquisite feeder, Paradise Creek, flowing into the Delaware at Stroudsburg; the Bushkill to the north; and the Lackawaxen—schooling grounds for author and ardent angler Zane Grey—entering the Delaware upstream at Shohola, have offered fine trout fishing for generations, as well as bass, walleye, and other species in the lower reaches. Lake Wallenpaupack, which drains into the Lackawaxen, contains some of the largest rainbow and brown trout (state record, 24 pounds) in the East, as well as muskies, bass, walleyes, and assorted panfish. Harveys and Crystal lakes, on the western edge of the Poconos, contain lake trout, kokanee, trout, bass, and panfish. To the north of Wallenpaupack in Wayne County is the beautiful, cold Upper Woods Lake, which provides angling for rainbows and kokanee in some of the most scenic country in Pennsylvania.

In the center of the state are a series of stream systems, tributaries of the West Branch of the Susquehanna, which offer fine trout fishing for browns and rainbows, as well as brookies in the forest headwaters. The Loyalstock enters the big river to the east of Williamsport at Montoursville. This stream and some of its tributaries, such as the Little Loyalstock and Elk Creek, contain good trout populations, including some large fish. Among the other fine trout streams flowing into the West Branch are the Big Pine Creek System, 15 miles west of Williamsport; Young Woman's Creek at Gleasonton near Hyner Run State Park, with 6 miles of fly fishing-only water on the right branch; Kettle Creek to the west at Westport; the vast Sinnamahoning Creek watershed which drains an immense, fan-shaped area—the First Fork produces lots of trophy browns; and the famous Bald Eagle Creek and its many noted feeder streams which spill into the Susquehanna just east of Lock Haven. The Bald Eagle yields eye-popping brown trout, as does its limestone tributary, Big Fishing Creek, whose rich, alkaline waters provide some superior fly fishing.

Another great trout stream is Penns Creek, a limestone stream complex rising in a ridge system a short distance to the south of Big Fishing Creek and running east into the main Susquehanna above Selinsgrove. Trophy browns await the skilled angler who hits the stream or its Elk and Pine Creek feeders at the right time.

South central Pennsylvania contains some world-famous limestone trout streams in the lush region surrounding the beautiful town of Carlisle. This is classic, pastoral fly fishing, reminiscent of the legend-

ary British chalk streams, the Test and the Itchen. Brown and rainbow trout grow long, deep, and heavy in these insect-rich waters, but their elusiveness increases with their weight. A whole school of American limestone fishing technique has arisen with special tackle and patterns suited to the demanding water conditions and insect hatches, and perfected by expert anglers such as Charles Fox and Vince Marinaro. The best known of these streams are the Letort, Yellow Breeches, and Big Spring creeks. It is advisable to be equipped with local patterns designed for these waters, because the fish are superselective. The Letort Cricket, the Jassid series, and the Leaf Hopper are a few examples of terrestrial flies which were developed for summer fishing on these exacting waters. Local fishing information and individual fly-fishing instruction in the area is provided by the famed *Yellow Breeches Fly Shop*, Box 200, Rte. 174, Boiling Springs 17007 (phone: 717-258-6752).

Lake Erie

The short shoreline exposure on Lake Erie furnishes Pennsylvania anglers with an opportunity to fish for steelheads, coho, and Chinook salmon, as well as for Great Lakes muskies, bass, walleyes, northern pike, and panfish. Some of the favorite spots for the spectacular lake-run trout and salmon are Presque Isle Bay at the city of Erie, and Trout Run, Elk, Walnut, and Twenty Mile creeks, all within 25 miles of Erie.

Muskellunge Waters

Muskellunge have been stocked throughout Pennsylvania in many streams, lakes, and ponds. Some of the better waters include Pymatuning Reservoir in the northwest on the Ohio border, nearby Conneaut Lake (state record), Canadohta Lake to the northeast, Tionesta Lake on the southwest rim of Allegheny National Forest, Juniata River and Conodoguinet Creek, north of Carlisle in south central Pennsylvania, and Raystown Lake, an impoundment on the Raystown Branch of the Juniata southeast of Altoona. Smallmouth bass are found in every part of the state and, like the musky, inhabit the major river systems as well as the major lakes. Conodoguinet Creek (state record), the Juniata River system, Youghiogheny Reservoir and River (muskies, northern pike, walleye, and trout too) in southwest Pennsylvania on the Maryland border, and Shenango Lake on the Ohio border near Sharon in northwest Pennsylvania are good bets, and the Shenango holds northerns and walleyes to complement the bronzebacks.

The Fish Commission publishes a free *Fishing and Boating Map* in cooperation with the Department of Transportation; it has the state road map on one side and a color-coded map on the reverse which indicates the principal streams, lakes, and boating access areas. The accompanying chart contains the following information for each of the 626 fishing spots on the map: location on both maps, type of ownership, type of fish present, and facilities. Fly fishing and fish-for-fun projects are listed along with mileage involved. This useful map can be used in conjunction with the *List of Pennsylvania Fishing Waters* mentioned earlier to gain an overview of the fishing possibilities.

Largemouth bass, panfish, and catfish are well distributed throughout Pennsylvania in the warmer waters. Channel and flathead catfish hot spots include the lower reaches of the major river systems and big, warm lakes and impoundments.

Pennsylvania Angler magazine is published by: Fish Commission (address above); it costs $3 per year or $7.50 for 3 years. The magazine contains articles about where to go, tackle and lures, conservation news, fishing tips, and various species of wildlife and is of real value to anyone who fishes the state's waters.

Hunting & Wildlife

Hunters invade the fields and forests of Pennsylvania by the hundreds of thousands each fall: well over 1 million hunting licenses are sold. Whitetail deer are the most prized game variety, and black bear are hunted in the most remote forest areas. Small-game species include wild turkeys, ruffed grouse, woodcock, pheasants, bobwhite quail, mourning doves, ducks, geese, rabbits, and squirrels. Write to: Game Commission, P.O. Box 1567, Harrisburg 17120, for a free *Pennsylvania Hunting Regulations* booklet which describes the seasons, species, bag limits, restricted areas, and special rules and provides a list of wardens, with their addresses and telephone numbers. The commission will also furnish a list of free department literature about various animals and game, conservation projects, wildlife areas, refuges, the hunting regions of the state, plants, and related topics; it also publishes the following free hunter's aids: *Hunting in Pennsylvania* series (Northwest, Northeast, Southwest, Southeast), *Duck Identification Chart*, *Vanishing Spitfire* (bobcat), *Keystone Bruin* (black bear), *Whitetail Deer, Woodchuck, Ruffed Grouse, Wild Turkey in Pennsylvania, American Woodcock, Beaver in Pennsylvania, After the Buck Season, List of Protected Species, Ten Commandments of Shooting Safety, Deer & Bear Harvest Map*, and the *Wildlife Notes* series (red fox, owl, varying hare, and so forth). Among other useful commission booklets and charts are *Big Game Records Book* ($1), *Whitetail Deer* (50¢), *Birdlife of Pennsylvania* ($2, waterfowl, wild turkey, and upland game-bird species), *Mammals of Pennsylvania* ($2.50), and a full-color *Bird Identification Chart* ($2) and *Mammal Identification Chart* ($2).

(For additional fishing and hunting information see individual state forest and "Allegheny National Forest" sections and "Wild & Trophy Fishing Waters Maps," "Boone & Crockett Club," "Fenwick Pennsylvania Fly Fishing Schools," and "State Game-Land & County Maps.")

Highways—Recreation & Scenic Routes

To determine the best route to your destination in Pennsylvania, consult the *Official Map of Pennsylvania*. Free copies may be obtained from: Bureau of Travel Development, Dept. of Commerce, South Office Bldg., Harrisburg 17120. The map shows all roads and highways, indicating accumulated mileage between selected points, highway markers, and approximate populations of towns and cities. It also shows airports, state forest lands, state game lands or game farms, state park lands, state or national forest natural areas, fish hatcheries, roadside rest areas, railroads, hiking trails, and other points of interest. There is a chart of public recreation areas showing their locations on the map and which facilities are available at which area.

Ski Touring Trails & Centers

Pennsylvania's vast state forest highlands, abandoned railroad beds, old logging roads, and extensive trail systems provide excellent opportunities for cross-country ski touring, snowshoeing, and winter camping. The major ski touring areas in the state include the Black Forest Ski Touring Trail, Appalachian Trail, Laurel Ride State Park, Pocono

Mountains, George B. Will Ski Touring Trail atop the 2,000-foot Allegheny Plateau, Long Yellow Trail, Hidden Valley Ski Area (Somerset 15501), and the Allegheny National Forest trails and Susquehannock Trail.

For descriptions of the state's major trail networks, see "Backpacking Trails & Primitive Camping." The 127-page *Ski Touring Guide* ($3.50), published by: Ski Touring Council, Troy, VT 05868, contains descriptions of the state's major cross-country skiing areas. A *Guide to the Susquehannock Trail* may be obtained from: Potter County Recreation, Box 245, Coudersport 16915. A *Black Forest Trail Map-Guide* may be obtained for $1 from: Bureau of Forestry, 423 E. Central Ave., South Williamsport 17701 (make check payable to Tiadaghton Forest Fire Fighters Assn.). Professional nordic instruction is provided by: *Ligonier Mountain Outfitters*, Box 175, Route 30, Laughlintown 15655; *Paul Wick Ski Shop*, 321 W. Woodland Ave., Springfield 19064; *Hidden Valley Ski Area*, Somerset 15501; *Apple Valley Ski Touring Center*, RD 1, Zionsville 18092 (215-967-2862); *Inn at Starlight Lake*, Starlight 18461 (717-798-2519); and *Mont St. Onge at Crystal Lake Camps*, RD 1, Hughesville 17737 (717-584-2698).

State Forest Reserves & Wild Areas

Pennsylvania's sprawling 1.9 million acres of state forest lands encompass some of the most scenic and wild limestone trout streams, virgin hemlock, cove hardwood, spruce fir forests, mountain swamps and bogs, beaver flows, remote lakes and ponds, and primitive trails in the eastern United States. These vast top-ranked fish and game lands offer unsurpassed fishing, backpacking, primitive camping, and hunting in season for whiteland deer, black bear, red fox, raccoon, snowshoe hare, wild turkey, crow, squirrel, and upland game birds. The north central forests of Elk, Clearfield, and Cameron counties are inhabited by a few protected elk—native to the state more than a century ago. Individual *State Forest Maps* may be obtained free by writing to: Game Commission, P.O. Box 1567, Harrisburg 17120.

The 70,000-acre *Buchanan State Forest* encompasses prime deer and upland game bird country in Fulton, Bedford, and Franklin county in

southcentral Pennsylvania, and includes the virgin hemlock and mixed oak forests of the 1,403-acre Sweet Root Natural Area; the virgin pine forests and abandoned farm settlements of the 568-acre Pine Ridge Natural Area; and the primitive camping areas of the 11,376-acre Martin Hill Wild Area.

The 71,387-acre *Delaware State Forest*, in Pike and Monroe counties, embraces the broad plateaus of the Pocono Mountains and nationally famous trophy brown trout waters of the Brodhead River and its Paradise Creek headwaters, Wallenpaupack Lake (home of the state record 24-pound brown trout), Spruce Run, Laurel Run, Rattlesnake Creek, and hundreds of remote lakes and ponds; the 67-acre Pine Lake Natural Area, a high mountain bog; the 2,845-acre wilderness of the glacial Bruce Lake Natural Area; the mountain swamps, rock ledges, and oak forests of the 471-acre Buckhorn Natural Area; the glacial swamps and spruce forests of the 1,931-acre Stillwater Natural Area; and the mountain swamps, sheep laurel, and mixed oak forests of the 936-acre Pennel Run Natural Area.

The beautiful valleys, meadows, bogs, beaver flows, and evergreen forests of the 172,308-acre *Elk State Forest* in Elk, Cameron, and Potter Counties in north central Pennsylvania form part of the 800,000-acre area known as the "Black Forest," which includes the 32-acre Lower Jerry Run Natural Area; the northern hardwood forests of the 1,245-acre Wykoff Run Natural Area; the old field white pines and abandoned farmlands of the 200-acre Pine Tree Trail Natural Area; the wildlands of the 15,682-acre Bucktail Natural Area; and the famous 46,163-acre Quehanna Wild Area and the Quehanna Trail.

The scenic *Moshannon State Forest* (derived from the Indian name Moss-hanne, meaning "Moose Stream") lies in the heart of the Allegheny Mountains in the "Black Forest" area and includes the Black Moshannon area, named for the color of its stream waters from decaying swamp vegetation—once one of the great logging centers of the state, noted for its giant virgin white pines; Bald Eagle Creek; the high mountain bogs, laurel thickets, and forests of the 917-acre Marion Brooks Natural Area; beautiful Black Moshannon Lake, noted for its muskellunge, chain pickerel, and yellow perch; and a portion of the Quehanna Wild Area.

The 85,138-acre *Rothrock State Forest* in the north-central portion of the state encompasses the famed trout waters of Spruce Creek, Standing Stone, Detweiler Run, Laurel and Shavers creeks; Indian Steps, an old Indian war-path; Bear Meadows, where black spruce, balsam fir, pitcher plant, and sundew grow in rare abundance; 185-acre Detweiler Run Natural Area and the laurel beds of the 142-acre Big Flat Laurel Natural Area; and the 1,757-acre Trough Creek Wild Area and the 1,757-acre Thickhead Mountain Wild Area in the Bear Meadows area.

The vast *Sproul State Forest* encompasses 256,000 acres of some of the most rugged and isolated wild country remaining in the state. The forest is located in western Clinton and Centre counties, and includes the 2,180-acre Burn's Run Wild Area; the 4,800-acre Fish Dam Wild Area; the 86-acre Tamarack Swamp Natural Area; the scenic northern hardwood and red pine forests of the 15,682-acre Bucktail Natural Area; the mountain swamps and old growth hemlocks of the 186-acre East Branch Swamp Natural Area; and the beaver dams, mountain bogs, and cranberry thickets of the 144-acre Cranberry Swamp Natural Area. The Bucktail Drive, which parallels the West Branch of the Susquehanna River, is considered the most scenic drive in the state.

The sprawling 275,961-acre *Susquehannock State Forest* is located in the heart of north central Pennsylvania's famed big-game lands in Potter, Clinton, and McKean counties, and includes the 1,500-acre

Beech Bottom Hemlocks Natural Area and the headwaters of the Allegheny River and Pine Creek.

The *Tiadaghton State Forest*—the name the Iroquois Indians gave to Pine Creek—encompasses 70,000 acres of prime trout waters and game lands in Sullivan and Lycoming counties, and includes the 3,727-acre Algerine Wild Area and the spruce-fir forests, sphagnum moss, and sundew of the Algerine Swamp; 7,032-acre Wolf Run Wild Area along Pine Creek; McIntyre Wild Area east of Ralston; the 4,000-acre high plateau country of the Miller Run Natural Area west of Pine Creek; and the old growth hemlocks at the Bark Cabin Run headwaters.

The rugged highlands of the 160,000-acre *Tioga State Forest*, named after a tribe of Seneca Indians, is located in Tioga and Bradford counties, and includes the renowned trout waters of Big Asaph Run, Elk Run, and Pine Creek—noted for its awesome 1,000-foot deep gorge, often referred to as Pennsylvania's "Grand Canyon"—and the 3,931-acre Asaph Wild Area; the old beaver meadows and conifer forests of the 308-acre Black Ash Swamp Natural Area; 5,720-acre Pine Creek Gorge Natural Area; and the high mountains bog and forests of the 1,302-acre Reynolds Spring Natural Area.

The *Wyoming State Forest* takes in 40,000 acres of wildly primitive conifer and northern hardwood forests, high plateaus and ridges, and deep stream canyons, and includes the nationally renowned trout waters of picturesque Loyalstock Creek and its tributaries; Eagles Mere, Mokoma, Splashdam, and Painter Den lakes; the Loyalstock Trail; the famed trout waters of the 774-acre Kettle Creek Gorge Natural Area; the High Knob Natural Area, and the beaver ponds and bogs of Spook Swamp.

Maps are also available from the Game Commission for Tuscarora, Forbes, Kittatinning, and Michaux state forests.

State Game-Land & County Maps

The Game Commission publishes county maps and state game-land topographic maps. The county maps are 17 × 22 inches and show roads, towns, and general locations of all state game lands and other public lands within each county. Because of the scale, details of the lands are not shown. Each map sells for 30¢. The state game-land maps sell for 25¢ each, are 8½ × 13 inches, and show individual game lands in green coloring, with contour lines, elevations, mountains, streams, roads, etc. The maps and a free map showing the location of Pennsylvania's famed state game lands by their designated numbers may be obtained by writing: Game Commission, P.O. Box 1567, Harrisburg 17120.

Wild & Trophy Fishing Waters Maps

An overview of the entire lengths and surrounding topography of the state's major canoe routes and fabled limestone trout streams, of which many, such as the Letort, Big Spring, Penns, and Yellow Breeches, offer superb fishing for trophy brook, rainbow, and brown trout up to 10 pounds, may be found on small-scale U.S. Geological Survey Maps for the following areas. *Allegheny River Headwaters* (including Portage Creek): Austin, Bullis Mills, Coudersport, Eldred, Port Allegany, Roulette, Sweden Valley; *Upper Allegheny River* (from the New York border to Franklin and the junction of French Creek): Clarendon, Cobham, Cornplanter Bridge, Cornplanter Run, Franklin, Oil City, President, Tidioute, Tionesta, Warren, West Hickory, Youngsville; *Aughwick Creek:* Aughwick, Burnt Cabins, Butler Knob, McConnellsburg, Orbisonia; *Bald Eagle Creek:* Bear Knob, Beech Creek,

Bellefonte, Julian, Mingoville, Port Matilda, Tyrone; *Bennett Creek* (including Trout Run): Dents Run, Driftwood, Huntley, Penfield, Rathbun, Weedville; *Big Spring Creek:* Carlisle 7.5, Mount Holly Springs; *Brodhead River* (including Paradise River and Promised Land Lake area): Buck Hill Falls, East Stroudsburg, Promised Land, Skytop, Stroudsburg; *Equinunk Creek* (including Lake Como): Lake Como, Long Eddy, Orson; *Fishing & Little Fishing Creek:* Beech Creek, Carroll, Loganton, Madisonburg, Mill Hall, Millheim, Mingoville; *Kettle Creek* (including Hammersley and Cress forks): Galeton, Hammersley Fork, Keating, Lee Fire Tower, Oleona, Renovo, Short Run, Tamarack; *Lackawaxen River & Headwaters:* Forest City, Aldenville, Honesdale, White Mills, Hawley, Rowland, Shohola; *Licking Creek:* Big Cove Tannery, Burnt Cabins, Cherry Run (WV), Hustontown, Meadow Grounds; *Loyalstock River* (including Wallis Run and Elk and Little Loyalstock creeks): Barbours, Bodines, Dinshore, Eagles Mere, Hillsgrove, Huntersville, Laporte, Lopez, Montoursville N., Montoursville S, Overton; *Lycoming Creek* (including Rearing, Rock, and Grays runs): Bodines, Canton, Cogan Station, Grover, Liberty, Ralston, Trout Run; *Penns Creek* (including Laurel Run): Barrville, Beavertown, Centre Hall, Coburn, Freeburg, Hartleton, Lewisburg, Middleburg, Spring Mills, Sunbury 7.5, Weikert; *Pine Creek* (including Cedar, Slate, and Little Pine Creeks): Cammal, Cedar Run, English Center, Jersey Shore, Keeneyville, Slate Run, Tiadaghton, Waterville; *Rattlesnake Creek:* Narrowsburg (NY), White Mills; *Raccoon Creek:* Aliquippa, Avella, Beaver, Burgettstown, Clinton; *First & East Forks Sinnamahoning River:* Austin, Ayers Hill, Conrad, First Fork, Sinnamahoning, Wharton; *Upper Susquehanna River* (from the New York border to Wilkes-Barre): Center Moreland, Jenningsville, Kingston, Laceyville, Meshoppen, Pittston, Ransom, Rome, Sayre, Towanda, Tunkhannock, Wilkes-Barre W, Waylusing; *Tioga River:* Blossburg, Gleason, Jackson Summit, Mansfield, Tioga; *Tionesta Creek & Reservoir:* Kelletville, Lynch, Mayburg, Sheffield, Tionesta, Tylersburg; *White Deer Creek* (including Spruce Run): Allenwood, Carroll, Loganton, Milton 7.5, Williamsport; *Yellow Breeches Creek* (including Letort Creek): Carlisle 7.5, Dickinson, Lemoyne, Mechanicsburg, Mount Holly Springs, Shippensburg, Steelton, Walnut Bottom; *Youghiogheny River* (one of the East's great wild rivers): Confluence, Connellsville, Dawson, Donora, Fayette City, Friendship, McKeesport, Mill Run, Ohiopyle, Smithton, South Connellsville; *Young Woman's Creek:* Oleona, Renovo E 7.5, Young Woman's Creek.

NEW JERSEY ENCYCLOPEDIA

Accommodations

For information on where to stay in New Jersey, whether it's a hotel, motel, resort, campsite, guesthouse, or anything in between, write to the local chambers of commerce of the areas you plan to visit or to: Chamber of Commerce, 54 Park Place, Newark 07102.

Appalachian National Scenic Trail

The New Jersey segment of this great trail winds from the New York border southwest along the crest of the scenic, rugged Kittatinny Mountains—meaning "big mountain," once home and hunting ground of the Leni-Lenape Indians—to the Delaware Water Gap, passing along its course through High Point State Park and Stokes and Wellington state forests.

The route of the trail in New Jersey passes through a variety of terrain —superb panoramas, quiet woodland paths, and serene rural roads. The traverse across Bear Mountain and Harriman state parks is particularly impressive, and the trip along the ridges of the Bellvale and Kittatinny mountains provides breathtaking views.

Anyone planning to hike the Appalachian Trail in New Jersey should obtain the comprehensive *Guide to the Appalachian Trail in New York and New Jersey* (including maps; $6.70), compiled by the New York-New Jersey Trail Conference. To obtain a copy, write to: Appalachian Trail Conference, P.O. Box 236, Harpers Ferry, WV 25425. Locations of lean-tos and other accommodations available to hikers are noted. The descriptions contain very detailed trail data and summaries of distances. In addition, there are sections on the development of the trail; facts you should be aware of before setting out, such as trail maintenance, trail registers, trail markers, trail precautions, and New Jersey forest fire and conservation laws. Helpful publications for Appalachian trail hikers (also published by the ATC) include *The Appalachian Trail* (25¢, publication #17), which contains a brief history of the trail and description of the route, including a map and a complete list of conference publications. *Suggestions for Appalachian Trail Users* (70¢, #15) contains information on planning your trip, precautions, maps, equipment, clothing, and food. *The Appalachian Trail* ($1.25, #5) contains a history of the Appalachian Trail, a list of trail-maintaining organizations, routes of the trail, and texts of legislation that has been instrumental in the construction and maintenance of the trail. *Mileage Facts* ($1.50) gives distances to shelters and certain post offices, stored water sources, lodging, etc. The ATC also publishes a New York-New Jersey color map (not included with the New York-New Jersey guidebook listed above), price $1.25. Trail hikers will also want to consult *Hiking Trails in New Jersey*, a 43-page compendium of federal, state, county, and municipal trail maps, available for $1 from: Division of Map & Publications Sales Office, Bureau of Geology, P.O. Box 2809, Trenton 08625.

The Appalachian Trail in New Jersey is listed on the following 7.5-minute U.S. Geological Survey Maps: Branchville, Bushkill (PA), Culvers Gap, Flatbrookville, Port Jervis S (NY), Portland (PA), Greenwood Lake (NY), Hamburg, Stroudsburg (PA), Unionville (NY), Wawayanda, Newton W.

A free *Map of Appalachian Trail Campsites* may be obtained along with free maps of the Worthington, Jenny Jump, and Stokes state forests and High Point State Park, from: Bureau of Parks, P.O. Box 1420, Trenton 08625, phone (609) 292–2797.

Camping & State Recreation Areas

State forests, park, and recreation areas which provide scenic eastern

woodland hiking, fishing, and camping areas are described in the *Guide to State Forests, Parks, Recreation Areas, Natural Areas, & Historic Sites*, available free, along with detailed camping and hiking information from: Bureau of Parks, P.O. Box 1420, Trenton 08625. The free, 40-page booklet *Campsites of New Jersey* contains listings and descriptions of all state-managed campgrounds. For info on privately owned campgrounds, write: New Jersey Private Campgrounds Assn., RD1, Box 14-H, Tuckerton 08087, phone (609) 296–8789. The camper and backpacker should send for the useful *Map of Open Spaces & Recreation Areas*, available free from: Bureau of Parks (address above). It shows major federal recreation areas, fish and wildlife lands, the Delaware Water Gap National Recreation Areas, Palisades Interstate Park, state parks and forests, and major county and public and private watershed areas, all color-keyed on the map for easy use.

Major state parks and recreation areas include the 9,020 acres of hardwood and spruce upland forests and lakes of *Wawayanda State Park* in Sussex County. This wild area, one of the state's premier hunting and fishing areas, is dominated by Lake Wawayanda—the Lenape Indian name meaning "water on the mountain"—once known as Double Pond. Lake Wawayanda, which produced the state record northern pike in 1971, provides excellent early and late season fishing for pickerel, pike, and largemouth bass up to 6 pounds, as does nearby, spring-fed Laurel Pond. The area is shown on a U.S. Geological Survey Map: Wawayanda.

Ringwood State Park in Passaic County (shown on U.S. Geological Survey Maps: Greenwood Lake (NY), Sloatsburg (NY) provides excellent backpacking opportunities and early season fishing in Shepherds Pond for rainbow, brook, brown, and tiger trout and late season fishing for largemouth bass and trophy-sized pickerel. The surrounding high country hardwood forests and meadowlands in the Bear Swamp Lake area provides excellent hunting in season for upland game birds and whitetail deer. The *Round Valley Reservoir State Recreation Area* (shown on U.S. Geological Survey Maps: Flemington, Califon) covers 4,003 acres of woodlands with numerous trails and semi-wilderness campsites, and the state's top-ranked fishing in the reservoir for trophy rainbows up to 8 pounds and brown trout in the 8-and-9-pound class. Nearby *Spruce Run State Recreation Area*, to the west, offers excellent camping and some of the state's finest fishing for lunker browns in the 8-to-10-pound range. Spruce Run Reservoir also holds some whopper

largemouth bass and northern pike. This 1,863-acre area (shown on U.S. Geological Survey Map: High Bridge) is bordered on the west by the Clinton Wildlife Management Area—one of the state's largest and most productive deer and upland game-bird hunting areas. *High Point State Park* covers 12,686 acres along the scenic high country of the Kittatinny Ridge in Sussex County. This outstanding backpacking and camping country, traversed by the Appalachian Trail, is shown on U.S. Geological Survey Map: Port Jervis S (NY).

Palisades Interstate Park, a state-designated natural area, encompasses 2,500 acres, extending for 13 miles along the Hudson River from Bear Mountain, New York, to Fort Lee. This scenic camping and backpacking area, named for the resemblance of the giant rock pillars along the Hudson to the palisades surrounding the old Indian villages, is shown on the following U.S. Geological Survey Maps: Haverstraw (NY), Sloatsburg (NY), Thiells (NY), Peekskill (NY), Yonkers (NY), Nyack (NY), Popolopen Lake (maps include Bear Mountain State Park and Seven Lakes Area).

Canoeing & Trout Stream Maps

New Jersey's premier wild canoe country is the seldom traveled Pine Barrens (see "Pine Barrens Wild Country & Canoe Trails"), with its 1.2-million-acre wilderness of shadowy cedar swamps, labyrinthian bogs, and pitch pine forests. Elsewhere in the state are Great Egg Harbor River, near Mays Landing, a winding canoe route surrounded by dark pine forests, swamps, and marshlands, with open blackberry fields and thick patches of laurel and lupine; and the Maurice River, near Malaga, which flows through the pine forests and cranberry bogs of the Wharton State Forest, with occasional carries around old wooden dams. The Mullica, Wading, and Batsto rivers flow through the cranberry bogs, pine forests, and cedar swamps of the Wharton and Lebanon state forests past several small abandoned villages. The Metedeconk River flows along the northern edge of the Pine Barrens through scrub oak and pine forests, marshes, and bogs. In northern New Jersey, the Ramapo River flows south from the Ramapo Mountains in New York through the scenic woodlands of the Ramapo Valley, with several carries over old dams. The stretch of river below the dam south of Darlington Bridge provides some good early season fishing for rainbow and brown trout. During July and August the mosquito is king: a good supply of insect repellent is strongly recommended.

Canoeists should consult an excellent book *Exploring The Little Rivers of New Jersey,* by James and Margaret Cawley ($6 cloth, $2.75 paper): Rutgers University Press, 30 College Ave., New Brunswick 08901. This book was first published in 1942 and has been revised by the authors, who have traveled the rivers and recorded the changes wrought by time. They have supplemented the photographs, updated the maps, and added a chapter on the Raritan Canal and the Delaware River. There is an index that provides information on places where canoes can be rented and a list of books on the history and lore of some of South Jersey's rivers.

A complete set of 10 *Outdoor Recreation Maps of the Delaware River* describe in detail the characteristics of the river along its entire nontidal main stem—a distance of 200 miles from Hancock, New York, in the western Catskill Mountains to Trenton, on the upstream edge of the tidal estuary that runs to the sea. Elevation of the river over this 200-mile reach drops from about 900 feet to zero. Shown are parks, forests, game lands, river launching locations and recreation areas; rapids, riffles, and pools; channel and water depths, and stream-flow characteristics. The maps point out the hazardous reaches of the river, including the rough waters below Lambertville and New Hope, Penn-

sylvania. You can obtain copies of these maps by sending $1 to: Delaware River Basin Commission, P.O. Box 360, Trenton 08603.

Canoe outfitters and rentals in the state include *Mick's Canoe Rental,* Route 563, Jenkins, Chatsworth 08019, (609) 726–1380; *Bel Haven Lake,* Route 542, Green Bank, RD2, Egg Harbor City 08215, (609) 965–2031; *Mullica River Boat Basin,* Route 542, Green Bank, RD2, Egg Harbor City 08215, (609) 865–2120; *Adams Canoe Rental,* Lake Dr., Atsion, RD2, Vincentown 08088, (209) 268–0189. *Mullica River Marina,* Weekstown Rd., Sweetwater, RD1, Hammonton 08036, (609) 561–4337; and *Pic-A-Lilli Canoe Rental,* Lake Rd., Atsion, RD2, Vincentown 08088, (609) 268–9831 or (609) 268–1236.

South Branch Canoe Cruises, P.O. Box 173, Lebanon 08833 (201–782–9700), offers expert instruction and guided canoe trips on the Lehigh, Juniata, Delaware, Shenandoah, South Branch of the Raritan, Millstone, and Schuylkill rivers, as well as in the legendary Pine Barrens, Ontario's Algonquin Provincial Park, and on Maine's St. Croix River.

The following U.S. Geological Survey maps show the entire lengths and surrounding topography of New Jersey's major canoe routes and trout streams. *Flat Brook* (including Big and Little Flat brooks and Kittatinny and Culver lakes): Culvers Gap, Flatbrookville, Lake Maskenza, Milford, Port Jervis S. (NY); *Maurice River:* Dividing Creek, Millville, Newfield, Pitman, Port Elizabeth, Port Norris; *Millstone River:* Bound Brook, Monmouth Junction, Princeton, Rocky Hill, Trenton E; *Mullica River:* Atsion, Egg Harbor City, Green Bank,

Hammonton, Medford Lakes, New Gretna; *Musconetcong River & Lake Hopatcong:* Bloomsbury, Easton (PA), Hackettstown, High Bridge, Riegelsville (PA), Stanhope, Tranquility, Washington; *Paulins Kill* (including Swartswood and Paulins lakes): Blairstown, Flatbrookville, Newton W, Portland (PA); *Pequannock River* (including Highland Green Pond and Beaver Lakes): Franklin, Newfoundland, Pompton Plains, Wanaque; *Pequest River:* Belvidere, Blairstown, Newton E, Newton W, Tranquility, Washington; *Pohatcong River:* Belvidere, Bloomsbury, Easton (PA), Washington; *Ramapo River:* Pompton Plains, Ramsey, Sloatsburg (NY), Wanaque; *Raritan River* (including North and South branches): Bound Brook, Califon, Chester, Gladstone, Hackettstown, High Bridge, Mendham, New Brunswick, Pittstown, Plainfield; *Wading River* (including West Branch and Oswego Lake and River): Chatsworth, Green Bank, Jenkins, New Gretna, Oswego Lake, Tuckerton, Woodmansie; *Wallkill River:* Franklin, Hamburg, Unionville (NY); *Wanaque River* (including Shepherds and Greenwood lakes, Wanaque Reservoir, and Norvin Green State Forest): Greenwood Lake, Sloatsburg (NY), Wanaque.

Delaware Water Gap National Recreation Area

The Delaware Water Gap National Recreation Area provides a well-managed, protected backcountry recreation area offering camping, hiking, and canoeing in an area of natural beauty and historical significance. The free-flowing Delaware River's white waters flow through the mountains and valleys of the Appalachian Plateau.

The rapids become more tame south of Port Jervis, New York, interspersed with quiet pools up to 20 feet deep. The river passes Bushkill Creek and enters Wallpack Bend, shored on the east by the forests of the Kittatinny Ridge. The famous Flatbrook Creek enters the river in this area. Below it is another stretch of riffles, and beyond them, a group of islands dot the river in an area of boulders deposited by glaciers. This upper, scenic section of the Delaware offers top-ranked fishing for big smallmouth bass, walleyes, rainbow trout, and muskellunge up to the state record 19 pounds.

There are no developed canoe camping areas along the river at present, but islands and shore areas offer a variety of natural campsites. Campers should be careful to choose sites protected from sudden changes in water level, which occur in this area even during relatively good weather. Group camping areas may be reserved by special permit from the park headquarters. Worthington State Park near the lower section of the national recreation area provides some campsites.

Check weather conditions before you start a canoe trip: foul weather and cold water can turn a pleasant trip into a dangerous and harrowing experience. Early spring and late fall trips require special preparation and knowledge of elementary rescue techniques.

The lands surrounding the river are cut by ravines; in some areas they are composed of rocky slopes, elsewhere of marshlands and swamps, and forests of oak, beech, and hickory trees and rhododendron and hemlock groves. Among the most beautiful areas here are the Pennsylvania Gorges north of Wallpack Bend carved out of the western side of the Delaware Valley. Old logging roads wind along the creek gorges. Trails also lead to Mounts Minsi and Tammany in the immediate vicinity of the divide. The Appalachian Trail runs through the recreation area. The Delaware Water Gap National Recreation Area and Upper Delaware River canoe route are shown on the following 7.5-minute U.S. Geological Survey Topographic Maps: Port Jervis S (NY), Milford, Lake Maskenozha, Flatbrookville, Bushkill (PA), Portland (PA), Stroudsburg (PA).

Fishing & Hunting in New Jersey

Although it is a small state, with only 7,836 square miles, and one of the nation's most populous, New Jersey is long famous for the quality of its deer, waterfowl, and upland game-bird hunting, and for its often amazing saltwater and freshwater fishing. The scenic highlands of the Appalachian Mountains cross the northwest corner of the state and include the Kittatinny Mountain and Valley. Crossing the Delaware River at the Delaware Water Gap and continuing in a southwest direction into Pennsylvania to the east are the famous lakes, streams, and hills of northern New Jersey, which include the renowned fishing waters of Lake Hopatcong and Wawayanda, Musconetcong River, and the Spruce Run and Round Valley reservoirs. To the south are the Watchungs and central New Jersey, the great game lands and fishing waters of the Pine Barrens, and the nationally renowned saltwater fishing meccas of the Jersey shore.

The remote wild country waters of the Pine Barrens, the famous big-lake waters of Hopatcong, Spruce Run, Round Valley, Greenwood, Wawayanda and Wanaque, and the hundreds upon hundreds of small backcountry and farm ponds and classic freestone streams offer often excellent fishing for pickerel, perch, largemouth bass, and trout—both stocked and a few holdovers. In 1912 New Jersey pioneered one of the first state hatcheries in the country, the Hackettstown Fish Hatchery, which expanded into one of the world's largest and implemented one of the first full-time trout float stocking programs.

The fishing potential of the state's lakes and streams is illustrated by a list of state record fish.

NEW JERSEY RECORD FRESHWATER FISH

	Lb.-oz.	Place	Year
Brook trout	6–8	Lake Hopatcong	1956
Brown trout	16–11	Greenwood Lake	1964
Rainbow trout	8–5½	Round Valley Reservoir	1970
Salmon (landlocked)	8	New Wawayanda Lake	1951
Smallmouth bass	6–4	Delaware River	1957
Largemouth bass	10–12	Mount Kimble Lake	1960
Muskellunge	19	Delaware River	1970
Northern pike	30–2	Spruce Run Reservoir	1977
Chain pickerel	9–3	Lower Aetna Lake	1957
Calico bass	3–5½	Alloway Lake	1961
Rock bass	1–2¼	Lake Hopatcong	1968
Channel catfish	28	Greenwood Lake	1918
White perch	2–8	Lake Hopatcong	1950
Yellow perch	4–3½*	Bordentown	1865
Bluegill	2	Farm Pond	1956
Walleyed pike	12–12¾	Delaware River	1934
Striped bass (landlocked)	23–8	Union Lake	1952
Brown bullhead	22–15	Spring Lake	1966
American shad	7–13½	Delaware River	1971
Carp	41–2	Delaware River	1971
White catfish	10–5	Raritan River	1976

*World's record.

Lake Hopatcong

Sprawling, irregular-shaped Lake Hopatcong, with its numerous bays, coves, islands, and deep river channels, is the focal point of northern New Jersey's lake country. This 2,685-acre lake, with its meandering shoreline and thick underwater vegetation, provides the state's premier fishing year in and year out for trophy-sized brook, brown, rainbow, golden, and tiger trout (a cross between a female brown trout and a male brook trout), and for big largemouth bass, walleye, and pickerel. The quality of the trout fishing in Hopatcong has been greatly improved over the years by the stocking efforts of the Knee-Deep Club. The best trophy fishing in the lake is for tackle-busting brown trout in the 8-to-12-pound class (particularly in the Nolan's Point area). Fly fishing from boats is productive along the shoreline during the early season. The most productive way to fish the lake is by drift fishing or slow trolling with a herring rig. Boat rentals, marinas, docking facilities, and launch sites are available at many locations along the shoreline.

Northern Lakes Country

The northern lakes country to the west of Lake Hopatcong offers good fishing for bass and pickerel: Swartswood, Owassa, Culvers, Kemak, Mohawk, Budd, Cranberry, Lackawanna, and Ginmill lakes and New Wawayanda Lake—home of the state record landlocked salmon. Brown and rainbow trout are found in Budd and Cranberry lakes and in Lake Ocquittunk in Stokes State Forest. The major bass and pickerel waters to the east of Lake Hopatcong include Morris, Beaver, Canister, Highland, Denmark, Splitrock, Echo, Clinton, Upper Greenwood, Shepherds, Wawayanda, and Greenwood lakes and Green Pond—the home of a longtime former world's record (8-pound) pickerel. The Wanaque Reservoir (fishing by permit only), surrounded by beautiful uplands and mixed hardwood and evergreen forests, holds some monster largemouth bass, pickerel, and rainbow and brown trout—which congregate at the Wanaque River during their fall migrations. Greenwood Lake, to the north of Wanaque, is famed for its trophy brown trout up to state record weight, as well as rainbow trout, largemouth bass, pickerel, and channel catfish to 20 pounds and over. Lake Wawayanda, surrounded by a wild backcountry of hardwood and spruce forests, holds lunker bass, pickerel, rainbow and brown trout, and northern pike to 20 pounds and over.

Round Valley & Spruce Run Reservoirs

The deep waters of Round Valley Reservoir in Hunterdon County, to the south of Lake Hopatcong, surrounded by scenic woodlands and rolling hills, hold large schools of landlocked alewifes (herring), which in turn produce fat trophy rainbows and hook-jawed browns in the 4-to-9-pound class. Round Valley is considered the state's top-ranked rainbow trout water. The deep, clear waters of this lake average 75 feet in depth with a maximum depth of 160 feet, and cover 2,350 acres. The reservoir also holds the state's largest lake population of acrobatic bronzeback smallmouth bass. Spruce Run Reservoir, almost due west of Round Valley, surrounded by scenic woodlands and the Clinton Fish and Wildlife Management Area, is renowned statewide for its superb fishing for trophy rainbow and brown trout to 8 and 10 pounds, and for its large population of big northern pike. Fly fishing for giant buckskin-flanked brown trout is often excellent during the fall spawning run up the lake's Mulhockaway and Spruce Run creeks and tributaries. Mulhockaway Creek is a state-designated natural trout fishing area, limited to dry flies, wet flies, bucktails, nymphs, and streamers. Spruce Run and Round Valley reservoirs are best fished by boat, either drifting or trolling along the drop-offs or old stream channel beds. For detailed info, regulations, and a free *Round Valley Reservoir and*

Spruce Run Reservoir Lake Contour Map, write: Round Valley-Spruce Run Recreation Areas, Van Syckels Rd., Clinton 08809.

Upper Delaware River

The majestic Upper Delaware River, which forms the western boundary of the state, flows south from the New York line through the scenic Upper Delaware Valley, rich in Indian lore, paralleled on the east by the historic Old Mine Road, forests, and beautiful thickets of mountain laurel, rhododendron, and dogwood, and the Appalachian Highlands. The Upper Delaware is the state's premier big-fish water above the Delaware Water Gap for trophy walleye up to 12 pounds, smallmouth bass up to 6 pounds, pickerel, and a few lunker rainbow and brown trout up to 4 pounds in the deep, swift-flowing pools and riffles. The Delaware produced the state record muskellunge. A complete set of 10 *Outdoor Recreation Maps of the Delaware River* showing forests and game lands, river launching sites and recreation areas, rapids, riffles and pools, channel and water depths, and stream-flow characteristics are available for $2 a set from: Delaware River Basin Commission, P.O. Box 360, Trenton 08603. The maps also pinpoint the rough waters below Lambertville and New Hope, Pennsylvania. Dunnfield Creek, a clear, rock-strewn tributary of the Delaware in Worthington State Forest, is one of the state's few streams supporting a population of wild brook trout. An abandoned road, departing from the Appalachian Trail, follows the creek for two-thirds of its length, then climbs a ravine to join the Appalachian Trail.

guide to
WILDLIFE MANAGEMENT AREAS

Division of Fish, Game and Shellfisheries

Big Flatbrook & the Musconetcong

Big Flatbrook, a tributary of the Delaware in Sussex County and New Jersey's top-ranked trout stream, flows southwest for 20 miles from its headwaters at High Point in the Kittatinny Mountains through the scenic high country woodlands and evergreen forests of Stokes State Forest and the Flatbrook Fish and Wildlife Management Area, through the fly fishing-only stretch in the famous Blewett Tract, to the beautiful historic Junction Pool at the confluence of Little Flatbrook and Big Flatbrook. Downstream from Junction Pool, Big Flatbrook enters its famed deepwater trophy trout area and flows through the lovely "Rhododendron Stretch" on past Flatbrookville to its marriage with the Delaware. The deep pools and riffles of Big Flatbrook hold large, extremely selective brown and rainbow trout up to trophy weights. Another famous tributary of the Delaware, the Musconetcong River, known locally as the "Musky," has a large holdover population of rainbow and brown trout. It flows from its headwaters near Lake Hopatcong southwest for 30 miles past the Hackettstown Fish Hatchery, over numerous small dams and Saxton Falls to its confluence with the Delaware at Riegelsville, Pennsylvania. The "Musky" has a good population of insect life as well as the state's only no-kill fishing area, near Hackettstown. Other premier rainbow and brown trout streams in northern New Jersey include the limestone stretches of the Pequest River, the Paulins Kill (immortalized by the fly pattern of this name created by Ray Bergman, author of *Trout,* an American fishing classic), and the wild, backcountry stretches of the Wallkill River in Sussex County and the Upper Wanaque and Ramapo rivers in Passaic and Bergen counties.

The historic South Branch of the Raritan River flows from its headwaters near Budd Lake south through pastoral farmlands, meadows, and woodlands and through the Lockwood Gorge Fish and Wildlife Management area, and winds on between Spruce Run and Round Valley reservoirs to its confluence with the North Branch. The deep, boulder-strewn holes, pockets, ledges, and the white-water stretches of the Ken Lockwood Gorge and the famed Trestle and Monument pools on the South Branch offer some of the state's premier fly fishing for rainbows and browns, a few up to lunker weights. The Ken Lockwood Gorge area is a state-designated fly fishing-only stretch.

The most effective early high-water fishing on northern New Jersey's trout streams is had using night crawlers, salmon eggs, spinners, and mayfly and Early Brown Stone Fly imitations. From late April through the end of the trout season, the most effective dry-fly patterns include the Quill Gordon, Light Cahill, Hendrickson, Adams, and Gray Fox; nymph patterns include the Brown Stonefly, March Brown, Hare's Ear, and Musky Shrimp. The most effective streamers include the Blacknosed Dace and the always reliable Muddler Minnow.

The useful, well-written 75-page *New Jersey Trout Guide* may be obtained for $2.95 from: Trout Unlimited, P.O. Box 581, Edison 08817. The New Jersey chapters of Trout Unlimited have contributed greatly to improving the quality of the state's premier trout waters. Membership in the New Jersey Council costs $15 a year (it includes national membership and a year's subscription to *Trout* magazine, national and chapter newsletters, and special bulletins).

Saltwater Fishing

The state's famed, year-round saltwater fishing and tidewater areas stretch from the renowned bluefish and striped bass Sandy Hook Bay, south along the Atlantic Coast past the surf-casting beaches, inlets, bays, jetties, and marina centers at Sea Bright, Long Branch, Deal, Asbury Park, Manasquan, Point Pleasant Beach, Mantoloking, Lavallette, Seaside Park, the scenic bluefish and striped bass surf-casting areas of Island Beach State Park, Barnegat Inlet, and Long Beach Island, to Atlantic City and Cape May. For detailed surf-fishing information and season permit, and four-wheel dune buggy use regulations on Island Beach State Park, write: Superintendent, Island Beach State Park, Seaside Park 08752.

The outstanding quality and diversity of the state's saltwater fishing is best summarized by the record fish caught on rod and reel (p. 543).

Detailed fishing and hunting regulations, and information about access, boating, seasons, and special permits may be obtained from: Division of Fish, Game, & Shellfisheries, P.O. Box 1809, Trenton 08625. The division publishes the following free publications: *Compendium of Game Laws, Compendium of Fish Laws, List of Stocked Trout Waters, Places to Fish in New Jersey,* and the *New Jersey Deer Season Map-Guide*—including deer management zone locations and permit quotas. *New Jersey Outdoors,* the official bimonthly magazine published by the division, contains invaluable info about the fishing waters and hunting areas of the state. A 1-year subscription is $3 (3

years for $8). For complete, comprehensive information on the state's wildlife management areas, send for the useful 112-page *Guide to Wildlife Management Areas* ($3) published by the Division.

NEW JERSEY RECORD SALTWATER FISH

	Lb.-oz.	Place	Year
Albacore	69–1	Hudson Canyon	1961
Red drum	46	Sandy Hook	1953
Black sea bass	6–4	Delaware Bay	1973
Striped bass	68	Off Sandy Hook	1970
Tautog (blackfish)	21–6	Cape May	1954
Bluefish	23–14	Off Cape May	1971
Atlantic cod	81	Brielle	1967
Black drum	92	Delaware Bay	1944
Summer flounder (fluke)	19–12	Cape May	1953
Pollack	43	Brielle	1964
Shortfin mako	322	Elberon	1952
Bluefin tuna	796	Off Long Branch	1973
Wahoo	93–10	Cape May	1969
Weakfish	17–8	Mullica River	1952
Blue marlin	620	Atlantic City	1964
White marlin	123	Ambrose Light	1968
Dolphin	48–15	Cape May	1969
Atlantic bonito	13–8	Sandy Hook	1945
Broadbill swordfish	530	Wilmington Canyon	1964
Winter flounder	3–2	Great Egg Harbor	1968
Cobia	45–2	Delaware Bay	1972
Scup (porgy)	4–6	Off Barnegat Light	1967
Yellowfin tuna	138–2	Hudson Canyon	1969
Atlantic mackerel	3	Atlantic City	1969
American shad	7	Great Bay	1967
Tarpon	42–8	Shrewsbury Rocks	1972
Spotted seatrout	9–8	Near Stone Harbor	1973

Hunting

New Jersey has over 300,000 acres of state-owned forests, recreation areas, and fish and wildlife management areas open to public hunting, ranging from scenic upland mixed hardwood and evergreen forests to swamps, bogs, vast stretches of wild pine barrens, and coastal plains and wetlands. Surprisingly, this crowded state has some magnificent pockets of wild backcountry and is one of the nation's top-ranked hunting areas for whitetail deer and waterfowl. The Garden State also provides some excellent hunting for bobwhite quail on the wildlife management areas and farmlands of the southern region, and for pheasant, ruffed grouse, and woodcock. Other game species include cottontails and a few snowshoe hares, gray squirrels throughout all woodlands and forests, raccoons, gray and red fox, and a few black bears in the Kittatinny Mountains.

Highway & Recreation Travel Guide

Anyone planning on driving in New Jersey should obtain the free *New Jersey Official Highway Map and Travel Guide* from: Dept. of Trans-
portation, 1035 Parkway Ave., Trenton 08618. The map shows all roads and highways, parks and forests, and recreation areas with and without campsites, winter sports areas, airports, railroads, state agencies, and other places of interest. The map provides a location index of towns and cities, a facility chart of state park, forest, and recreation areas, and a facility chart for fish and wildlife management areas. There is a list of New Jersey ski areas, also location-keyed, as well as brief descriptions of places of interest (monuments, museums, etc.).

Pine Barrens Wild Country & Canoe Trails

In the southern region of populous New Jersey, less than 100 miles south of New York, is one of the nation's most unusual wilderness areas. With its nearly 650,000 acres it is comparable in size to Yosemite and Grand Canyon national parks. This great wild country, known as the Pine Barrens, gives rise to the unspoiled tea-colored "cedar waters" of the Wading and Oswego, Batsto and Mullica rivers, which take twisting, tortuous, deep-flowing courses—similar to the rivers of Canada's Great North Woods canoe country—through dark canopies of white pine surrounded by quaking bogs, cranberry bogs, white cedar swamps of mosses and hummocks and fallen rotting logs, vast plains of stunted dwarf forests of scrub oak and pitch pine, and brush and thickets of foxtail mosses, giant fern, cat briar, blueberry, spaghnum moss, huckleberry, crowberry, greenbriers, bearberry, shadbush, poison sumac, orchids, sweet pepperbush, and once inhabited by panther, timber wolf, black bear, and bobcat. Today this paradise provides excellent hunting in season for whitetail deer, gray fox, and raccoon. The Mullica and Wading rivers and their innummerable sloughs, tributaries, and backwaters offer top-ranked fishing for largemouth bass and giant chain pickerel that grow to arm length in the seldom fished interior reaches.

More than 84 species of birds nest in the Pine Barrens, including Cooper's hawks, green herons, great horned owls, black ducks, whippoorwills, nighthawks, and bald eagles. In the deep swamps and ponds monster snapping turtles up to 50 pounds feed on ducks. Mink, otter, and muskrats inhabit the Barrens along with beaver, whose dams and ponds are often seen by the wilderness paddler. There are timber rattlers in the pines, along with puff adders and red-bodied corn snakes up to 5 feet long.

The Barrens encompass the Wharton, Penn, Bass River, and Lebanon state forests, and most of Atlantic, Ocean, and Burlington counties. Old sand roads and trails wind through the interior areas of the Barrens past several ghost towns to such interesting places as the Hog Wallow (bulls and hogs once ran wild here), the site of the old Lebanon Glass Works, and the Bear Swamp Observation Tower in the Penn State Forest—which provides an unbroken panorama of forest wilderness, broken by an occasional ribbon of flowing water and a few wildly scattered ponds, and of the eerie "dwarf" forests of the plains to the north. Several campsites are located along the trails. The longest pathway is the Batona Trail, which winds for 30 miles through the heart of the Pines, in the Batsto and Lebanon state forests, running parallel for most of its length to the twisting course of the Batsto River.

The 650,000-acre heart of the Pine Barrens is shown on the following 7.5-minute U.S. Geological Survey maps: New Egypt, Cassville, Lakehurst 7.5, Lakewood, Browns Mills, Whiting, Keswick Grove, Chatsworth, Woodmansie, Brookville, Indian Mills, Atsion, Jenkins, Oswego Lake, West Creek.

John McPhee, one of the nation's most accomplished authors, has written an engaging, fascinating book about this unusual region, *The Pine Barrens*. This 172-page paperback, packed full of facts about the history, lore, and wildlife of the region, may be obtained for 95¢ plus 25¢ handling from: Ballantine Cash Sales, P.O. Box 505, Westminster, MD 21157.

State Forest Reserves

The New Jersey forest areas offer outstanding hiking and canoe-camping opportunities, and good hunting in season for quail, pheasant, ruffed grouse, woodcock, waterfowl, gray squirrel, red fox, raccoon, and whitetail deer.

Bellephain State Forest, in Cape May and Cumberland counties, contains 11,223 acres. The Lake Mummy area is the main recreational area and has facilities for camping, hunting, and fishing. It can be found on the following U.S. Geological Survey Maps: Heislerville, Port Elizabeth, Tuckahoe, Woodbine. *Jenny Jump State Forest,* in Warren County, high on Jenny Jump Mountain, comprises 1,118 acres and offers outstanding panoramas of the surrounding country and the Delaware Water Gap. There are facilities for camping (shelters available), hiking, and hunting. It can be found on U.S. Geological Survey Maps: Blairstown, Tranquility, Washington. *Lebanon State Forest* is in southern New Jersey's Pine Barrens, in Burlington County. It is 27,304 acres in size and has excellent hunting facilities. There are also good facilities for camping and hunting. This extensive forest area, which includes the Batsto Wilderness Trail and the primeval swamps, bogs, and cranberry glades of the Pine Barrens, can be located on U.S. Geological Survey Maps: Browns Mills, Chatsworth, Whiting, Woodmansie. *Norvin Green State Forest* is a 2,296-acre woodland area of mixed hardwood and evergreen forests in Passaic County that is undeveloped except for hiking trails. Hunting is also permitted. It can be located on a U.S. Geological Survey Map: Wanaque.

Penn Forest comprises 3,666 acres of forest wilderness in the Pine Belt in Burlington County. It provides facilities for hiking, hunting and fishing, and contains Lake Oswego, which was developed from a cranberry bog. The forest is shown on U.S. Geological Survey Maps: Oswego Lake, Woodmansie.

Ringwood State Park can be located on U.S. Geological Survey Maps: Greenwood Lake (NY), Ramsey, Sloatsburg (NY). (These include Shepherd and Bear Swamp lakes.) *Stokes State Forest* (including High Point State Park) is on the Kittatinny Ridge in Sussex County. The 14,868-acre forest area has facilities for camping, hiking, fishing, and hunting. Tillman Ravine, a stunning natural gorge, is maintained as a natural area, not to be disturbed by man. This forest is an example of the fine mountain country New Jersey has to offer. There are outstanding scenic views from Sunrise Mountain. Stokes State Forest can be located on U.S. Geological Survey Maps: Branchville, Culvers Gap, Milford, Port Jervis S (NY). *Wharton State Forest,* in Atlantic, Burlington, and Camden counties, is crossed by Routes 206, 542, and 563; there are offices at Atsion and Batsto. This 150-square mile forest area is the state's largest, and is situated in the heart of south central New Jersey's Pine Barrens. It includes the Batsto Wilderness Trail, the Mullica, Batsto, and Wading rivers, and the primitive bogs and cranberry glades of the Pine Barrens. There are facilities for boating, camping, fishing, hunting, and hiking. The many miles of rivers afford excellent canoeing through wilderness areas. This forest area can be found on the following U.S. Geological Survey Maps: Atsion, Chatsworth, Egg Harbor City, Green Bank, Indian Mills, Jenkins, New Gretna, Oswego Lake, Woodmansie. The 5,830-acre *Worthington State Forest* can be reached via Route 80 at the Delaware Water Gap.

It contains 4 miles of land along the Delaware River and offers excellent hunting, fishing, hiking, and camping opportunities. Approximately 6 miles of Appalachian Trail follows the Kittatinny Ridge, which passes Sunfish Pond 4 miles northeast of the Delaware Water Gap. It can be located on the following U.S. Geological Survey Maps: Bushkill (PA), Flatbrookville, Portland (PA), Stroudsburg (PA).

Hikers in the state forest areas of New Jersey will want to explore the *Batona Trail,* which traverses the Pine Barrens in the Wharton and Lebanon state forests. The 30-mile trail, chartered and built in 1961 by the Batona Hiking Club in Philadelphia, passes through a vast wilderness area rich in historic lore as well as interesting flora, bird, and animal life, including white-tailed deer. This trail has no hardships and can be easily walked by anyone. Since the trail intersects many roads, it can be reached by car from many points and a variety of hikes can be planned.

Maps of the Batona Trail and all the other New Jersey state forests can be obtained at no charge from: Bureau of Parks, P.O. Box 1420, Trenton 08625. The maps show roads, footpaths, bodies of water, camping areas, recreation areas, etc. Some state forests that have particularly good hiking opportunities (Bass River, Jenny Jump, and Stokes) supply free trail guides for hikers, which outline and describe suggested hikes, pointing out features of special interest, such as flora and fauna or outstanding scenic views. Also available from the Bureau of Parks is the free booklet *Guide to New Jersey State Forests, Parks, Recreation Areas, Natural Areas, Historic Sites.* It contains capsule descriptions of these areas, with maps to illustrate their locations. The New Jersey Official Highway Map and Travel Guide (see "Highway & Recreation Travel Guide") shows state park and forest areas and includes a facilities chart for all state forests and parks. A helpful map to consult is the free Map of Open Spaces and Recreation Areas (see "Camping & State Recreation Areas").

Wilderness Adventure & Travel Service

Odyssey, the mountain travel agency of the eastern United States, offers guided trips with top-notch professionals throughout North America and the world. During the spring, summer, and fall it has a mountaineering school which runs wet-bend guiding and instruction in the Shawangunks and conducts 2-week summer climbing camps in the Bugaboos in British Columbia. From December through March it runs weekend cross-country ski trips (with certified instructors in Nordic skiing) to Lake Placid, New York, Vermont's Long Trail, and the White Mountains of New Hampshire, plus weeklong ski touring trips to Aspen, Yellowstone, and the Canadian Rockies.

The Canadian Rockies form the basis for the Odyssey summer program, which includes four backpacks, two mountaineering camps, and two 4-week Youthpack Wilderness Adventures. This renowned firm also offers the following guided trips: trekking in Nepal to the base of Mount Everest with Sherpa porters; cross-country skiing in the Canadian Laurentians; canoeing on the Shenandoah in Virginia's magnificent Blue Ridge Mountains; Grand Canyon combination backpack and raft trip; Mexican volcano climbing; mountaineering in the Bugaboos of British Columbia; and weekend canoeing trips and instruction on the Delaware from Bushkill down through the Water Gap, with camping on Tocks Island and hikes through historic Jockey Hollow—studded with Revolutionary War lore.

For detailed information, rates, and literature, write: Art Fitch or Denise Van Lear, *Odyssey,* 26 Hilltop Ave., Berkeley Heights 07922, phone (201) 322-8414.

Accommodations— Vacation Resorts & Lodges

For detailed information on vacation accommodations and travel in New York State, contact: New York State Vacation Information, 99 Washington Ave., Albany; for quick information on all aspects of vacation travel, call toll-free 800–342–3810. For daily winter ski reports call 518–474–5677 or 212–755–8100. A free travel and fishing guide describing accommodations, marinas, and docking facilities in the Thousand Islands, contact: 1000 Islands Bridge Authority, Alexandria Bay 13607.

For listings of major Adirondack lodges and resorts, see the "New York Travel & Recreation Guide" section.

Adirondack Mountain Club Wilderness Lodges

The Adirondack Mountain Club was founded in 1922 to promote and improve the forest conservation of the Adirondack Mountains and its camping, hiking, and canoeing opportunities. Today the 9,000-member club is dedicated to promoting a "forever wild" concept for the Adirondack Forest Preserve and to sponsoring outdoor recreation with conservation in mind.

The club's *Adirondak Loj* is located at Heart Lake 8 miles south of Lake Placid off Route 73 at the end of the Adirondak Loj Road (accessible by automobile). Trail heads near the lodge lead to the Adirondack High Peak Wilderness. The shortest trails to Mount Marcy (5,344 feet) and Mount Algonquin (5,114 feet) start here, as well as the trail to Indian Pass. The lodge houses dormitory-style overnight accommodations, a lounge with a fireplace, and a small library. The staff provides family-style meals and trail lunches. Nearby campgrounds include about 10 lean-tos and 40 campsites (trailer and camper sites are usually inaccessible during the winter). A campers and hikers building has hot showers and other facilities. Limited camping food supplies, candy, and Adirondack-oriented publications are available at a trading post. The 60-acre lake offers summer canoeing and fishing.

John Brooks Lodge is accessible by 3½ miles of foot travel in the Adirondack High Peak Wilderness Area. Parking arrangements should be made in Keene Valley on Route 73 about a mile below the trailhead. The main lodge, built in 1925, is open from late June to early September. It is staffed by hut boys and accommodates 28 people. The complex also includes Winter Camp, a 2-room cabin with cooking facilities, accommodates 12 people; Grace Camp, accommodates 6; and three open shelters, each accommodates 6 adults. Early weekend reservations are recommended for the cabins. Campers must pack in their own winter-weight sleeping bags, food, and supplies.

Many of the 46 major peaks (4,000 feet or over) are accessible from the lodges. Among the scenic destinations are the Great Range, Indian Falls, Lake Colden, Marcy Dam, and the MacIntyre Range. Trails for cross-country skiers and snowshoers radiate out from the lodges, including short, relatively flat loops for beginners and a vast system of trails through the mountains for experienced skiers. The trail system connects to the Mount Van Hoevenberg ski touring complex, one of the East's most extensive state networks. The two lodges are connected by the Klondike Trail.

NEW YORK ENCYCLOPEDIA

For reservations and information on both Adirondack Loj and John Brooks Lodge, write or call: P.O. Box 867, Lake Placid 12946, (518-523-3441).

For more information on the lodges, membership, and publications on travel through the Adirondack wilderness, write to: Adirondack Mountain Club, 172 Ridge Street, Glens Falls 12801. A leaflet describing and mapping *Adirondak Loj Ski Touring Trails* is available free (same address).

Appalachian National Scenic Trail

The Appalachian Trail is a continuous marked footpath following the crest of the Appalachian ranges from majestic Mount Katahdin in the central Maine wilderness south more than 2,000 miles to Springer Mountain, Georgia. The trail enters New York from Connecticut and winds southwest through the Taconic foothills east of the Harlem Valley and Fahnestock State Park to the tollgate at Bear Mountain Bridge.

The trail between Webatuck and Pawling passes Quaker Lake, named for the settlement founded there in 1750, used as a Revolutionary War hospital. In 1778–79 it served as Washington's headquarters. Much of the trail between Pawling and Holmes leads over little-used roads through oak and maple forests and old pastures. It ascends Mount Tom en route. From Hortontown the trail leads west, ascending Shenandoah Mountain and entering Fahnestock State Park along a series of ridges; hemlock and fruit trees are occasionally intermixed with oak and maple in this section, which is comprised of old wood roads and trails. Canopus Lake is a highlight of this section. South of Fahnestock State Park the trail passes Oscawana Lake.

West of the Hudson River the trail crosses a portion of Rockland County and the southern part of Orange County in New York before it leads across Sussex and Warren counties in New Jersey. Just beyond the Hudson the trail passes south through the Bear Mountain-Harriman section of the Palisades Interstate Park, past nearby Lake Tiorati, Monbasha and Walton lakes, Surprise Lake, Hessian Lake, Ramapo-Dunderburg Trail, Black Mountain, and Silver Mine Lake. The trail winds on through the beautiful Ramapo River Valley (known to the Indians as the "country of the slanted rocks"), Fingerboard Mountain, Green Pond Mountain, Cat Rocks, Eastern Pinnacles, Greenwood Lake Valley, and across the New Jersey line. This section of the trail leads through forested hills and valleys.

If you plan to walk the trail through New York, obtain the *Guide to the Appalachian Trail in New York & New Jersey* ($6), available from: Appalachian Trail Conference, P.O. Box 236, Harpers Ferry, WV 25425. The book describes the trail in depth throughout New York and New Jersey, noting topography, ground cover, distances between points, trail markings, special features nearby, and other information of interest to the hiker. The 247-page compact book includes an introduction to traveling the trail, noting rules and regulations in effect throughout this section, a short history of the trail, and 4 maps.

Also available from the conference is the quarterly publication *Appalachian Trailway News*, which contains reports on current trail conditions, activities of the Appalachian Trail Conference and member clubs, announcements, and news and issues relating to the trail and the lands it traverses. Cost is $2 per year. A free list of publications is also available.

U.S. Geological Survey Topographic Maps of the Appalachian Trail through New York include: Dover Plains, Greenwood Lake, Hamburg, Monroe, Oscawana Lake, Pawling, Peekskill, Popolopen Lake, Poughquag, Unionville, Warwick, Wawayanda, West Point.

Camping & Backpacking

New York State is blessed with thousands of miles of scenic and wild trails. Thousands of well-maintained family and primitive campsites dot the state, many of them easily accessible by car, others tucked deep in the backcountry pockets of New York and accessible only by trail. Public campgrounds are maintained by the Department of Environmental Conservation (DEC), the Office of Parks & Recreation, and other state, county, and municipal agencies. As an aid to hikers, canoeists, fishermen, and hunters on state-owned forestlands, the DEC maintains over 1,000 miles of trails and 200 open camps, or Adirondack lean-tos (log structures open on one side and designed primarily as a place to sleep in and as a shelter against storms) at many convenient points, free of charge. The DEC operates 45 public campsites in the forest preserves. Reservations can be secured for the regular camping season (May-September); most sites provide for limited day use. Some sites are available (no reservation) in the fall. Unless specifically prohibited, you can camp on state lands (other than developed campsites and wildlife management areas) for 3 days without a permit. For longer periods a permit must be obtained. Complete information can be obtained from DEC Regional Offices or: Bureau of Forest Recreation, DEC, 50 Wolf Rd., Albany 12233.

All public and private campgrounds in the state are described in the 32-page booklet *Camping in New York State*, available free from: Dept. of Commerce, 99 Washington Ave., Albany 12245. The guide gives address, fees, reservation information, facilities, and recreational opportunities for each campsite. The location information is keyed to a campground grid locater map. The campground descriptions are grouped by region.

For an overview of backpacking trails throughout the state, obtain a free leaflet on *Hiking Areas of New York State* from: Publications Distribution Unit, Dept. of Environmental Conservation, 50 Wolf Rd., Albany 12201. The publication covers canoeing waters, horse trails, off-trail hiking, and trails in the Catskills, Adirondacks, Long Island, Metropolitan New York City, western New York State, the Finger Lakes Trail, and the Appalachian Trail in New York and New Jersey. The author, A. T. Shorey, has hiked most of the trails he describes, and notes outstanding natural features and areas of historical interest along the way.

The DEC's free *Guide to Outdoor Recreation in New York State* outlines outdoor recreation possibilities throughout the state. It describes hunting and fishing areas by county, giving the size and location of each area, naming game available, and listing hunting regulations. It describes recreation facilities in the Catskill and Adirondack forest preserves, their locations, sizes, facilities, seasons of use, nearby waterways, and recreational opportunities. Also listed are winter sports areas (ski schools, ski touring trails, and snowshoeing trails are noted) and special use areas, including archery areas, environmental education centers, field trails, and sanctuary and recreation areas. A chart shows camping areas throughout the state park system, and their locations, facilities, and special features. The guide also lists and describes historic sites in the state, and includes information on canal parks, boating, recreational vehicles, and outstanding natural features throughout the state.

For the Summer Backpacker, For the Beginner Hiker, and *For the Winter Mountaineer* are available free if you send a self-addressed, stamped, business-size envelope for each to: Adirondack Mountain Club, 172 Ridge St., Glens Falls 12801. The useful guide *When You Are in the Woods*, by Fay Welch, is available free upon request from: State University of Forestry, Syracuse 12310.

Canoeing & Adirondack Wild Rivers

New York contains some of the eastern United States, finest wild and scenic canoe country, ranging from the large island-dotted lakes of the Big Moose-Fulton Chain country along the old Adirondack canoe route—surrounded by the towering evergreen spires of spruce and pine forests, extensive beaver meadows, cedar swamps, sandy jack pine plains, and thick undergrowths of huckleberry, dogwood, and tag alder—and the beautiful headwaters of the Hudson, with its rugged Hudson Gorge Primitive Area, to the historic Upper Delaware and Long Island's scenic Carmans River—a noted trophy brown trout stream. The New York State Wild, Scenic, & Recreational Rivers System, adopted in 1972 by the state legislature, called for the inclusion of the following rivers in the system: Ampersand Brook, AuSable (both the East and West branches), Bouquet (North and South forks), Boreas, Cedar, Cold, Hudson, Indian, Moose, Opalescent, East and West branches of the Sacandaga, and West Canada Creek in Adirondack Park; and the Carmans and Connetquot elsewhere on Long Island.

Detailed information about the Wild, Scenic, & Recreational Rivers System may be obtained from: Natural Rivers Program, Division Of Lands and Forests, DEC, 50 Wolf Rd., Albany 12233. Two free brochures, *Wild Rivers* and *Protecting Our Natural Rivers*, may be obtained from the same address.

A free *Canoe Trips* brochure, available from the DEC, Publications Distribution Unit, 50 Wolf Rd., Albany 12233, describes many of the state's wild and scenic canoe routes, including Black Creek, Cayuta Lake, Upper Mohawk River, West Canada Creek, the Kunjamuk, Fall Stream to Piseco and Vly lakes, Unadilla River, Upper Delaware River, Ramapo River, the Susquehanna, Chenango River, Upper Hudson River, Champlain Canal-Lake George, Allegheny River, West Branch of the Sacandaga River—a beautiful Adirondack meadowland stream—Oswegatchie River Primitive Area, Indian River, and Long Island's Nissequogue River. Canoe trips are keyed on a state map showing counties throughout the state. Outstanding features and fishing are noted.

In addition to its magnificent wild and scenic rivers, the north country is equally famous for its hordes of mosquitoes, black flies, no-see-ums, and deer flies—a good supply of bug dope is a must from the first week of June through August.

Fenwick Eldred Preserve Fly Fishing School

The Fenwick Corporation, the world-famous makers of quality fishing rods, operates 2-day schools of fly fishing instruction open to beginning through advanced fly fishermen from April through September at the Eldred Preserve in the southern Catskills. Eldred has lake and stream fishing for browns, brooks, and rainbows. Lodging is on the preserve or at nearby campsites. The Fenwick School teaches fly-line and rod-and-reel construction, how to choose the right tackle, and terminology. There is a class on entomology, which covers insect life cycles, what to look for, where and when, as well as artificial fly construction, identification, choices of flies and how to match the hatch, fly fishing knots, leader construction and uses, and how to read a stream. The Fenwick textbook is *Fly Fishing from the Beginning*, by Jim Green, former world champion fly caster and master fly fisherman. The instructors are all expert fly casters. For free literature and info on rates and registration, write: Director, Fenwick Fly Fishing School, Eastern Division, 2202 Glen Court, Rt. 7. Frederick, MD 21701 (301-663-3966).

Fishing & Hunting in New York

The vast reaches of the Empire State—with its more than 70,000 miles of streams, and 2,500 lakes and ponds surrounded by mixed hardwood, fir, and spruce forests inhabited by whitetail deer, black bear, and a variety of upland game birds—contain several of the nation's top fishing and hunting areas, stretching south from the famous trophy muskellunge, northern pike, and smallmouth bass waters of the St. Lawrence River, with its incredibly scenic maze of evergreen clad islands, to the northern forests, wild rivers, and remote gemlike wilderness lakes and windswept high peaks of the Adirondack Forest Preserve; the long, sinuous shoreline of beautiful Lake Champlain, which stretches along the northern New York-Vermont border for 130 miles; the trophy salmon and steelhead waters of Lakes Ontario and Erie and their deep-flowing tributary streams; the famed game lands and trophy trout waters of the Finger Lakes region; the classic, historic trout streams and wooded highlands of the Catskill Forest Preserve; and the renowned saltwater fishing and waterfowl hunting meccas of Long Island Sound.

The tremendous fishing potential and diversity of New York's lakes and streams is highlighted by a list of record freshwater fish caught on rod and reel, compiled by the progressive and innovative Department of Environmental Conservation.

NEW YORK RECORD FRESHWATER FISH

	Lb.-oz.	Place	Year
Brook trout	8–8	Punchbowl Pond	1908
Brown trout	21–5	Owasco Lake	1954
Lake trout	31	Follensby Pond	1922
Rainbow trout	21	Keuka Lake	1946
Splake	9–6	Lake Eaton	1976
Landlocked salmon	16–14	Lake George	1958
Chinook salmon	38–8	Cattaragus Creek	1976
Coho salmon	15–2	Salmon River	1975
Muskellunge	69–15*	St. Lawrence River	1957
Northern pike	46–2*	Sacandaga Reservoir	1940
Chain pickerel	6–8	Harrisburg Lake	1975
Largemouth bass	10–12	Chadwick Lake	1975
Smallmouth bass	9	Friends Lake Outlet	1925
Walleye	15–3	Chemung River	1952
Channel catfish	15–3	Lake Champlain	1975

*World's record.

Adirondack Forest Preserve

The spectacular north country wildlands of the Adirondack Mountain region, the ancient home and hunting grounds of the Iroquois Indians, undoubtedly qualifies as New York State's most historic and romantic outdoor recreational region. Other areas can compete in fish poundage and deer, but only the Adirondacks offer the numerous, tightly bunched domes of the High Peaks Wilderness, the great expanses of spruce, fir, and hardwood forests, the thousands of miles of foam-flecked white-water trout and canoe rivers, and the scores of lakes, seldom-fished wilderness ponds, and spring-fed beaver flows which are strung like glowing jewels across the face of the Adirondacks. The remote headwater lakes and streams of the Adirondack wilds are surrounded by highland bogs (known locally as "vlys" or "vlaies"), old

logging roads, beaver meadows, mosses and ferns, and carry trails, framed by deep, moist woods. The locations of these headwater ponds and "lost" lakes are shown on full-color topo maps and are accessible by old Indian trails and logging roads or by "bushwhacking" with map and compass.

Here, within the sprawling boundaries of the vast 2.2-million-acre Adirondack Forest Preserve are several of the East's top-ranked trout, landlocked salmon, northern pike, and smallmouth bass waters. The forest preserve is divided into two natural regions: the wild lake region in the west and north and the rugged mountains and high peaks which range across the eastern and southern regions. The scenic Lake Champlain watershed, which forms the eastern boundary of the preserve, offers some of the best angling opportunities in the state, both in the lake and its tributary streams. The shallow, narrow, weedy southern reaches of Lake Champlain yield largemouth bass, pike, and yellow perch. Smallmouth bass, walleye, lake trout, northern pike, crappie, yellow perch, and occasional musky and landlocked salmon are found in the deep, island-dotted waters of the lake's famed upper section. The mouth of the Great Chazy River, which enters the lake at the north tip of Isle La Motte, Vermont, is a top muskellunge hole. Lake Champlain's most noted tributary is the legendary Au Sable River, whose West Branch is ranked as the number one trout stream in the state. The boulder-filled runs and deep pools of the East and West branches of the Au Sable, which rise in the majestic High Peaks, hold trophy-sized brown and rainbow trout. The fabled West Branch flows for 7½ miles to Lake Placid and North Elba. The smaller East Branch has excellent fishing for all three species of trout from its headwaters in Upper Au Sable Lake, flowing northeast for 25 miles through beautiful Keene Valley to its confluence with the West Branch at Au Sable Forks. The lower main Au Sable flows through the Ausable Chasm to its mouth on Lake Champlain. Lake Placid, with its two large islands, Buck and Moose, lies in the shadow of Mount Whiteface and holds big lake trout, rainbow and brook trout, whitefish, smallmouth bass, and northern pike.

The wild, boulder-filled runs and beautiful evergreen, fringed pools of the legendary West Branch of the Au Sable provide shelter for some of the largest rainbow and brown trout in the Northeast. A topographic map will show you where the more inaccessible areas are, and it is in these rugged, sometimes precipitous stretches that superlative fishing can be found. Natural baits and deeply fished lures take a lot

of trout, but the fly fisherman comes into his own on these magnificent sections of the stream. The trout follow the hatch cycle in the spring, and the fortunate angler who is present during a major emergence of March browns or gray foxes will experience unforgettable fishing. This fork of the river produces well all summer, and during the fall the cooling waters encourage another feeding splurge. Fishing this great stream when crisp weather has turned the maples and birches into torches of crimson and yellow is a feast of the senses. Remember to include some large flies in your kit, such as the Muddler Minnow, Gray Ghost, Black Ghost, and assorted maribou patterns for those trophy trout, particularly the fall-spawning browns. Stonefly and Caddis imitations are particularly effective on this river, and big Stonefly nymphs account for numbers of lunker trout.

Other renowned Adirondack wild and scenic trout streams include the Bouquet River, rising in the lofty domes to the west of Keene Valley and boasting quite a reputation for trophy brown, rainbow, and brook trout; the beautiful and wild Boreas River, noted for its numerous white-water stretches interspersed with quiet deep pools and quality brook, brown, and rainbow trout; the brook, brown, and rainbow trout waters of the complex Black River system, surrounded by the interconnecting streams, lakes, ponds, wild tangled swamps, and beaver ponds of the Black River Wild Forest; the rainbow, brown, and brook trout waters of the Little Salmon and Great Chazy rivers, and the famed Saranac River and its North Branch; the rainbow and wild brown trout pools of the Chateaugay River and its Upper and Lower lakes, which hold smallmouth bass and lake, rainbow, brook, and brown trout; the brook and brown trout waters of the Trout River and its eastern branch, the Little Trout, which rise in the deep evergreen forests of the Owls Head Range; the famous brown trout waters of the Big Salmon River; the wild trout waters of the sprawling St. Regis River watershed, which drains a vast wilderness of evergreen forests and clear spring-fed ponds in the northern tip of the Adirondacks, and includes the East, West, and Middle branches of the St. Regis, the Deer River, and Big Fish, St. Regis, and Long ponds; the broad Raquette River system, which starts at Little Tupper Lake and flows north through the smallmouth bass, walleye, and northern pike waters of Round Lake, Big Tupper, Raquette Pond, and Carry Falls Reservoir into the St. Lawrence River; the wild, aptly named Cold River, which holds large brook trout in the rushing feeders which cascade down the steep, forested flanks of its wilderness headwaters; the famous wilderness brook waters of the Moose River and its Middle, North, and

South branches; the renowned trout waters of the wild and scenic Independence, Upper Hudson, Red, Opalescent, Indian, Jessup, Rock, Cedar, Boreas, Marion, Schroon, South Branch Grasse, and West Branch Sacandaga rivers; and the famed squaretail waters of West Canada Creek and the Silver Lake Wilderness.

The Adirondack lakes, with their many coves, bays, island- and evergreen-fringed, jagged shorelines offer some of the nation's top fishing for smallmouth bass, lake trout, rainbow trout, northern pike, landlocked salmon, and yellow perch. The major Adirondack lakes include the smallmouth bass haunts of island-dotted Cranberry Lake, bordered by the wild brook trout waters and beaver flows of the vast Five Ponds Wilderness and the Oswegatchie Primitive Area; Upper, Middle, and Lower Saranac lakes, which yield trophy smallmouth bass, northern pike, landlocked salmon (Upper Lake), and lake trout and are bordered by a vast network of remote streams, lakes, and ponds in the Saranac Wild Forest; Schroon Lake, famous for its landlocked salmon and lake and rainbow trout, bordered by the fragrant pine and spruce forests, bogs, and crystal-clear ponds of the Pharaoh Lake Wilderness; the sprawling Fulton Chain Lakes, which hold smallmouth bass, splake, landlocked salmon, and lake and rainbow trout; beautiful arrowhead-shaped Indian Lake and its smaller sister, Lewey Lake, which hold big smallmouth bass and northern pike to 20 pounds and over; narrow Long Lake, which stretches for 14 miles and holds smallmouth and largemouth bass, and some giant northern pike; jagged Piseco Lake, which produces lake trout, rainbows, whitefish, and smallmouth bass, bordered by the spruce and balsam swamp flats, beaver ponds, lakes, and rolling hills of the West Canada Lakes Wilderness; beautiful, island-dotted Lake George, whose deep, cold waters yield giant landlocked salmon up to 16 pounds, rainbows, lake trout, great northern pike, and smallmouth bass; and Great Sacandaga Reservoir, which produces giant northern pike—the water wolf of the north—as well as largemouth and smallmouth bass and hordes of panfish along the shallow weedy bays and coves of its lengthy arms. Other productive lakes nestled among the scenic rolling hills and conifer forests of the Adirondacks include the Cedar River flow, Beaver River Flow (Stillwater Reservoir), and Lila, Forked, Blue Mountain, Round, Catlin, Newcomb, Sanford, Meacham, Fern, Ampersand, Follensby Pond, Elk, Canachagala, Honnedaga, Pleasant, Big Moose, Wolf, Paradox, Eaton, Loon, Osgood, Canada, and Piercefield Flow. Due west of the forest preserve boundaries are the famous black bass waters of Butterfield, Bonaparte, and Black Lakes. Bonaparte Lake was named for Napoleon's older brother Joseph, who purchased more than 160,000 acres of Adirondack land, hoping to establish a New France for his exiled brother.

Guide to Trout Waters in the Adirondack Mountains ($1.50), by N. B. Cole: Outdoor Publications, Box 355, Ithaca 14850, describes the area contained in the park along with its history, sketches important facts about the principal trout species, provides helpful information about finding good public fishing areas in the park, and includes a review of the principal trout lakes, ponds, and streams. Of particular interest is a list of lakes and ponds which have been reclaimed and stocked with trout. Outdoor Publications has also issued the useful *Sportsman's Map of the Adirondack Mountains* ($2.50, 42 × 50 inches) and *Sportsman's Map of Hamilton Country* (the central Adirondacks, 16 × 24 inches $1), which show fishing access areas, public campsites, lean-to shelters, hiking and access trails, lookout towers, trout streams, lakes and ponds, roadways, and other features. The maps are printed in color. A useful *Adirondack Area Fishing Waters* guide may be obtained free upon request from the Adirondack Park Agency, Adirondack 12808.

For info on stream conditions and hatches, write or call: *Adirondack Sport Shop*, Wilmington 12997 (518–946–12997).

Great Lakes Salmon & Trout

To the west and south of the Adirondacks are the trophy salmon and trout waters of New York's wave-capped Great Lakes: Ontario and Erie. As a result of stockings begun in 1968, New York's Lake Ontario shoreline today produces some often spectacular fishing for coho and Chinook salmon as well as fat, trophy-sized brown and rainbow trout. During the fall spawning migration thousands of salmon and trout are caught in several Lake Ontario tributary streams, including the Salmon and Little Salmon rivers, South Sandy River, and Grindstone Creek. Steelhead migrate up Eighteen-Mile Creek, Oak Orchard Creek, and Sandy Creek. New York's Lake Erie shoreline offers a more varied bag, with smallmouth bass, muskellunge, and walleye found along with large hook-jawed Chinook and coho salmon, rainbow trout, brown trout, and steelhead. Lake Erie hot spots include the Eighteen-Mile Creek, Sturgeon Point, Cattaraugus Creek, Barcelona, Buffalo, Upper Niagara River, Athol Springs, Grand Island, and Van Buren Point areas. The major offshore fishing areas for smallmouth bass, walleye, and yellow perch are Sturgeon Point, Athol Springs, Van Buren Point, Dunkirk Harbor, and Barcelona. A useful guide to New York's Lake Erie and Lake Ontario waters and tributaries is contained in *The Complete Guide to Fishing the Great Lakes* (218 pp., $5.95), available from: Greatlakes Living Press, 3634 W. 216th St., Matteson, IL 60443.

Hudson River & Its Tributaries

The historic Hudson River rises from beautiful Lake Tear in the Clouds nestled in the Adirondack high peaks and flows south, gaining in size and strength as tributaries augment its flow and smallmouth and largemouth bass, northern pike, walleye, pickerel, and white and yellow perch replace the wild trout of its alpine headwaters. The fishing is good in the beautiful valley down to its confluence with the polluted Mohawk River at Troy. Several of the upper Hudson's feeder streams offer first-rate fishing for brook and brown trout, including the famed pools of the historic Battenkill, the Mettawee River, and Kayadosseras Creek. The upper Mohawk River in the Rome area has some good smallmouth and walleye fishing and the headwaters hold substantial populations of brown and brook trout, particularly above

Delta Reservoir, which contains smallmouth bass, northern pike, and walleye.

The middle course of the Hudson flows through one of the most scenic valleys in the East, past the dark, forbidding knobs of the Hudson uplands and the heart of Washington Irving's legendary Rip Van Winkle country. Henry Hudson, the great Dutch explorer who later died of starvation on the barren shores of Hudson Bay, marveled at the beauty of the forested peaks and ridges flanking the stream's southward course during his voyage of discovery in 1611. Its Kinderhook Creek and Rocliff-Jansen Kill tributaries—both top-ranked brown trout streams—flow in a westerly path to join the big river in the vicinity of Hudson in Columbia County.

The lower reaches of the Hudson constitute one of the world's great estuaries, containing a mixture of fresh- and saltwater fish. Major features include the bluffs of West Point, the beautiful Hudson uplands, the broad Tappan Zee, the sheer, rock face of the Palisades, a steep rampart extending along the west bank for 25 miles, New York Harbor, and the deep Hudson Canyon, a trench in the ocean floor which reaches out to the continental shelf. This part of the river contributes striped bass, bluefish, shad, sturgeon, and lesser species to the warmwater fish. The Hudson contains major spawning areas for stripers and shad, and vast schools of the latter ascend the currents to spawn during April and May.

The area between the estuary and the Connecticut border in Westchester and Putnam counties harbors a remarkable series of reservoirs and streams, the Croton-Kensico Watershed, which supplies the New York Metropolitan Area with water. Even though this system lies right on New York's doorstep, it offers some excellent fishing. From Putnam County south the reservoirs are Boyd Corners, West Branch of the Croton, Bog Brook, Croton Falls, Titicus, Amawalk, Muscoot, Cross River, New Croton, and Kensico. All these lakes contain largemouth bass, and panfish such as bluegill, crappie, white and yellow perch, and bullheads; most of them hold brown trout, smallmouth bass, and pickerel. The southernmost impoundment, Kensico, has a population of lake trout, some of which exceed 20 pounds in weight. All of this fishing is available within 60 miles of Times Square, and the reservoirs are ringed by a margin of forest, giving the outdoorsman relief from the noise and fumes of the city. Some of the tributary streams and reservoir outlets furnish decent trout fishing, particularly the East and West branches of the Croton River and the outlet of Amawalk.

Long Island Saltwater Fishing & Trout Streams

Stretching east from New York City for 120 miles is Long Island, an enormous glacial deposit, which forms a barrier between the parallel Connecticut shoreline and the foaming breakers of the Atlantic Ocean and which creates the popular fishing, boating, and sailing waters of Long Island Sound. The island is shaped like a giant fork, with Orient Point forming the tip of the north tine, and the famous bluffs of Montauk Point—the island's saltwater fishing capital—comprising the south tine. The space between the tines is filled by Big and Little Peconic, Southold, Nayack, Gardiners, and Napeague bays. A series of barrier beaches runs from Jamaica Bay, within New York City limits, east for almost 100 miles to Southampton. Great South, Moriches, and Shinnecock bays are a result of this formation.

Striped bass, hordes of powerful, savage bluefish, weakfish, mackerel, and fluke are found in the coastal waters, in the sound, along the beaches, and in the inlets and bays of the North and South shores. Popular bottom fish include cod, winter flounders, porgies, blackfish, and sea bass. Peconic Bay, inside of the Y at the east end of Long Island, is one of the great weakfishing spots along the East Coast. In May and June large schools of these iridescent, troutlike scrappers invade Peconic, and large "tide runners" of up to 12 pounds are taken on sea worms, squid, shrimp, jigs, and spoons. The inshore waters of Montauk Point rank among the great striped bass fisheries in America, with major migrations in the spring and fall, during which big bass up to 50 pounds are taken on plugs, eel rigs, spoons, feather lures, surgical tubes, spinner and bait combinations, and by "live lining," or drifting a live mossbunker, herring, or mackerel in the tide. Montauk has a big fleet of charter boats which take anglers offshore for tuna, broadbill swordfish, white and blue marlin, mako and other sharks, bonito, and a variety of less common species. Giant tuna, swordfish, blue marlin, and sharks reach weights in excess of 1,000 pounds, although the average is much smaller. Some skippers specialize in light-tackle fishing for stripers and blues. Party boats take fishermen for fluke, flounder, porgies, sea bass, blackfish, and cod.

Another top-ranked area, the awesome tidal race at Plum Gut, between Orient Point and Plum Island, is esteemed for its excellent striper and bluefish angling, and respected for the boiling, tortured currents that surge through the narrow channel when the tide is running. Don't try Plum Gut when a stiff wind is blowing against the tide, because this race can be a killer, with violent, choppy waves, small whirlpools, and vicious crosscurrents which capsize the unwary. Port Jefferson Harbor, Smithtown Bay, Cold Spring Harbor, Hempstead Harbor, Manhasset Bay, and the Westchester County shore are other popular fishing spots.

Freshwater fishing is rather limited on Long Island. On the North Shore, the Nissequogue River at Smithtown has some creditable brown trout angling, and there is always the chance of hooking a big sea-run fish. The famed Connetquot River, a beautiful alkaline stream which flows through the Woodlands State Park near Central Islip, holds some truly giant brown trout up to 6–8 pounds, as does Carmans River, a state-designated wild and scenic river, to the east near Shirley. Bass, pickerel, perch, bullheads, and bluegills are found in Lake Ronkonkoma adjacent to Long Island Expressway at Ronkonkoma, in the Peconic River at Riverhead, and in scores of private ponds on residential property and farmlands in the heavily populated length of Long Island. Fly fishing only is permitted on the Nissequogue and Connetquot within the state park areas of the same names. Fishing permits cost $5 for a half-day of angling. For reservations on the Connetquot, call (516–581–1005); for the Nissequogue, call (516–265–1054).

Catskill Forest Preserve

In the uplands to the west of the Hudson in southern New York lie the tradition-rich waters of the densely wooded Catskill Mountains Forest Preserve, the birthplace of modern American fly fishing. The revered Beaverkill, Willowemoc, Neversink, Esopus, and East Branch of the Delaware rise in a series of lofty green domes, including Double Top, Slide (the highest Catskill at 4,204 feet), Hemlock, Balsam, Balsam Lake, Pisgah, and Vly Mountains in the wild, high country of Ulster, Sullivan, Greene, and Delaware counties. Born as springs, gushing from beneath laurel-shaded rocks, these rills pick up strength as they race down the mountainsides into the steep, narrow valleys of their maturity, where the waters of countless feeder brooks produce riffles, waist-level runs, and deep, hemlock-fringed pools in which sly trophy browns take possession of the prime lies.

The Beaverkill River and Willowemoc Creek join at the town of Roscoe on Route 17. A legendary two-headed brown trout of immense proportions, the "Beamoc," is said to inhabit the Junction Pool, one head pointing up the waters of the Beaverkill, the other into the flow of the Willowemoc, destined by indecision to remain forever rooted in its hold.

The Big Beaverkill flows west from Roscoe through a series of beautiful pools (Ferdons, Horse Run, Wagon Wheel, Mountain, and Painter Bend, to name a few) to its confluence with the East Branch of the Delaware at the town of East Branch. The lower river holds some lunker browns, as well as rainbows and a few brookies. The bottom pools also yield some smallmouths.

The East Branch of the Delaware was one of the great trout streams of the East before the water demands of New York City raised havoc with the flow of cold water issuing from Pepacton Reservoir, impounding the waters of the East Branch at Downsville. At times the flow is reduced to a trickle, and the pools below the dam don't produce the great numbers of hefty browns which were once the trademark of this section of river. Above Pepacton, through the picturesque village of Margaretville, there is some quality trout water, and natives are found in the feeder brooks of the upper reaches. Pepacton Reservoir contains some of the most spectacular brown trout fishing in the East. Thick, deep-bodied lunkers roam the depths of the impoundment, and fish in excess of 15 pounds are not rare. Trolling, still fishing, and drifting with live bait produce a lot of big trout, 3 to 6 pounds in weight. Smallmouth bass, pickerel, and panfish contribute a lot of action too.

Other top-ranked Catskill trout waters include the upper West Branch of the Delaware; the upper Neversink, home river of the legendary Theodore Gordon, creator of the deadly Quill Gordon fly; Esopus Creek, which provides exciting fishing during the spring for big rainbows migrating up from Ashokan Reservoir; Schoharie Creek and its West Kill, Batavia Kill, and East Kill tributaries, which hold some good-sized browns; and Rondout and Kaaterskill creeks and the remote Catskill headwaters for fat, orange-bellied, native brookies. The upper reaches of the Delaware, below Hancock, yield trophy-sized smallmouth bass, walleye, and rainbow trout, as well as thousands of shad, known as the "poor man's salmon," during the May and June spawning run.

Outdoor Publications, Box 355, Ithaca 14850, publishes two booklets which are invaluable aides for anyone planning to fish in the Catskills. *Guide to Trout Streams in the Catskill Mountains* ($1.50), by Crane Hanover, describes the general area of the Catskills, the park, forest preserve, and principal watersheds, major roadways through the region, public fishing stretches, and access. The book includes tips on

securing permission to fish private lands, campsite information, and a thorough description of each major trout stream. A general schematic watershed map showing the internal road system is provided. For anyone planning to try the beautiful Catskill waters, this book will save hours of wasted time, and furnish a useful basic knowledge of the region and what is offered.

A companion book is *New York City Reservoirs in the Catskill Mountains* ($1.50), by C. Austin Glenn, which provides information about six major New York City reservoirs in the Catskills: Pepacton, Cannonsville, Neversink, Rondout, Ashokan, and Schoharie. Included in this very handy guide are details about the water system, license and permit requirements and how and where to secure them, reservoir regulations (pay attention—they are numerous and strictly enforced), boat ordinances—a boat is an enormous asset in fishing the big impoundments, but only one boat is allowed per permit and only for *one* specific lake—and a complete description of each reservoir. Individual impoundment sections contain a lake map and provide the location, access, species present, and fishing advice.

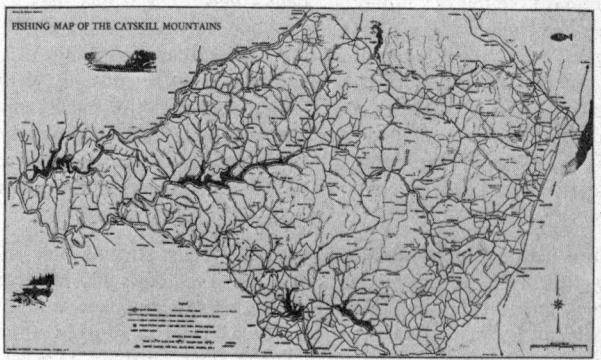

Outdoor Publications also publishes a valuable *Fishing Map of the Catskill Mountains* ($1.50, 22 × 37 inches), which shows more than 1,000 miles of mountain streams, lakes, ponds, and reservoirs, describes fishing rights areas and reservoirs open by permit, and pinpoints some 30 fishing hot spots; *Sportsman's Map of Pepacton Reservoir*, which shows water depths from 10- to 20-foot intervals, roadways, hollows, coves, and little-known fishing spots and feeder streams; *Sportsman's Map of the Central Catskill Mountains* ($2, 22 × 25 inches), showing all natural and man-made features, with contour lines; and a *Sportsman's Map of the Ashokan Reservoir* ($1, 18 × 30 inches), showing depth contours, roads, coves, and points favored by local guides and fishermen.

For info on Catskill lake and trout stream conditions and where-to-go advice, write or call: *Beaverkill Sportsman*, Roscoe 12776 (607–498–4677).

To the west of the Catskills, the walleye and smallmouth bass waters of the Susquehanna River system drain an extensive area in central and south-central New York, stretching from its headwaters in Otsego Lake at Cooperstown west to Canisteo River, south of the famed Finger Lakes region. The major lakes and streams of the Susquehanna system include Otsego Lake, which yields rainbow, brown, and lake trout, whitefish, both varieties of black bass, pickerel, and panfish; Canadargo Lake, noted for smallmouth and largemouth bass, trout, pickerel, and an occasional muskellunge; Schenevas Creek, one of the state's top 50 trout streams; and the trophy walleye, bass, and pickerel waters of the Chemung River and its Cohocton River tributary—another of the state's top 50 trout streams, particularly for browns along its upper reaches.

Finger Lakes Country

Occupying the area to the north of the sprawling Susquehanna watershed are Oneida Lake and the famous Finger Lakes region. Oneida, a long, wide body of water, covers over 50,000 acres and is the largest interior lake in the state. Located west of Rome and north of Syracuse, Oneida contains an unusually broad fish population, including trout, both kinds of bass, walleye, pike, pickerel, channel catfish, white and yellow perch, white bass, crappie, and bullhead. Oneida's Fish Creek and East Branch, and Limestone Creek tributaries are among the state's top 50 trout streams.

The Finger Lakes occupy a long arc of land in west central New York, stretching for about 100 miles east to west, and are nationally famous for their spectacular trout fishing, resorts, and wine vineyards. The lakes are deep glacial gouges set in the rolling Lake Ontario plain, and look as if a giant, multiclawed bear had raked the earth's surface from south to north. This scenic lakeland was once the home and hunting grounds of the Seneca Indians—among them were the great Seneca statesman Red Jacket, and Hiawatha, the Onondaga chieftain who inspired Longfellow's immortal poem—who believed that they lived atop the back of a giant turtle, with pools between the ridges of the turtle's back forming the great finger-shaped lakes. A group of the larger lakes (ranging from 11 to 40 miles long)—Canandaigua, Keuka, Seneca, Cayuga, Owasco, and Skaneateles—and the smaller ones, Conesus, Hemlock, Canadice, Honeoye, and Otisco, drain north to Lake Ontario, primarily through the Seneca and Genesee River networks. Seneca Lake reaches down to 618 feet and is one of the nation's deepest lakes.

These nationally renowned lakes and their feeder streams offer often spectacular fishing for big, metallic-flanked rainbows and lake trout which grow to the 10-to-20-pound class on the abundant schools of smelt and sawbellies, as well as trophy brown trout, landlocked salmon, walleye, smallmouth bass, muskellunge, and northern pike. The fishing quality of these great lakes is reflected in a listing of record fish caught in the region.

FINGER LAKES RECORD FISH

	Lb.-oz.	Place
Brown trout	21–5	Owasco Lake
Rainbow trout	21	Keuka Lake
Lake trout	26	Canandaigua Lake
Walleye	15–3	Chemung River
Smallmouth bass	7–4	Owasco Lake
Muskellunge	29–2	Waneta Lake
Northern pike	18	Seneca Lake

Seneca Lake, stretching north from the auto racing town of Watkins Glen for almost 40 miles, is one of the deepest bodies of water in the eastern United States, with depths exceeding 600 feet. Most anglers consider this the best member of the chain, and quantities of big lake trout, rainbows, smallmouth bass, and pike are taken from the clear waters. An incredible scene, reminiscent of a bargain basement sale, takes place on April 1 each year when the opening of the fishing season and the fabulous Catherine Creek rainbow run coincide. The creek, which runs through Watkins Glen, is not large to begin with and hordes of hopeful anglers assault the banks, jockey for the best spots, and bombard the stream with fish-roe imitations (spawn is prohibited) such as dyed vaseline balls and gumdrops, spinners, and night crawlers, in the hopes of hooking one of the enormous rainbows that reach weights to 20 pounds. Many trout of 5 pounds or better are caught during this period, and the great enthusiasm is understandable.

A useful *Finger Lakes Regional Travel Guide* (75¢), available from: Finger Lakes Assn., 309 Lake St., Rte. 54, Penn Yan 14527, describes the fishing, boating, and hunting opportunities available, as well as fishing and hunting vacation resorts, camping facilities, and tourist services.

To the west of the Finger Lakes lie the trout, walleye, and smallmouth bass waters of the Genesee River and its tributaries; the trophy muskellunge, walleye, northern pike, trout, largemouth and smallmouth bass waters of the Allegheny River and its great reservoir, formed by Kinzua Dam in Pennsylvania; Ischua Creek, an Allegheny tributary, rated as one of the state's top 50 trout streams, Cuba Lake, and Conewango Creek. The shallow, snag-filled waters of Chatauqua Lake at Jamestown, on the western edge of New York, has long held a reputation for being the top musky lake in the state, and fish up to 40 pounds are caught each year, although there are bigger ones in the lake. Chautauqua furnishes the number one opportunity to hook a musky, and substantial numbers of the large, barred Ohio or Chautauqua strain are boated each year on big plugs, bucktails, spinners, and live suckers.

Maps & Guides

A *Register of Guides* for fishing, hunting, and canoe-camping trips in the Adirondacks and Catskill forest preserves and outlying areas may be obtained by writing: Publications Distribution Unit, Dept. of Environmental Conservation, 50 Wolf Rd., Albany 12201. The department publishes several free maps, guides, and pamphlets of interest to the fisherman and hunter, including a *Sportfishing Guide* which contains all regulations, seasons, and license information, and shows the locations of state parks, campsites, boat access sites, public fishing streams, cooperative fishing areas, and fish and wildlife management areas; *Freshwater Fishing in New York*, which contains a list of the top 50 trout streams, a chart of major lakes, reservoirs, and rivers indicating fish species found in each, and a map showing the location of state fish hatcheries; *Big-Game Hunting Guide*, which contains hunting regulations, seasons, license info, and a color map showing state parks open to hunting, fish and wildlife management areas, special use areas, deer management units, and hunting zones; *Small-Game Hunting Guide*, which contains small-game and waterfowl hunting regulations, a chart of popular hunting areas, sunrise-sunset tables, and a map of state hunting areas and zones; *Wildlife Management Area and Fish-Wildlife Management Act Cooperative Area* brochures, which include a detailed map of each area, special regulations, and information on features, species available, and best seasons; *County Maps* (50¢ each), which show the location of all state lands, fire towers, campsites, logging roads, stocked trout streams, stream easements, boat-launching sites, and special use areas; *Outdoor Recreation Guide*, which contains additional information on state parks, hunting and fishing areas, and public campsites; *Public Use of New York's Forestlands*, which contains guidelines for outdoor recreation useage of all DEC-managed lands; and *Boat-Launching Sites*, which includes a list of all state boat access sites and gives details about the sites and how to locate them on a road map.

These and single copies of the following publications may be obtained free upon request from: Publications Distribution Unit, DEC, 50 Wolf Rd., Albany 12201: *Access Point Maps for the Catskill Forest Preserve, Great Lakes Salmon Sport Fishery, Leaping Rainbows of the Finger Lakes, Panfishes of New York, Red Salmon, Salmon in New York, Smelt, Trout Fishing in the Catskills, Marine Game Fish of New York, Sport Fishing for Cod, Catskill Forest Preserve, Wild Rivers,*

Weather and the Deer Population, Blackfly, Flytying, Surf Fishing, Tips for Getting a "Bow Buck," Ecology of a Bog, Survival, Big-Game Shots, Big-Game Cookery, Field Dressing a Deer, Care of Raw Furs, Trout Fishing in the Catskills, and *Return of the Wild Turkey.*

The Conservationist Magazine is the official publication of the DEC; it carries articles about outdoor recreation, natural history, regional history, conservation, interesting personalities who have had an impact on the New York wilderness, and related subjects. The magazine costs $3.50 per year, $6 for 2 years, or $9 for 3 years and is available from: Circulation Office, Conservation Magazine, P.O. Box 2328, Grand Central Sta., New York 10017.

Wildlife & Hunting

New York's once extensive north country wilderness areas were inhabited during the early 19th century by moose, elk, panthers, wolves, wolverines, and lynx. The last moose taken in the Adirondacks was in 1861 near Raquette Lake. It was an 800-pound female, 7 feet tall at the hump. Lynx, the silent hunter of the north, were once common throughout the north woods. In 1907, two lynx were killed in a barnyard at Willseyville, just south of Ithaca in Tioga County. In recent years several reports of lynx in the Adirondacks have been authenticated, but the occurrence is sporadic. The wapiti or American elk was once abundant in New York's southern tier and in Pennsylvania. A large bull elk was killed in Allegheny County in 1844, and several elk were killed in Genesee Valley between 1840 and 1843. A bull elk, a remnant from early introductions in the Big Moose region in the Adirondacks, was killed by a hunter in 1946 in Essex County. The mountain lion or panther once roamed the wild areas of the Adirondacks and Catskills. It was recorded by the Fish & Game Commission that between 1871 to 1894 the state paid a bounty on a total of 99 panthers taken in the Adirondack high country. The ferocious wolverine once roamed the dense evergreen forests in the north. The last authentic record is of a wolverine that was killed on the Raquette River in 1884. The last member of the once great packs of timber wolves was reportedly killed in St. Lawrence County in 1899. Bison, which once roamed eastward to the salt licks at Syracuse, disappeared before white settlement.

By 1900 the fur trade had all but exterminated the beaver, as well as otter, mink, marten, and fisher—which are found today in the remote wilderness boreal forests of the Adirondacks. Beaver were reintroduced throughout the Adirondacks in the early part of the century and today beaver dams dot the wilds and backcountry of the Adirondacks and Catskills. Some of the finest trout fishing in the state is to be found in the remote beaver ponds and flows scattered throughout the wilderness areas of the Adirondack Lake region for wild, orange-bellied brook trout. Many of these extensive beaver flows and meadows are accessible only by old logging roads and trails shown on large-scale U.S. Geological Survey Maps.

The Department of Environmental Conservation publishes informative, educational leaflets for many of the state's wildlife and bird species found throughout the high country, hardwood and boreal forests, lowlands, swamps, and bogs commonly traveled by the fisherman, hunter, backpacker, and wilderness canoeist. These useful free wildlife guides include: *Animals of New York, Bear Notes/Panther, Coyote, Fisher/Otter, Lynx/Wildcat, Mammals of New York—Past and Present, Rabbit Season, Skunk, Weasel Family, Wildlife Community, Birds' Eggs & Nests, Crows, Hawks and Eagles of New York, Marsh Waders of New York, Primary Waterfowl* and *Upland Game Birds and Water Birds.* Write: Publications Distribution Unit, DEC (address above).

The Empire State's vast forest lands, wetlands, and wildlife management areas today provide productive habitat for a variety of game species, including whitetail deer, wild turkey, ruffed grouse, woodcock, pheasants, bobwhite quail, cottontail rabbits, snowshoe rabbits, European hares, ducks, geese, snipe, rail, squirrels, and other small-game animals. Whitetail deer are found throughout the state, from the heavily forested slopes and ridges of the Adirondacks south through the mixed woodlands and farms of central and western New York, the Catskill Forest Preserve, and Long Island. Some of the largest trophy bucks are found in the farmlands and orchards adjoining the Catskill forest areas. *Guide to Deer Hunting in the Catskill Mountains* ($1.50), by Carl Oleberg, is published by: Outdoor Publications, Box 355, Ithaca 14850. The booklet describes the hunting opportunities in the four major counties: Delaware, Ulster, Greene, and Sullivan. Principal deer hunting areas are identified and discussed, and the publication furnishes hunting tips, access information, and other helpful material.

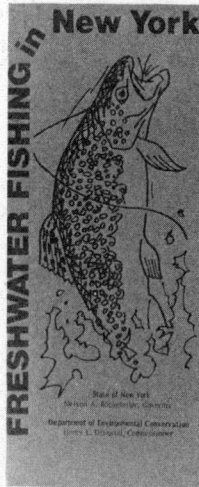

Black bears are found in the thick, tangled forests, bogs, and rugged high country areas of the Adirondacks, and in the interior Catskill and Allegheny ridges. Flocks of wild turkeys have been reestablished in their former strongholds, the southwest counties bordering Pennsylvania and the Catskills, and in some central Hudson Valley counties, where they can be found in ridge areas near open land, feeding on nuts, buds, wild fruits, seeds, and insects. These magnificent bronze trophies are worth the skill and patience needed to call or stalk them. Explosive ruffed grouse, the state's number one game bird, are found

throughout the state along forest borders which adjoin old orchards and farms, second-growth areas, alder thickets, and stream bottoms, where they can find seeds, fruits, buds, and insects. Thomapple and wild grape tangles are tops for these birds, and a good dog is of great value in locating and holding grouse in difficult cover. The brilliant autumn-painted forest fringes of the Catskills are among the best covers in the state. Woodcock and pheasant add to the state's mixed bag of upland game birds. Ducks and geese offer some of the finest hunting in the state along the Great Lakes shoreline, St. Lawrence River, and Long Island Sound, with their abundant marshes, islands, bays, coves, and inlets. There is some decoy hunting and jump shooting in the interior areas of the state, particularly along Lake Champlain, the Hudson and Mohawk valleys, and the many scattered lakes, ponds, marshes, and sluggish river stretches.

(For additional information, see "Wild River & Adirondack Wilderness Maps" and the "Travel & Recreation Guide" section.)

Highways—Recreation & Scenic Routes

New York's four-lane expressways include the Governor Thomas E. Dewey Thruway (Interstate 87 and 90), Adirondack Northway (Interstate 87), North-South Expressway (Interstate 81), Long Island Expressway (Interstate 495), and the partly completed Route 17-Southern Tier Expressway.

The New York Thruway runs from the state's western border 559 miles to New York City, inscribing an arc across the state and connecting with the Pennsylvania, Massachusetts, and Connecticut turnpikes, the Garden State Parkway, and other major highways. The thruway is a toll way. No accommodations are available on the highway, but there are accommodations just off most of the thruway's 103 interchanges.

The Adirondack Northway extends south from the Canadian border 176 miles to Albany, and is toll-free. Interstate 81 (also toll-free) runs from the Thousand Islands-St. Lawrence area and central New York 182 miles to the Pennsylvania line. The Long Island Expressway

(Interstate 495) runs from New York City's Queens Midtown Tunnel to eastern Long Island. Route 17-Southern Tier Expressway runs from Harriman to Allegany.

The Taconic State Parkway runs up the east side of the Hudson to connect with the Berkshire Spur of the thruway. The Palisades Interstate Parkway runs from the George Washington Bridge at New York City to Bear Mountain State Park. Other parkways include the Bronx River, Hutchinson, Sprain Brook, and Saw Mill River parkways in Westchester County, Robert Moses Parkway near Niagara Falls, and the Lake Ontario Parkway.

The Adirondack Trail (Route 30), which crosses the Adirondack Mountains between the Canadian border and the thruway at Amsterdam and Fultonville, is among the state's most scenic highways. For more information on it, write to: Hamilton Co. Publicity Bureau, Long Lake 12847. Among the scenic highways through the Catskills are the Shawangunk Trail (Route 52 from Newburgh), Minnewaska Trail (Routes 44 and 55 from Poughkeepsie), Onteora Trail (Route 28 from Kingston), Rip Van Winkle Trail (Route 23A from Catskill), and Mohican Trail (Route 23 from Catskill).

The Hawk's Nest Drive, a portion of Route 97 between Port Jervis and Hancock, offers spectacular views of the Delaware River Gorge. The Seneca Trail follows an old Indian trail from the Pennsylvania border through Limestone, Salamanca, Little Valley, Cattaraugus, and Gowanda to Hamburg. The St. Lawrence Scenic Highway (Route 12) runs along the river between Alexandria Bay and Morristown. Route 30 in Schoharie County is known as the Timothy Murphy Trail.

For a free full-color *Official New York State Road Map*, which shows all outdoor recreation areas, state parks and forest preserves, and a wealth of other useful information, write or call: New York State Vacation Information, 99 Washington Ave., Albany (800–342–3810 toll free).

Lake Contour Fishing Maps

The following detailed 8-½ × 11-inch maps showing depths and bottom contours, species of fish present, and lake characteristics, are available free from: Publications Distribution Unit, Department of Environmental Conservation, 50 Wolf Rd., Albany 12233: Ashokan Reservoir, Big Moose-Piseco, Black-Millsite, Canada-Chazy, Canadarago-Cuba, Caroga-Sacandaga-Pleasant, Carry Falls Reservoir-Rich, Cayuta-Loon (Steuben County), Chateaugay (Upper and Lower)-Fourth, Chautauqua, Conesus, Copake-Otsego, Cossayuna-Skaneateles, Cranberry, De Ruyter Reservoir-Rushford, Forked-Lake Eaton-South Pond-Long Lake-Indian Lakes, Fulton Chain, George (Lake), Indian (Dutchess County)-Greenwood, Keuka, Loon (Warren County)-Paradox, Luzerne (Lake)-Cross Lake, Mahopac Lake-Gilead-Glenida, Meacham-Tupper-Raquette Pond, Oneida-Canandaigua, Ontario, Owasco-Honeoye, Raquette-Blue Mountain, Sacandaga Reservoir, Saranac (Lower)-Fish Creek Pond-Rollins Pond, Saratoga, Burden, Butterfield, Bonaparte, Schroon-Brant, Seneca, Silver-Waneta-Lamoka Lakes, Seyder's-Crystal-Glass and Crooked Lake, Tsatsawassa-Kinderhook, and Thompson-Warners.

Moose River Plains Area

This 50,000-acre area in the Adirondack Forest Preserve is made up of the plains of the Moose and Red rivers, in Hamilton and Herkimer counties between Route 28 and the West Canada Lakes Wilderness. These flat zones of herb and grass vegetation contrast vividly with the

adjacent dense green forests. A maze of abandoned logging roads of the old Gould Paper Company wind through the region. Major features of this top whitetail deer and brook trout area include the Cedar River Flow, Moose River Cliffs, Mitchell Ponds, Lost Ponds, Icehouse and Helldiver ponds, Cedar Lakes, Brook Trout Lake, Indian River Canoe Trail, Beaver, Limekiln, Indian, Sly, and Wolf lakes, and the length of the South Branch of the Moose River.

Nearly 30 miles of access trails lead to the interior fishing and wilderness camping areas; these are open to foot travel only. The area is closed to snowmobile traffic until the close of the big-game hunting season, unless snow makes access roads impassable to other vehicles.

The main access roads to the Moose River Recreation Area include Cedar River Road off Route 28 running west from Indian Lake Village (entrance point is Cedar River Flow), and a road running south from Route 28 just east of the village of Inlet (entrance point is Limekiln Lake). The Cedar River entrance may be closed during bad weather. The recreation area is usually open to public use between June 1 and the close of deer season. Entry by foot trail is permitted at any time. All access roads are unimproved and narrow with steep grades in places. All persons who enter the recreation area must register with the caretaker at the gate.

A brochure describing the *Moose River Recreation Area* is available from: Division of Lands & Forests, Dept. of Environmental Conservation, 50 Wolf Rd., Albany 12233. The brochure describes the natural features of the area, access roads and trails, camping regulations, fishing and hunting regulations, and guidelines for hikers and campers. The brochure includes a map of the area on a scale of about 1 inch to 2 miles, showing primary roads, trails, road barriers, lean-tos, fire towers, camping areas, mountains, and water features.

Nautical Charts & Cruising Kits

New York's 1,647 square miles of water, including 800 miles of rivers and canals and hundreds of lakes, offer a wide spectrum of boating opportunities. Boat trailers are permitted on all state highways except a few parkways; for more information on restrictions, write to: Director of Operations, Thruway Authority, Box 189, Albany 12201.

Charts for *Chautauqua* ($3.50), *Cranberry* ($3), *George* ($4.50), *Great Sacandaga* ($4.50), *Long* ($3), *Owasco* ($3.50), *Placid* ($2), *Raquette* ($2.50), *Saranac Chain* ($2), *Schroon* ($2), *Tupper* ($3), and *Upper Saaranac* ($2.50) lakes are available from: Bureau of Marine & Recreational Vehicles, Parks & Recreation Dept., Albany 12238.

The bureau also issues three chart kits. Cruise'n Chart #1, *The Northwest Passage*, charts the waterways from New York City to the Canadian border via the Hudson River, Champlain Canal, and Lake Champlain. Cruise'n Chart #2, *The Grand Canal*, covers the Barge Canal and Oneida, Cayuga, and Seneca lakes between Albany, Buffalo, and Oswego. Cruise'n Chart #3, *The Inland Seaway*, covers the St. Lawrence River, Lake Ontario, the Welland Canal, and Lake Erie. Each of these chart kits is packaged in a waterproof carrier, and includes a full-color book of charts and a guide to marine facilities and points of interest along the way. They cost $7.50 each.

The 524-mile New York State Barge Canal System is another waterway open to cruises. The free pamphlet, *Cruising the Canals*, along with a canal map, is available from: Waterways Maintenance Subdivision, Dept. of Transportation, 1220 Washington Ave., Albany 12232. The pamphlet includes canal regulations.

Most waterways in the state have marinas and launching ramps. A free folder listing more than 75 small-boat launching sites throughout the state is available from: Bureau of Marine & Recreational Vehicles (address above).

Northville-Placid Trail to the High Peaks Wilderness

The famous Northville-Placid Trail, blazed by the Adirondack Mountain Club in 1922–23, passes through the heart of the Adirondack Forest Preserve wilderness along a northerly 133-mile-long course connecting the scenic lake-dotted southern Adirondack foothills with the majestic 219,750-acre High Peaks Wilderness to the north—dominated by Mount Marcy (5,344 feet), known as Tahawus ("cloud splitter") to the Iroquois, and the surrounding peaks of the MacIntyre Range and the Hudson-St. Lawrence Divide. The trail passes through several of the East's premier wilderness fishing, hunting, camping, and canoeing areas, including the 106,650-acre Silver Lake Wilderness— a wild country of low rolling hills, dense conifer forests, cedar swamps, and beaver flows dominated by the famed brook trout waters of the wild West Branch of the Sacandaga River; the 160,320-acre West Canada Lakes Wilderness, famous for its wild brook trout waters, spruce and balsam swamp flats, beaver meadows, and rolling hills, including the Moose River Plains, Pisceo Lake, Cedar Lakes, Jessup River Wild Forest, Spruce Lake, Cedar River Flow, and Indian River; and Blue Mountain Lake country and beyond, hugging the eastern shore of Long Lake through the heart of the Adirondacks along old logging roads to Lake Placid and the high peaks. Old tote roads and spur trails provide access to seldom explored game lands and remote high country lakes, many of which hold wild brook trout up to 5 pounds, northern pike, and smallmouth bass. There are several tent sites and Adirondack shelters along the trail.

The Northville–Placid Trail

DO NOT LITTER
If you carried it in—carry it out

A free guide to the *Northville-Placid Trail* is available from: Bureau of Forest Recreation, Department of Environmental Conservation, 50 Wolf Rd., Albany 12233. The guide describes the trail in depth, giving mileage information for each section of the trail, and noting landmarks, points of interest, fishing ponds and streams, campsites, lean-tos, and other information useful to the hiker.

The *Guide to Adirondack Trails* ($6) contains a section on the Northville-Placid Trail that includes even more detailed descriptions of the trail, as well as a map of the trail on a scale of about 1 inch to 10 miles,

showing water features, prominent topographic features, roads, camp-sites, and ranger cabins. The book is available from: Adirondack Mountain Club, 172 Ridge St., Glens Falls 12801.

These guides and maps should be used in conjunction with large-scale U.S. Geological Survey Topographic Maps for the trail route: Blue Mountain, Harrisburg, Indian Lake, Jackson Summit, Lake Placid, Lake Pleasant, Long Lake, Northville, Piseco Lake, Santanoni, Sara-nac Lake, West Canada Lake.

Ski Touring Trails & Centers

For many, a winter trek through the slopes and forests of the state sharpens the sense and deepens one's experience of the wilderness. Trails open the backcountry to the cross-country skier and snowshoer, and offer a landscape transformed by a magnificence of white.

The wildlands are at their most formidable during the winter months; the winter trekker should go prepared. Winter camping requires advanced planning, a knowledge of winter hazards, and wilderness travel experience. Be sure you take the proper equipment, including warm clothes (woolen underwear, not cotton), tent, winter sleeping bag, waterproof matches, hatchet, knife, repair kit for skis or snowshoes, first-aid kit, sunburn lotions, topographic map, compass, rope, small horn or whistle, mirror for signaling, toiletries, and water flask. Bring adequate food, including high-energy food such as granola and nuts. In extremely cold weather be sure to include foods that do not freeze.

Each year the backcountry claims the lives of those who underestimate the dangers of cold. Exposure can cause death at temperatures well above freezing if the victim is improperly dressed or wet. Brush excess snow from your clothing to avoid loss of heat caused by dampness. Be aware of the windchill factor, and its effect on exposed flesh for the temperatures you expect to experience on your trip. The chart below shows windchill temperatures for various wind velocities.

U.S. ARMY WINDCHILL INDEX

(Equivalent temperature in cooling power on exposed flesh in calm conditions)

Wind	30°	20°	10°	0°	−10°	−20°	−30°
10 mph	16	2	−9	−22	−31	−45	−58
15 mph	11	−6	−18	−33	−45	−60	−70
20 mph	3	−9	−24	−40	−52	−68	−81
25 mph	0	−15	−29	−45	−58	−75	−89
30 mph	−2	−18	−33	−49	−63	−78	−94
35 mph	−4	−20	−35	−52	−67	−83	−98
40 mph	−4	−22	−36	−54	−69	−87	−101

Wind speeds greater than 40 mph have little additional chilling effect.

Know how to read snow conditions. Avoid avalanche-prone areas. Plan your travel route ahead of time, and stick to it. Inform a friend of your plans and the time of your expected return before you leave, and give him the number of a local forest ranger to call in case of delay.

New York State forest preserves offer miles of scenic nordic skiing and snowshoeing trails. The Haines Falls Trail follows old 19th-century carriage roads, with vistas overlooking the Hudson. The Lake Trail takes you to the famous Mountain House, overlooking the Hudson Valley. Other trails in the northern Catskills include the Boulder Rock, Temper Mountain (advanced skiers only), Old Overlook Road (Woodstock area), and Diamond Notch trails.

In the southern Catskills, the Balsam Lake Mountain Trail, beginning at the junction of Millbrook Road and Pakatahan–Dry Brook–Ridge-Beaverkill Trail, the Neversink-Hardenburg Trail, the Slide Mountain Trail, and the Belleayre Mountain Trail offer ski touring possibilities.

In the foothills of the Adirondack High Peaks, trails approaching the mountains offer about 20 miles of easy ski touring. The Mount Van Hoevenberg Recreation Area offers another 12 miles of trails. The Mount Van Hoevenberg trails connect to the Adirondack Loj trail system, which offers some of the most scenic tours in the state. The Adirondak Loj Trails include the loop trip, hiking trail to Marcy Dam, truck trail to South Dam, and the Indian Pass Trail. The Mount Van Hoevenberg Recreation Area trailhead is 6 miles south of Lake Placid off Route 73, next to the first parking lot for the Olympic bobsled run. These trails were designed for ski touring, cross-country racing and training, and hiking in the summer. Another good trail in this area starts at Keene Valley and follows the Mount Marcy hiking trail to Bushnell Falls (John Brooks Trail).

Other Adirondack ski paths include the famous Northville-Placid Trail, The Crane Pond-Putnam Pond Trail in the Schroon Lake region, Otter Lake Truck Trail in the Old Forge region, and Cranberry Lake trails. For detailed information on Adirondack & Catskill ski touring centers, write: *Adirondak Loj*, P.O. Box 867, Lake Placid 12946 (518-523-3441); *Country Hills Farm*, Tully 13159; *Garnet Hill Lodge*, North River 12856; *Mount Van Hoevenberg* (Lake Placid), Dept. of Environmental Conservation, 50 Wolf Rd., Albany 12233; Adirondack and Catskill Forest Preserves, same address; Warren County Publicity (Lake George region), Lake George 12845; *Whiteface Chalet* (Whiteface Mountain region), Wilmington 12997; *Wills Run* (Schroon Lake region), Hoffman Rd., Schroon Lake 12870; *Bark Eater Lodge & Ski Touring Center*, Alstead Mill Rd., Keene 12942 (518-576-2221) in Lake Placid area, with access to Au Sable Lakes and Heart Lake trails, Old Military Road to Lake Placid, and Northville-Placid Trail; *Big Tupper Ski Area*, Box 820, Tupper Lake 12986 (518-359-3651); *Inlet Ski Touring Center*, South Shore Rd., Inlet 13360 (315-357-3453); *Paleface Lodge & Ski Center*, Rt. 86, P.O. Box 163, Jay 12941 (518-946-2272), with 25 miles of trails in the High Peaks area; *Lake Placid Club*, Lake Placid 12946 (518-523-3361), with 12 miles of trails at 1980 Olympic site; *Old Forge Ski Touring Area*, Central Adirondack Assn., Old Forge 13420 (315-369-6983), with 12 miles of trails and 20 miles at Inlet in Fulton Chain Lakes area; *Lake Minnewaska Ski Touring Center*, New Paltz 12561 (914-255-6000), with lodging, instruction, and 150 miles of trails high in the Shawangunk Mountains at 2,000-feet elevations; *Lake Mohonk Mountain House*, New Paltz 12561 (914-255-1000), with 65 miles of trails.

A schedule of group ski tours throughout the state ($2.75) and a *Ski Touring Guide* ($3.50) are available from: Ski Touring Council, Troy, VT 05868. The guide covers all facets of ski touring, including equipment, clothing, safety measures, trail cutting and maintenance, backpacking on skis, survival, avalanche protection, and how to start a ski touring program or a ski touring area. Besides listing ski touring areas, it is the only book which also covers snowshoeing possibilities, lists touring trails in New York and the East, and briefly outlines touring opportunities in other parts of the U.S. and in eastern Canada.

For detailed descriptions of ski touring trails throughout the state, write for a free copy of *Winter Hiking in the New York State Forest Preserve (Nordic Skiing and Snowshoeing).* The booklet describes location, landmarks, mileage, and other features of trails in the Catskill Mountains, Lake Placid and the Adirondack High Peaks Area, the Lakeville Placid Trail, Schroon Lake region, Old Forge region, and

Cranberry Lake region. Trails in most of the same areas are described and mapped in *Nordic Skiing and Snowshoeing Trails in New York Forest Preserves,* another free booklet from: Dept. of Environmental Conservation (address above).

Each year between Christmas and New Year's, the Adirondack Mountain Club runs schools in the Adirondacks which offer instruction in winter hiking and camping in co-operation with the Appalachian Mountain Club. For information, write: Winter School, AMC, 5 Joy St., Boston, MA 02108.

Wild River & Adirondack Wilderness Maps

The following full-color, large-scale U.S. Geological Survey Topographic Maps show the entire courses of the state's outstanding trout and salmon streams, canoe routes, and Adirondack wilderness and primitive areas (see the "Travel & Recreation Guide" section for additional listings). *Thousand Islands of the St. Lawrence:* Gananoque, St. Lawrence, Thousand Island Park, Alexandria Bay; *Salmon River & Headwaters:* Fort Covington, Constable, Malone, Chasm Falls, Owls Head; *Little Salmon River:* Bombay, Brushton, Bangor, Santa Clara, Lake Titus; *Great Chazy River:* Moffitsville, Ellenburg Mountain, Jericho, Altona, Mooers (7.5); *Indian River Canoe Country:* Old Forge, West Canada Lakes; *Jessup River:* Piseco Lake, West Canada Lakes, Indian Lake; *West Canada Lake Wilderness:* Indian Lake, Ohio, Old Forge, Piseco Lake, West Canada Lake; *Silver Lake Wilderness:* Canada Lake, Caroga Lake, Jackson Summit, Lake Pleasant, Piseco Lake; *McKenzie Mountain Wilderness:* Lake Placid, Saranac Lake; *Siamese Ponds Wilderness:* Harrisburg, Indian Lake, Thirteenth Lake; *Ha-De-Ron-Dah Wilderness:* McKeever, Number Four, Old Forge; *Giant Mountain Wilderness:* Elizabethtown, Mount Marcy; *Jordan River Wildlands:* Carey Falls Reservoir, Childwold, Mount Matumba, St. Regis; *Cedar River Wildlands:* Indian Lake, Blue Mountain, Newcomb; *Beaver River Wildlands:* Croghan, Belfort, Number Four; *Independence River Wildlands:* Lowville, Glenfield, Brantingham, Crystaldale, Number Four, Big Moose; *Opalescent River Wildlands:* Santanoni, Mount Marcy; *Grass River Canoe Country:* Tupper Lake, Childwold, Brother Ponds, Stark, West Pierrepont, Tooley Pond, Albert Marsh, Degrasse, Herman, Canton, Morley, Chase Mills, Louisville, Massena, Raquette River; *Sentinel Range:* Lake Placid; *Ampersand Lake Primitive Area:* Santanoni; *Boreas River Wildlands:* Mount Marcy, Newcomb, Schroon Lake, Thirteenth Lake; *Bouquet River:* Mount Marcy, Elizabethtown, Au Sable Forks, Port Henry; *Oswegatchie Primitive Area:* Brother Ponds, Cranberry Lake, Harrisville, Lake Bonaparte, Newton Falls, Oswegatchie, Remington Corners; *Cold River Wildlands:* Long Lake, Santanoni; *Pharaoh Lake Wilderness:* Brant Lake, Paradox Lake, Silver Bay; *Pigeon Lake Wilderness:* Big Moose, Raquette Lake; *Red River Wildlands:* Old Forge, West Canada Lakes; *Battenkill River:* Schuylerville, Cambridge, Cossayuna, Salem, Hartford, West Pawlet, Shashan; *Ischua River:* Sardinia, Arcade, Delevan, Franklinville, Hinsdale, Olean; *Nissequogue River:* St. James, Central Islip; *Carmans River:* Middle Island, Bellport.

Wilderness & Adventure Travel Service

Adventures Unlimited specializes in individually planned custom fishing, hunting, and family outdoor vacations anywhere in North America (or the world): the wild trout and salmon rivers of Alaska and British Columbia, Canada's big north fishing and hunting meccas, Wyoming's Rocky Mountain high country, Montana's blue-ribbon trout country, Michigan's Isle Royale, the Quetico-Superior canoe country, Cape Hatteras and the Outer Banks, the Florida Keys, Argentina's trophy trout highlands, Iceland's volcanic salmon rivers, or the Grand Canyon country, to name a few custom trips. They will take care of all your travel planning: plane flights, scheduling, and lodging. For trip planning assistance, call or write: Adventures Unlimited, 115 E. 57th St., New York 10022, phone (212-986-6686).

The long-established *Questers Tours & Travel, Inc.,* 257 Park Ave. S., New York, NY 10010 (212-773-3120) offers professionally guided nature tours throughout the Americas and the world, including the Everglades, Death Valley National Monument, Migratory Grey Whales-Baja California, Hawaiian Islands, Alaska, Superior-Quetico Wilderness, Idaho's Salmon River Wilderness, Alberta, Yukon, Northwest Territories, Southern Mexico and Yucatan, Galapagos Islands, Peru, Patagonia and Falkland Islands, Outer Islands and Highlands of Scotland, Northern India and Nepal, Africa, Oceania and Australasia.

NEW YORK TRAVEL & RECREATION GUIDE

Adirondack Park & Forest Preserve

Adirondack Park & Forest Preserve Topo Maps

U.S. Geological Survey Overview Maps (scale 1:250,000): Glens Falls, Lake Champlain, Ogdensburg, Utica.

Adirondack Canoe Route

Large-scale U.S. Geological Survey Topographic Maps: *(Fulton Chain of Lakes Section)* Old Forge, Big Moose, West Canada Lakes, Raquette Lake; *(Raquette Lake Section)* Raquette Lake, Blue Mountain; *(Long Lake Section)* Long Lake, Tupper Lake; *(Saranac Lake Section)* Long Lake, St. Regis, Saranac, Santanoni, Mount Marcy; *(Paul Smiths Section)* St. Regis, Saranac, Loon Lake.

Au Sable River Trophy Trout Waters & Canoe Route

Large-scale U.S. Geological Survey Topographic Maps (including East and West branches): Au Sable Forks, Keeseville, Lake Placid, Mount Marcy, Peru.

Blue Mountain Lake Region

Large-scale U.S. Geological Survey Topographic Maps: Blue Mountain, Indian Lake, Long Lake, Raquette Lake, West Canada Lakes.

Cranberry Lake Region & Five Ponds Wilderness

Large-scale U.S. Geological Survey Topographic Maps: Big Moose, Brother Ponds, Cranberry Lake, Five Ponds, Newton Falls, Oswegatchie, Remington Corners, Tooley Pond, Wolf Mountain.

High Peaks Region

Large-scale U.S. Geological Survey Topographic Maps: Long Lake, Mount Marcy, St. Regis, Santanoni, Saranac Lake.

Hudson River Canoe Trail & Hudson Gorge Primitive Area

Large-scale U.S. Geological Survey Topographic Maps: Conklinville, Johnsburg, Lake Luzerne, Newcomb, North Creek 7.5, Santanoni, Stony Creek, The Glen, Thirteenth Lake, Warrensburg.

John Brown Tract

Large-scale U.S. Geological Survey Topographic Maps: Raquette Lake, Big Moose, Old Forge, West Canada Lakes.

Lake George Region

Large-scale U.S. Geological Survey Topographic Maps: Lake George, Bolton Landing 7.5, Shelving Rock, Silver Bay, Putnam, Ticonderoga 7.5.

Moose River Canoe Country

Large-scale U.S. Geological Survey Topographic Maps: Port Leyden, Brantingham, McKeever, Old Forge, Big Moose, West Canada Lakes.

Raquette River Canoe Country

Large-scale U.S. Geological Survey Topographic Maps: Blue Mountain, Carry Falls Reservoir, Childwold, Cotton, Long Lake, Mount Matumba, Raquette Lake, Rainbow Falls, Stark, Tupper Lake.

Sacandaga Wild & Scenic River—West & East Branches

Large-scale U.S. Geological Survey Topographic Maps: *(West Branch)* Piseco Lake, Lake Pleasant; *(East Branch)* Lake Pleasant, Harrisburg, Thirteenth Lake.

St. Regis Wilderness Canoe Area

Large-scale U.S. Geological Survey Topographic Maps: Lake Ozonia, Meno, St. Regis, Saranac Lake.

Saranac Lakes Region

Large-scale U.S. Geological Survey Topographic Maps: (Upper Saranac Lake) St. Regis, Long Lake; (Lower Saranac Lake) Saranac Lake; (Saranac River) Saranac Lake, Lake Placid, Alder Brook, Redford, Moffitsville, Dannemora 7.5, Morrisonville, Plattsburgh 7.5.

Schroon Lake Region

Large-scale U.S. Geological Survey Topographic Maps: Chestertown, Schroon Lake, Paradox Lake.

Tupper Lake Region

Large-scale U.S. Geological Survey Topographic Maps: Tupper Lake, Long Lake.

The vast Adirondack Park and Forest Preserve embraces some 8,000 square miles of sprawling north country lakes, streams, ponds, wild brawling rivers, and high country trails, surrounded by extensive tracts of evergreen forests, bogs, rolling hills, and high peaks in northern New York State; it contains several nationally renowned fishing, hunting, backpacking, and wilderness canoe-camping areas. Indians once knew these coveted hunting grounds as "the Dark and Bloody Ground." They were the scene of repeated wars between the Iroquois and the Algonquin tribes of the north. Among the Algonquin tribes were the Montaignais Indians, who traveled a great distance to this land from the lower St. Lawrence. As the journey used up their supplies of fish and venison, they were forced to subsist on the buds of moosebushes and the bark of trees. The Mohawks scornfully labeled these unwelcome tribes the bark eaters; in Iroquois, that name was *Ad-i-ron-daks.*

The forest preserve lies, for the most part, within the boundaries of Adirondack Park, established in 1892 based on the explorations and surveys of Verplank Colvin (1847–1920). The park's 5,693,000 acres, or 8,895 square miles, make it larger than any other national or state park in the United States—larger in fact than Massachusetts. This magnificent north country paradise, first penetrated by the great French explorer Samuel de Champlain, and followed over the years by fur trappers, pioneers, lumbermen, miners, woodsmen, hordes of sportsmen, and such celebrated personalities as James Fenimore Cooper, Frederic Remington, Mark Twain, Nessmuk, and the members of the Philosopher's Camp—Louis Agassiz, James Russell Lowell, and Ralph Waldo Emerson—is protected for all time by New York State's "forever wild" statute of 1895.

The Adirondack Mountains form the southern tip of the ancient rock-bound plateau known as the Laurentian Upland or Canadian Shield. In the southeast lie the low hills and lakes of the Lake George resort country, the most highly developed region of the Adirondacks. The northeast contains the majestic High Peaks and the headwaters of the Hudson, the earliest settled villages, and the busy centers of Lake Placid and Saranac Lake. Low rolling hills, hundreds of ponds, beaver flows, meandering rivers, and beautiful lakes such as Cranberry Lake lie in the least traveled northwestern quarter. The network of lakes and waterways stretches deep into the southwestern portion of the region; here and there, low hills push up from the boggy land. The riches of this country lie within easy reach of the densely populated Northeast. The land would doubtless lie bereft of all natural beauty if not for the state-owned forest preserve encompassing half its 5 million acres.

The High Peaks of the Adirondacks lie roughly in the center of the region. Their height is obscured by their rounded, worn appearance, and the 1,500-foot plateau from which they rise. Of the mountains more than 100 rise more than 3,500 feet above sea level, and 46 more than 4,000 feet. Glaciers and erosion have scoured the peaks of much of their topsoil. Among the peaks, lakes are as common as valleys, and many of the mountains are interconnected above the 2,500-foot level.

More than a score of rivers lace the Adirondack country, among them the Hudson, Osgewatchie, Raquette, Grass, Black, and Saranac. The Hudson rises in the heights of Mount Marcy, in Lake Tear-of-the-Clouds. It begins as a small, clear-flowing stream before it opens into the course southward, a course that once bore the prize of the north country—its lumber. The Raquette River meanders along its course from Blue Mountain Lake through Long Lake and 170-odd miles to the St. Lawrence, though a straight line from its source to its junction with the St. Lawrence is only half this distance. The Moose River flows south from the Fulton Chain, connecting more than a hundred lakes and ponds. The Schroon, St. Regis, and the Osgewatchie attract trout fisherman in the spring. The smaller rivers of the region, among them the Cold, Chazy, Bog, Opalescent, Jordan, Cedar, and Chub, are the size of small mountain brooks over most of their lengths. Since the first large-scale lumbering of the region these rivers have shrunk in their water volume. Several of them supported log runs and boat travel during the 19th century, but most are virtually impassable by boat today.

The evergreen and mixed hardwood forests of the Adirondacks—once inhabited by herds of majestic elk, moose, timber wolves, fisher, marten, and the Indian "devil of the north," the wolverine—crown her mountain heights and border the shores of her rivers and lakes. The woods go on and on, surprisingly undaunted by the highways that have opened the area and the millions of visitors they have brought. The woods have changed since the first white explorers saw them. The once dominant great white pines and spruces have given way to hardwoods in many areas. Cherry, poplar, birch, and beech have reforested extensive stands decimated by lumbering or fire, and large areas are covered by scrub. Elsewhere maple and spruce have reseeded themselves. Ground pine, partridge and other berries, ferns and mosses form a luxuriant undergrowth, brightened by trilliums, lady's slippers, and other wildflowers in the spring.

The vast reaches of the forest preserve embrace several outstanding wilderness canoeing, camping, fishing, hunting, and high country backpacking areas. The major areas of the northern region include the De Bar Mountain Wild Forest, Raquette River Canoe Trail, Saranac Lakes country, and the St. Regis Wilderness Canoe Area. The De Bar Mountain Wild Forest is an outstanding hunting, fishing, and hiking tract in Franklin County. Backwoods trails and logging roads provide access to Meacham Lake, De Bar Mountain Wildlife Management Area, Deer River Flow, Mount Tom, Sable Mountains, Plumadore Pond, Elbow Range, and the Narrows Ragged Lake. Hays and Hatch brooks and the Osgood River offer excellent trout fishing, and the slopes of Sable, East, and De Bar mountains offer a challenge to the big-game hunter. The Salmon River, one of the state's top five trout streams, flows through the forest.

The 18,100-acre St. Regis Wilderness Canoe Area is in Franklin County in the northernmost hinterlands of the forest preserve. Often referred to as the Fish Creek area, the wilderness is noted for its clear spring-fed ponds, short carries, and tranquil beauty. The brook trout fishing is good in the St. Regis River, Turtle Pond, Long Pond, and Big Fish and St. Regis ponds. Other features of this area include Sylvan Falls, Allen Falls Reservoir, Azure Mountain, Stony Brook, and Lake Ozonia.

The sprawling St. Regis Watershed drains a vast, wild portion of the northern tip of the Adirondacks in the Saranac Lake-Paul Smiths region, liberally laced with lakes, wilderness trout ponds, and remote feeder brooks. Major forks include the East, West, and Middle branches of the St. Regis River, and the Deer River. This expanse in prime canoe country and a significant portion of the headwaters are contained in the St. Regis canoe area. Many of the ponds have been cleaned of undesirable fish and restocked with trout, and the wilderness paddler can add fresh squaretails to the many pleasures to be enjoyed on a canoe-camping trip through the silent forests of the canoe area. St. Regis Pond, the source of the West Branch, is a good producer of brookies, lake trout, and splake. The lower portions of the branches are stocked with brown and rainbow trout, as well as squaretails, and some big fish are taken out of the rocky, shaded pools. After the three branches join, the main river flows into the St. Lawrence through the St. Regis Indian Reservation, which nestles along the New York-Quebec border.

Scenic Saranac Lakes in southern Franklin County offer the outdoor enthusiast a vast network of streams, lakes, and ponds, including Follensby Clear Pond, Clear and Rainbow lakes, Osgood Pond, Two-bridge Brook, Wolf and Deer ponds, Oseetah Lake, Boot Bay Mountain, and a portion of the McKenzie Mountain Wilderness. The Saranac Lakes have fine canoeing and fishing for smallmouth bass, northern pike, landlocked salmon (in Upper Lake), and lake trout up to 30 pounds. The campgrounds at Fish Creek and Rollins ponds can serve as base camps for trips into the outlying wildlands.

Upper Saranac Lake, about 8 miles long by 1–3 miles wide, is connected to Round Lake (2 miles in diameter) by the Saranac River. The river flows from Round Lake on to Lower Saranac Lake and eventually empties into Lake Champlain at Plattsburgh. Lower Saranac is just slightly smaller than the upper lake of the chain. More than 50 islands rise from its waters. The lower lake is the scene of Martin's Hotel, once a famous center for camping, hunting, and fishing, John Brown, the

radical abolitionist who was hanged for his bid to erase slavery by starting a war against it, once managed a colony of freed slaves who settled in the Saranac Lakes region. He is buried here.

The Raquette River is among the most changeable of the Adirondack rivers, varying markedly in volume. The river rushes headlong through furious rapids and over plunging falls. It is navigable only by canoes and small boats that can be carried around these wild stretches. The river of this name rises at Raquette Lake in the midst of the park, but is connected by a continuous waterway to Eagle Lake, Utowana Lake, the Marion River, and Blue Mountain Lake. The Raquette flows northeast from Raquette Lake by way of Forked Lake and Long Lake and then swings northwest to Big Tupper Lake, where it changes direction again, this time to the north to the St. Lawrence. The river's course cuts through a mountainous plateau surrounded by lakes, swamps, and forest to Piercefield, where it begins a descent of some 1,500 feet to the St. Lawrence. This famous Adirondack canoe route flows through a wilderness of dense forests, rapids, falls, beaver meadows, cedar swamps, and flows. The major features shown on the maps of the river include Raquette Falls, Raquette Pond, Piercefield Flow, Sals Rapids, Mount Matumba, Burnt Island Rapids, Long and Halls rapids, Moody Falls, Moosehead Rapids, and Carry Falls Reservoir. Its seldom explored Jordan, Cold, and Bog River tributaries offer some of the most wild, unspoiled canoeing and fishing in the Adirondack north country.

In the low-lying lake-dotted west central plateau of the forest the outdoorsman will find several top-ranked fishing, hunting, and wilderness canoe-camping areas. Scenic, island-dotted Cranberry Lake, with 55 miles of shoreline, is the gateway to the vast 62,780-acre Five Ponds Wilderness on the south, and to the 16,920-acre Oswegatchie River Primitive Area on the northwest. The Oswegatchie River provides a wilderness canoe trail for 20 miles upstream from the lake. Beyond the network of trails and canoeing waters, unbroken forests stretch all the way south to the Beaver River country. The Five Ponds Wilderness is a low, rolling terrain broken by numerous ponds, swamps, and some of the few remaining virgin pine and spruce stands in the Northeast. The wilderness has for its northern boundary the Oswegatchie River and Cranberry Lake; eastern boundary, the lands near Grass Pond, Big Deer Pond, and Bog Lake; southern boundary, Beaver River Flow (Stillwater Reservoir); and western boundary, Hidden Lake, Brandy Pond, Bear Pond, Upper South Pond, and the Oswegatchie Primitive Area. Other features are "The Plains," Bog River Flow, Six-Mile Creek, Wolf Pond Outlet, Partlow Lake, Beaver River Lakes, Lila, Nehasane, Salmon, and Moshier ponds, and Raven Lakes. The wilderness has 5 lean-tos and over 60 miles of primitive trails.

At one time Cranberry Lake drew sportsmen from all over the East to fish for big squaretails in the lake and the river. Unfortunately, the introduction of yellow perch changed the balance of nature, and smallmouth bass are now the star attraction. Outlying ponds still offer some good brook trout fishing in unspoiled surroundings. The Oswegatchie and its tributaries produce trout fishing, and the Little River, which merges with the main stream about 15 miles below Cranberry Lake, is one of the state's better brown trout streams. For those who like to combine fishing with camping and canoeing, the East Branch of the Oswegatchie with its long reach of flat water offers great potential.

The Black River Wild Forest country, in the southwest corner of the preserve due west of the Adirondack Club lands (the club was originally the Philosopher's Camp, founded by Ralph Waldo Emerson and his coterie), is an outstanding hunting, fishing, and camping area. The forest is dominated by the Black River, which flows east to west through the heart of the area and includes Little Woodhull Creek,

South Lake, Black Creek Lake, Twin Lakes Stream, Mad Tom Brook, Pine Creek, and Hinckley and Forestport reservoirs. The headwaters of the Black flow from North Lake at the foot of Ice Cave Mountain, and this upper section yields good brook trout fishing. The river flows out of the park a short distance from North Wilmunt and spills into Kayuta Lake and Forestport Reservoir. Brown trout and rainbows replace the brookies as the Black leaves the Adirondacks behind.

The wild and scenic Moose River joins the Black at Lyons Falls and its drainage provides some of the best stream and wilderness pond fishing for brook trout in the Adirondacks, as well as fishing for trout, salmon, and splake. The South Branch begins in the shadow of steep Little Moose Mountain and flows through the heart of the wild Moose River Recreation Area. Wilderness brook trout fishing is available in the river and its numerous tributary streams and remote ponds. The Middle Branch drains the famous Fulton Chain before joining the South Branch above McKeever. This group of eight lakes, just north of the resort town of Old Forge on Route 28, all contain smallmouths; Second Fulton is the only one that does not hold trout. Rainbows are found in the other lakes, lakers in Third, Fourth, Seventh, and Eighth Fulton, and landlocked salmon and splake in Seventh. The North Branch flows out of Big Moose Lake, which holds lake trout and some brookies, and flows to the Middle Branch at Old Forge. This northerly fork contains excellent headwater squaretail fishing in magnificent surroundings.

The lakes, streams, swamps, beaver flows, and wild forests of the Moose River country surround the famous Fulton Chain canoe route, often referred to as the western gateway to the Adirondacks. The old Adirondack Canoe Trail starts at Old Forge, extends through the Fulton Chain and numerous lakes and interconnecting streams, and goes for nearly 100 miles to the northeast. The North Branch of the Moose River and its tributaries provide the greatest drainage of the region. The Independence River and Otter Creek flow into the Black River Valley, surrounded by the beaver meadows, and low rolling hills of the 26,600-acre Ha-De-Ron-Dah Wilderness. The Pigeon Lake Wilderness embraces 50,800 acres of brook trout ponds and vast expanses of swamplands adjacent to the Stillwater Reservoir. The famous John Brown Tract lies just southeast of the wilderness. The wetland of alder swamp, marsh, and beaver flows of the 14,600-acre Pepperbox Wilderness has for its southern boundary the Stillwater Reservoir and for its northern boundary the John Brown Tract. Major features of the region include the Big Otter Lake Trail, Moose River Mountain Trail, Big Moose Lake, Lost Creek Trail, Forked Lake, Marion River, Raquette Lake, Queer Lake Trail, and Brandreth, Utowana, Flatfish, Russian, Salmon, Windfall, Norridgewock, Snake, and Gull lakes. Campsites are located at Limekiln Lake, Browns Tract Pond, Nicks Lake, Golden Beach on Raquette Lake, Eighth Lake, and Alger Island.

Raquette Lake, although part of the Hudson system, lies a short distance to the northeast of Eighth Fulton Lake. Raquette is one of the largest lakes in the Adirondacks and produces excellent catches of lake trout, as well as rainbows, squaretails, whitefish, and smallmouth. The bass and trout seem to coexist in such a manner that both types of fish maintain strong, balanced populations. Beautiful, deep Blue Mountain Lake, connected to Raquette Lake by the Marion River and Utowana and Eagle lakes, lies nestled at the foot of its namesake, known to the Indians as the "hill of storms," in northern Hamilton County north of Indian Lake. About 25 islands rise from its 1,212 acres of water; the lake yields lake trout, smallmouth bass, and on occasion trophy rainbows and brook trout near the outlet of Minnow Pond.

Blue Mountain Lake is one of the most remote headwaters of the

Raquette River and is the gateway to a long chain of lakes and waterways stretching north for more than 80 miles. Scenic hiking trails, including a segment of the Northville-Placid Trail, Wilson Pond, Cascade Lake, Tirrell Pond, Owls Head, and Sargent Ponds trails, and old logging roads provide access to the Salmon River, Wolf Pond, Utowana Lake, Marion River, Eagle Lake, Lake Durant, Cedar River, South Pond, Long Lake, Fishing Brook Range, Wakely Mountain Primitive Area, Lake Kora, Eaton, Sagamore, and Forked lakes, and the Blue Mountain Wild Forest. The Blue Ridge Wilderness takes in 43,160 acres north and west of the Cedar River Flow, dominated by Blue Ridge—a height-of-land ranging from 2,700 to 3,497 feet. The Sargent Pond Wild Forest, east of Raquette Lake along the Raquette and Marion rivers, is a labyrinth of boreal swamp well known to canoeists, hunters, trappers, and fishermen.

Long Lake, to the north, was formed when the glaciers widened a stretch of the Raquette River. The town of Long Lake lies on both sides of the lake. The lake, which covers 3,929 acres, stretching over a length of about 14 miles, is an important link in the Fulton Chain; canoeists often take advantage of the many campgrounds and lean-tos along its shores. A short canoe journey from the north end of the lake up Cold River leads to a little-traveled area. Fishing on the lake is good for northern pike, particularly in the marshes near the middle portion of the lake. Smallmouth bass are taken from the lake's inlets and outlets, and an occasional trout, whitefish, walleye, or landlocked salmon is caught here.

West Canada Creek is born in the deep forests and domes of the south-central Adirondacks. The West Canada Lakes and West Canada, Baldface, and Spruce Lake Mountains give rise to this famous river, which vies with the Au Sable as the best trout water in New York State. The upstream section of the river splits into Main and South branches at Nobleboro, and both forks furnish good fishing for trophy brook trout in their inaccessible, primitive upper reaches. One section of the stream has been declared a wild river and can only be approached by foot, horse, or canoe. West Canada pours into the top of Hinckley Reservoir, which sits astride the Blue Line. From the impoundment of its mouth at Herkimer on the Mohawk River the creek provides exceptional angling for browns, rainbows, and a smattering of stocked brook trout. Even though Route 28 parallels the stream, lunker browns are taken every year, and the productivity of the water supports a resident population of big fish. East Canada Creek, a sister river, has good fishing, but in no way compares to the West Canada. Brook and brown trout are found in the stream but not in the same size or quantity. The East Canada joins the Mohawk near St. Johnsville and has some smallmouths in the lower end.

The scenic fishing, backpacking, and hunting area of the 160,320-acre West Canada Lakes Wilderness sprawls east and north to Indian Lake in Hamilton County. The topography varies from spruce and balsam swamp flats, beaver meadows, and rolling hills to steep mountains. The wilderness has for its northern boundary the Moose River Plains and private lands near Little Moose Lake, Squaw Brook, and Snowy Mountain; Route 30, International Paper Company lands, and the Spruce Lake-Piseco Trail form the southern boundary; West Canada Creek and private lands east of Honnedaga Lake form the western one. Old logging roads and trails lead to Cedar Lakes, West Canada Lakes, Indian River, Buell Brook Primitive Area, the renowned brook trout waters of the Jessup River Wild Forest, T Lake, Fort Noble Mountain and Pillsbury Lake primitive areas, the South Branch of the Moose River, and West Canada Mountain Primitive Area.

The Adirondack Forest Preserve section of the Hudson River drainage system includes some of the state's premier fishing and canoe-camping waters. The mighty Hudson stems from tiny rivulets in the secluded slopes and glens of the High Peaks. One feeder rises near the summit of soaring Mount Marcy at the outlet of Lake Tear-of-the-Clouds, the most alpine source of the great river. Another origin is the series of spring brooks feeding Lake Henderson, dominated by the imposing masses of Mount McIntyre, and the rugged Santanoni Range. The upper section of the Hudson provides wilderness brook trout fishing in both the Lake Henderson spur and the Opalescent River, which flows into it at Sanford Lake. The Opalescent receives Lake Tear-of-the-Clouds's outlet and begins a wild ride to the valley through a precipitous flume. This river derives its name from mineral-bearing rocks that catch the sun's rays and reflect brilliant bursts of color through the stream's clear waters. The Upper Hudson flows southeast from the High Peaks through the remote and spectacular "Little Grand Canyons" of the Hudson Gorge Primitive Area (lunker brown trout are occasionally caught along this stretch) to its confluence with the Boreas River, continuing south past Loon and Friends lakes, along the placid stretches to Corinth.

The majestic 219,570-acre High Peaks Wilderness ranges from small areas of low-lying swamplands along the Raquette and Saranac rivers to the highest point in New York, the summit of Mount Marcy, (5,344 feet), which was once known as Tahawus ("cloud splitter") to the Indians. Mount Marcy is surrounded by the other high peaks of the MacIntyre Range, which extends through the west central portion of Essex County. The Hudson-St. Lawrence River Divide passes over its summit. Lake Tear-of-the-Clouds lies at the base of Mount Marcy and is the highest lake source of the Hudson River. The Range Trail, which traverses a series of mountain summits above timberline from Mount Marcy and Mount Algonquin to the Keene Valley, has long been considered the most rugged and scenic trail in the state. More than 174 miles of trails, including a segment of the Northville-Placid Trail, provide access to the waterfalls and deep trout pools of the Opalescent River, Johns Brook Primitive Area, Flowed Lands, Cold Brook, Moose Creek, Hurricane Mountain Primitive Area, Dix Mountain Wilderness, Klondike Brook, Duck Hole, Cold River Wilderness Canoe Trail, Ampersand Primitive Area, and Sanford Lake. The trails to Mount Marcy from Adirondak Loj via Indian Falls or Lake Colden are perhaps the most heavily used trails in the Adirondacks. The wilderness contains 49 lean-tos. The region is a top-ranking deer and bear hunting area.

The densely forested 35,200-acre McKenzie Mountain Wilderness lies to the north of the High Peaks in western Essex County. The Saranac River forms its northern and western borders, and the West Branch of the Au Sable its eastern border. McKenzie Mountain dominates the area, which includes Lake Placid, Loch Bonnie, Moose Pond, Bartlett Pond, and Mounts Whiteface, Tamarac, Colburn, Lincoln Brook, and Esther. The Adirondack Mountain Club maintains a trail from Wolf Pond to the summit of Mount McKenzie. Beautiful Lake Placid, with its two major islands—Buck and Moose—and numerous coves, is one of the state's better producers of large lakers and rainbows.

Like many of the Adirondack lakes, Lake Placid is many-islanded; the islands stretch down the middle of the 5-mile-long lake (it is about 2 miles wide at its broadest point). Hills and mountains surround this lake, shielding it from the high winds and severe storms that whip over less protected areas. Many camps and resort hotels have sprung up along its irregular shores. This lake was once a major camping base for the Algonquins, who journeyed down from the lower St. Lawrence to hunt the Adirondacks. Later the Mohawks built stockaded bark houses near what are now Keene and Elizabethtown, and conquered their enemies from the north. About a thousand Mohawks live on the St. Regis Reservation, just north of the lake, today.

The rolling hills, lakes, evergreen forests, and wild rivers of the central Adirondacks lie to the southwest of the High Peaks, dominated by island-dotted Indian Lake, Cedar River Flow, Sacandaga Lake, Piseco Lake, and the West Branch of the Sacandaga, surrounded by some of the most remote and beautiful wild country in the forest preserve. The Siamese Ponds Wilderness embraces 107,740 acres of wild forests, rolling hills, beaver meadows, and bogs east of Indian Lake in Hamilton and Warren counties. More than 35 miles of trails and backcountry roads provide access to Thirteenth Lake, Puffer Pond, Siamese Ponds, Augur Falls on the East Branch of the Sacandaga River, John and Crotched ponds, Kings Flow, Big Range, Gore Mountain, Kunjamuk and Sacandaga rivers, Owl Pond, and County Line and Peaked Mountain brooks.

To the south are the outstanding hunting, fishing, camping, and canoeing areas of the vast Silver Lake Wilderness—a 106,650-acre area of low rolling hills, forests, conifer swamps, and beaver meadows in Hamilton County. The Northville-Placid Trail, which starts at the southern edge of the wilderness and winds north through the center of the area, and old tote roads provide access to Piseco Lake, the West Branch of the Sacandaga, Big Eddy, Black Cat Outlet, Oxbow Lake, Cathead Mountain, Clockmill and Kennels ponds, Lake Pleasant, Shaker Mountain Primitive Area, Hamilton and Sand lakes, the famed brook trout waters of Silver, Mud, and Rock lakes, and Ferris Lakes Wild Forest. One of the last of the old Adirondack dirt roads winds through the center of the forest for 17 miles from Route 10 near Piseco Lake to Stratford.

Piseco Lake was once an Indian camping ground; today state campgrounds lie along its shores. A high range juts up sharply 3,800 feet from its western shore; bald eagles can often be seen nesting in the rocky heights. The lake holds large lake trout (to 30 pounds), whitefish, smallmouth bass, perch, and a few pickerel along the major inlet at Fall Stream and the bay formed by Millhouse Dam. Piseco is about 6 miles long and 2 miles wide. Spy Lake, about one-eighth its size, lies directly across from it.

The famous lake-dotted fishing, hunting, and camping region surrounding Schroon Lake is due east of the central Adirondacks and west of Lake George. Schroon Lake is well known to anglers for its early season landlocked salmon and lake and rainbow trout. The 43,340-acre Pharaoh Lake Wilderness lies on the eastern side of Schroon Lake, and is made up of beautiful coniferous forests, marshes, and crystal-clear ponds surrounding Grizzle Ocean, Tub Mill Marsh, Glidden Marsh, Eagle, and Pharaoh lakes, Thunderbolt Mountain, Oxshoe Pond, and Desolate Brook. The Hoffman Notch Wilderness lies northwest of Schroon Lake and encompasses 35,200 acres of mountainous terrain dominated by Blue Ridge, Texas Ridge, Washburn Ridge, and Cheney Pond—a former flow used to drive logs down the Boreas River. Many hiking trails and old logging roads provide access to Peaked Hill, Pharaoh Mountain, Bald Ledge, and Crane Pond primitive areas, Otter and Goose ponds, Hammond Pond Wild Forest Area, Blue Ridge Range, and Lost, Spectacle, Gull, and Arnold ponds.

The country to the east and south is dominated by the beautiful island-dotted waters of deep Lake George, home of the state record 16-pound 14-ounce landlocked salmon, along with trophy rainbows, lake trout to 15 pounds, great northern pike, and smallmouth bass. More than 50 miles of trails provide access through the Lake George Wild Forest to the Tongue Mountain Range, Prospect Mountain, Black Mountain range, First Peak, Bumps Pond, Sleeping Beauty Mountain, and Fish Brook Pond. The summit of Black Mountain provides an awe-inspiring view of Lake Champlain, the Green Mountains of Vermont, Lake George, the Hudson Valley, and the Adirondack High Peaks. Hikers should keep an eye out for rattlesnakes.

Maps, Guides & Lodging

Several eminently useful map-guides of the Adirondack backpacking and canoeing areas are available free upon request from: Publications Distribution Unit, Dept. of Environmental Conservation, 50 Wolf Rd., Albany 12233. *Adirondack Canoe Routes* describes the famous 125-mile canoe route originally traveled by the Indians and trappers through the Fulton Chain, Raquette Lake, Long Lake, Tupper Lake, Saranac Lake, and Paul Smiths country; *Hiking Lesser-Known Adirondack Wilds* describes trails in the remote Pepperbox Wilderness, Tongue Mountain, Shaker Mountain Tract, and Soda Range areas; *Moose River Recreation Area* shows roads, trails, lean-tos, fire towers, and camping areas; *Trails in the Schroon Lake Region* shows and describes several primitive trails, including the Long Swing, Peaked Hill, Pharaoh Mountain Fire Tower, Berrymill Pond, and Pharaoh Lake trails; *Trails in the Lake George Region* shows and describes the Prospect Mountain, Tongue Mountain Range, and Black Mountain Fire Tower trails; *Trails in the Blue Mountain Lake Region* describes

the Northville-Placid, Cascade Lake, Sargent Ponds, and Tirrell Pond trails; *Trails in the Cranberry Lake Region* describes the Loop, Plains, Five Ponds-Wolf Pond-Sand Lake, Big Deer Pond, Buck Pond, and Cat Mountain trails; *Trails in the Old Forge-Big Moose Region* describes the Big Otter Lake, Moose River Mountain, Scenic Mountain, Cascade Lake-Queer Lake, and Windfall Lake trails as well as trails in the Beaver River flow region; *Trails to Marcy* describes the trails in the High Peaks country—including the northern approaches via the Van Hoevenberg, Avalanche Lake and Lake Colden, and Indian Pass trails, the trail to Scott and Wallface Ponds, the eastern approaches from Keene Valley via the John Brook, Hopkins, and Range trails, the southern approaches from Tahawus and Elk Lake, and western approaches from Tupper Lake. A detailed foldout *Map of the Mount Marcy Region* shows foot trails, roads, and lean-tos.

A free *Indian River Canoe Route Map* is available from: Indian River Lakes Chamber of Commerce, Theresa 13691. The map is on a scale of 1 inch to 1 mile, and shows put-in points, historic sites, towns, and riverside recreation areas.

The Adirondack Mountain Club publishes two useful canoeing guides to the Adirondacks. *Adirondack Canoe Waters—North Flow* (299 pp.), by Paul F. Jamieson, outlines canoe travel on the waterways of the Adirondack wilderness, describing excursions down the West, Middle, and East branches of the Oswegatchie River, Little River, Middle, North, and South branches of the Grass River, the Raquette River, Cold River, Bog River, Jordan River, West, Middle, and East branches of the St. Regis River, Osgood River, Deer River, Salmon River, and the Chateaugay River in the northwest watershed of the Adirondack area, and the Great Chazy, Saranac (North Branch), West, East, and Main Branches of the Au Sable River, the Bouquet River, and Lakes Champlain and George. The book relates the courses of each of these streams, describing rapids, falls, dams, obstructions, natural features, and flora and fauna of the rivers and their lands. The book is embellished with historical notes on the people who have inhabited the river country. It includes a chapter on canoe camping by Robert Bliss. The book costs $5.50 (when ordering by mail, be sure to include 50¢ per book for postage and handling). It is available from: Adirondack Mountain Club, 172 Ridge St., Glens Falls 12801.

The canoe waters of the south central Adirondacks are described in Barbara McMartin Patterson's 171-page *Walks and Waterways* ($4.75 plus 50¢ for postage and handling; same source). The portion of the Adirondack region covered by this book is the least known; it includes some of the wildest country in the state. Canoe routes de-

scribed include trips on the Big Bay, Piseco, Clockmill Pond, Fall Stream, Good Luck Lake, Kunjamuk Stream, North Flow of the East Canada, Piseco Outlet, Stewart's Landing, the West Branch of the Sacandaga (East), and the West Branch of the Sacandaga (North). Nearly 100 canoe routes, walks, and bushwhacks in the East Canada Creek and West Branch of the Sacandaga River regions are described; their natural features, wildlife, and plant life are noted. The book includes 5 simple maps, and should be used in conjunction with U.S. Geological Survey Topographical Maps.

The most important single source of information on trails of the High Peaks region is probably the *Guide to Adirondack Trails*, published by: Adirondack Mountain Club (address above, $6). It covers trails in the Keene Valley, St. Huberts, Upper Au Sable Lake, Elk Lake, Sanford Lake, Heart Lake, Cascade-Keene-Hurricane, Bouquet Valley, Lake Placid, and Saranac Lake regions, the outlying mountains of the High Peaks, and the trailless peaks. The book gives distances between points on the trails and identifies natural features, shelters, and camping areas along the way. Its introductory section describes the region, and includes information on preparation and essential camping skills. A topographical map shows trails of the High Peaks region on a scale of about 1 inch to the mile. The map shows water features, roads (heavy duty, medium duty, unimproved dirt, light duty), highways, horse trails, AMC lodges, other lodges, ranger stations, and public lean-tos.

The book also covers the Northville-Placid Trail, which leads north from the Adirondack foothills and the High Peaks through the heart of the Adirondack wilderness lowlands. It passes through about 133 miles of forest, shot through with myriad lakes and ponds and laced by streams which offer excellent trout fishing in the spring, and bass, pickerel, and pike fishing in the summer and fall. The Dept. of Environmental Conservation (address above) publishes a free leaflet on *The Northville-Placid Trail*. It describes the six major sections of the trails, features along these routes, and mileage between points.

Timberlock, Sabael 12864, phone (518) 648-5494, offers guided backpacking trips in the high peaks and Moose River wild country and guided canoe trips along the beautiful Fulton Chain Lakes.

For a complete listing of Adirondack fishing and hunting guides write for the *Register of Guides*, available free from: Bureau of Forest Recreation, DEC, 50 Wolf Rd., Albany 12233.

Several classic historical books on the forest preserve of interest to outdoorsmen are available from: Adirondack Life Books, Willsboro 12996; write for their free *Adirondack/Log Book Catalog*.

For detailed listings and descriptions of the hundreds of vacation lodges, resorts, and campgrounds in the Adirondacks, write: *Adirondack Park Association*, Adirondack 12808. Rustic lodgings on the famous West Branch of the Au Sable River are provided by *Whiteface Lodge*, known as the Adirondack fly fishing headquarters, Route 86, Wilmington 12997 (518-946-2392). Wilderness fishing, hunting, and canoeing fly-in service and sightseeing tours are provided by *Bird's Seaplane Service*, 6th Lake, Inlet 13360 (315-357-3631) and *Helms Aero Service*, Long Lake 12847 (518-624-3931). For additional fishing and hunting information, stream and lake conditions, hatches, and where-to-go advise, write or call the *Adirondack Sport Shop*, Wilmington 12997 (518-946-2605).

Several long-established Adirondack resorts and lodges provide four-season accommodations and services. *Bark Eater Lodge*, Alstead Mill Rd., Keene 12942, (518-576-2221), is in the Lake Placid area and is a jumping-off point for backpacking trips along the Northville-Placid Trail and High Peaks Wilderness. The famous *Adirondack Loj*, P.O. Box 867, Lake Placid 12946, (518-523-3441), is located eight miles

from Lake Placid on Heart Lake in the High Peaks Wilderness. The lodge has a New Camper's Building which offers food supplies, orientation publications, laundry facilities, and hot showers as well as a campground and inn with bunkrooms and dining facilities, and hot showers as well as a campground and inn with bunkrooms and dining facilities. The *John Brooks Lodge* (same address as the Adirondack Loj), is located in the High Peaks Wilderness and is accessible only by trail. Other lodges in the High Peaks Wilderness area include *Paleface Lodge*, P.O. Box 163, Jay 12941, (518–946–2272) and *Whiteface Chalet*, Wilmington 12997, (518–946–2207). The historic *Lake Placid Club*, Lake Placid 12946, (518–523–3361), long an exclusive private resort on the shores of Lake Placid, is now open to the public and offers some of the most beautiful, rustic vacation lodgings in the nation. Also on Lake Placid are *Placid Manor* (Box 879; 518–523–2573), and *The Homestead* (518–523–3359) and *Mirror Lake Inn* (518–523–2544), both on Mirror Lake. On the famed Au Sable River are the *Hungry Trout* (518–946–2217), *High Valley* (518–946–2355), and the nearby *Ledge Rock* (518–946–2302) and *Wilderness Inn* (518–946–2391), all Wilmington 12997. Saranac Lake to the west of Lake Placid is served by *Burke's Lake Flower* (518–891–2310) and *Cal Howard's Evergreen Camps* (518–891–9895), both Saranac Lake 12983. On Upper Saranac Lake is the *Wabeek Inn*, Tupper Lake 12986, (518–359–3800). Overlooking Tupper Lake is the *Timber Lodge*, Tupper Lake 12986, (518–359–3381). In the Central Adirondacks on the famous Fulton Chain of Lakes are *Alpine Lodges* (6th Lake; 315–357–2934), *The Crosswinds* (4th Lake; 315–357–4500), *Willis Lodges* (7th Lake; 315–357–3904)–all Inlet 13360; *Bear Paw Lodge* (315–735–6339; 1st Lake), *Big Rock Lodge* (4th Lake; 315–369–3713), *Burke's Waterfront Cottages* (rustic alpine and A-frame cottages on 1st Lake; 315–369–3337), *Crane's Camps* (Upper Joy Tract; 315–369–3010), *Four Season Lodge* (4th Lake; 315–369–6779), *The Homestead* (1st Lake; 315–369–6534), *Mingo Village* (4th Lake; 315–357–3143), *Mohawk Inn* (4th Lake; 315–357–2491), *Risley's Rush Point* (summers: Raquette Lake 13436), *Tee-O-Wana Lodge & Cottages* (4th Lake; 315–369–6546)–all Old Forge 13420; *Covewood Lodge* (Big Moose Lake; 315–357–9744), *Eagle Bay Villas* (4th Lake; 315–357–2411), *McKee's Evergreen Lodge* (4th Lake; 315–357–4383), *Torokan* (4th Lake)–all Eagle Bay 13331. Lodging on the Moose River is provided by *Hart's Whispering Falls Cottages*, P.O. Box 427, Old Forge 13420. *Geandreau's at Indian Lake*, Box 408, Indian Lake 12842, (518–648–5500), has modern cabins and access to the Abanakee Logs Trail system. Beautiful Blue Mountain Lake is served by *The Hedges* (one of the remaining old Adirondack estates; 518–352–7325), *Potter's* (518–352–7331), and the secluded *Hemlock Hall Lodge* (518–353–7706) –all Blue Mountain Lake 12812. On Long Lake 12847 are *Long View Lodge* (518–624–2862), *Camp Hilary Cottages* (518–624–2233), and *Sunset Point Lodge* (518–624–3781). Two remote wilderness lodges, the Log House Lodge and Big Shanty Lodge are nestled on the shore of 13th Lake; write: Garnet Hill Lodges, North River 12856, (518–998–2821). Schroon Lake 12870 is served by *Woods Lodge*, (518–532–7529). Lodges and resorts on Lake George include *Alpine Village* (Box 672; 518–668–2193), *Roaring Brook* (518–668–5767)–both Lake George 12845; *Trout House Village*, Box 42, Hague 12836, (518–543–2211); *Canoe Island Lodge*, Diamond Point 12824, (518–668–5191); *Twin Bay Village, Inc.* (518–644–9777) and the *Sagamore* (518–644–3121) a famous Adirondack resort on Green Island–both Bolton Landing 12814, and *Silver Bay Lodge*, Silver Bay 12874, (518–543–9976).

Access & Outfitting Centers

The Adirondack Park and Forest Preserve is reached via the scenic Adirondack Northway (Interstate 87), Interstate 90 and 81, and connecting New York 30, 10, 8, 28, 12, 3, 56, 73, and 86. Overnight

accommodations, guides, supplies, and equipment rentals are available at almost all Adirondack tours and resort villages, such as Lake George, Lake Luzerne, Indian Lake, North River, Warrensburg (known as the "queen village of the Adirondacks"), Schroon Lake, Lake Placid, Saranac Lake, Tupper Lake, Cranberry Lake, Raquette Lake, Piseco, Blue Mountain Lake, Old Forge, Big Moose, and Nehasane. A useful guide to accommodations and attractions, *Adirondack & Northway Travel Guide*, is available for $1.95 (postpaid) from: Adirondack & Northway Travel Guide, 314 Union St., Schenectady 12305. A useful *Adirondack Park Tour Auto Guide* is available free from: Publications Distribution Unit, DEC (address above).

Catskill Park & Forest Preserve

Catskill Park & Forest Preserve Topo Maps

U.S. Geological Survey Overview Maps (scale 1:250,000): Albany, Binghamton, Hartford, Scranton.

Ashokan Reservoir & Esopus Creek

Large-scale U.S. Geological Survey Maps: (*Ashokan Reservoir*) Ashokan, Kingston W, Bearsville W, Shokan; (*Esopus Creek*) Phoenicia, Shandaken.

Beaverkill River Historic Trout Waters

Large-scale U.S. Geological Survey Maps: Arena, Fishs Eddy, Horton, Lewbeach, Livingston Manor, Roscoe, Seager.

Delaware River Canoe Route

Large-scale U.S. Geological Survey Maps: Callicoon, Damascus (PA), Eldred, Hancock, Lake Como (PA), Long Eddy, Narrowsburg, Pond Eddy, Port Jervis N, Port Jervis S, Shohola (PA).

Neversink River & Headwaters

Large-scale U.S. Geological Survey Maps: Claryville, Peekamoose Mountain, Shandaken, West Shokan, Hartwood, Yankee Lake, Woodridge, Grahamsville, Liberty E, Willowemoc.

Pepacton Reservoir & East Branch of the Delaware

Large-scale U.S. Geological Survey Maps: (*Pepacton*) Downsville, Lewbeach, Arena, Margaretville; (*Upper East Branch Delaware*) Margaretville, Fleischmanns, Roxbury; (*Lower East Branch Delaware*) Downsville, Corbett, Readburn, Fishs Eddy, Hancock.

The Indians knew the beautiful rolling hills, swift flowing streams, and forests of the Catskills as *Onteora*, ("land in the sky," the dwelling place of the Great Spirit). They held Onteora sacred, and left its wilderness virtually untouched. By the 17th century Dutch settlers inhabited the eastern foothills. Eventually lumber companies entered the forest and blazed trails through its interior. The great hemlock stands of the forest had vanished by 1870 to supply the tanbark industry, but the dense mixed hardwoods remain today, painting the mountains and countryside brilliant red, orange, and crimson in the fall. A network of trails leads to most of the region's major peaks; highways serve the forest area, providing easy access.

Today the heart of the region is encompassed within the boundaries of the famous 250,000-acre Catskill Forest Preserve, which itself lies within the 650,000-acre Catskill State Park and contains several of the finest fishing, hunting, camping, and backpacking areas in the eastern United States. Its scenic mixed hardwood and conifer forests and thick undergrowths of huckleberry, alder, rhododendrons, mountain laurel, and wintergreen provide cover for whitetail deer, black bear, ruffed

grouse, a few wild turkey, and red fox. The ancient, glacially scoured mountains and forests are slashed by several of the nation's most historic trout streams which gave birth to American fly fishing: the famous Beaverkill, Neversink, Esopus, Willowemoc, and Schoharie, rising from springs in the hinterlands of the Catskill high country.

By the 1880s extensive lumbering and farm clearance had changed the watersheds, causing a substantial rise in median temperature. Coupled with better transportation and increased fishing pressure, warmer water spelled the end of the Catskills as prime brook trout waters. Toward the end of the decade brown trout were introduced from Europe to replace the diminishing population of native squaretails. Not only were the immigrants hardier, but they were far more wary than the naive brookies, and fishermen soon learned that the newcomers would not take such standard flies as the gaudy Parmachene Belles, Silver Doctors, and Scarlet Ibises which were so attractive to the natives. Encouraged by the British masters of the art, pioneer fly fishermen such as Theodore Gordon, Edward R. Hewitt, and George M. L. LaBranche developed techniques and patterns, including the then revolutionary dry fly, which were better suited to the selective, hatch-feeding habits of the brown trout. Bait fishermen, too, learned the delicate methods of presenting a wide range of naturals in a realistic manner. Generations of dedicated anglers have come to know and appreciate the deep, hemlock-shaded pools of these great trout streams, which at times will humble the most experienced fisherman, or conversely, amaze him with a sudden frenzy of feeding activity.

The Upper Delaware River at the western boundary of the Catskills forms the state's western border with Pennsylvania and New Jersey and offers top-ranked canoe camping and fishing for trout, smallmouth, bass, walleye, pickerel, shad, and panfish along the numerous riffles, pools, and eddies. Some of the best rainbow trout fishing in the East is found in this lengthy segment of river by those who know where and when to fish. The prime trout stretches produce rainbows, which average 15 inches, and fish to 24 inches are taken regularly. Fishing hot spots along the Upper Delaware are located at the Maples, Frisbie Island, Equimunk Eddy, Lordville Rift, Lacey's Bend Eddy, Baskett Riffle, Killams Bridge, Whitehouse Curve, and Plum Island areas. A small silver-bodied Adams is an effective dry fly, and when conditions are right the action is fast and furious. Shad are found in the main river and both branches and attract a great many fishermen in May, who take the big, silvery scrappers on beaded shad flies, shad darts, spinners, and small wobblers. The average fish weighs about 4 pounds, but a large number of fish reach 7 pounds. Walleye and bass occupy most stretches of the Delaware and furnish exciting angling. Live bait, such as small lampreys, spinner and worm combinations, hellgrammites, and live minnows are effective on both species, as well as standard spoons, jigs, and plugs. Fly fishermen score well with streamers, the deadly Muddler Minnow, and bass bugs, in quieter stretches.

The following maps and guides of the Upper Delaware are available from: Upper Delaware Publications, Rte. 97, Barryville 12719 (all prices postpaid). The *Upper Delaware River Recreation Map Set* ($2.60) is published in two sections; both show fishing access, boat rentals, boat-launching sites, fishing hot spots, springs, rapids, eel weirs, rock shelters, eddies, rifts, and streamflow characteristics. Section One ($1.50, 13 × 31 inches) shows the remote, wild section of the river from Hancock to Cochecton; Section Two ($1.50, 12 × 37 inches), the famous white-water and fishing areas of the river from Cochecton to Port Jervis. *Whitewater Boating on the Upper Delaware River* ($1.75) is the standard guide to canoeing, camping, and kayaking on the river (order from address above).

Canoe outfitting and guide service along the Upper Delaware is provided by: *Jerry's Canoe Rentals*, Rte. 97, Pond Eddy 12770; *Ten Mile River Lodge*, RD2, Narrowsburg 12764; and *Saddles & Paddles*, Box 188, Callicoon 12723.

Some of the East's top rainbow and brown trout fishing is found in the sprawling Pepacton and Ashokan reservoirs, in the heart of the forest preserve. Pepacton Reservoir impounds the once famous trout waters of the East Branch of the Delaware and is nationally renowned for its spectacular brown trout fishing. Giant, deep-bodied browns roam the depths of the reservoir; fish in excess of 15 pounds are frequently taken. Trolling, still fishing, or drifting with live bait produces a lot of big, buckskin-flanked browns in the 3-to-6-pound class. Pepacton also yields smallmouth bass, pickerel, and panfish. To the east, the Ashokan Reservoir contains a large population of big rainbows and browns as well as walleye, smallmouth bass, and pickerel. The spring rainbow run from Ashokan up the Esopus draws crowds of anglers, who take large numbers of the big lake-run trout.

Some of the finest fishing and wilderness camping opportunities in the forest preserve are found off the major trails by traveling cross-country with topo map and compass to the remote high country lakes, ponds, and streams in the central Catskill Mountains. Among the more challenging trails through the forest is the Devil's Path (Indian Head-Hunter Mountain Range Trail), which traverses the Catskill highlands from Platte Cove on the east over Indian Head, Twin, Sugarloaf, Plateau, and Hunter mountains to Spruceton Valley on the west.

Other trails through the Catskills (more than 200 miles of them) include the Wittenberg-Cornell-Slide Trail, John Burroughs's inspiration place; the Phoenicia-East Branch Trail; the Pine Hill-Eagle Mountain-West Branch Trail, with its many mountain byways; Seager-Big Indian Mountain Trail; the Delaware Trails, a network of trails through forest preserve lands south of the Pepacton Reservoir in Delaware County; the Mink Hollow Trail from Lake Hill north to the Platte Cove Highway; the Diamond Notch Trail from Lanesville to Spruceton; and the Escarpment Trail from Kaaterskill Creek on Route 23A north to East Windham on Route 23. All of these trails and others are described and mapped in detail in *Catskill Trails*, available free from: Information Office, Department of Environmental Conservation, 40 Wolf Rd., Albany 12201. The booklet gives the general location of each trail, then defines its course in greater detail, including mileage information. The trails are shown on a map, along with water features, public campsites, forest fire towers, and villages, on a scale of 1 inch to 1 mile. The booklet also includes a special map of the Delaware Trails on a scale of 1 inch to 2 miles, and small maps of the Escarpment Trail. In *Hiking Areas of New York State*, available from the same source, A. T. Shorey gives an overview of trail and cross-country travel in the Catskills, along with some backcountry history.

White Water Boating on the Upper Delaware River

A Guide to Canoeing, Kayaking and Camping.

Includes detailed map of the river's physical characteristics and available access areas.

By Aaron I. Robinson

Developed campgrounds and primitive campsites are scattered throughout the forest preserve. Thirty-three lean-tos or open camps lie along the trails. The Department of Environmental Conservation maintains 6 public campgrounds in the forest. The lands are open to winter use and offer many miles of trails for ski touring and snowshoeing. The Belleayre Mountain Ski Center is located near Pine Hill.

The DEC also publishes a free leaflet, *Catskill Forest Preserve*, which describes the tract, and includes information on the area's geology, history, wildlife, plant life, and recreational opportunities.

Several useful full-color maps of the Catskill country are published by: Outdoor Publications, Box 355, Ithaca 14850 (add 50¢ on all orders less than $6). *Sportsman's Map of the Catskill Mountains* ($1.50, 23 × 35 inches) locates some 250,000 acres of public land in Delaware, Sullivan, Ulster, and Greene counties and shows more than 300 miles of hiking and access trails, campsites, lean-to shelters, ski centers,

lookout towers, and 800 miles of trout streams, with stretches open to public fishing and state-stocked areas; *Sportsman's Map of Ulster County* ($1.50, 27 × 30 inches) shows all man-made and natural features in this heart of the Catskills; *Sportsman's Map of Delaware County* ($1.50, 27 × 27 inches) shows all major features, as do the *Sportsman's Map of Sullivan County* ($1, 28 × 30 inches), *Sportsman's Map of Greene County* ($1, 18 × 27 inches), and *Sportsman's Map of the Central Catskill Mountains* ($1, 18 × 30 inches). Outdoor Publications also publishes *Enjoying the Catskills* ($4.95), by Arthur C. Mack, which contains a wealth of useful information about access, geology, famous views, forest and wildlife, legends and history, wilderness areas, where to hike, major and outlying trails, camping, hunting and fishing, canoeable waters, and ski touring. (For listings of other Catskill maps and guides, see "Fishing & Hunting" in the "Encyclopedia" section.)

For additional fishing information, stream conditions, hatches, and where-to-go advice, write or call the *Beaverkill Sportsman*, Roscoe 12776 (607–498–4677).

Access & Outfitting Centers

The Catskill Park and Forest Preserve are reached via New York 44, 209, 28, and 23 off the New York State Thruway (Interstate 87) and spur roads off New York 17. The Catskill region contains literally hundreds of towns and rural hamlets which offer overnight accommodations, supplies, and equipment rentals.

NORTHERN APPALA-CHIAN STATES

Introduction

The Northern Appalachian States contain some of the wildest and most beautiful country east of the Rocky Mountains: sprawling glacial lakes dotting the lowlands as well as the high; mountains reaching above 5,000 feet, some still pathless; thousands of miles of wild and scenic rivers, strewn with giant boulders, rapids, chutes, and silent, deep-flowing pools; a rugged, wave-pounded coastline with many bays, islets, islands, and sand dunes broken by rocky headlands; and wide expanses of unbroken forests of northern hardwoods and conifers with colorful undergrowths which include hobblebush, holly, meadow sweet, alder, mountain ash, blueberry, starflower, heath shrubs, swamp candles, Indian cucumber root, painted trillium, skunk currant, shadbush, dogberry, and honeysuckle. The Northern Appalachians are an ancient range, bearing the marks of aeons of erosion. The great sheets of the Ice Age sculpted the rounded summits of the Green Mountains of Vermont that scoured the rugged White Mountains that sweep through New Hampshire and Maine. The famed Appalachian Trail and thousands of miles of spur trails and old logging roads climb along the summits and through the forests and valleys of the ancient chain, providing access to seldom explored fishing, hunting, and wilderness camping areas.

Although heavily populated and industrialized, the southern New England states—Connecticut, Massachusetts, and Rhode Island—offer some excellent camping, fishing, hunting, and backpacking opportunities in their extensive state forest reserves and wildlife management areas, as well as some of the nation's finest saltwater fishing along the rocky, deeply indented Atlantic coast and freshwater fishing in the hundreds of lakes, ponds, and swift-flowing freestone streams. Massachusetts's sprawling, island-dotted Quabbin Reservoir, surrounded by beautiful hardwood and evergreen forests, is one of the East's hot spots for trophy-sized landlocked salmon, brown trout, lake trout, northern pike, and walleye.

To the north, Vermont, the beautiful Green Mountain State, with its quaint New England villages and covered bridges, contains several outstanding outdoor recreation meccas, including huge, 110-mile-long Lake Champlain, with its islands, bays, coves, and fjordlike shores; the scenic forests, rolling hills, and trout streams of the Green Mountain National Forest, traversed by the famous 166-mile Long Trail, which climbs along the peaks and valleys of the range in a north-south course from the Vermont-Massachusetts border to the Canadian boundary; the nationally renowned fly fishing waters of the Battenkill River and the headwaters of Otter Creek; and the famous game lands and trophy fishing lakes of the Northeast Kingdom, dominated by the sprawling, island-dotted waters of Lake Memphremagog.

New Hampshire encompasses the beautiful White Mountain National Forest, dominated by the spectacular Presidential Range, with its towering peaks reaching up 6,000 feet, and arctic-like tundra above timberline. Old logging roads, abandoned railroad beds, and hundreds of miles of hiking trails provide access to the remote lakes, ponds, streams, and mountain bogs of the Pemigewasset Wilderness, Wild River area, Sandwich Range, Great Gulf Wilderness, Carter-Moriah Range, Franconia Notch, Carr Mountain Wilderness, and the Pilot and Pliny ranges in the Kilkenny Wilderness area. South of the White Mountains lies the famous Lakes Region, dominated by a cluster of the state's finest landlocked salmon, trout, and smallmouth bass lakes: Winnipesaukee, Squam, Ossipee, and Winnisquam. The remote, lightly traveled North Country Region of the Granite State is a vast wilderness of great evergreen and northern hardwood forests and rolling hills, broken by turbulent rivers and the sprawling blue headwater lakes of the Connecticut River.

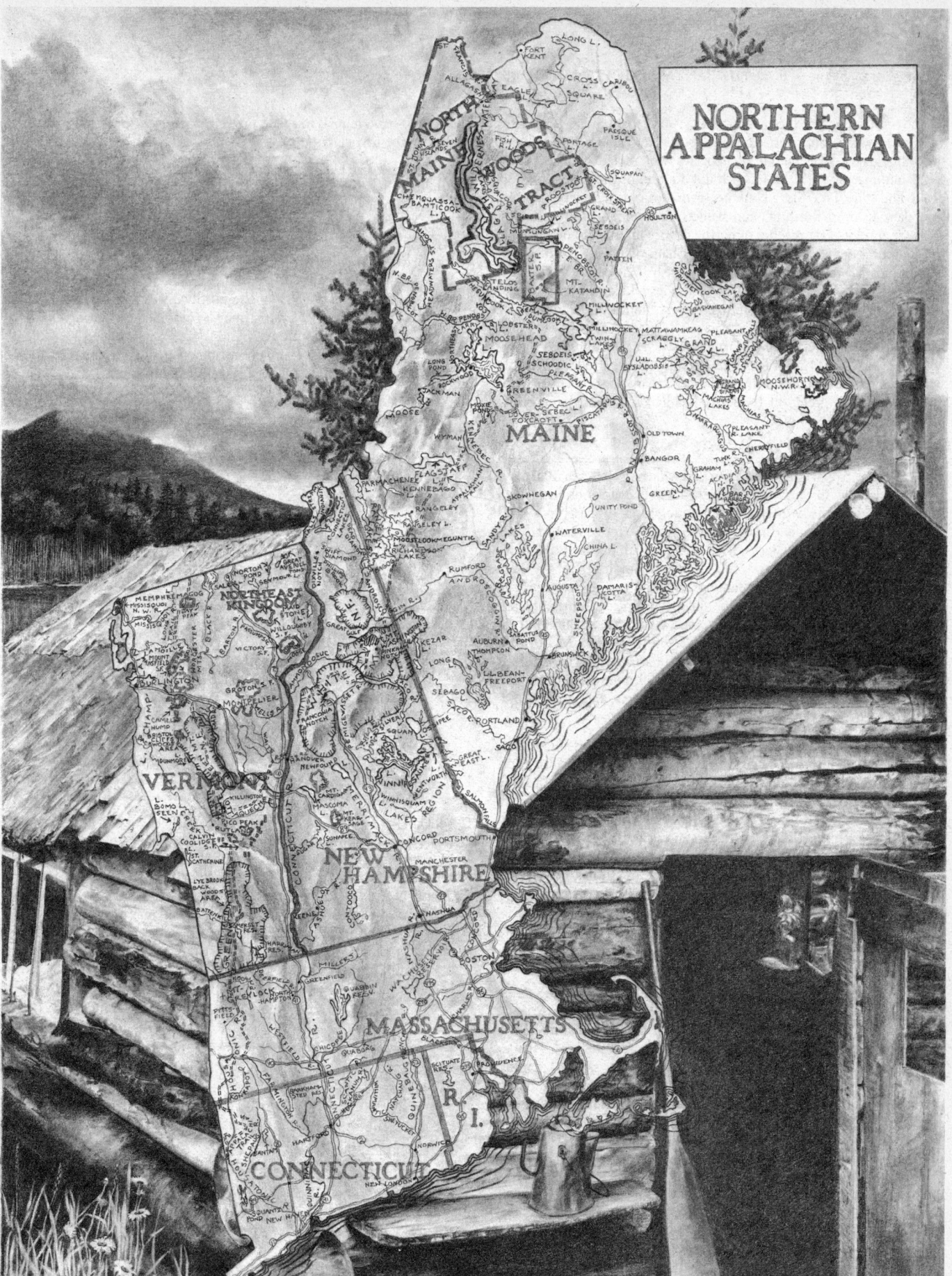

NORTHERN
APPALACHIAN
STATES

Maine—the largest of the six Northern Appalachian States—features a long rocky coastline, vast expanses of northern forests, wild rivers, sprawling glacial lakes, and wave upon wave of ancient rounded summits, culminating at 5,268-foot Mount Katahdin, the state's highest peak. The Pine Tree State contains several of North America's most legendary fishing, hunting, and wilderness camping and canoeing areas set amid its vast reaches of north country forests and mountains; the Chiputneticook Lakes, Fish River Chain of Lakes, Grand Lake Chain, North Maine Woods Tract, Allagash Wilderness Waterway, Mahoosuc Range, Machias River, Moosehead Lake, Mount Desert Island, Rangeley Lakes, St. John River, West Branch of the Penobscot River, Baxter State Park, Sebago Lake, Belgrade Lakes, Piscataquis Mountains, Kennebec River, Magalloway River, and the Red River, Musquacook, and Munsungan lakes country. Some 1,200 incredibly scenic conifer-clad islands, some little more than giant rocks, form an intricate maze of green off the rocky headlands of the Maine coast.

Weather, Bugs & Beasts

The Northern Appalachians encompass a wide range of climates corresponding largely to variations in elevation. The uplands have cool summers and severe winters, with temperatures dipping to −30°. Heavy precipitation falls throughout the year, with deep snows blanketing the area in winter. Coastal summers are famous for warm days and cool nights, although fogs, thunderstorms, and overcast days are not uncommon. During the summer the timberline areas of the White Mountains are notorious for violent electrical storms and sudden snow flurries. A useful full-color *Cloud Chart* may be obtained for 50¢ from: Appalachian Mountain Club, 5 Joy St., Boston, MA 02108. This handy chart will assist in forecasting the weather—which travels from west to east around the earth, about 600 miles each 24 hours, including warm fronts, cold fronts, thundershowers, and violent cold-front thunderstorms.

Potential wildlife hazards in the Northern Appalachians include an occasional camp-invading black bear in the deep North Country forests and a possible timber rattlesnake and copperhead. In the Maine North Woods the wilderness traveler should be alert for enraged bull moose during the fall rut. Mosquitoes, blackflies, no-see-ums, and an assortment of deerflies and moose flies can easily spoil your trip during the summer if you travel unprepared. Be sure to pack a good supply of insect repellent such as Cutters, Muskol, Mosquitone, or Off! (all of which contain a 50%-plus concentration of DEET, the most effective known chemical repellent).

Northern Appalachian Maps & Charts—How to Order

The topographic map kits listed throughout the Northern Appalachian States chapters will provide you with a full-color picture of the area you plan to visit: the mountain ranges, remote lakes, feeder streams, rivers, campsites, bogs, springs, wilderness shelters, rapids, falls, and chutes, as well as the gradient of the land and the boundaries of national forests and parks, wilderness areas, wildlife refuges and game management areas, and forest reserve tracts. All maps listed (unless otherwise noted) are U.S. Geological Survey Overview Maps with a scale of 1:250,000, or 1 inch to 4 miles ($2 each) or large-scale 7-½-minute and 15-minute maps ($1.25 each). These maps and free *Topographic Map Indexes* of the Northern Appalachian States may be ordered (along with a free *Map Symbol Chart* and *Topographic Maps* booklet) from: Eastern Distribution Branch, U.S. Geological Survey, 1200 S. Eads St., Arlington, VA 22202. Be sure to order your maps by their individual names (and indicate scale when ordering 1:

250,000-scale maps); to speed up delivery of your order, include extra money for first-class postage.

Useful large-size U.S. Geological Survey *State Topographic Maps* published with a scale of 1:500,000, or 1 inch to 8 miles, are available for all the Northern Appalachian States and may be ordered for $2 each from the above address. Beautiful U.S. Geological Survey *Shaded Relief Maps*, which are suitable for framing, are available at $2 each for all the Northern Appalachian States. Multicolor shading gives these maps a three-dimensional appearance as though the sunlight were striking the surface from the northwest. A free catalog, *Atlantic & Gulf Coasts Nautical Charts*, may be obtained by writing: National Ocean Survey, Distribution Division (C44), Riverdale, MD 20840. This catalog contains a complete listing of small-craft and recreational craft charts and Atlantic Coast nautical publications.

Full-color *Plastic Raised Relief Maps* of all 1:250,000-scale overview maps listed throughout the Northern Appalachian region may be ordered for $11.95 each from: Hubbard Scientific Co., 1946 Raymond Dr., Northbrook, IL 60062 (a free catalog is available upon request). These useful, attractive maps provide an actual three-dimensional model of the earth's surface and show all man-made and natural features. A useful 214-page handbook for wilderness travel, *Be Expert with Map & Compass*, by Bjorn Kjellstrom, the president and founder of Silva Compasses, may be obtained for $6.95 from: Charles Scribner's Sons, Bookstore Dept., 597 5th Ave., New York, NY 10017.

Accommodations

The State of Connecticut offers the traveler a wide variety of accommodations, ranging from resorts, hotels, motels, and guesthouses to camping areas of all kinds. For complete information on accommodations, write to the local Chamber of Commerce of the area you plan to visit or write to: Travel Director: Dept. of Commerce, 210 Washington St., Hartford 06106.

Appalachian National Scenic Trail

The Connecticut segment of this scenic highland trail enters the state at the Massachusetts border and winds for 55 miles through the Housatonic and Mohawk state forests, and parallels the Housatonic River for much of its length before it ascends to the New York border at the Schagticoke Mountain Indian Reservation.

Hikers planning to travel the Connecticut segment of this trail should be sure to purchase the *Guide to the Appalachian Trail in Massachusetts and Connecticut*. Order your copy ($5.85) from: Appalachian Trail Conference, Box 236, Harpers Ferry, WV 25425. This guide contains general information on the route of the trail in Connecticut, trail markings and maintenance, precautions, and some notes on the equipment you will need. There is a section on accommodations along the trail, and the trail sections in Connecticut are described in detail, from south to north and north to south. There is also a section on side trails in Connecticut.

The Appalachian Trail in Connecticut is shown on the following U.S. Geological Survey Maps: Amenia, Babish Falls, Cornwall, Dover Plains, Ellsworth, Kent, Sharon, South Canaan.

Camping & Backpacking

Campers have their choice of more than 1,500 campsites in 18 recreation sites located in the state park and forest reserve system. Campsite reservations are available for most campgrounds. For information and applications contact: Parks & Recreation Unit, Dept. of Environmental Protection, State Office Bldg., Hartford 06115. The state also has commercial campsites of all types, and a comprehensive listing of these areas can be found in an informative brochure, *Connecticut Campgrounds*. You can obtain a free copy by writing: Secretary, Connecticut Campground Owner's Assn., Woodstock 06281. The publication contains a listing and brief description of each camping area, and each area is location-keyed to the map provided on the reverse side of the brochure. The map will also show you how to get to the campsites, with major highways indicated. There is a chart showing the services provided at each campsite, along with information on rates.

For information on hiking trails in Connecticut, write to: Connecticut Forest & Parks Assn., 1010 Main St., East Hartford 06108, or consult their informative *Connecticut Walk Book* ($4.50).

Canoe Routes & Quality Fishing Waters

Connecticut offers some surprising scenic canoe routes and trout streams surrounded by beautiful upland forests of mixed hardwoods and conifers, meadows, rolling hills, beaver flows, and marshlands. It has over 500 lakes and ponds, and roughly 250 miles of coastline on Fishers Island and Long Island sounds. The state's major canoe routes are the Housatonic (the Indian name for "river beyond the mountains"), Connecticut, and Thames rivers, and the scenic 80-mile-long Farmington River, which provides excellent white-water runs. Al-

CONNECTICUT ENCYCLOPEDIA

though the state is heavily populated, there are many areas where the canoeist can enjoy smooth canoeing with scenic panoramas, or whitewater canoeing during the spring runoff. Anybody planning a canoe trip in Connecticut should send for the excellent *Connecticut Canoeing Guide,* available free from: Public Information & Education, Dept. of Environmental Protection, State Office Bldg., Hartford 06115. The beginner, even a person who has never set foot in a canoe, will find this booklet especially informative since it contains sections on canoeing safety, hints to the first-time canoeist, boating laws affecting canoeists, and basic canoeing techniques (river, lake, and sea and tidal river canoeing). There is a section listing lakes and ponds with public access that provide good waters for canoeing, with a brief description of each. A section on rivers is also included, describing the type of canoeing and its relative difficulty. Some interesting bits of historical information are included in this section. There is information on saltwater canoeing and overnight camping in state parks and forests (the traveler is urged to consult: Parks & Recreation Section, Dept. of Environmental Protection, State Office Bldg., Hartford 06115). There is an excellent bibliography at the end of the booklet.

Consult the *AMC River Guide Volume II: Central & Southern New England,* before setting out, which contains detailed descriptions of Connecticut rivers. It costs $6.00, and can be obtained from: Appalachian Mountain Club, 5 Joy St., Boston, MA 02108. *The Connecticut River Guide* ($4.50), Connecticut River Watershed Council, 125 Combs Rd., Easthampton, MA 01027, contains much information for the canoeist as well as three detailed maps of the Connecticut River. *The Farmington River and Watershed Guide* ($2.50), Farmington River Watershed Assn., 195 W. Main St., Avon 06001, is written primarily for canoeists and describes the scenic Farmington River system in detail. For the *Connecticut Walk Book* see "Camping & Backpacking." It covers wilderness areas that will help locate good scenic canoeing areas, even though it is written primarily for hikers and backpackers. *Public Access to Connecticut Fishing Waters* (free), Dept. of Environmental Conservation, State Office Bldg., Hartford 06115, gives directions to Connecticut public access areas. *Digest Of Connecticut Boating Laws* (free, same address), is a digest of current boating laws and regulations. A good text and workbook on safe boating and boating laws is *Better Boating,* obtainable free from the

same address, as is the *Connecticut Boating Manual* (free), which is used as a textbook in boat safety courses and contains detailed information on lifesaving devices.

Many of the streams and lakes offer good fishing for pickerel, bass, brook, brown, rainbow, and sea-run trout, the latter often reaching weights up to 5 pounds. Major trout streams and canoe trails are shown on the following U.S. Geological Survey Maps. *Connecticut River:* Broad Brook, Deep River, Essex, Glastonbury, Haddam, Hartford N, Hartford S, Manchester, Middle Haddam, Middletown, Old Lyme, Springfield S, Windsor Locks; *Farmington River:* Avon, Bristol, Collinsville, Hartford N, New Britain, New Hartford, Otis, Tariffville, Tolland Center, Windsor Locks, Winsted; *Five Mile River:* (one of Connecticut's finest canoe routes): Danielson, East Killingly, Oxford, Thompson; *Housatonic River* (from the Vermont border to its junction with the Shepaug River): Ashley Falls (MA), Cornwall, Danbury, Dover Plains, Ellsworth, Kent, New Milford, Newtown, and South Canaan; *Konkapot River:* Ashley Falls (MA), Great Barrington (MA), Monterey (MA); *Mattabesset River:* Hartford S, Meriden, Middletown, New Britain; *Naugatuck River:* Ansonia, Milford, Norfolk, Naugatuck, Thomaston, Torrington, Waterbury, West Torrington; *Quinebaug River:* Danielson, Jewett City, Norwich, Plainfield, Putnam, Webster (MA); *Quinnipiac River:* Branford, Meriden, New Haven, Wallingford; *Saugatuck River & Reservoir:* Bethel, Botsford, Sherwood Point, Westport; *Shepaug River:* Litchfield, New Preston, Newtown, Roxbury, West Torrington; *Shetucket River:* Norwich; *Mashapaug Pond* (including Break Neck and Bigelow ponds): Wales (MA); *Williams Pond:* Columbia.

Fishing & Hunting in Connecticut

For the angler and hunter, Connecticut is a state of many surprises —10-pound sea trout, 60-pound striped bass, 22-pound northern pike, 16-pound brown trout, 9-pound shad, rafts of scaup, black ducks, Canada geese, ruffed grouse, woodcock, 355-pound bucks, and rabbits. While no one would attempt to equate the Nutmeg State's outdoor potential with Maine, Michigan, Wyoming, Washington, or Quebec, a progressive, hard-working Department of Environmental Protection has done a creative job of protecting and maintaining the fishing and hunting opportunities, as well as introducing new, compatible species. Connecticut, of course, is very industrialized, urbanized, and heavily populated, containing more than 3 million people. However, there are numerous state forests and parks, the scenic Appalachian Trail, winding along the Housatonic River in the northwest section, and some exquisitely beautiful countryside. Parts of northwestern Connecticut look as though a giant hand had carved a slice out of Vermont and placed it there; and portions of the central, northern, and eastern regions are composed of rolling hills, forests, streams, and lakes of comparable quality. The southern margin of Connecticut rests on Long Island Sound, and the coastline area is famous for its beautiful sandy beaches, productive, rock-ribbed shoreline and points, tidal marshes, offshore islands, and the fish-filled sweep of the sound. There is much more to Connecticut than suburbia, factory whistles, and superhighways; yet many local sportsmen, unaware of the excellent opportunities right at their doorstep, pack up the station wagon and head for the Adirondacks, Maine, Canada, or other points.

The fishing potential of Connecticut's lakes and streams is reflected in the list of record freshwater fish, compiled by the Department of Environmental Protection (p. 573).

Awards are given annually for outstanding catches: forms are available from: Dept. of Environmental Protection, State Office Bldg., Hartford 06115, or sporting goods stores.

CONNECTICUT RECORD FISH

	Lb.-oz.	Place	Year
Brook trout	4–6	Housatonic River	1950
Brown trout	16–4	Mashapaug Lake	1968
Lake trout	29–13	Wononscopomuc Lake	1918
Rainbow trout	9–7	Saugatuck Reservoir	1962
Tiger trout	4–15	Farmington River	1972
Sea trout	9–10	Golden Spur	1968
Smallmouth bass	7–10	Mashapaug Lake	1954
Largemouth bass	12–14	Mashapaug Lake	1961
Walleye	14–8	Candlewood Lake	1941
Chain pickerel	7–14	Wauregan Reservoir	1969
Northern pike	22–4	Bantam Lake	1976
Shad (American)	9–2*	Connecticut River	1973
White perch	2–8	Connecticut River	1961
Yellow perch	2–13	Black Pond	1973
Black crappie	4	Pataganset Lake	1974
Bluegill	2	Waskewiscz Pond	1974
Rock bass	1–1	Highland Lake	1973
Common sunfish	0–14¼	Private Pond	1973
White catfish	9–13	Shaker Pines Lake	1973
Brown bullhead	2–14	Pritchard Pond	1968

*North American record.

Coldwater Fishing

Trout are found in every section of the state in streams, lakes, and ponds, and trophy fish are taken every season. Connecticut stocks more than 250 streams with trout, but because of watershed limitations and hot summer temperatures, a large percentage of the streams are "put and take," being reduced to trickles during July, August, and September. There are a number of all-season rivers, and these can provide some surprising sport throughout the state's long open fishing period. The Housatonic River, source of the state record 4-pound 6-ounce brook trout, dominates the western side of the state, winding its way from the Berkshire foothills of the northwest corner south to Long Island Sound. This verdant country furnishes some of Connecticut's finest trout fishing in the deep pools, swift runs, and riffles of the "Hous." The best water consists of the 20 or so miles between Kent and Lime Rock; the stream runs beside U.S. 7. Brown trout, rainbows, and brookies are stocked, and there are holdover browns to 7 or 8 pounds. The 2½ miles in the Housatonic Meadows State Park are for fly fishing only, and the energetic Housatonic Fly Fishermen's Association does an enormous amount of work, including stocking, to maintain the quality of the fishing. Some of the Housatonic's tributaries

produce good fishing, including the attractive Blackberry, Shepaug (a lot of private land is a problem on this one) flowing through Aspeterck, the excellent Pomperaug—an all-season producer—and the Pequonnock. These streams all yield some big holdover browns each season, in addition to the "stockers." Lake Lillinonah, an impoundment near Brookfield Center on Route 133, is a long sinuous section of the Housatonic which produces first-rate fishing for largemouth and smallmouth bass, pickerel, and panfish. Lake Zoar, another dammed-up stretch of the river a few miles upstream from Derby, is also a consistent producer of these species.

The great Connecticut River splits the state as it flows south to the sound at the picturesque towns of Old Saybrook and Old Lyme. The Connecticut is not a trout producer, but some of its tributaries are noted streams. The Scantic, above Hartford, yields good fishing throughout the season, and big browns are taken in the fall in the stretch near its confluence with the Connecticut. The Salmon River, which springs from feeder streams in the Salmon River State Forest, and its tributaries, such as Jeremy's River, Blackledge River, Fawn Brook, and Dickinson Creek, offer good spring fishing, and the main Salmon produces throughout the season.

The most famous Connecticut feeder is the beautiful Farmington River drainage, consisting of the West Branch, running south from the Massachusetts border through the trout-filled waters of the double impoundment of Colebrook River and Hogsback reservoirs, split by a dam, through a narrow, mixed hemlock, laurel, and hardwood forest valley, containing Peoples State Forest, to meet the flooded East Branch (Barkhamsted Reservoir) at Pine Meadow. This upper stretch and the main river down as far as Unionville furnish fine brook, brown, and rainbow trout fishing, and the Pine Meadow area, where the two branches meet, yielded the 4-pound 15-ounce record tiger trout. There are many picture-book pools with deep holes, ledges, and shallow, gravel-filled shoals. Below Unionville the river becomes a warmwater environment as it nears the Connecticut at Windsor, several miles north of Hartford, but there are a few awesome browns in the lower portions of the stream. The Farmington is part of the effort to restore Atlantic salmon to the Connecticut drainage.

Another fertile trout river complex is the group of streams consisting of the Willimantic River, the Natchaug-Mount Hope-Fenton-Shetucket system, and the Yantic River. The Willimantic is a long stream winding south from the Stafford Springs area to its junction with the Shetucket at Willimantic. The 6 or 7 miles below Stafford Springs are particularly fertile, and mayflies, caddis, and other stream insects come off the water in clouds during the cycle of hatches, causing the trout to go on a feeding binge. Some of the big holdover browns can be taken on dry flies when the large March Browns, Gray Foxes, and Green Drakes swarm on the surface. The Natchaug, Mount Hope, and Fenton rivers course south to meet at the Mansfield Hollow Federal Lease forest area. All three furnish good trout fishing from the Mansfield Hollow lease north until they become small brooks. The more inaccessible segments yield some large browns. The Yantic, another fine stream, spills into the Shetucket at Norwich and also contains an all-season trout population.

Two other popular rivers which hold up well during the season are the Hammonasset, noted for occasional browns to 5 pounds, which enters the sound at Clinton and is fished from Lake Hammonasset Dam south to the tidal area, and the Saugatuck River in Fairfield County. The Saugatuck receives heavy pressure during the spring, but as summer approaches, fewer anglers are seen. Evidently there are sufficient deep holes and springs to sustain the browns during the dog days, because late September sees the trout on the move again, and some

memorable hours are enjoyed by the relatively small autumn angling contingent. There are intermittent public stretches above and below Saugatuck Reservoir, including a fly fishing-only area in the lower end at Door's Mill Dam. This stream courses down a narrow, hemlock-shaded valley, and the scenery complements the angling.

Connecticut anglers have the opportunity to take sea trout, anadromous brown trout weighting up to 10 pounds, which inhabit several tidal streams. These beautiful silver, black-spotted battlers average about 3 pounds and have attracted a tight-lipped clique of devoted admirers; every once in a while a striper fisherman, trolling around the estuary of one of these sea trout rivers, gets a big surprise. The Connecticut Fisheries biologists noticed, over the years, that a few brown trout placed in streams such as the Hammonasset were migrating to salt water, returning to spawn in the fall. About 20 years ago, European sea trout (an anadromous brown trout) were imported from the Morrum and Dal rivers in Sweden and from waters in England, Scotland, and Denmark. These émigrés were planted in Latimer Brook to the north of Niantic, Whitfords Brook at Old Mystic, and the Hammonasset at Clinton. Populations are known to exist in the Eight Mile River at Hamburg on the Connecticut River, in the Farm River in East Haven, and in the Saugatuck at Westport. Occasional sea trout are taken in the Thames River below the Greenville Dam in Norwich, in the Housatonic below Derby Dam, and in several other small coastal brooks. Sea-run browns are seldom present in numbers, but their electrifying strike, enormous vitality, strength, and speed make them one of fishing's great prizes.

Much of the best all-season trout fishing can be found in the state's many lakes and ponds. Good trout ponds and lakes are found in every part of the state, including a group of reclaimed and heavily stocked "put and take" waters. There are a number of bodies of water which contain large holdover fish, and a significant proportion of these have been stocked with landlocked alewives and/or smelt to feed the big trout. East Twin Lake, in northwestern Connecticut near Salisbury, has some of the finest kokanee fishing in the East, with many fish near 2 pounds in weight, and offers excellent angling for brown and rainbow trout, bass, and panfish. Wononscopomuc, to the south at Lakeville, is another great producer in this beautiful section of New England villages and forested ridges. This lake holds the 29-pound 13-ounce record for lake trout, but lakers are now only an incidental catch. However, the excellent kokanee, brown, and rainbow populations make up for the laker's decline, and this body of water yields lunker trout, as well as largemouth and smallmouth bass, pickerel, and panfish. The Colebrook River-Hogsback reservoirs, a double impoundment, in the Algonquin-Tunxis State forest area near Colebrook, is a scenic piece of water bordered by Route 8. Rainbow trout create most of the excitement, but there are some big browns cruising the depths of this impoundment. Highland Lake, near Winsted, holds some lunker browns, and has fine angling for kokanee salmon, rainbow trout, both kinds of bass, pickerel, and panfish. West Hill Pond, a few miles southeast of Winsted, is considered by many knowledgeable Connecticut anglers to be the best trout lake in the state. Browns to 8 pounds are taken fairly regularly and there are some real busters in the cold depths, as well as some good-sized rainbows, kokanee, bass, pickerel, and panfish.

The area near the middle of the western border with New York State has two well-known Connecticut trout waters. Sprawling Candlewood Lake, paralleled by Routes 37 and 39, is a few miles north of Danbury. Even though its shoreline is clustered with cottages and docks and there is a lot of boating activity, early morning, evening, and nighttime angling can be surprisingly productive. Bass and panfish thrive in this deep lake, but it is the big rainbows and browns to weights in excess of 5 pounds that distinguish Candlewood. Many fishermen go out at night in a boat during the summer and use a lantern to attract night insects, minnows, and eventually, large hungry trout. Live bait and lures are used to take these hefty fish. Ball Pond, a few miles west, is a reclaimed lake that is heavily stocked with rainbow trout. Fertile and fairly deep water combine to promote fast growth, and some of the holdovers reach 3 pounds.

In south central Connecticut are three noted trout lakes. Higganum Reservoir, at the top of Cockaponset State Forest, is a scenic lake which furnishes good brown and rainbow trout fishing, and although many of the catches are of average size, there are some lunkers awaiting the fortunate angler. Quonnipaug Lake at North Guilford, above Long Island Sound, contains browns and rainbows and is a consistent producer of big fish weighing over 5 pounds. Bass, pickerel, and panfish are also present. Cedar Lake at Chester was reclaimed in 1961 and stocked with brown trout and alewives in 1965, and browns to 7 pounds are taken, as well as bass and panfish.

Near the Massachusetts border in the eastern half of the state is Crystal Lake at Stafford Springs. The nourishment potential of land-locked alewives is well illustrated here, because Crystal has recently produced a 13-pound brown and has a record of yielding outsized fish. Brookies and rainbows are also present, and the lake contains an excellent population of holdover trout. Smallmouths, largemouths, and pickerel add to the attraction of this fine scenic body of water. A short distance northeast, in Bigelow Hollow State Park, is Connecticut's premier producer of record fish, Mashapaug Lake. The champion brown (16 pounds 4 ounces), largemouth bass (12 pounds 14 ounces), and smallmouth bass (7 pounds 10 ounces) were taken here and big ones continue to appear.

New London County, in the southeast corner of the state, has some good trout ponds in an area noted for saltwater fishing. Rogers Lake, above Old Lyme, is one of Connecticut's quality waters, containing browns, rainbows, and a few brook trout. Browns of up to 5 pounds are taken, and Rogers also offers good bass, pickerel, and panfishing. Long Pond in North Stonington is the best big trout lake in southeast Connecticut and one of the outstanding waters in the state. Heavily stocked with browns, rainbows, and a few brook trout, it yields trophy browns to weights over 7 pounds. Bass, pickerel, and panfish are also caught in shallow, weedy areas. Lantern Hill Pond, just above Long Pond in Ledyard, also provides fine trout angling. Green Falls Reservoir at Voluntown in the Pachaug State Forest is a reclaimed water offering a combination of woodland scenery and above-average brown and rainbow trout fishing. There are other good trout lakes but many of these are town water supplies and are restricted to citizens by special permit or are closed.

Warmwater Fishing

Connecticut offers some of the best warmwater fishing in New England. There are hundreds of public and private lakes and ponds that produce largemouth bass to 9 or 10 pounds, and any fisherman can find a good, nearby bass lake where he is allowed to fish, or where permission can be secured. An exciting sport in which the state stands at the top of the list is fishing for swift, rugged shad, the "poor man's salmon." Shad are taken in rivers such as the Thames at Greenville Dam in Norwich, the Salmon and the Eight Mile rivers, both Connecticut River tributaries, and a few other rivers, but the best location in the state and probably in the United States is the Connecticut River above Hartford, including the mouth of the Farmington River, the Bissell Bridge area, the mouth of the Scantic River, the Windsor Locks area, and the finest shad stretch of all, Enfield Dam.

The Connecticut provides good fishing for other species too. White

perch and whitefish are found all along the river; striped bass are caught as far upstream as Enfield Dam. Largemouth bass, pickerel, and northern pike are caught at various points along the river. Pike are savage opponents in the Connecticut's currents and hit plugs, spoons, bucktail baits, minnows, and big spinners. Atlantic salmon restoration efforts are beginning to show some small victories, and it is hoped that the great expenditure of time, money, effort, and devotion of federal, state, and private groups will bear fruit.

Another great warmwater fishing area, also noted for northern pike, is Bantam Lake in northwest Connecticut, south of Litchfield. Pike were stocked in Bantam to thin out an overly abundant white perch population and the management step has worked out to the benefit of both species. A new state record 22-pound 4-ounce pike was taken in 1976, and other large specimens are taken throughout the season. Both kinds of bass, and pickerel and panfish, are abundant. Lake Wangumbaug at Coventry is considered to be one of the best, possibly the best smallmouth bass lake in the state, with little competition from other game fish. Other fine bass producers include Lake of Isles at North Stonington, which holds quantities of pickerel, perch, and crappies; Pachaug Pond on the edge of Pachaug State Forest, and Moodus Reservoir and Bashan Lake in East Haddam. Other exceptional warmwater fishing places are described in the descriptions of trout fishing above, being "two-story" lakes managed for both types of fish.

Saltwater Fishing

Connecticut has exceptional, unpublicized saltwater fishing, and fishermen passing through the state on their way to Cape Cod, Montauk Point, and other popular areas are overlooking some of the finest saltwater angling on the East Coast. Bluefish to 20 pounds and striped bass to 60 pounds are taken from the productive shores of Greenwich on the New York border at the west to the Pawcatuck River on the Rhode Island line to the east. The state's rocky shores, marshy coves, and rocky ledges provide optimum bass water, and the sound with its 250 miles of shoreline produces steady fishing during a long season. Bluefish appear in July and are present until fall storms drive them south; they are often caught along with stripers.

Weakfish (squeteague), mackerel, sea bass, porgies (scup), blackfish (tautog), fluke and winter flounders, cod, pollack, tomcods, and hordes of snappers (small bluefish) are other popular fish. The troutlike, iridescent weakfish has made a dramatic comeback after a long absence. These trim, orange-finned game fish weigh from about 2 to 12 pounds and prefer spoons, spinners, jigs, shrimptail lures, small bucktails, spinner and worm rigs, sea worms, squid, killies, spearing, and shrimp. Mackerel and snappers hit small chrome jigs, spoons, spinners, flies, bucktails, and minnows. The bottom fish take the baits described above, plus clams and small crabs—fiddlers and green crabs for blackfish. Cod and pollack hit jigs or other lures and can be taken on bait.

Angling Guides & Charts

Several publications of interest to the Connecticut fisherman and hunter are available free on request (single copies only) from: Dept. of Environmental Protection, State Office Bldg., Hartford 06115: *Public Access to Connecticut Fishing Waters, Connecticut Shad Fisher, Connecticut Trout Stocking Report, Hunting-Trapping & Sportfishing Regulations, Deer Season Field Guide, A Hunting Guide to Game Management Areas,* and *Waterfowl Hunting & Duck Identification Guide.* The useful large-format 202-page guide, *Trout and Salmon Fishing in New England Lakes and Ponds* ($8 postpaid), contains detailed descriptions and lake survey maps of East Twin,

Wononscopomuc, Mashapaug, and Crystal lakes and West Hill Pond. It may be ordered from: Partridge Press, Box 422, Camption, NH 03223.

Hunting

Connecticut offers a surprising amount of hunting, considering the size of the state, the population, and the heavy percentage of private land ownership. There are more than 122,000 acres in state forests, another 39,000 in state-owned or -leased game management areas, and nearly 62,000 acres in permit-required, cooperative private lands where hunters may secure permits to hunt the tracts.

Ruffed grouse, woodcock, pheasants, bobwhite quail, chukar (limited), squirrels, rabbits, and waterfowl are the most popular small-game species. Deer can be hunted in the state by shotgun, bow and arrow, and muzzle-loader but this sport is a somewhat involved process. There are different seasons for each type of weapon, and shotgun hunting on state lands is by application and draw for a permit. Fees are charged for permits, which are necessary for hunting deer by any method, either on state or private lands. A hunter may avoid the permit draw by securing permission to hunt on an unlimited number of private lands meeting specified size requirements, but must present consent forms to the DEP, signed by both applicant and landowner for each piece of land to secure a permit for that parcel. Deer are plentiful, having adjusted well to civilization, and the state's fields, gardens, and forest fringe areas make ideal habitat. In some areas deer have become pests, chewing up the family garden patch, farm produce, and grainfields. Hunter success, based on a recent season, ran about 10%, with the average buck weighing 163 pounds and the doe 127 pounds; a bow-and-arrow marksman killed a trophy 12-pointer which tipped the scales at 355 pounds. The prime areas are located in the southeast, northeast, and northwest, the latter being top choice. Housatonic State Forest at Sharon and Wyantenock State Forest at Cornwall account for almost 50% of the total deer kill in some seasons.

Ruffed grouse are the most important upland game species. As with deer, the rolling forested hills of Litchfield County contain some of the finest cover in the state, but partridge are well dispersed throughout Connecticut. Woodcock are found in many of the same places as partridge: alder thickets, stream bottoms, damp wooded areas, and wherever they can find earthworms. Fall is a beautiful time of the year in Connecticut, and a mixed bag of grouse and woodcock taken in one of the state's scenic forests or fields, vividly painted by autumn, makes a satisfying day. Pheasants are present, but generally on a put-and-take basis. Anyone who lives along the sound can tell you that ringnecks are commonly seen. Bobwhite quail, too, prefer the lands near the

moderating influence of salt water, but once again, public lands are very scarce. Chukar partridge are stocked but are very restricted in numbers; they are an incidental game bird. Cottontail rabbits are abundant all over the state except in the interiors of the forest tracts, and snowshoes are found in the dense wooded areas. Gray squirrels are common throughout the state, particularly in the oak, beech, and hickory woodlands. There is no season for the beautiful bronzed, majestic wild turkey, but these great game birds have been reintroduced into the state, particularly in the northwest, and the fortunate outdoorsman may see one of these spectacular natives in his journeys through the forestlands.

Some of Connecticut's prime hunting potential is found in Long Island Sound and the tidal river mouths. Scaup raft up off the shore by the thousands. The handsome drakes with their gray-striped back, whitish underside, glossy black head and chest, and characteristic slate-blue bill make quite a sight as they sweep across a decoy rig. These birds are the bread and butter of saltwater hunters. Black ducks are also abundant, along with mallard, whistlers (goldeneye), teal, and incidental flight birds. Canada geese are prevalent in the coastal area, and geese have taken up permanent residence in many of the suburban coastal towns in lakes, reservoirs, and residential zone ponds. When the winter nor'easters howl down the sound, sea-duck hunters come into their own and experience excellent shooting on rocky points, wind-lashed islands, and in dories on open water for the big, dark scoters (coot), old-squaws, and the occasional eider.

Besides duck hunting, the marshes of the Housatonic and Connecticut rivers have long been famous for rail hunting. Sora, king, clapper, and Virginia rails skulk in the reedy margins of these rivers, and some excellent shooting in September and October is largely neglected. Hunting out of a flat-bottomed poling skiff with a guide used to be a popular sport in the days when shorebirds were abundant and prized game. Inland duck hunting can be productive, and some of the public hunting lands are suitable for decoy and jump shooting. The marshy, slow, tidal portions of rivers such as the Connecticut, Housatonic, and

Thames offer opportunities, particularly for the boot hunter. Black ducks, teal, mallards, wood ducks, and Canada geese will furnish most of the gunning.

The *Citizens' Bulletin*, the official publication of the Department of Environmental Protection, appears 11 times a year. It publishes articles about fishing, hunting, outdoor recreation, wildlife, resources management, conservation, and other items of specific local interest. It costs $2.00 per year and provides a wealth of useful, interesting information about the Connecticut outdoors. Subscription requests should be mailed to: Editor, Citizens' Bulletin, Rm. 112, Department of Environmental Protection, State Office Bldg., Hartford 06115.

Highways & Scenic Routes

Connecticut's beautiful countryside—deep, wooded hills, stunning river valleys, charming old villages and towns, along with modern cities—offers many scenic routes that are resplendent with beauty throughout the year. The Dept. of Commerce, 210 Washington St., Hartford 06106, will send you a free information booklet, *Connecticut Scenic Tours*. Different types of tours are described. There is a 4-day scenic tour, a 2-day historical tour, a 3-day family trip, and a 2-day maritime tour. Explicit directions are provided for automobile travel, and there are small maps to aid the motorist. Distances between destinations are noted, and the booklet is attractively illustrated with photographs. The department will also send, at no charge, the official *Highway Map of Connecticut*, which shows all roads and highways; recreation features, such as state parks and forests, fishing areas, and ski areas; and miscellaneous features, such as airports, heliports, and fish hatcheries. There is a chart listing state parks and forests, location-keyed to the road map, showing what services are available at each area. Capsule information on fishing and hunting, and state parks and forests, is also shown. A list of public boat-launching sites, also location-keyed, is provided. For additional information on scenic routes and highways in Connecticut, write to: Dept. of Commerce (address above) for the

following publications: *Connecticut, So Much So Near, Points of Interest, Connecticut in Fall,* and *Connecticut in Winter.*

Lake Contour Fishing Maps

Depth contour maps for several of Connecticut's major lakes are available free (single copies only) from: Information Office, Dept. of Environmental Protection, State Office Bldg., Hartford 06115. These useful maps show depth contour intervals, which will allow the angler to determine his drifting and trolling patterns based on the lake's thermal stratification, and boat landings. Each map contains a detailed description of the lake's physical characteristics, fish species present, and fishing history and potential. Contour maps are available for the following lakes: *Wononscopomuc* (kokanee and trophy browns from 2 to 12 pounds), *West Hill Pond* (the former state record 31-inch, 13-pound brown trout was caught here in 1964), *Black Pond* (Meriden and Middlefield), *Quonnipaug* (largemouth bass and brown trout), *Mashapaug* (producer of state record fish), *Amos, Ball, Highland* (kokanee), *Silver, Cedar* (browns up to 7 pounds), *Dooley Pond, East Twin Lake* (considered the most productive kokanee lake east of the Rockies), *Pataganset* (trophy black crappie), *Bantam* (northern pike, trophy smallmouth and largemouth bass), *Beach, Billings, Black Pond, Crystal* (large holdover browns), *Gardner, Green Falls Reservoir, Halls Pond, Lantern Hill Pond, Long Pond* (New London County, trophy bass and browns up to 7 pounds), *Mohawk Pond, North Farms Reservoir, Pickerel Lake, Quaddick Reservoir, Rogers Lake* (large holdover browns up to 5 pounds), *Candlewood Lake.*

Outward Bound—North American Wilderness Instruction & Adventure

The renowned Outward Bound network of private nonprofit institutions—first begun in Wales during World War II by international educator Kirt Hahn to develop spiritual strength and the will to survive in young British seamen—operates a worldwide system of 30 schools for men, women, and young adults offering wilderness experience courses which include such skills as emergency first aid, map and compass, route finding, campcraft, rock climbing, rappelling, backpacking, white-water canoeing, solo cross-country travel, wilderness leadership, and search and rescue. Courses vary from region to region.

Information and literature can be obtained by writing to any of the following Outward Bound schools in North America: National Headquarters, Outward Bound, 165 W. Putnam Ave., Greenwich 06830, phone (203) 661-0797; *Northwest Outward Bound School,* 3200 Judkins Rd., Eugene, OR 97403; *Texas Outward Bound School,* 4603 W. Lovers La., Dallas, TX 75209; *Hurricane Island Outward Bound School,* P.O. Box 429, Rockland, ME 04841; *Colorado Outward Bound School,* P.O. Box 7247, Park Hill Sta., Denver, CO 80207; *North Carolina Outward Bound School,* P.O. Box 817, Morganton, NC 28655; Minnesota Outward Bound School, 1055 E. Wayzata Blvd., Wayzata, MN 55391; *Dartmouth Outward Bound Center,* P.O. Box 50, Hanover, NH 03755; *Outward Bound Mountain School,* P.O. Box 279, Keremeos, B.C. V0X 1N0; *Outward Bound British Columbia,* 1616 W. 7th Ave., Vancouver, B.C. V6S 1S5; *Canadian Outward Bound Wilderness School,* P.O. Box 1644, Kingston, Ont. K7L 5C8.

Ski Touring Trails & Centers

Connecticut's scenic state park and forest reserve trails provide unlimited cross-country skiing opportunities (see "State Forest Reserves & Wildlife Management Areas" for a list of topographic maps). The state's major cross-country skiing areas are described in detail in the *Ski Touring Guide* ($3) published by: Ski Touring Council, Troy, VT 05868. Major areas offering lodging, instruction, and tours include the *Copper Hill Ski Touring Center,* Granby 06035; *White's Woods* and the 500-acre "Topsmead" plateau, Litchfield 06759; *Peoples State Forest;* Powder Ridge Ski Area, Middlefield 06455, on the Mattabassett Trail, a segment of the Blue Trail System; *Candlelight Farms* in the Housatonic Mountains, New Milford 06776; the *Mount Riga Plateau,* Salisbury 06068; *Mohawk Mountain* (rentals and instruction), West Cornwall 06796.

The famous *Blackberry River Inn Ski Touring Center,* Rt. 44, Norfolk 06058 (203-542-5100), is the state's most popular nordic skiing area, with 25 miles of trails, instruction, rentals, and lodging. *Great World Inc.,* 250 Farms Village Rd., P.O. Box 250, W. Simsbury 06092 (203-658-4461), offers guided ski touring trips in the Adirondacks, New England, and the Colorado Rockies. The *Riverrun Touring Center,* Falls Village 06031 (203-824-5579), offers instruction, rentals, and 35 miles of scenic backcountry trails. The *Powder Ridge Ski Area,* Middlefield 06455 (800-243-3760), offers complete touring service and lodging at the Base Lodge Inn.

The invaluable *EMS Ski Touring Guide to New England* ($5.95) contains detailed descriptions, topo maps, and mileage charts of the state's major abandoned railroad beds and ski touring trails, including Tunxis State Forest, State Bridle Trail, McLean Game Refuge, and the Copper Hill area. It may be obtained by writing: Eastern Mountain Sports, 1047 Commonwealth Ave., Boston, MA 02215.

State Forest Reserves & Wildlife Management Areas

Connecticut's state forest reserves and wildlife management areas (WMAs) encompass a varied topography of mixed hardwoods and evergreens with laurel thickets, beaver flowage, meadows, wetlands, lakes, ponds, and streams, and offer excellent opportunities for back-

country hiking, camping, fishing, canoeing, cross-country skiing, and hunting in season for ruffed grouse, woodcock, gray squirrel, cottontails, raccoon, deer, woodcock, pheasant, and ducks and geese. The free 54-page *Hunting Guide to Wildlife Management Areas* may be obtained by writing: Wildlife Unit, Dept. of Environmental Protection, State Office Bldg., Hartford 06115. For information and hiking and wild country camping in the state forest reserves, write: Connecticut Forest and Parks Assn., 1010 Main St., East Hartford 06108.

The major man-made and natural features of the forest reserves and WMAs, including mountains, woodlands, marshes, ponds, streams, forest roads and trails, shelters, and campsites, are shown on the following 7.5-minute U.S. Geological Survey Maps. *Algonquin State Forest* (including Hogsback Dam Reservoir): Tolland Center, Winsted; *Cockoponset State Forest:* Clinton, Deep River, Essex, Haddam; *Housatonic State Forest* (including Mohawk SF, Macedonia Brook State Park, and Wononskopomuc, Wonon-Pakook, and Wagnum lakes: Ashley Falls, Babish Falls, Cornwall, Ellsworth, Sharon, South Canaan; *Nassahegan State Forest* (including Nepaug State Forest and Reservoir): Bristol, Collinsville; *Natchaug State Forest:* Eastford, Hampton; *Naugatuck State Forest:* Mount Carmel, Naugatuck; *Nehantic State Forest* (including Devils Hopyard State Park): Hamburg, Montville, Old Lyme; *Nipmuck State Forest:* Eastford, Southbridge (MA); *Pachaug State Forest* (including Hopeville Pond State Park, Assekonk Swamp State Forest, and Pachaug, Lake of Isles, Moosup, and Wyassup lakes): Ashaway (RI), Jewett City, Old Mystic, Oneco, Plainfield, Voluntown; *Paugussett State Forest* (including Kettletown State Park): Newtown, Southberry; *Peoples State Forest* (including Tunxis State Forest and Barkhamsted Reservoir): New Hartford, West Granville, Winsted; *Quaddick State Forest* (including Quaddick Reservoir and Wallum Lake): Oxford, Thompson; *Salmon River State Forest* (including Meshomasic State Forest and Terramuggus and Pocatopaug lakes): Glastonbury, Marlborough, Middle Haddam, Moodus; *Mattatuck State Forest WMA:* Waterbury; *Wyantenock State Forest WMA:* Kent, New Preston; *Nepaug State Forest WMA:* Collinsville; *Nye Holman State Forest:* Stafford Springs; *Shenipsit State Forest:* Ellington, Manson (MA); *Nathan Hale State Forest:* South Coventry;

Wilderness Travel Services

The Good Earth, Outdoor Travel Dept., 181 Meriden-Waterbury Rd., Southington 06489, phone (203) 634-4036, organizes backpacking trips of 2 to 14 days along the Connecticut segment of the Appalachian Trail, and in the White Mountains of New Hampshire, Maine's Baxter State Park, and the Adirondack Mountains. It also organizes canoe trips and white-water float trips through the Hudson River Gorge Primitive Area in the Adirondack Forest Reserve, with special 2-day instructional programs. *Riverrun Outfitters*, P.O. Box 33, Falls Village 06031, phone (203) 824-5579, provides canoe rentals, gear, and guide trips from its base on the banks of the Housatonic; and provides guided trips in the Okefenokee Swamp in Georgia and along Texas's Big Bend country of the Rio Grande.

Accommodations

The State of Massachusetts has travelers' accommodations of every type, including campsites, resorts, lodges, hotels, motels, and everything in between. They run the full gamut of price ranges and luxury standards, and local chambers of commerce can supply you with information on where to stay. Address your inquiries to: Dept. of Commerce & Development, Leverett Saltonstall Bldg., 100 Cambridge St., Boston 02202.

Appalachian Mountain Club—Outdoor Information Service, Instruction & Guided Hikes

The renowned Appalachian Mountain Club (AMC) provides a wide range of wilderness instruction, publications, workshops, guided hikes, and outdoor services. Information on hiking, backpacking, cross-country skiing, canoeing, and mountaineering in Massachusetts and throughout the Northeast is available by writing or calling: *AMC Information*, 5 Joy St., Boston 02108, phone (617) 523-0636. Questions about where to go, what to bring, equipment rental and retail, and how to obtain outdoor skill instruction are welcome. In addition, information on backcountry and wilderness use regulations as well as north country weather and snow conditions is kept as up to date as possible. The information service is open for Boston Headquarters Clubhouse visitors Monday through Friday from 9:00 to 5:00. A wide selection of trail and river guides and other outdoor activity books may be purchased, and a full collection of U.S. Geological Survey Maps is available for public use.

In addition to their authoritative guidebooks, the AMC publishes the semiannual, century-old journal *Appalachia*, which contains a wide range of articles on mountains and surrounding habitats, a quarterly public service magazine, the *Appalachia Bulletin*, and the *AMC Times*, a monthly paper listing organized trips, lectures, and workshops. For a publication price list or further information, write or call AMC Publications (address and phone above). The AMC's education department has available on a cost basis a number of pamphlets and posters dealing with aspects of hiking safety and ecologically sound camping practices. For additional information, write: Guidelines Project, c/o Education Dept., AMC (address above). The AMC recruits experienced mountain leaders for their Ridgerunner Program. Ridgerunners patrol the White Mountains advising hikers of forest regulations and assisting them if they require aid. Since 1958, the AMC's mountain leadership committee has sponsored a 5-day June workshop on the Presidential Range offering training in mountain leadership skills. A first-aid course is given immediately before the workshop. For info, write: *Mountain Leadership Workshop*, AMC (address above).

Each summer, guided natural history-oriented hikes in the White Mountains are led by experienced AMC personnel. Participants stay at AMC mountain huts. For further details, write: *Guided Hikes*, AMC, Pinkham Notch Camp, Gorham, NH 03581, phone (603) 466-3994. Workshops are run for the public on weekends throughout the year at Pinkham Notch Camp (see New Hampshire, "Travel & Recreation Guide" section). Topics covered have included winter ecology, mushrooms, orienteering, alpine flowers, mosses and lichens, spring natural history, equipment making, mountain medicine, photography, low-impact camping, astronomy, weather, ski touring, fall ecology, and outdoor sensitivity. For more information and a complete schedule, write: *Pinkham Notch Workshops*, AMC, Gorham, NH 03581. The education department places skilled naturalists in AMC mountain huts each summer and fall. For a schedule, write: *Resident*

Naturalist Program, Education Dept., AMC (address above). Each year, between Christmas and New Year's, the AMC, in conjunction with the Adirondack Mountain Club, runs schools in the White Mountains and the Adirondacks which offer instruction in winter hiking and camping. For more information, write: *AMC Winter School* (address above).

AMC membership information and fees may be obtained from the Boston office (address above).

Appalachian National Scenic Trail

This great mountain footpath winds through the backcountry of Massachusetts from the Vermont boundary over Mount Greylock south to Cheshire and along woodland roads to Dalton, Warner Hill, and Washington Town Hall before entering the scenic highlands of the October Mountain State Forest, beyond which it winds past Goose Pond and across Tyringham Valley, through the Beartown-East Mountain State Forest in the Berkshires to the Housatonic Valley and the Connecticut line.

Detailed mile-by-mile descriptions of the Massachusetts segment of the trail are contained in the *ATC Guide to the Appalachian Trail in Massachusetts & Connecticut* ($5.85), available from: Appalachian Trail Conference, Box 236, Harpers Ferry, WV 25425; and in the *AMC Massachusetts-Rhode Island Trail Guide* ($6.75), available from: AMC Books, 5 Joy St., Boston, 02108.

The major features of the trail in Massachusetts and the topography of the surrounding countryside are shown on the following U.S. Geological Survey Topo Maps: Bashbish Falls, Cheshire, East Lee, Egremont, Great Barrington, Monterey, Pittsfield E, Williamstown.

Camping & Backpacking

Massachusetts' scenic state forest lands and reservations provide numerous camping and backcountry hiking opportunities. An excellent brochure to consult is *Camping in Massachusetts*, available free from: Dept. of Commerce & Tourism, Box 1775, Boston 02105. It contains a listing and descriptions, regulations, and fee schedules for private campsites, state campgrounds, city and town campsites, and state day-use areas, whose locations are shown on easy-to-read maps. A free *Guide to Massachusetts Private Campgrounds* may be obtained by writing: Massachusetts Assn. of Campground Owners, Pinelake RD 1, Sturbridge, 01566.

Backpackers are advised to study the comprehensive *Fifty Hikes in Massachusetts* by Paul and Ruth Sadler ($5.95). Order from: New Hampshire Publishing Co., 15 Interstate Dr., Somersworth, NH 03878, or your local bookstore. This book takes you through the Bay State's best hiking country—Cape Cod's dunes and marshes, up mountains and down ravines in the Berkshires, to wildlife sanctuaries, fields, forests, and other beautiful countryside. There are helpful notes on rules, regulations, fitness, proper clothing, equipment, and food. The book provides maps showing the path of each hike, distances, and hiking time; each hike is classified according to the degree of ability required. (See also "Appalachian National Scenic Trail.")

The Appalachian Mountain Club, 5 Joy St., Boston 02108, publishes a free, informative little pamphlet entitled *So You Want to Take a Hike* . . . The beginner will find it extremely helpful, as it provides tips on planning your route and alternate routes, weather, equipment (a list of suggested clothing and supplies is included), first aid, tips that will be of interest when you are actually on the trail, and some facts about spending the night in the wilderness. A list of the excellent AMC guidebooks is also provided at no charge. The club has published the *AMC Guide to Country Walks Near Boston* within reach of public transportation. This guide to the undiscovered backcountry around Boston is of interest to the ski tourer, woods lover, birdwatcher, naturalist, or geologist. The guide is available for $4.95 from AMC Publications (address above). The *Guide to the Metacomet-Monadnock Trail in Massachusetts and New Hampshire* ($1), which describes the scenic route of this trail from Hanging Hills, Connecticut to the summit of Grand Monadnock in New Hampshire, may be ordered from: AMC, 5 Joy St., Boston 02108.

Free sketch maps of the Blue Hills, Breakheart, Middlesex Falls, and Stony Brook reservations are available from: Metropolitan District Commission, 20 Somerset St., Boston 02108. A Guide to the *Mount Everett Trails* may be obtained free (with stamped, self-addressed envelope) from: Superintendent, Mount Everett Reservation, RFD Copake Falls, NY 12517. *Taconic Crest Trail Maps* may be obtained for 50¢ from: Taconic Hiking Club, 50 Newark St., Cohoes, NY 12047. The *WOC Trail Guide* to Mount Greylock and other mountains in the Williamstown vicinity may be obtained for 75¢ from: Williams College Outing Club, Williamstown 01267.

For information on camping and backpacking in the state forests and parks, and for free state forest maps, write: Division of Forests & Parks, 100 Cambridge St., Boston 02202. Also write for the *MDC Recreational Facilities* guide, available free from: Recreation Section,

Metropolitan District Commission (address above). (See also "State Forest Reserves & Backcountry Area Maps" and "Appalachian National Scenic Trail.")

Canoeing Waters

There are many areas in Massachusetts where one can find good canoe trails and trout water. The canoeist would do well to consult the authoritative *AMC River Guide: Volume II Central & Southern New England*, ($6.00), published by: Appalachian Mountain Club, 5 Joy St., Boston 02108. It lists rivers arranged by watershed, except for coastal rivers which are arranged by areas. Rivers are described from source to mouth, since downstream travel is most common; but upstream travel has been indicated where it is necessary to make connections with other rivers. Lakes are described as parts of the watershed or stream in which they are located. There are maps included which will show the exact location of the river, and also describe the type of canoeing to be found. You will find detailed descriptions of the Housatonic ("river beyond the mountains") and Merrimack rivers, and the Rhode Island-Massachusetts coast.

Eastern Mountain Sports—Instruction & Adventure Travel Services

Eastern Mountain Sports—specialists in quality wilderness travel gear, clothing, and accessories, and publishers of the famous *EMS Catalog*—operate EMS Adventures—a year-round vacation service that provides a wide range of outdoor activities to wild and scenic areas throughout the world. Extensive experience is not required for EMS Adventures, but participants should be in good health and adaptable to the wilderness environment. Some preconditioning is highly recommended for any of these trips, and essential for the high-altitude treks in Nepal and Mexico. EMS Adventures include: Grand Canyon Combination Backpack & Raft Trip; Summer Backpacks in the Canadian Rockies; Canadian Rockies Youthpacks—a total wilderness experience for ages 14 to 19, with instruction in backpacking, wilderness skills, mountaineering, nature studies, and photography; Mountaineering in the Purcell Range of British Columbia—includes complete instruction in all phases of high climbing, including use of ice ax, rope management, glacier travel, snow and ice climbing, rock climbing, and safety; Backpacking in the North Cascades; Walking Photo Safari in Zambia, Africa; and Nepal Trek to Mount Everest Base Camp —trek follows the path of legendary explorers to Katmandu, the medieval capital city, Namche Bazar, the Thyanboche Monastary, the Khumbu Glacier, and the Everest Base Camp. For detailed information and rates, write: EMS Adventures, Vose Farm Rd., Peterborough, NH 03458 or phone (603) 924-7276.

Expert instruction in cross-country skiing and mountaineering is provided by the *Eastern Mountain Sports Nordic Ski Center*, Intervale, NH 03845, (603) 356-5606; *Eastern Mountain Sports Cross-Country Ski Touring Center*, North Conway, NH 03860, (602) 356-5433; and *Eastern Mountain Sports Climbing School*, North Conway, NH 03860. All EMS stores rent tents, packs, sleeping bags, ski-touring equipment, snowshoes, and mountaineering gear. For rental info and a copy of the full-color *EMS Catalog* ($1.00, 100-plus pages)—which is packed with the best in lightweight wilderness camping, ski touring, and mountaineering gear, clothing, accessories, books, and useful equipment selection charts and tables —write or call: EMS Boston, 1041 Commonwealth Ave., Boston 02215, (617) 254-4250.

Fishing & Hunting in the Bay State

Massachusetts, the most populous New England state, with over 5 million residents, provides some surprisingly good hunting and fishing in its varied topography, of which almost 70% is forest. Land types include the seacoast with its miles of scrub oak, pine, bayberry, sand plains, bays, and surf-pounded beaches, the rolling hills, river valleys, and farmlands of the central interior, and the Berkshire Highlands of the west, crowned by Mount Greylock at 3,491 feet and covered with a green forest mantle of pine, hemlock, white and yellow birch, beech, and maple. Bay State outdoorsmen have over 4,200 miles of streams and rivers, 1,100 lakes and ponds, wildlife management areas, state forests and parks, fisheries and wildlife private landowner cooperative tracts, and 2,000 miles of coastline and the island and reef-studded expanse of the Atlantic Ocean in which to pursue their favorite sport.

The state's freshwater fishing potential is illustrated by this list of record fish, compiled by the Division of Fisheries & Wildlife.

MASSACHUSETTS RECORD FISH

	Lb.-oz.	Place	Year
Brook trout	6–4	Otis Reservoir	1968
Brown trout	19–10	Wachusett Reservoir	1966
Lake trout	17–13	Quabbin Reservoir	1973
Rainbow trout	8–5	Quinnapoxet River	1976
Landlocked salmon	9–11	Quabbin Reservoir	1975
Smallmouth bass	7	Lovells Pond	1972
Largemouth bass	15–8	Sampson's Pond	1975
Northern pike	28–6	Onota Lake	1978
Chain pickerel	9–5	Pontoosuc Lake	1954
Walleye	11	Quabbin Reservoir	1973
Shad	8–12	South River	1975
Channel catfish	23	Quaboag River	1976

Several of the champion catches, such as the brown trout, largemouth bass, northern pike, and pickerel, are impressive by any standards, and many of the lunkers were landed in recent years. The Division of Fisheries & Wildlife annually awards bronze pins for outstanding catches, as well as special prizes for the heaviest specimen in each category. Minimum weights, in pounds, are as follows:

Brook trout	2	Walleye	5
Brown trout	6	Shad	6
Lake trout	7	Channel catfish	5
Rainbow trout	4	White perch	1⅜
Landlocked salmon	7	Yellow perch	1¼
Smallmouth bass	4	Crappie	2
Largemouth bass	7	Bluegill and pumpkinseed	1
Northern pike	10	Bullhead	1¾
Chain pickerel	4		

Fish must be registered at a sporting goods store which is designated as an official weighing station and an affidavit form is to be filled out, witnessed, and signed.

Quabbin Reservoir Trophy Waters

Massachusetts furnishes some excellent trout fishing, particularly in the many impounds, lakes, and ponds. The outstanding body of

water in the state is sprawling Quabbin Reservoir, in central Massachusetts, near Belchertown. The deep blue waters of this island-studded lake, the largest expanse of fresh water in the state, cover about 25,000 acres and are indented with long arms, bogs, and coves, which provide an ideal environment for a long list of game fish. This is the only lake in Massachusetts providing fishing for landlocked salmon (state record, 9 pounds 11 ounces) and lake trout (state record, 17 pounds 13 ounces), which grow to heavy weights in the cold, deep waters. Brown trout to 20 pounds and thick-bodied, metallic-striped rainbows are favorite quarry for many of the anglers who fish the big Swift River impoundment each season. Quabbin was primarily a bass and perch spot until the late 1950s, when the innovative Division of Fisheries & Wildlife correctly assumed that an excellent coldwater game-fish population could be established, and stocked the trout and salmon, plus smelts to feed them. The results have been spectacular, and Quabbin is one of the quality waters of New England, producing large gray lakers and trophy browns each season, as well as impressive salmon and rainbows. Superb large- and smallmouth bass, pickerel, walleye (state record, 11 pounds), and panfish angling round out the opportunities of this lake. An added dividend is the fact that Quabbin is surrounded by a large, beautiful forest tract which provides top-ranked whitetail deer and wild turkey hunting in season. The Swift River continues out of Quabbin at Windsor Dam, and the 4-mile stretch downstream to Bondsville, including a short piece of "fly fishing only water" from the dam to Route 9, offers some of the state's best trout fishing. The three branches of the Swift that flow into the top of Quabbin have good trout populations and also offer a chance at stream fishing for some of the enormous hook-jawed browns and rainbows which move in and out of the lower portions of these streams to feed on smelts and fly hatches. The spring spawning run of smelts and rainbows makes these feeders particularly attractive.

Otis & Onota Lakes

To the west of Springfield lie the productive waters of Otis Reservoir. Otis yields brook, brown, and rainbow trout, shelters some trophy fish in its deep blue waters, and produced the state record 6-pound 4-ounce squaretail. Smallmouth and largemouth bass and panfish are also present in large numbers and add variety to the angling in this prolific lake. Otis is a tributary lake of the West Branch of the Farmington River, and the stream provides good trout fishing from the town of Otis to the top of Hogsback Reservoir on the Connecticut border.

Onota Lake, a couple of miles northwest of Pittsfield near the middle of the border with New York, ranks close to Quabbin in the excellence and variety of its fishing; trophy browns and rainbows are taken every season. It provides the only fishing in the state for the landlocked, red kokanee salmon, and offers fine angling for bass, big northern pike (state record), pickerel, and panfish. Wachusett Reservoir (home of the state record brown trout), northeast of Worcester, holds big rainbows, smallmouths, and lots of browns in the 4–5-pound-and-over class.

Cape Cod Trout Ponds

Some of the best trout fishing in New England is found on Cape Cod. Because it is situated in the middle of a hotbed of saltwater angling, the Cape does not receive the pressure its quality would ordinarily attract. There are more than 50 "kettle" ponds, a heritage of the Ice Age, which provide exceptional angling in their cool, spring-fed depths. Among the best of these are the set of ponds at Nickerson State Park, near Orleans, composed of Cliff (brown and rainbow), Little Cliff (brook), Higgins (brook), and Flax (brook and rainbow). A brown trout tipping the scales at almost 20 pounds was found dead of old age on the shores of Cliff Pond! Mashpee Pond and its connected sister, Wakeby, are noted producers of brook and brown trout as well as smallmouth bass, perch, and pickerel. These two bodies of water are near Otis Air Force Base on Route 130 at the town of Mashpee. The Mashpee River, draining south to Popponesset Bay, is an excellent sea-run brook and brown trout stream, producing those big silver-bodied fish to weights of better than 2 pounds and occasional fish to 6 pounds. Other famous Cape Cod trout ponds include Gull Pond, Crystal Lake, Sheep, Shubael, Scargo, and Hamblin. Rivers containing stream and sea-run trout include the Pamet, Marston Mills, Quashnet, and Santuit rivers, and Scorton Creek, which flows north to Cape Cod Bay at Scorton Harbor. The sea trout are very wary and difficult to raise to a lure, fly, or bait. Flies and lures which imitate spearing, shrimp, killies, and other natural baits, as well as the naturals themselves, are preferred tackle.

In addition to the trout waters, the Cape has some excellent smallmouth and largemouth bass, pickerel, and perch ponds, as well as other trout ponds and streams. For a handy overview of Cape Cod fresh and saltwater fishing, write to: Cape Cod Chamber of Commerce, Hyannis 02601, for *Sportsman's Guide to Cape Cod*, a free folder which lists all of the trout, bass, pickerel, and perch ponds and streams by town, and lists the species present in each, the availability of boat-launching sites, and whether or not the pond is reclaimed.

Other popular trout lakes include Richmond Pond, a few miles southwest of Pittsfield, which contains large brown trout, both kinds of bass, pickerel, and panfish; Laurel Lake in the central Berkshires, which holds lunker browns, bass, pickerel, and panfish; the Congamond Lakes, on the Connecticut border below Southwick, which produce big browns and rainbows in the northern pond, and excellent smallmouths and largemouths, pickerel, and panfish in the other two sections; Asnacomet Pond, in central Worcester County, which has a reputation for good, steady brown and rainbow trout angling, and shelters bass, pickerel, and panfish to add variety; Quacumquosit Pond, southwest of Worcester, which produces browns and rainbows, its sister, Quaboag Pond, yielding bass and pickerel; the Quaboag River; the Chicopee River; and Lake Quinsigamond, east of Worcester, which is heavily stocked with brook, brown, and rainbow trout, and provides good warmwater fishing too.

In addition to these streams, Massachusetts has some scenic, productive rivers scattered about the state. The most famous trout river is the beautiful Deerfield, which rises in Vermont and meanders southeast through a heavily forested valley of mixed evergreens and hardwoods to the Connecticut at Greenfield. The lower part contains some trout, including an occasional trophy brown or brook trout, but the best fishing is from Shelburne Falls to the Vermont border at Sherman Reservoir. Power dams make the flow *highly* changeable, and you will have to watch the flow carefully or you may end up stranded on a midstream boulder for several hours, unless you are willing and able to swim for shore. The Deerfield is a beautiful piece of water to fish. Many of the Deerfield's tributaries, such as the east and west branches of the North River, yield good trout fishing; many of the little feeder brooks, rising high in the heavily wooded ridges, produce native trout for anyone willing to leg it up the steep, heavily forested slopes. The Green River rises in Vermont to the east of the Deerfield headwaters and flows south to meet the latter in Greenfield. Its limestone bed gives the Green a soft, emerald tint and the stream produces some enjoyable angling for all three stream trout. The many stretches of riffles found along the tight, hemlock-shaded river valley hold good-sized rainbows.

Two other Connecticut tributaries are popular with Bay State trout fishermen. The Westfield River drainage, that is, the Little River

(west, east, and middle branches), is productive from Huntington north and yields some fine creels of brook, brown, and rainbow trout. The Millers River, flowing west to the Connecticut at Millers Falls, provides good trout fishing from its headwaters to the Otter River State Forest in northern Worcester County. The Squannacook, which flows east from the central New Hampshire border near Ashby to the Nashua near West Groton, holds trout; some big browns are taken in the deep holes above the Nashua. The Ware River drainage parallels the east side of Quabbin Reservoir and consists of east and west branches. A glance at a map will show you how parts of the branches flow away from roads, and these sections have the best trout fishing. The Nisitissit, near the New Hampshire border in Middlesex County, and the suburban Ipswich, flowing through Middlesex and Essex counties, also receive a good deal of attention from trout fishermen.

Warmwater Fishing

Massachusetts offers excellent warmwater fishing opportunities throughout the state, including both species of black bass, northern pike, walleyes, pickerel, shad, white and yellow perch, crappies, bluegills, bullheads, and other panfish. Largemouth and small-mouth bass are present everywhere, from the ponds and brackish tidal basins of Martha's Vineyard and Nantucket Island to the forested upland waters of the Berkshires at the western border with New York. The Cranberry Bay area of southeastern Massachusetts in Plymouth County continues to produce outsized largemouths. The state record largemouth came from Sampson's Pond near South Carver, and in 1976 a 13-pounder was taken from Muddy Pond, a few miles north, which has a reputation for lunkers, even though it only covers 90 acres.

Many of the premier bass, pike, walleye, and pickerel waters were covered in the discussion of trout fishing above, but there are a number of productive spots that merit special mention. The Assawompset-Great Quitticas-Long Pond complex, at Lakeville, furnishes fine angling for both species of bass, trophy walleyes and pickerel, and panfish. To the northwest of Taunton lies Norton Reservoir, which consistently yields lunker smallmouth and largemouth bass—the latter to 10 pounds, pickerel, and panfish, big white and yellow perch, crappies, and bluegills. Lake Sabbatia, on the northern outskirts of Taunton, is considered another bass hot spot, and also holds pickerel and perch. Chauncy Lake at Westboro in eastern Worcester County provides some of the best smallmouth bass fishing in the state and has a healthy population of walleyes, in addition to largemouths and panfish. Singletary Pond, a few miles south of Auburn, is another exceptional bronzeback-largemouth producer and contains trout, pickerel, and panfish, with good fishing for all species.

On the Connecticut border near the town of Webster is Lake Chargoggagoggmanchaugagoggchaubunagungamaug (also known as Lake Webster, this is the famous "joke lake" which translates from the Indian dialect as "You fish on your side of the lake, I'll fish on mine, and nobody fishes in the middle"), which furnishes superb bass fishing for both species—some trout, pickerel, and panfish. The lake is somewhat off the beaten path and well worth the effort. East Brimfield Reservoir, an impoundment of the Quinebaug River at Sturbridge, produces bass, trout, pickerel, and panfish and also contains a few northern pike. At the northern tip of Worcester County, northwest of Fitchburg, are upper and lower Naukeag and Winnekeag lakes, which combine some fine scenery with bass, pickerel, and panfishing of top-notch quality.

In western Massachusetts, the Connecticut River produces shad to 10 pounds in the waters at the foot of the Holyoke Dam, in the Chicopee River at Chicopee, and in the Springfield area. Shad are also found in a few coastal rivers such as the South (state record) at Marshfield and the North at Scituate, both south of Boston. The best fishing in the Connecticut is from the Vermont border to Millers Falls where the Millers River enters. In this stretch of water paralleling I-91, smallmouths, largemouths, walleyes, northern pike, and assorted panfish are taken. Massachusetts is involved in the Atlantic salmon restoration program, and it is hoped that in the future silvery legions will again ascend the Connecticut. Pontoosuc Lake above Pittsfield once held the U.S. record for pickerel, and the 9-pound 5-ounce fish is still the state record. Bass, panfish, and a few trout are also taken. Nearby Onota Lake, discussed above as trout waters, draws much of the fishing interest; Pontoosuc receives less pressure. Cheshire Reservoir, a few miles northeast of Pontoosuc, has an excellent reputation for northern pike, and also yields bass, pickerel, and panfish. Stockbridge Bowl lies in the West Stockbridge-Tanglewood area and occupies one of the Berkshire's most scenic mountain regions. Bass, trout, pickerel, and panfish are caught in its scenic waters, perhaps to the strains of Gershwin, if the Boston Pops is playing at Tanglewood and the wind is just right. Other top-ranked Massachusetts lakes include Walden Pond near Concord, once Thoreau's base camp for his philosophical musings, which holds browns, rainbows, and smallmouths; Lake Mattawa in Franklin County, which holds rainbows and some giant browns; and Wallum Lake in the Douglas State Forest at the Rhode Island border, which holds some whopper brown trout.

Saltwater Fishing

Saltwater fishing is avidly pursued in many parts of the Bay State, which is not surprising, for the riches of the sea have been woven into Massachusetts history from its beginning, and a substantial portion of anglers look seaward rather than inland. The most prized species are the spectacular giant tuna, broadbill swordfish, and blue and white marlin—which are pursued from sleek charter boats, private cruisers, and console boats—the rugged striped bass, and that mobile meat grinder, the savage bluefish. Much of the offshore fishing is based on Cape Cod, which enables skippers to fish the Nantucket Sound-Block Island waters for the heavyweights, or on Cape Cod Bay and points north. Beautiful Ipswich Bay, on the north coast above Gloucester, is a renowned giant tuna ground, and charter boats are available in the area.

Cape Cod and the southeast shore of the state ranks as one of the best, if not *the* best, striped bass territories on either coast for fish up to 80 pounds. The Elizabeth Islands—including Naushon, Pasque, Nashawena, and fabled Cuttyhunk—with their reefs, boulder-girded shores, holes, and tidal rips are considered by many experts to be the finest stretch of bass water in existence. These superb striper islands are located off Cape Cod at Woods Hole. It was in Vineyard Sound, separating the Elizabeths from Martha's Vineyard, that the long-standing 73-pound world's record fish was taken in 1913 by trolling an eel. Martha's Vineyard and Nantucket Island also offer extraordinary striper fishing. Martha's Vineyard and Cuttyhunk have tradition-laden striper clubs; the preferred bait 70 years ago was lobster tail, with the rest of the animal used as chum—by the bushel! Evidently this practice is no longer followed, and stripers are now caught on plugs, surgical tube lures, bucktails, spoons, other artificials, and all sorts of live bait, including eels, squid, seaworms, live menhaden, herring, mackerel, other small bait fish, and clams. Martha's Vineyard is blessed with miles of beaches, including the excellent stretch under the multihued cliffs of Gay Head, whose minerals reflect blue, green, red, copper, and other colors in the sun. The numerous bays, salt

ponds with inlets, rocky shoals, and reefs make this ideal bass country. Light-tackle fans, including fly rodders, enjoy some memorable hours at the mouths of salt ponds, taking fish on light popping plugs and swimmers, lures, streamers, and popping bugs. Nantucket offers similar delights, and its beaches are famous throughout the East. Cape Cod itself takes a back seat to no area, and the Cape Cod Canal, the entire south shore including Monomoy Island, Chatham, the Cape Cod National Seashore, which takes up most of the northward "hook," and Race Point, Wellfleet, and Barnstable harbors, and much of the Cape Cod Bay shore produce fine striper fishing. The canal, separating the cape from mainland Plymouth County, receives enormous runs of bass, but the banks are lined with fishermen and this is not fishing for the dainty or timid. Buzzards Bay (the bay, not the town), between the Elizabeth Islands and New Bedford, offers great bass fishing along its beaches, points, reefs, bays, and in rivers such as the Acushnet, Westport, Taunton, and Weweantic. North from the canal to Boston, excellent striper fishing can be found in bays, such as historic Plymouth, along the beaches, and in rivers such as the North and South. Good fishing continues north of Boston through Marblehead, Gloucester, and Ipswich Bay to the area of the enormously productive waters of the Ipswich, Parker, and Merrimack rivers, Plum Island, and the Parker River National Wildlife Refuge. At times the stripers teem in the three rivers, offering opportunities for lighter tackle, and the Plum Island outer beach is excellent for surf casting.

Bluefish up to 20 pounds are found with stripers in all these coastal areas, and often herd up vast shoals of frantic bait fish such as mackerel, menhaden, and herring, turning the water blood-red as they attack the "balled-up" prey and reduce the fish to table scraps. When the unpredictable stripers turn sullen and refuse to hit, the voracious bluefish often save the day, whether the fisherman is on the beach or in a boat, on Cape Cod, the islands, or the mainland coast. The northern weakfish or squeteague has made a comeback and these gleaming, iridescent fish are taken on the beaches and in the bays. Troutlike in appearance, weaks run up to about 12 pounds and prefer natural baits, spoons, small bucktails, rubber or plastic-tailed jigs, and spinners.

Mackerel are taken from late spring until coldwater conditions in the fall and provide sport all along the Massachusetts shores. Bottom fish of one sort of another are taken throughout the year and include scup (porgies), tautog (blackfish), summer and winter flounders, tomcods, smelt, and lesser varieties, plus the offshore species halibut—which reach several hundred pounds—cod, haddock, pollack, hake, and ling. For information about saltwater fishing on Cape Cod see *Sportsman's Guide to Cape Cod*, described above, which lists some charter and party boats, along with the names and telephone numbers of their skippers, locations where charter boats are berthed, and the address of the *Cape Cod Charter Assn.*, P.O. Box 668, West Yarmouth 02673, where additional information and names can be obtained for those who want guides to take them out after stripers, blues, or big-game species. Local chambers of commerce, newspapers, magazines (such as the excellent *Saltwater Sportsman* published in Boston), and fishing tackle stores are other sources for guides and boats.

Maps & Guides

Bay State fishermen and hunters should write to: Division of Fisheries & Wildlife, Leverett Saltonstall Bldg., 100 Cambridge St., Boston 02202, for the following free publications: *Massachusetts Fish and Game Laws Folder, Migratory Birds Regulations, Public Access to Waters of Massachusetts*, and *Stocked Trout Waters of Massachusetts*. The Information & Education Section, Division of Fisheries & Wildlife, Westboro 01581, will send a free list of *Wildlife Manage-*

ment *Area Maps* available, which includes a majority of the tracts. Single copies of each map, not more than five areas per person, will be mailed free if the request for maps is accompanied by a stamped, self-addressed envelope. The eminently useful large-format 202-page guide, *Trout and Salmon Fishing in New England Lakes and Ponds* ($8 postpaid), contains detailed descriptions and lake survey maps of Quabbin Reservoir and Cape Cod Ponds. It may be ordered from: Partridge Press, Box 422, Campton, NH 03223.

Hunting

Massachusetts, with its wide range of terrain, offers hunting for deer, pheasants, ruffed grouse, quail, woodcock, waterfowl, rabbits, and gray squirrels, and has a severely restricted black bear season by limited permits. A few moose are known to exist in isolated parts of the northwest corner of the state, and wild turkeys have been reintroduced into appropriate areas, particularly the Quabbin forestlands and the Berkshires along the Appalachian Trail area northwest of Great Barrington, but there is currently no season for either species.

Deer are hunted in December during a very short 1-week season in which shotguns only are permitted. Bow hunters and muzzle-loaders are granted special seasons at other times. Whitetails are found all over the state, the best areas being the Berkshires, the northern portion of Worcester County, Franklin County, and Cape Cod.

An excellent information source for Massachusetts outdoorsmen is the bimonthly *Massachusetts Wildlife*, which is available free if you write: Information & Education Section, Division of Fisheries & Wildlife, Westboro 01581. Conservation, where-to-go, how-to, wildlife profiles, watershed studies, and wildlife management area developments are among the interesting topics covered, and Bay State outdoorsmen can glean plenty of useful tips from the articles.

Highways & Scenic Routes

The Bay State is filled with many beautiful scenic routes that will delight vacationers. For a guide to these, consult the *Official Massachusetts Transportation Map*, prepared by the Department of Public Works. You can get one free by writing: Massachusetts, Box 1775, Boston 02105. It is an excellent map of the state showing all highways and other roads. There is a chart showing recreational facilities (state forests, state parks, reservations, and beaches); the location of each area is shown. The chart indicates what facilities are available at each site. More information on scenic areas may be found in the free brochure *Vacationing in the Beautiful State of Massachusetts* (see "Camping & Backpacking"). This attractive publication has beautifully illustrated descriptions of suggested scenic trips in different areas of the state. It can be obtained by writing to the address above.

Lake Contour—Great Pond Maps

Great Pond Maps of the top-ranked fishing lakes, showing depth contours, boat-launching areas, locations of key structures, and areas where shore fishing is permitted, are available free (single copies) from: Information & Education Section, Division of Fisheries & Wildlife, Westboro 01581. Due to limited quantity, only single copies of up to five different maps will be furnished to each angler who sends a stamped, self-addressed, legal-sized envelope. Be sure to indicate the lake or ponds that you desire. Great Pond Maps are available for such renowned trout, salmon and bass waters as Land Pond, Lake Quacumquosit, Lake Nippenicket, Onota Lake, Otis Reservoir, Quabbin Reservoir, Mashpee-Wakeby Pond, Metacomet Lake, Nissitissit River, Pontoosuc Lake, Lake Beul, Lake Garfield, Lake Mattawa, Spy Pond, Lake Quannapowitt, Walden Pond—memorialized by Henry David

Thoreau—Watuppa Pond, Quaboag Pond, Furnace Pond, Manchaug Pond, and Assawompset, Packsha, and Great Quitticas Ponds. A free *Listing of Great Pond Maps* may be obtained from the Division of Fisheries & Wildlife (address above).

Ski Touring Trails & Centers

Massachusetts's state forest trails provide excellent cross-country ski touring and winter camping opportunities. The state's major ski touring areas include the Beartown State Forest; the *All Year Round Ski Touring Center*, Ipswich 01938; *Mount Tom Ski Area*, Holyoke 01040; *Broadmoor Little Pond Wildlife Sanctuary*, Natick 01760; the *School House Trail* in Otis State Forest, Otis 01253; *Williamstown Ski Touring Center*, Williamstown 02167; the Savoy State Forest in the Hoosac Range; *Pittsfield State Forest*, Pittsfield 01201; the beaver ponds, slopes, and ravines of the wild country at the Firecat Farm-Burt Hill Natural Area, Granville 01034; *Northfield Mountain Ski Touring Center*, RR 1, Box 377, Northfield 01360, with a 30-mile trail network recently designated as part of the National Trail System; *Cummington Farm Ski Touring Center*, South Rd., Cummington 01026, (413) 634-2111, with rustic backcountry cabins with woodburning stoves and 25 miles of trails in the heart of the Berkshire Mountains; *Jug End Resort*, S. Egremont 01258, (413) 528-0434, in the southern Berkshires with wooded groomed trails.

Detailed descriptions of the state's major cross-country skiing areas, including abandoned railroad beds, state forests and reserves, are con-

tained in the 127-page *Ski Touring Guide*, ($3.50), published by: Ski Touring Council, Troy, VT 05868, and in the *EMS Ski Touring Guide to New England* ($5.95), available from: Eastern Mountain Sports, 1047 Commonwealth Ave., Boston 02215.

State Forest Reserves & Backcountry Area Maps

The following U.S. Geological Survey Maps show the topography of the state's major forest reserves and game lands. These reserves provide excellent hiking, fishing, and canoe-camping opportunities, and good hunting in season for ruffed grouse, pheasant, quail, waterfowl, woodcock, whitetail deer, and a few wild turkey. *Ashburnham State Forest:* Ashburnham, Gardner; *Berkshire Hills & Beartown State Forest* (including Otis, Cookson, and East Mountain state forests): Colrain, Heath; *Holyoke Range:* Belchertown, Mount Holyoke; *Hoosac Range* (including Mount Greylock State Reservation, Williamstown Wildlife Management Area, and the Sayor Mountain, Clarksburg, Monroe, and Windsor state forests): Cheshire, North Adams, Williamstown, Windsor; *Hubbardston State Forest:* Barre, Gardner, Templeton, Wachusett Mountain; *Leominster State Forest:* Fitchburg, Sterling; *Mohawk Trail State Forest:* Plainfield, Rowe; *Miles Standish State Forest:* Plymouth, Wareham; *October Mountain State Forest* (including Peru Wildlife Management Area): Becket, East Lee, Peru (NY), Pittsfield E; *Quabbin Reservoir Forestlands* (including Swift River Wildlife Management Area and Mount Grace, Erving, Wendell, and Warwick state forests): Athol, Belchertown, Mount Grace, Orange, Palmer, Petersham, Quabbin Reservoir, Royalston, Shutesbury, Ware, Windsor Dam; *Townsend State Forest:* Ashley, Townsend; *Upton & Sutton State Forests:* Grafton, Milford; *Willard Brook State Forest:* Ashby, Fitchburg; *Willowdale & Georgetown-Rowley State Forests:* Georgetown, Salem; *Metacomet-Monadnock Trail:* Belchertown, Easthampston, Little Monadnock, Millers Falls, Mount Grace, Mount Holyoke, Mount Monadnock, Mount Tom, Northfield, Shutesbury, West Springfield.

Wilderness & Adventure Travel Service

Massachusetts has several good outfitters and organizers of wilderness expeditions. *The Infinite Odyssey,* 14 Union Park St., Boston 02118, phone (716) 542-0060, organizes hiking, canoeing, rafting, sailing, and mountaineering expeditions to many areas of the United States and abroad, including the Colorado Rockies, southern Alaska, and Wyoming's Wind River Range. Write or call for application forms and information on the latest trips. *Earthwatch* is an organization that involves "civilians" in scientific research. They help scientists who need people and funds to mobilize expeditions, and both are found by making the expeditions available to interested members of the public. Expeditions are taken to the far corners of the world to study such diverse subjects as the California sea otter, Great Basin ecology, Natural Trap-Bighorn Mountains, Amazon River study, and the Mammoth Graveyard in South Dakota. The costs are shared by the participants. The opportunities are in varied fields: natural sciences, marine sciences, and conservation. For further information, write: Earthwatch, 68 Leonard St., Box 127, Belmont 02178, phone (617) 489-3030. *Canoe Adventures NO'East* offers guided wilderness canoe trips in the Maine Northwoods and northern Canada. The firm also offers complete outfitting services, expert whitewater and flatwater instruction, and U.S. and Canadian canoe route topographic map service. Write: Canoe Adventures NO'East, Belmont 02178, phone (617) 484-6571.

RHODE ISLAND ENCYCLOPEDIA

Accommodations

Accommodations in Rhode Island are varied and plentiful. For information on where to stay, consult the useful *Guide to Rhode Island*, available free from: Dept. of Economic Development, 1 Weybosset Hill, Providence 02903, phone (401) 277-2614. This booklet contains a listing of accommodations arranged by region, including campgrounds and trailer parks. The traveler is advised to inspect the quarters upon arrival, and to obtain advance information from individual hostelries by phoning or writing in advance.

For further information, write to: Rhode Island Chamber of Commerce, 150 Francis St., Providence 02903.

Camping & Backpacking

Rhode Island has an excellent network of forest campsites and hiking trails. State camping facilities are available at Arcadia State Park, with 25 tent and trailer sites adjacent to a section of the Appalachian Trail; Arcadia Management Area, with 48 sleeping cabins; Burlingame State Park, 755 tent and trailer campsites in a wooded area bordering the shore of Watchaug Pond; Fisherman's Memorial State Park, 140 tent and trailer sites in a shore-meadow area overlooking Block Island and Rhode Island sounds; Frosty Hollow Area in Exeter, two Adirondack shelters on Shelter Trail off Frosty Hollow Road; George Washington Management Area, 60 tent and trailer sites in a wooded area overlooking Bowdish Reservoir; Horseman's Camping Area in West Greenwich, 30 tent and trailer sites; and the Ninigret Conservation Area in Charlestown, 50 sites for self-contained units. There are canoe campsites at the Burlingame Management Area on the shores of the Pawcatuck River, and at the Carolina Management Area on the Pawcatuck River. The privately owned Indian Acres Canoe Camp is on the Pawcatuck River, a day's paddle down the Wood River; write: LeRoy J. Edwards, 8 Friendship St., Westerly 02891. Reservations for state campgrounds are accepted at the Division of Park & Recreation, 83 Park St., Providence 02903.

A free *Camping in Rhode Island* describing all state-managed and commercial campgrounds may be obtained from: Dept. of Economic Development, 1 Weybosset Hill, Providence 02903. The state's major campsites and hiking trails, including the Inter-Park and Appalachian trails, are shown on the *Rhode Island Recreation Map* (See "Highway & Recreation Map.") Winter camping areas are described in the free publication *Winter in Rhode Island*, available free from: Dept. of Economic Development (address above). If you are planning to hike the Rhode Island backcountry be sure to consult the *AMC Massachusetts & Rhode Island Trail Guide* ($7.75), published by: Appalachian Mountain Club, 5 Joy St., Boston, MA 02108. It contains a detailed section on the state's Inter-Park trails, including the Arcadia, John B. Hudson, Breakheart, Narragansett, Mount Tom, Escoheag, Ben Utter, Tippecansett, and Walkabout trails, as well as Audubon sanctuaries and state parks.

Canoe Routes & Quality Fishing Waters

Rhode Island's major canoe trails and lakes are surrounded by a low rolling terrain of mixed hardwood woodlands, swamps, and a few beaver flows. The Wood, Beaver, and Moosup rivers provide good canoe-camping opportunities and hold some big, wary brown trout up to 5 pounds. The Pawcatuck, River which heads in the scenic woodlands of the Arcadia Management Area, is the state's major canoe route (see "Camping & Backpacking" for canoe campsites). The major canoe routes and quality fishing waters are shown on the follow-

ing 7.5-minute U.S. Geological Survey Topographic Maps. *Beaver River:* Carolina, Hope Valley; *Moosup River:* Coventry Center, East Killingly (CT), Oneco (CT); *Wood River:* Carolina, Hope Valley, Oneco (CT), Voluntown (CT); *Pawcatuck River:* Ashaway, Carolina, Kingston, Slocum, Watch Hill; *Pawtuxet River:* Clayville, Crompton, East Greenwich, North Scituate, Providence; *Pettaquamscutt River:* Narragansett Pier, Wickford; *Ponaganset River & Scituate Reservoir:* Chepachet, Clayville, North Scituate; *Watchaug Pond:* Carolina, Quonochontaug; *Worden Pond:* Kingston; *Indian Lake:* Narragansett Pier; *Beach Pond:* Voluntown (CT); *Yawgoog & Wincheck Ponds:* Voluntown (CT); *Quidnick Reservoir:* Coventry Center, Oneco (CT); *Flat River Reservoir:* Coventry Center, Crompton; *Pascoag Reservoir:* Chepachet; *Killingly Pond:* East Killingly (CT); *Bowdish Reservoir:* Thompson (CT); *Smith & Sayles Reservoir:* Chepachet; *Wallum Lake:* Thompson (CT), Oxford (CT); *Ponaganset Reservoir:* Clayville, Chepachet, Thompson (CT); *Slatersville Reservoir:* Chepachet; *Woonsocket Reservoir:* Georgiaville, Pawtucket; *Woonasquatucket Reservoir:* Georgiaville; *Pawtucket Reservoir:* Pawtucket, Georgiaville; *Falls & Flat Rivers:* Hope Valley, Voluntown (CT), Coventry Center, Oneco (CT).

Canoeists and fishermen should consult the *AMC River Guide: Volume II Central & Southern New England* ($6.00), available from: Appalachian Mountain Club, 5 Joy St., Boston, MA 02108, and the *Boating in Rhode Island* available free from: Dept. of Economic Development, 1 Weybosset Hill, Providence 02903.

Fishing & Hunting in Rhode Island

Rhode Island is the smallest, most densely populated state in America, yet it furnishes excellent saltwater angling, freshwater fishing for trout, bass, kokanee salmon, northern pike, pickerel, and panfish, and hunting for deer, upland game, and waterfowl. The state contains 1,214 square miles and offers the sportsman more than 400 miles of shoreline, island-filled bays, long tidal estuaries, game management areas, streams, and lakes. The Department of Natural Resources deserves a great deal of credit for managing and preserving inland wildlife resources under the most challenging conditions.

Saltwater Fishing

The productive waters of Narragansett Bay bite deep into the eastern interior of Rhode Island and contain three major islands, the largest of which gives the state its name. The bay, the adjacent coastal areas stretching west and east from its mouth, and the outstanding waters of Block Island, lying 15 miles due south of the mainland across the prolific sweep of Block Island Sound, constitute one of the East Coast's prime saltwater fishing areas. Giant tuna to weights of 1,000 pounds, school bluefins, white marlin, broadbill swordfish, and mako sharks are pursued in the bait-filled tides of Rhode Island and Block Island sounds and the trophy big-game Atlantic Ocean reaches that stretch from Block Island to New York's Montauk Point and the Gulf Stream eddy. Cod, pollack, and an occasional halibut are taken from the offshore reefs, ledges, and wrecks including Shark, Coxes', and Brown ledges. Heavy striped bass, bluefish, bonitos, weakfish (squeteague), fluke, winter flounders, sea bass, porgies (scup), mackerel, blackfish (tautog), tomcods, and other species provide great variety in the bays and estuaries, as well as along the shoreline and in sound waters.

Striped bass are probably the most popular game fish, followed by the savage bluefish, and are found along the beaches and rocky shores of the outer coastline, as well as in the interior waters of Narragansett Bay and the Sakonnet River. The long striper season extends from spring until late fall, and many of the trophy fish to 60 pounds are caught during the fall feeding spree when the linesides fatten up for a long, cold winter. Plugs, bucktails, eel rigs, surgical tubes, spinner and worm combinations, spoons, jigs, feather lures, and natural baits including live eels, menhaden, mackerel, squid, clams, herring, and sea worms are the most popular. Fly casting is gaining in popularity, and sheltered bays, estuaries, tidal rivers, and salt marshes provide ample opportunities to fish with streamers and popping bugs. Bass are well dispersed along the state's saltwater exposure, but inlets, known as breachways, are among the most productive areas and include the favorite channels at Weekapaug, Quonochontaug, Charlestown, Card Ponds, and Jerusalem-Galilee, which are all located west of the mouth of Narragansett Bay, and the various pond outlets at Little Compton to the east of the bay.

Bluefish, which attain weights of more than 20 pounds, are often found in the company of stripers, but are more inclined to pursue schools of menhaden and mackerel several miles offshore. Blues are taken from July until October or November on the same general lures as bass and are swift, powerful battlers. Weakfish have made an impressive comeback, following a severe low in their natural cycle, and once again are landed in weights up to 12 pounds. These spotted, iridescent scrappers, resembling trout in form, prefer bays, inlets, tidal marshes, and beach areas, striking at shrimptail jigs, spoons, spinners, bucktails, and spinner-and-worm combinations. Favorite natural baits include shrimp, sea worms, squid, and minnows, but weaks will also hit flies. Squeteague, as they are locally called, are present from May until low water temperatures in the fall drive them south.

The bottom varieties provide fishing all year long with scup, tautog, sea bass, and fluke available during the warmer months, and cod, pollack, tomcods, and winter flounder dominating the winter scene, as well as being taken in deeper cold water during the summer. Charter and party boat operations can be found at Jerusalem and Galilee, Wickford, Warwick, Pawtuxet, Sakonnet Harbor, world-famous Newport on the island called Rhode Island at the mouth of Narragansett Bay, and Block Island, which can be reached by ferry from Point Judith, Providence, or Newport.

Freshwater Fishing

The quality of the inland fishing is surprisingly good for a state with such a high population density. Write for the free *Rhode Island Fishing Laws* leaflet, which supplies the usual data on seasons, species,

limits, special regulations, and waters stocked with trout, to: Dept. of Natural Resources, Veterans Memorial Bldg., Providence 02903. The trout streams, lakes, and ponds are rated by trout present, trout habitat, and angling pressure. Some of the ponds are restricted to fly fishing only.

Stream trout fishing is somewhat limited because of the topography and demographics of the state. Most of the fast-water angling is put and take, because many of the watersheds are reduced to warm trickles during the summer heat. The best stream system in the state is the Wood River in southwest Rhode Island. The Wood flows out of Arcadia Management Area south for about 10 miles to Alton, where it meets the Pawcatuck. The entire length to Alton is stocked with brook, brown, and rainbow trout, and the Wood is by far the most consistent producer of holdover browns to 5 pounds. Tributaries such as Flat and Falls rivers and Breakheart, Roaring, and Parris brooks are also productive. Another Pawcatuck feeder, the Beaver River, furnishes trout fishing from the Pawcatuck at Shannock, upstream for about 4 miles. A few holdover browns are taken, especially near the confluence.

To the north of Arcadia Management Area are two other popular trout streams, both capable of producing an occasional large trout. The Moosup is near the center of the Connecticut border, and with its Bucks Horn Brook feeder provides more than 10 miles of fishing. The Ponaganset River, with its Dolly Cole and Windsor brooks tributaries, is similar in size to the Moosup Watershed and runs from Ponaganset impoundment into Barden Reservoir. The trout area is contained within Foster Township, and the large browns sometimes enter the river from Barden.

Some of Rhode Island's lakes and ponds supply good trout opportunities. Watchaug Pond, in the Burlingame Management Area in southwest Rhode Island, produces occasional browns to 6 pounds, stocked trout, and excellent fishing for both kinds of bass, pickerel, and panfish. Beach Pond, a few miles northwest on the Connecticut border at Beach Pond State Park, holds kokanee salmon, rainbows, browns, largemouths, smallmouths, pickerel, and panfish. The warmwater fish are abundant, but their growth rates are below standard. Beach Pond is shared with Connecticut under reciprocal arrangements. Wallum Lake straddles the Massachusetts border in the northwestern corner of Rhode Island and, like Beach Pond, is a reclaimed trout lake that became reinfested with warmwater species. Brook and rainbow trout, smallmouth bass, and panfish are the major species. Stafford Pond in the southeastern section near Tiverton is the most prolific smallmouth bass lake in Rhode Island, but also produces large quantities of rainbows through generous stocking, as well as pickerel and panfish. Other ponds on the fishing law list supply some good trout fishing; the town of each spot is provided, along with the spot's rating.

Warmwater possibilities are much greater, and there are many ponds, lakes, and brookish waters which have excellent largemouth populations. Both public and private areas produce well; in some cases, permission may be obtained to fish private property.

Worden Pond, skirting the Great Swamp Management Area near Tuckertown in the southeast section, is a marsh-bordered, primitive-looking expanse which lives up to its appearance, providing excellent fishing for largemouth bass, as well as good fishing for smallmouths, pickerel, and panfish. Northern pike are also present in this prolific lake and it is hoped that they will thrive and become a natural population. Nearby Tuckers Pond also boasts a reputation for fine bass fishing. Some other productive public bass, pickerel, and panfish wa-

ters include Bowdish, Pascoag, and Waterman reservoirs in West Glocester, Pascoag, and Greenville, respectively, Indian Lake at Mooresfield, Warwick Pond at Warwick, and Brickyard Pond at Barrington.

Hunting

Rhode Island may seem like a rather unlikely place to hunt, but deer, ruffed grouse, woodcock, pheasant, bobwhite quail, cottontail and snowshoe rabbits, gray squirrels, waterfowl, and other wildlife are found in the fields, woodlands, marshes, ponds, shorelines, and off-shore areas. Thirteen game management areas, ranging in size from Arcadia, 7,523 acres, in the southwest of the state, to Newton Swamp, 111 acres, also in the southwest, near Westerly, have a combined total of over 21,000 acres. These hunting lands are described in the Rhode Island *Recreation Map*, including size and principal game species, and are clearly identified on the map in bright green. Write for free *Rhode Island Game Laws* and *Waterfowl Hunting Laws* leaflets, which define seasons, species, bag limits, general and special regulations, and license provisions to: Dept. of Natural Resources, Veterans Memorial Bldg., Providence 02903. The hunter must remember that it is necessary to secure a permit to hunt any state-owned area, and that some areas may require daily permits. Permit requirements are spelled out in the game law leaflet and the Recreation Map, and permits may be obtained from the DNR at Providence or any field office, or from conservation officers or at checking stations.

Highway & Recreation Map

Anyone planning on participating in any kind of recreational activity in Rhode Island should send for the free *Rhode Island Recreation Map* to: Dept. of Natural Resources, Veterans Memorial Bldg., Providence 02903. Besides providing an excellent road map showing all major highways and other roads, it features a recreation guide legend, which indicates the following on the map: hunting checking stations, limits of stocked areas on trout streams, public boat-launching sites, guest moorings, public and private camping sites, charter boats, hiking trails, horseback trails, archery ranges, public rifle ranges, canoeing areas, areas where shellfishing is prohibited, and fish ladders. The map also features a recreation index showing saltwater beaches, freshwater beaches, yacht clubs, boatyards, yacht harbors and basins, trout ponds and streams (stocked), parks, view sites, and ski areas. All these are location-keyed to the map. The reverse side contains a wealth of recreational information. There is also safety information for boaters (whistle signals, rules for passing/overtaking, meeting head on, and crossing, storm warnings, and a channel buoy guide). Motorboat laws, waterskiing laws, and forestry and fire laws are provided, and there is, of course, an index showing cities, towns, and places of interest and their locations on the map.

Ski Touring Trails & Centers

Rhode Island trails in the forest management areas and parks offer opportunities for cross-country skiing and snowshoeing. For information on ski areas, there are two informative brochures available. *Winter in Rhode Island* is available free from: Dept. of Economic Development, 1 Weybosset Hill, Providence 02903, and *Where to Ski*, is obtainable at no charge from: Auto & Travel Club, National Headquarters, 888 Worcester St., Wellesley, MA 02181. Major Rhode Island ski areas offering instruction are Diamond Hill, Highway 114, Cumberland 02864, (401) 333-5400; *Pinetop*, off 1-95; Escoheag 02821, (401) 397-5656; *Ski Valley*, Highway 121, Cumberland 02864, (401) 333-6406; *Yawgoo Valley*, off Highway 2, Slocum 02877, (401) 295-5366. Call or write for further information on rates and type of trails. Those who are interested in snowmobiling should consult *Rhode Island's New Snowmobile and Recreational Vehicle Law*, a free pamphlet available from: Dept. of Natural Resources, Veterans Memorial Bldg., Providence 02903, which includes a list of areas where snowmobiling is permitted (only on designated trails).

VERMONT ENCYCLOPEDIA

Accommodations— Vacation Lodges & Resorts

The State of Vermont offers the outdoorsperson a great variety of accommodations, including hotels and motels, resorts, lodges, and all varieties of camping facilities. Prices vary according to the standard of luxury and extent of services offered. There are many helpful booklets that may be obtained free that will help you decide where to stay. The *Vermont Visitor's Handbook* (published yearly) is a handy 112-page pocket-sized guide containing a listing and complete descriptions of lodging, eating places, shops, and other attractions, conveniently broken down by region. You can get one free by writing to: Vermont Development Agency, Montpelier 05602. A similar booklet is *Vermont's Gazetteer,* which also lists lodgings, restaurants, cottages, ski areas, vacation and retirement homes, camping areas, and other attractions of interest by region. It may be obtained free by writing to: Vermont State Chamber of Commerce, Box 37, Montpelier 05602. For those who plan a more extended stay, *Vermont Four-Season Vacation Rentals* will be invaluable. This little booklet contains paid listings supplied by private individuals for housekeeping cottages, chalets, camps, and private homes for rent through the seasons. To order this free publication, write to: Agency of Development & Community Affairs, Montpelier 05602.

For more information on specific areas in Vermont, visit one of the many information booths located throughout the state or contact the appropriate local Chamber of Commerce.

For listings of many of the state's major vacation lodges and resorts, see the "Vermont Travel & Recreation Guide" section.

Appalachian National Scenic Trail

The Vermont section of this famous trail winds for 134 miles through scenic mixed hardwood and evergreen forests, rolling hills, valleys, meadows, and mountains, from Hanover, New Hampshire, through the scenic highlands and backcountry of the Green Mountain National Forest to the Massachusetts border. The last 95-mile stretch from Sherburne Pass follows south along the famous Long Trail segment, which is maintained by the Green Mountain Club.

The bible for hikers wishing to explore this scenic route is the Appalachian Trail Conference's *Guide to the Appalachian Trail in New Hampshire and Vermont* (publication #22). The format of the book is such that it may be conveniently taken apart so that you need only take with you the section pertaining to the part of the trail you are traveling. The book is packed with essential general information such as trail markings, trail allocations and maintenance, trail precautions, and a section on the equipment you will need. There is a section on the history of the trail, a list of individual trail sections, and a helpful treatise on accommodations along the trail. The chapter on "The Long Trail in Vermont" is broken down into five detailed sections, as are the other portions of the trail. You can send $6.60 for this book to: Appalachian Trail Conference, P.O. Box 236, Harpers Ferry, WV 25425. The *Dartmouth Outing Club Trail Guide* ($2.25, 110 pp., maps) provides a guide to trails in eastern Vermont, the Dartmouth region, and between Hanover, New Hampshire, and Mount Moosilauke. Write: Dartmouth Outing Club, Dartmouth College, Hanover, NH 03755.

The free pamphlet *Day Hiking in Vermont* also contains descriptions of some favorite summer and early fall hikes along the Vermont portions of the trail complete with times allotted for actual hiking.

This publication is available free from: Green Mountain Club, Box 94, Rutland 05701.

The Appalachian Trail is shown on the following large-scale U.S. Geological Survey Maps: Bennington, Delectable Mountain, Hanover (NH), Killington Park, Londonderry, Manchester, Pico Peak, Pownal, Quechee, Sunderland, Wallingford, Woodford, Woodstock N.

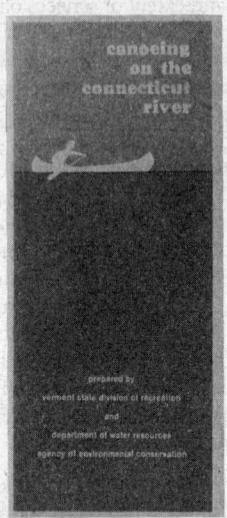

Camping & Backpacking

Excellent, well-maintained camping facilities are available throughout Vermont in state forest and park recreation areas and in the Green Mountain National Forest. The Department of Forests & Parks operates 36 campgrounds with 2,100 campsites. The campgrounds open officially the Friday preceding Memorial Day and close October 12. There are youth group camping areas at Kettle Pond in the Groton State Forest and at the Underhill Recreation Area in the Mount Mansfield State Forest on the western slope of Mount Mansfield. Special areas in the Groton and Coolidge state forests have been designated as primitive campsites accessible only by foot trails. Some of the campgrounds have Green Mountain lean-tos, which are roofed shelters closed on three sides and fully open on the fourth. They have a 10 × 13-foot wooden floor about 15 inches above the ground and will accommodate up to 5 persons. Detailed information about family camping, registration, time limits, campsite occupancy, pets, reserva-

tions, fees, regulations, youth group camping, primitive camping, and day use is contained in the *Vermont Guide to State Parks & Forest Recreation Areas*, available free from: Dept. of Forests & Parks, Montpelier 05602. The guide also contains a useful directory of state parks and forest recreation areas. *Day Hiking in Vermont*, a free guide published by the Green Mountain Club, Box 94, Rutland 05701, provides useful information on the Long Trail.

A useful *Map and Guide of Vermont Private Campgrounds* is available free from: Vermont Assn. of Private Campground Owners and Operators, Rd. #2, Box 113A, Bristol, 05443. The map-guide describes some 60 campgrounds, with a chart detailing the services offered at each.

Several useful publications are available from the Green Mountain Club (address above). A *Trail Map of the Mount Mansfield Region* is available for 50¢. The following GMC booklets describing trails and mountains outside the Long Trail system are available for 25¢ each, or 5 for $1: *Guide to the Lake Willoughby Area; Guide to Mount Cushman & Scraz Mountain; Guide to the Worcester Mountains; Guide to the Essex County Fire Tower Trails.*

Anyone planning a trek in the Vermont highlands should consult the information guide *Fifty Hikes in Vermont—Walks, Day Hikes, and Backpacking Trips in the Green Mountain State,* by Ruth and Paul Sadler, available for $5.85 from: New Hampshire Publishing Co., 15 Interstate Dr., Somersworth, NH 03878. A *Guide to the Trails of Ascutney Mountain* is available for $1.25 from: Ascutney Trails Assn., RFD 1, Windsor 05089. *New England Trails* ($1.00), issued annually by: New England Trail Conference, Box 145, Weston 05161, contains detailed reports of current trail conditions and shelters throughout New England. The conference also publishes the *Hiking Trails of New England Map* (50¢). (See also "Appalachian National Scenic Trail," the "Long Trail," and the "Travel & Recreation Guide" section.)

Canoe Trails & Outfitters

Vermont has several excellent canoe routes that provide white-water paddling, fishing, and backcountry camping opportunities. It should be noted, however, that low water flow during the summer months limits canoeing possibilities. Rivers and streams that were at full flow a few weeks earlier are often nothing more than a trickle during July and August, requiring the canoeist to walk his canoe through shallow stretches. The old Indian water trail formed by the Connecticut River, which forms the boundary between Vermont and New Hampshire, is the state's premier canoe route. Known to the Indians as *Quinatucquet* ("long estuary"), the Connecticut flows for 234 miles from its headwaters in New Hampshire's First Connecticut Lake near the Quebec border southward through scenic north woods country and many rapids and over several dams to the Massachusetts border. It offers varied "big-lake" canoeing and river paddling with a few unrunnable sections; 15 dams along the route require carries of varying lengths. The New England Power Company maintains canoe campsites along the Connecticut at Wilder, Bellows Falls, and Vernon ponds. For detailed information, contact: New England Power Co., 20 Turnpike Rd., Westborough, MA 01581.

Extended backcountry canoe trips may also be taken on Otter Creek, the longest river within the state, which rises in the town of Dorset and flows 90 miles northward into Lake Champlain; on the Winooski River from Middlesex through the great valley of the Winooski, where it cuts through the main range of the Green Mountains reaching depths of 4,000 feet, to Lake Champlain; the beautiful Lamoille River from Johnson to Lake Champlain; the Missisquoi (Indian for "much waterfowl and grass") from Richford to Lake Champlain; the White

River from Bethel to its junction with the Connecticut; and the West River from Townshend to the Connecticut. Many other streams mentioned in the *AMC River Guide: Volume II* (address below) and shown on the free Vermont Guide to Fishing Map provide 1- or 2-day trips. "Big-water" canoeing may be found on Lake Champlain, Lake Memphremagog, Lake Willoughby—which lies on a V-shaped trough formed by the downfaulting of a block of the earth's crust between Mounts Pisgah and Hor in the Northeast Kingdom—and on Lake Bomoseen, the largest natural body of water entirely within the state, with an area of 8 square miles.

The *Ledyard Canoe Club of Dartmouth,* Robison Hall, Hinman Box 6171, Hanover, NH 03755, offers canoe and kayak rentals for the Connecticut River (phone: 603-646-2753). Canoe trip information and rentals are provided by *Stowe Canoe Co.,* Rte. 100, Stowe 05672. Canoe rentals in the state are provided by *Burlington Rent-All,* 340 Dorset St., South Burlington 05401; *Canoe Imports,* 74 S. Willard St., Burlington 05401 (available for rent by the day, week, or month); *Chipman Point Marina & Campgrounds,* Chipman Point, Orwell 05760 (Lake Champlain, available by the day, week, month, or season); *Eddy's Marine and Sports Center,* Rte. 7 S., Brandon 05733 (day or week); *Sailing Winds,* Box 93, Wells 05774 (rent by day, week, or month); *Sports Shops,* 139 Lake St., St. Albans 05478 (day or week); *Tudhope Marine Co.,* Rte. 2, North Hero 05474 (day, week, month, or season); and *Waterhouses,* RFD, Salisbury 05769 (day, week, month, or season).

The handy brochure *Vermont Boating Guide* is a necessity for anyone planning to do any boating in Vermont. It provides essential information on canoe trips and fishing access areas. There is plenty of info on historic Lake Champlain, including a listing of marinas on the lake and the services offered by each, and sources of rentals of boating equipment, lodging and camping areas with boating facilities available only to guests, as well as other facilities with available boat rentals on Lake Champlain and elsewhere. This brochure can be obtained free from: Agency of Development & Community Affairs, Montpelier 05602. A very helpful booklet available at no charge from the Division of Recreation & Department of Water Resources, Agency of Environmental Conservation, Montpelier 05602, is *Canoeing on the Connecticut River.* This booklet contains info on everything you will need to know before starting your trip on this river—water conditions, camping, fishing, dams, and falls. The various stretches of the river are described, section by section, and for the convenience of the reader a map is provided on the page facing each section's description. The most comprehensive guide is the *AMC River Guide: Volume II Central & Southern New England.* This all-inclusive guide to the canoeable waterways of New England is published by: Appalachian Mountain Club, 5 Joy St., Boston, MA 02108 ($6.00). (For additional information see "Wild and Scenic Waters Maps.")

Fishing & Hunting in the Green Mountain State

Within Vermont's rugged borders is some of New England's most enjoyable fishing and hunting in surroundings famous for mountainous beauty. The lofty ridges of the Green Mountains form the spine of the state, running from the Massachusetts border north to Quebec, and contain scores of wilderness brook trout waters. Vermont also boasts one of the densest deer herds per square mile in America. Most of Vermont's western border lies on the great bass, pike, and walleye waters of sprawling Lake Champlain, while the east is bounded by the productive Connecticut River. The wild Northeast Kingdom occupies the corner at the top of the state where Vermont, New Hampshire,

and Quebec meet; it encompasses a large, unspoiled land of trout streams, beaver dams, salmon lakes, glacial bogs, and profuse wildlife. Rumors persist that remnants of the once plentiful mountain lion and wolf populations still exist in the vastnesses of this largely roadless area. Whether or not the region harbors these feared predators, it does shelter deer, bear, moose, and native trout, and marten, fisher, and Canada lynx prowl the thick forest of maple, birch, beech, spruce, fir, and tamarack (eastern larch) in search of prey.

The state has substantial amounts of public fishing and hunting land, considering its size. Occupying much of southern and central Vermont is the 240,000-acre Green Mountain National Forest. In addition, there are thousands of supplemental acres in state forests and parks, public hunting areas, wildlife management areas, and private tracts where the public is allowed, or where permission can be secured with a polite request. Prospecting with maps, especially the U.S. Geological Survey Topographic Maps, will allow the venturesome angler to hit the jackpot, because Vermont has many wilderness trout ponds, spring-fed, remote beaver ponds, and high country streams where excellent trout fishing can still be found if some boot leather is used.

Vermont's extensive fishing waters furnish a great variety of opportunities to suit every taste, as illustrated by these state records compiled by the Fish & Game Department.

VERMONT RECORD FISH

	Lb.-oz.	Place	Year
Brook trout	5–12	Paran Creek	1977
Brown trout	11–12	Little River	1974
Rainbow trout	12–½	Lake Dunmore	1975
Lake trout	27–8	Little Averill Lake	1971
Landlocked salmon	7–12	Lake Champlain	1977
Smallmouth bass	6–7	Harriman Reservoir	1969
Largemouth bass	8	Connecticut River	1977
Muskellunge	23–8	Missisquoi River	1970
Northern pike	30	Glen Lake	1977
Chain pickerel	6–4	Harriman Reservoir	1974
Walleye	12–6	Lake Memphremagog	1972
Yellow perch	1–5	Lake Hortonia	1975
Black crappie	1–2	Lake Bomoseen	1971
Smelt	0–11	Lake Champlain	1972
Mooneye	1–7	Lake Champlain	1971
Bullhead	1–8	Lake Hortonia	1969
Channel catfish	32–4	Lake Champlain	1974
Sheepshead	19	Lake Champlain	1974
Carp	29–4	Lake Champlain	1975
Bowfin	14–8	Missisquoi River	1977
Gar	5–4	Lake Champlain	1975
American eel	3–7½	Lake Champlain	1972

Most of the stream systems in Vermont flow east to the Connecticut River or west to Lake Champlain or New York State from the highlands of the central mountain backbone. The Green Mountains are the severely eroded stumps of an ancient range of towering peaks. Aeons of geological change drowned them in ancient seas, warped them through massive crustal upheavals, and ground the summits by the awesome force of the glaciers. Many of the streams are freestone,

while others, flowing through a watershed of marble and limestone, are alkaline, such as the beautiful Green River in the southern border area, an exquisite emerald-shaded trout creek flowing to the Connecticut River at Greenfield, Massachusetts.

Quality Trout Waters

Among Vermont's classic trout waters is the fabled Batten Kill in the southwestern part of the state which flows west to the Hudson River in New York State through Manchester, appropriately, home of the famous Orvis fly fishing tackle house. The upper reaches of the river lie in the shadow of Bromley Mountain, and, along with tributaries such as Roaring Brook, West Branch, and the Upper Green, provide brook and brown trout fishing. Browns, however, give the Batten Kill its mystique. The big river flows through a picturesque farmland valley surrounded by steep Green Mountain slopes and foothills. Swift runs are interspersed by deep, tree-shaded pools, and there are some covered bridges to complement the atmosphere. A majority of the trout that rise to the fly, spinner, or bait are small, many of which have been stocked. But beneath the snags and ledges lie those big, butter-sided cannibal browns of which fishermen's dreams are made. In the early season, spin-and-bait fishermen rule the stream, when the spring runoff swells and clouds the flow. As the level drops and the temperature rises, the fly caster comes into his own. The spring hatches bring dedicated anglers to the Batten Kill in hopes of tempting one of those 2-footers into an error of judgment. As summer progresses, terrestrials, midges, and spiders are preferred, and adventuresome anglers go astream at night with large, dark wet flies and take some trophy browns. Fall on the Batten Kill finds the fish on the move once again, and some of the most delightful fishing of the season is enjoyed as the hardwoods flame on the mountains.

Near the headwaters of the Batten Kill are the sources of two other great trout rivers, the Mettawee and the Otter. The Mettawee rises in the shadow of Dorset Peak and courses through a tight valley into New York and the Champlain-Hudson Canal. All three stream trout are found in the Mettawee, with rainbows very abundant near the state border. This river does not get as severe pressure as the Batten Kill and it, too, holds some large buckskin-flanked, hook-jawed browns. The Otter flows north through a long shallow valley, past Rutland and across the Champlain flatlands to the lake, and is the longest internal watershed in Vermont. The upper section runs through a series of headwater beaver flows and bogs and holds some large squaretails and rainbows. The feeder brooks and headwater ponds offer good fishing,

including Griffith Lake and its outlet, Big Branch, Little Rock Pond, and Clarendon and Cold rivers, all between Dorset, Wallingford, and Rutland. From Rutland downstream, bass, perch, and northern pike predominate, but again, some of the feeders have excellent trout fishing, such as Furnace Brook, Neshobe, Middlebury, and New Haven rivers, located between Rutland and Middlebury and spilling from the Green Mountains. Route 7 parallels the Otter for its entire length to Vergennes, where it flows into Lake Champlain north of Basin Harbor.

Below the Batten Kill is the productive Walloomsac, which flows through Bennington on Route 9. Along with its tributaries, Jewett Brook, South Stream, Furnace Brook, and the Sucker Pond Branch, the Walloomsac offers some excellent fishing for brookies, browns, and rainbows. The North and East branches of the Deerfield River have trout fishing and flow into Harriman Reservoir at Whitingham, which contains lakers, browns, rainbows, smallmouth bass (the state record 6 pounds 7 ounces), and pickerel. The Main Deerfield spills from the dam and enters Massachusetts through Sherman Reservoir, a good brown trout lake. Somerset Reservoir at the top of the East Branch is a good smallmouth bass impoundment.

Several lakes adjacent the Otter Creek flowage deserve mention. Lake St. Catharine, a Mettawee tributary on Route 149 at Wells, is noted for lake trout, northern pike, rainbows, both kinds of bass, and panfish. Lake Bomoseen, a tributary lake of the Carleton River at the town of Bomoseen, is an excellent northern pike lake, and holds rainbows, bass, and panfish. The Carleton is a fine trout stream, flowing south and then west along Route 4 to the New York border at Fair Haven. Browns are the major species, and there are some big ones, as well as brookies. Lake Hortonia to the north of Bomoseen is a great panfish producer and has bass and pike too.

Chittenden Reservoir at Chittenden in the Green Mountain National Forest to the west of the Long Trail, supplies fine trout fishing as do its feeders and adjacent ponds.

The extensive Winooski River watershed drains a large area of the Green Mountains in central and north central Vermont, and many of its tributaries, deep in the interior, are productive and scenic trout waters. The Winooski flows southwest from Molly Falls Reservoir on Route 2 at Marshfield and west from Montpelier along Interstate 89 to Burlington and Winooski where it spills into Lake Champlain. The big river has fishing for browns and rainbows all the way to Champlain, some of it excellent, particularly at stream mouths. The lower end of the Winooski contains bass and walleye and has a spring run of rainbows out of Lake Champlain. A tributary pond, Shelburne, south of Burlington, is top-rated for bass, pike, walleye, and panfish. Famous tributaries include the Mad and Dog rivers, which flow north to I-89 in and near Montpelier through scenic mountain valleys and offer good stream fishing for browns and rainbows with brookies found in the headwaters; North Branch, which flows south to Montpelier along Route 12; the Kingsbury Branch coursing south to Route 2 at Plainfield; and the Stevens and Jail branches south of Barre, all of which provide fine fishing for the three kinds of trout. Jail Branch yielded the state record brook trout and is considered an excellent brown trout stream.

The famous Lamoille River, like its neighbor to the south, the Winooski, rises deep in the mountains on the eastern side of the state and runs west to Champlain. Rising in Horse Pond above Greensboro Bend on Route 16 in north central Vermont, the Lamoille flows south to Route 15, picking up Caspian Lake's outlet. Caspian produces fine lake trout and landlocked salmon fishing. This upper stretch of river holds all three species of trout with brookies especially plentiful toward Horse Pond. From Hardwick on Route 15 the river heads west along

Routes 15, 104, and secondary roads to Milton, where it merges into Lake Champlain. The middle stretch has browns and rainbows, and toward Jeffersonville, walleyes, northern pike, and panfish. The state record muskellunge came from the western end of the river. Some of the tributaries are popular trout streams, including the Trout River and its two branches West Hill Brook and South Branch, the productive Tyler Branch flowing north along 108 to the Missisquoi near Enosburg Falls and Black Creek, meeting the Missisquoi a few miles west at Sheldon Junction. Lake Carmi, a few miles north of Enosburg Falls at East Franklin, contains big populations of smallmouths, pike, and panfish.

Lake Champlain

The sinuous 130-mile length of Lake Champlain forms the northern two-thirds of Vermont's border with New York. This magnificent inland sea ranks with any eastern lake in the beauty of its irregular, cove-filled shoreline, with mountains framing the background of both shores, the rocky, spruce-clad islands dotting the wide northern end, and the variety and productivity of its vast expanse of water. The shallow, weedy waters of the narrow southern end offer light tackle action for largemouth bass, northern pike, pickerel, walleye, and panfish from Whitehall, New York, north past the historic narrows of Fort Ticonderoga and Crown Point, Chimney Point, Basin Harbor, and the mouth of the Otter River and into the broad, deep upper segment of Lake Champlain. As one heads up the lake, smallmouth bass and walleye become more numerous, and lakers, ciscoes, and whitefish appear in the deep, cold waters off Burlington and up along the shores of Vermont's scenic Grand Isle. The mooneye, *Hiodon tergisus*, is a small herringlike fish which reaches about 2 pounds in weight and provides great sport on light tackle such as flies and small lures. These lightweight scrappers are abundant off Chimney Point. Occasional muskellunge, landlocked salmon, and big rainbow trout are taken from the lake by fortunate anglers. The incredible variety of species also includes smelt, sturgeon, channel catfish, assorted common panfish, barbot (freshwater cod), sheepshead, carp, bowfin, gar, eels, and suckers. Lake Champlain holds more state fish records than any other body of water in Vermont. Ice fishing is tremendously popular, and hardy winter anglers erect shanty cities on Champlain ice and take long strings of perch, walleye, smelt, barbot, whitefish, crappie, northern pike, and pickerel, as well as lake, brown, and rainbow trout.

Northeast Kingdom Trophy Waters

Lying astride the center of the border with Quebec is elongated Lake Memphremagog, most of which is in Canada. The fishing is centered at the town of Newport, through which the waters of the Clyde, Barton, and Black rivers feed into the lake. Landlocked salmon, rainbows, browns, walleyes, smallmouths, smelt, and panfish are the major species, and there are some real trophies in this lengthy body of water. Spring trolling draws big numbers of anglers who use long streamers to take large trout and landlocks. The Clyde River is famous for a run of sleek landlocks which pursue smelts in the early spring, and for a run of spawning walleyes in May. In the summer, after the trout and salmon have retreated into deep water, smallmouths furnish surface action for bait casters and bass bug enthusiasts. The Clyde watershed parallels Routes 5-A and 105 and offers a variety of fishing opportunities. Spectacle Pond, near Island Pond, at the top of the river, has salmon, lake trout, and bass. Pherrins River on Route 114 drains into the Clyde at Island Pond on Route 105 and holds brook trout. In the headwaters area of Pherrins is Norton Pond, a tributary lake of the Coaticook River which flows into Quebec. Norton, located on Route 114, is an excellent rainbow, brown, and brook trout lake, as is the short stretch of the Coaticook in Vermont. The Clyde broadens below the Pherrins River mouth and contains the three trout species, some of which run to size. The outlet of Seymour and Echo lakes enters the Clyde at East Charleston on Route 105, and these bodies of water are well-regarded salmon, lake trout, and smallmouth lakes. The river from the Echo outlet downstream holds some lunker browns. South of West Charleston, the Clyde flows into Lake Salem, which has a reputation for big landlocks and contains lake trout, smallmouths, and walleyes. The lower Clyde near Newport is mainly bass and walleye water, but some big browns, rainbows, and salmon are taken in the deep pools.

The Barton River, which runs beside Route 5 into Newport, is a great rainbow trout river, and also provides squaretails and browns. Parker Lake and Crystal Lake in its upper reaches produce excellent rainbow trout catches, but the star attractions are the Willoughby River and Lake, which enter the Barton about halfway to Newport at Orleans on Route 5. Lake Willoughby provides some of the best salmon, lake trout (to 20 pounds), and rainbow fishing in Vermont. The river, however, stages a spectacular wildlife display each spring when big metallic-flanked rainbows migrate out of Memphremagog up the Barton and into the Willoughby. Natural falls at Orleans force the big lake-run 'bows to leap the Whitewater Chute on their way to the spawning beds upstream, and people come from many miles around to see the trout, up to weights of 10 pounds, arching into the air over the spume. It follows that the banks are lined with less altruistic anglers, who assault the trophies with spawn sacks, spinners, wobblers, night crawlers, and flies. The scene is similar to the fireworks at Catherine's Creek, a tributary of the New York State Finger Lakes' big Seneca Lake. The third Memphremagog feeder, the Black, runs beside Routes 14 and 5, and while it does not provide the level of fishing found in the Clyde and Barton, it is a fine stream and contains some lunker browns and rainbows.

East of Memphremagog and south to the St. Johnsbury area lie the magnificent forests, monadnocks, ridges, swamps, beaver flowages, streams, and remote trout ponds of the Northeast Kingdom; bordered roughly by the Connecticut River on the east and Routes 5 and 5-A on the west, the tract contains all of Essex County. Although this gloriously wild expanse is not lake country, three of Vermont's best coldwater expanses are in the region: Great Averill, Little Averill, and Maidstone lakes. Great Averill and Little Averill are located on Route 114 a few miles from the Quebec border. These lakes have drawn several generations of anglers to troll streamers and lures for salmon, lake trout, rainbows, and brook trout at ice-out and are typically clear, deep north woods waters bordered by spruce, fir, pine, white birch, and maple. Maidstone is about forty miles to the south, off Route 102 a few miles west of the Connecticut River, and contains the same fish mixture with an emphasis on rainbows.

The Nulhegan River with its East, Black, Yellow, and North branches, rises just south of Island Pond on Route 105 and drains a primarily roadless section of the upper Northeast Kingdom. Brook trout are the dominant species in this clean, wilderness watershed until the stream approaches the Connecticut, where browns inhabit the lower stretches. Paul Stream, which receives Maidstone's outlet, is another excellent brook trout drainage and has some browns and rainbows near the confluence with the Connecticut. The Passumpsic River system tops a large part of the central and southern part of the Northeast Kingdom and lies south of Island Pond, Lake Willoughby, and Crystal Lake. The main stem flows along Routes 5 and 5-A. The upper feeders, Miller Run, Calendar Brook, Sutton River, West Branch, and East Branch, are all excellent brook trout streams, which hold browns and rainbows in the downstream areas. The Moose River tributary strikes deep into south and central portions of the Northeast Kingdom

through the wild tangles of Victory Bog. Squaretails and brownies inhabit the dark pools and eddies of this fine stream. Joe's Pond and Brook and Water Andric Brook flow to the Passumpsic, south of St. Johnsbury, and are productive trout waters. The Wells and Wait rivers enter the Connecticut at the towns of Wells River and Bradford, respectively, on Route 5 to the south of St. Johnsbury. Both stream systems have above-average fishing for the three major trout species and flow through green, wooded mountain valleys. The Wells is further distinguished by a feeder lake with the intriguing name of Ticklenaked Pond, which must have quite a tale to tell. A short drive to the south on Route 5 at Pompanoosuc is the Ompompanoosuc River, a scenic trout Connecticut tributary in the green rolling ridges just north of the Appalachian Trail.

White River Country

Several miles to the south at White River Junction is one of New England's classic trout streams, the brawling, rapid-strewn White River, which reaches deep into the heart of the Green Mountain National Forest and extends more than halfway across the state. The White and its vast tributary system race down out of the mountains through narrow forested valleys. Clear, swift water and a bed of white sand, gravel, cobblestones, and glacial boulders contribute to the visual pleasure of this picture-book stream. Deep, glassy pools, shaded runs, riffles, and waterfalls provide ample shelter for the hefty rainbows and browns which give the White its deserved reputation. Its tributaries, First, Second, Third, and West branches, Ayres, Brandon, Stony, Gilead, and Locust brooks, and the Tweed River, produce fine trout fishing and offer squaretails in the headwaters. Interstate 89 runs along the lower river and secondary roads give access to the upper river and feeders. Although the White is hard fished, the trophy trout are there, and they are wary! Canoeists rank the river among the best trips in New England, but with its falls, chutes, and rips it requires care, and during low-water periods it is a hull grinder. The area above White River Junction is a hot spot for big walleyes and acrobatic river smallmouths. Other major trout streams below the White, flowing to the Connecticut River, are the Ottauquechee with its spectacular gorge, the Black at Springfield, the Williams at Rockingham, Saxtons River at Bellows Falls, and the sprawling West River watershed. Route 100 runs across the upper sections of these rivers in or adjacent to the Green Mountain National Forest. These streams all contain some big trout, primarily rainbows and browns, and draw lunkers out of the Connecticut into cool tributaries where smallmouth bass appear. This portion holds some large browns and rainbows in the forested pools and deep, swift runs, particularly where streams feed in. Tributaries, such as Elmore and Wild branches and the Green, Gihon, Brewster, North Branch, and Seymour rivers, all on Route 15, have good trout fishing. The lower end of the Lamoille is primarily warmwater angling for bass, pike, walleye, pickerel, and panfish. The river is considered one of the East's great rainbow trout streams and flows through some of Vermont's outstanding mountain country.

The meandering Missisquoi River watershed lies a few miles north, and the stream begins life as a brook trout feeder near the Long Trail and Belvidere Mountain, to the south of Lowell. As the Missisquoi flows through its verdant mountain valley, it passes Sugarloaf and Jay Peak. Brown trout gradually replace squaretails as the river approaches Quebec, and the wooded pools and runs shelter some trophy fish, especially in the area of Big Falls north to the Quebec line at North Troy. The river returns to Vermont at East Richford and rambles west to Missisquoi Bay north of Swanton near the Canadian border. From East Richford downstream, warmwater fish gradually take over the water and offer excellent fishing for smallmouths, during the summer heat.

The Connecticut River is a productive brown and rainbow fishery from the Quebec border to the Bloomfield area. Below this point the great river provides some of the best smallmouth, walleye, and northern pike fishing in the East, and some heavy trout are present, particularly around the mouths of the rivers described above. Efforts are being made in conjunction with other Connecticut River Valley states to reestablish the Atlantic salmon in what was once its most prolific river. Streams such as the White are being used in this exciting project.

Fishing & Hunting Guides

For details about conservation efforts, useful fishing information, and area reports, write to: Fish & Game Dept., 5 Court St., Montpelier 05602, for the free booklet *Vermont's Fisheries Annual*. The following fishing and hunting publications may be obtained free upon request from the department: *Digest of Fish & Game Laws and Regulations; Vermont Guide to Fishing,* which contains a Fishing Map of Vermont and describes principal game-fish species, streams, lakes, ponds, and major information sources of interest to the outdoors enthusiast; *Vermont Guide to Hunting,* which includes deer and bear maps, descriptions of principal game species, and tips about planning a hunt, camping, and information sources; and *Vermont Hunting Season Camping List,* which describes and lists sites open for camping through the end of the deer season.

The informative, large-format 202-page guide, *Trout and Salmon Fishing in New England Lakes and Ponds* ($8 postpaid), contains detailed descriptions and lake survey maps of Crystal, Willoughby, Great Averill, Little Averill, Seymour, and Echo lakes. It may be ordered from: Partridge Press, Box 422, Campton, NH 03223.

Hunting & Wildlife

Vermont's mountain spine, rolling foothills, lake plains, and northern highlands provide food and shelter for many popular game species, including deer, bear, wild turkey, ruffed grouse, woodcock, pheasant, chukar, waterfowl, cottontail and snowshoe rabbits, squirrels, and assorted small animals.

Whitetail deer are so solidly entrenched in Vermont that many areas have too many animals for the available forage. Depending upon the severity of winter and cyclical factors, the deer herd exceeds 150,000 animals in years of peak abundance, which makes the state's relatively small area one of the nation's most productive regions in terms of deer per square mile. Deer kills are generally heaviest in the foothills of the Green Mountains, where the animals find the mixture of forest and farmland that provides optimum food and shelter. The most prolific hunting area is usually the belt of land between the Connecticut River and the Green Mountain spine from the Massachusetts border north to the St. Johnsbury area. The northeastern third of the state, encompassing the Northeast Kingdom, has a modest deer kill because of habitat and relatively light hunting pressure, but there are some trophy heads for those willing to hunt the wild country. The western foothills from the Massachusetts border north through the Batten Kill and upper Otter River watersheds is the second-best area in Vermont. The lake plains and territory north to the Quebec border between Lakes Memphremagog and Champlain produce modest hunter success, with a few local exceptions, but, again, the largest deer and racks are here for the hard-working rifleman. Vermont offers the deer hunter a magic combination of abundant animals and scenery to delight the heart of a landscape artist.

Bear populations are heaviest in the remote wilderness areas of the Green Mountains, and the northern highlands, including the Northeast Kingdom, which is the best bear range in Vermont.

The wily, bronze-tinted wild turkey has been successfully reestablished

in Vermont and is being spread throughout suitable habitat. Wild birds are trapped in areas of concentrated flocks and relocated. The eastern and western foothills, particularly the latter, contain the great majority of the prime cover.

The ruffed grouse is by far the most popular and numerous game bird in Vermont, and much of the state is good grouse cover. Pa'tridge, as they are called, are plentiful throughout most of the Green Mountain National Forest with the exception of high-altitude areas and deep, heavy evergreen forest patches. Grouse prefer hardwood ridges, forest/field margins, abandoned farms, old orchards, and second-growth alder thickets, stream bottoms, and stone fences. In such places they can find the seeds, buds, fruits, insects, and wild grape and thornapple tangles which provide their diet. The abandonment of subsistence farmlands has had the same beneficial effect on grouse that it has had on the turkey population. Almost all the public hunting land offers grouse hunting.

Woodcock, too, are plentiful and Vermont has a deserved reputation for productive timberdoodle cover. Woodcock prefer many of the same covers as grouse, with a bias toward damp areas where they can probe for their favorite delicacy, the earthworm. The best woodcock hunting is in southern and central Vermont, where a combination of premium terrain and migratory patterns produces the most birds, although plenty of woodcock are shot in the north. A good dog is a great asset for both partridge and woodcock, because both birds tend to flush wild as the season progresses. Many Vermont shotgunners have experienced the thrill of taking a mixed double in a sun-dappled thicket with the birches and maples flaming forth their warning of approaching winter.

Pheasant, quail, and chukar are listed in the game laws, but are marginal species at best.

The state has some good duck hunting areas, most notably the marshes and shoreline of Lake Champlain, Lake Memphremagog, the lower Connecticut River, and the larger lakes. Lake Champlain is by far the best area, and almost all of the geese killed are shot along its coastline.

Along Vermont's western border are seven waterfowl management areas, one state refuge and goose management area, Dead Creek Refuge and Management Area in the towns of Addison, Panton, and Bridgeport, and one national wildlife refuge, the Missisquoi at Missisquoi Bog, Swanton, in northwest Vermont. The Missiquoi refuge is a major nesting area for waterfowl, great blue heron, marsh hawks, peregrine falcons, and a few bald eagles. Waterfowl management areas such as Mud Creek at Alburg, Grand Isle County in Lake Champlain, Maquam at Swanton in Franklin County, and East Creek at Orwell and Benson, in Rutland and Addison counties are popular hunting spots.

The principal species shot are black ducks, mallards, teal, woodduck, goldeneye, scaup, and Canada goose.

Write to the Fish & Game Department for the free *Vermont's Game Annual* booklet, which provides plenty of information of interest and use to the hunter.

Highways—Recreation & Green Mountain Scenic Routes

Vermont's 2,294 miles of state highways wind through some of the most scenic highlands, valleys, evergreen forest and lake country, woodlands and farmlands in New England. The complete guide to the state's highway and road system is the *Vermont Official Transportation Map*, available free from: Dept. of Highways, Agency of Development & Community Affairs, Montpelier 05602. This attractive full-color map shows all highways and roads, interstate highways, historic sites, towns, museums, state parks and forests, wildlife management areas, campgrounds, state recreation areas, and natural features, including lakes, streams, and mountains.

Long Trail

The Long Trail is a scenic "wilderness" footpath that winds through beautiful high country forests of evergreens and mixed hardwoods

along the crest of the Green Mountains for 262 miles from the Massachusetts boundary north to the Quebec border. The trail passes close to 400 high country lakes and countless beaver ponds, many of which offer superb fishing for native brook trout, bass, and some arm-length chain pickerel. Nearly 100 approach and side trails supplement the Long Trail, creating a trail system of over 435 miles. This system traverses public lands, both state and federal, and also makes extensive use of private lands, thanks to cooperating landowners. Hikers can show their appreciation to all landowners by treating their property as carefully as they would their own.

The major features of the trail as it winds north from Shelburne Pass include Gifford Woods State Park, Deer Leap Trail, Willard Gap, South Pond Trail, Mount Carmel, Bloodroot Mountain, Farr Peak, Chittenden Brook Trail, Brandon Cooley Glen, Battel Trail, Monroe Skyline Area, Camels Hump, Mount Mansfield, Nebraska Notch, Cave of Winds, Lake of Clouds, Sterling Pond, Beaver Meadow, Whiteface Trail, French Camp, Ritterbush Pond, Hazan's Notch, Atlas Valley, Jay Peak, and Journey's End Trail.

Indispensable for Long Trail hikers is the 152-page *Guidebook of the Long Trail* ($3), available from: Green Mountain Club, P.O. Box 94, Rutland 05701. The GMC also publishes the following free leaflets: *Suggestions for Use of the Long Trail by Backpacking Groups* and *Suggestions for Use of the Long Trail in Winter*. The Appalachian Trail Conference's *Guide to the Appalachian Trail in New Hampshire and Vermont* (publication #22) also has an entire section devoted to the Long Trail. This guide may be ordered for $6.60 from: ATC, P.O. Box 236, Harpers Ferry, WV 25425.

The Long Trail is shown on the following large-scale U.S. Geological Survey Topographic Maps: Bolton Mountain, Bread Loaf, Chittenden, Huntington, Hyde Park, Jay Peak, Lincoln, Mount Carmel, Mount Ellen, Mount Mansfield.

Orvis Fly Fishing Schools

The manufacturers of the world-famous Orvis fly fishing gear conduct an intensive 3-day fly fishing school from April through August of each year on stocked trout ponds at the firm's Manchester national head-

quarters. The 3-day sessions include meals; a pleasant room at a mountain lodge; casting lessons and practice at the Orvis trout ponds with an expert instructor; illustrated lectures on fly selection and stream entomology; knot-tying instruction; lectures and demonstrations of rods, lines, and leaders; and a 3-day Vermont fishing license to fish the evening rises on the nearby Batten Kill. Fly casting instruction includes emphasis on the role of the rod hand, overhead cast, back cast, forward cast, line hand, casting in head winds, tail winds, and crosswinds, the double-haul, haul in a tail wind, roll cast, and the pickup, including the "snap" and "snake" pickups. Two additional schools are held during April at the Allenberry Resort on famous Yellow Breeches Creek in Boiling Springs, Pennsylvania. For additional information and the free full-color *Orvis Catalog* of fishing and outdoor gear, accessories, and clothing, write: Orvis Fly Fishing School, 10 River Rd., Manchester 05254, phone (802) 362-1300.

Orvis also conducts a Fly-Tying Workshop in conjunction with its Fly Fishing Schools under the leadership of John Harder, head of the Orvis fly department. This is a workshop, not a school; bring your tools and materials or use Orvis gear and supplies to refine your fly-tying techniques.

Ski Touring Trails & Centers

Vermont is blessed with hundreds of miles of trails, abandoned railroad beds, and old logging roads that wind through the Green Mountain National Forest and the state forest backcountry areas, as well as at special ski areas, winter lodges, and ski touring centers. The 288-page *EMS Ski Touring Guide to New England* describes Vermont's major ski touring areas. The EMS guide contains regional maps, trail mileages, and driving directions. It may be obtained for $5.95 (plus 50¢ postage and handling) from: Eastern Mountain Sports, 1041 Commonwealth Ave., Boston, MA 02215.

A detailed *Vermont Ski Guide* may be obtained free from: the Agency of Development & Community Affairs, Montpelier 05602. The Vermont State Chamber of Commerce in Montpelier maintains 24-hour-a-day ski reports; phone (802) 223-2957. A *New England Ski Touring Map* is available free by writing: New England Ski Touring Operators' Assn., Box 88, Rochester 05767. Most of Vermont's major touring trails are included in this useful new publication. For complete information, the *Ski Touring Guide* ($3.50) may be obtained from: Ski Touring Council, West Hill Rd., Troy 05868.

The state's major ski touring centers and outfitters, most of which provide lodging, instruction, and trails, include *Blueberry Hill*, Goshen 05733, (802) 247-6735, lodging, trails, instruction, orienteering, clinics, shelters; *Bolton Valley Resort*, Bolton Valley 05477, (802) 434-2131, lodging, instruction, rentals, 35 miles of trails; *Churchill House Inn*, Rte. 73, Brandon 05733, (802) 247-3300, provides 22 miles of farm trails; *Darion Inn*, East Burke 05832, (802) 626-5641, lodging, trails; *Edson Hill Manor Ski Touring Center*, RR 1, Edson Hill Rd., Stowe 05672, (802) 253-7371, trails over hundreds of woodland areas, professional instruction, rentals, snowshoes, inn accommodations; *Farm Motor Inn & Country Club*, Stowe Rd., Morrisville 05661, (802) 888-3525, groomed trails on open and wooded farmland, equipment rentals and sales, accommodations available at site; *Fox Run*, Ludlow 05149, (802) 228-8871, marked trails start at Lodge and run through beautiful terrain overlooking Okemo for 5-6 miles, supplies and equipment available at Tally-Ho Shop; *Green Mountain House*, Box 86, West Wardsboro 05360, (802) 896-8491, on Rte. 100, 5 miles north of Mount Snow, approximately 5 miles of trails, lodging and meals available, rentals, guided tours Saturday mornings, instruction; *Green Mountain Touring Center*, Green Mountain Stock Farm,

Randolph 05060, (802) 728–5861, offers family cross country skiing and lodging in central Vermont; *Green Trails Inn,* by the Floating Bridge, Brookfield 05036, (802) 276-2012, ski touring and sleigh ride center, 75 acres and 25 miles of marked scenic trails, shop, rentals, instructions and guided tours available; *Haystack,* Wilmington 05363, (802) 464-5321, approximately 25 miles of trails, equipment rentals nearby; *Highland Lodge,* Greensboro 05841, (802) 533-2647, ski touring in beautiful northern Vermont hill country, with complete touring centers—sales, rentals, instruction, guided tours. Miles of marked trails, accommodations; the *Inn on the Common,* Craftsbury Common 05827, (802) 586-9619, novice to expert trails, plush accommodations in beautiful country inn, instruction, guided tours and rentals available to guests; *Killington Ski Area,* Killington 05751, (802) 422-3333, 5 miles of marked trails for novice, intermediate, and expert, two classes daily teach all levels, half-day and full-day tours available, equipment rentals and sales; *Middlebury College Snow Bowl,* Rte. 125, Hancock, mailing address Middlebury 05753, (802) 388-4356, 25 miles of a variety of open and mountainous marked trails, rentals, instruction, base lodge; *Mountain Meadows Ski Touring Center,* Rte. 4, Killington 05751, (802) 775-7077, 40 miles of trails Killington Basin, including Vermont Ski Touring Trail, rentals, expert instruction, repairs; *Mountaintop Ski Touring Center,* Chittenden 05737, (802) 483-2311, 45 miles of maintained trails, rentals and guided tours, accommodations and dining at adjacent Mountaintop Inn; *Mount Snow,* Mount Snow 05356, (802) 464-3333, wide variety of ski touring on 40 miles of marked and groomed trails, 1,400-acre reservation, instruction, rentals, guided trips arranged; *Okemo Mountain,* RFD 1, Ludlow 05149, (802) 228-4041, complete daily touring program, instruction, guided tours, maintained trails, rentals; *Ski Hostel Lodge,* Waterbury Center 05677, (802) 244-8859, lodge, trails (not marked), accommodations and meals, guided tours and instruction available; *Smugglers Notch Ski Area,* Jeffersonville 05464, (802) 644-8851, village mountain complex includes extensive cross-country program, with 25 miles of scenic trails, surrounding Smugglers Notch village, instruction and clinics, rentals; *Stowe Touring Center, North American Nordic,* and the *Cross-Country Outfitters,* Box 1308, Stowe 05672, (802) 253-4592, area probably offers the widest range of touring trails in the East, novice to mountaineering, groomed to virgin powder, choice of lodging from hostel to hotel; *Stratton Mountain,* Stratton Mountain 05155, (802) 297-2200, complete program of instruction and guided trips at the Stratton Mountain Nordic Center; *Sugarbush Valley Ski Touring Center,* Warren 05674, (802) 583-2301, 40 miles of natural trails, rentals, Norwegian-certified instructor and coach; *Sugarhouse Touring Center at Burke Mountain,* East Burke 05832, (802) 626-3305, mountain blessed with endless terrain for its 32 miles of ski touring trails, novice to expert, certified instructors, weekend workshops, lectures, group tours, equipment sales and rentals; *Trapp Family Lodge,* Stowe 05672, (802) 253-8511, first ski touring center in the country, certified instruction, guided tours, equipment sales and rentals, 50-mile system of well-marked and -maintained trails; *Tucker Hill Lodge,* Rte. 17, Waitsfield 05673, (802) 496-3983, rentals, instructors and guides, approximately 4 miles of trails connect to approximately 20 miles of Sugarbush and Glen Ellen trails, accommodations; *Twin Mount Farm,* Peacham 05862, (802) 592-3579, natural trails through unspoiled countryside, lodging and meals; *Viking Ski Touring Center,* Londonderry 05148, (802) 824-3933, over 25 miles of trails, rentals, snowshoe and winter camping equipment rentals, warming hut, certified instruction; *West Mountain Inn,* Arlington 05250, (802) 375-6560, miles of marked trails for novice, intermediate, and expert overlooking the Batten Kill Valley, ski and snowshoe rentals, home-cooked meals, comfortable lodgings; *Wild Wings Ski Touring Center,* Peru 05152, (802) 824–6793, offers backcountry trails and access to primitive Green Mountain National Forest trails

in southern Vermont; *Woodstock Ski Touring Center,* Woodstock 05091, (802) 457-2112, over 40 miles of mapped and marked trails, equipment rentals and sales, certified instruction, ski packages with accommodations at Woodstock Inn.

Ski Tours of Vermont, RFD 1, Chester 05143, (802) 875–2631, offers guided package tours and ski adventures in the remote backcountry areas of the Green Mountains for adults and families, with survival instruction, and special Inn-to-Inn tours along the High Route and overnight Teepee tours accompanied by members of the National Nordic Ski Patrol.

State Forest Reserves & Maps

Vermont's scenic state forest lands provide excellent opportunities for fishing, backpacking, camping, cross-country skiing, and hunting in season for whitetail deer, small game, black bear, waterfowl, and upland game birds. *Groton State Forest* (U.S. Geological Survey Maps: East Barre, Woodsville) encompasses 19,957 acres midway between Montpelier and St. Johnsbury, with nine developed recreation areas, including the Big Deer Campground, Boulder Beach Day Use Area, Kettle Pond Youth Group Camping Area with 27 lean-tos, New Discovery Campground, Owls Head Area, Ricker Pond Campground, Stillwater Campground, and Seyon Fly Fishing Area. For information, write: Groton State Forest, Marshfield 05658. The *Maidstone State Forest* (U.S. Geological Survey Map: Guildhall) is 27 miles southeast of Island Pond on Maidstone Lake, in the Northeast Kingdom. Write: Maidstone NF, North Stratford, NH 03590. The renowned *Mount Mansfield State Forest* (U.S. Geological Survey Maps: Mount Mansfield 7.5, Hyde Park) at 27,377 acres is the largest state forest, with three major recreation areas: Little River Camping Area, Smugglers Notch Camping Area, and Underhill Recreation Area. For information write: Mount Mansfield SF, Stowe 05672. The *Townshend State Forest* (U.S. Geological Survey Map: Saxtons River) encompasses 856 acres, 17 miles northwest of Brattleboro. Write: Townshend SF, Newfane 05345. *Calvin Coolidge State Forest* (U.S. Geological Survey Maps: Pico Peak, Killington Peak, Plymouth, Woodstock S) is an outstanding scenic hiking and primitive area located in the heart of the Green Mountains 15 miles southeast of Rutland. For information, write: Assistant Park Operations Supervisor, Box 129, Rutland 05701. The *Camels Hump State Reserve* (U.S. Geological Survey Maps: Bottom Mountain, Huntington, Richmond, Waterbury) embraces 16,995 acres due southwest of Waterbury Village. The area is dominated by Camels Hump, a double-humped peak which rises 4,088 feet above the woodlands surrounding the Mad, Winooski, and Huntington river valleys. This high country backpacking area is traversed by a segment of the Long Trail, and the Forestry, Dean Callahan, Burrows, Allis, and Alpine trails. The *Granville Gulf Reservation* (U.S. Geological Survey Map: Hancock) takes in 1,171 acres, 20 miles south of Waterbury on Route 100. Its major features include Nosa Glen Falls and the Puddlelock ski touring trail.

For additional information, write for the *Vermont Guide to State Parks & Forest Recreation Areas,* available free from: Dept. of Forests & Parks, Agency of Environmental Conservation, Montpelier 05602.

Wild & Scenic Waters Maps

Lake contour charts for several of the state's major fishing waters, including Seymour, Willoughby, and Fairlee lakes, are available free from: Boat Division, Dept. of Public Safety, Montpelier 05602. The following large-scale U.S. Geological Survey Maps show Vermont's major trout streams and lakes and the topography of the surrounding countryside. These useful full-color maps show woodlands in green and contours, as well as all man-made and natural features such as bogs, rapids, falls, trails, campgrounds, mountains, shelters and cabins, orchards, and footbridges. *Batten Kill:* Arlington, Cambridge (NY), Cossayuna (NY), Manchester, Salem (NY), Schuylerville 15 (NY), Shushan (NY), Sunderland; *Black River:* Claremont (NH), Ludlow; *Connecticut River Canoe Route:* Averill, Guildhall, Whitefield (NH), Miles Pond, Littleton (NH) 7.5, Lower Waterford, St. Johnsbury, Woodsville (NH), Mount Cube, Hanover (NH), North Hartland, Hartland, Claremont (NH), Bellows Falls (NH), Keene (NH), Brattleboro, Northfield; *Lamoille River:* Fort Ethan Allen, Georgia Plains, Gilson Mountain, Hardwick, Hyde Park, Jeffersonville, Lyndonville, Milton 7.5; *Mad River:* Middlesex, Waitsfield, Warner, Waterbury; *Metawee River:* Dorset, Granville, Pawlet, Thornhill, Wells, Whitehall 7.5; *Missisquoi River:* East Alburg, Enosburg Falls, Highgate Center, Irasburg, Jay Peak, Memphremagog; *Otter Creek:* Brandon 7.5, Cornwall (NY), Middlebury 7.5, Port Henry (NY), Proctor, Rutland 7.5, Sudbury, Wallingford, West Rutland; *White River:* Barre, East Barre, Hancock, Randolph, Rochester 7.5, Essex Junction, Fort Ethan Allen, Huntington, Montpelier, Plainfield, Plattsburgh (NY), Richmond, Waterbury; (NY); *Lake Bomoseen:* Bomoseen, Poultney; *Knapp Brook Ponds:* Ludlow; *Ottauquechee River:* Pico Peak, Killington Peak, Plymouth, Woodstock S, Woodstock N, Quechee, Hartland, North Hartland; *Lakota Lake:* Delectable Mountain; *Lake Fairlee:* Mount Cube; *Ompompanoosuc River:* Stratford (NY), Mount Cube; *Waits River:* East Barre, Woodsville (NH), Mount Cube; *Wells River* (including Kettle Pond, Lake Groton and Ricker Pond): Plainfield, East Barre, Woodsville (NH); *Kingsbury Brook* (including Sabin, Curtis, and Worcester ponds, Lakes Mirror, Forest, Valley, Greenwood, and Buck, and Nichols and East Long ponds): Plainfield; *Molly Brook* (including Molly Falls and Peacham ponds): St. Johnsbury; *Maidstone Lake:* Guildhall; *Caspian Lake:* Hardwick; *Hosmer Ponds:* Hardwick; *Arrowhead Mountain Lake:* Milton; *Lake Carmi:* Enosburg Falls.

Wilderness Trail Camps & Instruction

The renowned *Killington Wilderness Trail Camp* offers summer adventure programs for teens and adults with initial training at the Killington Mountain base camp in central Vermont at the junction of U.S. 4 and Vermont 100 in Shelburne. Two-week camping expeditions for teens emphasizing minimum impact camping are conducted at several outstanding wilderness locations including: the Long Trail, from Wallingford Gulf to Stratton Area, with cave exploration and beginner's rock climbing sessions at Little Rock Pond; the Adirondacks, starting in Keene Valley to the spectacular high country around Mount Marcy and Lake Colden; the rugged Pemigewasset Wilderness in New Hampshire's White Mountain National Forest; and along the Appalachian Trail from Franconia Notch to Pinkham Notch, ending with a climb of 6,288-foot Mount Washington, New Hampshire. Killington also offers 3-week expeditions for experienced campers along the Long Trail from Killington to Mansfield, including rock

climbing at Deer Leap, Mount Horrid, and Mount Mansfield, and trekking along the spectacular Monroe Skyline section of the Long Trail; the Adirondacks; and New Hampshire from the Greeley Ponds Scenic Area over Tripyramid to the Sandwich Range, Sawyer Pond Scenic Area, the southern Presidential Range, the Pemigewasset Wilderness, and the Franconia Waterslides. The Killington Wilderness Trail Camp also offers a 1-week backpacking adventure for adults along the Long Trail and a wintertrek program of cold-weather backpacking and mountaineering in the high peak areas of the White Mountains or the Adirondacks. For detailed information and rates write: Killington Adventure, Killington 05751, (802) 422-333.

Overnight backpacking and wilderness camping trips on the Long Trail are also offered by *Rock & Rill,* RFD 1, Chester 05143, with an emphasis on cross-country travel and orienteering.

Eastern Fly-Fishing Workshop, P.O. Box 324, Lyndonville 05851 (802) 626-9232, offers a complete fly-fishing, camping, and conservation program for young adults, introducing them to the legendary trout streams of New England.

VERMONT TRAVEL & RECREATION GUIDE

Green Mountain National Forest

Green Mountain National Forest Topo Maps

U.S. Geological Survey Overview Maps (scale 1:250,000): Albany, Glens Falls, Lake Champlain.

Bristol Cliffs Wilderness

Large-scale U.S. Geological Survey Topographic Maps: Middlebury, South Mountain.

Lye Brook Backwoods Area

Large-scale U.S. Geological Survey Topographic Maps: Londonderry, Manchester, Sunderland.

Wallingford Pond Wilderness

Large-scale U.S. Geological Survey Topographic Map: Wallingford.

The northern and southern units of this magnificent forest embrace 240,000 acres of some of the finest backcountry camping, backpacking, and hunting areas in New England. Dominated by the scenic rolling hills of the Green Mountain Range, the terrain varies from the rugged heights of Mount Ellen to the quiet secluded hollows of the Lye Brook Backwoods area. The Long Trail winds along the crest of the Green Mountains for 88 miles along a north-south axis and provides access to seldom-explored wilderness camping areas and remote brook trout ponds and beaver flows surrounded by beautiful meadows and mixed hardwood and evergreen forests inhabited by whitetail deer, black bear, and upland game birds. The major lakes in the forest region—Somerset Reservoir, Stratton Pond, Chittenden Reservoir, Silver Lake, and Lake Dunmore—hold smallmouth and largemouth bass, northern pike, walleye, rainbow trout, and panfish. Lake Dunmore with its deep, clear waters is one of Vermont's top-ranked lakes for trophy smallmouth bass, northern pike, and a few landlocked salmon. The remote pools and runs of the White and Mad rivers and the headwaters of the Deerfield River provide fishing for rainbow brook and brown trout in a majestic north country setting. U.S. Forest service campgrounds are at Texas Falls, Chittenden Brook, Moosalamoo, White Rocks, Hapgood Pond, and Red Mill Brook.

The Lye Brook Backwoods area embraces 16,500 acres in the southern Green Mountain National Forest in Bennington County. The area acquired its name from Lye Brook, which flows northwesterly through the western half of the area. Remnants of old railroad grades and logging roads are found throughout the wilderness. Bourn Pond and numerous small beaver ponds and streams hold native populations of brook and brown trout. The Wallingford Pond Wilderness to the north, near the White Rocks area, embraces 20,000 acres of upland ridges, ponds, and beaver meadows. This outstanding primitive camping area is dominated by the beautiful blue waters of Wallingford Pond, the last large unspoiled natural pond in the state. The Bristol Cliffs Wilderness takes in 4,900 acres at the northern end of the Green Mountain National Forest. The cliffs on the western side of South Mountain provide a spectacular view of the Lake Champlain Valley and Adirondack Mountains in New York. Major features include the New Haven River and two remote natural ponds, North and Gilmore, that support beaver colonies. The backwoods is an outstanding hiking and hunting area for deer, black bear, and ruffed grouse.

The full-color *Green Mountain National Forest* map, available for 50¢ from: Forest Supervisor, Federal Bldg., 151 West St., Rutland 05701, shows highways, secondary roads, old logging roads, and major features of the outlying areas, including Okemo, Townshend, Grafton, Proctor, Piper, Rupert, Calvin Coolidge, George Aiken, West Rutland,

and Rothbury state forests as well as Lake Bomoseen, Lake Champlain, Lake St. Catharine, Connecticut River, and Wimona, Sunset, and Hortonia lakes. The Appalachian Trail is clearly marked, as are landing fields for planes, fire lookout towers, district ranger stations, spot elevation in feet, forest service recreation sites with and without camping facilities, other recreation sites without camping facilities, winter sports areas, boat access areas, points of interest, trail huts or cabins, trail shelters, forest supervisors' headquarters, and covered bridges.

The reverse side of the map contains detailed information on how to get to the Green Mountains. Some notes on the history of the area are provided—this area played a prominent role in the era of the pioneer timber harvests. In 1739 Vermont's first sawmill was making lumber of the virgin white pine, oak, and hemlock forests. By 1835 (12 years after the opening of the Champlain-Hudson River Canal) the towering forests on the slopes of the Green Mountains had been razed.

For specific fishing, hunting, camping, and cross-country skiing information and a free *Bristol Cliffs Wilderness Map & Guide*, write to: Forest Supervisor (address above).

Lodges and resorts in the Green Mountains region offering four-season vacation accommodations and services include: *The Churchill House Inn*, RD 3, Brandon 05733 (802-247-3300), a century-old country inn offering access to the Long Trail and central Vermont trout streams including the White River, Furnace Brook, and a privately stocked section of the Neshobe River; *Green Trails*, Floating Bridge, Brookfield 05036 (802-276-2012); *Norse Lodge*, Danby 05739 (802-293-5412), on Otter Creek and the National Forest; *Deer-Brook Lodge*, Pittsfield 05762 (802-746-5781); *Grey Bonnet Inn*, Killington 05751 (802-775-2537), on a scenic lake adjacent to Gifford Woods and Appalachian Trail; *Long Trail Lodge*, Sherburne Pass, Killington 05751, at junction of Long Trail and Appalachian Trail; *Mountain Meadows Lodge*, Killington 05751 (802-775-1010), adjoined by Kent Pond and Appalachian Trail; *Pico Peak Lodge*, Killington 05751 (802-773-6331); *Summit Lodge*, Killington 05751 (802-422-3535); *Keewaydin Camps*, Lake Dunmore, Salisbury 05769 (802-352-4247); *Sunset Lodge*, Lake Dunmore, Salisbury 05769 (802-352-4290); *The Rustics*, Bomoseen 05732 (802-273-2539); *Blue Gentian Lodge* (802-824-5908), *The Highland House* (802-824-3019), *The Post Horn*

(802-824-3131), and *White Pine Lodge* (on 10-acre tract adjacent to the National Forest; 802-824-3909)—all Londonderry 05148; *The Okemo Inn*, Ludlow 05149 (802-228-7151); *Green Mountain House*, Box 86, W. Wardsboro 05360 (802-896-8491); *Snow Lake Lodge*, Mt. Snow 05356 (802-464-3333); *The Lodge at Smuggler's Notch*, RR 1, Stowe 05672 (802-253-7311); *Notch Brook Resort*, Stowe 05672 (802-253-4882); *Trapp Family Lodge*, Stowe 05672 (802-253-8511); *West River Lodge*, Newfane 05345 (802-365-7745); *Killington Village*, Killington 05751 (802-422-3613).

Access & Outfitting Centers

The forest is reached via several of New England's most scenic auto routes, including the Calvin Coolidge Memorial Highway (U.S. 4), New England Heritage Trail (U.S. Highway 7), Vermont Routes 9, 100, 11, 125, and 73, and Interstate Routes 89 and 91. Overnight accommodations, supplies, meals, and equipment rentals are available at Rutland, Manchester Center, Middlebury, Rochester, and scores of scenic New England hamlets and rural villages.

Northeast Kingdom Fish & Game Region

Northeast Kingdom Topo Maps

Large-scale U.S. Geological Survey Topographic Maps: Memphremagog, Island Pond, Averill, Lyndonville, Burke, Guildhall.

Lake Memphremagog Trophy Trout & Smallmouth Bass Country

Large-scale U.S. Geological Survey Map: Memphremagog.

Lake Willoughby Fish & Game Area

Large-scale U.S. Geological Survey Topographic Maps: Lyndonville, Memphremagog.

Moose River Country

Large-scale U.S. Geological Survey Topographic Maps: Concord, Miles Pond, Burke.

Seymour Lake & Clyde River

Large-scale U.S. Geological Survey Topographic Maps: Memphremagog, Island Pond, Burke.

Victory State Forest & Wildlife Management Area

Large-scale U.S. Geological Survey Topographic Map: Burke.

The wild bogs, sprawling island-dotted lakes, ancient mountains, turbulent rivers, and fragrant north country spruce and fir forests of the Northeast Kingdom form one of New England's great fishing, hunting, and canoe-camping regions. This renowned fish and game country encompasses the northeast corner of Vermont, stretching south from the Quebec border; it contains the renowned trout, landlocked salmon, and smallmouth bass waters of Lake Memphremagog, Barton River, Brownington Pond, Clyde River, Echo Island, and Norton, Unknown, Holland, and Lewis ponds. Willoughby Lake is famous for its large lake trout up to 30 pounds, and the Averill, Salem, and Seymour lakes offer the best landlocked salmon waters in the state. The remote headwaters, ponds, and beaver flows provide exciting early season and early fall fishing for big, orange-bellied squaretails for the wilderness angler who is willing to travel the old logging roads and cross country using topo map and compass. Hunting for whitetail deer and black bear is good throughout the region, particularly in the wild Yellow Bogs area.

Beautiful island-dotted Lake Memphremagog, which sprawls for 32

miles across the Vermont-Quebec boundary, offers some of the East's top "big-lake" canoeing and early season fishing for big rainbow and brown trout up to 10 pounds, landlocked salmon, trophy smallmouth bass, walleye, pickerel, and a few gray lake trout up to 30 pounds in the deepwater areas. The 6,317-acre Vermont portion can be considered the second-largest body of water in the state. The greater portion of the lake, however, sprawls north into Quebec. The shallow waters of the Vermont section, with its numerous points, coves, and bays, contains the bulk of the lake's spawning beds, which provide often spectacular early season sport. The best fishing during July and August is at Gibraltar Rock, Long Island, Molson Island, Fitch Bay, Owl Head Mountain, Sable Point, Derby Bay, South Bay, Black Island, Horseneck Island, and Holbrook Bay areas.

There are several north-flowing Vermont tributaries of Lake Memphremagog: the Barton River rises in Shadow Lake and flows north for 20 miles into South Bay. It provides excellent early season fishing for big lake-run rainbows, as does its feeder, the Willoughby River. The Barton holds native rainbows and buckskin-flanked browns, as well as brook trout in the remote headwaters area. The lower stretches of the river meander through a broad floodplain surrounded by low, wooded hills. The Black River, which rises from a chain of lakes in its Orleans County headwaters, flows north into South Bay and holds some big browns and rainbows. The Clyde River flows northwest from its Island Pond headwaters for 24 miles through Pensioner, Salem, and Clyde ponds into Lake Memphremagog. The Clyde holds some big squaretails in its headwaters; brown trout in the lower stretches; and rainbow trout in the fast-water areas throughout its length. Island Pond, which covers 598 acres, holds rainbow and brook trout, smallmouth bass, and walleye. Pensioner Pond holds some trophy-sized smallmouths and pickerel. Neighboring Echo Lake and 1,732-acre Seymour Lake hold lake trout, landlocked salmon, rainbow trout, and smallmouth bass. Seymour Lake also holds big brown and brook trout and is renowned for its early season gray trout fishing. Clyde Pond, a dammed portion of the river, provides some excellent walleye and smallmouth bass fishing. To the east of Island Pond the Nulhegan River, a tributary of the Upper Connecticut River, flows through a remote, seldom-traveled high country wilderness of vast swamps, wooded hills, and mountains. The wild Nulhegan holds squaretails in its headwaters and some big browns in the boulder-studded pools and eddies along its lower reaches. The famed Averill Lakes to the north hold big lake trout, landlocked salmon, brook, and rainbow trout.

The remote Hurricane Brook Wildlife Management area, just south of the Quebec boundary at the head of the Pherrins River and northeast of Seymour Lake, offers some of the state's top-ranked hunting and unspoiled wilderness trophy brook trout fishing. This wild, roadless "big north" country is laced with a network of old logging trails which wind through dense northern hardwood and spruce and fir forests and provide access to Round and Beaver ponds—two of Vermont's best wild squaretail fisheries. Turtle Pond offers good chain pickerel fishing. Holland Pond, which covers 210 acres, holds some big brook, brown, and rainbow trout. Bow hunters will find good deer hunting along the game and hiking trails. Black bear are most often found along the extensive hardwood ridges. Upland bird hunters will find ruffed grouse and woodcock. Topo maps are a must in this big country.

Beautiful Lake Willoughby—surrounded by a magnificent north country wilderness dominated by Wheeler Mountain (2,371 feet), Mount Pisgah (2,751 feet), and Bald Mountain (3,315 feet)—is a deep, narrow body of water which covers 1,692 acres and offers top-ranked fishing for landlocked salmon, lake trout, and rainbow trout up to trophy weights. Narrow Crystal Lake to the west covers 712 acres

and holds big smallmouth bass, landlocked salmon, lake trout, and rainbow trout. Several scenic trails provide access to the remote headwater ponds and wilderness camping areas surrounding Lake Willoughby. The Wheeler Mountain trail climbs up over open rock and provides panoramic views of the northern Green Mountains and Lake Willoughby. The Mount Pisgah and North trails wind through scenic north woods and provide stunning views of Lake Memphremagog, northern Green Mountains, Lake Willoughby, and the Burke Mountain-Victory Bog wilderness.

The northern hardwood and conifer forests, sedge meadows, swamps, bogs, rocky mountaintops, old fields, brooks, streams, and ponds of the Victory State Forest and Victory Bog Wildlife Management Area are south of Lake Willoughby, ranging from the relatively developed Burke Mountain Area to the remote scenic wilderness of the Umpire Brook-Victory Bog area and the headwaters of the Moose River. Old logging roads, abandoned railroad beds, and primitive trails wind through the low-lying spruce and fir forests to remote fishing, hunting, and wilderness camping areas. The meadows, swamp areas and mountain summits are a naturalist's paradise, inhabited by marsh hawks, osprey, great blue heron, green heron, yellow-bellied sapsuckers, downy woodpeckers, northern water thrush, green heron, and rough-legged hawks, and carpeted by a lush understory of mountain holly, meadow sweet, hobblebush, partridge berry, dogberry, pink lady's slipper, shiny club moss, wild lily of the valley, goldthread, Indian cucumber root, wild sarsaparilla, Labrador tea, swamp candles, cayuga pondweed, painted trillium, starflower, wood sorrel, mountain ash, and dogberry. The evergreen forests are inhabited by deer, moose, black bear, coyote, lynx, marten, fisher, and weasel. Ruffed grouse and woodcock are often found along the hardwood ridges, while otter, beaver, mink, and muskrat inhabit the low-lying swamps and bogs. The Moose River provides scenic wilderness canoeing and fishing for brookies along its upper stretches and for brown trout in the lower reaches.

Public use maps of the *Victory State Forest-Wildlife Management Area* and *Hurricane Brook Wildlife Management Area* may be obtained free upon request from: Fish & Game Dept., Montpelier 05602. These useful maps show roads, trails, cross-country trails, and natural features.

Vacation lodges and sporting camps in the Northeast Kingdom include *Quimby Country*, Averill 05901 (802-822-5533), a 900-acre resort with 20 lakeshore cottages; *Highland Lodge*, Caspian Lake, Greensboro 05841 (802-533-2647); *Lakeview Cabins*, Crystal Lake, Barton 05822 (802-525-4463); *Lakeside*, Lake Willoughby, Barton 05822 (802-525-6639 or winter, 914-357-2246); *Burke Mountain Inn & Recreation, Inc.*, E. Burke 05832 (802-626-3305); *McGowan House-Lake Memphremagog*, Georgeville, Que. J0B 1T0 (819-843-2126), the fisherman's headquarters for half a century—member of Quebec Outfitters Assn., with rustic lodging, guide service, and trophy fishing.

Access & Outfitting Centers

The Northeast Kingdom is reached via Vermont Highways 100, 14, 54, and 114 and Interstate 91. Overnight accommodations, resorts, lodges, supplies, and boat and equipment rentals are available at Orleans, Barton, Newport, Island Pond, and many rural hamlets and villages.

NEW HAMPSHIRE ENCYLOPEDIA

Accommodations— Vacation Lodges & Resorts

The *Lodging in New Hampshire* accommodations guide, free from: New Hampshire Vacation Center, 1268 Ave. of the Americas, New York, NY 10020, gives an overview of available cabins and cottages, hotels, motels, resorts, and lodges throughout the state. It lists accommodations by city and region, with addresses and short descriptions. For more detailed information on accommodations in a specific region, write to one of the following addresses: Dartmouth-Lake Sunapee Region, Box 246, Lebanon 03766; Lakes Region Assn., Box 300, Wolfeboro 03894; Merrimack Valley Region Assn., Box 634, Manchester 03105; Monadnock Region Assn., Box 269, Peterborough 03458; New Hampshire Seacoast Regional Development Assn., Box 476, Exeter 03833; or the White Mountain Region Assn., Box A, Lancaster 03584. The White Mountains Attraction Assn. (Box 176, North Woodstock 03262) publishes a free guide to accommodations in the White Mountains area along with a brochure on the Lakes Region, along with publications on Lost River, Loon Mountain, and Franconia Notch State Park, and a highway map of the state.

For listing of many of the state's major vacation lodges, resorts, and sporting camps, see the "New Hampshire Travel & Recreation Guide" section.

Appalachian Mountain Club— White Mountain Huts & Camps

The most extensive network of trails in the country winds through the White Mountain National Forest backcountry, one of the last wildlands of the northeast and the home of New England's highest peaks. You can travel through these mountains for days without approaching civilization and yet avoid the rigors of a primitive backpacking experience by staying at the Appalachian Mountain Club huts in the forest. The club has spaced the huts 1 day apart among a myriad of trails of varying ease and difficulty. At each hut young people maintain the accommodations (bunkrooms with pillows and blankets), serve family-style meals at 7:00 A.M. and 6:00 P.M., and pack up food and supplies for the next day's trek.

Pinkham Notch Camp is the headquarters of the Northern New England regional office on U.S. Route 16, 11 miles north of Jackson. The camp is the hiking center of the White Mountains and a convenient base camp for hiking in the huts. The camp provides overnight accommodations, meals, and information. *Carter Notch Hut* neighbors Carter Lake, and can be reached by a 6.75-mile hike from Pinkham Notch Camp, and a 4.0-mile hike from the Wildcat Gondola's upper terminal over the Wildcat Ridge Trail.

The Old Jackson Road and the Madison Gulf Trail lead 6.1 miles from Pinkham Notch Camp to *Madison Spring Hut*. The hut can also be reached by a 7.3-mile hike from the *Lake of the Clouds Hut*. This hut lies above treeline in the rugged high country of the Washington-Monroe district, 1.5 miles from the Mount Washington summit by way of the Crawford Path. It can be reached from Pinkham Notch in a 4.5-mile hike. Be prepared for severe weather conditions in this area; some of the highest winds ever recorded were monitored in these mountains. These winds, low temperatures, and snow may preclude travel; never travel the high country in the face of a weather warning.

Five miles from the Lake of the Clouds Hut, on the side of Mount Clinton on the Webster Trail, is the *Mizpah Spring Hut*, which is 2.5 miles from Crawford Notch over the Crawford Path and the Mizpah

Cutoff. The *Zealand Hut* on Whitehall Brook can be reached by a 7-mile hike from the Crawford Notch, and 2.5 miles from the end of the Zealand Road from Zealand and Sugarloaf Camp grounds on U.S. 302. The Twinway Trail from Zealand Hut leads to *Galehead Hut* 7 miles away. Galehead can also be reached on the Garfield Ridge Trail by a 7.75-mile hike from Greenleaf Hut. *Greenleaf Hut* is above treeline 2.5 miles from Profile Clearing in an area of severe and sudden storms. The Franconia Ridge Trail from Whitehouse Bridge also leads to Greenleaf Hut. *Lonesome Lake Hut* is near a mountain pond 1.7 miles from Lafayette Place in Franconia Notch. The aerial tramway on Cannon Mountain also serves the hut.

Reservations are required for use of all the huts, as well as a $3.00-per-person-per-night deposit. For information on rates and to make reservations, write to: Reservations Secretary, Pinkham Notch Camp, Gorham 03581, (603) 466-2751.

The Appalachian Mountain Club also offers summer workshops in mountaineering, orienteering, skiing, mountain photography, nature study, and backpacking. For information on mountaineering workshops, write to: Brian Fowler, Workshop Director, RFD 5, Box 93E, Gilford 03246. Most workshops are based at Pinkham Notch camp on New Hampshire 16, 10 miles north of Jackson and 10 miles south of Gorham. For more information on these workshops, write to: Workshop Coordinator, Appalachian Mountain Club, Pinkham Notch Camp, Gorham 03581.

In addition to its White Mountains hut system, the AMC maintains several campgrounds and self-service facilities in New Hampshire. The three *Saco River Campgrounds,* easily reached from Boston, provide primitive tenting facilities and access to one of the finest unspoiled stretches of flatwater canoeing in New England. The *Moose Campground* is on the west bank of the Saco River near North Conway, with 10 large campsites plus room for overflow campers. AMC self-service facilities include *Harvard's Cabin,* on Route 16 in Mount Washington Valley, suitable for family vacations and responsibly led groups for day hiking, canoeing, skiing, and snowshoeing; and *Wonalancet Cabin,* located at the end of the Chinook Trail adjacent to the Hemenway State Forest near the southern border of the White Mountain National Forest, with accommodations for 12, and easy access to the trails in the Sandwich Range, Squam and Ossipee mountains and canoeing on the Swift, Bearcamp, and Chocorua rivers. For information, contact: AMC, 5 Joy St., Boston, MA 02108, (617) 523-0636.

The AMC also maintains several summer full-service facilities in the New Hampshire forests. The *Cardigan Lodge & Reservation* is a year-round facility in the Shem Valley of the Lakes Region about 10 miles west of Newfound Lake. Cardigan's 1,000-acre reservation adjoins some 1,000 acres of state park land which includes Mount Cardigan (3,121 ft.), its northern ridge Firescrew (3,040 ft.), and several smaller peaks. Activities include backpacking, fishing, canoeing, and cross-country skiing. Write: Cardigan Lodge, RFD, Bristol 03222, phone (603) 744-8011. The *Cold River Camp* includes single, double, and family cabins in the pine groves and meadowlands of Evans Notch Valley on the Maine-New Hampshire border on Route 113. Activities on this 40-acre site include hiking the treeline ridges of the Baldface Circle and fishing and canoeing on the beautiful Saco River. Contact AMC Cold River Camp, Evans Notch, North Chatham, or AMC Boston headquarters (address above) for info. The *Three-Mile Island Camp* is on a rocky, 43-acre island on sprawling Lake Winnipesaukee, with 47 screened 1-room cabins. The AMC centennial project of the camp is a comparison of wildlife found on the island today with a description compiled by AMC members 70 years ago. Activities include nature study, canoeing, fishing, and day cruises on the 19-mile-long lake. For info call AMC in Boston (address above).

Appalachian National Scenic Trail

In New Hampshire the great mountain footpath leads from Mount Carlo at the Maine line along the Mahoosuc Range and Peabody Brook trails. It then crosses the Androscoggin River into the White Mountain National Forest. Through the forest it follows the Rattle River and Kenduskeag, Wildcat, and Lost Pond trails to Pinkham Notch, climbs Mount Madison in the Presidential Range, and winds by the Gulfside Trail past Mounts Jefferson and Clay, and over Mount Washington (6,288 ft.—the highest peak in New England). The trail continues along the high Webster Cliff Trail and descends to Crawford Notch near Mount Jackson, crosses the Saco River, Mount Zeacliff, Buyot, South Twin, Garfield, and Lafayette, and leads on to Franconia Notch and the Appalachian Mountain Club huts at Lost River, renowned for its nature garden and spectacular geological exhibits. At Kinsman Notch the trail joins the Dartmouth Outing Club Trail network to Mount Moosilauke, and winds on to Glencliff and Mounts Cube, Smarts, and Moose to Hanover, where it crosses the Connecticut River into Vermont.

If you decide to hike the trail through New Hampshire, be prepared for weather conditions approaching arctic severity along the Presidential Range sections. This area of the White Mountains has claimed the lives of many who underestimated its hazards. The *Appalachian Trailway News,* published 3 times a year by: Appalachian Trail Conference, P.O. Box 236, Harpers Ferry, WV 25425, describes the condition of each section of the trail in its spring issue. (A yearly subscription costs $4.00.) It also reports developments and issues of interest relating to the trail.

The Appalachian Trail Conference publishes a number of other books for travelers of the Appalachian Trail, including the brief *Appalachian Trail* (publication #17, 25¢), containing a short history of the trail, a map of it, and a complete list of publications for sale by the conference; *Suggestions for Appalachian Trail Users* (publication #15, 70¢), including information on trip planning, accommodations, precautions, maps, equipment, clothing, and food; the *Appalachian Trail* (publication #5, $1.25), with a history of the trail, a list of trail-maintaining organizations, a description of the route of the trail, and a discussion of the legislation and regulations concerning the trail; *Mileage Facts* ($1.50), giving distances to shelters, stores, post offices, water sources, lodging, restaurants, and other service and supply points; and the *Guide to the Appalachian Trail in New Hampshire and*

Vermont ($5.85)—the comprehensive guide covers the general topics of the trail route, its marking, preparations and precautions, and necessary equipment; gives a list of the trail sections and a description of accommodations along the way, a detailed description of the trail through Vermont and New Hampshire, and maps of the trail sections.

U.S. Geological Survey Topographic Maps of the trail in New Hampshire include: Carter Dome, Crawford Notch, Franconia, Lincoln, Mount Cube, Mount Moosilauke, Mount Washington, Rumney, Shelburne, South Twin Mountain, Wild River.

Camping & High Country Trails

New Hampshire's mountains, lake country, and seacoast areas offer a variety of camping and backcountry experiences. About 360 miles of the AMC trails (see "Appalachian Mountain Club—White Mountain Huts & Camps") wind through the White Mountains. The club maintains a portion of the Appalachian National Scenic Trail in the mountains; the Dartmouth Outing Club maintains trails from Hanover to Littleton. The Forest Service and other clubs maintain many other trails through the state.

The *New Hampshire Four-Seasons State Camping Guide* lists privately and publicly operated campgrounds in each of the state's six regions, including location, facilities and services, recreational opportunities, and season rates. The guide is available free from: Lee Bosworth, New Hampshire Campground Owners Assn., Harbor Hill CA, Rte. 25, Meredith 03253. *The Clean Getaway* describes the state's 32 state parks and their camping facilities, recreational opportunities, and outstanding features. Order the guide from: Division of Parks, Dept. of Natural Resources, P.O. Box 856, State House Annex, Concord 03301. For information on camping in the White Mountain National Forest, write to: Supervisor, White Mountain National Forest, Laconia 03246.

An indispensable guide for those who plan on backcountry camping and backpacking through the White Mountains is the *Appalachian Mountain Club White Mountain Guide.* The book costs $8.00 (hardback), and is available from: Appalachian Mountain Club, 5 Joy St., Boston, MA 02108. Individual AMC maps of *Mount Chocorua, Mount Monadnock, Mount Cardigan, Waterville,* and the *Pilot Range* are available from the same source for 25¢ each; maps of *Mount Washington,* the *Franconia area,* and the *Carter-Mahoosuc Region* cost 50¢; and *Plastic-Coated Maps of the Franconia and Mount Washington Areas* cost $1.00 each. Daniel Dean's *Fifty Hikes in New Hampshire* is another detailed guide to hiking in the White Mountains. This 165-page book ($5.85, New Hampshire Publishing Co., Somersworth 03878), describes walks, day hikes, and backpacking trips in the White Mountains. It gives the distance, walking time, and vertical rise for each trip, and discusses the hiking area's outstanding natural features, flora and fauna, and history. Maps of each hike are included.

The *Dartmouth Outing Club Trail Guide* provides detailed descriptions of trails in the Dartmouth region, in eastern Vermont, and between Hanover and Mount Moosilauke. This guide is available from: Dartmouth Outing Club, Dartmouth College, Hanover 03755, for $2.25. The *Metacomet-Monadnock Trail Guide* covers this trail from Connecticut to Mount Monadnock. The book costs $1.00, and is available from: Walter Banfield, RFD 3, Pratt Corner Rd., Amherst, MA 01002. A contour trail map of *Mount Monadnock* is available from: Society for the Protection of New Hampshire Forests, 5 South St., Concord 03301, for 25¢. A contour map of *Randolph Valley and the Northern Peaks* costs 75¢, and may be ordered from:

Randolph Mountain Club, 97 Garden St., Cambridge, MA 02138. A *Squam Lake Area Trail Guide* is available from: Watson A. Rand, Squam Lake Assn., 71 Main St., Plymouth 03264, for $2.00 (extra maps cost 35¢ each). *Trails of the Wonalancet Outdoor Club,* including a map and brief guide to the trails on Mounts Paugus, Passaconaway, and Whiteface, is available from: Wonalancet Post Office, Wonalancet 03897, for 25¢.

Information on bicycling and walking trips throughout New England may be obtained from: American Youth Hostels, 251 Harvard St., Brookline, MA 02146. *New England Trails,* published annually in April, contains detailed reports of current shelter and trail conditions throughout New England. Order it ($1.00) from: New England Trail Conference, Box 145, Weston, VT 05161. The conference also publishes *Hiking Trails of New England,* a map of and guide to information sources on trails throughout the region. The map shows trails, highways, national forest land, water features, communities, and outstanding topographical features.

These maps and guides should be used in conjunction with U.S. Geological Survey Topographic Maps of the area in which you plan to hike. A map of the state showing these individual USGS quadrangles and the public lands and recreation areas within them is available free from: Dept. of Economic Resources & Development, Box 856, Concord 03301.

Canoeing & Wilderness Waters

New Hampshire offers a wide variety of wild and scenic canoe country ranging from the big, evergreen-fringed, island-dotted waters of the scenic Lakes Region, dominated by sprawling Lake Winnipesaukee, to the wild, turbulent mountain streams of the White Mountain National Forest and the far north wilderness, dominated by the majestic headwater lakes of the Connecticut River, which sprawl across the wilderness like a string of blue jewels. Here are several of New England's premier canoe routes, including the wild, upper stretches of the Connecticut River, and the Saco, Ammonoosuc, Androscoggin, Magalloway, Diamond, and the western reaches of the Rangeley Lakes Country. Anyone planning a summer canoe trip to the pine-fragrant north country should travel prepared for mosquitoes, no-see-ums, and black flies.

The state's major rivers are described in detail in *Summer Canoeing and Kayaking in the White Mountains of New Hampshire,* a free booklet available from: White Mountains Region Assn., Box K, Lancaster 03584. The booklet describes the major rapids in the main canoe and kayak streams, and lists larger lakes and ponds in the region which have public boat accesses.

The *AMC River Guide: Volume 1 Northeastern New England* ($6.00) is available from: Appalachian Mountain Club, 5 Joy St., Boston, MA 02108, and gives comprehensive descriptions of most of the canoeable waters in New England, including difficulty ratings, historical notes, and descriptions of features along the way. It includes a "Canoeist's Map of Vermont and New Hampshire," which shows ratings of rapids and the scenery of the areas surrounding the streams. The map also shows divides, communities, and major topographical features.

For information on canoe trips in the White Mountains, contact: Bruce and Helen Holt, *Scotlyn Yard,* Milan 03588; *Mad-Pemi Canoe and Kayak Club,* c/o 93 Realty, Campton 03223; *Androscoggin Canoe and Kayak Club,* Box 184, Berlin 03570; or Appalachian Mountain Club (address above). Information on water conditions, and canoe and kayak sales and rentals, are available from: *Canoe King of*

New England, Gralyn Sports Center, North Conway 03860; *Outdoor People,* Milan 03588; *White Mountain Canoe Co.,* 93 Motel, Rte. 3, West Thornton 03285; and Bruce and Helen Holt, *Scotlyn Yard* (address above).

Fishing & Hunting in the Granite State

New Hampshire's cloud-wreathed, glaciated mountain ranges, remote wilderness ponds, boulder-fringed lakes, swift, rocky streams, and fragrant northern forest tracts provide some of New England's outstanding fishing for landlocked salmon, lakers (togue), trout, and smallmouth bass, and hunting for deer, bear, and upland game birds in one of New England's spectacularly beautiful regions. The state contains four major divisions: the industrial valleys, foothills, and brief seacoast of the south; the lake-dotted landscape of the midsection uplands; the rugged summits of the White Mountains, interspersed by steep river valleys, culminating in the windswept crowns of the magnificent Presidential Range; and the vast, largely roadless evergreen expanse of New Hampshire's North Country, occupied by trophy deer, bear, beaver, native trout, and salmon. The outdoors traveler will find picturesque New England villages with treelined streets and neat colonial houses, high country peaks with tundra meadows containing alpine plants, and the brooding silences of the north woods, a land of impenetrable forest, spruce swamps, and pure watersheds stretching to the wild borders of Maine, Vermont, and Quebec.

The Granite State offers fishing to suit every taste, and the opportunities are limited only by the effort expended. You may troll for landlocks and togue on icy northern lakes, battle coho salmon in tidal currents, hike in to some spruce-fringed native trout pond, or dunk worms for perch from the end of a dock in a summer resort area. The quality of New Hampshire's waters is illustrated by the state fishing records.

NEW HAMPSHIRE RECORD FISH

	Lb.-oz.	Place	Year
Brook trout	9	Pleasant Lake	1911
Brown trout	15–4	Connecticut River	1953
Lake trout	28–5	Newfound Lake	1958
Rainbow trout	13	Dublin Lake	1953
Splake	8–5	White Lake	1963
Sunapee (golden trout)	11–5	Lake Sunapee	1954
Coho salmon	15	Lamprey River	1976
Landlocked salmon	18–5	Pleasant Lake	1942
Lake whitefish	5–1	Lake Winnipesaukee	1974
Largemouth bass	10–5	Lake Potanipo	1967
Smallmouth bass	7–9	Goose Pond	1970
Northern pike	17–14	Spofford Lake	1972
Chain pickerel	8	Plummer Pond	1966
Walleye	9	Merrimack River	1971
Yellow perch	2–4	Heads Pond	1969
White perch	3–8	Goose Pond	1977
Brown bullhead	2–8	Merrimack River	1924
Carp	27	Merrimack River	1968
American eel	*	Opechee Lake	1966

*41 inches.

The official angling rules and regulations booklet, *New Hampshire Freshwater and Saltwater Fishing Guide,* may be obtained free from: Fish & Game Dept. 34 Bridge St., Concord 03301; it provides the usual ordinances, a list of trout lakes and ponds, which are marked by an asterisk if reclaimed, a list of togue lakes, and special laws by county or border water. The Department also publishes the free *New Hampshire Fishing & Hunting* booklet which describes the fishing and hunting opportunities in the state, license details, seasons, and boat and snowmobile regulations and the free *Wildlife Management Area Guide* and *New Hampshire Game & Furbearers: A History.*

North Country Waters

The wild, beautiful North Country occupies the top third of the state. Encompassing most of Coos County and bordered by Maine to the east, Quebec to the north and northwest, Vermont to the west, and the Upper Ammonoosuc River to the south, this vast expanse of thick coniferous and hardwood forest, beaver flowages, deep, cold lakes, and hidden ponds offers wilderness trout fishing and exciting angling for aerial-minded landlocked salmon and stubborn, tenacious togue. The region is drained by the Connecticut and Androscoggin rivers, both famous in their own right. The headwaters of the former contain the three Connecticut Lakes and Lake Francis, which are all impoundments. Third Lake on the Quebec border is managed for brook and rainbow trout, Second holds squaretails, salmon, and togue, First harbors salmon and togue, and Francis yields rainbows and salmon. These scenic bodies of water are on U.S. 3 at the northern tip of the state at Pittsburg; the Glen East Inlet pond and stream, spilling into Second, Perry Stream, entering the Connecticut above Francis, Indian Stream, merging into the Connecticut below Pittsburg, and the Mohawk River, joining the big river at Colebrook, along with their tributaries offer some excellent brookie fishing. In addition, many of the small feeders of the lakes produce squaretails, and adjacent ponds such as Scott Bog, Big Brook Bog, Harris, and Round have been reclaimed and are fine brook trout water. As a general rule for the entire top half of New Hampshire, you should make use of the list of trout waters in *New Hampshire Fishing and Hunting;* it indicates the name, location, and trout species in scores of ponds, many of which are reclaimed, in conjunction with the appropriate U.S. Geological Survey Topographic Map. Not all the superior wilderness brookie ponds are on the list: you can find some excitement of your own, including beaver ponds, by prospecting with topo maps.

The Connecticut River between the lakes and from Pittsburg to the Stratford-North Stratford area provides some of New Hampshire's best river fishing for squaretails, rainbows, salmon (they tend to be small), and browns, the latter below the Pittsburg Dam. In the big water some of the fish run to large size, but be *careful,* because the water level fluctuates with the power demands on the lakes' generators and downriver flow needs, and the unwary risk an unexpected swim and trip down the fast water without benefit of a canoe. Many of the tributary systems entering the Connecticut between Pittsburg and the Upper Ammonoosuc at Groveton on U.S. 3 are good squaretail waters and include Bishop, Beaver, Simms, and Stratford Bog, the latter containing a productive pond. The Upper Ammonoosuc—not to be confused with the similarly named river draining the lower section of the White Mountain National Forest, is a fine brook trout stream, reaching east almost to Berlin. The headwaters are especially productive, and the tributaries, Phillips and Nash streams and ponds, also offer top-notch angling.

The brawling Androscoggin River Watershed tops the eastern section of the North County and provides some of its wildest country and best fishing. At the top of the drainage are the Dead Diamond and Swift

Diamond rivers, which form a Y and flow southeast and east respectively to meet and spill into the famed Magalloway River. Located in the swampy and mountainous Academic Grant country along the Maine border, this area is penetrated by a few dirt logging roads and provides some of New England's prime native trout fishing. Many of the feeders, flowing through tight valleys between domes up to 3,000 feet high, also hold wild brookies. Big and Little Diamond ponds at the head of the Swift Diamond, above Kidderville on Route 26, have fishing for rainbow trout; Big Diamond holds togue, while Little Diamond contains squaretails.

The Magalloway flows for a short, meandering distance along the New Hampshire-Maine border before spilling into Umbagog Lake. There are some lunker squaretails and landlocks in this stretch of the Magalloway, although this lowermost portion is full of warmwater fish, particularly yellow perch. Umbagog is rated by the state as a warmwater lake, but knowledgeable anglers take some big salmon in the spring, as well as an occasional togue, and a few landlocks run up the Magalloway in the fall to spawn.

The Androscoggin flows out of Umbagog through a dam at Errol and runs south for about 25 miles along Route 16 to Berlin. This piece of water is one of the great rainbow streams in the East, and holds a few brook trout and landlocks. From Berlin south the river is polluted, and several miles below the city it turns sharply to the east and enters Maine. Some of the tributary brooks and ponds below Errol, such as Big and Little Dummer, Munn, and Success ponds, and Clear and Chickwolnepy streams, are managed for brook trout.

White Mountain Lakes & Streams

Below the North Country is New Hampshire's magnificent White Mountain region, most of which is incorporated into the two sections of the White Mountain National Forest. The steep, granitic ramparts of this majestic Appalachian segment and the deep, narrow valleys which separate the peaks are not conducive to lake formation. With the exception of mountain tarns and beaver ponds, there is very little flat water in the area, except at the edges of the national forest. Running water, to the contrary, is found everywhere, and alpine rivulets race down the rocky, forested flanks of the domes, merge, and form river systems, topping the inner recesses of the ranges with an intricate network of feeders. Some of these streams have such precipitous gradients and scoured streambeds of boulders, cobblestones, and glacial debris that the conditions necessary to form the underwater chain of life are absent. Some of the most famous and scenic streams in the area belong to this category, and though a treat to the eye, are barren, or hold only marginal trout populations.

Other White Mountain rivers, however, offer some of the finest trout fishing in New England. Most of the northern segment of the national forest is drained by the previously-mentioned Upper Ammonoosuc with its remote headwaters striking deep into the region's innermost highlands. The Israel River system taps the southern and western fringes of this area and a small section of the big lower section. The Israel parallels U.S. 2; it flows west to the Connecticut at Lancaster and produces fishing for brook and rainbow trout. The lower section holds some big 'bows and browns which filter in from the Connecticut. Martin Meadow Pond, south of Lancaster on U.S. 3, is an excellent large- and smallmouth bass fishing spot and also produces rainbows. The Peabody River system enters the Androscoggin at Gorham, flowing north along Route 16 from the sweeping grandeur of Mounts Washington, Jefferson, Clay, and Madison, Carter Dome, and Wildcat Mountain. Brook trout and rainbows inhabit the clear, swift currents of this beautiful, peak-shaded stream. Another Androscoggin tributary, the Wild River, contains brook and rainbow trout and

occupies a marshy, forested valley filled with deer, bear, wildcats, and beaver.

The balance of the massive lower segment of the national forest is drained by three major rivers; the Saco, Pemigewasset, and Ammonoosuc. The Saco cuts diagonally across the center of the forest from Crawford Notch southeast to North Conway along U.S. 302. The upper river is brook trout water, and the lower section from Bartlett to the Maine border holds brown trout as well, some of which are large fish and occupy lies in the deep pools, ledges, and snag-filled slower stretches. Many of the Saco's wilderness tributaries are fine brook trout streams, including East Brandy and Ellis rivers, Wildcat River, Dry Brook, Miles Brook, and Rocky Branch, which parallel Route 16. The Swift River, which runs west along the Kancamagus Highway to the Saco, holds rainbows in addition to squaretails and is one of the area's most productive streams.

The Ammonoosuc River originates high in the peaks of the Presidential Range and runs west along U.S. 302 to the Connecticut at Woodsville. Brookies occupy the headwaters, to be joined by rainbows as the river broadens and matures on its path through the national forest. As the Ammonoosuc approaches the Connecticut, brown trout appear, and there are some lunkers, probably entering the stream from the big river. Many of its tributaries, such as the Wild, Ammonoosuc, and Gale rivers, offer good fishing, primarily for brook trout.

The large Pemigewasset River watershed drains most of the western side of the lower segment of the White Mountain National Forest and provides some of its best trout waters. Rising in the Franconia Notch area, the river flows south along U.S. 3 and I-93 through spectacular scenery and holds brookies and rainbows, but it is hard-fished. The squaretail waters of the East Branch course through the vast 100,000-acre Pemigewasset Wilderness, the largest roadless area contained in national forests along the Appalachian Mountain Chain, and meet the main stream at Lincoln. The Mad River, a squaretail and rainbow stream, races southeast between the peaks of Kancamagus and Osceola to the Pemigewasset, south of Campton Upper Village. The popular Baker River rises in the shadow of Mount Moosilauke and meanders in a southwesterly path to the Pemigewasset at Plymouth. The upper half of the stream is considered the best, but brookies and rainbows are taken all the way to Plymouth. Below this point, the river is big water and smallmouths and other warmwater fishes gradually replace trout as the dominant species.

The Lake Country

The famous Lake District sprawls across the state directly below the White Mountain National Forest and contains a group of New England's most popular salmon, trout, and bass lakes. Winnipesaukee, the largest lake in the state, lies east of the Pemigewasset at Wolfeboro and offers fishing for salmon, togue, large and smallmouth bass, whitefish, pickerel, and many varieties of panfish. Spring and fall fishermen take the coldwater species in shallow water, and bass fishermen do well on the shoals all season. In addition, this big body of water is an excellent ice-fishing spot and sprouts ice-shack cities during the winter months. Lake Wentworth at Wolfeboro is possibly the best smallmouth bass water in the state and produces exceptional fly fishing during a special season in May and June. Other notable lakes adjacent to Winnipesaukee include Big and Little Squam at Holderness, which yield landlocks, togue, smallmouths, and pickerel; Winnisquam at Laconia, which holds the same mixture plus largemouths; Merrymeeting Lake northeast of Alton on Route 11, which produces similar species to the Squams, as does Silver Lake Route at the village of Silver Lake; Dan Hole Pond, west of Center Ossipee, which provides brookies, salmon, togue, and panfish; and Ossipee Lake at Center Ossipee,

which furnishes angling for salmon, smallmouths, a few brook trout, and panfish. Two tributaries, the Bearcamp and Pine rivers, flowing southeast and northwest, respectively, to Ossipee along Routes 16 and 25 are top-rated trout streams. White Lake at West Ossipee on Route 16 supplies squaretails and splake, including the state record for the latter species, and Chocorua Lake, a few miles north on Route 16, is one of the state's prime smallmouth waters.

Great East Lake, straddling the Maine border near Wakefield, is a "sleeper" and is overshadowed by its better-known neighbors such as Winnipesaukee. This body of water has a substantial togue population and produces fish in excess of 20 pounds, and holds numbers of brown trout, including trophies to 15 pounds, as well as plenty of smallmouths. Intensive management efforts by Maine would seem to forecast an interesting future.

Newfound Lake, west of the Pemigewasset at Bridgewater, holds the state record for lake trout and produces landlocks, smallmouth bass, and panfish. Its outlet, the Newfound River, offers good fishing for brook trout and rainbows down to Bristol, where it enters the Pemigewasset. The Smith River, a short distance south of Newfound Lake and Bristol, flows west along Route 104 to the Pemigewasset and is a popular brook trout and rainbow stream.

The useful, large-format, 202-page guide, *Trout and Salmon Fishing* in New England lakes and ponds ($8 postpaid), contains detailed descriptions and lake survey maps of Silver, Winnipesaukee, Sunapee, Squam, Newfound, Ossipee, First Connecticut, and Winnisquam lakes. It may be ordered from: Partridge Press, Box 422, Campton 03223.

Sunapee Lake Country

Southwest of Bristol, adjacent to I-89, is the Sunapee Lake region centered in the towns of New London, Georges Mills, and Newbury. Sunapee was once famous as the home of the fabulous golden trout *Salvelinus aureolus*, an arctic char remnant population established during the glacial ages. Those rare, beautiful fish reached weights in excess of 12 pounds, but fishing pressure and changes in habitat caused their decline in this century. The lake does produce good angling for salmon, togue, brook trout, smallmouths, and panfish, and is enjoyable fishing, since it lies in a scenic area, surrounded by Mount Sunapee and other forested peaks. Pleasant Lake, in the towns of New London and Elkins, yielded both the state record 9-pound squaretail and 18-pound 5-ounce landlocked salmon, and offers fishing for smallmouths too. The Sugar River, which drains Sunapee, and its North and South branches, and the Blockwater River, issuing from Pleasant Lake, supply good stream fishing for brook, brown, and rainbow trout.

Southern Waters

Southern New Hampshire, below the Lakes Region, is more heavily populated, but because of its relatively rugged terrain it offers some fine fishing opportunities. South of Sunapee the Cold River flows west along Routes 123-A and 123 to the Connecticut River at the town of Cold River and provides brook, brown, and rainbow trout. The Ashuelot River, a Connecticut tributary in the extreme southwest corner of the state, is a well-known brown and rainbow trout stream in its upper reaches and runs south and then west along Routes 10 and 119 to the Connecticut at Hinsdale, just south of Pisgah State Park. Spofford Lake, a short distance north of the park at the town of Spofford, contains rainbows, both kinds of bass, and panfish, and yielded the state record northern pike. Several miles east of Keene on Route 112 is Nubanusit Lake, managed for salmon, lakers, and rainbows, which yields some impressive catches of these species. Bow Lake, in eastern

New Hampshire at Bow Lake Village, furnishes good angling for landlocks, lakers, and smallmouths.

The balance of the more industrialized southern tier is a well-drained region and there are some streams with productive, though relatively short, trout stretches and hundreds of ponds and lakes which offer bass, pickerel, and panfish, sometimes in combination with trout, and can yield some surprising catches. The lower portions of the Connecticut and Merrimack rivers provide, in certain stretches, excellent fishing for walleyes, bass, pickerel, and panfish; the former holds some hefty northern pike. The Contoocook, running north and east along U.S. 202 and then by secondary roads to Penacook, above Concord, on the Merrimack, has some trout fishing in its headwaters and smallmouths and walleyes in the lower sections. One of its tributaries, the Warner River, coursing east along Routes 103 and I-89, is a picturesque brook and rainbow trout stream in its upper reaches and is distinguished by a series of covered bridges along its scenic watershed. The Souhegan River crosses the center of the Massachusetts border and flows northeast for 31 miles through the towns of Greenville, Wilton, and Milford to the Merrimack River. The stream is stocked with brook, brown, and rainbow trout and provides good fishing from Wilton upstream. The Souhegan parallels Routes 123-A, 123, 31, and 101 in the trout fishing area.

Saltwater Fishing

New Hampshire offers excellent saltwater fishing on its short Atlantic coastline. Striped bass, bluefish, mackerel, tautog, cod, haddock, pollack, hake, flounder, and smelt are the most popular inshore species, and giant tuna are taken offshore. The biggest news on the coast is the introduction of coho salmon. The fish appear in the middle of July in coastal waters and provide exciting fishing in the tidal areas of rivers, particularly the Lamprey and the Exeter. The former produced a new

state record (15 pounds) in 1976. The best months for the silver salmon are September, October, and November. In addition to salmon, some of the tidal rivers and creeks are rumored to support runs of migratory browns, but as with sea trout fishing everywhere, information is jealously guarded, and it takes hard probing to learn anything of use. Headquarters for saltwater fishing, including boats, charters, bait, and tackle, can be found at towns located along Route 1-A, such as Seabrook Beach, Hampton, Rye Beach, Wallis Sands, and Portsmouth.

Hunting

New Hampshire provides hunters with abundant opportunities in some of the most varied scenic terrain in the East. There is plenty of public land to hunt in the White Mountain National Forest, public hunting areas and state forest and park hunting zones (limited). Many of the corporate owners of the several millions of acres of commercial forests grant responsible hunters access, as do smaller landowners, upon a polite request. Write: Fish & Game Dept. (address above) for the free *New Hampshire Hunting and Trapping Guide*, which provides the usual ordinances, seasons, limits, license information, sunrise and sunset hours, protected species, and a list of department officials and wardens, along with their addresses and telephone numbers. Upon request the state will mail you a nonresident license application so that you can save time and effort in securing a license.

New Hampshire has one of the healthiest deer herds in the East and it is spread throughout the state. Generally speaking, the best deer hunting is found in areas where thick forests border on fields, farmlands, and orchards. Deer will be most plentiful where there is abundant food, such as agricultural products, nuts, and field graze, as well as the relative safety of vast forest expanses where they can retreat during daylight hours, or when threatened. New Hampshire has settlements and abandoned farms throughout the northern half and these areas produce some of the best hunting in the state. The harsh climate of the upper mountain ridges and the lack of food makes extreme high country a poor choice for the deer hunter. The edges of the White Mountain National Forest are productive, and one of the very best

areas in the state is the Lakes Region of Carroll, Grafton, and Belknap counties, which provides the ideal combination of populated areas, farms, and dense forest cover. Some of the deer kills per square mile in this territory, which rests on the southern border of the national forest, are unusually high. However, good deer hunting is found everywhere in the state, and the Fish & Game Department has kept the herd in proper balance by allowing an either-sex season.

Black bear are firmly established in New Hampshire, and are found primarily in the three northern counties: Grafton, Carroll, and Coos. Bears prefer similar habitat to deer, but are better equipped to survive in more remote areas, where their powerful claws secure a wide range of food and their hibernation habits enable them to withstand the rigors of a severe environment.

The ruffed grouse, or "partridge," is well distributed throughout New Hampshire and is most abundant in field-forest fringe areas, abandoned farmlands, second growth, and stream bottoms and alder thickets where optimum food and cover balances occur. The Lakes Region, White Mountain National Forest, and North Country probably furnish the most birds, but there is plenty of prime cover in the southern tier, where the major problem is hunting pressure. Grouse are by far the most popular and plentiful game bird.

Woodcock run a close second to grouse in importance and are found in alder thickets, stream bottoms, and soft, moist forest cover all over the state. Migratory flights funnel in from Quebec on the north and from Maine on the east to augment the native population. Woodcock are often found with grouse, but are concentrated in damp areas where earthworm supplies are generous.

Although New Hampshire does not have extensive wildfowl marshes, the state provides some duck and goose hunting for those interested. Great Bay and the salt marshes along the brief shoreline provide good gunning, as do the many lakes, swamps, ponds, large slow rivers, and beaver flowages scattered around the state. Black ducks, goldeneyes, and wood ducks nest in the state, and mallards, teal, scaup, and other flight ducks pass through in season. Most of the Canada goose kills are made along the coast. In addition, sea ducks, including scoters or "coot," mergansers, old-squaws, and an occasional eider are shot from rocky points, islands, and open water. Refer to the waterfowl management area list in *New Hampshire Fishing and Hunting*, which gives the location, U.S. Geological Survey quadrangle, flooded acreage, and total area of the state's 37 wildfowl units.

Snowshoe rabbits are very abundant from the Lakes Region north to the top of the state. Spruce and cedar swamps are particularly good bets, and you will need snowshoes to hunt this swift animal once the snow piles up in the deep woods. Cottontail rabbits are found in southern New Hampshire, and good populations exist in the farmland fringes, swales, and brier tangles which cottontails prefer. Gray squirrels, too, are primarily southern tier residents; the animals are neither abundant nor popular.

Write to: Fish & Game Dept. (address above) for a subscription to *New Hampshire Natural Resources*, a semiannual magazine, and the companion monthly *Field Notes* newsletter; they provide articles on fishing, hunting, "where-to-go" and "how-to," wildlife species, and conservation. A subscription to both information sources costs $4.00 for one year or $7.50 for 2 years.

Golden Trout of the North Woods

The rare Sunapee trout *(Salvelinus aureolus)* is a remnant of the Arctic char which survived the great Wisconsin glacial age in a hand-

ful of once remote New England lakes and ponds. The beautiful, mysterious Sunapee—with its steel-green back, cream sides, and brilliant gold and ruby colored spots, and dazzling orange belly—was first discovered in the deep cold waters of Sunapee Lake, New Hampshire, in 1888. Toward the close of the 19th century, anglers reported catching a large number of big, deep-feeding Sunapee reaching weights of up to 12 pounds, with odd tales of this golden char reaching 15 to 20 pounds. As word of this rare and beautiful fish spread, fishermen came to the scenic, mountain-rimmed, blue waters of Sunapee, sporting camps and lodges sprang up, and the fishing for this fragile char rapidly declined with the increased pressure and interbreeding problems with lake trout.

The Sunapee was also reportedly caught in great numbers during the early 1900's in the deep glacial waters of kidney-shaped Little Averill Lake, surrounded by the evergreen-flanked mountains and ridges of Vermont's Northeast Kingdom. Today, the only thriving population of Sunapee left in its former range is found in Floods Pond near Ellsworth, Maine. Sunapee were stocked in the South Branch Ponds near Mount Kathadin in 1971. Primarily a smelt feeder, the Sunapee is found in shallow water for a brief two-week period after ice-out, then returns to the deeps until its spawning run in the autumn.

A fascinating publication, *The Sunapee—Maine's Rarest Trout* (B-208, 25¢) may be obtained by writing: Maine Dept. of Inland Fisheries & Wildlife, 284 State St., Augusta, ME 04333.

Highways—Recreation & White Mountain Scenic Routes

The *New Hampshire Official Highway Map* is distributed free by: Division of Economic Development, Concord 03301. The full-color map keys the locations of highways (express or interstate, U.S., primary state, secondary state), town or local roads, foot trails, historical markers, points of interest, cities and towns, public recreation areas, picnic areas, roadside rest areas, mountain passes or notches, airports, fire lookout stations, fish hatcheries, covered bridges, ski areas, high mountain peaks, and water features. A chart of public recreation areas gives the map locations, nearest towns, and types of available recreation for state parks, White Mountain National Forest, and other areas.

The Kancamagus Highway winds through the White Mountain National Forest for 34½ miles between Lincoln and Conway, offering marvelous views of towering mountain peaks, plunging mountain streams, and vistas of unspoiled wilderness. The Forest Service maintains recreation facilities, picnic sites, developed campgrounds, and scenic areas of outstanding natural beauty along the highway. Trails head along the highway for hikes ranging from an hour's to several days' duration. A free brochure on the *Kancamagus Highway* is available from: Forest Supervisor, White Mountain National Forest, Laconia 03246. The brochure describes the facilities and scenic areas along the highway, and includes a map of the highway showing the locations of national forest boundaries, campgrounds, picnic sites, scenic areas, overlooks, and water features.

Eight tours in the White Mountains are listed and mapped in a free brochure, *Shunpike Fall Foliage in New Hampshire's White Mountain Region.* The brochure is free from: White Mountain Region Assn., Lancaster 03584.

Lake Contour Fishing Maps

Special lake contour sounding maps of New Hampshire's major lakes are available for 50¢ each, or $2.00 for a package set of the larger lakes,

from: Fish & Game Department, 34 Bridge St., Concord 03301. These useful maps provide the angler with information about the composition of the lake bottom and show depths and contours, islands, feeder streams, and boat-launching sites. Individual maps are available for *Winnipesaukee, Winnisquam, Newfound, Ossipee, Dan Hole, First and Second Connecticut Lakes, Merrymeeting, Pleasant, Silver, Waukewan,* and *Nubanusit* lakes. The package set includes Winnipesaukee, Winnisquam, Newfound, Ossipee, Dan Hole, and First and Second Connecticut Lakes.

Ski Touring Trails & Centers

New Hampshire's majestic winter wilderness, with its whitened forests, fields, and slopes laced by hundreds of miles of trails, old logging roads, abandoned railroad beds, old carriage paths, and frozen lakes and streams, offers some of the nation's top cross-country skiing. The Granite State's major ski touring areas are described in the 288-page *EMS New England Ski Touring Guide*—including the abandoned railroad beds of the old Suncook Valley Railroad and Claremont and Concord Railroad. The EMS guide, which also contains regional maps, driving directions, ski trail mileages, and facilities, may be obtained for $5.95 (plus 50¢ postage) from: Eastern Mountain Sports, 1047 Commonwealth Ave., Boston, MA 02215.

For specific information about New Hampshire's ski touring trails, instruction, rentals, and lodging, write: *Village of Bretton Woods* 03575, (413) 783-4411, instruction, rentals, base camp for ski mountaineering treks up Mount Washington, Lealand Notch, or Jefferson Notch, and abandoned railroad beds and carriage paths; *Eastern Mountain Sports Nordic Ski Center,* Intervale 03845, (603) 356-5496, trail maps, instruction, rentals, 30 miles of trails in the Mount Washington Valley; *Jackson Ski Touring Foundation,* Box 90, Jackson 03846, (603) 383-9355, trail maps, guides, instruction, lodging, wilderness trails and logging roads in White Mountain National Forest; *Appalachian Mountain Club North Country System, Pinkham Notch Camp,* Gorham 03581, (603) 466-2727, ski touring trail information for the area, including Blanchard Loop, Lost Pond Trail, Mount Washington Auto Road (high winds, ice, and arctic weather conditions make this a hazardous tour), and Pinkham Notch Ski Trail; *Mitteraill Ski Area,* Cannon Mountain 03580, instruction, rentals, snowshoeing, and wilderness trails to Franconia Village in the northwestern corner of the White Mountain National Forest; *Waterville*

Valley Ski Touring Center, Waterville 03223, (603) 236-8311, at the head of the scenic Mad River Valley, surrounded by the White Mountain National Forest, instruction, rentals, guided trips, lodging, 35 miles of trails; *Summers Ski Tour Center*, Dublin 03444, (603) 563-8556, in the beautiful Mount Monadnock area, rentals, instruction, trails; *Temple Mountain Touring Center*, Peterborough 03458, (603) 924-6949, guided tours, winter camping, instruction, rentals, trails, base camp for treks up Mount Monadnock.

Other ski touring areas with instruction clinics include *Acworth Cross-Country Inn*, Acworth 03601, (603) 835-6869; *Attitash Ski Area*, North Conway 03860, (603) 374-2369; *Carroll Reed Ski Shops*, Campton 03223, (603) 726-3538; *Charmingfare Ski Touring Center*, Box 361, RFD 1, Manchester 03104; *Moose Mountain Cross Country Lodge*, Etna 03750, (603) 588-6345; *Pole & Pedal Shop*, Box 325, Henniker 03242, (603) 428-3242; *Gunstock Ski Area*, Laconia 03246, (603) 293-4342; *Loon Mountain*, on the Kancamagus Highway in White Mountain National Forest, Lincoln 03251, (603) 745-8111; *A & D Touring Center*, New Ipswich 03071, (603) 878-1863; *Emerson Hill Ski Touring Center*, New Ipswich 03071, (603) 878-1863; *Mount Sunapee*, Newbury 03255, (603) 763-2356; *The Skimobile*, Cranmore Mountain, North Conway 03860, (603) 356-5544; *North Conway Eastern Mountain Sports Shop*, North Conway 03860, (603) 356-5433; *The Nordic Skier* (maps and literature on request), Wolfeboro 03894, (603) 569-3724, known as the "ski touring center of the Lakes Region," surrounded by mountains on the eastern shore of Lake Winnipesaukee, with lodging and instruction; *Windblown*, New Ipswich 03071, (603) 878-2869, is a rustic retreat just north of the Massachusetts border with a 20-mile network of backcountry trails; *Franconia Inn Ski Touring Center*, Franconia 03580, (603) 823-5542, is located in the beautiful Easton Valley at the base of the Franconia Range, with 65 miles of scenic backcountry trails, instruction, and guided tours; *Grey Ledges*, Grantham 03753, (603) 863-9880, is a 213-year-old farm estate with over 100 miles of backcountry trails, lodging, bunkrooms, and a pioneer log cabin; *The Balsams*, Dixfield Notch 03576, (603) 255-3400, is a famous 15,000-acre north country resort in its 104th year, with more than 75 miles of marked and wilderness trails; *Norsk Ski Touring Center*, New London 03257, (603) 526-6040, is located at Mt. Kearsarge and operated at the facilities of the Lake Sunapee Country Club.

A free *Ski Accommodations* brochure listing hotels, motels, resorts, and campgrounds near ski areas accessible by way of New Hampshire 93, which runs north-south through the White Mountains, is available from: White Mountains 93 Assn., Lincoln 03251. The Ski Touring Council, Troy, VT 05868, publishes the useful *Ski Touring Guide* ($3.50), which provides a comprehensive listing and description of ski touring areas, instruction, and trails in the East. The council also publishes an *Annual Schedule* ($2.75) which lists workshops, tours, citizen races, and competitive events in the eastern United States and Canada.

White Mountain Wilderness Instruction Services

The *Eastern Mountain Sports Climbing School* offers the following instruction in various phases of technical rock, ice, and winter climbing at all levels of difficulty. Instruction on the intermediate and advanced levels is given on actual climbs in groups of no more than 2 students per instructor.

Winter climbing instruction will provide training in winter camping and navigation as well as technical snow and ice climbing. The emphasis will be on how to climb, live, and travel safely in the mountains under winter conditions. Technical climbing instruction will involve techniques and methods applicable to mountaineering in Alaska, Canada, the Andes, etc., as well as the shorter severe ice pitches and gullies found here in New England. Obviously opportunities for glacier travel and crevasse rescue practice are somewhat limited in this area, but weather and snow conditions do offer some severe technical problems. Register as early as possible. To guarantee space your reservation must be received at least 1 week in advance. Write or phone for rates and info: Eastern Mountain Sports Climbing School, Main St., North Conway 03860, phone (603) 356-5433.

The *International Mountain Climbing School*, North Conway 03860, phone (603) 356-5287, provides private and group instruction in the art of rock and ice climbing for all levels of experience, in the White Mountains. Services include Mount Washington climbs, winter camping, and package overnight trips and expeditions.

The *Appalachian Mountain Club* offers summer workshops in mountaineering, orienteering, skiing, mountain photography, nature study, and backpacking. For more information on the workshops, write to: Workshop Coordinator, Appalachian Mountain Club, Pinkham Notch Camp, Gorham 03581.

Wild & Scenic River Maps

The following large-scale U.S. Geological Survey Maps show the entire lengths of New Hampshire's premier canoe routes and trophy trout streams (see the New Hampshire and Maine "Travel & Recreation Guide" sections for additional listings). *Ammonoosuc River:* Littleton, Moosilauke, Mount Washington, Whitefield, Woodsville; *Upper Ammonoosuc River:* Guildhall (VT), Percy; *Ashuelot River:* Gileum Gorge, Pisgah Mountains; *Indian Stream:* Indian Stream, Moose Bog; *Swift River:* Crawford Notch, Ossipee Lake, Sebago Lake (ME); *Mad River:* Lincoln, Mount Chocorua, Mount Osecol, Plymouth; *Swift Diamond River:* Dixville, Errol; *Bearcamp River:* Plymouth, Mount Chocorua, Ossipee Lake; *Wild Ammonoosuc River:* Lisbon, East Haverhill, Mount Moosilauke; *Upper Connecticut River:* Indian Stream, Averill; *Androscoggin River & Umbagog Lake:* Errol, Milan, Berlin, Shelburn; *Israel River:* Mount Washington, Whitefield; *Pine River:* Ossipee Lake, Wolfeboro.

The Lakes Region

Lakes Region Topo Maps

Large-scale U.S. Geological Survey Maps: Plymouth, Mount Choco-rua, Ossipee Lake, Holderness, Winnipesaukee, Penacook, Gilman-ton, Alton, Wolfeboro.

South of the White Mountains is a group of famous landlocked salmon and lake trout waters, forming the largest and most beautiful of the state's 1,300 lakes, dominated by the jagged shoreline and blue island-dotted waters of Lake Winnipesaukee (the Indian name meaning "The Smile of the Great Spirit"), the second largest lake in New England. Algonquin Indians once fished these abundant lakes and hunted in the surrounding Squam, Ossipee, and Belknap mountains. The scenic mountain forests of this region harbor a variety of game, and provide good hunting for deer, woodcock, pheasants, and ducks. Smaller numbers of black bear and bobcat also roam the conifer and mixed hardwood forests surrounding the lakes.

The Indians who once inhabited these lands were of two confederacies: the Abenakis, "those living at the sunrise," and the Penacooks, "living at the bottom of the hill." Among the most powerful tribes of these confederacies were Winnipesaukees (Penacooks), and the Abenaki Ossipees. Winnipesaukees inhabited the fishing village of Aquadochtan at the weirs on the lake that bears their name; it lay on the north side of a stony stream that led to huge W-shaped fish traps made of stone and woven-together saplings. Here at the source of the Winnipesaukee River the Indians made great catches of shad, which were dried and stored for winter use.

New Hampshire's largest body of water, Lake Winnipesaukee, is 22 miles long and from 1 to 10 miles wide, with depths ranging to 300 feet, has a 240-mile shoreline and more than 250 scenic islands. Spring is naturally the best season for the coldwater salmon and trout. Winter fishing is also popular here; during the cold, snowy months hundreds of small ice-fishing huts dot the lake's frozen surface. Winnisquam Lake, covering 4,264 acres with a maximum depth of 154 feet, provides excellent fishing for lake trout and landlocked salmon, as well as for smallmouth and largemouth bass, and pickerel. Nearby Squam and Little Squam lakes, connected by a short, navigable neck of water, are known primarily for lake trout and landlocked salmon fishing.

The Ossipees fished beautiful Ossipee Lake and River, and the Pine and Bearcamp rivers. The remains of what was thought to be their burial place were found near the lake in the 1870s. Arrowheads, stone knives, and other artifacts lie along trails and in open fields throughout the area. Ossipee is a small lake, about 3.5 by 2 miles, with a pine-fringed shoreline. There are some summer homes around its shore. The lake holds large black bass, landlocked salmon, brook trout, and pickerel.

Mount Chocorua and its neighboring peaks tower above the forested shores of Big Squam Lake, one of the state's top-ranked salmon lakes, annually yielding landlocks up to 12 pounds. Both Big Squam and Little Squam dominate a scenic area known to the Indians as "Won-nasquamsaukee"—"the beautiful place surrounded by water." Other features of the region include the famous lake trout and landlocked salmon waters of Newfound Lake (known to the Indians as "Pas-quaney"—"the place where birch bark is found"), with its sheer 800-foot-high rock ledges and the Bearcamp River, Pine River, Pemigewas-set River, Merrymeeting Lake, Hemmenway and Belknap state reservations, and Sky Pond and Green Mountain state forests. White Lake State Park, near Tamworth, offers trout fishing and camping. Other state parks in the region are Ellacoya, on the southwest shore of Lake Winnipesaukee, and Wentworth, on the shore of the lake of

NEW HAMPSHIRE TRAVEL & RECREATION GUIDE

that name. Most of the state reserves have camping facilities. White Lake State Park, the largest camping area, limits stays to 2 weeks in the period July 1 to August 15. Reservations for White Lake camping should be made in person at the park office.

Hundreds of miles of scenic trails lace through the backcountry of the Squam, Ossipee, and Belknap mountains, good for hiking or ski touring. In addition, many towns and alpine ski areas have miles of marked cross-country trails.

Where to . . . in the Lakes Region of New Hampshire is a comprehensive 100-page guide to recreation, accommodations (motel, hotel, resorts, cabins, and camps), tourist services and facilities, campgrounds, and other features of the area. The guide describes most outfitting and supply centers in the region, gives detailed information on individual resorts and lodges, and includes special information on hunting and fishing seasons, scenic areas, and winter recreation. It also describes the history of the region. It is available free from: Lakes Region Assn., Wolfeboro 03894.

Vacation accommodations in the Lakes Region include the following resorts and lodges: *Clearwater Lodges* (603) 569-2370, *Piping Rock Cottages* (603) 569-1915, and *Winter Harbor Lodges* (603) 569-3596, all on Lake Winnipesaukee at Wolfeboro 03894; *Pick Point Lodge & Cottages*, Mirror Lake 03853, (603) 569-1338, on Lake Winnipesaukee; *Edwards on Wentworth*, Wolfeboro 03894, (603) 596-2124, on Crescent and Wentworth lakes; *Sandy Point Beach Resort* on Lake Winnipesaukee, Alton Bay 03810; *Lane's End* with 33 cabins and cottages on Lake Winnipesaukee, Melvin Village 03850, (603) 544-2641; *Red Cottage Colony* (Lake Winnipesaukee), Mirror Lake 03853, (603) 569-2726; *The Village at Winnipesaukee*, Weirs Beach 03246, (603) 366-2272; *Christmas Island* (603) 366-4378, *Flying Cloud* (603) 366-4993, *Grand View* (603) 366-0000, *Sweetwood Cottages* (603) 366-4680, all on Lake Winnipesaukee at Laconia 03246; *Kings Grant Inn & Chalets* on Lake Winnipesaukee, Gilford-Laconia 03246, (603) 293-4431; *Camp Laughing Bear* (603) 968-3819 and *Pine Shore Cottages* (603) 968-3871, both on Big Squam Lake at Holderness 03245; *Perkins Cabins* on Little Squam Lake, Holderness 03245, (603) 968-3680; *Little Switzerland Housekeeping Cottages* on Big Squam Lake, Holderness 03245, (603) 968-3807; *Pasquaney Inn* (603) 744-2712, *Bungalo Village* (603) 744-2220, and the *Whip-O-Will* (603) 744-2433, all on Newfound Lake at Bristol 03222; *Wagon Wheel Inn* (603) 744-3590 and *Sandybeach Bungalows* (603) 744-8473, both overlooking Newfound Lake at Bristol 03222.

Access & Outfitting Centers

Gilford, Laconia, Center Harbor, and Melvin Village on Lake Winnipesaukee, Holderness on Squam Lake, and West and Center Ossipee on Ossipee Lake are among the many outfitting and supply centers in the Lakes Region that offer boat and canoe rentals, fishing gear, and family vacation lodging. The area may be reached by driving north on State Routes 106 or 28, or U.S. 202/4. U.S. 3/Interstate 93 is the main artery entering the Lakes Region from the White Mountains National Forest to the north.

The North Country

North Country Topo Maps

U.S. Geological Survey Overview Maps (scale 1:250,000): Lewiston, Sherbrooke.

Connecticut Lakes Headwaters Country

The following large-scale U.S. Geological Survey Maps show First, Second, and Third Connecticut Lakes and Lake Francis: Moose Bog, Second Connecticut Lake, Indian Stream.

Dead Diamond River

Large-scale U.S. Geological Survey Topographical Maps: Second Connecticut Lake, Errol.

This magnificent evergreen forest and wilderness lake country includes the entire northern section of New Hampshire from the Upper Ammonoosuc River on the south to the Maine-New Hampshire border on the east, and the headwater lakes of the Connecticut River area along the Vermont and Quebec borders to the east and north. The vast North Country interior is among the northeast's last vestiges of wilderness. Few foot trails lead through the forests and rolling hills, but logging operations have created an intricate network of gravel roads that provide the fisherman, hunter, and camper with access to remote pockets of the hinterlands.

The Connecticut River finds its source near the Canadian boundary and flows southwest, forming a series of beautiful blue lakes as it flows south. The First Connecticut Lake, the largest of the lakes (5½ miles long), mirrors the unbroken fir and spruce forests of its northern and eastern shores, brilliant with color in the fall. Mountains rise up beyond the shores, among them the forested slopes of Magalloway Mountain (3,360 feet). Trails to Magalloway Mountain head on the eastern side of the lake, but directions from local inhabitants are necessary, and a guide would be helpful. The lake holds trophy landlocked salmon, and lake, rainbow, and brook trout. This majestic glacial lake is one of New England's premier landlocked salmon meccas. Back in the 1930's it was known for its population of chinook salmon, which reached weights of up to 12 pounds. Camping is available nearby. Several sporting lodges are located on the lake's western shore.

The Second Connecticut Lake lies among forested hills, 8 miles from the wide swells of Bosebuck (3,149 feet) and Rump (3,647 feet) mountains. Second Lake is framed on the west by the scenic conifers and hardwoods of the Connecticut Lakes State Forest. Third Lake, also known as Lake St. Sophia, surrounded by hills, embodies the primeval beauty of the northlands. Guides and trail information are available at nearby Pittsburg, the Glen or Camp Idlewild. The headwaters of the Connecticut River, where it flows from the Connecticut Lakes, downstream to North Stratford holds some lunker wild brook, brown, and rainbow trout.

The United States and Canada both claimed the Connecticut Lakes Region in the early years of its settlement. Finally the settlers formed their own government, and by 1829 the area was known as the Indian Stream Territory, named for the river which rises at the northern tip of the state and flows through this region. In 1832 the settlers formed the Republic of Indian Stream, with its own courts, constitution, council, and assembly. The republic died in 1836 when the New Hampshire militia occupied the region after a dispute with the Canadian authorities.

U.S. 3, one of three main highways in the whole of the North Country, provides access or near access to all the lakes but the Fourth. For the most part, even secondary roads are few and short in the North Country, and few of the mountains have trails. Inexperienced hikers should not attempt this sparsely settled, undeveloped region without guides; competent wilderness travelers will find it a challenge and a pleasure. The logging roads that run through the region alter their courses from year to year; for current trail information contact the state district chief conservation officer or the state district fire chiefs.

Some of the best areas for backcountry trekking and wilderness fly fishing in the Connecticut Lakes Region are old logging roads running from First Lake to Hell Gate on the Dead Diamond River, through the heart of the North Country woods; the Grouse Survey line from the Balsams Hotel in Dixville Notch to the dam at the lower end of Second Lake; Rump Mountain; and Deer Mountain Trail from Moose Campground north of Second Lake to the mountain summit. Both the Swift Diamond and Dead Diamond rivers hold large, wild brook trout. The Swift Diamond is fed by Big Diamond Pond in Coleman State Park and offers several miles of wild, deep-flowing water accessible by trail along its bank.

In the northernmost section of the state lies the Upper Androscoggin and Magalloway region, with logging roads winding through the areas of Cambridge Black Mountain (2,711 feet), Signal Mountain (2,673 feet), and the Diamond River, which has carved a stunning gorge between the Diamond Peaks on the north and Mount Dustan on the south. The remote stretches of the Dead and Swift branches of the Diamond offer some of the state's finest brook trout fishing.

South of the Connecticut Lakes lie the Dixville Mountains, including Mount Abenaki, Cave Mountain, Dixville Peak, Mount Gloriette, and Mount Sanguinari. The Balsams Hotel owns land in the Dixville Notch area, and manages the wilderness ski area on the western slopes of Dixville Peak. The Sanguinary Ridge trail winds from the Flume Picnic area of the Dixville Notch Waysider through the spruce and balsam forests of Mount Sanguinari. In the adjacent Upper Connecticut River region the West Side and Notch trails wind up the graceful slopes of the Percy Peaks. Sugarloaf Mountain in this area can also be scaled by trail.

The Crescent Range and the Moose River lie just north of the Presidential Range. Mount Crescent (3,230 feet) and Black Crescent Mountain (3,265 feet) offer some of the most challenging climbs in the area. Crescent Ridge Trail and Mount Crescent Trail ascend the mountain by that name, but Black Crescent to the north has no paths. Climbers can ascend Black Crescent from Pebomauk Fall or the head of the Ice Gulch, a deep, boulder-strewn chasm between these two mountains. Ice caves dot the canyon depths. The melting ice and springs feed the headwaters of Moose Brook. The Moosebank path follows the Moose River through nearby Randolph Valley. Durand Lake can be reached by the path; it holds salmon, rainbow trout, and brook trout. The path opens onto vistas of the northern peaks in the distance.

Beyond the Crescent Range to the north, in the small, isolated town of Randolph, lies the Pond of Safety, named for a handful of continental soldiers of the Revolutionary War who sought refuge here after deserting. Several trails lead to the pond.

Whitetail deer are found throughout the North Country. Black bears roam the remote clearings, slopes, and river valleys. Bobcat prowl the woods, seldom seen. The North Country also harbors red fox, snowshoe hare, raccoon, and a variety of upland game birds, and hawks.

Several state parks that lie within this region have public camping facilities. Coleman State Park, on little Diamond Pond in the Con-

necticut Lakes region, has 30 tent sites. There are 12 primitive camp-sites at Milan Hill State Park. The hilltop park overlooks the White Mountains, the Kilkenny Range, and the backcountry of southern Canada. Moose Brook State Park has more than 40 tent sites and is a good base for treks through the Randolph Range. The *New Hampshire Four-Seasons State Camping Guide* lists and describes public and private camping areas in the North Country and throughout the state. Order it from: Lee Bosworth, New Hampshire Campground Owners Assn., Harbor Hill CA, Rte. 25, Meredith 03253.

Vacation accommodations and services in the North Country are provided by the following fishing, hunting, and vacation resorts and lodges: *The Glen* (603) 538-6500, *John's Lodge & Log Cabins* (603) 538-6541, *Partridge Lodge & Cabins* (603) 538-6380, and *Timberland Camps* (603) 538-6613, all on First Connecticut Lake, Pittsburg 03592; *Tall Timber*, Pittsburg 03592, (603) 538-6651, with cabins and lodge on Back Lake; *The Balsams Hotel*, Dixville Notch 03576, (603) 255-3400, a famous 104-year old resort on 15,000 acres high in the northern White Mountains.

Access & Outfitting Centers

U.S. Highway 3 parallels the Connecticut River from Stewartstown northeast along the western shorelines of Lake Francis and Second Connecticut Lake where it merges into State Route 3 and enters the Connecticut Lakes State Forest, passing Second and Third Connecticut lakes to the Quebec border. Lodging, boat and canoe rentals, gear, supplies, and guides are available at Pittsburg, Stewartstown and the Glen. State Highway 26 passes through the heart of the North Country and provides access to Umbagog Lake, Dixville Wilderness Ski Area, Mohawk River, and Coleman State Park. The region is reached along the west via U.S. 3 and on the east via State Route 16 which parallels the Androscoggin River. The North Country's southern boundary is traversed by State Route 110.

White Mountain National Forest & The Presidential Range

White Mountain National Forest Topo Maps

U.S. Geological Survey Overview Maps (scale 1:250,000): Lewiston, Portland.

Caribou-Speckled Mountain Wilderness

Large-scale U.S. Geological Survey Topographic Maps: Speckled Mountain, Wild River.

Carr Mountain Wilderness

Large-scale U.S. Geological Survey Topographic Maps: Plymouth, Rumney.

Dry River—Rocky Branch Wilderness

Large-scale U.S. Geological Survey Topographic Maps: Crawford Notch, North Country.

Great Gulf Wilderness

Large-scale U.S. Geological Survey Topographic Maps: Carter Dome, Mount Washington.

Killkenny Wilderness

Large-scale U.S. Geological Survey Topographic Maps: Percy, Mount Washington.

Pemigewasset Wilderness

Large-scale U.S. Geological Survey Topographic Maps: Crawford Notch, Franconia, Lincoln, Mount Osceola, South Twin.

Presidential Range Mountains

Large-scale U.S. Geological Survey Topographic Maps: Berlin, Carter Dome, Crawford Notch, Mount Washington.

Sandwich Range Wilderness

Large-scale U.S. Geological Survey Topographic Maps: Mount Chocorua, Ossipee Lake, Plymouth.

Wild River Wilderness

Large-scale U.S. Geological Survey Topographic Maps: Carter Dome, Wild River.

The White Mountain National Forest encompasses New England's largest and most majestic fishing, backpacking, hunting, and wilderness camping area, covering 727,000 acres crowned by the towering peaks of the Presidential Range. The White Mountains, once the home and hunting grounds of the Algonquin Indians and known to them as *Waumbeck Methna* ("white rock"), sweep across more than 1,200 square miles in the northern half of the state into Maine, covered by forests of fir, hemlock, spruce, and lovely stands of mature white birch. The only higher mountains east of the Rockies are in North Carolina and Tennessee. Eight of the White Mountains are more than a mile high; 22 are 4,000 to 5,000 feet; and 26 3,000 to 4,000 feet high. Many of these mountains rise higher from the surrounding country than do the Rockies. The headwaters of four great rivers rise on the slopes and notches of the mountains. Hundreds of miles of forest roads and trails, including the Appalachian Trail from Kinsman Notch at the north base of Mount Moosilauke to the summit of Old Speck Mountain in Maine wind through the renowned high country fishing, hunting, and camping areas. Numerous spur trails, including the Diretissima, Crew-Cut, Nelson, Crag, Tuckerman Ravine, Lion Head, Boot Spur, Alpine Garden, and Lake-of-the-Cloud, provide access to the high peaks and surrounding valleys.

The crest of the great Presidential Range forms the backbone of the forest sweeping in a great arc from northeast to southwest through the peaks of Mount Madison (5,380 feet), the triple summits of the Adams Mountains (5,805 feet), Jefferson (5,725 feet), Clay (5,530 feet), Mount Washington (6,288 feet), the highest of the range, Monroe (5,390 feet), Pleasant (4,775 feet), Clinton (4,275 feet), Jackson (4,012 feet), and Webster (3,876 feet).

Great ridges stretch through the surrounding arcs of the White Mountains, bearing huge cirques, among them the outstandingly scenic King Ravine, the Great Gulf, Huntington, and Tuckerman, flanked by Lion's Head and Boot Spur to the east and Oakes to the south. The Montalban (white mountain), a 10-mile ridge, rises from the south. The most famous of the mountains in this ridge are the terraced Stairs (3,425 feet). The Rocky Branch parallels the Montalban to the east. The proposed Presidential Range Wilderness embraces some 26,000 acres of some of the most scenic geological relief in the northeast, with more than 8 miles of ridge above timberline. The wilderness is bordered on the north by the lower slopes of the northern peaks, on the west by Jefferson Notch and Mount Clinton roads, on the south by the Appalachian, Camel, and Boot Spur trails, and on the east by the Great Gulf.

The higher, wind-swept slopes of the Presidential Range, noted for weather conditions approaching arctic severity, have a number of alpine flora above the timberline, including ancient, gnomelike spruces, scrub birch, and mountain alder. Labrador tea is found frequently mingled with extensive patches of bilberry below the timberline along with large mats of colorful Greenland sandwort, beds of three-toothed cinquefoil, bearberry, moss campion, and alpine azalea.

High up on the summits of the Presidential Range are found arctic rushes, sedges, colorful lichens, and, infrequently, Lapland rosebay, an alpine relative of the great laurel. Lichens are so extensive on some of the high peaks that the color of the summit will occasionally change after a heavy rain, when lichens alter from brownish gray to green.

To the east of the Presidential Range beyond Pinkham Notch is the Carter-Moriah Range. Through Carter Notch to the south is Wildcat Mountain (4,415 feet). West of the Presidential Range across Crawford Notch are a group of lower mountains including Mount Willard and the Notch and Nancy (3,810 feet). Farther southwest rise the beautiful Franconias, crowned by the craggy summit of Lafayette (5,249 feet). Other great mountains of the Franconias are the Twins, Lincoln, and Little Haystack, all over 4,500 feet. Between the Franconias and the Kinsman Range lies the Franconia Notch. Profile Mountain is among the most impressive of this group. Its five granite ledges form the image of a man's profile 1,200 feet above the blue waters of Profile Lake, headwaters of the Pemigewasset River.

The proposed Pemigewasset Wilderness stretches through the mountain country, bisected by Kancamagus Highway. This renowned backpacking, fishing, and hunting area is the largest roadless area on the national forests of the Appalachian Mountain Chain, embracing 100,-000 acres surrounding the East Branch of Pemigewasset River—noted for its wild, orange-bellied brook trout. Several scenic trails wind through the backcountry and provide access to Black Pond, Franconia Brook, Cedar Brook, Thoreau Falls, Signal Ridge, Shoal Pond, Carrigan Notch, Sawyer River, Hancock Notch, Nancy Pond, Arethusa-Ripley Falls, and Lincoln Brook. The East Branch of the Pemigewasset is not recommended for canoeing because of its severe rapids.

The proposed Sandwich Range Wilderness area lies southeast of these highlands. This famous range rises abruptly from the surrounding lake country to towering 4,000-foot peaks, and extends for about 30 miles from Conway or the Saco River westward to Campton on the Pemigewasset. The wilderness area encompasses 60,000 acres of steep ridges, wooded valleys, glacial basins, passes, and remote uplands. Many trails wind to the summit of prominent Mount Chocorua (3,475 feet), the most accessible of which is the Piper Trail. More than 25 other trails ascend its surrounding peaks, including Scarred Whiteface (3,985 feet), Paugus (3,200 feet), and Sandwich Dome (3,993 feet).

The 5,552-acre Great Gulf Wilderness Area lies between Mount Washington and the northern peaks of the Presidential Range, embracing a huge valley 1,100 to 1,600 feet deep, formed by glacial action and drained by the West Branch of the Peabody River. A fairly accessible trail system leads through the rugged cirque. Waterfalls plunge down the steep walls of the gulf, and Spaulding and Star lakes sparkle in the uppermost reaches of the wilderness. Elevations range from 1,700 feet in the east to 5,800 feet near Mount Washington's summit. Spruce, fir, and northern hardwoods grow on the lower slopes. Frequent hurricanes and violent winds lash the barren high country.

Whitetail deer range the country to 3,500 feet, and snowshoe rabbit flourish here. Lynx, bobcat, mink, marten, fisher cat, ruffed grouse, and spruce partridge also inhabit the gulf. Hunting is difficult, however, because of the area's inaccessibility. The lower mile of Peabody River holds brook trout. Two backcountry shelters in the gulf are available on a first-come, first-served basis. A free *Great Gulf Wilderness Area Map/Brochure* is available from: Forest Supervisor, White Mountain National Forest, P.O. Box 638, Laconia 03246. The brochure describes the topography, history, and wildlife of the area, and gives trail and camping information. The map, on a scale of 1 inch to 1 mile, shows roads, trails, shelters, and water features.

The 29,000 roadless acres of the proposed Dry River-Rocky Branch Wilderness embrace the southern Presidential Range, large portions of the Dry River and Rocky Branch valleys, the above-mentioned Montalban Ridge, and some of the most spectacular "big mountain" terrain in the White Mountain National Forest. Dense hardwood forests cloak the river valleys and provide cover for good deer and black bear populations. Numerous trails wind through the rough landscape of the valleys, and five Appalachian Mountain Club shelters are located in the area. One of the most scenic of these footpaths is the Dry River Trail, which follows the river through a steep-walled chasm and winds over the headwall of Oakes Cirque to the Crawford path of Mount Washington. The AMC Mizpah Springs Hut and Lake of the Clouds Hut are located just outside the northern boundary of the wilderness.

The gorge of the Devil's Hopyard cuts through the dense forests of the proposed 24,000-acre Killkenny Wilderness Area, which embraces the Pilot and Pliny ranges in the northernmost part of the White Mountain Forest. This remote upland region contains the headwaters of the Upper Ammonoosuc River and a portion of the Israel River. Panoramic views of the surrounding White Mountain highlands can be had from the summits of Mount Cabot (4,180 feet) and Mount Waumbek (4,020 feet). Large herds of whitetails use the conifer stands throughout the area as winter yarding sites. The Killkenny Wildlife Management Area lies in the southeastern portion of the wilderness and has a large number of eastern coyote. The northern half of the area has seven small high country trout ponds, the largest being Unknown Pond in the shadow of the Horn, and a sizable beaver and moose population. Numerous hiking trails wind through the wilds to such scenic spots as Mount Crescent, Mount Forist and the frozen caves of Ice Gulch.

Hugging the New Hampshire-Maine border of the forest is a remote, roadless hiking, fishing, and hunting area embraced by the proposed 20,000-acre Wild River Wilderness, surrounding the beautiful Wild River. The Carter Range forms the western border and the mountains from North Baldface to West Royce form the eastern border. Many mountain streams flow out of these two ranges and converge at No-Ketchum Pond in the broad, gentle valley floor to form the Wild River. The marshy grasslands attract moose and beaver and provide fine open vistas of the surrounding mountains. Following the Wild River northward, the land changes from marsh to a dark climax forest of birch, balsam, and spruce. Except for a stand of virgin forest along the Black Angel Trail, most of the wilderness was either burned by the fire of 1903 or has been cut in logging operations. There are four shelters and 40 miles of primitive trails, including the Appalachian Trail, which follows the western boundary. Brook trout fishing is good along the broad, flat Wild River Trail. Wildlife includes deer, black bear, bobcat, fox, coyote, and fisher.

The proposed 10,000-acre Carr Mountain Wilderness Area includes Mount Carr and Mount Kineo, and the lowlands between the two mountains in the southwestern section of the White Mountain National Forest. To the west are many mountain brooks which drain into the Baker River. To the east, the brooks from Mounts Carr and Kineo empty into the marshy basin and form Three Ponds—tarns left by receding glaciers—and numerous beaver ponds. The Brown Brook

marshes are considered the best waterfowl habitat in the Pemigewasset ranger district. The brook trout fishing is at times excellent. There is a shelter at Three Ponds and an old logging road converted into a trail for access.

In the Maine portion of the Forest lies the proposed Caribou—Speckled Mountain Wilderness in the scenic Oxford Hills region, some 12 miles southwest of Bethel. This mountainous 12,000-acre area of heaths, stunted conifers and pine and spruce forests is a popular backpacking and hunting area, inhabited by whitetail deer, black bear, moose, upland game birds, and eastern coyote, or "brush wolves" as they are called locally.

Much of the White Mountain area is accessible by car, but vast expanses of undeveloped wilderness preserve the rugged beauty and the challenge of the mountains. Deer range the mountains below 3,000 feet; bear, partridge, ruffed grouse, and rabbits are other game animals of the forest. Among the better known hunting areas of the forest are the Killkenny, Wild River, Swift River, Zealand River, Sawyer River, Chatham, Jackson, and Waterville areas.

Many of the forest's rivers carve their paths through the remote backcountry areas; a canoe or kayak trip is one of the most pleasant ways to travel the undisturbed wildlands. The Magalloway, Androscoggin, Connecticut, Saco, Pemigewasset, and Ammonoosuc offer some of the best canoe water in the state. For general descriptions of the canoeable waters throughout the White Mountains, write to: White Mountains Region Assn., Lancaster 03584, for their free booklet *Summer Canoeing and Kayaking in the White Mountains of New Hampshire.*

Maps, Guides & Lodging

The forest includes more than 30 developed recreation sites, many of which include camping areas. Huts and trail shelters dot the mountain paths, and the backcountry areas have a wide variety of sites for primitive camping. The *White Mountain National Forest Map* (50¢) includes a directory of these recreation sites. Locations of the sites are shown on the full-color topographic map, as are wilderness areas, state forest areas, highways and roads (good, poor), trails (including the Appalachian trail), railroads, landing fields, ranger stations, campsites, recreation sites, winter sports areas, points of interest, and trail huts, cabins, and shelters. Order the map from: Eastern Region Office, U.S. Forest Service, 633 W. Wisconsin Ave., Milwaukee, WI 53203.

The forest requires wilderness permits for travel in the Great Gulf and Presidential Range areas. Applications for wilderness permits are available by mail from: White Mountain National Forest, Laconia 03246. Included with the application form is information on where within the forest you may obtain permits, rules and regulations for wilderness use, and a map showing entry points for the wilderness areas.

A map and text on *Off-Road Vehicle Conditions of Use* is available from: Forest Supervisor, White Mountain National Forest, Laconia 03246, which gives regulations for the use of such vehicles, and shows use areas.

A free *White Mountains Region Map-Guide* includes descriptions of the resort facilities, historic sites, settings of towns throughout the mountains, listings of accessible mountain notches in the higher mountains, mountain roads and highways, canoeable rivers in the region, and a large map showing more than 180 points of interest throughout the mountains. The map-guide is available from: White Mountains Region Assn., Box T, Lancaster 03584.

The association also distributes a free accommodation directory for the region, *Where to Stay in the White Mountains.* The guide de-

scribes locations, facilities, rates, recreation possibilities, and rates for campgrounds, cabins, motels, hotels, and resorts throughout the region. Accommodations are listed by town, and all the towns mentioned are shown on a map.

The *Mount Washington Valley Winter Vacation Guide* describes ski touring centers, downhill skiing areas, tourist services, special events, and overnight accommodations throughout the valley. It is available free from: Mount Washington Valley Chamber of Commerce, Box WB, North Conway 03860.

For more information on the *Appalachian Mountain Club Huts* of the White Mountains, write to: Reservations Secretary, Pinkham Notch Camp, Gorham 03581. These huts along the trails of the mountains offer lodging, meals, and supplies for backpacking. Reservations are required.

Perhaps the most important resource book for visitors to this region is the *AMC White Mountain Guide.* This 550-page guide describes the entire White Mountain region in detail, noting the topography and natural features, wildlife and plant life, and trails and cross-country routes to take through each area. The guide also describes skiing and rock-climbing areas, gives distances and times between points, and includes other information of interest to hikers, canoers, ski tourers, and campers. The guide includes contour maps of Mount Monadnock, Mount Cardigan, Chocorua-Waterville, Franconia, Mount Washington Range, Carter-Mahoosuc, and the Pilot Range. These show the locations of surfaced, unsurfaced, and abandoned roads, paths and trails, railroads, summits, camps, trail huts, shelters, abandoned buildings, abandoned trails, water features, and the Appalachian Trail. This compact, hardbound guide costs $8.00 and may be ordered from: AMC Books, 5 Joy St. Boston, MA 02108.

The club also publishes the *AMC Guide to Mount Washington and the Presidential Range* ($3.95). This eminently useful guide describes the mountain environment, weather, man's impact, management policies, accident reporting, camping facilities, and other wilderness information. The 160-page paperback book includes a map and is packaged in a waterproof bag.

Peter Randall's *Mount Washington,* $3.95 from: University Press of New England, Hanover 03755, offers a history of the mountain and its legends, and a guide to its rugged slopes. Diane M. Kostecke edited the *Franconia Notch* guide, which includes helpful facts for visitors, human history, natural history, major attractions in the area, rock climbing, fishing, winter activities, and hikes and trails. The 100-page guide ($2.95) is published by: Society for the Protection of New Hampshire Forests, 5 S. State St., Concord 03301. If you plan to hike the upper reaches of the mountains, L. C. Bliss's *Alpine Zone of the Presidential Range* ($1.50) will provide a helpful guide to the geology, climate, and flora and fauna of this area. This book and the others listed in this paragraph may be ordered by mail from: AMC Books (address above).

Write to: Forest Supervisor, P.O. Box 638, Laconia 03246, for additional trail, camping, wilderness use, and other recreational information. In addition, information on backcountry and wilderness use regulations, weather, and snow conditions may be obtained daily between 8:00 A.M. and 10:00 P.M. at the main desk in the trading post at the AMC Pinkham Notch Camp, Gorham 03581 phone (603) 466-3994.

Four-season vacation accommodations and services are provided by the following White Mountains lodges and resorts: *Campton Lodge* (603) 726-7001 and *Grey Fox Lodge* (603) 726-3224, both Campton 03223; *Darby Field Inn & Tavern* (603) 447-2181 overlooking the Mt.

Washington Valley and *Gateway Motel & Cottages* (603) 447-2645 set on 9 scenic acres along the Saco River, both Conway 03818; *Franconia Inn* (603) 823-8896, *Cannon Mountain House* (603) 823-9574, *Lovett's By Lafayette Brook* (603) 823-7761, *Mittersill Alpine Inn & Chalets* (603) 823-5511, *Flintlock Lodge* (603) 823-5562—all at Franconia 03580 overlooking the picturesque Franconia Valley; *Inn Unique & Hannah Crawford Camping Area,* Hart's Location, Bartlett 03812, (603) 374-2323; *The New England Inn,* Intervale 03845, (603) 356-5541, a 150-year-old inn with rustic cottages; *Christmas Farm Inn* (a complete family resort; (603) 383-4313, *Dana Place Inn* (Pinkham Notch; (603) 383-6822, *Eagle Mountain House* (603) 383-4264, *Iron Mountain House* (603) 383-6388, *The Inn Place* (603) 383-4232, *Thorn Hill Lodge* (village inn facing Mt. Washington; (603) 383-4242, *Jackson Lodge* (an elegant Victorian mansion and ski lodge; (603) 383-4226, *Wildcat Inn & Tavern* (ski touring and mountaineering center of Mt. Washington Valley; (603) 383-4245—all Jackson 03846 in the Mt. Washington Valley; *Indian Head Motel Resort* (603) 745-2480, *Kancamagus Motor Lodge* (one mile from Loon Mountain on highway, (603) 745-3365, *The Inn at Loon Mountain* (603) 745-8146, all Lincoln 03251; *Baker Brook Resort,* Littleton 03561, (603) 444-2147; *Cranmore Mountain Lodge & Barn,* Kearsarge 03847, (603) 356-2044; *Eastern Slope Inn* (famous ski resort; (603) 356-5533, *Forest Glen Inn* (603) 356-5346, *The Ledges* (ten rustic lodges at base of Moat Mountain Range, (603) 356-3732, all North Conway 03860; *Lime Kiln Camps,* North Haverhill 03774, (603) 989-5656; *Appalachian Mountain Club Pinkham Notch Camp,* Pinkham Notch 03581, (603) 466-2751; *Snowvillage Lodge,* Madison 03849, (603) 447-2818; *Lost River Lodge* (in renovated farmhouse surrounded by mountains), North Woodstock 03262, (603) 745-6653; *Mirror Lake Hamlet* (603) 726-7032, *The Robbins Nest* (on Pemigewasset River, (603) 726-3341, and *Waterville Valley Gateway* (603) 726-3724—all West Thornton 03285; *Abnaki Lodge* (603) 846-5714, *Ammonoosuc Campgrounds & Lodge* (603) 846-5527, and *Grand View Lodge* (603) 846-5731—all Twin Mountain 03595; *Snowy Owl Inn* (603) 236-8383, *Silver Squirrel Inn* (603) 236-8366, *The Resort at Waterville Valley* (603) 236-8686, and the *Waterville Valley Bunkhouse* (603) 236-8326—all in Waterville Valley 03223.

Access & Outfitting Centers

The forest is reached by way of U.S. Highway 302, and State Route 10 from the west, Interstate 93 from the south, and State Route 16/25 from the southeast. Outfitting and supply centers for the region include Berlin and Gorham to the north, Conway near the southeast boundary, Plymouth to the south on U.S. 3, and Littleton to the northwest on Interstate 93. Lodging, supplies, canoe rentals, and outfitters within the forest are available at Warren, Rumney, Benton, Woodstock, Waterville Valley, Bretton Woods, Jackson, Glen, Bartlett, Willey House, Intervale, Chatham, Shelburne, Gilead, and Stowe.

MAINE
ENCYCLOPEDIA

Accommodations—
Vacation Lodges & Sporting Camps

The Pine Tree State has hundreds of long established motels, camps, lodges, and vacation resorts of every description and price range. There are several guides that will help you select the accommodation that meets your taste and pocketbook. The *Maine Innkeepers Association Lodging and Food Guide* lists numerous motels, resorts, and hotels, all members of the association, alphabetically by city or town, and the booklet includes a small map showing where these townships are. For your free copy of the booklet, write to: Maine Innkeepers Assn., 105 Simmons Rd., South Portland 04106. For current information on rates, etc., it is best to check with the individual hotel or motel. Should you wish information about fishing, hunting, or other activities locally available, write to: Publicity Bureau, Gateway Circle, Portland 04103. The state's Publicity Bureau also publishes an excellent free guide, *Maine Camps and Cottages . . . for Rent.* This 56-page booklet, devoted entirely to listings of summer camps and cottages, presents its entries in alphabetical order by town or region. Each accommodation is described briefly; many of them are accompanied by black-and-white photographs. Names of proprietors, addresses, and phone numbers are provided. The booklet also includes handy tear-out cards to fill in if you desire further information on any of the camps or cottages listed in the guide. The motorist will also be interested in the *Innkeepers Map*, which can be obtained at no cost from: New England Innkeepers Assn., 25 Huntington Ave., Rm. 406, Boston, MA 02116. This is essentially a road map of New England, but it also lists, by state, a number of inns, motels, and resorts, indicating their locations on the road map and describing them briefly. Of course, addresses and phone numbers are provided.

For listings of the state's major vacation lodges and sporting camps, see the "Maine Travel & Recreation Guide" section.

Appalachian Mountain Club—
Campgrounds & Sporting Camps

The world-renowned Appalachian Mountain Club maintains group summer recreation camping sites for members and nonmembers (at slightly higher rates) that serve as convenient resting areas and base camps for the family camper, backpacker, naturalist, or wilderness paddler. Most of the camps are in scenic north woods backcountry and coastal areas. The *Swan's Falls Campground*, on the banks of the Saco River in Fryeburg, is a family campground in the White Mountains, with many remote, spacious campsites for families, individuals, and organized groups. The camp is open from June 19 through Labor Day and on weekends during the spring and fall. *Walker's Falls*, the most remote of the AMC Saco River campgrounds, is 14 miles downstream from Swan's Falls and is designed to serve as an overnight stop for canoeists, although many campers extend their visit to enjoy its idyllic wilderness setting. The camp is open June 15 through Labor Day. The *Beal Island Camp*, at Georgetown, accessible by canoe or boat from Bath, is 64 acres of scenic coastal woodlands surrounded by the tidal waters of the Sasanoa River. The island is a scenic wilderness retreat for canoeists of all levels of experience and ability.

The primitive *Knubble Bay Camp*, on Georgetown Island, is used by hikers, canoeists, and family vacationers. The idyllic *Fort Island Camp* on the Damariscotta River is open year round and provides the tidewater canoeist with a base camp from which he can explore the Maine coast from Pemaquid Point to Beal Island, 13 miles to the west. The *Swan Island Camp*, once the home of the Abenaki Indians and presently a wildlife refuge, is an ideal year round family campground

operated by the Island Fisheries & Game Commission on the Kennebec River. Canoeists can travel upriver with the tidal flow to the old Colburn House—a jumping-off point for Benedict Arnold's 1775 winter expedition to capture Quebec—or canoe down river with the ebb tide to Merrymeeting Bay, Bath, and Beal Island. This scenic island camp has 10 Adirondack shelters around a green meadow. A ferry will provide transportation to the island from the Steve Powell Game Management Area dock in Richmond. The *Echo Lake Camp*, Mount Desert 04660, (207) 244-3747, is in the beautiful coastal highlands of Acadia National Park near the south end of Echo Lake just off the road to Southwest Harbor. This is a scenic tent camp with excursions to outer islands and overnight trips to Mount Katahdin and Baxter State Park.

For complete information on these and other AMC camps (and for membership info and application forms), write: Appalachian Mountain Club, 5 Joy St., Boston, MA 02108, (617) 523-0636.

Appalachian National Scenic Trail & Maine Mountain Guides

This great mountain footpath winds across the Maine woods for 280 miles in a generally southwestern direction from its northern terminus at Baxter Peak on Mount Katadhin, passing through the wilderness lakes, streams and ponds in Baxter State Park, then crossing the Nesowadnehunk River and the West Branch of the Penobscot, winding past Rainbow, Nahmakanta, and Jo-Mary lakes, up White Cap Mountain, and crossing a road with side trails to the spectacular "Gulf Hagas." Then it continues on past Long Pond, over Columbus, Third, Fourth, and Barren mountains, through the abandoned forest village of Savage's Mills to the town of Monson, over Moxie Bald and Pleasant Pond mountains, past Wyman Lake, and crosses the Kennebec River at Caratunk. From the great bend of the Dead River the trail cuts across the Bigelow Range south of Flagstaff Lake and winds through the Rangeley Lakes region and into New Hampshire near the Old Speck Mountain-Grafton Notch area in the Mahoosuc Range.

The Appalachian Mountains, which are the principal mountain system of eastern Canada and the United States, are a nearly continuous chain of ranges stretching from the Long Range Mountains of Newfoundland to central Alabama, running roughly parallel to the Atlantic seaboard. The Appalachian Trail, which stretches 1,000 miles from Maine to Georgia, attracts thousands of hikers and campers each year. Mount Katahdin, at 5,268 feet, is the highest point of the trail in the state of Maine; in fact, one of the highest on the entire trail. The Appalachians are among the oldest mountains on earth, first formed by massive upheavals in the earth's crust, then sculpted by the eroding action of glaciers and rivers.

Anyone wishing to hike the trail in Maine can obtain information from excellent publications by the Appalachian Mountain Club and the Appalachian Trail Conference, two organizations involved in the support and maintenance of the trail. *Suggestions for Appalachian Trail Users* (ATC Publication No. 15) is available from: Appalachian Trail Conference, Box 236, Harpers Ferry, WV 25425, for 50¢. This 35-page booklet contains information for those contemplating trips over the Appalachian Trail. Subjects covered include the nature of the trail; the Appalachian Trail Conference; use of the trail; horse, bicycle, and motor vehicle guide; planning trips; maps; guidebooks, etc.; lean-to use; food and equipment; trail marking and maintenance; etc. *Guide to the Appalachian Trail in Maine* (Maine Appalachian Trail Club) is published in two volumes that can be purchased separately. *The Appalachian Trail in Maine* (356 pp., 9 maps) contains informa-

tion for planning trips in Maine, generalized description of the trail route, approaches to the trail, detailed trail data (24 sections) for the Appalachian trail in Maine reading in both directions, and a chapter on side trails. This volume is indexed, is issued in a loose-leaf format, and costs $7.25. The second volume, *Katahdin Section* (202 pp., 2 maps) is a complete guide to the Katahdin region, containing a description of the area, the approaches, trails, and accommodations, with chapters on the Katahdinauguoh and Deadwater mountains. This volume is also loose-leaf; it costs $2.50. The interesting *Annotated Bibliography of Katahdin* (ATC Publication No. 6), by Edward C. Smith and Myron C. Avery, is an extensive annotated bibliography of the Katahdin region, with chapters on place names, notable expeditions, photographs, and maps. It includes a 4-page supplement. This 78-page book costs $1.00. *The Map: The Katahdin Region* (MATC No. 3), 35¢, covers terrain between the East and West branches of the Penobscot River; it contains a sketch map of Katahdin trails.

The *AMC Maine Mountain Guide* contains summary trail mileages and mountain elevations in English and metric equivalents; durable, plastic pouch to carry books and maps, and other small hiking paraphernalia; and it has a soft, flexible, water-resistant binding. This volume contains about 290 pages and 5 maps, and costs $6.50. The *AMC Maine Mountain Guide* covers all trails in the Katahdin area, Aroostook, Mount Desert Island, East Branch of the Penobscot, Camden Hills, southwestern Maine, Oxford Hills, Grafton Notch area, Wild Region, Rangeley and Stratton area, Upper Kennebec and Piscataquis mountains. It is available from: Appalachian Mountain Club, 5 Joy St., Boston, MA 02108. Also available from the AMC are the following latex maps, at $1 each: Carter-Mahoosuc; Baxter Park-Katahdin; and Mount Desert Island. The following paper maps are available at 50¢ each: Carter-Mahoosuc/Monadnock/Cardigan; Carter-Mahoosuc/Rangeley-Stratton; and Mount Desert Island/Weld. Another AMC publication that will interest the trail hiker in Maine is *The AMC Trail Guide to Mount Desert Island* ($2). It is an excerpt from the Maine Mountain Guide, containing a complete description of trails and one map.

The strikingly beautiful *Phillips' Map of the Arnold Trail* shows the entire route of Benedict Arnold's historic trail from Madison to Eustice as well as the Appalachian Trail. This map shows all natural features, as well as gravel and logging roads, Forest Service and paper company campsites, public boat-launching ramps, and fish hatcheries. It may be ordered by mail for $1.50 (plus 40¢ postage) from Augustus D. Phillips & Son, Northeast Harbor 04662.

The Appalachian Trail in Maine is shown on the following U.S. Geological Survey Maps: Bingham, First Roach Pond, Harrington Lake, Greenville, Jo-Mary Mountain, Katahdin (also available in a beautiful shaded relief edition, $1.25), Little Bigelow Mountain, Norcross, Old Speck Mountain (also available in shaded relief), Oquossoc, Pierce Pond, Phillips, Rangeley, Sebec Lake, Stratton, The Forks.

Camping & Forest Service Campsites

The Maine Forest Service maintains hundreds of forest campsites scattered throughout the state, from the wave-pounded, rockbound coast, with its breathtaking scenic views, offshore islands, and jagged peninsulas, to the remote wild rivers, glistening mountain ponds, and sprawling, island-dotted glacial lakes of the North Maine Woods wilderness. A trip spent along one of the forest campsites will provide lasting memories of wind-swept blue lakes surrounded by the ancient rolling hills of the evergreen-carpeted Appalachians, wild deep-flowing streams and turbulent rivers, soaring gulls and hawks, and the fragrant smells of pine and wood smoke.

Most of the sites are available at no charge to the general public. A fee of $1 per party per night is charged at a few of the most heavily used campsites.

Access to the forest campsites may be over road, trail, or water. Most of the road access routes are privately owned and are open to the general public under a "multiple use" policy which is supported by the major paper companies and landowners in the area. Some roads are subject to nominal toll charges and others may be closed for reasons of fire protection and public safety. Recreationists are urged to respect the rules and regulations set up by the landowners regarding the use of these privately owned and maintained forest roads.

FOREST CAMPSITES

A Directory of Campsites Maintained by the
Maine Forest Service, Department of Conservation
in cooperation with the
Private Landowners
TWELFTH EDITION 1975

Additional detailed information may be obtained by contacting the following landowners: *Brown Co.*, Berlin, NH 03570; *Central Maine Power Co.*, Augusta 04330; *Dead River Co.*, Bangor 04401; *Diamond International Corp.*, Old Town 04468; *Georgia Pacific Corp.*, Woodland 04694; *Great Northern Paper Co.*, Millinocket 04462; *International Paper Co.*, Jay 04239; *Oxford Paper Co.*, Rumford 04276; *Prentiss and Carlisle Co.*, Bangor 04401; *Scott Paper Co.*, Winslow 04901; *St. Regis Paper Co.*, Bucksport 04416; *Seven Islands Land Co.*, Bangor 04401.

Maine Forest Service campsites have been provided as fire-safe areas for your convenience. Please use these sites whenever possible. If there are no campsites in the area that you wish to visit, you may obtain a fire permit from the forest ranger in that area. A fire permit may be issued depending upon (1) where you wish to build a fire, (2) prevailing weather conditions, (3) availability of campsites, and (4) duration of proposed trip.

Out-of-door fire permits may be obtained without charge by contacting: Forest Ranger, Forest Service, at the following locations: Allagash, Ashland, Brownville Junction, Caratunk, Cherryfield, Cupsuptic, Daaquam (PQ, Canada), Eustis, Greenville, Hay Lake, Island Falls, Masardis, Millinocket, Moose River, Old Town, Pittston Farm, Portage, Topsfield, Wesley.

There are other locations where permits may be obtained; however, they are not always manned. A telephone call to one of the above locations may save you the time and trouble of driving out of your way for a permit.

The Forest Service advises that every camper should have with him a compass and maps of the area he plans to visit. An ax, shovel, first-aid supplies, and fire chains are additional necessities. Registered guide service is available throughout the state—local fish and game wardens and forest rangers will advise you on where to contact the guides. Boats, canoes, and motors may be rented in most areas. Local chambers of commerce will supply information on whom to contact.

An excellent, informative free brochure entitled *Forest Campsites* can be obtained by writing: Forest Service, Dept. of Conservation, State Office Bldg., Augusta 04333. This brochure contains a map of Maine showing public and private roads, tollgates, North Woods, Forest Service campsites (free and those which charge), private campgrounds, Forest Service ranger stations, and other points of interest to campers. The reverse side contains a chart showing the Forest Service campsites broken down by district showing township, description, access routes, and available recreational facilities, and whether or not a fee is charged. The brochure also provides helpful information on fees, access, fire permits, forest and fire laws, equipment and services. The Forest Service welcomes requests for additional information.

A free 56-page booklet, *Camping in Maine*, can be obtained from: Publicity Bureau, 1 Gateway Circle, Portland 04102. This booklet contains brief descriptions of camping and tenting areas in Maine, organized by region. Each camping area's location is shown on a map, which also shows U.S. routes and turnpikes. Campers should write or phone individual camping areas that interest them to obtain information on rates, reservations, etc.

For additional information, you may wish to contact any of the following agencies: Publicity Bureau, 78 Gateway Circle, Portland 04102; Maine Vacation Center, 1268 Ave. of the Americas, New York, NY 10020; Information Center, Mount Royal Hotel, 1455 Peel St., Montreal, Que. H3A 1T5; Maine Campsites—Forest Service, State Office Bldg., Augusta 04333.

Canoeing & Wild Rivers

The mist-shrouded, boulder-studded pools, roaring rapids, rips, falls, eddies, and flat-water drifts of Maine's wild rivers and the windswept, island-dotted waters of the great North Maine Woods lakes provide some of the finest wilderness canoeing-camping opportunities in the nation. The old tramways, beaver dams, osprey, moose, logjams, bogs, legendary brook trout and togue, landlocked salmon, and fragrant evergreen forests found along the legendary canoe routes and Indian trails of the Allagash, St. John, West and East branches of the Penobscot, Fish River Chain of Lakes, Dead River, Aroostook River, Grand Lakes Chain, and the wild Machias River, which flows through a vast plateau of "blueberry barrens," combine to provide a wilderness canoeing paradise matched in the United States only by Minnesota's Boundary Waters Canoe Area. The North Maine Woods canoe country is also home to hordes of blackflies, mosquitoes, and cute little fellows known as "no-see-ums." If you forget to bring a good supply of insect dope you're sure to have a trip you'll long remember. (Detailed descriptions of Maine's great canoe routes and fishing waters are contained in the "Travel & Recreation Guide" section along with corresponding topographic maps.) If you are planning a canoe fishing trip, you will vastly improve your enjoyment, success, and knowledge of the Maine Woods by hiring the services of a registered guide. A listing of *Canoeing Guides* may be obtained by writing to: Dept. of Inland Fisheries & Game, State House, Augusta 04333.

The *AMC River Guide* vol. 1, *Northeastern New England* ($6), Appalachian Mountain Club, 5 Joy St., Boston, MA 02108, contains descriptions of the wild and scenic rivers in the Androscoggin, Kennebec, and Penobscot watersheds; the Allagash Wilderness Waterway, and the St. John, Mid-Coastal, and Eastern Coastal watersheds. Each stream is concisely described, indicating class, location, length of trip, surrounding wilderness, history, topographic maps. The book describes virtually every important Maine river in a clear, easy-to-read format. Maps show the locations. The helpful introduction contains notes on the format, explanation of terms, scenery descriptions, and river classifications, water levels, etc., that will aid you in getting the most out of this guide.

A free *Sportsman's Map of the Allagash, Chesuncook, and Chamberlain Canoe Country* may be obtained by writing: Great Northern Paper Co., 6 State St., Bangor 04401. A *Map of the Grand Lake Canoe Area* may be obtained free from: St. Croix Paper Co., Woodland 04694. A detailed *Map of Canoe Routes in the Rangeley Lakes-Azicoos Area* is free upon request from: Rangeley Lakes Region Chamber of Commerce, Rangeley 04970. A free *Map of the Moosehead & Upper Kennebec Waterways* may be obtained by writing: Scott Paper Co., Northwest Division, Winslow 04901. The *Allagash Wilderness Waterway* booklet with map may be had free from: Parks & Recreation Commission, Augusta 04330.

(For additional information, see "Camping & Forest Service Campsites" and "North Maine Woods Guides & Canoe Trip Outfitters.")

Charter Floatplane Service

The great Maine coastal and North Maine Woods wilderness fishing, canoe-camping, and hunting areas are served by several long established seaplane bases and charter wilderness fly-in services.

Higgins Marina Seaplane Base, L. W. Higgins, Higgins Sports Center, 65 N. River Rd., Auburn 04210, (207) 782-6481, offers air taxi, charter, rentals, scenic flights, and seaplane charter. *Old Seaplane Base*, Maine Coast Seaplane Service, 173 Park Row, Brunswick 04011, (207) 725-7323, runs aerial photo, air taxi, charter, seaplane charter, patrol, and scenic flights. *Wesserunsett Seaplane Base*, c/o Charles Gunther, RD4, Box 27, E. Madison Rd., Skowhegan 04976, (207) 474-5005, can supply aerial photos, courtesy car, scenic flights, and seaplane charter services. *Folsom's Air Service*, Greenville 04441, (207) 695-2821, will provide air taxi charter throughout Northern Maine, seaplane charter to Allagash and St. John sporting camps, scenic flights, and courtesy car. *Northern Maine Flying Service*, RFD1, Norridgewock 04957, (207) 634-3662, offers air taxi, charter, and seaplane charter services. *Lake Parlin Seaplane Base*, Young's Flying Service, Lake Parlin, West Forks 04985, (207) 688-3383, offers air taxi, scenic flights, and seaplane and other charter flight services. *Millinocket Lake Flying Service*, Millinocket 04662, offers air taxi, charter, seaplane charter, and scenic flights. *Porter's Flying Service*, Shin Pond, Patten 04765, (207) 528-2528, can supply air taxi, charter, rentals, seaplane charter, and scenic flight services. *Irving's Seaplane Base*, c/o Raymond Howland, RFD2, Page Rd., South Windham 04082, (207) 892-2007, provides charter and scenic flights. Naples Flying Service, phone James Build, (207) 693-6591, offers just scenic flights. *Central Maine Flying Service*, c/o Richard W. Leary, De Witt Field Municipal Airport, Old Town 04468, (207) 827-5911, offers air taxi, charter, seaplane charter, and scenic flights. *Portage Lake Flying Service*, Clair L. Moreau, Portage 04768, (207) 435-3301, offers seaplane charter flights. *Long Lake Seaplane Base*, c/o Mark Peterson, Sinclair 04779, (207) 543-7584, can provide air taxi, seaplane charter, and scenic flights. *Balch Pond Seaplane and Airport*, Verne H. Rogers, Balch Pond, West Newfield 04095, (207) 606-2114, provides charter, courtesy car, and scenic flights. *Moosehead Flying Service*, Greenville Junction 04442, also provides charter services; write for details. In the Rangeley Lakes Region, charter fly-in fishing and hunting trips and scenic flights are provided by *Rangeley Air Service* (207-864-3892) and *Steve's Air Service* (207) 864-3347, both Rangeley 04970.

Coastal Cruises & Islands

Maine's jagged 2,300-mile coastline angles northeast to southwest in a seemingly endless series of rocky islets and bays bordered by ancient spruce-clad mountains and valleys. More than 1,200 incredibly scenic islands, some little more than giant rocks, jut up from the waters off the wave-pounded, often fog-shrouded coastline. This labyrinth of isles lures thousands of family vacationers, backpackers, canoeists, and sailors each summer. The islands are inhabited by seals and a great variety of birds, including seagulls, terns, herons, great cormorants, Canadian geese, and ducks. Deer can often be seen feeding along the shore edges of the island forests. Red squirrel, fox, northern cottontail, woodchuck, otter, snowshoe hare, and many species of whale can be seen, as well as seals in the secluded rocks and ledges.

Several down east sailing firms operate summer schooner trips along the scenic Maine coast. These magnificent 19th-century sailing ships have been converted to the windjammer trade by the addition of staterooms, fully equipped galleys, and modern safety equipment. For information on these cruises, write to the following firms for rates and free literature: *Yankee Schooner Cruises*, Box 697, Camden 04843, (207) 236-4449, offers 6-day trips aboard the schooner *Adventure*. They will send you an attractive full-color brochure and a reservations form.

The schooner *Nathaniel Bowditch* sails the area from Boothbay Harbor to Bar Harbor, considered one of the world's finest sailing areas, with its snug harbors and picturesque villages. Some of the islands en route are excellent fishing spots. For a descriptive brochure and price information contact: Schooner Nathaniel Bowditch, Capt. Gilbert E. Philbrick, 16 Harrison Ave., Orono 04473, (207) 866-3592.

The schooner *Richard Robbins Sr.* sails the Penobscot and Blue Hill Bay area. An attractive full-color brochure is available describing the details of the cruise. The itinerary of the schooner *Lewis R. French* varies according to the wind and tide, but you won't fail to see some ruggedly beautiful coastline areas. For information on these two ships, contact *Schooner Richard Robbins/Schooner Lewis R. French*, Box 482, Rockland 04841, (207) 594-8007.

The *Victory Chimes* is the largest passenger sailing vessel under the American flag. She visits many of Maine's fascinating outer islands, such as Monhegan Island, Isle au Haut, Swans Island, and Mount Desert. An attractively illustrated color brochure and a reservations form can be obtained by writing: Maine Coast Cruises, Capt. Frederick B. Guild, Box 368, Rockland 04841; or you may phone (207) 596-6060 during the summer, (207) 326-8856 during the winter.

The modern-day schooner *Mary Day* (launched in 1962) offers trips to isolated places like Frenchboro, Isle au Haut, Matinicus, and Monhegan. For information and a descriptive full-color brochure, write: Coastal Cruises, Capt. H. S. Hawkins, Box 798, Camden 08483, (207) 236-2750.

The schooner *Stephen Taber* sails from Camden, and does not follow any predetermined route. The trip always includes island hopping and picturesque scenery. For a color brochure and reservations form, write: Capt. Mike Anderson, Yankee Packet Co., Box 736, Camden 04843, (207) 236-8873.

Casco Bay Lines offers a variety of interesting day trips around the 200 beautiful, rugged islands of the Casco Bay area. The area is rich in historical significance—it may have been visited by Leif Ericson as early as 1000 A.D. The first reliable map of the area was sketched by Captain John Smith. The islands were also a haven for pirates; it is believed that many treasures are buried in the bay. For complete information on cruise schedules, fares, etc., write or call: Casco Bay Lines, Custom House Wharf, Portland 04111, (207) 774-7871.

Fishing & Hunting in the Pine Tree State

The legendary Maine Woods conjure images of big orange-bellied native brook trout; spring-loaded, deep-shouldered landlocked salmon; massive, baleful bull moose; trophy whitetail bucks; vast green seas of spruce, fir, and pine; lean, rugged woodsmen, skilled with deer rifle, fishing rod, canoe paddle, and ax; icy, deep, boulder-girded lakes carving a jagged blue path into the forest; and pure white-water rivers, grinding tortured streambeds through the thick layers of glacial rock. These are some of the facets of the Maine outdoor experience that have attracted sportsmen for generations. Some of the finest fishing and hunting on the North American continent may be enjoyed in this beautiful state, which has almost 18 million acres of forestland. Maine is 90% wooded, harboring the largest expanses of wilderness in the East, and contains over 2,500 lakes and ponds, as well as more than 5,000 streams. The state occupies 33,215 square miles, almost exactly the same total as the rest of New England combined. Much of the northern half of Maine, which protrudes into Canada, including Washington County, is a wilderness of vast forests of spruce, fir, white pine, larch or tamarack, cedar, birch, beech, and maple, hundreds of lakes, ponds, and streams, few roads, and a sparse population. Paper companies and private landowners hold much of this territory, and individually, or through the North Maine Woods Association, maintain road networks—some of which may be driven by the public at no charge, while others require a modest fee.

Although 8-pound squaretails are no longer taken as a matter of course as was once the case, excellent fishing still exists, and the angler who is willing to exert some time and effort in reaching the "back-in" waters will experience fishing that compares with the quality taken for granted by 19th century "sports." In addition, many of the accessible waters that are considered run of the mill by local fishermen would be considered blue-ribbon fishing spots in most states. The state record fish roster gives an indication of what Maine offers.

It is interesting that only three of the champion fish come from the thinly populated, deep woods region of the top half of the state, indicating that trophies can be taken virtually anyplace in Maine. The state has sponsored the One That Didn't Get Away Club since 1939. A certificate signed by the governor of Maine and a blue-and-gold arm patch are given for the following species and minimum weights: Atlantic salmon, 15 lb.; Togue (lake trout), 15 lb.; Landlocked salmon, 8 lb.; Brown trout, 8 lb.; Rainbow trout, 6 lb.; Brook trout, 5 lb.; Smallmouth bass, 5 lb.; Largemouth bass, 5 lb.; Chain pickerel, 4 lb.; White perch, 2 lb. Entries should be mailed to the *Maine Sportsman*, a monthly magazine that maintains the club: P.O. Box 507, Yarmouth 04096.

MAINE RECORD FISH

	Lb.-oz.	Place	Year
Brook trout	8–5	Pierce Pond	1958
Brown trout	19–7	Sebago Lake	1958
Blueback trout	4–4	Basin Pond	1973
Togue (lake trout)	31–8	Beech Hill Pond	1958
Atlantic salmon	26–2	Narraguagus River	1959
Landlocked salmon	22–8	Sebago Lake	1907
Whitefish	7–8	Sebago Lake	1958
Smallmouth bass	8	Thompson Lake	1970
Largemouth bass	11–10	Moose Pond	1968
Chain pickerel	6–8	Sebago Lake	1969
White perch	4–10	Messalonskee Lake	1949
Cusk (burbot)	15–12	Sebago Lake	1977

Landlocked Salmon Waters

If Maine is famous for one fish, it is undoubtedly that valiant prince of freshwater game fish, the landlocked salmon. Landlocks are biologically indistinguishable from Atlantic salmon, differing only in their much smaller average size and in the fact that they do not have any inclination to migrate to salt water. Maine fish are native to only four watersheds; the Presumpscot (Sebago Lake, Cumberland County), the Union (Green Lake, Hancock County), the Penobscot's Piscataquis tributary (Schoodic and Sebec lakes, Piscataquis County), and the St. Croix (West Grand Lake, Washington County). Since the latter part of the 19th century, the silvery battlers have been widely introduced to waters in every part of the state. Thousands of New England anglers wait impatiently each spring for news that the ice is "out" on favorite lakes, where the grass is greening and salmon are chasing smelts in the rocky shallows. Sebago, home of the 22½-pound record, is the first major lake to shed its icy coat each spring—usually around the third week of April—and it still produces big landlocks every season. While salmon are distributed all over Maine, the cream of the fishing is generally found in the sparsely populated, colder northern half of the state. Among famous producers of bragging-sized landlocks are the Fish River Lakes Chain (Aroostook County), Moosehead Lake (Piscataquis and Somerset counties), Seboomook Lake (Somerset County), Chesuncook, Sebec, Schoodic, and Munsangan lakes (Piscataquis County), and East and West Grand lakes (Washington County). These prime fishing areas are located in the North Maine Woods, and pay the angler added dividends in the beauty of the scenery, which embraces cold, rocky lakes full of coves and islands, a

fragrant green forest mantle, and profuse wildlife, including moose, bear, and deer. High-flying clouds pushed by stiff northwesterly winds, cool evenings, and unpredictable weather remind the angler that the trackless solitude of the northern Canadian wilds is not so far away. One of the greatest thrills in landlock fishing is hooking a big, sky-climbing salmon in fast water. Anglers have enjoyed some great moments in noted streams such as the Magalloway and Rapid rivers in Oxford County near the top of the border with New Hampshire; the adjacent Kennebago River, a Rangeley Lakes tributary; the Moose River, feeding Moosehead Lake in Somerset County; Moosehead's East and West Outlets, and the upper Kennebec, which they form; the West Branch of the Penobscot, particularly the wild water below Ripogenus Dam at the foot of Chesuncook Lake; the fast water and thoroughfares of the Fish River chain; and Grand Lake Stream, which drains West Grand Lake. In addition the inlets and outlets of many productive salmon lakes offer short stretches of fast-water action, particularly during the spring smelt run and the fall spawning season.

Wilderness Squaretail Country

Maine offers more authentic wilderness brook trout fishing than any other state, because the vast corporate and individual timber holdings of the northern half of the state have preserved the critical watershed requirements of this fragile game fish. In certain locations it is still possible to enjoy some of the great fishing which attracted the influential and wealthy in the latter half of the 19th century. The squaretail is one of the most beautiful freshwater fishes, having an olive-tinted back with wormlike markings, sides of olive-brown, dappled with spots of gold and pinpoints of brilliant crimson fire surrounded by halos of pale blue, and fins of bright reddish orange trimmed with white borders. During spawning season colors intensify and the belly of the male blazes forth in deep hues of flame orange.

Rangeley fishermen still row the swift, graceful Rangeley boats of forest green in pursuit of squaretails, and while 8-to-12-pound squaretails are no longer taken, the lakes continue to produce fish in excess of 3 pounds. Beautiful, secluded Big and Little Kennebago lakes, the Kennebago River, and outlying ponds offer above-average sport in unspoiled surroundings; some impressive trout are taken in Rangeley, Mooselookmeguntic, upper and lower Richardson, Aziscohos, and Parmachenee lakes, and the Magalloway and wild Rapid rivers.

Washington County contains scores of headwater stream areas, swampy ponds, and beaver flowages which teem with brookies, some of which run to size, particularly in the Machias, St. Croix, and Narraguagus river basins. Many of the Washington County streams empty into the saltwater runs of sea trout, or salters, which have a larger average size than their inland brothers and a much more subdued coloration, lacking the brilliance of wild stream brook trout. Even some of the downstate waters continue to produce trophy brook trout, such as Messalonskee Lake in the Belgrades, and nearby Basin Pond at Fayette.

The great expanse of northern Maine, sweeping northeast from the Rangeley Lakes on the western border to the Quebec border and the Aroostook County potato lands, includes the state's greatest brook trout waters: the Kennebec River system area, taking in the Dead River, Pierce Pond (state record), King and Bartlett ponds, Spencer Lake and Stream, and other excellent spots; the Moosehead Lake and Jackman districts, offering the Moose River, Brassua Lake, Long, Attean, Wood, and Holeb ponds, the Yoke and Roach ponds, Kokadjo River, Jo-Mary Lake, and adjacent ponds; the drainage of the Penobscot's West Branch, including Caucomgomoc and Chesuncook lakes, the latter's Ripogenus Dam pool, which harbors some enormous squaretails in the deep ledges of the swift, black eddies; the glaciated

boreal streams and ponds of Baxter State Park, including famous Sourdnahunk Lake and Stream, Kidney Pond, Togue Ponds, and Wassataguoik Pond and Stream; the East Branch of the Penobscot and the Patten-Shin Pond area, the Allagash River basin, containing Chamberlain, Eagle, Churchill, Spider, Allagash, Round, Long, and Umsaskis lakes, and the fabled Musquacooks; the sprawling St. John River drainage area, Baker Lake, and the St. John Ponds; and the Fish River system, including the Red River lakes—Gardner, De Boullie, Pushiner, and Black.

All these areas are laced by productive streams, and thoroughly dotted with sparkling blue lakes and ponds. A glance at the map will show you that the Kennebec, Moosehead, Baxter, Allagash, and St. John regions contain an enormous amount of water. In addition to the well-known places, the upper half of Maine contains hundreds of secret, nameless, remote wilderness ponds and beaver flowages which produce trout fishing approaching the quality of Quebec's legendary squaretail waters. The keys to this fishing consist of long hours spent pouring over U.S. Geological Survey Topographic Maps, a lot of boot leather and sweat, and if you are lucky, a knowledgeable friend with a generous heart. Anyone who has made the effort to follow up promising hike-in possibilities gleaned from maps will tell you that time and energy are well spent. Be sure to take a reliable compass and be familiar with its use, or your trip of discovery may turn out to be longer than planned.

Trophy Lake Trout Waters

The togue, or lake trout, is the third member of the Big Three of Maine lakes, along with landlocks and squaretails. These big chars are well distributed in the state, and most lakes which have the necessary cold, oxygenated deep water contain togue. Lake trout, which are gray to brownish gray and mottled with yellow to cream spots, require colder water than trout or salmon, and chase smelts and minnows in the shallows for a few weeks after spring ice-out before returning to the 40°-50° water temperatures they prefer. During this time they can be taken on light tackle and hit big streamers, lures, sewn bait, and spinner and bait combinations. A big togue on a fly rod or light spinning rod is a rugged adversary, putting up a stubborn, bulldogging scrap interspersed with long, powerful runs.

Good lake trout waters are found in every part of Maine from Great East Lake on the southern end of the border with New Hampshire at the western edge of the state to the productive waters of East Grand Lake on the New Brunswick boundary and north through Sebec, Moosehead, Chesuncook, Chamberlain, Eagle, Churchill, and Spider lakes to Fish River Lake in Aroostook County. Beech Hill Pond near Otis in Hancock County produced the 31½-pound state record and continues to yield big togue, and there are many other excellent lake trout waters.

Brown & Rainbow Trout Waters

Brown and rainbow trout have been introduced into Maine to replace native trout where environmental changes and fishing pressure have made the habitat unsuitable for the unsophisticated brookie, which requires pure, cold water. Rainbows are not widely distributed, and the best fishing is found on the Kennebec River from Wyman Dam at Bingham. Wyman Lake above the dam and some of its tributaries contain rainbows, but they have to compete with landlocks, brown trout, and brookies. The second-best area is the upper Androscoggin tributary system from Rumford on U.S. 2 north. The Swift River at Rumford has a lot of small rainbows in its precipitous, rock-strewn flow, while the Ellis at Rumford Point and the Bear at Newry have some good fishing, and there are a few 'bows to 3 pounds. The Aroostook River in Aroostook County contains a modest population

of rainbows; most of the fish are taken from the river from the Ashland area on Route 11 downstream.

Brown trout, however, have been widely planted in southern Maine, as well as in a few waters in Hancock County in the eastern portion of the state, and Aroostook County. They are stocked where they will not compete with brook trout and landlocks, but the distribution is rather wide due to mix-ups that occurred in hatchery management many years ago. Because of this trout's tendency to assume a silvery, salmonlike coloration in many waters, browns are frequently mistaken for landlocks in lakes and streams where both species are present. In addition, many of the coastal rivers have sea-run browns, and they are almost indistinguishable from salmon, except to a trained biologist. Several Union tributary lakes, including Branch, the first water stocked with browns in the state (1885), Lower Patten, and Phillips, all contain browns. The Kennebec River both above and below Wyman Dam at Bingham has some very large fish. Many well-known lakes, such as Sabbathday, Sebago and Little Sebago, Kezar, Great East, Auburn, China, and the Belgrades, contain brown trout. One of the problems with this fish, particularly in lakes, is that even if it is present in healthy numbers not many fish are taken, since this European import is considerably more wary than the aggressive landlock or the guileless brookie. The most productive brown trout fishing is found in streams. Fishermen on their way to famous Maine fishing spots speed over a series of brown trout streams as they head north on U.S. 95, including the York, Kennebunk, Saco, Piscataquis, and Royal rivers. The Sandy River, noted for its beautiful, deep, boulder-studded pools, in the Farmington area, is one of the top-ranked fly fishing streams in the East for big, hook-jawed browns in the 5-to-9-pound class.

Smallmouth Bass Country

It is no secret that Maine offers some of the greatest smallmouth bass fishing in North America. Excellent bass angling is found everywhere with the exception of the Rangeley region and the area from the Moosehead and Baxter Park districts north to Canada. Most of the lakes in southern Maine have big populations of smallmouths and some hold largemouth as well. Well-known names include Long, Sebago, Thompson (state record smallmouth), and Great East lakes, Moose Pond (state record largemouth), and the Saco River. These waters are either next to or a short drive from Sebago Lake, 15 miles northwest of Portland, and most of the lakes in this area have bass fishing. Other popular spots include the Kennebec River from the Solon area downstream, the Belgrade-Winthrop lakes district near Augusta, China Lake, and the Piscataquis River, with its famous Sebec, Schoodic, and Seboeis tributary lakes, all of which produce bass, as well as coldwater fish. Many other lakes and ponds from the Winthrop lakes north to the Penobscot River in the Millinocket area have excellent bass fishing, as do many of the Hancock County lakes near Ellsworth.

The cream of the smallmouth fishing is found in the wild, snag-filled waters of Washington County. The St. Croix River and its tributary lakes produce angling that ranks with any bass fishing in the U.S. or Canada. Because the climate is cool and many of the best lakes are shallow, top-water fishing with surface plugs and fly-rod lures holds up well throughout the season, although early morning and evening hours are best when midsummer temperatures rise into the 80s for any length of time. Big Lake, Lewey, Grand Falls, Sysladobsis, Pocumcus, Baskahegan, and Spednic are just a few of the great bass lakes in this area, and the St. Croix produces superlative fast-water fishing.

The special single-hook artificials-only season from June 1 through June 20 has been repealed, and spawning bass are no longer protected.

If you are fortunate enough to hit right at this time, or again in the crisp days of fall, you may become a member of the 100-fish-a-day club. While most of the fish will run between 1½ and 3 pounds, bigger ones are there. When a 2-pounder dashes out from under a partly submerged cedar and smacks your popper you will agree, after several minutes of aerial fireworks, that his fierce heart adds weight to his performance.

In addition to the more popular game fish, Maine offers a grab bag of other species, including two seldom caught deepwater dwellers, the lake whitefish and the cusk, and hordes of pickerel, smelt, white and yellow perch, sunfish, and hornpout (bullhead). Some of the coastal rivers such as the Narraguagus and Sheepscott receive spawning migrations of the big American shad, but the run coincides with the peak of the Atlantic salmon season, and there is little interest.

Atlantic Salmon Rivers

Enormous runs of the aristocratic Atlantic salmon were common in the United States during the 19th century from Connecticut northward, but are now limited to a few Maine rivers. The most famous angling rivers were the Penobscot and the Kennebec, although other rivers such as the Androscoggin and the St. Croix supported enormous runs of fish. The great Bangor salmon pool on the Penobscot yielded thousands of fish per season; it was a long-standing tradition to send the first salmon taken from the pool to the president of the United States. The Kennebec River was such a prolific source of fish that "Kennebec salmon" became a generic term for the species on restaurant menus all over the eastern United States.

The nadir of the Atlantic salmon's fortunes was in the early 1950s. Since then, the Department of Inland Fisheries, the Atlantic Salmon Commission, and the federal government have invested substantial amounts of time, effort, and money to reverse the trend, and the

situation is improving. The six rivers which harbor meaningful runs include the Penobscot, Narraguagus, Machias, Dennys, Pleasant, and Sheepscott. Major improvements in the quality of the Penobscot may restore this great river to its former eminence, and fish are being taken above Bangor again as the beautiful game fish seek their vast, ancestral spawning grounds in the headwaters. Intensive management efforts and the major stocking program conducted by the U.S. Salmon Hatchery at Craig Brook, Orland, are showing positive results, and the future looks promising.

Salmon fishing in Maine is a great gamble: thousands of man-hours are spent beaching the 300 to 400 fish landed in a good season. The Narraguagus, Pleasant, Machias, and Dennys rivers, all in Washington County, flow through watersheds combining terrain of forest, blueberry barrens, and towns, and can be fished from the bank or by wading. Canoes are used only to reach the more inaccessible pools, particularly on the alder-shrouded Pleasant. Salmon anglers are a gregarious group and tend to congregate at the more popular spots; much of the potential fishing water in the upstream areas is seldom disturbed. Prospecting for secluded lies may prove productive for someone willing to devote the time and effort. Late May, June, and July are considered the best months and the success of the fishing depends heavily on the water level and temperature during the peak of the run. High water enables the fish to pass through the lower pools without much lingering, while low, warmwater conditions force the salmon to wait in the salt water for a freshet, which may not occur until late fall. The average fish weighs about 10 pounds; a few specimens exceed 20 pounds.

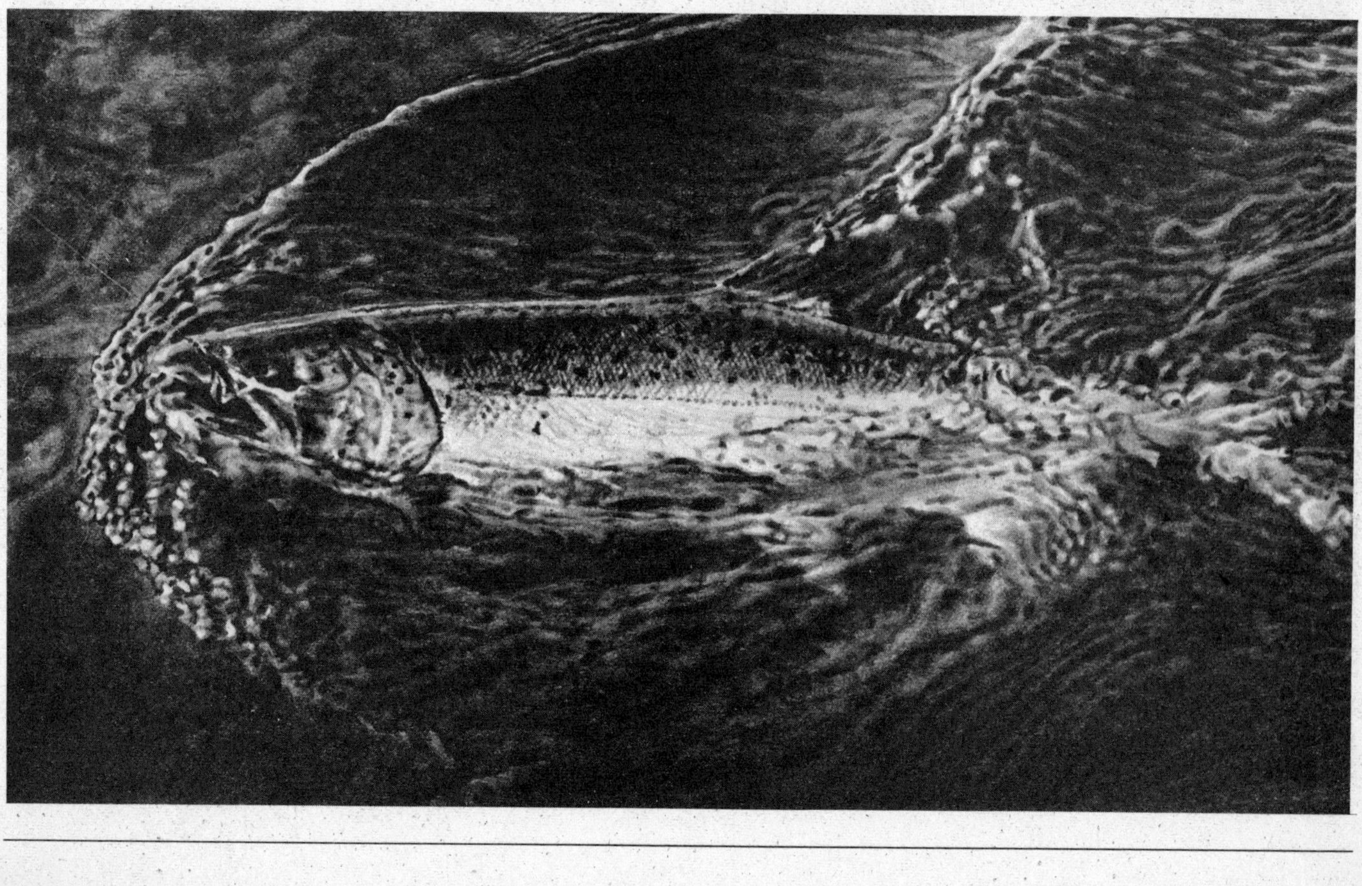

Maine salmon may be taken only by fly fishing: popular patterns include hair flies such as the Cosseboom, the Rat series, the Bomber, Muddler Minnow, Black Bear, and Hairy Mary, Classic Scottish ties including the Jock Scott, Black Dose, Dusty Miller, Silver Doctor, and

dries, particularly the Wulff series, palmers and bivisibles, clipped deer-hair flies (Ratfaced McDougal), and skatem. You will need wet- and dry-fly hook sizes ranging from #2 for high water to #8s and #10s for low-water conditions. Occasionally, when streams are very low and warm, salmon will rise to small wet and dry trout patterns down to #16. Less tradition-bound anglers have found that standard streamers and bucktails, such as the Gray Ghost and Mickey Finn, will attract fish.

Coastal Waters

Saltwater fishing is popular in Maine and ranges from the tiny smelt to giant tuna which weigh over 1,000 pounds. Striped bass, mackerel, halibut, cod, haddock, pollock, flounders, and smelt are the principal species. Charter boats and guides are available along the Atlantic coast and will take you out after stripers, tuna, and bottom fish. Party boats also take fishermen to the offshore grounds for bottom fish. Both kinds of craft can be found in the popular harbors and coastal resort areas. Local chambers of commerce can tell you where to locate boats and the names and telephone numbers of the skippers. Offshore fishing activities are centered in such areas as York Harbor, Ogunquit, Kennebunkport, Portland, Bailey Island (Maine's tuna capital), Boothbay Harbor, Cranberry Isles, Winter Harbor, and Bar Harbor.

Bluefish have appeared in Maine during the last few seasons, after an absence of many years, but 1976 was a poor season, and some fear that the cycle is at an end. Maine blues are caught on the same general equipment as striped bass and are cast to and trolled for in the same areas as stripers, but are also caught in bays. The *Maine Sportsman* has assumed operation of the Tacklebusters Club, which is similar in scope and intent to the One That Didn't Get Away Club; awards and patches are given for outstanding saltwater fish.

Maps & Guides

The following publications of interest to Maine-bound fishermen may be obtained from: Information & Education Division, Dept. of Inland Fisheries & Game, 284 State St., Augusta 04333, phone (207) 289–2871. *Maine Open Water Fishing Laws* and *Ice Fishing Regulations* are free; *Fishes of Maine* (A-6, $1.50¢) describes and color illustrates principal freshwater species; *Blueback Country* (B-110, 35¢), *Trout & Tributaries* (B-36, 25¢), *Discover Maine's Wilderness Trout Ponds* (B-308, 25¢), and *Orchids & Trout* (B-35, 25¢) supply basic facts about brook trout; *The Landlocked Salmon* (B-223, 35¢) is a nontechnical article which gives a good overview of the species; *Salmon on a Fly* (B-231, 35¢) is a guide to waters, patterns, and methods for taking landlocks with flies; *Rainbows Down East* (B-158, 35¢) discusses this trout's role in Maine waters; *Fishing & Hunting in Maine* (free) provides a useful guide to fish and game lands; *The Brown Trout* (B-128, 35¢) provides useful info on this fish's habits and biology; *Lake Trout* (B-97, 15¢) outlines the biology and habits of the gray trout, with tips on fishing techniques; *What About Togue Fishing* (B-211, 25¢) provides detailed tackle and angling information; *The Maine Smallmouth* (A-13, 50¢) is a handy guide to this fish's Maine history, biology, and habits of value to anglers; *Maine's Fighting Bronzebacks* (B-84, 35¢) provides useful information about bass and bass fishing; *Whitefish—Are Anglers Missing a Bet?* (B-24) and *Discover Whitefish* (15¢ each) furnish suggestions about fishing techniques and productive waters; and the useful *Maine's Warmwater Fishery Resources* (B-156, 35¢), *The Chain Pickerel* (B-4, 35¢), *The American Shad* (B-75, 25¢), *Maine's Most Versatile Fish—The Smelt* (B-338), *Zebra of the Lily Pads* (B-131, 35¢, the yellow perch), *Atlantic Salmon Fishing, Look Back* (B-39, 25¢), *Maine's Atlantic Salmon Sport Fishery* (B-50, 25¢), and *The Case for the Atlantic Salmon* (B-135, 25¢).

An eminently useful 225-page guide, *Trout and Salmon Fishing in New England Lakes and Ponds*, by Dick Devlin, may be obtained for $8 (postpaid) from Partridge Press, Box 422, Campton, NH 03223. It includes all you need to know about the trophy lakes, fishing techniques, bait fishing lures, fly patterns and colors for all six New England states, from the Maine North Woods to Connecticut and contains 35 detailed lake fishing maps showing boat launching sites and actual trolling routes in each for landlocks and trout.

Department of Inland Fisheries & Game publications of interest to the big-game, upland, gamebird, or waterfowl hunter include the following. *Hunting Regulations Summary* (free) includes a Wildlife Management and Township Divisions Map, sunrise and sunset tables, and tips on what to do if lost: A Wildlife Management Units Map is free; *A History of the White-Tailed Deer in Maine* (A-9, 75¢) contains a fascinating narrative of this animal's fortunes from the precolonial to the present, complete with old photos, graphs, and charts; *Field-Dressing Your Deer* (B-321), and *Venison—Handle With Care* (B-351) may be obtained for 25¢ each; *More on the Maine Deer* (B-280), and *Big Buck Odds* (B-74) are available for 35¢ each and provide useful info about where to go and hunting methods; *Deer Registration by County* (free) contains a map showing townships and kill in each; *15 Years of Big Bucks* (B-353, 15¢) summarizes the first 15 years of the Biggest Bucks of Maine Club; *Bear Hunting in Maine* (free) describes hunting in the major bear counties, provides listings of fall hunting accommodations and guides, and outlines the bruin's habits and favorite food staples; *Black Bear* (B-45, 35¢) provides insights into the animal and its habits; and *Maine's Dabbling Ducks* (B-127, 35¢), *Maine's Diving Ducks* (B-144, 25¢), *Honkers* (B-123, 35¢), *Blue-Wings* (B-245, 35¢), *The Ringneck* (B-303, 35¢), *Duck Identification for Hunters* (B-279, 35¢), *Waterfowl Identification Guide* (A-18, 35¢ duck, goose, and shorebirds), *Ruffed Grouse— Forest Drummer* (B-91, 15¢), *Ruffed Grouse—What Do They Eat?* (B-178, 25¢), and *Timberdoodlings* (B-63, 35¢, woodcock). Other Department hunting and wildlife publications include *Beaver Trappers* (B-225, 35¢), *Bald Eagle in Maine* (B-324, 25¢), *The Eastern Coyote* (B-376, 35¢), *The Lynx* (B-57, 15¢), *The Woodland Caribou* (B-120, 15¢) and *The Spruce Grouse* (B-155, 15¢).

Write: Dept. of Inland Fisheries & Game (address above) for their free *Publications Catalog*. Select subjects tailored to your particular needs and you will gain a great deal of helpful knowledge, including a wealth of where-to-go and technique information, because almost all of the articles are written by the department's in-the-field professionals. A subscription to the quarterly *Maine Fish and Wildlife* costs $2.50 for 1 year, $4.00 for 2 years, $5.50 for 3 years, and is an excellent way to keep current about the status of fishing and hunting, as well as projects affecting the future.

Hunting & Wildlife

Maine's millions of acres of thick, green forests, wild, tangled swamps and bogs, blueberry barrens, abandoned farms, woodland fringes, bays, and coastal shoreline provide some of the East's outstanding hunting for whitetail deer, black bear, ruffed grouse, woodcock, waterfowl, and snowshoe rabbits, as well as more limited gunning for pheasant, cottontails, and squirrels. Besides bear, hound enthusiasts pursue bobcats, coyotes and coydogs, and foxes. Among Maine's richly varied wildlife are protected species including woodland caribou, moose, wild turkey, marten (sable), Canada lynx, and timber wolf (which may be present again in the most remote wilderness areas). Caribou were stocked in Baxter State Park in 1963 and are seen occasionally by fortunate outdoorsmen, and the fish and game management hopes to reestablish this beautiful creature, which was once a common animal in northern Maine. Observant sportsmen on their travels through the woods, rivers, and lakes may see other interesting creatures such as the mink, otter, fisher, porcupine, weasel, loon, eagle, and osprey.

The whitetail deer undoubtedly ranks number one in importance and in the affections of Maine hunters, and the state has long been ranked at, or near, the top of the East's highest success regions. With an annual kill of more than 40,000 in a great year, deer kills are highest in the southern tier, particularly in the southwest corner and along the coast. The greatest success ratio, however, is found in the northern and

eastern counties where there are fewer hunters, though there are fewer animals in large parts of these ranges. These north country areas where the forest meets the edge of civilization offer some of the top deer hunting in the eastern United States.

The state for years sponsored the Biggest Bucks in Maine Club, which is now maintained and supported by the monthly *Maine Sportsman*. Entry cards are available from game wardens; to qualify for an award patch, the buck must dress out at 200 pounds *without* heart and liver. State records indicate that the champion buck weighed 351 pounds, field-dressed, and the top doe 178 pounds, "dressed." For other state record game and furbearers write: Dept. of Inland Fisheries & Game (address above) for the fact-filled article *Maine's Record Animals*, by Howard E. Spencer (B-252, 35¢), which contains the statistics and asks hunters and trappers to furnish reports of outstanding kills, which are both interesting and helpful in managing the state's wildlife. If you are sitting with your back against a gnarled old cedar in some secluded beaver swamp, and a big 12-point buck materializes out of a blowdown tangle, you will earn your patch when, after quieting your initial case of nerves, you bring him down with a well-placed shot. Your deer must then be registered at an official station and tagged in accordance with regulations.

Maine ranks number one among eastern black bear states and offers excellent hunting for this shy, unpredictable carnivore. The state record for a field-dressed animal is 540 pounds (1965); a bruin was killed in 1930 which weighed 465 pounds, field-dressed, a week after it was shot, according to *Maine's Record Animals*. Bear hunting is best in the northern portions of Penobscot County in the long rectangle paralleling Baxter State Park; in the central and southern portions

of Piscataquis County from Moosehead Lake west to Baxter Park and south to Dover-Foxcroft; in the wild lands of central Somerset County, west of Moosehead Lake and south to the Bingham area; in Franklin County on the abandoned farmlands lying to the south of Rangeley Lake and Sugarloaf Mountain; in Oxford County in the central and northern areas where the wilderness and populated areas meet, which includes the New Hampshire border territory from Aziscohos Lake to the White Mountain National Forest; in Aroostook County on the western edge of the agricultural lands where the deep forest begins, an area following Route 11 north to Fort Kent; and in the interior portions of Hancock and Washington counties. (These two counties abut each other in eastern Maine and are characterized by populated coastal margins and wild, beautiful interior sections.)

The ruffed grouse, the most popular small-game species, is present in quantity all over Maine, barring the vagaries of the population cycle. Tote and winter logging roads, trails, and second growth produced by lumber operations have improved the northern habitat; the farm/forest fringe, abandoned farms, second growth, and blueberry barrens of the southern and eastern regions provide ideal conditions. Bird hunters should remember that hunting pressure makes partridge wild, and they flush out of gun range at times. Some of the best opportunities require effort and legwork and are found in the remote deep woods. In the populated areas, dogs are very helpful and some of the most memorable grouse hunting days are spent in the orchards, stone fences, alder thickets, and fields of old farms. There are excellent grouse covers in every county in Maine, and they can be located by some local digging, especially by asking the area game warden.

Woodcock hunting in Maine ranks with the best anywhere. Maine supports a very substantial local or nesting population and receives an immense autumn invasion from the famous covers of New Brunswick. Washington and Hancock counties harbor the greatest number of birds and suffer relatively light hunting pressure. The best hunting is found south of the heavy forest cover in the alder thickets and damp places of the blueberry barrens, forest/field margins, and thickets. The portion of these counties stretching north to the potato lands of Aroostook is also productive. Coastal and southwestern Maine yields the bulk of the kill, but pressure is intense and hunter success not as high as in the east. The band of land running east from the New Hampshire and Quebec borders and passing to the south of Moosehead Lake and Baxter State Park and north of the population centers is also good gunning.

Waterfowl hunting has some ardent supporters in the state, and the unbelievable cannonading which takes place in Merrymeeting Bay on opening day is legendary. This expanse of water is the confluence of the mighty Androscoggin and Kennebec rivers, and when the legal shooting hour arrives, pellets really fly over the extensive marshes. Black ducks, blue- and green-winged teal, and wood ducks provide the bulk of the inland shooting; other species such as mallards, scaup, ring-necked ducks, whistlers (goldeneye), and other casual flight visitors make up the balance. Coastal gunners shoot the same general mix in the salt marshes; on the points, ledges, reefs, and open water are found eiders, mergansers, scoters (coot), oldsquaws, bufflehead, and other offshore divers. Write to: Dept. of Inland Fisheries & Game (address above) for a list of the game management areas devoted to wildfowling. The department has extensive programs to create new marsh and wildfowl management areas, as well as to protect the existing wetlands. Duck marshes are somewhat limited, aside from the food-rich margin of Merrymeeting Bay, but are found all along the coast. Some good shooting may be had on lakes, beaver flowages, logans (swampy ponds), and marshy stream mouths at the entrances into lakes. The Canada goose is found in the state, with the best

hunting being in Merrymeeting Bay and adjacent agricultural fields, in eastern Washington County near Moosehorn National Wildlife Refuge, adjacent to Calais and Eastport; and in the farmlands of Aroostook County.

(For additional regional information see "North Maine Woods Guides & Canoe Trip Outfitters" and the "Travel & Recreation Guide" section.)

Highways—Recreation & Scenic Routes

To get to your destination without getting lost, the *Maine Official Transportation Map* is indispensable. It shows the entire state, featuring all roads and highways (scenic highways are noted), route markers and access points, mileage between designated points, and approximate populations of cities and towns. Also shown are state boat-launching sites, seacoast ferry routes, highway rest areas and other lunch grounds, campsites, forest ranger headquarters, forest lookout stations, lighthouses, airports, state police stations, toll ferries and bridges, ports of entry, major ski areas, fish hatcheries, railroads, and state parks (indicating those places where camping is and is not permitted). This informative map may be obtained free from: Publicity Bureau, Gateway Circle, Portland 04102.

The state's Publicity Bureau also has available the free 100-page booklet *Motoring Through Maine*, a directory which contains a description of principal highway routes, along with an alphabetical gazeteer of towns and place names in Maine, including notes of interest on each, location on the *Official Maine Transportation Map*, and suggested places to shop and eat. A classified index of advertisers is also included. The booklet also provides handy lists of state and national parks. This is a fine companion publication that should be used with the road map to make getting around in Maine easy and enjoyable.

The most comprehensive road maps to Maine are in the excellent *Maine Road Atlas*. This large-format (18 × 25-inch) spiral-bound atlas is available for $6 from: Dept. of Transportation, Augusta 04333. General highway maps are provided for each county, as well as details of urban or congested areas. In addition to showing all roads and highways, airports, water features, boundaries, bridges, and city and village areas, the map also shows natural features, as well as scenic sites, campsites, tourist accommodations, camps or lodges, small state or municipal parks, roadside rest areas, ski areas, forest ranger stations, forest service towers, fish hatcheries, bird sanctuaries, game farms and preserves, and extensive recreational areas. The maps are printed in black and white and are clear and easy to read.

Prentiss & Carlisle Co., 107 Court Street, Bangor 04401, publishes excellent State of Maine County Maps, indispensable to campers, guides, tourists, fishermen, and hunters. These maps have a scale of 1 inch to 3 miles and are detailed and accurate. They show features such as roads and highways (including private roads), trails, railroads, town lines, state lookout stations, and bodies of water. The maps are priced from $1.25 to $1.75 depending on which county map you order. A complete set, flat for mounting, costs $12.50. Prices are subject to 5% sales tax for Maine residents, plus handling charge of 35¢ per order, prepaid. A current price list of the maps can be obtained from Prentiss & Carlisle.

Lake Survey Fishing Maps

Official lake survey maps, published by the Department of Inland Fisheries & Wildlife, are available for more than 1,000 Maine lakes and ponds, including Sabattus, Moosehead, Deboullie, East Grand, West Grand, Spednic, Fish River, Musquacook, Presque Isle, Chain of Ponds, Cupsuptic, Kennebago, Rangeley, Sysladobis, China, B. Pond, Azicoos, Green Parmachenee, Katahdin, Umbagog, Pemadumcook Chain of Lakes, Allagash, Caucomgomac, Chamberlain, Telos, Chemquasabamitook, Chesuncook, Big Eagle, Horserace Ponds, Millinocket, Nahmakanta, Penobscot, Munsungan, Machias, Meddybemps, Great East, Sebago, and hundreds more trophy landlocked salmon, lake trout, squaretail, and smallmouth bass waters. These useful maps show lake depth and major features and contain detailed descriptions of each lake along with lake bottom composition and fish species present. The maps cost 15¢ each and may be ordered from the *Maine Lakes Index,* available free from the Department of Inland Fisheries & Wildlife, 284 State St., Augusta 04333.

L. L. Bean—North Woods Clothing & Equipment Outfitters

Leon Leonwood Bean, known to outdoorsmen nationwide as L.L., launched his famous North Maine Woods empire in 1913 with a borrowed $400 and a practical, homely creation: the now legendary Maine hunting shoe. L.L. was tired of trekking home with wet and sore feet from wearing the heavy leather woodsman boot then in use. Rubber boots were too clammy and clumsy for all-day use. His new boot combined lightweight leather tops with all-rubber bottoms, incorporating the best features of both boots in use, and doing away with the disadvantages. Bean's business grew rapidly as fishermen and hunters discovered the comfort and warmth provided by this curious boot. For bare-ground walking it was light in weight, with a snug fit, cushioned innersole, and a chain tread outersole for traction. The waterproof bottoms proved ideal for hunting in wetlands and on snow. The revolutionary split backstay eliminated chafing.

Today the Maine hunting shoe is the most widely used sporting boot in the world. Its success launched the worldwide North Maine Woods mail-order business contained in the pages of the famous *L. L. Bean Catalog,* which is mailed four times a year to a million outdoor enthusiasts in 50 states and 70 foreign countries. This free, full-color 100-plus-page catalog has retained its old down east flavor over the years and today offers a wide range of boots (including the Maine guide shoe, fisherman shoe, woodsman boot, rubber moccasins, insulated hunting shoe, camp boot, and sheep-lined slippers), trousers, parkas, bush pants, shooting gloves, bush coats, Bean's Allagash hat, Maine guide shirt, and fishing, hunting, camping, canoeing, snowshoeing, ski touring, and backpacking gear. The Bean spring and fall catalog covers are full-color prints of beckoning north country fishing and hunting scenes. Bean's catalog service is legendary, and the prices are reasonable.

Bean's merchandise-packed, 10,000-square-foot retail salesroom is housed in a rambling wooden building in Freeport, accessible by two flights of stairs. The salesroom, visited annually by thousands of North Maine Woods-bound sportsmen and browsers, is open 24 hours a day, 365 days a year. During the peak summer months it's wall to wall with customers until 3:00 or 4:00 A.M. L. L. started keeping the store open all night in 1954 when he tired of being awakened at all hours of the night and early morning to serve newly arrived outdoorsmen and vacationers, who often traveled hundreds and even thousands of miles to visit this north country landmark.

A free copy of the *L. L. Bean Catalog* may be obtained by writing: L. L. Bean, Freeport 04032.

L. L. Bean and the *Maine Sportsman* magazine conduct an annual *Fly Fishing School* in May at the Bean Distribution Center in Freeport. Courses are taught by experienced instructors and include casting, knot tying, leaders, fishing tactics, entomology, equipment, and fly tying.

North Maine Woods Guides & Canoe Trip Outfitters

If you can afford a skilled Maine guide's hire, he will save you needless hours of wasted time and frustration in hunting or fishing new territory, or in canoeing unfamiliar, demanding rivers, as well as increasing your knowledge and appreciation of the north country. Write: Dept. of Inland Fisheries & Game, State House, Augusta 04333, for three free lists, *Maine Deer and Bear Hunting Guides, Maine Fishing Guides,* and *Maine Canoeing Guides.* The state does not evaluate the performance of the guides on the lists, and presents them only as a service. If you are staying at a sporting camp, the owner should be able to get a good guide if you let him know in advance. Chambers of commerce and game wardens are also productive sources, as are local newspaper rod-and-gun editors.

Maine has a large number of long established outfitters who provide guided wilderness canoe trips along the great north country rivers. *Sunrise County Canoe Expeditions,* Cathance Lake, Grove 04638, (207) 454-7708, in the heart of Washington County, provides outfitting services, instruction, canoe and accessories rentals, and runs trips on the Machias, St. Croix, Grand Lake Chain, East Machias, and Dennys rivers, ranging from smooth water to some of the most difficult white water in the East. Fishing is excellent throughout the region for trophy smallmouth bass, trout, and landlocked salmon, and the waters traveled include several of the last Atlantic salmon rivers in the country. The firm also runs two special 2-week boys' sessions with instruction in canoeing, camping, and woods skills, as well as a 10-day wilderness canoe trip. The *Maine Wilderness Canoe Basin,* Springfield 04487, (207) 989-3636, X 631, located on the northern shore of Pleasant Lake in Washington County, is a major outfitting center and gateway to the famous Grand Lake Chain, with more than 40 miles of wilderness waterways. The firm specializes in outfitting wilderness canoeists. Every essential item for camping and canoeing, along with food supplies and canoe pickup and delivery service, is provided. The canoe basin also provides a variety of accommodations—including wilderness tent sites, cabins, and deluxe tent cabins—as well as guided canoe trips along eastern Maine's wilderness waterways; fall hunting trips for partridge, black bear, and deer; young adult programs; and special instruction in white-water kayaking and canoeing. During the

winter, write or call: Capt. Carl Selik, 20 Bass Dr., Groton, CT 06340, (203) 536–7980.

In the North Maine Woods country, *Allagash Wilderness Outfitters*, Frost Pond, Star Rte. 76, Greenville 04441, (207) 764–0494, supplies canoe rentals and accessories, food, and shuttle transportation for trips on the St. John, Allagash, and West Branch of the Penobscot. *Allagash Canoe Trips*, 69 Winchester St., Presque Isle 04749, (207) 623–4429, offers guided and outfitted trips on the Allagash and St. John. Guided smooth- and white-water trips on the Allagash from Telos Lake to Allagash Village, with side trips to north country logging camps, are offered by: *Allagash River Canoe Trips*, 16 Woodside Rd., Augusta 04330, (207) 623–4429. Guide canoe fishing trips on the Allagash are also provided by *Earle N. Ahlquist*, 264 Beech Ridge Rd., Gorham 04038, (207) 839–4296, and by *Ray W. Jalbert*, RFD3, Fort Kent 04743, (207) 834–3265. *North Country Outfitters on Moosehead Lake*, P.O. Box 81, Rockwood 04478 (207–534–7305) offers complete outfitting service and guided trips on the Allagash, St. John, West Branch of the Penobscot, and Moose rivers.

For boys age 10–16 who want a canoeing and backpacking experience in the Maine wilderness, write: *Dirigo Wilderness Base*, P.O. Box 633, Auburn 04210, (207) 782–5209 in Auburn; (207) 998–4855 in Poland. This wilderness camp offers a fully operational base camp with special in-camp programs, flat-water, mountaineering, and backpacking pre-trip programs, and specially designed and pretested trail and canoeing equipment. The camper's summer stay will include basic and advanced canoeing skills, development of mountaineering skills, survival techniques, fancy trail cookery, swimming and lifesaving, fishing, and continuous on-the-trail program.

For whitewater rafting enthusiasts, guided trips down the wild upper Kennebec River and lower West Branch of the Penobscot are provided by *Northern Whitewater Expeditions*, Inc., P.O. Box 57, Rockwood 04478 (207) 534–7355. Saco River guided canoe trips, shuttle service, and rentals are provided by *Saco River Canoe & Kayak Inc.*, P.O. Box 111; Fryeburg 04037 (207) 935–2369.

(For additional information, see "Canoeing & Wild Rivers," "Fishing & Hunting," and the "Travel & Recreation Guide" section.)

Ski Touring Trails & Instruction

Maine, with its 33,040 square miles of mountainous forest terrain, is a veritable paradise for the winter sports enthusiast. The state's major ski touring areas—including the abandoned railroad beds of the "Old Eastern" and Greenville-Derby branch of the Bangor & Aroostock railroads and the Pleasant Mountain, Sunday River, Mount Blue State Park, Saddleback Mountain, Pineland Ski Club, Sugarloaf Mountain, Narrow Gauge Trail, University Forest, Bald Mountain, Acadia National Park, Appalachian Trail, Wolfe Neck Woods, Holbrook Hills, and Camden Hills State Park areas—are described in the *EMS Ski Touring Guide to New England*, along with regional maps, driving directions, ski trail mileages, and available facilities. This 288-page bible may be obtained for $5.95 (plus 50¢ postage) from: Eastern Mountain Sports, 1047 Commonwealth Ave., Boston, MA 02215.

For detailed information about the Pine Tree State's major cross-country skiing areas, instruction, and lodging, write: *Lost Valley Ski Area*, West Auburn 04210, (207) 784–1561, trails, instruction, and rentals; *Acadia National Park*, Bar Harbor 04609, (207) 288–2338; *Baker Mountain Ski Area*, Moscow 04920, (207) 672–9369, trails, rentals, instruction; *Pleasant Mountain Ski Area*, Bridgton 04009, (207) 647–2022, trails, rentals, instruction; *Spruce Mountain Area*,

Livermore Falls 04254, trails and instruction; *Hurricane Slope*, Falmouth 04105, (207) 797–4418, trails, rentals, instruction; *Saddleback Mountain Touring Center*, Rangeley 04970, (207) 864–3380, trails, maps, instruction, rentals, guided safaris, winter camping; *Chisholm Winter Park*, Rumford 04276, (207) 364–8977, trails and instruction; *Sunday River Ski Center*, Bethel 04217, (207) 824–2187, trails, instruction, lodging; *Sugarloaf Mountain*, Carrabassett Valley 04947, (207) 237–2000 or 237–2861—reservations, rentals, instruction, lodging at Deer Farm camps, and trails, including the Narrow Gauge Trail, once the nation's longest narrow-gauge railroad system, built to haul Maine timber; *Carrabassett Valley Touring Center*, Carrabassett Valley 04947, (207) 237–2205, instruction, rentals, and 50 miles of back-country trails with scenic views of Bigelow and Sugarloaf mountains and log cabin lodging at Caribou Pond; *Deer Farm Camps Ski Touring Center*, Kingfield 04947, (207) 265–2241, in western Maine, offers lodging, guided tours, instruction, and 26 miles of backcountry trails; *Squaw Mountain At Moosehead*, Greenville 04441, (207) 695–2272, offers deluxe lodging, rentals, instruction, trails, and touring across open fields, lakes, and ponds; *Titcomb Mountain Touring Center*, Farmington 04938, (207) 778–9384, offers lodging, instruction, groomed trails, and access to 20 miles of touring trails in the foothills of the beautiful Longfellow Mountains.

For more information on where to go ski touring, snowmobiling, or snowshoeing, consult the excellent *Maine for Winter Vacations*. This 28-page booklet is available free from: Publicity Bureau, Gateway Circle, Portland 04102. It contains a listing and description of Maine winter recreation areas, as well as where to stay, eat, and shop.

Thoreau's Great Wilderness Canoe Journey to Mount Katahdin

The summer of 1846 was on the wane when Henry David Thoreau set out for the Maine Woods, a wilderness yet unmapped. Between that time and this, white men have explored the deepest interior of the wild country, and settled along the banks of its many waterways. Paper companies have harvested the wealth of the forests, and laced the woods with logging roads. But the wilderness remains for those who are willing to seek it out in the great tracts of boreal forests, the remote lakes accessible only by canoe or foot travel, and the frothing wild waters of its great rivers.

Thoreau's goal on this epic journey, described in his famous book, *The Maine Woods*, was majestic Mount Katahdin (he spelled it Ktaadn), the second-highest mountain in New England (5,268 feet), and surrounded, now as then, by some of the most beautiful country in the eastern United States. In the 20th century it became the northern terminus of the Appalachian Trail. The mountain lies within Baxter State Park (see "Moosehead Lake & Mount Katahdin Region" in the "Travel & Recreation Guide" section), a preserve of some 200,000 acres. Today the park area is accessible by road through Greenville, Millinocket, and Patten, and the mountain by numerous trails.

For Thoreau, however, the waterways of the Maine wilderness were the only route to Ktaadn. He started from a small settlement on the Mattawamkeag River 56 miles beyond Bangor. The two seasoned woodsmen who took him to Moosehead Lake and up the West Branch of the Penobscot River, through the Pemadumcook Lakes to the foot of Ktaadn in their bateau were men of a breed that has become legendary; their handmade boats, part dory, part canoe, have disappeared from the great northeastern rivers, supplanted by motorboats and the network of logging roads that have opened the woods. Tho-

reau and his guides covered the first few miles of the trip on foot, and set out by boat near the mouth of the Millinocket River, where a town has grown up around the power plants that draw their energy from the river. Just upstream are the Grand Falls of the Penobscot, where the waters' 60-foot plunge demands a portage by today's river travelers, as it did on Thoreau's trip.

For him, the wilderness began at Quakish Lake, where "the spruce and cedar on its shores, hung with gray lichens, looked at a distance like the ghosts of trees. Ducks were sailing here and there on its surface, and a solitary loon . . . laughed and frolicked, and showed its straight leg, for our amusement . . . We had our first, but a partial view of Ktaadn, its summit veiled in clouds, like a dark isthmus in that quarter, connecting the heavens with the earth."

Today, the river lands and the lakes through which the stream passes are quiet and unpopulated, although between Thoreau's time and the 1920s, its waters were among the most heavily traveled in Maine. During those years they provided the major means of access to the East Branch of the Penobscot, the St. John, and the Allagash. Logging roads reduced this flow of water traffic, and provided access to the river at many points (most access roads start at Greenville and Millinocket).

Thoreau's route took him up the river, his guides poling up the stretches of white water, and carrying around the river's several large falls. The lakes and dead waters along the stream offered easier passage. One can canoe down the river at any season, although several stretches are dangerous at high water and the most difficult white-water runs must be carried in the spring. The trip offers vistas of Katahdin and its surrounding forests, unmarred by civilization.

In the area of the North Twin Lake and above, the white waters become less frequent and the true lake country begins. Upstream from the Pemadumcook Lakes lies Ambajejus Lake, with the great flat summit of Katahdin rising beyond. Even along this portion of the river, however, the lakes are interspersed with rapids and falls, among them the Ambajejus Falls, the Passamagamet Falls, Debsconeag Falls (a ¼-mile carry), Pockwockamus Falls, Abol Falls, and Sourdnahunk Falls. Abol and Pockwockamus falls can be run only during summer low water. The Sourdnahunk Falls must be carried.

Thoreau's party camped in this area, on the Sourdnahunk Deadwater, at the mouth of Murch Brook and the Aboljacknagesic (Abol Stream), a stream running down from Katahdin. From here they hiked to the mountain's summit. Today the mountain is usually approached by trail through Baxter State Park. Access roads run from Greenville, Millinocket, and Patten. The Abol Trail, heading at the Abol Campground off the Millinocket-Nesowadnehunk Tote Road, is the oldest known trail up the mountain.

The view from atop Katahdin embraces hundreds of lakes, many connected by the waters of the Penobscot, and the hills of Mounts Camden and Desert to the south. The view today is much like Thoreau's: "Immeasurable forest for the sun to shine on . . . Countless lakes, Moosehead in the southwest, forty miles by ten, like a gleaming silver platter at the end of the table, Chesuncook, eighteen long by three wide, without an island; Millinocket, on the south, with its hundred islands, and a hundred others without a name . . ."

Thoreau started his second journey through the Maine woods in the midst of the lake country, at Moosehead Lake. Joe Aitteon, a Penob-

scot Indian, took Thoreau through the swamplands and down the Penobscot River to Chesuncook Lake. The notes Thoreau makes of Aitteon's special mixture for pitching the canoe, his methods of applying and checking the canoe for its watertightness, the Indian's unequaled tracking prowess, and his familiarity with the animals of the woods preserve something of a culture that has virtually vanished, as the Indians' ways of life became white men's legends. Thoreau writes of Joe's tracking a wounded moose: "We all landed at once . . . The Indian fastened his birch, threw off his hat, adjusted his waistband, seized the hatchet, and set out. He told me afterward, casually, that before we landed he had seen a drop of blood on the bank, when it was two or three rods off. He proceeded rapidly up the woods, with a peculiar, elastic, noiseless, and stealthy tread, looking to the right and left on the ground, and stepping in the faint tracks of the wounded moose, now and then pointing in silence to a single drop of blood on the handsome, shining leaves . . ."

But it is not until his third trip through the Maine woods that Thoreau realizes the pathetic and sometimes hilarious inadequacy of his own woodcraft before the competency of his guide, on this trip a Penobscot named Joe Polis. After seeing fox fire for the first time, he says he is prepared "to hear of the most startling and unimagined phenomena witnessed by 'his [Thoreau's guide's] folks,' they are abroad at all hours and seasons in scenes so unfrequented by white men. Nature must have made a thousand revelations to them which are still secrets to us." His respect for the Indians deepens as he learns of his guide's ability to make his way through the pathless woods without a compass, his considerable knowledge of edible roots, berries, and herbs, and the finely wrought art of his handmade canoe.

At one point Polis walks ahead of Thoreau and his companion with the canoe, instructing them to follow his tracks and keep to the main path. Soon the two are hopelessly lost, slogging through the blackfly-ridden swamp on an abandoned trail, up to their knees in mud. Polis finally locates them, wondering at their ignorance. The same pitfalls which complicated Thoreau's journey lie in wait for the wilderness traveler today, and they are not as humorous when experienced firsthand. Cross-country travel through these roadless areas is hazardous at best, and should be avoided or kept to a minimum. Most carries and logging roads are well marked; keep to them. Before you set out on your trip, provide yourself with the necessary equipment and maps.

Much of the land here is privately owned by various paper companies which have cut logging roads. Each company has special rules on use of the roads, and some require travelers to obtain their permission before using them. The *AMC Maine Mountain Guide* lists the names of the companies. For a copy of the *Sportsman's Map of Northwestern Maine* and information on regulations pertaining to use of paper company land, write to: Paper Industry Information Office, 133 State St., Augusta 04330.

Wild & Scenic River Maps

The following full-color, large-scale U.S. Geological Survey Topographic Maps show the entire lengths of the Pine Tree State's nationally renowned wild and trophy fishing waters and the topography of the surrounding wilderness (see the "Travel & Recreation Guide" section for additional listings): *Musquacook Lakes & Stream:* Allagash Falls, Musquacook Lake; *Allagash Stream & Lake:* Allagash Lake, Churchill Lake; *St. Francis River & Headwaters:* Allagash, Beau Lake, St. Francis, Rocky Brook; *Red River Lakes:* Fish River Lake; *Aroostook River Country:* Ashland, Caribou, Fort Fairfield, Grand Lake Seboeis, Mars Hill, Millinocket Lake, Oxbow, Presque Isle, Spider Lake; *Moose River:* Attean, Brassua Lake, Long Pond, Moosehead

Lake, Skinner (7.5); *East Branch of the Penobscot:* Millinocket, Shin Pond, Spider Lake, Stacyville, Telos Lake, Traveler Mountain; *West Branch of the Pleasant River:* First Roach Pond, Sebec, Sebec Lake; *Baskahegan Lake and Stream:* Danforth, Scraggly Lake; *Dennys River:* Calais, Gardner Lake, Pembroke (7.5); *Narraguagus River:* Cherryfield, Harrington (7.5), Lead Mountain, Tunk Lake; *Union River:* Ellsworth, Great Pond, Lead Mountain, Tunk Lake; *St. Croix River:* Calais, Danforth, Devils Head (7.5), Forest, Kellyland, Red Beach (7.5), Robinson (7.5), Vanceboro, Waite; *Machias River & Headwater Lakes:* Machias (7.5), Machias Bay (7.5), Lead Mountain, Nicatous Lake, Tug Mountain, Wabassus Lake, Wesley, Whitneyville; *Pleasant River:* Addison (7.5), Cherryfield, Columbia Falls, Tug Mountain; *Dead River-Main Branch:* Little Bigelow Mountain, Pierce Pond, The Forks; *Dead River—North Branch:* Arnold Pond, Chain of Ponds, Jim Pond (7.5), Stratton, Tim Pond (7.5); *Dead River-South Branch:* Quill Hill (7.5), Phillips, Rangeley, Stratton, Tim Pond (7.5); *Kennebago River:* Arnold Pond, Cupsuptic, Kennebago Lake (7.5), Oquossoc; *Magalloway River:* Cupsuptic, Errol (NH), Oquossoc, Second Connecticut Lake (NH); *Rapid River:* Errol (NH), Oquossoc; *Sandy River & Ponds:* Farmington (7.5), Farmington Falls (7.5), Kingsfield, New Sharon (7.5), Norridgewock, Phillips, Rangeley; *Saco River:* Biddeford (7.5), Brownfield (7.5), Buxton, Cornish (7.5), Crawford Notch (NH), North Conway (NH), Old Orchard Beach (7.5), Ossipee Lake (NH), Sebago Lake, Whitefield (NH).

Eastern Maine Fish & Game Region

Eastern Maine Topo Maps

U.S. Geological Survey Overview Maps (scale 1:250,000): Bangor, Eastport, Fredericton (N.B.), Millinocket.

Acadia National Park & Mount Desert Island

U.S. Geological Survey Map (size 23 × 27 inches, scale 1:62,500): Acadia National Park & vicinity.

Chiputneticook Lakes

U.S. Geological Survey Large-scale Maps: Amity, Danforth, Forest, Vanceboro.

Grand Lake Chain

U.S. Geological Survey Large-scale Maps: Big Lake, Kellyland, Nicatous Lake, Scraggly Lake, Springfield, Wabassus Lake, Waite.

Moosehorn National Wildlife Refuge

U.S. Geological Survey Large-Scale Maps: Calais, Devil's Head, Gardner Lake, Pembroke (7.5), Red Beach (7.5), Whiting (7.5).

Washington County, on Maine's and the nation's easternmost border, has been blessed with an abundance of natural riches and is an outdoors enthusiast's paradise. The 5,000-square-mile region is bordered on the south by the jagged, spruce-clad, rocky Atlantic coastline, on the north by the pastoral potato lands of Aroostook County, on the west by the Penobscot River, and on the east by the Maine-New Brunswick border. Within this area lies the greatest variety of fish and game species and terrain in the state. Graceful, aristocratic Atlantic salmon, acrobatic landlocked salmon, pugnacious smallmouth bass, native brook trout, lunker togue (lake trout), voracious pickerel, and white and yellow perch await the fisherman, and you can fish for more species of game fish in a single day than in any other place in Maine. The smallmouth bass fishing is so good that landing 50 fish a day weighing over 1½ pounds each is possible in many of the better waters. There are also a few bronzebacks here, exceeding 5 pounds in weight.

The topography is richly varied and includes the beautiful fjord- and island-studded coast, the cool, deep spruce and fir forests, thousands of acres of fish-laden lakes and ponds, many miles of productive streams and canoe trails, the fragrant blueberry barrens, granite mountains, and glacial bogs. The growing moose herd finds the swamps particularly to its liking, and some of the finest deer and black bear hunting in the East is found here. Ruffed grouse, woodcock, pheasant, wildfowl, and small game abound, and the observant outdoorsman may see beaver, otter, mink, bobcat, marten, fisher, ospreys, and eagles. *Maine Fishery Regions: Grand Lake* (B-162, 45¢) will give you a good basic knowledge of the region, and where to find your favorite fish. In addition, lake survey maps are available for the important waters at a cost of 15¢. Three free paper company maps show area campsites, public and private roads, fire towers, land holdings, and much other useful information. *Eastern Maine Timberlands Sportsman's Map* is produced by the Dead River Company and Eastern Woodlands Division of Standard Packaging Corporation. This excellent map covers most of Hancock and Washington counties and the lower part of Aroostook County and is packed with a great deal of valuable material. The publication describes the area, facilities, fishing, hunting, and camping details, and can be obtained from: Dead River Co., 55 Broadway, Bangor 04401, or Standard Packaging Corp., Brewer 04412. Write to: Penobscot Development Co., Great Works 04468, for the *Sportsman's Map, Penobscot Tree Farm*, which covers 20 townships in the Nicatous Lake-Penobscot River area and includes

MAINE TRAVEL & RECREATION GUIDE

an interesting history of the company. Woodland Division, Georgia Pacific Corp., Mill St., Woodland 04694, produces the free, colorful, informative *Sportsmen's Map of Washington County and Western New Brunswick*.

Nestled on the Maine-New Brunswick border in the northeast corner of the region are the irregular-shaped shorelines of the Chiputneticook Lakes, East Grand and Spednic, which are also the headwaters of the St. Croix River. Sprawling, rocky East Grand is one of the blue-ribbon landlocked salmon and togue lakes in Maine and one of the least

known, considering the quality fishing it offers. Salmon and togue run big, with some salmon topping 5 pounds and togue exceeding 10 pounds. The outlet spills through a dam and runs into Spednic, and offers the chance to hook one of these big, silvery acrobats in fast water. Jagged Spednic has a well deserved reputation for big bass and lots of them, and offers some excellent salmon fishing as well.

The St. Croix River, a famous canoeing and fishing stream, spills through a dam on the end of Spednic at Vanceboro and flows southeast for about 100 miles to the sea, forming the border between Maine

and New Brunswick. Fishing is good for landlocks and bass, and the many miles of white water will test the wilderness paddler's skills. Among the popular stretches are Elbow, Mile, Joe George's, and Hall's rips and the dangerous class IV rapids at Little Falls. *Maine Rivers: The St. Croix* (B-241) is available for 45¢ from: Dept. of Inland Fisheries & Game, State House, Augusta 04333, and gives a description of the watershed and a chart of the principal lakes and the fish species found in each.

The Grand Lake Chain, which is the inundated West Branch of the St. Croix, merges with the main river at Grand Falls Flowage. Names that are dear to the hearts of smallmouth bass fans include Sysladobsis, Junior, Scraggly, Big, Long, Lewey, Pocumus, Pocamoonshine, Clifford, and Wabassus lakes. When conditions are right you can hook bass until your arms won't take any more, and there are a number of fish weighing more than 3 pounds. Paddling along the dri-ki-strewn shore of these waters, your solitude will be broken only by the cry of a loon, the malevolent gaze of a feeding moose, or the electrifying strike of a lunker smallmouth. Some of the heftiest pickerel to be found in the United States add variety to the day's fishing. West Grand Lake, one of the original homes of the landlocked salmon, provides excellent fishing for this species, as well as for togue. Its outlet, Grand Lake Stream, which runs into Big Lake, offers superb fly fishing for landlocks, if you are there at the right time. The Musquash Lakes are also good salmon waters, as are Sysladobsis, Scraggly, and Junior lakes, where bass and salmon seem to tolerate each other. Tomah Stream is famous for brook trout and gave its name to the beautiful Tomah Jo fly. Adjacent waters which are famous for fishing include Nicatous and Gassabias lakes and the Pistol group, all of which are part of the Passadumkeag River headwaters, and Crawford and Meddybemps lakes to the south of Grand Falls Flowage.

Moosehorn National Wildlife Refuge, in the southeast corner of Washington County, consists of the Baring Unit (16,065 acres) near Calais, and the Edmunds Unit (6,600 acres) on Cobscook Bay near Dennysville. The topography bears witness to the awesome force of the glaciers during the Ice Age. The effects of thousands of years of massive weight and grinding can be seen in the rocky outcroppings, hills, boreal forests, lakes, streams, bogs, and marshes of the refuge. The tidal bores exceed 20 feet and are the greatest to be found in the United States, with the exception of Alaska's Cook Inlet. Moosehorn is primarily managed for migratory birds such as woodcock, ducks, and geese. Harbor seals chase fish in the turbulent waters along the shore, moose, deer, and bear find the rugged inland to their liking, and there is an abundance of small-game animals and birds, such as snowshoe hares and ruffed grouse. For a change of pace the nature lover will find some good fishing for brook trout, smallmouth bass, and pickerel. A free leaflet, *Moosehorn National Wildlife Refuge*, is available from: Refuge Manager, Moosehorn National Wildlife Refuge, Calais 04619. This informative publication provides an interesting, concise description of the area and its inhabitants. Lists of bird and animal species and other information can be obtained from the refuge manager.

Maine is the only state where the spectacular Atlantic salmon can still be caught in its original habitat. The Dennys, Machias, Pleasant, and Narraguagus, four Washington County rivers, are managed for salmon, and a great deal of effort and expense has been employed by the state and federal governments and concerned sportsmen. The runs seem to be on the increase, and the commitment has been worthwhile. The Dennys River drains Meddybemps Lake and joins the sea near Dennysville. Fly fishermen try their luck in the beautiful rocky pools of this exquisite little river, especially during June and July. Canoeists will enjoy the exciting trip of about 20 miles and will encounter some

rugged white-water stretches, most notably the formidable Little Falls.

The rapid-strewn Machias River, a few miles to the west of the Dennys on U.S. 1, is another popular salmon and canoeing stream. An awesome natural ravine, the Machias Gorge at the tideline in the town of Machias, hinders the upstream migration of salmon, except during periods of low stream flow. The hordes of fish at the foot of the ravine were easy pickings for the nets of Indians and colonists 200 years ago. Those who know the river take salmon on local fly patterns year after year, and there is some fine trout fishing, particularly around the mouths of feeder brooks. Fifth Machias Lake in the headwaters produces good squaretail fishing. Fourth, Third, Second, and First Machias Lakes offer warmwater species. Mopang Lake at the head of Mopang Stream, a feeder, has a sizable population of scrappy landlocks. Canoeists will find the Machias a worthwhile challenge, particularly in the early season. The long Wigwams Rapids and Carrot and Boot rips will test your mettle. Upper Holmes Falls, a 30-foot drop through a canyon, and Little Falls must be portaged or lined. The Machias is a river for experienced canoeists, and the trip is well worth the effort, because you will pass through some wild, lonely country in which surprising a moose or black bear are distinct possibilities. *Maine Rivers: The Machias* (B-194, 10¢) describes the river and its watershed. It devotes substantial space to discussing the Atlantic salmon management program.

The Pleasant River lies about 15 miles west of the Machias and is the least known of the salmon waters. The Pleasant rises in Pleasant River Lake, a good spot for landlocks and trout, and meanders through the blueberry barrens and the evergreen forests to join the sea at Addison. Those who fish this river keep quiet about the results, but rumor says that this is a productive river, and that many more fish are taken than are reported. The Pleasant is a delightful canoe trail and lives up to its name. The observant paddler will see much wildlife on his trip down this gentle stream. Moose, bear, deer, and beaver are plentiful, and eagles and ospreys watch for unwary fish in the depths.

The neighboring Narraguagus is the most noted and productive Atlantic salmon river in Maine. (The state record fish was taken by veteran guide Harry Smith, the originator of the bear-hair salmon fly, in 1959.) In good years almost 200 magnificent fish fall to anglers' rods. The Narraguagus flows through the blueberry barrens and forests to the north and west of the picturesque town of Cherryfield, which is at the head of the tide on the river. The *Belgrade*, a full-rigged bark that carried 56 local men around Cape Horn to California in the days of the gold rush, was built in this once active shipbuilding community. Tributaries and lakes, such as Narraguagus and Schoodic, provide good fishing for landlocks and trout. Tunk, Pleasant, and Lead mountains loom in the distance across the colorful, almost treeless expanse of the blueberry barrens. Atlantic salmon are taken right in the middle of Cherryfield, at the Academy Pool. If you are fortunate enough to hook a fish, enthusiastic onlookers will make you feel like a star, and you won't lack for advice. *Maine Rivers: The Narraguagus* (B-157, 10¢), is an informative Department of Inland Fisheries & Wildlife Publication about the river, its watershed, and, of course, the Atlantic salmon. Anyone planning to use the region should write for it (address above). The Narraguagus offers good canoeing early in the season and gives the paddler a chance to see moose, bear, and deer, as well as the beaver, which is particularly abundant in the watershed. Plan to be surprised by the electrifying crack of an alarmed beaver's tail as you canoe this beautiful, game-rich area.

Between Cherryfield on the western edge of Washington County and the Penobscot River lies fine fishing for landlocks and togue; Tunk Lake is rumored to have produced a 20-pound landlocked salmon during the 1920s. It is the deepest lake in eastern Maine, with a

maximum depth of 222 feet. With its boulder-strewn shoreline set in an area of forested hills and mountains, Tunk is a beautiful place. Beech Hill Pond, near Ellsworth, produced the state record togue in 1958, which is remarkable when one thinks of all of the famous remote togue waters in Maine. Green and Branch lakes are neighboring waters which produce good catches of salmon and togue. Floods Pond has the only population in Maine of the rare Sunapee trout, a relative of the arctic char. Sprawling Graham Lake has superb fishing for bass, pickerel, and perch, as do many other lakes and ponds in Hancock County. Brown trout have been selectively stocked in places like the Union River, and some browns find their way to the ocean to return later as sea trout.

 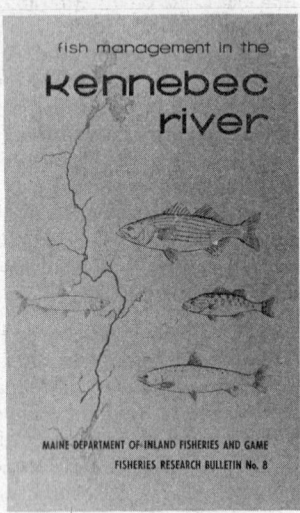

Three beautiful large-size maps of the Eastern Maine Region, *Phillips' Map of Washington County, Phillips' Map of Hancock County,* and *Phillips' East of Katadhin Map* ($1.50 each, plus 40¢ postage) show all man-made and natural features, including trails, portages, gravel roads and highways, Forest Service and paper company campsites, fly-in services, fish hatcheries, and boat-launching sites. They may be ordered from Augustus D. Phillips & Son, Northeast Harbor 04662.

Acadia National Park (33,000 acres) is a magnificent expanse of rugged, glacial seacoast indented by fjords, fir-clad mountains, sparkling lakes and ponds, rushing streams, and forested valleys; it is crisscrossed by an excellent network of trails. The major section of the park is located on Mount Desert Island, which is dominated by Cadillac Mountain (1,580 feet), the highest point on the New England coast. The fjord of Somes Sound divides the park into eastern and western sections. The island was named by the great French explorer Samuel de Champlain in 1604, who incorrectly thought the land was inhabited. The famous summer resort town of Bar Harbor is found on the eastern side of the island in the shadow of Cadillac Mountain. Two additional segments, Schoodic Point on the mainland and Isle au Haut to the southwest, complete the park. Major features include Long Pond, Eagle Lake, Big Heath, the Black Woods, Penobscot Mountain, Jordan Pond, and the Bubbles.

Summer resort activities are blended with outstanding hiking and naturalist pursuits, and bird-watchers, botanists, and geologists find plenty to keep them occupied. There is some trout, salmon, bass, and pickerel fishing available, and the quality is fairly good, considering the numbers of people. *Acadia National Park,* a free brochure from:

Acadia National Park, RFD1, Box 1, Bar Harbor 04609, colorfully describes the park and its many enticements, and includes a map. A free *Camping and Campsite* leaflet is also furnished by the park and tells about the two park campsites, their facilities, regulations, fees, and activities. A free hiking map, *Acadia National Park,* another park offering, shows the roads and hiking trails, and grades the latter by degree of steepness. *Wintertime Activities,* free from the park, provides the snowshoe, cross-country skiing, and snowmobile routes. Included are the regulations and some useful cold weather information, such as a windchill chart and frostbite precautions. For detailed information about the park, write to the park for the free *Eastern Park and Monument Association Publications List.* There are books and articles on every subject from blueberries to seals. A handy *AMC Trail Guide to Mount Desert Island and Acadia National Park* may be obtained by sending a check or money order for $2 to: Appalachian Mountain Club Books, 5 Joy St., Boston, MA 02108.

The Washington County region is served by several well-established fishing and hunting camps and lodges. *Robinson's Log Housekeeping Cottages* on the Dennys River provides accommodations and fishing for Atlantic salmon, smallmouth bass, pickerel, and fall deer hunting; for literature and rates write: G. Raymond Robinson, Dennysville 04628. *Play-Stead Lodge & Cottages,* Princeton 04668, on Lewey Lake, connecting Long Lake, Big Lake, Grand Lake and St. Croix waters, offers some of the finest bass fishing in the east. *Rideout's Lodge-Cottages,* Danforth 04424, is on scenic East Grand Lake on the New Brunswick border. *Leen's Lodge,* Grand Lake Stream 04637, has cottages and resort facilities with amphibious floatplane service. *Grand Lake Lodge,* Grand Lake Stream 04637 (write for literature and rates), on the shore of West Grand Lake, offers housekeeping cottages, canoe and boat rentals, and guide service. The *Down River Camps,* in the heart of smallmouth bass country on the Grand Falls Flowage of the St. Croix River, offers comfortable housekeeping cabins with full services. *Pocomoonshine Lake Lodges* provide fully equipped cabins for fishermen and hunters, boaters, and guides. Write: Gene Moriarty, Alexander, Baring 04610. *Weatherby's—the Fisherman's Resort,* Grand Lake Stream 04637, offers deluxe accommodations and services in a rustic setting. *Chet's Camps on Big Lake,* Princeton 04668, offers cabins, boats, and guides. *Long Lake Camps,* Princeton 04668, is a hunting and fishing camp with cabin accommodations, guides, and boats. *Tripp's Lodge & Camps,* Princeton 04668, is in the Grand Lake, Big Lake, and St. Croix River area. *Spruce Lodge & Cabins* is on Sysladobsis Lake near famous Scraggly Lake and West Grand Lake in the St. Croix River chain. Write: RD1, Springfield 04487. Canoe rentals in eastern Maine are provided by *Maine Wilderness Canoe Basin,* Pleasant Lake, Box P, Springfield 04487, and *Franklin Woodcraft Co.,* Rte. 182, Franklin 04634.

Vacation resorts in the Penobscot-Acadia region include *Wantalfego Lodge & Cabins,* RD1, Franklin 04634, on Webb Pond in Eastbrook; *Breezemere Farm,* South Brooksville 04617; *Goose Cove Lodge,* Sunset 04683, on Deer Isle in the East Penobscot Bay region; Oakland House, Sargentville 04673; *Hiram Blake Camp,* Harborside 04642, a recreational vacation resort on Penobscot Bay; *Sunset Lodge,* c/o Ray Hale, Box 404, 2 Canal Plaza, Portland 04111, on the eastern shore of Green Lake near Ellsworth. For information on accomodations and services in Bar Harbor and Acadia National Park, write: Chamber of Commerce, Bar Harbor 04609.

Access & Outfitting Centers

The eastern Maine region is reached by U.S. 95 or U.S. 1 and is crossed by Maine 9, called the Airline, and by Maine 6. Lodging, supplies, guides, and outfitters are available at the towns of Calais, Eastport, Lubec, Machias, Dennysville, Whiting, Northfield, Wesley,

Cooper, Grove, Meddybemps, Baring, Woodland, Princeton, Waite, Topsfield, Brookton, Forest City, Danforth, Forest Station, Cherryfield, Debois, Great Pond, Franklin, Eastbrook, Waltham, Green Lake, Ellsworth, Bucksport, and Dedham.

Moosehead Lake & Mount Katahdin Region

Moosehead Lake & Mount Katahdin Region Topo Maps

U.S. Geological Survey Overview Maps (scale 1:250,000): Lewiston, Millinocket, Presque Isle, Quebec, Sherbrooke.

Baxter State Park

U.S. Geological Survey large-scale maps: Harrington Lake, Katahdin (also available in a stunning shaded relief edition), Telos Lake, Traveler Mountain.

Moosehead Lake

U.S. Geological Survey large-scale maps: Brassua Lake, Greenville, Moosehead Lake, North East Carry.

West Branch of the Penobscot & Chesuncook Lake

U.S. Geological Survey large-scale maps: Caucomgomoc Lake, Chesuncook, Harrington Lake, Jo-Mary Mountain, Katahdin, Millinocket, Norcross, North East Carry, Ragged Lake, Seboomook Lake.

This vast northern lakes and forests region encompasses huge Piscataquis, the "county of lakes," and the northern parts of Somerset and Penobscot counties. The Moosehead Lake country, one of the great, historic fishing, canoeing, camping, and hiking areas in the Northeast, is dominated by Maine's largest lake, Moosehead, 40 miles long and 20 miles wide, the Kennebec and Penobscot watersheds, and Baxter State Park. This territory is bordered to the north by the North Maine Woods tract, to the south by a line drawn between Stratton and Millinocket, to the west by the Maine-Quebec border, and to the east by Baxter State Park and the East Branch of the Penobscot. Within this region lie over 5,000 square miles of cold, deep, rockbound lakes, gouged out by the great glacial ice cap, wilderness trout ponds, hundreds of miles of classic canoeing water, thick evergreen forests, and scores of mountains dominated by majestic Mount Katahdin. The lakes and river waters hold brook trout and landlocked salmon of better than 7 pounds and togue well in excess of 15 pounds. Some of the famous names are Spencer, Brassua, Chesuncook, Lobster, Penobscot, Schoodic, Canada Falls, and Sebec lakes. Schoodic is one of the original homes of the landlocked salmon, and Schoodic fish have been stocked all over the state. Pierce Pond is the home of Maine's record brook trout, taken in 1958. The state record blueback was taken at nearby Basin Pond in 1973. The fragrant balsam and spruce mantle is the habitat of bear, moose, deer, ruffed grouse, marten, wildcat, lynx, fisher, beaver, mink, otter, loon, osprey, and eagle. Miles of hiking trails, such as the famed Appalachian, afford a good opportunity to view some of these natives. Other, less friendly, natives were the Abenaki Indians, who made their home in the Moosehead-Kennebec area. Their raids on coastal settlements made much of Maine uninhabitable for more than 100 years. This area is also one of the earliest centers of Maine's immense timber industry. In season, pulpwood drives still fill some of the rivers bank to bank with seething masses of 4-foot-long "sticks."

Moosehead Lake has attracted sportsmen since the early 19th century. This greatest of all New England lakes cuts through the north Maine wilderness for a stretch of about 35 miles, hemmed by rugged mountains and flanked by dense forests. In the center of the lake Mount Kineo thrusts itself above the waters and far-flung forests of the lake's eastern shores. The mountain is composed of flint. Many of the New England Indian tribes came here for flint and it is believed that this mountain was also the source of iron pyrites used by the ancient Red Paint People for firestones. When Henry David Thoreau made a trip into the Moosehead-Katahdin region in 1846, his party remarked on the size, abundance, and voracity of the trout. The philosopher's comrades did not observe the niceties of angling, however, and harvested their squaretails with salt pork and stout lines. The lake holds sizable populations of trout, togue, and salmon. You can enjoy the recreational activities of one of Moosehead's many luxury resorts one minute, and in half an hour be fly casting on a remote trout pond. Write: Dept. of Inland Fisheries & Game, State House, Augusta 04333, for an excellent pamphlet, *Maine's Fishery Regions: Moosehead* (B-270, 45¢), which describes the lake, its drainage area, the fishery, and the fishing. It tells about the major species, primarily coldwater fish, including the scarce blueback trout, a handsome fellow with a blue back and round red spots. This fish is a relative of the arctic char and is found in Penobscot Lake and a few ponds. The pamphlet also includes interesting, useful information about the region and its history.

Scott Paper Company produces an excellent free map and brochure titled *Maine USA and Scott Paper Company Timberlands*. This colorful publication includes a map of the area around Moosehead Lake and west to Coburn Gore and contains a wealth of detail about the private road network, campsites, boat-launching sites, ski areas, gasoline locations (in remote areas), landing strips, fish species in principal waters, and much other valuable data. The brochure portion tells about the company, its timberlands, and its recreational programs and facilities. The information and regulations section describes the forest fire laws, where to write for fire permits, snowmobile rules, and landowner liability. Of particular value is a commonsense article about being lost in the woods, and how to handle the situation. Specific instructions and survival hints will take the panic out of a trying experience, if followed, and enable the lost outdoorsman to return safely to civilization. To obtain this worthwhile brochure, write to: Paper Industry Information Office, 133 State St., Augusta 04330.

The Great Northern Paper Co., Millinocket 04462, produces a free pamphlet, *Your Road Guide to the West Branch Region*, which traces the GNP road system around Moosehead, Lobster, Seboomook, Caucomgomoc, Chesuncook, and Telos lakes and the western approaches to Baxter State Park. Rules of the road, safety regulations, registration, and forestry management are discussed too.

The Kennebec River discharges from the East and West Outlets of Moosehead, which drain into a dammed lake, Indian Pond. The East Outlet offers 3½ miles of heavy rapids before it flows into Indian Pond. The river holds some good trout and salmon all the way to Wyman Lake at Bingham. One of its tributaries, the Dead River, was the scene of Benedict Arnold's ill-fated march to Quebec in 1775. Fans of novelist Kenneth Roberts will recall his account of the epic. An interesting Dept. of Inland Fisheries & Game publication (address above), *Maine Rivers: The Kennebec* (B-275, 45¢), describes the Kennebec fishery, fish management, the effects of logging, and other information.

To the north, northeast, and east of Moosehead lie the wilderness waterways of the West and East Branches of the Penobscot, which include Baxter State Park. The West Branch, one of America's famed canoe trails, has two major segments. The top portion from Seboomook Lake to Chesuncook is mostly easy going. It passes close to

Lobster Lake, a truly great salmon and togue spot, picking up its outlet, receives the two Ragmuff streams, and merges with Chesuncook for the final paddle to Ripogenus Dam, 92 feet high at the head of West Branch Gorge. The swift Penobscot currents at the foot of the dam hold some salmon of better than 7 pounds and some eye-popping trout. The fisherman may find himself with the trophy of a lifetime or some smashed tackle, depending on his brand of luck.

The upper stretch of the West Branch (from Seboomook Lake Dam downstream past the North East Carry to Chesuncook Lake) and huge Chesuncook Lake offer some of Maine's finest trophy fishing for landlocked salmon up to 9 pounds. The major fishing pools along the upper West Branch, bordered by a dense northern forest of spruce, pine, poplar, and tamarack, include the Big Island area, the legendary Fox Hole with its sheer granite cliffs, and the boulder-studded Rocky Rips area near the mouth of Pine Stream (an excellent early season stream which yields big squaretails from its meandering, tea-colored waters). The top fishing areas in Chesuncook Lake include the rock ledges along beautiful Gero Island, mouth of Red Brook, Togue Point, and the Caribou Lake area.

The nearby lakes and streams of Chesuncook Country—which is dominated on the east by majestic Mount Katahdin, and is believed to be the Algonquin word for "land of many waters"—provide some excellent early and late season fishing for salmon and squaretails up to trophy weights. The most productive waters (particularly during the early season smelt run for 10 days after ice out for salmon, during the May spawning run of suckers for squaretails, and during the upstream spawning migration of landlocked salmon from late August to October 1st) which feed into Chesuncook Lake are Duck Pond—a perennial hotspot for squaretails up to 4–6 pounds, Cuxabexis Stream and Lake, Umbazooksus Stream, beautiful Caucomgomac Lake and Stream, and remote Loon Lake—one of the state's least explored trophy salmon waters.

The wilderness traveler in Chesuncook Country—one of the state's most productive trapping, logging, and big game and upland game bird hunting areas—will often see osprey, the phantom-like goshawk, red-tailed and sharp-shinned hawks, pine marten, loons, grebes, mergansers, teal, ruffed grouse, woodcock, river otter, beaver, red fox, goldeneye, moose, whitetail deer, and the sign of black bear, lynx, and the large eastern coyote, known locally as "brush wolves," which are descended from the Ontario timberwolf and reach weights up to 120 pounds.

The legendary Chesuncook Country and the headwaters of the Allagash to the north are shown on the *North Maine Woods Guide Map* available free from: North Maine Woods, Box 552, Presque Isle 04769.

The lower West Branch from Chesuncook to Ambajejus Lake, an arm of sprawling Pemadumcook, is quite different from the upper portion. This is a trip for experts. Here the West Branch is full of boiling rapids, falls, chutes, and everything an experienced canoeist could desire. The tongue-twisting names are indicative of the brawling nature of the water: Ambejackmockamus, Nesowadnehunk, and Pockwockamus Falls, as well as Horserace Rapids.

The formidable East Branch spills from Grand Lake Matagamon at the northeast corner of Baxter State Park. It is considered more fearsome, if less well known, than the West Branch. The name of some of the stretches tell the story; Grand Pitch, the Hulling Machine, Spencer Rips, and Grindstone Falls. These are not names to inspire confidence in the inexperienced or timid. Rampaging white water, seething currents, falls, and jagged rocks await the expert. This river segment is considered by many knowledgeable enthusiasts to be the finest canoe run in the eastern United States.

Baxter State Park, a magnificent tract of more than 200,000 acres, is the gift of former Governor Percival P. Baxter. The park is a magnificent expanse of evergreen-clad mountains, cold glacial lakes, remote ponds, and streams famous for trout, togue, and salmon fishing, dense forests, and rugged alpine bogs. The park is crowned by Maine's highest mountain, Katahdin (5,268 feet), known to the Abenaki Indians as Ktaadn, the "Greatest Mountain." Mount Katahdin (shown in three dimensions on a beautiful full-color, shaded relief U.S. Geological Survey Map of Katahdin) is a perfect example of a monadnock, a single remnant of a former highland which rises as an isolated rock mass above a plain, and is said to be the first point on which the morning sun shines in the continental United States. The mountain is one of the highest points east of the Rockies and dominates a vast expanse of territory whose lakes and streams are famous among fishermen and whose forest depths outside the park are among the best deer, black bear, and upland game bird hunting grounds in the state.

Katahdin, the eastern terminus of the Appalachian Trail, was climbed in 1804 by Charles Potter, a Boston surveyor, who so far as is known was the first white man to stand on its summit. Forty-two years later, Thoreau wrote of the view from the summit that "the surrounding world looked as if a huge mirror had been shattered, and glittering bits thrown on the grass." There are 46 peaks in Baxter which exceed 3,000 feet. Major features surrounding Mount Katahdin include Grand Lake Matagamon, Nesowadnehunk (Sourdnahunk) Lake and Stream, the Wassataquoik watershed (the lake contains some bluebacks), Kidney Pond, Upper Togue, Daicey, and Chimney ponds, the Klondike, the Cross Range, and Traveler Mountain. The rare Sunapee golden trout, a relative of the arctic char, was stocked in the South Branch Ponds in 1971. Woodland caribou, long absent from Maine, were reintroduced (unsuccessfully) into the park in 1973. One hundred and forty miles of trails, including the old Hunt and Abol Trails, spread through Baxter, ranging in length from ½ to 22 miles; they afford every degree of hiking difficulty. You can take a short Sunday stroll to a quiet pond, or tackle imposing Mount Katahdin. Campgrounds are conveniently located, except for two sites, which require a hike. An informative Dept. of Inland Fisheries & Game publication, *Baxter State Park—Its Waters and Their Management*, by Paul R. Johnson, (B-49, 45¢), will prove valuable in acquiring useful knowledge of the park and its fish life. He describes the physical details of the park and its watersheds, then provides helpful information about the fishery and fishing. Interesting historical facts add flavor to the article, and a small map illustrates the various points of reference.

Two other essential free information pieces are the *Baxter State Park Leaflet* and the *Baxter State Park Rules and Regulations Bulletin.* Both may be obtained from: Reservations Clerk, Baxter State Park, Millinocket 04462, phone (207) 723-5140. You can telephone ahead for up-to-the-minute park conditions. The leaflet contains a schematic map which shows the park features, road and trail network, campground locations, access, park history; it lists all of the trails and their lengths. The bulletin gives the rules and essential information, such as fees, registration, length-of-stay regulations, reservations, and other details of park use. You are advised to place reservations months in advance of your trip.

Two beautiful, useful maps, *Phillips' Map of Northern Maine's Moosehead-Allagash Region: Headwaters of the Kennebec, St. John & Penobscot* and *Phillips' Map of Baxter Park* ($1.50 each, plus 40¢ postage) may be ordered from Augustus D. Phillips & Son, Northeast Harbor 04662. Both maps show all man-made and natural features, including trails, portages, logging roads, fly-in services, and Forest Service and paper company campsites.

The Moosehead-Katahdin region is dotted with many renowned and long established fishing and hunting camps. *Attean Lake Resort,* on a beautiful island, one of 42 in the lake, has 23 log cabins with baths, and a central dining room, with canoeing and fishing for landlocked salmon and trout. The resort has boats and canoes on 17 lakes in the area and outfits the famous Bow Trip, a 3-day, 40-mile canoe and trout fishing trip along the Moose River. For literature and rates write: The Langdon Holdens, Jackman 04945. The *Sky Lodge* is 2 miles north of Jackman on the picturesque Arnold Trail. Write: E. R. Landgraf, Moose River 049451. *Shin Pond Lodge,* Rte. 159, Patten 04765, is on the gateway to Baxter State Park and the Allagash Wilderness Waterway. Other camps include *Wilson's on Moosehead Lake,* Moosehead 04442; *Horseshoe Pond Camps,* for fly-in trout fishing with Folsom's Air Service, Greenville 04441; *Chesuncook Lake House,* Chesuncook Village 04441, a rustic lodge at the head of Chesuncook Lake with boat and guide service, and access to some of the state's finest salmon and wilderness trout waters; *Bulldog Camps on Enchanted Pond,* the Forks; *Lobster Lake Camps,* North East Carry 04441; *Nahmakanta Lake Camps,* Millinocket 94462; *Libby's Camps,* Ashland 04732; *Russell Pond Camps,* operated by Folsom's Air Service, Greenville 04441; *Packard's Camps,* Sebec Lake 04482, with outpost camps on Lobster and Moosehead. *Chalet Moosehead,* Greenville Junction 04442, on Moosehead Lake; *Spencer Pond Camps,* c/o The Howes, RFD, Greenville 04441; *Camp Phoenix,* Box 210-M, Millinocket 04462, for remote brook trout fly fishing in the northern wilderness; *Buckhorn Camps,* Millinocket 04462, in the Katahdin wilderness; *Kidney Pond Lodge & Camps,* Box 300, Millinocket 04462, at the foot of Mount Katahdin with excellent fly fishing, birdwatching, canoeing, and mountain climbing; *Penobscot Lake Lodge,* P.O. Box 45, Greenville 04441, offers rustic accommodations and fishing for squaretail and rare blueback trout at the wilderness headwaters of the West Branch of the Penobscot; and *Katahdin Lake Wilderness Camp,* with rustic accommodations, packhorse and seaplane service, and top-ranked fishing for brook trout and hunting in season for deer and bear. Write: Embert G. Stevens, P.O. Box 398, Millinocket 04462. *Millinocket Lake Camps & Trading Post,* P.O. Box 98, Millinocket 04462, provides North Maine Woods sporting camp accommodations and services. Canoe rentals in the region are provided by *D. T. Sanders & Son,* Moosehead's old country store in Greenville 04441; *Allagash Wilderness Outfitters,* Frost Pond, Star Route 76, Greenville 04441; *Folsom's Air Service,* Greenville 04441; *Smith Hardware,* Box 278, Jackman 04945; and *Smith Pond Camping,* Baxter State Park Rd., Box 34, Millinocket 04462. For a listing of accommodations, plane service, and fishing, hunting, and mountain

climbing opportunities in the free booklet *Mount Katahdin and Millinocket,* write: Chamber of Commerce, Millinocket 04462.

Access & Outfitting Centers

The Moosehead Lake and Katahdin region is reached via U.S. Highway 201, Interstate 95 and Maine Highways 6–15, 11, and the Baxter State Park Road. Lodging, guides, supplies, and outfitters are available at Jackman—the "Switzerland of Maine"—Medway, Millinocket, Moosehead, Tarratine, Greenville, Rockwood, Kokadjo, and Grindstone.

North Maine Woods & The Allagash

North Maine Woods Tract Topo Maps

U.S. Geological Survey Overview Maps (scale 1:250,000): Edmundston, Presque Isle, Quebec.

Allagash Wilderness Waterway

Large-scale U.S. Geological Survey Topographic Maps: Allagash, Allagash Falls, Allagash Lake, Caucomgomoc Lake, Chesuncook, Churchill Lake, Musquacook Lake, Round Pond, Spider Lake, Telos Lake, Umsaskis Lake.

Fish River Chain of Lakes

Large-scale U.S. Geological Survey Topographic Maps: Eagle Lake, Fish River Lake, Frenchville, Portage, Square Lake, Stockholm, Winterville.

St. John River Wilderness Canoe Country

Large-scale U.S. Geological Survey Topographic Maps: Allagash, Baker Lake, Beaver Pond, Clayton Lake, Norris Brook, Rocky Mountain, Round Pond, St. John Pond, Seven Islands. Tributary Maps: Beau Lake, Depot Lake, Hardwood Mountain, Little East Lake, Rocky Brook, St. Zacharie. Downstream Maps: Eagle Lake, Fort Kent, Frenchville, Grand Isle, St. Francis, Stockholm, Van Buren.

The legendary North Maine Woods tract occupies 2.5 million acres of evergreen forest in the northernmost portion of the state and is cut by two great wild rivers, the Allagash and the St. John. The Fish River Lake Chain, renowned for trophy landlocked salmon, has its headwaters in the tract. For centuries the NMW area was the prized fishing and hunting ground for the Abenaki Indians, who harvested the abundant fish and game, especially moose, bear, and woodland caribou. The region is bordered to the south by Baxter State Park and the Moosehead country, to the west by the Quebec border, to the east by Maine Route 11, which is Aroostook Country's Potatoland Highway, and to the north by Maine's northernmost point, the Quebec border at Estcourt, Quebec. Hundreds of miles of maintained roads, jeep trails, and rugged logging roads provide access to the remote fishing, hunting, and canoeing areas. The lakes and ponds are justly famous for superb fishing for trout, togue, and whitefish. The streams offer some of the greatest brook trout fishing in the United States. Chamberlain, Churchill, Eagle, Spider, Munsungan, Haymock, Umsaskis, Ross, Chase, Priestly, and Telos are well known. The Musquacook Lakes hold brook trout in excess of 6 pounds and are considered by many fishermen to be the best trout waters in the state. Big Reed Pond, south of Munsungan, holds a sizable population of blueback trout. Lake surveys are available for the important waters at a cost of 15¢ each from: Dept. of Inland Fisheries & Game, State House, Augusta 04333. *Maine's Fishery Regions: Fish River Lakes* (B-340, 55¢) discusses the entire fishery region, which includes most of the NMW. This publication is free and provides a helpful overview of the region, including general canoeing information. The fishery and fishing is

discussed in depth, including useful information about fish species, fishing spots, habits, and techniques. Wildlife of the North Maine Woods includes moose, bear, deer, marten, fisher, mink, otter, lynx, bobcat, ruffed grouse, loon, eagle, and osprey.

The North Maine Woods tract became a reality when the increased construction of timber roads and public recreational desires necessitated centralized control, in keeping with Maine's multiple use concept. The land is owned primarily by family groups, partnerships, and paper companies. Some families acquired their holdings as far back as 1820, when the new state needed operating funds. The free *Welcome to North Maine Woods Guide/Map*, including the "Sportsman's Map of the North Maine Woods," and the annual *Information, Rules, and Regulations Folder* are available by writing to: North Maine Woods, Box 552, Presque Isle 04769 (phone: 207–764–0016). Anyone who contemplates visiting the area should obtain these two publications. *The Sportsman's Map* shows the area boundaries, the checkpoints through which you must pass, the road network, and the lakes, ponds, and streams. A legend shows manmade features, such as NMW campsites, customs stations, forest ranger stations, and sporting camps. The regulations and information section describes general regulations, NMW road distances, land ownerships, general information about the tract and its history, campsite facts, and quotas. Incidentally, there are several hundred camping locations, both NMW and Forest Service facilities. For further details, write to the NMW and to: Forest Service, Dept. of Conservation, State Office Bldg., Augusta 04333.

The annual *Information, Rules, and Regulations Folder* gives the specifics: registration, checkpoint and customs locations and their hours, camping rules and fees, fly-in requirements, road use, equipment restrictions, and other essential data. The North Maine Woods tract is very tightly controlled for the protection of visitors, the land, and its employees. Everyone is logged in and out and must have an NMW registration, which is good for the season. The folder suggests that you write at least 30 days in advance of your trip to expedite entry into the area. There are special regulations for the hunting season, and many exceptions to general rules, depending on particular areas, road, or access points.

The Allagash Wilderness Waterway was established in 1966 by an act of the legislature, thus protecting forever this historic river. The wilderness contains about 200,000 acres, of which roughly 30,000 acres are water. One section of the law establishes a zone along the water where no cutting or building may be done. The Allagash region has been a major source of timber for over 100 years. Great virgin white pines, which once grew to heights in excess of 150 feet with girths of 20 feet, were logged out by the fabled Allagash rivermen, "Moosetowners" as they were called, for the coastal shipbuilders. The "Telos War" in 1846 was a dispute over the use of waterways for the transport of logs to the market. The remains of a 6,000-foot-long tramway on the piece of land separating Chamberlain and Eagle lakes can still be seen. The abandoned Eagle Lake and Umbazookus Railroad, with its two enormous locomotive hulks, is a popular sight. The NMW has attracted sportsmen for many years. Henry David Thoreau visited the Allagash headwaters in 1857; he was the first of many naturalists to recognize the great beauty and value of the Allagash country.

The Allagash, the Abenaki Indian word for "bark cabin," flows north for about 100 miles to its confluence with the St. John River. The trip can start at Telos Lake or at more northerly access points, and will take you through some magnificent country: granite-hemmed blue lakes, a deep green forest, and white-water river segments. The river flows through Telos, Chamberlain, Eagle, and Churchill lakes, through the exciting Chase Rapids—9 miles of fast water—Umsaskis and Long lakes, Round Pond, past Musquacook Stream, and on to the impassable 40-foot-high Allagash Falls. The Allagash meets the St. John 14 miles downstream from the falls at Allagash Village. The river is not particularly difficult. It is a blend of fast water, dead water, lakes, and ponds. There are few dangerous places. The Bureau of Parks and Recreation, Augusta 04330, publishes the free *Allagash Wilderness Waterway Map-Brochure* and *Laws, Rules, and Regulations for the*

Allagash Wilderness Waterway. The canoeist should write for both. The map guide folder gives the history and general information of the route, registration and checkpoints, winter use, gear suggestions, and a mileage chart, point to point. Included is a useful map of the river with a legend of features and a list of the appropriate topographic maps. The *Allagash Rules and Regulations* leaflet presents the hard details of usage, including check-in and -out requirements—you must do both—fees, camping regulations, boating structures, aircraft landing sites—only seven allowable places—conduct, and winter rules. *The Allagash* (B-133, 35¢) is a Dept. of Inland Fisheries & Game publication (address above); it describes the fishing and fishery, as well as topography, history and general information.

During the brief period between ice-out and the end of June, the Allagash waterways offer often spectacular fishing for coasting lake trout and voracious squaretails up to 5 pounds. The most productive "big-river" fishing on the Allagash is found along the pools and eddies of Chase's Rapids, in the 14-mile stretch below Allagash Falls, in the deep holes around the abandoned Long Lake logging dam, and at the mouths of feeder streams, using streamers, nymphs, or worms. There are few portages along the Allagash. Park rangers operate a portaging service at the 5-mile Chase's Carry below Churchill Dam. Other portages include a 100-yard trail around Lock Dam at the head of Chamberlain Lake and at Allagash Falls, near journey's end.

The St. John Wilderness Canoe Trail offers over 100 miles of prime canoeing and trout fishing water. In the early season fishermen have a good chance of hooking squaretails of better than 4 pounds. The river flows in a northeasterly direction through remote forest areas, where you are more likely to see a moose than another human, from its headwaters in the St. John Ponds to its meeting with the Allagash, where the upper portion ends. There is a good deal of heavy water in the early season, but the river drops quickly as summer starts and can become a real hull scraper. Highlights of the journey include Poplar, Priestly Brook, Big Black, Long, School House, Fox Brook, Poplar, and Big Rapids. Other points of interest are Depot Lake, Burntland Pond, Clayton Lake, Big Black River, Little East Lake, and Musquacook Mountain. For detailed access and canoe-camping information on the river and a free *St. John River Map-Brochure,* write North Maine Woods, Box 552, Presque Isle 04769.

Canoe rental and return transportation for people and canoes in the Allagash-St. John country is provided by *Wilmer Hafford,* Box 149, Allagash Village 04774; *McBreairty's Service,* Box 134, and *Ernest Chamberlain & Son,* Route 161, Box 105, both Allagash Village 04774. Canoe rentals for both the Fish River Chain of Lakes and the Allagash are provided by *Pierre Freeman,* 47 W. Main St., Fort Kent 04743.

The Fish River Chain of Lakes lies partly in the NMW tract and offers some of the finest landlocked salmon fishing in the state, as well as good trout fishing. These lakes have yielded salmon of better than 20 pounds. There are eight major lakes in the chain: Fish River, the farthest upstream, followed by Portage, St. Froid, Eagle, Square, Cross, Mud, and Long lakes. Most of the big fish come from the downstream lakes. The Fish River and the thoroughfares between Eagle, Square, Cross, Mud, and Long lakes offer good fishing in the spring during the smelt run and in the fall during the spawning season. Several landlocked salmon weighing 18 pounds were taken out of these waters in the fall of 1936. Seventeen small ponds on the headwaters of the Red River provide un-

surpassed fishing for lunker squaretails. Canoeists will enjoy the Fish River in early season, but the level drops quickly and the river soon becomes impassable. The area is well known for its fall deer and bear hunting. On fishing and hunting trips in this region, guides will frequently call attention to beaver dams and houses, which are particularly numerous in the vicinity of Portage Lake, 60 miles from St. Agatha, a terminus of the Fish River Chain of Lakes canoe trip. The *Maine Rivers: The Fish River Drainage* (B-96, 35¢) gives a concise description of the fishing and fish management. The blueback trout is found in Gardner, Deboullie, Pushineer, and Big Black lakes in the Red River area. The publication *Maine Rivers: The Aroostook* (B-372, 45¢) describes the watershed of the Aroostook, Maine's fifth-largest river. Included in the article are details of the fish and fishing in lakes such as Munsungan, Millinocket, Millimagassett, and Squapan. It notes that Millimagassett yielded a 16-pound togue in 1973, the first known to be caught there. Spring trout fishing is good for trout to 3 pounds in the Aroostook and such tributaries as the Machias, Munsungan Stream, and Mooseluk Stream.

Three extremely useful large-size maps, *Phillips' Map of the St. John-Allagash Wilderness, Phillips' East of the Allagash Map* and *Phillips' Map of Northern Maine's Moosehead-Allagash Region* ($1.50 each, plus 40¢ postage) may be ordered from Augustus D. Phillips & Son, Northeast Harbor 04662. These beautiful maps show all man-made and natural features, including trails, portages, fly-in services. Forest Service and paper company campsites, and logging roads.

Sporting Camps & Access

The North Maine Woods Tract and Allagash Country are reached by charter float-plane service (which see) and via State Forest Service roads off Maine highways 6/15 and 11. For info on Allagash and St. John water conditions and wilderness travel, contact: Maine Forest Service, Allagash Village 04774 (207-398-3196). Wilderness sporting camp accommodations in the region are provided by: *Jalbert's Allagash Camps,* c/o Willard Jalbert, Fort Kent 04743 (207-834-5015), with camps at Round Pond on the Allagash; *Bradford's Camps,* Patten 04765 (207-225-3057), a fly-in camp on Munsungan Lake with outpost camps; *Libby's Sporting Camps,* Ashland 04732 (207-435-4202), a fly-in camp on beautiful Millinocket Lake at the headwaters of the Aroostook River; *Moose Point Camps,* Portage 04768 (207-435-4091), on Fish Lake; and *Red River Camps,* Portage 04768 (207-435-6000 or 207-764-1256 in winter), a superb fishing and hunting retreat in the heart of the fabled Red Lakes country.

Rangeley Lakes Region

Rangeley Lakes Region Topo Maps
U.S. Geological Survey Maps (scale 1:250,000): Lewiston, Sherbrooke.

Rangeley Lakes Waterways
U.S. Geological Survey large-scale Maps: Arnold Pond, Black Mountain 7.5, Cupsuptic, Errol (NH), Kennebago Lake 7.5, Milan (NH), Old Speck Mountain, Oquossoc, Quill Hill 7.5, Rangeley, Tim Pond 7.5.

The beautiful Rangeley Lakes region occupies the western corner of

Maine where its border joins with those of New Hampshire and Quebec. Known as the Switzerland of Maine, this scenic area is dominated by the spruce and fir-clad peaks of the Mahoosuc Mountain Range to the southwest, the Blue Mountain Range to the east, the Kennebago Mountains to the north, and by the cold deep waters, rich in trout and landlocked salmon, of the Rangeley Lakes. This 2,500-square-mile area is covered by a thick northern forest of spruce, fir, pine, birch, and maple, and contains hundreds of miles of fast-flowing streams, and many shimmering blue lakes and wilderness trout ponds. In the fall the crimson of the maples and the bright yellow of the birches are framed in brilliant contrast against the rich green background of balsam, spruce, tamarack, and pine, making a breathtaking sight on a clear blue day. Bear, moose, and deer find the dense forest to their liking, and you may see bobcat, lynx, marten, fisher, mink, otter, grouse, eagles, and ospreys in your travels on forest paths or along a rapid-filled stream. Hunters come back every year to try for deer and bear, and wing shots pursue the abundant partridge and woodcock.

The Rangeley Chain of Lakes descend like a series of steps from Kennebago Lake on the north to Rangeley, Mooselookmeguntic, the largest of the chain, and its arm, Cupsuptic, and Upper and Lower Richardson lakes. Rapid River, which spills through Middle Dam, the outlet of Lower Richardson, is 4 miles of wild pitches, chutes, ledges, and rips, interrupted by Pond-in-the-River, a 1½-mile pond in the upper third of the river. Rapid River drops 300 feet in elevation between Middle Dam and its foam-flecked merger with Umbagog Lake, the source of the Androscoggin River. Standing on the rock-ribbed bank you can look upstream and see the sharp pitch of the riverbed. This river is reputed to be the fastest piece of white water, for its length, in the East. The final 2 miles are not for the canoeist, and have only been run once in high water, by two professionals

standing up in a freight canoe. Kayakers find the river a great challenge, and enjoy facing rugged stretches such as Hedgehog Pool and the boulder-studded Devil's Hopyard. The 14 deep, magnificent pools scattered the length of Rapid River have drawn fly fishermen for over 100 years to try for trout and landlocked salmon. If you hook a big fish in this heavy water, be prepared to do some fancy acrobatic footwork. The famous Maine author Louise Dickinson Rich and her family lived for many years at Forest Lodge, an old fishing camp on the river below the dam at Pond-in-the-River and wrote of her adventures in the moving 1943 best-seller *We Took to the Woods.*

Squire Rangeley, for whom the region is named, built and operated sawmills in the area in 1825. The great pine, spruce, and balsam forests lured woodsmen to the region throughout the early 19th century, and dams were built at Rangeley, Mooselookmeguntic, Lower Richardson, Pond-in-the-River, and Umbagog Lake to sluice the logs down through the chain to the Androscoggin River and the many lumber and paper mills along its banks. Logs were "boomed" or rafted in vast floating seas of wood and hauled down each lake by picturesque streamboats with raffish names such as the "*Alligator*." The booms were sluiced through each dam down into the next lake to their ultimate destinations on the Androscoggin. The log drive era, which continued into the 1930s, attracted some hard-bitten lumberjacks of various nationalities, and when these rivermen hit towns such as Berlin, New Hampshire, or Rumford after weeks on the lakes, the townspeople groaned, shuttered their houses, and stayed at home, while their respective communities reverted to the old West for a few days, and the loggers "let 'er rip."

The Rangeleys are famed as the home of a giant strain of brook trout which grew to weights of 12 pounds. Fed by the hordes of their smaller cousin, the blueback trout, the size and numbers of these great fish were unequaled in the United States, and 19th-century experts argued over whether these outsized trout were indeed squaretails. R. G. Allerton, in *Brook Trout Fishing* (1869), tells about a week's catch by his party of eight in June of that year. The 30 largest fish weighed from 4 to 9 pounds and averaged 6¼ pounds. By the 1850s word started to spread about the incredible sport to be had in the lakes, particularly at Upper Dam Pool, between Mooselookmeguntic and Upper Richardson, a short piece of fast water at the foot of the dam. The wealthy and famous soon followed, and private railroad cars became a common sight at sidings in Bemis and Rangeley. Some of the well-appointed fishing lodges which sprang up to take care of the creature comforts of the gentleman sportsmen survive to this day. Third- and fourth-generation descendants still return to favored sporting lodges or family camps such as Lakewood Camps at Middle Dam. By the 1870s, fishing for the pressure-vulnerable squaretails had started a long, slow decline, although remarkable catches continued into the 1940s. Not content with the trout bonanza, the Oquossoc Angling Association stocked landlocked salmon in 1875. The more active, aggressive salmon preyed on the bluebacks to such an extent that by 1905 these fish, once so plentiful that farmers loaded wagons with them for use as fertilizer, were extinct in the chain. The bluebacks outlasted, by 50 years, the Abenaki Indians, who used the small char as a food staple. Smelts were introduced in the late 19th century to replace the fading blueback population, and still fuel the trout and salmon in the lakes. Although the fishing is not what it once was, good catches continue to be made, and every once in a while a fisherman will have his sturdy leader shattered by the incredibly powerful strike of one of the remnants of the native strain of giant squaretails.

Brook trout have contributed to the fame of several adjacent lakes and streams. Parmachenee Lake to the northwest of the Rangeleys was an exclusive club for many years and produced some superior fishing. The

famed Parmachenee Belle fly was named in the lake's honor. Nearby Aziscohos Lake and its outlet, the Big Magalloway River, have drawn anglers for over 100 years, including President Eisenhower, to try for trout and landlocks. Kennebago Lake and River to the north of Mooselookmeguntic produce great trout and salmon fishing in the spring and fall. The beautiful lake is set in a bowl in the mountains surrounded by peaks, such as East Kennebago (3,791 feet), which exceed 3,000 feet. The scenic Kennebago River rises in the Island Ponds to the north of Kennebago lake and flows south through a ruggedly mountainous forest area, passing through Little Kennebago Lake, picking up Kennebago's outlet, and flowing through two dams to its mouth at Mooselookmeguntic. In early season canoeists like to run the river and enjoy the exquisite scenery and abundant wildlife. Some vicious, boiling rapids, particularly those below Kennebago Lake, require portaging, but the trip is well worth the effort. The Sandy River rises in the Sandy River Ponds just to the south of Rangeley Lake and flows southeast through Phillips and Farmington to the Kennebec River below the town of Anson. This stream is noted for excellent brown trout fishing and is a popular canoe trip. Write: Dept. of Inland Fisheries & Game, State House, Augusta 04333, for *Maine's Fishery Regions: Rangeley Lakes* (B-343, 45¢), which describes the area and its fishing, and gives some fascinating historical information and Indian lore. For example, Oquossoc, the Abenaki name for Rangeley Lake, means "slender blue trout," and the publication gives the Indian names for all of the chain and their translations.

The Mahoosuc Mountain Range, dominated by Old Speck Mountain (4,180 feet), and the Blue Mountain Range, crowned by Saddleback (4,116 feet) are crisscrossed by trails, including the famed Appalachian, and give the hiker the chance to travel through some exceptionally beautiful scenery and challenge some difficult mountain trails, which ascend most of the peaks. Stunning, panoramic views of the wild mountainous terrain will reward your efforts. In the winter, the mountains and surrounding areas, such as the Sugarloaf complex near Kingfield, offer excellent alpine and cross-country skiing.

The beautiful, large-size *Phillips' Map of the Rangeley Lakes Region* shows all man-made and natural features, including logging roads, portages, fly-in services, fish hatcheries, Forest Service and paper company campsites, boat-launching ramps, and the Appalachian Trail. It may be ordered for $1.50 (plus 40¢ postage) from Augustus D. Phillips & Son, Northeast Harbor 04662.

A *Rangeley Lakes Region Trail Map* from the high country near the Quebec border to Richardson Lakes and the Appalachian Trail may be obtained free by writing: Rangeley Lakes Region Chamber of Commerce, Rangeley 04970. This useful map contains a list of accommodations in the Rangeley region.

There are several long established sporting camps and resorts in the Rangeley Lakes region. Rangeley Lake is served by *Birchwood Housekeeping Cottages; Lakeview Cabins; Rangeley View Camps*, Box 166; *Hunter Cove Cottages; North Camps;* and *Rangeley Lake Lodge;* all are Rangeley 04970. *Saddleback Lake Lodge*, Rangeley 04970, is a charming mountain resort on a scenic, crystal-clear lake nestled at the base of Saddleback Mountain. The scenic shores of Mooselookmeguntic Lake are dotted by *Bald Mountain Camps; Wildwind Lodge & Camps;* and *Pleasant Island Lodges & Cottages. Grant's Kennebago Camps* offers rustic lodging and fly fishing only for native trout and landlocked salmon. (These are all Oquossoc 04964.) *Cobb's Bosebuck Mountain Camps*, Wilson's Mills 04293, are located on Aziscohos Lake in the heart of a 200,000-acre wilderness with access to the Magalloway River and Parmachenee Lake and fly-fishing for salmon and squaretails. Rustic accommodations are also available at the *Parmachenee Club* (on Parmachenee Lake) and *Lakewood*

Camps (at Middle Dam on the Rapid River), both Rangeley 04970. Rustic accommodations, fly fishing, and guide service are provided by *Quimby Pond Camps,* Rangeley 04970. For fishing information on lakes and streams in the Rangeley Region and guide service info, write or call: *Rangeley Region Sports Shop,* Box 850, Rangeley 04970, (207) 864-3309.

Access & Outfitting Centers

The Rangeley Lakes region is reached from the south by Maine Highway 4 or Maine Highway 26 and local roads; from east and the west by U.S. Highway 2 and local roads; and from the north by Maine Highway 16. Lodging, supplies, canoes, boats, and guides for fishing and big-game hunting are available at the towns of Oquossoc, Rangeley, Kennebago Lake, Stratton, Andover, Byron, Upton, Wilsons Mills, and Pleasant Island.

Southern Maine Vacationland

Southern Maine Vacationland Topo Maps

U.S. Geological Survey Overview Maps (scale 1:250,000): Bangor, Bath, Lewiston, Portland.

Belgrade Lakes

U.S. Geological Survey large-scale Topographic Maps: Augusta, Norridgewock, Waterville.

Sebago Lake

U.S. Geological Survey large-scale Topographic Maps: Gray, Norway, Sebago Lake.

The southern Maine vacationland offers traditional summertime vacation activities in populated areas, and at the same time some surprisingly good fishing and hunting, canoeing, camping, and hiking in the famous Sebago Lake area, Belgrade Lakes, Oxford Hills, and the Androscoggin River and the lower sections of the Kennebec and Penobscot rivers—the three largest rivers in Maine, which drain the area. The region contains sizable forest areas, hundreds of lakes, ponds, and streams, and rolling green hills and mountains.

The crystal-clear waters of Sebago, the second-largest lake in Maine at 14 miles long and 11 miles wide, reach a depth of 400 feet and are the native habitat of acrobatic landlocked salmon, brook trout, and black bass. On the shore of Sebago in North Windham, where one of the largest Indian burial grounds in the United States was discovered and thousands of Indian relics have been collected, the storied Songo River connects Sebago Lake to the north with Long Lake. Scores of other lakes and ponds, such as Little Sebago, Panther Pond, Crescent Lake, Thomas and Moose ponds, and Pleasant, Highland, and Woods lakes, dot this area. Sebago Lake is one of the original homes of the landlocked salmon, and has been honored by the fish's Latin name, *Salmo salar sebago*. The state record landlock was taken in Sebago Lake in 1907. A giant 36 pound landlock was netted by Fish

& Game officials during the previous year. Sebago holds more state records than any other body of water in Maine: landlocked salmon, brown trout, chain pickerel, and whitefish. Moose Pond, a close neighbor, yielded the record largemouth bass. Easterners look forward to the news each spring that the ice has gone out on Sebago, and another Maine fishing season has begun. *Maine's Fishery Regions: Sebago* (B-288, 45¢), published by: Dept. of Inland Fisheries & Game, State House, Augusta 04333, discusses the fishing in the area waters, including Sebago. Salmon, brook trout, browns, togue, smallmouth and largemouth bass, pickerel, and perch waters are identified and described. The Sebago fishery region occupies all of southern Maine to Brunswick and north to Rumford in the Oxford Hills, so there is much useful information. Major lakes, streams, and canoe trails include Long Lake, Little Sebago, the Songo and Saco rivers, and Lake Pennesseewassee. Lovewell Pond is named for a Captain Lovewell who was killed by Indians, after a savage battle in 1725, the so-called Lovewell's War. A more fortunate colonist was a fellow named Frye who, when chased by Indians, scaled down a steep cliff on Sebago's Frye Island, dropped to the beach, and escaped from the amazed war party. The Indians made pictographs on the cliff's face to commemorate the event.

The Saco River is described in *Maine's Rivers: The Saco*, (B-165, 35¢), a bulletin which gives a good account of the fishing and canoeing opportunities on this popular river. *Maine Rivers: The Presumpscot* (B-315, 35¢), another Department of Inland Fisheries & Game publication, contains an interesting account of this river and its history of Indian trouble. The Presumpscot, Sebago's outlet, was dammed in 1739 and the salmon run was blocked, which caused the Aucisco tribe to object. Skirmishes finally led to a battle in 1756 when the chief, Polin, was killed, and hostilities ceased. Trout and warmwater fishing on the river and its tributaries is discussed.

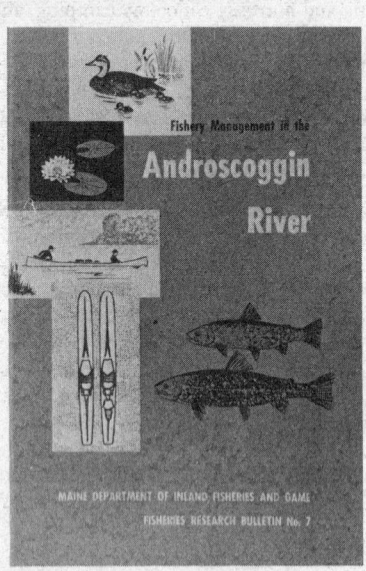

The scenic Belgrade Lakes region is located just north of Augusta and near the lower Kennebec River. The Belgrades area has been a popular fishing, canoeing, and vacationing spot for many years. Great, North, East, Ellis, Long, and McGrath ponds and Messalonskee Lake make up the scenic chain. Messalonskee holds the state record for white perch, a hefty 4 pounds 10 ounces. Warmwater species such as bass, pickerel, and perch predominate, and they run to large size. Some big landlocks and trout are taken from a few of the waters, particularly Messalonskee. *Maine Fishery Regions: Belgrade* (B-312, 45¢), is an

excellent article that will tell you a great deal in 5 pages about fish, fishing, and where to go. Pictures of a 9-pound salmon taken at Parker Pond and an 8-pound largemouth from Cobbosseecontee affirm your chances of hooking a big one. Cobbosseecontee, Maranacook, and Annabessacook lakes lie just to the south of the Belgrades. Lake surveys are available for all of the major waters in the southern Maine region.

The Sheepscott River, east of the Belgrades, is the most westerly of Maine's revitalized Atlantic salmon rivers and a popular canoe route. *Maine Rivers: The Historic Sheepscott* (B-125, 35¢) is another Department of Inland Fisheries & Game publication; it gives an interesting account of the colonists' stormy relations with the Sagamore Indians. Periodic wars led to several razings of the town of Sheepscott over a 75-year period. The booklet discusses fishing for Atlantic salmon, trout, and warmwater species.

The Oxford Hills region occupies the western border of Maine between the Androscoggin River to the north and Sebago Lake to the south. This mountainous area is dotted with lakes, ponds, streams, and bogs. Major features of the Oxford Hills include the Evans Notch segment of the White Mountain National Forest on the New Hampshire border: Mounts Abram, Black, Caribou, Tir'em, Speckled, Royce, Ames, and Zircon, Lake Kezar, Little Concord Pond, the Bryant Ponds, and the Androscoggin River. The *AMC Maine Mountain Guide* will tell you what you need to know about the extensive trail system in this famous hiking country. Hunting is good in season for deer, ruffed grouse, snowshoe rabbits, and woodcock. Bass, pickerel, and perch are found in most lakes and ponds. Kezar Lake has a good population of salmon and brown trout, as well as warmwater species. Worthley Pond, near Rumford, produces some hefty brown trout exceeding 6 pounds, but they are extremely wary. Lake surveys are available for most of the lakes and ponds. For information on the lower Androscoggin, Kennebec, and Penobscot rivers, read *Maine Rivers: The Androscoggin* (B-191, 35¢), *Maine Rivers: The Kennebec* (B-275, 45¢), and *The Penobscot* (B-85, 35¢).

Fishing camps and vacation resorts on the shores of Lake Sebago include *Goodwin's Lodge & Cottages*, North Sebago 04029; *Sebago Lake Camps*, Box 36, North Sebago 04029; *Burton's Lake Shore Cottages*, North Windham 04062; *Weislander's Cottage Homes*, c/o The Weislanders, 26 Seeley Ave., Portland 04103. The *Chute Homestead Cottages*, Naples 04055, and *Sandy Cove Cottages*, RFD2, Bridgton 04009, are on Long Lake. *Pleasant Mountain Inn*, Bridgton 04009, is at Moose Pond. *Brookline Cottages* and *Stone's Lakeside Cottages*, both Bridgton 04009, are on Highland Lake. Kezar Lake is served by *Quisisana Lodge & Cottages*, c/o Ralph Burg, Center Lovell 04016; *Kinapic Cottages*, Lovell 04051; and *Hewnoaks Cottages*, Center Lovell 04016. The Belgrade Lakes are served by *Crystal Spring Camps*, Belgrade Lakes 04918, on Great Pond; *Long Lake Cottages*, Box 275A, Belgrade Lakes 04918; *Whisperwood Lodges & Cottages*, North Belgrade 04959, on Salmon Lake; *Mace's Lakeside Cottages*, on Lake Maranacook, c/o R. E. Mace, Winthrop 04364; *Castle Island Camps*, Box 70, Belgrade Lakes 04918, on Long Lake; *Bear Spring Camps*, Oakland 04963, on Belgrade Lake, *Snug Harbor Camps*, North Belgrade 04959, on Great Lake; *Alden Camps*, Oakland 04963, on East Lake, the headwaters of the Belgrade Lakes.

Access & Outfitting Centers

The southern Maine vacationland is reached via Interstate 95 and U.S. Highways 2, 202, and 302. Lodging, supplies, guides, canoes and boats, and gear are available at the hundreds of towns and villages scattered throughout the Sebago-Long Lake region, Belgrade Lakes region, and Oxford Hills.

PART TWO
CANADA AND THE
GREAT NORTH WOODS

NORTHERN CANADA

NORTHERN
CANADA

Introduction

Sweeping east and south across the top of Canada are the remote wilderness expanses of the Yukon and Northwest Territories—one of North America's last great outdoor frontiers. From the barren lands and polar bear hunting grounds of the Arctic Ocean this area spreads across thousands of square miles of tundra, permafrost, and stunted dwarf forests of spruce, pine, and muskeg. The north is broken by brawling wild rivers, huge lakes surrounded by the ancient cliffs and rock outcroppings of the Canadian Shield, and dotted by a vast mosaic of countless small lakes and ponds. The Northwest Territories encompass all of Canada north of the 60th parallel, except for the Yukon and a portion of Quebec's Ungava Plateau, forming a vast wilderness of 1.4 million square miles.

Here, in this land of the northern lights and "midnight sun," you will find the fabled grayling, lake trout, and northern pike waters of Great Bear Lake and Great Slave Lake—the headwaters of the Mackenzie River, surrounded by stark cliffs and boreal forests; the legendary big-game ranges of the Mackenzie and Richardson Mountains; the historic island-dotted waters of the Mackenzie River—the "Great River of the North"; the remote, wilderness canoeing and char waters of the treacherous Coppermine, Back, Tree, Horton, Arctic, Hornaday, Camsell, and Hanbury Rivers; and the great barren ground canoe routes and muskox and caribou country of the mysterious sub-arctic oasis known as the Thelon Game Preserve.

The Yukon takes in 207,076 square miles, bordered on the west by Alaska and the eastern Brooks Range, on the east by the Northwest Territories and the Mackenzie Mountains, on the north by the frozen expanse of the Beaufort Sea, and on the south by British Columbia and the northernmost reaches of the Rocky Mountains. The rugged interior plateau is cut by the mighty Yukon River and its wild tributaries and surrounded by the towering snow-capped peaks of the massive St. Elias Range in the southwest, the Ogilvie Range and British Mountains in the northwest, and the legendary big-game lands of the Cassiar Mountains in the south and Mackenzie Mountains in the east.

The historic Yukon River flows in a northwest direction through the Territory and winds on through Alaska to its mouth on the Bering Sea —some 2,000 miles distant from its headwaters. The mountainous

Yukon wilderness is slashed by the deep valleys of the Ross, Stewart, Peel, Porcupine, Wind, Pelly, and Teslin Rivers and shelters the huge blue wind-swept waters of Kluane, Watson, Teslin, Laberge, Dezadeash, Bennett, Marsh, Tagish, and Frances Lakes—famed for their giant lake trout and great northern pike.

The interior boreal forest stretches northward to the "land of little sticks" and the treeline, beyond which are the gently rolling tundra lands of the far north. During the brief, but warm, summer months, fields of brilliant wildflowers—such as poppies, blue lupine, Labrador tea, and red and white heath—carpet the tundra, alpine meadows, mountain slopes and bogs of the northern wilderness. During July, fireweed, the territorial flower of the Yukon, turns the meadows, forests, river bars, and burned-over areas a glowing pink. The remote high country regions of the Yukon and Northwest Territories are a botanist's paradise, with many as yet unidentified plants awaiting discovery and classification (a handsome, 218-page color illustrated book, *The Alaska-Yukon Wild Flowers Guide*, $7.95, is available from Alaska Northwest Publishing Co., Box 4-EEE, Anchorage, AK 99509).

Weather, Bugs, Beasts & "Circle of the Great Bear"

The Yukon and Northwest Territories, notorious for their extreme variations in climate, are divided into the arctic and sub-arctic climatic zones. The arctic is the area where the average mean daily temperature does not exceed 50° F. Most of the Yukon and Northwest Territories lie within the sub-arctic zone, including all of the Mackenzie Valley, where the summer climate is similar to that of the southern prairies. On the arctic tundra, one of the world's great deserts, precipitation runs 2–10 inches yearly. It is a region of continual daylight during June and early July when sunset blends into the sunrise; outdoor activities can be pursued for the full 24 hours of each day in the land of the midnight sun. At Fort Smith, near Wood Buffalo National Park, summer temperatures have reached 103° F—hotter than has ever been recorded in Canada's southernmost cities. And Resolution Island, in the arctic archipelago of the northernmost District of Franklin, has an average January temperature higher than that of Winnipeg, located some 800 miles to the south.

The boundary between the arctic and sub-arctic zones bears no relation to the Arctic Circle—the latitude above which the sun does not set during a certain time in the summer, known as the midnight sun. The Arctic Circle was named by the ancient Greeks. These fearless mariners noticed during their voyages that as they traveled northward the circles that girdle the stars seemed to become larger and larger and that the stars had fixed orbits about a fixed pole in the heavens. They also noticed that some stars came and disappeared with the rhythms of the seasons. They divided the fixed stars from the varying stars by drawing a circle through the constellation Arktos—the constellation of the Great Bear.

A useful guide to the weather, cloud formations, and forecasting in the Yukon and Northwest Territories called *Weather Ways*, is available for $2 from the Canadian Hydrographic Service, Department of the Environment, Ottawa, Ontario K1A 0E8.

The Yukon Territory and the Mackenzie Mountains are grizzly country. The fisherman, hunter, wilderness paddler, and camper is well advised to to be on the alert for a mother bear with cubs or for a "sorehead"—a bear with an old body wound or impacted tooth. Anyone planning a trip to this majestic wild country should read, prior to his departure, Andy Russell's brilliant classic *Grizzly Country*

($7.95, available from Alfred A. Knopf Inc., Mail Order Books, 400 Hahn Rd., Westminster, MD 21157), as well as William Pruitt's great classic, *Animals of the North* ($9.95, available from Harper & Row, Mail Order Division, 10 E. 53rd St., New York, NY 10022). The Yukon grizzly, present in both the cinammon brown and blond color phases, is notorious for its generally ill-tempered disposition. Other potential wildlife hazards include camp-invading black bears and moose during the fall rut. The moose can charge with the impact of a one-ton freight train. The most ferocious critter of this north country, however, is the mosquito. A healthy supply of insect repellent is a must—use *Muskol, Mosquitone, Off!*, or *Cutters*. All contain a 50 percent plus concentration of DEET. Also bring along a wide-brimmed hat, a heavy, light-colored cotton shirt, a head net, good quality sun glasses, and rain gear. If you plan an extended trip into the wilderness, a recommended dosage of 50 mg/day of Vitamin B-1 for the week prior to your exposure to insects and about 10 mg a day each day during your trip is an effective preventive against the clouds of mosquitoes and black flies you may encounter. (Check with your physican for his recommended dosage and advice.)

Northern Canada Maps & Lake Charts—How to Order

The fabled fishing, big-game hunting, canoeing, and wilderness camping areas of the Yukon and Northwest Territories are shown on the full-color Canadian National Topographic Maps listed throughout the "Encyclopedia" and "Travel & Recreation Guide" sections. All topo maps listed are printed at a scale of 1:250,000 (1 inch to 4 miles) or 1:50,000 (1¼ inch to 1 mile) and show man-made and natural features, including contours, forests, lakes and streams, mountain ranges, roads, towns, trails, marshes, bogs, portages, rapids and falls, open muskeg, fur-trading posts, campgrounds, national and provincial parks, game preserves, direction of water flow, wilderness cabins, and the magnetic declination of the compass. The topo maps (and free *Yukon and Northwest Territories Map Indexes* and a *Map Symbols Chart*) are available for $1.50 each, plus a 50¢ handling charge, from the Canada Map Office, Surveys Mapping Branch, Department of Energy, Mines, & Resources, Ottawa, Ont. K1A 0E9, (613) 994–9663. When ordering, be sure to list the individual map names and code, and make your check payable to: Receiver General of Canada. The Canada Map Office publishes a useful 362-page *Catalogue of Published Maps* ($3.50), which lists all topographic and national park maps available, as well as aeronautical charts and photo, alpine, and glacier maps. In addition, the Canada Map Office publishes a beautiful, full-color shaded-relief map, *Northwest Territories & Yukon Territory* (MCR 36, $2). This map is 42 × 52 inches with a scale of 1: 4,000,000 and includes all of Hudson Bay, the Ungava barren lands, northern British Columbia, as well as man-made and natural features, including Kluane and Nahanni national parks, Peel River Preserve, Thelon Game Preserve, Wood Buffalo National Park, trading posts, seaplane bases, bathymetric contours, and airports. Free hydrographic chart catalogs, *Canadian Arctic—Information Bulletin 15, Hudson Bay—Information Bulletin 11*, and *Northwestern Canada—Mackenzie River Basin*, are available from the Hydrographic Chart Distribution Office, Department of the Environment, Room 512, Federal Bldg., Victoria, British Columbia V8W 1Y4. Hydrographic charts *Great Bear Lake* (6390) and *Great Slave Lake* (6370) are available for $2 each. (Make checks payable to Receiver General of Canada.)

Anyone planning a trip to the Big North should send for the *Canada Maps & Wilderness Canoeing Guide* (MCR-107) available free upon request from the Canada Map Office (address above). This valuable publication contains a text written by Eric Morse, one of the intrepid pioneers of recreational canoeing in Canada's Far North. Subjects discussed include planning your trip, making a trip profile, making a schedule, map symbols, barren land maps, navigating in the far north, use of maps, types of map scales, how to order aerial photographs, and use of compass on a canoe trip. This full-color illustrated guide contains a "Canada 1:250,000 Scale Map Index."

Vacation Travel Maps, Information & CB Radio Permits

A handsome full-color *Vacation Planning—Topographic Highway Map of Western Canada* showing all major man-made and natural features of the Yukon and Northwest Territories is available free upon request from the Canadian Government Office of Tourism, 150 Kent St., Ottawa, Ontario K1A 0H6. The useful free booklet *Canada Ferries, Bridges & Cruises* and the indispensible 36-page *Canada Travel Information Handbook* contain everything you need to know about such things as airlines, customs regulations, hunting and fishing regulations, insurance, and weather, with temperature and time-zone charts. Canadian license applications for free citizen-band radio permits may be obtained by writing: Regional Superintendent, Telecommunications Branch, Department of Communications, Financial Bldg., 10621 100th Ave., Edmonton, Alberta T5J 0B1.

For information on Canadian train vacations, rates, schedules, itineraries, hotels, and package tours, write: *VIA Rail Canada*, P.O. Box 8117, Montreal, Quebec H3C 3N3 or contact your local travel agent. VIA Rail Canada manages Canadian National and Canadian Pacific passenger train services.

YUKON TERRITORY ENCYCLOPEDIA

Accommodations—Vacation Lodges & Sporting Camps

Although the Yukon Territory is true frontier country, it offers a diversity of hotels, motels, wilderness lodges, and hunting and fishing outpost camps. The great majority of the Yukon's lodges are located along the highway system and along the Alaska Highway in particular; they are seldom more than 25 miles apart. A free guide to accommodations and campgrounds, *Travel Yukon,* is available from the Department of Travel and Information, Box 2703, Whitehorse Y1A 2C6. It lists and describes the facilities and recreation activities for all motels, lodges, and public and private campgrounds located along the Alaska Highway, Haines Road, Whitehorse-Carcross-Alaska Highway Loop, Klondike Route, Top of the World Highway, Dempster Highway, Stewart Crossing-Mayo-Keno Highway, Campbell Highway and Canol Road, and contains a *Yukon Campgrounds Map.* Yukon territorial campgrounds are spacious enough for campers, trailers, and tents. Privately operated campgrounds can provide plug-in facilities for water and electricity and/or centrally located showers and laundry facilities.

Fly-in wilderness vacation lodging and services are provided by *Air-In Fishing Lodge,* Box 158, Watson Lake; *Kluane Wilderness Lodge,* General Delivery, Whitehorse; and *Northern Wilderness Fishing Lodge,* Box 264, Watson Lake.

Airlines & Wilderness Fly-in Services

The magnificent Yukon wilderness of densely forested mountain areas, tree-lined lakes, and spectacular scenery is served daily by jetliners from eastern Canada and major U.S. cities, Europe, and the Orient. The territory has its own network of scheduled air carriers and charter airlines serving Yukon communities and wilderness fishing areas. *International Jet Air, Ltd.,* P.O. Box 3180, Station B, Calgary, Alta. T2M 4L7, has service from Whitehorse to northern points. *Northward Airlines Ltd.* has service from Whitehorse to points north. *CP Air,* 200 Granville St., Vancouver, B.C. V6C 2R1, has service between Vancouver, Edmonton, and Whitehorse. *Fly Yukon Road and Air Facilities Map* is available from the Department of Tourism and Information, Box 2703, Whitehorse. This useful full-color map shows all settlements, highways, airports and airstrips, seaplane bases, campgrounds, and accommodations, and contains a complete listing of Yukon landing fields, tips on mountain flying, a survival kit, and a ground-air emergency code chart. A free booklet, *Air Tourist Information,* is available from the Ministry of Transport, Canadian Air Transportation Administration, Aeronautical Information Services, Ottawa, Ont. K1A 0N8.

Charter fly-in services for Yukon wilderness fishing, hunting, and canoeing trips are provided by *British Columbia-Yukon Air Services Ltd.,* Box 68, Watson Lake Y0A 1C0; *Dalziel Hunting Ltd.,* Watson Lake Y0A 1C0; *Frontier Helicopters Ltd.,* Box 10, Watson Lake Y0A 1C0; *Mayo Helicopters Ltd.* Box 130, Mayo Y0B 1M0; *Watson Lake Flying Services,* Box 7, Watson Lake Y0A 1C0; *Yukon Airways Ltd.,* Box 4428, Whitehorse Y1A 3T5; and *Trans North Turbo Air Ltd.,* Box 4338, Whitehorse Y1A 3T5, with floatplane service throughout the Yukon and sightseeing flights in Kluane National Park.

Camping & Backpacking

The great snow-covered peaks and thousands upon thousands of wild lakes and rivers, alpine meadows, and tundra of the Yukon wilderness offer a wide variety of camping, backpacking, and mountain climbing

opportunities. Territorial campsites and campgrounds are conveniently located along the Alaska Highway, Haines Road, Whitehorse-Carcross-Alaska Highway Loop, Klondike Route, Top of the World Highway, Dempster Highway, Stewart Crossing-Mayo-Keno Highway, Campbell Highway, Canol Road, and Nahanni Range Road. These well-maintained campsites include outdoor privies, tables, and water supply from a well, lake, or stream, enclosed kitchen shelters, and barrel stoves. None, however, have water or sewer connections for camper or trailer. An annual campground maintenance fee of $5 is charged throughout the Yukon and can be paid at visitor information centers. The development of territorial campgrounds began as part of a fire prevention program when the Alaska Highway was opened to public travel in 1946.

Kluane National Park and the great St. Elias Range offer many hiking and climbing opportunities. Few people realize that the St. Elias Range is the home of some of the most spectacular high peaks in the world. Mount Logan at 19,850 feet towers over a dozen other peaks above 10,000 feet. Mountaineers from around the world use the St. Elias peaks as a final training ground before taking on the great peaks of the Himalayas. For information on obtaining a permit for climbing, contact the office of the Territorial Secretary, Box 2703, Whitehorse. The National and Provincial Parks Association of Canada offers a *Northern Wilderness Backpacking Trip* in Kluane National Park to study and experience the northern tundra-taiga mountain environment. The trip is from July 5 to July 15 and begins and ends at Whitehorse or Haines Junction. Participants will be expected to carry their own gear and a portion of the group's food supply, and to contribute to camp chores. Write: NPPAC, 47 Colborne St., Suite 308, Toronto, Ont. M5E 1E3. For information on Yukon wilderness backpacking and pack trips write to *Outfitted Pack Trips*, W. G. Brewster, Mile 1,016 Alaska Highway, Haines Junction and *Yukon Wilderness Unlimited*, Box 4126, Whitehorse. A free guide, *Hiking in the Yukon,* is available from the Department of Travel Information, Box 2703, Whitehorse. It describes the Cottonwood Creek Trail, Gribbles Gulch Trail, and Dalton Post-Bates River Trail in the Haines Road area, the Stony Creek Trail in Kluane National Park, and the Whitehorse-Canyon City Trail and Grey Mountain Trail in the Whitehorse area. An *Outdoor Guide for Hikers and Backpackers, Climbers, Canoeists and Kayakers* may be obtained free from the Yukon Conservation Society, P.O. Box 4163, Whitehorse Y1A 3S9.

Canoeing & Wilderness Waters Outfitters

The hundreds of wild rivers in the Yukon come plunging out of the high glacial peaks of the St. Elias Range and Mackenzie Mountains, flowing through moose pastures and dense boreal evergreen forests, and past rotting, abandoned gold-rush settlements into the land of the beaver, wolverine, and caribou. The Department of Travel Information, Box 2703, Whitehorse, publishes extremely useful wild river surveys, available free to the canoeist. A *Yukon River Survey and Chart* is available for the Upper Yukon from Whitehorse to the Alaska boundary. *Yukon Wild River Surveys* are available free for the following wilderness canoe routes: Firth, Pelly, Ross, Macmillan, Bell, Porcupine, Klondike, Sixty-Mile, White, Bennett-Nares, Tagish-Atlin, Marsh Lakes, Big Salmon, Ogilvie, Peel, Nisling, Stewart, and Teslin rivers. The invaluable *A Boater's Guide to the Upper Yukon River,* available from the Alaska Northwest Publishing Co., Box 4-EEE, Anchorage, AK 99509, for $3.95, contains sectional maps covering the historic 2,000-mile Yukon from Bennett Lake to the Bering Sea, photographs of the historic relics of gold-rush days, and information on the river: where to find drinking water and campsites, transportation for your gear, supplies, and river conditions. Emphasis is given to

river travel between Whitehorse, Yukon Territory, and Fort Yukon, Alaska.

The wilderness paddler should prepare carefully for a Yukon canoe trip. During July and August it can get pretty cold on the rivers and downpours may be encountered. Suitable clothing and gear are essential: a waterproof jacket or poncho, sweater, long underwear, wool socks, lightweight foot gear, gloves, brimmed hat, sunglasses, first-aid kit, strong bug dope, fishing gear, and a good quality sleeping bag and lightweight tent fitted with a groundsheet should be packed for the trip. Expedition canoes should be 17–18-foot, good-quality construction. Food, supplies, and canoe rentals are available in Whitehorse. Gas and general supplies are obtained at settlements indicated on the Yukon road map. The Yukon has several wilderness canoeing and river outfitters: *Yukon Wilderness Unlimited* and *Wilderness Waterways,* John Lammers, P.O. Box 4126, Whitehorse; *Yukon Canoe Rental,* 507 Alexander St., Whitehorse; *Yukon Outdoor Adventures Ltd.,* P.O. Box 4164, Whitehorse; *Karl's Outdoor Living,* Carcross Corner Cut-off, P.O. Box 4643, Whitehorse; *Dawson Trail Services,* Box 20, Mackenzie, RR1, Whitehorse; *Yukon Rafting Ltd.,* Box 23, Dawson City; and *Mr. Paul Lucier,* 507 Alexander St., Destruction Bay Y0B 1H0. For your protection you are advised to report your plans and estimated time of departure and return to the nearest Royal Canadian Mounted Police detachment. RCMP detachments are located in Beaver Creek, Carcross, Carmacks, Dawson City, Faro, Haines Junction, Mayo, Old Crow, Ross River, Teslin, Watson Lake, and Whitehorse. (See "Wilderness & Trophy Fishing Waters.")

Dawson City & the Klondike

(Pop. 800). This historic town lies 165 miles south of the arctic circle, surrounded by the Moosehide Hills at the confluence of the Yukon River and Klondike—known to the Indians as the Thronduik River —meaning "hammer water"—about 333 miles northwest of Whitehorse. Its old weather-beaten buildings and boardwalks keep alive the rich, bawdy memory of the gold-rush days and the famous adventurers who walked its roller-coaster streets—from Diamond Tooth Gertie and Nellie the Pig—so named because she once bit off a bartender's ear—to Jack London, Robert W. Service, and Rex Beach. Dawson City was the largest settlement north of San Francisco and west of Winnipeg at the height of the boom in 1900. Today its streets are lined with old deserted hotels and gambling houses, saloons and dance halls—once packed with prospectors and treasure seekers from all corners of the globe. The news of the great discovery of gold in 1896 at Rabbit Creek, a tributary of the Klondike, by George Carmack and the two Indians from his salmon fishing camp, Skookum Jim and Tagish Charlie, spread like wildfire and initiated the great gold rush of 1896–99. Gold seekers by the thousands headed north for Dawson City, enduring incredible hardships and tragedy along the Trail of '98 over Chilkoot or White Pass, Dalton Trail over the Chilkat Pass, Shushana Trail from Alaska, the Peace River Trail, and along the all-water route from the Bering Sea at the mouth of the 2,000-mile-long Yukon River, then upriver by stern-wheeler to Dawson. By 1904 the great placer mines of the Klondike, such as Bonanza, Eldorado, Hunker, and Dominion, had produced $100 million in gold. In 1903, stampedes to Nome and the Alaskan goldfields turned Dawson into a ghostly relic of its former glory. Today, Dawson City is a national historic complex and tourist mecca, with tours to the Klondike goldfields departing from the old Palace Grand theater and Yukon River tours aboard the stern-wheeler S.S. *Keno* to the mouth of the Klondike and the old Indian villages of Moosehide, Sisters Island, and Dog Islands. Dawson is the outfitting and jumping-off point for many canoe trips along the Yukon River and Fortymile River Wilderness Canoe Trail. The town is reached via the Klondike Highway and Northward Airlines. Northwest of Dawson City lies the ghost town of Forty Mile, reached by a 4-mile hike from the Clinton Creek Road off the Klondike Highway along the bank of the Forty Mile River. It was here, at Forty Mile, that the first claims on Bonanza Creek were registered and it was from here that the news of the discovery spread. Pierre Berton's great classic, *The Klondike Fever* ($8.95, available from Alfred A. Knopf, Inc., Mail Order, 400 Hahn Rd., Westminster, MD 21157), provides the complete epic story of the great gold rush in all its grandeur and sweep.

Fishing & Hunting in the Yukon Wilderness

The thousands of deep, blue lakes, wild, turbulent rivers, and towering snow-covered peaks, alpine meadows, and tundra of the Western Highlands and the St. Elias Range offer some of the finest fishing and big-game hunting in Canada. Much of the 207,076 square miles of the Yukon, larger than all the New England states combined, is still the same wild country traveled by the explorer-fur trader John Bell when he hiked across the divide from the Northwest Territories to the Yukon in 1847 and canoed down the Bell and Porcupine rivers to reach the large waterway the Indians of the interior called *Youcon*, meaning "great river." The topography of the Yukon varies with the three regions of the Western Highlands, sweeping westward from the majestic, glacier-studded peaks of the Selwyn Mountains along the eastern boundary of the Yukon and the Northwest Territories: the Yukon Plateau, Peel Plateau, and Porcupine Plain.

The Yukon Plateau is the largest of the regions, dominated by North America's third longest river. The Yukon rises in the coastal mountains of British Columbia within 15 miles of the Pacific Ocean and empties into Alaska's Bering Sea after a journey of 2,000 miles. The highlands of the Yukon Plateau are walled off by the rugged Ogilvie Mountains to the north, the 18,000-foot summits and glaciers of the St. Elias Range to the west, and the northernmost buttresses of the Cassiar and Coastal ranges to the south. The Peel Plateau and Porcupine Plain occupy the highlands north of the brooding Ogilvie Mountains and are dominated by rivers bearing their names, walled in by the Richardson Mountains to the east and by the British Mountains on the north. Boreal evergreen forests occupy most of the highlands, apart from alpine tundra in the high country and the drowned muskegs of the Porcupine Plain far to the north.

Trophy Fishing Waters

Trophy fishing can be found in the Yukon for record lake trout, arctic grayling, northern pike (called jacks locally), rainbow trout, Dolly Varden, arctic char, whitefish, Chinook (king), silver (coho), and chum (dog) salmon. Great runs of salmon come thousands of miles from the Pacific and the Bering Sea up the main stream of the Yukon to spawn in its tributaries and headwater lakes. Record lake trout up to 60 pounds are found in most of the large, deep lakes, with particularly good fishing in beautiful Kluane Lake and Teslin, Aishihik, Laberge, Wolf, Frances, Quiet, Kusawa, Ethel, Mayo, Finlayson, and Tagish lakes. Great northern pike, up to 50 pounds, are found in the weedy bays and shoals of the large lakes and in the countless small tundra and muskeg lakes. Excellent arctic grayling fishing is present in most of the wilderness areas along the Yukon Highways in the tributary streams of the great rivers. Guides are highly recommended for extended wilderness fishing trips and for the large lakes, where sudden gale winds can create treacherous waves for the small-craft fisherman. Bush pilots provide charter fly-in service to the great northern wilderness of the Yukon, renowned for spawning runs of huge arctic char in the Firth, Babbage, and Blow rivers of the arctic coast and for record sheefish, arctic grayling, and northern pike in the Bell, Miner, Whitestone, Caribou, Ogilvie, Bonnet Plume, Snake, Hart, Wind, and Eagle rivers of the interior.

A useful guide called *Hunt & Fish Yukon* is available free from the Department of Travel & Information, Whitehorse. It describes the fish and game species of the Yukon, tells where to go, lists regulations, fees, limits, and seasons, and contains an angler's guide to the lakes, streams, and fish species present along the Alaska Highway, Haines Road, Mayo and Dawson roads, Carcross Area, and Watson Lake.

Guides and wilderness fly-in fishing services are provided by Mr. G. F. Mahoney, Teslin; Wesley Doe, *Fox Point Lodge*, Mile 806, Alaska Highway; Leslie Allen, *Johnson's Crossing Lodge*, Mile 837, Alaska Highway (Teslin Lake and River); *Amato's Boat Rental*, Tagish; *Tagish Fishing Tours*, Lloyd Reid, Tagish; *Marsh Lake Resort*, Mile 883 Alaska Highway, P.O. Box 4216, Whitehorse; Mabel and Art Brewster, Mile 1,016 Alaska Highway, Haines Junction; Ted Yardley, *Cortino Lodge*, Mile 135 Haines Road, Haines Junction; R. J. White, Destruction Bay (Kluane Lake). Guided fishing-canoe trips are offered by *Atlin Lake Canoe Tours*, P.O. Box 14, Atlin, B.C., and *Dawson Trail Services*, P.O. Box 20, RR1, Whitehorse. Guide services generally include boat, motor, and fishing gear, and some will also arrange for shore lunches. Burning permits (free) are required if you plan on using open fires. They may be canceled if the fire hazard potential becomes too great. A *Hunting and Fishing Regulations Guide* and *Yukon Territory Guide Management Zone Map* can be obtained free from the Yukon Department of Travel and Information, Box 2703, Whitehorse Y1A 2C6.

Hunting & Photography

The great Yukon mountain ranges, boreal forest, and tundra areas of the far north offer some of the finest hunting in North America, with camera, bow, or gun, for black and grizzly bear, woodland and barren-ground caribou, Dall, Stone, and Fannin sheep, mountain goat, and moose. There are a few deer in the south and west. Photographers are encouraged to visit the Fishing Branch Preserve due north of the Peel River in the far north, the Peel River Preserve in the Richardson Mountains, the McArthur Game Sanctuary south of Mayo, and the Kluane National Park and Game Sanctuary. In addition to the big-game species, the preserves offer the opportunity to view wolf, coyote, wolverine, lynx, peregrine, and gyrfalcons. Keep in mind that Yukon grizzlies have a well-earned reputation for being tough, short-tempered fellows. Polar bears are found along the arctic coastline, but only Eskimos are allowed to hunt them. The best hunting for the slope-shouldered Alaska-Yukon, or Alaskan moose *(Alces alces gigas)* is in the boreal forest areas of central Yukon. A trophy Yukon moose may stand 7½ feet high, weigh close to 1,700 pounds, and carry an antler spread of more than 6 feet.

A nonresident big-game hunter must be accompanied by a licensed guide. The Yukon is divided into 22 guiding areas, with one registered outfitter in each having exclusive guiding rights. *Yukon Registered Outfitters and Guides* may be obtained from the Director of Game,

Box 2703, Whitehorse Y1A 2C6. Outfitters generally prefer to book hunts of at least 14 days. They are usually booked at least a year in advance, so it's wise to plan your trip early. Many Yukon outfitters book photographic safaris during the off-season. Permits are required for all commercial photographers who plan to take pictures in wilderness areas. To obtain a free permit write to the Director of Game, Box 2703, Whitehorse. Although Yukon summers are generally mild, the wilderness traveler is well advised to come prepared for cold, rainy overcast days and to carry an amply supply of insect repellent to ward off mosquitoes and black flies.

Highways—Recreation & Scenic Routes

The Alaska Highway and Yukon's other gravel-surfaced, all-weather territorial highways offer access to many of the outstanding outdoor recreation areas and major settlements. The two main approaches to the Alaska Highway are via Edmonton, Alberta, then north to Dawson Creek, British Columbia, at Mile 0 on the 1,523-mile road to Fairbanks, Alaska. From Seattle you can drive north to Vancouver and on to Prince George where you continue northeast to Dawson Creek or head west on Highway 16 connecting with the Inner Passage and the Alaska Marine Highway System. British Columbia ferries offer service for passengers and vehicles from Kelsey Bay on Vancouver Island to Prince Rupert, British Columbia. Alaska state ferryliners at Prince Rupert connect with the Alaska ports of Skagway or Haines, and the Alaska Highway via the Haines Road. The free booklet *Traveling Yukon* provides useful information on Yukon highways, vehicle requirements, climate, and highway safety, plus a detailed road map,

available from the Department of Travel and Information, Box 2703, Whitehorse Y1A 2C6. The full-color, free *Official Yukon Territory Road Map* published by the Department of Travel and Information shows all highways, roads, ferries and boatlines, settlements and towns, campgrounds, airports, landing strips, and floatplane bases. Yukon road condition reports are broadcast daily on CKNL Fort St. John, British Columbia (dial 560), CKRW (610), and CFWH (570) in Whitehorse. Station CFWH (Canadian Broadcasting Corporation) has repeater stations at Fort Nelson, British Columbia (1110), Watson Lake (990), Cassiar, British Columbia (1340), Swift River (970), Teslin (940), Haines Junction (860), Destruction Bay (940), Beaver Creek (690), Clinton Creek (990), Dawson City (560), Mayo (1230), Elsa (560), Carmacks (990), and Faro (1230). The Canadian National Topographic Survey Map kits listed below are printed in full-color at a scale of 1:250,000, or 1 inch to 4 miles, and provide the outdoor

traveler with an excellent overview of the famous wilderness recreation areas surrounding Yukon Territory's major highways.

Alaska Highway

The 630-mile Yukon portion of the Alaska Highway, originally known as the Alcan Highway, starts at Mile 588 near Watson Lake and winds its way northwest, crossing the British Columbia-Yukon border seven times, traversing dozens of streams and wild rivers which are part of the great Mackenzie and Yukon watershed, and runs parallel to the massive St. Elias Range to enter Alaska near Beaver Creek. Major features seen along the highway include the Liard River, Watson Lake, the Cassiar Mountains, Teslin and Tagish lakes, Whitehorse and Haines Junction—nestled among the towering mountains, glaciers, and tundra meadows of Kluane National Park. Territorial campgrounds are located at Watson Lake, Big Creek, Rancherina River, Swift River, Morley River, Teslin Lake, Judas Creek, Squange Lake, Tagish Bridge, Marsh Lake, Wolf Creek, Mendenhall Creek, Pine Creek, Sulphur Lake, Goose Bay, Burwash Flats, Lake Creek, and Snag Junction. Canadian National Topographic Survey Maps: Coal River 95-D, Watson Lake 105-A, Rabbit River 94-M, Jennings River 104-O, Wolf Lake 105-B, Teslin 105-C, Whitehorse 105-D, Dezadeash 115-A, Mount St. Elias 115-B, Kluane Lake 115-G.

Campbell Highway, Robert

Yukon Highway 9 was opened in 1968 and provides an alternate route to the Klondike, winding for 372 miles through the peaks and valleys of the Campbell Range and Big Salmon Range Mountains. The highway begins at Watson Lake and runs northwest for 230 miles to the historic settlement of Ross River and a side road to the mining community of Faro. Highway 9 continues westward for 105 miles, joining the Klondike Highway just north of Carmacks. The Campbell Highway is a well-maintained gravel road that follows closely the original trail blazed by Robert Campbell—the first white man to penetrate what is now known as the Yukon Territory—along the upper Liard, Frances, Finlayson, and Pelly rivers during his 1840 expedition. Campbell traveled through the Yukon wilderness by canoe and portage from Fort Simpson on the Mackenzie River to Frances Lake, where he established a Hudson's Bay Company fur trading post. Campgrounds are located along the highway at Simpson Lake, Frances River, Ross River, Fisheye Lake, Drury Creek, and Little Salmon. Please note that there are no services of any kind from Watson Lake along the 231-mile stretch to Ross River. Canadian National Topographic Survey Maps: Watson Lake 105-A, Frances Lake 105-H, Finlayson Lake 105-G, Quiet Lake 105-F, Tay River 105-K, Glenlyon 105-L, Carmacks 115-I.

Canol Road

The map kit shows the entire length of Yukon Highway 8, built during wartime to parallel the oil pipeline from Norman Wells, Northwest Territories, on the Mackenzie River to Whitehorse. The pipeline has been abandoned, but the highway has been improved with a campground established at Quiet Lake. It runs northward at Mile 836 of the Alaska Highway, joining the Campbell Highway at Mile 220 and winds on for another 129 miles to the Northwest Territories border in the Mackenzie Mountains. Complete outfitting and supply services are available at Ross River—a historic trading post located on the southwest bank of the Pelly River. There are no facilities or services available on the 138-mile trip from Johnsons Crossing on the Alaska Highway to Ross River, and beyond to the Yukon-Northwest Territories border. This is a rugged gravel, summer road, recommended only for the experienced wilderness motorist. Canadian National Topographic Survey Maps: Teslin 105-C, Quiet Lake 105-F, Tay River 105-K, Sheldon Lake 105-J, Nahanni 105-I.

Dempster Highway

Highway 11 winds north from its juction with the Klondike Highway near Dawson through the rugged big-game hunting grounds of the Ogilvie Mountains to its present terminus north of the Peel River at the arctic circle. The highway will eventually extend through the Richardson Mountains to Fort McPherson on the Peel River—a tributary of the Mackenzie—in the Northwest Territories. The highway runs through the dense spruce forests, mountains, and treeline tundra in the heart of trophy caribou, grizzly, and Dall sheep hunting and arctic grayling fishing country and leads over the height of land between the Yukon and Mackenzie watershed. The route is named in honor of Inspector W. J. D. Dempster of the Royal Canadian Mounted Police, who traveled 400 grueling miles by dog team from Dawson City through the Ogilvie Mountains and the headwaters of the Peel River to Fort McPherson to determine the fate of a lost police patrol. This gravel-surfaced road has no services or facilities. Territorial campgrounds are located high in the hills near the north fork of the Klondike River and at Milepost 122 at the Ogilvie River—the northernmost campsite in the Yukon. Canadian National Topographic Survey Maps: Dawson 116-B, Ogilvie River 116-G, Porcupine River 116-J.

Haines Road

The map kit shows the entire length of Highway 4 and the surrounding high country wilderness as it climbs northward along the old Dalton Trail from the coastal forests of Haines, Alaska, at the head of the Lynn Canal through the magnificent peaks of the St. Elias Range, across the northwestern tip of British Columbia and into the Yukon, past the historic salmon-trapping Indian village of Klukshu, across the Dalton Trail past Dezadeash and Kathleen Lakes to Haines Junction at Mile 1,016 of the Alaska Highway in the valleys of the Yukon Basin. Klukwan at Mile 21 was the headquarters of the Chilkat tribe of the Tlingit Indians, famous for their chilkat blankets woven from the long hair of mountain goats and cedar bark fibers. Territorial campgrounds are located at Portage Cove, Chilkoot Lake, Mosquito Lake, and Kathleen Lake. The Haines Highway offers access to the finest wilderness steelhead and salmon fishing in the Yukon, in the Tatshenshine and Klukshu rivers; also, to trophy lake trout in Dezadeash Lake. Canadian National Topographic Survey Maps: Skagway 104-M, Tatshenshine River 114-P, Dezadeash 115-A.

Klondike Highway

The Klondike route begins at the picturesque town of Carcross and Mile 866 on the Alaska Highway at the north end of Bennett Lake and runs northwesterly to Dawson and the Klondike goldfields. Carcross was formerly known as Caribou Crossing because of the herds of caribou which migrated through the narrows between Bennett and Nares lakes. From Carcross the highway leads north through the smallest desert in the world back to the Alaska Highway and into the capital city of Whitehorse on the banks of the Yukon. The Klondike Highway begins again at Mile 925 of the Alaska Highway and runs north past Lake Laberge, the famous setting for Robert W. Service's poem "The Cremation of Sam McGee," and continues past the historic village of Carmacks and across the Pelly and Stewart rivers to Dawson City at the confluence of the Yukon and Klondike rivers and the legendary Klondike goldfields. The "Top of the World Highway 3" continues on to Tetlin Junction in Alaska where it rejoins the Alaska Highway at Mile 1,301. Territorial campgrounds are located at Wolf Creek, Lake Laberge, Fox Lake, Twin Lakes, Tachun Creek, Moose Creek, and the Klondike and Yukon rivers. Canadian National Topographic Survey Maps: Whitehorse 105-D, Laberge 105-E, Carmacks 115-I, McQuesten 115-P, Dawson 116-B & C.

Nahanni Range Road

This gravel summer road, known as Yukon Highway 10, runs for 125 miles northwest from Mile 67 of the Campbell Highway through the Selwyn Mountains to the Northwest Territories mining community of Cantung and the Canada Tungsten mine. There are no facilities or services on the road or at the mine site. Canadian National Topographic Survey Maps: Frances Lake 105-H, Nahanni 105-I, Flat River 95-E.

Whitehorse & the Yukon Riverboats

(Pop. 12,000). This historic town, the capital of the Yukon Territory, is located south of Lake Laberge on the Upper Yukon in Canada's subarctic, surrounded by scenic lakes, mountains, and boreal forests. Prospectors by the thousands once landed here after running the famous Whitehorse Rapids to dry out and repack their supplies before heading northwest to the fabled Klondike goldfields. Whitehorse came into being as the northern terminus of the White Pass and Yukon Railroad, which was completed in 1900, connecting Skagway with the Yukon River and the Klondike and outlying settlements as far west as the outfitting point of St. Michael on the Bering Sea. The famed Yukon River boats connected the railhead with Dawson City and the gold fields along the Trail of '98. During the Klondike boom there were over 250 stern-wheelers operating in the Yukon. Today some of the most famous of the old Yukon riverboats may be found along the river, their timber black with age and their paddlewheels crumbling to bits, with the most famous riverboat graveyard downstream and across the river from Dawson City. In Whitehorse, the

riverboat *Klondike* has been restored as a museum piece. Grant McConachie, famed Yukon bush pilot and the founding president of Canadian Pacific Airlines, leased the old freighter and spent a small fortune transforming her into a floating hotel, with a cabaret and a cocktail lounge decorated with murals of the dance-hall days; he organized a Klondike Tour from Whitehorse to Dawson City. The S.S. *Klondike* has since been converted into a national historic site. The old weekly *Whitehorse Star* published the early verses of Robert W. Service, whose *Songs of a Sourdough*, containing his three best-known poems, "The Law of the Yukon," "The Shooting of Dan McGrew," and "The Cremation of Sam McGee," was written before he ever set foot in the Klondike. The MacBride Museum in Whitehorse houses a fine collection from Yukon's past, as does the Old Log Church Museum. Area attractions include the "log skyscrapers," the cabin of Sam McGee, the old log tramway, and the Golden Horn mine, which provides a chance to pan for gold and study placer mining equipment. The surrounding wilderness areas offer fishing for large lake trout up to 60 pounds, northern pike and arctic grayling in Tagish Lake (an 87-pound lake trout was caught here by net) and Tagish River, Marsh and Atlin Lakes, Lake Bennett, Kathleen Lake, and Carcross and Six Mile rivers. Camping facilities are located at Robert Service Park, Wolf Creek Campground, Pioneer Camper Trailer Park, and Jackson Lake Campground. Seaplane dock and Yukon boat tours are located at Schwatka Lake. Whitehorse is reached via the Alaska Highway, White Pass and Yukon Railroad, and scheduled airline service. Yukon river tours and canoe-camping outfitting services are provided by *Goldrush River Tours*, P.O. Box 4835, Whitehorse Y1A 2S3.

White Pass & Yukon Railroad

This privately owned narrow-gauge (36-inch) railroad links the coastal forests of Skagway, Alaska, with Whitehorse and the Klondike country. The route winds along one of the steepest railroad grades in North America on the eastern side of the Coast Range Mountains, climbing from sea level at Skagway to 2,885 feet at White Pass in only 20 miles of track. The railroad reaches its highest point at Log Cabin, British

Columbia, where it reaches an elevation of 2,916 feet. At Rocky Point, just out of Skagway, the railroad crosses the famous Trail of '98, visible 300 feet below at the floor of the Skagway River Gorge. The train continues past Black Cross Rock where two men were buried under the rock by blasting operations during construction of the railroad, past the cataracts of Bridal Veil Falls and the ghost town of White Pass City, which had a population of 10,000 during the gold rush. At Inspiration Point, at an altitude of 2,400 feet, is a monument to the thousands of packhorses that died during the gold rush. The train climbs over White Pass at an elevation of 2,885 feet, and winds on to Log Cabin, formerly the headquarters for the old Northwest Mounted Police and the Canada customs in the gold-rush days, and the jumping-off point for the Fan Tail Trail to the Atlin Lake of British Columbia. From Log Cabin the train passes through scenic moose and caribou country to Lake Bennett, Carcross, and Whitehorse, where it ends its 110-mile journey. Today the mainstay of the route is shipment of freight and mining concentrates, and summer tourists who wish to retrace the Trail of '98. The White Pass and Yukon has a 1-day adventure tour out of Skagway to Lake Bennett and return. It also has arrangements for travelers who want to take their car or camper from Skagway to Whitehorse, or vice versa. For information and a free brochure write: White Pass and Yukon Route, P.O. Box 2147, Seattle WA 98111, (206) 623-2510. The White Pass and Yukon route and the surrounding wilderness are shown on *Canadian National Topographic Survey Maps*, at a scale of 1:250,000: Skagway 104-M, Whitehorse 105-D.

Wilderness & Trophy Fishing Waters

The Canadian National Topographical Survey Map Kits listed below are at a scale of 1:50,000 and 1:250,000 and provide an excellent overview of the lakes, streams, and wild rivers of the Peel River Plateau, Porcupine Plain, and the Yukon Plateau and Liard River Headwaters region. The remote Peel River in the far north is unusual in that it flows eastward through a gap between the Richardson and Selwyn mountains to join the Mackenzie. The Porcupine River, farther north, flows westward into Alaska where it eventually joins the ancient Yukon near Fort Yukon. The Bell and Porcupine rivers were once part of a major Hudson's Bay Company canoe route used as a "freshwater northwest passage" to connect Fort Simpson on the Mackenzie River with the more remote outposts of La Pierre House, Rampart House, and Fort "Youcon." Many of the lakes and streams of the far north are completely unexplored and offer excellent opportunities for the fly-in angler. If you plan on using your own boat or canoe keep in mind that on the large lakes, a sudden wind can kick up sealike waves very suddenly. Guides may be hired at most frontier settlements. A competent guide will keep you from getting lost, do the lion's share of paddling and portaging, and provide an opportunity for you to learn northern canoe, fishing, and woodcraft techniques. The chief disadvantage in having a guide, aside from the expense, occasional inconvenience and difficulties in making arrangements, is the loss of a sense of self-reliance. If you decide to travel without a guide, be sure to have a companion, map kit, and compass. Topographic maps are an absolute essential for travel through an unfamiliar area, for without them it is possible to become completely lost among the maze of channels, bays, and islands of northern lake and river country.

Rapids are shown on the maps by the letter *R* or *F*, for falls; the length of the rapids may be shown by a number of wavy lines across the river. Portage trails connecting lakes, around rapids, between lakes and rivers, or across peninsulas are usually shown on maps as dotted or broken lines with the designation *P*. Occasionally an approximation of their length measured in chains (1 chain = 66 feet) is given. Make

sure to check the variation of contour interval on each of the 1: 250,000 series maps. The ability to correlate the natural features seen on the land with their representation on a map enables the wilderness traveler to know where he is and to direct and plot his progress. A good compass is essential on a wilderness canoe trip. Even if you become temporarily confused among the maze of islands that are found in many northern lakes, with the aid of a compass it's possible to follow a reasonably accurate course across a lake and establish your exact position from distinctive landmarks when you reach the far shore.

The major Yukon lakes and rivers are shown on the following Canadian National Topographic Survey Maps, scale 1:250,000. *Upper Yukon River:* Laberge 105-E, Glenlyon 105-L, Carmacks 115-I, Snag 115-J, Stewart River 115-O, Whitehorse 105-D, Dawson 116-C; *Teslin Lake & River:* Atlin 104-N, Teslin 105-C, Laberge 105-E; *Quiet Lake:* Quiet Lake 105-F; *Liard River & Watson Lake:* Finlayson Lake 105-G, Wolf Lake 105-B, Watson Lake 105-A; *Tagish-Marsh-Bennett Lakes:* Skagway 104-M, Whitehorse 105-D; *Kathleen Lakes:* Kathleen Lakes 115-A/11 (1:50,000 scale); *Kluane Lake* (1:50,000 scale): Serpenthead Lake 115-G/10, Burwash Landing 115-G/7, Duke River 115-G/6; *Alsek River & Aishihik Lake:* Aishihik Lake 115-H; *Peel River:* Ogilvie River 116-G, Hart River 116-H, Wind River 106-E, Martin House 106-K, Trail River 106-L, Fort McPherson (N.W.T.) 106-M; *Porcupine River:* Ogilvie River 116-G, Porcupine River 116-J, Eagle River 116-I, Bell River 116-P, Old Crow 116-N & O; *Bell River:* Bell River 116-P, Blow River 117-A.

YUKON TERRITORY TRAVEL & RECREATION GUIDE

Kluane National Park

Kluane National Park Topo Maps

Canadian National Topographic Survey Maps, scale 1:250,000: Dezadeash 115-A, Mount St. Elias 115-B & C, Kluane Lake 115-F & G.

This scenic 5-million-acre wilderness preserve embraces a rugged country of alpine tundra, dense boreal forests, and lakes in the southwestern corner of the Yukon, dominated by the towering peaks of the Kluane Range and St. Elias Mountains. Kluane (pronounced Kloo-aw-nee) country once served as a trading corridor between the coastal Chilkat Indians and the Yukon interior tribes or "Stick" Indians; many overland trails and canoe routes in the park region were used. The Kluane Range, near the route of the Dalton Trail, was actively propected by sourdoughs at the turn of the century with the main activity centered in Silver City, now a ghost town located outside the park on Kluane Lake.

The dominant feature of Kluane are the two major mountain chains running parallel as the Front Range, bordering the Alaska Highway in a nearly unbroken chain of 8,000-foot summits overshadowing large valleys, cut by the Donjek, Slims, Alsek, Sockeye, and Alder rivers. The Duke Depression, a narrow trough consisting of several large plateaus and valleys, separates the Kluane Range from the St. Elias Range to the west. The towering St. Elias Range reaches its greatest heights at Mount St. Elias (18,008 feet), Kings Peak (16,971 feet), and Mount Vancouver (17,700 feet). A vast ice-covered plateau 8,000–10,000 feet high, known as the Ice-Field Range, forms the world's largest nonpolar glacier system at the base of the St. Elias Range. These great fields of ice and snow are maintained by moist Pacific air flowing over the mountains.

Free guides, *Kluane National Park, Accommodation and Visitor Facilities in Kluane National Park,* and *You Are in Bear Country,* may be obtained by writing the Supervisor, Kluane National Park, Mile 1,019 Alaska Highway, Haines Junction Y0B 1L0. Wildlife in Kluane includes a large population of Alaska-Yukon moose along the alluvial flats of the Donjek River, caribou in the Duke River region, and grizzlies in the Alsek River Valley. Wolf, coyote, red fox, wolverine, lynx, beaver, otter, and snowshoe hare are found throughout the boreal forest areas of the park. Dall sheep and mountain goats roam the rocky slopes and cliffs of Sheep Mountain and the highlands in the south. Trails in Kluane are not maintained or marked and generally follow old mining, trapping, and game trails along the river valleys. You are well advised, when hiking in the Kluane country, to bring a compass, a topographical map kit, and a companion. Overnight hikers and mountain climbers must register with a park warden and obtain a campfire permit. Cross-country hikes provide excellent opportunities to view and photograph a great variety of wildlife and birdlife, including the upland plover, mountain bluebird, and sharp-tailed grouse.

Groups planning an expedition in the great St. Elias Range must apply in writing to the park superintendent, at least 3 months in advance. Fishing in the park and surrounding areas is generally excellent for grayling, northern pike, and lake trout up to 58 pounds in Kluane Lake, renowned for its wild and desolate beauty, and Kathleen, Bates, Much, Dezadeash, Pine, and Kloo lakes.

Access & Lodging

Kluane National Park is reached via the Alaska Highway and the Haines Road. Outfitters, lodges, and supplies are found at Burwash Landing on Kluane Lake, Destruction Bay, and Haines Junction. Photo guiding service is offered by *Haines Junction Inn*, Mile 1,016 Alaska Highway. Fishing guides are available at *Kluane Fishing Tours*, Mile 1,064 Alaska Highway. Vacation lodging in the park and fishing for lake trout, northern pike, and grayling are provided by *Kluane Lake Camp*, c/o Bob White, Destruction Bay.

NORTHWEST TERRITORIES ENCYCLOPEDIA

Accommodations— Vacation Lodges & Sporting Camps

A complete listing of all vacation lodges, fishing and hunting camps, motels, and hotels is contained in the *Explorer's Guide* to Canada's Arctic, available free from Travel Arctic, Yellowknife X1A 2L9. Listings and descriptions of all major lodges and sporting camps in the Northwest Territories are contained in the "Travel & Recreation Guide" section.

Airlines & Charter Fly-in Services

Air Canada and CP Air serve the northern gateway airports of Edmonton, Winnipeg, and Montreal. CP Air serves Whitehorse and the Yukon Territory as well. A number of United States and foreign airlines serve the Canadian international airports. There are connecting flights at the gateway airports to the Northwest Territories. Scheduled airline service to the major settlements of the Northwest Territories is provided by *Austin Airways*, P.O. Box 4000, Timmins, Ont. P4N 7H9, to Cape Dorset from arctic Quebec subject to traffic demand; *Nordair Ltd.* has daily jet service from Montreal to Frobisher Bay with connecting flights to several Baffin Island communities; *Northward Airlines Ltd.*, P.O. Box 356, Yellowknife X0E 1H0, has scheduled flights using Twin Otter aircraft from Inuvik to Tuktoyaktuk, Sachs Harbor, Johnson Point, Holman Island, Coppermine, and Yellowknife, and from Inuvik to communities in the Yukon and Mackenzie River Delta and valley with F-27 and Twin Otter aircraft and from Cambridge Bay to Gjoa Haven, Spence Bay, Pelly Bay, and Igloolik; *Northwest Territories Airways Ltd.* has scheduled DC-3 service available from Yellowknife to Port Radium, Coppermine, Lady Franklin, and Cambridge Bay; *Pacific Western Airlines Ltd.*, 9th Floor, Edmonton Inn Tower, 119th St., Kingsway Ave., Edmonton, Alta. T5G 0X5, has scheduled flights from Edmonton to Yellowknife, Inuvik, Norman Wells, Fort Smith, Fort Simpson, Cambridge, and Resolute; *Ptarmigan Airways Ltd.* has regular service to Snowdrift, Rae-Edzo, Lac La Martre, and Rae Lakes; *St. Felicien Air* serves Port Burwell from Fort Chimo with connections to Montreal and Frobisher Bay via Nordair; *Transair Ltd.*, Winnipeg International Airport, Winnipeg, Man. R3J 0H7, has scheduled Fokker F-28 jet service from Winnipeg via Churchill to Yellowknife, with connecting flights from Churchill to Eskimo Point, Whale Cove, Rankin Inlet, Chesterfield Inlet, Baker Lake, Repulse Bay, Coral Harbor, and Resolute. Wilderness charter service into and within the Northwest Territories is provided by *Kenn Borek Aviation*, 10401 10th St., Suite 216, Dawson Creek, B.C., via Twin Otter Unit Toll Service to Arctic Bay, Igloolik, Grise Fjord, and Pond Inlet and via DC-3 and Twin Otter charter service throughout the Northwest Territories from their base at Resolute Bay; *Klondike Helicopters*, #3 Hangar, McCall Field, Calgary, Alta., has a base at Inuvik; *Lambair*, Box 808, The Pas, Man., has a base at Rankin Inlet; *Survair Limited*, Box 469, RR5, Hunt Club Rd., Ottawa, Ont. K1G 3N3, has charter service from Great Whale River, Quebec, to Sanikiluaq and Belcher Islands; *Gateway Aviation Ltd.*, Box 880, Yellowknife X0E 1H0, from bases at Calgary, Norman Wells, and Yellowknife; *Keewatin Air Ltd.*, 1129 Sanford St., Winnipeg, Man. R3E 3A1, using Cessna 185 and Beaver from base at Rankin Inlet; *Koenen's Air Service Ltd.*, Box 233, Yellowknife X1E 1H0; *Mackenzie Air Ltd.*, Box 2489, Yellowknife X0E 1H0; *Nahanni Air Services*, Box 123, Norman Wells X0E 0V0; *Wolverine Air Ltd.*, Box 316, Fort Simpson X0E 0N0, serving the Mackenzie and Liard River areas with Cessna 185's; *Nahanni Helicopters Ltd.*, Box 32, Fort Simpson X0E 0N0; *Northwest Territorial Airways Ltd.*, Box 100, Yellowknife X1E 1H0; *Buffalo Airways Ltd.*, Box 168, Fort Smith

X0E 0P0; and *Slave Air Services,* Box 262, Pine Point X0E 0W0. Charter rates vary according to the aircraft's capacity. Rates are higher north of the arctic circle and in the remoter outlying areas. Fuel and crew surcharges may apply in addition to distance rates. For information on flying private aircraft in the Northwest Territories write: Travel Arctic, Yellowknife X1A 2L9. Official aeronautical charts and VFR chart supplements may be obtained from Flight Information Publications, Canada Map Office, Dept. of Energy, Mines, & Resources, Ottawa, Ont. K1A 0E9. A free booklet, *Air Tourist Information,* is available from the Ministry of Transport, Canadian Air Transportation Administration, Aeronautical Information Services, Ottawa, Ont. K1A 0N8.

Arctic Char Fishing & Outpost Camps

The remote coastal rivers of the Northwest Territories offer the finest arctic char fishing in North America. The world's record 29-pound-11-ounce char was caught in the Arctic River in 1968. The fish was 39¾ inches long and had a girth of 26 inches. Fish in the 8–20-pound class are caught each year in the famous Tree and Kaugunyauk rivers and in the Victoria Island, Baffin Island, and Koluktoo Bay regions. The handsome bright red or orange char *(Salvelinus alpinus)* will readily take a brightly colored wet fly (such as a Gray Ghost, Light Tiger, or Supervisor), or small spinners or wobblers, during their upstream spawning runs in the late summer or early fall. The arctic char is renowned for the rapierlike speed of its run and spectacular jumps. Fishing for char, as for salmon, is generally hit or miss because of their mercurial, migratory nature. Several established fishing outfitters operate lodges and outpost camps specializing in arctic char fishing on the remote coastal rivers and arctic islands. The *Clearwater Fjord Camp* is located 200 miles north of Frobisher Bay on Cumberland Sound. The camp is open mid-July to the end of August, and accommodates 12 in tents. Write: Consolidated Tours, Suite 480, 550 Sherbrooke St. W, Montreal, Que. *Ikaluvik Arctic Camp* offers fishing for arctic char near Frobisher Bay. Write: Bill Mackenzie, Box 400, Frobisher Bay, X0A 0H0. *Koluktoo Bay Camp* is located 70 air miles southwest of Pond Inlet on the Robinson River with accommodations for 12 and excellent fishing. Local attractions include ancient Eskimo campsites and narwhal calving grounds. Camp is open August 8–September 15. Write: Toonoonik Sahoonik Co-operative, Pond Inlet, X0A 0S0. *Arctic Outpost Camps Ltd.* is located 52 miles northeast of Cambridge Bay and 2 miles southwest of Albert Edward Bay on Victoria Island, about 225 miles north of the arctic circle. The camp accommodates 24 in heated framed tents, plus a modern main lodge, 2–4 per cabin. Facilities include showers, smokehouse and fish freezer, and floatplanes, guides, boats, and motors. Regular side trips to Hadley Bay and the Kent Peninsula. Season is July 1–September 1. Write: Arctic Outpost Camps Ltd., Box 1104, Edmonton, Alta. The *Belcher Islands Char Camp* is located in Hudson Bay. Camp accommodates 6, with separate bedrooms, running water, and electricity, and has guides, boats, and motors. Area attractions include arctic owls, Canada geese, white whales, seals, polar bear, and high-arctic birdlife. The camp is reached by air charter from Chapleau, Wawa, or Timmins, Ontario. Write: Theirault Air Service, Box 269, Chapleau, Ont. *High Arctic Sportfishing Camps* has a tent camp on Merkley Lake on Victoria Island with an outpost camp near Namayuak Lake for arctic char and lake trout. Area wildlife includes musk-ox, caribou, and polar bear. Rates include accommodations, meals, boats, motors, guides, and floatplane flights. Write: High Arctic Sportfishing Camps, Box 5035, Fort McMurray, Alta. T9H 3E7. *Plummer's Tree River Char Camp* (world record caught here) offers first-class accommodations and services. Write: Great Bear Lodge Ltd., 1110 Sanford St., Winnipeg, Manitoba R3E 2Z9.

Barren Grounds

The vast zone of treeless tundra of Canada's north that the explorer Samuel Hearne named the barren grounds (also commonly referred to as the barrenlands) stretches across the top of Canada, covering a million square miles from the wooded Mackenzie Valley on the west to Hudson Bay and the northern portions of the Yukon, the Ungava Plateau of Labrador and Quebec, and the treeless islands of the remote arctic archipelago. For centuries the awesome mystery and majesty of the barrens has haunted and beckoned the men who have explored the north country. The mainland barren grounds of the Northwest Territories embrace close to half a million square miles of rolling, lake-dotted plains, broken here and there by ancient, worn-down hills. Viewed by an observer in a bush plane, the barrens appear to be a mosaic of untold thousands of lakes and rivers wrought by the ebb and flow of the great ice sheets, with desolate rolling tundra covered with strewn boulders, rubble, and a thick carpet of grayish white caribou moss and colorful lichens, pocked by countless tundra pools, or kettle ponds, discolored by organic stains of sepia, burnished copper, shimmering green, and burning red muskeg water. The wild, twisting barren-ground rivers roar through deep canyons, flow through great chains of deep, clear irregularly shaped lakes, and slowly meander through stretches of chocolate-brown muskeg and between silver-gray moraines and sandy eskers. The eskers, casts of long dead rivers that once flowed beneath the great ice sheets, wind at times for hundreds of miles across the barrens, giving the land a haunting, dreamlike appearance.

The great watershed of the barren lands lies trapped in a granite-hard floor of permafrost which reaches, in some areas, to a depth of 1,200 feet. If the permafrost ever melts due to the gradual warming trend of the climate, the barrens will become a desert of gray rock and sand. These great northern plains are actually anything but "barren." Each

summer the barrens become an arctic rock garden bursting with millions of brightly-colored lousewort, white lichen, map lichen, amica, wintergreen, and arctic willow, as well as poppy, cotton grass, mountain heather, arctic crocus, purple saxifrage, white heather and rhododendron, grasses, sedges, mushrooms, dwarf shrubbery, stunted willows, alder, and ground birch. Raw peat, particularly heath turf and sphagnum moss, is found everywhere and is an important source of fuel.

One of the most awesome sights in the far north, equal to the magical dance of the green and white waves of the northern lights across the night sky, is the mysterious herds of migrating caribou, drifting like grayish-white specters across the taiga of the barren lands on their annual trek to the treeline, the land of lichen, in a phenomenon known as *la foule*, or "the throng," moving in seemingly endless single-file lines along deeply furrowed trails often no more than 6–12 inches wide. Where they go and why they leave the treeline was long one of the mysteries of the north. Recent studies show that they are in search of browse such as berry bushes, dwarf willow, and birch, and the thick whitish lichen, sometimes more than 2 feet thick, that forms a rumpled carpet on the tundra during the spring and summer months.

The thousands of kettle ponds and lakes are famous breeding grounds for ducks, geese, and wading birds; the dry and rock tundra is the habitat of the northern grouse, or ptarmigan, and snowy owls which nest on the grass flats, along with roughlegged hawks, peregrine falcons, gray jays, plover, tufted puffin, murres, and ravens, as well as butterflies, bees, arctic fox, wolves, hordes of voracious black flies and mosquitoes, and the gaudy orange-colored ground squirrel. Until a few decades ago, the barren-ground grizzly bear roamed the tundra west of Hudson Bay with millions of musk-ox, caribou, and arctic wolves.

With the brutal slaughter of the great herds of musk-ox and caribou at the turn of the century, the barren-ground grizzly and the people of the caribou diminished in numbers. When J. B. and J. W. Tyrell, the renowned explorers of the western tundra, entered the barrenlands of Keewatin in 1893 there were approximately 2,000 Eskimos who lived in the interior and were exclusively a people of the caribou. By 1970 there was not one resident Indian or Eskimo to be found in the great interior, except at Baker Lake village near the mouth of the Thelon River.

The barrenlands have always intrigued and lured the great northern explorers. It was at Montreal Island, near the mouth of the treacherous Back River, that Sir John Franklin and his crew of 125 men began their ill-fated trek inland to die of starvation, scurvy, exposure, and drowning. Samuel Hearne, the author of *Journey to the Northern Ocean 1795*, Mackenzie, and Franklin came here by canoe and moccasin to navigate the unknown lengths of the Coppermine and Mackenzie rivers. In 1834 George Back set out with Dr. Richard King, two carpenters, and a shipwright from Great Slave Lake to locate the headwaters of the tongue-twisting *Thlew-ee-choh-desseth*, or "Great Fish River," which the Indians said flowed in a northeasterly direction to the frozen Arctic Ocean. They tackled the maniacal fury of the Great Fish and "arrived at the mouth of the Thlew-ee-choh-desseth, which, after a violent-tortuous course of 530 geographical miles, running through an iron-ribbed country without a single tree on the whole of its banks, expands into fine, large lakes with clear horizons . . . and breaks into falls, cascades and rapids to the number of no less than 83." (Sir George Back, *Narrative of the Arctic Land Expeditions to the Mouth of the Great Fish River.)* The Great Fish is today known as the Back River.

Camping & Territorial Parks

Several well-maintained territorial park campgrounds are located at scenic points, near swift-flowing rivers, picturesque waterfalls, and stately jackpine ridges, along the Mackenzie Highway System. They include areas for tenting or trailer parking, sanitary facilities, picnic tables, fireplaces, and covered camp kitchens. Be sure to ask about the facilities ahead at the 60th Parallel Visitor Information Center (open May 15–September 15). It may be 100 miles from one supply center to the next. In addition to the highway system, territorial park campgrounds are located at Pangnirtung and Frobisher Bay on Baffin Island. Camping permits, required for use of the park campgrounds, are available for $5 from the 60th Parallel Visitor Information Center, at Travel Arctic in Yellowknife, and from park offices in Hay River and Yellowknife. Permits are valid for the year April 1–March 31. Maximum length of stay in a campground is 14 days per year. The territorial park campgrounds are shown on the free *Northwest Territories Official Travel Map*, available from Travel Arctic, Yellowknife X1A 2L9. *Arctic Camping Tours* to Pangnirtung and the Cumberland Sound region of Baffin Island amid a wilderness of wild rivers, streams, rolling hills, and steep-sided fjords are offered by Consolidated Tours, Suite 480, 550 Sherbrooke St. W, Montreal, Que. H3A 1B9.

Canoeing the Great Barren-Ground Rivers

The thousands upon thousands of wild, churning barren-ground rivers and unexplored lakes of the Northwest Territories offer some of the most challenging canoe water in North America. These great subarctic rivers should be attempted only by the experienced, thoroughly prepared canoeist. The mighty Mackenzie River—known as the "Mississippi of the North"—and its tributaries offer a staggering amount of wilderness canoe country. The Slave River, reached from Fort Smith at Wood Buffalo National Park, flows through the notorious Slave River rapids—Cassette, Pelican, Mountain, and the Rapids of the Drowned—into Great Slave Lake, the headwaters of the Mackenzie. About 1,300 air miles from Great Slave Lake lies Jolly Lake and the height of land into the Mackenzie River watershed. The renowned Hanbury and Thelon flow east of Jolly Lake along a rugged 500-mile course through the barrenlands to Hudson Bay. The short, swift Hanbury roars through Dickson Canyon and over the thunderous 60-foot Helen Falls to its junction with the Thelon River. There are numerous caribou trails along the Hanbury that aid in portaging. The Thelon flows from its headwaters through the Thelon Game Sanctuary, an oasis of deep wooded valleys and green meadows of an ancient sea bottom, to its junction with the Hanbury and continues east along the edge of the taiga through Aberdeen Lake—where high waves can travel 40 miles—to Baker Lake and Hudson Bay. Canoes rented from Hudson's Bay Company can be left at the HCB Baker Lake outpost. To the west of the Jolly Lake height of land is the treacherous Snare River, which flows through deep canyons and cataracts into Great Slave Lake, and the Camsell River, an important link in the old Indian fur trade route between Great Slave and Great Bear lakes. The Camsell winds through a chain of lakes and forested banks into the massive Great Bear Lake, whose shores are lined by stark granite cliffs. The Great Bear River forms the western outlet of the lake and flows along a swift, shallow course to its confluence with the Mackenzie near Fort Norman. The infamous boiling fury of the 615-mile Back River is the barrenlands' premier canoe route. The Back, known to the Indians as "Great Fish River," rises at Aylmer Lake and flows over some 80 falls, cascades, and rapids through Pelly and Macdougal lakes in the heart of caribou and musk-ox country to its mouth on the Arctic Ocean.

Other well-known barren-ground canoe trails include the Horton, Anderson, Coppermine, Burnside, Dubawnt, Kazan, and Yellowknife rivers.

The useful free booklet *Canoe Canada's Arctic* provides the nitty-gritty on the great wilderness routes of the Northwest Territories and describes the barren-ground rivers. The booklet and detailed trip-planning info on individual rivers is available from Travel Arctic, Yellowknife X1A 2L9. *Northwest Expeditions* offers guided canoe trips down the Coppermine to the Arctic Ocean and down the south Nahanni River from Watson Lake, Yukon. Write: Northwest Expeditions, Box 1551, Edmonton, Alta. T5J 2N7. *Canoe Arctic* offers remote guided trips north and south of the treeline. These trips are guided by Alex Hall, wildlife biologist, and provide opportunities to photograph caribou, white wolves, musk-ox, and bird-life at close range. Complete outfitting is included. For a free brochure write: Alex M. Hall, 9 John Beck Crescent, Brampton, Ont. L6W 2T2. (See "Hudson's Bay Company Outfitting Posts & Canoe Service.") *Wild River Surveys* are available free from Information Services Conservation Group, Department of Indian Affairs & Northern Development, 400 Laurier Ave. W, Ottawa, Ont. K1A 0H4 for the Hanbury and Thelon rivers, South Nahanni River, South Redstone River, and Hare Indian River. The surveys are invaluable aids to the canoeist for information about access and egress, flora, wildlife, history, and a thorough description of the canoe route.

Fishing & Hunting in Canada's Arctic

The Northwest Territories encompass a sprawling wilderness of untold thousands of remote lakes and cold, clear rivers—more than a million square miles (more than half the size of the continental United States) stretching across the top of the continent from Hudson Bay to the Yukon, north of the 60th parallel. It is so huge that it's divided into three districts: the Mackenzie District in the west; the Keewatin District, which lies between the Mackenzie District and Hudson Bay, and embraces the great barrenlands; and the Franklin District, which takes in the remote islands of the arctic archipelago.

Trophy Fishing Waters

The Northwest Territories offer some of the finest frontier fishing in North America for arctic char, grayling, and sheefish in the barren-

ground rivers and their tributaries; and trophy northern pike, walleye, and world's record lake trout in the deep, cold waters of the legendary Great Bear Lake and Great Slave Lake regions. The arctic grayling *(Thymallus arcticus)* is the premier game fish of the wilderness lakes and streams. Grayling up to weights of 5 pounds are caught annually in the world-renowned Great Bear and Great Slave lakes and in the Mackenzie, Coppermine, Anderson, Thelon, and Back River watersheds. This slender, graceful fish, distinctly more colorful than grayling of southern waters, is noted for its long, high dorsal fin marked with bright blue or red spots or bands reflecting shades of lilac or gold. Grayling vary in color from dark, almost black, to a silvery bright pearl color. The male's dorsal fin and overall size is larger than that of the female grayling. The fish generally reaches trophy size only in the cold, clear streams and lakes of the north, up to the 21-inch, 5-pound world's record caught in Great Slave Lake. A gregarious fish, the grayling travels in schools, and will readily take a dark fly in black, gray, or brown such as a March Brown, Black Ant, Dark Cahill, or Black Gnat.

Fishing the remote wilderness waters generally calls for fly-in charter service, a guide, and proper clothing and gear. A complete listing of Northwest Territories angling regulations, charter fly-in services, outfitters, and wilderness outpost fishing and hunting camps is found in the useful 56-page *Explorer's Guide to Canada's Arctic*, available free from Travel Arctic, Yellowknife X1A 2L9. The trophy fish of the great subarctic lakes, such as Great Bear and Great Slave, are extremely slow growing and very long lived. A lake trout of 60 pounds caught in Great Bear or Great Slave lake may be as old as 60 years; a 30-pounder has probably lived there for about 40 years. The best fishing is usually found along the shallow bays, coves, and shoals where the sun shines long enough and hard enough during the few ice-free months to create the vital chain of plants, insects, and small bait fish.

Hunting

The wilderness hunting zones of the Northwest Territories have some of the best big-game hunting in the world for Dall sheep, mountain goat, grizzly and black bear, moose, woodland and barren-ground caribou, wild bison, and polar bear. The famous Mackenzie Mountains embrace a hunter's paradise: 60,000 square miles of 9,000-foot peaks, wild rivers, deep, dark gorges, and soft upland meadows extend-

ing due west of the Mackenzie River to the Yukon Highlands, and northward from the swift blue Liard River to the Peel River Game Preserve south of the arctic coast. For decades the Mackenzie Mountains lay unhunted while the wildlife population multiplied and grew to trophy sizes. A fairly stable population of the snow-white, golden-horned Dall sheep *(Ovis dalli dalli)* are found high among the alpine meadows and ridges. Grizzly bear are found in the forests of the Mackenzie Mountains and along the low, scattered foliage of the barrenlands, where they feed on fish, ground squirrels, and berries. The Mackenzie black bear *(Ursus americanus hunteri)* roams in considerable numbers throughout the Northwest Territories south of the treeline. Moose belonging to the northwestern race *(Alces alces andersoni)* range throughout the Great Slave Lake, Great Bear Lake, Mackenzie River Valley, and Mackenzie Mountains regions, from the 60th parallel to the arctic circle, and are found scattered across the southern portion of the Keewatin District. Barrenland caribou are common throughout the Northwest Territories from the 60th parallel to the Arctic Ocean, while the larger woodland caribou occur south of the treeline in the Mackenzie Mountains. The swift, agile polar bear *(Ursus maritimus)*, often weighing up to half a ton, prefers the far northern arctic and Hudson Bay coastlines and on the barren islands of the arctic archipelago. Scientists estimate that approximately one-half of the world's population of these huge, paddle-footed animals roam Canada's arctic regions. This monarch of the north has unbelievable power and is as agile as a cat. Polar bear licenses and experienced Eskimo guides and outfitters are found in a limited number of Eskimo settlements along the arctic coast. For information and polar bear hunting license applications, write: Superintendent of Game, Yellowknife. A complete listing of nonresident big-game hunting regulations, outfitter areas, and a *Northwest Territories Game Zone Map* are found in the *Explorer's Guide to Canada's Arctic*, available free from Travel Arctic, Yellowknife X1A 2L9.

Big-Game Hunting Guide Services

All nonresident big-game hunters are required to hire the services of a licensed outfitter. The *Nahanni Butte Outfitters* offer 2-week fly-in, backpack hunts from July 15 to October 6 for Dall sheep, grizzly bear, and wolf in the Mackenzie Mountains (zone 12). For info write: Don Turner, Box 307, Fort Nelson, B.C. *Rex Logan*, Box 484, Sundre, Alta., operates in the Mackenzie Mountains from August 1 to October 15 for Dall sheep, grizzly, caribou, moose, and wolf. The *South Nahanni Outfitters*, Box 586, Cardston, Alta., offers 15-day hunts from July 18 to September 17 in the Mackenzie Mountains for Dall sheep, grizzly, caribou, wolf, moose, and mountain goat. The *Mackenzie Mountain Outfitters Ltd.*, Box 123, Norman Wells X0E 0V0, offers 10-day hunts from July 15 through August 15 and from August 15 to September 30 in the Mackenzie Mountains for Dall sheep, grizzly, woodland caribou, moose, and the elusive wolf. *Redstone Mountain Trophy Hunts*, Box 608, Banff, Alta. T0L 0C0, operates in the Mackenzie Valley for all big-game species. Other licensed outfitters operating camps in the Mackenzie Mountains include: *Skyline Outfitters Ltd.*, Box 224, Gleichen, Alta.; *Arctic Red River Lodge Ltd.*, Box 1932, Hay River X0E 1G0; and *Gana River Outfitters*, Box 1791, Hay River. The Northwest Territories also offer superb waterfowl and upland game-bird shooting. The barren grounds are the world's greatest nesting area for the Canada goose, snow and blue goose, whistler swan, ducks, rails, and coots. Upland game birds, including ruffed, spruce, and sharptail grouse and arctic ptarmigan, are found on the lichen-carpeted barrens, and in the snowgrass pastures and brushy woodlands of the Mackenzie Valley and the Great Slave Lake region.

Clothing & Gear

Your choice of clothing and gear for wilderness fishing and big-game hunting trips in the Northwest Territories requires as much careful planning and thought as does your choice of guide. A recommended clothing list for, say, a 2-week Mackenzie Mountain hunt would include a couple of pairs of light duofold underwear, heavy cotton gloves, wool or heavy cotton pants, heavy long underwear, 2 heavy woolen shirts and a couple of wool sweaters, flannel shirts, 1 pair of rubber-bottom shoepacks with vibram soles, camp shoes (try to avoid rubber soles that will absorb water), sturdy ankle-fit lightweight hip boots, 1 lightweight woolen jacket, a knee-length raincoat and hooded down jacket, and a hat with ear flaps. If you are planning a late September or October hunt, remember to pack a pair of warm down-filled mittens, insulated boots, a skullcap, and a heavy down-filled coat with a hood. Bring along a good supply of bug dope and woolen socks, heavy cotton handkerchiefs, sunglasses, a down-filled sleeping bag, pocket compass and hunting knife, and a set of topo maps. A lightweight aluminum frame packboard with a packsack or light rucksack will prove an invaluable aid for carrying your lunch, camera and film, raingear, insect dope, fishing gear, ammunition, and game meat.

Great River of the North

In 1789 when Alexander Mackenzie completed his 2,500-mile voyage and exploration to the mouth of the great river that was eventually to bear his name, in search of the Pacific Ocean and the fabled Northwest Passage, he stood on the shore of the great Arctic Ocean and gazed upon a desolate land of naked islands, shallow silt-filled ponds, meandering channels, alluvial mud and silt of the river's delta, and then wearily set back with his mutinous Indian guides to face the backbreaking portages, storms, and recriminations of his colleagues at Fort Chipewyan, far to the south.

The Mackenzie flows through a broad forested valley to its mouth, draining its waters from high country lakes and rivers thousands of wilderness miles away; from the distant headwaters of the Athabasca River in Jasper National Park; from the floor of the Rocky Mountain Trench and the mighty Peace, Finley, Hay, Peel, and Liard rivers; from the roaring, wild rivers and streams of the Mackenzie Mountains; from the rivers and headwater lakes of the Canadian Shield Country in northern Saskatchewan; and from the deep, cold waters of huge Lake Athabasca and Great Slave and Great Bear lakes. Ten thousand years ago the Keewatin Ice Sheet was stopped, momentarily, by the great wall of the Mackenzie Mountains, and was forced to turn north, plowing a channel hundreds of miles wide to the Arctic Ocean. This channel was soon filled by the waters of what was to become the Great River of the North, fed by the waters of the huge lakes the glacier had gouged around the granite rim of the Canadian Shield.

A voyage down the Mackenzie will take you from its headwaters at Great Slave Lake, past Fort Providence and the Mackenzie Bison Sanctuary, past the Jean Marie River village to its confluence with the blue waters of the Liard at Fort Simpson. The great river continues on flowing through a deeply wooded valley and around numerous large, spruce-covered islands, surrounded by foothills of the Mackenzie Mountains on the west and by the Franklin Mountains on the east, past Wrigley and Fort Norman—where it picks up the cold, clear waters of Great Bear Lake via the Great Bear River outlet. Northwest of Fort Norman the Mackenzie flows past Fort Good Hope, Arctic Red River village and the northernmost portion of the Peel River Reserve, and enters the great delta where it widens and separates in

numerous broad channels as it meanders past the Eskimo villages of Aklavik and Inuvik and the reindeer grazing reserve in its mouth on the Arctic Ocean.

Boat rentals, guides, cruises, wilderness cabins, fly-in fishing and air charters on the Mackenzie are provided by *Snowshoe General Store*, Fort Providence X0E 0L0. River transportation is provided by *Northern Transportation Co. Ltd.*, 9945 108 St., Edmonton, Alta. T5K 2G9, (403) 423-9201. Vacation accommodations are provided by *Brabant Lodge*, located on an island in the Mackenzie 32 air miles from Hay River, with guide service and fishing for grayling, walleye, and northern pike. Write or call Territorial Hotels Ltd., 1609 14 St., SW, Calgary, Alta. T3C 1E4, (403) 245-4342.

Highways—Traveling the Mackenzie Route

The six major sections of the all-weather gravel Mackenzie Highway system wind north from the Alberta border through the beautiful northland wilderness of the Northwest Territories, from the connecting communities around Great Slave Lake and the upper Mackenzie River Valley, and Alberta. The six major sections of the system include Mackenzie Route Highway 1, Hay River Highway 2, Yellowknife Highway 3, Ingraham Trail Highway 4, Fort Smith Highway 5, and Fort Resolution Highway 6. The hundreds of miles of wilderness gravel road, dust, insects, and long stretches between service stations present a challenge to the traveler that requires thoughtful planning and care. Campsites and scenic picnic areas are conveniently located for the wilderness motorist. The price of gasoline along the Mackenzie Highway ranges from 75¢ to 85¢ per gallon depending on the distance and cost of haulage from main distribution centers. Remember that gasoline stations in Canada use the imperial measure, which is one-

fifth greater than the U.S. measure. Visitors are advised to drop in at the 60th Parallel Visitor Information Center for the latest info on road conditions, fishing hot spots, and a cup of hot coffee. If you plan to venture off the highway, you are advised to register with the nearest Royal Canadian Mounted Police detachment. Drivers are well advised to take a few precautions such as using headlight protectors and rubber gas-tank protectors for the all-gravel highways. Passing should be done

on the dust-controlled passing zones along the highways. Free ferry service operates on the Mackenzie and Liard rivers in season, and after freeze-up in late fall there are ice bridges.

The *Official Travel Map Northwest Territories* showing all towns and settlements, paved and gravel highways, ferry crossings, campgrounds, picnic areas, national parks, and points of interest is available free from Travel Arctic, Yellowknife X1A 2L9. The Mackenzie Route Highway System and the surrounding wilderness and recreation areas are shown on the following 1:250,000 scale Canadian National Topographic Survey Maps: Fort Smith 75-D, Little Buffalo River 85-A, Fort Resolution 85-H, Buffalo Lake 85-B, Tathlina Lake 85-C, Kakisa River 85-D, Falaise Lake 85-F, Rae 85-K, Yellowknife 85-J, Hearne Lake 85-I, Mills Lake 85-E, Fort Simpson 95-H.

Hudson's Bay Company Outfitting Posts & Canoe Service

The Northwest Territories outpost stores of the Hudson's Bay Company carry food supplies, gear, and ammunition required for wilderness hunting, fishing, and canoeing. Keep in mind, however, that the remote HBC Posts may not necessarily carry a full range of supplies. It's best to place your order a couple of months in advance in writing for pick up when you arrive. For information on canoe rentals and a free *HBC U-Paddle Service* map/brochure, rates and reservations write: Hudson's Bay Company, Northern Stores Department, 800 Baker Center, 10025 106th St., Edmonton, Alta. T5J 1G7, or phone (403) 424–8113. HBC outpost supply stores are found scattered

throughout the Northwest Territories at Fort Liard in the Nahanni Country; Fort Rae, Fort Providence, Hay River, Fort Resolution, Yellowknife, and Fort Smith in the Great Slave Lake region; Fort Simpson, Fort Norman, Fort Good Hope, Fort McPherson, Aklavik, Arctic Red River, Inuvik, and Tuktok in the Mackenzie River Valley and Delta; Fort Franklin on Great Bear Lake; Pangnirtung, Frobisher Bay, Lake Harbor, and Cape Dorset on Baffin Island; and Eskimo Point, Rankin Inlet, Chesterfield Inlet, and Baker Lake in Keewatin District. Several of the outpost stores are equipped with HBC radiotelephone service. Additional canoe and boat rental services are offered in the Northwest Territories: *Yellowknife River Boat Rentals* has 16-foot canoes, 17-foot freighters, and motorboats, including life jackets, paddles, and gas. Write: Box 1343, Yellowknife X0E 1H0; *North Cruise*, Box 2794, Yellowknife X0E 1H0, has charter service for Great Slave Lake; *Norlan Rentals*, Box 1760, Inuvik X0E 0T0; *The Sportsman*, Box 162, Yellowknife X0E 1H0, and *R.A.M. Enterprises Ltd.*, Box 342, Hay River X0E 0R0.

Thelon Game Sanctuary— The "Oasis of the Barrens"

The great Thelon Game Sanctuary is located in the northeast portion of the Northwest Territories, straddling the border between the tundra and the treeline and the districts of Mackenzie and Keewatin, and preserves the soul of the north and a beauty that few men have experienced. The sanctuary was established in 1929 and embraces the deep, wooded valley of the Thelon River from its confluence with the Hanbury to Beverly Lake, surrounded by boulder-strewn tundra with its dry brown grass, apple-green lichen, and glacial rubble. The treeline and the tundra merge here in dramatic relief, and beavers, marten, and fisher share their territory with musk-ox, grizzly bear, and barren-ground caribou; robins are often seen feeding beside Lapland longspurs. One of the north's largest herds of musk-ox are found here, concentrated at Grassy Island, where the broad valley of the Thelon widens into marshlands. The musk-ox *(Ovibos moschatus)* is a member of the family Bovidae, to which our domestic cattle, sheep, and goat belong. It's one of the hardiest of animals, withstanding extreme variations in temperature and subsisting on grasses, dwarf willows, forbs, and sedges. The adult musk-ox weighs 500–900 pounds and is easily recognized by its long, silky brown coat, which hangs like a shirt of hair nearly to its feet, and by its broad flat horns with curved tips pointed forward. When attacked by wolves musk-ox will form a circle with their heads pointed outward. The musk-ox nearly became extinct during the last century when whalers slaughtered the animals by the thousands for their meat, which tastes much like a good beefsteak. They have been protected by law since 1917.

Until the recent advent of scientific exploration in the sanctuary, and during the trapping era of the 1920s when white fox furs were in demand for high fashion, the great oasis had few visitors, except for J. B. Tyrell, who canoed down the Valley of the Thelon between 1892 and 1900, and wanderers such as James Anderson in 1855, Roderick Mackenzie in 1857, David Hanbury in 1901–2, and John Hornby, who left his starved bones and those of two companions in a small cabin on the bank of the Thelon oasis in 1927. When the bodies were discovered, the journal of young Edgar Christan, a 27-year-old ex-Royal Air Force pilot who was the last to die, was found on the cook's stove, and is one of the most graphic and detailed descriptions of the agonies of starvation in existence. The graves of the three men can still be seen on the wooded banks of the Thelon. Present-day wilderness travelers planning a journey through the game sanctuary are required

to secure a permit from the Game Management Division, Government of the Northwest Territories, Yellowknife X1A 2L9. Inquiries or applications for scientific research may be sent to the Science Adviser, Government of the Northwest Territories, Yellowknife. The Thelon Game Sanctuary is shown on the following 1:250,000 scale *Canadian National Topographic Survey Maps:* Hanbury 75-P, Baillie River 76-A, Tammarvi River 66-D, Beverly Lake 66-C, Clarke River 65-M, Dubawnt Lake 65-N, Tebesjuak Lake 65-O, Aberdeen Lake 66-B, Duggan Lake 76-H, Jervoise River 66-E, and Pelly Lake 66-F.

Wild & Trophy Fishing Waters Map Kits

The following full-color 1:250,000 scale Canadian National Topographic Survey Maps show the major Northwest Territories trophy fishing waters and wilderness canoe routes (see the Travel & Recreation Guide for additional listings). *Coppermine River:* Lac des Gras 76-D, Winter Lake 86-A, Sloan River 86-K, Dismal Lakes 86-N, Coppermine 86-O; *Yellowknife River:* Hearne Lake 85-J, Wecho River 85-O, Carp Lakes 85-P; *Artillery Lake:* Fort Reliance 75-K, Lynx Lake 75-J, Walmsey Lake 75-N, Artillery Lake 75-O; *Kasba & Snowbird Lakes:* Ennadai Lake 65-C, Snowbird Lake 65-D; *Nueltin Lake:* Kasmere Lake 64-N, Munroe Lake 64-O, Nueltin Lake 65-B; *Hare Indian River:* Fort Good Hope 106-I, Lac Belot 96-L, Lac Des Bois 96-K; *Redstone River:* Wrigley Lake 95-M, Dahadinni River 95-N, Fort Norman 96-C; *Carcajou River:* Mount Eduni 106-A, Carcajou Canyon 96-D, Norman Wells 96-E, Sans Sault Rapids 106-H; *Horton River:* Franklin Bay 97-C, Simpson Lake 97-B, Erly Lake 97-A, Horton Lake 96-O, Bloody River 96-P; *Hornaday River:* Brock River 97-D, Erly Lake 97-A, Bloody River 96-P; *Great Bear River:* Fort Norman 96-C, Mahony Lake 96-F, Fort Franklin 96-G; *Snare River:* Marian River 85-N, Wecho River 85-O, Indin Lake 86-B; *Burnside River:* Nose Lake 76-F, Contwoyto Lake 76-E, Kathawachaga Lake 76-L, Mara River 76-K, Arctic Sound 76-N; *Snowdrift River:* Snowdrift 75-L, Reliance 75-K, Lynx Lake 75-J; *Tazin River:* Tazin Lake 74-N, Hill Island Lake 75-C, Fort Smith 75-D; *Taltson River:* Fort Smith 75-D, Taltson Lake 75-E, Nonacho Lake 75-F; *Thoa River:* Hill Island Lake 75-C, Abitau Lake 75-B; *Slave River:* Fitzgerald 74-M, Fort Smith 75-D, Little Buffalo River 85-A, Fort Resolution 85-H.

Wilderness Fishing & Adventure Trips

Established package tours and expeditions are available into and within the Northwest Territories. It is recommended that you contact Travel Arctic, Yellowknife X1A 2L9, phone (403) 873–7319 for up-to-the-minute developments. *Mackenzie River Tour* is offered by Arctic Cruise Ltd., Box 1155, Hay River X0E 0R0, aboard the luxury cruise ship *Norweta*. Visit the historic settlements along the great 1,200-mile water route to Canada's western arctic. Package includes airfare from Edmonton, Alberta, meals, shipboard accommodations, 7 days northbound, 8 days southbound: 20 passengers for each of 18 departures, mid-June to early October. *Ferguson Travel*, Box 1990, Hay River X0E 0R0, has customized tours of the surrounding country or to the entire Northwest Territories, and fishing trips to area lodges and Wood Buffalo National Park. *Arctic Adventure Tour*, offered by Horizon Holidays of Canada, 44 Victoria St., Toronto, Ont. M5C 1Y9, is a fully escorted holiday consisting of 14 days by air, rail, cruise ship, and private motorcoach to Yellowknife, Inuvik, Tuktoyaktuk, Dawson City, Whitehorse, and Skagway, plus a cruise of the Inside Passage aboard Canadian Pacific *Princess Patricia*. Tour departures June, July, and August from Montreal, Toronto, Edmonton, and Vancouver. Maximum of 40 persons for each 16 departures. *Eastern Arctic Safari* is also offered by Horizon Holidays (address above), consisting of a 10-day tour with chartered aircraft visiting the north magnetic pole, Eureka on Ellesmere Island, Koluktoo Bay, Resolute, and Pangnirtung. *South Nahanni River Tour*, offered by Northwest Expeditions Ltd., Box 1551, Edmonton, Alta. T5J 2N7, consists of a float down the South Nahanni River in large inflatable rubber rafts, through Nahanni National Park, with spectacular views of Rabbitkettle, Hotspring, and Virginia Falls, canyons, and wildlife. Guests participate in paddling, portages, and wilderness camping. Departures from Watson Lake, Yukon Territory, June 22, July 6, July 20, and August 3. CP Air serves Watson Lake from Edmonton or Vancouver. The *Coppermine River Tour*, also operated by Northwest Expeditions, is a 13-day raft tour down the Coppermine River, crossing the arctic circle to the Arctic Ocean with views of the barren grounds, Bloody Falls, and a wide variety of arctic wildlife, and fishing for arctic char and grayling. Guests participate in paddling and wilderness camping. Departures from Edmonton on July 13 and July 27. *Baffin Island Tour*, offered by Thomas Cook Travel, 45 Berkley St., London, England WIA IEB or offices in U.S.A. or Canada, consists of one departure for a 25-day tour to Baffin Island, visiting Frobisher Bay, Pangnirtung, Auyuittuq National Park, and Pond Inlet. This is an extensive hiking and camping trip amid the spectacular mountains and fjords, with an opportunity to photograph the flora and fauna of the arctic. *Canadian Rockies and Northwest Territories Tour*, offered by Holtz Tours & Travel, 4018 Piedmont Ave., Oakland, CA 94611, is an 18-day motor-coach tour which includes southern British Columbia, Banff and Jasper national parks, northern Alberta, and the Great Slave Lake Region of the Northwest Territories, visiting Yellowknife, Hay River, Fort Providence, and return to Vancouver via the British Columbia interior. Holtz Tours also sponsors the *Arctic Explorer Tour*, consisting of one departure for a 17-day tour of the Great Slave Lake and Mackenzie River region of the Northwest Territories, Yukon Territory, and southeastern Alaska. Several modes of transportation are used on this trip. Departure date is July 11 for 19 passengers. The *Arctic Waters Tours*, sponsored by Arctic Divers Ltd., Box 2812, Yellowknife, is an expedition for qualified divers operating out of Bathurst Inlet Lodge during the month of August. A 7-day all-inclusive tour from Yellowknife to Bathurst Inlet Lodge includes use of tanks and weight belts. Divers must supply their own dry volume suit or wet suit. The *North of Sixty Tour*, operated by UTL Holiday Tours, 22 College St., Toronto, Ont. M5G 1Y7, consists of 13 days, 12 nights visiting Edmonton, Yellowknife, Inuvik, Tuktoyaktuk, Dawson City, Haines, Skagway, Whitehorse, and Vancouver. Travel is by air, rail, ferry, and private motor coach. Tour departs from Edmonton every Sunday from June 27 to August 8 inclusive. All departures are fully escorted with maximum group size of 28 persons. *Northwest Territories, Yukon, & Alberta Tour*, sponsored by Questers Tours and Travel, 257 Park Ave. S, New York, NY 10010, consists of 2 weeks to Edmonton, Whitehorse, Dawson City, Inuvik, Tuktoyaktuk, Yellowknife, Fort Smith, and Hay River. Includes a boat trip through the maze of lakes and tributaries of the Mackenzie River Delta, air charter visit to Tuktoyaktuk and Herschel Island, private motor-coach tour to Alexandra Falls, Wood Buffalo National Park, and the 150-year-old log cabin community of Fort Resolution, plus a cruise on Great Slave Lake. Departures on June 19, July 10, and August 14 from Edmonton. Pacific Western Airlines, Vancouver International Airport, Vancouver, British Columbia, sponsors wilderness river expeditions, fishing trips, and naturalist excursions in the Northwest Territories. The *South Nahanni River Expedition*, Pacific Western Airlines, is a 7-night trip to Nahanni National Park and Virginia Falls on the South Nahanni River. Six departures plus air fare to Fort Simpson. *Arctic Star Lodge* fishing trip on the north shore of Great Slave Lake, for arctic grayling, northern pike, and lake trout: 7 nights, Pacific Western Airlines, air fare to Yellowknife. Departures from June 26 to September 1. *Brabant Lodge* is located on an island where the mighty Mackenzie River flows

out of Great Slave Lake. Fishing for 2–7 nights, plus Pacific Western air fare to Hay River. Departures from June 15 to October 7. *Frontier Fishing Lodge* is located 115 miles east of Yellowknife at Great Slave Lake near the village of Snowdrift. Fishing for northerns, lake trout, and grayling. A 7-night trip, plus Pacific Western air fare to Yellowknife. Departs weekly from June 12 to September 18. *Bathurst Inlet Naturalist Lodge* is a small and exclusive naturalist's paradise north of the arctic circle that caters to bird-watchers, photographers, rockhounds, artists, and underwater enthusiasts. It offers spectacular scenery, a rare opportunity to observe arctic flora and fauna, and the traditions and customs of the Inuit Eskimos; 7 nights, plus Pacific Western air fare to Yellowknife. *Carcajou Mountains Naturalist Camp* is located at beautiful Porter Lake in the land of the midnight sun, about 12 miles from the Canol pipeline in the heart of the Carcajou (Wolverine) Mountains—a subrange of the Mackenzie Mountains. Activities include hiking and backpacking trips from base camp. Photography of Dall sheep, moose, barren-ground grizzlies, and birdlife: 6 nights plus Pacific Western air fare to Norman Wells. *Arctic Explorers,* sponsored by Consolidated Tours, Suite 480, 550 Sherbrooke St. W, Montreal, Que. H3A 1B9, consists of a wide variety of tours to Baffin Island and Greenland in the spring and summer. Tours are 7–15 days. Explore Baffin Island during spring breakup, view ancient Thule Eskimo campsites and visit Auyuittuq National Park, bird sanctuaries and high arctic settlements such as Pond Inlet, Pangnirtung, and Frobisher Bay. *Headless Valley Tour,* operated by Wilderness Expeditions, 9511 63d Ave., Edmonton, Alta., is by jet boat up the South Nahanni River to Virginia Falls and Nahanni National Park: 8-day trips from Fort Simpson; Pacific Western air fare to Fort Simpson; departures mid-June to September. (See "Travel & Recreation Guide" section for additional information on wilderness outfitters and facilities.)

Wilderness Travel & Exploration

The Royal Canadian Mounted Police, distinctive in their maroon parkas and blue breeches, operate a voluntary registration program to protect the traveler going into the Northwest Territories wilderness areas. Registration can mean the difference between life and death in an emergency, and is useful in relaying urgent messages. If you are planning to leave the highways for a canoe or boat trip, or a hiking or fishing journey, you are advised to register with the RCMP post nearest to your point of departure and to check in upon your return. You must obtain the proper hunting and fishing licenses before leaving your departure point. Travel permits from the Game Management Division, Yellowknife, are required before traveling through the Thelon Game Sanctuary.

Yellowknife—Outfitting Center for Great Slave Lake

(Pop. 9,100). This famous mining and outfitting center, located on the north arm of Great Slave Lake, was born in the late 1930s at the height of the greatest gold boom in the world's history. There were actually two Yellowknife gold booms, and there are separate towns to mark them. The old Yellowknife is a picturesque frontier town of frame shacks and log cabins located on the Precambrian cliffs overlooking the lake. The new Yellowknife is a modern town that marks the site of the second boom in 1945 with the opening of the Giant Yellowknife Mine. The town has been the capital of the Northwest Territories since 1967. The Yellowknife region was first explored by Samuel Hearne, the Marco Polo of the Canadian barrenlands, in 1771. Hearne was one of the world's great adventurers, who set out in 1769

at the age of 24, with his indispensable Indian guide Chief Matonabbee, to explore more than a quarter of a million square miles of the barrenlands. Today Yellowknife is the outfitting center for the world-famous lake trout and grayling waters of Great Slave Lake and the outlying wilderness areas. Fly-in charter service headquartered in Yellowknife is provided by *Aero Arctic Ltd.,* Box 1496: *Gateway Aviation Ltd.,* P.O. Box 880; *Koenen's Air Service Ltd.,* Box 233; *La Ronge Aviation Ltd.* (Mackenzie Air Ltd.), Box 2489, with additional bases in Hay River and in Edmonton, Alberta; *Latham Island Airways,* Box 791; *Ptarmigan Airways Ltd.,* P.O. Box 66; and *Wardair Canada Ltd.,* P.O. Box 610, X0E 1H0. Yellowknife is reached via Highway 2 of the Mackenzie Road System and via Northward, NWT Air, Pacific Western, Ptarmigan Airways, and Transair.

NORTHWEST TERRITORIES TRAVEL & RECREATION GUIDE

Baffin Island & the Arctic Highlands

Auyuittuq National Park

Canadian National Topographic Survey Maps, scale 1:250,000: Pangnirtung 26-I, Clearwater Fjord 26-J, Nedlukseak Fjord 26-O, Okoa Bay 26-P.

Northward, across the Ungava barrenlands of Quebec and the Hudson Strait, on Baffin Island in the remote land of the northern explorers, lies the upper portion of one of the world's great mountain ranges. The range sweeps in a great arc from the top of Ellesmere Island southward for 1,900 miles to form the bleak, snowcapped hornlike mountain peaks of northern Labrador—the foreboding Torngat Mountains, which derive their name from the Eskimo word for "sorcerer." Few people are aware that this great range of mountains exists. It does not even have a name.

On the southwestern portion of Baffin Island, the range includes the Everett Mountains of the Meta Incognita Peninsula and the unnamed ranges of the Hall Peninsula, separated from each other by Frobisher Bay—a 150-mile-long neck of the sea stretching inland and named in honor of Martin Frobisher, England's first sea lord, who believed that here he had discovered King Solomon's Mines. At Cumberland Peninsula the Icy Mountains arc northwesterly in a welter of 8,000-foot peaks, massive glaciers, and deep fjords, forming the eastern coast of Baffin Island. The great range continues its arc, gaining in breadth and height, soaring to 10,000-foot peaks at the Agassiz Ice Cap and British Empire Range on Ellesmere Island. North of Ellesmere, the range is swallowed up by the sea and continues as a submarine range, passing through the north pole, and then marches south until it emerges off the arctic coast of the Soviet Union as the New Siberian Islands.

Baffin Island is the fourth-largest island in the world, excluding Greenland, which lies due east. Once a submerged land mass when the weight of the Pleistocene glaciers forced it beneath the surface of the sea, the island emerged with the melting of the glaciers and is still emerging from its ocean slumber. Marine deposits are found 700 feet and more above sea level, and strange stone rings that mark the ancient dwellings of the extinct Eskimo culture known as the Thule are 20–30 feet higher than present-day Eskimo settlements along the coast. The natural phenomena of Baffin Island have been a mecca for a long procession of explorers since the days of Frobisher and his fellow Elizabethan seafarers. In Baffin's interior they discovered two great lakes in the drab swampy land near the Great Plain of the Koudjuak. One of these lakes, Nettilling, measures more than 100 miles across. Other discoveries include hot springs 3 acres in size; mountain peaks that soar into the clouds; and rivers of solid ice. Admiralty Inlet, the world's longest fjord, more than 240 miles long, is guarded by a sheer 1,000-foot wall known as the Giant's Castle, whose great ancient pillars, columns, caves, gateways, and giant caldrons have been carved and sculptured for aeons by fierce winds and waves; also worth mentioning are the Barnes Ice Cap, a massive remnant of the Pleistocene Age, which measures 90 miles long and 40 miles across and is a quarter of a mile thick; and, at Mary's River, one of the world's largest deposits of iron ore, of such richness that neither concentration nor "beneficiation" is required—it can be fed straight into a blast furnace.

The village of Pangnirtung, the gateway to the new Auyuittuq National Park (formerly known as Baffin Island National Park), lies in a valley surrounded by steeply rising mountains and is known as the Switzerland of the arctic. Pangnirtung is the terminus of one of the two main passes and the dogsled route through the Icy Mountains to the park. The village is located on the northwest shore of Cumberland

Island at the mouth of Pangnirtung Fjord. The settlement was established by the Hudson's Bay Company in the 1920s, and the local areas had been explored as early as 1585 and 1616 by John Davis and William Baffin. The Eskimos survive by fishing for arctic char in the great rivers and hunting the caribou, walrus, small ringed or jar seal *(Pusa hispida)* and large bearded or square-flipper seal *(Erignathus barbatus),* the latter reaching mature weights of up to 700 pounds. In the spring, Eskimo hunters travel by dogsled over ice that is still safe despite 14–18 hours a day of warm sunlight and temperatures above freezing. When a seal is spotted, by his breathing hole, the difficult stalk begins. Sealskins are used for clothing, boots, and boats; the meat, for food; and the fat, for lighting and heating fuel.

Auyuittuq National Park encompasses 8,290 square miles of spectacular fjords, deeply carved mountains, and the 7,000-foot glacier-studded Penny Highlands. Dominating the highlands is the Penny Ice Cap, which covers 2,200 square miles and is one of the largest ice caps in the northern hemisphere. The largest of the many long glaciers that extend from the cap is the 20-mile-long Coronation Glacier. The highlands are surrounded by a rolling hilly land littered by huge boulders and moraine. A free *Auyuittuq Map-Brochure* to the park and detailed trip planning information can be obtained from the Supervisor, Auyuittuq N.P., Pangnirtung X0A 0R0.

Package tours to Baffin Island are provided by *Consolidated Tours,* Suite 480, 550 Sherbrooke St. W., Montreal, Quebec H3A 1B9, (514) 849-1259 and *Horizon Holidays of Canada Ltd.,* 44 Victoria St., Toronto, Ontario M5C 1Y9, (416) 366-8985.

Access & Outfitting Centers

Several wilderness outfitters for exploration, photography, and some of the world's finest arctic char fishing are headquartered on Baffin Island. *Baffin Kamutauyait Outfitters* offers photo safaris, and backpacking from Frobisher Bay to Lake Harbor, for 8 persons, and summer boat cruises around Frobisher Bay; it also offers fishing trips for arctic char in the wild arctic rivers and fjords. Write: Box 575, Frobisher Bay

X0A 0H0. *Baffin Travel & Charter Service,* Box 711, Frobisher Bay X0A 0H0, offers sightseeing and wildlife tours. *Aqvik Ltd.,* Pangnirtung, Baffin Island X0A 0R0, offers transportation and guiding services and camping supplies for the backpacker and mountain climber. *Consolidated Tours* (address above), has arctic exploring, camping, and arctic char fishing expeditions each summer on the Pangnirtung and Cumberland Sound region of Baffin Island. Nordair provides scheduled air service to Frobisher Bay and Pangnirtung.

Great Bear Lake Region

Great Bear Lake Country Topo Maps

Canadian National Topographic Survey Maps, scale 1:250,000: Johnny Hoe River 96-A, Blackwater Lake 96-B, Grizzly Bear Mountain 96-H, Fort Franklin 96-G, Mahony Lake 96-F, Lac des Bois 96-K, Kilkale Lake 76-J, Cape MacDonnell 96-I, Takaatcho River 86-L, Sloan River 86-K, Calder River 86-F, Leith Peninsula 86-E.

Camsell River

Canadian National Topographic Survey Maps, scale 1:250,000: Marian River 85-N, Hardisty Lake 86-C, Rivière Grandin 86-D, Leith Peninsula 86-E, Calder River 86-F.

Tree River Trophy Arctic Char Waters

Canadian National Topographic Survey Maps, scale 1:250,000: Takiyuak Lake 86-I, Mara River 76-K, Arctic Sound 76-N.

Great Bear Lake, like its sister lakes Great Slave and Athabasca to the south, was gouged out of the hard granite of the Precambrian Shield millions of years ago by the huge Keewatin Ice Cap. Great Bear covers 12,000 square miles, or more than three times the area of Lake Ontario, and is located some 60 miles east as the crow flies from the Mackenzie River in the "land of the little sticks" surrounded by the barren, eroded crags of the Precambrian Shield. The lake is a world-

renowned sportfishing preserve (commercial fishing is prohibited) and annually produces lake trout up to world's record size. Fly-fishing with streamers and bucktails from boats along the stark, cliff-lined shores on the east and along the wooded hills of the western shores is usually quite effective for grayling and coasting lake trout. The arctic circle —the circle of Arktos, or the Great Bear—bisects the northern half of the lake, which is located just south of the northernmost limit of trees. Because of the lake's great depth and frigid waters, almost all fishing is done on the surface off the numerous islands and shoals in the five great arms of the lake: McTavish Arm in the east; McVicar and Keith arms in the south; and Dease and Smith arms in the north and west. Great Bear is an enormous biological desert whose dark blue waters are icebound until mid-July and are never more than a few degrees above freezing. The lake is so cold that no plankton live in its deepest waters and fish seldom leave the sun-warmed shallows along the shoreline. Great Bear Country is a rugged land of desolate, barren shores and islands, cold windy bays, deeply cut fjords, and high cliffs colored by red, white, pink, and green metallic oxides.

The renowned Camsell River, an ancient Indian trading and exploration route between Great Bear and Great Slave lakes, flows into Great Bear at its southernmost shore after a tortuous, winding journey from its headwaters at Sarah Lake north through a crazy-quilt chain of lakes formed by Faber, Rae, Hardisty, Hottah, Grouard, Clut, and Conjuror lakes. At the southwestern outlet of the lake, the Great Bear River races along its short, swift course to join the silt-colored Mackenzie River.

Several wilderness fishing outfitters and lodges are located on the shores of Great Bear and the surrounding lakes and rivers. *Great Bear Trophy Lodge* is located at Ford Bay of Smith Arm on the western side of the lake near the arctic circle. The lodge accommodates up to 40 people in 20 rooms with bath, twin beds, and electricity, including radiophone, boats, motors, and guides and a 4,800-foot airstrip. Write: Box 9000, Ponoka, Alta. *Great Bear Lodge* is located at Sawmill Bay with accommodations for 54 at the main lodge and outpost camps. A charter flight leaves for the lodge from Minneapolis every Saturday from June 5 to September 6. Side trips are offered for fishing the coastal rivers to the north for arctic char. Write: 707 E. 41st St., Sioux Falls, SD 57105. *Plummer's Great Bear Lake Lodge*, located on Dease Arm of the lake, is open July and August with accommodations for 54 in 16 cabins with showers. Facilities and services include boats, motors, fuel, guides, gear, cold storage, and dining room, and float-plane trips to the famous Tree River for arctic char. Write: 101 Airport Hotel, Winnipeg, Man. R3H 0B7. *Branson's Lodge*, located in scenic protected waters on the east side of Great Bear, 5 miles from Port Radium, has accommodations for 40 through July and August. Offers side trips for arctic char, grayling, and lake trout and visits to Eskimo villages and abandoned mines. Write: P.O. Box 130, Wanham, Alta. T0H 3P0. *Arctic Circle Lodge*, Box 503, Edmonton, Alta. T5J 2K1, is located on Great Bear, 14 miles south of the arctic circle. It has accommodations for 34, plus boats and motors. *Colville Lake Lodge* is located on the south end of Colville Lake, some 36 miles north of the arctic circle and Great Bear Lake. The main lodge, which accommodates 6, is located in the Hareskin Indian Village. The outpost camp farther north has 2 cabins, and boats and motors. Offers fishing for lake trout and grayling, canoeing, and camping. Write: Mr. Bern Will Brown, Colville Lake (via Fort Good Hope) X0E 0H0. *Kelly Lake Outfitting* offers fishing trips and naturalist tours of the Kelly and Brackett lakes area, Great Bear River, and the Mackenzie near Fort Norman. Trip length and destination are tailored to your plans. Write: Mr. Alfred Lennie, Tulita Tserequi Tours, Fort Norman X0E 0K0. *Drum Lake Lodge* is located on Wrigley Lake with accom-

modations for 6 near Fort Norman. Has a private 1,000-foot airstrip and fishing for lake trout, grayling, and arctic char. Write: Mr. Paul Wright, Fort Norman X0E 0K0.

Access & Outfitting Centers

Seaplane bases on Great Bear are located at outfitting and supply centers of Echo Bay, Sawmill Bay, and Fort Franklin, and at Fort Norman, Norman Wells, and Fort Good Hope on the Mackenzie River. Access is via scheduled airline service.

Great Slave Lake Region

Great Slave Lake Country Topo Maps

Canadian National Topographic Survey Maps, scale 1:250,000: Little Buffalo River 85-A, Buffalo Lake 85-B, Tathlina Lake 85-C, Mills Lake 85-E, Falaise Lake 85-F, Sulphur Bay 85-G, Fort Resolution 85-H, Taltson Lake 75-E, Snowdrift 75-L, Fort Reliance 75-K, Rae 85-K, Yellowknife 85-J, Hearne Lake 85-I, Marian River 85-N, Wecho River 85-O, Carp Lakes 85-P.

Wood Buffalo National Park

Canadian National Topographic Survey Maps, scale 1:250,000: Fort Chipewyan (Alta.) 74-L, Fitzgerald 74-M, Lake Claire 84-I, Whitesand River 84-O, Peace Point 84-P, Little Buffalo 85-A.

The famous trophy fishing waters of huge Great Slave Lake, which forms the headwaters of the Mackenzie River, are located due north of Wood Buffalo National Park and the Alberta border, some 550 miles north of Edmonton. The irregular-shaped shoreline of this great lake is formed by sheer cliffs and scattered spots of poplar and spruce. Great Slave, although fished commercially, is renowned for its populations of large lake trout, arctic grayling, northern pike and whitefish, and sheefish or inconnu. Sheefish are most often caught during spawning runs in tributary streams such as the Yellowknife, Hay, Little Buffalo, and Taltson rivers. The major fishing areas of Great Slave include the west shore near Big Island and Slave Point, North Arm, Caribou Island, Gros Cap and Preble, Blanchet and Ethen islands, and the 2,000-foot-deep, island-dotted waters of Christie and McLeod bays.

Several established trophy fishing outfitters and wilderness outpost camps are found scattered throughout the Great Slave Lake Region. *Trophy Lodge*, located at Fort Reliance, 160 miles east of Yellowknife on McLeod Bay, has accommodations in housekeeping cabins with showers and fully equipped kitchens, and boats, motors, gas, fish freezing, and tackle shop. The lodge offers fishing for lake trout, arctic grayling, and outings to Parry Falls south of Artillery Lake. Write to: Trophy Lodge, Box 670, Yellowknife X0E 1H0. *Taiga Sports Fishing Lodge* has new housekeeping cabins on Blatchford Lake east of Yellowknife. Write: Don Carlieux, Box 1288, Yellowknife X0E IH0. *Frontier Fishing Lodge*, located at the mouth of the Snowdrift River on the east arm of Great Slave Lake, has a 2,300-foot airstrip and accommodations for 24 in lodge and cabins. Facilities include dining room, sauna, walk-in freezing facilities, guides, motors, and boats. An Indian village is located nearby. Write: Jerry Bacher, Box 4495, Edmonton, Alta. T6E 4T7. *Great Slave Lake Lodge*, located 900 miles east of Yellowknife at Taltheibei Narrows, has a 5,200-foot airstrip and accommodations for 44. Offers meals, guides, boats, motors, gas, modern plumbing, two-way radio, dining room, and care of fish. Fishing for lake trout, grayling, northern pike, and fly-fishing in nearby lakes for walleye. Write: Chummy Plummer, Airliner Motor Hotel, Winnipeg, Man. R3H 0B7. *Snowshoe General Store*, at Fort Providence X0E 0L0 on the headwaters of the Mackenzie on the western shore

of Great Slave, specializes in arctic grayling, walleye, and great northerns. Offers charter fly-in services, boats, motors, and guides. *Indian Mountain Lodge,* located on Thompson Landing on the east arm of Great Slave, has accommodations for 10 persons in 5 cabins. Facilities include a float base, dining room, boats, motors, guides, radiophone, and fishing for lake trout and arctic grayling. Write: Bernie Spencer, Box 2793, Yellowknife X0E 1H0. *Prelude Lodge,* Box 4262, Yellowknife X0E 1H0, is located on Prelude Lake about 20 miles east of Yellowknife. The lodge has accommodations for 12 guests in 2- and 3-bed housekeeping cabins. Includes ice, tackle shop, licensed dining lodge, and hikes to falls on nearby Cameron River. *Pilot Lake Cabins* are reached by charter aircraft to Pilot Lake about 35 miles from Fort Smith. Boats, motors, and guide service available. Write: Pilot Lake Cabins, Box 52, Fort Smith. *Rutledge Lake Lodge,* with a modern, fully equipped cabin is located 170 miles east of Hay River, south of the east arm of Great Slave Lake. Services include boats, motors, life jackets, sleeping bags. Write: Rutledge Lake Lodge, Box 342, Hay River X0E 0R0. *Nonacho Lake Camp* is located on the Taltson River, 200 miles east of Hay River due south of the east arm of Great Slave Lake. Offers cabin accommodations and fishing for lake trout and northern pike. Write: Merlyn Carter, Carter Air Service Ltd., Box 510, Hay River X0E 1G0. *Lady Grey Lake Outfitters,* Box 364, Fort Smith X0E 0P0 has lodgings 70 miles northeast of Fort Smith on the Taltson River lakes chain. Facilities and services include guides, cabins, boats, motors. Accommodates 6, guests supply own food. Winter season, January 1–March 15, offers dog-team trips along a working trapline. *Hearne Lake Lodge,* Box 271, Yellowknife X0E 1H0, located on Hearne Lake, 42 miles from Yellowknife, offers cabin accommodations for 6. *Hanging Ice Fishing Lodge,* Box 415, Fort Smith X0E 0P0, is located northeast of Fort Smith. New lodgings and fishing for lake trout, walleye, and northern pike. *Dogface Lake Fishing Lodge,* Box 1480, Hay River, has fly-in cabins on an island in Dogface Lake north of the Alberta border and Cameron Hills. Room for 10 guests in comfortable log cabins. *Adventure North Ltd.,* 108 Lower Eastgate Mall, Sherwood Park, Alta., operates fishing camps on Harding Lake, 32 miles east of Yellowknife. Facilities include cook, licensed lounge, baths, and showers. *Beaulieu River Camps,* located on Consolidation Lake 42 miles east of Yellowknife, have accommodations for 6 and fishing for lake trout, arctic grayling, and northern pike. Write: Box 880, Yellowknife X1E 1H0.

Great Slave Lake charter boat service is offered by *Great Slave Cruises,* Box 1400, Yellowknife, featuring two 36-foot cabin cruisers for luxury voyages anywhere on the lake. Meals and sleeping accommodations on board for overnight trips. Cruises of Yellowknife Bay and and islands with special stops for fishing and photography. *N.W.T. Wilderness Cruise Lines,* Box 2547, Yellowknife X0E 1H0, operates trips on Great Slave Lake and the Mackenzie River, including photographic and naturalist tours of the East Arm via freighter canoes and small boats; accommodations in tents. *North Cruises,* Box 2794, Yellowknife X0E 1H0, offers boat cruises on Great Slave, with stops for bird-watching, rock hunting, and fishing. Seaplane bases on Great Slave are located at Hay River, Rae, Yellowknife, Reliance, and Fort Resolution.

Wood Buffalo National Park encompasses 17,300 square miles of wilderness straddling the Northwest Territories and the Alberta border, due south of Great Slave Lake. Two-thirds of its area is in Alberta. The park was established in 1922 to protect Canada's only remaining herd of wood bison. When the killing of wood bison was prohibited in 1893 it was estimated that fewer than 500 remained, all in the region now encompassed by the park. By 1922 their numbers had grown to an estimated 1,500. Wood bison *(Bison bison athabascae)* are slightly larger, darker, northern relatives of the plains buffalo.

Shortly after the establishment of the park more than 6,000 plains bison were moved from southern Alberta to the park. The two species interbred and grew to 10,000–12,000 in number. Other wildlife in the park are moose, woodland caribou and beaver, muskrat, and black bear. Barren-ground caribou once traversed the region in large numbers during the southward winter migration, but in recent years they have passed 50 miles northeast of the park.

Wood Buffalo
National Park

Alberta & N.W. Territories

A free *Wood Buffalo National Park Map-Brochure* showing roads, trails, lakes, rivers, patrol cabins, campgrounds, and fire towers is available free from the park headquarters at Fort Smith X0E 0P0. Geographically, the park lies on the eastern interior plains and has several topographic regions. The Birch Mountains in the southwest and the Caribou Mountains in the west are round-to-oval erosion plateaus, rising abruptly from almost flat plains to heights of 2,500–3,200 feet. The plateaus have numerous swift streams, which have cut deep, rugged gullies. The major area of the park is the large, almost flat, glacial outwash plain known as the Alberta Plateau. It is a dismal area of meandering streams, shallow lakes and bogs, sand dunes, and eskers deposited by the retreating glaciers. The park contains hundreds of huge collapsed areas or sinkholes, some 120 feet across and 80 feet deep. Pine Lake, which is 3 miles long and 70 feet deep, was formed by several huge sinkholes. East of the Alberta Plateau are the vast salt plains of the Salt River area, a century-old source of salt for Indians, explorers, and fur traders. The mighty Peace River meanders through the park past several abandoned Hudson's Bay Company posts to its confluence with the Slave River, due north of Fort Chipewyan on the western shore of huge Lake Athabasca. The Peace occupies a wide, flat valley with very little drop along its course, which causes the river to meander and change its course from time to time. Davidson's Lake and Big Slough are remnants of old river courses. Just above Fort Smith, the Slave River marks the boundary between the old, eroded formations of the Precambrian Shield and the younger sedimentary rocks of the Great Central Plains. The great Peace-Athabasca Delta, the staging ground for North America's four major waterfowl flyways, lies in the Kazan Uplands and the Athabasca Plains of the Canadian Shield and the Great Slave Plain.

The Athabasca, Peace, and Slave rivers, leading to Great Slave Lake and the Mackenzie, served for centuries as the water highway to the north. Alexander Mackenzie traveled down the Slave River in 1789 on his trip to the Arctic Ocean, up the Mackenzie, which he called the "River of Disappointment," and up the Peace River on his way to the Pacific in search of the Northwest Passage a few years earlier. Simon Fraser also traveled up the Peace; he visited the original Fort Chipewyan, built in 1788. Charles Camsell, during his extensive travels in the area, made the first recorded canoe voyage through the park from Great Slave Lake to the Peace River.

The Alberta record 12-pound brook trout was caught in Pine Lake. Great northern pike and walleye are found in many of the shallow lakes and sluggish streams, along with goldeye, whitefish, and sheefish.

Customized fishing trips to Wood Buffalo National Park and area lodges are provided by *Ferguson Travel*, Box 1990, Hay River X0E 0R0, (403) 874-6878 or Box 44, Fort Smith, (403) 872-2645.

Access & Outfitting Centers

Great Slave Lake country is reached via the Mackenzie Highway System from Alberta and by scheduled air service to the outfitting and supply centers of Yellowknife, Fort Smith, Hay River, Fort Resolution, Fort Providence, and Fort Chipewyan. Wood Buffalo N.P. can also be reached by boat on the Peace and Athabasca rivers, but should not be attempted except in seaworthy boats with experienced guides.

Keewatin Barrenlands

Back River Country

Canadian National Topographic Survey Maps, scale 1:250,000: Nose Lake 76-F, Aylmer Lake 76-C, Healy Lake 76-B, Beechey Lake 76-G, Duggan Lake 76-H, Jervoise River 66-E, Pelly Lake 66-F, Deep Rose Lake 66-G, Amer Lake 66-H, Montresor River 66-I, Mistako River 56-L, Lower Hayes River 56-M.

Dubawnt River Country

Canadian National Topographic Survey Maps, scale 1:250,000: Wholdaia Lake 75-A, Snowbird Lake 65-D, Boyd Lake 65-E, Carey Lake 65-L, Kamilukuak Lake 65-K, Dubawnt Lake 65-N, Tebesjuak Lake 65-O, Aberdeen Lake 66-B.

Hanbury-Thelon River Country

Canadian National Topographic Survey Maps, scale 1:250,000: Artillery Lake 75-O, Hanbury 75-P, Healy Lake 76-B, Lynx Lake 75-J, Beaverhill Lake 75-I, Clarke River 65-M, Tammarvi River 66-D, Beverly Lake 66-C, Aberdeen Lake 66-B, Schutz Lake 66-A, Baker Lake 56-D, MacQuoid Lake 55-M, Gibson Lake 55-N, Chesterfield Inlet 55-O.

Kazan River Country

Canadian National Topographic Survey Maps, scale 1:250,000: Ennadai Lake 65-C, Ennadai 65-F, Kamilukuak Lake 65-K, Tulemalu Lake 65-J, Ferguson Lake 65-I, Thirty Mile Lake 65-P, MacQuoid Lake 55-M.

The ancient barrenlands of the Keewatin District form the geographic center of Canada, encompassing the entire northeast portion of the mainland Northwest Territories. Keewatin country is one of the last remaining great wilderness fishing, hunting, and canoeing regions left in North America. One million years ago the region was covered by the great Keewatin Ice Cap. The ice cap reached depths of 12,000 feet and radiated north beyond the arctic circle, grinding west to the

Rockies and south to the Missouri and Mississippi. When the ice cap eventually melted it left a topsy-turvy barrenland here of thousands on thousands of irregular-shaped lakes, great twisting rivers, and rolling tundra plains that have long beckoned and haunted explorers and adventurers.

The major topographic and recreation features of the Keewatin include the great coastal arctic char rivers and polar bear hunting grounds, and, inland, the caribou hunting grounds and exploration and canoe routes of the wild Back, Hanbury, Thelon, Dubawnt, and Kazan rivers. In 1893 the great 19th-century Canadian explorers J. B. and J. W. Tyrell set out to investigate the unknown barrenlands of Keewatin. They journeyed by snowshoe, canoe, and moccasin to the southern headwaters of the unknown Dubawnt River and lakes chain and in a tortuous voyage of 3,500 miles explored it north, then east, to Baker Lake. The following year, Joseph Tyrell paralleled the Dubawnt route farther to the east, canoeing down the unexplored Kazan River. Then, 6 years later, his brother James left Great Slave Lake and explored the oasis of the Thelon River valley east to Baker Lake.

Today, during the summer months, the population of Baker Lake is swollen by an assortment of weary canoeists who have completed exhausting trips down the Hanbury, Thelon, and Dubawnt rivers. Canoe trips on the great barren-ground rivers should be carefully planned and attempted only by the experienced wilderness paddler. This is not tenderfoot country. Canoe trips here can quickly turn into a nightmare with blinding hordes of mosquitoes and black flies, icy water, backbreaking scouting, lining, and portaging, and a proximity to the magnetic pole that plays havoc with compass readings. The rewards are equal, however, to the possible hazards. During the warm summer months the barren-ground canoeists will travel through thick carpets of caribou moss, brilliant arctic wildflowers, white heather, and red and yellow lichens and may see herds of caribou, arctic moles, musk-ox, barren-ground wolves, ground squirrels, snowy owl, and soaring rough-legged hawks and peregrine falcon. Arctic char are found in the coastal rivers and large lake trout, grayling, whitefish, and northern pike are found in the secluded lakes in scenic areas below the treeline and out on the vast barrenlands.

Wilderness fishing outfitters and outpost camps are scattered throughout Keewatin District. *Kasba Lake Lodge* is located at Kasba Lake—the headwaters of the Kazan River system—265 miles northwest of Lynn Lake, Manitoba. The lodge has accommodations for 12 in tents. All meals are served in a main dining room. The camp is located below the treeline in a heavily forested, picturesque setting with fishing for lake trout, arctic grayling, and northern pike. Write: D. E. Hill, Box 96, Parksville, B.C. V0R 2S0. *Snowbird Lake Lodge*, located at Snowbird Lake in caribou country, 273 miles north of Lynn Lake, Manitoba, offers cabin accommodations with dining room and licensed lounge, guides, boats, and motors. Access is via floatplane from Lynn Lake. Write: Snowbird Lake Lodge, 2717 Highland Dr., Burnsville, MN 55337. *Smalltree Lake Camp* has accommodations for 6 on a sheltered narrow point of land which juts into island-dotted Smalltree Lake, and has fishing for lake trout, northern pike, and grayling. *Mosquito Lake Lodge* is located in the heart of the barrenlands, near Dubawnt Lake. Includes boats, motors, guides, sleeping bags, and transportation by twin-engine Beechcraft. Accommodations for 12 in 3 cabins with central dining facilities. Write: Northwestern Flying Services, Ltd., Box 6, Nestor Falls, Ont. Other Keewatin sporting camps include the *Chantrey Inlet Camp* (Rainy Lake Airways, Box 79, Fort Francis, Ontario) at the mouth of the Back River; *Dubawnt Lake Outpost Camp* (Keewatin Arctic Camp Co., 931 Centennial St., Winnipeg, Manitoba R3N 1R6), accommodating six in tent camps; and *Nueltin Narrows Sub Arctic Camp* (P.O. Box 1821, The Pas,

Manitoba R9A 1L5) at the outlet of sprawling Nueltin Lake for trophy lake trout, grayling, and northern pike. Fly-in canoe-fishing trips on the wild Dubawnt River are provided by Northwestern Flying Services Ltd., Box 6, Nestor Falls, Ontario.

Access & Outfitting Centers

Transair flights from Winnipeg and Churchill, Manitoba, are the main access route to the barrenlands of Keewatin. Sanikiluaq on the Belcher Islands, the eastern side of Hudson Bay, is serviced via Great Whale River, Quebec. There are three Nordair flights weekly to Great Whale from Montreal, with charter service to the Belcher Islands. Air charter fly-in service in the Keewatin District is offered by Lambair and Transair out of Churchill and Keewatin Air bases in Rankin Inlet. The major Keewatin outfitting and supply centers are Baker Lake, Repulse Bay, Coral Harbor on Southampton Island, Chesterfield Inlet, Rankin Inlet, Whale Cove, and Eskimo Point.

Nahanni
National Park

Northwest Territories

Nahanni National Park & Wild River

Nahanni National Park and South Nahanni River Topo Maps

Canadian National Topographic Survey Maps, scale 1:250,000: Nahanni 105-I, Flat River 95-E, Virginia Falls 95-F, Sibbeston Lake 95-G, Glacier Lake 95-L.

The Nahanni country—a haunting Indian name meaning "people over there, far away"—with its weird limestone pinnacles, fantastic cliffs, sunless valleys, and raging rapids and canyons, has given birth over the years to dark legends of lost gold mines, tropical hot spring valleys and semihuman monsters who roam the dark valleys and canyon floors. The legends began early in the present century when two half-Indian brothers named McLeod vanished, seeking placer gold in the limestone crags of the Canyon Ranges surrounding the wild South Nahanni River in the southwest corner of the Northwest Territories. The discovery, several years later, of their headless skeletons gave birth to the legend of Headless Valley and subsequent rumors of prehistoric animals; there were also several real murders and mysterious deaths. Before the arrival of the prospectors and white explorers the inhabitants of the region were the Slavey tribe of the Athabascan Indians. The Slaveys lived a nomadic existence in the Nahanni country until the early 19th century, when the Northwest Company and later the

Hudson's Bay Company set up fur trading posts along the Liard and Mackenzie rivers.

Nahanni National Park encompasses 1,840 square miles dominated by the limestone peaks of the Canyon Ranges and the 200-mile-long, wild South Nahanni River, which rises below peaks 9,000 feet high and rages southeastward to the Liard, roaring over Virginia Falls in a drop of 294 feet. The river flows through a land whose topography varies from towering mountains and deep gorges to wide flat valleys. In the headwaters area the river flows by 8,000–9,000-foot ice-capped peaks of the Ragged Range and Rabbitkettle Hot Springs, an outstanding mineral spring deposit located a short walk from the right shore. Between Rabbitkettle and Virginia Falls the river meanders through a 1-mile-wide floodplain of spruce forest and tamarack bogs. From the 294-foot-high Virginia Falls the river flows through Hell's Gate, also referred to as the Figure of Eight Rapids, the Gate, and Deadman's Valley, and three 5,000-foot-high steep-walled canyons. Numerous limestone caves and colorful sedimentary rock formations are found in all the canyons. The Kraus Homestead, located at the mouth of the First Canyon, is used as a summer base for the national park staff and marks the site of a hot spring. Below the canyon runs, the river flows through rolling terrain and a wide, marshy floodplain to its junction with the Liard River at the Slavey Indian settlement of Nahanni Butte.

The South Nahanni should be attempted only by experienced wilderness paddlers. Campsites are located on many sandbars and islands along the river. Occasionally snowmelt or rain will raise water levels by a foot or more overnight. Try to plan daily travel to avoid camping in the canyons, and remember to cache food supplies out of reach of bears. Driftwood for campfires is abundant along most stretches of the river. Drinking water may be obtained from the cool, clear feeder streams or from the South Nahanni, which although silty is potable. The upper valley is plagued by frequent upstream winds in the late afternoon and stiff downstream breezes in the evening. Fishing in the river is generally poor. Allow 9–15 days for the trip plus days for rest or exploration side trips to the outlying areas such as the limestone caves in the canyon areas. Another 3–5 days should be scheduled to travel down the Liard to Fort Simpson on the Mackenzie River.

Access & Outfitting Centers

The headwaters of the South Nahanni are reached by air, either by floatplane or helicopter from Fort Simpson, or Watson Lake in the Yukon Territory. Several outfitters provide services into the roadless wilderness of the park. *Deadman's Valley Outfitters* offer boat trips up the South Nahanni to Virginia Falls. The trip takes 6 days; all gear is supplied except sleeping bags and clothing. Operates from May 20 to June 1 and from June 15 to September 1. Write: Rod Norwegian, Box 152, Fort Norman X0E 0K0. *South Nahanni River Ltd.*, Box 426, Fort Nelson, B.C. V0C 1RO, has river trips via jet-powered boats through the Headless Valley to Virginia Falls, as does *Francis Bitsaka* of Nahanni Butte, via Fort Simpson. A *Nahanni National Park Map-Brochure* is available free from the Supervisor, Nahanni National Park, Fort Simpson.

WESTERN CANADA

Introduction

Canada's western provinces, British Columbia and Alberta, form one of the world's great fishing, hunting, canoeing, and wilderness camping regions. This area is famous for majestic, towering snow-capped mountain ranges, vast boreal and coastal rain forests, tundra, wild river valleys, and thousands of remote blue lakes and turbulent streams. British Columbia, the westernmost and third largest of Canada's provinces, covers 366,255 square miles of dramatic relief. Here are the world-renowned salmon, trout, and trophy steelhead waters of Vancouver Island and the mist-shrouded Queen Charlotte Islands. The fabled Kispiox, Dean, and Babine Rivers cut through deep mountain valleys on their journeys to the Pacific through the Coastal Mountains and dense rain forests. The western hemlock and Sitka spruce are scattered with stands of mountain hemlock, red elder, black cottonwood and alder, with thick understories of dwarf blueberries, red huckleberry, copperbush, salal, salmonberry, and the treacherous devil's club. The province's vast interior plateau shelters hundreds of deep blue lakes including Babine, Chilko, Morice, François, Stuart, and Tatla Lakes, inhabited by giant lake trout, rainbow and Dolly Varden trout. The interior plateau is hemmed on the east by the legendary big-game hunting ranges and wilderness camping areas of the Northern Rocky Mountains, with their beautiful alpine lakes and meadows, great rock walls, and glacier-studded 10,000-foot spires.

The Northern Rockies march down the entire easternmost side of the province, forming the central and southern British Columbia-Alberta boundary. The Rocky Mountain Trench forms a narrow valley that extends up from Flathead Lake in Montana for 1,000 miles through British Columbia to the Yukon. Flat-bottomed in some places, rolling in others, with steep box-like sides, the Rocky Mountain Trench embraces the headwaters of the mighty Liard, Peace, Columbia and Fraser Rivers. The great boreal forests, wild rivers, and lakes of the Interior Plateau, which embraces the Fraser Plateau in the south and the remote Nechako Plateau in the central region, lies between the Rocky Mountain Trench on the east and the snow-capped Coast Range on the west. The famous big-game ranges of the Skeena Mountains lie to the northwest of the Nechako Plateau, the Ominecas to the northeast. These ranges flatten out into the volcano-studded Stikine Plateau in the far northwest portion of the province. Beyond the fabled rain forests and steelhead streams of the Coast Range lie the rocky beaches of the Pacific Ocean, with its mild Japan Current and countless islands, bays, spits, and inlets of the labyrinthine archipelago known as the "Inside Passage."

Alberta contains 255,285 square miles and the greatest variety of topography of any of Canada's provinces. Like its western neighbor, Alberta offers some of the finest fishing, hunting, backpacking, and wilderness canoeing areas in North America. The Rocky Mountain-Great Divide high country is an awesome beauty with its alpine meadows, headwater lakes, turbulent mountain streams, massive glaciers, ice fields, and deep valleys protected within the boundaries of Waterton Lakes, Banff, and Jasper national parks and the Willmore Wilderness. The big-game hunting and wilderness camping areas and trophy rainbow trout waters of the foothills region in the Rocky Mountain Forest Reserve are located due east of the Continental Divide. The mixed hardwood and conifer forests, ridges, and broad valleys are formed by the Old Man, Red Deer, Battle, and North Saskatchewan Rivers in the Central Parklands. There are vast stretches of muskeg, boreal forests, moose pasture, rolling hills and lakes of the north country, drained by the historic fur-trade and exploration routes of the Athabaska and Peace Rivers. The deep, cold trophy lake trout, walleye, and northern pike lakes of the Canadian Shield country

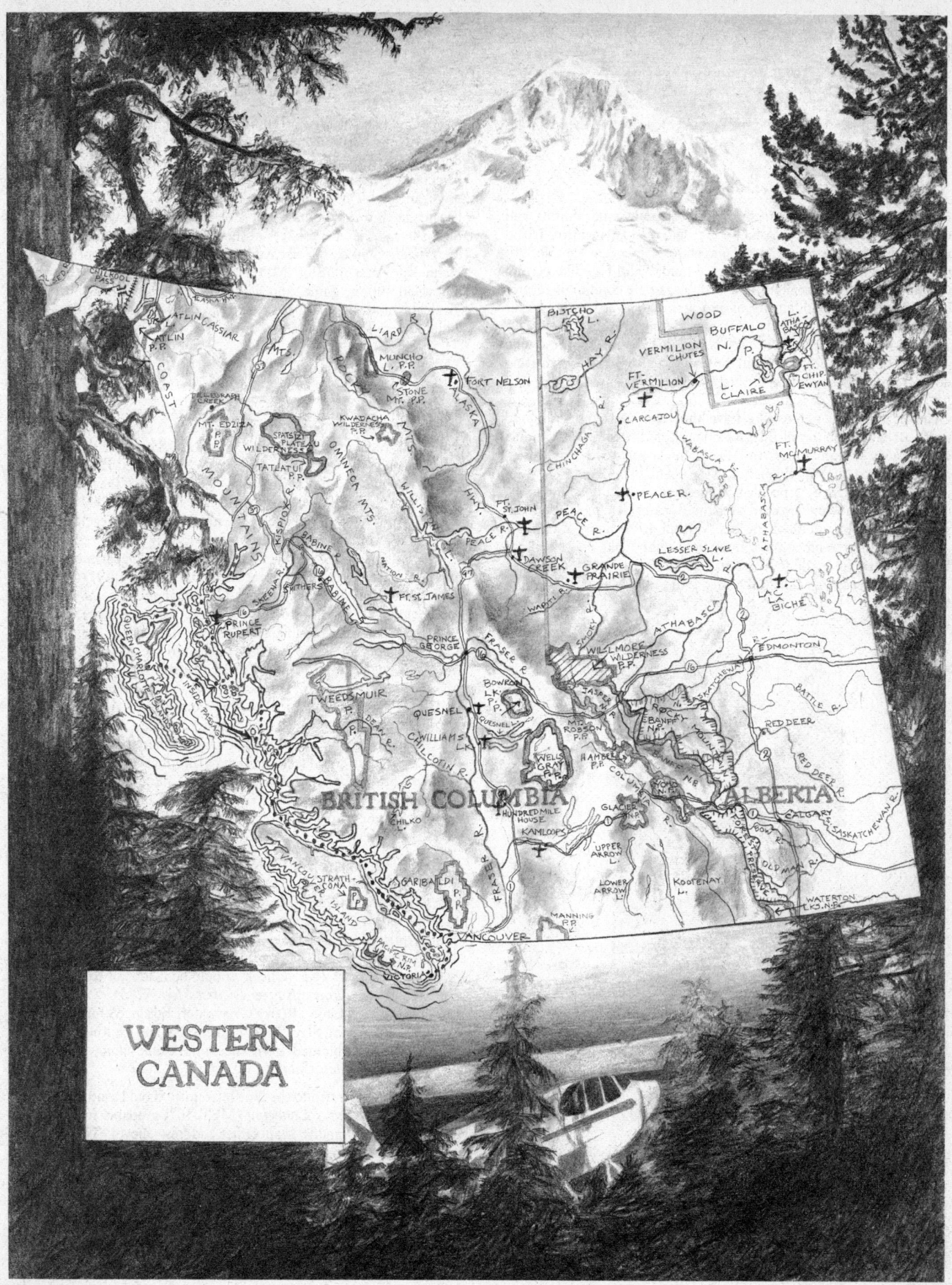

WESTERN CANADA

are in the northeast, and the broad prairie steps of the Cypress Hills country, in the southeast.

Weather, Bugs & Beasts

British Columbia's weather consists of generally mild winters and warm fall days along the Coastal Forest regions and Vancouver Island warmed by the Japan Current. Temperatures range in the 50s–70s during the summer months with heavy rainfall and fog. The central interior and northern regions have unstable, severe conditions regardless of the season. Sudden storms and periods of wet weather occur frequently in the high country areas. Summer nighttime temperatures are cool, dropping into the low 40s and to freezing in the alpine valleys. The first light snowfalls in the Canadian Rockies begin drifting down from the peaks during the first two weeks of September. Beautiful Indian summer days are the rule during late September and early October. Ice does not usually leave the lakes of the interior and northern canoe country of British Columbia and Alberta until middle to late May. Summer days in Alberta, nicknamed the "sunshine" province, are warm but seldom hot, with cool nights. Alberta's weather is strongly affected by a peculiar feature known as the "chinook"— a warm wind blowing eastward over the Rockies that replaces colder southward-moving arctic air masses. Within a few hours, a chinook can raise winter temperatures from unbearably cold to well above freezing. A useful guide to Western Canada's weather, cloud formations, and forecasting, called *Weather Ways*, is available for $2 from the Canadian Hydrographic Service, Department of the Environment, Ottawa, Ontario K1A 0E8.

If you are planning a summer fishing, camping, backpacking, or wilderness canoeing trip to one of the two western provinces, be sure to take a good supply of Muskol, Mosquitone, Off!, or Cutters insect repellent. (All contain a 50 percent plus DEET content.) Also bring a wide-brimmed hat, light-colored cotton shirt with long sleeves, a head net, and a pair of good quality sun glasses to cut water glare. If you are planning an extended trip into the interior wilderness areas,

a recommended dosage of 50mg/day of Vitamin B-1 for the week prior to your exposure to insects and about 10 mg a day each day during your trip will build up an excellent natural defence against blackflies, mosquitoes, chiggers, and no-see-ums. (Check with your physican for his recommended dosage and advice.) Other potential hazards in British Columbia and Alberta include grizzlies, black bears, moose in rut, and rattlesnakes in the southernmost areas of the Rockies. *Grizzly Country* ($7.95, available from Alfred A. Knopf, Inc., 400 Hahn Rd., Westminster, MD 21157) by Andy Russell, the world-renowned author, guide, and wildlife photographer, will provide an invaluable and spellbinding guide to grizzly behavior and the British Columbia and Alberta high country.

Western Canada Maps & Charts—How to Order

The remote fish and game regions, wild rivers, mountain ranges, and wilderness reserves of Western Canada are shown on the full-color Canadian National Topographic Survey Maps listed throughout the British Columbia and Alberta "Encyclopedia" and "Travel & Recreation Guide" sections. The maps, with a scale of 1:250,000 (1 inch to 4 miles) or 1:50,000 (1¼ inch to 1 mile), cost $1.50 each, plus 50¢ service and handling charge per order, and may be ordered from the Canada Map Office, Surveys Mapping Branch, Department of Energy, Mines, & Resources, Ottawa, Ontario K1A 0E9, (613) 994-9663. Free *Map Indexes of British Columbia and Alberta* and a free *Map Symbol Chart* may be obtained from the same address. Be sure to make all checks payable to: Receiver General of Canada. The Canada Map Office also publishes a handy 362-page *Catalogue of Published Maps* ($3.50) which lists all available topographic, national park, and specialty maps. The 4-color *British Columbia Province Map* (MCR 3, $1.50, size: 31×42 inches) and 8-color *Alberta Province Map* (MCR 83, $4, size: 42×68 inches, 2 sheets) are available from the Canada Map Office. Catalogs of nautical charts—*Southern British Columbia Coast & Vancouver Island* (Information Bulletin 13) and *Northern British Columbia Coast & Queen Charlotte Island* (Information Bulletin 14)—are available free from the Canadian Hydrographic Service, Marine Sciences, Directorate, Room 512, Federal Bldg., Victoria, B.C. V8W 1Y4.

Useful topographic maps of Alberta's *Rocky/Clearwater Provincial Forest* (Clearwater sheet, 36×43 inches) and *Bow/Crow Provincial Forest* (Crowsnest sheet, 21×32 inches) showing contours, ranger stations, forestry cabins, access roads, trails, towns, and logging roads may be ordered for $1.50 each from the Director, Technical Division, Alberta Energy & Natural Resources, Natural Resources Bldg., Edmonton, Alta. T5H 2E1. (Checks should be made out to the Provincial Treasurer.) A *Forest Ranger District Map* ($2, 31½×52 inches) showing the Bow-Crow, Rocky-Clearwater, Edson, Whitecourt, Lac La Biche, Athabasca, Slave Lake, Peace River, and Footner Provincial Forests may be obtained from the same source along with a free 27-page *Alberta Map Catalog*.

Anyone planning a trip to the North Country should send for *Canada Maps and Wilderness Canoeing* (MCR-107) available free upon request from the Canada Map Office (address above). This valuable publication contains a text written by Eric Morse—among the intrepid pioneers of recreational canoeing in Canada's Far North. Subjects discussed include planning your trip, making a trip profile, making a schedule, map symbols, barren land maps, navigating in the far north, use of maps, types of map scales, how to order aerial photographs, and use of compass on a canoe trip. This full-color illustrated guide contains a "Canada 1:250,000 Scale Map Index."

Vacation Travel Maps, Information & CB Radio Permits

An attractive full-color *Vacation Planning—Topographic Highway Map of Western Canada*, showing all man-made and natural features, may be obtained free upon request from the Canadian Government Office of Tourism, 150 Kent St., Ottawa, Ontario K1A 0H6, along with two free booklets, *Canada Ferries, Bridges & Cruises* and the 36-page *Canada Travel Information Handbook*—an indispensible guide to everything you need to know about airport services, customs regulations, insurance, fishing and hunting regulations, and weather, with temperature and time-zone charts. Canadian license applications for free citizen-band radio permits may be obtained from the Regional Superintendent, Telecommunications Branch, Department of Communications at the following addresses: Financial Bldg., 10621 100th Ave., Edmonton, Alta. T5J 0B1 and Granville St., Vancouver 2 B.C.

For information on Canadian train vacations, routes, rates, itineraries, hotels, and package tours, write: *VIA Rail Canada*, P.O. Box 8117, Montreal, Quebec H3C 3N3 or contact your local travel agent. VIA Rail Canada manages Canadian National and Canadian Pacific passenger train services.

BRITISH COLUMBIA ENCYCLOPEDIA

Accommodations—Vacation Lodges & Sporting Camps

A complete listing of accommodations, including motels, auto courts, year-round resorts, lodges, dude ranches, beach cottages, bungalows, cabins, trailer parks, and hunting and fishing camps is contained in the *British Columbia Tourist Directory,* available free on request from the Department of Travel Industry, 1117 Wharf St., Victoria V8W 1T7. The descriptions include rates, units, reservations, service, and facilities. A 110-page directory of *Canadian Indian Tourist Outfitting & Outdoor Recreation Facilities* is available free from the Information Office, Department of Indian & Northern Affairs, Centennial Tower, 400 Laurier W, Ottawa, Ont. This booklet contains a complete listing of Indian-operated fishing and hunting lodges, campgrounds, and facilities in British Columbia and describes type of establishment, location, services and facilities available, and fishing, hunting, and area attractions. Lodges and resorts for the important fishing, hunting, and wilderness vacation areas are listed in the "Travel & Recreation Guide" section.

Airlines & Charter Fly-in Services

British Columbia is served by major international and domestic airlines with scheduled flights daily to Vancouver International Airport. Several airlines provide scheduled and charter fly-in service to the remote wilderness lodges and outpost fishing and big-game hunting camps. A complete *Listing of Charter Aircraft Services* may be obtained by writing: Fish and Wildlife Branch, 1019 Wharf St., Victoria. Scheduled and air charter service within the province is provided by *Island Airlines Ltd.,* P.O. Box 1510, Campbell River, with flights throughout the province; *Alert Bay Air Services Ltd.,* P.O. Box 317, Campbell River V9W 5B1, has service from Port Hardy; *Trans-Mountain Air Services Ltd.,* P.O. Box 1451, Campbell River V9W 5C7, has service between Campbell River and province points and between Qualicum Beach, Vancouver, and Port Alberni; *Trans-Provincial Airlines Ltd.,* P.O. Box 310, Terrace V8G 4B3, has flights between Prince Rupert and British Columbia coastal points and Ketchikan, Alaska; *Pacific Western Airlines,* Vancouver International Airport, Central V7B 1V2, has service from Vancouver to Victoria, Seattle, Calgary, Kamloops, Grand Forks, Kelowna, Penticton, Prince George, Campbell River, Comox, Powell River, Sandspit, Cranbrook, and Castlegar; *Northern Thunderbird Air Ltd.,* Box 1510, Prince George, has charter and scheduled service from Prince George, Fort St. James, and Mackenzie to Lee Creek, Lovell Cove, Bulkley House, Bear Lake, Mosque River, Chipmunk, Mesilinka, Factor, Ross, Ingenika, Johanson Lake, Moose Valley, and Germansen Landing; *Tyee Airways Ltd.,* Porpoise Bay Rd., P.O. Box 640, Sechelt V0N 3A0, has scheduled service from Vancouver and Nanaimo to Pender Harbor, Nelson Island, Jervis Inlet, and charter and scenic tours; *Cougar Air Inc.,* P.O. Box 2385, Sidney V8L 3Y3, offers bush-style float-plane charter service for the British Columbia coast and Vancouver Island; *CP Air,* 1004 W. Georgia St., Vancouver V6E 2Y2, has scheduled flights from Vancouver to Prince George, Fort St. John, Dawson Creek, Fort Nelson, Watson Lake, and Whitehorse; *Harrison Airways Ltd.,* Vancouver International Airport, Vancouver, has scheduled flights to Vanderhoof, Fort St. James, Burns Lake, Smithers, Burrage, Shaft, Dease Lake, and Atlin; *Airwest Airlines Ltd.,* 468 Cowley Crescent, Vancouver International Airport S, Vancouver V7B 1C1, has float and land charters from Nanaimo and Powell River and scheduled flights to Victoria Harbor, Duncan, Texada Island, and Nanaimo Harbor; *Air Canada,* 905 W. Georgia St., Vancouver V6E 2K4, has daily service from Vancouver to Victoria; *North Coast Air*

Services Ltd., P.O. Box 610, Prince Rupert, charter service to Port Simpson and the Queen Charlotte Islands; *Arrow Aviation*, P.O. Box 235, International Airport, Abbotsford V2S 4N9, has service between Revelstoke and wilderness points; *Wilderness Airlines Ltd.*, P.O. Box 4659, Williams Lake V2G 2V6, has service from Bella Coola to remote northern recreation areas. Charter floatplane service for the far northern reaches of the province is provided by *British Columbia-Yukon Air Service Ltd.*, Box 68, Watson Lake, Yukon Y0A 1C0; *Fort St. John Aviation Ltd.*, Box 688, Fort St. John V0C 2P0; *Kenn Borek Air Ltd.*, 10401–10 St., Dawson Creek V1G 3T8; *Knight Air Ltd.*, 10516 Alaska Rd., Fort St. John V1J 1B3; *North Cariboo Flying Services Ltd.*, Box 1558, Fort St. John V0C 2P0; and, *Watson Lake Flying Services*, Box 7, Watson Lake, Yukon Y0A 1C0.

For visitors with private aircraft, the publication *Air Tourist Information* is available on request from the Aeronautical Information & Publications Office, Ministry of Transport, Place de Ville, Tower C, Ottawa, Ont. K1A 0N5. The booklet contains a listing of Canadian aeronautical information publications and charts and a list of authorized customs airports and airports of entry and exit. A *British Columbia Air Facilities Map* is available free from the British Columbia Aviation Council, 208, 438 Agar Dr., International Airport S, Vancouver V7B 1A3. It contains information on airstrips and floatplane landing facilities. The map lists authorized customs ports of entry and exit, and tips on flying in mountain country. *Fly Beautiful British Columbia*, published by the Department of Travel Industry, 1019 Wharf St., Victoria V8W 2Z2, gives pilots helpful information on weather, mountain flying, maps and charts, and land and water.

British Columbia Recreational Atlas

A basic tool for the outdoorsman planning a visit to British Columbia is the 97-page *British Columbia Recreational Atlas*, designed to provide specific information about the locations of a wide variety of recreation areas throughout the province, and to serve as the definitive description of the new British Columbia Wildlife Management Units. The atlas contains full-color topographic maps at a scale of 1:600,000 of every recreation area, including Vancouver Island, Garibaldi-Golden Ears parks, Manning Provincial Park, Kokanee Glacier Park, Mount Revelstoke and Glacier National Park, Bugaboo Glacier Park,

Purcell Wilderness Conservancy Area, Yoho and Kootenay national parks, Tweedsmuir Park, Wells Gray Park and the Murtle Lake Nature Conservancy Area, Bowron Lake Park, Mount Robson Park, Queen Charlotte Islands, Mount Edziza Park, Tateatui Park, Kwadacha Wilderness, Muncho Lake-Stone Mountain parks and Atlin Park and Recreation Area. The atlas's maps show highways, logging and four-wheel drive roads, trails, railway lines, airports, floatplane bases, villages, ranger stations, resource region boundaries, wildlife management unit boundaries and number, major conservation reserves, recreation areas, parks, nature conservancy areas, provincial and federal fisheries facilities, spawning channels, recreational shellfish areas, boat-launching ramps, ski areas, glaciers, and historic monuments. The atlas may be obtained for $5.95 from the Information & Education Branch, Department of Recreation and Conservation, 512 Fort St., Victoria.

Camping & Wilderness Trails

The thousands of square miles of alpine wilderness of British Columbia's Selkirk, Purcell, Cariboo, and Rocky mountains offer some of the most spectacular high country and hiking country in the world. The remote wilderness trails of British Columbia's mountain country were blazed by the Indian guides, fur traders, and explorers who opened the land west of the Great Divide for the Hudson's Bay and Northwest Company and for the construction of the Canadian Pacific Railway. Thousands of miles of high country trails wind through the mountain passes, past towering glacier-studded peaks, through lush alpine meadows, and along turbulent mountain streams and wild rivers to remote lakeshore campsites, including the Glacier Crest and Avalanche Crest trails in Glacier National Park; the beautiful Jade Lakes Trail in Mount Revelstoke Park; the Simpson River, Ottertail Pass, Paint Pots, and Verendrye Creek trails in Kootenay National Park; the Yoho Valley and Lake O'Hara trails in Yoho National Park; and the spectacular Great Divide Trail along the backbone of the Rockies running north from the international boundary at Waterton Lakes, Alberta, to Mount Robson, British Columbia. Most wilderness travelers camp at roadside campsites within the ranges and at primitive campsites or alpine huts maintained by the Alpine Club of Canada. The wilderness camper should be prepared for sudden storms and periods of wet weather, particularly during the "monsoon season" in late May and June. Summer temperatures range from the 70s during the day dropping into the 40s and even to freezing in the high country. Anyone planning overnight wilderness camping expeditions must register with the Warden Service in the national park system. The extremely useful *Canadian Rockies Trail Guide* ($4.95), published by Summerthought Publications, Box 1420, Banff, Alta., is available at most information centers in Glacier, Revelstoke, Kootenay, and Yoho national parks. The free 30-page *Accommodation Guide to Western Canada's National Parks* is available from Park Canada, Department of Indian Affairs & Northern Development, 400 Laurier Ave. W, Ottawa, Ont. K1A 0H4. The guide lists and describes all public and commercial accommodations and campgrounds in Mount Revelstoke, Glacier, Kootenay, and Yoho national parks. (See descriptions of provincial and national parks in the "Travel & Recreation Guide" section.)

Canoeing & Wild Rivers

Many of the remote wild rivers of British Columbia are virtually unchanged from the days when they were traveled by the canoes of the great explorers and fur traders of the Hudson's Bay Company and the old Northwest Company. When Alexander Mackenzie, Simon Fraser, and John Stuart and their company of adventurers unrolled the map of Canada up to the Great Divide of the Rocky Mountains and

entered the distant territory then known as New Caledonia and the Columbia Department, they discovered a rugged, scenic high country of steep gradients and wild torrential rivers. Today in the faraway wild rivers of the interior only deeply worn portage trails, campsites, and an occasional prospector's or trapper's cabin bear witness to the legions who, over the centuries, have passed by on their journeys through the north country. The canoeist planning a trip to the British Columbia wilderness should know at least the fundamentals of northern canoe navigation. A set of topographical maps and a compass are absolute essentials for travel through unfamiliar areas; without such maps one can become thoroughly lost among the maze of channels, bays, and islands of northern lake and river country. Grizzlies, boiling rapids, falls and chutes and often backbreaking portages, and the occasional sealike waves of big lake country present constant hazards to the inexperienced wilderness paddler. Guides may be hired at most of the historic frontier settlements, such as Fort Nelson, Fort St. John, Hudson Hope, Fort St. James, and 100 Mile House. A competent guide will keep you from getting lost, do much of the heavy work of paddling and portaging, and provide an opportunity for you to learn northern canoe and woodcraft techniques.

Canadian Wild River Surveys, which provide complete descriptions of British Columbia's great wilderness canoe routes including access, geography, flora, fauna, and history, are available for the *Liard, Kechika, Dease, Stikine, Bowron, Salmon, Willow, Stuart, Nechako, Blackwater, Chilcotin, Fraser, Chilko, Cariboo, Smoky, Quesnel,* and *Gataga* rivers. They may be obtained free by writing: Conservation Study Group, Parks Canada, Department of Indian Affairs & Northern Development, 400 Laurier Ave. W, Ottawa, Ont. K1A 0H4. The free 24-page *Wild Rivers* booklet is available upon request from the British Columbia Wildlife Federation, 17655 57th Ave., Cloverdale. It describes the proposed Gitnadoix Wild River, a winding, scenic tributary of the Skeena River, which flows for 15 miles through near vertical cliffs of a deeply cut glacial valley from its confluence with the Skeena to beautiful Alastair Lake high in the Coast Range Mountains; the proposed Chilko-Chilcotin scenic river system, which flows through alpine highlands, dense evergreen forests, deep-cut rocky canyons, and arid bunchgrass benchlands past the ancient Indian dwellings known as the "Keekwilly Holes" and Battle Mountain, the scene of an Indian tribal massacre; and the world-famous steelhead, salmon, cutthroat, and brown trout waters of the proposed Cowichan Recreational River system on Vancouver Island. Beautiful Westwater scroll

maps (produced by the famed mapmaker Leslie Allen Jones, Star Route Box 13, Heber City, UT 84032) showing every bend, islands, rapids, falls, campsite, contour, and cross-sectional view of the river's gradient, as well as brief descriptions, scouting advice for the more difficult rapids and falls, water-flow information, and historical notes, are available for the *Fraser River* ($5, waterproof $13.50), *Canoe River* ($2.50, waterproof $5), and *Columbia River* from Golden to Revelstoke ($5, waterproof $15.20). A complete listing of *Canoe Clubs in British Columbia* may be obtained from the Department of Travel Industry, 1117 Wharf St., Victoria V8W 2Z2. The useful *Canoe Trip Guide to British Columbia* is available for $2.75 from Canoe British Columbia, 1606 W. Broadway, Vancouver V6J 1X7. (See "Hudson's Bay Company Outfitting Posts & Canoe Service"; also "Travel & Recreation Guide" section, for descriptions of British Columbia's wilderness canoe country.)

Chilkoot Trail of '98

For years the forbidding alpine heights of the Chilkoot Pass, the gateway to the Yukon Valley and the great goldfields of the Klondike, was jealously guarded by the squat, heavy-shouldered Chilkoot Indians to protect their lucrative trade with the "Stick Indians" of the interior, whom they held in virtual slavery. The Chilkoots defended their pass successfully against the Hudson's Bay Company and ill-fated prospectors. George Hold, a vague and shadowy figure in the annals of Klondike history, was the first white man to scale the ice-covered, boulder-strewn 1,000-foot climb over the pass to British Columbia and the Yukon Territory, somehow missing the eagle eyes of the Chilkoot guardians. In 1878 Holt surfaced in Sitka, the frontier capital of Alaska's Panhandle, with two small gold nuggets and tales of goldfields that launched a hot-blooded posse of 20 prospectors, protected by a U.S. gunboat, and convinced the Chilkoot chief Hole-in-the-Face that the pass should be opened after firing a couple of blank rounds from a Gatling gun. Soon the deluge began. In the spring of '98, thousands upon thousands of souls suffered, many tragically, the single-file hike over the pass to Dawson City and the Klondike.

The Chilkoot Trail Pass has been maintained in excellent condition and is a popular hike for backpackers who wish to experience a few of the hardships of the sourdoughs. A free publication, *The Chilkoot Trail: Bennett, Nares, Tagish, Atlin, and Marsh Lakes Survey*, is available from the Conservation Group, Information Services, Department of Indian Affairs and Northern Development, 400 Laurier W, Ottawa, Ont. K1A 0H4. The Chilkoot Trail starts at Dyea, Alaska, at the head of the Lynn Canal and winds for 35 miles through a scenic alpland wilderness to the waters of the Yukon River. The major features passed on the trail include the Sheep Camp and the Scales—where the Klondike stampeders' grubstakes were weighed by Canadian customs officials—Crater and Deep lakes, interior lodgepole pine flats, and Bennett, Atlin, Tagish, and Marsh lakes. The trail is usually in best condition from late July to early September, when the ground is at its driest in the coastal forest between Sheep Camp and Dyea. Foggy weather is common, with clear, sunny skies occurring infrequently. *Klondike Safaris*, P.O. Box 1898-A, Skagway, AK 99840, provides guided hikes over the pass and along the Chilkoot Pass to the headwaters of the Yukon, from July to September.

Ferries of the Coastal & Inland Waterways

Several coastal and inland ferries provide scheduled passenger and vehicle service year round between the mainland and scenic coastal islands along the protected fjordlike Inside Passage, and along the great inland rivers and lakes. *British Columbia Ferries Corporation* provides daily service along the island-studded "Inside Passage" from Vancouver Island to Victoria, and Nanaimo to Langdale, Saltery Bay, and Bowen Island on the Sunshine coast; to the Gulf Islands ports of Long Harbor, Fulford Harbor, and Vesuvius Bay on Saltspring Island; to Prince Rupert and Beaver Cove. Reservations for both vehicles and stateroom are recommended. For information write: 816 Wharf St., Victoria V8W 1T3. *Black Ball Transport Inc.*, 814 Wharf St., Victoria V8W 1T3, has scheduled service from Victoria to Port Angeles, Washington. Capacity, 100 cars, 900 passengers. *CP Rail Ferry*, Marine Operations, Pier B-C, Vancouver V6C 2R3, has scheduled service from Vancouver to Nanaimo. Capacity, 155 cars, 1,030 passengers. *British Columbia Department of Highways*, Parliament Bldgs., Victoria V8V 1X4, operates scheduled coastal ferryliners from Nanaimo to Gabriola Island, Buckley Bay to Denman Island, Denman Island to Hornby Island, Chemainus to Thetis Island, Little River to Westview, Campbell River to Quadra Island, Cortes Island, Woodfire, Texada Island, Malcolm Island, and Cormorant Island from Vancouver Island and to Digby Island from Prince Rupert. The Department of Highways has scheduled inland ferry service on the Fraser River, Francis Lake, Nechako River, Thompson River, Shuswap Lake, Arrow Lake, Columbia River, Kootenay Lake, Kootenay River, Peace River, and Skeena River. The *Alaska Division of Marine Transportation*, Pouch "R" Juneau, AK 99801, has scheduled service from Prince Rupert, British Columbia, to Skagway, Alaska, with ports of call at Ketchikan, Wrangell, Petersburg, Juneau, Haines, and Sitka. Route time is 34 hours each way. *Washington State Ferries*, Seattle Ferry Terminal, Seattle, WA 98104, has scheduled service from Victoria to Anacortes, Washington, with ports of call along the scenic San Juan islands wilderness, capacity, 160 autos, 2,000 passengers.

Fishing & Hunting in British Columbia

This westernmost province of Canada offers some of North America's finest steelhead, salmon, and trout fishing and big-game hunting for deer, moose, elk, mountain goat, Dall and bighorn sheep, grizzly and black bear, mountain lion, wolf, and upland game birds. The province encompasses 366,255 square miles, much of it rugged logging country and high country wilderness, ranging from the magnificent forests and coastal streams of the Vancouver Island and Gulf Islands district to the historic hunting grounds and fishing waters of the rugged canyon and plateau country of the Horsefly, Chilcotin, and Chilko regions of the Cariboo District; the famous salmon and steelhead waters and coastal highlands of the Central Coast region; the interior ranges, lakes, and wild rivers of the Wells Gray, Bonaparte, Nicola, and North Thompson regions of the Kamloops District; the Rocky Mountain Highlands and Big Bend region of the Kootenay District; the great boreal forests, northern Rockies, and vast interior plains of the Peace, Finlay-Parsnip, Stuart-Nechako, and Upper Fraser regions of the Northern Interior District; and the coastal mountains and forests, wild rivers and volcanic highlands of the Atlin-Stikine, Skeena, North Coast, and Queen Charlotte Islands regions of the Northern Coast Fish and Game District.

Trophy Fishing Waters

Many of the remote stretches of the world-famous salmon, trout, and steelhead streams, such as the Dean, Babine, Kispiox, Stuart, Skeena, and Driftwood rivers and the isolated high country lakes, are accessible only by floatplane, primitive logging roads, canoe, jet-powered riverboat, or packtrain. The wise nonresident angler will hire the services of a local guide to help him navigate the potentially hazardous wildlands of the outlying areas. The *British Columbia Sport Fishing Regu-*

lations and *Regional Angling Guides* (which describe in detail the lakes and streams, quality of the fishing and fish species present within British Columbia's fish and wildlife districts) are available free from the following Fish & Wildlife Branch Regional Offices: *Vancouver Island Region*, 324 Terminal Ave., Nanaimo; *Mainland Coast Region*, 4529 Canada Way, Burnaby; *Kamloops Region*, 1959 E. Trans-Canada Highway, Kamloops; *Okanagan Region*, P.O. Box 638, Penticton; *Kootenay Region*, 320 Ward St., Nelson; *Cariboo Coast Region*, 540 Borland St., Williams Lake; *Northern Interior Region*, 1777 Third Ave., Prince George; *Northern Coast Region*, Courthouse, Smithers.

The premier sport fish of British Columbia is the acrobatic, hard-fighting sea-run steelhead and the resident rainbow or Kamloops trout, followed by the coho salmon and Chinook salmon caught up to weights of 90 pounds in saltwater. The province's world-famous steelhead rivers include the Morice, Zyometz, Telkwa, Babine, Sustut, Lakelse, Copper, Bulkley, and Kispiox—the world's record 36-pound steelhead was caught here in 1954—in the Skeena River watershed northeast of Prince Rupert; the beautiful Bella Coola, Dean, Squamish, and Powell rivers in the central coast region; the clear, swift-flowing Thompson River and the Nahatlatch (Salmon), Chilcotin,

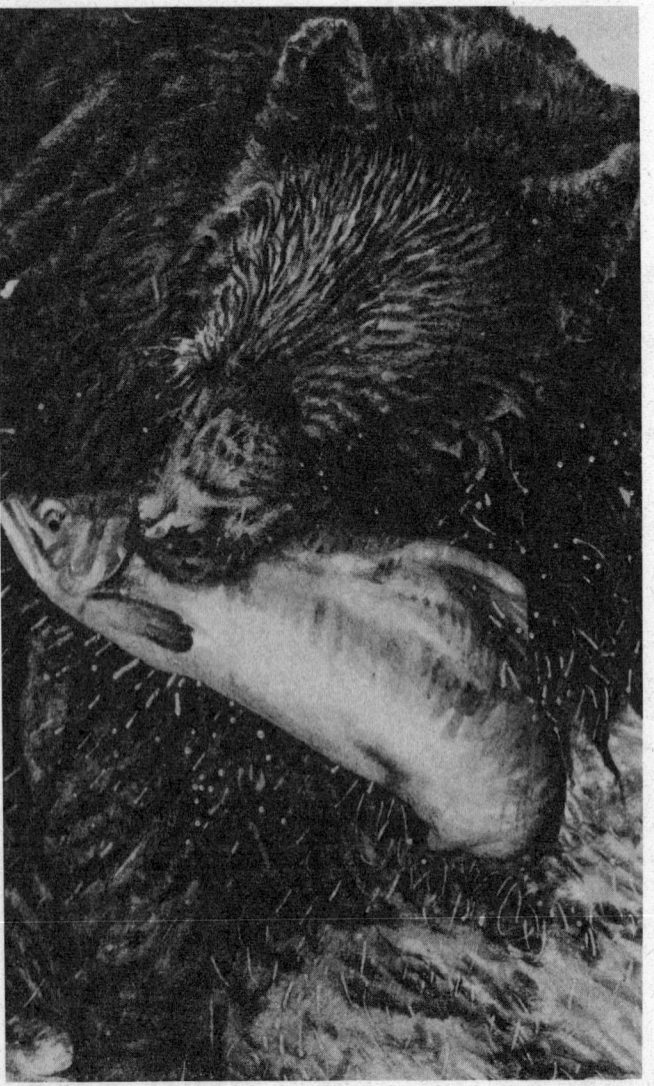

and Chilko rivers in the Southern Interior Region with large hook-jawed steelhead to 20 pounds; the Copper, Tlell and Yakown rivers on scenic Queen Charlotte Islands; the famous Ash, Stamp, Cowichan, and Campbell rivers on Vancouver Island; and, in the Lower Mainland Region, the Vedder, Chehalis, Coquitham, Alouette, Capilano, and Seymour rivers. In 1913 two huge Kamloops or resident British Columbia rainbow trout, one 56 pounds and the other 48 pounds, were taken from Jewel Lake in the Kootenay District (but were not caught by rod, however). Today, trophy Kamloops trout tipping the scales up to 25 pounds are caught in hundreds of large, high country lakes throughout the province. The Kootenay, Upper and Lower Arrow, Christina, and Jewel are some of the better-known lakes in the Kootenays. In the Okanagan District, Kalamalka and Okanagan lakes have produced some large Kamloops trout. In the renowned Kamloops District, Shuswap, the largest lake in the area, produces large Kamloops to 25 pounds; trophy fish are also caught in Adams Lake and River and in the Lac La Hache area. Hundreds of remote, little-known lakes of the Quesnel-Chilcotin District and huge Quesnel, Horsefly, and the wilderness lakes of Wells Gray Provincial Park hold trophy rainbows. The remote lakes and wild rivers of the Burns Lake area and Tweedsmuir Provincial Park wilderness hold lunker rainbow, lake trout, and Dolly Varden. Resident rainbows are also found in the large steelhead streams along the upper and lower coast and on Vancouver Island. Cutthroat trout are found in almost all lakes and streams along the British Columbia coast up to lake-caught weights of 17 pounds. Coastal sea-run cutthroats of 1–4 pounds are found in most of the steelhead waters, entering their spawning streams in late November. The handsome Yellowstone cutthroat is found in most streams and alpine lakes of the Rocky Mountains in southeastern British Columbia. Kokanee, landlocked sockeye salmon, are present in most of the larger lakes on the mainland and Vancouver Island; the delicious red-fleshed kokanee, also known as the "little red fish," Kikininee, or silver trout, averages about a pound in Lac La Hache, for example, up to a 9½-pounder caught in Kootenay Lake. Gray lake trout to 60 pounds are found in the deep cold-water lakes in the large lakes of the interior from Shuswap Lake northward to the lakes of the Yukon River system. Lake trout are not found in the Columbia River country. Dolly Varden, up to 29 pounds in Kootenay Lake, are common throughout the province with the exception of the Okanagan country. Brook trout, transplanted to the province in 1908, are now found on Vancouver Island and in the lakes and streams in the southeastern part of the mainland. The beautiful arctic grayling inhabits the clear, cold waters of Atlin, Teslin, and other lakes and streams of the far north headwaters of the Yukon River and in the Peace River country in the northeast. For the free *British Columbia Tidal Waters Sportfishing Guide*, information, and regulations on fishing for salmon in the tidal salt waters of the province, write: Fisheries Service, Department of the Environment, 1090 W. Pender St., Vancouver V6E 2P1. For a free brochure, *British Columbia Fly Fishing Only & Motorless Craft Waters*, write: Fish & Wildlife Branch, Parliament Bldgs., Victoria V8V 1X4.

Hunting & Wildlife

The high country wilderness of British Columbia has long been famous for the variety and excellence of its big-game hunting. The Stikine Plateau, the Interior Plains, and the Cassiar, Coast, Omineca, and northernmost Rocky Mountains of northern British Columbia are known to sportsmen throughout the world for Stone sheep, mountain and Osborn caribou, goat, grizzly bear, and Alaskan and British Columbia moose. Elk and Dall sheep are found in a few areas of the north country. The Prince George region offers good hunting for moose, mule deer, mountain caribou, and goat in the renowned Stuart Lake fish and game area and Hogem, Swanell, Bait, Sicintine, Babine, and

Bulkley mountain ranges and the Tweedsmuir wilderness to the south and west. The Cariboo Mountains-Chilcotin region has excellent hunting for moose, goat, grizzly and black bear, and mule deer. Moose hunters who cannot manage the trip to Prince George or the Peace River are advised to outfit at some point along the Cariboo Highway, either at Clinton, Horsefly, Likely, Quesnel, Williams Lake, 100 Mile House, or 150 Mile House, where licensed guides are available. The Kamloops moose country in the Thompson and Wells Gray Park wilderness areas is a day's drive by car from Vancouver on Trans-Canada Highway 1. The valleys and forests of the Okanagan region provide excellent mule and whitetail deer hunting and good hunting for blue, ruffed and Franklin grouse, mourning dove, pheasant, and California quail. The Rocky, Purcell, and Selkirk mountains, and valleys and forests of the Kootenay region, contain the province's largest herds of elk as well as Rocky Mountain bighorn sheep, grizzly, goat, whitetail and mule deer, and Shiras or Yellowstone moose. The extensive uplands of the upper Columbia River and Creston areas provide good duck and goose hunting. Other wildlife and furbearers found in the British Columbia wilderness include wolverine, wolves and coyote, bobcat, fox, raccoon, snowshoe hare, and sea lions and hair seals along the coastal regions.

All nonresident hunters must be accompanied by a licensed guide while hunting big game. No guide is required for hunting game birds. The free guide *Hunting in British Columbia* is published by the Fish & Wildlife Branch, Parliament Bldgs., Victoria V8V 1X4. It provides complete info on hunting and fishing licenses for nonresidents, guides, trophy fees, dogs, aircraft, border regulations, firearms and fishing tackle, and export permits, and contains a *Game Management Boundaries Map*. The free guides *Cougar in British Columbia, Deer in British Columbia, Mountain Sheep in British Columbia, Moose in British Columbia, Elk in British Columbia,* and *Mountain Goats in British Columbia* are available free upon request from the Information Branch, Department of Recreation and Conservation, 512 Fort St., Victoria. (See "British Columbia Recreational Atlas," "Guides & Wilderness Outfitters," "Airlines & Charter Fly-in Services," and the "Travel & Recreation Guide" section.)

Fort St. James—Gateway to the North

(Pop. 5,000). This famous wilderness outfitting center, located at the southeastern shore of Stuart Lake in the Omineca gold-mining country of central interior British Columbia, was founded in 1806 by Simon Fraser. This early Northwest Company trading post was the capital of New Caledonia, and subsequently became an important fur trading center for the Hudson's Bay Company. Some of the finest trophy fishing and big-game hunting in the province is found due north of Fort St. James in the Stuart, Trembleur, Babine, Inzana, Tezzeron, Tchentlo, Chuchi, Great Beaver, and Takla lakes areas, Nation and Driftwood rivers, and in the Hogem, Swanell, and Bait mountains. The major points of interest in the area include Chief Quaivo's grave, Mount Pope Indian etchings, and the Necoslie Indian Reserve. The *Stuart River Campground*, Box 141, Fort St. James V0J 1P0, provides camping facilities, boat rentals, and river cruises. Lodging, guides and wilderness outfitting services in the Fort St. James region, zip code V0J 1P0, are provided by *Culchoe Nu Lodge*, Box 70, on Stuart Lake; *Takla Lake Lodge*, Box 558; *Cinnabar Resort* on Tezzeron Lake, Box 76; *Trayta Lodge*, Fort St. James. Fort St. James is reached via Highway 27, 39 miles from Vanderhoof (pop. 3,000) and Yellowhead Highway 16. Highway 27 continues on past Fort St. James for 189 miles along the shoreline of Stuart Lake to Tachie. From Vanderhoof the Kenny Dam Road provides access to the Nechako River bird sanctuary and several fishing and hunting camps

including the *Nulki Lake Resort*, Box 148; *Tachick Fishing Camp*, Box 530; and *Nechako Lodge and Resort*, Box 839, Vanderhoof V0J 3A0. Northwest of Vanderhoof on the Yellowhead Highway are the renowned fishing and big-game hunting outfitting centers of Fort Fraser, Fraser Lake, and Burns Lake, and the world-famous Endako Mines, the renowned steelhead fly-fishing waters of the Stellako River, the Tintagel cairn, historic Telegraph Trail, Deadman's Island, and Pinkut artificial fish spawning grounds; Tweedsmuir Provincial Park wilderness canoe routes and the famous salmon and steelhead trout waters of the Babine, Kitimat, Morice, and Copper rivers. The entire region lies within the Stuart-Nechako wildlife management area, which offers some of the finest high country hunting in the province for moose, goat, caribou, deer, wolf, black and grizzly bear, ruffed grouse, and waterfowl.

Guides & Wilderness Outfitters

The *British Columbia List of Guide Outfitters* is available on request from the Fish & Wildlife Branch, Department of Recreation and Conservation, 1019 Wharf St., Victoria. All nonresidents are required to be accompanied by a licensed guide while hunting deer, mountain sheep, mountain goat, moose, caribou, elk, cougar, wolf, grizzly bear, and black bear. Guides are not required while hunting game birds, migratory game birds, or coyote. Guide outfitters set their own guiding fees, and we recommend that you write to several outfitters in the area of your choice to obtain full particulars regarding reservations, rates, services provided, and recommended hunting times. For additional information on guides and outfitters write: Secretary-Manager, *West-*

Moose in British Columbia

Elk in British Columbia

Mountain Goats in British Columbia

ern Guides & Outfitters Association, 213, 1717 3d Ave., Prince George. Most British Columbia lodges and sporting camps offer guide service and outfitting for boats and gear. A complete listing and description of British Columbia Indian-operated hunting and fishing camps and canoe outfitters is contained in the 110-page directory of Canadian Indian Tourist Outfitting & Outdoor Recreation Facilities, available free from the Information Branch, Department of Indian Affairs and Northern Development, 400 Laurier Ave. W, Ottawa, Ont. K1A 0H4.

BEAUTIFUL
BRITISH COLUMBIA
ROAD MAP
CAMPGROUND & ANGLING GUIDE

Highways—Recreation & Scenic Routes

British Columbia has about 9,000 miles of paved roads and more than 11,000 miles of good gravel roads that provide access to the major outdoor recreation areas and the more remote wilderness regions. Most road regulations, signals, and road signs are the same as those in the United States and elsewhere in Canada. The official British Columbia Road Map is available free from the Department of Travel Industry, 1019 Wharf St., Victoria V8W 2Z2. This full-color map shows all paved and gravel highways, logging roads, trails, marine highway routes, federal and provincial campgrounds, Red Cross outposts, ski areas, points of interest, airports, time-zone boundaries, fish hatcheries, ports of entry, dams, mountain passes, waterfalls, railroads, and towns. It contains hunting and fishing license information, a complete listing and description of provincial campgrounds, and a complete "Angling Guide" that tells where to go for steelhead, Kamloops, brown trout, coastal & Yellowstone cutthroat trout, and kokanee, lake trout, Dolly Varden, brook trout, and salmon. The Canadian National Topographic Survey Maps listed below are printed in full color at a scale of 1:250,000, or 1 inch to 4 miles, and provide an excellent overview of the famous recreation and wilderness areas surrounding British Columbia's major roadways.

Alaska Highway

This map kit is a must for the outdoorsman who uses the Alaska Highway during his journey through the wildlands of northern British Columbia. Once known as the Alcan Highway, the great gravel highway was constructed during World War II as a land route for shipping war material and equipment. The 1,523-mile gravel highway was completed in March 1942 when the U.S. Army Corps of Engineers reached Mile 0 and "arrived at the end of the steel" at the remote frontier settlement of Dawson Creek. Today this great northern road has been widened and the primitive log bridges have been replaced by steel. The map kit shows the entire British Columbia segment of the highway and the surrounding wilderness from Mile 0 at Dawson Creek northwest to Watson Lake in the Yukon Territory. The major features shown along the route include the Interior Plains; Hudson's Hope Loop Road, developed from the original Telegraph Trail of 1918; Peace River Valley, Fort St. John, where Alexander Mackenzie camped in 1793 on his journey west to the Pacific Ocean; Sikanni Chief River, which holds northern pike and grayling; the former trading post of Fort Nelson; the arctic grayling and Dolly Varden waters of the Racing and Toad rivers and Muncho Lake Provincial Park; and the historic Hudson's Bay Company trading post and Indian village of Lower Post, located near the confluence of the Dease and Liard rivers. Other features shown on the map kit include the unbroken wilderness of boreal evergreen forest, lakes, alpine tundra, and wild rivers of the Cassiar and Northern Rockies and Stone Mountain and Kwadacha wilderness provincial parks. Provincial campgrounds and wayside areas are located at Kiskatinaw, Charlie Lake, Buckinghorse River, Prophet River, Kledo Creek, Stone Mountain Park, N5 Creek, Racing River, Muncho Lake, Liard Hot Springs, and Hyland River. Canadian National Topographic Survey Maps: Dawson Creek 93-P, Charlie Lake 94-A, Halfway River 94-B, Trutch 94-G, Fort Nelson 94-J, Tuchodi Lake 94-K, Toad River 94-N, Rabbit River 94-M, Watson Lake 105-A.

Cariboo & John Hart-Peace River Highway

This map kit shows paved Highway 97 as it passes through the famous Cariboo country of the immense Interior Plateau—a rolling parklike country, similar to parts of Wyoming, dotted with thousands of remote blue lakes and sagebrush areas renowned for its old West ranches, cattle ranges, frontier roadhouses, and big-game hunting and fishing. The highway winds north from Hope to its junction with the Alaska Highway at Dawson Creek. The major features and points of interest along the route include the settlement of Cache Creek; Fraser and Thompson rivers; Green Lake; 100 Mile House, a former outfitting center during the gold-rush days of the Cariboo Trail; the trophy arctic char, lake trout, and rainbow trout waters of Lac La Hache, Canim Lake, and McIntosh Lakes; the famous outfitting town of Williams Lake, named after the Shuswap Indian chief Willyum; Quesnel and to the east the ghost towns of the old Cariboo road and the famous big-game hunting, fishing, and wilderness canoeing areas at Bowron Lake and Wells Gray provincial parks and Quesnel and Horsefly lakes; Prince George, a famous jumping-off center for big-game hunting and steelhead and rainbow trout fishing trips in the Interior; Carp Lake Provincial Park; John Hart-Peace River Highway from Highway 97 north along Williston Lake to Finlay Forks; and the Hudson's Hope Loop from Chetwynd on the Cariboo Highway north past Moberly Lake and Hudson Hope—the original site of Rocky Mountain Portage, a trading post established in 1805 by Simon Fraser —and then to the Alaska Highway and Fort St. John and Dawson Creek. Public campgrounds are located at Emory Creek, Skihist, Goldpan, Green Lake, Lac La Hache, Ten Mile Lake, Bowron Lake, Cottonwood River, Crooked River, Whisker's Point, and Moberly Lake. Canadian National Topographic Survey Maps: Ashcroft 92-I, Taseko Lake 92-O, Bonaparte Lake 92-P, Quesnel Lake 93-B, Prince George 93-G, McLeod Lake 93-J, Pine Pass 93-O, Halfway River 94-B, Charlie River 94-A, Dawson Creek 93-P.

Cassiar Highway

This map kit shows the entire length of the scenic Highway 37 from its junction with the Alaska Highway at Watson Lake in the Yukon Territory, southwest through the boreal forests and big-game highlands of the Cassiar Mountains, Stikine Plateau, and Skeena Mountains to Stuart at the head of the Portland Canal in the Coast Range, and south along restricted logging roads to Terrace, Kitwanga, Cedarvale, and New Hazelton where it connects with Yellowhead Highway 16. The major points of interest along the route include the confluence of the Skeena and Bulkley rivers at Hazelton, once a trading post and winter quarters for sourdoughs during the early gold-rush days; the totem poles at Kitwanga, which means the "place of the rabbit people"; the brilliant green and blue glacier and icefalls at Bear Pass; the gold-rush boomtown of Stewart and the salmon and steelhead waters of the Meziadin and Nass rivers; the Bell Irving River and old Telegraph Trail; the 2,500-foot-high Stikine-Nass river divide; the volcanic highlands surrounding 9,143-foot Mount Edziza, a potentially active volcano; the trophy rainbow and lake trout waters of Kinaskan, Eddontenajon, Morchura, and Dease lakes and the grayling waters of Tanzilla River; the ghost town of Laketon and the rugged, scenic spur route along the historic Telegraph Creek Road. Wildlife found along the river valleys and in the wilderness highlands includes moose, grizzly, caribou, wolf, Dall and Stone sheep, and bald and golden eagles. Campgrounds are located at Lava Lake, Tatogga Lake Resort, Stikine River Bridge, Sixteen Mile Creek, Dease Lake, Iskut, Kinaskan Lake, Rainy Creek Park, Meziadin Lake, 'Ksan and Dragon Lake. Canadian National Topographic Survey Maps: Smithers 93-L, Hazelton 93-M, Nass River 103-P, Bowser Lake 104-A, Iskut River 104-B, Telegraph Creek 104-G, Spatsizi 104-H, Dease Lake 104-J, Cry Lake 104-I, McDame 104-P, Watson Lake 104-A.

Trans-Canada Highway

This map kit shows the scenic British Columbia segment of Highway 1 from Banff National Park in Alberta westward through the Rockies and the Interior Plateau to Vancouver. The major scenic and recreation area features shown along the route include beautiful Lake Louise in Banff Park; the Kicking Horse River and the scenic peaks and glaciers of Yoho National Park west of the Great Divide; the logging, fishing, and big-game country surrounding Golden; Big Bend Highway and the high country emerald lakes and snowcapped peaks of Glacier and Mount Revelstoke national parks; Columbia River and the Selkirk and Monashee mountains; the famous Kamloops and lake trout waters of huge Shuswap, Adams, and Mara lakes near the town of Salmon Arm; Kamloops Lake and the town of Cache Creek. Other features shown on the maps include Garibaldi, Golden Ears, and Manning provincial parks. Public campgrounds are located at Kicking Horse, Hoodoo Creek, Chancellor Peak, Takakkaw Falls, Lake O'Hara, and Ottertail Group Camp in Yoho National Park; Illecillewaet, Loop Creek, and Mountain Creek in Glacier National Park; and along the Trans-Canada Highway recreation areas at Yard Creek, Cinnemousun Narrows at Shuswap Lake, Shuswap Lake, Paul Lake, Goldpan, Skihist, Emory Creek, Sasquatch, and Rolley Lake. Canadian National Topographic Survey Maps: Calgary 82-O, Golden 82-N, Vernon 82-L, Ashcroft 92-I, Hope 92-H, Vancouver 92-G.

Yellowhead Highway

This useful full-color map kit shows Yellowhead Highway 16 and the surrounding scenic wilderness and recreation areas from Jasper National Park west through the Interior Plateau to Prince Rupert and Yellowhead Highway 5 from its junction with Highway 16 at Tête Jaune Caché, southwest to Kamloops. This interprovincial highway crosses the Canadian Rockies at 3,760-foot Yellowhead Pass (the

terminus of the old Carlton Trail, used by westward-bound explorers, fur traders, and settlers, which ran along a winding rugged course for 1,160 miles from Fort Gary at Lake Winnipeg to Yellowhead Pass), named after an Iroquois trapper and guide, Tête Jaune ("Yellow Head" in French), who worked for the Hudson's Bay Company. The major scenic high country wilderness and recreation areas shown on the map kit include Jasper National Park; Fraser River; Prince George; Fort St. James—the former fur trading capital of New Caledonia founded by Simon Fraser, a major outfitting center for fishermen and

big-game hunters heading north to Stuart, Takla, Chuchi, Trembleur, and Inzana lakes and the Hogem, Swanell, and Bait mountain ranges; Vanderhoof and Fraser Lake; Burns Lake and Babine Lake and Tweedsmuir Provincial Park; and the outfitting and supply centers of Smithers, Moricetown, New Hazelton, and Hazelton, which provide guide service, lodging, and access to the world-famous steelhead and salmon waters of the remote Kispiox River (Indian for "the people who hid"), Morice River, and the Bulkley, Babine, Suskwa, Copper, Kitwanga, Telkwa, Kitwancool, and Lakelse rivers. Yellowhead winds on through ancient lava beds and the Coast Range mountains along the great Skeena River, which produced the world's record 92½-pound king salmon, to its terminus at the city of Prince Rupert, the "gateway to Alaska" located due south of the massive Alexander Archipelago of Alaska's Panhandle. Public campgrounds along Yellowhead Highway 16 are located at Mount Robson Park, Purden Lake, Beaumont, Babine Lake, Topley Landing, Maclure Lake, Seeley Lake, Kleanza Creek, Lakelse Lake, Exchamsiko River, and Prudhomme Lake. The Yellowhead Highway 5 segment from Tête Jaune Caché south to Kamloops winds through the scenic Columbia Mountains past Canoe River, Blue River, Wells Gray Provincial Park wilderness canoeing and fishing area, and the North Thompson and Clearwater rivers. Public campgrounds along Highway 5 are located at Spahats Creek, North Thompson River, and Wells Gray Park. Canadian National Topographic Survey Maps. *Yellowhead Highway 16:* Canoe River 83-D, Mount Robson 83-E, McBride 93-H, Prince George 93-G, McLeod Lake 93-J, Fort Fraser 93-K, Smithers 93-L, Terrace 103-I, Prince Rupert 103-J; *South Yellowhead Highway 5:* Canoe River 83-D, Seymour Arm 82-M, Bonaparte Lake 92-P, Ashcroft 92-I.

Hudson's Bay Company Outfitting Posts & Canoe Service

The British Columbia northern outpost stores of the Hudson's Bay Company carry food supplies, gear, and ammunition needed for wilderness hunting, fishing, and canoeing trips. Hudson's Bay Company supply posts and merchandise stores in British Columbia are located at Vancouver, 100 Mile House, Fort St. James, Kitimat, Kitwanga, Hazelton, Mackenzie, Dawson Creek, Fort St. John, and Fort Nelson. A free *Hudson's Bay Company U-Paddle Service Map-Brochure* and information are available upon request from the HBC, Northern Stores Department, 800 Baker Center, 10025 106th St., Edmonton, Alta. T5J 1G7, or phone (403) 424–8113. A listing of *Canoe Rentals in British Columbia*, which describes the canoe outfitters and types of canoes and gear available, can be had by writing: Department of Travel Industry, 1019 Wharf St., Victoria V8W 2Z2.

Railway Services

The major recreation access and outfitting centers of British Columbia are served by several major railroads which travel through scenic wilderness high country and provide excellent service. The *British Columbia Railway* operates a scenic route from North Vancouver to Prince George with waypoints at Clinton, 70 Mile House, Lone Butte, Exeter, Lac La Hache, Williams Lake, Macalister, Quesnel, and Stoner; and from North Vancouver to Lillooet with waypoints at Sunset Beach, Squamish, Cheakamus, Garibaldi, Alta Lake, Pemberton, D'Arcy, MacGillivray Falls, and Seton Portage. For reservations, time schedules, and recreation travel information, write: 1311 W. 1st St., North Vancouver V7P 1A7. *Canadian National Railways* runs from Vancouver to Edmonton, Alberta, with connecting services and waypoints at Boston Bar, Kamloops Junction, Clearwater, Vavenby, Blue River, Valemount, and Jasper; and from Prince Rupert to Edmonton with connecting services and waypoints at Terrace, Kitwanga, New Hazelton, Smithers, Houston, Burns Lake, Vanderhoof, Prince George, McBride, Red Pass, and Jasper. For travel information write: 1150 Station St., Vancouver V6A 2X7. *CP Rail*, Granville and Cordova Sts., Vancouver V6A 2R3, runs from Vancouver to Toronto and Montreal via Mission City, Agassiz, Kamloops, Salmon Arm, Revelstoke, Lake Louise, Banff, and Calgary. The *Esquimalt & Nanaimo Railway* operates from Victoria to Courtenay with connecting service and waypoints at Shawnigan, Cobble Hill, Cowichan, Duncan,

Chemainus, Ladysmith, Cassidy, Nanaimo, Wellington, Parksville, and Qualicum Beach. For info write: 325 Esquimalt Rd., Victoria. The scenic, narrow-gauge (36-inch-track) *White Pass & Yukon Railway*, P.O. Box 2147, Seattle, WA 98111, (206) 623-2510, runs through the Coast Range along the old Trail of '98 from Skagway, Alaska, through British Columbia to Whitehorse, Yukon, with waypoints at Bennett and Carcross.

Wild & Trophy Fishing Waters Maps

The following Canadian National Topographic Survey Maps (scale indicated) show the major British Columbia wilderness camping, canoeing, and trophy salmon, trout, and steelhead waters (see the "Travel & Recreation Guide" section for additional listings). *Horsefly Lake* (1:50,000): Beaver Creek 93A-5, Horsefly 93A-6; *Canim & Mahood Lakes* (1:50,000): Canim Lake 92P-15, Mahood Lake 92P-16; *Lac La Hache* (1:50,000): Lac La Hache 92P-14; *Chilko Lake & River* (1:250,000): Tchaikazan River 92O-4, Chilko Mountain 92N-1, Stikelan Creek 92N-8, Tatlayoko Lake 92N-9; *Dean River* (1:50,000): Kimsquit 93D-15, Sigutlat Lake 93D-16, Ulkatcho 93C-13, Carnlick Creek 93C-14, Christensen Creek 93C-11, Anahim Lake 93G-6, Satan Mountain 93C-7, Chantslar Lake 93C-2; *Bella Coola River* (1:50,000): Charlotte Lake 93C-3, Atnarko 93C-5, Stuie 93D-8, Bella Coola 93D-7; *Stuart Lake & River* (1:250,000): Fort Fraser 93-K, McLeod Lake 93-J, Prince George 93-G; *Bulkley River & Morice Lake* (1:250,000): Hazelton 93-M, Smithers 93-L, Whitesail Lake 93-E; *Nation River & Lakes Chain* (1:250,000): Pine Pass 93-O, Manson River 93-N; *Shuswap & Adams Lake* (1:250,000): Seymour Arm 82-M, Vernon 82-L; *North Thompson River* (1:250,000): Canoe River 83-D, Seymour Arm 82-M, Bonaparte Lake 92-P, Ashcroft 92-I.

Wilderness Fishing, Canoeing & Backpacking Trips

Several great Canadian wilderness adventure package trips to famous British Columbia recreation areas are operated by Air Canada and Pacific Western Airlines. The *Beaverdam Guest Ranch* trip consists of 8 days serviced by Pacific Western Airlines to Kamloops, at one of the last old-time ranches in the Cariboo country. Includes all meals, horses, guides, accommodations in rustic log cabins and transportation from Kamloops. The *Bowron Lake Wilderness Park Canoe Trip* consists of 8 days serviced by Pacific Western to Quesnel, at the Bowron Lake Lodge with canoeing and fishing in the scenic Bowron Lake chain, photographic safaris, backpacking to the 90-foot Cariboo River falls, and wilderness camping. It includes surface transfer from Quesnel to Lodge, all meals and 2 night accommodations at Lodge, and all food and gear for canoe trips. *Backpack in the Queen Charlotte Islands* trip, serviced by Pacific Western to Sandspit, consists of 7 days in the Misty Islands, 50 miles off the mainland coast and 40 miles south of Alaska, backpacking along wild beaches and across tundralike peat bogs on a pioneer trail. It includes transportation from airport and return, food, backpack, and 2-man mountain tent, group cooking equipment, and guide. *Chilcotin River Whitewater Rafting Adventure* consists of 7 days river rafting, hiking, and trail riding. Includes all food while on river, rafts (16–18-foot oar-powered), 2 nights hotel accommodation, and transfers. Pacific Western Airlines also services several Great Canadian fishing adventure trips to British Columbia. *April Point Lodge* at Quadra Island offers 8 days fly-fishing for coho and Chinook salmon overlooking Discovery Passage opposite the mouth of the Campbell River at the world-famous April Point Fly Fishing Club. The trip is serviced by Pacific Western to Campbell River; it includes transfers, accommodations at lodge, boats and

motor, and guide. The *Brentwood Bay Fishing Resort* trip consists of 3 days of salmon fishing in cabin cruisers, accommodations at Brentwood Inn on Vancouver Island, gear, and Pacific Western service to Victoria. *Hoeya Sound Lodge,* located at Knight Inlet, 60 miles north of Campbell River, includes 6 days of salmon fishing, transfer, meals, tackle, boats, and guide. The *Haida Inn* on the Campbell River offers 3 days salmon fishing in the waters of Discovery Passage, accommodations, guides, boat, and gear. *Good Hope Cannery Lodge,* serviced by Pacific Western to Rivers Inlet, offers 4 days of salmon fishing on the rugged north coast, accommodations, meals, gear, guides, and boats. *Wilderness Lodge,* Quesnel Lake, serviced by Pacific Western to Williams Lake, offers fishing for lake trout, Dolly Varden, rainbow, and kokanee, accommodations, air charter, meals, boats, and motors. For information and literature contact your local travel agent or write: Tour Division, Pacific Western Airlines, Vancouver International Airport, Central V7B 1V2.

Chilcotin Mountain Adventures Ltd., based at the rustic Chilko Lake Wilderness Ranch in the Cariboo-Chilcotin region, provides guided wilderness canoe trips in Tweedsmuir Provincial Park; raft trips down the Chilko, Chilcotin, and Fraser rivers; backpacking and trail riding trips to the Coast Range; salmon and steelhead fishing and hunting trips. For literature and info, write: Box 4750, Williams Lake V2G 1H6; phone (604) 398-8828.

Fly-in wild river expeditions on the Chilcotin, Fraser, and Stikine are provided by *Canadian River Expeditions,* 845 Hornby St. Vancouver; phone (604) 926-4436. This firm is the largest and oldest operation of its kind in Canada. Guides, equipment, and services are all first class.

BRITISH COLUMBIA TRAVEL & RECREATION GUIDE

Atlin-Stikine Wilderness & the Cassiar Mountains

Atlin Provincial Park & Recreation Area

Canadian National Topographic Survey Maps, scale 1:250,000: Skagway 104-M, Atlin 104-N.

Cassiar Mountains

Canadian National Topographic Survey Maps, scale 1:250,000: Jennings River 104-O, McDame 104-P, Dease Lake 104-J, Cry Lake 104-I, Kechika 94-L, Toodoggone River 94-E, Spatsizi 104-H, Telegraph Creek 104-G.

Mount Edziza Provincial Park

Canadian National Topographic Survey Map, scale 1:250,000: Telegraph Creek 104-G.

Tatlatui Provincial Park

Canadian National Topographic Survey Maps, scale 1:250,000: McConnell Creek 94-D, Toodoggone River 94-E.

This huge, remote mountain region is famous the world over for its outstanding hunting for Stone and Fannin sheep (the Fannin or saddleback sheep is a cross between a Stone and Dall sheep), mountain goat, grizzly bear, and moose. Elk and Dall sheep are hunted, but only in certain areas. Moose reach enormous size, and the Osborn caribou found here is the finest of its species for body growth and antler size. Hunting parties planning to fly into the Cassiars are recommended to charter aircraft at Prince George, Watson Lake, or Whitehorse in the Yukon Territory. Guides and complete outfits are available at Telegraph Creek, Dease Lake, and Atlin. The region encompasses the Atlin-Stikine wildlife management unit, and is bordered on the north by the Yukon Territory, on the west by the Alaska Panhandle and the Coast Range Mountains, and on the east by the great plain of the Liard River. Big-game hunting trips can be combined with excellent fishing for fat, deep-bodied rainbows, Dolly Varden to 20 pounds, arctic grayling and char, salmon, and giant northern pike. The top hundred Boone and Crockett entries for Stone sheep came from British Columbia and are noted for horns that are slightly heavier and more severely broomed than Dall or Rocky Mountain sheep. The pure strain of Stone sheep are blackish brown to almost blue-black and range from the Yukon east to the Mackenzie Mountains, and south into British Columbia to the Stikine River area. Wild sheep are noted for their ability to bound as high as 17 feet and, of all big-game species, only the antelope is known to surpass the sheep in keenness of vision. The rams are often seen in the highlands gathered in bachelor bands, and at the turn of the century as many as 200 Stone rams were reported sighted on a single mountain. The joy of hunting in this remote, barren region of glaciers, lakes, towering peaks, and wild rivers is the long, rigorous stalk among the high ridges and slopes. The wilderness traveler in the north country is likely to see the tracks and scat of wolves, grizzly bear, fox, mink, marten, fisher, beaver, and the Indian devil of the north, the wolverine. Canada geese frequent the channels of the Stikine and Dease rivers along with mergansers, mallards, and harlequin ducks. Hawks, bald eagles, ravens, cliff swallows, loons, lesser yellowlegs, terns, spotted sandpipers, seagulls, and a few rufous hummingbirds are often sighted.

Forty miles north of Juneau, just east of the Alaska border, 575,000 acres of the rugged Tagish Highlands have been preserved as the Atlin Provincial Park. Access to the park is by air or water across Atlin Lake. The only trails are the Indian and game trails of deer, bear, and

caribou. The nearest road is the Atlin-Carcross Road to Atlin which winds south from the Alaska Highway past Little Atlin Lake and scenic Mount Minto and along the shore of Atlin Lake—one of the largest natural lakes in the province at 307 square miles. The 95,000-acre Atlin Recreation Area is adjacent to the park on the west. The major features of the park and recreation area include the 274-square-mile Llewellyn Glacier, Tagish and Fantail lakes, and the towering peaks of the Florence Range. A boat-launching ramp and seaplane base are located at Atlin on the east shore of the lake. A free *Atlin Provincial Park* Map-Brochure is available from the Parks Branch, Department of Recreation & Conservation, 1019 Wharf St., Victoria V8W 2Y9. *Atlin Wilderness Charters*, Box 41, Atlin V0W 1A0, located on the east shore of Atlin Lake, has wilderness fishing camps for salmon, Dolly Varden, grayling, and pike with guided wildlife photography and scenic charters.

From its Dease Lake headwaters the Dease River flows through a short chain of glacial lakes flanked by peaks of the Cassiar Mountains (soaring to 7,000 feet) and subarctic forests to its confluence with the Blue River, where it flows northeasterly across the Liard Plain to join the historic Liard River across from Lower Post. Historically the Dease was an important waterway linking Wrangell, Alaska, via the Stikine River to Telegraph Creek, overland to Dease Lake and the Yukon. In 1873 gold was discovered at the present site of McDame, an Indian reservation which was a Hudson's Bay fur trading post during the great Klondike gold rush of '98; the Dease was important as a link with the Liard River and for its deposits of placer gold. The rotting hulls of large freight boats can still be seen along the shores of Dease Lake, which, before the completion of the Alaska Highway during World War II, served as an important freight route to the northern interior of British Columbia and the Yukon. West of Dease Lake the wild Stikine River flows from its headwaters at Tuya Lake, southwest through the Cassiar and Coast ranges and the barren outcroppings of the Spatsizi Plateau, Stikine Range, Eaglenest, and Three Sisters Range mountains and the spectacular Grand Canyon of the Stikine, to its mouth near Wrangell in the Alaska Panhandle. The Dease and Upper Stikine rivers hold fat bull Dolly Varden, lake and rainbow trout, arctic grayling, and char. Below the Grand Canyon the Stikine is a spawning area for Chinook and coho salmon.

During the early 18th century the Russian-American Fur Company established an island outpost 10 miles from the mouth of the Stikine. Fort Dionysus, where Wrangell now stands, boomed with the international demand for otter and fur seal pelts. While the Russians dominated the coastal region, the Hudson's Bay Company sent John McLeod to establish a post at Dease Lake, which failed because of competition from the Russians. A horde of laborers, sourdoughs, and adventurers headed up the Stikine during the building of the ill-fated Telegraph Trail and the gold rush of 1873 and during the great Klondike gold rush of 1897–98.

The forbidding wilderness of beautiful Mount Edziza Provincial Park and Recreation Area encompasses 570,000 acres south from the Grand Canyon of the Stikine in the Tahltan Highlands, west of the Cassiar Mountains. The park takes in some of the most spectacular scenery in North America and one of the most significant volcanic regions in Canada. Volcanic activity—according to Tahltan and Tsimshian Indian lore, confirmed by scientific studies—has occurred as recently as a century ago. Mount Edziza, which means "cinders" in the Tahltan dialect, erupted violently over 1 million years ago, spreading volcanic ash over most of northern British Columbia. The wilderness surrounding glacier-rimmed Edziza Peak is a great plateau built up by subsequent lava flows and 30 smaller lava and cinder cones,

domes, vents, and pumice fields. Raspberry Pass to the south separates the more recent area of volcanic activity from the brilliantly colored rainbow hues of the ancient Spectrum Mountains. The remains of the old Telegraph Trail, built to link North America with Asia and Europe by telegraph (only to be abandoned in 1866 with the successful laying of the transatlantic cable), and evidence of the line cabins that stood along the route can still be seen in the Raspberry Pass area and along the Mess Creek Gorge. Rainbow and lake trout are found in Buckley Lake northwest of Mount Edziza and in the chain formed by the beautiful Mowdade, Mowchilla, Kakiddi, and Nuttlude lakes along the eastern boundary and in the Little Iskut River. Access is via a rugged wilderness hike from Telegraph Creek or by floatplane charter. This remote wilderness preserve is for the experienced wilderness traveler. The *Mount Edziza Provincial Park and Recreation Area Map-Brochure* is available free from the Parks Branch, 1019 Wharf St., Victoria V8W 2Y9.

MOUNT EDZIZA PROVINCIAL PARK

and RECREATION AREA

In the heart of the Skeena Mountains, southeast of Mount Edziza, is the remote Tatlatui Provincial Park. The park embraces 261,500 acres, dominated by Tatlatui, Kitchener, and Stalk lakes, whose crystal-clear blue waters mirror the towering 7,000-foot summits of the Tatlatui Range. This scenic wilderness reserve is accessible only by floatplane or canoe up the Finlay and Firesteel rivers. For travel information write: Parks Branch, 1019 Wharf St., Victoria V8W 2Y9. The wilderness traveler in the Tatlatui Range and the surrounding Skeena-Cassiar netherlands should be prepared for extremely variable weather conditions during the summer months, with rainstorms and strong midafternoon headwinds common.

Access & Outfitting Centers

The Atlin-Stikine region is reached by charter aircraft, the Chilkoot Trail, the Whitehorse and Yukon Railroad, and the Alaska Highway. The Cassiar Mountains and Stikine River areas are reached by Cassiar Highway 37 and charter aircraft. Wilderness outfitters, guides, and supplies are available at Telegraph Creek, Dease Lake, Watson Lake (Yukon), Haines (Alaska), Stewart, Atlin, and Carcross (Yukon).

Cariboo-Chilcotin Country

Bowron Provincial Park

Canadian National Topographic Survey Maps, scale 1:50,000: Lanzei Lake 93H-2, Spectacle Lakes 93H-3, Cariboo Lake 93A-14, Indian-point Lake 93H-6, Goat River 93H-7.

Chilko Lake & Chilcotin River.

Canadian National Topographic Survey Maps, scale 1:250,000: Mount Waddington 92-N, Anahim Lake 93-C, Quesnel 93-B, Taseko Lakes 92-O.

Wells Gray Provincial Park

Canadian National Topographic Survey Maps, scale 1:250,000: McBride 93-H, Quesnel Lake 93-A, Canoe River 83-D, Bonaparte Lake 92-P, Seymour Arm 82-M.

The Cariboo-Chilcotin plateau country, a scenic wilderness of deep forests of spruce, fir, red cedar, western hemlock, and lodgepole pine, alpine tundra, glaciers, ancient volcanic craters and lava flows, deep-cut canyons, wild rivers and lonely gemlike lakes, encompasses the Chilko, Central Coast, Chilcotin, and Horsefly wildlife management units. The region is famous for its excellent hunting for moose, mule deer, grizzly, and black bear.

The northernmost peaks of the Cariboo Mountains lie near the Fraser River in the Bowron Provincial Park, some 70 miles east of Quesnel. The park is a magnificent wilderness of more than 304,000 acres, roughly rectangular in shape and dominated by a chain of lakes that includes Kibbee, Indian Point, Issac, McLeary, Lanezi, Babcock, Sandy, Spectacle, and Bowron, and the Bowron and Cariboo rivers, as well as several portages. Anyone planning to canoe the wilderness lakes chain can expect to experience conditions similar to the hazards and hardships of frontier travel. At least 7–10 days should be planned to complete the trip. It's quite common to be stormbound for several days. There are seven portages around the lakes chain, with numerous log jams, rapids, boils, chutes, and eddies along the Bowron and Issac rivers. Be sure to bring along plenty of insect dope and waterproof

footwear and outer garments, since the park lies within the Interior West Belt and has frequent rainy spells. Light hip waders are particularly useful where the canoe must be lined and pulled over numerous beaver dams. Canoe rests are located along most portages. The wilderness canoe route passes through thick forests, aquatic moose pastures and beaver meadows, and deep valleys, dominated by the towering snow-covered peaks of McCabe Ridge, Tidiko Peaks, Mowdish Road, and Needle Point Ridge, rising to elevations of 8,200 feet. The park is a game sanctuary, and hunting for caribou, mountain goat, grizzly, and moose is forbidden. The lakes and rivers hold lunker Kamloops, Dolly Varden, lake trout, and kokanee salmon. There are several shelters and campsites along the canoe route. Preparations and guide arrangements should be made well in advance of your trip.

The *Bowron Lake Provincial Park Map-Brochure* is available free from the Supervisor, Bowron Lake Provincial Park, Box 33, Barkerville. It shows trails, campsites, patrol cabins, shelters, trail heads, falls, portages, and log jams and chutes, and lists canoe route distances and describes the wilderness canoe circuit, the Issac River, and camping areas, equipment, aircraft entry, and accommodations. The camping areas have 5–10 cleared tent spaces, fireplace rings, and pit toilets. The shelters are log cabins, generally in poor condition, intended for emergency use or to dry out. A *Bowron Lake Park Contour Map*, scale 1:63,360, is available for $1 from the Map Production Division, British Columbia Lands Service, Parliament Bldgs., Victoria V8V 1X5. A canoe float and small-boat-launching site are located near the park headquarters at Bowron Lake. Lodging and canoe outfitting are provided by *Becker's Canoe Outfitters & Lodge*, Box 129, Wells V0K 2R0; *Bowron Lake Lodge & Resorts* and *Chain of Lakes Canoe Outfitters & Lakeshore Campsite*, 740 Vaughan St., Quesnel V2J 2T5. The park is reached from Quesnel and the Cariboo Highway 97 via Highway 26 to Wells and the Barkerville gold-rush ghost town; a forest access road leads to the park headquarters.

The Cariboo region was originally the home and hunting grounds of the Carrier Indians, who in later times have adopted the name Tukulli. The area was called New Caledonia in the late 18th and early 19th centuries, during the fur trade era. Gold was discovered at Keithley Creek in 1859 and within a year the famous gold rush up the Cariboo Trail was at its peak. From 1874 to 1954, more than $27 million worth of gold was mined. The settlement of Quesnel Forks was the capital of British Columbia for a brief time, and was used as a stopover en route to the boomtown of Barkerville on the Cariboo Trail. At the height of the gold rush more than 10,000 prospectors flocked to Barkerville; they stayed for two summers, living mostly in tent camps erected around the mouth of the creek on Cariboo Lake. After the main gold rush of 1859–60, the Chinese carried on most of the mining and prospecting in place of the sourdoughs.

Guided helicopter mountaineering tours of the spectacular Cariboos are provided by Canadian Mountain Holidays. The firm operates the beautiful *Cariboo Lodge*, a rustic alpine resort, high in the range, built by mountain guides and craftsmen. For literature and rates, write or call: Canadian Mountain Holidays, P.O. Box 1660, Banff, Alta. T0L 0C0, (403) 762-4531.

South of Bowron Lake Provincial Park, in the southernmost Cariboos, are the Wells Gray Mountains and the remote 1.3-million-acre wilderness of the Wells Gray Provincial Park, about 240 air miles northeast of Vancouver. The Wells Gray wilderness is dominated by five huge, finger-shaped lakes—Hobson, Azure, Clearwater, Murtle, and Mahood—and contains the entire upper drainage of the Clearwater River. Hunting is permitted in the northern areas of the park for moose, mule deer, mountain caribou, goat, black and grizzly bear,

WELLS GRAY *Provincial* PARK

PROVINCIAL PARKS BRANCH

wolf, cougar, coyote, grouse, and ptarmigan. The southern region of Wells Gray is protected within the Murtle Lake nature conservancy area. The park is a famous wilderness camping and canoeing area. Many of the canoe routes, however, are extremely hazardous and should be attempted only by seasoned voyageurs. One of the most popular and scenic routes is the 64-mile trip along the Clearwater and Azure lakes waterway. The park's wilderness canoe routes, portages, falls, shelters, and campgrounds are shown on the *Wells Gray Provincial Park Map-Brochure* available free from Supervisor, Wells Gray Provincial Park, Box 297, Clearwater. Supplies, food, and lodging are available at the park headquarters on the south shore of Mahood Lake. Access to the Wells Gray region is by gravel road 25 miles north of Yellowhead Highway 5 and Clearwater; by gravel road and trail from Blue River on Yellowhead Highway 5, along the eastern shore of Murtle Lake; and via Cariboo Highway 97 and a 55-mile-long gravel road to huge Mahood Lake.

The scenic big-game hunting and wilderness camping areas among the 10,000-foot peaks and V-shaped valleys of the famous Premier Range lie due east of Wells Gray, bordered by Camp Creek and the Albreda, North Thompson, Raush, Fraser, McLennan, and Canoe rivers. West of Wells Gray Park lies Canim Lake, which at 21 miles long is the largest lake on the Cariboo Plateau, draining the greater part of this high moose and deer country. Canim's deep waters are famous for their giant Kamloops and lake trout up to 35 pounds. Fly-fishermen will find some great action on the Mahood and Canim rivers after the spring runoff for rainbow trout in the 3–5-pound class. North of Wells Gray are glacier-fed Quesnel and Horsefly lakes, renowned for their trophy rainbow and lake trout. Huge Quesnel Lake reaches depths of 1,500 feet, with its main body over 30 miles long, its north arm 28 miles long, and its east arm some 70 miles long. Wilderness lodging and guide service are provided by *Northern Lights Lodge*, Box 33, Likely V0L 1N0; *Wilderness Lodge Quesnel Lake*, P.O. Box 4701, Williams Lake V2G 2V7; *Loury's Lodges Ltd.*, Box 40, Horsefly V0L 1L0, on Quesnel Lake; *Horsefly Landing Resorts*, Box 125, Horsefly V0L 1L0; *North Country Lodge*, Box 100, Horsefly V0L 1L0; *Mahood Lake Resort*, RR1, Lone Butte, V0K 1X0.

West of Bowron Lake and Wells Gray provincial parks and the Cariboo Plateau frontier country is the vast wilderness of the Chilcotin Plateau. The gravel route of wilderness Highway 20 winds through the Chilcotin Country for 296 miles, past remote lakes, wild rivers, and valleys bordered on the west by the Coast Range, the ancient home and hunting grounds of the Carrier Indians, to Bella Coola and the Pacific Ocean. The major features of this beautiful region include Chilko Lake, the Fraser Plateau, Homathko Icefield, the southern portion of Tweedsmuir Provincial Park, Taseko Lakes, Tatla Lake, Nazko and West Road (Blackwater) rivers, Nimpo Lake, Chilcotin River, and the world-famous coastal salmon, steelhead, and resident rainbow trout waters of Dean and Bella Coola rivers. The large 45-mile-long Chilko Lake, rimmed by scenic mountains, has good fishing at the mouths of its feeder streams for bull Dolly Varden and rainbow trout. The cold deep water of Nimpo Lake, dotted by 7 islands, is one of the region's best producers of trophy rainbow trout. The Chilcotin Plateau is one of British Columbia's finest mule deer and moose hunting regions.

The scenic, wild Chilcotin flows from its headwaters through parklands, Douglas fir and lodgepole pine forests with patches of birch grass, sagebrush, black hawthorn, chokeberry, and mock orange, high lava ridges, deep valleys, and canyons marked by pillars of sandstone and cliffs to its confluence with the historic Fraser River. The salmon and steelhead of the Chilcotin and its major tributary, the Chilko, and

the moose, mule deer, and Dall sheep found in the surrounding highlands once fed the ancient "People of the Blue Water," as the Chilcotin Indians were called. The Chilcotins lived in covered pit houses known as Keekwilly Holes, which today can be seen along the Chilcotin River. Today the native Indians still net salmon from rock ledge "dipping stands" as their ancestors have done since time immemorial for their winter's food supply. The wild West Road or Blackwater River offers superb fishing for rainbow trout of 1–8 pounds and for lake trout and kokanee in its remote headwater lakes located high in the Ilgachuz Range Mountains. Alexander Mackenzie named the river the West Road as he followed its banks along the ancient Indian trail through the Chilcotin Plateau to its headwaters at Eliguk Lake and over the Coast Range to the Great Indian Village at the head of the Dean Channel, near present-day Bella Coola. The best way to reach the headwaters of the Chilcotin and West Road rivers is by floatplane charter.

Many of the wilderness lodges and hunting and fishing camps in the Chilcotin Region are fly-in by floatplane or land plane. Accommodations, campgrounds, big-game hunting and fishing guides, and boats and floatplane charter services are provided by *Chilcotin Lodge*, Riske Creek V0L 1T0, 30 miles west of Williams Lake on Highway 20; *Mons Lake Hunting & Fishing Camp*, Big Creek Post Office V0L 1E0; *Hitching Post*, Alexis Creek V0L 1A0; *Willow Springs Guest Ranch*, Alexis Creek V0L 1A0; *Barney's Lakeside Resort*, Chilanko Forks V0L 1H0; *Puntzi Lake Resort*, Chilanko Forks V0L 1H0; *Clearwater Lake Resort*, Kleena Kleene V0L 1M0; *Fred Hansen Hunting & Fishing Camp*, Clearwater Lake, Kleena Kleene V0L 1M0; *Pine Point Resort*, Nimpo Lake V0L 1R0; *Wilderness Rim Hunting & Fishing Camp*, Nimpo Lake V0L 1R0; *Dean River Resort Fishing Camp*, Nimpo Lake V0L 1R0; *Stewarts Lodge & Fishing Camps*, Nimpo Lake V0L 1R0; *Rainbow Lodge*, Nimpo Lake V0L 1R0; *Nimpo Lake Resort*, Nimpo Lake V0L 1R0; *Frontier Inn*, Anahim Lake V0L 1C0; *Escott Bay Fishing & Hunting Resort*, Anahim Lake V0L 1C0; *Anahim Lake Resort*, Anahim Lake V0L 1C0; *Tweedsmuir Lodge*, on the Atnarko River with steelhead and salmon fishing, 40 miles east of Bella Coola, write Stuie via Bella Coola; *Hunlen Wilderness Camp*, Box 308, Bella Coola V0T 1C0, fly-in from Nimpo Lake to Turner Lake with canoe trips on a 7-lake chain and cutthroat trout fly-fishing with canoe and tent rentals.

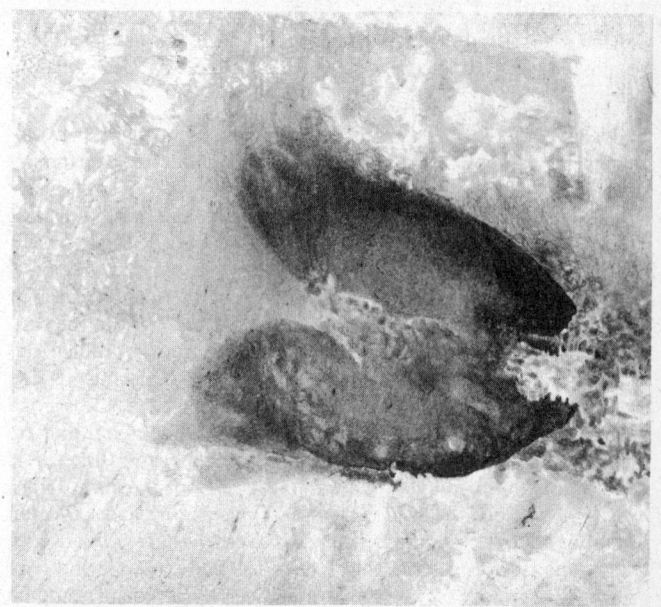

Chilcotin fly-in vacation accommodations are provided by *Chilko Lake Wilderness Ranch* (P.O. Box 4750, Williams Lake V2G 1H6; phone 604-398-8828), one of British Columbia's outstanding year-round lodge-resorts offering rustic facilities, airstrips, and guided fishing, hunting, canoeing, and backpacking trips throughout the Chilcotin-Coast Range region; *Bear Track, Chaunigan Lake & Twin Lake Lodges* (Box 4099, Williams Lake V2G 2V2); and the rustic *Tsuniah Lake Lodge* (Box 4685, Williams Lake V2G 2V7).

Access & Outfitting Centers

The Cariboo-Chilcotin country is reached by scheduled and charter aircraft service from major British Columbia cities, Canadian National Railroad, and Cariboo Highway 97, Yellowhead Highway 5 South, Yellowhead Highway 16, and Chilcotin Highway 20. Major outfitting and supply centers in the Cariboo Region include the towns of Williams Lake, 100 Mile House, Blue River, Quesnel, Mahood Lake, and Clearwater; outfitting and supply settlements along the Chilcotin Road include Williams Lake, Chilanko Forks, Tatla Lake, Nimpo Lake, Anahim Lake, Kleena Kleene, and Bella Coola.

Great Interior & the North Coast

Babine Lake & River Trophy Waters

Canadian National Topographic Survey Maps, scale 1:50,000: Kisgegas 93M-12, Gunanoot Lake 93M-11, Nilkitkwa River 93M-10, Netalzul Mountain 93M-7, Harold Price Creek 93M-2, Old Fort Mountain 93M-1, Fulton Lake 93L-16, Topley 93L-9, Tochcha 93K-13, Pendelton Bay 93K-12, Cunningham Lake 93K-11, Decker Lake 93K-5, Taltapin Lake 93K-6.

Fort St. James-Stuart Lake Area

Canadian National Topographic Survey Maps, scale 1:250,000: McLeod Lake 93-J, Fort Fraser 93-K, Manson River 93-N, Hazelton 93-M.

Kispiox River Trophy Waters

Canadian National Topographic Survey Maps, scale 1:50,000: Hazelton 93M-5, Kisgegas 93M-12, Kispiox River 103P-9, Cranberry River 103P-10, Brown Bear Lake 103P-15.

Tweedsmuir Provincial Park

Canadian National Topographic Survey Maps, scale 1:250,000: Whitesail Lake 93-E, Nechako River 93-F, Bella Coola 93-D, Anahim Lake 93-C.

The Great Interior and North Coast regions encompass the world-famous big-game hunting, fishing, and wilderness canoe-camping areas of the Upper Fraser, Finlay, Parsnip, Stuart-Nechako, Peace River, Skeena, and North Coast wildlife management units. This vast wilderness stretches from the Pacific shoreline and dense fir, cedar, and pine forests of the North Coast through the unbroken boreal forests, alpine tundra, wild rivers, and lakes of the Central Interior Plateau to the Peace River plains and Upper Fraser River on the east. Moose, mountain caribou, sheep, black and grizzly bear, mule deer, wolf, and wolverine are found in the remote highlands of the Omineca, Babine, Hogem, Sicintine, Bulkley, Hazelton, Coast, and Rocky mountains. Elk are making a comeback in the interior, but are rarely seen. Furbearers are abundant and include beaver, fisher, fox, lynx, marten, mink, muskrat (known to the early fur traders as "musquash"), otter, and weasel. Canada geese, merganser, and harlequin ducks are often seen by the wilderness traveler. Ospreys, kingfishers, golden and bald eagles, and black terns fish and scavenge the river valleys. Cliff swallows and warblers nest along the riverbanks, and on higher ground, back from the alder and willow stands. Franklin grouse are abundant.

The mighty Skeena River system takes in a 15,000-square-mile wilderness in the western central portion of the province. Although the Skeena is seldom fished because of discoloration from glacial runoff, its tributaries, such as the Kispiox, Sustut, Bulkley, Morice, Babine, Zyometz, and Kitwanga rivers, are renowned for their trophy Chinook, coho, and steelhead fishing. These wild, mercurial rivers produce a unique strain of giant sea-run rainbows that often reach weights of 30 pounds and over. Rugged logging roads provide access to many of the best holding pools and riffles along these "big fish" tributaries. The remote waters of the Sustut and Babine, however, are reached only by float plane or jet boat. Yellowhead Highway 16, east of Prince Rupert, provides access to jumping-off points as it winds close by the Skeena between Hazelton and Terrace. Near the scenic 9,000-foot Seven Sisters the highway passes through a spectacular canyon area of the Coast Range. The beautiful Kispiox River, located due north of the Yellowhead Highway and the Indian village of Kispiox, flows from its headwaters high in the Skeena Mountains through a large plateau dotted by remote blue lakes for 50 miles to its confluence with the Skeena. The Kispiox has densely forested banks with deep holding pools and riffles. The old world's record 36-pound steelhead was caught here in October 1954. The Kispiox steelhead average 12–18 pounds of explosive, acrobatic fury. The upper stretches of the river are reached by gravel and dirt access roads. Guides and lodging are provided by the *Kispiox Steelhead Camp*, RR1, Hazelton; *Sportsman's Kispiox Lodge*, RR1, Kispiox Rd., Hazelton; and *Raven Wood Resort*, Kispiox Valley Rd., Hazelton V0J 1Y0.

The famous Babine River flows out of its namesake lake to its confluence with the Skeena in the Babine Range, and offers top-ranked fly-fishing for salmon, steelhead, and native rainbows. One of the best spots to fish is at the head of the river when the giant Kamloops trout move into the river from Babine Lake to feed on the millions of sockeye salmon fry. The beautiful deep blue waters of Babine Lake, British Columbia's largest natural body of water (covering 250 square miles), hold trophy rainbow and lake trout to 40 pounds. The surface of the lake can be extremely treacherous and guides with safe, sturdy boats to withstand sealike waves are a must. Access to the lake and river is via secondary roads from the Yellowhead Highway. Campgrounds, boat-launching sites, and seaplane bases are located at Topley Landing and Pendelton Bay. Guides, supplies, lodging, and wilderness big-game outfitters are provided by *Babine Lodge*, Topley Landing; *Totem Resort & Marina*, Box 1, Topley Landing V0J 2Y0; and *Babine Lake Resort*, Box 64, Burns Lake V0J 1E0. First-class rustic accommodations and guides on the powerful Babine, protected as a provincial "trophy river" where giant steelhead average 15-20 pounds, are provided by Bob Wickwire's remote *Babine River Steelhead Resort Ltd.* (Box 3040, Smithers V0J 2N0) reached by a 7-mile jet boat trip down river from the Salmon Fishery Weir and by the *Babine River Rainbow Lodge* (Box 3399, Smithers V0J 2N0). Rustic accommodations and guide service on the Sustut River are provided by *Suskeena Enterprises Ltd.*, P.O. Box 596, Kamloops V2C 5L7.

High in the Laskinia Mountains far to the north of Babine Lake lies Thutade Lake, the headwaters of the wild Finlay River. The Finlay flows from the lake for 250 miles through some of the finest wilderness and big-game country in North America before it flows into Williston Lake to form the historic waters of the mighty Peace River, known to the Indians as Unjagah. The upper Finlay is a fly-fisherman's paradise for arctic grayling, rainbows, and Dolly Varden to 10 pounds. The Finlay is reached by floatplane, packtrain, or riverboat. The remote Nation River and lakes chain lies high in moose and grizzly country

about 115 miles north of Fort St. James. The Nation offers wilderness fishing for arctic char, grayling, rainbow, and lake trout. Fort St. James, established by the Hudson's Bay Company in 1806, is the outfitting center and jumping-off point for outdoorsmen heading into the 200-mile-long chain of lakes and rivers stretching from Stuart Lake north along the powerful Tachie River for 19 miles to beautiful Trembleur Lake, famous for its 5–16-pound rainbow trout, across Trembleur to the peaceful marshes and beaver meadows of the Middle River moose country to Takla Lake, and on through a spectacular fjord, north to the beckoning wild Driftwood River and its Bear Lake headwaters high in the Driftwood Range. The entire region, especially the Middle River area, is considered the best moose country in British Columbia. Great Beaver Lake and the wild Salmon and Musky rivers flow through the dense lodgepole pine, Douglas fir, and spruce forests east of Fort St. James; and to the south are the wilderness canoe routes along the Stuart and Nechako rivers. Set in the remote Omineca Mountains on 8-mile long Tutizzi Lake are the *Omineca Wilderness Lodges* with a rustic main lodge and A-frame cabins, guide service, and trophy fishing for rainbow, Dolly Varden, and lake trout. Write: Dawson Creek V1G 3M4, (604) 782-8205.

The rugged untamed wilderness of Tweedsmuir Provincial Park encompasses 2.5 million acres, roughly triangular in shape, bounded on the north and northwest by the huge Ootsa-Whitesail Lakes reservoir, on the west and southwest by the Coast Mountains, and on the east by the Interior Plateau. In the northern section of the park is the Eutsuk nature conservancy area and the Quanchus Range; and in the south is the Rainbow nature conservancy area and the glowing reds, brilliant yellows, grays, and lavenders of the Rainbow Mountains—*Tsitsutl* in Carrier Indian dialect, meaning "painted mountains," surrounded by lush green meadows and snowfields. In the northern section, Eutsuk and Pondosy lakes offer stiff big-lake canoeing opportunities. High winds and waves, unmarked reefs, and shoals provide constant hazards. The giant 200-mile-long circular chain formed by Eutsuk, Pondosy, Tetachuck, Natakuz, Ootsa, and Whitesail lakes should be traveled only with an experienced guide. The alpine meadows and parks, slopes, and open valleys of Tweedsmuir are famous as a hunting reserve where moose, mountain caribou, mule deer, and black and grizzly bear may be taken in season. Guides and outfitters will provide access to the outstanding big-game regions in the Whitesail Mountains, Quanchus Range, Fawnie Range, and Coast Range Mountains.

The *Tweedsmuir Provincial Park Map-Brochure,* available free from the Parks Branch, 1019 Wharf St., Victoria, V8W 2Y9, shows all major topographic features including Tzeetsaytsul Peak, named by the Carrier Indians for the rumble and boom of its glacier; Hunlen Falls on the famous steelhead waters of the Atnarko River; the rapids and pools of the Bella Coola and Dean Rivers; and Lonesome Lake, framed in a book by Leland Stowe, *Crusoe of Lonesome Lake,* the saga of Ralph Edwards, who settled at Lonesome Lake just after the turn of the century, many years before the park was established. The Tweedsmuir map also shows nature conservancy boundaries, roads, portages, trails, and areas closed to bear hunting. Ill-defined Indian and game trails, suitable for packhorse and wilderness hiking, provide access to remote high country lakes; in the southern portion is the ancient overland Indian trail traveled by Alexander Mackenzie to the great village of the Bella Coola Indians and the Pacific Ocean—known to the Carrier Indians of the interior as the "stinking lake." Here, in July 1793, Mackenzie became the first European to traverse the continent, after a soul-searing journey from Fort Chipewyan on Lake Athabasca up the Peace River to the headwaters of the wild Parsnip River at the Continental Divide, down through the interior wilderness in the an-

cient home and hunting grounds of the Carrier Indians—named after their custom of having widows carry the bones of their husbands on their backs during the mourning period—to the Pacific and the opulent, complex culture of the Coastal Indian tribes.

The Burnt Bridge and Atnarko River campgrounds are located on Chilcotin Highway 20, which runs through the southern section of the park. Lodging, guides, and boat and canoe rentals are provided by *Tweedsmuir Lodge,* write Stuie via Bella Coola V0T 1C0 and the *Hunlen Wilderness Camp,* Box 308, Bella Coola V0T 1C0. Tweedsmuir is reached via Yellowhead Highway 16 and gravel access roads from Vanderhoof to the Kenny Dam, Burns Lake, the François Lake ferry to the settlement of Cotsa Lake, Houston, Chilcotin Highway 20 on the south, and the Canadian National Railway.

Vacation lodges and salmon fishing resorts along the coastal fjords, flanked by the Coast Range, include *Good Hope Cannery Lodge* (Rivers Inlet), 3740 Highway, West Vancouver; *River's Lodge* fishing resort, Rivers Inlet, Dawsons Landing V0N 1M0; *Rivers Inlet Resort* (a top-ranked fly-in fishing vacation resort), P.O. Box 25787, Seattle, WA 98125.

The *Copper River Ranch,* located by the shores of McDonell Lake on the headwaters of the Copper River, approximately 28 miles west of Smithers, specializes in family recreation during the summer months and steelhead fishing and big game hunting during the fall months. The ranch accommodations are rustic cabins with wood heat. There is a log cook cabin for serving meals family style. Write: Box 2047, Smithers V0J 2N0.

Access & Outfitting Centers

The North Coast region is reached via Yellowhead Highway 16, the Canadian National Railway, British Columbia Marine Ferries, scheduled and charter air service, and Cariboo Highway 97 and Chilcotin Highway 20 to the Bella Coola Valley; guides, supplies, lodging, and wilderness fly-in services are located at Bella Coola, Ocean Falls, Kitimat, and Prince Rupert. The Great Interior and Peace River area is reached via Yellowhead Highway 16, Highways 37 and 27, the John Hart-Peace River Highway, the Canadian National Railway, and scheduled and charter aircraft. Guides, supplies, outfitters, lodging,

and wilderness fly-in service are provided at Hazelton, Smithers, Houston, Burns Lake, Fraser Lake, Fort St. James, Vanderhoof, Prince George, Mackenzie, Chetwynd, Hudson Hope, and Dawson Creek.

Liard River Country & the Northern Rockies

Kwadacha Wilderness Provincial Park

Canadian National Topographic Survey Maps, scale 1:250,000: Tuchodi Lakes 94-K, Ware 94-F.

Liard River

Canadian National Topographic Survey Maps, scale 1:250,000: McDame 104-P, Rabbit River 94-M, Toad River 94-N, Maxhanish Lake 94-O, Fort Liard 95-B, Sibbeston Lake 95-G, Fort Simpson 95-H.

Muncho Lake & Stone Mountain Provincial Parks

Canadian National Topographic Survey Maps, scale 1:50,000: Trout River 94-N4, Muncho Lake 94-K13, Upper Toad River 94-K12, Toad Hotsprings 94-K14, Racing River 94-K11, Stone Mountain 94-K15, MacDonald Creek 94-K10.

This far north region is located in northeastern British Columbia and encompasses the northernmost Rocky Mountains and the Liard and Interior plains. The region falls within the Liard wildlife management unit, and is bordered on the north by the Yukon Territory, on the east by Alberta, and on the south and west by the Peace River and Cassiar Mountains. The great boreal evergreen forests, plains, brawling wild rivers, and majestic highlands form one of North America's finest big-game hunting, fishing, and wilderness canoe-camping areas. Leaving Fort Nelson, the Alaska Highway winds through the Northern Rockies and the Interior and Liard plains northwestward for 200 miles to Watson Lake, Yukon Territory. The highway is the primary access route in the Liard River country. Guides, outfitters, supplies, and accommodations are available at the milepost lodges located along the route.

The historic Liard (pronounced *Leeard*), which means "poplar" in French on account of the numerous poplar stands along its banks, is a major tributary of the Mackenzie River. It drains the eastern slope of the Northern Rockies and flows across the northern plain and joins the Mackenzie River at Fort Simpson in the Northwest Territories.

The Liard, the Athabasca, and the Peace rivers were the great water highways for the early explorers and northmen of the fur trade. The mouth of the Liard was first sighted by Alexander Mackenzie in 1789 (who named it the "River of the Mountains"), while on his historic canoe voyage down the Mackenzie to the great "Frozen Ocean." The remote tributaries of the Liard offer some superb fishing for Dolly Varden and arctic grayling up to 4 pounds in the Red, Toad, Grayling, Rabbit, and Beaver rivers.

The spectacular alpine grandeur of the isolated northernmost Rockies is big-game hunting country for grizzly, mountain caribou and goat, Stone sheep, and moose. The Northern Rockies contain hundreds of gemlike headwater lakes drained by the Gataga and Kechika rivers on the northwest, the Racing and Muskwa rivers on the east, and the Finlay, Parsnip, and Fox rivers along the great Rocky Mountain Trench to the west, which stretches for 1,100 miles from Montana's northwest to the Liard River and the Yukon in a great diagonal swath 5–10 miles wide. This huge trough has served as the Great North Trail for trappers, fur traders, explorers, pioneers, and Indians since the days of early North American man.

The major features of the region include the Great Snow Mountain area, Battle of Britain Range, Tower of London Range, and Kwadacha Wilderness—a 414,000-acre provincial reserve dominated by the Lloyd George Ice Field, and Quentin and Haworth lakes—the headwaters of the wild Kwadacha, Tuchodi, Muskwa, and Warneford rivers. Access is by bush plane or floatplane from the Churchill Mine Airstrip. The glacial alpine lakes and rivers hold big Dolly Varden and arctic grayling. Up north, the Alaska Highway passes through the east section of Muncho Lake Provincial Park at Mile 456 and continues southeast through the heart of beautiful Stone Mountain Park at Mile 390. The deep blue-green waters of Muncho Lake, surrounded by dense evergreen forests and towering Rocky Mountain highlands, hold lake trout up to over 50 pounds and whitefish and grayling up to 3 pounds. Wildlife sometimes seen along the shores of Muncho Lake includes mountain caribou and goat, beaver, black bear, and Stone sheep. Liard River country is one of the province's top hunting areas for caribou. Unlike the keen-eyed wild sheep, the caribou has an unusually poor sense of smell and vision for an open-country animal, and more than one story has been told in the north country of a bull caribou trying to add a lady packhorse to his harem. Caribou are daylight feeders; the most likely places to spot them are above the timberline on high slopes, snow patches, gravel ridges, and along riverbanks and ponds during the warm summer months. The climate in these netherlands is often frightfully cold and frequently there is still snow until the spring storms during April and May. The rivers are usually high in June and July, and the summers are often cool and rainy. August and September are the best months to drive or fly into this area. Bush planes or floatplanes can be chartered in Fort Nelson to get into the remote alpine hunting and fishing areas.

Lodging and guide service are provided by *Toad River Lodge*, Mile 937, Alaska Hwy.; *Muncho Lake Lodge*, Mile 463, Alaska Hwy.; *Wiebe's Wilderness Motel & Fishing Camp*, Mile 463.3 Alaska Hwy.; and *Lower Liard River Lodge*, Mile 496, Alaska Hwy. Wilderness fly-in service is provided by *AG Air Ltd.*, Box 1022 and *Kenn Borek Air Ltd.*, both of Dawson Creek V1G 3T8.

Access & Outfitting Centers

Liard River country is reached by scheduled air flights to Fort Nelson and via the Alaska Highway from Dawson Creek or Watson Lake. Food, supplies, lodging, guides, and fly-in service are located on the Alaska Highway at Fort Nelson, Toad River, Muncho Lake, Liard River, Smith River, and Lower Post.

Okanagan & the Kamloops Country

Garibaldi & Golden Ears Provincial Parks

Canadian National Topographic Survey Maps, scale 1:50,000: Coquitlam 92G-7, Pitt River 92G-10, Squamish 92G-11, Mamquam Mountain 92G-15, Cheakamus River 92G-14, Alta Lake 92J-2, Brandywine 92J-3, Pemberton 92J-7.

Kamloops Lake Country

Canadian National Topographic Survey Maps, scale 1:50,000: Kamloops 92I-9, Cherry Creek 92I-10, Tranquille River 92I-15, Heffley 92I-16.

Lillooet Range

Canadian National Topographic Survey Maps, scale 1:250,000: Vancouver 92-G, Hope 92-H, Ashcroft 92-I, Pemberton 92-J.

Manning & Cathedral Provincial Parks

Canadian National Topographic Survey Maps, scale 1:50,000: Manning 92H-2, Ashnola 92H-1.

The Okanagan-Fraser Canyon region is located in south central British Columbia and takes in the Similameen, Okanagan, Nicola, Bonaparte, and Squamish-Harrison wildlife management areas. The region is well known for its wilderness camping and hunting for mule and whitetail deer, black bear, elk, moose, mountain goat, grizzly bear, bighorn sheep, and upland game birds including blue, ruffed, and Franklin grouse, morning dove, pheasant and California quail in the Beaverdell Range, and Christina and Midway ranges in the Okanagan Highlands on the east and in the Cascade and Coast ranges on the west. The Okanagan is one of the finest waterfowl areas in the Pacific Northwest. Okanagan Lake, a narrow 60 miles long, is the largest lake in the region and has good fishing for kokanee and Kamloops trout of 3–25 pounds. The Kamloops country north of Okanagan offers some of the best fishing in interior British Columbia for Dolly Varden, kokanee, and Kamloops trout in 16-mile-long Kamloops Lake and in Lac Le June, known as the "Lake of the Jumping Fish" for its acrobatic strain of rainbow trout known to leap 2–3 feet in the air when hooked, beautiful Knouff Lake, the temperamental Lac des Roches, the fly-fishing waters of Hihium Lake (Indian for "Lake of Plenty"), Bonaparte Lakes, and hundreds of scenic alpine lakes such as Mile High and the 4,000-foot-high Aurora Lakes chain and Loopin chain of lakes.

Southeast of the great Fraser River Canyon, which forms a natural barrier between the snowcapped peaks of the Coast Range and Cascade Mountains, is Manning Provincial Park. The park encompasses 176,000 acres of remote hiking trails and wilderness camping and fishing areas in the heart of the North Cascades, stretching north from the Washington-British Columbia border. The major features of Manning Park include the wild Skagit, flowing west and south to the Pacific Ocean, and the Similameen, which enters the Okanagan, a major tributary of the Columbia, the Skyline Trail to Shadow and Nepopekum Falls, Heather Trail to Three Lakes Chain, and the northern terminus of the Pacific Crest National Scenic Trail, stretching from the California-Mexico boundary north through the High Sierras, Oregon, and Washington to Monument 78 at the British Columbia-Washington international boundary. The park is the eastern terminus for the 120-mile-long Centennial Trail from Vancouver. Ultimately this footpath will be extended through the Okanagan region to the Rocky Mountains, if plans are successful to revive the century-old Dewdney Trail. The park also has primitive trails blazed centuries ago by the Indians and later by fur brigades and sourdoughs.

The *Manning Provincial Park* Map-Brochure, available free from the District Superintendent, Manning Provincial Park, Manning V0X 1R0, (604) 840-8836, shows all nature trails, hiking trails, wilderness camps and shelters, campgrounds, paved and gravel roads, and major features of the park. The Superintendent's Office also publishes a free *Manning Provincial Park Ski Touring Trails Map.* Ski and road reports may be obtained during the season by phoning (604) 929-2358 or 929-2359 in Vancouver. There are four campgrounds in the park: Hampton, 80 units; Mule Deer, 49 units; Coldspring, 68 units; and the Lightning Lake Campground, 91 units. Each camping unit consists of a parking spur, cleared tent space, fireplace, and picnic table. Overnight lodging is available at the *Manning Park Lodge* and *Gateway Lodge*, both Manning Park V0X 1R0. Park access is via Highway 56 from Hope or Princeton.

Cathedral Provincial Park, about 20 miles to the east of Manning, embraces 18,000 acres of lake-dotted alpine wilderness. The dominant features of the park are the beautiful cluster of sparkling gemlike lakes, Ladyslipper, Quiniscoe, Lake of the Woods, Scout, Pyramid, and Glacier, and the surrounding alpine meadows and crags of the Sawtooth Range. The interior highland lakes and the Ashnola River hold rainbow and cutthroat trout. Cathedral is linked to Manning Provincial Park by trail along Wall Creek, the Ashnola River, and Easygoing Creek, connecting with the U.S. Forest Service Trail in Manning Park at Monument 83. A small campground is located at the park entrance near the footbridge spanning the Ashnola River. The free *Cathedral Provincial Park Map*, and wilderness camping and hiking info, may be obtained by writing District Superintendent, Parks Branch, Box 318, Summerland V0H 1Z0.

Due west of the historic lower Fraser River, with its overlapping spawning runs of salmon, steelhead, and sea-run cutthroat trout, are the great Coast Range peaks, majestic glaciers, cascading rivers, and jewellike lakes of Garibaldi and Golden Ears provincial parks. The major features of Garibaldi Park include the volcanic wildlands within the Black Tusk nature conservancy area, dominated by the Diamond Head, Panorama Ridge, Helm Glacier, and Barrier and Garibaldi lakes. The roads, hiking trails, campgrounds, lava flows, and major features of Garibaldi Park's 484,000 acres are shown on the *Garibaldi Provincial Park Map*, available free along with wilderness camping and

travel information from Parks Branch, 1019 Wharf St., Victoria. Primitive campsites are located around beautiful glacier-fed Cheakamus Lake, with the mile-high summits of the Coast Range towering above its thickly forested shores. The Red Heather Campground and Diamond Head Campground are located along Paul Ridge. Access to the main routes into the park is by Highway 99 and the British Columbia Railway along the western boundary. Extending southward from Garibaldi is the rugged 137,000-acre Coast Range wilderness of Golden Ears Provincial Park—named for the twin peaks of Golden Ears Mountain, the region was once the site of the province's greatest railroad logging operations. Hiking trails provide access to the alpine camping areas and to the steelhead, cutthroat, kokanee, and Dolly Varden waters of Alouette Lake and River, Mike Lake, Gold Creek, Pitt Lake and River, and Stave Lake adjacent to the eastern park boundary. There are boat-launching sites at most lakes. The Alouette Lake Campground and Gold Creek Campground are located near Alouette Lake. The park is reached from access roads off Highway 7 from Vancouver. Wilderness camping and fishing information and the free *Golden Ears Provincial Park—Alouette Lake Area Trails Map* may be obtained by writing Regional Supervisor, Golden Ears Provincial Park, Box 7000, Maple Ridge.

Rustic vacation lodging in Garibaldi Park is provided by *Garibaldi Lodge* and *Alpine Lodge*, both Highway 99, Garibaldi Highlands V0N 3G0.

Access & Outfitting Centers

The Okanagan and Fraser Canyon region is reached via the Canadian National Railroad and British Columbia Railway, by car along Highways 5, 3, 7, 99, 97, 8, and 12, and along the Trans-Canada and Yellowhead Highway 5. Scheduled airlines flights serve major towns and cities. Lodging, guides, outfitters, and charter fly-in services are available in Vancouver, Squamish, Lillooet, Vernon, Kelowna, Summerland, Penticton, and Osoyoos.

Queen Charlotte Islands

Queen Charlotte Islands Topo Maps

Canadian National Topographic Survey Maps, scale 1:250,000: Dixon Entrance 103-K, Prince Rupert 103-J, Graham Island 103-F, Hecate Strait 103-G, Moresby Island 103-B & C.

Naikoon Provincial Park

Canadian National Topographic Survey Maps, scale 1:50,000: Tow Hill 103G-4, Eagle Hill 103G-13, Tlell 103G-12, Port Clements 103F-9, Masset Sound 103F-16.

The Queen Charlotte Islands, known as the Misty Islands, have changed little since they were first visited by explorers two centuries ago. These often fog-shrouded islands, once the home and hunting grounds of the proud Haida Indians, consist of five main islands, Langara, Moresby, Graham, Kunghit, and St. James, grouped in a triangular shape 156 miles long and 52 miles at their greatest width. The Queen Charlotte archipelago consists of some 150 islands and islets located in the Pacific about 80 miles west of Prince Rupert and the mainland north coast. The scenic, rugged fjords, long sandy beaches, inlets, wild coastal rivers and impenetrable forests, and alpine highlands of the Queen Charlotte Range Mountains offer some of the finest steelhead and salmon fishing, wilderness camping, and big-game hunting for black bear, elk, and blacktail deer in British Columbia, and a profusion of coastal wildlife including bald eagle, seabirds, and migrating waterfowl traveling the Pacific Flyway. Indigenous mammals such as marten and otter and introduced species like the Roosevelt elk and beaver are common. Cutthroat and Dolly Varden trout are found in Mayer Lake; some of the other lakes and streams with the rivers,

especially the serpentine Tlell, provide good steelhead fishing. Weather conditions are extremely variable and overcast skies, fog, and high winds are commonplace.

A Guide to the Queen Charlotte Islands published by the Alaska Northwest Publishing Co., Box 4-EEE, Anchorage, AK 99509 ($2.95), provides a detailed description of the recreation areas and major features of Graham and Moresby islands, including the adjacent Langara, Louise, Kunghit, and St. James islands as well as info on weather, clothing, camping, hunting, and fishing. One of the fascinating features of the Misty Islands is the abandoned villages and totem poles of the once powerful Haida Indians. Before British Columbia was explored and settled by Europeans, and for some years afterward, Haida warriors, braving the violent seas in dugout cedar war canoes, swooped south to the mainland and west to Vancouver to raid and plunder rival Indian villages and returned to their mist-shrouded isles with slaves. Near the rare golden spruce, a tall and shapely tree with golden needles growing along the Yakoun River, lies an uncompleted dugout canoe nearly 50 feet long, abandoned for some unknown reason over a century ago by the Haida craftsmen. Old logging roads crisscross the island and provide excellent hiking trails to the remote scenic lakes, abandoned Haida longhouses and whaling stations, and towering limestone spires along the rugged coastal inlets. A working knowledge of the tides is essential for anyone contemplating travel in the coastal areas. No attempt should be made to hike the coastal areas at high tide or when tides are flooding. High-topped leather or rubber boots should be carried and proper hiking boots should be worn.

Naikoon Provincial Park covers 179,000 acres of coastal wilderness along the northeast corner of Graham Island, the largest and most populous of the Queen Charlotte Islands. Naikoon, which means "long nose" in the Haida dialect, is the Haida name for Rose Point, one of the important recreational features of the park. The major features of the park include the broad expanses of surf-pounded beach nearly 300 yards wide on McIntyre Bay, and the cutthroat and Dolly Varden waters of Mayer and Hickey lakes and in the northern section of the Argonaut Plain, a wildland of stunted pines, muskeg, meandering oxbow streams, meadows, and low flat-topped hills. The *Naikoon Provincial Park Map-Brochure* and travel information are available from the District Superintendent, Parks Branch, Box 119, Terrace V8G 4A2. (Note that special permission is needed to visit certain abandoned Indian villages. Be sure to check with local authorities.)

Access & Lodging

Wilderness outfitting, hunting and fishing guides, and lodging are provided by the *Copper Bay Lodge*, Box 52, Sandspit V0T 1T0; *Richardson Ranch*, Box 10, Tlell V0T 1Y0; *Tanoo Lodge*, General Delivery, Tlell V0T 1Y0; and *Tlell River Lodge*, Box 28, Tlell V0T 1Y0. The Queen Charlotte Islands are served by regularly scheduled airlines and by ferries operated by the *Misty Islands Transportation Company*, Box 8, RR 1, Queen Charlotte City V0T 1S0; *Northland Navigation Co., Ltd.*, 2285 Commissioner St., Vancouver V5L 1A9; and *Rivtow Straits Ltd.*, 2215 Commissioner St., Vancouver V5L 1A8. A highway connects the coastal towns of Queen Charlotte City, Tlell, Port Clements, Masset, and Tow Hill along the northern boundary of Naikoon Provincial Park.

Rocky Mountains & the Great Divide Wilderness

Glacier National Park

Canadian National Topographic Survey Map, scale 1:126,720: Glacier Park 82N/SW.

lands of the park and moose are found along the Moose and Fraser rivers and in the marshes at the east end of Moose Lake. Mountain goat and grizzly are found in the highlands surrounding Yellowhead Lake and mule deer, elk, and black bear are found throughout the subalpine forests of white and black spruce, fir, red cedar, balsam, and alder. Developed campgrounds are located at Robson Meadows (127 sites), Robson River (19 sites), and Lucerne (32 sites). Wilderness camping shelters are located along the Berg Lake Trail at the north

end of Kinney Lake, in the Valley of the Thousand Falls, and at Berg Lake. Lodging and accommodations are available at the *Mount Robson Motor Village* and *Mount Robson Ranch* near the western boundary of the park. Access is via the Yellowhead Highway at Tête Jaune Caché on the Fraser River at the western gateway and at Yellowhead Pass, the eastern gateway. Tête Jaune, French for "Yellowhead," is the nickname of a blond fur trader and trapper of mixed Iroquois blood who crossed the Rockies in the early 19th century through the pass that bears his name. He is thought to be either Pierre Hatsinaton, who guided Iroquois fur hunters into the area in 1820, or François Decoigne, a trapper employed by the Hudson's Bay Company in 1814.

Yoho National Park, known as the "roof of the Rockies," lies to the south of Mount Robson, encompassing 507 square miles along the west slope of the Great Divide, bordered on the east by Alberta's Banff

Park and on the south by Kootenay National Park. Thousands of years before the explorers, fur traders, and railroad surveyors of the Palliser expedition discovered the great alpine wilderness surrounding the Kicking Horse Pass that is now preserved within the park, Cree Indian tribes had set up camps around Emerald Lake and explored the Yoho Valley—named after a Cree expression meaning "awe." Scenic wilderness hiking trails such as the Highline, Avalanche, and Beaver Dam trails wind through the remote alpine valleys and meadows, and along high ridges and glacial stream banks to McArthur Pass, Beaverfoot River, Opabin Glacier, the Elizabeth Parker huts on the Lake O'Hara Meadows, Presidential Range Peaks, Yoho Lake, Morning Glory Lakes, Ice River, and the Des Poilus Glacier. The cross-country wilderness traveler must register with park officials. Tent and trailer campgrounds are located at Kicking Horse, Hoodoo Creek, and Chancellor Peak; tents only are allowed at the Lake O'Hara and Takakkaw Falls campgrounds. Advance reservations are required. Dolly Varden, rainbow, cutthroat, and brook trout are found in lakes and streams free of glacial silt. Wilderness travel and camping info, and the free *Yoho National Park Map-Brochure* showing roads, campgrounds, hiking trails, warden stations, fire towers, shelters, and topography, may be obtained by writing Superintendent, Yoho National Park, Box 99, Field. Access is via Trans-Canada Highway 1.

Stretching for 65 miles parallel to the Continental Divide are the alpine lakes, glaciers, deep canyons, hot springs, and ocher beds in the 543-square-mile wilderness of Kootenay National Park. Kootenay is from the Indian word *K'tunaxa*, which means "people from beyond the hills." Long before the first white explorers and trappers visited the area, Kootenay Indians from the upper Columbia and Kootenay River valleys and Stony and Blackfoot Indians from the Rocky Mountain foothills and plains of Alberta traveled here to collect ocher from the "paint pots" and ocher beds near the Vermilion River southwest of Marble Canyon for use in painting their bodies for war, tepees, clothing, and pictographs on rock faces. According to the Stony Indians, they used to hear flutelike sounds or war songs from the big animal spirit or thunder spirit in the paint pots around the outlets of the mineral springs. The red ocher collected from the paint pots, or *Usna Waki-Cagubi* (Indian dialect for "where the red clay spirit is taken"), was mixed with fish oil and melted bear or deer fat. During times of war the Kootenays used the ocher to paint red human hands on the shoulders of their horses so that their "enemies might fall in front of them and raise their hands for mercy." Ancient ocher rock paintings on limestone ledges in Sinclair Canyon at the southwestern end of the park depict wapiti or elk, bighorn sheep, bear, horses, and spirits. In the 1840s George Simpson explored the area in search of a freight route through Rockies over what is now known as Simpson Pass, to the Columbia River.

The *Kootenay National Park Map-Brochure*, the free publications *Birds of Kootenay*, *Bighorn Sheep*, *Wapiti*, and *Banff-Windermere Parkway*, and wilderness camping, hiking trails, and travel information are available from the Superintendent, Kootenay National Park, Box 220, Radium Hot Springs V0A 1M0. Wilderness hiking trails wind through forests of fir and spruce in the Columbia and Kootenay valleys, and above the timberline at approximately 7,000 feet, through windswept meadows covered with red and white mountain heather, dwarf willow, and bog laurel. The backcountry trails provide access to the major features of the Kootenay, including Sinclair Canyon, Kindersley Pass, Cobb Lake, Kootenay River, Floe Lake, Simpson River, the paint pots, Marble Canyon, Vermilion River, Ottertail Pass, and Kaufman Lake. Big-game animals in the Kootenay Park include elk, mule deer, mountain goat, and bighorn sheep; a few grizzly roam the remote high country regions. Banff-Windermere Parkway 93 travels

the length of the park and is the gateway to Yoho and Banff national parks. Campgrounds are located at McLeod Meadows, Marble Canyon, and Redstreak.

Mount Assiniboine Provincial Park embraces 96,500 acres of spectacular alpine scenery, dominated by the craggy heights of 11,870-foot Mount Assiniboine, in a roughly arrowhead shape between the Great Divide and Banff National Park on the east and Kootenay National Park on the west. Long before the arrival of the explorers of the Northwest and Hudson's Bay Company, the Stoney or Assiniboine Indians, meaning "those who cook by placing hot stones in water," migrated northwest along the Great North Trail from the great plains to the area dominated by Mount Assiniboine. At the lower elevations the park is covered by a green boreal forest of spruce mixed with stands of alpine fir and lodgepole pine; and in the clearings and forest meadows, by scattered patches of false azalea, buffalo berries, white rhododendron, and a few stands of red elder. Above timberline is a ground cover of red and white heather and grouseberries, stunted white-bark

High in the ancient Selkirk Mountains due west of Yoho National Park and the Continental Divide are the spectacular alpine wilderness areas of Glacier and Mount Revelstoke national parks, flanked on the east by the Purcell Mountains and on the west by the Monashee Range. Because of their constant avalanche threat, rugged topography, sparseness of game, and the ancient legends and superstitions connected with them, the Selkirks were seldom traveled by the Indians, except through Rogers Pass on occasional journeys to distant hunting grounds. Walter Moberly was the first white man to explore the Selkirks, during his search for a lowland route from Shuswap Lake to Kicking Horse Pass in 1865. Shortly after the completion of the Canadian Pacific Railway over Rogers Pass and the establishment of Glacier National Park in 1886, the famed Glacier House was built. For more than 25 years this great lodgelike hotel in the wilderness was a mecca for the world's leading mountaineers, naturalists, and geographers. Glacier House was torn down in 1929 after two destructive fires and the shifting of the railroad's interest to Lake Louise. Glacier embraces 333,440 acres of classic alpland wilderness with soaring

pine, stands of alpine larch, some of them 5,000–6,000 years old, willow and bog birch along the mountain streams and headwater lakes. Along the rocky slopes and ridges and alpine meadows are brilliant wildflowers such as Indian paintbrush, fireweed, columbine, mountain daisies, and spring beauty. Lake Magog, the largest in the park, lies at the northern base of Mount Assiniboine, surrounded by nearby Gog Lake and the beautiful Cerulean and Sunburst lakes nestled in Sunburst Valley. Dolly Varden, cutthroat, and brook trout are found in most of the lakes and in Simpson, Vermilion, and Cross rivers, tributaries of the Kootenay River. As in most glacial waters, the lakes and streams do not support large fish populations.

An 11-page *Mount Assiniboine Park Map-Brochure* is available free from the Parks Branch, Department of Recreation & Conservation, 1019 Wharf St., Victoria. The only access into the interior of the Mount Assiniboine wilderness is by trailheads along the Simpson and Vermilion rivers, at Spray Reservoir and the Sunshine Ski Village. Within the park, numerous trails provide access from Lake Magog to Og Lake, and from Sunburst Lake to Elizabeth and Wedgewood lakes. The main campsite is located on a benchland above the western shore of Lake Magog, and 4 alpine shelters are located on the east side of Lake Magog. Overnight accommodations are provided by the *Mount Assiniboine Lodge*, Box 368, Banff, Alta.

peaks, massive snowfields, dense coniferous forests, and high glaciers. Hundreds of miles of wilderness hiking trails lead off through majestic western red cedar and hemlock forests to the highlands and the famous Nakimu caves of Cougar Valley—one of the largest labyrinths of limestone subterranean passages in Canada, the Bonney Mountains, Purity Mountains, Battle Range, Beaver River, and the Illecillewaet and Avalanche glaciers. The timberline is lower and the growing season is shorter in the Selkirks than in the Rockies because of heavy snowfalls. The hiking trails, railroads, lakes and streams, glaciers, wardens' cabins, accommodations, and campgrounds are shown on the *Glacier National Park Map-Brochure* available free from the Superintendent, Glacier National Park, Revelstoke. The park superintendent's office also publishes the free *Abandoned Rails Trail Guide*, which describes the trail along the abandoned tracks once used by the spark-belching steam engines of the Canadian Pacific Railway at Rogers Pass. Campgrounds are located at Mountain Creek, Illecillewaet, and Loop Creek. The park is reached via the Trans-Canada Highway from Revelstoke on the west and from Golden on the east.

Mount Revelstoke National Park is located 12 miles west of Glacier, encompassing 64,000 acres on the western edge of the Selkirk Mountains stretching north of the Trans-Canada Highway. The park is

dominated by the clustered peaks of the Clachacudainn Range Mountains, which lie between Carnes and Woolsey creeks on the north and east and the Illecillewaet and Columbia rivers on the south and west. The major peaks of the range include Mount La Forme (8,400 feet), Mount St. Cyr (8,520 feet), Mount Coursier (8,680 feet), and a ridge of sharp towers and pinnacles known as the Inverness Peaks. Hiking trails lead to the trout waters of Eva Lake, where there is a small cabin, and to the Jade Lakes, Lake Millar, and the "icebox," a snow-filled crevice sheltered among heaped masses of colorful lichen-covered rocks. There are no overnight camping or lodging facilities in Revelstoke Park. Write: Superintendent, Mount Revelstoke National Park, Revelstoke V0E 2S0, for wilderness camping and hiking info.

The Bugaboo alpine recreation area and the Purcell wilderness conservancy area and Fry Creek Canyon recreation area are located in the heart of the massive Purcell Range, which contains some of the most spectacular spires in Canada. The Bugaboo Glacier and the spires of the Four Squatters, Howser Towers, Hounds Tooth, Snowpatch, Pigeon, and Crescent are reached by trail head in the Bugaboo Valley. Access to beautiful Cobalt Lake between Northpost and the Cobalt Lake Spire is by trail through the "Black Forest" to the highland open plateau country. The map kit shows the entire Purcell Range including the Toby, Leaning Tower, and Findlay peaks—the glacial source of the Columbia River—located in the Purcell wilderness conservancy area. Due west of the Purcell Wilderness and Kootenay Lake—famous for its trophy Kamloops trout to 30 pounds and Dolly Varden to 25 pounds—is the 63,000-acre wilderness preserved within Kokanee Glacier Provincial Park. Kokanee, a Kootenay Indian word meaning "red fish," refers to the landlocked salmon of Kokanee Lake and its tributaries. The *Kokanee Glacier Provincial Park Map-Brochure* shows gravel roads, foot trails, ranger cabins, campgrounds, glaciers, major points of interest, and topographic features including the Giant's Kneecap and Kokanee Glacier, Caribou Glacier, and Sunset, Nalmet, Kokanee, Kalso, and Natanek lakes. The park has no developed campgrounds. Camping is restricted to sites between Gibson and Kaslo lakes and near Slocan Chief Cabin—a sturdy log shelter which accommodates up to 20 campers.

The great forests, highlands, wild rivers, and lakes of the Kootenay region are famous for salmon, steelhead, Dolly Varden, and Kamloops fishing in the huge Arrow Lakes, Trout Lake, Adams and Shuswap lakes, and the Seymour, Adams, and North Thompson rivers, and for its large population of Rocky Mountain elk, bighorn sheep, black bear, mountain goat, grizzly, mule deer, and moose. The extensive wetlands of the upper Columbia River are renowned for their superb waterfowl shooting. Some of the finest wilderness camping and big-game areas in the region are the sharp, rugged peaks and alpine meadows of the Monashee Range located between the Columbia River on the east, the North Thompson River and Adams Lake on the west, and the Canoe Reach on the north and south to Upper Arrow Lake. The central part of the range embraces a heather-covered alpland dotted with remote, sparkling blue lakes. Access to the Monashees is by logging road, waterway, or bush plane, as trails are few. The major features of the range include the Scrip Range, which is one of the most inaccessible of the interior ranges, extending for 60 miles south of Bone Creek and the Shuswap Mountains, the Gold Range in the logging country along the west bank of the Columbia River, and the Dominion Peaks.

A complete listing and descriptions of campgrounds, motels, hotels, vacation lodges and mountain resorts in British Columbia's Rocky Mountain national parks is contained in the *Western Canada National Parks Accommodations Guide*, available free from: Parks Canada, Western Region, 134–11th Ave. SE, Calgary, Alta. T2G 0X5.

The major vacation lodges in Kootenay National Park (write to lodge, c/o Radium Hot Springs V0A 1M0) include: *Radium Hot Springs Lodge, Addison's Bungalows, Blakely's Bungalows, Mount Farnham Bungalows,* and *Vermilion Crossing Bungalow Camp.* Yoho National Park (write to lodge, c/o Field V0A 1G0) is served by: *Cathedral Mountain Chalets, Emerald Lake Chalet, Lake O'Hara Lodge, Wapata Lodge, Field Hotel, Twin Falls Chalet,* and *Whiskey Jack Youth Hostel.* Glacier National Park is served by the *Northlander Motor Hotel* (located at Rogers Pass), Revelstoke V0E 2S0. There are no accommodations in Mount Revelstoke National Park.

Access & Outfitting Centers

The Kootenay and Rocky Mountains regions are reached by scheduled airlines to major towns and cities, charter aircraft, Canadian National Railway, Highways 95, 93, 6, and the Trans-Canada and Yellowhead highways. Wilderness outfitters, canoe rentals, guides, lodging, and charter fly-in services are provided at Tête Jaune Caché, Jasper (Alberta), Chase, Salmon Arm, Revelstoke, Golden, Banff (Alberta), Nakusp, Nelson, Invermere, Kimberley, Cranbrook, Creston, Castlegar, Fernie, and Trail.

Vancouver Island & the Pacific Rim

Vancouver & Gulf Islands Topo Maps

Canadian National Topographic Survey Maps, scale 1:250,000: Victoria 92-B, Cape Flattery 92-C, Vancouver 92-G, Alberni 92-F, Nootka Sound 92-E, Bute Inlet 92-K, Cape Scott 102-I.

Cowichan Wild & Scenic River

Canadian National Topographic Survey Maps, scale 1:50,000: Duncan 92B-13, Cowichan Lake 92C-16.

Pacific Rim National Park

Canadian National Topographic Survey Maps, scale 1:50,000: Carmanah 92C-10, Pachena Point 92C-11, Ucluelet 92C-13, Barkley Sound 92C-14, Nitinat 92C-15.

Strathcona Provincial Park

Canadian National Topographic Survey Maps, scale 1:50,000: Forbidden Plateau 92F-11, Great Central 92F-6, Bedwell 92F-5, Buttle Lake 92F-12, Upper Campbell 92F-13.

Vancouver Island lies parallel to the southern mainland of British Columbia bordered by the inner coastal passage on the east and by the Pacific Ocean on the west, with the Gulf Islands, like a school of fingerlings, sheltering on its lee side. The topography is mountainous, with many scenic lakes, such as Upper Campbell, Buttle, Great Central, Sproat, Cowichan, and Shawnigan, pocketed in the narrow, alplike valleys. The great mountains, dense coastal forests, and wild salmon and steelhead streams of the island were first explored by Captain Cook, who landed at Nootka in 1778. Spanish explorers followed Cook into the region; as a result, many coastal features of the island bear Spanish names. Juan de Fuca Strait, Quadra Island, and Alberni Inlet are examples. The island is named after Captain George Vancouver, who conducted much of the early exploration of the Island in 1791–1795. The island's major industries are mining, fishing, logging, and forest products.

The turbulent coastal streams that flow from scenic headwater lakes high in the interior uplands provide migration routes for steelhead, sea-run cutthroat, and salmon. Roderick Haig-Brown, author of the *River of No Return*, has referred to the tidal waters of the Gulf of Georgia on the leeward side of the island as the "Great Salmon Lake"

for the tremendous runs of Chinook salmon in the 40–60-pound range. The island has good hunting for elk, blacktail deer, and black bear. There is excellent waterfowl shooting in the spring and fall in the coastal bays and coves, and wing shooting in the upland meadows and along logging roads for grouse. At the center of the island lies Strathcona Provincial Park, a 500,000-acre alpine wilderness dominated by Elkhorn Peak and Golden Hinde Peak rising to 7,000 feet, and below timberline, by the small lakes and meadows of the Forbidden Plateau—which has the roots of its name in ancient Indian legend. The plateau was believed, according to the legend, to be inhabited by evil spirits who consumed women and children who dared wander into the area. Scenic highland trails wind through the wild areas to remote Kwai Lake, Moat Lake, Mount Albert Edward, Cruikshank Canyon, Lake Beautiful, Marble Meadows, Panther and Hairtrigger lakes, Della Falls, and Cream Lake. There are access routes into the Forbidden Plateau by way of the Cruikshank River and Paradise Meadows, over Crown Zellerbach logging roads to the trail heads. (Permission must be obtained from the company before using these routes.) Three roadless areas, the Big Den, Central Strathcona, and Comox Glacier nature conservancy areas, cover a total area of 302,000 acres within the park.

Pacific Rim
National Park

British Columbia

The *Strathcona Provincial Park Map-Brochure,* available free from the Parks Branch, Department of Recreation & Conservation, 1019 Wharf St., Victoria, shows park boundaries, topographic features, paved and gravel roads, trail routes, glaciers and ice fields, nature conservancy boundaries, boat-launching sites, and campgrounds. Provincial campgrounds are located at the north end of Buttle Lake and at Ralph River along the Buttle Lake Road. The park is reached via Highway 28, which connects Campbell River on the east with Gold River on the west coast of the island, and passes through the northern section of the park and the cutthroat, rainbow, and Dolly Varden waters of the Buttle Lake area. (The lake is named after Commander John Buttle, who explored the area in the 1860s.) The Forbidden Plateau is reached by 12 miles of gravel road from Courtenay, about 140 miles north of Victoria.

Great Central Lake lies to the south of the Comox Glacier nature conservancy area and the Forbidden Plateau and holds trophy cutthroat and rainbow trout to 11 pounds, as well as Dolly Varden, sockeye, and coho salmon. Great Central is reached by gravel road from Alberni and by logging roads along the north shore. A trail winds from the head of the lake upstream for 12 miles to the spectacular 1,580-foot-high Stella Falls—the highest falls in Canada. The largest river on Vancouver Island is the famous Campbell River, noted for its rapids, deep holding pools, and large runs of winter steelhead up to 25 pounds. The fly-fishing is generally excellent year round for resident rainbow and cutthroat trout. In August the river has a run of big Chinook salmon. The enchanting 3-mile-long Cowichan River, located at the south end of the island, is one of the world's great fly-fishing streams. The Cowichan is one of the most beautiful rivers in British Columbia, noted for the dense forests of Douglas fir, spruce, and lodgepole pine that crowd to its banks, deep-cut canyons, gravel bars, and deep holding pools and riffles found along its course from its headwaters at Cowichan Lake down to its mouth on Georgian Bay. The river has superb fishing for steelhead, sea-run cutthroat, Chinook and coho salmon, and brown trout to 10 pounds. The Cowichan is one of the few rivers in western Canada where the brown trout has found an ideal habitat, due to mild winter water temperatures. The Cowichan River Footpath provides hiking access to the middle section of the river and along the beautiful fly-fishing stretches near Skutz Falls, which holds the largest population of trophy browns. The trail covers 19 miles of river, winding through magnificent scenery, and provides access for the sportsman and naturalist alike. The *Cowichan Footpath & Map* may be obtained from the Cowichan Fish and Game Association, Box 445, Duncan, for $2.00. Cowichan Lake, 26 miles long, is the island's top producer of big Dolly Varden and rainbow trout. Other renowned steelhead and salmon streams found throughout the island include the Nimpkish, Muchalat, Kennedy, Quinsam, Salmon, Iron, Ash, and Oyster rivers.

The island's remote coastal areas are wildlands of rocky headlands, placid lagoons, crashing surf, and sandy low-strewn beaches surrounded by upland forests of hemlock and pine spruce, with forest floors covered by moss, huckleberry, red alder, blueberry, copperbush, devil's club, and salal. The coastal and interior parks are shown on the map/guide *Provincial Parks on Vancouver Island,* available free from the Parks Branch, Department of Recreation & Conservation, 1019 Wharf St., Victoria. This publication contains an attractive shaded-relief map of the island and a complete listing and description of provincial campgrounds and parks.

Stretching along the southwest coast of the island is scenic Pacific Rim National Park—a wilderness hiker's paradise with its long, sandy beaches, surf-swept headlands, quiet estuaries and lakes, rocky islands, and impenetrable rain forests. The treacherous waters off Vancouver Island's west coast, once known as the Graveyard of the Pacific, have accounted for some 240 shipwrecks since 1803. The famous Lifesaving Trail between Bamfield and Port Renfrew was constructed to aid sailors shipwrecked along this dangerous 45-mile-long stretch of coast. For maps and travel info write: Superintendent, Pacific Rim National Park, Box 280, Ucluelet V0R 3A0. Vacation accommodations are provided by *Wickaninnish Inn,* Ucluelet V0R 3A0.

Vancouver Island vacation lodges and fishing camps include: *Pacific Sands Resort,* Box 237, Tofino V0R 2Z0; *Clayoquot Lodge* (Stubbs Island), Box 188, Tofino V0R 2Z0; *Eaglecrest Lodge, The Qualicum Arms Inn,* and *St. Andrews Lodge,* all Qualicum Beach V0R 2T0; *Bates Beach Fishing Resorts,* Courtenay V9N 5M9; *Oyster River Resort,* Campbell River V9W 3S4; *The Breaker's Resort,* Campbell River V9W 3S4; *Campbell River Lodge,* 1760 Island Highway,

Campbell River V9W 2E7; *Painter's Lodge & Fishing Resort*, Box 460, Campbell River V9W 5C1; *April Point Lodge & Fishing Resort* (Quadra Island), Box 1, Heriot Bay V0P 1H0; *Taku Resort* (Quadra Island), Box 1, Heriot Bay V0P 1H0; *Silva Bay Resort*, Gabriola V0R 1X0; *Salishan Resort*, Galiano V0N 1P0; *Hornby Island Lodge*, Hornby Island V0R 1Z0.

Access & Outfitting Centers

Transportation to and from Vancouver Island is by British Columbia ferries and scheduled flights to Victoria and other points on the island. Major highways and secondary roads provide access along the eastern coastline. Road access across the island is available at Shawnigan Lake, Campbell River, and Port Alberni. The west coast is primarily a coastal forest wilderness with extremely limited access other than by chartered aircraft or four-wheel-drive vehicles. Lodging, guides, supplies, hunting and fishing outfitting, and charter fly-in services are available at Victoria, Shawnigan Lake, Duncan, Crofton, Chemainus, Lake Cowichan, Honeymoon Bay, Ladysmith, Youbou, Nanaimo, Parksville, Qualicum Beach, Port Alberni, Comox, Courtenay, Campbell River, Kelsey Bay, Gold River, Tofino, Ucluelet, Bamfield, Port Renfrew, and Jordan River. The Gulf Islands are served by ferries, with water taxi service available to the smaller islands not having scheduled service.

ALBERTA ENCYCLOPEDIA

Accommodations— Vacation Resorts & Lodges

A comprehensive listing of recreation accommodations, in alphabetical sequence according to city, town, or village, is contained in the useful 80-page *Alberta Vacation Guide*, available free from Travel Alberta, Box 2500, Edmonton T5J 2Z4, (403) 427-4321. The 30-page *National Parks Accommodation Guide*, which lists and describes all resorts, motels, hotels, and wilderness lodges in Banff, Jasper, Waterton Lakes, and Wood Buffalo national parks, may be obtained free by writing to the Western Regional Office, Parks Canada, 134 11th Ave. SE, Calgary T2G 0X5. The *Alberta Great West Country Vacations Guide* lists accommodations, locations, rates, and detailed information about Alberta's famous ranch and farm vacation facilities, primarily for children and teens. The guide may be obtained free by writing to Alberta Great West Country Vacations Association, Box 185, Bentley T0C 0J0. The Canadian Youth Hostels Association operates 10 hostels open July and August for young hikers and backpackers in Banff and Jasper national parks. Hostels include simple overnight accommodations, common kitchen, bunk, mattresses, and blankets. Membership and information can be obtained by writing: CYHA, Mountain Region, 455 12th St. NW, Calgary, or CYHA, Northwest Region, 10922 88th Ave., Edmonton. The Young Men's Christian Association operates two alpine lodges in Banff and Jasper national parks. The *Y Mountain Chalet Banff* has 47 rooms, central lavatory, restaurant, and fireplace in living room, Write: 414 Muskrat St., Banff. The *Lake Edith Lodge* in Jasper National Park, operated by the YMCA of Edmonton, has 20 units with central showers and toilets, recreational facilities, and free boats and canoes for guests. Write: after May 15, Lake Edith Lodge, Box 607, Jasper; after mid-September, Edmonton YMCA, 10030–102 A Ave., Edmonton T5J 0G5. Hunting and fishing packtrain trips, trail riding, jeep trips, backcountry hiking, and camping excursions are provided by *PB Guest Ranch*, on the east boundary of Jasper National Park (write: J. Bond, Brule); *Crowsnest Guest Ranch & Health Resort*, Box 97, Coleman, in the Rockies; *Timber Ridge Lodge*, Box 94, Nanton, in the foothills; and *Brewster's 3 Circle Guest Ranch*, Seebe, 43 miles west of Calgary on the banks of the Bow River.

For additional listings of Alberta's major lodges, resorts, and sporting camps, see "Mountain Camps & Pack Trains," "Far North Fly-in Fishing & Hunting Lodges," and the "Travel & Recreation Guide" section.

Airlines & Charter Fly-in Services

Alberta's major cities are served by Air Canada, Canadian Pacific Airlines, Pacific Western Airlines, Western Airlines, Hughes Air West, Northwest Orient Airlines, Time Air, and Bayview Air Services. Scheduled service to major outdoor recreation centers within the province is provided by *Northward Airlines Ltd.*, Slave Lake T0G 2A0, with service between Slave Lake and northern Alberta points; and *Time Air Ltd.*, P.O. Box 423, Lethbridge T1J 3Z1, with service between Lethbridge, Calgary, Red Deer, Edmonton, and Medicine Hat, and between Lethbridge and Great Falls, Montana. A complete listing of *Charter Airlines Operating in Alberta* may be obtained by writing: Alberta Aviation Council, 201 Terminal Bldg., Industrial Airport, Edmonton. The listing includes names, addresses, and phone numbers of wilderness bush and floatplane fly-in services. For owners of private aircraft, details of air regulations, navigation orders, radio aids, and sources of air maps and relevant material are available on request from the Air Regulations Superintendent, Federal Bldg., 9820 170th St., Edmonton.

Charter fly-in services for fishing, hunting, and canoeing trips include: *Alberta Central Airways Ltd.*, Box 518, Lac La Biche T0A 2C0; *Alert Aviation*, Box 715, Fort McMurray; *Alpine Helicopters Ltd.*, Hangar 13, International Airport, Calgary; *Aurora Aviation Ltd.*, 7611-141 Ave., Edmonton T5C 2N4; *Bow Helicopters Ltd.*, Hangar 10, International Airport, Calgary; *Chinook Air Ltd.*, Hangar 57, Industrial Airport, Calgary; *Crowsnest Helicopters Ltd.*, Box 705, Blairmore; *La Ronge Aviation Services Ltd.*, Hangar 6A, Industrial Airport, Edmonton; *MacKenzie Air Ltd.*, Hangar 3, Industrial Airport, Edmonton T5G 2Z3; *Noralta Flights Ltd.*, Box 365, Fort Chipewyan; *Peace Air Ltd.*, Box 1357, Peace River T0H 2X0; *Rocky Mountain Helicopters Ltd.*, Box 90, Invermere, B.C. V0A 1K0; *Points West Outfitters*, Box 5175, Fort McMurray; and *Wapiti Aviation Ltd.*, RR 2, Grande Prairie T8V 2Z9.

Big-Game Ranges & Wildlife Maps

Alberta's great forest reserves and mountain ranges offer some of the best big-game hunting and wildlife photography in North America. The tundra region of the far north is the summer range of the barren-ground caribou; during the winter months they migrate into Alberta's open and sparsely timbered rock and moss country. The larger woodland caribou are found in northern Alberta in the Athabasca River region and roam as far south as Lesser Slave Lake and Cold Lake and into Banff National Park. Trophy moose are found throughout the boreal evergreen forest regions and in the muskeg and wetland regions of the north. A small herd is found in the Cypress Hills Provincial Park in the southeast of the province. Majestic Rocky Mountain elk are found in the open woodlands of the foothills and along the scenic highlands of the eastern slope of the Great Divide. Small herds are found scattered in Cypress Hills and Elk Island National Park, northeast of Edmonton. The white rumps of the brownish gray mule deer are seen throughout the mountains, foothills, and brush country of Alberta, and the handsome whitetail are found in open parklands and grasslands. Bighorn sheep are found in the Rockies in the high meadows above the timberline; the white mountain goat ranges in the Rockies and the foothills of the east slope of the Great Divide. Grizzly bear in color phases from tawny to yellowish brown, ranging in weights from 400 to 900 pounds, inhabit the remote high country of the Rockies and the Swan Hills. The giant Swan Hills grizzly, believed to be a remnant of the extinct plains grizzly, is a member of the most inland race of large grizzly bears found in the coniferous forests of north central Alberta. Swan Hills grizzly and wolves have been reported to prey on moose in the area. Black bear (grizzlies in the Swan Hills area have also been known to prey on black bear during their hibernation period) inhabit the northern coniferous forest and the foothills of the Rocky Mountains. The elusive tawny mountain lion is found in the Rockies and occasionally along the river systems of southern Alberta.

The useful *Cloven-Hoofed Animals of Alberta Map & Guide* provides descriptions, full-color illustrations, and an ecosystem map and life-zone distribution maps for the bison, pronghorn antelope, woodland caribou, barren-ground caribou, Rocky Mountain sheep, goat, mule deer, whitetail deer, wapiti (elk), and moose. The *Large Carnivores of Alberta Map & Guide* contains descriptions, full-color illustrations, and life-zone and track maps for the Great Plains wolf, Montana gray wolf, British Columbia wolf, northern timber wolf, Saskatchewan timber wolf, coyote, British Columbia red fox, northern plains red fox, cougar, Canada lynx, bobcat, grizzly, and black bear. The map guides may be obtained free from the Information Branch, Department of Lands & Forests, Natural Resources Bldg., Edmonton.

The important big-game ranges in Alberta are found within the 10 great provincial forest reserves, which cover a total of 150,000 square miles. A free *Trees of Alberta Map & Guide* (write: Information Branch, Department of Lands & Forests) contains a description of the forest regions in Alberta and principal tree species, and full-color illustrations and distribution maps for the pin cherry, chokecherry, limber and whitebark pine, black spruce, white or canoe birch, tamarack, aspen and balsam poplar, and Douglas and balsam fir.

Camping

A comprehensive listing of Alberta's provincial and commercial campgrounds and trailer parks is contained in the *Alberta Provincial Parks Guide* and 80-page *Travel Alberta Vacation Guide*, available free upon request from Travel Alberta, Box 2500, Edmonton T5J 2Z4. The travel guide describes the size, fees, number of campsite units, trailer sites, hookups, stoves, toilets, water, picnic areas, recreation, boat-launching sites, boat rentals, sewage facilities for all commercial campgrounds and trailer parks, provincial park campgrounds, national park campgrounds, the Alberta Forest Service recreation areas, and the Alberta highway campsites. The use of campgrounds and trailer sites maintained by the provincial park and highway service and national park service in Banff, Jasper, and Wood Buffalo national parks is on a first-come, first-served basis and reservations are not accepted. In the national and provincial parks, visitors may not camp outside designated areas unless they obtain permission from the Warden Service. All electrical services in campgrounds are 60-cycle. Wood fuel is supplied free in many of the campgrounds. A small fee is charged in the national park campgrounds; the use of Alberta Forest Service, highway service, and provincial park sites is seasonal and free of charge. The 30-page *National Parks Accommodation Guide*, which lists and describes all campgrounds and accommodations—resorts, lodges, motels, hotels—in Banff, Jasper, Waterton Lakes, and Wood Buffalo national parks, may be obtained free from Western Regional Office, Parks Canada, 134 11th Avenue SE, Calgary T2G 0X5. *Alberta Camping Association Directories* are available free from the Alberta Camping Association, c/o 332 6th Ave. SW, Calgary T2P 0R5.

Canoeing & Wilderness Waters

Alberta offers a great diversity of wild rivers and historic canoe routes traveled for centuries by the Cree, Beaver and Rocky Mountain Indians and by the great northern, explorers and north men of the fur trade. Romantic names on the land—Fort Chipewyan, Caribou Hills, Fort Vermilion, Vermilion Chutes, Rocky Mountain House, Athabasca Landing, Slave Lake, Jasper House—beckon the wilderness paddler along water trails blazed by Peter Pond, Alexander Mackenzie, Anthony Henaday, and David Thompson in the northern lake country of the Canadian Shield, Rocky Mountain headwaters and foothills, parklands and plains. The large 38 × 20-inch *Canoe Alberta Map*, published in full-color shaded relief, shows the major canoe routes with color-coded keys indicating falls, lakes subject to sudden dangerous windstorms, streams directly below dams subject to changes in water level and velocity, federal and provincial campsites adjacent to classified streams, and mileages. Streams are shown according to five classifications: (1) clear channels with minor obstructions; (2) clear channels, fairly numerous rapids; (3) narrow clear channels, numerous rapids; (4) obstructed channels with extended difficult rapids; and (5) not navigable. Continuous long and violent waves, rocks and boiling eddies, ledges and obstructed passages are indicated by a graded scale of rapids. The *Canoe Alberta Map* outlines some 65 explored trips and

may be obtained free from Travel Alberta, Box 2500, Edmonton T5J 2Z4, (403) 427-4321.

Companion guidebooks which provide detailed descriptions of the 65 major canoe routes as well as info about hydrography, duration of voyage, total distance, gradient, stopover and access points, and camping, portages, and rapids, may be obtained for $1 each from the Queen's Printer, 11510 Kingsway Ave., Edmonton. The guides are printed on waterproof paper for use on the river. The 40-page *Canoe Alberta North—Book 1* describes the Hay River canoe route from its headwaters at Rainbow Lake in northwest Alberta as it flows northeast through coniferous forest and muskeg, winding past Zama Lake and Meander River, Steen River, Indian cabins, and across the Northwest Territories border to the mouth on Great Slave Lake. The 140-mile *Peace and Slave Rivers Canoe Route* is described from Peace Point on the Peace River through the Peace-Athabasca Delta, and Wood Buffalo National Park along the wide, meandering, island-dotted Peace River past Carson and Sweetgrass Landings to its confluence with the Rivière des Rochers (the western outlet of Lake Athabasca) to form the mighty north-flowing Slave River—named after the Beaver Indians who were enslaved by the powerful Cree Indians, and were known thereafter as the Slavey Indians. The Slave twists its way north through the Salt Plains and muskeg through the Demicharge Rapids, past Hay Camp, Smith Landing, and Fitzgerald Settlement, through the notorious Rapids of the Drowned, and Cassette, Pelican, and Mountain rapids, into the Northwest Territories to its mouth on Great Slave Lake. The historic Slave River forms the western boundary of the Precambrian Shield. The 316-mile Peace River route from Dunvegan Bridge to Fort Vermilion flows past Verte Camp and Long Islands to Peace River settlement, where it bends northward and flows past the wolf, black bear, moose, and caribou country of the Hawk and Buffalo Head hills, past the Indian village of Carcajou (Cree for "Indian devil," also known as the wolverine) to the historic fur trade settlement of Fort Vermilion. The Peace River route from Fort Vermilion to Peace covers 192 miles, flowing past Beaver Ranch, John d'Or Prairie, and Donnelly Island, through the treacherous Vermilion Chutes and Falls past the Caribou Mountains and Fox Lake into Wood Buffalo National Park, where it meanders slowly past Garden Creek and Big Island, numerous sloughs and oxbows to Jackfish River, through the Boyer Rapids and spectacular white cliffs to Peace Point settlement. The Peace River country is the home of the north country's most ferocious big-game species—the mosquito, and in hordes, with maddening no-see-ums as a backup. Travel prepared! A mosquito-proof tent and a large supply of fly dope are necessities. *Book 1* also describes the wild Smoky River route from Grande Cache to Highway 34 bridge; the Little Smoky River route and the Wabasca River route from North Wabasca Lake through the Slave Lake Forest wilderness to Fort Vermilion or Jean d'Or Prairie on the Peace River. The Wabasca is for the experienced wilderness paddler—there are 27 dangerous rapids, marshlands, clouds of mosquitoes, poor campsites, and muskeg-stained water.

The 48-page *Canoe Alberta North—Book 2* describes the famous Athabasca River country canoe routes. The Athabasca River route runs from its headwaters in Jasper National Park northeast through the Edson, Whitecourt, Lac La Biche, and Athabasca provincial forests to its mouth at the southwest end of Lake Athabasca. The major features shown on the topo maps of this historic water trail, originally

known to the Indians as the Elk River, include Athabasca Falls, Colin and Jacques ranges, Jasper Lake (notorious for its sandbars), Brulé Lake, Fort Assiniboine—once the northern terminus of the overland route from Edmonton to the Athabasca River, established in 1825 by Sir George Simpson to facilitate the movement of supplies from Cumberland House to the Pacific—Lesser Slave River and Lake, Athabasca, Calling River and Lake, Upper Wells, the Pelican Rapids and the historic Pelican Portage, House River Indian cemetery, and Grand Rapids and the dangerous stretch of rapids along the limestone ledges of the Thickwood Hills—including the Brulé, Boiler, Middle, Long, Crooked, Rock, Little Cascade, and Mountain rapids—and the Forks at Fort McMurray, Fort MacKay Settlement, the Fort Hills, Dawsens Landing, Firebag Ranger Station, Point Brulé, Kenny Woods, Embarras; and near its mouth on the Athabasca Delta marshlands is the ancient Embarras Portage ("embarras" was the French-Canadian voyageurs' term for debris of driftwood and uprooted trees), Big Eddy, Richardson Lake, Big Point Ranger Station, and the Chipewyan Lake Athabasca Indian Reserve at the mouth on Lake Athabasca. The stretch from Athabasca to Fort McMurray was a major route to the Klondike goldfields and is one of the most exciting and hazardous wilderness canoe trips in Alberta; the stretch through the Athabasca Tar Sands from Fort McMurray to Fort Chipewyan requires expert camping and navigation skills. *Book 2* also describes the famous tributaries of the Athabasca, including the white-water and open boat stretches of the Miette River, the white-water "flowing staircase" of the Maligne River, McLeod River of the Rocky Mountain Foothills with its logjams and sweepers, the historic Clearwater River and the famous 12-mile Methye Portage, and the scenic Wildhay River and Berland River route to Hudson Bay camp. Scenic Clearwater River was the major link along the voyageurs' highway between Fort Chipewyan and the Mackenzie River system and the easterly flowing Churchill River to Norway House and York Factory. The historic Methye Portage and the spacious parklike campsite near Lac La Loche, known as "the rendezvous" of the La Loche and Mackenzie brigades of the Hudson's Bay Company, was discovered by Peter Pond of the Northwest Company in 1777. From Lac La Loche in Saskatchewan, Pond hiked across the Methye Portage north to the Clearwater, which he descended west through the Whitemud Rapids into Alberta Territory to the Athabasca River and Lake Athabasca (then known as Lake of the Hills), where he built Fort Chipewyan—a wintering post for the northwesters. The Athabasca and its northern tributaries hold large northern pike, walleye, and arctic grayling. The Rocky Mountain tributaries of the upper Athabasca hold cutthroat, Dolly Varden, rainbow, and brook trout.

The 32-page *Canoe Central Alberta* describes the historic North Saskatchewan River and its tributaries, from its headwaters in Banff National Park northeasterly to Edmonton. The major features shown on the map kit of the route include the Alexandra River, Glacier Lake, White Goat and Siffleur wilderness areas, Kootenay Plains natural area, Abraham Lake and the Bighorn Dam, the Stone Indian Reserve and Saskatchewan Crossing (David Thompson's exploration party was attacked in this area in 1810 by a group of Piegan Indians and was saved by the sudden appearance of three grizzlies whom the Indians believed to be spirit protectors of Thompson, enabling the explorer and his group to escape), the braided maze of channels, Gap Rapid, the haystacks of the Devil's Elbow, Fisher's Rapid, Grier and Brierly rapids, Ram River, and Rocky Mountain House—established by the Northwest Company in 1799, Brazeau River confluence, and the winding island-dotted stretch west of Edmonton. *Canoe Central Alberta* also describes the white-water Clearwater River canoe route through the foothills from Seven Mile Campground to Rocky Mountain House; the fast-flowing Brazeau River; and the Wolf, Sand, and

Beaver rivers in the Lac La Biche region. The Beaver River was once a fur trade route from the Churchill River and Lac Île La Crosse to the Athabasca River and Fort Chipewyan.

The 50-page *Canoe Alberta South—Book 1* covers rugged foothills, Indian country, badlands, parklands, and plains of the South Saskatchewan River country. The scenic South Saskatchewan River canoe route from Grand Forks and the confluence of the Oldman and Bow rivers east to Estuary flows through rolling, grass-covered hills, steep cliffs and canyons, rapid narrows, and badlands. Pigeon and sparrow hawks, golden eagles, marsh hawks, great horned owls, beaver, and rattlesnakes are commonly seen along the route. In addition the guide describes the scenic Bow River from the headwaters and Lake Louise in Banff National Park to its confluence with the Oldman River at Grand Forks to form the South Saskatchewan; the Ghost River canoe route with its logjams, sweepers, and ledges; the Kananaskis River canoe route; the Elbow River canoe route; the notorious canyons, ledges, and logjams of the treacherous Highwood River; the beautiful Oldman River (named for Napa, meaning "old man," the tribal god of the Blackfeet Indians) canoe route which flows through the Rocky Mountain foothills through the haystacks and ledges of the Gap and several series of rapids, past the site of Fort Kipp which was burned to the ground by Blood Indians in 1873 and the notorious Fort Whoop-up, abandoned with the arrival of the Northwest Mounted Police in 1874; and the scenic Waterton River, which flows from its glacial headwaters in the Waterton Lakes (known to the Indians as *Omok-Sikkima*, which means "beautiful water") through numerous canyons and 6-foot waves to Waterton Dam. The 32-page *Canoe Alberta South—Book 2* describes the spectacular scenery of the Red Deer River canoe route from Mountain Aire to Estuary, and the Panther River and Blindman River canoe routes.

Wild River Maps

The following Canadian National Topographic Survey Maps show the entire length of Alberta's major wilderness canoe-camping routes and the topography of the surrounding bush. These full-color maps show all contours, gradients, rapids, falls, chutes, cascades, marshes, swamps, bogs, forests, canyons and woodlands, shelters, and campsites. Map scales are at 1:50,000 and 1:250,000. *Hay River:* Zama Lake 84-L, Mount Watt 84-K, Steen River 84-N, Tathlina Lake 85-C; *Peace River:* Clear Hills 84-D, Grande Prairie 83-M, Peace River 84-C, Bison Lake 84-F, Mount Watt 84-K, Vermilion Chutes 84-J, Lake Claire 84-I, Peace Point 84-P, Fitzgerald 74-M, Fort Chipewyan 74-L; *Rivière des Rochers & Slave River:* Fort Chipewyan 74-L, Fitzgerald 74-M, Fort Smith 75-D, Little Buffalo River 85-A; *Wabasca River:* Lesser Slave Lake 83-O, Peerless Lake 84-B, Algar Lake 84-A, Wadlin Lake 84-G, Vermilion Chutes 84-J; *Athabasca River:* Edson 83-F, Iosegun Lake 83-K, Whitecourt 83-J, Lesser Slave Lake 83-O, Tawatinaw 83-I, Pelican 83-P, Algar Lake 84-A, Waterways 74-D, Bitumount 74-E, Fort Chipewyan 74-L; *Smoky River:* Mount Robson 83-E, Wapiti 83-A, Grande Prairie 83-M, Winagami 83-N, Peace River 84-C; *Miette & Maligne River:* Jasper Park MCR-205; *McLeod River:* Edson 83-F, Wabamun Lake 83-G, Whitecourt 83-J; *Clearwater River & Methye Portage:* La Loche (Sask.) 74-C, Waterways 74-D; *Wildhay River:* Mount Robson 83-E, Edson 83-F; *Wildhay & Berland Rivers:* Edson 83-F, Iosegun Lake 83-K; *North Saskatchewan River:* Rocky Mountain House 83-B, Wabamun Lake 83-G, Edmonton 83-H, Tawatinaw 83-I, Vermilion 73-E; *Brazeau River:* Brazeau 83-C, Rocky Mountain House 83-B; *Wolf & Sand Rivers:* Sand River 73-L; *Beaver River:* Tawatinaw 83-I, Sand River 73-L, Waterhen River 73-K, Green Lake 73-J; *South Saskatchewan River:* Foremost 73-E, Medicine Hat 72-L, Prelate 72-K; *Bow River:* Golden 82-N, Calgary 82-O, Gleichen 82-I, Medicine Hat 72-L, Foremost 72-E;

Ghost River: Wildcat Hills 82O-7, Lake Minnewanka 82O-6; *Kananaskis Range:* Kananaskis Lakes 82-J, Calgary 82-O; *Elbow River:* Bragg Creek 82J-15, Calgary 82O-1; *Highwood River:* Mount Rae 82J-10, Mount Head 82J-7, Stimson Creek 82J-8, Turner Valley 82J-9, High River 82I-12, Dalemead 82I-13; *Oldman River:* Fernie 82-G, Lethbridge 82-H, Foremost 72-E; *Waterton River:* Calgary 82-O, Rocky Mountain House 83-B, Drumheller 82-P, Red Deer 83-A, Oyen 72-M; *Panther River:* Burnt Timber Creek 72O-11; *Blindman River:* Sylvan Lake 83B-8, Rimbey 83B-9, Red Deer 83A-5. (See "Wild River Voyageur Routes Guide.")

Far North Fly-in Fishing & Hunting Lodges

The famous Canadian Shield trophy lakes country of the Lac La Biche and Athabasca provincial forest reserves offers some of the finest moose, black bear, and caribou hunting and walleye, arctic grayling, and northern pike fishing in Canada. Several remote hunting and fishing outpost lodges provide accommodations, guide services, and floatplane services. *Christina Lake Lodge* is a fly-in fishing retreat 80 miles north of Lac La Biche. Accommodations and facilities include 4 cabins and dining room to accommodate up to 14 guests. There is fishing for arctic grayling up to 3 pounds, northern pike, lake trout, and walleye (called "pickerel" locally) in Christina Lake in the heart of the Lac La Biche, Lloydminster, and Fort McMurray. For info write: F. W. Thom, Conklin. *Birch Mountains Sportsman's Lodge* offers floatplane fly-in hunting and fishing from its camp in the remote Birch Mountains, dominated by the renowned Legend, Namus, Gardiner, and Eaglenest trophy lakes, south of Wood Buffalo National Park in the Athabasca Provincial Forest. These deep, cold lakes hold record lake trout, walleye, and northern pike. Write: 40 Orchard Green, Red Deer. *Gristhaven Fishing and Hunting Lodge* offers fly-in fishing on remote Grist Lake, just south of Winefred Lake trophy waters in the Lac La Biche Provincial Forest, 75 miles north of Cold Lake. Accommodations consist of a main lodge and 12 cabins with dining room and lounge in lodge. Fishing with experienced guides for lake trout, walleye, northern pike, and arctic grayling in Grist and Winefred lakes. Hunting season open May 1-December 1; fishing, May 15-October 30. Special off-season arrangements may be made for big-game hunting trips for moose, mule deer, caribou, or black bear. Lodge maintains a 3,000-foot landing strip for private planes. Charter air service from Edmonton. Write: Gristhaven Lodge Ltd., Box 266, Cold Lake. Some of the finest lake trout, walleye, northern pike, and arctic grayling fishing in Alberta is offered by the remote *Andrew Lake Fishing Lodge,* located in the far northeast corner of the province, on the Andrew Lake trophy waters due north of huge Lake Athabasca near the Northwest Territories and Saskatchewan boundaries. For information write: Box 5846, Station L, Edmonton.

Fenwick Bow River Fly Fishing School

The Fenwick Corporation's Alberta School of Fly Fishing is located on the banks of the famous Bow River—ranked as one of the best rainbow and brown trout rivers in North America. The school's curriculum, limited to fly fishermen with some previous experience, includes fly casting; fly line, rod and reel construction; how to choose the proper tackle and terminology; insects and their life cycles; artificial fly construction; choice of flies and how to match the hatch; knots; leader construction and uses; fly presentation; stream lore and wading. One of the main attractions of the area is The Tree Farm with its beautiful outdoor-indoor recreational facilities. Accommodations are at the Elbow Lodge in Calgary. For free literature, rates, and info, write: School Coordinator, Fenwick Fly Fishing Schools, P.O. Box 729, Westminster, CA 92683.

Fishing & Hunting in Alberta

Alberta contains the greatest variety of geographical features of any province, and like its neighbor, British Columbia, offers some of the finest wilderness fishing and big-game hunting in North America. The province is a giant plateau 2,200 feet above sea level, stretching 760 miles from north to south, and 182–404 miles east and west for a total area of 255,285 square miles. Alberta is divided roughly into four general areas: (1) the Rocky Mountains and foothills of the southwest along the British Columbia border. (2) From the Alberta-Montana border to a point approximately 200 miles north, the land is a rolling prairie, a productive agricultural area fed by extensive irrigation reservoirs. (3) The central parklands form a succession of wide ridges and

broad valleys with a number of lakes and streams and mixed forests. (4) The whole northern half of the province is a region of great lakes, rivers, and boreal forests, broken by tracts of open prairie and the broad sweeping terraces of the Peace River Valley. Within the province are 6,485 square miles of lakes ranging in size from several acres to over 800 square miles and varying from the deep, cold lakes of the Canadian Shield to shallow bodies of water of the prairie.

Trophy Lakes, Streams, & Wild Rivers

The Alberta Department of Recreation Parks and Wildlife, Natural Resources Bldg., Edmonton, publishes a free useful *Fish of Alberta Map & Guide* which contains full-color illustrations, descriptions, and color-coded distribution maps of the province's sportfish species. The *Alberta Guide to Sportfishing Regulations* contains a fish and wildlife management areas map and a map showing trophy lakes and stocked lakes, reservoirs, and ponds. The guide may be obtained from the Fish and Wildlife Division, Natural Resources Bldg., Edmonton. Alberta's angling records illustrate the wide variety of fishing available to the wilderness traveler planning a trip to the provinces.

ALBERTA RECORD FISH

	Lb.-oz.	Length (inches)	Place	Year
Brook trout	12–14		Wood Buffalo National Park	1967
Brown trout	12–5		Lake Edith	1939
Cutthroat trout	8–15		Lower Kananaskis Lake	1950
Dolly Varden	25–13		Muskeg River	1947
Golden trout	4–7		Barnaby Ridge Lakes	1965
Rainbow trout	15	34½	Mami Lake	1967
Lake trout	52–8		Cold Lake	1928
Arctic grayling	2–13		Embarras River	1966
Mountain whitefish	5–1	19	Athabasca River	1963
Lake whitefish	8–8		Buck Lake	1972
Walleye	14–5		Red Deer River	1970
Yellow perch	2–4	15	Tucker Lake	1967
Northern pike	37–8	48½	Milk River Ridge Reservoir	1974
Goldeye	4–2	20	Battle River Dam	1974

The *Fish of Alberta Map & Guide* also provides a thorough description of each fish species, as well as valuable comments on angling techniques. Rainbow trout are the premier game fish and, since 1949, have been introduced throughout the province. Rainbows introduced in the province's "pothole lakes" grow at a rate of up to 5 pounds in 2 years. The best rainbow trout fishing, however, is found in the swift runs and riffles of the large streams of the Rocky Mountains and scenic foothills. Two of the finest rainbow trout streams on the continent are the Bow River for approximately 25 miles downstream from Calgary and in the Oldman River as it winds through the foothills northwest of the town of Pincher Creek. Catches of "bows" of 2–6 pounds are not uncommon. Rainbow trout are native to the Athabasca River system from the headwaters area near the Jasper National Park boundary to the south slopes of the Swan Hills wildlands. Rainbows are found throughout the alpine lakes and white-water streams of Banff and Jasper national parks and in the great wild rivers of the Rocky

Mountain foothills, including the Belly, Castle, Highwood, Sheep, Elbow, Dogpound, Red Deer, Clearwater, upper North Saskatchewan, Nordegg, Brazeau River and Reservoir, Berland, Wildhay, McLeod, and the Athabasca tributaries of the eastern Swan Hills wilderness.

Guided float fishing trips down the trophy rainbow and brown trout waters of the wild, picturesque Bow River are provided by the *Bow River Company*, 76 Beaverbrook Crescent, St. Albert T8N 2L1, (403) 458-0326.

Lake trout up to 50 pounds are most abundant in the deep cold lakes of the Canadian Shield in the extreme northeastern section of the province. Lake trout fishing in Alberta is mostly by wilderness charter fly-in to Peerless Lake in the Slave Lake Forest, Grist and Cold lakes in the Lac La Biche Forest region, Namur Lake in the Birch Mountains and Lake Athabasca, and Wentzel and Margaret lakes in the Peace River system in Footner Lake Forest due west of Wood Buffalo National Park. Lake trout are also found in the deep Rocky Mountain lakes of Waterton Lakes, Banff and Jasper national parks, and Spray Reservoir and Ghost Reservoir in the foothills. Lake trout are most active immediately after spring breakup and again in the fall when the fish are found "coasting" in relatively shallow water. Cutthroat are native to headwater lakes and streams from the international boundary north to the Bow River system including the Castle, Belly, Sheep, Highwood, and Elbow rivers and the northwest branch of the Oldman and Livingston rivers. Cutthroat were successfully introduced into the Ram River system (which contained no other trout due to several impassable falls) in 1955. The handsome cutthroat, which seldom jumps when hooked, is taken on dry flies, nymphs, wet flies, bucktails, spinners, spoons, and worms, with a marked preference for flies that imitate shrimp or local forage fish. California golden trout were introduced to several alpine lakes southwest of Pincher Creek in the South Castle wildlands areas in 1959. The wilderness fly-fisherman will do best in the high country lakes with small dry flies, bucktails, or streams and nymphs on No. 14 or No. 16 hooks which imitate caddis larvae.

Fat brook trout or "squaretails" up to 7 pounds are caught in the lakes and streams of the Rocky Mountains and foothills including Prairie Creek, Upper Stony Creek, Alford and Lookout creeks, and Bovin, Rat, Elbow, and Muskiki lakes. Pine Lake in Wood Buffalo National Park, which straddles the northern Alberta-Northwest Territories border, is one of North America's top-ranked trophy brook trout fisheries. Brookies often favor flies such as the Black Gnat, Black Moose, Royal Coachman, Silver Doctor, Parmachenee Belle, and Montreal. Trophy squaretails go for big, rough-looking flies such as the Burlap, Fledermaus, or Silver Shrimp on No. 2–6 hooks. Brown trout have been successfully introduced to the Raven River, Athabasca River, Peace River, Waterton River, and to Beaver, Stauffer, Fallen Timber, Alford, Dogpound, and Shundra creeks in the west central foothills and parklands. These streams are ideal brown trout habitat with gentle flow rates, moderately cool water temperatures, sunken logs, and tangles of tree roots with abundant forest cover along the banks. Dolly Varden trout up to 15 pounds are found in headwater streams and lakes throughout the province from the Peace River country south through the south Saskatchewan River system. Trophy Dolly Varden waters include the Cardinal, Muskeg, Berland, and Wildhay rivers. The remote wilderness tributaries of the Athabasca and Peace rivers, as well as the headwaters of the Wapiti and Smoking rivers, hold virgin populations of arctic grayling up to 3 pounds. Grayling are found in the rapids of the Swan, Freeman, Prairie, Goose, and Little Smoky rivers and Snipe Lake in the Swan Hills wilderness (prime grizzly country—watch yourself here); Lesser Slave, Utikuma, Wabasca,

Fawcett, Calling, and Peerless lakes and Wabasca River in the Slave Lake Provincial Forest; Winefred, Namur, and Claire lakes and the MacKay, Steeplank, Firebag, and Christina lakes in the Athabasca Provincial Forest; Margaret and Wentzel lakes in Footner Lake Provincial Forest; and Wapiti, Saddle, Cutbank, Kakwa, Berland, Wildhay, and McLeod rivers in the Edson, Grand Prairie, and Whitecourt provincial forests and in the Athabasca headwaters in Jasper National Park.

Deep-feeding walleye up to 12–14 pounds are taken in the Athabasca and Pembina, Peace, Beaver, and Red Deer rivers and throughout the north country, particularly in the Lac La Biche and Lesser Slave Lake regions and in the Lake Athabasca area. Schools of walleye are most often caught near or on sandbars or shoals which provide a good feeding area close to deep water. Northern pike are found in lakes and rivers throughout the prairies and northern forest regions of Alberta; trophy-sized pike up to 35 pounds are caught in famous Seibert Lake in the Lac La Biche Provincial Forest and in Lesser Slave, Utikuma, Wabasca, Peerless, Zama, Bistcho, Margaret, Wentzel, Claire, and Namur lakes and in huge Lake Athabasca. Other sportfish found in Alberta are kokanee, lake and mountain whitefish, goldeye, and yellow perch. Yellow perch up to 2 pounds are commonly caught in Beaver Lake near Lac La Biche.

Big-Game Hunting & Wildlife Guides

Alberta ranks first with British Columbia among the Canadian provinces for the number, quality, and diversity of its big-game animals. Hunting regulations, license information, and hunting maps showing game zones, wildlife management units, Indian reserves, no-hunting areas, and restricted wildlife areas are contained in the *Alberta Summary of Game-Bird Regulations* and *Alberta Summary of Big-Game Regulations*, available free from the Fish & Wildlife Division, Depart-

ment of Lands and Forests, Natural Resources Bldg., Edmonton. The big-game regulations summary also contains a "Big Game Field Guide," hunting hints and techniques, and a "Field Guide to Trophy Sheep." The Information Branch, Department of Lands & Forests, Natural Resources Bldg., Edmonton, T5K 2E1 publishes a free series of illustrated, full-color wildlife map-guides, including *Owls of Alberta, Falcons & Eagles of Alberta, Broadwinged Hawks of Alberta, Geese, Swans & Cranes, Diving Ducks of Alberta, Puddle Ducks of Alberta,* and *Upland Game Birds of Alberta*. A fascinating study of Alberta's world-famous big-game hunting, *Alberta Trophy Hunting*, by John G. Stelfox, wildlife biologist, may be obtained free by writing: Fish & Wildlife Division, Department of Lands & Forests, Edmonton T5K 2E1.

Through the years Alberta has consistently produced trophy big game in the Boone & Crockett world's record class, including the world's record mountain lion, shot near Trout Creek. The province's top hunting areas for bighorn sheep include Oyster Creek, Burnt Creek, Panther Creek, Brazeau River, and Coalbranch areas in the Rocky Mountains and foothill wilderness areas. Rocky Mountain goat inhabit the mountain and foothill areas, particularly in the Rock Lake and Corral and Sheep creeks and Sulphur River areas. Wapiti or elk are found in woodlands throughout the foothills and eastern slopes of the Rocky Mountains, with the greatest concentration of trophies taken in the Smoky River, Ram River, and Rock Lake areas. Woodland (mountain) caribou range throughout the Athabasca River system of northern Alberta with the greatest number of trophy animals taken in the Sheep Creek and Wildhay River areas. Woodland caribou may be found as far south as Banff National Park. Grizzly bear roam the remote Rocky Mountain highlands and the interior woodlands of the Swan Hills; Alberta trophy grizzlies are found in the Swan Hills, Sheep Creek, Berland, and Smoky river areas in Willmore Wilderness Park. Black bear are found throughout the province, with the largest animals coming from the Smoky River, Rocky Mountain House, and Peace River areas. Mountain lion (cougar) range throughout the Rocky Mountains and foothills, especially in the Clearwater River and Dutch, Solomon, and Flat Creek areas. Record mule deer range throughout the parklands and are most common in the mountains, foothills, and Smoky and Peace River areas. Whitetail deer are found throughout the parklands and open grasslands and occasionally in the mountain country of the eastern slope of the Rockies. Moose are found throughout the northern coniferous forest regions and in the foothills. Some of the finest big moose country is found in the Whitecourt, Edson, and Grande Prairie provincial forests. Recently constructed logging and carry roads in northern bushlands and in the Lesser Slave Lake, Swan Hills, and foothills regions provide access to remote big-game areas previously accessible only by charter bush plane. (See "Big-Game Ranges & Wildlife Maps," "Outfitters & Guides," and the "Alberta Travel & Recreation Guide.")

Fort Chipewyan

(Pop. 717). Located in the far northeast of Alberta on Lake Athabasca, shown on the early maps of the fur traders as "Lake of the Hills," Fort Chipewyan was for many years one of the most important fur trading posts of the Northwest Company. It was founded by Roderick Mackenzie (cousin to Sir Alexander) in 1788 on a rocky point projecting into the shore. Eleven years later the post was relocated to its present site on the north shore peninsula of the lake near its western end. In 1821, after the merger of the two companies, the post was taken over by the Hudson's Bay Company and operated in place of Fort Wedderburn. Its name is derived from the local tribe of Chipewyan Indians and means, appropriately for a major fur trade center, "pointed skins."

A library was established there by Roderick Mackenzie, and the fort was accordingly dubbed "Little Athens" because it offered a tiny haven of civilization in the wilderness. It was from Fort Chipewyan that Sir Alexander Mackenzie embarked on his famous voyage to the Arctic Ocean in June 1789, up the Great River of the North that was later to bear his name. The settlement is reached by scheduled and charter aircraft and provides access to Lake Claire and Wood Buffalo National Park, Andrews Lake, Rivière des Rochers and Slave River, and the world-famous waterfowl shooting on the Peace-Athabasca Delta.

Great Divide Trail

The Great Divide Trail (several sections are still under construction) follows the backbone of the Continental Divide for 350 miles across the top of the Canadian Rockies from the south end of Banff Park through Mount Assiniboine, Kootenay, Yoho, Jasper, and Mount Robson parks and the White Goat Wilderness. Plans call for the construction of primitive alpine shelters every 10 miles or so apart, and for extending the trail south along the Great Divide through Waterton Lakes National Park to the Montana border and the Rocky Mountain Trail. The Great Divide Trail winds along high ridges near and above timberline at altitudes of 4,000–9,000 feet through a rugged alpine wilderness. Overnight campers using the trail are required to register with the national park wardens. Primitive campsites are located along the entire length of the trail. The major features shown on the trail maps, from north to south, include Palliser Pass, Upper Spray River, Sunshine-Egypt Lake area, Mount Assiniboine, Floe Creek, Wolverine Pass, Goodsir and McArthur passes, Tumbling Glacier, 1,200-foot Helmet Falls, Lake O'Hara, fossil beds, Mount Burgess, Little Yoho and Amiskwi valleys, the caribou trail segment from Norman Creek to tranquil Maligne Lake, Yellowhead Pass, Moose and Robson passes, Berg Lake, and 12,972-foot Mount Robson. Numerous spur trails and loop routes wind through scenic alpine valleys and passes along remnants of old Indian and trapper trails. The wilderness traveler is advised to have good lightweight equipment and be prepared for occasional violent weather conditions in the high country. The Great Divide Trail country is shown on the following Canadian National Topographic Survey overview maps: Fernie 82-G, Kananaskis Lakes 82-J, Calgary 82-O, Golden 82-N, Brazeau 82-C, Canoe River 83-D, Mount Robson 83-E.

Highways—Recreation & Scenic Routes

The major outdoor recreation areas of Alberta are served by an excellent network of well-maintained scenic highways and secondary access roads. For the official *Alberta Road Map* write: Travel Alberta, Box 2500, Edmonton T5J 2Z4. This useful full-color map, at a scale of 1 inch to 25 miles, shows all paved, gravel, and unimproved roads, trails, provincial and national parks, campgrounds, scheduled airline stops, time-zone boundaries, and ports of entry. The Canadian National Topographic Survey Map Kits listed below for each highway are printed in full color at a scale of 1:250,000, or 1 inch to 4 miles; they provide an excellent overview of the topography of the famous fishing, camping, hunting, and canoeing areas surrounding Alberta's major roadways.

Alberta Forestry Trunk Road System

This 640-mile gravel route, constructed primarily for forest protection, runs largely through the spectacular scenery and world-famous fishing, big-game hunting, and wilderness camping areas of the great Rocky Mountain Forest Reserve, from Crowsnest Pass on Highway 3 in the south to Goodwin, 21 miles east of Grande Prairie on Highway 34 in the north. With proper care, all vehicles, including those towing light trailers, can readily negotiate the route. Be sure to carry maps, emergency food, blankets, and a good first-aid kit. Service stations providing mechanical services and gas are located along the Trunk Road at Highwood Junction, 69 miles north of Blairmore; Red Deer River Crossing, 53 miles north of Highway 1A; and Muskeg station, 65 miles north of Entrance. Food supplies are available at Highwood Junction, Red Deer Junction, Nordegg, Muskeg, Robb, and Hinton. The major features shown along the route on the map kit include the Gap and the Livingstone Mountain Range, Old Man River; Livingston Falls, about 18 miles north of the Gap Ranger Station; Plateau Mountain, Highwood River, Kananaskis Lakes and River, Spray Lakes Reservoir, Bow Valley Provincial Park, Panther River, Ghost River Wilderness, Clearwater and Ram rivers, Abraham Lake and the Bighorn Dam, Siffleur Wilderness, Bighorn River, White Goat Wilderness, Elbow Sheep Wilderness, Pulp Company Lease, the 1,774-square-mile Willmore Wilderness Park at the north end of Jasper National Park, Pierre Gray's lake and trading post just south of the Grande Cache Turnoff, and the Muskeg and wild Smoky rivers. The Forestry Trunk winds through the mixed subalpine, grassland, aspen parkland, and boreal forests of the Rocky Mountain foothills and the Bow-Crow, Rock-Clearwater, Edson, and Grand Prairie provincial forests. Provincial forest service tent and trailer campsites are located along the entire length of the Forestry Trunk Road and are shown on the *Recreation Areas of the Foothills Map*, which may be obtained free by writing: Alberta Department of Lands & Forests, Natural Resources Bldg., Edmonton T5K 2E1. Drinking water is available at hand pumps, and toilets are the pit privy type. Individual unit services or hookups are not available. The tent units consist of a back-in stall, with drive-through stalls for trailer units. Pickup campers and tent trailers may be accommodated in either type of unit. Boat-launching sites are available at most lakeshore campsites. Canadian National Topographic Survey Maps, scale 1:250,000: Fernie 82-G, Kananaskis Lakes 82-J, Calgary 82-O, Rocky Mountain House 83-B, Brazeau 83-C, Edson 83-F, Mount Robson 83-E, Wapiti 83-L, Grande Prairie 83-L.

Alberta Highway (2)

This paved route is the largest south-north highway in Alberta, running for 480 miles from Carway (on the Montana border) north through Cardston, Fort Macleod, Calgary, Edmonton, Athabasca, Slave Lake, Peace River, Dunvegan, Spirit River, Grande Prairie, Beaverlodge, and west into British Columbia at Tupper. North of Edmonton Highway 2 passes through the boreal evergreen forests of the Slave Lake, Peace River, and Grande Prairie provincial forests. The major recreation areas shown along the route include the Rocky Mountain foothills, St. Mary River, Beaver and Highwood rivers, Sylvan and Gull lakes, Red Deer River Badlands, known for their dinosaur fossil rocks, the historic Athabasca River, and the famous trophy fishing waters of Lesser Slave Lake—the largest body of water in Alberta—Heart River, Saddle Hills, Bear Lake, and Smoky and Wapiti rivers. West of Slave Lake the highway passes through some of the finest big moose country and elk, whitetail deer, and black bear hunting areas in the province. Provincial campsites are located near Stand Off, Fort Macleod, Willow Creek Provincial Park, Nanton, Bowden, Red Lodge Province Park, Red Deer, Sylvan Lake, Gull Lake, Pigeon Lake, Dapp Lake, Athabasca, Lawrence Lake, Fawatt Lake, Lesser Slave Lake, Peace River, Cardinal Lake, Woking, Swan Lake, and Saskatoon Island Provincial Park. Canadian National Topographic Survey Maps, scale 1:250,000: Lethbridge 82-H, Gleichen 82-I, Calgary 82-O, Drumheller 82-P, Red Deer 82-A, Edmonton 83-H, Tawatinaw 83-I, Pelican 83-P, Lesser Slave Lake 83-O, Winagami 83-N, Peace River 84-C, Grande Prairie 83-M.

Alberta Highway (36)

This 424-mile partly paved highway begins at Warner, 24 miles north of the Montana border on Highway 4. It crosses Highways 3, 1, and 16 on its way north through the short grass prairies and fertile aspen parklands to the vast spruce and poplar evergreen forests and trophy fishing lakes of the Canadian Shield surrounding Lac La Biche. The major features shown on the map kit include the Chin Lakes, Oldman River, Lake Newell, Dowling and the Chain Lakes, Sullivan Lake, Battle River, Lac Santé, North Saskatchewan River, and the renowned moose country surrounding the trophy lake trout, northern pike, and walleye waters of Whitefish Lake, Beaver Lake and River, and Touchwood, Pinehurst, Siebert, Ironwood, Frenchman, and Missawaiwi lakes. Provincial campsites are located along Highway 36 at Taber Provincial Park, Castor, Two Hills, Lac Sante, Therien Lake, Vincent Lake, Garner Lake Provincial Park, Missawaiwi Lake, Lac La Biche, and along the shore of Ironwood, Fork, Pinehurst, and Siebert lakes. Canadian National Topographic Survey Maps, scale 1:250,000: Lethbridge 82-H, Gleichen 82-I, Medicine Hat 72-L, Oyen 72-M, Wainwright 73-D, Vermilion 73-E, Sand River 73-L, Tawatinaw 83-I.

Alberta Highway (63)

This paved all-weather route winds north from Highway 46 and Lac La Biche through the boreal wilderness of spruce and poplar forests, rolling hills, and swamplands of the Lac La Biche and Athabasca provincial forests to Fort McMurray at the confluence of the Athabasca and Clearwater rivers. The wildlands surrounding the highway offer some of the finest moose and woodland caribou hunting in the province. The major features shown on the route include the arctic grayling, walleye, and northern pike waters of the La Biche River, Corrigall and Lyle lakes, House River, Gregoire Lake, and Hangingstone and Horse rivers. North of Fort McMurray are the great oil deposits of the Athabasca tar sands. Charter aircraft at Fort McMurray provide access to the 17,300-square-mile wilderness of the Wood Buffalo National Park and Lake Athabasca to the north. Provincial campgrounds are located along the highway near Wandering River, Mariana Lake, Hangingstone River, and Gregoire Lake Provincial Park. Canadian National Topographic Survey Maps, scale 1:250,000: Tawatinaw 83-I, Pelican 83-P, Winefred Lake 73-M, Waterways 74-D, Algar Lake 84-A.

David Thompson Highway (11)

This route is named after David Thompson, the great Northwest Company explorer and mapmaker who discovered the Athabasca Pass in the Rocky Mountains in 1810. Before 1810 the trade route from Rocky Mountain House to the Pacific was through House Pass to the Columbia River. In 1810 the bloody rivalry between the Piegan and Flathead Indians blocked access to this route. Discovery of an alternative pass at the headwaters of the Athabasca River by Thompson followed. The modern Highway 11 runs from its junction with Highway 2 near Red Deer, westward past the historic fur trading post at Rocky Mountain House and Nordegg, over the Kootenay Plains to the Saskatchewan River and the Bighorn Dam and Abraham Lake, through the White Goat and Siffleur Wilderness areas, to its junction with the Ice Fields Parkway in Banff National Park. Campgrounds are located at Jarvis Bay Provincial Park, Crimson Lake Provincial Park, Nordegg, and Abraham Lake. Canadian National Topographic Survey Maps, scale 1:250,000: Red Deer 83-A, Rocky Mountain House 83-B, Brazeau 83-C.

Ice Fields Parkway (93)

Known as the show window of the Rockies, the Ice Fields Parkway is one of the greatest "highroads" in the world. It winds for 142 miles through the breathtaking scenery of the Canadian Rockies from the serene alpine waters of Lake Louise in Banff National Park north to Jasper. The highway follows the old packtrain route past majestic peaks and mountain passes named for such wilderness explorers as Hector, Collie, Wilcox, and Outram, and their alpine guides and packers—Peyto, Sarbach, and Kaufmann. Other features along the route bear place names from the fur trade era, Canadian Pacific Railroad surveys, and Indian names such as Sunwapta, which means "turbulent river," or Mistaya River, "grizzly bear." The major topographic features, accommodations, campgrounds, hiking trails, warden stations, fire towers, and railroads are shown on the *Ice Fields Parkway Map*, available free from the Superintendent, Banff National Park, Banff. The major features from Lake Louise (formerly known as Laggan—a departure point for packtrains heading beyond the headwaters of the Bow River) to Saskatchewan Crossing include a chain of large glacier-fed jewellike lakes; the broad, heavily forested Mistaya Valley; and the scenic blue-green waters of Peyto Lake, named for Bill Peyto, a renowned packer and guide and self-taught geologist who became a park warden at Banff. The parkway winds north from Saskatchewan Crossing past the 120 square miles of the Columbia Ice Fields, which form the headwaters of the Athabasca (765 miles long), Saskatchewan (1,205 miles long), and Columbia (1,210 miles long) rivers, and the 12,294-foot summit of Mount Columbia. Rocky Mountain sheep, elk, moose, and black bear are seen from time to time in the highlands surrounding the parkway. Camping facilities are located south from Jasper at Whisters Campground (Mile 1.4), Wapiti Campground (Mile 2.7), Mount Kerkeslin Campground (Mile 21.8), Honeymoon Lake Campground (Mile 31.8), Jonas Creek Campground (Mile 48.0), Columbia Ice Field and Wilcox Creek Campgrounds (Mile 66.2); Cirrus Mountain Campground (Mile 79.2), Rampart Creek Campground (Mile 88.1), Waterfowl Lake Campground (Mile 106.7), and Mosquito Creek Campground (Mile 127.9). Canadian National Topographic Survey Maps: Calgary 82-O, Golden 82-N, Brazeau 83-C, Canoe River 83-D.

Mackenzie Highway (35)

This great highway, named for Alexander Mackenzie, forms the gateway to Alberta's far north and the Northwest Territories. It extends for 289 miles north from Grimshaw, 13 miles west of Peace River, to the Northwest Territories border. The Mackenzie route passes through the Peace River and Footner Lake forests. The major features shown on the map kit include the great Peace River Canyon, the walleye and northern pike waters of Cardinal Lake, Notikewin River, Hay and Steen rivers, and the remote moose, grizzly, and caribou territory in the Cameron Hills. The grave of "Twelve-Foot" Davis, pathfinder, pioneer, miner, and trader, lies in the town of Peace River. During the Cariboo gold rush in British Columbia, Davis discovered an overlooked 12-foot strip between previously staked claims which produced more than $15,000 in gold. Nearby, in the Peace River Canyon, are huge dinosaur tracks dating back more than 100 million years. The Mackenzie Highway is paved for the first 189 miles north to High Level, with gravel surface on the remaining 100 miles to the Northwest Territories boundary. Provincial campgrounds are located near Peace River, Hotchkiss, Twin Lakes, Paddle Prairie, High Level, Meander River, Steen River, and Cameron Hills. Canadian National Topographic Survey Maps, scale 1:250,000: Peace River 84-C, Bison Lake 84-F, Mount Watt 84-K, Steen River 84-N.

Southern Trans-Provincial Highway (3)

This paved route winds for 202 miles starting at Medicine Hat and running southwesterly through the dry open prairie grasslands, aspen parklands, and southeast slopes of the Rocky Mountain foothills—key wintering ranges for Rocky Mountain elk and bighorn sheep. The

highway passes through the southern frontier once patrolled by the Rocky Mountain Rangers and Steele's Scouts during the Riel Rebellion of 1885, defeating Chief Big Bear and his Cree rebels at Frenchman's Butte. The major features shown along the route include Old Man River, Lethbridge, Fort Macleod, Beaver River, and Pincher Creek. Provincial campgrounds are located near Bow Island, Taber, Chin, Fort Macleod, and Beauvais Lake Provincial Park. Canadian National Topographic Survey Map Kits, scale 1:250,000: Medicine Hat 72-L, Foremost 72-E, Lethbridge 82-H.

Trans-Canada Highway (1)

The 333-mile Alberta segment of the 5,000-mile Trans-Canada Highway, one of the world's longest, stretching from Newfoundland to Vancouver Island, British Columbia, begins at the Saskatchewan border, 2 miles east of Walsh, then passes northwest through Medicine Hat, Calgary, Canmore, Banff, and Lake Louise, over the Great Divide at Kicking Horse Pass at 5,405-feet elevation into British Columbia's Yoho National Park. Major features along the route include Lake Newell, Bow River, Kananaskis River, and Lake Minnewanka. Provincial campgrounds are located near Redcliff, Suffield, Kinbrook Island Provincial Park, Tillebrook Trans-Canada Campsite, Brooks Bow Valley Provincial Park, Exshaw, Kananaskis, Canmore, Banff, and Lake Louise. Canadian National Topographic Survey Maps, scale 1:250,000: Medicine Hat 72-L, Gleichen 82-I, Calgary 82-O, Golden 82-N.

Yellowhead Highway (16)

The Alberta section of the Yellowhead, named for a blond trapper of mixed Iroquois Indian blood who traveled across the Rockies into the Kootenay Country of British Columbia, runs for 399 miles from Lloydminster west through Elk Island National Park, Edmonton, Edson, and Jasper National Park, over the spectacular 3,760-foot Yellowhead Pass on the Great Divide, into British Columbia's Mount Robson Provincial Park. Major features along the route include Beaverhill Lake, Wabamun Lake, Chip Lake, McLeod River, Brulé and Jasper lakes, Snake Indian, and Athabasca River. The Yellowhead passes through the aspen parklands, boreal evergreen forests, and spectacular Rocky Mountain foothills and the high rugged backbone of the Great Divide. West of Edmonton the highway runs through the famous big-game hunting, fishing, and wilderness canoe-camping areas of the Whitecourt and Edson provincial forests. Provincial campgrounds are located at Kenilworth Lake, Vermilion Provincial Park, Birch Lake, Vegreville, Elk Island National Park, Wabamun Lake Provincial Park, Pembina River Provincial Park, MacKay, Carrot Creek, Edson, Obed Lake, Brulé Lake, and Jasper National Park. Canadian National Topographic Survey Maps: Vermilion 73-E, Edmonton 83-H, Wabamun Lake 83-G, Edson 83-F, Canoe River 83-E.

Hudson's Bay Company Outfitting Posts & Canoe Service

The western divisional headquarters of the Hudson's Bay northern stores department is in Edmonton, where the white palisades of Fort Edmonton, on the left bank of the Saskatchewan River, once served as a great supply center and jumping-off point for explorations across the Rockies into British Columbia. The northern outpost stores carry food supplies, gear, and ammunition needed for hunting, fishing, and wilderness canoeing. The HBC U-Paddle Canoe Service rents 17-foot standard 75-pound Grumman paddling canoes. Each canoe is equipped with a carrying yoke and 3 paddles. The service is available to experienced canoeists only. HBC supply posts in Alberta are located at Fort McMurray, Fort MacKay, Fort Chipewyan, Fox Lake, Garden River, John d'Or Prairie, Fort Vermilion, Meander River, Assumption, Peace River, Grande Prairie, Atikameg, Wabasca, Desmarais, Lac La Biche, Grande Cache, and Rocky Mountain House. For a free *HBC U-Paddle Service Map-Brochure*, rates, and reservations write: Hudson's Bay Company, Northern Stores Department, 800 Baker Center, 10025 106th St., Edmonton T5J 1G7, or phone (403) 424–8113. Keep in mind that the remote HBC posts do not necessarily carry a full range of supplies. It's best to place your order in writing a couple of months in advance.

Mountain Camps & Pack Trains

High in the spectacular alpine wilderness of Banff and Jasper national parks are several famous mountain camps which provide guided pack-train trips, hiking, photography, and fishing excursions along the old hunting trails of the Stone Indians and the Great Divide exploration routes of the early fur traders. Packtrains—the classic symbol of the Canadian Rockies; boat rentals, fishing guides, and accommodations are provided by *Tonquin Valley Chalets* in Jasper National Park. Facilities include 5 rustic cabins and 4 tent cabins, a main lodge and dining room, located in the beautiful Tonquin Valley, 14 miles by

packhorse from View Point at Mount Edith Cavell or from the Portal Creek Trail. For information write: Box 1175, Jasper. The *Tonquin Valley-Skyline Trail Camps* operate packtrain trips to remote alpine areas of Jasper National Park and Willmore Wilderness Park, to Tonquin Valley on the Great Divide, and to the Skyline-Maligne Lake area. The gemlike emerald lakes, green meadowlands, and spectacular peaks and glaciers of Tonquin Valley form one of the finest alpine regions in North America. Services include guided alpland riding, wildlife photographic safaris, trout fishing, and trophy big-game hunts. For info write: Box 508, Jasper (summer), or Brulé (winter). Mountain camps and packtrain trips in the Lake Louise area of Banff National Park and the three valleys near the lake—Louise, Paradise, and Moraine—are provided by the *Mount Temple Chalet,* with accommodations for 14. Write: Village Lake Louise Ltd., Box 5, Lake Louise. The famous *Skoki Lodge* is located in the scenic Skoki Valley of Banff National Park, surrounded by the spectacular wilderness of lakes, peaks, mountain passes, windswept tundra and fir, and larch-laced meadows of the Slate Range. The lodge is reached by trail with accommodations for 24 people. For guided packtrain and hiking trips to the Wall of Jericho, Merlin's Castle, Skoki Lakes, Fossil Mountain, Red Deer Lakes, Boulder Pass, and Hidden Lake, write: Timberline Tours Ltd., Skoki Lodge, Box 12, Lake Louise T0L 1E0. Guided packtrains in the Intersection Mountain area of the Willmore Wilderness are operated by Rocky Mountain Trail Rides. For information, rates, and the free publication *Wilderness Trail Rides,* write: Edward Sodergren, c/o Travel Alberta, Box 2500, Edmonton T5J 2Z4. *Warner & Mackenzie Guiding & Outfitting Ltd.,* Box 448, Banff T0L 0C0, specializes in pack trips and fishing trips in the Banff National

Park high country. *Canadian Mountain Holidays Ltd.,* P.O. Box 1660, Banff T0L 0C0, offers guided 8-day cross-country ski trips in the Canadian Rockies near Lake Louise. This renowned firm also runs *The Ski School of the Canadian Rockies* and the *CMH Climbing School & Guide Service.* Write for their free *Heli-Skiing Handbook.* Phone (403) 762-4531.

Outfitters & Guides

A *Listing of Guide Outfitters* for wilderness fishing and big-game hunts in the Canadian Rockies and foothills of the Rocky Mountains Forest Reserve and in the Edson, Whitecourt, Peace River, Slave Lake, Lac La Biche, Athabasca, and Footner provincial forests may be obtained from the Fish & Wildlife Branch, Natural Resources Bldg., Edmonton T5K 2E1. Much of the hunting in the highlands of the Rockies is done by packhorse along the old Stoney and Kootenay Indian game trails used by trappers and explorers during the fur trade era. Hunting from horseback allows the hunter to reach the remote alpine areas with a minimum of exertion up the steep slopes, across the cold, deep streams and through heavy brush tangles that might prove impenetrable on foot. The homing instinct of the horse will carry the outdoorsman safely to camp after sunset. Big-game animals frequently allow a horse to approach at close range, allowing the hunter or wildlife photographer a better shot than if he were traveling on foot. The packhorse will pack out game easily and will easily carry extra gear that would prove troublesome on foot. A code of ethical standards and a free *Western Guides & Outfitting Listing* for the Canadian Rockies may be obtained by writing: Western Guides & Outfitters Association, 213–1717 3d Ave., Prince George, B.C. The guide listing contains useful advice in choosing a guide-outfitter. Indian guide and outfitting service is provided by the *Ghost River Indian Guide Service,* about 10 miles west of Morley in the Rocky Mountain foothills with 10 tents at headquarters camp and 6 outpost tent camps. The service caters to big-game hunters willing to rough it in primitive wilderness settings, with guided hunts for moose, elk, black bear, bighorn sheep, and goat; facilities and services include boats, canoes, gear, guides, and horses; alpine fishing for rainbow and cutthroat trout. For information write: Wallace Snow, P.O. Box 52, Morley. The *R. Makinaw Guiding & Outfitting Center* is 74 miles west of Rocky Mountain House with service for fishermen, big-game hunters, and tourists. Operates the *Rocky Mountain Bush School* (brochure on request) and trail rides in the high country. Accommodations include 10 tents at headquarters camp and 10 outpost tent camps. Big-game hunts for moose, elk, mule deer, bear, goat, Rocky Mountain sheep, wolf, and cougar. Write: R. Makinaw, P.O. Box 1209, Rocky Mountain House.

For detailed information on guided fishing, big-game hunting, photography, wild river, and packhorse trips, write to the following members of the Alberta Professional Guides & Outfitters Federation: *Wilderness Alberta,* 7215 Whitemud Rd., Edmonton; *Trophy Guide Service,* Box 687, Sylvan Lake; *Getaway Guide Service,* Box 3312 Sta. D, Edmonton; *Timber Mountain Pack Train,* Box 511, Claresholm; *North West Outfitters,* 10525-162 St., Edmonton; *Gristhaven Lodge,* Box 266, Cold Lake. For additional listings and information, write: *Alberta Professional Guides & Outfitters Federation,* Box 177, St. Albert.

Railway Services

The main lines of the Canadian National Railways and the Canadian Pacific Railways pass through Edmonton and Calgary, with a network of lines serving most of the province. The Northern Alberta Railways,

operated jointly by the CN and CP railways, provides access to the major outfitting and supply centers in the famous big-game hunting, fishing, and wilderness canoe-camping country in the northern part of the province. For travel information and rates write: *Northern Alberta Railway Co.*, 13025 St. Albert Trail, Edmonton T5L 4L4; *Canadian National Railways*, 935 Lagauchetière St. W, P.O. Box 8100, Montreal, Que. H3C 3N4; and *CP Rail*, Windsor Sta., Montreal, Que. H3C 3E4.

Rocky Mountain Forest Reserve Map

An attractive, extremely useful *Recreation Areas of the Foothills* map and guide to the famous wilderness recreation areas of the Rocky Mountains Forest Reserve and the 620-mile-long Forestry Trunk Road may be obtained free from Alberta Recreation, Natural Resources Bldg., 9833 109th St., Edmonton T5K 2E1. This full-color map shows the forestry recreation areas, Alberta transport campsites, ranger stations, forestry lookout stations, service stations, railways, and provincial parks. The guide section describes the famous forest service recreation areas in the Bow-Crow Forest, such as Indian Graves, Chinook, Burnt Timber, Beaver Mines Lake, and Spray Lakes; the wild Brazeau River, Kootenay Plains, and North Ram River recreation areas in the Rocky-Clearwater Forest; the Berland and Cardinal River recreation areas in the Edson Forest; and the forest service recreation areas in the big-game hunting and wilderness fishing country of the Whitecourt, Grande Prairie, Peace River, Footner Lake, Slave Lake, and Lac La Biche provincial forests. Other features shown on the map include the wilderness hiking and camping areas of the Willmore Wilderness Park, White Goat Wilderness, and Siffleur and Ghost River wilderness areas.

Vacation Travel Information

The *Travel Alberta Vacation Guide* contains the nitty-gritty about transportation, car rentals, gasoline, ice, propane, border crossing info, ports of entry, currency, firearms, fishing tackle and gear, pets, and alcoholic beverage outlets. The 80-page guide is available free from Travel Alberta, Box 2500, Edmonton T5J 2Z4, (403) 427-4321. A handsome 64-page *Alberta Adventure Guide* is packed with beautiful full-color photographs, maps, and detailed descriptions of the provincial tourist regions: the Gateway Zone, Big Country, land of David

Thompson, Battle River region, the Lakeland, Evergreen Zone, Land of the Mighty Peace, Jasper, Calgary, Edmonton, Banff, big-game country, land of the midnight twilight. The adventure guide is published free by Travel Alberta.

Wild River Voyageur Routes Guide

One of the most useful publications available to the wilderness paddler and fisherman planning a trip to Alberta is the 72-page *Alberta Wild Rivers Guide* published by the Wild Rivers Survey, Parks Canada, Department of Indian Affairs & Northern Development. It may be purchased by mail for $1.50 from Information Canada, 171 Slater St., Ottawa, Ont. The guide contains a map of the wild rivers of Alberta, information about the climate and how to plan your canoe voyage, thorough descriptions of access and egress, geography, flora and fauna, and the canoe route for the Brazeau River from Nigel Pass to the Brazeau Reservoir; Clearwater River, from Trident Lake to Rocky Mountain House; Smoky River, from Grande Cache to the Peace River; North Saskatchewan River, from Alexandra River to Edmonton; and the Red Deer River, from the Rocky Mountains to the Saskatchewan River. The North Saskatchewan River was one of the major access routes during the fur trade era to Fort Edmonton, Rocky Mountain House, and Fort Chipewyan at Lake Athabasca. York boat brigades plied the waters of the North Saskatchewan, bringing supplies west and transporting furs east to York Factory and Hudson for shipment to England. David Thompson traveled from Lake Superior to the Pacific along the "voyageurs' highway" via the Saskatchewan and North Saskatchewan rivers, and in 1806–7 used Rocky Mountain House as a base during his search for a trade route over the Rockies to the Columbia River and the Pacific. (See "Canoeing & Wilderness Waters.")

Far North Trophy Lakes Country

Birch Mountains Lake Chain

Canadian National Topographic Survey Maps, scale 1:250,000, shows Legend, Namur, Gardiner, and Eaglenest lakes: Namur Lake 84-H, Bitumount 74-E.

Lac La Biche Trophy Lakes Area

Canadian National Topographic Survey Maps, scale 1:50,000, includes Touchwood, Seibert, Pinehurst, Beaver, Ironwood, Wolf, Marguerite, Burnt, May, Marie, and Cold lakes: Plamondon 83P-16, Lac La Biche 73L-13, Touchwood Lake 73L-14, Wolf River 73L-15, Medley River 73L-16, Beaver Lake 73L-12, Pinehurst Lake 73L-11, Marguerite Lake 73L-10, Marie Lake 73L-9, Cold Lake 73L-8, Cold River 73K-12.

Lake Athabasca

Canadian National Topographic Survey Maps, scale 1:250,000: Fort Chipewyan 74-L, Fitzgerald 74-M, Tazin Lake 74-N, William River 74-K, Fond du Lac 74-O.

Lesser Slave Lake

Canadian National Topographic Survey Maps, scale 1:50,000: Grouard 83N-9, High Prairie 83N-8, Salt Creek 83O-12, Driftpile 83O-5, Narrows Creek 83O-11, Kinuso 83O-6, Slave Lake 83O-7.

In Alberta's far north, in the great boreal forest and Precambrian Shield country of the Athabasca, Slave Lake, and Lac La Biche provincial forests, are a group of deep, cold lakes famous for their large lake trout and great northern pike that have been protected as trophy fishing lakes by the Alberta Division of Fish & Wildlife. To fish these lakes a trophy lake license is required in addition to the regular angling license; the use or possession of a gaff and the use of bait fish are prohibited. A "Map of Trophy Fishing Lakes" is contained in the *Guide to Sportsfishing Regulations*, available free from the Fish & Wildlife Division, Natural Resources Bldg., Edmonton T5K 2E1. Due east of the outfitting and fly-in center of Lac La Biche are the trophy waters of Seibert and May lakes, part of the historic Beaver River system. Seibert Lake is famous for the large northern pike in the 20–35-pound range taken over the years. Other outstanding lakes in the area are Cold, Marie, Wolf, Muriel, and Touchwood. To the north lie the remote lake trout, pike, walleye, and arctic grayling waters of large island-dotted Winefred Trophy Lake, surrounded by a thick forest of spruce and poplar. On the southern shore of Winefred stands the Winefred Lake Ranger Station next to a carry road that winds southeast through the evergreen stands to Grist Lake. Far to the northwest, due north of Peerless Lake in the Trout Mountain country of the Slave Lake Forest, are the trophy walleye, lake trout, and pike waters of little God's Lake, which appears on the map as a mere speck of blue in a vast sea of forest green. Due northeast as the crow flies of God's Lake are the game-famous lake-dotted Birch Mountains (hills, actually) and Namur and Gardiner trophy lakes in the ancient hunting and trapping grounds of the Chipewyan Indians. Although not trophy lakes, nearby Legend and Eaglenest lakes offer equally good cold-water fishing.

If you were to fly north to the last remaining trophy lake, you would pass along the old fur trade route of the Athabasca River (known back then to Mackenzie and Company as the Elk) and the tar sands which stretch for 100 miles along the river, and on over Peter Pond's Fort Chipewyan and huge Lake Athabasca, and the notorious Slave River rapids and lowlands, to small Andrew Lake, tucked into the northeastern corner of the province. The trophy lakes are reached by floatplane from Edmonton, Fort McMurray, and Lac La Biche. Big-game hunt-

ALBERTA TRAVEL & RECREATION GUIDE

ing is good throughout the Athabasca, Slave Lake, and Lac La Biche Forest regions for caribou, black bear, and moose, as well as in the historic Peace River and Footner Forest regions to the west. Both the Athabasca and Peace rivers and their tributaries hold Dolly Varden, grayling, and walleye up to 10 pounds. Lake Athabasca, straddling the boundary between Alberta and Saskatchewan, is the home of giant northern pike and lake trout reaching weights of up to 72 pounds. (See "Far North Fly-in Fishing & Hunting Lodges" in the "Encyclopedia" section.)

NORTHERN ALBERTA

TRAVEL GUIDE TO A NEW SCENIC LAND OF THE MIGHTY PEACE

Access & Outfitting Centers

The far north regions are reached by floatplane from major outfitting centers and via Alberta Highways 63 and 36 on the east and Macken-zie Highway on the west. Major outfitting, guide, and supply centers include Lac La Biche, Medley, Cold Lake, Fort McMurray, Slave Lake, and Peace River.

Rocky Mountains Forest Reserve & the Foothills

Rocky Mountains Forest Reserve Topo Maps

Canadian National Topographic Survey Maps, scale 1:250,000: Edson 83-F, Wabamun Lake 83-G, Brazeau Lake 83-C, Rocky Mountain House 83-B; Calgary 82-O, Kananaskis Lakes 82-J, Gleichen 82-I, Fernie 82-G, Lethbridge 82-H.

Rocky Mountains Foothills

Canadian National Topographic Survey Maps, scale 1:250,000: Fernie 82-G, Lethbridge 82-H, Kananaskis Lakes 82-J, Calgary 82-O, Rocky Mountain House 83-B, Brazeau 83-C, Edson 83-F, Mount Robson 83-E, Iosegun Lake 83-K, Wapiti 83-L, Grande Prairie 83-M, Winagami 83-N.

Bow-Crowsnest Forest Reserve

Canadian National Topographic Survey Maps, scale 1:250,000: Calgary 82-O, Kananaskis Lakes 82-J, Fernie 82-G, Lethbridge 82-H.

Ghost River Wilderness

Canadian National Topographic Survey Maps, scale 1:50,000: Lake Minnewanka 82O-6, Mount Eisenhower 82O-5.

Siffleur Wilderness

Canadian National Topographic Survey Maps, scale 1:50,000: Mistaya River 82N-15, Siffleur River 82N-16, White Rabbit Creek 83C-1.

White Goat Wilderness

Canadian National Topographic Survey Maps, scale 1:50,000: Cline River 83C-2, Job Creek 83C-7, Sunwapta 83C-6.

The Rocky Mountains Forest Reserve embraces some of the most spectacular wilderness camping and big-game hunting country in North America. The forest reserve encompasses white and Engel-mann spruce forests, wild rivers, valleys, alpine meadows, and lakes of the foothills along the eastern slope of the Great Divide from the trophy moose and elk country of the Edson Forest south through the highlands of the Rocky Mountain-Clearwater Forest and the Bow-Crowsnest Forest. The famous Forestry Trunk Road system runs the entire length of the reserve from Crowsnest Pass in the south, north through the Grande Prairie region. This rugged wilderness travel route is maintained by the Alberta Forest Service and provides access to the remote fishing, hunting, and camping regions in the ancient hunting grounds of the Stone and Kootenay Indians in the scenic high country of the Flathead, Livingstone, Porcupine, Highwood, Elk, Opal, Kananaskis, Fisher, Goat, First, Miette, and Hoff Range mountains. The wilderness high country areas are reached by hiking and packtrain along old Indian and game trails used over a century ago by the explorers and fur traders during their westward crossings from Fort Chipewyan and Rocky Mountain House.

In the Bow-Crowsnest Forest, south of Banff National Park, are the majestic wildlands of the upper Kananaskis recreation area along the British Columbia border, at the head of the popular Kananaskis Valley. The major features of the area (named during the 1858 Palliser expedition after Kananaskis, Palliser's Indian guide, who is said to have made a miraculous recovery from a severe blow he received from an ax) include the beautiful brook and cutthroat trout waters of Kananaskis, Aster, Three Isle, and Maude lakes, the upper Kananaskis River, large areas of old burns, and the mountain goat range of the 10,000-foot peaks and glaciers of the Great Divide Peaks. The Kananaskis, Elk, White Man, and Simpson passes were used by the Kootenay Indians to reach their favored elk hunting range surrounding the Kananaskis Lakes. Wildlife includes a few elk around Maude and Lawson lakes, black bear, and bighorn sheep. A segment of the Great Divide Trail winds along the upper Kananaskis River to the alpine lakes and over the North Kananaskis Pass into British Columbia and the Palliser River. Several campsites are located in the wildlands, and a Forest Service campsite is located at upper Kananaskis Lake.

The Elbow-Sheep Wilderness encompasses some 560 square miles, due east of the Kananaskis Lakes, surrounding the scenic headwaters of the Jumping Pound Creek (named for a high steep bank near its mouth, a buffalo "pound" where buffalo were driven over by the Indians and killed), Elbow, shown as the "Hokaikshi" or Moose River on Arrow-Smith's map of 1859, and Sheep and Highwood rivers. Ancient Stone and Kootenay Indian hunting trails run through the wilderness, including the famous "Stony Trail" which ran the entire length of the foothills from west of Rocky Mountain House south to Waterton Lakes and the Montana border. The Palliser expedition traveled along an old Indian trail from Waterton Lakes north through the area to their camp at Old Bow Fort and on over the Great Divide

into the Kootenay Valley of British Columbia. In the remote upper stretches of the Highwood River is the reputed site of the legendary Lost Lemon mine, where the famous Blackjack was murdered by his partner Lemon after discovering a rich deposit of gold. The major recreation features of the Elbow-Sheep wildlands include the Opal, Fisher, and Highwood ranges, Canyon Creek, Elbow Falls, Beaver Flat, Sheep Falls, Sibbald Lake, Gooseberry Flat, and the rainbow, cutthroat, Dolly Varden, brook trout, and Rocky Mountain whitefish waters of the Bow, Jumping Pound, and Sheep rivers and Elbow and Picklejar lakes. The parklands and forests of the lowlands and the alpine tundra and lush meadows and islands of alpine fir, Engelmann spruce, and alpine larch of the high country support some of the finest big-game hunting in the province for bighorn sheep, Rocky Mountain goats, elk, black and grizzly bear, moose, mule, and whitetail deer. The wilderness is also home for a band of wild horses (known as feral horses), the beautifully marked harlequin duck, and the silent hunters of the north country, the lynx and marten.

A detailed study of the region, *Elbow Sheep Wilderness,* may be obtained for $3 from the Alberta Wilderness Association, Box 6398, Station D, Calgary T2P 2E1. Camping facilities are located at the Eau Claire Campsite, Ribbon Creek Campsite and Youth Hostel, Cat Creek Campsite, Highwood Campsite, and the adjacent Kananaskis Lakes Campsite on the west and Bragg Creek Provincial Park on the east. Forest Service recreation area campgrounds are located along the forestry road at Beaver Flat, Gooseberry, Paddy's Flat, Evans-Thomas, and Sibbald Flat.

Ghost River Wilderness embraces 59 square miles approximately 50 miles northwest of Calgary in the Bow River Forest. The wilderness is bordered on the west and south by Banff National Park and on the north and east by the Burnt Timber and Waiparous Creek wildlands. The Ghost River area is a renowned wintering area for bighorn sheep and a major range for mountain goat in the Aylmer Pass, Mount Aylmer, and Apparition Mountain areas of the Palliser and Front Range Mountains. The forests of spruce, subalpine fir, and lodgepole pine, forest floors carpeted with twinflower, bunchberry, and feather mosses, and alpine meadows and valleys support populations of wolf, mountain lion, elk, grizzly and black bear, and the rarely seen Indian devil of the north, the wolverine, marten, and lynx. The Ghost River and its tributaries hold brook and cutthroat trout. Access is by trail over Aylmer Pass from the north side of Lake Minnewanka in Banff

National Park and from the Forestry Trunk Road west for 12 miles up the Ghost River Valley. The *Ghost River Wilderness Area Map* may be obtained free by writing: Recreation, Parks, & Wildlife Division, Department of Lands & Forests, Natural Resource Bldg., Edmonton T5K 2E1.

The famous pack trail and big-game hunting areas of the Burnt Timber-Waiparous wildlands (key hunting grounds of the Stone Indians, who used to trade their bighorn sheep trophies with white travelers in the 1890s) encompass 139 square miles between the Ghost River Wilderness and the Forestry Trunk Road embracing bighorn sheep, moose, and mountain goat country surrounding the headwaters of the Burnt Timer and Waiparous (aptly named by the Stone Indians for "Crow Indian scalp") rivers. The major features include excellent moose country in the muskeg and sloughs north of Margaret Lake, Ghost River, Truck Trail, Devil's Head and Black Bear mountains, Burnt Timber River Trail, Otuskwan Peak, numerous burns, and an old trappers' trail. The hiking and packtrain trails provide access to the remote interior areas which offer some of the finest hunting in the Bow River Forest for trophy bighorn sheep, elk, mule deer, black bear, and grizzly. The muskeg pastures northeast of Margaret Lake are good photography and hunting areas for moose in the southern Alberta Rockies. Wild horses are often seen along the foothill ridges east of the Front Range. The Burnt Timber and Waiparous Creek Forest Service campsites are located along the eastern boundary of the wildlands on the Forestry Trunk Road. North of the area are the Panther and Red Deer River canoe routes and to the south is the Bow River route along Deadmans Flat and the Bow Valley.

South of the Bow River Forest are the famous trout waters and big-game ranges of the Livingstone and Flathead mountains in the incredibly scenic Crowsnest Forest. One of the most remote trout fishing and big-game hunting areas in the province is the South Castles wildlands, which takes in more than 100 square miles of towering peaks, alpine lakes, and wild rivers north of Waterton Lakes National Park on the British Columbia-Alberta border. The South and West Castle rivers are two alpine fishing streams in the Canadian Rockies noted for cutthroat and Dolly Varden. The colorful exotic golden trout, eastern brook, and rainbow trout are found in the cold high country waters of Bovin, West, North, and East Scarp and South Fork lakes. Fat golden trout in the 1½-pound range have been caught in the South Fork Lakes. Several primitive hiking and pack trails provide access to the big-game areas near Castle River Pass, Sage Mountain, the huckleberry patches near Middle Kootenay Pass, Three Lakes, Ruby Lake, and Whistler Mountain. The South Castle wildlands are among the most productive mule deer and grizzly ranges in the province. Elk, moose, bighorn sheep, black bear, cougar, and a few mountain goat also roam the South Castle highlands. Upland game birds include the slate-gray blue grouse, the brownish sharp-tailed grouse, ruffed and spruce grouse, and white-tailed ptarmigan.

North of the Castle River wildlands, along the east slope of the Great Divide, are the headwaters of the Old Man River surrounded by the peaks of the Great Divide Range and Livingstone Range mountains. The Blackfoot Indians believed the Old Man to be a deity second in power only to the Great Spirit who gave them knowledge of games and war paint. Ancient Indian hunting and game trails crisscross the 100-square-mile wilderness along the north-flowing Highwood River, Cummings and Lost creeks, the south-flowing Old Man River, and along the Dutch, Hidden, Cache, and Beehive creeks. Wilderness outfitters and packtrains provide access to the high country mule deer, elk, and bighorn sheep areas surrounding 10,000-foot Tornado Mountain, Mount Farquhar, Old Galena Mine, Gould Dome, and the Old Slaker Creek cabin. East of the Old Man Headwaters and the Great

Divide are the Porcupine Hills, with their unique mixture of Montana, boreal, and subalpine forests of Engelmann spruce, lodgepole pine, alpine fir, and majestic stands of Douglas fir reaching heights in excess of 100 feet and diameters of 4 feet. The hills were called *Ky-es-Kaghp-ogh-suy-iss,* the "porcupine's tail," by the Piegan Indians. The wilderness hiker who follows the old Indian and game trails in the area will see remnants of early Indian activities, including buffalo jumps, tepee rings, and stone fire circles. Renegade whiskey traders from Fort Whoopup sought refuge in the Porcupines from the Canadian mounties. The hills and grassy savannahs are the habitat for mule and whitetail deer, elk, moose, black bear, lynx, and mountain lion. Campgrounds are located at Indian Grave, Livingstone Falls, Old Man River, and Racehorse forest service sites located along the Forestry Trunk Road.

The famous cutthroat and rainbow trout waters, big-game ranges, and wilderness areas of the Rocky Mountains-Clearwater River Forest encompass the rugged foothills north of the Crowsnest and Bow River forests. The major topographic features of the forest, shown on the Rocky Mountain Forest Reserve Map Kit, include the Clearwater, Ram, North Saskatchewan, and Bighorn, Brazeau river canoe routes, First Range, the Siffleur and White Goat wilderness areas, and the headwaters of the Ram and White Rabbit rivers. The Siffleur Wilder-

ness is located along the eastern border of Banff National Park, north of the Siffleur River headwaters about 145 miles west of Red Deer on David Thompson Highway 11. Trails from Banff and the David Thompson Highway provide access to the scenic wilderness camping, hiking, and trout fishing areas along the Main and Front ranges, Siffleur River, Porcupine Lake, Escarpment River, and Dolomite Pass at 5,900 feet, 10,566-foot Mount Loudon, and Spreading and Porcupine creeks. The major features, magnetic declination, boundaries, trails, logging roads, thrust faults, burns, and campgrounds are shown on the annotated *Siffleur Wilderness Area Map,* available free from Alberta Recreation, Parks & Wildlife, Natural Resources Bldg., 9833 109th St., Edmonton. The beautiful Kootenay Plains and Thompson Creek Forest Service recreation areas and campgrounds are due north of the wilderness along Highway 11. East of the Siffleur Wilderness are the 447 square miles of the Ram-White Rabbit headwaters wildlands between the Abrahams Lake area of the North Saskatchewan River and the Clearwater River. Running north and south through the region is the Forestry Trunk Road and the Peppers Creek, Elk Creek, Ram Falls, and North Ram River Forest Service recreation areas and campgrounds.

The famous wilderness camping and alpine fishing areas of the scenic White Goat Wilderness are located along the eastern boundary of

726 · THE BANTAM GREAT OUTDOORS GUIDE

Jasper and Banff national parks, north of the Cline River and the Kootenay Plains of the North Saskatchewan River Valley. Hiking trails wind through the valleys and alpine meadows and along the high ridges, following old Indian hunting and game paths to the bighorn sheep and mountain goat ranges of the 10,000-foot White Goat Peaks, to the Dolly Varden waters of Pinto and Wilson lakes, and the woodland caribou, grizzly, black bear, and moose country along the Brazeau and Cline River marshlands, MacDonald Creek, the Hoodoos, Mount Cline, Shoe Leather Creek, Lioness Peak, and Landslide Lake. Wilderness furbearers include wolverine and marten. The *White Goat Wilderness Area Map* may be obtained free from Alberta Recreation, Parks & Wildlife, Natural Resources Bldg., 9833 109th St., Edmonton. The map shows relief, major features, trails and logging roads, horse trails, boundaries, fords, and magnetic declination. The Forestry Trunk Road winds on north of the White Goat Wilderness and the David Thompson Highway past the Goldeye Lake, Upper Shundra Creek, and Brazeau River Forest Service recreation areas. It continues through the Rocky Mountain foothills and the Edson and Grande Prairie forests to its terminus at Goodwin, due east of Grand Prairie. The major features shown on the maps covering the Edson Provincial Forest include the Pembina, McLeod, Athabasca, and Berland River canoe routes and the Whitehorse Creek, McLeod River, Forks, Cardinal River, Pickle Lake, Rocky Lake, Big Berland, and Pierre Grey Forest Service recreation areas and campgrounds. Arctic grayling and bull Dolly Varden to 10 pounds are found in the Athabasca, Berland, Cardinal, McLeod, and Pembina rivers. An eminently useful 123-page guide, *Alberta's Eastern Slope: Wildlands for Recreation*, complete with 50 detailed maps, trail guides, and illustrations, is available for $4 from the Alberta Wilderness Association, Box 6398, Station D, Calgary T2P 2E1.

Guided float fishing trips down the trophy rainbow and brown trout waters of the wild Bow River are provided by the *Bow River Company*, 76 Beaverbrook Crescent, St. Albert T8N 2L1, phone (403) 458-0326.

Access & Outfitting Centers

The primary access routes to the Rocky Mountains Forest Reserve and Forestry Trunk Road include Alberta Highway 2, David Thompson Highway, Trans-Canada Highway, and Yellowhead Highway. Outfitters, guides, supplies, and accommodations are available at Calgary, Cochrane, Canmore, Nanton, Claresholm, Fort Macleod, Pincher Creek, Rocky Mountain House, Robb, Edson, Hinton, Grande Cache, and Grande Prairie.

Rocky Mountains National & Wilderness Parks

Banff National Park

Canadian National Topographic Survey Maps: Banff Park MCR-200 (shaded relief, scale 1:50,000), Banff 82O-4, Lake Louise 82N-8.

Jasper National Park

Canadian National Topographic Survey Maps: Jasper Park North MCR-204, Jasper Park South MCR-205 (shaded relief).

Waterton Lakes National Park

Canadian National Topographic Survey Map: Waterton Lakes Park MCR-211 (shaded relief).

Willmore Wilderness Park

Canadian National Topographic Survey Maps, scale 1:50,000: Holmes River 83E-5, Twintree Lake 83E-6, Blue Creek 83E-7, Rock Lake 83E-8, Moberly Creek 83E-9, Adams Lookout 83E-10, Hardscrabble Creek 83E-11, Pauline Creek 83E-12, Dry Canyon 83E-13, Grande Cache 83E-14, Pierre-Grey Lakes 83E-15.

Alberta's great mountain parks form a chain of spectacular alpine fishing, hiking, and wilderness camping reserves along the eastern slope of the Canadian Rockies and bordering the Great Divide, from the southernmost Waterton Lakes National Park adjoining Glacier National Park in Montana, northwest through Banff and Jasper national parks to Willmore Wilderness Park. Together with Kootenay and Yoho national parks on the British Columbia side of the Continental Divide, they form a wilderness of windswept ridges, towering summits, lush alpine meadows and remote blue lakes, wild rivers and deep-cut valleys, more than twice the size of Yellowstone Park or more than 8,000 square miles. As with all mountain country, unstable weather rules. Sudden electrical storms and periods of wet weather during the summer, as well as snowfalls above timberline, must always be reckoned with. A 20-page guide, *Canada's Mountain National Parks*, contains useful descriptions of Waterton Lakes, Banff, and the British Columbia national parks. The guide may be obtained free by writing: Parks Canada, Western Region, 134 11th Ave. SE, Calgary T2G 0X5.

Waterton Lakes National Park, once the little-known stronghold of the Blackfoot Confederacy until Lieutenant Thomas Blakiston of the Palliser expedition explored the area in 1858, lies along the eastern slope of the Rockies adjoining Montana's Glacier National Park. The *Waterton Lakes National Park Map-Brochure*, showing accommodations, campgrounds, primitive campgrounds, hiking trails, warden stations, and patrol cabins, may be had along with wilderness camping and travel information from the Superintendent, Waterton Lakes National Park, Waterton Park T0K 2M0. One of the most useful and attractively designed maps published by the Canadian National Topographic Survey is the *Waterton Lakes Shaded Relief Map* (MCR-211). The full-color, 38 × 27-inch map gives the appearance of the sunlight striking the surface from the northwest and is designed with painstaking detail showing contours in brown, glaciers, marshlands, lakes, rapids, falls, dams, deciduous and coniferous trees, campsites, gravel pits, foreshore flats and sand, cabins, shelters, bridges, cart tracks and trails, roads, and magnetic declination. Map annotations provide trail information indicating termination points, hiking time, and difficulty—all trails in the park can be traveled by foot or horseback except the Bears Hump trail, Lineham Cliff, and Crypt Lake Tunnel, which are restricted to foot travel. The Waterton Lakes map also contains, on the reverse side, a detailed "Map of Glacial and

Postglacial Features"; a "Chart of Fishing Lakes & Rivers" showing location, access, size and depth of lake, elevation, and fish species present; and "Trail Profile" line drawings showing the Bertha Lake, Alderson-Carthew, South Kootenay Pass, Rowe Lakes, Lone Lake, Pecks Basin, Twin Lakes, Lost Lake, Castle River Divide, Great Divide, and Goat Lake trails. The "Trail Profiles" are designed to assist the wilderness hiker in map reading. Each profile shows where the trail passes through tree vegetation, which will provide shade during the midday heat; and shows the locations of water supplies along the trail, campsites, and horse corrals, as well as ground distances in miles along the trail. The wilderness traveler should use the "Trail Profiles" on the shaded relief map along with the *Trails of Waterton* guide available for 50¢ from the Park Superintendent along with the free guides *Birds of Waterton, Red Rock Canyon, History Notes—the Waterton Valley, Wapiti, Bighorn Sheep,* and *Bison,* and the *Townsite Campground* and *Crandell Mountain Campground* guides. The major features shown on the Waterton shaded relief map include the rainbow, cutthroat, brook, and lake trout and northern pike waters of upper, middle, and lower Waterton Lakes; the alpine trout waters of Lineham, Goat, Maskinonge, Giant's Mirror, Carthew, Lone, Twin, and Buffalo Creek lakes; and the Border Mountains, Boundary Mountains, Indian Springs Ridge, Horseshoe Basin, Red Rock Canyon, Waterton River, Lewis Range, Rocky Mountain foothills, and Blood Indian Reserve. The park is inhabited by bighorn sheep, mule deer, grizzly bear, bison, Yellowstone moose and elk. Migrations of elk from

Glacier National Park and the Flathead Lake and Valley areas in Montana have considerably increased the park's population since the first authentic record of elk was made in 1920. The forest cover is composed of alpine larch, whitebark pine, alpine fir, and spruce at the higher elevations and Douglas fir, lodgepole pine, and poplar at the lower elevations and lowlands. Waterton Park is reached via scenic Chief Mountain Highway 6 from Montana.

Banff National Park embraces 2,546 square miles of spectacular alpine wilderness north of Waterton Lakes, about 75 miles west of Calgary. Banff shares a common boundary with Jasper National Park to the north and with Yoho and Kootenay parks on the west along the Great Divide for 150 miles. The park came into existence in 1885 when the federal government took over the ownership of the hot springs at the base of Sulphur Mountain, which were discovered during the construction of the Canadian Pacific Railway. Two businessmen took over the hot springs and were charging admission when a dispute arose over ownership and the government stepped in. More than 700 miles of trails provide access by foot or horse to the remote wilderness camping, hiking, and fishing areas along the Sundance Range, Sawback Range, Lake Minniwanka, Palliser Range, Valley of the Ten Peaks, the massive 130-square-mile Columbia Ice Field—reaching depths of 2,000–3,000 feet—the Towers, Gloria and Marvel lakes, Goat Range, Pharaoh Peaks, Slate Mountains, Hector Lake, Waputik Range, Bow Lake and River, Plain-of-the-Six Glaciers, Kicking Horse Pass at 5,339 feet (the pass and Kicking Horse River were named in 1858, when the

eminent geologist and physician of the Palliser expedition, Sir James Hector, was kicked by an ill-tempered packhorse), and the Panther, Red Deer, Clearwater, Mistaya, Pipestone, Spray, and the braided headwaters of the North Saskatchewan and Howse rivers. Overnight hikers and campers are required to register with the warden service or at information centers before and after every trip. Permits for the use of alpine huts and shelters in remote areas of the park must be obtained from the warden's offices at Banff or Lake Louise. The *Banff National Park Shaded Relief Map* (MCR-200), published by the Canadian National Topographic Survey at a scale of 1¼ inches to 1 mile, shows all fire roads, trails, railways, glaciers in blue, sand or gravel,

contours in brown, telegraphic offices, warden's cabins, camera stations, park boundaries, elevations, and declination of the compass needle. The *Banff National Park Map-Brochure* and the guides *Silver City, Fenland Trail, Birds of Banff, Cave and Basin, Peyto Lake Viewpoint, Ice Fields Parkway, Angling Regulations,* and *Skier's Guide* are available free from the Superintendent, Banff National Park, Banff T0L 0C0. A number of campsites are located in the park on a first-come, first-served basis. There is semiserviced winter camping at Tunnel Mountain, Lake Louise, and Mosquito Creek from mid-October to May 1. Wildlife seen by the wilderness traveler may include grizzly bear, bighorn sheep, mountain goat, golden eagle, magpie, elk, deer, and moose, as well as the tracks of the rarely seen

wolf, lynx, and marten. The National and Provincial Parks Association of Canada sponsors summer wilderness backpacking trips in Banff and Jasper national parks. The treks are moderately strenuous and participants are required to contribute to camp chores. For the NPPAC summer outings *Wilderness Canoeing & Backpacking Trips* brochure write: NPPAC, 47 Colborne St., Suite 308, Toronto, Ont. M5E 1E3.

The beginnings of Jasper National Park date back to the early 19th century when 3 log structures (known as Jasper House, after Jasper Hawse of the Northwest Company, who was earlier in charge of a trading post of the same name located on Brulé Lake) were built as a stopover and provisioning place for fur traders traveling over the Athabasca and Yellowhead passes en route to the Big Bend of the Columbia and the Pacific Ocean. The awesome beauty of Jasper Park, preserved as a national park by the federal government in 1907, encompasses 4,200 square miles of remote emerald lakes, massive summits and glaciers, wild mountain streams, and tranquil alpine valleys along the eastern slopes of the Rockies, bordered on the west by Mount Robson Provincial Park and the Great Divide, on the south by Banff Park, and on the north by Willmore Wilderness Park. Jasper Park has more than 750 miles of primitive wilderness trails and well-developed backpacking trails such as the famous Skyline Trail from tranquil Maligne Lake to the Maligne Canyon Road and the Tonquin Valley Trail to Amethyst Lakes and the Ramparts. The remote high country wilderness trails follow old Indian, trapper, and game trails to Bald Hills, Opal Hills, Angel Glacier, Geraldine Lakes, Valley of the Five Lakes, Colin Range, Berg Lake, Snake Indian River, Moosehorn Creek, Smoky River, and Yellowhead and Athabasca passes along the old route of the fur traders up the Whirlpool River to the headwaters of the Athabasca River at the committee's punchbowl—a small tarn in Athabasca Pass 5,736 feet up. The wilderness trails, campsites, cart tracks, cabins, fire towers, contours, magnetic declination, and topography of the Starlight Range, Victoria Cross Range, Ancient Wall, DeSmet Range, and the Queen Elizabeth, Maligne, Colin, Miette, Le Grand, and Winston Churchill mountain ranges are shown on the beautiful full-color *Jasper National Park Shaded Relief Map* (MCR-204) published by the Canadian National Topographic Survey. The *Jasper National Park Map-Brochure* and the *Athabasca Glacier, Birds of Jasper, Bighorn Sheep, Wapiti, Angling Regulations, Whistlers Campground, Wapiti Campground, Wabasso Campground,* and *Snaring River Overflow Campground* guides are available free along with wilderness camping and travel information from the Superintendent, Jasper National Park, Jasper T0E 1E0. Jasper and Banff parks are traversed north and south by the majestic Ice Fields Parkway 93 with access via Trans-Canada Highway 1, David Thompson Highway 11, and Yellowhead Highway 16.

During the early days of the fur trade, northern traders laden with lynx, marten, and beaver pelts trapped by the Athabasca Indians traveled up the Smoky River Valley by packhorse to Grande Cache (named for its large fur depot) and continued on through the famous fur and game country that is today preserved as the Willmore Wilderness Park along the Smoky Valley to Jasper House in what is now Jasper National Park. The Willmore Wilderness encompasses 1,775 square miles of rugged spruce and fir forests, lowlands, alpine tundra and meadows, and remote mountain ranges north of Jasper National Park. The wilderness is one of Alberta's finest big-game ranges for woodland caribou, grizzly bear, bighorn sheep, mountain goat, and cougar. The park is reported to contain at least 50 percent of Alberta's mountain goats and 20 percent of the bighorn sheep population concentrated in the Hoff, Berland, and Persimmon ranges. Mountain caribou are found in the old-growth forests where they feed on ground mosses and hanging tree lichen known as "old man's beard." Elk are found in broad valleys of the Smoky and Wildhay rivers, and grizzlies

are found concentrated in the Sheep Creek area and in the headwaters area of Muskeg Creek and Berland River. Wolves follow the caribou, elk, moose, and mule deer along the river valleys. The Willmore Wilderness, long famous for its big-game hunting outfitters and trappers, today supports 13 outfitters who guide hunters into the remote interior wildlands by packhorse along the old Indian and fur trade trails. The Willmore region has produced some of Alberta's finest big-game trophies since the early days of hunting. (See "Fishing & Hunting" in the "Encyclopedia" section.) A detailed recreation map and guide to the Willmore Wilderness is contained between the covers of the large-format 42-page *Willmore Wilderness Park* guide published by the Alberta Wilderness Association. The guide contains detailed descriptions of history, geology, vegetation, wildlife, and climate; it may be obtained for $3 from the Alberta Wilderness Association, Box 6398, Station D, Calgary T2P 2E1. The Willmore Wilderness recreation map shows cabins, roads, logging and coal exploration roads, campgrounds with shelters, fire lookouts, and foot and horse trails such as the Snow, Sheep Creek, Mountain, Indian, Berland River, and Muskeg River. Trail-riding outfitters operate in the park in July and August for short trips or extended excursions from base camps in the interior wilderness areas. Willmore Park is reached via the Forestry Trunk Road and Yellowhead Highway 16.

A complete listing of Banff, Jasper, and Waterton national parks campgrounds, motels, hotels, lodges and mountain resorts is contained in the *Western Canada National Parks Accommodations Guide*, available free from: Parks Canada, Western Region, 134–11th Ave. SE, Calgary T2G 0X5.

The major vacation lodges in Banff National Park (for literature, rates, and information, write to the lodge, c/o Banff T0L 0C0) include: *Aspen Lodge, Aylmer Lodge, Banff Springs Lodge, Cascade Inn, Chateau Lake Louise, Deer Lodge, King's Domain, Moraine Lake Lodge, Mount Temple Chalet, Mountainview Village, Num-Ti-Jah Lodge, Paradise Lodge, Pipestone Lodge, Rainbow Chalets, Skoki Lodge, Storm Mountain Lodge, Sunshine Village*—winter only, *Swiss Village Lodge, Voyageur Inn.* The major Jasper National Park lodges (write to the lodge, c/o Jasper T0E 1E0) include: *Alpine Village, Athabasca Hotel, Columbia Ice Fields Chalet, Jasper House Bungalows, Jasper Park Lodge, Miette Hot Springs Bungalows, Mount Robson Hotel, Tekarra Lodge, Whistler's Youth Hostel.* Vacation lodges in Waterton National Park (write to the lodge, c/o Waterton Park T0K 2M0) include: *Kootenai Lodge, Northland Lodge, Prince of Wales Hotel, Waterton Bungalows.*

Access & Outfitting Centers

Alberta's Rocky Mountain parks are reached via the Chief Mountain International Highway from Montana, Highway 95 from Idaho, Alberta Highway 2, Forestry Trunk Road, Trans-Canada Highway, David Thompson Highway 11, and Yellowhead Highway 16. Lodging, supplies, and outfitter and guide services are available at Cardston, Pincher Creek, Calgary, Banff, Lake Louise, Hinton, and Grande Cache.

CENTRAL CANADA

Introduction

Saskatchewan and Manitoba, often referred to as the "prairie provinces," together form one of Canada's most popular outdoor vacation regions. Found within their borders are vast stretches of prairie grasslands, parklands, and a great north country wilderness of countless island-dotted lakes and wild rivers surrounded by boreal forests, great rock outcroppings of the Canadian Shield, and forested valleys. Here are several of Canada's top-ranked moose and waterfowl hunting areas; trophy northern pike, walleye, arctic grayling, lake and brook trout waters; and historic fur-trade canoe routes first traveled by the great northern explorers including Alexander Mackenzie, Samuel Hearne, and the infamous Peter Pond. The major waterway in this colorful "land of the voyageur" is the great Churchill River which flows eastward through both provinces forming an endless series of lakes, conifer-clad islands, falls, and mist-filled rapids to its mouth on the bleak shores of Hudson Bay. The wild, free-flowing Upper Churchill, which rises near the Alberta border and crosses virtually the entire province of Saskatchewan, was the major waterway for the north men of the Hudson's Bay Company fur empire: the Lower Churchill, near Manitoba, however, has seldom been traveled and has recently been diverted for hydroelectrical power by re-routing its flow through South Bay, into the Rat and Burntwood Rivers, and into the Nelson River and Hudson Bay.

Saskatchewan contains within its rectangular-shaped 251,700 square miles the huge trophy northern pike, lake trout, and walleye waters of huge Lac La Ronge, located just south of the Churchill River. In the far north, there are the wilderness trophy fishing waters of huge Lake Athabasca—known to Alexander Mackenzie as the "Lake of the Hills"—and the historic Fond du Lac River, Clearwater River, Careen Lake and Black Birch River, Cree Lake, and the vast island-dotted waters of Wollaston and Reindeer Lakes. Saskatchewan is flanked on the west by Alberta, on the east by Manitoba, and on the north and south by the barren lands of the Northwest Territories, and the states of Montana and North Dakota.

Manitoba is often referred to as the "keystone" province because it links the western and eastern regions of Canada. Manitoba's 251,000 square miles are bordered on the west by Saskatchewan, on the north and northeast by the Northwest Territories and the western shores of Hudson Bay, and on the east and south by Ontario and Minnesota. Originally called the Red River Colony, and controlled by the Hudson's Bay Company, Manitoba contains a great diversity of terrain and some of North America's legendary fishing, hunting, wilderness canoeing areas. Here are the renowned trophy squaretail waters of Gods River Country; the prolific goose hunting grounds of the "great muskeg" of the Hudson Bay Lowlands surrounding York Factory and Churchill; the legendary voyageur routes and fishing waters of the big, turbulent Hayes, Nelson, Grass, and Churchill Rivers and Southern Indian Lake; the famous wilderness fishing waters of Gods, Island, Molson, Oxford, Kississing, and Athapapuskow Lakes; the top-ranked moose country surrounding the wilderness outfitting centers of Flin Flon and The Pas; and the remote seldom-visited arctic grayling and trout waters of the South Knife, Seal, and Wolverine Rivers. To the east of the Manitoba Escarpment—a plateau of forests and rolling hills, including the Porcupine, Duck, and Riding Mountains—are the famous goose and duck hunting grounds of the central Manitoba Lowlands and the huge wind-swept waters of Lakes Manitoba, Winnipegosis and Winnipeg. Eastward of Lake Winnipeg is a remote north country fishing, hunting, and canoeing paradise known as the Atikaki Wilderness, dominated by the rocky upthrusts of the Canadian Shield.

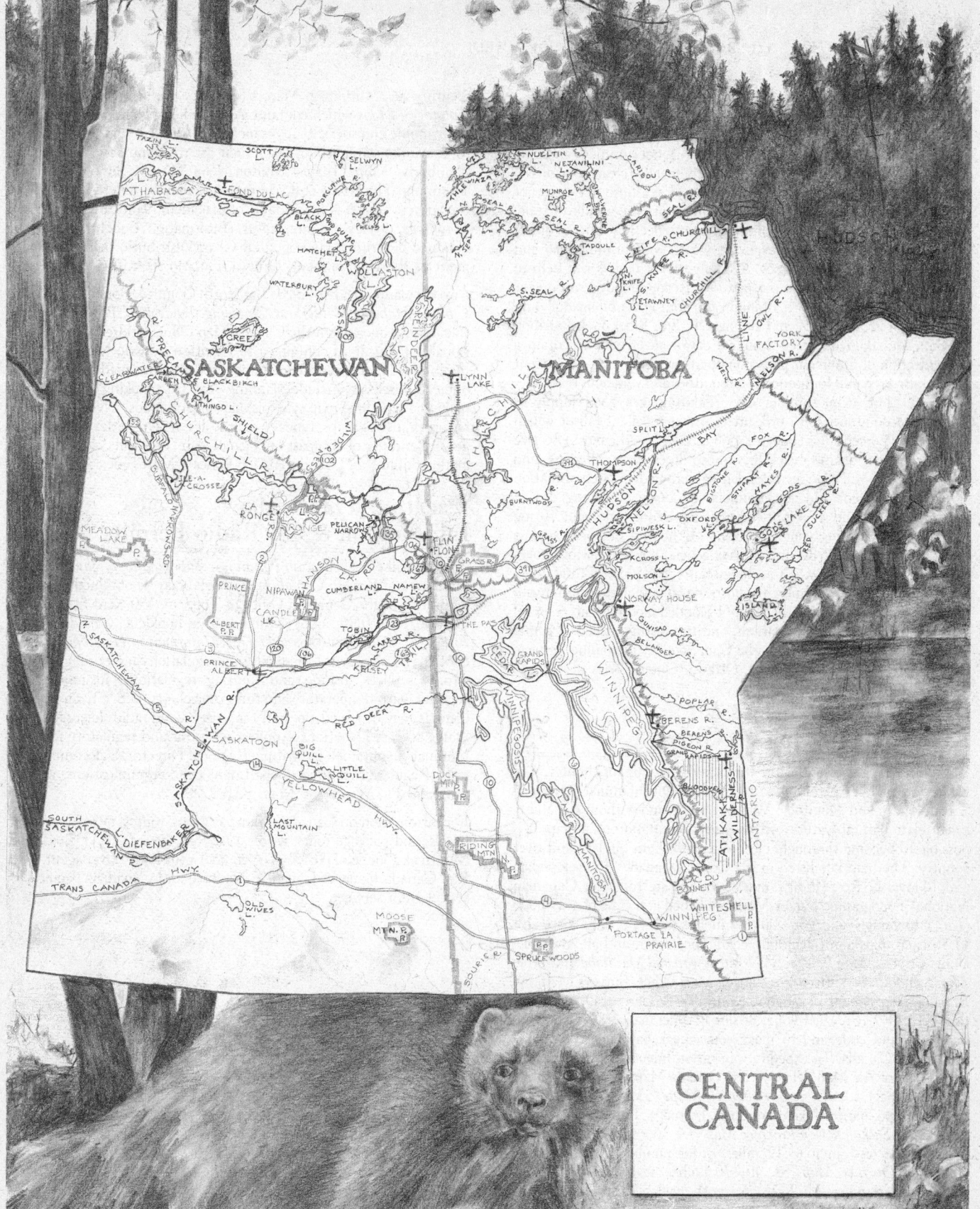

CENTRAL
CANADA

Weather, Bugs & Beasts

Saskatchewan and Manitoba have a typically continental climate characterized by low precipitation, relatively short, hot summers, and long cold winters. The long summer days and generally clear skies of the northern reaches result in high total hours of sunshine. Ice does not generally leave the lakes in the north country until the middle of June. Watch out for bad sunburns from the bright reflecting surfaces of the big lakes and rivers. To avoid exposure, wear a wide-brimmed hat and a pair of top-quality sun glasses. A supply of salt tablets will help to restore sodium lost through perspiration. Recommended sunscreens include A-Fil (opaque, with titanium dioxide) and non-opaque sunscreens such as Almay Deep Tanning Oil, Sun Block Gel, Pabanol, Pre-Sun, and Bain de Soleil Suntan Foam—all of which contain a concentration of 5 percent para-aminobenzoic acid in 50–70 percent ethanol. Be prepared for hordes of mosquitoes and voracious black flies during the hot, calm summer days. Take along a good supply of Muskol, Mosquitone, Off!, or Cutters insect repellent (all of which contain a 50 percent plus concentration of DEET—the most effective known repellent against black flies, mosquitoes, ticks, chiggers, and no-see-ums). If you plan an extended wilderness trip, a combination of DEET repellent and a recommended dosage of 50 mg/day of Vitamin B-1 for the week prior to your departure and about 10 mg a day each day during your trip is one of the best defences against north country insects. Be sure to pack a head net and cotton gloves for those bad bug days when nothing seems to work with total effectiveness. Other potential north country hazards include camp-invading black bears and, during the fall, hot-blooded moose in rut. A useful guide to weather, cloud formations, and forecasting, called *Weather Ways*, is available for $2 from the Canadian Hydrographic Service, Department of the Environment, Ottawa, Ontario K1A 0E8.

Central Canada Maps & Lake Charts—How to Order

Suitable maps are essential for the fisherman, camper, hunter, and wilderness paddler planning to travel through unfamiliar terrain in Saskatchewan and Manitoba. Without them, and without the ability to correlate natural features with their representation on a map, it is possible to become thoroughly lost in the northern big lake and river country. The map kits listed in the Central Canada "Encyclopedia" and "Travel & Recreation Guide" sections are full-color Canadian National Topographic Survey Maps published at a scale of 1:250,000 (1 inch to 4 miles) and 1:50,000 (1¼ inches to 1 mile). The maps cost $1.50 each, plus a 50¢ handling charge per order, and are available, along with free *Map Indexes of Saskatchewan and Manitoba* and a free *Map Symbol Chart*, from the Canada Map Office, Surveys Mapping Branch, Department of Energy, Mines, & Resources, Ottawa, Ontario K1A 0E9, (613) 994-9663. Be sure to order maps by their individual name and code and to make your check payable to: Receiver General of Canada. To expedite your order, include extra money for First Class or Air Mail delivery. The Canada Map Office publishes a useful 362-page *Catalogue of Published Maps* ($3.50), which lists all available topo, national park, and specialty maps. Two excellent overview maps, *Saskatchewan Province Map* ($4, 36×40 inches, 5-colors, with a scale of 1 inch to 12 miles; order number, MCR-45) and *Manitoba Province Map* ($4, 40×70 inches, scale of 1 inch to 12 miles; order number, MCR-26), are both available from the Canada Map Office. The *Lake Athabasca Hydrographic Chart* and *Lac La Ronge Hydrographic Chart* are available for $2 each from the Saskatchewan Lands and Surveys Branch, 8th Ave. and Toronto St., Regina. The Manitoba Surveys, Mapping, and Lands Branch, 1007 Century St., Winnipeg, Man. R3H 0W4, publishes a free 30-page *Catalog of Maps* which contains a comprehensive index and listing of topographic and specialty maps including *Lake Contour Depth Charts* for the important fishing lakes such as Athapapuskow, Cormorant, Cranberry, Knife, Island, Molson, Paint, Snow, Simonhouse, and Tramping. The charts cost 25¢ each and may be ordered direct from the address above. A free catalog of Canadian Nautical Charts, *Lake Winnipeg & Lake Winnipegosis* (Information Bulletin 4) may be obtained by writing: Hydrographic Chart Distribution Office, Department of the Environment, Ottawa, Ontario K1A 0E6.

Anyone planning a trip to the Big North Country should send for the *Canada Maps & Wilderness Canoeing Guide* (MCR-107) available free upon request from the Canada Map Office (address above). This valuable publication contains a text written by Eric Morse—among the intrepid pioneers of recreational canoeing in Canada's Far North. Subjects discussed include planning your trip, making a trip profile, making a schedule, map symbols, barren land maps, navigating in the far north, use of maps, types of map scales, how to order aerial photographs, and use of compass on a canoe trip. This full-color illustrated guide contains a "Canada 1:250,000 Scale Map Index."

Vacation Travel Maps, Information & CB Radio Permits

A useful full-color *Vacation Planning—Topographic Highway Map* of *Western and Eastern Canada* (two sheets) may be obtained free upon request from the Canadian Office of Tourism, 150 Kent St., Ottawa, Ontario K1A 0H6, along with two free booklets, *Canada Ferries, Bridges & Cruises* and *Canada Travel Information Handbook*, which contain the nitty-gritty about customs regulations and border crossing, airport services, fishing and hunting regulations, insurance, and weather, with temperature and time-zone charts. U.S. citizens visiting Canada may be issued a permit for citizen-band radios licensed in the States as class D stations. Application forms and regulatory information may be obtained by writing: Regional Director, Telecommunications Regulation Branch, Department of Communications, 2300–1 Lombard Pl., Winnipeg, Man. R3B 2Z8.

For infromation on Canadian train vacations, routes, rates, itineraries, hotels, and package tours, write: *VIA Rail Canada*, P.O. Box 8117, Montreal, Quebec H3C 3N3 or contact your local travel agent. VIA Rail Canada manages Canadian National and Canadian Pacific passenger train services.

Accommodations—Vacation Lodges & Sporting Camps

The 60-page *Saskatchewan Travel Guide* contains a comprehensive listing of motels, hotels, resorts, lodges, and outpost camps from A to Z with brief descriptions of facilities and services, including canoe outfitters, fishing and big-game outfitters, and game-bird outfitters. The guide may be obtained free from the Department of Tourism & Renewable Resources, P.O. Box 7105, Regina S4P 0B5. Major resorts and lodges in the important outdoor recreation areas are listed in the "Encyclopedia" and "Travel & Recreation Guide" sections. Most northern Saskatchewan lodges and wilderness fly-in camps rent boats, motors, and canoes, and supply guide service.

If you are planning an extended fishing, hunting, canoeing, or camping trip to the north country, it's best to make reservations several months in advance. The northern Saskatchewan fly-in lodges, with their renowned grayling, walleye, lake trout, and northern pike fishing and fall big-game hunting, have generally limited accommodations, often booked up to a year in advance. Be sure to request detailed information on local fish and game conditions, type of food service, guide service and equipment, and fly-in services.

Airlines & Floatplane Fly-in Services

Saskatchewan is served by scheduled Air Canada flights to Regina and Saskatoon. *Norcanair*, P.O. Box 850, Prince Albert S6V 5S4, has scheduled service between Prince Albert and Collins Bay, Cluff Lake, Deschambault Lake, Flin Flon, Fond du Lac, Île-à-la-Crosse, Kinoosao, La Ronge, Pelican Narrows, Regina, Sandy Bay, Saskatoon, Southend, Stony Rapids, Uranium City, and Wollaston Lake. *Miksoo Aviation Ltd.*, Box 1492, Meadow Lake, has nonscheduled service between Saskatoon, North Battleford, Meadow Lake, Beauval, Île-à-la-Crosse, Buffalo Narrows, La Loche, Cluff Lake, and Uranium City. Charter fly-in service to wilderness hunting, fishing, and canoe-camping areas is provided by *Athabasca Airways*, Box 100, Prince Albert, which has floatplane bases at Buffalo Narrows, La Ronge, Stony Rapids, and Uranium City; *Chieftain Flying Services*, Indian Head; *Miksoo Aviation Ltd.*, Box 1492, Meadow Lake; *Gateway Aviation*, Uranium City; *Interprovincial Airways Ltd.*, Lloydminster; *La Ronge Aviation Services*, Box 320, La Ronge, with bases at Lynn Lake, Manitoba, and Missinipe; *Nipawin Air Services Ltd.*, Box 1540, Nipawin, which has wheel, ski, and float aircraft, with base at Missinipe; *Carrot River Airways Ltd.*, Carrot River; *Parson's Airways Northern Ltd.*, Flin Flon, Man.; *Ray's Flying Service Ltd.*, Saskatoon; *Three*

Lakes Camp Air Service Ltd., Box 206, Flin Flon, Man., base at Jan Lake. For Air Canada travel and flight information contact local office or write: 1 Place Ville Marie, Montreal, Que. H3B 3Y8. For owners of private aircraft, an air facilities map which lists landing strips and facilities is available for $2 at a scale of 1 inch to 16 miles from the Lands & Surveys Branch, Department of Tourism & Renewable Resources, P.O. Box 7105, Regina S4P 0B5. The free booklet *Air Tourism Information* is available from Aeronautical Information Services, Ministry of Transport, Transport Canada Bldg., Place De Ville, Ottawa, Ont. K1A 0N5. It contains a listing of Canadian aeronautical information publications and charts, customs airports and aerodromes of entry and exit, and other items of interest to air tourists.

Big-Game & Wildlife Guides

The diversity of wildlife that inhabit the short- and long-grass prairies, poplar bluff prairies, mixed woodlands, and great northern coniferous forests are described in a useful series of free booklets published by the Department of Tourism & Renewable Resources, Box 7105, Regina S4P 0B5. The 15-page guide *Big-Game Animals of Saskatchewan* describes the range and physical characteristics of the bison, mule deer, moose, wapiti or elk, woodland and barren-ground caribou, and pronghorn antelope. The moose is the province's most-sought-after big-game species. Moose range throughout the mixed woodlands and southward through the areas of heavy popular. They are not as numerous in the boreal evergreen forest, except when there is abundant browse. One of the finest moose ranges is the Cumberland House-Pasquia Hills region, characterized by its remote rolling hills with birch and pine forests, poplar stands, swamps, hay meadows, and lakes, where the moose feed on the rootstocks of water lilies. Great herds of barren-ground caribou winter along the northern shore of Lake Athabasca and range southward as far as the southern end of Reindeer Lake on the east and the upper Clearwater River on the west. The handsome woodland caribou, which once roamed in great numbers throughout the Churchill River Country, are now quite scarce. Pronghorn antelope inhabit the open prairies and sagebrush flats in the southwestern corner of the province from north of Swift Current westward to the Cypress Hills. In the great lake country and coniferous forests of the north, Indian trappers still run their traplines during the lonely winter months in search of gray wolf, lynx, river otter, marten, fox, and beaver, whose fur they sell to the northern outposts of the Hudson's Bay Company. The still active Cumberland House, founded by Samuel Hearne in 1774, was the first inland trading post of the Hudson's Bay Company and for a long time the principal fur warehouse for the Saskatchewan country. The fascinating 16-page guide *Furbearing Animals of Saskatchewan* contains line drawings and descriptions of the beaver, muskrat, red squirrel, marten, fisher, ermine, mink, wolverine, river otter, striped skunk, badger, lynx, bobcat, red fox, coyote, gray wolf, black bear, raccoon, white-tailed jackrabbit, and snowshoe rabbit. The guide, which also contains a history of trapping in the province, is available free along with the guides to *Swans, Geese, Ducks, and Cranes of Saskatchewan* and *Winter Birds of Saskatchewan* from the Department of Tourism & Renewable Resources, P.O. Box 7105, Regina S4P 0B5. Each wildlife guide contains a map of Saskatchewan showing life zones. (See "Wolverine—'Indian Devil' of the North" and "Fishing & Hunting.")

Canoeing & North Country Waters

The great rockbound lakes and wild rivers of Saskatchewan's northern forest and Canadian Shield country provide some of the finest wilderness canoe-camping opportunities in North America. Few people are

aware that the province has more than 10,000 lakes ranging from tiny potholes in the Great Sand Hills of the Southwest to the deep, cold waters of huge Lake Athabasca in the northwest which covers 3,050 square miles and has produced giant lake trout up to 102 pounds. The lakes and rivers of the province cover 31,000 square miles of water, the greater part of it in the sparsely populated northern half of the province, once the home and hunting grounds of the Cree and Chipewyan Indians, surrounded by lowlands covered with alder, willow, and tamarack, and on higher ground, by spruce, birch, fir, and jack pine. The remote lakes of the Canadian Shield are typified by rocky, cliff-lined shores and numerous scenic spruce-covered islands. In the far north the wilderness paddler will pass by a variety of magnificent sandstone cliffs, granite walls, sandy beaches, and spectacular waterfalls and rapids. The great northern forests are inhabited now, as in the old days of the Indian hunter, fur trader, and explorer, by moose, black bear, woodland and barren-ground caribou, timberwolf, fox, lynx, deer, and wolverine. During the evening hours the quiet of the campfire is often broken by the haunting howl of the gray wolf and loon. Whisky jacks are the northman's constant camp companions, and on the water trail, the fascinating lodges of the beaver dot the feeder streams and moose pastures. The Saskatchewan River, known to the Cree Indians as *Kisiskatchewan*, "the river which flows swiftly," was the main east-west water route of the early fur traders. Henry Kelsey first explored this region of Rupert's Land in 1691, followed by Samuel Hearne, who established Cumberland House in 1774, and in 1772 Thomas Frobisher, who established a post at Île-à-la-Crosse on the Churchill River. In 1777–79 Peter Pond discovered the Methye Portage to the Clearwater River and Lake Athabasca and built a trading post at Lac La Ronge, where he was accused of murdering Étienne Wadin. Pond was replaced by his ambitious young assistant, Alexander Mackenzie. Today much of the Churchill River canoe country remains virtually unchanged from the fur trade days.

If you are planning or thinking about taking a canoe trip along the Churchill River system or in the far north, be sure to write for the 25-page *Canoe Saskatchewan Guide*, available free from the Department of Tourism & Renewable Resources, P.O. Box 7105, Regina S4P 0B5. The guide contains useful info about Churchill River and north country canoe routes, camping, safety, equipment and supplies, food, fishing, access, and outfitters. In addition to the Canadian topographic series of maps, a *Canoe Route Series of Maps* have been published by

the Department of Tourism & Renewable Resources. There are five maps in the series covering the Churchill and Sturgeon-Weir River systems and the southern half of Reindeer Lake, all with a scale of 4 inches to 1 mile. Two more maps of the Lac La Ronge area have been prepared at 1 inch to 1 mile. The Lac La Ronge maps are available in a waterproof version. These specialty maps show roads, trails, portages, water elevation, buildings, bridges, Indian reserves, marshes or swamps, and magnetic declination of the compass needle. Cost is $1; for the series of five maps, it is 50¢ apiece. The waterproof maps go for $3 each ($1 if not waterproofed). A complete set of topographic maps of the area you intend to canoe, and a working knowledge of the compass, are absolute necessities for the north country wilderness. The full-color Canadian topo maps show contours, gradient, rapids, falls, swamps, islands, trails, wilderness cabins, and shelters (see "Travel & Recreation Guide" section for topo map kits of the Wilderness Canoe Routes). When camping on islands in northern Saskatchewan near Indian reserves and settlements, keep in mind that Indians often leave their dogs on small islands all summer and fall, feeding them only occasionally. Scout the island thoroughly before setting up camp. A pack of hungry wild dogs can wreak havoc in short order. Do not disturb fish drying poles, or nets, traps, snowshoes, and dog harnesses hung in bushes. These essential items are used by the Indians during their winter trapping season and their loss or destruction may have a serious effect on their livelihood. With proper precautions taken, islands generally make ideal campsites, with fewer mosquitoes than inland or lakeshore sites. Prevailing winds in the Churchill River country are from the northwest. Try to allow 15–20 miles per day paddling, and be prepared for such unforeseen events as being wind-bound or delayed by rain. You are advised to check in with the Royal Canadian Mounted Police or with the Department of Northern Saskatchewan (Legislative Bldgs., Regina) giving them your route and expected time of arrival. Be sure to take along lengths of strong rope for lining and hauling and a pair of high-cut running shoes to absorb the abuse of rocks and constant wetness. (See "Voyageur Wilderness Canoe Trips," "Portage Trails & Lob Pines," "Wild Rivers & Fur Trade Routes Guide," "Hudson's Bay Company Outfitting Posts & Canoe Service," and "North Country Outfitters & Guides.")

Fishing & Hunting in Saskatchewan

Saskatchewan's 251,700 square miles of huge lakes and wild rivers, rocky northern evergreen forests, rolling wooded hills, parklands, and prairies contain some of the continent's finest wilderness fishing and canoeing waters and big-game hunting for moose, black bear, mule deer, whitetail deer, and upland game birds and waterfowl. The province is entirely landlocked, with man-made boundaries dividing it east and west from Alberta and Manitoba, and from the barrenlands and tundra of the Northwest Territories and the states of North Dakota and Montana on the north and south, respectively. The southern two-thirds of the province, sloping from an altitude of 3,000 feet at the Cypress Hills in the southwest to 1,500 feet in the Canadian Shield country in the northeast, falls well within the Great Plains region of North America. Although usually known as one of the "prairie provinces" along with Manitoba, there is little true prairie in Saskatchewan, since a large part of its acreage consists of rolling farmlands and parklands. The famous fishing, canoeing, and moose country of the northern third of the province, part of the Canadian Shield, is characterized by thousands of remote blue lakes ranging from small moose ponds to huge Lake Athabasca, large wild rivers such as the Fond du Lac and Churchill, and large areas of swamp, muskeg, boreal evergreen forests, and rock outcroppings. The famous walleye waters of the North and South Saskatchewan rivers drain most of the

Canadian plains before joining near Prince Albert and emptying into Lake Winnipeg in Manitoba.

North Country Lakes & Wild Rivers

The legendary lakes and wilderness rivers of Saskatchewan's north country—the Churchill, Sturgeon-Weir, Clearwater, Wollaston, Lac La Ronge, Reindeer, Fond du Lac, Athabasca—hold great northern pike, lake trout, walleye, and arctic grayling in the world's record class. The deep, cold lakes of the Lac La Ronge-Churchill River country, such as Nemeiben, Wapawekka, Besnard, McIntosh, Nipiew, Crean, and Kingsmere lakes in Prince Albert National Park, hold trophy-sized walleye and pike. Lake trout up to 50 pounds are caught in Kingsmere, Lac La Ronge, Lac La Plonge, Cold and Tazin lakes, Lake Athabasca, and Wollaston and Reindeer lakes in the far north. The beautiful arctic grayling is found in the cold, clear, swift-flowing streams of the far north. The most famous fly-in grayling waters are the Fond du Lac, Cree, Black Birch, and Reindeer rivers. Brook trout were successfully introduced into Saskatchewan in the 1920s in the Cypress Hills area. Today "squaretails" up to 4–5 pounds are caught in Echo Creek, Sand Lake, Nipawin Lake, Lonepine Creek, and Fir and Prairie rivers in the Pasquia Hills, Meadow Lake, and Fort-à-la-Corne areas. The original

ancestral home of the brook trout *(Salvelinus fontinalis)* is the turbulent mountain streams of the Appalachian chain of northeastern North America north and west to the Churchill, Knife, Seal, and Nelson rivers of northern Manitoba. The exotic rainbow trout has been successfully introduced in a number of Saskatchewan lakes and streams. The province's number one rainbow hot spot is Piprell Lake, north of Candle Lake and due west of Nipawin Provincial Park. In a 5-year period the lake produced 16 of the province's 13–18-pound trophy rainbows. Wary brown trout up to 15 pounds are caught in the Cypress Hills region in Little Frenchman, Cypress, and Bone Creeks. Walleye and great northern pike are found throughout the province. Trophy pike up to 40 pounds are caught yearly in Lake Athabasca, Lac La Ronge, Reindeer, Cree, Wollaston, and Hatchet lakes. A recent listing of Saskatchewan's trophy fish (includes record and second-place listing) reflects the potential of its lakes, streams, and wild rivers.

SASKATCHEWAN TROPHY FISH

	Lb.-oz.	Place	Year
Lake trout	51–10	Kingsmere Lake	1958
	46–12	Lake Athabasca	1967
Brook trout	5–12	Echo Creek	1968
	5–9	Echo Creek	1968
Brown trout	15–8	Duncairn Dam	1951
	10	Harris Reservoir	1971
Rainbow trout	18	Piprell Lake	1967
	16–8	Piprell Lake	1969
Arctic grayling	4–5	Fond du Lac River	1966
	4–4	Fond du Lac River	1965
Northern pike	42–12	Lake Athabasca	1954
	39–8	Black Lake	1962
Walleye (pickerel)	13–9	South Saskatchewan River	1953
	13–3	South Saskatchewan River	1963

Maps & Guides

Of great help to outdoorsmen planning a fishing trip to Saskatchewan are the free guides and booklets published by the Department of Tourism & Renewable Resources, P.O. Box 7105, Regina S4P 0B5. The *Saskatchewan Fishing* guide contains maps and descriptions of the Hanson Lake Road-Hudson Bay, Meadow Lake-La Loche, Lac La Ronge-Churchill River, and Southern trophy fishing areas, as well as details on the game-fish species, licenses, guides, seasons, and accommodations. The *Saskatchewan Anglers Guide* contains the lowdown on district offices of the departments of Tourism & Renewable Resources and Northern Saskatchewan, fishing rules, species guide, regulations, a management area map, and a chart showing prime fishing waters and species present. A complete list of waters stocked with trout is contained in the folder *Stocked Trout Waters*, which may be obtained upon request from Extension Services, Department of Tourism & Renewable Resources, Regina. There are almost 200 drive-in and fly-in fishing camps located throughout the province, with more than half of them beyond roads' end in the northern coniferous forest zone. Licensed big-game hunting guides, outfitters, and lodges are located throughout the province, with the greatest concentration of lodging and services found in the moose, deer, caribou, and black bear country of northern Saskatchewan's Canadian Shield and boreal forest zone. The *Saskatchewan Big-Game Guide*, available free from the Department of Tourism & Renewable Resources (along with hunting guides listed below), P.O. Box 7105, Regina S4P 0B5, contains useful info about license fees, game management programs, regulations, vehicle control, and a game management zone map, describing game management zones and wildlife management units with open hunting for whitetail deer, mule deer, elk, woodland and barren-ground caribou, moose, antelope, and black bear. Guided moose hunting licenses are available from the Department of Northern Saskatchewan, Box 539, La Ronge. The services of a licensed guide are required while hunting moose. Be sure to respect trapline rights while hunting in the northern fur conservation trapping areas. Never interfere with traps or trapline cabins. Some of the finest upland game-bird, duck, and goose shooting in North America is found in the province. The *Saskatchewan Game-Bird Guide* contains detailed info about license fees, regulations, sunrise and sunset times, and a game management zone map and chart for sharp-tailed grouse, Hungarian partridge, ruffed grouse, ptarmigan, deep-forest spruce grouse, pheasant, ducks, coots, Wilson's snipe, sandhill cranes, and geese. Great numbers of ducks, merganser, geese, swans, and cranes breed in the barren grounds of the far north along the coast, in river estuaries, and on the massive islands of the arctic archipelago. During the fall tremendous flocks wing south to the prairies and later converge on the Mississippi and Central flyways which take them to their southern wintering grounds. The Department of Tourism & Renewable Resources also publishes the free guides *Upland Game Birds, Moose in Saskatchewan*, and *Whitetail Deer in Saskatchewan*. (See "Big-Game & Wildlife Guides" and "North Country Outfitters & Guides.")

Fond du Lac

Fort Fond du Lac (a voyageur's term meaning the end of a waterway, a place where a river flows in or out of a lake) was founded by the Hudson's Bay Company around 1820 at the east end of Lake Athabasca on a low point of sand and rock where the lake is only 2 miles wide. Soon after, the 3 inhabitants of the post were killed by Chipewyan Indians. At the same time the Northwest Company operated a post on the opposite shore a little farther east, which they moved to the south after the murders. Both companies soon abandoned the area until 1845 when the Hudson's Bay post was rebuilt by José Mercredi, a French half-breed who ran the business for the next 47 years. The post is on a principal line of travel for the barren-ground caribou in their annual migrations and is still in operation. Access is by charter aircraft from Uranium City on Lake Athabasca. Lake Athabasca and Black Lake, located due east as the crow flies on the Fond du Lac River, offer some of the province's finest wilderness fishing for lake trout, northern pike, and arctic grayling.

Highways—Recreation & Scenic Routes

Saskatchewan's scenic northern big-lake country and the famous fishing, hunting, and canoe-camping areas and lodges are well served by a network of modern paved and gravel highways. Information about road conditions during the summer months is available Monday through Friday, 8:30 a.m. to 5:00 p.m., for the Swift Current District (306) 773-2955, Regina District (306) 522-2666, Yorkton District (306) 783-2400, Saskatoon District (306) 374-9300, North Battleford District (306) 445-3825, and Prince Albert District (306) 764-5100. The free *Department of Highways Construction Map*, available from the Department of Travel & Renewable Resources and most tourist information booths, shows major construction projects, with details of traffic accommodations through the projects. Sask Travel, an in-province toll free telephone service, provided by the Dept. of Tourism & Renewable Resources, supplies up-to-date information on the availa-

bility and services of all Saskatchewan parks and campgrounds. The Sask Travel service operates from June 1 to September 1. For cities within the province dial toll-free (1–800) 667–3674 and for other nonurban areas dial (112–800) 667–3674. The free *Saskatchewan Official Highway Map* shows all paved, gravel and graded roads, municipal grid roads, resource development roads, railways, ports of entry, ferries, historic parks, provincial campgrounds, regional parks, Indian reservations, fly-in fishing camps (base camps only), and landing strips for wheeled airplanes. The official highway map also contains full-color charts showing trading posts and forts, Northwest Mounted Police stations and historical trails; wildlife zones for moose and elk, bear, whitetail and mule deer, antelope, pheasant, sharptail and ruffed grouse, ducks, and geese; and natural vegetation zones of the subarctic forest and tundra, northern coniferous forest, mixed woodlands, aspen parklands, and prairies. The following Canadian National Topographic Survey Maps, at a scale of 1:250,000, show the entire length of Saskatchewan's scenic highways and the topography of the surrounding recreation and wilderness areas in full color. The maps are an invaluable aid to anyone planning a vacation fishing, hunting, or canoeing trip.

Buffalo Narrows Road

This map kit shows gravel Highway 155 from the settlement of Green Lake at the junction of Highway 55 northwest through the northern evergreen forest past the Brazeau River, Canoe Lake, and Lac La Plonge, the Churchill River at Lac Île-à-la-Crosse, Churchill Lake, and Peter Pond Lake to the village of La Loche and Lac La Loche and the famous Methye Portage of the fur trade era. North of Peter Pond

Lake a graded spur road leads to the renowned northern pike, walleye, and big moose country at Turnor and Frobisher Lakes. Lodging, guides, supplies, and government campgrounds are located along the highway at Green Lake, Canoe Lake, Canoe Narrows, Lac La Plonge, Île-à-la-Crosse, and Buffalo Narrows at Peter Pond and Churchill lakes. Canadian National Topographic Survey Maps: Shellbrook 73-G, Green Lake 73-J, Île-à-la-Crosse 73-O, Buffalo Narrows 73-N, La Loche 74-C.

Hanson Lake Road

This 225-mile gravel Highway 16 winds through the evergreen forests of northeastern Saskatchewan from its junction on Highway 55 (from Prince Albert) north and east through Nipawin Provincial Park and the Cub Hills, past Big Sandy Lake and the Wapawekka Uplands, Deschambault Lake, Hanson Lake, and Amisk Lake to Creighton and the Manitoba border at the famous outfitting town of Flin Flon. Highway 135 branches off the Hanson Lake Road near Leaf Rapids and Jan Bay and runs northeast through the famous fishing and big-game hunting areas surrounding Sandy Narrows, Mirond Lake, Pelican Narrows, Attitti Lake, and Island Falls and Sandy Bay on the Churchill River. The Candle Lake Road (Highway 120) is all all-weather gravel route that connects with the Hanson Lake Road near the Fishing Lakes, connecting with forest access roads to Whiteswan, White Gull, Piprell, and East Trout lakes. Highway 167 from Creighton connects Amisk Lake and Denare Beach with the Hanson Lake Road and Manitoba Highway 10. The Hanson Lake Road country is one of the province's best fishing regions for northern pike, lake trout, and walleye. Fall big-game hunting is good throughout the region for

moose, woodland caribou, and black bear. Lodging, guides, supplies, and government campgrounds are located at or near Big Sandy Lake, Deschambault Lake, Jan Bay, Mirond Lake, Pelican Rapids, Island Falls, Sandy Bay, Leaf Rapids, Denare Beach, Creighton, and Whelan Bay. Fly-in floatplane bases are located at Deschambault, Pita, and Attitti lakes. Several of the resort operators along the Hanson Lake Road have DNS (two-way) radios, permitting fast communication with southern points. Anyone wishing to contact one of the resort operators along the road can phone Smeaton Service in Smeaton and the message will be relayed to the resort, or telephone the DNS Service in Prince Albert (306) 764–4741 or 763–3048. Canadian National Topographic Survey Maps: Prince Albert 73-H, Wapawekka 73-I, Amisk Lake 63-L, Pelican Narrows 63-M.

Kelsey Trail—Hudson Bay-Cumberland Lakes Road

Highway 163 was named in honor of Henry Kelsey, the first European to explore this northeastern region of Saskatchewan. Kelsey followed the Saskatchewan River, passing close to the present-day sites of The Pas, Nipawin, Prince Albert, and Battleford before turning back to the Hudson's Bay post at York Factory. He is believed to be the first white man to view the great central plains and to see the buffalo and grizzly. Kelsey made his historic journey to the interior in 1690, accompanied by Stone Indian guides. Today the Kelsey Trail winds southwest from The Pas, Manitoba, through a magnificent wilderness dominated by the Pasquia Hills, Carrot River, the 40,000-acre Wildcat Hill Wilderness area and Red Earth and Shoal lakes, to its terminus at Nipawin. The ancient Pasquia Hills were once an island in Lake Agassiz. Fossilized shark teeth and the partial skeleton of a triceratops have been unearthed here. Lakes and streams of the Pasquia Hills area hold northern pike, walleye, and brook trout. The Kelsey Trail provides access to Highway 123 due east of Nipawin. This highway, known as the Hudson Bay-Cumberland Lakes Road, winds past Tobin Lake and the Squaw Rapids hydroelectric station and heads east along the Saskatchewan River past the Birch River, Cut Beaver Lakes, and Pemmican Portage to the historic Hudson's Bay post at Cumberland House on the shores of Cumberland Lake. Resort lodging, outfitters, guides, and supplies are available at The Pas, Nipawin, Pemmican Portage, and Cumberland House. Six government campground facilities are located along the route. Please note that there are no towns along the entire length of the Kelsey Trail. Canadian National Topographic Survey Maps: The Pas 63-F, Pasquia Hills 63-E, Amisk Lake 63-L.

Saskatchewan Wilderness Highway (2–102–105)

This map kit shows Highways 2, 102, and 105 from Prince Albert, north past Montreal Lake, Thunder Hills, and Prince Albert National Park to scenic, island-dotted Lac La Ronge and the famous northern gateway outfitting centers of Stanley Mission, La Ronge, Mountain Portage, and Missinipe. Lac La Ronge is one of Canada's greatest sportfishing centers. Anglers annually catch more than 200,000 pounds of lake trout, northern pike, and walleye from its deep blue waters, dotted by a labyrinthine maze of more than 1,000 islands. Lac La Ronge is the jumping-off point for wilderness canoe-camping, fishing, and moose and caribou hunting trips along gravel Highway 102 and 105, which begins where Highway 2 ends, winding north past Otter Rapids of the Churchill River, McLennan Lake, Brabant Lake, Southend and huge Reindeer lakes, and the Geikie River to its terminus at the Gulf Minerals mine on the western shore of Wollaston Lake. Eleven government campgrounds are located along Highways 2, 102, and 105. Fly-in floatplane bases are located at Lac La Ronge, Otter Lake, McIntosh Lake, McTavish Lake, Shadd Lake, Reindeer

Lake and Wollaston Lake. Canadian National Topographic Survey Maps: Prince Albert 73-H, Wapawekka 73-I, Lac La Ronge 73-P, Foster Lake 74-A, Reindeer Lake South 64-D, Reindeer Lake North 64-E, Wollaston Lake 64-L.

Trans-Canada Highway

Saskatchewan's 408-mile section of Highway 1 passes near many famous vacation areas such as Moose Mountain Provincial Park, the historic Qu'Appelle Valley, Last Mountain Lake, and Cypress Hills Provincial Park, and intercepts the major north-south routes that run into the renowned fishing, hunting, and wilderness canoeing regions of the northern forest zone. The 4,000-foot cobblestone crest of the Cypress Hills is the highest point of land in the province. The Cypress Hills contain lodgepole forests found nowhere else in the province. These hills, in the southwestern corner of the province, were deposited more than 30 million years ago by a river flowing eastward from the Rocky Mountains, and were lifted into prominence by the erosion of the surrounding strata. The major towns and features shown on the maps of the Trans-Canada Highway include Moosomin, Regina, Swift Current, Missouri Coteau, Lake Chaplin, Old Wives Lake, Crane and Bigstick lakes, and the Great Sand Hills. The highway passes through the aspen parklands, midgrass prairies, and short- or mixed-grass prairies of southern Saskatchewan. Provincial campgrounds are located at Moosomin, McLean, Buffalo Pound Lake, Caron, Beverly, and Maple Creek. Canadian National Topographic Survey Maps: Riding Mountain 62-K, Melville 62-L, Regina 72-I, Swift Current 72-J, Prelate 72-K, Cypress 72-F.

Yellowhead Highway

This map kit shows the route Highways 14 and 5 follow through the rolling central parklands of the province. The major features shown on the maps of the route from east to west include Yorkton, Good Spirit Lake Provincial Park, Foam and Fishing lakes, Big Quill Lake, Wolverine Lake, Saskatoon, North Saskatchewan River, North Battleford, Jackfish Lake, Battle River, and Lloydminster. There are provincial campgrounds at Kuroki, Good Spirit Lake, and Lanigan. Canadian National Topographic Survey Maps: Yorkton 62-M, Duck Mountain 62-N, Rosetown 72-O, Wynard 72-P, Saskatoon 73-B, North Battleford 73-C, St. Walburg 73-F.

the Bay
U-Paddle Canoe Service

Shooting rapids on the Coppermine River – Picture by Eric W. Morse

Hudson's Bay Company

Hudson's Bay Company Outfitting Posts & Canoe Service

Hudson's Bay northern supply stores carry food supplies, gear, and ammunition needed by the wilderness fisherman, hunter, and canoe camper in Saskatchewan's north country. Hudson's Bay supply posts are located at Black Lake, Stony Rapids, Fond du Lac, and Uranium City at Lake Athabasca; Southend on Reindeer Lake; Pelican Narrows, Stanley, La Ronge, Patuanak, Île-à-la-Crosse, Cumberland House, Dillon, Buffalo Narrows, Beauval, and Portage-la-Loche in the Churchill River Country; and Green Lake. The Hudson's Bay Company U-Paddle canoe service is available at outpost stores along the old historic fur trade routes in Saskatchewan. For rates, info, and a free HBC *U-Paddle Canoe Service* map and brochure, write: Northern Stores Department, Hudson's Bay Company, 800 Baker Center, 10025 106th St., Edmonton, Alta. T5J 1G7, or phone (403) 424–8113. Keep in mind that the remote HBC posts do not necessarily carry a full range of supplies. It's best to place your order in writing a couple of months in advance.

Lac La Ronge Wilderness Outfitting Center & Trophy Fishing Waters

Lac La Ronge, a world-famous fishing mecca, is located 147 miles north of Prince Albert via Highway 2. Connecting gravel roads lead north to Nemeiben Lake and the Churchill River canoe country and beyond to McLennan and Reindeer lakes. La Ronge (pop. 898), located on the southwestern shore of Lac La Ronge on Highway 2, is the gateway to the 450 square miles of Lac La Ronge. The lake is one of Canada's great sport fisheries, where anglers annually catch more than 200,000 pounds of lake trout, northern pike, and walleye. The lake is renowned for the scenic beauty of its thousands of spruce-covered islands and hidden bays, surrounded by coniferous forests to the north and sedimentary rock and hardwood forests to the south. The wilderness canoeist and fisherman is advised to carry a compass to navigate through the endless maze of islands. *Lac La Ronge Provincial Park* takes in 381,440 acres of lakes, bogs, and boreal evergreen forests along the northern shoreline. The historic settlements of Stanley Mission, Missinipe, and Mountain Portage are located in Lac La Ronge Park. The Stanley Mission is at the southeast end of Lake Otter and is accessible by boat from a nearby tourist lodge. The principal attraction of the mission is the Church of the Holy Trinity, constructed between 1853 and 1860 under the direction of two English missionaries, the Reverend and Mrs. Robert Hunt. Built of local lumber and adorned with stained glass imported from England, the church is an old-world building set in a new world of forest and wilderness, a standing testimony to the white man's determination to make his faith prevail among the Indians.

Athabasca Airways, La Ronge Aviation, and Norcanair operate wheel- and floatplane bases on the lake for wilderness fly-in fishing and big-game hunting trips. The Lac La Ronge Campground Museum exhibits the history and geology of the Lac La Ronge area. *Viking Water Charters, Ltd.*, P.O. Box 1568, Prince Albert S6V 3B4, provides water taxi service in fast enclosed cruisers from La Ronge dock facility to any lodge or point on the lake. There are 4 government campgrounds on Highway 2 along the western shore of the lake. Several hunting and fishing lodges, guides, and outfitters are located at Lac La Ronge. *Heglands Fishing Camp*, La Ronge S0J 1L0, provides lodging, canoe, boats, motors, and guides with outpost camps at Hunters Bay and Wapawekka Lake. *Camp Kinisoo Ltd.*, Box 120, La Ronge S0J 1L0, is a licensed outfitter for fishing, with lodging, freezing, and filleting facilities, boats, motors, and outpost camps located at Hunters Bay, Trout Lake, and Wapawekka Lake. *Lindy's Cabins*, Box 270, La Ronge, is a licensed outfitter for fishing and big-game hunting with cabins, boats, motors, guides, and outpost camps at Hunters Bay, Wapawekka Lake, and Stoney Narrows. *Reds Camps Ltd.*, Box 67, La Ronge, has full lodging and outfitting services with outpost camps at Hunters Bay, Besnard Lake, and Costigan Lake. *Alpaha Hunting & Fishing Camps Ltd.*, c/o R. Boyer, Wee-Ma-Tuk Hills, Rt. 2, Canton, IL 61520, has lodging and outfitting and guide service on English Bay of Lac La Ronge, as does *English Bay Cabins*, Box 591, La Ronge S0J 1L0. *Pickerel Bay Cabins*, Box 259, La Ronge, is a fly-in base camp located on Hunters Bay with lodging, DNS radio service, and canoe rentals; it is a licensed outfitter for fishing, and big-game and upland bird hunting. *Van's Camp*, 35 11th St. E, Prince Albert, is a fly-in base camp on Hunters Bay with lodging, outfitting, and guide services. The outpost camp is on Iskwatikan Lake. Athabasca Airways operates a two-way radio at camp, with call letters VYD 43, frequency 5025. The *Rapid River Lodge*, Box 318, La Ronge S0J 1L0, is a base camp with access via Athabasca Airways. *Coopers Wadin Bay Outfitters*, Box 94, La Ronge, is 18 miles north of town at Wadin Bay. Lodging and licensed outfitters are located at nearby Nemeiben Lake, which holds trophy walleye, lake trout, and northern pike to 35 pounds. *Lindwood Lodge*, Box 114, La Ronge S0J 1L0, is a base camp with lodging, guides, and outpost camps at Clam and Setter lakes. *Sunset Island Lodge*, Box 151, La Ronge, has licensed outfitters and guides, accommodations with Norcanair radio at camp (call letters XOY 787, frequencies Sask-Tel-Channels 1, 2, 3, and 4, Norcanair 5167). Package plan includes lodging, meals, boat, motor, guide, and return boat transportation from Department of Northern Saskatchewan campground. Nemeiben Lake is just west of Lac La Ronge with access via Highway 2 and forest access road. The Lac La Ronge region is shown on Canadian National Topographic Survey Maps: Wapawekka 73-I, Lac La Ronge 73-P.

Lake Contour Fishing Maps

Lake contour (bathymetric) maps are available for over 350 lakes in Saskatchewan. The maps are very useful to the fisherman planning a trip to one of the north country lakes, showing islands, bottom contours, depths, reefs, shoals, cliff depths, and sandbars. The maps will assist the angler to determine the most productive feeding areas of walleye, northern pike, and lake trout based on a thorough study of the lake map. Lake contour maps are available for most of the famous lakes in the Churchill River country wilderness and far north including Lake Athabasca, Beaverlodge Lake, Peter Pond Lake, and Big Sandy, Birchbank, Piprell, Black, Candle, Careen, Churchill, Cumberland, Hatchet, Île-à-la-Crosse, Iskwatikan, Lac des Îles, Lac La Loche, Lac La Plonge, Lac La Ronge, Montreal, Mistohay, Namew, Nipekamew, Nistowiak, Reindeer, Sturgeon, Waterhen, Wollaston, Amisk, and Waskesiu. The maps cost 50¢ each and are available along with a *Listing of Lake Maps* from the Lands & Surveys Branch, Department of Tourism & Renewable Resources, 8th Ave. and Toronto St., Regina.

North Country Communications

Several of the larger north country settlements, including many fishing and hunting camps, are connected to the long-distance telephone network by high-frequency radio. For information and connections call the northern radiotelephone operator at Prince Albert (area code 306). Remote far north settlements and fishing camps not having telephone service may be reached by sending a radiogram over the

two-way radio network operated by the communications division of the department of Northern Saskatchewan. Messages may be sent by telephoning the principal station in Prince Albert at (306) 764–4741.

North Country Outfitters & Guides

Outdoorsmen planning a fishing, hunting, or canoe-camping trip to the boreal evergreen forests, remote island-dotted lakes, and wild rivers of northern Saskatchewan may obtain a comprehensive listing of hunting and fishing resorts, wilderness lodges, and outpost camps from the Secretary-Treasurer, Northern Ontario Outfitters Association, 316 10th Street E, Prince Albert. The *Saskatchewan Outfitters & Guide Listing,* available free from the Department of Tourism & Renewable Resources, Regina S4S 0B5, lists all licensed guides and outfitters, including descriptions of specialty and management zones in which they operate. Canoe outfitting and trip-planning facilities are provided by the following major northern Saskatchewan outfitters. The *Churchill River Canoe Outfitters Ltd.,* operates a base camp at Otter Lake near Missinipe and the Otter Rapids of the Churchill River. Services include planning and complete or partial outfitting of small or large groups. Transportation is arranged for canoeists and gear at start and finish of the trip (8-canoe maximum per road trip). Rentals include complete canoe outfit or individual items, 17-foot canoes, freeze-dried and dehydrated foods, and lightweight camping equipment. Accommodations are available at the rustic Otter Lake Lodge. For complete details write: Peter Whitehead, Manager, Box 26, La Ronge S0J 1L0. At Lac La Ronge, *Coopers Wadin Bay Outfitters,* Box 94, La Ronge, provides complete canoe outfitting services; *Keighley's Camp,* Box

191, La Ronge S0J 1L0, on Nunn Lake, and the *Rapid River Lodge*, Box 318, La Ronge S0J 1L0, offer fly-in canoe outfitting services, as do *Jacobsen Bay Outfitters*, Box 4, Christopher Lake S0J 0N0, on Anglin Lake in the Prince Albert area; *Johnson's Camp*, P.O. Box 61, Île-à-la-Crosse, with base camps at Synik, Alstead, and Big Sandy lakes; *Morbergs Wilderness Fishing Lodge*, on Black Lake in the far north, with base camps at Riou, Small Tree Lake, Northwest Territories, and Selwyn Lakes, write: 601–2345 Portage Ave., Winnipeg, Man. R3J 0M7; *Meadow Lake Outfitters*, Box 1149, Meadow Lake S0M 1V0, with outpost camps in the far north, serving Complex, Cup, Haultain, and Holt lakes; *Northern Lights Lodge*, Box 832, Flin Flon, Man., on Deschambault Lake; *Jan Lake Lodge*, Box 62, Flin Flon, Man.; *Troxel's Resort*, Lac La Plonge; *Lloyd Lake Resort*, Box 86, Buffalo Narrows S0M 0J0, in the far north with an outpost camp at Forrest Lake; *Katche Camp*, on Nipekamew Lake; write: 1102 Lancaster Blvd., Saskatoon S7M 3V5; *Tawaw Cabins*, on Waterhen Lake, write: Box 10, Dorintosh S0M 0T0. A complete listing of Indian outfitters, guides, and facilities in Saskatchewan is contained in the 110-page *Canadian Indian Tourist Outfitting & Outdoor Recreation Facilities* directory available free from Information Branch, Department of Indian Affairs & Northern Development, Centennial Tower, 400 Laurier Ave. W, Ottawa, Ont. K1A 0H4. (See "Travel & Recreation Guide" section for listings and descriptions of fishing and big-game hunting lodges and outpost camps.)

Pelican Narrows

(Pop. 108). This old fur-post was established by the Hudson's Bay Company in 1798 at the north end of Pelican Lake near Pelican Narrows, between Pelican Lake and Mirond Lake (enlargements of the Sturgeon-Weir River) about 30 miles from Frog Portage. The post is still maintained by the company. Access is via Highway 135 from the Hanson Lake Road (Highway 106). The post is surrounded by top-ranked moose, deer, and black bear country. Lodging, guides, and outfitting services are provided by *Pelican Narrows Fly-in Ltd.*, P.O. Box 1888, Melfort S0E 1A0, on Pelican Lake; *Great North Lodge*, Box 237, Flin Flon, Man. R8A 1M9, due south on scenic Jan Lake; *Jan Lake Lodge*, Box 62, Flin Flon, Man., on Jan Lake; *Martin's Cabins*, P.O. Box 453, Flin Flon, Man. R8A 1N3; *Three Lakes Camp Ltd.*, Box 206, Flin Flon, Man., on Jan Lake with outpost camps at Kamatsi, Kiaska, Pagato, Pekuskium, Rita, and Wintego lakes; *Newmart Resort*, Box 463, Flin Flon, Man., on Mirond Lake; *Angell's Motel and Marina*, Box 342, Flin Flon, Man., on Amisk Lake; and *T & D Amisk Cabins*, Box 161, Creighton S0P 0A0.

Portage Trails & Lob Pines

The packed, centuries-old portage paths along the great rivers of the northern forest are the combined work of moose, caribou, and man. The voyageurs of the fur trade packed 3–4 tons of gear, bundled in 90-pound pieces, with each man carrying 2 pieces of goods—180 pounds—over the ancient portage trails of the Churchill River system. The voyageurs took several trips across the portage; each trip was broken into posés of about a third of a mile each done at a dogtrot. On a posé, loads were carried partway; the voyageur returned for another piece before going on. The historic portage trails along the great lakes chain of the Churchill River—the Methye Portage, Stony Mountain Portage, and Frog Portage—and the canoe routes were marked by lob pines, the voyageur's landmark, usually a tall pine tree on a prominent point, visible for a great distance against the skyline. The voyageur would climb the pine and strip or "lob" off the center branches, leaving a tuft or broom at the top or bottom. The lob pines of the fur trade days marked the canoe routes from Montreal to Lake

Athabasca. It is said that some of these trees are still standing. The Canadian National Topographic Survey Maps show portage trails as dotted or broken lines marked "P," connecting lakes, around rapids and falls, and between lakes and rivers or across peninsulas. Well-traveled portage trails are generally visible from 50 yards or more from the river or lake, appearing as a break in the shoreline forest cover, with lighter green patches of grass, blazed trees, and poles or tree boughs on the rocks if the landing is rough. When the trail head of a portage cannot be found, it's often advisable to walk inland using compass routing to intersect the probable line of the trail. It has been said that the voyageurs dogtrotted their supplies along the old portage trails to avoid the annoying mosquitoes and black flies that swarm thick in the quiet inland glades and forest meadows—so remember to apply insect repellent before starting the portage.

Vacation Travel Information

The *Saskatchewan Travel Guide* contains detailed trip-planning information about border crossing, Canadian government tourism offices, climate, customs, trailer-camping stations, ferry crossings, mobile home courts, parks, ski areas, transportation, campgrounds, and much more. This 160-page guide may be obtained free, along with detailed travel information, from the Department of Tourism & Renewable Resources, Box 7105, Regina S4P 0B5. For specific travel information and hunting, fishing, and canoe-camping info for trips in northern Saskatchewan write: Department of Northern Saskatchewan, Government Administration Bldg., Regina S4S 0B1. For detailed travel counseling and info on campsite availability and activities, sites, and attractions call *Sask Travel*, operated by the Department of Tourism & Renewable Resources, (112–800) 667–3674, toll-free within the province, or (306) 565–2300 (long-distance charges applicable).

Voyageur Wilderness Canoe Trips

The Department of Tourism & Renewable Resources publishes 50 *Canoe Trip Guides* which describe the famous voyageur routes of the fur trade from Cumberland House north along the continual rapids of the Sturgeon-Weir River to Frog Portage and the mainstream of the Churchill River in Trade Lake. The voyageurs of the Hudson's Bay Company used to paddle down the Churchill River—actually an immense chain of scenic interconnected lakes in the rugged boreal forest country of the Canadian Shield—to Île-à-la-Crosse; from Île-à-la-Crosse the Athabasca Brigade pushed off for Lac La Loche and the famous "Rendezvous" of the Methye Portage, to the Clearwater River, which carried them down to the Athabasca River and Fort Chipewyan on the western shore of huge Lake Athabasca (then known as "Lake of the Hills"). The canoe-trip guides listed below may be obtained free from the Department of Tourism & Renewable Resources, P.O. Box 7150, Regina S4P 0B5. (When ordering, be sure to indicate both place name and code number of the guide you want.) They describe the length of trip, time required to complete trip, number of portages, access to starting point, maps, and description of the canoe route. Before starting out all wilderness paddlers are requested to obtain a voyageur permit at the Visitor Information Center at La Ronge; or Department of Northern Saskatchewan offices in La Ronge, Prince Albert, Green Lake, Beauval, Île-à-la-Crosse, Buffalo Narrows, La Loche, Pelican Narrows, Weyakwin, Creighton, or Department of Tourism & Renewable Resources offices in Prince Albert, Saskatoon, Pierceland, Meadow Lake Provincial Park, Loon Lake, and Nipawin. Almost all the routes are accessible by road, and fly-in routes can be reached by charter floatplane from any of the 10 northern Saskatchewan outfitting centers listed above.

VOYAGEUR CANOE TRIP GUIDES

Guide No.	Miles	Days	Portages
SASKATCHEWAN RIVER(S)			
15 Cumberland House—(Saskatchewan River)—The Pas, Manitoba	83	2–3	0–1
19 Saskatoon—(South Saskatchewan River, Saskatchewan River)—Nipawin	220	5	None
25 Squaw Rapids—(Saskatchewan River)—Cumberland House	70	2–3	None
44 Amisk Lake—Sturgeon-Weir River—Namew Lake—Cumberland House	50	3–4	3
MEADOW LAKE (PROVINCIAL PARK) DISTRICT			
23 Pierce Lake—Lac des Îles (Waterhen River)	22	1–2	None
24 Waterhen River—Beaver River (considerable wading required)	23–70	1–4	None
LAC LA RONGE AND DISTRICT			
16 Nemeiben Lake—Trout Lake—Churchill River—Otter Lake	63	4–6	13–15
17 Nemeiben Lake—Besnard Lake—Churchill River—Otter Lake	100	7–9	19
18 Nemeiben Lake—Besnard Lake—Black Bear Island Lake—Trout Lake—Nemeiben Lake	103	5–8	18
20 Lynx Lake—Sulphide Lake—Contact Lake—Kuskawao Lake	13	1–2	7
21 Lynx Lake—Sulphide Lake—Freda Lake—Freestone Lake—Hebden Lake—Contact Lake—Sulphide Lake—Lynx Lake	33	2–4	19
43 Lac La Ronge—Wapawekka Lake—Deschambault River—Ballentyne Bay	105	7–9	17
LAC LA RONGE TO CHURCHILL RIVER and CHURCHILL RIVER TO LAC LA RONGE			
2 Otter Lake (Churchill River)—Stanley—Iskwatikan Lake—Hale Lake—Lac La Ronge—La Ronge	75	5	5
3 Otter Lake (Churchill River)—Stanley—Iskwatikan Lake—Thomas Lake—Hunter Bay	90	6–7	7

Guide No.	Miles	Days	Portages
(Lac La Ronge)—Lac La Ronge—La Ronge			
4 Otter Lake (Churchill River)—Mountain Lake—Hunt Lake—Stroud Lake—Lac La Ronge—La Ronge	62, 70, 78	4–6	6–9
6 La Ronge—Lac La Ronge—Lynx Lake—Sulphide Lake—Freda Lake—Otter Lake (novices should use alternate starting point of Lynx Lake)	57	4–5	12
7 La Ronge—Iskwatikan Lake—Churchill River—Pelican Narrows—Deschambault Lake—Highway 106, Mile 146	175	8–10	13–14
8 La Ronge—Iskwatikan Lake—Churchill River—Pelican Narrows—Jan Lake (Doupe Bay)	148	6–8	12
9 La Ronge—Iskwatikan Lake—Churchill River—Pelican Narrows—Mirond Lake—Sturgeon River—Mile 190, Highway 106	151	7–10	15
10 Wadin Bay (Lac La Ronge)—Hunter Bay—Nunn Lake—Big Whitemoose Lake—Whitemoose River—Churchill River—Iskwatikan Lake—Lac La Ronge—Wadin Bay	126	7–10	14
11 La Ronge (Lac La Ronge)—Stroud Lake—Hunt Lake—Nistowiak Lake—Iskwatikan Lake—Lac La Ronge—La Ronge	106	6	7
12 La Ronge—Lynx Lake—Sulphide Lake—Freda Lake—Otter Lake—Stanley—Nistowiak Lake—Iskwatikan Lake—Lac La Ronge—La Ronge	120	8–10	17
CHURCHILL RIVER (West of Otter Lake)			
1 Village of Île-à-la-Crosse (Churchill River)—Otter Lake	240	14–18	13–19
CHURCHILL RIVER (East of Otter Lake)			
5 Otter Lake (Churchill River)—Stanley—Frog Portage—Pelican Narrows	100	6–7	13

Guide No.	Miles	Days	Portages
7 La Ronge—Iskwatikan Lake—Churchill River—Pelican Narrows—Deschambault Lake—Highway 106, Mile 146	175	8–10	13–14
8 La Ronge—Iskwatikan Lake—Churchill River—Pelican Narrows—Jan Lake (Doupe Bay)	148	6–8	12
9 La Ronge—Iskwatikan Lake—Churchill River—Pelican Narrows—Mirond Lake—Sturgeon-Weir River—Mile 190, Highway 106	151	7–10	15
28 Pelican Narrows—Frog Portage—Churchill River—Sandy Bay	115	8–10	13–16
29 Otter Lake—Churchill River—Sandy Bay	140	9–12	16–19
30 Otter Lake—Grandmother Bay—French Lake—Ducker Lake—Rattler Creek—Otter Lake	22	1–2	3

INTO AND ON CHURCHILL RIVER
(Highways 102, 106, 135)

Guide No.	Miles	Days	Portages
27 Brabant Lake—Kakabigish Lake—Kemp Lake—Mountain Lake—Otter Lake (Missinipe)	77	5–6	14
32 McLennan Lake—Davis Lake—Versailles Lake—Settee Lake—Mountain Lake (Guncoat Bay)—Otter Lake	68	5–6	18
34 Brabant Lake—Wapiskau River—Steephill Lake—Reindeer River—Churchill River—Sandy Bay	140	10–14	21–25
36 Paull Lake—Paull River—Churchill River—Otter Lake	50	4–5	16–17
37 Paull Lake—Paull River—Churchill River—Kavanagh Lake—Bassett Lake—Bartlett Lake—MacKay Lake	55	5–6	20–21
39 Southend (Reindeer Lake)—Reindeer River—Churchill River—Sandy Bay	125	8–12	9–13
45 Tyrrell Lake—Kipahigan Lake—Sisipuk Lake—Bonald Lake—Pukatawagan	105	7–9	11

Guide No.	Miles	Days	Portages
46 Tyrrell Lake—Kipahigan Lake—Sisipuk Lake—Loon Lake—Wasawakasik Lake—Sandy Bay	132	9–11	12
47 Sandy Bay—Churchill Bay—Pukatawagan	65	4–5	5
48 Southeast Arm, Deschambault Lake—Pelican Narrows—Wunehikun Bay—Attitti Lake—Kakinagimak Lake—Nemei Lake—Nemei River—Sandy Bay	72	5–6	18
49 Southeast Arm. Deschambault Lake—Pelican Narrows—Wunehikun Bay—Attitti Lake—Belcher Lake—Mukoman Lake—Ohoo Lake—Mukoman River—Sokatisewin Lake—Sandy Bay	71	5–6	15
50 Mile 20½, Highway 135—Tomahawk Lake—Tommy Lake—Churchill River—Sokatisewin Lake—Sandy Bay	32	3–4	8

NORTH OF THE CHURCHILL RIVER

Guide No.	Miles	Days	Portages
26 Black Lake (Saskatchewan)—Chipman Lake—Bompas Lake—Selwyn Lake—Flett Lake (Northwest Territories)	105	7–11	12
31 McLennan Lake—MacLean Lake—Versailles Lake—Davis Lake—McLennan Lake	28	2–3	8
32 McLennan Lake—Davis Lake—Versailles Lake—Settee Lake—Mountain Lake (Guncoat Bay)—Otter Lake	68	5–6	18
33 Brabant Lake—Kakabigish Lake—Settee Lake—Colin Lake—Versailles Lake—Davis Lake—McLennan Lake	58	4–5	12
34 Brabant Lake—Wapiskau River—Steephill Lake—Reindeer River—Churchill River—Sandy Bay	140	10–14	21–25
35 Brabant Lake—Wapiskau River—Steephill Lake—Reindeer River—Southend (Reindeer Lake)	70	5–7	15–16

Guide No.	Miles	Days	Portages
36 Paull Lake—Paull River—Churchill River—Otter Lake	50	4–5	16–17
37 Paull Lake—Paull River—Churchill River—Kavanagh Lake—Bassett Lake—Bartlett Lake—MacKay Lake	55	5–6	5–6
38 Big Sandy Lake—Geikie River—Highway 105	55–65	4–8	4
39 Southend (Reindeer Lake)—Reindeer River—Churchill River—Sandy Bay	125	8–12	9–13

LAC LA RONGE to STURGEON-WEIR RIVER

Guide No.	Miles	Days	Portages
43 Lac La Ronge—Wapawekka Lake—Deschambault River—Ballentyne Bay	105	7–9	17

STURGEON-WEIR RIVER (Highway 106)

Guide No.	Miles	Days	Portages
13 Mile 146, Highway 106—Deschambault Lake—Pelican Narrows—Mirond Lake—Sturgeon-Weir River—Mile 190, Highway 106	94	5–6	4–5
14 Mile 190, Highway 106—Sturgeon-Weir River—Amisk Lake—Denare Beach	53	3–4	4–5
22 Pelican Narrows—Wunehikun Bay, Mirond Lake—Waskwei Lake—Attitti Lake—Kakinagimak Lake—Wildnest Lake—Granite Lake—Sturgeon-Weir River—Mile 190, Highway 106	74	5–6	14
41 Missi Island Loop on Amisk Lake	30	2–3	None
42 Meridian Creek—Bootleg Lake—Wekach Lake—Mystic Lake—Table Lake—Amisk Lake—Denare Beach	34	2–3	13
43 Lac La Ronge—Wapawekka Lake—Deschambault River—Ballentyne Bay	105	7–9	17
44 Amisk Lake—Sturgeon-Weir River—Namew Lake—Cumberland House	50	3–4	3
45 Tyrrell Lake—Kipahigan Lake—Sisipuk Lake—Bonald Lake—Pukatawagan	105	7–9	11
46 Tyrrell Lake—Kipahigan Lake—Sisipuk Lake—Loon Lake—Wasawakasik Lake—Sandy Bay	132	9–11	12

Guide No.	Miles	Days	Portages
47 Sandy Bay—Churchill River—Pukatawagan	65	4–5	5
48 Southeast Arm, Deschambault Lake—Pelican Narrows—Wunehikun Bay—Attitti Lake—Kakinagimak Lake—Nemei Lake—Nemei River—Sandy Bay	72	5–6	18
49 Southeast Arm, Deschambault Lake—Pelican Narrows—Wunehikun Bay—Attitti Lake—Belcher Lake—Mukoman Lake—Ohoo Lake—Mukoman River—Sokatisewin Lake—Sandy Bay	71	5–6	15
50 Mile 20½, Highway 135—Tomahawk Lake—Tommy Lake—Churchill River—Sokatisewin Lake—Sandy Bay	32	3–4	8

CLEARWATER RIVER (Near Careen Lake)

Guide No.	Miles	Days	Portages
40 Warner Rapids (56° 54' × 109° 01') (Clearwater River)—Fort McMurray, Alberta	125	8–10	9–14

Wild Rivers & Fur Trade Routes Guide

The wild rivers of Saskatchewan offer the wilderness traveler the rare combination of superb fishing, magnificent north country forests, and the beckoning lure of exploring the historic water trails and portages of the fur trade era. An eminently informative and useful 68-page guide, *Wild Rivers Saskatchewan*, is available for $1.50 from Information Canada, 171 Slater St., Ottawa, Ont. The guide contains detailed maps and descriptions of the length, access and egress, maps, geography, flora and fauna, history, and canoe route and portages for the *Clearwater River:* from Lloyd Lake to Virgin River; Virgin River to the Descharme River; Descharme River to Contact Rapids, including Gould Rapids and Simonson Rapids; Contact Rapids to Fort McMurray, Alberta, including Methye Portage, Whitemud Falls, Pine Rapids, Bigrock Rapids, Long Rapids, Cascade Rapids, and Fort McMurray. The historic *Fond du Lac River* Canoe Route, discovered in 1796 by David Thompson of the Hudson's Bay Company, is described by map and word from Wollaston Lake to Redbank Falls, including Wollaston Lake, Hatchet Lake, Corson Lake, Cascade Rapids to Crooked Lake, the sandstone formations along the Poplar Rapids, Demicharge Rapids, Flett Rapids, Redbank Falls; Otter Lake to Brink Rapids, including detailed descriptions of Otter Lake, Thompson Rapids, and Manitou Falls; Brink Rapids to Black Lake, including Brink Lake, Brassy Rapids, North Rapids, Perch Rapids, Burr Falls, Woodcock Rapids, Woodcock Falls, and the settlement of Stony Rapids. The famous 500-mile *Churchill River* canoe-trip map and description begins at the Department of Natural Resources "camp kitchens" at Île-à-la-Crosse to Sandfly Lake and includes description of the Shagwenaw Rapids, Drum Rapids, Leaf Rapids, Deer Rapids, Dipper Rapids, Crooked Rapids, Knee Rapids, Snake Rapids, Sandfly Lake to Dead Lake, including Sandfly Lake, Needle Rapids, Black Bear Island Lake, Birch Portage, Trout Lake to Stack Lake, Rock

Trout Portage, Mountney Lake, Dead Lake; Dead Lake to Trade Lake, including the Little Devil Portage, Stony Mountain Portage, Mountain Portage, Mountain Lake (home of Saskatchewan's oldest church, built in 1850), the Hudson's Bay post at Stanley, Stony Rapids Portage, Nistowiak Lake, Drinking Lake, Keg Lake, Keg Falls, and Grand Rapids; Trade Lake to Sandy Bay, including descriptions of Kettle Falls, Iskwatikan Lake to Wapumon Lake, Wintego Lake, Pita Lake, and Sokatisewin Lake. The historic *Sturgeon-Weir River* canoe trip begins at the Frog Portage at Trade Lake and flows through a beautiful country of mixed woodlands, open aspen glades, rock cliffs, and small sand beaches to the Hanson Lake Road bridge at Maligne Lake. The wild river guide describes the route from Frog Portage to Pelican Narrows, including Wood Lake with its winding waterways, islands, and superb rock formations, Grassy Narrows, Medicine Rapids, Pelican Narrows to Maligne Lake, Corneille Portage, Dog Rapids, and Birch Portage. Moose and black bear, and a large variety of ducks, geese, and other birds including eagles are often seen along the great northern Saskatchewan canoe routes. The fishing is often excellent for arctic grayling, walleye, northern pike, and lake trout.

Wolverine—"Indian Devil" of the North

The solitary wolverine *(Gulo luscus)* was known to the Cree as *Carcajou,* "Indian devil"; it inhabits the lake and river country of the great northern coniferous forests of Canada, Alaska, and the remote northern wilderness of the United States. The wolverine is the largest member of the weasel family, often weighing up to 40 pounds at maturity. The "Indian devil" possesses keen sight and smell with a broad, flat head, small fierce eyes, jaws filled with sharp teeth and massive fangs, and a stocky, powerful body with incredibly strong legs and claws and a thick, bushy tail. Larger carnivores such as cougar and wolves steer a clear path of this brutal hermit of the northlands. The wolverine has a sleek, brown coat, highly prized by Indian trappers because the hairs are resistant to moisture and frost will not readily collect on the pelt. The coat has a pair of light-colored lateral stripes which run down each side of the upper back and merge again at the tail. It is primarily a terrestrial animal but is an agile climber when the need arises. When the wolverine invades a trapper's cabin, it often befouls the provisions and gear with a foul-smelling scent produced by glands located in the anal cavity. The carcajou will feed on almost anything from field mice to deer, with a fondness for carrion. Like its cousin the fisher, it has acquired the knack of dining on belly-up porcupine without coming-up second best. During its constant prowl for food, the wolverine covers many miles a day with its loping walk until it makes a substantial kill. It is a favorite character in the timeless sagas and legends of the north, often representing cunning and ferocity. Because it is so ingenious in avoiding set traps, except to rob them, and wreaks calculated havoc on the northman's supplies and possessions, the Indians and Eskimos believe the wolverine to possess supernatural powers. It was known to the French-Canadian trappers as *loup-garou,* or "evil spirit," and at times, it does seem possessed, so deliberate is its harassment of the solitary woodsman. To protect food and supplies from this fellow, the northmen build a cache—an elevated storage locker built on posts inside the camp. The posts are sheathed with metal to prevent the wolverine from climbing up to the food and gear. (See "Big-Game & Wildlife Guides.")

Churchill River
Wilderness Canoe Country

Churchill River Wilderness Canoe Country Topo Maps

Canadian National Topographic Survey Maps, scale 1:250,000: La Loche 74-C, Mudjatik 74-B, Buffalo Narrows 73-N, Île-à-la-Crosse 73-O, Lac La Ronge 73-P, Wapawekka 73-I, Pelican Narrows 63-M, Amisk Lake 63-L, Cormorant Lake 63-K.

Meadow Lake Provincial Park

Canadian National Topographic Survey Maps, scale 1:150,000: Cold River 73K-12, Pierceland 73K-5, Goodsoil 73K-6, Dorintosh 73K-7, Island Hill 73K-8, Waterhen Lake 73K-9, Flotten Lake 73K-10.

Sturgeon-Weir River & Frog Portage

Canadian National Topographic Survey Maps, scale 1:50,000: Trade Lake 63M-5, Manawan Lake 63M-6, Sandy Narrows 63M-3, Marchel Lake 63M-7, Pelican Narrows 63M-2, Birch Portage 63L-15, Hanson Lake 63L-10, Denare Beach 63L-9, Leonard Lake 63L-8.

The famous northern Saskatchewan section of the Churchill River flows east from the historic height of Land at Lac La Loche (known as the Methye Portage where the waters flow north to the arctic and east to Hudson Bay) through a majestic northern wilderness of huge blue lakes and vast evergreen forests that were once the home and hunting grounds of the Cree, Chipewyan, Yellow Knife, and Dog Rib Indians to Cumberland House, more than 500 miles away. The unspoiled wilderness along the Churchill and its great island-dotted lake chains is one of Saskatchewan's top-ranked trophy walleye and northern pike fishing and hunting regions for moose, caribou, whitetail deer, and black bear. The wilderness canoeist will often see loons, ducks, and geese, and in certain areas pelicans, bald eagles, and golden eagles are present. The geography of the river is typical of those in the Canadian Shield with a low-level surrounding landscape that is uneven and hummocky with rock outcroppings common east of Dipper Lake and on the islands and shorelines of Sandfly and Black Bear Island lakes. Joseph Frobisher of the Northwest Company was the first white explorer to travel the Churchill. His journey from the Saskatchewan River up the Sturgeon-Weir River and over Frog Portage to the Churchill established a trade route that was to eventually link Fort Chipewyan on Lake Athabasca and the northern interior to the Hudson's Bay Company post at York Factory. The map kit of the Churchill shows it as less a river than a chain of interconnected lakes characterized by turbulent rapids, waterfalls, and long stretches of quiet water. The major features shown on the route as it flows east from its headwaters at Lac La Loche, Peter Pond, and Churchill lakes include 40-mile-long Lac Île-à-la-Crosse, and Knee, Sandy, Otter, Pine House, Sandfly, Black Bear Island, Trout, Snake, McIntosh, Nipiew, Nistowiak, La Ronge, Key, Trade, Peta, Okipwatsikew, and Loon lakes, and the Foster, Reindeer, and Sturgeon-Weir rivers. The Churchill River system, which continues through Manitoba to Hudson Bay, is one of the few great wilderness canoeing and fishing areas left in North America.

If you are planning or dreaming of a canoe trip down the Churchill, you'll be interested in reading Sigurd F. Olsen's classic, *The Lonely Land* (available for $7.95 plus 50¢ postage from Alfred A. Knopf, Mail Order Books, 400 Hahn Rd., Westminster, MD 21157 U.S.A.). The author captures the romance and history of this great wilderness as he describes his voyage along the Churchill from Île-à-la-Crosse through the land of the Shield to the White Horses, Dipper Lake, Marshes of Haultain, Valley of the Snake, Trout Lake Falls, Lake of the Dead,

Stanley Post, Nistowiak, Frog Skin Portage, Pelican Narrows, Sturgeon Weir, Red Cliffs of Amisk, Goose Creek Camp, Chimneys of Namew, and Cumberland House.

Several fishing and hunting lodges with guides and outfitting services are located along the river. *Kingfisher Lodge*, Sandy Bay, is a fly-in camp on Okipwatsikew Lake, operating as licensed outfitters for fishing and big-game hunting. *Three Lakes Camp Ltd.*, Box 206, Flin Flon, Man., is a licensed outfitter for fishing, big-game, and game-bird hunting with fly-in outpost camps located on the shores of remote Pikusikun, Tabberman, Wintego, and Pita lakes. The *Birchwood Drinking Falls Lodge*, 22–15 Assiniboine Drive, Saskatoon, is a fly-in camp at Drinking Falls Lake with an outpost camp at Planinshek Lake, north of Lac La Ronge. Its package plan includes lodging, meals, boat, motor, guide, return air transportation from La Ronge to camp, and fish filleting and freezing. *La Ronge Lodge*, La Ronge, located at Mountain Portage on Otter Lake, is licensed as an outfitter for fishing with lodging, meals, boat, motor, guides, and filleting and freezing facilities. *Churchill River Canoe Outfitters*, Box 26, La Ronge, provides complete or partial outfitting for small or large groups on the Churchill River system, from a base camp with excellent lodging facilities on Otter Lake. *Churchill River Lodge-Thompson's Camps Ltd.* (306) 425-2347, Box 419, La Ronge, are licensed fishing and big-game hunting outfitters on Otter Lake near Missinipe, with outpost camps at Black Bear Island, Hickson, Highrock, Maucon, Oliver, and lower and upper Foster lakes, *Tamarack Lodge*, Box 562, La Ronge, is on McLennan Lake and specializes in lake trout fishing. *Lindwood Lodge*, Box 114, La Ronge, is a fly-in camp on Settee Lake. *Sportman's Lodge*, P.O. Box 20212, Oklahoma City, OK 73120, is a licensed fishing fly-in camp on the shore of McIntosh Lake. *Camp Kinisoo Ltd.*, Box 120, La Ronge, is an outpost fly-in camp at Trout Lake. Moving west toward the headwaters of the Churchill lakes chain, we find the *Shadd Lake Cabins*, P.O. Box 503, La Ronge; *Camps Ltd.*, Box 419, La Ronge, on Black Bear Island Lake; *Besnard Lake Lodge*, Box 295, La Ronge; *Reds Camps Ltd.*, Box 67, La Ronge, on Besnard Lake; and *Turnor Lake Tourist Development*, Box

175, Buffalo Narrows, a licensed outfitter for fishing, big-game, and game-bird hunting with an outpost camp at Frobisher Lake. The Churchill River fishing camps provide access to some of the finest big-lake fishing on the continent for trophy-sized lake trout, walleye, and northern pike.

Frog Portage at Trade Lake on the Churchill River, due east of Lac La Ronge Provincial Park, is the historic east-west overland trail to the famous Sturgeon-Weir River. It was one of the chief portages traveled by the fur traders crossing the height of land separating the Nelson and Saskatchewan rivers from the Churchill River system and was the gateway from eastern Canada to the west and northwest. After reaching Sturgeon Landing at Cumberland Lake, the voyageurs paddled up the Sturgeon-Weir through Mirond, Pelican, and Lake of the Woods to Churchill River, and westward up the Churchill through Lac Île-à-la-Crosse, Peter Pond Lake, and Lac La Loche to the Methye Portage and the wild Clearwater River to the Athabasca River up to Fort Chipewyan and Lake Athabasca. Frog Portage was named for the Cree Indians' peculiar habit of leaving a stretched frog's skin at this location to ridicule the way the Chipewyans dressed and stretched their beaver skins. The portage was first traveled in 1774 by Joseph and Thomas Frobisher and Alexander Henry, who afterward formed the Northwest Company. A fort known as Fort La Traite, or Frogskin Portage, was built by the free traders nearby on the Churchill River at the mouth of the Reindeer River. The Sturgeon-Weir flows through an exceptionally scenic chain of lakes past beautiful wooded islands and superb rock outcroppings and cliffs. The surrounding wilderness country is covered with birch and poplar stands and spruce forests, open aspen glades, and small sand beaches. Special care should be taken along the Sturgeon-Weir River rapids between Maligne and Amisk lakes, and along the 30-mile stretch of rapids between Amisk Lake and Sturgeon Landing at Namew Lake. The voyageur's route continues through the Narrows of Namew to the shallow waters of Cumberland and the historic fur depot and supply post at Cumberland House. Never enter a stretch of unfamiliar rapids unless its end

can be seen and there is no doubt that it's safe. Remember the adage, "No one ever drowned making a portage." The Sturgeon-Weir chain of lakes holds large lake trout, walleye, northern pike, and whitefish. Several wilderness hunting and fishing lodges with guide and outfitting services are located in the region at Pelican Narrows, Mirond Lake, Amisk Lake, and Sturgeon Landing.

Meadow Lake Provincial Park embraces 881,440 acres of boreal jack pine, aspen, tamarack, and black and white spruce forests along the Waterhen River in northwest Saskatchewan. There are several scenic wilderness canoe routes here with good fishing for coho salmon, brook and rainbow trout, and recently introduced splake, as well as northern pike and walleye in Pierce, Lac des Îles, Craig, Waterhen, and Cold Lake trophy waters. There are 7 government campsites and several remote hiking trails in the area. Outside of the park, some great fishing for northern pike and walleye can be found in Dore Lake, Lac Île-à-la-Crosse, Lac La Plonge, and the Lac La Loche headwaters of the Churchill River near Highway 155 and Canoe and Keeley lakes, accessible by Highway 104. The surrounding coniferous forests are a top-ranked moose, whitetail deer, caribou, black bear, and upland game-bird hunting zone.

Access & Outfitting Centers

The Churchill River country is reached by scheduled and charter aircraft and Highways 21, 104, 55, 155, 2, 120, 106, and 135. There are accommodations, supplies, and outfitting services at Meadow Lake, Green Lake, Canoe Narrows, Beauval, Lac La Plonge, Île-à-la-Crosse, Buffalo Narrows, La Loche, Pine House, La Ronge, Missinipe, McLennan Lake, Mountain Portage, Island Falls, Sandy Bay, Pelican Narrows, Mirond Lake, Jan Bay, Leaf Rapids, Creighton, Denare Beach, and Sturgeon Landing.

Far North Grayling & Caribou Country

Careen Lake & Blackbirch River

Canadian National Topographic Survey Map Kit, scale 1:250,000: La Loche 74-C, Mudjatik 74-B.

Clearwater River Country

Canadian National Topographic Survey Map Kit, scale 1:250,000: Lloyd Lake 74-F, La Loche 74-C, Waterways 74-D.

Cree Lake Country

Canadian National Topographic Survey Map Kit, scale 1:250,000: Cree Lake 74-G, Livingston Lake 74-J, Pasfield Lake 74-I.

Fond du Lac River & Wollaston Lake

Canadian National Topographic Survey Map Kit, scale 1:250,000: Reindeer Lake North 64-E, Wollaston Lake 64-L, Pasfield Lake 74-I, Stony Rapids 74-P, Fond du Lac 74-O.

Lake Athabasca Country

Canadian National Topographic Survey Map Kit, scale 1:250,000: Fond du Lac 74-O, Tazin Lake 74-N, William River 74-K, Fort Chipewyan (Alta.) 74-L, Fitzgerald 74-M.

Reindeer Lake Country

Canadian National Topographic Survey Map Kit, scale 1:250,000: Granville Lake 64-C, Reindeer Lake South 64-D, Brochet (Man.) 64-F, Reindeer Lake North 64-E, Wollaston Lake 64-L, Whiskey Jack Lake 64-K.

Saskatchewan's far north is an immense lonely land with countless thousands of lakes, great wild rivers, unnamed waterways, and distant forest valleys known only to the soaring eagle and the descendants of the ancient people of the moose and caribou. Three great lakes, Reindeer, Wollaston, and Athabasca, gouged out of the ancient granite of the Precambrian Shield by the massive Keewatin Ice Cap, form a necklace of blue across the very top of the province. The deep, cold waters of these great lakes and the boiling rapids and placid pools of the remote wild rivers hold northern pike, lake trout, and arctic grayling up to world's record weights. The legendary Fond du Lac River flows for 170 miles from its great headwaters at Wollaston Lake, northwest through the black spruce forest of the Canadian Shield and magnificent sandstone cliffs, sandy beaches, over spectacular waterfalls, and stark granite walls to pour its waters at journey's end into huge Lake Athabasca. The river's cold, deep-flowing waters provide some of the finest grayling, walleye, and northern pike fishing in Canada. The surrounding boreal wildlands are inhabited by moose, black bear, and wolves, and form the winter range of barren-ground caribou from the northern shore of Lake Athabasca southward as far as the southern end of Reindeer Lake on the east and the upper Clearwater River on the west. The major lakes formed by the Fond du Lac include Hatchet, Corson, Crooked, Kosclaw, Otter, Black, and Stony. From the outlet at Black Lake, the Fond du Lac cascades over Elizabeth Falls for 110 feet and forms the Woodcock and Stony Rapids. The deep waters of huge Lake Athabasca cover 3,050 square miles, straddling the Saskatchewan-Alberta boundary. The irregular, jagged granite shoreline of Athabasca is surrounded by stands of black and white spruce; near its center, the lake reaches depths of 400 feet. The lake no doubt holds lake trout far greater in size than the current over-60-pound world's record; in fact, one of the largest lake trout ever taken in a commercial net was caught here. The giant trout tipped the scales at 102 pounds, and was estimated to have been close to 100 years old. Lake Athabasca, Wollaston Lake, and the Fond du Lac River are accessible by scheduled airline service to Uranium City on Lake Athabasca and Stony Rapids with charter floatplane service to wilderness outpost fishing and hunting camps. Lodging and guides are pro-

vided by *Athabasca Lake Lodge*, 870 Avord Tower, Saskatoon S7K 3H1. Guides, lodging, and fishing and big-game hunting outfitting services at Black Lake are provided by two fly-in outposts, *Camp Grayling Ltd.*, P.O. Box 1393, Edmonton, Alta., and *Morbergs Wilderness Fishing Lodge*, 203-2639 Portage Ave., Winnipeg, Man., R3J 0P7, with outpost camps at Riou and Selwyn lakes. At Wollaston Lake, *Hopps Nekweaga Bay Camp*, P.O. Box 146, La Ronge, and *Wollaston Lake Lodge*, Box 2106, Prince Albert, provide lodging, guides, outfitting, and floatplane service. *Tazin Lake Lodge*, Box 128, Uranium City, provides lodging and outfitting and guide service

for fishing and big-game hunting. Tazin Lake is famous for trophy lake trout up to 44 pounds and large northern pike. Rustic *Hatchet Lake Lodge*, on the Fond du Lac River system, offers first-class accommodations, services, and trophy fishing for northern pike, lake trout, walleye, and grayling. For literature and rates, write: Hatchet Lake Lodge Ltd., Sub Post Office 55, Calgary, Alta. T3B 0H0, (403) 286-2717.

The headwaters of the famous Clearwater River lie due south of Lake Athabasca and east of the Firebag Hills surrounded by jack-pine forests which grow in the dry Athabasca sand covering this portion of the Canadian Shield. Downstream from the Lloyd Lake headwaters the jack pines give way first to spruce and, still farther downriver, to stands of large poplar. The Clearwater is a totally isolated wilderness river and flows for 185 miles through spectacular sandstone and limestone gorges and over numerous falls and brawling rapids. The Clearwater, like all far north wild rivers, should be attempted only by the experienced canoeist, if possible, with the services of a qualified guide. The fisherman and wilderness paddler will see moose, beaver, ducks, golden eagles, geese, and the tracks of fox, wolf, lynx, and deer. The river is renowned for its northern pike, walleye, and arctic grayling up to 4 pounds. The far north is also prime blackfly and mosquito country. Be sure to bring along an ample supply of repellent. It may be some consolation to know that the blackfly is a major portion of the grayling's diet. During the fur trade era the Clearwater was a major link connecting the east-flowing Churchill River route with the north-flowing Athabasca River and the high-quality beaver pelts of the Mackenzie River country. The two watersheds were connected by the historic Methye Portage, also known as Portage-la-Loche, of the Athabasca Brigade of the Hudson's Bay Company. The major features along the Clearwater include scenic Lloyd Lake, Careen Lake, and the famous grayling water of the Virgin River Gorge near its junction with the Clearwater and the Descharme rivers, and Fort McMurray on the Athabasca River. The Lloyd Lake headwaters can be reached by charter floatplane from La Loche and Buffalo Narrows, and from Fort McMurray, Alberta, Fly-in fishing, lodging, guide, and outfitting service are available at *O'Brien's Grayling Lodge*, Box 789, Biggar, on Careen Lake; *Ithingo Lake Lodge*, Box 131, Buffalo Narrows; *Black Birch Camp*, Green Lake, just east of Careen Lake; and *Lloyd Lake Resort*, Box 86, Buffalo Narrows, with an outpost camp at Forrest Lake and canoe outfitting services available.

The famous grayling, northern pike, and whitefish waters of Cree Lake and River lie to the east of the Clearwater River headwaters in the geographical center of Saskatchewan's northern coniferous forest and Canadian Shield country. Cree is a large irregular-shaped lake with 6 scenic spruce-covered islands and a reputation for record-sized grayling up to 4 pounds and northern pike to 36 pounds. The lake is surrounded by spruce and poplar forests and lowland brush of labrador tea, dwarf birch, willow, bunchberry, bluejoint grass, dwarf raspberry, northern reed grass, and sedge. Licensed outfitters for fishing, moose and black bear hunting, lodging, guides, and supplies are provided by *Cree Lake Lodge*, a fly-in camp with floatplane transportation from Lac La Ronge and Lynn Lake. For information and literature write: Box 1074, Saskatoon. Wilderness fly-in and hunting camps located south of Cree Lake are operated by *Meadow Lake Outfitters Ltd.*, Box 1149, Meadow Lake, with outposts at Complex, Haultain, Soaring, Cup, and Holt Lakes. Package plan includes charter floatplane service from Keeley Lake, Lac La Plonge, or Meadow Lake to the south. *Precambrian Safari Ltd.*, Box 116, La Ronge, operates a fly-in camp on Banyard Lake south of Cree Lake. Far to the east of Cree Lake is wilderness Highway 105 and the sprawling blue waters of huge Reindeer Lake, one of the province's top fishing spots for trophy northerns, lake trout to 40 pounds, and walleye. The old Fort Caribou, built by the Northwest Company in the 1780s, once thrived at Vermilion Point on the western shore. Today outfitters, guides, lodging, and fly-in charters are provided by *Lawrence Bay Lodge*, Box 583, La Ronge; *Reindeer Lake Trout Camp*, Southend; and *Wilson's Lodge*, P.O. Box 429, Lynn Lake, Man. At the Indian village of Southend, off Highway 105 on Numabin Bay at the southern end of Reindeer Lake, is *Nordic Lodge*, Box 2082, Saskatoon, licensed outfitters for fishing and moose hunting trips. *Brabant Lake Hunting and Fishing Camp*, Box 605, La Ronge, and *McKenzies Camps* are on Brabant Lake off Highway 102.

Access & Outfitting Centers

The remote fly-in camps of the far north are accessible by chartered aircraft from Prince Albert, La Ronge, La Loche, Buffalo Narrows, Meadow Lake, Missinipe, Jan Lake, Pelican Narrows, Uranium City, and Flin Flon or Lynn Lake, Manitoba. Scheduled air services are available through La Ronge, Stony Rapids, and Uranium City. Pacific Western flies from Edmonton to Uranium City. Saskatchewan Highways 102 and 105 are a wilderness gravel route that runs north from Lac La Ronge Provincial Park past Brabant and Reindeer lakes to the Gulf Minerals mine at Wollaston Lake. The far north fly-in fishing and hunting camps are shown on the *Official Saskatchewan Highway Map*, available free from the Department of Tourism & Renewable Resources, P.O. Box 7105, Regina S4P 0B5.

Prince Albert National Park & Nipawin Country

Prince Albert National Park

Canadian National Topographic Survey Map, scale 1:125,000: Prince Albert Park MCR-210.

Nipawin Provincial Park & the Wapawekka Uplands

Canadian National Topographic Survey Maps, scale 1:250,000: Wapawekka 73-I, Prince Albert 73-H.

Thunder Hills & Montreal Lake

Canadian National Topographic Survey Maps, scale 1:250,000: Green Lake 73-J, Wapawekka 73-I.

Prince Albert National Park encompasses 957,440 acres of open grassy prairies, boreal forests, moose bogs, aspen parklands, and hundreds of lakes and streams in the geographic center of the province. The prairies are located in the extreme southern portion of the park along the Sturgeon River. Northward are the aspen groves, beaked hazelnut, dogwood, high bush cranberry, and wild sarsaparilla of the parklands and the white and black spruce, jack pine, white birch, and tamarack of the boreal forest zone. The major features of the park include the renowned lake trout, walleye, northern pike, and whitefish waters of Kingsmere (the Saskatchewan record 51-pound 10-ounce lake trout was caught here), Waskesiu, Namekus, Halkett, Crean, Wasaw, Wassegam, Lavallee, Strange, Tibiska, and Bladebone lakes, the Waskesiu Hills, and the Sturgeon, Spruce, Crean, Smoothstone, Waskesiu, and

MacLennan rivers. The *Bagwa Canoe Route* guide describes the canoe-camping journey from the Kingsmere Lake outlet near Grey Owls Cabin through Bagwa, Lily, and Clare lakes and the Kingsmere River to Waskesiu Lake. The *Prince Albert National Park Topographic Map* (MCR-210) is 30 × 40 inches and shows all natural features in color, with contours in brown, lakes in blue, and woodlands in green as well as trails, warden stations, fish ladders, campgrounds, trails, portages, wagon roads, seaplane anchorage, fire towers, and magnetic declination.

The *Prince Albert National Park Map-Brochure*, *Mammals of Prince Albert Park*, *Boundary Bog Nature Trail*, *Bagwa Canoe Route* guides and the 30-page *Western Canada National Parks Accommodation Guide* may be obtained free from the Superintendent, Prince Albert National Park, Waskesiu Lake S0J 2Y0. Camping facilities are located at Waskesiu, Beaver Glen, and the Narrows. Wilderness campsites are located on the shores of Crean, Kingsmere, Namekus, Trappers, and Halkett lakes. Rowboats and canoes are permitted on most of the larger lakes and ponds. Motorboats are restricted to Waskesiu, Sandy, Heart, Crean, and Kingsmere lakes. Boat-launching and docking facilities are located on Waskesiu, the Narrows, and Hanging Heart lakes, with a launching ramp only at Halkett Lake. Fishing permits must be obtained at the park administration building, camping registration points, or boat rental offices. Primitive trails provide access to the wildlife and wilderness camping areas of the interior. Birdlife is abundant along the waterways. The hiker, fisherman, or canoeist may frequently see loons, mallards, blue-winged teals, terns, herring gulls, marsh hawks, cormorants, bald eagle, osprey, and on Lavallee Lake, white pelicans.

The lakes, streams, and boreal evergreen forests of the Thunder Hills to the north of Prince Albert Park and the Wapawekka and Cub hills to the east are one of the province's most productive moose and upland game-bird hunting areas. Northern pike, walleye, and lake trout grow to record size in Lakes Montreal, Candle, Whiteswan, Piprell, Weyakwin, Little Bear, Big Sandy, and Wapawekka, and in the Fishing Lakes surrounded by the Cub Hills and jack-pine forests of 161,280-acre Nipawin Provincial Park. Piprell Lake and the swift, cold streams of the Nipawin area hold record rainbows to 18 pounds and squaretails to 4–5 pounds. Lodging, guides, supplies, and fishing and hunting outfitting services are provided at the Fishing Lakes in Nipawin Provincial Park by *Caribou Creek Lodge*, Box 157, Smeaton S0J 2J0, and *N & D Cabins*, Box 135, Ridgedale S0E 1L0; at Little Bear Lake by *Bear Lake Cabins*, Box 38, Prince Albert S6V 5R4, *Trout Haven* Resort, Box 189, Smeaton S0J 2J0, and *Moose Hour Lodge*, Mile 68, Hanson Lake Road; at Mile 87 on the Hanson Lake Road is Big Sandy Lake, which is served by the *Big Sandy Resort*, Mile 62, Hanson Lake Road S6V 5Z5, via Prince Albert. The famous Candle Lake area is served by *Candle Lake Lodge Ltd.*, Box 28, RR 1, Meath Park; *Holiday Acres Ltd.*, RR 1, Candle Lake; *Paul's Cabins*, Box 20, Meath Park; *Tel-Win Beach*, Box 11, RR 1, Meath Park S0J 1T0. The *Whiteswan Lodge*, Box 83, Meath Park, is located at Whiteswan Lake on the resource road north of Candle Lake as is the *Pine Grove Resort*, 714 East Dr., Saskatoon S7J 2X7 at East Trout Lake, *Katche Camp*, 1102 Lancaster Blvd., Saskatoon S7M 3V5 at Nipekamew Lake, and *Rainbow Lodge*, Box 40, Meath Park on the shore of Piprell Lake. Angling Lake, located just outside the eastern boundary of Prince Albert National Park, is served by the *Beaver Store*, Christopher Lake S0J 0N0, and *Jacobsen Bay Outfitters*, Box 4, Christopher Lake S0J 0N0. Christopher Lake is serviced by *Northern Production Ltd.*, Christopher Lake.

Access & Outfitting Centers

Prince Albert National Park is reached via Highway 2 from Prince Albert. Hanson Lake Road 106 and Highway 120 provide access to the Nipawin country government campgrounds. Lodging, guides, and supplies are located at Prince Albert, Christopher Lake, Montreal Lake, Weyakwin, Molanosa, and Timber Bay off Highway 2 and at Candle Lake, Whelan Bay, East Trout Lake, and Big Sandy Lake along the Hanson Lake Road.

MANITOBA ENCYCLOPEDIA

Accommodations—Vacation Lodges & Sporting Camps

Manitoba has a wide variety of accommodations ranging from rustic north country fly-in fishing camps to deluxe hotels. The 32-page *Manitoba Accommodation Guide* contains a comprehensive listing of hotels, motels, trailer courts, resorts, lodges, and fly-in outpost camps. The accommodations are listed in a region-by-region format with descriptions of facilities and services offered. The guide also contains a listing of Manitoba farm vacation hosts. For detailed info about the province's farm vacations write: Manitoba Farm Vacations, 347 Assiniboine Ave., Winnipeg. The provincial government, in addition, publishes the 64-page *Manitoba Vacation Guide*, which contains a complete listing and descriptions of fly-in lodges, hotels, motels, boat-launching facilities, campgrounds, picnic sites, beaches, horseback-riding services, historic sites, museums, and points of interest for the northern, western, eastern, and central regions and for the city of Winnipeg. The Manitoba accommodation and vacation guides may both be obtained free by writing: Manitoba Government Travel, 200 Vaughan St., Winnipeg R3C 1T5.

Listings and descriptions of Manitoba's major vacation lodges, resorts, and sporting camps are found throughout the "Encyclopedia" and "Travel & Recreation Guide" sections.

Airlines & Floatplane Fly-in Services

Manitoba's major cities and northern settlements are served by 6 national and international airlines and by regional and charter aircraft companies. *Air Canada*, Place Ville Marie, Montreal, Que. H3B 3Y8, has service daily between Winnipeg and New York; *Northwest Airlines*, Winnipeg International Airport, Winnipeg, has service between Winnipeg and Fargo and Grand Forks, North Dakota; *Midwest Airlines Ltd.*, Winnipeg International Airport, Winnipeg, has service between Winnipeg and northern Manitoba points; *Calm Air Ltd.*, P.O. Box 818, Lynn Lake R0B 0W0, serves northern Manitoba points; *Lambair Ltd.*, P.O. Box 808, The Pas R9A 1K8, has service from Churchill to points on Hudson Bay and between Thompson and northern Manitoba points; *Ilford-Riverton Airways Ltd.*, Winnipeg International Airport, Winnipeg R2R 0T1, has service from Winnipeg and Thompson to northern Manitoba settlements; *Transair Ltd.*, Winnipeg International Airport, Winnipeg R2R 0S6, has daily service between Winnipeg and The Pas, Flin Flon, Thompson, Churchill, between Churchill and Northwest Territories settlements, and between Winnipeg and Red Lake, Ontario, and Kenora, Dryden, Thunder Bay, Sault Ste. Marie, and Toronto. Additional air charter and wilderness fly-in services to northern Manitoba fishing, hunting, and canoe-camping areas are provided by *Aerial Spray and Charter Ltd.*, Neepawa; *Aero Trades* (Western Ltd.), Winnipeg International Airport; *Air Park Ltd.*, Lac du Bonnet; *Cross Lake Air Services Ltd.*, Wabowden; *Gem Air Ltd.*, 4239 Main W St. Paul, Winnipeg; *Helair Ltd.*, 405–203 Portage Ave., Winnipeg; *Keewatin Air Ltd.*, Winnipeg International Airport and Ilford, *La Ronge Aviation Services Ltd.*, Eldon and Lynn lakes; *Maple Leaf Aviation Ltd.*, Hangar 1, Brandon Airport, Brandon; *Northland Ltd.*, Thompson Riverbase, Thompson; *Northway Aviation Ltd.*, Box 72, Arnes; *Parsons Airways Northern Ltd.*, Schist Lake and Flin Flon; *Perimeter Aviation Ltd.*, Hangar 2, Winnipeg International Airport; *St. Andrews Airways Ltd.*, St. Andrews, Island Lake and Norway House; *Silver Pine Air Service Ltd.*, Pine Falls; *Whiteshell Air Service*, 450 Dufferin W, Portage la Prairie. Pilots planning to fly their own aircraft in the province are advised to write for the *Manitoba Flight Information Map*, Surveys Branch, 1007 Century Ave., Winnipeg (price $2). For the convenience of visiting

pilots the publication *Air Tourist Information* is available free on request from the Aeronautical Information Service, Ministry of Transport, Canada Bldg., Place De Ville, Ottawa, Ont. K1A 0N5.

Camping & North Country Trails

Manitoba's provincial park system covers a total area of over 3,000 square miles in which approximately 5,000 public campsites are maintained ranging from primitive wilderness sites to full-service campgrounds. Another 5,000 public campsites are run by commercial establishments. The commercial tourist campgrounds are inspected annually by accommodation development counselors to see that they provide essential and standard conveniences. A comprehensive listing of all provincial and commercial campsites as well as boat-launching sites in the central, eastern, western, and far northern regions—from famous Whiteshell Provincial Park north of Lake of the Woods in the southeast to the remote Paint Lake provincial recreation area in the northern forest—is contained in the 64-page *Manitoba Vacation Guide,* available free from Manitoba Government Travel, 200 Vaughan St., Winnipeg R3C 1T5. The *Manitoba Official Highway Map* shows the locations of government campsites by green triangular symbols. Camping permits are required in all provincial campgrounds. Provincial campsites are open to the public by the third week in May and generally close on the last weekend of September, although those on the Trans-Canada Highway stay open until the last week in October. Oversize trailers may be moved only with special permits, which are available free from the Highways Department, 1075 Portage Ave., Winnipeg R3G 0S1, or at provincial weigh scales at West Hawk Lake, Emerson, and Headingley.

There are scenic and wilderness hiking trails maintained by the provincial government within all major parks and forest reserves. Trail guides published by the Parks Branch for the major trail systems may be obtained free by writing: Manitoba Department of Tourism, Recreation, & Cultural Affairs, 200 Vaughan St., Winnipeg R3C 1T5. Among scenic north country trails in Whiteshell Provincial Park, the *Pine Point Trail* is a 4-mile trek along a picturesque old portage located off Provincial Road 307, north of Highway 44 near Betula and Nutimuk lakes; the *Amisk Trail* runs through typical Canadian Shield country between Brereton Lake and the Rennie River off Provincial Road 307 at the north end of Brereton Lake; the *Bear Lake Wilderness Trail* runs along rock ridges and jack-pine and spruce swamps to the scenic waters of Bear Lake, located off Provincial Road 44, 8 miles

east of the Whiteshell Park headquarters at Rennie; the *Assinika Trail* is located off Provincial Road 312, between the renowned smallmouth bass waters of West Hawk and Caddy lakes; the *McGillivray Falls Trail* is off Provincial Highway 44, 2 miles east of the Lily Pond; the *Cedar Bog Trail* in Birds Hill Provincial Park, on Highway 59 about 20 miles northeast of Winnipeg, runs through groves of aspen, poplar, shrub thickets, and open grasslands and through a typical cedar bog environment. Pamphlets are also available for *Shining Stone Trail,* Duck Mountain Provincial Park, and the *Ox-Bow Lake, Isputinaw,* and *Spirit Hill* trails, Spruce Woods Provincial Park. The scenic *North Star Trail* winds through the 184,920 acres of timberlands that make up the Belair Provincial Forest, just south of Lake Winnipeg's Traverse Bay. In Spruce Woods Park the naturalist may also follow the scenic trails described by Ernest Thompson Seton in his novel *The Trail of the Sandhill Stag.* (See "Riding Mountain National Park.")

Canadian Shield

All those who have traveled along the ancient trails used by the northern explorers, fur traders, and Indian trappers through the country of the great shield have experienced the sameness and loneliness of its immense spruce and jack-pine forests, remote, seemingly endless chains of oddly shaped lakes and wild rivers, granite outcroppings, and thick carpets of caribou moss, muskeg, dwarf willow, lichens, and Labrador tea. To the Norse explorer Leif Ericson the shield was Helluland, "the land of the flat stone." The Canadian Shield (also known as the Precambrian Shield) is a vast V-shaped area of low elevation surrounding Hudson Bay, covering nearly half of Canada, or about 1,850,000 square miles. The shield extends from Great Bear Lake in the northwest to the Strait of Belle Isle on the east and to the Great Lakes in the south. Northward it reaches as far as Baffin Island. Portions of the shield extend below Canada to include small areas in New York state as well as areas to the west and south of Lake Superior in Michigan, Wisconsin, and Minnesota. The great shield is so named because most of the area is composed of ancient Precambrian, crystalline rocks of great hardness and strength—granites, gneisses, and veins of snowy quartz. The age of greenstone, which is among the oldest rocks in the world, in areas such as the Labrador Coast and Great Bear Lake has been estimated at 2.5 billion years.

In Quaternary times great ice sheets covered the country of the shield, and when the ice melted away, huge lakes remained. Eventually these enormous glacial lakes drained away, leaving clay flats and huge gravel beaches. Millions of small, oddly shaped lakes were also formed; the shield is believed to contain more lakes than all the rest of the world. At one time high mountain ranges marked the landscape, only to be worn down by the great ice sheets to form a characteristic surface of low, rounded hills and valleys. Because the topography of the shield is so strikingly uniform, the scenery of much of the Northwest Territories is nearly indistinguishable from that of Quebec's Ungava Plateau or northern Ontario. Along its eastern edge, however, the shield thrusts upward and majestic fjordlike coasts are dominated by spectacular ancient mountain ranges, cliffs, and massive glaciers and ice caps. The shield is rich in forests and mineral deposits. In fact, many of the world's greatest deposits of iron, copper, nickel, gold, and uranium are found here. Anyone planning to travel through the land of the shield is advised to read two classic books, Sigurd Olson's *The Lonely Land,* which brings to life the romance and history of the great Churchill River wilderness, and Pierre Burton's *The Mysterious North,* a more wide-ranging but equally enthralling and informative portrait of the northland and the great shield. Both books are published by Alfred A. Knopf, Inc., New York.

Canoeing & Wilderness Waters

Manitoba's wild north woods lakes and rivers were traveled for centuries by Indians, voyageurs, explorers, fur traders, trappers, and missionaries. The legendary adventures of the northmen who traveled the water trails and portages can be shared today by the wilderness paddler who is willing to endure the hardships, treacherous rapids, headwinds, mosquito-infested portages, and backbreaking work experienced by all who travel through the northern bush. Anyone who is planning a canoe trip on one of Manitoba's historic canoe routes which lead to the great fur forests of the northwest is advised to read Eric W. Morse's *Fur Trade Canoe Routes of Canada: Then and Now.* This

book may be obtained for $3.75 from Information Canada, 171 Slater St., Ottawa, Ont. (make checks payable to the Receiver General of Canada). This 125-page bible contains historic canoe-route maps and illustrations and describes Canada's fur trade waterways and portages, including Manitoba's famous Winnipeg River, "Upper Track" and "Middle Track" canoe routes. The historic Upper Track route used by Indian coureurs de bois ran from Cumberland House in Saskatchewan up the Sturgeon-Weir and Goose rivers and over Cranberry Portage to the Grass River, which flows through a labyrinth of lakes to the Nelson River and on to Hudson Bay and York Factory. In 1766, Samuel Hearne, a Hudson's Bay Company explorer, traveled along the Upper Track from York Factory up the treacherous Nelson River and the 450-mile Grass River to Cumberland Lake (then known as Pine Island Lake), where he established Cumberland House, which remains in operation to this day. The Grass River country was known over 2 centuries ago as *Le Pays du Rat,* or muskrat country. The famous Middle Track country was used by Indian middlemen prior to the building of Cumberland House on their journeys between York Factory and the Saskatchewan River along the Hayes River. The indispensable publication *Canoe Trips in Manitoba,* available free from the Tourist Branch, Department of Tourism, Recreation, & Cultural Affairs, 200 Vaughan St., Winnipeg R3C 1T5, provides detailed descriptions of major waterways including the Red River canoe route; Whiteshell-Caddy Lake route; the Norway House to York Factory Route, along the Hayes River between Lake Winnipeg and Hudson Bay; the Cranberry Lake to Wekusko route, which flows for 120 miles from Cranberry Portage to Wekusko Lake through a complex lakes chain and the Grass River; the 90-mile Wekusko to Wabowden canoe route along the Grass River; the famous 140-mile Pukatawagan Falls-Churchill River canoe route; the scenic Pineroot chain of lakes canoe

route from Whitefish Lake, north of Cranberry Portage, to Aimee and Wobishkok—regarded as a fisherman's paradise where large lake trout and walleye are commonly caught; and the Poplar River, Headwater Lake-McPhail River, and Assapan River canoe routes located in the remote Atikaki Wilderness area, east of Lake Winnipeg. In addition, the Tourism Branch, Department of Tourism, Recreation, & Cultural Affairs, publishes several free illustrated canoe-route guides. The *Manigotagan River Guide* describes the challenging 50-mile trip starting on the shore of Long Lake, east of Bissett, to the settlement of Manigotagan; the *Bloodvein River Guide* describes a wild 200-mile route in the Atikaki Wilderness; there is also a *Souris River Guide.*

The provincial government also publishes several magnificently illustrated and annotated maps of Manitoba's historic fur trade canoe routes. These large maps, designed and illustrated by the artist Réal Bérard, show the entire canoe route with detailed descriptions annotating every portage, rapid, falls, trapper's cabin, fish camp, Indian archaeological site and petrograph, historical site, and dam. Each map contains detailed descriptions and line drawings of Indian and voyageur artifacts, wildlife, and fascinating biographies and anecdotes about the great explorers and Indian guides. These beautiful, informative maps may be obtained for 50¢ each from: Surveys Branch, 1007 Century St., Winnipeg R3H 0W4, for the following fur trade routes: the *Sasaginnigak Canoe Country Map,* showing the remote network of rivers and lakes located in the Atikaki Wilderness along the eastern shore of Lake Winnipeg; the *Kautunigan Canoe Route Map,* showing the 300-mile Atikaki Wilderness canoe route along the Wanipigow, Broadleaf, Gammon, Bloodvein, Sasaginnigak, and Berens rivers; the *Rivière aux Rats Canoe Route Map,* showing the 140-mile voyage from La Montagne de Cypres to Winnipeg; the *Mistik Creek Canoe Route Map,* showing 50 miles of wilderness streams and lakes stretching east of Flin Flon, Cranberry Portage, and The Pas; the *Grass River Canoe Route Map,* showing the historic route from Cranberry Portage northeast to Paint Lake, located due south of the mining settlement of Thompson, a distance of 450 miles; the *Middletrack & Hayes River Canoe Route Map,* showing the rugged 500-mile route from The Pas to the historic Hudson's Bay Company post of York Factory near the mouth of the Hayes River; the *Winnipeg River Canoe Route Map,* showing the famous 510-mile fur trade route down the Winnipeg River to Traverse Bay, where the route follows the east shore of Lake Winnipeg (known to the Indians as *Win-nipiy,* or "murky waters"), to the mouth of the Red River, and up the Red to its confluence with the Assiniboine River; and the *Little Grand Rapids Canoe Route Map,* showing the rugged 110-mile Atikaki Wilderness route along the Pigeon, Berens, Poplar, and Assinika rivers. The Boy Scouts of Canada have published a booklet covering the following routes: Caddy Lake, Whitemouth Lake and River, Assiniboine River, and Red River. The booklet costs 50¢ and may be obtained from the Scouts Office, 148 Colony St., Winnipeg R3C 1V9. The National & Provincial Parks Association of Canada sponsors an 8-day summer canoe trip through the Atikaki Wilderness areas of eastern Manitoba and northern Ontario. For trip particulars and literature write: Outings Coordinator, NPPAC, 47 Colborne St., Suite 308, Toronto M5E 1E3. (See "Outfitting & Guide Service.")

Churchill & the Journeys of Samuel Hearne—Explorer

(Pop. 1,678). Manitoba's subarctic seaport is located at the mouth of the Churchill River on Hudson Bay. The port was discovered in 1619 when Captain Jens Munch, who was searching for the legendary northwest passage to the East Indies, was forced to spend the winter about 5 miles from the entrance to the harbor. In the years that followed Churchill became the site of Fort Prince of Wales, a Hudson's Bay Company post that served as a base for Samuel Hearne's expeditions to the mouth of the Coppermine River in the Northwest Territories. Today Churchill serves as the arctic gateway to the grain harvests of Canada's west, with wheat as the principal commodity. The surrounding Hudsonian and arctic life zones are a naturalist's rendezvous and are one of the world's greatest polar bear denning areas and goose hunting regions. The nearby fly-in waters of the famous Seal, North and South Knife, and Churchill rivers hold brook trout, arctic char, and grayling. The Churchill Whaling Center and several hotels provide a wide range of accommodations. Fort Prince of Wales has been partly restored and is maintained in a 50-acre national park. A unique way to visit the fort is by Jane's Dogsled Taxi (ice and weather conditions permitting). Arrangements for fishing trips, hunting, or sightseeing may be made by contacting the *Churchill Whalers Cooperative,* Box 593, Churchill R0B 0E0. Churchill is reached via scheduled air service from Winnipeg, by the Hudson Bay line of the Canadian National Railway, or via Churchill or Hayes River wilderness canoe routes.

The amazing adventures of Samuel Hearne (who was born in London in 1745 and became a midshipman in the Royal Navy at the age of 11) began in 1766 when he entered the service of the Hudson's Bay Company and worked as a mate for 3 years before coming ashore and being given command of exploring expeditions inland from Hudson Bay. An amateur naturalist, self-styled nonconformist, and great admirer of Voltaire, Hearne was only 24 when he set out in 1769 from Fort Prince of Wales with a small band of Chipewyan Indians in search of the El Dorado of copper rumored to exist at the mouth of a river flowing into the Arctic Ocean. After he had walked about 200 miles he was deserted by his unreliable Indian guides and forced to make his own way back. A second expedition proved equally futile. After spending a desperate 9 months in the wilds, during which his supplies were plundered by Indians, his quadrant was smashed, and his dogsled team froze to death, Hearne returned half starved and half frozen but determined to try again.

On the third expedition Hearne took along an Indian guide named Matanabbee and several other stout Chipewyan braves. The party was also accompanied by Matanabbee's seven wives, who took care of the cooking, sewing, tent pitching, and pack carrying. The group walked as much as 20 miles a day over spongy muskeg. Bouts of starvation (at one point Hearne boiled and ate his own boots) alternated with orgies of hunting when game was abundant. In his journal Hearne reported watching the Indians slay an elk: too hungry to wait until the beast was cooked, they ripped open its stomach and devoured the raw entrails. When the band reached the banks of the Coppermine, the Indians discovered a village of Eskimos camped beside a waterfall. Inflamed with an unreasonable hatred for these people, Matanabbee was determined to lead his band in a savage massacre. Hearne, after seeking in vain to dissuade his guide, stood hopelessly by while his Indian companions swooped down on the sleeping Eskimo camp and slaughtered all of them. The setting for this brutal scene was known forever after as Bloody Falls.

Disenchanted and heartsick, Hearne proceeded down the Coppermine River to its mouth at the Arctic Ocean. Further disappointment awaited him when he discovered no copper at all. An extensive search yielded no more than a 4-pound chunk of metal. It was little consolation to Hearne that he was the first white man to reach the Arctic Ocean from Hudson Bay. Two years later, when the Hudson's Bay

Company decided to establish its first inland post, Hearne led the expedition up the Hayes River and founded Cumberland House on Pine Island. He settled down to a life of administrative duties and in 1776 was given command of Prince of Wales Fort. He was still in charge of the post when it was captured by the French under La Pérouse in 1782. Hearne was taken to France as a prisoner but returned a year later to reestablish the fort on the Churchill. He remained there for 4 years until poor health forced him to return to England. His last years were spent preparing the remarkable journal of his travels, one of the great classics of the north, *A Journey to the Northern Ocean.*

Fishing & Hunting in Manitoba

A glance at the map of northern Manitoba's almost roadless wilderness indicates that here, in the boreal forests of the Canadian Shield, with its great wild rivers and complex lake chains, you will find some of the finest fishing and hunting on the continent. To the north of the shield is a strip of land, about 100 miles wide, known as the Hudson Bay Lowlands, bordering on Henry Hudson's huge bay. This flat, almost treeless plain of muskeg and tundra, where the elevation rarely exceeds 500 feet, is one of the most spectacular goose hunting (and mosquito-breeding) grounds in the world. To the southwest of the Canadian Shield, which occupies almost the entire northern third of the province's 250,000 square miles, lies the prairie country—a triangular-shaped tract containing some of the most fertile land in the province. The beautiful scenic valleys of the Assiniboine, Pembina, Shell, Swan, and Red rivers provide stunning breaks in the predominatly flat plain. To the west and north of the plains, along the Saskatchewan border, are Manitoba's highlands. Here the Riding, Duck, and Porcupine mountains form the Manitoba escarpment, where Baldy Mountain in the Duck Mountain Range reaches an elevation of 2,727 feet. The lowlands of central Manitoba held an immense prehistoric sea, known as Lake Agassiz, which covered some 200,000 square miles, the remains of which are held by Manitoba's three great lakes: Winnipeg, Manitoba, and Winnipegosis. Lake Winnipeg, with an area of 9,094 square miles and a total length of 250 miles, is the largest of these lakes and also the 13th largest in the world.

North Country Trophy Lakes & Wild Rivers

North of Manitoba's 53rd parallel are the renowned lake trout, northern pike, and walleye waters of the Grass River lakes chain, Churchill River system, the great Nelson River (which is the outlet of Lake Winnipeg and bears the full force of the Saskatchewan and Winnipeg rivers), and the famous Middle Track and Hayes River country. Here are seemingly endless networks of great lakes of astounding beauty and wild twisting rivers, and the world-famous brook trout waters of the Gods River and Island Lake River country. In the northernmost part of the province, in the land of the caribou, are the remote arctic grayling, lake trout, char, and brook trout waters of the Nejanilini, Nueltin, Munroe, and Bain lakes and the wild Wolverine, Caribou, Seal, and North and South Knife rivers which flow through this ancient country of the Cree Indians into Hudson Bay. Lake Athapapuskow near Flin Flon is probably the best-known lake trout water in the northland, with Gods, Clearwater, Nueltin, Reed, Southern Indian, and Kississing lakes running a close second. The Manitoba record 63-pound lake trout, caught in 1935 in Lake Athapapuskow, held the world record for 35 years; since then it has been broken twice. Northern Manitoba's top grayling waters include the Owl, Deer, Silcox, Cochrane, Seal, and Wolverine rivers, and the record 3.2-pound grayling was taken from the remote fly-in waters of the South Knife River. Trophy-sized northern pike up to 36 pounds and walleye to 14 pounds

are caught each year in the famous north country waters at Gods Lake, Churchill and Grass rivers, and Cranberry, Kississing, Molson, Athapapuskow, Simonhouse, Reed, Cross, and Paint lakes. Splake, a hybrid of lake trout and brook trout, is caught up to 8 pounds in the Laurie River and Lake area.

South of the 53rd Parallel

Southeast of the 53rd parallel, between the eastern shoreline of Lake Winnipeg and the Ontario boundary, lies a vast roadless Precambrian country of interconnected lakes and wild rivers known as the Atikaki Wilderness. Here, in the remote, seldom fished waters of the Sasaginnigak Lake and River system, in the Bloodvein, Poplar, Etomami, Berens, and Dogskin rivers, and in Lakes Family, Viking, Fishing, Aikens, and Assinika, are record-sized walleye, lake trout, and northern pike. The famous Interlake region, between Lake Winnipeg on the east and Lakes Manitoba and Winnipegosis on the west, annually produces walleye up to 14 pounds in the Lake Manitoba Narrows and Waterhen Lake areas. The mouth of the Saskatchewan River at Grand Rapids on Lake Winnipeg, some 125 miles north of the Lake Manitoba Narrows, forms Cross and Cedar lakes, both famous for large walleyes and northern pike up to 30 pounds, in the shallow weedy bays and coves. The Winnipeg River, in the southeastern corner of the province, is one of Canada's finest northern pike, smallmouth bass, and walleye fishing waters. The Winnipeg flows from its headwaters in Lake of the Woods and arcs for 100 miles through Whiteshell Provincial Park and the rocky upthrusts of the Canadian Shield, its banks bordered by scenic boreal forests and stands of canoe birch and burr oak, into Traverse Bay of Lake Winnipeg. A comprehensive listing of the province's master angler annual award winners and record fish is contained in the free *Manitoba Master Angler Award* booklet, available from Manitoba Government Travel, 200 Vaughan St., Winnipeg R3C 1T5. Manitoba's all-time fishing records, by species, illustrate the fishing potential and diversity of its lakes and streams.

MANITOBA RECORD FISH

	Lb.-oz.	Place	Year
Lake trout	63	Lake Athapapuskow	1930
Sturgeon	119	Winnipeg River	1964
Arctic char	6	Churchill River	1961
Northern pike	41–2	Fishing Lake	1969
Walleye	18–8	George Lake	1954
Muskellunge	26–0	Steep Rock Lake	1970
Brook trout	9–8	Gods River	1972
Rainbow trout	13–4	William Lake	1977
Arctic grayling	3–9	South Knife River	1974
Splake	9–1	Childs Lake	1975
Brown trout	7–7½	Lake Winnipeg-Penniac Bay	1961
Smallmouth bass	7–10	Netley Creek	1977
Whitefish	11–4	Lake Winnipeg-Cross Bay	1975

The Manitoba Department of Mines, Resources, & Environmental Management publishes several essential guides for the outdoorsman planning a Manitoba fishing or hunting trip. These booklets may be obtained free by writing: Box 9, 989 Century St., Winnipeg R3H 0W4. The *Manitoba Sport Fishing Guide* contains fishing area maps and information about angling seasons, regulations, and the master angler awards. The beautifully illustrated and useful 20-page booklet

A Look at Trout & Grayling contains full-color drawings and descriptions of the species and Manitoba hot spots of for brook, brown, rainbow, and lake trout, arctic grayling and char, and splake. *Fishes of Manitoba* is an attractive full-color wall chart which illustrates all the major fish species and the types of habitats they frequent, with capsule descriptions for each species. The *Manitoba Stocked Waters* booklet lists stocking locations throughout the province in alphabetical order. The booklet is profusely illustrated with detailed maps, and colored symbols indicate fish types "planted" and give their map locations. The 32-page booklet *How to Catch Fish in Fresh Water* is packed with information of interest to anglers with tips on what makes a good fishing spot, merits of different types of lures, and how to handle fish. The 130-page *Freshwater Fishes of Manitoba* guide contains comprehensive descriptions and illustrated keys to identifying the freshwater fishes found in the province's lakes, rivers, streams, and marshes. The 38-page *Manitoba Game-Bird & Big-Game Seasons* is published annually and contains hunting zone maps and season and bag limit information for hunters. The 38-page booklet *Field Handling of Game* is a valuable aid to hunters and fishermen which illustrates proper methods of handling game, including deer, moose, bear, game birds, and fish. Equipment and various methods of cleaning, dressing, and storing are discussed. The *Upland Game Birds and Big Game of Manitoba* guide is illustrated with color photographs and drawings, with descriptions of the habitats and life cycles of the whitetail deer, black bear, moose, elk, woodland and barren-ground caribou, ruffed grouse, sharp-tailed and spruce grouse, rock and willow ptarmigan, and gray or Hungarian partridge. The *Manitoba Waterfowl* guide contains color photographs and descriptions of flyways and some of the common waterfowl including the Canada and white-fronted goose, snow and blue goose, ruddy duck, mallard, wood duck, and canvasback. The 24-page *Ducks at a Distance Identification Guide* contains useful color drawings that show the birds in flight and at rest, with brief notes on their habits, range, and preferred habitats. The useful *Ducks Unlimited* wall chart contains full-color drawings and descriptions. An illustrated guide, *Birds & Mammals of Delta Marsh*, contains a useful description of this world-famous waterfowl hunting area.

Big-Game Hunting

Manitoba's northern coniferous forests and mixed woodlands, which cover some 50% of the total land area, offer excellent big-game and upland game-bird hunting opportunities. Whitetail deer are the most prolific big-game animals in the province; their range extends 600 miles north-south from the 49th parallel at the United States border to well beyond the northernmost tip of Lake Winnipeg at the 54th parallel. Scattered herds of mule deer, once plentiful throughout the southern region, inhabit the Porcupine and Duck Mountain provincial forests and Riding Mountain National Park. Substantial moose populations are found in the second-growth forests in the northwestern part of the province, in the north central bush, and south through the Interlake region and east of Lake Winnipeg in the Atikaki Wilderness. A limited number of moose licenses have been allocated to Manitoba lodges and outfitters. North country fly-in moose hunting lodges are located in the Cranberry Portage, Flin Flon, and The Pas areas and at Gods Lake, Kississing Lake, Cormorant Lake, Reed Lake, and at Dogskin Lake and Fishing Lake in the Atikaki Wilderness. To acquire a moose license, you must purchase a complete package plan of not less than 4 days and make your reservations directly with the lodge or outfitter of your choice. A free *Moose Hunting Zone Map* and a *Listing of Nonresident Moose Hunting Lodges & Outfitters* may be obtained by writing: Manitoba Government Travel, 200 Vaughan St., Winnipeg R3C 1T5.

In recent years, moose and black bear have generally been the only big-game species open to nonresident hunters. The best spring and fall black bear hunting is found in Whiteshell Provincial Park, the Lac du Bonnet area, and in the Duck Mountain Provincial Forest. Elk, which once roamed the southern part of the province in great numbers, are now restricted to a few small herds along the slopes and valleys of the Duck and Riding mountains, and in the Porcupine and Spruce Woods provincial forests and the Interlake region. Woodland caribou roam through much of their ancestral range (although their numbers have been reduced drastically to an estimated population of 5,000 animals) in the Cormorant Lake, Cranberry Portage, Snow Lake, and Shamattawa-Gods River areas and in small herds near Norway House and Island Lake. Barren-ground caribou of the Manitoba-Keewatin herd winter in the vast boreal forests north of the Churchill River. As spring approaches so begins their great annual migration north, once again, out from the taiga and onto the summer feeding grounds of the arctic tundra, beginning their trek back to the treeline during the month of August.

Waterfowl Hunting

Manitoba's 39,000 square miles of lakes and rivers, bordered by large marshlands and extensive rice beds, and the famous pothole region in the south central part of the province, together with the thousands of acres of grain and stubble fields in the central and southern regions, have long been referred to as the "duck factory of North America." Manitoba's physiographic regions form one of the most important breeding grounds on the continent for ducks and geese. In addition, three of North America's main waterfowl flyways—the Central, Mississippi, and Atlantic—converge here. The province's world-famous autumn shooting areas include the pothole country; the stubble fields in the Brandon, Minnedosa, and Oak lakes areas; the entire Lake Winnipeg basin, particularly for redheads and mallards in the Netley and Hecla Island marshes; Lake Winnipegosis, and the renowned Delta Marshes at the southernmost tip of Lake Manitoba; the Interlake Region; and the Whiteshell Provincial Park and Winnipeg River country in the southeast for bluebills and mallards; and in the north country, the extensive marshes surrounding The Pas. Manitoba's famous goose hunting areas include Hecla Island, The Pas, and the Hudson Bay lowlands surrounding York Factory and Churchill. (See "Outfitting & Guide Service," "Manitoba's Great Northern Wilderness Map," "Indian Outfitters—Goose Hunting & Fishing Camps," "Wilderness Travel Guides," "Hudson's Bay Company Outfitting Posts & Canoe Service," and "Gods Lake & River Trophy Trout Country.")

Flin Flon & Cranberry Portage Outfitting Centers

(Pop. 9,344). Flin Flon is on the Manitoba-Saskatchewan border on Highway 10, some 91 miles north of The Pas; its unusual name was acquired in 1915 when prospectors in the area found a novel, *The Sunless City,* on a portage near the Churchill River. The town's name is taken from the name of Professor Josiah Flintabbety Flonation, the hero of the novel who discovered a city of gold in the center of the earth. Rich deposits of silver, gold, copper, and zinc were discovered in the early part of the 19th century. Essentially a mining town, with mines in operation since 1927, Flin Flon also relies on lumbering and fishing to support its population. The town is a famous fishing, hunting, and canoeing outfitting center and every July holds the renowned Flin Flon trout festival, with cash prizes for anglers who bring in the largest lake trout and northern pike. To the east of Flin Flon is

Cranberry Portage, a small community at the divisional point of the Lynn Lake-Flin Flon lines of the Canadian National Railway. The town is a popular hunting, fishing, and wilderness canoeing outfitting center with some commercial trapping carried on in the winter. The Flin Flon-Cranberry Portage area is a famous jumping-off spot for the Mistik Creek and Grass River wilderness canoe routes. Trophy-sized lake trout, northern pike, and walleye are found in Lakes Athapapuskow, Goose, Egg, and Kisseynew in the Flin Flon area between Grass River Provincial Park and the Saskatchewan border and, to the north, in famous Kississing Lake. Several hunting and fishing camps and outfitters serve the area and 9 government campsites are located here along Explorers Highroad 10. Daily (except Sunday) air service serves Flin Flon from Winnipeg as well as railroad and bus lines. The wilderness fish and game region surrounding Flin Flon is shown on a beautiful full-color shaded-relief map (no. 63K/NW), available for $1.50 from the Canada Map Office, Ottawa, Ontario.

Gods Lake & River Trophy Trout Country

Far to the northeast of Lake Winnipeg, in the heart of the evergreen wilderness of the Canadian Shield, are the legendary brook trout waters of the Gods River. Here, in the remote hunting and trapping grounds of the Swampy Cree Indians, are the deep, fertile waters of Gods Lake, which covers 400 square miles and the scenic, aptly named Island Lake, whose irregular, jagged shoreline and island-dotted waters cover an area of some 375 square miles. The brook trout of the region

are of a native strain that grow to phenomenal size in these cold turbulent headwaters. The Gods River and Island Lake River squaretails are equally famous for their brilliant coloration and markings. Gods Lake, particularly in the Gods Narrows Area, is one of Canada's greatest producers of large lake trout (and giant northern pike), as the listing of Manitoba's top 10 record lake and brook trout illustrates so well.

	Lb.-oz.	Place	Year
Lake trout	63–0	Lake Athapapuskow	1930
	53–4	Gods Lake	1966
	52–0	Gods Lake	1963
	51–4	Gods Lake	1961
	50–4	Gods Lake	1959
	50–2	Gods Lake	1960
	50–1	Gods Lake	1959
	49–10	Gods Lake	1964
	49–8	Gods Lake	1962
	49–8	Gods Lake	1964
Brook trout	9–8	Gods River	1972
	8–7	Gods River	1959
	8–3	Gods River	1954
	8–3	Weir River	1951
	8–0	Island Lake River	1969
	7–11	Gods River	1967
	7–8	Gods River	1968
	7–8	Gods River	1968
	7–8	Gods River	1964
	7–8	Gods River	1961

The Gods River is as infamous for its violent rapids as it is famous for its trophy fish. Eric Sevareid, the nationally famous television journalist, has a spellbinding account of his canoe journey down the Gods River in his book *Canoeing with the Cree* (available for $4.75 plus 50¢ postage from Waters Inc., 111 E. Sheridan St., Ely, MN 55731 U.S.A.). Indian guides who know every pocket of water on the river are available for hire at several of the fly-in fishing camps in the area. Lodging, transportation, and fly-in service, guides, canoes, boats, motors, meals, and goose hunting trips are provided in the Gods River country by *Gods River Lodge*, Box 714, Winnipeg R3C 2K3, with a floatplane base on Gods River and an outpost camp on the Kaskattama River; the *Narrows Lodge*, Gods Lake Narrows R0B 0M0, on Gods Lake; *Gods Lake Elk Island Lodge*, 500 Henderson Hwy., Winnipeg R2K 2H8, on Gods Lake, with a 4,200-foot airstrip and 15 fully modern cabins, offering a complete package plan and guided moose and goose hunting trips, with an outpost camp located on the Gods River; *Island Lake Lodge*, c/o St. Andrews Airways, Box 15, Group 6A, RR 1, Winnipeg R3C 2E4 with a remote outpost on Island Lake River, noted for its boiling rapids, chutes, falls, and giant square-tails. See the "Manitoba Travel & Recreation Guide" for map information.

Great White Bears

For thousands of years the solitary polar bear *(Ursus maritimus)*, known to the Eskimos as *Nanook*, has been hunted by the natives of Hudson Bay and respected for its courage, cunning, and great strength. The great white bears hunt and rear their young along the broken line of arctic ice pack and open water from Manitoba's Hudson Bay coastline northward. In 1969 one of the world's largest polar bear

denning areas was discovered in Manitoba between Churchill and the mouth of the Nelson River in the Broad River-Owl River systems in the Hudson Bay Lowlands—a region of extensive muskeg, stunted black spruce, and tamarack with old rolling beaches, ice outcroppings, and bleak tidal flats. These summer denning areas—which offer cool retreats for the bears—went undetected by Eskimos, Crees, and European explorers and fur traders until the recent discovery. Most of the world's population of polar bears are found in Canada; they have been placed on the world list of endangered species by the International Union for Conservation of Nature in Switzerland. Each fall up to 100 bears frequent the Churchill townsite, occasionally wandering into the center of town. The polar bear is an awesomely powerful animal with little fear of man. A mature male may stand 7½ feet and weigh 1,100 pounds or more. The heaviest Canadian bear recorded weighed 1,450 pounds. The world's largest polar bears are found, however, in the Kotzebue area of Alaska. A fascinating and informative study of the polar bear, *The Great White Bears*, by Robert W. Nero, may be obtained free by writing: Department of Mines, Resources, & Environmental Management, Box 9, 989 Century St., Winnipeg R3H 0W4. This beautifully illustrated booklet contains 8 large-format photographs, several in full color, of the bears, and a map showing the polar bears' range and denning areas in Manitoba.

THE GREAT WHITE BEARS

Highways: Recreation & Scenic Routes

Manitoba's outdoor recreation areas are served by well-maintained paved and gravel highways stretching from the Manitoba-United States boundary to Lynn Lake, the province's northernmost settlement 500 miles northwest of Winnipeg. The highway system and scenic routes are shown on the full-color *Manitoba Official Highway Map*, available free from Manitoba Government Travel, 200 Vaughan St., Winnipeg R3C 1T5, which shows all major paved and gravel routes, ports of entry, airports, ferries, town populations, cities and settlements, points of interest, Indian reserves, national and provincial parks, and forest reserves. The map also lists public recreation areas with map location keys, customs border offices, and the locations of Royal Canadian Mounted Police detachments. Detailed information about fishing, hunting, camping, and accommodations along the major highways and recreation routes may be obtained by writing: Tourist Information Office, Legislative Bldg., Winnipeg, or by phoning (204) 946–7131. A free full-color *Topographic Map of Western Canada* may be obtained by writing: Canadian Government Office of Tourism, 150 Kent St., Ottawa, Ont. K1A 0H6. U.S. citizens visiting Canada may be issued a permit for citizen band radio stations licensed in the United States as class D stations. Free license application forms

and regulatory information may be obtained upon request by writing: Regional Director, Telecommunications Regulation Branch, Department of Communication, 2300–1 Lombard Pl., Winnipeg R3B 2Z8. For a complete listing of ferry, bridge, and cruise services, write: Canadian Government Office of Tourism, 150 Kent St., Ottawa, Ont. K1A 0H6, for the free booklet *Canada Ferries, Bridges, & Cruises*. The following Canadian National Topographic Survey Map Kits at a scale of 1:250,000 show the entire lengths and the topography of the surrounding countryside.

Explorers Highroad (10)

This map kit shows the Manitoba segment of this international route north from the Minnesota boundary following Highway 12 and the Trans-Canada Highway northwest to Winnipeg. From Winnipeg, the Explorers Highroad follows the Trans-Canada west to Brandon, where it turns north on Manitoba Highway 12 and winds through Riding Mountain National Park and Duck Mountain and Porcupine provincial forests past Lake Winnipegosis to The Pas. The Highroad runs on from The Pas past Clearwater Provincial Park, Cranberry Portage, and Grass River Provincial Park to Flin Flon, where it swings across the border into Saskatchewan. Canadian National Topographic Survey Maps: Roseau 52-D, Kenora (Ont.) 52-E, Winnipeg 62-H, Brandon 62-G, Neepawa 62-J, Riding Mountain 62-K, Duck Mountain 62-N, Swan Lake 63-G, The Pas 63-F, Cormorant Lake 63-K, Amisk Lake 63-L.

Interlake Highway (6)

This map kit shows Manitoba Highway 6 from Winnipeg north through the scenic Interlake Region, surrounded by Lake Manitoba and Lake Winnipegosis on the west and by Lake Winnipeg on the east, to its junction with wilderness Highway 391 near the remote settlement of Button—named after the explorer Thomas Button, who in 1612–13 searched the far north near the mouth of the Nelson River for a trace of the ill-fated Henry Hudson and for a passage to the Orient. The major features and points of interest along Highway 6 and the Interlake include the Lake Manitoba Narrows, Waterhen Lake and River, Warpath River, Chitek Lake, Cross Lake, Grand Rapids, Limestone Lake, and Minago River. Canadian National Topographic Survey Maps: Winnipeg 62-H, Selkirk 62-I, Neepawa 62-J, Dauphin Lake 62-O, Waterhen Lake 63-B, Grand Rapids 63-G, Wekusko Lake 63-J.

Trans-Canada Highway

This kit shows the entire Manitoba segment of Highway 1, from the Ontario boundary west across the province to Saskatchewan. The major features shown along the route include Shoal Lake, Whiteshell Provincial Park, Agassiz and Sandilands provincial forests, Northwest Angle Provincial Forest, Winnipeg, Portage la Prairie, Spruce Woods Provincial Park and Forest, and the Assiniboine River. Canadian National Topographic Survey Maps: Kenora (Ont.) 52-E, Winnipeg 62-H, Brandon 62-G, Virden 62-F.

Wilderness Highway (391)

This map kit shows the entire length of gravel Highway 391 and the surrounding wilderness of the Canadian Shield from Cranberry Portage north to the mining settlements of Thompson and Lynn Lake past historic exploration and fur trade routes, pine and spruce forests, bogs, large lakes, and granite cliffs. The major features shown along the route include the Grass River canoe route, Snow Lake, Paint Lake provincial recreation area, Nelson House, Granville Lake, Leaf Rapids, Barrington Lake, the Laurie and Keewatin rivers, Southern Indian Lake, and Lynn Lake. The map kit shows the primitive extension from Lynn Lake along Highway 394 to Kinoosao at Reindeer Lake near the

Saskatchewan border. Canadian National Topographic Survey Maps: Cormorant Lake 63-K, Wekusko Lake 63-J, Nelson House 63-O, Uhlman Lake 64-B, Granville Lake 64-C.

Yellowhead Highway

This map kit shows the Manitoba segment of Highway 4 from its origin at Portage la Prairie, northwest across the province to the Saskatchewan boundary. The major features shown along the route include Neepawa and the Fort Ellice Trail, Minnedosa, Riding Mountain National Park, and the Assiniboine River. Canadian National Topographic Survey Maps: Brandon 62-M, Neepawa 62-J, Riding Mountain 62-K.

Hudson's Bay Company Outfitting Posts & Canoe Service

The historic northern supply posts and merchandise stores of the Hudson's Bay Company, known throughout Canada as "the Bay," are located throughout Manitoba's famous wilderness hunting, fishing, and canoe-camping regions. The northern outposts carry food supplies, ammunition, and gear often needed by the wilderness traveler. HBC stores in Manitoba are located at Churchill on Hudson Bay, Brochet on Reindeer Lake, South Indian Lake, Lynn Lake, Split Lake and Gillam on the Nelson River, Nelson House and Thompson on the Burntwood River, Pukatawagan and Leaf Rapids on the Churchill River, Oxford House on the shores of Oxford Lake on the Hayes River, Gods Narrows, Red Sucker Lake, and Shamattawa on Gods River, Rossville and Norway House on Playgreen Lake, Island Lake, Wassagomach and St. Theresa Point, The Pas, Poplar River, and Berens River on the eastern shore of Lake Winnipeg, and Little Grand Rapids in the Atikaki Wilderness. For an *HBC U-Paddle Canoe Rental Service* map and brochure and reservations and information, write: Hudson's Bay Co., Northern Stores Dept., 800 Baker Center, 10025 106th St., Edmonton, Alta. T5J 1G7, or phone (403) 424–8113.

Indian Outfitters—Goose Hunting & Fishing Camps

The Hudson Bay lowlands in northeastern Manitoba are one of the great goose-hunting regions in North America, the habitat of the majestic Canada goose—and the snow goose (known to the Cree Indians as *Wa-Ha*), whose Latin name, *Chen hyperborea*, means "goose beyond the north wind." Here, and in the Nelson, Hayes, and Gods River country to the south, are 4 famous fishing and hunting

outpost camps run by the Cree Indians. The *York Factory Goose Camp*, P.O. Box 1210, Thompson, is on Hudson Bay's west coast near the mouth of the Hayes River. The camp has several cabins with accommodations for 12, with boats, canoes, motors, ammunition, and guides. The facility is inspected annually by the provincial government and is of the highest quality. Package plan includes meals and air service from Winnipeg. The *Masamagoes Lodge*, c/o Dept. of Indian Affairs, Box 1210, Thompson, is a fly-in camp located 450 miles north of Winnipeg at the Red Sucker Rapids on the Gods River. Accommodations include 1 lodge and 5 cabins. The fishing season for brook trout, northern pike, and walleye runs from June through September. The *Churchill Whaler Cooperative* operates two wilderness outpost camps, one at the North Knife River, about 30 miles west of Churchill, and one at the Seal River, approximately 40 miles north. The camps offer excellent fishing for arctic grayling and brook trout, in addition to goose shooting and tundra hunts for swift-flying, explosive ptarmigan. The two camps have full services and accommodate up to 20 guests. The goose season here runs from September through November. The useful booklet *Indian Outfitters of Manitoba* may be obtained free from the Department of Indian Affairs, Gillam.

Manitoba's Great Northern Wilderness Map

If you're planning a trip to the northern Manitoba wilderness, be sure to write for the free 24 × 25-inch *Manitoba North of 53° Map* published by the Tourist Branch, Department of Tourism, Recreation, & Cultural Affairs, Legislative Bldg., Winnipeg R3C 1T5. The map is printed at a scale of 1 inch to 20 miles and shows the locations of all wilderness fly-in hunting and fishing camps, provincial parks, airfields and air water-landing sites, campsites, highways, settlements, and regional airline flight routes. In addition the map shows the routes of Samuel Hearne's expeditions and historic fur trade canoe routes along the Hayes, Bigstone, Fox, Burntwood, and Gods rivers. The seaplane bases and outpost camps shown on the map are located at the remote lake trout, walleye, and northern pike waters of Lakes Molson, Gods, Island, Washahigan, Playgreen, Wintering, Split, Moose Nose, Setting, Wekusko, Waskaiowaka, Southern Indian, Oxford, Brochet Bay of Reindeer Lake, Bain, Munroe, South Knife, Nejanilini, Nueltin, Vandekercove, Eldon, Reed, Athapapuskow, and Cranberry, also York Factory on Hudson Bay and Kettle Rapids on the Hayes River.

North Country Trophy Fishing Lakes & Wild Rivers

The following 1:250,000 scale Canadian National Topographic Survey maps show the major Manitoba trophy lakes (for additional listings, see the "Travel & Recreation Guide" section). *Aikens Lake:* Aikens Lake 52M-3 (1:50,000 scale); *Family & Fishing Lakes:* Deer Lake 53-D, Carroll Lake 52-M; *Kississing Lake:* Kississing 63-N; *Athapapuskow Lake:* Cormorant Lake 63-K; *Southern Indian Lake:* Uhlman Lake 64-B, Big Sand Lake 64-G; *Cochrane River:* Brochet 64-F, Whiskey Jack Lake 64-K, Wollaston Lake 64-L; *Gunisao River:* Norway House 63-H; *Berens River:* Berens River 63-A, Deer Lake 53-D, Carroll Lake 52-M; *Bloodvein River:* Hecla 62-P, Carroll Lake 52-M, Pointe Du Bois 52-L; *Cobham River:* Deer Lake 53-D, Island Lake 53-E, Opasquia Lake 53-F.

Outfitting & Guide Service

Manitoba's important fishing, hunting, and wilderness canoeing areas are well served by competent licensed guides and outfitters. The names and addresses of government-licensed guides may be obtained by writing one of the following regional offices: Regional Director, Northern Region, Box 2550, The Pas R9A 1M4; Regional Director, Western Region, 120 1st Ave. NE, Dauphin R7N 1A5; and Regional Director, Eastern Region, Box 22, 1495 St. James St., Winnipeg. A *Listing of Lodges & Outfitters Catering to Nonresident Moose Hunters* may be obtained by writing: Manitoba Government Travel, 200 Vaughan St., Winnipeg R3C 1T5. The famous moose hunting, goose shooting, fishing, and canoe-camping areas of the province are served by the following outfitting services: *Big John's Landing Outfitting Service*, Grand Rapids R0C 1E0; *Kistum Outfitters*, Box 143, The Pas R9A 1K3; *Sportsmen Expeditions Ltd.*, Box 1821, The Pas R9A 1L5; *Northern Outfitters Ltd.*, 514 McKeen Ave., Flin Flon R8A 1J0, with complete canoe-outfitting service as well as guided hunting and fly-in fishing package for northern pike, walleye, and lake trout. *Flin Flon Outfitters*, Box 101, Flin Flon, has complete outfitting, fly-in service, and package hunting and fishing trips. *Sharron's Outfitting Service*, Sherridon R0B 1L0, is at Kississing Lake and outfits fall moose hunting trips. Most lodges, resorts, and wilderness camps in northern Manitoba provide guide service. *Churchill River Outfitters*, Leaf Rapids, offers boats, motors, and guided fly-in fishing trips on the Churchill River system. If, however, you require other guiding service, the following associations can provide trained, licensed guides: *Cranberry Portage Guide Association*, contact D. S. Michelle, Cranberry Portage R0B 0H0; *Moose Lake Guide Association*, contact V. J. Martin, Moose Lake R0B 0Y0; and *Grand Rapids Guide Association*, contact Mr. A. Cook, Grand Rapids R0C 1E0. Outfitting services in central Manitoba are provided by *Big Rock Fishing & Hunting*, St. Martin R0C 2T0, at Lake St. Martin; *Lake St. Martin Tourist Camp*, Gypsumville R0C 1J0; *Anderson's Outfitting Service*, Box 91, Gypsumville R0C 1J0, at Dauphin River, with guided trips to Mantagao, Warpath and Jumping rivers, and Lynx Harbor; *Hunter's Outfitting Service*, Dauphin River, Box 71, Gypsumville R0C 1J0; and *Sturgeon Bay Outfitting Service*, Gypsumville R0C 1J0. For licensed guide info write: *Interlake Guide Association*, contact Mr. K. Desjarlais, Deer Horn R0C 0T0.

Railway Services & the Hudson Bay Line

Manitoba's 251,000 square miles are crisscrossed by the main lines of the Canadian Pacific and Canadian National Railway systems serving Winnipeg, Portage la Prairie, and Brandon, and by Canadian National

lines from Winnipeg to the northern regions of the province through Dauphin and The Pas to Thompson and Churchill on Hudson Bay, via the old Hudson Bay Railway line now operated by the Canadian National Railway. The Hudson Bay line runs through the heart of northern Manitoba's boreal forests and Canadian Shield country past some of the best lake trout, walleye, and northern pike lakes, brook trout rivers, moose hunting areas, and wilderness canoe routes in the province. The CNR Hudson Bay line knifes through the iron-ribbed wilderness of the shield for 510 miles from The Pas to the historic northern port of Churchill; it is often used by fishermen, hunters, and wilderness paddlers as an alternative to the more expensive air charter fly-in. The Hudson Bay line will drop you off along with your gear and canoes and pick you up at any point on the line. Just wave with a shirt or piece of cloth and she'll pull to a stop. The major wilderness recreation areas and settlements along the line include Setting Lake and Halfway River, Wintering Lake, Grass River canoe route, Thompson, Moose Nose Lake, Nelson and Kettle rivers, Weir River, and the famous goose hunting lowlands surrounding Hudson Bay at Churchill. The Canadian National Railway line running between The Pas and Lynn Lake is another route often used by moose hunters, canoeists, and fishermen en route to Kississing Lake, Pukatawagan Lake and the Churchill River, Laurie River, Anson Lake, and the Huges River. For info and rates write: Canadian National Railways, Depot Ticket Office, Broadway & Main, Winnipeg; Canadian Pacific Railway, Ticket Office, 181 Higgins Ave., Winnipeg.

Riding Mountain National Park

This famous recreation and nature reserve encompasses 1,150 square miles of evergreen and hardwood forests, prairies, rolling hills, valleys, and lakes and streams on a rolling plateau that forms part of the Manitoba Escarpment, some 60 miles north of Brandon. The western-most sections of the park are covered by meadows and windswept grasslands. The *Riding Mountain National Park Map* (MCR-207) may be purchased for $1 from the Canada Map Office or from the park office. The map shows the location of wardens' cabins, lookout towers, woodlands, marshlands, bogs and open muskeg, elevations, and the declination of the compass needle. The *Riding Mountain National Park Map-Brochure* is available free from the Superintendent's Office, Riding Mountain National Park, Wasagaming R0J 2H0; it shows natural and man-made features and contains a useful description of the park's topography and recreation facilities. Several useful guides and booklets may also be obtained free by writing the Superintendent's Office: the 20-page *Cross-Country Skiing & Snowshoeing Guide* describes the several ski touring trails and contains detailed topographic maps showing the trail heads and routes; the 30-page *Western Canada National Parks Accommodations Guide* provides descriptions and addresses of the park campgrounds and resort lodges; The *Mammals, Birds, Reptiles, & Amphibians* checklist guides will prove useful to the naturalist and backpacker; the 16-page *Riding Mountain National Park Trail Guide* contains maps and descriptions of the Ominnik Marsh, Clear Lake, Loon's Island, Arrowhead, Brulé, Grey Owl, Escarpment, Muskrat Lake, Kelwood, Gorge, Packhorse Creek, Moon Lake, and Cowan Lake trails.

Riding Mountain Park is well known for the deep, cold northern pike, walleye, and lake trout waters of Clear Lake. Rainbow trout and brookies inhabit Lake Katherine and Deep Lake. The park's wildlife population includes black bear, elk, moose, whitetail deer, and bison. A network of hiking and riding trails provides access to the remote interior camping areas. The Escarpment Trail winds along the crest of the Manitoba Escarpment for 40 miles past scenic creeks, beaver meadows, and high country ridges. Campgrounds are located at scenic

areas in the park and range from fully serviced to primitive wilderness sites. Wasagaming Campground has 86 fully serviced sites for trailers and 395 unserviced sites. Lake Katherine Campground has 118 unserviced sites. Group camping areas are located at Camp Manito and

Camp Kippechewin—an unserviced tenting camp. Other sites are located at Moon Lake, Lake Audy, Whirlpool Lake, Glen Beag, Birches, Spruce, Aspen, Firth Beach, Clear Spring, Dead Ox Creek, and Grayling Lake. The Wasagaming service center near the park entrance contains a wide range of cabins, motels, and lodges.

The Pas Wilderness Outfitting Center

(Pop. 6,062). This famous fishing, hunting, and wilderness canoe-outfitting center is in northwest Manitoba on Explorers Highroad 10, due south of the Clearwater Provincial Park and Cormorant Provincial Forest, on the bank of the Saskatchewan River. A Hudson's Bay post was established here in 1775. The Pas is an abbreviation of the old French Fort Basquia or Pascoyac, which was located nearby. A cairn here honors Henry Kelsey, the Hudson's Bay Company fur trader and explorer who traveled inland from York Factory to the Saskatchewan River via The Pas. Kelsey was known to his Assiniboine Indian companions as *Miss-Top-Ashish*, the "little giant of the prairies." The Pas sponsors the northern Manitoba trappers' festival, one of the most important events in Manitoba, featuring a 150-mile dogsled race. The town is surrounded by one of the finest wilderness fishing and hunting regions in Manitoba. Clearwater Provincial Park lies in the heart of the wilderness, embracing 147,000 acres. Clearwater Lake, known to the Indians as Atikameg, is one of the three clearest lakes in the world and is deservedly famous for its trophy-sized lake trout. Bush pilots have reported being able to see pebbles on the lake's bottom from an altitude of 1,500 feet. Cormorant Lake Provincial Forest adjoins Clearwater Park on the north. The country from The Pas east to the Summerbury River marshes and mud flats is an excellent moose hunting, and duck and goose shooting, area. Other major features in the region include the famous fishing waters of Namew, Root, Rocky, Reader, Saskeram, and Kelsey lakes and the Carrot River. Lodging, guides, and outfitting services are provided by the following provincial park fishing and hunting resorts, all on Clearwater Lake: *Evergreen Lodge*, Box 1796, The Pas R9A 1L5; *Clearwater Lodge*, Box 695, The Pas R9A 1K7; and *Vickery's Lodge*, Box 756, The Pas R9A 1K8, with lodge-owned aircraft for fly-in fishing and hunting trips. Clearwater

Provincial Park and Cormorant Provincial Forest are shown on Canadian National Topographic Survey Maps: The Pas 63-F, Grand Rapids 63-G, Cormorant Lake 63-K, Wekusko Lake 63-J.

Wilderness Travel Guides

All who plan to travel through Manitoba's wilderness country should write the Department of Mines, Resources, & Environmental Management for their useful wildlife and nature guides. These booklets, which may be obtained free by writing: Box 9, 989 Century St., Winnipeg R3H 0W4, should prove of equal interest to the hiker, camper, canoeist, fisherman, and hunter. The 66-page *Field Guide to the Native Trees of Manitoba* provides illustrations and descriptions of all 24 of the province's native trees. The 26-page *Manitoba Wildflowers* booklet contains full-color photographs and descriptions of blue flag, showy lady's-slipper, fringed gentian, bunchberry, wild rose, prairie crocus, bog laurel, hoary puccoon, Indian pipe, pitcher plant, wild bergamot, Labrador tea, and prairie lily. The 18-page guide *Some Edible & Poisonous Berries* describes Alberta, Saskatchewan, and Manitoba berries which the wilderness traveler is likely to come in contact with, with line drawings of each plant. The handy guide *Mushroom Collecting for Beginners* points out important differences between edible and poisonous mushrooms. The booklets *Birds Protected in Canada* and *Endangered Wildlife in Canada* describe and list all bird species protected under federal law and the various species that are in danger of becoming extinct. The beautifully illustrated booklet *A Glimpse of Wild Nature* provides an intimate study of the life-styles of the screech owl, osprey, short-eared owl, great gray owl, and peregrine falcon.

Wolves of the Great North Woods

Few animals captured the imagination of the northern Indians and explorers and so well symbolize the great north woods as the caribou wolves and timber wolves of the northern coniferous forest. At one time the wolves' range in North America stretched from Mexico to the Arctic Ocean. Today, however, wolves are extinct in Mexico and much of the United States except for Alaska and a few northern regions in Minnesota, Wisconsin, and Michigan, and for the smaller red wolf *(Canis niger)* found in some southern states. In Canada's interior fur-trapping areas there are probably more wolves today than during the days of the voyageurs. Many of the Indians' and white men's legends and fear of this gray ghost of the north woods stem from their elusiveness. Woodsmen have lived for years in north country regions where wolf and its sign are abundant without ever having seen one. Today, with our ever diminishing wilderness, to hear the lonely howl of a wolf in the wild country is a memory to be treasured. A fascinating guide to the wolves of Manitoba, *The Wild Dogs*, may be obtained free by writing: Department of Mines, Resources, & Environmental Management, Box 9, 989 Century St., Winnipeg R3H 0W4. The booklet is illustrated with paintings, drawings, and unfinished studies from the sketchbooks of the wildlife artist Clarence Tillenius.

Manitoba has two subspecies of wolves, the timber wolf *(Canis lupus knightii)* and caribou wolf *(Canis lupus hudsonicus)*. The caribou wolf is the most plentiful, ranging across thousands of square miles of boreal forests, mostly north of the 58th parallel, that serve as the wintering grounds for the Manitoba-Keewatin barren-ground caribou herd. Caribou wolves are large, averaging about 100 pounds, and range in color from black to pure white. One wolf caught in the far north of Manitoba is reported to have tipped the scales at 175 pounds. The great northern explorer Samuel Hearne observed during his journey to the Coppermine River and the northern ocean that hungry wolves often followed the Indian guides for several days, but always kept at a distance. The wolves were mortal enemies to the Indian dogs and would frequently kill and devour those that were heavily loaded and could not keep up with the team. Hearne observed that the northern Indians would never kill a wolf, believing that it possessed supernatural

powers. The Indians believed that the wolf never ate its meat raw but possessed a power to cook the meat without fire (!). The timber wolf is found in the heavier timbered areas of the province and is such a rarity that in the 1920s a wolf shot in the Porcupine Mountains was put on display in a store window at Birch River. The timber wolf's range is usually 50 to 60 square miles, which must provide him with enough big game to keep him alive. Timber wolves have been known to travel as far as 60 miles in a day in search of a moose. The wolf's competence as a master hunter has been greatly exaggerated; he will rarely chase any animal unless the chance of success is very high. The wolf usually preys upon the older, sickly, or wounded animals. The Indian knew well that the caribou kept the wolves strong and that the wolves kept the caribou strong by killing off the weaker members of the herd.

MANITOBA TRAVEL & RECREATION GUIDE

Atikaki Wilderness

Atikaki Wilderness Topo Maps

Canadian National Topographic Survey Maps, scale 1:250,000: Berens River 63-A, Deer Lake 53-D, Hecla 62-P, Carroll Lake 52-M, Pointe du Bois 52-L.

Poplar River Country

Canadian National Topographic Survey Maps, scale 1:250,000: Berens River 63-A, Deer Lake 53-D.

Sasaginnigak Canoe Country

Canadian National Topographic Survey Maps, scale 1:250,000: Berens River 63-A, Deer Lake 53-D, Hecla 62-P, Carroll Lake 53-M, Selkirk 62-I, Pointe du Bois 52-L.

The Atikaki Wilderness area stretches eastward from the shoreline of Lake Winnipeg to the Ontario boundary, dominated by the rugged boreal forests and granite outcroppings of the Canadian Shield. This huge remote region, accessible only by charter aircraft or canoe and portage, is completely roadless and has only two settlements: one at Berens River and one at Little Grand Rapids, on the western shore of Family Lake. The Atikaki Wilderness is a top-ranked moose hunting zone and fly-in fishing region for trophy-sized lake trout, northern pike, and walleye in Sasaginnigak, Aikens, Dogskin, Family, Moar, Fishing, and Harrop lakes.

Lodging, guides, outfitting, and meals are provided by several fly-in hunting and fishing camps. *Aiken's Lake Lodge*, P.O. Box 20, Pine Falls, has 7 cabins and 4 motel units with a capacity of 30 people, with an outpost camp located at No Name Lake for brook trout fishing. *Sasaginnigak Lodge*, Box 72, Arnes, has 7 housekeeping cabins on the shore of Sasaginnigak Lake with outpost camps located at Charron and Apisko lakes. *Dogskin Lake Lodge*, Box 157, Lac du Bonnet R0E 1A0, has 17 units to accommodate 40 guests. An all-inclusive package plan includes meals, lodging, boat and motor, guide, fish processing, and air transportation from Lac du Bonnet and Winnipeg. *Little Grand Rapids Lodge*, Box 403, Winnipeg R3C 2H6, maintains a lodge and two housekeeping cabins with accommodations for 16 guests. The lodge is adjacent to a 2,400-foot government airstrip. A fishing package includes air transportation from Winnipeg and return. *Norse Lodge*, Box 37, Winnipeg R3C 2G1, is on Moar Lake with 10 cabins and fishing for lake trout, northern pike, and walleye. *Fishing Lake Lodge*, Box 403, Winnipeg R3C 2H6, has 9 cabins on famous Fishing Lake, home of Manitoba's record 41-pound northern pike. An all-inclusive hunting package is available which includes air transportation from Winnipeg and return. *Harrop Lake Lodge* has 4 housekeeping cabins with fly-out service from base camp to surrounding wilderness fishing and hunting areas. For info write: R. Polinuk, 504 Sutherland Ave., Selkirk R1A 0M7.

The remote wild rivers of the Atikaki Wilderness are among the most challenging canoe routes in the province. The historic Sasaginnigak canoe country flows through this spruce and pine logging and Indian trapping country with numerous rapids, falls, portages, Indian rock paintings, scenic channels, island-dotted lakes, beaver dams, trapper's cabins, old fishing camps and Indian graves, and forestry stations found along the canoe routes. The Sasaginnigak canoe route follows the Broadleaf, Gammon, Bloodvein, Sasaginnigak, Dogskin, and Leyand rivers, part of the Wanipigow River, and dozens of lakes including Wallace, Aikens, Sasaginnigak, Carroll, Family, and Fishing lakes. The southernmost portion of the route may be reached by the gravel Provincial Road 304, which provides access to the Wanipigow River

and Wallace Lake. The Kautunigan canoe route starts at Wallace Lake and proceeds down the Wanipigow and Broadleaf rivers to Aikens Lake, down the Gammon and Bloodvein rivers up to Cabin Point, up the Sasaginnigak River to Sasaginnigak Lake, to Shining Falls Pass, through Family Lake past Little Grand Rapids Indian settlement (which includes a forestry station, general stores, and a nursing station), and down the Berens River to its mouth at the Berens River Indian Reservation on Lake Winnipeg. The Kautunigan route is a good 3-week journey covering some 300 miles. The rugged Little Grand Rapids canoe route follows the Pigeon River for about 110 miles, the Berens River for about 80 miles, and the Poplar and Assinika rivers for about 160 miles. Completely outfitted and guided canoe trips in the Atikaki Wilderness are provided by *Sasaginnigak Trippers Ltd.*, Box 9, G.P. 384, RR3, Winnipeg R3C 2E7. Good camping spots are found along this route. The southernmost portion of the Atikaki Wilderness is served by the *Wanipigow Lake Campground*, 15 miles east of Manigotagan, with 40 unserviced sites; the *Caribou Landing Campground*, 11 miles southeast of Bissett Road, with canoe rentals and 30 unserviced sites; and the *Wallace Lake Campground*, some 17 miles east of Bissett, with supplies, gear, and 60 unserviced sites.

Great Northern Wilderness

Churchill River & Indian Lakes Country
Canadian National Topographic Survey Maps, scale 1:250,000: Kississing 63-N, Granville Lake 64-C, Uhlman Lake 64-B, Big Sand Lake 64-G, Northern Indian Lake 64-H, Herchmer 54-E, Churchill 54-L.

Gods Lake & River
Canadian National Topographic Survey Maps, scale 1:250,000: Oxford House 53-L, Gods River 53-N, Hayes River 54-C.

Grass River Provincial Park & Canoe Route
Canadian National Topographic Survey Maps, scale 1:250,000: Cormorant Lake 63-K, Wekusko Lake 63-J, Nelson House 63-O, Sipiwesk 63-P, Split Lake 64-A.

Island Lake & River
Canadian National Topographic Survey Maps, scale 1:250,000: Island Lake 53-E, Opasquia Lake 53-F, Oxford House 53-L.

Middle Track & Hayes River Country
Canadian National Topographic Survey Maps, scale 1:250,000: Grand Rapids 63-G, Wekusko Lake 63-J, Cross Lake 63-I, Oxford House 53-L, Knee Lake 53-M, Gods River 53-N, Hayes River 54-C.

Molson Lake & River
Canadian National Topographic Survey Maps, scale 1:250,000: Cross Lake 63-I, Oxford House 53-L.

Nueltin Lake & "The Great Fish" River
Canadian National Topographic Survey Maps, scale 1:250,000: Kasmere Lake 54-N, Munroe Lake 64-O, Nueltin Lake 65-B, Edehon Lake 65-A, Hyde Lake 55-D.

Red Sucker Lake & River
Canadian National Topographic Survey Maps, scale 1:250,000: Stull Lake 53-K, Gods River 53-N.

Seal River System
Canadian National Topographic Survey Maps, scale 1:250,000: Whiskey Jack Lake 64-K, Kasmere Lake 64-N, Munroe Lake 64-O, Tadoule Lake 64-J, Shethanei Lake 64-I, Churchill 54-L, Caribou River 54-M.

South Knife Lake & River
Canadian National Topographic Survey Maps, scale 1:250,000, includes the North Knife River and Lake: Northern Indian Lake 64-H, Shethanei Lake 64-I, Churchill 54-L.

Wolverine River & Nejanilini Lake
Canadian National Topographic Survey Maps, scale 1:250,000: Munroe Lake 64-O, Nejanilini Lake 64-P.

Northern Manitoba's vast boreal forests, wild rivers, and thousands of remote blue lakes, many of them as yet unnamed, form one of the finest fishing, hunting, and wilderness canoe-camping regions in Canada. Here hard-rock miners, fishermen, Indian trappers, woodsmen, and bush pilots travel through one of the few remaining pioneering regions in North America. The famous outfitting and supply centers of The Pas, Cranberry Portage, Flin Flon, Norway House, Thompson, Lynn Lake, and Churchill or Hudson Bay provide access to the remote fish and game areas. Manitoba's northern region is dominated by the world-famous northern pike, lake trout, and walleye waters of the powerful Nelson River system and the remote big-lake chains formed by the Churchill, Grass, Hayes, Red Sucker, and Gods rivers. The immense wildlands north of the Churchill River, the hunting and trapping grounds of the Cree Indians, contain virgin evergreen forests, vast moose bogs, and countless lakes and waterways, dominated by the arctic char, grayling, and lake trout waters of deep, cold Nueltin Lake, which sprawls across the Manitoba-Northwest Territories boundary,

and by the wild Cochrane, Caribou, Seal, Wolverine, and North and South Knife rivers.

There are far north wilderness fly-in fishing camps at Nueltin, Bain, Munroe, Nijamiliou, and South Knife lakes. The *Bain Lake Lodge,* Box 1152, Lynn Lake, has a main lodge and 4 cabins with complete services and guides for lake trout, grayling, and northern pike fishing. An inclusive package plan, including meals, lodging, boat, motor, gas, and guide is provided with air transportation from Lynn Lake. Open from June 1 to September 7 to the northeast of Bain Lake and the Seal River is the *Blue Chip Lodge,* on Munroe Lake. The lodge has full services and 3 cabins which accommodate 12 guests. For info and rates write: A. Kacy, 8010 Holmes Ave., Detroit, MI 48210. Northeast as the crow flies from Munroe Lake, at the headwaters of the wild Wolverine River, is the *Nejalini Lodge,* at Caribou Settlement on the shore of Little Duck and Nejalini lakes, surrounded by the taiga and eskers of the Canadian Shield. The Nejalini Lodge has a dining-room lodge, 4-room cabins to accommodate 16 people, and fish-processing facilities. An all-inclusive package plan includes air charter from Winnipeg and return via Gods River Lodge. For info and rates write: Box 714, Winnipeg R3C 2K3. The famous trophy lake trout waters of island-dotted Nueltin Lake, located in the heart of Manitoba's caribou and wolf country, are served by the *Treeline Lodge,* operated by Sportsmen Expeditions Ltd., Box 1821, The Pas R9A 1L5. Services include canoe rental and complete outfitting, with air charter from Lynn Lake (Manitoba's northernmost mining town) to Nueltin. Far

to the southeast of Nueltin Lake, at the headwaters of the famous South Knife River, is the *South Knife Lake Lodge.* There is one main lodge here, with 2 cabins to accommodate 16 people. Its package plan includes all services, plus air charter from Churchill. The South Knife River is one of the province's top producers of arctic grayling and char.

Anyone planning a solo canoe trip into this far north wilderness should bear in mind that this is an isolated remote region with no roads or settlements; only wild twisting rivers, caribou trails, glacial debris, mile upon mile of winding eskers, and huge complex lakes with hundreds of islands, points, bays, and coves. This "land of little sticks," seldom traveled since Samuel Hearne's visit to the shores of Nueltin Lake in 1770, is a beckoning challenge to the experienced wilderness paddler. Nueltin Lake forms the major headwaters of the infamous Thlewiaza or "Great Fish" River—one of the Far North's great wild rivers.

The historic Churchill River system, which generally marks the southernmost migration of the Manitoba-Keewatin caribou herd, flows northeast from Saskatchewan through a series of huge, clearwater lakes, and the wildlands of the Canadian Shield, to its mouth at Churchill on Hudson Bay. The major features shown on the Churchill River Map Kit include Pukatawagan Lake, Highrock Lake, the Laurie River canoe route, and the huge chain of trophy lake trout, northern pike, and walleye waters formed by Granville and Southern and Northern Indian lakes. The Churchill is one of Manitoba's finest producers of large northern pike and, in its lower reaches, of arctic char. The

140-mile-long Churchill River canoe route from Pukatawagan Falls to the Upper Twin may be reached by the Canadian National Railway from The Pas or Cranberry Portage to Pukatawagan Station. The canoeist should keep in mind that the Churchill has been known to rise as much as 4 feet overnight and should select his campsite accordingly. Due west of Granville Lake is the Laurie Lake and River, home of the Manitoba record 12-pound rainbow trout and large lake trout. The *Laurie River Lodge* has 4 cabins, with guided moose hunting trips and a fishing package which includes air transportation from Lynn Lake and return. For info and rates write: 3012 Silver Lake Rd., Minneapolis, MN 55418 (winter address), or Box 550, Lynn Lake R0B 0W0 (summer address). The *Wolverine Lodge*, Box 568, Lynn Lake R0B 0W0, is on Vandekercove Lake, with 5 cabins to accommodate 30 guests and fishing for lake trout, walleye, and northern pike.

The Pas, Cranberry Portage, and Flin Flon country, located due south of the Pukatawagan Falls area of the Churchill River, is one of Manitoba's premier fishing, moose and waterfowl hunting, and wilderness canoeing regions. Lake trout to 60 pounds, northern pike to 36 pounds, and walleye in the 10-pound range are caught in the deep, clear waters of Athapapuskow, Kississing, Squall, Snow, Wekusko, Setting, Elbow, Reed, and Cranberry lakes. Grass River Provincial Park, located just east of Flin Flon and Cranberry Portage, encompasses 565,000 acres of boreal forests and lakes in the heart of the Precambrian Shield country. The wilderness reserve is dominated by the famous headwater lakes of the Grass River canoe route, which flows for some 450 miles through the historic "Pays du Rat"—Muskrat country—of the voyageurs from Cranberry Portage to Paint, south of the mining and outfitting settlement of Thompson. The major features along this rugged, incredibly scenic wilderness waterway include the Cranberry Lakes, Reed Lake, the Tramping Lake petrographs, Wekusko Lake (Cree Indian word meaning "sweet grass or herb"), Setting Lake, Paint and Wintering lakes, and numerous falls and rapids, including the 18-foot Kanisota Falls, Pisew (one Indian word for "Lynx") Falls, the Thicket and Cross Portages, and several trapper's cabins and Indian cemeteries. The famous Tramping Lake petrographs are red ocher paintings of humans, snakes, fish, birds, and moose found on granite outcroppings along the northwest shore. Camping facilities, boats, canoes, motors, and guides in Grass River Provincial Park are provided by the *Viking Lodge* and *Caribou Lodge*, both at First Cranberry Lake, Cranberry Portage R0B 0H0.

Several renowned fishing and hunting camps are located at trophy fishing lakes in the region, surrounded by scenic spruce and pine forests and rugged granite cliffs and outcroppings of the shield. The *Overflowing River Sport & Tourist Camp*, Box 576, The Pas R9A 1K6, offers guided fishing and hunting and charter lake cruises. Famous Lake Athapapuskow is served by the *Ptarmigan Lodge*, Cranberry Portage R0B 0H0; *Athapap Lodge*, Cranberry Portage, with outpost camps located on the Churchill River and File Lake; *Constable's Lakeside Lodge*, Box 308, Flin Flon R8A 1N1, with a fly-in outpost fishing camp; *Tonepah Lodge*, Cranberry Portage R0B 0H0; *Pine Point Lodge*, Box 354, Flin Flon R8A 1N1; and *New Paradise Lodge*, Box 777, Flin Flon R8A 1N6 (summer), or Box 1750, Aspen, CO 81611 (winter), 14 miles north of Cranberry Portage. Wilderness fishing and hunting camps in Grass River Provincial Park include the *Caribou Lodge* and *Viking Lodge* at First Cranberry Lake; *Elbow Lake Lodge*, Cranberry Portage R0B 0H0, and *Ashdown Camp*, Cranberry Portage R0B 0H0, both at Elbow Lake; *Mistik Lodge*, Cranberry Portage, on Payuk Lake on the Mistik Creek canoe route; *Flintoba Lodge*, Box 98, Flin Flon R8A 1M6, at Bakers Narrows; the *Westwood Lodge*, Box 66, Flin Flon R8A 1M6, at Lake Manistikwan, with hunting and outfitting service, and an outpost camp at Kisseynew Lake; *Grass River Lodge*, Box 1680, The Pas R9A 1L5, on Reed Lake,

with outpost camps located on Morton and File lakes by short portage; and *Reed Lake Lodge*, Box 1648, The Pas R9A 1L4, on Four Mile Island 4 miles from the government dock on Reed Lake. Wilderness fly-in hunting and fishing lodging and guide service at the famous northern pike, lake trout, and walleye waters of Kississing Lake is provided by *Kississing Lake Redwood Lodge*, c/o Neil Knight, Sherridon R0B 1L0, and *Glunz's Kississing Lodge*, 1420 Renaissance Dr., Park Ridge, IL 60068, with complete outfitting service and canoe trips, and outpost fly-in camps on Hassett, Kisseynew, and Gwilliam lakes.

East of The Pas and Grass River Provincial Park are the Lake Winnipeg headwaters of northern Manitoba's two greatest rivers: the Nelson and the Hayes. The Nelson is a big, awe-inspiring river which flows from Playgreen Lake at Norway House through Pipestone, Cross, Sipiwesk, and Split lakes to its mouth at Hudson Bay, due east of York Factory. The Nelson is an extremely dangerous river and should be attempted only by the experienced canoeman. The Middle Track and Hayes River canoe route is a 1,255-mile journey from The Pas going downstream via the Middle Track to York Factory and returning upstream via the Hayes River route to The Pas. The Middle Track route follows the Summersberry River through South Moose Lake to the Minago River through Hill, Drunken, Cross, Rabbit, and Cotton lakes, and continues along the Bigstone River through Bear and Bigstone lakes to the Fox and Hayes rivers. The historic Hayes River route between Norway House and York Factory is an exciting, never-to-be-forgotten journey through virgin wilderness. Major features shown on the Hayes River map include the Echimamish River (from a Cree Indian word meaning "water flowing both ways") and Oxford, Knee, and Swampy lakes. Norway House, at Playgreen Lake, may be reached in summer by plane from Winnipeg. Supplies must be taken on at Oxford House, the last outpost on the way to York Factory. The return trip can be via chartered plane on the Hudson Bay Railway, which crosses the Limestone River about 70 miles from the mouth of the Nelson River. The canoe trip around Marak Point, the peninsula which divides the Hayes and Nelson rivers, must be made against a 4-knot tide. On clear days seals, beluga whales, and polar bears may be observed, as well as various old shipwrecks in the old port of Nelson. Fishing along the Hayes and Nelson River lake chains and tributaries is generally good to excellent for lake trout, walleye, and northern pike—and for brook trout in the world-famous Gods River and Island Lake River country. There are fly-in fishing camps at Molson, Island, and Gods lakes and Gods River. The *Washakigan Lodge*, c/o Sportrip, Inc., 1106 W. Market St., York, PA 17404, operates an outpost camp on Beach Lake, with an inclusive fishing package that includes air transportation from Winnipeg. The *Bolton Lake Lodge*, c/o C. & W. Wood, St. Theresa Point R0B 1J0, has accommodations for 14, including guides, fish processing, and air transportation. Famous Molson Lake, at the headwaters of the Hayes River, is served by *Molson Lake Lodge*, Box 493, West Fargo, ND 58078, (701) 282-7154. The lodge is a fly-in affair, 45 minutes northeast of Norway House at the head of Lake Winnipeg, with first-class services and accommodations. The camp also outfits fall moose hunting trips. Molson Lake is deep, clear and holds record-sized northern pike, lake trout, and walleye.

For additional information on Manitoba's Great Northern Wilderness, see "Gods Lake & River Trophy Trout Country," "Indian Outfitters—Goose Hunting & Fishing Camps," and "Manitoba's Great Northern Wilderness Map" in the "Encyclopedia" section.

Access & Outfitting Centers

Outfitters, guides, supplies, and accommodations north of Manitoba's 53d parallel are located at The Pas, Cranberry Portage, Flin Flon,

Norway House, Oxford House, Churchill, Thompson, and Lynn Lake. Access is via scheduled and charter aircraft or by Provincial Highways 10 and 391.

Interlake Fish & Game Region

Interlake Topo Maps

Canadian National Topographic Survey Maps, scale 1:250,000: Selkirk 62-I, Neepawa 62-J, Hecla 62-P, Dauphin Lake 62-O, Berens River 63-A, Waterhen Lake 63-B, Grand Rapids 63-G.

Lake Manitoba Narrows

Canadian National Topographic Survey Maps, scale 1:50,000: Ebb and Flow 62O-2, Alonsa 62J-15.

Manitoba's Interlake country is a vast region of lakes, rivers, evergreen forests, and world-famous waterfowl marshes between Lake Winnipeg on the east and Lakes Manitoba and Winnipegosis on the west. The rivers emptying into Lake Manitoba and the Narrows—the waterway connecting the northern and southern sections of the lake—are renowned for record-sized walleyes. The Interlake region's other premier northern pike and walleye waters include the Dauphin River and Lake St. Martin, Dog Lake, Mantagao River, Reedy Lake and Warpath River, St. George Lake, Waterhen Lake and River, Chitek, Sisib, Kawinaw, Katimik, and Beaverdam lakes, and Cross Lake and the Saskatchewan River at Grand Rapids. The entire Lake Winnipeg basin, particularly the great Nettey Marshes at the south end of the lake, the marshes on Hecla Island, and the world-famous Delta Marsh, located at the southern end of Lake Manitoba, are among the finest waterfowl hunting areas on the continent. Moose and black bear roam the remote, sparsely settled regions of the Interlake.

The incredibly scenic Grindstone provincial recreation area and Hecla Provincial Park are located in the southern portion of Lake Winnipeg. Hecla Park encompasses some 200,000 acres on Hecla, Black, and Deer islands. This beautiful, seldom visited reserve is described in the full-color 32-page booklet *Hecla*, available free from the Tourist Branch, Department of Recreation, Tourism, & Cultural Affairs, Legislative Bldg., Winnipeg. Hecla Island, once known as New Iceland, is today largely uninhabited, with cleared fields giving way in the

interior to dense forests of spruce, aspen, balsam, jack pine, and tamarack mingled with vagrant stands of birch and poplar. To the south the pastures and forests give way to reedy island marshes, which are inhabited during the summer months by some 50,000 ducks, Canada geese, and snow and blue geese. Other wildlife found on Hecla includes moose, deer, badger, fisher, lynx, black bear, cougar, beaver, and muskrat. The breathtaking beauty of Hecla's granite and limestone cliff-lined shores offers some of the finest camping and wilderness hiking opportunities in the province. The *Gull Harbor Lodge*, on Provincial gravel Road 233 on Hecla Island, has 4 housekeeping units with fishing and hunting for waterfowl and upland game birds. The *Gull Harbor Campground* is on the northern tip of Hecla Island, with 118 unserviced sites. Year-round full service facilities on Manitoba's wilderness island are provided by the beautiful *Gull Harbor Resort Hotel*, General Delivery, Riverton R0C 2R0.

Hunting and fishing resorts providing accommodations, supplies, guides, and outfitting services are located at the important Interlake fish and game areas. The *Lake Manitoba Narrows Lodge*, c/o P. Stasiuk, Oakview R0C 2K0, has 7 housekeeping cabins, with boat and motor rentals. At the famous Delta Marsh, *Hextall's Shooting Lodge*, on Provincial Road 430, has 8 rooms in the main lodge and 2 cabins, with canoe and decoy rentals and guide service. For information write: Bryan Hestall, Poplar Point R0H 0Z0. The *Anama Bay Tourist Camp*, Box 15, Gypsumville R0C 1J0, is on the Dauphin River with 6 housekeeping cottages and 35 unserviced campsites. At Lake St. George, the *White Birch Lodge*, Dallas R0C 0S0, has 4 housekeeping units with outfitting services. In the Grand Rapids and Saskatchewan River region, the *Moak Lodge* has 6 units with boats, canoes, and guide service. For info write: Northern Diver Resort, Grand Rapids R0C 1E0. *River View Cabins*, Grand Rapids R0C 1E0, has 6 housekeeping cabins with boat rental and guide service. *Pine Grove Cabins*, Grand Rapids R0C 1E0, is located at the famous northern pike and walleye waters of Cross Lake, formed by a widening of the Saskatchewan River, with outpost camps at Sugar Island and Cedar Lake.

Access & Outfitting Centers

The primary access routes in the Interlake Region include Provincial Highways 6, 7, 8, and 9. Accommodations, supplies, guides, and outfitting service are available at Moosehorn, Gypsumville, Meadow Portage, Easterville, and Grand Rapids.

Winnipeg River Country

Whiteshell Provincial Park

Canadian National Topographic Survey Maps, scale 1:50,000: Waugh 52E-11, McMunn 52E-12, Caddy Lake 52E-14, Whitemouth 52E-13, Crow Duck Lake 52L-3, Pinawa 52L-4, Ryerson Lake 52L-6, Pointe du Bois 52L-5.

Winnipeg River Canoe Route

Canadian National Topographic Survey Maps, scale 1:50,000: Crow Duck Lake 52L-3, Ryerson Lake 52L-6, Pinawa 52L-4, Molson 62I-1, Lac du Bonnet 62I-8, Pointe du Bois 52L-5, Pine Falls 62I-9.

The historic Winnipeg River, once the most majestic main-line fur trade canoe route of the voyageurs between Lake Superior and Lake Athabasca, dominates this southeastern corner of the province. Today, with its power harnessed by several power dams, the Winnipeg is more famous for its outstanding northern pike and walleye fishing than as a wilderness canoe route. The Winnipeg rises in Lake of the Woods near Kenora, Ontario, and sweeps northwesterly in a giant arc, picking up the waters of the English River system and flowing through the

northernmost portion of Whiteshell Provincial Park to Seven Sisters Falls, where it turns northward and broadens to form Lac du Bonnet in a northwesterly direction past Great Falls, Silver Falls, and Pine Falls to its mouth at Lake Winnipeg.

The Winnipeg flows for its entire length through the rugged Precambrian rock of the Canadian Shield, surrounded by scenic evergreen forests and stands of canoe birch and burr oak. Rock formations discovered along the Winnipeg have been dated by geologists as among the oldest in the world—some 2½ billion years old. These formations are believed to be the roots of ancient mountains worn down by successive waves of ice caps before the Rockies began to form. Most fishing on the Winnipeg is done from boats, which can be rented in the area, for smallmouth bass, walleye, northern pike, sturgeon, and goldeye. The Winnipeg annually produces northern pike in the 30-pound-plus class, walleye to 13 pounds, and smallmouth bass to 5 pounds. The Manitoba record 119-pound sturgeon was caught here in 1964. The famous Bird River to the north, a tributary of the Winnipeg, is one of Manitoba's finest fishing streams for smallmouth bass and walleye to 14 pounds. Caddy and Falcon lakes in Whiteshell Park to the south hold record smallmouth bass. The Winnipeg River country and the Whiteshell wilderness compose one of the province's best hunting regions for whitetail deer, black bear, moose, and waterfowl. Popular duck and goose shooting areas include Lakes George, Echo, and Saddle; there are extensive wild rice beds in Whiteshell. Pass shooting is a popular fall sport between Heart, Betula, White, Red Rock, and Jessica lakes. Ruffed grouse are found as far north as the Winnipeg River with medium to heavy concentrations found along Provincial Road 315 near the Bird River.

The famous Whiteshell Provincial Park embraces 1,065 square miles southward from the Winnipeg River. The park is one of Canada's most popular wilderness canoeing, fishing, hiking, hunting, and vacation areas. The *Whiteshell Guide*, available free from the Tourist Branch, Department of Tourism, Recreation, & Cultural Affairs, Legislative Bldg., Winnipeg R3C 1T5, contains a park map which shows the locations of tent and trailer campgrounds, tourist accommodations, boating facilities, aircraft landing sites and seaplane bases, canoe routes, hiking trails, horseback-riding facilities, Indian boulder mosaics, and game preserves. Primitive wilderness campsites are located along most of the canoe routes.

There are several rustic family fishing and vacation lodges within the Whiteshell with outfitting and some guide services. In the southern portion of the park the *Falcon Motor Hotel*, Falcon Beach R0E 0N0, has 21 units with full services and access to riding stables and fishing for northern pike, walleye, splake, and smallmouth bass and waterfowl hunting; the *El'Nor Resort*, Falcon Beach R0E 0N0, is a family resort on Falcon Lake with 16 housekeeping units; *Penguin Motel & Camp*, Falcon Beach R0E 0N0, has 15 housekeeping units, 11 cabins, and 4 motel units on Falcon Lake; the *Toniata Lodge*, Falcon Beach R0E 0N0, is a family fishing resort on Falcon Lake with 12 housekeeping cabins and 12 units. At famous Caddy Lake, lodging, canoes, boat rentals, and gear are provided by *Caddy Lake Camp*, Whiteshell R0E 2H0, and *Green Bay Cabins*, Whiteshell R0E 2H0. At West Hawk Lake several family resorts provide accommodations, equipment, and fishing for lake trout, walleye, and northern pike: *Lakeside Cabins*, Whiteshell R0E 2H0; *Keystone Motel and Cabins*, Whiteshell R0E 2H0; *West Hawk Motel*, Whiteshell R0E 2H0; *Crescent Beach Cabins and Motel*, Whiteshell R0E 2H0; and *Kenwin Cabins*, Whiteshell R0E 2H0. The *Riverview Lodge*, Seven Sisters Falls R0E 1Y0, is on Eleanor Lake, with 8 housekeeping cabins and full services. The *Otter Falls Resort*, Seven Sisters Falls R0E 1Y0, is on scenic Margaret Lake. The *Pinewood Lodge & P.W. Ranch*, Seven Sisters Falls R0E 1Y0,

is on Dorothy Lake, as is the *Barrier Bay Lodge*, Seven Sisters Falls R0E 1Y0, with fly-in hunting and fishing service.

In the central and northern regions of Whiteshell Provincial Park, lodging, outfitting, and supplies are provided by the *Nutimik Lodge*, Seven Sisters Falls R0E 1Y0, on Nutimik Lake; *Betula Lake Resort*, Seven Sisters Falls R0E 1Y0, with fly-in service to remote lakes available; *Rainbow Falls Lodge*, Rennie R0E 1R0, on White Lake; *Jessica Lake Lodge*, Rennie R0E 1R0, with fly-in service and boat and motor rentals at Malloy Lake; *Red Rock Lake Camp*, c/o F. Deppendorf, 279 Scotia St., Winnipeg R2V 1V7; *Inverness Falls Camp*, Rennie R0E 1R0, on Brereton Lake with hunting and fishing fly-in service; *Whiteshell Inn*, Rennie R0E 1R0, on Brereton Lake; *De Caigny's Fishing Lodge*, Rennie R0E 1R0, on Big Whiteshell Lake with guide and fly-in service; *Big Whiteshell Lodge*, Rennie R0E 1R0, on Big Whiteshell Lake, with fly-in service and jeep service to Crow Duck Lake; *Castaway Cabins*, Rennie R0E 1R0, on an island in Big Whiteshell Lake; and *Crowduck Lake Camp*, c/o K. MacKenzie, 598 Erin St., Winnipeg R3G 2V9, which has guest pickup at Big Whiteshell Lake landing with transportation to camp by boat and jeep. Several fishing and hunting resorts are located along the Winnipeg River, including the *Trail End Lodge*, Box 122, Pointe du Bois R0E 1N0; *Kendall Point Lodge*, c/o W. T. Kendall, 62 Leighton Ave., Winnipeg R2K 0H9; *Pine Island Lodge*, Box 107, Pointe du Bois (winter address: 106 Fairlane Ave., Winnipeg R2Y 0B1), accessible by air or boat; *Eagle Nest Lodge*, Box 74, Pointe du Bois R0E 1N0, a fishing and hunting resort on the Winnipeg River with pickup boat service at Pointe du Bois or fly-in from Kenora or Winnipeg. If you plan to fish or hunt along the Winnipeg River, please note that the *Whiteshell Guide* map shows all islands, tramways, portage trails, and forestry towers along the river as well as the location of Lamprey Falls, Slave Falls powerhouse and dam, Sturgeon Falls, Otter Falls, Whitemouth Falls, and the Pinawa Channel.

There are several hunting and fishing resorts in the Canadian Shield wilderness north of the Winnipeg River. The *Tall Timber Lodge*, Box 157-D, Lac du Bonnet R0E 1A0, is on the famous smallmouth bass and walleye waters of the Bird River. The lodge has a 5,000-foot private landing strip with fly-in service and outpost camps located at Black Lakes and Cole and Stonehouse lakes. *Lodge Oiseau*, c/o 1079B St. Marys Rd., Winnipeg R2M 3T2, is on Bird Lake. *Camp Hide-Away*, Box 640, Lac du Bonnet R0E 1A0, is a full-service lodge on the Lee River, a tributary of the Winnipeg. Farther north along wilderness Highway 304, just south of the Atikaki Wilderness, is the *Wallace Lake Lodge*, a fishing and hunting resort, with wilderness canoe trip outfitting, boat-launching, and fly-in service to remote lakes. The lodge operates an outpost camp on Gammon River and Craven Lake. For info and rates write: Box 59, Bissett R0E 0J0. The *Windsock Lodge*, c/o 274 Vermillion Rd., Winnipeg R2J 2Y8, is a fishing resort on Long Lake at the end of Highway 304. *Advent's Lodge*, Bissett R0E 0J0, is at Caribou Lake on the Manigotagan River.

Access & Outfitting Centers

Primary access to the Winnipeg River country is via the Great River Road and the Trans-Canada Highway. The interior wilderness areas of Whiteshell Provincial Park are reached via Provincial Roads 207 and 309. The Bird River country and Wanipigow River wilderness to the north are reached via Provincial Roads 314, 315, and 304. Accommodations, supplies, guides, and outfitting service are available at Falcon Lake, West Hawk Lake, Pinawa, and Pointe du Bois in Whiteshell Provincial Park, and at Lac du Bonnet, Manigotagan, and Wallhope.

EASTERN CANADA

Introduction

Ontario and Quebec offer over 1 million square miles containing countless remote blue lakes and wild rivers, vast evergreen forests, muskeg, tundra, mountains, glaciers, and several world-renowned fishing, big-game and waterfowl hunting, boating, camping, and wilderness canoeing areas. Within Ontario's boundaries are found some 250,000 lakes and innumerable streams, including the trophy smallmouth bass, muskellunge, and walleye waters of scenic Lake of the Woods, with its 14,000 evergreen-clad islands; the famed canoeing, fishing, and moose hunting areas of the Quetico Provincial Park; the remote, wild Albany and Moose River Canoe Country; the island-dotted trophy salmon, trout, bass, and muskellunge waters of Lake Huron's Georgian Bay and the North Shore wilderness of Lake Superior; the beautiful highlands and remote lakes and streams of Algonquin Provincial Park; the tundra and muskeg of Polar Bear Provincial Park in the far north along the shores of Hudson Bay; and the Mattawa Wild River and the "big fish" waters of Lac Seul.

The topography of Quebec, with its one million lakes and streams and wild rivers, encompasses the Gaspé Peninsula, featuring world-renowned Atlantic salmon, brook trout, ouananiche waters, wilderness camping, canoeing, and moose, bear and waterfowl hunting areas set among majestic highlands; Anticosti Island; the incredibly scenic North Shore and Mingan Coast of the St. Lawrence River; the rugged peaks of the Laurentians; and the famous fish and game regions north of the 4,000-foot Laurential Divide; the sprawling lakes of the Great Mistassini, Chibougamau, and Assinica Provincial Reserves; the wild Broadback and Rupert Rivers; the prolific goose-hunting grounds of the James Bay Lowlands; and the wind-swept tundra lands of the great Ungava Plateau salmon and caribou country, noted for its broad brawling rivers and thousands of unnamed headwater lakes and streams located north of the 51st parallel.

Ontario contains 412,582 square miles bordered on the west by Manitoba, on the north by Hudson and James Bays, on the east by Quebec, and on the south by the wave-swept waters of the Great Lakes: Superior, Huron, Ontario, and Erie. The great northern part of the province lakes and outcroppings of the Canadian Shield are surrounded by dense boreal forests. The Canadian Shield stretches north from the rugged height of land along the North Shore of Lake Superior across vast tracts of roadless wilderness to the "great muskeg" of the Hudson Bay Lowlands. In the southeast, the province is dominated by farmlands, major population centers, and mixed Laurentian forests of the St. Lawrence Lowlands.

The great outdoor recreation lands contained within Quebec's sprawling 594,861 square miles are bordered on the north by the arctic barren lands of Ungava Bay and Hudson Strait, on the west by James Bay and Ontario, on the east by the largely unexplored Torngat Mountains and the great Labrador Plateau, and on the south by the Gulf of St. Lawrence and Strait of Belle Isle, and across the St. Lawrence River by northern New York, Vermont, New Hampshire, Maine, and the province of New Brunswick. Northwards from the St. Lawrence and the northern Appalachian highlands of the Gaspé Peninsula are the 4,000-foot summits of the ancient Laurentian Plateau and the vast boreal forests of the Canadian Shield. Beyond are the taiga barren grounds of the vast Ungava Plateau—a mysterious land of stunted, wind-swept "little sticks," countless lakes, and the brawling courses of the Ungava Bay rivers: the renowned Kaniapiscau, Whale, George, Leaf, Koksoak, and Delay Rivers. These rivers hold trophy Atlantic salmon up to 20 pounds, landlocked salmon to 12 pounds, lake trout, arctic char, and wild, red-bellied squaretails up to 6 pounds. The tree line of the far north, which corresponds with the border between the

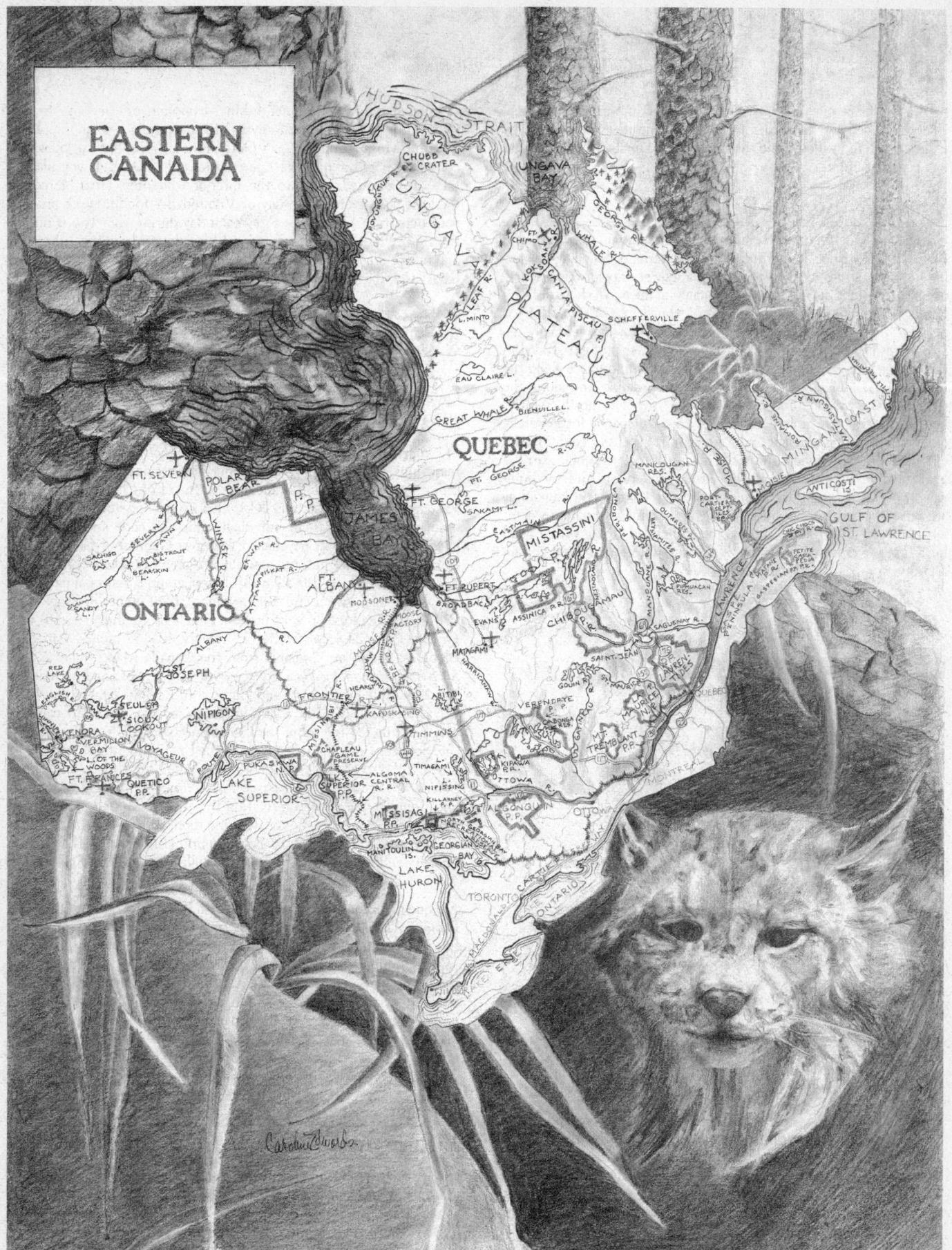

EASTERN CANADA

tundra and taiga, gives way first to dense shrub thickets of resin birch, alders, and willows, then to spongy tundra meadows dominated by sedges, scattered willows, and dwarf birch, and finally to marshes and wet coastal tundra.

Weather, Bugs & Beasts

Ontario and Quebec have an enormous weather range. June, July, and August are the true summer months, with warm, occasionally blistering hot days, and cool nights. Unseasonably wet or cold weather may occur throughout the north country and along the north shore of frigid Lake Superior and the north shore of the St. Lawrence. Rain is heaviest along the eastern shore of Lake Superior and gradually decreases toward James and Hudson Bays. Weather prohibits travel in the far north regions before June 20th. Fog is commonplace along the Hudson Bay, James Bay, and Ungava Bay Lowlands, and along the Gulf of St. Lawrence and Strait of Belle Isle. The north-country-bound outdoorsman is well advised to travel prepared for generally chilly temperatures at night and for occasional spells of cold, inclement weather. Sportsmen visiting the far north regions should carry at least medium-weight woolen or thermal underwear and medium-weight parkas. Even in the middle of summer, light-weight long johns are a must because of the chill mornings and evenings; medium-weight woolen shirts and trousers are also recommended (along with a good head net, gloves, sturdy rain gear, life jacket, water-proof flashlight, an accurate compass and topo maps).

The Ungava Peninsula, a plateau 2,000 feet above sea level and almost devoid of natural obstacles, is swept by gale winds known as the "attuarnek" to the Eskimos, occasionally reaching speeds of up to 100 miles an hour. July is the only frost-free month in the remote, starkly beautiful land of Ungava. A useful guide to weather, cloud formations, and forecasting, called *Weather Ways*, is available for $2 from the Canadian Hydrographic Service, Department of the Environment, Ottawa, Ont. K1A 0E8.

Anyone planning a summer fishing, camping, or canoeing trip to Ontario or Quebec is well advised to take along a good supply of Muskol, Mosquitone, Off!, or Cutters insect repellent (all of which contain concentrations of 50 percent plus of DEET). If you plan to take an extended trip into the interior wilderness areas, a recommended dosage of 50 mg/day of Vitamin B-1 for the week prior to your departure and 10 mg a day each day during your trip is one of the most effective repellents against blackflies, mosquitoes, chiggers, and no-see-ums. Other potential hazards include camp-invading black bears, and, during the fall, marauding hot-blooded bull moose in rut.

Eastern Canada Maps & Charts—How to Order

A set of full-color topographic maps will provide the Quebec and Ontario bound outdoorsman with a complete physical inventory of the area he plans to fish, hunt, camp, or canoe. All Canadian National Topographic Survey maps are available (along with free *Map Indexes of Ontario and Quebec* and a free *Map Symbol Chart*) for $1.50 per map, plus a 50¢ handling charge per order, from the Canada Map Office, Surveys Mapping Branch, Department of Energy, Mines, and Resources, Ottawa, Ontario K1A 0E9, (613) 966-9663. Be sure to order your maps by their individual name and code and make your check or money order payable to: Receiver General of Canada. The Canada Map Office puts out a useful 362-page *Catalogue of Published Maps* ($3.50) which lists all available topographic, national park, and specialty maps. Two useful overview maps, the *Ontario Province Map* (MCR-39, 5-colors, 36×40 inches, 1 inch to 16 miles, $1.50) and *Quebec Province Map* (MCR-42, 5-colors, 40×45 inches, 1 inch to 16 miles, $1.50) are available from the Canada Map Office. A free *Map of Hydrographic Basins of Quebec* may be obtained by writing: Ministry of Tourism, Fish, and Game, 150 E. Boul. St. Cyrille, Quebec City G1R 2B2. The following Canadian nautical chart catalogs may be obtained free from the Canadian Hydrographic Service, Marine Services Branch, Department of the Environment, Ottawa, Ont.: *Great Lakes & Adjacent Waterways including the Rideau and Trent-Severn Waterways, Ottawa River, Lake Nipissing, Night Hawk Lake, and Boundary Waters* (Information Bulletin 1); *Rainy Lake, Lake of the Woods, Boundary Waters* (Information Bulletin 4); *St Lawrence River from Île d'Anticosti to Lake Ontario* (Information Bulletin 5); *Hudson and James bays* (Information Bulletin 11); *North Shore of the Gulf of St. Lawrence* (Information Bulletin 7).

Anyone planning a trip to the Big North Country should send for the *Canada Maps & Wilderness Canoeing Guide* (MCR-107) available free upon request from the Canada Map Office (address above). This valuable publication contains a text written by Eric Morse—among the intrepid pioneers of recreational canoeing in Canada's Far North. Subjects discussed include planning your trip, making a trip profile, making a schedule, map symbols, barren land maps, navigating in the far north, use of maps, types of map scales, how to order aerial photographs, and use of compass on a canoe trip. This full-color illustrated guide contains a "Canada 1:250,000 Scale Map Index."

Vacation Travel Maps, Information & CB Radio Permits

An attractive full-color *Vacation Planning—Topographic Highway of Eastern Canada,* showing all major man-made and natural features, is available free upon request from the Canadian Government Office of Tourism, 150 Kent St., Ottawa, Ont. K1A 0H6, along with the two free booklets, *Canada Ferries, Bridges & Cruises* and the 36-page

Canada Travel Information Handbook, which contain indispensable info about customs regulations, airport and airline services, bus lines, insurance, fishing and hunting regulations, and weather, with temperature and time-zone charts. Free citizen-band radio permit applications and regulatory information may be obtained by writing: Regional Director, Telecommunications Regulations Branch, Department of Communications, 55 St. Clair Ave., E., Toronto M4T 1M2.

For information on Canadian train vacations, routes, rates, itineraries, hotels, and package tours, write: *VIA Rail Canada,* P.O. Box 8117, Montreal, Quebec H3C 3N3 or contact your local travel agent. VIA Rail Canada manages Canadian National and Canadian Pacific passenger train services.

ONTARIO ENCYCLOPEDIA

Accommodations—Vacation Lodges & Sporting Camps

Ontario offers the outdoor sportsman a wide range of places to stay: motels, motor courts and inns, big resorts, individual lodges, and furnished housekeeping camps. Costs are determined by the standard of luxury, location, convenience, and season. Costs quoted by wilderness hunting and fishing camps vary greatly. Some camps include guide services, equipment rental, fly-in transportation, and other services as part of the full package price. Check the camp operator's literature and establish by correspondence exactly what you're getting for your dollar. Be sure to ask for past guests' names and addresses and write to them for verification of the camp's quality. You'll learn a lot doing this. The thick *Ontario Accommodation Guide*, a useful 241-page full-color booklet with maps and charts, is available free from the Information Branch, Ministry of Industry & Tourism, Parliament Bldgs., Toronto M7A 2E5. This guidebook lists all Ontario establishments—from the near north to the James Bay frontier—including location, telephone number, facilities, rates, guides, fly-in camps, and hunting and fishing package plans. If you're planning a trip to northern Ontario, be sure to write: Northern Ontario Tourist Outfitters, Alban P0M 1A0, for a free 90-page *Northern Ontario Outfitters Directory*.

Listings and descriptions of major vacation lodges and sporting camps are found throughout the "Ontario Travel & Recreation Guide."

Airlines & Charter Fly-in Services

Air Canada offers direct flights to Toronto from New York City, Cleveland, Los Angeles, Dallas-Fort Worth, Houston, Miami, and Tampa. Canadian Pacific flies to Toronto and Ottawa from San Francisco. You can also fly to Ontario via Allegheny, American, Eastern, North Central, or United Airlines. Air Canada and Canadian Pacific provide passenger service to Ontario from all major centers in Canada. From Toronto, Air Canada has jet service direct to North Bay, Sudbury, Sault Ste. Marie, Timmins, and Thunder Bay. From Ottawa you can fly direct to Sudbury or Thunder Bay. Province-wide air service with experienced bush pilots provides fly-in service to the most remote wilderness fishing and hunting, and canoeing, regions from the major outfitting centers. Scheduled and charter service within Ontario is provided by *Austin Airways Ltd.*, Toronto Island Airport, with service between Timmins and Moosonee and points on Hudson Bay, and between Nakina and north central Ontario points; *Great Lakes Airlines Ltd.*, Sarnia Airport, 1972 Sarnia Rd., Sarnia, with service between Sarnia and Ontario points; *NorOntair*, Bradley Air Services Ltd., Carp Airport, Carp K0A 1L0, with service between Kapuskasing and Timmins, Kirkland Lake, Earlton, North Bay, Sudbury, Chapleau, and Sault Ste. Marie; *Ontario Central Airlines Ltd.*, Box 1248, Gimli, Man. R0C 1B0, with service between Kenora and points to the north and west, and between Red Lake and north central Ontario points; *Hooker Air Service Ltd.*, P.O. Box 1248, Gimli, Man. R0C 1B0, with service between Sioux Lookout, Pickle Lake, and other northern Ontario points. For trip planning information from the major airlines write: Air Canada, Promotion Distribution Department, 130 Bloor St. W, Toronto, or CP Air, Regional Sales Office, 69 Yonge St., Toronto. A fascinating history of the Ontario Provincial Air Service by Bruce West, *The Firebirds—How Bush Flying Won Its Wings*, 272 pages, with numerous photos and drawings of bush planes, is available for $6.95 from the Ministry of Natural Resources, Parliament Bldgs., Toronto M7A 1W3. (See "Northern Ontario Wilderness Outfitters & Floatplane Fly-in Services.")

Aurora Borealis—the Northern Lights

The northern lights, a luminous meteoric phenomena appearing at night in the northern hemisphere, are caused by electrically charged particles from the sun which are diverted toward the earth's magnetic poles where they collide with gases in the atmosphere and change their electrical charge. Displays are most frequent around times of greatest sunspot activity. At full intensity the aurora will cover the entire night sky with erratic, shifting curtains of brilliant white light and dancing, curved bands of green or rose. The aurora borealis was known as *Ed Thin,* meaning "deer," among the Chippewa Indians. Their legends say that far up in the northern skies the fur of a celestial deer was stroked by a mystical hand activating sparks and creating the wondrous phenomena they observed. Several explorers and northmen have told in their journals of being able to actually hear the brilliant aurora whisper and crackle during its dance across the winter night sky of the far north. Samuel Hearne, the great northern explorer, in his classic book *A Journey to the Northern Ocean* wrote of the northern lights that "I can positively affirm, that in still nights I have frequently heard them make a rustling and crackling noise, like the waving of a large flag in a fresh gale of wind."

Boating & North Country Waterways

Ontario has some of the most magnificent scenic inland waterways in North America. A 100-page *Ontario Boating Guide* is available free from the Ministry of Industry & Tourism, Parliament Bldgs., Toronto M7A 2E5. It has detailed descriptions and maps of the famous Rideau Waterway, St. Lawrence River, Georgian Bay, Lake of the Woods, and Trent-Severn Waterway as well as a complete listing of marinas with lake or river location, fuel, launch facilities, anchorage, services, repairs, rentals, supplies, charted waterways, and Canadian hydrographic chart numbers for the waterways mentioned above and for Lake Nipissing, Lake Huron, Muskoka Lakes, Ottawa River, Lake Superior, Lake of Bays, Lake Ontario, Bay of Quinte, Lake Simcoe, and Rainy Lake.

Boreal Forest

The boreal evergreen forest covers about three-quarters of Ontario's forest land. The word "boreal" comes from Greek mythology, after *Boreas,* the personification of the north wind. The forest stretches in a continuous belt of varying width from Manitoba to the Quebec border north of Lake Superior. Trees of the boreal forest are mostly coniferous, with white and black spruce the most common. Other trees include tamarack, balsam fir, and jack pine. A few broadleaf species occur widely, the most common being white birch and balsam poplar; there are also scattered stands of dogwood. Stands of black spruce and tamarack increase as one moves north and the climate and soil conditions become harsher. At the northernmost limits, the dark canopy of the boreal forest gives way to open lichen woodlands, and at the treeline, to tundra. The eastern portion of the forest contains a sprinkling of trees from the Great Lakes-St. Lawrence region. The Cree Indians used the bud gum of balsam poplar, which grows on sunlit riverbanks and on the flooded parts of islands in the great rivers of the north, to toughen string for their bows, snowshoes, and cloth-

ing. If you should run out of pipe tobacco in the north country, dogwood leaves will make a good substitute. The Crees also used the gum of balsam fir to heal skin injuries. A free guide, *Canada's Eight Forest Regions,* and a 172-page book, *Forest Regions of Canada* ($2.50), may be obtained by writing: Publishing Division, Information, Canadian Forestry Service, Department of the Environment, Ottawa K1A 0H3.

Camping & North Country Trails

The bible for the camper, backpacker, or wilderness paddler planning a trip north is the free 173-page *Ontario Camping Guide,* published by the Ministry of Industry & Tourism, Parliament Bldgs., Toronto M7A 2E5. The booklet is illustrated with full-color photos, charts, and maps. It contains hiking maps and descriptions of the Ganaraska Trail, Bruce Trail, and Rideau Trail; maps and information about Algonquin and Quetico provincial parks; a complete listing of canoe outfitters and packaged canoe trips; provincial park fees; listing of Ministry of Natural Resources district field offices; sewage pump-out facilities for trailers; and a complete listing of Ontario campgrounds including info about highway access, site name, adjacent lake or river, acres, number of sites, camp facilities, water facilities, address and location, and telephone number. A free map, *Overnight Camping in Northwestern Ontario,* may be obtained by writing: Information Branch, Ministry of Natural Resources, Parliament Bldgs., Toronto M7A 1W3. A great little how-to booklet, *So You Want to Go Camping,* may be had free by writing: Information Branch, Department of Lands & Forests, Whitney Block, Toronto M7A 1W3. It was written by the woodsmen who staff Ontario's provincial parks and tells how to use campgrounds, equipment, and tools. It includes many interesting details on planning, making camp, food and storage, cooking, clothing, bears, firearms, boat trailers, and interior camping permits. The Information Branch of the MNR (address above) also publishes an informative free booklet, *How to Survive in the Woods.*

The famous Bruce Trail winds for 430 miles along the Niagara Escarpment from Niagara Falls north to Tobermory at the northern tip of the Bruce Peninsula at Georgian Bay, passing through a great variety of scenery and terrain with numerous campsites located along the route. Travel info, membership applications, and copies of the *Bruce Trail Guidebook* ($5 to nonmembers) can be obtained from the Bruce Trail Association, 33 Hardale Crescent, Hamilton L8T 1X7. The

guide contains detailed trail maps and info on general stores, water supplies, and campsite locations. The Ganaraska Trail winds through a great diversity of geological formations and flora from Port Hope on Lake Ontario northwest through the Kawartha Lakes and Huronia resort area to join the Bruce Trail at Glen Huron. Several sections of the trail, Ontario's newest hiking trail, are still being blazed. Maps and membership information are available from the Ganaraska Trail Association, Box 1136, Barrie L4M 5E2. The Rideau Trail meanders north for 200 miles along the route of the historic Rideau Canal through lake-dotted forests and placid countryside, from the marshes of the Little Cataraqui on the shore of Lake Ontario to the Chaudière Falls at Ottawa. For trail information write: Rideau Trail Association, P.O. Box 15, Kingston K7L 4V6.

Canoeing & Wilderness Waters Outfitters

Ontario is the wilderness paddler's dream: Quetico, Lake of the Woods, and the Albany, Winisk, Mattawa, and Moose rivers beckon to the modern voyageur from a vast network of 250,000 lakes and as many more streams which provide a wide range of water, forest, and geological conditions. An experienced guide should be hired for all journeys from Highway 11 north to Hudson and James bays. An experienced guide in this isolated rugged country may well save your life—in addition to increasing your enjoyment and knowledge of the northland. *Northern Ontario Canoe Routes* and an information kit are available for 50¢ from the Ministry of Natural Resources, Parliament Bldgs., Toronto M7A 1W3, or from the district field offices. This publication is a must for the Ontario-bound canoeist. It contains an overview map of the northern canoe routes and detailed route descriptions of the Ottawa River watershed, Lake Huron, Moose River, Albany River-Attawapiskat-Winisk-Ekwan River systems, Severn and Winnipeg River systems, Lake of the Woods, and Lake Superior watersheds. The publication also provides detailed info about fishing, archaeology, Indian rock paintings and carvings, weather and clothing, pack load, canoes, tools, restricted travel zones, topo maps, portages, bears, insect and animal hazards, campsite care, safety, and distress signals. The National & Provincial Parks Association of Canada, 47 Colborne St., Suite 308, Toronto M5E 1E3, has detailed literature about summer trips on the Albany and Missinaibi rivers and in the Atikaki Wilderness areas of Manitoba and northwest Ontario. Packaged canoe trips are available from *Wilderness Canoe Tours,* Box 219, Moose Factory; *Wilderness Tours,* Box 661, Pembroke; *Canoe Canada Outfitters,* Box 388, Atikokan; *Algonquin Waterways Wilderness Trips,* 271 Danforth Ave., Toronto M4K 1N2; *Headwaters,* P.O. Box 288, Temagami P0H 2H0; and *Heyden Crafts Co. Ltd.,* RR 2, Sault Ste. Marie.

Ontario's famous canoe-camping regions are well served by outfitters offering complete wilderness canoe-trip services. The Quetico Provincial Park wilderness waters are served by *Wilderness Canada Trips Inc.,* P.O. Box 388, Atikokan; *Camp North Ontario Ltd.,* Box 1510, Atikokan, with base at Niobe Lake; *Voyageur Wilderness Program,* Box 1210, Atikokan, at Nym Lake; *Adventure Canoe Trails,* Box 208, Atikokan, at Lerome Lake; *Clearwater West Lodge,* Box 790, Atikokan, with base on Clearwater Lake; *Powell Lake Resort,* Box 1526, Atikokan; *Canadian Quetico Outfitters,* Box 910, Atikokan, at Eva Lake; *Caribou Resort,* Box 1390, Atikokan, at Sylvan Lake; *North Country Wilderness Outfitters,* Box 850, Atikokan, at Nym Lake; *Quetico North Tourist Services,* Box 100, Atikokan, at Eva Lake; and *Canoe Canada Outfitters,* Box 388, Atikokan. The scenic Rainy River District is served by *Wickstrom's Camp,* 512 Church St., Fort Frances, at Lake Despair; *Nestor Falls Canoe Outfitters,* Box 247,

Nestor Falls; *Northern Wilderness Outfitters,* Box 637, Fort Frances, at Rainy Lake; and *Clearwater Pipestone Portage,* Box 48, Emo. To the north, the Red Lake District and Sioux Lookout area are served by *Canadian Canoe Routes,* Box 70, Cochenour P0V 1L0; *Voyageurs North Canoe Outfitters,* Box 507, Sioux Lookout, at Abram Lake; and *Albany Outfitters,* Osnaburgh House P0V 2H0, at the Albany River headwaters. The James Bay and Moose River country is served by *James Bay Outfitters,* P.O. Box 1866, Cochrane. The Chapleau Forest Preserve region is served by *Windermere Camp,* Lakefield College School, Lakefield K0L 2H0; and *Coeur du Bois,* Chapleau P0M 1K0. *Canoes North Ogoki Outfitters,* Box 56, Caribou Lake Rd., Armstrong P0T 1A0, serves the Nipigon region. The famous Algonquin Provincial Park canoe country is serviced by *Bartlett Lodge,* 2 Avalon Blvd., Scarborough, at Cache Lake; the *Portage Store,* Algonquin Park P0A 1B0, at Canoe Lake; *Kish-Kaduk Lodge,* Brent, at Cedar Lake; *Killarney Lodge,* Algonquin Park P0A 1B0, at scenic Lake of Two Rivers; *Openongo Outfitting Store,* Whitney K0J 2M0, at Openongo Lake; *Algonquin Outfitters,* RR 1, Dwight P0A 1H0, at Ortongue Lake; and *Northern Wilderness Outfitters,* Box 665, Station B, Willowdale M2K 2P9, at Kawawaymog Lake. (See "Indian Outfitters—Fishing & Hunting Camps," "Hudson's Bay Company Outfitting Posts & Canoe Service," and "Wild Rivers & Voyageur Route Maps.")

Fishing & Hunting in Ontario

Ontario's wilderness forests and waters offer some of North America's finest moose hunting and fishing for trophy northern pike, walleye, muskellunge, and lake, rainbow, and brook trout. Hard-hitting great northern pike up to 40 pounds are caught each year in the "big-fish" waters of Georgian Bay, French River, Missinaibi Lake, Savant Lake, Eagle Lake, and the rivers in the Kapuskasing-Geraldton-Sioux Lookout regions; savage, fighting muskellunge (known locally as maskinononge, or "ugly fish" in the Ojibway Indian dialect) up to weights of 58 pounds are caught in the trophy waters of Georgian Bay and the North Channel, St. Lawrence River (the world's record 69-pound muskie was caught here), Lake St. Clair, eastern Lake Nosbonsing, Trent and Crowe rivers, Lake of the Woods, and Eagle Lake in the Kenora region; walleye, known in Ontario as "yellow pickerel," up to weights of 18 pounds are caught throughout the province with northern Ontario rivers such as the Moose, Abitibi, Albany, and their tributaries the best bets for this delicious fellow; hot spots for brook trout up to 8 pounds are the deep cold waters of the Algonquin Highlands, Mattawa Wild River Reserve, and the remote wilderness waters of the Severn, Sutton, Winisk, and Albany rivers; beautiful hook-jawed, lake-run rainbow or steelhead trout up to 20 pounds are

found in the cold swift rivers of the Great Lakes and Georgian Bay; lake trout up to 30 pounds are found in the deep, cold boulder-strewn lakes of the Precambrian Shield; lake-run coho and Chinook salmon are found in the stream of Lakes Superior, Ontario, and Huron, reaching weights of up to 20 pounds; smallmouth bass hot spots are Lake of the Woods, St. Lawrence River, Georgian Bay and the French River, and the waters of the Temagami, Sault Ste. Marie, and Thunder Bay regions.

The quality of Ontario's fishing is illustrated by the list of record fish compiled by the Ministry of Natural Resources.

ONTARIO RECORD FISH

	Lb.-oz.	Length (inches)	Girth (inches)	Place	Year
Brook trout*	14–8	31½	23	Nipigon River	1916
Lake trout	63–2	51½	32¾	Lake Superior	1952
Brown trout	19–11	36½	22¾	Lake Huron-Manitoulin	1974
Rainbow trout	29–2	38½	25	Nottawasaga River	1975
Muskellunge	61–9	59	31	Eagle Lake	1940
Walleye	22–4	36½	21	Niagara River	1943
Northern pike	42–2	—	—	Delaney Lake	1946
Smallmouth bass	9–13½	24	24	Birch Bark Lake	1964
Atlantic salmon (landlocked)	19–6	—	—	Trout Lake	1967

*World's record.

The more remote wilderness fishing and big-game areas are best reached by float-equipped bush planes from jumping-off points such as Fort Frances, Kenora, Sioux Lookout, Red Lake, Pickle Lake, Thunder Bay, White River, Wawa, Sudbury, North Bay, or Kapuskasing. Although a good deal of romantic hoopla has been written about the bush pilot, cruising over the Ontario wilderness with one of these knowledgeable gents can often be worth the price of the trip itself. All fishermen and hunters in Ontario must be licensed. It's illegal to bring pistols, revolvers, or full or semiautomatic weapons—or in fact, any working firearm under 26 inches in length.

An indispensable book, *The Hunter's & Fisherman's Ontario,* can be obtained free by writing: Information Branch, Ministry of Industry & Tourism, Queens Park, Toronto M7A 2E5. This 80-page book is packed with full-color photos, maps, and charts. It describes airline service and northern Ontario air routes, and has a complete listing of bush pilots and fly-in services. It provides information about the highways and railroads. It tells when and where to hunt for small game and waterfowl, moose, deer, black bear, and what gear to bring. This Ontario guidebook recommends that the well-equipped hunter's pack include a rifle-cleaning kit and spare cartridges; an ax and wedge or bucksaw to take care of trail and woodcutting, as well as some butchering; a skinning/dressing knife, whetstone, aluminum foil, cheese cloth, and block and tackle for meat preparation; pepper to keep insects off meat; and a plastic bag for skins. All big-game skins should be left at the nearest Ministry of Natural Resources field office where they are turned over to Indian leather craftsmen. The guide has a complete listing of Ontario fish and game regulations, a fishing guide, and a comprehensive listing of hunting and fishing camps and lodges. The information branch of the Ministry of Natural Resources also publishes *Fish Ontario* ($1), a 76-page illustrated booklet with maps and charts. For a summary of hunting and fishing regulations, an Ontario hunting zone map, and a 46-page *Wildlife Management Areas* booklet write: Ministry of Natural Resources, Parliament Bldgs., Toronto M7A 1W3. Two useful booklets, *The Whitetail Deer in Ontario* and *The Beaver in Ontario* may be obtained free from the Information Branch, Ministry of Natural Resources at the above address.

Highways—Recreation & Scenic Routes

Ontario's well-engineered highways provide access to most of the major outdoor recreation areas and wilderness outfitting villages and jumping-off points to the interior big-game hunting and fishing regions. MacDonald-Cartier Freeway 401 provides access to southern Ontario with up to 12 lanes. It extends 510 miles from Windsor in the southwest to the Quebec border. The famous Trans-Canada Highway 17 runs from eastern Ontario west through Sudbury, Sault Ste. Marie, Thunder Bay, Fort Frances, Rainy River, with the alternate Northern Route 11 through Timmins, Dryden, and Kenora to the Manitoba border. Listed below are the major scenic, recreation, big-game hunting, and fishing region routes and wilderness highways in northern Ontario and their corresponding Canadian topographic maps at a scale of 1:250,000, or 1 inch to 4 miles.

Trans-Canada Highway (11): Frontier Route.

This is the northern segment of the Trans-Canada Highway, 1,000 miles long. It links the gold, silver, and lumbering communities of the north—North Bay, Temagami, Cobalt, Timmins, Cochrane, Kapuskasing, Hearst, Geraldton—with the town of Nipigon at the north shore of Lake Superior where it joins Highway 17 to Dryden and Kenora at the Manitoba border. Highway 11 provides access to some of northern Ontario's premier wilderness canoeing, camping, fishing, and big-game hunting for moose and black bear. The major topographic features and recreation areas shown on the maps are Lake Nipissing, Algonquin Provincial Park, Kirkland Lake, Lake Abitibi, Remi Lake Provincial Park, Long Lake, Lake Nipigon, and the wild Mattagami, Abitibi, and Missinaibi rivers. Canadian National Topographic Survey Maps: Huntsville 31-E, North Bay 31-L, Ville Marie (Que.) 31-M, Timmins 42-A, Cochrane 42-H, Kapuskasing 42-G, Hornepayne 42-F, Longlac 42-E, Nipigon 52-H, Fort William 52-A.

Trans-Canada Highway (17): Voyageur Route.

This historic 1,300-mile route follows the trails of the explorers and voyageurs along the Ottawa Valley and Lake Superior segments of Highway 17. It links Hawkesbury, Ottawa, Sudbury, Sault Ste. Marie, Thunder Bay, and Kenora. Terrain varies from the rolling hills of Ottawa Valley to the rugged Precambrian Shield country along the north shore of Lake Superior. The major features and recreation areas shown on the topographic maps are White Lake, Snake River, Bonnechere and Algonquin provincial parks, Mattawa Wild River Provincial Reserve, Quetico Wilderness Provincial Park, Rainy Lake, Sioux Narrows, Mississagi Provincial Park, Lake Superior Provincial Park, Puskaskwa National Park, and Lake of the Woods. Canadian National Topographic Survey Maps: Pembroke 31-F, Ottawa 31-G, Deep River 31-K, North Bay 31-L, Ville Marie (Que.) 31-M, Sudbury 41-I, Blind River 41-J, Sault Ste. Marie 41-K, Michipicoten 41-N, White River 42-C, Schreiber 42-D, Fort William 52-A, Quetico 52-B, Ignace 52-G, Dryden 52-F, Kenora 52-E.

Wilderness Highway (101)

This route travels through the heart of Canadian Shield fish and game country from its junction at Trans-Canada Highway 17 at Wawa northeast past Windemere Lake, Chapleau-Nemegosenda Wild River Reserve, Groundhog and Ivanhoe rivers, Kemogamissi Lake, Timmins, Iroquois Falls, and Lake Abitibi to the Quebec border. Canadian National Topographic Survey Maps: Timmins 42-A, Foleyet 42-B, Chapleau 41-O, Michipicoten 41-N.

Wilderness Highway (105)

This highway travels from its junction at Vermilion Bay on Trans-Canada Highway 17 northward past the remote outfitting and supply posts of Camp Robinson, Perrault Falls, and Goldpines to its terminus at the wilderness mining towns of Red Lake and Balmertown in northwest Ontario. The major topographic and recreation areas shown on the maps are Lac Seul, Pakwash Lake Provincial Park, Chukuni River, and Ranger and Trout lakes. This region offers excellent moose hunting and angling for northern pike, walleye, and lake trout up to 30 pounds. Canadian National Topographic Survey Maps: Dryden 52-F, Lac Seul 52-K, Trout Lake 52-N, Carroll Lake 52-M.

Wilderness Highway (144)

This popular northern Ontario route winds northwest from Sudbury past Onaping Lake and Discotasi, Rush, Rice, Mattagami, Kemogamissi, and Kapiskong lakes to its junction with wilderness Highway 101 west of the mining center of Timmins. Canadian National Topographic Survey Maps: Timmins 42-A, Gogama 41-P, Sudbury 41-I.

Wilderness Highway (599–808)

This gravel, oil-topped trail travels due north from Ignace through the Sioux Lookout-Ojibway country past the famous northern pike, walleye, muskie, and lake trout waters of the English River, Sturgeon Lake, Savant Lake, Marchington River, Lake St. Joseph, and the headwaters of the Albany River, on past Kapkich Lake, Central Patricia, Pickle, Crow, Meneko Lake, and the remote Otoskwin River. This is a top-ranked region for moose and black bear. Canadian National Topographic Survey Maps: Ignace 52-G, Sioux Lookout 52-J, Lake St. Joseph 52-O.

Looking at the official *Northern Ontario* road and recreation map, you will notice that a good three-quarters of northern Ontario is completely roadless. This immense wildland is accessible for the most part only by floatplane or canoe. The free northern Ontario map is the best available; it is a large, full-color map packed with detailed fishing, hunting, and camping info and shows all highways, provincial campgrounds, Indian reserves, gravel roads, wild reserve boundaries, and seaplane bases, and has handy insert maps of provincial park campground areas and full-color charts of northern Ontario game fish. The map may be obtained by writing: Department of Transportation & Communications, Downsview. Ontario's highways are patrolled by the Ontario provincial police, who are there to help out when needed. Road condition information for all highways in the province is available 24 hours a day at (416) 248–3561. A detailed *Official Ontario Road Map* is available free from the Ministry of Industry & Tourism, Parliament Bldgs., Queens Park, Toronto. *Ecotour Maps,* ecological interpretive maps, provide information about the ecozones, the natural and human history, that have shaped the appearance of the country surrounding portions of the Trans-Canada Highway. They may be obtained free by writing: Public Information Unit, Canadian Forestry Service, Department of the Environment, Ottawa K1A 0H3.

Hudson Bay & the "Great Muskeg"

Henry Hudson's huge inland sea is slowly shrinking. In preglacial times the bay was a great river flowing over a plain. It is believed that the Missouri River once flowed into it before the massive ice barriers

dammed the river off and diverted it south to its present-day course. When the invading Wisconsin ice cap ground down from the north, its massive weight compressed the land beneath it, forcing it some 1,200 feet lower. With the passage of time the ice retreated and the land slowly began to expand, like a sponge, rising 250–800 feet over the centuries. Eskimo dwellings originally built near the shoreline of Hudson Bay are now 30–80 feet above sea level. Ages hence, the bay will once again be a river surrounded by a land of a thousand lakes and vast expanses of muskeg.

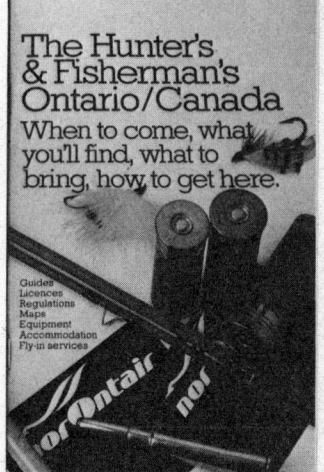

Hudson Bay is surrounded by a physical region of Canada known as the Hudson Bay lowlands or "great muskeg," which forms a dramatic mosaic of lichen and muskeg, broken by patches of stunted spruce and thousands of small kettle ponds, extending for 800 miles along the southwestern coast and inland for 40–240 miles.

Hudson's Bay Company Outfitting Posts & Canoe Service

Fishermen, hunters, and wilderness paddlers interested in the *Hudson's Bay Company's U-Paddle Canoe Service* in Ontario should write for free literature, rates, and info, to: HBC, Northern Stores Department, 800 Baker Center, 10025–106 St., Edmonton, Alta. T5J 1G7, or phone (403) 424–8113. The company's northern supply posts are

situated at strategic wilderness travel locations in Northern Ontario at Moosonee, Hearst, Hornepayne, Gogama, Wawa, White River, Manitouwadge, Longlac, Nakina, Geraldton, Nipigon, Armstrong, Sioux Lookout, Atikokan, Dryden, Red Lake, Hudson, Albany, Ogoki, Fort Hope, Pickle Lake, New Osnaburgh, Cat Lake, Landsdowne House, Wunnummin Lake, Round Lake, Trout Lake, Bearskin Lake, Winisk, Severn, Pikangikum, Lac Seul, and Grassy Narrows. Please note that many of the remote HBC posts do not necessarily carry a full range of provisions and gear. It's advisable to place your order by writing a couple of months in advance for pick-up upon your arrival.

Indian Outfitters— Fishing & Hunting Camps

Some of Ontario's finest wilderness fishing, hunting, and canoe camping is to be had with the services of licensed Indian outfitters and guides. Indian lodges and camps are located at strategic sites along the Winisk River—noted for its excellent speckled trout fishing, goose hunting, and wild river canoeing; Constance Lake and Kabinakagami River, for moose and bear hunting and canoe routes; Hawley Lake and Sutton River, for geese, speckled trout, lake trout, and walleyes; Attawapiskat River, Kapuskau River, and the mouth of the Albany River,

for Canada goose and duck hunting and canoeing; Kesagami River, for wilderness canoeing and fishing; Moose and French rivers; Kettle Point Indian Reserve on Lake Huron; Cape Croke Indian Reserve on Georgian Bay; West Bay Indian Reserve on Manitoulin Island; and Fort Albany Reserve. Fly-in services will take you into the most remote camps. A free 110-page *Directory of Canadian Indian Tourist Outfitters & Outdoor Recreation Facilities,* illustrated with maps, is available from the Department of Indian Affairs & Northern Development, 400 Laurier Ave. W, Ottawa K1A 0H4. Please note that you may not hunt, fish, camp, canoe, or travel on Indians' reserve lands without their permission.

For literature and travel information write the following Indian-operated fishing, hunting, and canoeing base camps: *Winisk Goose Camp,* General Delivery, Cochrane, 5 miles from the village of Winisk on Hudson Bay; *Chookomolin Camp,* Hawley Lake, via Moosonee; *Attawapiskat Goose Camp,* General Delivery, Cochrane; *Kapuskau Goose Camp,* General Delivery, Cochrane; *Kashechewan Goose Camp,* General Delivery, Cochrane, at Fort Albany Indian Reserve at the mouth of the Albany River; *Tidewater Goose Camp,* General Delivery, Cochrane, at the mouth of the Missisicabbi River; *Big Trout Lake Camp,* c/o Department of Indian Affairs, Big Trout Lake via Central Patricia, 180 air miles north of Sioux Lookout; *Fort Severn Goose Camp,* c/o Ministry of Natural Resources, P.O. Box 309, Sioux Lookout; *Keewatin Kinoshao,* Moose Factory, at Kesayami Lake, 65 air miles south of James Bay; *French River Canoe Trips,* Moose Factory, at Moose and French rivers; *Papamotao Goose Camp,* P.O. Box 81, Moose Factory, on James Bay by canoe from Moosonee; *Fort Hope Camps,* north of Nakina along the Albany River and *Ogoki Camps,* at Sturgeon Lake, Ogoki, and Nottick on the Albany River north of Nakina; and the *Winisk River Camps* and *Lansdowne House Camps* on the Attawapiskat River, all c/o Ojibway Country Indian Camps, Fort Hope (via Nakina) P0T 2H0.

Indian Rock Paintings & Carvings

The ancestors of the Chippewa, Ojibway, and Cree Indians of the Lake of the Woods country believed in a world of spirits existing in the wind and water, rocks, birds and bear, sun and moon. These symbols and graceful, haunting representations of men, canoes, moose, and loons are found painted and carved on vertical cliffs along the shores of the wilderness lakes in Quetico Provincial Park and elsewhere throughout the province. The figures, called petroglyphs, were painted while standing on the thwarts of canoes using pigments made from berries and bark. The rock paintings are believed to represent the dreams of *Mi-shi-pi-zhiw,* the Chippewa god of water, while fasting to communicate with the guardian spirits. Three useful books of interest to the wilderness traveler in Quetico country are published by the University of Toronto Press, 33 E. Tupper St., Buffalo, NY 14203. *Indian Rock Paintings of the Great Lakes,* by Selwyn Deurtney and Kenneth Kidd ($10), describing the results of an exciting quest to discover and record Indian rock paintings of northern Ontario and Minnesota, and *Quetico-Superior Country,* by Bruce M. Littlejohn ($1.50), may be used in conjunction with the handy guidebook *Canoe Trails Through Quetico,* by Keith Denis ($5), a remarkable combination of early Canadian history and practical guidance about the wilderness canoe routes in Quetico Provincial Park.

Lake of the Woods & the World's Oldest Freshwater Fish

Before the turn of the century Ontario's lakes and rivers teemed with one of the largest and longest-lived of fish: the sturgeon. Lake of the Woods, in northwest Ontario, was known as the "greatest sturgeon pond in the world." Early accounts mention sturgeon being transported piled like cordwood on railroad flatcars. The largest sturgeon caught in Lake of the Woods weighed 234 pounds and was 90 inches long. This fish, caught by gill net, was about 120 years old. The oldest recorded sturgeon taken from Lake of the Woods was 152 years old; this is believed to be the oldest recorded age for a freshwater fish in the world. It was 81 inches long and weighed 215 pounds. It is likely that record giant sturgeon, born before the American Civil War, swim the depths of the lake to this very day.

Loon—the Great Northern Diver

The long, ghostly cry of the loon, piercing the quiet of the night, is the haunting symbol of the northern lake country. The Cree Indians believed that it was the cry of a dead warrior who had been forbidden entry into heaven. At any rate, the loon *(Gavia immer)* or great northern diver, as it is also known, can dive 200 feet down and swim faster than most fish. It eats its catch quickly and its bill is often empty when it returns to the surface, although 10 fish might be in its stomach. If something frightens it, the loon can swim submerged with only its beak out of the water; it is then invisible if the wind is forming a ripple on the lake. Takeoff is a definite problem for our friend, for its webbed feet push it forward, but not upward. So it has to get into the air by making a long run along the surface, climbing gradually until completely airborne. Every fall a few loons get trapped by staying too long on their favorite lakes, letting a quick freeze-up reduce the space of open water overnight.

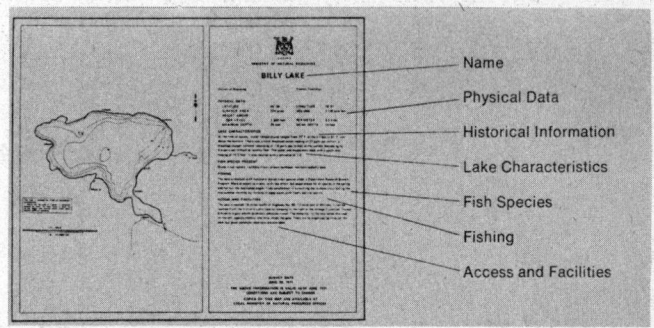

Maps—Fishing & Hunting

A free catalog of *Lake Contour Fishing Maps* is available from the Map Office, MNR, Parliament Bldgs., Toronto M7A 1W3. It lists 484 of Ontario's major trout, walleye, pike, muskellunge, and smallmouth bass lakes in alphabetical order by region. The maps are lithographed on water-resistant paper and include detailed information about physical characteristics, origin of lake name, fish species present, lake characteristics, where and when to fish, access, and facilities. Each map in this series costs $1; and a few maps of the larger lakes sell for $2 each. Free color-coded *Hunting Maps* clearly outlining private lands and major roads are published by the Ministry of Natural Resources (MNR) for the region above a line running from the north shore of Lake Huron to just south of Sioux Lookout. A large, attractive, annotated *Trout & Salmon Migratory Routes Map* can be obtained for $1 by writing: Information Branch, Ministry of Natural Resources, Parliament Bldgs., Toronto M7A 1W3. It provides detailed illustrations and descriptions of the history, distribution, weight, and migration routes for lake-run brown trout, rainbow trout, splake, and coho, Chinook, and kokanee salmon in the Great Lakes of southern Ontario.

Moose—the "Monarch of the North"

In his travel journals, David Thompson, the famous northern explorer, described the moose as "the noblest animal in the forest . . . the flesh of a moose in good condition contains more nourishment than that of any other deer, 5 pounds of this meat being held equal in nourishment to 7 pounds of any other meat . . . . The nose of the moose, which is very large and soft, is accounted a great delicacy. It is very rich meat. The bones of its legs are very hard and several things can be made of them and its skin makes the best of leather." Ontario is the most important moose hunting region in North America. The moose population is spread over most of the province, except for the southern lowlands and the western shores of Hudson and James bays. The best hunting is found in the boreal forests and lake country of the Canadian Shield from Quebec to the Manitoba border, most of which can be reached along Trans-Canada Highways 11 and 17. Moose live where coniferous forests are mingled with deciduous growth, preferring logged or burned areas where new forest growth provides a plentiful supply of browse, since they eat an average of 50 pounds a day. In the northern muskeg country they are most often found along wooded riverbanks and ridges. One of the most unusual features of the moose —other than his overall appearance—is the odd-looking appendage which hangs below the throat on both the male and female and is known as the dewlap or bell. It's formed of flesh and gristle covered with hair, and its significance is not understood. Among the many guesses which have been made, one is that it provides the throat with protection from wolves. It may also help a large moose to establish a kind of social status. A moose hunter's crest—embossed with the year of kill—is presented to each hunter who turns in the lower jaw of his moose to the Ministry of Natural Resources district office for research. An interesting 28-page booklet, *The Moose in Ontario*, describing physical characteristics, history, life cycles, habits, population and range, and hunting methods—as well as the moose's nemesis, the wolf —is available free by writing: Information Branch, Ministry of Natural Resources, Parliament Bldgs., Toronto M7A 1W3.

Moosonee & Moose Factory

(Pop. 1,000). This Hudson's Bay Company outpost town, surrounded by the ancient home and hunting grounds of the Cree Indians, is 187 miles north of Cochrane, at the mouth of the Moose River, which flows into the arctic tidewaters of James Bay. At Moosonee the river is more than 3 miles wide, although a labyrinth of spruce-covered islands conceal all but the main channel. Expeditions to the outlying islands can be a rewarding experience. On Fossil Island you'll find ancient fossils of the Devonian period—that's only 350 million years ago. Moose Factory Island is the site of the Hudson's Bay Company's second-oldest trading post, erected in 1673. Or you can travel in one of the giant Rupert House freighter canoes through the mouth of the Moose River, past marsh flats and the wreck of the good ship *Eskimo* to Shipsands Island with its teeming waterfowl and fossils. The *Polar Bear Lodge*, Box 305, Moosonee, provides lodging with fishing and goose hunting trips arranged and airport facilities. The *James Bay Goose Camp*, Box 173, Weston, operates a goose and duck hunting lodge on the west shore of James Bay, about 20 miles north of Moosonee, with landing strip at camp. The *Hannah Bay Goose Camp*, operated by the Ontario Northland Transportation Commission, 195 Regina St., North Bay, is 45 miles east of Moosonee on the Harricanaw River. Full-service accommodations are provided by the *Moosonee Lodge*, Ontario Northland, 805 Bay St., Toronto M5S 1Y9. Boat services are available between Moosonee and Moose Factory Island and to Shipsands Island. Charter sightseeing flights are also available. For detailed information and literature about outpost camps, outfitters, and fly-in fishing, hunting, and canoeing in the 50,000-square-mile wilderness south from the James Bay Lowlands, write: *James Bay Frontier*, Box 1162, Timmins P4N 7H9; phone (705) 264–9589. Ask for their free *James Bay Frontier Hunting & Fishing Guide* and *James Bay Frontier Vacation Planning Guide*.

Northern Ontario Wilderness Outfitters & Floatplane Fly-in Services

Northern Ontario's famous hunting, fishing, and wilderness canoeing outfitters are the inheritors of a tradition dating back half a century to the days when almost all hunting was done with a canoe, a guide, and the camping equipment and food necessary for wilderness living. The gear was supplied by a depot operator who used his stores to outfit the hunting and fishing parties. The operators gradually became known as tourist outfitters and their early depots evolved into today's well-established camps. The outfitters listed below are members of the Northern Ontario Tourist Outfitters Association. For a comprehensive listing of lodges and camps, many of which offer partial outfitting services, write: NOTOA, Alban, for the free 90-page *Northern Ontario Tourist Outfitters Directory*. The individual outfitters will usually supply descriptive literature and information upon request. *Algonquin Outfitters*, RR 1, Dwight, provides complete outfitting for canoe and fishing trips in Algonquin Park and neighboring areas; *James Bay Outfitters*, Box 1866, Cochrane, operates the Little Abitibi Lodge, Yesterday Lodge, and Albany River Goose & Duck Camp with wilderness outfitting and air charter from Timmins and Cochrane; *Kap Outfitters*, P.O. Box 129, Moonbeam, operates fishing and hunting fly-in camps; *Archie's Outfitting Depot*, P.O. Box 627, Geraldton, has fly-in camps for fishing and moose hunting, and complete outfitting for canoe trips; *Con McGuire Professional Guiding*, 379 E. Amelia St., Thunder Bay, provides air charters and hunting and fishing trips on Lake Nipigon; *Canoes North*, Armstrong, offers complete canoe outfitting and custom planned trips for the Albany River system; *Northland Outfitters*, Nakina, has fly-in fishing camps and complete outfitting for canoe trips; *O'Sullivan Lake Outfitters*, Nakina, has outpost camps on Esnagami and Stinger lakes; *Sportsmen's Outfitting*, Box 85, Nakina, serves Smoothrock Lake and the Ogoki and Nipigon watersheds; *Upper Twin Outfitters*, Box 8, Nakina, outfits for fishing, hunting, and canoeing; *Northern Trails Outfitters*, 867 William Ave., Sudbury, outfits fishing, moose, and black bear hunting trips; *Ranger Lake Holidays Ltd.*, P.O. Box 145, Sault Ste. Marie, has fly-in outposts and complete canoe outfitting; *Nipigon Trout Outfitters*, RR 1, Nipigon, has guiding services for Nipigon River; *Oslon's Camp Quetico*, Box 100, Atikokan, outfits fishing and canoe trips into the Quetico wilderness; *Canadian Quetico Outfitters*, Box 910, Atikokan, has complete canoe outfitting; *Caribou Resort & Quetico Wilderness Outfitters*, Box 1390, Atikokan, offers complete outfitting for Quetico canoe trips; *Quetico North Tourist Services Ltd.*, Box 100, Atikokan, outfits canoes for the north country and Quetico Park; *Voyageurs North Canoe Outfitters*, Box 507, Sioux Lookout, is known as the "farthest north canoe outfitters," with train transportation to remote put-in spots and unique train-in or plane-out routes; *Black Bear Portage Camp*, Minaki, is on the Winnipeg River with canoe safaris and fly-in service to remote outposts; *Canadian Wilderness Camps & Outfitters Ltd.*, 305 2d St., Kenora, has a new Sandlake camp on Harbor Island, with fly-in service to outpost hunting and fishing camps and guides;

Nestor Falls Canoe Outfitters, Box 247, Nestor Falls, has complete canoe outfitting and fishing and hunting trips in the Lake of the Woods area; *The Sanctuary*, Box 158, Sioux Narrows, makes plane pickups at camp for canoe trips to remote lakes; *Cathart's Canoe Rentals*, Box 483, Fort Frances; *Bill Zup's Lac La Croix Fishing Camp*, Crane Lake, MN 55725, is a canoe and boat outfitter at the southwestern entrance to Quetico Park. Complete canoe outfitting sevice and fly-in fishing trips in the Quetico and White Otter Wilderness are provided by *Canoe Canada*, Box 388, Atikokan.

The members of the Northwest Ontario Air Carriers Association are experienced bush pilots with thousands of flying hours logged serving northern Ontario from the Manitoba border on the west to the Quebec boundary on the east. All flying charges are government regulated and every aircraft is regularly inspected by government-licensed engineers. Association members can fly you to any point in Canada and to any camp. They can fly in your gear or see that equipment is available at the site you select. Descriptive literature and detailed info are available upon request from individual association members. *Canadian Voyageur Airlines Ltd.*, Box 507, Fort Frances, has wilderness fly-in services and 5-day package trips for goose hunting and brook trout fishing on Hudson Bay; camp-out or 1-day fishing trips are arranged at your convenience. *Gibson's Thousand Lakes Resort & Airways*, Upsala, has a modern base lodge at Lac des Mille Lacs, with outpost fly-in services, moose hunting, and sightseeing charter flights. *Northwestern Flying Services Ltd.*, P.O. Box 6, Nestor Falls, has bases at Nestor Falls, Sioux Narrows, and Clearwater, Twin Buck, Beaver, and Found Lakes, with Cessna aircraft servicing outpost camps, fly-in camping, and sightseeing trips. *Nuttall Charter Fly-in Service*, Hur-

kett, provides fly-in hunting, fishing, and sightseeing service. *Pioneer Airways Ltd.*, Box 357, Atikokan, provides fly-in services, canoe outfitting, and outpost camps in Quetico Provincial Park Wilderness. *Lac La Croix Quetico Air Services Ltd.*, Crane Lake, MN 55725, provides canoe rentals, outpost camps, complete outfitting, and wilderness fly-in fishing in Quetico Provincial Park with quick access to Beaverhouse Ranger Station (Cirrus, Quetico, Dean, and Sturgeon lakes), Lac La Croix Ranger Station (McAree, Minn, Crooked, and Darby lakes), Three Mile, and other lakes from pickup points in Crane Lake and Ely, Minnesota. *Rusty Myers Flying Service Ltd.*, Box 668, Fort

Frances, serves camps in northwestern Ontario and Manitoba with a fleet of radio equipped Beechcraft, Norsemen, Beavers and Cessna 180's with fly-in camping, fishing, goose and moose hunting. *Rainy Lake Airways, Ltd.*, Box 790, Fort Frances, offers wilderness fly-in service and fishing, hunting, and canoeing trips throughout the Lake of the Woods-Quetico region. *Severn Enterprises Ltd*, Box 428, Sioux Lookout, has base camps at Sioux Lookout and Pickle Lake with fly-in package plan fishing, moose and goose hunting trips arranged. *Slate Falls Airways*, Box 188, 31 Wellington St., Sioux Lookout, provides air service for hunting and fishing. *Stan's Flying Service*, Box 8, Ear Falls, has fly-in fishing and hunting, and tent camps. *Superior Airways Ltd.*, P.O. Box 52, Postal St. F, Thunder Bay, has northern bases at Rossport, Nakina, Armstrong, Pickle Lake, Sioux Lookout, and Albany River Sportsmen's Lodge, with package plan fishing and moose hunting trips. *Swan Air*, P.O. Box 297, Dryden, provides fly-in fishing and hunting in the Dryden area and outposts via Cessna, Norseman, and twin-engine Piper. *Wilderness Air*, Group A, Box 83, Vermilion Bay, has wilderness fly-in fishing and moose hunting. *Theriault Air Services Ltd.*, Box 269, Chapleau, provides complete fly-in and outfitting services with bases at Wawa, Chapleau, and Foleyet. *Ignace Airways Ltd.*, Ignace, provides wilderness fly-in hunting and fishing from a floatplane base. *Leunberger Air Service & Wilderness Outfitters Ltd.*, P.O. Box 22, Nakina, has fly-in fishing and moose hunting service and package fly-in trips to over 30 remote lakes. *Wings Aviation Ltd.*, P.O. Box 218, Red Lake, services fly-in outpost camps. *Kenora Air Service*, Kenora, serves northwestern Ontario from bases at Kenora and Minaki via Otter, Goose, Beaver, and Cessna aircraft. *Green Airways Ltd.*, Red Lake, provides fly-in service with outpost hunting and fishing camps at Nungesser, Mamakwask, Birch, and Haggart lakes. *Gogama Air Services*, P.O. Box 159, Gogama, offers fly-in camping service and arctic fishing in the Hudson Bay region. (See "Ontario Travel & Recreation Guide.")

Provincial Parks & Campgrounds

A complete map and campground recreation guide, *Ontario Provincial Parks*, details Ontario's network of 100 provincial and primitive parks, widely scattered across the province from the shores of Lake Ontario to the vast wilderness of Polar Bear Provincial Park on the shores of Hudson Bay. It is available free from Information Branch, Ministry of Natural Resources, Parliament Bldgs., Toronto. The map-guide

provides useful background info about Mattawa Wild River Park and Quetico, Lake Superior, Algonquin, and Killarney provincial parks. In wilderness parks like Algonquin and Quetico, canoe campers are required to have an interior camping permit, a form on which the canoe route is described as accurately as possible. In an emergency this permit assists park rangers to find the wilderness paddler more quickly. Interior permits are obtained at park entry points.

Railway Services & the "Polar Bear Express"

Trains provide efficient access to some of the finest outdoor recreation areas in Ontario. The Canadian Pacific and Canadian National railways link most of the major cities in the province. Both lines connect with Amtrak and other U.S. rail lines at border crossings. The Algoma Central Railway offers an awesome scenic journey north from Sault Ste. Marie for 114 miles through vast forests, dramatic ravines and hills, past sparkling lakes and streams through the spectacular Agawa Canyon to the town of Hearst—known as "the moose capital of the world." At the canyon, it drops you off for a 2-hour fishing or exploration jaunt. The Algoma line operates one-day wilderness tours mid-May through mid-October and also runs regularly between Sault Ste. Marie and Hearst. The "Polar Bear Express" is operated by the Ontario Northland Railway from Cochrane, where it links up with the Canadian National. The express rolls 186 miles from Cochrane, north through Moose River country fur trading and lumberjacking regions, to Moosonee at James Bay and the famous Cree goose hunting camps. The Hudson's Bay Company village of Moose Factory is a canoe trek away. The engineer will drop you off along the route to hunt or fish, and he'll take you back the same day (or whenever) if you stand by the tracks and holler a bit. For literature and rates contact: Ontario Northland Transportation Commission, 195 Regina St., North Bay P1B 2J6, (705) 472-4500; Canadian National Railway, Passenger Sales & Service, 20 York St., Room 1454, Toronto; or Canadian Pacific Railway, Passenger Department, Room 108, Union Station, 61 Front St. W, Toronto. Write: Algoma Central Railway, Passenger Sales Department, Sault Ste. Marie, or phone (705) 254-4331.

St. Lawrence Islands

The Canadian government has protected 17 scenic islands and 8 rocky islets in the upper St. Lawrence River as the St. Lawrence Islands National Park. The Thousand Islands region between Kingston and Brockville is one of Ontario's most popular recreation areas. As well as being a highly developed tourist area, the Thousand Islands area is famous for its early and late season smallmouth bass and muskellunge fishing. The world's record 69 pound 15 ounce muskellunge was caught here in 1957. The fish was 64½ inches long and had a 31¾-inch girth. For fishing, camping, hiking, boating, and vacation travel information write: Eastern Ontario Travel Association, Reynolds Rd. & 1000 Islands Pkwy., Lansdowne K0E 1L0, or Superintendent, St. Lawrence Islands National Park, Mallorytown.

Wild River & Voyageur Route Maps

Ontario's famous wilderness canoe routes were once the main portage canoe trails of the Northwest Company and Hudson's Bay Company voyageurs to the great interior Indian trapping grounds. The important canoe routes of the Northwest Company led from Montreal to Fort Moose (now Moose Factory) by way of the Ottawa River, Lake Abitibi and Abitibi River, and Moose River. The second route to Fort Moose was by the Ottawa River to Mattawa to Lake Nipissing, Georgian Bay, Lake Superior to Fort Michipicoten, and up the Michipicoten River to the Missinaibi and Moose rivers. The canoe route to Fort Albany on Hudson Bay led from Lake Nipigon at the outlet of the Nipigon River across the lake to the Ogoki River, a tributary of the Albany, and on down the Albany River to the fort. The canoe trails from Lake Superior to the Far West and Fort Chipewyan on the shore of huge Lake Athabasca began at Grand Portage along the Pigeon River; then went through the beautiful boundary lakes and what is now known as the Quetico-Superior wilderness to Rainy Lake, and followed the Rainy River to Lake of the Woods—the headwaters of the Winnipeg River. Lake of the Woods (known to the Blackstone Indians as "Lake of the Assiniboines") was described by Jacques de Noyon, who discovered the Kaministiquia canoe route in 1688, as being on its south side "lined with barren expanses, while on the north side it is covered with woods and fringed with islands. At the end of this lake is a river [the Winnipeg] that flows into the Western sea," according to Indian legends. After recognition of the independence of the United States, the headquarters of the Northwest Company were moved from Grand Portage, Minnesota, to Fort William at the mouth of the Kaministiquia River on Lake Superior. This route followed the Kaministiquia River through the scenic lakes chain in the Quetico Wilderness to Lac La Croix and Rainy Lake to the Rainy River and Lake of the Woods, then to Rat Portage and the Winnipeg River. Canadian wild river surveys describing access and egress, geography, history, flora and fauna, and canoe routes, are published for the *Upper Albany River*, from Lake St. Joseph to the Albany and Ogoki confluence; *Ogoki and Albany Rivers*, from Kayedon Lake to Ghost River; *Attawapiskat River*, from Missisa River to the village of Attawapiskat on Hudson Bay; *Fawn and Severn Rivers*, from Angling Lake to Fort Severn; and *Missinaibi-Moose Rivers* and *The French River*. Copies of the surveys may be obtained free by writing: Information Services, Conservation Group, Department of Indian Affairs & Northern Development, Ottawa K1A 0H4.

The following Canadian National Topographic Survey Maps, scale 1:250,000, show the entire lengths of northern Ontario's premier wild rivers and lake chains (see the "Ontario Travel & Recreation Guide" for additional listings). *Attawapiskat River & Lake:* Wunnummin Lake 52-P, Lansdowne House 43-D, Missisa Lake 43-C, Matateto River 43-F, Kapiskau River 43-B; *Asheweig River:* Asheweig River 53-H, Winiskisis Channel 43-E, Clendenning River 43-L; *Fawn River & Big Trout Lake:* Makoop Lake 53-G, Asheweig River 53-H, Fawn River 53-I, Clendenning River 43-L, Fort Severn 43-M, Dickey River 53-P; *Pipestone River:* North Caribou Lake 53-B, Wunnummin Lake 52-P, Lansdowne House 43-D, Winiskisis Channel 43-E; *Severn River:* Opasquia Lake 53-F, Makoop Lake 53-G, Thorne River 53-J, Fawn River 53-I, Dickey River 53-P, Fort Severn 43-M; *Little Current River:* Nakina 42-L, Kenogami River 42-K; *Kenogami River:* Longlac 42-E, Nakina 42-L, Kenogami River 42-K; *Missinaibi River:* Foleyet 42-B, Kapuskasing 42-G, Smoky Falls 42-J, Moose River 42-I; *Mattagami River:* Timmins 42-A, Cochrane 42-H, Kapuskasing 42-G, Smoky Falls 42-J, Moose River 42-L; *Groundhog River:* Chapleau 41-O, Foleyet 42-B, Kapuskasing 42-G, Cochrane 42-H.

ONTARIO TRAVEL & RECREATION GUIDE

Albany River Wilderness Canoe Country

Albany River & Lake St. Joseph Headwaters

Canadian National Topographic Survey Maps, scale 1:250,000: Sioux Lookout 52-J, Lake St. Joseph 52-O, Miminiska Lake 52-P, Fort Hope 42-M, Ogoki 42-N, Ghost River 42-O, Kapiskau River 43-B, Fort Albany 43-A.

Ogoki River

Canadian National Topographic Survey Maps, scale 1:250,000: Nakina 42-L, Fort Hope 42-M, Ogoki 42-N, Armstrong 52-I.

The large, fast-flowing Albany is one of northern Ontario's great wilderness waterways, offering superb fishing, canoeing, and the romance of history. It was once the major fur trade route from York Factory on Hudson Bay to Lake of the Woods and Fort Gary on the shores of Lake Winnipeg. The Hudson's Bay Company still operates active posts at Osnaburgh House on Lake St. Joseph, Fort Hope, Ogoki, and Fort Albany along the river. The river cuts a line through the center of northern Ontario, flowing from its headwaters at Lake St. Joseph north of Sioux Lookout through a remote chain of scenic lakes surrounded by thick spruce forests and the rocky uplands of the Canadian Shield, on past fur trading outposts and Indian camps. This upper stretch of the river has numerous turbulent rapids and falls. Gradually the river widens and carves its way through the 30-foot-high dazzling white clay banks of the Hudson Bay lowlands, through a labyrinth of spruce-covered islands to its mouth at Fort Albany on James Bay.

The Albany and its tributaries, the Kenogami, Nagagami, Kabinakagami, Little Current, and Ogoki rivers, drain an area of 53,000 square miles. Upstream on the Albany from Martin Falls, canoeists can still use the wide portages shown on the maps. They were constructed for large fur trade York boats which were moved on rollers around the chutes and rapids. The Albany and its tributaries flow through top-ranked moose and black bear country, and hold trophy-size northern pike, walleye, and some large brook trout up to 6 pounds in the deep, cold pools at the bottom of rapids and falls. A handy free guide for the fisherman and canoeist, the *Albany River Canoe Route*, complete with maps and detailed info, is available from the Geraldton or Sioux Lookout district offices of the Ministry of Natural Resources.

On your journey down the Albany you'll see campsites where Indians have camped during their winter trapping season, scattered with trapping gear, stretching frames, snowshoes, traps, and toboggans. Do not depart with any of these items. The Indians return every winter to set and run their traplines; loss of their precious tools will cause great hardship. Please note that canoeing the Albany is not a trip for the tenderfoot. It can be extremely dangerous due to the almost total isolation that will be experienced. The enjoyment and knowledge of even the most seasoned wilderness veteran will be enhanced by the services of an Indian guide. For info write: Department of Indian Affairs & Northern Development, Box 388, Geraldton.

Lodging, guides, and package fly-in vacations are offered by the following Northern Ontario resort operators. Write for literature and rates, and be sure to make your reservations well in advance. (Cochrane) *Albany River Goose & Duck Camp*, Box 1866. (Sudbury) *Andersons Fort Albany Goose Camp*. (Nakina) *Esnagami Lodge; Leunberger Air Service*, Box 22; *Nakina Outpost Camps*, Box 126; *Northern Lakes Outfitters*, Box 73; *Sportsmens Outfitting*, Box 85; *The Wilderness Outfitters*, Box 22; *Upper Twin Outfitters*, Box 8; *Viking Outfitters*, Box 142. (Jellicoe) *Kyros Albany River Airways*; and Albany River *Fort*

Hope Camps and *Ogoki Camp*, c/o Ojibwuay Country Indian Camps, Fort Hope (via Nakina) P0T 2H0. Deluxe fly-in accommodations on the Albany are provided by *Winkelmann's Makokibatan Lodge*, Box 132, Nakina P0T 2H0 (winter: 27 Creery Ave., Sault Ste. Marie P6B 1G7, (705) 949-6100.

Access & Outfitting Centers

Transportation to Albany River Country is primarily a fly-in operation, although supplies are still moved to some communities during the long winter months by tractor-train across the frozen lakes and snow-covered forest trails. The famous fishing waters of the upper tributaries may be reached by secondary highways and forest access roads running north from the northern rate of Trans-Canada Highways 11 and 17. The major outfitting and supply centers are Geraldton, Sioux Lookout, Hearst, Longlac, and Nakina.

Publications & Information Sources

Write the Ministry of Natural Resources district offices listed for the nitty-gritty about fly-in services, guides, canoe outfitters, hunting, fishing, and camping information, a free catalog of waterproof lake contour fishing maps ($1 each), and free canoe route guides. For *Recreation in Nagagamisis Uplands Area Guide, Hearst District Canoe Routes, Limestone Rapids to Fort Albany Canoe Route, Nagagamisis Provincial Park, Morrison River Canoe Route*, and *A Trip to James Bay* write: Hearst District Office, MNR, Box 460, Hearst P0L 1N0. For lake contour fishing maps for all major lakes in the district, such as Long, O'Sullivan (2 maps), Pagwachwan, and Wintering Lakes, write: Geraldton District Office, MNR, Box 640, Geraldton P0T 1M0. For travel info write: North of Superior Travel Association, 200 S. Syndicate Ave., Thunder Bay.

Algonquin Highlands

Algonquin Provincial Park Topo Maps

Canadian National Topographic Survey Overview Maps, scale 1:250,-000: North Bay 31-L, Deep River 31-K, Huntsville 31-E, Pembroke 31-F. Maps, scale 1:50,000: Wilberforce 31E-1, Kawagama 31E-7, Whitney 31E-8, Opeongo Lake 31E-9, Algonquin 31E-10, Burk's Falls 31E-11, South River 31E-14, Burntroot Lake 31E-15, Lake Lavielle 31E-16, Round Lake 31F-12, Des Joachims 31K-4, Brent 31L-1, Kiosk 31L-2, Achray 31F-13.

Algonquin Provincial Park is one of the most famous brook trout fishing and canoe-camping areas in Ontario. This scenic reserve embraces 2,910 square miles of lakes, streams, and forests straddling the renowned wilderness highlands between Georgian Bay and the Ottawa River, 110 miles north of Toronto. By the time the park was established in 1893 most of the original great white pine trees had been logged out by pioneers, and fires, fueled by pine slash, had ravished large areas. The park contains numerous remnants of the camboose logging camps and river drives. The western highlands consist of hundreds of deep, clear lakes and wild streams surrounded by dense forests of sugar maple, beech, spruce, red and white pine, cedar, and hemlock; the lower, drier eastern portion is a land of deep-flowing rivers, extensive glacial sand deposits, and forests of white, red, and jack pine.

The interior wilderness regions of Algonquin are a fisherman's and canoeist's paradise of rolling maple-covered hills, rocky ridges, spruce bogs, and thousands of lakes, ponds, and streams dominated by the deep, clear waters of Hogan, Opeongo, Happy Isle, Big Trout, Burnt Island, North Tea, Lavielle, and Big Crow lakes. The interior wildlands offer some of Ontario's finest fishing for trophy splake, and lake

and brook trout. One of the unusual features of the interior headwaters country is the absence of northern pike, muskellunge, walleye, and smallmouth bass. If you're planning a fishing or canoeing trip be sure to send for the useful 40-page full color guide *Fishing in Algonquin Provincial Park* ($1). The book provides complete details for 230 Algonquin lakes and streams. Write: Superintendent, Algonquin Provincial Park, Whitney K0J 2M0.

The 1,000 miles of Algonquin wilderness canoe routes are shown in detail on the full-color, 38 × 38-inch *Algonquin Provincial Park Canoe Routes* map ($1). This indispensable annotated map (available from the Park Superintendent's Office, above) describes the history of the park and provides detailed info about 131 canoe routes along the famous interior rivers and lakes, including the headwaters of the Petawawa, Bonnechere, Madawaska, Oxtongue, and Amable du Fond rivers—all remnants of the glacial spillways that fed ancient Lake Algonquin and the Champlain Sea. The map shows access points, highways, gravel roads, portages, campsites, dams, rapids, bogs, and seaplane bases, and provides fascinating historical annotations showing the precise location where the last logging drive occurred on the Petawawa River in 1945 when 150 lumberjacks worked from April to September driving logs 155 miles down the Ottawa River; the site of the Brent Crater—still visible 450 million years after the explosion of a giant meteorite; the site at Catfish Lake of machinery from an alligator—a steam warping tug used for towing log booms; the site of rare ferns on the spectacular 300-foot-high cliffs of the Notch above the Notch Rapids on the Petawawa River; the deepest lake in Algonquin, Eustache, ringed by 80-foot cliffs which continue down through its crystal-clear waters for another 300 feet; the huge wild bogs of Hailstorm Creek, which supports moose and several field birds rare to the park; the tall red pine at Dickson Lake, over 300 years old; and the site of Fossmill Outlet, where the Upper Great Lakes drained through about 10,000 years ago. The park is also shown on two shaded-relief maps published by the Canada Map Office in Ottawa. These beautiful maps give the appearance of the sunlight striking the surface from the northwest. They cost $1.50 each. Ask for maps: 31E/NE and 31L/SE.

Complete canoe outfitting services and supplies and a free guide, *Canoe Tripping in Algonquin Park*, are provided by the Portage Store and Opeongo Store, both Algonquin Park P0A 1B0. The stores also offer equipment drop-off, shuttle, and water taxi services. For inquires and reservations for either store phone (705) 633-5622. The *Portage Store* is located on Canoe Lake in the heart of the park. Canoeists have used Canoe Lake for decades as a jumping-off place for trips into the interior wilderness. The *Opeongo Store* is located 25 miles to the east on Sproule Bay at the south end of Opeongo Lake. Smaller than the Portage Store, it serves solely as an outfitting center for canoeists and fishermen. Specific inquiries for Opeongo, regarding fishing conditions and water taxi, may be obtained by calling (705) 637-2831. Canoe outfitting services and guided trips are also provided by *Algonquin Outfitters*, RR1, Dwight P0A 1H0.

The lunker muskie, walleye, and smallmouth bass lakes of the Haliburton Highlands and the Kawartha Lakes lie to the south of Algonquin Provincial Park. The Muskoka Lakes are located to the southeast along the rocky shores of the beautiful, island-dotted Georgian Bay of Lake Huron.

Lodging facilities and guide service in the Park are provided by *Bartlett Lodge*, Cache Lake, Algonquin Park P0A 1B0; *Killarney Lodge*, Huntsville P0A 1K0; and *Arowhon Pines Resort*, Huntsville P0A 1K0.

Access & Outfitting Centers

Access is via Trans-Canada Highways 11 and 17, and Highway 60, which travels 37 miles through the park. Outfitting, supplies, and lodging at Whitney, North Bay, Pembroke, Barry's Bay, and Dwight.

Publications & Information Sources

For free Algonquin Provincial Park map & brochure, *Algonquin Provincial Park Canoe Routes Map* ($1), *Birds of Algonquin Provincial*

Park (40 pp., 50¢), *Fishing in Algonquin Park* (40 pp., $1.60), and the trail guides *Highland Hiking Trail* (free) and *Western Uplands Trail* (free), *Hardwood Lookout Trail* (10¢), *Peck Lake Trail* (10¢), *Hemlock Bluff Trail* (10¢), *Two Rivers Trail* (10¢), *Lookout Trail* (10¢), *Booth's Rock Trail* (10¢), *Spruce Bog Boardwalk* (10¢), and *Beaver Pond Trail* (10¢), write: Algonquin Provincial Park, Ministry of Natural Resources, Whitney K0J 2M0. (Algonquin waterproof lake contour fishing maps are also available ($1 each), for Aylen, Balfour, Big Cauliflower, Billy, Booth, Cache, Cedar Crotch, Grand, Kingscote, Lake of Two Rivers, Louisa, Opeongo, Shirley, St. Andrews, Smoke, and Transverse lakes.) For lake contour fishing maps ($1) of Baptiste, Farquhar, Fishtail, Looncall, Weslemkoon, and Wollaston lakes, and other region lakes, write: Bancroft District Office, MNR, Bancroft K0L 1C0. For the free guides *Black Lake Canoe Route*, *Wild Cat Canoe Route*, *South Muskoka River Canoe Route*, and lake contour fishing maps for Lake of Bays, Ontangue, Troutspawn, and other district lakes, write: Bracebridge District Office, MNR, Box 1138, Bracebridge P0B 1C0. For the free *Burnt River Canoe Routes Guide* and lake survey fishing maps for all major district lakes, including Big Hawk, Mississauga, and Red Pine, write: Minden District Office, MNR, Minden K0M 2K0. For the free *Gibson & McDonald Canoe Routes* and *Georgian Bay Canoe Routes* guides, and for lake contour fishing maps for Threelegged, Trout, and Otter lakes, and others, write: Parry Sound District Office, MNR, 4 Miller St., Parry Sound P2A 1S8. For the *Mississippi Canoe Route* guide and waterproof lake contour fishing maps for the major district lakes, write: Pembroke District Office, MNR, Box 220, Pembroke K8A 6X4. For travel information write: Georgian Bay Travel Association, 73 Mississauga St. E, Orillia, and Central Ontario Travel Association, 139 George St. N, Peterborough K9J 6Z3.

Lac Seul-Sioux Lookout Country

English River & Lac Seul Country

Canadian National Topographic Survey Maps, scale 1:250,000: Pointe du Bois 52-L, Lac Seul 52-K, Sioux Lookout 52-J, Ignace 52-G, Dryden 52-F, Carroll Lake 52-M, Trout Lake 52-N.

Eagle Lake Country

Canadian National Topographic Survey Maps, scale 1:250,000: Lac Seul 52-K, Dryden 52-F.

Red Lake Country

Canadian National Topographic Survey Maps, scale 1:250,000: Carroll Lake (52-M), Trout Lake (52-N).

Winnipeg River Voyageur's Route

Canadian National Topographic Survey Maps, scale 1:250,000: Kenora 52-E, Pointe du Bois 52-L.

The Sioux Lookout-Lac Seul country, ancestral home of the nomadic Ojibway Indians, is located north of the Lake of the Woods region in the heart of the vast boreal forests and thousands of irregular-shaped lakes of the Canadian Shield. The region is dominated by the famous lake trout and northern pike waters of huge Lac Seul and the sparkling maze of lakes along the English River and its tributaries. The English River is the largest tributary of the Winnipeg River. It was explored by Alexander Mackenzie and once formed a vital link of the Hudson's Bay Company's fur trade route via the Albany River from Fort Albany on James Bay to Fort Gary on Lake Winnipeg in Manitoba. The English and its tributaries, the Chukuni, Sturgeon, Wabigoon, Longlegged, and Cedar rivers, hold large northern pike, walleye, muskellunge, and a few lunker squaretails at the mouths of feeder streams. Sprawling Eagle Lake and the Vermilion Lakes offer some of Ontario's top-ranked fishing for trophy muskellunge up to 50 pounds. The region is a top-ranked hunting zone for moose and black bear.

Lac Seul, known to the Indians as the "lake of the white pine narrows," is the major headwaters of the English River and drains a large lake basin. The topography of the country surrounding Lac Seul varies from the ice-scoured, rocky ridges of the Canadian Shield and mixed forests of jack pine, white and black spruce, balsam, poplar, and white birch to the clay flats of ancient Lake Agassiz, created during the retreat of the last glacier. Up to the north, at the end of wilderness Highway 105, is the iron ore and gold-mining district of Red Lake. The discovery of gold at Red Lake in 1926 kicked off the biggest gold rush since the Klondike in '98 and stimulated the building of highways in this wilderness region. Until the construction of Highway 105 to connect Red Lake with the railroads to the south, all the heavy equipment and supplies were transported by barge from Sioux Lookout, along Lac Seul and up the Chukuni River to Red Lake. A fascinating 48-page photo history of mining throughout the province, *Ontario Mining,* can be obtained free from the Information Branch, Ministry of Natural Resources, Toronto.

Lodging, guides, and package fly-in vacations are offered by the following Northern Ontario resort operators. Write for free literature and rates. (Dryden) *Big Sandy Camps,* Box 268; *Bonny Bay Camps,* Box 4 RR 1; *Camp Caribou,* Box 310; *Gold Rock Lodge; Green Island Lodge,* Box 239. (Eagle River) *Big Eagle Muskie Camp,* Box 12; *Lindmeiers North Shore Lodge; Maylings Eagle Lake Camp; Robertsons Fin & Feather Lodge.* (Ear Falls) *Golden Eagle Resort,* Box 244; *Golden Fawn Lodge,* Box 218; *Fawn Lodge,* Box 218; *Goose Bay Camp,* Box 68; *Little Beaver Lodge,* Box 8; *Merls Lac Seul Lodge,* Box 375; *Oak Lake Camp,* Box 120; *Twiggs Canada North Lodge,* Box 279. (English River) *Browns of English River.* (Ignace) *Ignace Airways Outpost Camps,* Box 244; *Jorgensons Lodge,* Box 126; *Miminiska Sportsmans Lodge,* Box 244; *Moose Point Lodge,* Box 359. (Red Lake) *Bow Narrows Camp,* Box 217; *Canadian Fly-In Fishing,* Box 184; *Cat Island Lodge,* Box 857; *Dons Hinterland Lodge,* Box 744; *Freys West Deer Lake Lodge,* Box 887; *Sandy Beach Lodge; Trout Lake Lodge,* Box 918; *Vans Red Lake Lodge,* Box 159. (Sioux Lookout) *Andersons Camp,* Box 1058; *Fireside Lodge,* Box 218; *Hidden Bay Lodge,* Box 248; *Mackenzie Camps,* RR 1; *Moosehorn Lodge,* Box 579; *Patricia Air Transport,* Box 428; *Pickerel Arm Camp,* Box 458; *Slate Falls Airways,* Box 188; *Sturgeon River Camp,* Box 447;

Sunset Lodge, Box 399. (Savant Lake) *White Sands Camp.* (Vermilion Bay) *Big Canon Lake Lodge; Little Norway Camp,* Box 144; *Myers Camp,* Box 58; *North Star Camps,* RR 1; *South Shore Lodge,* Box 9; *Weavers Lodge,* Box 187. (Minaki) *Bayview Lodge; Black Bear Portage Camp; Caribou Falls Lodge,* Box 22. (Camp Robinson) *Lost Bay Resort.* Full-service vacation accommodations on Eagle Lake are provided by *Eagle Lake Lodge, Big Eagle Lodge,* and *Ramier's Island View Lodge,* all Eagle River P0V 1S0. The area is also served by the *Eagle Lake Sportsmen's Camp,* Box 96, Vermilion Bay P0V 2V0. Wilderness outpost camps throughout the northwest are operated by *Central Patricia Outfitters, Ltd.,* Box 5, Central Patricia. First-class accommodations on Wabigoon Lake are provided by *Muskie Bay Lodge,* Box 546, Dryden P8N 2Z2.

Access & Outfitting Centers

The English River-Lac Seul Country is reached by Trans-Canada Highways 11 and 17, wilderness Highways 105 and 72, and numerous forest access and logging roads. Outfitters, supplies, rentals, and lodging are available at Red Lake, Kenora, Ear Falls, Dryden, Sioux Lookout, Ignace, Savant Lake, Hudson, Central Patricia, and Vermilion Bay.

Publications & Information Sources

For details on guides, outfitters, fishing, hunting, canoeing, camping, a free catalog of waterproof lake contour fishing maps ($1 each), and color-coded hunting maps, write the following district offices of the Ministry of Natural Resources. For the free guides *English River Canoe Routes* and *Albany River Headwaters,* and contour fishing maps of all major lakes, including Lac Seul (3 maps), Minnitaki (2 maps), and Vermilion (2 maps), write: Sioux Lookout District, MNR, Box 309, Sioux Lookout P0V 2T0. For contour maps of major lakes, including Confederation (3 maps), Longlegged (2 maps), Red (2 maps), and Sydney (2 maps), write: Red Lake District Office, MNR, Forestry Rd., Red Lake. For contour fishing maps of major lakes, including Eagle (2 maps) and Sturgeon (2 maps), write: Dryden District Office, MNR, Highway 17, Ignace. For additional travel information, maps, and brochures write: Northwest Ontario Travel Association, P.O. Box 725, Dryden.

Lake Huron Country

Killarney Provincial Primitive Park

Canadian National Topographic Survey Maps, scale 1:50,000: Whitefish Falls 41I-4, Lake Panache 41I-3, Collins Inlet 41H-14.

Manitoulin Island

Canadian National Topographic Survey Overview Maps, scale 1:250,000: Alpena 41-G, Tobermory 41-H. Maps, scale 1:50,000: Meldrum Bay 41G-14, Silver Water 41G-15, Great Duck Island 41G-10, Kagawong 41G-16, Providence Bay 41G-9, Little Current 41H-13, Manitowaning 41H-12.

Mississagi Provincial Park & Wild River Reserve

Canadian National Topographic Survey Maps, scale 1:50,000. *Provincial Park:* Rawhide Lake 41J-10, Elliot Lake 41J-7. *Wild River Reserve:* Rocky Island Lake W. 41H-14, Rocky Island Lake E. 41J-15, White Owl Lake 41O-2, Indian Lake 41O-1, Biscotasing 41O-8.

North Georgian Bay Provincial Reserve

Canadian National Topographic Survey Overview Maps, scale 1:250,000: Blind River 41-J, Sudbury 41-I, Tobermory 41-H. Maps, scale 1:50,000: Algoma 41J-2, Elliot Lake 41J-7, Whiskey Lake 41J-8, Span-

ish 41J-1, Espanola 41I-5, Whitefish Falls 41I-4, Lake Panache 41I-3, Collins Inlet 41H-14, Delamere 41I-2, Key Harbor 41H-15, Naiscoot River 41H-10, Pointe-au-Baril 41H-9, Parry Sound 41H-8, Noganosh Lake 41H-16.

The Lake Huron region, known to the Huron Indians as "Ouendake" or "One Land Apart," is without a doubt Ontario's most scenic fish and game region. The Lake Huron country is formed by a southward-tilting strip of the Canadian Shield, which extends 75 miles inland from the shores of the North Channel, and the Thirty Thousand Islands region of Georgian Bay. The region is dominated by the rocky, gnarled, log-strewn beaches, shoals, reefs, bays, and cliffs, and a maze of spruce-covered islands and blue waters of Lake Huron. A majestic wilderness sprawls inland from the north shore characterized by dense forests of spruce, jack pine, balsam, white birch, and poplar. There are hundreds of remote lakes and wild rivers, including the Mississagi, Boland, Spanish, Abinadong, and Vermilion, and the rugged snow-white quartz summits of La Cloche Mountains. The island-dotted waters of Georgian Bay are world-renowned for their trophy fishing for muskellunge, northern pike, lake and rainbow trout, walleye, smallmouth bass, and coho and Chinook salmon. The region is also a top-ranked hunting zone for whitetail deer, black bear, moose and ducks.

The North Georgian Bay Recreational Reserve contains 4,500 square miles of forests and waterways stretching between Parry Sound and Algoma. The reserve includes the scenic cliffs, islands, and bays of the Thirty Thousand Islands and, inland, a primitive canoeing, hunting, and fishing country dotted with thousands of interconnected lakes and streams. A useful free 34-page guide, *North Georgian Bay Recreational Reserve Canoe Routes*, is published by the Department of Lands & Forests. It contains thorough descriptions of the major canoe routes including George Lake to Carlyle Lake and Killarney, Threenarrows, Bell, Tyson, Panache, and Wahwashkesh lakes, the Whitefish and Wanapitei rivers, and the historic fur trading route of the French River. The North Channel and Georgian Bay make for extraordinarily beautiful canoeing. The prevailing wind is westerly, and the paddler is well advised, like the voyageurs of old, to hug the mainland and to take advantage of the screen of islands, often a mile wide. The great mass of Manitoulin and Great Cloche islands forms a natural divide between the waters of the north shore and Georgian Bay. Manitoulin Island has a rugged landscape dotted with hundreds of lakes and

streams which offer excellent rainbow and brook trout and salmon fishing. Access is via Highway 68 or by ferry from Tobermory at the tip of the Bruce Peninsula, which is traversed by the northernmost segment of the 430-mile-long Bruce Trail. The 5.4-square-mile Georgian Bay National Park lies just off the tip of the peninsula.

Killarney Provincial Park encompasses 84,990 acres of wilderness on the north shore of Georgian Bay, due north of Manitoulin Island. The park is located on the southern portion of the 2-billion-year-old Canadian Shield. To the north lie the 1,000-foot quartzite summits of La Cloche Mountains. The interior campsites can be reached by 46 miles of portages linking deep, clear lakes nestled in forest valleys, including Bell, David, Johnnie, Threenarrows, and Killarney lakes. A Killarney Provincial Park brochure and canoe-camping-fishing information is available from the Superintendent, Killarney Provincial Park, Killarney P0M 2A0.

The Mississagi Provincial Park contains 153 square miles of the Canadian Shield country, 16 miles north of the mining town of Elliot Lake, known as the uranium capital of the world. The park contains mature forests of sugar maple, yellow birch, red and white pine, remote lakes, beaver ponds, and meadows dominated by Flack and Semiwite lakes and the Boland River. Campgrounds are located near the center of the reserve on Semiwite Lake. The Mississagi Wild River Reserve winds due north of the park through the brook trout, walleye, and northern pike waters of Rocky Island, Bark, Red Elk, White Owl, Spanish, Swallow, and Biscotasing lakes.

Lodging, guide service, and vacation package fly-in services are offered by the following Northern Ontario resort operators. Write for free literature and rates. (Blind River) *Log Chateau Lodge*, Box 1228. (Elliot Lake) *Blue Fox Camp*, Box 367; *Laurentian Lodge*, Box 141. (Little Current) *Okeechobee Lodge*, Box 100. (Parry Sound) *Glen Burney Lodge*, Box 187. (Killarney) *Killarney Mountain Lodge*. (Sault Ste. Marie) *Camp Millwood*, Box 1016; *Fullers Patter Lake Camp*; *Kwagama Lake Camp*, Box 32; *Winklemanns Trout Camps*, Box 416. (Sudbury) *Blue Mountain Lodge*. (Sturgeon Falls) *Sturgeon Lodge*, Box 510. (Metagama) *Shooting Star Camp*. (Thessalon) *Limberlost Lodge*, RR3; *Mashagama Lodge*, RR3; *The Outpost*, RR3.

Access & Outfitting Centers

The region is well serviced by the Lake Superior route of Trans-Canada Highway 17, Chapleau Route Highway 129, Highway 144, and numerous secondary and forest roads. Mississagi Provincial Park is reached via Highways 108 and 546; Killarney Provincial Park via Highway 637 off of Highway 69; and the Bruce Peninsula and Georgian Bay National Park via Highway 6. Air charter service is available throughout the region. Outfitting and supply centers are located at Sault Ste. Marie, Thessalon, Blind River, Elliot Lake, Massey, Espanola, Little Current, Wikwemikong, Sudbury, Parry Sound, Chapleau, and North Bay.

Publications & Information Sources

For hunting, fishing, canoeing, and camping information, waterproof lake contour fishing maps ($1), and free guides write the following district offices of the Ministry of Natural Resources. For contour fishing maps of major lakes, including Matinenda (3 maps) and Wakwekobi, and the free guides *Mississagi Wild River*, *Dunlop Lake to Mace Lake Loop*, *Boland River Canoe Route*, *Mississagi Provincial Park Reserve Canoe Routes*, *Aubinadong River Canoe Route*, *Wenebegon Canoe Route*, and *Mississagi Provincial Park Trail Guides* write: Blind River District Office, MNR, Box 190, 62 Queen St., Blind River P0R 1B0. For lake contour fishing maps and the free guides *Montreal River Canoe Route* and *Wakami River Canoe Route* write: Chapleau District Office, MNR, 34 Birch St., Chapleau P0M 1K0. For lake contour fishing maps and the free guides *Magnetawan River Canoe Route* and *French River Canoe Route* write: Parry Sound District Office, MNR, 4 Miller St., Parry Sound P2A 1S8. For lake contour maps of major lakes write: Sault Ste. Marie District Office, MNR, Box 130, Aerodrome Bldg., Sault Ste. Marie P6A 5L5. For the free guides *North Georgian Bay Recreational Reserve Canoe Routes, Sturgeon River Canoe Route A, Chiniguchi & Sturgeon Rivers Canoe Route D, Sturgeon River Canoe Route B, Wanapitei River Canoe Route E, Vermilion River Canoe Route F, Onaping River Canoe Routes G & H,* and *Spanish River Canoe Route* write: Sudbury District Office, MNR, 174 Douglas St. W, Sudbury P3E 1G1. For hiking info and maps for the Bruce Trail write: Bruce Trail Association, 33 Hardale Crescent, Hamilton L8T 1X7. For travel planning information write: Algoma-Kinniwabi Travel Association, Suite 3, 553 Queen St. E, Sault Ste. Marie; or Rainbow Country Travel Association, 43 Frood Rd., Sudbury P3E 4N3; or Georgian Bay Travel Association, c/o Ministry of Industry & Tourism, 73 Mississauga St. E, Orillia.

Lake of the Woods—Quetico Country

Lake of the Woods Region Topo Maps

Canadian National Topographic Survey Maps, scale 1:250,000: Kenora 52-E, Dryden 52-F, Rosseau 52-D. Hydrographic Charts: 6202, 6203, 6204, 6205.

Lac La Croix

Canadian National Topographic Survey Maps, scale 1:250,000: International Falls 52-C, Quetico 52-B.

Manitou Lakes Chain

Canadian National Topographic Survey Maps, scale 1:250,000: International Falls 52-C, Kenora 52-E, Dryden 52-F.

Northern Lite Lake Canoe Route

Canadian National Topographic Survey Maps, scale 1:50,000: Saganaga Lake 52B-2, Mowe Lake 52B-7, Marks Lake 52B-8, Shebandowan 52B-9.

Quetico Provincial Park Wilderness

Canadian National Topographic Survey Overview Maps, scale 1:250,-000: Quetico 52-B, International Falls 52-C. Maps, scale 1:50,000: Saganaga Lake 52B-2, Knife Lake 52B-3, Basswood Lake 52B-4, Poobah Lake 52B-5, Kawnipi Lake 52B-6, Mowe Lake 52B-7, Lac La Croix 52C-8, Pipe Lake 52C-9, Quetico Lake 52B-12, Pickerel Lake 52B-11, Burchell Lake 52B-10, Atikokan 52B-13, Sapawe 52B-14, Bedivere Lake 52B-15.

White Otter Wilderness Reserve

Canadian National Topographic Survey Maps, scale 1:250,000: Ignace 52-G, Dryden 52-F.

Lake of the Woods and the Rainy Lake and Quetico wilderness areas to the east are among the finest canoe-camping and fishing regions in North America. Lake of the Woods is located due east of the Manitoba border in the southern portion of northwest Ontario and dominates the region with its glacier-formed irregularly shaped shoreline and 12,000 spruce-covered islands. The islands house many Indian rock paintings and are the only nesting ground of the white pelican in Ontario. The lake is surrounded by the boreal forests of the Canadian Shield country and its thousands upon thousands of sparkling blue lakes, streams, and interconnecting waterways. The Lake of the

Woods watershed drains 27,000 square miles of the surrounding wilderness waters and is actually the southernmost portion of the Winnipeg River system. The rivers in this system flow south and west into the Rainy River waterway along the international boundary waters that divide Minnesota and Ontario before flowing into Lake of the Woods. The lake is one of Canada's hot spots for record-sized muskellunge up to 58 pounds, great northern pike, walleye, smallmouth bass, and lake trout. The Ministry of Natural Resources publishes a useful 48-page fishing guide, *The Fisheries of Lake of the Woods.* It costs $1 and contains maps, charts, and info about the lake's bays, islands, and fishing areas.

In the 19th century Lake of the Woods became the crossroads of the growing northwest fur trade empire with the shift of operations from Montreal to York Factory of Hudson Bay. The new route along the Albany River to Lake of the Woods and Fort Gary replaced the long and costly haul the northmen had to make around the violent cascades of the lower Pigeon River at Grand Portage and the difficult Kaministikwia River route through the Quetico wilderness. An interesting guide to the historic Grand Portage Trail, the *Pigeon River Hiking Trail,* is available free from Thunder Bay District Office, Ministry of Natural Resources, Thunder Bay.

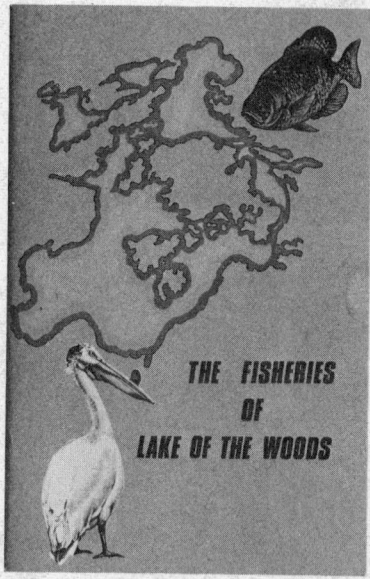

The canoe country of the Quetico Provincial Park is north of the boundary waters between Minnesota and Ontario. It is still a wild and primitive country, much as it was during the days of the voyageur. Indian summer is the best canoeing season here when the woods are colored orange, yellow, and red; and bays of the deep, clear lakes seem to burst with activity. Along the 900 miles of Quetico canoe trails the paddler will often see tracks of the elusive timber wolf; beavers pushing branches homeward on quiet ponds in the forest meadows; golden eagles soaring above the rocky, cliff-lined lake shores; and giant pike swirling in the shallow sunlit bays. He will paddle on through turbulent rapids, portage around innumerable falls and cascades, and cruise across the large island-dotted lakes with the autumn sun high in the clear noon sky as the winds guide his canoe toward the distant headlands. The beauty, romance, and history of the Quetico Country is captured in Sigurd Olsen's classic *Runes of the North* and *The Singing Wilderness,* both available for $7.95 (plus 50¢ postage) from Alfred A. Knopf, Mail Order Books, 400 Hahn Rd., Westminster, MD 21157 U.S.A.

A 38 × 38-inch *Quetico Provincial Park Map* is available free from the Ministry of Natural Resources. It is printed in full color and is quite attractive. It shows all portages with length in yards, seaplane bases, entry points and park stations, Canadian customhouses, and the adjacent wildlands of the Neguagon Indian Reserve, huge Lac la Croix, and the oddly shaped boundary waters. The map-guide gives information about the history of the region, canoeing, fishing, Indian rock paintings, geology, wildlife and flora, access, and the Dawson Trail Campgrounds. A handbook to the map, the 50-page *Quetico Provincial Park Canoe Routes* is available free from the Ministry of Natural Resources. It describes such historic wilderness water trails as the Olifaunt, Maligne-Beaverhouse, and Quetico lake loops, to mention a few.

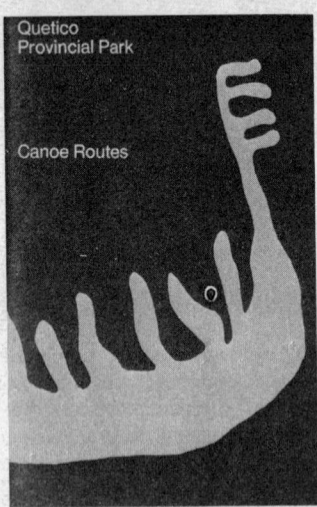

The glacial wilderness of the remote White Otter Reserve takes in 66,000 acres of prime canoeing and fishing country about 30 miles northwest of Atikokan. The reserve is dominated by beautiful White Otter Lake, reached by 30-mile wilderness canoe journey. For a free *White Otter Reserve Map*, write to: Ministry of Natural Resources, White River P0M 3G0. An odd feature of the area is a 40-foot log castle built by an old trapper for his bride in Scotland—who, by the way, never showed up.

Lodging, guides, and package fly-in vacations are offered by the following Lake of the Woods—Quetico Country resort operators. Write for free literature and rates. (Atikokan) *Caribou Resort*, Box 1390; *Clearwater West Lodge*, Box 790; *Eddies Island Camp*, Box 881; *Eva Lake Resort*, Box 1209; *Morris Camp*, Box 550; *Pioneer Airways*, Box 730; *Powell Lake Resort*, Box 1526. (Fort Frances) *Bill Zups Fishing Camps*; *Bowes Manion Lake Camp*; *Camp Manitou*, Box 127; *Campbells Cabins*; *Hales Bay Resort*; *Northern Lite Camps*, Box 579; *Northern Lite Manitou Lake Camp*, Box 579; *Northland Tent Camps*; *Rinas Outpost Camps*, Box 451; *Shannons Camp*, Box 784; *Silver Muskie Lodge*, Box 116; *Tang of the North Lodge*, Box 668. (Kenora) *Crow Rock Muskie Camp*, Box 291; *Dogtooth Resort*, Box 437; *Grassy Lodge*, Box 120; *Hide-A-Way Resort*; *McKeevers Portage Bay Camp*, RR1; *Reids Stork Lake Camp*, Box 120; *The Chalet*, Box 5. (Nestor Falls) *Atikwa Lake Camp*, Box 149; *Bull Moose Lodge*, Box 69; *Clarke & Crombie Camps*, Box 34; *Deer Lake Portage Camp*; *Greens Camp*, Box 37; *Crawfords Resort*, Box 97; *Crow Lake Lodge*, Box 34; *Hector Lake Camp*, Box 279; *Helliars Resort*, Box 39; *Hook'n Horn Lodge*; *Lake of the Woods Lodge*; *Larssons Camp*, Box 190; *Moose Point Lodge*, RR2; *Slippery Winds Resort*; *The Marina*, Box 36; *Youngs Wilderness Camp*, Box 129. (Rainy River) *Windy Bay Lodge*, RR1. (Sioux Narrows) *Caribou Lodge*, Box 38; *Crawfords Sioux Narrows Camp*, Box 330; *Lebrons Long Bay Camp*, Box 54; *Red Indian Lodge*, Box 270; *Sioux Narrows Lodge*, Box 90; *The Rod & Reel*, Box 119; *White Birch Lodge*, Box 300; *Woodland Resort*, Box 370.

Access & Outfitting Centers

Lake of the Woods country is reached by Trans-Canada Highways 11 and 17 to Fort Frances and Kenora. The main entry point to Quetico Park is on Highway 11 at the Dawson Trail Campgrounds on French Lake 30 miles east of Atikokan. There are 5 water entry stations on Quetico's southern perimeter: Beaverhouse Lake, Lac La Croix Cabin, Prairie Portage and Ottawa Island (cabin 16) on Basswood Lake, and Cache Bay cabin on Saganaga Lake. Travelers from the United States must clear Canadian customs and immigration. Landings for floatplanes must be made at one of the airports on the park boundaries: Dawson Trail at French Lake, Lac La Croix, Ottawa Island on Basswood Lake, and Cache Bay. The major outfitting and supply centers are Fort Francis, Sioux Narrows, Kenora, Vermilion Bay, Atikokan, and Thunder Bay.

Publications & Information Sources

For the nitty-gritty about provincial parks, campgrounds, canoe outfitters, hunting, fishing, and camping, waterproof lake survey fishing maps ($1 each), as well as free maps, guidebooks, and color-coded hunting maps, write the following district offices of the Ministry of Natural Resources. For the free 50-page *Quetico Provincial Park Canoe Routes* booklet and 38 × 38-inch *Quetico Provincial Park Map* (No. 56A) write: Atikokan District Office, MNR, Atikokan P0T 1C0. For a free *Rainy River District Map*, and free guides and maps for the *Rainy Lake Loop*, *Big Canoe River*, *Caliper Lake to Kishkutena Lake*, *Vickers Lake to Lower Manitou*, *Manitou River*, *Caliper Lake to Burditt Lake via Pipestone Lake*, *Burditt Lake Loop*, and *Lower Seine River* canoe routes, write: Fort Frances District Office, MNR, 922 Scott St., Fort Frances P9A 1J4. For free guidebooks and maps of *Pigeon River Hiking Trail*, *Northern Light Lake Canoe Routes* (booklets 1–10), *Kaministiquia River Fur Trade Route*, and contour fishing maps of all major lakes in this district, including Arrow (2 maps), Lac des Mille Lacs (2 maps), Northern Light (3 maps), and Shebandowan (3 maps), write: Thunder Bay District Office, MNR, 14 N. Algoma St., Thunder Bay P7A 4Z3. For contour fishing maps of the important lakes, including Lower Black Sturgeon (3 maps) and Separation (2 maps), write: Kenora District Office, MNR, P.O. Box 1080, Kenora P9N 3X7. Two guidebooks, *The Fisheries of Lake of the Woods* and the 118-page *Geology & Scenery: Rainy Lake and East to Lake Supe-*

rior, are available for $1 each from the Ministry of Natural Resources, Parliament Bldgs., Toronto. For additional travel information about Lake of the Woods country write: Northwest Ontario Travel Service, P.O. Box 725, Dryden. For a free 48-page *Lake of the Woods* brochure, write: Regional Information Center, 1500 Highway 17E, Kenora.

Lake Superior Country

Lake Nipigon Region

Canadian National Topographic Survey Maps, scale 1:250,000: Nipigon 52-H, Fort William 52-A, Nakina 42-L, Longlac 42-E, Schreiber 42-D.

Lake Superior Provincial Park

Canadian National Topographic Survey Overview Maps, scale 1:250,000: Michipicoten 41-N. Maps, scale 1:50,000: Agawa Bay 41N-7, Gray Owl Lake 41N-8, Blackspruce Lake 41N-9, Gargantua Harbor 41N-10, Michipicoten Harbor 41N-15.

Pukaskwa National Park

Canadian National Topographic Survey Maps, scale 1:250,000: Schreiber 42-D, White River 42-C, Michipicoten 41-N.

The famous fish and game country of the Canadian Shield of the north shore of Lake Superior, stretching from Sault Ste. Marie to Thunder Bay, is the most rugged in Ontario. The entire region is dominated by Lake Superior, known to the Ojibway as *Keckegumme,* "the mother of all lakes," a vast inland sea more than 400 miles long and 1,300 feet deep in spots, which holds record rainbow and lake trout and Chinook and coho salmon. This is a land of dense forests of black and white spruce, jack pine, aspen, white birch, and balsam fir, which supports a number of paper mills. There are massive rock-covered hills and cliffs, gravel ridges, and 2,000-foot-high mountains; short, brawling rivers with numerous falls and rapids flow south from the height of land along the rim of the Canadian Shield, located 60 miles inland from the spectacular 500-foot cliffs, deep bays, boulder-strewn beaches, and scenic, often fog-covered islands of the Superior shoreline.

The moose and black bear hunting lands of the Nipigon Provincial Forest and the brook trout meccas and canoe routes surrounding huge Lake Nipigon, which covers 1,870 square miles, are located north of Lake Superior's Thunder Bay. Lake Nipigon is known for its large spruce-covered islands and trophy fishing for brook trout up to 10 pounds, lake trout up to 30 pounds, great northern pike up to 43 pounds, and fat walleye up to 12 pounds. A number of Hudson's Bay Company fur trading posts were once active along its rocky shores, and York boats traveled its waters on the route from Lake Superior to Fort Albany on James Bay. The renowned Nipigon River annually produced brook trout in the 6–9-pound class and, in 1916, produced the world's record 14 pound 6 ounce squaretail. In his famous book *A Trout & Salmon Fisherman for 75 Years,* Edward R. Hewitt, one of the founders of fly fishing in America, reports of Indians netting tons of giant squaretails in the 10 to 12 pound range, reaching weights of up to 19 pounds, in the spawning beds at the head of Lake Nipigon during the late 1800's.

The scenic, rugged wilderness of the recently established Pukaskwa National Park lies due east of Lake Nipigon, north of Michipicoten Island in Lake Superior. The park takes in 464,000 acres of wild streams, mountains, hundreds of remote lakes, and dense green forests, stretching 50 miles along the Superior shoreline with its massive, rocky headlands, secluded bays, islets, and islands between the White and Pukaskwa rivers. Ancient pitlike structures are found along the boulder-strewn beaches where shamans and wabenos, custodians of the Ojibway Indian customs, came to honor and appease the spirits of the land, water, and skies. Two useful guides, *Pukaskwa National Park* and *The Coastal Trip,* a fascinating guide to canoe travel along the Pukaskwa shoreline of Superior from the Pic River to Michipicoten, are available free from the Superintendent, Pukaskwa National Park, P.O. Box 550, Marathon P0T 2E0. The notoriously unpredictable fog and squalls—known to the voyageurs of Lake Superior as *la vieille*—rule the canoeists. Access within the park is limited to gravel jeep trails and cross-country hiking.

Lake Superior Provincial Park, a 601-square-mile wilderness reserve, stretches inland from the shores of Old Woman Bay, 75 miles north of Sault Ste. Marie between the Michipicoten and Montreal rivers. The interior of the park is a rugged country of dense forests, lakes, glacial spillways, lava flows, kames, kettles, eskers, and faults dominated by the deep, cold lake trout waters of Mijnemungshing Lake and the lake-run rainbow and brook trout waters of Agawa, Baldhead, and Rabbit Blanket rivers. There is controlled logging within the park as well as trapping for marten, wolverine, beaver, fisher, and mink and a 1-month moose hunting season. Campsites are located at Crescent Lake, Agawa Bay, and Rabbit Blanket Lake.

Vacation lodging, guides, and package fly-in holidays are offered by the following Northern Ontario resort operators. Write for free literature and rates, and be sure to make reservations well in advance. (Armstrong) *Bear Paw Lodge,* Box 37; *Caribou,* Box 128; *Caribou Lake Lodge,* Box 57; *Ferring & Nuttalls Camp; Nipigon Lodge; Obonga Cottages,* Box 94. (Geraldton) *Wild Goose Lake Resort,* Box 520. (Hornepayne) *Granite Hill Lake Resort,* Box 448. (Longlac) *Klotz Lake Camp,* Box 305. (Nipigon) *Chalet Lodge,* Box 97; *North Shore Lodge,* Box 203. (White River) *Dellair Enterprises,* Box 220; *Norm-An-D Lodge,* Box 338; *Olivers Fly-in Camp,* Box 1191. (Hawk Junction) *Konika Lodge.*

Access & Outfitting Centers

The Lake Superior country is reached by Trans-Canada Highway 17. A gravel road extension of Highway 627, off the Trans-Canada, passes through the Pic River Indian Reserve to the mouth of the Pic River at Pukaskwa National Park. Trans-Canada Highway 11 and Highways 800 and 585 provide access to the Lake Nipigon region. Numerous gravel secondary and forest roads provide access to the interior fish and game areas. Outfitting and supply centers are located at Nipigon, Red Rock, Armstrong, Geraldton, Longlac, Manitouwadge, Schreiber, Terrace Bay, Marathon, White River, Wawa, Michipicoten, and Sault Ste. Marie.

Publications & Information Sources

For hunting, fishing, camping, and canoeing information, and waterproof lake contour fishing maps ($1 each) and canoeing guides, write the following district offices of the Ministry of Natural Resources. For free canoe-route guides, *Gull River, Nipigon District Canoe Routes,* and *Kopka River* and contour fishing maps for all major lakes, including Black Sturgeon (2 maps), Northwind, and Trapnarrows, write: Nipigon District, MNR, Box 729, Nipigon P0T 2J0. For *A Guide to Fishing, A Guide to Hunting, Batchawana River Canoe Route, Ranger Lake Area Canoe Route, Lake Superior Provincial Park, Michipicoten River Canoe Route,* all free, and contour fishing maps for all major lakes in the region write: Sault Ste. Marie District, MNR, Aerodrome Bldg., Box 130, Sault Ste. Marie P6A 5L5. For information and contour fishing maps of all major lakes, including White Otter and Dickison, write: Terrace Bay District, MNR, Terrace Bay P0T 2W0.

For info and lake contour fishing maps of Manitowik (2 maps), Oba (2 maps), and Wabatongushi (2 maps) write: Wawa District, MNR, Box 1160, Wawa P0S 1K0. For lake contour fishing maps, the free *White River District Fishing Lakes* guide, and the free *White River, Tedder River-Wawigami Lake, Hammer Lake-Obatanga Lake,* and *Knife Lake-University River-Hammer Lake* canoe-route guides write: White River District, MNR, White River P0M 3G0. For travel information, booklets, and brochures write: Algoma-Kinniwabi Travel Association, 553 Queen St. E, Suite 3, Sault Ste. Marie.

Moose River Country & the James Bay Frontier

Moose River & the James Bay Frontier Topo Maps

Canadian National Topographic Survey Maps, scale 1:250,000: Timmins 42-A, Kapuskasing 42-G, Cochrane 42-N, Moose River 42-I, Smoky Falls 42-J, Moosonee 42-P.

Chapleau Forest Reserve Headwaters

Canadian National Topographic Survey Maps, scale 1:250,000: Chapleau 41-O, Foleyet 42-B.

This renowned northeast Ontario fishing, moose hunting, and canoe-camping region takes in the lake-dotted boreal forests, string bogs, tundra, and turbulent rivers along the historic Hudson's Bay Company fur brigade routes of the Moose River and its major tributaries: the Abitibi, Mattagami, Missinaibi (a fast-packet route used by the Hudson's Bay Company to get messages quickly from Moosonee to Lake Superior), Kapuskasing, and Groundhog rivers. The Moose stretches from the trophy brook trout waters of the headwater lakes of its tributaries located along the height of land in the Chapleau Forest Reserve, northward through the jack-pine stands and moose country of the Canadian Shield and the forests of spruce and tundra of the Hudson Bay lowlands at its mouth on James Bay.

The adventurous outdoorsman will find good moose and black bear hunting along the route traveled by the Polar Bear Express operated by the Ontario Northland Railway between the towns of Cochrane and Moosonee at James Bay. The wilderness paddler and fisherman will find walleye and lunker great northern pike up to 36 pounds in the weedy bays and shoals of the Moose and its tributaries. During the warm summer months the banks of these great northern rivers are a rainbow of colors with clusters of wild rose, aster, goldenrod, blue iris, and lily of the valley in vivid contrast to the woodland greens and browns. Traveling north down the Moose to its mouth at James Bay, the canoeist will find an extremely dangerous coast of boulder-strewn mud flats which extend miles from shore at low tide. Near its mouth the Moose has a canallike character and is surrounded by mixed spruce and poplar forests. Away from the river the forest gradually thins out to the open lowland bogs with hummocks of stunted black spruce and tamarack and hollows of sedge and cottongrass.

String bogs which are alternating low vegetated ridges and long narrow pools which lie crosswise to the slight slope of the land are the dominant feature of the Hudson Bay lowlands. Cross-country travel over the mire of the lowlands during the summer months is a nightmare beset with hordes of vicious blackflies and mosquitoes. All summer travel other than by air and railway is done on the rivers and along the coast. Canoe travel on James Bay is always uncertain—even in the large Rupert House canoes a light east or north wind will create a rough sea and hazardous travel conditions. Travel must be gauged for high tide to ride the shoals at Shipsands Island at the mouth of the Moose. The tide moves so fast that it's extremely difficult to run against it. Two useful and interesting booklets, *The Land of the Cree* and *Tides of James Bay,* are available free from the Moosonee District office of the Ministry of Natural Resources. The Cree Indian hunting camps along the tidal flats of James Bay offer some of the finest goose hunting in North America. The thousands of small pools with their islands and peninsulas provide important breeding sites for Canadian geese. Additional information may be obtained by writing: Cree Indian Goose Camps, Ministry of Natural Resources, P.O. Box 190, Station A, Moosonee.

Lodging, guides, and package fly-in vacations are provided by the following Northern Ontario resort operators. (Chapleau) *Chapleau Lodge,* Box 640; *Chapleau Outpost,* Box 487; *Rollo Lake Lodge,* Box 567. (Cochrane) *James Bay Outfitters,* Box 1866; *Lindbergs Air Service,* Box 998. (Foleyet) *Horwood Lake Lodge,* Box 141; *Ivanhoe Lodge,* Box 37; *Moose Land Resort,* Box 70; *Red Pine Lodge.* (Hearst) *Forde Lake Lodge,* Box 417; *Mooseland Outfitters,* Box 1329. (Moonbeam) *Kap Outfitters,* Box 129. (Moose Factory) *Keewatin Kinoshao Sports Camp,* Box 26; *Papamotao Goose Camp.* (Moosonee) *Hannah Bay Goose Camp.* (Timmins) *James Bay Goose Camp,* Box 162; *New Bromley Lodge,* Box 1021.

Access & Outfitting Centers

The Moose River country is reached by Trans-Canada Highway 11, the Polar Bear Express, and bush plane from major outfitting centers. The Chapleau Forest and Game Reserve region is reached via Highway 101. Major outfitting centers are Chapleau, Timmins, Iroquois Falls, Cochrane, Kapuskasing, Hearst, and Moosonee.

Publications & Information Sources

For additional information about fishing, hunting, canoeing, guides and outfitters, free guidebooks, and lake contour fishing maps ($1 each) of the major lakes, printed on waterproof paper, write the following district offices of the Ministry of Natural Resources. For contour survey maps of the major regional lakes, including Big Missinaibi (2 maps), Five Mile, Ivanhoe, and Wakami, write: Chapleau District Office, MNR, 34 Birch St., Chapleau P0M 1K0. Free *Canoe Route Travelog* guides which provide complete route descriptions,

rapids, falls, portages, mileage, access, and regional history are also available: *Aguasuk-Kwataboahegan-Moose River Canoe Route Guide, Chapleau-Nemogesenwikda River Guide, Groundhog River Guide, Kormak to Foleyet Guide, Partridge River Guide, Shoals Loop Guide,* and *Sakatawi Route Guide.* For contour fishing maps ($1 each) of the major lakes, including Commanda, Dora, Little Abitibi, Pierre, and Trail lakes, and the free guides *Fishing Opportunities in Cochrane District, Hunting in the Cochrane District,* and *Mattagami & Moose River Canoe Trip from Smooth Rock to James Bay* write: Cochrane District Office, MNR, 140 4th Ave., Box 730, Cochrane P0L 1C0. For contour fishing maps of Canoeshed Lake, Hart Island and Muskasenda lakes and the free 20-page *Mattagami River Canoe Route Guide, Abitibi River Fur Brigade Water Trail,* and *Missinaibi River Guide* write: Timmins District Office, MNR, 896 Riverside Dr., Timmins P4N 3W2. Four fascinating guidebooks, *Birds of Tidewater, Plants of Tidewater, The Land of the Cree,* and *Tides of James Bay,* can be had free by writing: Moosonee District Office, MNR, Moosonee P0L 1Y0. For survey fishing maps of Cantin, Inlet, Opasatika, Penelton, Remi, Rufus, Sagamash, and Usnac lakes and for the free *Kapuskasing River to James Bay Guide* write: Kapuskasing District Office, MNR, 6 Government Rd., Kapuskasing P5N 2W4. For travel information write: Cochrane Timiskaming Travel Association, P.O. Box 1162, Timmins P4N 7H9.

Ottawa River Country

Lady Evelyn Wild River Reserve

Canadian National Topographic Survey Maps, scale 1:50,000: Lady Evelyn Lake 41P-8, Obabika Lake 41P-1, Elk Lake 41P-9.

Lake Nipissing Region

Canadian National Topographic Survey Maps, scale 1:250,000: Sudbury 41-I, North Bay 31-L.

Lake Temagami Country

Canadian National Topographic Survey Maps, scale 1:50,000: Obabika Lake 41P-1, Lake Temagami 41I-16, Glen Afton 41I-9, Temagami 31M-4, Ingall Lake 31L-12, Marten Lake 31L-12.

Mattawa Wild River Reserve

Canadian National Topographic Survey Maps, scale 1:50,000: Mattawa 31L-7, North Bay 31L-6, Kiosk 31L-2, Powassan 31L-3.

The iron, silver, and copper mining and logging country of the upper Ottawa River includes the Mattawa, Montreal, and Lady Evelyn rivers and Lake Timiskaming—a widening of the Ottawa. The famous lake trout and walleye fishing waters of sprawling, island-dotted Lake Temagami and its wilderness headwaters, and the trophy muskellunge waters of Lake Nipissing, although they flow into Lake Huron, are included here because they are most accessible from the Ottawa River country.

During the fur trade era the Ottawa and Mattawa rivers were major water trails to the upper Great Lakes and the Northwest Company's headquarters at Grand Portage where the voyageurs met the smaller, fur-laden canoes from Lake Athabasca. The Ottawa and Montreal River system was the fur traders' link route to James Bay. White-pine lumber replaced beaver pelts as the most important trade item in the region. Remnants of the once majestic stands of red and white pine, which grow over 200 feet tall in these rocky uplands, may still be seen. Following extensive forest fires and logging operations over the past half century, most of the original pine stands have been replaced by a typical Great Lakes forest of jackpine, balsam, poplar, and white and

yellow birch. Construction of the T & NO (Temiskaming & Northern Ontario) Railway, later to become known as the Ontario Northland, was the major factor leading to the discovery of minerals and the subsequent development of the boomtown mining centers at Temagami and Cobalt. Big-game animals and wildlife found in the wilderness forests include moose, black bear, wolf, red fox, fisher, marten, beaver, wolverine, bald eagle, and waterfowl.

The upper Ottawa River, described once as a "strange wild river of seething white, lashing among gray-capped, dark greenish boulders," was used by the French and later by the Northwest Company as the route to Lake Timiskaming and the height of land to the Moose River and James Bay. Hudson's Bay Company posts were located at Frederickhouse, Abitibi, Kenogamissi, and Ground lakes. The famous brook trout fishing waters of the Mattawa River, Ojibway for "place where the rivers meet," lies in an ancient geological fault noted for its sheer cliffs soaring to heights of 100 feet. The Mattawa was used by the voyageurs as a route connecting the Ottawa River to Lake Nipissing and the upper Great Lakes. It was traveled by Étienne Brulé as early as 1608 and later by other explorers, missionaries, and traders including Champlain, Nicolet, Radisson, La Vérendrye, Marquette and Joliet, and Mackenzie. Canoe trips begin downstream at Explorer's Point on the Ottawa River or at Samuel de Champlain Provincial Park. A 25-mile stretch of the river has been recently established as a wild river reserve by the Department of Lands & Forests. The interesting free guides *Mattawa Wild River Provincial Park* and *Samuel de Champlain Trail Guide* are available from the North Bay District Office of the Ministry of Natural Resources.

Vacation lodging, guides, and package fly-in holidays are offered by the following Northern Ontario resort operators. Write for free literature and rates, and be sure to make your reservations well in advance. (Gowganda) *Auld Reekie Camp,* Box 99; *Gowganda Hunt & Fish Camp.* (Marten River) *Fish Richfield; Marten River Lodge; O-Pee-Chee Camp; Pozniaks Camp.* (Mattawa) *Papineau Lodge,* Box 99. (Noelville) *Fish Tale Lodge,* RR 1; *North Channel Camp,* Box 95. (North Bay) *Casa Blanca Lodge.* (Nipissing) *Nipissing Lodge,* RR 1; *Meadow Creek Lodge.* (Temagami) *Angus Lake Lodge,* RR 1; *Bambi Lodge,* Box 94; *Camp Andorra,* Box 156; *Camp Ket-Chun-Eny Lodge,* Box 7; *Camp Wanapitei; Centura Wilderness Resort,* Box

444; *Keewaydin Camps; Loon Lodge; Temagami Lodge*, Box 326; *White Gables Camp*, Box 21. (French River) *Hass Camp*, RR 2.

Access & Outfitting Centers

The region is serviced by Trans-Canada Highway 11, which runs parallel to the Ottawa and Mattawa rivers, and by Trans-Canada Highway 17, which runs northward from Lake Nipissing past the headwaters of tributary streams of Temagami, Anima, Nipissing, and Lady Evelyn lakes to Cobalt, New Liskeard, and Kirkland Lake. Secondary and forest service roads provide access to many of the remote interior fish and game areas. The Ontario Northland Railway runs north through Temagami to Cochrane and Moosonee. Air charter service is available throughout the region. Outfitting and supply centers are at Esker Lakes, Restoule, Samuel de Champlain, Antoine, Marten River, Finlayson Point, and Kapkigiwan provincial parks.

Publications & Information Sources

Write the following district offices of the Ministry of Natural Resources for waterproof lake contour fishing maps, hunting, fishing, camping, and canoeing info, and free guides. For contour fishing maps of the major district lakes, including Ducan (3 maps) and Watabeag, and the free guides *Esker Lakes Provincial Park, KapKigIwan Provincial Park, KapKigIwan-Sylvan Valley Trail Guide, Lonesome Bog-Esker Lakes, KapKigIwan-Trail of the Beavers, KapKigIwan-Hell's Gate Trail Guide, Esker Lakes-Trapper's Trail,* and *Kirkland Lake District Canoe Routes:* Montreal, Englehart, Larder, Misema River Chain, Magusi, and Lady Evelyn rivers write: Kirkland Lake District Office, MNR, Swastika P0K 1T0. For contour fishing maps of major lakes, including Nobonsing and Restoule lakes, and the free guides *Mattawa Wild River, Samuel de Champlain Trail Guide, Restoule Provincial Park, Restoule River Trail, Restoule & Upper French Canoe Route, Dokis Canoe Route, Marten River Provincial Park, Early Log-*

ging, and *Forest Hiking Trail* write: North Bay District, MNR, P.O. Box 3070, North Bay P1B 8K7. For contour fishing maps of the major lakes, including Temagami (4 maps), Thieving Bear, and Anima Nipissing, and the free guides *Temagami District Fishing Lakes, Whitefish of Lake Temagami,* and *Temagami Canoe Routes* write: Temagami District, MNR, Box 38, Temagami P0H 2H0.

Winisk Wild River & Polar Bear Provincial Park

Polar Bear Provincial Park

Canadian National Topographic Survey Maps, scale 1:250,000: Lakitusaki River 43-J, Sutton Lake 43-K, Cape Henrietta 43-O, Winisk 43-N, Clendenning River 43-L, Fort Severn 43-M.

Winisk Wild River & Provincial Park

Canadian National Topographic Survey Maps, scale 1:250,000: Wunnummin Lake 53-A, Lansdowne House 43-D, Winiskisis Channel 43-E, Clendenning River 43-L, Sutton Lake 43-K, Winisk 43-N.

The Winisk, one of Ontario's great northern rivers, flows north for 270 miles from its headwaters at Winisk and Shibogama lakes in the northwestern portion of the province to its mouth at Wabuk Point on Hudson Bay. Downstream from the headwaters it forms two branches, both of which have numerous boiling rapids, falls, and long stretches of fast water. The two branches of the Winisk merge about 150 miles upstream from its mouth. The upper stretch of the river is a pure boreal forest wilderness of dense stands of black spruce and tamarack and jutting ridges of rock. The Winisk changes its mood and character as it nears Hudson Bay, flowing through the towering white limestone canyons of the lowlands past numerous spruce-covered islands and

great heaps of shimmering ice-covered gravel along the banks in Polar Bear Provincial Park to its mouth at the Indian village of Winisk. The fishing is particularly good in the upper reaches for voracious northern pike and lunker brook trout at the mouths of tributaries. Unless you are a seasoned wilderness traveler it would be wise to arrange for the services of a guide and gear at the Cree Indian trapping and fishing village of Webequie (pop. 300), on the shores of Winisk Lake. In addition to making your trip more enjoyable, he will add immeasurably to your store of woodcraft and knowledge of the surrounding wildlands. The Crees maintain 8 outpost cabins located at strategic sites along the river, outfitted with canoes, motors, and camp equipment. For information write: *Winisk River Camps*, c/o Ojibway Country Indian Camps, Fort Hope (via Nakina) P0T 2H0.

The Asheweig River, a remote, turbulent tributary of the Winisk, is one of Canada's great untapped trophy brook trout fisheries, often yielding squaretails up to 6, 7, and 8 pounds. The Asheweig is best fished by setting up a fly-in wilderness base camp. Charter floatplane services for the region are based at Nakina.

The lower stretch of the Winisk flows through Polar Bear Provincial Park, on the western shorelines of James and Hudson bays, some 250 miles northwest of Moosonee. This 9,300-square-mile primitive reserve is one of the most southerly extensions of arctic tundra in the world. In the Cape Henrietta region to the east it is a country of bare, disintegrated limestone ridges, grasslands, coastal flats, and numerous small kettle ponds seldom more than 2 feet deep. The park is the denning ground of the polar bear and the subarctic breeding ground for huge colonies of snow geese, and is the habitat of arctic and red fox, wolf, otter, bearded seal, moose, beaver, and caribou. A free 20-page *Polar Bear Provincial Park Guide* is available from the district Ministry of Natural Resources office.

The remote Ekwan, Sutton, and Attawapiskat rivers to the east of the Winisk and the Severn and Fawn River systems to the west offer good fishing for virgin populations of trophy brook trout, walleye, lake trout, and northern pike. The Cree Indians operate a camp and guide service for canoe routes on the Fawn and Severn at Big Trout Lake. For fly-in camping rates write: Department of Indian Affairs & Northern Development, Big Trout Lake, via Central Patricia. The Fort Severn Band of Indians operate a goose hunting camp at the mouth of the Severn on Hudson Bay. Information can be obtained from the Ministry of Natural Resources, P.O. Box 309, Sioux Lookout. For literature and rates on the *Lansdowne House Camps* on the Attawapiskat River, write to Ojibway Country Indian Camps (address above).

Access & Outfitting Centers

Scheduled air transportation is available between the coastal communities of Winisk, Fort Severn, and Attawapiskat from Moosonee. Supplies and communications are available at Hudson's Bay Company posts inland at Winisk Lake and Lansdowne House and on the coast at Winisk and Attawapiskat. Be sure to allow time in your trip (sometimes days) for the occasional blanket of coastal fog. In the Severn and Fawn River region to the west, regular scheduled air service is available from Pickle Lake on Highway 599 to Big Trout Lake.

Publications & Information Sources

For the nitty-gritty info about guides, outfitters, canoe services, hunting, fishing, and camping write: Moosonee District Office, Ministry of Natural Resources, P.O. Box 190, Moosonee (also ask for the guides *Polar Bear Provincial Park* and *Winisk Wild River Canoe Route)*; Department of Indian Affairs & Northern Development, Moosonee; Geraldton District Office, MNR, P.O. Box 640, Geraldton; Sioux Lookout District, MNR, P.O. Box 309, Sioux Lookout.

QUEBEC
ENCYCLOPEDIA

Accommodations—Vacation Lodges & Sporting Camps

In Quebec hospitality is proverbial. An 83-page guide to lodges, motels, and hotels, *Hotels of Quebec,* is available free from the Ministry of Tourism, Fish, & Game, 150 E. Boul. St. Cyrille, Quebec City G1R 4Y3. The guide provides the outdoor traveler with a comprehensive listing and rating of the quality of service for all lodging establishments in Quebec. It includes the address of each establishment, rates, and facilities and services offered. For additional information and listings of major vacation lodges and sporting camps, see "Indian Outfitters" and "Outfitters, Guides, & Bush Pilots" in this section, and the "Quebec Travel & Recreation Guide." Fishing and hunting vacation travel service for many of the top lodges and sporting camps in Northern Quebec and Labrador is provided by *Sportravel Ltd.,* 2150 Berthier St., Duvernay H7E 1G8; phone (514) 669-1309.

Airlines & Charter Fly-in Services

Air service from the major cities of the United States and Canada to Montreal is provided by Air Canada, CP Air, Eastern Airlines, Allegheny, and Delta Air Lines. For rates and flight schedules contact your local travel agent or the information office of the airline you plan to fly. Air service within Quebec to the major outdoor recreation areas is provided by several airlines. *Golfe Air Quebec, Ltd.,* P.O. Box 96, Hauterive G5C 2S8, has scheduled flights between Baie Comeau and points on the north and south shores of the St. Lawrence River. *Quebecair Inc.,* Montreal International Airport, Montreal H4Y 1C1, has scheduled flights between Baie Comeau and points on the north and south shores of the St. Lawrence between Quebec City and Val d'Or. *Northern Wings, Ltd.,* P.O. Box 2012, Sept-Îles, offers flights between Sept-Îles and the North Shore towns as far east as Blanc Sablon at the Labrador border. *Nordair Ltd.,* Montreal International Airport, Montreal H4Y 1B8, has scheduled flights between Montreal, Chibougamau, and the Ungava Bay region. *St. Félicien Air Service Ltd.,* P.O. Box 910, St. Félicien G0W 2N0, has service between Fort Chimo on Ungava Bay and northern points. *Air Gaspé Inc.,* P.O. Box 69, Gaspé Harbor G4R 4L9, has scheduled flights between Gaspé and St. Lawrence River points, including Anticosti Island. Visiting pilots are advised to write for the free publication *Air Tourist Information,* available from the Aeronautical Information Services, Ministry of Transport, Transport Canada Bldg., Place de Ville, Ottawa, Ont. K1A 0N5. It contains lists of Canadian aeronautical information publications and charts, authorized customs airports, and aerodromes of entry and exit. (For additional information on fly-in services and bush pilots see "Outfitters, Guides, & Bush Pilots" and the "Travel & Recreation Guide" section.)

Atlantic Salmon Fishing in Quebec

Quebec has some of the finest Atlantic salmon fishing rivers in the world. Many of the province's great salmon rivers, however, are under lease by private fishing clubs. The best salmon rivers are found in three regions: the North Shore, Gaspé Peninsula, and the subarctic barren grounds of Ungava Bay. One of the mysteries of the Atlantic salmon in Quebec is the origin of their presence in the great Ungava Bay rivers. It is believed by some authorities that they established themselves in Ungava by a migration route around Cape Chidley at Labrador's northern tip; others believe they swam through Lake Michikamau in Labrador at the height of land on the Ungava Plateau and found their way down the headwaters of the George River to Ungava Bay. The renowned *Atlantic Salmon Journal* is required reading for

the serious Atlantic salmon fishing enthusiast. It is published in a beautiful full-color format 4 times a year and contains useful, authoritative articles about Atlantic salmon fishing throughout Canada and the world. A subscription is included with an annual membership fee of $15 in the Atlantic Salmon Association, 1405 Peel St., Suite 409, Montreal H3A 1S5. The Association also publishes a useful 36 × 24-inch *Atlantic Salmon Rivers Map of Canada* ($5), which shows all Atlantic salmon rivers in Quebec and the Atlantic provinces; private waters, rivers open to the public or controlled by an outfitter, provincial reserve waters, waters closed to fishing; number and types of nets, airports, ferries, power dams with and without fishways, logging booms, fish hatcheries, and outfitters. (For information about outfitters and guides see "Outfitters, Guides, & Bush Pilots" and the "Travel & Recreation Guide" section.)

 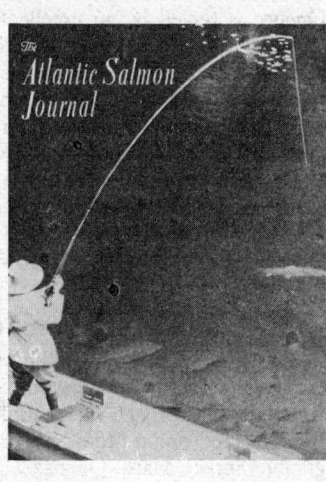

Beaupré Coast, Charlevoix, & the North Shore

The Tourism Branch, Parliament Bldgs., Quebec City G1A 1R4, publishes a free, useful 83-page guidebook, *Beaupré-Charlevoix-North Shore*, to the famous trophy brook trout and Atlantic salmon rivers, moose and waterfowl hunting areas, and wilderness reserves of the incredibly scenic region known as the Beaupré coast, north shore, and Mingan coast and lower North Shore, stretching east as the crow flies from Quebec City to Labrador along the north shore of the St. Lawrence River and Gulf. It contains detailed area maps of Highway 138 and descriptions of the principal localities and provincial parks, ferries, airports and seaplane bases, campgrounds, fish and game species, and special features. Part of the Beaupré coast is a sanctuary for the greater snow geese *(Chen hyperborea atlantica)*, which stop in large flocks to rest on the mud flats off the coast during their spring migration to the arctic nesting grounds and during their fall return to their southern haunts. (See "Mingan Coast & Archipelago"; also "North Shore Fish & Game Region" in the "Travel & Recreation Guide" section.)

Boating

The Tourism Branch, Parliament Bldgs., Quebec City G1A 1R4, publishes the free 48-page guide *Pleasure Boating in Quebec*, which contains a map of the navigable waters into Quebec and a complete listing of marinas and their locations, facilities and services, accommodations, launching ramps, and recreation activities for the St. Lawrence, Ottawa, Richelieu, Yamaska, and St. Francis rivers and the St.

Maurice Valley, Saguenay-Lac St. Jean, Laurentides-Outaouais, Southern Quebec, Northwest Quebec, lower St. Lawrence, and Gaspé canals. For information about the Quebec canals system write: Superintending Engineer, Quebec Canals, 200 Churchill Blvd., Greenfield Park J4V 2M4.

Camping in Quebec Province

Most Quebec campgrounds are run by private concerns. There are 40 campgrounds located throughout the province and in the great hunting and fishing reserves and parks administered by the Quebec Department of Tourism, Fish, & Game. The best private campgrounds are members of the Quebec Camping and Caravaning Grounds Association, 8775 Lacordian Blvd., St. Leonard. All Quebec campgrounds are visited once a year by inspectors of the Department of Tourism, Fish, & Game, which publishes a free 72-page guide, *Camping Quebec*, listing all campgrounds by numerical order of highway and describes services, facilities, outdoor recreation activities, and rates. Write: Ministry of Tourism, Fish, & Game, 150 E. Boul. St. Cyrille, Quebec City G1R 4Y3. For a complete description of provincial park campsites write the Parks Branch at the same address for the free 62-page guide *Parks of Quebec—Activities and Rates*. There are 60 campgrounds under the jurisdiction of the Parks Branch. Reservations are not required except at Lake Albanel in the Mistassini Reserve and Lake Normand in the St. Maurice Reserve. Site permits cost $2–$5 per day. Only 1 car is allowed per site with a maximum 14-day stayover. There are hundreds of primitive wilderness campsites found throughout the park system which offer basic facilities and latrines. (See "Provincial Wilderness Reserves & Parks.")

Canoeing & Wilderness Waters

The forests of Quebec are laced with over a million lakes and thousands of remote wild rivers which flow through some of the most scenic and rugged country in North America. The province is drained by the rivers of three great watersheds: (1) the St. Lawrence River and its historic tributaries, such as the Ottawa, Chaudière, Jacques Cartier, St. Maurice, Moisie, and Matabetchouane; (2) the James Bay Watershed and its mighty tributaries, such as the Broadback, Rupert, Eastmain, Nottaway, Great Whale, Sakami, and Harricanaw rivers; and (3) the far north arctic char and Atlantic salmon rivers of Ungava Bay such as the Whale, Koksoak, George, and Kaniapiskau, and their remote big-lake headwaters which stretch along the ancient height of land of the Ungava Plateau. The wilderness canoeing country of Quebec is heavyweight mosquito and blackfly country. Much of it is marshy; dry campsites are hard to find. Look for high rises covered with white caribou moss, which makes a dry, comfortable bed. The rivers of Ungava and James Bay, 100–400 yards wide, are infamous for their turbulent rapids, whirlpools, chutes, numerous islands, and steep canyons. Portages in the northern Quebec wilderness can be extremely arduous, although caribou trails are often found along the river valleys. The trails of the far north have been used for centuries by Indian hunters, explorers, and trappers. For literature and rates on wilderness canoe trips along the wild Dumoine River, which flows into the Ottawa River from the southern edge of the Laurentian Highlands, and in the famous Kipawa Forest Reserve, write: Outings Coordinator, National & Provincial Parks Association, Suite 308, 47 Colborne St., Toronto, Ont. M5E 1E3. For detailed trip information about specific rivers write: Information Branch, Ministry of Tourism, Fish, & Game, 150 E. Boul. St. Cyrille, Quebec City G1R 4Y3. (See "Hudson's Bay Company Outfitting Posts & Canoe Service" and "Wild & Scenic River Maps.")

Chubb Crater of the Ungava

It wasn't until as recently as 1950 that anyone knew of the existence of the great Chubb, or Ungava-Quebec Crater as it is also known, with its mysterious lake of dark emerald green, hidden away in the northernmost tip of the vast, black wildlands of the Ungava Peninsula. The crater was created by a giant meteorite some 4,000 years ago which exploded into the surface of the Ungava Peninsula with the mightiest blast known to man. Its force was that of a thousand Hiroshima atom bombs. The crater is 3 miles across and 1,203 feet deep with a rim 333 feet above sea level. The green waters of Ungava Lake at its center are surrounded by numerous smaller lakes.

Fishing & Hunting in Quebec

The great barren grounds, boreal evergreen forests, and rolling southern woodlands of Quebec offer some of Canada's finest hunting for trophy caribou (north of the 50th parallel in Nouveau-Québec), moose, black bear, whitetail deer, ruffed grouse (or partridge, as it is locally known), spruce grouse in the moist spruce bogs of the north, sharptail grouse in the muskeg and brushy openings of the James Bay region, ptarmigan (known as the grouse of the arctic tundra), lynx and bobcat, arctic hare, wolf, and fox. There is excellent hunting in the James Bay and St. Lawrence regions for ducks, Canada and snow geese, and snipe. Hunting is strictly forbidden for polar bear and musk-ox, found in the Ungava and James Bay regions. *Quebec Hunting & Summary of Regulations*, a 56-page booklet, describes hunting seasons and regulations, lists shot sizes recommended for small game and for skeet and trap shooting, calibers recommended for big-game hunting, and contains a foldout *Map of Quebec's Hunting Zones*. It is available free from the Ministry of Tourism, Fish, & Game, 150 E. Boul. St. Cyrille, Quebec City G1R 4Y3. The ministry also publishes an 80-page *Summary of Sport Fishing Regulations in Quebec*, which contains a foldout *Map of Quebec's Sport Fishing Zones* and *Salmon Rivers Map*. The million lakes and remote, wild rivers of Quebec offer the experienced angler the chance to tangle with record brook or speckled trout, found throughout the province as far north as Ungava and Hudson's Bay regions; Quebec red trout in the turbulent streams of the North Shore; arctic char in the mouths of the great James, Hudson, and Ungava bays; lake trout in the deep, cold lakes of the Canadian Shield; Atlantic salmon in the rivers of Ungava Bay, North Shore, Gaspé Peninsula, and Anticosti Island; ouananiche, or landlocked salmon, in the Lac St. Jean and New Quebec regions; and smallmouth bass in the St. Lawrence and Ottawa watersheds and throughout Eastern Townships, particularly in Lake Memphremagog and Missisquoi Bay. Walleye and great northern pike are found throughout Quebec. Fat rainbow and brown trout are found in Lake Memphremagog and the North River, and world's record muskellunge cruise the St. Lawrence and Ottawa. The 52-page guidebook *Sportfishing in Quebec* contains beautiful full-color plates of Quebec sportfishes and wet and dry flies, describes where and when to fish, recommends gear, and lists fish recipes à la québecoise such as pike chowder, salmon bisque, and poached walleye with beer sauce. It may be obtained free by writing: Ministry of Tourism, Fish, & Game, 930 Chemin Ste. Foy, Quebec City. (See "Atlantic Salmon Fishing in Quebec" and "Ouananiche & the Quebec Red Trout.")

Highways—Recreation, Wilderness, & Scenic Routes

Quebec is served by an excellent network of scenic highways and secondary roads which provide access to many of the major outdoor recreation areas. The whole of the Ungava Plateau and New Quebec north of the 51st parallel is roadless, except for gravel Highway 109, which runs north from Mattagami to Fort George on James Bay. The *Official Quebec Road Map* is available free from the Information Branch, Ministry of Tourism, Fish, & Game, 150 E. Boul. St. Cyrille, Quebec City G1R 4Y3. This full-color map shows all highways, paved and gravel roads, forest roads, provincial campsites, hydroplane bases, ferries, roadside tables, provincial parks, and hunting and fishing reserves.

Trans-Canada Highway (20)

This kit of topo maps shows the whole length of Highway 20 and the topography of the surrounding country of southern Quebec from Montreal east through the beautiful St. Lawrence Valley and Gaspé Peninsula to Edmundston, New Brunswick. Canadian National Topographic Survey Maps: Quebec 21-L, Baie St. Paul 21-M, Montreal 31-H, Trois Rivières 31-I, Edmundston (N.B.) 21-N.

Wilderness Highways (117 & 113)

This kit shows connecting Highways 117 and 113 from Montreal north to the remote wilderness of the great Mistassini Hunting & Fishing Reserve. The major features shown along the highways are the Labelle-Papineau, Joliette, Mont Tremblant and La Vérendrye provincial parks, Lakes Senneterre, Parent, Waswanipi, Goeland, and Mattagami, and the Assinica, Chibougamau, and Mistassini provincial reserves. Canadian National Topographic Survey Maps: Montreal 31-H, Ottawa 31-G, Mont Laurier 31-J, Deep River 31-K, Grand Lake Victoria 31-N, Senneterre 32-C, Waswanipi 32-F, Chibougamau 32-G, Assinica Lake 32-J, Mistassini Rivière N. 32-I.

Wilderness Highway (138) —the North Shore Route

This kit shows the whole route of Highway 138 and the famous North Shore wilderness. The highway runs parallel to the breathtakingly beautiful scenic shoreline of the St. Lawrence River from Trois Rivières northeast along the Beaupré Coast, past hundreds of quaint fishing villages, Port Cartier-Sept-Îles Provincial Park, and the world-famous North Shore Atlantic salmon rivers. Canadian National Topographic Survey Maps: Trois Rivières 31-I, Quebec 21-L, Baie St. Paul 21-M, Edmundston (N.B.) 21-N, Rimouski 22-C, Baie Comeau 22-F, Cap Chat 22-G, Sept-Îles 22-J, Manitou Lake 22-I.

Wilderness Highway (155)

This kit shows the whole length of Highway 155 from Trois Rivières, north, past Maurice and St. Maurice provincial parks, the St. Maurice River, Borgia River, Grand Lac Bostonnais, Lac des Commissaires, and the Ouiachouane River to its terminus at Lac St. Jean. Canadian

LA PÊCHE SPORTIVE
AU QUÉBEC
SPORTFISHING
IN QUÉBEC

GOUVERNEMENT DU QUÉBEC

National Topographic Survey Maps: Trois Rivières 31-I, La Tuque 31-P, Roberval 32-A.

Wilderness Highways (175–169–167)

This kit shows the whole length of connecting Highways 175, 169, and 167 from Quebec City on the north shore of the St. Lawrence River northwesterly through the mountainous lake country of Laurentides Provincial Park, Lac St. Jean country, and the Chibougamau Provincial Hunting and Fishing Reserve, to the outfitting village of Chibougamau. Canadian National Topographic Survey Maps: Quebec 21-L, Baie St. Paul 21-M, Chicoutimi 22-D, Roberval 32-A, Chibougamau 32-G, Rivière Mistassini S. 32-H.

Wilderness Highway (389)
—the Hydro-Quebec Road

This kit shows the whole length of Highway 389 and the gravel extension route from Baie Comeau north through rugged evergreen forestlands along the Manicouagan River and its great dams to Lac Manicouagan, and on past Gagnon to the mining center of Fremont at the Labrador-Quebec border. The highway is a harsh wilderness road to be traveled only by the experienced and well-prepared outdoorsman. Canadian National Topographic Survey Maps: Baie Comeau 22-F, Lac Berte 22-K, Lac Manicouagan 22-N, Lac Fouquet 22-O, Opocopa Lake 23-B.

Hudson's Bay Company
Outfitting Posts & Canoe Service

The Quebec northern outpost stores of the Hudson's Bay Company carry food supplies, gear, and ammunition needed for wilderness hunting, fishing, and canoeing. For a free *HBC U-Paddle Service Map-Brochure*, rates and reservations write to: Hudson's Bay Company, Northern Stores Department, 800 Baker Center, 10025–106 Street, Edmonton, Alberta T5J 1G7, or phone (403) 424–8113. HBC Northern Stores in Quebec are located at the fishing and hunting outfitting centers of Mattagami, Senneterre, Chapais, Chibougamau, Mistassini, Schefferville, Port Cartier, Gagnon, Sept-Îles, Baie Comeau, Forestville, Rupert House, Eastmain, Fort George, Great Whale River, Payne Bay and Fort Chimo. Be sure to write several months in advance for gear and supplies.

Indian Outfitters—Far North
Fishing & Hunting Camps

Several Indian-operated fishing and hunting camps in the remote subarctic wilderness of the James Bay Provincial Reserve provide access to some of the finest goose hunting and brook trout fishing on the continent. Indian hunting and fishing camps in the ancient Precambrian wilderness of the Ungava Bay region provide an opportunity for trophy barren-ground caribou and Atlantic and landlocked salmon fishing. The *Diamond Brothers Goose Camp,* c/o Den Austin, P.O. Box 520, Rawdon, on the Jack River north of Rupert House in the James Bay Reserve, has 5 cabins for 20 guests. Camp has modern facilities and boats, canoes, motors, camp equipment, and guide services. The guides are Cree Indians who have lived all their lives on the James Bay Coast. Shotgun shells are available in camp. The camp has radio communication to Rupert House and Val d'Or. Hunting season is September 15–October 15 for blue and snow geese, Canada geese and ducks. The *Julian Lake Sports Fishing Camp,* c/o Den Austin, P.O. Box 520, Rawdon, is at Julian Lake, 60 miles north of Fort George; it has 2 outpost cabins with accommodations for 10. The camp is accessible only by air, via Fort George; it offers excellent

fishing for brook trout, lake trout, northern pike, and whitefish. *Dead-Duck Bay Goose Camp,* c/o Den Austin, P.O. Box 520, Rawdon, 20 miles south of Fort George in the James Bay Reserve, has a main lodge with 5 motel-style units which accommodate 20 guests. The camp has modern facilities and complete outfitting services. There are special canoe routes for those who wish to explore the coast and fish for brook trout in nearby lakes. Hunting from September 1 to October 1 for Canada, blue, and snow geese, and ducks. The *Cape Jones Goose Camp,* P.O. Box 520, Rawdon, is in the James Bay Reserve, with complete facilities and outfitting services. The camp is a consistent producer of good goose hunting, with Canada geese the predominant species. *Paul's Bay Goose Camp,* P.O. Box 520, Rawdon, is 20 miles north of Fort George in the James Bay Reserve. This is a good isolated camp, offering goose and duck hunting. The *Roggan River Goose & Fishing Camp,* P.O. Box 520, Rawdon, is at the mouth of the Roggan

River, 45 miles north of Fort George in the James Bay Reserve. The camp provides comfortable accommodations and good brook trout fishing and goose hunting. *Club Chambeaux*, P.O. Box 520, Rawdon, has a main lodge and 4 outpost camps on the Kaniapiskau River in the Ungava Region, with guided caribou hunting September 1 to October 1 and fishing for brook trout, ouananiche, lake trout, and northern pike from June 15 to September 15. The *Finger Lake Lodge*, P.O. Box 520, Rawdon, is a wilderness fly-in camp just off Ungava Bay, with guided fishing for arctic char, lake trout, and brook trout. The *Alkalu Lodge*, P.O. Box 520, Rawdon, is on the famous George River in the Ungava Bay region with a main lodge, 4 cabins, and an outpost cabin. The camp is operated by Eskimos from Fort Chimo and offers guided caribou hunts September 1–28 and fishing for Atlantic salmon, arctic char, sea trout, and brook trout July 1–September 20. (See "Outfitters, Guides, & Bush Pilots" and the "Travel & Recreation Guide" section.)

Laurentians, Gatineau, & Outaouais

The scenic Laurentians, located between the Ottawa and Saguenay rivers to the south of the Canadian Shield, are the oldest chain of mountains in the world. The Laurentides, as the region is known in Quebec, is renowned for its 3,000-foot peaks, thousands of sparkling blue lakes and streams, and dense forests. A useful, free 87-page guidebook, *Laurentians-Gatineau-Outaouais*, is published by the Ministry of Tourism, Fish, & Game, 150 E. Boul. St. Cyrille, Quebec City G1R 4Y3; it contains detailed highway maps and descriptions of the principal localities and recreation areas in the heart of the Laurentians and along the Lièvre, Gatineau, and Ottawa rivers. The famous Outaouais region encompasses the great valley of the Ottawa River, originally the Grand Rivière, which later became known as the Ottawa in English and as the Outaouais in French. To the Iroquois the river was known as the "Meeting Place"; the Hurons knew it as Portage River. To the fur traders, pushing off from the Lachine Rapids near Montreal in their big "canots de maître" about the first of May, the Ottawa was the great river route to the fur empire of the northwest. The great valley of the Outaouais covers some 35,000 square miles and contains about 50,000 lakes, 24 rivers, and the renowned outdoor recreation areas of the Pontiac Reserve, Papineau Reserve, and Gatineau Park—an old Algonquin and Iroquois domain preserved in its natural state. A full-color *Shaded Relief Map of Gatineau Park* can be obtained for $1.50 from the Map Office, Surveys Mapping Branch, Department of Energy, Mines, & Resources, Ottawa, Ont. K1A 0E9. (See "Laurentians" in the "Travel & Recreation Guide" section.)

Lower St. Laurent & the Gaspé

The incredibly beautiful Gaspé Peninsula, called *Gaspeg* ("land's end") by the Indians, is a thick tongue of land reaching out into the Gulf of the St. Lawrence at the southeastern part of the province. The northern shore of the Gaspé borders the "river of great waters," or *Magtogock*, as the Micmac and Malecite Indians called the lower St. Lawrence. The Gaspé is, geologically, one of the oldest lands on earth. It is dominated by the wooded plateau and naked peaks of the Chic-Chocs Mountains and the deep green valleys of the great Gaspé salmon rivers such as the Matapédia, Grand Cascapédia, Port Daniel, and Bonaventure. The highlands are the home of the endangered woodland caribou *(Rangifer caribou)* and unusual alpine flora including ancient 12-foot firs. The rugged woodlands of the Gaspé are a top-ranked moose and whitetail deer hunting zone. A full-color 104-page guidebook, *Lower Saint-Laurent and the Gaspé*, is available free from the Ministry of Tourism, Fish, & Game, 150 E. Boul. St. Cyrille, Quebec City G1R 4Y3, providing a complete description of the principal localities and provincial parks in the lower St. Laurent, Grand Portage, Gaspé, Magdalen Islands, and Matapédia Valley. The guide contains detailed maps and lists all ferries, campgrounds, airports, seaplane bases, launching ramps, covered bridges, fish hatcheries, Indian villages, geological phenomena, falls and cascades, fish and game species, and trails for each area. (See "Gaspé Peninsula & Lower St. Lawrence" in the "Travel & Recreation Guide" section.)

Lynx—Silent Hunter of the North

The lynx *(Lynx canadensis)* is one of Quebec's most interesting fur-bearers. These solitary, silent hunters are found in the great spruce forests of Quebec. From their unique light-gathering eyes comes their name—"one who sees well in dim light"—and their advantage over the game they stalk. Their extremely large feet, covered with thick hair, serve as snowshoes, allowing them to travel easily over deep snow or a thin crust. Although most lynx are solitary and prefer to hunt alone, several families have been known to fan out through the forest in search of snowshoe hare, ground-nesting birds, and small rodents. Winter coats of this valuable furbearer are soft, thick and bluish gray, usually speckled with faint brown. The lynx inhabits the boreal evergreen regions throughout Quebec and Canada and ranges down into some of the northeastern states and along the Cascades and the Rocky Mountains. Other furbearers of Quebec's boreal forests are the snowshoe hare, wolf, beaver, wolverine, mink, river otter, bobcat, marten, fisher, red fox, weasel, and in the far north, the white or arctic fox.

Mingan Coast & Archipelago

This remote eastern stretch of the north shore of the St. Lawrence has some of the province's finest Atlantic salmon and trophy brook trout fishing rivers. The small village of Mingan, far to the east of Moisie, was an old fishing and trading post under the French regime. Due west of Mingan is the renowned St. Jean River, which has about 75 salmon shoals along a 28-mile stretch. To the east, the Great Natashquan River and the sandy promontory of Pointe Natashquan (Parent) forms a natural frontier between the Mingan coast and the lower North Shore. The Mingan coast was once the crossroads of Indian civilization; it marked the southern limit of Eskimo penetration and was the site of many bloody tribal battles between the Eskimos, Iroquois, and Montagnais. Raiding parties of Micmac Indians arrived regularly from the Gaspé Peninsula across the "great river" to collect scalps. The ships of the Norsemen are thought to have sailed these parts in search of whales as early as the year 1000 A.D. Later, in the 16th century, the

Mingan coast was one of the fishing haunts of the Spanish Basques. The beautiful islands of the Mingan Archipelago stretch along the coast for 45 miles. Anticosti Island lies to the south. Anticosti is noted for its Atlantic salmon and brook trout fishing and hunting for deer, duck, and Canada goose. Air Gaspé links Anticosti Island with the mainland. The Mingan coast and lower North Shore are shown on Canadian National Topographic Survey Maps, scale 1:250,000: Manitou Lake 22-I, Havre St. Pierre 12-L, Musquard 12-K, Harrington Harbor 12-J, St. Augustin 12-O, Blanc Sablon 12-P. Anticosti Island is shown on Port Menier 22-H, Anticosti Island 12-E, Box Bay 12-F. (See "North Shore Fish & Game Region" in the "Travel & Recreation Guide" section.)

Northern Quebec & the Ungava Plateau

Northern Quebec (also known as "Nouveau" or "New" Quebec) takes in the great roadless wilderness region north of the 51st parallel and encompasses the Quebec portion of the Ungava Plateau. The plateau is bordered on the west by James Bay, on the north by Ungava Bay and Hudson Strait, and on the east by the bare, jagged 5,000-foot peaks of the Torngat Mountains and the mountains running south along the Labrador-Quebec border. The Ungava Plateau (also referred to as the Ungava-Labrador Plateau) is the ancient mountain country of the Canadian Shield—a land of thunderous, turbulent rivers and long thin lakes radiating in glacial troughs formed by the path of the Labrador Ice Cap. The Breton explorer Jacques Cartier called it "the land God gave to Cain." To the Eskimos Ungava was the word meaning "faraway." The vast barren grounds of the plateau are carpeted with a foot-thick blanket of caribou moss and lichen. The great Ungava Atlantic salmon rivers flow from their headwaters at the height of land north of the Laurentian Scarp northward to their mouths at Ungava Bay through a crazy-quilt pattern of thousands upon thousands of irregularly shaped lakes, gorges (such as the Manitou Gorge on the Kaniapiskau River) reaching depths of 1,000 feet and surrounding wildlands of low hills, hummocks and hollows, deposits of rough brown sand, and stands of black stunted spruce. The roofless abandoned Fort McKenzie and the rotted freighter canoes lying nearby at Lac Le Moyne near the confluence of the Kaniapiskau and Swampy Bay rivers is one of the few signs of human settlement found in the great Ungava interior from the tableland headwaters to

Fort Chimo at the mouth of the Koksoak River on Ungava Bay. The great Labrador iron trough, once the arm of an ancient sea, runs north and south through the plateau for almost 600 miles to the very tip of Ungava. The Labrador trough is one of the world's greatest iron-ore deposits. At Schefferville the Iron Ore Company of Canada is mining and hauling millions of tons of high-grade ore annually south to the port of Sept-Îles on the St. Lawrence. One of the most unusual and fascinating features of the Ungava Plateau is the enormous desert of burned country in the tableland above the Moisie River. Henry Youle Hind, an explorer of subarctic forests, believed that these great burns were created by vast areas of smoldering caribou moss, ignited by spontaneous combustion or lightning and the cause of the mysterious "dark days" that fell over eastern Canada in the early 19th century.

Ouananiche & the Quebec Red Trout

The savage fighting ouananiche *(Salmo salar)*, known for its spectacular leaps and runs, is a primitive landlocked race of Atlantic salmon which was trapped inland thousands of years ago as the waters of the Wisconsin Ice Age receded. It spends its entire life cycle in the great wilderness lakes and rivers of northern Quebec, growing to record weights in the rivers and tributaries of New Quebec and Ungava Bay and in the Lac St. Jean region. The ouananiche is distinguished from the Atlantic salmon by its longer body, darker color, and markings of black spots or dark brown crosses. The handsome Quebec red trout or red char *(Salvelinus marstoni)* is found in the turbulent wilderness streams of the North Shore, through to some lakes near Hull and to the western limits of the Gatineau Valley and a few streams of the Gaspé Peninsula. The Quebec red is distinguished from the brook trout by its brilliant red coloring, the shape of its fins, and the absence of wavy, wormlike markings.

Outfitters, Guides, & Bush Pilots

In the New Quebec wilderness all nonresident hunters and fishermen are required to hire the services of an outfitter. The Ministry of Tourism, Fish, & Game, 150 E. Boul. St. Cyrille, Quebec City G1R 4Y3, publishes a free 256-page *List of Outfitters*. This eminently useful directory is a must for all Quebec-bound outdoorsmen: it lists all qualified outfitters and fly-in services and describes the services,

facilities, and fish and game species present for every fishing and hunting camp and club located in the lower St. Laurent, Quebec, Maurice, Lac St. Jean, Montreal, Eastern Townships, Laurentides, New Quebec-James Bay, Outaouais, Témiscamingue, Abitibi, and North Shore fish and game districts. The Department of Tourism, Fish, & Game exercises strict surveillance of all establishments operated by outfitters. A free 110-page *Directory of Canadian Indian Tourist Outfitting & Outdoor Recreation Facilities*, which provides a complete listing of Indian-operated hunting and fishing camps in Quebec, is available from the Department of Indian Affairs & Northern Development, Centennial Tower, 400 Laurier Ave. W, Ottawa, Ont. K1A 0H4.

For listings of the major outfitters, floatplane services, and fishing and hunting camps, see the "Quebec Travel & Recreation Guide."

Provincial Wilderness Reserves & Parks

Quebec's great parks and wilderness reserves cover 51,000 square miles, more than three times the size of Switzerland, stretching from the vast subarctic wilderness of the James Bay Reserve south to the majestic valley of the St. Lawrence and the scenic highland parks of the Gaspé. For access rights and reservations for campgrounds, boats, canoes, lodging, and Atlantic salmon fishing on waters operated by the Parks Branch, write: Reservations Office, Parks Branch, P.O. Box 8888, Quebec City G1K 7W3, or call from Quebec the toll-free number (1–800) 462–5349. Outside Quebec, call collect 1–418–643–5349. A free 64-page guidebook, *Quebec Parks*, is published by the Ministry of Tourism, Fish, & Game, 150 E. Boul. St. Cyrille, Quebec City G1R 4Y3. It contains 12 pages of maps and thorough descriptions of 22 major parks and wilderness reserves, full-color photographs, and detailed information about access, lodging, supplies, topography, wildlife, hunting, fishing, boats, canoe routes, and information address for each park. The Parks Branch also publishes the free booklet *Activities and Rates*, which describes the outdoor recreation activities—canoeing, camping, moose hunting, deer and small-game hunting, hiking, cross-country skiing, and salmon fishing—in all rivers operated by the Parks Branch and Anticosti Island and in each park, as well as access rights, rates, and fees.

Railway Services

The *Canadian National Railroad* provides the outdoor traveler with access to some of the province's best canoeing, camping, and fishing and big-game hunting areas. For recreation travel information write: Rail Travel Bureau, Canadian National Railroad, 935 Lagauchetière St. W, Box 8100, Montreal H3C 3N4. The *Quebec North Shore & Labrador Railroad* runs north from Sept-Îles 360 miles across the rugged Canadian Shield to the famous iron-ore mining center of Schefferville. It passes through the great Laurentian Scarp, a huge granite barrier 3,000 feet high which walls off the interior of the Ungava Plateau from the North Shore wilderness and winds north past the canyon of the Moisie River through a primeval land of boiling rivers, sheer black cliffs, and thousands of lakes surrounded by muskeg, moss, lichen, and stunted spruce. The train winds past the famous brook trout waters of Lac Achouanipi and Menihek, Astray, Petit-stikapau, and Attikamagen lakes and their tributaries. During its rugged journey through Labrador to its final destination at Schefferville the railroad is used to haul thousands of tons of iron ore, supplies, and personnel in and out of this great mining region. For travel permits and information write: Quebec North Shore & Labrador Railroad, 1245 Sherbrooke St. W, Montreal.

Southern Quebec & the Sugar Camps of the Bois Francs

The Bois Francs (hardwoods) region of southern Quebec near Sherbrooke with its maple groves and sugar camps is one of the most beautiful areas in the Eastern Townships. The rolling woodlands of the Eastern Townships were once the tribal lands and hunting grounds of the Abnakis, from a Wabanaki word meaning "Indians of the eastern lands." The Abnaki Indian Reserve at Lac St. Pierre is an exceptional duck hunting area. The more remote woodlands, hills, and marshes of southern Quebec have excellent hunting for whitetail deer, black bear, upland game birds, and waterfowl. Lac Megantic and Lakes Massawippi and Memphremagog—meaning "great stretch of water"—hold trophy brook, brown, and rainbow trout, northern pike, walleye, and ouananiche (landlocked salmon) up to 10 pounds. A handy full-color 136-page guidebook, *Southern Quebec*, can be had free by writing: Ministry of Tourism, Fish, & Game, 150 E. Boul. St. Cyrille, Quebec City G1R 4Y3. It contains detailed highway maps and descriptions of the principal localities and recreation areas and lists campgrounds, airports, fish and game species, and topography. The major features and recreation areas of the scenic Chaudière Valley and Appalachian Highlands of the Beauce region are described in a free 40-page guidebook, *La Beauce*, published by the Ministry of Tourism, Fish, & Game at the address listed above. The features of southern Quebec and La Beauce are shown on Canadian National Topographic Survey Maps: Montreal 31-H, Sherbrooke 21-E, Quebec 21-L, Trois Rivières 31-I.

Wild & Scenic River Maps

Canadian Wild River Surveys which describe access and egress, geography, history, flora and fauna, and the canoe routes are available for the following Quebec historic fur trade routes and wilderness waterways: *Rupert River, Kipawa River, Moisie River, Manitou River, Romaine River, Dumoine River,* and the *Perch, Chef,* and *Chamouchouane* rivers. The surveys are an invaluable aid to the wilderness paddler planning a trip down one of these wild rivers. The surveys may be obtained free from Information Services, Conservation Group, Department of Indian Affairs & Northern Development, 400 Laurier Ave. W, Ottawa, Ont. K1A 0H4.

Gaspé Peninsula & Lower St. Lawrence

Gaspé Peninsula Topo Maps

Canadian National Topographic Survey Maps, scale 1:250,000: Rimouski 22-C, Cap Chat 22-G, Matane 22-B, Port Menier 22-H, Gaspé 22-A.

Forillon National Park

Canadian National Topographic Survey Maps, scale 1:50,000: Petit Cap 22H-1, Gaspé 22A-16.

Gaspesian Provincial Park

Canadian National Topographic Survey Maps, scale 1:50,000: Lac Raudot 22A-12, Lac Madeleine 22A-13, Big Berry Mountains 22B-9, Mount Albert 22B-16.

Matane Provincial Park

Canadian National Topographic Survey Maps, scale 1:50,000: Boutet 22B-10, St. Vianney-Cuoq 22B-11, Sayabec 22B-12, Matane 22B-13.

Port Daniel Provincial Park

Canadian National Topographic Survey Maps, scale 1:50,000: Port Daniel 22A-2, New Carlisle 22A-3, Honorat 22A-6, Chandler 22A-7.

Rimouski Provincial Park

Canadian National Topographic Survey Maps, scale 1:50,000: Wild Goose Lake 21N-16, Lac des Chasseurs 22B-4, Lac Prime 22C-1.

The lower St. Lawrence region is the gateway to the majestic panoramas and world-famous Atlantic salmon fishing, camping, and backpacking areas of the rugged Gaspé Peninsula. Here, Rimouski Provincial Park—from an Indian name meaning "land of the moose"—preserves 299 square miles of lakes, streams, and mixed maple, fir, and white birch forests along the edge of the Horton Reserve. Moose are abundant throughout the park, along with hare, ruffed and spruce grouse, and whitetail deer. Brook trout are found in most of the streams and lakes; there is a provincial campground at Rimouski Lake; and housekeeping cottages are located at Plate River and Lacs Kedhivick, Castor, and Blanc. For park information and reservations write: Bureau of Reservations, Park Division, 150 E. Boul. St. Cyrille, Quebec City G1A 1R3.

The Gaspé Peninsula, called *Gaspeg* ("land's end") by the Indians, is due east of the lower St. Lawrence, stretching out into the Gulf of St. Lawrence at the southeastern extremity of the province. The Gaspé is the northernmost extension of the ancient Appalachian mountain chain forming a thick tongue of land extending from the beautiful Matapédia Valley to Cape Gaspé. The peninsula is dominated by the deep, scenic woodland valleys of some of the world's greatest Atlantic salmon rivers and by the famous Chic-Chocs Mountains, called *Sigsoog* by the Micmac Indians, meaning "rocky mountains." The Chic-Chocs form a long wooded plateau with naked peaks among the highest in eastern Canada. The woodlands, valleys, and high country regions offer some of the finest moose, deer, and upland game-bird hunting in eastern Canada. The Chic-Chocs are also inhabited by woodland caribou and hold the headwater lakes of the great Atlantic salmon rivers.

The magnificent peaks, valleys, and woodlands of the Chic-Chocs are preserved within two of Quebec's most scenic parks, the Matane and Gaspesian provincial reserves. Matane Park, which adjoins Gaspesian Park on the east, was established in 1962 with the acquisition of the Hammermills lumber company lands located in the valley of the Matane River. The park embraces some 417 square miles dominated by the Chic-Chocs peaks, deep valleys, and dense forests of black

spruce, balsam fir, and white birch. The major features of the park include the famous Atlantic salmon waters of the Matane River, the deep valley of the Cap Chat River, 3,725-foot high Mount Logan, and the brook and lake trout waters of Lac Matane, Lac Duviver and the Bonjour River and Rivière à la Truite. The park is inhabited by caribou, deer, moose, and black bear. One of the greatest concentrations of moose in Quebec is found at Étang de la Truite. The Matane River is the most popular salmon river in the Gaspé region. Its deep pools are the annual mecca of anglers from all over eastern Canada and the United States. The Cap Chat River is a small, swift river rising in the Chic-Chocs Mountains about 45 miles east of the Matane. Park information, fishing and camping info, and a free *Matane Provincial Park Map* and *Salmon Fishing Maps of the Matane & Cap Chat Rivers* may be obtained by writing: Matane Park, 263 St. Jerome Ave., Matane G4W 3A7. Campgrounds are located at Barrière John and Étang de la Truite. Cottages are available for summer fishing and fall hunting for moose and small game.

The famous Gaspesian Provincial Park, one of Quebec's most spectacular wilderness hiking, camping, and Atlantic salmon fishing areas, encompasses some 498 square miles surrounding the peaks of the Chic-Chocs. The major features of the park include the McGerrigle Peaks, ancient rocky, volcanic formations, and the gorges and valleys of the Ste. Anne, Cascapédia, Marsoui, and Madeleine rivers and Rivières à Claude and à Pierre. Caribou, moose, deer, and black bear share the same range. During the summer months caribou may be seen in the 4,160-foot-high Mont Jacques Cartier area. Numerous wilderness hiking trails, including the Des Chutes, Du Diable, Mont Albert, and De la Rivière trails provide access to the remote high country brook trout lakes, and to the massive granite peaks and moss, lichen, and alpine tundra. A panoramic road, first constructed to provide access to mines in the region, encircles the McGerrigle Peaks, winding for 55 miles through a wild country of unsurpassed beauty. The Ste. Anne River, one of the finest public Atlantic salmon rivers in the Gaspé, is 11 miles east of Cap Chat. Ste. Anne salmon average

about 15 pounds and usually start running the first week of July. Wilderness hiking, camping, and fishing information, and the *Gaspesian Park and Chic-Chocs Reserve Map* and *Atlantic Salmon Fishing Maps of the Little Cascapédia and Ste. Anne Rivers* may be obtained by writing: Superintendent, Gaspesian Park, Ste. Anne des Monts G0E 2G0. The Little Cascapédia River Provincial Park takes in 200,-000 acres adjacent to the southern boundary of Gaspesian Park. The Little Cascapédia is renowned for its sea-run brook trout in 6-pound-and-over class. The sea trout, as well as Atlantic salmon, enter the river toward the end of July. Gaspesian Park campgrounds are located at Lac Madeleine and Mont Albert. The park maintains 13 fisherman's cabins and 12 resort cabins available for public rental.

Forillon National Park encompasses 92 square miles at the eastern end of the Gaspé Peninsula. The park occupies a small scenic peninsula which juts out from the Gaspé into the blue waters of the Gulf of St. Lawrence, between the mouth of the St. Lawrence River and the Bay of Gaspé. The Forillon coastline is dominated by 600-foot sculptured escarpments, sandy beaches, and small caves nestled between rocky headlands. In the western corner of the park a series of lake-dotted hills rise to an altitude of 1,800 feet. During the summer months double-crested cormorants, black-legged kittiwakes, black guillemots, and herring gulls nest along the sheer coastal cliffs of the park. Harbor seals and pilot whales are often seen along the shore. The inland forests are inhabited by deer, moose, black bear, red fox, beaver, and lynx. Campgrounds are located at Cap Bon Ami and Petit Gaspé. For travel information, a free *Map of Forillon National Park*, and campground and trail guides write: Superintendent, Forillon National Park, P.O. Box 1220, Gaspé G0C 1R0.

Due west of Forillon National Park are the Atlantic salmon waters of the Dartmouth River, until recently a private fishing club, now open to the public. To the southwest of Forillon is the Port Daniel River, a portion of which is encompassed by the 25-square-mile Port Daniel Provincial Park. The Port Daniel flows through a beautiful valley, surrounded by forests of spruce with a sprinkling of white birch. Rolling hills rise to heights of 1,000 feet. A small run of Atlantic salmon enters the Port Daniel during August and the fishing is at its peak when the season closes in mid-September. At the easternmost end of the Gaspé is the beautiful Matapédia River, known as the "river of the 222 rapids." This famous salmon river is deeply embanked and flows through a deep valley that seperates the massive Chic-Chocs Mountains on the east from the highland zone to the west. The Matapédia is a big-fish river which annually yields several salmon in the 35-pound-and-over class. Wading is almost impossible due to the river's large size and deep, boulder-strewn pools. The Quebec Parks Division office in Matapédia and Causapscal Mountains has a list of guides and boats for hire. It's strongly recommended to make your reservations and arrangements well in advance of your trip. *Maps of Rimouski and Port Daniel Provincial Parks* and *Atlantic Salmon Fishing Maps of the Matapédia, St. Jean, and Port Daniel* may be obtained by writing: Parks Division, Ministry of Tourism, Fish, & Game, Bldg. G, Cité Parlementaire, Quebec City G1A 1R3. Several hunting and fishing camps are located on the Gaspé. *Camps Lebreux*, C.P. 88, Cloridorme, maintains 14 camps with brook trout fishing and hunting for moose and deer. The *Gaspesian Fish & Game Club*, C.P. 282, Ste. Anne des Monts, maintains camps on the Madeleine River for brook trout fishing and fall moose and deer hunting. The *Ash Inn Fishing Club*, C.P. 160, Gaspé, operates camps on the St. Jean and York rivers for Atlantic salmon and brook trout fishing.

Access & Outfitting Centers

The Gaspé Peninsula is reached via scheduled airline service and ferry from the North Shore towns of Baie Comeau and Godbout. The major recreation areas on the peninsula are reached by Provincial Highways 132, 195, 299, and 198. Guides, outfitters, supplies, lodging, and provincial campground are available at Ste. Flavie, Grand Netis, Netis sur Mer, Baie des Sables, St. Ulric, Matane, Ste. Félicité, Cap Chat, Ste. Anne des Monts, St. Joachim de Tourelle, Rivière à Claude, Mont St. Pierre, Anse Pleureuse, Gros Morne, Manche d'Épée, Rivière Madeleine, Grande Vallée, Cloridorme, L'Anse à Valleau, Anse au Griffon, Cap aux Os, Gaspé, Douglas, St. Georges de Malbaie, Barachois, Bridgeville, Percé, Grand Rivière, Pabos, Newport, Anse aux Gascans, Port Daniel, New Carlisle, Bonaventure, Caplan, New Richmond, Maria, Carleton, St. Omer, Nouvelle, Escuminac, Pointe à la Croix, Matapédia, Mont Joli, and Causapscal.

James Bay Region

James Bay Provincial Reserve

Canadian National Topographic Survey Maps, scale 1:250,000: Fort Rupert 32-M, Eastmain 33-D, Fort George 33-E, Pointe Louis XIV 33-L, Belcher Islands South 33-M, Poste de la Baleine 33-N.

Assinica Provincial Reserve

Canadian National Topographic Survey Maps, scale 1:250,000: Waswanigi 32-F, Chibougamau 32-G, Assinica Lake 32-J, Lake Evans 32-K.

Broadback River

Canadian National Topographic Survey Maps, scale 1:250,000: Assinica Lake 32-J, Lake Evans 32-K, Nemiscau Lake 32-N, Fort Rupert 32-M.

Eastmain River

Canadian National Topographic Survey Maps, scale 1:250,000: Lac Naocacane 23-D, Lac Rossignol 33-A, Lac Baudeau 32-P, Lac Mesgouez 32-O, Lichteneger Lake 33-B, Opinaca Lake 33-C, Eastmain 33-D.

Forillon National Park

Quebec

Great Mistassini Provincial Reserve

Canadian National Topographic Survey Maps, scale 1:250,000: Mistassini River N. 32-I, Assinica Lake 32-J, Lac Baudeau 32-P, Lac Mesgouez 32-O.

Rupert River

Canadian National Topographic Survey Maps, scale 1:250,000: Lac Baudeau 32-P, Lac Mesgouez 32-O, Nemiscau Lake 32-N, Fort Rupert 32-M.

Sakami River

Canadian National Topographic Survey Maps, scale 1:250,000: Sakami Lake 33-F, Frigate Lake 33-G, Lac Sauvolles 33-H, Lac Rossignol 33-A.

The vast Precambrian wilderness of the James Bay watershed is drained by some of the finest brook trout waters and canoe routes in North America. The great Mistassini and Assinica provincial reserves, north of the 50th parallel, give rise to two mighty rivers that flow westward for hundreds of miles through forests of black spruce and palsa bogs into James Bay. The Mistassini Reserve covers 13,123 square miles in north central Quebec, dominated by huge Lakes Mistassini and Albanel, which form the headwaters of the famous Rupert River. The relatively flat land surface of the reserve is studded with lakes which provide some of the best trophy fishing in the province for northern pike, walleye, and lake and brook trout. The major features of the reserve, established to protect the trapping grounds of the Cree Indians, include the wilderness fishing and canoe-camping routes along the Chalifour, Rupert, Naococane, Mistassini, Daniel, and Témiscamie rivers. The Mistassini region, and the headwaters of the great Broadback River in the Assinica Reserve to the southwest, are world-famous for trophy brook trout fishing. Cree Indians have been reported to have netted squaretails up to 20 pounds from these remote wild rivers. Wildlife found in this sparse land of string bogs, ancient rock outcroppings, and a forest undercover of caribou moss and Labrador tea includes beaver, moose, wolf, caribou, and black bear.

The *Musgoun Fishing Club*, Reserve de Mistassini, Baie du Poste via Chibougamau, is a tent camp reached by floatplane from Chibougamau with accommodations for 16 guests. The camp offers wilderness fishing for speckled and lake trout, northern pike, and walleye. The *Figaro Fishing Lodge, Inc.*, is on Lac Albanel with a lodge and 10 camps, and accommodations for 40 guests. The camp, which offers fishing for trophy brook and lake trout, northern pike, and walleye, is reached by floatplane from Chibougamau to the Témiscamie seaplane base on Lac Albanel. The Figaro Lodge outpost camps have pioneered trophy fishing on the Sakami River and headwaters of the Eastmain River in the remote Otis Mountains for giant lake trout, northern pike, and squaretails. Write: P.O. Box 161, Chibougamau G8P 2K6; (819) 276-2232.

Great migrations of brook trout up to weights of 12 pounds begin to move out of Lakes Mistassini and Albanel during the latter part of August into the Toqueco, Témiscamie, Chalifour, Wabassinon, and Papaskwasati rivers. Fly-in outpost camps are accessible by arrangement from the Vieux Poste Lodge.

The small island where Vieux Poste, the park headquarters, is located, was formerly called Fort Mistassini, an important Hudson's Bay Company post that commanded the freighter canoe route to Rupert House on James Bay. Campsites in the Mistassini Reserve are located at Penicouane Bay on Lake Mistassini, Chalifour River, and Lac Albanel. Outboard motors are available for campground guests who have retained the services of a guide. The park reserve maintains 6 cottages

for rental at *Waconichi Lodge* and 23 lodges at three different sites for 3–6 each. Twelve of these lodges are actually shelters with wooden walls and floors and canvas rooftops. Waconichi Lake camp is reached by automobile via Provincial Highway 167 and secondary roads; *Louis Joliet Lodge*, on the Rupert River, is reached by seaplane from the base at Témiscamie, about 5 miles before the end of Highway 167; *Vieux Poste Lodge*, in the north sector of Mistassini Lake, is reached by seaplane from the Témiscamie base. The fishing season in the reserve runs from June 4 to September 6. For additional information about fishing, camping, wilderness canoe routes, lodges, and a free full-color *Mistassini Provincial Reserve Map*, write: Mistassini Reserve, 951, rue Hamel, Chibougamau; phone (819) 276-6144.

The famous Rupert River wilderness canoe route is a 378-mile journey from Mistassini Post on the crystal-clear waters of Lake Mistassini (which means "big rock" in Cree) to Rupert House at the river's mouth on James Bay. (Rupert House is the oldest trading post of the Hudson's Bay Company, built in 1668 by the Sieur des Groseilliers.) The Rupert River flows from Lake Mistassini, noted for its bottom covered with smooth round stones and the large boulders of granite jutting above the lake's surface, through a Precambrian valley bordered by low hills, eskers, sandbars, and glacial debris. In the distance from Lake Mistassini, barren, worn-down mountains rise to heights of 3,600 feet. The major features shown on the map kit of the Rupert include Baie du Portage, Lac Capichinatun, picturesque Woollett Lake surrounded by 600-foot mountains, Lac Bellinger, beautiful crystal-clear Lac Mesgouez, Lac Nemiscau—renowned for its sand beaches, abundant sturgeon, and historic view of an ancient Cree Indian settlement—75-foot Oatmeal Falls, Portage du Chat, and the Plum Pudding Rapids. The Rupert is a wild river with dangerous rapids, falls, chutes, canyons, gorges, and about 25 portages; it is a top-ranked river for walleye and northern pike to 25 pounds. The wilderness paddler will see numerous loons, geese, moose, beaver, and river otter. Rupert House, today the center of a 7,000-acre mink farm, is built on a sandy hill on the marshy barrier shores of James Bay. Scheduled flights are available from Rupert House to Moosonee, Ontario, across the bay, where you can take a connecting flight or the Polar Bear Express train homeward bound. During the height of the fur trade days Broadback River was used on the return voyage from Rupert House to Lake Mistassini.

The Broadback River and the Chibougamau River, both renowned for trophy-sized brook trout, walleye, and northern pike, rise in the sprawling headwater lakes of the vast 2-million-acre Assinica Provincial Reserve, which adjoins the Mistassini Reserve on the southwest. The other features of the reserve include Lakes Assinica, Cachisa, Opotaca, and Frotet. Big game and furbearers include moose, black bear, beaver, caribou, and wolf. The famous *Broadback River Fishing Camps*, reached by Air Fecteau from Chibougamau, operates 7 camps on the Broadback in the Assinica Reserve. The camp provides guides and top-ranked fishing for brook trout up to 10 pounds, and for northern pike and walleye. For information and rates write: René Demers, C.P. 190, Chibougamau. The *Square Tail Fishing Club* has 3 camps on Frotet and Troilus Lakes in the reserve. Access is via plane, train, or auto to Chibougamau and by seaplane to the camp. For information and rates write: Robert D. White, RR2 Mont Castor, Sainte Agathe des Monts.

The James Bay Provincial Reserve lowlands, surrounding the mouths of such great far north rivers as the Great Whale, Fort George, and Eastmain, is one of the finest goose and duck hunting regions in North America. Several well-established goose hunting and fishing camps are at the mouths of the major James Bay rivers. (For a complete listing, see "Indian Outfitters—Far North Fishing & Hunting Camps," in

the "Encyclopedia" section.) The *Cabbage Willows Club, Inc.*, operates a lodge and 3 camps in the James Bay Reserve with guided hunting for duck and lesser snow goose. For information and rates write: André Bureau, Suite 312, 3 Place Ville-Marie, Montreal H3B 3Y1. *Lakeshore Air Service Reg'd.* provides fly-in fishing trips to Burton Lake in the James Bay Reserve for lake and brook trout, and northern pike, Guests are accommodated in the James Bay Mission. For information write: S.S. Albulet, 42 Oxford Rd., Baie d'Urfe (Île de Montréal). *Mrs. Kathleen Maclean-Gowell* operates a lodge and 3 camps in the James Bay Reserve with accommodations for 22 guests. The camp specializes in guided fishing trips for brook trout and walleye and hunting for duck and lesser snow goose. Write: Box 208, Prospect, KY 40059. *La Sarre Air Service*, La Sarre, provides fly-in service to sporting camps at lakes Mistauao, Lucie, and Seal and to Rupert House.

Travelers in the James Bay Region should be aware that the massive Hydro-Quebec $16 billion hydroelectric project—the biggest construction project in the world—is developing an area bigger than Iowa, diverting the waters of the lower Eastmain, La Grande, and Kaniapiskau rivers and filling reservoirs half the size of Lake Erie.

Access & Outfitting Centers

Scheduled air service and bush plane fly-in service are available at the following James Bay Region outfitting and supply centers: Chibougamau, Mattagami, Senneterre, Fort Rupert, Eastmain, Fort George, and Poste de la Baleine. The Mistassini and Assinica provincial reserves may also be reached by car along Provincial Highways 113 from the west and 167 from the east. Fly-in service is available at the Lac Cache seaplane base in Chibougamau or from the Témiscamie River seaplane base. Charter fly-in service for wilderness fishing, hunting, and canoeing trips throughout the James Bay region is provided by *Air Fecteau Ltd.*, C.P. 220, Senneterre J0Y 2M0, (819) 737-2262 with bases at Chibougamau, Témiscamie, Rupert House, Fort George, and Mattagami.

Laurentians

Laurentians Topo Maps

Canadian National Topographic Survey Maps, scale 1:250,000: Mont Laurier 31-J, Kempt Lake 31-O, La Tuque 31-P, Trois Rivières 31-I.

Joliette Provincial Park

Canadian National Topographic Survey Maps, scale 1:50,000: Ste. Émélie de l'Énergie 31I-5, St. Michel des Saints 31I-12, St. Donat de Montcalm 31J-8, St. Guillaume N. 31J-9.

La Maurice National Park

Canadian National Topographic Survey Maps, scale 1:50,000: Shawinigan 31I-10, Lac au Sorcier 31I-11, Eveleen Lake 31I-14, Mattawin 31I-15.

Mont Tremblant Provincial Park

Canadian National Topographic Survey Maps, scale 1:50,000: L'Annonciation 31J-7, St. Donat de Montcalm 31J-8, St. Guillaume N. 31J-9, L'Ascension 31J-10, Lac Maison de Pierre 31J-15, Lac Charland 31J-16, Pine Lake 31O-2, Lac Troyes 31O-1.

Papineau-Labelle Provincial Park

Canadian National Topographic Survey Maps, scale 1:50,000: Low 31G-13, Chénéville 31G-14, Duhamel 31J-3, Bouchette 31J-4, Maniwaki 31J-5, Nominingue 31J-6.

St. Maurice-Mastigouche Provincial Parks

Canadian National Topographic Survey Maps, scale 1:50,000: Shawinigan 31I-10, Eveleen Lake 31I-14, Mattawin 31I-15, Steamboat Rock Lake 31P-3, Lac au Sorcier 31I-11, St. Michel des Saints 31I-12, Reservoir Taureau 31I-13, Ste. Émélie de l'Énergie 31I-5, St. Gabriel de Brandon 31I-6.

The majestic Precambrian peaks of the Laurentian mountains and the surrounding forests and thousands of remote lakes and wild whitewater rivers form one of the outstanding fishing, camping, hiking, hunting, and wilderness canoeing areas in North America. Towering south of the Canadian Shield, the peaks of the Laurentians have been worn down over millions of years by wind, weather, and glaciers. During the autumn hunting season the Laurentians blaze with an unforgettable spectacle of reds, orange, yellows, browns, and green. The wilderness heartlands of the range are preserved in several famous parks and provincial reserves. The westernmost reserve is the Papineau-Labelle Park, which encompasses 671 square miles in the geological region of Grenville, overlooking the Montreal-Ottawa clay plains. Brook trout, walleye, lake trout, and northern pike are found in Lakes Pimodan, Sound, Echo, Gagnan, Montjoie, Sept-Frères, Minerve, and Preston. The Petite Nation River is a challenging wilderness canoe-camping route. The surrounding forests of yellow birch and white, red, and gray pine are inhabited by moose, whitetail deer, and partridge. Campgrounds are located at Sept-Frères, Du Sound, and Preston. The park maintains cabins for fishermen, hunters, and resort living. For park maps and information write: Chief, Park Office, Papineau-Labelle Provincial Park, Val des Bois.

Mont Tremblant and Joliette provincial parks lie due east of Papineau-Labelle Park. Mont Tremblant embraces 990 square miles of mixed hardwood and evergreen forests, hundreds of sparkling blue lakes and wild rivers, and in the southern section of the park, massive peaks reaching heights of 2,800 feet. The major features of this famous camping, hiking, canoeing, and fishing reserve include the Du Diable River canoe route, the wild Mattawin River, and Lakes Forbes, Jamet, Mosquic, and Rossi, Lac du Diable, and Lacs des Mocassins. The scenic Mattawin is one of Quebec's top-ranked wilderness canoe routes. The river roars for 60 miles through a series of awesome rapids, falls, gorges, and chutes. The remote lakes and rivers hold brook and lake trout, northern pike, and walleye. The De la Roche and De la Corniche trails provide access to interior scenic areas. Park campgrounds are located at Lacs Monroe and Lajoie. There are park cabins available for public rental at Lacs Gesseron and Mattawin. For information and a *Mont Tremblant Provincial Park Map* and *Du Diable River Canoe Route Map* write: Superintendent, Parc du Mont Tremblant, via Lac Supérieur, Comte de Terrebonne. Joliette Provincial Park joins Mont Tremblant Park on the east, embracing some 187 square miles of the Laurentian Plateau. The park is renowned for its scenic undulating valleys, mountains, sheer rock cliffs, and the deep gorges of the Ouareau and Voire rivers and the Rivière l'Assumption. The park's waters hold brook trout, northern pike, and walleye. The park maintains cabins for fishermen, small-game hunters, and resort living. For information and a *Joliette Provincial Park Map* write: Joliette Provincial Park, 5075 Fullum St., Montreal.

The wilderness fishing, canoe-camping, and hiking areas of the St. Maurice and Mastigouche provincial parks and the La Maurice National Park lie due east of Mont Tremblant and Joliette parks in the rugged Trois Rivières region. Mastigouche Provincial Park, the name derived from the Montagnais Indian words *mistik* ("wood") and *ush* ("small" or "bear"), encompasses 678 square miles of lakes, coniferous forests, and undulating hills of the Laurentian Plateau reaching heights of 2,000 feet. The park is renowned for its rugged fishing,

810 · THE BANTAM GREAT OUTDOORS GUIDE

canoe-camping, and hiking areas. Landlocked salmon are caught in scenic Lac au Sorcier; brook trout and lake trout are found in Grand Lac des Îles, Lac au Sable, and Lac Bigoine. The Du Loup River is a top-ranked wilderness canoe route. Wildlife inhabiting the park includes moose, black bear, and partridge. Park cabins are available for rental by fishermen, small-game hunters, and cross-country skiers. For park information and a *Mastigouche Provincial Park Map* and *Du Loup Canoe Route Map* write: Mastigouche Provincial Park, C.P. 297, St. Alexis des Monts, Maskinongé County.

La Maurice National Park adjoins Mastigouche Park on the east, encompassing some 132,474 acres of rugged glaciated wilderness along the wild St. Maurice River. The park wildlands, once the fishing and hunting grounds of the Attikameg Indians, is a renowned canoeing, camping, and fishing area for lake trout, northern pike, and small-mouth bass. The dense evergreen forests, rolling hills, and wild bogs are inhabited by moose, timber wolves, black bear, deer, lynx, and red fox. Developed campgrounds are located within the park and lodging may be secured at nearby Shawinigan and Grand'Mère. Park information, a free *La Maurice National Park Map Folder* and *Canoe Route Map of La Maurice National Park*, the free guide *Get on the Track* (an illustrated guide to animal tracks), and *Trails of La Maurice National Park* may be obtained by writing: Superintendent, P.O. Box 758, Shawinigan G9N 6V9. The attractive La Maurice canoe route map shows the Lac à la Pêche-Berube, Attikameg, Laurentian, and Metaberoutin canoe routes, as well as gravel and forest roads, boat rentals, launching ramps, wilderness campsites, semiserviced campsites, rapids, portages, and portage length. The vast wilderness hunting and fishing region of St. Maurice Provincial Park adjoins La Maurice National Park on the north. This rugged lake-dotted wilderness reserve occupies 678 square miles of territory leased by hunting and fishing clubs since 1886 and is today managed for public use by the Shawinigan Sportsmen's Group. The parks, lakes, and remote wild rivers hold trophy brook and lake trout and are surrounded by scenic coniferous forests, bogs, and mountains. Campgrounds are located at Dunbar, Inman, Normand, Tousignant, and Wessonneau lakes. The park maintains 43 cabins for fishermen, small-game hunters, and cross-country skiers. For maps and information write: St. Maurice Provincial Park, 175 6th Rue, Edifice Hotel de Ville, Box 36, Shawinigan.

Access & Outfitting Centers

Papineau-Labelle Provincial Park is reached via Provincial Highways 307, 309, and 117; there are guides, supplies, lodging, and outfitters at Mont Laurier, Lac du Cerf, Nominingue, Lac Desert, Duhamel, Buckingham, and Val des Bois. Mont Tremblant and Joliette provincial parks are reached via Provincial Highways 117, 125, 329, and 131; outfitting centers include La Macaya, Mont Tremblant, Lac Supérieur, St. Sonat, St. Guillaume, St. Jovite, and St. Michel des Saints. Mastigouche Provincial Park access is via Provincial Highways 347, 131, and 349; outfitting centers are St. Ignace du Lac, St. Gabriel, and St. Alexis. St. Maurice Provincial Park and La Maurice National Park are reached via Highways 55, 351, and 155; outfitters, guides, and lodging are available at Shawinigan, Grand'Mère, and Mattawin.

North Shore Fish & Game Region

North Shore Region Topo Maps

Canadian National Topographic Survey Maps, scale 1:250,000: Baie Comeau 22-F, Cap Chat 22-G, Lac Berte 22-K, Lac Manicouagan 22-N, Lac Eouquet 22-O, Sept-Îles 22-J.

Anticosti Island Reserve

Canadian National Topographic Survey Maps, scale 1:50,000: Port Menier 22H-16, Rivière aux Becs Scies 22H-9, Lac Faure 12E-13, Squaw Cove 12E-14, Gun River 12E-12, Jupiter River 12E-11, Gibbons Cove 12E-5, Rivière Galiote 12E-6, Rivière Chicotte 12E-3, Carleton Point 12E-10, Natiskotek River 12E-7, Rivière de la Chaloupe 12E-2, Tower Point 12E-9, Broom Bay 12E-8, Bagot Bluff 12E-1, Table Head 12F-5, Heath Point 12F-4.

Moisie River

Canadian National Topographic Survey Maps, scale 1:50,000: Opocopa Lake 23B-10, Lac Felix 23B-7, Opocopa Lake (1:250,000) 23-B, Rivière La Ronde 22O-15, Whitefish Lake 22O-16, Lac Brochet 22O-9, Grand Lac aux Sables 22O-8, Nipissis Lake 22O-1, Lac à l'Eau Dorée 22J-16, Rivière Vallée 22J-9, Lac des Rapides 22J-8, Sept-Îles 22J-1.

Port Cartier-Sept-Îles Provincial Park

Canadian National Topographic Survey Maps, scale 1:50,000: Sept-Îles 22J-1, Clark City 22J-2, Lac Vermette 22J-3, Lac Ste. Anne 22J-4, Lac Beaudin 22J-5, Walker Lake 22J-6, Lac Asquiche 22J-7, Lac Attacaupe 22J-10, Lac Rond 22J-11, Lac Bouffard 22J-12, Lac Fortin 22J-13, Grand Lac Nord 22J-14, Lac Dollard 22J-15.

Quebec's North Shore, world renowned for its beauty and wilderness fishing and hunting areas, is the name given to the left bank of the St. Lawrence River and Gulf, from the mouth of the Saguenay to the eastern end of Provincial Highway 138 at the coastal village of Moisie. The North Shore Highway winds along the scenic coast of the St. Lawrence through a historic wilderness dotted by picturesque 18th-century whaling, fishing, and fur trade villages. The highway is linked along its whole length by ferry service to the Gaspé Peninsula. At Sept-Îles, near the end of Highway 138, is the old trading post of Sept-Îles, a magnificent reconstruction of the first fur trading fort on the bank of the Vieux Fort River. *Navigation Nutak*, 312 Brochu Ave., Sept-Îles, offers cruises through the scenic 7 islands of the Sept-Îles Archipelago. Port Cartier-Sept-Îles Provincial Park encompasses some 3,000 square miles of subarctic forest, lakes, and wild rivers within the vast Saguenay Beaver Reserve, organized in 1955 to assure the conservation of beaver and to permit its trapping for the benefit of the Montagnais Indians in the territory. The reserve offers some finest brook trout fishing on the continent in the Ste. Marguerite, Asquiche,

Schmon, Gravel, Pentecôte, MacDonald, and Couleuvres rivers. Moose and black bear inhabit the virgin stands of black spruce and white birch, and the wet bogs surrounding the scenic, turbulent rivers and Lakes Walker, Posteur, Morin, and Arthur. The park is magnificent country for fly-fishermen, with Quebec red trout found in most of the rivers along with brook trout up to 7 pounds. There are campgrounds at the Toulnustouc and Ste. Marguerite rivers and at Lakes Walker, Nord-Est, and Arthur. Thirteen cottages are located at 3 sites within the reserve for public rental. For additional information and a free *Port Cartier-Sept-Îles Park Map* write: Port Cartier-Sept-Îles Reserve, 818 avenue Laure, Sept-Îles, (418) 962-9876.

The famous North Shore rivers and the wild, remote rivers of the Mingan coast to the east are among the finest Atlantic salmon fishing waters in Quebec. The famous Moisie River is a big salmon river that is impossible to fish without a boat; for nonresidents, a guide is a necessity. No reservations are necessary in Moisie Park, however, and there is no limit to the number of rods. The Moisie is also one of Quebec's great wilderness canoe routes, flowing southward from its Ungava headwaters at Opocopa Lake through a deep, steep-sloped scenic valley some 300 miles to its mouth on the St. Lawrence at the village of Moisie. This river, as well as being one of the world's great salmon rivers, is among the most beautiful of the North Shore rivers; it passes through majestic landscapes, gorges, canyons, waterfalls, rapids, and dense forests of white and black spruce, balsam fir, trembling aspen, and jack pine. Large game common to the banks of the Moisie and the North Shore includes moose and woodland caribou. Anglers should note that the Moisie is leased by private clubs upstream from

Moisie Provincial Park. For detailed info, write: District of North Shore, 818 avenue Laure, Sept-Îles, (418) 962-9876.

Several wilderness outfitters operate moose hunting and salmon fishing camps along the remote North Shore rivers. The St. Paul River is leased by Jon Pollack of the *St. Paul River Salmon Club* and is accessible only by floatplane. Reservations can be made by writing: P.O. Box 122, Quebec City. The Du Vieux Fort River is accessible by floatplane only and is outfitted by *Henry Fequet*, 488 Perreault Ave., Sept-Îles. The *Mecatina Lodge* is on the Mecatina River, with fishing for Atlantic salmon and trophy brook trout. Write: Norman Bobbitt, 1343 Meadowlands Dr., Ottawa, Ont. K2E 7E8. *Mabec Ltd.*, C.P. 10, Baie Comeau, operates 5 camps on the Étamamiou River. The Kégaska River is accessible by plane or boat and is outfitted by *Leslie S. Foreman*, Kégaska. The wild, remote Natashquan River, on the Mingan coast, is accessible by Quebecair or the Maritime Agency. For information and reservations write: *Natashquan Outfitters Inc.*, Suite 3160, 630 Dorchester Blvd., Montreal. The upper stretches of the renowned Godbout River are served by *Gabou Lodge*, 7780 Yves Prevost Blvd., Ville d'Anjou, Montreal. Other hunting and fishing outfitters serving the North Shore wilderness and territory north of the 51st parallel include: *Omer Gallienne*, 630 Gamache, Sept-Îles; *Raymond Buffitt*, Mutton Bay; *Camps-Trio*, c/o Bob Peel, 204 Rue Evangeline, C.P. 550, Sept-Îles; *Antoine Cormier*, C.P. 267, Gagnon; *Club de Pêche d'Iberville, Inc.*, 495 Rue Iberville, Sept-Îles, with fishing north of the 51st parallel on Kerbadot, Le Prevost, and Ponterel lakes and the Kaniapiskau River; *Club Outarde*, 80 Rue Ronchamps, Micoua; the *Eaton Canyon Club Ltd.*, c/o Laurentides Air

Service, C.P. 1540, Schefferville, operating 4 camps north of the 51st parallel for caribou and landlocked salmon and lake and brook trout; *Étamamiou Fishing Club*, C.P. 10, Baie Comeau; *Fongava Ltd.*, C.P. 1950, Schefferville; *Manitou Fishing Camps*, Baie Comeau Company, C.P. 10, Baie Comeau, operates camps on the famous brook trout waters of scenic Manitou Lake and River; *Club de la Rivière au Lac, Inc.*, C.P. 301, Forestville; and the *St. Lawrence Fishing & Hunting Club, Inc.*, operating hunting and fishing camps on the Mingan coast for caribou, and brook trout and ouananiche—write: Gordon W. Blair, 245 Welsh Rd., Huntingdon Valley, PA 19005.

Some of Quebec's finest salmon fishing is to be found on beautiful Anticosti Island, located in the Gulf of St. Lawrence due south of the rugged Mingan coast. The island has 15 excellent Atlantic salmon rivers including the famous Bec Scie, Loutre, and Jupiter rivers. The island was recently bought by the Quebec government from the Consolidated Bathurst Paper Company and the rivers are accessible by air to the public. The Anticosti Island Reserve has campsites and lodges open for salmon fishing from June through August and fall moose and deer hunting. The best salmon fishing is to be had in July before the water temperature rises. For information and reservations write: Anticosti Reserve, Port Menier, Ile d' Anticosti, P.Q.

The historic fishing and trading posts of the remote Mingan coast and the lower North Shore, stretching from the village of Moisie at the end of Provincial Highway 138 to the seacoast village of Blanc Sablon at the Newfoundland-Quebec border, are accessible only by boat or scheduled and charter aircraft. The Great Natashquan (derived from the Indian word *Moutascouan*, "remarkable bear hunting") and Romaine are two of the province's finest wilderness canoe routes and salmon and brook trout waters. The *Fort Mingan*, a ship of the *Maritime Agency*, Rimouski, links Sept-Îles to Blanc Sablon with stopovers at Mingan, Havre St. Pierre, Baie Johan Beetz, Natashquan, Kégaska, Romaine, Harrington, Tête à la Baleine, Baie des Moutons, Tabatiere, St. Augustin, and Rivière St. Paul. These coastal villages are also served by scheduled Quebecair flights. *Air Gaspé* has scheduled flights to Rivière au Tonnerre, Mingan, and Havre St. Pierre. Charter fly-in service is provided by *Ailes du Nord*, *Northern Helicopter*, and the *Sept-Îles Flying Club*, all in Sept-Îles.

Access & Outfitting Centers

The North Shore is served by scheduled airline service to the major coastal villages and by Provincial Highway 138. Outfitters, guides, lodging, supplies, and provincial campgrounds are available at Tadoussac, Grandes Bergeronnes, Escoumins, Sault au Mouton, Sainte Anne de Portneuf, Forestville, Îlets Jeremie, Betsiamites, Ragueneau, Chute aux Outardes, Hauterive, Manicouagan-Outardes, Baie Comeau, Franquelin, Godbout, Îlets Caribou, Port Cartier, Sept-Îles, and Moisie. Charter fly-in services for fishing, hunting, and wilderness canoeing trips throughout the North Shore region are provided by *Air Fecteau Ltd.*, CP 220, Senneterre J0Y 2M0, (819) 737-2262, from bases at Sept-Îles, Havre St. Pierre, and Gagnon.

Northwest Quebec

Kipawa Provincial Reserve

Canadian National Topographic Survey Maps, scale 1:250,000: Deep River 31-K, North Bay 31-L, Ville Marie 31-M.

La Vérendrye Provincial Park

Canadian National Topographic Survey Maps, scale 1:250,000: Mount Laurier 31-J, Deep River 31-K, Kempt Lake 31-O, Grand Lake Victoria 31-N, Ville Marie 31-M.

Quebec's northwest encompasses the scenic fishing, hunting, and canoe-camping areas in the Abitibi and Témiscamingue regions. The Abitibi region takes in the upper corner of the northwest from Lake Abitibi on the Ontario-Quebec border east to the wilderness mining and big-game hunting and fishing lands surrounding the outfitting and supply centers of Mattagami and Senneterre. The vast boreal evergreen forests of the Abitibi are famous for big-game hunting for moose, black bear, caribou, and upland game birds and outstanding fishing for great northern pike, walleye, and brook and lake trout to record sizes, which are found in the thousands of lakes and wild rivers. The Abitibi and Témiscamingue are dominated by forests of black spruce, red pine, and white pine with vagrant stands of white birch and white cedar. Maples and ash become predominant as one descends out of the highlands toward the Ottawa River. During the 19th century logging camps were established in the region to log out the huge virgin white pines needed for the masts of the British fleet. Today huge white pine stumps, old log chutes, and remnants of lumber camps may be found along several of the wild rivers that flow into the Ottawa River from the Laurentian Highlands. The scenic Témiscamingue region is an ancient lake bed gouged out of the Laurentian Plateau between La Vérendrye Provincial Park and Lake Témiscamingue—a widening of the Ottawa River. The major topographic features of the region include Lacs des Quinze, aux Sables, des Sables, and Simard, Pommeroy, Bois Franc, Guepe, Big Birch, Grand, Long, Kikwissy, Prevost, Watson, and Fraser lakes and the famous canoeing, fishing, and moose hunting areas of the Kipawa Reserve wilderness.

The Kipawa Provincial Reserve embraces 1 million acres of elongated, irregularly shaped lakes with countless bays and islands dominated by the 1,000-mile shoreline of spider-shaped Lake Kipawa. This huge body of water sprawls out between high wooded shores and sheer Precambrian cliffs and is dotted by hundreds of spruce-covered islands, including Mackenzie Island, which is 12 miles long and has 6 lakes of its own. Lake Kipawa, which derives its Indian name—meaning "lake without an outlet"—from its long narrow bays, is never over 5 miles wide and is one of the finest wilderness canoeing and lake trout, smallmouth bass, northern pike, and walleye fishing areas in the province. The provincial campground at the woodland village of Kipawa has 125 sites. There is a marina on Plongeurs Bay of Lake Kipawa and a seaplane base at Kipawa. Several wilderness hunting and fishing

camps are within the reserve. Kipawa Air Service, Kipawa, provides fly-in service for hunters and fishermen to outfitter organizations located within the reserve and for campers and canoeists to wilderness territories.

The following camps in the Kipawa Provincial Reserve and Témiscamingue region are members of the Quebec Outfitters Association, and provide outfitting and guide service for lake trout, northern pike, and walleye fishing trips and hunting for moose, black bear, and upland game birds. *Carniels Lodge & Cabins*, Guerin, Témiscamingue, operates a lodge and 8 camps on Lac des Quinze and Guepe Lake. *Doce Lodge*, C.P. 33, Angliers, maintains 10 camps with accommodations for 42 guests on Lac des Quinze. *Driftwood Lodge*, Kipawa, Témiscamingue, operates camps on Kipawa and Grassy lakes in the Kipawa Reserve. *Camp Grassy Narrows*, Moffet J0Z 2W0, is on Lac des Quinze with accommodations for 45 guests. *Hauleminn Camps, Ltd.*, RR 3, Orillia, Ont., maintains 9 camps in the Kipawa Reserve. *J.J. Camps*, C.P. 247, Stenhouse Bay, Lake Kipawa, Témiscamingue, operates 6 wilderness camps on Kipawa Lake. *Club Trout Lake*, C.P. 57, Belleterre, Témiscamingue, maintains 14 camps with accommodations for 68 guests on Lac à la Truite. *Two Moon Lodge*, c/o Kenneth Mullins, 21 Summit Dr., North Bay, Ont., has accommodations for 35 guests on Lake Kipawa. *White Pine Fish & Game Club*, Box 626, Orillia, Ont., is an Ottawa River outfitter, with 4 camps and accommodations for 20 hunters or fishermen. *Maple Leaf Lodge*, c/o Leonard Grace, Laniel, Témiscamingue, runs 9 camps on Kipawa Lake.

La Vérendrye Provincial Park, due east of the Kipawa Reserve, encompasses 3.2 million acres of Canadian Shield wilderness in the Abitibi region. The park is named in honor of Sieur de La Vérendrye, discoverer of the Rocky Mountains, and is at the northernmost limit of the Laurentians. The park's yellow birch, spruce, and red pine forests and deep, swift-flowing streams plus hundreds of large blue lakes form one of the province's outstanding fishing and canoe-camping meccas. Major lakes and waterways include Grand Lake Victoria, the Dozois and Cabonga reservoirs, lakes Renault, Jean Père, Lambert, Byrd, Poulter, and Kondiaronk, and the upper Ottawa, Chochocouane, and Dumoine rivers. For information, campsite reservations, and a free *La Vérendrye Provincial Park Map* write: Parks Branch, Ministry of Tourism, Fish, & Game, Hotel du Gouvernement, Quebec City. The park map shows canoe camping routes, portages with distance marked, rapids, tracking, dams, beaver dams, falls, currents, trails, roads, cart tracks, and campgrounds. There are maintained campsites at Lac La Vieille, Savary, and Dozoie, and wilderness campsites at Lac Leamy, Roland, Cabonga Road, Lake Rapide, Larouche, Barrage, Camatose, Whiskey River, Lac des Neuf Miller, Elbout, Denain, Camille Roy, Granet, and Victoria, L'Epinette River, Lac Andow, Lakes Rodin and Grand Poigan, Ottawa River, and Lac Joncas. Moose hunting in the park is open to residents of Quebec only.

Outfitting, lodging, and hunting and fishing guide service in the La Vérendrye Park and Abitibi region are provided by these members of the Quebec Outfitters Association: *Berthelot Lake Lodge*, C.P. 925, Senneterre; *Club Cesar Ltd.*, 7602 Boul. Marie Victorin, Ville Brossard, with camps on Cesar, Choquette, Baldwin, Beryl, Bolduc, Taylor, and Mary lakes; *Club Lac Faillon*, c/o 132 Villeneuve, Val d'Or; *Gueguen Lake Lodge*, Louvicourt, in La Vérendrye Park; *Camps Ratte*, Miquelon, on Waswanipi and Pusticamica lakes; *Ferns Cabins*, C.P. 98, Duparquet, at Lac Duparquet with accommodations for 36; and *Rosaire Delisle Pourvoyeur, Inc.*, St. Laurent de Galichan, with camps on Lakes Matis, Garneau, Plamondon, and Joanette and the Samson River. Fly-in service in Northwest Quebec is provided by *Tamarac Air Services*, Clova, Abitibi Co., Quebec G0A 1P0 (819) 662–0019.

Access & Outfitting Centers

The Kipawa Provincial Reserve is reached via charter aircraft by Canadian Pacific Railway from Montreal, and by car along Ontario Highway 63 and Quebec Highway 101. La Vérendrye Provincial Park is traversed by Provincial Highway 117. In the Témiscamingue region, outfitters, supplies, and lodging are available at Rouyn Noranda, Ville Marie, Laniel, and Témiscamingue—outfitting, supplies, guides, and lodging in the Abitibi region are available at Val d'Or, Le Domaine, Mont Laurier, Rouyn Noranda, La Sarre, Amos, Malartic, Duparquet, Mattagami, and Senneterre. Charter fly-in service for fishing, hunting, and wilderness canoeing trips throughout the region is provided by *Air Fecteau Ltd.*, CP 220, Senneterre J0Y 2M0, (819) 737-2262, from bases at Val d'Or, Senneterre, and Mattagami.

Saguenay & Lac St. Jean Region

Chibougamau Provincial Reserve

Canadian National Topographic Survey Maps, scale 1:250,000: Roberval 32-A, Réservoir Gouin 32-B, Chibougamau 32-G, Rivière Mistassini S. 32-H.

Lac St. Jean Country

Canadian National Topographic Survey Maps, scale 1:250,000: Roberval 32-A, Chicoutimi 22-D.

Laurentides Provincial Park

Canadian National Topographic Survey Maps, scale 1:250,000: Baie St. Paul 21-M, La Tuque 31-P, Chicoutimi 22-D.

Portneuf Provincial Park

Canadian National Topographic Survey Maps, scale 1:50,000: Tabot 31P-1, Lac Chat 31P-2, La Tuque 31P-7, Beaudet 31P-8.

Chibougamau Provincial Reserve encompasses 4,257 square miles of some of Quebec's finest canoe-camping and fishing waters. The park's wilderness waters are part of the Lac St. Jean basin and are surrounded by a lowland of rolling hills, vast moose bogs, beaver meadows, and forests of white pine and birch. The renowned Chef and Chamouchouane rivers drain much of the Chibougamau wilderness, flowing through a region known as the Laurentian massif south into Lac St. Jean. Trophy-sized lake trout, walleye, and northern pike are found in Lakes Postrincourt, Rohault, Marquette, Aigremont, Denalt, Chiqoubicke, d'Esglia and Chamouchouane—Indian for "where moose can be heard." The wild Chamouchouane River canoe route, one of the most challenging in the province, once served as the return route of expeditions to Hudson Bay and Lake Mistassini. Portage trails along the Perche, Chef, and Chamouchouane rivers are often easily traveled, as they are frequently used by Indians operating traplines in the region. The canoe route flows through beautiful scenic valleys and pine forests, marked by many, often dangerous rapids, falls, and chutes. Brook trout are found along the canoe route and in the Pemonka and Vermilion rivers and Rivière du Cran. Campsites are at Lake Argenson and Lac du Milieu. There are housekeeping cottages at 6 sites in the park. For park information and reservations write: Chibougamau Provincial Reserve, 748 Boul. Marcotte, Roberval. *Club Chasse & Pêche Hotel/Hotel des Laurentides* operates a lodge and 10 camps in the Chibougamau area with fishing for lake and brook trout and hunting for moose and black bear. Write: T. R. Levesque, 350 Boul. Ste. Anne, Beauport.

The scenic 100-mile shoreline of Lac St. Jean, due southeast of the Chibougamau Reserve, and its tributaries are famous for record-sized brook trout, ouananiche (landlocked salmon), northern pike, and wall-

eye. The migrating ouananiche offer some spectacular summer and early fall fishing in Lake Tchitagama and in the Ashwapmuchwan, Chamouchouane, Mistassini, Mistassibi, and Manouane rivers. Lac St. Jean, called *Piekouagami* ("flat lake") by the Indians, is surrounded by the Saguenay hollows. The surrounding woodlands are one of Quebec's top-ranked moose, black bear, woodland caribou, and partridge hunting regions. The historic Jesuits' Trail linked Fort Metabetchouan, built in 1676, to Quebec along the Metabetchouan River, the Jacques Cartier Valley, and other wild rivers and portages through the vast wilderness that was to become Laurentides Park. A provincial campground is located at Val Jalbert, a ghost town with a breathtaking view of Lac St. Jean, at the mouth of the Quiatchouane River (Montagnais Indian word for "small whirlpool")—a top-ranked landlocked salmon river. Provincial campgrounds elsewhere in the region are along Highway 169 at Hébertville, St. Jérôme, Desbiens, Chambord, Lac des Commissaires, Roberval, Pointe Bleue Indian Reservation, and St. Félicien.

Several wilderness hunting and fishing outfitters operate camps in the Lac St. Jean region. The *Bellevue Air Service, Inc.*, 2 Boul. Sacré Coeur, St. Félicien, maintains a lodge and 3 camps for moose hunting and lake trout, Quebec red trout, and northern pike fishing. *Camping Rocher Percé*, Chambord, operates fishing and hunting camps on Lac St. Jean. *Club Colonial, Inc.*, 1151 Rue Bellevue, St. Félicien, has 2 lodges and 2 camps on Lacs Meilleur and Damville for moose hunting and fishing for brook and lake trout, northern pike, and walleye. *Club Ouananiche*, 1170 W. Rue Gauthier, Alma, operates 3 chalets on Lac St. Jean. Lodging in the reserve is available at Pemonka and lakes Charron, d'Église, la Truite. For detailed info and maps, write: Chibougamau Reserve, Administration Bldg., 50 Harvey Blvd., Jonquière-Kénogami G7X 7W4.

Lac St. Jean is the headwaters of the majestic Saguenay River—a sinuous arm of the sea a mile wide and 65 miles long, banked by steep fjordlike cliffs occasionally 1,500 feet in height. Jacques Cartier named the river in 1535 after the Montagnais Indian word *Sakini*, "from where the water comes." The world-famous fish and game areas of the Saguenay wilderness surround the Chicoutimi headwaters of the Ste. Marguerite River (known as the jewel of the north) and Lakes Portneuf, Pipmuacon, Onatchiway, La Mothe, and Betsiamites. The Ste. Marguerite River, famous for its magnificent scenery and Atlantic

salmon fishing, is reached from the village of Sacré Coeur on Highway 172. There are provincial campgrounds and lodges along the north shore on Highway 172 at the outfitting and supply centers of Alma, St. Ambroise, Chicoutimi Nord, Sacré Coeur, and Tadoussac. The south shore of Saguenay fjord is paralleled by Quebec Highway 170. The incredibly scenic south shore wilderness is served by the city of Chicoutimi, once a main fur trading post of the king's domain, located due north of Laurentides Provincial Park.

Laurentides Provincial Park embraces a 4,000-square-mile wilderness of dense coniferous forests, wild white-water streams, and countless blue lakes in central Quebec in what was once the hunting and trapping territory of the Montagnais and Huron Indians. The park stretches north of Quebec City to the Lac St. Jean region. The reserve was established to protect the remnants of the great herds of caribou that once roamed throughout the region. Caribou, fortunately, have been successfully reintroduced into the reserve. The multitude of sparkling gemlike lakes and remote streams offer some of the finest wild brook and Quebec red trout fishing and canoeing water in the province. The major features of the park include the 4,000-foot peaks of the Laurentian Mountains and the famous brook trout waters of the Picaula, Metabetchouane, Chicoutimi, Ecores, Mallaie, Ha Ha, Mars, Cyriac, Jeanette, Bostonnais, Jacques Cartier, and Montmorency rivers—major fur trading routes to the far north. Wildlife in the park includes moose, black bear, wolf, and lynx. The remote Kikissink Wilderness, which adjoins the park on the west, holds record-sized brook trout and landlocked salmon. There are inns at the villages of Le Relais and Le Gîte du Berger, and park campgrounds at Mare du Sault, with 112 units at the Montmorency River; La Loutre, with 146 camping units; and Lac Athabaska and Belle Rivière. Laurentides Park has 41 fishermen's camps and light winter sports camps, with lodges at Le Montagnais and Les Portes de l'Enfer. Fishing, canoeing, camping, and lodging information and the free *Laurentides Provincial Park Map* and *Canoe-Route Map* may be obtained by writing: Superintendent, Laurentides Provincial Park, Édifice de la Faune, Box 7200, Charlesbourg G1G 5H9. Information for Portneuf Provincial Park, which includes 186,800 acres just southwest of Laurentides Reserve, may be obtained by writing the same address.

Access & Outfitting Centers

The Saguenay, Chibougamau, and Lac St. Jean regions are reached by scheduled and charter aircraft, by Canadian National Railway, and by automobile along Provincial Highways 155, 170, and 167. The north shore of the Saguenay River is reached via Highway 172 from Tadoussac, at the mouth of the Saguenay on the St. Lawrence. Laurentides Provincial Park is reached via Highway 175 northbound from Quebec City. Major outfitting and supply centers include Quebec City, Chicoutimi, Jonquière, Arvida, Kénogami, Alma, Roberval, Dolbeau, Mistassini, St. Félicien, Chibougamau, and Tadoussac. *Air Fecteau Ltd.*, CP 220, Senneterre J0Y 2M0 (phone: 819-737-2262) provides charter fly-in service for fishing, hunting, and canoeing trips throughout the region from seaplane bases at Chibougamau and Senneterre.

Ungava Salmon & Caribou Country

George River

Canadian National Topographic Survey Maps, scale 1:250,000: George River 24-I, Lac Ralleau 24-J, Lac Henrietta 24-H, Lac Brisson 24-A, Whitegull Lake 23-P.

Koksoak & Kaniapiskau Rivers

Canadian National Topographic Survey Maps, scale 1:250,000: Fort Chimo 24-K, Lac Herodier 24-F, Cambrian Lake 24-C, Rivière

Serigny 23-N, Lac Clairambault 23-K, Lac Hurault 23-L, Lac Vermen 23-F.

Leaf River & Lake Minto

Canadian National Topographic Survey Maps, scale 1:250,000: Lac Dufreboy 24-L, Lac Potherie 34-I, Nedluk Lake 34-H, Lake Minto 34-G.

Whale River

Canadian National Topographic Survey Maps, scale 1:250,000: Lac Ralleau 24-J, Lac Saffray 24-G, Lac Jeannin 24-B, Lac Brisson 24-A.

The Ungava, named after an Eskimo word meaning "faraway," is a lowland of Precambrian rock, dwarf willows, and stunted larch trees, crossed by some of North America's greatest Atlantic salmon rivers. This vast, partly unexplored wilderness is a land of austere beauty bounded on the north and east by the 4,000-foot peaks of the ancient Torngat Mountains, whose horn-shaped peaks are named after the Labrador Eskimo word for "sorcerer." The Ungava Bay watershed is dominated by the world-famous Atlantic salmon and ouananiche waters of Koksoak, Leaf, and Whale rivers and the 400-mile-long George River, renowned for its rugged, barren beauty, boiling rapids, falls, and deep, boulder-strewn pools. The surrounding Ungava wildlands also offer some of the finest trophy barren-ground caribou hunting on the continent. Anyone planning a trip to one of the wilderness fishing or hunting camps in the Ungava is advised to come prepared for cold rainy days, constant strong winds, and generally rugged conditions. This is also trophy bug country and a good supply of mosquito repellent is a must. Paired with the rugged, demanding weather and climate are the beauties of this far north region: the thick white carpets of caribou moss, the rose-yellow-green waves of the northern lights as they shift in a wavering three-dimensional effect across the brilliant night sky, and the great seasonal rhythms of the migrating caribou herds and geese and the spawning run of the Atlantic salmon.

The 400-mile subarctic watershed of the George rises in the glittering linear lakes of the White Gull wilderness and flows north along its tortured course through a sheltered valley into Ungava Bay. In addition to salmon, which enter the river each August on the primordal ebb and flow of the tide, the George holds trophy-size brook trout, arctic char, and lake trout. The major features shown on the maps of the George River, long the most famous of the Ungava salmon waters, include Helen Falls, Hades and Bridgeman Hills, Indian House Lake, Whitegull Lake, and the Mistinibi, Goelands, Tudor, and Michekanou lakes headwaters.

The George is served by several well-established fishing and hunting camps. The *Big Bend Camp* is reached by Nordair Ltd. from Montreal to Fort Chimo, at the mouth of the George on Ungava Bay. The camp has a main lodge and 4 camps with boats and guide for salmon, arctic char, and brook trout fishing and hunting in season for caribou, black bear, and wolf. For information and rates write: Mr. Bob May, Fort Chimo, Nouveau-Québec. The *George River Lodge*, a member of the Quebec Outfitters Association, is reached by plane from Schefferville, and has accommodations for 24 guests with guided fishing for salmon, arctic char, and lake and brook trout, and caribou hunts. Write: Henri Culos, C.P. 1238, Schefferville. The *Montagnais Hunting & Fishing Club, Inc.*, also a member of the Quebec Outfitters Association, operates 6 camps on the George with accommodations for 20 guests. The camp offers guided hunts for caribou, wolf, and bear and fishing for landlocked salmon, Atlantic salmon, lake trout, northern pike, and brook and Quebec red trout. Write: Fritz Gregor, C.P. 112, Sept-Îles. The *Pyramid Mountain Camp*, on the George, is accessible by Nordair Jet Service from Montreal to Fort Chimo and by

seaplane to camp. Facilities include a lodge and 5 camps. For information write: Johnny May, Fort Chimo, Nouveau-Québec. The *Tuktu Fish & Game Club, Inc.*, a member of the Quebec Outfitters Association, has a lodge and 4 camps on the George, reached by plane from Schefferville. Services include boats and guided fishing and hunting trips. Write: Gerry Poitras, C.P. 398, Sept-Îles. The *Twin River Lodge Ltd.* is a member of the Quebec Outfitters Association with 4 camps on the George for guided trophy fishing and hunting for barrenground caribou, black bear, and wolf. For information and rates write: Kenneth G. MacDonald, 74 Braeman Dr., Wayne, NJ 07470. *Arctic Anglers, Inc.*, is accessible by plane to Fort Chimo and has camps on the George for 14 guests with guided fishing for arctic char and Atlantic salmon. For information and rates write: Willis L. Littleford, Nemacolin Farm, PA 15437.

Some of the finest Ungava salmon and ouananiche fishing and caribou hunting are found along the Koksoak River and its Kaniapiskau and Delay River tributaries. The Koksoak, Kaniapiskau, and Delay rivers are served by *Laurentian-Ungava Outfitters Ltd.*, c/o Peter Schock, Box 818, RR5, Ottawa, Ont., or C.P. 1540, Schefferville. The *Kaniapiskau River Fishing Camps, Inc.*, is reached by Quebecair from Montreal to Labrador and by Laurentian Air Services seaplane to camp. Facilities include 7 camps with accommodations for 16 guests, with fly-fishing only at 3 camps for trophy landlocked salmon and brook and lake trout. For information write: *Laurentian Air Service*, Schefferville G0G 2T0, (418) 585-3475, which provides charter fly-in services to the most remote, unexplored lakes and rivers of the Ungava Plateau in both Quebec and Labrador. You can fly in, set up your wilderness base camp, and Laurentian will fly you out on a pre-designated date. Write or call the Schefferville office or the head office: Box 127, Aylmer East J9H 5E5, (819) 684-0330.

The full length of the famous Whale River is shown on the map kit including the Lac Champdore headwaters, Jeannin and Privert lakes, and Tunulic River. A number of outfitters offer salmon fishing and caribou hunting trips along the Whale. *Whale River Outfitters Ltd.* operates a lodge and 5 camps with accommodations for 40 guests. For rates and information write: Stanley Karboski, Camp Twelve Pines Rd., Parish, NY 13131. *Ungava Atlantic Salmon Outfitters*, operated by the Quebec Eskimo Indian Outfitters, C.P. 520, Rawdon, runs 6 camps on the Whale with accommodations for 12 guests and guided caribou hunting and Atlantic salmon fishing trips. The *Tunulik River Fishing Camp* is reached by Nordair Jet Service from Montreal and chartered seaplane to camp. Write: *Arctic Adventures*, c/o Bill Tait, 880 Begin, St. Laurent, (514) 332–0880. Arctic Adventures also operates the *Payne Bay Camp* and offers caribou hunting at their *Upper Tunulik River Camp*, goose hunting on James Bay at their *Paint Hills Goose Camp*, and fishing in the Hudson Bay area at their *Kovik Bay Fishing Camp*.

As most fishing on the large, powerful Ungava River is done from boat or freighter canoe, lightweight leather-topped and rubber-bottomed boots are suggested. If you plan on wading these boulder-strewn waters, the waders or hip boots should be fitted with cleats or felt soles. Good raingear, an insect-proof head net, and cotton gloves are also recommended.

Access & Outfitting Centers

The Ungava Bay region is reached via scheduled air service from Montreal to Schefferville, Labrador City, and Fort Chimo on Ungava Bay, and then by charter floatplane service to your designated hunting or fishing camp. Guides are mandatory for nonresidents in New Quebec. Supplies, ammunition, and gear may be purchased at Schefferville, and to a limited extent at Fort Chimo.

ATLANTIC CANADA

Introduction

Atlantic Canada encompasses the provinces of Newfoundland and Labrador, Nova Scotia, Prince Edward Island, and New Brunswick—a group, commonly referred to as the "Maritime Provinces." Newfoundland, the easternmost province, is divided into two parts: the 43,359 square-mile island of Newfoundland, said to be the 10th largest island in the world; and the 112,826 square miles of Labrador, separated from the island by the scenic Strait of Belle Isle—also known as the "Isle of Demons."

The rocky 4,000-mile coast of Newfoundland lies in the Atlantic across the Gulf of St. Lawrence and Cabot Strait from the eastern coasts of Quebec and Nova Scotia. The island is cut by several Atlantic salmon rivers, including the famed Humber, Exploits, Gander, and River of Ponds, which form large island-studded bays at their mouths. Inland, this magical island is a land of fog-shrouded moors and boreal forests, dotted with blue lakes, and slashed by wild foaming rivers. Much of the island is a rolling plateau with elevations ranging between 500 and 1,000 feet. The majestic Long Range Mountains, the northernmost extension of the great Appalachian Chain, run parallel to the western coast and reach heights of more than 3,000 feet. Just east of the Long Range are the innumerable lakes, forests, and moose bogs—including huge Red Indian Lake and Grand Lake—of a high 1,500-foot plateau known as the "Great Barrens." All of the land above 1,000 feet is taiga and tundra, with rocky stretches supporting little more than stunted spruce, alpine flowers, caribou moss, and colorful orange, white, brown, and yellow lichens.

The coast of Labrador to the north, also referred to as "Mainland Newfoundland," forms the northeast corner of the continent and is bordered on the west by Quebec, on east by the Northern Atlantic, and on the north by Ungava Bay and Hudson Strait. For centuries after its discovery by the Vikings in 986 A.D., it was thought to be part of Greenland, until Henry Hudson explored its Atlantic Coast into Hudson Bay and mapped this great peninsula. Inland, Labrador is a vast plateau with an average altitude of 2,000 feet. There are chains of interconnected lakes in the west—among them are Ashuanipi, Lobstick, and Michikamau; the deep-flowing pools and rapids of the Hamilton and Churchill rivers; and the world-renowned trophy brook trout and Atlantic salmon waters of the Minipi and Eagle Rivers. In the panhandle-shaped northern reaches of the province is a great sub-arctic wilderness containing thousands of unexplored lakes and trophy arctic char and brook trout streams. This area is hemmed on the west by the Torngat or "Devil" Mountains and on the east by the coastal Kiglapaits or "Dog-toothed" Mountains and Kaumajets or "Shining Tops" Mountains.

Beautiful Nova Scotia, a peninsula connected to New Brunswick on the north, is situated southwest of the island of Newfoundland across the Cabot Strait. The province, often called the "Wharf of North America" because of its numerous harbors and rustic fishing villages, contains 21,425 square-miles. Here are the majestic highlands of Cape Breton Island, separated from the mainland by the Strait of Canso, and first discovered by the explorer John Cabot in 1497. The rocky, scenic coast of Nova Scotia is dotted by quaint "old-world" fishing villages and is famous for its huge tides, which average more than 40 feet at the Bay of Fundy.

New Brunswick is the largest of the four eastern Maritime Provinces. The 28,000-square-mile province is famous for its Atlantic salmon fishing, giant bluefin tuna, landlocked salmon and trophy smallmouth bass, moose hunting, northwoods backpacking, canoeing, and camping areas. It is bordered on the west and north by the great lake chains and forests of Maine and the magnificent highlands of Quebec's

Gaspé Peninsula, and Chaleur Bay; on the south by the great tidal flats of the Bay of Fundy and Nova Scotia; and on the east by the Gulf of St. Lawrence and Prince Edward Island. The Appalachian Highlands of Maine are continued in the western half of New Brunswick where the historic Atlantic salmon waters of the famed Restigouche, St. John, and Miramichi Rivers and their tributaries flow through the evergreen forests of the Central and Northern highlands—a great wilderness plateau at 1,500 to 2,000 feet elevation. The eastern half of the province includes part of a large basin that extends into Nova Scotia, rimmed by 600-foot high limestone ridges.

Prince Edward Island, Canada's smallest province, is called the "Garden of the Gulf." Famous for summer vacation lands and off-shore tuna-fishing the island lies in the Gulf of St. Lawrence, separated from Nova Scotia and New Brunswick by the Strait of Northumberland. The interior acadian forests of the Atlantic Provinces, dominated by red spruce, are described in detail in the free publication *Canada's Eight Forest Regions*, available upon request from the Information Branch, Environment Canada, Ottawa, Ontario.

Weather, Bugs, Beasts & the Labrador Current

Canada's Maritime Provinces have what is usually described as a continental climate, but the influence of the frigid Labrador Current and variations in weather among different regions, produce unexpected variations in temperature. Winters are cold and harsh, with heavy snowfall. In summer, along the coastal areas, June and July tend to be foggy with moderate temperatures. Inland, however, summer is usually warm, occasionally hot, with cool evenings. The spectacular "Indian Summer" days during autumn are generally long, clear, and sunny, with brisk, damp evenings. Contrary to popular notion, Newfoundland is not perpetually locked in fog. The southeast coast of Nova Scotia, for example, is more likely to have mist and fog than the island of Newfoundland. Labrador summers along the coast are often chilly and foggy due to the southward drifting of the Labrador Current. Further inland, summers tend to be hotter and winters considerably colder because of air masses traveling north and east from interior Quebec. A useful guide to weather, cloud formations, and forecasting in the Atlantic Provinces, called *Weather Ways*, is available for $2 from the Canadian Hydrographic Service, Department of the Environment, Ottawa, Ontario K1A 0E8.

Anyone planning a summer fishing, camping, or canoeing trip to one of the Atlantic Provinces is well advised to take along a good supply of Muskol, Mosquitone, Off!, or Cutters insect repellent. (All contain 50 percent plus DEET concentration.) Bring along a wide-brimmed hat, a heavy, light-colored safari shirt, a head net, and good quality sun glasses to cut water glare. If you plan an extended trip into the interior wilderness areas, a recommended dosage of 50 mg/day of Vitamin B-1 for the week prior to your exposure to insects and about 10 mg a day each day during your trip is one of the best natural defences against blackflies, mosquitoes, chiggers, and no-see-ums. (Check with your physician for his recommended dosage and advice.) Other potential wildlife hazards include black bears, and moose during the fall rutting season.

Atlantic Canada Maps & Nautical Charts—How to Order

A set of full-color topographic maps will provide the Atlantic Canada outdoorsman with an invaluable physical inventory of the region where he plans to fish, hunt, camp, or canoe. All Canadian National Topo-graphic Survey Maps are available for $1.50 per map, plus a 50¢ handling charge from the Canada Map Office, Surveys Mapping Branch, Department of Energy, Mines, and Resources, Ottawa, Ont. K1A 0E9, (613) 994-9663. (Be sure to order by individual map name and code, and make your check or money order payable to Receiver General of Canada.) To expedite your shipment include extra money for First Class postage. Free *Indexes of Topographic Maps* for the Atlantic Provinces and a *Map Symbol Chart* may be obtained from the same address. Useful overviews of the individual provinces are provided by the 7-color *Newfoundland and Labrador Map* (MCR-30, $1.50), 42×51 inches, with a scale of 1 inch to 8 miles; *Nova Scotia & Prince Edward Island Map* (MCR-37, $1.50), 38×50 inches, scale of 1 inch to 8 miles; *New Brunswick Province Map* (MCR-29, $1.50), 38×50 inches, scale of 1 inch to 8 miles. *New Brunswick County Maps* at a scale of 1 inch to 3 miles are available for $1.08 each for Restigouche, Madawaska, Victoria, Gloucester, Northumberland, Kent, Carleton, Sunbury, Queens, and Charlotte counties from the Lands Branch, Department of Natural Resources, Centennial Bldg., Fredericton, New Brunswick. The following Canadian nautical chart catalogs may be obtained free from the Hydrographic Chart Distribution Office, Department of the Environment, Ottawa, Ontario: *Nova Scotia, New Brunswick & Prince Edward Island* (Information Bulletin 8); *Island of Newfoundland & North Shore of the Gulf of St. Lawrence* (Information Bulletin 7); and *Labrador Coast* (Information Bulletin 9).

Anyone planning a trip to the Big North Country should send for the *Canada Maps & Wilderness Canoeing Guide* (MCR-107) available free upon request from the Canada Map Office (address above). This valuable publication contains a text written by Eric Morse—among the intrepid pioneers of recreational canoeing in Canada's Far North. Subjects discussed include planning your trip, making a trip profile, making a schedule, map symbols, barren land maps, navigating in the far north, use of maps, types of map scales, how to order aerial photographs, and use of compass on a canoe trip. This full-color illustrated guide contains a "Canada 1:250,000 Scale Map Index."

Vacation Travel Maps, Information & CB Radio Permits

A beautiful full-color *Vacation Planning—Topographic Highway Map of Eastern Canada*, showing all major natural and man-made features, including lakes and streams, mountain ranges, national and provincial parks, towns, cities, and highways, is available free upon request from the Canadian Government Office of Tourism, 150 Kent St., Ottawa, Ontario K1A 0H6, along with the indispensable free booklets *Canada Ferries, Bridges & Cruises* and *Canada Travel Information Handbook* (36 pp.), which contain everything you need to know about customs regulations, airport services, hunting and fishing regulations, insurance, and weather, with temperature and time-zone charts. Citizenband radio permit applications and regulatory information may be obtained for Newfoundland from the Regional Director, Telecommunications Regulations Branch, Department of Communications, 2085 Union Ave., Montreal, Quebec H3A 2C3; for Nova Scotia, Prince Edward Island, and New Brunswick, from the Regional Director, Telecommunications Regulation Branch, Department of Communications, Terminal Plaza Bldg., 1222 Main St., Moncton, New Brunswick E1C 8P9.

For information on Canadian train vacation, routes, rates, itineraries, hotels, and package tours, write: *VIA Rail Canada*, P.O. Box 8117, Montreal, Quebec H3C 3N3 or contact your local travel agent. VIA Rail Canada manages Canadian National and Canadian Pacific passenger train services.

Accommodations—Vacation Lodges & Sporting Camps

A wide range of accommodations and fishing and hunting camps throughout the island of Newfoundland and the mainland (Labrador) part of Newfoundland Province are described in the free 42-page accommodation guide called *Newfoundland: Where to Stay*. The guide contains complete descriptions of services and facilities of government licensed establishments and may be obtained by writing: Department of Tourism, Confederation Bldg., St. John's, Nfld. The guide will prove an invaluable aid for anyone planning a trip to the province. (See the "Travel & Recreation Guide" section for listings of sporting camps and lodges.)

Airline & Charter Fly-in Services

Eastern Provincial Airways, P.O. Box 5001, Gander, Nfld. A1V 1W9, has regularly scheduled jet flights daily from Montreal to St. John's with stops at Charlottetown, Halifax (N.S.), Sydney (N.S.), Stephenville, Deer Lake, and Gander, and additional daily flights between Wabush, Churchill Falls, Goose Bay, Deer Lake, Stephenville, Gander, and St. John's. *Air Canada*, 1 Place Ville Marie, Montreal, Que. H3B 3Y8, has regularly scheduled flights from the United States and Canadian mainland points to Stephenville, Gander, and St. John's. *Newfoundland & Labrador Air Transport Ltd.*, Box 3, Corner Brook, Nfld., operates a year-round scheduled service between Deer Lake and Blanc Sablon (Que.) (Forteau-Pinware Rivers), St. Anthony, and Port aux Choix, as well as operating a charter fleet of 12 float- and ski-planes and helicopters of several sizes throughout Labrador and the island of Newfoundland. The Labrador charter fleet base is located at Goose Bay: Bay 171, Happy Valley, Nfld. *Labrador Airways Ltd.*, P.O. Box 219, Goose Bay, Nfld. A0P 1C0, has year-round scheduled flights out of Goose Bay to all towns on the Labrador coast between Forteau on the south coast to Nain on the north coast. Labrador Airways also operates a fleet of 15 charter aircraft from their bases at Goose Bay and St. Anthony. *Quebecair*, Montreal International Airport, P.O. Box 490, Dowal, Que. H0Y 1B5, operates a scheduled service from Montreal to Wabush and Churchill Falls. *Gander Aviation Ltd.*, Gander, Nfld., provides charter flights from Gander to all points in Newfoundland and Labrador using 10-passenger Otters, 6-passenger Beavers, and 3-passenger Cessnas with floats, wheels, and skis.

Atlantic Salmon Fishing & Maps

Newfoundland and Labrador's wild rivers provide some of the finest Atlantic salmon fishing in eastern Canada. The province's scheduled salmon rivers are shown on the *Atlantic Salmon Rivers Map of Canada*, available for $5 from the Atlantic Salmon Association, 1405 Peel St., Suite 409, Montreal H3A 1S5, Que. The map shows all Atlantic salmon rivers in Newfoundland and Labrador including the Forteau, Pinware, Eagle, Naskaysi, Hawke, and Adlatok rivers in Labrador and the Grand Codroy, Serpentine, Torrent, Main, and Humber rivers and the River of Ponds on the island of Newfoundland. The map also shows private waters; rivers open to the public or controlled by an outfitter; provincial reserve waters; waters closed to fishing; number and types of nets, airports, ferries, power dams with and without fishways, logging booms, fish hatcheries, and outfitters. Salmon in Newfoundland and Labrador may be taken by artificial fly only and the open season is from late May to September 15. Nonresidents fishing for salmon must be accompanied by licensed guides, except when fishing ¼ mile upstream or ¼ mile downstream from Trans-Canada Highway bridges crossing scheduled streams. Licensed guides

NEWFOUNDLAND & LABRADOR ENCYCLOPEDIA

are required for all types of fishing in Labrador. Among the most popular Atlantic salmon flies for the rivers of the province are the Jack Scott, Silver Doctor, Silver Wilkinson, Black Dose, Silver Gray, Blue Charm, Patfaced McDougals, Thunder & Lightning, Cosseboom, Dusty Miller, Green Highlander, Marlodge, Black Doctor, Moose Hair, March Brown, Ross Special, and Black Pennell in sizes 6, 8, and 10, with some size 4 for high water. The renowned *Atlantic Salmon Journal* is required reading for the serious salmon fishing enthusiast. The magazine is published in a beautiful full-color format 4 times a year and contains authoritative and useful articles. A subscription is included with an annual membership fee of $15 in the Atlantic Salmon Association, 1405 Peel St., Suite 409, Montreal H3A 1S5, Que.

Canoeing & Wilderness Waters

The wild rivers of Newfoundland and Labrador are among the most challenging and remote canoe routes in North America. *Canadian Wild River Surveys* for the rivers described below may be obtained free by writing: Information Services, Conservation Group, Department of Indian Affairs & Northern Development, Ottawa, Ont. K1A 0H4. The *Kanairiktok River* lies in middle Labrador and flows for 185 miles from its headwaters in Ethyl and Morris lakes near the Quebec border through numerous lakes, string bogs, and evergreen forests. Good camping sites occur frequently along the course of the river. The *Lloyds-Exploits River* system is one of the most important in Newfoundland, flowing for about 265 miles to the Bay of Exploits on the northeast coast. The major features shown on the maps of this canoe route include the Annieopsquotch Mountains, King George IV Lake, Lloyds Lake, Red Indian Lake—at 37 miles the second-largest lake in the province—and Grand Falls. The barren grounds surrounding King George IV Lake and the Annieopsquotch Mountains offer excellent fly-in caribou hunting and moose hunting in the river valleys. The *Goose River* flows through the Labrador wilderness for 100 miles to empty into Goose Bay on Lake Melville. The remote *Vajoktok River* system flows through the Labrador wilderness above the 55th parallel with numerous canyons, rapids, waterfalls, and chutes along the route. The wild *Naskaupi River* flows from Lake Michikamau through the Labrador Plateau into Grand Lake. The major features along the route include Orma and Caribou lakes, the scenic Rainbow Hills, the "Narrows," Seal Lake, the cobbled shoreline of Naskaupi Lake, and the

North Pole Rapids. The scenic *Main River* flows east from the Long Range Mountains in the Great Northern Peninsula for 33 miles. The headwater lakes provide excellent brook trout fishing and are spawning grounds for Atlantic salmon. The Main is a scheduled salmon river and offers excellent fishing during the inland run. The famous *Humber River* flows for 110 miles from the Osmond Pond headwaters through scenic spruce and white birch forests and a deep valley to its mouth on Deer Lake. The Humber is a renowned Atlantic salmon river and provides excellent fishing for brook trout and landlocked salmon. The river flows through moose and caribou country.

The useful publication *Newfoundland Canoe Trips* may be obtained free by writing: Department of Tourism, Confederation Bldg., St. John's, Nfld. This publication describes the Grand Lake-Sandy Lake and Birchy Waterways, Indian River, upper Humber River, Terra Nova River, Northwest Gander River, Exploits River, and lower Gander River canoe routes. It also contains topographic maps of each canoe route. During the period the Forest Travel Restricted Area order is in effect, usually from June 1 to September 7, a nonresident may not travel over any forest land in the province without a permit unless accompanied by a licensed guide or resident. Forest travel permits may be obtained from any Forest Service official or by writing direct to the Department of Forestry, Confederation Bldg., St. John's, Newfoundland. The following 1:50,000 and 1:250,000 scale Canadian National Topographic Survey Map Kits show the major Newfoundland and Labrador wild rivers. *Lloyds-Exploits River:* King George IV Lake 12A-4, Puddle Pond 12A-5, Howley Lake 12A-6, Star Lake 12A-11, Lake Ambrose 12A-10, Buchans 12A-15, Badger 12A-16, Grand Falls 2D-13; *Kanairiktok River:* Kasheshibaw Lake 13-L, Snegamook Lake 13-K, Hopedale 13-N; *Humber River:* Gros Morne 12H-12, Silver Mountain 12H-11, Cormack 12H-6, Deer Lake 12H-3, Pasadena 12H-4, Corner Brook 12A-13; *Main River:* Silver Mountain 12H-11, Jackson's Arm 12H-15, Main River 12H-14; *Ugjoktok River:* Mistastin Lake 13-M, Hopedale 13-N; *Goose River:* Winokapau Lake 13-E, Goose Bay 13-F; *Naskaupi River:* Kasheshibaw Lake 13-L, Snegamook Lake 13-K, Goose Bay 13-F.

Fishing & Hunting in Newfoundland and Labrador

Newfoundland and Labrador's 156,185 square miles of virgin forests, 13,000 square miles of wilderness lakes and streams, and rugged coastal waters are a unique sportsman's paradise with big-game hunting for moose, barren-ground and woodland caribou, fishing for Atlantic salmon and near world's record brook trout, landlocked salmon, sea trout, rainbow trout, arctic char, and northern pike, and offshore coastal fishing for giant bluefin tuna. Labrador, with its undulating granite surface, is a large plateau 1,000–3,000 feet in elevation which forms part of the northeastern area of the Canadian Shield. Vast regions of muskeg and swamp, bare rocky ridges, and innumerable lakes, many as yet unnamed, characterize its stark, generally barren landscape. In the extreme north are the Torngat Mountains, rising to over 5,000 feet north of the Eskimo village of Saglek. The rugged Labrador seacoast with its numerous scenic fjords and sheer cliffs rising to dizzying heights of 3,000 feet is almost unnavigable. A long sandy beach near Cape Porcupine interrupts the generally wild coast and has been identified by some as the strand where Norsemen first touched land in North America over 1,000 years ago. While Labrador falls within the Canadian Shield, the island of Newfoundland is the northernmost extension of the Appalachian Mountain chain which reaches far south into the United States. The island is volcanic in origin, featuring a low rolling surface, with the highest elevations along the Long Range Mountains in the Gros Morne region. The New-

foundland coastline is fringed with innumerable bays, small islands, caves, and rocky harbors. The eastern and southern coasts are the rockiest and most barren, but on the west coast amply wooded hills and valleys provide scenic panoramas. In the interior wilderness moors and moose bogs prevail and thousands of lakes and streams form a network of outstanding fishing waters. Grand Lake, with an area of 140 square miles, is the largest body of fresh water in the province. The Exploits, Gander, and Humber are the major rivers.

A complete list of fishing camps and descriptions of Newfoundland and Labrador's 100 scheduled Atlantic salmon rivers, and the major lakes and rivers which hold landlocked salmon, brook trout, arctic char, and sea-run squaretails, browns, and rainbows are contained in the invaluable 54-page *Newfoundland Fishing Guide*, available free from Tourist Services Division, Department of Tourism, Confederation Bldg., St. John's, Nfld. The federal Department of the Environment, Fisheries, & Marine Service, Bldg. 302, P.O. Box 5667, Pleasantville, Nfld., will answer your inquiries requesting specific information on the various species of game fish and their general location, and detailed information on any river (including weekly catch reports). A description of seasons, limits, and regulations is contained in the 54-page fishing guide. Inland fishery licenses for trout and salmon may be obtained by writing: Wildlife Division, Department of Tourism, Confederation Bldg., St. John's, Nfld.

The most effective trout flies in the provincial waters are Silver Doctor, Parmachene Belle, Cow Dung, Black Zulu, Terra Nova (silver body), Dark Montreal, Jenny Lind, Bumble Bee, Marlodge, Royal Coachman, and March Brown in sizes 10, 12, and 14. Warm clothing for the cool evenings, waterproof jackets, and waders are recommended. A good supply of insect repellent and a head net are a must.

Moose, caribou, and black bear roam the boreal forests of Newfoundland and Labrador's interior wilderness in large numbers. Vast tracts of taiga still remain virtually unexplored and accessible only by fly-in charter aircraft. Nonresidents may hunt caribou in Newfoundland in the La Poile area, western Labrador, Grey River, and Buchans Plateau regions. Bull moose may be hunted by nonresidents in all moose management areas except the Agnuille Mountains. Nonresident hunters must be accompanied by a licensed guide. In western Labrador the fishing and hunting seasons overlap by 3 weeks, providing the sportsman with the opportunity of combining top-ranked caribou hunting with trophy brook trout, lake trout, and ouananiche (landlocked salmon) fishing. The invaluable *Newfoundland Hunting Guide* may be obtained free by writing: Tourist Service Division, Department of Tourism, Confederation Bldg., St. John's, Nfld. This 24-page booklet contains the nitty-gritty about age limits, aircraft, caribou hunting, customs regulations, clothing requirements, dogs, export of meat, guides, hunting weapons, license fees, moose hunting, small game, and a comprehensive where-to-hunt guide describing hunting outfitter services and facilities by area. Nonresident caribou and moose licenses are available through licensed outfitters. (See "Atlantic Salmon Fishing & Maps" and the "Travel & Recreation Guide" section for listings of hunting and fishing outfitters.)

"Grand Banks" & Bluefin Tuna Fishing

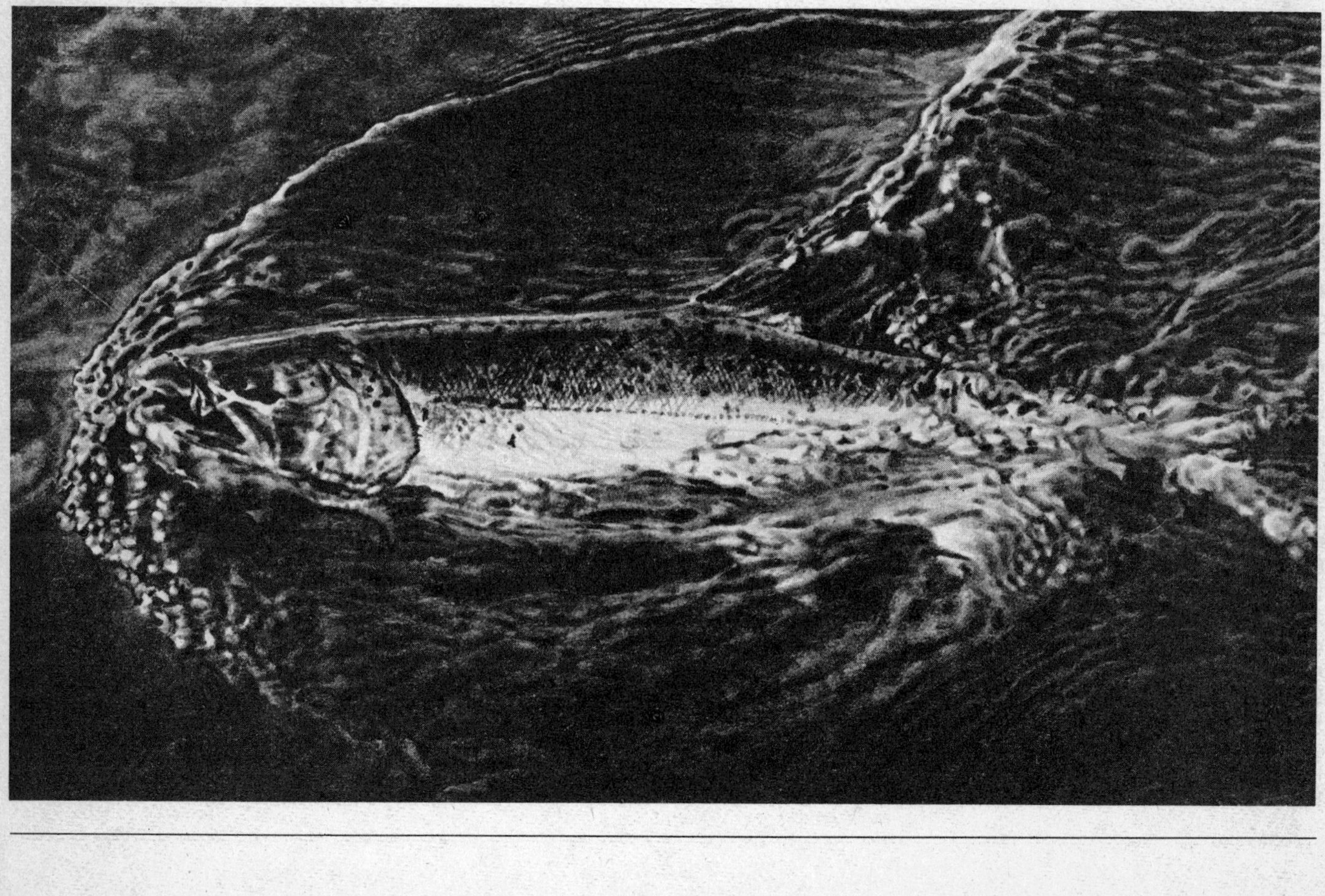

Newfoundland is surrounded by a number of large banks or submarine plateaus frequented by great numbers of cod, lobster, herring, Atlantic salmon, and tuna. The most famous of these plateaus are the famous Grand Banks of Newfoundland, fished for centuries by the great fleets of bankers, or line fishing vessels, from the world over. These great fleets, with the exception of Portugal's ships, have been replaced by

large fleets of trawlers, many of them operating from European bases. Large schools of giant bluefin tuna move inshore along Newfoundland coastal waters from mid-June to mid-October. Each year huge schools of tuna appear in such world-famous coastal bays as Conception, Notre Dame, and Trinity bays. The Newfoundland record bluefin tuna, caught on September 18, 1973, weighted 877 pounds. Detailed information on tuna charter boat services and rates may be obtained by writing: Tourist Services Division, Department of Tourism, 5th Floor, Confederation Bldg., St. John's, Nfld.

Highways—Recreation & Scenic Routes

Newfoundland's outdoor recreation areas are served by well-maintained paved highways and gravel roads. Labrador, however, is for all practical purposes completely roadless. The extremely useful *Newfoundland Transportation & Roads Guide* describes all local and regional roads, unleaded gas station and diesel pump locations, traffic regulations, gravel highways, winter travel, and car rental facilities. This 32-page guide and the *Newfoundland & Labrador Official Road Map* may be obtained free from the Tourist Services Division, Newfoundland Department of Tourism, Confederation Bldg., St. John's, Nfld. The official road map shows paved and gravel roads, forest roads and private roads, ferry lines, airports, hospitals, fishing camps, points of interest, historic sites, towns and settlements, and hunting camps. The Department of Tourism also publishes the free booklet *Newfoundland and Labrador*, a guide to resources, towns, recreation, and transportation. The 1:250,000 scale Canadian National Topographic Survey map kits below show Newfoundland's major recreation highways.

Great Northern Peninsula Highway (430)

This map kit shows the entire length of Provincial Highway 430 and the surrounding wildlands of the Great Northern Peninsula from Deer Lake northeastward along the coastline of the Gulf of St. Lawrence to St. Anthony. The major features shown along the route include Gros Morne National Park and the interior wilderness surrounding the rugged Long Range Mountains and the famous Atlantic salmon and brook trout waters of Portland Creek, Blue Ponds, Ten Mile Lake and the Upper Humber, Main, Torrent, and Cloud rivers, and River of Ponds. The highway passes through the heart of one of the finest moose and caribou hunting regions in North America. Canadian National Topographic Survey Maps: St. Anthony 2-M, Sandy Lake 12-H, Port Saunders 12-I, Blanc Sablon (Que.) 21-P.

Trans-Canada Highway (1)

This map kit shows the entire 565-mile length of Newfoundland Highway 1 from Channel Port aux Basques as it winds across the province to the capital, St. John's, on the Avalon Peninsula. The major features shown along the route include the Burnt Islands, Codroy, Exploits, Barachois, Harrys, Serpentine, Humber, and Gander rivers, Terra Nova National Park, Middle Ridge, Annieopsquotch and Topsails mountains, and the vast 2,450-square-mile wilderness surrounding the Meelpaeg, Island, Granite, Round, and Great Burnt lakes moose and caribou country. Canadian National Topographic Survey Maps: St. John's 1-N, Bonavista 2-C, Gander Lake 2-D, Botwood 2-E, Port aux Basques 11-O, Red Indian Lake 12-A, Stephenville 12-B, Sandy Lake 12-H.

Hubbard-Wallace Labrador Expedition—Journey to Ungava

Labrador is a land of fierce and lonely beauty. Its vast reaches hold yet the mystery of the unknown—a wilderness compelling, inspiring, and on occasion, cruel. It was all of these things to Leonidas Hubbard, a writer and wilderness lover who set out in the midsummer of 1903 to chart the course of the largely unexplored Naskaupi River. He planned to ascend the river to its source in Lake Michikamau and continue thence down the wild George River through the Barren Grounds to the old Hudson's Bay Company post at Ungava. Shortly before he left the outpost at Hamilton Inlet for the wilderness he wrote in his journal, "Awoke from bad dream of trouble getting somewhere to realize that I was at a post. Mighty good awakening." Three months later he died of starvation, lost in the far interior.

Confused by the reports of the Hamilton Inlet outpost inhabitants and inaccuracies on the official map of the region, he had mistaken the smaller Susan River for the Naskaupi. The shoals and brawling rapids of the wild river slowed the expedition's progress and often forced the three men to portage their heavy load, while the hellish flies of the northcountry tortured them. But the tracks of the caribou were many, and the hoped-for migration of the reindeer at the height of the land beckoned. The men caught scores of trout, and it seemed certain that larger fish would be abundant further on. They shot wild geese and partridge, enough to sustain them if not to store for tomorrow. The promises of the austere land were many: the stars shone, the fir trees sang in the wind above their lonely campground, and they went on, stirred by hope, fascinated by the waters of their uncharted path.

On August 11 Hubbard wrote of desperate hunger. But before it could drive him to the admission of failure and the necessity of the retreat, he shot a caribou. And so the trip continued. They followed the dwindling rapids through the barren mountainland, and the river finally ended in a maze of lakes with no obvious outlet. Unknown to the men, these were the lakes of the interior plateau; a short portage from those they reached led to Michikamau. Instead, the party retraced their path to the last rapid of the Susan and set off along a narrow creek valley through the bleak mountain tundra.

The trek was long and arduous. Finally, within sight of the lake, alarm overtook ambition and they retreated. But the caribou and the geese had already fled before the winter, and the fish lay dormant beneath the ice. The snow and wind overtook them. As the days grew short, his companions were forced to leave Hubbard behind. They managed to reach civilization, but the rescue party reached Hubbard too late. He had died within one day's hike from safety.

It seemed that Hubbard's dream would go unfulfilled. But his wife had shared his dream, and was determined to achieve it. She left her mirror and her bustle at home and set out two years later with George Wallace, who had accompanied her husband, and three Indian guides. Her goal, like her husband's, was Ungava.

Hunger and hardship had masked the glories of the stern land from her husband, but they were revealed to her. She wrote of the furious Naskaupi River: "Through a narrow opening in the hills farther up, the river came pouring from between dark, perpendicular walls of the evergreen in a white, tossing rapid, widening again to one only less turbulent. A heavy cloud hung over us, throwing a deeper shade on the hills and turning the water black save for the white foam of the rapids, while down the valley came a gale of hot wind like a blast from a furnace." She watched the fish eagles plunge to their prey, or ride the winds above the rust brown moss of the riverbanks. The blues and white of violets, pink of the twinflowers, and yellow of the dandelion brightened the vast reaches of the land. Several days upstream the river plunged 50 feet through a narrow chasm of slick, gleaming rock. Above it the river roared through an even higher falls, and a mile-long course of falls, chutes, and rapids. Spruces and a few balsams lined the stream banks. Beyond them, everywhere, stretched the white reindeer moss.

At Michikamau rocky island and great ice masses dotted the wind-whipped waters. Fifteen and 20-pound namaycush (lake trout) rose to their bait. A lone caribou forded the icy waters. It caught their scent too late, and replenished their dwindling food stores. Then another deer appeared, and another; beyond them thousands more teemed across the Barren Grounds toward their wintering place, the greatest spectacle of the North.

The party found the divide beyond the lake, and started the journey out through the sparsely wooded, boggy lake country of the Upper George. This second wild river led them to a settlement of the Montagnais Indians and a Naskapi camp. Both peoples greeted them in friendship, and listened intently to their story of sighting the caribou, central to their own existence. The Indians marveled at the route by which the expedition had arrived; prior to this time the native peoples had navigated only about half the length of the George.

But the party had yet to reach their goal, and the tortuous rapids of the George had stretched on farther than they had thought possible. It seemed that they were seriously behind schedule. The Montagnais Indians had known little about the distance to Ungava, and their praise of the party's achievement thus far could not guarantee their goal. Had the Naskapis heard of a place called Ungava, and did it lie within the reach of summer? These, the people of the Barren Grounds Hubbard had dreamed of meeting, gave the second party the good news: the rapids beyond them were fierce, but passable, and three sleeps down the river, where the mountains swept out toward the sea, the expedition would reach its goal.

Marine Ferry System

Canadian National Railways operates a daily car and passenger ferry service between North Sydney, Nova Scotia, and Port aux Basques and Argentia, Newfoundland. For info on rates, schedules, and reservations write: Passenger Service Supervisor, Canadian National Ferry Terminal, North Sydney, N.S. *Newfoundland Transportation Company*, Portugal Cove, Nfld., operates a ferry service between Portugal Cove and Bell Island. *Fogo Transport Ltd.*, Fogo Island, Nfld., operates a ferry service between Carmanville and Fogo Island. The *Puddister Trading Company Ltd.*, P.O. Box 5353, St. John's, Nfld., runs a ferry service between St. Barbe and Blanc Sablon, Que. For informa-

tion, schedules, and rates for the Bonne Bay ferry service write: *Clarence V. Laing*, P.O. Box 92, Norris Point, Nfld. Additional information can be obtained from the Department of Transportation & Communication, Confederation Bldg., St. John's, Nfld.

Provincial Parks & Campgrounds

Newfoundland's provincial parks and campgrounds are located throughout the province at such famous recreation areas as Barachois Pond, Grand Codroy River, Indian River, Pinware River, and River of Ponds. Vehicle park entry permits and camping permits are required of all overnight visitors. The maximum stay at a park campground is 10 consecutive days. The free *Newfoundland and Labrador Provincial Parks* guide may be obtained by writing: Parks Division, P.O. Box 9340, St. John's, Nfld. This useful 20-page booklet contains a reference map and information table, and descriptions of all provincial parks and regulations.

NEWFOUNDLAND AND LABRADOR TRAVEL & RECREATION GUIDE

Central Newfoundland Wilderness & the Avalon Peninsula

Annieopsquotch Mountains

Canadian National Topographic Survey Maps, scale 1:50,000: Puddle Pond 12A-5, Victoria Lake 12A-6, Star Lake 12A-11, Lake Ambrose 12A-10, Buchans 12A-15, Little Grand Lake 12A-12.

Avalon Peninsula

Canadian National Topographic Survey Maps, scale 1:250,000: Trepassey 1-K, St. Lawrence 1-L, Belleoram 1-M, St. John's 1-N, Bonavista 2-C.

Terra Nova National Park

Canadian National Topographic Survey Maps, scale 1:50,000: Sweet Bay 2C-5, Eastport 2C-12, Port Blandford 2D-8, Glovertown 2D-9.

The great interior boreal wilderness of central Newfoundland and the scenic coastal regions of the eastern sections of the province, once the hunting and fishing grounds of the ancient Beothuk and Micmac Indians, provide some of the finest Atlantic salmon and trout fishing, caribou and moose hunting, and canoe-camping opportunities in North America. Incredibly scenic waterways such as the Indian River and the Exploits, Gander, White Bear, and Grey rivers are a wilderness paddler's dream and are noted for their annual runs of salmon and sea trout. The valley of the Exploits River—the largest river in the province—was the winter hunting grounds of the Beothuks, the Red Indians, and it was near this area that Shanawdithit, the last Beothuk survivor, was captured in 1823. The banks of the Exploits and the shores of Red Indian Lake formed the main hunting grounds for the now extinct tribe. Hunting camps are located in the interior forests of white birch, larch, black spruce, balsam fir, and alder at the woodland caribou and moose hunting grounds in the Annieopsquotch Mountains along the Lloyds River and Red Indian Lake and at the remote shores of Peter Strides, White Bear, Stag, Antler, Buck, Spruce, and Burnt lakes and the headwaters of the Robinson River. (The *Newfoundland Hunting Guide* and *Newfoundland Fishing Guide* contain a complete listing of hunting and fishing camps in central and eastern Newfoundland.)

Many of the large lakes of northern Canada, such as Red Indian Lake (the largest on the island) were reportedly fishless at the turn of the century. Several of these lakes were found to harbor a large population of freshwater ling (a remnant of an earlier geological period, noted for its sharp, massive teeth and enormous mouth) which reached weights up to 100 pounds and devoured the resident trout population. The interior wilderness regions of Newfoundland were once the range of the now extinct Newfoundland wolf, a subspecies of the arctic wolf, named *beothucus* after the extinct Beothuk Indians. The last recorded Newfoundland wolf was shot in 1911, just north of the valley of the Indian River near the Topsails Mountains. The scenic Topsails were once the terminus of an old Micmac Indian trail. The Micmacs traveled inland during the summer to hunt caribou and would cache the dried meat on the hunting grounds. In late fall the squaws would return to the cache for the tribe's supply of winter meat.

Located along the rugged eastern seacoast are the world-famous Newfoundland sealing grounds and the 153-square-mile coastal wilderness of Terra Nova National Park—a forested landscape of rocky points, fjords or "sounds," and ancient rolling hills located on Bonavista Bay, 48 miles southeast of Gander. The park—the most easterly of Canada's national parks—was once the site of sawmills and pulpwood camps and is today thickly covered by a boreal forest dominated by

black spruce and balsam fir, with numerous bogs matted with wet, spongy sphagnum moss carpeted by bog laurel, leatherleaf rhodora, Labrador tea, and bog orchids. The rocky coastal shores are covered with Irish moss, bladderwrack, and sea bootlace. Wildlife occasionally seen in the interior wildlands includes moose—introduced to the province from Nova Scotia in 1878 and again in 1904—black bear, beaver, snowshoe hare, lynx, fox, bald eagle, and osprey. Seals and pothead whales are often seen frolicking in the coastal waters along the park shoreline. The interior lakes and streams hold brook trout, arctic char, and landlocked salmon. Southwest and Big brooks are restricted to fly-fishing only. The topographic features of the park are shown on the attractive full-color *Terra Nova National Park* map (MCR-214), available from the Canada Map Office, Ottawa, Ont. The map is printed in shaded relief and shows all roads, trails, bridges, warden's stations and patrol cabins, campgrounds, wharfs, fire towers, contours, foreshore flats, marshes, forests and cabins, and magnetic declination. Park campgrounds are located at Newman Sound and Alexander Bay. Two unserviced primitive campgrounds are accessible only by boat. Park canoe routes provide access to the remote interior wilderness camping areas. For detailed park info and for the free *Terra Nova National Park Map-Guide, Hiking & Canoeing Guide*, and *Campground Guides*, write: Superintendent, Terra Nova National Park, Glovertown, Nfld.

Due south of Terra Nova are the Atlantic salmon and sea trout waters of the scenic Avalon Peninsula, surrounded by the world-famous bluefin tuna fishing waters of Trinity, Conception, Trepassey, St. Mary's, and Placentia bays. Large sea-run brown trout caught at the mouths of the peninsula's major Atlantic salmon rivers, including the Trepassey, Salmonier, Colinet, and Placentia, reach weights of up to 28 pounds. Bluefin tuna in 400–800-pound range are caught in the Conception and Trinity bays. Conception Bay is reached by auto from the colorful seaport and capital, St. John's. Brook trout migrate to the sea in May and can be taken in coastal waters close to the mouths of scheduled rivers without a license. A few of the more popular fishing areas are Biscay Bay, Little Salmonier, Barachois, Come by Chance, Trouty, and Swift Current.

Access & Outfitting Centers

The major fishing, hunting, and canoe-camping areas of central and eastern Newfoundland and the Avalon Peninsula are accessible via the Trans-Canada Highway and provincial spur Highways 370, 360, 330, 340, 320, 210, 80, 90, and 10. Charter fly-in service from the major outfitting centers provides access to the interior wilderness moose and caribou hunting camps. Guides, outfitters, supplies, and lodging are available at Deer Lake, Springdale, Badger, Windsor, Grand Falls, Bishop's Falls, Gander, Glovertown, Bonavista, Grand Bank, Argentia, and St. John's.

Labrador Salmon, Trout, & Caribou Country

Ashuanipi River Country

Canadian National Topographic Survey Maps, scale 1:250,000: Opocopa Lake 23-B, Lac Joseph 23-A, Shabogamo Lake 23-G, Schefferville (Que.) 23-J.

Eagle River Country

Canadian National Topographic Survey Maps, scale 1:250,000: Cartwright 13-H, Lake Melville 13-G, Upper Eagle River 13-B.

Forteau-Pinware River Country

Canadian National Topographic Survey Maps, scale 1:250,000: Blanc Sablon (Que.) 12-P, Battle Harbor 13-A.

Minipi River Trophy Brook Trout Country

Canadian National Topographic Survey Map, scale 1:250,000: Minipi Lake 13-C.

Labrador forms a roughly triangular portion of the continental mainland north of the island of Newfoundland and encompasses some 112,826 square miles of the finest brook trout and Atlantic salmon fishing country left in North America. The thousands of square miles of northern coniferous forests of the Canadian Shield, untold thousands of remote lakes and wild rivers, and barren-ground caribou feeding grounds are accessible only by floatplane or canoe. In recent years western Labrador has had an open caribou season for nonresident hunters. The Canadian National Railways operates a fleet of passenger freighters which call at many of the old fishing villages along the scenic, rugged Atlantic coastline of Labrador. There is heavy seasonal demand for the limited amount of cabin space on each vessel, and reservations must be requested well in advance of the summer season by contacting the Passenger Sales Office, Canadian National Railways, St. John's, Nfld.

Several wilderness outfitters operate remote hunting and fishing camps in the inland caribou and trout country, and along the famous coastal Atlantic salmon rivers. The *Forteau Salmon Lodge*, on the Forteau River which empties into the Strait of Belle Isle, has modern accommodations for 12 fishermen. Guides and riverboats are provided to cover the river's 2-mile chain of pools. The Coffin Pool, located near the river's headwaters at the foot of a scenic spraying cataract, is the most productive. For info and rates write: Harvey Sheppard, P.O. Box 307, Corner Brook, Nfld., or Edwin Sharpe, Pasadena, Nfld. The Forteau and nearby Pinware rivers can be reached by charter aircraft and by road from Port aux Basque to St. Barbe and from there by ferry to Blanc Sablon, Quebec. The Pinware River is 50 miles long with deep, boulder-strewn pools. The County Cat River enters the Pinware at the head of a large rapid about 8 miles from the mouth of the Pinware. The most productive fishing is found at the foot of a high falls about 7 miles from the forks. The *Pinware Lodge Ltd.* provides

accommodations for up to 12 fishermen near the confluence of the Pinware and County Cat rivers. For information and rates write: Elmer Lovett, 4527 Du Bois Blvd., Brookfield, IL 60513. The *Lucky Strike Lodge* on the Pinware accommodates up to 14 fishermen. For info and rates write: Hedley Normore, L'Anse au Loup, Nfld. The *Matimek Lodge* on Anne Marie Lake, 55 miles southwest of Goose Bay, has modern accommodations for 8 fishermen, serving some 20 miles of interconnected waterways which hold brook trout averaging 4 pounds and running up to 8 pounds. *Minonipi Lodge,* at Minonipi Lake on the same branch of the upper Minonipi River as Anne Marie Lake, provides modern accommodations for 8 fishermen. The largest brook trout caught to date in this region was caught in 1973 and weighed 8 pounds 4 ounces. The camps are reached by charter aircraft from Goose Bay. For info and rates write: Ray Cooper, Box 8, North West River, Nfld.

The famous 150-mile-long Eagle River, reached only by floatplane from Goose Bay, empties into Sandwich Bay and is one of Labrador's most productive Atlantic salmon rivers. *Goose Bay Outfitters Ltd.,* Box 171, Happy Valley, Nfld., provides excellent accommodations for 6 at their lodge at the Eagle River Falls, with additional camps located at Little Minipi Lake and Eagle Lake on the headwaters of the Eagle River. The Eagle, with its renowned smooth-flowing Back and Pratfall Rock pools, and the turbulent, swirling Bathtub Pool, is one of the half dozen or so great salmon rivers of the world. The number of salmon that make up the Eagle's average run is unknown, but figures supplied by Canada's Department of Fisheries suggest that the run is tremendous. The *Eagle River Falls Lodge* provides access to the beautiful White Bear River, some 3 miles north of the Eagle. Historically, the season begins either side of July 10 through September 15, the last day of fishing in Labrador. Goose Bay Outfitters recommend that salmon fishermen come equipped with waders (felt soles recommended), plenty of warm clothing, rainwear, Polaroid glasses to protect your eyes from stream glare, and a fly box well stocked with the following wet and dry patterns: Black Fitchtail, Hairwing Highlander, Orange Blossom, Gray Wulff, White Wulff, Rat-Faced McDougall, and Hairwinged Black Gnat. The world-famous Minipi River watershed, some 60 miles by floatplane from Goose Bay, encompasses beautiful wild lakes and rivers that harbor a virgin strain of brook trout which, for average size and beauty, is unequaled in the world. The average brook trout caught by anglers at the *Little Minipi Brook Trout Camp* weighs 4 pounds. The largest brook trout taken from the Minipi waters (1972)

weighed 9½ pounds. Squaretails in the 6- and 7-pound class are common. The brook trout in Little Minipi Lake share a delicately balanced ecosystem with landlocked arctic char up to 10 pounds and voracious northern pike (the brook trout's main predator), up to 20 pounds and over. Little Minipi's outlet is a medium-sized stream that's ideal for wading; it resembles the classic freestone streams of the northeastern United States with its smooth deep slicks, riffles, and deep, swirling pools. The waters of the Minipi region are rich in insect life, with stone flies, mayflies, and caddis flies present throughout the year; along with a small snail, they form the brook trout's diet. *Eagle Lake Camp,* operated by Goose Bay Outfitters at the headwaters of the Eagle River, is, along with the Minipi River, one of the last fly-fishing frontiers in North America for squaretails up to 8 pounds, large lake trout, and landlocked arctic char.

Several other outfitters operate salmon and trout fishing camps in the Eagle River and Minipi River wilderness. The *Igloo Lake Lodge* on the Eagle River has accommodations for 4 guests. For info and rates write: John G. Pomphrey, Highlands, Nfld. *Labrador Wilderness Camps* is at Parke Lake, a tributary of the Eagle River some 60 miles by floatplane from Goose Bay Airport. The camp has 3 comfortable cabins with accommodations for 12 fishermen, with fly-in charter via Labrador Airways. Parke Lake is renowned for its fat, wild brook trout averaging 3–6 pounds. For info and rates, write: William J. Coish, P.O. Box 484, Happy Valley, Nfld. To the northeast, *Voisey's Bay Fishing Lodge,* near the mouth of the Kogaluk River, has accommodations for 8 fishermen. For information telephone: Labrador Services, (709) 722–0711, ext. 258. Float-equipped aircraft serving the wilderness fishing camps in the region are headquartered at the Goose Bay military and commercial airport, established during the Second World War on the inner reaches of Hamilton Inlet. Eastern Provincial Airways operates daily Boeing 737 jet service between Montreal and Goose Bay. Wilderness trophy fly fishing for brook trout in the 4 to 8 pound class is offered by Ray Cooper's famous *Northern Labrador Camps,* P.O. Box 8, North West River, Labrador, phone (709) 946–8236. The two camps, the Matimek Lodge and Minonipi Lodge, are located on the Minipi River with fly fishing only for trophy squaretails.

In western Labrador, *Frontier Fishing & Hunting Ltd.,* P.O. Box 55, Labrador City, Nfld. A2V 2K3, operates wilderness caribou hunting and fishing camps with accommodations for 6 sportsmen at Atikonak River and Lake, and a cabin for 4 on Kepimets Lake. These camps are in the heart of caribou and trophy brook trout country some 100 miles east of Wabush and 200 miles north of Sept-Îles, Quebec. *Minnehaha Hunting & Fishing Service,* P.O. Box 353, Gander, Nfld., operates a caribou hunting and fishing camp on the Kepimets River near Atikonak Lake. The fishing is for large brook trout, landlocked salmon, and lake trout. The camp has accommodations for 6 guests; floatplane transportation between Labrador City and the camp and guides are included in the rates. *Menihek Camps,* c/o Box 1371, Schefferville, Que. is on the wild Ashuanipi River, 1½ miles downstream from the Menihek Dam, with accommodations for 20 fishermen.

Far to the northeast of Goose Bay are some of Labrador's most remote and productive Atlantic salmon rivers. The Big River, 120 miles northeast of Goose Bay, provides good fishing for salmon up to 22 pounds and sea trout up to 7 pounds. The modern *Lakeland Lodge,* 5 miles upstream from the mouth of the Big River, provides guided fishing in the river and at Lake Edith, one of the large lakes that form the headwaters of the Big River, for record-sized brook trout, landlocked salmon, and pike. For info and rates write: R. W. Skinner, Pasadena, Nfld. *Northern Labrador Outfitters,* Box 250, Gander, Nfld., operates a lodge with accommodations for 12 fishermen on the Michael River,

fishing in
LABRADOR
the last frontier
Your Hosts:
Goose Bay
Outfitters, Ltd.

ARCTIC CHAR
SPECKLED TROUT
ATLANTIC SALMON

some 140 miles northeast of Goose Bay. The Michael River has good-sized runs of Atlantic salmon, sea trout, and arctic char. The *Sand Hill River Fishing Lodge* is about 160 miles east of Goose Bay on an island in the Sand Hill River. The river is 60 miles long and provides good fishing for salmon and trout. Write: W. J. Bennett, P.O. Box 250, Gander, Nfld. Some 300 miles north of Goose Bay are the newly discovered arctic char waters of Umiakovik Lake. Peter Paor of *Goose Bay Outfitters Ltd.*, Box 171, Happy Valley, Nfld., operates a comfortable tent camp on the shores of the lake.

Access & Outfitting Centers

Access to the Labrador mainland is via ferry from the island of Newfoundland, and by scheduled airline service to Blanc Sablon, Quebec, Goose Bay, Wabush, Labrador City, and Schefferville, Quebec. These towns provide outfitting, guide, and charter fly-in service to the hunting and fishing camps and to the remote headwaters of the wilderness canoe routes. Air Canada operates a daily service between Montreal and Sept-Îles, and Quebecair operates daily, except Sunday, between Montreal, Wabush, and Schefferville. The North Shore & Labrador Railroad connects Sept-Îles, Quebec, with the Ungava Plateau mining center of Schefferville. The hundreds of remote lakes and rivers between Sept-Îles and Schefferville hold virgin populations of record-sized brook trout, lake trout, landlocked salmon, northern pike, and whitefish.

Fly-in Lakes & Rivers Topo Maps

Canadian National Topographic Survey Maps, scale 1:250,000. *Sand Hill River:* Cartwright 13-H; *White Bear River:* Cartwright 13-H, Lake Melville 13-G; *St. Lewis & Alexis Rivers:* Battle Harbor 13-A; *Hamilton River & Lake Melville:* Schefferville (Que.) 23-J, Michikamau Lake 23-I, Ossokmanuan Lake 23-H, Winokapau Lake 13-E, Goose Bay 23-F, Lake Melville 13-G; *Atikonak Lake & River:* Lac Joseph 23-A, Ossokmanuan Lake 23-H; *Michael Lake & River:* Rigolet 13-J, Grosswater Bay 13-I; *Big River & Lake Edith:* Rigolet 13-J; *Lake Michikamau Country:* Michikamau Lake 23-I, Kasheshibaw Lake 13-L, Ossokmanuan Lake 23-H, Winokapau Lake 13-E; *Umiakovik-Arctic Char Lake:* Umiakovik Lake 14E-7.

Western Newfoundland & the Great Northern Peninsula

Great Northern Peninsula

Canadian National Topographic Survey Maps, scale 1:250,000: St. Anthony 2-M, Sandy Lake 12-H, Port Saunders 12-I, Blanc Sablon (Que.) 12-P, Bay of Islands 12-G.

Gros Morne National Park

Canadian National Topographic Survey Maps, scale 1:50,000: Skinner Cove 12G-9, Trout River 12G-8, Lommond 12H-5, Gros Morne 12H-12, St. Paul's 12H-13.

Humber River & Headwaters

Canadian National Topographic Survey Maps, scale 1:50,000: Corner Brook 12A-13, Serpentine 12B-16, Bay of Islands 12G-1, Deer Lake 12H-3, Pasadena 12H-4, Cormack 12H-6, Silver Mountain 12H-11, Main River 12H-14, St. Paul's Inlet 12H-13.

River of Ponds

Canadian National Topographic Survey Map, scale 1:50,000: Bellburns 12I-6.

The scenic, deeply cut river valleys, rounded hills, fjordlike bays, coastal barrens, raised beaches, heaths, bogs, coniferous forests, and remote blue ponds and lakes of western Newfoundland and the Great Northern Peninsula provide some of the finest fishing, hunting, and wilderness camping areas in the province. The ancient Long Range Mountains, the most northerly components of the Appalachian mountain range that extends south to the state of Georgia, dominate the moose, black bear, and woodland caribou country from the Codroy Region north to the top of the Great Northern Peninsula. The mountains appear as a rolling plateau, shaped for millions of years by the movements of glaciers and weathered by the strong coastal winds and water. These fierce coastal winds reach gale force of up to 100 miles per hour and have been known to lift railroad cars off the tracks. The granite hills of the Long Range, which form a portion of the Canadian

Shield, tower above the weatherbeaten forests and windswept treeless barrens near the sea, contrasting with the sheltered river valleys and fir and birch forests inland.

Gros Morne National Park encompasses 716 square miles of scenic rolling mountain plateaus, jagged coastal cliffs, sheltered coves, bogs, tundra barrens, and deep "fjord ponds" hemmed in by towering vertical cliffs stretching inland from the Gulf of St. Lawrence in the southwest portion of the Great Northern Peninsula. The park received its name from Gros Morne Mountain—part of the Long Range, and at 2,644 feet the highest peak in the park—an old French name meaning "big gloomy." Gros Morne is located on Bonne Bay and is dominated by sheer 2,000-foot cliffs and the barren lunar landscapes of the Serpentine tablelands. Wildlife occasionally seen along the primitive trails includes moose, caribou, black bear, arctic hare, lynx, beaver, otter, and pine marten tracks. The park's major Atlantic salmon and brook trout waters are Rex Lake, Western Brook Pond, and the Trout River. Trout River Pond lies in a long slim glacier-carved trough known as a finger lake to geologists and plunges to depths of 400 feet. The pond is used as a migratory route by sea trout during their spawning runs in late summer. Several wilderness hiking trails provide access to the remote interior areas, including the summit of Gros Morne Mountain and Western Brook Pond. Local fishermen will rent their boats for exploration cruises and fishing expeditions along the coast. The park is reached via the Trans-Canada Highway and Highway 430 at Deer Lake. One of the unique local features seen along the coastal auto tours is the impenetrable tangled tree layers pruned by the wind, called tuckamore. Gros Morne Park campgrounds are located at Green Point and Western Brook. For detailed park and travel info, and free copies of the *Gros Morne National Park Map-Guide, Car Caravan Guide,* and *Birds of Gros Morne Check List,* write: Superintendent, Gros Morne National Park, Rocky Harbor,

Nfld. The National & Provincial Parks Association of Canada sponsors an annual summer wilderness camping and backpacking trip on the interior plateau of Gros Morne Park above the spectacular fjords. The trip is recommended for fairly experienced backpackers. For detailed information and the *Wilderness Camping and Backpacking Trips* brochure write: NPPAC, 47 Colborne St., Suite 308, Toronto, Ont. M5E 1E3.

The vast wilderness areas of western Newfoundland and the Great Northern Peninsula are served by several outfitters who operate fishing and hunting camps along the famous Atlantic salmon fishing rivers and in the remote moose and caribou hunting zones. The renowned Grand Codroy River and its north and south branches are among the finest salmon rivers in the province, with fish up to 40 pounds. The Grand Codroy is 25 miles from Port aux Basque. Outfitters operating camps on the river include *Tompkins House & Cabins,* phone (709) 955–2826; *Chignic Lodge & Cabins,* P.O. Box 9, Doyles, Nfld.; and *Wall's Cabins,* South Branch, Nfld. Harry's River, one of the largest and most productive salmon rivers in the province, noted for its large run of fish and deep holding pools, is outfitted by *Dhoon Lodge,* Route 460, P.O. Box 39, Stephenville Crossing, Nfld., with accommodations for 8 fishermen. Harvey Sheppard, Box 307, Corner Brook, Nfld., operates a cabin for 4 on the Little Rapids of the famous Humber River, and will arrange trips to the upper pools of the river. The Humber, one of the largest in the province, produces fish in the 6–40-pound range. *St. Paul's Big Pond Camp,* at the headwaters of the Main River, is operated by Sam's Fishing & Hunting Camps, Portland Creek, Nfld. The Main produces brook trout up to 4 pounds and Atlantic salmon up to 8 pounds. *Eagle Mountain Camp,* located at the headwaters of the Main, is operated by Gene Manion, Box 3, Corner Brook, Nfld. Angus Wentzell, Parsons Pond, Nfld. (winter address: 193 East Valley Rd., Corner Brook, Nfld.) runs the *Four Ponds Cabins* near the headwaters of the Main River and the *Angus Lake Cabin* in the interior of the Great Northern Peninsula at the headwaters of the Humber River. The romantically named River of Ponds, located 137 miles from the outfitting center of Deer Lake, has large runs of Atlantic salmon and sea trout up to 30 pounds. Rendell C. Wentzell, Portland Creek, Nfld., operates 5 cabins on the banks of the scenic river. Portland Creek, rated as one of the best rivers in the province, is 96 miles by road from Deer Lake, and is served by *Sea Pool Cabins,* operated by A. Neaman Wentzell, P.O. Box 9, Corner Brook, Nfld. For a comprehensive listing and description of the hunting and fishing camps in western Newfoundland and the Great Northern Peninsula, write for the *Newfoundland Hunting Guide* and *Newfoundland Fishing Guide,* available free from the Department of Tourism, Confederation Bldg., St. John's, Nfld.

Access & Outfitting Centers

The major hunting, fishing, camping, and hiking areas of western Newfoundland and the Great Northern Peninsula can be reached via the Trans-Canada Highway and Provincial Highways 430 and 431. Guides, outfitters, supplies, lodging, and charter fly-in service are available at Port aux Basque, Stephenville, Corner Brook, Deer Lake, and St. Anthony.

NOVA SCOTIA &
PRINCE EDWARD ISLAND
ENCYCLOPEDIA

Accommodations &
Provincial Campgrounds

A comprehensive listing and descriptions of motels, hotels, inns, and lodges offering hunting, fishing, hiking, boating, and saltwater fishing, and provincial and commercial campgrounds are contained in the 84-page *Nova Scotia Accommodation & Campgrounds Guide*, available free from the Department of Tourism, P.O. Box 130, Halifax, N.S. The guide includes rates and descriptions of facilities and recreation services of lodges, resorts and campgrounds, and the province's scenic recreation highways, including the Lighthouse Route, Evangeline Trail, Glooscap Trail, Sunrise Trail, Cabot Trail, and Marine Drive. The 80-page *Prince Edward Island Accommodations Guide*, available free from the Tourist Information Division, P.O. Box 940, Charlottetown, P.E.I. C1A 7M5, contains a comprehensive listing of hotels, motels, lodges, inns, resorts, cabins, and farm vacation homes, and includes rates and descriptions of facilities and recreation services. The Tourist Information Division also publishes the free 30-page *Prince Edward Island Camping Guide*, which contains a complete listing and descriptions of provincial and commercial campsites and trailer parks. The division will assist you with vacation planning and reservations; write, or telephone (1–902) 892–2457 (not toll-free).

Airlines & Charter Fly-in Services

The international airport in Halifax, Nova Scotia, hosts many of the major international and domestic airlines. The airport offers, through franchised operators, bus, limousine, and taxi service to major city centers. Bus service from Halifax Airport to major recreation centers throughout the province is provided by *Acadian Lines*, 6040 Almon St., Halifax, N.S. B3K 1T8. *Eastern Provincial Airways Ltd.*, P.O. Box 5001, Gander, Nfld. A1V 1W9, serves the major outfitting and supply centers on Nova Scotia from its base at Charlottetown, Prince Edward Island. Nova Scotia's well-developed system of highways and relative absence of vast tracts of primitive wilderness areas preclude the use of charter fly-in services. For the convenience of visiting pilots the publication *Air Tourist Information-Canada* is available on request from the Aeronautical Information Services, Ministry of Transport, Transport Canada Bldg., Place de Ville, Ottawa, Ont. K1A 0H5. The booklet contains a listing of Canadian aeronautical information publications and charts, and of authorized customs airports and aerodromes of entry and exit.

Atlantic Salmon Fishing in Nova Scotia

The scenic, crystal-clear rivers of eastern Nova Scotia and Cape Breton Island host large annual runs of Atlantic salmon. The average annual angling catch of salmon in the provinces, outside Cape Breton Highlands National Park, is about 8,000. The most productive Nova Scotia salmon rivers are the Medway, St. Mary's, Stewiacke, Grand, La Have, Moser, Gold, North, and Ecum Secum. The beautiful Margaree River in the Cape Breton highlands is well known for its late season run of large fish. The province's scheduled salmon rivers are shown on the *Atlantic Salmon Rivers Map of Canada*, available for $5 from the Atlantic Salmon Association, 1405 Peel St., Suite 409, Montreal H3A 1S5, Que.—publishers of the world-famous *Atlantic Salmon Journal* (a subscription is included with an annual association membership fee of $25). The salmon river map shows private waters; rivers open to the public or controlled by an outfitter; provincial reserve waters; waters closed to fishing; number and types of nets; airports, ferries, power dams, and fishways; logging booms, fish hatcheries, and outfitters. Atlantic salmon fishing in Nova Scotia is re-

stricted to fly-fishing. A complete listing of salmon rivers, guides, and seasons is contained in the *Nova Scotia Freshwater Fishing Guide*, available free from the Department of Tourism, P.O. Box 130, Halifax, N.S. (See "Fishing & Hunting in Nova Scotia.")

Canoeing & Wilderness Waters

Nova Scotia's scenic rivers flow through a gentle rolling terrain of wilderness forests of red spruce, balsam fir, and yellow and sugar maple. The most popular canoeing regions are in the vast wilderness tracts of the Tobeatic Game Sanctuary and Kejimkujik National Park in the western part of the province and in the Cape Breton highlands in the easternmost section. The canoe routes of the province, once the water trails of the Micmac Indians, are described in the booklet *Canoe Routes of Nova Scotia*, available for $2 plus 50¢ handling charge from the Nova Scotia Camping Association, Box 1622, Halifax, N.S. The canoe routes that run through the Acadian forests, swamps, and lake chains in the Tobeatic Game Sanctuary and surrounding wildlands are outfitted by *Maritime Canoe Outfitters*, RR1, Shelburne, N.S. B0T 1W0, who will arrange and outfit your party with food and 17-foot fiberglass tripper canoes, tents, sleeping bags, stove, fuel, cooking gear, rainwear, packsacks, waterproof pouch, ax, compass and maps, flashlight, life jacket, fishing gear, and waterproof match containers. Tobeatic Game Sanctuary permits will be arranged before your arrival. Drop-off and pickup service can be arranged. The major features shown on the maps of the Tobeatic canoe country include the Roseway and Jordan rivers, Fields of the Forest, Baron Hills, Gander Way, the scenic Woods of Clyde and the Clyde River, Tamawa Woods, and Tobeatic and Mickchickchawagata lakes. The Tobeatic canoe country is shown on Canadian National Topographic Survey Maps, scale 1:50,000: Shelburne 20P-14, Tusket 20P-13, Wentworth Lake 21A-4, Lake Rossignol 21A-3. (See "Cape Breton Island & the Northern Highlands" and "Kejimkujik National Park.")

Cape Breton Island & the Northern Highlands

Cape Breton Island, the easternmost part of Nova Scotia, is one of the great outdoor recreation areas in North America and is world-renowned for its majestic beauty. Triangular in shape and indented with numerous bays, the island at its maximum dimensions is 100

miles north to south and 85 miles wide. The northern highlands, coastal cliffs, dense evergreen forests, and deep-flowing crystal-clear rivers of the island are separated from the Nova Scotia mainland by the Strait of Canso. The major features of the island, shown on the *Cape Breton Island Map*, available free from the Cape Breton Tourist Association, 20 Keltic Dr., Sydney, N.S., include magnificent coastal hills broken by the deep valleys of the western shore, warmed by the summer water of the Northumberland Strait; the renowned Atlantic salmon and trout waters of the scenic Margaree River and Lake Ainslie; the Acadian Trail, built by the Canadian Youth Hostel Association, and the beautiful hills and valleys of the Mabou highlands; the rolling northern highlands traversed by the famous Cabot Trail, one of the most scenic drives in North America, and the hundreds of fishing villages nestled between the highlands and the rugged coastline; the canoeing and trout waters of the highland streams, including the Chéticamp, North, Aspy, Indian, and Barachois rivers; the famous sailing waters of the central Bras d'Or Lakes, a vast inland sea surrounded by highlands that nearly divides the island in two; and the canoeing and fishing waters of the Baddeck, Denys, and Mira rivers —the Mira is the largest river in Nova Scotia. The 32-page *Cape Breton Island* guidebook, available free from the Cape Breton Tourist Association (address above) contains useful info about beaches, boating, canoeing, fishing, recreation and sports, historic sites, and points of interest.

Cape Breton Highlands National Park encompasses 367 square miles of ancient Appalachian highlands, rugged coastal cliffs, rocky beaches, streams, lakes, Acadian forests, treeless barrens, and bogs. The scenic highlands reach an altitude of 1,747 feet, the highest point in Nova Scotia, and spectacular cliffs rise to 1,000 feet above the park's western shore in contrast to the more gentle slopes along the eastern coastline; also, a long eastward facing cliff runs along a fault north beyond the North Aspy River valley. Deep river valleys of incredible beauty cut through the highland plateau reaching depths of 1,000 feet in the valley of the Chéticamp River. The park's central plateau region is a near treeless wilderness of small ponds and lakes, heath barrens of muskeg covered with reindeer lichen, sheep laurel, and stunted spruce trees similar to the subarctic forest regions of Labrador. Wildlife in the region includes moose, black bear, red fox, red squirrel, deer, otter, mink, lynx, pine marten and snowshoe rabbit, spruce and ruffed grouse, bald eagle, red-tailed hawk, and barrel owl. The Chéticamp is a top-ranked Atlantic salmon river; sea trout and brook trout are found in most of the wilderness rivers and lakes. The park's major features and hiking trails, warden's cabins, campgrounds, viewpoints, and fire towers are shown on the *Cape Breton Highlands National Park Map-Brochure*, available free from the Superintendent, Cape Breton N.P., Ingonish Beach, N.S. The park is accessible via the Cabot Trail, which circles the northern portion of the island and leads to both the Ingonish Beach and Chéticamp entrances. The Cabot Trail passes through some sections of the park and is considered one of the most scenic drives in North America, particularly in the northern region where the highlands tower above the blue waters of the Gulf of St. Lawrence and Cabot Strait. *Hiking Trail Maps* of the eastern and western sections of the park and guides to the Chéticamp, Broad Cove, and Black Brook campgrounds may be obtained by writing the Superintendent's Office (address above). Vacation accommodations in and adjacent to the park are provided by *Cape Breton Highlands Bungalows* (Ingonish B0C 1K0); *Glenghorn Resort* (Ingonish B0C 1K0); *Keltic Lodge* (Ingonish B0C 1K0); *Margaree Lodge* (Margaree Forks B0E 2A0). Cape Breton Highlands National Park is shown on the following Canadian National Topographic Survey Maps, scale 1:50,000: Ingonish 11K-9, Chéticamp River 11K-10, Chéticamp 11K-11, Pleasant Bay 11K-15, Dingwall 11K-16.

Fishing & Hunting in Nova Scotia

The scenic woodlands, ancient rolling Appalachian hills and high-lands, and wilderness lakes and streams of Nova Scotia provide challenging big-and small-game hunting and fishing for Atlantic salmon, landlocked salmon, brook trout, sea trout, and rainbow, brown, and lake trout (known locally as gray trout or togue). The *Nova Scotia Freshwater Fishing Guide* describes and lists the outstanding fishing waters as well as seasons, limits, and angling methods for the major sportfish; it lists the names, addresses, and telephone numbers of many of the more than 600 licensed guides located throughout the province. The fishing guide and *Summary of Sportfishing Regulations* are available upon request from the Department of Tourism, P.O. Box 130, Halifax, N.S. The *Nova Scotia Sport Fisheries Newsletter*, available free from Forest Resources Education, P.O. Box 68, Truro, N.S. B2N 5B8, contains articles on fish and how to find them, results of sport fisheries research, and statistics on angling. Nova Scotia's best brook trout fishing is found off the beaten track in seldom fished waters deep in the remote wilderness areas. The total annual catch of sea-run brook trout in recent years is reported as 394,000. The most productive sea trout waters include the Musquodoboit River and Moser, Salmon, Ecum Secum, Gaspereaux, St. Mary's, Margaree, Clyburn, and North rivers. Hard-hitting rainbow trout up to 5 pounds are caught in Sunken, Rumsey, Levers, and Clearwater lakes. Brown trout, introduced to the province in 1923, are found in the Milford Haven, Salmon, Cornwallis, East, Mersey, Kilkenny, and Waugh rivers. Native lake trout up to 15 pounds are caught chiefly in Pockwock and Sherbrooke lakes. *Scotian Manor Inn, Ltd.*, Clyde River, Nova Scotia, phone (902) 637–2789, provides lodging and outfitting service for freshwater trout and Atlantic salmon fishing, as well for big game, small game, upland birds, ducks, and geese. Guide service and access to the St. Mary's and Ecum Secum and Idian rivers may be arranged through the beautiful *Liscomb Lodge*, Liscomb B0J 2A0, which offers vacation lodging in secluded, rustic A-frame chalets equipped with fireplaces. The lodge also arranges deep-sea fishing trips.

Moose, whitetail deer, and black bear make up Nova Scotia's three big-game species. Caribou were once common to the province, but became extinct during the 1920s. Transplanted caribou from Quebec were reintroduced into Cape Breton Island in 1968. A nonresident big-game license and a guide are required to hunt deer and black bear in the province. Moose are hunted only under special license, and only a limited number of such licenses are issued each year. Whitetail deer is the most abundant big-game species, found in nearly all the wooded areas of the province. Black bear are widely scattered throughout Nova Scotia, but are much more common in the wilderness areas of the western part of the province. Upland game birds and waterfowl include ruffed and spruce grouse, pheasant, Hungarian partridge, woodcock, Wilson's snipe, and geese and ducks. Seasons, limits, regulations, and a complete listing of big-game hunting guides may be found in the *Nova Scotia Hunting Guide* and *Summary of Hunting Regulations*, available upon request from the Department of Tourism, P.O. Box 130, Halifax, N.S. (See "Atlantic Salmon Fishing in Nova Scotia" and "Outfitters & Guide Service.") The following are Canadian National Topographic Map Kits, scale 1:50,000, for Nova Scotia's major fishing waters. *Chéticamp River:* Chéticamp River 11K-10, Chéti-camp 11K-11; *Ecum Secum River:* Ecum Secum 11D-16, Liscomb 11E-1; *Margaree River:* Lake Ainslie 11K-3, Margaree 11K-6, St. Ann's 11K-7; *Musquodoboit River:* Musquodoboit 11D-14, Tangier 11D-15, Upper Musquodoboit 11E-2; *St. Mary's River:* Ecum Secum 11D-16, Liscomb 11E-1, Lochaber 11E-8; *Salmon River:* Guysborough 11F-5; *Stewiacke River:* Shubenacadie 11E-3.

Highways—Recreation & Scenic Routes

Nova Scotia's woodland and coastal recreation areas can be reached by some of the most spectacular scenic highways in the world. The major highway systems are thoroughly described in the useful 136-page *Nova Scotia Highway Tour Book*, available free from the Department of Tourism, P.O. Box 130, Halifax, N.S.; it describes the towns and fishing villages, historical sites, provincial parks, recreation areas, and points of interest along the Evangeline Trail, Lighthouse Route, Glooscap Trail, Sunrise Trail, Marine Drive, and the incredibly scenic Cabot Trail on Cape Breton Island. In addition, the tour book contains a listing of scenic lookoffs, a glossary of place names, and descriptions of flowers and flowering shrubs, forest trees, and mammals of Nova Scotia. The official *Nova Scotia Highways & Byways Map* serves as a trip companion to the highway tour book and may be obtained free by writing the Department of Tourism in Halifax. The *Prince Edward Island Official Road Map & Tourist Guide*, available free from the Tourist Information Division, P.O. Box 940, Charlottetown, P.E.I. C1A 7M5, shows all towns and fishing villages, highways and roads, railway lines, airports and landing strips, ski areas, provincial and commercial campgrounds, beach access areas, bluefin tuna fishing zones, and the Lady Slipper Drive, Blue Heron Drive, and Kings Byway. The Nova Scotia Recreation & Scenic Highways topographic maps will provide the visiting outdoorsman with an invaluable guide to the Nova Scotia fish and game areas, showing all contours, salmon and trout streams, lakes, mountains, national and provincial parks, forests, and highways including the scenic drives and Trans-Canada Highway. The province is shown on the following 1:250,000 Canadian National Topographic Survey Maps: Shelburne 20-O&P, Eastport 21-B, Annapolis 21-A, Amherst 21-H, Truro 11-E, Halifax 11-D, Canso 11-F, Sydney 11-K, Magdalen Islands (Que.) 11-N, Glace Bay 11-G. (See "Cape Breton Island & the Northern Highlands" and "Prince Edward Island.")

Kejimkujik National Park

Kejimkujik, from a Micmac Indian word meaning "place that swells," is in western Nova Scotia and encompasses 145 square miles of interconnected lakes and streams surrounded by a dense Acadian forest of mixed hardwoods and evergreens, inhabited by whitetail deer, black

bear, river otter, red squirrel, and beaver. The park's rolling landscape is dominated by Kejimkujik Lake, some 5 miles long and 3 miles wide. A large, shallow, rocky area of the lake is known to local fishermen as "the granite barrens." Major features shown on the *Kejimkujik National Park Map-Brochure* include the Mersey River, Big Dam Lake, Rocky Falls Portage, Frozen Ocean Lake, Northwest River, Mountain Lake Portage, and Loon and Beaverskin lakes. The park map-guide shows roads, hiking trails, wooden cabins, campgrounds, boat launching and rental sites, canoe portages, and fire towers. It may be obtained along with the free *Kejimkujik Canoe Route-Hiking Trails Guide* from the Superintendent's Office, Kejimkujik National Park, Maitland Bridge, N.S. The Jeremy Bay Campground has 320 sites for tents or trailers and 10 walk-in campsites. The park is shown on a Canadian National Topographic Survey Map, scale 1:50,000: Kejimkujik Lake 21A-6. The park is reached via Highway 8, which runs north-south from Annapolis Royal to Liverpool.

Marine Ferry Service

Nova Scotia and Prince Edward Island are served by marine car and passenger ferry liners ranging from 1–2-hour voyages to overnight cruises. The M.V. *Bluenose* sails between Bar Harbor, Maine, and Yarmouth, Nova Scotia, with daily service from early June to mid-September and 3 times weekly from mid-September to early June. For rates and reservations write: Canadian National Railways, Bar Harbor, ME, or Yarmouth, N.S., or call toll-free from the U.S., (1–800) 341–7981; from Canada call collect anytime, (902) 742–3513. The M.S. *Prince of Fundy* and *Bolero* sail daily between Portland, Maine, and Yarmouth, Nova Scotia. Write: Prince of Fundy Line, P.O. Box 4216, Sta. A, Portland, ME 04101, or Port Agent, Canadian National Railways, Yarmouth, N.S., or call toll-free from the U.S. (May 1-September 15) at (1–800) 341–7540 or call collect, (207) 775–5616; from Canada call collect anytime, (514) 845–9842. The *Princess of Acadia* sails daily between St. John, New Brunswick, and Digby, Nova Scotia. For reservations and info write: Manager, Bay of Fundy Services, P.O. Box 3589, Postal Sta. B, St. John, N.B. E2M 4Y2, or call toll-free,

Prince Edward Island National Park

Prince Edward Island

(1–800) 561–9742. Northumberland Ferries Ltd., Wood Islands, P.E.I., sails daily between Wood Islands and Caribou, Nova Scotia. The CN East Coast Marine Ferry Service operates daily between Cape Tormentine, New Brunswick, and Borden, Prince Edward Island; between Port aux Basques, Newfoundland, and North Sydney, Nova Scotia; and between North Sydney, Nova Scotia, and Argentia, Newfoundland, during the summer months.

Outfitters & Guide Service

All nonresidents planning to hunt or fish in Nova Scotia are required to hire the services of a licensed guide or Nova Scotia resident who has received written permission from the Minister of Lands & Forests to act as a guide for a given period of time. No more than 3 nonresident hunters or fishermen may employ a guide at one time. A comprehensive listing of fishing and big-game hunting guides and outfitters in Annapolis, Antigonish, Cape Breton, Colchester, Cumberland, Digby, Guysborough, Halifax, Hants, Inverness, Kings, Lunenburg, Pictou, Queens, Richmond, Shelburne, Victoria, and Yarmouth counties is contained in the *Nova Scotia Hunting Guide* and *Nova Scotia Fishing Guide*, available free from the Department of Tourism, P.O. Box 130, Halifax, N.S. When required, guide service fees include the use of riverboats or canoes.

Prince Edward Island

Prince Edward Island is 140 miles long and lies about 9 miles offshore from both Nova Scotia and New Brunswick, surrounded on the north by the blue waters of the Gulf of St. Lawrence and on the south by Northumberland Strait. The island, a world-famous outdoor recreation area, is reached by ferry from Cape Tormentine, New Brunswick, and from Caribou, Nova Scotia. Air Canada provides daily service direct to the island from Toronto via Ottawa; Eastern Provincial Airlines has jet service from Montreal and Halifax to Charlottetown. The island's streams, such as the Cardigan, Seal, and Mitchell rivers, hold brook and rainbow trout up to 6 pounds. Scenic indented bays and tidal rivers provide good fishing for sea-run brook trout, known locally as satters. The island's coastal waters are becoming increasingly popular for bluefin tuna fishing. The world record 1,120 lb. bluefin tuna was caught off the coast of the province in 1973. Tuna-fishing charter boat operator info, fishing, camping, and lodging information, and a free *Prince Edward Island Official Road Map* may be obtained by writing: Tourist Information Division, P.O. Box 940, Charlottetown, P.E.I. C1A 7M5 or by telephoning (1–902) 892–2457. Prince Edward Island National Park forms a narrow 25-mile-long strip along the island's north shore, embracing a scenic area of high coastal cliffs, sand dunes, woodlands, bogs, and ponds. The vast sand beaches and broad, shallow bays of the eastern section of the park contrast to the towering sandstone cliffs of the western section. The *Prince Edward Island National Park Map-Brochure*, available free from the Superintendent's Office, P.O. Box 487, Charlottetown, P.E.I., shows hiking trails, campgrounds, beaches, roads, and lodges. Park campgrounds are located at Stanhope, Rustico Island, and Cavendish. Resort lodging is available at Cavendish and Delvay Beach. Green Gables House, immortalized by Canadian author Lucy Maud Montgomery in her classic novel *Anne of Green Gables*, is located in the Cavendish section. The national park is shown on a Canadian National Topographic Survey Map, scale 1:50,000: Rustico 11L-6. Prince Edward Island is shown on the following 1:250,000 scale topo maps: Truro (N.S.) 11-E, Charlottetown 11-L, Moncton (N.B.) 21-I, Sydney (N.S.) 11-K.

Saltwater Fishing & Charter Boat Operators

Nova Scotia's scenic, island-studded Atlantic coastland, joined to the mainland only by the isthmus of Chignecto, provides some of the finest fishing in the Maritime Provinces for giant bluefin tuna, broadbill swordfish, halibut, cod, hake, haddock, pollack, and sea-run brook and brown trout. A boat and crew, equipped and experienced in saltwater fishing, may be hired for a reasonable price in the hundreds of scenic fishing villages nestled in the lee and protected headlands along the coast of the province. A complete listing and description of charter boat operators in the Yarmouth, Digby, Annapolis, Shelburne, Lunenburg, Halifax, Guysborough, Cumberland, Pictou, Inverness, Victoria, Richmond, and Cape Breton Island coastal areas is contained in the useful *Nova Scotia Saltwater Fishing Guide*, available free from Department of Tourism, P.O. Box 130, Halifax, N.S. The average day's cost for a charter boat is about $75; for tuna fishing the average daily cost is $100. Schools of giant bluefin tuna move into the offshore feeding grounds in July, August, September, and October. The record tuna caught by rod and reel in Nova Scotia waters weighed 1,065 pounds; it was boated on November 19, 1970, in George Bay. Nova Scotia's outstanding coastal waters, which frequently produce bluefin tuna in the 800-pound class, include Cape St. Mary in Digby County, Wedgeport coastal area in Yarmouth County, St. Margaret's Bay in Halifax County, and the Halifax and Strait of Canso-George Bay coastal waters. The International Tuna Cup match, established in 1937, is held each September in the Cape St. Mary and Wedgeport areas off Nova Scotia's southwestern tip. Teams from foreign nations, including Scandinavians, Australians, New Zealanders, Italians, and Americans, compete for the coveted Alton B. Sharpe trophy. Descriptions of angling methods, recommended gear, and outstanding coastal fishing locations for the major saltwater game-fish species are contained in the saltwater fishing guide.

Accommodations & Provincial Campgrounds

The hunting, fishing, and vacation areas of New Brunswick are well served by a wide variety of accommodations, including motels, hotels, cottages, and fishing and hunting lodges and camps. The 62-page *New Brunswick Accommodation Guide* contains a complete listing of accommodations and provincial parks and campgrounds. The guide describes facilities, services, and recreation activities available, including trailer disposal, beaches, boat ramps, equipment, boats, and canoes; and salmon, trout, and striped bass fishing and game-bird, deer, and black bear hunting. The guide may be obtained free by writing: Department of Tourism, P.O. Box 1030, Fredericton. (See "Sporting Camps & Lodges.")

Airline & Railway Service

New Brunswick has three major airports, at Moncton, Fredericton, and St. John, served daily by Air Canada and Eastern Provincial Airways. For flight schedules, rates, and connecting flights contact the local airline office or travel agent, or write: Air Canada, 1 Place Ville Marie, Montreal, Que. H3B 3Y8, or Eastern Provincial Airways, Head Office, Gander, Nfld. Both the Canadian National and Canadian Pacific railways serve the province; for time schedules and tour and hotel information write: C.P. Rail, Windsor Station, Montreal, Que. H3C 3E4, or Canadian National Railways, 935 Lagauchetière St. W, P.O. Box 8100, Montreal, Que. Visiting pilots should write for the publication *Air Tourist Information-Canada*, available upon request from the Aeronautical Information Services, Ministry of Transport, Transport Canada Bldg., Place de Ville, Ottawa, Ont. K1A 0H5. It contains a listing of Canadian aeronautical information publications and charts. For charter aircraft fly-in services contact: New Brunswick Department of Tourism, P.O. Box 1030, Fredericton.

Atlantic Salmon Fishing & Maps

New Brunswick's world-famous Atlantic salmon rivers, notably the Miramichi and Restigouche River systems, are renowned for their large runs of salmon in the 8½-pound range and acrobatic grilse weighing 2½–5 pounds. The province's salmon rivers are shown on *Atlantic Salmon Rivers Map of Canada* (available for $5 from the Atlantic Salmon Association—publishers of the *Atlantic Salmon Journal*—1405 Peel St., Suite 409, Montreal H3A 1S5, Que.) and include the Restigouche, Kedgwick, Upsalquitch, Charlo, Jacquet, Tetagouche, Middle, Nepisiguit, Tabusintac, Caraquet, Northwest Miramichi, Sevogle, Little Southwest Miramichi, Renous, Dungarvon, Southwest Miramichi, Cains, Tobique, St. John, Big and Little Salmon, Petitcodiac, Buctouche, and Kouchibouguac rivers. Provincial reserve waters are located on the Nepisiguit, Little Southwest Miramichi, Tobique, N.W. Miramichi, Sevogle, Restigouche, and Upsalquitch rivers. The Atlantic salmon river map shows private waters; rivers open to the public or controlled by an outfitter; waters closed to fishing; number and type of river-mouth nets; airports, ferries, power dams with and without fishways; logging looms, fish hatcheries, and location of outfitters. Salmon fishing in New Brunswick is restricted to fly-fishing; the services of a guide are required. Detailed information on salmon fishing and lodges, particularly in the Miramichi River system, may be obtained by writing: Manager, Miramichi Salmon Association, Inc., Boiestown.

Fishing Guidebooks, published by the Lands Branch, Department of Natural Resources, Centennial Bldg., Fredericton, contains detailed maps showing salmon pools, lodges and fishing camps, freehold and

NEW BRUNSWICK ENCYCLOPEDIA

private waters, forest roads, trails, and crown open waters; they are available for the following Atlantic salmon rivers: *Main Southwest Miramichi River*, Boiestown to Renous ($1.08); *Little Southwest Miramichi* ($1.08); *Northwest Miramichi* ($1.08); *Cains River* ($1.08); *Tracadie River* (25¢); *Big Salmon River* (25¢); *Nashwaak River* ($1.08); *Renous River* ($1.08); *Dungarvon River* ($1.08); *Bartholomew River* ($1.08); *Tobique River* ($1.08); and *Jacquet River* ($1.08). The maps in these guides will provide the New Brunswick-bound Atlantic salmon fisherman with useful trip planning and reference information. (See "Fishing & Hunting" and "Sporting Camps & Lodges.")

Canoeing & Wilderness Waters

New Brunswick's major canoe waters are located in the rugged, scenic Central Highlands, the Miramichi and Cains River region, and the Chiputneticook Lakes and Magaguadavic canoe country in the southwestern part of the province. The canoe routes of the Central Highlands wilderness, including the Nictau and Nepisiguit lakes, Restigouche and Miramichi rivers, Serpentine, Mamogekel, Little Tobique, and Tobique rivers, and Trousers and Long Lakes, flow through majestic wildlands dominated by the highland summits of North Pole Mountain and Mounts Carleton, Webster, McNair, Big Bald, and Bald Peak, and dense evergreen forests. This interior wilderness region provides some of the finest and most picturesque scenery in the province and is renowned for its brook trout fishing and wilderness camping opportunities. The highland canoe routes differ from most other canoe country waters in that very few portages are necessary. Black bear, moose, and beaver are occasionally seen, and whitetail deer are found along the stream banks and at numerous natural mineral licks. The canoe routes of the Central Highlands were once the trade and war trails of the ancient Micmac Indians, a hunting people with warlike characteristics who were renowned for the excellence of their birchbark canoes, including the Micmac Woods canoe, Big River canoe, Ocean canoe and Rough-Water canoe. In the southwest corner of New Brunswick, adjacent to the Maine border, are the famous Chiputneticook Lakes and Magaguadavic canoe country, once the hunting and fishing grounds of the warlike Malecite and Passamaquoddy Indians. This scenic canoe country is dominated by the waters of the scenic St. Croix, Digeguash, and Magaguadavic rivers and Lakes Grand, Spednic, North, Musquash, Palfry, Canoose, Skiff, and Magaguadavic. Wilderness canoe outfitting service in the Central Highlands is provided by *Tobique Trails Outfitters*, who will assist you in planning wilderness canoe trips suited to your particular interests. It has a "put-in" and "take-out" service and will provide expert guides who are professional woodsmen, canoe handlers, and woods cooks. This wilderness outfitting package includes fully equipped canoe, lightweight tents, sleeping bags and accessories, packs, and cooking gear. Rustic accommodations and meals are provided at Riley Brook and Nictau for the first and last days of the journey, or for the entire visit. The nearest commercial airport is at Presque Isle, Maine, about 80 miles from Riley Brook. For info and rates write: Tobique Trails Outfitters, RR1, Plaster Rock, phone (506) 356–2496. (See "Atlantic Salmon Fishing & Maps" and "Fishing & Hunting in New Brunswick.")

Fishing & Hunting in New Brunswick

New Brunswick's scenic rivers, valleys, and gently undulating woodlands offer some of the world's most productive fishing for aristocratic Atlantic salmon and brook trout, and fine fall hunting for whitetail deer, black bear, ruffed grouse—known locally as birch partridge because of its fondness for birch buds along woodland trails and burrs

—spruce grouse, woodcock, and abundant migratory populations of black duck, scaup, Canada geese, and brant along the lower St. John, Chiputneticook Lakes region and St. Croix River, Bay of Fundy, Tabusintac River region, and the Tantramar Marshes in the southeast. The province, which is almost rectangular in shape, extends 200 miles from north to south and 150 miles from east to west; it is bordered on the north by the province of Quebec, the Restigouche River, and Chaleur Bay; on the east by the Gulf of St. Lawrence and Northumberland Strait; on the south by the Bay of Fundy and Chignecto Bay and the isthmus of Chignecto, which joins the province with Nova Scotia; on the west the province is bordered by the state of Maine and the famous landlocked salmon and smallmouth bass waters of the Chiputneticook Lakes chain and the St. Croix River, and in the extreme northwest, by the province of Quebec.

Geographically, about 88 percent of the province is covered by Acadian forests—half of them public crown land. The northern regions are dominated by ancient Appalachian highlands wilderness, reaching the highest point of 2,690 feet at Mount Carleton, located due west of Nepisiguit Lakes in Mount Carleton Provincial Reserve. The central interior wilderness is mostly scenic rolling highland plateau and beautiful deep river valleys formed by the Tobique, Miramichi, Renous, Dungarvon, Bartholomew, and Cains River systems. These scenic Atlantic salmon rivers and the mighty St. John River were once the major water routes of the Micmac Indians. The province's major lakes and most important smallmouth bass, lake trout, and landlocked salmon waters are in the lower St. John and St. Croix River systems in the southwest and include Grand, Chiputneticook, Magaguadavic, and Oromocto Lakes.

Fishing and hunting information and copies of *New Brunswick Angling and Hunting Laws* may be obtained by writing: Fish & Wildlife Branch, Centennial Bldg., Fredericton. All nonresident hunters and Atlantic salmon fishermen must be accompanied by a guide. Numerous outfitters are available to guide the hunter and fisherman into the interior wilderness areas by charter fly-in service or canoe. Most of the province's salmon rivers are under lease to operators of fishing and hunting camps, who restrict the fishing to their guests with a preregulated number of rods per mile of stream, hoping to avoid overcrowding. The province's scenic coastal waters offer excellent fishing for pollack and bluefin tuna. (For additional information see "Atlantic Salmon Fishing & Maps," "Sporting Camps & Lodges," and "Tuna Fishing & Charter Boat Operators.")

New Brunswick's important Atlantic salmon, brook trout, smallmouth bass, and landlocked salmon waters and the surrounding wilderness areas are shown on Canadian National Topographic Survey Maps, scale 1:50,000. *Grand Lake Country:* Codys 21H-13, Shipman 21I-4, Minto 21J-1, Grand Lake 21G-16; *Chiputneticook Lakes Region:* Fosterville 21G-13, Forest Lakes 21G-12, McAdam 21G-11; *Magaguadavic Canoe Country:* Rollingdam 21G-6, McAdam 21G-11, Forest City 21G-12, Fosterville 21G-13, Canterbury 21G-14; *Big Salmon River:* Salmon River 21H-6, Waterford 21H-11; *Little South-*

west Miramichi: Newcastle 21I-13, McKendrick Lake 21L-16, Big Bald Mountain 21O-1; *Northwest Miramichi River:* Newcastle 21I-13, Big Bald Mountain 21O-1, California Lake 21O-8, Sevogle 21P-4, Nepisiguit Falls 21P-5; *Southwest Miramichi & Cains Rivers:* Newcastle 21I-13, Blackville 21I-12, Doaktown 21J-9, Boiestown 21J-8, Napadogan 21J-7, Hayesville 21J-10, Juniper 21J-11, Plaster Rock 21J-14; *Nepisiguit River:* Nepisiguit Lakes 21O-7, California Lake 21O-8, Nepisiguit Falls 21P-5, Bathurst 21P-12; *Restigouche River Country:* Grand River 21I-5, Gounamity River 21O-12, Kedgwick

21O-11, Sisson 21O-6, Upsalquitch Forks 21O-10, Tetagouche Lakes 21O-9, Menneval 21O-14, States Brook 21O-13; *Jacquet River:* Tetagouche Lakes 21O-9, Charlo 21O-16; *Tabusintac River:* Nepisiguit Falls 21P-5, Tabusintac River 21P-6; *Tracadie River:* Tracadie 21P-10, Burnsville 21P-11; *St. John River:* Aroostook 21J-13, Andover 21J-12, Florenceville 21J-5, Coldstream 21J-6, Woodstock 21J-4, Millville 21J-3, Canterbury 21G-14, Fredericton 21G-15, Grand Lake 21G-16, Hampstead 21G-9, St. John 21G-8; *Tobique River:* Aroostook 21J-13, Plaster Rock 21J-14, Riley Brook 21O-3, Sisson 21O-6, Nepisiguit Lakes 21O-7, Upsalquitch Forks 21O-10.

Fundy & Kouchibouguac National Parks

Fundy National Park embraces 80 square miles of jagged coastline along the Bay of Fundy and extends inland over a rolling forested plateau cut by deep valleys and swift-flowing streams. The tides along the Bay of Fundy are the highest in the world, reaching heights up to 53 feet. The park's wave-sculptured coastal cliffs reach heights of up to 200 feet, slashed at intervals by streams flowing into the bay through deep scenic valleys. Inland are the lakes, bogs, forests, and swamps of a rolling plateau—a remnant of an ancient range of mountains. Black bear and moose are found in the highland areas and whitetail deer are often seen along the coastal areas. The park is reached by car from St. John, about 80 miles to the southwest via Highways 1, 2, and 114, and from Moncton via Highway 114. The free *Fundy National Park Map-Brochure, Shaded Maples Guide, Checklists of Birds and Mammals,* hiking trail guides, and travel and camping information may be obtained by writing: Superintendent, Fundy National Park, Alma E0A 1B0. Fully serviced campgrounds are located at park headquarters, Pointe Wolfe, Chignecto, and Wolf Lake. The *Alpine Chalets* and *Fundy View Motel* are 1 mile west of park headquarters; the *Fundy Park Chalets* are at the headquarters, with 29 cottages.

Kouchibouguac National Park takes in 93 square miles of Atlantic coastline and Acadian forest, salt marshes, bogs, swamps, and sand dunes along Kouchibouguac Bay of the Gulf of St. Lawrence. The major features of the park are shown on the *Kouchibouguac National Park Map-Brochure,* available free along with camping and fishing info and hiking trail guides from the Superintendent, Kouchibouguac National Park, Kent Co. Park nature and hiking trails provide an opportunity to view the coastal environment and large populations of sandpipers, terns, gulls, bitterns, plovers, herons, and kingfishers. The inland swamps, fields, and woodlands are populated by crows, hawks, ospreys, ruffed grouse, woodcocks, grackles, woodpeckers, and eastern kingbirds, and by moose, deer, black bear, beaver, river otters, and seals along the rocky coastal headlands and spits. There is a 55-site temporary campground at Callander's Beach, and 144 semiserviced sites with accommodations for tents, tent trailers, and small camping trailers at the South Kouchibouguac campground. Access to the park is via the Acadian Trail and Highways 11 and 117.

Highways—Recreation & Scenic Routes

New Brunswick's scenic and recreation highways, including the famous Nashwaak-Miramichi Trail, Acadian Trail, River Route, and Fundy Trail, are shown on the *Official New Brunswick Highway Map,* available free from the Department of Tourism, P.O. Box 1030, Fredericton. The map shows all major and secondary roads, customs offices, airports, ferries, Indian reservations, and rest areas. Toll-free river ferries are part of the provincial highway system and operate during daylight hours, mainly along the St. John River. Blacks Harbor is the mainland terminal for the Grand Manan Ferry, while Deer Island, also in the isles of Fundy, is reached by ferry from Letete. A shuttle ferry service operates between Deer Island and Campobello Island during the summer months. A ferry at Dalhousie connects the province with Quebec at Miguasha. Canadian National Topographic Survey Map Kits listed below, scale 1:250,000, show the topography of the outdoor recreation areas surrounding New Brunswick's major highways.

Acadian Trail

This incredibly scenic trail winds for 375 miles from Moncton to Shediac and on along the coast of the Northumberland Strait, Miramichi Bay, and Chaleur Bay of the Gulf of St. Lawrence to Dalhousie and Campbellton, then winds through the hunting and Atlantic salmon fishing country of the Restigouche River to St. Leonard on the Maine-New Brunswick border. The scenic woodlands and mountains surrounding the far-famed Restigouche River were once the hunting and fishing grounds of the Micmac Indians. Restigouche is Micmac for "five fingers," after the five tributaries of the river: the famous Matapédia, Upsalquitch, Patapédia, Kedgwick, and Little Main Restigouche. The Acadian Trail follows Provincial Highways 6, 15, 11, and 17. Canadian National Topographic Survey Maps: Moncton 21-I, Bathurst 21-P, Campbellton 21-O, Edmundston 21-N.

Fundy Trail

This scenic route winds along the Bay of Fundy coastline for much of its 190-mile length from St. Stephen, the southwestern gateway of New Brunswick, to Moncton, known as the hub of the Maritimes. The trail, which is formed by Highways 1, 111, and 114, offers spectacular views of the Bay of Fundy, and the ebb and flow of its mighty tides—among the highest in the world. The trail passes through St. Andrews to the famous fishing and vacation grounds of Deer, Grand Manan, and Campobello islands, and winds on to St. John, Canada's oldest incorporated city, past inland towns and villages to Fundy National Park and Hopewell Cape, renowned for its tide-sculptured rocks, to Moncton, the site of the Tidal Bore and Magnetic Hill. Canadian National Topographic Survey Maps: Fredericton 21-G, Amherst 21-H, Moncton 21-I.

Nashwaak-Miramichi Trail

This renowned hunting, Atlantic salmon, and logging country route winds for 140 miles from Fredericton to Escuminac, Quebec, through the geographical center of New Brunswick at Boiestown on the Southwest Miramichi River and on to Newcastle and Chatham. The major features along the route, which follows Highways 8 and 420, include the rolling forested hills of the Nashwaak River valley, the famous Atlantic salmon fishing and hunting outfitting villages that dot the banks of the Southwest Miramichi River, including Boiestown, Ludlow, McNamee, Doaktown, Blissfield, Upper Blackville, and Blackville, and the logging and mining center of Newcastle. Canadian National Topographic Survey Maps: Fredericton 21-G, Woodstock 21-J, Moncton 21-I.

St. John River Route

This route follows Highway 2 and 102 for 250 miles from Edmundston, known as the capital of the "republic of Madawaska," south along the scenic St. John River to the city of St. John and the Bay of Fundy. The St. John was once a major Indian trail, known as "Oa-las-tuk," the "goodly river" connecting the Bay of Fundy with the St. Lawrence River. The major features along the route include the town of Grand Falls, named for the 75-foot waterfall and sheer-walled gorge on the St. John River, the famous fishing and hunting outfitting center of Woodstock, Kings Landing, Mactaquac Provincial

Park and Campground, the historic city of Fredericton, known as the "Poet's Corner of Canada," Fort Nashwaak, Oromocto Indian Reservation, and St. John. Canadian National Topographic Survey Maps: Edmundston 21-N, Campbellton 21-O, Woodstock 21-J, Fredericton 21-G, Amherst 21-H.

Sporting Camps & Lodges

The famous Atlantic salmon and trout fishing country and big-game and upland game-bird hunting areas of New Brunswick are served by a good number of first-class hunting and fishing camps. The following outfitters cater to nonresident hunters and fishermen and are fully licensed. The outfitters will provide you with complete details on accommodations, rates, salmon water leases, boats—and guides, which are required for nonresident Atlantic salmon license holders. Carleton County is served by *Governors Table Camps*, Hartland, and *Miramichi Camps*, Juniper, on Provincial Highway 107; and by *Henderson's Camps*, RR1, Hartland, on Highway 575. *Loon Bay Lodge*, P.O. Box 601, St. Stephen, off Highway 745 in Charlotte County, has full services for hunting and fishing for Atlantic salmon, trout and small-mouth bass. *Tabusintac Camps Ltd.*, Tabusintac, is on Highway 11 with hunting and guided service for salmon, trout, and tuna. In Northumberland County, the famous Southwest Miramichi River is served by the following Atlantic salmon fishing camps on Highway 11: *Curtis Fishing Camps*, RR1, Upper Blackville; *Gilks House*, RR2, Doaktown; *Maple Leaf Salmon Lodge*, Blackville; *Micmac Salmon Club* (off Highway 11), Box 43, Tabusintac; *Millet's Fishing Lodge*, Blackville, and *Millets Cains River Fishing Camp*, Cains River; *Porter's Kove Kamps*, Ludlow; *Riverside Guest Home*, Doaktown; *Lyon's Den*, Doaktown; *Wilson's Sporting Camps Ltd.*, McNamee; *Burnt Church Indian Co-op Ltd.-Tabusintac Camps*, Burnt Church, RR2, Lagaceville; and *Myles L. Wishart Bird Hunting & Fishing Camps*, RR2, Tabusintac, the latter two on Highway 11; *Cains River Enterprises Ltd.*, R. R. W. Brown, 775 Hillsborough Rd., Riverview E1B 3W1; *Campbell's Fishing Camps*, Bird Holdings, P.O. Box 1090A, Fredericton; *Hunter's Fishing Lodge*, Box 35, Boiestown; and *Miramichi Salmon Club Ltd.*, Doaktown. The Restigouche River country in Restigouche County is served by the *Upsalquitch Salmon Club Ltd.*, Robinsonville off Highway 117.

The Tobique River country in Victoria County reached via Highway 385 is served by the *Northern Wilderness Lodge*, Box 385, Plaster Rock; *Barkers Sporting Camps*, RR1, Plaster Rock; *Tobique & Serpentine Camps*, RR1, Plaster Rock; *Tobique Trails Outfitters Ltd.*, Plaster Rock; *Spruce Grove Camps*, RR2, Plaster Rock; *North View Hunting Camp*, RR2, Plaster Rock; *Tobique Lodge*, RR1, Plaster Rock; *Johnson's Camps*, Plaster Rock; *Long Lake Hunting & Fishing Camps*, Plaster Rock; *McAskill Hunting & Fishing Camp*, Plaster Rock; and *Cuffley Hunting Lodge*, RR1, Arthurette. York County outfitters include *Bell's Hunting Lodge*, Canterbury, on Highway 122; *Long Meadow Cabins*, Harvey Station, on Highway 3; *Lodge Spensella*, RR1, Canterbury, on Route 122; *Hide-Away Lodge & Camps*, Fosterville, on Grand Lake and on Highway 122; and *Palfrey Lake Hunting & Fishing Lodge*, Box 41, McAdam, off Highway 4.

Tuna Fishing & Charter Boat Operators

New Brunswick's northeastern area is one of the world's newest hot spots for giant bluefin tuna. Since 1974 giant bluefins averaging 800 pounds have been landed in the eastern end of Chaleur Bay and on the east coast from Tabusintac to Miramichi Bay. Charter boats with experienced crews are available at several ports including Bathurst, Caraquet, Miscou Island, and Tabusintac. Passengers must bring their own lunches. Only tea and coffee are provided on board. In accordance with Maritime Provinces tradition, all tuna caught belong to the boat's captain. For additional information and a listing of charter boat operators write: New Brunswick Tuna Sport Fishing Association, 14 Birch St., Moncton E1C 5T3.

BIBLIOGRAPHY

The bulk of the source materials used in the writing of *The Bantam Great Outdoors Guide* are listed within the main text. The selected sources that follow are listed as a guide to readers who wish to obtain additional information. Although many of the reference titles are out of print, you may obtain them through the permission of public, state, federal, or university and college libraries.

PART ONE
THE UNITED STATES

ALASKA—"THE LAST FRONTIER"

Dall, William Healey. *Alaska and Its Resources.* Boston: Lee Shepard, 1870.

A Guide to Alaska, Last American Frontier. Federal Writers' Project (Works Progress Administration). New York: Macmillan Publishing Co., 1941.

Leopold, Aldo. *Wildlife in Alaska.* New York: Ronald Press Co., 1953.

Marshall, Robert. *Alaska Wilderness: Exploring the Central Brooks Range.* Berkeley: University of California Press, 1970.

Muir, John. *Travels in Alaska.* Boston: Houghton Mifflin Co., 1915.

Queeny, Edgar Monsanto. *Cheechako: The Story of an Alaskan Bear Hunt.* New York: Charles Scribner's Sons, 1941.

Sheldon, Charles. *The Wilderness of Denali.* New York: Charles Scribner's Sons, 1960.

Teichman, Emil. *A Journey to Alaska in the Year 1868.* New York: Argosy Antiquarian, 1963.

Woolen, William Watson. *The Inside Passage to Alaska, 1792–1920.* Glendale, CA: Arthur H. Clark Co., 1924.

PACIFIC CREST STATES

Bingaman, John. *The Ahwahneechees: A Story of the Yosemite Indians.* Lodi, CA: End-Kian Publishing Co., 1966.

Bolton, Herbert E. *Anza's California Expeditions.* Berkeley: University of California Press, 1930.

California: A Guide to the Golden State. Federal Writers' Project (Works Progress Administration). New York: Hastings House, 1939.

Farquhar, Francis P. *History of the Sierra Nevada.* Berkeley: University of California Press, 1972.

Frémont, John Charles. *Geographical Memoir upon Upper California.* San Francisco: Book Club of California, 1964.

King, Clarence. *Mountaineering in the Sierra Nevada.* New York: Charles Scribner's Sons, 1911.

Muir, John. *The Mountains of California.* New York: Century Co., 1904.

———. *Yosemite and the Sierra Nevada.* Boston: Houghton Mifflin Co., 1948.

Nevada: A Guide to the Silver State. Federal Writers' Project (Works Progress Administration). Portland, OR: Binfords & Mort, 1940.

Oregon: End of the Trail. Federal Writers' Project (Works Progress Administration). Portland, OR: Binfords & Mort, 1940.

Peale, Titian Ramsey. *Diary of California Overland Journey, September and October, 1841.* Los Angeles: Glen Dawson, 1957.

Roth, Hal. *Pathway in the Sky: The Story of the John Muir Trail.* Berkeley, CA: Howell-North Books, 1965.

Russell, Osborne. *Journal of a Trapper.* Portland, OR: Oregon Historical Society, 1955.

Sheldon, Charles. *The Wilderness of the North Pacific Coast Islands.* New York: Charles Scribner's Sons, 1912.

Travis, Helga (Anderson). *The Umatella Trail.* New York: Exposition Press, 1951.

Washington: A Guide to the Evergreen State. Federal Writers' Project (Works Progress Administration). Portland, OR: Binfords & Mort, 1941.

Wright, William. *The Big Bonanza.* New York: Alfred A. Knopf, 1947.

ROCKY MOUNTAIN STATES

Anderson, William Marshall. *The Rocky Mountain Journals of William Marshall Anderson: The West in 1834.* Ed. Dale L. Morgan and Eleanor T. Harris. San Marino, CA: Huntington Library, 1967.

Arnold, Lloyd R. *High on the Wild with Ernest Hemingway.* Caldwell, ID: Caxton Printers, 1968.

Bailey, Robert G. *Hells Canyon.* Lewiston, ID: R. Bailey Printing Co., 1943.

————. *River of No Return.* Lewiston, ID: Bailey-Blake Printing Co., 1935.

Beal, Merrill, and Wells, Merle W. *History of Idaho.* New York: Lewis Historical Publishing Co., 1959.

Berry, Gerald. *The Whoop-up Trail.* Edmonton, Alta: Applied Art Products, 1953.

Bischoff, Hermann. *Deadwood to the Big Horns.* Bismarck, ND, 1931.

Borland, Hal. *Rocky Mountain Tipi Tales.* Garden City, NY: Doubleday & Co., 1924.

Brandon, William. *The Men and the Mountains: Frémont's Fourth Expedition.* New York: William Morrow & Co., 1955.

Burlingame, Merrill Gildea. *The Montana Frontier.* Helena, MT: State Publishing Co., 1942.

Chisholm, James. *South Pass 1868: James Chisholm's Journal of the Wyoming Gold Rush.* Ed. Lola M. Homsher. Lincoln: University of Nebraska Press, 1960.

Colorado: A Guide to the Highest State. Federal Writers' Project (Works Progress Administration). New York: Hastings House, 1941.

Grinnell, George Bird. *When Buffalo Ran.* Norman: University of Oklahoma Press, 1966.

Guernsey, Charles Arthur. *Wyoming Cowboy Days.* New York: G. P. Putnam's Sons, 1936.

Idaho: A Guide in Word and Picture. Federal Writers' Project (Works Progress Administration). Caldwell, ID: Caxton Printers, 1937.

The Idaho Encyclopedia. Federal Writers' Project (Works Progress Administration). Caldwell, ID: Caxton Printers, 1938.

Montana: A State Guide Book. Federal Writers' Project (Works Progress Administration). New York: Viking Press, 1939.

Moomaw, Jack Clifford. *Recollections of a Rocky Mountain Ranger.* Longmont, CO: Times-Call Publishing Co., 1963.

Murie, Margaret E. *Wapiti Wilderness.* New York: Alfred A. Knopf, 1966.

Murney, Nolie. *The Teton Mountains, Their History and Tradition.* Denver: Artcraft Press, 1947.

Neihardt, John S. *The Mountain Men.* New York: Bison Books, 1971.

Nelson, Bruce Opie. *Land of the Dacotahs.* Minneapolis: University of Minnesota Press, 1946.

Randall, Leslie Watson. *Footprints Along the Yellowstone.* San Antonio, TX: Naylor Co., 1961.

Russell, Osborne. *Journal of a Trapper.* Portland: Oregon Historical Society, 1955.

Triggs, J. H. *History of Cheyenne and Northern Wyoming.* Laramie, WY: Powder River Publishers, 1955.

Utah: A Guide to the State. Federal Writers' Project (Works Progress Administration). New York: Hastings House, 1941.

Welch, Charles A. *History of the Big Horn Basin.* Salt Lake City: Desert News Press, 1940.

Willard, John. *Adventure Trails in Montana.* Helena: Montana Historical Society, 1964.

Wolle, Muriel. *Montana Pay Dirt: A Guide to the Mining Camps of the Treasure State.* Denver: Sage Books, 1963.

Wyoming: A Guide to Its History, Highways and People. Federal Writers' Project (Works Progress Administration). New York: Oxford University Press, 1941.

Zimmerman, William. *The Fort Hall Story: An Interpretation.* Philadelphia: Indian Rights Association, 1959.

SOUTHWEST STATES

Arizona: A State Guide. Federal Writers' Project (Works Progress Administration). New York: Hastings House, 1940.

Darrah, William Culp. *Powell of the Colorado.* Princeton, NJ: Princeton University Press, 1951.

Hafen, LeRoy H. *The Overland Mail 1849–69.* Glendale, CA: Arthur H. Clark Co., 1926.

Lockwood, Francis Cummins. *Pioneer Days in Arizona.* New York: Macmillan Publishing Co., 1932.

Mitchell, John D. *Lost Mines of the Great Southwest.* Phoenix, AZ: Journal Co., 1933.

New Mexico: A Guide to the Colorful State. Federal Writers' Project (Works Progress Administration). New York: Hastings House, 1940.

Oklahoma: A Guide to the Sooner State. Federal Writers' Project (Works Progress Administration). Oklahoma City: Tribune Publishing Co., 1938.

Rockefellow, John A. *Log of an American Trailblazer.* Tucson, AZ: Acme Printing Co., 1933.

Sibley, Marilyn McAdams. *Travelers in Texas, 1761–1860.* Austin: University of Texas Press, 1967.

Sitgreaves, Lorenzo. *Report of an Expedition Down the Zuni and Colorado Rivers in 1851.* Chicago: Rio Grande Press, 1962.

Texas: A Guide to the Lone Star State. Federal Writers' Project (Works Progress Administration). New York: Hastings House, 1940.

GREAT PLAINS STATES

Brown, Dee. *Bury My Heart at Wounded Knee.* New York: Bantam Books, 1970.

Crawford, Lewis F. *History of North Dakota.* Chicago: American Historical Society, 1931.

Kansas: A Guide to the Sunflower State. Federal Writers' Project (Works Progress Administration). New York: Viking Press, 1939.

Nebraska: A Guide to the Cornhusker State. Federal Writers' Project (Works Progress Administration). New York: Viking Press, 1939.

North Dakota: A Guide to the Northern Prairie State. Federal Writers' Project (Works Progress Administration). Fargo, ND: Knight Printing Co., 1938.

A South Dakota Guide. Federal Writers' Project (Works Progress Administration). Pierre, SD: State Publishing Co., 1938.

Williams, Mary A. *Origins of North Dakota Place Names.* Washburn, ND, 1959.

GREAT LAKES STATES

Blackbird, Andrew J. *History of the Ottawa and Chippewa Indians of Michigan.* Harbor Springs, MI: Babcock & Darling, 1897.

Bolz, J. Arnold. *Portage into the Past.* Minneapolis: University of Minnesota Press, 1960.

Brown, Charles Edward, ed. *Paul Bunyan Classics.* Madison: Wisconsin Folklore Society, 1945.

Burroughs, Raymond Darwin. *Peninsular Country.* Grand Rapids, MI: Wm. B. Eerdmans Publishing Co., 1965.

Gray, James. *Pine, Stream and Prairie: Wisconsin and Minnesota in Profile.* New York: Alfred A. Knopf, 1945.

Henry, Alexander. *Massacre at Mackinac.* Ed. David A. Armour. Mackinac Island, MI: Mackinac Island State Park Commission.

Kinzie, Juliette A. *Wau-bun: The Early Days of the Northwest.* Ed. Louise Phelps Kellogg. New York: Derby & Jackson, 1930.

Larsen, Erling. *Minnesota Trails.* Minneapolis: T. S. Denison & Co., 1958.

Michigan: A Guide to the Wolverine State. Federal Writers' Project (Works Progress Administration). New York: Oxford University Press, 1941.

Minnesota: A State Guide. Federal Writers' Project (Works Progress Administration). New York: Viking Press, 1938.

The Minnesota Arrowhead Country. Federal Writers' Project (Works Progress Administration). Chicago: Albert Whitman & Co., 1941.

Wellman, Paul Iselin. *Portage Bay.* Garden City, NY: Doubleday & Co., 1957.

Wisconsin: A Guide to the Badger State. Federal Writers' Project (Works Progress Administration). New York: Duell, Sloan and Pearce, 1941.

CENTRAL STATES

Arkansas: A Guide to the State. Federal Writers' Project (Works Progress Administration). New York: Hastings House, 1941.

Illinois: A Descriptive and Historical Guide. Federal Writers' Project (Works Progress Administration). Chicago: A. C. McClung & Co., 1939.

Indiana: A Guide to the Hoosier State. Federal Writers' Project (Works Progress Administration). New York: Oxford University Press, 1941.

Iowa: A Guide to the Hawkeye State. Federal Writers' Project (Works Progress Administration). New York: Viking Press, 1938.

Kentucky: A Guide to the Bluegrass State. Federal Writers' Project (Works Progress Administration). New York: Harcourt Brace Co., 1939.

Missouri: A Guide to the "Show Me" State. Federal Writers' Project (Works Progress Administration). New York: Duell, Sloan and Pearce, 1941.

The Ohio Guide. Federal Writers' Project (Works Prog-

ress Administration). New York: Oxford University Press, 1940.

GULF COAST STATES

Alabama: A Guide to the Deep South. Federal Writers' Project (Works Progress Administration). New York: R. R. Smith, 1941.

Florida: A Guide to the Southernmost State. Federal Writers' Project (Works Progress Administration). New York: Oxford University Press, 1939.

Louisiana: A Guide to the State. Federal Writers' Project (Works Progress Administration). New York: Hastings House, 1941.

Mississippi: A Guide to the Magnolia State. Federal Writers' Project (Works Progress Administration). New York: Viking Press, 1938.

SOUTHERN APPALACHIAN STATES

Callahan, North. *Smoky Mountain Country.* New York: Duell, Sloan and Pearce, 1952.

Georgia: A Guide to Its Towns and Countryside. Federal Writers' Project (Works Progress Administration). Athens: University of Georgia Press, 1940.

McQueen, Alexander Stephens. *History of Okefenokee Swamp.* Clinton, SC: Press of Jacobs and Co., 1926.

North Carolina: A Guide to the Old North State. Federal Writers' Project (Works Progress Administration). Chapel Hill: University of North Carolina Press, 1939.

South Carolina: A Guide to the Palmetto State. Federal Writers' Project (Works Progress Administration). New York: Oxford University Press, 1941.

Tennessee: A Guide to the State. Federal Writers' Project (Works Progress Administration). New York: Viking Press, 1939.

Terres, John K. *From Laurel Hill to Siler's Bog.* New York: Alfred A. Knopf, 1969.

Wigginton, Eliot, ed. *The Foxfire Book.* Garden City, NY: Doubleday & Co., 1972.

MID-APPALACHIAN STATES

Delaware: A Guide to the First State. Federal Writers' Project (Works Progress Administration). New York: Viking Press, 1938.

Maryland: A Guide to the Old Pine State. Federal Writ-

ers' Project (Works Progress Administration). New York: Oxford University Press, 1940.

New Jersey: A Guide to Its Present and Past. Federal Writers' Project (Works Progress Administration). New York: Viking Press, 1939.

New York: A Guide to the Empire State. Federal Writers' Project (Works Progress Administration). New York: Oxford University Press, 1940.

Pennsylvania: A Guide to the Keystone State. Federal Writers' Project (Works Progress Administration). New York: Oxford University Press, 1940.

Virginia: A Guide to the Old Dominion. Federal Writers' Project (Works Progress Administration). New York: Oxford University Press, 1940.

West Virginia: A Guide to the Mountain State. Federal Writers' Project (Works Progress Administration). New York: Oxford University Press, 1941.

Wilderness Chronicles of Northwestern Pennsylvania. Federal Writers' Project (Works Progress Administration). Harrisburg: Pennsylvania Historical Commission, 1941.

NORTHERN APPALACHIAN STATES

Connecticut: A Guide to Its Roads, Lore, and People. Federal Writers' Project (Works Progress Administration). Boston: Houghton Mifflin Co., 1938.

Coolidge, Philip Tripp. *History of the Maine Woods.* Bangor, ME: Furbush-Roberts Printing Co., 1963.

Doucette, Earle. *The Fisherman's Guide to Maine.* New York: Random House, 1951.

Hoagland, Edward. *Walking the Dead Diamond River.* New York: Random House, 1973.

Maine: A Guide "Down East." Federal Writers' Project (Works Progress Administration). Boston: Houghton Mifflin Co., 1937.

Massachusetts: A Guide to Its Places and People. Federal Writers' Project (Works Progress Administration). Boston: Houghton Mifflin Co., 1937.

Morison, Samuel Eliot. *The Story of Mount Desert Island, Maine.* Boston: Little, Brown and Co., 1960.

New Hampshire: A Guide to the Granite State. Federal Writers' Project (Works Progress Administration). Boston: Houghton Mifflin Co., 1938.

Rhode Island: A Guide to the Smallest State. Federal

Writers' Project. (Works Progress Administration). Boston: Houghton Mifflin Co., 1937.

Thoreau, Henry David. *Canoeing in the Wilderness.* Boston: Houghton Mifflin Co., 1916.

————. *The Maine Woods.* Boston: Ticknor and Fields, 1864.

Vermont: A Guide to the Green Mountain State. Federal Writers' Project (Works Progress Administration). Boston: Houghton Mifflin Co., 1937.

Weygandt, Cornelius. *The White Hills.* New York: Holt Co., 1934.

PART TWO
CANADA & THE
GREAT NORTH WOODS

NORTHERN CANADA

Berton, Pierre. *The Klondike Fever: The Life and Death of the Last Gold Rush.* New York: Alfred A. Knopf, 1958.

Butler, W. F. *The Wild North Land.* London: Marston, Low & Searly, 1874.

Campbell, Robert. *Discovery and Exploration of the Yukon.* Winnipeg, Man., 1885.

Chapman, John Wight. *A Camp on the Yukon.* Cornwall-on-Hudson, NY: Idlewild Press, 1948.

Fountain, Paul. *The Great Northwest and Great Lake Region of North America.* London: Longmans, Green & Co., 1904.

Gates, O. M., ed. *Five Fur Traders of the Northwest.* St. Paul: Minnesota Historical Society, 1965.

Sheldon, Charles. *The Wilderness of the Upper Yukon.* New York: Charles Scribner's Sons, 1911.

Tyrell, J. W. *Across the Sub-Arctics of Canada.* Toronto, Ont., 1908.

WESTERN CANADA

Fraser, Simon. *Letters and Journals, 1806–1808.* Toronto, Ont.: Macmillan Co. of Canada, 1960.

Hardy, W. G., ed. *Alberta: A Natural History.* Edmonton, Alta.: Hurtig Publishers, 1967.

Hoagland, Edward. *Notes from the Century Before: A Journal of British Columbia.* New York: Random House, 1969.

MacGregor, James G. *Behold the Shining Mountains: An Account of the Travels of Anthony Benday, 1754–5, the First White Man to Enter Alberta).* Edmonton, Alta. Applied Arts Products, 1954.

Mitchell, B. W. *Trail Life in the Canadian Rockies.* New York: Macmillan Publishing Co., 1924.

Sprague, Marshall. *The Great Gates: The Story of the Rocky Mountain Passes.* Boston: Little, Brown and Co., 1964.

Stanwell-Fletcher, Theodora Morris. *Driftwood Valley.* Boston: Little, Brown and Co., 1946.

Woodcock, George. *Ravens and Prophets: An Account of Journeys in British Columbia, Alberta and Southern Alaska.* London: A. Wingate, 1952.

CENTRAL CANADA

Dawson, Simon James. *The Red River Expedition of 1870.* Toronto, Ont.: Canadiana Library Service, 1967.

Morton, William Lewis. *Manitoba: A History.* Toronto, Ont.: University of Toronto Press, 1967.

Stanwell-Fletcher, Theodora Morris. *The Tundra World.* Boston: Little, Brown and Co., 1952.

Warkentin, John. *Manitoba Historical Atlas: A Selection of Facsimile Maps, Plans and Sketches from 1612 to 1969.* Winnipeg: Historical and Scientific Society of Manitoba, 1970.

EASTERN CANADA

Davies, Blodwen. *Saguenay, "Sagginawa": The River of Deep Waters.* New York: Dodd, Mead & Co., 1930.

Guillet, Edwin Clarence. *Pioneer Travel in Upper Canada.* Toronto, Ont.: University of Toronto Press, 1966.

Rowlands, John J. *Cache Lake Country: Life in the North Woods.* New York: W. W. Norton & Co., 1947.

Saunders, Audrey. *Algonquin Story.* Toronto, Ont.: Dept. of Lands and Forests, 1963.

Umfreville, Edward. *Nipigon to Winnipeg: A Canoe Voyage Through Western Ontario in 1784.* Ottawa, Ont.: R. Douglas, 1929.

ATLANTIC CANADA

Clarke, George Frederick. *Someone Before Us: Our Maritime Indians.* Fredericton, N.B.: Brunswick Press, 1970.

Ellis, Mina Benson Hubbard. *A Woman's Way Through*

Unknown Labrador: An Account of the Exploration of the Nascaupee and George Rivers. London: J. Murray, 1908.

Horwood, Harold. *Newfoundland.* New York: St. Martin's Press, 1969.

Leechman, John Douglas. *Eskimo Summer.* London: Museum Press, 1950.

Rowland, John T. *North to Adventure.* New York: W. W. Norton & Co., 1963.

Russell, Franklin. *The Secret Islands.* New York: W. W. Norton & Co., 1965.

GENERAL SUBJECTS

TALES OF ADVENTURE & EXPLORATION

Allen, Paul. *History of the Expedition of Lewis and Clark.* New York: Bradford and Inskeep, 1814.

Amundsen, Roald. *The Northwest Passage.* New York: E. P. Dutton & Co., 1908.

Ballantyne, R. M. *Hudson Bay.* London: T. Nelson & Sons, 1876.

Bell, William Abraham. *New Tracks in North America.* New York: Soiebner, Welford & Co., 1870.

Bigsby, J. J. *The Shoe and Canoe.* London: Chapman & Hall, 1850.

Bossu, Jean-Bernard. *Travels in the Interior of North America, 1751–1762.* Ed. Seymour Feiler. Norman: University of Oklahoma Press, 1962.

Brebner, John Bartlett. *The Explorers of North America, 1492–1806.* New York: Macmillan Publishing Co., 1933.

Butler, W. F. *The Great Lone Land.* London: Marston, Low & Searle, 1850.

Clemens, Samuel Langhorne (Mark Twain). *Roughing It.* Chicago: F. G. Gilman & Co., 1872.

Cushman, Dan. *The Great North Trail.* New York: McGraw-Hill Book Co., 1966.

De Voto, Bernard A. *Across the Wide Missouri.* Boston: Houghton Mifflin Co., 1964.

———. *The Course of Empire.* Boston: Houghton Mifflin Co., 1952.

Ferguson, Harvey. *Rio Grande.* New York: Alfred A. Knopf, 1933.

Frémont, John Charles. *The Expeditions of John Charles Frémont.* Ed. Donald Jackson and Mary Lee Spence. Urbana: University of Illinois Press, 1970.

Goetzman, William H. *Exploration and Empire.* New York: Alfred A. Knopf, 1967.

Hebard, Grace Raymond. *The Bozeman Trail.* Glendale, CA: Arthur H. Clark Co., 1922.

———. *The Pathbreakers from River to Ocean: The Story of the Great West from the Time of Coronado to the Present.* Glendale, CA: Arthur H. Clark Co., 1932.

Henry, Alexander, *Alexander Henry's Travels and Adventures in the Years 1760–1776.* Ed. Milo Milton Juaife. Chicago: R. R. Donnelley & Sons Co., 1921.

Irving, Washington. *The Adventures of Captain Bonneville, U.S.A., in the Rocky Mountains and the Far West.* New York: G. P. Putnam's Sons, 1850.

———. *Astoria, or Anecdotes of an Enterprise Beyond the Rocky Mountains.* Philadelphia: Carey, Lea & Blanchard, 1836.

———. *A Tour on the Prairies.* Philadelphia: Carey, Lea & Blanchard, 1835.

Kipling, Rudyard. *"Captains Courageous": A Story of the Grand Banks.* New York: Century Co., 1897.

———. *Land and Sea Tales for Scouts and Guides.* London: Macmillan, 1923.

Lefroy, Sir John Henry. *In Search of the Magnetic North.* Ed. George Stanley. Toronto, Ont.: Macmillan Co. of Canada, 1955.

Lewis, Meriwether, and Clark, William. *Original Journals of the Lewis and Clark Expedition, 1804–1806.* Ed. Reuben Gold Thwaites. 8 vols. New York: Dodd, Mead & Co., 1904.

Markham, Sir Clements. *The Lands of Silence.* Cambridge, England: Cambridge University Press, 1921.

Mirsky, Jeannette. *To the Arctic! The Story of Northern Exploration from Earliest Times to the Present.* New York: Alfred A. Knopf, 1948.

———. *The Westward Crossings: Balboa, Mackenzie, Lewis and Clark.* New York: Alfred A. Knopf, 1946.

Morison, Samuel Eliot. *The European Discovery of America.* New York: Oxford University Press, 1971–74.

Morse, Eric Wilton. *Fur Trade Canoe Routes—Then and Now.* Ottawa, Ont.: Queen's Printer, 1969.

Mowat, Farley. *Canada North.* Boston: Little, Brown and Co., 1967.

———. *The Snow Walker*. Boston: Little, Brown and Co., 1975.

———. *Tundra: Selections from the Great Accounts of Arctic Land Voyages*. Toronto, Ont.: McClelland & Stewart, 1973.

———. *Westviking: The Ancient Norse in Greenland and North America*. Boston: Little, Brown and Co., 1965.

Nuttal, Thomas. *A Journal of Travels into the Arkansas Territory During the Year 1819*. Philadelphia: T. H. Palmon, 1821.

Pike, Warburton. *Through the Subarctic Forest*. London: E. Arnold, 1896.

HISTORY & INDIANS

Anderson, Anita Melva. *Fur Trappers of the Old West*. Chicago: Wheeler Publishing Co., 1946.

Bagley, Clarence B. *Indian Myths of the Northwest*. Seattle: Lowman & Hartford Co., 1930.

Caesar, Gene. *King of the Mountain Men: The Life of Jim Bridger*. New York: E. P. Dutton & Co., 1961.

Canfield, William Walker. *The Legends of the Iroquois*. New York: A. Wessels Co., 1902.

Campbell, Marjorie Elliot. *The North West Company*. New York: St. Martin's Press, 1957.

Catlin, George. *Letters and Notes on the North American Indians*. Ed. Michael Macdonald Mooney. New York: Clarkson N. Potter, 1975.

Chittenden, Hiram Martin. *The American Fur Trade of the Far West*. New York: F. P. Harper, 1902.

———. *Yellowstone National Park, Historical & Descriptive*. Cincinnati: Stewart, 1912.

Coues, Elliot, ed. *New Light on the Early History of the Greater Northwest. (The Manuscript Journals of Alexander Henry and David Thompson.)* Minneapolis: Ross & Haines, 1965.

Glasscock, Carl Burgess. *The Big Bonanza: The Story of the Comstock Lode*. Indianapolis: Bobbs-Merrill Co., 1931.

Grinnell, George Bird. *Blackfeet Indian Stories*. New York: Charles Scribner's Sons, 1913.

Hafen, LeRoy Reuben. *The Mountain Men and the Fur Trade of the Far West*. Glendale, CA: Arthur H. Clark Co., 1965.

Haines, Francis. *Red Eagles of the Northwest: The Story of Chief Joseph and His People*. Portland, OR: Scholastic Press, 1939.

McClintock, Walter. *The Old North Trail: Life, Legends and Religion of the Blackfeet Indians*. London: Macmillan, 1910.

Morison, Samuel Eliot, and Commager, Henry Steele. *The Growth of the American Republic*. New York: Oxford University Press, 1962.

———. *The Oxford History of the American People*. New York: Oxford University Press, 1965.

———. *Samuel de Champlain, Father of New France*. Boston: Little, Brown and Co., 1972.

Mowat, Farley. *People of the Deer*. Boston: Little, Brown and Co., 1952.

Ormsby, Margaret A. *British Columbia: A History*. Toronto, Ont.: Macmillan Co. of Canada, 1958.

Rich, Edwin Ernest. *The Fur Trade and the Northwest to 1857*. Toronto, Ont.: McClelland & Stewart, 1967.

Ross, Alexander. *The Fur Hunters of the Far West*. Ed. Kenneth A. Spaulding. Norman: University of Oklahoma Press, 1956.

Ruxton, George Frederick. *Life in the Far West*. Ed. LeRoy H. Hafen. Norman: University of Oklahoma Press, 1951.

———. *Mountain Men*. New York: Holiday House, 1966.

Schultz, James Willard. *Blackfeet and Buffalo: Memories of Life Among the Indians*. Ed. Keith C. Steele. Norman: University of Oklahoma Press, 1962.

Severin, Timothy. *Explorers of the Mississippi*. London: Routledge & Kegan Paul, 1967.

Stuart, Granville. *Forty Years on the Frontier*. Ed. Paul C. Phillips. Glendale, CA: Arthur H. Clark Co., 1957.

Sunder, John Edward. *The Fur Trade on the Upper Missouri, 1840–1865*. Norman: University of Oklahoma Press, 1965.

Vestal, Stanley. *Jim Bridger, Mountain Man*. New York: William Morrow & Co., 1946.

Wallace, William Stewart. *The Pedlars from Quebec, and Other Papers on the Nor'westers*. Toronto, Ont.: McGraw-Hill Ryerson, 1954.

· THE BANTAM GREAT OUTDOORS GUIDE

WILDERNESS SPORTS & WILDLIFE

Bradner, Enos. *Northwest Angling.* Portland, OR: Binfords & Mort, 1969.

Dice, Lee Raymond. *The Biotic Provinces of North America.* Ann Arbor: University of Michigan Press, 1943.

Elman, Robert. *The Hunter's Field Guide.* New York: Alfred A. Knopf, 1974.

Carpenter, Robert R. Morgen. *Game Trails in Idaho and Alaska.* N.P., c. 1940.

Grey, Zane. *Tales of Fishes.* New York: Harper & Row, 1919.

———. *Tales of Freshwater Fishing.* New York: Harper & Row, 1928.

Marsh, Othniel Charles. *Dinocerata: A Monograph of an Extinct Order of Ancient Mammals.* Washington, DC: U.S. Geological Survey, 1884.

Murie, Margaret E. *Two in the Far North.* New York: Alfred A. Knopf, 1963.

Murie, Olaus J. *The Elk of North America.* Harrisburg, PA: Stackpole Books, 1951.

———. *A Field Guide to Animal Tracks.* Boston: Houghton Mifflin Co., 1954.

———. *Journeys to the Far North.* Palo Alto, CA: American West Publishing Co., 1973.

Olson, Sigurd F. *The Hidden Forest.* New York: Viking Press, 1969.

———. *Listening Point.* New York: Alfred A. Knopf, 1958.

———. *Sigurd F. Olson's Wilderness Days.* New York: Alfred A. Knopf, 1972.

Peterson, Roger Tory. *A Field Guide to the Birds.* Boston: Houghton Mifflin Co., 1934.

Rutstrum, Calvin. *The New Way of the Wilderness.* New York: Macmillan Publishing Co., 1958.

———. *North American Canoe Country.* New York: Macmillan Publishing Co., 1964.

Sheldon, Charles, and Grinnell, George Bird. *Hunting and Conversation.* New York: Arno Press, 1970.

Voelker, John Donaldson (Robert Traver). *Laughing Whitefish.* New York: McGraw-Hill Book Co., 1965.

———. *Trout Madness.* New York: St. Martin's Press, 1960.

INDEX